THE MIDDLE EAST AND NORTH AFRICA
1975-1976

A survey and directory of Afghanistan, Algeria, Bahrain, Cyprus, Egypt, Iran, Iraq, Israel, Jordan, Kuwait, Lebanon, Libya, Morocco, Oman, Qatar, Saudi Arabia, Spanish North Africa, Sudan, Syria, Tunisia, Turkey, United Arab Emirates, Yemen Arab Republic and Yemen People's Democratic Republic.

THE
MIDDLE EAST
AND
NORTH AFRICA

1975-76

TWENTY-SECOND EDITION

EUROPA PUBLICATIONS LIMITED
18 BEDFORD SQUARE LONDON WC1B 3JN

Previous Editions:

1948	1950	1953
1955	1957	1958
1959	1961	1962
1963	1964	1965
1966	1967	1968
1969	1970	1971
1972	1973	1974

© EUROPA PUBLICATIONS LIMITED 1975

ISBN 0 900 36287 1

Library of Congress Catalog Card Number 48-3250

AUSTRALIA AND NEW ZEALAND
James Bennett (Collaroy) Pty. Ltd., Collaroy, N.S.W., Australia

INDIA
UBS Publishers' Distributors Pvt. Ltd., P.O.B. 1882, 5 Ansari Road, Daryaganj, Delhi 6

JAPAN
Maruzen Co. Ltd., 6 Tori-Nichome, Nihonbashi, Tokyo 103

Printed and bound in England by
STAPLES PRINTERS LIMITED
at The Stanhope Press, Rochester, Kent.

Foreword

DURING the past year the Middle East has continued to be at the centre of the world economy and of world politics. The increase in the price of oil has played an important part in stimulating the inflation which the Western world has been experiencing, and every country in the world has an interest in resolving the Arab-Israeli conflict. An important step in this direction was taken in September 1975 with the signing of the interim agreement between Egypt and Israel over Sinai (*see* Late Information, page xx). Much remains to be settled before peace comes permanently to the Middle East, and the 22nd edition of THE MIDDLE EAST AND NORTH AFRICA provides up-to-date information for all who are concerned about this rich but troubled area.

Once again we would like to thank the numerous individuals and organizations who have sent us both revised and new information for inclusion in this edition of THE MIDDLE EAST AND NORTH AFRICA. Without their assistance the book could not have become a recognized authority on the region.

September 1975.

Acknowledgements

We express our thanks for much help and information kindly supplied by many Foreign Ministries and National Statistical Offices and by the following embassies and other bodies.

Afghan Embassy, London
Algerian Embassy, London
Arab League
Arab Report and Record
Arabian American Oil Company
Bahrain Embassy, London
British Embassy, Kuwait
Central Treaty Organization
Cyprus High Commission, London
French Embassy, London
Imperial Iranian Embassy, London
Institute of Petroleum Information Service, London
Iraq Ministry of Information, Baghdad
Israel Embassy, London
Jordan Embassy, London
Kuwait Embassy, London
Kuwait Oil Company
Lebanese Embassy, London
Libyan Embassy, London
Michael Rice Group Middle East
Middle East Economic Digest
National Bank of Egypt, Cairo
Moroccan Embassy, London
Oman Embassy, London
Organization of Arab Petroleum Exporting Countries (OAPEC)

Organization of Petroleum Exporting Countries (OPEC)
Palestine Liberation Organization, Beirut
Private Information Center on Eastern Arabia, Belgium
Qatar Embassy, London
Regional Co-operation for Development
Saudi Arabian Embassy, London
Spanish Embassy, London
Syrian Embassy, London
Sudanese Embassy, London
Tunisian Embassy, London
Turkish Embassy, London
Embassy of the United Arab Emirates, London
United Nations Information Centre, London
United Nations Economic Commission for Africa
United Nations Economic Commission for Western Asia
United Nations Relief and Works Agency for Palestine Refugees in the Near East
Embassy of the Yemen Arab Republic, London
Embassy of the Yemen People's Democratic Republic, London

We also acknowledge with thanks the co-operation of the International Institute for Strategic Studies, 18 Adam Street, London, WC2N 6AL, in permitting us to use data on defence manpower and finance from *The Military Balance 1974–1975*, and the Israel Embassy, London for the use of two maps of the disengagement agreements between Israel and Egypt (1974) and Israel and Syria.

Contents

PART ONE
General Survey

PART TWO
Regional Organizations

PART THREE

Country Surveys

CONTENTS

ix

PART FOUR
Other Reference Material

Maps

Abbreviations

A	..	Ambassador
AAHO	..	Afro-Asian Housing Organization
AAPSO	..	Afro-Asian People's Solidarity Organization
Acad.	..	Academy
accred.	..	accredited
AD ..	..	Algerian Dinars
A.D.C.	..	Aide-de-camp
Admin.	..	Administrative; Administration; Administrator
Admin.-Gen.		Administrator-General
ADMA	..	Abu Dhabi Marine Areas
ADOCO	..	Abu Dhabi Oil Company
ADPC	..	Abu Dhabi Petroleum Company
AfDB	..	African Development Bank
Afs...	..	Afghanis
AIWO	..	Agudath Israel World Organization
ALF	..	Arab Liberation Front
ALN	..	Armée de Libération Nationale (National Liberation Army of Algeria)
Amb.		Ambassador
AMINOIL	..	American Independent Oil Company
AMOSEAS	..	American Overseas Petroleum Ltd.
AOC	..	Arabian Oil Company
AOF	..	Afrique Occidentale Française (French West Africa)
API	..	American Petroleum Institute
approx.	..	approximately
apptd.	..	appointed
A.R.	..	Arab Republic
Aramco	..	Arabian-American Oil Company
A.R.E.	..	Arab Republic of Egypt
ARGAS	..	Arabian Geophysical Survey Company
ASFEC	..	Regional Centre for Functional Literacy in Rural Areas for the Arab States
Ass...	..	Assembly
Asscn.	..	Association
Assoc.	..	Associate
Asst.	..	Assistant
ATAS	..	Anatolian Refinery Company
ATUC	..	African Trade Union Confederation
AUA	..	Austrian Airlines
AUXERAP		Société Auxiliaire de la Régie du Pétrole
Ave.		Avenue
b. ..	..	born
B.A.	..	Bachelor of Arts
BAPCO	..	The Bahrain Petroleum Company Ltd.
bbl(s).	..	barrel(s)
BD ..	..	Bahrain Dinars
Bd. ..	..	Board
Bde.	..	Brigade
B.Lit(t).	..	Bachelor of Letters
Blvd.	..	Boulevard
B.P.	..	Boîte Postale (Post Office Box)
BP ..	..	British Petroleum
BPC		Basrah Petroleum Company
br(s).		branch(es)
B.Sc.	..	Bachelor of Science
B.S.T.	..	British Standard Time
BUSHCO		Bushire Petroleum Company
CA ..	..	Chargé d'Affaires
CAFRAD	..	Centre Africain de Formation et de Recherches Administratives pour le Développement
CAMEL		Compagnie Algérienne du Methane Liquid
cap...	..	capital
Capt.	..	Captain

CARE	..	Co-operative for American Relief Everywhere
CENTO	..	Central Treaty Organization
CEP	..	Compagnie d'Exploration Pétrolière
CEPT	..	Conférence Européenne des Administrations des Postes et des Télécommunications
CFP	..	Compagnie Française des Pétroles
Chair.	..	Chairman
Cie. ..	..	Compagnie (Company)
c.i.f...	..	cost, insurance, freight
C.-in-C.	..	Commander-in-Chief
Co. ..	..	Company
Comm.	..	Commission
Commdr.	..	Commander
Commdt.	..	Commandant
Commr.	..	Commissioner
Conf.	..	Conference
Contrib.	..	Contributor; Contribution
COPE	..	Compagnie Orientale des Pétroles
COPEFA	..	Compagnie des Pétroles France-Afrique
Corpn.	..	Corporation
CPA	..	Compagnie des Pétroles d'Algérie
CREPS	..	Compagnie de Recherches et d'Exploration de Pétrole du Sahara
CRNA	..	National Council of the Algerian Revolution
CRUA	..	Revolutionary Council for Unity and Action (now FLN)
ČSA..	..	Československé Aerolinie
Cttee.	..	Committee
Del...	..	Delegate; Delegation
Dem...	..	Democratic
dep...	..	deposits
Dept.	..	Department
Devt.	..	Development
Dir...	..	Director
Div...	..	Division
DPA	..	Deutsche Presse-Agentur
Dr. ..	..	Doctor
DUP	..	Democratic Unionist Party (Sudan)
d.w...	..	dead weight
ECOSOC	..	Economic and Social Council (UN)
ECWA	..	Economic Commission for Western Asia
ed. ..	..	Educated
Edn.	..	Edition
Educ.	..	Education
EEC	..	European Economic Community
EFTA	..	European Free Trade Association
EOKA	..	National Organization of the Struggle for Freedom of Cyprus
ERAP	..	Entreprise des Recherches et d'Activités Pétrolières
est. ..	..	estimate(d)
excl.	..	excluded; excluding
Exec.	..	Executive
Extra.	..	Extraordinary
f. ..	..	founded
FAO	..	Food and Agriculture Organization
FCM	..	Federation of Muslim Councillors
Fed.	..	Federation; Federal
FFS..	..	Socialist Forces Front
FIDES	..	Fonds d'Investissement pour le Développement Economique et Sociale de la France d'Outre-Mer

FLN	..	Front de Libération Nationale (National Liberation Front)
FLOSY	..	Front for the Liberation of Occupied South Yemen
fmr...	..	former
f.o.b.	..	free on board
ft. ..	..	feet; foot
gal. ..	..	gallons
GDA	..	Gas Distribution Administration
G.D.P.	..	Gross Domestic Product
Gen. Man.	..	General Manager
GFCM	..	General Fisheries Council for the Mediterranean
G.H.Q.	..	General Headquarters
G.M.T.	..	Greenwich Mean Time
G.N.P.	..	Gross National Product
G.O.C.-in-C.	..	General Officer Commanding-in-Chief
Gov.	..	Governor
Govt.	..	Government
GPRA	..	Gouvernement Provisoire de la République Algérienne (Provisional Government of the Republic of Algeria)
GUPCO	..	Gulf of Suez Petroleum Company
ha. ..	..	hectares
H.E.	..	His Eminence; His Excellency
H.I.M.	..	His Imperial Majesty
Hist.	..	Historical
H.M.	..	His (or Her) Majesty
Hon.	..	Honourable; Honorary
HOPECO	..	Hormuz Petroleum Company
H.Q.	..	Headquarters
IAEA	..	International Atomic Energy Authority
IATA	..	International Air Transport Association
IBRD	..	International Bank for Reconstruction and Development
ICAO	..	International Civil Aviation Organization
ICATU	..	International Conference of Arab Trade Unions
ICFTU— AFRO	..	International Confederation of Free Trade Unions—African Regional Organization
ICOO	..	Iraqi Company for Oil Operations
IDA	..	International Development Association
IFC ..	..	International Finance Corporation
ILO..	..	International Labour Organization
IMF	..	International Monetary Fund
IMINOCO ..	..	Iranian Marine International Oil Company
Inc...	..	Incorporated
incl...	..	included; including
Ind...	..	Independent
Insp.	..	Inspector
Inst.	..	Institute; Institution
Int. ..	..	International
INOC	..	Iraq National Oil Company
IOP..	..	Iranian Oil Participants
IPAC	..	Iran-Pan American Oil Company
IPC..	..	Iraq Petroleum Company
IPO..	..	Iranian Plan Organization
IRCAN	..	Iran Canada Oil Company
IROPCO	..	Iranian Offshore Petroleum Company
ITU..	..	International Telecommunications Union
JAL	..	Japan Airlines
JAT	..	Jugoslovenski Aerotransport
kg. ..	..	kilogram
KFAED	..	Kuwait Fund for Arab Economic Development
kl. ..	..	kilolitre
KLM	..	Koninklijke Luchtvaart Maatschappij NV

km. ..	..	kilometres
KNPC	..	Kuwait National Petroleum Company
KOC	..	Kuwait Oil Company
KSPC	..	Kuwait Spanish Petroleum Company
kWh.	..	kilowatt
L ..	..	Legation
LAPCO	..	Lavan Petroleum Company
lb. ..	..	pounds (weight)
LINOCO	..	Libyan National Oil Corporation
LL.B.	..	Bachelor of Laws
LN ..	..	League of Nations
LOT	..	Polskie Linie Lotnicze
Ltd...	..	Limited
M ..	..	Minister
m. ..	..	million
M.A.	..	Master of Arts
Maj.	..	Major
Maj.-Gen.	..	Major-General
Malev	..	Magyar Légyar Légiköz-lekedési Vállalat
Man.	..	Manager; Managing
M.B.E.	..	Member of the (Order of the) British Empire
M.D.	..	Doctor of Medicine
MEA	..	Middle Eastern Airlines
Mem(s).	..	Member(s)
MEOC	..	Middle East Oil Company
Mgr.	..	Monseigneur; Monsignor
Mil. ..	..	Military
Min...	..	Minister; Ministry
MNA	..	Mouvement Nationale Algérienne (Algerian National Movement)
M.P.	..	Member of Parliament
MPC	..	Mosul Petroleum Company
MRP	..	Mouvement Républicain Populaire
M.Sc.	..	Master of Science
MSS.	..	Manuscripts
MTA	..	Mineral Research and Exploration Institute of Turkey
MTLD	..	Mouvement au Triomphe des Libertés Démocratiques (Movement for the Triumph of Democratic Liberties in Algeria)
n.a. ..	..	not available
Nat.	..	National
NATO	..	North Atlantic Treaty Organization
NDRC	..	National Defence Research Council
NECCCRW	..	Near East Christian Council Committee for Refugee Work
n.e.s.	..	not elsewhere specified
n.i.e.	..	not included elsewhere
NIOC	..	National Iranian Oil Company
NLF	..	National Liberation Front (People's Democratic Republic of Yemen)
no. ..	..	number
NUP	..	National Unionist Party (Sudan)
N.Y.	..	New York (City)
OAPEC		Organization of Arab Petroleum Exporting Countries
OAS	..	Secret Army Organization (Algeria)
OAU	..	Organization for African Unity
O.B.E.	..	Officer of the (Order of the) British Empire
OCAM	..	Organisation Commune Africaine, Malgache et Mauricienne
OCRA	..	Clandestine Organization of the Algerian Revolution
OECD	..	Organisation for Economic Co-operation and Development

ORP	..	Organisation de la Résistance Populaire (Organization of Popular Resistance in Algeria)
OPEC	..	Organization of Petroleum Exporting Countries
Parl.	..	Parliament; Parliamentary
PDFLP	..	Popular Democratic Front for the Liberation of Palestine
PDO	..	Petroleum Development Oman
PDP	..	People's Democratic Party (Sudan)
PDR	..	People's Democratic Republic
PEGUPCO.	..	Persian Gulf Petroleum Company
Perm.	..	Permanent
Perm. Del.	..	Permanent Delegate
Perm. Rep	..	Permanent Representative
PFLO	..	Popular Front for the Liberation of Oman
PFLP	..	Popular Front for the Liberation of Palestine
Ph.D.	..	Doctor of Philosophy
PIA	..	Pakistan International Airlines
PLA	..	Palestine Liberation Army
PLO	..	Palestine Liberation Organization
P.O.B.	..	Post Office Box
Pres.	..	President
Prof.	..	Professor
Prop.	..	Proprietor
PSD	..	Parti Socialiste Destourien (Tunisia)
PPA	..	Parti des Peuples Algériennes (Party of the Algerian People)
P.R.	..	People's Republic
p.u.	..	paid up
Publ(s).	..	Publication(s)
QPC	..	Qatar Petroleum Company
R.A.F.	..	Royal Air Force
RCC	..	Revolutionary Command Council (Libya)
RCD	..	Regional Co-operation for Development
Rd.	..	Road
RDA	..	Rassemblement Démocratique Africain
reg.	..	registered
Rep.	..	Representative; Represented
resgnd.	..	resigned
retd.	..	retired
R.P.	..	Révérend Père (Reverend Father)
RPP	..	Republican People's Party
Rt. Hon.	..	Right Honourable
Rt. Rev.	..	Right Reverend
SAS	..	Scandinavian Airlines System
SCAP	..	Supreme Command Allied Powers
SDF	..	Sudan Defence Force
Sec.	..	Secretary
Sec.-Gen.	..	Secretary-General
SEHR	..	Société d'Exploitation des Hydrocarbons de Hassi—R'Mel
SIRIP	..	Société Irano-Italienne des Pétroles
SNPA	..	Société Nationale des Pétroles d'Aquitaine
SNREPAL.	..	Société Nationale de Recherche et d'Exploitation des Pétroles en Algérie
Soc.	..	Society; Société
SOFIRAN	..	Société Française des Pétroles d'Iran

SONATRACH		Société Nationale pour la Recherche, la Production, la Transformation et la Commercialisation des Hydrocarbures
SOPEG	..	Société Pétrolière de Gérance
Sq.	..	Square
St.	..	Street
TAL	..	Trans-Alpine Line
Tapline	..	Trans-Arabian Pipeline Company
TAROM	..	Transporturile Aeriene Române
THY	..	Türk Hava Yollari
TMA	..	Trans Mediterranean Airways
TPAO	..	Turkish Petroleum Corporation
trans.	..	translated; translation
TRAPES	..	Société de Transport de Pétrole de l'Est Saharien
TRAPSA	..	Compagnie de Transport par Pipe-line au Sahara
TWA	..	Trans World Airlines
U.A.E.	..	United Arab Emirates
U.A.R.	..	United Arab Republic
UBAF	..	Union des Banques Arabes et Françaises
UDMA	..	Union Démocratique du Manifeste Algérienne (Democratic Union of the Algerian Manifesto)
UGTA	..	Union Générale des Travailleurs Algériens (Algerian General Workers Union)
U.K.	..	United Kingdom
UN	..	United Nations
UNDOF	..	United Nations Disengagement Observation Force
UNDP	..	United Nations Development Programme
UNEA	..	Union National des Etudiants Algériennes (National Union of Algerian Students)
UNEF	..	United Nations Emergency Force
UNESCO	..	United Nations Educational, Scientific and Cultural Organization
UNFICYP	..	United Nations Peace-Keeping Force in Cyprus
UNFP	..	Union National des Forces Populaires (National Union of Popular Forces in Morocco)
UNICEF	..	United Nations International Children's Emergency Fund
Univ.	..	University
UNMEM	..	United Nations Middle East Mission
UNRWA	..	United Nations Relief and Works Agency for Palestine Refugees in the Near East
UNTSO	..	United Nations Truce Supervision Organization
UPAF	..	Union Postale Africaine (African Postal Union)
U.P.	..	University Press
UPI.	..	United Press International
U.S.A. (U.S.)		United States of America (United States)
USIS	..	United States Information Services
U.S.S.R.	..	Union of Soviet Socialist Republics
UTA	..	Union de Transports Aériens
vols.	..	volumes
VSO	..	Voluntary Service Overseas Limited
WEPCO	..	Western Desert Petroleum Company
WFTU	..	World Federation of Trade Unions
WHO	..	World Health Organization

TRANSCRIPTION OF ARABIC NAMES

The Arabic language is used over a vast area. Though the written language and the script are standard throughout the Middle East, the spoken language and also the pronunciation of the written signs show wide variation from place to place. This is reflected, and even exaggerated, in the different transcriptions in use in different countries. The same words, names and even letters will be pronounced differently by an Egyptian, a Lebanese, or an Iraqi—they will be heard and transcribed differently by an Englishman, a Frenchman, or an Italian. There are several more or less scientific systems of transliteration in use, sponsored by learned societies and Middle Eastern governments, most of them requiring diacritical marks to indicate Arabic letters for which there are no Latin equivalents.

Arabic names occurring in the historical and geographical sections of this book have been rendered in the system most commonly used by British and American Orientalists, but with the omission of the diacritical signs. For the convenience of the reader, these are explained and annotated below. The system used is a transliteration—i.e. it is based on the writing, which is standard throughout the Arab world, and not on the pronunciation, which varies from place to place. In a few cases consistency has been sacrificed in order to avoid replacing a familiar and accepted form by another which, though more accurate, would be unrecognisable.

Consonants:

d   represents two Arabic letters. The second, or emphatic d, is transliterated ḍ. It may also be represented, for some dialects, by dh and by z, e.g. Qāḍī, qadhi, qazi.

dh   in literary Arabic and some dialects pronounced like English th in this. In many dialects pronounced z or d.

gh   A strongly guttural g—sometimes written g, e.g. Baghdād, Bagdad.

h   represents two Arabic letters. The second, more guttural h, is transliterated ḥ, e.g. Husain, Husein.

j   as English j in John, also represented by dj and g. In Egypt this letter is pronounced as a hard g, and may be thus transcribed (with u before e and i), e.g. Najib, Nadjib, Nagib, Naguib, Neguib.

kh   as ch in Scottish loch, also sometimes represented by ch and h, e.g. Khalīl, Chalil, Halil.

q   A guttural k, pronounced farther back in the throat. Also transcribed ḳ, k, and, for some dialects, g, e.g. Waqf, Wakf, Wakf, Wagf.

s   represents two Arabic letters. The second, emphatic s, is transliterated ṣ. It may also be represented by ç, e.g. Sālih, Saleh, Çaleh.

t   represents two Arabic letters. The second, emphatic t, is transliterated ṭ.

th   in literary Arabic and some dialects pronounced as English th in through. In many dialects pronounced t or s, e.g. Thābit, Tabit, Sabit.

w   as in English, but often represented by ou or v, e.g. Wādī, Vadi, Oued.

z   represents two Arabic letters. The second, or emphatic z, is transliterated ẓ. It may also be represented, for some dialects, by dh or d, e.g. Hāfiz, Hafidh, Hafid.

A glottal stop, as in Cockney 'li'l bo'ls'. May also represent the sound transliterated ʿ, a deep guttural with no English equivalent.

Vowels

The Arabic script only indicates three short vowels, three long vowels, and two diphthongs, as follows:

a   as in English hat, and often rendered e, e.g. balad, beled, emir, amir; with emphatics or gutturals usually pronounced as u in but, e.g. Khalīfa, Baghdād.

i   as in English bit. Sometimes rendered e, e.g. jihād, jehād.

u   as in English good. Often pronounced and written o, e.g. Muhammad, Mohammad.

In some Arabic dialects, particularly those of North Africa, unaccented short vowels are often omitted altogether, and long vowels shortened, e.g. Oued for Wādī, bled for balad, etc.

ā   Long a, variously pronounced as in sand, dart and hall.

ī   As ee in feet. In early books often rendered ee.

ū   As oo in boot. The French transcription ou is often met in English books, e.g. Mahmūd, Mahmood, Mahmoud.

ai   Pronounced in classical Arabic as English i in hide, in colloquial Arabic as a in take. Variously transcribed as ai, ay, ei, ey and ê, e.g. sheikh, shaikh, shaykh, etc.

aw   Pronounced in classical Arabic as English ow in town, in colloquial Arabic as in grow. Variously rendered aw, ew, au, ô, av, ev, e.g. Tawfīq, Taufiq, Tevfik, etc.

TURKISH ORTHOGRAPHY AND PRONUNCIATION

Turkish has been written in Roman characters since 1928. The following pronunciations are invariable:

c   hard j, as in majority, jam.

ç   ch, as in church.

g   hard g, as in go, big.

ğ   not voiced, or pronounced y; Ereğli is pronounced erayly.

ı   short vowel, as the second vowel of 'centre', or French 'le'.

i   i sound of Iran, bitter (NOT as in bite, might).

o   o, as in hot, boss.

ö   i sound of 'birth', or French 'oeuvre'.

u   as in do, too, German 'um'.

ü   as in burette, German 'Hütte'.

The Year in the Middle East—July 1974-75

W. B. Fisher

During the twelve months from July 1974 the Middle East certainly maintained its reputation as one of the most troubled, sensitive and critical areas of the world: assassination, local warfare, shuttle and U-turn diplomacy, and the increasingly ramifying problems of world-wide significance deriving from changes in the price of oil. High Summer 1974 was dominated by the Cyprus confrontation, with Turkish forces extending their occupation of the island from their original base in the north around Kyrenia to reach the outskirts of Nicosia, and much of the south and east of Cyprus: nearly 40 per cent of the total area, from Morphou to Famagusta. After several abortive attempts a ceasefire came into effect late in August, with small numbers of prisoners exchanged during September, and a United Nations peacekeeping force interposed. A UN estimate suggested that 226,000 Cypriots in all had been displaced from their homes by the fighting, out of a total population of 675,000, of whom 180,000 were Greek speaking. Many refugees (mainly Greek Cypriots) had sought refuge in the British sovereign bases, and Britain later in the year came under severe criticism from Greece and Greek Cypriot leaders for not facilitating the return of these refugees to their former homes: the British view was that until definite arrangements had been made (since most of the Greek Cypriots had come from what was now Turkish-occupied territory), any attempt to force the refugees back would merely aggravate the situation—the awful consequences of a rather similar occurrence in Palestine in the late 1940s was certainly in the minds of some.

The United States showed displeasure at the Turkish action by suspending military and other aid to Turkey, against the wishes of President Ford; Turkey responded by bringing into question the status and future of the American air bases in Turkey. It was also by no means a fortuitous incident that, during July, Turkey re-legalized the growing of opium, prohibited some years earlier in deference to American wishes. Besides the legally controlled Turkish crop, there had been extra, illegal cultivation; and the view at the earlier time was that it was easier to control a totally illegal situation than one which was partly legal, partly not.

During the rest of the year Turkey consolidated her hold of the north by announcing plans for the expansion of Turkish-Cypriot agriculture and industry, including a Turkish-Cypriot oil company; and there have since been suggestions that Turks from the mainland have been settled in Cyprus in order to raise the pre-1974 proportion of Turkish Cypriots, which was about 18 per cent. A referendum held in June 1975 among Turkish Cypriots both in the north and in the south produced a 99 per cent majority (with a turnout of 70 per cent) in favour of a separate Turkish Cypriot state, that could, if necessary, form a federated unit alongside a similar Greek Cypriot

state. This was countered by Greek Cypriots, who now propose a multi-unit single state, the units to have an ethnic base, and the Turks, as a minority, would have only a small number of these. Effective power of decision, however, remains largely in Turkish hands.

Elsewhere, the two major and fundamental problems of the Middle East continued to rumble on: the Arab-Israeli confrontation, and the matter of oil revenues. A distinctly new element this year is, however, a distinct shift of position by the U.S.A. Whether or not this could be regarded as deriving from the importance of the Arabs as oil producers, it became clear during the year that America was no longer to be regarded as the single-minded champion of Israel, and, in the words of President Ford, a re-assessment of American policy in the Middle East could be expected. Over the last few months pressure has been put on Israel by the U.S. to make an interim peace agreement with Egypt and Syria. An essential first element in this policy of *détente* would be pulling back by the Israeli forces from the western Sinai, where they now hold the two strategically commanding routes through the centre of the Peninsula. In return, some, possibly three, years of peace would be offered during which longer term agreements could be negotiated. This new "even-handed" American policy, put during a partly inconclusive period of shuttle diplomacy by Dr. Kissinger, and received with dismay and some anger in Israeli circles, led to Israeli withdrawal in March from the talks with Egypt, and indicates a distinct shift not only in American, but in world opinion generally. There is now a greater disposition to appreciate the Arab point of view, and a corresponding view of Israel as intransigent. This may be a crude piece of geopolitical response deriving from the world situation, or it may, hopefully, be an attempt to see the Arab-Israeli issue in better perspective—but its appearance is a very clear and definite part of 1974–75. It is currently the Israeli hope to receive specific U.S. support on particular issues: financial and military supplies, and diplomatic backing; in return, Israel would seem at the time of writing prepared to make concessions in the Sinai (*see* Late Information, page xx).

In mid-1974 there was considerable apprehension over the impact on world economy of the higher prices for oil: would the new wealth swamp world markets? Wild statements such as "there may not be enough money in the world to meet the new prices", and fears expressed of massive "Arab" share and property take-overs produced a few weeks of alarm in the West; but since the summer of 1974 it has been clearly shown on the one hand that the OPEC states are determined to use their wealth wisely and moderately, and on the other, in the light of this moderation, that the world currency system can absorb the new funds. In very general terms, some 30–40 per cent of the new wealth has been retained at home to be applied to internal development; another third (estimated in January 1975 at U.S. $4,000 to 5,000 million) has been placed abroad in long- or short-term loans, or through minority purchase of equity stocks (for example, in Lonhro, Nippon Steel, or Krupp), in sound property ownership, and on short-term deposit (chiefly in London, where interest rates are highest). The remainder of oil funds has been offered for foreign development: loans on a large scale to other less wealthy Middle Eastern countries (especially Egypt), and as aid to Third World states. Thus the massive penetration and takeovers feared by some a year ago have not materialized, though some capital has moved into western industry (for example, Britain borrowed $1,200 million from Iran for her nationalized industries, and Italy negotiated a $3,000 million "oil for technology" deal with Iraq). Some resistance to OPEC investment has occurred in the U.S.A., where bankers have attempted to block OPEC buying of stocks, and the Government has introduced legislation to protect military defence industries from foreign share participation.

The year has also seen a marked trend for oil-producing states to increase their own shareholding in producer companies. In some instances there has been total takeover by decree (Bapco of Bahrain and Kuwait companies, both in March 1975), and some partial (though majority) acquisition designed in certain cases as a preliminary stage to total ownership. Aims differ: some governments prefer full nationalization (for example, Libya), whereas others remain content with a partial holding because they are not in a position to handle technical and "downstream" problems: the United Arab Emirates demanded total control of their oil companies late in 1974 but altered this to a partial participation in April 1975.

Going "downstream" in the oil industry has so far mainly meant setting up tanker operations—for example, in Abu Dhabi, Kuwait and Libya. But there is already a 15–20 per cent world surplus of tanker capacity, with many idle ships moored off the Gulf coasts—though the special privileged position as producer/owner may count for a good deal. Price rises for oil came into effect on December 20th, aiming at the reduction of operating company profits, which had greatly risen with the increase of oil prices generally in 1973–74. As well, companies were in some instances subjected to higher local taxation. At present, opinion among producer governments is divided as to the feasibility of further increases, with, for example, Iran much in favour and Saudi Arabia not. Middle Eastern states also hold strongly that the fourfold price rise of 1974 was largely to counter price rises in imports from outside, which, comprising essential imports of capital goods, machinery, vehicles and foodstuffs, had become much more costly, though gradually. Raising of oil prices is consequently merely a form of indexing to keep pace with the terms of trade that until 1973 worked very much to the detriment of the OPEC states. This is clearly the view, for instance, of the Shah of Iran.

Parallel with these price changes, there has been a sharp decline in oil production: 3 per cent overall by the end of 1974, and now between 15–20 per cent, with further falls occurring (up to 25 per cent) in May–June 1975. This is in response to various factors: overproduction generating revenues that could not be absorbed (as declared by Qatar in April); deliberate reduction made by western oil companies to induce concessions by national governments (for example, in the U.A.E., February); desire to conserve stocks which might well become even more valuable in a period of world monetary inflation (Kuwait, Libya); and response to a general fall-off in world demand, estimated by mid-1975 (following two mild winters) at 17 per cent. Another response to the changed financial situation is the desire of the Middle Eastern states to avoid dependence on the American dollar, which for various reasons has shown increasing weakness over the past two years. In February 1975 Iran valued the rial in terms of SDRs instead of the U.S. dollar, and in the following month Saudi Arabia followed suit, with Kuwait revaluing its dinar in terms of six international currencies rather than the dollar.

One small facet of the confrontation between consumers and producers of petroleum emerged in January 1975, when a few loquacious officers of the Sixth U.S. Fleet, eagerly reported by French TV and American news magazines, hinted at possible contingency plans involving military action by the U.S. to take over, by invasion, certain Middle Eastern oilfields. Though relatively little attention was paid to these remarks in Europe and the U.S., the impact in certain Gulf states (Kuwait especially, which had been mentioned as a target) was considerable. Perhaps the incident was merely indicative of strained nerves; perhaps there was more to it and there *is* a plan. It has left some unpleasantness and mistrust that will take time to dissipate, and maybe we should classify the whole incident as Talleyrand might have done— worse than a crime, a blunder.

The shift in Egyptian policy away from Soviet links continued at an accelerating pace during the year. The visit of President Ford to the Middle East, later talks between President Ford and President Sadat in Salzburg (June 1st–2nd) with suggestions (not yet fully substantiated) of very considerable U.S. aid to Egypt, produced Soviet reaction postponing the projected visit of Mr. Breznev to Egypt (June 4th), and closer Soviet cultivation of relations with Libya. The tortuous pattern of Egyptian-Libyan relations took a distinctly graver turn during the year, reaching what was described as "almost breaking point" in April, with both countries hurling abuse, general and personal, at each other, and one head of state describing his opposite number as "a psychiatric case, a terrorist". Egyptian anger was further roused when, after acute disappointment during the year over the scale and quality of arms supplied by the U.S.S.R. to Egypt (and the financial terms proposed), the U.S.S.R. negotiated a massive arms deal with Libya during May following a personal visit by the Soviet Prime Minister, Mr. Kosygin. Previously, Egyptian-Libyan tension had grown over a variety of issues: accusations by Libya that Egypt, in negotiating with Israel and the Americans, was "selling out" the Arab cause; the minor but extra irritant of Libya supporting the Turks over Cyprus, whilst Egypt, conscious of its commercial links with the Greek south, was much more pro-Greek Cypriot; treatments of respective nationals in each other's country—both complained of discrimination and harassment; and finally, the reopening of the Suez Canal, described by Libya as "treason to the Arab cause". Further, Libya was accused by Egypt of fomenting civil unrest within Egypt, and an assassination plot against President Sadat, with further designs to detach the western desert area and incorporate it in Libya. Counter-accusations were made of Egyptian espionage through the large numbers of Egyptian professionals working in Libya, and of a subversion plot in reverse, so to speak, aimed at taking over eastern Libya with its oilfields. In short, from the honeymoon of projected union of only a year or two ago, Egyptian-Libyan affairs have reached the lowest level possible short of actual hostilities.

Economically, Egypt has in some ways experienced a good year. Loans on a massive scale were offered: from the OPEC states (chiefly but not entirely Iran and Kuwait), from various European countries, including Yugoslavia, and from the U.S., which according to a London report on June 3rd offered $2,000 million as an aid fund. In consequence, extensive plans have been drawn up to develop industry in the lower Delta area, and resettle the devastated towns along the Gulf of Suez; and Iranian sources announced that another sum of $2,000 million would be invested in trade and industrial activities in the Port Said area, including participation in the proposed Suez-Port Said oil pipeline.

The reopening of the Suez Canal on June 5th after eight years of closure was a further fillip to Egypt; and it was significant that the only foreign vessel to take part in the formal ceremony was an American cruiser, whilst the Iranian Crown Prince with two Iranian vessels was in the first north-bound convoy. Canal dues are set at approximately 90 per cent above 1967 rates, and within one month Egypt had received nearly $15 million in transit royalties. A somewhat less favourable matter was that, despite the movement of Egyptian policy towards the capitalist West, designed, in the words of President Sadat, "to counter-act the excesses of socialist nationalization under the Nasser régime", little foreign capital of a private nature has been invested in Egypt.

Within Libya there has been a somewhat confused pattern of events. The embargo on sales of oil to the U.S. was lifted, but royalties generally declined —by at one time as much as 25 per cent. Overall, however, Libya had a record trade surplus. Colonel Gaddafi has demonstrated at times an extreme pro-Moslem and pro-radical attitude: over Cyprus, as we have seen; as a major supporter of the Palestine Liberation Front, in sharp rejection of any negotiation with Israel; and latterly, in Oman. The Libyan Prime Minister stated in June that, unless British, Iranian and Jordanian elements fighting with Omani government forces against dissidents in Dhofar withdrew,

Libya would intervene. Considerable point was added to this statement by the massive arms deal negotiated during May with the U.S.S.R. (as mentioned above), which according to President Sadat involved the sum of $12,000 million and would entail the build-up for 20 years at least of Soviet military and technical personnel to train Libyans in the use of the highly sophisticated weapons promised. With the opening of the Suez Canal, and the establishment of a Soviet base at Berbera at the southern end of the approaches to the Red Sea, it is now possible to see how intervention in Dhofar might be possible: by no means good news for Oman. During June it was also stated that the U.S.S.R. had agreed to supply a nuclear reactor to Libya, in order to produce power for irrigation, using reserves of water known to occur at depth in various parts of Libya. Continuing its programme of socialist austerity, the Government confiscated all recordings of western popular music on sale in Tripoli.

Another small-scale but none the less acute issue of the past year was the fate of the Kurds. As a minority within three states, the Kurds have had particularly difficult relations with Iraq, claiming autonomy and at least partial self rule in what is one of the richest areas of Iraq—the oilfield area round Kirkuk. After many years of minor disturbance punctuated by temporary settlements, the Iraq Government undertook a major military campaign during the winter to reduce Kurdish armed revolt. Hitherto the Kurds have had support—moral and in small arms—from Iran, with which Iraq has had strained relations for over 40 years. One principal element in this coolness was the frontier between Iraq and Iran, which, lying along the eastern bank of the Shatt el Arab and not down the centre of the channel (the thalweg) has increasingly hampered Iranian port development in this area. Suddenly it was announced that adjustments to the frontier would be made in Iran's favour, closer to the thalweg; and simultaneously Iran ceased to support the Kurds and closed her frontier in the area of fighting, thus cutting off sources of military and other supplies to the Kurds, who could no longer offer effective resistance to the Iraqi forces. Kurdistan was overrun early in 1975, and some 10,000 Kurds are said to have died in these operations, together with civilians who attempted to cross the mountains and died of privation at the severest time of winter. Over 90,000 Kurdish refugees may have remained in Iran at the end of June.

Iraq had further disputes on her hands: one in the south with Kuwait over frontier details, partly on land and partly at the entrance to the Shatt el Arab. Accommodation over these difficulties was announced in June. The other dispute concerns Syria and her use of the waters of the Euphrates river. With the completion of a massive barrage at Tabqa above the Syria-Iraqi frontier, river-flow has been greatly reduced, to the marked detriment of Iraqi irrigated agriculture. Matters reached a crisis during April, with troop movements on both sides to the Euphrates area; but the issue was referred to an emergency meeting of Arab League Ministers, and, following mediation by Saudi Arabia, a *modus vivendi* has been worked out. During the year economic prospects in Iraq (despite the Euphrates difficulty) markedly improved; and at the same time there has been a slight drift towards improvement of economic relations with non-communist states, France especially, and a corresponding move away from the previous very close dependence on the U.S.S.R.

Prospects of better things also appeared in the Sudan. The régime of President Nimeiri, increasingly strongly based, is consequently more able to exercise a firm policy of balance and selectivity between "western" economic patterns and the reliance upon the U.S.S.R. that had been a feature of the recent past. As a result, the wealthier OPEC states, conscious of the limited opportunities for agriculture in their own countries, are now beginning to make serious appraisals of agricultural potential in the Sudan as a source of food and industrial materials, given its enormous unused areas of well-watered, fertile soil. As a preliminary, the long-delayed scheme of improving the sudd (marsh) areas of the Nile by a major diversion canal at Jonglei now looks like achieving reality.

Apprehension was felt throughout the Middle East when King Faisal of Saudi Arabia was assassinated on March 25th by a member of his own family; but it soon became clear that no international or factional conspiracy was involved. Nevertheless, the loss to Saudi Arabia and the Middle East generally is considerable. Monarchy came to an end during the year in Ethiopia with the deposition of the Emperor Haile Sellassie on September 12th by a revolutionary Armed Forces Committee. For some time impatience had been manifest at the unprogressive rule of the Emperor, and combined with severe regional drought during 1973–75 in many parts produced severe tension, exacerbated by misuse of relief funds, and a Christian-Moslem confrontation in the Awash and Afar regions of the north and east.

In great contrast, Iran demonstrated massive economic advancement and stability. For some years annual growth has exceeded 15–20 per cent; but this is estimated for last year at 43 per cent. In political terms there is a considerable spin-off in that Iran is more and more accepted as a dominant unit and major patron of the whole Middle East: what other Moslem country could openly recognize and trade with Israel, and yet be gratefully counted a pillar of Moslem Asia? Saudi Arabia, with broadly equivalent income, has a far smaller population, whilst Egypt and Turkey, with similar sized populations, are much less prosperous, and grateful for Iranian loans. By settling a number of border disputes including an accommodation with Turkey to assist in development of communications and raw materials supplies, Iran has emerged as leader and patron of a wide area, by no means confined to the Gulf. Western countries have shown eagerness as suppliers and as minority participants in Iranian business and industry (with West Germany and the U.S.A. in the lead). However, with the recent drop in oil exports (currently down nearly

20 per cent), development cannot continue at its recent headlong rate; and on June 15th Iran announced a system of priorities and cutbacks in development projects: otherwise, the Plan Organization Direction stated, Iran would have a shortfall of income within a very few years.

A crisis of considerable importance, which could conceivably destroy the country, developed in the Lebanon during April. Originally formed as an independent state in the 1940s to recognize majority Christian Arab aspirations, the Lebanon has so far survived as a remarkable example of religious tolerance, economic *laisser faire*, and political democracy. A complex *modus vivendi* was worked out which gives major political influence to Christian groups whilst allowing effective power sharing with Moslems and others. As a result, though lacking major economic resources other than reasonable rainfall and scenic attraction, the Lebanon has built up a remarkably high standard of living. However, the remarkable consensus underlying this has recently shown ominous signs of breaking down. It is now clear (though no real census of population has taken place for over 30 years) that Moslems are now in a majority; and it is also apparent that, whilst certain areas (mainly but not solely Christian) are relatively well off, other parts, particularly the Shi'a Moslem extreme south, are not, with conspicuously lower living standards that appear all the more striking when set against the prosperous centre round Beirut, and even the Israelis to the south.

Besides these growing internal problems, there are external ones—the pressure of many Palestinian refugees who form bases for Moslem guerrilla activities, particularly in the south adjacent to Israel, and in the relatively remote north-east, close to Syria—both predominantly Moslem areas. Counter-guerrilla strikes by Israel across the frontier in response to Arab terrorist acts in Israel have become more numerous, especially during the past year: villages and crops are damaged and random civilian deaths occur. Parts of south Lebanon are thus becoming a "no-man's land" as the result of these attacks from Israel on what Israelis describe as "Palestinian terror bases" that also attract militant Arab support from outside.

During April fighting broke out chiefly in Beirut between Phalangist (i.e., Christian) groups and Palestinians on the issue of whether the dominant (and elected) Christian groups were to remain in control of the country, or whether the Lebanon could be increasingly mobilized as a base by Palestinian dissidents in order to carry on the struggle with Israel. After an uneasy truce, fighting broke out again in May, this time mostly between Lebanese (generally right wing) and groups of left wing connection, some with non-Lebanese affiliations: for example, Syrian Socialists and Nasserists. A third phase of fighting which began towards the end of June seemed more to be a direct confrontation between left and right, with far more bloodshed and deliberate destruction of property, especially the luxurious kind, of which there is a good deal round Beirut. Some 300–400 are reported killed, and several thousand severely injured in this last period of warfare, to which more significance attaches than to the others, not so much because of the higher number of casualties (which so far exceed those suffered in the previous sectarian violence in the 1950s and 60s, but for two underlying aspects. The first is that for the first time in Lebanon, intercommunity fighting was in its latest (and bitterest) phase more on a class basis (i.e., rich and poor) rather than on purely sectarian lines; the second distinctive factor is that the scale of weaponry used suggests outside subvention and support: quite possibly from Libya, Iraq and Syria in support of the left, and from the U.S.A. on the right, where many Lebanese Christian emigrants now live, and in quite a number of cases maintain Lebanese nationality.

A final point on the year in the Middle East must be that, as well as being undoubtedly the most prosperous ever (for many), it was also the one in which more armaments—and in particular of a very sophisticated kind—were bought than ever before. Between 25–30 per cent of many national incomes now goes on weapons and defence systems, with higher figures in some states; and the Middle East is now the main world buyer. One-third of all production from major suppliers (certainly the U.S.A. and probably the U.S.S.R.) now finds its way to the Middle East, accompanied, as has been admitted in one instance, by bribery. As well, four countries: Egypt, Iran, Israel and Libya have or are likely to have nuclear energy plants—devoted wholly of course so far to peaceful uses. Preparations for war, civil and external, are understandably but regrettably taking an increased share of the higher incomes of Middle Eastern states.

Second Interim Peace Agreement Between Egypt and Israel

After several days of shuttle diplomacy by the U.S. Secretary of State, Dr. Henry Kissinger, a second interim peace agreement between Egypt and Israel was initialled on September 1st, 1975, and signed in Geneva three days later. Both Egypt and Israel agreed to refrain from using force during the three years of the agreement.

Israel agreed to evacuate about 2,590 square miles of occupied Sinai, including the Abu Rudais oilfields and the Mitla and Giddi passes. (The position of the Mitla and Giddi passes can be seen on the map of the January 1974 disengagement agreement on page 63.) Israel agreed to withdraw to the eastern end of the Mitla and Giddi passes, but to the south the boundary line will run across the mountains, giving Israel defensive positions on the high ground. In order to regain the Abu Rudais oilfields Egypt will occupy a narrow coastal strip along the Gulf of Suez from the area around Sudr to Abu Rudais. As in the previous agreement a UN buffer zone will be interposed between two limited-force zones. This does not apply, however, to the strip of land between Sudr and Abu Rudais, which will be under Egyptian civilian administration.

Practical questions of implementing the agreement will be worked out in Geneva and incorporated in a protocol which is to become an integral part of the agreement.

The U.S.A. undertook to provide 200 civilian technicians to supervise and man early-warning stations for both sides.

Free passage of non-military cargoes through the Suez Canal to or from Israel is guaranteed. Egypt also renounces the use of blockades.

The agreement states that the UN Emergency Force is essential and shall continue its functions and its mandate shall be extended annually. It is reported that a secret clause adds that this will continue for at least three years. Egypt and Israel are also establishing a joint military commission to resolve any differences in implementation of the pact.

The agreement concludes by stating that it is regarded by the parties "as a significant step towards a just and lasting peace. It is not a final peace agreement. The parties shall continue their efforts to negotiate a final peace agreement within the framework of the Geneva Peace Conference in accordance with Security Council Resolution 338" (*see* Documents on Palestine, page 60).

PART ONE

General Survey

The Middle East and North Africa:
An Introduction

W. B. Fisher

Definition of the Area

The term, "Middle East and North Africa" is a cumbersome, and, possibly to some, even a misleading description. Besides already embracing part of northern Africa, "Middle East" has the further objection of meaning different things to different people. Some would apply it to areas much farther east, and not to Africa at all—which is geographically more logical—but then Libya and Egypt would no longer be in the "Middle East", a nonsense for some others. Perhaps only when we come to consider alternatives do the merits, such as they are, of our present title begin to emerge. "Muslim World" is too extensive in that it could reach as far as Pakistan, Malaysia and Indonesia; whilst reference to "Arab" only would exclude Turkey, Iran, Cyprus (80 per cent Greek) and, logically to one way of thinking, the Berber areas of Tunisia, Algeria and Morocco.

We can trace popular use of "Middle East" back to the Second World War. It developed in a casual, almost haphazard, manner following the territorial expansion of a unified military command that was originally based on countries lying east of the Suez Canal. In this way, the British and American publics grew accustomed to the association of Jerusalem, Damascus, Cairo and then Benghazi and even Tripoli with the collective description "Middle East" (now increasingly shortened in America, to "Mid East"); and, in the writer's view, the expression has come to have a validity based on popular usage which it is now difficult to challenge. There are, however, numerous geographers and historians who are unwilling to abandon the older concept of southern Asia as divisible into a Near, Middle and Far East; and in 1946 the Royal Geographical Society protested against the British Government's continued official usage of "Middle East" to indicate Palestine, Egypt and countries further west. If we talk of a Middle East, the logical argument runs, there is also implied a Near East; and in fact this term was once in great vogue, as referring to the territories along the seaboard of the eastern Mediterranean. It was, moreover, a useful collective geographical description for the lands of the former Ottoman Empire.

However, usage of "Middle East" in the present volume may be justified on several grounds. (a) Few definitions of a Near East ever agreed—some authors extended it eastwards to include Afghanistan, others terminated it at the coastal ranges of Syria and Palestine; and some included Egypt, whilst others did not. (b) "Near East" is convenient to apply, in an historical sense only, to the now defunct Ottoman Empire. (c) Nowadays, for the English-speaking public at least, the term "Middle East" would have no validity if applied, in a strictly logical sense, to Afghanistan, Pakistan and India. (d) The term can be taken as denoting a single geographical area in which occur broadly similar features of physical environment and ways of life.

We thus arrive at the definition of the Middle East as given on the title-page of earlier editions of this volume—the highland countries of Turkey and Iran; Cyprus; the Arab-speaking states of the eastern Mediterranean seaboard; Israel; the Arabian peninsula; the valley of the Tigris-Euphrates (chiefly but not entirely comprising Iraq), the Nile Valley (Egypt, and also Sudan); and Libya. This, in no sense an ideal or unassailable solution, has at least considerable sanction in popular usage and technical utility. Subsequently, the addition of chapters on north-western Africa and on Afghanistan has extended the range of the present volume beyond many but by no means all of the numerous definitions of the "Middle East" which have been proposed. North-western Africa (Tunisia, Algeria and Morocco) spoken of by Arab geographers as "Jeziret al Maghreb" ("island of the west", or "setting sun"), or usually nowadays just "Maghreb" ("west"), surrounded as it is to the south by deserts and on its remaining sides by sea, may be looked on in many ways as linked to the Middle East both by environment and culture, whilst retaining something of the separateness indicated by the term "island".

Physical Background

STRUCTURE

Geologically speaking, the entire area can be regarded as deriving from two distinct provinces. The south consists largely of continental massifs (increasingly spoken of today as "plates") that would appear once to have been joined in one large mass, known as Gondwanaland. To the north of this mass there has been throughout most geological time a trough or geosyncline. This, a zone of crustal weakness, has mostly been occupied by deep seas of varying extent (at some periods more extensive than now) and in these seas lived the immense numbers of living creatures whose bodies after death decayed to form the oil deposits now so characteristic of the central Middle East. Alternate periods of quiescence and geological disturbance occurred. During quiescent phases, material eroded from the neighbouring continental masses accumulated in the oceanic deeps of the geosyncline, rapidly covering the fatty bodies of dead sea organisms to allow petroleum formation; then periods of contraction occurred, heaving up marine sediments in enormous flexures or fold-structures to produce mountain chains. Sometimes the flexures were relatively simple, like hogs' backs; in other instances they were much more intense, giving rise to tightly packed, highly distorted folds, with extremes where shearing and total deformation of the structures produced an overthrust ("nappe") rather than a recognizable fold.

From various parts of the geosyncline has emerged a great series of fold-mountain chains that are traceable from Western Europe and North-West Africa as far as Northern India. This is the so-called "Alpine" or Tertiary fold system, since it is the latest in geological time of three major mountain-building periods. The Pyrenees and Sierra Nevada of Spain, the Alps, Appennines, and Carpathians in Europe, and the massive Atlas Mountains of Africa are all part of this system. Further east many of the mountain chains of Asia Minor, the Caucasus, the Zagros and Elburz Ranges of Iran, and the complex of ridges that form the Afghan Pamir are all part of this "Alpine" system—geologically young in age, and relatively uneroded and therefore high in altitude.

This is by no means the whole story. Besides the actual fold ranges, simple and complex, there are often embedded between them portions of older, more resistant structures. Some of these are remnants of the first two mountain building phases: Palaeozoic (or Caledonian) and Mesozoic (Hercynian), the latter now being found extensively in central Europe. Parts of these remnant structures, certainly of Hercynian age and possibly also Caledonian, are found in western Morocco, the central Atlas, Asia Minor, the interior of Iran, and western Afghanistan. One cannot trace any simple pattern in the arrangement of the folds, which may occur in straight parallel ranks, or sinuous arcs and garlands that may alter trend abruptly.

North Africa is a good example of the complexity of conditions. Generally speaking, the entire highland zone consists of a series of parallel-fold mountain chains of Tertiary age running east-west or north-east/south-west, and separated by tablelands or narrow trough-like valleys. In the extreme west, however, areas of Palaeozoic and Mesozoic remnant structures are prominent. The whole mountain system is higher and wider in the west (Morocco) and diminishes considerably in width towards the east (Tunisia), as well as declining in height. Much discussion centres on how far the Tertiary Atlas fold structures can be regarded as continuations of the fold mountains of southern Spain and Italy: whether there is in fact an almost continuous ring of folds enclosing the entire western Mediterranean basin, and breached only by the Straits of Gibraltar and the narrows between Tunis, Sicily and Italy.

Somewhat different conditions obtain in Asia Minor, where much larger interior plateaux, often eroded into sumps or basins, are surrounded by Tertiary fold ranges. Of this kind are the Taurus and Anti-Taurus Ranges of the south, and the coastal ranges of the north, which continue into the Caucasus and Iranian mountains. Within Iran the interior basins (composed in part of Hercynian nuclei) are even more developed,

so that, with minor variations, the whole country can be regarded as saucer-shaped, a rim of Tertiary fold mountains very clearly framing and defining a series of interior basins—which are hardly plains, since most are above 2,000 ft. in altitude.

Further east still, in Afghanistan, the Tertiary folds again develop into enormous dominating ridges that bunch together eastwards and northwards to form a formidable, though relatively narrow, mountain complex that presents a major barrier between central and southern Asia. The first portion of it is the Pamir "knot"—a "swag" or bunch of mountain ranges enclosing tenuous and restricted valleys. Intervening blocks or interior plateaux, present in the west on a small scale, disappear entirely towards the east, with topography passing unbroken into the main Himalaya.

The southern geological province of the Middle East contrasts markedly with that of the north as just described. It consists essentially of the platform (or basement) of extremely ancient rocks, some amongst the oldest known in the world (Precambrian and Archaean). These—chiefly granites, schists and quartzites—most likely once made up the enormous Gondwana continent, which included much of Australia, southern India, Arabia, most of Africa, and parts of South America. Whilst generally rigid and resistant to the pressures that rucked up the sediments of the geosyncline, this ancient mass was from time to time, especially on its northern fringe, overrun by shallow seas, which deposited thin, often horizontal layers of limestones and sandstones. In addition, wind- and water-eroded silts and sands from the surface became consolidated in similar thin, level strata. Thus the basement area of the south, whilst generally flat and fairly uniform in character, is not wholly so, since much of its surface is covered by these deposits, which erode differentially, the harder bands standing out as ridges and the less resistant as vales. The whole aspect of this southern basement/platform is one of a vast open plateau diversified here and there by small-scale hill-systems and shallow valleys. Much is occupied by sand deposits in the form of major dunes or as irregular shifting masses—the "sand-seas" of the Sahara and inner Arabia.

One major feature of considerable importance—part, in fact, of a world-wide process—is the drift apart of the two major platforms of Arabia and Africa, which once, as noted, formed a single larger continent. Extensive fissuring (faulting) in the area of the Red Sea and Gulf of Aden led to the separation of Arabia from northern Africa and the tilting of the entire block of Arabia, uplifting the west (Red Sea coast) and downwarping the east (Persian/Arabian Gulf). At first, the foundering of the Red Sea trough was thought to represent a simple rifting process—the downletting of a segment between two parallel sets of faults. Latest research suggests, however, that the situation is somewhat more involved. Once crustal weakness developed through fissuring and rifting, the sea floor of the Red Sea began to "spread", due to the rise of deep-seated strata from the lower parts of the earth's crust. In this way, Arabia and Africa were forced apart, a process that may well still be continuing.

Sketch of structural elements.

The zone of fissuring and faulting continues southwards into the Great Rift Valley of East Africa, and northwards on a diminishing scale through the Jordan valley, the Lebanon and western Syria as far as southern Turkey.

The areas where extensive folding and fissuring occur (e.g. the Maghreb, Asia Minor, Iran and Afghanistan, with offshoots into Syria, Lebanon, Jordan and Israel) are obviously zones of crustal weakness, where from time to time adjustment and movement take place, giving rise to earthquakes of varying severity. Minor tremors are frequent (they are described for the Jordan area in the Bible), and in the Istanbul area as many as fifty to one hundred minor tremors are recorded per year. At longer intervals severer shocks of greater amplitude occur, causing on occasion severe loss of life. The latest, killing nearly 1,000, occurred in southern Iran early in 1972. Another feature of these zones of weakness has been the rise of liquid magma from the interior of the earth. Amongst the northern fold ranges enormous volcanic cones have been formed, producing the highest peaks in the Middle East (Mt. Ararat, 17,000 ft., Mt. Demavend, 19,000 ft.). Farther south, in Syria, Jordan, Libya and parts of southern Algeria, the lava has emerged in sheets rather than cones, and whole areas are covered by basalt of very recent deposition, giving a barren, desolate, and inhospitable landscape. Despite this widespread extension of lava outpourings in geologically very recent times, there are today, however, no really active volcanoes in the Middle East, although in a number of areas there are still emissions of hot gases and mud—the last phases of igneous activity.

Within the last five to seven years, a novel concept has been worked out that explains many, but not all, of the geological features of the area. This is the idea of "plate tectonics", now accepted widely in Britain, but with more reserve by American geologists. The continents are regarded as comprising a stiff, but rather shallow, brittle "plate". From time to time, differential heating at depth in the earth's crust, due to phases of radioactivity, generates "convection currents" in the relatively plastic deep layers. The surface plates overlying the plastic layers (the continents) are then cracked from below by these currents, and there occurs a process termed sea-floor spreading, where, along the central line of some major seas and oceans, an upwelling of plastic material gradually takes place, forcing the continental masses apart. These "plate movements" are thought to have occurred very rapidly as geological time goes, producing tearing apart and the opening of new seas in some areas (e.g., the Red Sea and Gulf of Aden) and impinging of plates one against another—over-riding, crushing and shattering, and in so doing producing fold mountain ranges, sunken troughs and garland structures that are so characteristic of the Middle East. Supporters of the plate tectonics theory believe that one original large plate comprising most of what is now Arabia, Egypt and the Sudan was first cracked by convectional currents in the lower earth mantle to produce a number of smaller plates.

Two of these were forced westwards, producing first a narrow Red Sea trough which was rapidly enlarged by spreading along its floor to its present size. Then further migration of the second, more southerly plate, this time more southward, as well as westward, produced the Gulf of Aden; and the process still continues, with Africa still drifting away south and west from Arabia. The Arabian plate itself may be impinging northwards against a larger Asian plate: it is certainly downtilted from west to east, giving the shallow Persian Gulf and Gulf of Oman; and it is sometimes believed that impingement of these two plates with the Arabian one driven down under the Asian one can be held to have given rise to the Zagros fold mountains. Asia Minor equally is regarded as a smaller plate that is being pushed or "extruded" westwards between larger plates to the north and southwest, thus producing the tectonic weakness lines already mentioned as characterizing Asia Minor. Part of the same process has also produced a lateral shear in the Jordan valley area, where according to proponents of the plate theory, the plate west of Jordan (mainly present-day Israel) has been displaced southwards by 60–80 miles in relation to the plate now forming the eastern Jordan area.

Minerals

Often associated with volcanic outpourings, especially in the north, are veins of metallic minerals, antimony, cobalt, chromium, copper, iron, lead, molybdenum, silver and zinc—and also asbestos, barytes, coal, and emery, together with marble which is produced by the "baking" of strata by underground heat. These minerals are fairly widespread, and important new discoveries have been made over the last few years, so that the total reserves in some instances (copper at Chesmeh in Iran, iron in Egypt and Syria) are now far higher than was at one time thought likely. Often, however, individual deposits tend to be of irregular occurrence, of varying quality, and sometimes in remote, difficult districts. The lack of fuel for treatment has also been a disadvantage, so that commercial exploitation has not always been possible. On the other hand, rises in world prices since 1940 and again in the 1970s have had a highly stimulating effect. World shortages, or threats of shortage, plus political attitudes (e.g., over Rhodesia and Chile) have led to increased interest in Middle Eastern minerals. Moreover, local governments will sometimes prefer to exploit national resources at higher cost rather than be dependent upon imports. Hence mineral exploitation has growing importance, with Turkey ranking second as a world producer of chromium and Cyprus a significant producer of asbestos, copper and iron ore. Egypt has recently begun to develop on an extensive scale the important iron deposits near Aswan, using hydro-electric power from the High Dam; and other iron deposits occur between the Nile Valley and the north-west coast of the Red Sea, and in the Behariya oasis due west of the Nile. Another important discovery of iron not yet producing is at Rajo, near Aleppo, in Syria. North Africa is distinctly richer in minerals than most of the Middle East proper. Besides extensive deposits of phosphate (which make Morocco the second largest world producer), there are important deposits of iron ore, with smaller, but highly significant quantities of lead, zinc, antimony, cobalt, molybdenum and barytes.

Elsewhere in the Middle East, other mineral resources are found, but on a scale somewhat smaller than in North Africa: phosphate in Israel, Jordan and Syria—all of these deposits are exploited commercially; manganese in the Sinai peninsula; and small deposits of copper and natural gas in Israel. There is increasing use of soluble salts found in such lakes as the Dead Sea and the Wadi Natrun west of Cairo, chiefly (in the case of the Dead Sea) as sources of bromine. Very small quantities of alluvial gold are still produced, mainly from Saudi Arabia.

On the southern flanks of the fold mountains, rock strata are tilted into great domes, in which have accumulated the vast deposits of petroleum that now make the Middle East the leading oil province in the world with some 60 per cent of proven world reserves. The vast bulk of this—over half the world's oil—lies around and under the shores of the Persian/Arabian Gulf. More will be said later about these deposits, but it may here be noted that the occurrence of oil is closely dependent upon a certain kind of geological structure. There must be first an alternation of porous and impermeable strata, with the latter uppermost so as to act as a seal, and prevent the oil from running away; and there must also be a slight degree of disturbance enough to produce the domes in which the oil can collect, but not sufficient to produce cracks which will allow oil to escape. Such factors can explain why oil is restricted in occurrence to a few zones, and why its discovery is such a chancy affair, with many disappointments—for every boring that produces oil, at least nine others are made without success.

CLIMATE

One basic reason for the distinctive character of the Middle East and North Africa is the special and unusual climate. Most parts of the world experience their rainfall either mostly during summer (the warm season) or distributed throughout the year. Only in a very few areas is there a maximum in winter (the cold season). This is the so-called "Mediterranean" climate, giving a long intensely hot summer, and a relatively mild, rainy winter, with occasional cold spells. The distinction does not seem very important, but it "conditions" plant life to a remarkable degree, and thus also agriculture and general ways of life. Native plants "rest" in the hot season, not in the cold one, which is the opposite to what happens in cooler temperate climates. Some indigenous plants, such as cereals, mature quickly in order to complete a rapid growth cycle before the onset of hot weather; others, chiefly bulbs, flower in spring or autumn; whilst some, such as the citrus, bear fruit in winter. All this has a marked effect on agricultural routines and general living habits. One obvious result is the summer "siesta", which involves breaking the day into two rest periods, with a very early morning start, and continuance of work well into the evening.

Weather conditions are dominated by the long, hot and dry summer, which then quickly gives way to a relatively rainy winter that is mild near the coast but can be surprisingly cold inland. Autumn is warm and sunny, and spring changeable and liable to cold spells —both are short, merely intermediate, seasons. Because of the absence of cloud during summer (away from the coast there can be days without any cloud whatever) the sun beats down uninterruptedly, and the temperatures reached are far higher than those at the Equator. Day maxima of 100° to 115° F. are usual, and a figure of over 125° F. is known. Parts of the interior of Arabia, Algeria, Libya and Iran may experience the highest temperatures occurring in the world.

In winter, though frost is uncommon actually at sea level, the land interior can be cold, especially at higher altitudes. Snow can fall as far south as central Morocco and Algeria, Aswan, the Yemen A.R. and southern Iran, whilst the presence of high mountains has the effect of intensifying winter cold. The plateaux of Turkey and Iran in particular, and to a slightly lesser degree of the Atlas region, experience severe winters, with several months of frost, and up to 120 days of snow cover—a reminder of their geographical position adjacent respectively to Russia and to Spain, which is surprisingly cold in winter. Considerable seasonal change is thus the keynote of Middle Eastern climate, with 40° to 50° F. of temperature range between one part of the year and another (cf. the 26° F. range in London). Wide changes of temperature as between day and night are also characteristic of the interior, but not close to the coast.

The second characteristic of Middle Eastern climate is the scantiness and irregularity of rainfall (*see* pages 8 and 9). Much of the entire region has less than 10 ins. (250 mm.) annually, and this deficiency is intensified by the highly sporadic and irregular nature of the actual fall—for instance, in 1972 Kuwait and parts of the Gulf coast had unprecedented floods that washed away parked cars, whilst the Yemen A.R. in the opposite corner of the Arabian peninsula was just ending seven years of drought. As much as three to four inches have been known to fall in a single day; there can be heavy rain in one locality and none a few kilometres away; and years may go by in some places without any substantial fall. On the other hand, there are a few regions where special circumstances produce annual totals of 30-40 ins. (750-1000 mm.). These are usually upland areas close to large seas— northern Israel and Jordan, the Lebanon and western Syria, south and west Turkey, the north of Iran close to the Caspian Sea, and the higher parts of the North African mountain zones, in Morocco and as far east as northern Tunisia. The extreme south and east of Arabia can, as it were, be "brushed" by the monsoonal current from the Indian Ocean, and thus have a local summer rainfall: parts of the interior of the Yemen A.R., the Yemen P.D.R. and Oman are influenced in his way.

Normally, the winter rains begin in October, with a series of storms (the "Former Rains" of the Bible).

[*continued on p.* 10

7

Rainfall: North Africa.

Rainfall: Middle East.

continued from p. 7]

Heaviest rain falls during January in the west, and February or March in the east. Towards the end of April there may be a final onset of rain (the "Latter Rains"), and then from June to September no rain whatever falls in the south, and only very small amounts in the north.

Two other phenomena may be mentioned: the occurrence from time to time of hot, and sometimes dust- or sand-laden, winds from desert areas, and the prevalence of high atmospheric humidity near the coasts. The sand winds—known as *Khamsins, Simooms* (Iran) *Chehili* (Morocco) or *Ghibli* (Libya)— are unpleasant visitations that can last up to 48 hours, and their main effect, apart from personal inconvenience and mental irritation among humans, is to wither growing crops on a large scale. High humidity, especially in summer, makes living conditions difficult in such areas as the Persian/Arabian Gulf, the Red Sea, and parts of the Lebanon and Asia Minor, so that the wealthier sections of the community try to pass this season in hill stations. Though, as we have seen, the summer is almost rainless, humidity in coastal areas may be highest at the hottest time of the year. One other effect is the intense evaporation from water surfaces, due not only to the high temperatures, but also to the windiness of much of the region, again more pronounced in summer.

The effects of climate are now increasingly mitigated by modern technology. Irrigation and, in a few places, large-scale distillation of sea water allows crops to be grown throughout the summer and new towns to develop. Temperature and humidity difficulties can be reduced by air conditioning, which is spreading rapidly, at least among the better-off classes. Public demand for electricity is now at a peak in summer because of air-conditioning.

At the present, we may be experiencing a minor phase of climatic oscillation, with the increased tendency of the northern part of the Middle East to experience slightly more unsettled conditions, with rather cooler temperatures, and increased but still highly sporadic rainfall. On the southern side, warm desert conditions have tended to creep southwards, producing the devastating droughts now occurring in Ethiopia, parts of Sudan, and much of north central Africa (Mali, Upper Volta, Mauritania). This may be no more than a minor fluctuation that may last only for a few years, but its economic and social effects are considerable.

Social Geography

The lands of the Middle East occupy a unique geographical position as lying between and linking the three continents of the Old World. We may therefore expect that cultural influences from all three continents will be strongly represented. At the same time, whilst some parts of the Middle East are easy of access, and have thus acted for centuries as transit zones, thereby acquiring a mixed culture, there are also extensive areas of difficult terrain—mountain, desert, and swamp, where invaders do not often penetrate, and where ancient languages, religions, and ways of life still persist, largely unaltered and undisturbed.

This contrast between seclusion and openness to outside influence is highly characteristic of the Middle East, and explains why in some parts the population is extremely mixed in racial origin (for example, the "Levantine" of the coasts), and why in other districts it is racially pure (e.g. the Bedouin Arabs or Armenians); and why in some regions there is a modernity of outlook existing alongside ways of life that have persisted with little change since Biblical days. Rapid transition from one way of life to another within a small region is thus a marked feature, and there can be groups of people with traditions, language, religion and racial origins radically different from those of near neighbours. The most outstanding example of this is to be found in the heart of Arabia, where a number of desert tribes living less than 500 miles from Mecca itself remained, until quite recently, only slightly affected by the Muslim faith, though Islam itself had reached out centuries before to overrun and influence countries as far away as Spain, India, and Central Africa.

RACIAL GROUPING

In recent years there has been a revaluation of ideas on racial questions. Previously the trend had been towards devising increasingly elaborate and subtle groupings based on finer and finer measurements of physical characteristics: bodily physique, hair and skin qualities, especially colour. But we are now aware that some, though not all of these, may be induced or modified by diet, upbringing as children, and social customs. At the same time, investigation of genetic differences, as partly evidenced by blood serum character, has demonstrated a whole new field of possible biological relationships that often bear little or no concordance with observed "racial" characters, but can be traceable in certain ways to geographical location and environment—for example, the perpetuation of certain physical traits and genetical characters through seclusion in a remote area with interbreeding, or the opposite in an "open" area subject to much human movement and interchange. Whilst it would be idle to deny that differences between various groups of the human race certainly exist—some are darker- or lighter-skinned, or with slight physical and anatomical differences—it would appear far less possible than was once thought to devise meaningful categories of racial groupings. Some authorities now speak only of a very few distinctive groups: "caucasoid" or white, "brown", "yellow" etc., and then distinguish minor variations as arising from the influences of genetical inheritance, geographical location, and cultural experience.

Thus, earlier typologies such as "Alpine", "Armenoid", or "Mediterranean" are increasingly abandoned in favour of a more detailed but in one sense restricted approach based on precisely measurable elements such as blood grouping or other genetic qualities, discarding what are now recognized as variable and partially subjective criteria such as bodily build.

The Middle East offers special difficulties partly because of its location, as just described, between major world zones, and partly owing to a dearth of information, for example, on blood groupings. At the present, given this unsatisfactory situation, it is perhaps best to limit our survey to noting that (a) there is, as might well be expected, evidence of considerable intermixture and variation, with African, Asian and other elements represented, alongside an indigenous "brown" racial type, from very dark to blond skin colour; and (b) there is evidence of persistence of special genetical factors (and hence of physical characters) in some groups, and much less in others. Variation of type is thus prominent.

LANGUAGE DISTRIBUTION

This is far clearer than the racial pattern. Arabic, the language of Muhammad, and of comparatively recent origin, was spread rapidly by the Islamic conquests of the seventh to ninth centuries A.D., and has now become universal in Egypt, the Sudan, Arabia, Jordan, Syria, Lebanon, and Iraq. There is a classical form, now understood with some difficulty and (as the language of the Koran) used for religious observance and broadcasting; and various regional dialects. Some of these latter are close to each other in syntax but differ in pronunciation (i.e. differences are of the order of those in English, spoken let us say, in London, Lancashire and Glasgow, or Massachusetts, Georgia and Nebraska). But in other instances the colloquial forms of Arabic can differ as widely, as say, French, Spanish or Italian, so that intercommunication is difficult.

Farther north, Turkish, a central Asiatic language brought in by the Turkish conquerors of the eleventh century A.D., is current over most of Asia Minor, with extensions into Iran and the U.S.S.R. Turkish was for many centuries written in Arabic characters, but as the sounds of Turkish are not easily adaptable to Arabic letters, Roman (i.e. European) characters were introduced by government decree in 1928. Persian is an Indo-Aryan language with affinities to some European forms of speech, but it is by no means universally spoken throughout Iran—probably by only one-half or at most two-thirds of the population. It is written in Arabic script. A variation known as Dari Persian is spoken in Afghanistan, as is the Pashtu language. The hill country from Asia Minor as far east as the Indian frontier is a mosiac of different dialects spoken by various tribal groups. Some of these dialects are remnants of ancient forms of speech that were once more widely current; some are of fairly recent origin; whilst some show relationships to languages of central and eastern Asia. Aramaic, the language of Palestine at the time of Christ, now persists in a modern and altered form only in a few villages near Damascus and Mosul; Kurdish has a fairly wide extension in the hills from central Turkey as far as south-west Iran; and Armenian, owing to the perse-

cution and dispersal of Armenians from their homeland, is spoken in many large towns. Greek is the chief language of Cyprus. In Israel, Hebrew and Arabic are the two official languages, the former predominating. Berber is dominant in parts of the hill country and adjacent areas of Morocco, Algeria and Tunisia, with a few offshoots into Libya. Prior to invasion by the Arabs in the tenth and eleventh centuries, Berber was the major language in what is now Tripolitania, but it survives today in only a few towns—Aujila, Zuara and Garian.

Language and Educational Problems

Variation of language, as between written and spoken forms of the same dialect and as between families of languages, presents a serious problem at the present time, and is an important factor in the isolation and retarded economic level of several Middle Eastern states. In education, the problem is more complicated, because for a long time practically all modern scientific and technological works were written in English, French, German or Russian, with higher teaching often in the hands of foreigners. To the complication of having several indigenous languages within one country was thus added the difficulty of having higher instruction carried on by foreigners in their own tongue. Thus school and university teaching was frequently enmeshed in the toils of language, and timetables heavily weighted towards language teaching, as an essential preliminary to any other work. Because of the lack of contact, and the smallness of the potential market, which rarely make translation of serious works into Arabic, Turkish or Persian a commercial proposition, only a minority of standard texts from Europe or America could, until very recently, be read in the native languages of the Middle East. This has been a considerable, but not recognized, factor in the cultural and educational separation which has for long existed between the Middle East and other countries. Within the last few years certain governments, notably those of Egypt, Iran and Turkey, have tackled the problem, by sponsoring translation; and UNESCO has also been active in this connection. Another significant change is that with the expansion of general education, there is a greater flow of Middle Easterners abroad, and many of these have now returned as teachers, technicians and officials. In addition, locally trained Arabic-speaking personnel, chiefly Egyptian, but also Palestinian and Syrian Arab, have tended to take up appointments in less developed Arab countries. Thus there is much more specialist instruction in Arabic as compared with, say, twenty years ago. Nationalist feeling in itself, and the reduced openings for expatriates also foster this tendency. A few universities still use English as the main medium of instruction, but opinion is divided as to whether this should continue. To some it appears that fuller use of Arabic will allow more effective teaching; to others, that it will reduce the reading of textbooks (a number of which are available only in a foreign language) and limit yet further the possibility of employing expatriate staff.

NOMADS

With much of the Middle East arid or semi-arid, animal rearing plays an important part in the life of the region, with numerous migratory tribes moving regularly in search of fresh pasture. Though the actual numbers of people who live as pastoral nomads are relatively small and now declining, their way of life is of great significance, and contrasts sharply with that of the townspeople and peasant cultivators. The impact of desert life and ideas upon neighbouring peoples has from time to time been immense, through invasion and destruction, but also in more positive, ways often leading to cultural progress. particularly in the fields of religion and abstract thought. The Old Testament deals continually with the theme of desert against town; and we may also recall the words of T. E. Lawrence that the edge of the desert is littered with the relics of religions and ideas developed from the interaction of nomadic and sedentary ways of life. Many of these movements have perished, but a few have gained strength enough to affect the whole world.

The unit among nomads is the tribe—a group that ensures a certain advantage in numbers, yet is small enough to exist within the limits set by a hard environment. Tribal discipline is strong, and direction is in the hands of a leader whose right to rule is based partly on hereditary descent, and partly on personal merit. This system of rule may to some extent explain the general importance of leaders and persons, rather than principles and party doctrines, in the general political life of the present-day Middle East.

The mobility of the nomads, their predilection for raiding and skirmishing, and their scanty material possessions for long made them difficult subjects for any national government that attempted to impose its rule. An unusually vigorous head of state, such as Reza Shah in Iran, could from time to time successfully break or limit the power of the tribes; but a better policy (followed by the Ottomans, and by several present-day governments) has been to let the nomads go their way, with a minimum of interference. This was the situation until very recently, but the exploitation of oil has been a powerful solvent of ancient custom. Thus many former nomads have found sedentary occupations within oilfields, or in towns, or as semi-settled cultivators using irrigation water paid for or supplied largely by oil revenues. Now, nomadism and tribalism are in rapid decline, and it is the stated policy of certain governments to encourage sedentarization. Twenty years ago, perhaps 10 per cent of the population of the Middle East and North Africa was in the main nomadic, now the figure is about 1–2 per cent: half a million in Saudi Arabia, 400,000 in the rest of the Arabian Peninsula, 350,000 in Turkey, 300,000 in Iran and also in Iraq, 200,000 in Syria; 70,000 in Jordan, 50,000 in Egypt, and in Libya; and 18,000 in Israel. There are also uncertain numbers of nomads in the Sudan who move relatively short distances to escape annual floods.

One important feature in the sedentarization of nomads has been land-reform schemes by which plots of agricultural land, sometimes even with houses, have been made over to former pastoral nomads, e.g. in parts of the Nile valley, northern Syria and in north-east Iran; for such schemes to be successful, education in cultivation methods, and the provision of facilities and agricultural credit schemes are essentials.

RELIGIOUS DIVERSITY

Religious divisions are still strong, though now declining, within the Middle East; and for many persons religious and sectarian fidelity even replaces nationality, so that it is frequently possible, on asking an Arab to what country he belongs, to receive the answer, "I am a follower of Islam". A remarkable feature of the area, possibly connected with its geographical function as a meeting-place of peoples and ideas, is that three great religions of the modern world —Judaism, Christianity and Islam—have arisen within its limits; and that others, notably Zoroastrianism (now confined almost entirely to the Parsees of Bombay), Manichaeism, and Mithraism (of great influence in the later Roman Empire) should also be associated with the Middle East. The most recent example is the rise of Baha'i.

Judaism

All three of the modern religions have various branches or sects. Little need be mentioned concerning Judaism, except to note that one of the main social problems of the State of Israel is to absorb Jewish immigrants of widely differing backgrounds and religious traditions. Because of the dispersals of Jews in various continents, there have developed Hebrews of Oriental and African affinities, besides the two European groups of northern (Ashkenazim) and southern (Sephardim) Jews. Since the establishment of the State of Israel divergence of view as to the part religion should play in everyday life, and its general relationship with politics have proved intractable questions in the Israel Parliament, and have led to several Cabinet crises. Because of greater levels of immigration and a generally higher birthrate Israelis of "Oriental" descent now outnumber those of "European" origin.

Christianity

Christianity in the Middle East is even more widely divided. Geographical separation and the development of regional feeling during and after the end of the Roman Empire resulted in the rise of many cults that varied greatly in dogma, ritual and opinion; and despite the efforts of the early Fathers of Christianity, it proved impossible to reconcile all conflicting views, and maintain the unity of Christian peoples. There arose the Greek (or Orthodox) Church; the Roman Catholic Church (called the Latin Church in the Middle East); the Nestorians. who were once widespread from Mesopotamia and Asia Minor as far as India and China; the Armenians (or Gregorians); Copts; Abyssinians; Jacobites (or Syrian followers of Jacob Baradeus); and the Maronites (adherents of St. John Maroun). All of these sects came in time to possess complete autonomy, but following the rise of Islam in the seventh century A.D. the fortunes of many of them declined. Numbers of Armenians, Copts,

Greeks, Jacobites, Nestorians and others (and the entire Maronite Church) were driven to accept aid from Rome, but at the price of recognizing the Pope as their titular Head. Thus we have what are termed the Uniate Churches—Armenian, Coptic, Nestorian Catholics, etc.—which further reduced the strength of the older autonomous groups, most of which managed to continue, though no longer of great importance. At present, therefore, we have more than twenty separate Christian sects, some powerful and world wide, others purely local in allegiance. The appearance of Protestant missionaries in the nineteenth century and after has added further to the religious bodies represented, although the number of converts is small.

Islam

Division in Islam began on the death of Muhammad. As the prophet designated no successor, most followers agreed that leadership of Islam could pass from any individual to another, according to merit and circumstance. This group came to be known as the *Sunni*, or Orthodox, and numbers about 90 per cent of all Muslims. A minority supported the claims of the next male relative of Muhammad, and these Muslims took the name of *Shi'a*, or Party. Shi'a adherents are dominant in Iran and the Yemen Arab Republic; in southern Iraq, where they form a large majority of the inhabitants; and as minorities in Syria, the Lebanon, and Turkey. Many sub-sects of the Shi'a are known, representing different forms of belief; and one such group was for a time a warlike military order, with much power in Syria and Iran. Its head was finally forced to take refuge in India, where his direct descendant is today the Aga Khan. Groups of his followers still remain in Iran and Syria. Many Muslims believe that there will one day arise a Mahdi (Messiah) who will conquer the world for Islam, and this circumstance has led to the appearance at various times of leaders who have claimed to be the long-awaited incarnation—for example, the Mahdi in the Sudan in the late nineteenth century.

The revival during the present century of Wahhabi power may briefly be noticed. The Wahhabis, by reason of their dislike of ostentation in religious observance, and their desire to revive the earlier, simpler tenets of the Faith, have been termed the Puritans of Islam. Under the vigorous and skilled leadership of their late head, King Ibn Saud of Arabia, they rose from obscurity as a desert people to control of most of the Arabian peninsula, and hence domination of the holy cities of Mecca and Medina. One factor in the present Arab disunity is the division on general religious grounds between the Wahhabis, who tend to despise the Muslims of Egypt, Jordan and Syria as lax in observance, and as backsliders in the Faith, and who are in turn criticized as primitive reactionaries. There have also been acute personal differences involving King Ibn Saud, who in conquering Mecca displaced the former ruler, Sharif Husain, a direct descendant of the Prophet. A descendant of the former Sharif rules in Jordan (as also until 1958 in Iraq), hence something of the animosity displayed

between Saudi Arabia and its northern neighbours owed its origin to personal feuds. This, like other religious causes, is tending to disappear, however, in the light of the current new situations confronting Middle Eastern states.

Political Complications

There are other questions of a general political nature that stem from religious differences within the Middle East. The willingness of outside nations to support various religious groups in their struggle against each other has from time to time led to large-scale intervention. France has championed the cause of the Latin and Uniate Churches, basing many of her claims to influence and territory within Syria and the Lebanon on her long connection with the Uniates, who form the largest single sect in the latter country.

Russia, under Tsarist and Soviet rule alike, has maintained a link with the Orthodox Church, and from time to time Russian bishops visit Jerusalem, where the larger part of Christian shrines are owned by the Orthodox Church. Within the last few years Russia has strongly supported, by means of legal and diplomatic action, Orthodox claims to ownership of property and privileges; and whatever the position within the U.S.S.R., Soviet policy is firmly directed to maintaining the rights and position of the Orthodox Christians within the Middle East. Because of its territorial ownership within Old Jerusalem, Russia could in some respects make a good case for trusteeship of the Christian Holy Places. Britain, rather curiously, has at times supported Muslim groups—sometimes orthodox, sometimes dissident. American interest, though of long standing (as much as a century in one or two localities) has generally been much less direct, but over the last ten to fifteen years has greatly expanded. There are now within the Middle East a number of American educational institutions of great influence and standing (for example, the American University of Beirut and the American Colleges of Istanbul). Most of these were founded as Protestant missionary activities, but have since developed into secular institutions covering a wide range of subjects.

One final effect of religious differences may be noted. With the possibilities of appeal to outside assistance, and the internal vigorousness of religious feeling, it has happened that a political *modus vivendi* can be achieved only by a distribution of offices and appointments among the interested religious sects. This is most obvious in the Lebanon, where ever since independence the President of the Republic has been a Maronite, and the Prime Minister a Sunni Moslem, with a close eye kept on the balance of religious parties represented in the Cabinet. In Iraq Muslims, certainly until 1958, had a major influence in Cabinet policy, though the majority of the population is Shi'a in adherence.

It is, however, necessary to state that the pattern of religious life in the Middle East is at the present time rapidly altering. Among many, there is a marked decline of religious belief and impatience with its influence on political and social life, with a parallel growth of secular and materialist outlook. This is still perhaps not quite so marked as in contemporary Europe, but it is now increasingly significant. Yet it is also true to say that an entirely opposite tendency prevails in certain groups. Religious brotherhoods of an extremist character, dedicated to subversion and fanaticism have come into prominence over the last few years, and a number of these—the *Ikhwan* of Egypt, *Fidaiyai* of Iran, and *Tijaniya* of Turkey—exert growing political influence. At the same time, however, the traditionally close relationship of religion and politics is tending slowly to change in character, with secular nationalism becoming more and more a feature.

CITY LIFE IN THE MIDDLE EAST

From very early times, long before Plato commended the city-state as an ideal form of political organization, town life has exercised a predominant influence in lands of the Mediterranean; and this predominance, amounting to a marked disproportion, has been particularly characteristic of the Middle East. Here, towns stand out as islands of relative wealth, culture and progress in a poor and backward countryside; and it is significant that the two centres that dispute the title of the oldest, continuously inhabited site in the world are Damascus and Aleppo, whilst the oldest undoubted port is Byblos (modern Jbeil, 20 miles north of Beirut), which from its trade in papyrus gave us the word Bible.

There have been several contributing factors in the precocious growth of Middle Eastern cities. Firstly, because of a wide variety in geographical environment—rich oasis or coastal plain, mountain, desert, steppe and forest—there soon arose a diversity of economic production, and hence a need for exchange and market centres. Then too, with frequent warfare and invasion, defence became a necessity, and strong points on mounds or peaks, commanding corridors, defiles and river passages soon developed and gathered around them a township. Examples of former simple tribal strongholds that have evolved into great cities are Aleppo, Ankara, Jerusalem, Mosul and Tabriz, the third city of Iran. Another feature of the Middle East is the number of "planted" towns—sites deliberately planned or designated to be important. Of this nature is Teheran, which before it was chosen as a new capital by the Qajar rulers in 1788 had few functions other than that of a wintering spot for pastoral nomads. Amman was largely uninhabited for several centuries previous to 1880, though the site (Philadelphia) had held importance in Roman times; and there are other towns whose origins can be clearly traced to planned development in early Arab, Roman or Classical Greek times. Alexander the Great, and especially his successors, fostered many new towns and extended others.

The City in Conquest

It is a feature of Middle Eastern history that, time and time again, small but energetic groups of people seized power, and for a limited period ruled a large territory. The Hyksos Kings of Egypt, the Medes, Assyrians, Macedonian Greeks, Romans, Arabs, and Ottomans can all be cited as examples; and for each conqueror there soon arose the acute problem of maintaining a hold on defeated but numerically superior subject races, and of spreading the language, religion and traditions of the minority ruling group.

Most conquerors found that it was usually easier to dominate the cities, partly for the reason that military operations could be undertaken with more success against the inhabitants of a closely packed town, rather than against the nomads or peasants of trackless steppes, deserts, or mountains; partly because the towns with their trade could easily be taxed to support military rule; and partly because the population of the cities, polyglot in origin and in touch with outside conditions, could be more often induced to accept a new idea, a new language, or even a new religion. It is no accident that the great evangelical religions of the modern world should have extended from towns—that men first called themselves Christians in Antioch, or that Muhammad could feel that his cause had succeeded when Mecca and Medina acknowledged his rule, or that Jewish ritual should include the phrase "Next year in Jerusalem". We also have the curious position that the towns of the Middle East may often be strikingly different in wealth, in outlook and even in language and religion, as compared with the immediately surrounding countryside. The most famous example may be cited from the New Testament, as when the inscription on the Cross of Christ indicated the presence of a Latin-speaking ruling class, a Greek-speaking town and professional class, and an Aramaic-speaking peasantry. Such contrasts are apparent even today, though, of course, involving different languages.

Economic and Political Dominance

Another feature of Middle Eastern cities is their economic dominance, amounting almost to a stranglehold, in the life of each country. Town merchants are in touch with world markets and can control or "corner" the produce of the rural areas in their own district, for which, owing to the difficulties of transport, they are the only outlet. The strength of the merchants is indicated by the fact that in many Middle Eastern countries there is relatively little, or even in a few instances no, direct taxation, most governmental revenue being raised by indirect imposts.

We also find that in many cities there is an important community of wealthy absentee landlords. Unlike that of Europe, the Middle Eastern countryside offers few amenities—rather is it a stronghold of poverty, discomfort and disease. Hence landowners tend to remain most of the time in the towns, and visit their estates only rarely, sometimes merely to collect the rents, for which, occasionally, an armed guard may be necessary. The same can be said of religious communities, Christian and Muslim, many of which possess landed estates, or which actually control the exploitation of land by tenant farmers. In either case, there is a general flow of money, derived from the country, but spent in the towns, and this provides a living not only for the wealthy, but for artisans, domestic servants, and shopkeepers, though land reform operations have recently diminished the importance and wealth of some absentee landlords, these have by no means disappeared, partly because a new group of landlords has arisen as the result of the reform. Also, with depreciation of currencies and share prices, the ownership of land still remains a useful (though not now "gilt-edged") outlet for capital gains.

Another feature of town life in the Middle East until recently was the absence, or relatively slight development, of traditions of civic government and responsibility. There was little to parallel the growth of the burgher class that became so prominent in parts of Europe, and hence less of a corporate pride and pattern of local, as distinct from provincial or national, interest in problems of rule. The situation is changing markedly in some localities; but the absence of a bourgeois outlook (in its best sense) is still a feature.

Lastly, it is interesting to observe that towns have long tended to dominate Middle Eastern political life. The lure of greater wealth attracts the energetic, dissatisfied, and sometimes turbulent elements from the countryside. Many such immigrants, together with the occupants of city slums who become periodically unemployed because of trade slumps, and also a third element, inexperienced secondary school and university students, form a very dangerous combination—the Middle Eastern city mob. Mob violence, awakened at first over a political matter, sometimes assumes a religious complexion directed against minorities and foreigners, and among the demonstrators are often groups with few political or religious convictions, but whose aim is to spread disorder so that shops can be broken open and looted. Most Middle Eastern shops in the cities carry iron shutters that can cover the whole of the shop-front at the slightest sign of trouble. A restless, underfed proletariat, excited by political and religious issues, and inflamed by student agitators, can be very menacing in close, narrow streets. Even politicians themselves may ultimately go in fear of the tide of disorder that they themselves have had a hand in provoking. Over and over again in Middle Eastern affairs, demonstrators in the streets have swayed or brought about a total change of government; and, as in 1951 (Egypt), 1956 (the Lebanon), 1958 (Iraq), 1960 (Turkey) and 1963 (Iraq, Syria and Jordan), the dilemma of Pontius Pilate—how far to give way to turbulence in the streets—arises in an acute form at unhappily frequent intervals. The swift explosion of anti-American and anti-British feeling, expressed through mob violence in centres as far apart as Kuwait, Benghazi and Tunis, was a feature of June 1967.

Urban Growth

A further considerable problem now arises from the exceedingly rapid physical growth of a few urban centres. Cairo, with a population of about 5½ million, is not only the capital of Egypt but the largest town of the Mediterranean area and by far the largest city in Africa. "Greater" Teheran is now over 3½ million, and Baghdad 2–2½ million in population. Beirut and Casablanca each (with their suburbs) have more than one million, Algiers about one million, and about one-fifth of the country's population live in Tunis. This rapid and accelerating growth—placed at six to ten per cent per annum for many large towns—is leading to a concentration of economic power, political influence, and social prestige which poses acute problems of two kinds. Besides the difficulties of providing adequate amenities and methods of administration—the demand for electricity in Beirut is doubling at present every five years, and the traffic problems are monumental—there is also a retrogression of provincial life, with stagnation in more distant parts. The problems associated with the "drift to London" in Britain are repeated in another highly acute form in parts of the Middle East and regeneration of regional centres is now being taken up as an urgent matter in those countries that have oil revenues to support expansion plans or programmes.

Economic Geography

By far the greater part of the land surface in the Middle East is either mountain, desert, or swamp, and cultivated areas are extremely small in extent, covering no more than 5 to 7½ per cent of the total area. Nevertheless, agriculture is the main occupation of a large majority of the inhabitants; and a further proportion of the people is employed in processing the products of agriculture, as cotton and tobacco packers, fruit driers, or canners of fruit, vegetables, and olive oil. It is obvious therefore, that the remaining activities in the Middle East are of relatively restricted extent. Pastoral nomadism is found in many districts, as the only possible way of life in an arid or mountainous environment; but few people are involved, and the nomads live mainly a self-sufficient existence, so that their contribution to general economic activity is on the whole small. Because of this relatively low level, we have the apparent paradox that, whilst in many (though not all) countries of the Middle East most of the inhabitants are engaged in agriculture or pastoralism, the total contribution of these two activities to Gross National Product is often well under 50 per cent—oil exports and transit trading accounting for the larger share.

AGRICULTURE
Cereals

The chief food crops grown in the Middle East are wheat, barley and rye in the north, and millet, maize and rice in the south. Wheat, the chief crop of Turkey, Syria, the Lebanon, Jordan, Israel, Algeria and Tunisia, is of the hard variety, planted in autumn, and harvested in late spring or early summer. The use of Mexican strains of high-yielding wheat has spread over the past few years, with good, sometimes dramatic, results. Barley is more important than wheat in Libya, Iraq, Morocco and parts of Iran, since it is hardier and more resistant to insects. Rye (with some oats) is restricted to the colder and hillier parts of Turkey and Iran, whilst rice though much prized as a luxury, and also for its very high yield per unit of farm land, needs much heat and abundant water, and is grown only in a few specially fertile and favoured localities—Lower Egypt, southern Iraq, the valleys of southern Turkey, and a few parts of North Africa, especially Morocco. In some countries, because of its demands on irrigation water, and its tendency to spread malaria (owing to the flooded ground), the cultivation of rice is limited by law. Maize is the chief cereal in Egypt, and its cultivation is also being greatly extended in Israel. Farther south, towards Arabia and the Sudan, millets of various species become of increasing importance.

Cotton and Tobacco

In addition to these food crops, which, except for barley, are mostly of indifferent quality and are grown for home consumption only, there is increasing emphasis on cash crops, as communications develop and an export market can be found. Some of the finest cotton in the world is grown in Egypt, where about 20 per cent of the agricultural land is given over to its production, and four-fifths of the total exports are in the form of raw cotton. The same crop is also a chief export of the Sudan. Elsewhere, quality is much lower, but cultivation is spreading, especially in the Seyhan plain of southern Turkey around Adana, in the Aleppo and Jezireh districts of Syria, and in parts of Iran.

Production of tobacco, introduced into the Middle East during the sixteenth century, is considerable, mainly in the Black Sea and Aegean coastlands of Turkey, and in Cyprus. Pure Turkish tobacco is no longer in favour among British and American smokers, but most "Virginian" cigarette and pipe tobaccos contain a small admixture of Turkish leaf; and Central Europe still prefers the unmixed Turkish variety. Many Arab farmers grow small quantities for their own use, but here quality is generally low, except in the district of Latakia, from which there is some export.

Fruit

The Middle East has an extremely wide variety of fruit. Vines are found both wild and cultivated, and besides their use in Turkey and Cyprus for currants and sultanas, much local wine is made, the best probably coming from Cyprus, the Lebanon and Israel. North Africa is especially favourable for wine-growing, which immigrants from France did much to foster. As a result, quantities of *vin ordinaire* are sold abroad, to France especially, where the local product had to some extent been superseded by the cheaper Algerian wine, until pressure from domestic growers forced the government to reduce imports. The U.S.S.R. has recently become a large-scale importer.

Citrus fruits are of increasing importance along the north-eastern Mediterranean coast, whilst apricots, figs, peaches and plums are widespread. Olives form a very important part of Middle Eastern diet, since animal fats are scarce, and the poorer fraction of the oil also serves as a domestic illuminant and for soap-making. Other products of some importance are hazel nuts, liquorice, and dates.

Dates are a principal article of food in the arid areas of the south—Arabia, southern Iran, and parts of the Sudan. In addition, there is export on a large scale from the Basra district of southern Iraq, which produces 80 per cent of the world's supply. Nearness to the sea, allowing cheap transport by water, gives Basra a considerable advantage over its competitors in North Africa—though it must also be stated that Algerian dates, and especially those from Biskra, are superior in quality to those from Iraq. Mention must also be made of bananas, citrus fruit and apples, the importance of which has greatly increased in the last few years following expansion of export markets, and demands from the oilfields. In contrast to the "soft" fruits already discussed, the three latter types of fruit can be more easily transported without damage, and are also less likely to be carriers of human disease. A feature of the last few years also has been considerable development of market gardening (fruit and vegetables) near larger towns.

Narcotics

Finally, reference may be made to the cultivation of narcotics—opium and hashish—the first of which is the source of morphine and heroin; and also of qat, which has a very local market. There is a legal and strictly controlled world trade in morphine, and about one-half of the legal supplies come from Turkey; but in addition, quantities above the legal maximum are grown illicitly in the Lebanon, Syria, and Iran, since prices are very high, and supervision lax. There is consequently much temptation in the way of a poor peasant farmer to grow a few plants for sale to the illicit buyer. Qat is grown only on the hill slopes of south-west Arabia, in the Yemen A.R. and near Aden, and when chewed induces a feeling of euphoria. It can only be used fresh, so for long its consumption was closely limited to the environs of where it could be grown. But now, air transport has allowed wider consumption and production, reaching as far as East Africa, and cultivation has increased. Opinion is divided as to the dangers of qat—some hold that it can be regarded as no more than a harmless addiction, whilst others believe it to be a dangerous drug. At one time the Government of Aden prohibited its production and sale.

YIELDS AND LEVELS OF PRODUCTION

Though there are several conspicuous exceptions, with production per unit area amongst the highest in the world, levels of production and quality of crops are not in general at a satisfactory level: it is estimated that the Middle Eastern farmer is no more than one-eighth to one-quarter as efficient a producer as his counterparts in Western Europe or the U.S.A. This is particularly true as regards basic food grains, and so despite much emphasis on farming and self-subsistence, some populations are among the poorest fed in the world. There is the paradox that quite often, although agriculture is the livelihood of the largest group of the people (in some countries over 50 per cent), the contribution of agriculture to G.N.P. is often far less than this.

Natural vegetation.

Woodland (scrub to forest)

Mediterranean type

S. Arabian–Ethiopian type

Steppeland

Desert

Tropical Savanna

Riverine (including Sudd)

Reasons for this situation are to be sought first in the obvious handicaps of heat and aridity, together with the resulting effects of this climatic régime upon soil character. Many Middle Eastern soils are lacking in humus; and another difficulty is that when watered copiously by artificial means (e.g. by irrigation) certain soils that would appear to be capable of bearing heavy crops can turn saline and sterile. This is at present a problem in the Nile Delta, where heavy irrigation is tending to induce soil salinity; and a number of large irrigation schemes, notably round Konya in Anatolia, and along the Karun River of south-west Iran, have failed to achieve success for the same reason. In 1949 it was estimated that for the whole of Iraq some 60 per cent of all irrigated land had become salinated to a certain degree; and that about 1 per cent of area is abandoned each year. Relatively little would appear to have been done to alter this general situation; though the development of the Wadi Tharthar drainage scheme could have some effect when it is fully in operation. The Tigris and Euphrates carry double the quantity of salts near their mouth as compared with upstream above Baghdad. The best remedy is to have extensive underground drains in the fields, to prevent accumulation of excess water. This is, however, expensive and adds greatly to the overall cost of irrigation schemes.

Another limiting factor is the unusually high soil temperature during summer—of the order of 130° to 180° F., which has the effect of destroying organic material within the soil itself, and of preventing the efficient use of fertilizers. There is a fundamental problem, as yet not solved, of maintaining soil fertility by artificial means, because the techniques successful in wetter and colder parts of the world do not always answer in the Middle East.

Pests and Diseases

One other source of agricultural loss occurs in the pests and diseases that affect both plants and man. As much as 60 per cent of a year's crops may be destroyed by locusts, which breed in the deserts of Arabia, Africa and Somalia, and move as swarms into cultivated areas. In Iraq and Iran the much smaller *sunna* fly causes periodic devastation—one reason for the emphasis on barley growing is that it ripens faster, and hence can be harvested before the arrival of the *sunna* insect in late summer. Scale diseases, rusts, and mildew are other handicaps. An encouraging feature is the expansion of activity on an international scale directed towards locust control. Faced with growing annual losses, Middle Eastern governments are now co-operating not only with neighbours but also with such organizations as FAO and UNESCO in preventive measures.

Equally severe, if not actually more damaging, are the diseases of man himself. In Egypt, rates of incidence of serious maladies were not long ago up to 70-75 per cent of the whole population, and there are still a few areas in districts of Iraq, Turkey, the Sudan and the Yemen A.R. where malaria affects over half the population. Plague was endemic, whilst Turkey,

owing to its colder winter climate, has long been a stronghold of tuberculosis. Eye diseases, chiefly trachoma, are rife, and in some areas produce blindness in up to 20 per cent of the population. Smallpox, typhoid and venereal diseases are still prevalent, and from time to time there are outbreaks of cholera, sometimes minimized or "played down" by local governments. The Sudan has a particularly poor level of public health, especially in the south, where diseases are not only endemic but spread easily from tropical Africa. The riverine areas of Egypt and Iraq are particularly notorious for parasitic infections—ankylostomiasis, bilharzia and hookworm—which, most unfortunately, tend to spread with the expansion of irrigation. Dysentery (usually of a relatively mild form) is an almost ubiquitous feature, especially affecting newcomers. Despite this depressing list, it is also true to say that very considerable changes have been brought about in many areas by better public health measures—control of insect and animal disease vectors, provision of cleaner drinking water, and improved medical care. In a few regions (e.g. Kuwait) hospital services are among the best in the world. Thus incidence of many diseases, especially in towns, has shown a marked drop over the past decade.

The high incidence of disease was for long, and still remains in some areas, an important contributing factor to low agricultural efficiency: besides reducing physical capacity, mental alertness may also be reduced, thus retarding the introduction of new techniques. Until recently, one could speak of a "vicious circle"—the peasant was diseased and could not work hard, yields were thus precarious leading to malnutrition which in turn pre-disposed to disease. Malaria alone has in the recent past been cited as a major cause of backwardness, including also the decay of the earlier brilliant Arab civilization. Over the past twenty years malaria has successfully been eradicated in most, though not all parts of the Middle East: down to the 1950s, mosquito nets were found in the better hotels of most cities, now they are rarely to be seen. However, it would seem that in a few areas, species of mosquito more resistant to modern pesticides are now appearing, and strains of the disease itself also appear less susceptible to eradication by drugs: this is becoming something of a new problem in the southern areas of the Middle East.

Land Tenure

Yet more factors in agricultural backwardness are the methods of land holding and forms of tenancy. Full ownership, with the possibility of applying long-term methods of improvement, is not frequent among Middle Eastern farmers. Instead, there are various forms of share-cropping or tribal ownership, which collectively tend to perpetuate old, wasteful methods, to emphasize conservatism in outlook, and to make it extremely difficult for an individual to introduce any innovation. Holdings are often small and scattered, so that modern ploughs, tractors, or reaping machinery cannot easily be introduced; and owing to extremely high rents and dues, amounting in some instances to 65 per cent of the total yield of the holding, the peasant farmer is entirely lacking in capital for improvements, and remains dependent on his landlord for seed and even implements. Land-reform schemes now in progress in several countries, notably Iran, Iraq, Syria and Egypt, are altering this picture, but they do not affect all areas. When they do become more widespread there is a risk that production will decline initially, owing to the lack of capital and knowledge of new techniques of the new owners.

A further feature of Middle Eastern farming has been the existence of numerous absentee landlords, who invest money in land purely as a safe outlet for surplus capital, and have no real interest in farming itself. Such owners live mainly in the towns, and delegate control of their agricultural estates to overseers, being satisfied if the same level of production is maintained from one year to another. Such owners are not often willing to sink capital in new methods or machines, but are content to perpetuate existing methods. Because of the lack of outlet for investment in most Middle Eastern countries—movable property may be stolen, paper securities may be repudiated, and foreign currency, particularly the franc, lira, and pound sterling have depreciated—real property represents a fairly safe long-term investment that cannot easily depreciate.

In recent years, many Middle Eastern governments have made attempts to improve the position by redistribution of holdings, and enactments limiting the total area of land held by one individual. This has had some good effect, but in some cases the laws have been loosely applied, or even remained a dead-letter; and ways of ignoring or circumventing them have further reduced their efficiency. Extensive handing over of Crown land to peasant ownership in Iran, followed by the redistribution to peasant ownership on a national scale of all large estates, and the organization of Liberation Province in Egypt, mainly from expropriated and irrigated land, are outstanding but by no means the only large-scale examples of reallocation of big estates, which has also been energetically pursued in Iraq. In Iran, the process has been so fully pursued as to invite the description "White Revolution": during the period 1962–72 some 700,000 peasant families received land for the first time as full owners.

It is also necessary to state that despite all the handicaps noted above considerable progress has been achieved in certain areas of the Middle East. In parts of the Nile Valley, yields per acre of one or two crops are among the highest in the world; and in Israel a remarkable development of mixed farming, based on cereals, vegetables and animal husbandry, has transformed conditions in many areas. Much the same could be said of parts of Cyprus, Syria and Lebanon. The influence of French and Italian settlers in North Africa and Libya respectively was to demonstrate what might be done to improve yields and methods. Iran and Turkey, too, have experienced considerable agricultural development in certain directions over the last twenty to thirty years. Such ameliorations stand, however, in sharp contrast to conditions elsewhere in the Middle East.

INDUSTRIAL ACTIVITIES

In medieval times Middle Eastern industrial products had a high reputation. Steelwork, silverware, pottery, leather, and above all, textiles (from Damascus and Mosul, giving the words damask and muslin) found their way into many parts of Europe. At the present time, however, the scale of Middle Eastern industries is small; lack of fuel (particularly of coal and hydro-electric power), scarcity of mineral ores and some other raw materials, and the poverty of local markets being severe limiting factors. There is only one coalfield of any great importance—this is in north-west Turkey, at Ereğli (Heraclea), and production is only 4–5 million tons per annum; whilst very much smaller amounts are produced from fields in the region of Teheran.

In recent years a significant degree of industrial development has, however, taken place in Egypt, Turkey, Israel and Iran, with some industry on a smaller scale in Iraq, the Lebanon and Syria. Some industrial activity, on a smaller scale, and related chiefly to production of building materials, processing of agricultural produce, or the limited treatment of mineral ores for export, has developed in North Africa. Textiles—chiefly cotton, but also silk, wool and mohair—are important, together with the transformation of agricultural products (sugar, tobacco, fruit processing and distilling) and the making of cement and bricks, for which there is a considerable local demand.

A further feature has been the growth of light consumer industries. Acute shortages during the Second World War impelled many Middle Eastern governments to try to develop local manufactures, even where local conditions were not outstandingly favourable; and over the last fifteen years there has been a marked growth of new power stations, factories and mills (detailed instances of which can be found in the economic surveys of the individual countries). Heavy capital goods such as machinery and vehicles are still imported on a large scale, though there are now assembly plants for motors and electrical machinery in Turkey, Iran, Israel and Egypt, with plans for similar plants, e.g. in the Lebanon, Syria and Iraq. Since 1960, however, there have been the beginnings of local manufacture of motors (in Egypt, Iran and Israel) and other machinery. Industrial expansion is marked in Egypt, Israel, Turkey, the Lebanon and Iran, and especially in the first two; and the last fifteen years have seen the start of petro-chemical industries in Egypt, Israel, Kuwait and Iraq, based on local supplies of oil. In many places, however, restricted size of the potential market, and competition of foreign produced goods (it is cheaper to import Indian cement, for instance, in parts of the Oman Gulf) inhibit industrial development on a large scale.

Over the past few years, a number of smelting plants have been constructed: for iron and steel in Egypt, Israel, Turkey and Iran; and for aluminium in Bahrain and elsewhere.

PETROLEUM RESOURCES

The general geological factors involved in the occurrence of petroleum have already been touched on; but it remains to add that there are a number of features special to the Middle East. Exploration has been retarded by the presence of what may be described as misleading surface structures—in some places, the possibility of finding oil was at first entirely discounted (as in Saudi Arabia); whilst in others, leakages of oil to the surface have given rise to optimism that has not always been justified. Moreover, the oilfields are often of extraordinarily large size, and the oil is held under considerable pressure, so that very few wells need be sunk to tap a large area, and the crude oil often rises of itself without much pumping—factors that allow an unusually low cost of production. The open nature of the country, as compared with the jungle of the East Indies, and the mangrove swamps of Venezuela, has been another favourable circumstance. Hence the cost of production of Middle Eastern oil is distinctly lower than that of oil from the U.S.A., the Caribbean, and from South-east Asia, both in terms of actual production costs and in terms of capital investment. As the selling price of most oil is based on American costs, this disparity in costs has meant a higher rate of profit on Middle East oil for the exploiting companies. (Petroleum development is dealt with in more detail in a later chapter.)

One important factor in oilfield development has been the utility of pipelines. Broadly speaking, as compared with sea transport via the Cape, or, before 1967, the Suez Canal, a pipeline can move oil more cheaply from the Persian Gulf to the Mediterranean, and hence countries through which pipelines pass have been able to exact substantial royalties and other payments. Increasing demands of this nature (together with political troubles) have led to suggestions of developing alternative routes (e.g. through Turkey), events since 1956 having demonstrated the vulnerability of European consumers dependent on a single pipeline route. Use of larger tankers has, however, diminished the margin of profitability in using pipelines, and in 1972 the Iraq Petroleum Co. stated that it had become commercially cheaper to exploit fields closer to the Persian Gulf and export via the Cape, rather than move oil from the northern fields by pipeline to the Mediterranean.

Present-Day Problems

In the context of a rapid survey, it is possible to do no more than hint at a few acute issues which exert a profound influence on current trends in the Middle East. These issues may be summarized as population pressure, the question of finding a reasonably equitable basis for the distribution of wealth between social classes, political leadership, and the cultural crisis within Islam.

POPULATION PRESSURE

The population problem arises as the result of a high birth-rate, together with a fairly high death-rate which is now in some parts declining rapidly, as the result of improvements in public health. There is, in consequence, an increasing number of survivors, producing a population growth of the order of 2.5 per cent annually in Turkey, and 2.3 per cent in Egypt (cf. 0.1 per cent in England and Wales). Between 1900 and 1970 the population of Turkey grew from approximately 9 million to 36 million, producing an annual increase now of just under one million. Even an increase of 2 per cent per annum in population can, if unchecked, lead to a doubling of numbers in less than forty years. So long as food supplies can be increased at a commensurate rate, either by farming within the country, or by an expansion of industry and commerce that can pay for imported food, the position is without danger; but it is in fact difficult to maintain a continuous improvement in agriculture and industry of 2 per cent per annum, particularly under Middle Eastern conditions. Hence, there are signs of severe pressure of numbers on resources—in a few parts of the Nile Valley there are now over 6,000 persons per square mile living by agriculture—with a resulting decline in standards of living. As regards Turkey, FAO has said that the situation calls for a "truly heroic" agricultural programme, and that "many farm animals are so seriously underfed that it is surprising they stay alive". Another economist suggests that the production of foodstuffs has actually fallen within Egypt during the last thirty years, despite a growth in population numbers. Under such conditions it is not difficult to suggest a possible relationship between the current demographic situation of an underemployed, underfed but increasing proletariat, and the disturbed political conditions of many parts of the Middle East.

EXTREMES OF WEALTH

A second group of problems arises from the social inequality that is a feature of many Middle Eastern countries. There is the large mass of the poor, and a small number of wealthy families, with few of a "middle" class. At present it is fair to say that the gap between the groups is widening rather than closing, as the standard of living of the poor remains the same, or even falls, and that of the rich rises rapidly, owing to profits from high world prices in cotton, tobacco, and, above all, in petroleum. Equally significantly, the appearance of western luxuries—large automobiles, radios, refrigerators, furs, and luxury hotels—tends to increase the visible gap between rich and poor. Until 1918, an Arab who lived ostentatiously risked the vigorous attentions of the Ottoman tax-collector; today, the wealthy Arab is himself often closely connected with the government, and can manipulate its fiscal policy closely to his advantage. We have noted that the larger proportion of the revenues of Middle Eastern states is usually derived from indirect taxation of necessities such as food and clothing—a system that bears heaviest on the poorer classes.

AUTHORITARIAN RULE

A third problem concerns the political organization in certain Middle East states. By temperament and experience, many Middle Easterners incline to personal and authoritarian forms of rule. Nomadic and pastoral ways of life tend to throw up individuals of much prestige and personal leadership; and even in religion —as indicated by the importance of prophetic revelation in Islam and Christianity—there is a tendency to respect the man equally with, if not more than, the principle. In consequence the idea of parliamentary democracy, introduced after 1920 partly in deference to the Western European views, has had a limited and uncertain extension. The average man has tended to be impatient of rule by general consent, as expressed through Western democratic methods, preferring to follow a single individual of superior appeal and ability. Where such a figure has not been forthcoming, there has been acquiescence in rule by a caucus or oligarchy. In this situation, the importance of armed services is very great. As the final repository of physical power—only artillery, tanks, and aircraft can really control a large dissident mob—the army leaders especially come often to be the final arbiters in a struggle for power. Moreover, as something of a meritocracy in which able officers can most easily rise from humble origins to positions of power, the armed forces in the Middle East have often come to a centre of evolved middle-class, or even radical, opinion essentially different from the bourgeois attitude of the merchant groups.

Saudi Arabia and the Gulf states are ruled by absolute monarchs. For the twenty years preceding 1940 Turkey and Iran were ruled by despots. In more recent times, there has been a partial rejection of democracy on the Western pattern in countries where parliaments existed, and the last few years have seen a tendency towards a recrudescence of personal rule, the outstanding instances being in Egypt and Iraq. Parliamentary government seemed fairly strongly developed in Turkey until about 1955, but later events have suggested a return to the now normal pattern within the Middle East. A few years ago, it was perhaps widely felt that, eventually, monarchy would be largely displaced by a rising tide of republicanism, as actually has happened in Egypt, Iraq and Libya. But latterly, partly due to increased oil revenues, monarchs have shown considerable leadership and resilience, whilst republicanism is rather less successful.

MODERNIZING ISLAM

The widest problem of all concerns the cultural crisis within modern Islam. Until the end of the Middle Ages, Islamic culture was vigorous, and in many respects more advanced than that of Europe. Islamic thought greatly influenced the West, with a parallel superiority, or at least equality, in the political sphere. Since that time, however, there has been a considerable decline in power and intellectual strength: large-scale political penetration and domination from Europe began in the nineteenth century, and for several centuries material standards of life have no longer approximated to those of the West. There has, as a result, been much speculation in the Arab world upon the reasons for this decline. Three broad points of view can be discerned. There are those

who see no good prospect in a continuance of Islamic traditions, and so wish to follow new ways of life— either Christian and western, or, less clearly, new materialistic doctrines, one ultimate expression of which may be Communism. At the opposite extreme are those who suggest a return to a stricter form of Islam; and this policy is followed at the present time to a varying extent in Saudi Arabia and Algeria. Then there is a third group of intermediates, whose position is perhaps the most difficult of all, since they wish to combine modernity with a maintenance of internal traditions. How far exactly can one go in this respect? And too often an attempt at combining widely diverse elements leads to superficiality, a rejection of fundamentals and a real understanding of neither aspect. We therefore have the phenomenon of the 'angry young Arab'—given more and more to rejection of existing ways and now actively critical of the failure of leadership over Palestine, and of inequalities in and lack of opportunity for economic advancement.. He has an increasing sense of frustration which becomes more and more vocal with the spread of literacy. A further development, reflecting the special position of the Middle East between East and West, is the emergence of a specifically "Arab" socialism: neither Soviet nor Maoist communism, according to some Arab intellectuals, and certainly not "western" socialism, but reflecting the special social traditions of Islam.

Summing Up

Having made a cursory survey of Middle Eastern lands and their resources, it is now possible to attempt a summary of conclusions. We may recall once again what was said concerning the geographical position of the Middle East as the land connexion between three continents; from this situation has arisen its main role in the world—as an intermediary between the nations of Europe, Asia, and Africa, both in the economic and cultural spheres. Sometimes this historic function has been discharged purely, so to speak, as an agent or middlemfan, without any indigenous contribution—as when, or example, silk, sugar, citrus fruit, paper, gunpowder, and the compass were introduced from Further Asia into Europe. At other times, a technique or an idea has been received or developed in the Middle East, expanded there into a great movement, and transmitted elsewhere. One may cite, for example, the system of garden irrigation brought by the Arabs to Spain, which is still a highly productive element in Spanish agriculture, or the religions of Christianity and Islam, or the scientific ideas of the Greeks and Hindus, which were preserved throughout the Dark Ages of Europe and later made available to the West through the works of Muslim commentators.

With the discovery of the sea route to India in the fifteenth century, the importance of the Middle East as a transit area greatly declined, but following the opening of the Suez Canal, and the later growth of air communications, the situation has once more altered.

There has been a return to something of the ancient position, with air and sea routes now contributing again to outstanding prosperity, even though the Suez Canal, re-opened in 1975, cannot recapture all its former traffic unless it is enlarged.

Beirut early emerged as a world centre for air traffic—it was one of the first airports to be designed for jet aircraft—and because of its central geographical location, a climate that is exceptionally favourable for air navigation, and the topographical and political difficulties in regions further north and south, the Middle East has become a world nodal centre of air traffic. In a broader sense still there has very recently been a major shift of political and economic influence within the world. For several centuries, wealth and hence power were concentrated in north-western Europe; but since about 1900 the rise of America and Russia, the independence of India and black Africa, revival of China, and growing dependence of Europe on foodstuffs and primary materials imported from Australasia and Africa brought about an expansion of global relations. The Middle East, situated at the cross-roads of the world, has increasingly profited from what is now a central geographical position. Over and above this have been the dramatic effects first from the fact of having more than half the world's proven reserves of oil, and in 1974 awakening by Middle East governments to the implications of this commanding geopolitical situation. In only a few weeks during 1974 the dominance of Middle Eastern oil suppliers was demonstrated, with effects that will last for decades. A question anxiously debated since the quadrupling of oil revenues in 1973–74 is how far the Middle East will play a much greater financial and hence political role in world affairs. Concern, even alarm, in early 1974 over whether the new revenues would overturn or disrupt world markets has subsided, as it becomes clearer that the Middle East oil states are (very broadly) using one-third of their revenues for internal development, one-third in loans outside (often to Arab countries), and the remaining third for short-term deposit or longer-term investment in world stock markets. The political effects of the new wealth remain to be experienced: one so far is certainly the tendency of the U.S.A. to push Israel more strongly towards seeking political accommodation with its Arab neighbours.

Returning to more modest horizons, it is useful to notice one other feature of the Middle East, due in large part to its geography: potential as a tourist centre. It is probable that currently north-west Europe is experiencing a small climatic oscillation towards cooler, rainier summers; hence with "guaranteed" sunshine, excellent beaches, and considerable archaeological and human interest, certain parts of the Middle East have been able to develop a growing tourist attraction. New hotels, amenities and sports stadia are under construction; and given stable political conditions, this activity could well develop much further in the next few years, not merely for one season, but through a large proportion of the whole year.

POLITICAL OUTLINE

Similarly, there have been shifts in political fortune since the First World War. In 1916 the allocation of almost the entire Middle East as spheres of influence for European powers—Britain, France, Russia, Italy and Greece—had been agreed on. Treaties were actually in existence envisaging a territorial division which would have left only a fraction of Asia Minor under autonomous local rule.

From that apparent high water mark of Western influence, there has been a considerable decline; but the interest of external powers in the Middle East continues, fostered by the petroleum resources and strategic geographical location of the area.

At the same time there has been a parallel rise in nationalist feeling, helped on partly by differences among interested European powers and the skill with which these were exploited by Middle Eastern governments, and partly by the growth of internal wealth in the states themselves. This process became particularly vigorous after 1940, when from being a small marginal producer of in the main low-quality commodities, the Middle East became an important world supplier of petroleum, cotton, tobacco, wool and cereals.

The main element in the present-day politics of the Middle East is the existence of the state of Israel. To most Arabs, the creation first of a National Home for Jews and later of a Jewish State was a clear demonstration of hostility toward the Arab world on the part of Britain, France and the U.S.A.—a view which the events of 1956, and then of 1967, seemed only to confirm. As the Arabs see it, Western patronage of Zionism was a Machiavellian device to disrupt the Arab Middle East; and there can be no real friendship or understanding with the West until support for Zionism is disavowed. Moreover, uncertain of their own strength, Arab governments have increasingly turned to the U.S.S.R. for support against Zionism and its patrons. At times too it has been possible to take advantage of American divergence in policy from that of Britain and/or France (e.g. over oil concessions, Algeria, Cyprus and Suez). Moreover, the Middle East may offer a counterpoise to the forces balanced within the other southern extremity of Asia—in Viet-Nam especially. Thus the present situation in many ways resembles that of the pre-1914 Balkans, with a number of small and antagonistic states manoeuvering between independence and "protection" from a great power in the background. But the Balkans never possessed more than half the world's oil.

ECONOMIC TRENDS

In the economic sphere, it is more difficult to present a clearly defined picture. There is the unique asset of petroleum, which has already transformed ways of life in areas where it is exploited, and brought unexpected wealth to port terminals such as Abadan, Bahrain, Tripoli (Lebanon), Baniyas, Sidon, Kuwait and Benghazi. A striking inequality has consequently developed between various countries. Those actually producing oil have substantial extra wealth, and can embark on schemes of improvement, with at some time the possibility of a relatively unfettered foreign policy. Next in order come the non-producers with locational advantages—pipelines, good harbours or oil refineries. These countries can profit in a minor way from petroleum exploitation, but a ceiling is set by the cost of alternative transport. If too much is demanded by way of transit dues, the oil traffic could be re-routed either via Suez (when the Canal is open), the Cape of Good Hope, or even by alternative pipeline routes, such as that from Eilat on the Gulf of Aqaba to Haifa, or from Iran to the Mediterranean via Turkey, or the proposed one from Suez to Alexandria.

The relationships of foreign exploiting companies have undergone much change since the 1920s, when approximately only 16 per cent of oil revenue was paid over to native governments, and companies had almost extra-territorial legal and fiscal rights. One problem remains—the corroding effect upon native society (especially at highest levels) of sudden and easy wealth.

As regards agriculture and industry, the position is less satisfactory. Though there are certainly richly endowed spots (especially parts of the Nile Valley), the Middle East is on the whole a poor area, condemned by aridity and scantiness of resources to a marginal place as a producer. Nevertheless, the last twenty years have seen highly significant increases, particularly in Egypt, Iran and Turkey, which are now undoubtedly in numbers and wealth the leading states of the Middle East.

Turkey

Though an agricultural country, Turkey in 1920 imported almost one-half of her foodstuffs: most of the few public utilities were foreign-owned; and modern industry could hardly be said to exist. Following several phases of development (the last of which from 1947 onwards amounting almost to an agricultural revolution) Turkey is almost self-sufficient in food, and in favourable years since 1950 has even exported wheat. Foreign ownership has been very greatly reduced, and a variety of light industry created. At first much of this activity was state-sponsored and owned, but since 1950 there has been a partial de-nationalization of industry.

Egypt

Progress in Egypt has also been considerable. The careful use of river barrage systems has made the lower Nile valley one of the most productive agricultural areas in the world, with highest unit yields in maize and sugar, and highest quality in cotton. Intensity and quality of farming are unrivalled elsewhere in the Middle East, though there are ominous signs that future progress will be difficult—almost all the Nile water is now in use, and more and more fertilizers must be imported. Also, war periods greatly stimulated the growth of local industry, which, until the 1952 revolution, had always been on a capitalist, *laissez faire*, basis. Textiles are most important, but the increased wealth of the upper and middle classes has provided a market for light consumer goods that is now largely supplied within the country. An outstandingly important development is the full implementation of the Aswan High Dam project which, besides adding one-third to the present total of cultivated land in Egypt, provides electric power for heavy and light industry on a very considerable scale, at prices comparable with those of Europe.

Israel

Israel had certain advantages when it began the desperate task of attempting to support relatively large numbers in a poor environment at high standards of life. There were the energy and skill of its European-trained population; an overriding determination to make a success from unpromising beginnings, much machinery imported from Europe (Hitler allowed refugees from Nazi Germany to take plant, but not capital), and financial support from outside, chiefly the U.S.A. The country is not richly endowed—though mineral deposits (oil, natural gas, copper and phosphates) on a relatively small scale have recently been discovered—and transport is difficult. Moreover, most of the south is arid, and good agricultural land is everywhere severely restricted. A further handicap has been the determination to maintain European rather than Arab levels of wages—a matter in which powerful trade unions are involved. The advances achieved both in agriculture and industry have been very great but some restriction of consumption of food and clothing is still necessary, and there is a severe adverse balance of trade with exports amounting to only one-half or in some recent years, one-quarter of imports. In consequence, despite stringent controls, and great efforts to expand production, loans from abroad are still vital to the Israel economy, and unemployment on a moderate scale had come to be a problem before the 1967 War. Since then, however, the Israeli economy has enjoyed a sustained boom.

Iran

Iran has a long tradition of craft industry, especially in wool; and there are varied mineral deposits, including coal. With the exception of petroleum, however, these deposits are scattered, small in amount, often of low grade. Within the last few years, however, there has been a considerable degree of industrial growth in Teheran city, which now has an industrial quarter that produces a wide range of consumer goods and building materials, especially bricks. The construction of a gas-grid from Gach Saran to Shiraz, and then farther north, is a further impetus to development, and a large steel-making plant is now being built at Isfahan. Overall, Iran now claims a 15 per cent annual growth rate, one of, if not the highest, in the world.

Iraq

Until recently there was hardly any industry of any kind in Iraq, in distinct contrast to many of its neighbours. But since 1945 oil revenues have been allocated to a national Development Board, which has fostered the development of communications and agriculture, and begun to plan some industrial activity. Now, in addition to the processing of agricultural products, there is some textile manufacturing (chiefly cotton and rayon), a little light engineering, and a small chemical industry. Plans are in hand to expand these, especially the last. Agriculture is less developed than in Egypt, owing in part to the difficult nature of the two rivers, which have been more difficult to control and develop for irrigation. Since 1954, however, with the completion of Wadi Tharthar and other flood control and irrigation projects, the situation has changed, and large areas of good land which have hitherto remained unused can now be developed.

Syria, Lebanon, Jordan

At one time, Syria was the most industrialized province of the Ottoman Empire, with Aleppo second only to Constantinople in size. Loss of markets since 1918 has hampered but not destroyed the textile and metal manufactures of Aleppo and Damascus, and there are a small number of other industrial activities. Agriculturally, Syria has developed greatly since 1945. The irrigated "Fertile Crescent" has been expanded, and parts of the Euphrates valley brought back into cultivation for the first time in many centuries. Syria is self-sufficient in cereals, and exports these, together with raw cotton, to her less well-placed neighbours, the Lebanon and Jordan. The cotton is used both in the Middle East and in central Europe and Japan. The building of a dam across the Euphrates at Tabqa east of Aleppo (begun 1968 with German interests involved) will, when completed shortly, greatly assist Syrian development.

The Lebanon, like Israel, has severe natural handicaps. The rugged nature of the hills, which occupy most of the country, and aridity in the east greatly limit cultivation, and there are no mineral resources. Dependent on the import of foodstuffs, the country nevertheless has a considerable transit traffic, with the intelligence, adaptability and highly developed commercial sense of its people as the chief assets of the country. There is an international trade in gold, and Beirut (with four universities) has become a major cultural centre for the entire Middle East. Tourism could also become much more important.

Jordan, with almost no sea outlet, is in a very different situation. Most of the country is either arid or covered by bare sheets of lava—the only cultivable areas are west of the Jordan (Israeli-occupied since June 1967), in the Judaean uplands, and around Amman. Nomadic pastoralism is the only possible activity over much of the country—though the exploitation of substantial phosphate deposits provides a further source of occupation. An artificial territorial unit, with very few resources, Jordan is hardly viable, and has depended on outside subsidies, at present provided by Britain, the U.S.A. and, for varying periods since 1967, by Saudi Arabia, Kuwait and Libya.

Libya

A somewhat similar situation obtained in Libya until very recently where, despite the imposing size of territory, cultivated land is restricted to certain districts near or along the coast, together with a few inland oasis settlements. Now, discoveries of oil on a large scale are rapidly transforming the situation, and there is marked growth, especially in towns such as Benghazi and Tripoli.

Arabia

The Arabian peninsula is, so to speak, a stage beyond Libya. Before 1940 the territory was possibly the poorest in all the Middle East—only scattered oases with a largely nomadic population. Now the economic situation has been completely transformed; Saudi Arabia and Kuwait are, with Iran, the largest oil producers in the area by a considerable margin, and some of the small sheikhdoms along the Persian Gulf are also becoming major contributors. The immense oil revenues have financed lavish public works and welfare programmes, but the ease with which all imports needed for the small population can be paid for has reduced the incentive to develop the peninsula's other resources.

Cyprus

Though small, Cyprus prior to the troubles of 1974 had a very sound agricultural system, with over 55 per cent of the total land area used—a figure far higher than in any other Middle Eastern country. There are also small but useful deposits of iron, copper and asbestos; with a growing tourist trade. Since 1974, however, agriculture has been disrupted by the exchange of populations, with crops in some areas untended.

The Maghreb

Lastly, North Africa is still suffering from the effects of colonial rule. The efforts of prolonged and bitter warfare, the withdrawal of French "colons" who contributed in predominant measure to the more highly developed economic activities, and the resulting disequilibrium in an economy that until independence was strongly integrated with that of France—all these will take time to dissipate. Whilst over and above, there is the desperate need to provide for the rapidly growing numbers of inhabitants, with the concomitant problem of greater imbalance between urban and rural areas—a declining countryside, resulting in a fall-off in agricultural production, and congestion at declining levels of subsistence in the larger towns.

The most hopeful element is the presence of substantial mineral resources. Oil and gas could be used in part directly as fuel for industry; and revenues from exports might be directed to an expansion both of home manufacturing and improved agricultural techniques. Hydro-electricity is another possible source of energy, and this could foster *inter alia* more methodical exploitation and treatment of metallic mineral resources. At long term, the problem is also one of transferring the liability of an underemployed and growing population into the economic asset of a large pool of labour and consumer demand.

The Religions of the Middle East and North Africa

Islam

R. B. Serjeant

Islam is a major world religion and the faith predominating throughout the Middle East (with the exception of Lebanon the population of which is approximately half Muslim and half Christian) and North Africa. There are substantial Christian minorities in some countries and communities of oriental Jews and other faiths, for centuries integrated with the Muslim majority. Islam is not only a highly developed religious system but an established and distinctive culture embracing every aspect of human activity from theology, philosophy, literature to the visual arts and even man's routine daily conduct. Its characteristic intellectual manifestation therefore is in the field of Islamic law, the *Shari'ah*. Though in origin a Semitic Arabian faith, Islam was also the inheritor of the legacy of classical Greek and Roman civilization and, in its major phase of intellectual, social and cultural development after its emergence from its Arabian womb, it was affected by Christian, Jewish and Persian civilization. In turn, Greek scientific and philosophical writings—direct translations into Arabic or forming a principal element in the books of Arab scholars began to enter medieval Europe in Latin renderings about the early 12th century from the brilliant intellectual circles of Islamic Spain, and formed a potent factor in the little Renaissance of western Europe.

Islamic civilization had, by about the 18th century, clearly lost its initiative to the ascendant West and has not since regained it.

HISTORY

The founder of the religion of Islam was the Prophet Muhammad b. 'Abdullah, born about A.D. 570, a member of the noble house of Hashim, belonging to the 'Abd Manaf clan, itself a part of the Quraish tribal confederation of Mecca. 'Abd Manaf may be described as semi-priestly since they had the privilege of certain functions during the annual pilgrimage to the Meccan Ka'bah, a cube-shaped temple set in the sacred enclave (*haram*). Quraish controlled this enclave which was maintained inviolate from war or killing, and they had established a pre-eminence and loose hegemony even over many Arabian tribes which they had induced to enter a trading alliance extending over the main Arabian land routes, north and south, east and west. With the powerful Quraish leaders in Mecca, temple guardians, chiefs, merchant adventurers, Muhammad clashed, when, aged about 40, he began to proclaim the worship of the one God, Allah, as against their multiplicity of gods. These Quraish leaders were contemptuous of his mission.

While his uncle Abu Talib, head of the house of Hashim, lived, he protected Muhammad from physical harm, but after his death Muhammad sought protection from tribes outside Mecca—they would not accept him even when he asked only to remain quietly without preaching—Thaqif of Taif drove him roughly away. Ultimately pilgrims of the Aws and Khazraj tribes of Yathrib (Medina), some 200 miles north of Mecca, agreed to protect him there, undertaking to associate no other god with Allah and accepting certain moral stipulations. Muhammad left Mecca with his Companion Abu Bakr in the year 622—this is the year of the *hijrah* or hegira.

Arriving in Yathrib, Muhammad formed a federation or community (*ummah*) of Aws and Khazraj, known as the "Supporters" (*Ansar*), followed by their Jewish client tribes, and the "Emigrants" (*Muhajirun*), his refugee Quraish adherents, with himself as the ultimate arbiter of the *ummah* as a whole, though there remained a local opposition covertly antagonistic to him, the Munafiqun, rendered as "Hypocrites". Two internal issues had now to be fought by Muhammad—the enforcement of his position as theocratic head of the federation, and the acquisition of revenue to maintain his position; externally he took an aggressive attitude to the Meccan Quraish.

In Yathrib his disposal of the Jewish tribes who made common cause with the "Hypocrites" improved his financial position. The Meccan Quraish he overcame more by skilful political manoeuvre than through the occasional armed clashes with them, and in year 8 he entered Mecca without fighting. Previously he had declared Yathrib a sacred enclave (*haram*), renaming it Medina, the City (of the Prophet)—the two cities known as al-Haraman have become the holy land of Islam. Muhammad was conciliatory to his defeated Quraish kinsmen, and after his success against Taif, south of Mecca, deputations came from the Arabian tribes to make terms with the new Prophet—the heritor of the influence of the Meccan Quraish.

Early Islam

The two main tenets of Islam are embodied in the formula of the creed, "There is no god but Allah and Muhammad is the Apostle of God." Unitarianism (*tawhid*), as opposed to polytheism (*shirk*) or making partners with God, is Islam's basic principle, coupled with Muhammad's authority conferred on him by God. Muhammad made little change to the ancient Arabian religion—he abolished idolatry but confirmed the pilgrimage to the Ka'bah; the Koran, the sacred Book in Arabic revealed to Muhammad for his people, lays down certain social and moral rules. Among these are the condemnation of usury or interest (*riba*) on loans and prohibition of wine (*khamr*)—both ordinances have always been difficult to enforce. On the whole the little change involved seems to have made it easy for Arabia to accept Islam. While there is incontrovertible evidence of Muhammad's contact with Judaism, and even with Christianity, and the Koran contains versions of narrative known to the sacred books of these faiths, yet these are used to point purely Arabian morals. The limited social law laid down by the Koran is supplemented by a body of law and precept derived from the *Hadith* or Tradition of Muhammad's practice (*Sunnah*) at Medina, and welded into the Islamic system, mainly in its second and third centuries.

Subsequent History

Immediately after Muhammad's death in 632, Abu Bakr delegated by him to lead the prayer during his last indisposition became his successor or Caliph. Some Medinan supporters had attempted a breakaway from Quraish overlordship but Abu Bakr adroitly persuaded them to accept himself to follow Muhammad. But office in Arabia, generally speaking, is hereditary within a family group, though elective within that group, and Abu Bakr's action had taken no account of the claims of 'Ali, the Prophet's cousin and son-in-law—the house of Hashim to which Muhammad and 'Ali belonged was plainly aggrieved that a member of a minor Quraish clan should have snatched supreme power. Muhammad's Arabian coalition also showed tendencies to dissolve, the tribes particularly objecting to paying taxes to Medina, but Abu Bakr's firm line held it together. The expansionist thrusts beyond Arabia during his Caliphate, continued under his successor 'Umar and part of the reign of the third Caliph 'Uthman, diverted tribal energies to profitable warfare in Mesopotamia, Palestine-Syria, Egypt and Persia. Muslim armies were eventually to conquer North Africa, much of Spain, parts of France, and even besiege Rome, while in the east they later penetrated to Central Asia and India.

During 'Uthman's tenure of office the tide of conquest temporarily slackened and the turbulent tribes, now settled in southern Iraq and Egypt, began to dispute the Caliph's disposal of booty and revenue, maintaining that he unduly favoured members of his own house. A delegation of tribal malcontents from Egypt murdered 'Uthman in the holy city of Medina, and in the resultant confusion 'Ali, Muhammad's cousin was elected Caliph with the support of the tribesmen responsible for murdering 'Uthman. This raised grave constitutional problems for the young Muslim state, and is regarded as the origin of the greatest schism in Islam.

If Legitimist arguments were the sole consideration 'Ali's claims to succession seem the best, but he had previously lost it to 'Uthman—whose father belonged to the Umaiyah clan which had opposed Muhammad, but whose mother was of Hashim. 'Uthman naturally appointed Umaiyah men loyal to him to commands in the Empire, notably Mu'awiyah as governor of Syria—the son of that very Abu Sufyan who headed Quraish opposition to Muhammad at Mecca—though later reconciled to him. Mu'awiyah demanded 'Uthman's murderers be brought to justice in accordance with the law, but 'Ali, unable to cope with the murderers, his supporters, was driven by events to take up arms against Mu'awiyah. When they clashed at Siffin in Syria 'Ali was forced, against his better judgement to submit to the arbitration of the Koran

and Sunnah, thus automatically losing the position of supreme arbiter, inherited by the Caliphs from Muhammad. Though history is silent as to what the arbiters actually judged it was most likely as to whether 'Ali had broken the law established by Muhammad, and that he was held to have sheltered unprovoked murderers. The arbiters deposed him from the Caliphial office though the historians allege trickery entered into their action.

'Ali shortly after was murdered by one of a group of his former supporters which had come out against the arbitration it had first urged upon him. This group, the Khawarij, is commonly held to be the forerunner of the Ibadis of Oman and elsewhere. Mu'awiyah became Caliph and founder of the Umaiyad dynasty with its capital at Damascus. The ambitions of the Hashim house were not however allayed, and when Umaiyad troops slew 'Ali's son Husain at Karbala' in south Iraq they created the greatest Shi'ah martyr.

The house of Hashim also included the descendants of 'Abbas the Prophet's uncle, a relative, in Arabian eyes, as close as 'Ali to him, but 'Abbas had opposed Muhammad till late in the day. The 'Abbasids made common cause with the 'Ali-id Shi'ah against the Umaiyads, but were evidently abler in the political field. In the Umaiyad empire the Arabian tribes formed a kind of military élite but were constantly at factious war with one another. The Hashimites rode to power on the back of a rebellion against the Umaiyads which broke out in Khurasan in east Persia, but it was the 'Abbasid branch of Hashim which assumed the Caliphate and ruled from the capital they founded at Baghdad.

The 'Abbasid Caliphate endured up to the destruction of Baghdad in 1258 by the devastating Mongol invaders of the eastern empire, but the Caliphs had long been mere puppets in the hands of Turkish and other mercenaries, and the unwieldy empire had fragmented into independent states which rose and fell though they mostly conceded nominal allegiance to the 'Abbasid Caliphs.

The Mongol Ilkhanid sovereigns, now turned Muslim, were in turn displaced by the conquests of Tamlerlane at the end of the 14th century. In fact the Islamic empire had largely been taken over by Turkic soldiery. The Mameluke or Slave rulers of medieval Egypt who followed the Aiyubid (Kurdish) dynasty of Saladin were mainly Turks or Circassians. It was they who checked the Mongol advance at 'Ain Jalut in Palestine (1260). The Ottoman Turks captured Constantinople in 1453, and took Egypt from the Mamelukes in 1516, following this up by occupying the Hejaz where the Ashraf, descendants of the Prophet, ruled in Mecca and Medina, first under Mameluke then Turkish suzerainty. In 1533 the Turks took Baghdad and Iraq became part of the Ottoman Empire. The Ottoman Sultans assumed the title of Caliph—though in Islamic constitutional theory it is not easy to justify this. The Ottoman Caliphs endured till the Caliphate was abolished by Mustafa Kamal in 1924. The Turks have always been characterized by their adherence to Sunni orthodoxy.

Throughout history the 'Ali-ids have constantly asserted their right to be the Imams or leaders of the Muslim community—this in the religious and political senses, since Islam is fundamentally theocratic. The Shi'ah or followers of 'Ali and his descendants were in constant rebellion against the 'Abbasids and came to form a distinct schismatic group of Legitimist sects—at one time the Fatimid Shi'ah rulers of Egypt were near to conquering the main part of the Islamic world. The main Shi'ah sects today are the Ithna-'asharis, the Isma'ilis, and the near-orthodox Zaidis of the Yemen. The Safavids who conquered Persia at the beginning of the 16th century brought it finally into the Shi'ah fold. Sunni Hashimite dynasties flourish today in Jordan and Morocco as they did till fairly recently in Iraq and Libya, and the Shi'ah Zaidi ruler of Yemen was only displaced in 1962. The main difference between Sunnis and Shi'ah is over the Imamate i.e. the temporal and spiritual leader of Islam, for whereas Sunnis while they respect the Prophet's house, do not consider the Imam *must* be a member of it—the Shi'ah insist on an Imam of the descendants of 'Ali and Fatimah his wife, the Prophet's daughter.

It has been too readily assumed that, during the later Middle Ages and long Turkish domination, the Islamic Middle East was completely stagnant. The shift in economic patterns after the New World was discovered, and the Cape route to India, coupled with widening Western intellectual horizons and the development of science and technology did push European culture far ahead of the Muslim Middle East. It was confronted by a vigorous and hostile Christianity intent on proselytising in its very home-lands. Muslims had to face the challenge of the ideas and attitudes of Christian missionaries. Muslim thinkers like Muhammad 'Abduh (1849–1905) of Egypt and his school asserted that Islam had become heavily overlaid with false notions—hence its decline; like earlier reformers they were convinced that present difficulties could be solved by reversion to and (idealized) pure primitive Islam. Sometimes, in effect, this meant re-interpreting religious literature to suit attitudes and ideas of modern times—as for instance when they saw the virtual prohibition of polygamy in the restrictions which hedge it about. Since the earlier modern days political leaders like Mustafa Kamal of Turkey have often taken drastic measures, secularizing the state itself even up to the sensitive field of education, and accusing the more conservative forms of Islam of blocking progress. Today the Islamic Middle East has régimes ranging from the strong supporters of traditional Islam—like Sa'udi Arabia and Libya—to the anti-religious Marxist group controlling Aden.

ISLAMIC LAW

Orthodox Sunni Islam finds its main expression in *Shari'ah* law which it regards with great veneration. The Sunnis have crystallized into four "schools" (*madhhab*) or "rites", all of which are recognized as valid. Though in practice the adherents of one school can sometimes be at loggerheads with another, in modern times it is claimed that the law of any one of the rites can be applied to a case. The schools, named after their founders, are the Hanbali, regarded as the strictest, with adherents mainly in Sa'udi Arabia, the Shafi'is, the widest in extent with adherents in Egypt, Syria-Palestine, Egypt, South Arabia, and the Far East, the moderate Hanafi school which was the official rite of the Ottoman Turkish empire and to which most Muslims in the Indian sub-continent belong, and the Malikis of the North African states, Nigeria, and the Sudan. The Shi'ite sects have developed their own law, and give prominence to *ijtihad*, the forming of independent judgement, whereas the Sunnis are more bound by *taqlid* or following ancient models. However as the law of Sunnis, the moderate Shi'ah, and the Ibadis is basically derived from the same sources the differences are generally more of emphasis than principle.

Civil Courts. In the modern states of the Islamic world there exists, side by side with the *Shari'ah* court (judging cases on personal status, marriage, divorce, etc.), the secular court which has a wide jurisdiction (based on Western codes of law) in civil and criminal matters. This court is competent to give judgment irrespective of the creed or race of the defendant.

Islamic Law as Applying to Minorities. In cases of minorities (Christian or Jewish) residing as a community in Muslim countries, spiritual councils are established where judgment is passed according to the law of the community, in matters concerning personal status, by the recognised head of that community.

Tribal Courts. In steppe and mountain areas of countries where a proportion of the population is still tribal, tribal courts administer law and justice in accordance with ancient custom and tribal procedure.

Awqaf. In Muslim countries the law of Awqaf is the law applied to religious and charitable endowments, trusts and settlements. This important Islamic institution, found in all Eastern countries, is administered by the *Shari'ah* courts. Awqaf, or endowments, are pious bequests made by Muslims for the upkeep of religious institutions, public benefits, etc.

SUFIS

As in other religions, many Muslims find their emotional needs are not satisfied by observing a code of law and morals alone, and turn to mysticism. From early times Islamic mystics existed, known as Sufis, allegedly from their wearing a woollen garment. They seek complete identification with the Supreme Being and annihilation of the self—the existence of which latter they call polytheism (*shirk*). The learned doctors of Islam often think ill of the Sufis, and indeed rogues and wandering mendicants found Sufism a convenient means of livelihood. Certain Sufi groups allowed themselves dispensations and as stimulants even used hashish and opium which are not sanctioned by the Islamic moral code. The Sufis became organized in what are loosely called brotherhoods (*tariqah*), and have to a large extent been incorporated into the structure of orthodox Islamic society. Some *tariqahs* induce ecstatic states by their performance of the *dhikr*, meaning, literally, the mentioning (of Allah). Today there is much disapproval of the more extravagant manifestations of the Sufis and in some places these have been banned entirely.

The completely Islamic state as the theorists envisage it, run in conformity with the rules of the *Shari'ah* has probably never been achieved, and people's practice is often at variance with some or other requirements of *Shari'ah*. The imprint of Islam is nevertheless unmistakably evident on every country in this volume.

BELIEF AND PRACTICE

"Islam" means the act of submitting or resigning oneself to God, and a Muslim is one who resigns or submits himself to God. Muslims disapprove of the term "Muhammadan" for the faith of Islam, since they worship Allah, and Muhammad is only the Apostle of Allah whose duty it was to convey revelation, though he is regarded as the "Best of Mankind". He is the Seal (*Khatam*) of the Prophets, i.e. the ultimate Prophet in a long series in which both Moses and Jesus figure. They are revered, but, like Muhammad the Prophet, they are not worshipped.

Nearly all Muslims agree on acceptance of six articles of the faith of Islam: (i) Belief in God; (ii) in His angels; (iii) in His revealed books; (iv) in His Apostles; (v) in the Resurrection and Day of Judgement; and (vi) in His predestination of good and evil.

Faith includes works, and certain practices are obligatory on the believing Muslim. These are five in number:

1. The recital of the creed (*Shahadah*)—"There is no god but God (Allah) and Muhammad is the Apostle of God." This formula is embodied in the call to prayer made by the muezzin (announcer) from the minaret of the mosque before each of the five daily prayers.

2. The performance of the Prayer (*Salat*) at the five appointed canonical times—in the early dawn before the sun has risen above the horizon, in the early afternoon when the sun has begun to decline, later when the sun is about midway in its course towards setting, immediately after sunset, in the evening between the disappearance of the red glow in the west and bedtime. In prayer Muslims face towards the Ka'bah in Mecca. They unroll prayer mats and pray in a mosque (place of prostration), at home, or wherever they may be, bowing and prostrating themselves before God and reciting set verses in Arabic from the Koran. On Fridays it is obligatory for men to attend congregational Prayer in the central mosque of the quarter in which one lives—women do not normally attend. On this occasion formal prayers are preceded by a sermon.

3. The payment of the legal alms (*Zakat*). In early times this contribution was collected by officials of the Islamic state, and devoted to the relief of the poor, debtors, aid to travellers and other charitable and state purposes. Nowadays the fulfilment of this religious obligation is left to the conscience of the individual believer.

4. The thirty days of the fast in the month of Ramadan, the ninth month in the lunar year. As the lunar calendar is shorter by 11 days than the solar calendar Ramadan moves from the hottest to the coldest seasons of the solar year. It is observed as a fast from dawn to sunset each day by all adults in normal health, during which time no food or drink may be taken. The sick, pregnant women, travellers and children are exempt; some states exempt students, soldiers and factory workers. The fast ends with one of the two major Muslim festivals, 'Id al-Fitr.

5. The pilgrimage (*Hajj*) to Mecca. Every Muslim is obliged, circumstances permitting, to perform this at least once in his lifetime, and when accomplished he may assume the title, *Hajji*. About a million pilgrims go each year to Mecca, but the holy cities of Mecca and Medina are prohibited to non-Muslims.

Before entering the sacred area around Mecca by the seventh day of Dhu 'l-Hijjah, the twelfth month of the Muslim year, pilgrims must don the *ihram*, consisting of two unseamed lengths of white cloth, indicating that they are entering a state of consecration and casting off what is ritually impure. The pilgrims circumambulate the Ka'bah seven times, endeavouring to kiss the sacred Black Stone. Later they run seven times between the near-by twin hills of Safa and Marwa, thus recalling Hagar's desperate search for water for her child Ishmael (from whom the Arabs claim descent). On the eighth day of the month the pilgrims leave the city for Mina, a small town six miles to the east. Then before sunrise of the next day all make for the plain below Mount 'Arafat some twelve miles east of Mecca where they pass the day in prayers and recitation until sunset. This point is the climax of the pilgrimage when the whole gathering returns, first to Muzdalifah where it spends the night, then to Mina where pilgrims stone the devil represented by three heaps of stones (*jamrah*). The devil is said to have appeared to Abraham here and to have been driven away by Abraham throwing stones at him. This day, the 10th of Dhu 'l-Hijjah is 'Id al-Adha, the Feast of the Sacrifices, and the pilgrims sacrifice an animal. usually a sheep, and have their heads shaved by one of the barbers at Mina. They return to Mecca that evening.

The Holy War (*Jihad*) against the infidel was the means whereby Arab Muslim rule made its immense expansion in the first centuries of Islam, but despite pressures to do so it has never been elevated to form a sixth Pillar of Islam. Today many theologians interpret *jihad* in a less literal sense as the combatting of evil.

The Koran (*Qur'an*, "recital", "reading") is for Muslims the very Word of God. The Koran consists of 114 chapters (*surah*) of uneven length, the longest coming first after the brief opening chapter called *al-Fatihah*. (The Koran is about as long as the New Testament). *Al-Fatihah* (The Opener) commences with the words, "*Bismillahi 'l-Rahmani 'l-Rahim*, In the name of God, the Compassionate, the Merciful", and forms part of the ritual five prayers (*salat*). Other special verses and chapters are also used on a variety of occasions, and of course Muslim children are taught to recite by heart a portion of the Koran or, preferably, the whole of it. The Koran has been the subject of vast written commentaries, but translation into other languages is not much approved by Muslims, though inter-linear translations (a line of Koran underneath which is a line of translation) are used, and a number of modern translations into English exists. The earlier (Meccan) chapters of the Koran speak of the unity of God and his wonders, of the Day of Judgement and Paradise, while the Medinan chapters tend to be occupied more with social legislation for marriage, divorce, personal and communal behaviour. The definitive redaction of the Koran was ordered by the Caliph 'Uthman (644–56).

HOLY PLACES

Mecca: Hijaz province of Sa'udi Arabia. Mecca is centred around the Ka'bah, the most venerated building in Islam, traditionally held to have been founded by Abraham, recognized by Islam also as a Prophet. It stands in the centre of the vast courtyard of the Great Mosque and has the form of a cube; its construction is of local grey stone and its walls are draped with a black curtain embroidered with a strip of writing containing Koran verses. In the eastern corner is set the famous Black Stone. The enlarging of the Great Mosque commenced under the second Caliph 'Umar. Both the Ka'bah and Great Mosque have undergone many renovations, notably recently since 1952. Mecca is the centre of the annual pilgrimage from all Muslim countries.

Medina (*The City*, i.e. of the Prophet): Hijaz province of Sa'udi Arabia. Medina, formerly called Yathrib, was created a sacred enclave (*haram*) by Muhammad who died there in the year 11 of the *hijrah* and was buried in the Mosque of the Prophet. Close to his tomb are those of Abu Bakr and 'Umar and a little further away that of his daughter Fatimah. Frequently damaged, restored and enlarged, the mosque building was extensively renovated by the Sa'udi Government in 1955.

Jerusalem (Arabic *al-Quds* or *Bait al-Maqdis, The Hallowed/Consecrated*): Jordan (currently annexed by Israel). Jerusalem is Islam's next most holy city after al-Haraman (Mecca and Medina), not only because it is associated with so many pre-Islamic prophets, but because Muhammad himself is popularly held to have made the "Night Journey" there. Jerusalem contains the magnificent Islamic shrine, the Dome of the Rock (688–91), built by the Caliph 'Abd al-Malik, and the famous al-Masjid al-Aqsa recently severely damaged by arson.

Hebron (Habrun): Israel-occupied Jordan. The Mosque of Abraham, called al-Khalil, the "Friend of God" is built over the tomb of Abraham, the Cave of Machpelah; it also contains the tombs of Sarah, Isaac, Rebecca, Jacob, and Leah. The shrine is revered by Muslims and Jews, and is also important to Christians.

Qairawan: Tunisia. The city is regarded as a holy place for Muslims, seven pilgrimages to the Great Mosque of Sidi 'Uqbah b. Nafi' (an early Muslim general who founded Qairawan as a base for the Muslim invaders of North Africa) being considered equivalent of one pilgrimage to Mecca.

Muley Idris: Morocco. The shrine at the burial-place of the founder of the Idrisid dynasty in the year 687, at Walili.

* * *

Every Middle Eastern country has a multitude of shrines and saints' tombs held in veneration, except Wahhabi states which consider saint cults to be polytheism (*shirk*). In Turkey, however, the policy of secularization led to Aya Sofya Mosque (St. Sophia) being turned into a museum.

The following shrines are associated with the Shi'ah or Legitimist sects of Islam.

Mashhad (Meshed): Iran. The city is famous for the shrine of Imam 'Ali al-Rida/Riza, the eighth Imam of the Ithna'ashari group, which attracts some hundred thousand pilgrims each year. The shrine is surrounded by many buildings with religious or historical associations.

Qum: Iran. A Shi'ah centre, it is venerated as having the tomb of Fatimah the sister of Imam al-Rida/Riza and hundreds of saints and kings including Imams 'Ali b. Ja'far and Ibrahim, Shah Safi and Shah 'Abbas II.

Najaf: Iraq. Mashhad 'Ali, reputed to be constructed over the place where 'Ali b. Abi Talib, the cousin and son-in-law of Muhammad is buried, is a most venerated Shi'ah shrine drawing many pilgrims.

Karbala': Iraq. The shrine of Husain b. 'Ali where, at Mashhad Husain, he was slain with most of his family, is today more venerated by the Shi'ah than the Mashhad 'Ali. 'Ashura Day (10th Muharram) when Husain was killed is commemorated by passion plays (*ta'ziyah*) and religious processions when the drama of his death is re-enacted with extravagant expressions of emotion.

Baghdad: Iraq. The Kazimain/Kadhimain Mosque is a celebrated Shi'ah shrine containing the tomb of Musa al-Kazim/Kadhim, the 7th Imam of the Ithna'asharis.

RELIGIOUS GROUPINGS

Sunnis

The great majority, probably over 80 per cent of Muslims, is Sunni, followers of the *Sunnah*, i.e. the way, course, rule or manner of conduct of the Prophet Muhammad; they are generally called "Orthodox". The Sunnis recognize the first four Caliphs (Abu Bakr, 'Umar, 'Uthman, 'Ali) as Rashidun, i.e. following the right course. They base their *Sunnah* upon the Koran and "Six Books" of Traditions, and are organized in four Orthodox schools or rites (*madhhab*), all of equal standing within the Orthodox fold. Many Muslims today prefer to avoid identification with any single school.

Wahhabis

The adherents of "Wahhabism" strongly disapprove of this title by which they are known outside their own group, for they call themselves Muwahhidun or Unitarians. In fact they belong to the strict Hanbali school following its noted exponent, the 13th/14th century Syrian reformer Ibn Taimiyah. The founder of "Wahhabism", Muhammad b. 'Abd al-Wahhab of Arabian Najd (1703–87), sought to return to the pristine purity of early Islam freed from all accretions and what he regarded as innovations contrary to its true spirit, such as saint worship, lax sexual practices, and superstition. His doctrine was accepted by the chief Muhammad b. Sa'ud of Dar'iyah (near al-Riyadh). Ibn Sa'ud and his son 'Abd al-'Aziz—who proved a capable general—conquered much of Arabia. Medina fell in 1804 and Mecca in 1806 to Sa'ud son of 'Abd al-'Aziz, but after his death in 1814 the Wahhabis were gradually broken by the armies of the Pasha of Egypt, Muhammad 'Ali acting nominally on behalf of the Ottoman Sultan of Turkey. After varying fortunes in the 19th century the Wahhabis emerged as an Arabian power in the opening years of the 20th century. By the close of 1925 they held the Holy Cities and Jeddah and are today the strongest power in the Arabian Peninsula. Though Wahhabism remains the strictest of the Orthodox groups, Sa'udi Arabia has made some accommodation to modern times.

The Tariqahs or Religious Orders

In many Middle Eastern countries the Religious Orders (*Tariqahs*) have important political cum religious roles in society. There are the widely spread Qadiriyah who with the Tijaniyah are found in North Africa, the Khatmiyah in the Sudan, the Rifa'iyah in Egypt and Syria to pick out a few at random. The West has no organizations exactly equivalent to these Sufi orders into which an individual has to be initiated, and in which, by dint of ascetic excercises and study he may attain degrees of mystical enlightenment—this can also bring moral influence over his fellow men. The Orders may be Sunni or Shi'ah; some few Orders are even so unconventional as to be hardly Islamic at all. It was the Orthodox reformist Sanusi Order that has played the most significant role in our time. The Grand Sanusi, Muhammad b. 'Ali, born at Mustaghanem in Algeria of a Sharif family, founded the first *zawiyah* or lodge of the Sanusis in 1837. The Sanusi *Tariqah* is distinguished for its exacting standards of personal morality. The Sanusis set up a network of lodges in Cyrenaica (Libya) and put up strong resistance to Italian colonization. The Grand Sanusi was recognized as King Idris of Libya in 1951, but lost his throne at the military revolt led by Colonel Gaddafi in 1969.

Shi'ah

The Legitimist Shi'ah pay allegiance to 'Ali as mentioned above. 'Ali's posterity which must number

at least hundreds of thousands, scattered all over the Muslim world, are customarily called Sharifs if they trace descent to his son al-Hasan, and Saiyids if descended from al-Husain, but while the Sharifs and Saiyids, the religious aristocracy of Islam, traditionally are accorded certain privileges in Islamic society, not all are Shi'ah, many being Sunnis. By the 9th century many strange sects and even pagan beliefs had become associated with the original Shi'ah or Party of 'Ali, but these extremist sects called *ghulat* have mostly vanished except a few, often practising a sort of quietism or dissimulation (*taqiyah*) for fear of persecution. All Shi'ah accord 'Ali an exalted position, the extreme (and heretical) Shi'ah at one time according him a sort of divinity even. Shi'ite Islam does not in the main differ on fundamental issues from the Sunni Orthodox since they draw from the same ultimate sources, but Shi'ah *mujtahids* have, certainly in theory, greater freedom to alter the application of law since they are regarded as spokesmen of the Hidden Imam.

The Ithna'asharis (Twelvers)

The largest Shi'ah school or rite is the Ithna'ashariyah or Twelvers, acknowledging twelve Imams. From 1502 Shi'ism became the established school in Iran under the Safavid ruler Sultan Shah Isma'il who claimed descent from Musa al-Kazim (see below). There are also Ithna'ashariyah in southern Iraq, al-Hasa, Bahrain and the Indian sub-continent.

The last Shi'ah Imam, Muhammad al-Mahdi, disappeared in 878, but the Ithna'asharis believe he is still alive and will re-appear in the last days before the Day of Judgement as the Mahdi (Guided One)—a sort of Messiah—who will rule personally by divine right.

The twelve Imams recognized by the Twelver, Ithna'ashari Shi'ah are:

(1) 'Ali b. Abi Talib, cousin and son-in-law of the Prophet Muhammad.

(2) Al-Hasan, son of 'Ali.

(3) Al-Husain, second son of 'Ali.

(4) 'Ali Zain al-'Abidin, son of Husain.

(5) Muhammad al-Baqir, son of 'Ali Zain al-'Abidin.

(6) Ja'far al-Sadiq, son of Muhammad al-Baqir.

(7) Musa al-Kazim, son of Ja'far al-Sadiq.

(8) 'Ali al-Rida, son of Musa al-Kazim.

(9) Muhammad al-Taqi, son of 'Ali al-Rida.

(10) 'Ali al-Naqi, son of Muhammad al-Taqi.

(11) Al-Hasan al-Zaki, son of 'Ali al-Naqi, al-'Askari.

(12) Muhammad al-Mahdi, son of al-Hasan b. 'Ali, al-'Askari, known as al-Hujjah, the Proof.

Isma'ilis

This group of the Shi'ah does not recognize Musa al-Kazim as seventh Imam, but holds that the last Imam visible on earth was Isma'il, the other son of Ja'far al-Sadiq. For this reason they are also called the Sab'iyah or Seveners. There is however much disagreement among the Seveners as to whether they recognized Isma'il himself as seventh Imam, or one of his several sons, and the Fatimids of Egypt (10th–12th centuries) in fact recognized a son of Isma'il's son Muhammad. Schismatic off-shoots from the Fatimid-Isma'ili group are the Druzes, the Musta'lians first settled in the Yemen but now with their main centre in Bombay—where the Daudi section is known as Bohoras, and the Nizari Isma'ilis of whom the Aga Khan is the spiritual head. The sect has a secret literature embodying its esoteric philosophy. Small groups of Isma'ilis are to be found in north-west Syria, Iran, Afghanistan, East Africa and Zanzibar, and larger numbers in India and Pakistan.

'Alawis (Nusairis)

The 'Alawis believe Muhammad was a mere forerunner of 'Ali and that the latter was an incarnation of Allah. This Shi'i extremist sect established in the ninth century has also adopted practices of both Christian and pagan origin. Most of its members today live in north-west Syria.

Druze

The Druzes are heretics, an off-shoot of the Fatimid Isma'ilis (see above), established in Lebanon and Syria. Their name (Duruz) derives from al-Darazi, a missionary of Persian origin who brought about the conversion of these Syrian mountaineers to the belief of the divine origin of the Fatimid Caliph al-Hakim. The origins of this sect and its subsequent expansion are still obscure. Hamzah b. 'Ali, a Persian contemporary of al-Darazi is the author of several of the religious treatises of the Druze. This community acknowledges one God and believes that he has on many occasions become incarnate in man. His last appearance was in the person of the Fatimid Caliph al-Hakim (disappeared 1020). The Druze have played a distinctive role in the political and social life of their country and are renowned for their independence of character.

Zaidis

The Zaidis are a liberal and moderate sect of the Shi'ah close enough to the Sunnis to call themselves the "Fifth School" (*al-madhhab al-khamis*). Their name is derived from a grandson of al-Husain b. 'Ali called Zaid b. 'Ali whom they recognize as fifth Imam. They reject religious dissimulation (*taqiyah*) and are extremely warlike. Zaidism is the dominant school of Islam in the Yemen Arab Republic, but Shafi'is form roughly half the population.

Ibadis

The Ibadis are commonly held to have their origins in the Khawarij who disassociated themselves from 'Ali b. Abi Talib when he accepted arbitration in his quarrel with Mu'awiyah, but this is open to question. They broke off early from the main stream of Islam and are usually regarded as heretics though with little justification. Groups of the sect, which has often suffered persecution, are found in Oman where Ibadism is the state religion, Zanzibar, Libya and Algeria, mainly in the Mzab.

Christianity

DEVELOPMENT IN THE MIDDLE EAST

Christianity was adopted as the official religion o. the Roman empire in A.D. 313, and the Christian Church came to be based on the four leading cities, Rome, Constantinople (capital from A.D. 330), Alexandria and Antioch. From the divergent development of the four ecclesiastical provinces there soon emerged four separate churches: the Roman Catholic or Latin Church (from Rome), the Greek Orthodox Church (from Constantinople), the Syrian or Jacobite Church (from Antioch) and the Coptic Church (from Alexandria).

Later divisions resulted in the emergence of the Armenian (Gregorian) Church, which was founded in the fourth century, and the Nestorian Church, which grew up in the fifth century in Syria, Mesopotamia and Iran, following the teaching of Nestorius of Cilicia (d. 431). From the seventh century on followers of St. Maron began to establish themselves in northern Lebanon, laying the foundations of the Maronite Church.

Subsequently the Uniate Churches were brought into existence by the renunciation by formerly independent churches of doctrines regarded as heretical by the Roman Church and by the acknowledgement of Papal supremacy. These churches—the Armenian Catholic, the Chaldean (Nestorian) Catholic, Greek Catholic, the Coptic Catholic, the Syrian Catholic and the Maronite Church did, however, retain their Oriental customs and rites. The independent churches continued in existence alongside the Uniate Churches with the exception of the Maronites, all of whom reverted to Rome.

HOLY PLACES

Bethlehem: Israeli-occupied Jordan. The traditional birthplace of Jesus is enclosed in the Basilica of the Nativity, revered also by Muslims. Christmas is celebrated here by the Roman and Eastern Rite Churches on December 25th, by the Greek Orthodox, Coptic and Syrian Orthodox Churches on January 6th and 7th, by the Ethiopian Church on January 8th, and by the Armenian Church on January 19th. The tomb of Rachel, important to the three faiths, is just outside the town.

Jerusalem: Jordan (but annexed by Israel). The most holy city of Christianity has been a centre for pilgrims since the Middle Ages. It is the seat of the patriarchates of the Roman, Greek Orthodox and Armenian Churches, who share the custodianship of the Church of the Holy Sepulchre and who each own land and buildings in the neighbouring area.

The Church of the Holy Sepulchre stands on the hill of Golgotha in the higher north-western part of the Old City. In the central chamber of the church is the Byzantine Rotunda built by twelfth century crusaders, which shelters the small shrine on the traditional site of the tomb. Here the different patriarchates exercise their rights in turn. Close by is the Rock of Calvary, revered as the site of the Crucifixion.

Most pilgrims devoutly follow the Way of the Cross leading from the Roman Praetorium through several streets of the Old City to the Holy Sepulchre. Franciscan monks, commemorating the journey to the Crucifixion, follow the course of this traditional route each Friday; on Good Friday this procession marks a climax of the Easter celebrations of the Roman Church.

Outside the Old City stands the Mount of Olives, the scene of Jesus' Ascension. At the foot of its hill is the Garden of Gethsemane which is associated with the vigil on the eve of the Crucifixion. The Cenaculum or traditional room of the Last Supper is situated on Mount Zion in Israel.

Nazareth: Israel. This town, closely associated with the childhood of Jesus, has been a Christian centre since the fourth century A.D. The huge, domed Church of the Annunciation has recently been built on the site of numerous earlier churches to protect the underground Grotto of the Annunciation. Nearby the Church of St. Joseph marks the traditional site of Joseph's workshop.

Galilee: Israel. Many places by this lake are associated with the life of Jesus: Cana, scene of the miracle of water and wine, which is celebrated by an annual pilgrimage on the second Sunday after Epiphany; the Mount of Beatitudes; Tabgha, scene of the multiplication of the loaves and fish; and Capurneum, scene of the healing of the Centurion's servant.

Mount Tabor: Israel. The traditional site of the Transfiguration, which has drawn pilgrims since the fourth century, is commemorated by a Franciscan Monastery and a Greek Basilica, where the annual Festival of the Transfiguration is held.

Jericho: Israeli-occupied Jordan. The scene of the baptism of Jesus; nearby is the Greek Monastery of St. John the Baptist.

Nablus (*Samaria*): Israeli-occupied Jordan. This old town contains Jacob's Well, associated with Jesus, and the Tomb of Joseph.

Qubaïbah (*Emmaus*): Israeli-occupied Jordan. It was near this town that two of the Disciples encountered Jesus after the Resurrection.

'Azariyyah (*Bethany*): Israeli-occupied Jordan. A town frequented by Jesus, the home of Mary and Martha, and the scene of the Raising of Lazarus.

Mount Carmel: Haifa, Israel. The Cave of Elijah draws many pilgrims, including Muslims and Druzes, who celebrate the Feast of Mar Elias on July 20th.

Ein Kerem: Israel. Traditional birthplace of John the Baptist, to whom a Franciscan church is dedicated; nearby is the Church of the Visitation.

Ephesus: Turkey. The city, formerly a great centre of pagan worship, where Paul founded the first of the seven Asian Churches. The recently restored Basilica, built by Justinian, is dedicated to John the Evangelist, who legend claims died here; a fourth century church on Aladag Mountain commemorating Mary's

last years spent here now draws an annual pilgrimage in August.

Judaism

There are two main Jewish communities, the Ashkenazim and the Sephardim, the former from east, central and northern Europe, the latter from Spain, the Balkans, the Middle East and North Africa. The majority of immigrants into Israel were from the Ashkenazim, and their influence predominates there, though the Hebrew language follows Sephardim usage. There is no doctrinal difference between the two communities, but they observe distinct rituals.

HOLY PLACES

Wailing Wall: Jerusalem. This last remnant of the western part of the wall surrounding the courtyard of Herod's Temple, finally destroyed by the Romans in A.D. 70, is visited by devout Jews, particularly on the Fast Day of the 9th of Av, to grieve the destruction of the First and Second Temples which had once stood on the same site.

Mount Zion: Israel. A hill south-west of the Old City of Jerusalem, venerated particularly for the tomb of David, acknowledged by Muslims as abi Dawud (The Jebuzite hill on which David founded his Holy City is now known as Mount Ophel, and is in Jordan, just to the east of the modern Mount Zion). Not far from the foot of the hill are the rock-cut tombs of the family of King Herod.

Cave of Machpelah: Hebron, Israeli-occupied Jordan. The grotto, over which was built a mosque, contains the tombs of Abraham and Sarah, Isaac and Rebecca, Jacob and Leah.

Bethlehem: Israeli-occupied Jordan. The traditional tomb of Rachel is in a small shrine outside the town, venerated also by Muslims and Christians.

Mount Carmel: Israel. The mountain is associated with Elijah, whose Cave in Haifa draws many pilgrims. (*See* Christianity section).

Safad: Israel. Centre of the medieval Cabbalist movement, this city contains several synagogues from the sixteenth century associated with these scholars, and many important tombs, notably that of Rabbi Isaac Louria.

Meiron: Israel. The town contains the tombs of Shimon bar Yohai, reputed founder in the second century of the medieval Cabbalist movement, and his son Eleazer. A yearly Hassidic pilgrimage is held to the tomb to celebrate Lag Ba'Omer with a night of traditional singing and dancing in which Muslims also participate.

Tiberias: Israel. An ancient city containing the tombs of Moses Maimonides and Rabbi Meir Baal Harness. Famous as an historical centre of Cabbalist scholarship, it is with Jerusalem, Safad and Hebron, one of the four sacred cities of Judaism, and once accommodated a university and the Sandhedrin.

Other Communities

ZOROASTRIANS

Zoroastrianism developed from the teaching of Zoroaster, or Zarathustra, who lived in Iran some time between 700 and 550 B.C. Later adopted as the official religion of the Persian empire, Zoroastrianism remained predominant in Iran until the rise of Islam. Many adherents were forced by persecution to emigrate, and the main centre of the faith is now Bombay, where they are known as Parsees. Technically a monotheistic faith, Zoroastrianism retained some elements of polytheism. It later became associated with fire-worship.

Yazd: Iran. This city was the ancient centre of the Zoroastrian religion, and was later used as a retreat during the Arab conquest. It contains five fire temples and still remains a centre for this faith, of which some 35,000 adherents live in Iran.

BAHA'IS

Baha'ism made its appearance in Persia during the middle of the nineteenth century. It was founded by Baha'ullah, who, after a revelation in Baghdad in 1863, declared himself to be the "Promised One". A member of the Persian nobility he devoted his life to preaching against the corruption endemic in Persian society and as a result spent many years in exile; he died at Acre in Palestine in 1892. The Sect was administered by his descendants until 1957; the 56 national branches now elect the present governing body, the Universal House of Justice.

Baha'ism claims complete independence from all other faiths. Its followers believe that the basic principles of the great religions of the world are in complete harmony and that their aims and functions are complementary. Other tenets include belief in the brotherhood of man, the abolition of racial and colour discrimination, the equality of the sexes, progress towards world government and the use of an international language, monogamy, chastity and the encouragement of family life. There is no Baha'i priesthood, and asceticism and monasticism are discouraged. Most of the Middle Eastern adherents of the faith live in Iran or Israel.

Haifa: Israel. Shrine of the Bab and gardens, world centre of the Baha'i faith. Pilgrims visit this centre, and one in Acre where Baha'ullah was imprisoned, on the anniversaries of the birth and death of Bab and Baha'ullah.

SAMARITANS

Mount Gerazim: Jordan. The mountain is sacred to this small sect, who celebrate Passover here. The Samaritan High Priest lives at Nablus.

The Arab-Israeli Confrontation 1967-75

Michael Adams

Introduction

Israel's decisive victory over the Arab states in the Six Day war of 1967 raised hopes that at last it would be possible to reach a definitive settlement of the Arab-Israeli conflict. Instead it soon became apparent that the conflict had merely been complicated by the occupation of further Arab territory, the displacement of still more refugees and the aggravation of the sense of grievance felt by the Palestinians and now shared more widely than ever in the rest of the Arab world. For six years, during which an uneasy condition of "no peace and no war" persisted in the area, accompanied by extreme tension and frequent outbreaks of guerrilla activity and even limited warfare, there was no material change in the situation. The Arabs, immediately after their defeat in 1967, were unwilling to consider negotiations; by the time they had modified this refusal, the Israelis had so hardened their position that there appeared to be no basis for an acceptable compromise. With diminishing conviction the United Nations, the superpowers and other intermediaries tried to devise a settlement, but without success. In May 1973 the Israelis celebrated the twenty-fifth anniversary of the birth of the Jewish state with a military parade in Jerusalem which symbolized Israel's strength and determination. With the Arab states apparently divided and in disarray, the surprise was all the greater when, on October 6th, the armies of Egypt and Syria launched a surprise attack on Israel which was to upset completely the power balance in the Middle East and to lead to important repercussions in the rest of the world.

During the six years between the June war of 1967 and the October war of 1973 there had been five main attempts from outside the area to provide an acceptable basis for agreement between the parties in the Middle East. The first of these was made at the United Nations in the autumn of 1967 when the Security Council, after anxious debate, adopted a unanimous resolution dealing with all the points at issue between Israel and her Arab neighbours. As a result of this resolution (No. 242 of November 22nd, 1967) a Swedish diplomat, Dr. Gunnar Jarring, was appointed as the Special Representative of the Secretary-General of the United Nations, with the task of establishing contact with the conflicting parties and helping them to reach agreement. The fact that the resolution was supported by all the major powers gave it a strength which enabled it to survive as the basis for a potential settlement; but, despite the patient efforts of Dr. Jarring, the varied interpretations placed upon the resolution prevented its implementation.

The second initiative was taken early in 1969 at the suggestion of the French Government, in the conviction that Dr. Jarring would be unable to make any progress until the major powers agreed on a single interpretation of the Security Council resolution. Accordingly, Four-Power talks were started in New York between the representatives at the UN of the United States, the Soviet Union, Britain and France and these were later superseded by bilateral talks between the United States and the Soviet Union. The stumbling-block continued to be the interpretation of the clause in resolution 242 which provided for Israeli withdrawal "from territories occupied" in the conflict of June 1967 and by the end of the year it was clear that the two super-powers had failed to reach agreement.

The American Secretary of State, Mr. William Rogers, then took the third initiative, putting forward in December 1969 a series of proposals which came to be known as the "Rogers Plan". The plan left the details of a settlement to be negotiated between the interested parties, but made it clear that the American Government envisaged only minor rectifications in the pre-June 1967 borders between Israel and her Arab neighbours and favoured granting to the Palestinians the right so often promised in UN resolutions to choose between returning to Palestine or receiving compensation for their lost properties.

The Rogers proposals were badly received by all parties and although they continued to be discussed throughout 1970 the United States Government finally abandoned them in favour of a less ambitious plan to achieve a partial settlement between Israel and Egypt. Aimed at achieving the reopening of the Suez Canal in exchange for a limited withdrawal by the Israelis, this fourth initiative again failed and was replaced towards the end of 1971 by a fifth, coming this time from the Organization for African Unity. A committee of ten African Heads of State was formed and in November 1971 a delegation of four African leaders visited Israel and Egypt to put forward proposals which included the reactivation of Dr. Jarring's mission, the reopening of the Suez Canal, an Israeli withdrawal and international guarantees for secure borders and the freedom of navigation. Once again there was no result and the fifth anniversary of the June War was reached with Dr. Jarring's mission still in suspense and with a settlement no nearer than it had been on the day of his appointment in 1967.

Thereafter the unresolved conflict in the Middle East continued to preoccupy the diplomats at the United Nations and, increasingly, those responsible for the oil supplies of Europe, the United States and Japan. However, the United States, whose position as the protector and supplier of Israel gave it an influence in the Middle East which no other power could match, showed itself more interested in achieving a détente with the Soviet Union (one condition for which appeared to be a tacit agreement not to disturb the precarious balance of power in the Middle East) than in using this influence to produce a settlement between Israel and the Arabs. To the Arabs this apparent collusion between the superpowers threatened to perpetuate a situation in the Middle East which the Arabs found intolerable; it strengthened their conviction that only a renewal of the war against Israel would galvanize the United States into a serious attempt to promote a settlement in the Middle East by enforcing an Israeli withdrawal. In October 1973, by resorting to war against an enemy supremely confident of its strength, the Arabs took a tremendous risk; but events were to justify the strategy of a limited war for political ends.

The October war set in motion a series of developments whose effects were felt far beyond the Middle East. The unexpectedly effective use by the Arabs of the oil weapon, as well as the sharp increase in oil prices which accompanied the limitations on output, precipitated a world-wide energy crisis. No government remained unaffected by the crisis, nor could any government afford to overlook its implications for the future relationship between the developed and the under-developed countries of the world. As far as the Arab-Israeli confrontation was concerned, one thing appeared certain: that in their oil and in the tremendous financial power with which it endowed them, the Arabs—who so short a time ago had seemed powerless—were now in possession of a weapon whose strength was incalculable. Much would depend on how they would use it—and what reaction it might provoke.

In the immediate aftermath of the October war and of the restrictions on the production and export of oil, the Arabs appeared to have achieved the objective they had set themselves in going to war: to remind the superpowers of their responsibilities and to restore a sense of urgency to the search for a settlement of the Arab-Israeli conflict. In a burst of activity the U.S. Secretary of State, Dr. Henry Kissinger, took the initiative in arranging disengagement agreements between Israel and its principal Arab antagonists, while the U.S. and Soviet governments co-operated in sponsoring a peace conference at Geneva in December, at which the first of these agreements was signed between Israeli and Egyptian representatives in January 1974. The second agreement, between the Israelis and the Syrians, proved much harder to negotiate but it was eventually signed four months later, on May 30th. On both fronts a complex series of provisions were agreed whose essential features were the separation of the armed forces of the two sides and the interposition between them of UN forces in a narrow neutral zone. On both fronts, also, the agreements called for minor withdrawals by the Israeli forces, which were to be followed, under the terms of two resolutions adopted by the UN Security Council in October 1973 (resolutions 338 and 339, *see* Documents on Palestine p. 60), by further steps to implement the provisions of resolution 242 for the settlement of the conflict in the Middle East.

The course of events after June 1967

As soon as a ceasefire had brought an end to the fighting in June 1967 a series of international consultations began with the aim of bringing to a final conclusion the nineteen year old conflict between Israel and her Arab neighbours.

Once the ceasefire was in operation, the Security Council's next step was to pass a resolution (No. 237, of June 14th, 1967), calling on Israel to facilitate the return of the new refugees who had fled (and were still fleeing) from the areas occupied by Israel during the war. The resolution also called on Israel to ensure the safety, welfare and security of the inhabitants of the "Occupied Areas".

President Johnson, who had announced on the outbreak of the war the United States' neutrality and support for the territorial integrity of all states in the Middle East, invited Mr. Kosygin, who was attending the United Nations session, to meet him to discuss "five great principles for peace". These were: the right of every state to exist in security; justice for the refugees; the right of free navigation in international waterways; the dangers of an arms race: and the need to recognize the political independence and territorial integrity of all states in the area. The two leaders met at the "Glasboro Summit" from June 23rd to 25th and agreed on the urgency of the need for action; but the dividing line which was to bedevil all efforts to achieve a settlement began to appear. The Russians, who had started to replace the arms lost by Egypt during the war, insisted that an Israeli withdrawal must be the preliminary to negotiations. The Americans upheld the right of the Israelis to maintain their occupation of Arab territory until the Arabs should recognize Israel and agree to negotiate directly with her.

An emergency meeting of the UN General Assembly reiterated on July 4th the Security Council's call for the return of the refugees and on the same day it declared "invalid" the Israeli decision to annex the Arab sector of Jerusalem; but the Assembly failed to produce an agreed resolution on the basis for a settlement. A plan put forward later in the month by President Tito of Yugoslavia, calling for an Israeli withdrawal to the pre-war frontiers and a guarantee of those frontiers by the international community, was rejected by Israel on the ground that to recreate the pre-war situation would endanger that country's security.

The deadlock became total when an Arab summit conference, held in Khartoum between August 29th and September 3rd, 1967, confirmed earlier decisions not to negotiate directly with Israel, not to accord her recognition and not to sign a peace treaty. The Israeli Government, for its part, announced its refusal to undertake any but direct negotiations; if no such negotiations developed, Israeli forces would maintain their occupation of the Arab territories conquered during the war.

RESOLUTION 242

It was against this background that the UN Security Council met in the autumn of 1967 to consider the situation. A number of draft resolutions were submitted but failed to gain approval, either because (in the eyes of the supporters of the Arabs) they condoned the acquisition or occupation of territory by military force, or because (in the eyes of the supporters of Israel) they contained no adequate guarantee for Israel's security.

Finally, on November 22nd, 1967, the Security Council unanimously adopted a resolution put forward by the British delegate, Lord Caradon, and supported by the United States on the ground that it was entirely consistent with the five principles stated by President Johnson. The resolution, which was to remain the basis of all subsequent peace initiatives during the next five years, emphasized in its preamble "the inadmissibility of the acquisition of territory by war and the need to work for a just and lasting peace in which every state in the area can live in security". It then stated that such a peace should involve the withdrawal of Israeli armed forces "from territories occupied in the recent conflict" and the termination of the state of belligerency, with acknowledgment of the right of every state in the area to live in peace "within secure and recognized boundaries, free from threats or acts of force". The resolution affirmed the necessity to guarantee freedom of navigation through international waterways, to achieve a just settlement of the refugee problem and to guarantee the territorial integrity and political independence of every state in the area. Finally, the resolution requested the Secretary-General to appoint a Special Representative who would make contact with the parties in the Middle East and "assist efforts to achieve a peaceful and accepted settlement" on the basis of the provisions of the resolution.

This, the famous Resolution 242 of November 1967, precariously bridged the gap between the Arab and Israeli positions, which were also the positions adopted by their super-power supporters, the Soviet Union and the United States. By emphasizing the inadmissibility of the acquisition of territory by war, the resolution satisfied the demand of the Arabs and the Russians for an Israeli withdrawal. By being less than categorical about the extent of that withdrawal, it became acceptable to the Israelis and the Americans. All the subsequent arguments which developed centred around the question of whether the Israelis, in return for a definitive peace treaty, would have the right to retain parts of the Arab territories occupied during the war.

PALESTINIAN RESISTANCE

Even before these arguments developed, and during the interval of nearly six months which elapsed between the ceasefire and the adoption of the Security Council's resolution, events on the ground had hardened the positions of both sides. In the immediate aftermath of the fighting, despite the Israeli Prime Minister's declaration on the eve of the war that Israel had no intention of annexing "even one foot of Arab territory", the Israeli Knesset had legislated the "reunification" of Jerusalem,* which amounted in fact to the annexation of the Arab sector of the city. The Israelis had also destroyed a number of Arab villages, notably the three villages of Imwas, Beit Nuba and Yalu in the Latrun area, and had expelled their inhabitants. These actions, which appeared to confirm Arab accusations of Israeli expansionism, greatly encouraged the rise of a Palestinian resistance movement, already stimulated by the failure of the Arab governments and the humiliation which that failure had brought on the Arab world. When the Israelis began, as early as September 1967, to establish Jewish settlements in the occupied territories,† at a time when the stream of Arab refugees set in motion by the June war was still flowing eastward at the rate of several hundred a day, support for the resistance movement became widespread in the Arab world. It was strengthened when the Israelis, after agreeing in response to United Nations resolutions to allow the return of these new refugees, arbitrarily closed the border again after only 14,000 had been allowed to re-enter Palestine, out of 150,000 who had filed applications with the Red Cross to do so.

The situation, then, was deteriorating even before Dr. Gunnar Jarring, whom the Secretary-General had appointed as his Special Representative in accordance with Resolution 242, went to the Middle East to undertake his mission at the end of 1967. During the first half of 1968 there were increasingly frequent breaches of the ceasefire along the Suez Canal (which remained blocked to traffic), while Palestinian guerrilla raids led to heavy Israeli reprisal actions in the Jordan valley. After the first anniversary of the June war, and while Dr. Jarring was patiently pursuing his contacts with both sides, the trend towards violence accelerated. In July 1968 guerrillas of the Popular Front for the Liberation of Palestine carried out the first hijack operation in the Middle East, diverting an Israeli airliner to Algiers. President Nasser in the same month warned that another explosion in the area was inevitable if a stalemate which left Israel in occupation of territory belonging to three of its neighbours was allowed to continue indefinitely. In the course of artillery duels across the Canal the towns of Suez and Ismailia were virtually destroyed by the Israelis and their populations had to be evacuated into the interior of Egypt.

PHANTOMS FOR ISRAEL

The governments of Egypt and Jordan had accepted Resolution 242, while Syria rejected it. Israel, while not rejecting the resolution, said it could not be a substitute for specific agreements between the parties. When the UN General Assembly met in the autumn of 1968, Israel put forward a nine-point plan for a Middle East settlement which made no

---

* For a discussion of the Jerusalem issue, *see* p. 46.

† Between June 1967 and October 1973 nearly fifty of these settlements had been established by the Israelis in the occupied areas of the West Bank of Jordan, the Gaza Strip, the Golan Heights in south-west Syria, and Sinai.

mention of withdrawal, speaking instead of "a boundary settlement compatible with the security of Israel and the honour of the Arab states". This produced no response from the Arab governments, which were shocked when President Johnson at the height of the American election campaign, announced that the United States was considering the sale of Phantom aircraft to Israel. A month later Richard Nixon was elected as President Johnson's successor and sent Governor William Scranton on a fact-finding mission to the Middle East. Mr. Scranton was reported as saying that the United States should adopt "a more even-handed policy in the Middle East", but the sale of fifty Phantoms to Israel was confirmed at the end of December and marked an important stage in the escalation of the arms race in the Middle East.

The day after the sale of Phantoms was announced, Israeli parachutists raided Beirut airport, in reprisal for an Arab guerrilla attack on an Israeli airliner in Athens, and destroyed thirteen aircraft. This incident, which for the first time directly involved the Lebanon in the Arab-Israeli confrontation, brought about renewed diplomatic activity to arrest the worsening situation. After the Security Council had unanimously condemned Israel for the Beirut raid, the Soviet Government took up an earlier French proposal that there should be Four-Power talks between the Soviet Union, the United States, Britain and France to obtain agreement between the major powers over the implementation of Resolution 242.

FOUR-POWER TALKS

Dr. Jarring withdrew from the scene while the "Big Four" tried to reconcile the conflicting interpretations of the Security Council resolution. At first the prospects seemed encouraging, with President Nixon eager to register an initial success in the field of foreign affairs and with general agreement that the drift to war in the Midddle East threatened the peace of the world. At the beginning of February 1969, President Nasser declared his willingness to enter into direct negotiations once Israeli forces had withdrawn from Arab territory. Mr. Eshkol, the Prime Minister of Israel, stated his readiness to meet President Nasser and declared that Israel was prepared to be flexible about all the occupied territories except Jerusalem and the Golan Heights (captured from Syria in 1967). But as the year wore on, spasmodic fighting continued along both the Suez Canal and the Jordan fronts, until in July 1969 President Nasser publicly gave up hope of a peaceful settlement, forecasting that a long "war of attrition" would be necessary to dislodge Israel from the occupied territories. A month later a severe fire at Al Aqsa mosque in the Old City of Jerusalem, for which an Australian immigrant to Israel was later blamed, caused a further dangerous increase in tension.

THE ROGERS PLAN

The Four-Power talks were suspended while Soviet and American representatives engaged in bilateral contacts. There was a moment of optimism when it appeared likely that a formula had been found for "Rhodes-style" negotiations (on the pattern of the talks conducted in Rhodes which led to the armistice agreements between Israel and the Arab states in 1949), but the optimism faded when an Israeli suggestion that this would amount to direct negotiations led the Arabs to reject the formula. Instead the American Secretary of State, Mr. William Rogers, produced on December 9th, 1969, a set of proposals which came to be known as the Rogers Plan. The proposals represented an attempt to steer a middle course between the Arab view, that the Security Council resolution should be implemented *in toto* and did not call for negotiation, and the Israeli preference for direct negotiations which would decide where the new borders should be drawn. The most important aspect of the plan was that it made clear the American view that there should only be minor rectifications of the pre-June 1967 boundaries. This ensured Israeli hostility to the plan, since despite the insistence of the Israeli Foreign Minister, Abba Eban, that "everything is negotiable", it had now become clear that his cabinet colleagues were deeply divided on this crucial question.

President Nasser, impatient with what he saw as the hypocritical attitude of the American Government, also rejected the plan, which in any case was presently swept aside by a serious renewal of hostilities in January 1970, when the Israelis initiated a series of deep penetration bombing raids (using the new American Phantom aircraft) on targets inside Egypt. General Dayan announced at the beginning of February that the Israeli bombing attacks had three aims: to force the Egyptians (who had been sustaining heavy casualties along the Canal front) to respect the ceasefire, to prevent Egyptian preparations for a new war and to weaken the Egyptian régime. In practice, the raids (which caused heavy civilian casualties) had three results: they strengthened Egyptian support for President Nasser; they damaged Israel's image in the outside world; and they drew the Russians into providing further assistance to Egypt. In March 1970 the first reports appeared of the installation in Egypt of Soviet SAM-3 anti-aircraft missiles in the vicinity of Cairo, Alexandria and key targets in the Nile delta, while the number of Soviet military advisers in Egypt rose to an estimated 6,000.

International concern over these developments paved the way for a renewal of diplomatic efforts. In April 1970 the American Assistant Secretary of State, Joseph Sisco, visited the Middle East to explain the objectives of the Rogers Plan. Israeli requests for more Phantoms were not granted and it appeared that the immediate American objectives were to obtain a renewal of the ceasefire and to extract from the Israeli Government an undertaking to withdraw from the greater part of the occupied territories as part of an overall peace settlement. President Nasser, in a speech on May 1st said that "despite Phantoms and napalm" he was keeping the door open to the American initiative. The Israelis made no public commitment on withdrawal, but their response in private was sufficiently encouraging for Mr. Rogers to relaunch his proposals, with the backing of the four major powers. After a variety of bilateral contacts between the various parties, President Nasser announced in a speech on July 23rd, 1970, Egypt's acceptance of the American proposal for a renewal of the ceasefire, followed by negotiations through Dr. Jarring for the implementation of Resolution 242. A week later, the Israeli Government, after receiving assurances on the future supply of arms from the United States, also agreed to the American proposal, with the proviso that Israel would never return to the pre-war boundaries and that none of its troops would be withdrawn from the ceasefire lines until a binding peace agreement had been signed. Even so, the price of Israel's qualified acceptance of the Rogers proposals was a cabinet crisis which resulted in the resignation from Mrs. Golda Meir's cabinet of the right-wing Gahal party led by Mr. Menachem Begin.

The renewed ceasefire along the Suez Canal front came into operation on the night of August 7th/8th, with a duration of ninety days, during which the two sides were to engage in indirect negotiations under the auspices of Dr. Jarring. Two fresh developments, however, frustrated the movement towards an overall settlement. After a single meeting with Dr. Jarring in New York, the Israeli representative was recalled to Jerusalem and the Israeli Government protested that the ceasefire had been violated by the movement of Soviet missiles behind the Egyptian lines. The confused American reaction suggested that there had been a genuine misunderstanding about the conditions agreed to, but the negotiations in New York had not been renewed when a serious crisis in Jordan distracted the attention of all the parties concerned.

KING HUSSEIN AND THE PALESTINE GUERRILLAS

On September 6th, 1970, Palestine guerrillas of the Popular Front for the Liberation of Palestine hijacked two airliners and flew them to a desert airfield in Jordan. A third airliner was taken to Cairo and destroyed on the airfield there. Three days later a fourth aircraft was hijacked and joined the two in the desert near Zerqa, where the guerrillas, after releasing a number of passengers, held some three hundred others as hostages, demanding in exchange for them the release of a substantial number of Palestinians held prisoner in Israel.

This episode, which marked the high point of guerrilla activity, proved also the last straw as far as the Government of Jordan was concerned. During the previous two years, as the strength of the guerrilla movement increased, the Jordan Government had faced a dilemma. If it allowed the guerrillas freedom of movement in Jordan, it invited retaliation from Israel—and the retaliation had been heavy, in the form of ground and air raids which had depopulated the East Bank of the Jordan river and caused severe casualties in Irbid, Salt and other towns and villages of east Jordan. If the Government tried to control or suppress the activities of the guerrillas, it faced the possibility of civil war in Jordan.

The relationship between the Government and the guerrillas was linked to the question of a political settlement with Israel. The Palestine resistance movement, whose declared objective was the reconstitution in Palestine of a democratic state open to Jews and Arabs alike, opposed the idea of a political settlement with Israel, since this would involve the recognition and the perpetuation of a Zionist state. King Hussein had followed the lead of President Nasser in accepting the Rogers Plan and was thus committed to the principle of a political settlement involving the recognition of Israel. So long as a political settlement was not in prospect, it had been possible for the King and the guerrillas to pursue their diverse objectives without coming into open conflict, but as soon as such a settlement became a serious possibility the uneasy coexistence between them was threatened. On several previous occasions in 1969 and 1970 the Jordan Government and the guerrillas had come close to a confrontation and after the renewal of the ceasefire in August 1970 and the acceptance by the Jordan Government of the Rogers Plan, a clash became inevitable.

The multiple hijack operation by the PFLP, which explicitly challenged the authority of the Jordan Government, provided the spark and on September 16th King Hussein appointed a military government in Jordan which next day set about the liquidation of the resistance movement. After ten days of heavy fighting in Amman, mediation efforts by other Arab governments, and in particular by President Nasser, brought about a truce, which was signed in Cairo on September 27th, 1970. On the following day President Nasser suffered a heart attack and died almost immediately.

As far as a settlement between Israel and the Arabs was concerned, it looked as though the position so painstakingly established in August had been undermined. The ceasefire along the Suez Canal endured, though precariously; but the negotiations through Dr. Jarring were not renewed and until President Nasser's successor had had time to consolidate his position, it seemed unlikely that they would be. Jordan was faced with the task of overcoming the effects of an inconclusive civil war and only Israel, which had achieved its objective of a renewal of the ceasefire, had any reason to feel satisfied with the turn of events. Miraculously, all of the hostages held in Amman throughout the fighting were released unharmed (indeed, they praised their captors for the care they had taken to protect them), although the three airliners were blown up by the guerrillas.

PRESIDENT SADAT AND THE CEASEFIRE

There was both surprise and relief, therefore, when the new President of Egypt, Anwar Sadat, established himself without opposition and showed himself willing to take up the search for a settlement where it had been left by his predecessor. He agreed to renew the ceasefire for a further 90 days and, after intensive consultations between Israeli and American leaders and the extension to Israel of American credits worth $500 million, Israel agreed to return to the Jarring talks. Preliminary discussions took place in New York and in January 1971 Dr. Jarring visited Israel and Egypt, where both sides restated their positions to him on all the points at issue. When the ceasefire agreement was again coming to an end, on February 5th, 1971, President Sadat once more agreed to renew it, this time for 30 days, adding the proposal that Israel should begin to withdraw its forces from the east bank of the canal, in which case Egypt would be able to clear the canal for navigation. This was to constitute the first stage in the implementation of Resolution 242; but, as things turned out, this new suggestion was to provide the pretext for delaying further movement towards an overall settlement.

On February 8th Dr. Jarring wrote to the Governments of Israel and Egypt, expressing his optimism about the desire of both parties for a settlement and inviting each of them to give firm commitments which would resolve the central deadlock. Israel, Dr. Jarring suggested, should agree on certain stated conditions (providing guarantees for security and freedom of navigation) to withdraw to the international boundary between Egypt and the Palestine of the British Mandate. Egypt should give a parallel undertaking to conclude a peace agreement explicitly ending the state of belligerency and recognizing Israel's right to exist in peace and security. In other words, both parties were asked formally to accept the principal obligations laid on them by Resolution 242.

The Egyptian reply gave the undertaking called for by Dr. Jarring, provided that Israel did the same and agreed to withdraw its forces to the international border. The Israeli reply stated firmly that, while Israel would be prepared to withdraw its forces to "secure, recognized and agreed boundaries to be established in the peace agreement", it would in no circumstances withdraw to the pre-June 1967 lines.

This official confirmation of Israel's insistence on territorial expansion as part of a peace settlement embarrassed the American Government, which had first withheld and then granted military and economic assistance to Israel, in the attempt to persuade the Israeli Government to accept only "minor rectifications" of the armistice lines. The Americans made one further attempt when Mr. Rogers, at a press conference on March 16th, 1971, urged the Israelis to accept international guarantees in place of territorial gains, adding that security did not "necessarily require additions of territory" and that in the American view "the 1967 boundary should be the boundary between Israel and Egypt".

PROPOSAL FOR A "PARTIAL SETTLEMENT"

When this too met with an Israeli refusal, the American Government took up instead President Sadat's suggestion of an Israeli withdrawal for some distance in Sinai to allow the reopening of the Suez Canal. But the opportunity had been lost and the new proposal for a partial settlement quickly became bogged down in arguments over the extent of the Israeli withdrawal and the question of whether it should be seen as the first step in a complete withdrawal or not. The arguments dragged on through most of 1971 until the proposal was finally dropped by the Americans on November 22nd—the fourth anniversary of the passage of Resolution 242.

Before this a new initiative had been launched, this time by the Organization for African Unity, which on June 22nd, 1971, had come out in support of Dr. Jarring's mission and had adopted a strong resolution calling for an Israeli withdrawal and the full implementation of Resolution 242. A committee of ten African Heads of State was formed to undertake a peace mission and in November 1971 four members of this committee visited the Middle East for discussions with the contending parties. They submitted to President Sadat and Mrs. Meir proposals based closely on the provisions of Resolution 242 and appeared for a time to have some hopes of narrowing the gap between the two sides. In the growing mood of frustration and disillusionment which had by now gripped the Arab world, and with the Israelis confident that, with an election less than a year away in the United States, they could count on American benevolence, such hopes seemed over-optimistic and before the end of the year the OAU initiative had quietly foundered.

In December the UN General Assembly, in a resolution reaffirming the "inadmissibility of the acquisition of territory by war" and calling for an Israeli withdrawal, also urged Israel to "respond favourably" to the proposals made by Dr. Jarring in February. Only seven states voted against the resolution (Israel and six Latin American states) and it was noted that the United States, which in the past had always voted in support of Israel on territorial questions, abstained, reflecting the American view that Israel should withdraw from all but insubstantial portions of the occupied territories. However, no action followed and the year ended with President Sadat in a dangerously weakened position. He had taken considerable risks in going so far in pursuit of a political settlement and had promised the Egyptian people that 1971 would be the "year of decision". He blamed the lack of progress on American "political manoeuvring", and when the American Government ushered in the new—election—year by promising Israel a further 42 Phantom and 90 Skyhawk aircraft, there was little likelihood that a fresh American suggestion of indirect talks between Israeli and Egyptian representatives in New York would come to anything.

In February 1972 the Israelis launched a large-scale incursion into the Lebanon, stating that its aim was the elimination of guerrilla bases near Israel's northern border. When there was a revival of guerrilla action in May and June, in the form of another hijacking and an attack by Japanese gunmen (acting for the PFLP) on Lydda airport, there was speculation about further Israeli action against the Lebanon (where the PFLP had established its headquarters after being driven out of Jordan). In June a further Israeli raid on the Lebanon was condemned by the Security Council after more than 70 civilians had been killed or wounded by what the Israeli Deputy Prime Minister described as an "error".

Before this, in March 1972, King Hussein had announced a plan for the reorganization of his kingdom along federal lines, with the Palestinians on the West Bank enjoying autonomy. The plan was conditional on an Israeli withdrawal and so had no immediate significance. It was nevertheless denounced on all sides, by the Palestinian resistance organizations, by the other Arab governments (Egypt went so far as to break off relations with Jordan on account of it) and by Israel, whose Prime Minister vied with the Arab leaders in the strength of her criticisms. When the storm had abated, there were signs in Israel, in the occupied territories and in the rest of the Arab world that on second thoughts many people were prepared to take a less jaundiced view of the King's proposals.

An unexpected development followed when President Sadat, in July 1972, called for the withdrawal from Egypt of the large contingent of Soviet advisers engaged on the reorganization of Egypt's defence system. This surprise move, which gravely damaged Egypt's defensive capability—to say nothing of its capacity to launch an attack against the forces of Israel—was interpreted as a final appeal to the American Government to bring pressure to bear on Israel to accept a settlement involving an Israeli withdrawal from Sinai. If this was its intention, the move was ill-timed, since the approach of the Presidential election made it virtually certain that no American politician would advocate a course of action so unwelcome to Zionist opinion in the United States. There was in fact no American response to President Sadat's gesture before the election in November; nor, after it, apart from generalized statements about the need for a new initiative to restore peace in the Middle East, was there any sign of a reappraisal of American policy towards the area. Even the painful conclusion, early in 1973, of the Paris agreement putting an end to the United States' involvement in Viet-Nam, which had been widely envisaged as the precursor to an attempt to reach a settlement in the Middle East, brought no fresh move from Washington.

In Europe, however, partly out of a feeling that an important opportunity was being allowed to slip and partly as a reflection of a sense of disillusionment with American leadership, a reappraisal of Middle Eastern policy was taking place. In preparation for Britain's entry into the European Community (which took place on January 1st, 1973) an attempt was being made to concert a European approach to important questions of foreign policy. The attempt found expression in the voting at the end of the annual Middle East debate in the General Assembly of the United Nations when, with the single exception of Denmark, all the members of the Community followed the lead of Britain and France in voting for a resolution strongly critical of Israel. (The United States again abstained.)

TERROR AND COUNTER-TERROR IN THE MIDDLE EAST

The cease-fire along the Suez Canal was maintained, but along the northern borders of Israel and Israeli-held territory there was a renewal of violence in the second half of 1972, accompanied by a mounting series of terrorist attacks by both Israelis and Palestinians in various parts of the world. In July and August 1972, a number of Palestinian leaders were killed or seriously injured by explosive devices sent to them in Beirut. In September, during the Olympic Games in Munich, Palestinian guerrillas captured a number of Israeli athletes and held them hostage in an attempt to obtain the release of Palestinians held captive in Israel. The attempt failed when West German police, after promising the Palestinians safe conduct out of Germany, opened fire on them at Munich airport, whereupon the guerrillas killed the hostages and were themselves either killed or captured. (The three Palestinians who survived were later released when a West German airliner was hijacked and flown, with the guerrillas on board, to Libya.)

The Munich attack was followed by heavy Israeli ground and air raids into the Lebanon, which the Israeli Government held responsible for the activities of guerrillas whose bases (since their expulsion from Jordan in 1970 and 1971) were in the refugee camps of the Lebanon and in Beirut. The fact that many civilians were killed in these raids, among them women and children in the refugee camps, provoked a confused international response and a growing sense of alarm as the unsettled conflict in the Middle East sparked violence in countries far from the conflict itself. Letter bombs were posted to Israeli representatives in various countries—an attaché at the Israeli Embassy in London was killed by one in September 1972—and after the Israeli Prime Minister, Mrs. Meir, had announced that "we have no alternative but to strike at the terrorist organizations wherever we can locate them", representatives of the Palestine Liberation Organization were attacked by gunmen or with explosive devices in Rome, Stockholm, Paris and Nicosia.

For a brief period at the beginning of 1973 it looked as though an effort would be made to take the conflict out of the hands of the terrorists and return it to the political arena. In rapid succession Mr. Hafez Ismail (President Sadat's political adviser), King Hussein of Jordan and Mrs. Meir visited Washington for talks with President Nixon. But the frail hopes aroused by this diplomatic activity were dashed when, in February 1973, a heavy Israeli attack on guerrilla installations in a refugee camp in North Lebanon was followed immediately by the shooting down by Israeli fighters of a Libyan airliner whose French captain had strayed over occupied Sinai in a sandstorm. The two incidents caused the death of 150 people—almost all of them civilians—within twenty-four hours and provoked an unprecedented wave of criticism of the Israelis on the eve of Mrs. Meir's arrival in Washington. Before she left, however, Palestinian guerrillas had diverted international indignation onto themselves by attacking the Saudi Arabian Embassy in Khartoum, where they held hostage and eventually murdered the American Ambassador and two other diplomats, one American and the other Belgian. A month later, following an abortive Palestinian attack on the Israeli Embassy in Nicosia, Israeli commandos mounted a carefully planned and ruthlessly executed attack in Beirut, penetrating into a residential district in the heart of the Lebanese capital and killing, among a number of other people, three leading members of the PLO.

CRISIS IN LEBANON

The Israeli raid provoked a serious crisis in the Lebanon, where fighting broke out between Palestinian guerrillas and Lebanese Government forces. The agreement signed in Cairo between representatives of the PLO and the Lebanese Government in 1969, which had regulated relations between the two sides ever since, was called in question and for a time it looked as though the Lebanese Government might follow the example of King Hussein of Jordan and try to suppress guerrilla activity in the Lebanon altogether. However, the Lebanese instinct for compromise asserted itself and a fresh agreement was reached in May 1973 which imposed further restrictions on guerrilla activity. Heavy casualties had been caused during the fighting, in which the Lebanese Government had ordered airstrikes against guerrilla positions in the refugee camps on the outskirts of Beirut, and the resulting bitterness on both sides inevitably threw doubt on the durability of the new agreement.

On May 7th, 1973, the twenty-fifth anniversary of the creation of the State of Israel was celebrated with a massive military parade in Jerusalem. The parade symbolized Israel's commanding military position but was widely criticized, both inside and outside Israel, as an indication of the Israeli Government's refusal to consider any compromise formula which might lead to peace with the Arabs. Public opinion polls in Israel, as well as the pronouncements of leading figures in the Israeli political and military establishment, indicated a significant hardening of Israeli attitudes over the crucial question of withdrawal from the territories occupied in 1967.

ENERGY CRISIS

A new factor which affected international attitudes towards the Arab-Israeli conflict began to make itself felt during the first half of 1973. This was the prospect of a serious energy crisis arising out of the rapidly increasing demand for oil products in Europe, the United States and Japan. In the United States in particular, the realization that industrial expansion in the following decade was likely to become much more dependent on imports of oil and natural gas from Middle Eastern producing countries caused serious concern at a time when America's support for Israel made the United States a particular target for criticism throughout the Arab world.

STALEMATE

In the autumn of 1973, the Arab-Israeli conflict appeared to be further than ever from solution. The Israelis, confident that their military supremacy over the Arabs had if anything increased, remained in control of all the territories they had occupied in 1967 and had established in these territories some fifty civilian and paramilitary settlements. The Egyptian and Jordanian Governments—though not yet the Syrian—had long since modified their earlier refusal to negotiate a settlement and had clearly indicated their willingness to recognize the State of Israel; but they still refused to envisage a peace settlement which did not provide for the return of all the occupied territories. The United Nations, despite the passage every year of resolutions calling for an Israeli withdrawal, found all its efforts to devise a settlement blocked by Israel's refusal to relinquish its 1967 conquests. A dangerous mood of frustration enveloped the Middle East, while for the outside world anxiety over a possible renewal of the conflict was compounded by apprehensions about the maintenance of vital oil supplies.

More than ever, the key to the situation rested in the hands of the United States, which found itself isolated in support of Israel and yet faced with the prospect of becoming increasingly dependent on Arab oil. America's allies, for whom dependence on Arab oil was already a fact, were growing increasingly impatient with the American Government's Middle East policy, which seemed to be aimed at maintaining Israel's overall supremacy without seeking in return any concessions from the Israeli government over the occupied territories or the other necessary ingredients of a peace settlement. The Watergate scandal in Washington appeared to make it even less likely than before that the Nixon administration would risk unpopularity with the Zionist lobby by proposing any fresh initiative to break the deadlock in the Middle East. The isolation of the United States was emphasized during the debate in the Security Council in the summer of 1973. After prolonged discussion, the Council considered a resolution put forward by eight non-aligned members which was strongly critical of Israel's continued occupation of Arab territory. The United States found it necessary to use its veto to prevent the passage of the resolution, which obtained the affirmative votes of all the other Council members except China, which abstained.

This American decision played its part in convincing the Arabs that only by a renewal of the war could they hope to break the stalemate in the Middle East and look forward to the recovery of their lost territories. They had no illusions about their ability to recover them by defeating Israel; but they judged that, unless the superpowers were brought to face with the danger of a fresh round of fighting which would threaten their own interests, they would not exert themselves to obtain a settlement. They were influenced in forming this judgment by the American decision (announced in March, shortly after President Sadat's special envoy had visited President Nixon) to furnish another forty-eight jet fighters to Israel, and by the progress towards détente between the United States and the Soviet Union (symbolized by the meeting between President Nixon and Mr. Brezhnev in June). From both it appeared plain to the Arabs that the stalemate in the Middle East was to be preserved at their expense.

RENEWAL OF THE WAR

The attack which was launched on two fronts by the Egyptian and Syrian forces on October 6th took everyone by surprise. Unusual activity behind the lines had been observed by Israeli and American intelligence agencies west of the Suez Canal and east of the cease-fire line on the Golan Heights; but in each case its importance was discounted because of the Israeli conviction (shared by military experts elsewhere) that the Egyptian army was incapable of the elaborate operation required to cross the canal and breach the chain of Israeli fortifications known as the Bar-Lev line on the east bank. Their success in guarding the secret of the attack won for the Egyptian and Syrian forces on both fronts a substantial initial advantage, which was enhanced by the fact that October 6th was Yom Kippur, the Day of Atonement in the Jewish calendar, when all public services were suspended, which made it unusually difficult for the Israelis to mobilize their forces rapidly to meet the emergency. By midnight on the first day of the war, four hundred Egyptian tanks had crossed the canal, the Bar-Lev line had been out-flanked and a massive Syrian tank attack beyond the Golan Heights had only been stemmed by a masterly rearguard action by greatly outnumbered Israeli armour, aided by costly air strikes.

During the fighting that followed and which continued for three weeks (despite a United Nations cease-fire on October 22nd) before all operations ceased, the Syrians were driven back beyond the old cease-fire line and Israeli forces counter-attacking on the Suez front effected a westward crossing of the canal, to establish a wide bridgehead on the edge of the Nile delta. At the end of the war, the military advantage lay with the Israelis, who had occupied a further area of Syrian territory and were threatening Damascus, while their units west of the canal had isolated an Egyptian army in Suez, cutting its communications with Cairo. Meanwhile, however, largely as a result of the intervention of the Arab oil-producing states, the political objectives of the Arabs had been achieved and the whole context of the confrontation with Israel had been decisively altered.

To begin with, the legend of Israeli invincibility had been shattered. Making unexpectedly efficient use of new weapons (especially portable anti-tank missiles) the Arab armies demonstrated that since 1967 they had significantly narrowed the technological gap between themselves and the Israelis. By doing so, they exposed the fallacy on which Israeli strategy had been based since the Six Day War: the fallacy that the control of wide buffer zones (in the shape of the territories occupied since 1967), together with the military supremacy of which they felt assured, rendered the Israelis immune to Arab attack. This assumption had encouraged in the Israeli leaders the dangerous conviction that since they were in no danger from the Arabs they could afford to disregard the mounting pressure of world opinion calling for an

Israeli withdrawal as the essential condition for a negotiated settlement with the Arabs.

THE OIL WEAPON

Soon after the outbreak of the war, there were calls within the Arab world for measures to deny Middle East oil to the supporters of Israel. On October 17th a meeting in Kuwait of representatives of the Arab oil producers resulted in an agreement to reduce output; two days later Abu Dhabi took the lead in stopping altogether the export of oil to the United States. In adopting and presently intensifying these measures, the Arab oil-producing states showed an unexpectedly determined sense of solidarity. This had an evident effect on the Governments of Western Europe, conscious of their dependence on the free flow of oil from the Middle East. On November 6th the nine member states of the Common Market endorsed in Brussels a statement calling for an Israeli withdrawal from the territories occupied in 1967 and asserting that, while all states in the Middle East should enjoy the right to secure boundaries, the legitimate rights of the Palestinians should be taken into account in any settlement (*see* Documents on Palestine, page 61. This provoked accusations from the Israelis to the effect that the Europeans were giving in to Arab "blackmail", but these took too little account of the fact that for several years past (as shown by the yearly votes at the United Nations) the Europeans had been dissociating themselves from United States policy and registering their growing impatience with Israel's refusal to make any concession. Relations became strained within the Atlantic Alliance when the Americans complained of desertion by their European allies and the Europeans countered with accusations that the Americans had not consulted them before putting their nuclear forces throughout the world on alert as a warning against Soviet involvement in the Middle East crisis.

AMERICAN INITIATIVE

These developments underlined the central point which the Arabs had sought to make by their resort to war: the point that neither the Israelis nor those countries which were dependent on Middle East oil would be safe if they allowed a situation to continue in the Middle East which left large areas of Arab territory under Israeli occupation. The Americans, who alone possessed the influence that could induce the Israelis to withdraw—and who now found themselves inconvenienced much more by the oil embargo than they had anticipated—accepted the need to use their influence to bring about a settlement. The American Secretary of State, Dr. Kissinger, who had been active in obtaining Soviet co-operation over a cease-fire, now embarked on a dramatic series of visits to the capitals of the contestants in the Middle East, out of which there resulted disengagement agreements between Egypt and Israel (signed on January 18th 1974) and—after much more protracted and intricate exchanges—between Syria and Israel (signed on May 30th 1974). In the middle of June 1974 President Nixon, whose domestic position had become dangerously insecure on account of the protracted investigations into the Watergate scandal, embarked on a triumphant tour of the Middle East, forecasting a new era of co-operation between the United States and the Arab world, while reassuring the Israelis of continuing American support. Thanks largely to the personal success achieved by Dr. Kissinger with both Arab and Israeli leaders, this American initiative was generally well received, except by some Israelis who foresaw mounting pressure on Israel to make concessions inconsistent with her security, and by the extreme wing of the Palestinian resistance movement, which engaged in a series of terrorist attacks on targets in northern Israel in an effort to frustrate a settlement inconsistent with their aim of total liberation in Palestine. Otherwise, despite reservations about the future of President Nixon's administration and the continuity of American policy in the event of his resignation, Mr. Nixon's visit revealed a strong desire on the part of the Arab governments concerned to restore friendly relations between themselves and the United States. Diplomatic relations between Washington and Damascus were re-established and the embargo on the export of Arab oil to the United States was lifted in recognition of Dr. Kissinger's efforts to promote a satisfactory settlement in the Middle East.

CHANGE IN THE BALANCE OF POWER

This Arab-American reconciliation was one of the most striking results of the October war; it was a reminder of the greatly increased influence of the Arab states so long as they continued to act in concert. Conversely, Israel's international position had been much weakened by the failure of her pre-war policies and by the revelation of the extent to which the rest of the world was dependent on Arab goodwill. The Government headed by Mrs. Golda Meir, in which General Dayan had been the very influential defence minister, was widely blamed both for provoking the October war by its policy of "creeping annexation" and for being caught unawares when the war came. After winning a narrow victory in a general election at the end of 1973, Mrs. Meir finally abandoned the attempt to rebuild her coalition in April 1974. She was succeeded as leader of the Labour party and prime minister by General Itshak Rabin, who had been Chief of Staff at the time of the 1967 war and later Israeli ambassador in Washington. In the Arab world, the effect of the war was to strengthen the position of the régimes in Cairo and Damascus and to give new authority to King Faisal of Saudi Arabia, whose control of the greatest share of the oil reserves of the Middle East made him a dominant figure in Arab politics. The fact that the disengagement agreements arranged with the help of Dr. Kissinger involved small but significant Israeli withdrawals from Arab territory gave satisfaction throughout the Arab world; but the central problem of the future of the Palestinians remained unsolved. The difficulty of finding a solution to this problem which would prove acceptable both to the Israelis and to the Palestine Liberation Organization (which the Arab governments, meeting in Algiers in November 1973, had recognized as "the sole legitimate representative of the Palestinian people") posed a continuing threat to the stability of the disengagement agreements entered into in 1974.

Despite the general awareness of the new strength of the Arab world, the movement towards a settlement in the Middle East gradually lost momentum during the second half of 1974 and a mood of apprehension developed in which a further outbreak of war at times seemed imminent. The disengagement agreements were carried out and UN forces were inserted between the combatants in Sinai and on the Golan front, but mutual recriminations were exchanged between the Syrians and the Israelis over the ill-treatment of prisoners and the destruction of the Syrian town of Kuneitra, demolished by the Israelis on the eve of their withdrawal. The arms lost by both sides during the October war were rapidly replaced, although the Egyptians complained that the Soviet Government had restricted supplies to Egypt while making good all Syria's losses. During the year following the October war the United States Government committed $3,000 million of military aid to Israel, whose leaders claimed that the country was stronger at the end of 1974 than it had been before the Egyptians crossed the Suez Canal on October 6th, 1973.

While the optimism generated by the disengagement agreements was dissipated by the renewal of the stalemate between the Arab governments and Israel, the Palestinians saw their central role in the conflict strikingly endorsed. On September 21st, 1974, the UN General Assembly voted to include "the Palestine Question" on its agenda for the first time since the establishment of the state of Israel in 1948. (Only four governments opposed this decision: Israel, the United States, the Dominican Republic and Bolivia.) On October 14th the General Assembly invited the Palestine Liberation Organization to take part in the debate and a month later the Chairman of the PLO, Yasser Arafat, outlined to the Assembly the PLO's design for a "democratic, secular state" in Palestine in which Jews and Arabs would coexist on terms of equality, specifying that "all Jews now living in Palestine who choose to live with us there in peace and without discrimination" were included in this design. At the end of October a meeting of Arab Heads of State in Rabat confirmed that the PLO was the "sole legitimate representative of the Palestinian people", with the right to speak for the Palestinians at any future Middle East peace talks and to establish an independent national authority in any part of Palestine liberated from Israeli occupation.

These decisions greatly strengthened the hand of the Palestinians and of the PLO as their representative. However, they also deepened the impasse over movement towards a settlement because the Israeli Government adamantly refused to have any dealings with the PLO, dismissing it as a terrorist organization which Israel would meet, in Prime Minister Rabin's words, "only on the battlefield". The position of the PLO was also complicated by internal divisions over the objective which the organization should pursue. Although Yasser Arafat at the United Nations had spoken only of the PLO's goal of a unitary Palestine (whose achievement would mean the elimination of the state of Israel), he was under pressure from the Arab governments to accept the limited objective of a Palestinian state on the West Bank and the Gaza Strip, whose establishment could only be envisaged (if at all) in the context of a compromise settlement incuding the recognition of Israel within its pre-1967 borders. A majority within the PLO appeared at the end of 1974 to be moving towards acceptance of this formula, but the minority rejected any thought of compromising with the long-term goal of the total liberation of Palestine. This "rejection front", which had the backing of the governments of Iraq and Libya, made it difficult for the PLO openly to align itself with those Arab governments (notably the government of President Sadat in Egypt) which were prepared to exchange recognition of Israel for an Israeli withdrawal from the territories occupied in 1967, including Arab Jerusalem, and the creation of a Palestinian state on the West Bank.

This was in effect the pattern for a settlement which had been envisaged in the Security Council's resolution 242 in November 1967 and which had provided the basis for all the international initiatives undertaken, with diminishing prospects of success, between 1967 and 1973. These initiatives had failed because the Israelis, before October 1973, had felt confident of their ability to retain control of at least substantial parts of the occupied territories and to hold off any Arab attempt to recover them by force. The October war, by undermining this confidence, had made more evident the Israelis' total dependence on American support; and the initial efforts of Dr. Kissinger immediately after the war had encouraged the Arabs to believe that American influence would at last be used to promote a settlement based on an Israeli withdrawal. It was this belief which had brought about the restoration of diplomatic relations between Washington and both Cairo and Damascus and the lifting of the Arab oil embargo.

The Arab-American reconciliation, in which President Sadat had taken the lead and to which he totally committed himself during 1974, had failed by the end of the year to produce any results beyond the initial disengagement agreements. Apart from the tiny areas of territory conceded by Israel under those agreements, the Israeli occupation was maintained in Sinai, the Golan Heights (including the plateau up to the outskirts of Kuneitra), the West Bank (including the Old City of Jerusalem) and the Gaza Strip, with no relaxation of the ban on political activity by the Arab population or of the repressive measures enforced against that population by the occupation authorities. None of the fifty-odd Jewish settlements established in the occupied territories before October 1973 had been given up; indeed, the Israeli Government, under pressure from the right-wing opposition and the religious parties in the Knesset, continued to announce plans to extend the pattern of Jewish settlement. In the wake of Yasser Arafat's appearance

at the United Nations in November 1974 there were demonstrations on the West Bank in support of the PLO, to which the Israelis responded by widespread arrests of Palestinians and the deportation of a number of leading citizens, among them the President of Bir Zeit College, Dr. Hanna Nasir.

These developments caused growing impatience in the Arab world, symbolized by rioting in Cairo in January 1975, over the lack of progress towards a settlement. The tension was heightened by a series of widely advertised statements by American leaders, including Secretary of State Kissinger, hinting at the possibility of armed intervention by American forces in the event of a fresh oil embargo by the Arab oil-producing states. Although these statements were later discounted as somewhat heavy-handed propaganda, those Arab leaders, like President Sadat, who had pinned their faith to American sincerity in the search for a settlement and had nothing to show for it, found themselves under heavy pressure. It was in these circumstances that Dr. Kissinger announced his intention to use his own brand of personal diplomacy to carry the process of disengagement between Israel and Egypt a stage further. When he returned to the Middle East in March it was widely assumed that Dr. Kissinger had obtained prior assurances from both sides of their willingness to conclude a bargain; but after two weeks of intensive "shuttle diplomacy" he had to admit failure when the Israelis refused to withdraw from the Mitla and Giddi passes in Sinai and from the oilfield at Abu Rudeis without an explicit undertaking of future non-belligerency from President Sadat. The latter demand was clearly unrealistic, since to satisfy it would have confirmed Arab suspicions that the Egyptians were prepared to abandon their allies and envisage a separate peace with Israel. There was therefore little surprise when the American Secretary of State (and later President Ford) let it be known that they blamed Israeli obstinacy for the breakdown of the negotiations and announced that the United States would embark on a "reassessment" of its Middle East policy. This was held to mean that the latest Israeli request for increased military and economic aid from the United States would not be granted until the Israelis showed a more conciliatory attitude.

The breakdown of Dr. Kissinger's mission coincided with the assassination in Riyadh of King Faisal of Saudi Arabia, whose prestige and authority had been greatly strengthened as a result of his support for the Arab war effort during and after the October war. Together, the two events brought renewed anxiety about the stability of the Middle East; and this anxiety was increased by the simultaneous and abrupt collapse of American policy in Indochina, where the capitals of Cambodia and South Viet-Nam fell in rapid succession to communist forces.

Even before the failure of his mission, Dr. Kissinger's critics had pointed to two weaknesses in his "step-by-step" approach to peace-making in the Middle East. In concentrating on limited territorial issues, they said, he had ignored the real heart of the problem, which was the future relationship between

Israel and the Palestinians. And by using his personal style of diplomacy, he had excluded the Soviet Government from participation in the negotiations for a settlement which they too would eventually be expected to accept and endorse. When his mission broke down, the Soviet and Egyptian governments at once called for the resumption of the Geneva peace conference, which had met briefly at the time of the Egyptian-Israeli disengagement agreement at the end of 1973 but had been in abeyance ever since. In the absence, however, of any real prospects for progress at Geneva until the gap between the positions of the two sides had been narrowed, none of the parties showed real enthusiasm for reconvening the conference and the Soviet Government tacitly agreed to let the Americans make one more effort to break the deadlock. President Ford had arranged to meet the Egyptian President in Salzburg at the beginning of June, while the Israeli Prime Minister was due to visit Washington ten days later. Until it could be seen whether these contacts would bring the two sides to the dispute any closer, it was agreed to postpone any further session of the Geneva conference until the autumn of 1975.

Two practical steps were taken on the Arab side which helped to allay the anxieties aroused by the breakdown of the peace-making mission of Dr. Kissinger. In May the Syrian Government unexpectedly agreed to renew for a further six months the mandate of the UN force separating the two sides on the Golan front; and on June 5th the Egyptian Government reopened the Suez Canal, eight years to the day after the outbreak of the June war which led to its closure in 1967. Besides offering the Egyptians some hope of relief from their pressing economic problems, this step was taken to indicate President Sadat's continuing preference for a political settlement with Israel rather than a further round of war.

However, further exchanges between the Egyptian and Israeli governments, again using Dr. Kissinger as intermediary, failed to produce agreement over the terms for a new interim settlement before the mandate for the UN force in Sinai expired on July 24th. As this date approached there was renewed anxiety when President Sadat announced his unwillingness to allow the force to remain unless the Security Council took. action to enforce Israel's withdrawal. At the last minute President Sadat relented, enabling the Security Council to renew the force's mandate for a further three months, but declaring that he did so on the understanding that the Israeli withdrawal should start before the mandate expired again on October 24th.

The Jerusalem Issue

Michael Adams

The Arab sector of Jerusalem, including the old walled city, was captured during the June War in 1967 by Israeli forces, which went on to occupy all the Jordanian territory lying west of the River Jordan. Theoretically, there was no difference in status between Jerusalem and the rest of the West Bank; both were occupied territory. In practice, the Israelis immediately removed the walls and barriers dividing the western (Israeli) and eastern (Arab) sectors of the city and at the end of June 1967 the Knesset passed legislation incorporating the Arab sector into a reunited Jerusalem under Israeli sovereignty. At the same time the boundaries of the municipal area of Jerusalem were greatly extended, reaching to near Bethlehem in the south and incorporating Kalandia airport (close to Ramallah) in the north.

Juridically speaking, the status of Jerusalem was already complicated. The plan for the partition of Palestine adopted by the General Assembly of the United Nations in 1947 had envisaged separate Arab and Jewish states, with the city and environs of Jerusalem constituting an international enclave. In the war of 1948, Israeli and Jordanian forces had fought for possession of Jerusalem and the armistice of April 1949 had left each in control of part of the divided city. The international community had never recognized this *de facto* arrangement, which endured for 18 years until the June War of 1967.

Faced with Israel's effective annexation of the Arab sector, the General Assembly on July 4th, 1967, ruled, by 99 votes to none, that the annexation was invalid and called on Israel not to take any measures to alter the status of the city. Ten days later the Assembly adopted a second resolution "reiterating" the earlier one and "deploring" Israel's failure to implement it.

Before the first of these resolutions was passed, the Israeli authorities had embarked on a series of structural alterations and demolitions in the Old City of Jerusalem, which aroused strong Arab protests and whose continuation was to lead to considerable international controversy. In clearing the area in front of the Western (Wailing) Wall, they expropriated 50 Arab families at very short notice and demolished their houses, while in the Jewish Quarter they dispossessed a further 200 Arab families. In all, and before the end of June 1967, some 4,000 Arabs in Jerusalem had lost their homes. In some cases, but not all, they were provided with alternative accommodation.

In November 1967 the UN Security Council passed its unanimous resolution number 242 setting out the basis for an overall settlement between Israel and its Arab neighbours. The resolution spoke of "withdrawal of Israeli armed forces from territories occupied in the recent conflict", but made no specific mention of Jerusalem, where the anxiety of the Arab population was increased by the growing signs of Israel's intention to exclude the city from the scope of any eventual negotiations. In January 1968 the Israeli authorities expropriated more than 800 acres of land in the Arab sector and announced plans for the construction of housing estates on the slopes of Mount Scopus, overlooking the Old City. A joint protest signed by fifty leading members of the Muslim and Jewish communities in Jerusalem had no result, beyond provoking the expulsion by the Israelis of the Mayor of Arab Jerusalem, but in May 1968, after the Israelis had held (in defiance of a unanimous resolution by the Security Council) a military parade in Jerusalem to commemorate the foundation of the State of Israel, the Security Council passed its first resolution dealing specifically with the Jerusalem issue.

The resolution (No. 252 of May 21st, 1968) deplored Israel's failure to comply with the two General Assembly resolutions of July 4th and 14th, 1967, confirmed that any measures taken by Israel to alter the status of Jerusalem were invalid and called on Israel to rescind all such measures and to refrain from similar action in the future. The effect was only to increase the haste with which the Israelis set about changing the face of the city. Bulldozers had been at work on Mount Scopus since February and soon the first of the new housing estates began to take shape beside the Nablus Road leading northwards out of Jerusalem. In the absence of any progress towards a peace settlement, it became clear that the Israeli Government intended to forestall, by establishing a physical presence in the Arab sector of Jerusalem, any future attempt to challenge their sovereignty over the whole of the municipal area.

Meeting again to consider the question in July 1969, the Security Council adopted, this time by a unanimous vote (in the previous year the United States had abstained from voting on the Jerusalem resolution), an even stronger resolution (No. 267 of July 3rd, 1969). Reaffirming its earlier stand and deploring "the failure of Israel to show any regard" for the previous resolutions both of the General Assembly and of the Security Council, the Council "censured in the strongest terms" all measures taken by Israel to change the status of Jerusalem, confirmed that all such measures were "invalid" and again called on Israel to desist from taking any further action of the same kind. The Israelis formally rejected the resolution and the Israeli Minister of Information stated in Jerusalem that it could not influence the "facts" which had been intentionally created by Israel "after due consideration of the political danger involved".

The situation in Jerusalem itself was further aggravated in August 1969 by a disastrous fire in Al Aqsa mosque, which at first sight appeared to confirm the fears of the Arabs for the safety of the Muslim and Christian shrines in the Old City. Israeli investigations showed that the fire had been caused by a deranged Australian religious fanatic and the Australian was later brought to trial; but from that moment the concern of Muslim communities throughout the world reinforced the Arab sense of grievance at the loss of the Holy city.

In the following year Christian concern also began to make itself felt, especially after the publication of an Israeli "master plan" for the future of Jerusalem. This plan envisaged the doubling of the Jewish population of the city by 1980 and an eventual total population of 900,000. An international conference of town planners, convoked by the Israeli municipal authorities at the end of 1970 to consider the plan, was almost unanimous in condemning its aesthetic implications. Early in 1971 a dispute also developed between the United Nations and the Israeli Government over the intention, announced in the master plan, to build another housing estate in the neighbourhood of Government House, the headquarters in Jerusalem of the United Nations. In March 1971 articles in the official Vatican newspaper *L'Osservatore Romano* and in the English Catholic weekly *The Tablet* revealed the strength of Catholic feeling over developments in the Holy City, and these feelings were strengthened when it became known that in the same month the Israelis had destroyed an Arab village on the hill of Nebi Samwil, north-west of Jerusalem, in preparation for the building on Arab land of yet another housing estate for immigrant Jews.

Israeli opinion was divided over the future of Jerusalem. Only a small minority of Israelis were in favour of relinquishing Israeli sovereignty over the Arab sector of the city, if negotiations for an overall settlement of the Arab-Israeli conflict should ever materialize. In the absence of any sign of such negotiations, the issue remained a hypothetical one and the Israeli Government made no secret of its determination to establish a hold on Jerusalem which would prove unbreakable. A further resolution by the Security Council (No. 298 of September 25th, 1971— see Documents on Palestine, p. 60) was rejected as brusquely as the previous ones and even the provision in the resolution that the Secretary-General, "using such instrumentalities as he may choose", should report to the Council within 60 days on the implementation of the resolution, failed to achieve any result since the Secretary-General had to report at the end of that period that he had been unable to execute his mission, for lack of co-operation from the Israeli authorities.

On purely aesthetic grounds, however, many Israelis were disturbed by the physical changes overtaking Jerusalem. Within five years of the June War of 1967 the construction of large housing estates had transformed the appearance of Mount Scopus, where the Old City (and the whole of the Arab sector) was dominated by a row of apartment blocks breaking the historic skyline. There were acute disagreements between the Mayor of Jerusalem and the Ministers of Housing and of Tourism over some of the implications of this building programme, but continuing uncertainty over the prospects for a political settlement with the Arabs gave encouragement to the "activists" in Israel, and the creation of "facts" continued, in Jerusalem as in the rest of the occupied territories, throughout 1972 and up to the eve of the war in October 1973.

Anxiety over the future of Jerusalem and resentment at the Israelis' treatment both of the Arab population and of the physical fabric of the city played a part in provoking the Arab decision to resort to war in 1973. In particular, these feelings influenced King Faisal to throw Saudi Arabia's weight behind the attempt to enforce Israel's withdrawal from the occupied territories, including Arab Jerusalem. Henceforth the restoration to Arab sovereignty of the Old City became one of the principal conditions demanded by the Arabs for a comprehensive peace settlement with Israel.

Immediately after the October war political and economic conditions in Israel combined to slow down for a time the work of demolition and construction by which the face of the city was being transformed. In the course of 1974, however, the same general pattern as before was maintained, resulting in the steady eviction from the Old City of Arabs whose houses were demolished and replaced by dwellings for Jewish immigrants. Protests from the international community, stimulated by anxiety over the continuing exodus from Jerusalem of Christian Arabs, became more frequent and achieved some publicity, but no practical result.

Similar protests over excavations being conducted by the Israeli authorities in the vicinity of Muslim and Christian holy places in the Old City of Jerusalem brought to a head criticisms which had been voiced for more than five years within UNESCO. Recalling that urgent appeals previously addressed to the Israeli Government to suspend these excavations had been ignored, the Executive Board of UNESCO, in June 1974, voted "to condemn the persistent violation by Israel of the resolutions and decisions adopted by the General Conference and the Executive Board". In its turn the General Conference of UNESCO, meeting in November 1974, condemned Israel's attitude as "contradictory to the aims of the Organization as laid down in its Constitution" and resolved to withhold assistance in the fields of education, science and culture until Israel agreed to respect previous Conference resolutions in the matter; it also refused Israel's application for membership of the European regional grouping within UNESCO. These decisions, which were widely misrepresented as amounting to the "exclusion" of Israel from the activities of UNESCO, were criticized by many international figures in the world of the arts and sciences on the ground that UNESCO had allowed itself to be diverted from its proper field of activity into the political arena. The decisions, however, were maintained and seemed likely to acquire historic significance as the first practical expression of international impatience with Israel's behaviour in Jerusalem.

Documents on Palestine

DECLARATION OF FIRST
WORLD ZIONIST CONGRESS

The Congress, convened in Basle by Dr. Theodor Herzl in August 1897, adopted the following programme:*

The aim of Zionism is to create for the Jewish people a home in Palestine secured by public law.

The Congress contemplates the following means to the attainment of this end:

1. The promotion on suitable lines, of the settlement of Palestine by Jewish agriculturists, artisans and tradesmen.

2. The organization and binding together of the whole of Jewry by means of appropriate institutions, local and general, in accordance with the laws of each country.

3. The strengthening of Jewish sentiment and national consciousness.

4. Preparatory steps towards obtaining government consent as are necessary, for the attainment of the aim of Zionism.

McMAHON CORRESPONDENCE†

Ten letters passed between Sir Henry McMahon, British High Commissioner in Cairo, and Sherif Husain of Mecca from July 1915 to March 1916. Husain offered Arab help in the war against the Turks if Britain would support the principle of an independent Arab state. The most important letter is that of October 24th, 1915, from McMahon to Husain:

. . . I regret that you should have received from my last letter the impression that I regarded the question of limits and boundaries with coldness and hesitation; such was not the case, but it appeared to me that the time had not yet come when that question could be discussed in a conclusive manner.

I have realized, however, from your last letter that you regard this question as one of vital and urgent importance. I have, therefore, lost no time in informing the Government of Great Britain of the contents of your letter, and it is with great pleasure that I communicate to you on their behalf the following statement, which I am confident you will receive with satisfaction:

The two districts of Mersina and Alexandretta and portions of Syria lying to the west of the districts of Damascus, Homs, Hama and Aleppo cannot be said to be purely Arab, and should be excluded from the limits demanded.

With the above modification, and without prejudice to our existing treaties with Arab chiefs, we accept those limits.

As for those regions lying within those frontiers wherein Great Britain is free to act without detriment to the interests of her ally, France, I am empowered in the name of the Government of Great Britain to give the following assurances and make the following reply to your letter:

(1) Subject to the above modifications, Great Britain is prepared to recognize and support the independence of the Arabs in all the regions within the limits demanded by the Sherif of Mecca.

(2) Great Britain will guarantee the Holy Places against all external aggression and will recognize their inviolability.

(3) When the situation admits, Great Britain will give to the Arabs her advice and will assist them to establish what may appear to be the most suitable forms of government in those various territories.

(4) On the other hand, it is understood that the Arabs have decided to seek the advice and guidance of Great Britain only, and that such European advisers and officials as may be required for the formation of a sound form of administration will be British.

(5) With regard to the *vilayets* of Bagdad and Basra, the Arabs will recognize that the established position and interests of Great Britain necessitate special administrative arrangements in order to secure these territories from foreign aggression, to promote the welfare of the local populations and to safeguard our mutual economic interests.

I am convinced that this declaration will assure you beyond all possible doubt of the sympathy of Great Britain towards the aspirations of her friends the Arabs and will result in a firm and lasting alliance, the immediate results of which will be the expulsion of the Turks from the Arab countries and the freeing of the Arab peoples from the Turkish yoke, which for so many years has pressed heavily upon them. . . .

ANGLO-FRANCO-RUSSIAN AGREEMENT
(SYKES—PICOT AGREEMENT)
April-May 1916

The allocation of portions of the Ottoman empire by the three powers was decided between them in an exchange of diplomatic notes. The Anglo-French agreement‡ dealing with Arab territories became known to Sherif Husain only after publication by the new Bolshevik government of Russia in 1917:

1. That France and Great Britain are prepared to recognize and protect an independent Arab State or a Confederation of Arab States in the areas (A) and (B)

---

* Text supplied by courtesy of Josef Fraenkel.

† British White Paper, Cmd. 5957, 1939.

‡ E. L. Woodward and Rohan Butler (Eds.). *Documents on British Foreign Policy 1919–1939.* First Series, Vol. IV, 1919. London, H.M.S.O., 1952.

marked on the annexed map, under the suzerainty of an Arab Chief. That in area (A) France, and in area (B) Great Britain shall have priority of right of enterprises and local loans. France in area (A) and Great Britain in area (B) shall alone supply foreign advisers or officials on the request of the Arab State or the Confederation of Arab States.

2. France in the Blue area and Great Britain in the Red area shall be at liberty to establish direct or indirect administration or control as they may desire or as they may deem fit to establish after agreement with the Arab State or Confederation of Arab States.

3. In the Brown area there shall be established an international administration of which the form will be decided upon after consultation with Russia, and after subsequent agreement with the other Allies and the representatives of the Sherif of Mecca.

4. That Great Britain be accorded

(*a*) The ports of Haifa and Acre;

(*b*) Guarantee of a given supply of water from the Tigris and the Euphrates in area (A) for area (B).

His Majesty's Government, on their part, undertake that they will at no time enter into negotiations for the cession of Cyprus to any third Power without the previous consent of the French Government.

5. Alexandretta shall be a free port as regards the trade of the British Empire and there shall be no discrimination in treatment with regard to port dues or the extension of special privileges affecting British shipping and commerce; there shall be freedom of transit for British goods through Alexandretta and over railways through the Blue area, whether such goods are going to or coming from the Red area, area (A) or area (B); and there shall be no differentiation in treatment, direct or indirect, at the expense of British goods on any railway or of British goods and shipping in any port serving the areas in question.

Haifa shall be a free port as regards the trade of France, her colonies and protectorates, and there shall be no differentiation in treatment or privilege with regard to port dues against French shipping and commerce. There shall be freedom of transit through Haifa and over British railways through the Brown area, whether such goods are coming from or going to the Blue area, area (A) or area (B), and there shall be no differentiation in treatment, direct or indirect, at the expense of French goods on any railway or of French goods and shipping in any port serving the areas in question.

6. In area (A), the Baghdad Railway shall not be extended southwards beyond Mosul, and in area (B), it shall not be extended northwards beyond Samarra, until a railway connecting Baghdad with Aleppo along the basin of the Euphrates will have been completed, and then only with the concurrence of the two Governments.

7. Great Britain shall have the right to build, administer and be the sole owner of the railway connecting Haifa with area (B). She shall have, in addition, the right in perpetuity and at all times of carrying troops on that line. It is understood by both Governments that this railway is intended to facilitate communication between Baghdad and Haifa, and it is further understood that, in the event of technical difficulties and expenditure incurred in the maintenance of this line in the Brown area rendering the execution of the project impracticable, the French Government will be prepared to consider plans for enabling the line in question to traverse the polygon formed by Banias-Umm Qais-Salkhad-Tall 'Osda-Mismieh before reaching area (B).

8. For a period of twenty years, the Turkish customs tariff shall remain in force throughout the Blue and Red areas as well as in areas (A) and (B), and no increase in the rates of duties and no alteration of *ad valorem* duties into specific duties shall be made without the consent of the two Powers.

There shall be no internal customs barriers between any of the areas mentioned above. The customs duties to be levied on goods destined for the interior shall be collected at the ports of entry and remitted to the Administration of the area of destination.

9. It is understood that the French Government will at no time initiate any negotiations for the cession of their rights and will not cede their prospective rights in the Blue area to any third Power other than the Arab State or Confederation of Arab States, without the previous consent of His Majesty's Government who, on their part, give the French Government a similar undertaking in respect of the Red area.

10. The British and French Governments shall agree to abstain from acquiring and to withold their consent to a third Power acquiring territorial possessions in the Arabian Peninsula; nor shall they consent to the construction by a third Power of a naval base in the islands on the eastern seaboard of the Red Sea. This, however, will not prevent such rectification of the Aden boundary as might be found necessary in view of the recent Turkish attack.

11. The negotiations with the Arabs concerning the frontiers of the Arab State or Confederation of Arab States shall be pursued through the same channel as heretofore in the name of the two Powers.

12. It is understood, moreover, that measures for controlling the importation of arms into the Arab territory will be considered by the two Governments.

BALFOUR DECLARATION

November 2nd, 1917

Balfour was British Foreign Secretary, Rothschild the British Zionist leader.

Dear Lord Rothschild,

I have much pleasure in conveying to you on behalf of His Majesty's Government the following declaration of sympathy with Jewish Zionist aspirations, which has been submitted to and approved by the Cabinet.

"His Majesty's Government view with favour the establishment in Palestine of a national home for the Jewish people, and will use their best endeavours to facilitate the achievement of this object, it being clearly understood that nothing shall be done which may prejudice the civil and religious rights of existing non-Jewish communities in Palestine, or the rights and political status enjoyed by Jews in any other country."

I should be grateful if you would bring this declaration to the knowledge of the Zionist Federation.

Yours sincerely,
Arthur James Balfour

HOGARTH MESSAGE*
January 4th, 1918

The following is the text of a message which Commander D. G. Hogarth, C.M.G., R.N.V.R., of the Arab Bureau in Cairo, was instructed on January 4th, 1918, to deliver to King Husain of the Hejaz at Jeddah:

1. The *Entente* Powers are determined that the Arab race shall be given full opportunity of once again forming a nation in the world. This can only be achieved by the Arabs themselves uniting, and Great Britain and her Allies will pursue a policy with this ultimate unity in view.

2. So far as Palestine is concerned, we are determined that no people shall be subject to another, but—

(a) In view of the fact that there are in Palestine shrines, Wakfs and Holy places, sacred in some cases to Moslems alone, to Jews alone, to Christians alone, and in others to two or all three, and inasmuch as these places are of interest to vast masses of people outside Palestine and Arabia, there must be a special régime to deal with these places approved of by the world.

(b) As regards the Mosque of Omar, it shall be considered as a Moslem concern alone, and shall not be subjected directly or indirectly to any non-Moslem authority.

3. Since the Jewish opinion of the world is in favour of a return of Jews to Palestine, and inasmuch as this opinion must remain a constant factor, and, further, as His Majesty's Government view with favour the realization of this aspiration, His Majesty's Government are determined that in so far as is compatible with the freedom of the existing population, both economic and political, no obstacle should be put in the way of the realization of this ideal.

In this connection the friendship of world Jewry to the Arab cause is equivalent to support in all States where Jews have political influence. The leaders of the movement are determined to bring about the success of Zionism by friendship and co-operation with the Arabs, and such an offer is not one to be lightly thrown aside.

ANGLO-FRENCH DECLARATION†
November 7th, 1918

The object aimed at by France and Great Britain in prosecuting in the East the war let loose by the

ambition of Germany is the complete and definite emancipation of the peoples so long oppressed by the Turks and the establishment of national Governments and Administrations deriving their authority from the initiative and free choice of the indigenous populations.

In order to carry out these intentions France and Great Britain are at one in encouraging and assisting the establishments of indigenous Governments and Administrations in Syria and Mesopotamia, now liberated by the Allies, and in the territories the liberation of which they are engaged in securing and recognizing these as soon as they are actually established.

Far from wishing to impose on the populations of these regions any particular institutions they are only concerned to ensure by their support and by adequate assistance the regular working of Governments and Administrations freely chosen by the populations themselves. To secure impartial and equal justice for all, to facilitate the economic development of the country by inspiring and encouraging local initiative, to favour the diffusion of education, to put an end to dissensions that have too long been taken advantage of by Turkish policy, such is the policy which the two Allied Governments uphold in the liberated territories.

RECOMMENDATIONS OF
THE KING—CRANE COMMISSION‡
August 28th, 1919

The Commission was set up by President Wilson of the U.S.A. to determine which power should receive the Mandate for Palestine. The following are extracts from their recommendations on Syria:

1. We recommend, as most important of all, and in strict harmony with our Instructions, that whatever foreign administration (whether of one or more Powers) is brought into Syria, should come in, not at all as a colonising Power in the old sense of that term, but as a Mandatory under the League of Nations with the clear consciousness that 'the well-being and development', of the Syrian people form for it a 'sacred trust'.

2. We recommend, in the second place, that the unity of Syria be preserved, in accordance with the earnest petition of the great majority of the people of Syria.

3. We recommend, in the third place, that Syria be placed under one mandatory Power, as the natural way to secure real and efficient unity.

4. We recommend, in the fourth place, that Amir Faisal be made the head of the new united Syrian State.

5. We recommend, in the fifth place, serious modification of the extreme Zionist programme for Palestine of unlimited immigration of Jews, looking finally to making Palestine distinctly a Jewish State.

---

* British White Paper, Cmd. 5964, 1939.

† Report of a Committee set up to consider Certain Correspondence between Sir Henry McMahon and the Sherif of Mecca in 1915 and 1916, March 16th, 1939 (British White Paper, Cmd. 5974).

‡ U.S. Department of State. *Papers Relating to the Foreign Relations of the Untied States. The Paris Peace Conference 1919.* Vol. XII. Washington, 1947.

(1) The Commissioners began their study of Zionism with minds predisposed in its favor, but the actual facts in Palestine, coupled with the force of the general principles proclaimed by the Allies and accepted by the Syrians have driven them to the recommendation here made.

(2) The Commission was abundantly supplied with literature on the Zionist program by the Zionist Commission to Palestine; heard in conferences much concerning the Zionist colonies and their claims; and personally saw something of what had been accomplished. They found much to approve in the aspirations and plans of the Zionists, and had warm appreciation for the devotion of many of the colonists, and for their success, by modern methods in overcoming great, natural obstacles.

(3) The Commission recognised also that definite encouragement had been given to the Zionists by the Allies in Mr. Balfour's often-quoted statement, in its approval by other representatives of the Allies. If, however, the strict terms of the Balfour Statement are adhered to—favoring 'the establishment in Palestine of a national home for the Jewish people', 'it being clearly understood that nothing shall be done which may prejudice the civil and religious rights of existing non-Jewish communities in Palestine'—it can hardly be doubted that the extreme Zionist program must be greatly modified. For 'a national home for the Jewish people' is not equivalent to making Palestine into a Jewish State; nor can the erection of such a Jewish State be accomplished without the gravest trespass upon the 'civil and religious rights of existing non-Jewish communities in Palestine'. The fact came out repeatedly in the Commission's conference with Jewish representatives, that the Zionists looked forward to a practically complete dispossession of the present non-Jewish inhabitants of Palestine, by various forms of purchase.

In his address of July 4th, 1918, President Wilson laid down the following principle as one of the four great 'ends for which the associated peoples of the world were fighting': 'The settlement of every question, whether of territory, of sovereignty, of economic arrangement, or of political relationship upon the basis of the free acceptance of that settlement by the people immediately concerned, and not upon the basis of the material interest or advantage of any other nation or people which may desire a different settlement for the sake of its own exterior influence or mastery.' If that principle is to rule, and so the wishes of Palestine's population are to be decisive as to what is to be done with Palestine, then it is to be remembered that the non-Jewish population of Palestine—nearly nine-tenths of the whole—are emphatically against the entire Zionist program. The tables show that there was no one thing upon which the population of Palestine were more agreed than upon this. To subject a people so minded to unlimited Jewish immigration, and to steady financial and social pressure to surrender the land, would be a gross violation of the principle just quoted, and of the people's rights, though it kept within the forms of law.

It is to be noted also that the feeling against the Zionist program is not confined to Palestine, but shared very generally by the people throughout Syria, as our conferences clearly showed. More than 72 per cent—1,350 in all—of all the petitions in the whole of Syria were directed against the Zionist program. Only two requests—those for a united Syria and for independence—had a larger support. This general feeling was duly voiced by the General Syrian Congress in the seventh, eighth and tenth resolutions of their statement.

The Peace Conference should not shut its eyes to the fact that the anti-Zionist feeling in Palestine and Syria is intense and not lightly to be flouted. No British officer, consulted by the Commissioners, believed that the Zionist program could be carried out except by force of arms. The officers generally thought that a force of not less than 50,000 soldiers would be required even to initiate the program. That of itself is evidence of a strong sense of the injustice of the Zionist program, on the part of the non-Jewish populations of Palestine and Syria. Decisions requiring armies to carry out are sometimes necessary, but they are surely not gratuitously to be taken in the interests of serious injustice. For the initial claim, often submitted by Zionist representatives, that they have a 'right' to Palestine, based on an occupation of 2,000 years ago, can hardly be seriously considered.

There is a further consideration that cannot justly be ignored, if the world is to look forward to Palestine becoming a definitely Jewish State, however gradually that may take place. That consideration grows out of the fact that Palestine is the Holy Land for Jews, Christians, and Moslems alike. Millions of Christians and Moslems all over the world are quite as much concerned as the Jews with conditions in Palestine, especially with those conditions which touch upon religious feelings and rights. The relations in these matters in Palestine are most delicate and difficult. With the best possible intentions, it may be doubted whether the Jews could possibly seem to either Christians or Moslems proper guardians of the holy places, or custodians of the Holy Land as a whole.

The reason is this: The places which are most sacred to Christians—those having to do with Jesus— and which are also sacred to Moslems, are not only not sacred to Jews, but abhorrent to them. It is simply impossible, under those circumstances, for Moslems and Christians to feel satisfied to have these places in Jewish hands, or under the custody of Jews. There are still other places about which Moslems must have the same feeling. In fact, from this point of view, the Moslems, just because the sacred places of all three religions are sacred to them, have made very naturally much more satisfactory custodians of the holy places than the Jews could be. It must be believed that the precise meaning in this respect of the complete Jewish occupation of Palestine has not been fully sensed by those who urge the extreme Zionist program. For it would intensify, with a certainty like fate, the anti-Jewish feeling both in Palestine and in all other portions of the world which look to Palestine as the Holy Land.

In view of all these considerations, and with a deep sense of sympathy for the Jewish cause, the Commissioners feel bound to recommend that only a greatly reduced Zionist program be attempted by the Peace Conference, and even that, only very gradually initiated. This would have to mean that Jewish immigration should be definitely limited, and that the project for making Palestine distinctly a Jewish commonwealth should be given up.

There would then be no reason why Palestine could not be included in a united Syrian State, just as other portions of the country, the holy places being cared for by an international and inter-religious commission, somewhat as at present, under the oversight and approval of the Mandatory and of the League of Nations. The Jews, of course, would have representation upon this commission.

ARTICLE 22 OF THE COVENANT OF THE LEAGUE OF NATIONS

1. To those colonies and territories which as a consequence of the late War have ceased to be under the sovereignty of the States which formerly governed them and which are inhabited by peoples not yet able to stand by themselves under the strenuous conditions of the modern world, there should be applied the principle that the well-being and development of such peoples form a sacred trust of civilization and that securities for the performance of this trust should be embodied in this Covenant.

2. The best method of giving practical effect to this principle is that the tutelage of such peoples should be entrusted to advanced nations who by reason of their resources, their experience or their geographical position can best undertake this responsibility, and who are willing to accept it, and that this tutelage should be exercised by them as Mandatories on behalf of the League.

3. The character of the Mandate must differ according to the stage of the development of the people, the geographical situation of the territory, its economic conditions and other similar circumstances.

4. Certain communities formerly belonging to the Turkish Empire have reached a stage of development where their existence as independent nations can be provisionally recognized subject to the rendering of administrative advice and assistance by a Mandatory until such time as they are able to stand alone. The wishes of these communities must be a principal consideration in the selection of the Mandatory.

7. In every case of Mandate, the Mandatory shall render to the Council an annual report in reference to the territory committed to its charge.

8. The degree of authority, control, or administration to be exercised by the Mandatory shall, if not previously agreed upon by the Members of the League, be explicitly defined in each case by the Council.

9. A permanent Commission shall be constituted to receive and examine the annual reports of the Mandatories and to advise the Council on all matters relating to the observance of the Mandates.

MANDATE FOR PALESTINE*

July 24th, 1922

The Council of the League of Nations:

Whereas the Principal Allied Powers have agreed, for the purpose of giving effect to the provisions of Article 22 of the Covenant of the League of Nations to entrust to a Mandatory selected by the said Powers the administration of the territory of Palestine, which formerly belonged to the Turkish Empire, within such boundaries as may be fixed by them; and

Whereas the Principal Allied Powers have also agreed that the Mandatory should be responsible for putting into effect the declaration originally made on November 2nd, 1917, by the Government of His Britannic Majesty, and adopted by the said Powers, in favour of the establishment in Palestine of a National Home for the Jewish people, it being clearly understood that nothing should be done which might prejudice the civil and religious rights of existing non-Jewish communities in Palestine, or the rights and political status enjoyed by Jews in any other country; and

Whereas recognition has thereby been given to the historical connection of the Jewish people with Palestine and to the grounds for reconstituting their National Home in that country; and

Whereas the Principal Allied Powers have selected His Britannic Majesty as the Mandatory for Palestine; and

Whereas the Mandate in respect of Palestine has been formulated in the following terms and submitted to the Council of the League for approval; and

Whereas His Britannic Majesty has accepted the Mandate in respect of Palestine and undertaken to exercise it on behalf of the League of Nations in conformity with the following provisions; and

Whereas by the afore-mentioned Article 22 (paragraph 8), it is provided that the degree of authority, control or administration to be exercised by the Mandatory, not having been previously agreed upon by the Members of the League, shall be explicitly defined by the Council of the League of Nations;

Confirming the said Mandate, defines its terms as follows:

ARTICLE 1. The Mandatory shall have full powers of legislation and of administration, save as they may be limited by the terms of this Mandate.

ARTICLE 2. The Mandatory shall be responsible for placing the country under such political, administrative and economic conditions as will secure the establishment of the Jewish National Home, as laid down in the preamble, and the development of self-governing institutions, and also for safeguarding the civil and religious rights of all the inhabitants of Palestine, irrespective of race and religion.

ARTICLE 3. The Mandatory shall, so far as circumstances permit, encourage local autonomy.

---

* British White Paper, Cmd. 1785.

ARTICLE 4. An appropriate Jewish Agency shall be recognized as a public body for the purpose of advising and co-operating with the Administration of Palestine in such economic, social and other matters as may affect the establishment of the Jewish National Home and the interests of the Jewish population in Palestine, and, subject always to the control of the Administration, to assist and take part in the development of the country.

The Zionist organization, so long as its organization and constitution are in the opinion of the Mandatory appropriate, shall be recognized as such agency. It shall take steps in consultation with His Britannic Majesty's Government to secure the co-operation of all Jews who are willing to assist in the establishment of the Jewish National Home.

ARTICLE 5. The Mandatory shall be responsible for seeing that no Palestine territory shall be ceded or leased to, or in any way placed under the control of, the Government of any foreign Power.

ARTICLE 6. The Administration of Palestine, while ensuring that the rights and position of other sections of the population are not prejudiced, shall facilitate Jewish immigration under suitable conditions and shall encourage, in co-operation with the Jewish Agency referred to in Article 4, close settlement by Jews on the land, including State lands and waste lands not required for public purposes.

ARTICLE 7. The Administration of Palestine shall be responsible for enacting a nationality law. There shall be included in this law provisions framed so as to facilitate the acquisition of Palestinian citizenship by Jews who take up their permanent residence in Palestine.

ARTICLE 13. All responsibility in connection with the Holy Places and religious buildings or sites in Palestine, including that of preserving existing rights and of securing free access to the Holy Places, religious buildings and sites and the free exercise of worship, while ensuring the requirements of public order and decorum, is assumed by the Mandatory, who shall be responsible solely to the League of Nations in all matters connected herewith, provided that nothing in this Article shall prevent the Mandatory from entering into such arrangements as he may deem reasonable with the Administration for the purpose of carrying the provisions of this Article into effect; and provided also that nothing in this Mandate shall be construed as conferring upon the Mandatory authority to interfere with the fabric of the management of purely Moslem sacred shrines, the immunities of which are guaranteed.

ARTICLE 14. A special Commission shall be appointed by the Mandatory to study, define and determine the rights and claims in connection with the Holy Places and the rights and claims relating to the different religious communities in Palestine. The method of nomination, the composition and the functions of this Commission shall be submitted to the Council of the League for its approval, and the Commission shall not be appointed or enter upon its functions without the approval of the Council.

ARTICLE 28. In the event of the termination of the Mandate hereby conferred upon the Mandatory, the Council of the League of Nations shall make such arrangements as may be deemed necessary for safeguarding in perpetuity, under guarantee of the League, the rights secured by Articles 13 and 14, and shall use its influence for securing, under the guarantee of the League, that the Government of Palestine will fully honour the financial obligations legitimately incurred by the Administration of Palestine during the period of the Mandate, including the rights of public servants to pensions or gratuities.

CHURCHILL MEMORANDUM*

June 3rd, 1922

The Secretary of State for the Colonies has given renewed consideration to the existing political situation in Palestine, with a very earnest desire to arrive at a settlement of the outstanding questions which have given rise to uncertainty and unrest among certain sections of the population. After consultation with the High Commissioner for Palestine the following statement has been drawn up. It summarizes the essential parts of the correspondence that has already taken place between the Secretary of State and a Delegation from the Moslem Christian Society of Palestine, which has been for some time in England, and it states the further conclusions which have since been reached.

The tension which has prevailed from time to time in Palestine is mainly due to apprehensions, which are entertained both by sections of the Arab and by sections of the Jewish population. These apprehensions, so far as the Arabs are concerned, are partly based upon exaggerated interpretations of the meaning of the Declaration favouring the establishment of a Jewish National Home in Palestine, made on behalf of His Majesty's Government on November 2nd, 1917. Unauthorized statements have been made to the effect that the purpose in view is to create a wholly Jewish Palestine. Phrases have been used such as that Palestine is to become "as Jewish as England is English." His Majesty's Government regard any such expectation as impracticable and have no such aim in view. Nor have they at any time contemplated, as appears to be feared by the Arab Delegation, the disappearance or the subordination of the Arabic population, language or culture in Palestine. They would draw attention to the fact that the terms of the Declaration referred to do not contemplate that Palestine as a whole should be converted into a Jewish National Home, but that such a Home should be founded *in Palestine*. In this connection it has been observed with satisfaction that at the meeting of the Zionist Congress, the supreme governing body of the Zionist Organization, held at Carlsbad in September 1921, a resolution was passed expressing as the official statement of Zionist aims "the determination of the Jewish people to live with the Arab people on terms

* Palestine, Correspondence with the Palestine Arab Delegation and the Zionist Organization (British White Paper, Cmd. 1700), pp. 17–21.

of unity and mutual respect, and together with them to make the common home into a flourishing community, the upbuilding of which may assure to each of its peoples an undisturbed national development."

It is also necessary to point out that the Zionist Commission in Palestine, now termed the Palestine Zionist Executive, has not desired to possess, and does not possess, any share in the general administration of the country. Nor does the special position assigned to the Zionist Organization in Article IV of the Draft Mandate for Palestine imply any such functions. That special position relates to the measures to be taken in Palestine affecting the Jewish population, and contemplates that the Organization may assist in the general development of the country, but does not entitle it to share in any degree in its Government.

Further, it is contemplated that the status of all citizens of Palestine in the eyes of the law shall be Palestinian, and it has never been intended that they, or any section of them, should possess any other juridical status.

So far as the Jewish population of Palestine are concerned, it appears that some among them are apprehensive that His Majesty's Government may depart from the policy embodied in the Declaration of 1917. It is necessary, therefore, once more to affirm that these fears are unfounded, and that that Declaration, re-affirmed by the Conference of the Principal Allied Powers at San Remo and again in the Treaty of Sèvres, is not susceptible of change.

During the last two or three generations the Jews have recreated in Palestine a community, now numbering 80,000, of whom about one-fourth are farmers or workers upon the land. This community has its own political organs; and elected assembly for the direction of its domestic concerns; elected councils in the towns; and an organization for the control of its schools. It has its elected Chief Rabbinate and Rabbinical Council for the direction of its religious affairs. Its business is conducted in Hebrew as a vernacular language, and a Hebrew Press serves its needs. It has its distinctive intellectual life and displays considerable economic activity. This community, then, with its town and country population, its political, religious and social organizations, its own language, its own customs, its own life, has in fact "national" characteristics. When it is asked what is meant by the development of the Jewish National Home in Palestine, it may be answered that it is not the imposition of a Jewish nationality upon the inhabitants of Palestine as a whole, but the further development of the existing Jewish community, with the assistance of Jews in other parts of the world, in order that it may become a centre in which the Jewish people as a whole may take, on grounds of religion and race, an interest and a pride. But in order that this community should have the best prospect of free development and provide a full opportunity for the Jewish people to display its capacities, it is essential that it should know that it is in Palestine as of right and not on sufferance. That is the reason why it is necessary that the existence of a Jewish National Home in

Palestine should be internationally guaranteed, and that it should be formally recognized to rest upon ancient historic connection.

This, then, is the interpretation which His Majesty's Government place upon the Declaration of 1917, and, so understood, the Secretary of State is of opinion that it does not contain or imply anything which need cause either alarm to the Arab population of Palestine or disappointment to the Jews.

For the fulfilment of this policy it is necessary that the Jewish community in Palestine should be able to increase its numbers by immigration. This immigration cannot be so great in volume as to exceed whatever may be the economic capacity of the country at the time to absorb new arrivals. It is essential to ensure that the immigrants should not be a burden upon the people of Palestine as a whole, and that they should not deprive any section of the present population of their employment. Hitherto the immigration has fulfilled these conditions. The number of immigrants since the British occupation has been about 25,000. . . .

REPORT OF PALESTINE ROYAL COMMISSION PEEL COMMISSION*

July 1937

The Commission under Lord Peel was appointed in 1936. The following are extracts from recommendations made in Ch. XXII:

Having reached the conclusion that there is no possibility of solving the Palestine problem under the existing Mandate (or even under a scheme of cantonization), the Commission recommend the termination of the present Mandate on the basis of Partition and put forward a definite scheme which they consider to be practicable, honourable and just. The scheme is as follows:

The Mandate for Palestine should terminate and be replaced by a Treaty System in accordance with the precedent set in Iraq and Syria.

Under Treaties to be negotiated by the Mandatory with the Government of Transjordan and representatives of the Arabs of Palestine on the one hand, and with the Zionist Organization on the other, it would be declared that two sovereign independent States would shortly be established—(1) an Arab State consisting of Transjordan united with that part of Palestine allotted to the Arabs, (2) a Jewish State consisting of that part of Palestine allotted to the Jews. The Mandatory would undertake to support any requests for admission to the League of Nations made by the Governments of the Arab and Jewish States. The Treaties would include strict guarantees for the protection of minorities. Military Conventions would be attached to the Treaties.

A new Mandate should be instituted to execute the trust of maintaining the sanctity of Jerusalem and Bethlehem and ensuring free and safe access to them

---

* *Palestine Royal Commission: Report,* 1937 (British Blue Book, Cmd. 5479).

for all the world. An enclave should be demarcated to which this Mandate should apply, extending from a point north of Jerusalem to a point south of Bethlehem, and access to the sea should be provided by a corridor extending from Jerusalem to Jaffa. The policy of the Balfour Declaration would not apply to the Mandated Area.

The Jewish State should pay a subvention to the Arab State. A Finance Commission should be appointed to advise as to its amount and as to the division of the public debt of Palestine and other financial questions.

In view of the backwardness of Transjordan, Parliament should be asked to make a grant of £2,000,000 to the Arab State.

WHITE PAPER*
May 1939
The main recommendations are extracted below:

10. . . . His Majesty's Government make the following declaration of their intentions regarding the future government of Palestine:

(i) The objective of His Majesty's Government is the establishment within ten years of an independent Palestine State in such treaty relations with the United Kingdom as will provide satisfactorily for the commercial and strategic requirements of both countries in the future. This proposal for the establishment of the independent State would involve consultation with the Council of the League of Nations with a view to the termination of the Mandate.

(ii) The independent State should be one in which Arabs and Jews share in government in such a way as to ensure that the essential interests of each community are safeguarded.

(iii) The establishment of the independent State will be preceded by a transitional period throughout which His Majesty's Government will retain responsibility for the government of the country. During the transitional period the people of Palestine will be given an increasing part in the government of their country. Both sections of the population will have an opportunity to participate in the machinery of government, and the process will be carried on whether or not they both avail themselves of it.

(iv) As soon as peace and order have been sufficiently restored in Palestine steps will be taken to carry out this policy of giving the people of Palestine an increasing part in the government of their country, the objective being to place Palestinians in charge of all the Departments of Government, with the assistance of British advisers and subject to the control of the High Commissioner. With this object in view His Majesty's Government will be prepared immediately to arrange that Palestinians shall be placed in charge of certain Departments, with British advisers. The Palestinian

heads of Departments will sit on the Executive Council, which advises the High Commissioner. Arab and Jewish representatives will be invited to serve as heads of Departments approximately in proportion to their respective populations. The number of Palestinians in charge of Departments will be increased as circumstances permit until all heads of Departments are Palestinians, exercising the administrative and advisory functions which are at present performed by British officials. When that stage is reached consideration will be given to the question of converting the Executive Council into a Council of Ministers with a consequential change in the status and functions of the Palestinian heads of Departments.

(v) His Majesty's Government make no proposals at this stage regarding the establishment of an elective legislature. Nevertheless they would regard this as an appropriate constitutional development, and, should public opinion in Palestine hereafter show itself in favour of such a development, they will be prepared, provided that local conditions permit, to establish the necessary machinery.

(vi) At the end of five years from the restoration of peace and order, an appropriate body representative of the people of Palestine and of His Majesty's Government will be set up to review the working of the constitutional arrangements during the transitional period and to consider and make recommendations regarding the Constitution of the independent Palestine State.

(vii) His Majesty's Government will require to be satisfied that in the treaty contemplated by sub-paragraph (i) or in the Constitution contemplated by sub-paragraph (vi) adequate provision has been made for:

(*a*) the security of, and freedom of access to, the Holy Places, and the protection of the interests and property of the various religious bodies;

(*b*) the protection of the different communities in Palestine in accordance with the obligations of His Majesty's Government to both Arabs and Jews and for the special position in Palestine of the Jewish National Home;

(*c*) such requirements to meet the strategic situation as may be regarded as necessary by His Majesty's Government in the light of the circumstances then existing.

His Majesty's Government will also require to be satisfied that the interests of certain foreign countries in Palestine, for the preservation of which they are at present responsible, are adequately safeguarded.

(viii) His Majesty's Government will do everything in their power to create conditions which will enable the independent Palestine State to come into being within ten years. If, at the end of ten years, it appears to His Majesty's Government that, contrary to their hope, circumstances require the postponement of the establishment of the independent State, they will consult with representatives

---

* British White Paper, Cmd. 6019.

of the people of Palestine, the Council of the League of Nations and the neighbouring Arab States before deciding on such a postponement. If His Majesty's Government come to the conclusion that postponement is unavoidable, they will invite the co-operation of these parties in framing plans for the future with a view to achieving the desired objective at the earliest possible date.

11. During the transitional period steps will be taken to increase the powers and responsibilities of municipal corporations and local councils.

14. ... they believe that they will be acting consistently with their Mandatory obligations to both Arabs and Jews, and in the manner best calculated to serve the interests of the whole people of Palestine by adopting the following proposals regarding immigration:

(i) Jewish immigration during the next five years will be at a rate which, if economic absorptive capacity permits, will bring the Jewish population up to approximately one-third of the total population of the country. Taking into account the expected natural increase of the Arab and Jewish populations, and the number of illegal Jewish immigrants now in the country, this would allow of the admission, as from the beginning of April this year, of some 75,000 immigrants over the next five years. These immigrants would, subject to the criterion of economic absorptive capacity, be admitted as follows:

(a) For each of the next five years a quota of 10,000 Jewish immigrants will be allowed, on the understanding that a shortage in any one year may be added to the quotas for subsequent years, within the five-year period, if economic absorptive capacity permits.

(b) In addition, as a contribution towards the solution of the Jewish refugee problem, 25,000 refugees will be admitted as soon as the High Commissioner is satisfied that adequate provision for their maintenance is ensured, special consideration being given to refugee children and dependants.

(ii) The existing machinery for ascertaining economic absorptive capacity will be retained, and the High Commissioner will have the ultimate responsibility for deciding the limits of economic capacity. Before each periodic decision is taken, Jewish and Arab representatives will be consulted.

(iii) After the period of five years no further Jewish immigration will be permitted unless the Arabs of Palestine are prepared to acquiesce in it.

(iv) His Majesty's Government are determined to check illegal immigration, and further preventive measures are being adopted. The numbers of any Jewish illegal immigrants who, despite these measures, may succeed in coming into the country and cannot be deported will be deducted from the yearly quotas.

15. His Majesty's Government are satisfied that, when the immigration over five years which is now

contemplated has taken place, they will not be justified in facilitating, nor will they be under any obligation to facilitate, the further development of the Jewish National Home by immigration regardless of the wishes of the Arab population.

16. The Administration of Palestine is required, under Article 6 of the Mandate, "while ensuring that the rights and position of other sections of the population are not prejudiced," to encourage "close settlement by Jews on the land," and no restriction has been imposed hitherto on the transfer of land from Arabs to Jews. The Reports of several expert Commissions have indicated that, owing to the natural growth of the Arab population and the steady sale in recent years of Arab land to Jews, there is now in certain areas no room for further transfers of Arab land, whilst in some other areas such transfers of land must be restricted if Arab cultivators are to maintain their existing standard of life and a considerable landless Arab population is not soon to be created. In these circumstances, the High Commissioner will be given general powers to prohibit and regulate transfers of land. These powers will date from the publication of this statement of Policy and the High Commissioner will retain them throughout the transitional period.

17. The policy of the Government will be directed towards the development of the land and the improvement, where possible, of methods of cultivation. In the light of such development it will be open to the High Commissioner, should he be satisfied that the "rights and position" of the Arab population will be duly preserved, to review and modify any orders passed relating to the prohibition or restriction of the transfer of land.

BILTMORE PROGRAMME*
May 11th, 1942

The following programme was approved by a Zionist Conference held in the Biltmore Hotel, New York City:

1. American Zionists assembled in this Extraordinary Conference reaffirm their unequivocal devotion to the cause of democratic freedom and international justice to which the people of the United States, allied with the other United Nations, have dedicated themselves, and give expression to their faith in the ultimate victory of humanity and justice over lawlessness and brute force.

2. This Conference offers a message of hope and encouragement to their fellow Jews in the Ghettos and concentration camps of Hitler-dominated Europe and prays that their hour of liberation may not be far distant.

3. The Conference sends its warmest greetings to the Jewish Agency Executive in Jerusalem, to the Va'ad Leumi, and to the whole Yishuv in Palestine, and expresses its profound admiration for their steadfastness and achievements in the face of peril

* Text supplied by courtesy of Josef Fraenkel.

and great difficulties. The Jewish men and women in field and factory, and the thousands of Jewish soldiers of Palestine in the Near East who have acquitted themselves with honour and distinction in Greece, Ethiopia, Syria, Libya and on other battlefields, have shown themselves worthy of their people and ready to assume the rights and responsibilities of nationhood.

4. In our generation, and in particular in the course of the past twenty years, the Jewish people have awakened and transformed their ancient homeland; from 50,000 at the end of the last war their numbers have increased to more than 500,000. They have made the waste places to bear fruit and the desert to blossom. Their pioneering achievements in agriculture and in industry, embodying new patterns of cooperative endeavour, have written a notable page in the history of colonization.

5. In the new values thus created, their Arab neighbours in Palestine have shared. The Jewish people in its own work of national redemption welcomes the economic, agricultural and national development of the Arab peoples and states. The Conference reaffirms the stand previously adopted at Congresses of the World Zionist Organization, expressing the readiness and the desire of the Jewish people for full cooperation with their Arab neighbours.

6. The Conference calls for the fulfilment of the original purpose of the Balfour Declaration and the Mandate which *"recognizing the historical connexion of the Jewish people with Palestine"* was to afford them the opportunity, as stated by President Wilson, to found there a Jewish Commonwealth.

The Conference affirms its unalterable rejection of the White Paper of May 1939 and denies its moral or legal validity. The White Paper seeks to limit, and in fact to nullify Jewish rights to immigration and settlement in Palestine, and, as stated by Mr. Winston Churchill in the House of Commons in May 1939, constitutes "a breach and repudiation of the Balfour Declaration". The policy of the White Paper is cruel and indefensible in its denial of sanctuary to Jews fleeing from Nazi persecution; and at a time when Palestine has become a focal point in the war front of the United Nations, and Palestine Jewry must provide all available manpower for farm and factory and camp, it is in direct conflict with the interests of the allied war effort.

7. In the struggle against the forces of aggression and tyranny, of which Jews were the earliest victims, and which now menace the Jewish National Home, recognition must be given to the right of the Jews of Palestine to play their full part in the war effort and in the defence of their country, through a Jewish military force fighting under its own flag and under the high command of the United Nations.

8. The Conference declares that the new world order that will follow victory cannot be established on foundations of peace, justice and equality, unless the problem of Jewish homelessness is finally solved.

The Conference urges that the gates of Palestine be opened; that the Jewish Agency be vested with control of immigration into Palestine and with the necessary authority for upbuilding the country, including the development of its unoccupied and uncultivated lands; and that Palestine be established as a Jewish Commonwealth integrated in the structure of the new democratic world.

Then and only then will the age old wrong to the Jewish people be righted.

UN GENERAL ASSEMBLY RESOLUTION ON THE FUTURE GOVERNMENT OF PALESTINE (PARTITION RESOLUTION)

November 29th, 1947

The General Assembly,

Having met in special session at the request of the mandatory Power to constitute and instruct a special committee to prepare for the consideration of the question of the future government of Palestine at the second regular session;

Having constituted a Special Committee and instructed it to investigate all questions and issues relevant to the problem of Palestine, and to prepare proposals for the solution of the problem, and

Having received and examined the report of the Special Committee (document A/364) including a number of unanimous recommendations and a plan of partition with economic union approved by the majority of the Special Committee,

Considers that the present situation in Palestine is one which is likely to impair the general welfare and friendly relations among nations;

Takes note of the declaration by the mandatory Power that it plans to complete its evacuation of Palestine by August 1st, 1948;

Recommends to the United Kingdom, as the mandatory Power for Palestine, and to all other Members of the United Nations the adoption and implementation, with regard to the future government of Palestine, of the Plan of Partition with Economic Union set out below;

Requests that

(a) The Security Council take the necessary measures as provided for in the plan for its implementation;

(b) The Security Council consider, if circumstances during the transitional period require such consideration, whether the situation in Palestine constitutes a threat to the peace. If it decides that such a threat exists, and in order to maintain international peace and security, the Security Council should supplement the authorization of the General Assembly by taking measures, under Articles 39 and 41 of the Charter, to empower the United Nations Commission, as provided in this resolution, to exercise in Palestine the functions which are assigned to it by this resolution;

(c) The Security Council determine as a threat to the peace, breach of the peace or act of aggression, in accordance with Article 39 of the Charter, any attempt to alter by force the settlement envisaged by this resolution;

(*d*) The Trusteeship Council be informed of the responsibilities envisaged for it in this plan;

Calls upon the inhabitants of Palestine to take such steps as may be necessary on their part to put this plan into effect;

Appeals to all Governments and all peoples to refrain from taking any action which might hamper or delay the carrying out of these recommendations, and

Authorizes the Secretary-General to reimburse travel and subsistence expenses of the members of the Commission referred to in Part 1, Section B, paragraph 1 below, on such basis and in such form as he may determine most appropriate in the circumstances, and to provide the Commission with the necessary staff to assist in carrying out the functions assigned to the Commission by the General Assembly.

Official Records of the second session of the General Assembly, Resolutions, p. 131.

UN GENERAL ASSEMBLY RESOLUTION 194 (III)

December 11th, 1948

The resolution's terms have been reaffirmed every year since 1948.

11. . . . the refugees wishing to return to their homes and live at peace with their neighbours should be permitted to do so at the earliest practicable date, and that compensation should be paid for the property of those choosing not to return and for the loss of or damage to property which, under principles of international law or in equity, should be made good by the Governments or authorities responsible;

Official Records of the third session of the General Assembly, Part 1, Resolutions, p. 21.

UN GENERAL ASSEMBLY RESOLUTION ON THE INTERNATIONALIZATION OF JERUSALEM

December 9th, 1949

The General Assembly,

Having regard to its resolution 181 (II) of November 29th, 1947 and 194 (III) of December 11th, 1948,

Having studied the reports of the United Nations Conciliation Commission for Palestine set up under the latter resolution,

I. Decides
In relation to Jerusalem,

Believing that the principles underlying its previous resolutions concerning this matter, and in particular its resolution of November 29th, 1947, represent a just and equitable settlement of the question,

1. To restate, therefore, its intention that Jerusalem should be placed under a permanent international regime, which should envisage appropriate guarantees for the protection of the Holy Places, both within and outside Jerusalem, and to confirm specifically the following provisions of General Assembly resolution 181 (II): (1) The City of Jerusalem shall be established as a *corpus separatum* under a special international regime and shall be administered by the United Nations; (2) The Trusteeship Council shall be designated to discharge the responsibilities of the Administering Authority . . .; and (3) The City of Jerusalem shall include the present municipality of Jerusalem plus the surrounding villages and towns, the most eastern of which shall be Abu Dis; the most southern, Bethlehem; the most western, Ein Karim (including also the built-up area of Motsa); and the most northern, Shu'fat, as indicated on the attached sketchmap; . . . [*map not reproduced: Ed.*]

Official Records of the fourth session of the General Assembly, Resolutions, p. 25.

TEXT OF UN SECURITY COUNCIL RESOLUTION
November 22nd, 1967

The Security Council,

Expressing its continued concern with the grave situation in the Middle East,

Emphasizing the inadmissibility of the acquisition of territory by war and the need to work for a just and lasting peace in which every state in the area can live in security,

Emphasizing further that all Member States in their acceptance of the Charter of the United Nations have undertaken a commitment to act in accordance with Article 2 of the Charter

1. *Affirms* that the fulfilment of Charter principles requires the establishment of a just and lasting peace in the Middle East which should include the application of both the following principles:

(i) Withdrawal of Israel armed forces from territories occupied in the recent conflict;

(ii) Termination of all claims or states of belligerency and respect for and acknowledgement of the sovereignty, territorial integrity and political independence of every State in the area and their right to live in peace within secure and recognized boundaries free from threats or acts of force.

2. *Affirms further* the necessity

(*a*) For guaranteeing freedom of navigation through international waterways in the area;

(*b*) For achieving a just settlement of the refugee problem;

(*c*) For guaranteeing the territorial inviolability and political independence of every State in the area, through measures including the establishment of demilitarized zones;

3. *Requests* the Secretary-General to designate a Special Representative to proceed to the Middle East

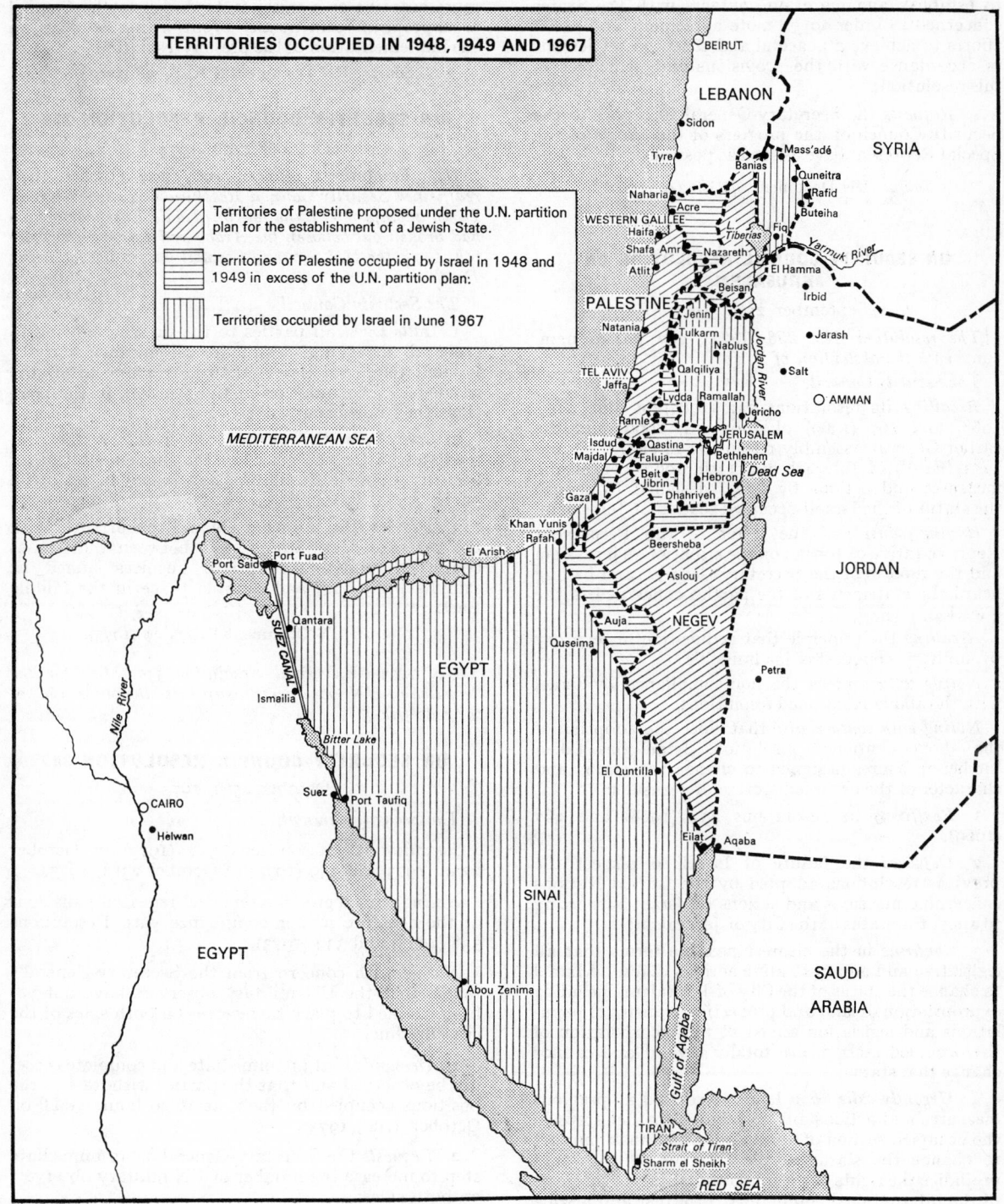

TERRITORIES OCCUPIED IN 1948, 1949 AND 1967

Territories of Palestine proposed under the U.N. partition plan for the establishment of a Jewish State.

Territories of Palestine occupied by Israel in 1948 and 1949 in excess of the U.N. partition plan:

Territories occupied by Israel in June 1967

The expansion of Israel. See also the maps on page 63.

to establish and maintain contacts with the States concerned in order to promote agreement and assist efforts to achieve a peaceful and accepted settlement in accordance with the provisions and principles in this resolution;

4. *Requests* the Secretary-General to report to the Security Council on the progress of the efforts of the Special Representative as soon as possible.

Source: UN Document S/RES/242 (1967).

UN SECURITY COUNCIL RESOLUTION ON JERUSALEM

September 25th, 1971

The resolution, No. 298 (1971), was passed nem. con., *with the abstention of Syria.*

The Security Council,

Recalling its resolutions 252 (1968) of May 21st, 1968, and 267 (1969) of July 3rd, 1969, and the earlier General Assembly resolution 2253 (ES-V) and 2254 (ES-V) of July 4th and 14th, 1967, concerning measures and actions by Israel designed to change the status of the Israeli-occupied section of Jerusalem,

Having considered the letter of the Permanent Representative of Jordan on the situation in Jerusalem and the reports of the Secretary-General, and having heard the statements of the parties concerned in the question,

Recalling the principle that acquisition of territory by military conquest is inadmissible,

Noting with concern the non-compliance by Israel with the above-mentioned resolutions,

Noting with concern also that since the adoption of the above-mentioned resolutions Israel has taken further measures designed to change the status and character of the occupied section of Jerusalem.

1. *Reaffirms* its resolutions 252 (1968) and 267 (1969);

2. *Deplores* the failure of Israel to respect the previous resolutions adopted by the United Nations concerning measures and actions by Israel purporting to affect the status of the City of Jerusalem;

3. *Confirms* in the clearest possible terms that all legislative and administrative actions taken by Israel to change the status of the City of Jerusalem, including expropriation of land and properties, transfer of populations and legislation aimed at the incorporation of the occupied section, are totally invalid and cannot change that status;

4. *Urgently calls upon* Israel to rescind all previous measures and actions and to take no further steps in the occupied section of Jerusalem which may purport to change the status of the City, or which would prejudice the rights of the inhabitants and the interests of the international community, or a just and lasting peace;

5. *Requests* the Secretary-General, in consultation with the President of the Security Council and using such instrumentalities as he may choose, including a representative or a mission, to report to the Council as appropriate and in any event within 60 days on the implementation of the present resolution.

Source: UN Document S/RES/298 (1971).

UN SECURITY COUNCIL RESOLUTION 338

October 22nd, 1973

UN Resolutions between 1967 and October 1973 reaffirmed Security Council Resolution 242 (see above). In an attempt to end the fourth Middle East war, which had broken out between the Arabs and Israel on October 6th, 1973, the UN Security Council passed the following Resolution:

The Security Council,

1. *Calls upon* all parties to the present fighting to cease all firing and terminate all military activity immediately, not later than 12 hours after the moment of the adoption of the decision, in the positions they now occupy;

2. *Calls upon* the parties concerned to start immediately after the ceasefire the implementation of Security Council Resolution 242 (1967) in all of its parts;

3. *Decides that*, immediately and concurrently with the ceasefire negotiations start between the parties concerned under appropriate auspices aimed at establishing a just and durable peace in the Middle East.

Source: UN Document PR/73/29 (1973).

UN Security Council Resolution 339 called for the despatch of UN Observers to supervise the observance of the ceasefire.

UN SECURITY COUNCIL RESOLUTION 340

October 25th, 1973

The Security Council,

Recalling its Resolutions 338 (1973) of October 22nd, 1973 and 339 (1973) of October 23rd, 1973,

Noting with regret the reported repeated violations of the ceasefire in non-compliance with Resolutions 338 (1973) and 339 (1973),

Noting with concern from the Secretary-General's report that the UN military observers have not yet been enabled to place themselves on both sides of the ceasefire line,

1. *Demands* that an immediate and complete ceasefire be observed and that the parties withdraw to the positions occupied by them at 16.50 hours GMT on October 22nd, 1973;

2. *Requests* the Secretary-General as an immediate step to increase the number of UN military observers on both sides;

3. *Decides* to set up immediately under its authority a UN emergency force to be composed of personnel drawn from member states of the UN, except the permanent members of the Security Council, and

requests the Secretary-General to report within 24 hours on the steps taken to this effect; (*Details of the UN Emergency Force are given in the Chapter "United Nations in the Middle East and North Africa"— Editor*)

4. *Requests* the Secretary-General to report to the Council on an urgent and continuing basis on the state of implementation of this Resolution, as well as Resolutions 338 (1973) and 339 (1973);

5. *Requests* all member states to extend their full co-operation to the UN in the implementation of this Resolution, as well as Resolutions 338 (1973) and 339 (1973).

Source: UN Document PR/73/31 (1973).

DECLARATION OF EEC FOREIGN MINISTERS ON THE MIDDLE EAST SITUATION

November 6th, 1973

The Nine Governments of the European Community have continued their exchange of views on the situation in the Middle East. While emphasizing that the views set out below are only a first contribution on their part to the search for a comprehensive solution to the problem, they have agreed on the following:

1. They strongly urge that the forces of both sides in the Middle East conflict should return immediately to the positions they occupied on October 22nd in accordance with Resolutions 339 and 340 of the Security Council. They believe that a return to these positions will facilitate a solution to other pressing problems concerning prisoners-of-war and the Egyptian Third Army.

2. They have the firm hope that, following the adoption by the Security Council of Resolution 338 of October 22nd, negotiations will at last begin for the restoration in the Middle East of a just and lasting peace through the application of Security Council Resolution 242 in all of its parts. They declare themselves ready to do all in their power to contribute to that peace. They believe that those negotiations must take place in the framework of the United Nations. They recall that the Charter has entrusted to the Security Council the principal responsibility for international peace and security. The Council and the Secretary-General have a special role to play in the making and keeping of peace through the application of Council Resolutions 242 and 338.

3. They consider that a peace agreement should be based particularly on the following points:

(i) the inadmissibility of the acquisition of territory by force;

(ii) the need for Israel to end the territorial occupation which it has maintained since the conflict of 1967;

(iii) respect for the sovereignty, territorial integrity and independence of every state in the area and their right to live in peace within secure and recognized boundaries;

(iv) recognition that in the establishment of a just and lasting peace account must be taken of the legitimate rights of the Palestinians.

Article 4 calls for the despatch of peace-keeping forces to the demilitarized zones.

Source: Bulletin of the European Communities Commission, No. 10, 1973, p. 106.

EGYPTIAN-ISRAELI AGREEMENT ON DISENGAGEMENT OF FORCES IN PURSUANCE OF THE GENEVA PEACE CONFERENCE

(signed by the Egyptian and Israeli Chiefs of Staff, January 18th, 1974)

A. Egypt and Israel will scrupulously observe the cease-fire on land, sea and air called for by the United Nations Security Council and will refrain from the time of the signing of this document from all military or para-military actions against each other.

B. The military forces of Egypt and Israel will be separated in accordance with the following principles:

1. All Egyptian forces on the east side of the canal will be deployed west of the line designated as line A on the attached map (*reproduced below*). All Israeli forces, including those west of the Suez Canal and the Bitter Lakes, will be deployed east of the line designated as line B on the attached map.

2. The area between the Egyptian and Israeli lines will be a zone of disengagement in which the United Nations Emergency Force (UNEF) will be stationed. The UNEF will continue to consist of units from countries that are not permanent members of the Security Council.

3. The area between the Egyptian line and the Suez Canal will be limited in armament and forces.

4. The area between the Israeli line (B on the attached map) and the line designated as line C on the attached map, which runs along the western base of the mountains where the Gidi and Mitla Passes are located, will be limited in armament and forces.

5. The limitations referred to in paragraphs 3 and 4 will be inspected by UNEF. Existing procedures of the UNEF, including the attaching of Egyptian and Israeli liaison officers to UNEF, will be continued.

6. Air forces of the two sides will be permitted to operate up to their respective lines without interference from the other side.

C. The detailed implementation of the disengagement of forces will be worked out by military representatives of Egypt and Israel, who will agree on the stages of this process. These representatives will meet no later than 48 hours after the signature of this Agreement at kilometre 101 under the aegis of the United Nations for this purpose. They will complete this task within five days. Disengagement will begin within 48 hours after the completion of the work of the military representatives and in no event later than seven days after the signature of this Agreement. The process of disengagement will be completed not later than 40 days after it begins.

D. This Agreement is not regarded by Egypt and Israel as a final peace agreement. It constitutes a first step toward a final, just and durable peace according to the provisions of Security Council Resolution 338 and within the framework of the Geneva Conference.

DISENGAGEMENT AGREEMENT BETWEEN SYRIAN AND ISRAELI FORCES AND PROTOCOL TO AGREEMENT ON UNITED NATIONS DISENGAGEMENT OBSERVER FORCE (UNDOF)

(signed in Geneva, Friday, May 31st, 1974)

(Annex A)

A. Israel and Syria will scrupulously observe the cease-fire on land, sea and air and will refrain from all military actions against each other, from time of signing this document in implementation of the United Nations Security Council Resolution 338 dated October 22nd, 1973.

B. The military forces of Israel and Syria will be separated in accordance with the following principles:

1. All Israeli military forces will be west of a line designated line A on the map attached hereto (*reproduced below*), except in Quneitra (Kuneitra) area, where they will be west of a line A-1.
2. All territory east of line A will be under Syrian administration and Syrian civilians will return to this territory.
3. The area between line A and the line designated as line B on the attached map will be an area of separation. In this area will be stationed UNDOF established in accordance with the accompanying Protocol.
4. All Syrian military forces will be east of a line designated as line B on the attached map.
5. There will be two equal areas of limitation in armament and forces, one west of line A and one east of line B as agreed upon.

C. In the area between line A and line A-1 on the attached map there shall be no military forces.

D. This agreement and the attached map will be signed by the military representatives of Israel and Syria in Geneva not later than May 31st, 1974, in the Egyptian-Israeli Military Working Group of the Geneva Peace Conference under the aegis of the United Nations, after that group has been joined by a Syrian military representative, and with the participation of representatives of the United States and the Soviet Union. Precise delineation of the detailed map and plan for implementation of the disengagement of forces will be worked out by the military representatives of Israel and Syria in the Egyptian-

Israeli Military Working Group who will agree on the stages of this process. The Military Working Group described above will start their work for this purpose in Geneva under the aegis of the United Nations within 24 hours after the signing of this Agreement. They will complete this task within five days. Disengagement will begin within 24 hours after completion of the task of the Military Working Group. The process of disengagement will be completed not later than 20 days after it begins.

E. Provisions of paragraphs A, B and C shall be inspected by personnel of the United Nations comprising UNDOF under the Agreement.

F. Within 24 hours after the signing of this Agreement in Geneva all wounded prisoners of war which each side holds of the other, as certified by the International Committee of the Red Cross, will be repatriated. The morning after the completion of the task of the Military Working Group, all remaining prisoners of war will be repatriated.

G. The bodies of all dead soldiers held by either side will be returned for burial in their respective countries within ten days after the signing of this Agreement.

H. This Agreement is not a peace agreement. It is a step towards a just and durable peace on the basis of the Security Council Resolution 338 dated October 22nd, 1973.

*   *   *

The following is the Protocol to the Disengagement Agreement *(Annex B)*:

Israel and Syria agree that:

The function of UNDOF under the Agreement will be to use its best efforts to maintain the ceasefire and to see that it is scrupulously observed. It will supervise the Agreement and the Protocol thereto with regard to the areas of separation and limitation. In carrying out its mission, it will comply with the generally applicable Syrian laws and regulations and will not hamper the functioning of local civil administration. It will enjoy freedom of movement and communications and other facilities that are necessary for its mission. It will be mobile and provided with personal weapons of a defensive character and shall use such weapons only in self defence. The number of UNDOF shall be about 1,240, who will be selected by the Secretary-General of the United Nations in consultation with the parties from members of the United Nations who are not permanent members of the Security Council.

UNDOF will be under the command of the United Nations, vested in the Secretary-General under the authority of the Security Council.

UNDOF shall carry out inspections under the Agreement, and report thereon to the parties, on a regular basis not less often than once every 15 days, and, in addition, when requested by either party, it shall mark on the ground the respective lines shown on the map attached to the Agreement.

[*continued on page 64.*

Disengagement Agreement of May 30th, 1974, between Israel and Syria.

Disengagement Agreement of January 18th, 1974, between Israel and Egypt.

Israel and Syria will support the Resolution of the United Nations Security Council, which will provide for UNDOF contemplated by the Agreement. Initial authorization will be for six months subject to renewal by further Resolution of the Security Council.

RESOLUTION OF CONFERENCE OF ARAB HEADS OF STATE

Rabat, October 28th, 1974

The Conference of the Arab Heads of State:

1. *Affirms* the right of the Palestinian people to return to their homeland and to self-determination.

2. *Affirms* the right of the Palestinian people to establish an independent national authority, under the leadership of the PLO in its capacity as the sole legitimate representative of the Palestine people, over all liberated territory. The Arab States are pledged to uphold this authority, when it is established, in all spheres and at all levels.

3. *Supports* the PLO in the exercise of its national and international responsibilities, within the context of the principle of Arab solidarity.

4. *Invites* the kingdom of Jordan, Syria and Egypt to formalize their relations in the light of these decisions and in order that they be implemented.

5. *Affirms* the obligation of all Arab States to preserve Palestinian unity and not to interfere in Palestinian internal affairs.

Sources: Le Monde; *Problèmes Politiques et Sociaux*, March 7th, 1975; *Arab Report and Record*.

UN GENERAL ASSEMBLY RESOLUTION 3236 (XXIX)

November 22nd, 1974

The General Assembly,

Having considered the question of Palestine,

Having heard the statement of the Palestine Liberation Organization, the representative of the Palestinian people,

Having also heard other statements made during the debate,

Deeply concerned that no just solution to the problem of Palestine has yet been achieved and recognizing that the problem of Palestine continues to endanger international peace and security,

Recognizing that the Palestinian people is entitled to self-determination in accordance with the Charter of the United Nations,

Expressing its grave concern that the Palestinian people has been prevented from enjoying its inalienable rights, in particular its right to self-determination,

Guided by the purposes and principles of the Charter,

Recalling its relevant resolutions which affirm the right of the Palestinian people to self-determination,

1. *Reaffirms* the inalienable rights of the Palestinian people in Palestine, including:
   (a) The right to self-determination without external interference;
   (b) The right to national independence and sovereignty;

2. *Reaffirms also* the inalienable right of the Palestinians to return to their homes and property from which they have been displaced and uprooted, and calls for their return;

3. *Emphasizes* that full respect for and the realization of these inalienable rights of the Palestinian people are indispensable for the solution of the question of Palestine;

4. *Recognizes* that the Palestinian people is a principal party in the establishment of a just and durable peace in the Middle East;

5. *Further Recognizes* the right of the Palestinian people to regain its rights by all means in accordance with the purposes and principles of the Charter of the United Nations;

6. *Appeals* to all States and international organizations to extend their support to the Palestinian people in its struggle to restore its rights, in accordance with the Charter;

7. *Requests* the Secretary-General to establish contacts with the Palestine Liberation Organization on all matters concerning the question of Palestine;

8. *Requests* the Secretary-General to report to the General Assembly at its thirtieth session on the implementation of the present resolution;

9. *Decides* to include the item "Question of Palestine" in the provisional agenda of its thirtieth session.

Source: UN Document BR/74/55 (1974).

Palestine Organizations

Palestine Liberation Organization (PLO)

The Palestine Liberation Organization was founded in 1964 at the first Arab Summit Meeting, and the Palestine Liberation Army was established in the same year. The supreme organ of the PLO is the Palestine National Assembly (*see* below), while the Palestine Executive Committee, consisting of 14 members, deals with the day-to-day business. Fatah (the Palestine National Liberation Movement) joined the Palestine National Assembly in 1968, and all the guerrilla organizations joined the Assembly in 1969. The Palestine Executive Committee controls the following eight departments, and a member of the Executive Committee is at the head of each department:

(i) Military Department, which includes Palestine Liberation Army.

(ii) Cultural and Educational.

(iii) Political and International Relations.

(iv) Palestine National Fund.

(v) Social Affairs (includes Palestine Red Crescent).

(vi) Occupied Territories.

(vii) Information and National Guidance.

(viii) Popular Organizations (Trade Unions, Students, Workers, Women, etc.).

The PLO has offices and representatives in every Arab country except Saudi Arabia, as well as in non-Arab states such as U.S.A., U.S.S.R., China, Cuba, Yugoslavia, Switzerland and Britain. The Rabat Arab Summit, in October 1974, affirmed the right of the Palestinian people to establish an independent national authority, under the leadership of the PLO in its capacity as the sole legitimate representative of the Palestine people, over all liberated territory (*see* Documents on Palestine, p. 64). In November 1974 Yasser Arafat addressed the UN General Assembly, and on November 22nd the UN General Assembly passed a resolution acknowledging and reaffirming the PLO position (*see* Documents on Palestine, p. 64). On the same day the PLO was granted permanent observer status at the General Assembly of the UN and at international conferences sponsored by the UN.

Chairman: 1964-67   Ahmed Shukairi.

            1967-68   Yahya Hammouda.

            1968-   Yasser Arafat.

Main Regional Offices:

Beirut: Dir. SHAFIQ HOUT.

Damascus: Dir. MAHMOUD KHALIDI.

Kuwait: Dir. ALI YASSIN.

Cairo: Dir. JAMAL SOURANI.

Algiers: AHMED WAFI.

Tripoli: SULEIMAN SHURAFA.

New York: SAA'DAT HASAN.

Moscow: ABDUL RAZAK YAHYA.

Peking: HAMAD ABDEL-AZIZ AIDI.

PALESTINE NATIONAL ASSEMBLY

It has 180 members and meets once a year in Cairo. As well as the guerrilla organizations, the other PLO bodies, trade and student unions, etc. are represented. Of the 180 members, 85 represent guerrilla organizations.

Chairman: KHALED FAHOUM.

CENTRAL COUNCIL

It is appointed by the Palestine National Assembly; consists of the members of the Executive Committee, 20 other members, and the Chairman of the Palestine National Assembly. For details of affiliated organizations *see* page 66.

EXECUTIVE COMMITTEE

This is elected by the Palestine National Assembly and is responsible for the running of the PLO in between meetings of the Council. In September 1974 the PFLP withdrew from the Executive Committee and Central Council of the PLO because it rejected PLO policies which recognized the existence of Israel. This "rejectionist front" was later joined by the PFLP--General Command, the Arab Liberation Front and the Front for the Popular Palestinian Struggle, and in practice their members are not at present serving on the Executive Committee and Central Council listed below, although they are still members of the Palestine National Assembly.

Chairman: YASSER ARAFAT (Fatah).

Members: FAROUK KADDOUMI (also known as "ABU LUTF"—Fatah—Head of Political Dept.), ZUHEIR MUHSEN (Saiqa—Head of Military Dept.), ABDUL WAHHAB KAYYAL (ALF—Head of Dept. of Cultural Affairs and Education), AHMED YAMANI (also known as "ABU MAHER"—PFLP—Head of Dept. of Popular Organizations), YASIR ABDOU RABBOU (PDFLP—Head of Information Dept.), ZOHDI EL NACHACHIBI (independent—Sec. of Exec. Cttee. and Head of Admin. Dept.), HAMED ABOU SETTEH (independent—Head of Occupied Territories Dept.), TALAL NAJI (PFLP—General Command), ELIA KHOURY (independent), ABDEL AZIA WAGIH (Palestine Liberation Army—Deputy Sec. of Exec. Cttee. responsible for Admin. Affairs), MOHSEN ABU MAYZER (independent, pro-Fatah—Head of Social Affairs and Refugee Dept. and official spokesman), ABDEL JAWAD

SALAH (independent, pro-Fatah—Deputy Head of Occupied Territories Dept. responsible for interior affairs), WALID KAMHAWEH (independent—Chairman of Palestine National Fund).

PALESTINE LIBERATION ARMY (PLA)

Commander-in-Chief: YASSER ARAFAT.

Chief of Staff: Brig.-Gen. WALID JAMOUS.

The PLO is preparing for the establishment of a joint military and political command with Syria.

PALESTINE NATIONAL FUND

The fund is financed by a contribution of between 3 and 6 per cent from the income of every Palestinian and also aid from Arab and friendly countries.

Chairman: Dr. WALID KAMHAWEH.

Director: DARWICHE ABYAD.

PALESTINE PLANNING CENTRE

Director: Dr. NABIL SHAATH.

PALESTINE RED CRESCENT

President: Dr. ABDULLAH ABU HASSAN.

PALESTINE RESEARCH CENTRE

Director: Dr. ANIS SAYEGH.

PRESS AND RADIO

Falastine Al-Thawra: Beirut; newspaper of the Palestine Liberation Organization.

Al Hadaf: Beirut; organ of the Popular Front for the Liberation of Palestine; weekly.

Voice of Palestine: official radio station of Palestine Liberation Organization; broadcasts from Cairo, Baghdad and Algiers, and also from the Yemen Arab Republic.

Palestine News Agency: Beirut; official PLO news agency.

CENTRAL COUNCIL OF THE PALESTINE RESISTANCE MOVEMENT

It was created early in 1970 and represents all the guerrilla groups. The most important guerrilla organizations are:

Fatah (The Palestine National Liberation Movement): leader YASSER ARAFAT; deputy leader SALAH KHALAF (also known as "ABU IYAD").

Popular Front for the Liberation of Palestine (PFLP): leader Dr. GEORGE HABASH.

Popular Front for the Liberation of Palestine— General Command: leader AHMED JEBRIL.

Saiqa (Vanguard of the Popular Liberation War): Syrian-backed; leader ZUHEIR MUHSEN.

Popular Democratic Front for the Liberation of Palestine (PDFLP): leader NAIF HAWATMEH.

Arab Liberation Front (ALF): Iraq-backed; leader Dr. ABDUL WAHHAB KAYYALI.

"Black September" is a hard-core group which draws its support from a variety of organizations. The "Rejectionist Front" consists of four organizations who reject any settlement which recognizes Israel (see under Executive Committee, p. 65).

THE PALESTINIAN NATIONAL CHARTER

(Palestine Liberation Organization)*

1. Palestine is the homeland of the Palestinian Arab people; it is an indivisible part of the Arab homeland, and the Palestinian people are an integral part of the Arab nation.

2. Palestine, with the boundaries it had during the British mandate, is an indivisible territorial unit.

3. The Palestinian Arab people possess the legal right to their homeland and have the right to determine their destiny after achieving the liberation of their country in accordance with their wishes and entirely of their own accord and will.

4. The Palestinian identity is a genuine, essential and inherent characteristic; it is transmitted from parents to children. The Zionist occupation and the dispersal of the Palestinian Arab people, through the disasters which befell them, do not make them lose their Palestinian identity and their membership of the Palestinian community, nor do they negate them.

_____
* Decisions of the National Congress of the Palestine Liberation Organization held in Cairo July 1st–17th, 1968.

5. The Palestinians are those Arab nationals who, until 1947, normally resided in Palestine regardless of whether they were evicted from it or have stayed there. Anyone born, after that date, of a Palestinian father—whether inside Palestine or outside it—is also a Palestinian.

6. The Jews who had normally resided in Palestine until the beginning of the Zionist invasion will be considered Palestinians.

7. That there is a Palestinian community and that it has material, spiritual and historical connection with Palestine are indisputable facts. It is a national duty to bring up individual Palestinians in an Arab revolutionary manner. All means of information and education must be adopted in order to acquaint the Palestinian with his country in the most profound manner, both spiritual and material, that is possible. He must be prepared for the armed struggle and ready to sacrifice his wealth and his life in order to win back his homeland and bring about its liberation.

8. The phase in their history, through which the Palestinian people are now living, is that of national

struggle for the liberation of Palestine. Thus the conflicts among the Palestinian national forces are secondary, and should be ended for the sake of the basic conflict that exists between the forces of Zionism and of imperialism on the one hand, and the Palestinian Arab people on the other. On this basis the Palestinian masses, regardless of whether they are residing in the national homeland or in diaspora, constitute—both their organizations and the individuals—one national front working for the retrieval of Palestine and its liberation through armed struggle.

9. Armed struggle is the only way to liberate Palestine. Thus it is the overall strategy, not merely a tactical phase. The Palestinian Arab people assert their absolute determination and firm resolution to continue their armed struggle and to work for an armed popular revolution for the liberation of their country and their return to it. They also assert their right to normal life in Palestine and to exercise their right to self-determination and sovereignty over it.

10. Commando action constitutes the nucleus of the Palestinian popular liberation war. This requires its escalation, comprehensiveness and the mobilization of all the Palestinian popular and educational efforts and their organization and involvement in the armed Palestinian revolution. It also requires the achieving of unity for the national struggle among the different groupings of the Palestinian people, and between the Palestinian people and the Arab masses so as to secure the continuation of the revolution, its escalation and victory.

11. The Palestinians will have three mottoes: national unity, national mobilization and liberation.

12. The Palestinian people believe in Arab unity. In order to contribute their share towards the attainment of that objective, however, they must, at the present stage of their struggle, safeguard their Palestinian identity and develop their consciousness of that identity, and oppose any plan that may dissolve or impair it.

13. Arab unity and the liberation of Palestine are two complementary objectives, the attainment of either of which facilitates the attainment of the other. Thus, Arab unity leads to the liberation of Palestine; the liberation of Palestine leads to Arab unity; and work towards the realization of one objective proceeds side by side with work towards the realization of the other.

14. The destiny of the Arab nation, and indeed Arab existence itself, depends upon the destiny of the Palestine cause. From this interdependence springs the Arab nation's pursuit of, and striving for, the liberation of Palestine. The people of Palestine play the role of the vanguard in the realization of this sacred national goal.

15. The liberation of Palestine, from an Arab viewpoint, is a national duty and it attempts to repel the Zionist and imperialist aggression against the Arab homeland, and aims at the elimination of Zionism in Palestine. Absolute responsibility for this falls upon the Arab nation—peoples and governments —with the Arab people of Palestine in the vanguard. Accordingly the Arab nation must mobilize all its military, human, moral and spiritual capabilities to participate actively with the Palestinian people in the liberation of Palestine. It must, particularly in the phase of the armed Palestinian revolution, offer and furnish the Palestinian people with all possible help, and material and human support, and make available to them the means and opportunities that will enable them to continue to carry out their leading role in the armed revolution, until they liberate their homeland.

16. The liberation of Palestine, from a spiritual point of view, will provide the Holy Land with an atmosphere of safety and tranquillity, which in turn will safeguard the country's religious sanctuaries and guarantee freedom of worship and of visit to all, without discrimination of race, color, language, or religion. Accordingly, the people of Palestine look to all spiritual forces in the world for support.

17. The liberation of Palestine, from a human point of view, will restore to the Palestinian individual his dignity, pride and freedom. Accordingly the Palestinian Arab people look forward to the support of all those who believe in the dignity of man and his freedom in the world.

18. The liberation of Palestine, from an international point of view, is a defensive action necessitated by the demands of self-defence. Accordingly, the Palestinian people, desirous as they are of the friendship of all people, look to freedom-loving, justice-loving and peace-loving states for support in order to restore their legitimate rights in Palestine, to re-establish peace and security in the country, and to enable its people to exercise national sovereignty and freedom.

19. The partition of Palestine in 1947 and the establishment of the state of Israel are entirely illegal, regardless of the passage of time, because they were contrary to the will of the Palestinian people and to their natural right in their homeland, and inconsistent with the principles embodied in the Charter of the United Nations, particularly the right to self-determination.

20. The Balfour Declaration, the mandate for Palestine and everything that has been based upon them, are deemed null and void. Claims of historical or religious ties of Jews with Palestine are incompatible with the facts of history and the true conception of what constitutes statehood. Judaism, being a religion, is not an independent nationality. Nor do Jews constitute a single nation with an identity of its own; they are citizens of the states to which they belong.

21. The Palestinian Arab people, expressing themselves by the armed Palestinian revolution, reject all solutions which are substitutes for the total liberation of Palestine and reject all proposals aiming at the liquidation of the Palestinian problem, or its internationalization.

22. Zionism is a political movement organically associated with international imperialism and antagonistic to all action for liberation and to progressive movements in the world. It is racist and fanatic in its nature, aggressive, expansionist and colonial in its

aims, and fascist in its methods. Israel is the instrument of the Zionist movement, and a geographical base for world imperialism placed strategically in the midst of the Arab homeland to combat the hopes of the Arab nation for liberation, unity and progress. Israel is a constant source of threat *vis-à-vis* peace in the Middle East and the whole world. Since the liberation of Palestine will destroy the Zionist and imperialist presence and will contribute to the establishment of peace in the Middle East, the Palestinian people look for the support of all the progressive and peaceful forces and urge them all, irrespective of their affiliations and beliefs, to offer the Palestinian people all aid and support in their just struggle for the liberation of their homeland.

23. The demands of security and peace, as well as the demands of right and justice, require all states to consider Zionism an illegitimate movement, to outlaw its existence, and to ban its operations, in order that friendly relations among peoples may be preserved, and the loyalty of citizens to their respective homelands safeguarded.

24. The Palestinian people believe in the principles of justice, freedom, sovereignty, self-determination, human dignity, and in the right of all peoples to exercise them.

25. For the realization of the goals of this Charter and its principles, the Palestine Liberation Organization will perform its role in the liberation of Palestine in accordance with the Constitution of this Organization.

26. The Palestine Liberation Organization, representative of the Palestinian revolutionary forces, is responsible for the Palestinian Arab people's movement in its struggle—to retrieve its homeland, liberate and return to it and exercise the right to self-determination in it—in all military, political and financial fields and also for whatever may be required by the Palestine case on the inter-Arab and international levels.

27. The Palestine Liberation Organization shall cooperate with all Arab states, each according to its potentialities; and will adopt a neutral policy among them in the light of the requirements of the war of liberation; and on this basis it shall not interfere in the internal affairs of any Arab state.

28. The Palestinian Arab people assert the genuineness and independence of their national revolution and reject all forms of intervention, trusteeship and subordination.

29. The Palestinian people possess the fundamental and genuine legal right to liberate and retrieve their homeland. The Palestinian people determine their attitude towards all states and forces on the basis of the stands they adopt *vis-à-vis* the Palestinian case and the extent of the support they offer to the Palestinian revolution to fulfill the aims of the Palestinian people.

30. Fighters and carriers of arms in the war of liberation are the nucleus of the popular army which will be the protective force for the gains of the Palestinian Arab people.

31. The Organization shall have a flag, an oath of allegiance and an anthem. All this shall be decided upon in accordance with a special regulation.

32. Regulations, which shall be known as the Constitution of the Palestine Liberation Organization, shall be annexed to this Charter. It shall lay down the manner in which the Organization, and its organs and institutions, shall be constituted; the respective competence of each; and the requirements of its obligations under the Charter.

33. This Charter shall not be amended save by (vote of) a majority of two-thirds of the total membership of the National Congress of the Palestine Liberation Organization (taken) at a special session convened for that purpose.

Oil in the Middle East and North Africa

Michael Field

INTRODUCTION

If 1973 was the year of crisis in the Middle Eastern oil industry, with the Organization of Petroleum Exporting Countries quadrupling the price of oil in the space of two and a half months, and the Arabs using production cuts and embargoes as a political weapon, the past 18 months (up to the middle of 1975) have been a period of reappraisal, in which both the producers and the consumers have been taking stock of their own and each others' strength and weaknesses. As yet this reappraisal has produced no definite indication of the future trend of prices and supplies—taking place as it has against a background of apparently contradictory movements in the oil maıket, with demand falling and, in 1974 at least, the cost of oil in the Gulf continuing to rise.

Right from the beginning of 1974 the consumers split into two camps in their interpretation of the permanence of the price rise. The Americans took the view that the increase announced in December 1973 (which took the Saudi Arabian light "marker" crude from $5.12 to $11.65) was intolerable, and that the industrial countries could and should force the price down again. They felt that the consumers ought not only to avoid doing anything to accommodate the effects of the higher prices (by sponsoring massive official recycling operations through the International Monetary Fund, for instance) which might give the impression that the new levels had been tacitly accepted, but should also combine in an attempt to cut their consumption, develop alternative energy sources, and present a united front to OPEC. The U.S. Government had some limited success in winning the other consumers over to these views in February 1974, when it was agreed at the Washington Energy Conference that the industrial countries should avoid competing for oil supplies, and should establish the International Energy Agency as a forum for co-ordinating their policies.

In contrast to America, the European countries and Japan, which would have been very much more vulnerable than the U.S.A. in the event of a confrontation policy backfiring, initially responded to the crisis by rushing to conclude bilateral deals with the producers—involving the exchange of arms and capital goods for specific quantities of oil. In the event only one of the proposed deals, a small Anglo-Iranian exchange, was ever brought to fruition, and subsequent deals, reflecting the concensus at the Washington conference, have excluded reference to oil supplies. But the Europeans and Japanese have remained noticeably more moderate than the Americans in their policies—treating the rise in oil prices as inevitable, and putting the emphasis on trying to accommodate their effects with a minimum of disruption, while promoting a dialogue with the producers.

During the later months of 1974 and the first half of 1975 the consumers moved closer together. The U.S. Government seemed gradually to accept that it had no immediate means of forcing a price reduction, and although different members of the administration continued the sabre-rattling tactic (designed partly for internal consumption, and partly to draw a response from the producers which might give an indication of their determination to stand up to the consumers in a confrontation), in concrete terms American policy by the end of the year had come down to promoting three schemes which it was felt were the only immediate and acceptable means of strengthening the consumers' position. These were: the establishment of a common loan and guarantee recycling facility (commonly known as the Kissinger facility) which would be financed entirely by consumers running a current or capital account surplus, and would not require the participation of OPEC states; the institution by each consumer state of its own conservation programme, designed to effect a further cut in consumption on top of that already caused by the high price; and an agreement on a "minimum energy price" (the "floor price") which would encourage the development of alternative oil and other energy sources without companies fearing a future collapse of the OPEC cartel making their investment uneconomic. The last of these schemes ran into opposition, both from Congress and from consumers such as Italy and Japan, which felt that the floor price would benefit only those countries with big indigenous resources—the U.S.A., the United Kingdom and Canada.

Despite having achieved only partial success with its proposals, the U.S.A. eventually agreed to join in the producer-consumer conference held in Paris in April—though it took a notably tougher line than the other consumers at this meeting, insisting that discussions on the indexation of oil prices and related issues be preceeded by a price reduction, and it was felt that, of the consumers taking part, the U.S.A. bore the greatest share of responsibility for the conference's failure.

However, the fact that the 18 months following the oil crisis saw at least some narrowing of differences among the industrial nations, was a reflection of the increasingly accurate analyses being made by the consumers both of OPEC's determination to maintain prices in the face of declining demand, and of their own potential for saving fuel and diversifying their energy sources.

In the early part of 1974 there was a widely held belief, inherent in President Nixon's Project Independence (a plan to make the U.S. virtually self-sufficient in energy by 1980), that the consumers might find it relatively easy to diversify their energy sources, and that their dependence on OPEC would be a short-lived phenomenon. But during the following months the evidence began to point against this theory. Estimates of the cost and technical difficulty of producing "alternatives" (coal, tar sands, shales and nuclear power) and conventional crude oil within the consuming areas rose at a terrifying rate—as shown by Britain's own experience in the North Sea. In Canada several companies actually pulled out of their Athabasca tar sand leases, and in the U.S.A. the development of nuclear power plant was impeded by the fall in electricity demand causing a drop in orders from the utilities companies. Gulf and Shell were forced to reschedule and scale down their work on one of the most promising of the new systems—the High Temperature Reactor. At the same time, under the stimulus of the decontrol of prices on new oil wells, there was a significant increase in drillings in the U.S., from 27,000 wells in 1973 to 33,000 in 1974, but only 2 per cent of these produced finds of 0.5/1 million barrels or more judged to be commercial. In offshore areas along the U.S. east coast, environmental opposition and disputes between the federal and state authorities caused delays in working out leasing arrangements, and although in March 1975 the federal authorities won their case in the Supreme Court, it was thought that it would take another year before east coast leases were granted, and at least ten years before any oil discoveries would be brought on stream. Elsewhere there were a few discoveries, greeted with much enthusiasm by the media, in such places as Mexico—but although these finds were useful, the North Sea remained the only new oil province with real potential for taking up a significant part of the anticipated increment in Free World demand in the later 1970s and early 1980s.

The second part of the consumers' strategy for lessening their dependence on OPEC—cutting consumption—met with only slightly greater success. In response to the price rises and the energy saving measures introduced with varying degrees of seriousness in different industrial countries, Free World oil consumption fell by 2.9 per cent in 1974, from 47.8 million b/d in 1973 to 46.5 million b/d, with the U.S.A. cutting its consumption by 4 per cent, Western Europe by 6.6 per cent and Japan by 2.7 per cent. In the first quarter of 1975, as the recession took root, Free World consumption fell still further to 45 million b/d. But with the public in most countries apparently unwilling to make real sacrifices, big savings, on a scale which might have broken the OPEC cartel, seemed to elude the consumers.

This was particularly so in the U.S.A., where, much against the trend in the other industrial nations, oil consumption in the first 4 months of 1975 actually increased by 2.1 per cent over the equivalent period of 1974. Equally disappointing for the U.S. Government, which in view of its strong line policy on OPEC prices was somewhat embarrassed at putting up a poorer conservation performance than the European countries, was that domestic production in January–April 1975 dropped by 5.6 per cent while imports increased by 11.6 per cent, and seemed likely to reach 6.7 million b/d by the end of the year. It was calculated that this performance would push average U.S. imports in 1975 to 6.2 million b/d—compared with a record 6.26 million b/d in 1973.

Throughout 1974 and the first half of 1975 the U.S. Congress' approach to oil conservation was marked by a lack of urgency and a general unwillingness to take unpopular measures. No progress was made with such aspects of the President's conservation programme as the opening up of Navy reserves for civilian use, the decontrol of natural gas prices in non-producing states, and the encouragement of power stations to burn more domestic coal; while those parts of the plan which Mr. Ford pushed most vigorously met with consistent Congressional opposition. The relaxation of the $5.25 fixed price on "old" oil (from wells producing before the crisis) was voted down, though it was expected that in August 1975 the President would use his own authority to remove the control; and the imposition of the second and third $1 instalments of the $3 tax on imported oil was continually postponed while the President waited for Congress to produce its own energy saving proposals— something which it eventually proved unable to do. Domestic exploration was further discouraged in March 1975 (after the increase in drillings in the previous year) by the removal of the Depletion Allowance, which had recognized oil in the ground as an asset, and had enabled the companies to depreciate it as if it were industrial plant.

Just as the aftermath of the crisis led to strains in the ranks of the consuming nations, the achievement by the producers of their long held ambitions of raising oil prices and controlling output brought to the fore differences in political philosophy and economic interest among the OPEC states themselves. These differences were apparent in their approach to the producer-consumer conference, with Algeria arguing in favour of the inclusion of other underdeveloped countries and other commodities in the discussions as part of a revolutionary drive to create a new world economic order, and Saudi Arabia suggesting a more limited and less ambitious programme.

More fundamental were the differences that emerged over the Saudis' campaign during the spring and summer of 1974 for a reduction of prices. In part the Saudi policy stemmed from King Faisal's anxiety to avoid severely damaging the Western economies, but at the same time the Saudis, with an eye on their own self-interest, and bearing in mind the colossal size of their oil reserves and their limited immediate development potential, clearly felt that the maintenance of too high a price in the short term might eventually lead to a serious drop in demand for their oil and a price collapse. At the opposite extreme Iran (which at the beginning of the year was the leading price hawk in OPEC) and Algeria, both of which had immediate development potential but limited reserves in relation to their current levels of output, made it their policy to export the maximum amount of oil at the highest possible price, and trust that when prices fell and/or their production started running down they would be sufficiently developed to be able to live off their own industrial and agricultural output.

In the event the Saudi price campaign failed, and as the months passed, the Saudis' attitude towards a reduction became steadily more ambivalent, and their statements more contradictory, so that by mid-1975, although officially still opposed to any regulation of production designed to support prices artificially, they appeared to accept existing price levels.

Despite the drop in consumption and the low level of bids put in at auctions of government crude, production in the OPEC states was held up in 1974 by restocking, which kept overall demand in the Free World at 48.5 million b/d, or roughly 2 million b/d above the level of consumption. At the same time, although posted prices in the Middle East states remained static and were reduced in the North African countries, the average cost of OPEC oil to the consumer was increased by the 60 per cent government participation backdated to the beginning of the year, and the imposition of higher taxes and royalties on the companies' remaining 40 per cent of production known as equity crude.

It was only in the early months of 1975 that market pressure for a price reduction became really strong. The effects of the recession and a mild winter, and a run-down of stocks at a rate of 2 million b/d, reduced Free World demand for new supplies in the first quarter of 1975 to 43 million b/d—or some 5.5 million b/d below the average level of 1974. The brunt of this reduction fell on OPEC, where production declined to 26 million b/d compared with 30 million b/d in the second half of 1974, and naturally enough the states worst affected were those which had exploited the boom period of late 1973 to push their prices up too far relative to the Saudi Arabian light marker crude. With the consumers showing themselves unwilling to pay extra for light grades of low sulphur oil, Abu Dhabi in February 1975 was forced to cut its gravity and sulphur premiums by some 24–58 cents, while the short haul Mediterranean producers, Libya and Algeria, affected by the collapse of freight rates (which led to the complete closure of Saudi Arabia's Tapline) made similar reductions.

Throughout this period of early 1975 the "marker" crude price stayed conspicuously immune from market pressures, and at no point did it appear that Gulf prices were in danger of collapsing. Indeed it was thought in mid-1975 that the economic upturn expected in the autumn or in the early part of 1976, and the necessity for a new period of restocking in the last two quarters of 1975, would remove the downwards pressure on prices altogether.

The belief that prices would probably not collapse was strengthened by the evolution of thinking on OPEC's need for revenues and its consequent ability to stand reductions in output. Immediately after the crisis it was widely thought that OPEC's revenues would be unspendable until well into the 1980s, that the deficits of the consumers would be incurable for the same period, and that there would have to be a massive official intervention in the recycling process if the world was to avoid a major international depression. During the latter part of 1974, OPEC's proof of its ability to spend far more than originally anticipated, and the appearance of trade surpluses in some consumer countries, led to predictions that within two or three years some of the producers would

be in deficit and that by 1980 the group as a whole would be in equilibrium. But in the early summer of 1975 the pendulum swung back slightly against these predictions, as it came to be realized that a large number of industrial projects announced in the previous year were being abandoned, and that the OPEC states, in talking of their running short of money (in order to destroy the popular impression that they had "more money than they knew what to do with") were including in their "spending" such items as aid and commitments to the IMF and the World Bank, which would normally have been regarded as part of their surplus. Thus it seemed that OPEC's ability to cut production in order to maintain prices was somewhat greater than had been assumed at the beginning of 1975. At the same time Saudi Arabia's abandonment of its price-lowering campaign seemed to re-emphasize OPEC's solidarity in defence of its gains—a solidarity which was reinforced by the Organization's memory of the disunity which led to the abysmal failure of its previous attempt to raise prices by controlling output in the 1960s.

In mid-1975, with the future subject to so many imponderables—not least the date of the economic recovery and the development of the political situation in the Middle East—few organizations or governments were prepared to make hard predictions on the future movement of prices. But overall it seemed that, with the industrial countries having been unable to cut consumption by enough to force a reduction of prices in early 1975, time was beginning to run against the consumers. The OPEC governments, led on this issue by the Shah of Iran, were talking confidently of a 35 per cent price rise to offset the effects of inflation when the freeze decided upon at the beginning of the year came to an end in October; while in London Shaikh Ahmed Zaki Yamani, in a speech reminiscent of those he made before the crisis in 1973, referred to the belief that "supplies should not be determined by producing capacities, but by producers' requirements"—adding significantly that although Saudi Arabia had authorized a production level of 8.5 million b/d, its requirements did not exceed 3.5 million b/d.

OWNERSHIP OF THE INDUSTRY

Concessions

Until the end of 1972 the bulk of the Middle East's and North Africa's output was produced under the traditional concession agreements. The first of the concessions was granted in 1901 in Iran by Muzzaffareddin Shah to William Knox D'Arcy, a wealthy prospector who had made a fortune out of gold mining in Australia, in return for £20,000 in cash and the promise of a further £20,000 in shares. After a number of dry holes and an acute financial crisis, oil was finally discovered in 1908 at Masjid-i-Sulaiman, and just before the beginning of the First World War, the Anglo-Persian Oil Company (renamed the Anglo-Iranian Oil Company in 1935 and British Petroleum in 1954), which had been formed to take over the concession, began exports through the port of Abadan.

During the 1920s and 1930s further concessions were granted in Iraq and in the states of the Arabian Peninsula—and in every case the concessionaire companies were made up chiefly by members of the seven major oil companies which have dominated the world oil business throughout this century. In approximate order of size these were: Standard Oil of New Jersey (which changed its name to Exxon in 1972 and markets its products under the name Esso), the Royal Dutch-Shell group, Texaco, Standard Oil of California (known as Socal and marketing as Chevron), Mobil, Gulf and British Petroleum. The only other company to participate in the early days was Compagnie Française des Pétroles (marketing as Total), which is considerably smaller than the big seven, but is often regarded as an eighth major company because of the world-wide spread of its operations.

Under the original terms of their concessions, these companies were given exclusive rights for drilling, production, sales and the construction of pipelines, the ownership at the wellhead of all oil produced, and immunity from taxes and customs dues. The governments' receipts, apart from an initial downpayment and a rental, came in the form either of a percentage royalty on sales (which was how Iranian income was worked out at first) or of a fixed royalty of four gold shillings a ton (about 22 cents a barrel).

In view of the vast amounts of oil discovered during the 1930s and 1940s, and the extremely low cost of production, the Middle Eastern governments by the later 1940s no longer felt that the companies had been as generous as they had originally believed, and with the growing sophistication of the local populations in this period, all aspects of the concessions began to come under attack. The main complaints, apart from criticism of the financial terms, were that the concessions were too large in area and their duration too long, that they were run almost entirely by foreign nationals, that the companies had appropriated for themselves a quasi-colonial authority, and that the host governments had no control over the amount of drilling carried out nor the volume of exports. The strength of the producers' feelings was only reinforced when Kuwait in 1948 and Saudi Arabia in 1949 granted concessions in their respective halves of the Neutral Zone (now known as the Partitioned Zone) to American independent companies, Aminoil and Getty, on conditions which were very much more favourable than those obtained earlier from the Kuwait Oil Company (BP and Gulf) and Aramco (Exxon, Socal, Texaco and Mobil).

The major change in the financial terms of the concessions which followed did not, however, stem from events in the Middle East, but from Venezuela, where, after the first free elections in the country's history, the Acción Democratica party in November 1948 passed an income tax law giving the Government 50 per cent of the companies' profits. A year later the Venezuelans sent a delegation to the Gulf to explain the advantages of the new legislation, and the companies, realizing that such a revolutionary change could not be confined to one country, and that they would be able to deduct tax payments made abroad

from tax paid in their home countries, promptly offered the same deal to the Middle Eastern governments. Under the new system, introduced in Saudi Arabia at the end of 1950 and in Iraq and Kuwait a few months later, the companies' "profits", arrived at by deducting the production cost per barrel from the posted price, were divided equally between the companies and the governments. Assuming that no special discounts off the posted price were given, this arrangement increased the producers' revenue per barrel from 22 cents to about 80 cents.

The only country not to receive the 50-50 profit split at this time was Iran. Despite various revisions in concession terms during the inter-war years, relations between Anglo-Iranian and the Government were bedevilled not only by financial disputes, but also by the Iranian population's view of the company as the symbol of their country's subjugation to foreign influence and of Britain's colonial power—which had involved Iran being invaded in 1941 (so that the allies could secure a supply route to the Soviet armies in the Caucasus) and Reza Shah being deported to Mauritius. In 1949, Anglo-Iranian and the Government resolved their differences in a Supplemental Agreement which gave Iran royalty and profit-sharing terms as good as those concluded in the Arab states a year and a half later. But the Iranian National Assembly was dissatisfied with the deal, and during the following months, Dr. Mohammed Mossadeq, an extreme nationalist demagogue and chairman of the Assembly's Oil Committee, managed to discredit the Agreement totally in the eyes of the Iranian people. In December 1950, the Government, which had hoped that it would be able to solve the issue peacefully by negotiating minor revisions, was forced to renounce the Agreement altogether. Anglo-Iranian immediately suggested further talks leading to a 50-50 settlement, while Mossadeq in February 1951 suggested nationalization, and, with Iran slipping into a state of internal chaos, the Shah on May 1st was forced to give his assent to the nationalization bill and appoint Mossadeq as Prime Minister.

Over the next two years, Mossadeq refused all compromise solutions offered to him, Iranian oil exports, embargoed by all the companies, came rapidly to a halt, and the economy collapsed. In July 1953, having tried to dismiss Mossadeq, the Shah was forced to flee to Rome; but within a few days, Mossadeq was overthrown by a *coup*, and the Shah returned in triumph. In the subsequent negotiations, the principle of nationalization was recognized, but the National Iranian Oil Company was forced to grant a lease (which was a concession in all but name) incorporating the 50-50 profit split to Iranian Oil Participants (known as "The Consortium") made up of BP, Shell, CFP and the five U.S. majors—who were later obliged by the U.S. Government to give a 5 per cent shareholding to a group of U.S. independents.

The Mossadeq debacle provided a reminder of the strength of the majors and although in 1961 the revolutionary government of General Kassem expropriated more than 99.5 per cent of the concession held by the Iraq Petroleum Company group (BP,

OIL FIELDS AND LOADING TERMINALS IN THE GULF

TURKEY

Karatchouk

Rumelan

to Homs.

Souedia

Ain Zalah

Butmah
(ICOO)

SYRIA

Quyarah

Bai Hassan

Kirkuk
(ICOO)

to Tripoli/Banias

Jambur

IRAN

Naft-i-Shah
(NIOC)

Khanaqin
(INOC)

IRAQ

Cheshmeh
Khush

Lab-e-Safid

to Sidon

Lali

Karun

Masjid-i-Sulaiman

Par-e-Siah

Naft Safid

Kuh-i-Rig

Mullasani

TAPLINE

Buzurgan
(ERAP)

Haft Kel

Kupal

Marun

Susangerd

Ahwaz

Paris

Nahr Umr
(INOC)

Shadegan

Karanj

Abteymur

Ramshir

Agha Jari

Zubair (BPC)

Mansuri

Pazanan

Rumaila
(INOC/BPC)

Gach Saran

KUWAIT

Mutribah

Rag-i-
Safid

Bibi Hakimeh

Binak

Kilur Karim

Gulkhari

Bushgan

South Umm Guadir
(AMINOIL)

Burgan

Hout
(AOC)

Khafji

Wafra
(GETTY)

Zuluf

Safaniyah

Marjan

Maharah

Karan

Jana

Juraybait

Abu Hadriah

Khursaniyah

Berri

Abu Safah

SAUDI ARABIA

Fadhili

Qatif

Dammam

Awali
(BAPCO)

Abu Musa
(BUTTES)

Fazran

Abqaiq

QATAR

Fatah
(DPC)

Khurais

Dukan (QPC)

Um Shaif
(ADMA)

Zakum

Abu Jifan

Qirdi

Ghawar

Murban
(ADPC)

Sahil

UNITED ARAB
EMIRATES

Mazalij

Harmaliya

Bu Hasa
(ADPC)

Abujidu

Natih (PDO)

Zarrara

Shah
Dome

Fahud (PDO)

Yibal (PDO)

Shaybah

Huwaisah (PDO)

Siah Rawl (PDO)

OMAN

OIL FIELDS

1 Raudhatain
2 Sabriya
3 Bahrah
4 Minagish
5 Umm Guadir
6 Nowruz (SIRIP)
7 Bahregan (SIRIP)
8 Cyrus (IPAC)
9 Darius (IPAC)
10 Fereidoun (IPAC)
11 Lavan (LAPCO)
12 Rostam (IMINOCO)
13 Sassan/Abu Al Bu Koosh
      (LAPCO/Abu Al Bu Koosh Group)
14 Maydan Mahzan (Shell)
15 Idd Al Shargi (Shell)
16 Bul Hanine (Shell)
17 Al Bunduq (Al Bunduq Co.)
18 Mubarraz (ADOCO)

LOADING TERMINALS

A Abadan
B Fao
C Khor Al Amaya
D Sea Island
E Mina Al Ahmedi
F Mina Abdullah
G Ras Al Khafji
H Maharah
I Jumayah
J Ras Tanura
K Sitra
L Umm Said
M Jebel Dannah
N Mina Al Fahal
O Halul Island
P Das Island
Q Lavan Island
R Kharg Island
S Bahregan

Proven oil fields (owner/operator);
Not all fields shown are producing.

All Iranian onshore fields (except
Naft-i-Shah) operated by OSCO.

All onshore and offshore fields of
Saudi Arabia operated by ARAMCO.

All Kuwaiti fields operated by KOC.

O   Loading Terminal

| Long distance Pipeline

Shell, CFP, Exxon, Mobil and Gulbenkian), on the grounds that this area was not being exploited by the companies, no Middle Eastern government again nationalized an important productive operation until 1971—when Algeria seized a majority share of the local operations of CFP and the French state company, ERAP.

Partnership, contracts and production sharing

Although, at the time, the nationalization of AIOC was a disaster for Iran, the dispute did at least mark the end of the period in which Middle Eastern governments gave 75 or 95 year concessions, covering their whole country, to a single group. What new concessions were signed in the Arabian Peninsula states during the later 1950s and 1960s had a duration of 35 to 45 years, covered much smaller areas, and contained relatively tough terms, with bigger signature bonuses and provisions for the rapid relinquishment of acreage. Even in Libya, where the financial terms of the concessions let at the end of the 1950s were considerably more generous than those applying in the Gulf, the available acreage was divided among more than ten different groups.

From 1957 the concession concept itself began to be replaced by new arrangements giving the state a degree of direct participation, and placing heavier financial burdens and greater risks on the companies—which the producers discovered the American independents and the European national companies were prepared to accept for the sake of gaining a foothold in the Middle East. The first of the new arrangements was the partnership of Société Irano-Italienne des Pétroles (SIRIP) between the National Iranian Oil Company and the Italian state concern ENI, under which ENI's subsidiary, AGIP, agreed to bear the whole exploration cost (only to be repaid if oil was found), and guaranteed to spend not less than $22 million on exploration. It was arranged that half of any oil produced would be owned by NIOC and sold by AGIP on the Iranians' behalf, while half would be owned by the Italian company and taxed at the normal 50 per cent rate—giving the Government a 75-25 profit split, together with valuable experience.

One year later the Iranians substantially improved their terms in a partnership with Amoco (a subsidiary of Standard Oil of Indiana), and during the early 1960s, they signed further partnerships containing cash bonuses, production bonuses, minimum exploration guarantees and minimum development expenditure guarantees. With certain variations the Iranians' example has been followed in the allocation of new acreage by Saudi Arabia and Kuwait in the Neutral Zone (where in 1957, a few months after the formation of SIRIP, the two countries obtained a stake of 10 per cent each when offshore acreage was let to a group of Japanese companies), by Kuwait on its own territory, by Algeria (where all acreage let since 1973 has been on a partnership basis), and by Egypt. In other countries, Saudi Arabia, Qatar, Abu Dhabi, Tunisia and Kuwait (with its offshore areas granted

to Shell), the governments have concluded carried interest arrangements, where acreage has been let originally as a concession, with the proviso that the state has the right to negotiate a shareholding once oil is discovered—a right which in Abu Dhabi's case has not been exercised. In all countries, the tax terms have been adjusted to reflect current OPEC rates.

In 1966 Iran led the way again by introducing the still more radical idea of service contracts when it let relinquished Consortium acreage to a French group, SOFIRAN. Like the foreign companies in partnership arrangements, SOFIRAN agreed to bear the whole cost of exploration; but if oil was struck it was to be refunded completely, and NIOC was also to provide all capital for development. NIOC was to be the sole owner of all oil produced, while the foreign contractor was to act as a broker for the national company on a commission of 2 per cent of the realized price, being paid by the guaranteed purchase of between 35 per cent and 45 per cent of production at cost plus 2 per cent. Fifty per cent of the difference between this sum and the realized price was to be payable as income tax—though when oil is brought on stream (expected to be in 1975), the financial terms will be adjusted.

Since 1966 Iran has signed a further seven service contracts, the most recent (in 1974) allowing the foreign companies to purchase about half of production at discounts of up to 5 per cent; and Iraq has signed three contracts, one of which, involving ERAP, is bringing the Buzurgen field on stream. None of the other Middle Eastern or North African states has concluded contracts, but not dissimilar production sharing arrangements, on modified Indonesian lines, have been concluded by Egypt (which invited Western companies to bid for new acreage in 1973, following a period in which oil exploration had been given over to the Soviet Union), by Libya (in 1974), and most recently (in 1975) by Syria and Lebanon. There are considerable variations in this type of agreement, but in most cases the foreign company is compensated for its share of expenditure in cash or kind, or by favourable tax terms, while production is divided in a ratio of between 75-25 and 85-15 in favour of the state.

The drive for participation, and Algerian takeovers

Parallel with the development of partnerships and contracts on new acreage, the 1960s saw a growing desire on the part of the producer governments for participation in existing concessions. This idea was originally put by Saudi Arabia to Aramco in 1964, and in 1968 it was given formal voice in OPEC's Declaratory Statement of Petroleum Policy. Apart from being satisfactory on nationalist grounds, and giving the producers a more direct say in such matters as the relinquishment of acreage, the employment of nationals, production rates and investment in new capacity, the governments felt that participation would give them a foothold in the oil industry, which would later enable them to mount their own crude oil sales operations, or expand their national companies downstream into the tankering, refining and marketing business. The producers, however, did not feel strong enough to press their claim until after the appearance of a sellers market and their success in the Teheran price negotiations of February 1971; and so it was not until OPEC's Twenty-fifth Conference in Vienna in July 1971 that the members announced that they were going to call the companies to formal talks on participation.

By this time a precedent had already been set by Algeria. For political reasons Algeria had nationalized its American concessionaires and Shell in 1967, without causing itself economic harm. This left the French companies, CFP and ERAP, which were responsible for most of the country's production, and were in a special position under the 1965 Franco-Algerian Evian Agreement. Hopes of a satisfactory relationship under this agreement were not fulfilled, and in 1969, under the terms of the agreement, Algeria opened negotiations for higher prices. The talks were inconclusive, and in July 1970 Algeria increased its prices unilaterally. Then, after further fruitless discussions, it seized 51 per cent of the two French companies on February 24th, 1971. The French sponsored a highly effective boycott, but in June CFP settled its differences with the Government—Algeria agreeing to pay $60 million compensation, while CFP paid $40 million backpayments and accepted a higher price. Five months later, ERAP also came to terms, handing over the remaining 49 per cent of its local operations, and agreeing that compensation and backpayments should be cancelled out.

The takeover of CFP and ERAP was not directly related to the formal OPEC participation demand, being very much a Franco-Algerian affair, having its roots in the colonial past and the aftermath of the country's independence—but it nevertheless increased the confidence of the other producers when they began negotiations with the companies in Geneva in January 1972. The countries concerned in these negotiations were just the five Arab producers in the Gulf (Venezuela and Indonesia having already achieved a degree of participation, and Iran, Libya and Nigeria having made it clear that they would pursue their own negotiations), and in practice the talks were conducted by Shaikh Ahmed Zaki Yamani of Saudi Arabia, representing the producers, and Aramco, representing the companies. Yamani's initial demand was for an immediate 25 per cent share rising to 51 per cent, with compensation to be at net book value, and that part of the government share of production sold back to the companies to be priced between the posted price and the tax paid cost (government revenue plus production cost). The companies' counter proposal, offering 50-50 joint ventures on new acreage, showed how big the gap between the two sides was at this point. In March, however, the companies agreed in principle to surrender 20 per cent of their operations, and in October, by which time Iraq, having nationalized IPC five months earlier, was no longer concerned in the negotiations, an outline agreement was reached in New York.

The General Agreement of 1972

The details of the General Agreement on Participation were finalized in December 1972, and ratified by Saudi Arabia, Qatar and Abu Dhabi at the turn of the year. Under the Agreement the producers took an immediate 25 per cent stake in the concessionaire companies. The earliest date for majority participation laid down was January 1st, 1982, with the initial shareholding rising by 5 per cent in 1978, 1979, 1980 and 1981 and by 6 per cent in 1982. This timetable, designed to make for a smooth transition and to enable all the companies to adjust their supply arrangements over the following decade, reflected a major difference of interest, which emerged in the later stages of negotiations between the Aramco partners (Exxon, Socal, Texaco and Mobil) whose concession had vast potential for making up any production that was lost to the Saudi Government, and the other majors (Gulf, Shell, BP and CFP) whose concessions in the other producing states had far less potential for expansion or were subject to production freezes, as in Kuwait. The result had been a compromise: the companies conceded an initial 25 per cent rather than the 20 per cent offered originally, but the timetable for majority control was extended beyond the date that the producers had wanted and Aramco had been prepared for.

The need to ease company problems also accounted for the complex arrangements for pricing and disposing of the states' 25 per cent share of production. The 75 per cent companies entitlement, which became known as "equity crude" remained subject to the provisions of the Teheran Agreement of February 1971, but the balance belonging to the producing states was divided into three categories, each of them priced in a different way. First there was a small proportion of production (only 10 per cent of the states' share or 2.5 per cent of total output in 1973) which the governments undertook to sell on the open market themselves for whatever price they could get. Secondly, there was "bridging crude" which the producing states were obliged to sell to the companies to help them meet supply commitments. This was priced at the "Quarter Way Price" (a quarter of the way between the tax paid cost and the posting) plus a certain number of extra cents a barrel depending on the quality and freight advantage involved, and was to account for 75 per cent of the states' quarter share of production in 1973, 50 per cent in 1974, and 25 per cent in 1975. And finally there was "phase-in crude" which the producer states could oblige the companies to purchase if they were unwilling or unable to market the crude themselves. The maximum percentages of the governments' share which could be passed back as phase-in crude were to rise as bridging crude declined, and then fall as follows: 1973, 15 per cent; 1974, 30 per cent; 1975, 50 per cent; 1976, 70 per cent; 1977, 65 per cent; 1978, 60 per cent; 1979, 50 per cent; 1980, 40 per cent; 1981, 30 per cent; and 1982, 10 per cent. Phase-in crude was priced at the tax paid cost, plus an additional few cents according to the type of oil, with the cost to the companies working out lower than the cost of bridging crude. Both categories of buy-back crude were of course priced at a higher level than the companies' 75 per cent equity crude entitlement, which effectively meant an erosion of the five-year Teheran Agreement. Furthermore, within nine months of the General Agreement coming into effect, the Gulf producers decided that both bridging and phase-in crude should be treated on the same basis, and costed at 93 per cent of the posting—this being the price Saudi Arabia had obtained in the sale of its own 2.5 per cent crude entitlement in May. (At the same time Saudi Arabia, having originally notified Aramco that it would be required to take the maximum phase-in crude, asked the company to drastically reduce the amount, because the Government realized that it would be able to sell much more itself sooner than it had anticipated.)

For compensation under the General Agreement the criteria adopted was "updated book value" which took account of the cost of replacement of the companies' assets. This was a compromise between the producers' demand for compensation to be on a net book value basis (i.e. after depreciation) and the companies' efforts to obtain a formula which would repay them for some of the value of the proven reserves discovered in their concessions. In the event, the system adopted involved Saudi Arabia paying Aramco $500 million, Abu Dhabi paying $162 million in almost equal parts to Abu Dhabi Marine Areas and the Abu Dhabi Petroleum Company, and Qatar paying $28 million to the Qatar Petroleum Company and $43 million to Shell.

Iraqi nationalization

Iraq ceased to have any involvement with the participation negotiations in 1972, when it nationalized the Iraq Petroleum Company. For 20 years relations between the Government and the company had not been good. In the later 1950s, a dispute had arisen over the fact that IPC and its sisters, the Basrah Petroleum Company in the south and the Mosul Petroleum Company in the north, had developed only a very minor part of their 160,000 square mile concession, and, combined with disagreements over the group's accounting procedures, this led to Law 80 of 1961 expropriating more than 99.5 per cent of the group's acreage. The companies never accepted the expropriation, and although several attempts were made to settle this and any other outstanding differences over the next 10 years, the two parties were forced to accept a position of stalemate, in which Iraqi production expanded very slowly.

In June 1971, as part of the agreement on Iraqi Mediterranean crude prices which followed the Teheran pact in February, the IPC group gave commitments for increases in production, but in the following spring, the company found itself obliged to cut the throughput of its pipeline from Kirkuk to the Mediterranean terminals of Banias (Syria) and Tripoli (Lebanon). The company explained that in a period of low Gulf/Europe freight rates, the high prices negotiated for all Mediterranean crudes in the previous years made it uneconomic for its owners to run the pipe at more than half capacity. The Iraqi Government claimed that the cut-back was politically motivated, and presented IPC with alternatives: either the company was to restore Kirkuk production to normal levels and hand the extra production over to the Government, or it was to surrender the field entirely and concentrate production on BPC's acreage in the south. This conflict was further exacerbated by IPC's threats of legal action to prevent the sale of the Iraq National Oil Company's crude from North Rumaila (in expropriated BPC acreage), and by a number of old issues, including an Iraqi claim for royalty backpayments dating from 1964, which IPC had refused to pay until it received the compensation it was claiming for the acreage expropriated in 1971. On May 31st, IPC presented its answers to the Iraqi ultimatum. These did not satisfy the Government, and on the next day, IPC was nationalized. The affiliates, BPC and MPC, were not immediately affected.

In mid-July, negotiations got underway, with Nadim Pachachi, then Secretary-General of OPEC, and M. Jean Duroc-Danner of CFP, acting as mediators. IPC promptly announced that it would not pursue legal action against buyers of Kirkuk crude while mediation efforts were in progress, and the Iraqis were then able to sell substantial amounts of oil—including a deal in February 1973 under which CFP agreed to take 23.75 per cent of Kirkuk's output (equivalent to the company's stake in IPC) over ten years. On February 28th, 1973, IPC and the Government finally reached agreement. IPC accepted the expropriations of 1961 and the nationalization of the Kirkuk producing area, and at the same time handed over MPC and paid the Government $141 million of outstanding royalty backpayments. In return it was promised 15 million tons of oil in two batches in 1973 and 1974, and was given some assurance of the long-term security of its investment and growth of output from BPC's southern fields, where it agreed to more than double production from 640,000 b/d in 1972 to 1,626,000 b/d in 1976.

In the event, it was only seven months before BPC suffered the seizure, during the October war, of the holdings of Exxon and Mobil, and 60 per cent of Shell's share (a proportion relating to the Dutch-registered part of the group) as a political gesture against the U.S.A.'s and the Netherlands' association with Israel. Later the 5 per cent share of the Participations and Explorations Corporations (owned by the Gulbenkian family) was seized on the grounds that the company was registered in Portugal, which was pursuing racist policies in Africa. BPC did not accept these measures, and being a London-registered company, the distribution of its shares technically remained as it always had been; but for practical purposes the seizures gave the Government a stake of 43 per cent in the company's concession. The Government regarded this holding as quite separate from any participation it might be entitled to under the General Agreement (which it rejected as inadequate), or the 60 per cent participation régime evolved in the other Gulf states in 1974, and it appeared to be awaiting the outcome of the Gulf states' move towards a 100 per cent participation before deciding its future policy towards BPC.

Iranian Sales and Purchase Agreement

Although it was clear from the beginning of the Saudi Arabian-Aramco participation negotiations in January 1972 that Iran was not interested in the type of participation envisaged by the other Gulf states, it was not until June 24th, 1972, that the Shah announced that Iran was negotiating with the Consortium an agreement which would extend its lease while giving the National Iranian Oil Company large amounts of crude to sell on its own. For the rest of the year, as the Iranians watched the progress of Shaikh Yamani's negotiations, their scheme remained in abeyance; but by the beginning of 1973, it had become clear that they were seeking somewhat more radical arrangements than those which they had proposed originally. On January 23rd, 1973, the Shah gave the Consortium an ultimatum: under no circumstances would Iran extend its lease, and the companies could either continue under existing arrangements until the expiry of the lease in 1979 and then become ordinary arms-length buyers, or they could negotiate an entirely new agency agreement immediately. The Consortium opted for the latter plan, and, under the Iranian Sales and Purchase Agreement, signed in Teheran in May, NIOC took formal control of the management of the Consortium's entire production operation and the Abadan refinery. The Agreement laid down that NIOC would provide the capital for expanding production, in return for the companies advancing 40 per cent of the funds needed in the first five years (the period of greatest expansion) as prepayment for crude oil. Iran argued that this deal did not amount to nationalization, because full ownership of all assets had been secured in 1951, and technically the Consortium had only leased the assets back from NIOC. The lease was, however, due to run until 1974, and thereafter, under the terms of the agreement finally reached in 1954, it was renewable for three more five-year periods at the companies' option.

Under the Sales and Purchase Agreement, though NIOC became owner/manager, the Consortium members established a service company, the Oil Service Company of Iran (OSCO), to carry out operations for an initial period of five years, which could be renewed. NIOC undertook to raise total installed production capacity to 8 million b/d by October 1st, 1976. The national company is entitled to take the oil needed for internal consumption and a "stated quantity" for export, which is to rise from 200,000 b/d in 1973 to 1.5 million b/d in 1981, and thereafter, except in certain cases of *force majeure*, will remain in the same proportion to total crude available for export as 1.5 million b/d represents to oil available for export in 1981. The balance of crude production goes to the Consortium members, which have been guaranteed security of supply for 20 years.

With regard to financial terms, the Agreement stated that the price and government revenue should be "no less favourable than those applicable (at present or in future) to other countries in the Persian Gulf". This has meant that Iranian revenues per barrel are calculated in almost exactly the same way as revenues in the Arab Gulf states, even though the participation situation which led to the evolution of the revenue formula used in the Arab countries in 1975 does not apply in Iran.

Libya asserts 51 per cent control

It was only a matter of weeks after OPEC had made its formal call for participation in July 1971 that Libya, ever anxious to be first among the producers in militancy and to upstage any participation agreement negotiated by Saudi Arabia, let it be known that it would be interested in nothing less than an immediate 51 per cent share. Four months later, at the beginning of December 1971, Libya nationalized outright BP's half-share of the Sarir field, but this was a purely political gesture (against alleged British connivance in the Iranian invasion of the Tumbs Islands some 24 hours before Britain's withdrawal from the Gulf)—and for the next year the Libyan Government made no move while it awaited the outcome of the participation negotiations in the Gulf.

Talks on Libya's demand for majority control eventually began in early 1973, with the Government adopting its usual policy of negotiating on a company by company basis; but they made no progress. In June Libya nationalized outright the U.S. independent Nelson Bunker Hunt, which had been BP's 50 per cent partner in the Sarir field. Colonel Gadaffi, the Libyan leader, represented the seizure of Bunker Hunt as an anti-U.S. gesture, but he more correctly characterized it as "a warning to the companies to respond to the demands of the Libyan Arab Republic" —which in Bunker Hunt's case had involved not only majority participation, but also a demand that the company should market the share of Sarir output formerly belonging to BP. The régime apparently concentrated its pressure on Bunker Hunt because of the fact that the company possessed direct access to no other oil outside the U.S. and therefore appeared to be very dependent on Libyan supplies. In fact the company, being a private concern, was able to show firm resistance, because its owners were not answerable to shareholders, and were confident in the Libyan operators' secret agreement, under which the companies had promised to meet the supply commitments of any one of their number whose concession was expropriated. From circumstantial evidence it seems that Libya fully decided on nationalizing Bunker Hunt when it concluded that it would have no difficulty in selling the oil to markets apart from the East bloc. This followed the judgement of a local court in Sicily which dismissed a suit brought by BP against the importers and refiners of its expropriated Sarir oil.

Following its nationalization of Bunker Hunt, the Libyan Government proceeded in August to seize 51 per cent of Occidental's operations. Faced with the threat of having the rest of its assets seized and being deprived of its most vital source of oil outside the U.S., Occidental announced its "acquiescence" in the measure. For the other companies the significance of this "acquiescence" lay in the fiscal terms. The companies had in fact been prepared to offer Libya a nominal 51 per cent on the condition that the financial results gave parity with those deriving from the participation agreements with the Gulf producers and Nigeria—but this was not the case in the terms settled with Occidental. Compensation was agreed on at book value, rather than the updated book value formula used in the Gulf, and the buy-back price was set above the posting, rather than between the posting and the tax paid cost.

Five days after the Occidental seizure, three independent companies in the Oasis group, Continental, Marathon and Amerada Hess, accepted a majority takeover on similar terms, though Shell, the only major in Oasis, did not comply with the measure. Then in September the Government announced 51 per cent takeovers of all the other significant producing groups. Gelsenberg, a German concern in partnership with Mobil, and W. R. Grace, a small shareholder in the Esso Sirte venture, agreed to Libya's terms; but Atlanti : Richfield (another partner in Esso Sirte) and the majors, Mobil, Esso (which held a concession on its own as well as the biggest share in Esso Sirte) and the Texaco-Socal company, Amoseas, joined Shell in resisting any sort of arrangement which might have undermined their participation agreements in the Gulf.

Libya's next move came in February 1974 when it seized all of the remaining assets of Texaco, Socal and Atlantic Richfield; and in the following month, Shell too was nationalized. Finally Mobil, in March, and Esso, in April, accepted the 51 per cent seizure of the previous September.

Gulf States achieve 60 per cent participation

The General Agreement on Participation concluded at the end of 1972 had satisfied the Kuwaiti Government, and had been signed by the Minister of Finance and Oil, Mr. Abdel-Rahman Atiqi, at the beginning of January 1973; but the Kuwait National Assembly refused its approval. The determination of the handful of radicals lending opposition to the measure was strengthened by Iraq's success in settling its dispute with IPC in February and by the signature of Iran's Sales and Purchase Agreement in May; and by the summer of 1973, it had become clear that the Government would not, as it had originally hoped, be able to rally sufficient support to get the General Agreement accepted. On June 13th, the Ruler formally requested a revision of the accord, and during the autumn, when Libya announced its series of 51 per cent takeovers, the other Gulf producers followed Kuwait's example. In November Shaikh Ahmed Zaki Yamani announced that Saudi Arabia would not be satisfied with a simple majority holding, and it was subsequently made clear early in 1974 that the Saudi Government would be negotiating a complete takeover of Aramco's operations.

Negotiations between the Kuwait Government and the Kuwait Oil Company shareholders, BP and Gulf, during the winter, resulted at the end of January in the state g ining a holding of 60 per cent, which, after several months of further wrangling in the National Assembly, was ratified on May 14th, 1974. The new

agreement was made valid from January 1st, meaning that the companies had given way on the principle of retroactivity on which they had held so firm in the past, and was to last for six years—though in explaining the terms, Mr. Atiqi was insistent about the Government's right to call fresh negotiations at any point before the end of 1974. The compensation formula agreed was net book value (giving KOC $112 million) rather than updated book value, but there was no settlement of buy-back terms, with the volume and price of oil being left for more hard bargaining over the summer. In fact Kuwait did not conclude a buy-back deal with BP and Gulf until after it had rejected all bids put in for its 60 per cent crude share at an auction in July. For the third quarter of the year, the Government then sold rather over 55 per cent of its entitlement to the two companies at 94.8 per cent of the posted price; and for the last quarter, BP and Gulf bought two-thirds of the state's crude at 93 per cent of the posting.

Three months before the ratification of the Kuwaiti participation agreement, Qatar concluded a similar accord with its concessionaires (the Qatar Petroleum Company and Shell) in February, and in April it settled buy-back arrangements for the following six months. These involved the two companies purchasing 60 per cent of the state entitlement (about 36 per cent of total output) at 93 per cent of the posted price— the same level as that agreed in September 1973 in the original modification of the terms of the General Agreement. Then in June, after the Kuwaiti ratification, Saudi Arabia concluded an "interim" 60 per cent participation agreement with Aramco. No details emerged about the buy-back arrangements, but one immediate effect of the agreement was to make available to Saudi Arabia a large volume of crude which it could threaten to sell on the market at a relatively low price as part of its campaign to lower prices. Finally, in September, Abu Dhabi negotiated a 60 per cent share in the Abu Dhabi Petroleum Company and Abu Dhabi Marine Areas, which like all the other revised participation agreements of 1974 was backdated to the beginning of the year.

Towards complete ownership

Although Saudi Arabia had originally decided that it would be asking for more than a simple majority stake in Aramco in November 1973, it was not until early 1974 that it finally became clear that the government was seeking a complete takeover, linked to sales and contracting arrangements similar to that concluded between Iran and the Consortium in May 1973. Within a matter of weeks, the two sides were reported to be close to clinching the deal, but over the next six months they made very little further progress. The main sticking points concerned the volume of oil to be guaranteed to Aramco and the fee, in the form of a discount, which Aramco was to be given for continuing its role as an operator—though it was also known that the company's owners (Exxon, Socal, Texaco and Mobil) were anxious that any change in the fiscal arrangements should not involve their losing the U.S. tax advantages which had traditionally derived from their being able to have the main cost element in their oil attributed to "tax" rather than "royalties" or "purchase price".

During the summer, Saudi Arabia showed no signs of wanting to hurry the deal, but by the autumn of 1974, when the Government was anxious to see the introduction of a single price system for Gulf oils (which it was felt should be based on the fiscal terms incorporated in the new arrangements with Aramco) there were signs of growing Saudi annoyance with the slow progress of negotiations. In September, the Government suggested that Aramco should agree to the principle of a takeover first, and settle the details later, and demanded that buy-back oil under the 60 per cent participation agreed in June, should be priced at 94.8 per cent of postings. Throughout this period the Saudis, together with the other producers, were placing increasing emphasis on cutting back the "excessive" profits being made by the majors, and, with a view to putting additional financial pressure on Aramco, in October the Government suddenly decided that the group should pay retroactively the royalty and tax increases agreed at OPEC meetings in June and September, which Saudi Arabia had previously refused to implement. At the end of November, Aramco finally gave way and conceded the principle of a complete takeover, and in December it was understood that the two parties had reached agreement on a compensation formula—which had been one of the less contentious issues in the talks. The figure decided was between $1,500 and $2,000 million for 75 per cent of the group's assets (which had expanded considerably since 1972) at net book value.

On March 5th, 1975, the initiative was taken up by Kuwait which announced that as of that date it had taken over all assets of the Kuwait Oil Company, and would be beginning negotiations to settle the terms with BP and Gulf retroactively. The Kuwaitis made it clear that they wanted a continuing relationship with the KOC owners, but that they felt quite capable of running the production operations themselves. Given that geological and topographical conditions make Kuwaiti oil extremely cheap and easy to produce, and that the state has been fairly thoroughly explored and will not be requiring large-scale new exploration or development work, the continued presence of the major companies was very much less necessary for Kuwait than it was for Saudi Arabia and Abu Dhabi, where there are large potentially oil-bearing areas still to be opened up. For this reason it was felt at the time of the announcement that Kuwait might have decided on a complete takeover after consultation with the other Gulf producers —wanting to use Kuwait's negotiations to gauge what conditions the major companies might eventually be prepared to accept.

As with the Saudi negotiations, however, Kuwait's talks with KOC stuck on the issues of the value of oil to be lifted by BP and Gulf, and the price of supplies. It was assumed that whatever the outcome of negotiations the KOC partners' share of future output would be radically reduced, because Kuwait was already concluding big long-term contracts with a number of other companies, including BP's and Gulf's former customers, Exxon and Shell. At the same time, it appeared that Kuwait was intending to sell to BP and Gulf at its normal third party customers price of $10.365 (93 per cent of postings) rather than at the $10.16 "acquisition price" at which BP and Gulf were getting their crude in the first quarter of 1975. A month later, in April, a third problem was added to the negotiations by disagreements over compensation formulae. The Government was offering compensation at net book value, which worked out pro-rata with the $112 million paid for 60 per cent of the company in 1974, should have given KOC $74 million while the companies were demanding better terms to compensate for their loss of access to cheaper crude.

In Saudi Arabia and Kuwait negotiations between governments and companies resumed in May, but in both states the talks were marked by a lack of urgency—and in Saudi Arabia's case it was believed that the Government might have been considering leaving the four American companies with a small stake in Aramco. The general reappraisal of the benefits of a complete takeover which appeared to be in progress was caused by the big reduction in liftings experienced by the Gulf producers in the early part of the year, and by the added security in terms of a guaranteed volume of offtake in each state (and hence ultimately of price), which it seemed could be gained from continuing a partnership with the major companies. This reappraisal was naturally most evident in those producers which had experienced the biggest drop in output. Abu Dhabi, which had announced in December 1974 that it would be taking complete ownership of ADPC and ADMA within a few weeks, decided in early 1975 to shelve the idea of a takeover indefinitely; and Qatar, which in April and May had all but finalized takeover arrangements with QPC and Shell, was holding back from implementing its decision. Libya meanwhile had expressed itself satisfied with its 51 per cent participation formula as it stood, and in Iraq the subject of increased participation in the Basrah Petroleum Company had hardly been mentioned since 1974.

THE DEVELOPMENT OF PRICES

The 1940s and 1950s

In the years before the introduction of the 50-50 profit split in 1950 and 1951, when most of the producers received their revenues on the basis of the fixed royalty arrangements (22 cents a barrel) the development of prices was of only academic interest to the Middle Eastern governments. For all of the 1930s, and the first half of the 1940s, the pricing formula applied was the "U.S. Gulf Plus" system, which was worked out by the chairmen of Shell, Standard of New Jersey and Anglo-Persian when they drew up their famous cartel agreement at Achnacarry House in 1928. The U.S. Gulf Plus system laid down that the price of oil in every export centre throughout the world should be the same as that obtaining in the Gulf of Mexico, but that the price at the point of delivery should be made up of the Gulf of Mexico price plus the cost of freight to that point from the

Gulf of Mexico. It made no difference to the buyer where the oil actually came from. If a buyer in Bombay, for example, placed an order with a cartel company, the oil would probably be supplied from Persia, but he would still be charged the same freight cost as if the oil had been brought from the United States—and the saving, known as "phantom freight" would go to the cartel company. This system could also work in reverse. A shipment of Persian oil to London, which was nearer to the U.S. than to the Middle East, would still be priced at the Gulf of Mexico price plus freight from the Gulf of Mexico to London—leading to the company accepting an element of "freight absorption". The explanation for this peculiar system lay in the fact that the major companies, as a group, had their biggest and most valuable investments in the U.S., and therefore had an interest in maintaining the biggest possible market for American oil.

Given that all of the other major companies and most of the larger American independents joined the cartel, the U.S. Gulf Plus system continued to operate successfully until near the end of the Second World War, when the British Government objected to paying phantom freight for bunker fuel supplied to the navy in the Indian Ocean, and forced the companies to institute a Persian Gulf base. Under the new system, crudes f.o.b. the Persian Gulf were given the same price as similar crudes f.o.b. the Gulf of Mexico, and at the point of delivery only real freight was levied on top. This resulted in crude oils from the two producing areas finding their natural markets (which met in the Mediterranean near Italy)—though if Middle East oil was landed in north-west Europe, the company would, of course, still have to bear an element of freight absorption if its oil was to be competitive.

It was not long, however, before the Persian Gulf Base system itself began to come under attack from the governments of the importing countries. Immediately after the war, the U.S.A. swung rapidly round from being a big net exporter to being a small net importer (a position it maintained for the next 25 years), and as soon as domestic price controls were removed in 1946, prices in the Gulf of Mexico climbed fast. Persian Gulf prices followed automatically, and because the production cost of Middle Eastern oil was very much lower than that of Texan oil, the companies made enormous profits. Despite the freight disadvantage they were able to import Middle Eastern oil into the U.S. and undercut domestic oil as far inland as the mid-West. In 1948 the companies, influenced in part by criticism from the U.S. Government, lowered their Persian Gulf prices so that the delivered prices of Middle Eastern and Texan oil equalized at London; and in 1949, the Director of the Economic Co-operation Administration (which had been established under the Marshall Plan to finance sales of oil and other vital products to Europe) objected to the companies selling oil to the ECA at higher prices than they seemed to be charging to their American affiliates, and forced a further cut in the Persian Gulf so that the delivered prices of Texan and

Middle Eastern oil were made to equalize at New York. This reduction, of course, affected only the profits of the companies in their sales to third parties, and made no difference to the profits made on the large volumes of oil passing down their integrated chain of affiliates.

The large profits made by the companies in this period were a major factor behind the Middle Eastern governments' demands in the late 1940s for better financial terms—demands which were met in 1950 and 1951 by the introduction of the 50-50 profit split (*see* "Concessions" above). The new financial terms (which increased government revenues on Saudi Arabian Light from some $0.22 a barrel to about $0.80—depending on the fluctuations of prices in Texas) served to make the producers price conscious. In retrospect they did not fail to notice that the price adjustments of the later 1940s had been to their considerable disadvantage, and they have since claimed that the movement of the equalization point to New York was not justified in view of the fact that at the time the American market accounted for only 10 per cent of their total exports.

The producers also noticed soon after the introduction of 50-50 that the profit split was not quite as even as it seemed, because the companies were always able to press them into giving discounts off the posted price—like the marketing allowance (which was hardly justified when almost all production was sold to affiliates of the operator or to major companies under long-term contracts) and volume discounts. In fact, Abdullah Tariki, the radical Saudi Oil Minister during the 1950s, calculated soon after 50-50 came into force that the effective split of profits was 32-68 in favour of the companies.

Worse still, the price discrepancies between Texan, Venezuelan and Gulf crudes continued to expand. In 1953 $0.25 was added to the price of Texan and Venezuelan crudes, while Gulf crudes went up by only $0.22, and two years later the Venezuelan price was increased by $0.25. These adjustments destroyed the principle of the three crudes equalizing at New York, and ushered in a new era in which the price of Gulf crudes was to be determined by the supply and demand situation in Europe rather than in America—which directly or indirectly had been the basis for all quotations for Gulf crudes since 1929. In these new circumstances, the growing availability of production capacity in the Middle East, and increasing competition in the European market, led the companies to start giving their own discounts off the posted price for sales to third parties. It was at this stage that posted (or tax reference) prices and f.o.b. (or market) prices in the Gulf began to part company. Given that the 50-50 profit split was still worked out on the basis of the posting, this meant that the producer government's effective share of profits began to climb back towards the 50 per cent it was always supposed to have been.

Then in 1957, after the closure of the Suez Canal, all prices went up—and although in the Middle East the increase was smaller than in Texas or Venezuela, the new price of $2.12 represented the highest posting for Saudi Arabian Light since 1948. These levels were maintained until February 1959, when there was a general reduction, in which Gulf crudes fell by more than the others. Two months later, the Venezuelan price was lowered again, and in August 1960, the Gulf price was reduced without any parallel reduction being made elsewhere. Thus the discrepancy between Arabian Light and Texan crude had expanded from zero in 1948 (when both crudes were priced at $2.68) to $1.20 in 1960—when Texan crude stood at $3.00 and the Saudi Arabian Light posting at $1.80.

From the point of view of the governments in the Middle Eastern capital and Caracas, the price cuts of 1959 and 1960 (about which they were never consulted) were very damaging—affecting the size of their budgets and their development prospects. In April 1959, at the first Arab Petroleum Congress in Cairo (to which Iranian and Venezuelan representatives were invited as observers), the oil ministers of Saudi Arabia and Venezuela, Abdullah Tariki and Perez Alfonso, sponsored the formation of the Oil Consultation Commission. Then in September 1960, a month after the further reduction of Middle Eastern prices, the ministers of Iran, Iraq, Saudi Arabia, Kuwait and Venezuela met again in an atmosphere of crisis in Baghdad. The Oil Consultation Commission was already defunct, having run into opposition from Iran and Iraq who objected to the inclusion of Egypt, and the ministers decided to create a permanent and stronger institution. The body that emerged was OPEC —the Organization of Petroleum Exporting Countries.

Since OPEC's formation, the original five members have been joined by Qatar in 1961, Libya and Indonesia in 1962, Abu Dhabi in 1967, Algeria in 1969, Nigeria in 1971, Ecuador in 1973 and Gabon—as an associate member in 1973 and a full member in 1975.

OPEC in the 1960s

At first the major companies ignored OPEC. In accordance with a resolution passed at the Organization's fourth conference in June 1962, the members addressed protests to the companies against the price cuts of August 1960, and demanded that prices be restored to their previous level. But the companies refused to enter into any collective negotiations, and in their individual replies, they argued that the development of prices did not depend on their own will, but was determined by economic factors over which they had no control.

OPEC realized that the only way to achieve a restoration of posted prices would be to force up market prices, and this the producers decided would best be done by limiting the annual growth in their output. So over two years (from mid-1965 to mid-1967) the members worked out a joint production programme. In both years they over-estimated the overall growth in demand for their oil, and at the same time certain members, notably Libya and Saudi Arabia, and, to a lesser extent, Iran, made no effort to keep within their quotas. The obvious conclusion was that in a period when prices were low enough to cause a tight budgeting condition in some states, those countries which were either new exporters

and/or had big oil reserves and expensive development programmes, would not be willing to make a temporary sacrifice, and await an improvement in the unit price of their oil, but would be tempted to increase revenues by maximizing the volume of their output.

However, OPEC did manage to increase its members' effective share of profits during the 1960s. First in 1963 the companies accepted a cut in the marketing allowance (which they were able to deduct as an expense before making the profit split) from some $0.01–0.02, depending on arrangements in different states, to a uniform half-cent throughout the Gulf; and secondly, and more important, the Organization negotiated two agreements on the expensing of royalties. These agreements the Middle Eastern members saw as removing an anomaly in their fiscal arrangements, and as bringing their taxes into line with the system prevailing in Venezuela. Although the producers' revenues since 1950 had nominally been made up of a royalty of 12.5 per cent of the posted price (as payment for the oil itself) and income tax (representing the 50 per cent tax on the profits from the sale of this oil), payments made under the heading of royalties had always been totally deducted from tax. The producers, referring to the normal internationally accepted arrangements, under which the royalty payer was entitled to deduct the royalty only from his gross income when computing his tax liability, wanted royalties to be treated as an expense in their own countries also—and in 1964 this was what was agreed. As part of a package deal the companies received various further discounts off the posted price in respect of "royalty expensing" and "gravity differential". These discounts were set to be reduced each year—this process being accelerated by a second agreement in 1968, which arranged for the complete disappearance of the royalty expensing discount in 1972 and of the gravity allowance in 1975. Under the new system the companies deducted their production cost, the 12.5 per cent royalty, and the applicable allowances and discounts from the posted price, then split the remainder 50-50, and then added the royalty on to the government's share. For Arabian Light, the royalty expensing agreements and the reduction of the marketing allowance increased government take from $0.84 at the end of 1960 to about $0.90 in 1968.

It was not, however, OPEC's achievements in improving its members' share of profits that were to be of the greatest long-term significance for the oil industry in the 1960s. In 1957, oil had been found in Libya. Unlike the governments in the Gulf, Libya had not awarded all its acreage to a single group, and as the discoveries were brought on stream in the early 1960s, it became clear that some of the largest fields lay in concessions held by American independent companies. These companies had originally ventured out of the U.S. in the late 1940s with the intention of finding new supplies for their marketing operations at home, but when the U.S. Government imposed import controls in 1959, they were forced either to launch themselves downstream in Europe, as Occidental (marketing as VIP or Oxy) and Continental (marketing as Conoco or Jet) did, or to sell their crude to others, as Marathon and Amerada Hess did.

Libya proved to be an ideal source of crude for such operations. Its oil yielded a high proportion of high value products such as gasoline and heating oils, and had a low sulphur content. The country's position gave its crude a big freight advantage over Gulf crudes (an advantage only enhanced by the closure of the Suez Canal in 1967), concession terms were uniquely generous, and for the first half of the decade the profit split was made not on posted prices, but on the much lower realized prices. In the mid-1960s these advantages were somewhat reduced when Libya seized the occasion of the first royalty expensing agreement as an opportunity to renegotiate its profit split on the basis of postings. The majors in Libya, who did not favour the independents having access to crude on terms so much more generous than those applying to their own production in the Gulf, agreed to Libya's request in 1965, but the independents only gave in in 1966, after a bitter struggle in which the Government threatened to stop exports or nationalize their assets. Even with these new terms, Libyan crude was still very competitive with Gulf crudes in Europe, because its posted prices, while higher than those in the Gulf, only partially reflected its freight advantage.

Given the relatively low price, Libyan production expanded extremely fast—from 20,000 b/d in 1962 to 3.3 million b/d in 1970—and throughout the decade prices in Europe fell. The majors' response to the independents' sales and marketing operations was to seek economies of scale in building ever larger tankers, refineries and storage and distribution facilities; but because larger units become most attractive when operated at near full capacity, this led the majors themselves to look for the highest possible market share, and led to an acceleration of price cutting. Although this process was most apparent at the downstream end of the industry, there was also an erosion of market prices in the Gulf, and because the existence of OPEC prevented a lowering of postings, the majors' margins were squeezed. The net earnings per barrel on the seven majors' eastern hemisphere operations dropped from $0.60 in 1958 to $0.33 in 1970, while the effective profit split in the Gulf climbed to something in the region of 70/30 in favour of the governments.

Teheran and Tripoli Agreements

In 1970 the marginal surpluses which had been so strong a feature of the previous decade suddenly disappeared. A combination of higher than expected demand as the Western economies entered a period of upturn, a shortage of tankers and a growing tightness of European refinery capacity, led to an ususually tight supply situation, which left the oil industry with very little flexibility to deal with any disruption which might occur in the Middle East.

These conditions coincided with a series of negotiations in Libya, where in January the new revolutionary régime of Colonel Gadaffi had started pursuing a claim, originally formulated by King Idris' government in 1969, for higher prices which would reflect the true freight advantage enjoyed by Libyan crude

since the closure of the Suez Canal, and would incorporate a premium for the oil's high quality. During the early months of 1970, the Government took a notably moderate stance, but negotiations made rather slow progress, and although it seemed that they might still be brought to a satisfactory conclusion, by the beginning of the summer, the Government's position had hardened. In part the régime's determination stemmed from an agreement in the spring to co-ordinate its efforts with the Algerians, who were engaged in similar negotiations with their French concessionaires, but at the same time, the Libyans could see that their bargaining position as a short-hand supplier was being considerably strengthened by events in the tanker market. The economic upturn in Europe was resulting in a rapid rise in demand for industrial fuel oils of the type derived from the heavier Gulf crudes, and this additional pull on long-haul supplies increased the demand for tanker charters. The strain was only made worse by the loss of several of the new class of mammoth tankers in mysterious explosions early in the year; and in May the situation deteriorated further when a Syrian bulldozer broke Tapline, running from Saudi Arabia to the Mediterranean port of Sidon, and deprived the industry of 480,000 b/d of short-haul crude.

In the same month, the Libyans ordered Occidental, a particularly vulnerable independent which derived nearly a third of its earnings from its Libyan concession, to cut back its production. Whether this decision was made for conservation reasons, or because the Government realized what chaos a further reduction in the supply of short-haul crude would cause, remains unclear—but either way the Libyans soon appreciated the value of production cuts as a lever in their price negotiations, and they quickly imposed further reductions on Occidental and on the other companies. By the beginning of September, the industry had lost about one million b/d of Libyan production, and freight rates soared as extra supplies had to be brought in from the Gulf. One by one the companies surrendered—led, naturally, by Occidental and followed by the other independents in the Oasis group. The majors held out a bit longer, but finally Texaco and Socal broke ranks, and then Esso, Mobil and, eventually, Shell gave in too. The Libyans achieved a price rise of $0.30, rising to $0.40 over the next five years, and their tax rate raised from 50 per cent to amounts varying from 54 to 58 per cent in payment for what the Government claimed should have been higher prices since 1965.

Although in theory these changes were made only to reflect the freight and quality advantages of Libyan crudes, the majors realized that they would be bound to result in higher prices in the Gulf, and they promptly decided to pay the Gulf producers a higher tax rate of 55 per cent and an extra $0.09 on heavier crudes (which although normally regarded as of lower quality, were in particularly high demand in 1970). Then in December 1970, at OPEC's Twenty-first conference, in Caracas, the members decided that the Gulf countries should press for a further round of price increases.

The oil industry, with the support of the consumer governments, formed itself into a united front combining majors, independents and European national companies. When talks with the producers' representatives began in Teheran in January 1971, the companies agreed in principle to a price revision, but insisted that negotiations should cover all OPEC states, so as to avoid the leapfrogging of the past few months. The companies were forced to give in on this point and a parallel series of negotiations was begun in Libya. During the second half of January the gap between the Gulf producers and the companies was gradually narrowed, but on February 2nd, the talks broke down. OPEC then held an extraordinary conference, and all members resolved to legislate a price increase if the companies did not respond to their minimum demands by February 15th. But none of the parties wanted a confrontation, and one day before the OPEC deadline, the companies gave in. The producers were given: and immediate $0.33 basic increase, $0.02 for freight disparities, half a cent for every degree API by which any crude fell below 40° API, the elimination of all remaining discounts and allowances, and provision for prices to increase by 2.5 per cent and $0.05 on June 1st, 1971, and January 1st, 1973, 1974 and 1975. This took 34° API Saudi Arabian Light from $1.80 to $2.18. In return, the companies were guaranteed that there would be no further claims until after December 31st, 1975, no more leapfrogging if the Mediterranean producers concluded better terms, and no embargoes.

Later, in March, negotiations were resumed in Libya, and on April 2nd an agreement was signed giving Libya $0.90, a uniform 55 per cent tax rate, and provision for annual price increases of 2.5 per cent and $0.07. Subsequent negotiations secured similar terms for Iraqi and Saudi crude arriving at Mediterranean terminals through the IPC pipe and Tapline

The price explosion

It was hoped that the Teheran and Tripoli Agreements would give a full five years of price stability—but it was only a matter of months before they began to come under strain. In August 1971, President Nixon's decision to float the dollar (leading to a formal devaluation in December) produced OPEC claims for compensation—though in a notably moderate tone. The claim was settled on January 20th, 1972, when the companies agreed in Geneva to an immediate price rise of 8.49 per cent in the Gulf; and later, in May, after rather tougher negotiations, the same was agreed for Libya.

In February 1973, the dollar was devalued a second time by 10 per cent, and under the terms of the Geneva Agreement, prices were duly raised by 5.8 per cent on April 1st. The OPEC states were disappointed by the time the adjustment mechanism took to operate, and by the small size of their compensation, and, after a further series of discussions with the companies, on June 1st a second dollar compensation agreement was signed in Geneva. The producers obtained an 11.9 per cent increase (which included the 5.8 per cent increase in April plus

compensation for the further slide in the dollar's parity during May) and it was agreed that prices would in future be adjusted monthly according to a weighted average movement of 11 major currencies against the dollar. This formula resulted in further rises in August and September and a reduction in October.

The companies presented the Geneva Agreements as supplementary to the Teheran Agreement—although they both involved a significant rise in revenues, and could equally be characterized as a breach of the five-year price programme. Similarly, the participation arrangement negotiated in 1972 meant a significant increment in government receipts and a modification of the fiscal structure; and a still more drastic alteration came in September 1973 when Saudi Arabia agreed with Aramco that both categories of buy-back crude should be priced at 93 per cent of postings—this being the price obtained by the Saudis in May at the first auction of their own direct crude entitlement.

In the summer of 1973, there were, however, much more fundamental forces undermining the Teheran Agreement than the dollar compensation adjustments or the modification of buy-back terms. As production in the U.S.A. began to fall after 1970, the world's biggest consumer began to look to the Eastern Hemisphere not only to make up for its declining domestic output, but also for an annual increment in supplies that was nearly as big as the annual increase demanded by the whole of Western Europe. United States imports from the Arab countries and Iran grew from 0.6 million b/d in 1971, to 1.0 million b/d in 1972, and to 1.7 million b/d in 1973. It was in 1973 that U.S. demand became really noticeable in the Middle East, and prices on the open market began to move up accordingly.

The OPEC states profited from this situation in as much as they received bids close to postings for the small amounts of crude they were selling on the market themselves; but, with the fiscal terms applied to the bulk of their production still tied to modified 1971 prices, they were for the most part excluded from sharing in the boom, and the main benefit went to the companies. The producers calculated that the effective profit split had changed from about 80-20 in their favour at the time of the Teheran Agreement to about 64-36, and they suggested that the companies were making excessive profits, and that the whole set of prices negotiated two years earlier had become out of date. These arguments were backed up by the producers pointing out that the small annual increments agreed at Teheran were not keeping up with the rate of world inflation.

At the OPEC conference in Vienna on September 15th–16th, the members agreed to call the companies to negotiations in the following month, and to seek a sizable lump increase in posted prices to bring them sufficiently above market realizations to permit them to resume their function as a realistic tax reference, while establishing a mechanism whereby the desired differential between posted and realized prices could be maintained in future. The six Gulf members of the

Organization began meetings with a company delegation in Vienna on October 8th, but the two sides' positions were far apart, with the producers demanding an increase of some 70 per cent and the companies offering only 20 per cent. At the end of the week, the companies requested a fortnight's adjournment. The producers immediately held a meeting of their own, and decided to hold a conference in Kuwait four days later on October 16th "to decide on a course of collective action to determine the true value of the oil they produced".

When the producers met again, they quickly abandoned the idea of holding any further consultations with the companies, and raised their posted prices by 70 per cent. For the Arabian light "marker" crude, the posting rose from $3.01 to $5.12, while government take went up by a slightly larger proportion from $1.77 to $3.05. Subsequently, Libya raised its price by 94 per cent from $4.60 to $8.92, thereby widening further the differential between Gulf and Mediterranean crudes. The new prices were designed to be 40 per cent above the market price for any given crude as determined by the direct sales of governments to third parties, and OPEC gave notice that the movement of prices would in future be determined by actual market realizations. Both the size of the October increase and the fact that it was made unilaterally were unprecedented, and signalled the final complete transfer of control over the price system, which until 1971 had been in the hands of the companies, into the hands of the producers—after a transitional three and a half year period of negotiated prices.

The price increase of October 16th was an important milestone in oil politics, but immediately, for the world economy, the meeting of Arab producers in Kuwait on the following day was far more cataclysmic. Gathering under the aegis of the Organization of Arab Petroleum Exporting Countries, they decided to use the "oil weapon" in support of Egypt and Syria in their war with Israel. With Iraq opting out, the other nine members of OAPEC decided upon a policy of 5 per cent cumulative monthly cuts in production from the levels of September—to continue until the political objective of Israeli withdrawal from the territories occupied in 1967 and the "restoration of the rights of the Palestinians" had been achieved. The meeting was far from being an occasion of complete unanimity, and the decision on 5 per cent cuts was taken with a degree of hesitancy on the part of some members and amounted to something of a compromise. But once the cuts had started, they escalated rapidly. Within days all of the Arab producers (including Iraq) placed embargoes on the U.S.A. and the Netherlands and reduced their production by equivalent additional amounts, while Saudi Arabia and Kuwait also incorporated the 5 per cent reduction scheduled for November in their initial cutback. Irritated by the lack of response from the West, the Arab producers then decided at a further meeting in Kuwait on November 4th to reduce output across the board by 25 per cent of the September level, and gave notice of a further 5 per cent cut

in December. But in practice, the cutback again turned out to be rather larger than it appeared to be on paper, and by the middle of November, output in the two biggest Arab producers, Saudi Arabia and Kuwait, was down by between 30 per cent and 40 per cent.

With winter setting in, the Arab cuts had a dramatic effect on the market. Cargoes of Algerian and Nigerian short-haul crude fetched as much as $16 a barrel, and in December the National Iranian Oil Company in an auction of its crude entitlement under the Sales and Purchase Agreement got the staggering price of $17.40. In these conditions, the OPEC Economic Commission's search for a market price on which could be based the quarterly revision of postings became impossible, and the views of company representatives, who suggested in November in a brief exchange in Vienna that no changes should be made until the market had become more stable, were brushed aside. When the Gulf producers met in Teheran on December 22nd, the new price level set was an arbitrary one dictated largely by the Shah of Iran, who intervened directly in the ministers' deliberations. The Shah suggested a price of $14, while Shaikh Ahmed Zaki Yamani, the Saudi Oil Minister, argued for a price of about $7.50—though he did not, perhaps, put his plea for restraint as strongly as King Faisal would have wished. The other ministers gave Yamani little backing, although they resented the way in which the Shah took control of the meeting, and it was eventually decided that the market price should be increased by nearly 130 per cent from $5.11 to $11.65—taking the government revenue from $3.05 to $7.00. The Libyan price rise which followed was rather more modest in percentage terms—from $8.92 to $15.76.

1974—a dual pricing system

The OPEC conference at Geneva on January 17th–19th, 1974, revealed the full extent of Saudi Arabia's opposition to the price increase announced in the previous month—although in the conference chamber itself, Yamani did not raise a formal objection. As it was members endorsed the new prices, while deciding on a three-month freeze. At the next OPEC conference, in March, the split in the producers ranks became more open, with most members favouring an increase and Saudi Arabia threatening to lower its own prices unilaterally if the other countries had their way, but eventually a compromise decision was reached to freeze postings for a further quarter.

Coinciding with the OPEC conference in March, was another review by the Arabs of their embargo policy. In effect the cuts had come to an end in December, when the Arabs announced that they would not be imposing a further 5 per cent reduction in January, and reclassified most of the EEC and Japan as "favoured nations" for which they were prepared to run production as normal. But it was not until their meeting in March, by which time Dr. Kissinger had arranged the Egyptian-Israeli disengagement, that they lifted the embargo on the U.S. (with Libya and Iraq temporarily dissenting) and only in July was the embargo on the Netherlands lifted. The resumption of normal exports to the U.S. was accompanied by a decision to restore output to September 1973 levels, and Saudi Arabia, with an eye on the coming price battle within OPEC, which it saw would not be settled without reference to actual market realizations, let it be known that it would raise its output somewhat above September levels.

Inevitably, market prices weakened over the following months. A slackening of demand has been evident as early as February, when the Kuwaitis at an auction of participation crude failed to receive any bids coming up to their minimum demand of the posted price, and subsequently sold only 20 per cent of the crude on offer when they lowered the asking price to 93 per cent of postings. In March bids for participation crude put on the market by Abu Dhabi fell well short of the posting, and twice in April Libya lowered its asking price, first from $16.00 to $14.00 and then to $12.75/13.00, with Nigeria and Algeria following suit. By May Iraqi exports at Mediterranean terminals, for which the price was pegged at $12.20, were running at only half the capacity of the pipeline system, and in June Tunisia dropped its asking price from $15.20 to $13.00. Finally in August, in the biggest single sale of 1974, the Kuwaitis failed to sell any of their 60 per cent of production at the 97 per cent of postings demanded—though for the third quarter of the year they subsequently sold rather over 55 per cent of the oil on offer to BP and Gulf at 94.8 per cent of postings.

As the Saudis had hoped in March, the excess of supply assumed a critical importance in the struggle within OPEC over pricing policy. Although King Faisal's wish to lower the price had been known since the beginning of the year, it was not until early in June that Yamani indicated the extent of the reduction sought when he formally proposed that the marker crude posting should be lowered by $2.50. When OPEC held its third meeting of the year at Quito in June, the other members vigorously opposed the Saudi policy, and argued for the adoption of one of the different price and tax formulas presented by OPEC's Economic Commission, which would have raised the cost of oil to the consumers by anything up to the region of $1.50. Saudi Arabia again threatened a unilateral lowering of prices, and a cheap auction of its participation crude entitlement, and the result was a stalemate in which it was decided (with the Saudis dissenting) to increase the royalty rate on the companies' 40 per cent crude entitlement (known as equity oil) from 12.5 to 14.5 per cent.

Although within OPEC in the summer of 1974 a major battle was being fought over the level of postings, there was at the same time a considerable (and unopposed) increase in government take (and therefore in the cost of oil to the consumers) coming about as a result of the 60 per cent participation agreements, concluded in the middle of the year but backdated to the beginning of 1974. In that the states' participation crude was either sold back to the companies at a level well above the governments' take on equity crude, or was sold on the open market at roughly similar prices,

the average government revenue over their whole production was increased, even though on participation crude the governments had to bear the production cost themselves. In 1973, under the 25 per cent régime, the overall effect of participation was fairly small—increasing average government revenues by about $0.10 in the first nine months of the year and by $0.15/20 from September, when the 93 per cent of postings buy-back price came into force. But in mid-1974, under the 60 per cent participation régime, the weighted average revenue worked out, in theory, at some $2 above the government revenue on equity crude (which after the December 1973 increases was about $7.00). In practice, however, there were considerable variations between the different producers in the amount by which the weighted average revenue exceeded the take on equity crude, and in every case, the actual weighted average was lower than it appeared to be in theory. A relatively small factor in determining the variations between the states was the different percentages of postings (93 or 94.8 per cent) charged to the companies for buy-back crude. Much more important was that, following the failure of their auctions (or, in Saudi Arabia's case, in the event of their not holding an auction) the governments kept part of their crude entitlement in the ground, and thus lowered the proportion of participation crude in their overall output, and reduced their weighted average revenues. In Kuwait, for instance, during the third quarter of the year, the ratio of the two types of crude was 65 per cent equity and 35 per cent participation.

One of the consequences of this dual pricing system was that the companies got their crude on average at a price well below that demanded by governments for their direct sales, and the OPEC states realized that the companies' own sales of this relatively cheap crude to third parties were not only undercutting state prices and causing the failure of the auctions, but were also giving the companies large windfall profits. It was with these problems in mind that the producers met in Vienna for OPEC's fourth meeting of 1974 on September 12th–13th. The dispute between Saudi Arabia and the other members had mellowed considerably by this time, but the Saudis still argued that any increase in government take brought about by higher levies on the companies' equity crude should be offset by a reduction of postings, which would not only leave the average cost of oil to the consumers unchanged, but would also be the most effective way of narrowing the margin between the weighted average cost to the companies and the prices demanded at state sales. The Saudis did not accompany their arguments with threats as they had done at Quito, but they again dissented from the eventual OPEC decision, which was to effect a 3.5 per cent increase in average government take in the final quarter to offset the effects of inflation—calculated to be running at four times this level, or 14 per cent over the whole year. This was achieved by a further increase in the royalty rate on equity crude to 16.67 per cent, and by an increase in the tax rate on equity crude from 55 per cent to 65.65 per cent. Although

OPEC did not mention the fact in its communique, the tax and royalty adjustments only had the effect of raising overall take by 3.5 per cent if it was assumed that the equity-participation crude ratio was in practice 40 : 60, and that the producers had previously been charging a buy-back price of 94.8 per cent of postings and would in future be charging 93 per cent. Shortly after the OPEC meeting Kuwait did indeed lower the buy-back paid by BP and Gulf to 93 per cent, but its equity-participation crude ratio had not previously been anything like 40 : 60, and because the Government simultaneously took steps to raise the ratio to 50 : 50 (selling two-thirds of its 60 per cent back to BP and Gulf in the fourth quarter of 1974), the overall increase in government revenue and the cost to the consumer of its oil as from October 1st, 1974, rose by considerably more than 3.5 per cent.

1975—a single price system

During the late autumn of 1974, Saudi Arabia's determination to lower prices appeared to weaken further, and there emerged a marked discrepancy between the government's statements on the subject and its actions, which included the indefinite postponement of its long-promised auction, and its decision in October to call on Aramco for back-payments covering the royalty and tax rate adjustments agreed at Quito and Vienna. At the same time, the Saudis, along with the other producers, remained irritated by the "excessive" margin of profits made by the companies on sales of crude. To remedy this situation, Saudi Arabia, Abu Dhabi and Qatar held their own meeting at Abu Dhabi early in November, and agreed with effect from the beginning of that month to cut $0.40 off their postings while raising the royalty rate on equity crude to 20 per cent and the tax rate to 85 per cent.

When OPEC met in Vienna for its fifth and final conference of 1974, on December 13th–14th, the other members endorsed the new arrangements, and decided that from January 1st, 1975, (the date to which it was assumed the final takeover of Aramco will be back-dated) all of the Gulf states would apply the new weighted average cost to all of their production exported by their concessionaire companies, and that the new price levels should be frozen for nine months. The distinction between equity and participation crude, and the possibility in variations in the weighted average cost being caused by alterations in the ratio between the two crudes, therefore ceased to exist—even though the notion of a 40 : 60 split was still used to work out the new cost, known henceforth as the "acquisition price". The new single price system involved a big jump in government revenue, not only because it was based in part on the higher tax and royalty rates agreed at Abu Dhabi (which more than offset the drop in postings) but also because it was based on a 40 : 60 equity-participation crude ratio which had not existed before. The government revenue on the "marker" crude rose to $10.13, and the acquisition price for the companies to $10.25 (reflecting the "marker" production cost of $0.12), while the gap between the acquisition price and the 93 per cent of postings, $10.46, which remained the

official state sale price, was narrowed to $0.21. (Although throughout 1974 and 1975 OPEC continued to refer to "the marker crude" as the basis of all its calculations, the figures used did not reflect the calculations applied to Saudi Arabian Light in practice—because, even disregarding the problem of equity-participation crude ratios, the production costs applied by OPEC in 1974 and 1975 were lower than the real production costs. The marker therefore became a "notional" crude oil, and is used as such above.)

By the time OPEC held its next meeting in Vienna, at the end of February 1975, the nine-month price freeze was already under pressure—as a result of the depreciation of the dollar in the early part of the year, and calls by Kuwait and other producers for some different unit of account to be used for denominating oil prices. At the same time there were suggestions that OPEC might work out a joint production programme to support prices against the continued fall n demand, which had caused Libya to cut its prices in February to $11.50/12.00, and Abu Dhabi to reduce its sulphur and gravity premiums by $0.24/58 backdated to January 1st. (Subsequently, in April, Abu Dhabi made a further price cut, also backdated to January 1st, by changing the notional equity-participation crude ratio used in calculating its acquisition price from 40 : 60 to 50 : 50.) In the event, the Organization made no decision on production programming, and referred the matter of units of account to the OPEC Economic Commission.

When OPEC met again at Libreville on June 9th–11th, it was proposed that oil prices should be denominated in terms of the IMF's Special Drawing Rights, which are based on a basket of major trading currencies. Algeria, Iraq and Nigeria urged that the new formula be put into effect on July 1st, and that the new price should reflect the $-SDR rate of October 1974. Iran took a middle-of-the-road position, agreeing with Algeria as to the date of implementation, but suggesting that the $-SDR rate of December 1974 might be used. But it was Saudi Arabia, with the tacit support of Venezuela, that won the day—insisting that the producers should wait until the price freeze came to an end at the beginning of October (so that the new unit of account could be neatly incorporated into the general revision of prices scheduled for that date) and that the SDR parity to be used should be decided at OPEC's next meeting in Vienna in September.

The Saudis by this time clearly felt that the erosion of the real value of oil prices had made the existing levels acceptable—and part of the reason for their moderate stance was that they wished to provide a further opportunity for a revival of the producer-consumer dialogue, for which the agenda included a long-term formula to protect oil prices against inflation. However, together with the other producers, the Saudis made it clear at the end of the Libreville meeting, that there would be a significant price increase in October 1975, reflecting both a change in the unit of account, and (whatever the outcome of the producer-consumer dialogue) the world wide rate of inflation—and that thereafter the price of oil would remain indexed.

Oil Statistics

(compiled by Michael Field)

CRUDE OIL PRODUCTION

(million barrels per day)

	1964	1972	1973	1974	1973/74 % Change
Middle East OPEC:					
Saudi Arabia	1.730	5.730	7.345	8.210	11.8
Kuwait	2.115	3.000	2.755	2.275	−17.3
Partitioned Zone[1] . . .	0.360	0.565	0.535	0.545	2.0
Iran	1.170	5.050	5.895	6.060	2.7
Iraq	1.255	1.465	2.020	1.935	− 4.2
Abu Dhabi	0.185	1.050	1.305	1.415	8.5
Qatar	0.215	0.485	0.570	0.520	− 9.1
North Africa OPEC:					
Libya	0.860	2.240	2.180	1.525	−29.9
Algeria	0.565	1.070	1.095	1.040	− 5.3
Other OPEC:					
Venezuela	3.395	3.305	3.460	3.060	−11.6
Nigeria	0.120	1.820	2.055	2.330	13.3
Indonesia	0.470	1.080	1.335	1.390	4.5
Ecuador	0.008	0.064	0.240	0.158	−22.6
Gabon	0.022	0.126	0.162	0.200	23.5
Other Middle East and North Africa:					
Oman	—	0.280	0.295	0.295	0.3
Dubai	—	0.152	0.220	0.242	10.0
Sharjah	—	—	—	0.021	—
Bahrain	0.048	0.076	0.068	0.066	− 2.9
Syria	—	0.116	0.110	0.134	21.8
Egypt[2]	0.122	0.352	0.259	0.240	− 7.3
Tunisia	—	0.080	0.076	0.080	5.3
Morocco	0.002	0.001	0.001	0.001	—
Other producers:					
U.S.A.	8.770	11.185	10.950	10.485	− 4.3
Canada	0.850	1.830	2.115	2.000	− 5.6
Mexico	0.355	0.505	0.550	0.625	14.1
Trinidad and Tobago . .	0.135	0.140	0.165	0.180	8.4
Colombia	0.170	0.195	0.185	0.170	− 7.6
Argentina	0.275	0.435	0.420	0.415	− 1.4
Brazil	0.090	0.165	0.165	0.175	4.8

[continued on next page]

CRUDE OIL PRODUCTION—*continued*]

	1964	1972	1973	1974	1973/74 % CHANGE
U.S.S.R.	4.485	7.890	8.455	9.055	7.1
China	0.190	0.630	0.845	1.050	24.5
Eastern Europe	0.300	0.345	0.345	0.350	1.2
WORLD TOTAL	29.520	52.980	57.845	57.970	0.2
FREE WORLD TOTAL	24.545	44.115	48.200	47.515	− 1.4
OPEC TOTAL[3]	11.570	26.860	30.952	30.663	− 0.9
OPEC % FREE WORLD TOTAL[3]	47.1	60.9	64.2	64.5	0.3
MIDDLE EAST AND NORTH AFRICA TOTAL	8.627	21.716	24.729	24.604	− 0.5
MIDDLE EAST AND NORTH AFRICA % FREE WORLD TOTAL	35.1	49.2	51.3	51.8	0.5

[1] Partitioned Zone production is shared equally by Kuwait and Saudi Arabia.
[2] Includes output of fields in Israeli-occupied Sinai.
[3] OPEC total production and OPEC percentage contribution to total Free World production is based only on the production of countries which were members of the Organisation in the year for which each set of figures is given. In 1964 Abu Dhabi, Algeria, Nigeria, Ecuador and Gabon were not members of OPEC. In 1972 Ecuador and Gabon were not members. In 1973 and 1974 Gabon was only an associate member (becoming a full member in 1975), but its production in 1973 and 1974 is regarded in this table as being part of the OPEC total.

Conversion factors based on world average crude oil gravity:

1 long ton = 7.42 barrels   1 barrel = 35 imperial gallons
1 metric ton = 7.30 barrels   1 barrel = 42 U.S. gallons
1 short ton = 6.63 barrels

To convert metric tons a year into b/d divide by 50.0
To convert long tons a year into b/d divide by 49.2

PROVEN PUBLISHED WORLD CRUDE OIL RESERVES AS AT JANUARY 1st, 1975

('000 million barrels)

MIDDLE EAST AND NORTH AFRICA	RESERVES	YEARS OF PRODUCTION AT 1974 LEVELS	OTHER LEADING PRODUCERS	RESERVES	YEARS OF PRODUCTION AT 1974 LEVELS
Saudi Arabia	164.5	55	Other OPEC		
Kuwait	72.8	88	Venezuela	15.0	13
Partitioned Zone	17.3	87	Nigeria	20.9	24
Iran	66.0	30	Indonesia	15.0	29
Iraq	35.0	50	Ecuador	2.5	43
Abu Dhabi	30.0	58	Gabon	1.8	25
Qatar	6.0	32			
Bahrain	0.3	12	TOTAL OPEC	485.0	40
Dubai	2.4	27	Rest of World:		
Sharjah	1.5	196	U.S.A.	35.3	9
Oman	6.0	56	Canada	9.4	13
Syria	1.5	31	Mexico	13.6	60
Algeria	7.7	20	United Kingdom	15.7	*
Libya	26.6	48	Norway	7.3	*
Egypt	3.7	42	U.S.S.R.	83.4	25
Tunisia	1.1	38	Eastern Europe	3.0	23
			China	25.0	65
MIDDLE EAST AND NORTH AFRICA TOTAL	442.4	49	WORLD TOTAL	715.7	34

* Not applicable.

Source: Oil and Gas Journal.

Note: Reserve figures are subject to wide margins of error, and there are considerable differences between sources—including oil companies and governments.

RESERVES OF BIGGEST OIL FIELDS[1]
('ooo million barrels)

	Year of Discovery	Cumulative Production to end-1973	Estimated Remaining Reserves Jan. 1st, 1974
Saudi Arabia			
Ghawar	1948	9.0	66.5
Safaniyah	1951	2.7	12.6
Abqaiq	1940	4.5	7.8
Kuwait:			
Burgan	1938	5.0	56.1
Iran:			
Agha Jari	1938	5.6	4.5
Gach Saran . . .	1928	3.1	8.1
Marun	1964	1.8	8.9
Bibi Hakimeh . . .	1961	1.0	7.2
Ahwaz	1958	1.0	8.1
Iraq:			
Kirkuk	1929	6.0	9.7
Rumaila	1953	1.8	11.9
Libya:			
Sarir	1961	0.8	7.6
Other OPEC producers:			
Venezuela:			
Bachaquero . . .	1930	4.6	2.0
Lagunillas . . .	1926	8.0	2.5
Indonesia:			
Minas	1944	1.7	5.6
Other producers:			
United States:[2]			
Wilmington (Cal) . .	1932	1.5	0.8
East Texas . . .	1930	4.2	1.8
Prudhoe Bay (Alaska) .	1968	—	10.0
Norway:			
Ekofisk	1970	0.03	2.0
Statfjord	1973	—	3.0
United Kingdom:			
Forties	1970	—	2.0
Brent	1972	—	2.0

[1] By normal international standards a big field is considered to be one with reserves of more than one thousand million barrels.

[2] Wilmington, East Texas and Prudhoe Bay are by far the biggest fields in the U.S.A. Few other U.S. fields have ever contained more than 300 million barrels.

GOVERNMENT OIL REVENUES
(million U.S. dollars)

	1965	1966	1967	1968	1969	1970	1971	1972	1973*	1974*
Iran . . .	522	593	737	817	938	1,093	1,870	2,308	5,600	22,000
Saudi Arabia . .	655	777	852	966	1,008	1,200	2,160	3,107	7,200	29,000
Kuwait . . .	671	707	718	766	812	895	1,395	1,657	2,800	8,000
Iraq . . .	375	394	361	476	484	521	840	575	1,900	6,000
Abu Dhabi . .	33	100	105	153	191	233	431	551	1,200	4,300
Qatar . . .	69	92	102	110	115	122	198	255	600	1,650
Libya . . .	371	476	631	952	1,132	1,295	1,766	1,598	3,000	6,000
Algeria . . .	102	145	200	262	299	325	320	700	1,100	3,500

* Estimated; 1973 and 1974 figures include revenues paid and *due* for production in those years.

EVOLUTION OF PRICES FOR MAIN GULF CRUDE OIL VARIETIES
($ per barrel)

	Production Cost	API°	Percentage Sulphur Content	Pre-November 14th, 1970 p.p.	g.r.	January 1st, 1971 p.p.	g.r.	February 15th, 1971 p.p.	g.r.	January 20th, 1972 p.p.	g.r.	June 1st, 1973 p.p.	g.r.	October 16th, 1973 p.p.	g.r.	January 1st, 1974 p.p.	g.r.	October 1st, 1974 p.p.	g.r.	January 1st, 1975 p.p.	g.r.
Arabian Light	1970-71 0.11 / 1972-73 0.10 / 1974 0.16 / 1975 0.25	34°	1.7	1.80	0.91	1.80	0.99	2.18	1.26	2.48	1.45	2.90	1.70	5.12	3.05	11.65	6.98	11.65	9.69	11.25	10.00
Arabian Medium	1970-71 0.11 / 1972-73 0.10 / 1974 0.16 / 1975 0.25	31°	2.4	1.59	0.80	1.68	0.93	2.09	1.20	2.37	1.38	2.78	1.63	4.90	2.92	11.56	6.92	11.56	9.62	11.16	9.92
Arabian Heavy	1970-71 0.11 / 1972-73 0.10 / 1974 0.16 / 1975 0.25	27°	2.85	1.47	0.72	1.56	0.84	1.96	1.11	2.24	1.30	2.62	1.54	4.63	2.75	11.44	6.85	11.44	9.52	11.04	9.81
Iranian Light	1970-74 0.12 / 1975 0.16	34°	1.35	1.79	0.90	1.79	0.98	2.17	1.25	2.47	1.43	2.88	1.68	5.34	3.17	11.88	7.13	11.88	9.92	11.48	10.29
Iranian Heavy	1970-74 0.12 / 1975 0.16	31°	1.6	1.63	0.82	1.72	0.94	2.13	1.22	2.42	1.40	2.83	1.65	4.99	2.96	11.64	6.99	11.64	9.71	11.24	10.07
Kuwait	1973-75 0.06 / 1974-75 0.07	31°	2.5	1.59	0.83	1.68	0.96	2.09	1.23	2.37	1.41	2.78	1.65	4.90	2.94	11.55	6.96	11.55	9.68	11.15	10.08
Abu Dhabi Murban	1970-73 0.15 / 1974 0.165 / 1975 0.25	39°	0.75	1.88	0.92	1.88	0.01	2.24	1.27	2.54	1.46	2.79	1.72	6.05	3.58	12.64	7.57	12.64	10.52	11.69	10.36
Abu Dhabi Marine (Umm Shaif)	1970-71 0.20 / 1972-73 0.30 / 1974 0.46 / 1975 0.60	37°	1.3	1.86	0.89	1.86	0.97	2.23	1.24	2.53	1.39	2.96	1.65	5.34	3.19	12.09	7.07	12.09	9.80	11.45	9.81
Abu Dhabi Zakum	1973 0.30 / 1974 0.46 / 1975 0.60	40°	0.95	NOT POSTED								2.87	1.67	5.96	3.45	12.57	7.37	12.57	10.21	11.59	9.94
Iraq Basrah	1974-73 0.12 / 1974-75 0.15	35°	1.95	1.72	0.86	1.72	0.93	2.16	1.24	2.45	1.42	2.87	1.67	5.06	3.00	11.67	6.99	11.67	9.72	11.27	10.15
Qatar Dukan	1970-71 0.12 / 1972 0.14 / 1973 0.17 / 1974-75 0.25	40°	1.17	1.93	0.96	1.93	1.05	2.28	1.32	2.59	1.49	3.03	1.74	5.83	3.44	12.41	7.39	12.41	10.26	12.01	10.69
Qatar Marine	1970-71 0.25 / 1972 0.30 / 1973 0.22 / 1974-75 0.26	36°	1.4	1.83	0.85	1.83	0.92	2.20	1.20	2.50	1.35	2.92	1.65	5.50	3.22	12.01	7.14	12.01	9.91	11.61	10.32

NOTES

1. p.p. = posted price; g.r. = government revenue.

2. Arabian Light has been designated as the "Marker" crude, forming the basis for the prices of all other Gulf crudes. From January 1st, 1974, to January 1st, 1975, other Gulf crudes were priced at Arabian Light plus or minus:

(a) API Gravity Differential—set at minus 3 cents per degree below 34° API and plus 6 cents per degree above 34° API.

(b) Sulphur Premium—for all crudes with a sulphur content lower than that of Arabian Light.

(c) Freight Differential—involving crudes loaded nearer the entrance of the Gulf (nearer the markets) being given a marginal price differential over those loaded at the top of the Gulf.

During February and March 1974 the Gravity Differentials and Sulphur Premiums of Abu Dhabi crudes were reduced—the reductions being backdated to January 1st. In July 1975 the differentials affecting all other Gulf crudes remained as in 1974.

In the official OPEC calculations during 1974 and 1975 the production costs applied to the marker crude, being used to illustrate movements in government revenue, were notional figures somewhat lower than the real production costs. In the table the figures used are the higher real costs applied in practice.

3. Prior to October 16th, 1973, Abu Dhabi Zakum had no separate posting. The price and government take were derived by escalation from Umm Shaif.

4. Government revenue for the period 1970–January 1st, 1974, has been calculated as follows:

(a) For pre-November 1970: posted price, minus expensed 12.5 per cent royalty, production cost and appropriate discounts; taxed at 50 per cent with royalty added.

(b) For January 1st, 1971: posted price, minus expensed 12.5 per cent royalty, production cost and appropriate discounts; taxed at 55 per cent with royalty added.

(c) For February 14th, 1971–January 1st, 1974: posted price, minus expensed 12.5 per cent royalty and production cost; taxed at 55 per cent with royalty added.

5. During 1973, in which year the governments had a 25 per cent participation (or in the case of Iran whole ownership but financial terms equivalent to those in the Arab states) average government revenues per barrel were somewhat higher than those shown in the table above, which for 1973 gives only government revenues from the companies' equity crude. A small percentage of participation crude was sold by governments on the open market, at prices only slightly below, or exceeding, the postings, and a further proportion of participation crude (amounting to rather more than 20 per cent of total production) was sold back to the concessionaire companies at a price between the tax paid cost (i.e. government revenue on equity crude plus production cost) and the posting.

For the first eight months of the year, under the buy-back terms of the original participation agreement (*see text*), the effect of the 25 per cent participation was to increase government revenues, on a weighted average basis, by about 10 cents a barrel. From September 16th, when the companies' buy-back cost was fixed at 93 per cent of postings, government revenues averaged some 15–20 cents above the levels shown for June in the table; and from October 16th government revenues averaged about 35–45 cents more than shown in the table.

6. During 1974, in which year the governments took a 60 per cent participation backdated to the beginning of January, revenues per barrel were based on a weighted average of the taxes and royalties received from the companies' equity crude (40 per cent of production) and the proceeds (minus production costs) of the sale of participation crude (60 per cent of production) back to the companies at a small discount off the posting.

This pricing formula is not reflected in the figures given for January 1st, 1974, which denote only government revenue from equity crude. In practice, during the first nine months of 1974, the effect of participation was to increase the governments' revenues by some $2.20–2.40 a barrel. The weighted average formula is, however, reflected in the figures given for October 1st, 1974—which assumes that the buy-back price paid by the companies for participation crude before that date was 94.8 per cent of postings, and after that date 93 per cent of postings. Government revenues for equity crude in October 1974 have been calculated on the basis of: posted price, minus expensed 16.66 per cent royalty and production cost; taxed at 65.75 per cent, with royalty added.

In practice all of the weighted average figures are notional: partly because during the year the division between equity crude and participation crude was often nearer 50–50 than 40–60, and partly because there were variations at different times and in different states in the percentage of postings charged to the companies for buy-back crude. This percentage varied from 93 to 94.8 per cent of postings.

7. Government revenues for January 1st, 1975, are based on the weighted average of a 20 per cent royalty and an 85 per cent tax rate for equity crude (40 per cent of production), and a 93 per cent buy-back price for participation crude. As from January 1st, 1975, this formula was applied to the pricing of 100 per cent of production, so in practice the price distinction between equity crude and participation crude ceased to exist, even if the notions of equity crude and participation crude were still used in working out the single price level.

8. The cost of crude to the consumer is government revenue plus production cost.

9. The dates in the table denote changes in price and tax formula (*see text* for details) as follows:
Pre-November 14th, 1970: before price increase for heavy crudes (27° and 31° API).
January 1st, 1971: after November 1970 tax and price increases, and introduction of 55 per cent tax rate.
February 15th, 1971: after Teheran Agreement price increases and elimination of all price discounts and gravity adjustment discounts.
January 20th, 1972: after first Teheran inflation/escalation increment (June 1st, 1971) and First Geneva Agreement for dollar compensation.
June 1st, 1973: after second Teheran inflation escalation increment (January 1st, 1973), dollar compensation increment under First Geneva Agreement (April 1st, 1973), and Second Geneva Agreement for dollar compensation.
October 16th, 1973: after dollar compensation adjustments under Second Geneva Agreement (July 1st, August 1st and October 1st), and first OPEC unilateral increase.
January 1st, 1974: after second OPEC unilateral increase.
October 1st, 1974: after July 1st royalty rate adjustment for equity crude (agreed at Quito in June), and royalty and tax rate adjustments for equity crude agreed at Vienna in September.
January 1st, 1975: after royalty and tax rate adjustment for equity crude and posted price reduction agreed in Abu Dhabi in November, and introduction of single price structure in Vienna in December. Also after reductions in Abu Dhabi crudes' sulphur and gravity differential premiums announced in February and March 1975, and made retroactive to January 1st, 1975.

91

REFINERY CAPACITY AND OWNERSHIP[1]
('ooo barrels per day)

STATE	REFINERY	CAPACITY	STATE TOTAL	OWNERSHIP
Iran	Abadan	414		National Iranian Oil Co.
	Kermanshah	15		,, ,, ,, ,,
	Shiraz	40		,, ,, ,, ,,
	Teheran	100	569	,, ,, ,, ,,
Iraq	Daurah	73		Government Oil Refineries Admin.
	Basra	70		,, ,, ,, ,,
	Kirkuk	18		,, ,, ,, ,,
	Alwand (Khanaqin)	12.4		,, ,, ,, ,,
	Haditha/K3	6		,, ,, ,, ,,
	Muftiah (Basra)	4.2		,, ,, ,, ,,
	Qaiyera (Mosul)	2.2	185.8	,, ,, ,, ,,
Kuwait	Shuaiba	121.6		Kuwait National Petroleum Co.
	Mina al Ahmedi	272		Kuwait Oil Co.
	Mina Abdullah	144	537.6	American Independent Oil Co.
Saudi Arabia	Ras Tanura	415		Aramco
	Riyadh	13.6		Petromin
	Jeddah	40.6	487.2	,,
Partitioned Zone	Mina Saud	50		Getty
	Ras al Khafji	27	77	Arabian Oil Co.
Bahrain	Sitra	250	250	Bahrain Petroleum Co.
Qatar	Umm Said	6	6	National Oil Distribution Co.
Yemen, P.D.R.	Aden	158	158	British Petroleum
Lebanon	Tripoli	30		Government
	Sidon	17.4	47.4	MEDRECO (Caltex & Mobil)
Jordan	Zerqa	15.6	15.6	Jordan Petroleum Refining Co.
Syria	Homs	59	59	General Petroleum Authority
Egypt	Mex-Alexandria	64		Alexandria Petroleum Co.
	Suez[2]	30		Suez Oil Processing Co.
	Tanta (Nile Delta)	14		,, ,, ,,
	Al Amiriyah (Alexandria)	36	144	El Nasr Petroleum Co.
Sudan	Port Sudan	22	22	British Petroleum & Shell
Libya	Marsa el Brega	8.2		Esso Sirte
	Zavia	60	68.2	Libyan Government
Algeria	Hassi Messaoud	2		REPAL
	El Harrach (Maison Carrée)	50		Sonatrach-Raffinerie d'Alger
	Arzew	53.2	105.2	,, ,, ,,
Tunisia	Bizerta	25	25	Soc. Tunisio-Italienne de Raffinage
Morocco	Sidi Kacem	14.4		Soc. Cherifienne des Pétroles
	Mohammedia	45	59.4	Marocaine-Italienne de Raffinage
MIDDLE EAST AND N. AFRICA TOTAL			2,816.4	
Venezuela			1,490	
U.S.A.			14,970	
United Kingdom			2,985	
Italy			3,890	
France			3,330	
Germany, Fed. Rep.			2,985	
Japan			5,095	

[1] Excludes topping plants. [2] The Suez refinery was destroyed after 1967. It is now being recommissioned to give a **capacity of 100,000 b/d by the end of 1975.**

IMPACT OF OIL PRICE INCREASES ON DEMAND AND PRODUCTION PROJECTIONS
(million barrels per day)

DEMAND		PROJECTIONS OF 1973[4]					PROJECTIONS OF 1975[3]	
	1970[1]	1973[1]	1975	1980	1985	1980	1985
U.S.A.	14.4	16.9	17.8	21.6	25.5	18.0	19.5
W. Europe	12.7	15.2	16.7	21.8	28.5	15.4	18.4
Japan	4.0	5.5	6.5	9.0	12.0	6.6	7.9
Free World Total	39.5	47.8	52.3	70.0	91.5	52.2	57.5
PRODUCTION	1970[1]	1973[1]	1975	1980	[2]	1980	[2]
Saudi Arabia	3.6	7.3	8.7	17.5		9.5	
Iran	3.8	5.9	7.4	8.0		5.8	
Abu Dhabi	0.7	1.3	2.4	4.1		1.5	
Total Gulf Area	13.8	21.1	27.0	39.7		23.0	
Free World Total	39.9	48.2	52.3	70.0		52.2	

[1] Actual figures. Projections made in 1973 for the later 1970s and 1980s generally assumed that demand and production in 1973 would be lower than it turned out to be.

[2] Projections for production in 1985 are not included because it is not possible to forecast future oil discoveries, and therefore the sources of production, for more than five years ahead—this being the time taken to bring recent big discoveries on stream.

[3] Demand and production in 1975 was, in the middle of the year, expected to be slightly lower than in 1973.

[4] Projections of 1973 given in the table fall towards the lower end of the range of projections made in that year. Some forecasts anticipated total Free World demand in 1985 of 100 million b/d.

Oil Groups Producing and Exploring in the Gulf

Iran

OIL SERVICE COMPANY OF IRAN (OSCO)

CONTRACTOR: As from May 1973 the state-owned National Iranian Oil Company took over the administration of all fields formerly run by Iranian Oil Participants (the Consortium). Under a twenty-year agreement the Consortium companies became privileged buyers of Iranian crude. The companies established a new contracting concern, OSCO. This replaced the Consortium's previous operator, the Iranian Oil Exploration and Producing Company.

PRODUCTION (1974): 5.542 million b/d.

OWNERSHIP:
British Petroleum					40%
Royal Dutch/Shell					14%
Exxon					7%
Standard Oil of California					7%
Texaco					7%
Gulf					7%
Mobil					7%
Compagnie Française des Pétroles (CFP)					6%
Iricon Agency					5%
Atlantic Richfield (Arco)				4/12%	
Reynolds				2/12%	
Charter Company				2/12%	
Getty				2/12%	
Continental				1/12%	
Standard Oil Ohio (Sohio)				1/12%	

NATIONAL IRANIAN OIL COMPANY (NIOC)

Operations at Naft-i-Shah: The state company has developed a field at Naft-i-Shah, on the border between Iraq and the province of Kermanshah.

PRODUCTION (1974): 18,000 b/d.

SOCIÉTÉ IRANO-ITALIENNE DES PÉTROLES (SIRIP)

PARTNERSHIP: Signed 1957. Twenty-five years from start of sales—1962. Three areas totalling 22,900 sq. km.: offshore northern Gulf, east-central Zagros, Gulf of Oman coast. All except producing areas now relinquished. Original exploration obligation $22 million. No bonuses.

PRODUCTION (1974): 36,000 b/d.

OWNERSHIP:
National Iranian Oil Company				50%
AGIP S.p.A.				50%

IRAN PAN-AMERICAN OIL COMPANY (IPAC)

PARTNERSHIP: Signed 1958. Twenty-five years from start of commercial production. Two areas totalling 16,000 sq. km. offshore. All except producing areas now relinquished. Original exploration obligation $82 million. Cash bonus $25 million.

PRODUCTION (1974): 132,000 b/d.

OWNERSHIP:
National Iranian Oil Company				50%
Standard Oil of Indiana (Amoco)				50%

IRANIAN MARINE INTERNATIONAL OIL COMPANY (IMINOCO)

PARTNERSHIP: Signed 1965. Twenty-five years from start of commercial production. Four areas totalling 7,960 sq. km. offshore. Most now relinquished. Original exploration obligation $42 million. Expenditure guarantee $24 million. Cash bonus $34 million. Production bonus $10 million.

PRODUCTION (1974): 58,000 b/d.

OWNERSHIP:

National Iranian Oil Company.	50%
AGIP S.p.A.	16⅔%
Phillips Petroleum.	16⅔%
Oil and Natural Gas Commission of India.	16⅔%

LAVAN PETROLEUM COMPANY (LAPCO)

PARTNERSHIP: Signed 1965. Twenty-five years from start of commercial production. Three areas totalling 8,000 sq. km. offshore. Most now relinquished. Original exploration obligation $15 million. Expenditure guarantee $12 million. Cash bonus $25 million. Production bonus $6 million.

PRODUCTION (1974): 195,000 b/d.

OWNERSHIP:

National Iranian Oil Company.	50%
Atlantic Richfield (Arco).	12½%
Murphy Oil	12½%
Sun Oil.	12½%
Union Oil of California (Unocal).	12½%

IRAN NIPPON PETROLEUM COMPANY (INPECO)

PARTNERSHIP: Signed 1971. Twenty years from start of commercial production. Area in Lurestan of 8,000 sq. km. Twenty-five per cent relinquished. Exploration obligation $52 million. Expenditure guarantee $21 million. Cash bonus $40 million. Production bonus $10 million. Exploration in progress.

OWNERSHIP:

National Iranian Oil Company.	50%
Teijin Ltd. & North Sumatra Oil Development Corporation	33.3%
Mitsui & Co., Mitsubishi Shoja Kaisha, & Mobil.	16.7%

BUSHIRE PETROLEUM COMPANY (BUSHCO)

PARTNERSHIP: Signed 1971. Twenty years from start of commercial production. Area of 3,715 sq. km. offshore near port of Bushire. Twenty-five per cent relinquished. Exploration obligation $22 million. Expenditure guarantee $13 million. Cash bonus $5 million. Production bonus $6 million. Exploration in progress.

OWNERSHIP:

National Iranian Oil Company.	50%
Amerada Hess	50%

HORMUZ PETROLEUM COMPANY (HOPECO)

PARTNERSHIP: Signed 1971. Twenty years from start of commercial production. Area of 3,500 sq. km. offshore near the Straits of Hormuz. Twenty-five per cent relinquished. Exploration obligation $20 million. Expenditure guarantee $8 million. Cash bonus $2 million. Production bonus $10 million. Exploration in progress.

OWNERSHIP:

National Iranian Oil Company.	50%
Mobil.	25%
Petrobras (Brazilian)	25%

SOCIÉTÉ FRANÇAISE DES PÉTROLES D'IRAN (SOFIRAN)

SERVICE CONTRACT: Signed 1966. Twenty-five years from start of commercial production. Onshore and offshore areas totalling 45,000 sq. km. Onshore and most of offshore areas now relinquished. Exploration obligations expressed in areas to be surveyed and numbers of wells to be drilled. No bonuses. Oil expected on stream in 1975.

OWNERSHIP:

Entreprise de Recherches et d'Activités Petroliers (ERAP)	48%
Aquitaine	12%
Mitsubishi	40%

EUROPEAN GROUP OF COMPANIES (EGOCO)

SERVICE CONTRACT: Signed 1969. Twenty-five years from start of commercial production. Area of 27,260 sq. km. plus territorial waters. Half now relinquished. Exploration obligations three wells and $10 million in first five-year phase. No bonuses. ERAP operator. Exploration in progress.

OWNERSHIP:

ERAP.	32%
AGIP S.p.A..	28%
Hispanoil	20%
Petrofina (Belgian).	15%
Österreichische Mineraloelverwaltung (OMV)	5%

PHILLIPS PETROLEUM (PHILIRAN)

SERVICE CONTRACT: Signed 1969. Twenty-five years from first commercial production. Onshore area of 32,860 sq. km. Forty per cent now relinquished. Exploration obligations three wells and $8 million in first five-year phase. Cash bonus $5 million during first five years. Production bonus $1–5 million depending on production levels. Exploration in progress.

OWNERSHIP:

Phillips.	50%
Continental (Conoco)	25%
Cities Service.	25%

TOTAL

SERVICE CONTRACT: Signed 1973. Onshore area of 8,000 sq. km. in Lar region. Exploration obligation $40 million in first five years. Cash bonus $6 million. Total may purchase 45 per cent of production for 15 years at 5 per cent discount. Exploration in progress.

OWNERSHIP:

Total (CFP).	100%

ULTRAMAR

SERVICE CONTRACT: Signed 1973. Area of 20,000 sq. km. in Lar region. Exploration obligation $14 million in first five years. Cash bonus $4.5 million. Ultramar may purchase half of production below 100,000 b/d at 5 per cent discount, reduced to 4 per cent if production exceeds 100,000 b/d. Exploration in progress.

OWNERSHIP:

Ultramar	100%

DEMINEX

SERVICE CONTRACT: Signed 1973. Areas of 14,500 sq. km. in Abadan and Shiraz regions. Denimex may purchase 30–45 per cent of production at 3–3.8 per cent discount. Exploration in progress.

OWNERSHIP:

Deminex (German).	100%

ASHLAND OIL PARTNERSHIP

SERVICE CONTRACT: Signed 1973. Acreage in Lar region. Exploration obligation $25 million. Contractors may purchase 50 per cent of production for 15 years at 3.5–5 per cent discount. Exploration in progress.

OWNERSHIP:

Ashland Oil.	50%
Pan-Canadian Petroleum	50%

AGIP

SERVICE CONTRACT: Signed 1973. Area of 7,150 sq. km. in Lar region. Exploration obligation $20 million. AGIP may purchase 50 per cent of production for 15 years at 5 per cent discount. Exploration in progress.

OWNERSHIP:
AGIP S.p.A. 100%

Iraq

IRAQ NATIONAL OIL COMPANY (INOC)

Production and Exploration operations: INOC, the Iraqi state company, runs two production operations—the small Khanaqin field (formerly operated by BP) on the Iranian border, and the northern part of the Rumaila field, in the south of the country, which came on stream in 1972. INOC also manages the marketing of Rumaila crude. With the assistance of Russian and Hungarian drilling concerns INOC is appraising a number of other promising finds.

PRODUCTION (1974): 160,000 b/d.

IRAQI COMPANY FOR OIL OPERATIONS (ICOO)

Production operations: The state-owned ICOO was formed in June 1972 to take over the production operations of the nationalized Iraq Petroleum Company. ICOO manages production from the Kirkuk, Jambur and Bai Hassan fields on former IPC acreage, and from the Ain Zalah and Butmah fields on former acreage of the Mosul Petroleum Company (dissolved by the IPC group in early 1973). Marketing is managed by INOC.

PRODUCTION (1974): 896,000 b/d.

ENTREPRISE DES RECHERCHES ET D'ACTIVITÉS PETROLIERS (ERAP)

SERVICE CONTRACT: Signed 1968. Areas totalling 10,800 sq. km. onshore and offshore. Most relinquished. Production is expected from the Buzurgan field.

OWNERSHIP:
ERAP 60%
Sumitomo, Mitsubishi, Idemitsu and other Japanese interests 40%

PETROBRAS

SERVICE CONTRACT: Signed 1973. Area of 3,050 sq. km. Exploration obligation $12 million. Exploration in progress.

OWNERSHIP:
Petrobras 100%

INDIAN OIL AND NATURAL GAS COMMISSION

SERVICE CONTRACT: Signed 1973. Onshore acreage near Neutral Zone. Exploration in progress.

OWNERSHIP:
Oil and Natural Gas Commission of India . 100%

BASRAH PETROLEUM COMPANY (BPC)

PARTNERSHIP: Originally a concession of seventy-five years from 1938, expiring 2013. Confined to producing areas west of Basra since expropriation measures of 1961. The Iraqi Government did not take a share in BPC as a result of the 1972 Participation Agreement—rejecting an initial 25 per cent holding as inadequate. During the October War of 1973 the State nationalized the holdings of the Near East Development Corporation (Exxon and Mobil), as well as 60 per cent of Shell's

holding (that part relating to the company's Dutch registration). The expropriation of the Partex share followed. These expropriations are not officially accepted by BPC, which is a London registered company with shares still distributed between BP, Shell, CFP and the Near East Development Corporation with 23¾ per cent each, and Partex with 5 per cent. For practical purposes the ownership of the BPC concession is now as listed below.

PRODUCTION (1974): 878,000 b/d.

OWNERSHIP:
British Petroleum 23¾%
Royal Dutch/Shell 9½%
Compagnie Française des Pétroles (CFP) . . 23¾%
Iraq Government 43%

Kuwait

KUWAIT OIL COMPANY (KOC)

Production operations: In March 1975 it was announced that Kuwait had taken a 100 per cent of the assets of KOC, which had originally been owned by Gulf and BP. The original concession covered all of Kuwait including territorial waters to a six-mile limit, though areas totalling 11,414 sq. km. were relinquished in 1962, 1967 and 1971. The concession was signed in 1934 for seventy-five years, and was extended in 1951 to expire in 2026. The Kuwait National Assembly rejected the first participation agreement (for a 25 per cent state share) in 1973. The state took a 60 per cent stake in 1974. The details of the 100 per cent take-over in March 1975 were left to be settled by negotiation.

PRODUCTION (1974): 2.276 million b/d.

KUWAIT SHELL PETROLEUM DEVELOPMENT

CONCESSION: Forty-five years from 1961. Area of 1,500 sq. miles offshore. Drilling began in 1962, but was abandoned in the following year as a result of a still unresolved boundary dispute.

OWNERSHIP:
Royal Dutch/Shell 100%

KUWAIT SPANISH PETROLEUM COMPANY

PARTNERSHIP: Signed 1968. Thirty-five years with the option of a five-year extension. Area of 9,270 sq. km. on relinquished KOC acreage including some territorial waters. Drilling revealed shows of oil, but not commercial possibilities, and has been suspended since 1973.

OWNERSHIP:
Kuwait National Petroleum Company . . 51%
Hispanoil 49%

Partitioned Zone

AMERICAN INDEPENDENT OIL COMPANY (AMINOIL)

PARTNERSHIP: Originally a concession of sixty years from 1948, expiring in 2008. All of Kuwait's half of the Partitioned Zone, including territorial waters and islands. Agreement on 25 per cent state participation was ratified in 1973.

PRODUCTION (1974): 82,000 b/d.

OWNERSHIP:
R. J. Reynolds Industries 75%
Kuwait Government 25%

GETTY OIL COMPANY

PARTNERSHIP: Originally a concession of sixty years from 1949, expiring in 2009. All of Saudi Arabia's half of the Partitioned Zone including territorial waters and islands. Agreement on 25 per cent participation was ratified in 1973.

PRODUCTION: (1974): 82,000 b/d.

OWNERSHIP:
Getty	75%
Saudi Arabian Government	25%

ARABIAN OIL COMPANY (AOC)

PARTNERSHIP: All areas offshore the Partitioned Zone outside the six-mile limit. Under original terms, signed in 1957, the Saudi Arabian and Kuwaiti governments were given a stake of 10 per cent each. This was increased to 12½ per cent each in 1973. Revenues are shared equally between Saudi Arabia and Kuwait.

PRODUCTION (1974): 381,000 b/d.

OWNERSHIP:
Japan Petroleum Trading Company . . .	75%
Kuwait Government	12½%
Saudi Arabian Government	12½%

Saudi Arabia

ARABIAN AMERICAN OIL COMPANY (ARAMCO)

PARTNERSHIP: Originally two concessions of sixty-six years from 1933 and sixty-six years from 1939, expiring in 1999 and 2005. Covering most of Eastern Province and other onshore and offshore areas. In 1973 Saudi Arabia took a 25 per cent participation, and in 1974, as an interim measure pending the negotiation of a 100 per cent take-over, a 60 per cent stake.

PRODUCTION (1974): 8.211 million b/d.

OWNERSHIP:
Saudi Arabian Government	60%
Exxon	12%
Standard Oil of California	12%
Texaco	12%
Mobil	4%

TENNECO

PARTNERSHIP: Signed 1965. Three areas totalling 26,000 sq. km. onshore and offshore along Red Sea Coast. Gas has already been struck in the northern Red Sea and exploration is continuing.

OWNERSHIP:
Petromin (Saudi state company) . . .	10%
Tenneco	90%

Bahrain

BAHRAIN PETROLEUM COMPANY (BAPCO)

PARTNERSHIP: Originally a concession of ninety-five years from 1929, expiring 2024. All onshore areas, territorial waters and islands. Areas relinquished. In 1973 the Government took a 25 per cent participation, which was increased to 60 per cent in 1974.

PRODUCTION (1974): 67,000 b/d.

OWNERSHIP:
Bahrain Government	60%
Caltex (Texaco & Socal 50–50) . . .	40%

SUPERIOR OIL COMPANY BAHRAIN

CONCESSION: Signed 1970. Thirty-five years. Area 1,307 sq. miles offshore relinquished by BAPCO. Exploration in progress.

OWNERSHIP:
Superior Oil	100%

Qatar

QATAR PETROLEUM COMPANY (QPC)

PARTNERSHIP: Originally a concession of seventy-five years from 1935, expiring in 2010. Onshore Qatar territory excluding large areas relinquished in the north and east. In 1973 the Government took a 25 per cent share in the operation, and in 1974 a 60 per cent share.

PRODUCTION (1974): 223,000 b/d.

OWNERSHIP:
Qatar Government	60%
Qatar Petroleum Company	40%
British Petroleum . . . : .	9½%
Royal Dutch/Shell	9½%
Compagnie Française des Pétroles (CFP)	9½%
Near East Development Corpn. (Exxon & Mobil)	9½%
Participations and Explorations Corpn. (Gulbenkian)	2%

SHELL QATAR

PARTNERSHIP: Originally a concession of seventy-five years from 1952, expiring 2027. Offshore north-east of Qatar peninsula. In 1973 the government took a 25 per cent stake in the operation, and in 1974 a 60 per cent stake.

PRODUCTION (1974): 295,000 b/d.

OWNERSHIP:
Qatar Government	60%
Royal Dutch/Shell	40%

Qatar/Abu Dhabi

AL BUNDUQ COMPANY

CONCESSION: Granted in 1970 to develop the offshore al Bunduq field, on the median line between Qatar and Abu Dhabi. Revenues to be divided equally between Abu Dhabi and Qatar. Expected on stream August 1975.

OWNERSHIP:
British Petroleum	33⅓%
Compagnie Française des Pétroles (CFP) .	33⅓%
Japanese group: ADOCO, Fuji, Kansai, Kansai Electric Power, Tokyo Electric Power, North Slope Oil, Alaska Oil	33⅓%

Abu Dhabi

ABU DHABI PETROLEUM COMPANY (ADPC)

PARTNERSHIP: Originally a concession of seventy-five years from 1939, expiring 2014. Includes onshore acreage and a three-mile belt of territorial waters, minus areas relinquished. In 1973 the Government took a 25 per cent share in the operation, and in 1974 negotiated 60 per cent participation.

PRODUCTION (1974): 920,000 b/d.

OWNERSHIP:

Abu Dhabi Government	60%
Abu Dhabi Petroleum Company	40%
British Petroleum	$9\frac{1}{2}$%
Royal Dutch/Shell	$9\frac{1}{2}$%
Compagnie Française des Pétroles (CFP)	$9\frac{1}{2}$%
Near East Development Corpn. (Exxon & Mobil)	$9\frac{1}{2}$%
Participations and Explorations Corpn. (Gulbenkian)	2%

ABU DHABI MARINE AREAS (ADMA)

PARTNERSHIP: Originally a concession held by BP (two-thirds) and CFP (one-third) running from 1953 to 2018, and covering areas of the continental shelf beyond the three-mile limit. In December 1972 BP sold part of its stake to a large group of Japanese industrial companies (OPC). In 1973 the government took a 25 per cent stake, and in 1974 negotiated a 60 per cent participation.

PRODUCTION (1974): 362,000 b/d.

OWNERSHIP:

Abu Dhabi Government	60%
British Petroleum	$14\frac{2}{3}$%
Compagnie Française des Pétroles	$13\frac{1}{3}$%
Overseas Petroleum Corporation (OPC)	12%

ABU DHABI OIL COMPANY (ADOCO)

CONCESSION: Forty-five years from 1967 to 2011. Two offshore areas totalling 4,416 sq. km. relinquished by ADMA. A government participation option was written into the agreement. The company's first field, Mubarraz, was brought on stream in May 1973 at a rate of 20,000 b/d.

PRODUCTION (1974): 14,000 b/d.

OWNERSHIP:

Maruzen	$33\frac{1}{3}$%
Daikyo	$33\frac{1}{3}$%
Nippon Mining	$33\frac{1}{3}$%

ABU AL BU KOOSH GROUP

CONCESSION: Company formed in December 1972 to operate a small portion of LAPCO's Iranian field, Sassan, which extends into Abu Dhabi waters, where it is known as Abu al Bu Koosh. Oil on stream June 1974 at 45,000 b/d.

OWNERSHIP:

Compagnie Française des Pétroles	51%
New England Petroleum (Nepco)	$24\frac{1}{2}$%
Sunningdale	$12\frac{1}{4}$%
Amerada Hess	$12\frac{1}{4}$%

MIDDLE EAST OIL COMPANY (MEOC)

CONCESSION: Granted in 1966. Two areas relinquished by ADPC onshore totalling 15,566 sq. km. Exploration in progress.

OWNERSHIP:

Mitsubishi	100%

PHILLIPS/AGIP

CONCESSION: Granted in 1965. Three areas relinquished by ADPC onshore totalling 9,000 sq. km. Exploration in progress.

OWNERSHIP:

Phillips	$41\frac{2}{3}$%
AGIP S.p.A.	$41\frac{2}{3}$%
Aminoil (R. J. Reynolds)	$16\frac{2}{3}$%

AMERADA GROUP

CONCESSION: Two offshore blocks relinquished by ADMA totalling 3,150 sq. km. Exploration in progress.

OWNERSHIP:

Amerada Hess	$31\frac{1}{2}$%
Pan Ocean	$31\frac{1}{2}$%
Bow Valley Industries	20%
Wington Enterprises	17%

SUNNINGDALE

CONCESSION: Two offshore blocks covering 2,820 sq. km. relinquished by ADMA. Term: eight years for exploration and thirty years for production. Government has a participation offer of 51 per cent. Exploration in progress.

OWNERSHIP:

Sunningdale	100%

Dubai

DUBAI PETROLEUM COMPANY (DPC)

CONCESSION: Sixty years from 1952, expiring 2012. Continental shelf area beyond the three-mile limit. The ownership of the concession, originally held by BP and CFP as Dubai Marine Areas, has changed several times. Under arrangements existing in 1973–75 the concession is held by the companies listed below, with DPC, a wholly owned subsidiary of Conoco, as operator.

PRODUCTION (1974): 242,000 b/d.

OWNERSHIP:

Continental (Conoco)	30%
Deutsche Erdol (Texaco)	10%
Compagnie Française des Pétroles	25%
Hispanoil	25%
Sun	5%
Wintershall	5%

TEXAS GROUP

CONCESSION: Granted 1974 for onshore and offshore areas totalling 1.5 million acres. Exploration in progress.

OWNERSHIP:

Texas Pacific	50%
Union Texas	25%
Louisiana Land and Exploration	10%
Quintana	$7\frac{1}{2}$%
Natomas	$7\frac{1}{2}$%

Sharjah

BUTTES GROUP

CONCESSION: All Gulf coast offshore areas including islands and territorial waters awarded in 1969. Production began in 1974 from a structure within the twelve-mile territorial waters of the island of Abu Musa. Until Sharjah extended its limit this far in 1970, the structure had been outside Abu Musa waters and within the offshore concessions granted by Umm al Qaiwain to Occidental. In December 1971, Iran occupied half the island and announced an agreement with Sharjah whereby Abu Musa came under joint sovereignty. Revenues from the field are now shared equally. Subsequently Sharjah agreed that Umm al Qaiwain should receive 30 per cent of its half share. The Abu Musa field came on stream in August 1974, and up to December production averaged 50,000 b/d.

OWNERSHIP:

Buttes Oil and Gas.	25%
Ashland Oil	25%
Skelly Oil	25%
Kerr-McGee	12½%
Cities Service	10%
Juniper Petroleum	2½%

CRYSTAL GROUP

CONCESSION: Granted 1974, for 2,200 sq. km. onshore. Exploration in progress.

OWNERSHIP:

Crystal Oil	65%
Norsk Hydro	30%
Parisbas Associates	5%

RESERVE OIL

CONCESSION: Granted 1974. Area of 1,500 sq. km. in the Gulf of Oman off Sharjah's east coast. Expenditure obligation $1 million over two years. Exploration in progress.

OWNERSHIP:

Reserve Oil and Gas	100%

Ajman

UNITED REFINING

CONCESSION: Signed 1974. Thirty-five years. Area of 600 sq. km. representing entire onshore and offshore acreage, formerly held by Occidental. In 1975 Asamera took 25 per cent. Exploration in progress.

OWNERSHIP:

United Refining	75%
Asamera	25%

Umm Al Qaiwain

UNITED REFINING

CONCESSION: Signed 1974 for 1,920 sq. km. offshore areas formerly held by Occidental. Exploration in progress.

OWNERSHIP:

United Refining	30%
Asamera	20%
Canadian Superior	25%
Kewanee	10%
Zapata	15%

Ras Al Khaimah

CRYSTAL GROUP

CONCESSION: Originally held by Union Oil of California, which made a non-commercial discovery in deep water offshore, and in 1973 gave up both onshore and offshore rights. Onshore rights of 2,000 sq. km. went to Peninsula Petroleum, which, in 1974, transferred concession to Crystal group. Exploration in progress.

OWNERSHIP:

Crystal Oil	65%
Norsk Hydro	35%

VITOL GROUP

CONCESSION: Originally held by Unocal (*see* above), which, in 1973, gave up its offshore rights to Vitol Exploration of Holland. In 1974 Vitol transferred half of its interest to Weeks Associates. In 1975 a group of European, U.S. and Canadian companies took half of the interests of both Vitol and Weeks. The companies were planning to start drilling in 1975.

OWNERSHIP:

Vitol Exploration	25%
Weeks Associates	25%
European, U.S. Canadian group: SIR, Deutsche Schachtbau, United Refining, Canadian Superior, Asamera, Kewanee	50%

Fujairah

RESERVE OIL

CONCESSION: Signed in 1974 for offshore area totalling 2,300 sq. km. in Gulf of Oman. Expenditure guarantee $1 million over two years. Exploration in progress.

OWNERSHIP:

Reserve Oil and Gas	100%

Oman

PETROLEUM DEVELOPMENT OMAN (PDO)

PARTNERSHIP: Originally a concession of seventy-five years from 1937, expiring 2012. Onshore areas, originally covering northern provinces, now including Dhofar. Government took a 25 per cent share in 1973, and increased this to 60 per cent in 1974.

PRODUCTION (1974): 295,000 b/d.

OWNERSHIP:

Oman Government	60%
Royal Dutch/Shell	34%
Compagnie Française des Pétroles	4%
Participations and Explorations Corpn. (Gulbenkian)	2%

SUN OIL

CONCESSION: Offshore areas of 13,000 sq. km. south of Masirah Island. Awarded to a group composed of Sun Oil, Home Oil of Canada, Canadian Industrial Gas and Oil, Deutsche Schachtbau. Sun Oil is the operator. Area awarded was part of a larger offshore concession awarded to Wendell Phillips and later revoked by the Oman Government in 1971. Exploration in progress.

ELF/SUMITOMO

CONCESSION: Signed 1975 for onshore area of 7,000 sq. km. in Butabul region. Exploration in progress.

OWNERSHIP:

Elf (France)	50%
Sumitomo	50%

Oil Groups Producing and Exploring in North Africa and Syria

Algeria

SONATRACH

With the 51 per cent nationalization of French oil companies in February 1971, Sonatrach, the state oil concern, took full control of the bulk of the country's production, as well as ownership of all pipelines and the country's natural gas production. Sonatrach is responsible for the operation of the Gassi Touil, Rhourde el Baguel, Zarzaitine, Edjeleh and Tinfouye fields amongst others.

COMPAGNIE FRANÇAISE DES PÉTROLES

Total Algérie, CFP's affiliate, operates the Hassi Messaoud North field as 49 per cent minority partner with Sonatrach in Société Algérienne d'Exploration Petrolière (ALREP), in accordance with the nationalization settlement reached in 1971.

ELF-ERAP

Elf-ERAP, the French state oil corporation, as the 49 per cent minority partner of Sonatrach, operates the Hassi Messaoud South field.

GETTY OIL

Alone of the U.S. companies operating in Algeria, which were nationalized in 1967, Getty has been allowed to maintain its interests—5.6 per cent of the Rhourde el Baguel and Messdar fields. It also joined a new exploration venture as a minority partner, on a 49–51 per cent basis, in 1968—but this was abandoned in 1973 after the company had failed to find oil.

Since the beginning of 1973 Algeria has concluded a number of joint exploration agreements with foreign partners on a 51–49 per cent basis for limited periods. Under the pattern established the foreign partners undertake to bear the whole cost of exploration as well as, in several cases, making payments for geophysical work already carried out by Sonatrach. The state company will repay 51 per cent of costs in cash or kind in the event of production. Partners' offtake is subject to standard fiscal obligations.

Sun Oil: Under agreement of March 1973 the company is to explore 4,100 sq. km. in the Ouargla region and 5,375 sq. km. in the Grand Erg Oriental (south of the el Borma field). Sun Oil paid Sonatrach $14 million for work already carried out, and undertook a total exploration commitment of $17.5 million.

Compagnie Française des Pétroles: Under agreement of June 1973 the company is to explore four blocks covering some 12,700 sq. km. Two are in the Ouargla area, and two are south of the Erg Oriental. A minimum exploration expenditure commitment was set at $33.5 million. A subsequent agreement covered the exploration of offshore waters.

Hispanoil: Under agreement of July 1973 Hispanoil is to explore three blocks totalling 10,200 sq. km., two in the Ouargla region and one in the Touggourt region for periods of three and four years respectively. Oil has been discovered in one of these blocks. The company paid Sonatrach $6.5 million for work already carried out, and undertook a minimum expenditure of $18.5 million.

Kopex: Under agreement of October 1973 the Polish state concern undertook to spend $32 million exploring an area of 8,500 sq. km.

Deminex: Under agreement of November 1973 the German group undertook to explore six blocks totalling 28,500 sq. km. over a two to four-year period, with a minimum spending commitment of $103 million and with production sharing in the event of a commercial discovery to last twelve years. Under a subsequent agreement of January 1974 Deminex committed another minimum of $60 million exploring four blocks covering 19,700 sq. km. in the Eastern Sahara.

Elf-ERAP: Under agreement of January 1974 the French state concern undertook to explore three blocks covering an area of 8,450 sq. km. spending a minimum of $31 million. This is in addition to the exploration acreage of 4,325 sq. km. involved in the December 1971 settlement with the Algerian Government.

Standard Oil of Indiana (AMOCO): Under agreement of 1974 the American independent undertook to explore an area of 6,562 sq. km. in the Illizi region south-east of the Hassi Messaoud field, with a minimum spending commitment of $33.5 million.

Tunisia

SOCIÉTÉ ITALO-TUNISIENNE EXPLOITATION PETROLIÈRE

A fifty-fifty partnership between the state and AGIP, the affiliate of the Italian state concern ENI. Oil has been on stream from the El Borma field on the Algerian border since 1966.

PRODUCTION (1974): 40,000 b/d (est.).

AQUITAINE-SEREPT

A seventy-thirty partnership between Aquitaine and SEREPT—Société de Recherches et d'exploitation des Pétroles en Tunisie (56.93% ERAP, 23.87% Tunisian Government, 10.94% CFP, 5.49% REPFRANCE, 2.77% COFIREP). The group operates two small onshore fields, El Douleb and Tamesmida, which were brought on stream in 1968.

PRODUCTION (1974): 9,500 b/d (est.).

COMPAGNIE FRANÇAISE DES PÉTROLES

A fifty-fifty partnership between the state and CFP. Operates the small onshore field, Sidi Litayem which was put into production in 1972.

PRODUCTION (1974): 4,000 b/d (est.).

AQUITAINE—ELF-ERAP

A fifty-fifty partnership between the state and Aquitaine-Elf-ERAP. Production from the Ahstart field off the Gulf of Gabes near the Kerkenna Isles since December 1973.

PRODUCTION (1974): 30,000 b/d (est.).

AGIP-SHELL

Partnership between AGIP, Shell, Amoco (Standard of Indiana), and Total (CFP). Discovered Isis field offshore. Expected on stream in 1976.

Other exploration licences, announced in the past two years, have been awarded to: Shell, Santa Fe, Gulf, A. P. Moeller (Danish), Buttes, Conoco, Panocean-Sunningdale and Bow Valley.

Egypt

AL NASR OILFIELDS

Owned by the Egyptian General Petroleum Corpn. (EGPC). Area of Sinai adjacent to the northern end of the Gulf of Suez. The company operated a group of fields until the 1967 operation by the Israelis, who concentrated their efforts on the Abu Rudais field of COPE (*see* below). Formerly Anglo-Egyptian Oilfields, in which BP and Shell had a 39 per cent holding until their nationalization in 1964.

COMPAGNIE ORIENTALE DES PÉTROLES D'EGYPT (COPE)

Partnership of EGPC and International Egyptian Oil Company (91.73% ENI) on fifty-fifty basis. Area of Sinai coast towards southern end of Gulf of Suez. The company was responsible for operating the fields onshore and offshore. Since 1967 Abu Rudais has been exploited by Israel.

GULF PETROLEUM COMPANY

Fifty-fifty partnership between EGPC and Amoco (Standard of Indiana). Area offshore south-east of Suez. Original exploration permit granted in 1964 for thirty-year concession. Production mainly from El Morgan field.

FAGHUR PETROLEUM COMPANY

Fifty-fifty partnership between EGPC and Amoco. Areas of the Western Desert in the Agila and Rayoum regions. Exploration permit originally granted in 1963 over 6,500 sq. km. territory. Abu Gharadiq and Razzak fields.

WESTERN DESERT PETROLEUM OPERATING COMPANY (WEPCO)

Partnership between EGPC with 50 per cent, Phillips Petroleum with 35 per cent and Hispanoil with 15 per cent. Area of the Western Desert between the Nile and the Libyan border, including coastal waters. Production from El Alamein and Yidma fields.

GENERAL PETROLEUM CORPORATION

Owned by EGPC. Coastal area on the Western side of the Gulf of Suez. A number of small fields including Ras Gharib. In 1974 production from the July field was started at a rate of 30,000 b/d, and output from three smaller structures also began at 7,500 b/d.

DELTA PETROLEUM COMPANY (DELPCO)

Owned by EGPC (50%), International Egyptian Oil Company (25%) and Conoco (25%). Originally exploration over territory covering 24,000 sq. km. in Nile Delta. No oil discoveries, but natural gas has been found and is being exploited.

Since the spring of 1973 Egypt has concluded a number of joint exploration and production agreements with foreign oil companies. Under all but one of them, 40 per cent of output is set to repay the cost of production (though if the market proceeds from this proportion exceed production expenses in any one year the partner will repay the difference in cash). Thereafter production is to be split on an 80–20 or 75–25 basis in favour of the state. However, for most agreements the exact arrangements have not been revealed. Also involved are signature bonuses and exploration commitments from the partners, while EGPC is to bear all taxes and bonuses payable to the state.

Braspetro: 18,000 sq. km. in the Nile Delta, the Eastern Desert and the Western Desert. Exploration commitment by the Brazilian company $14.4 million over eight years. A 50–50 joint venture.

Transworld: 100 sq. km. in the Gulf of Suez offshore. Exploration commitment $5.6 million over four years. 80–20 production sharing.

Transworld International: 7,300 sq. km. in the Gulf of Suez offshore. Exploration commitment $9 million over six years.

Mobil: 6,500 sq. km. offshore the Nile Delta. Exploration commitment $23 million over eight years.

Mobil: 2,250 sq. km. in the Gulf of Suez offshore. Exploration commitment $21.5 million over eight years.

Mobil: 5,300 sq. km. in the Sallum area of the Western Desert. Exploration commitment $8.25 million. 80–20 production sharing.

Exxon: 15,000 sq. km. offshore the Nile Delta. Exploration commitment $50 million over twelve years.

Exxon: 12,000 sq. km. Red Sea. Exploration commitment $48 million over twelve years. 70/80–30/20 production sharing depending on water depth.

Deminex: 2,000 sq. km. in the Gulf of Suez. Exploration commitment $22 million over eight years. Production sharing 80–20.

Conoco: 8,500 sq. km. in the southern part of the Nile Delta. Exploration commitment $23 million over ten years.

Conoco-International Egyptian Oil Company (93% *ENI*): 13,000 sq. km. offshore and the Nile Delta. Exploration commitment $20 million over eight years. Production sharing 75–25 onshore and 70–30 offshore.

Pexpach LVO Corpn.: 3,000 sq. km. in the Western Desert south-west of Cairo. Exploration commitment of $9 million over eight years. Production sharing 75–25 at the outset rising to 80–20 if production rises above 125,000 b/d.

Chevron (Standard Oil of California): 7,000 sq. km. in the Western Desert, north of WEPCO's El Alamein field. Exploration commitment $17 million.

Atlantic Richfield: acreage in the Mersa Matruh area along the Mediterranean in the Western Desert. Exploration commitment $17 million.

Shell: 15,000 sq. km. in the Western Desert. Expenditure commitment $35.5 million over four years.

Shell-British Petroleum-Deminex: 1,500 sq. km. offshore in the north-east of the Gulf of Suez. Expenditure commitment of $12 million over three years.

Amoco: 100 sq. km. of offshore acreage in the Gulf of Suez north of the Ras Ghareb field.

Amoco: 600 sq. km. in the Gulf of Suez. Expenditure commitment $20.5 million over seven and a half years. Production sharing 85–15.

Amoco: 1,350 sq. km. in the Gulf of Suez. Exploration commitment $29 million over seven and a half years.

Union Oil of California: 3,850 sq. km. in the Benas area along the Red Sea coast. Expenditure commitment $30 million over ten years.

Petroswede: 4,000 sq. km. in the Natrun area of the Western Desert. Exploration commitment $10.5 million over eight years. Production sharing 80–20.

Phillips-Hispanoil: 12,000 sq. km. in the Red Sea and the Quseir region onshore. Exploration commitment $45 million over seven to nine years. Production sharing 80–20.

Santa Fe: 4,500 sq. km. east of Cairo. Exploration commitment $18 million over seven years. Production sharing 80–20.

Epedeco: 527 sq. km. west coast Gulf of Suez, near Bakr field. Exploration commitment $15 million over six years. Production sharing 85–15 rising to 87.5–12.5 if production exceeds 50,000 b/d.

Elf-ERAP: 2,200 sq. km. offshore Alexandria. Exploration commitment $28 million over six years. Production sharing 85–15/75–25.

Libya

ESSO STANDARD LIBYA

AREA: Original territory included nine concessions granted in 1955 and 1956 covering 52,000 sq. km., now reduced by relinquishments. Most production comes from the Zelten field from which the 172 km. pipeline runs to the Mersa el Brega terminal on the Gulf of Sirte. Esso accepted the Government's 51 per cent nationalization in the spring of 1974.

PRODUCTION (1974): 183,000 b/d.

OWNERSHIP:
Libyan Government	51%
Exxon	49%

OASIS OIL COMPANY

AREA: Original territory included twelve concession areas granted in 1955 and 1956 covering 150,000 sq. km. subsequently reduced by relinquishments. Production comes from the Dhara, Defa, Bahi, Waha, Samah and Zaggut fields connected to the terminal at Es Sidr. Original concessions held by Continental, Marathon and Amerada Hess, which sold half its share to Shell. The three U.S. independents accepted Libya's 51 per cent nationalization, but Shell did not—losing its stake by nationalization in March 1974.

PRODUCTION (1974): 550,000 b/d.

OWNERSHIP:
Libyan Government	$59\frac{1}{8}$%
Continental	$16\frac{1}{8}$%
Marathon	$16\frac{1}{8}$%
Amerada Hess	$8\frac{1}{8}$%

OCCIDENTAL PETROLEUM

AREA: The Sirte Basin where the company made discoveries in concessions, granted in 1966, which had previously been relinquished by another company. Fields are connected to the Zuetina terminal by a 217 km. pipeline.

PRODUCTION (1974): 321,000 b/d.

OWNERSHIP:
Libyan Government	51%
Occidental	49%

ARABIAN GULF EXPLORATION COMPANY

AREA: South-east Cyrenaica deep in the desert. Production from the Sarir field (the biggest in Libya) which was discovered and developed by the Bunker Hunt-British Petroleum fifty-fifty partnership in a concession granted in 1957. The BP interest was nationalized in December 1971 and Bunker Hunt in June 1973. The Sarir field, whose crude has a remarkably high wax content and is difficult to produce, is now run by AGEC, a subsidiary of the National Oil Company.

PRODUCTION (1974): 87,000 b/d. (1973): 248,000 b/d).

OWNERSHIP:
Libyan Government	100%

AMERICAN OVERSEAS PETROLEUM COMPANY (AMOSEAS)

AREA: Nine concessions granted in 1956, 1959 and 1966 totalling 60,000 sq. km., subsequently reduced by relinquishments. The Beda and Nafoora fields connect separately with the Mobil pipeline systems which have their terminal at Ras Lanuf. The owners of Amoseas, Texaco and Standard Oil of California, were nationalized in February 1974 following their refusal to accept the Government's 51 per cent take-over measure. Fields now run by NOC.

PRODUCTION (1974): 93,000 b/d.

OWNERSHIP:
Libyan Government	100%

AGIP-NOC

AREA: Eastern Cyrenaica towards the Egyptian border. Fifty-fifty partnership between AGIP and the state dating from 1969. Production from the Abu Tiffel field is pumped through a 110 km. spur line to the Occidental system.

PRODUCTION (1974): 107,000 b/d.

OWNERSHIP:
Libyan Government	50%
AGIP	50%

MOBIL-GELSENBERG

AREA: Eleven concessions granted in 1956 and 1957 totalling 47,000 sq. km. Production mainly from the Hofra field, which is linked by a 138 km. pipeline to the Ras Lanuf terminal. A second pipeline carries the oil of the Amal field to the same outlet. Gelsenberg agreed to a 51 per cent state take-over in September 1973, and Mobil in April 1974.

PRODUCTION (1974): 104,000 b/d.

OWNERSHIP:
Libyan Government	51%
Mobil	$31\frac{17}{20}$%
Gelsenberg	$17\frac{3}{20}$%

ESSO SIRTE

AREA: Two concession areas in Sirte basin granted in 1955. Production is from the Raguba field, which is connected to Esso's pipeline to Mersa el Brega by a 90 km. spur. Atlantic Richfield's stake in the operation was nationalized in February 1974 because of its refusal to accept the government's 51 per cent take-over.

PRODUCTION (1974): 27,000 b/d.

OWNERSHIP:
Libyan Government	63%
Exxon	$24\frac{1}{2}$%
W. R. Grace	$12\frac{1}{2}$%

AQUITAINE GROUP

AREA: Four concessions granted in 1968, one neighbouring the Sorite Basin and three in Western Libya. The field is operated by Aquitaine, an affiliate of CFP.

PRODUCTION (1974): 9,000 b/d.

OWNERSHIP:
Aquitaine	28%
Hispanoil	42%
Murphy Oil	12%
Elf-ERAP	14%

AMOCO LIBYA

AREA: Originally six areas totalling 76,000 sq. km., now reduced by relinquishments to four areas totalling 2,000 sq. km.

PRODUCTION (1974): 5,500 b/d.

OWNERSHIP:

Amoco (Standard Oil of Indiana) . . . 100%

Having established the principle of 51 per cent majority participation, the Libyan Government in 1974 began entering into production sharing agreements with foreign concerns, which have set the pattern for joint ventures in the future with the National Oil Company, which holds all acreage relinquished from the original concessions of the 1950s and 1960s. Under the production sharing agreements the foreign companies undertake expenditure commitments over a set period for exploration—the cost of which they bear in full. In the event of commercial discoveries output is to be split 85–15 or 81–19 in favour of the state. The government is to provide the funds for development, which the partner repays on easy terms. The latter will not be liable to taxation on their share of the agreement.

NOC-Occidental: Nineteen blocks covering 49,000 sq. km. in the Sirte basin, the Jebel Akhdar, east of Benghazi, and the Fezzan district in the south-west of the country. Expenditure commitment $90 million over five years. Production sharing 81–19.

NOC-AGIP: Two offshore blocks totalling 44,000 sq. km., one of which is west of Tripoli bordering Tunisian waters; and two onshore blocks of 100,000 sq. km. in the west of the country—one in the Sirte basin and the other in the Kufra area. Expenditure commitment $70 million over five years. Production sharing 85–15.

NOC-Mobil: Area of 30,000 sq. km. including six onshore blocks in the Sirte basin and one onshore in the Gadames basin, as well as one deep-water offshore area in the west and another offshore area in the east. Expenditure commitment $70 million over six years. Production sharing 85–15 offshore, and 81–19 onshore.

NOC-Exxon: Unspecified acreage onshore and offshore. Expenditure commitment $90 million over five years. Production sharing 85–15 offshore, and 81–19 onshore.

NOC-CFP: Areas and production split unspecified. Expenditure commitment $90 million over five years.

NOC-Aquitaine-Elf: Agreement changed arrangements with affiliates of CFP and ERAP for one block offshore granted in 1968 on old style concessionary terms, and three others in east and central Libya granted in the same year on a joint venture basis. Expenditure commitment $45 million. The French companies have also undertaken to put into operation two fields hitherto considered uncommercial.

NOC-Petrobras: Two areas totalling 30,000 sq. km. in the Sirte basin and the Marzuq basin. Expenditure commitment $35 million over five years. Production sharing 85–15. If no oil is found within five years, Petrobras, under a thirty-year agreement, has the right to negotiate another area.

Syria

From 1964 to 1975 all oil rights were vested exclusively in the hands of government agencies under the overall control of the General Petroleum Authority. The main oil fields are at Suweidiya, Rumelan and Karatchuk in the extreme north-east of the country, where the aim is to increase production to 300,000 b/d in 1975. The GPA has been assisted by foreign expertise under contract. Following the nationalization of the Iraq Petroleum Company in 1972, Syria took over the company's installations in the country—in particular the pipeline to the Mediterranean. Transit dues were subsequently negotiated with Iraq. In 1975, in a major reversal of its previous policy, the government decided that it would in future allow in foreign companies on a production sharing basis, similar to that applied by Egypt and Libya.

Tripco Petroleum: Under agreement of March 1975, 6,000 sq. km. of continental shelf. Production sharing 80–20 rising to 85–15 if production exceeds 200,000 b/d.

Lebanon

Soon after the conclusion of the Syria-Tripco agreement the Lebanese Government concluded a similar agreement with Tripco.

Tripco Petroleum: Under agreement of April 1975, offshore areas between Beirut and Syrian border. Production sharing 80–20, rising to 85–15 if production exceeds 200,000 b/d.

The Arms Trade with the Middle East and North Africa

Hanns Maull

The Middle East is today—judging by the percentage share of military expenditure in Gross Domestic Products—the most highly militarized area in the world. It is also one of the areas most plagued by military conflict and war.

There are two geographical areas in the Middle East and North Africa which are at the centre of political and military conflict in this region: Palestine and the Persian Gulf. In Palestine, the issue is the struggle between Jewish and Arab (Palestinian) nationalism over the same territory; in the Persian Gulf, there are various rivalries, conflicts and tensions which all appear at least connected with the main source of wealth in this zone: oil. Both areas have also seen an unparalleled military build-up in two major arms races: the Arab-Israeli arms race, dominated by Israel, Egypt and Syria, but also including other countries; and the arms race in the Persian Gulf in which Iran, Saudi Arabia and Iraq are the main participants. Here, as well, the arms race has shown a tendency to spill over to other countries in the area. There is also a certain link between the two zones: the financial, military and above all the political support (in the form of the oil weapon) which the Arab Gulf producers gave to the countries fighting against Israel is clear evidence of this now strongly established connection between the Persian Gulf and the Arab-Israeli zone.

However, the past year has seen a distinct movement towards greater co-operation in the Persian Gulf, especially among the three major powers Iran, Iraq and Saudi Arabia: Iran and Iraq concluded a comprehensive agreement to settle the various disputed issues between them, and a similar compromise was negotiated between Saudi Arabia and Iraq with regard to the territorial dispute over the neutral zone between the two states. While the momentum of the negotiation process in the Arab-Israeli conflict has slackened somewhat in 1974/75, the opportunity for a political solution still exists. These hopeful signs are, however, not yet reflected in a slow-down in the military build-up in both areas, and while the possibility of open military conflicts in the Gulf seems at present remote, another war between Israel and the Arabs cannot be excluded.

THE NATURE OF THE ARMS RACES

Arms races tend to develop quantitative and qualitative aspects, and both are strongly at work in the Middle Eastern arms races. The *quantitative* aspect is apparent in the rapid growth of the armed forces (in terms of manpower, tanks, aircraft, artillery etc.). In the 1967 war, Israel could muster some 1,050 tanks and 290 combat aircraft, while Egypt and Syria together had some 1,650 tanks and 550 aircraft. In 1974, two bitter and costly wars later, the military power of Israel stood at 2,260 tanks and 437 combat aircraft, while Egypt and Syria together possessed 3,870 tanks and 820 combat aircraft. The *qualitative* aspect is reflected by the rapid growth in destructive power of each weapon system and the deployment of totally new systems which replace old, outdated systems. This qualitative change means that less complex and sophisticated weapons are replaced by more sophisticated and therefore more expensive weapons. Impressive as the quantitative arms build-up in the Middle East may be, it is surpassed by the speed of qualitative changes. The gap between the arms technology of the Great Powers and the Middle Eastern countries has been gradually closed, with important thresholds being the deployment of supersonic jet fighters (between 1956 and 1967) and the large-scale introduction of missiles and electronic warfare (between 1970 and 1973). As far as conventional warfare is concerned, the main participants in the two Middle Eastern arms races now command weapon systems which are the most modern available for the Great Powers themselves; a development strongly underlined by American commitments to supply Iran with advanced Grumman F-14 *Tomcat* fighters and by the appearance of the Soviet counterpart to this aircraft, the MiG-23, in Iraq, Syria and Egypt. This means that both weapon systems will have arrived in the Middle East within two years of being deployed by the Superpowers themselves. Besides, Israel has sought up to 48 F-15 fighters from the United States—the final approval by Washington, however, is still outstanding. The qualitative arms race also took a new turn in the last year in the area of surface-to-surface missiles: Israel received the American *Lance* missile (with a range of 70 miles), while both Egypt and Syria have been supplied by the Soviet Union with *Frog* (range: 30 miles) and *Scud* missiles (range: 185 miles). Both the *Lance* and the *Scud* are thought to be capable of delivering nuclear warheads, and this has once more focused attention on the last remaining qualitative difference between Middle Eastern and Superpower weapon systems: the nuclear threshold. While Israel certainly has had a nuclear option for some years, and would be capable of assembling nuclear warheads within a relatively short period, should she desire to do so, the growing interest of other Middle Eastern countries in nuclear technology and reactors poses the question whether some of these countries might also eventually try to develop nuclear weapons. Nuclear reactors produce plutonium which, after separation and enrichment, could be used to assemble atomic warheads. Countries to receive reactors and/or to develop some form of co-operation with nuclear powers or countries with considerable know-how and capabilities in nuclear technology (threshold powers such as Argentina or Germany) include at present Egypt, Iran, Iraq, Saudi Arabia and Libya. It has been estimated that Iran and possibly also Egypt could in theory become nuclear powers in about ten years. Iran, however, has ratified the Non-Proliferation Treaty and repeatedly denied any intention to "go nuclear", while Egypt has signed, but not ratified the Treaty.

Arms races of such dimensions in a third world area necessarily mean heavy reliance on imported weapons. True, Iran and Egypt both have indigenous arms industries producing small arms and ammunition. Recently, several Arab countries have launched a new effort to develop an indigenous arms industry in a joint venture, using the oil revenues of Saudi Arabia, Qatar and the United Arab Emirates and the existing know-how in Egypt. In this connection, Egypt reached an agreement to build British *Lynx* helicopters and *Hawk* aircraft under licence. But only Israel's arms industry is of military significance, and even she has to rely heavily on arms imports.* Table 1 shows the amount of arms imports by Middle Eastern countries and (by comparison with *total* expenditure on arms imports from 1961 to 1971) the financial implications of quantitatively and qualitatively rapidly expanding arms races.

THE MOTIVES FOR THE ARMS RACES

Arms races (a competitive military build-up) are predominantly fuelled by a feeling of insecurity and a (real or imagined) threat to vital foreign policy objectives among the participants. There are, however, other factors which make for higher military expenditures or facilitate military build-ups. Generally speaking, external objectives include not only the obvious one—military forces sufficient to guarantee the security of the state against a threat from outside. They may also include the intention to expand the influence of the state beyond its boundaries by the explicit or implicit threat and the application of force to achieve certain objectives. Military power also serves as a symbol of national independence and status. Prestige expenditure like Abu Dhabi's small airforce of Mirage 5 fighters (at present manned and serviced by Pakistani personnel) or Libya's air defence system hardly have any military function but serve mainly as show-pieces in parades.

Another set of motives for increasing military strength is internal: some of the Middle Eastern and

North African régimes are politically unstable and still have to enforce the central power of the Government against the return or threat of tribal and minority challenges. Oman is a typical example of a state whose arms purchases are designed to resist an internal threat, the rebellion in Dhofar (*see* table).

Many Middle Eastern and North African countries are ruled by military régimes or governments whose main source of support is the armed forces. Consequently, the armed forces form an influential pressure group, whose demands have to be taken into account. Since the rulers of these countries depend on the loyalty of the army they will try to keep this by dispensing various benefits and privileges. A good example here is Libya: in the last year of its existence, the monarchy embarked on a modernization programme for the armed forces in order to appease the growing discontent in the officer corps; after the coup, military expenditure rose dramatically, and it is difficult to say whether the Libyan interest in the Arab-Israeli conflict under the new leadership in fact caused this increase or was a justification for it.

These external and internal factors fuel the demand for higher military expenditure and consequently for increased arms imports. The various mechanisms of arms races (worst-case assumptions of defence planners and the trend towards over-insurance: Israel, for instance, will plan for a contingency of a large Arab coalition of armed forces and attempt to provide forces appropriate to it while Egypt might try to achieve parity with Israel by itself) actually cause these factors to interlock so that internally motivated arms purchases might induce the opponent to increase his force level as well.

Of crucial importance for the actual development of the arms race are factors of availability—the resources available for military expenditure, and the interest of Great Powers in particular countries or groups. High oil revenues enable the oil producers (and other Arab countries as well) to buy weapons, and the involvement of the United States and the Soviet Union in the Arab-Israeli zone and in the Persian Gulf allowed countries in the region to receive weapons even without the financial burden this would normally constitute (reduced or suspended payment, favourable conditions for repayment).

Let us now take a closer look at some countries. In the Arab-Israeli zone, one could draw a distinction between defensive and offensive objectives of a military build-up. Israel relies on military strength to deter any attack on its territory and to induce the Arabs to comply with its demands—e.g. in reprisal attacks against the Lebanon to force the suppression of Palestinian raids from her territory, or in the threat to intervene in the Jordanian civil war in 1970. Egypt and Syria, on the other hand, relied on an offensive military strategy to break the stalemate in the Arab-Israeli conflict. Though in the aftermath of the October war the emphasis has shifted away from an exclusively military strategy, military power will continue to play an important role in the present situation as a bargaining card and a means to keep momentum in the negotiating process.

---

* Today, Israel produces two light transport airplanes, the *Arava* and the *Westwind*, and recently also started production of a new fighter, *Kfir* (based on French *Mirage* design and an American engine, the General Electric J-79) in addition to the *Barak*, another indigenous, less powerful Israeli version of the *Mirage* which had been already used in combat in 1973. Israel also manufactures air-to-air missiles (*Shafir*) and ship-to-ship missiles (*Gabriel*) as well as missile boats and (under concession) the Sabra medium tank. Egypt's plans to develop military aircraft and ground-to-ground missiles did not pass the prototype stage, apart from the jet trainer HA-200 (*al-Kahira*) produced under license from Spain.

THE PERSIAN GULF

While the Arab-Israeli conflict is essentially clear-cut, the Persian Gulf is characterized by a much more complex structure of varied, partly overlapping tensions. The most important country at the moment is Iran—which can also be considered the initiator of the present Gulf arms race. The country now appears about to move into a new stage of strategic objectives. In recent years, Iran's main concern was the establishment of a dominating influence in the Persian Gulf as a means to secure her vital trade routes. These trade routes were in the eyes of Teheran potentially threatened by countries and forces hostile to Iran and possibly through a Soviet co-ordination of these hostile forces. Iran's suspicion of Soviet "encirclement" has been aggravated by the Soviet-Iraqi and Soviet-Indian treaties, by Soviet support for the rebellion in Oman and the growing naval presence of Russian vessels in the Indian Ocean. Iraq was viewed in Teheran as the main opponent of Persian hegemony in the Gulf; the two states were at loggerheads over a wide range of conflicting claims and issues such as the mutual support for dissident movements in Kurdistan (supported by Iran with arms, troops and logistics) and Arabistan/Khuzistan (which Iraq regarded as part of the Arab nation); disputed demarcation lines off-shore; and the shipping rights in the Shatt al-Arab waterway. Iraq rejected the Iranian bid for dominance in the Gulf area and tried to match Teheran's growing military power through a parallel build-up. Whether the recent agreement between the two governments will have a lasting impact on this major source of the Persian Gulf arms race remains to be seen.

Another potential danger for Iran lies in the radical threat to the conservative régimes on the opposite shore of the Gulf. The Shah is trying to prevent the spread of such régimes in the sheikhdoms through military support for the Sultan of Oman in his struggle against the PFLO. Besides, military co-operation with Oman enables Teheran to exert virtual control over both sides of the Strait of Hormuz, strategically the most sensitive point in the Gulf. It is not surprising, therefore, that the two states have developed a close alliance.

Iran's military presence in Oman indicates that the Shah regards the protection of the present political order on the western shore of the Gulf as a vital aspect of Iranian security, and with large helicopter and hovercraft fleets the Persian armed forces have deliberately developed the potential to intervene on the other side of the Gulf, especially against insurgency-type challenges.

The agreement between Baghdad and Teheran appears to mark Iraqi acceptance of Iranian dominance in the Gulf—a dominance founded on clear and growing military superiority. It was, however, not only Baghdad which tried to challenge the Iranian military build-up by parallel measures of her own: Saudi Arabia has also embarked on a massive programme of expansion and modernization of her armed forces. The external motivations for this programme are presumably a certain distrust of Iranian intentions as well as fear of the radical régime in Baghdad and the ambition to play an even more prominent role in Middle Eastern affairs.

Iran and Saudi Arabia have a common interest in preserving the present situation in the Persian Gulf, and they are united in their hostility to radical forces such as the PFLO and South Yemen. Both states have a long tradition as American allies, and the strategic importance of both Iran and Saudi Arabia has grown considerably in recent years. For both countries, vastly increased oil revenues provide the necessary means for their military ambitions. But in spite of the continuing amassment of military power, both governments have shown their desire to reduce the likelihood of conflict in the Middle East by launching diplomatic offensives to settle regional disputes. So, Saudi Arabia mediated between Iraq and Syria, and Iraq and Kuwait, and Iran further improved her relations with Arab states not only in the Gulf area, but also in the Mediterranean.

Since late 1972, Iran has also shown growing interest in the Indian Ocean. Plans to quadruple the strength of the Iranian navy; the purchase of highly sophisticated U.S. destroyers and of British aircraft carriers, and of advanced aircraft and air tankers; and finally the construction of the large Chah Bahar naval and air base on the shore of the Indian Ocean underline Iranian ambitions. Presumably, the role of a regional power to which Iran aspires also serves a useful internal purpose: it satisfies nationalist aspirations and helps to divert the attention of the population.

Apart from the three major powers in the Gulf, the arms race in the Gulf has also affected the smaller states. As a result of border skirmishes between Iraqi and Kuwaiti troops, Kuwait has in recent years embarked on a massive rearmament programme, and the smaller sheikhdoms have also stepped up their purchases of arms (*see* table 1).

THE EFFECT OF INCREASED ARMS

The vast amount of highly sophisticated weapons flowing into the Middle East and North Africa often transcends the capacity of the armed forces to absorb these weapons. Highly skilled personnel are needed to man and to maintain them—but in most countries this is a valuable and desperately scarce resource. Long training periods will be needed to operate those weapons effectively, and training can to a large extent only be provided by foreigners. A country then has to send either a great number of soldiers abroad or alternatively provide for training teams. Already, foreign military advisors can be found in many Middle Eastern and North African countries (Americans in Saudi Arabia and Iran, Russians in Syria, Indians in Iraq, Pakistanis in Abu Dhabi and Libya).

These technical problems will prove a formidable and sometimes extremely difficult barrier on the way towards a highly effective military force. To overcome this barrier will mean a heavy drain on precious and scarce resources in terms of manpower and for the

Table 1

MAJOR ARMS DEALS, JULY 1974–MAY 1975

Recipient	Value of Total Arms Imports 1961–71 (million current U.S. $)	Supplier Approx. Date of Agreement	Name of System	Approx. Quantity	Comments
Egypt	2,197	France, late '74	*Mirage* III-E	38	Fighter; 3 delivered late 1974; paid by Saudi Arabia
		France, Jan. '75	*Mirage* F-1C/E (M53)	44	Fighter bomber; delivery from 1978
			AMX-30, add. arms	n.a.	Medium tank; value of total deal est. at $2,300 million
		France/U.K., n.a.	SA-341 *Gazelle*	42	Transport helicopter
		U.K., 1975	BAC *Lightning*	n.a.	Interceptor; paid by Saudi Arabia
		U.S.S.R., late '74	MiG 23	50	Fighter
Israel	936	U.S.A., Sept. '74	F-4 *Phantom*	50	Fighter; delivery from 1975
			M-60	200	Main battle tank
		U.S.A., Nov. '74	*Lance*	110	Surface-to-surface missile; range 70 miles; delivery from 1974
		U.S.A., Nov. '74	TOW/*Redeye*/Strike	n.a.	Anti-tank missile, delivered 1974/infra-red guided air-to-air missile/radar-guided air-to-surface missile
		U.K., 1974	*Centurion*	400	Medium tank; to be modernized in Israel; value £30 million; delivered 1974–75
Jordan	289	U.S.A./Iran	F-5E *Tiger II*	24	Fighter; transferred from Iran early 1975 as gift
		U.S.A., May '75	Air defence system (radar, AA guns, HAWK surface-to-air missiles)		Value $350 million; delivery to start Sept. 1975; held up by U.S. Congress.
Syria	443	U.S.S.R., n.a.	MiG 23	45	Fighter
			SU-7	25	Fighter
			Mi-5	n.a.	Helicopter
			OSA class patrol boat	3	Fast patrol boat, armed with ship-ship missiles
Iran	1,091	U.S.A., mid-'74	F-33C *Bonanza*	19	Trainer; delivery 1975; in addition to previous orders
		U.S.A., Aug. '74	DD 963 *Spruance* class	6	Destroyer, each $110 million
		U.S.A., Oct. '74	F-4E *Phantom*	36	Fighter
		U.S.A., 1974	MK-105	n.a.	Helicopter-towed mine counter-system; value $6 million
		U.S.A., 1974	Chukar 11 & Shelduck	n.a.	Target drones; value $8.4 million
		U.S.A., 1974	Boeing 707 CJ9C	6	Air refueller; value $103 million
		U.S.A., 1975	Complete intelligence system (computer, aircraft, radar, possibly satellite)	1	Value $500 million; delivery over 5–10 years
		U.S.A., n.a.	S-65A/CH 53	6	Heavy assault helicopter; delivery 1976

[continued on next page

MAJOR ARMS DEALS—*continued*]

RECIPIENT	VALUE OF TOTAL ARMS IMPORTS 1961–71 (million current U.S.$)	SUPPLIER APPROX. DATE OF AGREEMENT	NAME OF SYSTEM	APPROX. QUANTITY	COMMENTS
Iran		France, '74–75	*La Combattante II*	18	Fast patrol boat armed with *Exocet* and *Harpoon* missiles; 3 orders
		U.K., Sept. '74	BAC *Rapier, Blindfire*	n.a.	Surface-to-air missile system; Iranian share in development cost
		U.K., May '75	*Chieftain*	800	Main battle tank; in addition to previous order of 800; est. value $1,000 million
		U.K., 1975	Through-deck cruiser	2	Small aircraft carrier
			Harrier	n.a.	Vertical take-off fighters; total value £550 million
Iraq	760	France, 1974	*Alouette* III	31	Helicopter, armed with SS.11 anti-tank missile
		U.K., 1974	Landrover	1,000 }	Value £55 million
			Range Rover	300 }	
		U.S.S.R., 1974	Tu-22	n.a.	Bomber; delivered 1974
			MiG 23	n.a.	Fighter; delivered 1974
			OSA class patrol boat	2	Fast patrol boats armed with *Styx* ship-ship missiles; delivered 1974.
Kuwait	46	U.S.A., mid-'74	A-4 *Skyhawk*	36	Fighter; delivery 1975–76; value $250 million
		U.S.A., Sept. '74	Improved *Hawk*	n.a.	Surface-to-air missile; value $125 million
		Singapore, n.a.	Fast patrol boat	1	Patrol
			Landing craft	1	Supply; total value £350,000
Oman	n.a.	U.K., 1974	Fast patrol boat	4	Value £6 million
		U.K., 1974	Britten-Norman *Defender*	8	Counter-insurgency aircraft; delivered 1974; value £1 million
		U.K., 1974	BAC *Rapier*	28	Surface-to-air missile system; value of deal £47 million
		U.K., 1974	*Saladin*	40	Armoured cars; delivered 1974
		U.K., 1974	*Saladin*	28	Gift from Abu Dhabi
		U.K./France, 9/74	*Jaguar*	12	Fighter, ground attack; value of deal £44 million
		Netherlands, 1974	Minesweepers	2	Refitted, for coastal patrol; value £665,000
		Italy, 1974	AB 205A	10 }	Helicopters
			AB 214A	5 }	
Qatar	n.a.	France/U.K., 1974	SA-341 *Gazelle*	2	Transport helicopter
		U.K., 1974	Westland *Commando*	2	Transport helicopter
		Brazil, 1974	EE-9 *Cascavel*	20	Armoured cars
Saudi Arabia	322	U.S.A., 1974	Development of Navy (incl. 26 destroyer, missile boats)		Value of deal $850 million–1.5 billion
		U.S.A., Jan. '75	Armoured personnel carriers	250 }	Equipment and training for National Guard; value of total deal $828 million
			M-60 A1 medium tank	n.a. }	
			Anti-tank missiles, air-to-surface missiles, artillery	n.a. }	
		U.S.A., Jan. '75	F-5E *Tiger II*	60 }	Fighter/trainer; delivery 1976; value $750 million
			F-5F	}	

[*continued on next page*

MAJOR ARMS DEALS—*continued*)

RECIPIENT	VALUE OF TOTAL ARMS IMPORTS 1961–71 (million current U.S. $)	SUPPLIER APPROX. DATE OF AGREEMENT	NAME OF SYSTEM	APPROX. QUANTITY	COMMENTS
Saudi Arabia		France, Dec. '74	AMX-30	200	Medium tank
			AMX-10	250	Light tank
			Crotale	n.a.	Surface-to-air missile; value of deal $800 million; delivery 1975–79
		Pakistan, n.a.	Warships	8	
U.A.E.	—	U.S.A., 1974	Bell 205A	4	Anti-tank helicopter; delivery mid-1975
		U.K., 1974	BAC *Rapier*	n.a.	Surface-to-air missile system; value £35 million
		Italy, 1974	MB-326K	3	Counter-insurgency/trainer aircraft; delivery 1974–75
			MB-326L	1	
Libya	210	France, 1974	*Mirage* F-1	38	Fighter
			SS.11/12	n.a.	Anti-tank missile
			SFCN-PR 72	n.a.	Fast patrol boat
		U.S.S.R., May '75	MiG 23	29	Fighter
			Tu-22 (?)	n.a.	Bomber
			SAM; armoured personnel carriers	n.a.	Surface-to-air missiles; value est. at $800 million
		Italy, April '75	*Corvette*	4	Fast patrol boat
Morocco	125	France/U.K., n.a.	SA-330E *Puma*	40	Helicopters
		Italy, n.a.	C-119 *Fairchild*	6	Transport aircraft; delivery 1974
		U.S.A., 1975	AA guns	n.a.	
			Armoured personnel carriers	334	Total value $145 million
			Lorries	753	
Tunisia	n.a.	U.S.A., n.a.	F-5 *Tiger* II	12	Fighter; value $53.6 million
		Italy, n.a.	5F-260W *Warrior*	12	Trainer; delivery 1974–75; value $2.4 million

Sources: IISS, SIPRI, *Middle East Economic Digest*, Newspaper reports.

Table 2

CUMULATIVE VALUE OF ARMS TRADE TO THE MIDDLE EAST AND NORTH AFRICA
BY MAJOR SUPPLIERS, 1961–71
(million current U.S. $)

	TOTAL	U.S.A.	U.S.S.R.	FRANCE	U.K.
Algeria	311	negligible	286	8	2
Egypt	2,197	negligible	2,080	—	—
Iran	1,091	733	235	2	69
Iraq	760	14	632	5	20
Israel	936	694	—	96	68
Jordan	289	221	—	3	47
Kuwait	46	2	negligible	—	38
Lebanon . . .	70	6	2	54	3
Libya	210	50	60	47	42
Morocco . . .	125	50	10	29	negligible
Saudi Arabia . . .	322	172	—	26	84
Syria	443	—	388	—	—
Tunisia	46	34	—	7	1
Yemen A.R. . . .	86	negligible	77	—	—
Yemen P.D.R. . .	17	—	15	—	1

poor countries also in terms of capital. But the influx of modern weapons is also likely to have social and political consequences: It will strengthen the power of the military elites and increase their size. The officer classes in the Middle East and North Africa in many countries have proved themselves highly politicized, and their increased power could be accompanied by or lead to more involvement in politics.

THE ARMS SUPPLIERS

The international arms trade has become a competitive business; for some countries, one could talk about a buyers' market. As table 1 shows, some countries have successfully attempted some degree of diversification in their sources of arms supply. In 1974, the most important suppliers of arms to the Middle East and North Africa were the U.S.S.R., the United States, Great Britain and France. Other developed countries also exported weapons into this region, but on a lower scale. Table 2 gives a survey of the main suppliers of each country during the decade 1961 to 1971.

Two distinct sets of objectives and motivations can be discerned which induce the industrialized countries to encourage and even actively promote arms exports into the area: political and economic. The political objectives in arms sales to the third world aim at gaining influence in the importing country and in the area. Arms exports can be used to strengthen a ruling group vis-à-vis external or internal threats, and if an exporting and importing country pursue similar foreign policy objectives in the area the latter can fulfill certain strategic functions which otherwise might require some form of military presence of the supplier himself. The supplier might also try to gain access to ports and receive naval and air facilities in exchange for arms sales. The leverage obtained by the exporting country consists basically of two factors: First, the buyer becomes dependent on a continuous flow of spares and the threat to cut this flow and thereby eventually reduce the military strength of the importing country might provide some influence on his behaviour. Second, and more important, sophisticated weapon systems require large-scale training and assistance by the exporting countries which allows the seller to gain access to the officer corps and therefore to one very influential group within the political framework of most importing countries. Political objectives have been predominant in the arms supply policies of the Superpowers, the U.S. and the U.S.S.R., and also China, and often arms deals are concluded to pre-empt arms sales by the rival Superpower (this gives the importing country some leverage to press for new supplies). The most recent example of such a politically-motivated arms supply strategy appears to be behind the U.S. military assistance agreement negotiated and concluded with Saudi Arabia. U.S-Saudi deals comprise not only considerable arms sales but also demonstrate the desire to back up the present régime by providing for arms deliveries and training for the National Guard, a military body which predominantly serves to protect the present régime

against internal threats and to guard oil installations. It is on the National Guard the monarchy relies domestically, rather than on the army which in the past was considered to have only limited reliability. Attempts to gain political influence through arms sales, however, are not necessarily limited to states— as Soviet support for the PLO and the PFLO has demonstrated.

Unlike the Superpowers, the arms export policies of France and Britain and other suppliers are dominated by economic considerations—considerations which are of growing importance even for the U.S.A. and the Soviet Union (for the U.S.S.R., weapons can either be bartered for oil or—if sold—contribute welcome foreign exchange earnings). For Western countries, including the United States, the prevailing economic reason for arms exports is its positive impact on the balance of payments, which the recent oil price increases have worsened for almost all Western industrialized countries. Arms sales help to offset the balance of payments deficits vis-à-vis oil exporting countries either directly (if oil producers and arms importers are identical) or indirectly (through increased export earnings).

Arms exports, however, are also vital for the economic viability of sophisticated arms industries in smaller industrialized countries such as France and Britain. Advanced weapon systems, with their enormous research and development costs, can hardly be produced on an economic scale on the basis of the comparatively small domestic military requirements of these countries: the costs would be prohibitive. Exports enable longer production runs, which reduce the cost per unit, and they can also make up for fluctuations in domestic demand which would otherwise have to be rescheduled according to economic rather than military requirements (this is done by Sweden, for example). Exports mean that labour and capital can be kept fully employed. It is not surprising, therefore, that the Governments of both Britain and France actively support and encourage arms exports by providing official sales' assistance and credit facilities and also design their own military requirements partly with the export potential of certain weapon systems in mind.

There is, however, also a restrictive side to arms exports, stemming in principle from the desire of exporting countries not to become unintentionally involved in local or international conflicts through their role as arms suppliers. All suppliers have some form of governmental say in the export decisions and licensing systems, and some of them have made exports conditional upon certain requisites, e.g. not to re-sell the weapons. There have also been repeated attempts to control the flow of arms in crisis areas by embargoes against certain countries or regions (such as the British embargo on combatant states in the Middle East war in 1973, which was lifted in January 1974). The most comprehensive attempt to control and limit the arms trade with the Middle East was the Tripartite Declaration of the U.S., France and Britain in 1950 which broke down with large-scale French sales to Israel and the appearance of the Soviet Union as arms supplier for Egypt in 1955.

The Suez Canal

The Suez Canal joins the Mediterranean and Red Seas between Port Said and Suez, in Egypt. It was closed during the Arab-Israeli war of June 1967 and was not re-opened until June 5th, 1975. Between June 1967 and October 1973 the canal formed the demarcation line between Egypt and the Israeli-occupied Sinai peninsula. After the disengagement of forces agreement which followed the October 1973 Arab-Israeli war, Israeli forces withdrew to a line about 13 miles east of the canal. After 13 months of clearing the canal of obstacles, it was re-opened by President Sadat on June 5th, 1975. Transit rates were fixed at a level which represented an increase of more than 90 per cent on the rates before the closure in June 1967.

PRINCIPAL FACTS

Length: 107 miles including approach fairways.

Maximum Depth: 50 ft.

Maximum Width: 660 ft.

Minimum Width: 600 ft.

Transit Time: Average transit time was fifteen hours in 1967.

CHRONOLOGY

1854 Ferdinand de Lesseps granted building concession.

1859 Excavation began.

1869 Canal opened.

1875 Ismail Pasha of Egypt sold his shares in the French Suez Canal Company (44% of total to the British Government for nearly £4m.).

1888 Convention of Constantinople declared Canal open to vessels of all nations.

1956 President Nasser of Egypt nationalized Canal. Canal closed following invasion of Egypt.

1957 Canal re-opened under the control of the Egyptian Suez Canal Authority (April).

1959 World Bank lend Authority U.S.$56.5m.

1961 UN surcharge of 3% on transit dues, levied in 1958 to pay for clearing the Canal, was lifted (March).

1964 Loan of £E9.8m. granted by Kuwait Fund for Arab Development for dredging and widening operations. Permissible draught increased to 38 ft.

1965 Transit rates increased 1%, July.

1966 Transit rates increased 1%, July.

1967 Canal closed (June) during war with Israel.

1975 Canal re-opened (June).

IMPROVEMENT SCHEMES

In the years following the opening of the Canal the depth of the channel was 26.2 ft. (8 m.) and its breadth at the bottom 72.2 ft. (22 m.), with a wet cross-sectional area of 3,272 sq. ft. (304 sq. m.). The average gross tonnage of transiting vessels was then 1,700 tons and the highest

ORGANIZATION

Suez Canal Authority (*Hay'at Canal Al-Suess*): Ismailia, Egypt; Chair. MASHHOUR AHMED MASHHOUR; Dir.-Gen. EZZAT ADEL; Chief Pilot KAMAL HAMZA. The Suez Canal Authority manages the Canal on behalf of the Government of Egypt.

authorized draught was 24.6 ft. (7.5 m.). Navigation speed was 6.21 miles (10 km.) per hour.

NASSER PROJECT

Seven programmes of improvement were executed between 1876 and 1954. The eighth programme had started before nationalization, was modified thereafter to achieve better results and is now called the Nasser Project. Under this scheme the Canal was widened and deepened to take large tankers. New navigational aids and dockyard facilities were built and tug and salvage services improved. A Research Centre has been founded at Ismailia.

Under the first stage, finished in 1961, the Canal was widened and deepened to take vessels of 37 ft. draught. Under the second stage, finished in 1964, the Canal was widened and deepened to take vessels of 38 ft. draught. The installation of two salvage stations and a system of direct radio between vessels and the traffic control station at Ismailia were finished during 1962.

SUEZ AREA REDEVELOPMENT

After the war of October 1973 Egypt announced a plan to re-open the Suez Canal and generally develop the canal area. The canal was re-opened in June 1975 with a permissible draught of 33 ft., increased to 38 ft. in July 1975. Under a widening and deepening plan it is hoped to increase the permissible draught to 53 ft. by 1978–79, thus allowing loaded passage of ships of 150,000 tons, and to 67 ft. by 1981–82, allowing passage of ships of 250,000 tons fully laden. Port Said and Suez harbours will be enlarged to accommodate the largest vessels and the dock facilities at Port Fuad and Port Tewfik will be modernized. Five tunnels, carrying railway tracks, motorways, electricity cables and water are to be built under the canal.

STATISTICS

SUEZ CANAL TRAFFIC

YEAR	SHIPS		MERCHANDISE ('ooo tons)		NUMBER OF PASSENGERS	TOTAL TRANSIT RECEIPTS (E £'ooo)
	NUMBER	DISPLACEMENT ('ooo net tons)	NORTHBOUND	SOUTHBOUND		
1957 Apr./Dec. . .	10,958	89,911	67,219	14,104	188,361	24,514
1958 . . .	17,842	154,479	114,430	24,943	342,404	42,157
1959 . . .	17,731	163,386	121,749	26,505	326,446	44,536
1960 . . .	18,734	185,322	139,630	29,253	366,562	50,408
1961 . . .	18,148	187,059	139,599	32,795	322,842	51,088
1962 . . .	18,518	197,837	151,190	31,207	269,685	53,958
1963 . . .	19,146	210,498	159,482	34,050	297,955	71,294
1964 . . .	19,943	227,991	172,463	38,518	269,569	77,697
1965 . . .	20,289	246,817	183,441	42,001	291,085	85,792
1966 . . .	21,250	274,250	194,168	47,725	299,557	95,187

NORTHBOUND GOODS TRAFFIC
('ooo tons)

	1964	1965	1966
Crude petroleum .	132,685	143,664	154,092
Petroleum products	11,976	11,422	12,626
Ores and Metals	6,745	7,116	6,490
Cereals . .	2,601	2,665	1,787
Oil Seeds .	1,587	1,367	1,588
Textile fibres .	1,918	1,861	1,838
Rubber . .	1,289	1,417	1,387
Oil seed cake .	1,559	1,436	1,484
Sugar . .	1,270	1,287	1,338
Fruits . .	850	973	941
Wood . .	980	949	891
Tea . .	430	455	397
Others . .	8,573	8,829	9,309
TOTAL .	172,463	183,441	194,168

SOUTHBOUND GOODS TRAFFIC
('ooo tons)

	1964	1965	1966
Crude petroleum .	2,255	2,140	2,893
Petroleum products	3,881	5,768	6,060
Fabricated metals .	5,096	4,727	5,015
Fertilizers . .	3,897	5,168	6,748
Cereals . .	8,190	8,042	9,738
Cement . .	1,760	1,215	1,407
Machinery and parts	1,421	1,506	1,464
Chemical products .	974	1,040	1,017
Wood-pulp and paper	764	681	675
Sugar . .	1,122	1,695	1,231
Salt . .	606	544	412
Lubricating oils .	579	493	577
Ores and Metals .	n.a.	404	925
Others . .	7,973	8,578	9,563
TOTAL .	38,518	42,001	47,725

DISTRIBUTION OF NORTHBOUND CRUDE OIL 1966
('ooo tons)

COUNTRY OF ORIGIN	To EUROPE	To AMERICAN COUNTRIES	To AFRICA	To OTHERS
Kuwait . . .	56,624	1,881	160	24
Saudi Arabia . .	33,052	1,819	392	53
Iran . .	28,535	5,168	415	125
Abu Dhabi . .	9,210	185	—	—
Iraq . .	6,781	823	—	—
Qatar . .	5,730	—	—	—
U.A.R. (Egypt) .	1,148	211	59	—
Indonesia .	225	—	—	—
Bahrain . .	188	—	—	—
Others . .	1,240	44	—	—
TOTAL .	142,733	10,131	1,026	202

FLAG DISTRIBUTION OF NET TONNAGE
('ooo tons)

	1965		1966	
	TANKERS	ALL VESSELS	TANKERS	ALL VESSELS
United Kingdom . .	26,881	41,494	31,301	45,580
Liberia . .	46,126	48,390	53,260	56,455
Norway . .	33,852	37,450	40,282	43,840
France . .	13,255	16,082	13,730	16,517
Italy . .	10,712	14,368	11,394	15,231
Greece . .	7,879	12,673	6,930	12,554
Netherlands . .	6,104	9,685	5,457	9,106
Germany . .	4,069	8,136	3,825	7,904
U.S.A. . .	2,168	6,998	1,816	6,686
Sweden . .	5,674	6,862	6,992	8,196
Panama . .	6,332	7,358	6,530	7,755
U.S.S.R. . .	4,327	8,619	5,335	10,156
Denmark . .	4,668	5,881	5,325	6,775
Japan . .	1,383	2,945	4,104	5,896
Others . .	9,765	19,876	9,851	21,599
TOTAL . .	183,195	246,817	206,132	274,250

CARGO BY DESTINATION AND ORIGIN

NORTH OF CANAL
('ooo tons)

	1964	1965	1966
North and West Europe and U.K. . .	100,589	99,387	98,887
Baltic Sea	4,828	4,119	4,584
North Mediterranean . . .	53,110	66,637	78,034
East and South Mediterranean . .	4,624	4,308	4,084
West and South Mediterrranean . .	4,423	4,332	4,464
Black Sea	11,176	12,604	13,848
America	21,649	22,595	26,234
Other	10,582	11,460	11,758
TOTAL	210,981	225,442	241,893

SOUTH OF CANAL
('ooo tons)

	1964	1965	1966
Red Sea	8,124	7,132	6,523
East Africa and Aden . .	5,835	6,107	6,295
India, Pakistan, Burma and Ceylon	23,400	24,722	26,263
Persian Gulf . . .	139,191	151,184	163,105
South-East Asia . . .	7,144	7,566	8,583
Far East	14,742	16,230	19,532
Australia	5,792	5,963	5,292
Other	6,753	6,538	6,300
TOTAL	210,981	225,442	241,893

PART TWO

Regional Organizations

The United Nations in the Middle East and North Africa

MEMBERS, CONTRIBUTIONS, YEAR OF ADMISSION

(% contribution to UN Budget for 1974-76)

Country	%	Year	Country	%	Year
Afghanistan	0.02	1946	Morocco	0.06	1956
Algeria	0.08	1962	Oman	0.02	1971
Bahrain	0.02	1971	Qatar	0.02	1971
Cyprus	0.02	1960	Saudi Arabia	0.06	1945
Egypt	0.12	1945	Sudan	0.02	1955
Iran	0.20	1945	Syria	0.02	1946
Iraq	0.05	1945	Tunisia	0.02	1956
Israel	0.21	1949	Turkey	0.29	1945
Jordan	0.02	1955	United Arab Emirates	0.02	1971
Kuwait	0.09	1963	Yemen Arab Republic	0.02	1947
Lebanon	0.03	1945	Yemen, People's Democratic Republic	0.02	1967
Libya	0.11	1955			

MEMBERSHIP OF THE UNITED NATIONS AND RELATED AGENCIES IN THE MIDDLE EAST AND NORTH AFRICA

	UN	IAEA	ILO	FAO	UNESCO	WHO	IBRD	IFC	IDA	IMF	ICAO	UPU[1]	ITU[2]	WMO	IMCO	GATT[3]	WIPO	UNCTAD
Afghanistan	X	X	X	X	X	X	X	X	X	X	X	X	X	X				X
Algeria[3]	X	X	X	X	X	X	X			X	X	X	X	X	X	X	X	X
Bahrain[3]	X			X	X	X	X				X	X	X					X
Cyprus	X	X	X	X	X	X	X	X	X	X	X	X	X	X	X	X	X	X
Egypt	X	X	X	X	X	X	X	X	X	X	X	X	X	X	X		X	X
Iran	X	X	X	X	X	X	X	X	X	X	X	X	X	X	X			X
Iraq	X	X	X	X	X	X	X	X	X	X	X	X	X	X	X			X
Israel	X	X	X	X	X	X	X	X	X	X	X	X	X	X	X	X		X
Jordan	X	X	X	X	X	X	X	X	X	X	X	X	X	X	X		X	X
Kuwait	X	X	X	X	X	X	X	X	X	X	X	X	X	X	X	X		X
Lebanon	X	X	X	X	X	X	X	X	X	X	X	X	X	X	X			X
Libya	X	X	X	X	X	X	X	X	X	X	X	X	X	X	X			X
Morocco	X	X	X	X	X	X	X	X	X	X	X	X	X	X	X		X	X
Oman	X			X	X	X	X				X	X	X					X
Qatar[3]	X		X	X	X	X	X				X	X	X					X
Saudi Arabia	X	X		X	X	X	X	X	X	X	X	X	X	X	X			X
Sudan	X	X	X	X	X	X	X	X	X	X	X	X	X	X	X		X	X
Syria	X	X	X	X	X	X	X	X	X	X	X	X	X	X	X		X	X
Tunisia[3]	X	X	X	X	X	X	X	X	X	X	X	X	X	X	X	X	X	X
Turkey	X	X	X	X	X	X	X	X	X	X	X	X	X	X	X	X	X	X
United Arab Emirates	X		X	X	X	X	X				X	X	X			X	X	X
Yemen Arab Republic	X		X	X	X	X	X	X	X	X	X	X	X	X				X
Yemen, People's Democratic Republic[3]	X		X	X	X	X	X		X	X	X	X	X	X				X

[1] The Spanish Province in Africa (Spanish Sahara) is also a member of UPU.

[2] The Spanish Province in Africa (Spanish Sahara) is also a member of ITU.

[3] The following countries have special forms of relationship with GATT: *Acceded provisionally:* Tunisia; *applying GATT de facto pending final decisions as to their future commercial policy:* Algeria, Bahrain, Qatar, People's Democratic Republic of Yemen.

PERMANENT MISSIONS TO THE UNITED NATIONS
(with Permanent Representatives)

Afghanistan: 866 United Nations Plaza, 4th Floor, New York, N.Y. 10017; (vacant).

Algeria: 750 Third Ave., 14th Floor, New York, N.Y. 10017; ABDELLATIF RAHAL.

Bahrain: 747 Third Ave., 19th Floor, New York, N.Y. 10017; Dr. SALMAN MOHAMED AL SAFFAR.

Cyprus: 820 Second Ave., 12th Floor, New York, N.Y. 10017; ZENON ROSSIDES.

Egypt: 36 East 67th St., New York, N.Y. 10021; Dr. AHMED ESMAT ABDEL MEGUID.

Iran: 622 Third Ave., 34th Floor, New York, N.Y. 10017; FEREYDOUN HOVEYDA.

Iraq: 14 East 79th St., New York, N.Y. 10021; ABDUL KARIM AL-SHAIKHLY.

Israel: 800 Second Ave., New York, N.Y. 10017; CHAIM HERZOG.

Jordan: 866 United Nations Plaza, Room 550–552, New York, N.Y. 10017; SHERIF ABDUL HAMID SHARAF.

Kuwait: 235 East 42nd St., 27th Floor, New York, N.Y. 10017; ABDALLA YACCOUB BISHARA.

Lebanon: 866 United Nations Plaza, Room 533–535, New York, N.Y. 10017; EDOUARD GHORRA.

Libya: 866 United Nations Plaza, New York, N.Y. 10017; (vacant).

Morocco: 757 Third Ave., 23rd Floor, New York, N.Y. 10017; DRISS SLAOUI.

Oman: 605 Third Ave., Room 3304, New York, N.Y. 10016; (vacant).

Qatar: 747 Third Ave., 22nd Floor, New York, N.Y. 10017; JASIM YOUSIF JAMAL.

Saudi Arabia: 6 East 43rd St., 26th Floor, New York, N.Y. 10017; (vacant).

Sudan: 757 Third Ave., 24th Floor, New York, N.Y. 10017; MUSTAFA MEDANI.

Syria: 150 East 58th St., Room 1500, New York, N.Y. 10022; HAISSAM KELANI.

Tunisia: 40 East 71st St., New York, N.Y. 10021; RACHID DRISS.

Turkey: 866 Second Ave., 15th Floor, 2 Hammarskjöld Plaza, New York, N.Y. 10017; OSMAN OLCAY.

United Arab Emirates: 866 Second Ave., New York, N.Y. 10017; Dr. ALI HUMAIDAN.

Yemen Arab Republic: 211 East 43rd St., Room 2402, New York, N.Y. 10017; Dr. HASSAN MOHAMED MAKKI.

Yemen, People's Democratic Republic: 211 East 43rd St., Room 903, New York, N.Y. 10017; ABDALLA SALEH ASHTAL.

UN INFORMATION CENTRES

Afghanistan: Shah Mahmoud Ghazi Watt, Kabul; P.O.B. 5.

Algeria: 19 Avenue Claude Debussy, Algiers; P.O.B. 823.

Egypt: Sh. Osiris, Tagher Building, Garden City, Cairo; P.O.B. 262 (also covers Saudi Arabia and Yemen).

Iran: Off Takhte Jamshid, 12 Kh. Bandar Pahlavi, Teheran; P.O.B. 1555.

Iraq: House 167/1 Abu Nouwas St., Bataween, Baghdad; P.O.B. 2398, Alwiyah.

Lebanon: Information Service, UN Economic Commission for Western Asia, P.O.B. 4656 Apt. No. 1 Fakhoury Bldg., Montée Baim Militaire, Beirut (also covers Jordan, Kuwait and Syria).

Morocco: "Casier ONU", Angle Charia Moulay Hassan et Zankat Assafi, Rabat.

Sudan: House No. 9, Block 6.5.D.E., Nejumi St., Khartoum; P.O.B. 1992.

Tunisia: 61 Boulevard Bab Benat, Tunis; P.O.B. 863 (also covers Libya).

ECONOMIC COMMISSION FOR AFRICA—ECA

Africa Hall, P.O. Box 3001, Addis Ababa, Ethiopia

Telephone: 447200.

Initiates and takes part in measures for facilitating Africa's economic development. Member countries must be independent, be members of the UN and within the geographical scope of the African continent and the islands bordering it. ECA was founded in 1958 by a resolution of ECOSOC as the fourth UN regional economic commission.

MEMBERS

Algeria	Gabon	Malawi	South Africa*
Botswana	The Gambia	Mali	Sudan
Burundi	Ghana	Mauritania	Swaziland
Cameroon	Guinea	Mauritius	Tanzania
Central African Republic	Guinea-Bissau	Morocco	Togo
Chad	Ivory Coast	Niger	Tunisia
Congo People's Republic	Kenya	Nigeria	Uganda
Dahomey	Lesotho	Rwanda	Upper Volta
Egypt	Liberia	Senegal	Zaire
Equatorial Guinea	Libya	Sierra Leone	Zambia
Ethiopia	Madagascar	Somalia	

* Suspended by ECOSOC since 1963.

ASSOCIATE MEMBERS

(a) Non-Self-Governing Territories situated within the geographical scope of the Commission.

(b) Powers other than Portugal responsible for the international relations of those territories (France, Spain and the United Kingdom).

Associate Members may take part in the Commission's activities but may not vote.

ORGANIZATION

(as of April 1975)

COMMISSION

Executive Secretary: ADEBAYO ADEDEJI (Nigeria).

The Commission has held twelve sessions since its inception.

(a) *Conference of Ministers* which is vested with full powers to consider matters of general policy and the priorities to be assigned to the programme and other activities of the Commission. It reviews programme implementation and examines and approves the proposed programme of work, and considers reports submitted to it by the Executive Committee and the Technical Committee of Experts. The Conference of Ministers holds its meetings every two years. The first meeting was held in Tunis in February 1971; the second was held in Accra early in 1973 and the third in Nairobi in February 1975.

(b) *Technical Committee of Experts* which meets once a year. It is composed of senior officials of member states concerned with economic affairs, and it examines studies prepared by the ECA Secretariat and assists in the formulation of the work programme. It held its fifth meeting in Addis Ababa in February 1975.

(c) *Executive Committee* which is composed of representatives of 16 member states and which assists the Executive Secretary in the implementation of the resolutions and the work programme of the Commission, and provides links between the Secretariat, member states and the sub-regions. The Executive Committee meets at least twice a year. Its twelfth meeting was held in November 1974.

Subsidiary Bodies. The Commission is empowered, under its terms of reference, to establish subsidiary bodies. Those now in existence and actively functioning are the *Conference of African Statisticians*, the *Conference of African Planners* and the *Conference of African Demographers*, each of which meets once every two years.

Sub-Regional Offices: Lusaka, Niamey, Tangier, Kinshasa.

ACTIVITIES

Objectives. The work of the Commission is determined by decisions of its plenary sessions. The Commission is charged with the responsibility for promoting and facilitating concerted action for the economic and social development of Africa; for maintaining and strengthening the economic relations of African countries, both among themselves and with other countries of the world; for undertaking or sponsoring investigations, research and studies of economic and technological problems and developments; for collecting, evaluating and disseminating economic, technological and statistical information; and for assisting in the formulation and development of co-ordinated policies promoting economic and technological development in the region.

Relations with Other Organizations: WHO maintains a liaison office at ECA. In co-operation with ITU work has begun on a pan-African telecommunications system. ECA also runs a Joint Agricultural Division in conjunction with FAO, and since 1974 a Joint ECA/UNIDO Division. UNDP's Regional Representative in Addis Ababa has special liaison duties with ECA.

Co-operation between ECA and the Organization of African Unity started with the signing of a UN/OAU agreement by the then Secretary-General of the United Nations, U Thant, and the then Secretary-General of the OAU, Diallo Telli, on November 15th, 1965. An ECA/OAU/UNESCO Inter-Secretariat Meeting was held in September 1972, and the eighth ECA/OAU Joint Meeting on Trade and Development was held in Geneva during August 1973.

The Conference of Ministers of Industry held in October 1973 was co-sponsored by ECA, OAU and UNIDO. ECA and OAU have also co-operated in creating the Association of African Trade Promotion Organizations.

PUBLICATIONS

Economic Bulletin for Africa (twice yearly).
The Statistical Newsletter (quarterly).
Foreign Trade Newsletter (quarterly).
Agricultural Economic Bulletin (twice yearly).
Social Welfare Services in Africa (thrice yearly).
Natural Resources, Science and Technology Newsletter (quarterly).
Foreign Trade Statistics for Africa, Series A: Direction of Trade (quarterly).
Foreign Trade Statistics for Africa, Series B: Trade by Commodities (thrice yearly).
African Target (quarterly).

Planning Newsletter (bi-monthly).
Statistical Bulletin for Africa (quarterly).
Social Work Training Newsletter (quarterly).
Training Information Notice (quarterly).
Statistical Yearbook.
Survey of Economic Conditions (annual).
Statistical and Economic Information. Bulletin for Africa (quarterly).
Population Newsletter (quarterly).
Rural Development Newsletter (quarterly).
Investment Promotion Newsletter.

AFRICAN INSTITUTE FOR ECONOMIC DEVELOPMENT AND PLANNING

Dakar, Senegal

An autonomous organ of the ECA opened in 1963 with Special Fund assistance to train senior African officials in techniques of development planning and to serve as a clearing house and documentation centre on all African development questions.

Director: SAMIR AMIN (Egypt).

ECONOMIC COMMISSION FOR WESTERN ASIA—ECWA

UN Building, P.O.B. 4656, Bir Hassan, Beirut, Lebanon

Established to commence operations in 1974 by a resolution of ECOSOC as the fifth regional Economic Commission of the UN, ECWA provides facilities of a wider scope for those countries previously served by the UN Economic and Social Office in Beirut (UNESOB).

MEMBERS

Bahrain	Kuwait	Qatar	United Arab Emirates
Iraq	Lebanon	Saudi Arabia	Yemen Arab Republic
Jordan	Oman	Syria	Yemen, People's Democratic Republic

ORGANIZATION

(as of June 1975)

COMMISSION

Meets once a year at headquarters to discuss the programmes of work and the policies and institutions of ECWA. The first session was held in June 1974 and the second session in May 1975.

Chairman: JAWAD HASHEM (Iraq).

SECRETARIAT

Whilst the site of a building for ECWA headquarters is still to be determined, the Commission is to make use of the building formerly housing the UN Economic and Social Office in Beirut (UNESOB). The staff of UNESOB have also been integrated into the Secretariat of ECWA.

Executive Secretary: MOHAMMED SAID AL-ATTAR (Yemen Arab Republic).

COUNTRIES PARTICIPATING ON A CONSULTATIVE BASIS

Austria	Federal Republic of Germany	Netherlands	U.S.S.R.
Belgium	Hungary	Pakistan	United Kingdom
France	Ireland	Poland	U.S.A.
German Democratic Republic	Italy	Spain	Yugoslavia

SECOND SESSION

All member countries participated except for the two Yemens; several other countries participated in a consultative capacity and the Palestine Liberation Organization was accepted as a permanent observer. Representatives of 11 UN organizations, the Arab Fund for Economic and Social Development, the Kuwaiti and Abu Dhabi Funds, the Arab Labour Office, the Arab Economic Unity Council and the Organization of Arab Petroleum Exporting Countries participated as observers.

The session considered a policy statement from the Executive Secretary, and reports on: the work programme and priorities for 1976–77, a mid-term plan for 1976–79, and work and activities since the first session.

The main resolutions recommended: a voluntary trust fund, as requested by the member states, enabling the Commission to provide advisory service; a programme of studies on the Arab world, with collaboration from the ECA or other organizations; expansion of ECWA's statistical activities; and a standing committee to give advice for preparation for Commission sessions and other ECWA meetings.

WORK PROGRAMMES

Inherited from UNESOB, ECWA's 1974 programme included: agriculture; a review of economic and social conditions within the framework of the 2nd UN Development Decade; a seminar on manpower; environment; industrial development; population; public administration; science and technology; external trade; and transport.

It was agreed at the first two sessions that the priorities for the future should be water resources development; the food deficit; the fertilizer industry; industrial training and management; tourism; public finance and investment; natural resources; population; urban settlement; social attitudes and values in development; availability of domestic skills; electricity; new means of co-operation among existing regional organizations.

BUDGET

ECWA has been granted a budget of U.S. $2,422,000
by the General Assembly for the biennium 1974–75.

INTERNATIONAL BANK FOR RECONSTRUCTION AND DEVELOPMENT—IBRD (WORLD BANK)

INTERNATIONAL DEVELOPMENT ASSOCIATION—IDA

1818 H Street, N.W., Washington, D.C. 20433, U.S.A.

The World Bank was established in 1945. It aims to assist the economic development of member nations by making loans, in cases where private capital is not available on reasonable terms, to finance productive investments. Loans are made either direct to governments, or to private enterprises with the guarantee of their governments. The IDA began operations in 1960. An affiliate of the World Bank, it advances capital on more flexible terms to developing countries.

President: ROBERT S. McNAMARA (U.S.A.).

Regional Vice-President, Europe, Middle East and North Africa: MUNIR P. BENJENK (Turkey).

LOANS AND CREDITS TO MIDDLE EASTERN AND NORTH AFRICAN COUNTRIES
(July 1974–June 30th, 1975)

	PROJECT	IBRD LOAN (U.S. $'000)	IDA CREDIT (U.S. $'000)
Afghanistan . . .	Agricultural Credit II		13,000
	Water supply		9,000
Algeria	Rural development	8,000	
	Development finance company	40,000	
Egypt	Suez Canal rehabilitation	50,000	
	Industrial and agricultural recurrent imports	35,000	35,000
	Tourah cement expansion	40,000	
	Railways II	37,000	
	Telecommunications		30,000
Iran	Agricultural Development Bank III	40,000	
	Fisheries I	12,500	
Israel	Development finance company	35,000	
Jordan	Irrigation and rural development		7,500
	Education		6,000
	Electricity supply		5,000
	Pilot potash project		1,000
Morocco	Development finance company	30,000	
	Irrigation and rural development	18,500	
	Agricultural development		14,000
Sudan	Education		10,000
	Power		23,000
	Irrigation (supplement)		20,000
Syria	Power expansion	8,600	
	Mehardeh power	72,000	
Tunisia	Phosphate development	23,300	
	Irrigation and rehabilitation	12,200	
	Urban sewerage I	28,000	
Turkey . . .	Development finance company	65,000	
	Industry-fertilizer expansion	18,000	
	Rural development	75,000	
Yemen Arab Republic .	Agriculture, S. Uplands		10,000
	Highways		9,000
	Water supply and sewerage		8,100
Yemen, P.D.R. . . .	Education I		5,400
	Fisheries (supplement)		1,600
	Highway		15,500

COUNTRY TOTALS IN U.S. $'000 FROM ESTABLISHMENT TO JUNE 30th, 1975

	BANK LOANS	IDA CREDITS		BANK LOANS	IDA CREDITS
Afghanistan . . .		65,000	Morocco . . .	471,700	50,800
Algeria	310,500		Oman . . .	8,400	
Cyprus	77,100		Sudan . . .	134,000	134,000
Egypt	218,500	216,075	Syria . . .	96,600	119,300
Iran	1,210,700		Tunisia . . .	258,900	69,800
Iraq	145,700		Turkey . . .	906,700	178,100
Israel	249,000		Yemen Arab Republic .		65,300
Jordan		59,800	Yemen, P.D.R. . .		28,160
Lebanon	66,600				

INTERNATIONAL FINANCE CORPORATION—IFC

1818 H Street, N.W., Washington, D.C. 20433, U.S.A.

Founded in 1956 as an affiliate of the World Bank to encourage the growth of productive private enterprise in its less-developed member countries.

Director of Investments, Africa and Middle East: GUNTER H. KREUTER (Federal Republic of Germany).

IFC COMMITMENTS IN MIDDLE EASTERN AND NORTH AFRICAN COUNTRIES
(up to June 30th, 1975—U.S. $)

COUNTRY	TYPE OF BUSINESS	FISCAL YEAR	AMOUNT*
Iran . .	Ceramic tiles	1959	300,000†
	Steel products	1969, 1974	7,738,805
	Textiles	1971	4,500,000†
	Pulp and paper	1972	14,193,443
	Food products	1973	1,250,000†
	Carbon black	1973	3,553,333
	Automobiles	1973	11,000,000
Israel . .	Pesticides	1974	3,500,000
Jordan . .	Ceramics	1974	1,825,834
	Fertilizer	1975	3,215,513
Lebanon .	Textiles	1971	930,000
	Textiles	1975	3,900,000
	Ceramic tiles	1971	1,200,000
	Home financing	1975	1,250,000
Morocco . .	Development financing	1963	1,495,774
	Food processing and canning	1966	1,388,486
Sudan . .	Textiles	1964, 1972	2,211,795
Tunisia . .	Fertilizers	1963	3,500,000
	Development financing	1966, 1970	1,208,231
	Tourism financing	1969	110,247,899
	Tourism	1973	1,929,619
	Tourism	1973, 1975	3,246,489
	Aluminium fluoride	1974	718,659
Turkey . .	Development financing	1964,1967,1969,1972, 1973, 1975	38,606,998
	Textiles	1966,1969,1971,1972,	4,568,272
	Pulp, paper and paper products	1970, 1971	3,168,889
	Glass and glass products	1970	11,583,330
	Aluminium sheet and foil	1971	8,371,429
	Tourism	1973	602,857
	Steel pipe	1974	4,036,508
	Synthetic fibres	1974	10,000,000
	Cement	1975	10,600,000
	Steel	1975	8,871,841
	Textiles	1975	1,300,000
	Chemicals	1975	15,000,000

* Includes standby and underwriting commitments.   † Fully cancelled, terminated, written off, sold, redeemed or repaid.

UNITED NATIONS DEVELOPMENT PROGRAMME—UNDP
United Nations, New York, U.S.A.

Established in 1965 to replace the Expanded Programme of Technical Assistance and the UN Special Fund.

Aden: Resident Rep. of UNDP in the People's Democratic Republic of Yemen, P.O.B. 1188, Tawahi, Aden, Yemen P.D.R.

Algiers: Resident Rep. of UNDP in Algeria, B.P. 823 B.P., Algiers, Algeria.

Amman: Resident Rep. of UNDP in Jordan, P.O.B. 565, Amman, Jordan.

Ankara: Resident Rep. of UNDP in Turkey, P.K. 407, Ankara, Turkey.

Baghdad: Resident Rep. of UNDP in Iraq, P.O.B. 2048, Alwiyah Post Office, Baghdad, Iraq.

Beirut: Resident Rep. of UNDP in Lebanon, P.O.B. 3216, Beirut, Lebanon.

Cairo: Resident Rep. of UNDP in Egypt, P.O.B. 982, Cairo, Egypt.

Damascus: Resident Rep. of UNDP in the Syrian Arab Republic, P.O.B. 2317, Damascus, Syria.

Jerusalem: Resident Rep. of UNDP in Israel, 39 Jabotinsky St., Komemiut (Talbieh), Jerusalem, Israel.

Kabul: Resident Rep. of UNDP in Afghanistan, P.O.B. 5, Kabul, Afghanistan.

Khartoum: Resident Rep. of UNDP in the Sudan, P.O.B. 913, Khartoum, Sudan.

Kuwait City: Resident Rep. of UNDP in Kuwait, P.O.B. 2993, Kuwait City, Kuwait.

Manama: Deputy Regional Rep. of UNDP in Bahrain, P.O.B. 814, Manama, Bahrain (also covers Qatar and the United Arab Emirates).

Muscat: Asst. Regional Rep. of UNDP in Oman, F.O.B. 87, Muscat, Oman.

Nicosia: Resident Rep. of UNDP in Cyprus, P.O.B. 3521, Nicosia, Cyprus.

Rabat: Resident Rep. of UNDP in Morocco, Casier ONU, Rabat-Chellah, Rabat, Morocco.

Riyadh: Regional Rep. of UNDP in Saudi Arabia and the Gulf Area, P.O.B. 558, Riyadh, Saudi Arabia. (Gulf Area consists of Bahrain, Oman, Qatar and the United Arab Emirates).

Sana'a: Resident Rep. of UNDP in the Yemen Arab Republic, P.O.B. 551, Sana'a, Yemen Arab Republic.

Teheran: Resident Rep. of UNDP in Iran, P.O.B. 1555, Teheran, Iran.

Tripoli: Resident Rep. of UNDP in Libya, P.O.B. 358, Tripoli, Libya.

Tunis: Resident Rep. of UNDP in Tunisia, B.P. 863, Tunis, Tunisia.

SELECTED NATIONAL PROJECTS CURRENTLY ASSISTED BY THE UNDP IN THE MIDDLE EAST AND NORTH AFRICA, AND EXECUTING AGENCIES

Algeria: Allocation of $1,791,276 for Hydrometeorological Institute for Training and Research (WMO).

Bahrain: Allocation of $494,236 for Assistance to Teacher Training Colleges (UNESCO).

Cyprus: Allocation of $1,151,475 for Hotel and Catering Institute, Nicosia (ILO).

Egypt: Allocation of $1,126,415 for Engineering and Industrial Design Development Centre, Nasser City (UNIDO).

Iraq: Allocation of $1,231,726 for Animal Health Institute (FAO).

Israel: Allocation of $658,800 for Electrodialysis Pilot Plant, Mashabei Sade (UN).

Jordan: Allocation of $1,364,960 for Dryland Farming (FAO).

Kuwait: Allocation of $701,810 for Shuwaikh Industrial Training Centre (ILO).

Lebanon: Allocation of $1,113,173 for Hydro-Agricultural Development (FAO).

Libya: Allocation of $1,438,573 for National Institute of Public Administration, Tripoli (UN).

Morocco: Allocation of $1,082,788 for Mineral Survey in the Anti-Atlas (UN).

Oman: Allocation of $573,500 for Port Management and Operations (UNCTAD).

Saudi Arabia: Allocation of $1,167,768 for Telecommunications and Broadcasting Training Centre, Jeddah (ITU).

Sudan: Allocation of $1,138,975 for National Public Health Laboratory Service (WHO).

Syria: Allocation of $1,707,452 for Euphrates Pilot Irrigation Project (FAO).

Tunisia: Allocation of $1,334,529 for Reforestation Institute, Tunis (FAO).

Turkey: Allocation of $2,938,126 for Research and Training Centres for the Production, Processing and Marketing of Fruit and Vegetables (FAO).

Yemen Arab Republic: Allocation of $1,530,067 for Food and Nutrition Programme (FAO).

Yemen, People's Democratic Republic: Allocation of $1,662,671 for Soil and Water Utilization and Conservation in the Wadi Tuban Watershed Area (FAO).

National projects are also in progress, among them:

African Training and Research Centre in Administration for Development, Tangiers (UN): Allocation of $1,592,600.

Survey of Groundwater Resources in the Northern Sahara (UNESCO): Allocation of $1,252,850.

Maritime Transport Institute (IMCO): Allocation of $2,360,046.

UNITED NATIONS RELIEF AND WORKS AGENCY FOR PALESTINE REFUGEES IN THE NEAR EAST—UNRWA

Museitbeh Quarter, Beirut, Lebanon

Began operations in 1950 to provide relief, health, education and welfare services for Palestine refugees in the Near East.

REGIONAL OFFICES

Gaza Strip: UNRWA Field Office, P.O.B. 61, Gaza.
East Jordan: UNRWA Field Office, P.O.B. 484, Amman.
West Bank: UNRWA Field Office, P.O.B. 19149, Jerusalem.
Lebanon: UNRWA Field Office, P.O.B. 947, Beirut.
Syria: UNRWA Field Office, 19 Salah Eddin el Ayoubi St., Abou Rummaneh, Damascus.

Egypt: UNRWA Liaison Office, 2 Dar el Shifa, Garden City, P.O.B. 277, Cairo.
Europe: UNRWA Liaison Office, Palais des Nations, 1211 Geneva 10, Switzerland.
United States: UNRWA Liaison Office, Room 1801, United Nations, New York.

ORGANIZATION

Commissioner-General: Sir JOHN S. RENNIE, G.C.M.G., O.B.E. (United Kingdom).

Deputy-Commissioner-General: THOMAS W. MCELHINEY (U.S.A.).

UNRWA is a subsidiary organ of the United Nations General Assembly, and began operations in May 1950; it employs an international staff of 126 and 15,461 local staff, mainly Palestine refugees. The Commissioner-General is assisted by an Advisory Commission consisting of representatives of the governments of:

Belgium	Jordan	Turkey
Egypt	Lebanon	United Kingdom
France	Syria	U.S.A.
Japan		

STATISTICS

REFUGEES REGISTERED WITH UNRWA
(as at March 31st, 1975)

COUNTRY OR FIELD	IN CAMPS	NOT IN CAMPS	TOTAL
East Jordan . .	156,919	461,665	618,584
West Bank . .	73,700	217,295	290,995
Gaza . .	198,268	133,003	331,271
Lebanon . .	100,066	95,201	195,267
Syria . .	51,306	131,360	182,666
TOTAL . .	580,259	1,038,524	1,618,783

DISPLACED PERSONS

Apart from the Palestine refugees of 1948 who are registered with UNRWA and who are UNRWA's main concern (*see* table at left), considerable numbers of people have, since 1967, been displaced within the UNRWA areas of operations, and others have had to leave these areas. According to government estimates there are 210,000 displaced persons in East Jordan and 125,000 in Syria.

NUMBER OF REFUGEE PUPILS RECEIVING EDUCATION IN UNRWA/UNESCO SCHOOLS
(October 1974)

FIELD	NUMBER OF SCHOOLS	PUPILS IN ELEMENTARY CLASSES			PUPILS IN PREPARATORY CLASSES			TOTAL NUMBER OF PUPILS
		Boys	Girls	Total	Boys	Girls	Total	
East Jordan . . .	182	42,905	40,163	83,068	14,398	10,898	25,296	108,364
West Bank . . .	92	12,436	13,530	25,966	3,971	3,358	7,329	33,295
Gaza	121	28,369	24,503	52,872	8,229	7,564	15,793	68,665
Lebanon	82	15,162	13,868	29,030	4,910	4,278	9,188	38,218
Syria	99	15,207	13,143	28,350	5,966	4,920	10,886	39,236
TOTAL . .	576	114,079	105,207	219,286	37,474	31,018	68,492	287,778

Additionally in the 1974–75 school year an estimated number of 60,000 refugee children received education in government schools and an estimated 8,800 in private schools in the host countries, partly with grants paid by UNRWA.

ACTIVITIES

SERVICES FOR PALESTINE REFUGEES

Since 1950, UNRWA has provided relief (including food), health and education services for the needy among the Palestine refugees in Lebanon, Syria, east Jordan, the West Bank and the Gaza Strip. For UNRWA's purposes, a Palestine refugee is one whose normal residence was in Palestine for a minimum of two years before the 1948 conflict and who, as a result of the Arab-Israeli hostilities, lost his home and means of livelihood. To be eligible for assistance, a refugee must reside in one of the "host" countries in which UNRWA operates and be in need. A refugee's children and grandchildren who fulfil certain criteria are also eligible for UNRWA assistance. In March 1975, the registered refugee population numbered 1,618,783, including 580,259 in 63 refugee camps.

Whereas the vast majority (1.4 million) of the refugees are eligible for health services and, in the appropriate age-groups, for education, only 51 per cent receive rations. Over the years an effective community health service has been built up with technical guidance from WHO and there has never been a major epidemic among the refugees in UNRWA's care. An education system has been developed with technical guidance from UNESCO and in the 1974–75 school year there were 287,778 children in 576 elementary and preparatory schools operated by UNRWA. More than 20,000 refugees have already passed through UNRWA's eight vocational centres (capacity: 4,424 trainees) for training either as teachers or in a variety of industrial and semi-professional skills; UNRWA has become one of the most important channels for this type of technical assistance in the Middle East. Since 1950 UNRWA has also served 315 million meals to young children and distributed about 33,000 tons of clothing.

AID TO DISPLACED PERSONS

After the renewal of Arab-Israeli hostilities in the Middle East in June 1967, hundreds of thousands of people fled from the fighting and Israeli-occupied areas to east Jordan, Syria and Egypt. UNRWA provided emergency relief for displaced refugees and was additionally empowered by a UN General Assembly resolution to provide "humanitarian assistance, as far as practicable, on an emergency basis and as a temporary measure" for those persons other than Palestine refugees who were newly displaced and in urgent need. In practice, UNRWA has lacked the funds to aid the other displaced persons and the main burden of supporting them has fallen on the Arab governments concerned. The Agency, as requested by the Government of Jordan in 1967 and on that Government's behalf, distributes rations to displaced persons in east Jordan who are not registered refugees of 1948. In May 1975, for example, 204,500 displaced persons in east Jordan were issued with rations.

With the agreement of the Israeli Government, UNRWA has continued to provide assistance for registered refugees living in the Israeli-occupied territories of the West Bank and the Gaza Strip.

RECENT DISTURBANCES

Refugees have been affected and UNRWA's services disrupted by recent events such as: the September 1970 clashes between the Jordanian army and the *fedayeen*; the renewal of Arab-Israeli hostilities in October 1973; Israeli attacks in south Lebanon in 1974 and 1975; and civil strife in Lebanon in 1975.

FINANCE

BUDGET

As at May 30th, UNRWA's budget for 1975 was $124.3 million.

For the most part, UNRWA's income is made up of voluntary·contributions, almost entirely from governments, the remainder being provided by voluntary agencies, business corporations and private sources. However, the cost of the Agency's 126 international staff is funded by the UN, WHO and UNESCO.

In recent years financial crises have posed serious threats of cuts in services, and in 1975 the Agency faced a budget deficit of extraordinary magnitude. The rise in prices of all supplies, the continued appreciation of three of the local currencies against currencies of major importance in the Agency's income, and local increases in the cost of living (which in 1974 ranged from 11 per cent in Syria to 47 per cent in the Gaza Strip), have resulted in an estimated deficit of $30 million in 1975. As of mid-year the deficit had been reduced but not eliminated and cuts in or suspension of the Agency's programmes appeared increasingly imminent, with serious implications for the search for peace in the Middle East.

ESTIMATED EXPENDITURE, 1975

(as at May 30th, 1975; these figures are subject to change)

	ESTIMATED EXPENDITURE (U.S. $'000)	PERCENTAGE
Relief Services:		
Basic Rations	39,868	—
Supplementary Feeding	6,028	—
Shelter	472	—
Special Hardship Assistance . . .	1,043	—
Share of Common Costs* . . .	7,001	—
TOTAL RELIEF SERVICES . .	54,412	43.8
Health Services:		
Medical Services	8,045	—
Environmental Sanitation . . .	3,229	—
Share of Common Costs* . . .	2,206	—
TOTAL HEALTH SERVICES . .	13,480	10.8
Education Services:		
General Education . . .	40,515	—
Vocational and Professional Training . .	7,402	—
Share of Common Costs* . . .	5,424	—
TOTAL EDUCATION SERVICES .	53,341	42.9
Other Extraordinary costs . .	3,094	2.5
GRAND TOTAL	124,327	100

* Includes general administration, other internal services, supply and transport services.

PUBLICATIONS

Annual Report of the Commissioner-General of UNRWA.

UNRWA—a survey of United Nations Assistance to Palestine Refugees (every 2 years).

Palestine Refugees Today—the UNRWA Newsletter (quarterly).

UNITED NATIONS TRUCE SUPERVISION ORGANIZATION—UNTSO

Headquarters: Government House, Jerusalem

Set up in 1948 to supervise the truce called for by the Security Council in Palestine.

Chief of Staff: Maj.-Gen. BENGT LILJESTRAND (Sweden).

COMPOSITION

As at June 1975 there were 298 Military Observers from the following countries:

Argentina	Denmark	New Zealand
Australia	Finland	Norway
Austria	France	Sweden
Belgium	Ireland	U.S.S.R.
Canada	Italy	U.S.A.
Chile	Netherlands	

ACTIVITIES

Military observation duties have been carried out since 1948, and UNTSO has assisted in the application of the 1949 Armistice Agreements.

The military observers are deployed along the Israeli and Syrian Forward Defended Localities in the Golan Heights, where they now operate as part of the United Nations Disengagement Observer Force (UNDOF), and in the Sinai peninsula in the area of the zone of disengagement, in conjunction with the United Nations Emergency Force (UNEF).

Since April 1972 observers have been placed in southern Lebanon to carry out observation duties with regard to the cease-fire in the Israel-Lebanon sector.

UNTSO maintains field stations and liaison offices in Amman, Beirut, Cairo, Damascus, Gaza and Tiberias.

FINANCE

UNTSO expenditures are covered by the regular budget of the United Nations. For the biennial period 1974-75, a sum of $18,883,000 was appropriated by the General Assembly.

UNITED NATIONS EMERGENCY FORCE—UNEF

Headquarters at Ismailia, Egypt

Set up in October 1973 by Security Council resolution to supervise the ceasefire and troop withdrawals called for by the Council in the Egypt-Israel sector. The original mandate of the Force had effect for six months and has since been extended by Security Council resolutions until October 24th, 1975.

Commander: Maj.-Gen. E. SIILASVUO (Finland).

Deputy Commander and Chief of Staff: Brig.-Gen. E. A. ERSKINE (Ghana).

COMPOSITION OF FORCE

(April 1975)

Canada	842
Finland	506
Ghana	501
Indonesia	400
Poland	878
Senegal	402
Sweden	500
TOTAL	4,029

ACTIVITIES

The initial task of the Force was to supervise the cease-fire and to ensure a return of Egyptian and Israeli forces to the position held on October 22nd, 1973.

In accordance with the provisions of the Agreement on Disengagement of January 18th, 1974, UNEF subsequently supervised the withdrawal of Israeli forces east of the zone of disengagement established by that Agreement and handed over to Egyptian forces territory west of that zone.

The Force continues to supervise the cease-fire and to man, patrol and control the zone of disengagement and, with the assistance of UNTSO Military Observers, it conducts regular and special inspections of the Israeli and Egyptian areas of limited armaments and forces, as well as inspections of other areas agreed by the parties.

FINANCE

In addition to previous expenditure totalling $79.8 million up to October 1974, the General Assembly appropriated $40 million for both UNEF and UNDOF from October 25th, 1974, to April 24th, 1975, and authorized expenditures not to exceed $6,666,667 per month from April 25th to October 31st, 1975.

UNITED NATIONS
DISENGAGEMENT OBSERVATION FORCE—UNDOF

Headquarters at Damascus, Syria

Established for an initial period of six months by a Security Council resolution on May 31st, 1974, following the signature in Geneva of a disengagement agreement between Syrian and Israeli forces. The mandate has since been extended by the Security Council until November 30th, 1975.

Officer-in-Charge: HANNES PHILIPP (Austria).

COMPOSITION OF FORCE
(May 1975)

Austria	518
Peru	348
Canada	152
Poland	85
UNDOF military observers (transferred from UNTSO)	89
UNDOF headquarters staff on secondment from UNEF	6
	1,198

ACTIVITIES

The initial task of the Force was to take over territory evacuated in stages by the Israeli troops, in accordance with the disengagement agreement, to hand over territory to Syrian troops, and to establish an area of separation.

UNDOF continues to man the area of separation, from which Syrian and Israeli forces are excluded; it carries out inspections of the areas of limited armaments and forces, and it uses its best efforts to maintain the cease-fire. The area of separation has been placed under Syrian civil administration.

FINANCE

UNDOF finances are treated in conjunction with those of UNEF (*see* above).

UNITED NATIONS PEACE-KEEPING FORCE IN CYPRUS—UNFICYP

P.O.B. 1642, Nicosia, Cyprus

Set up in March 1964 by Security Council resolution, for a three-month period, subsequently extended to December 1975 by 27 successive resolutions.

Special Representative of the Secretary-General: LUIS WECKMANN-MUÑOZ (Mexico).
Commander: Lt.-Gen. D. PREM CHAND (India).

COMPOSITION OF FORCE
(December 1974)

	Military	Police
Australia	—	34
Austria	320	55
Canada	859	—
Denmark	420	23
Finland	599	—
Ireland	6	—
Sweden	569	40
United Kingdom	1,410	—
TOTAL	4,183	152

FUNCTIONS

The purpose of the Force has been to keep the peace between the Greek and Turkish Cypriot communities pending a resolution of outstanding issues between them, to help maintain law and order, and to promote a return to normal conditions. UNFICYP now also performs functions in relation to the supervision of the cease-fire between the armed forces of Turkey and Cyprus, and in providing humanitarian assistance to refugees and to villages isolated behind military lines. The United Nations High Commissioner for Refugees acts as Co-ordinator of UN humanitarian assistance for Cyprus.

FINANCE

The estimated cost to the United Nations for maintaining the Force during the period from December 15th, 1974, to June 15th, 1975, is $13.7 million. The total costs from the beginning of the operation in March 1964 to December 15th, 1974, were $186.4 million.

OTHER UN ORGANIZATIONS AND RELATED AGENCIES

UNITED NATIONS CHILDREN FUND—UNICEF

New York, N.Y. 10017, U.S.A.

Office of the Director for the Eastern Mediterranean: P.O.B. 5902, Beirut, Lebanon (covers Cyprus, Israel, Jordan, Lebanon, Saudi Arabia and Syria).

Office of the Director for Europe and North Africa: Director, European Office, UNICEF, Palais des Nations, CH-1211 Geneva 10, Switzerland.

FOOD AND AGRICULTURE ORGANIZATION—FAO

Rome, Italy

FAO Regional Office for the Near East: FAO Regional Rep., P.O.B. 2223, Cairo, Egypt.

FAO Regional Office for Africa: FAO Regional Rep. P.O.B. 1628, Accra, Ghana.

Regional Councils and Commissions

Commission for Controlling the Desert Locust in the Near East: c/o UNDP Resident Representative, P.O.B. 3216, Beirut, Lebanon; f. 1965 to carry out all possible measures to control desert locust plagues within the Middle East and to reduce crop damage. Mems.: 9 states.

Commission on Wheat and Barley Improvement and Production in the Near East: to strengthen national programmes on wheat and barley improvement through advice on breeding procedures, seed multiplication and distribution, training, supply of outstanding sources of germ plasma, etc.

FAO Commission on Horticultural Production in the Near East and North Africa: c/o FAO Regional Office for the Near East, P.O.B. 2223, Cairo, Egypt; f. 1966 to promote international collaboration in the study of technical problems and the establishment of a balanced programme of horticultural research at an inter-regional level. Mems.: 21 states.
Chair. T. ElWakeel; Sec. Y. Salah.

General Fisheries Council for the Mediterranean—(GFCM): Viale delle Terme di Caracalla, 00100 Rome, Italy; f. 1952 to formulate oceanographical and technical aspects of developing and utilizing aquatic resources, to encourage and co-ordinate research in the fishing and allied industries, to assemble and publish information, and to recommend the standardization of scientific equipment, techniques and nomenclature. Mems.: 18 governments.
Chair. C. Maurin. Publs. *Session Reports* (biennially), *GFCM Circulars* (irregularly), *Studies and Reviews* (irregularly).

Near East Commission on Agricultural Planning: f. 1963 to review and exchange information and experience on agricultural plans and planning, and to make recommendations to members on means of improving their agricultural plans. Mems.: 17 states.

Near East Commission on Agricultural Statistics: f. 1962 to review the state of food and agricultural statistics in the region and advise member countries on the development and standardization of agricultural statistics. Mems.: 20 states.

Near East Forestry Commission: c/o FAO Regional Office for the Near East, P.O.B. 2223, Cairo, Egypt; first Session 1955; purpose: to advice on formulation of forest policy and to review and co-ordinate its implementation at the regional level; to exchange information and advise on suitable practices and action regarding technical and economic problems; mems. 21 countries.
Chair. Eng. Mahmoud Awad al-Jabouri; Sec. K. Hamad (FAO Regional Forestry Officer for the Near East).

Near East Plant Protection Commission: c/o FAO Regional Office for the Near East, P.O.B. 2223, Cairo, Egypt; f. 1963 to advise member countries on matters relating to the protection of plant resources in the region. Mems.: 15 states.

Near East Region Animal Production and Health Commission: c/o FAO Regional Office for the Near East, P.O.B. 2223, Cairo, Egypt; f. 1966 to provide a means of initiating and promoting agricultural development with special reference to the field of animal production and health. Mems.: FAO member nations in the Near East region.
Chair. Dr. Sultan Haidar; Sec. Dr. D. E. Faulkner.

Regional Commission on Land and Water Use in the Near East: c/o FAO Regional Office for the Near East, P.O.B. 2223, Cairo, Egypt; f. 1967 to study land and water use in the region and the problems concerning the development of land and water resources. Mems.: 16 states.
Chair. H. A. Eltobjy.

Regional Project on the Improvement and Production of Field Food Crops in the Near East and North Africa: c/o FAO Regional Office for the Near East, P.O.B. 2223, Cairo, Egypt; f. 1971 (replacing the Technical Committee on Cereal Improvement and Production in the Near East); aims to increase overall crop production in the region through research, co-operative investigations and other forms of international action. Mems: 22 states.

WORLD HEALTH ORGANIZATION—WHO

Geneva, Switzerland

WHO Regional Office for the Eastern Mediterranean: The Director, P.O.B. 1517, Alexandria, Egypt.

WHO Regional Office for Africa: The Director, P.O.B. 6, Brazzaville, People's Republic of Congo.

INTERNATIONAL CIVIL AVIATION ORGANIZATION—ICAO

Montreal, Canada

ICAO Regional Office for the Middle East and Eastern Africa: 16 Hassan Sabri, Zamalek, Cairo, Egypt.

ICAO Regional Office for Africa: P.O.B. 2356, 15 boulevard de la République, Dakar, Senegal.

REGIONAL ORGANIZATIONS

INTERNATIONAL LABOUR ORGANIZATION—ILO
Geneva, Switzerland

ILO Regional Office for Africa: P.O.B. 2788, Addis Ababa, Ethiopia.

ILO Regional Office for the Middle East and Europe: CH-1211 Geneva 22, Switzerland.

ILO Area Office in Algiers: B.P. 226, Algiers, Algeria.

ILO Area Office in Beirut: B.P. 4656, Beirut, Lebanon.

ILO Area Office in Cairo: 9 Sharia Willcocks, Zamalek, Cairo, Egypt.

ILO Area Office in Istanbul: Gümüşsuyu Caddesi 96, Ayazpaşa, Istanbul, Turkey.

Country Representative in Kuwait: P.O.B. 20275 Safat, Kuwait, Kuwait.

Representative in Teheran: P.O.B. 1555, Teheran, Iran.

UNITED NATIONS EDUCATIONAL, SCIENTIFIC AND CULTURAL ORGANIZATION—UNESCO
Paris, France

Africa Division.   **Arab States Division.**

Regional Centre for Functional Literacy in Rural Areas for the Arab States (ASFEC): Sirs-el-Layyan, Menoufia, Egypt; f. 1952 for the training of specialists, production of prototype educational materials, research in functional literacy and literacy teaching; advisory service to member states.

Dir. Dr. BASHIR AL-BAKRI.

UNESCO Regional Office for Science and Technology in the Arab States: 8 Sh. el Salamlik, Garden City, Cairo, Egypt.

Head of Office CHAUDHURI KAMAL REHEEM.

UNESCO Regional Office for Education in the Arab Countries (*Bureau Régional de l'Unesco pour l'education dans les pays arabes*): B.P. 5244, Avenue de la Cité Sportive, Bir Hassan, Beirut, Lebanon; f. 1973; part of the Secretariat of Unesco, the Regional Office trains education personnel (especially planners and administrators), provides advisory services, information and documentation, and carries out studies and research.

Dir. CHIKH BEKRI. Publs. *Review Education* (quarterly), *Bulletin du Liaison*.

The Arab League

Midan Al Tahrir, Cairo, Egypt

The League of Arab States is a voluntary association of sovereign Arab states designed to strengthen the close ties linking them and to co-ordinate their policies and activities and direct them towards the common good of all the Arab countries. It was founded in March 1945.

MEMBERS

Algeria	Lebanon	Palestine (*see* below)	Syria
Bahrain	Libya	Qatar	Tunisia
Egypt	Mauritania	Saudi Arabia	United Arab Emirates
Iraq	Morocco	Somalia	Yemen Arab Republic
Jordan	Oman	Sudan	Yemen People's Democratic
Kuwait			Republic

MEMBERSHIP AND FUNCTIONS

While it is a prerequisite that members must be Arab states that are fully independent, the activities of the League also often include Arab countries which are not independent. Palestine is considered an independent state, as explained in the Charter Annex on Palestine (reproduced on page 136), and therefore a full member of the League.

The Arab League itself is an international body with its own independent statutory powers and general objectives.

MAIN ORGANS

Provided for in the Charter, or else legally considered among the main organs of the League:

COUNCIL

The supreme organ of the Arab League. Meets in March and September. Consists of representatives of the twenty member states, each of which has one vote, and a representative for Palestine. Unanimous decisions of the Council shall be binding upon all member states of the League; majority decisions shall be binding only on those states which have accepted them.

The Council may, if necessary, hold an extraordinary session at the request of two member states. Invitations to all sessions are extended by the Secretary-General. The ordinary sessions are presided over by representatives of the member states in turn.

Sixteen committees are attached to the Council:

Political Committee: studies political questions and reports to the Council meetings concerned with them. All member states are members of the Committee. It represents the Council in dealing with critical political matters when the Council is meeting. Usually composed of the Foreign Ministers.

Cultural Committee: in charge of following up the activities of the Cultural Department and the cultural affairs within the scope of the secretariat; co-ordinates the activities of the general secretariat and the various cultural bodies in member states.

Economic Committee: complemented by the Economic Council since 1953.

Communications Committee: supervises land, sea and air communications, together with weather forecasts and postal matters.

Social Committee: supports co-operation in such matters as family and child welfare.

Legal Committee: an extension of the Nationality and Passports Committee abolished in 1947; studies and legally formulates draft agreements, bills, regulations and official documents.

Arab Oil Experts Committee: for study of oil affairs; also investigates methods to prevent the smuggling of Arab oil into Israel; and for co-ordination of oil policies in general.

Information Committee: studies information projects, suggests plans and carries out the policies decided by the Council of Information Ministers.

Health Committee: for co-operation in health affairs.

Human Rights Committee: studies subjects concerning human rights, particularly violations by Israel; collaborates with the Information and Cultural Committees.

Permanent Committee for Administrative and Financial Affairs.

Permanent Committee for Meteorology.

Committee of Arab Experts on Co-operation.

Arab Women's Committee.

Organization of Youth Welfare.

Conference of Liaison Officers: co-ordinates trade activities among commercial attachés of various Arab embassies abroad.

GENERAL SECRETARIAT

The administrative and financial offices of the League. The Secretariat carries out the decisions of the Council, and provides financial and administrative services for the personnel of the League. There are a number of departments: economic, political, legal, cultural, social and labour affairs, petroleum, finance, Palestine, health, information, communications, protocol. The most recently formed department deals with African affairs.

The Secretary-General is appointed by the League Council by a two-thirds majority of the member states. He appoints the Assistant Secretaries and principal officials, with the approval of the Council. He has the rank of Ambassador, and the Assistant Secretaries have the rank of Ministers Plenipotentiary.

Secretary-General: MAHMOUD RIAD (Egypt).

Assistant Secretaries-General: Dr. S. NOFAL (Egypt), Dr. AHMED EL SAIED HAMAD (Sudan), ASSAAD EL ASSAAD (Lebanon), SELIM EL YAFI (Syria), Dr. M. EL FARRA (Jordan).

Assistant Secretary-General for Military Affairs: Gen. MOHAMMED ALI FAHMY (Egypt).

DEFENCE AND ECONOMIC CO-OPERATION

Groups established under the Treaty of Joint Defence and Economic Co-operation, concluded in 1950 to complement the Charter of the League:

Arab Unified Military Command: Cairo; f. 1964 to co-ordinate military policies for the liberation of Palestine.

Economic Council: to compare and co-ordinate the economic policies of the member states; the Council is composed of Ministers of Economic Affairs or their deputies. Decisions are taken by majority vote. The first meeting was held in 1953.

Joint Defence Council: supervises implementation of those aspects of the treaty concerned with common defence. Composed of Foreign and Defence Ministers; decisions by a two-thirds majority vote of members are binding on all.

Military Advisory Organization.

Permanent Military Commission: Established 1950; composed of representatives of army General Staffs; main purpose: to draw up plans of joint defence for submission to the Joint Defence Council.

OTHER INSTITUTIONS OF THE COUNCIL

Other bodies established by resolutions adopted by the Council of the League:

Academy of Arab Music.

Administrative Tribunal of the Arab League: Cairo; f. 1964; began operations 1966.

Arab Authority for Exhibitions: f. 1964 to co-ordinate the planning and holding of international exhibitions and fairs in the member states of the League; has a Council of representatives appointed by the member states.

Arab Centre for Industrial Development: 22 Dr. Taha Hussein St., Zamalek, Cairo, Egypt; created in 1968 in compliance with a decision of the League Economic Council; the Arab states are represented at the Centre by an official representative and an alternative; the secretariat includes departments for technical and economic studies and aid for the promotion of industrial information; began operations in 1970.

Arab Institute of Forestry: Latakia, Syria.

SPECIALIZED AGENCIES OF THE LEAGUE

All member states of the Arab League are also members of the Specialized Agencies, which constitute an integral part of the Arab League.

Arab Centre for the Study of Dry Regions and Arid Territories: Damascus, Syria.

Arab Educational, Cultural and Scientific Organization: Baghdad, Iraq; f. 1964 when the Ministers of Education of Arab Countries (excluding Lebanon) issued the Charter of Arab Cultural Unity and laid down the Statute of the organization; the organization was approved by the League Council in the same year; aims: to promote intellectual unity of the Arab countries by means of Education; to raise cultural standards; to enable the Arab countries to participate in technical development; to establish specialized institutes; to train experts for research in Arab civilization. Each member submits an annual report on progress in education, cultural matters and science.

The Arab League has a Permanent Delegation at UNESCO which may act on behalf of Arab states that are not members of the world body.

The first session of the General Conference was held in Cairo in 1970. Dir.-Gen. Dr. ABDEL-AZIZ EL SAYED IBRAHIM.

There are five institutions within the framework of the Arab Educational, Cultural and Scientific Organization:

Institute for Arab Studies and Research Work: f. 1953 for specialization by graduates of Arab universities; provides for studies in contemporary Arab affairs, including national and international affairs, economics, social studies, history, geography, law, literature and linguistics. A special department of the Institute is devoted to Palestinian affairs, to research into the Arab cause; the Institute aims to develop the understanding of Arab nationalism.

Arab Regional Literacy Organization: Cairo, Egypt.

Institute of Arab Manuscripts.

Permanent Bureau for Arabization: Rabat, Morocco.

Museum of Arab Culture: Cairo, Egypt.

Arab Fund for Economic and Social Development: P.O. Box 21923, Kuwait; f. 1971; finances economic and social development projects in Arab countries; Pres. SAYEB JAROUDI.

Arab Health Organization.

Arab Institute of Petroleum Research.

Arab Labour Organization: 7 Midan El Misaha, Cairo; established in 1965 for co-operation between member states in labour problems; unification of labour legislation and general conditions of work wherever possible; research; technical assistance; social insurance; training, etc.; the organization has a tripartite structure: governments, employers and workers; first meeting March 1971; Gen Dir. Dr. TAYEB LAHDIRI. Publs. _Bulletin_ (monthly), _Arab Labour Review_ (quarterly).

Arab Organization for Administrative Science: 8 Salaheldin Street, Cairo, Egypt; created in accordance with an approval of the League Council in 1961, commencing activity in 1969 soon after ratification of the agreement by four Arab states (Egypt, Iraq, Syria, Kuwait); to ensure co-operation in promoting administrative science, to improve the standard of administrative staff in the Arab states.

Arab Organization for Agricultural Development: Khartoum, Sudan; proposed in 1969 by a decision of Arab Ministers of Agriculture, which was approved by the Economic Council in 1970 and ratified by the League Council; to contribute to co-operation in agricultural activities, and in the development of natural and human resources for agriculture.

Arab Organization for Specifications and Standards: 11 Mohamed Marashly Street, Zamalek, P.O.B. 690, Cairo, Egypt; created 1965 after the Economic Council had approved an agreement for its creation by twenty Arab states as a specialized institution in the field of economic, commercial and industrial co-operation; began activity in 1968 to unify technical terms and standard specifications for products such as food, cloth, fertilizers, building materials, oil, minerals, electrical products; also deals with technical drawing and packaging; assists in the establishment of national bodies and collaborates with international standards activities; Sec.-Gen. Dr. MAHMOUD MOHAMAD SALAMA (Egypt); publs. _Annual Report_ (French and English), _Quarterly Bulletin_ (Arabic and English), _Standard Specification_ (Arabic, English and French) and information pamphlets.

Arab Postal Union: 28 Adly Street, Cairo, Egypt; f. 1954; Aims: to establish more strict postal relations between the Arab countries than those laid down by the Universal Postal Union, to pursue the development and modernization of postal services in member countries; Sec.-Gen. Dr. ANOUAR BAKIR. Publs. _Bulletin_ (monthly), _Review_ (quarterly), _News_ (annual) and occasional studies.

Arab States Broadcasting Union: 23 Kasr el Nil St., Cairo; f. 1969 to promote Arab fraternity, to acquaint the world with the Arab nation, co-ordinate and study broadcasting subjects, to exchange expertise and technical co-operation in broadcasting by establishing permanent bodies and forming permanent or temporary study committees. Mems.: 19 Arab radio and TV stations and four foreign associates; Sec.-Gen. SALEH ABDEL KADER. Publs. _Arab Broadcasts_ (monthly, in Arabic), _ASBU Review_ (quarterly, in English), _Broadcasting Studies and Researches_ (irregular), _Broadcasting Reports_ (irregular).

Arab Telecommunications Union: 83 Ramses Street, Cairo, Egypt; f. 1958; to co-ordinate and develop telecommunications between member countries; to exchange technical aid and encourage research. Sec.-Gen. Dr. MAHMOUD MUHAMMAD RIAD. Publs. _Economic and Technical Studies; Arab Telecommunications Union Journal_ (quarterly).

Civil Aviation Council of Arab States: 10 El Nil St., El Giza, Arab Republic of Egypt; created 1965, began operations 1967; aims to develop the principles, techniques and economics of air transport in the Arab World; to co-operate with the International Civil Aviation Organization and to attempt to standardize laws and technical terms; deals also with Arab air rates; Pres. M. S. EL-HAKIM. Publs. _Air Transport Activities in Arab Countries, Lexicon of Civil Aviation Terminology_ (Arabic); _Unified Air Law for Arab States_ (Arabic and English).

Council of Arab Economic Unity: created under the Arab Economic Unity Agreement (reproduced on page 137) which was drawn up by the League Council in June 1962; the Council of Arab Economic Unity was formed in June 1964, when five states had ratified the Agreement, namely Egypt, Iraq, Jordan, Kuwait and Syria; it supervises implementation of the Agreement, which aims to form a single economic system combining all the Arab states; common external tariffs, freedom of movement of labour and capital, and common economic policies are to be introduced. In August of the same year the five states ratified a further resolution, establishing a Common Market of the Arab States, although Kuwait withdrew in July 1965.

The Arab Economic Unity Agreement was also signed by Morocco, Yemen and the Sudan; it was ratified by Yemen in 1967 and by the Sudan in 1969.

In January 1971 a further common market agreement between Egypt, Iraq and Syria came into force.

International Arab Organization for Social Defence against Crime: f. 1965 at League Headquarters by the League Council to study causes and remedies for crime and the treatment of criminals; Sec.-Gen. Dr. ABDEL-WAHHAB EL-ASCHMAOUI; the organization consists of three bureaux:

International Arab Bureau for Narcotics: Cairo; Dir.-Gen. AHMAD ALHADIQAH (Egypt).

International Arab Bureau for Prevention of Crime: Baghdad; Dir.-Gen. AMER AL-MUKHTAR (Iraq).

International Arab Bureau of Criminal Police: Damascus; Dir.-Gen. Col. ASHDEK ALDEIRY (Syria).

Joint Arab Scientific Council for the Utilization of Atomic Energy.

EXTERNAL RELATIONS

Arab League Offices and Information Centres abroad.

Set up by the Arab League to co-ordinate work at all levels among Arab embassies abroad. The Arab League Office in New Delhi has been given full diplomatic status.

Argentina: Officina de la Liga de los Estados Arabes, Calla 0 1319, Buenos Aires.

Belgium: Bureau de la Ligue des Etats Arabes, 108 Ave. F.D. Roosevelt, Brussels 1050.

Brazil: Missao de Liga dos Estados Arabes, Sqs. 105, Bloco K, Apt. 201, 70000 Brasília, D.F.

Canada: Arab Information Centre, 170 Laurier Ave. West, Suite 709, Ottawa, Ontario.

Chile: Representación de la Liga de Los Estados Arabes, Gallard 2175, Santiago de Chile.

France: Bureau de la Ligue des Etats Arabes, 138 blvd. Haussman, Paris 8.

Federal Republic of Germany: Delegation von der Liga der Arabischen Staaten, Friedrich Wilhelm Strasse 2A, Bonn-53.

India: League of Arab States Mission, 62 Golf Links, New Delhi.

Italy: Arab League Office, Piazzale Belle Arti no. 6, Rome.

Japan: Office of the League of Arab States, 1-1-12 Moto Azabu, Minato-ku 106, Tokyo.

Spain: Officina de la Liga de los Estados Arabes, c/Alcala 89-20 Derecha, Madrid 9.

Switzerland: Délégation de la Ligue des Etats Arabes, 7 Ave. Krieg, Geneva.

United Kingdom: Arab Information Office, 1-11 Hay Hill, London, W.1.

U.S.A.: Arab Information Center, 747 Third Ave , 25th Floor, New York, N.Y. 10017.

Arab Information Center, 18 South Michigan Ave., Chicago, Illinois 60603.

Arab Information Center, Suite 1302, Hartford Bldg., Dallas, Texas.

Arab Information Center, World Trade Center, Ferry Bldg , San Francisco, California 94111.

Arab Information Center, 1875 Connecticut Ave , N.W., Suite 1110, Washington, D.C. 20009.

Arab League Representatives:

Kenya: Arab League Representative, c/o The Embassy of the Arab Republic of Egypt, Total Bldg., Koinange St., Nairobi.

Nigeria: Arab League Representative, Post Box 6916, 55 Ademola St., Ikoyi, Lagos.

Senegal: Arab League Representative, c/o L'Ambassade du Liban, 18 Ave. de la République, Dakar.

BUDGET

CONTRIBUTIONS (%)
(1973)

Egypt	14.00	Sudan	3.80
Kuwait	14.00	Tunisia	3.00
Saudi Arabia	11.50	Lebanon	2.50
Libya	11.00	Syria	2.50
Iraq	10.00	Jordan	1.30
Morocco	6.40	Bahrain	1.00
Algeria	6.00	Oman	1.00
United Arab Emirates	6.00	Yemen A.R.	1.00
		Yemen P.D.R.	1.00
Qatar	4.00		
			100.00

EXPENDITURE 1973-74

	£E	$
General Secretariat	310,734	1,857,487
Industrial Development Centre	126,445	255,310
Arab Organization for Social Defence against Crime	10,099	58,140
TOTAL	447,278	2,170,937

RECORD OF EVENTS

1945   Pact of the Arab League signed, March.

1946   Cultural Treaty signed.

1950   Joint Defence and Economic Co-operation Treaty.

1952   Agreements on extradition, writs and letters of request, nationality of Arabs outside their country of origin.

1953   Formation of Arab Telecommunications and Radio Communications Union.
Agreements for facilitating trade between Arab countries.
Formation of Economic Council.

Convention on the privileges and immunities of the League.

First Conference of Arab Education Ministers, Cairo, December.

1954   Formation of Arab Postal Union.
Nationality Agreement.

1956   Agreement on the adoption of a Common Tariff Nomenclature. Establishment of the Arab Potassium Company.
Sudan joins Arab League.

1957   Agreement on the creation of Arab Financial Institution for Economic Development, June.

Cultural Agreement with UNESCO signed, November.

1958   Co-operation Agreement between the Arab League and the International Labour Organisation.

1959   First Arab Oil Congress, Cairo, April.

1960   Inauguration of new Arab League HQ at Midan Al Tahrir, Cairo, March.

1961   Kuwait joins League.

Syrian Arab Republic rejoins League as independent member.

Agreement on the establishment of the Arab Organization for Administrative Sciences.

Agreement with WHO on exchange of medical information, May.

1962   Arab Economic Unity Agreement.

U.A.R. announced intention of leaving Arab League.

1963   U.A.R. resumes active membership of League, March.

Agreement to establish an Arab Navigation Company, December.

Agreement on establishment of an Arab Organization on Social Defence against Crime.

1964   Cairo conference of Arab Kings and Presidents, called by Gamal Abdul Nasser, January.

First session of the Council of Arab Information Ministers, Cairo, March.

First meeting of Economic Unity Council, June.

Arab Common Market approved by Arab Economic Unity Council, August.

Second Summit Conference welcomes establishment of Palestine Liberation Organization, September.

First Conference of Arab Ministers of Communications, Beirut, November.

1965   Arab Common Market established, January.

Third Summit Conference, May. Tunisia absent. Intergrated plan approved to defend Palestine in the UN.

Establishment of Arab Air Carriers' Organization. Agreement on Arab Co-operation for the Peaceful Uses of Atomic Energy.

Establishment of Arab Union of Automobile Clubs and Tourist Societies, October.

1966   Cairo Conference of Arab leaders, March. Tunisia absent.

Cairo Conference of Arab Foreign Ministers, September. Tunisia absent.

First session of Arab League Administrative Court, September.

1967   Meeting of Arab Foreign Ministers, Kuwait, June. Cairo meeting of Heads of State of Algeria, Iraq. Sudan, Syria, U.A.R., July.

1967   Meeting of Arab Foreign Ministers, Khartoum, August. Discussion of Arab oil embargo against the U.S.A. and the United Kingdom.

Fourth Summit Conference in Khartoum, August. Decision to resume oil supplies to the West. Syria absent.

Establishment of Civil Aviation Council of Arab States.

Agreement to establish an Arab Tanker Company, December.

1968   First Conference of Arab Tourist Ministers, Cairo, February.

Arab League approves Industrial Development Centre.

Economic Council approves establishment of Arab Fund for Economic and Social Development.

1969   Permanent Council of Co-operation Experts established to promote co-operative movement in Arab States, January.

First Session of the Arab States Broadcasting Union (ASBU), Khartoum, February.

Fifth summit Conference, Rabat. Call for mobilization of all Arab Nations against Israel.

Industrial Development Centre for the Arab States starts activities.

First Conference of Arab Health Ministers, Cairo.

1970   Establishment of the Arab Organization for Agricultural Development.

Establishment of the Arab Educational, Cultural and Scientific Organization.

1971   First meeting of Arab Labour Organization.

Bahrain, Qatar and Oman admitted to Arab League, September.

1972   First Arab Traffic Conference, May.

Mahmoud Riad succeeds Abdel Khalek Hassouna as Secretary-General, June.

Conference on Arab Women and National Development, Cairo, September.

Meeting of the Arab Agricultural Development Organization, Khartoum, October.

1973   Treaty for Technical Co-operation between the Afro-Asian Rural Reconstruction Organization (AARRO) and the Arab League signed, May.

Declaration issued defining Arab demands for settlement of the Middle East conflict.

Sixth summit conference in Algiers, November; approval of three institutions to help Africa in the oil crisis: Arab Loan Fund for Africa, Arab Bank for Development in Africa, and Arab Fund for Technical Assistance.

Mauritania admitted to Arab League, December.

1974   Arab oil ministers endow Arab Loan Fund for Africa with $200 million, January.

Somalia admitted to Arab League, February.

Twenty-third ordinary session of council of Arab Economic Unity, June. The main proposals discussed were a joint petrochemical fertilizer

1974
cont. company, an Arab League development fund and a commission to supervise the pharmaceuticals industry in the member states.

Agreement to establish permanent joint commission for economic co-operation with EEC.

Joint Defence Council meeting, July. Decisions

concerning political, financial and military assistance to ensure the defence of Lebanon.

Seventh summit conference in Rabat, October. Replenishes Arab Loan Fund with further $200 million.

1975   Arab Bank for Development in Africa established.

PUBLICATIONS

Information Department: *Information Bulletin* (Arabic and English); also bulletins of treaties and agreements concluded among the member states.

New York Office: *Arab World* (monthly), and *News and Views*.

Geneva Office: *Le Monde Arabe* (monthly), and *Nouvelles du Monde Arabe* (weekly).

Buenos Aires Office: *Arabia Review* (monthly).

Paris Office: *Actualités Arabes* (fortnightly).
Brasília Office: *Oriente Arabe* (monthly).
Rome Office: *Rassegna del Mondo Arabo* (monthly).
London Office: *The Arab* (monthly).
New Delhi Office: *Al Arab* (monthly).
Bonn Office: *Arabische Korrespondenz* (fortnightly).
Ottawa Office: *Spotlight on the Arab World* (fortnightly), *The Arab Case* (monthly).

THE PACT OF THE LEAGUE OF ARAB STATES

(March 22nd, 1945)

Article 1

The League of Arab States is composed of the independent Arab States which have signed this Pact.

Any independent Arab state has the right to become a member of the League. If it desires to do so, it shall submit a request which will be deposited with the Permanent Secretariat-General and submitted to the Council at the first meeting held after submission of the request.

Article 2

The League has as its purpose the strengthening of the relations between the member states; the co-ordination of their policies in order to achieve co-operation between them and to safeguard their independence and sovereignty; and a general concern with the affairs and interests of the Arab countries. It has also as its purpose the close co-operation of the member states, with due regard to the organization and circumstances of each state, on the following matters:

(a) Economic and financial affairs, including commercial relations, customs, currency, and questions of agriculture and industry.

(b) Communications: this includes railways, roads, aviation, navigation, telegraphs and posts.

(c) Cultural affairs.

(d) Nationality, passports, visas, execution of judgments, and extradition of criminals.

(e) Social affairs.

(f) Health problems.

Article 3

The League shall possess a Council composed of the representatives of the member states of the League; each state shall have a single vote, irrespective of the number of its representatives.

It shall be the task of the Council to achieve the realization of the objectives of the League and to supervise the execution of agreements which the member states have concluded on the questions enumerated in the preceding article, or on any other questions.

It likewise shall be the Council's task to decide upon the means by which the League is to co-operate with the international bodies to be created in the future in order to guarantee security and peace and regulate economic and social relations.

Article 4

For each of the questions listed in Article 2 there shall be set up a special committee in which the member states of the League shall be represented. These committees shall be charged with the task of laying down the principles and extent of co-operation. Such principles shall be formulated as draft agreements, to be presented to the Council for examination preparatory to their submission to the aforesaid states.

Representatives of the other Arab countries may take part in the work of the aforesaid committees. The Council shall determine the conditions under which these representatives may be permitted to participate and the rules governing such representation.

Article 5

Any resort to force in order to resolve disputes arising between two or more member states of the League is prohibited. If there should arise among them a difference which does not concern a state's independence, sovereignty, or territorial integrity, and if the parties to the dispute have recourse to the Council for the settlement of this difference, the decision of the Council shall then be enforceable and obligatory.

In such a case, the states between whom the difference has arisen shall not participate in the deliberations and decisions of the Council.

The Council shall mediate in all differences which threaten to lead to war between two member states, or a member state and a third state, with a view to bringing about their reconciliation.

Decisions of arbitration and mediation shall be taken by majority vote.

REGIONAL ORGANIZATIONS

The Arab League

Article 6

In case of agression or threat of aggression by one state against a member state, the state which has been attacked or threatened with aggression may demand the immediate convocation of the Council.

The Council shall by unanimous decision determine the measures necessary to repulse the aggression. If the aggressor is a member state, his vote shall not be counted in determining unanimity.

If, as a result of the attack, the government of the State attacked finds itself unable to communicate with the Council, that state's representative in the Council shall have the right to request the convocation of the Council for the purpose indicated in the foregoing paragraph. In the event that this representative is unable to communicate with the Council, any member state of the League shall have the right to request the convocation of the Council.

Article 7

Unanimous decisions of the Council shall be binding upon all member states of the League; majority decisions shall be binding only upon those states which have accepted them.

In either case the decisions of the Council shall be enforced in each member state according to its respective basic laws.

Article 8

Each member state shall respect the systems of government established in the other member states and regard them as exclusive concerns of those states. Each shall pledge to abstain from any action calculated to change established systems of government.

Article 9

States of the League which desire to establish closer co-operation and stronger bonds than are provided by this Pact may conclude agreements to that end.

Treaties and agreements already concluded or to be concluded in the future between a member state and another state shall not be binding or restrictive upon other members.

Article 10

The permanent seat of the League of Arab States is established in Cairo. The Council may, however, assemble at any other place it may designate.

Article 11

The Council of the League shall convene in ordinary session twice a year, in March and in September. It shall convene in extraordinary session upon the request of two member states of the League whenever the need arises.

Article 12

The League shall have a permanent Secretariat-General which shall consist of a Secretary-General, Assistant Secretaries, and an appropriate number of officials.

The Council of the League shall appoint the Secretary-General by a majority of two-thirds of the states of the League. The Secretary-General, with the approval of the Council, shall appoint the Assistant Secretaries and the principal officials of the League.

The Council of the League shall establish an administrative regulation for the functions of the Secretariat-General and matters relating to the Staff.

The Secretary-General shall have the rank of Ambassador and the Assistant Secretaries that of Ministers Plenipotentiary.

The first Secretary-General of the League is named in an Annex to this Pact.

Article 13

The Secretary-General shall prepare the draft of the budget of the League and shall submit it to the Council for approval before the beginning of each fiscal year.

The Council shall fix the share of the expenses to be borne by each state of the League. This share may be reconsidered if necessary.

Article 14

The members of the Council of the League as well as the members of the committees and the officials who are to be designated in the administrative regulation shall enjoy diplomatic privileges and immunity when engaged in the exercise of their functions.

The building occupied by the organs of the League shall be inviolable.

Article 15

The first meeting of the Council shall be convened at the invitation of the head of the Egyptian Government. Thereafter it shall be convened at the invitation of the Secretary-General.

The representatives of the member states of the League shall alternately assume the presidency of the Council at each of its ordinary sessions.

Article 16

Except in cases specifically indicated in this Pact, a majority vote of the Council shall be sufficient to make enforceable decisions on the following matters:

(*a*) Matters relating to personnel.

(*b*) Adoption of the budget of the League.

(*c*) Establishment of the administrative regulations for the Council, the Committees, and the Secretariat-General.

(*d*) Decisions to adjourn the sessions.

Article 17

Each member state of the League shall deposit with the Secretariat-General one copy of every treaty or agreement concluded or to be concluded in the future between itself and another member state of the League or a third state.

Article 18
(deals with withdrawal)

Article 19
(deals with amendment)

Article 20
(deals with ratification)

Annex Regarding Palestine

Since the termination of the last great war the rule of the Ottoman Empire over the Arab countries, among them Palestine, which had become detached from that Empire, has come to an end. She has come to be autonomous, not subordinate to any other state.

The Treaty of Lausanne proclaimed that her future was to be settled by the parties concerned.

However, even though she was as yet unable to control her own affairs, the Covenant of the League (of Nations) in 1919 made provision for a regime based upon recognition of her independence.

Her international existence and independence in the legal sense cannot, therefore, be questioned, any more than could the independence of the other Arab countries.

Although the outward manifestations of this independence have remained obscured for reasons beyond her control, this should not be allowed to interfere with her participation in the work of the Council of the League.

The states signatory to the Pact of the Arab League are therefore of the opinion that, considering the special circumstances of Palestine and until that Country can effectively exercise its independence, the Council of the League should take charge of the selection of an Arab representative from Palestine to take part in its work.

Annex Regarding Co-operation with Countries which are not Members of the Council of the League

Whereas the member states of the League will have to deal in the Council as well as in the committees with matters which will benefit and affect the Arab world at large;

And whereas the Council has to take into account the aspirations of the Arab countries which are not members of the Council and has to work toward their realization;

Now therefore, it particularly behoves the states signatory to the Pact of the Arab League to enjoin the Council of the League, when considering the admission of those countries to participation in the committees referred to in the Pact, that it should do its utmost to co-operate with them, and furthermore, that it should spare no effort to learn their needs and understand their aspirations and hopes; and that it should work thenceforth for their best interests and the safeguarding of their future with all the political means at its disposal.

ARAB ECONOMIC UNITY AGREEMENT

The Economic Unity Agreement between the member states of the Arab League was drawn up in Cairo on June 6th, 1962, and subsequently came into effect on April 30th, 1964. The Agreement was signed in 1962 by Jordan, Kuwait, Morocco, Syria and Egypt, in 1963 by Iraq and the Yemen Arab Republic, and in 1968 by the Sudan. It was ratified by Kuwait (1962), Egypt (1963), Iraq, Jordan and Syria (1964), the Yemen Arab Republic (1967) and the Sudan (1969). The Unity Council held its first meeting in Cairo on June 3rd, 1964.

The Agreement is summarized below.

OBJECTS

Preamble

The Governments of the member-states of the Arab League, desirous of organizing between them and unifying their relations on bases accommodating to the natural and historical ties between them, and for the purpose of creating the best conditions for the growth of their economy, for promoting their riches, and for ensuring the prosperity of their peoples, have agreed on creating a complete unity between them, to be achieved gradually with the maximum possible speed ensuring the transition to the desired situation without causing harm to their essential interests.

Article 1

The main objective of the Agreement is to attain complete Arab Economic Unity. The Arab State will thus have a unified, integrated, proportionate Arab economy guided by one single economic policy for all the component parts. The member-states and their nationals are guaranteed equality in the following:

(1) Freedom of movement of persons and capital.

(2) Freedom of exchange of domestic and foreign goods and products.

(3) Freedom of residence, work, employment, and exercise of economic activities.

(4) Freedom of transport and transit and of using means of transport, ports and civil airports.

(5) Rights of ownership, of making one's will, and of inheritance.

METHODS

Article 2

The Arab states are required to work for accomplishing the following:

(1) The Arab states should be made one customs zone subject to a single administration. Customs tariffs, legislations, and regulations applied in these states should be standardized. This is to be achieved by gradual abolition of customs duties between the Arab states for ensuring the exchange of Arab-made goods and the eventual removal of duties altogether. In addition customs duties should be adjusted between the Arab states so as to arrive at standard rates in respect of the outside world. In this way, the Arab states would be converted into one market where both home-produced and imported goods could move without being subject to any duties other than those imposed in respect of the outside world.

(2) The Arab states should work for standardizing their import-export policies and all relevant regulations. It is a prerequisite for the creation of one Arab market to have import-export policies and regulations unified and co-ordinated.

(3) Standardizing transport and transit systems. As the means of transport will enjoy freedom of movement between all parts of the Arab homeland, they should necessarily become subject to standard regulations.

(4) Trade agreements and payments agreements with outside countries are to be concluded collectively by the Arab states. The creation of one Arab market makes it necessary to have such agreements concluded jointly. Relations with the outside world will be unified.

(5) Policies related to agriculture, industry and internal trade should be co-ordinated. Economic legislation should be standardized in a manner ensuring equal terms to all nationals of the contracting countries in respect of work in agriculture, industry, or any other calling. The co-ordination of these policies and legislations is an inevitable sequence to the creation of the United Arab Market where Arab nationals are to be guaranteed the right of taking up any profession or any economic activity anywhere in the Arab world.

(6) Steps should be taken to co-ordinate labour and social legislation. In so far as Arab workers are to enjoy the freedom of working anywhere they please in the Arab homeland, it is necessary to make them all subject to one labour law and to the same social security rules.

(7) (a) Steps should be taken to co-ordinate legislation concerning government and municipal taxes and duties and all other taxes pertaining to agriculture, industry, trade, real estate, and investments in a manner ensuring equal opportunities.

(b) Measures should be taken to prevent the duplication of taxes and duties levied on the nationals of the contracting countries.

(8) The monetary and fiscal policies and all relevant regulations of the contracting countries should be co-ordinated before the standardization of currency.

(9) Standardizing the methods of the classification of statistics.

(10) All necessary measures should be taken to ensure the attainment of the goals specified in Articles 1 and 2 of the Agreement.

It is however possible to by-pass the principle of standardization in respect to certain circumstances and certain countries—this being made with the approval of the Arab Economic Unity Council.

ORGANIZATION

Articles 3–10

Article 3 provides for the establishment of a body with the name of "The Arab Economic Unity Council" This Council will have its centre in Cairo and will be composed of a full member from each of the contracting parties. Decisions are taken by a two-thirds majority. Each state has one vote.

The Council has been vested with all necessary powers for implementing the rules of the Agreement and its protocols, for running the subsidiary committees and establishments and for appointing members of staff and experts.

Branching from the Unity Council are a number of permanent and provisional committees.

The permanent committees are:

(1) The Customs Committee, whose task will be to handle customs technical and administrative affairs and transit affairs.

(2) The Monetary and Financial Committee. This Committee will undertake the handling of affairs pertaining to monetary matters, banking taxes, duties and other financial affairs. Two Sub-Committees have been formed:

(a) Sub-Committee on Financial and Taxation Affairs;

(b) Sub-Committee on Monetary Affairs.

(3) The Economic Committee. It will be the duty of this Committee to handle matters pertaining to agriculture,

industry, trade, transport, communications, labour and social affairs. Five Sub-Committees have been formed:

(a) Agricultural Growth Sub-Committee; (b) Industrial Co-ordination and Mineral Wealth Development Sub-Committee; (c) Planning and Trade Co-ordination Sub-Committee; (d) Planning and Transport and Communications Co-ordination Sub-Committee; (e) Social Affairs Sub-Committee.

The Council and its subsidiaries enjoy financial and administrative autonomy. The Council will have a special budget to which the member-states will subscribe at the rate of their subscriptions to the budget of the Secretariat-General of the Arab League. The Council has been entrusted with the tasks of formulating regulations and legislations aiming at the creation of a unified Arab customs zone and at co-ordinating foreign trade policy. The conclusion of trade agreements and of payments agreements has been made subject to the approval of the Council. The Council is also entrusted with the task of co-ordinating economic growth, laying down programmes for the attainment of common economic development plans, co-ordinating policies for agriculture, industry and external trade, working out transport and transit regulations and unification of regulations on labour and social security, and harmonizing financial and monetary policies with the purpose of standardizing currency. It will also formulate all other legislation necessary for the achievement of the purposes of the Agreement.

IMPLEMENTATION

Articles 11–20, Protocols

The implementation of the Agreement is to take place in successive stages and in the shortest possible time. The Council has been required to draw up a practical plan for the stages of implementation and to define the legislative, administrative and technical measures necessary for each stage taking into consideration the appendix concerning the necessary steps for the realization of Arab Economic Unity, which is attached to the Agreement and constitutes an integral part of it. Article 15 stipulates that any two or more of the contracting parties have the right to conclude

agreements for economic unity wider than that provided for under the Agreement.

The Council shall exercise its powers in accordance with resolutions which it will pass, which will be executed by the member-states in accordance with their constitutional rules.

The Governments of the contracting parties have pledged not to promulgate any laws, regulations or administrative decisions of a nature which might conflict with the Agreement or its Protocols. However, the contracting parties have been given the freedom, under the Agreement's

First Protocol, to conclude bilateral economic agreements, for extraordinary political or defensive purposes, with outside parties, provided that such bilateral agreements contain nothing prejudicial to the objectives of this Agreement.

The Agreement's Second Protocol places limitations on the powers of the Arab Economic Unity Council. In the course of an initial period not exceeding five years (but which can be renewed for up to ten years) the Council is required to study the necessary steps for co-ordinating the economic, financial and social policies and for the attainment of the following objectives:

(*a*) The freedom of the movement of persons and the freedom of work, employment, residence, ownership, making one's will, and inheritance.

(*b*) Giving unrestricted and unqualified freedom to the movement of transit goods without any restrictions in respect of the type or nationality or the means of transport.

(*c*) Facilitating the exchange of Arab goods and Arab products.

(*d*) The freedom of exercising economic activities—it should be understood that this should cause no harm to the interests of some of the contracting parties at this stage.

(*e*) The freedom of using ports and civil airports in a manner guaranteeing activation and development.

———————

At its first session held in Cairo from June 3rd–6th, 1964, the Economic Unity Council decided to interpret the time periods suggested in the Second Protocol in such a manner as to speed up the accomplishment of the various phases. Thus the Council considered the five-year period proposed as a maximum limit for the completion of the necessary studies. The Council also resolved to benefit from the rule established in Article 4 of the Protocol, which provided for the following:

"Two parties or more can, if they so desire, agree on ending the introductory stage or any other stage, and move directly to comprehensive economic unity."

The Council has therefore begun by studying the practical steps to be taken for the achievement of economic unity. It was decided that the Arab Common Market project should be accomplished as quickly as possible. A Technical Committee was assigned with the study of the subject, and its detailed report was debated and approved by the Council at its second meeting on August 7th, 1964.

The resolution passed at that meeting called for exempting from customs duties all agricultural and animal products as well as natural resources and industrial goods exchanged between the members of the Arab Market. This exemption will be either complete or gradual. It was also resolved that, in the case of gradual exemption, the rate should be ten per cent in respect of industrial goods and twenty per cent for agricultural products, to be effective from the beginning of 1965.

Central Treaty Organization—CENTO

Eski Büyük Miilet Meclisi Binası, Ankara, Turkey

The Central Treaty Organization aims to provide mutual security and defence for member countries and seeks the peaceful economic development of the region through co-operative effort. CENTO replaced the Baghdad Pact Organization (formed in 1955) after the withdrawal of Iraq in March 1959.

MEMBERS

Iran   Pakistan   Turkey   United Kingdom

The United States is a member of the Organization's Military, Economic, and Counter-Subversion Committees, and signed bilateral agreements of military and economic co-operation with Iran, Pakistan and Turkey in Ankara in March 1959.

ORGANIZATION

THE COUNCIL

Ministerial Level: Meets normally once each year in rotation at CENTO country capitals. Attended by Foreign Ministers or senior Cabinet Ministers, and an observer from U.S.A.

Deputies Level: Meets fortnightly in Ankara under the Chairmanship of the Secretary-General. Attended by Ambassadors resident in Ankara, a senior representative from the Turkish Ministry of Foreign Affairs and an observer from U.S.A.

Committees of the Council: (1) Military Committee, (2) Counter-Subversion Committee, (3) Liaison Committee, (4) Economic Committee.

SECRETARIAT

There are four divisions: Political and Administration, Economic, Public Relations, and Security.

Secretary-General: M. BAYÜLKEN (Turkey).

PERMANENT MILITARY DEPUTIES GROUP

Composed of five senior officers who represent the Military Committee; advises the Military Committee on the current military problems in the area and provides direction to the Combined Military Planning Staff.

COMBINED MILITARY PLANNING STAFF

Chief of Staff: Maj.-Gen. COLIN C. HAMILTON (U.S.A.); has an international staff of officers from three services of the five member nations of the Military Committee. There are three divisions: Intelligence; Plans, Training and Operations; and Logistics.

GROUPS REPORTING TO THE ECONOMIC COMMITTEE

Sub-Committee on Agriculture: increased production, development policy, banking and credit, forestry, pest control, land classification and soil survey, irrigation systems, improved annual breeding and control of virus and parasitic diseases of livestock.

Council for Scientific Education and Research: development of science and technology and the peaceful uses of atomic energy; undertakes research in all three countries of the region.

TECHNICAL ASSISTANCE PROGRAMME

Training fellowships in specialized subjects in all three countries, visits and tours of experts, working and travelling seminars and conferences of experts are financed by the Multi-lateral Technical Co-operation Fund (MTCF) of approximately U.S. $315,000 per year, and by the Multi-lateral Scientific Fund, of approximately U.S. $66,000 per year.

Advisory Group on Minerals Development: concerned with locating resources, and finding means of using them.

Sub-Committee on Health: development of public health in the CENTO region, eradication of malaria, control of smallpox, teaching of preventive medicine, environmental sanitation, hospital administration, health education, family planning, etc.

Sub-Committee on Communications and Public Works: development of improved communications by rail, sea, road and air in the region.

SECRETARIAT BUDGET

(1974–5)

£500,000 (approx.)

ECONOMIC DEVELOPMENT PROGRAMME

ROAD PROJECTS

Completed or due for completion in 1975

Pakistan-Iran road link joining Karachi, Kunnar, Khuz-dar, Quetta, Baratagzai, Zahedan, Kerman, Bad and Kashan.

Pakistan-Iran road linking Karachi, Bela, Pishin, Sarbaz.

Turkey-Iran road linking Iskenderun, Urfa, Diyarbakir, Bitlis, Gurpinar, Yuksekova, Esendere, Serow, Rez-aiyeh. Original route was abandoned in 1974 because of weather and terrain difficulties. This route is an improvement and upgrading of an existing National Highway.

ROAD PROJECTS UNDER CONSTRUCTION

Iran: road linking Zahedan and Char Bahar. The project to link Pishin and Bandar Abbas by road was abandon-ed.

Turkey: road linking Trabzon with the main highway at Erzurum. This is a widening and straightening of an existing road.

COMPLETED PROJECTS

Turkey-Iran rail link (including a ferry across Lake Van) joining Muş, Tatvan, Van, Qotur and Tabriz.

Development of the ports of Trabzon and Iskenderun.

CENTO Airway; U.S.A. and the United Kingdom have contributed towards improved navigational and other aids for regional air traffic.

High-frequency radio telecommunication links between London and key regional stations, i.e. Istanbul, Ankara, Teheran and Karachi. First stage completed in 1964; in full operation 1968.

Ankara–Teheran–Karachi microwave links project, in-volving 88 relay stations and 13 air navigation stations, opened 1965, completed 1966. Teheran Control Centre opened 1969. Currently being updated in Turkey to accept three times as much traffic. The other sections to be improved later.

RECORD OF EVENTS

1955 Baghdad pact signed; international secretariat established.

1956 United States joined Economic and Counter-Subversion Committees of the Pact.

1958 Pact's Headquarters and staff moved to Ankara.

1959 Bilateral defence agreements signed between the United States, Turkey, Pakistan and Iran, March. Iraq withdrew from the Pact, March. Opening of Nuclear Centre in Teheran, June. Name of Organisation changed to CENTO, August.

1960 Permanent Military Deputies Group established. U.S.A. Development Loan Fund lent $6 million to Turkey for Turkey-Iran railway.

1961 High-Frequency Telecommunication link opened between London, Istanbul, Ankara and Teheran, June. Contract for $16,490,000 awarded by U.S. Govern-ment to build microwave telecommunications system.

1963 Development of the port of Trabzon completed, aided by a grant of £181,000 from U.K.

1964 U.S.A. Development Loan Fund lent over $18 million for completion of Turkey-Iran railway. Permanent Military Telecommunication System linking Ankara, Teheran and Rawalpindi opened: cost of over $2 million provided by U.S.A. British

contribution to CENTO raised to £1 million annually. First section of Turkey-Iran railway, Muş to Tatvan (100 km.) opened.

1965 CENTO Microwave Telecommunications system opened.

1966 First section of Turkey-Iran road, Sirelan to Rezaiyeh, opened.

1969 Decision to set up an Industrial Development Wing within the CENTO Secretariat.

1971 Turkey-Iran railway link opened completely.

1972 Development of Iskenderun harbour completed.

U.S.-CENTO Scientific Fund inaugurated (July).

U.S. Government transferred the responsibility for administering U.S.-sponsored seminars, conferences, etc. to the CENTO Secretariat (July).

1974 First Annual Meeting of University Rectors and Vice-Chancellors from CENTO regional countries, Teheran (June).

Appointment of Senior Industrial Development Adviser.

21st Session of the Council of Ministers held in Washington (May).

1975 22nd Session of the Council of Ministers held in Ankara (May).

CENTO Road and Railway Projects, May 1975.

PACT OF THE CENTRAL TREATY ORGANIZATION

(February 24th, 1955)

Article 1

Consistent with Article 51 of the United Nations Charter the High Contracting Parties will co-operate for their security and defence. Such measures as they agree to take to give effect to this co-operation may form the subject of special agreement with each other.

Article 2

In order to ensure the realization and effect application of the co-operation provided for in Article 1 above, the competent authorities of the High Contracting Parties will determine the measures to be taken as soon as the present Pact enters into force. These measures will become operative as soon as they have been approved by the Governments of the High Contracting Parties.

Article 3

The High Contracting Parties undertake to refrain from any interference whatsoever in each other's internal affairs. They will settle any dispute between themselves in a peaceful way in accordance with the United Nations Charter.

Article 4

The High Contracting Parties declare that the dispositions of the present Pact are not in contradiction with any of the international obligations contracted by either of them with any third state or states. They do not derogate from, and cannot be interpreted as derogating from, the said international obligations. The High Contracting Parties undertake not to enter into any international obligation incompatible with the present Pact.

Article 5

This Pact shall be open for accession to any member state of the Arab League or any other state actively concerned with the security and peace in this region which is fully recognized by both of the High Contracting Parties. Accession shall come into force from the date of which the instrument of accession of the state concerned is deposited with the Ministry of Foreign Affairs of Iraq.

Any acceding State Party to the present Pact, may conclude special agreements, in accordance with Article 1, with one or more states Parties to the present Pact. The competent authority of any acceding State may determine measures in accordance with Article 2. These measures will become operative as soon as they have been approved by the Governments of the Parties concerned.

Article 6

A Permanent Council at Ministerial level will be set up to function within the framework of the purposes of this Pact when at least four Powers become parties to the Pact.

The Council will draw up its own rules of procedure.

Article 7

This Pact remains in force for a period of five years renewable for other five-year periods. Any Contracting Party may withdraw from the Pact by notifying the other parties in writing of its desire to do so, six months before the expiration of any of the above mentioned periods, in which case the Pact remains valid for the other Parties.

Article 8

This Pact shall be ratified by the Contracting Parties and ratifications shall be exchanged at Ankara as soon as possible. Thereafter it shall come into force from the date of the exchange of ratifications.

The European Economic Community and the Middle East and North Africa

THE MEDITERRANEAN POLICY OF THE EUROPEAN COMMUNITY

In June 1972 the Council of Ministers of the European Community asked the Commission to draw up proposals for a "global" or overall approach in all the Community's relations with Mediterranean countries. The Commission drew up these proposals at the end of September 1972.

Broadly, the Commission proposed that the European Community should follow up and amplify the trade relations that had been created with Mediterranean countries (*see* below), and that a start should be made on a consistent programme of aid and co-operation in the region.

Under the Commission's proposals, new agreements would be negotiated removing all obstacles to free trade between the Community and each Mediterranean country. Industrial goods should move freely—except for certain sensitive goods—between the Community and the more developed countries by July 1st, 1977. Less advanced countries would take a longer period. Agricultural products, being sensitive ones for both the Community and the Mediterranean countries, should be freed gradually, the concessions varying according to the product in question.

The Council decided to begin by negotiating agreements with six countries—Spain, Israel, Morocco, Algeria and Tunisia (with whom trade, technical co-operation and aid relations were envisaged), and Malta, with whom the same matters were to be discussed apart from trade. The negotiations began in June 1973 with Spain, Israel and the Maghreb countries.

The discussions with the three Maghreb countries were concerned chiefly over their exports of refined petroleum products to the Community, and with provisions for the welfare of their migrant workers in the Community. Concessions for agricultural exports from all five countries were to be improved.

These efforts, however, were inconclusive, and were not resumed until October 1974. Meetings were held in the last quarter of 1974 with the Maghreb countries, and again in March 1975 with Tunisia and Morocco, and in April with Algeria. Negotiations with Israel moved at a faster pace, and a preferential trade agreement was signed in May 1975, coming into effect in July. Israel's industrial exports to the EEC are to be granted free entry, and tariffs on farm goods will be generally reduced.

As regards other Mediterranean countries, the Commission proposed in January 1975 to open negotiations with Egypt, Syria, Lebanon and Jordan with a view to concluding similar co-operation agreements within the global policy for the Mediterranean, in accordance with the requests these countries had made. The agreements should be on the same basis as those envisaged for the Maghreb countries. As regards trade, industrial products would be affected more than agricultural goods, partly in consideration of the concessions granted elsewhere in the Mediterranean.

EXISTING EEC AGREEMENTS WITH MEDITERRANEAN COUNTRIES

The agreements in existence or being negotiated between the EEC and countries in the Middle East and North Africa fall into two categories: preferential and non-preferential agreements.

I. PREFERENTIAL AGREEMENTS

These are either association agreements under the terms of Article 238 of the Treaty of Rome or agreements under the terms of Article 113 of the Treaty.

A. Agreements concluded under Article 238 of the Treaty

COUNTRY	DURATION	DATE OF COMING INTO FORCE	DATE OF EXPIRY	OPENING OF NEGOTIATIONS
Turkey . .	unlimited	1.12.64		
Tunisia . .	5 years	1.9.69	31.8.74*	
Morocco . .	5 years	1.9.69	31.8.74*	End 1972 End 1972
Algeria . .		negotiations in progress		
Cyprus . .	9½ years	1.6.73	30.11.82	

* Agreements being extended provisionally until new arrangements enter into force.

B. Agreements concluded under Article 113 of the Treaty

There are preferential agreements between the Community and Israel, Egypt and Lebanon. The content of these agreements with Egypt and Lebanon is the same as that laid down for the first phases of the agreements concluded with Tunisia and Morocco. The movement of goods is subject to rules of origin and conditional on certificates of origin. The agreement with Israel is of a new type; it is the hope of the Community that similar agreements will be made with other Mediterranean countries.

Country	Duration	Date of Coming into Force	Date of Expiry	Date of Opening Negotiations
Israel . .	—	1.7.75	—	1.4.74
Egypt . .	5 years	1.11.73	31.12.77	1.7.76
Lebanon .	5 years	—	—	—

SUMMARIES OF AGREEMENTS*

TURKEY

Signature: Ankara, September 12th, 1963.

Date of coming into force: December 1st, 1964.

Type: Association Agreement concluded by the Community and the Member States.

Legal basis: Article 238.

Duration: Unlimited.

Object: The phased establishment of a customs union between Turkey and the EEC, with the long-term possibility of full Turkish membership of the Community.

A customs union will be established in three phases. These are:

(a) *Preparatory phase.* It was provided that Turkey would strengthen its economy with help from the Community during this phase so as to achieve a level of development adequate for assuming the obligations involved in the transitional and final phases. Thus, Turkey received help from the EEC in the form of loans of 175 million units of account over a five-year period under the first financial protocol. Preferential tariff quotas were granted for four agricultural products accounting for 40 per cent of Turkey's exports to the EEC: unmanufactured tobacco, dried raisins, dried figs and nuts.

(b) *Transitional phase,* in force January 1st, 1973 after all Member States and Turkey had ratified the Additional Protocol to the Ankara Agreement (signed on November 23rd, 1970). This protocol laid down the detailed arrangements for implementing the transitional period. A new Financial Protocol has also been signed. An Interim Agreement, signed on July 27th, 1971, brought into force on September 1st, 1971, the commercial provisions of the Additional Protocol before the completion of the ratification procedures. The Interim Agreement has subsequently been renewed at the beginning of each year until the present.

The Additional Protocol provides for the gradual establishment of a customs union during the course of a transitional phase of 12 to 22 years, depending on the product. Turkish industrial exports enjoy immediate duty and quota free entry to the EEC, except for petroleum products and three textile products. The EEC will grant Turkey concessions on 90 per cent of its agricultural exports to the EEC. Turkey will dismantle its tariffs on EEC imports over a 12-year period, but for a list of products accounting for 45 per cent of its imports from the EEC the period will be 22 years.

As for agriculture, the Association Council will lay down the provisions necessary to achieve the free movement of agricultural products between the Community and Turkey at the end of a 22-year period and will also adopt procedures for implementing the provisions relating to freedom of establishment, freedom to provide services, transport and approximation of economic policies.

Financial help to be granted under the Financial Protocol amounts to 195 million units of account over a period of five-and-a-half years, and this was increased under the second Financial Protocol of June 1973, with the extension of the Association to the new member states, to 242 million units of account. The European Investment Bank may supplement this with loans amounting to 25 million units of account from its own resources.

Further arrangements concerning the accession of the three new member states to the EEC are as follows: regarding industrial products, the new member states have from January 1st, 1974 removed their customs duties and quotas with a small number of exceptions; their exports to Turkey, however, are subject to tariffs which will be reduced by stages to the same level as those in force for the rest of the Community's exports.

Turkey's agricultural exports to the Community have been encouraged by the bringing forward by one year of the dates for regular review of the EEC preferential scheme, as well as by the introduction of certain new preferences and the improvement of some existing ones.

---

* All the agreements described on these pages have been supplemented by protocols making adjustments occasioned by the accession to the European Community of Denmark, Ireland and the United Kingdom.

(c) *Final phase.* The transitional stage will be followed by a final situation in which the customs union will develop towards full economic union with the EEC through intensified co-ordination of economic policies. Article 28 of the agreement provides for the possibility of accession to the Community in due course.

The Association Council, with equal Community and Turkish representation, is responsible for examining progress under the agreement, and during the transitional stage is able to take decisions regarding concerted action not provided for in the agreement which may appear necessary for the attainment of the association's objectives, both parties being required to implement such decisions. The Joint Parliamentary Committee, consisting of 15 members of the European Parliament and 15 members of the Turkish parliament, is responsible for facilitating contact and co-operation between the two parliaments.

TUNISIA AND MOROCCO

Signature: Tunis, March 28th, 1969; Rabat, March 31st, 1969.
Date of coming into force: September 1st, 1969.
Date of expiry: September 1st, 1975.
Date for the opening of further negotiations: not later than September 1st, 1972.
Type: Association Agreement concluded by the Community on the basis of Article 238.
Object: The Tunis and Rabat Agreements are at present restricted to trade. The movement of goods is subject to control over origin.

These "partial association" agreements grant duty and quota free entry to the EEC for Moroccan and Tunisian industrial products (with the exception of a few sensitive products) and *ad hoc* reductions (100 per cent, 80 per cent and 50 per cent) on a variety of agricultural products accounting for 35 per cent of Morocco's exports to the Community and about 70 per cent of Tunisia's.

In return Morocco and Tunisia grant the Community a number of tariff and quota concessions.

Although these are purely commercial agreements they are regarded as constituting an important step towards the negotiation of agreements which will associate Morocco and Tunisia more fully with the Community.

Negotiations are in progress for a wider type of agreement, in the overall approach of the Community to the Mediterranean. Although the present agreements expired formally in September 1970, they are to be extended in practice until new agreements come into force.

The operation of each agreement is supervised by an Association Council comprising members of the Moroccan Government or the Tunisian Government and members of the EEC Council and Commission.

ISRAEL

Signature: May 11th, 1975.
Date of coming into force: July 1st, 1975.
Duration: Unlimited.
Type: This is the first agreement to be concluded under the global policy of the Community for Mediterranean Countries.
Legal basis: Article 113.

The objective of the agreement is the progressive establishment of a free-trade area between the Contracting Parties, and an introduction of economic co-operation as a factor complementary to the commercial exchanges.

In industrial sectors, tariffs and related obstacles to free trade are to be removed on both sides. This will be achieved for Israel's exports to the EEC by July 1977, for 60 per cent of EEC exports to Israel by 1980 and for the remaining 40 per cent by 1985.

As regards agriculture, the EEC will reduce its tariffs substantially for products accounting for 85 per cent of Israel's exports to the EEC; these include products which the community has traditionally imported from Israel, for example some vegetables and fruit juices.

Review meetings have been arranged, to be held in 1978 and 1983, at which possible improvements to the agreement might be discussed; if necessary, the dates might be postponed by up to two years for Israel's removal of tariffs on EEC industrial goods, which is to be completed by 1989 in the present arrangement.

A Joint Committee will supervise the operation of the agreement and study the possibilities of economic co-operation. The objects of this would be: to diversify the pattern of trade, assist the transfer of technology, encourage private investment and increase contacts between industries in Israel and the EEC, including scientific and technical co-operation.

This agreement replaces one signed in June 1970, which thus ceased to apply.

ALGERIA

Exploratory talks between the Community and Algeria on the possibility of concluding a preferential agreement took place in March 1970. As a result of Algerian reluctance to negotiate a first-stage, purely commercial agreement, similar to those in force with Morocco and Tunisia, in March 1972 the Council agreed to opening negotiations with Algeria on an overall agreement, involving not only preferential trading relations, but economic and financial co-operation as well.

The broad commercial contents of the agreement to be negotiated have been defined. Algerian industrial projects would benefit from intra-Community treatment, except for petroleum products. Limited concessions would apply to processed farm products. The EEC would operate the same system as the one already in force for Morocco and Tunisia concerning fishery products, olive oil, durum wheat, preserved fruit and vegetables and citrus fruit. For wine, a 60 per cent tariff reduction is proposed, subject to reference-price conditions and a prohibition on blending. In the commercial sphere, Algeria's interests lie mainly in the pursuit of a solution to the problem of disposal of its wines. Algeria wants a multi-national agreement assuring its disposal of minimum quantities on the Community markets.

The EEC asks for certain tariff preferences and for the consolidation of preferences, as well as for the binding of liberalization measures and certain guaranteed quotas. The EEC will also demand a non-discrimination clause, as in the agreements negotiated with Egypt and Lebanon.

Measures for economic and financial co-operation will be introduced in the framework of Community policy for development co-operation.

Under the agreements in force with Morocco and Tunisia re-negotiations began in the latter months of 1972. The Council of Ministers informed Tunisia and Morocco that it was prepared to begin re-negotiations with a view to an overall agreement at the same time as negotiations began with Algeria. These negotiations were opened in July and October of 1973. They resulted in a number of proposals made by the Commission to the Council; the main problem was that of diversifying the trading patterns of the Maghreb countries, as hitherto the French market had been their only significant contact with Europe. A proposal to widen the range of imports to Europe was designed to counterbalance difficulties that might arise in this way. Further amendments were proposed to the Community's offers on: the price and quantity of imports of petroleum products from Algeria, the import of Algerian wine, the question of discrimination in employment and social security, and co-operation to promote industrial activity in the Maghreb countries.

CYPRUS

Signature: Brussels, December 19th, 1972.
Date of Coming into force: June 1st, 1973.
Type: Association Agreement concluded by the European Community on the basis of Article 238.
Object: the phased establishment of a customs union between the Community and Cyprus.

The first phase of negotiations with a view to reaching an agreement with Cyprus began in January 1972.

The agreement is aimed at the removal of nearly all barriers to trade between Cyprus and the Community, and is scheduled to be achieved in two phases over a period of nine and a half years. The first stage runs until mid-1977. Details of the second stage are to be worked out in negotiations to be begun eighteen months before the end of the first stage.

Under the agreement the Community makes an immediate 70 per cent tariff cut in the industrial sector, except for petroleum products, and agrees to a 40 per cent preference for Cypriot citrus fruit and a 100 per cent preference for carob beans.

Cyprus reduces its tariffs by 15 per cent immediately, by 25 per cent at the beginning of the third year and by 35 per cent at the beginning of the fifth year. Some Cypriot products will continue to enjoy protection, to help certain sectors of the economy that are not sufficiently competitive and also to maintain privileges of a fiscal character.

An additional protocol to the agreement provides that Cyprus, as a Commonwealth country, remains entitled to some of its existing trade preferences in the British and Irish markets, particularly with regard to its sherry exports.

In October 1973 negotiations were proposed by the Commission to include Cyprus among those countries to be considered under the Community's "global approach" towards the Mediterranean basin. These would affect the agreement as regards agricultural produce, and some new provisions for co-operation in economic development were also envisaged.

LEBANON AND EGYPT

Signature: Brussels, December 18th, 1972.
Date of coming into force: Egypt: January 1st, 1973; Lebanon: not yet ratified.
Type: Preferential trade agreement concluded on the basis of Article 113.
Object: To promote increased trade between the European Community and Egypt and Lebanon, and thereby to contribute to the development of international commerce.

Initial negotiations with a view to concluding five-year preferential agreements between the Community and Lebanon and Egypt began in September 1970. For a fairly long period, however, negotiations remained interrupted over the inclusion of a non-discrimination clause: the EEC was unable to accept discrimination against its companies because of their trade with Israel—which has special links with the Community—whereas the two Arab countries were not willing explicitly to give up the principle of a boycott. However, in April 1972 a pragmatic compromise solution satisfying both EEC and Arab governments was found and a non-discrimination clause has been successfully negotiated.

Under the two agreements 45 per cent of Egypt's industrial products and 58 per cent of Lebanon's benefit from tariff concessions. In both cases the reduction in tariffs amounts to 55 per cent, 45 per cent being taken off on the coming into force of the agreements, while the further 10 per cent was deducted on January 1st, 1974.

For certain products, such as vehicles and aluminium products, the concessions are less, ranging from 35 to 41 per cent. Other products for which there exist agreed quotas—cotton fabrics and petroleum products in the case of Egypt, and cotton fabrics alone in the case of Lebanon—come into the same category.

Other products, still, are not covered by the agreement. These include veneers, wood laminates and certain textile products, and in the case of Lebanon petroleum products. Agricultural produce already regulated by the Common Agricultural Policy of the European Community is also outside the scope of the agreements.

In the agricultural sector, cuts are to be made in customs duties or import levies for citrus fruits, onions and garlic cloves and, additionally, in the case of Egypt, rice, and, in the case of Lebanon, crude olive oil.

In return, Egypt grants concessions on machinery, electrical equipment, organic and inorganic chemical products and certain agricultural produce. Lebanon grants concessions on these products and also on certain textile products.

Fresh negotiations are planned in order to apply to Lebanon and Egypt the "global approach" foreseen by the Community. The Egyptian Government requested negotiations for an agreement on an extended basis at the first meeting of the Joint Committee of the present agreement, held in May 1974.

JORDAN, IRAN AND SYRIA

Jordan and Iran have opened exploratory talks with the EEC with a view to opening negotiations towards a preferential agreement. In January 1975 the Commission proposed that the negotiations should begin; Syria, as she had requested, is also to negotiate a preferential agreement.

II. NON-PREFERENTIAL AGREEMENTS

(1) Iran: a trade agreement, signed on October 14th, 1963, came into force on January 1st, 1964. Its renewal has, however, been delayed indefinitely.

(2) Lebanon: the Community's first trade and technical co-operation agreement, signed on May 21st, 1965, came into force on July 1st, 1968.

IRAN

A limited 3-year renewable trade agreement between the EEC and Iran—the Community's first purely commercial agreement on the basis of Articles 111 and 114 of the Treaty of Rome—came into force on January 1st, 1964. It was renewed on an annual basis until it last expired in November 1973. The agreement provided for limited reductions in the common customs tariff for imports of carpets, dried grapes, dried apricots and caviar as well as for a non-discriminatory tariff quota for dried grapes. This agreement was amended in 1967 to provide further limited concessions for Iran.

The Community has been examining possibilities for developing relations with Iran further, both by enlarging trade links and by eventually extending its contractual obligations to technical, economic and financial co-operation. Since Iran's manufactured exports to the Community already benefit from the system of "generalised preferences", it seems that an improvement in relations between the Community and Iran must focus on oil and natural gas and on financial and technical co-operation.

LEBANON

The 3-year renewable trade and technical co-operation agreement between the Community and Lebanon was signed on May 21st, 1965, and came into force on July 1st, 1968. Following its expiry in June 1971, the agreement has been renewed annually since then.

This is a "mixed" agreement in that some of the points in the agreement regarding technical co-operation are under the jurisdiction of the individual Member States.

With regard to trade, the agreement provides that the two parties shall grant each other "most-favoured-nation" treatment, under certain conditions: the "most-favoured-nation" clause does not, for example, include the special advantages granted by Lebanon to Arab League states nor to advantages granted by either party with a view to establishing a free trade area or a customs union.

Under the agreement, which is notable chiefly for its technical assistance provisions, Member States shall co-ordinate the action they take as regards technical co-operation with Lebanon. This technical co-operation includes:

(a) sending experts, specialists or teachers to public bodies or research or teaching institutions in Lebanon;

(b) the technical training of Lebanese subjects at public bodies, educational institutions, industrial, agricultural, commercial or banking concerns in the Member States of the Community;

(c) the preparation of studies and enquiries into making the most of the resources of Lebanon;

(d) if need be, supplying technical equipment to research on teaching institutions in Lebanon.

A mixed group on technical co-operation was set up and this body is responsible for examining Lebanese applications for technical assistance and for supervising the execution of approved schemes. By May 1972 the technical provisions had been given no real content, although Lebanon recently put forward suggestions on restarting technical co-operation. Technical co-operation is subject to joint agreements reached through a bilateral procedure between each of the Member States and Lebanon, bearing in mind the conclusions arrived at by the mixed group.

A new preferential type of trade agreement has been negotiated between the Community and Lebanon (*see* above), to co-exist with the present agreement; this has been signed by both parties but not yet ratified by Lebanon.

THE EUROPEAN-ARAB DIALOGUE

The Euro-Arab dialogue was opened as a result of the Declaration made by the Nine in November 1973 (*see Documents on Palestine*, page 61), the Arab summit held also in November 1973 and the meeting in Copenhagen in December 1973 between the Heads of Government and envoys from the Arab League.

By March 1974 a general plan for a political approach to Euro-Arab co-operation had been formed; the Community suggested long-term arrangements in economic, technical and cultural matters.

The first meeting was held in Paris in July 1974; the Nine were represented by Jean Sauvagnargues, President of the Council, and François-Xavier Ortoli, President of the Commission. It was agreed that a Euro-Arab General Commission and a number of working parties would be set up. Preparatory talks for the meeting of the General Commission began in October 1974, between the Community and the Arab League, in Cairo.

Progress was delayed after this by disagreement whether Palestine should be represented on the General Commission; in the short term it was resolved by forming a joint delegation of Arab Representatives including Palestinian officials, the question of representation thus being avoided.

The dialogue was resumed in June 1975 in Cairo. The two sides met for four days, and decided to establish tangible co-operation in the spheres originally envisaged; a steering committee is to meet regularly to supervise these activities. This progress, it was hoped, would "develop common interests between the Arab world and Europe and prepare favourable circumstances for developing the whole Arab world and narrowing the technological gap between the Arab and European countries".

In July a three-day conference was held in Rome. EURABIA (European Co-ordinating Committee of Friendship Societies with the Arab World) was founded in April 1972, and the Parliamentary Association for Euro-Arab Co-operation was founded in March 1974. For details *see* entries under *Other Regional Organizations*, page 165.

Federation of Arab Republics

The establishment of the Federation of Arab Republics was approved by the electorates of Egypt, Libya and Syria in referenda on September 1st, 1971. Of the total electorate in all three countries, 98.1 per cent voted in favour of the Federation.

PRESIDENTIAL COUNCIL

Col. MUHAMMAD ANWAR SADAT (Egypt) (Chair.), Col. MUAMMAR AL-GADDAFI (Libya), Lt.-Gen. HAFIZ AL-ASSAD (Syria).

FEDERAL MINISTERIAL COUNCIL
(formed December 24th, 1971)

Chairman, Federal Ministerial Council: AHMED EL KHATIB (Syria).

Speaker, Federal National Assembly: Dr. KHAIRY AL SOUGHAYAR (Libya).

Secretary-General, Presidential Council: MOHAMED AHMED (Egypt).

Minister of State, Chairman, Council of Scientific Research Affairs: SALAH HEDAYAT (Egypt).

Minister of State, Chairman, Council of Economic and Planning Affairs: SAMY SOUFAN (Syria).

Minister of State, Chairman, Council of Transportation and Communication Affairs: Eng. ALI EL SAYYED (Egypt).

Minister of State, Chairman, Council of Foreign Affairs: Dr. MOHAMED FATHALLAH EL KHATIB (Egypt).

Minister of State, Chairman, Council of Service Affairs: MOHAMED EL KHAWAGA (Egypt).

Minister of State, Chairman, Council of Information Affairs: ABDULLA QUWAIRI.

Minister of State, Chairman, Council of Educational and Cultural Affairs: Dr. ALI FAHMY KHSHIM (Libya).

FEDERAL NATIONAL ASSEMBLY

Twenty members elected from each Republic by its People's Assembly. The Federal Assembly has a four-year term, with two ordinary sessions a year, and met for the first time in March 1972. The most recent session of the Assembly was held in May 1975.

CONSTITUTIONAL COURT

A Federal Constitutional Court was the fourth and last major institution provided for in the Statutes; it should be appointed by the Presidential Council and consist of two members representing each republic. It should be concerned with deciding on the constitutionality of laws and with settling disputes between the institutions and the authorities of the Federation and the Republics.

FUNCTIONS

(From the Declaration on the setting up of the Federation, signed by the three Presidents, Benghazi, April 1971.)

The Federation of Arab Republics shall be concerned with the following:

(a) Working out the bases of foreign policy.

(b) Questions of peace and war.

(c) Regulating and commanding the defence of the Federation of Arab Republics in the presence of a military command responsible for training and operations. Forces shall be transferred between the Republics by decision of the Presidential Council or such quarters as it will invest with this power during operations.

(d) Defending national security, and the formulation of bases whereby to regulate measures to safeguard the Federation. In the event of disorders from within or without, in any Republic, which endangers its security, or threatens the safety of the Federation, the government of such Republic shall immediately advise the Federal Government to take the necessary measures within the limits of its powers to preserve peace and order. In cases where the government of any member Republic is in no position to apply for aid from the Federal Government, or where the security of the Federation is jeopardized, the Federal authorities concerned may intervene without request to restore order.

(e) Planning the national economy, the formulation of joint general development plans, and the direction of the economic institutions of federal character.

(f) The introduction of an educational policy aimed at the building of a loyal Arab national socialist generation.

(g) The institution of a federal information policy serving the targets and the strategy of the Federal State in peace and war.

(h) The establishment of a unified policy of scientific research, and to co-ordinate its agencies in the Republics.

(i) The admission of new members to the Federation by a unanimous vote of the Federation's Presidential Council.

FINANCE

The Presidential Council approved a budget of £E33.7 million for 1974.

Islamic Conference

Secretariat-General, Kilo 6, Mecca Rd., P.O.B. 179, Jeddah, Saudi Arabia

Formally established in May 1971 following a summit meeting of Moslem Heads of State at Rabat, Morocco, in September 1969, and the Islamic Foreign Ministers' Conference in Jeddah in March 1970, and in Karachi, Pakistan in December 1970.

MEMBERS

Afghanistan	Guinea-Bissau	Morocco	Syria
Algeria	Indonesia	Niger	Tunisia
Bahrain	Iran	Oman	Turkey
Bangladesh	Jordan	Pakistan	Uganda
Cameroon	Kuwait	Qatar	United Arab Emirates
Chad	Lebanon	Saudi Arabia	Upper Volta
Egypt	Libya	Senegal	Yemen Arab Republic
Gabon	Malaysia	Sierra Leone	Yemen, People's Democratic
Gambia	Mali	Somalia	Republic
Guinea	Mauritania	Sudan	

Secretary-General: MOHAMED HASSAN MOHAMED AL-TOHAMY (Egypt).

CONFERENCES

Sept.	1969	Summit Meeting of Islamic Heads of State, Rabat.
March	1970	First Islamic Conference of Foreign Ministers, Jeddah.
Dec.	1970	Second Islamic Conference of Foreign Ministers, Karachi.
April	1971	Conference on International Islamic News Agency, Teheran.
June	1971	Conference on Islamic Cultural Centres, Rabat.
June	1971	Conference on the Charter, Jeddah.

Feb./March	1972	Third Islamic Conference of Foreign Ministers, Jeddah.
Aug.	1972	Inaugural Conference on the establishment of an International Islamic News Agency, Kuala Lumpur.
March	1973	Fourth Islamic Conference of Foreign Ministers, Benghazi.
Feb.	1974	Second Summit Meeting of Islamic Heads of State and Government preceded by Islamic Conference of Foreign Ministers, Lahore, Pakistan.
June	1974	Fifth Islamic Conference of Foreign Ministers, Kuala Lumpur, Malaysia.

AIMS

1. To promote Islamic solidarity among member states;
2. To consolidate co-operation among member states in the economic, social, cultural, scientific and other vital fields, and to arrange consultations among member states belonging to international organizations;
3. To endeavour to eliminate racial segregation and discrimination and to eradicate colonialism in all its forms;
4. To take necessary measures to support international peace and security founded on justice.
5. To co-ordinate all efforts for the safeguard of the Holy Places and support of the struggle of the people of Palestine, and help them to regain their rights and liberate their land;
6. To strengthen the struggle of all Muslim people with a view to safeguarding their dignity, independence and national rights; and
7. To create a suitable atmosphere for the promotion of co-operation and understanding among member states and other countries.

ACTIVITIES

1. The establishment of the International Islamic News Agency (IINA).
2. The establishment of an Islamic Development Bank in Jeddah, Saudi Arabia (*see* entry in section entitled *Other Regional Organizations*, p. 165).
3. Efforts to consolidate the activities of the Islamic Cultural Centres in non-Muslim countries.

SECOND SUMMIT MEETING, LAHORE 1974

Coincided with the diplomatic recognition of Bangladesh by Pakistan. The Lahore Declaration, issued after the Conference, re-affirms demands for Israel's withdrawal from all territories occupied in the recent wars; it also pledges that Arab countries will find ways to offset the recent rise in petroleum prices and to promote economic development in poorer countries, especially those in the Arab world.

FINANCES

The Conference is financed by contributions and donations from member states.

PUBLICATIONS

News bulletin, issued three times a week by the International Islamic News Agency (IINA).

The Maghreb Permanent Consultative Committee

(COMITÉ PERMANENT CONSULTATIF DU MAGHREB)

Rue Oued Hitti, Mutuelleville, Tunis, Tunisia

A permanent committee for economic co-ordination, established at Tunis in October 1964 by the Economic Ministers of the member countries.

MEMBERS *

Algeria   Mauritania   Morocco   Tunisia

* Libya withdrew from all Maghreb institutions in 1970. Mauritania joined in 1974.

FUNCTIONS

The Maghreb Permanent Consultative Committee has the general aim of studying the whole network of problems bearing on economic co-operation in the Maghreb, and of proposing to the Conference of Economic Ministers, either upon the demand of the latter or in the context of the programme outlined by it, all measures designed to strengthen such co-operation and realize the construction of a Maghreb Economic Community.

The Conference of Economic Ministers is the supreme embodiment of the Maghreb economic organization. It comprises the Economic Ministers of the Maghreb countries and is assisted by delegations of senior officials.

The Maghreb Permanent Consultative Committee exercises tutelar authority over the commissions and specialized organs of which it co-ordinates and directs the activities. The President and Vice-President are both from the same country and come from each of the member countries in turn.

Relations are maintained with the UN organizations (ECA, UNDP, UNIDO, UNCTAD, ILO, FAO), the OAU and the Arab League organizations (chiefly the Arab Economic Council and the Arab States Industrial Development Centre). In its external affairs the committee is represented by the President.

Languages: Arabic and French.

ORGANIZATION

(as of June 1975)

(For the composition of the Maghreb Permanent Consultative Committee and the rules governing its conduct *see* the *Statutes* below.)

Secretariat: f. 1965; headed the by Secretary, who provides services for meetings of the Conference of Ministers, the Permanent Committee and the Maghreb Commissions and Committees listed below. He is responsible for administrative aspects of the Committee's work, and directs the personnel and financial affairs of the Committee. Each country nominates one delegate for administrative duties to work permanently at the Headquarters of the Committee; Sec. MUSTAPHA FILALI; budget provided by equal donations from the member states.

DEPENDENT BODIES

Maghreb Centre for Industrial Studies: Tangier, Morocco; originally f. 1968 in Tripoli, but transferred to Tangier in 1971, following the withdrawal of Libya; Dir. MOHAMED DAYA (Tunisia).

Maghreb Alfa Bureau: Algiers, Algeria; f. 1965; Dir. LABOUT BELABBES (Algeria).

Maghreb Committee on Tourism: Tunis, Tunisia; f. 1966.

Maghreb Committee on Postal and Telecommunications Co-ordination: location varies; f. 1964.

Maghreb Commission for Transport and Communications: Tunis, Tunisia; f. 1965; has four subsidiary committees.

Maghreb Committee for Air Transport, Rabat.

Committee for Maghreb Railways, Algiers.

Maghreb Committee on Shipping.

Maghreb Committee on Road Transport.

Maghreb Committee on National Accounts and Statistics: f. 1965.

Maghreb Committee on Administrative Studies and Research: f. 1970.

Maghreb Committee on Employment and Labour: Rabat; f. 1970.

Maghreb Committee on Normalisation: Algiers; f. 1970.

Maghreb Committee on Insurance and Re-insurance Rabat; f. 1970.

Maghreb Committee for Pharmaceutical Products: f. 1973.

Maghreb Committee for Electric Energy: f. 1974.

Maghreb Committee on Stockbreeding: f. March 1974.

RECORD OF EVENTS

1964
October

First meeting of the Economic Ministers of the four Maghreb countries, Tunis. The creation of the permanent consultative committee was decided upon, and the principal of co-ordinating export and industrial policies was affirmed.

November

Second Conference of Ministers, Tangier. The decision was taken to establish a centre for industrial studies and it was recommended that Maghreb co-ordination on tourism, transport, posts and telecommunications, manpower and development finance should be developed.

1965
March

First meeting of the Permanent Consultative Committee, Algiers. Three commissions appointed, for an economic survey of the member countries, for foreign trade and for co-ordination of industry.

May

Third meeting of the Maghreb Economic Ministers, Tripoli. Plans agreed for the co-ordination of exports of citrus fruits, wines, esparto and olive oil. An esparto bureau established in Algiers to handle the exports of all four countries. Special commissions set up for statistics, accounting, and the steel industry, and it was agreed to study improvement of telecommunication links. Protocol signed agreeing to study co-ordination in the spheres of trade fairs and insurance.

1966
February

Fourth meeting of the Maghreb Economic Ministers, Algiers. Plans agreed for establishment of a permanent secretariat in Tunis. The Ministers requested the Committee to examine the obstacles hindering the development of inter-Maghreb trade. Reports drawn up by the Committee on tourism, national accounts and statistics, and transport and communications were adopted.

1967
January

Meeting of Permanent Consultative Committee, Rabat; discussion of possible negotiations with EEC and inter-Maghreb trade relations.

November

Fifth meeting of Economic Ministers in Tunis. Decision to draft a new five-year agreement on general economic co-operation. The agreement to be based on the reduction of trade barriers, the harmonization of customs policies towards third countries and an agreed list of industries whose products would benefit from freedom of movement and from a common external tariff.

1970
July

Sixth Conference of Economic Ministers held in Rabat. Meeting held without participation of Libya, who later in summer announced withdrawal from the organization. The Ministers agreed to readjust and strengthen the whole Maghreb project. Programme for 1970–71 drawn up: studies on co-operation in tourism, national infrastructures, transport, export policies, etc. The Conference decided to create specialized committees on normalization, insurance and reinsurance, employment and labour, and compensation. Mauritania attended the meeting as an observer.

1975
May

Seventh Conference of Economic Ministers, Algiers; the Committee was requested to undertake studies of industrial, agricultural and professional activity in order to identify possible areas for free exchange and movement, and for preferential advantages within the Maghreb countries, during the period 1976-81.

STATUTES

Signed at Tunis, October 1st, 1964, by the Economic Ministers of the four member-states.

Article 1. The Permanent Consultative Committee is an organism in which representatives of the four countries of the Maghreb are brought together. It is composed of a President and eight members, of whom four are titulary representatives and four are deputies.

Article 2. The President of the Permanent Consultative Committee must have the rank of Minister. The Presidency is entrusted to each of the member states in turn for the duration of one year.

Article 3. The President may arrange to be assisted by a Vice-President who will be the titulary representative of the country which is holding the Presidency.

Article 4. The Government of each of the countries of the Maghreb will appoint a deputy titulary member with the rank of Director of Central Administration.

The representatives of each country will be able to command the help of these experts in case of need.

Article 5. The Permanent Consultative Committee is provided with a Permanent Secretariat headed by an Administrative Secretary appointed by the President.

The location of the Secretariat will vary according to the location of the Presidency.

Article 6. The Permanent Consultative Committee will have correspondents in each member state appointed by the government concerned. These correspondents must establish a Central Administration, and preferably some organizations and services with the object of planning economic programmes.

Article 7. Meetings of the Permanent Consultative Committee will be held at least once every three months when called by the President. At the same time as the President calls members of the Committee to meetings, he will present them with a programme embodying the proposals which he has received from the member countries.

Article 8. The proceedings of every session of the Permanent Consultative Committee must be recorded in Minutes drawn up by the President in office. These minutes must receive the unanimous approbation of the members of the Committee.

Article 9. The President will supply each of the members of the Committee with a copy of all documents brought to his attention, as well as any document likely to be of value to the Committee.

Article 10. The President will submit the budget planned to cover the expenses of the Permanent Consultative Committee for the approbation of the Maghreb Council of Economic Ministers.

Organization of Arab Petroleum Exporting Countries—OAPEC

P.O.B. 20501, Al-Soor Street, Kuwait City, Kuwait

Established 1968 to safeguard the interests of members and determine ways and means for their co-operation in various forms of economic activity in the petroleum industry. *See* also OPEC (p. 156).

MEMBERS

Algeria	Kuwait	Saudi Arabia
Bahrain	Libya	Syria
Egypt	Qatar	United Arab Emirates
Iraq		

ORGANIZATION

(as at May 1974)

COUNCIL

Supreme authority of the Organization, responsible for drawing up its general policy, directing its activities and laying down its governing rules. Meets twice yearly as a minimum requirement and may hold extraordinary sessions. Chairmanship on annual rotation basis.

Chairman: H.E. Shaikh AHMED ZAKI YAMANI (Saudi Arabia).

BUREAU

Assists the Council to direct the management of the Organization, approves staff regulations, reviews the budget, and refers it to the Council, considers matters relating to the Organization's agreements and activities and draws up the agenda for the Council. Each member country is represented on the Bureau. Chairmanship of which is by rotation. The Bureau convenes four times a year as a minimum requirement.

Draft Budget (1974): 300,000 Kuwait dinars.

Chairman: JAMAL JAWA (Saudi Arabia).

SECRETARIAT

Secretary-General: Dr. ALI AHMAD ATTIGA.

Assistant Secretary-General: ABDUL AZIZ AL-TURKI.

Besides the Office of the Secretary-General, which assists the Secretary-General in following up resolutions and recommendations of the council, there are five departments: the Administration and Financial Department, the Technical Department, the Legal Department, the Economic Department and the Information and Public Relations Department.

RECORD OF EVENTS

1968

Sept. First meeting of the Council, Kuwait.

Dec. First meeting of the National Oil Companies, Riyadh.

1969

Jan. Second meeting of the Council, Kuwait.

March Second meeting of the National Oil Companies, Tripoli.

July Third meeting of the Council, Vienna.

1970

Jan. Fourth meeting of the Council, Kuwait.

May Extraordinary meeting of the Council to consider applications for membership of Abu Dhabi, Algeria, Bahrain, Dubai, and Qatar. The applications were approved. Held in Kuwait.

June Fifth meeting of the Council, Algeria, at which decision was taken to establish a dry dock for large crude carriers.

Dec. Sixth meeting in Kuwait failed to admit Iraq as a member of the Organization. Members agreed to create a jointly owned tanker company and petroleum services company.

1971

June Seventh meeting of Council in Kuwait ended early after disagreement on Iraq's proposed admission, support to be given to Algeria in dispute with France, and policy towards EEC and EFTA.

Oct. Meeting in Kuwait postponed until December because of dispute over Iraq's proposed admission.

Dec. Eighth meeting of Council in Abu Dhabi. Decided to alter constitution to allow membership of Egypt and Syria.

1972

May Members sign agreement establishing an Arab Maritime Petroleum Transport Company.

June Second extraordinary meeting held in Beirut to assist Iraq and Syria in their dispute with the Iraq Petroleum Company.

Nov. Ninth Council meeting held in Kuwait.

1973

Jan. Council met in Kuwait as the constituent General Assembly of the Arab Maritime Petroleum Transport Company.

1973
June Tenth Council meeting held in Damascus.
Sept. Third extraordinary meeting of the Council, Kuwait; Council expressed support for the partial nationalization of oil companies operating in Libya.
Dec. Eleventh Council meeting held in Kuwait. Founding agreement of the Arab Shipbuilding and Repair Company signed.
1974
July Twelfth Council meeting passed a resolution creating the Arab Petroleum Investments Company.
October Agreement with EEC Commission to have regular contacts and to exchange technical information.
1975
April Committee of experts meeting in Kuwait on the exploitation of energy resources and the search for new ones.
May Agreement to form the Arab Petroleum Services Company. Thirteenth Council meeting, Libya; decision to establish marine academies in Jeddah (Saudi Arabia), Doha (Qatar) and Basra (Iraq).

JOINT UNDERTAKINGS

Arab Maritime Petroleum Transport Company: f. January 1973 in Kuwait to undertake transport of crude oil, gas, refined products and petrochemicals, and thus to increase Arab participation in the tanker transport industry; authorized capital: $500 million; subscribed capital: $100 million. Mems.: Algeria, Bahrain, Iraq, Kuwait, Libya, Qatar, Saudi Arabia, United Arab Emirates.

Chairman: Dr. Abdul Hadi Taher.
Managing Director: Abdul Rahman Sultan.

Arab Shipbuilding and Repair Company: f. December 1973 in Kuwait to undertake all activities related to repairs, service and eventually construction of vessels for the transport of hydrocarbons. The company will begin by building a dry dock in Bahrain. Authorized capital: $100 million; subscribed capital: $30 million.

Arab Petroleum Investments Company: created July 1974 to finance petrochemical plants in the Arab World. Authorized capital: $1,100 million.

Arab Petroleum Services Company: approval for establishment given in May 1975; the company to be formed in Libya, with a capital of $300 million.

Meetings of Arab Ministers of Petroleum were held in Kuwait in October, November and December 1973, at which cuts in oil production, export restrictions and the embargo imposed on certain countries, were decided on. These meetings, however, were not held under the auspices of OAPEC, which was thus not involved with the decisions taken.

On July 10th, 1974, the Ministers of Petroleum met at Cairo, deciding unanimously to lift the embargo on petroleum exports to the Netherlands.

Organization of the Petroleum Exporting Countries—OPEC

Dr. Karl Lueger-Ring 10, 1010 Vienna, Austria

Established 1960 to unify and co-ordinate members' petroleum policies and to safeguard their interests generally. *See* also OAPEC (p. 154).

MEMBERS

Algeria	Kuwait	United Arab Emirates
Ecuador	Libya	Venezuela
Indonesia	Nigeria	Gabon (Associate member)
Iran	Qatar	
Iraq	Saudi Arabia	

ORGANIZATION

THE CONFERENCE

Supreme authority of the Organization, responsible for the formulation of its general policy. It consists of representatives of member countries, decides upon reports and recommendations submitted by board of governors. Meets at least twice a year. It approves the appointment of governors from each country and elects the chairman of the board of governors. It works on the unanimity principle.

THE BOARD OF GOVERNORS

Directs management of the Organization; implements resolutions of the Conference; draws up an annual Budget. It consists of one Governor for each member country, and meets at least twice a year.

Chairman (1975): ALI KHALIFA AL-SABAH (Kuwait).

THE ECONOMIC COMMISSION

A specialized body operating within the framework of the Secretariat, with a view to assisting the Organization in promoting stability in international oil prices at equitable levels; consists of a Board, national representatives and a commission staff; the Board meets at least twice a year.

SECRETARIAT

Secretary-General (1975–76): Chief MESCHACH FEYIDE (Nigeria).

Administration Department: Deals with personnel matters, budget and accounting, filing and archives, conference services, general correspondence and clerical services.

Economics Department: Consists of Financial, Supply and Demand, and General Economics Sections; is responsible for all economic studies and reports.

Information Department: Responsible for a programme of general and technical publications and periodicals, appropriate relations with other oil industry institutions with a view to expanding the Information Centre of the Organization.

Legal Department: Consists of Concessions and Special Studies sections; is responsible for all legal studies and reports.

Technical Department: Carries out studies mainly on petroleum technical matters, including exploration, production and processing.

Statistics Unit: Collects, edits, collates and analyses statistical information from both primary and secondary sources.

Office of the Secretary General: Assists him in matters of protocol and implementation of the recommendations and decisions of the Conference calling for action by member countries.

ACTIVITIES

Technical and economic guidance for member countries and co-ordination of their petroleum policies.

FINANCE

1975 budget: 41,986,703 Austrian schillings, contributed in equal parts by members.

RECORD OF EVENTS

1971

January Teheran Meeting between OPEC and the oil companies to negotiate Gulf oil prices. Negotiations break down and OPEC members prepare to legislate unilaterally to set posted prices and tax rates.

February Teheran Twenty-second OPEC Conference. Resolutions passed made public on February 7th: OPEC threatens oil companies with total embargo if the minimum requirements of the Gulf states are not met by February 15th. Five-year agreement between 23 international oil companies and the six producing countries in the Gulf.

July Vienna Twenty-third OPEC Conference (extraordinary). Discussion on measures to implement a Joint Production Programme.
Twenty-fourth OPEC Conference. Nigeria admitted as eleventh member.

September Beirut Twenty-fifth OPEC Conference (extraordinary). Approved recommendations by the Ministerial Committee for preparatory moves towards state participation in existing concessions.

December Abu Dhabi Twenty-sixth OPEC Conference. Discussion on securing member governments' participation in their respective oil concessions and on new oil prices following dollar devaluation.

1972

January Geneva Meetings held between OPEC and the international oil companies. Oil companies agreed to adjust the oil revenues for six of the largest oil producing countries of the Middle East after changes in currency exchange rates.

March Beirut Twenty-seventh OPEC Conference (extraordinary). Resolution adopted that in case any oil companies fail to comply with any action taken by a member country in accordance with decisions of OPEC, the Organization shall take appropriate action against said company.

June Beirut Twenty-eighth OPEC Conference (extraordinary). Resolution adopted supporting the Iraqi nationalization of the Iraq Petroleum Company.

Vienna Twenty-ninth OPEC Conference.

1972

October Riyadh OPEC discusses the agreement reached between five Arab oil exporting states and Western oil companies on government participation in the oil industry.

November Lagos Thirtieth OPEC Conference establishes a $22m. fund to aid member states encountering difficulties concerning their oil policy. Support for Iraq's policy reaffirmed.

1973

March Beirut OPEC members meet to discuss demands for compensation following the 10 per cent devaluation of the U.S. dollar.

April Cairo OPEC members and oil companies meet to discuss the OPEC demand for compensation for the devaluation of the dollar.

Vienna An OPEC Ministerial Committee meets oil company representatives to discuss increases in oil prices. No agreement reached.

May Tripoli OPEC members have talks with oil companies on increases in oil prices. No agreement reached.

Vienna Extraordinary conference of OPEC to discuss the deadlock in the oil price talks with the oil companies.

Geneva Negotiations with the oil companies reopen and are successfully concluded (on June 1st) by an agreement under which the posted prices of crude oil are raised by 11.9 per cent and a mechanism is installed whereby prices are adjusted monthly in future.

June Vienna Thirty-fourth OPEC Conference. Resolution admitting Ecuador as an Associate Member. The Conference formed a Ministerial Committee to review the world energy situation continuously, and adopted a statement of policy.

September Vienna Thirty-fifth OPEC Conference (Extraordinary). Discussed possible amendments to the Teheran, Tripoli and Lagos Agreements, and decided to negotiate with the oil companies about these amendments. Gulf states propose collective talks with the oil companies to revise the Teheran Agreement. These talks subsequently broke down. Conference also expressed support for Libya and Abu Dhabi in their current dispute with the oil companies.

1973

October	Kuwait	The six Gulf states increased market price of Arabian crude oil by 17 per cent to $3.65 a barrel. Price of other crudes fixed accordingly. This action meant a rise in posted prices from $3.02 to $5.11 a barrel.
November	Teheran	Ministers from six Gulf oil states had talks with oil company representatives on ways of implementing 17 per cent increase announced in October. No definite results. Later all 11 members of OPEC met to discuss establishment of a new market price system. Ecuador became a full Member and Gabon an Associate Member of OPEC.
December	Vienna	OPEC members decided to raise the posted price of oil to $11.651 a barrel from January 1st, 1974.

1974

January	Geneva	Oil-producing states announced that they would hold prices at their current level until April 1st, 1974. Abu Dhabi's membership transferred to United Arab Emirates.
March	Vienna	Special OPEC conference at which OPEC Economic Commission was instructed to embark upon a study of organization of oil production in the light of oil market conditions. Oil prices to be frozen for a further three months.
April	Vienna	Special Funds inaugurated to provide "soft" loans and other credit facilities to help developing countries affected by the rise in oil prices. Six-nation working party to draw up articles of agreement in August.
June	Quito	Ordinary conference on oil prices. Posted price frozen for third quarter of the year, but royalties charged to the oil companies were raised, though only by 2 per cent, by all member states except Saudi Arabia.
September	Vienna	Forty-first OPEC conference (Extraordinary). Taxes and royalties levied were raised by 3.5 per cent while maintaining the freeze on the basic posted price of crude oil until the end of 1974 by all member states except Saudi Arabia.
December	Vienna	Oil ministers agreed on prices to be fixed for the first nine months of 1975. A standard price is to be introduced in all major countries which achieve full state ownership of their oil industries.

1975

February	Vienna	Oil ministers' meeting; Kuwait, Iran and Algeria reported to be sponsoring a plan to limit crude production, possibly by forming a supervisory agency within OPEC; no further action reported.
March	Algiers	Conference of Heads of State issues a Solemn Declaration calling for true co-operation from the developed countries in establishing a new international economic order.
April	Paris	Preparatory meeting between oil producers and consumers held by French Government. No agreement reached on holding a full conference later in the year.
June	Libre-ville, Gabon	Forty-second OPEC conference; the price of oil to be linked to the SDR of the International Monetary Fund, instead of the U.S. dollar, from October. An indexation scheme is also likely to be introduced in order to compensate for the world rate of inflation.

Regional Co-operation for Development—RCD

5 Vassal Shirazi, North of Boulevard Elizabeth, P.O. Box 3273, Teheran, Iran

Telephones: 638614, 636152, 638045.

Established in 1964 as a tripartite arrangement aiming at closer economic, technical and cultural co-operation and promoting the economic advancement and welfare of over 150 million people of this region.

MEMBERS

Iran   Pakistan   Turkey

ORGANIZATION

(as at June 1975)

MINISTERIAL COUNCIL

Established 1964 as the highest decision-making body of the RCD; composed of the Foreign Ministers of the three countries; considers and decides on measures for regional co-operation among the three countries.

REGIONAL PLANNING COUNCIL

Established 1964; composed of the Heads of the three Planning Organizations; makes recommendations to the Ministerial Council on measures for regional co-operation among the three countries.

Working Committees: Industry, Petrol and Petrochemicals, Trade, Transport and Communications, Technical Co-operation and Public Administration, Social, Cultural and Informational Co-operation, Co-ordination Committee.

SECRETARIAT

Permanently established in Teheran in 1965; staff consists of Secretary-General, three Deputy Secretaries-General, six Directors and supporting staff, drawn from nationals of the member countries.

Secretary-General: Dr. AHMAD MINAI (Iran).

ACTIVITIES

INDUSTRY AND STANDARDIZATION

In an agreement of November 1967 the three members agreed to collaborate in joint-purpose enterprises, and guidelines were laid down.

Materials, skills and, if possible, capital were to be pooled; national markets would be shared and industrial specialization encouraged; long-term agreements (off-take guarantees) were to be negotiated for the specific enterprises, ensuring that the partner countries provide a market for the products, and through fiscal arrangements the products would be protected against imports from outside the region.

About fifty enterprises were identified of which ten were in production by April 1975. Three of these have equity participation by the member countries:

(a) Iranian Aluminium Company, Takht-e-Jamshid Avenue, Teheran.

(b) Bank note and Security Paper, Pakistan Security Printing Corporation Limited, Karachi.

(c) Ball Bearings Aizad Industries Limited, Palace Cinema Building, Civil Lines, Karachi.

Those without equity participation include the Ultramarine Blue Project and the Shock Absorbers Project in Pakistan, and the following Projects in Turkey: Tungsten Carbide, Borax and Boric Acid, Centrifugal and Special Filters for Chemical Industries, High Tension Insulators and Tetracycline.

There are also provisions for common RCD Standards, twenty-four of which have been so far established in the region.

PETROLEUM AND PETROCHEMICALS

Projects include the Glycerine Plant in Pakistan, which exports its products to Turkey, the Polystyrene project in Turkey and the Carbon Black Project in Iran.

There have been other joint activities in this field: a chain of filling stations has been formed. Iran-air has a contract with Turkey for all the airline's fuel supplies, and there is a special programme for the exchange of trainees and experts.

TRADE

RCD hopes to introduce a system of regional trade preferences, and a special Experts Group has held six meetings on trade liberalization and expansion. A meeting of Economy and Commerce Ministers will be called when a protocol has been finalized. Two agreements have already been signed, on RCD Trade and on a Multilateral Payments Arrangement. It is also hoped to revive the traditional international trade route from Europe to Asia through Trabzon in Turkey, which could substantially assist regional transit trade.

There has also been in existence since 1966 an RCD Chamber of Commerce and Industry. The secretarial work of this body has been taken over by the Secretariat as from 1973.

INSURANCE

Five re-insurance pools have been created by RCD, for Accident, Engineering, Marine, Aviation and Fire. Forty-four companies had joined the Pools by 1973, with a total annual premium income of $1.5 to $2.0 million. Since the beginning of 1975, they have been merged into a single agency designed to pave the way for the establishment of an RCD re-insurance company. An RCD International School of Insurance has also been active in Teheran since 1970.

The RCD Insurance Centre has its headquarters in Karachi; it undertakes research and disseminates information on insurance activities in the region.

TRANSPORT

RCD Shipping Services began operation in 1966, both within the region and to the United States. The organization has its office in Istanbul.

The RCD Highway is now nearing completion, linking the three member countries along a 5,180 km. route.

The rail link between Pakistan and Iran is to be completed by 1980. Iran and Turkey were linked by rail in 1971.

COMMUNICATIONS

Postal, telephone and telegraph rates within the region have been reduced and Operator Trunk Dialling has been introduced between Teheran, Ankara and Karachi.

TECHNICAL CO-OPERATION

Up to 1975, 1,600 trainees, 1,000 students and 68 experts have visited the region under RCD programmes. Also, thirty-eight seminars and seven joint courses on public administration have been held under the aegis of the tripartite arrangement.

CULTURAL AND INFORMATION

The RCD Cultural Institute in Teheran is engaged in research into the common historical and cultural heritage of the member countries. It has a library housing over 4,500 books. The Institute brings out a quarterly journal and has hitherto published fifty books, including original works and translations.

The Cultural Exchange Programme for 1975 includes exchange visits of artists, painters and eminent personalities. There is also a Sports Calendar. A seminar will discuss the status of women, and six scholarships will be awarded to women's organizations.

Study tours will be arranged for journalists, as well as the Fourth RCD Seminar of Journalists scheduled to be held in Turkey.

The three national Radio/Television and News Agencies also co-operate under RCD programmes.

RECORD OF EVENTS

1964 **July**	Meeting of Foreign Ministers of the three countries, Ankara. Agreement on collaboration in communications, agriculture, industry, mineral resources, education, health, and regional development, outside the framework of CENTO.
	Meetings of the Heads of State of Iran, Pakistan and Turkey at Istanbul. Agreement on economic and cultural co-operation. Ministerial Council and Regional Planning Council established.
August	Meeting of working committees, Teheran. Fields of study: trade, shipping, air transport, road and rail transport, telecommunications, petroleum, banking, cultural affairs, tourism.
September	Meetings of Regional Planning Council and Ministerial Council, Teheran. Agreement to set up a joint international airline, a joint shipping company, joint petroleum organizations, and a regional cultural institute. Asphalt roads and rail links to be completed by 1968. Reduction planned of postal charges, insurance rates, and tariffs. Joint action to be taken to develop regional tourism. Secretariat established in Teheran. New committees on joint industrial ventures and technical co-operation set up.
1965 **March**	Meetings of Regional Planning Council and Ministerial Council, Islamabad, Pakistan.

Agreement to set up a tripartite Shipping Conference. Air mail surcharges on letters between the countries to be reduced to the internal level. General agreement on technical co-operation. Joint industrial enterprises identified. Agreements on establishment of an RCD Chamber of Commerce, collaboration between news agencies.

July	Meetings of Regional Planning Council and Ministerial Council, Ankara. RCD Joint Chamber of Commerce and Industry established in Teheran. RCD Insurance Centre established in Karachi.
1966 **May**	RCD Shipping Services started operations on intra-regional routes.
August	Iran and Pakistan signed agreement providing for setting up of a joint aluminium plant.
1967 **January**	Meeting of Regional Planning Council and Ministerial Council, Ankara. Agreement to set up a joint Bank Note Paper project in Pakistan. Decision to form a Payments Union among the three countries.
March	The following three Regional Reinsurance Pools started operations: *Accident*, managed by Iran; *Marine (Hull and Cargo)*, managed by Pakistan; *Fire*, managed by Turkey.
April	Agreement providing for the RCD Union for Multilateral Payments Arrangements signed at Ankara.

1967	
July	Summit conference held at Ramsar, Iran.
November	Agreement signed on public and private investment in joint enterprises.
1968 April	Eighth Session of the Council of Ministers and the Regional Planning Council, Teheran.
	Two more Regional Reinsurance Pools, *Aviation* and *Engineering*, started operations.
June	Operator Trunk Dialling System introduced between Ankara, Teheran and Karachi.
November	Agreement to establish joint Tungsten Carbide Plant in Turkey.
December	Summit Conference, Karachi.
1969 February	Meeting of Heads of Iran Air, PIA and Turkish Airlines at Karachi to consider feasibility of forming a joint airline.
March	Agreement signed on the establishment of an Ultra-Marine Blue project in Pakistan.
July	Agreement signed between IRANAIR and PIA for pooling traffic in Karachi-Teheran sector.
December	Establishment of joint purpose enterprise for production of High-Tension Porcelain Insulators agreed; to be sited in Turkey.
1971 March	Mr. Masarrat Husain Zuberi completed his term as Secretary-General of RCD.
May	Mr. Vahap Asiroglu took over as Secretary-General of RCD.
September	First railway link between Iran and Turkey inaugurated.
1973 August	Experts Group meeting on the establishment of RCD Halls in each member country, Karachi.

1974 January	Meeting of Experts Group on recognition and equivalence of university degrees, Islamabad.
May	Ambassador Vahap Asiroglu of Turkey completed his term as Secretary-General of RCD and was succeeded by Dr. Ahmad Minai of Iran.
July	Celebration of first decade of RCD with commendations from Heads of State of the three member countries.
October	RCD Secretary-General Dr. Ahmad Minai participated as Observer in IMF/IBRD annual meetings.
November	Tour of the region by a team of experts on telecommunications and electronics.
	Committee on Petroleum and Petrochemicals.
	Committee on Trade.
	Committee on Industry and Standardization.
December	Committee on Cultural Affairs and Information.
	Council of the RCD Chamber of Commerce and Industry.
	Committee on Transport and Communications
	Committee on Technical Co-operation and Public Administration.
	Governing Body of the Cultural Institute meeting.
1975 February	RCD Secretary-General Dr. Ahmad Minai participated in 31st session of UN ESCAP (Economic and Social Commission for Asia and the Pacific), New Delhi.
March/ April	RCD Ministerial Council, Regional Planning Council and Co-ordination Committee meetings in Turkey.

PUBLICATIONS

The RCD Magazine (quarterly), *RCD Newsletter* (monthly).

AIMS OF REGIONAL CO-OPERATION FOR DEVELOPMENT

Enunciated in Istanbul, July 23rd, 1964, by the Foreign Ministers of the Member States

1. The emergence of regional economic groupings enjoying a community of interest is an outstanding feature of our time for accelerating the pace of economic growth. Efforts directed towards regional economic collaboration have gained international acceptance and the present move to promote collaboration amongst countries of the region is directed towards the same aim, *viz.*, the strengthening of their development efforts through active and sustained collaboration on a regional basis. This is particularly true in the case of Iran, Pakistan and Turkey since the desire and basis for such a close collaboration and co-operation exist amongst them and will continue in view of the cultural and historic ties of friendship amongst the peoples of the three countries, and further because increasing regional economic co-operation has become a necessity. Economic and cultural collaboration amongst them is therefore most desirable, and should be raised to the highest possible level.

There are great possibilities for such collaboration to the mutual benefit of the three countries which should be achieved expeditiously.

Measures

2. The measures for economic collaboration suggested in the following paragraphs may be broadly divided into two categories—(*a*) Those which can be worked out and implemented forthwith and (*b*) Those which will require detailed study and scrutiny by Regional Planning Council.

3. A Regional Planning Council composed of the Heads of the Planning Organizations is established. It will be assisted by advisers and could meet in any of the regional countries, preferably by rotation.

4. The Council will study the development plans and production potential of countries of the region with a view *inter alia* to making recommendations on joint purpose

projects and long-term purchase agreements. Joint purpose projects will feed the requirements of the three countries. There are several projects for which none of these countries can provide a sufficient domestic market yet they can be valuable projects if the total requirements of the three countries are taken into consideration.

5. The Council may also make proposals regarding the harmonization of the national development plans in the wide interest of accelerated regional development.

6. The Council will submit its reports to the Ministerial meetings. The first report is to be submitted to the next such meeting.

7. Efficient and effective means of communication and transport are essential for the promotion of the regional economic and cultural collaboration. The preparation of recommendations in this field and their implementation should be given the highest priority.

Air Transportation

8. A Committee on air transportation is set up to study measures required to—(a) improve the transport services in the region so that quick and frequent movement of passengers and freight within the region be possible; (b) establish a strong and competitive international airline among the three countries; (c) foster co-operation among the civil and commercial aviation authorities of the three countries.

The report of the Committee should be available for the next Ministerial meeting.

Shipping

9. Collaboration among the countries of the region in shipping is highly desirable. A Committee on shipping is set up to investigate the possibility of securing a close co-operation in this field including the establishment of a joint maritime line.

Roads and Railways

10. Committees on road, railways and telecommunications are established immediately. The Committee will *inter alia* study and report on the following:

(a) The measures which should be taken to complete expeditiously the rail and road links among the countries of the region.
(b) Whether any additional rail and road links are considered necessary.
(c) Reduction of telephone rates.
(d) Establishment of P.T.T. offices in border areas.
(e) Feasibility of providing services such as direct dialling between the countries of the region and telecommunication, etc.

11. It is agreed that the postal and telegraph rates among Iran, Pakistan and Turkey be reduced to the levels of internal rates within the respective countries. The implementation of this decision is entrusted to the P.T.T. authorities of the three countries.

12. The construction of roads from the western and central parts of Iran to Zahidan and from Karachi to Zahidan should be given consideration by Iran and Pakistan so that the two countries are effectively linked by road. The Zahidan-Kashan rail link should be given further consideration with a view to developing it as early as possible.

Trade

13. Economic collaboration should provide for effective measures to build up and promote trade since expansion of inter-regional trade, apart from being highly desirable, in itself tends further to promote regional economic growth and amity.

14. A Committee on trade is established to study, report and recommend *inter alia* on the following measures on which agreement in principle has been reached:

(a) Free or freer movement of goods among the countries of the region through practicable means such as the conclusion of trade agreements, etc.;
(b) transit trade arrangements;
(c) establishment of closer collaboration between existing chambers of commerce and establishment of a joint chamber of commerce;
(d) establishment of halls and showrooms, provision of special customs facilities for exhibitions and increased participation in each other's fairs;
(e) dissemination of information on a large scale of the export and import potential of the three countries and investigation of the possibilities of joint publicity and joint marketing policy outside the region for similar exportable products.

Petroleum

15. A Committee on petroleum is established to consider measures for co-operation among the three countries in the field of petroleum and natural gas and for their exploration drilling; exploration; refining; transportation; distribution, etc. Collaboration in this field could be developed to mutual advantage.

Petrochemicals

16. A Committee on petrochemical industries is established for development of these industries in the region.

Tourism

17. A Tourist Agreement will be signed at an early date among the countries of the region with a view to promoting tourist traffic among themselves and to increase the flow of tourists from other countries. A Committee on tourism should be established immediately to prepare an agreement on tourism which should *inter alia* cover co-operation in publicity, group or package tourist arrangements. Promotion of inter-regional travel, substitutes of passports by documents valid for travelling in the three countries. Efforts with the aim of exchanging and training of tourist personnel, technicians, tourist investments, tourist propaganda and utilization of the services and facilities of their tourist organizations, travel bureaux and other agencies in their countries and abroad. As economic collaboration grows, inter-regional travel should increase considerably; it does however need a special effort if it is to be developed to a substantial degree in the immediate future.

Abolition of Visas

18. The abolition of visas for travel purposes by their nationals in the three countries is accepted in principle; the procedure for the implementation of this decision should be worked out by the Committee on tourism.

Banking and Insurance

19. A Committee on Banking and Insurance is established for collaboration in these fields.

Technical Co-operation

20. The countries of the region should provide technical assistance to each other in the form of exports and training facilities. Such a programme will, apart from intrinsic utility, promote regional understanding and harmony. The Planning Council will be directly responsible for progress in this matter.

Joint Purpose Enterprises

21. The Committee carries out feasibility studies in regard to the development of some industries on a joint purpose basis.

Cultural Co-operation

22. Iran, Pakistan and Turkey are bound to one another by historical and cultural ties, they share a common heritage. Their cultural ties go far back in history and their

national cultures owe much to continuous exchanges which have gone on for centuries. In the modern world they must integrate their traditional cultures with the new scientific outlook.

23. Co-operation in the field of education, science and culture is necessary to develop consciousness of the common cultural heritage and to promote social and economic development and political collaboration.

24. During the last few years a certain measure of progress has been achieved in cultural relations through bilateral programmes. However, there is considerable scope for further action. At the same time there is strong need for a joint sponsorship of many cultural activities under a regional programme.

Cultural Relations

25. The programme of cultural relations should be particularly oriented towards the following aims: (*a*) creating mass consciousness of the common cultural heritage. To this end the three countries should jointly sponsor an institute for initiating studies and research in this field and bringing out clearly those traditions which bind the people of the region together. Further, school books should be carefully reviewed to eliminate misleading interpretations of history and to promote greater understanding of their common interests; (*b*) disseminating information about history, civilization and culture of the people of the region. To this end each country should consider: (1) establishment of chairs for the study of its language, history, civilization and culture in universities of the other countries; (2) increasing substantially the number of scholarships for the students of other countries to enable them to study together in their educational institutions; (3) establishment of cultural centres in the other two countries; (4) provision as far as possible of facilities for the teaching of international language in the schools of other member countries; the media of mass communications, radio, films, television, etc., should be extensively used for the propagation of information and ideas aimed at a closer understanding of the people of the region.

26. Cultural co-operation may also be extended through: (a) exchanges in the field of fine arts; (b) exchanges of visits by teachers, scientists, educational administrators, writers, artists, journalists, etc.; (c) exchanges of information on educational techniques, experiences, and programmes; (*d*) collaboration in regard to programmes for radio, films and television; (*e*) elimination of obstacles in the way of free exchange of books, films and other printed materials of an educational and cultural character; (*f*) organization of regional tournaments; (*g*) co-operation in the field of joint production of films.

Organization

27. The organizational arrangements for planning and promoting economic and cultural collaboration amongst Iran, Pakistan and Turkey should be simple and effective. As the scope of co-operation widens these arrangements could be modified as required.

28. The highest decision-making body for regional co-operation shall be a Council of Ministers consisting of the Ministers nominated by each of the three countries concerned. It shall consider and decide upon measures for regional economic and cultural co-operation. It will also follow the programmes in the implementation of its decisions. The Council shall meet once in four months and more frequently if necessary. The Chairman of the Council shall be the Head of State or Head of Government of the host country.

29. The Council will be assisted by a Regional Planning Council composed of the Heads of the three Planning Organizations. They will deal with work relating to regional collaboration including detailed preparatory negotiations and preparation of recommendations for submission to the Council. The Committee will be assisted by Sub-committees which will report to it. If necessary the Committee may engage expert consultants to examine particular subjects for regional co-operation.

30. The host country will for the time being provide secretarial facilities (including office accommodation, etc.). The officials of the countries deputed by their Governments to serve on the Secretariat will draw their emoluments and allowances from their own Governments.

31. After 12 months the Council of Ministers will review the position and decide upon the setting up of a permanent Secretariat.

Other Regional Organizations

AGRICULTURE, FORESTRY AND FISHERIES

African Agricultural Credit Commission: Rabat, Morocco, f. 1966 to study agricultural finance problems. Mems.: Algeria, Ivory Coast, Libya, Morocco, Senegal, Tunisia, Upper Volta and Zaire.

Afro-Asian Rural Reconstruction Organization (AARRO): C/117-118, Defence Colony, New Delhi-3, India; f. 1962 to launch concrete and wherever possible co-ordinated action to reconstruct the economy of the rural peoples of Afro-Asian countries and to revitalize their social and cultural life. Mems.: governments of 11 African and 12 Asian countries.

Prés. Philippines; Vice-Pres. Egypt, Republic of Korea; acting Sec.-Gen. S. M. OSMAN (Egypt); Dir. and Co-ordinator of Programmes M. R. KAUSHAL (India). Publ. *Rural Reconstruction* (quarterly).

International Olive Growers' Federation (*Fédération internationale d'oléiculture*): Agustina de Aragón 11, Madrid 6, Spain; f. 1934 to promote the interests of olive growers and to effect international co-ordination of efforts to improve methods of growing and manufacturing and to promote the use of olive oil. Mems.: organizations and government departments in Algeria, Argentina, France, Greece, Israel, Italy, Lebanon, Libya, Morocco, Portugal, Spain, Syria, Tunisia.

Pres. CHARILAOS CARYOTAKIS (Greece). Publs. *Informations oléicoies internationales* (quarterly).

THE ARTS

Afro Asian Writers' Permanent Bureau: 104 Kasr el-Aini St., Cairo, Egypt; f. 1958 by Afro-Asian Peoples' Solidarity Organization; conferences of Asian and African writers have been held at Tashkent (1958), Cairo (1962), Beirut (1967), New Delhi (1970), Alma Ata (1973). Mems.: 78 writers' organizations.

Sec.-Gen. YOUSSEF EL-SEBAI (Egypt). Publ. *Lotus Magazine of Afro-Asian Writings* (quarterly in English, French and Arabic), *Afro-Asian Literature Series* (in English, French and Arabic).

ECONOMICS AND POLITICS

African Institute for Economic Development and Planning: (*see* under ECA in the chapter *UN in the Middle East and North Africa*).

Afro-Asian Organization for Economic Co-operation (AFRASEC): Chamber of Commerce Building, Midan al Falaki, Special P.O. Bag, Cairo, Egypt; f. 1958 to speed up industrialization and implement exchanges in commercial, financial and technical fields. Mems.: Central Chambers of Commerce in 45 countries.

Pres. ZAKAREYA TEWFIK; Sec.-Gen. FARID AHMED MOSTAFA. Publ. *Afro-Asian Economic Review*.

Afro-Asian Peoples' Solidarity Organization (AAPSO): 89 Abdel Aziz al Saoud St., Manial, Cairo, Egypt; f. 1957 as the Organization for Afro-Asian Peoples' Solidarity; acts as a permanent liaison body between the peoples of Africa and Asia and aims to ensure their economic, social and cultural development. Mems.: national committees and affiliated organizations in 75 countries.

Sec.-Gen. YOUSSEF EL-SEBAI (Egypt). Publs. *Afro-Asian Bulletin* (monthly), *Afro-Asian Women's Bulletin* (irregular), etc.

Arab Bank for African Development: f. Oct. 1974 by the summit conference of Arab states, Rabat; first assembly held in January 1975, Cairo.

Dirs. SHADLI AYARI (Tunisia), RAOUF BOUHOULA (Kuwait).

Arab Common Market: (*see* chapter *The Arab League*).

Arab Economic Council: (*see* chapter *The Arab League*).

Council of Arab Economic Unity: (*see* chapter *The Arab League*).

EURABIA (European Co-ordinating Committee of Friendship Societies with the Arab World): 16 rue Augereau, 75007 Paris, France; f. April 1972 to achieve greater co-operation between European organizations working for friendship with the Arab world; sponsors meetings and seminars to improve understanding of political, social, economic and cultural aspects of the Arab world, including the need to recognize the national rights of the Palestinian people.

Chair. LUCIEN BITTERLIN (Association de Solidarité Franco-Arabe); Admin. Sec. ROBERT SWANN (U.K.). Publs. *Fortnightly. Bulletin* (in French), *Quarterly Review* (in English, French and German).

Islamic Development Bank: Jeddah, Saudi Arabia; f. August 1974; capital $900 million, subscribed by 24 Arab and Islamic nations; the bulk of this finance will come from the oil producing countries.

Jewish Agency for Israel: P.O.B. 92, Jerusalem, Israel; f. 1897 as an instrument through which world Jewry could build up a national home. Is now the executive arm of the World Zionist Organisation. Mems.: Zionist federations in 61 countries.

Chair. Executive Cttee. LEON DULZIN; Chair. Board of Governors MAX M. FISHER; Dir.-Gen. MOSHE RIVLIN. Publs. *Israel Digest* (fortnightly), *Israel Features Service* (weekly).

Parliamentary Association for Euro-Arab Co-operation: 16 rue Augereau, 75007 Paris, France; f. March 1974 as an association of parliamentarians of the Europen Community to promote friendship and co-operation between Europe and the Arab world; a joint conference was held with the Arab Interparliamentary Union in Damascus, September 1974; at a meeting in Strasbourg in June 1975 the Association passed a resolution calling on EEC governments to recognize the Palestine Liberation Organization as the sole representative of the Palestinian people.

Joint Chair. RAYMOND OFFROY (France), LENELOTTE VON BOTHMER (Federal Republic of Germany); Gen. Sec. ROBERT SWANN (U.K.).

Union de Banques Arabes et Françaises—UBAF (*Union of French and Arab Banks*): "La France", 4 rue Ancelle, 92 Neuilly S/Seine, France; f. 1970 to group together 25 banks of 19 Arab countries (with 60 per cent of share capital), the Crédit Lyonnais of France (32 per cent share capital) and the Banque Française du Commerce Extérieure (8 per cent share capital) with the aim of contributing primarily to the development of financial, commercial, industrial and economic relations between the Arab countries on the one hand and Europe, and in particular France, and the international financial markets on the other.

Chair. MOHAMED MAHMOUD ABUSHADI; Gen. Man. BERNARD THIOLON.

World Zionist Organisation (*see* entry *Jewish Agency for Israel*, above).

EDUCATION AND DEVELOPMENT

Afro-Asian Housing Organization (AAHO): 28 Ramses St., Cairo, Egypt; f. 1965 to promote co-operation between African and Asian countries in housing, reconstruction, physical planning and related matters. Sec.-Gen. ABDEL HAMID EL ZANFALY (Egypt).

Alliance Israélite Universelle: 45 rue La Bruyère, F. 75425 Paris CEDEX 09, France; f. 1860 to work for the emancipation and moral progress of the Jews; maintains 62 schools in the Mediterranean area; library of 100,000 vols. Mems.: 12,000 in 40 countries; local committees in six countries.

Pres. RENÉ CASSIN (France); Sec.-Gen. EUGENE WEILL (France). Publs. *Cahiers de l'Alliance Israélite Universelle*, *The Alliance Review*, *Les Nouveaux Cahiers*, *La Revista de la Alliance*.

Arab Cities Organization: P.O.B. 4954, Kuwait; f. 1967; deals with the scientific, cultural and social aspects of town development, planning, administration, etc.; holds conferences every two years—last Conference Tunis, summer 1971; the main Arab Town Councils are members; 44 were represented at the First Conference in Beirut.

Dir. TALEB AL-TAHER.

Arab Fund for Economic and Social Development: (*see* chapter *The Arab League*).

Association of Arab Universities: Scientific Computation Centre, Tharwat St., Orman P.O.-Giza, Egypt; f. 1964. Mems.: 32 universities.

Publs. bulletin, directory of Arab universities.

Board for the Utilization of the River Jordan and its Tributaries: Cairo; f. 1964 to regulate the utilization of the River Jordan and its tributaries, whose basin lies within the territories of more than one state; main projects include the Mukhaiba Dam on the River Yarmuk (Jordan), to be linked by tunnel to the East Ghor Irrigation Scheme, and to serve as a storage dam for water diverted from rivers farther north (Latani, Hasbani, Wazzani and Banias); the activities of the Board have been interrupted as a result of Israel's occupation of the west bank of the river and other territories.

Centre Africain de Formation et de Recherches Administratives pour le Développement (CAFRAD) (*African Training and Research Centre in Administration for Development*): 19 rue Abou Alla El Maari, B.P. 310, Tangier, Morocco; f. 1964 by agreement between Morocco and UNESCO, final agreement signed by 23 African states; undertakes research into administrative problems in Africa, documentation of results, provision of a consultation service for governments and organizations; holds frequent seminars; aided by UNESCO and the UN Development Programme; library of 10,000 vols.

Pres. LOUAFI SKALLI; Dir.-Gen. J. E. KARIUKI. Publs. *Cahiers Africains d'Administration Publique* (twice a year), *Abstracts* (quarterly), *Information Bulletin* (8 times a year), *CAFRAD News* (irregularly in English and French).

International Institute for Adult Literacy Methods: P.O.B. 1555, Teheran, Iran; f. 1968 by UNESCO and the Government of Iran; carries out comparative studies of the methods, media and techniques used in literacy programmes; maintains documentation service and library on literacy; arranges seminars.

Dir. Dr. JOHN W. RYAN. Publs. *Literacy Discussion* and *Literacy Work* (quarterlies in English and French), *Literacy Documentation* (3 times a year in English).

International Planned Parenthood Federation: Middle East and North Africa Office, P.O.B. 1567, Beirut, Lebanon; aims to advance planned parenthood through education and scientific research and to attain a favourable balance between population and natural resources; Regional Office covers Afghanistan*, Algeria,

the Arabian peninsula, Cyprus*, Egypt*, Iran*, Iraq*, Jordan*, Lebanon*, Libya, Morocco*, Sudan*, Syria, Tunisia* (member asscns. with asterisk).

Near East Foundation, 54 East 64th St., New York 21, N.Y., U.S.A.; f. 1930. Aims: to conduct agricultural and educational programmes and demonstrations in order to improve standards of living in underdeveloped areas of the world, primarily the Near East, with technicians at work in Asia and Africa.

Chair. CLEVELAND E. DODGE; Vice-Chair. J. B. SUNDERLAND; Pres. HERRICK YOUNG; Exec. Dir. Dr. DELMER J. DOOLEY.

LABOUR

Arab Federation of Petroleum, Mining and Chemicals Workers (*Fédération arabe des travailleurs du pétrole, des mines et des industries chimiques*): 5 Zaki St. Cairo, Egypt; f. 1961; owns and manages the Arab Petroleum Institute for Labour Studies, Cairo; 18 affiliated unions in 11 countries.

Pres. GHAZI NASSIF (Syria); Sec.-Gen. ALI SAYED ALI (Egypt). Publ. *Arab Petroleum* (monthly; English, Arabic and French editions).

International Confederation of Arab Trade Unions (ICATU): 70 El Gomhorya St., Cairo, Egypt; f. 1956; mems.: 14 unions in 14 countries.

Sec.-Gen. ABDEL LATIF BOLTEYA (Egypt). Publs. *Arab Worker* (Arab, French, English, Spanish editions, monthly).

International Institute for Development, Co-operation and Labour Studies: P.O.B. 16201, Tel-Aviv, Israel; established by Afro-Asian Institute of Histadrut, 1960. Aims: advanced training of union workers, co-operators, government executives and higher education teachers in the theory and practice of economic and social development problems, labour economics, trade unionism and co-operation; English-speaking courses: Aug.-Nov.; French-speaking courses: Jan.-April; special courses on request: May-July.

Chair. Dr. ELIAHU ELATH; Principal AKIVA EGER.

MEDICINE

Middle East Neurosurgical Society: Dr. FUAD S. HADDAD, Neurosurgical Department, Orient Hospital, Beirut, Lebanon; f. 1958; mems. in Egypt, Greece, India, Iraq, Jordan, Lebanon, Pakistan, Syria and Turkey.

Society of Haematology and Blood-Transfusion of African and Near Eastern Countries: Tunis, Tunisia; f. 1965 for the promotion and co-ordination of scientific research in the field of haematology.

Pres. Dr. SY BABA (Ivory Coast); Vice-Pres. Dr. BENABADJY (Algeria); Sec.-Gen. Dr. ALI BOUJNAH (Tunisia).

MILITARY AFFAIRS

Arab Joint Defence Council (*see* chapter *The Arab League*).

Arab Permanent Military Commission (*see* chapter *The Arab League*).

PRESS, RADIO AND TELECOMMUNICATIONS

African Postal Union (*Union postale Africaine—UPAF*) 5 26th July St., Cairo, Egypt; f. 1961 to improve postal services between member states, to secure collaboration between them and to create other useful services. Mems.: Algeria, Egypt, Ghana, Guinea, Mali Morocco and Sudan.

Sec.-Gen. ABDUL AZIZ SHAKER (Egypt). Publ. *African Postal Union Review* (quarterly).

Arab Postal Union: (*see* chapter *The Arab League*).

Arab States Broadcasting Union (*see* chapter *The Arab League*).

Arab Telecommunications Union (*see* chapter *The Arab League*).

Federation of Arab News Agencies: Beirut; f. 1965; this Federation will work on the establishment of an Arab Central News Agency.

Union of African News Agencies (UANA): Algérie Presse Service, 7 blvd. de la République, Algiers, Algeria; f. 1963; meets annually; has proposed the creation of a Pan-African News Agency within aegis of OAU.
  Pres. MUHAMMAD BOUZID (Algeria); Sec.-Gen. HAMED SGHAL (Tunisia).

RELIGION

Agudath Israel World Organization (AIWO) (*Organisation mondiale Agudas Israel—OMAI*): Hacheruth Square, P.O.B. 326, Jerusalem; f. 1912 to protect the interests of Jewish communities and to further religious education, in the spirit of traditional Judaism; Mems.: affiliated organizations totalling 300,000 mems. in 21 countries.
  Chair. (Israel) Rabbi P. LEWIN (Jerusalem); Chair. (Europe) Rabbi L. GURWICZ (Gateshead); Chair. (U.S.A.) Rabbi Dr. I. LEWIN (New York); Sec.-Gen ABRAHAM HIRSCH (Jerusalem).

Bahá'i International Community: Office of UN Representative, 345 East 46th St., New York, N.Y. 10017, U.S.A.; f. 1844 in Persia to promote the teachings of the Bahá'í religion; to promulgate the unity of the human race; to work for the elimination of all forms of prejudice and for equality of men and women; to establish basic education schools for children; to maintain adult programmes in basic literacy and community training. Mems. in 72,000 centres in 335 countries and territories. Governing body: The Universal House of Justice, Bahá'í World Centre, Haifa, Israel.
  Rep. to UN Dr. VICTOR DE ARAUJO (U.S.A.); Alternate Mrs. ANNAMARIE HONNOLD (U.S.A.). Publs. *The Bahá'í World* (quadrennial), *Bahá'í News* (monthly); 16 Bahá'í Publishing Trusts in countries throughout the world; publications in over 598 languages and dialects.

International Council of Jewish Women: Rio Bamba 1020, Buenos Aires, Argentina; f. 1912 to promote friendly relations and understanding among Jewish women throughout the world. It exchanges information on community welfare activities, promotes volunteer leadership, sponsors field work in social welfare and fosters Jewish education. It has consultative status with UN, ECOSOC and with the UNICEF Executive Board, also information and consultative status with UNESCO. Mems.: 25 affiliates, 24 countries grouping about 1,000,000 members.
  Pres. Dra. ROSA S. DE HERCZEG (Argentina); Sec. Dra. DEBORAH SCHLESINGER (Argentina). Publ. *Newsletter* (3 a year, English and Spanish).

International Hebrew Christian Alliance, The: Shalom, Brockenhurst Rd., Ramsgate, Kent, England; f. 1925. Objects: to unite Hebrew Christians throughout the world, to maintain and extend the Christian faith among those of Hebrew birth and to help them and their families in need.
  The Alliance is at work in Great Britain, America, Argentina, South Africa, Iran, Israel and many European countries.
  Pres. HABIB YUSEFZADEH; Exec. Sec. and Treas. Rev. HARCOURT SAMUEL. Publ. *The Hebrew Christian* (quarterly).

International Muslim Union (*Union Musulmane Internationale*): Grande Mosquée de Paris, Place du Puits de l'Ermite, Paris 5e, France; f. 1968. Objects: to assist the needy, defend the Muslim community, spread the knowledge of Islamic civilization and to organize Islamic worship wherever necessary.
  Sec.-Gen. Dr. DALIL BOUBAKEUR.

World Jewish Congress (*Congrès Juif Mondial*): 1 rue de Varembé, Geneva, Switzerland; f. 1936. It is a voluntary association of representative Jewish bodies, communities and organisations throughout the world. Aims: to assure the survival and to foster the unity of the Jewish people. Mems.: Jewish communities in over 60 countries.
  Pres. Dr. N. GOLDMANN; Sec.-Gen. Dr. GERHART M. RIEGNER. Publs. *World Jewry* (bi-monthly, London), *L'Information Juive* (monthly, Paris), *Jewish Journal of Sociology* (bi-annual, London), *Gesher* (Hebrew quarterly, Israel).

World Sephardi Federation: New House, 67-68 Hatton Garden, London, EC1N 8JY; f. 1951 to strengthen the unity of Jewry and Judaism among Sephardim, to defend and foster religious and cultural activities of all Sephardi Communities and preserve their spiritual heritage, to provide moral and material assistance where necessary and to co-operate with other similar organizations. Mems.: 50 communities and organizations in 30 countries.
  Sec. MICHAEL MARCHANT.

SCIENCE AND TECHNOLOGY

Arab Engineering Union: 81 Ramses St., Cairo; co-operates with the Arab League in matters concerning the engineering profession; holds a conference on scientific engineering studies every two years.

International Meteorological Institute: Cairo; f. 1966 to carry out meteorological research and to provide training for Middle Eastern and African personnel engaged in meteorological work; the building of this project is being executed by World Meteorological Organization (WMO).

Mediterranean Social Sciences Research Council: American University of Beirut, Beirut, Lebanon; f. 1960 to promote research on problems concerning the social and economic development of the land and peoples of the Mediterranean Basin. Mems.: Research Centres and individuals in 19 countries.
  Chair. Prof. D. J. DELIVANIS (Greece); Sec.-Gen. Prof. N. ZIADEH (Lebanon).

Middle Eastern Regional Radioisotope Centre for the Arab Countries: Sh. Malaeb El Gamaa, Dokki, Cairo, Egypt; f. 1963; trains specialists in the applications of radioisotopes, particularly in the medical, agricultural and industrial fields; conducts research in hydrology, tropical and subtropical diseases, fertilisers and entomology; promotes the use of radioisotopes in the Arab countries.

SOCIAL SCIENCES

Congress of Arab and Islamic Studies (*Congrès des études arabes et islamiques*): c/o Prof. F. M. Pareja, Juan XXIII, 5, Madrid 3, Spain; f. 1962; eighth congress, Aix-en-Provence, 1976.
  Sec.-Gen. Prof. F. M. PAREJA (Spain).

European Union of Arabic and Islamic Scholars (*Union Européenne d'Arabisants et d'Islamisants—U.E.A.I.*): Juan XXIII 5, Madrid 3, Spain; f. 1970 to organize a Congress of Arabic and Islamic Studies. Mems.: about 120.
  Sec. Prof. F. M. PAREJA (Spain).

TRADE AND INDUSTRY

General Union of Chambers of Commerce, Industry and Agriculture for Arab Countries (*Union générale des chambres de commerce, industrie et agriculture des pays arabes*): P.O.B. 11-2837, Beirut, Lebanon; f. 1951 to foster Arab economic collaboration, to increase and improve production and to facilitate the exchange of technical information in Arab countries. Mems.: 20 Chambers of Commerce in 20 countries.

Pres. FARAJANI BEN HAJAMMAR (Tunisia); Gen. Sec. BURHAN DAJANI. Publ. *Arab Economic Report* (Arabic and English).

TRANSPORT AND TOURISM

Arab Air Carriers' Organization (AACO): 707 South Bloc, Starco Bldg., Rue Omar Daouk, Lebanon; f. 1965 to co-ordinate and promote co-operation in the activities of Arab airline companies.

Pres. 1974–75 ABDEL AZIZ ZUNAIDI; Sec.-Gen. SALIM A. SALAAM.

Arab Association of Tourism and Travel Agents— A.A.T.T.A.: P.O.B. 5196, Beirut, Lebanon; f. 1952; groups Tourist and Travel Agents operating in the Arab world to promote tourism in the region. Mems.: 250.

Pres. MOHAMMED S. GIABER; Senior Vice-Pres. SALIM KHEIREDDIN; Gen. Man. SALIM ISSA. Publ. *Arab World Tourism* (monthly).

Arab Tourism Union: P.O.B. 2354, Amman, Jordan; f. 1954. Mems.: Nat. Tourist orgs. of 20 Arab states, and 4 Assoc. mems. in private sector; 7 members form the Executive Committee for a term of three years.

Sec.-Gen. ABU RABAH (Jordan). Publs. *Arab Tourism* (bi-monthly, Arabic), *Research Supplement* (bi-monthly Arabic), *Press Bulletin* (bi-monthly, Arabic and English).

Arab Union of Automobile Clubs and Tourist Societies: 8 Kasr El Nil St., Cairo; f. 1965.

Trans-Sahara Liaison Committee: c/o Ministry of Public Works, 135 rue Didouche Mourade, Algiers, Algeria; f. 1964; mems.: Algeria, Mali, Niger and Tunisia; this technical committee was formed to study the proposed trans-Saharan road route, the favoured scheme being a road from El Golea to Tamanrasset in Algeria branching towards Gao in Mali and In Gall in Niger. Tunisia will have access to the route via existing communications. The estimated cost for a tarred road 7 metres wide, 2,900 km. long, is U.S. $86.0 million and the road will take about eight years to build. The pre-feasibility study of the whole route has been completed under the auspices of the UN Development Programme. The construction of the El Golea—In Salah section in Algeria was started in September 1971 and was expected to be completed in about 3 years.

PART THREE
Country Surveys

Afghanistan

PHYSICAL AND SOCIAL GEOGRAPHY

W. B. Fisher

Occupying an area of approximately 250,000 square miles (estimates range between 240,000 and 270,000 square miles) Afghanistan has the shape of a very irregular oval with its major axis running N.E.-S.W. and extending over roughly 700 miles, and the minor axis at right angles to this, covering about 350 miles. The country is in the main a highland mass lying mostly at an altitude of 4,000 ft. (1,200 metres) or more, but it presents a highly variable pattern of extremely high and irregular mountain ridges, some of which exceed 20,000 ft. (6,000 metres); ravines and broader valleys, parts of which are very fertile; and an outer expanse of undulating plateau, wide river basins, and lake sumps.

Politically, Afghanistan has two frontiers of major length: one on the north with the Turkmen, Uzbek and Tadzhik Republics of the U.S.S.R., the other (on the south and east) with Pakistan.

This frontier follows what was once termed the Durand Line (after the representative of British India, Sir Mortimer Durand, who negotiated it in 1893 with the Ruler of Afghanistan). So long as the British occupied India, it was generally accepted as forming the Indo-Afghan frontier, but in 1947 with the recognition of Pakistan as a successor to the British, the Afghan government recalled that for much of the eighteenth century, Peshawar and other parts of the Indus Valley had formed part of a larger Afghan state, and were moreover occupied largely by Pashtuns, who are of closely similar ethnic character to many Afghans. Accordingly, the Durand Line frontier was denounced by Afghanistan, and claims were made that the territories as far as the line of the Indus, including Chitral, Swat, and Peshawar, and continuing as far as the Pashtun areas of the North-west Frontier Province and Baluchistan, ought to be recognized as an autonomous state, "Pashtunistan". This remains a topic of dispute between Afghanistan and Pakistan.

There are shorter but no less significant frontiers on the west with Iran, and on the north-east with Kashmir and with China. This last was fully agreed only in 1963, and the precise location of others in the south and west has not been fully delimited: an indication of the extreme difficulties of terrain, and an explanation of the uncertainty regarding the actual area of Afghanistan. It is noteworthy that, in order to erect a "buffer" between the then competing Empires of Russia and India, under the Durand treaty of 1893 the Wakhan district, a narrow strip of land 200 miles long and under 10 miles wide in its narrowest part, was attached to Afghanistan. This strip controls the Baroghil pass over the Pamir, and avoids having a Russian-Indian joint frontier.

PHYSICAL FEATURES

The main topographical feature of Afghanistan is a complex of irregular highlands that is relatively broad and low in the west, and very much higher and also narrower towards the east. In this eastern part the mountains form a group of well-defined chains that are known by the general name of the Hindu Kush (Hindu destroyer), and are linked further eastward first to the Pamirs and then to the main Himalaya system. The Eastern Hindu Kush ranges form the southern defining limit of the Wakhan strip whilst a short distance to the north and east, a small but high ridge, the Little Pamir, forms the topographic link between the Hindu Kush and the main Pamir. From maximum heights of 20,000–24,000 ft. (6,000–7,000 metres) the peaks decline in altitude westwards, attaining 15,000–20,000 ft. (4,500–6,000 metres) in the zone close to Kabul. Further west still, the ridges are no more than 12,000–15,000 ft. (3,500–4,500 metres) and in the extreme west they open out rather like the digits of a hand, with the much lower Parapamisus ridges (proto-Pamir) forming the last member of the mountain complex. The various ridges are distinguished by separate names. The Hindu Kush, which has a general altitude of about 15,000 ft. (4,000 metres) with peaks 7,000–10,000 ft. higher still, is however narrow, and crossable by quite a number of passes, some of which are indirect and snow-bound for much of the year.

In geological structure, Afghanistan has close affinities both to Iran further west, and, as has just been stated, to the massive Himalayan system further east. Development of present-day land-forms has been greatly influenced by the existence of several large, stable masses of ancient rocks, which have acted as cores around which rock series of younger age first developed and were then closely wrapped as fold structures. Most important of these ancient massifs, or "shield" areas so far as Afghanistan is concerned, is the plateau of the Deccan, the effect of which was to "bunch" a series of tight folds in a double loop or garland on its northern side. In this way can be explained the existence of the "knot" or "bunch" of fold structures lying partly in Afghanistan, and comprising the Pamir which forms the eastern limb and the Hindu Kush that makes up the western segment of the "garland". The abrupt change of direction and swinging of the fold structures from an east-west to, in some places, a north-south direction are a direct result of the presence of the resistant mass of the Deccan. The fold ranges themselves are composed in part of sediments mainly laid down under water, and include limestones with some sandstones, and are of Cretaceous and later age, Eocene especially. Extensive heat and pressure in some regions have metamorphosed original series into schists and gneiss; and there has been much shattering and cracking of the rock generally, with the consequent development of fault-lines and overthrust zones. A further feature in much of Afghanistan has been a good deal of differential earth movement, uptilting, downwarping and local adjustment which make the region particularly susceptible to earth tremors, which occur frequently, usually on a small scale. Occasionally, however, a major disaster occurs, the latest being at Tashkent just north of Afghanistan in 1965.

As a consequence of frequent crustal disturbance, the rise of magma from the earth's interior has produced lava-flows, and minor volcanos. Most of these are in a stage of old age—being merely fissures from which emanate gas, steam and mud flows; and the presence of soft volcanic debris adds considerably in places to soil fertility.

As far as river drainage is concerned, Afghanistan forms a major watershed, from which rivers flow outward. The Amu Darya (Oxus) rises on the north side of the Hindu Kush and flows northwestwards into the U.S.S.R. Here, away from the mountains the presence of loess (a yellowish soil of high fertility) in small pockets offers scope for agriculture. The Hari Rud rises a short distance only from the Amu Darya, but flows westward through Herat to terminate in a salt, closed basin on the Iranian frontier. From the south and west of the Hindu Kush flow a number of streams that become tributaries of the Indus; and in the extreme south-west the Helmand river flows through to end like the Hari Rud in a closed basin that is partly within Iranian territory. The Helmand basin is of interest in that because of a curious balance in water-level at its lowest part, the river here reverses its flow seasonally, and remains for much of its length non-brackish instead of becoming progressively more saline, as is normal when there is no outlet to the sea. The Helmand basin thus offers distinct potential for agricultural improvement, and in fact schemes for irrigation are in process of development. But political difficulties (part of the lower basin is Iranian territory) and remoteness are inhibiting factors.

The areas of lower, and in the main more densely peopled areas occur either as a series of peripheral zones to north and south, or as a series of interior valleys and basins between the main mountain ridges of the centre. Largest of these areas is the piedmont lying on the northern flanks of the mountains, and dropping northwards in altitude to merge into the steppelands of Russian Central Asia. This is Bactria, a region of, in places, light yellowish loessic soils. An interior situation, shut off from the sea by mountains means that rainfall is deficient, and falls mainly over the mountains. Streams fed partly by mountain snow-melt straggle across the plain, to lose themselves in the sand, feed salt swamps, or in a few cases, join others to form larger rivers such as the Hari Rud. Much of Bactria thus consists of semi or full desert with sheets of sand and gravel in many places, with, nearer the mountains, outwash of larger, coarser scree. Given stable political conditions this area with its areas of highly fertile loess soils and moderate

water supplies offers much scope for economic development. For long inhabited by pastoral nomads, and disputed politically between various claimants: Afghan, Iranian and Russian, this northern zone is now developing rapidly with irrigated cotton growing as a main element. Links with the U.S.S.R. are considerable, and the two chief towns of Herat in the west and Mazar-i-Sharif in the north have grown considerably in size over the past few years.

On the south, towards the east, is the Kabul basin, which is a relatively flat zone hemmed in closely by steep mountain ridges. Some distance away to the north-west, and reachable through two major passes is the narrower Vale of Bamian; whilst south-east of Kabul occurs another fertile lowland zone around Jellalabad. Here lower elevation and southerly situation produce warmer conditions, especially in winter, as compared with most of the rest of Afghanistan.

In the south-west, extending through Ghazni as far as Kandahar, there is another series of cultivated zones; but the extent of this piedmont area is much smaller than the corresponding one we have just described as Bactria. To the west, aridity, the price of declining altitude, increases, so the lowland passes into the desert areas of Registan and the Dasht-i-Mayo. Registan has seasonal flushes of grass, which support relatively large numbers of pastoral nomads, who however, are becoming increasingly sedentarized following irrigation development on the Helmand and Arghandab rivers.

Two other regional units may be mentioned. South of the Parapamisus and Kuh-i-Baba mountain ranges are a number of parallel but lower massifs, with narrow valleys between. Here because of altitude there is relatively abundant rainfall, but owing to topography, the region is one of remoteness and difficulty. This is the Hazarat, so called from the name of the Hazara inhabitants; and it still remains despite a central position one of the least known and visited parts of the country. Another equally remote highland, this time located north-east of Kabul, is Nuristan, again high and mountainous, but wellwooded in places, and supporting a small population of cultivators and pastoralists who use the summer pastures of the high hills, and move to lower levels in winter.

CLIMATE

Climatically, Afghanistan demonstrates a very clear relationship with Iran and the Middle East, rather than with Monsoon Asia, in that it has an almost arid summer, a small amount of rainfall which is largely confined to the winter season, and considerable seasonal variation in temperature. The monsoonal condition of heavy summer rainfall does not occur, despite Afghanistan's nearness to India. Annual rainfall ranges from 4-6 in. (10-15 cm.) in the drier, lower areas of the west and north, to 10-15 in. (25-40 cm.) in the east; and on the highest mountains there is more still. Kabul, with an average of 13 in. per annum, is typical of conditions in the east, and Herat with 5 in. typical of the west. Almost all this falls in the period December to April, though there can be a very occasional downpour at other times, even in summer, when a rare damp monsoonal current penetrates from the Indian lowlands. Temperatures are best described as extreme. In July, the lowlands experience temperatures of 110°F., (43°C.) with 120° not uncommon—this is true of Jellalabad on the edge of the Indus lowlands. But the effects of altitude are important, and Kabul, at an elevation of 6,000 ft. does not often experience temperatures of over 100°F. (38°C.). Winter cold can be bitter, with minima of –10° to –15°F. (–22° to –26°C.) on the higher plateau areas; and as a result there are heavy blizzards in many mountain areas. The January mean at Kabul is 25°F. (–4°C.). Generally speaking, a seasonal temperature range of 80-100°F. is characteristic of many areas (cf. 26°F. for London). A further difficulty is the prevalence of strong winds, especially in the west, where a persistent and regular wind blows almost daily from June to September and affects especially the Sistan area of the lower Helmand basin, where it is known as the *Wind of 120 Days*.

With highly varied topography and climate, Afghanistan has a wide range of plant life—a good deal of which is not yet fully recorded. Conditions range from Arctic and Alpine type flora on the highest parts to salt-tolerant arid zone species in the deserts. Woodland occurs in a few areas, but much has been used for fuel in a country that has cold winters.

PEOPLE AND ACTIVITIES

The considerable variation in the types of terrain, and the considerable obstacles imposed by high mountains and deserts, have given rise to marked ethnic and cultural differences, so that heterogeneity in human populations is most characteristic. The Pashtuns live mainly in the centre, south and east of the country, and are probably numerically the largest group. The Ghilzais, also of the areas adjacent to Pakistan, are thought to be of Turkish origin, like the Uzbeks who live in the north, mainly in the Amu Darya lowlands. Another important element are the Tadzhiks or Parziwans who are of Persian origin, and in the opinion of some represent the earliest inhabitants of the country. Other groups, such as the Hazara (who are reputed to have come in as followers of Ghenghis Khan), and the Chahar Aimak may have Mongol ancestry, but they now speak Persian and the Hazara are Shi'a Muslims. In the north-east, the presence of fair-haired groups has suggested connection with Europe. Another possibly indigenous group of long-standing, is the Nuristani or Kafirs, now small in number. Most Afghans (the Hazara and Qizilbash of Kabul excepted) are Sunni.

For long a difficult topography, extreme climate with a generally deficient rainfall, and political instability inhibited economic progress. Small communities lived by cultivation where water and soil were available, and there were relatively numerous pastoralists, mostly nomads, who formed an important section of the community. Even today, it is estimated that about 15 per cent of the population is nomadic, and tribal organization is strong.

Two major handicaps, arising directly from its geography, have long been the fragmented nature of the settlement pattern and the difficulties of physical communications between the various communities. Scale of production and size of markets have consequently been very limited: local standards often prevail and the central government does not find it easy to develop full control. So inherently strong is this fact of regional subdivision and diversity that the improvement of infrastructure (roads, airfields, radio and telephonic communication), undertaken with vigour over the past few years, has largely resulted in the intensification of regionalism.

Over the last few years developments have taken place on a significant scale. A series of three Five-Year Development Plans, 1956-72, gave encouragement to cereal cultivation (wheat, barley and maize), olive cultivation in the eastern provinces, sericulture in the north, and the improvement of commercial crops such as cotton and sugar beet. As part of a general attempt to improve animal husbandry fodder crops (alfalfa and lucerne) are given prominence, and improved strains of traditional fruit and vegetables (apricots, apples, peaches, melons, vines, squashes, potatoes, etc.) are replacing the older species in many areas.

In common with other countries of south-west Asia, Afghanistan experienced severe drought between 1968-72: this is thought to have been due to a major cyclical climatic shift that is traceable over a very wide area of the Northern Hemisphere. The economic consequences of this drought have been considerable, though varied regionally within Afghanistan, not only for the 80 per cent or so of the population who still live directly by agriculture, but, as well, through restriction on water supplies for developing manufacturing and other activities. Consequently, the Third Five-Year Plan (1967-71) failed to realize its full objectives; but nevertheless it would seem that it did achieve enough to keep roughly level with population increase, despite the drought, so that living standards, at least, did not fall.

As a result, the Fourth Plan, inaugurated in 1972, has more modest objectives: retrieval and improvement of defects and failures in infrastructure projects, and improvement in existing agriculture and industry, rather than the introduction of major new construction. So far the Plan appears to have achieved a 6 per cent annual growth rate. Much of this has come from a distinct upturn in mid-1973 from agricultural yields, especially in cotton, rice and wheat, production of the last more than meeting home demands. World price rises in commodities exported by Afghanistan (e.g. hides, skins and carpets) have also had a markedly beneficial effect, but these price levels are highly erratic, so that they may not be a permanent factor. One highly important influence has been the disturbed political situation. Apart from the direct effects, there has been a slight fall-off in tourism, and a decline in outside aid; Afghanistan has drifted into closer financial dependence on the U.S.S.R. Given a moderate political "line", however, and freedom from drought, there are reasonably good prospects of further and consistent development, though very far below those of the neighbouring oil-rich states to the west.

Irrigation has developed markedly within the last ten years. The major scheme so far is in the Helmand basin where two storage dams and a series of distributary canals offer potential development for about a quarter of a million acres (100,000 hectares) of arid land. Irrigation development is also taking place on the Arghandab river in the same region. Other schemes are in existence near Jellalabad, and on the Amu Darya; and there is a much more ambitious scheme for this last river which will involve both extension of irrigation and large-scale generation of electric power, in co-operation with the U.S.S.R.

Because of Afghanistan's former location as a buffer between Russia and British India, railways approached from various sides, but none actually penetrated the country, and so Afghanistan is one of the few parts of the world still to be totally without railways. During 1975 possibilities of constructing a railway with Indian assistance have been discussed. The plan is to link Kabul, Kandahar, Herat and Islamqala (on the Iranian frontier) with a line that would be 1,000 miles in length and cost £500 million. A possible extension from Kabul to Zahidan in Iran and the Pakistan border is also under consideration. The narrowness (despite the great height) of the mountain barrier as compared with the Himalayas, has made Afghanistan a traditional routeway between north and south, and at present, helped by various foreign agencies and governments, there is a programme for considerable road improvement and development. Given the difficulties of terrain, Afghanistan now possesses a reasonably good road system, with some very good sections. Air transport is also an increasingly important factor. Better accessibility has also resulted in the growth of a small, but far from insignificant tourist traffic.

HISTORY

M. C. Gillett

(Revised by the Editor, 1975)

It will be convenient to refer to Afghanistan throughout this essay, though the word (which means "The Country of the Afghans"—i.e. Pashtuns or Pathans) only goes back to 1747 and the name Afghan first appears in the tenth century. A better name would be "The Country of the Hindu Kush". For this range not only gives our area, where Central Asia, India and Persia meet, its special character but also helps to elucidate much of its history. The Hindu Kush forms a boundary between the nomadic and the settled lands: a boundary, but not a barrier. For at its eastern end are several practicable passes of the order of 10,000 feet above sea level and it can be turned at its western end near Herat. It serves as a backbone that encourages the formation of states astride itself. And it is the reservoir of the area: it is the winter snows in the Hindu Kush that provide the water for irrigation so vital to settled life in an area with an average annual precipitation of less than twelve inches. Further, the rivers rising in the Hindu Kush provide convenient routes of communication much frequented by traders and invaders during the ages when land transport predominated. In conjunction with the east-west ways along the Oxus valley and the passes through the Hindu Kush these routes explain why Afghanistan is at the centre of Professor Toynbee's *Central Asian Roundabout*. The valley of the Hari Rud turns the Hindu Kush to the west. The Helmand-Arghandab-Tarnak system leads from the frontiers of Persia to within a hundred miles of the headwaters of the Kabul river. And the line of the Kabul river provides the easiest access to the Indian sub-continent from the north and west. French excavations at Mundigak near Kandahar (virgin soil about 3,000 B.C.) suggest these routes were of importance already in prehistoric times; and they fitted into that great Eurasian caravan route sometimes called "The Silk Road". They were probably used by the Aryans, and certainly used by Alexander and by the Sakas, on their way to India. Though the Hindu Kush is now but a key to India it was formerly *the* key; and the holders of this key seldom failed to use it, lured on, often to the detriment of their interests in Afghanistan, by the great wealth of the sub-continent.

EARLY HISTORY

Afghanistan first appears in history during the reign of Darius I (6th century B.C.) not as a political entity, but divided among at least three of the Achaemenian satraps. It remained under the Achaemenians till the defeat of Darius III by Alexander at Guagamela in 331 B.C. After Darius's death a sort of national resistance to the Greeks developed in Afghanistan and Transoxiana.

Greeks: Alexander, Seleucids, Graeco-Bactrians

Alexander spent three years in and about Afghanistan pacifying and organizing the country, where he established five cities. He marched on India in 327 B.C. and did not return to Afghanistan. During the confused period that followed Alexander's death in 323 B.C. Afghanistan was at first controlled by Antigonus Cyclops but by 305 B.C. it had come into the hands of Seleucus, another of Alexander's generals. The main centre of power then lay to the west so the Seleucids tended to neglect their eastern territories. In 302 B.C. Seleucus himself ceded south-eastern Afghanistan to the Maurya emperor Chandragupta in exchange for the five hundred elephants that contributed to the important victory at Ipsus in the following year. Southeastern Afghanistan remained under Maurya control till that empire declined after the death of Asoka, the encourager of Buddhism. Seleucid preoccupation with the west encouraged their

Satrap of Bactria, Diodotus, to declare himself independent of Antiochus II in about 255 B.C. Diodotus and the Graeco-Bactrian rulers who succeeded him (they were not all of his blood: three frequently inimical families of rulers are known) were tough, able men who were able to maintain their independence. And helped by the weakening of the Seleucid and Maurya empires they enlarged their kingdom till it extended from the Zarafshan to the Punjab. But their quarrels weakened them. The rise of Parthia cut them off from the west. And the lure of India was strong. So their guard on their nomadic frontier ultimately failed. Between 140 and 130 B.C. Bactria fell to the nomads, and the Kabul region and the rest of southern Afghanistan (Parthia had already occupied Herat and western Afghanistan) followed suit a century later. Greek influence persisted well into the Christian era, and petty kings of Greek descent probably continued to rule for at least as long in inaccessible places.

Kushans

Between 177 and 170 B.C. the nomadic Hsiungnu, or Huns (probably proto-Turk) inflicted two crushing defeats on the Yüehchih, a nomadic Indo-European people in what is now the Kansu-Ninghsia border area. The Yüehchih fled west driving before them the Saka tribes living astride the Alai mountains (another Indo-European people). What actually happened when the Greek kingdom of Bactria fell to the nomads is not clear. But we do know the Yüehchih ultimately occupied the Balkh region. And the Sakas turned the Hindu Kush to the west, occupied Seistan (Seistan is but a corruption of Sakasthan) and spread up the river system mentioned in paragraph one towards northern India. The chronology of this period is uncertain, but it was probably in the first century A.D. that the Kushans became the leading tribe in the Yüehchih confederacy. Under King Kujula Kadphises they moved south of the Hindu Kush, splitting the Sakas in two and driving part of them down into India. Under some able kings, prominent among whom was Kanishka, the Kushans built up an empire extending from the Oxus to Mathura (Muttra). They were an interesting people who developed a considerable degree of culture. They adapted Greek letters for writing the language they used in Afghanistan. The stability their empire afforded greatly facilitated trade along the "Silk Road" and its important feeder down to India at a time when only the Kushans and the Parthians lay between flourishing Han China and the Roman Empire. From Kanishka onwards the Kushan kings became patrons of Buddhism, probably from policy as much as from conviction, for the southern parts of their empire had been strongly Buddhist ever since Asoka's time. Under them Buddhism spread along the trade routes northwards across the Hindu Kush then eastwards through Central Asia towards China. The Kushan empire, with its capital at Peshawar, started to decline about the middle of the third century. The Sassanians, who replaced the Parthians in Persia in 226, came to control western Afghanistan (including Seistan) and, according to some, may even have exercised suzerainty over the later Kushans. And about the middle of the fifth century the Kushans were replaced in our area by the Kidarites (also of Yüehchih stock) who controlled the country south of the Oxus between Balkh and Merv.

Hephthalites

At the beginning of the fifth century High Asia was controlled by two powerful Turco-Mongol confederacies, both apparently under Mongol leadership. In the east were the Juanjuan; to the west, centred on the Altai, were the Hephthalites, who seem to have been always in some sort vassals of the Juanjuan. During the second quarter of the fifth century the Hephthalites (also known as "Huna" and "White Huns" though with little connection with Attila and his tribes) started to expand westwards. They occupied Soghdia, replaced the Kidarites in Bactria, and in 484 attacked Persia and killed the Sassanian King Firuz. Then, while continuing to harry Persia, they turned to the south-east, occupied Afghanistan and invaded north-west India. The Hephthalites remained nomadic and barbaric, destroyed much, and were particular enemies to Buddhism.

Tuchüeh

When the Juanjuan ruler Anakuei put a slight upon one of his vassals, Bumin, Chief of the Tuchüeh, or Turks, they revolted and, with the help of the Turkish rulers of north China (Wei dynasty), defeated the Juanjuan in 552. Bumin died in the year of this victory and the Turks divided into two: the Eastern Turks under Bumin's son; and the Western Turks under Bumin's able brother, Istämi. The two confederacies continued friendly for a while, but later were often at enmity. About 565 the Western Turks allied themselves with the Sassanians and smashed the Hephthalites, who disappeared as a political entity. Their territory was divided between the allies, roughly along the line of the Oxus, and Afghanistan became part of the Sassanian empire for some twenty years. Later the Turks split with the Sassanians (profits from the transit trade along the "Silk Road" contributed to the quarrel) and allied themselves with Byzantium. The Turks invaded Bactria in 558/9 and by 597/8 they controlled the whole of Afghanistan. Their power was at its peak in 630, when the celebrated Chinese pilgrim Hsüan Tsang passed through their territories. Many Turks adopted Buddhism, which the Hephthalites had failed to eradicate. And some Turks seem to have become partially sedentary in Afghanistan.

Chinese

Between 659 and 661 T'ang China, who had already defeated the Eastern Turks in 630, crushed the Western Turks. The Chinese took over the Turkish territories and started to set up an administration in them, which never had time to develop as the Tibetans occupied the Tarim basin for twenty-four years after 670 and thus cut China off from her westernmost dependencies.

THE COMING OF ISLAM

The Arabs, in their astonishing expansion, now enter our area. At the battle of Nehavend in 642 they completed the destruction of the Sassanians. In 651, they occupied Herat, and the following year they raided Balkh. Civil wars halted this Arab expansion for a time, but it was renewed early in the eighth century under Qutayba b. Muslim, the Ommayad Viceroy of Khorassan. The Western Turks never recovered from their defeat by the Chinese. The Eastern Turks had briefly revived their empire between about 683 and 743 but were never in a position to help their western congeners. And, though the Chinese had recaptured the Tarim basin by 694 and were able to start a forward policy again by 715 (the year of Qutayba's death), they suffered a crushing defeat on the Talas in July 751. So the rulers of Afghanistan, not all of whom were Turks had no outside help in their resistance to the Arabs. They put up a tough struggle: parts of eastern Afghanistan were not converted to Islam till the ninth century, and the centre not till the beginning of the eleventh century. But ultimately the bulk of Afghanistan became part of the Abbassid Caliphate.

Tahirids, Saffarids and Samanids

By the time of the Abbassids the dilution of the Arab element in Islam by conquests and conversions was already marked. This dilution continued to increase; and the Abbassids came to rely more and more on mercenary armies chiefly composed of Turkish Ghulams, or slaves, rather than on Arabs. And with the decline of the Caliphate there was an increasing tendency for the formation of local dynasties owing but nominal allegiance to the Caliph. Such, in our area, were the Tahirids who ruled Khorassan for about fifty years from 820; the Saffarids from Seistan who overthrew the Tahirids in the second half of the ninth century and added Herat and Balkh to their dominions; and, most important, the Samanids who established their capital in Bokhara in 874, subjugated the Saffarids about 900, and at the height of their power controlled Transoxiana, the greater part of Persia, and much of Afghanistan. The Samanids were brought down by the Qarakhanid Turks in 999.

Ghaznavids

Under the Samanid, Abdalmalik I, a Turkish Ghulam called Alptegin was Captain of the Guard. By shrewd use of the political arts of the time he had made himself Governor of Khorassan and was in the way of becoming the most powerful man in the kingdom when the death of Abdalmalik and the accession of Mansur I ruined his prospects. In 962 he fled to Ghazni, displaced the local ruler, became himself almost independent, and founded the important Ghaznavid dynasty which lasted for 200 years. The greatest Ghaznavid was Mahmud who, building on the foundations laid by his grandfather Alptegin and his father Sabuktegin (977-997), extended his sway till he controlled much of Persia, most of Afghanistan, and northern India. Moved largely by religious zeal, Mahmud aimed at an annual winter campaign in India, into which he made

seventeen expeditions, exacting vast treasures in tribute. Towards the north he was less successful but though he was unable to take Transoxiana from the Qarakhanids he managed to hold his own against them and against the Ghuzz. Mahmud adopted the title of Sultan. His court was a brilliant one, frequented by people such as Firdausi, the poet, and Al Biruni, the polymath. Mahmud died in 1030. His successors lacked his abilities and they were under constant pressure from the Seljuks, a tribe of the Ghuzz, to whom the Ghaznavids ultimately became tributary. In 1152 Sultan Bahram Shah was defeated by Alauddin of Ghor, who sacked Ghazni. And Bahram Shah's son Kusru, the last of the Ghaznavids to rule in Afghanistan, was forced down to India by the Ghuzz.

Seljuks

Towards the end of the tenth century a nomadic Turkish people, the Oghuz or Ghuzz, appear in Transoxiana, moving slowly towards the south and west and playing their part in the fighting that accompanied the decline of the Samanids. The bulk of them remained nomadic, as their descendants, the Turcomans, have remained to this day. But one clan, the Seljuks, appreciated the advantages of civilization, became orthodox muslims and ultimately became sedentary. Under Toghrul Beg the senior branch of the Seljuks took Khorassan from the Ghaznavids between 1038 and 1040, when they defeated Masud near Merv. Toghrul Beg's brother occupied Khwarezm. By the middle of the century the Seljuks were the masters of most of Persia; and in 1058 Toghrul Beg displaced the Shi'a Buyids to become Temporal Vicar of the Abbassid Caliph. With the help of an able Persian Vizier known as Nizam-ul-Mulk (the friend of Omar Khayyam) Toghrul Beg's two successors Alp Arslan (1063-72) and Malik Shah (1072-92) were able to hold onto their possessions in Persia and to deal with the traditional fissiparous tendencies of their people. Malik Shah took Balkh from the Ghaznavids. His son, Sultan Sinjar, who became ruler of Khorassan in 1095, played an important part in our area and in 1117 reduced the Ghaznavids to vassalage. He died in 1157, after trouble with the untamed Ghuzz in the Balkh area, without being able to establish a stable Turco-Persian kingdom.

Ghorids

The hill-country up the Hari Rud from Herat, known as Ghor, for long remained in isolation because of its poverty and difficulty of access. The Achaemenians seem to have penetrated there. And Masud, while Governor of Khorassan under his father Mahmud of Ghazni, undertook the systematic reduction of the area to vassalage, and its conversion. At that time the country was divided among a number of *Maliks*, or petty kings. But by the end of the eleventh century a central authority had developed and in 1099 Masud III of Ghazni was able to recognize one Izzuddin Hussain as Prince of Ghor. Izzuddin, who died about the middle of the twelfth century, managed to balance fairly successfully the often conflicting claims of his Ghaznavid suzerains and the powerful Seljuks in Khorassan. His son and successor,

Saifuddin Suri, delegated some of his power to two half-brothers. Fakhruddin got Bamian where he founded the Shanshabanid dynasty, which lasted till the Mongol invasion; and Qutbuddin got the hill country. Some family quarrel drove Qutbuddin down to Ghazni where he was poisoned by Sultan Bahram Shah in 1146. Saifuddin marched on Ghazni to avenge his brother, took the town and held it for a couple of years, when he assumed the title of *Sultan*. But in 1149 Bahram Shah drove him out of Ghazni, captured him and ignominiously executed him. A fourth brother died on the way to attack Ghazni. It was left to the fifth brother, Alauddin Hussein (1149-56), to rout Bahram Shah at Taginabad on the Helmand and to sack Ghazni, which earned him the epiteth of *Jahansoz*, or *World Burner*. Alauddin did not hold Ghazni, and Bahram Shah reoccupied it till his death. Alauddin was less successful against the Seljuks, by whom he was defeated in 1152 and held prisoner a while. His son and successor was killed in 1163 near Merv while attacking the Ghuzz and the army gave allegiance to his nephew Ghiyasuddin. This was the Ghiyasuddin who built the beautiful minaret near Jam. Closely supported by his brother Muizuddin (also known as Mohammed Ghori) Ghiyasuddin brought Ghor to its brief period of glory, with an empire stretching from Herat to Ajmir in India. Muizuddin, who had been made Sultan of Ghazni on driving the Ghuzz out of that town in 1173, proved unequal to ruling alone after Ghiyasuddin died in 1203. In 1204 he was defeated by the Khwarezm Shah near Andkhui. And when he was assassinated in 1206 while returning from dealing with a revolt in the Punjab the Ghorid empire collapsed. The Indian territories became independent, and the rest of the kingdom was incorporated in the Khwarezmian empire between 1206 and 1215.

Khwarezm Shahs

The rulers of the Khiva oasis long made use of the title of Khwarezm Shah, which was later appropriated by the Seljuk governors of Khorassan. Shah Atsiz (1127/8-56), son of a Seljuk governor of Khorassan and grandson of a Turkish slave, tried to declare his independence of the Seljuks but was defeated by Sinjar in 1138. In 1141 the Qarakhitai defeated Sinjar and invaded Khwarezm. These Qarakhitai were a strongly sinicized Mongol *élite* who had been driven from Peking some twenty years before by a revolt of their vassals, the Tungusic Jurchen. They fled westward and founded a new state at the expense of the Qarakhanid Turks of Transoxiana and Sinkiang. They were not muslims. Khwarezm remained tributary to the Qarakhitai till the reign of Shah Atsiz's grandson, Alauddin Mohammed (1200-20); and it was with the help of his overlords that he defeated Muizuddin, as related above. Between 1207 and 1210 this Muhammad of Khwarezm threw off the yoke of the Qarakhitai, whose *Gurkhan*, or ruler, Yeh-Liu Ch'e-Lu-Ku was having trouble with rebellion in the east. The Khwarezm Shahs had got control of Khorassan towards the end of the twelfth century, occupied Transoxiana after defeating the Qarakhitai, and by taking Ghazni in 1215-16 completed their occupation of Afghanistan. So by 1217 Muhammad of Khwarezm seemed to have effected the task in which Sinjar had failed: the creation of a strong Turco-Persian state in eastern Islam. But the strength of this empire was illusory. It was based on locally-powerful landowners and a mercenary army, and depended for its strength chiefly on the character of the ruler. Mohammed of Khwarezm was unequal to his task. He offended Genghiz Khan in 1218, and by the time he died, two years later, a broken-hearted fugitive, his empire had disintegrated.

Mongols

Genghiz Khan, the great Mongol leader, had consolidated his power over Mongolia by 1206 and then started to expand. By 1216 he had defeated the Qarakhitai in what is now Sinkiang so his territories marched with those of the Khwarezm Shah. Genghiz Khan, seemingly impressed by the apparent strength of the Khwarezm Shah, was willing to enter into commercial and diplomatic relations. But in 1218 the Khwarezmian governor of Otrar pillaged a Mongol caravan and massacred its muslim merchants and the Mongol envoy accompanying it. The Khwarezm Shah refused any reparation so the following year Genghiz Khan attacked. The Khwarezmians put up little effective resistance, though Mohammed's son Jalaluddin did inflict two defeats on the Mongols in Afghanistan before being finally defeated himself. By 1222 Afghanistan was in Mongol hands. The towns were destroyed, the urban population massacred, the dams on the Helmand wrecked, and the country became a sort of no-man's-land without any proper government. It took one hundred and fifty years before Afghanistan even started to recover from these disasters. Some sort of administration was set up in Möngkä's reign (1251-59) when Afghanistan was divided, the western parts going to the Ilkhans of Persia and the eastern parts forming part of the Jaghatai Khanate. Afghanistan further suffered in the Mongol dynastic wars when the Ilkhans supported the Great Khan Kublai while the Jaghataids did not.

Karts

In 1245 one Shamsuddin Kart, related on his mother's side to Ghiyasuddin of Ghor, inherited the rulership of Ghor, which had suffered less from the Mongols than the rest of Afghanistan. In 1251 he was invested by Möngkä with the province of Herat under the suzerainty of the Ilkhan Hülägü. Shamsuddin laid such solid foundations during his reign of twenty-five years that, despite many difficulties, the Kart dynasty for one hundred and thirty years ruled from Herat over a territory that at its greatest extent comprised western Afghanistan and much of Khorassan.

Timurids

Eastern Afghanistan, as we have seen, formed part of the Ulus of the Mongol prince Jaghatai. When, at the beginning of the fourteenth century, the Jaghatai Khan, Kebek, discovered the delights of urban life in Transoxiana and his successor adopted Islam the Khanate was split in two: in the east Mogholistan, where the Mongols continued their nomadic traditions, and Transoxiana in the west, where the ancient Turkish nobility, notably the Amir Qazghan, held the real power. From this nobility there arose the Barlas Turk known as Tamerlane. By 1365 he had secured control of Transoxiana from the Jaghataids and by 1370 he controlled eastern Afghanistan. For ten years Tamerlane was preoccupied elsewhere but in 1381 he took Herat from the Karts and in the next three years he completed his control over Afghanistan including Seistan. Most of Tamerlane's astonishing career lies outside the scope of this note. He died in 1405 and by 1407 his fourth son Shah Rukh emerged victor from the struggle for succession and for forty years ruled from Herat over the bulk of the Timurid empire—west Persia had been lost to the Black Sheep Turcomans—either directly, or as suzerain over his nephews. Timurid decline began under Ulugh Beg, Shah Rukh's scholarly son, who was murdered by his son in 1449, when the Timurid territories were under serious threat from the Uzbegs. These were a predominantly Turkish horde under Mongol leadership who had started moving southwards in 1428. Within twenty years the Timurid empire had disintegrated under pressure from the Uzbegs in the north and the White Sheep Turcomans in the west. All that remained was Khorassan and parts of western Afghanistan ruled by Hussain Baiqara from Herat till his death in 1507. Hussain Baiqara's court was of great intellectual and artistic brilliance, but he was little of a statesman. His son, the last Afghan Timurid, was driven from Herat by the Uzbegs in 1507.

Safavids, Mughals, Uzbegs

For the next two hundred years the history of Afghanistan is the arid and confusing story of struggles of the Safavids with the Uzbegs for Khorassan and Herat and with the Mughals for Kandahar. The Safavids were a national dynasty that arose in Persia at the beginning of the sixteenth century. The Mughal empire was founded by that fascinating character Babur, Timurid prince of Ferghana who had been driven out of his patrimony by the Uzbegs. He was unable to persuade Hussain Baiqara to join him against the Uzbegs. But in 1502 he occupied Kabul (where he is buried), in 1522 he took Kandahar, and at the battle of Panipat in 1526 he laid the foundation of the Mughal empire.

MODERN HISTORY

Between 1708 and 1730 occurred the first, though brief, emergence of the Pashtuns as a political power when the Ghilzai Mir Wais revolted from the declining Safavids and for a short time he and his successors ruled Persia itself.

Nadir Shah of Persia

The Safavids were helped against the Ghilzais by Nadir Kuli Khan, a bandit chief, who proclaimed himself ruler of Persia in 1736 Within two years he had extended his rule over southern Afghanistan.

In 1739 he carried out his great raid into India and sacked Delhi. And in 1740 he took northern Afghanistan from the Uzbeg ruler of Bokhara. He was assassinated in 1747.

Durranis

Sadozais. Unlike the Safavids, Nadir Shah encouraged Afghans in his service. In the confusion following his assassination an Afghan of the Sadozai clan (the Khan Khel, or Royal Clan) of the important Abdal tribe rallied his countrymen and led them back to Kandahar. Here the chiefs elected him King with the style of Dur-i-Duran (Pearl of the Age), from which the Abdals are now known as Durranis. This Ahmed Shah was a very capable man and created the Afghanistan we now know. His dominions included Afghanistan, Kashmir and north-west India, and Khorassan, Sind and Baluchistan became tributary to him. He undertook regular winter campaigns into India but, though he smashed the Marathas at Panipat in 1761, they brought him little permanent extension of territory, and he met with increasing trouble from the Sikhs. On Ahmed Shah's death he was succeeded by his son Timur who during a reign of twenty years was able to hold the territories he had inherited and who moved the capital from Kandahar to Kabul. But he left more than twenty sons, whose unedifying struggle for the throne brought about the dissolution of the Sadozai kingdom. Zaman, Mahmud, Shuja-Ul-Mulk, and again Mahmud occupied the throne in succession. The Uzbeg north and much other territory fell away from the Sadozais. Mahmud acquired the throne a second time with the help of Fatteh Khan, leader of another important clan, the Barakzais (or Mohammedzais). When Mahmud and his son Zaman barbarously murdered Fatteh Khan his brothers united and drove the Sadozais to Herat, where Sadozai rule came to an end with the death of Kamran in 1842.

Barakzais (Mohammedzais). When the Sadozais were driven west in 1818 Dost Mohammed, youngest of the twenty-one Barakzai brothers, was allotted Ghazni, to which he soon added Kabul. His position was difficult. His brothers were not readily submissive. The Sikhs took Peshawar in 1823. And the British, who had become the leading power in a still nominally Mughal India were inevitably interested in Afghanistan, the key to India. This interest led to the First Afghan War (1838–42) when the British thought they could best secure their northwestern approaches against the Russian threat by replacing Dost Mohammed by the Sadozai, Shuja-ul-Mulk, on the throne of Kabul. The project was ill-conceived, ended in a major disaster, and left an understandable legacy of bitterness. When the British evacuated Afghanistan in 1842 they released the Dost, who returned to Kabul and set about extending his control over the whole country. He died at Herat in 1863 soon after completing his task by taking the town. The Dost appealed particularly to the Afghans, who call him Amir-i-Kabir (The Great Amir). For the last eighteen years of his reign he maintained friendship with the Government of India. He nominated his third son, Shere Ali, to succeed him. The two older brothers, and Abdurrahman, son of the eldest brother, did not accept this and it was not till 1868 that Shere Ali was secure.

At first he continued his father's old policy of friendship with Britain, but as time went on a coolness developed and in 1878 the Second Afghan War started. The underlying cause was again British fear of Russian intentions. The actual crisis came when the Afghans refused to accept a British mission but publicly accepted a Russian one. Shere Ali fled before the invaders and died in Mazar in February 1879. His younger son, Abdullah Jan, who had been named to succeed him, had died in 1878, and it was the elder son, Yakub, who was out of favour with the people, who took over the vacant seat of power. In May 1879 Yakub signed the Treaty of Gandamak, which gave the British most of what they wanted. But when the envoy whom Yakub had agreed to accept was massacred together with his escort, the British had to return. When they occupied Kabul in November Yakub gave himself up. Though British arms were generally successful, despite the Maiwand disaster (July 27th, 1880), the political situation was unsatisfactory, particularly after a change of ministry in London led to the abandonment of the Forward Policy. So when Shere Ali's nephew, Abdurrahman, returned from exile early in 1880 the British took a gamble (which succeeded) and recognized him as Amir of Kabul.

The British evacuated Kabul early in 1881. They, wisely, no longer insisted on a resident envoy in Afghanistan; but they gained some territory (including the Khyber Pass) and agreed to help the Amir against unprovoked foreign aggression provided he followed their advice on foreign policy. After the British left Abdurrahman spent ten years imposing a despotic centralized government on Afghanistan. In 1895 he occupied, and forcibly converted, Nuristan. Abdurrahman thought Afghanistan's interests were best served by loyal friendship with Britain even though this led to certain difficulties with Russia. Accordingly, he consented to sign the Durand treaty, which attempted, albeit incompletely, to demarcate the boundaries between Afghan and British territories. When he died in 1901 his son, Habibullah, succeeded without any civil war. During his reign Anglo-Russian tension over Afghanistan was lessened as part of a wider diplomatic settlement. But he had to face the complications caused by the First World War. Habibullah was assassinated in 1919, being succeeded after a brief struggle, by his third son Amanullah, one of whose first acts was to raid India. The attack failed militarily but was a success inasmuch as, for other reasons, the British offered favourable peace terms. By the treaty of August 1919 freedom of action in foreign affairs was restored to Afghanistan, which entered into diplomatic relations with several countries, including the U.S.S.R. and Britain in 1921. Amanullah was an erratic character and his precipitate zeal for reform alienated powerful tribes and religious leaders. In May 1929 he fled the country. Kabul was briefly held by Tadzhik a bandit leader known as Bachha-i-Saqao.

Mohammedzai (Yahya Khel). In October, 1929, Nadir Khan, a cousin of Amanullah and a former Minister of War, returned from exile and with the help of his equally able brothers Hashim Khan, Shah Wali Khan and Mahmud Khan *(the Musahiban Brothers)* defeated the Bachha and occupied Kabul. He was soon elected as King Nadir Shah. He was making good progress towards restoring conditions in Afghanistan when he was assassinated in 1933 and was succeeded by his son, Mohammed Zahir Shah.

In the period up to the end of the Second World War King Zahir Shah had the benefit of a wise and experienced Prime Minister in his uncle, Sardar Hashim Khan. The next Prime Minister, Sardar Shah Mahmud, for all his ability and integrity, was not at home in the changed situation after the war, marked by the British abdication in India and the emergence of the two super-powers, the U.S.S.R., which has a long common frontier with Afghanistan, and the U.S.A., half the world away. At this time the royal family was still effectively the ruling authority in Afghanistan, and the democratic institutions laid down in Nadir Shah's constitution were chiefly consultative. The younger members of the royal family thought that Shah Mahmud was not dealing with Afghanistan's two major problems forcibly enough.

These men were part of the first generation of Afghans to have received some of their education in the west. By the autumn of 1953 they had generated sufficient support within the family to secure the resignation of Shah Mahmud and his replacement by his nephew, Sardar Daud. Internally Daud's administration was less liberal than its predecessor. It kept a firm grip on the country and had little trouble except for some tribal disturbances in the Khost area and a nasty, but short-lived riot in Kandahar. The important problem of modernization was attacked with energy and success. A Ministry of Planning was set up, with Daud holding the portfolio, and a series of Five-Year Plans was initiated. Much of the finance for the Plans came from abroad. In 1955 the U.S.S.R. began loans and the U.S.A. and other powers were not long in following this example. Under the Plans due attention was paid to social services, including education. And in 1959 Daud was successful in abolishing the compulsory veiling of women in public. In foreign affairs Daud had his younger brother Sardar Naim as Foreign Minister, who pursued an active and generally successful policy. Diplomatic relations were entered into with many countries and full use was made of the facilities of the United Nations. Politically Afghanistan has usually voted with the non-aligned countries. A UN Technical Assistance Mission was also accepted. In another sphere considerable importance was attached to the question of the Pashtun tribes living in Pakistan. These had been separated from Afghanistan in the nineteenth century, first by Sikh and then by British action, but had remained of interest to the predominantly Pashtun Government of Afghanistan. Indeed a right to such interest had been implied in the treaty signed with the British in 1921. In 1947, when the sub-continent was being partitioned, it had been hoped that something might be done about these tribes. However, they were given the sole choice of acceding to either India or Pakistan, a circumstance which caused resentment in Afghanistan. The Daud administration campaigned, therefore, for the creation of a quasi-independent area of "Pashtunistan" within Pakistan. Friction between the two governments came to a head in 1955 when, after the embassies and consulates of both countries had been the scenes of disorderly demonstrations, Pakistan briefly cut off Afghanistan's transit facilities. Relations returned to normal but the Pashtunistan issue was not forgotten and continuing coolness in Afghanistan's relations with Pakistan extended to its relations with the West generally. Consequently, from 1955 onwards, Soviet aid to Afghanistan increased, especially in military fields. In 1959 the Pashtunistan campaign was stepped up again and diplomatic relations between Afghanistan and Pakistan were broken off in 1961. Transport facilities through Pakistan were once again denied to Afghanistan, this time for a longer period and with more serious economic results. Meanwhile, pressure for political reform had been growing within Afghanistan. The Daud administration made attempts to put through constitutional reforms but considered that, while the dispute with Pakistan remained unsettled, it was not able to take political initiatives on the scale required. Accordingly, the administration resigned in March 1963.

The man now invited to be the Prime Minister, Dr. Yusuf, was not only not a member of the royal family, he was not even a Pashtun. His first administration was generally well-received. Its chief achievement was the promulgation of a new, and moderately liberal, constitution on October 1st, 1964. It also made possible a resumption of relations with Pakistan. Dr. Yusuf's second administration, elected under the new constitution, was not so successful. There were troubles, including student riots in Kabul, which led to his resignation. He was replaced by Mr. Maiwandwal, in 1965. In 1967 Mr. Maiwandwal resigned on grounds of ill-health and was succeeded by Mr. Nur Ahmed Etemadi. There has been considerable progress in modernization. In this Afghanistan has been helped by substantial aid from both Communist countries and the West.

Political development has inevitably been slower. For democratic rights granted from above are never so easy to work as those won from below, particularly in a country where scarcely half the population has any tradition of the public discussion of public affairs. The Pashtuns have their *Jirgas* where such discussions take place; the other peoples are accustomed to live under authority. The result of this was that the three Prime Ministers who succeeded Sardar Daud were all administrators rather than politicians, while the elected legislators have tended to be critical rather than constructive. And so far no political parties have

been formed, as permitted by the 1964 Constitution, though Mr. Maiwandwal was on the way to creating a "tail", rather than a political party as we understand it, when he retired. Ever since the fall of Dr. Yusuf's administration students have been very conscious of their political power: this led to the University and colleges being closed for a while during 1969. One important step forward has been made. The Supreme Court, envisaged in the 1964 Constitution and intended primarily to administer secular law rather than the muslim *shariat* has now been set up. Elections were held in October 1969 which resulted in the re-appointment of Nur Ahmed Etemadi as Prime Minister.

Parliamentary crises and severe drought led to political instability between 1969 and 1972, causing the resignations both of Etemadi in May 1971 and of his successor, Dr. Abdul Zahir, in December 1972. A turn towards economic and political stability in Afghanistan began under the administration of Mr. Musa Shafiq, a former Foreign Minister who had been a leading figure in the formation of the new constitution of 1964. Mr. Shafiq's principal achievements were in the field of foreign policy, where he ended an age-old dispute with Iran over the waters of the Helmand river by signing a mutually beneficial treaty, and also enhanced Afghan-Indian relations, culminating in the visit to Kabul of the Indian Vice-President, Gopal Pathak, in June 1973. The treaty with Iran was not, however, ratified, as a result of the subsequent developments in Afghanistan.

On July 17th, 1973, came a totally unexpected, although successful, *coup d'état*, led by Lt.-Gen. Mohammad Daud, the King's brother-in-law and former Prime Minister, with the support of the young army officers. With the abdication of King Zahir Shah in August 1973, the monarchy and most of the 1964 constitution were abolished, and Afghanistan declared a Republic. Both houses of the Shura were suspended and Daud retained for himself the positions of President, Prime Minister, Foreign Minister and Defence Minister. Following an abortive counter-revolution in October 1973 President Daud has been concerned to free himself from dependence on the young army officers who initiated the July *coup* and establish a personal basis of power. The régime has been preoccupied with security and efforts to instil confidence in the Republic. Proposed social and economic reforms have therefore been delayed although some progress has been made in the fields of taxation, land reform and education. The promised constitution has still to emerge.

Support for the Pashtuns and Baluchis of Pashtunistan has been restored to a central place in Afghanistan's foreign policy and relations with Pakistan have rapidly deteriorated. Closer ties have been established with Iran and India and relations with the Soviet Union were strengthened by President Daud's visit to Moscow in June 1974 and by the conclusion of several economic agreements.

ECONOMIC SURVEY

Arthur Paul

(Extensively revised by G. F. ACHIKZAD, 1975)

About 18 million people live in the Republic of Afghanistan. A full census of the population has yet to be completed, but the round figure cited is one that is based on official estimates. These indicate that from 1963 to 1973 the population increased from 14.5 to 18.3 million. The calculations used for these estimates assume an annual rate of increase of 2.3 per cent.

Of the total population, 85 per cent live in rural areas. Rural migration is augmenting the natural increase in population in urban areas so that this percentage may soon change. Nearly 70 per cent of the people live in villages scattered throughout the mountain or desert countryside. They are too remote from the urban centres to take much part in the market economy. This 70 per cent includes about 2,800,000 kuchies, many of whom are nomads.

Kabul, the capital city, with a rapidly increasing population that has reached over 500,000, is the dominant financial and commercial centre of the country. Other large cities are Herat, a trading centre near the Iranian border, with a population of 106,000 people and Kandahar, in the wool and fruit producing area of the south-west, with 136,000 inhabitants. The smaller provincial centres include Mazar-i-Sharif, in the northern karakul country where natural gas has recently been found, Kunduz and Pul-i-Kumri in the cotton country, and Jalalabad in the east. Only in recent years have these and other urban centres been linked to each other and with the capital city by adequate transportation and communication systems. A more unified national economy is now emerging from what had been a group of relatively isolated trading centres located in provincial areas largely devoted to agriculture carried on at close to a sub-sistence level. These areas were, nevertheless, nearly self-sufficient.

Afghanistan's economy has in the past been based almost entirely on agricultural production. Probably two-thirds of the agricultural production still does not enter the market economy. Of the other third, roughly half is sold for urban consumption and the other half for export. The mainstays of the economy and the chief earners of foreign exchange are wool, karakul skins (obtained from a unique breed of sheep that graze in the northern provinces) and cotton. Natural gas, fresh and dried fruit and hand-woven carpets, are also important factors in the Afghan economy.

Industrial production in the modern sense started in Afghanistan with the establishment of a cotton textile plant in 1934. This industry expanded rapidly and is today the largest in the country. It was followed by the building of wool factories, sugar refineries, cement plants, and other processing industries. Engineering industries are small and relatively new. Excluding handicrafts and utilities, industrial produc-tion accounts for only about 5–8 per cent of the total production of the country.

Although the existence of large mineral resources has been known for many years, it is only recently that economic exploitation of some of these resources has become possible. This is due to the discovery of natural gas in the northern part of Afghanistan and to the building of facilities for making use of the large reserves of this new source of energy. The export of natural gas started in 1967 and shipments through a pipeline to the U.S.S.R. accounted for 11.2 per cent of the country's total export earnings in 1972–73.

Sufficient statistical data are not available to make more than rough estimates of the gross domestic pro-duct (G.D.P.) of Afghanistan. Two separate studies for the year 1959 produced estimates varying from Afs. 28,000 million to 39,000 million. The most recent comparable information furnished by Afghan authori-ties is that the G.N.P. (gross national product) for the year 1971–72 was the equivalent of U.S. $2,000 million at the official exchange rate of Afs. 45 to U.S. $1. The rate of growth in real G.N.P. is estimated to have amounted to some 7–8 per cent in 1972–73. On the basis of the above information, the *per capita* income in 1972–73 would amount to U.S. $120.

AGRICULTURE

In past years Afghanistan produced enough food to fill the needs of its own people and to supply substan-tial amounts, particularly of fresh and dried fruits, to the Indian sub-continent. But in recent years, the population has grown at a more rapid rate than food production, so that it became necessary to import large quantities of wheat, sugar and vegetable oils. Some shifting in the use of land from wheat to cotton has contributed to this change in the pattern of agricultural production.

Of the total land area, which is 64.7 million hectares, only 22 per cent, or 14 million hectares, is suitable for cultivation. Of this, 7.8 million hectares are today considered crop land, 6.0 million hectares are irrigable, but only 60 per cent of this irrigable land is actually cropped because of lack of water. Some of the non-irrigable crop land is dry farmed, but not all of it.

Grain Crops

Grains are the most important crops. Estimates of production (in metric tons) for 1973–74 were: wheat, 2,750,000 tons; maize, 760,000 tons; barley, 360,000 tons; and rice, 450,000 tons. The wheat crop has varied by large amounts from year to year. This is partly due to periodic recurrences of rust damage and to the shifting of land to cotton. The low yields of wheat obtained in Afghanistan are attributable to a steady reduction in soil fertility and to the primitive methods of cultivation that have been used throughout the country. In recent years, the introduction of improved seeds and the use of chemical fertilizers have increased the yields of wheat and other crops in some areas. 1971–72 was a year of drought so that it was necessary to import 226,000 tons of wheat, but in 1972–73 domestic production of wheat exceeded consumption.

Cotton

Cotton is a major crop in the northern provinces, but in recent years its cultivation has commenced in the Helmand Valley and near Herat. A well planned and intensive effort to encourage cotton cultivation was very effective during the period of 1962-1965. This resulted in a doubling of the production of raw cotton in a remarkably short time. It rose from 52,000 tons in 1961 to 110,000 tons in 1963. But ginning capacity became a bottleneck; furthermore, diseases and seed degeneracy were encountered. Together with the shift in land use, the combination of these factors caused a falling off in the production of cotton, which dropped back to 55,000 tons by 1967. However, in 1973–74 cotton production reached a record level of 105,000 tons.

More than half of Afghanistan's ginned cotton is exported, with the largest shipments going, under barter contracts, to the U.S.S.R.

Other Crops

The estimated production of other important crops in 1973–74 was: sugar beet, 63,600 tons; sugar cane, 22,000 tons; and vegetable oil seeds (excluding cotton seeds) 42,500 tons. None of these crops are sufficient to meet the needs of the country, so that substantial amounts of sugar and vegetable oils are being imported.

The climate of Afghanistan is very favourable for the production of a wide variety of fruits. Grapes are the most important of the fruits and account for more than half of the estimated total of 840,000 tons of fruits produced in 1973–74. Afghan fruits are exported in both the fresh and dried states. Traditionally India and Pakistan were the markets for these goods, but shipments now go to the U.S.S.R. and China, and more recently to Germany, Iran, Iraq, Kuwait and other Gulf countries. The installation of modern facilities for cleaning and packing raisins has made it possible for Afghanistan's dried fruits to enter the European market.

Vegetable production has been neglected in the past, but the use of new seeds and better methods of cultivation are increasing the level of production, which was estimated at 680,000 tons in 1973–74. With the installation of new facilities for handling vegetables, including canning and cold storage plants, vegetable crops will be more important in the future and may even enter the European market.

Afghan melons are famous for their flavour, but the ratio of weight to value and the hazards of spoilage in transit make it impossible to export them except to nearby Pakistan. Pomegranates are also an important crop and have been exported to Pakistan and Iran. The use of concentrated pomegranate juice as a blend in soft drinks is an interesting new export possibility. Pistachios and almonds grow in widely scattered areas and substantial quantities are exported.

Livestock

Two of Afghanistan's leading exports, karakul skins and wool, depend on the raising of sheep. The sale of karakul skins to European and American buyers alone accounts for a large part of the convertible foreign exchange earnings of the country. Karakul, which is more popularly known as Persian lamb, is widely used in the manufacture of fur coats and other garments. Afghan skins generally command a higher price than competing products, which come from Namibia and the U.S.S.R. The number of karakul sheep is estimated to be 6.8 million, all located in the northern provinces. In recent years the foreign exchange obtained from the export of karakul skins has ranged from U.S. $10 million to U.S. $21 million annually. This industry is very important to the Afghan economy but it is not expanding; in fact, considerable efforts are needed to maintain the present volume. In 1972–73 export sales amounted to U.S. $16.8 million.

The number of sheep in Afghanistan, excluding the karakul flock, was estimated in 1973 to be roughly 15 million. Sheep are the main source of meat for the country, and they produce enough wool to export from 5,000 to 6,000 tons annually, most of which is sent to the U.S.S.R. under barter agreements.

To help make up a deficiency of protein in the Afghan diet, there are important projects for increasing poultry production which is today quite small. A fisheries programme has also been started. In addition, great efforts are being made to improve the local breeds of cattle in order to increase the very low output of dairy products. A livestock project aiming to promote exports of mutton in Herat has recently been started with a credit from the International Development Association.

A basic problem of the livestock industries of Afghanistan is the limited amount of pasture land and the difficulties which over-grazing causes. The demand for meat and dairy products is expanding much more rapidly than the supply of these products.

MINERAL RESOURCES

Exploratory drilling carried on with Soviet assistance has located supplies of petroleum in the northern provinces, but the commercial production of oil is not yet possible. This exploration work is continuing, and the search for oil has been extended to the southern part of the country as well.

The situation in regard to natural gas is very different. There are proven reserves of more than 60,000 million cubic metres in a large field near Mazar-i-Sharif. The estimate of the total of all reserves is 300,000 million cubic metres.

The availability of natural gas in Afghanistan will have far-reaching effects on the economy of the country. The construction of a pipeline to carry natural gas to the U.S.S.R. made it possible to start exporting this commodity in 1967. Contracts with the U.S.S.R. called for delivery of 1,700 million cu. metres in 1968–69, but actual exports were only about half of that amount. By 1972–73 total exports had risen to 2,750 million cu. metres and the income from this resource amounted to U.S. $18 million. Relatively small amounts of natural gas have as yet been allocated for domestic uses, which could include the supply of energy for thermal electric plants and for the manufacture of chemical fertilizer.

Iron Ore: unexploited deposits

The discovery of natural gas in Afghanistan raises important questions regarding its uses, one of which could be as a source of energy for the reduction of iron ore and its conversion to steel. The major iron ore deposits are in the Hajigak area, 125 km. west of Kabul and directly south of the natural gas field. The ore is too distant from the sea to be sold competitively on the international market, but efficient, low-cost reduction or conversion to steel prior to shipment would change the economic factors that determine its marketability.

The estimates of the extent of the iron ore deposits are that the proven reserves amount to 10 million tons. In addition, there are 314 million tons of partially drilled reserves, and the general geological prognosis is that the total deposits exceed 2,000 million tons. Analysis of the ore indicates that it is high grade and of a type suitable for reduction by natural gas.

Other mineral resources that have been located, but which are not yet exploited, include deposits of copper, lead, zinc, beryl, gold, barytes and sulphur.

Coal, Salt, Lapis Lazuli

Commercial mining operations have so far been confined to the production of coal, salt and lapis lazuli.

Coal mining was started in 1939 and is entirely a governmental activity. The production of the Karkar and the Ishpushta coal mines, both near enough to Kabul to supply most of the needs of the capital city and its industrial environs, reached 149,000 tons in 1972–73. But the reserves of these mines are relatively small, 13 million tons in the case of Karkar, and 2 million tons for Ishpushta. The largest deposits of coal are in the north at the Darrah-i-Soof mines, which have proven reserves of 75 million tons and where the actual reserves may be several hundred million tons. Another coal deposit is at the Sabzak mines near Herat, where the known reserves are 3 million tons. These mines are being prepared for active production and are expected in the near future to add 30,000 tons each to the country's annual production of coal. Because of the size of its reserves, the Darrah-i-Soof mine will play a large role in the future.

Afghanistan produces much of the salt that it consumes, but the methods used for this production are still primitive. New mines equipped for modern methods will soon be in operation and may eliminate any need for importing salt. In 1972–73 salt production reached a level of 42,000 tons.

Afghanistan's lapis lazuli is famous throughout the world. The mining of these gem stones has been carried on for thousands of years. The chief deposits are in the province of Badakhshan. About 3,000 kilograms of lapis lazuli were produced in 1971–72.

ENERGY

At the present time the consumption of energy in Afghanistan is, by Western standards, very low. A calculation based on 1970 estimates shows that the *per capita* use of energy in the United Kingdom was 200 times that of Afghanistan. Nearly two-thirds of the total energy available is supplied by imported petroleum products. These provide the fuel for transportation, and small quantities of oil are also used in diesel plants producing electricity. In 1964, the imports of petroleum products, most of which came from the U.S.S.R., exceeded 150,000 tons and the amounts purchased are increasing yearly.

Hydroelectric Power

Hydroelectricity is next in importance as a source of energy. Total electric power production in 1972–73 reached 525.4 million kWh. Several new hydroelectric projects are now nearing completion so that the country's energy capacity will further increase.

Other Sources

Coal and wood are the other sources of energy used in the country. In 1964 about 100,000 tons of each were consumed for fuel. There are extensive plans for increasing coal production. The target set for the early 1970s is 350,000 tons. However, the supply of wood, which is still extensively used for cooking and heating, is steadily decreasing because of the destructive lumbering practices employed in the few remaining forests.

INDUSTRY

Afghanistan's first modern industrial venture, a cotton textile plant started at Jebel-i-Seraj in 1934, has grown into a large and important enterprise. This business, which is partly owned and managed by the Banke Millie, a private commercial bank, now operates two large-scale spinning and weaving plants, one at Pul-i-kumri and the other, a quite modern plant, at Gulbahar, where it has also installed finishing equipment for dyeing and printing cloth. The basic equipment for textile production now installed in these plants is 77,000 spindles and 2,100 power looms, more than half of which are automatic. Another large cotton textile plant has recently been built with the help of the Chinese Government in Bagrami, near Kabul. In 1972–73, the production of cloth (cotton and rayon) was 76.6 million metres, which is still below the needs of the people. Imports in excess of 35 million metres yearly have added to the supply, but the demand for cloth is not fully satisfied. Consequently the production of the Gulbahar plant has been expanded, and plans have been made to build new textile plants which will be located in different provinces throughout the country.

Woollen textiles have been produced in small quantities for many years, but this industry has not yet become important. Annual production was 133,400 metres in 1972–73.

Processing Industries

Cement production, which was started on a small scale by the Afghan Cement Company at Jebel-i-Seraj in 1958, has been expanded by the building of a large government-owned plant near Pul-i-kumri. In 1972–73 the combined production of the two plants was 135,000 tons. Plans have been made to construct a third plant, for which Herat will be the site.

There are a number of newly established industrial plants for processing agricultural products. Many raisin cleaning plants are now in full operation. The Spinzar Company operates a large cotton ginning plant at Kunduz with branches throughout the cotton producing provinces. It produces vegetable oil as a by-product, and a new oil extraction plant has been constructed in the Helmand Valley, at Bost. In Kandahar there is a plant for handling and preserving fresh fruits. Other processing or handling industries include leather tanning, the preparation of casings for export, and cold storage and refrigeration facilities for vegetables, fruits and meat.

Sugar refining was started many years ago. The present annual production of beet sugar is only 8,000 tons, but total output of refined sugar is planned to reach more than 20,000 tons.

Other Industries

Among the smaller industries are some plants producing consumer goods such as wine, soft drinks, soap and detergents, pharmaceuticals, pottery, glassware, plastics, shoes and knitted goods, but the production of these articles is small.

The most important handicraft industry is the weaving of carpets and rugs. Handwoven Afghan carpets are well known in western and other markets and command high prices because of their quality and distinctive designs. Federal Germany and the United Kingdom 'are the largest customers. This trade earns about U.S. $14 million of foreign exchange annually and is therefore important to the economy of the country. To improve the quality of Afghan carpets, a plant for washing carpets locally, before export, has been built.

The engineering industries of Afghanistan have confined their operations to the repair of automotive equipment and some assembly work on trucks and motors. Plans for the development of metallurgical industries await the completion of studies of the feasibility of building an iron smelter.

Stimulation of Industrial Expansion

In 1967, a new Foreign and Domestic Private Investment law was passed. This has stimulated interest in industrial enterprises. By 1971, out of 188 investment applications submitted under the law, 153 had been approved and 61 new industrial concerns were already in operation. An Industrial Development Bank was established in 1972. It is expected that the operations of this institution will hasten the expansion of many industries in Afghanistan.

TRANSPORT AND COMMUNICATIONS

By using a substantial portion of the foreign aid received in recent years on the building of roads and airports, Afghanistan has greatly expanded and vastly improved its transportation system. Nearly 2,000 km. of asphalt and concrete roads were completed between the years 1957 and 1967. Good roads now connect all of the main cities of the country with Kabul and with each other. The most dramatic achievement of the programme was the reduction of time needed to travel by automobile and for truck services between Kabul and the northern provinces. This has been accomplished by building a high altitude tunnel near the Salang Pass of the Hindu Kush mountain range. A journey from Kabul to Kunduz that formerly required several days of rough driving now takes six or seven hours on a fine road. To complete this project was a spectacular feat of engineering, carried out with Soviet aid and Soviet technical assistance.

Important extensions and spurs for the roads constructed recently are open for transport. These include the Herat to Islam Qala road which joins Afghanistan's highway system with Iran's. Another important project is the building of a direct road from Herat to Kabul through the central provinces; this will eventually be part of the Asian Highway sponsored by the United Nations.

There are large modern airports at Kabul and Kandahar which can accommodate jet traffic. Local airports are now in use in Faizabad, Mazar-i-Sharif, Maimana and 33 other cities in the country.

Ariana Airlines, the Afghan national line, in which Pan American Airways has a minority interest and a management contract, provides passenger and cargo services to Iran, Beirut, New Delhi, Moscow, Istanbul, Paris, Rome, Frankfurt and London. Bakhtar Airlines has weekly services to various cities of Afghanistan.

There are no railroads in Afghanistan. However, plans are under way to build a railroad connecting Mashad (Iran) and Kabul.

Telephone Communications

Automatic telephones were installed in Kabul in 1950. The initial 5,000 line exchange has been replaced by one with 13,000 lines. Other automatic exchanges taking 7,000 lines have recently been put in operation in various provinces and installations will be considerably expanded in the near future. Most of the telephone equipment is of German origin, the Afghan Government's communications programme having been assisted by the Federal Republic of Germany.

Access to the Sea

Afghanistan is a land-locked country. The shortest land routes to the sea are through Pakistan to the port of Karachi. There is a rail line from Chaman which runs across western Pakistan to Karachi, a distance of 950 km. A spur of 8 km. from Chaman to the new rail head at Spin Baldack inside the Afghan border near Kandahar will connect this line with the present Afghan highway system. Goods shipped from Kabul usually go by truck to Peshawar and thence by rail to Karachi.

Afghanistan's foreign trade is dependent on transit rights through neighbouring countries. When political difficulties caused the closing of the border between Afghanistan and Pakistan in the early 1960s, it became necessary to use different routes to the sea. One of these was through Iran to the port of Khorramshahr on the Persian Gulf; the other was across Russia to the Baltic sea. Since the reopening of the border, the shorter and less costly routes through Pakistan are again in use.

New transit agreements recently concluded with Turkey and with Iran have already made through transportation by truck possible from Western Europe to Afghanistan.

FOREIGN TRADE AND BALANCE OF PAYMENTS

The cost of the imported goods and services which Afghanistan requires in order to sustain an economic development programme that will create a modestly rising standard of living exceeds the current value of exports by substantial amounts. In 1962–63 imports cost U.S. $115.9 million, whereas the proceeds from the sale of exports were only $58.9 million. By 1973–74 imports had risen to $193 million and exports to $159 million. The export-import gap, which had widened to nearly $72 million in 1967–68, amounted to $34 million in 1973–74.

The balance of payments problems created by this gap have been met by Afghanistan's reserves and by commodity loans and grants from aid-giving countries, chiefly the United States and the U.S.S.R. Short-term credits obtained from the International Monetary Fund have also helped to ease the financial difficulties caused by an unfavourable balance of payments situation. But the present indications are that the trade gap will shrink for 1975.

Afghanistan's pattern of export trade has shown only minor variations in recent years. More than one-third of the exports were delivered under barter contracts (mainly to the U.S.S.R.) which provide for payments by credits usable only in the country to which the goods were shipped. Exports to India and Pakistan accounted for 30 per cent of the total. Payments for these shipments were made in rupees the use of which was restricted under bilateral agreements. The remaining exports were sold in western markets for convertible currencies. The chief purchasers were the United Kingdom, Federal Germany and Switzerland.

MONEY AND BANKING

Due to a succession of fiscal deficits, the supply of money (bank notes and demand deposits) in Afghanistan increased from a total of Afs. 3,205 million in March 1962 to Afs. 10,160 million in 1972–73. The growth rate of the monetized sector of the economy has in recent years exceeded the rate of increase in money supply. The volume of credit extended to both the public and private sectors of the economy also increased substantially. In the past, the growth rates for both monetary supply and credit have not been excessive, and, in general, the fiscal and monetary policies of the country have been conservative. The most recent figures, however, show evidence of inflationary pressures within the economy.

The chief banking institution in Afghanistan is Da Afghanistan Bank, a government-owned central bank, which also engages in commercial operations. As of March 1973, its international reserves amounted to U.S. $58.8 million. In addition to its main offices in Kabul, it has 57 provincial branches as well as offices in London and New York.

There are two other commercial banks in Afghanistan, the older of which is the Banke Millie (Afghan National Bank), founded in 1932. It conducts a commercial banking business and acts as a holding company with controlling interests in some of the leading industries, including the Textile Company. The other commercial bank, the Pashtany Tejaraty Bank, is affiliated to the Da Afghanistan Bank. It started its commercial operations in 1954, and as of March 1971 had total resources of Afs. 2,249 million and capital and reserves of Afs. 356 million. No foreign banks have been permitted to open branches in Afghanistan.

PUBLIC FINANCE

Government revenues have risen from Afs. 2,120 million in the fiscal year 1962–63 to Afs. 7,892 million in 1972–73 (not including loans from the Central Bank and grants from foreign countries). More than half of the revenues are raised by taxes on business transactions, customs duties on imports being by far the largest source. Income taxes on individuals and corporations account for less than 10 per cent of the total revenue. Direct taxes on land are nominal.

The ordinary expenses of government plus the developmental expenditures incurred by the Government of Afghanistan was about Afs. 3,000 million in 1962–63. By 1972–73 the figure had risen to around Afs. 9,000 million, which included about Afs. 1,500 million for national defence. Deficits have been financed by credits from the Central Bank, by expansion in the supply of money, and by the sale of commodities supplied under foreign aid grants and loans.

For many years the funds for developmental projects have far exceeded the amounts charged as expenditures in Afghanistan's fiscal accounts. The additional costs were covered by funds received from foreign countries in the form of loans and grants.

FOREIGN AID

Foreign aid to Afghanistan started in 1950 when the Export-Import Bank of the U.S. granted a loan for the development of the Helmand Valley. The U.S. has continued to support this land development programme which has included extensive irrigation and hydroelectric projects.

Up to June 30th, 1968, the total aid furnished by the U.S. to Afghanistan amounted to nearly U.S. $400 million. Forty-five per cent of the American aid was used to improve transportation, mainly road building; 25 per cent was spent in the Helmand Valley, and 12 per cent on education. Smaller amounts were used for technical assistance in agriculture, government management and planning.

Soviet aid has exceeded the amounts furnished by the U.S. Details of its use are not available, especially those in respect of military assistance, which has been substantial. The most spectacular Soviet projects are the building of the tunnel through the Hindu Kush mountain range at the Salang Pass, the erection of giant-sized silos in Kabul for the storage of wheat and the Nangahar hydroelectric and rural development projects.

During the period covered by the Second Five-Year Plan (1962 to 1966–67), Afghanistan received a total of U.S. $362 million in the form of project loans and grants from foreign countries. Of this amount, 65 per cent came from the U.S.S.R., 23 per cent from the U.S.A. and 9 per cent from the Federal Republic of Germany.

In addition to these project loans and grants, the Government of Afghanistan realized U.S. $71.1 million from the sale of commodities furnished under grants and loans. Of the total, 47 per cent (almost entirely in the form of grants) came from the U.S., 37 per cent (all under loan agreements) came from the U.S.S.R. and 13 per cent (grants) from Germany. Technical assistance furnished during this period in the amount of U.S. $50 million brings the total aid received by Afghanistan for its Second Five Year Plan to U.S. $483 million. Debt service paid to donor countries during the period amounted to $28.1 million. Annual debt service now amounts to around $32 million.

Starting in 1969 the World Bank has extended a series of credits to Afghanistan which totalled U.S. $40.8 million on December 31st, 1974.

By the end of the Third Five-Year Plan in 1972, the total foreign aid received by Afghanistan since 1950 was estimated at over U.S. $1,600 million of which about $1,000 million came from the U.S.S.R.

The United Nations has maintained a large staff in Afghanistan which has furnished a wide variety of technical assistance, which has been especially effective in the field of public health.

Afghanistan is counting heavily on the continuance of foreign aid in order to achieve its developmental objectives. A serious problem for the future is the steadily increasing size of the requirements for debt service payments.

STATISTICAL SURVEY

AREA AND POPULATION

TOTAL AREA	ESTIMATED MID-YEAR POPULATION				DENSITY (per sq. km.) 1973
	1970	1971	1972	1973	
250,000 sq. miles (647,497 sq. km.)	17,087,278	17,480,280	17,882,326	18,293,841	28.2

Note: Population estimates are derived by assuming a steady rate of growth from 1965, when the country's population was conjectured. Some authorities believe that the official estimates overstate the size of the population.

ETHNIC GROUPS (1963)

Pashtuns or Pathans	Tadzhiks	Uzbeks	Hazarahs	Nomads
8,800,000	4,300,000	800,000	444,000	650,000

PROVINCES*
(1970)

	AREA (sq. km.)	POPULATION	DENSITY (per sq. km.)	CAPITAL (with population)
Uruzgan . . .	34,000	513,100	15.1	Tareenkoot (48,200)
Badghis . . .	24,700	329,500	13.3	Qala-i-nau (78,400)
Bamian . . .	19,200	356,200	18.5	Bamian (46,200)
Badakhshan . . .	42,600	354,600	8.3	Faizabad (64,700)
Baghlan . . .	18,600	641,800	34.5	Baghlan (103,600)
Balkh . . .	15,100	364,100	24.1	Mazar-i-Sharif (44,500)
Parwan . . .	5,600	913,300	163.0	Charikar (93,800)
Paktia . . .	17,600	859,100	48.8	Gardiz (40,300)
Takhar . . .	11,800	508,800	43.1	Taluqan (68,600)
Jawzjan . . .	24,700	442,100	17.9	Sheberghan (56,500)
Zabul . . .	20,000	368,600	18.4	Qalat (51,200)
Samangan . . .	16,000	213,400	13.3	Uiback (39,500)
Ghazni . . .	31,400	1,136,400	36.1	Ghazni (44,700)
Ghour . . .	35,100	333,000	9.5	Cheghcheran (62,700)
Fariab . . .	22,900	447,500	19.5	Maimana (57,100)
Farah . . .	57,800	323,500	5.6	Farah (29,600)
Kunduz . . .	7,400	417,400	56.4	Kunduz (82,500)
Kandahar . . .	45,100	763,100	16.9	Kandahar (130,800)
Kabul . . .	4,500	1,330,100	295.7	Kabul (513,000)
Kapisa . . .	5,800	354,900	78.4	Mahmoodraqi (72,700)
Kunarha . . .	10,300	339,300	32.9	Asadabad (28,900)
Laghman . . .	9,100	229,100	25.2	Meterlam (74,700)
Logar . . .	4,500	318,300	70.7	Pulialam (27,500)
Nangarhar . . .	7,600	842,100	110.8	Jelalabad (50,400)
Neemroze . . .	50,000	125,400	2.5	Zarunj (17,400)
Wardak . . .	10,300	427,900	41.5	Maidan (55,900)
Herat . . .	41,500	706,100	17.0	Herat (73,700)
Helmand . . .	59,700	325,800	5.5	Bost (29,200)
TOTAL . .	652,900†	14,284,500	21.9	

* Population figures refer to settled inhabitants only, excluding kuchies (nomads), estimated at 2,801,800 for the whole country in 1970.

† Other sources give the total area as 250,000 square miles (647,497 sq. km.).

Source: Department of Statistics, Ministry of Planning, *Statistical Pocket-Book of Afghanistan.*

PRINCIPAL CITIES
(estimated population at July 1st, 1973)

Kabul (capital) .	. 534,350	Herat .	.	. 108,750
Kandahar .	. 140,024	Tagab .	.	. 106,777
Baghlan .	. 110,874	Charikar .	.	. 100,443

Source: Central Statistics Office, Prime Ministry, Kabul.

Births and Deaths: Average annual birth rate 50.5 per 1,000; death rate 26.5 per 1,000 (UN estimates for 1965–70).

EMPLOYMENT*

	1971/72	1972/73
Agriculture . . .	3,120,000	3,200,000
Manufacturing (incl. Handicrafts) . . .	280,000	300,000
Construction and Mining .	110,000	120,000
Transport and Communications . . .	30,000	30,000
Other Production Industries	330,000	350,000
Education and Health Services .	30,000	40,000
Government Institutions .	70,000	70,000
Commerce . . .	110,000	110,000
Unknown . . .	110,000	110,000
TOTAL LABOUR FORCE .	4,190,000	4,330,000

*Excluding kuchies (nomads).

Source: Central Statistics Office, Prime Ministry, Kabul.

Total economically active population (1970): 6,000,000, including 4,890,000 in agriculture (ILO and FAO estimates).

AGRICULTURE
LAND USE, 1968
('000 hectares)

Arable Land	7,844
Permanent Crops	136
Permanent Meadows and Pastures .	6,020
Forest Land	2,000
Other Areas	48,750
TOTAL	64,750

Source: FAO, *Production Yearbook 1971.*

PRINCIPAL CROPS
(twelve months ending March 20th)

	AREA ('000 hectares)			PRODUCTION ('000 metric tons)		
	1971/72	1972/73	1973/74	1971/72	1972/73	1973/74
Wheat . . .	2,350	2,891.1	2,236	1,915	2,450	2,750
Maize . . .	315	320	322	670	720	760
Rice (paddy) . .	200	210	210	350	400	450
Barley . . .	500	460	470	355	350	360
Cotton . . .	54	51.6	74.8	63	58	105
Sugar beet . .	4.4	4.6	5.3	60	63	63.6
Sugar cane . .	2.5	0.5	0.7	50	17.3	22.2
Vegetables . .	91	92	92	725	658	680
Fruits . . .	136	136.5	136.7	650	820	840

Source: Central Statistics Office, Prime Ministry, Kabul.

LIVESTOCK
('ooo)

	1969–70	1970–71	1971–72*	1972–73*
Cattle	3,608	3,700	3,750	3,812
Sheep†	21,880	22,900	23,000	23,644
Goats	3,219	3,300	3,350	3,400
Horses	414	370*	360	385
Asses	1,360	1,275*	1,200	1,225
Mules	33	30*	25	27
Buffaloes	33	35*	35	38
Camels	301	300	300	300

* FAO estimate.   † Including Karakul sheep, numbering 6.8 million in 1971.

Source: FAO, *Production Yearbook 1973.*

LIVESTOCK PRODUCTS
('ooo metric tons—FAO estimates)

	1970	1971	1972	1973
Beef, Veal and Buffalo Meat† .	32	40	41	42
Mutton, Lamb and Goats' Meat†	118	106	106	109
Cows' Milk . . .	311	318	323	335
Sheep's Milk . . .	218	278	278	289
Goats' Milk . . .	51	66	67	68
Buffaloes' Milk . .	4	3	3	3
Hen Eggs . . .	12	13	13.3	13.7
Wool: Greasy . . .	30	31	31.5	33.1
Clean . . .	16.5	17.1	17.3	18.2

Source: FAO, *Production Yearbook 1973.*

FORESTRY
('ooo cubic metres)

	ROUNDWOOD REMOVALS*			SAWNWOOD PRODUCTION		
	1969	1970	1971	1969	1970	1971
Coniferous (soft wood) . .	1,310	1,455	1,600	550	630	655
Broadleaved (hard wood) . .	6,085	6,275	6,600	163	154	168
TOTAL . . .	7,395	7,730	8,200	713	784	823

* Unofficial figures.

Source: FAO, *Yearbook of Forest Products 1970*; United Nations *Statistical Yearbook 1972.*

OTHER FOREST PRODUCTS
(metric tons)

	1968	1969	1970
Bark and other tanning materials	200	220	242
Materials for plaiting (excluding bamboo) . . .	n.a.	320	n.a.

Source: FAO, *Yearbook of Forest Products.*

Inland Fishing (1964–71): Total catch 1,500 metric tons each year (FAO estimate).

INDUSTRIAL AND MINERAL PRODUCTION

(Twelve months ending March 20th)

		1969/70	1970/71	1971/72	1972/73
Ginned Cotton . . .	'ooo tons	27.0	30.5	16.8	25.0
Cotton Fabrics . . .	million metres	49.4	57.1	62.0	76.5
Woollen Fabrics . .	'ooo metres	663.4	433.3	284.0	133.4
Rayon Fabrics . . .	,, ,,	2,520.0	8,272.0	10,547.0	13,438.0
Cement	'ooo tons	103.5	94.3	73.0	135.0
Electricity	million kWh	358.8	395.0	422.6	525.4
Wheat Flour . . .	'ooo tons	40.4	51.2	92.3	48.4
Sugar	,, ,,	6.1	8.6	8.5	7.4
Vegetable Oil . . .	,, ,,	2.8	4.1	4.0	4.2
Coal	,, ,,	136.6	164.4	135.0	149.0
Natural Gas . . .	million cu. metres	2,029.0	2,583.0	2,635.4	2,735.0

Sources: Department of Statistics, Kabul, *Survey of Progress 1971–72*, and Central Statistics Office, Prime Ministry, Kabul.

FINANCE

100 puls (puli) = 2 krans = 1 afghani.

Coins: 25 and 50 puls; 1, 2 and 5 afghanis.

Notes: 10, 20, 50, 100, 500 and 1,000 afghanis.

Exchange rates (April 1975): £1 sterling = 105.9 afghanis (official rate) or 135.3 afghanis (free rate);

U.S. $1 = 45.00 afghanis (official rate) or 57.50 afghanis (free rate).

1,000 afghanis = £7.39 = $17.39 (free rates).

Note: Multiple exchange rates were in operation before March 1963. Between 1956 and 1963 the official base rate was U.S. $1 = 20.00 afghanis. Since March 1963 there has been a single official rate of $1 = 45.00 afghanis. In terms of sterling, the official exchange rate was £1 = 108.00 afghanis from November 1967 to August 1971; and £1 = 117.26 afghanis from December 1971 to June 1972. Some trade takes place at the official rate; some at rates determined by discounts or premiums; and some at free market rates, which fluctuate widely.

BUDGET

(million afghanis, twelve months ending March 20th)

REVENUE	1972/73	1973/74	1974/75*	EXPENDITURE	1972/73	1973/74	1974/75*
Direct Taxes . . .	573	819	1,023	Administration . .	517	540	444
Indirect Taxes . . .	2,939	3,593	4,969	Defence, Security . .	1,731	1,885	2,030
Revenue from monopolies				Social Services . .	1,230	1,412	1,439
and other enterprises .	928	721	750	Economic Services .	442	448	456
Natural Gas Revenue .	727	771	900				
Revenue from other property				TOTAL MINISTRIES .	3,900	4,285	4,369
and services . .	496	602	692				
Other Revenue . .	503	604	594	Foreign Debt Service .	1,035	1,411	1,840
				Subsidies (exchange etc.) .	721	835	1,341
TOTAL REVENUE .	6,166	7,110	8,928	TOTAL ORDINARY .	5,650	6,531	7,550
				Development Budget .	2,387	1,986	2,250

* Estimates.

Source: Statistical Information about Afghanistan 1350–1352, Department of Statistics, Office of the Prime Minister, Kabul.

GOLD RESERVES
BANK OF AFGHANISTAN
('ooo U.S. dollars at March 21st)

1972	.	.	35,920
1973	.	.	39,350
1974	.	.	39,350
1975	.	.	40,940

Source: IMF, *International Financial Statistics.*

CURRENCY IN CIRCULATION
(million afghanis at March 21st)

1971	.	.	6,532
1972	.	.	6,785
1973	.	.	8,180
1974	.	.	9,057

February 21st, 1975: 10,050 million afghanis.

Source: IMF, *International Financial Statistics.*

COST OF LIVING
INDEX NUMBERS OF CONSUMER PRICES
(Twelve months ending March 20th.   Base: 1961/62 = 100)

	1969/70	1970/71	1971/72	1972/73	1973/74	1974/75
All Items	208	265	313	267	246	280
Cereals	219	318	401	307	233	278
Meat	215	223	204	245	311	356
Fruits	235	215	228	261	351	372
Vegetables . . .	242	248	241	218	294	282
Other Food Articles . .	146	147	162	203	206	213
Non-Food Items . .	115	117	120	123	133	144

Source: Central Statistics Office, Prime Ministry, Kabul.

NATIONAL ACCOUNTS
NET DOMESTIC PRODUCT BY ORIGIN
(million afghanis, at 1965 market prices)

ECONOMIC ACTIVITY	1967	1968	1969
Agriculture, Forestry and Fishing . . .	28,300	29,050	29,117
Mining	280	540	700
Manufacturing	5,707	5,777	6,200
Construction . . .	860	900	990
Transportation, Communication, Utilities .	1,481	1,630	1,820
Wholesale and Retail Trade* . .	7,122	7,350	7,650
Ownership of Dwellings . . .	4,673	4,800	4,900
Public Administration and Defence . .	2,890	3,150	3,528
Other services	2,174	2,200	2,300
NET DOMESTIC PRODUCT . . .	53,487	55,397	57,205

* Including storage, hotels and restaurants.

Source: United Nations, *Quarterly Bulletin of Statistics for Asia and the Far East,* December 1971.

BALANCE OF PAYMENTS
(U.S. $ million, twelve months ending March 20th)

	1971/72	1972/73
Merchandise trade:		
Exports	95.9	121.0
Imports	−125.1	−138.0
Trade balance	− 29.2	− 17.0
Adjustment between customs and exchange records	5.7	− 6.4
Adjusted trade balance	− 23.5	− 23.4
Tourism*	6.4	6.9
Project assistance (services component) .	− 6.0	− 7.2
Foreign grants and loans . . .	49.8	55.7
Foreign debt service	− 28.1	− 29.5
Net residual transactions (including errors and omissions	12.5	− 4.6
Allocation of IMF Special Drawing Rights .	4.3	—
BALANCE (net monetary movements) .	+ 15.4	− 2.2

* Provisional figures.

Sources: Bank of Afghanistan; Ministries of Finance, Commerce and Planning, Kabul.

FOREIGN AID
(U.S. $ million, twelve months ending March 20th)

SOURCE	1971/72	1972/73	1973/74
Import of commodities aid	22.9	26.1	8.0
Other grants	11.3	5.9	7.3
Foreign project and non-project loans . .	47.2	40.1	53.2
TOTAL	81.4	72.1	68.5

Source: Central Statistics Office, Prime Ministry, Kabul.

EXTERNAL TRADE
(million afghanis, twelve months ending March 20th)

	1968–69	1969–70	1970–71	1971–72	1972–73	1973–74
Imports*	9,267	9,410	6,271	14,155	12,645	n.a.
Exports	5,348	6,180	7,160	8,427	10,046	9,556

*Including imports under commodity loans and grants from foreign countries and international organizations. In recent years the value of these imports (in million afghanis) was: 4,383.5 in 1968–69; 3,940.1 in 1969–70.

PRINCIPAL COMMODITIES

Imports (U.S. $'000)	1972/73	1973/74
Commercial Imports:		
Sugar	9,597.8	13,071
Tea	9,603.7	10,143
Other food products . .	1,962.6	2,472
Petroleum products . .	6,518.3	8,387
Medicinal products . .	5,048.5	4,982
Chemical products . .	3,567.3	5,838
Rubber tyres and tubes . .	8,334.9	11,611
Textiles . . .	8,930.5	13,241
Non-metallic minerals . .	11,744.3	18,744
Metals and metal manufactures	3,332.4	5,434
Machinery	4,330.8	6,668
Motor vehicles . . .	4,383.1	5,262
Other transportation equipment . . .	4,202.3	4,238
Total (incl. others) .	96,219.4	127,558
Non-project Loan and Grant Financed Imports:		
Wheat . . .	19,135.3	10,292
Petroleum products . .	2,940.0	2,721
Chemical fertilizers . .	5,607.8	16,801
Total (incl. others) .	31,795.8	} 55,293
Project Loan and Grant Financed Imports . . .	29,083.4	
Total . . .	157,098.6	182,851

Exports (million afghanis)	1972/73	1973/74
Casings	151.3	92.2
Fresh fruits . . .	847.4	1,272.1
Dried fruits and nuts . .	2,522.9	2,869.8
Apricot kernels . .	122.5	135.4
Hides and skins . . .	252.9	339.9
Karakul skins . . .	1,269.8	960.5
Oil seeds	197.1	214.3
Wool and other fine animal hair .	476.5	343.5
Raw cotton . . .	910.2	429.6
Natural gums . . .	192.9	147.8
Medicinal herbs . . .	63.2	147.8
Natural gas . . .	1,378.7	1,110.4
Carpets and rugs . . .	877.2	889.2
Fur coats . . .	405.1	117.1
Total (incl. others) . .	10,045.6	9,556.3

PRINCIPAL TRADING PARTNERS

Imports (U.S. $'000)	1972/73	1973/74
Czechoslovakia . .	534.9	727
Germany, Fed. Republic .	14,254.4	11,165
India	11,730.1	18,885
Japan	24,187.1	31,704
Pakistan . . .	6,348.8	5,465
U.S.S.R. . . .	34,043.9	38,321
United Kingdom . .	5,654.4	7,689
U.S.A. . . .	16,475.8	21,954
Total (incl. others) .	157,098.6	182,851

Exports (million afghanis)	1970/71	1971/72	1972/73
Czechoslovakia . .	49.9	111.8	226.5
Germany, Fed. Republic	366.9	730.2	614.7
India	1,134.2	401.0	2,446.1
Lebanon . . .	125.2	456.4	293.8
Netherlands . . .	114.3	297.9	52.4
Pakistan . . .	512.7	439.3	428.1
Switzerland . . .	329.5	392.2	391.9
U.S.S.R. . . .	2,752.6	3,256.1	2,929.5
United Kingdom . .	1,155.1	1,670.7	1,610.7
U.S.A. . . .	212.6	182.1	200.0
Total (incl. others) .	7,160.1	8,427.2	10,045.6

Source: Various Afghan government and USAID documents.

TOURISM
INTERNATIONAL TOURIST ARRIVALS BY COUNTRY

	1970	1971	1972	1973	1974
Australia	2,072	2,703	2,614	2,974	3,349
France	6,536	8,130	7,649	6,442	8,541
Germany, Federal Republic . .	5,472	7,524	7,020	7,516	7,157
Pakistan	51,250	51,792	49,121	28,470	26,864
United Kingdom . . .	9,309	10,117	9,067	8,875	10,112
U.S.A.	9,572	11,965	11,630	12,769	10,369
Others	16,022	20,878	23,137	24,616	29,830
TOTAL	100,233	113,109	110,238	91,662	96,222

Receipts from Tourism: U.S. $4.3 million in 1969; $7.8 million in 1970; $11 million in 1971.

Source: Central Statistics Office, Prime Ministry, Kabul.

TRANSPORT
CIVIL AVIATION
(twelve months ending March 20th)

	1970/71	1971/72	1972/73	1973/74
Kilometres flown ('000) . . .	3,022	4,032	3,604	3,595
Passengers carried	69,132	74,236	81,669	80,317
Passenger-km. ('000) . . .	200,621	202,620	203,300	198,000
Total ton-km. ('000) . . .	8,587	9,974	15,107	16,100
Cargo . . .	8,349	9,676	14,744	14,900
Free luggage . . .	138	148	163	1,000
Mail	100	150	200	200

Source: Central Statistics Office, Prime Ministry, Kabul.

ROAD TRAFFIC
Motor Vehicles in Use.

	1969	1970	1971
Passenger cars .	34,200	36,200	38,400
Commercial vehicles	23,800	24,400	26,100

Source: United Nations, *Statistical Yearbook.*

COMMUNICATIONS MEDIA

Telephones in use: 20,492 in 1973/74.
Radio sets in use: 450,000 in 1973.
Books published: 83 titles in 1969.
Daily newspapers: 18 in 1970 (total circulation 101,000).

EDUCATION
(1973/74)

	INSTITUTIONS	PUPILS
Primary Schools . .	1,345	482,194
Village Schools . . .	1,882	139,728
Middle Schools . . .	517	108,795
Lycées	197	51,663
Commercial, Agricultural and Technical Schools .	14	4,444
Teacher Training Colleges .	10	5,086
Religious Schools . .	13	4,165
Universities and Higher Institutes . . .	13	8,011

Note: Teachers in all institutions totalled 18,158 in 1970.

Source: Central Statistics Office, Prime Ministry, Kabul.

THE CONSTITUTION

In July 1973, a special ordinance abolished most of the 1964 Constitution. On August 24th, 1973, the Head of State announced that a commission would be established to put forward proposals for a new Constitution.

THE GOVERNMENT

HEAD OF STATE

Lt.-Gen. MOHAMMAD DAUD.

CABINET

(August 1975)

Head of State, Prime Minister, Minister of Foreign Affairs, Minister of National Defence: Lt.-Gen. MOHAMMAD DAUD.

Deputy Prime Minister: Dr. MOHAMMAD HASSAN SHARQ.

Minister of Justice: Dr. ABDUL MAJID.

Minister of Finance: SAID ABDUL ELLAH.

Minister of the Interior: FAIZ MOHAMMAD.

Minister of Education: ABDUL KAYOUM.

Minister of the Frontiers: (to be appointed).

Minister of Mines and Industries: (to be appointed).

Minister of Communications: (to be appointed).

Minister of Public Health: Dr. NAZAR MOHAMMAD SEKANDAR.

Minister of Information: Dr. ABDUR RAHIM NAWIN.

Minister of Agriculture: GHULAM JAILANI BAKHTARI.

Minister of Planning: ALI AHMED KHORAM.

Minister of Commerce: MOHAMMAD KHAN JALALAR.

PARLIAMENT

Prior to the *coup* of July 17th, 1973, the Shura (Parliament) consisted of the Meshrano Jirgah (House of Elders) and the Wolesi Jirgah (House of the People). The Shura was dissolved on July 28th, 1973.

POLITICAL PARTIES

No political parties had been officially authorized before the *coup* of July 17th, 1973.

DIPLOMATIC REPRESENTATION

EMBASSIES ACCREDITED TO AFGHANISTAN

(Kabul unless otherwise stated)

(E) Embassy.

Argentina: Teheran, Iran (E).

Australia: Islamabad, Pakistan (E).

Austria: Zarghouna Wat (E); *Chargé d'affaires a.i.:* Dr. R. F. KREUTEL.

Bangladesh: Wazir Akbar Khan Mena (E); *Ambassador:* M. SULTAN.

Belgium: Teheran, Iran (E).

Brazil: Teheran, Iran (E).

Bulgaria: Wazir Akbar Khan Mena (E); *Ambassador:* IVAN HRISTOV KARATZANOV.

Burma: New Delhi, India (E).

Canada: Islamabad, Pakistan (E).

China, People's Republic: Shah Mahmoud Ghazi Wat (E); *Ambassador:* KAN YEH-TAO.

Czechoslovakia: Taimani Wat, Kale Fathullah (E); *Ambassador:* JAN SUCHANIK.

Denmark: Teheran, Iran (E).

Egypt: Wazir Akbar Khan Mena (E); *Ambassador:* AHMAD MUHAMMAD ABU ZAID.

Finland: Ankara, Turkey (E).

France: Nedjat Wat (E); *Ambassador:* EUGÈNE WERNERT.

German Democratic Republic: Teheran, Iran (E).

Germany, Federal Republic: Wazir Akbar Khan Mena (E); *Ambassador:* Dr. J. HOFFMAN.

Ghana: New Delhi, India (E).

Greece: Teheran, Iran (E).

Hungary: Teheran, Iran (E).

India: Malalai Wat (E): *Ambassador:* RAM PRATRAP SINGH.

Indonesia: Wazir Akbar Khan Mena (E); *Ambassador:* ABDUL HABIR.

Iran: Malekyar Wat (E); *Ambassador:* HUSSEIN DAOUDI.

Iraq: Malalai Wat, Shar-e-Nau (E); *Ambassador:* N. A. KADER HADISSI.

Italy: Khwaja Abdullah Ansari Wat (E); *Ambassador:* VALERIO BRIGANTI COLONNA ANGELINI.

Japan: Wazir Akbar Khan Mena (E); *Ambassador:* JUNJI YAMADA.

Jordan: Teheran, Iran (E).

Korea, Democratic People's Republic: Wazir Akbar Khan Mena (E); *Chargé d'Affaires a.i.:* KIM WON BOK.

Korea, Republic: Wazir Akbar Khan Mena; *Chargé d'Affaires a.i.:* CHANG HWAN KIM.

Kuwait: Teheran, Iran (E).

Lebanon: Teheran, Iran (E).

Malaysia: Teheran, Iran (E).

Mexico: New Delhi, India (E).

Mongolia: Moscow, U.S.S.R. (E).

Morocco: Teheran, Iran (E).

Nepal: New Delhi, India (E).

Netherlands: Teheran, Iran (E).

Norway: Teheran, Iran (E).

Pakistan: Zarghouna Wat (E); *Ambassador:* ALI ARSHED.

Philippines: New Delhi, India (E).

Poland: Guzargah Wat (E); *Ambassador:* TADEUSZ MARTYNOWICZ.

Qatar: Teheran, Iran (E).

Romania: Teheran, Iran (E).

Saudi Arabia: Wazir Akbar Khan Mena (E); *Ambassador:* MOHAMMAD AL-AHMAD AL-SHOBAILI.

Senegal: Teheran, Iran (E).

Spain: Teheran, Iran (E).

Sri Lanka: New Delhi, India (E).

Sudan: Islamabad, Pakistan (E).

Sweden: Teheran, Iran (E).

Switzerland: Teheran, Iran (E).

Syria: New Delhi, India (E).

Thailand: New Delhi, India (E).

Turkey: Shah Mahmoud Ghazi Wat (E); *Ambassador:* FARUK ŞAHINBAŞ.

U.S.S.R.: Dar-ul-Aman Wat (E); *Ambassador:* M. POZANOV.

United Kingdom: Parwan Mena (E); *Ambassador:* J. K. DRINKALL.

U.S.A.: Khwaja Abdullah Ansari Wat (E); *Ambassador:* T. ELLIOT.

Yugoslavia: Wazir Akbar Khan Mena (E); *Ambassador:* BORISLAV SAMONIKOV.

Afghanistan also has diplomatic relations with Algeria, Tunisia and the United Arab Emirates.

JUDICIAL SYSTEM

Prior to the *coup* of July 17th, 1973, the judiciary of Afghanistan consisted of the Supreme Court, the highest judicial authority, three High Courts, a Court of Appeal, 28 Provincial Courts, 216 Primary Courts and a number of Special Courts. On July 28th, 1973, the powers of the Supreme Court, which include administrative powers within the framework of the judicial organization, were transferred to a council set up within the Ministry of Justice.

RELIGION

The official religion of Afghanistan is Islam. The great majority (almost 90 per cent) are Muslims of the Sunni (Hanafi) sect, and the remainder belong to the Shi'a sect. About 20,000 Hindus are living in different parts of the country.

THE PRESS

PRINCIPAL DAILIES

Anis (*Friendship*): Kabul; f. 1927; evening; Independent; news and literary articles; Persian and Pashtu; circ. 25,000; Editor-in-Chief IBRAHIM ABBOSSI.

Badakshan: Faizabad; f. 1945; Persian and Pashtu.

Bedar: Mazar-i-Sharif; f. 1920; Persian and Pashtu; circ. 1,500.

Daiwan: Sheberghan.

Ettifaqi-Islam: Herat; f. 1920; Persian and Pashtu; circ. 1,500.

Ettehadi-Baghlan: Baghlan; f. 1921; Persian and Pashtu.

Helmand: Bost; f. 1953; twice weekly; Pashtu.

Heywad: Kabul; f. 1949; Pashtu; Editor MOHAMMED SHAFIQ WEJDAN; circ. 5,000.

Jamhouryat (*Republic*): Kabul; f. 1973; official organ; Dari and Pashtu; Editor-in-Chief Dr. ASIF SOHAIL; circ. 25,000.

Kabul Times: Kabul; f. 1962; English; circ. 5,000.

Nangarhar: Jelalabad; f. 1918; Persian and Pashtu; circ. 1,500.

Seistan: Farah; f. 1947; twice weekly.

Tuloi-Afghan: Kandahar; f. 1924; circ. 1,500.

Wolanga: Gardiz; f. 1941; Pashtu; circ. 1,000.

PERIODICALS

Adab: Kabul; f. 1953; organ of the Faculty of Literature, Univ. of Kabul.

Afghan Journal of Public Health: Institute of Public Health, Ansari Wat, Kabul; 2 per month; Editor A. SATAR AHMADI, M.D.

Afghan Tebbi Mojalla: Faculty of Medicine, Kabul University; monthly.

Afghanistan: Kabul; f. 1946; quarterly; English and French; historical and cultural; Historical Society of Afghanistan, Kabul.

Akhbare Erfani: Ministry of Education, Kabul; f. 1952; fortnightly.

Aryana: Kabul; f. 1943; quarterly (Pashtu and Dari); cultural and historical; produced by the Historical Society of Afghanistan; Editor Dr. A. KH. WAFAI.

Badany Rauzana: Department of Physical Education, Kabul University; quarterly.

Eqtesad: Afghan Chamber of Commerce and Industry, Darul Aman Watt, Kabul; monthly; Editor PAINDA MOHAMMED MOHEBZADA.

Hawa: Afghan Air Authority, Kabul; f. 1957.

Irfan: Ministry of Education, Kabul; f. 1923; monthly; Persian.

Jamhouryat: Kabul; every two months; Editor MOHAMMED ASSEF SOHIL.

Kabul: Pashtu Tolana, Kabul; f. 1931; 2 per month; Pashtu; literature, history, social sciences; Editor MOHAMMED MOHEM PATWAL.

Kabul Pohantoon: Kabul University; monthly.

Karhana: Kabul; f. 1955; monthly; produced by the Ministry of Agriculture; circ. 2,500; Editor M. Y. AINA.

Kocheniano Zhaqh: Ministry of Education, Kabul; f. 1957; monthly.

Mairmun: Kabul; f. 1955; Persian and Pashtu; produced by the Women's Welfare Association.

Mokhaberet: Ministry of Communications, Kabul; f. 1957; monthly.

Pamir: Kabul; f. 1951; organ of the Municipality; fortnightly.

Pashtun Zhaqh: Ansari Wat, Kabul; f. 1940; programmes of broadcasts; issued by Kabul Radio; 2 per month.

Payame Haq: Ministry of Information, Kabul; f. 1953; monthly.

Sera Miasht: Red Crescent Society, Kabul; f. 1958.

Talim wa Tarbia: Kabul; f. 1954; monthly; published by Institute of Education.

Urdu: Kabul; f. 1922; monthly; military journal; issued by the Ministry of National Defence.

Zhwandoon: Kabul; Persian; illustrated; Editor NAJEE-BULLAH RAHEQ; circ. 10,000.

Zeru: Pashtu Tolana, Kabul; f. 1949; weekly.

NEWS AGENCIES

Bakhtar News Agency: Kabul; f. 1939; Pres. MOHAMMED KAZIM AHANG.

FOREIGN BUREAUX

The following Foreign Agencies are represented in Kabul: Agence France-Presse (AFP), Deutsche Presse-Agentur (DPA), and Tass.

PRESS ASSOCIATION

Journalists' Association: c/o Department of Press and Information, Sanaii Wat, Kabul.

PUBLISHERS

Afghanistan Publicity Department: c/o Kabul Times, Kabul; publicity materials; answers enquiries about Afghanistan.

Afghan Kitab: Kabul; f. 1969 by K. Ahang; books on various subjects and translations of foreign works on Afghanistan.

Baihaqi Book Publishing Institute: Kabul; f. 1971 by Government Press, Ministry of Information and Culture.

Book Publishing Institute: Kabul; f. 1966 by co-operation of the Government Press, Bakhtar News Agency and leading newspapers.

Book Publishing Institute: Herat; f. 1970 by co-operation of Government Press and citizens of Herat; books on literature, history and religion.

Book Publishing Institute: Kandahar; f. 1970 by citizens of Kandahar, supervised by Government Press; mainly books in Pashtu language.

Educational Publications: Ministry of Education, Kabul; text-books for primary and secondary schools in the Pashtu and Dari languages; also two monthly magazines, one in Pashtu and the other in Dari.

Government Press: Kabul; f. 1870 under supervision of the Ministry of Information and Culture; four daily newspapers in Kabul, one in English; weekly, fortnightly and monthly magazines, one of them in English; books on Afghan history and literature, as well as textbooks for the Ministry of Education; thirteen daily newspapers in thirteen provincial centres and one journal and also magazines in three provincial centres.

Historical Society of Afghanistan: Kabul; f. 1931 by Department of Press and Information; mainly historical works and two quarterly magazines; *Afghanistan* (English and French), *Aryana* (Dari); Head Dr. M. YAKUB WAHIDI.

Institute of Geography: Faculty of Letters, Kabul University; geographical and related works.

Kabul University Press: Kabul; publishes textbooks for Kabul and Nangarhar Universities, College Journals, etc.

Pashto Tolana: Kabul; f. 1937 by the Department of Press and Information; research works on Pashtu language.

RADIO

Radio Afghanistan: P.O.B. 544, Kabul; Pres. ABDUL KARIM ATTAHI; Prog. Chief S. Y. WASEEP; the Afghan Broadcasting station is under the supervision of the Ministry of Information; Home service in Dari, Pashtu, Uzbaki, Pashahi and Balochi; Foreign service in Urdu, English, Russian, German, Dari and Pashtu.

Number of radio receivers: 450,000 in 1973.

There is no television.

FINANCE

(cap. =capital; p.u. =paid up; res. =reserves; m. =million; Afs. =Afghanis.)

BANKING

CENTRAL BANK

Afghanistan Bank (Da): Jadeh Ibne Sina Wat, Kabul; f. 1939; the central bank; main functions: banknote issue, foreign exchange control and operations, credit extensions to banks and leading enterprises and companies, government and private depository, government fiscal agency; 58 local brs.; cap. Afs. 480m.; dep. 8,915m. (August 1974); Gov. MOHAMMED HAKIM (acting); Deputy Gov. FAQIR MOHAMMED MUNIF; Sec. (vacant).

Overseas Corporations:

The Trading Company of Afghanistan Inc.: 122–126 West 30th St., New York, N.Y. 10001, U.S.A.

The Trading Company of Afghanistan Ltd.: Riverbank House, 67 Upper Thames St., London, EC4V 3AH, England.

Pashtany Tejaraty Bank (*Afghan Commercial Bank*): Mohammad Jan Khan Wat, Kabul; f. 1954 to provide long- and short-term credits, forwarding facilities, opening letters of credit, purchase and sale of foreign exchange, transfer of capital, issuing travellers' cheques; cap. p.u. Afs. 250m.; total resources Afs. 2,249m. (March 1971); Pres. GUL-AHMED NOURI; 17 brs. in Afghanistan and abroad.

Agricultural Development Bank of Afghanistan: Kabul; f. 1955; makes available credits for farmers, co-operatives and agro-business; aid provided by IBRD and UNDP; auth. share cap. Afs. 1 billion; Pres. A. AFZAL; Gen. Man. J. DVESTER.

Banke Millie Afghan (*Afghan National Bank*): Head Office: Jadae Ibn Sina, Kabul; f. 1932; brs. throughout Afghanistan and in Pakistan; London Office: (as Afghan National Bank Ltd.) 22 Finsbury Square, E.C.2; offices in New York and Hamburg; cap. Afs. 500m.; dep. 1,284m. (March 1973); Pres. MOKHTAR-ZADA.

Mortgage and Construction Bank: 2 Jade' Maiwand, Kabul; f. 1955 to provide short and long term building loans; cap. Afs. 60m.; Pres. ESMATOLLAH ENAYAT SERAJ.

Industrial Development Bank of Afghanistan: Kabul; f. 1973; provides financing for industrial development; Pres. Dr. NOUR ALI.

There are no foreign banks operating in Afghanistan.

INSURANCE

There is one national insurance company:

Afghan Insurance Co.: P.O.B. 329, 26 Mohd. Jan Khan Wat, Kabul; f. March 1964; marine, aviation, fire, motor and accident insurance; cap. p.u. Af. 15m.; Pres. ABDUL RASHID; Gen. Man. N. H. SIMONDS.

Three foreign insurance companies are operating in the country: *Ingosstrakh* (Soviet National Company); the *Commercial Union Group* (Head Office: 24 Cornhill, London, E.C.3, England) and the *Sterling General Insurance Co. Ltd.* (Head Office: Scindia House, P.O.B. 12, New Delhi 1, India) maintain branch offices.

TRADE AND INDUSTRY

CHAMBER OF COMMERCE

Afghan Chamber of Commerce: Darul Aman Wat, Kabul; Pres. Dr. MOHAMMAD AKBAR OMER.

TRADING CORPORATIONS

Cotton Export Corporation: Kabul; formed to facilitate cotton production, improve methods of cultivation, install modern ginning and pressing plants, and export cotton.

Kandahar Woollen Factory: Kandahar; formed for the export of wool.

Livestock Improvement Organization: Kabul; f. 1952; formed to improve the quality of Karakul, campaign against animal diseases and to fix buying prices in the interests of producers.

Pashtoon Food Processors Inc.: P.O.B. 3025, Kabul; f. 1946; processes and exports Red Afghan raisins; 64 mems.; Pres. A. MOOSA.

Textile Company: Kabul; manufactures yarn and fabrics from cotton, rayon and other synthetic fibres at its three mills.

Herat Pistachio Company: Herat; formed for the export of pistachio nuts.

Balkh Union: export and import agency handling exports of wool, hides and karakul.

Wool Company: deals with wool exports.

Carpet Export Company: Kabul.

State Co-operative Depot: Kabul; deals with export and imports of all commodities.

Government Officials' Co-operative: Kabul; export and import company.

Office S. M. Azam Azimi: P.O.B. 498, Kabul; f. 1972; carries out import-export transactions.

TRADE UNIONS

There are no trade unions in Afghanistan.

TRANSPORT

There are no railways in Afghanistan.

ROADS

Ministry of Communication and Ministry of Public Works: Kabul; in 1971 there were about 6,000 km. of all-weather tarmac and gravel roads. All-weather highways now link Kabul with Kandahar and Herat in the south and west, Jelalabad in the east and Mazar-i-Sharif and the Oxus in the north. Road development continues with the aid of Soviet and American loans.

Afghan Motor Service and Parts Co.: Zendabanon Workshops, P.O.B. 86, Kabul; passenger services in Kabul; long-distance freight and passenger services from Kabul to most parts of the country; trucking services in all towns; Pres. HAFIZULLAH RAHIMI; Vice-Pres. KHAWJA MOENODDIN.

INLAND WATERWAYS

River ports on the Oxus are linked by road to Kabul.

CIVIL AVIATION

Civil Aviation Authority: Ansari Wat, Kabul; Pres. SULTAN MAHMOUD GHAZI.

There are modern international terminals at Kabul and Kandahar.

NATIONAL AIRLINE

Ariana Afghan Airlines Co. Ltd.: P.O.B. 76, Kabul; f. 1955; international services to Amritsar, Beirut, Damascus, Frankfurt, Istanbul, London, New Delhi, Paris, Rome, Tashkent, and Teheran; Chair. Sultan MAHMOUD GHAZI; Pres. AMINULLAH NAJIB; Exec. Vice-Pres. CHARLES H. BENNETT; Comptroller S. G. HAZRAT; Dir. of Operations AZIZ A. MALIKYAR; Commercial Dir. EHSAN GRAN.

The following airlines also operate services to Afghanistan: Aeroflot, IAC, Iran Air, Pakistan International Airways, TMA (cargo).

Air France, KLM, Lufthansa, TWA, British Airways, SAS and Pan American are also represented in Kabul.

Bakhtar Afghan Airlines: Ansari Wat, P.O.B. 3058, Kabul; f. 1968; internal services between Kabul and 17 regional locations; Pres. A. A. ETEMADI; Dir. of Operations Capt. R. NAWROZ.

TOURISM

Afghan Tourist Organization: Mohammad Jan Khan Wat. Kabul; f. 1958; Pres. M. O. SERADJ; Vice-Pres. R. A, SULTANI. Publishes monthly Afghan Travel News (in English) and a quarterly Statistical bulletin.

Afghan Tour: Kabul; official travel agency; Gen. Man. M. A. BABA.

ATOMIC ENERGY

Atomic Energy Commission: Faculty of Science, Kabul University, Kabul; Pres. of Commission and Dean of Faculty Dr. A. G. KARKAR.

DEFENCE

Armed Forces: (1974) Total strength 86,500; army 78,500; air force 8,000; reserves total 162,000 and para-military forces comprise 14,000 gendarmes; military service lasting two years is compulsory for every able-bodied man.

Equipment: The army's equipment and training are very largely provided by the Soviet Union. The air force has 150 Russian-built combat aircraft.

Defence Expenditure: Estimated Defence expenditure in 1973–74 was 2,022 million afghanis (U.S. $45 million).

EDUCATION

The traditional system of education in Afghanistan was religious instruction by mullahs in the mosques, leading to higher religious education in the Ulema schools. These centres are still active, but a modern educational system has been built up over the past sixty-five years.

Since 1933 primary, middle and secondary schools have been opened all over the country. The development of education since 1961 has been rapid especially at the primary level where enrolment has risen from 231,000 to 621,922 by 1973. In 1973 there were 3,227 primary and village schools. By 1973 the number of middle schools had risen to 517, and the number of lycées had risen to 197. The number of vocational schools has been falling but this has been compensated for by an expansion of other forms of technical education.

Teacher training began on an organized scale in the early 1950s. The University of Kabul was founded in 1932 when the Faculty of Medicine was established. It now has 11 Faculties. In 1972 a second university was founded in Jelalabad, Nangarhar province; again the nucleus was provided by a Medical Faculty.

Progress is also being made in women's education, and girls' schools are now found in all major cities.

UNIVERSITIES

Kabul University: Kabul; 1,027 teachers, 8,994 students.

University of Nangarhar: Jelalabad; 61 teachers, 410 students.

BIBLIOGRAPHY

GENERAL

AFGHAN TRANSPORT & TRAVEL SERVICE. Afghanistan—Ancient Land with Modern Ways (London, 1961).

CAROE, OLAF. The Pathans.

GRASSMUCK, GEORGE, and ADAMEC, LUDWIG (editors) Afghanistan: Some new approaches (Center for Near Eastern and North African Studies, University of Michigan, 1969).

GREGORIAN, VARTAN. The Emergence of Modern Afghanistan (Stanford University Press, Stanford, 1969).

GRIFFITHS, JOHN C. Afghanistan (Pall Mall Press, London, 1967).

KESSEL, FLINKER and KLIMBURG. Afghanistan (photographs, 1959).

KING, PETER. Afghanistan, Cockpit in Asia (Bles, London, 1966, Taplinger, N.Y., 1967).

KLIMBURG, M. Afghanistan (Austrian UNESCO Commission, Vienna, 1966).

SHALISI, PRITA K. Here and There in Afghanistan.

WATKINS, MARY B. Afghanistan, an Outline (New York, 1962).

Afghanistan, Land in Transition (Van Nostrand, Princeton, N.J., 1963).

WILBER, DONALD N. Afghanistan (New Haven, Conn., 1956).

Annotated Bibliography of Afghanistan (New Haven, Conn., 1962).

TOPOGRAPHY AND TRAVELS

BURNES, Sir ALEXANDER. Cabool (John Murray, London, 1842).

BYRON, ROBERT. Road to Oxiana.

ELPHINSTONE, M. An Account of the Kingdom of Caubul and its Dependencies in Persia, Tartary and India (John Murray, London, 1815).

FERRIER, J. P. Caravan Journeys.

HAHN, H. Die Stadt Kabul und ihr Umland (2 vols., Bonn, 1964–65).

HAMILTON, ANGUS. Afghanistan (Heinemann, London, 1906).

HUMLUM, J. La Géographie de l'Afghanistan (Gyldendal, Copenhagen, 1959).

MASSON, CHARLES. Narrative of various journeys in Balochistan, Afghanistan and the Punjab (Bentley, London, 1842).

MOHUN LAL. Journal.

WOLFE, N. H. Herat (Afghan Tourist Organization, Kabul, 1966).

WOOD, JOHN. A Personal Narrative of a Journey to the Source of the River Oxus by the Route of Indus, Kabul and Badakshan (John Murray, London, 1841).

HISTORY

ADAMEC, LUDWIG W. Afghanistan 1900–1923 (University of California, Berkeley, 1967).

Afghanistan's Foreign Affairs to the Mid-Twentieth Century (University of Arizona Press, Tucson, 1974).

BOSWORTH, C. E. The Ghaznavids (Edinburgh University Press, 1963).

CAMBRIDGE HISTORY OF INDIA, Vols. I, III, IV, V, VI.

DOLLOT, RENÉ. Afghanistan (Payot, Paris, 1937).

DUPREE, LOUIS, and LINNET, ALBERT (Editors). Afghanistan in the 1970s (Praeger, New York, 1974 and Pall Mall Press, London).

FLETCHER, ARNOLD. Afghanistan, Highway of Conquest (Cornell and Oxford University Presses, 1965).

FRASER-TYTLER, Sir W. KERR. Afghanistan (Oxford University Press, 1950, 3rd edn., 1967).

GOVERNMENT OF INDIA. The Third Afghan War, 1919 (Calcutta, 1926).

GREGORIAN, VARTAN. The Emergence of Modern Afghanistan—Politics of Reform and Modernization 1880–1946 (Stanford University Press, 1970).

GROUSSET. L'Empire des Steppes.

KHAN, M. M. S. M., Editor. The Life of Abdur Rahman, Amir of Afghanistan (John Murray, London, 1900).

KOHZAD, A. A. Men and Events (Government Printing House, Kabul).

MACRORY, PATRICK. Signal Catastrophe (Hodder & Stoughton, London, 1966).

MASSON, V. M., and ROMODIN, V. A. Istoriya Afghanistana (Akad. Nauk, Moscow, 1964–65).

MOHUN LAL. Life of the Amir Dost Mohammed Khan of Kabul (Longmans, London, 1846).

NORRIS, J. A. The First Afghan War, 1838–42 (Cambridge University Press, 1967).

SYKES, Sir PERCY. A History of Afghanistan (Macmillan, London, 1940).

TATE, G. P. The Kingdom of Afghanistan (London, 1911).

ECONOMY

ASIAN CONFERENCE ON INDUSTRIALIZATION. Industrial Development: Asia and the Far East (Report of Manila Conference, 1965, published by ECAFE, Bangkok).

MALEKYAR, ABDUL WAHED. Die Verkehrsentwicklung in Afghanistan (Cologne, 1966).

RHEIN, E. and GHAUSSY. A. GHANIE. Die wirtschaftliche Entwicklung Afghanistans, 1880-1965 (C. W. Leske Verlag, Hamburg 1966).

Algeria

PHYSICAL AND SOCIAL GEOGRAPHY

D. R. Harris

Algeria is the largest of the three countries in north-west Africa that comprise the Maghreb, as the region of mountains, valleys and plateaux that lies between the sea and the Sahara desert is known. It is situated between Morocco and Tunisia with a Mediterranean coastline of nearly 1,000 km. and a total area of some 2,381,741 sq. km., over four fifths of which lies south of the Maghreb proper and within the western Sahara. Its extent, both from north to south and west to east, exceeds 2,000 km. The Arabic name for the country, *al Jazair* (the Islands), is said to derive from the rocky islands along the coastline, which have always constituted a danger to ships approaching the harbours.

In the 1966 census the population was 11,821,679 and the overall density was 5.0 per sq. km. However, a vast majority of the inhabitants live in the northern part of the country, particularly along the Mediterranean coast where both the capital, Algiers (population, with suburbs, now over one million), and the second largest town, Oran (about 325,000), are located. The population is almost wholly Muslim, of whom a majority speak Arabic and the remainder Berber, the language of the original inhabitants of the Maghreb. Most educated Algerians, however, speak French. Nearly all the European settlers, who numbered about 1 million in 1960, have left the country since it attained its independence from France in 1962.

PHYSICAL FEATURES

The primary contrast in the physical geography of Algeria is between the mountainous, relatively humid terrain of the north, which forms part of the Atlas mountain system, and the vast expanse of lower, flatter desert to the south, which is part of the Saharan tableland. The Atlas Mountains trend from south-west to north-east across the whole of the Maghreb. Structurally they resemble the "Alpine" mountain chains of Europe north of the Mediterranean and, like them, they came into existence during the geologically recent Tertiary era. They are still unstable and liable to severe earthquakes, such as that which partially destroyed Orléansville (now El Asnam) in 1954. They consist of rocks, now uplifted, folded and fractured, that once accumulated as submarine deposits beneath an ancestral Mediterranean sea. Limestones and sandstones are particularly extensive and they often present a barren appearance in areas where a cover of soil and vegetation is only thin or absent altogether.

In Algeria the Atlas mountain system is made up of three broad zones running parallel to the coast: the Tell Atlas, the High Plateaux and the Saharan Atlas. In the north, and separated from the Mediterranean by only a narrow and discontinuous coastal plain, is the complex series of mountains and valleys that comprise the Tell Atlas. Here individual ranges, plateaux and massifs vary in height from about 500 to 2,500 metres, and are frequently separated from one another by deep valleys and gorges which divide the country into self-contained topographic and economic units. Most distinctive of these are the massifs of the Great and Little Kabyle between Algiers and the Tunisian frontier, which have acted as mountain retreats where Berber ways of village life persist.

South of the Tell Atlas lies a zone of featureless plains known as the High Plateaux of the Shotts. To the west, near the Moroccan frontier, they form a broad, monotonous expanse of level terrain about 160 km. across and over 1,000 metres high. They gradually narrow and fall in height eastward and end in the Hodna basin, a huge enclosed depression, the bottom of which is only 420 metres above sea-level. The surface of the plateaux consists of alluvial debris derived from erosion of the mountains to north and south, and only here and there do minor ridges project through the thick mantle of alluvium to break the monotony of the level horizons. The plateaux owe their name to the presence of several vast basins of internal drainage, known as shotts, the largest of which is the Hodna basin. During rainy periods water accumulates in the shotts to form extensive shallow lakes which give way, as the water is absorbed and evaporated, to saline mud flats and swamps.

The southern margin of the High Plateaux is marked by a series of mountain chains and massifs that form the Saharan Atlas. They are more broken than the Tell Atlas and present no serious barrier to communications between the High Plateaux and the Sahara. From west to east the chief mountain chains are the Ksour, Amour, Ouled Naïl, Ziban and Aurès. The latter is the most impressive massif in the whole Algerian Atlas system and includes the highest peak: Djebel Chelia, 2,328 metres. The relief of the Aurès is very bold, with narrow gorges cut between sheer cliffs surmounted by steep bare slopes, and to the east and north of the Hodna basin its ridges merge with the southernmost folds of the Tell Atlas. North-eastern Algeria forms, therefore, a compact block of high relief in which the two Atlas mountain systems cease to be clearly separated. Within it there are a number of high plains studded with salt flats but their size is insignificant compared with the enormous shotts to the west.

CLIMATE AND VEGETATION

The climate of northernmost Algeria, including the narrow coastal plain and the Tell Atlas southward to the margin of the High Plateaux, is of "Mediterranean" type with warm wet winters and hot dry summers. Rainfall varies in amount from over 100 cm. annually on some coastal mountains exposed to rain-bearing winds to less than 13 cm. in sheltered, lee situations, and most of it occurs during the winter when depressions most frequently pass across the western Mediterranean most frequently. Complete drought lasts for three to four months during the summer and at this time too, the notorious sirocco occurs. It is a scorching, dry and dusty south wind blowing from the Sahara and is known locally as the Chehili. It blows on 40 or more days a year over the High Plateaux but nearer the coast its frequency is reduced to about 20 days. When it sets in, shade temperatures often rise rapidly to over 40°C. and vegetation and crops, unable to withstand the intensity of evaporation, may wither and die within a few hours. As a result of low and uneven rainfall combined with high rates of evaporation the rivers of the Tell tend to be short and to suffer large seasonal variations in flow. Many dry out completely during the summer and are only full for brief periods following heavy winter rains. The longest perennially flowing river is the Oued Chélif which rises in the High Plateaux and crosses the Tell to reach the Mediterranean east of Oran.

Along the northern margin of the High Plateaux, which approximately coincides with the limit of 40 cm. mean annual rainfall, "Mediterranean" conditions give way to a semi-arid or steppe climate in which summer drought lasts from five to six months and winters are colder and drier. Rainfall is reduced to between 20 and 40 cm. annually and tends to occur in spring and autumn rather than in winter. It is, moreover, very variable from year to year, and under these conditions the cultivation of cereal crops without irrigation becomes quite unreliable. South of the Saharan Atlas annual rainfall decreases to below 20 cm. and any regular cultivation without irrigation becomes impossible. There are no permanent rivers south of the Tell Atlas and any surface run-off following rain is carried by temporary watercourses towards local depressions, such as the shotts.

The soils and vegetation of northern Algeria reflect the climatic contrast between the humid Tell and the semi-arid lands farther south, but they have also suffered widely from the destructive effects of over-cultivation, over-grazing and deforestation. In the higher, wetter and more isolated parts of the Tell Atlas relatively thick soils support forests of Aleppo pine, cork-oak and evergreen oak, while the lower, drier, and more accessible slopes tend to be bare or covered only with thin soils and a scrub growth of thuya, juniper and various drought-resistant shrubs. Only a few remnants survive of the once extensive forests of Atlas cedar which have been exploited for timber and fuel since classical times. They are found chiefly above 1,500 metres in the eastern Tell Atlas. South of the Tell there is very little woodland except in the higher and wetter parts of the Saharan Atlas. The surface of the High Plateaux is bare or covered only with scattered bushes and clumps of esparto and other coarse grasses.

SAHARAN ALGERIA

South of the Saharan Atlas, Algeria extends for over 1,500 km. into the heart of the desert. Structurally, this huge area consists of a resistant platform of geologically ancient rocks against which the Atlas Mountains were folded. Over most of the area relief is slight, with occasional plateaux, such as those of Eglab, Tademaït and Tassili-n-Ajjer, rising above vast spreads of gravel such as the Tanezrouft plain and huge sand accumulations such as the Great Western and Eastern Ergs. In the south-east, however, the great massif of Ahaggar rises to a height of 2,918 metres. Here erosion of volcanic and crystalline rocks has produced a lunar landscape of extreme ruggedness. Southward from the Ahaggar the massifs of Adrar des Iforas and Aîr extend across the Algerian frontier into the neighbouring countries of Mali and Niger.

The climate of Saharan Algeria is characterized by extremes of temperature, wind and aridity. Daily temperature ranges reach 32°C. and maximum shade temperatures of over 55°C. have been recorded. Sometimes very high temperatures are associated with violent dust storms. Mean average rainfall is everywhere less than 13 cm., and in some of the central parts of the desert it falls to less than one cm. It is, however, extremely irregular and often torrential; a fall of several cm. in one day may be followed by several years of absolute drought. These rigorous conditions are reflected in the extreme sparseness of the vegetation and in a division of the population into settled cultivators, who occupy oases dependent on permanent supplies of underground water, and nomadic pastoralists who make use of temporary pastures which become available after rain.

HISTORY

Algeria as a political entity is a phenomenon of the last four hundred years: the history of its peoples, however, is of considerably greater antiquity. Little is known of the origin of the Berber people who have comprised the majority of the population of this part of Africa since the earliest times, but they had long been established there in numerous nomadic tribes when, at the time of the Punic Wars, the first ephemeral state-organizations may be distinguished in the area. The most important of these states was Numidia (208–148 B.C.), established by the chieftain Masinissa, which occupied most of present-day Algeria north of the Sahara. With the destruction of Carthage in 146 B.C., Numidia, greatly reduced in extent, was transformed into a Roman vassal-state. By the time of Augustus, Numidia was merely a senatorial province of the empire, while the rest of the area formed a loose confederacy of more or less independent tribes. Roman rule lasted until the fifth century. In the coastal centres of trade and culture a certain degree of assimilation to Roman ways took place, but in the mountains and deserts of the interior the Berber tribes maintained their independence by frequent revolt.

The adoption of Christianity as the official religion of the Roman Empire, in the early part of the fourth century, provided a convenient ideological framework for Berber separatism: in particular, their adherence to the Donatist heresy provoked violent civil war and religious strife throughout this period. Under the impact of barbarian invasions, the Roman Empire in the west slowly disintegrated in the course of the fifth century, towards the end of which its rule in North Africa was replaced by the transient dominion of the Vandals. A nomadic people of Germanic origin, they established themselves in the east of present-day Algeria, but failed, like the Romans before them, to gain any real control over the Berber tribes of the hinterland. In A.D. 531, Roman, or rather Byzantine, rule was restored in North Africa, with the conquest by the emperor Justinian of the provinces of Africa (the modern Tunisia) and Numidia, and the establishment of a tenuous hold on the coast as far west as the region of modern Algiers. Elsewhere the Berber confederacies, centred in the Aurès and the Kabyle, maintained their independence.

The rise of Islam in Arabia, and its rapid expansion after the death of the Prophet (632), leading to the Arab conquest of Syria and Egypt, was quickly followed by the penetration of North Africa. The first Arab raids into North Africa (or the Maghreb, as the region comprising the present states of Morocco, Algeria, and Tunisia now came to be called) took place about the middle of the seventh century. The foundation of Kayrawan in 670 provided a permanent base for their operations, which remained for a time little more than raids. The towns remained under Byzantine control, while the Berber tribes, uniting against the invaders, killed the Arab leader, Ukba ibn Nafi (682), and set up a Berber state centred in the eastern Maghreb. Increasing Arab immigration towards the end of the seventh century finally put an end to Berber resistance, under its heroic and legendary warrior-queen Kahina (692). At the same time the last Byzantine garrisons were dislodged from their coastal strongholds, and the whole of the area was incorporated into the Ummayad Empire. The Berbers, for their part, became converted *en masse* to Islam, and, enrolling in its armies, went on with them to the conquest of the western Maghreb and of Spain.

BERBER UNREST

This new-found Islamic unity of North Africa did not long endure. Dissatisfied with their inferior position as non-Arabs in what was in fact an Arab empire, the Berbers adopted Muslim heresies as eagerly as they had previously embraced Christian ones.

The first signs of unrest appeared early in the eighth century, part of a general movement of discontent among the non-Arab peoples of the empire, which in the course of the succeeding years was to bring about the downfall of the Ummayad dynasty (750). By this time the Berbers had become converted to Kharijism, an esoteric radical Muslim sect, and in 756 under its auspices they destroyed completely the authority of the recently-established Abbasid Caliphate throughout the Maghreb. In the east of the area imperial authority was restored in 761, ushering in a period of forty years' anarchy and civil war. In the centre and west of the Maghreb, an area comprising much of present-day Algeria, a number of small, mostly heretical states arose. Later, in the ninth century, the focal point of Berber Kharijism was transferred from Tlemcen to Tiaret. Meanwhile, in the west, the authority of the caliphs had been superseded by that of an independent dynasty, the Aghlabids, who, ruling from Kayrawan, attempted to extend their control into the central Maghreb. In opposition to their rule the Berbers of the Kabyle now embraced Shi'i doctrines—in contrast with their previous adoption of Kharijism—a move which led in 910 to the establishment of the Fatimid dynasty in the central Maghreb. Fatimid rule, however, was not undisputed. From 943 to 947 they were faced with the terrible revolt of Abu Yazid, known as "The man with a donkey", and from then on Fatimid interest in and power over the central Maghreb declined. After several attempts the capital of the dynasty was in 973 transferred to Egypt, while power in the Maghreb was again disputed between various Berber confederacies. In the centre and the east the Sinhaja tribes, the successors to the Kutama who had established the Fatimids, supported the minor dynasty of the Zirids; in the west the more nomadic Zenata established themselves under the remote suzerainty of the Spanish Ummayads. In the early eleventh century the Sinhaja Banu Hammad rose to the status of a local dynasty, ruling as neighbours of the kingdom of Kayrawan.

An event of some importance in the history of the

Maghreb occurred c. 1050: the invasion of the Banu Hilal, a confederation of Arab tribes dislodged from Egypt. These nomads severely damaged the economy of North Africa, and represent the only considerable Arab immigration into the Maghreb since the original Arab conquest of the area. A period of anarchy ensued, but some order was restored by the Berber dynasty of the Almoravids who, coming from Morocco, brought the area of modern Algiers and Oran under their rule. The Banu Hammad, meanwhile, had become established at Bougie. Almoravid power rapidly declined, and c. 1147 they were succeeded by the Almohads. This dynasty, perhaps the most important to rule in North Africa in the medieval Islamic period, unified the whole of the Maghreb together with Muslim Spain. This was a time of cultural and economic prosperity for North Africa, especially at Tlemcen, and witnessed the expansion of trade with the northern shores of the Mediterranean, but the precarious unity of the Maghreb was short-lived. By 1250 the area was again in a condition of political chaos and instability, with the Zenata Banu 'Abd al-Wad exercising such power as existed. A general decline set in, which was to last for over two centuries, during which time the general prevalence of the Berber language gradually gave way to Arabic, a further legacy of the Hilali invasions.

Throughout this period the chief seat of political power was at Tlemcen. In the interior various minor princes asserted their independence, while the coastal towns, including the minor port of Algiers, organized themselves into independent republics, the chief support of which came from piracy. This state of affairs, which lasted throughout the fourteenth century, was terminated by the sudden involvement of Algiers in matters of more than local significance.

OTTOMAN RULE

The Spanish monarchy, bringing to completion its task of driving Muslim power from the Iberian peninsula with the conquest of Granada in 1492, now carried its crusade across the Mediterranean to North Africa. The fragmented political state of that area offered little obstacle to its progress. Mers el-Kebir was captured in 1505, Oran in 1509, and Bougie in 1510, while Algiers, at that time a small port of little importance except as a centre for piracy, was reduced to submission in the same year. On the death of Ferdinand of Castile in 1516 the Algerines, in an attempt to throw off Spanish rule, sent envoys to the Turkish corsair Aruj, seeking his assistance. Aruj took possession of the town, together with other places on the littoral and Tlemcen in the interior, and caused himself to be proclaimed sultan. In 1518 Aruj was killed and was succeeded by his brother Khaye al-Din, Barbarossa, who, in order to consolidate his position, placed all the territories which he controlled under the protection of the Ottoman sultan. This decisive act, which brought together under a single jurisdiction the whole of the coast of North Africa and its immediate hinterland between Constantine and Oran, may be said to mark the emergence of Algeria as a political concept. Meanwhile, the struggle for North Africa,

one aspect of the conflict between Ottoman and Hapsburg which ranged from the western Mediterranean to Hungary and the Indian Ocean, continued. In 1529 Khayr al-Din drove the Spaniards from the Peñon, the fortified rock which overlooks Algiers, while throughout the next decade constant Spanish efforts were made to re-establish their position in the area. Finally, in 1541, a great expedition led by the Emperor Charles V in person, failed miserably in its objectives, and after that Algeria was left for three centuries to the Muslims. Ottoman rule in Algiers had already been further strengthened. In 1533 Khayr al-Din had been summoned to Istanbul to take charge of the Ottoman fleet. In his place a more regular administration was set up, under a succession of *beylerbeys* responsible directly to the sultan. The regime of the *beylerbeys* lasted in Algiers until 1587, when it was replaced by a government headed by a series of *pashas*, who were appointed for a term of three years. These again were succeeded in power in 1659 by the *aghas* (or commanders) of the corps of janissaries, replaced later by the *deys*, who retained their power until the French occupation in 1830. All these changes were, however, very much on the surface. From the mid-sixteenth century actual Ottoman supervision of Algerian affairs became increasingly a convenient fiction, perpetuated in the interests of both the Algerines themselves and the imperial authorities at Istanbul. The real power in Algiers gradually came into the hands of two main bodies. One, the nominal representative of Ottoman power, was the janissary corps, who were for the most part of Anatolian origin; the other, the so-called *taife-i ruesa*, was the guild of corsair captains, men of widely differing origins, who for over three centuries were the main financial support of the state.

The Regency of Algiers reached the peak of its prosperity in the course of the seventeenth century. During this period the rulers of the state entered into diplomatic relations with the leading maritime states of western Europe—England, Holland and France, while these countries maintained their consuls or agents at Algiers. The profitable trade of piracy flourished throughout the century, bringing to Algiers great wealth in the form of captured ships, cargoes and men, and great notoriety as the centre of the North African slave trade. Throughout the seventeenth and eighteenth centuries Algiers looked outwards to the sea. Despite some early Turkish attempts to control the interior, many of the Berber tribes, especially in the Aurès and the Kabyle, maintained their independence throughout the period of Turkish rule; others, more accessible to Algiers, paid to the *dey* a grudging tribute, or unwillingly recognized his suzerainty. With the eighteenth century, and the growth of European seapower in the Mediterranean, conditions became less favourable for corsair activity, and a period of decline set in. From a former figure of 100,000, the population of the city itself dropped to less than thirty thousand at the beginning of the nineteenth century, while in the interior, never firmly controlled by the Turks, the tribal chiefs extended their authority and a period of relative economic prosperity ensued.

In the period of the Napoleonic wars piracy and the economy of Algiers both underwent a certain revival, but this renewal of prosperity was shortlived. On the restoration of peace the European powers called upon the *dey* to abandon piracy, and in 1816 the British fleet bombarded Algiers. It was obvious that before long one of the European powers would take advantage of the growing anti-slavery movement in Europe, and the increasing weakness of Algiers itself, to go beyond naval demonstrations, and to land forces in the country. In the event, the conquest of Algiers was the work of France.

THE FRENCH CONQUEST

The excuse for intervention was an insult offered by the *dey* to the French consul in 1827: the real cause was the pressing need of Polignac, the chief minister under Charles X, to secure some credit for his administration in the eyes of the French public. On July 5th, 1830, Algiers fell to a French expedition, the *dey* and most of the Turkish officials being sent into exile. But the Polignac administration was unable to gather the fruits of its triumph, for before further plans for the consolidation of French rule, and its extension to other coastal towns, could be put into effect, the Bourbon dynasty and its government were overthrown by revolution. A further casualty in the revolution was Polignac's plan for handing over the rest of the country, and the decision on its future, to a European congress; instead, for four years, the problem of what to do with Algiers now that it was in French hands was left to mark time. Away from Algiers itself the absence of any central authority strengthened still further the prestige of the tribal chiefs. Finally, in 1834, following the report of a special commission, the further conquest and annexation of Algeria was decided upon, and a governor-general appointed to put the new plans into effect.

The history of Algeria for the next quarter of a century is mainly concerned with the gradual reduction of the country by France, against bitter and continuing opposition. Constantine, the last stronghold of Turkish rule, was captured in 1837, and by 1841 French rule had been consolidated in most of the ports and their immediate environs. By 1844 most of the eastern part of Algeria had been brought under French control, but in the west the conquerors were faced with the formidable power of Abd el-Kadir. This Berber leader, a skilful diplomat and a military commander of genius, had at first concluded treaties with the French, which consolidated his position as leader of the Berber confederacies in the west. But in 1839 he declared war on France, achieving widespread unity between Berbers and Arabs against the invaders. He held out until 1847, when he was finally defeated by the persistence and ruthless tactics of the French general Bugeaud, the real architect of French rule in Algeria. During the late 1840s and 1850s the tribes on the edge of the Sahara were pacified, while the virtual end of the conquest was achieved by the submission of the hitherto independent Berber confederacies of the Kabyle, in 1857. Further rebellion was to occur, however, throughout the nineteenth century, and

especially after France's defeat at the hands of Prussia in the war of 1870–71.

Meanwhile, a policy of colonization, with widespread confiscation of land and its transference to settler groups, had been pushed forward. Bugeaud had at first encouraged colonization in the coastal plains; after 1848 the influx of colonists was much increased, with the approval of the governments of the Second Republic and, in its early years, the Second Empire. A further stimulus to colonization was provided by the widespread confiscation of lands resulting from the unsuccessful rebellion of 1871. By 1860 much of the best land in Algeria was in French hands, and was the scene of considerable subsequent agricultural development, while the French settlers themselves rapidly became the dominant power in the land. This was well seen some ten years later. Napoleon III had been favourably disposed towards the Algerian Muslim population, and had taken steps to protect tribal lands against settler encroachments, at the same time securing for Muslims the right to acquire French nationality. These measures had provoked strong opposition among the settlers, and in 1870, in the confusion of the Franco-Prussian War, the French colonists in Algeria expelled the imperial agents and set up a revolutionary commune.

After the confusion of the period of "commune" rule, and the subsequent Muslim revolt of 1871, the situation was regularized by the new French administration under Thiers. A civil administration with the status of a French *département* was set up for much of Algeria, while the amount of territory under military rule steadily declined. From then until the end of the nineteenth century Algeria was the scene of considerable economic progress, and increasing European immigration, especially from Italy. A feature of this period was the growth of large-scale agricultural and industrial enterprises, which concentrated still more power in the hands of the most powerful members of the settler groups. In 1900 Algeria secured administrative and financial autonomy, to be exercised through the so-called "Financial Delegations", composed of two-thirds European and one-third Muslim members, and empowered to fix the annual budget and to raise loans for further economic development.

In seventy years the Muslim people of Algeria had been reduced from relative prosperity to economic, social and cultural inferiority. Three million inhabitants had died, tribes had been broken up and the traditional economy altered during the prolonged "civilizing" campaigns. In particular, the production of wine for export had replaced the traditional production of cereals for home consumption. The settlers, however, experienced a high level of prosperity and economic progress in the years before the First World War. For the present, the French ascendancy seemed assured.

BIRTH OF NATIONALISM

The spirit of nationalism was spreading throughout the Middle East, however, and it emerged among the Algerian Muslims as a force to be reckoned with after the First World War. Nationalist aspirations began to be voiced not only by Algerian veterans of the war in Europe but also by Algerians who went to France to study or take up employment. In 1924 one of these students, Messali Hadj, founded in Paris the first Algerian nationalist newspaper, in collaboration with the French communist party; the link with the communists was severed in 1927, however. Messali Hadj and his movement were driven underground by the French Government, but reappeared in 1933 as sponsors of a congress on the future of Algeria which called for total independence, the recall of French troops, the establishment of a revolutionary government, large-scale reforms in land ownership and the nationalization of industrial enterprises.

More moderate doctrines were put forward in the post-war years by an influential body of French-educated Muslims, formalized in 1930 as the Federation of Muslim Councillors. Under the leadership of Ferhat Abbas, this group called for integration with France on a basis of complete equality. The victory of the Popular Front in the French elections of 1936 gave rise to the hope that at least some of these aspirations might be peaceably achieved. The Blum-Viollet Plan, which would have granted full rights of citizenship to an increasing number of Algerian Muslims, was, however, dropped by the French Government in the face of fierce opposition from the French settlers and the Algerian civil service.

The years immediately prior to World War II were marked by growing nationalist discontent, in which Messali Hadj, released from prison in 1936, played a significant part with the formation of the Party of the Algerian People (PPA). The outbreak of war in 1939 temporarily put an end to the nationalists' activities, but the war greatly strengthened their hand for the future. Although the Vichy administration in Algeria, strongly supported by the French settlers, was antipathetic to nationalist sentiment, the Allied landings in North Africa in 1942 provided an opportunity for the Algerian nationalists to put forward constitutional demands. A group headed by Ferhat Abbas on December 22nd, 1942, presented to the French authorities and the Allied military command a memorandum calling for the post-war establishment of an Algerian constituent assembly, to be elected by universal suffrage. No demand was made for Algerian independence outside the French framework, however.

These proposals, to which the French authorities remained unresponsive, were followed early in 1943 by the "Manifesto of the Algerian People", which called for immediate reforms, including the introduction of Arabic as an official language. Further proposals submitted in May envisaged the post-war creation of an Algerian state with a constitution to be determined by a constituent assembly, and looked forward to an eventual North African Union, comprising Tunisia, Algeria and Morocco. The newly-established Free French administration in Algiers rejected the Manifesto and the subsequent proposals out of hand.

In the face of growing Muslim discontent, and following a visit to Algiers by General de Gaulle, a new statute for Algeria was put into effect in March 1944. It was an attempt at compromise which satisfied neither the Algerian nationalists nor the European settlers. Membership of the French electoral college was opened to 60,000 Muslims, but there were still 450,000 European voters, and in the event only 32,000 Muslims accepted inscription. The Muslim share of the seats in the *communes mixtes* was restricted to 40 per cent. All further discussion of Algeria's future relationship with France was ruled out.

Ferhat Abbas shortly afterwards founded the Friends of the Manifesto of Freedom (AML), to work for the foundation of an autonomous Algerian republic linked federally with France. The new movement was based mainly on the support of middle-class Muslims, though it also gained a certain following among the masses. At the same time, Messali Hadj's PPA gained many followers among the masses during 1944 and 1945.

FRENCH INTRANSIGENCE

All possibility of an evolutionary settlement was destroyed by blunders of post-war French policy and the opposition of the French settlers to any concessions to Muslim aspirations. The ruthless suppression of the riots at Sétif in May 1945, which claimed the lives of some 15,000 Muslims, and the subsequent arrest of Ferhat Abbas and the dissolution of the AML drove many of the nationalist leaders to regard force as the only means of gaining their objective.

Nevertheless, attempts to reach a compromise solution continued for some time. In March 1946 Ferhat Abbas, released under an amnesty, launched the Democratic Union of the Algerian Manifesto (UDMA), with a programme providing for the creation of an autonomous, secular Algerian state within the French Union. Despite successes in elections to the French Assembly, the UDMA failed to achieve any of its objectives. It withdrew from the Assembly in September 1946 and refused to participate in the next elections. The breach was filled by the more radical Movement for the Triumph of Democratic Liberties (MTLD), the party formed by Messali Hadj at the end of the war, which demanded the creation of a sovereign constituent assembly and the evacuation of French troops—aims which stood no chance of adoption.

In another attempt at compromise the French Government introduced a new constitution which became law on September 20th, 1947. This gave French citizenship, and therefore the vote, to all Algerian citizens, including women, and recognized Arabic as equal in status to French. The proposed new Algerian Assembly, however, was to be divided into two colleges, each of 60 members, one to represent the 1½ million Europeans, the other the 9 million Muslims. Other provisions ruled out all possibility of anti-European legislation.

The new constitution was never brought fully into operation. Following MTLD successes in the municipal elections of October 1947, the elections to the Algerian Assembly were openly and clumsily interfered with, many candidates being arrested, election meetings forbidden and polling stations improperly operated.

As a result only a quarter of the members returned to the second college in April 1948 were MTLD or UDMA; the remainder, nominally "independent", were nonentities. Such methods continued to be employed in local and national elections during the next six years, as well as in the Algerian elections to the French National Assembly in June 1951. Some of the ameliorative provisions of the 1947 constitution were never put into effect. The aim was to destroy, or at least render harmless, opposition to French rule; the result was to drive the main forces of nationalism underground.

As early as 1947 several of the younger members of the MTLD had formed the "Secret Organization" (OS), which collected arms and money from supporters and built up a network of cells throughout Algeria in preparation for armed insurrection and the establishment of a revolutionary government. Two years later the OS felt itself strong enough to launch a terrorist attack in Oran. The movement was subsequently discovered and most of its leaders were arrested. A nucleus survived, however, in the Kabyle region, ever a stronghold for dissident groups, and the organizer of the attack, Ben Bella, escaped in 1952 to Cairo.

A decisive split was taking place in the ranks of the MTLD, and the veteran Messali Hadj, now embracing nebulous doctrines of pan-Arabism, was gradually losing control of the party organization to more activist members. The first open breach occurred in 1953, and in March the following year nine former members of the OS set up the Revolutionary Council for Unity and Action (CRUA) to prepare for an immediate revolt against French rule.

WAR OF INDEPENDENCE

Plans for the insurrection were worked out at a series of CRUA meetings in Switzerland between March and October 1954. Algeria was divided into six *wilaya* (zones) and a military commander appointed for each. When the revolt was launched on November 1st the CRUA changed its name to the National Liberation Front (FLN), its armed forces being known as the National Liberation Army (ALN). Beginning in the Aurès, the revolt had spread by early 1955 to the Constantine area, the Kabyle and the whole of the Moroccan frontiers west of Oran. By the end of 1956 the ALN was active throughout the settled areas of Algeria.

Ferhat Abbas and Ahmed Francis of the more bourgeois UDMA and the religious leaders of the Ulema joined the FLN in April 1956, making it representative of all shades of Algerian nationalist feeling apart from Messali Hadj's Algerian National Movement (MNA). In August a secret congress of the FLN, held at Soummam in the Kabyle, formed a central committee and the National Council of the Algerian Revolution; drew up a socialist programme for the future Algerian republic; and approved plans for the launching of a terrorist offensive in Algiers.

In the early stages of the war the French Government was convinced that only external support kept the FLN offensive going. The Foreign Minister was therefore despatched to Cairo in an attempt to persuade President Nasser to withdraw his support for the Algerian revolution. This mission was in vain, and Guy Mollet, the French Prime Minister, then resorted to collusion with the Israelis and the British in the abortive invasion of Egypt at the end of October 1956. The Suez operation not only did not topple Nasser, nor stop the Algerian struggle, it actually strengthened the FLN's position by increasing support from newly independent and non-aligned states.

Between September 1956 and June 1957 bomb explosions engineered by the FLN caused much loss of life. This terrorism was brought to a stop only by severe French repression of the Muslim population, including the use of torture and internment, measures which aroused condemnation of French policy both at home and abroad. Guerrilla activities continued but electrified barriers were set up along the Tunisian and Moroccan borders and ALN bands attempting to cross into Algeria met with heavy losses.

In June 1957 the Bourges-Manoury administration in France, which had replaced that of Mollet the previous month, put forward legislation intended to link Algeria indissolubly with France, but the bill was never passed. Following the Soummam conference, a joint Moroccan-Tunisian plan had been put forward for the establishment of a North African federation linked with France. FLN leaders began negotiations in Morocco in October 1957. However, Ben Bella and his companions were kidnapped on their way from Morocco to Tunisia, when the French pilot of their plane, which the Sultan of Morocco had chartered for them, landed it at Algiers. The French authorities could hardly reject this *fait accompli*, and the hijacked leaders were arrested and interned in France. Neither the internment of FLN leaders nor the bombing by French aircraft, in February 1958, of the Tunisian border village of Sakhiet, in which 79 villagers were killed, had any effect on the FLN's capacity to continue fighting, and the failure of these desperate measures only made the possibility of French negotiations with the FLN more likely. This in turn provoked a backlash from the Algerian Europeans (only half of whom were of French origin).

In May 1958 they rebelled and set up committees of public safety in the major Algerian towns. Supported by the army and exploiting the widespread fear of civil war, the colonists caused the overthrow of the discredited Fourth French Republic and General De Gaulle's return to power, believing that he would further their aim of complete integration of Algeria into France. They were very soon to be bitterly disappointed. Although De Gaulle did step up military action against the FLN by the 500,000 French troops in Algeria, this was only at the cost of increased terrorism in Algiers and of growing tension on the Tunisian and Moroccan borders. The FLN responded in August 1958 by establishing in Tunis the Provisional Government of the Algerian Republic (GPRA), headed by Ferhat Abbas and including Ben Bella and the other leaders who had been interned in

France. De Gaulle was already beginning to recognize the strength of Algerian nationalism and was moving cautiously towards accepting FLN demands.

NEGOTIATIONS AND THE COLONISTS' LAST STAND

Initially De Gaulle's public statements on Algeria were vague. When he did make an unequivocal pronouncement, in September 1959, and upheld the right of Algerians to determine their own future, the colonists did not take long to react. In January 1960 they rebelled again, this time against De Gaulle, and erected barricades in Algiers streets. However, without the support of the army the insurrection collapsed within nine days. The first exploratory talks between French and FLN delegates took place in secret near Paris in the summer of 1960 but were abortive.

In November de Gaulle announced that a referendum was to be held on the organization of government in Algeria, pending self-determination, and in December he visited Algeria himself to prepare the way. In the referendum the electorate were asked to approve a draft law providing for self-determination and immediate reforms to give Algerians the opportunity to participate in government. There were mass abstentions from voting in Algeria, however, and in February 1961 new French approaches to the FLN were made through the President of Tunisia. Secret talks led to direct negotiations between French and FLN representatives at Evian, on the Franco-Swiss border. These began in May but were finally broken off in August over the question of the Sahara and because of the French attack on Bizerta.

Europeans in Algeria and segments of the French army had meanwhile formed the Secret Army Organization (OAS) to resist a negotiated settlement and the transfer of power from European hands. On April 22nd, 1961, four generals, Chalel, Zeller, Jouhaud and Salan, organized the seizure of Algiers, but this attempt at an army *putsch* proved abortive, most regular officers remaining loyal to de Gaulle. Offensive operations against the Algerian rebels, which had been suspended when the Evian talks began, were resumed by the French Government in response to rebel pressure, and fighting continued, though on a reduced scale. At the same time the OAS began its campaign of indiscriminate terrorism against native Algerians. The Mayor of Evian had already been killed by an OAS bomb, and attacks were now also mounted in Paris.

Secret contacts between the French government and the FLN were re-established in October. Negotiations were resumed in December 1961 and January 1962 in Geneva and Rome, the five members of the GPRA interned in France taking part through a representative of the King of Morocco. Meetings at ministerial level were held in strict secrecy in Paris in February and the final stage of the negotiations was concluded at Evian on March 18th with the signing of a ceasefire agreement and a declaration of future policy. The declaration provided for the establishment of an independent Algerian state after a transitional period, and for the safeguarding of individual rights and liberties. Other declarations issued the following day dealt with the rights of French citizens in Algeria and with future Franco-Algerian cooperation. In the military sphere, France was to retain the naval base at Mers el Kebir for 15 years and the nuclear testing site in the Sahara, together with various landing rights, for five years.

In accordance with the Evian agreements a provisional government was formed on March 28th, with Abderrahman Farès as provisional President and an executive composed of FLN members, other Muslims and Europeans. Ben Bella and the other detained Algerian leaders had been released on March 18th and flown to Morocco. The Soviet Union, the East European and many African and Asian countries quickly gave *de jure* recognition to the GPRA.

The signing of the Evian agreements was the signal for a final desperate fling by the OAS. A National Council of French Resistance in Algeria was set up, with General Salan as Commander-in-Chief, and OAS commando units attempted by attacks on the Muslim population and the destruction of public buildings to provoke a general breach of the ceasefire. After the failure of the OAS to establish an "insurrectional zone" in the Orléansville area and the capture of General Salan on April 20th, and with a renewal of FLN terrorist activity and reprisals, increasing numbers of Europeans began to leave Algeria for France. Abortive secret negotiations by OAS leaders with the FLN, aimed at securing guarantees for the European population, which began in May, disclosed a split in the OAS which heralded the virtual end of European terrorist activity. By the end of June over half the European population of Algeria had left.

The final steps towards Algerian independence were now taken. In a referendum on July 1st, 91 per cent of the electorate voted for independence, which was proclaimed by General de Gaulle on July 3rd, 1962.

THE INDEPENDENT STATE

The achievement of power by the FLN revealed serious tensions and weaknesses within the government, while the problems facing the new state after eight years of civil war were formidable.

The dominant position in the GPRA of the "centralist" group, headed by Ben Khedda and consisting of former members of the MTLD, was threatened by the release of the five GPRA members who had been detained in France—Ben Bella, Mohammed Khider, Mohammed Boudiaf, Ait Ahmed and Rabah Bitat. Boudiaf and Ait Ahmed rallied temporarily to the support of Ben Khedda, while the others formed yet another opposition faction besides that of Ferhat Abbas, who had been dropped from the GPRA leadership in 1961.

The ALN leadership was also split. The commanders of the main armed forces in Tunisia and Morocco were opposed to the politicians of the GPRA, and the commanders of the internal guerrilla groups were opposed to all external and military factions.

Serious differences had appeared when the National Council of the Algerian Revolution (CRNA) met in Tripoli in May 1962 to consider policies for the new state. A commission headed by Ben Bella produced a programme which included large-scale agrarian reform, involving expropriation and the establishment of peasant cooperatives and state farms; a state monopoly of external trade; and a foreign policy aimed towards Maghreb unity, neutralism and anti-colonialism, especially in Africa. Despite the opposition of Ben Khedda's group, the Tripoli programme became the official FLN policy.

When independence came on July 3rd the GPRA cabinet, with the exception of Ben Bella, flew to Algiers, where they installed themselves alongside the official Provisional Executive, and Ben Khedda attempted to reassert control over the ALN by dismissing the Commander-in-Chief, Col. Boumedienne. Ben Bella, however, flew to Morocco to join Boumedienne and on July 11th they crossed into Algeria and established headquarters in Tlemcen. Here Ben Bella set up the Political Bureau as the chief executive organ of the FLN and a rival to the GPRA. After negotiations he was joined by some of the GPRA leaders; this left Ben Khedda isolated in Algiers, with Boudiaf and Ait Ahmed in opposition.

Several of the *wilaya* leaders, however, felt that, having provided the internal resistance, they represented the true current of the revolution, and they were opposed to the Political Bureau and Boumedienne. While ALN forces loyal to the Bureau occupied Constantine and Bône in the east on July 25th, Algiers remained in the hands of the leadership of *wilaya* IV, who refused the Bureau entry. When Boumedienne's forces marched on Algiers from Oran at the beginning of September there were serious clashes with *wilaya* IV troops. Total civil war was averted, however, partly because of mass demonstrations against the fighting which were organized by the Algerian General Workers' Union (UGTA).

The struggle for power had gone against Ben Khedda. Before the elections were held on September 20th, 1962, a third of the 180 candidates on the single list drawn up in August were purged, including Ben Khedda himself, and their places filled with lesser-known figures. Although the elections failed to produce much public enthusiasm, some 99 per cent of the electorate were declared to have voted in favour of the proposed powers of the Constituent Assembly. The functions of the GPRA were transferred to the Assembly when it met on September 25th, and Ferhat Abbas was elected its President. The Algerian Republic was proclaimed and the following day Ben Bella was elected Prime Minister, with a cabinet drawn from his personal associates and former ALN officers.

BEN BELLA IN POWER

The new government immediately set about consolidating its position. Messali Hadj's PPA (formerly the MNA), the Algerian Communist Party, largely discredited because of its role in the war, and Boudiaf's Party of the Socialist Revolution were all banned in November; the *wilaya* system was abolished the following month, and, apart from the UGTA, all organizations affiliated to the FLN were brought firmly under control.

The economic plight of the country was severe. Some 90 per cent (one million) of the Europeans, representing virtually all the entrepreneurs, technicians, administrators, teachers, doctors and skilled workers had left the country. Factories, farms and shops had closed, leaving 70 per cent of the population unemployed. Public buildings and records had been destroyed by the OAS. At the end of the war, in which over a million had died, there had been two million in internment camps and 500,000 refugees in Tunisia and Morocco. Food, money and clothing were sent by many countries to alleviate the immediate suffering. In December 1962 an emergency austerity plan was drawn up and the government was enabled to continue functioning by large loans and technical assistance from France.

By packing the first UGTA congress with FLN militants and unemployed, the FLN managed in January 1963 to gain control of the UGTA executive, which had been opposed to the dictatorial nature of the new government. The decrees of March legalized the workers' committees which, aided by the UGTA, had taken over the operation of many of the deserted European estates in the summer and autumn of 1962. The system of workers' management known as *autogestion*, under which the workers elected their own management board to work alongside a state-appointed director, became the basis of "Algerian socialism".

In April 1963 Ben Bella increased his powers by taking over the post of general secretary of the FLN, ousting Mohammed Khider, who later went into exile but retained control of FLN funds in Switzerland. In August Ben Bella secured the adoption by the Assembly of a draft constitution providing for a presidential régime, with the FLN as the sole political party. The new constitution was approved in a referendum and on September 13th Ben Bella was elected President for a period of five years, assuming the title of commander-in-chief as well as becoming head of state and head of government.

These moves towards dictatorial government aroused opposition. Ferhat Abbas, the leading spokesman for a more liberal policy, resigned from the presidency of the Assembly and was subsequently expelled from the FLN. In the Kabyle, where discontent was accentuated by Berber regionalism, a revolt broke out during the late summer led by Ait Ahmed's Front of Socialist Forces (FFS) and former *wilaya* chief Col. Mohand Ou El Hadj. After some clashes Ben Bella reached agreement with Mohand but Ait Ahmed remained in the *maquis*. In October, partly in an attempt to regain popularity, Ben Bella nationalized the remaining European estates, placing them under *autogestion*, and suppressed the remaining French-controlled newspapers.

Long-standing disputes between Algeria and Morocco over areas on their common frontiers deteriorated into open conflict in October 1963, a fact which had made the need for agreement with Col.

Mohand Ou El Hadj all the more pressing. The hostilities, near the strategic posts of Hassi-Beida and Tinjoub, were not on a large scale and were soon brought to an end through the mediation of interested African states, but they left a legacy of bitterness between the two countries. The tension between Algeria and its neighbours lessened, however, as a result of the Arab summit conference in Cairo in January 1964 and the implementation of an agreement settling the border dispute between Algeria and Morocco in March.

THE FALL OF BEN BELLA

In the last year of its existence the Ben Bella régime appeared to be achieving both a certain measure of internal stability and an improvement in the country's external relations. In April 1964 Ben Bella visited the Soviet Union where he obtained financial aid for the construction of a metallurgical plant at Bône and assistance for other technical and educational projects. A World Bank loan towards the cost of the Arzew gas liquefaction plant, to exploit the extensive resources of natural gas beneath the Sahara, was also obtained. The plant was opened in September and the following month the first cargo of liquefied methane gas was discharged in England, under a trade agreement.

Relations with Morocco improved during 1964. Prisoners were exchanged in April; a demilitarized zone was delimited by a joint commission drawn from Ethiopia and Mali; the border was reopened in June; and, following discussions on economic and technical cooperation, a trade agreement with Morocco was signed on November 25th. The heads of state of Algeria, Morocco and Tunisia had met together for the first time at the Organization of African Unity conference in Cairo in July, and in November their economic ministers decided in Rabat to establish a permanent joint consultative committee to coordinate economic policies.

At the long-awaited first Congress of the FLN in April 1964, despite opposition from the right and silence from army delegates, Ben Bella secured acceptance of the "Algiers Charter", which criticized past mistakes of the FLN, defined relations between party, state and army, and attempted to formulate a theoretical basis for "Algerian socialism", centred on *autogestion*. This was the last occasion on which most of the "historic chiefs" met together. Soon afterwards Ait Ahmed's FFS again led a revolt in the Kabyle and Col. Chabaani, the army commander in the south, also rebelled against the Government. Both Chabaani and Ait Ahmed were eventually captured; the former was executed but the latter was reprieved in view of his popularity. Most of the other "historic chiefs" were eliminated from public life during 1964.

In the early months of 1965 the Algerian Government was preoccupied with preparations for an Afro-Asian conference, planned for the tenth anniversary of the Bandung Conference and due to open in Algiers on June 29th, when Ben Bella was to stand revealed both as the undisputed leader of Algeria and a force to be reckoned with in Afro-Asian affairs. The

conference was not to take place. On June 19th Ben Bella was deposed and arrested in a swift and bloodless military *coup d'état*, led by Col. Houari Boumedienne whose army had brought Ben Bella to power in 1962.

The *coup* successfully pre-empted Ben Bella's own plans for a political takeover to coincide with the opening of the Afro-Asian conference. Ben Bella's takeover would have brought a shift to the left and the introduction of Marxist structures of political control. Ait Ahmed would have been freed and some right-wing ministers and Boumedienne detained. Ben Bella had been preparing for this for some time; he had announced that a popular militia was to be created, and he had dismissed Medeghri, the Minister of the Interior and one of Boumedienne's supporters. Finally, at the end of May, he had attempted to force the resignation of Bouteflika, the Foreign Minister, who was closely associated with Boumedienne. In the face of Algeria's poor economic situation and Ben Bella's dictatorial tendencies, many administrators and politicians were not averse to the *coup*, and his elimination of most of the traditional leaders, his repeated attacks on the UGTA and his failure to turn the FLN into a broadly-based party left him without organized support once the army had turned against him.

Bereft of its leader, the FLN accepted the *coup*, and the UGTA, while expressing no real support for Boumedienne, did not oppose it. A number of known left-wingers, including former officials of the banned Algerian Communist Party, were arrested in September 1965 and the most militant of the opposition groups, the Organization of Popular Resistance was broken up. Although rapid Chinese recognition of the new régime had given rise to conjectures of a move to the left in Algeria's international relations, this did not materialize. Relations with Cairo, with which Ben Bella's links had been close and where concern for his safety had been voiced, became more distant, though not unfriendly.

THE BOUMEDIENNE RÉGIME

Supreme political authority in Algeria was taken over by a Council of the Revolution, consisting mostly of military figures and presided over by Col. Boumedienne. Under the Council's authority a new Government of 20 members was announced on July 10th, with Boumedienne as Prime Minister and Minister of Defence, besides being President of the Council; Rabah Bitat as Minister of State; and Bouteflika continuing as Foreign Minister. Nine members of the Government, which included technocrats and members of the radical wing of the FLN, had held office under Ben Bella. To ensure a satisfactory relationship between the government and the FLN, a five-man party secretariat under Cherif Belkacem was set up on July 17th.

The aims of the new régime, as described by Boumedienne, were to re-establish the principles of the revolution, to remedy the abuses of personal power associated with Ben Bella, to end internal divisions, and to create an "authentic socialist society" based on a sound economy. To those who feared that it was intended to nationalize land under private ownership and to abolish private property he was reassuring, stating that the traditional sector of the economy would be modified only by the formation of non-compulsory cooperative societies. In international relations a policy of non-alignment would be pursued and support for people struggling for freedom and independence would continue. Beyond this, Algeria was committed to the realization of Mahgreb and Arab unity and to the strengthening of ties with the socialist camp.

The remainder of 1965 was taken up with domestic consolidation and attempts to break out of the diplomatic isolation which had followed the *coup*. The conclusion of a treaty with France on July 23rd providing for the exploitation of Algeria's oil and natural gas was followed by a visit to Paris by Bouteflika for talks with President de Gaulle on future cooperation. Boumedienne visited Moscow in December 1965, and in January 1966 American aid, in surplus wheat and technical assistance, which had been in abeyance since June 1965, was resumed.

Although the army remained the basis of Boumedienne's power, an attempt was made in 1966 to strengthen the FLN party organization and, despite general apathy, to recruit new members. Boumedienne stated that under the one-party system contradictions between army and government should not arise, the task of the FLN being to "animate and direct". Feeling against the new régime, shown in demonstrations and student strikes in Algiers in January and February, became less apparent, particularly after a number of arrests of trade union leaders in July.

Signs that discord remained, however, were provided by the defection in August of Hadj Smain, Minister of Reconstruction and Housing before his resignation in April, and of Ahmed Mahsas and Bechir Boumaza, Ministers of Agriculture and Information respectively, in September and October. Slimane Rebba, national secretary of the UGTA, also defected in October. Ait Ahmed, in detention since 1964, had escaped from Algeria in April. Boumedienne nevertheless dismissed the opposition groups in exile as "out of circulation". When Mohammed Khider was assassinated in Madrid in January 1967, it was suggested that he had been killed to prevent him handing over the FLN funds under his control to three of these groups.

Apart from preparations for elections to the Communal Councils, the régime showed no signs of seeking a popular mandate and the Algerian National Assembly remained in abeyance. New penal and civil legal codes were promulgated in 1966, the judiciary was Algerianized and tribunals to try "economic crimes" with powers to impose the death penalty were set up in July. New conditions of service and training schemes for public employees were introduced with the aim of improving the standard of administration. A new university, at Oran, was opened in December.

In accordance with its socialist policies, the régime increased state participation during 1966 in fields previously left to private enterprise. A state-owned construction company was set up, and it was decided in March that the distribution of the income of the oil and gas industry, both inside and outside Algeria, should be subject to government supervision. In May the nationalization was announced of eleven foreign-owned mines and of property of absentee owners, and all insurance activities were placed under state control. A National Bank of Algeria, specializing in short-term credit for the nationalized sector of the economy, was inaugurated in July.

Industrial activity continued at a low level and the country remained heavily dependent on external aid for industrial development. A mission from the World Bank investigated development possibilities and bilateral agreements were signed with several countries in 1966. A new investment code, designed to attract both domestic and foreign capital and promulgated in September, contained assurances of indemnification in the event of nationalization. Agriculture was depressed and a poor wheat harvest made necessary substantial purchases on the world market. State loans were made available in October to peasant farmers and cooperatives for the purchase of seed and equipment in an attempt to increase production, and land redistribution was postponed.

CAUTION IN FOREIGN POLICY

The need to consolidate and build up national strength which influenced its domestic policies also caused Boumedienne's Government to conduct Algeria's foreign relations with caution, although it remained committed to "anti-imperialism" and a militant stand on the Palestine question.

The relationship with France, Algeria's main customer and the source of substantial assistance, remained paramount. In April 1966 an agreement was concluded which provided for French technical and educational assistance for 20 years. Another agreement with France in July covered the setting-up of a new television system. Oil prospecting in the Sahara by the joint French-Algerian oil concern, ASCOOP, resulted in a new find in November. On December 23rd an agreement was signed which cancelled Algeria's pre-independence debts and reduced indebtedness to France to DA 400 million. Relations with France subsequently deteriorated, however. Domestic pressures caused the French government to revoke the 1964 agreement on Algerian wine exports in 1967, there was increasing Algerian criticism of French petroleum interests because of the slow growth of Algerian oil production, and French fears of the Soviet navy being allowed to use the Mers el Kebir base, handed over by France on January 31st, 1968, led to the cancellation of a visit of the French Foreign Minister towards the end of the year.

The following year saw an improvement: French relations with the Arab world in general were growing more cordial and Algeria seemed to desire a continuation of its links with the former colonial power, possibly as a counterbalance to growing Soviet influence. The French cultural influence remained:

there were still many French teachers, although the teaching of Arabic was being extended in the schools; large numbers of Algerians worked in France; there was a preference for such French consumer goods as were still being imported; and France continued to give assistance, including training and equipment for Algeria's armed forces.

Algerian involvement in the six-day Palestine war in June 1967 was small. Several squadrons of MiGs and some troops were sent to Egypt, and, when it was falsely alleged that Britain and the United States were militarily involved in support of Israel, action was taken against their interests in Algeria. When the ceasefire came, however, there were street demonstrations against Nasser's "treason" and also against the Soviet Union for lack of support for the Arab countries. At the Khartoum conference and also at the United Nations, Algeria's voice was one of the most belligerent, calling for a people's war such as had been fought against the French, and as a token of support detachments of Algerian troops were maintained in the Suez Canal area until August 1970.

Boumedienne visited Moscow after the Palestine war in an attempt to get a clearer understanding of Soviet policy over Israel. Algeria's economic and military ties with the Soviet Union were growing closer. Soviet advisers were playing a leading role in the development of Algeria's small industrial base and its considerable mineral resources, and Soviet agreement in 1968 to take approximately half the country's wine exports was a major relief for the agricultural sector. The Algerian army was receiving training and equipment from the U.S.S.R., while Soviet naval units made use of the harbours of Algiers and Oran and the Soviet air force enjoyed access to facilities in the interior formerly used by the French, the base at Tamanrasset in the south being especially useful as a staging post.

A highly critical, often openly hostile attitude to the United States was maintained, and diplomatic relations were severed in 1967. Nevertheless, American oil expertise was respected and, as a substantial American investment in Algeria's oil industry remained, and a contract to sell liquefied natural gas to the United States was signed in 1969.

In Africa the Boumedienne Government took a consistently anti-colonial line, breaking relations with Britain over Rhodesia in 1965 (but restoring them in 1968), and providing training and other facilities for the liberation movements of southern Africa, as well as to the Eritrean Liberation Front and the National Liberation Front of Chad. A determined effort was made to improve relations with neighbouring countries in the Mahgreb. In January 1969 President Boumedienne paid his first official visit to Morocco for talks with King Hassan, and the following June frontier posts were reopened for the first time since 1963. In May 1970 King Hassan and President Boumedienne signed an agreement at Tlemcen settling the long-standing border dispute and pledging mutual cooperation on the question of the Spanish presence in North Africa. Further agreements were signed between the two leaders in

June 1972, one defining the Algerian—Moroccan border, the other providing for joint exploitation of the Gara-Djebilet mines in the border regions. Algeria ratified her border settlement with Morocco in May 1973. An agreement with Mauritania was signed in December 1969 and a friendship treaty with Tunisia agreeing on common borders in January 1970. Whilst Algeria welcomed the Libyan revolution in 1969, the subsequent orientation of the Libyan leaders towards Egypt and the Sudan rather than the Mahgreb, was not conducive to close relations between the two régimes; nevertheless, an agreement to coordinate oil policies was signed.

INTERNAL OPPOSITION OVERCOME

The uneasy alliance between opponents of Ben Bella which had enabled Boumedienne to take over in 1965 broke down in 1967. Boumedienne's main support came from the "Oujda group"—Bouteflika, Medeghri, Kaid Ahmed and Cherif Belkacem; ex-members of the GPRA, such as Ben Yahia, Lamine Khane and Belaid Abdessalam; and the new professionals in the administration and the army. Opposition came from certain left-wing ministers, such as Ali Yahia and Abdelaziz Zerdani, the UGTA, the students, and some sections of the army, notably the former *wilaya* leaders. These feared the imposition of a technocratic and centralized form of socialism, different from the syndicalist concepts embodied in *autogestion*, and felt that collegial rule was being supplanted by the dictatorship of the small group round Boumedienne.

During the first half of 1967 the conflict was muted. There was student unrest in February and May, and in the communal elections in February, in which the opposition elements urged abstention, although a turn-out of 71 per cent was officially claimed there were reports of low polls in the Kabylie and Oran regions and of no more than a 50 per cent poll in the Algiers region. Unity brought about by the Palestine war was short-lived. When Abdessalem, Minister of Industry and Energy, attacked union officials and left-wing employees in the socialist sector at the end of June, the UGTA threatened to call a general strike, which was averted only by Boumedienne's mediation and the appointment of a committee of enquiry. In the autumn Ali Yahia resigned from the Ministry of Agriculture over the refusal of Kaid Ahmed, Minister of Finance to supply funds to help the *autogéré* sector of agriculture. A demand by former *wilaya* leaders for a meeting of the Council of the Revolution was refused by Boumedienne, who was uncertain of getting a majority. In December Kaid Ahmed was put in charge of the FLN, replacing the executive of Cherif Belkacem and several former *wilaya* leaders.

On December 14th, 1967, Col. Tahar Zbiri, army chief of staff and a prominent former *wilaya* leader, launched an armed rising in the Mitidja. It was put down two days later, but Zbiri was not captured and was joined in hiding by Abedlaziz Zerdani, the Minister of Labour, and other supporters. Cols. Mohand Ou El Hadj, Salah Boubnida and Katib

Youcef also disappeared. The rising had failed because the key posts in the army were held by the younger professionals loyal to Boumedienne, and it was followed by a wave of arrests in the unions and the administration, and selective dismissals in the FLN and the army in order to secure his position. On March 7th Boumedienne appointed three well-known supporters to vacant ministerial offices: Cherif Belkacem (Finance), Tayebi Larbi (Agriculture) and Mohand Said Mazouni (Labour).

Opposition to Boumedienne was by no means crushed, however. FLN attempts in February 1968 to impose a new loyal student committee at Algiers University provoked a long strike by students and teachers, and in the spring there were numerous reports of guerrilla activity in the Aurès and the Kabyle. The Organization of Popular Resistance (ORP) appeared to be active both in these areas and among the students. An attempt to assassinate Boumedienne was made on April 25th in Algiers, but he escaped with only minor injuries.

In the latter part of 1968 there were signs that the Government's position had strengthened and President Boumedienne made several visits to the provinces without special security precautions. In March 1969 a number of secret trials were held and numbers of less important prisoners were subsequently released. The second stage of the reform of governmental institutions (the first being the 1967 communal elections) was put into operation in May 1969 when elections were held for the 15 administrative districts (*wilaya*) and 72 per cent of the electorate voted for candidates on a single FLN list. In June 1970, following the celebration of his first five years in power, Boumedienne undertook an extensive tour of western Algeria, and when cabinet changes were made in July, his key colleagues retained their places, a fact which served to emphasize the regime's stability. On the anniversary of the revolution in November 1970 he felt able to amnesty 100 people, including three close associates of Ben Bella arrested in 1965— Hadji Ben Alla, Mohamed Nekkache and Abderahmane Sherif; Ben Bella himself remained in detention, however. Others freed included three leaders of the ORP, one being Bachir Hadj Ali, former secretary of the Communist Party, and more recent opponents of the régime who had been tried in 1969. The release of these former enemies gave some indication of the weakness of the underground opposition.

Only among school and university students did discontent remain in evidence. A school strike in December led to violent clashes with the police, and in January 1971 the arrest of eight Algiers university students resulted in a strike at the university, the dissolution by the government of the National Union of Algerian Students (UNEA), the introduction of a university security force and the banning of all meetings, demonstrations and distributions of leaflets on the campus. Six of the students arrested were accused of having connections with the Party of the Socialist Vanguard (PAGS) formed from the remnants of the ORP. The attitude of many students otherwise sympathetic to the aims and achievements of the FLN was doubtless affected by poor employment prospects.

TAKE-OVER OF FRENCH OIL INTERESTS

The improvement in President Boumedienne's position at home enabled him to adopt a more militant attitude towards France. He could afford to demand more for Algerian oil, and the resultant dispute over the price to be paid by the French oil companies culminated in the decision to take control of them by nationalization.

The two companies concerned, the Compagnie Française de Pétroles (CFP) and the Compagnie de Recherches et d'Activités Pétrolières (ERAP), were responsible for some two-thirds of Algeria's total production. In the first half of 1970 the Algerian government pressed them to accept an increase in the price at which each barrel exported was assessed for fiscal purposes (the tax reference price). Negotiations broke down and in July the government unilaterally decided on a new price of $2.85 per barrel, 77 cents above the former level. Talks were resumed at government level in September but, given Algeria's determination to become a "Mediterranean Cuba" rather than submit to what she regarded as French neo-colonialism, no progress was made and they were abandoned on February 4th, 1971. After the agreement of February 14th in Teheran between the international oil companies and the Gulf states, which raised posted prices by only 35 cents, the French thought they were in a stronger position, but on February 24th Boumedienne announced the takeover by the Algerian government of a 51 per cent holding in CFP and ERAP and the complete nationalization of the companies' gas and pipeline interests.

The French Government regarded this move as a breach of the 1965 agreement but could only ask for fair compensation. The subsequent Algerian offer was found unacceptable and in April 1971 France discontinued negotiations. Relations appeared to have reached their lowest ebb. It was announced that many French technicians and teachers were to leave Algeria, and attacks were made on some of the 700,000 Algerians in France. The French Government applied a boycott against Algerian oil and tried to get other major consumers to do the same. Talks between the two French companies and SONATRACH, the Algerian state oil concern, were resumed, however, and agreements were reached in June and September under which the role of CFP and ERAP became that of minority partners of the Algerian state in return for guaranteed oil supplies. After approval by the two governments a final agreement, which also provided for compensation and reduced back claims of taxes, was signed on December 15.

The agreement was the culmination of Algerian measures to gain control by nationalization of all major French industrial and commercial interests in the country and the "privileged relationship" between Algeria and France, provided for in the 1962 Evian agreements, was at an end. In addition, by the end of 1971, the Boumedienne government had nationalized or otherwise assumed control of other foreign oil, industrial and commercial interests in Algeria, including those of Britain and the United States.

In 1973 and early 1974 the Foreign Ministers of Algeria and France exchanged visits in an attempt to re-establish good relations. Some progress was made with issues left over from the War of Independence and the nationalization dispute. SONATRACH and French oil companies signed new agreements for joint exploration and the settlement of compensation. Relations between the two countries were disturbed, however, when an outbreak of racialist violence against Algerian workers in France led the Algerian Government to suspend emigration to France in September 1973.

In December 1974 the French Minister of the Interior, Michel Poniatowski, visited Algeria accompanied by the Minister responsible for immigration, who discussed the immigrant question with the Algerians. After the visit Poniatowski announced that there were no unresolved differences between the two countries. In April 1975, Valéry Giscard d'Estaing became the first French President to visit Algeria since independence. According to Boumedienne, this event marked the definitive reconciliation of the French and Algerian peoples.

THE PALESTINE QUESTION

The Boumedienne Government's stand on the Palestine question remained uncompromisingly militant. Algeria accepted neither the 1967 UN resolution nor the ceasefire, and when, after the hostilities along the Suez Canal in 1969 and 1970, a further ceasefire was agreed in August 1970, Algerian troops were withdrawn. Radio stations of Palestine liberation movements banished from Cairo in July 1970 were allowed to broadcast from Algiers and relations with Jordan were broken off in June 1971 after the final destruction of Palestinian guerrilla bases in Jordan by King Hussein's forces. During the October War in 1973 Algeria was active on the diplomatic front, encouraging African countries to break off relations with Israel. It participated fully with other Arab oil-producing states in cut-backs in production and boycotts aimed at countries regarded as hostile to the Arab cause. Relations with Jordan were restored after the dispatch of Jordanian troops to the Syrian front, but Algeria continued to support the Palestinians against any Jordanian territorial claims.

Despite Algeria's policy towards Palestine and the welcome accorded to almost any exiled foreign opposition group, it continued to co-operate in the economic field with any state willing to do so. Fears that Algeria might fall under Soviet dominance proved groundless. Despite strong disagreements with the U.S.A. over Viet-Nam and the Palestinian question, full diplomatic relations were restored at the end of 1974 and trade between the two countries increased dramatically.

During 1973 Algiers was the scene of two important conferences, the fourth Non-Aligned Conference in September and the meeting of Arab Heads of State in November. Colonel Boumedienne chaired both meetings, which gave an indication of Algeria's leading role among the developing nations. In April 1974 Boumedienne addressed the UN General Assembly, calling for the nationalization of natural resources throughout the world and a new economic system to redistribute wealth from the rich to the poor nations. He reiterated this theme in discussions with world leaders and at the Developing Nations' Conference held in Algiers during February 1975.

Relations with Morocco were troubled in 1974 by the reopening of the Spanish Sahara question. Morocco accused the Algerians of supporting Saharan liberation movements hostile to Moroccan claims on the territory. In May 1975, at the International Court of Justice, Algeria denied any self-interest in the matter but affirmed a desire to see genuine decolonization and liberation of the region.

HOME AFFAIRS

By 1971 Boumedienne's Government felt strong enough to initiate a more active social policy. The choice of capital-intensive export industry as the basis for economic development and of centralized bureaucratic state-control as the mode of organization had saddled Algeria with many of the same problems as countries dominated by foreign capitalism. The lives of the majority of the population, especially in the rural areas and the backward regions of the country, were untouched by the economic progress. There was mass unemployment and considerable inequality in the distribution of wealth. In 1971 a programme of agrarian reform, known as the Agrarian Revolution, was initiated. The reform was to proceed in three phases, the redistribution of state-owned and foreign land, the redistribution of private estates, and the transformation of the lives of the pastoral nomads. At the same time the government resolved to develop workers' control in industry and to reanimate the FLN as a radical force. Elected workers' councils have slowly spread through nationalized industries, but the reorganization of the FLN was a failure. In 1972 Kaid Ahmed, the leader of the party, resigned because of his lack of success. The initiative in promoting the Agrarian Revolution passed to a student *volontariat*, in which the more radical students participated enthusiastically. Boumedienne's determination to build a socialist society encountered resistance from conservative sectors of the population, especially after the redistribution of private estates and the nationalization of food distribution. Conflict came into the open in May 1975 when there were clashes at Algiers University between radical students devoted to the Agrarian Revolution and conservative students wishing to give priority to Arabization. Boumedienne came out strongly in favour of the radicals.

The personal authority of Boumedienne grew in the 1970s. The death of Ahmed Medeghri in 1974 and Belkacem's dismissal from the cabinet in July 1974 left only Bouteflika as a figure of comparable stature in the government. Encouraged by the success of local and provincial elections since 1967 and 1969 respectively, Boumedienne announced in June 1975 that national elections for an assembly and a president would be held within a year. It was widely expected that Boumedienne himself would be the only candidate for the presidency.

ECONOMIC SURVEY

Algeria covers an area of 2,381,741 square kilo-metres of which a large part is desert. At the census of 1966 the population (including Algerians abroad) was returned at 12.1 million and it grew to an estimated 16.3 million by mid-1974. The great majority of Europeans had returned to France by the early 1960s. Almost two-thirds of the population still live in rural areas but about 100,000 peasants migrate every year to the towns in search of work. About 900,000 Algerians live abroad, mainly in France. The largest towns are Algiers, the capital (1,200,000, including the suburbs), Oran (440,000 with its suburbs), Constantine (324,000), Annaba (Bône) (180,000) and Sidi-Bel-Abbès (105,000). The population is growing at an estimated rate of 3.4 per cent a year, and could reach 24.6 million by 1986 in view of the current birth rate of 48 per thousand. In an effort to reduce the flow of peasants to the towns, the Government is undertaking a far-reaching programme of land reform and redistribution.

Algeria has varied natural resources. In the coastal region are highly fertile plains and valleys, where profitable returns are made from cereals, wine, olives and fruit. However, the rest of the country serves little agricultural purpose, though in the mountains, grazing and forestry bring a small income for the population, and dates are grown in the oases of the Sahara. Mineral resources are abundant and are now the mainstay of Algeria's foreign trade. Revenues from oil and gas are being used to finance ambitious industrialization plans, although the majority of the population is still engaged in agriculture.

GOVERNMENT STRATEGY

Since independence in 1962 Algerian governments have sought to gain control of the economy and promote economic growth as a foundation for a future socialist society. They have either taken over completely or taken a controlling interest in most foreign-owned companies. In 1966 the government nationalized foreign-owned mines, unoccupied lands deserted by Europeans at independence, and insurance companies. It took control of the whole of the hydrocarbon sector in the spring of 1971.

Heavy industries are all state-run, while consumer goods industries are still largely in private hands, although parts of the textile, leather and food industries have already been nationalized. In brief, all key sectors are run by the state, which intends eventually to control all internal transport, domestic wholesale trade and foreign trade.

The Government's strategy for development involves a high degree of austerity, with heavy restrictions placed on the importation of "luxury" goods. The first Four-Year Plan, 1970–73, emphasized the establishment of a capital-intensive sector, involving the hydrocarbon, iron and steel, chemical and engineering industries, which was to serve as a basis for economic growth. During the period of the Plan, a 9 per cent annual growth rate was achieved. About 34,000 million dinars were invested, while the original target was only 26,400 million dinars (only 4,200 million dinars were invested in the initial Three-Year Plan, 1967–69).

The new Four-Year Plan, 1974–77, while still paying attention to the heavy industry base, will lay more emphasis on housing and health and on training, as well as on labour-intensive projects, small and medium-sized industries and improved agricultural methods, with the aim of achieving a greater degree of self-sufficiency in foodstuffs. Industry will receive 43.5 per cent of total investment, infrastructure 14 per cent, social services and housing 13.3 per cent and agriculture 10.9 per cent. The high level of investment (40 per cent of G.D.P.) is expected to be maintained in the new Plan and an average annual growth rate of 10 per cent is aimed at. Total expenditure, originally put at 52,000 million dinars, is now estimated at 110,000 million dinars, on the basis of the large increase in income expected as a result of oil price rises. The Plan is to be financed 90 per cent by Algeria's oil and gas exports.

The country's gross domestic product, at current prices, rose from 13,300 million dinars in 1964 to 26,865 million dinars in 1973. Per capita income in 1970 was about 1,500 dinars which the Government aims to increase to 2,500 dinars by 1980.

According to the last census in 1966, the active work force was 2.5 million, of which 1.5 million (55 per cent) were in the agricultural sector, while 200,000 were employed by industry. It is estimated that about 20 per cent of the urban population and 60 per cent of the rural population are unemployed or underemployed. However, the Government aims to create 450,000 new jobs outside agriculture during the second Four-Year Plan, and it hopes to have solved the unemployment problem by 1980.

AGRICULTURE

Algeria is still mainly an agricultural country. Over nine-tenths of the land consists of arid plateaux, mountains or desert, supporting scattered herds of sheep, goats or camel. Only the northern coastal strip, 100-200 km. wide, can be used for arable purposes. There are about 6.8 million hectares of cultivable land, representing less than one hectare per rural inhabitant. Forests cover about 2.4 million hectares. Most of the Sahara is devoted to semi-desert pasturage. The most valuable crop is the grape harvest, which represents 66 per cent of total agricultural exports by value; whilst wheat, barley and oats, grown for local consumption, cover a large area. Other crops include maize, sorghum, millet, rye and rice, as well as citrus fruit, olives, figs and dates, and tobacco. Agricultural development is restricted by problems such as erosion, adverse weather conditions, especially drought and flood, primitive methods of production, and underemployment.

Over half the country's workforce is employed in agriculture but this sector contributes only 10 per cent of G.D.P. The 1974–77 Plan allocates just over 15 per cent of total investment to agriculture, agricultural development and water projects. This apparently rather small proportion is offset by the fact that the Agrarian Reform programme, with its own budget, is to be intensified. There is an urgent need to increase food production since foodstuffs at present account for about one quarter of Algeria's total imports bill. The Government's aim is to achieve self-sufficiency in basic foodstuffs by 1980. The second Four-Year Plan aims at bringing a further 110,000 hectares of land under irrigation, and at improving a total of 500,000 hectares of land. The Plan envisages increasing cereal production by 20 per cent, milk by 20 per cent, meat by 25 per cent and market garden produce by 55 per cent by the end of 1977.

LAND REFORM

The first regulations, under which settlers were able to hold and transfer land, were introduced in October 1962. From that date the state took over any property declared vacant; at the same time all property transactions were made illegal in order to prevent profiteering by Muslims. Under French Government pressure a guarantee fund was set up to provide compensation for expropriated settlers.

Under the first decree, the settlers remained the legal owners of the land, while the state "used" it. However, in March 1963, another Government decree declared that the state was taking over ownership of abandoned land. A number of large French landowners subsequently had their land taken away, although it was still occupied. In May 1966 all remaining unoccupied property which had been evacuated by settlers was finally taken over by the state. These expropriated lands were turned into State farms run by workers' committees (*comités de gestion*).

After the total nationalization of French land in October 1963, state farm land accounted for 2.3 million ha., roughly half the cultivable land in Algeria. The modern, "self-managed" agricultural sector represents one-third of the total agricultural area, provides work for only about 135,000 in permanent employment and about 100,000 in seasonal work, but its revenue is twice that of the "traditional" private sector, which provides a living for more than 5 million people. It enjoys a number of benefits provided by the state, such as special credit facilities.

In July 1971 President Boumedienne announced an agrarian reform programme which provided for the break-up of large, Algerian-owned farms and their re-organization into co-operatives. The first stage of its implementation, the registration of land ownership, began in March 1972. The Government has made great efforts to explain the programme to the rural population and is proceeding cautiously to avoid stirring up discontent. By the end of 1974, out of a total of 5 million hectares of public land, 788,000 hectares of land had been redistributed to 54,000 families of landless peasants, or *fellahs*, and 1,748

co-operatives had been created. Of the 1.4 million hectares still to be redistributed in this first phase, only 75,000 hectares are cultivable, the remainder being unimproved land.

A census begun in September 1972 showed that a quarter of cultivable land was in the hands of 16,500 large landowners who represented only 3 per cent of the total number of farmers. In 1973 the Agrarian Revolution entered its second phase, that of redistributing over 650,000 hectares of private land to 60,000 families of landless peasants. Those receiving land under the scheme will be granted permanent use of it but they must belong to one of the new co-operatives being set up. Through these they will be given state loans and assistance in the form of seed, fertilizers and equipment. By the end of 1974, 494,101 hectares had been nationalized under the second phase of the reform and, of these, 353,196 hectares had been redistributed. As part of the land reform programme, the Government plans to resettle the rural population in 1,000 co-operative villages, of which over 200 had been completed by the end of 1974. Under the *volontariat* scheme, young people are encouraged to spend their vacations working and teaching in rural areas.

The third phase of the agrarian reform programme, launched in January 1975, aims at increasing livestock production in the steppe areas. About 20 million hectares of pasturage, mostly in southern Algeria, will be nationalized, large herds and flocks broken up, and nomads settled.

CROPS

The coastal areas of the Mediterranean produce grapes. Vines have been grown in Algeria since antiquity merely for local consumption; however, after the coming of the French in 1830, vine growing received substantial encouragement and wines still represent the principal agricultural export. Production has fallen sharply from 18.6 million hectolitres in 1960 to 5 million hectolitres in 1975.

The Boumedienne régime regards agricultural dependence on wine as incompatible with real political independence. Thus it is tearing up the least productive vines and converting the land to cereal and dairy farming, and to forestry. The target for 1980 is 140,000 hectares under vines, compared with the present total of 250,000 hectares. The tendency will be for better quality wines, and dessert grapes to be produced.

Foreign ownership of wheat land was particularly resented by the Algerian peasantry. Grown principally in the Constantine, Annaba, Sétif and Tiaret areas, wheat in 1972 covered 2,403,000 hectares. Production has fluctuated considerably since independence, falling as low as 700,000 tons in drought years. In 1972 it was 1,692,000 tons. The area under barley in 1972 was 781,000 hectares. Production was only 500,000 tons in 1970, but reached 720,000 tons in 1972. Rice, maize and sorghum are also grown. Average cereal production is 2 million tons, whereas national consumption is about 2.7 million tons.

Olives are grown in the western coastal belt. Production fluctuates because of the two-year flowering cycle of the olive. In 1973 an estimated 12,500 tons of table olives were produced, and 20,000 tons of olive oil. It is hoped to increase olive yields from 1.5 tons a hectare to 2.4 tons by 1976, with improved techniques and new varieties.

The citrus crop, grown in the coastal districts, totalled 630,000 tons in 1972. Production of potatoes reached 350,000 tons in 1972–73, double the figure for 1968–69. Also in 1972–73, 46,000 tons of dried vegetables were produced. Market gardening is being encouraged, with the aim of finding a ready export market for Algerian produce in Western Europe. Algeria is the world's third largest date producer, with an average of 110,000 tons a year.

Tobacco is the main industrial crop, employing about 13,000 people. An estimated 6,000 tons of tobacco was produced in 1972, against 3,862 tons in 1970.

LIVESTOCK, FORESTRY AND FISHING

Sheep, goats and cattle are raised but great improvements will have to be made in stock-raising methods, grassland, control of disease and water supply if the increasing demand for meat is to be met. At present, a large part of Algeria's requirements in dairy products have to be imported. In 1972 there were 863,000 head of cattle, 8,420,000 sheep and 2,200,000 goats.

The area covered by forests has dropped from 3.04 million hectares in 1961 to only 2.4 million hectares in 1970, and the Government plans to re-afforest 335,000 hectares and to rehabilitate 30,000 hectares, partly to protect cultivable land against erosion. A vast "green wall" of forest, 20 km. wide, is being planted along 1,500 km. on the northern edge of the Sahara from the Moroccan to the Tunisian frontier. Though largely brushwood, there are large areas of cork-oak trees, Aleppo pine, evergreen oak and cedar; dwarf palm is grown in the plains and alfa on the table-land.

The Government feels that Algeria is not exploiting its fishing potential and hopes to raise annual production to over 40,000 tons. The catch in 1973 was 31,000 tons. Sardines, anchovies, sprats and tunny fish are caught.

SUMMARY

Algerian agriculture suffers considerably from bureaucratic control that is both excessive and inefficient. However, the Agrarian Reform programme is regarded by the Government as a necessary prelude to improving the productivity of this sector and to integrating it into the modern economy.

MINERALS

Algeria has rich mineral resources and, since before the petroleum era, Algeria had mined and exported high-grade iron ore, phosphates, lead, zinc, and antimony. Mining is now controlled by the state enterprise SONAREM.

Iron ore is mined at Beni-Saf, Zaccar, Timezrit and near the eastern frontier at Ouenza and Bou Khadra. The average grade of ore is between 50 and 60 per cent. Production has fluctuated greatly since independence but reached nearly 4 million tons in 1974. The deposits at Ouenza represent 75 per cent of total production. Exploitation will begin by 1977 of deposits at Gara Djebelit and at Kenadza, in the west. The Gara Djebelit reserves are estimated at 2,000 million tons, over half of which are on the surface. Local consumption of iron ore was 602,800 tons in 1974. Italy is the biggest customer, followed by the United Kingdom. Production of bituminous coal, mined at Colomb Béhar-Kenadza and Ksiksou, dropped steadily from 153,000 tons in 1958 to 15,000 in 1970, but mining of deposits at Abadla, in the same region, is to begin soon.

The most important zinc deposit is found on the Algerian-Moroccan frontier at El-Abed-Oued Zounder, which is an extension of the Moroccan deposits. Production in 1973 was 26,000 tons of zinc concentrates, and most of the output is exported. A zinc oxidising plant is being built at El-Abed to feed the electrolysis plant under construction at Ghazaouet.

Exploitation of large phosphate deposits at Djebel-Onk, 340 km. from Annaba, began in 1960 and reached an estimated 1.13 million tons in 1973. It is planned to increase it to 2.40 million tons a year by 1980. The deposits are used to feed the Arzew fertilizer plant and the surplus is exported, mainly to France and Spain.

Lead is mined at El Abed on the Moroccan border; production in 1973 was 5,800 tons of concentrates. Other mineral resources include antimony, tungsten, manganese, mercury, copper and salt. An aluminium smelter is planned and a mercury mine and refinery are being developed at Ismail.

PETROLEUM AND NATURAL GAS

Production of crude oil in the Sahara on a commercial scale began in 1958. The original principal producing areas were at Hassi Massaoud in Central Algeria and round Edjeleh-Zarzaitine in the Polignac Basin near the Libyan frontier. In 1966 production was boosted by substantial quantities of crude from fields at Gassi Touil, Rhourde el Baguel and Rhourde Nouss with the opening of the third pipeline to the coast. Subsequent discoveries of oil have been made at Nezla, Hoaud Berkaoui, Ouargla, Mesdar and El Borma, and more recently at Hassi Keskessa, Guellala, Tin Fouyé and El Maharis. In 1969 Algeria joined the Organization of Petroleum Exporting Countries (OPEC).

From 1.2 million tons in 1959, Algerian production of crude oil rose to a ceiling of 26 million tons in 1964 and 1965, limited by the capacity of the two pipelines to the coast, one from the eastern fields through Tunisia to La Skhirra, and the other from Hassi Messaoud to Bejaia on the Algerian coast. The Hassi Messaoud pipeline also serves other fields further inland. The combined capacity of these two pipelines is now over 30 million tons, as a result of the installation of additional pumping stations. The government set up its own company, *Société Nationale pour la Recherche, la Production, le Transport, la Transformation et la Commercialisation des Hydrocarbures* (SONATRACH) to be responsible for the construction of a third pipeline from Hassi Messaoud to Arzew on the coast. This pipeline came into operation early in 1966, reaching its maximum capacity of 22 million tons per year in 1970. The new pipeline permitted a steady increase in total production to 47.3 million tons in 1970. Production in 1971 dropped to 36.4 million tons because of the dispute with French companies and nationalization of French oil interests. Production of crude oil reached 50.1 million tons in 1972 and 51.2 million tons in 1973 but by 1974 this had fallen to 47.2 million tons, due to cutbacks in output imposed by Algeria in connection with the Middle East crisis. By the end of the year the production rate was about 900,000 barrels a day, 18 per cent lower than in late 1973. Algeria is the seventh largest Midddle East oil producer and in 1974 was responsible for about 3.9 per cent of total output in the region.

Algeria's fourth oil pipeline, from Mesdar to Skikda, was completed in May 1972 with an initial capacity of 12 million tons a year which may be increased to 30 million tons a year.

In 1966 SONATRACH bought BP's distribution network and its share in the Algiers refinery. A year later the Esso and Mobil marketing organizations were nationalized, and in May 1968 the nine remaining networks (mostly French except for *Shell Algérie*) were also taken over and SONATRACH became the sole domestic distributor. SONATRACH acquired majority control of the Algiers refinery (capacity 2.5 million tons per year) in 1969, when it took over Total's holding. It has since gained complete control by taking over the Algerian operations of the other shareholders, CFP and Shell. Crude supplies are delivered by a 135 km. spur from the main pipeline to Bejaia. A small 100,000 tons per year refinery at Hassi Messaoud supplies the Saharan market. Refineries at Arzew (built by a Japanese consortium and completed in June 1973; annual capacity 2.5 million tons) and Skikda (under construction) are both owned by SONATRACH. The Skikda refinery will have an annual capacity of 15 million tons and is being built by SNAM Progetti, subsidiary of the Italian state-owned ENI. Algeria's fourth major refinery is to be built at Bejaia by British and Italian firms. It will go on stream in 1979 with a capacity of 7.5 million tons a year, bringing the country's total refining capacity up to 30 million tons a year.

Natural gas will become more valuable to Algeria than oil and by 1980 it is likely to be the world's biggest natural gas exporter. Reserves are currently estimated at three million million cubic metres. In 1974, output was nearly 6,000 million cubic metres. A pipeline from Hassi R'Mel, one of the world's largest gas fields, to Arzew, Algiers and Oran was opened in 1961. The *Cie. Algérienne du Méthane Liquide* (CAMEL) has a liquefaction plant at Arzew, and shipments of natural gas in liquefied from in specially constructed tankers to the U.K. began in October

1964 and to France in March 1965. Natural gas is currently produced from fields at Hassi R'Mel, Hassi Messaoud, Nord In Amenas and Rhourde el Baguel. In March 1968 a new field with estimated reserves of 30,000 million cubic metres was discovered at Gassi-El-Adem, some 60 miles south of Hassi Messaoud.

Contracts for sales of natural gas to Western Europe and the U.S.A. have shown a spectacular increase in size in recent years and should total more than 80,000 million cubic metres a year by 1980. Major contracts have been with the U.S. company El Paso (1970, for 15,000 million cubic metres a year for 25 year from 1975), with a consortium of European companies (1972 for 15,500 million cubic metres a year for 20 years from 1977) and with West Germany (for 12,000 million cubic metres a year).

To fulfil these commitments Algeria is investing heavily in pipelines, liquefaction plants and tankers. Major liquefaction plants have been built at Skikda and Arzew and in May 1972 the 40-inch pipeline from Hassi R'Mel to Skikda was opened. The pipeline, 577 kilometres long, will have a capacity of 12,700 million cubic metres a year by the end of 1975. The El Paso deal alone involves the building of pipelines and of a second Arzew liquefaction plant and the purchase of nine l.n.g. tankers. An under-sea pipeline for natural gas is being constructed, linking Skikda with Italy, via Cap Bon (Tunisia) and Sicily. Another is planned to Spain. Algeria has ordered four l.n.g. carriers, each with a capacity of 125,000 cubic metres, with a $200 million loan arranged in November 1973 with an international banking consortium. These carriers, to be built in France, will join Algeria's 40,000 cubic metre tanker, which went into service in 1972 between Skikda and France.

In June 1970 the local interests of Shell, Phillips, Elwerath, and AMIF were nationalized, following protracted negotiations which failed to achieve agreement on tax reference prices. The four companies, which together produced about 5 million tons of crude annually, were merged into SONATRACH, which thus became Algeria's largest producer.

In February 1971, Algeria nationalized the French oil companies operating in the country, as well as pipeline networks and natural gas deposits. In April 1971 President Boumedienne issued a decree laying down the conditions under which foreign oil companies could operate in Algeria. Concession-type agreements were banned. Talks were held with the French companies on compensation terms and on the future mode of their activity in Algeria, the negotiations ended in an agreement with CFP at the end of June and a settlement with Elf-ERAP in November. The basic provisions of these agreements were that the companies would provide some investment funds and technical help in exchange for oil and that compensation payments were largely cancelled out by the tax debts of the companies to Algeria. SONATRACH now directly controls 77 per cent of Algeria's oil production, compared with only 31 per cent in 1970.

Despite a law of April 1972 requiring companies wishing to explore in Algeria to form a joint company with SONATRACH, in which the latter should have a controlling interest, co-operation with foreign oil firms is increasing. The U.S. firm, Getty Oil, has operated effectively as a minority partner of SONATRACH since 1968. Under the terms of the 1972 law, agreements have been signed with Sun Oil of the U.S.A., Hispanoil of Spain, Petrobras of Brazil, Total-Algérie (a subsidiary of CFP), Copex of Poland, Elf-ERAP of France, Deminex of West Germany and Amoco of the U.S.A.

INDUSTRY

Industrialization is the keynote of the government's economic policy and the major investment effort in the 1970–73 plan was devoted to this end. Under the second Four-Year Plan, industry will receive about 43.5 per cent of total allocations.

At the time of independence the Algerian industrial sector was very small, being confined mainly to food processing, building materials, textiles and minerals. The departure of the French entailed loss of demand, capital and skill, thereby slowing down the industrialization process.

Foreign firms became increasingly reluctant in the 1960s to invest in Algeria because of the danger of nationalization. In May and June 1968 over 40 companies in the food, chemical, mechanical and construction material sectors were taken over. The installations of seven French explosives manufacturers were nationalized in April 1974.

The iron and steel industry are basic to the development of other industries and very large investments have been made in the El Hadjar complex at Annaba. The smelter and tube-mill were opened in 1969 after several delays. The steelworks, mainly Russian-built, did not go into operation until May 1972. Two converters are now in operation, producing 800,000 tons of laminated steel, and two more will be operating by 1977, bringing production up to between 1.5 million and two million tons. The furnaces are now fired by natural gas. The complex uses one-third of the total 3 million tons of iron ore produced in the Ouenza mines. Output should eventually cover most of the domestic market's requirements of steel, which are now about 1 million tons per year. A giant 10 million ton steel works is planned to be built on the coast in the west of the country. If realized, it will make Algeria a significant exporter of steel.

During the 1970–73 Plan, great emphasis was laid on the development of the hydrocarbon sector, including the building of refineries and natural gas liquefaction plants. A vast petrochemical complex being built at Skikda by SNAM Progetti of Italy and Toyo Engineering of Japan will produce polyethylene, PVC, caustic soda and chlorine and is due to come into operation by early 1976. A fertilizer plant utilizing natural gas was opened in 1970 at Arzew, where there is also a complex for the manufacture of intermediate petrochemical products. At Annaba, a 550,000 tons a year plant for phosphate fertilizers was opened in 1972 and a further plant is planned, to use the Djebel Onk phosphate deposits. Four new plants

for the production of ammonium nitrates for fertilizers are planned. In March 1974 SONATRACH and Sapiem, a subsidiary of the Italian state-owned ENI, agreed to set up a joint company, Alcip, to carry out projects in the petrochemical and natural gas sectors.

Algeria is expanding its vehicle and farm machinery industries rapidly. At Constantine, a factory producing 4,000 tractors and 9,500 diesel engines a year has recently begun operating and the West German firm Diag is building a large farm machinery plant at Sidi Bel Abbès, to commence production early in 1976. A heavy vehicle assembly plant built by Berliet at Rouiba will have a capacity of 4,550 vehicles a year by 1976 and 9,000 a year by 1980. Two-thirds of the parts used by the plant are manufactured in Algeria. At Guelma there is a plant manufacturing 30,000 motor cycles, 15,000 bicycles and 5,000 small motors annually. Pumps and irrigation equipment are produced at Médéa. International tenders have been invited for a 100,000 cars a year plant at Senia, near Oran. Firms interested include Renault, Peugeot, French Chrysler, Fiat, Nissan and Toyota.

The Government intends to establish a major shipyard at Oran and a metal works was opened at Meftah in January 1972. West German firms are setting up an electrical goods factory at Tizi Ouzou and have built a battery factory at Setif. Other growth areas are the paper industry, textiles and building materials. Three cement works are being built by West German, Japanese, and Belgian and French firms.

A paint factory was opened at Bakhdaria in September 1972, and two plastics factories at Setif. Work is under way on a 55 million dinar printing complex, which will be the largest in Africa. Following the signing of an agreement in February 1974, Algeria is to manufacture Pall Mall cigarettes under licence from the British American Tobacco Company.

In 1973, 2,374 million kWh of electricity were produced, compared with 2,019 million kWh the previous year.

TRADE

Since 1948, with two exceptions, Algerian foreign trade figures have consistently shown a surplus of imports over exports; this feature was reversed only in 1967 and 1968. The collapse of the domestic market after the departure of the French army and most of the French settlers reduced imports sharply. In 1962 petroleum exports were included in Algerian figures for the first time, i.e. after the two Saharan departments joined Algeria. Oil and natural gas exports have transformed the pattern of Algerian exports, previously limited to agricultural products and some minerals. Main exports in the past were wine, citrus fruit and iron ore, but export markets for wine are now difficult to find. Other exports include vegetables, tobacco, hides and skins, dates and phosphates. Imports of consumer goods are severely restricted. Hydrocarbons now account for more than 83 per cent of all exports. Agricultural and food products rose from 9 per cent in 1972 to 12 per cent in 1973, mainly because of renewed wine sales to France. Finished capital goods make up 36 per cent of the total value of imports; semi-finished goods 27 per cent and consumer goods account for only 17 per cent.

Algerian exports used to be about 2,000 million dinars but in 1973 totalled 7,479 million, while imports reached 8,876 million dinars, compared with 1971 figures of 4,207.5 million dinars for exports and 6,027 million dinars for imports. In 1973 the trade deficit grew by 64 per cent and the rate of coverage of imports by exports dropped to about 85 per cent from 88 per cent in 1972 (less than 70 per cent in 1971). For 1974 a small trade surplus was achieved and estimated total volume of trade was 40 million dinars, compared with 16.3 million dinars in 1973 (10.2 million dinars in 1971). The large increase in trade in 1974 is due partly to the oil price rises but also to higher prices for imported foodstuffs, raw materials and industrial goods.

Before independence France took 81 per cent of Algeria's exports and provided 82 per cent of its imports. This dominance declined steadily, particularly at the time of the 1971 oil nationalization crisis, and France's share of Algerian trade in 1972 dropped to only 21 per cent of exports and 35 per cent of imports. However, following the visit to France in 1973 of Algeria's Foreign Minister, Abdelaziz Bouteflika, trade between the two countries began to pick up again. In 1973, the EEC accounted for 67 per cent of all Algeria's imports, and 65 per cent of its exports. France was still Algeria's main supplier, followed by West Germany, the United States and Italy. Main customers were West Germany, France, the United States, Spain and Italy. The U.S.S.R. is Algeria's main trading partner in the socialist bloc but accounts for only 3 per cent of imports and about 4 per cent of exports. Trade is growing at a significant rate with Spain, Switzerland, Sweden, Morocco, Czechoslovakia, Denmark, Canada, Japan and Brazil.

About 90 per cent of exports and 75 per cent of imports are handled by State trading agencies, which operate on a commercial basis and are not backed by the automatic guarantee of the Algerian Government.

Since 1973 negotiations have been under way with the European Economic Community, with which Algeria wants to sign a long-term preferential trade agreement. A major obstacle has been the opposition of France and Italy to Algeria's demands for special terms of entry for its wines and its fruit and vegetables.

FINANCE

Until independence, Algeria was mostly dependent on France for its central banking and monetary system, though some of the usual central banking functions were carried out by the *Banque d'Algérie*. The *Banque Centrale d'Algérie*, the sole bank of issue of the new Algerian franc, which started its operations on January 1st, 1963, has all the usual central banking powers. The Algerian Dinar which in 1964 replaced the franc, remained at par with the French franc, until the devaluation of the French franc in 1969, when the parity of the Algerian dinar remained unchanged. After the dollar devaluation of December 1971, the parity of the dinar to gold was left unchanged at AD 1.0=180 milligrams of gold. The banking system has been largely taken over by the state, various restrictions having discouraged private banks (almost all of which were foreign owned, most being subsidiaries of French companies) from continuing their operations in the country. A state monopoly on all foreign financial transactions was imposed in November 1967; this followed a similar monopoly imposed on insurance in June 1966. The Banque Nationale d'Algérie deals in particular with finance for agriculture. The Crédit Populaire d'Algérie and the Banque Extérieure d'Algérie are concerned with the financial interests of industry, commerce and transport. In 1974 an Algerian-Libyan bank, the Banque Internationale Arabe, was opened in Paris to finance trade and investment between France and Arab countries.

In 1974 there was a budget surplus of 9,000 million dinars, due to the fact that oil receipts were more than double those originally estimated. Other receipts rose by only 17 per cent over 1973. The 1975 budget envisages revenue of 21,995 million dinars and expenditure of 21,854 million dinars, giving a surplus of 141 million dinars. Capital expenditure will amount to 8,685 million dinars. Public spending will be up 54 per cent on 1974. Of the recurrent budget, 33 per cent is allocated to education and training, reflecting the importance attached to this aspect of development by the Government. Oil revenues are expected to reach 13,500 million dinars, representing 61 per cent of total revenue.

The Government is proud of the fact that much of Algeria's investment is financed by domestic saving. However, Algeria's political stability and its oil revenues have made many countries and international financial institutions willing to lend it money. During 1973 Algeria borrowed about U.S. $1,600 million on the Eurodollar market and there were fears that this might bring about a dangerous rate of inflation, in view of the floating interest rates attached to Eurodollar loans. Major foreign loans contracted during 1974 included a U.S. $700 million soft-term loan granted jointly by West Germany and the Arab Fund for Economic and Social Development, for the construction of a tanker port near Arzew; U.S. $157.5 million granted by the World Bank for the port of Bethiouia, railways and electricity production; 100 million Deutschmarks for a cement works at Sétif, granted by West Germany; a £20 million loan from Lloyd's Bank for construction of the Hassi R'Mel to Skikda gas pipeline; a £17 million loan from National Westminster Bank for studies for expanding output at the El Hadjar steel complex. Nevertheless, not more than 25 per cent of finance for the 1974–77 Plan is to be brrowed abroad. Late in 1974 Algeria embarked on a programme of early repayment of about U.S. $520 million of its Eurodollar loans. Its foreign debts early in 1975 amounted to about 11,000 million dinars, debt servicing representing about 8 per cent of total value of exports.

In 1974 Algeria had a 2,000 million dinar surplus on balance of payments, due to increased value of oil and gas sales but also to the large foreign loans it has contracted and also to repatriated income from abroad. Nevertheless, in 1975 Algeria will still have to borrow abroad in order to finance investment.

International reserves at the end of September 1974 stood at U.S. $1,987 million, compared with U.S. $472 million at the end of June 1973, but by the end of March 1975 they had dropped to U.S. $1,083 million.

STATISTICAL SURVEY

AREA AND POPULATION

AREA	CENSUS	POPULATION				
		MID-YEAR ESTIMATES†				
	April 4th, 1966	1970	1971	1972	1973	1974
2,381,741 sq. km.*	11,821,679	14,330,000	14,769,000	15,270,000	15,772,000	16,275,000

* 919,595 square miles.

† Including Algerian nationals living abroad, numbering 268,868 at the 1966 census.

In 1972 over 700,000 Algerians were estimated to be living in France.

LANGUAGES*
(1966 Census)

	MALES	FEMALES	TOTAL	PERCENTAGE
Arabic	4,908,100	4,826,000	9,734,100	80.43
Berber	1,123,200	1,144,100	2,267,300	18.73
French	37,500	40,100	77,600	0.64
Others	8,500	8,900	17,400	0.14
Unknown . . .	2,600	3,000	5,600	0.05
TOTAL . .	6,079,900	6,022,100	12,102,000	100.00

* Rounded provisional figures, including Algerian nationals abroad.

POPULATION BY DEPARTMENTS
(1966 Census)

Algiers . . .	1,629,019		Oran . . .	946,567
Annaba . . .	939,378		Saida . . .	236,338
Aurès . . .	748,970		Saoura* . . .	209,850
Constantine . .	1,469,106		Sétif . . .	1,164,636
El Asnam . .	775,692		Tiaret . . .	360,920
Médéa . . .	864,799		Tizi-Ouzou . .	776,588
Mostaganem . .	766,216		Tlemcen . . .	432,225
Oasis* . . .	501,375			

* Enumeration took place between December 22nd, 1965, and January, 20th, 1966

CHIEF TOWNS

POPULATION (1966 Census)

Algiers (capital) .	903,530*	Skikda . . . 88,000‡
Oran . .	327,493†	Mostaganem . . 74,876
Constantine .	243,558	El Asnam . . 69,580
Annaba . .	152,006	Batna . . 68,856
Sidi Bel Abbès .	105,000‡	Bejaia . . . 65,012
Sétif . .	98,384	Biskra . . . 59,052
Tlemcen . .	96,072	Médéa . . 53,951
Blida . .	93,000‡	Tizi Ouzou . 53,291

* 1973 estimate 1,200,000 (including suburbs).
† 1973 estimate 325,000.   ‡ Estimates.

BIRTHS, MARRIAGES AND DEATHS

	LIVE BIRTHS*		MARRIAGES		DEATHS*	
	Number	Rate (per 1,000)	Number	Rate (per 1,000)	Number	Rate (per 1,000)
1966 . . .	561,528	46.2	61,981	5.1	122,999	10.1
1967 . . .	534,904	42.7	59,549	4.7	118,325	9.4
1968 . . .	529,806	39.3	n.a.	n.a.	134,160	9.9

* Data exclude live-born infants dying before registration of birth. Death registration is estimated to be between 40 and 60 per cent complete. According to United Nations estimates, the average annual death rate was 16.9 per 1,000 in 1965–70.

ECONOMICALLY ACTIVE POPULATION*
(1966 Census)

	MALES	FEMALES†	TOTAL†
Agriculture, Forestry, Hunting and Fishing .	1,270,098	23,315	1,293,413
Mining and Quarrying	21,456	414	21,870
Manufacturing	148,506	14,496	163,002
Construction	128,012	690	128,702
Electricity, Gas and Water Supply . .	9,752	391	10,143
Commerce	148,500	3,775	152,275
Transport, Storage and Communications .	85,580	2,316	87,896
Services	286,134	51,778	337,912
Other Activities (not adequately described) .	83,104	2,655	85,759
TOTAL	2,181,142	99,830	2,280,972

* Excluding Algerian nationals abroad, military personnel in barracks and 283,691 persons (274,068 males and 9,623 females) seeking work for the first time.

† Excluding about 1,200,000 females, mainly occupied in agriculture.

AGRICULTURE
LAND USE, 1970
('000 hectares)

Arable Land	6,240
Under Permanent Crops . . .	552
Permanent Meadows and Pastures . .	37,416
Forest Land	2,424
Other Land and Inland Water . .	191,542
TOTAL AREA	238,174

Source: FAO, *Production Yearbook 1973.*

PRINCIPAL CROPS
('000 metric tons)

	1971	1972	1973
Wheat	1,235	1,956	1,100*
Barley	340	720	450*
Potatoes	274	300*	300*
Onions (dry) . . .	40*	40*	42*
Tomatoes . . .	86	130*	130*
Grapes	1,200*	1,150*	1,200*
Olives	170.0*	174.9	150.0*
Oranges	380*	380*	383*
Tangerines and mandarines .	130*	130*	132*
Dates	130.0	160.1	170.0
Figs	50*	51	58*
Tobacco	4.3	6.0	6.2*

* FAO estimate.

LIVESTOCK
('000)

	1970/71	1971/72*	1972/73*
Sheep . . .	8,164	8,165	8,000
Goats . . .	2,473	2,470	2,300
Cattle . . .	922	925	950
Horses . . .	144	145	145
Camels . . .	184	185	185
Chickens . . .	14,400*	15,000	15,500

* FAO estimates.

LIVESTOCK PRODUCTS
('000 metric tons—FAO estimates)

	1971	1972	1973
Beef and veal . .	29	29	29
Mutton, lamb and goats' meat . .	50	50	49
Poultry meat . .	28	29	30
Cows' milk . .	332	333	333
Sheep's milk . .	117	117	114
Goats' milk . .	121	121	113
Hen eggs . . .	11.9	11.9	12.2
Wool . . .	6.3	6.3	5.9

Source: FAO *Production Yearbook 1973.*

FISHING
('000 metric tons)

1970 . .	25.7
1971 . .	23.7
1972 . .	28.3
1973 . .	31.2

Source: FAO *Yearbook of Fishery Statistics 1973.*

MINING

		1969	1970	1971	1972
Coal	'000 metric tons	17	15	14	n.a.
Iron Ore	,, ,, ,,	1,599	1,537	1,698	1,978
Antimony	metric tons	60*	60*	60*	60*
Lead Ore	,, ,,	7,900	6,500	4,700	7,000*
Zinc Ore	,, ,,	20,900	17,000	16,400	17,000
Phosphate Rock . . .	'000 metric tons	420	492	491	370
Crude Petroleum . . .	,, ,, ,,	43,860	47,250	36,410	50,100
Natural Gas†	million cu. metres	8,724	15,260	13,426	16,700

Crude petroleum: (1973) 51,200,000 metric tons; (1974) 47,192,056 metric tons.

* Estimates.

† This series reported in Algerian publications is different from the one given in the UN *Statistical Yearbook, 1972.*

Sources: United Nations, *Statistical Yearbook 1972,* and *The Growth of World Industry 1972.*

INDUSTRY
SELECTED PRODUCTS

		1969	1970	1971	1972
Olive oil, crude	'ooo metric tons	15	15	25	15
Flour	,, ,, ,,	426	422	n.a.	n.a.
Wine	'ooo hectolitres	8,711	8,692	8,250	8,400
Cigarettes	million	5,127	5,890	6,818	7,912
Paints	metric tons	14,500	15,000	n.a.	n.a.
Washing powder and detergents .	,, ,,	15,550	18,144	19,439	n.a.
Motor spirit	'ooo metric tons	507	514	570	598
Kerosene and jet fuel . . .	,, ,, ,,	209	203	234	269
Distillate fuel oils	,, ,, ,,	813	961	960	977
Residual fuel oils	,, ,, ,,	496	640	745	862
Liquefied petroleum gas . . .	,, ,, ,,	88	107	112	n.a.
Cement	,, ,, ,,	927	924	964	n.a.
Car assembly	'ooo units	13	71	n.a.	n.a.
Electricity	million kWh.	1,782	1,989	2,126	2,270
Manufactured gas	million cu. metres	63	52	50	n.a.

Source: United Nations, *The Growth of World Industry, 1972.*

FINANCE

100 centimes = 1 Algerian dinar.

Coins: 1, 2, 5, 10, 20 and 50 centimes; 1 dinar.

Notes: 5, 10, 50 and 100 dinars.

Exchange rates (April 1975): £1 sterling = 9.116 dinars; U.S. $1 = 3.874 dinars.

100 Algerian dinars = £10.97 = $25.81.

Note: The Algerian dinar was introduced in April 1964, replacing (at par) the new Algerian franc. From January 1960 the Algerian franc (equal to the French franc) was valued at 180 milligrammes of gold. Until August 1971 the dinar was thus valued at 20.225 U.S. cents (U.S. $1 = 4.937 dinars). Between December 1971 and February 1973 the dinar's value was 21.991 U.S. cents ($1 = 4.537 dinars); from February 1973 to January 1974 it was 24.435 U.S. cents ($1 = 4.093 dinars). Since January 1974 the Algerian authorities have allowed the dinar to "float" on foreign exchange markets. In terms of sterling, the exchange rate between November 1967 and June 1972 was £1 = 11.849 dinars.

BUDGET
(million AD)

	1974	1975
Current Budget . . .	7,673.0	13,168.8
of which:		
Defence . . .	874.3	1,030.0
Interior . . .	482.3	622.3
Agriculture and Agrarian		
Reform . . .	414.5	387.5
Primary and Secondary		
Education . . .	1,609.9	2,106.1
Higher education and		
scientific research .	298.4	417.5
Public health . .	564.8	725.9
Public works . .	228.1	270.0
Labour and social affairs	145.1	172.8
Finance . . .	206.5	268.0
Veterans . . .	400.4	432.1
Youth and sports .	133.0	175.0
Expenditure in common .	1,612.0	5,703.0
(Incl. price subsidies) .	(—)	(3,200.0)
Development Budget . .	6,500.0	8,685.0
TOTAL EXPENDITURE .	14,173.0	21,853.8

DEVELOPMENT PLAN 1974–77
EXPENDITURE (million AD)

Industry	48,000
Agriculture	12,005
Dams and water . . .	4,400
Tourism	1,500
Fishing	115
Economic infrastructure . .	15,521
Education and training . .	9,947
Social services . . .	14,610
Administration	1,399
TOTAL (incl. others) . .	110,217

EXTERNAL TRADE
(million AD)

	1967	1968	1969	1970	1971	1972	1973
Imports .	3,154	4,023	4,981	6,205	6,028	6,694	8,876
Exports .	3,572	4,098	4,611	4,980	4,208	5,854	7,479

PRINCIPAL COMMODITIES
('ooo AD)

IMPORTS	1970	1971	1972
Dairy products	133,591	162,790	266,952
Cereals and flour	144,577	282,735	351,636
Sugar . . . . —	111,488	168,127	228,379
Chemicals and parachemicals .	347,947	375,124	498,322
Semi-finished textiles and leather goods	269,001	255,468	337,521
Iron and steel	779,219	638,768	546,391
Technical equipment . . .	270,047	280,534	349,501
Transport equipment . . .	591,926	483,254	568,478
Machinery	1,397,359	1,452,182	1,442,498
Pharmaceutical products . .	186,570	187,254	190,131

EXPORTS	1970	1971	1972
Fruit and vegetables . . .	153,608	143,954	133,159
Wine and beverages . . .	728,749	301,790	336,107
Crude petroleum . . .	3,287,550	2,972,194	4,627,170
Natural gas	144,496	132,768	138,623
Iron ore and concentrates . .	87,294	95,250	119,923
Metal products . . .	128,283	79,053	59,871
Transport equipment . .	48,744	115,571	68,841

PRINCIPAL COUNTRIES
('ooo AD)

IMPORTS	1970	1971	1972
Belgium-Luxembourg . . .	215,631	167,687	315,507
Canada	78,955	166,294	122,863
France	2,631,278	2,273,449	2,020,468
Germany, Federal Republic .	619,807	567,910	865,397
Italy	451,509	515,285	689,671
Netherlands	140,880	163,616	220,692
Spain	200,461	166,071	306,631
U.S.S.R.	224,591	242,204	229,396
United Kingdom . . .	207,488	331,126	352,778
U.S.A.	497,948	502,982	468,087

EXPORTS	1970	1971	1972
Belgium-Luxembourg . . .	101,464	205,930	287,625
Brazil	99,060	153,642	152,632
Bulgaria	64,088	94,310	113,633
France	2,667,180	991,119	1,362,900
Germany, Federal Republic .	640,296	1,013,863	1,122,034
Italy	209,737	317,293	450,211
Netherlands	43,375	191,188	178,494
Spain	124,624	169,787	493,750
U.S.S.R.	242,045	277,639	288,328
United Kingdom . . .	204,784	153,315	238,153
U.S.A.	40,360	77,207	494,898

TRANSPORT
RAILWAYS

	1972	1973	1974
Passengers Carried ('000) . . .	n.a.	6,900	8,000
Freight Carried ('000 metric tons) . .	n.a.	6,650	7,683
Passenger-km. (million)	1,016	944	1,057
Freight ton-km. (million)	1,536	1,790	1,817

ROAD TRAFFIC
(motor vehicles in use at December 31st)

	1971	1972	1973
Passenger cars	154,231	165,022	176,898
Commercial vehicles	86,144	90,771	96,676

Source: IRF, *World Road Statistics 1969–73.*

SHIPPING
SEA-BORNE FREIGHT TRAFFIC
('000 metric tons, international and coastwise)

	GOODS LOADED			GOODS UNLOADED		
	1968	1969	1970	1968	1969	1970
Algiers	1,579	2,142	2,256	3,488	3,665	4,240
Annaba	3,089	2,838	2,331	461	768	1,130
Arzew	19,269	20,568	20,141	134	190	199
Bejaia	15,557	15,371	16,683	158	287	638
Oran	495	662	786	918	908	1,076
TOTAL (incl. others) .	40,037	41,680	44,260	5,752	5,820	8,085

Source: UN *Monthly Bulletin of Statistics,* December 1972 and February 1974.

CIVIL AVIATION
SCHEDULED SERVICES

	1969	1970	1971	1972
Kilometres Flown ('000) . .	8,696	10,353	12,439	14,000
Passengers Carried ('000) . .	448	563	715	844
Passenger-km. (million) . .	418	515	634	699
Freight ton-km. ('000) . .	2,586	3,078	3,663	4,200
Mail ton-km. ('000) . .	621	647	697	700
Total ton-km. ('000) . .	40,782	49,983	61,354	68,000

Source: UN *Statistical Yearbook 1973.*

TOURISM
Number of Tourist Arrivals: (1970) 235,900, (1971) 367,700.

EDUCATION*
(1973–74)

	Schools	Pupils	Teachers
Primary		2,376,344	55,844 (of whom
Secondary	8,087	397,837	52,956 Algerians)
University	3	30,070	4,041†

* State institutions only.   † 1974-75 figure.

Source (unless otherwise stated): Direction Générale du Plan et des Etudes Economiques, Ministère de l'Economie Nationale, Algiers.

THE CONSTITUTION
(*Approved by popular referendum, September* 1963)

Articles 1–11; *Main Aims and Principles*

Algeria is a Democratic and Popular Republic. It forms part of the Arab Maghreb, the Arab World and of Africa. Islam is the official religion, but the State guarantees freedom of opinion and belief and free expression of religion. Arabic is the official language of the State. The capital of Algeria is Algiers, headquarters of the National Assembly and the Government. The National Popular Army ensures the defence of territory and takes part in the country's social and economic activities. The basic administrative unit of the Republic is the Commune.

The main aims of the Republic are to build a socialist democracy; to fight discrimination, in particular that based on race or religion and to strive for peace in the world. The Republic conforms to the Universal Declaration of the Rights of Man.

Articles 12–22; *Fundamental Rights*

All citizens of both sexes have the same rights and the same duties. All citizens over 19 years have the right to vote. Domicile cannot be violated and secrecy of correspondence is guaranteed to all citizens. No one can be arrested or tried except for legal offences and according to legal procedure. The Family, main unit of society, is under State protection. Education is compulsory. The Republic guarantees freedom of the Press and other means of information, freedom of association, freedom of speech and public discourse and freedom to hold meetings. Trade unionism, the right to strike, and the participation of workers in the administration of business will be upheld within the framework of the relevant laws. The Republic guarantees political asylum to all who fight for freedom.

The rights and freedoms referred to may not be used to hinder national independence, or to affect territorial integrity, national unity, the institution of the Republic, the socialist aims of the people or the principle of unity of the F.L.N.

Articles 23–26; *The National Liberation Front (F.L.N.)*

The F.L.N. achieves the objectives of the revolution and establishes socialism in Algeria.

Articles 27–38; *Sovereign Rights—The National Assembly*

Sovereign rights belong to the people. They are exercised by representatives in the National Assembly, nominated by the F.L.N. and elected for five years by direct and secret ballot.

The President of the National Assembly occupies the second highest position in the State.

The President of the Republic and Members of the Assembly have the power to initiate laws. All members of the Government have the right to attend debates and to address the Assembly. Control over Government acts is exercised by: hearings of Ministers in Committees; written questions; oral questions with or without debate.

Articles 39–59; *The Executive*

The executive power lies with the Head of State, the President of the Republic. He is nominated by the Party, and is elected by universal direct and secret ballot, for a five-year term. Any Moslem of Algerian origin having all civil and political rights and being 36 years of age or older, may be elected President of the Republic.

The President: signs, ratifies (in consultation with the Assembly) and ensures the execution of Treaties and other International Agreements; is Supreme Leader of the Armed Forces; declares war and draws up terms for peace, with the approval of the National Assembly; presides over the Higher Councils of Defence and the Law; exercises the right to grant a legal reprieve; nominates Ministers, of whom two-thirds must be members of the Assembly; has sole responsibility before the Assembly; defines and directs Government policies; proclaims and publishes Laws and ensures that they are executed; appoints all civil servants and defence personnel.

The President must promulgate Laws within ten days of their formal transmission by the National Assembly. Within this time limit the President can ask the Assembly to deliberate a second time, and this request cannot be refused. The period of ten days can be reduced at the request of the Assembly in matters of urgent necessity. If the President of the Republic does not proclaim the Laws within the time limit, the President of the Assembly shall do so.

A motion of censure may be tabled against the President if signed by one-third of the members of the Assembly. A majority vote in the Assembly on such a motion shall entail the resignation of the President and the automatic dissolution of the Assembly. This vote by public ballot shall take place after five clear days have expired from the time of tabling the motion.

In the case of emergency, the President can take

exceptional measures to safeguard national independence and the Institutions of the Republic. The National Assembly then has the full right to meet automatically.

Articles 60–62; *Justice*

Judges obey only the Law and the interests of the Socialist Revolution. Their independence is guaranteed by Law and by the existence of a Higher Council of Law.

Articles 63–64; *The Constitutional Council*

The Constitutional Council consists of the President of the Supreme Court, the Presidents of the Civil and Administrative Chambers of the Supreme Court, three nominated members of the National Assembly and a member nominated by the President of the Republic.

Articles 65–70; *Higher Organizations*

The Higher Council of the Law consists of the President, the Minister of Justice, the President and Attorney General of the Supreme Court, a Lawyer of the Supreme Court, two Magistrats, one of whom is a judge, elected by their colleagues, and six Members of the Assembly elected by the permanent Committee of Justice.

The Higher Council of Defence consists of the President, the Ministers of National Defence, the Interior, and Foreign Affairs, the President of the Assembly's Commission for National Defence, and two Members nominated by the President of the Republic.

The Higher Economic and Social Council consists of five Members of the Assembly, the Director of Economic Planning, the Governor of the Central Bank of Algeria, members of the national organizations and representatives of major national economic and social activities appointed by the President. It elects its own President

Articles 71–74; *Constitutional Alterations*

The initiative for altering the Constitution lies jointly with the President of the Republic and the National Assembly. Two readings and two votes with absolute majority must be given at an interval of two months, to draft any bill. This draft shall then be submitted for approval to the People by referendum. A bill approved by the People shall be proclaimed Law within eight days of the referendum.

Articles 75–78; *Temporary Measures*

The national hymn is *Kassamen* until such time as an extra-constitutional law shall fix a new national hymn.

The use of French in education shall continue only until the realisation of all-Arabic education becomes possible.

After approval of the Constitution by popular referendum it shall be promulgated within eight days. The election of the President of the Republic shall take place within one month of the approval of the Constitution.

THE GOVERNMENT

REVOLUTIONARY COUNCIL

Set up in June 1965 following the arrest of President Ben Bella. With Col. HOUARI BOUMEDIENNE as its President the Council has the following members:

AHMED BELHOUCHET	Col. BOUHEDJAR BENHADDOU	ABDELAZIZ BOUTEFLIKA	YAHYAOUI MOHAMMED SALAH
MOHAMMED BEN AHMED	CHEDLI BENJEDID	Col. AHMED DRAIA	SALAH SOUFI
Col. AHMED BENCHERIF	ABDERRAHMAN BEN SALEM	TAYEBI LARBI	

COUNCIL OF MINISTERS

(July 1975)

Head of Government, President of the Council of Ministers and Minister of Defence: Col. HOUARI BOUMEDIENNE.

Minister of State for Transport: RABAH BITAT.

Minister of the Interior: Col. MOHAMMED BEN AHMED.

Minister of Justice: BOUALEM BEN HAMOUDA.

Minister of Industry and Energy: BELAID ABDESSELAM.

Minister of Foreign Affairs: ABDELAZIZ BOUTEFLIKA.

Minister of Finance: ISMAIL MAHROUG.

Minister of Agriculture and Agrarian Reform: TAYEBI LARBI.

Minister of Primary and Secondary Education: ABDELKRIM BEN MAHMOUD.

Minister of Higher Education and Scientific Research: MOHAMMED BEN YAHIA.

Minister of Indigenous Education and Religious Affairs: MOULOUD KASSEM.

Minister of Health and Population: OMAR BOUDJELLAB.

Minister of Public Works: ABDELKADER ZAIBEK.

Minister of Posts and Telecommunications: SAID AÏT MESSAOUDENE.

Minister of Commerce: LAYACHI YAKER.

Minister of Labour and Social Affairs: MOHAND SAID MAZOUZI.

Minister of Youth and Sports: ABDALLAH FADEL.

Minister of Tourism: ABDELAZIZ MAAOUI.

Minister for Ex-Servicemen: MAHMOUD GUENNEZ.

Minister of Information and Culture: AHMED TALEB.

Under-Secretary of State for Planning: KAMEL ABDULLAH KHODJA.

Under-Secretary of State for Hydraulics: ABDULLAH ARBAOUI.

ASSEMBLIES

The Algerian political system provides for elected assemblies at three levels, communal, provincial and national. The communal assemblies (*assemblées populaires communales*) were created in 1967. They are headed by an elected president and are renewed by democratic vote every four years. The provincial assemblies (*assemblées populaires de wilayas*) were created in 1969 and are renewed every five years. The chief of the executive, the wali, is a

government appointee. The national assembly (*assemblée nationale populaire*) was first elected in 1964 and has not met since 1966. In June 1975, however, Boumedienne announced that national elections would be held within a year. Elections for all assemblies are made from a single-party list presented by the FLN, but a choice of candidates is offered within the list.

POLITICAL PARTY

Government is based on a one-party system.

Front de Libération Nationale (FLN): place Emir Abdel-kader, Algiers; f. 1954; socialist in outlook, the party is divided into a Secretariat, a Central Committee, Federations, Dairas and Kasmas; Head MOHAMED CHERIF MESSADIA.

Under the aegis of the FLN there exists a number of mass political organizations, including *Jeunesse du Front de Libération Nationale* (JFLN) and the *Union Nationale des Femmes Algériennes* (UNFA).

There are several small opposition groups; all are proscribed and in exile in France or in other Arab countries.

DIPLOMATIC REPRESENTATION

EMBASSIES ACCREDITED TO ALGERIA

(In Algiers unless otherwise stated)

Afghanistan: Cairo, Egypt.

Albania: 50 rue Oukil Mohammed, Birmandréis; *Ambassador:* RIZA TAUSHANI (also accred. to Mauritania).

Argentina: 7 rue Hamani; *Ambassador:* MANRIQUE FERNÁNDEZ MORENO (also accred. to Tunisia).

Austria: Cité Dar el Kef, rue Shakespeare, El Mouradia; *Ambassador:* MANFRED SCHEICH.

Bangladesh: 141 blvd. Salah Bouakouir; *Chargé d'Affaires:* ARSHAD UZ ZAMAN (also accred. to Tunisia).

Belgium: 18 ave. Claude Debussy; *Ambassador:* VICTOR NIJS.

Brazil: 48 blvd. Mohammed V; *Ambassador:* DAVID SILVEIRA DA MOTA.

Bulgaria: 13 blvd. Bougara Mohammed; *Ambassador:* VENELINE KOTZEV.

Cambodia: 52 rue Parmentier, Hydra; *Ambassador:* SNGUON CHEM.

Cameroon: 26 chemin Sheikh Bachir Brahimi; *Ambassador:* FERDINAND LEOPOLD AYONO.

Canada: 27 *bis* rue d'Anjou, Hydra; *Ambassador:* ROBERT ELLIOTT.

Central African Republic: 14 rue Jean Rameau, Bellevue; *Ambassador:* CHRISTOPHE MAIDOU (also accred. to Tunisia).

China, People's Republic: 34 blvd. des Martyrs; *Ambassador:* LIN CHING.

Congo People's Republic: 6 rue Cheick el Kamel Kouba; *Ambassador:* RAPHAEL ELENGA.

Cuba: 14 rue ibn Batran, Mouradia; *Ambassador:* GIRALDO MAZOLA.

Czechoslovakia: Villa Malika, Parc Gatliff; *Ambassador:* VÁCLAV PLESCOT.

Denmark: 23 blvd. Zirout Youcef; *Ambassador:* HANS SEVERIN MOLLER.

Egypt: chemin de la Madeleine, Hydra; *Ambassador:* MOHAMED MUSTAPHA LOFTI.

Finland: 2 blvd. Mohammed V.; *Ambassador:* OSOMO OKEMIS.

France: rue Larbi Alik, Hydra; *Ambassador:* GUY DE COMMINES DE MARSILLY.

Gabon: 136 blvd. Salah Bouakouir; *Ambassador:* ETIENNE M'BOUMBA MOUDOUNGA.

German Democratic Republic: 16 rue Payen, Hydra; *Ambassador:* SIEGFRIED KAMPF.

Germany, Federal Republic: 165 Chemin Findja; *Ambassador:* KARL HEINZ VESPER.

Ghana: 62 rue Parmentier, Hydra; *Ambassador:* CHARLES KWASHIE MAWUENYEGAH.

Greece: 38 rue Didouche Mourad; *Ambassador:* JEAN GREGORIADIS.

Guinea: 43 blvd. Central Said Hamdine, Hydra; *Ambassador:* SEKOU CAMARA (also accred. to Tunisia).

Guinea-Bissau: *Ambassador:* LUÍS D'OLIVEIRA SANGA.

Hungary: 18 ave. Lyautey; *Ambassador:* ZSIGMOND ZOLTAN (also accred. to Tunisia).

India: 119 rue Didouche Mourad; *Ambassador:* SAYEB SHUHABADDIN.

Indonesia: rue Etienne Baillac, Mouradia; *Ambassador:* SOE MARMAN (also accred. to Morocco and Tunisia).

Iran: 60 rue Didouche Mourad; *Ambassador:* ASSAD K. SADRY.

Iraq: 4 rue Areski, Abri-Hydra; *Ambassador:* FAYEQ AT-TAKRITI.

Italy: 37 chemin Sheikh Bachir Brahimi; *Ambassador:* UBERTO BOZZINI.

Ivory Coast: Parc Paradou, Hydra; *Ambassador:* EDMOND ZEKBAHI.

Japan: 3 rue du Lucien Reynard; *Ambassador:* YOSHITO SHIMODA.

Jordan: 6 rue Chenoua; *Ambassador:* NAIF AS-SAAD AL-BATAYANA.

Kenya: Cairo, Egypt.

Korea, Democratic People's Republic: 49 rue Salvandy; *Ambassador:* KANG MAN SOU.

Kuwait: 1 rue Didouche Mourad; *Ambassador:* YOUSOUF AL MONAYES.

Lebanon: 9 rue Kaid Ahmed el Biar; *Ambassador:* KHALIL ITANI.

Libya: 15 chemin Bachir Brahimi; *Ambassador:* ABDEL FATAH MOHAMMED AN-NAAS.

Madagascar: rue Abdelkadir Aouis; *Ambassador:* JUSTIN RAKOTONIAINA (also accred. to Tunisia).

Mali: Paris, France.

Mauritania: 5 rue de la Révolution, Mouradia; *Ambassador:* SAAD BOUH KANE.

Mexico: Cairo, Egypt.

Mongolia: rue Belkacem Amani, Hydra; *Ambassador:* BAYARYN JARGALSAIKHAN (also accred to Mauritania).

Morocco: 6 rue des Cèdres; *Ambassador:* AHMAD SENOUSSI.

Nepal: Cairo, Egypt.

Netherlands: 23 blvd. Zirout Youcef; *Ambassador:* GERHARD WOLTER BENTINCK.

Niger: 136 blvd. Salah Bouakouir; *Ambassador:* KARIM ALIO (also accred. to Morocco and Tunisia).

Nigeria: 27 rue Blaise Pascal; *Ambassador:* LAMIDI MALIKI.

Norway: Rabat, Morocco.

Oman: *Ambassador:* IBRAHIM HAMED SULAIMAN AL-HARITHI.

Pakistan: 14 ave. Souidani Boudjemâa; *Ambassador:* S. A. B. BOKHARI.

Peru: 127 rue Didouche Mourad; *Ambassador:* E. DE HABICH Y PALACIO (also accred to Morocco and Tunisia).

Philippines: *Ambassador:* PACIFICO CASTRO.

Poland: 37 ave. Mustafa Ali Khodja, El Biar; *Ambassador:* ANTONI KARAS.

Romania: 24 rue Si Areski, Hydra; *Ambassador:* MIHAT G. STEFAN.

Saudi Arabia: 7 chemin des Glycines; *Ambassador:* ABDALLAH AL MOULHAQ.

Senegal: 60 ave. Souidani Boudjemâa; *Ambassador:* CHARLES DELGARO.

Somalia: 11 blvd. des Martyrs; *Ambassador:* ABDELHAMID ALI YOUCEF.

Spain: 10 rue Azil Ali; *Ambassador:* R. SOBREDO-RIOBOO.

Sri Lanka: Cairo, Egypt.

Sudan: 27 rue de Carthage, Hydra; *Ambassador:* SALAH AHMED IBRAHIM.

Sweden: 4 blvd. Mohammed V; *Ambassador:* HARALD EDEL STAM.

Switzerland: 27 blvd. Zirout Youcef; *Ambassador:* ETIENNE VALLOTON.

Syria: chemin de la Madeleine, El Biar; *Ambassador:* AHMAD MADANIYA.

Tanzania: Paris, France.

Tunisia: 11 rue du Bois de Boulogne, Hydra; *Ambassador:* MAHMOUD MAAMOURI.

Turkey: Villa dar el Ouard, blvd. Colonel Bougara; *Ambassador:* FAIK MELEK.

Uganda: Cairo, Egypt.

U.S.S.R.: chemin du Prince d'Annam, El Biar; *Ambassador:* VASSILY NAZAROVICH RYKOV.

United Arab Emirates: *Ambassador:* ISSA KHALFAN.

United Kingdom: 7 chemin des Glycines; *Ambassador:* J. A. ROBINSON.

U.S.A.: 4 chemin Bachir Brahimi; *Ambassador:* RICHARD PARKER.

Upper Volta: Hydra le Paradou, Immeuble du Bosquet; *Ambassador:* (vacant).

Vatican: 1 rue de la Basilique; *Pro-Nuncio:* Mgr. SANTE PORTALUPI.

Venezuela: 38 rue Jean Jaurès, Mouradia; *Ambassador:* ALFREDO MONCH.

Viet-Nam, Democratic Republic: 30 rue de Chenoua, Hydra; *Ambassador:* VAN BA KIEM.

Yemen Arab Republic: 74 rue Bouraba; *Ambassador:* ABDELWAHEB JAHAF (also accred. to Tunisia).

Yemen, People's Democratic Republic: 105 ave. Mustapha Ali Khodja, El Biar; *Chargé d'Affaires:* SAEED HADI AWAD.

Yugoslavia: 7 rue d'Anjou, Hydra; *Ambassador:* DUSAN VEJNOVIC.

Zaire: 12 rue A, Les Crêtes, Hydra; *Ambassador:* MUTUALE TSHIKANKE.

Zambia: Cairo, Egypt.

Algeria also has diplomatic relations with Australia, Chad, Costa Rica, Dahomey, Ecuador, Ireland, Laos, Portugal, Qatar, Trinidad and Tobago and South Viet-Nam.

JUDICIAL SYSTEM

The highest court of justice is the Supreme Court in Algiers. Justice is exercised through 132 courts grouped on a regional basis. Three special Criminal Courts have been set up in Oran, Constantine and Algiers to deal with economic crimes against the state. From these there is no appeal. In April 1975 the Government decided to establish a *Cour de sûreté de l'état*, composed of magistrates and high-ranking army officers, to try all cases involving state security.

President of Supreme Court: M. GATY.

Procurator-General: M. MOSTEFAI.

RELIGION

Islam is the official religion and the whole Algerian population, with a few rare exceptions, is Muslim.

President of the Superior Islamic Council: AHMED HAMANI; place Cheik Abdelhamid ibn Badis, Algiers.

The Europeans, and a few Arabs, are Christians, mostly Roman Catholics.

Archbishop of Algiers: H.E. Cardinal LEON-ETIENNE DUVAL; 13 rue Khelifa Boukhalfa, Algiers.

SUFFRAGAN BISHOPS

Constantine: JEAN SCOTTO.

Laghouat: JEAN-MARIE RAIMBAUD.

Oran: HENRI TEISSIER.

THE PRESS

DAILIES

al Chaab: 1 Place Maurice Audin, Algiers; f. 1962; national information journal in Arabic.

al Joumhouria—La République: 6 rue Benjenouci Hamida, Oran; f. 1962; French language; Editor BACHIR REZZOUG; circ. 80,000.

el Moudjahid: 20 rue de la Liberté, Algiers; f. 1965; FLN journal in French; circ. 130,000.

an Nasr: 100 rue Larbi Ben M'Hidi, Constantine; f. 1963; Arabic language.

WEEKLIES

Algérie Actualité: 20 rue de la Liberté, Algiers; f. 1965; French language weekly; Dir. R. C. YOUCEF FERHI.

el Hadef: 100 rue Larbi ben M'Hidi, Constantine; f. 1972; sports; in French.

el Moudjahid: 20 rue de la Liberté, Algiers; f. 1965; FLN journal in Arabic.

Révolution Africaine: 7 rue du Stade, Hydra, Algiers; F.L.N. journal in French; Socialist.

Révolution et Travail: 48 rue Khelifa Boukhalfa, Algiers; journal of U.G.T.A. in Arabic and French editions.

PERIODICALS

al Acala: Algiers; f. 1970; published by the Ministry of Education.

al Chaab al Thakafi: Algiers; f. 1972; cultural monthly; Arabic.

el Chabab: 2 rue Khelifa Boukhalfa; journal of the JFLN; bi-monthly; French and Arabic.

el Djazairia: Villa Joly, ave. Franklin Roosevelt, Algiers; f. 1970; organ of the UNFA; monthly; French and Arabic.

el Djeich: Office de l'Armée Nationale Populaire, 3 chemin de Gascogne, Algiers; f. 1963; monthly; Algerian army review; Arabic and French.

Journal Officiel de la République Algérienne Démocratique et Populaire: 7, 9 and 13 ave. A. Benbarek; f. 1962; French and Arabic.

al Kitab: 3 blvd. Zirout Youcef, Algiers; f. 1972; bulletin of SNED; every two months; French and Arabic.

al Thakafa: Algiers; f. 1970; published by the Ministry of Information and Culture.

PRESS AGENCIES

Algérie Presse Service (A.P.S.): 6 blvd. Ché Guévara, Algiers; f. 1962; Dir. MOHAMED BOUZID.

FOREIGN BUREAUX

Algiers

ANSA: 1 Chemin du parc Gatliff; Bureau Chief BERHANE GEBRE EGZIABHIER.

Associated Press: B.P. 769; Bureau Chief MICHAEL GOLDSMITH.

Bulgarian Telegraph Agency (BTA): Zaatcha 5, Muradia; Bureau Chief GORAN GOTEV.

Middle East News: 10 ave. Pasteur, B.P. 800.

Novosti: B.P. 24, Muradia.

The following are also represented: Agence France-Presse, Deutsche Presse-Agentur (DPA), Maghreb Arabe Presse, Prensa Latina, Reuters, Tass, UPI.

PUBLISHING

All privately owned publishing firms have been replaced by a single national organization:

Société Nationale d'Edition et de Diffusion (SNED): 3 blvd Zirout Youcef, Algiers; f. 1966; publishes books of all types, and is sole importer, exporter and distributor of books and periodicals; also holds state monopoly for commercial advertising.

RADIO AND TELEVISION

RADIO

Radiodiffusion Télévision Algérienne (R.T.A.): Imm. RTA, 21 boulevard des Martyrs, Algiers; Government controlled; Dir. ABDERRAHMANE CHERIET.
Arabic Network: stations at Algiers, Oran, Constantine.
French Network: stations at Algiers, Constantine, Oran
Kabyle Network: station at Algiers.
Supplementary Network: stations at Bouira, Tlemcen, Sétif, Souk Ahras, Batna, Bejaia, Touggourt, Laghouat, Ghardaïa, Aïn Salah and Tamanrasset.
There are 3,000,000 radio receivers.

TELEVISION

Radiodiffusion Télévision Algérienne (R.T.A.): 21 blvd. des Martyrs, Algiers; stations at Algiers, Oran, Tizi-Ouzou, Chrea and Constantine; the national network

was completed during 1970. Television is taking a major part in the national education programme. Dir. ABDERRAHMANE CHERIET.

There are 121,000 television receivers.

FINANCE

(cap. = capital; dep. = deposits; m. = million; AD = Algerian dinars; Fr. = French francs.)

BANKING

CENTRAL BANK

Banque Centrale d'Algérie: 8 blvd. Zirout-Youcef, Algiers; f. 1963; cap. 40m. AD; central bank of issue; Gov. SEGHIR MOSTAFAÏ.

NATIONALIZED BANKS

From November 1967 only the following nationalized banks were authorized to conduct exchange transactions and to deal with banks abroad, and by May 1972 these three banks had absorbed all foreign and private banks.

Banque Extérieure d'Algérie: 11 blvd. Colonel Amirouche, Algiers; f. 1967; cap. 110m. AD; chiefly concerned with foreign trade transactions and the financing of industrial development in Algeria; brs. in Algiers and 17 other principal cities in Algeria; Pres. and Gen. Man. BOUASRIA BELGHOULA.

Banque Nationale d'Algérie: 8 blvd. Ernesto Ché Guévara, Algiers; f. 1966; cap. 20m. AD; dep. 3,161m. AD; 138 brs.; Pres. and Gen. Man. ABDELMALEK TEMAM.

Crédit Populaire d'Algérie: 2 blvd. Colonel Amirouche, Algiers; f. 1966; cap. 45m. AD; re-grouping of former credit banks; brs. in Algiers, Constantine, Oran and Annaba.

SAVINGS BANK

Caisse Nationale d'Epargne et de Prévoyance: 40-42 rue Larbi Ben M'Hidi, Algiers.

INSURANCE

A state monopoly on insurance transactions was introduced in 1966.

Caisse Algérienne d'Assurance et de Réassurance: 48 rue Didouche Mourad, Algiers; f. 1963 as a public corporation; Admin.-Gen. A. BELBAY.

Caisse Nationale de Mutualité Agricole: 24 blvd. Victor Hugo, Algiers; Dir. O. LARFAOUI.

Société Algérienne d'Assurances: 5 blvd. de la République, Algiers; f. 1963; state sponsored company; Chair. and Man. Dir. MOHAMED BENSALEM.

TRADE AND INDUSTRY

CHAMBERS OF COMMERCE

Chambre de Commerce et d'Industrie d'Alger: Palais Consulaire, Place des Martyrs, Algiers; Administrator HACHEMI LARABI.

Chambre de Commerce et d'Industrie d'Annaba: Palais Consulaire, 4 rue du Cénra, Annaba; Pres. AMARA AMAR.

Chambre de Commerce de Bejaia: B.P. 105, Bejaia; f. 1892; 11 mems.; Pres. BENCHEIKH ABDERRAHMANE; Sec.-Gen. MAHDI YOUNÉS.

Chambre de Commerce et d'Industrie de Constantine: 2 ave. Zebane, Constantine; Pres. BEN MATTI ABDESSELAM.

Chambre de Commerce et d'Industrie d'Oran: 8 boulevard de la Soummam, Oran; Pres. TAÏEB BRAHIM MOKHTAR; Sec.-Gen. ABDELHAK NOR'EDDINE; publs. *Rapport Economique Mensuel.*

Chambre de Commerce et d'Industrie de Mostaganem: avenue Bénaïed Bendehiba, Mostaganem; f. 1901; 8 mems.; Pres. MOHAMED BELHADJ; Sec.-Gen. HARRAG BENBERNOU.

Chambre de Commerce Espagnole: 8 rue Amjère, Algiers.

Chambre de Commerce Italienne: 6 rue Hamami, Algiers.

Chambre Française de Commerce en Algérie: 1 rue du Languedoc, Algiers; Pres. M. J. BERNARD; Dir. M. G. FAULX-BRIOLE

Jeune Chambre Economique d'Alger: rue de Nîmes, Algiers; Pres. M. DONNEAUD.

There are also Chambers of Commerce at Colomb-Béchar, Ghordaia and Tlemcen.

EMPLOYERS' ORGANIZATION

Union Générale des Commerçants Algériens: Place des Martyrs, Algiers.

PRINCIPAL TRADE UNIONS

Union Générale des Travailleurs Algériens—UGTA: Maison du Peuple, Algiers; f. 1956; 300,000 mems.; Sec.-Gen. ABDELKADER BENIKOUS; publ. *Révolution et Travail* (weekly).

AFFILIATES

Fédération du Bois, du Bâtiment, des Travaux Publics et des Activités Annexes (*Federation of Building Trades Workers*): Maison de Peuple, Algiers; f. 1964; 17,000 mems.; Gen. Sec. BELHADJ BUKIR.

Fédération Nationale des Cheminots (*National Federation of Railwaymen*): 3 rue Alexandre Dumas, Algiers; Sec.-Gen. AZZI ABDELMOUDJID.

Fédération Nationale de l'Energie Electrique et du Gaz d'Algérie—FNEEGA (*National Federation of Utility Workers*): Maison du Peuple, Place du 1er Mai, Algiers; f. 1963; 5,000 mems.; Gen. Sec. CHABANE LABOU.

Fédération Nationale de la Santé (*Federation of Hospital Workers*): Maison du Peuple, Algiers; f. 1962; 15,000 mems.; Gen. Sec. DJEFFAL ABDELAZIZ.

Fédération Nationale des Travailleurs du Pétrole, du Gaz et Assimilés (*Federation of Oil and Gas Workers*): 21 blvd. Colonel Amirouche, Algiers; f. 1964; 45,000 mems.; Gen. Sec. ALI LASFER.

Fédération Nationale des Travailleurs de la Terre—FNTT (*Federation of Farm Workers*): 4 rue Arago, Algiers; f. 1964; Gen. Sec. BENMEZIANE DAOUD.

Fédération des Ports, Docks et Aéroports (*Federation of Dock and Airport Workers*): Maison du Peuple, Algiers; f. 1964; 2,500 mems.; Gen. Sec. SAID OUKALI.

Fédération des Postes et Télécommunications (*Federation of Postal and Telecommunications Workers*): Maison du Peuple, Algiers; f. 1964; 6,000 mems.; Gen. Sec. YSSAAD ABDELKADAR.

Fédération des Travailleurs de l'Alimentation et du Commerce (*Federation of Food and Commerce Workers*): Maison du Peuple, Algiers; f. 1965; 14,000 mems.; Gen. Sec. DJEBIENE MAHMOUD.

Fédération des Travailleurs de l'Education et de la Culture—FTEC (*Federation of Teachers*): Maison du Peuple, Algiers; f. 1962; 13,000 mems.; Gen. Sec. BOUAMRANE CHAIKH.

Fédération des Travailleurs des Mines et Carrières (*Federation of Mine and Quarry Workers*): Maison du Peuple, Algiers; f. 1965; Sec.-Gen. OUALI MAHOUD KAHAR.

Fédération des Travailleurs Municipaux d'Algérie (*Federation of Municipal Employees*): Maison du Peuple, Algiers; 15,000 mems.; Gen. Sec. AHMED ZITOUNI.

Union nationale des paysans algériens (UNPA): f. 1973; 700,000 mems.

DEVELOPMENT

Banque Algérienne de Développement: Immeuble Joly, 38 ave. Franklin Roosevelt, Algiers; f. 1963; cap. 100m. AD; Government-sponsored development fund to finance industrial and commercial enterprises and excercise credit control by means of medium and long-term credits in the private sector.

Caisse Centrale de Coopération Economique (C.C.C.E.): 22 rue Larbi Alik, Hydra, Algiers; f. 1968; Dir. JEAN GAMBETTE.

Société Centrale pour l'Equipment du Territoire—S.C.E.T. International: 8 rue Sergent Addoun, Algiers; Dir. A. GAMBRELLE.

Société Nationale d'Etudes de Gestion, de Réalisations et d'Exploitations Industrielles—S.N.E.R.I.: 50 rue Khélifa Boukhalfa, Algiers.

NATIONALIZED INDUSTRIES

A large part of Algerian industry is nationalized. The following are some of the most important nationalized industries:

Office Algérien des Pêches: 1 place de la Pêcherie, Algiers; f. 1969; state trawling and canned sea-food organization.

Société Nationale Algérienne de Constructions Mécaniques (SONACOME): Route Nationale 1, Birkhadem; f. 1967; sole manufacturer and importer of motor vehicles, agricultural equipment and allied products.

Société Nationale de Constructions Métalliques (SN METAL): 38 rue Didouche Mourad, Algiers; f. 1968; production of metal goods.

Société Nationale des Industries Textiles (SONITEX): 4–6 rue Patrice Lumumba, Algiers; f. 1966; 10,107 employees; Dir. Gen. BENALY CHERIF.

Société Nationale des Lièges et du Bois (SNLB): 1 rue Aristide Briand, Algiers; f. 1973; production of cork and wooden goods.

Société Nationale des Matériaux de Construction: Algiers; f. 1968; building materials.

Société Nationale des Peaux et Cuirs (SONIPEC): 14 rue Amane Ramdane, Algiers; f. 1967; hides and skins.

Société Nationale de Recherches et d'Exploitations Minières (SONAREM): 127 Blvd. Salah Bouakouir, Algiers; mining and prospecting; Dir.-Gen. MOHAMED AMIROUCHE.

Société Nationale des Semoules, Pâtes Alimentaires et Couscous (SN SEMPAC): 6 blvd. Zirout Youcef, Algiers; f. 1965; semolina, paste, flour and couscous.

Société Nationale de la Sidérurgie (SNS): 5 rue Abou Moussa, Algiers; f. 1963; cast iron and products.

Société Nationale des Tabacs et Alumettes (SNTA): 40 rue Hocine Nourredine, Algiers; monopoly of manufacture and trade in tobacco, cigarettes and matches.

STATE TRADING ORGANIZATIONS

Since 1972 all international trading has been carried out by state organizations, of which the following are the most important:

Office Algérien Interprofessionel des Céréales (OAIC): 5 rue Ferhat Bousaad, Algiers; f. 1962; monopoly of trade in wheat, rice, maize, barley and products derived from these cereals.

Office des Fruits et Légumes d'Algérie (OFLA): 21 rue Larbi Ben M'Hidi, Algiers; f. 1969; division of the Ministry of Agriculture and Agrarian Reform; collects the produce from worker-controlled farms, and exports vegetables, fresh and dried fruit and associated by-products of Europe.

Office National de Commercialisation (ONACO): 21 rue Larbi Ben M'hidi, Algiers; f. 1963; monopoly of bulk trade in basic foodstuffs except cereals; brs. in over 40 towns.

Office National de Commercialisation des Produits Viti-Vinicoles (ONCV): 112, Quai-Sud, Algiers; f. 1968; monopoly of importing and exporting products of the wine industry; Dir.-Gen. A. KARA TERKI.

Other state buying organizations exist for dairy products, wood and wood products, textiles, footwear and hides and skins, and more are being set up.

TRADE FAIR

Foire Internationale d'Alger: Palais des Expositions, Pins Maritimes, B.P. 571, Algiers; annual; fortnight in September.

OIL

Sonatrach (*Société nationale pour la recherche, la production, le transport, la transformation et la commercialisation des hydrocarbures*): Immeuble Maurétania, Agha, Algiers; f. 1963; state-owned organization for exploration, exploitation, transport, refining and marketing of oil and gas and their products. In 1973 it accounted for 78 per cent of output and 67 per cent of exports, operating through a number of subsidiary companies formed in association with foreign oil companies; Dir. SID AHMED GHOZALI.

TRANSPORT

RAILWAYS

Société Nationale des Chemins de Fer Algériens: 21 blvd. Mohammed V, Algiers; f. 1959; 4,074 km. of track, of which 319 km. are electrified; daily passenger services from Algiers to the principal provincial cities, and a service to Casablanca via Oran; Dir. Gen. SADDEK BENMEHDJOUBA.

ROADS

There are about 82,000 km. of roads and tracks, of which 18,500 km. are main roads and 19,000 km. are secondary roads. The total is made up of 55,000 km. in the north, including 24,000 km. of good roads, and 27,000 km. in the south, including 3,200 km. with asphalt surface. The French administration built a good road system, partly for military purposes, which since independence has been allowed to deteriorate in parts, and only a small percentage of roads are surfaced. New roads have been built linking the Sahara oil fields with the coast, and the trans-Saharan highway is a major project. Algeria is a member of the Trans-Sahara Road Committee, organizing the building of this road, now renamed the "Road of African Unity". The first 360-km. stretch, from Hassi Marroket to In Salah, was opened in April 1973, and work has begun on the next section, which will include 420 km. inside Algeria and run into Niger.

Société Nationale des Transports Routiers: 27 rue des 3 Frères, Bouaddon, Algiers; f. 1967; holds a monopoly of goods transport by road; Dir.-Gen. HAOUSSINE EL-HADJ.

Société Nationale pour le Transport des Voyageurs: 27 rue des 3 Frères, Bouaddon, Algiers; f. 1967; holds monopoly of passenger transport by road.

MOTORISTS' ORGANIZATION

Touring Club d'Algérie: 1 rue El Idrissi, Algiers.

SHIPPING

Algiers is the main port, with 23–29 metres anchorage in the Bay of Algiers, and anchorage for the largest vessels in Agha Bay. The port has a total quayage of 8,380 metres in three basins; the Old Port with 2.4–12 metres depth alongside, Mustapha Basin 7–11 metres depth alongside, and the Agha Basin.

Annaba's 48 hectare harbour has 9–11 metres depth with 140 metres of quayage for petrol tankers. The Inner Port (Grande Darse) has 1,850 metres of quayage with 9 metres depth alongside. Oran's 120 hectare harbour has 2,800 metres of quayage with 6–12 metres depth alongside, accommodating vessels of up to 167 metres. Arzew has 1,850 metres of quayage of which a third has 8 metres depth alongside. There are also important ports at Bedjaia, Djidjelli, Ghazaouet, Skikda (for oil), and Mostaganem.

Compagnie Nationale Algérienne de Navigation (CNAN): quai d'Ajaccio, B.P. 280, Algiers; f. 1964; State-owned company managing its own fleet and vessels on time charter; concerned in the transport of oil, gas, wine, early fruit and other goods; 33 vessels; agencies and monopoly of handling facilities in all Algerian ports; office in Marseilles and reps. in Paris, all French ports and the principal ports in many other countries.

Office National des Ports: 2 rue d'Angkor, B.P. 830, Algiers; responsible for management and growth of port facilities and sea pilotage.

Société Nationale de Manutention (SONAMA): B.P. 147, Algiers; monopoly of port handling.

CIVIL AVIATION

Algeria's main airport, Dar el Beïda at Algiers, is a class A airport of international standing. At Constantine, Annaba and Oran are smaller modern airports able to accommodate jet aircraft, and there are also 65 aerodromes of which 20 are public, and a further 125 air-strips connected with the oil industry.

Air Algérie: 1 place Maurice Audin, B.P. 858, Algiers; f. 1946; internal services and extensive services to Europe, North and West Africa, Middle East and Asia; fleet of 3 Caravelles, 4 Convair 640, 4 Boeing 727-200, 8 Boeing 737-200, 5 Nord 262; Pres. MOHAMED BOUZADA.

FOREIGN LINES

The following foreign airlines operate services to Algiers: Aeroflot, Air France, Alitalia, Aviaco, Balkan, ČSA, EgyptAir, Interflug, Royal Air Maroc, Saudi Arabian Airlines, Swissair, Tunis Air.

TOURISM

Office National Algérien du Tourisme (ONAT): 25 rue Khélifa Boukhalfa, Algiers.

Société Nationale Algérienne de Tourisme et d'Hotellerie (SONATOUR): 8 rue du Dr. Saadane, Algiers.

THEATRE

Théâtre National Algérien: 10 rue Hady Oman, Algiers; performances in Arabic and French in Algiers and all main cities.

ATOMIC ENERGY

Institut d'Etudes Nucléaires d'Alger: B.P. 1147, Algiers; f. 1958; research into nuclear physics, solid and electronic physics; two Van de Graaff accelerators, 3 MeV and 2 MeV; one Sames accelerator 600 KeV and one isotope separator of the Saclay type; Dir. Prof. M. ALLAB.

DEFENCE

Commander-in-Chief of the Armed Forces: Col. HOUARI BOUMEDIENNE.

Defence Budget (1974): 1,600 million dinars.

Military Service: compulsory national service for both sexes since 1969.

Total Armed Forces: 63,000: army 55,000; navy 3,500; air force 4,500.

Paramilitary Forces: 10,000.

EDUCATION

Education in Algeria continues broadly to follow the pattern laid down during the French administration, but its scope has been greatly extended. About 30 per cent of school-age children still receive no schooling at all, but current plans envisage education facilities for all by 1978. By 1974, well over two million children attended primary schools, compared with about 800,000 in 1962. Facilities for secondary education are still limited, although they, too, have improved greatly in the decade, and accommodated about 400,000 pupils in 1974 compared with 45,800 in 1962. Whereas before independence most teachers were French, now over 90 per cent of the primary school staffs are Algerians, as are over 50 per cent of staffs in secondary and higher education, where teaching is still mostly in French. By the end of the 1972–73 school year all French teachers had left, to be replaced eventually by Algerians. In the meantime the complement is being made up by teachers from Egypt, Syria, Tunisia and other Arab countries. For several years Arabic has been used increasingly in primary education, and this has been made possible by the recruitment of foreign Arabic-speaking teachers and of Algerian *moniteurs*. At higher levels scientific and technical subjects are being given priority. There are a number of technical colleges and three main universities, at Oran, Constantine and Algiers, the latter being the oldest in North Africa. At the end of 1974 a supplementary university opened in Algiers, and there are plans for a Technical University in Oran, a university at Annaba and a *centre universitaire* at Tlemcen. Several thousand students go abroad to study, especially to France. Adult illiteracy is being combatted by a large-scale campaign, in which instruction is given in some cases by young people who have only recently left school, and in which the broadcasting services are widely used.

UNIVERSITIES

Université d'Alger: 2 rue Didouche Mourad, Algiers; 500 teachers, 9,500 students.

Université d'Oran: rue du Colonel Lotfi, Oran.

Université de Constantine: rue Ben M'hidi, Constantine; 1,200 teachers, 8,500 students.

BIBLIOGRAPHY

ALAZARD, J. and others. Initiation à l'Algérie (Paris, 1957).

ALLAIS, M. Les Accords d'Evian, le référendum et la résistance algérienne (Paris 1962).

AMIN, SAMIR. The Maghreb in the Modern World: Algeria, Tunisia, Morocco. (Penguin, Harmondsworth, 1970).

ARON, RAYMOND. La Tragédie Algérienne (Paris, 1957).

BALOUT, L. Algérie Préhistorique (Algiers, 1958).

BEHR, EDWARD. The Algerian Problem (London, 1961).

BOURDIEU, PIERRE. The Algerians (Boston, 1962). Sociologie de l'Algérie (Que Sais-je, Paris, 1958).

BRACE, R. and J. Ordeal in Algeria (New York, 1960).

CHALIAND, G. L'Algérie, est-elle Socialiste? (Maspéro, Paris, 1964).

DE GAULLE, CHARLES. Mémoires d'espoir: Le Renouveau 1958–1962 (Plon, Paris, 1970).

DE GRAMMONT, H. Histoire d'Alger sous la Domination Turque (Paris, 1887).

ENCYCLOPAEDIA OF ISLAM. Algeria (New Edition, Vol. I. London and Leiden, 1960).

FANON, FRANZ. Les Damnés de la Terre (Maspéro, Paris, 1961).

FAVROD, CH.-H. Le F.L.N. et l'Algérie (Paris, 1962).

FERAOUN, MOULOUD. Journal, 1955-1962 (Paris, 1963).

FIRST, RUTH. The Barrel of a Gun: Political Power in Africa and the Coup d'Etat (Allen Lane, The Penguin Press, London, 1970).

FISHER, G. Barbary Legend (Oxford, 1957).

GILLESPIE, JOAN. Algeria (Benn, London, 1960).

GORDON, DAVID. North Africa's French Legacy, 1954-1963 (London, 1963). The Passing of French Algeria (Oxford, 1966).

HENISSART, PAUL. Wolves in the City: The Death of French Algeria (Hart-Davis, London, 1971).

HUMBARACI, ARSLAN. Algeria—A Revolution that Failed (Pall Mall, London, 1966).

IBRAHIMI, A. TALEB. De la Décolonisation à la Révolution Culturelle (1962–72) (S.N.E.D., Algiers, 1973).

JEANSON, C. and F. L'Algérie hors la Loi (Paris, 1955).

JEANSON, F. La Révolution Algérienne; Problèmes et Perspectives (Milan, 1962).

JOESTEN, JOACHIM. The New Algeria (New York, 1964).

JULIEN, CHARLES-ANDRÉ. Histoire de l'Algérie contemporaine, conquête et colonisation, 1827-1871 (Presses Universitaires de France, Paris, 1964).

KRAFT, JOSEPH. The Struggle for Algeria (New York, 1961)

LACHERAF, MOSTEPHA. L'Algérie Nation et Société (Maspéro, Paris, 1965).

LAFFONT, PIERRE. L'Expiation: De l'Algérie de papa à l'Algérie de Ben Bella (Plon, Paris, 1968).

LEBJAOUI, MOHAMED. Vérités sur la Révolution Algérienne (Gallimard, Paris, 1970).

LESCHI, L. Algérie Antique (Algiers, 1952).

MANDOUZE, ANDRE. La Révolution Algérienne par les Textes (Paris, 1961).

MANSELL, GERARD. Tragedy in Algeria (Oxford, 1961).

MARÇAIS, G. Algérie Médiévale (Algiers, 1957).

MARTIN, CLAUDE. Histoire de l'Algérie Française 1830–1962 (Paris, 1962).

MOUILLESEAUX, LOUIZ. Histoire de l'Algérie (Paris, 1962).

M'RABET, FADELA. Les Algériennes (Maspéro, Paris, 1967).

NYSSEN, HUBERT. L'Algérie en 1970 (1970).

O'BALLANCE, EDGAR. The Algerian Insurrection 1954–62. (Archon, Hamden, Conn., and Faber, London, 1967).

OPPERMANN, THOMAS. Die Algerische Frage (Frankfurt, 1960).

OTTAWAY, DAVID and MARINA. Algeria. The Politics of a Socialist Revolution (Berkeley, University of California Press, 1970).

OUZEGANE, AMAR. Le Meilleur Combat (Julliard, Paris, 1962).

QUANDT, WILLIAM B. Revolution and Political Leadership: Algeria, 1954–1968 (M.I.T. Press, 1970).

REUDY, JOHN D. Land Policy in Colonial Algeria: The Origins of the Rural Public Domain (University of California Press, Berkeley, 1967.).

ROBSON, P. and LURY, D. The Economies of Africa (Allen & Unwin, London, 1969).

ROY, JULES. The War in Algeria (New York, 1961).

SA'DALLAH, A. Q. Studies on Modern Algerian Literature (Al Adab, Beirut, 1966).

SOUSTELLE, J. Le Drame Algérien et la Décadence Française: Réponse à Raymond Aron (Paris, 1957).

SULZBERGER, C. L. The Test, de Gaulle and Algeria (London and New York, 1962).

THOMAS, BENJAMIN E. Trade Routes of Algeria and the Sahara (London, 1958).

Bahrain

GEOGRAPHY

The Bahrain Archipelago lies near Qatar off the west coast of the Gulf.

The total area of the Bahrain group of islands is 255 square miles. Bahrain itself, the principal island, is 30 miles long and 10 miles wide. To the north-east of Bahrain, and linked to it by a causeway and motor road, lies Muharraq island, which is approximately 4 miles long. The archipelago comprising the State of Bahrain consists of thirty-three islands, including Nabih Salih, Jeddah, Hawar and Umm Suban.

The total population is 250,000. The port of Manama, the capital and seat of government, has a population of approximately 90,000 (including several hundred foreigners, mainly businessmen). The town of Muharraq has a predominantly Arab population of approximately 38,000. Both Sunni and Shi'ite Moslems are represented in the indigenous population, the Ruling Family belonging to the Sunnis.

HISTORY

After several centuries of independence Bahrain passed firstly under the rule of the Portuguese (1521 to 1602) and then it occasionally came under Iranian rule (1602 to 1782). The Iranians were expelled in 1783 by the Utub tribe from Arabia whose paramount family, the Al-Khalifas, became the independent Sheikhs of Bahrain and have ruled Bahrain ever since, except for a short break before 1810. Iranian claims based on the Iranian occupation of the islands in the seventeenth and eighteenth centuries nevertheless continued to be made from time to time.

In the nineteenth century European powers began to interest themselves in the Gulf area, and Britain was principally concerned to prevent French, Russian and German penetration towards India, and to suppress the slave and arms trades. In 1861, in consequence of political claims put forward by Iran and Turkey, the Sheikh of Bahrain undertook to abstain from the prosecution of war, piracy and slavery by sea in return for British support against aggression. In 1880 and 1892 the Sheikh further undertook not to cede, mortgage or otherwise dispose of parts of his territories to anyone except the British Government, nor to enter into any relationship with a foreign government other than the British without British consent.

Bahrain was naturally affected by the general post-war ferment in the Arab world. A tentative step towards democratic institutions was taken in February 1956, when elections were held for members of an Education and Health Council, the first election in Bahrain being held in 1919 for the Municipal Council. Shortly afterwards there was a strike in the oil refinery, said to be partly a protest against the paternalistic attitude of the British adviser to the Sheikh. There were further disturbances at the time of the Suez crisis. Meanwhile, further symbols of Bahrain's growing independence were the establishment of Bahraini as opposed to British legal jurisdiction over a wide range of nationalities (1957), the issue of Bahrain's own stamps (1960), and the introduction of a separate currency (1965). A small-scale distribution of village lands was started in 1960, and among economic developments the construction of a new town, Isa Town built to Western standards of amenity, has been prominent; its first stage was completed and formally inaugurated in November 1968, and eventually the town will have 35,000 people living in 2,500 houses. Bahrain also pioneered free education and health services in the Gulf, and good electricity and water services are available. There was another major strike in 1965 lasting from March 19th to April 30th, the principal cause being a fear of redundancies in the oil companies. In May 1966 Britain announced that her principal base in Arabia would be transferred from Aden to Bahrain in 1968, and a more realistic rent was agreed with the Bahrain Government for the military establishment. However, in 1968 the British government announced that all forces "East of Suez"—including those in the Gulf—would be withdrawn by the end of 1971, a decision which was subsequently implemented. However, the year's notice given by the Bahrain government in October 1973 to the U.S. Navy, whose ships have docking facilities in Bahrain, was not carried out and in March 1975 it was announced that the United States had agreed to a 600 per cent increase in rent for the port facilities.

Extensive administrative and political reforms came into effect in January 1970. A twelve-member Council of State became the State's supreme executive authority, this being the first formal delegation of the sheikh's powers. Only four of the initial twelve "Directors" were members of the royal family, but all were Bahrainis, and the British advisers were officially reduced to civil servant status. Equal numbers of Sunni and Shi'ite Muslims were included (the royal family apart) to represent Bahrain's religious balance. The reform was claimed to bring Bahrain closer to the Kuwait form of government rather than that in the Trucial sheikdoms. In August 1971 the Council of State became the Cabinet of the State of Bahrain, authorized to direct the internal and external affairs of the State.

After 1968 Bahrain was officially committed to membership of the embryonic Federation of Arab Emirates, but with over half the Federation's population and high educational and social welfare standards built up over 40 years, Bahrain disagreed with the richer but more backward sheikdoms further down the Gulf over the terms of the federal constitution (especially those relating to method of government), the allocation of common finances, etc. Bahrain's position was strengthened in May 1970 when Iran accepted the United Nations' report on Bahrain's future. The UN representatives visited the island in April and found that popular opinion overwhelmingly favoured a complete independence rather than union with Iran.

By the summer of 1971 Bahrain was ready to go it alone. On August 14th, 1971, full independence was proclaimed, the treaty arrangements with Britain being terminated, and a new treaty of friendship was signed with Britain the next day. On August 17th Sheikh Isa took the title of Amir. In September Bahrain became a member of the Arab League and the UN. In December 1972 elections were held for a Constituent Assembly, whose first task was to study proposals for, and produce within six months, a draft Constitution. This task was completed on June 2nd, 1973, and, in accordance with the new Constitution, elections to a National Assembly took place on December 8th, 1973 (see National Assembly, page 241). In June 1974 industrial unrest occurred, and the delay in allowing trade unions to be set up, although provided for in the constitution, was thought to be responsible, together with a large increase in the cost of living.

ECONOMY

Agriculture and cattle breeding are practised throughout the islands, the main crops being vegetables, lucerne, fodder crops and some dates. Traditional occupations such as dhow building, fishing and pearling continue but on a much smaller scale than before. In recent years several soft drink factories and brick making plants have been established. The Bahrain Fishing Company, 40 per cent British owned and 60 per cent Bahraini, has now been operating successfully for several years, exporting frozen prawns to the U.S.A. and Japan.

Oil in commercial quantity was found in 1932. The Bahrain Petroleum Company (BAPCO), which has been the main concessionaire, was formerly owned jointly by the Standard Oil Company of California and Texaco Inc. In November 1974 an agreement giving 60 per cent participation to the Bahrain Government was reached, and in March 1975 the Bahrain Government announced that it intended to take over full ownership of BAPCO. A new agreement implementing this is under negotiation. The State will then control not only crude production, which averaged 66,000 barrels per day in 1974, but also the BAPCO refinery which handles large supplies of crude by submarine pipeline from Saudi Arabia and also future exploitation of natural gas.

In common with other Arab oil-producing countries, Bahrain cut back its oil production and placed an embargo on the export of oil to the U.S.A. and the Netherlands after the October 1973 war with Israel. The embargo on the export of oil to the U.S.A. was lifted in March 1974 and to the Netherlands in July 1974. It is estimated that the known oil reserves can only be exploited for about another 20 years.

The second largest refinery in the Middle East is at Bahrain. In 1974 it refined a total of over 89 million barrels; although this figure includes crude oil piped from Saudi Arabia, the Bahrain Petroleum Company itself produced 24.6 million barrels in 1974. In 1972 plans were laid for the construction of a £26 million desulphurization plant as part of a general expansion programme for the refinery. This plant was brought into commission in the autumn of 1973, and can process up to 50,000 barrels per day. It should help meet the growing world demand for low sulphur fuels. Production from Abu Saafa, an offshore field between Bahrain and Saudi Arabia, began in 1968 at the rate of 1,500,000 tons per annum.

In December 1971 the new Bahrain International Airport Terminal Building was opened. The first Terminal designed specifically for Jumbo Jets, this building can handle the passengers of two 747s simultaneously and is equipped with four airbridges and all the equipment required for the handling of the largest aircraft planned from now until the end of the century. Further expansion is planned. A four-lane causeway and bridge joins the two main islands of Bahrain.

In the first half of 1962 new port installations were completed at Mina Sulman, which enables the port to handle up to six vessels of 30 ft. draught simultaneously. The port has, unlike the majority of other Gulf ports, never had any surcharge imposed by International Shipping Conferences. It also has storage and refrigeration facilities for the transit trade. Mina Sulman is to be extended under a World Bank project, and a master plan has been prepared by British consultants Rendel, Palmer & Tritton. A slipway and modern marine and engineering workshops adjacent to the port and under separate commercial management were completed during 1963. Bahrain has a free zone in which many British, American and local concerns have their headquarters; the island is a major entrepôt market for the neighbouring Gulf states.

A dry dock project, backed by the Organization of Arab Petroleum Exporting countries and costing £74 million, has been planned and should be completed by the end of 1975. Known as AGRY (Arabian Gulf Repair Yards) the ship repair centre and dry dock will take tankers up to 400,000 tons and should be in full operation in 1977.

The Ministry of Development and Engineering Services offers inducements to foreign investors in industrial and commercial projects, notably in the form of relief from taxation, freedom to repatriate profits, and cheap power (Bahrain has a large surplus of low cost natural gas). The concern for industrial development is stronger than in the other Gulf states, owing to the greater educational advancement of the population and the small scale of the islands' oil production and reserves. The majority of new industrial concerns established under this programme have been built in the Free Zone. Besides the ship repair facilities and the fishing company referred to above, other companies are now producing offshore oil wellhead structures, manufactured domestic and industrial plastic products, assembly of air-conditioning units and furniture assembly.

A £60 million aluminium smelter, under construction since 1969, began production in 1970 and it now has a capacity of 120,000 tons per annum. By June 1975 the Bahrain Government had secured a 52.4 per cent share in the consortium, Aluminium Bahrain (ALBA); the rest of the capital had been subscribed by a variety of European and American interests. Under a twenty-year contract production of natural gas was begun in 1971 by the Bahrain Petroleum Company to provide fuel for the turbine complex of the plant. Another long-term contract was signed with Western Australian interests to provide alumina for the Smelter. Ancillary industries are now being established—a factory to produce aluminium powder (Bahrain Atomizers) is now in production and plans for an extrusion plant were approved by the Ministry of Finance at the beginning of June 1975.

STATISTICAL SURVEY

AREA AND POPULATION

Area sq. km.	Population (Census of April 3rd, 1971)		
	Total	Manama (capital)	Muharraq Town
369.6	216,815	89,399	37,732

Estimated Population: 250,000 (July 1974).

EMPLOYMENT
(1971)

Agriculture and fishing	3,990
Mining and Manufacturing . . .	4,152
Oil	4,312
Public Utilities	1,705
Construction	10,404
Wholesale and retail trade, and catering .	7,706
Transport, storage and communications .	7,743
Finance, insurance, property and business services	1,084
Community, social and personal services .	13,182
Public administration and defence . .	5,206
Other	817
Total	60,301

CRUDE OIL PRODUCTION
('000 metric tons)

1970	1971	1972*	1973*	1974*
3,847	3,761	3,471	3,395	3,380

Source: Petroleum Times.

REFINERY PRODUCTION
(Output in million barrels)

1970	1971	1972	1973
91.4	93.3	85.9	89.6

Note: 1 metric ton equals approx. 7.3 barrels.

Industry: Building materials, clothing, soft drinks, plastic products, industrial gases, boat building, air conditioning manufacture, flour mills and an aluminium plant.

FINANCE

1,000 fils = 1 Bahrain dinar (BD).
Coins: 1, 5, 10, 25, 50 and 100 fils.
Notes: 100, 250 and 500 fils; 1, 5 and 10 dinars.
Exchange rates (July 1975): £1 sterling = 863.29 fils; U.S. $1 = 394.74 fils.
100 Bahrain dinars = £115.84 = $253.33.

Note: The Bahrain dinar was introduced in October 1965, replacing the Persian Gulf Indian rupee at the rate of 1 dinar = 10 rupees = 15 shillings sterling (£1 = 1.333 dinars). Until August 1971 the dinar was valued at U.S. $2.10 ($1 = 476.19 fils). Between December 1971 and February 1973 the dinar was worth U.S. $2.28 ($1 = 438.60 fils). The present dollar valuation has been effective since February 1973. In terms of sterling, the value of the Bahrain dinar between November 1967 and June 1972 was 17s 6d. (87½ new pence), the exchange rate being £1 = 1.143 dinars.

BUDGET
('000 Bahrain dinars)

Revenue	1975-76	Expenditure	1975-76
Oil Payments	111,000	Amiri Expenditure	6,000
Government Dues	9,000	Finance and National Economy . .	4,335
Public Services	6,000	Development and Engineering Services .	11,310
Miscellaneous	8,240	Education	9,582
		Health	6,857
		Defence	5,600
		Consumer Subsidies . . .	6,000
		Development Expenditure . .	61,264
		Other	23,292
Total	134,240	**Total**	134,240

Currency in Circulation (December 1974): BD 19,337,547.

EXTERNAL TRADE

(B.D. '000)

	1972	1973	1974*
Imports	100,102	127,769	178,032
Exports and Re-exports (excl. oil) . .	32,292	32,011	70,083

* Estimate.

COMMODITIES

IMPORTS	1971	1972	1973
Food and live animals	14,536.3	14,992.8	19,635.3
Beverages and tobacco . . .	2,531.8	2,932.1	3,986.9
Inedible raw materials (not fuels) . .	1,424.9	1,355.1	1,726.2
Mineral fuels, lubricants etc. . .	1,125.2	1,318.6	2,375.5
Animal and vegetable oils and fats .	178.8	186.7	178.4
Chemicals	7,134.7	6,287.3	16,017.0
Basic manufactured goods . .	30,624.5	26,669.2	29,194.8
Machinery and transport equipment .	33,332.0	30,539.4	36,071.9
Miscellaneous manufactured articles .	13,983.3	15,723.1	18,379.5
Unclassified groups and transactions .	133.4	166.9	202.9
TOTAL	105,004.9	100,101.7	127,768.9

EXPORTS AND RE-EXPORTS	1971	1972	1973
Cereals and cereal preparations . . .	1,306.8	1,734.9	2,414.3
Coffee, tea, cocoa and spices . . .	1,307.0	1,090.7	1,130.1
Textile yarn, fabrics, etc. . . .	7,443.8	6,759.3	5,652.9
Machinery, other than electric . .	3,232.7	3,795.9	3,265.9
Electric machinery, etc. . . .	1,038.5	761.8	758.6
Transport equipment	1,162.6	1,397.4	772.5
Clothing	3,014.1	4,232.9	5,622.4
Footwear	1,498.8	1,628.9	1,763.8
Scientific instruments, optical and photographic goods, watches and clocks . .	1,703.3	1,480.0	499.0
TOTAL (including others) . .	28,404.7	32,291.8	32,011.7

PRINCIPAL COUNTRIES

IMPORTS	1970	1971	1972	1973
Australia	1,108	2,590	5,978	13,184
China, People's Republic . .	4,091	5,867	6,594	7,561
France	902	1,229	1,597	2,407
Germany, Federal Republic .	2,684	4,155	4,678	5,150
Hong Kong . . .	2,495	2,790	2,537	2,820
India	3,347	3,031	2,835	3,544
Italy	1,580	3,204	1,853	3,886
Japan	9,972	12,793	14,869	15,119
Netherlands . . .	3,817	5,671	2,393	2,501
Pakistan	2,915	2,438	1,958	3,617
United Kingdom . .	24,904	31,754	21,194	24,147
U.S.A.	5,812	12,630	13,079	17,647

COUNTRIES—*continued*

EXPORTS AND RE-EXPORTS	1971	1972	1973
Saudi Arabia	14,016	16,523	16,592
Qatar	1,648	1,833	1,461
Iran	1,043	1,916	1,875
Dubai	1,442	2,204	2,691
Abu Dhabi	639	569	1,292
Kuwait	3,518	2,146	1,235
United Kingdom . .	711	860	911

TRANSPORT

ROAD MOTOR VEHICLES
(number registered)

TYPE OF LICENCE	1970	1971	1972	1973
Private Cars . . .	8,960	10,400	12,389	15,228
Taxi Cabs . . .	915	908	837	895
Vans and Lorries . .	2,999	3,439	4,267	5,156
Private Buses . . .	381	419	491	545
Public Buses . . .	142	145	175	184
Motor Cycles . . .	1,529	1,772	1,966	2,286
TOTAL . . .	13,397	17,083	20,125	24,294

EDUCATION

GOVERNMENT EDUCATION, 1973-74

	SCHOOLS/ COLLEGES	STUDENTS
Primary	79	38,562
Intermediate	28	8,016
Secondary	8	6,397
Technical, Commercial, Religious	1	1,626
Higher (incl. Teacher Training Colleges)	2	386
TOTAL . . .	118	54,987

Source: Statistical Bureau, Finance Department, Bahrain Government.

THE CONSTITUTION

A new 108-article constitution was ratified in June 1973. It states that "all citizens shall be equal before the law" and guarantees freedom of speech, of the Press, of conscience and religious beliefs. Other provisions include the outlawing of the compulsory repatriation of political refugees. The constitution also states that the country's financial comptroller should be responsible to Parliament and not to the Government, and allows for national trade unions "for legally justified causes and on peaceful lines". Compulsory free primary education and free medical care are also laid down in the constitution. It is to remain in force for a minimum of five years. The constitution provides for a National Assembly, composed of the members of the Cabinet and 30 members elected by popular vote.

THE GOVERNMENT

Amir: Sheikh ISA BIN SULMAN AL-KHALIFA, K.C.M.G.

Heir Apparent: Sheikh HAMAD BIN ISA AL-KHALIFA.

THE CABINET
(*July* 1975)

Prime Minister: Sheikh KHALIFA BIN SULMAN AL-KHALIFAH.

Minister of Defence: Sheikh HAMAD BIN ISA AL-KHALIFAH.

Minister of Finance and National Economy: SAYED MAHMOOD AL-ALAWI.

Minister of Foreign Affairs: Sheikh MOHAMED BIN MUBARAK AL-KHALIFA.

Minister of Education: Sheikh ABDUL AZIZ MUHAMED AL-KHALIFA.

Minister of Health: Dr. ALI MOHAMED FAKHRO.

Minister of Interior: Sheikh MOHAMED BIN KHALIFA BIN HAMAD AL-KHALIFA.

Minister of Information: TARIQ ABDAL-RAHMAN AL-MUAYYAD.

Minister of Justice: Sheikh ISA BIN MOHAMED AL-KHALIFA.

Minister of Development and Engineering: YOUSIF AHMED AL-SHIRAWI.

Minister of Labour and Social Affairs: IBRAHIM MOHAMED HASAN HUMAYDAN.

Minister of Municipalities and Agriculture: Sheikh ABDULLA BIN KHALID AL-KHALIFA.

Minister of State for Judicial Affairs: Dr. HUSSAIN MOHAMED AL-BAHARNA.

Minister of State for Cabinet Affairs: JAWAD SALIM AL-URRAYED.

NATIONAL ASSEMBLY

In December 1972 22 members were elected to seats in the 44-member Constituent Council. The remaining 22 seats were occupied by nominees of the Amir and members of the cabinet. During the first six months of 1973 the Constituent Assembly drew up the new constitution, which was ratified in June 1973. In accordance with this constitution elections to a National Assembly took place on December 8th, 1973, and the Amir opened the Assembly on December 16th, 1973. About 30,000 electors elected 30 members for a four-year term. Since political parties are not allowed, all 114 candidates stood as independents, but in practice the National Assembly is divided about equally between conservative, moderate and more radical members. In addition to the 30 elected members, the National Assembly also contains 12 members of the cabinet.

DIPLOMATIC REPRESENTATION

EMBASSIES ACCREDITED TO BAHRAIN
(Manama unless otherwise stated)

Afghanistan: Baghdad, Iraq (E).

Belgium: Abu Dhabi, United Arab Emirates (E).

Canada: Teheran, Iran (E).

Egypt: 3105/7 Adliya, P.O.B. 818 (E); *Ambassador:* MOHAMED G. ABDUL-SALAM.

France: P.O.B. 1034 (E); *Ambassador:* J. BOURGOIN.

Germany, Federal Republic: Kuwait City, Kuwait (E).

Guinea: Jeddah, Saudi Arabia (E).

India: Sh. Isa Road 2299/7, Ad Adlia Area (E); *Ambassador:* P. M. S. MALIK.

Iran: Sh. Isa Road 1018/7 (E); *Ambassador:* MANUCHEHR SEPAHBODY.

Iraq: Almutanbi Road 911/8, Al-Mahouz (E); *Ambassador:* K. AL HADEETHI.

Ireland: London, England (E).

Italy: Kuwait City, Kuwait (E).

Japan: Kuwait City, Kuwait (E).

Jordan: Sh. Isa Rd. (E); *Ambassador:* MOUSSA AL KILANI.

Kuwait: Bani Atba Road 2105/7, Qudhaibiyya, nr. the new Palace (E); *Ambassador:* GHAZI MOHAMMED AMIN AL RAYYIS.

Lebanon: Kuwait City, Kuwait (E).

Morocco: Kuwait City, Kuwait (E).

Netherlands: Kuwait City, Kuwait (E).

Norway: Teheran, Iran (E).

Pakistan: Sh. Essa Rd. (E); *Ambassador:* GHOULAM GHOUTH KHAN.

Saudi Arabia: Delmon Road, Branch of Sh. Isa Road (E); *Ambassador:* Sheikh ABDULLAH SALEH AL-FADHEL.

Senegal: Teheran, Iran (E).

Somalia: Jeddah, Saudi Arabia (E).

Spain: Kuwait City, Kuwait (E).

Sudan: Kuwait City, Kuwait (E).

Switzerland: Jeddah, Saudi Arabia (E).

Tunisia: Kuwait City, Kuwait (E).

Turkey: Kuwait City, Kuwait (E).

United Kingdom: Al-Mathaf Square (E); *Ambassador:* ROBERT M. TESH, C.M.G.

U.S.A.: Sh. Isa Road, P.O.B. 431 (E); *Ambassador:* JOSEPH TWINAM.

Yemen Arab Republic: Kuwait City, Kuwait (E).

Bahrain also has diplomatic relations with Chad, Denmark, the Democratic People's Republic of Korea, Libya, Malaysia, Mongolia, Niger, Oman, Qatar, Syria, the U.S.S.R. and the United Arab Emirates.

JUDICIAL SYSTEM

Minister of Justice: Sheikh ISA BIN MOHAMED AL-KHALIFA.

Since the termination of British legal jurisdiction in 1971, intensive work has been in progress on the legislative requirements of Bahrain. The Criminal Law is at present contained in various Codes, Ordinances and Regulations.

Judges, both Bahraini and Arab, are all fully qualified, as are the lawyers that appear before the courts.

All nationalities are subject to the jurisdiction of the Bahrain Courts which guarantee equality before the Law irrespective of nationality or creed.

RELIGION

The great majority of the people are Muslims of the Sunni and Shi'ite sects. The ruling family is Sunni.

Religious affiliation (1971 Census):

Muslims	206,708
Christians	6,590
Others	2,780
TOTAL	216,078

PRESS, RADIO AND TELEVISION

Al Bahrain Al-Yom (*Bahrain Today*): P.O.B. 253, Manama; weekly; Arabic; published by the Ministry of Information; Manama; Editor SALMAN TAKI; circ. 4,000.

al Adhwaa: Arab Printing and Publishing Establishment, P.O.B. 224, Old Palace Rd., Manama; f. 1965; Arabic; weekly; Editor MAHMOUD ALMARDI, circ. 5,000.

Arab Markets: P.O.B. 604, Bahrain; monthly; English and Arabic; Editor ABDU F. BUSHARA.

Awali Evening News: Published by the Bahrain Petroleum Co. Ltd.; daily; English; circ. 1,000.

Awali Magazine: Published by the Bahrain Petroleum Co. Ltd.; monthly; English; circ. 1,000.

Bahrain Trade Directory: P.O.B. 524, Manama; annual; Publisher and Man. Dir. A. E. ASHIR.

al Hiya al Tijariya (*Commerce Review*): P.O.B. 248, Manama; monthly; Arabic; published by Bahrain Chamber of Commerce and Industry.

Al-Mujtama Al-Jadid: P.O.B. 590; Editor MUSTAFA.

Gulf Weekly Mirror: P.O.B. 455, Manama; f. 1971; weekly; English; also circulates in Oman, Qatar, United Arab Emirates and eastern Saudi Arabia; Editor STEFAN KEMBALL; circ. 8,500.

al Jarida al Rasmiya (*Official Gazette*): Information Department, Government of Bahrain, Manama; f. 1957; Arabic; weekly.

al Mawaquf: P.O.B. 1083, Manama, f. 1973; weekly; Arabic; world news, politics, arts, religion; Owner ABDULLA MADANI.

al Murshid: Arabian Printing and Publishing House, P.O.B. 553, Bahrain; monthly guide, including "What's on in Bahrain"; English and Arabic; Editor M. SOLIMAN.

al Najma al Asbuia (*Weekly Star*): Awali; Arabic; weekly; published by The Bahrain Petroleum Co. Ltd.; circ. 8,000.

The New Society: P.O.B. 590, Manama; weekly.

Sada Al Usbou: P.O.B. 549, Bahrain; f. 1969; Arabic; weekly; Owner and Editor-in-Chief ALI SAYYAR.

NEWS AGENCY

Reuters: P.O.B. 1030, Manama.

RADIO AND TELEVISION

Bahrain Broadcasting Station: P.O.B. 253, Manama; f. f. 1955; state-owned and operated enterprise; two 10kW. transmitters; programmes are in Arabic only, and include news, plays and talks; Dir. of Broadcasting IBRAHIM KANOO.

R.T.V. Bahrain: commenced colour TV broadcasting in 1973. The station takes advertising; taken over by Bahrain Government, February 1975.

English language programmes broadcast by the U.S. Air Force in Dhahran and by ARAMCO can be received in Bahrain, as can the television service provided by the latter. The station is currently being expanded and its power increased.

In 1974 there were approximately 100,000 radio receiving sets.

FINANCE
BANKING

(cap. = capital; dep. = deposits; m. = millions; B.D. = Bahrain Dinars)

CENTRAL BANK

Bahrain Monetary Agency: Manama; f. 1973 and became fully operative January 1975; controls issue of currency, exchange control, organization and control of banking system and bank credit; Dir.-Gen. A. E. MOORE.

COMMERCIAL BANK

National Bank of Bahrain: P.O.B. 106, Manama; f. 1957; commercial bank with Government of Bahrain as major shareholder; total assets (Dec. 1974) B.D. 82.12m. Chair. AHMED ALI KANOO; Gen. Man. A. S. WOOD.

FOREIGN BANKS

Algemene Bank Nederland: Amsterdam; Manama.

Arab Bank Ltd.: Amman, Jordan; P.O.B. 395, Manama; Man. AHMED I. JABER.

Bank Melli Iran: Teheran; Government Rd., P.O.B. 785, Manama; 1 br.

Bank of America: New York; Manama.

Bank of Bahrain and Kuwait: P.O.B. 597, Manama; cap. p.u. 2m. B.D. subscribed by Bahraini citizens and six leading finance institutions in Kuwait.

Bank of Cairo: P.O.B. 815, Manama.

Bank Saderat Iran: Teheran; Manama.

British Bank of the Middle East: London; P.O.B. 57, Manama; Man. D. A. BAGE.

The Chartered Bank: London; P.O.B. 29, Manama; Chief Man. for the Gulf V. R. WINTON.

Chase Manhattan Bank: New York; P.O.B. 368, Manama; Man. JOHN HOUSE.

Continental Illinois National Bank and Trust Co. of Chicago: Chicago; Manama.

First National City Bank: New York; P.O.B. 548, Manama, 1 br.; Gen. Man. GEORGE E. BARNES.

Grindlays Bank Ltd.: London; P.O.B. 793, Manama.

Habib Bank (Overseas) Ltd.: Karachi; Government Road, P.O.B. 566, Manama; Man. M. H. PASHMI.

National Westminster Bank: London; P.O.B. 820, Manama.

Rafidain Bank: Baghdad; f. 1969; P.O.B. 607, Manama; Man. T. AL-KHATIB.

Union Bank of Switzerland: Zurich; P.O.B. 795, Manama.

United Bank Ltd.: Karachi; Government Road; P.O.B. 546, Manama; Man. S. M. AKHTAR.

INSURANCE

Bahrain Insurance Co.: P.O.B. 179, Manama; f. 1971; general accident, fire and life insurance; cap. B.D. 300,000; $66\frac{2}{3}$ per cent Bahrain owned; $33\frac{1}{3}$ per cent Iraq owned.

About fifteen foreign insurance companies are represented.

TRADE AND INDUSTRY

Bahrain Chamber of Commerce and Industry: P.O.B. 248, Manama; f. 1939; 1,200 mems.; Pres. MUHAMMAD YOUSUF JALAL; Dir. YUSUF MUHAMMAD SALEH.

Michael Rice Group—Middle East: P.O.B. 551, Manama; consultants to the Governments of Bahrain and Oman and to numerous local and foreign businesses trading in Bahrain, the Gulf area, Saudi Arabia and Kuwait.

There are no Trade Unions in Bahrain.

OIL

The Bahrain Petroleum Company (BAPCO) Ltd.: Awali; the sole oil producer in Bahrain; owned jointly by Texaco and Standard Oil of California; a participation agreement, giving 60 per cent state participation to the Bahrain Government, was reached in September 1974; a new agreement, by which the Government will take over full ownership of BAPCO, is under negotiation; also operates the Bahrain refinery and holds a contract to supply natural gas to the ALBA aluminium smelter; Pres. W. O. STOLZ.

TRANSPORT

ROADS

Most inhabited areas of Bahrain are linked by bitumen-surfaced roads. Public transport consists of taxis and privately owned bus services. A new national bus company is being developed to provide public services throughout the country. A modern network of dual highways is being developed.

SHIPPING

Director-General of Customs and Ports: Sheikh DAIJ BIN KHALIFA AL-KHALIFA.

Port Operations Manager: BARRY METCALFE.

Cargo Manager: HASSAN SHAMS.

Numerous shipping services link Bahrain and the Gulf with Britain and with Europe (Strick Line, V.N.S. "Kerk" Line, Hansa Line, Nationale Compagnie Havraise Peninsulaire and Compagnie Maritime Belge, Kuwait Shipping Company, Iraqi Maritime Transport Corporation, Lauro Line, Yugo-Linea, Polish Ocean Lines); with the East and West Coasts, of U.S.A. (Concordia Line, Nedlloyd Line); with Pakistan, India, Japan and the Far East and Australia P & O, British & India Steam Navigation Company, Maersk Line, Everett Johnson Line, "K" Line of Japan, etc.). Though predominantly cargo operators, most of the foregoing lines have some passenger accommodation available; the British India Line operates a mail service between Bombay, Karachi, Bahrain and other Gulf Ports, carrying passengers in Saloon and Deck classes; the Mogul line operates mail and passenger services between Bombay and the Gulf, and the Pan Islamic Steamship Co. between Karachi and the Gulf ports.

The deep water harbour of Mina Sulman was opened in April 1962; it has six berths capable of taking vessels of draughts up to 9 metres. In the vicinity are two slipways able to take vessels of up to 1,016 tonnes and 73 metres in length, with services available for ship repairs afloat. Further development for Mina Sulman is planned. A trawler basin is the centre of a flourishing shrimping industry, the packaged produce being exported primarily to Europe, North America and Japan.

In November 1972 OAPEC approved Bahrain as the site for a £40 million dry dock large enough to accept super-tankers of up to 375,000 d.w.t. By December 1974, when work had begun, estimated costs had risen to £74 million and capacity was increased to 400,000 tons. The scheme should be completed in 1977.

CIVIL AVIATION

Bahrain Airport has a first-class runway, capable of taking the largest aircraft in use. A new jumbo jet airport terminal was opened in December 1971 and expansion is still in progress.

Gulf Air: P.O.B. 138, Bahrain; f. 1950; jointly owned by the governments of Bahrain, Qatar, United Arab Emirates and Oman; services linking Bahrain, Doha, Abu Dhabi, Dubai, Sharjah, Salalah and Muscat with London, Beirut, Cairo, Kuwait, Dharan, Shiraz, Bandar Abbas, Karachi, Bombay, Basra, Baghdad, Amman and Athens; fleet consists of five VC-10, four BAC 1-11, three F27, four Skyvans, two Islanders, two Beechcraft B80.

Bahrain is served by the following foreign airlines: Air India, Alia, British Airways, British Caledonian Egyptair, Iran Air, Iraqi Airways, KLM, Kuwait Airways, MEA, Singapore International Airlines, PIA (Pakistan), Qantas, Saudia, TMA, Sudan Airways, UTA.

EDUCATION

Education is free in Bahrain. From the ages of six to twelve children attend primary school. The next intermediate stage lasts two years and the secondary stage three years. There are three higher educational establishments, a Men's Teacher Training College, a Women's Teacher Training College and the Gulf Technical College. Expenditure on education was BD 5.9 million in 1973, 17.9 per cent of total government expenditure.

Gulf Technical College: Isa Town, Bahrain; f. 1969; 240 full-time and 480 part-time students.

BIBLIOGRAPHY

ADAMIYAT, FEREYDOUN. Bahrain Islands: A Legal and Diplomatic Study of the British-Iranian Controversy (New York, Praeger, 1955).

ALBAHARNA, H. M. The Legal Status of the Arabian Gulf States (Manchester University Press, 1968).

BUSCH, B. C. Britain and the Persian Gulf 1894–1914 (University of California Press, 1967).

FACT SHEETS ON EASTERN ARABIA (Private Information Center on Eastern Arabia, Heldenplein, 12-1800 Vilvoorde, Belgium).

FAROUGHBY, ABBAS. The Bahrain Islands (New York, 1951).

HAKIMA, A. M. The Rise and Development of Bahrain and Kuwait (Beirut, 1965).

HAY, SIR RUPERT. The Persian Gulf States (Middle East Institute, Washington, 1959).

MARLOWE, JOHN. The Persian Gulf in the 20th Century (Cresset Press, London, 1962).

MILES, S. B. The Countries and Tribes of the Persian Gulf (3rd edition, Cass, London, 1970).

WILSON, SIR A. T. The Persian Gulf (Oxford University Press, 1928).

Cyprus

PHYSICAL AND SOCIAL GEOGRAPHY

W. B. Fisher

The island of Cyprus, some 3,572 sq. miles in area, is situated in the north-eastern corner of the Mediterranean Sea, closest to Turkey (which is easily visible from its northern coast), but also under 100 miles from the Syrian coast. Its greatest length, including the long, narrow peninsula of Cape Andreas, is 140 miles. The population was estimated at 634,000 in 1973, including 488,000 Greeks and 116,000 Turks.

PHYSICAL FEATURES

Cyprus owes its peculiar shape to the occurrence of two ridges that were once part of two much greater arcs running from the mainland of Asia westwards towards Crete. The greater part of these arcs has disappeared, but remnants are found in Cyprus and on the eastern mainland, where they form the Amanus Range of Turkey. In Cyprus the arcs are visible as two mountain systems—the Kyrenia Range of the north, and the much larger and imposing Troödos Massif in the centre. Between the two mountain systems lies a flat lowland, open to the sea in the east and west and spoken of as the Mesaoria. Here also lies the chief town, Nicosia.

The mountain ranges are actually very different in structure and appearance. The Kyrenia Range is a single narrow fold of limestone, with occasional deposits of marble, and its maximum height is 3,000 ft. As it is mainly porous rock, rainfall soon seeps below ground; and so its appearance is rather arid, but very picturesque, with white crags and isolated pinnacles. The soil cover is thin. The Troödos, on the other hand, has been affected by folding in two separate directions, so that the whole area has been fragmented, and large quantities of molten igneous rock have forced their way to the surface from the interior of the earth, giving rise to a great dome that reaches 6,000 ft.

above sea-level. As it is impervious to water, there are some surface streams, rounder outlines, a thicker soil, especially on the lower slopes, and a covering of pine forest.

CLIMATE

The climate in Cyprus is strongly "Mediterranean" in character, with the usual hot dry summers and warm, wet winters. As an island with high mountains, Cyprus receives a fair amount of moisture, and up to 40 in. of rain falls in the mountains, with the minimum of 12 to 15 inches in the Mesaoria. Frost does not occur on the coast, but may be sharp in the higher districts, and snow can fall fairly heavily in regions over 3,000 ft. in altitude. In summer, despite the nearness of the sea, temperatures are surprisingly high, and the Mesaoria in particular can experience over 100° F. A feature of minor importance is the tendency for small depressions to form over the island, giving a slightly greater degree of changeability in weather than is experienced elsewhere in the Middle East.

Relatively abundant rainfall together with high average temperatures were in the past responsible for a heavy incidence of malaria in the island. After World War II, however, an energetic campaign was waged against mosquitoes, and Cyprus is now entirely free from the disease.

Cyprus is noteworthy in that between 50 and 60 per cent of the total area is under cultivation—a figure higher than that for most Middle Eastern countries. This is partly to be explained by the relatively abundant rainfall; the expanses of impervious rock that retain water near the surface; and the presence of rich soils derived from volcanic rocks which occur round the Troödos Mountains. The steadily developing tourist trade and the export markets in wine and early vegetables add to the incentives to development.

HISTORY

EARLY HISTORY

Cyprus first became important in recorded history when the island fell under Egyptian control in the second millennium B.C After a long period during which the Phoenicians and the people of Mycenae founded colonies there, Cyprus, in the eighth century B.C., became an Assyrian protectorate, at a time when the Greeks of the mainland were extending their settlements in the island. From the sixth century B.C. it was a province of the Persian empire and took part in the unsuccessful Ionian revolt against Persian rule in 502 B.C. Despite the Greek triumph over Xerxes in 480 B.C., subsequent efforts by the Greek city states of the mainland to free Cyprus from Persian control met with little success, largely because of dissension amongst the Greek cities of Cyprus itself. For more than two centuries after 295 B.C the Ptolemies of Egypt ruled in Cyprus until it became part of the Roman Empire.

Under the enlightened rule of Augustus the island entered upon a long period of prosperity, for trade flourished while the Romans kept the seas clear of piracy. When Jerusalem fell to the Emperor Titus in A.D. 70,

many Jews found refuge in Cyprus where they became numerous enough to undertake a serious revolt in A.D. 115. Christianity, apparently introduced into the island in the reign of Emperor Claudius (A.D. 41-54), grew steadily in the next three centuries, during which Cyprus, isolated from a continent frequently ravaged by barbarian inroads, continued to enjoy a relative degree of prosperity. From the time of Constantine the Great, Cyprus was a province governed by officials appointed from Antioch and formed part of the diocese of the East. In the reign of Theodosius I (379-395) the Greek Orthodox Church was firmly established there and in the fifth century proved strong enough to resist the attempt of the Patriarchs of Antioch to control the religious life of the island.

The Arab attack of 649 began a new period in the history of Cyprus which now became, for more than three hundred years, the object of dispute between the Byzantines and the Muslims. In the time of the Caliph Abd al-Malik (685–705) the revenues of the island were divided between the two Empires but in 691 hostilities were renewed after large numbers of Christians from Cyprus had moved to a new settlement on the shores of the Hellespont. In 747 the Byzantines crushed a determined Muslim effort to seize the island but were less successful in repelling serious attacks in the reign of the Emperor Nicephoras I (802–811). For a brief space Byzantium recovered effective possession of the island in the time of Basil I (867–886) but, whenever the Byzantine fleet was weak, Cyprus remained a doubtful possession of the Empire. From the decisive Byzantine reconquest of 964–5 Cyprus now enjoyed for more than two centuries a period of relative calm disturbed only by occasional revolts.

WESTERN RULE

Only with the Third Crusade did Cyprus begin a new chapter of its long story. In 1192 Richard Coeur-de-Lion, having conquered the island from the Greek usurper Comnenus, bestowed it on Guy de Lusignan, formerly King of Jerusalem. There now began almost four hundred years of Western rule, which saw the introduction of Western feudalism and of the Latin Church into a land which hitherto had been Greek in its institutions and Orthodox in its religious beliefs.

In the period from 1192 to 1267 (when the direct line of the Lusignan house became extinct) the new régime was gradually elaborated. The Lusignan monarchy was limited in character, for the royal power was effective only in the military sphere, all other important business of State being decided in a High Court which consisted of the nobles, the fief-holders, and the great officers of State. This Court applied to the island a highly developed code of feudal law derived from the Assizes of Jerusalem, the Cypriots being allowed to retain their own laws and customs in so far as these did not conflict with the feudal law. The period is also marked by the determined efforts of the Latin clergy, supported by the Papacy, to establish a complete control over the Orthodox Church, a policy carried out with much harshness which the Crown and the feudal nobility often sought to mitigate in order to keep the loyalty of the subject population. The dominance of the Latin Church was finally assured by the Bulla Cypria of Pope Alexander IV (1260).

During the second half of the thirteenth century the kingdom of Cyprus (now ruled by the house of Antioch-Lusignan) played an important role in the last struggle to maintain the Latin States in Syria against the Mamluk offensive. The influence of the monarchy was further strengthened in this period, and when in 1324 Hugues IV became king, the great age of feudal Cyprus had begun. Cyprus was now of great importance in the commerce which the Italian republics maintained with the East, and Famagusta became a flourishing port. The Papacy, however, always anxious to weaken the power of Mamluk Egypt, placed on the trade of the Italian republics with that State severe limitations and charged Cyprus and Rhodes with their enforcement. Thus began a conflict between the kings of Cyprus and the great republics of Venice and Genoa which did not endanger Cyprus so long as the Papacy could mobilize sentiment in the West to support the crusading State of the Lusignans. When, as the fourteenth century advanced, the Papacy lost its power to command such support in the West, Cyprus was left to face unaided the ambitions of Genoa and Venice, which she was powerless to withstand.

Before this decline began Cyprus enjoyed, in the mid-fourteenth century, a brief period of great brilliance under her crusading King Peter I (1359–69). In 1361 he occupied the port of Adalia on the south coast of Asia Minor, then held by the Turkish emirate of Tekke; and in the years 1362–65 toured Europe in an effort to win adequate support for a new crusade. His most memorable exploit came in 1365 when he captured Alexandria in Egypt, sacking it so completely that even as late as the sixteenth century it had not recovered its former splendour. In 1366 he repelled a Turkish attack on Adalia and in the next year ravaged the coast of Syria, seizing and pillaging Tripoli; but, seeing at last that no help was to be expected from the West, he made peace with Egypt. With his assassination in 1369 the great period of the Lusignan house was ended.

The reign of King Janus I (1398–1432) was a long struggle to drive out the Genoese, who had seized Famagusta during the war with Cyprus in 1372–74, and to repel the attacks of Mamluk Egypt, which had become weary of the repeated sea-raids undertaken from the ports of Cyprus. After plundering Larnaca and Limassol in 1425 the Mamluks crushed the army of Cyprus in a battle at Khoirakoitia in 1426, King Janus himself being captured, and his capital Nicosia sacked. The King was released in 1427, when he had promised the payment of a large ransom and of an annual tribute. The last years of Lusignan power were marked by dissension in the ruling house and by the increasing domination of Venice which, with the consent of Caterina Cornaro, the Venetian widow of the last Lusignan king, annexed Cyprus in 1489.

TURKISH RULE

Venice held Cyprus until 1570 when the Ottoman Turks began a campaign of conquest which led to the fall of Nicosia in September 1570 and of Famagusta in August 1571. The Turks now restored to the Orthodox Greek Church its independence and ended the former feudal status of the peasantry. The Cypriots paid a tax for their freedom to follow their own religion and were allowed to cultivate their land as their own and to hand it to their descendants on payment of a proportion of the produce, which varied from one-fifth to one-tenth according to the locality. About thirty thousand Turkish soldiers were also given land in the island, thus forming a Turkish element in the population which was later reinforced by a certain amount of immigration from Asia Minor.

The seventeenth and eighteenth centuries were a melancholy period in the history of Cyprus. Repeated droughts and ravages of locusts preceded a famine in 1640 and an outbreak of plague in 1641. In 1660 the Ottoman government, in order to limit the extortions of its officials and of the tax-farmers, recognized the Orthodox Archbishop and his three suffragans as guardians of the Christian peasantry, but this step did not prevent revolts in 1665 and 1690. A great famine in 1757–58 and a severe attack of plague in 1760 reduced the numbers of the peasantry very considerably, causing a widespread distress which culminated in the revolt of 1764–66. Cyprus from 1702 had been a fief of the Grand Vizier who normally sold the governorship to the highest bidder, usually for a period of one year. This practice created opportunities of financial oppression which were rarely allowed to pass unused. Perhaps the most striking development of the period was the continued rise in the power of the Orthodox bishops whose influence was so great in the late eighteenth century that the Turkish administration depended on their support for the collection of the revenues. The Turkish elements in Cyprus, who resented the dominance of the Orthodox bishops, accused them in 1821 of having a secret understanding with the Greeks of the Morea who had revolted against Turkish rule, and carried out a massacre of the Christians at Nicosia and elsewhere, which brought the supremacy of the bishops to an end.

In 1833 the Sultan granted Cyprus to Muhammad Ali, Pasha of Egypt, who was forced, however to renounce possession of it in 1840 at the demand of the Great Powers. During the period of reforms initiated by Sultan Mahmud II (1808–39) and continued by his immediate successors, efforts were made to improve the administration of the island. The practice of farming out the taxes was abolished (although later partially reintroduced) and the Governor now became a salaried official ruling through a divan half-Turkish and half-Christian in composition.

BRITISH RULE

In 1878 Great Britain concluded an agreement with the Sultan by which Cyprus was given over to British control. Great Britain intended to use the island as a base from which the Ottoman Empire might be protected against the ambitions of Russia, a defence then all the more important in that the opening of the Suez Canal (1869) had made the East Mediterranean an area of great strategic importance. Under the agreement of 1878 Cyprus remained legally a part of the Ottoman Empire, to which a tribute was paid consisting of the surplus revenues of the island, calculated at a sum rather less than £93,000 per annum.

From 1882 until 1931 the island had a Legislative Council partly nominated and partly elected. Various reforms were carried out in this first period of British rule: the introduction of an efficient judicial system and of an effective police force, and considerable improvements in agriculture, roads, education and other public services.

Cyprus was offered to Greece in 1915 provided Greece joined the Allies in the war, but the offer was refused and did not remain open. In 1925 the island became a Crown Colony, at a time when the discontent of the Greek Cypriots was beginning to assume more serious proportions.

In the period since 1931 the desire to achieve self-government within the Commonwealth grew stronger, but the *Enosis* movement remained a strong influence in the political life of the island. Cypriot troops performed valuable services in the war of 1939–45, for example in Libya under Lord Wavell and in the Greek campaign of 1941. Later Cyprus was used as a place of detention for illegal Jewish immigrants into Palestine, the last of such detention camps being closed in 1949.

CONSTITUTIONAL PROPOSALS

In July 1954 Great Britain made known its intention to prepare a restricted form of constitution for Cyprus, with a legislature containing official, nominated and elected members. The Greek Cypriots, insisting that their ultimate goal was *Enosis*, viewed the proposed constitution with disfavour, whereas the Turkish Cypriots declared their readiness to accept it. The Greek Government at Athens now brought the problem of Cyprus before the UN. Great Britain, however, urged that the question was one with which she alone was competent to deal. The result was that, in December 1954, the UN resolved to take no immediate action in the matter.

The more extreme advocates of *Enosis*, grouped together in the EOKA (National Organization of the Struggle for the Freedom of Cyprus) now began a campaign of terrorist activities against the British administration. A conference including representatives from Great Britain, Greece and the Turkish Republic met in London in August 1955. The British offer of substantial autonomy for Cyprus failed to win the approval of Greece, since it held out no clear prospect of self-determination for the island, and the conference therefore ended in frustration.

A new and more violent wave of terrorism swept Cyprus in November 1955. A state of emergency was declared on November 27th whereby the death penalty was imposed for the bearing of arms, life imprisonment for sabotage and lesser sentences for looting and the harbouring of terrorists. All public assemblies of a political nature were forbidden; the British troops in Cyprus (about 10,000 in all) assumed the status of active service in war time. The Governor now ruled the island through an executive council consisting of four officials from the administration, two Greek Cypriots and one Turkish Cypriot.

At the beginning of 1956 the Governor, Sir John Harding, discussed the situation with Archbishop Makarios, head of the Greek Orthodox Church in the island. Since Great Britain was now willing to accept the principle of ultimate independence for Cyprus, agreement seemed to be within reach. In March 1956, however, the discussions were broken off and Archbishop Makarios, implicated in the activities of the EOKA, was deported to the Seychelles Islands.

THE RADCLIFFE PROPOSALS

Great Britain, confronted with a general strike in Cyprus, with a renewed and more intense campaign of terrorism and with the first ominous signs of strife between the Greek and Turkish communities in the island, now appointed Lord Radcliffe, in July 1956, as Commissioner for Constitutional Reform. His report, published in December of that year, proposed that defence, foreign affairs and internal security should be reserved to the Governor, other spheres of rule being under the control of a cabinet of Cypriot Ministers responsible to an elected legislature. Lord Radcliffe laid down careful safeguards for the Turks in Cyprus—no laws affecting the domestic affairs of the Turks would be valid without the consent of two-thirds of the Turkish members in the legislature.

Meanwhile, in June 1956, Greece appealed once more to the United Nations. Great Britain, asserting that the internal affairs of Cyprus fell solely within her own competence, complained to the UN in October about the aid forthcoming from Greece for the EOKA terrorists. There were, however, talks at Athens and Ankara in December 1956, but to no effective end, since Greece rejected the proposals of Lord Radcliffe for constitutional reform in Cyprus. The UN, in February 1957, adopted a resolution urging that a peaceful and democratic settlement be found for the Cyprus problem.

RELEASE OF MAKARIOS

In March 1957 Archbishop Makarios was released from detention in the Seychelles and, since he was not allowed to return to Cyprus, went in fact to Athens. The British authorities also relaxed some of the emergency laws—e.g. the press censorship and the mandatory death penalty for the bearing of arms. These measures facilitated the holding of further discussions, but the progress made by the end of the year was inconsiderable.

The tide of violence ran high in Cyprus during the first half of 1958. EOKA carried out an intensive campaign of sabotage, especially at Nicosia and Famagusta. At the same time strife between the Greek Cypriots and the Turkish Cypriots was becoming more frequent and severe, the outbreaks in June 1958 being particularly serious. There was increased tension, too, between the governments at Athens and at Ankara.

BRITAIN'S SEVEN-YEAR PLAN

It was in this situation that Great Britain, on June 19th, 1958, made public a new scheme for Cyprus. The island was to remain under British control for seven years; full autonomy in communal affairs would be granted, under separate arrangements, to the Greek Cypriots and the Turkish Cypriots; internal administration was to be reserved for the Governor's Council which would include representatives of the Greek Cypriot and Turkish Cypriot communities and also of the Greek and Turkish governments at Athens and Ankara. This scheme came into force on October 1st, 1958.

THE ZÜRICH AND LONDON AGREEMENTS

Negotiations between Greece and the Turkish Republic soon carried the Cyprus problem towards an agreed solution. As the result of a conference held at Zürich, it was announced on February 11th, 1959, that the two states had devised a compromise settlement. A further conference at London led to a full and formal publication of the details.

Cyprus was to become an independent republic with a Greek Cypriot President and a Turkish Cypriot Vice-President. There would be a Council of Ministers (seven Greeks, three Turks) and a House of Representatives (70 per cent Greek, 30 per cent Turkish) elected by universal suffrage for a term of five years. Communal Chambers, one Greek, one Turkish, were to exercise control in matters of religion, culture and education. The Turkish inhabitants in five of the main towns would be allowed to establish separate municipalities for a period of four years.

Cyprus was not to be united with another state, nor was it to be subject to partition. Great Britain, Greece and the Turkish Republic guaranteed the independence, the territorial integrity and the constitution of Cyprus. Greece received the right to station a force of 950 men in the island, and the Turkish Republic, a force of 650 men. Great Britain retained under her direct sovereignty two base areas in Cyprus—at Akrotiri and at Dhekelia.

In November 1959 agreement was attained in regard to the delimitation of the executive powers to be vested in the President and Vice-President of Cyprus. A further agreement defined the composition of the Supreme Constitutional Court. On December 4th, 1959, the state of emergency (in force since 1955) came to an end. Archbishop Makarios, on December 13th, 1959, was elected to be the first President of Cyprus. After long negotiations concluded on July 1st, 1960, Great Britain and Cyprus reached agreement over the precise size and character of the two military bases to be assigned to British sovereignty.

INDEPENDENCE

Cyprus became formally an independent republic on August 16th, 1960, and, on September 20th, a member of the United Nations. The Conference of Commonwealth Prime Ministers, meeting at London, resolved on March 14th, 1961, that Cyprus be admitted as a member of the Commonwealth.

A team of experts from the United Nations visited Cyprus in the autumn of 1960. Its official report was made public on April 5th, 1961. On August 21st, 1961, Archbishop Makarios submitted to the Cyprus House of Representatives the outline of a five-year plan based on the UN report. The Archbishop laid particular emphasis on reform in land-tenure and agrarian methods, on the conservation of existing and the development of new water supplies and on the introduction of long-term loans to farmers.

CONSTITUTIONAL PROBLEMS

As Cyprus entered thus into its independence, serious problems began to arise over the interpretation and working of the constitution. There was divergence of opinion between Greek Cypriots and Turkish Cypriots over the formation of a national army, as laid down in the Zürich agreement of 1959 (2,000 men: 60 per cent Greek, 40 per cent Turkish), the main point of dispute being the degree of integration to be established between the two racial components. On October 20th, 1961, the Turkish Vice-President, Dr. Küçük, used his power of veto to ban full integration which President Makarios favoured at all levels of the armed forces.

Difficulties arose also over the implementation of the 70 per cent-30 per cent ratio of Greek Cypriot to Turkish Cypriot personnel in the public services. There was friction too in the House of Representatives, about financial affairs—e.g. customs duties and income tax laws.

The year 1962 saw the growth of a serious crisis over the system of separate Greek and Turkish municipalities in the five main towns of Cyprus—Nicosia, Famagusta, Limassol, Larnaca and Paphos. On December 29th, 1962, the Turkish Communal Chamber passed a law maintaining the Turkish municipalities in the five towns from January 1st, 1963, and also establishing a similar municipality in the predominantly Turkish town of Lefka. President Makarios now issued a decree stating that from January 1st, 1963, Government-appointed bodies would control municipal organizations throughout the island—a decree which the Turkish Cypriots denounced as an infringement of the constitution.

The Constitutional Court of Cyprus, sitting in judgement on the financial disputes, ruled in February 1963 that, in view of the veto exercised by the Turkish members of the House of Representatives since 1961, taxes could be imposed on the people of the island, but that no legal machinery existed for the collection of such taxes. In April the court declared that the Government had no power to control the municipalities through bodies of its own choosing and that the decision of the Turkish Communal Chamber to maintain the separate Turkish municipalities in defiance of the Cyprus Government was likewise invalid.

Negotiations between President Makarios and Vice-President Küçük to resolve the deadlock broke down in May. Accordingly in November Archbishop Makarios put forward proposals for a number of reforms—e.g. that the President and Vice-President of Cyprus should lose their right of veto over certain types of legislation; that separate Greek Cypriot and Turkish Cypriot majorities in the House of Representatives should not be required for financial legislation; and that single municipal councils, with both Greek and Turkish Cypriot members, should replace the separate municipalities in the five chief towns of Cyprus. These proposals proved to be unacceptable to the Turkish Cypriots.

CIVIL WAR

Meanwhile, underground organizations, prepared for violence, had come into being both among the Greek and the Turkish communities. In December 1963 serious conflict broke out. On December 25th Great Britain suggested that a joint force composed of British, Greek and Turkish troops stationed in Cyprus should be established to restore order. The governments at Nicosia, Athens and Ankara gave their assent to this scheme. At this same moment the forces of the Turkish Republic serving in the island occupied, north of Nicosia, a strong position which gave them control of the important road to Kyrenia on the northern coast of Cyprus—a road which was to become the scene of much conflict in the future. As a result of the December crisis co-operation between the Greek Cypriots and the Turkish Cypriots in government and in other sectors of public life came almost to an end.

The general situation was now becoming extremely tense. There was renewed violence in February 1964, especially at Limassol. Arms in considerable quantities were being brought secretly into the island for both sides and the number of armed "irregulars" was increasing rapidly. These developments also gave rise to sharp frictions between Athens and Ankara.

ESTABLISHMENT OF
UN PEACE-KEEPING FORCE

Cyprus, in January 1964, had asked the UN to send a representative to the island. On January 16th U Thant, the Secretary-General of the United Nations, nominated Lieutenant-General Prem Gyani of India to act in this role. Later in the same month the Cyprus Government informed U Thant that it would be glad to see a UN force established in the island. The UN Security Council debated the Cyprus question on February 18th, finally adopting a resolution on March 4th authorizing the creation of a United Nations peace-keeping force for Cyprus. U Thant, on March 6th, appointed Lieutenant-General Gyani to command this force. Advance units of the Canadian contingent reached the island later in the month and by May 22nd the UN Headquarters at Nicosia controlled some 7,000 men.

U Thant, on March 25th, announced the appointment of Mr. S. Tuomioja, the Finnish Ambassador to Sweden, as United Nations mediator in Cyprus. Later, on May 11th, U Thant nominated Dr. Galo Plaza, of Ecuador, to be his special representative in the island. After the death of Mr. Tuomioja Dr. Galo Plaza was to become, in September 1964, the UN mediator in Cyprus, Senhor Carlos Bernardes, of Brazil, taking his place as U Thant's Special Representative. The exploratory consultations of the UN officials—at Nicosia, at Athens and at Ankara—failed to achieve real progress in the summer of 1964.

There was more fighting between Greek and Turkish Cypriots in March and April 1964—above all for control of the Nicosia-Kyrenia road, which the troops of the Turkish Republic stationed in Cyprus controlled in the south, near Nicosia, and which Turkish guerrillas operating from St. Hilarion Castle, high in the mountains close to Kyrenia, dominated in the north. The fighting was severe at Ktima on March 7th–9th, 1964. On June 1st the Cyprus House of Representatives passed a Bill establishing a National Guard and making all male Cypriots between the ages of 18 and 59 liable to six months of service in it. Only members of the National Guard, of the regular police and of the army forces would now have the right to bear arms. One purpose of the Bill was to suppress the irregular bands which, as extremist sentiment grew stronger, tended more and more to escape from the control of the established régime.

Under the agreements concluded for the independence of Cyprus in 1959–60 the Turkish Republic maintained a contingent of troops in the island, the personnel of this force being renewed from time to time on a system of regular rotation. A new crisis arose in August-September 1964 when the Government at Nicosia refused to allow such a rotation of personnel. After much negotiation through the UN officials in the island the Cyprus Government agreed to raise its existing blockade of the Turkish Cypriots entrenched in the Kokkina district and to allow the normal rotation of troops for the Turkish force stationed at Cyprus. The Government at Ankara now consented that this force, which dominated the Nicosia-Kyrenia road, should come under the United Nations command in Cyprus.

LEGISLATIVE MEASURES

Towards the end of 1964 the Cyprus House of Representatives passed a number of important measures—a Bill for the creation of unified municipalities in Nicosia, Larnaca, Limassol, Famagusta and Paphos; a law restoring to the Government the right to exact income tax (a right inoperative since 1961 as a result of the veto of the Turkish Cypriot members in the House); and a Bill extending compulsory service in the National Guard for Greek Cypriots from six to twelve months. In July 1965 a new law was approved for unified elections on the basis of a common electoral roll, the communal distinction between Greek Cypriots and Turkish Cypriots being thus abolished.

The UN mediator in Cyprus, Dr. Galo Plaza, resigned in December 1965. A special envoy from U Thant, Señor José Rolz-Bennett, reached Cyprus in February 1966 with the aim of discovering local views on the continuation of the UN mediation effort and to examine the position of the UN peace-force in Cyprus. Little had been done towards mediation since Dr. Galo Plaza published a detailed report in March 1965. Moreover, no clear indication existed at this time as to where the funds would be found to continue the existence of the UN forces in the island. The United Nations was in fact to renew the mandate of these forces in June 1966 and again in December 1966. In addition the UN Secretary-General, U Thant, announced in January 1967 that he had chosen Señor Bibiano Osorio-Tafall, of Mexico, to be his personal representative in Cyprus, Senhor Carlos Bernardes, of Brazil, having resigned the appointment for personal reasons.

GENERAL GRIVAS

There was further tension in Cyprus during March 1966 over the position of General Grivas, the former head of EOKA. The General had returned to the island in June 1964 at a time when it was felt that he might be able, with his high personal prestige, to bring to order the small "private armies" and "irregular bands" which had emerged among the Greek Cypriots and which were violently defying the Cyprus Government.

President Makarios now, in March 1966, attempted to limit the functions of General Grivas in Cyprus and so to end a situation which saw political control vested in himself, while command of the armed forces, both the Greek Cypriot National Guard and also the "volunteer" Greek troops stationed in Cyprus, rested with the General, who took his orders from Athens. The President suggested that the National Guard should be transferred to the control of the Cyprus Minister of Defence—a proposal which found favour neither with General Grivas nor at Athens, where it provoked a sharp political crisis. The whole affair underlined the distrust separating President Makarios and General Grivas and the doubts existing at Athens as to the ultimate intentions of the President.

Meanwhile negotiations in secret had begun anew between Athens and Ankara in June 1966 and continued throughout the rest of the year.

Great Britain, in November 1966, announced her intention to reduce her military establishment in Cyprus. Some 2,000 servicemen would be brought back to Great Britain by the summer of 1967. At the same time there was to be a scaling down in the amount of stores held at the Dhekelia base. The Royal Air Force station at Nicosia had already been run down to care and maintenance status, leaving Akrotiri to function still as a large R.A.F. headquarters.

The shipment of small arms and machine-guns from Czechoslovakia for specialized units of the Cypriot police force during the winter of 1966–67 gave rise to another crisis. Turkey declared its concern for the safety of the Turkish community, and urged the United Nations Peace-Keeping Force (UNFICYP) to take control of the arms. The Greek government persuaded the Cypriot authorities to store the arms under the custody of the Greek troops in Cyprus.

The military *coup* in Greece in April 1967 was followed by a brief improvement in Greco-Turkish relations. The Prime Ministers and Foreign Ministers of Greece and Turkey met in Thrace in September 1967, but failed to come to an agreement on Cyprus, Greece rejecting any form of partition, which was implicit in the Turkish proposal to accept *Enosis* in return for military bases and ten per cent of the island's territory.

In November 1967 Greece and Turkey came near to war when the Greek Cypriot National Guard attacked the Turkish Cypriot villages of Kophinou and Ayios Theodoros, killing 24 Turkish Cypriots. Popular feeling in Turkey was in favour of war, and the Turkish army was mobilized in preparation for landings in Cyprus and an invasion of Greek Thrace. The immediate crisis was resolved, in large measure due to the recall of General Grivas to Greece and the intervention of Cyrus R. Vance, the emissary of President Johnson of the U.S.A. A settlement was reached, whereby Turkey demobilized and dispersed the invasion fleet, and both countries withdrew from Cyprus troops in excess of the agreed contingents.

TURKISH CYPRIOT ADMINISTRATION

On December 29th, 1967 the Turkish Cypriot community announced the establishment of a "Transitional Administration" to administer their affairs until the provisions of the 1960 Constitution were implemented. Measures were approved to establish separate executive, legislative and judicial authorities, and Dr. Fazil Küçük, Vice-President of Cyprus, was appointed President of the Transitional Administration, with Rauf Denktaş as Vice-President. A legislative body was set up, consisting of the Turkish Cypriot members of the House of Representatives elected in 1960 and the members of the Turkish Communal Chamber. The Executive Council's nine members functioned as the administration. President Makarios described the Transitional Administration as "totally illegal", but it continued to function as the *de facto* government of the Turkish community in Cyprus.

INTER-COMMUNAL TALKS

Between January and April 1968 the Cypriot Government gradually relaxed the measures it had taken against the Turkish community. With the exception of the Turkish area in Nicosia, freedom of movement for Turkish Cypriots was restored, checkpoints were removed and unrestricted supplies to Turkish areas were allowed. In April Rauf Denktaş, the Vice-President of the Turkish Cypriot Administration, was permitted to return from exile, and in May he began talks with Glavcos Clerides, the President of the House of Representatives. These talks were intended to form the basis of a settlement of the constitutional differences between the Greek and Turkish communities, but very little progress was made. After years of intermittent discussion, there was still an impasse, the Turks demanding local autonomy, the Greeks rejecting any proposals tending towards a federal solution, fearing that it might lead to partition. In June 1972 Dr. Kurt Waldheim, the UN Secretary-General, attended the talks, stressing the need for a peaceful settlement and expressing a hope that UNFICYP might be withdrawn in the near future. By the end of 1973 the Greek Cypriot representative seemed to have accepted the principle of local autonomy, but the talks still dragged on, with no acceptable compromise having been found on the scope of local automony or the degree of control to be exercised by the central government over local authorities. A statement by Mr. Ecevit, Prime Minister of Turkey, calling for a federal settlement of the constitutional problem, caused the talks to break down in April 1974. The Greek and Cypriot governments claimed that the talks had been conducted on the understanding that any solution would be in terms of a unitary state, Mr. Denktaş that federation would not necessarily mean partition. Mr. Denktaş also feared that the Greek Government was giving support to the *Enosis*

movement. Each side accused the other of trying to sabotage the talks.

TERRORISM AND ELECTIONS

While the talks between the Greek and Turkish communities were drifting on, there was a marked reduction in intercommunal violence, but the Greek population of the island was split between supporters of Makarios and his aim of an independent unitary state and those who demanded union with Greece. In 1969 the National Front, an organization calling for immediate *Enosis*, embarked on a campaign of terrorism, raiding police stations to steal arms, bombing British military buildings and vehicles, shooting and wounding the chief of police and making several unsuccessful bomb attacks on Government ministers. Mr. Papadopoulos, the Greek Prime Minister, denounced terrorism in Cyprus and the National Front in particular.

On March 8th, 1970 there was an attempt to assassinate President Makarios, attributed to the National Front. The President escaped unhurt. A week later, Polycarpos Georghadjis, a former Minister of the Interior, was found shot dead. At the trial of the President's would-be assassins, Georghadjis was named as a member of the conspiracy.

Despite the activities of the National Front, the Government decided to hold a general election on July 5th, 1970. The dissolved House of Representatives had been in existence since 1960, and the elections which should have been held in 1965 according to the Constitution had been postponed from year to year due to the continuing crisis. The continued absence of the 15 Turkish members, who met as part of the Turkish Legislative Assembly, meant that the Greek Cypriot House of Representatives contained only 35 members. Fifteen of the Greek Cypriot seats were won by the Unified Party, led by Glavcos Clerides, with a policy of support for President Makarios and a united independent Cyprus. The Communist party AKEL won nine seats, to become the second largest in the House. None of the candidates of DEK, the Democratic National Party, which stands for *Enosis*, won a seat. The elections held at the same time by the Turkish Cypriots resulted in a victory for the National Solidarity Party, led by Rauf Denktaş.

RETURN OF GRIVAS AND EOKA-B

The ideal of *Enosis* was still very attractive to many Greek Cypriots, despite the lack of success for pro-*Enosis* candidates in the election. Greek Cypriot students condemned President Makarios' policy of an independent unitary state, and called for an end to the inter-communal talks. General Grivas attacked the President in an article in an Athens newspaper, calling for his resignation on the grounds that, by abandoning *Enosis*, the President had betrayed EOKA's struggle for freedom.

At the beginning of September 1971 General Grivas returned secretly to Cyprus and began to hold meetings with the leaders of the National Front and his followers in the EOKA movement of the 1950s. President Makarios threatened to arrest the General for setting up armed bands, and declared his opposition to the achievement of *Enosis* by violent means. His opponents, pro-*Enosis* Greek Cypriots, condemned the inter-communal talks and rejected the idea of a negotiated compromise with the Turkish community. The Cyprus Government imported a considerable quantity of arms from Czechoslovakia as a precautionary measure, but after protests from the Greek and Turkish Foreign Ministries that the distribution of these arms would serve only to aggravate an already tense situation, the consignment was placed under the custody of UNFICYP. In April 1972 President Makarios expressed his support for the Turkish Prime Minister's suggestion that each community should gradually disarm, but nothing came of this move.

The President had been under pressure from the Greek Government to dismiss ministers considered hostile to Athens for some time. In February 1972 it was suggested in Athens that a Cypriot government of national unity should be formed, including moderate representatives of General Grivas. For some months the President resisted this pressure, and it seemed that the Greek Government, in alliance with dissident bishops and General Grivas, was intent on forcing his resignation. In May Spyros Kyprianou, the Foreign Minister who had been the main target of Greek hostility and one of the President's closest collaborators, resigned, and in June the President gave way and carried out an extensive reorganization of his cabinet.

General Grivas organized a new guerilla force, which became known as EOKA-B, and launched a series of attacks on the Makarios Government similar to those against British rule in the 1950s. While the Committee for the Co-ordination of the *Enosis* Struggle, his political front organization, demanded a plebiscite on *Enosis* and rejected inter-communal agreement as a means of settling the future of Cyprus, EOKA-B raided police stations, quarries and warehouses, stealing arms, ammunition, dynamite and radio transmitters.

PRESIDENTIAL ELECTIONS

The demand for a plebiscite from supporters of General Grivas was put forward as an alternative to the election for the presidency, called by President Makarios as a test of strength. The President's speech of February 8th, 1973 explained his position. While believing in *Enosis*, he considered that talks with the Turkish community on the basis of an independent Cyprus were the only practical possibility. He condemned terrorism and violence as counter-productive, likely to lead to Turkish intervention and unsupported by the Greek and Cypriot authorities. The Greek Government also repudiated terrorism and expressed its support for a constitutional solution.

On February 8th, 1973 Makarios was returned unopposed for a third five year term as President, and in the Turkish quarter of Nicosia Rauf Denktaş was declared elected Vice-President following the withdrawal of Ahmet Berberoğlu.

EOKA-B continued its terrorist activities throughout 1973, concentrating on bombings and raids on police stations. On July 27th the Minister of Justice, Christos Vakis, was kidnapped, and there were over 80 bomb explosions throughout Cyprus on the three following nights. The President refused to give in to violence or to blackmail, rejecting the terms put forward by Grivas for the release of Mr. Vakis. Numerous police and National Guard officers, suspected of being Grivas sympathizers, were dismissed, and Mr. Vakis was released on August 26th. Action by security forces against secret EOKA bases resulted in many arrests, the seizure of quantities of munitions and the discovery of plans to assassinate the President. President Papadopoulos of Greece publicly condemned the activities of "the illegal organization of General Grivas", which undermined the Greek policy of "support for the finding of a solution to the Cyprus problem through the enlarged local talks aimed at ensuring an independent, sovereign and unitary state."

MAKARIOS AND THE BISHOPS

On March 2nd, 1972 the three bishops of the Orthodox Church of Cyprus—Anthimos of Kitium, Yennadios of Paphos and Kyprianos of Kyrenia—called on Archbishop Makarios to divest himself of the temporal power of the Presidency, on the ground that his political role was incompatible with his ecclesiastical position under the rules of the Church. This provoked massive popular demonstrations and a resolution in the House of Representatives in support of the President. It appeared that the bishops had the support and protection of General Grivas. When the President rejected their demand for his resignation, they charged him with abandoning the ideal of *Enosis*, tolerating the growth of Communism and permitting the rise of anti-Greek attitudes.

The clergy of the diocese of Paphos voted Bishop Yennadios out of office in June 1972, but he and the other two bishops refused to accept this decision and continued their campaign against Archbishop Makarios. In March 1973 they held what they called a Holy Synod of the Church of Cyprus, and announced that in view of the Archbishop's refusal to resign the presidency they would strip him of his episcopal titles. Makarios disregarded this move and the bishops' declaration in April that he had been reduced to the rank of layman. While the bishops were attempting to gain control of the administration and finances of the Church, claiming that Yennadios had been appointed to the vacant archiepiscopal throne, Makarios was taking counter-measures. He called an election for the diocese of Paphos in succession to Yennadios, and in July 1973 held a synod of the Orthodox Churches in Nicosia. The synod, presided over by the Patriarch of Alexandria, gave its support to Archbishop Makarios. It ruled that the Presidency and the Archbishopric were not incompatible under canon law, that the bishops' attempt to depose the Archbishop was invalid and that the bishops were guilty of schism. The dissident bishops were replaced.

MILITARY COUP

Following the deposition of the three bishops, and the demonstrations of popular support for the President which their actions provoked, the Cypriot Government was able to take strong measures against other supporters of General Grivas. Forces loyal to the President waged guerrilla war against EOKA—B, and carried out a purge of the armed forces and police, some of whose members had collaborated with EOKA and helped their raids on police stations in search of arms. The Grivas campaign of terrorism seemed to have been checked by the beginning of 1974, and when General Grivas died of a heart attack on January 27th, 1974 the President granted an amnesty to 100 of his imprisoned supporters, hoping to restore normality in Cyprus.

In June 1974 President Makarios ordered a purge of EOKA supporters in the police, civil service, schools and National Guard, and on July 2nd wrote to President Ghizikis of Greece, accusing the Greek military régime of giving arms and subsidies to EOKA and using the Greek army officers attached to the Cyprus National Guard as a centre of subversion. The President demanded that the Greek officers who had collaborated with EOKA should be withdrawn, and began to take steps to ensure that the Guard should be loyal to Cyprus rather than to Greece and *Enosis*. The National Guard, apparently with Greek support, then staged a *coup*. On July 15th former EOKA gunman Nicos Sampson was appointed President. Makarios fled to Britain, the resistance of his supporters was crushed, and Greece sent more officers to reinforce the National Guard.

Rauf Denktaş, the Turkish Cypriot leader, called for military action by Britain and Turkey, as guarantors of Cypriot independence, to prevent Greece imposing *Enosis*. Having failed to induce Britain to intervene, Turkey acted unilaterally. Turkish troops landed in Cyprus on July 20th, and seized the port of Kyrenia and a corridor connecting it to the Turkish sector in Nicosia. A ceasefire on July 22nd did not prevent further Turkish advances, and the UN Peace-Keeping Force had little success in its efforts to interpose itself between the two Cypriot communities. Massacres and other atrocities were reported from many bi-communal villages, reinforcing the hostility between Greeks and Turks.

TURKEY OCCUPIES NORTHERN CYPRUS

The successful Turkish invasion had foiled Greek plans to take over Cyprus using the National Guard, and when the military government of Greece resigned on July 23rd, Nicos Sampson did likewise. Glavcos Clerides, the moderate Speaker of the House of Representatives who had led the Greek Cypriot delegation to the intercommunal talks, was appointed President, and began negotiations with Rauf Denktaş. In Geneva, Britain, Greece and Turkey also held talks, seeking a settlement, but negotiations broke down following Turkish demands for the establishment of a cantonal federation giving almost a third of the area of Cyprus to the Turkish Cypriots.

On August 14th, the day after the Geneva talks ended, the war was renewed. Turkish forces seized the whole of Cyprus north of the Attila Line, running from Morphou through Nicosia to Famagusta, and the new civilian government in Greece announced its inability to intervene. Turkey announced that, by this *fait accompli*, the boundaries of an autonomous Turkish Cypriot administration had been established, while Mr. Denktaş spoke of establishing a completely independent Turkish Cypriot state north of the Attila Line and of encouraging the immigration of Turkish Cypriots from areas still under Greek Cypriot control, to produce a permanent ethnic and political partition of the island. Dr. Kurt Waldheim, the UN Secretary-General, succeeded in arranging talks between Mr. Clerides and Mr. Denktaş, but was unable to bring about any constructive results from these negotiations. Possibly the most crucial round of peace talks on the Cyprus problem began in Vienna between Mr. Clerides and Mr. Denktaş in January 1975 under the aegis of Dr. Waldheim. The success of the talks hinged on whether the two sides could reach agreement on the political future of the island: the Turkish Cypriots wanting a Greek-Turkish bi-regional federation with strong regional governments, whereas the Greeks, whilst not ruling out a bi-zonal solution, favoured a multi-regional or cantonal federation with strong central government. Both parties stressed the need for an independent, non-aligned, demilitarized Cyprus.

Negotiations were postponed in February following the Turkish Cypriots' unilateral declaration of a Turkish Federated State of Cyprus in the northern part of Cyprus. Greece denounced this move as a threat to peace and declared that the issue would be taken to the UN Security Council where a resolution was passed, on March 13th, regretting the unilateral decision to set up a Federated Turkish State. Talks were resumed in April and the foundation laid for intercommunal reconciliation and co-operation, when the Cypriot leaders agreed to form an expert committee, under the auspices of Dr. Luis Weckmann-Muñoz, Special Representative of the UN Secretary-General, to consider the powers and functions of a central government for Cyprus and present their findings in June to the Cypriot negotiators in Vienna.

The flight of Turkish Cypriots to British bases after the National Guard *coup* and the withdrawal of Greek Cypriot civilians before the advancing Turkish army had produced a major problem in Cyprus. In August 1974 the United Nations estimated that there were some 225,600 refugees in Cyprus, of whom 183,800 were Greek Cypriots. In the southern part of Cyprus, under Greek Cypriot control, were 198,800 of these refugees, of whom 35,000 were Turkish Cypriots, including prisoners of war. The future of many of these refugees still remained uncertain in mid-1975, although 9,000 Turkish Cypriots were given the opportunity to move to the northern sector in August 1975.

By September 1974, the Greek Cypriot community was showing a tendency to divide into mutually hostile factions. Supporters of Archbishop Makarios, Communists and the right wing favouring *Enosis* were arming and training paramilitary groups, and EOKA was capitalizing on the discontent produced by the Turkish occupation, leading a demonstration in which the U.S. Ambassador was killed and threatening Acting President Clerides' position. In December 1974 Archbishop Makarios returned to Cyprus, and resumed the Presidency. In January 1975 Britain decided to permit the resettlement of over 9,000 Turkish Cypriot refugees from the British Sovereign Base at Akrotiri. The problem of population exchanges threatened to provoke a new crisis between Greek and Turkish Cypriots in July 1975; about 10,000 members of each community were still in each other's territory, unable to travel. In retaliation for the alleged ill-treatment of Turkish Cypriots still living in Greek areas and in order to force a decision on the release of the refugees and their resettlement, the Turks threatened to expel all remaining Greek Cypriots in northern Cyprus and launched a massive scheme to colonize the area, bringing thousands of farmers and peasants from mainland Turkey and settling them in Greek-owned property. Before the Turkish invasion of July 1974, Cyprus' 650,000 population was 18 per cent Turkish Cypriot and about 80 per cent Greek Cypriot. The Greek Cypriots claimed that Turkey planned to ship some 120,000 mainland Turks to Cyprus by the end of 1975, increasing the Turkish portion of the population to 30 per cent, thus strengthening the Turkish Cypriots' position on the island. The Cyprus Government alleged in July that Turkish forces in the North of the island were making "intensive military preparations".

With the establishment of the Turkish Cypriot Federated State in 1975 it appeared that the two national communities of Cyprus could not live together, but only side by side. It remained to be seen in July 1975 whether the Greek and Turkish Cypriot communities could reach a settlement on the balance of power in Cyprus without further bloodshed.

ECONOMIC SURVEY

Geographically Cyprus may be divided into four regions distinguished by their natural and climatic features. These are the north coastal belt including the narrow Kyreria mountain chain; the central plain, known as the Mesaoria, from Famagusta and Larnaca to Morphou Bay; the mountainous area of the south centre, dominated by the Troödos massif with its highest point of Mount Olympus (6,400 feet); and the coastal plain of the south running from a point west of Larnaca to Limassol and Paphos.

Of these areas the most significant in the island's economy are the central plain, which is the most densely populated and the centre of the island's grain production, the mountains, in which are situated the mineral deposits, which form the basis of the important extractive industries, the vineyards and the state forests, and the coastal plain, whose beaches form the principal tourist attraction on Cyprus.

The population of Cyprus increased rapidly in the period since the island passed under British rule, and had reached 639,000 by June 1974. The population rise has been mainly the result of a fall in the death rate due to advances in public health. The emergence of a young, mostly literate population, unable to be contained by the old agricultural economy, has been at the root of most of the island's political and economic problems in the last two decades. G.D.P. per head has risen from $575 in 1963 to $1,419 in 1973.

Since the middle of 1974, however, the economy has been gravely disrupted by the political *coup*, the intervention of the Turkish army and the effective partition of the island. As well as the physical damage caused by the fighting, the flight of more than a third of the population as refugees and the collapse of essential services in many areas reduced economic activity to a low level. Crops were not harvested, and the citrus groves suffered from lack of irrigation. Buildings and plant were destroyed or lost their workforce. The delay in arriving at a political settlement, which had still not been reached by June 1975, is very discouraging for the economy.

AGRICULTURE

Agriculture is the most important single economic activity in Cyprus. In 1973 it employed 30 per cent of the labour force. Wheat and barley account for 25 per cent of crop production, but the island is a net importer of cereals.

The principal exports are food (£29.8 million in 1973—mainly citrus fruits and potatoes), and beverages and tobacco (£6.8 million in 1973). Exports dropped in 1974, owing to the political situation. Agricultural exports accounted for 60 per cent of total exports in 1973. In recent years there has been a tendency towards production of "exotic" vegetables such as asparagus, green peppers, aubergines and artichokes. Viticulture has been an outstanding success in recent years, with steadily increasing exports of wine, grape juice and raisins as well as fresh grapes.

About 60 per cent of the land area is cultivated but only 5 per cent of this is irrigable in the hot summer, and because of the extensive fallow system in use on a third of the land only one crop in two years is produced in these areas. A five-year water study completed in 1968 by the UN revealed that the discovery of any new underground water supplies is unlikely. Already uncontrolled pumping has caused an incursion of sea water into some citrus areas.

Until 1974, when political troubles intervened, agricultural production had been on the increase. Production of citrus fruits rose from 257,000 tons in 1971 to 298,000 tons in 1973 but fell to 230,000 tons in 1974. Production of potatoes, which had been more than 170,000 tons in 1971 and 1972, fell to 150,000 tons in 1974. Cereal production, however, which had been affected by bad harvests in 1972 and 1973, was 195,000 tons in 1974, almost up to the 1971 level of 205,000 tons. Despite Government encouragement, livestock production is insufficient for the island's needs. Rising standards of living and the influx of tourists have raised demand for meat, and it is hoped to introduce intensive methods of animal husbandry.

Since agriculture is the most important sector of the Cyprus economy, substantial efforts have been made by the government to strengthen it. In March 1969 the House of Representatives passed the Land Consolidation Law, aimed at putting an end to land fragmentation and at establishing economically viable land holdings through the unification and redistribution of existing small plots. Laws and customs of inheritance have led to fragmentation of ownership on a vast scale. The new Law envisaged the creation of a Central Land Consolidation Authority which will direct, organize and co-ordinate *all* activities pertaining to land consolidation. At the end of 1972 land consolidation was being applied in seven different regions. The expectations were that when fully applied, land consolidation will raise the island's agricultural output by 20 per cent, but the process is rather slow, and much depends upon the conclusion of a political settlement.

Consolidation is not to be confined only to forming viable units as far as area is concerned. The construction of irrigation channels designed to conserve the use of water, new roads to provide ease of access (farmers and shepherds in many cases have to pay for the right to cross other owners' properties to reach their own), encouragement of terracing in hill farm areas, anti-erosion measures and the provision of windbreaks will be carried out in conjunction with the programme. The mechanization of agriculture is progressing, and the Ministry of Agriculture leases machinery to farmers.

INDUSTRY

Most manufacturing industry in Cyprus is limited to the production of basic consumer goods and the processing of agricultural raw materials. The manufacturing sector grew rapidly during the 1960s, concentrating on import substitution, and is characterized by the predominance of small productive units with an average of five employees. Despite structural inefficiencies and a shortage of skilled labour, manufacturing's share of the GDP grew to 12.5 per cent in 1972, due mainly to gains in the production of construction materials, particularly cement, as building expanded. The production of shoes and cigarettes also rose, and a number of new industries were established. An oil refinery was inaugurated in 1972, saving some £1.5 million a year in foreign exchange. In 1973, 13.6 per cent of the working population was employed in manufacturing and 10.3 per cent in construction. Most industrial production fell in 1974, owing to the political disturbances, but the production of cigarettes rose from 2.3m. lb. in 1973 to 3.2m. lb. in 1974.

The mining sector has been declining in importance for some years. Its contribution to GDP decreased from 4.9 per cent in 1971 to 3.8 per cent in 1972, and the labour force also decreased, partly as a result of mechanization. Export earnings from minerals fell from £13.97 million, 34.9 per cent of total exports in 1970 to £8.56 million, 19.2 per cent of total exports in 1972. Mineral deposits are depleting, and a fall in international copper prices in 1971–72 reduced the profitability of exploiting low grade ores. Despite rising prices in 1973, production of iron pyrites, cupreous concentrates and cupreous pyrites continued to fall, a decline which continued in 1974. Only asbestos production showed a significant increase. Heavy demand in the building and construction sector has produced a growing demand for quarrying materials.

TRADE

Cyprus had a trade deficit of £92m. in 1974, £5m. less than in 1973. This was mainly due to the curtailment of trade by the political crisis. Exports in 1974 fell to £55.2m. (£60.5m. in 1973), while imports fell to £148m. (£157m. in 1973).

Although improvements have been made to the island's principal port of Famagusta, it has been in Turkish hands since 1974. Nicosia international airport, which ceased to operate in the summer of 1974, had still not been re-opened by the end of June 1975, in spite of many political discussions about its re-opening.

Most of the island's trade is with the U.K., the other EEC countries and eastern Europe. In 1974 the U.K. took some 38 per cent of exports and 21 per cent of imports came from the U.K. Negotiations began early in 1971 to study the island's relationship with the EEC and the possibility of an association. In December 1972 an association agreement with the EEC was signed which came into force on June 1st, 1973. The agreement provides for the elimination of almost all trade barriers during two stages spread over 9½ years. During the first stage, ending on June 30th, 1977, the Community undertakes to reduce import tariffs on Cypriot industrial goods by 70 per cent and on citrus products by 40 per cent. These reductions, together with complete removal of duties on carobs, were to be effective immediately, while Cypriot tariffs on imports of industrial products from the Community were to be reduced by 35 per cent in three stages over a four-year period. Under a separate protocol, trade arrangements between Cyprus on the one hand and the U.K. and the Republic of Ireland on the other are to be maintained during the first stage. It was agreed that Cyprus will be permitted to export 200,000 hectolitres of sherry to the U.K. and the Republic of Ireland each year during 1973 and 1974, without having to respect Community reference prices. This arrangement will continue until the last of the 1974 vintage has been sold.

Diversification of export markets is official policy. Cyprus has trade and payments agreements with most of the east-European countries, and trade with this area has shown a steady and balanced growth.

The large trade deficit has been more than offset by invisibles and capital inflow, notably tourism, U.K. and other military expenditure and Cypriot expatriate remittances and capital inflows. In 1972 Cyprus's foreign exchange reserves had risen to £121 million, but with political uncertainty and the loss of tourist revenue, they had fallen to about £30m. by March 1975.

Tourism has been a major growth industry. The number of visitors to Cyprus has more than trebled between 1967

(68,379) and 1972, when the figure reached over 228,000. In addition many cruise passengers visit the island for short periods. Tourist expenditure reached £19 million in 1972, having shown a steady growth from £2.2 million in 1965. The growth continued in 1973, when foreign visitors totalled more than 264,000, bringing in £24m. The political troubles of 1974, however, brought a fall in the number of tourists to 150,000, with a consequent drop in tourist earnings to £14m. The potential for tourist development is there, however, as the number of hotel beds rose from 10,796 in 1973 to 13,050 in 1974.

The purchase of villas or plots of building land by expatriates has become increasingly common in some parts of the island. The buyers are mainly British and the villas are used as homes for retirement or as holiday cottages. Strong demand meant that high prices were paid, and this inflow of foreign capital has helped strengthen the balance of payments, but further growth in this direction depends on a political settlement.

The U.K. military presence in Cyprus is reckoned to benefit the economy to the extent of £15 million. Dependence on this (and expatriate remittances) is regarded as a structual weakness in the external accounts and growth in exports and tourist revenue is designed to counteract this.

DEVELOPMENT

There was no overall economic planning under British rule, and the first comprehensive Five-Year Plan was launched only in August 1961. By 1966 both unemployment and underemployment in rural areas had been reduced, and the annual rate of growth for G.N.P. and for gross domestic fixed capital formation increased.

The second Five-Year Plan (published in 1968) envisaged an annual growth rate of 7 per cent on the total investment of £200 million. Of this figure government expenditure was to be £57 million with £9.6 million contributed from public corporations. The private sector was to contribute £13.6 million. In contrast to the previous Five-Year Plan, only 9 per cent of the investment was to be derived from foreign sources.

The principal objectives of the 1967–71 Plan were to improve the balance of payments and to expand production in agriculture and in manufacturing and services. Improvements in communications and accelerated tourist development were sought as Cyprus aimed to lessen dependence on the British military presence as a source of foreign exchange. The third Five-Year Plan was to have come into operation in 1972, but its start was delayed until 1973. Expenditure of £360 million is involved.

The political situation obviously poses great problems for the future of the Cyprus economy. In July 1975 Cyprus was, in practical terms, a divided island, with the population polarizing into a Turkish north and a Greek south. With talk of plans to settle 40,000 Turks from the mainland in the Turkish zone of Cyprus to make up for the shortage of labour, it is obvious that if this division continues and hardens, the whole structure of the economy will permanently change.

STATISTICAL SURVEY

AREA AND POPULATION

AREA (square miles)		"DE JURE" POPULATION (1973 estimates)			
TOTAL	CULTIVATED	TOTAL	GREEKS	TURKS	NICOSIA (capital)
3,572	2,300	634,000	518,000*	116,000	116,100

Limassol 79,000, Famagusta 39,100, Larnaca 19,700, Paphos 9,000, Kyrenia 3,900. Immigrants: nil; Emigrants: 1,312. Estimated Population, June 30th, 1974: 639,000 (excluding tourists and British Sovereign Base Areas).

* Includes 29,800 other minorities.

BIRTHS AND DEATHS

	BIRTH RATE (per '000)	DEATH RATE (per '000)
1970	19.1	9.7
1971	18.7	9.6
1972	18.4	9.6
1973	18.2	9.5

ECONOMICALLY ACTIVE POPULATION
(1973)

	TOTAL
Agriculture, forestry, hunting and fishing	93,900
Mining and quarrying	3,700
Manufacturing	38,100
Construction	28,600
Electricity, gas, water and sanitary services	1,700
Commerce	21,900
Transport, storage and communications .	11,600
Services	41,800
Other activities (not adequately described)	38,400
TOTAL	279,700

AGRICULTURE

PRODUCTION
('000 tons)

	1972	1973	1974		1972	1973	1974
Wheat . . .	80	4	90	Olives . . .	20	2	8
Barley . . .	80	3	105	Grapes . . .	165	95	145
Potatoes . . .	172	160	150	Oranges . .	145	190	155
Carrots . . .	17	12	15	Grapefruit . .	57	67	57
Carobs . . .	38	14	6	Lemons . .	36	41	18

EXPORTS (tons)

	1972	1973	1974
Citrus Fruit . .	184,340	235,358	177,645
Potatoes . .	147,827	134,183	130,472
Carrots . . .	13,538	9,706	12,250
Grapes . . .	11,090	6,850	6,009
Raisins . . .	4,269	1,349	91

EXPORTS OF CITRUS FRUIT (tons)

	1972	1973	1974
Oranges . .	115,766	149,659	125,148
Grapefruit . .	42,813	53,842	40,015
Lemons . .	24,487	29,365	12,006
Others . . .	1,274	2,492	476

Livestock (1973): 430,000 sheep, 340,000 goats, 163,000 pigs, 33,000 cattle, 3,100,000 poultry.

Fishing: Value of catch: (1971) £632,000; (1972) £683,000; (1973) £884,000.

MINING

EXPORTS
(tons)

	1971	1972	1973	1974
Asbestos	22,255	27,546	28,541	36,579
Chromite	42,273	23,318	29,907	24,453
Cupreous concentrates . . .	50,633	64,737	63,978	45,737
Cement copper	9,056	5,744	6,440	2,317
Cupreous pyrites	73,336	45,980	32,875	22,965
Iron pyrites	602,177	452,901	358,026	282,625
Gypsum	530	114	22,875	10,564
Terra umbra	6,883	10,265	14,491	11,124
Yellow ochre	474	862	630	596
Other minerals	13,844	12,361	9,632	7,039

INDUSTRY

PRINCIPAL PRODUCTS OF MANUFACTURING INDUSTRIES

	UNIT	1972	1973	1974
Cement	'ooo metric tons	422.5	451.3	338.4
Bricks	million	46.4	46.7	23.8
Tiles	'ooo sq. metres	1,001	1,156	740
Cigarettes . . .	'ooo lb.	2,236	2,323	3,219
Shoes*	'ooo pairs	2,042	2,008	1,608
Beer	million litres	12.3	14.7	12.5
Wines	,, ,,	39.7	46.9	42.6
Intoxicating Liquors . . .	,, ,,	2.9	3.3	2.3

* Excluding plastic and semi-finished shoes.

Gross Output: (1972) Cyprus £96,726,000; (1973) Cyprus £110,639,000.

FINANCE*

1,000 mils = 1 Cyprus pound.

Coins: 1, 3, 5, 25, 50 and 100 mils.

Notes: 250 and 500 mils; 1 and 5 pounds.

Exchange rates (July 1975): £1 sterling = 800.3 mils; U.S. $1 = 366.0 mils.

Cyprus £100 = £124.95 sterling = $273.26.

Note: From November 1967 to August 1971 the par value of the Cyprus pound was U.S. $2.40 ($1 = 416.7 mils). Between December 1971 and February 1973 the Cyprus pound was valued at U.S. $2.6057 ($1 = 383.8 mils). From February to July 1973 the exchange rate was Cyprus £1 = U.S. $2.8952 ($1 = 345.4 mils). The Cyprus pound was at par with the pound sterling until the latter was allowed to "float" in June 1972; and it has itself been "floating" since July 1973.

* Since 1974 Turkish currency has been in use in the Turkish Cypriot area, as there is a shortage of Cypriot currency. The exchange rate has been fixed at Cyprus £1 = 38 Turkish liras.

BUDGET 1974
(Cyprus £)

REVENUE		EXPENDITURE	
Direct Taxes	13,662,649	Agriculture and Forests	969,201
Indirect Taxes	22,710,036	Water Development	367,460
Fees, Charges and Reimbursements	6,492,474	Public Works	1,023,091
Interest on Public Money	2,101,648	Cyprus Army and Tripartite Agreement	162,357
Rents and Royalties	677,558	Customs and Excise	474,314
Fines and Forfeitures	117,466	Public Debt Charges	4,145,950
Lotteries	880,810	Pensions and Grants	2,113,456
Miscellaneous	864,007	Cost of Living Allowances	7,716,892
Sales of Immovable Property	28,638	Medical	3,549,117
		Police	3,872,783
		Subsidies, Subventions and Contributions	11,356,083
		Education Grants	5,631,489
		Other	19,457,839
TOTAL	47,535,286	TOTAL	60,840,032

1975 Budget: Revenue £46,600,000; Expenditure £64,500,000.

DEVELOPMENT BUDGET
(Cyprus £)

	1972	1973	1974
Water Development	1,884,735	1,875,800	1,628,973
Road Network	1,462,666	1,283,664	1,184,692
Harbours	2,385,751	2,153,144	1,139,619
Agriculture	1,504,027	2,286,613	2,127,672
Commerce and Industry	512,188	557,902	367,520
Airports	352,603	262,341	96,739

1975 Development Budget: Total expenditure £14,900,000.

NATIONAL ACCOUNTS
(Cyprus £ million)

	1970	1971	1972	1973
GROSS DOMESTIC PRODUCT AT FACTOR COST .	208.2	240.8	273.2	302.5
of which:				
Agriculture, etc.	35.6	46.0	48.4	40.5
Manufacturing	25.5	29.9	37.9	43.3
Construction	16.9	19.8	23.0	28.7
Wholesale and retail trade . . .	32.3	36.8	42.4	48.4
Income from abroad	7.4	8.0	8.9	9.2
GROSS NATIONAL INCOME . . .	234.1	269.6	305.8	338.0
Less depreciation allowances . . .	—10.5	—12.1	—13.8	—15.2
NET NATIONAL INCOME . . .	223.6	257.5	292.0	322.8
Indirect taxes less subsidies . . .	18.5	20.8	23.7	26.3
NET NATIONAL PRODUCT . . .	205.1	236.7	268.3	296.5
Depreciation allowances . . .	10.5	12.1	13.8	15.2
GROSS NATIONAL PRODUCT . . .	215.6	248.8	282.1	311.7
Balance of exports and imports of goods and services, and borrowing . . .	21.7	19.8	22.0	41.9
AVAILABLE RESOURCES . . .	237.3	268.6	304.1	353.6
of which:				
Private consumption expenditure . .	171.6	194.1	219.3	248.4
Government consumption expenditure .	21.6	25.5	29.6	37.0
Gross fixed capital formation . .	53.3	58.5	67.2	80.2
Increase in stocks	1.9	3.3	2.8	5.1

CURRENCY IN CIRCULATION
December 31st, 1974: £39,654,000.

May 31st, 1975: £35,858,000.

GOLD RESERVES
1974: £6,246,000.

RETAIL PRICE INDEX
(1967=100)

	1971	1972	1973	1974*
All Items . .	113.29	118.77	128.05	113.66
Food and Drinks . .	115.43	123.18	133.65	115.57
Rent . . .	113.53	119.92	126.99	103.35
Fuel and Light . .	102.38	102.81	103.58	128.34
Household Equipment .	118.15	120.99	132.31	111.74
Household Operations .	115.93	119.94	125.65	125.26
Clothing and Footwear .	106.95	111.46	119.97	109.56
Miscellaneous . .	116.89	120.65	132.08	118.69

* Average for January–June 1974 (base: 1973=100). Series discontinued in July 1974.

BALANCE OF PAYMENTS
(£ million)

	1970	1971	1972	1973
Exports f.o.b.	41.3	44.8	47.9	57.2
Imports f.o.b.	−86.0	−94.5	−108.2	−140.5
TRADE BALANCE	−44.7	−49.7	−60.3	−83.3
Invisible Receipts	64.7	75.4	87.8	96.7
Invisible Payments	−27.2	−29.5	−33.4	−40.9
Invisible Balance	37.5	45.9	54.4	55.8
CURRENT ACCOUNT BALANCE	−7.2	−3.8	−5.9	−27.5
Short-term Capital	2.4	3.8	3.1	7.5
Long-term Loans	4.6	0.6	−0.5	3.8
Other Private Long-term Capital	6.1	12.0	14.4	13.0
Other Official Long-term Capital	0.2	1.7	0.2	—
Net Capital Movement	13.3	18.1	17.2	24.3
Net Errors and Omissions	4.4	3.6	−3.9	−1.3
OVERALL BALANCE	10.5	17.9	7.4	−4.5

EXTERNAL TRADE
(£'000)

	1968	1969	1970	1971	1972	1973	1974
Imports*	70,944	86,462	98,229	106,869	121,480	157,442	148,028
Exports	36,959	40,903	45,189	47,276	51,305	60,474	55,287

* Excluding NAAFI imports.

COMMODITIES (£'000)

IMPORTS*	1972	1973	1974
Food	16,224	32,668	24,084
Beverages and Tobacco	2,591	2,012	2,037
Crude Materials, Inedible	2,787	3,325	3,392
Mineral Fuels and Lubricants	8,432	8,774	19,021
Petroleum Products	3,176	3,000	5,583
Animal and Vegetable Oils and Fats	1,659	2,082	2,538
Chemicals	9,366	11,725	11,106
Manufactures	34,032	43,250	43,067
Iron and Steel	7,026	9,955	10,234
Machinery and Transport Equipment	36,277	40,150	32,770
Non-electric Machinery	13,011	14,181	15,024
Electrical Machinery	8,992	9,987	9,794
Transport Equipment	14,274	15,982	7,951
Miscellaneous Manufactures	8,581	11,533	9,248
Other Items, n.e.s.	1,531	1,923	765
TOTAL	121,480	157,442	148,028

EXPORTS	1972	1973	1974
Food	26,732	29,831	23,178
Oranges	6,685	8,777	6,963
Potatoes	7,092	5,941	5,066
Beverages and Tobacco	5,906	6,813	7,057
Crude Materials, Inedible	9,537	11,578	11,389
Iron Pyrites	1,061	727	699
Cupreous Concentrates	3,827	4,760	4,971
Copper Cement	1,176	1,759	1,003
Mineral Fuels and Lubricants	184	34	221
Animal and Vegetable Oils and Fats	160	178	76
Chemicals	703	602	364
Manufactures	1,191	1,403	3,744
Machinery and Transport Equipment	3,807	5,949	4,752
Miscellaneous Manufactures	2,831	3,269	3,847
Other Items, n.e.s.	254	817	659
TOTAL	51,305	60,474	55,287

* Excluding NAAFI imports.

COUNTRIES (£'ooo)

IMPORTS*	1972	1973	1974		EXPORTS	1972	1973	1974
Austria . . .	1,338	1,593	1,609		Belgium . . .	274	1,055	185
Belgium . . .	2,603	3,823	2,776		Czechoslovakia . .	1,487	2,068	1,445
France . . .	6,821	10,344	9,716		Denmark . . .	521	429	579
Germany, Fed. Republic	9,087	14,048	13,674		France . . .	1,516	1,418	457
Greece . . .	6,530	8,978	9,743		German Dem. Republic	991	516	553
India . . .	984	645	746		Germany, Fed. Republic	3,212	4,523	3,283
Israel . . .	2,486	2,865	2,579		Greece . . .	1,781	1,936	1,862
Italy . . .	9,662	12,392	11,509		Israel . . .	642	664	479
Japan . . .	6,120	5,965	5,356		Italy . . .	1,379	1,613	1,178
Lebanon . . .	1,498	1,477	1,879		Lebanon . . .	1,006	1,133	2,519
Netherlands . .	3,806	4,350	3,775		Netherlands . .	1,171	2,658	1,221
Portugal . . .	731	412	289		Spain . . .	1,323	779	804
Sweden . . .	2,323	2,522	2,256		Sweden . . .	404	517	469
Turkey . . .	818	1,746	1,718		Turkey . . .	1,370	434	254
U.S.S.R. . . .	3,566	4,044	5,753		U.S.S.R. . . .	3,251	2,570	3,928
United Kingdom . .	33,915	39,251	30,652		United Kingdom . .	21,234	24,152	21,099
U.S.A. . . .	7,290	10,568	9,383		U.S.A. . . .	565	729	533
Yugoslavia . . .	757	758	848					

* Excluding NAAFI imports.

TRANSPORT

ROADS

	1971	1972	1973	1974
Cars . . .	60,351	72,662	75,075	66,094
Taxis . . .	2,941	3,435	2,984	2,972
Lorries . . .	15,760	18,149	17,477	17,267
Motor Cycles .	13,647	14,935	14,880	15,274
Tractors .	7,782	8,067	7,479	7,332
TOTAL .	100,481	117,248	117,895	108,939

SHIPPING

	1971	1972	1973	1974
Vessels* Entered ('ooo net reg. tons) .	4,716	4,869	5,152	3,310
Goods Loaded ('ooo tons) . .	1,338	1,235	1,149	1,000
Goods Unloaded ('ooo tons) . .	1,505	1,781	2,121	1,382

* Steam or motor vessels and sailing vessels.

CIVIL AVIATION
CYPRUS AIRWAYS

	1971	1972	1973	1974
Kilometres flown . . .	3,474,000	4,465,000	5,727,302	2,894,313
Passenger arrivals . .	237,724	309,697	351,434	190,976
Passenger departures .	238,691	310,002	352,165	194,525
Freight landed (tons) .	2,053	2,596	2,551	1,524
Freight cleared (tons) .	6,863	8,460	5,561	3,783

Passenger kilometres: (1971) 187,983,000; (1972) 254,153,000.
Cargo ton-kilometres: (1971) 19,006,000; (1972) 25,374,000.

TOURISM

FOREIGN VISITORS BY COUNTRY OF ORIGIN*

	1971	1972	1973	1974
Greece	12,327	12,816	15,017	9,614
Israel	7,957	8,322	5,863	3,592
Lebanon	10,708	10,392	10,067	7,581
United Kingdom . .	78,062	98,136	116,026	52,938
United States . .	13,880	15,177	14,808	6,721
TOTAL (incl. others) .	178,598	228,309	264,066	150,478

* Excluding one-day visitors.

Tourist Earnings: (1970) £8.1m.; (1971) £13.6m.; (1972) £19m.; (1973) £24m.; (1974) £14m.
Number of Hotel Beds: (1970) 7,823; (1971) 9,413; (1972) 8,420; (1973) 10,796; (1974) 13,050.
Number of Tourist Nights: (1970) 658,322; (1971) 890,952; (1972) 1,167,963; (1973) 1,334,490; (1974) 740,143.

EDUCATION

(1973–74)

	GREEK			TURKISH	
	Establishments	Teachers	Pupils	Establishments	Pupils
Elementary . . .	554	2,219	62,465	167	16,014
Secondary (Public) . .	45	1,620	33,827	} 18	7,190
Secondary (Private) .	38	551	11,169		
Technical and Vocational .	8	338	4,672	6	753
Teacher Training . .	1	14	170	1	13
Other Post-Secondary .	6	74	679	—	

Source: Ministry of Finance, Department of Statistics and Research, Nicosia.

THE CONSTITUTION

The Constitution entered into force on August 16th, 1960, on which date Cyprus became an independent republic. In March 1961 Cyprus was accepted as a member of the Commonwealth.

ARTICLE 1

The State of Cyprus is an independent and sovereign Republic with a presidential regime, the President being Greek and the Vice-President being Turkish, elected by the Greek and the Turkish Communities of Cyprus respectively as hereinafter in this Constitution provided.

ARTICLES 2–5

The Greek Community comprises all citizens of the Republic who are of Greek origin and whose mother tongue is Greek or who share the Greek cultural traditions or who are members of the Greek Orthodox Church.

The Turkish Community comprises all citizens of the Republic who are of Turkish origin and whose mother tongue is Turkish or who share the Turkish cultural traditions or who are Moslems.

Citizens of the Republic who do not come within the above provisions shall, within three months of the date of the coming into operation of this Constitution, opt to belong to either the Greek or the Turkish Community as individuals, but, if they belong to a religious group, shall opt as a religious group and upon such option they shall be deemed to be members of such Community.

The official languages of the Republic are Greek and Turkish.

The Republic shall have its own flag of neutral design and colour, chosen jointly by the President and the Vice-President of the Republic.

The Greek and the Turkish Communities shall have the right to celebrate respectively the Greek and the Turkish national holidays.

ARTICLES 6–35
Fundamental Rights and Liberties

ARTICLES 36–53
President and Vice-President

The President of the Republic as Head of the State represents the Republic in all its official functions; signs the credentials of diplomatic envoys and receives the credentials of foreign diplomatic envoys; signs the credentials of delegates for the negotiation of international treaties, conventions or other agreements; signs the letter relating to the transmission of the instruments of ratification of any international treaties, conventions or agreements; confers the honours of the Republic.

The Vice-President of the Republic as Vice-Head of the State has the right to be present at all official functions; at the presentation of the credentials of foreign diplomatic envoys; to recommend to the President the conferment of honours on members of the Turkish Community which recommendation the President shall accept unless there are grave reasons to the contrary. The honours so conferred will be presented to the recipient by the Vice-President if he so desires.

The election of the President and the Vice-President of the Republic shall be direct, by universal suffrage and secret ballot, and shall, except in the case of a by-election, take place on the same day but separately.

The office of the President and of the Vice-President shall be incompatible with that of a Minister or of a Representative or of a member of a Communal Chamber or of a member of any municipal council including a Mayor or of a member of the armed or security forces of the Republic or with a public or municipal office.

The President and Vice-President of the Republic are invested by the House of Representatives.

The President and the Vice-President shall hold office for a period of five years.

The Executive power is ensured by the President and the Vice-President of the Republic.

The President and the Vice-President of the Republic in order to ensure the executive power shall have a Council of Ministers composed of seven Greek Ministers and three Turkish Ministers. The Ministers shall be designated respectively by the President and the Vice-President of the Republic who shall appoint them by an instrument signed by them both.

The decisions of the Council of Ministers shall be taken by an absolute majority and shall, unless the right of final veto or return is exercised by the President or the Vice-President of the Republic or both, be promulgated immediately by them.

The executive power exercised by the President and the Vice-President of the Republic conjointly consists of:

Determining the design and colour of the flag.

Creation or establishment of honours.

Appointment of the members of the Council of Ministers.

Promulgation by publication of the decisions of the Council of Ministers.

Promulgation by publication of any law or decision passed by the House of Representatives.

Appointments and termination of appointments as in Articles provided.

Institution of compulsory military service.

Reduction or increase of the security forces.

Exercise of the prerogative of mercy in capital cases.

Remission, suspension and commutation of sentences.

Right of references to the Supreme Constitutional Court and publication of Court decisions.

Address of messages to the House of Representatives.

The executive power exercised by the President consists of:

Designation and termination of appointment of Greek Ministers.

Convening and presiding of the meetings of the Council of Ministers.

Right of final veto on Council decisions and on laws or decisions of the House of Representatives concerning foreign affairs, defence or security.

Right of recourse to the Supreme Constitutional Court.

Publication of the communal laws and decisions of the Greek Communal Chamber.

Prerogative of mercy in capital cases.

Addressing messages to the House of Representatives.

The executive power exercised by the Vice-President consists of:

Designation and termination of appointment of Turkish Ministers.

Asking the President for the convening of the Council of Ministers and being present and taking part in the discussions.

Right of final veto on Council decisions and on laws or decisions of the House of Representatives concerning foreign affairs, defence or security.

Right of recourse to the Supreme Constitutional Court.

Publication of the communal laws and decisions of the Turkish Communal Chamber.

Prerogative of mercy in capital cases.

Addressing messages to the House of Representatives.

ARTICLES 54–60
Council of Ministers

The Council of Ministers shall exercise executive power in all matters, other than those which are within the competence of a Communal Chamber, including the following:

General direction and control of the government of the Republic and the direction of general policy.

Foreign affairs, defence and security.

Co-ordination and supervision of all public services.

Supervision and disposition of property belonging to the Republic.

Consideration of Bills to be introduced to the House of Representatives by a Minister.

Making of any order or regulation for the carrying into effect of any law as provided by such law.

Consideration of the Budget of the Republic to be introduced to the House of Representatives.

ARTICLES 61–85
House of Representatives

The legislative power of the Republic shall be exercised by the House of Representatives in all matters except those expressly reserved to the Communal Chambers.

The number of Representatives shall be fifty:

Provided that such number may be altered by a resolution of the House of Representatives carried by a majority comprising two-thirds of the Representatives elected by the Greek Community and two-thirds of the Representatives elected by the Turkish Community.

Out of the number of Representatives 70 per cent shall be elected by the Greek Community and 30 per cent by the Turkish Community separately from amongst their members respectively, and, in the case of a contested election, by universal suffrage and by direct and secret ballot held on the same day.

The term of office of the House of Representatives shall be for a period of five years.

The President of the House of Representatives shall be a Greek, and shall be elected by the Representatives elected by the Greek Community, and the Vice-President shall be a Turk and shall be elected by the Representatives elected by the Turkish Community.

ARTICLES 86–111
Communal Chambers

The Greek and the Turkish Communities respectively shall elect from amongst their own members a Communal Chamber.

The Communal Chambers shall, in relation to their respective Community, have competence to exercise legislative power solely with regard to the following:

All religious, educational, cultural and teaching matters.
Personal status; composition and instances of courts dealing with civil disputes relating to personal status and to religious matters.
Imposition of personal taxes and fees on members of their respective Community in order to provide for their respective needs.

ARTICLES 112–121, 126–128
Officers of the Republic

ARTICLES 122–125
The Public Service

The public service shall be composed as to 70 per cent of Greeks and as to 30 per cent of Turks.

ARTICLES 129–132
The Forces of the Republic

The Republic shall have an army of two thousand men

of whom 60 per cent shall be Greeks and 40 per cent shall be Turks.

The security forces of the Republic shall consist of the police and gendarmerie and shall have a contingent of two thousand men. The forces shall be composed as to 70 per cent of Greeks and as to 30 per cent of Turks.

ARTICLES 133–164
The Courts
(See section Judicial System)

ARTICLES 165–199
Financial, Miscellaneous, Final and Transitional Provisions

Note: The following measures have been passed by the House of Representatives since January 1964, when the Turkish members withdrew:

1. The amalgamation of the High Court and the Supreme Constitutional Court.
2. The abolition of the Greek Communal Chamber and the creation of a Ministry of Education.
3. The unification of the Municipalities.
4. The unification of the Police and the Gendarmerie.
5. The creation of a military force by providing that persons between the ages of eighteen and fifty can be called upon to serve in the National Guard.
6. The extension of the term of office of the President and the House of Representatives by one year intervals from July 1965 until elections in February 1968 and July 1970 respectively.
7. New electoral provisions; abolition of separate Greek and Turkish rolls; abolition of post of Vice-President, which was re-established in 1973.

THE GOVERNMENT
HEAD OF STATE
President: Archbishop MAKARIOS III.

In the presidential elections of February 1973 Archbishop Makarios was re-elected unopposed. Following the *coup d'état* of July 15th, 1974, Archbishop Makarios fled from Cyprus, and Glavcos Clerides, as President of the House of Representatives, became acting President. In December 1974 Makarios returned, and resumed the presidency.

COUNCIL OF MINISTERS
(*August* 1975)
Minister of Foreign Affairs: IOANNIS CHRISTOPHIDES.
Minister of the Interior and of Defence: CHRISTODOULOS VENIAMIN.

Minister of Agriculture and Natural Resources: FRIXOS KOLOTAS.
Minister of Labour and Social Insurance: MARCOS SPANOS.
Minister of Communications and Works: GEORGE TOMBAZOS.
Minister of Education: Dr. ANDREAS MIKELLIDES.
Minister of Justice: GEORGE IOANNIDES.
Minister of Finance: ANDREAS PATSALIDES.
Minister of Health: CHRISTOS VAKIS.
Minister of Commerce and Industry: MICHAEL COLOCASSIDES.

PARLIAMENT

HOUSE OF REPRESENTATIVES

The House of Representatives originally consisted of 50 members, 35 from the Greek community and 15 from the Turkish community, elected for a term of five years. In January 1964, the Turkish members were forced to withdraw and set up the Turkish Legislative Assembly of the Turkish Cypriot Administration.

President: GLAVCOS CLERIDES.

Vice-President: TASSOS PAPADOPOULOS.

ELECTIONS FOR THE GREEK REPRESENTATIVES
(July 5th, 1970)

PARTY	SEATS
Unified Party	15
AKEL (Communist Party)	9
Progressive Front	7
EDEK (Unified Democratic Union)	1
Independents (Pro-Government)	3
TOTAL	35

POLITICAL PARTIES

Unified Party (*Enieon*): Diagoras St., Chanteclair Building, Nicosia; f. 1960; Greek; supporters of Archbishop Makarios; maintains the Hellenic character of the state, right of private ownership; 15 seats in the House of Representatives; Chair. GLAVCOS CLERIDES.

AKEL—Progressive Party of the Working People (*Anorthotikon Komma Ergazomenou Laou*): Akamantos St., P.O.B. 1827, Nicosia; f. 1941; the Communist Party of Cyprus; over 14,000 mems.; 9 seats in the House of Representatives; Sec.-Gen. EZEKIAS PAPAIOANNOU; publ. *Haravghi.*

Progressive Front (*Proodeftiki Parataxis*): Dionyssios Solomos Sq., Nicosia; f. 1970; sponsored by the right-wing farmers' union; pro-Government; 7 seats in the House; Gen. Sec. ERACLIS HADJERACLEOUS.

EDEK—Unified Democratic Union of the Centre (*Eniea Democratiki Enosis Kentrou*): f. 1969; the Socialist Party of Cyprus; supports independent, non-aligned, unitary, demilitarized Cyprus; stands for a socialist structure; Chair. Dr. VASSOS LYSSARIDES; Publs. *Ta Nea* (daily), *Anexartitos* (weekly).

DEK—Democratic National Party (*Demokratikon Ethnikon Komma*): Archbishop Makarios Ave., Nicosia; f. 1968; opposition party, pledged to a policy of union with Greece (*Enosis*); secured 9.8 per cent of votes in the 1970 elections; Chair. TAKIS EVDOKAS.

EDON-United Democratic Youth Organization (*Eniaia Demokratiki Organosis Neolaias*): P.O.B. 1986, Nicosia; f. 1959; 16,000 mems.; Pres. MICHAEL PAPAPETROU; Gen. Sec. ANTONIS CHRISTODOULOU; Org. Sec. DIMITRIS CHRISTOFIAS.

DIPLOMATIC REPRESENTATION

EMBASSIES, HIGH COMMISSIONS AND LEGATION ACCREDITED TO CYPRUS

(In Nicosia, except where otherwise stated.)

(E) Embassy; (HC) High Commission; (L) Legation.

Argentina: Rome, Italy (E).

Australia: Athens, Greece (HC).

Austria: Athens, Greece (E).

Belgium: Beirut, Lebanon (E).

Brazil: Tel Aviv, Israel (E).

Bulgaria: 15 St. Paul St. (E); *Ambassador:* CONSTANTIN POPOV.

Canada: Tel-Aviv, Israel (HC).

China, People's Republic: (E); *Ambassador:* TAI LU.

Colombia: Jerusalem, Israel (E).

Cuba: Halkydonos 9 (L); *Chargé d'Affaires:* Dr. JOSÉ LUIS GALBE.

Czechoslovakia: 5 Glavcos St. (E); *Ambassador:* JOSEPH GREGR.

Denmark: Beirut, Lebanon (E).

Egypt: 3 Egypt Ave. (E); *Ambassador:* JHAIRY RAGHEB EL-AYOUTI.

Finland: Rome, Italy (E).

France: 43 Savvas G. Rotsides St. (E); *Ambassador:* ALAIN CHAILLOUS.

German Democratic Republic: (E); *Ambassador:* KARL WILDAU.

Germany, Federal Republic: 10 Nikitaras St. (E); *Ambassador:* Dr. HEINRICH SARTORIUS.

Greece: 8–10 Byron Ave. (E); *Ambassador:* MICHAEL DOUNTAS.

Hungary: Athens, Greece (E).

India: Beirut, Lebanon (HC).

Iraq: Beirut, Lebanon (E).

Israel: 27 Androcleous St. (E); *Ambassador:* NISSIM YOSHA.

Italy: 7 Alexander Diomedes St. (E); *Ambassador:* VITTORIANO MANFREDI.

Ivory Coast: Jerusalem, Israel (E).

Japan: Beirut, Lebanon (E).

Lebanon: 1 Queen Olga St. (E); *Ambassador:* MUNIR TAKKIEDIN.

Libya: Nicosia (E); *Ambassador:* ABDUL WAHAB EL-ZENTANI.

Malta: (HC); *High Commissioner:* ARTHUR SCERRI.

Netherlands: Beirut, Lebanon (E).

Nigeria: Rome, Italy (HC).

Norway: Tel-Aviv, Israel (E).

Pakistan: Beirut, Lebanon (E).

Poland: Athens, Greece (E).

Romania: 8 Catsonis St. (E); *Chargé d'Affaires:* ION ANGHEL.

Spain: Damascus, Syria (E).

Sweden: Beirut, Lebanon (E).

Switzerland: Tel-Aviv, Israel (E).

Syria: 28 Stassinos Ave. (E); *Chargé d'Affaires:* MOHAMMAD KHODOR.

Turkey: 10 Server Somuncuoğlu St. (E); *Ambassador:* ASAF INHAN.

U.S.S.R.: 4 Gladstone St. (E); *Ambassador:* SERGEY T. ASTAVIN.

United Kingdom: Alexander Pallis St. (HC); *High Commissioner:* Sir STEPHEN OLVER.

U.S.A.: Therissos St. (E); *Ambassador:* WILLIAM CRAWFORD.

Vatican: 2 Victoria Rd. (Apostolic Nunciature); *Apostolic Pro-Nuncio:* WILLIAM ALQUIN CAREW.

Yugoslavia: 2 Vasilissis Olgas St. (E); *Ambassador:* NICOLA MANDIC.

Cyprus also has diplomatic relations with Chile, Ethiopia, Ghana, Kuwait, Mongolia, Portugal, Somalia, Uganda, Uruguay and Zaire.

JUDICIAL SYSTEM

Supreme Court: Nicosia.

President: Hon. Mr. Justice M. A. TRIANTAFYLLIDES.

Judges: Hon. Mr. Justice A. S. STAVRINIDES, Hon. Mr. Justice L. N. LOIZOU, Hon. Mr. Justice T. HADJIAN-ASTASSIOU, Hon. Mr. Justice A. N. LOIZOU, Hon. Mr. Justice Y. CH. MALACHTOS.

The Supreme Court is the final appellate court in the Republic and the final adjudicator in matters of constitutional and administrative law, including recourses on conflict of competence between state organs on questions of the constitutionality of laws, etc. It deals with appeals from Assize Courts and District Courts as well as from the decisions of its own single judges when exercising original jurisdiction in certain matters such as prerogative orders of *habeas corpus, mandamus, certiorari*, etc., and in admiralty and certain matrimonial causes.

Assize Courts and District Courts:

As required by the Constitution a law was passed in 1960 providing for the establishment, jurisdiction and powers of courts of civil and criminal jurisdiction, i.e. of six District Courts and six Assize Courts.

Ecclesiastical Courts:

There are seven Orthodox Church tribunals having exclusive jurisdiction in matrimonial causes between members of the Greek Orthodox Church. Appeals go from these tribunals to the appellate tribunal of the Church.

Supreme Council of Judicature: Nicosia.

The Supreme Council of Judicature is composed of the Attorney-General, the President and the two senior Judges of the Supreme Court, the senior District Court President, the senior District Court Judge and a practising advocate of at least twelve years practice.

It is responsible for the appointment, promotion, transfer, etc., of the judges exercising civil and criminal jurisdiction in the District Courts and the Assize Courts.

TURKISH FEDERATED STATE OF CYPRUS

The Turkish intervention in Cyprus in July 1974 saw the establishment of a separate area in northern Cyprus under the control of the Autonomous Turkish Cypriot Administration with a Council of Ministers, and separate judicial, financial, military and educational machinery serving the Turkish community.

On February 13th, 1975, the Turkish-occupied zone of Cyprus was declared a Turkish Cypriot Federated State and Rauf Denktaş named president. At the second joint meeting held by the Executive Council and Legislative Assembly of the Autonomous Turkish Cypriot Administration it was decided to set up a Constituent Assembly which would prepare a Constitution for the Turkish Federated State of Cyprus within 45 days. This constitution, which was approved by the Turkish Cypriot population in a referendum held on June 8th, 1975, is regarded by the Turkish Cypriots as a first step towards the Federal Republic of Cyprus. Article 2 of the Constitution provides that the Turkish Federated State of Cyprus shall exercise all powers except for those expressly given to the Federal Republic of Cyprus. Also, Transitional Article 2 provides that when the Constitution of the Federal Republic comes into force the necessary amendment shall accordingly be made to the Constitution of the Turkish Federated State of Cyprus.

Vice-President of the Republic and President of the Turkish Federated State of Cyprus: RAUF R. DENKTAŞ.

COUNCIL OF MINISTERS

Vice-President of the Turkish Federated State of Cyprus and Minister of Defence: OSMAN ÖREK.

Minister of Finance and Budgetry Affairs: RÜSTEM TATAR.

Minister of the Interior: ORHAN ZİHNİ BİLGEHAN (Acting).

Minister of Health: Dr. NİYAZİ MANYERA.

Minister of Labour, Rehabilitation and Social Services: İSMET KOTAK.

Minister of Agriculture: OĞUZ RAMADAN.

Minister of Communications and Works: EROL KÂZIM.

Minister of Education and Teaching: ORHAN ZİHNİ BİLGEHAN.

Minister of Commerce and Industry: TUNCER ARİF.

Minister of Power and Natural Resources: Prof. KENAN ATAKOL.

Minister of Planning and Co-ordination: TUNCER ARİF (Acting).

Minister of Tourism and Information: ÇAĞLAR YASAL.

Minister of State for Foreign Affairs: VEDAT ÇELİK.

TURKISH CONSTITUENT ASSEMBLY
(LEGISLATIVE)

A 50-member Assembly was set up in February 1975, composed of 25 members of the former Legislative Assembly and representatives of trade unions, professional, academic and commercial organizations.

President: RAUF R. DENKTAŞ.

Vice-President: Dr. NEJDET ÜNEL.

POLITICAL PARTIES

Cumhuriyetçi Türk Partisi (*Republican Turkish Party*): Mirata Flats, First Floor, Osman Paşa Avenue, Nicosia; f. 1970 by members of the Turkish community in Cyprus; social democratic principles with left of centre stand; district organizations at Famagusta, Kyrenia, Lapithos, Morphou and Lefka; Leader A. M. BERBEROĞLU.

Ulusal Dayanışma (*National Solidarity*): Nicosia; national organization with political and economic programme under which 1970 elections were held; Leader RAUF R. DENKTAŞ.

JUDICIAL SYSTEM

Supreme Court: Ataturk Square, Nicosia.

President: Hon. Mr. Justice M. NECATİ MUNİR.

Judges: Hon. Justices ULFET EMİN, AHMED IZZET, SHAKİR S. İLKAY.

In the areas governed by the Turkish Federated State of Cyprus the Supreme Court exercises the powers vested in the Supreme Council of Judicature and the Supreme Court by the 1960 Constitution. It is the final appellate court dealing with appeals from Assize and District Courts and from the decisions of its own judges when exercising original jurisdiction. It is the final adjudicator in matters of constitutional and administrative law. Judges are appointed and promoted by the President of the Turkish Federated State of Cyprus on the recommendation of the Supreme Court, and the Court is responsible for the transfer, leave and discipline of judges.

Assize Courts and District Courts:

The courts of civil and criminal jurisdiction, established by the law of 1960, amended by the Turkish Legislative Assembly in 1968.

Turkish Communal Courts:

Civil disputes relating to the personal status of members of the Turkish community are dealt with by two Communal Courts. There is also a communal appellate court to which appeals may be made from the courts of first instance.

BRITISH SOVEREIGN BASE AREAS

AKROTIRI and DHEKELIA

Administrator: Air Marshal Sir JOHN AIKEN, K.C.B., R.A.F.

Chief Officer of Administration: W. C. CURTIS.

Senior Judge of Senior Judge's Court: W. A. SIME, M.B.E., Q.C.

Resident Judge of Judge's Court: E. R. HARLEY, C.B.E.

Under the Cyprus Act 1960, the United Kingdom retained sovereignty in two sovereign base areas and this was recognized in the Treaty of Establishment signed between the U.K., Greece, Turkey and the Republic of Cyprus in August 1960. The base areas cover 99 square miles. The Treaty also conferred on Britain certain rights within the Republic, including rights of movement and the use of specified training areas.

UNITED NATIONS PEACE-KEEPING FORCE IN CYPRUS

(UNFICYP)

P.O.B. 1642, Nicosia, Cyprus

Set up for three months in March 1964 (subsequently extended at intervals of three or six months) to keep the peace between the Greek and Turkish communities and help to solve outstanding issues between them.

Commander: Lieut.-Gen. D. PREM CHAND (India).

Special Representative of the UN Secretary-General: Dr. LUIS WECKMANN-MUÑOZ (Mexico).

See page 127.

RELIGION

Greeks form 80 per cent of the population and most of them belong to the Orthodox Church. Most Turks (18 per cent of the population) are Muslims.

Greek Orthodox	449,000
Muslims (Turks)	104,000
Armenian Apostolic	3,500
Maronite	3,000
Anglican	
Roman Catholic }	18,000
Other	

(1960 census).

The Orthodox Church of Cyprus: Archbishopric of Cyprus, P.O. Box 1130, Nicosia; f. 45 A.D.; the Autocephalous Orthodox Church of Cyprus is part of the Eastern Orthodox Church; the Church is independent, and the Archbishop, who is also the Ethnarch (national leader of the Greek community), is elected by universal suffrage; 500,000 members.

Archbishop of Nova Justiniana and all Cyprus: Archbishop MAKARIOS III.

Metropolitan of Paphos: Bishop CHRYSOSTOMOS.

Metropolitan of Kitium: Bishop CHRYSOSTOMOS.
Metropolitan of Kyrenia: Bishop GREGORIOS.
Metropolitan of Limassol: Bishop CHRYSANTHOS.
Metropolitan of Morphou: Bishop CHRYSANTHOS.
Suffragan Bishop of Salamis: Bishop BARNABAS.

Islam: Most of the adherents in Cyprus are Sunnis of the Hanafi Sect. The religious head of the Muslim community is the Mufti.
The Mufti of Cyprus: Dr. R. M. RIFAT.

Roman Catholic Church: Archbishopric of Cyprus of the Maronite rite, subject to the Sacred Congregation for the Oriental Churches; 78 parishes, 54 educational institutes, 109 resident priests, 86,000 Catholics in a total population of 940,000 (December 1972 estimate by Catholic church).
Archbishop of Cyprus: Mgr. ELIE FARAH, Maronite Archbishopric, Antelias, Lebanon (winter); Cornet-Chahouane, Lebanon (summer).

Other Churches: Armenian Apostolic, Roman Catholic and Church of England.

THE PRESS

DAILIES

Agon (*Struggle*): 238 Ledra St., P.O.B. 1417, Nicosia; f. 1964; morning; Greek; Independent; Owner and Editor N. KOSHIS; circ. 12,000.

Apogevmatini (*Afternoon*): P.O.B. 1094, Nicosia; f. 1972; afternoon; Greek; pro-Government; Editor M. HADJI-EFTHYMIOU; circ. 5,000.

Bozkurt (*Grey Wolf*): 142 Kyrenia St., P.O.B. 324, Nicosia; f. 1951; morning; Turkish; Independent; Editor SADI C. TOGAN; circ. 5,000.

Cyprus Bulletin: Nicosia; f. 1964; English; published by the Cyprus Public Information Office; circ. 8,000.

Cyprus Mail: P.O.B. 1144, 24 Vasiliou Voulgaroctonou St., Nicosia; f. 1945; English; Independent; Editor C. H. W. GOULT; circ. 5,740.

Eleftheria (*Freedom*): P.O.B. 1050, 30 Plutarch St., Nicosia; f. 1906 as bi-weekly, 1936 daily; Greek; Independent; Editor G. J. HADJINICOLAOU; circ. 13,250.

Ethniki (*National*): Nicosia; f. 1959; organ of *Enosis* movement; Greek; Editor CH. M. CHARALAMBOUS; circ. 8,000.

Halkin Sesi (*Voice of the People*): 172 Kyrenia St., P.O.B. 339, Nicosia; f. 1942; morning; Turkish; Independent Turkish Nationalist; Editor HASAN FAIZ; circ. 5,000.

Haravghi (*Dawn*): P.O.B. 1556, Bouboulinas 25, Nicosia; f. 1956; organ of AKEL (Communist Party); Greek; Editor ANDREAS FANTIS; circ. 13,500.

Makhi (*Battle*): P.O.B. 1105, Grivas Dighenis Ave., Nicosia; f. 1960; morning; Greek; Owner and Editor N. SAMPSON; circ. 12,000.

Mesimvrini: 25D Diagoras St., P.O.B. 1543, Nicosia; f 1970; Greek; afternoon; Editor G. HADJINICOLAOU.

Philelephtheros (*Liberal*): Tryfou Building, P.O.B. 1094, Nicosia; nationalist; Greek; morning; Chief Editor CHR. KATSAMBAS; circ. 15,000.

Special News Bulletin: Nicosia; f. 1963; morning; English; published by Public Information Office of Turkish Federated State of Cyprus; circ. 1,500.

Ta Nea (*The News*): 23 Constantine Palaelogos Ave., P.O.B. 1064, Nicosia; organ of EDEK party; Greek; morning; f. 1970; Editor CHR. SAVVIDES; circ. 4,000.

Zaman (*Times*): 43 Yediler St., Nicosia; f. 1973; Nationalist; Chief Editor RAIF R. DENKTAS; circ. 3,500.

WEEKLIES

Alithia (*Truth*): P.O.B. 1605, 26 Apollon St., Nicosia; f. 1951; Greek; Pancyprian; Liberal; Editor ANTONIOS PHARMAKIDES; circ. 14,500.

Anexartitos: Nicosia; Greek; organ of EDEK party.

Athlitiki (*Athletics*): 15A Mnassiades St., Nicosia; Greek; Editor A. TSIALIS; circ. 12,000.

Asyrmatos (*Wireless*): P.O.B. 2082, 26 Apollon St., Nicosia; Greek; Editor NT. CONSTANTINIDES; circ. 7,400.

Ergatiki Phoni (*Workers' Voice*): 35 Zenonos St., Limassol; f. 1946; Greek; organ of Cyprus Workers' Confederation; Editor CHR. A. MICHAELIDES; circ. 5,300.

Ergatiko Vima (*Workers' Tribune*): P.O.B. 1885, Volonaki St., Nicosia; f. 1956; Greek; organ of the Pancyprian Federation of Labour; Editor-in-Chief PAMBOS VARNAVA; circ. 8,300.

Kypros (*Cyprus*): P.O.B. 1491, 10 Apostle Barnabas St., Nicosia; f. 1952; Greek; non-party; circ. 12,000; Editor J. KYRIAKIDIS.

Nei Keri (*New Times*): P.O.B. 1963, 8 Vasiliou Voulgaroktonou St., Nicosia; Greek; Editor LYSSANDROS TSIMILLIS; circ. 7,300.

Official Gazette: Printing Office of the Republic of Cyprus, Nicosia; f. 1960; Greek; published by the Government of the Republic of Cyprus.

Patris (*Fatherland*): P.O.B. 2026, 1 Androcleous St., Nicosia; f. 1964; Greek; right wing; Editor K. KONONAS; circ. 7,500.

Philathlos: P.O.B. 1543, Nicosia; Greek; sports; Editor C. J. SOLOMONIDES; circ. 4,400.

Synagermos: P.O.B. 1061, 217 Ledra St., Nicosia; f. 1964; Greek; Owner and Editor PH. CONSTANTINIDES; circ. 4,000.

Tharros (*Courage*): P.O.B. 1105, Grivas Dighenis Ave., Nicosia; f. 1961; Greek; Independent; Propr. and Editor N. SAMPSON; circ. 9,200.

PERIODICALS

Apostolos Barnabas: Cyprus Archbishopric, Nicosia; twice monthly; organ of the Orthodox Church of Cyprus; Dir. Dr. ANDREAS N. MITSIDES; circ. 1,200.

Countryman: Nicosia; f. 1943; every two months; Greek; published by the Cyprus Public Information Office; circ. 9,000.

Cyprus Medical Journal: P.O.B. 93, Nicosia; f. 1947; monthly; English and Greek; Editor Dr. G. N. MARANGOS.

Cyprus Today: c/o Ministry of Education, Nicosia; f. 1963; every two months; published in English by the Public Information Office for the Ministry of Education; cultural and general information; Chair. Editorial Board P. CHR. SERGHIS; Chief Editor N. PANAYIOTOU.

Dimossios Ipallilos: 2 Andreas Demetriou St., Nicosia; fortnightly; published by the Cyprus Civil Servants' Trade Union; circ. 8,000.

Eğitim Bülteni (*Education Bulletin*): Nicosia; f. 1972; monthly; Turkish; published by Office of Member for Education and Teaching of Turkish Cypriot Administration; circ. 2,000.

International Political Review: 21A Nicodimou Mylona, Nicosia; Editor A. KANNAOUROS; circ. 2,400.

Kooperatif (*Co-operative*): Nicosia; f. 1970; monthly; Turkish; published by Co-operative Development Dept. of Turkish Cypriot Administration; circ. 2,000.

Kypriacos Logos: 10 Kimon St., Engomi, Nicosia; f. 1969; twice monthly; Editor P. STYLIANOU; circ. 4,000.

Mathitiki Estia (*Student Hearth*): Pancyprian Gymnasium, Nicosia; f. 1950; twice a year; Greek; organ of the Pancyprian Gymnasium students; Editor GEORGE PRODROMOU.

Nea Epochi: 11 Stassandrou St., P.O.B. 1581, Nicosia; f. 1959; every two months; Greek; literary material; Editor ACHILLEAS PYLIOTIS; circ. 2,500.

Öğretmen (*Teacher*): Nicosia; f. 1972; monthly; Turkish; organ of Cyprus Turkish Secondary Schools Teachers Ascn.; circ. 1,200.

Paediki Hara: 18 Archbishop Makarios III Ave., Nicosia; monthly; published by the Pancyprian Union of Greek Teachers; Editor THEOCHARIS ARISTODEMOU; circ. 18,000.

Panta Embros: P.O.B. 1156, Nicosia; monthly; published by the Cyprus Scouts' Association; Greek; circ. 3,700.

Pnevmatiki Estia: Nicosia; f. 1960; Greek; literary; monthly.

Radio Programme: Cyprus Broadcasting Corpn., P.O.B. 4824, Nicosia; fortnightly; published by the C.B.C.; radio and TV programme news; Editor TAKIS G. MAGOS; circ. 25,000.

Synergatistis (*The Co-operator*): P.O.B. 4537, Nicosia; f. 1961; monthly magazine; Greek; official organ of the Pancyprian Confederation of Co-operatives; Editor G. I. PHOTIOU; circ. 4,300.

Trapezikos: P.O.B. 638, Nicosia; f. 1960; bank employees' magazine; Greek; monthly; Editor G. S. MICHAELIDES; circ. 17,500.

Türk Sen (*Turkish Trade Unions*): 13-15 Mufti Ziai St., P.O.B. 829, Lefkoşa, Mersin 10, Turkey; f. 1971; monthly; Turkish; organ of Cyprus Turkish Trade Unions Federation; circ. 5,000.

NEWS AGENCY

Turkish News Cyprus: f. 1973.

RADIO AND TELEVISION

Cyprus Broadcasting Corporation: P.O.B. 4824, Nicosia; Chair. LOUKIS PETRIDES; Dir. Gen. A. N. CHRISTOFIDES; Deputy Dir. Gen. I. HADJIOSSIF; Chief Engineer P. ASTREOS; Head of Radio Programmes G. MITSIDES; Head of Television Programmes CH. PAPADOPOULOS; publ. *Radio Programme*.

Radio: f. 1952; programmes in Greek, Turkish, English and Armenian; two medium wave transmitters of 20 kW in Nicosia, relay stations at Paphos and Limassol, four 20 kW VHF transmitters on Mount Olympus and Mount Sina Oros; international service in English and Arabic; relays Radio Monte Carlo to the Middle East from a station on Cape Greco.

Television: f. 1957; two Band III 40/8 kW transmitters on Mount Olympus and Mount Sina Oros, giving almost full coverage of the island, transposer stations at Tsada, Platres, Kakopetria.

Radio Bayrak: Ataturk Sq., Nicosia; home service in Turkish, overseas services in Turkish, Greek and English; Dir.-Gen. H. SÜHA; Dir. of Programmes MEHMET FEHMİ.

British Forces Broadcasting Service, Cyprus: British Forces Post Office 53; 120 hours per week in English; Station Controller R. W. MORGAN; Engineer-in-Charge E. C. O'GORMAN.

Türkiye Radyo Televizyon (**T.R.T.**): Turkish television programmes are transmitted to the Turkish sector of Cyprus.

In December 1973 there were 205,000 radio receivers and 80,000 television receivers in use in Cyprus.

FINANCE

(br. = branch; cap. = capital; p.u. = paid up; dep. = deposits; m. = million)

BANKING

CENTRAL BANK

Central Bank of Cyprus: P.O.B. 1087, 36 Metochiou St., Nicosia; f. 1963; became the Bank of Issue in 1966; cap. p.u. £100,000; dep. £66.1m. (Dec. 1974); Gov. C. C. STEPHANI; publ. *Report* (annual), *Bulletin* (every two months).

CYPRIOT BANKS

Bank of Cyprus Ltd.: P.O.B. 1472, 86-90 Phaneromeni St. 86-90, Nicosia; f. 1899; cap. p.u. £6,000,000; dep. £95.1m. (Dec. 1973); Gov. Dr. REGHINOS THEOCHARIS, PH.D.; Chair. C. D. SEVERIS; 44 branches throughout Cyprus.

Co-operative Central Bank Ltd.: P.O.B. 4537, Nicosia; banking and credit facilities to member societies; Dir. R. ELERIDES.

Cyprus Popular Bank Ltd.: P.O.B. 2032, Archbishop Makarios III Avenue, Nicosia; f. 1901; cap. p.u. £1,000,000; dep. £15.9m. (Dec. 1974); Chair. EVAGORAS C. LANITIS; Gen. Man. KIKIS N. LAZARIDES; 6 brs.

Cyprus Turkish Co-operative Central Bank, Ltd.: P.O.B. 1861, Mahmout Pasha St., Nicosia; banking and credit facilities to member societies, bodies and individuals; Gen. Man. MEHMET ESHREF.

N.J. Dimitriou Ltd.: P.O.B. 18, 30 D.N. Dimitriou St., Larnaca; f. 1943; cap. £50,000; private company, balance sheets not published; Man. Dirs. NICOS G. DIMITRIOU, DIMITRIOS G. DIMITRIOU.

Turkish Bank Ltd.: P.O.B. 1742, Kyrenia St. and Turkish Bank St., Nicosia; f. 1901; cap. p.u. £200,000; dep. £7.5m. (Dec. 1973); Chair. UMIT SULEYMAN; Gen. Man. MADJID M. FERDİ; 5 brs.

DEVELOPMENT BANK

Cyprus Development Bank, Ltd., The: Nicosia; f. 1963; cap. p.u. £1,000,000; provides medium and long term loans for productive investments, particularly in manufacturing and processing industries, tourism and agriculture, and technical managerial and administrative assistance and advice; performs related economic and technical research; Chair. CHR. G. PAPADOPOULOS; Gen. Man. A. M. PIKIS; Operations Man. L. D. SPARSIS; Economics Man. J. JOANNIDES.

OTHER BANKS

Barclays Bank International Ltd.: 54 Lombard St., London EC3P 3AH; Local Director's Office, P.O.B. 2081, Metaxas Sq., Nicosia; branches in Nicosia (Metaxas Sq., Ataturk Sq., Nicosia Airport Rd.), two brs. each in Famagusta, Limassol, and other brs. in Larnaca, Morphou, Akrotiri, Dhekelia, Kyrenia and Episkopi; Local Dir. C. CAROLIDES.

The Chartered Bank: P.O.B. 1047, Evagoras Ave., Nicosia; 15 brs. throughout Cyprus; Cyprus Man. D. A. WEATHERSON.

Grindlays Bank Ltd.: 23 Fenchurch St., London, E.C.3; General Manager's Office, P.O.B. 2069, Nicosia; 26 brs. throughout Cyprus; General Man. in Cyprus K. O. DANCEY.

Lombard Banking (Cyprus) Ltd.: 31 Lombard St., London, E.C.3; General Manager's Office, P.O.B. 1661, Mitsis Building, Metaxas Square, Nicosia; owns a subsidiary, Lombard (Cyprus) Ltd., specializing in hire purchase business; brs. in Nicosia, Limassol, Larnaca and Famagusta; Gen. Man. H. M. KEHEYAN.

National Bank of Greece, S.A.: Athens, Greece; Regional Manager's Office, P.O.B. 1191, Makarios III Ave., Nicosia; three brs. in Nicosia, two in Limassol and other brs. in Famagusta, Larnaca, Paphos and Morphou; Regional Man. TILEMAHOS GOURZIS.

Türkiye Cumhuriyeti Ziraat Bankası (*Agricultural Bank of Turkey*): Ankara, Turkey; Cyprus branch Kyrenia; Man. DOĞAN ERDOĞAN; acts as central bank for Turkish area of Cyprus.

Türkiye İş Bankası: Ulus Meydanı, Ankara, Turkey; Cyprus office P.O.B. 1817, 9 Kyrenia St., Nicosia; br. at Famagusta.

INSURANCE

General Insurance Company of Cyprus Ltd., The: Bank of Cyprus Bldg., P.O.B. 1668, Nicosia; f. 1951; Chair. M. S. SAVIDES; Vice-Chair. G. C. CHRISTOFIDES.

TRADE AND INDUSTRY

CHAMBERS OF COMMERCE

Cyprus Chamber of Commerce and Industry: Hadjisavva Bldg. (6th Floor), Metaxas Square, P.O.B. 1455, Nicosia; Pres. M. SAVIDES; Vice-Pres. GEORGE ROLOGIS, CHR. MAVROUDES; Sec.-Gen. S. THEOCHARIDES.

Famagusta Chamber of Commerce and Industry: P.O.B. 777, Famagusta; temporary address: P.O.B. 347, Limassol; Pres. PHANOS N. EPIPHANIOU; Vice-Pres. ANDREAS DJORDJIS; Sec.-Gen. PAUL VANEZIS.

Larnaca Chamber of Commerce and Industry: 30 D.N. Dimitriou, P.O.B. 18, Larnaca; Pres. A. FRANCIS; Vice-Pres. Dr. N. A. ONISSIFOROU; Hon. Sec. C. PIERIDES.

Limassol Chamber of Commerce and Industry: Spyros Araouzos St., P.O.B. 347, Limassol; Pres. KYRIACOS HAMBOULLAS; Vice-Pres. NICOS ROSSOS; Hon. Sec. JOHN VRYONIDES.

Paphos Chamber of Commerce and Industry: 18-20 Grivas Dhigenis Ave., P.O.B. 68, Paphos; Pres. LOIZOS M. HAVOUZARIS; Vice-Pres. MATHEOS CHARALAMBIDES; Hon. Sec. CARLIS AGROTIS.

Nicosia Chamber of Commerce and Industry: Hadjisavva Building (6th Floor), Metaxas Square, Nicosia; Pres. A. AVRAAMIDES; Vice-Pres. N. K. SHAKOLAS; Hon. Sec. L. TRYFON.

Turkish Cypriot Chamber of Commerce: 99 Kyrenia Ave., Nicosia, P.O.B. 718; Chair. AHMET RAŞIT MUSTAFA; Vice-Chair. AGÂH M. NECAT.

EMPLOYERS' ORGANIZATIONS

Cyprus Employers' Federation: Charalambides Bldg., Grivas-Dhigenis Ave., P.O.B. 1657, Nicosia; f. 1960; 11 member Trade Associations, 300 direct and 550 indirect mems.; Acting Dir.-Gen. TAKIS CHRISTOFIDES; Chair. CONSTANTINOS LORDOS; publ. *Bulletin.*

There are also ten independent employers' associations, among the largest of which are:

Cyprus Building Contractors' Association: 2 Voulgari St., Nicosia; 217 mems.; Sec. G. PARASKEVAIDES.

Limassol Enterprises Contractors' Association: 18 Ipiros St., Limassol; 57 mems.; Sec. O. ECONOMIDES.

Employers' Union of Car Owners: 1 Menandrou St., Nicosia; 1,107 mems.

Turkish Employers' Association: Müdüroğlu Apartments, 3 Ortakeuy, Nicosia; f. 1961; 60 mems.; Pres. EFRUZ SAMİ MÜDÜROĞLU; Vice-Pres. MUSTAFA TURKOĞLU.

TRADE UNIONS

Cyprus Civil Servants' Trade Union: 2 Andreas Demetriou St., Nicosia; f. 1949, registered 1966; restricted to persons in the civil employment of the Govt.; 6 brs. with a total membership of 9,000; Pres. A. PAPANASTASIOU; Gen. Sec. G. IACOVOU; publ. *Dimosios Ipallilos* (Public Servant), fortnightly.

Demokratiki Ergatiki Omospondia Kyprou (*Democratic Labour Federation of Cyprus*): 10 Kimonos St., Engomi, Nicosia; f. 1962, registered 1962; 4 unions with a total membership of 3,500; Hon. Pres. PETROS STYLIANOU; Gen. Sec. STAVROS STAVRINIDES; publ. *Ergatikos Agonas* (fortnightly).

Kıbrıs Türk İşçi Sendikaları Federasyonu (*Cyprus Turkish Trade Unions Federation*): 13–15 Mufti-Ziai St., P.O.B. 829, Lefkoşa; Mersin 10, Turkey; f. 1954, registered 1955; 14 unions with a total membership of 5,915; affiliated to ICFTU and the Federation of Trade Unions of Turkey; Gen. Sec. NECATI TASHKIN; publ. *Türk Sen* (Turkish Trade Unions), monthly.

Pankypria Ergatiki Omospondia (*Pancyprian Federation of Labour*): 32–35 Archemou St., Nicosia; f. 1946, registered 1947; previously the Pancyprian Trade Union Committee f. 1941, dissolved 1946; 16 unions and 225 brs. with a total membership of 48,500; affiliated to the World Federation of Trade Unions; Gen. Sec. A. ZIARTIDES; publs. *Ergatiko Vima* (Workers' Forum), weekly, *Ergasia* (Labour), quarterly.

Pankyprios Omospondia Anexartition Syntechnion (*Pancyprian Federation of Independent Trade Unions*): 1 Menadrou St., Nicosia; f. 1956, registered 1957; has no political orientations; 7 unions with a total membership of 1,008; Pres. COSTAS ANTONIADES; Gen. Sec. KYRIACOS NATHANAEL.

Synomospondia Ergaton Kyprou (*Cyprus Workers' Confederation*): 23 Athanasiou Diakou St., P.O.B. 1138, Engomi, Nicosia; f. 1944, registered 1950; 7 Federations, 5 Labour Centres, 41 unions, 13 branches with a total membership of 30,168; affiliated to the Greek Confederation of Labour and the ICFTU; Gen. Sec. MICHAEL IOANNOU; publ. *Ergatiki Phoni* (Workers' Voice), weekly.

On December 31st, 1972, there were 21 employers' associations with 1 branch and a total membership of 2,194, 105 unions with 254 brs. and 8 Unions Federations and 5 Confederations with 10 brs. and a total membership of 87,655.

TRADE FAIRS

Cyprus International (State) Fair: P.O.B. 3551, Nicosia; first season scheduled for May-June 1976.

Cyprus International Trade Fair: P.O.B. 1094, Nicosia; annually in September.

TRANSPORT

There are no railways in Cyprus.

ROADS

There are 8,319 kilometres of roads, of which 623 kilometres are main roads. There is an extensive network of bus services between Nicosia and the major towns and most villages, and between district centres and villages in each area. There are also taxi services between the principal towns.

Cyprus Automobile Association: Flat 101, Pedhieos Building, Louki Akrita Ave., P.O.B. 2279, Nicosia; f. 1933; Chair. M. S. AGROTIS.

SHIPPING

Famagusta is the main cargo port of the island and has a natural harbour; vessels of an overall length of 120 metres and a maximum draught of 6.8 metres can be accommodated alongside the quay in the inner harbour; ships with a maximum draught of 9.15 metres can be accommodated in the outer harbour. In 1972 461,733 metric tons were loaded there and 711,991 metric tons unloaded. Breakwater ports at Larnaca and Limassol were completed in 1973; 168,563 metric tons were loaded and 324,649 unloaded in 1972. The harbour of Paphos offers good anchorage to small vessels and is used mainly for exports, 107,300 metric tons being loaded in 1972 and only 11,912 unloaded. Kyrenia's small harbour is now used chiefly by fishing boats and yachts, but since it came under Turkish Cypriot control the expansion of the harbour for trade with Turkey has been undertaken.

Most of the island's oil passes through Larnaca (705,423 metric tons in 1972), although large quantities are discharged at Dhekelia, Karavostassi, Moni and Akrotiri for use in power stations and cement factories. Minerals are exported mainly through Vassiliko, Latchi and Karavostassi, where a total of 565,000 metric tons was loaded in 1972.

In recent years the number of merchant vessels registered in Cyprus has risen sharply from 314 (1,575,702 g.r.t.) in 1970 to 876 (3,637,679 g.r.t.) in 1973.

Limassol is the main passenger port in Cyprus with 17,335 arrivals and 19,515 departures in 1972. In the same year the figures for Famagusta were 11,080 and 10,498 and for all other ports 631 and 598 respectively.

Allied Industries Ltd.: Nicosia; part of Chandris Group, London, U.K.; one cargo vessel, one tanker.

Evelpis Shipping Co. Ltd.: Nicosia; London agents Lemos Bros. Co. Ltd.; one cargo vessel.

Hellespont Shipping Co. Ltd.: 28c Maria Synglitiki St., Famagusta; two cargo vessels.

Kavalaris Shipping Co. Ltd.: Famagusta; worldwide tramping services; one cargo vessel; Dirs. S., M., P., G. and A. KOLAKIS.

Kornos Shipping Co. Ltd.: Nicosia; cargo services; one cargo vessel; Gen. Man. N. M. PAPAIONNOU.

Marifoam Shipping Co. Ltd.: Nicosia; part of Chandris Group, London, U.K.; one tanker.

CIVIL AVIATION

There is an international airport at Nicosia, which can accommodate all types of aircraft, including jets. It was closed in July 1974 following the Turkish invasion.

Cyprus Airways: Head Office: 21 Athanasiou Diakou St., P.O.B. 1903, Nicosia; f. 1946; jointly owned by Cyprus Government, British Airways and local interests; charter subsidiary Cyprair Tours; Chair. G. ELIADES; Gen. Man. E. SAVVA; routes from Nicosia to Ankara, Athens, Beirut, Brussels, Cairo, Frankfurt, Istanbul, London, Manchester, Paris, Rome and Tel Aviv; fleet of two Trident 2E and two Trident 1E (some reported damaged following Turkish invasion).

Under normal conditions Cyprus is also served by the following foreign airlines: Aeroflot, ALIA, Alitalia, Balkan, British Airways, ČSA, Egyptair, El Al, Interflug, KLM, LOT, MALÉV, MEA, Olympic, Sabens, Swissair, Syrian Arab Airlines, TAROM, THY and Zambian Airways.

TOURISM

Cyprus Tourism Organization: Zena Building, 18 Th. Theodotou St., P.O.B. 4535, Nicosia; there are 116 established hotels with 13,000 beds.; Chair. FRIXOS PETRIDES; Dir.-Gen. A. ANDRONICOU.

CULTURAL ORGANIZATIONS

E. Ka. Te: Pancyprian Chamber of Fine Arts, P.O.B. 2179, Nicosia; f. 1964; Pres. A. SAVVIDES; Sec. Gen. A. LADOMMATOS; publ. *Bulletin* (monthly).

TH.OK.: Cyprus Theatrical Organization; Dir. YACOVOS PHILIPPOU.

FESTIVALS

There are numerous religious feasts, celebrated with processions, dancing, fairs and the display of icons. The orange, peach, fig and grape harvests are occasions for local festivals, parades and dancing. Carnivals, exhibitions and dances are organized by the larger towns. During June the ancient theatres of Curium and Salamis are used for open-air folk-dancing, concerts and performances of ancient and modern drama. The Pan-Cyprian Cultural Festival takes place in Larnaca in September.

EDUCATION

Until 31st March, 1965, each community in Cyprus managed its own schooling through its respective Communal Chamber. Intercommunal education had been placed under the Minister of the Interior, assisted by a Board of Education for Intercommunal Schools of which the Minister was the Chairman. On 31st March, 1965, the Greek Communal Chamber was dissolved and a Ministry of Education was established to take its place. Intercommunal education has been placed under this Ministry.

Greek-Cypriot Education

Elementary education is compulsory and is provided free in six grades to children between 6 and 14 years of age. In some towns and large villages there are separate junior schools consisting of the first three grades. In some large rural centres there are schools where children can take a two-year post-elementary course if they are not proceeding to a secondary school. Apart from schools for the deaf and blind, and the Lambousa School for juvenile offenders there are also 7 schools for handicapped children. The Ministry runs 9 kindergartens for children from low-income families; most pre-primary education is privately run.

Secondary education is free as from 1972-73 for the first grade of the lower cycle and is fee-paying for the rest, but over 25 per cent of pupils are wholly or partially exempt from payment. There are two types of six-year schools: the Gymnasion-Lykeion (classical, science and economic sections) and the Agricultural Gymnasion. There are five-year vocational (trade) schools and six-year technical schools. There are also 9 foreign-run schools (formerly called "intercommunal") with 208 teachers and 3,750 pupils, and 29 private schools, with 343 teachers and 7,419 pupils.

Post-Secondary education is provided at the Pedagogical Academy, which organizes three-year courses for the training of elementary school teachers, and at the Higher Technical Institute, which provides three-year courses for technicians in civil, electrical and mechanical engineering. There is also a two-year Forestry College (administered by the Ministry of Agriculture) and a three-year Nurses School and one-year School for Health Inspectors (Ministry of Health). Adult education is conducted through Youth Centres in rural areas, Foreign Language Institutes in the towns and an apprenticeship scheme for young workers (in co-operation with the Ministry of Labour).

Turkish-Cypriot Education

The Ministry of Education of the Turkish Federated State of Cyprus caters for some 18 per cent of the islands' population and administers 10 kindergartens, 167 elementary schools (16,014 pupils), 18 secondary schools (7,190 pupils), 6 technical schools (735 pupils) and 1 teacher-training college (13 students). There are 43 evening institutes for adult education.

BIBLIOGRAPHY

ALASTOS, D. Cyprus in History (London, 1955).

ARNOLD, PERCY. Cyprus Challenge (London: Hogarth Press, 1956).

BARKER, DUDLEY. Grivas (London, Cresset Press, 1960).

BYFORD-JONES, W. Grivas and the Story of EOKA (London, Robert Hale, 1960).

CASSON, S. Ancient Cyprus (London, 1937).

EMILIANIDES, ACHILLE. Histoire de Chypre (Paris, 1963).

ESIN, EMEL. Aspects of Turkish Civilization in Cyprus (Ankara University Press, Ankara, 1965).

FOLEY, CHARLES. Island in Revolt (London, Longmans Green, 1962).
Legacy of Strife (Penguin, London, 1964).

FOOT, SYLVIA. Emergency Exit (Chatto and Windus, London, 1960).

FOOT, Sir HUGH. A Start in Freedom (London, 1964).

GRIVAS (DIGHENIS), GEORGE. Guerilla Warfare and EOKA's Struggle (London, Longmans, 1964).
Memoirs of General Grivas (London, Longmans, 1964).

HARBOTTLE, MICHAEL. The Impartial Soldier (Oxford University Press, 1970).

HILL, Sir GEORGE. A History of Cyprus (4 vols., London, 1940-1952).

JENNES, D. The Economics of Cyprus (Montreal, 1962).

KYRIAKIDES, S. Cyprus—Constitutionalism and Crisis Government (Philadelphia, University of Pennsylvania Press, 1968).

LAVENDER, D. S. The Story of Cyprus Mines Corporation (San Marino, Calif., 1962).

LUKE, Sir H. C. Cyprus under the Turks 1571-1878 (Oxford, 1921).
Cyprus: A Portrait and an Appreciation (London, Harrap, 1965).

MEYER, A. J. (with S. VASSILIOU). The Economy of Cyprus (Harvard University Press, 1962).

NEWMAN, PHILIP. A Short History of Cyprus (1940).

PAPADOPOULLOS, T. The population of Cyprus (1570–1881) (Nicosia, 1965).

PURCELL, H. D. Cyprus (London, Benn, 1969).

RICHARD, J. Chypre Sous les Lusignan (Paris, 1962).

ROYAL COMMONWEALTH SOCIETY. Notes on Conditions in Cyprus (London, 1973).

SPYRIDAKIS, Dr. C. A. Brief History of Cyprus (Nicosia, 1964).

STORRS, Sir RONALD. A Chronology of Cyprus (Nicosia, 1930).

STYLIANOU, A. and J. Byzantine Cyprus (Nicosia, 1948).

THURSTON, HAZEL. The Traveller's Guide to Cyprus (Jonathan Cape, London, 1967).

XYDIS, S. G. Cyprus—Conflict and Conciliation 1945-58 (Ohio State University Press, Columbus, Ohio, 1967).

OFFICIAL BOOKS OF REFERENCE:
Cyprus: Documents relating to Independence of Cyprus and the Establishment of British Sovereign Base Areas (Cmnd. 1093, H.M.S.O., London, July 1960).

Cyprus: Treaty of Guarantee, Nicosia, August 16th 1960.

Egypt

PHYSICAL AND SOCIAL GEOGRAPHY

W. B. Fisher

SITUATION

The Arab Republic of Egypt occupies the north-eastern corner of the African continent, with an extension across the Gulf of Suez into the Sinai region which is usually, but not always, regarded as lying in Asia. The area of Egypt is approximately 386,700 sq. miles (1,001,000 sq. km.); but of this only 4 per cent can be said to be permanently settled, the remainder being desert or marsh. Egypt lies between Lat. 22° and 32° N.; and the greatest distance from north to south is about 674 miles (1024 km.), and from east to west 770 miles (1240 km.), giving the country a roughly square shape, with the Mediterranean and Red Seas forming respectively the northern and eastern boundaries. Egypt has political frontiers on the east with Israel, on the south with the Democratic Republic of the Sudan, and on the west with the Libyan Arab Republic. The actual frontiers run in general as straight lines drawn directly between defined points and do not normally conform to geographical features. Between June 1967 and October 1973 the *de facto* frontier with Israel was the Suez Canal. The *de facto* frontier now runs approximately 13 miles to the east of the Suez Canal.

Egypt occupies an almost unique place in the world as a region where, in all probability, the earliest developments of civilization and organized government took place. Though many archaeologists would not wholly subscribe to the view of Egypt as actually the first civilized country, there can be no doubt that from very early times the lower Nile Valley has been prominent as possessing strongly marked unity, with a highly specialized and characteristic way of life. Empires with fluctuating boundaries and with varying racial composition have arisen in neighbouring lands of the Middle East, but Egypt has seemed able to stand relatively unchanged, with the facility of absorbing immigrants and outside ideas, of surviving military occupation and defeat, and of maintaining her own culture, finally shaking clear of foreign influence and rule.

PHYSICAL FEATURES

The reasons for this remarkable persistence of cultural cohesion amongst the Egyptian people may be found in the geography of the country. Egypt consists essentially of a narrow, trough-like valley, some 2 to 10 miles wide, cut by the River Nile in the plateau of north-east Africa. At an earlier geological period a gulf of the Mediterranean Sea probably extended as far south as Cairo, but deposition of silt by the Nile has entirely filled up this gulf, producing the fan-shaped Delta region (8,500 sq. miles in area), through which flow two main distributary branches of the Nile—the eastern, or Damietta branch (150 miles

long), and the western, or Rosetta branch (146 miles), together with many other minor channels. As deposition of silt takes place large stretches of water are gradually impounded to form shallow lakes, which later became firm ground. At the present there are four such stretches of water in the north of the Delta: from east to west, and, in order of size, Lakes Menzaleh, Brullos, Idku and Mariut.

Upstream from Cairo the Nile Valley is at first 6 to 10 miles in width, and, as the river tends to lie close to the eastern side, much of the cultivated land, and also most of the big towns and cities, lie on the western bank. Towards the south the river valley gradually narrows until, at about 250 miles from the frontier of the Sudan, it is no more than 2 miles wide. Near Aswan there is an outcrop of resistant rock, chiefly granite, which the river has not been able to erode as quickly as the rest of the valley. This gives rise to a region of cascades and rapids which is known as the First Cataract. Four other similar regions occur on the Nile, but only the First Cataract lies within Egypt. The cataracts form a barrier to human movement upstream and serve to isolate the Egyptian Nile from territories farther south. In Ancient Egypt, when river communciations were of chief importance, there was a traditional division of the Nile Valley into Lower Egypt (the Delta), Middle Egypt (the broader valley above the Delta), and Upper Egypt (the narrower valley as far as the cataracts). Nowadays it is usual to speak merely of Upper and Lower Egypt, with the division occurring at Cairo.

The fertile strip of the Nile Valley is isolated on the south by the cataracts and by the deserts and swamps of the Sudan; on the north by the Mediterranean Sea; and to east and west by desert plateaux, about which a little more must be said. The land immediately to the east of the Nile Valley, spoken of as the Eastern Highlands, is a complex region with peaks that rise 6,000 to 7,000 ft., but also much broken up by deep valleys that make travel difficult. Owing to aridity the whole region is sparsely populated, with a few partly nomadic shepherds, one or two monasteries and a number of small towns associated chiefly with the exploitation of minerals—petroleum, iron, manganese and granite—that occur in this region. Difficult landward communications mean that contact is mostly by sea, except in the case of the ironfields. The Sinai, separated from the Eastern Highlands by the Gulf of Suez, is structurally very similar, but the general plateau level is tilted, giving the highest land (again nearly 7,000 ft. in elevation) in the extreme south, where it rises in bold scarps from sea-level. Towards the north the land gradually slopes down, ultimately forming the low-lying sandy plain of the Sinai desert which fringes the Mediterranean Sea. Because of its low altitude and accessibility, the Sinai, in spite of its desert nature, has been for many centuries an important corridor linking Egypt with Asia. It is now crossed only by a motor road, the railway having been torn up in 1968 by occupying Israeli forces.

West of the Nile occur the vast expanses known as the Western Desert. Though by no means uniform in height, the land surface is much lower than that east of the Nile, and within Egypt rarely exceeds 1,000 ft. above sea-level. Parts are covered by extensive masses of light shifting sand that often form dunes; but in addition there are a number of large depressions, some with the lowest parts actually below sea-level. These depressions seem to have been hollowed out by wind action, breaking up rock strata that were weakened by the presence of underground water, and most hollows still contain supplies of artesian water. In some instances (as for example, the Qattara depression, and the Wadi Natrun, respectively south-west and south-east of Alexandria) the subterranean water is highly saline and consequently useless for agriculture; but in others—notably the oases of the Fayyum, Siwa, Dakhla, Behariya, and Farafra—the water is sufficiently sweet to allow use for irrigation, and settlements have grown up within the desert.

CLIMATE

The main feature of Egyptian climate is the almost uniform aridity. Alexandria, the wettest part, receives only 8 inches of rain annually, and most of the south has 3 inches or less. In many districts rain may fall in quantity only once in two or three years, and it is apposite to recall that throughout most of Egypt, and even in Cairo itself, the majority of the people live in houses of unbaked, sun-dried brick. During the summer temperatures are extremely high, reaching 100-110°F. at times and even 120° in the southern and western deserts. The Mediterranean coast has cooler conditions, with 90° as a maximum; hence the wealthier classes move to Alexandria for the three months of summer. Winters are generally warm, with very occasional rain; but cold spells occur from time to time, and light snow is not unknown. Owing to the large extent of desert, hot dry sand-winds (called *khamsin*) are fairly frequent particularly in spring, and much damage can be caused to crops; it has been known for the temperature to rise by 35° in two hours, and the wind to reach 90 m.p.h. Another unusual condition is the occurrence of early morning fog in Lower Egypt during spring and early summer. This, on the other hand, has a beneficial effect on plant growth in that it supplies moisture and is a partial substitute for rainfall.

IRRIGATION

With a deficient rainfall over the entire country, human existence in Egypt depends closely on irrigation from the Nile; in consequence it is now necessary to consider the régime of the river in some detail. More detailed reference to conditions outside Egypt is made in the section on the geography of Sudan (below); but it may here be stated in summary that the river rises in the highlands of East Africa, with its main stream issuing from Lakes Victoria and Albert. In the southern Sudan it wanders sluggishly across a flat open plain, where the fall in level is only 1:100,000. Here the shallow waters become a vast swamp, full of dense masses of papyrus vegetation, and this section of the Nile is called the Sudd (Arabic for "blockage"). Finally, in the north of the Sudan, the Nile flows in a well-defined channel and enters Egypt. In Upper Egypt the river is in process of cutting its bed deeper into the rock floor; but in the lower part of its course silt is deposited, and the level of the land is rising—in some places by as much as 4 inches per century.

The salient feature of the Nile is, of course, its regular annual flood, which is caused by the onset of summer rains in East Africa and Ethiopia. The flood travels northward, reaching Egypt during August, and within Egypt the normal rise in river level was at first 21 feet, which had declined to 15 feet as irrigation works developed. This cycle of flood had been maintained for several thousand years until, in 1969, construction of the Aswan High Dam made it a feature of the past (see the section on the High Dam below) so far as Egypt is concerned.

Originally, the flood waters were simply retained in specially prepared basins with earthen banks, and the water could then be used for three to four months after the flood. Within the last century, building of large barrages held water all the year round, allowing cultivation at any season. The old (basin system) allowed one or two crops per holding per year, the newer (perennial) system, three or even four. In the past, barley and wheat were the main crops; under perennial irrigation maize and cotton, which can tolerate the great summer heat provided they are watered, take first and second place.

Changeover from basin to perennial irrigation allowed a considerable population increase in Egypt, from about 2½ million in 1800 to about 37 million in 1975, giving rural densities of over 6,000 per square mile in some areas; and as 99 per cent of all Egyptians live within the Nile valley (only 4 per cent of its area) there is considerable pressure on the land.

With most Egyptians entirely dependent upon Nile water, the point has now been reached that almost all the water entering Egypt is fully utilized. However, there are enormous losses by evaporation which at present amount to some 70 per cent of the total flow. A political problem is concerned with the effects devoting an increased area of the Nile Valley to the growing of commodities for export: cotton, rice and vegetables. Such a change from agricultural self-sufficiency to a cash economy involves the purchase abroad of fertilizers and even foodstuffs, and is inducing considerable social changes within the country. Moreover, so long as only one or two crops were taken per year, the silt laid down by the annual floods maintained soil fertility, but now that three or four crops are taken the import of fertilizer is essential. Hence Egypt has become increasingly sensitive to world trade prices. The position of the merchant and capitalist has greatly improved, often at the expense of the peasant farmer.

Difficulties and opportunities over use of Nile water are exemplified in the High Dam scheme at Aswan, which has created a lake 350 miles (500 km.) in length and 6 miles (10 km.) wide that has extended southwards across the Sudanese frontier and inundated the town of Wadi Halfa, whose 55,000–60,000 inhabitants were re-settled at Kashm el Girba, a district lying south east of Khartoum, whilst displaced Egyptians were settled in 33 villages around Kom Ombo: total costs of re-settlement were about £14 million. Prior to 1959 technical and political objections delayed the High Dam scheme; and as the cost of the dam (estimated at £345–400 million) could not be met by the Egyptian Government alone, application was made to the World Bank, America and Britain for a loan, This was refused (Sudanese opposition being one, but only one, factor in this refusal), whereupon Egyptian reaction was to expropriate the Suez Canal Company, in order to finance part of the Aswan scheme.

Soviet offers to assist were made and accepted; and in 1959 a first Soviet credit of £33 million allowed preliminary work to begin in December of the same year. In 1960 further agreement was reached by which the U.S.S.R. supplied credits up to £81 million (making a total of £194 million) together with technical and material assistance; and in 1964 further proposals for credit and loans were made by Mr. Khrushchev. Egypt must thus find at least £200 million in addition to repayments at a later stage of the Russian credits.

In May 1964 the first phase of the High Dam was inaugurated by President Nasser and Mr. Khrushchev. The High Dam is 3,600 metres across, with a girth of 980 metres at the river bed and 40 metres at the top. It holds back the largest artificial lake in the world, and makes possible large scale storing of water from year to year, and a regular planned use of all Nile water independently of the precise amount of annual flood. Its irrigation potential is 2 million feddans for Lower Egypt alone, and the total for the Nile valley (including Upper Egypt) is adding 30 per cent to the total cultivable area of Egypt. Twelve generator units incorporated in the dam give considerable quantities of low-cost electric power (lower than costs in much of Europe and less than 50 per cent of that of electricity in London). This power is already a most important aid to industrialization, especially for the new metal industries. Started in January 1960, the Dam was completed in July 1970 and officially inaugurated in January 1971.

Some relatively minor adverse effects have been noticed: scouring of the Nile bed below the dam; increased salinity in the lower stretches; reduced sedimentation below the dam and heavy deposition within the basin; effects of blowing sand on the electric power lines; and, perhaps more seriously, the disappearance of fish (particularly sardines) off the Mediterranean coast of Egypt. It is hoped that this last can be compensated by new fishing within Lake Nasser.

RACE

The racial origins of the Egyptian people present certain problems. In the deserts to east and west of the Nile Valley the population is of unmixed Mediterranean strains; but within the Nile Valley itself there is a special native Egyptian type that would seem to have developed partly from intermixture. The Egyptian peasant is more heavily built and muscular than the nomadic Bedouin, and his colouring is intermediate between the lighter brown of Syrian and Palestinian Arabs and the dark skins of the negroid peoples of the Sudan and Abyssinia. Facial features show some resemblance to those of other Arabs, but despite this there is often more than a hint of the features depicted in ancient monuments. It might thus be reasonable to suggest that there seems to have developed within Egypt a special racial sub-type, basically Mediterranean, with smaller elements both from the south and the north, but also greatly affected by local indigenous conditions which have given rise to a specific Egyptian racial type.

LANGUAGE

Arabic is the language of almost all Egyptians, though there are very small numbers of Berber-speaking villages in the western oases. Most educated Egyptians also speak either French or English, often with a preference for the former. This is a reflection of the traditional French interest in Egypt, which is reciprocated: governmental decrees are sometimes published in French, as well as Arabic, and newspapers in French have an important circulation in Cairo and Alexandria. Small colonies of Greeks and Armenians are also a feature of the larger Egyptian towns. It should perhaps be noted that the Arabic name for Egypt, Misr, is always used within the country itself.

HISTORY

Geography has influenced the history of Egypt from the earliest times. The narrow strip of cultivable land along the banks of the Nile between the First Cataract and the Delta is distinct from the extensive and fertile plain of the Delta itself, but the resultant tendency to separatism has been counterbalanced by the dependence of the people on the annual Nile flood: the control and exploitation of the water and silt have necessitated co-operation and obedience to routine and authority. The eastern and western deserts seal off the lower reaches of the Nile Valley from the neighbouring territories in Africa and Asia. Until recent times communication with the outside world was largely restricted to the route up the river into Nubia, the sea route across the Mediterranean to Syria and the land route to Palestine across the northern fringe of Sinai. The effect of Egypt's relative isolation has been to produce a high degree of cultural individuality.

PHARAONIC EGYPT TO 671 B.C.

Traditionally Egyptian history begins with the semi-legendary Menes, the first ruler of the united kingdom of Upper and Lower Egypt at the end of the fourth millenium B.C. But the flowering of the Old Kingdom came in the third millenium under the IVth Dynasty, which had its capital at Memphis, near the apex of the Delta. The technical and engineering progress of this period is witnessed by the pyramids. These and other works indicate a powerful monarchy commanding great resources.

This efflorescence was followed by a decline. Not until the XIth and XIIth Dynasties (c. 2000 B.C.) does the resurgence of a united Egypt in the Middle Kingdom become clear. The powerful provincial nobles were slowly brought under royal control. Improved conditions were reflected in reclamation works in the Fayyum and temple building at numerous sites. Egyptian armies penetrated into Nubia, a land at that time rich in gold, and the conquest of the region to a point above the Second Cataract was accomplished.

Another obscure period followed and the course of Egyptian history was interrupted by the invasion from Palestine of the Hyksos who established themselves as rulers in the Delta. Although they adopted Egyptian customs, they were never assimilated. About 1620 B.C. a revolt began under a southern prince and ultimately the Hyksos were expelled and Egypt was reunited.

Under the XVIIIth Dynasty, ancient Egypt reached her zenith. This period of the New Kingdom has left its mark up and down the land especially around the capital, Thebes, near the modern Luxor. Abroad the name of the pharaoh was feared in western Asia. The greatest of the conquerors was Thothmes III who established an Egyptian empire in Syria. Egyptian rule was restored and extended in Nubia.

The empire decayed during the reign of Akhenaten (c. 1380–1362), whose religious innovations antagonized the powerful priesthood of Thebes. On his death the old polytheism was restored. The outstanding figure of the XIXth Dynasty was Rameses II (c 1300–1234). He fought the rising power of the Hittites in Syria for twenty years and was both a great builder and a usurper of other men's works.

After him Egypt passed into decline. The XXth Dynasty closed with a long series of insignificant pharaohs and under their successors Egypt was divided between a ruler in the Delta and a priest-king at Thebes. In the eighteenth century B.C. a dynasty originating from Nubia held Upper Egypt and even for a time the Delta. But Egypt was soon to pass under completely alien domination.

EGYPT UNDER FOREIGN RULERS:
671 B.C.–A.D. 640

In 671 the Assyrians conquered Egypt and drove out the Nubian pharaoh. The Assyrians, however, did not long maintain their hold and a native ruler succeeded in reuniting the country. The dynasty which he founded encouraged Greek traders and was supported by Greek mercenaries.

This last native dynasty came to an end in 525, when Persia conquered Egypt. The Persian kings patronized the religion of their subjects and were officially regarded as pharaohs. Darius I (522–485) completed the work of an Egyptian predecessor in cutting a canal linking the Nile and the Red Sea. His successors fought native pretenders to keep Egypt within their empire.

Under Alexander the Great another change of masters occurred. The Persian satrap surrendered in 332 and Alexander was recognized as pharaoh. His visit to the oracle at Siwa shows his fascinated interest in Egyptian religion, while by founding the city of Alexandria he conferred on Egypt a lasting benefit. After Alexander's death, Egypt fell to his general, Ptolemy. The Ptolemaic Dynasty was Greek in origin and outlook. Its capital was Alexandria, which was in effect a Greek rather than an Egyptian city. Egypt was the private estate of the Ptolemies, who taxed its people through a competent bureaucracy.

When Cleopatra committed suicide in 30 B.C., Egypt passed under Roman rule. Although the emperors were regarded as successors of the pharaohs the country sank into a mere province of a great Mediterranean empire. Egyptian Christianity had a distinctive doctrinal character and, by fostering monasticism, originated an important institution. In the dogmatic disputes of the Byzantine period, the adherence of the Coptic church of Egypt to monophysite beliefs in face of the official theology was a form of national self-assertion.

ARAB EGYPT: 640-969

In the early seventh century two great powers dominated the Middle East: the Byzantine empire and the Sasanian empire of the Persians. In 616 the Sasanian army invaded Egypt but Byzantine supremacy was soon restored. Meanwhile a third power was arising, the Arabs, summoned by Muhammad to belief in Islam.

The Prophet's death in 632 was followed by wars against the Byzantines and Sasanians. Egypt, the granary of the Byzantine Empire, soon attracted the Muslim warriors. In the reign of the Caliph Umar I an Arab army under 'Amr ibn al-As took the invasion route from Syria. The frontier towns fell after short sieges and in April 641 the key-fortress near the head of the Delta was captured. Alexandria, the capital, surrendered and was evacuated by the Byzantine garrison. A camp-city at Al-Fustat, again in the strategic position near the apex of the Delta, became the headquarters of the Muslim army and the new capital.

For some centuries Egypt remained an occupied rather than a Muslim country. The Copts, who disliked Byzantine rule, had not opposed the conquest. Under the Arabs they found less oppression and paid lower taxes at first than under Constantinople. In course of time, however, Egypt became an Arabic-speaking country with a Muslim majority. But to this day the Coptic Christian minority remains and uses the ancient language in its liturgy.

For over two centuries Egypt was administered as a province of the Arab Empire. By the middle of the ninth century the remoter territories were slipping from the grasp of the Abbasid caliphs of Baghdad. Egypt was obviously well-fitted to be the domain of an autonomous governor. Two short-lived Sunnite Dynasties, founded by men of central Asian origin, the Tulunids and the Ikhshidids, ruled in virtual independence of the caliph between 868 and 969. Each rapidly degenerated after the death of its founder. Ahmad ibn Tulun in 877 occupied Syria and thus once again created an empire based on Egypt.

THE FATIMIDS AND AYYUBIDS: 969-1250

Ikshidid rule was terminated in 969 by an invasion from Tunisia. Here the rival caliphate of the Fatimids had been set up by Muslims of the Shia sect, who believed that the caliphate could only pass through the direct descendants of 'Ali, the husband of Muhammad's daughter, Fatima. The fourth of these anti-caliphs, Al-Mu'izz, was made the master of Egypt by his general, Jawhar. Jawhar laid out a new capital, just outside Al-Fustat, which has developed into the modern city of Cairo, and was the founder of the mosque of Al-Azhar, the greatest centre of Islamic theological learning.

Under the early Fatimids Egypt enjoyed a golden age. The country was a well-administered absolute monarchy and it formed the central portion of an empire which at its height included North Africa, Sicily, Syria and western Arabia. Agriculture and industry were encouraged. Trade with Europe and India brought prosperity to the land and wealth to the ruler.

Soon, however, Fatimid rule began to decay. Ali Hakim (996–1021) departed from the tolerant policy towards Christians and Jews which was normal in Muslim states. The long reign of Al-Mustansir (1035–94) witnessed the break-up of the Fatimid Empire and the growing insubordination of the slave-soldiery. In 1073 the caliph was obliged to send for Badr al Jamali, the governor of Acre, to take control of the country. This he did and Egypt passed under the government of a military autocracy who kept the Fatimid caliphs under their tutelage. Thus the collapse of the Fatimid state was postponed for nearly a century but, after the death of Al-Mustansir, the six succeeding caliphs had no power.

Meanwhile a new enemy was on the threshold—the Crusaders who after 1098 established feudal, Christian states along the Syrian coast. Neither the Abbasids nor the Fatimids were capable of resisting them but in the later twelfth century the tide began to turn. The Muslim reconquest of Syria was largely due to the energy and ability of the Kurdish leader, Salah al-Din ibn Ayyub, known in European history as Saladin. In 1169 he became minister to the Fatimid caliph. In 1171 the last Fatimid was quietly deposed and Egypt restored to Sunni orthodoxy. The remainder of Saladin's life was a struggle against the crusading states but when he died in 1193 he was sultan over Egypt and practically the whole of the former Crusader territory.

Saladin's Empire was divided amongst his heirs, one branch of which, the Egyptian Ayyubids, reigned in Cairo. Dynastic struggles weakened the family and the Crusaders were able to recover some lost ground. Louis IX of France led an attack directly on Egypt. Damietta was occupied in 1249 but the advance of the Crusaders through the difficult and pestilential Delta was stopped at the battle of Al-Mansura in 1250. Louis was made prisoner but subsequently regained his liberty on paying a ransom and restoring Damietta.

THE MAMLUK SULTANATE: 1250-1517

During this Crusade the Ayyubid sultan, al-Malik al-Salih, died. This was virtually the end of the dynasty. After a short confused period the commander of the forces, a certain Aybak became the first of the Mamluk sultans who ruled Egypt from 1250 to 1517. These sultans were of slave origin. The Ayyubids had built up bodyguards of slave-troops, whose power increased as that of their masters declined. The earlier Mamluks, until 1390, were mainly of Turkish and Mongol origin, while their successors, originally the bodyguard of the former, were mostly Circassians. The Mamluk sultans did not form a dynasty in the hereditary sense but a caste from which successive rulers emerged after election or a struggle for power. The ranks of the Mamluks were replenished by fresh purchases.

The Mamluks were thus an alien element which was never fully assimilated in Egypt. They exploited the land for their own benefit and the Egyptians played a passive role under their domination. Nevertheless they protected Egypt and Syria against the Mongols and the Crusaders. The Mongol threat developed in the middle of the thirteenth century when Hulagu, the grandson of Jenghiz Khan, advanced through Persia. Baghdad was taken and the Abbasid caliphate extinguished in 1258. From Northern Syria the Mongol army advanced southwards until at Ain Jalut, near Nazareth, it was overwhelmed in 1260 by the Mamluk Sultan, Baibars. Spared from the ravages of the Mongols, Egypt became the principal centre of Arab culture. The change in the centre of gravity of Islam was symbolized when Baibars brought to Cairo an 'Abbasid prince, who was formally recognized as titular caliph.

This victory also ensured that the Mamluk sultans would rule over a combined empire of Egypt and Syria. The remaining pockets of Crusader territory were regained by Baibars and his successors. Baibars also intervened in the affairs of the Christian kingdom of Nubia and virtually established a protectorate.

The numerous mosques and public works of the Mamluk period indicate the wealth of Egypt. But from the middle of the fourteenth century the condition of the country declined owing to plague and civil war, while heavy taxation oppressed all classes of the native Egyptians. Another Mongol invasion under Tamerlane in 1401 devastated Syria, although Egypt itself was again spared. The valuable transit trade through Egypt was subjected to a close monopoly, which diminished its flow. Finally Vasco da Gama's voyage to India around the Cape (1496–99) sounded the doom of Egyptian prosperity. European ships henceforward by-passed Egypt and traded directly with the east, while the Portuguese destroyed the Mamluk fleets and harried Arab shipping in the Indian Ocean, Red Sea and Persian Gulf.

OTTOMAN EGYPT: 1517-1798

At the beginning of the sixteenth century a powerful state was created in Persia under the Safavid dynasty, while Anatolia and the Balkan peninsula were ruled by the Ottomans. The Mamluks were by comparison a declining power and sought by a secret understanding with the Persian Shah to hold their own against the expansionist and militant Ottomans.

In 1516 at the battle of Marj Dabiq north of Aleppo the Ottoman Sultan, Selim I, defeated the Mamluks and advanced southwards. A second battle in January 1517, outside Cairo, resulted in the overthrow of the last Mamluk sultan. The whole of his empire fell into Selim's hands and Cairo sank to a provincial status. The Turkish conquest together with the change in international trade-routes marked the beginning of a period of political and economic insignificance. The great mosque of Al-Azhar retained its primacy among the theological schools of Islam but its teaching was set in a conservative tradition that remained unbroken until the nineteenth century.

Selim recognized the individuality of Egypt and his successors usually interfered but little with the administration. The Mamluk soldiery and their leaders,

the beys, were allowed to continue receiving their revenues. A garrison of Turkish janissaries was stationed in Egypt but in the course of a few generations they became useless as a military force, while constant recruiting from the slave-markets kept the Mamluks in unimpaired vigour. Ottoman governors were appointed but for the most part they were utterly dependent on the Mamluk beys.

From time to time Mamluk grandees were virtually sovereign in Egypt. The most famous of these was Ali Bey, who ruled from 1761 to 1766, was then driven into exile, but regained power from 1767 to 1772. He made an alliance with a Syrian Arab chief, and contacted a Russian squadron, which was then cruising in the eastern Mediterranean, during the course of hostilities against the Ottoman Empire. A Mamluk force attacked Damascus, and drove out the Ottoman governor, but Ali's general betrayed him, and returned to Egypt. Ali fled to his Syrian friend, but was defeated in an attempt to reconquer Egypt in 1773 and died a prisoner.

Ali Bey's career illustrated the weakness of the Mamluks. They had no roots in Egypt and the Egyptians viewed with indifference their struggles for mastery. Their power to achieve their ambitions was limited by the difficulty of financing their factions and they became unpopular by the extortions which they practised on the native Egyptians. At the end of the century a shock from Europe was to reveal the hollowness of their power.

THE FRENCH IN EGYPT: 1798-1801

During the eighteenth century, the British obtained the chief share of Eastern commerce. With the outbreak of the Revolutionary War between Britain and France, the French decided that the occupation of Egypt and the revival of the transit trade might lead to the disruption of British commerce and the overthrow of British rule in India. Bonaparte landed at Alexandria in July 1798.

His aim was to colonize Egypt, break the Mamluk hold and introduce Western ideas. Although he professed sympathy with Islam, his expedition was essentially inspired by the nationalist and secular ideology of the French Revolution. The Egyptians saw in it a new crusade and Bonaparte's attempts to win support by appeals to Muslim sentiment miscarried.

Defeated in the decisive "Battle of the Pyramids" on July 21st, the Mamluks fled and the sudden collapse of their administration was followed by disorder and pillage in Cairo until the entry of French troops. The following month, however, Bonaparte was cut off from France by the destruction of his fleet by Nelson in the "Battle of the Nile". In September the Ottoman Sultan declared war and news of this, combined with Mamluk intrigues and hostility towards the alien French, led in October to a serious revolt in Cairo, centred around Al-Azhar which was subjected to an artillery bombardment.

Early in 1799 Bonaparte invaded Syria to attack the combined forces of the Mamluks and the Ottomans under the governor of Acre. The latter was supported by a British naval squadron and after besieging Acre for two months Bonaparte withdrew to Egypt, his forces much reduced by fighting and disease. He repulsed a Turkish landing near Alexandria in July and succeeded in August in getting away to France with a few companions. His army held out until 1801 when a British force, subsequently joined by Ottoman troops, compelled them to capitulate.

The shock to Egypt of the French occupation was great. The Mamluk ruling caste was unseated, Egyptian Muslim leaders were associated with the administration and consulted on public matters, and the Copts were placed on an equal footing with the Muslims. The immediate effect was to confuse and irritate Egyptian opinion, but the way to future developments had been opened.

The French did not abandon the idea of gaining control over Egypt and their interest in Egyptian affairs was maintained. French scholars who had accompanied Bonaparte produced monographs which became the basis of modern studies of the country. In the hands of Champollion, the Rosetta Stone was to be the key to the hieroglyphs.

MUHAMMAD ALI PASHA AND HIS SUCCESSORS: 1805-63

The expulsion of the French was followed by a struggle for power in which the victor was an Albanian officer in the Ottoman forces, Muhammad Ali. In 1805 he was recognized by the Sultan as Governor of Egypt. In 1807 he defeated a British force which had occupied Alexandria. In 1811 the Mamluk chiefs were massacred in Cairo. His prestige was increased by the success of his forces in a campaign in Arabia, undertaken between 1811 and 1818 at the request of the Sultan, against the Wahhabi conquerors of the Hijaz, led by the family of Saud, who threatened the Fertile Crescent. Between 1820 and 1822 his army conquered most of the northern Sudan, the source of gold and slaves.

The gaps in his army resulting from these campaigns were made up first by slaves, who were found unsuitable because of their high mortality, and then by the conscription—unprecedented, brutal and unpopular—of native Egyptians. The new army had Turks, Albanians and Circassians for officers and was trained by European military instructors.

In 1824 Muhammad Ali sent his son Ibrahim with an Egyptian force to assist the Sultan to suppress the Greek revolt, but European intervention in 1827 led to the destruction of the Turkish and Egyptian fleets at Navarino. On the rejection by the Sultan of Muhammad Ali's demand that Syria should be given to him in recompense, Ibrahim invaded that country in 1831. War with the Ottomans followed and Ibrahim advanced into Anatolia. A convention in 1833 gave Muhammad Ali the Syrian provinces, which were ruled by Ibrahim for seven years as his viceroy. A second Ottoman war then broke out, and international intervention once again resulted in Ibrahim's defeat.

Muhammad Ali's dominions were restricted to Egypt and the Sudan but his governorship was made hereditary. He died in 1849, having been predeceased by Ibrahim.

Within Egypt Muhammad Ali reformed the administration and controlled the national wealth. An ambitious educational system was organized under European teachers, and Egyptian students were sent abroad, especially to France. A press was set up, primarily for the production of textbooks and manuals. Towards the end of his reign a Western-educated class was emerging and the ferment of ideas characteristic of modern Egyptian intellectual life had begun.

Muhammad Ali was succeeded by his grandson, Abbas I (1849–54), under whom the westernizing trend was reduced, and he by Said (1854–64), Muhammad Ali's surviving son.

THE MAKING OF THE SUEZ CANAL: 1854-69

During Muhammad Ali's reign, Egypt regained importance as a link between Europe and the East. The overland route via Alexandria, Cairo and Suez, which was improved with the construction of a railway by British enterprise, reduced the passage between England and India from five months to forty days. This route was used by passengers and mail but heavy merchandise continued to go by the Cape. The scheme for a maritime canal, regarded by the British Government as a threat to India, was backed by France but Muhammad Ali refused to grant the necessary concession, seeing a canal as a threat to the independence he sought.

Said proved more pliant and in 1854 granted a concession to de Lesseps which included an undertaking to supply labour but which required ratification by the Sultan. This was delayed owing to British opposition and work did not begin until 1859, in anticipation of ratification after de Lesseps had gained the support of Napoleon III.

Said was succeeded by Ismail, Ibrahim's son, who inherited something of his grandfather's imagination and his father's energy. At his insistence the concession (and particularly the clause concerning the provision of labour) was modified, but he was obliged to pay £3 million in compensation to the Suez Canal Company after the matter had been submitted to the arbitration of Napoleon III. The canal was opened with great festivities.

At first the British Government tried to ignore the canal and none of the 80,000 shares reserved for Britain (one-fifth of the total) were bought. Ismail, who had originally been allotted 64,000 shares, took up these and others which remained unsubscribed, bringing his total holding to 182,023 shares. Said and Ismail had together paid about £11½ million in connection with the canal which cost approximately £16 million to cut. Ismail was to receive 15 per cent of the net profits, in addition to the interest on his shares.

THE KHEDIVE ISMAIL AND INTERNATIONAL CONTROL: 1863-81

As part of the Ottoman Empire, Egypt was bound by the Capitulations—treaties with European powers giving European communities in Ottoman territories a considerable degree of autonomy under the jurisdiction of their consuls. Originally they had applied to small groups of merchants but with the growth of trade with Egypt in the nineteenth century consular protection came to be enjoyed by sizeable foreign communities, who were exempt from Egyptian jurisdiction and largely free of Egyptian taxation. After prolonged negotiations Mixed Courts, which reduced the scope of consular jurisdiction, were introduced in 1875; these, however, had a majority of European judges and were not insensitive to diplomatic pressures.

Ismail was to deliver Egypt into far greater international control. His ambitions made him careless of financial considerations, and high cotton prices during the American Civil War gave him a false idea of his country's wealth. In 1866 he obtained the title of Khedive. He extended his Sudanese dominions, cut canals, built railways and constructed telegraph lines. No distinction was drawn between the debts of the state and those of the ruler, whose personal expenses were high, and between 1863 and 1876 Egyptian indebtedness rose from £7 million to nearly £100 million. Much of this was in the form of loans from European financial houses at steep rates of interest.

In 1875 Ismail staved off a financial crisis by selling his Suez Canal shares to the British Government for nearly £4 million, a profitable investment by Disraeli who sought to prevent French control. The crisis came in 1876 when Ismail suspended payment of his treasury bills, a declaration of bankruptcy which led to international control. A khedival decree of May 1876 established the "Caisse de la Dette Publique", administered by four foreign members—British, French, Austrian and Italian—to provide for the service of Egyptian debts. When this arrangement proved unsuccessful the French insisted on reform of the fiscal system to provide for repayment of the debts and in 1878 Ismail was forced by France and Britain, in return for a new loan, to surrender his powers and revenues to a ministry, headed by Nubar Pasha, which included a British and a French minister. Ismail chafed under foreign control, aligned himself with Egyptian opposition to it and in May 1879 dismissed the ministry. The French and British Governments retaliated by securing his deposition by the Ottoman Sultan.

Ismail was succeeded by his son Tawfik, who, ostensibly, governed through a responsible Egyptian ministry. Strict financial control was exercised, however, by a French and a British controller, and under the law of liquidation of 1880 an international Debt Commission, consisting of two French and two British members together with one German, one Austrian and one Italian, administered 66 per cent of the country's revenue for the benefit of foreign creditors. Furthermore, a maximum was laid down for government expenditure and the Commissioners were empowered to draw on any surplus administrative revenue. Such was the burden laid upon the Egyptian people by Ismail's improvidence.

THE ARABI EPISODE: 1881-82

Meanwhile a nationalist outlook was developing among those classes who had been touched by Western influences, particularly the younger Egyptian army officers whose way to promotion was barred by Turks and Circassians. Liberal reformers led by Cherif Pasha resented Turkish overlordship and wanted a Western-style constitution. Moslem leaders were opposed to the spread of Christian influence. The great landowners, many of whom were, like the ruling house, Turkish in origin, fought to retain their privileges which were threatened by foreign control. The peasantry, who had been squeezed to pay for Ismail's schemes were being squeezed again to pay his debts. The Khedive, Tawfik, was revealed as a puppet maintained by France and Britain.

By 1881 the country seethed with unrest and a climax was reached in February when, in protest against cuts imposed on the army, a group of officers led by Arabi Pasha forced Tawfik to dismiss his Circassian War Minister. In September, after surrounding his palace, they compelled him to agree to the formation of a new ministry, and to summon the Chamber of Notables, a consultative body originally set up by Ismail. France was opposed to any concession to moderate Egyptian opinion, Britain agreed rather than risk a split with France, and a Franco-British note was sent proclaiming the resolve to maintain the Khedive and the established order.

The effect of the note was to align the Chamber of Notables with Arabi against foreign intervention. In February 1882 the Khedive was forced to dismiss the ministry led by Cherif Pasha and appoint a nationalist ministry with a supporter of Arabi as Prime Minister and Arabi himself Minister for War. The Dual Control ceased to exist and, although anxious to avoid sending an expedition to Egypt, the British and French Governments in May sent naval squadrons to Alexandria as a demonstration. On their arrival Egyptian opinion became so inflamed that in June fanaticism took control and riots broke out in Alexandria and other places in which numbers of Europeans were killed.

At a conference in Constantinople neither Germany nor Turkey would support the sending of an expeditionary force and the French Chamber of Deputies refused to sanction French intervention. On July 11th, the Egyptians having refused to cease work on the fortifications of Alexandria, the British squadron bombarded the forts. The town was evacuated by the Egyptian army, while the Khedive placed himself under British protection and subsequently proclaimed Arabi a rebel. The French ostentatiously dissociated themselves from the British action. A British expeditionary force landed at Ismailia and routed the Egyptian army at Tel el Kebir. Cairo was occupied and Tawfik's prerogatives were restored, to be subsequently exercised under British control.

THE RULE OF CROMER AND HIS SUCCESSORS: 1883-1914

The British Government hoped to set Egyptian affairs in order and then to withdraw, but the execution of this policy was frustrated. The Arabi episode had brought Egypt once again to the verge of bankruptcy. Difficulties were increased by a cholera epidemic, a poor Nile, the Mahdist revolt in the Sudan and the unremitting hostility of France. Evacuation was repeatedly deferred and the occupation gradually assumed the character of a veiled protectorate.

From 1883 to 1907 the Egyptian Government was dominated by the British Agent and Consul-General, Sir Evelyn Baring, who in 1891 became Lord Cromer. He was in title only the equal of the other consuls-general and British control was established with diplomatic care, German support being canvassed to counterbalance French obstruction. A policy of severe economy was necessary to satisfy foreign bondholders. In spite of the limitation on his freedom of action, Cromer obtained remarkable results. An international convention in 1885 eased the financial strain by permitting a further loan and modifying the rigidity with which Egyptian revenues were assigned. British financial advisers brought about increased revenues, solvency was restored and taxation reduced. Irrigation works were improved and paid labour replaced the corvée for the annual clearance of the canals. The Aswan dam was constructed. A new Egyptian army was trained by British officers.

In 1892 Tawfik died. He was succeeded by his son, Abbas II, who was barely eighteen at his accession and soon resented Cromer's authority. The possibility of a conjunction between Abbas and a new nationalist movement led by Mustafa Kamil, a young lawyer who had been trained in France, caused the British some anxiety but the Khedive's attempts to assert himself resulted in humiliation which further embittered him against Britain. A series of puppet governments preserved a façade of constitutionalism but educated youth turned increasingly to opposition.

At the turn of the century Britain gained a freer hand in Egypt. The Sudan was reconquered between 1896 and 1898. A clash between British and French at Fashoda on the Upper Nile was narrowly averted and the liquidation of this problem led ultimately to the Entente Cordiale of 1904 and the diminution of French opposition in Egypt. At the same time senior British officials, who had increased in number from about 100 in 1885 to over 1,000 in 1905. were out of touch with the growing strength of nationalist feeling.

Cromer was succeeded in 1907 by Sir Eldon Gorst, who managed to establish better relations with the Khedive and adopted an attitude of informality which contrasted with Cromer's proconsular pomp. On his death in 1911 he was followed by Lord Kitchener, who, as conqueror of the Sudan, was treated with more deference than had been grudgingly accorded to Gorst and whose arrival marked a return to more autocratic methods. Nevertheless a Legislative Assembly was created in 1913 which provided a platform from which the voice of nationalism could make itself heard with constitutional propriety, and it is to the credit of British rule throughout this period that the press was uncensored and the expression of opinion free.

THE FIRST WORLD WAR AND ITS CONSEQUENCES: 1914-22

After Turkey entered the First World War in November 1914 on the side of Germany, Egypt, still nominally a province of the Ottoman Empire, was declared a British protectorate and Britain assumed responsibility for the defence of the Suez Canal. On December 20th Abbas II was deposed and the British Government offered the title of Sultan to Husain Kamil, the brother of Tawfik. When Husain died in 1917 he was succeeded by his brother Fuad.

Under the protectorate the combination of British and Egyptian officials in the administration continued. Kitchener was succeeded by Sir Henry McMahon, the first High Commissioner, and he in turn was succeeded in 1917 by Sir Reginald Wingate, who had served in the Egyptian army under Kitchener and had since 1899 been Governor-General of the Sudan.

The Constantinople Convention of 1888 provided that the Suez Canal should be "always free and open, in time of war as in time of peace, to every vessel of commerce or war, without distinction of flag", but, by a blockade against enemy shipping outside the three-mile limit covered by the Convention, Britain was able to deny the use of the Canal to enemy shipping.

The pressure of military necessity was increasingly felt by the Egyptians. Martial law, censorship, the dearth of officials of good quality, the forcible recruitment of labour and the requisition of animals for the advance into Palestine, rising prices and profiteering all combined to intensify opposition to the protectorate. The nationalist movement, antagonistic to both the British administration and the Sultan, fed on popular discontent and at the end of the war, in November 1918, a delegation, headed by Saad Zaghlul, presented Wingate with a demand for autonomy. The British Government's refusal to deal with the nationalists and the deportation of Zaghlul and three of his associates resulted in riots and murders early in 1919 and order had to be restored by military action.

Wingate, who had given warning of the danger, was superseded by Allenby, fresh from his successful campaign against the Turks. Allenby made overtures to Egyptian opinion and Zaghlul and his friends were released, only to fail to get a hearing at the Peace Conference and to be rebuffed by the recognition of the British protectorate by the United States. Known now as the *Wafd* (i.e. Delegation), they set to work to organize support in Egypt and boycotted the British mission under Lord Milner, sent to report on the situation. Britain was prepared to negotiate a treaty in exchange for the abolition of the protectorate, and discussion between Milner and Zaghlul subsequently took place in Paris. After inciting further unrest in Egypt, Zaghlul was again deported, however.

On February 28th, 1922, the British Government issued a declaration unilaterally announcing the abolition of the protectorate and the recognition of Egypt as an independent sovereign state. Four matters were absolutely reserved to the discretion of the British Government, pending the conclusion of negotiated agreements. These were: the security of the communications of the British Empire in Egypt; the defence of Egypt; the protection of foreign interests and of minorities in Egypt; and the Sudan.

In March 1922 the Sultan, Fuad, took the title of King of Egypt and in April a committee was set up to draft a constitution.

THE TRIANGULAR STRUGGLE: 1922-39

The period after the declaration of independence saw a triangular struggle in Egypt between the King, the Wafd and the British Government. The Wafd was organized to carry out a revolution, not to direct affairs of state. The King owed his throne to the British and his presence guaranteed their interests, yet obvious subservience to them might have enabled the Wafd to rob him of his throne.

The new constitution, which made Egypt a parliamentary monarchy on the Belgian model, was promulgated in 1923. The Wafd triumphed in the elections which were then held and Saad Zaghlul became Prime Minister for a brief period in 1924. In the succeeding years political instability continued as the struggle for power between the Wafd and the throne went on. Elections usually gave the Wafd a majority but a Wafd ministry was unacceptable to King Fuad and in this he normally had the concurrence of the British Government. Hence Palace influence was predominant in the ministries appointed and at times legislation had to be enacted by decree. In 1928 the Parliament was suspended for three years, in 1930 modifications were made to the constitution which altered the electoral law, but in 1935 the original provisions were restored and in elections the following year the Wafd again obtained a majority. The month before the elections King Fuad had been succeeded by his son, Farouk, a minor. The new Prime Minister was Nahas Pasha, who had led the Wafd since Zaghlul's death in 1927.

Until 1936 negotiations for an Anglo-Egyptian treaty invariably broke down over questions of defence and the Sudan. The continued presence of British troops was regarded by Egyptians as denying the reality of independence. The Egyptians also felt that they had been ousted by Britain from dominion over the Sudan and control over their water supply. When the Governor-General of the Sudan was assassinated in Cairo in 1924, Allenby demanded the withdrawal of Egyptian troops from the Sudan, and also the unlimited extension of the irrigation of the Sudan Gezira. Although these demands were later modified, the Egyptian share in the Condominium was to remain nominal.

In 1929 the Nile Waters Agreement allotted the respective shares of Egypt and the Sudan, to Egypt's advantage. The deadlock over a treaty ended in 1936 when the rise of Italian power threatened British and Egyptian interests alike. On August 26th an Anglo-Egyptian treaty of twenty years duration was signed which formally terminated British occupation but empowered Britain to station forces in the Suez Canal zone until the Egyptian army was in a position to ensure the security of the Canal. The Sudan was to continue to be administered as in the past. The protection of foreign interests and of minorities in Egypt was recognized as the exclusive responsibility of the Egyptian Government. The abolition of the Capitulations was secured by the Convention of Montreux in May 1937. In the same month Egypt was admitted to the League of Nations.

THE SECOND WORLD WAR AND ITS CONSEQUENCES: 1939-52

In the Second World War Egypt was a vital strategic factor as the British base in the Middle East. Her treaty obligations were fulfilled but the ruling classes were by no means committed to the Allied cause and on occasions popular support for Germany became manifest. Nevertheless the presence of British forces ensured co-operation.

The young King Farouk, who had assumed full royal powers in 1937, was a popular national figure but as determined as his father to avoid domination by the Wafd. Although still the dominant political party, the Wafd was losing its revolutionary fervour and its appeal to youth was diminishing. Fascist influence appeared in the Greenshirt organization, while the Muslim Brotherhood, a puritanical religious body, developed a terrorist wing and threatened the established authorities.

The critical year was 1942. Alamein had not yet been fought, the King was disposed to appease the Axis powers and the government was under Palace influence. The Wafd, however, favoured co-operation with Britain. In February the British Ambassador, supported by an armed escort, entered the Palace and insisted on the formation of a Wafdist government. Threatened with deposition, Farouk acquiesced and Nahas Pasha became Prime Minister and Military Governor of Egypt.

Nahas held office until 1944. During this period Nuri al-Said, the Prime Minister of Iraq, and King Abdulla of Transjordan separately put forward proposals for a union of Arab states in the Fertile Crescent. These were opposed by Egypt as they seemed to favour Iraqi hegemony. Nahas took the initiative, proposing a broader league of Arab states, and a conference was held which in October 1944 produced the Alexandria Protocol. On this the Arab League was founded the following year. From the beginning Egypt held a position of leadership in the League, which was bitterly hostile to the idea of establishing a Jewish state in Palestine. Previously, preoccupied with her own national problems, Egypt had shown little interest in the Palestine problem.

By 1944 the danger to Egypt had passed. Nahas was no longer indispensable and his government fell, discredited by co-operation with the British and by the corruption which had flourished during its tenure of office. The struggle between the Wafd and the

Palace revived. Communism, made attractive, especially among students, by the Russian successes in the war, gained new adherents, and the Muslim Brotherhood continued its subversive activities. Negotiations in the immediate post-war years for a new treaty with Britain broke down over the questions of the British occupation of the Canal Zone and the future of the Sudan.

In Palestine Britain's renunciation of the Mandate on May 14th, 1948, was followed immediately by the declaration of the State of Israel and military action by Egypt, Iraq, Syria and Jordan. The Egyptian army was badly defeated. Although the fact was long concealed from the Egyptian public, it eventually recoiled on the ruling classes. The King's early popularity had vanished; military failure and the scandal of the supply of faulty arms, in which members of the Palace clique were implicated, undermined the loyalty of the army, which was his last support.

The fall of the discredited regime did not come immediately. The Communists, although widespread, lacked the means to capture the administration. A terrorist campaign by the Muslim Brotherhood was suppressed and the organization driven underground in 1949. Nahas, again in power, made a last bid for royal and popular support in 1951 by abrogating the Treaty of 1936 and the Condominium Agreement and proclaiming Farouk "King of Egypt and Sudan". New British proposals on the Sudan were rejected, as also were proposals on defence, involving the creation of an Allied Middle East Command with Egyptian participation, put forward jointly by Britain, France, Turkey and the United States. Terrorism and economic sanctions were then employed in an attempt to force the withdrawal of British forces from the Canal Zone. Clashes occurred, resulting in many deaths, and on January 26th, 1952, an anti-British demonstration in Cairo developed into rioting, looting and a conflagration, brought to an end only by army intervention.

THE REVOLUTION: 1952-56

On July 23rd, 1952, a group of young army officers, the "Free Officers", who had long been planning a *coup d'état*, seized power in Cairo. They invited the veteran politician, Ali Maher, to form a government under their control, and secured the abdication of King Farouk in favour of his infant son, Ahmed Fuad II, on July 26th. Farouk sailed to exile.

General Muhammad Neguib, an associate of the Free Officers who had incurred the enmity of King Farouk and who had earlier made himself popular by his condemnation of the British action in 1942, was made Commander-in-Chief of the armed forces and head of the military junta. A Council of Regency was formed in August. On September 7th, after an attempt by the Wafd and other parties to resume the political battle on their own terms, a new cabinet with General Neguib as Prime Minister was substituted for that of Ali Maher. Real power, however, lay with the nine officers who formed the Revolutionary Command Council.

The Revolution soon gained momentum. In September 1952 land ownership was limited to 300 acres in any one family and the power of the feudal class which had for so long dominated Egyptian political life was destroyed. Land owned by the royal family was confiscated. On December 10th the constitution was abolished and on January 16th, 1953, all political parties were dissolved. It was announced that there would be a three-year transition period before representative government was restored. On June 18th the monarchy was abolished and Egypt declared a republic, with Neguib as President and Prime Minister as well as Chairman of the Revolutionary Command Council. Colonel Gamal Abdel Nasser, who, although leader of the Free Officers, had hitherto remained in the background, became Deputy Prime Minister and Minister of the Interior, and Abdel Hakim Amer was appointed Commander-in-Chief of the armed forces.

A struggle for power soon developed between General Neguib, whose personal tendencies were Islamic and conservative, and Colonel Nasser. On February 25th, 1954, Neguib was relieved of his posts as President, Prime Minister and Chairman of the Revolutionary Command Council and accused of having attempted to concentrate power in his own hands. Nasser became Prime Minister and Chairman of the Revolutionary Command Council in his place for a few days but Neguib was restored as President and took back both the other posts, only to be ousted again as Prime Minister by Nasser in April. Neguib had suffered a defeat and his liberal measures were rescinded. When in October a member of the Muslim Brotherhood attempted to assassinate Nasser, its leaders and several thousand alleged supporters were arrested and in subsequent trials a number of death sentences were passed. On November 14th, 1954, General Neguib was relieved of the office of President and accused of being involved in a Muslim Brotherhood conspiracy against the regime. He was placed under house arrest and Colonel Nasser became acting head of state.

A settlement of the Sudan and Suez problems had been facilitated by the expulsion of King Farouk. The claim to the joint monarchy of Egypt and the Sudan was dropped and negotiations with Sudanese leaders were helped by the fact that Neguib himself was half-Sudanese and popular in the Sudan. An Anglo-Egyptian agreement, signed on February 12th, 1953, ended the Condominium and offered the Sudanese the choice of independence or union with Egypt. Egyptian expectation that they would choose the latter was disappointed; the overthrow of Neguib and the suppression of the Muslim Brotherhood fed the century-old suspicion of Egyptian motives.

An Anglo-Egyptian agreement on Suez was signed on October 19th, 1954; this provided for the withdrawal of British troops from the Canal Zone within twenty months. The agreement recognized the international importance of the Suez Canal (which was described as "an integral part of Egypt") and expressed the determination of both parties to uphold the 1888 convention.

Under Nasser Egypt began to assert her importance in world affairs. He sought influence in three circles: the Islamic, the African and the Arab, and his visit to the Bandung conference in 1955 added a fourth: the "non-aligned". Egypt led the opposition among certain Arab states to the Baghdad Pact (on which was founded the Central Treaty Organization). In October 1955 Egypt concluded defence agreements with Syria and with Saudi Arabia and in April 1956 a military pact was signed between Egypt, Saudi Arabia and the Yemen. Tension with Israel remained high, and raids and counter-raids across the border of the Gaza Strip called for unceasing vigilance on the part of the United Nations observers stationed on the frontier. In September 1955 Nasser announced an arms deal with Czechoslovakia which was to supply large quantities of military equipment, including Soviet tanks and aircraft, in return for cotton and rice.

In 1956 a constitutional basis for Colonel Nasser's authority was established. A new constitution providing for a strong presidency was proclaimed in January and on June 23rd approved in a plebiscite in which the citizens of the Egyptian Republic also elected Nasser as President.

THE SUEZ CRISIS AND ITS CONSEQUENCES: 1956-57

President Nasser's policy of non-alignment, which implied willingness to deal with both power blocs, was followed in the Egyptian attempt to obtain funds for the ambitious High Dam project at Aswan. By this project the Egyptian Government aimed to increase cultivable land and generate electricity for industrialization, which was seen as the main solution to Egypt's increasing population problem. Following offers of assistance from the United States and Britain and, separately, by the U.S.S.R., the International Bank for Reconstruction and Development offered a loan of $200 million in February 1956, on condition that the United States and Britain lent a total of $70 million and that the agreement of the riparian states to the scheme was obtained; Egypt was to provide local services and material.

The last British troops were withdrawn from Egypt in June 1956, in accordance with the 1954 agreement. Relations with the West were not helped, however, by Egyptian opposition to the Baghdad Pact and strong propaganda attacks on Britain, France and the United States. On July 20th the United States and Britain withdrew their offers of finance for the High Dam, pointing out that agreement between the riparian states had not been achieved and that Egypt's ability to devote adequate resources to the scheme was doubtful. The U.S.S.R. made no compensating move. On July 26th President Nasser announced that the Suez Canal Company had been nationalized and that revenue from the Canal would be used to finance the High Dam.

Britain, France and the United States protested strongly at this action and after an international conference had met in London in August a committee under the chairmanship of Mr. Menzies, the Prime

Minister of Australia, went to Cairo to submit proposals for the operation of the Canal under an international system. These were rejected by the Egyptian Government. At a second London conference, in September, a Suez Canal Users' Association took shape and was later joined by sixteen states. On October 13th the UN Security Council voted on an Anglo-French resolution embodying basic principles for a settlement agreed earlier between the British, French and Egyptian Foreign Ministers in the presence of the UN Secretary-General. The first part of this, setting out the agreed principles, was adopted unanimously; the second, endorsing the proposals of the first London conference and inviting Egypt to make prompt proposals providing no less effective guarantees to users, was vetoed by the U.S.S.R.

Britain and France, thus frustrated in their attempts to retain some measure of control over the Suez Canal, at this stage reached a secret understanding with Israel involving military action. Following the disclosure on October 24th that a unified military command had been formed by Egypt, Jordan and Syria, Israeli forces on October 29th crossed into Sinai, ostensibly to attack Egyptian *fedayeen* bases, and advanced towards the Suez Canal. On October 30th France and Britain called on Israel and Egypt to cease warlike action and withdraw their forces from either side of the Canal; Egypt was requested to agree to an Anglo-French force moving temporarily into key positions at Port Said, Ismailia and Suez. Israel agreed but Egypt refused. The same day in the UN Security Council Britain and France vetoed United States and Soviet resolutions calling for an immediate Israeli withdrawal and calling on all UN members to refrain from the use of force or the threat of force.

Anglo-French air operations against Egypt began on October 31st but paratroops and seaborne forces landed in the Port Said area only on November 5th. Meanwhile, on November 2nd, the UN General Assembly called for a cease-fire and two days later adopted a Canadian proposal to create a United Nations Emergency Force to supervise the ending of the hostilities. On November 6th, following heavy United States pressure, the British Prime Minister, Sir Anthony Eden, announced that, subject to confirmation that Egypt and Israel had accepted an unconditional cease-fire, the armed conflict would end at midnight.

The organization of the UN force was rapidly put in hand and the first units reached Egypt on November 15th. The withdrawal of the Anglo-French forces was completed the following month. The Israelis, who had occupied the entire Sinai peninsula, withdrew from all areas except the Gaza strip, which they wished to prevent becoming a base for more raids, and Sharm el-Sheikh at the entrance to the Gulf of Aqaba, which commanded the seaway to the port of Eilat. These areas were returned to Egyptian control in March 1957 after pressure on Israel by the United States.

The Suez Canal, which had been blocked by the Egyptians, was cleared by a UN salvage fleet and reopened at the end of March 1957. The Egyptian Government rejected in February a plan proposed by

Britain, France, Norway and the United States, for the Canal to be operated by Egypt but the tolls collected by an outside agency. The Egyptian terms, announced on March 18th, which users of the Canal were subsequently obliged to accept, were full control by the Egyptian Canal Authority and respect for the Constantinople Convention of 1888. Disputes would be settled in accordance with the UN Charter or referred to the International Court of Justice.

UNION OF EGYPT AND SYRIA

Elections to the Egyptian National Assembly, provided for in the 1956 constitution, were held in July 1957. Only candidates approved by President Nasser and his colleagues were permitted to stand and it was clear that the 350 members elected (who included women) were not expected to exert much influence on the government.

Following the defence agreement in 1955, discussions had been held in the following two years on union between Egypt and Syria. Both countries were aligned against the West and looked to the U.S.S.R. and other Communist states for support, and in Syria pro-Egyptian elements were in the ascendant. On February 1st, 1958 the union of Egypt and Syria under the title of the United Arab Republic (U.A.R.) was announced. Both parliaments then formally approved the union and seventeen principles on which the constitution of the U.A.R. would be based were proclaimed. A plebiscite, held in both countries on February 21st, confirmed the union and made Nasser the first President of the United Arab Republic

The implementation of the union took time, and it was not until July 21st, 1960, that the first National Assembly of the U.A.R. was opened in Cairo by President Nasser. It consisted of 400 deputies from Egypt and 200 from Syria, appointed by him from candidates nominated by the National Union. Over half the deputies were former members of the dissolved national assemblies of Egypt and Syria. Early in 1961 the President entrusted the National Assembly with the task of drawing up a permanent constitution for the U.A.R.

EXTERNAL RELATIONS: 1958-61

During this period President Nasser was actively concerned with changes in the rest of the Arab world.

An invitation was extended to other Arab states to join the new Union and in March 1958 the U.A.R. and the Yemen entered into a loose association referred to as the United Arab States. This association did not prosper, however, and was terminated by the U.A.R. in December 1961.

The reaction of the Hashemite monarchies of Iraq and Jordan to the new relationship between Egypt and Syria (both of which had been accused of complicity in an attempted *coup d'état* in Jordan in 1957) was immediately to form a federation themselves, styled the Arab Union. This was subjected to U.A.R. propaganda attacks which stigmatized its formation as a hostile move inspired by the West. It did not survive the revolution in Iraq in July 1958.

The military revolution in Iraq in July, in which the royal family and the Prime Minister, Nuri al-Said, were murdered, destroyed the only Arab regime in the Middle East to have identified itself explicitly with the West. The immediate dispatch of American troops to the Lebanon and British forces to Jordan drew strong protests from the U.A.R. which were echoed by the U.S.S.R. The U.S.A. and Britain gave warning of the grave consequences of any conflict between their forces and those under the control of Egypt and Syria. President Nasser visited Moscow and on his return received in Damascus a delegation from the new republican regime in Baghdad. A joint communiqué on July 19th declared that the U.A.R. and Iraq would assist each other to repel any foreign aggression. A United Nations resolution sponsored by Arab states in August, which welcomed assurances that they would refrain from action calculated to change each other's system of government, prepared the way for the withdrawal of the British and American forces.

U.A.R. propaganda voiced support for a revolt which broke out at Mosul in Iraq in March 1959, and there were mass demonstrations in Cairo and Damascus in sympathy with the rebels. The Iraqi Government of General Kassem countered with the accusation that the revolt had been engineered from Syria. The political committee of the Arab League met at Beirut in April in an attempt to reduce the prevailing tension but Iraq took no part in the principal activities of the League until 1960 when relations with the U.A.R. improved.

Diplomatic relations between the U.A.R. and Jordan, severed at the time of the Iraqi revolution, were resumed in August 1959, but there were further violent propaganda exchanges in 1960, the U.A.R. criticizing Jordan for continuing to accept aid from Britain and the United States and Jordan accusing the U.A.R. of complicity in the assassination of the Jordanian Prime Minister in Amman.

Agreement between Egypt and the Sudan on the sharing of the Nile waters after the completion of the Aswan High Dam was reached in November 1959 and a trade and customs convention was also signed.

President Nasser's hostility to the West found favour with the U.S.S.R., with which the U.A.R. established closer ties during these years. In addition to purchases of arms and industrial equipment, Soviet aid for the construction of five airfields and for industrial projects in Egypt was announced in December 1958 and the same month an agreement was concluded which ensured Soviet assistance for the building of the Aswan High Dam. Nevertheless, President Nasser was not inhibited from denouncing Communist activities in the Syrian region and from taking measures to circumscribe them. Work on the first stage of the High Dam began in January 1960 and it was announced that the U.S.S.R. had agreed to participate in the second stage, due to begin in 1962. Soviet assistance for shipyard construction at Alexandria and for industrial projects, including steel and engineering plants, irrigation schemes, and oil, chemical, food and textile enterprises, was announced early in 1960.

Relations with the West improved during 1959 and 1960. Through the mediation of the International Bank for Reconstruction and Development an agreement with Britain was signed on March 1st, 1959, providing for the payment by the U.A.R. of £27½ million as compensation for British private property taken over at the time of the Suez crisis in 1956. Diplomatic relations with Britain were resumed at chargé d'affaires level in December 1959 and raised to ambassadorial level early in 1961. A $56.5 million loan from the International Bank was announced in December 1959 for improvement to the Suez Canal. Financial aid agreements between the U.A.R. and the U.S.A. were signed in March 1960, providing for the supply of surplus U.S. farm products and loans totalling $32.5 million for economic development.

SYRIAN WITHDRAWAL FROM U.A.R.

President Nasser replaced the two Regional Executive Councils and the Central Cabinet of the U.A.R. with a single Central Government in August 1961. By this time, however, the increasing subordination of Syria was breeding resentment and the issue of decrees in July of that year nationalizing most large-scale industrial and commercial concerns had provoked further Syrian discontent. Colonel Seraj, a Syrian Vice-President of the U.A.R., resigned on September 26th and on September 28th the Syrian army seized control in Damascus and Syria withdrew from the U.A.R. President Nasser at first called for resistance to the Syrian *coup d'état* but, when the rebels were seen to be in firm control, said on October 5th that he would not oppose recognition of Syria's independence.

The loss of Syria was a bitter blow to President Nasser and his Egyptian colleagues who now set about a re-examination of their policies which resulted in a renewal of revolutionary fervour.

The U.A.R. Government (Egypt retained the full title) was re-formed on October 18th and a National Congress of Popular Forces, consisting of 1,750 delegates, representing not geographical areas but economic and professional interests and other social groups, met in Cairo on May 21st, 1962. President Nasser presented the National Congress with a draft National Charter outlining his programme for developing the U.A.R. on Arab socialist lines. The Charter stated that imperialists must be evicted, the power of feudalists destroyed and state control of finance and industry established. A new democratic system of government was proposed, based on the Arab Socialist Union (replacing the National Union) and including popular councils at least half the members of which would be workers or *fellahin*. The National Congress approved the Charter on June 30th and then dispersed.

MORE ATTEMPTS AT UNION

The Syrian *coup d'état* had been preceded by the overthrow in February 1963 of the regime of General Kassem in Iraq. These changes in power brought Syria and Iraq into closer alignment with Egypt and it was announced on April 17th that agreement had been reached on the formation of a federation of the three countries under the name of the United Arab Republic. Rivalries, however, arose in both Baghdad and Damascus between supporters of the Baath Party and "Nasserists" and by August President Nasser had withdrawn from the agreement, claiming that the Baathists had set up one-party dictatorships in Syria and Iraq and ignored his insistence on wider nationalist representation.

A month later President Arif of Iraq called for a Baathist union of the three countries, but after the expulsion of Baath leaders from Iraq in November 1963 and the consolidation of power in Arif's hands the unity movement between Iraq and Syria fell apart and Iraq and Egypt again moved closer together. An agreement was concluded on May 25th, 1964, to establish a joint Presidency Council, consisting of the two Presidents and six members from each country, with a secretariat and committees in Cairo. A Unified Political Command was set up in December 1964 to bring about political unity and co-ordinate foreign policy, the armed forces, national security, economic planning and education.

The first meeting of the Unified Political Command was held in Cairo in May 1965 but the succeeding year saw little progress towards unity, and the Unified Political Command did not meet again until March 1966. There were signs that the new Iraqi Government preferred a looser relationship with Egypt to the integration favoured by Iraqi "Nasserists". Suspicions of Egyptian intentions were strengthened in June 1966 when Abdul Razzaq attempted a second *coup*, which, like the first one, failed but which provided evidence of Egyptian complicity.

President Nasser took an important initiative in Arab League affairs following the announcement by Israel in 1963 of her intention to take water for irrigation purposes from the River Jordan where it runs through Lake Tiberias. Neighbouring Arab states had for a number of years refused to agree, on political grounds, to the planned use of the Jordan waters and Israel had proceeded unilaterally with a major irrigation project. At President Nasser's invitation a conference of Arab heads of state met in Cairo in January 1964 to discuss what should be done to counter the Israeli move. This Arab summit conference recommended Arab diversion of the Jordan headwaters, and at the same time agreed that Arab states should follow a policy of "live and let live" among themselves.

A second Arab summit meeting, held in Alexandria in September 1964, decided that a dam should be built on the Yarmuk River, a tributary of the Jordan forming the border between Jordan and Syria, and an irrigation scheme developed in Jordan. A fund would be established to strengthen the armies of Syria, the Lebanon and Jordan over the next five years against possible Israeli reprisals. The U.A.R., Saudi Arabia, Libya, Morocco and the Yemen were to make annual financial contributions for this purpose and the three armies were to have a unified command under the Egyptian General Ali Amer, although movement across the frontiers of friendly states was not to be an automatic right. A further £E 1 million was set aside for the formation of a Palestine Liberation Organization.

The Arab reconciliation and presentation of a united front lasted until the spring of 1965. Iraq, Kuwait, Yemen (Republic), Algeria and the Lebanon continued to follow President Nasser's lead, only Syrian critics complaining that U.A.R. policy was not sufficiently anti-Israeli. U.A.R. relations with Jordan improved strikingly and, after a conference of heads of Arab governments in Cairo in January 1965 to discuss co-ordination of Arab policies, King Hussein, previously the object of U.A.R. attacks and derision, himself paid a visit to Cairo. State visits to Cairo were made by President Bourguiba of Tunisia in February and King Hassan of Morocco in March. Only King Faisal of Saudi Arabia remained aloof, seeing the presence of Egyptian troops in the Yemen, in support of the republicans in the civil war which had begun in 1962, as evidence of U.A.R. expansionism and a threat to the Saudi position as the dominant power in the Arabian peninsula.

The general atmosphere of cordiality was shattered in April 1965 by President Bourguiba who criticized Arab policy on Israel as unrealistic and suggested negotiation with Israel on the basis of the 1947 UN partition plan (which would have involved Arab recognition of Israel, Israeli withdrawal to the borders proposed in the plan and the return of the Palestinian Arab refugees). This was attacked by the U.A.R. as a betrayal of the agreement at Alexandria in 1964 that the Arabs should work in concert. Further statements by President Bourguiba, who was not supported on this issue by any other Arab state, were followed by riots in Cairo and Tunis and the breaking of diplomatic relations with U.A.R.

At the third Arab summit conference, at Casablanca in September 1965, President Nasser found himself on the defensive, in the face of charges made by President Bourguiba (who did not attend the conference) of attempting to dominate the Arab world and interfering in the internal affairs of other Arab states. The conference re-emphasized the need for Arab solidarity and called upon Arab countries not to interfere in each other's domestic affairs by encouraging subversive movements or by attacks in the press.

In the Yemen, despite Egyptian support, the republican regime seemed no closer to victory over the royalists, who held the mountainous regions of the north-east and were assisted by Saudi Arabian finance and supplies of arms. This military stalemate and the financial burden of maintaining some 50,000 troops in the Yemen moved President Nasser to attempt to disengage. On August 24th, 1965, after a two-day conference at Jeddah, he and King Faisal reached agreement on a peace plan to end the civil war. A cease-fire was to be declared immediately, a national conference of Yemeni leaders was to meet to form a provisional government, Saudi Arabia was to cease supplying arms to the royalist forces, and Egyptian troops were to be withdrawn by November 1966.

The conference of republicans and royalists at Haradh in November 1965 ended in deadlock, however, owing to republican intransigence, and the Egyptian troops remained in the Yemen. On February 22nd, 1966, the day the British Government announced that British forces would leave Aden and South Arabia when that territory became independent in 1968, President Nasser stated that Egyptian troops would not be withdrawn until the revolution in the Yemen could "defend itself against the conspiracies of imperialism and reactionaries"

CHANGES OF INTERNATIONAL ALIGNMENT

The years 1964 and 1965 saw a deterioration of U.A.R. relations with the West and increasing dependence on the Soviet Union.

Relations with the United States were adversely affected by U.A.R. support for the Stanleyville rebels in the Congo during the winter of 1964–65, and following the airlift of Belgian paratroops in U.S. aircraft in the Stanleyville rescue operation the U.S.I.S. library in Cairo was burned down. This led to an embargo by the U.S. Government on supplies of surplus wheat, badly needed by the U.A.R. Diplomatic relations with Britain, already worsened by Egyptian encouragement of dissident elements in South Arabia, were severed by the U.A.R. in December 1965 over the Rhodesia issue, in common with eight other members of the Organization of African Unity. The new elasticity of Gaullist policy led to improved relations between the U.A.R. and France, however, and in 1965 official visits were exchanged and French financial aid was made available.

With West Germany relations deteriorated after the discovery of an arms agreement between that country and Israel. When in February 1965 the East German Premier, Herr Ulbricht, visited the U.A.R., where he was accorded full honours, West Germany reacted by stopping further economic aid to the U.A.R. and entering into diplomatic relations with Israel. In retaliation the U.A.R. broke off diplomatic relations with West Germany, and established relations with East Germany.

Relations with the U.S.S.R. had been strengthened in May 1964 when the Soviet Premier, Nikita Khruschev, made a sixteen-day visit to Egypt to attend the ceremony marking the completion of the first stage of the Aswan High Dam, being built with Soviet aid. President Nasser paid his third visit to the U.S.S.R. in August 1965 and (Khruschev having been overthrown) the new Soviet Premier, Alexei Kosygin, visited the U.A.R. in May 1966, expressing support for U.A.R. policies and again demonstrating Soviet interest in the Middle East.

DOMESTIC TROUBLES

Although President Nasser obtained over 99 per cent of the votes cast in the presidential referendum in March 1965, there were subsequently more signs of discontent in the U.A.R. than at any time since he had come to power. In a speech to Arab students during his visit to Moscow in August 1965, he disclosed that a plot against his life had been discovered, in which the banned Muslim Brotherhood was thought to have been involved.

In September 1965 a new government headed by Zakaria Mohieddin replaced that of Ali Sabri, who became Secretary-General of the Arab Socialist Union. Thereafter, administrative changes were made and the security system was tightened up. Taxation was increased and measures of retrenchment were introduced because of increasing economic difficulties particularly the acute shortage of foreign exchange. United States wheat supplies were continued, credits from France, Japan and Italy and a loan from Kuwait were obtained and there were increased drawings from the International Monetary Fund. Nevertheless the level of imports, particularly food to feed the growing population, and the debt service burden resulting from the first five-year plan caused a continuing drain on foreign exchange reserves and the U.A.R. faced a balance of payments crisis. A mission from the International Bank for Reconstruction and Development, which visited Cairo in January 1966, subsequently made recommendations for stabilization and missions of Egyptian bankers and finance officials visited Western countries, including Britain, to discuss credits and debt repayment. The second five-year plan was revised and extended over seven years and President Nasser gave public warnings that sacrifices were necessary in every field as Egypt lacked the foreign currency to pay for imports. He refused, however, to abandon the expensive commitment in the Yemen. Zakaria Mohieddin's replacement in September 1966 by Sidki Soliman (a technocrat who retained his post as Minister of the High Dam) was seen as the outcome of disagreement over retrenchment measures. When the U.A.R. defaulted on repayments due to the International Monetary Fund in December 1966, the country was seen to be on the verge of bankruptcy.

WIDENING RIFT WITH SAUDI ARABIA

The year 1966 saw a rapprochement between the U.A.R. and Syria. A trade, payments and technical co-operation agreement was concluded in July and on November 4th a five-year joint defence agreement was signed. This provided for a joint defence council and a joint command, military operations being under the overall control of the U.A.R. Chief of Army General Staff, and stated that armed aggression against either country would be considered as aggression against both.

The rift between the U.A.R. and Saudi Arabia widened. President Nasser in February 1966 expressed opposition to an Islamic grouping which King Faisal was promoting, and in the succeeding months propaganda warfare between the two countries was intensified. In the middle of the year the President gave notice that he would not attend an Arab summit conference with Saudi Arabia and Jordan, both of whom he stigmatized for obtaining British and United States military aid, and called for the indefinite postponement of the conference planned for September.

A majority of Arab states agreed, but in October Tunisia broke off relations with the U.A.R. over continued differences on Arab League policies.

In the Yemen Egyptian forces had been withdrawn from northern and eastern areas and concentrated in the triangle between Sana'a, Hodeida and Taiz. Egyptian control over the republican armed forces and administration was increased and when, in September 1966, after President Sallal had returned to the Yemen from a year's absence in Cairo, the republican Prime Minister, Hassan al-Amri, and seven senior members of his cabinet visited Egypt to make a plea for greater independence, they were arrested and detained there. The following month about 100 senior Yemen officials were dismissed and arrests and executions were carried out.

In November 1966 Egyptian aircraft carried out raids on Saudi Arabian villages near the Yemen border. In January 1967, after air attacks with bombs and rockets on royalist-held areas in the Yemen, the village of Kitaf was bombed and over 100 deaths caused, allegedly, by poison gas.

February 1967 saw the closing of two Egyptian banks in Saudi Arabia and the seizure of Saudi property (including King Faisal's) in the U.A.R. In the same month, following President Nasser's accusation that Jordan and Saudi Arabia were "lackey and reactionary regimes" serving the interests of imperialism and allied with the Muslim Brotherhood in Egypt, the Jordanian ambassador was withdrawn from Cairo.

WAR WITH ISRAEL

The events of May 1967 were to transform the Middle East scene. There had been an increase of Syrian guerrilla activities in Israel during the previous six months and on April 7th the tension had led to fighting in the Tiberias area in which six Syrian aircraft had been shot down. Israeli warnings to the Syrian Government, culminating on May 12th in the threat by Premier Eshkol of severe reprisals if terrorist activities were not controlled, evoked Syrian allegations that Israel was about to mount a large-scale attack on Syria. President Nasser, who had been reproached for not aiding Syria in the April fighting in accordance with the mutual defence agreement, responded immediately, moving large numbers of troops to the Israel border, He secured the dissolution of the UN Emergency Force, whose presence on the Egyptian side of the frontier depended on Egyptian permission, and re-occupied the gun emplacement at Sharm el Sheikh on the Straits of Tiran. He later justified these steps by claiming that he had received Syrian and Soviet warnings that Israeli troops were concentrated on the Syrian border (an allegation subsequently disproved by reports of UN truce observers) and an invasion of Syria was imminent.

When on May 23rd President Nasser closed the Straits of Tiran to Israeli shipping, thereby effectively blockading the Israeli port of Eilat, his prestige in the Arab world reached an unparalleled height. Britain and the United States protested that the Gulf of Aqaba was an international waterway; Israel regarded the blockade of the Straits as an unambiguous act of war. A British attempt to produce a declaration by the maritime powers on freedom of passage through the Straits met with little enthusiasm when it became clear that only by force would the blockade be lifted. As tension increased, with frequent belligerent pronouncements from Arab leaders and the threat by President Nasser that any aggressive act by Israel would lead to an all-out battle in which the Arab aim would be Israel's destruction, King Hussein of Jordan concluded a mutual defence pact with the U.A.R. which was immediately joined by Iraq. Gestures of support were made to Nasser by all Arab leaders, including President Bourguiba and King Faisal.

On the morning of June 5th Israel launched large-scale air attacks on Egyptian, Jordanian, Syrian and Iraqi airfields and Israeli ground forces made rapid advances into the Gaza Strip, Sinai and western Jordan; there was also fighting on the Israeli-Syrian border. The outcome was decided within hours by the air strikes, which destroyed the bulk of the Arab air forces, and the Israeli ground forces were everywhere successful. By June 10th, when all participants had accepted the UN Security Council's call for a cease-fire, Israeli troops were in control of the Sinai peninsula as far as the Suez Canal (including Sharm el Sheikh), the west bank of the Jordan (including the Old City of Jerusalem), the Gaza Strip and Syrian territory extending twelve miles from the Israel border. The Suez Canal was blocked by Egypt in the course of the fighting.

On June 9th, the day after he had accepted the cease-fire, President Nasser announced his resignation in a speech in which he assumed full responsibility for the nation's plight, but the following day, in response to huge street demonstrations of popular support, he agreed to continue in office. A number of senior army officers were immediately replaced and on June 19th Nasser took over the duties of Prime Minister and Secretary-General of the Arab Socialist Union.

The implications of the catastrophe were only gradually realized. It was estimated that the loss of revenue from the Suez Canal, from oil produced in Sinai and from tourism amounted to some £12.5 million a month, or almost half Egypt's foreign currency earnings. Also, the withdrawal of a large part of the Egyptian force in the Yemen reduced Nasser's ability to influence affairs both in that country and in Aden and South Arabia (which became independent as the Republic of Southern Yemen on November 30th, 1967, after the withdrawal of British troops).

The Soviet Union, which had given the Arab cause strong verbal support throughout the crisis, continued to take a strong pro-Arab stand at the United Nations and President Podgorny paid a lengthy visit to Cairo to discuss future Egyptian policy. Although the Soviet resolutions were rejected in both the Security Council and the General Assembly, Soviet assistance took the more concrete form of quickly replacing about half the lost Egyptian aircraft and providing other military supplies. By the end of October it was estimated that about 2,500 Russian military instructors had been

sent to Egypt. Despite this military aid, Soviet leaders seemed anxious to discourage hopes of a resumption of hostilities, however. Further economic assistance was also offered by the Soviet Union and in May 1968 an agreement was announced for the construction of a steel complex at Helwan.

Israel demanded direct negotiations with the Arab states for a peace settlement but the fourth conference of Arab heads of state, held in Khartoum at the end of August 1967, decided against recognition or negotiation with Israel. At this conference, in which Syria did not participate, it was agreed that the embargo on oil supplies to Western countries (applied the previous June) should be lifted, that the Suez Canal should remain closed until Israeli forces were withdrawn, and that Saudi Arabia, Kuwait and Libya should give special aid of £95 million a year to the U.A.R. (and also £40 million a year to Jordan) until the "effects of the aggression" were eliminated. King Faisal and President Nasser announced their agreement on a peace plan for the Yemen under which Egyptian troops were to be withdrawn within three months and Saudi Arabia was to stop supplying the royalists; the withdrawal was subsequently completed by December (President Sallal being deposed by republican leaders in November).

After repeated violations of the cease-fire by both sides, the UN Security Council on November 22nd, 1967, adopted a British resolution laying down the principles for a just and lasting peace in the Middle East and authorizing the appointment of a special UN representative to assist in bringing about a settlement. This was Resolution 242 (*see* Documents on Palestine, page 58) which has since formed the basis of almost all attempts to restore peace to the Middle East. Dr. Gunnar Jarring was appointed special UN representative, and quickly began discussions with Arab and Israeli leaders which continued for a number of years.

U.A.R. AFTER THE JUNE WAR

Meanwhile President Nasser faced daunting economic difficulties and a disturbed political situation in Egypt. An austerity budget had been framed in July 1967. The cost of re-equipping the armed forces forced a cut in investment, in spite of Soviet aid and assistance from other Arab governments. Socialist policies were still followed, as was shown by the decision to nationalize the wholesale trade, announced in October. The continuing shortage of foreign exchange made desirable an improvement in the U.A.R.'s relations with the West and in December diplomatic relations with Britain were resumed. A bridging loan from British, West German and Italian banks, obtained in February 1968, enabled the U.A.R. to make the repayments to the International Monetary Fund which had been due since the end of 1966, and in March the IMF approved further drawings. Another hopeful development was the increased production of oil from Egyptian oilfields, which made up for the loss of Sinai.

As a result of the military débâcle the Egyptian army was subjected to major reorganization, involving the dismissal of large numbers of officers. The reaction of Field-Marshal Abdel Hakim Amer was to plan a *coup d'état*, but his intentions became known. His arrest, together with other senior army officers, on August 30th was followed by the arrests of a former Minister of the Interior, Abbas Radwan, and the chief of the central intelligence department. The suicide of Amer was announced by the U.A.R. Government on September 15th. At the end of October senior officers of the air force were put on trial and in February 1968 the former air force commander was imprisoned for fifteen years; other senior air force officers also received prison sentences. In January 1968 the armed forces supreme command was reorganized.

Widespread demonstrations of students and workers took place in Cairo, Helwan and other main centres, towards the end of February. Initially in protest at the leniency of sentences on air force officers, they revealed widespread popular disillusion and discontent to a degree unprecedented since the revolution of 1952. A number of persons were killed in clashes with police, and the universities were closed; nevertheless President Nasser realized the need for immediate conciliatory action. Re-trials were ordered and sweeping cabinet changes announced, a number of civilian experts in various fields being brought in. Ali Sabry, who had been reinstated as Secretary-General of the Arab Socialist Union in January, was also included but Zakaria Mohieddin left the government. President Nasser continued to exercise the functions of Prime Minister.

On March 30th President Nasser announced a new plan for building a modern state in Egypt based on democracy, science and technology. The single party would remain but there would be free elections from top to bottom of the Arab Socialist Union and changes were promised among leaders in all spheres. An announcement of the distribution to the people of land taken over by the state or reclaimed was made on April 6th. In a plebiscite on May 2nd the "Declaration of March 30th" was overwhelmingly approved. The first Arab Socialist Union elections were held in June; the 75,000 persons chosen then elected a national congress in July; this in turn chose a central committee which then chose the party's higher executive. These proceedings however, did not appear to arouse much public interest. President Nasser dissolved the U.A.R. National Assembly on November 14th and elections for a new Assembly were held on January 8th 1969.

November 1968 saw further student riots, resulting in many injuries and some deaths, in Alexandria and Mansoura. The universities were again closed. Although these disturbances were officially attributed to the activities of an Israeli agent arrested by the police and to indignation at the continued occupation of Sinai by Israeli forces, they were seen by many observers as further evidence of frustration with the restrictions imposed by President Nasser's government and of disillusion with its performance, particularly in relation to Israel. Moreover, in uncertain health, his popularity diminished, the President appeared in 1968 to be increasingly isolated and exposed.

Deprived of foreign exchange by the continued closure of the Canal and the drop in the tourist trade, the U.A.R. remained dependent on the regular aid payments from Saudi Arabia, Kuwait and Libya and on Soviet assistance, both humiliating to a people strongly nationalist in outlook. There were signs that the civilian economic ministers favoured some relaxation of over-rigid state control in industry and more encouragement of private enterprise and foreign investment. Military expenditure in 1968 and 1969 remained high. Soviet arms deliveries continued, as also did the presence of about 3,000 Russian military advisers and instructors.

The efforts of Dr. Jarring, the representative of the UN Secretary-General, to bring Israel, the U.A.R. and Jordan closer together had, by the end of 1968, yielded little success. In April 1969, following initiatives by the U.S.S.R. and France, those two countries together with Britain and the United States, as permanent members of the Security Council, began talks at the United Nations in New York in an attempt to promote a settlement. These talks, after a recess between July and December 1969, were resumed in December 1969, but no settlement was reached.

A pattern of sporadic action, involving artillery duels across the Suez Canal, commando raids and air combat developed throughout 1969 and into 1970, with growing Soviet involvement in Egypt's defence. In the summer of 1970 the U.S. Secretary of State, Mr. William Rogers, put forward a set of proposals for solving the continuing Middle East crisis. After lengthy negotiations and a visit by President Nasser to Moscow, both Egypt and Israel agreed to a 90 days ceasefire in August 1970. Talks between the U.A.R. and Jordan on the one hand and Israel on the other began later in August in New York under the guidance of the UN mediator Gunnar Jarring. They soon broke down following accusations from both sides of violations of the ceasefire agreement, but despite this the ceasefire was renewed, on its expiry, for another three months.

EGYPT AFTER NASSER

Although President Nasser had had his differences with the Palestinian guerrillas over their rejection of the U.S. peace proposals and the hijackings of the western airliners at the beginning of September, one of his last acts was to secure agreement in Cairo between King Hussein and Yassir Arafat for an end to the fighting between the Jordanian army and the guerrillas.

Nasser's death on September 28th, 1970 came as a profound shock and it was feared by many that it would materially lessen chances of achieving peace in the Middle East. However, his death made it easier for the Jordanian government to proceed with crushing the Palestine commando bases throughout the rest of 1970 and the first half of 1971.

A close associate of Nasser, and Vice-President at the time of his death, Anwar Sadat, was immediately appointed provisional president by the Cabinet and Party, being later elected President in a national referendum, and by mid-1971 he was firmly in control of the government of Egypt.

Meanwhile, the ceasefire on the Suez Canal was extended in February 1971 for only thirty days, but on its expiry fighting was not resumed. Although Egypt was ostensibly preparing for war and, for example, formed a military union with Syria, she also maintained diplomatic efforts to secure a basis for peace negotiations which, in the spring and summer of 1971, centered on various proposals for reopening the Suez Canal as a first step towards a settlement.

In November 1970 President Sadat (whose mother is Sudanese) had agreed to the federation of the U.A.R. with Sudan and Libya. Sudan, however, later postponed her membership of a union and it was Syria who in April became the third member of the Federation. The federation proposals, together with Sadat's plan for the reopening of the Canal, precipitated a crisis in the leadership which led to a comprehensive purge by Sadat of opponents at all levels of the government. Ali Sabri, one of the two Vice-Presidents, and strongly pro-Moscow, was the first to go, on May 2nd, just before U.S. Secretary of State, William Rogers, arrived in Cairo. On May 13th, President Sadat, convinced of an impending coup, dismissed six other ministers and important Party and National Assembly members. In July new elections were held, not only for all levels of the Party, but also for trade unions and professional bodies. A new constitution, the first permanent one since the 1952 revolution, was voted in September. It contained important clauses governing personal freedoms and discarded at last the name of United Arab Republic, the state being known henceforward as the Arab Republic of Egypt.

The year 1971 was marked by repeated Egyptian declarations of the intention to fight Israel—but only when the time was ripe—and Egypt mounted an extensive diplomatic campaign to state her case in the West. One result of this activity was a move towards reconciliation with West Germany. In September 1971 came the first large-scale military operations on the canal since the August 1970 ceasefire and in December the UN passed a resolution calling for the resumption of the Jarring peace mission.

Dr. Mahmoud Fawzi, who was appointed Prime Minister in October 1970, resigned in January 1972 and was made a joint Vice-President. His successor was Dr. Aziz Sidqi, who had been First Vice-Premier since September 1971.

Egypt was becoming increasingly dependent on the U.S.S.R., both militarily and economically. In spite of Russian assurances that aid would be continued, the Egyptians were becoming very dissatisfied. This was partly because they felt the arms deliveries were not up to standard, and partly because of the frustration engendered in the country by the prolonged state of uncertainty. Student riots at the beginning of 1972 brought assurances from President Sadat that an armed confrontation with Israel was definitely in-

tended. Against this background of increasing internal uneasiness Egypt intensified efforts to diversify sources of development aid and armaments. The Suez-Alexandria (Sumed) pipeline received promises of Western backing and in May 1972 a five-year preferential trade agreement was concluded with the EEC. Relations with West Germany, too, on the whole improved.

CRISIS IN EGYPTIAN-SOVIET RELATIONS

The most striking event of 1972 was the dismissal of Soviet military advisers from Egypt in July and the manning of installations by Egyptians. This did not lead to a rupture in Egyptian-Soviet relations but neither did it result in any significant rapprochement with the West, anti-American feeling remaining very strong. A new round of diplomatic visits to state Egypt's case, particularly in the West and the Far East, was embarked upon and arms supplies requested from France and Britain. With the announcement on August 2nd, 1972, of Egypt's plan to merge with Libya, France stated that supplies of Mirage fighters to Libya would continue, Libya not being in direct conflict with Israel.

Contacts with the U.S.S.R. continued and economic relations appeared unaffected by the events of July but it was clear that the U.S.S.R. was looking elsewhere to maintain its presence in the Mediterranean. Prime Minister Aziz Sidqi visited Moscow in October but no conclusive results came of his visit. It was unclear to what extent Sadat's hand had been forced in ordering the Soviet withdrawal. The dismissal in November of the War Minister, General Sadeq, and other high-ranking officers in the armed forces pointed to disagreements between the military and Sadat and to a desire for reconciliation with the U.S.S.R.

INTERNAL UNREST

A law passed in August 1972 provided for penalties up to life imprisonment for offences endangering national unity, including opposing the Government by force and inciting violence between Muslims and the Coptic minority. Clashes between these two communities were growing more frequent and, along with increasing student unrest, were seen as an expression of dissatisfaction with the state of "no-peace-no-war". The Government resorted to repeated assurances of military preparations. In December 1972, Sadat in fact ordered preparations for fighting, after strong criticism in the People's Assembly of the Government's policies. Another cause of uneasiness was the proposed merger with Libya, which many people felt might give Colonel Gaddafi too much control over Egypt's destiny.

January 1973 saw violent clashes between police and students and the universities had to be closed for a short time. In February a number of left-wing elements, among them many journalists, were expelled from the ASU, student unrest continued and in March President Sadat took over from Aziz Sidqi as Prime Minister. The new administration's policies were approved by the People's Assembly but the Government was criticized for failing to follow a clear-cut economic policy, particularly with regard to the five-year plan.

RELATIONS WITH LIBYA

Egypt and Libya had agreed on a programme of full union by stages at a meeting between the two Heads of State in Benghazi in August 1972, and a merger of the two countries was planned to take place on September 1st, 1973. The Libyan leader, Colonel Gaddafi, showed more enthusiasm than President Sadat for total union, and in July 1973 Gaddafi organized a march of 40,000 Libyans on Cairo in order to bring pressure to bear on Egypt. The march was turned back about 200 miles from Cairo, however, and Sadat, although showing support for eventual union, stated that "enthusiasm and emotional impulses are not a sufficient basis for unity." An agreement in principle was nevertheless signed on August 29th, but few practical steps were taken to implement the agreement.

Relations between Egypt and Libya have since deteriorated. Gaddafi was very critical of Egypt's strategy in the early days of the October war, and when, in April 1974, a terrorist attack took place on the Military Technical Academy at Heliopolis, outside Cairo, it was suspected in Egyptian circles that the attack was the beginning of an attempted *coup* in which Libya was implicated. Throughout 1974 and early 1975 relations between the two countries deteriorated to such an extent that President Sadat asserted in a press interview in April 1975 that Gaddafi was "100 per cent sick". At the time Libya had been threatening to take action against Egyptians working in Libya. In spite of the apparent temporary success in May 1975 of attempts by a mission from the National Assembly of the Federation of Arab Republics to mediate between Sadat and Gaddafi, relations soon worsened when a large Soviet-Libyan arms deal was revealed later in the month. President Sadat hastily accused Libya and the Soviet Union of conducting an international campaign against him and his Middle East policy.

THE OCTOBER WAR AND ITS AFTERMATH

Between the June 1967 war and October 1973 Egyptian leaders frequently stated that the war against Israel would be resumed, but when Egyptian forces crossed the Suez Canal on October 6th, 1973, it came as a surprise to Israel and to the rest of the world. The course of the war, and the political questions involved, are dealt with in the chapter "The Arab-Israeli Confrontation 1967–74", pages 34–45. For President Sadat the war was a considerable triumph. It appeared to end the years of stalemate with Israel, and his personal reputation was greatly enhanced. As a result of the Disengagement Agree-

ment which Israel and Egypt signed on January 18th, 1974, Egyptian forces regained a strip of territory to the east of the Suez Canal (see map on page 63).

After the war extensive and far-reaching changes took place in Egypt. An amnesty was extended to many important political prisoners in January 1974, and in April an amnesty was extended to more than 2,000 persons who had been imprisoned for political or criminal offences. Press censorship was lifted in February, and in April about 8.5 million voters gave a 99.95 per cent endorsement to a programme of economic and social reform which concentrated on reconstruction, attracting foreign investment, limiting police interference in everyday life, and the introduction of a private enterprise sector in the economy while still maintaining the public sector (*see* Economic Survey).

One result of the October war was Egypt's improved relations with the U.S.A. Diplomatic relations between Egypt and the U.S.A. were restored in November 1973 and the U.S. Secretary of State, Dr. Henry Kissinger, had a cordial relationship with President Sadat during the disengagement talks. American initiatives in peacemaking were generally welcomed by Egypt, while the Americans were now conscious of the extent of their dependence on Arab oil. It was in this atmosphere of *rapprochement* that President Nixon visited Cairo in June 1974, and the U.S.A. and Egypt agreed to set up a Joint Co-operation Commission and to begin negotiating an agreement for co-operation in the field of nuclear energy.

RETURN TO STALEMATE

The euphoria which the crossing of the Suez Canal had produced began to disappear during 1974. Increases in the cost of living, and the slowness with which the promised economic reform was proceeding, led to riots in Cairo on January 1st, 1975, and to further disturbances among textile workers in March 1975, when the textile complex at El Mahalla el Kubra was closed for several days after violent clashes over pay demands. Inflation was estimated at the time to be running at an annual rate of about 24 per cent.

As a result of these disturbances Dr. Abdel Aziz Higazy, who had taken over the premiership from President Sadat in September 1974, resigned as Prime Minister and was replaced in April 1975 by Gen. Mamdouh Muhammad Salem, the former Minister of the Interior and Deputy Prime Minister. On May 1st, 1975, President Sadat announced that all lower-paid public-sector employees would receive additional cost-of-living allowances equal to 30 per cent of their pay, and later in May, in a speech to the People's Assembly, the new Prime Minister promised that steps would be taken to ensure that the economic programme of 1974 would be implemented and that foreign investors, whether from Western countries or from the Eastern bloc would be given every facility.

During the first half of 1975 relations with Israel were still unsettled. President Sadat had put his faith in Dr. Kissinger to achieve a settlement, but after considerable "shuttle diplomacy" by Dr. Kissinger, negotiations broke down in March 1975. The whole question was complicated by the position of the Palestine Liberation Organization, who at the Rabat Arab summit in October 1974 and later at the UN General Assembly, had achieved the status of the "sole legitimate representative of the Palestinian people". President Sadat himself set out on an Arab-solidarity tour of Syria, Iraq, Kuwait and Jordan in mid-May 1975. Fuller details of the attempts to reach a settlement can be found in the article on "The Arab-Israeli Confrontation" on page 48.

By mid-July 1975 it seemed probable that an initial settlement with Israel might soon be achieved whereby Israel made certain withdrawals from the Giddi and Mitla passes in the Sinai peninsula and also from the Abu Rudais oilfield in Sinai. A hopeful sign had been the re-opening of the Suez Canal in June 1975 and the thinning out of Israeli forces in the area nearest the canal which took place at about the same time.

ECONOMIC SURVEY

The Egyptian economy remains very weak, a position which only a final Arab-Israeli peace settlement or the discovery of oil in vast quantities can remedy. President Sadat revealed in 1974 that nearly a third of gross national product was being spent on defence. Although aid from Arab oil states, particularly since the 1973 war, has been substantial, the economy still needs other sources of foreign exchange to replenish its seriously depleted reserves. The re-opening of the Suez Canal will bring some relief with $500 million in dues expected in the first year of operation. Oil may supply the answer in the next five years, but for the moment, though a sizeable producer, Egypt is still a net importer. Cotton also cannot provide the answer, since at least half the crop goes to the Soviet and East European bloc under barter arrangements. Though reconstruction is proceeding in the canal region, and ambitious plans have been drawn up for its development, commitments by foreign investors have been far less than initial interest might have suggested. Most foreign companies interested in setting up business in a "free zone" have been daunted by bureaucratic delays and the inadequacy of basic infrastructure. Above all, most people expect another war with Israel in the next year or so.

With food supply barely keeping pace with population growth and with the psychological successes of the October war fading, Egypt faced severe problems in the winter of 1974/75 bringing popular protests against the government, notably at the beginning of January in Cairo. The riots resulted in panic measures by the government, including the importing of basic foods like beans, rice and lentils, and eventually in its fall, to be replaced by one headed by a policeman.

Thus Egypt joined the thin ranks of the United Nations' "Most Seriously Affected" countries in April 1975, the qualification for which is a balance of payments deficit of more than 5 per cent of the total import bill, and President Sadat's gamble on the October war, which looked like succeeding at first, now seemed to be failing.

The October war was part of President Sadat's strategy to "open up" the economy, which dates from the cabinet reshuffle in March 1973. Ultimately the policy of "liberalization" or "desocialization" can be traced back to Sadat's assumption of the Presidency on the death of Nasser in September 1970. It was March 1973, however, that saw the inauguration of the new economic policy. Then Sadat took on the Premiership in addition to the Presidency and Abdel-Aziz Higazi was made economic overlord with the portfolio of Economy & Foreign Trade, as well as a Deputy Premiership, added to his existing post at the Finance Ministry. His task was to prepare the country for a war which had the fairly limited objective of recovering territory on the east bank of the Suez Canal so that the canal could be reopened, reconstruction in the Canal zone begun, the transit trade revived, foreign investment encouraged, popular morale restored and a new lease of life given to the economy, which had been stagnating under the pressure of population on the limited supply of agricultural land. The limited objective of the war also won the support of Saudi Arabia, Kuwait and Qatar. This not only mobilized the oil "weapon" during and after the war but also assured Egypt of finance for development after the war.

Higazi reorganized his department in June to give greater scope to the foreign trade sector and to control more closely all aspects of economic policy. Then at the end of July he announced a major reorganization of foreign-exchange and trade policy designed to "open-up" the economy. A "parallel" market for foreign exchange dealings, offering an incentive rate of exchange, was created with effect from September 1st to attract Arab and foreign capital for development projects, and to lead eventually to the abolition of restrictive trade agreements, mainly with communist countries. Guarantees and encouragement were given to foreign investors in August, when an agreement on the protection of investments in Egypt was signed with the Swiss and when new emphasis came to be placed by the Government on the Arab Capital Investments and Free Zones Law which had been promulgated in September 1971 but had been mostly inoperative since then.

The role of the private sector in Egypt's economic development was also the subject of discussion in political circles before the October war though it was December before a People's Assembly committee recommended offering up to 49 per cent of the capital of state enterprise for sale to private investors and reviving the Cairo stock exchange.

After the war the Government's overriding pre-occupation became reconstruction and a separate ministry was established. Sadat appointed Othman Ahmad Othman, head of one of the Arab world's biggest construction firms and one of Egypt's most successful businessmen, Minister of Reconstruction, and he soon produced a plan that not only laid down the obvious areas for rebuilding but also outlined ambitious development schemes in Sinai, the Western Desert, Cairo and Alexandria. Many of these schemes predated even the June 1967 war and probably had a lot to do with the Government's desire to assure Western Governments and investors of Egypt's long-term peaceable intentions and to rally popular enthusiasm in a difficult post-war period.

The most pressing part of the reconstruction plan was to restore and reopen the Suez Canal. The clearance of mines and military debris was started in April 1974 by U.S. and British teams of military experts, and they were later joined by French and Soviet experts. In March 1975 the Suez Canal Authority pronounced the canal ready for reopening. No-one expected the step to be taken, however, before the Israelis had made a further withdrawal into Sinai, but after the failure of U.S. Secretary of State Henry Kissinger's step-by-step approach to peace-making President Sadat took the bold decision to seize the initiative and announce that the waterway would be reopened on June 5th, 1975, the eighth anniversary of the outbreak of war which led to its closure in 1967. Sadat himself sailed in the leading ship of a convoy down the canal to mark the official reopening. The next stage will be to restart the interrupted programme of expansion of the canal, which is scheduled to take six years to complete. Such expansion has been made even more urgent because of the vast increase in oil-tanker sizes since June 1967 which the closure of the canal then helped provoke. The existing dimensions of the canal allow the passage of ships of 70,000 dwt or 200,000 dwt in ballast. The first part of the development programme would allow 150,000 dwt tankers to pass through fully loaded, and the second part would enable tankers of up to 260,000 dwt fully laden or 290,000 dwt partly laden to pass. A Japanese company, the Penta-Ocean Construction Company, has been contracted to begin the work of widening and deepening the canal at a cost of £72 million, backed by a Japanese Government loan, but no date has been set for work to begin. The present state of utter depression in the tanker market seems to make such a programme an investment with doubtful returns for the foreseeable future. The state of the tanker market also means that the impact of the reopening on the oil trade is marginal for the moment, though for dry cargo the advantages of the shorter Suez route over the Cape route are much clearer. The Canal Authority set the dues for ships using the canal 90–100 per cent higher than in 1967. They are calculated in the Special Drawing Rights of the International Monetary Fund, although actual payment is in dollars. Egyptian estimates of revenues from dues in the first year are around $500 million. Losses from the closure of the canal are estimated at £E 1,300 million, of which £E 950 is lost revenue.

Reconstruction of the canal cities, some of them up to 80 per cent destroyed, and resettlement of refugees was the other immediate task, and this is progressing as rapidly as finance and the availability of materials, equipment and technical expertise will allow.

The cost of reconstruction is enormous—up to £E 3,000 million—and the Egyptians are hoping to pay for it by using the increased interest in the Arab world which the industrialized world has shown since its realization of the economic power, based on oil, and the economic potential, of the Arabs.

Japan, among the most dependent of the industrial nations on outside sources of energy, was the first to make concrete offers of aid. So far they have granted loans of about U.S. $390 million, mainly for work on the canal, and they are also involved in studies for a monorail in Cairo, a microwave telecommunications network and a clothing factory.

After President Nixon's visit to Egypt in 1974 U.S. investment, agreed or under discussion, was put at $2,000 million. U.S. aid, finally approved by Congress in January 1975, amounted to $250 million for the fiscal year 1974/75, and another $250 million is said to be under discussion for 1975/76. While many U.S. firms are eager to take advantage of the new climate for foreign investment in Egypt, they, like other foreign businesses, are finding Egyptian bureaucracy hard to cope with, and the lack of basic infrastructure, especially in the field of telecommunications and transport, is also hindering attempts to get projects off the ground.

Iran promised $750 million in aid and investment in May 1974 and a further loan of $120 million in March 1975. Various joint projects and companies are also to be set up, but the Iranians too have apparently found the Egyptians ill-prepared to absorb the investment, and during the Shah's historic visit to Egypt in January 1975 few further details of the projects decided seven months earlier could be revealed. West Germany is providing credit of over £83 million sterling for the purchase of German goods for reconstruction and development purposes, and progress has been made on the allocation of French aid of up to about $100 million agreed in August 1974. Italy, Britain, Denmark and the Netherlands are also providing loans, credits and investment.

Despite political differences, the U.S.S.R. continues to provide substantial aid to the Egyptian economy, mainly for heavy industry, and industrial delegations have gone back and forth between Moscow and Cairo despite Sadat's public upbraiding of the Soviet leadership. East Germany, Czechoslovakia, Romania and Poland have agreed to help in agricultural, metallurgical, textile and transport projects. Most of these developments have been announced since the beginning of 1974.

But other Arab states, particularly oil-rich Saudi Arabia, Kuwait and Qatar, have been the major benefactors. The Arab summit in Rabat in October 1974 pledged $1,000 million a year in grants to Egypt, most of it coming from the Gulf states. The late King Faisal of Saudi Arabia made separate gifts of $100 million, $100 million and $300 million in 1974 and 1975; the Saudi Development Fund made available loans totalling $161 million in November 1974; and various lines of credit and joint investments have been agreed. Investment in or loans for projects costing $1,300 million were agreed with Kuwait in December 1974. The United Arab Emirates and Qatar have also been generous—the U.A.E. gave $60 million in 1975 for Egyptair to buy Boeings—and Egypt has built up ties with Iraq leading to discussions on projects involving investment of around $1,200 million.

All this has been aided by the law on the investment of Arab and foreign capital and on free zones which was finally approved in June 1974. The 57-article law lays down incentives and guarantees for foreign investors and provides the legal framework for the establishment of free zones on the Mediterranean coast and in the canal zone where foreign concerns can set up businesses completely free of customs or financial controls.

GENERAL

The total area of Egypt is about 1,001,000 square km., but 96 per cent of the country is desert. With no forested land, and hardly any permanent meadows or pastures, the arable land available is greatly overcrowded. Relating the population, numbering 35.6 million in 1973, to the inhabited area, a density of over 1,000 persons per square kilometre gives 5.5 persons per acre of arable land, representing one of the highest man/land ratios in the world. At the root of Egypt's poverty lies its expanding population, which had an annual growth rate between 1965 and 1972 of 2.5 per cent, though the head of family planning in Egypt said in May 1975 that this was now down to 2.1 per cent. Another official Egyptian source estimated early in 1975 the present population total to be 37 million. The International Development Association in November 1973 granted a $5 million interest-free credit towards a $10.5 million health and family-planning project in Egypt. The World Bank gave Egypt's G.N.P. per head as $240 in 1972.

Despite this low level of income, certain aspects of the Egyptian economy indicate a relative state of advance, but overpopulation still tends somewhat to neutralize the effects of social and economic progress. Among the comparatively advanced areas of the Egyptian economy are the infrastructure of communications, the irrigation system, public administration and education. Although the illiteracy rate remains high (the 1960 population census showed an illiteracy rate of 69.7 per cent among people of over ten years of age) both secondary and higher education are quite developed and Egypt is a net exporter of skills, especially to other Arab countries. The diet of the average Egyptian is poor and contains little animal protein.

From 1918–39 when the Egyptian pound was tied to sterling and a fairly free trade policy was being pursued, manufacturing industry had little chance of developing and agricultural production, though expanding, could not keep up with the rapidly rising population. A gradual deterioration of living standards set in. This trend did not change direction until the immediate post-war period, when cotton prices improved. These reached their greatest heights during the Korean boom of 1951–52, when "soft-currency cotton", including Egyptian cotton, enjoyed high premia over dollar-cotton. But the collapse of the boom, the easing up of the world dollar scarcity and the beginning of American subsidization of cotton exports in the mid-1950s, marked a turning point in raw cotton terms of trade which, until quite recently, showed a declining trend.

The régime which assumed power in 1952 and ended the monarchy gave urgent attention to Egypt's economic problems. Its policies included measures of agrarian reform, land reclamation, the High Dam, and a programme of industrialization which was accelerated in 1960 by the formation of a comprehensive social and economic development plan.

Egypt's first five-year plan aimed at increasing real national income by 40 per cent between 1960 and 1965, this being advertised as the first lap of a ten-year programme to double real national income by 1970. The five-year growth target was virtually fulfilled, so that the second lap was initially replaced by a more ambitious plan to double real income in seven years (i.e. by 1972). Lack of finance, however, frustrated this new plan, and after two years of uncertainty, a three-year "accomplishment" plan, beginning July 1967, was proclaimed. This was to aim at a target growth rate of 5 per cent per annum (compared with 7.2 per cent under the first five-year plan) with a total investment of £E1,085 million (against £E1,513 million in 1960–65), and would concentrate on completing projects already started, rather than initiating new ones. This plan was dropped as a result of the 1967 war and was substituted by annual development appropriations (£E320 million in 1968–69 and £E350 million in 1969–70). Apart from a few select new projects, the whole emphasis of Egyptian planning was turned towards rationalizing the existing industries, and introducing incentives to improve their performance.

This plan was, however, to be superseded by a more ambitious ten-year scheme under a Programme of National Action, proclaimed by President Sadat in July 1971. The ten-year programme was to be implemented under two consecutive five-year plans, the first starting in July 1972. The target of the Programme was to double national income within ten years to £E5,000 million, with investments totalling £E8,400 million of which 3,200 million were to be spent on the first Five-Year Plan. Industry was due to receive 31.2 per cent of the five-year allocations, agriculture 12.5 per cent, transport and communications 21.9 per cent, electric power 6.3 per cent, housing 10.2 per cent, public utilities 4.1 per cent and social services 7 per cent.

The ten-year plan was never put into operation, however, and the Government reverted to annual development appropriations. The development budget for 1971–72 was set at £E 350 million and was intended to raise G.D.P. in real terms by 5 per cent. The plan was extended until the end of 1972 to aid the changeover to a calendar fiscal year. The 1973 development plan provided for £E 430 million in investments, in addition to £50 million to be invested in the private sector. Its aim was less ambitious than the 1971–72 plan, which is believed to have been only partly fulfilled; despite greater investment the projected growth rate of the 1973 plan was only 3 per cent. Fixed and current investments in the 1974 budget amount to £E 564.3 million.

In mid-1974 a transitional plan was announced to prepare the ground for a new full-scale five-year plan to begin in 1976. The transitional plan envisaged total investment up to the end of 1974 of £E 454 million and in 1975 of £E 1,165.6 million, of which all but about £E million was to be in the public sector. The foreign component of the plan total is set at £E 467.7 million.

AGRICULTURE

Agriculture's contribution to G.D.P. has remained fairly constant at around 30 per cent with industry accounting for 20–21 per cent and services 20–22 per cent over the decade 1959/60–1969/70. Agriculture still employs about 52 per cent of the labour force and earns, through cotton exports, most of the country's foreign exchange. In spite of the diminishing stress on agriculture in Government plans, the volume of agricultural production has been increasing, although population growth has cancelled out most of the benefits of this increase. Preliminary FAO figures for 1973 show that, with the 1961–65 average as a base of 100, agricultural production in 1973 reached 132, only one per cent up on the previous year. The *per capita* figures give an even worse picture, having declined by two per cent from 1972 back to the base level of 100.

The entire arable land available is just under 6 million feddans (one feddan=1.038 acres). The extension of this area through reclamation has been slow difficult and costly. The increasing pressure of people on the land has led to an intensification of cultivation almost without parallel anywhere. Dams, barrages, pumps and an intricate network of canals and drains (in 1960 there were 25,000 km. of canals and 13,000 km. of drains) bring perennial irrigation to almost the whole area. The strict pursuit of crop rotation, lavish use of commercial fertilizer and pesticides, and the patient application of manual labour, not only make multiple cropping possible, but also raise land yields to exceptionally high levels.

Some 979,000 feddans of land were reclaimed between 1952 and mid-1973, in addition to 880,000 feddans of basin land. By mid-1975 it is planned that a total of 1,299,000 feddans should have been reclaimed with priority being given to the Delta, the region with the most productive potential, where Lake Manzala is to be partly drained to improve 600,000 feddans. The targets for reclamation were recently scaled down and there have been attacks on reclamation policy by members of the People's Assembly. A Cairo press report in February also pointed to another form of pressure on cultivable land—housing. It estimated the annual loss in this way at 25,000 feddans. The IBRD and the World Food Programme are financing drainage schemes in the delta and Upper Egypt.

As the yields of land are already very high, increased use of manual labour, or practically any other means of production with the exception of land, encounters rapidly diminishing returns. Since the expanding industrial sector, with its use of modern capital-intensive techniques, can offer relatively few opportunities for increased employment, the incidence of both unemployment and under-employment in the economy at large is likely to grow as the economy advances, at least for some time. There has been a steady flow of workers from the countryside into the cities, though nearly 50 per cent of the labour force is still employed in agriculture with only some 11 per cent in industry. But if employment in the towns is far from full, agriculture too suffers from a surfeit of unnecessary labour. The growth of redundant labour is a constant threat to labour productivity, not only in agriculture, but also in manufacturing industry and service activity. Emigration out of Egypt has recently intensified, but the number of people involved (several thousands every year) is relatively small. The emigrants, however, tend to be highly qualified professionals whom the economy can ill afford to lose.

The bulk of agricultural production is intended for the market place and not for subsistence. Nearly three-quarters of agricultural income comes from field crops, the remainder deriving from fruit, vegetables, live-stock and dairy products. Long-staple cotton is the most important field crop; it absorbs a great deal of the available labour, occupies about a quarter of the arable land and provides up to 40 per cent of the value of field crops and 50–60 per cent of the proceeds of visible exports.

Rice is another important crop and now comes second to cotton as a foreign currency earner. Rice yields have also been improving steadily and more is being cropped in spite of lower acreage. By 1970 Egypt had become the world's third largest rice exporter after the United States and Thailand. Other important grain crops grown include wheat, maize, millet and barley. Population pressure has resulted in Egypt becoming a net importer of cereals, mostly wheat.

Another high-yielding crop is sugar-cane. It is nurtured by an expanding sugar industry, supplying the bulk of national requirements. Other crops include lucerne, a nitrogen-fixing fodder, beans, potatoes and onion and garlic.

The many kinds of fruit, vegetables and horticultural products grown are capable of great expansion and are potentially important as exports. Special efforts are being made to promote the production of these items, especially citrus fruit, and special areas are being allocated along the Mediterranean coast for their cultivation. Recent attention has been given to animal husbandry in an attempt to raise dairy and meat production. Egypt has become a net importer of

meats and only fairly recently were restrictions on
meat consumption, imposed in 1967, removed.

Egypt is the world's principal producer of long-
staple cotton, followed by Sudan and Peru. Many
factors combine to give the high yields and excellent
quality of Egyptian cotton. Among these should be
mentioned climatic, soil and labour conditions, and a
long experience with careful planting, watering and
picking. Government assistance, which has increased of
late, has always been important. The development of
new varieties, seed distribution, area selection, timing
of farm operations and marketing are all carried out
under strict government supervision. Fertilizers and
pesticides have long been distributed through the
government-sponsored Agricultural Credit Bank,
lately converted into a public organization; more
recently this task has been undertaken by govern-
ment-administered agricultural co-operatives which
are multiplying and expanding their area of activity.
All the cotton ginning industry and the cotton
exporting business had been nationalized by 1963.The
cotton exchanges were closed, and the Government
undertook to guarantee prices to regulate internal
trade. A public organization for cotton has been set
up to regulate all aspects of cotton growing, marketing
and manufacturing. Plantings for the 1975–76 season
are down again on previous seasons—1.2 million
feddans compared with 1.48 million feddans in 1974–75
and 1.5 million feddans in 1973–74 —as more land is
turned over to food production. Exports in the calendar year 1973 stood at £E 191.9 million for raw
cotton, £E 44.2 million for cotton yarn, £E 16.7 million
for cotton fabrics and £E 22.2 million for cotton waste,
giving a total of £E 275 million. The yield per acre in
1969–70 was 709 lb., compared with 441 in the United
States.

Egypt produces between 33 and 40 per cent of the
world crop of long-staple cotton (1⅛ in. and longer).
Demand for this type of cotton has been shifting
away towards man-made fibres, a fact which has
tended to weaken Egypt's previous position of pre-
eminence, and consequently the premia Egyptian
cotton commanded over rival cottons. For many years
the government has operated a system of price supports and the farmers find cotton cultivation highly
profitable. The shortage of land, however, together
with the increasing requirements of the domestic
textile industry (190,000 tons in 1970–71 or 38 per
cent of production) set a limit on the quantity available for export. It is noteworthy that average annual
exports of raw cotton from Egypt have remained
roughly constant since the turn of the century when
population was less than a third of its present level.

About half of Egypt's cotton exports has gone to
Communist countries in recent years under various
bilateral agreements. Egyptian preference for trading
with the Western countries, with which Egypt has a
balance of payments deficit, has tended to be frustrated by a number of factors, including U.S. trade
restrictions (on raw cotton imports), the decline of
the high-grade sections of the European cotton
industries, political considerations and shortage of
finance. The availability of credits (to finance imports)

from the Communist countries and the flexibility with
which these countries conduct their relations with
Egypt, have also tended to divert Egyptian foreign
trade towards the Communist states.

AGRARIAN REFORM

Immediately after the Egyptian Revolution of 1952
an experiment in land reform was started. This has
been among the more successful of such attempts,
though only the very large estates were dismembered
while medium-sized estates remained untouched.
Among other measures, a limit of 200 feddans was
imposed on individual ownership of land. This limit
was lowered to 100 feddans in 1961 and again to 50
feddans in 1969. The primary aim of this reform was
the destruction of the feudal power of the old politicians, an aim which was easily realized. In 1952,
5.8 per cent of all landowners held 64.5 per cent of
the total area, but only a quarter of the national
acreage (some 1.5 million feddans) was in plots of
over 100 acres each. By 1961, however, this area
had dwindled to about 1 million feddans, nearly
all of which had been appropriated by the Ministry
of Agrarian Reform and redistributed to landless
peasants. The 1969 land reform affected a further
1.13 million feddans owned by some 16,000 landowners.

Other measures of agrarian reform included rent
control; the regulation of land tenure; consolidation of
fragmented holdings for production purposes; and the
drive to build co-operatives. Under Government
supervision both the number and activities of agricultural co-operatives increased. By 1963 there were
4,897 such co-operatives (compared with 1,727 in
1952) which offered more than £E46 millions in loans
to 920,000 borrowers. The value of services provided
by the agrarian reform co-operatives (set up to help
the recipients of land under the land reform programme) increased more than fivefold between 1958
and 1965 and the activities provided covered the
supply of seeds, sacks, fertilizer, insecticides and pest-
control machinery. However, co-operatives were not
a complete success since they readily lent themselves
to corruption. Also in the process of dispossessing the
large landowners and promoting co-operatives, the
authorities unwittingly helped to eliminate many
highly efficient medium-sized farmers. On balance,
however, the redistribution of land was accompanied
by improved land productivity and not the reverse.

Since land reform affected only about one-sixth of
the total land, the main structure of land-ownership
remained unaffected; in 1965, 5.4 per cent of the
owners still held 49.3 per cent of the land while 94.6
per cent of the owners shared the other half. But the
average ownership of the first group was only 18.05
feddans, and the national average, 1.95 feddans. The
fundamental land tenure problem was not so much
one of distribution but an overall scarcity.

Given the land shortage, special attention has
naturally been paid to increasing the arable area.
In view of the fact that the land to be reclaimed is
often arid desert, reclamation is a costly process
requiring substantial capital outlays, and the question

has to be asked whether new investment should not be directed to the development of manufacturing industry instead, where returns to the scarce capital may well be higher.

THE HIGH DAM

The decision to invest more than £E400 million in the High Dam project (including initial Russian credits of £E113 million, supported subsequently by another loan of £E81 million for the later stages) was, therefore, taken with an eye also on the development of cheap hydro-electric energy for industry. The official estimate of the dam's contribution to the increase in national production was £E234 million. By 1974 revenue from the dam had exceeded the cost of its construction. The project was started in January 1960, completed in July 1970, and officially inaugurated in January 1971. From 1964 onwards various parts of the project matured, but all work ceased when the last of the twelve turbines in the dam's power station had been installed. The station's generating capacity, at 10,000 million kWh. exceeds by a considerable margin the 6,012 million kWh. produced in all Egypt in 1967 mostly from thermal stations with some hydro-electric energy from the old Aswan dam. Transmission lines carry the current from the Dam site to Cairo and further north, and a major scheme aiming at the complete electrification of Egypt's villages has already started. The storage lake behind the dam, which is 500 km. long and 10 km. wide, is the centre of a developing fishing industry which is expected to replace the sardine catch in the Mediterranean, lost as a result of building the dam.

As much as 144,000 feddans were reclaimed annually in the period 1960–65; by the end of 1972 another 1.2 million feddans should have been reclaimed and 700,000 feddans have already been converted from basin (i.e. cultivated once a year) to perennial irrigation. By 1980 a total of 465,000 feddans will have been reclaimed in the Nubariyya region including 300,000 feddans with Russian assistance. The Public Organization for Desert Development is also carrying out an ambitious programme of land reclamation in the Western Desert with the help of underground water. Despite all these activities the man/land ratio is unlikely to improve in the foreseeable future in view of the rapid growth of population.

MANUFACTURING INDUSTRY

Excluding the attempts at industrialization in the early nineteenth century, the history of Egypt's manufacturing industry may be said to begin with World War I. Isolation and increased demand gave rise then to a number of small-scale industries, but many of these had to close down in the face of foreign competition during the 1920s when international trade was resumed. When the commercial treaties holding Egypt to a virtually free-trade policy came to an end in 1930, a protective tariff was established to give shelter to a widening spectrum of nascent industry. The establishment of Bank Misr, and the group of companies it supported in the twenties, coincided with a rising tide of Egyptian nationalism and it became

patriotic to buy Egyptian industrial products. A number of manufacturing industries, mainly catering for domestic consumption and with cotton textiles at their head, came to be established and grew rapidly. On the eve of World War II local industry satisfied a substantial part of the domestic demand for textiles, cement, sugar, edible oils, soap and other consumer products. In 1937 industrial employment in establishments employing 10 persons and over totalled 155,000; two years later, however, the contribution of mining, manufacturing and public utilities to the national product was still only about 8 per cent.

The war greatly stimulated Egyptian industry which, in conditions of acute shortages, especially of equipment and raw materials, strove to meet the expanded demand. A wide variety of goods came to be produced and sometimes exported to neighbouring countries. Considerable expansion took place in the production of textiles, chemicals, building materials and processed foods, while entirely new industries sprang up, including rubber and pharmaceutical manufacturing. By 1947, and in spite of some decline in activity, industrial employment in establishments employing 10 persons and over had risen to 278,000. Industrial growth slowed down after the war owing to a period of relatively free trade, although industry was immensely encouraged by the opening up of foreign sources of machinery. Industrial production continued to expand, however, and in 1951 it reached about 140 per cent of its level in 1938. Throughout the decade of the 1950s industrial production grew steadily at an average rate of about 7 per cent per annum, helped by the chronic deficit which developed in the balance of external payments. The exchange controls that have ruled during most of the post-war period have given Egyptian industry added protection. A great drive toward self-sufficiency after the 1956 war resulted in an intensive industrialization programme which began tentatively in 1957, but was later incorporated in the first five-year economic and social development plan, 1960–65. In the six years from 1959–60 to 1965–66, gross value added by industry and mining rose, at constant prices, at an average rate of 9.5 per cent per annum.

In recent years manufacturing industry has been held back by lack of foreign exchange, and some excess capacity has resulted from shortages of spare parts and raw materials. An acute recession hit the industrial sector in the latter half of 1967, but recovery has been rapid since then. The total value of industrial production (including mining and electricity) has been increasing steadily and reached £E 1,500 million in 1971. Food processing and textiles still dominate the industrial sector, contributing 55–60 per cent of the total value of industrial output. At the end of 1971 a total of 632,528 persons were employed by 2,434 industrial establishments with 25 or more employees. The value added in these establishments totalled £E 699.8 million. Official data for employment in 1969–70 indicate a work force of 916,100 in mining and manufacturing industry, 22,800 in electricity and 387,900 in construction, totalling 16 per cent of employed labour compared with 48.9 per cent for agriculture.

Although the Government has abandoned the ten-year plan under which £E3,000 million was to be invested in industrial development, the annual development allocations still have the increase of industrial output as their prime aim and the drive to encourage foreign investment is directed particularly towards industry. Even without the ten-year plan the major projects to be completed remain the same. The expansion of the iron and steel complex at Helwan is going ahead. The first stage of the complex was completed in December 1973 when the third blast furnace was officially opened and production will now be able to expand up to 900,000 tons a year. Further expansion up to 2 million tons is planned by 1982, the end of the old plan period. The complex has so far cost £E150 million.

Another long-standing project is the Nag Hammadi aluminium complex which should open some time in 1975. Production for the first three months will be around 40,000 tons, after which it should rise to its full capacity of 100,000 tons. Australian and Guinean bauxite will be used. The establishment of a phosphorous complex awaits the start of exploitation of the Hamrawein phosphate deposits with Romanian assistance which has been postponed from 1973 to 1976. Phosphate reserves at Abu Tartur have been estimated at 1,000 million tons, but plans for their exploitation are at an early stage.

A major fertilizer project will be at Talkha which will cost $130 million and will use $88 million in loans from the IDA, the KFAED, the AFESD, Libya, Qatar and Abu Dhabi. The plant will be fed with gas from the Abu Madi field and will have a capacity of 570,000 tons of urea fertilizer a year.

The Tourah cement plant near Cairo is to be expanded from an annual capacity of 1.4 million tons to 2.1 million tons. Loans are also being sought from the IDA and AFESD.

Other heavy industry plans include sponge iron plants, a steel pipe plant, a glass factory and a second iron and steel plant at Alexandria, which would be Soviet-assisted.

In manufacturing industry textiles still account for over a third of total output. The Government has embarked on a three-stage rehabilitation of the cotton-ginning industry costing $40.4 million and assisted by an $18.5 million loan from the IDA.

The Government is studying various offers from foreign companies to set up factories in free zones, notably British Leyland, Honda, and Massey-Ferguson.

The needs of heavy industry, and the plan to extend electric power to all Egypt's rural communities by 1982, has underlined the need for more power generation than that supplied by the High Dam. Hence, plans to implement the Qattara Depression scheme to generate energy by flooding the depression with waters from the Mediterranean have been speeded up, and the potential for nuclear energy is being explored, notably as part of the agreement with the U.S.

OIL AND GAS

Crude oil production in 1974 is estimated to have been about 150,000 barrels per day, a further decline from the 165,706 b/d of 1973 and 208,902 b/d of 1972. The 1974 figure excludes the 80,000 b/d estimated to have been produced in the Israeli-occupied Sinai fields. A list of oil companies in Egypt can be found in "Oil in the Middle East & North Africa", page 100. The value of oil production in 1974 was over £E 152 million, nearly £E 50 million over the target figure and almost £E 60 million up on 1973, according to official sources. Total sales rose from £E 254 million in 1973 to £E 329 million in 1974. The main producing fields remain Morgan and July in the Gulf of Suez, now supplemented by the new field, Ramadan. These are operated by the Gulf of Suez Petroleum Company, a joint venture between the state Egyptian General Petroleum Corporation (EGPC) and Amoco of the U.S., as are all the operating companies in Egypt.

Production was said by the Petroleum Ministry in April 1975 to be running at about 220,000 b/d. Morgan, with about 80,000 b/d, is still way below its peak of some 360,000 b/d in 1963, but the water-injection programme is continuing and output should be raised to around 120,000 b/d in 1976.

Some compensation for Morgan's disappointment comes from a neighbouring field offshore in the Gulf— July— which came on stream in April 1974.

Like Morgan, July has a very low sulphur content. It also has another advantage in that there is no need to duplicate facilities because of its proximity to those of Morgan. In addition its oil will be able to be used to bunker tankers unloading at the nearby terminal of the Suez-Mediterranean pipeline, now under construction. July's reserves are estimated at 600 million barrels, worth about $6,000 million at current prices. Three wells producing about 30,000 barrels per day together are operating at present, though production is expected to rise to 150,000 barrels per day.

Ramadan, GUPCO's new field in the Gulf of Suez, was officially opened in February 1975. It is remarkable for producing all of its 35,000 b/d from one well, and the Government thinks that it will be able to reach 100,000 b/d some time in 1976.

North of Morgan and July and offshore or in Sinai are the fields that formerly provided Egypt with over 60 per cent of its oil before the June 1967 war brought Israeli seizure of them. These fields include Belayim, which used to account for the bulk of the Sinai output and Abu Rudeis which, until the beginning of 1974 when fire broke out in three of the wells, was supplying about 60 per cent of Israel's crude needs. Total output from these Israeli-held fields was estimated at about 80,000 barrels per day in 1974.

WEPCO's Alamein field, discovered at the end of 1966, got off to a promising start and early in 1970 was producing 43,000 barrels per day, but its output has since declined considerably and by 1973 WEPCO's average, including production from a more recent discovery, Yidma, was only 15,130 barrels per day.

The Abu Gharadeq field which came on stream in 1973 has been disappointing for oil but its operator, FAPCO, has struck it rich in gas. The Razzaq field, operated by NIPCO, the other Amoco-EGPC venture in the Western Desert, has more potential than Abu Gharadeq and estimates of eventual production range up to 60,000 barrels per day. The field is already linked to the Mediterranean by pipeline.

The fields of the GPC on the west coast of the Red Sea are expected to raise their output during 1974 from 27,500 barrels per day to 42,000 barrels per day. In June 1974 the Minister of Petroleum opened three new fields belonging to the GPC in that area: Amer (onshore and offshore), producing 3,500 barrels per day; Uyun (onshore), producing 3,500 barrels per day and projected to rise to 6,000 barrels per day; and Khair, producing 500 barrels per day and projected to rise to 700 barrels per day.

Foreign companies are now queueing up to prospect for oil in Egypt. Between March 1973 and June 1975 the EGPC signed 27 exploration agreements with various companies. Another eight are expected to be concluded by the end of 1975, bringing total expenditure commitments to $800 million. The Government is committing £E 250 million to the oil sector over the next five years, with the aim of achieving production of 50 million tons per year by 1982. These commitments reflect the Government's belief that oil is one of the best hopes for earning valuable foreign exchange.

Apart from Phillips, Amoco and Hispanoil, the Italian state concern ENI and Conoco of the U.S. are involved in Egyptian oil through the International Egyptian Oil Company, which partners EGPC in the Delta Petroleum Company (Delpco), a joint venture operating company. Braspetro, the Brazilian state monopoly, is involved in several areas, notably in the Western Desert. Deminex of West Germany has a separate agreement with the EGPC covering 2,000 square kilometres in the Gulf of Suez, as well as a joint agreement with Shell and BP and the EGPC in the same area concluded in July 1974. Elf-Aquitaine of France and the Egyptian Petroleum Development Company, a Japanese company, both signed agreements with EGPC in 1975. All the other foreign participants with the EGPC are American— Transworld (Tripco), Mobil, Exxon, Union, Pexamin Pacific (Pexpac)/LVO, Sante Fe International, Chevron and Atlantic Richfield. Some of the companies— for instance, Amoco, Conoco and Mobil—have more than one agreement, most of which are of the production-sharing type. Under this, the company undertakes to invest a certain amount in exploration over a specified period and pays a signature bonus. If oil is discovered and produced, the company takes 40 per cent of output as reimbursement for its expenses and the remaining 60 per cent is split between the EGPC and the company, usually 80–20 in the EGPC's favour. Thus the EGPC gets 48 per cent of total output and the company 52 per cent.

The Egyptians believe that the Western Desert contains an overlap from the giant Libyan field and the interest shown by foreign companies in this area, previously unsuccessfully explored by the U.S.S.R., seems to justify their confidence. Delta and offshore Mediterranean areas are being rapidly opened up for exploration too, but it is the virgin areas of the Red Sea and Eastern Desert which are now attracting most interest as the map gradually becomes filled in with a maze of lines showing areas allotted and areas under offer. U.S., Japanese and German firms are also understood to have expressed interest in exploring in Sinai, pending an Israeli withdrawal.

There are six oil refineries at Suez (two), Musturud near Cairo, Amiriyah and Mex both near Alexandria, and Tanta. The two refineries at Suez, of 85,000 b/d and 55,000 b/d capacity, were closed between 1969 and 1975. They are located where the bulk of the crude was produced and their closure caused great problems. Under the reconstruction plan petroleum and petrochemical industries are to be established at Suez. The Mex refinery has been enlarged to a capacity of 75,000 barrels per day and the Amiriyah refinery, opened in 1972, has a capacity of 32,000 barrels per day. The Tanta refinery, designed to meet the needs of lower Egypt and with a capacity of only 15,000 barrels per day was opened in August 1973. There is a good network of product pipelines.

A major crude pipeline is being built from Ain-Sukhna on the Gulf of Suez to Sidi-Krer, west of Alexandria. This Suez-Mediterranean pipeline (Sumed) has been under discussion for several years. Originally a French-led West European consortium of companies won the contract to build the pipeline but disagreement over cost-inflation resulted in the contract passing to the U.S. firm, Bechtel, backed by American public and private finance, in October 1973. Strengthening of the dollar at the end of 1973 led in turn to a request by Bechtel to raise the agreed costs, and the contract again changed hands in April 1974, going to a consortium of Italian state enterprises, led by Montubi, who had been part of the original consortium. Bechtel was given a face-saving supervisory role in the contract which was now worth $348 million. Construction work began in 1974. At the end of 1973 Egypt formed with Saudi Arabia, Kuwait, Qatar and Abu Dhabi the Arab Company for Oil Pipelines-Sumed to finance the pipeline. Egypt's share in this is 50 per cent or $200 million. Of this, $80 million has been raised in the Eurodollar markets by Chase Manhattan and Orion Bank, based in London. Chase's role in this predates the October war and was largely the result of personal contact between the bank's Chairman, David Rockefeller, and President Sadat. The loan, subscribed by 18 international banks, is seen as a big breakthrough for Egypt as it is the first for a specific project.

The pipeline's capacity will initially be 40 million tons a year but a second stage will take it to 80 million a year and there is the possibility of expansion up to 120 million. By April 1973 ten foreign oil companies had contracted to put through a total of 60 million tons of crude a year, the minimum to ensure the pipeline's viability. Sumed is not expected to compete with a reopened Suez Canal for oil shipments. The Government expects the two to be complementary. A crude oil pipeline from Suez to Port Said has also been mentioned as part of the Egyptian-Iranian investment package, but this is thought to be fairly low on the list of priorities.

Plans for an export refinery, with a capacity of 500,000 barrels a day, in Alexandria's free zone to process crude transported through Sumed are still at an early stage, though the Arab oil states, especially Saudi Arabia, have reportedly promised finance for it.

The first of Egypt's gas-fields to come on stream was Abu Madi, in the Nile Delta, in October 1974. Its capacity is 3.5 million cubic metres a day or one million tons of oil equivalent a year. Reserves are estimated at some 20 million tons. Abukir, offshore near Alexandria, and Abu Gharadeq in the Western Desert, should both start producing in 1976. They are said to have the same producing capacity and reserves as Abu Madi. Abu Madi is to be linked with the industrial centres of the Delta, in particular with the fertilizer plant being built at Talkha, and Abu Gharadeq with the industrial centre of Helwan and notably the iron and steel complex. Abukir will eventually supply fertilizer and sponge iron plants in the Alexandria region.

FINANCE

British Treasury bills were used as a cover to the Egyptian currency issued by the National Bank of Egypt, then the bank of issue before 1947, when the sterling connection was severed completely. Since 1948 Egyptian government securities have complemented the gold reserves as currency backing, and Egypt has followed a policy of money management based on a separation between the balance of payments and domestic money supply.

The most recent series of reorganizations of the banking system, in late 1971, resulted in three of the banks merging into others and each of the rest being entrusted with specialized functions. The National Bank of Egypt was entrusted with foreign trade, the Bank of Port Said merged into Misr Bank which was to deal with home trade, including agricultural finance, the Industrial Bank merged into the Bank of Alexandria which was to deal with manufacturing, the Mortgage Credit Bank merged with the *Credit Foncier Egyptien* and was to deal with construction and housing and the Bank of Cairo left to deal with operations of the public sector. A new bank, the Nasser Social Bank has been created to deal with pensions and other forms of social security. The Egyptian International Bank for Foreign Trade and Development was also created in 1971 to promote foreign trade and attract foreign investment but was later transformed into the Arab International Bank for Foreign Trade and Development with each of Egypt and Libya holding £10 million of its £30 million capital and the rest offered to other Arab investors. These banks are additional to the Central Bank of Egypt, which was created from the issue department of the National Bank of Egypt in 1960, and the Public Organization for Agricultural Credit and Co-operatives, which the *Crédit Agricole* became in 1964.

Compared with an average rate of growth for the real economy of 5–7 per cent a year in the 1960s, money supply was increasing on average by about 9 per cent a year. But in the first half of 1974 the increase was 13.3 per cent, compared with 9.8 per cent and 2.4 per cent in the corresponding periods of 1973 and 1972. This reflected the rapid inflation since the October war which has produced rises in the cost of living estimated at 30–50 per cent. The increase in money supply has been accompanied by a growing share in the economic life of the community of the public sector which has proved to be a great user of means of exchange. The traditional anti-inflationary devices (e.g. devaluation, used in 1962 to bring the Egyptian pound down to $2.30 from $2.838) have had little effect on effective demand and hence the balance of payments disequilibrium, since most of the credit created by the banking system is for use by the public sector. There were two dollar devaluations, one in 1971 and one in 1972, but a revaluation against the dollar in February 1973 brought the Egyptian pound up to $2.56.

Egypt's foreign debts are enormous and repayment of them is one of the biggest hindrances to economic development plans. By 1975 Egypt was having to borrow on a longer-term basis just to pay off the more pressing shorter-term debts. Without grants from Saudi Arabia, Qatar, the UAE and other rich Arab states, Egypt would have been in serious default on its debts. The military debt alone is estimated at $8,000–10,000 million, much of it owed to the Soviet Union. Non-military debts to the U.S.S.R. are estimated to have been around $1,000 million by the end of 1973. Egyptian efforts to get a 10-year moratorium on Soviet debts had not succeeded by mid-1975, as the Soviet leadership continued to show its displeasure at Egyptian co-operation with the U.S. in Middle East peace efforts.

Total debts to the West amount to about $3,000 million, but rescheduling was agreed to after the October war.

BUDGET

Egypt draws up six budgets—the current services budget, the public authorities' current budget, the economic organizations' current budget, the special finance fund's current budget, the investment budget and the emergency fund—but in practice they can be grouped together. The calandar year has been the fiscal year since the end of 1972 when a July-December budget was drawn up to aid the changeover. The 1973 budget total was not publicly revealed until December 1973 when the 1974 budget was announced. This was because the 1973 budget included a secret "battle budget".

The 1975 budget totals £E 5,000 million, compared with £E 4,187 million in 1974 and £E 3,233 million in 1973. The exact figure for defence spending is not known but is certainly more than the official total of £E 1,000 million of 1974. Reconstruction has been allocated £E 500 million and food subsidies £E 640 million.

FOREIGN TRADE AND PAYMENTS

The external trade deficit has persisted almost without interruption for the whole of the past two decades. According to the IMF, the visible trade deficit was $524.1 million in 1972, $576.3 million in 1973 and no less than $1,527.2 million in 1974. However, financial grants turned the deficit into a surplus in 1973 and grants of $1,033.3 in 1974 left a current deficit of only $325.2 million. The Government keeps a constant vigil on all external payments, permitting only the most essential imports, but the pressure of population on resources helps to keep the balance of external payments in a critical state. The problem is unlikely to be solved without a breakthrough in the pattern of imports and exports which may be brought about by the development of the petroleum sector.

Imports in 1974 totalled $3,194.6 million, compared with $1,586.9 million in 1973. Machinery, vehicles, metal products, fuels, chemicals and other raw materials, and food products formed the majority of imports. The value of exports in 1974 was $1,667.4 million, compared with $1,010.6 million in 1973.

In 1971, 33 per cent of imports and 60 per cent of exports were traded with Eastern European countries, compared with 29 per cent and 56 per cent respectively in the previous year. It should be noted, however, that Egyptian trade figures include Greece, Turkey, Finland and Cyprus under this heading. Communist Eastern Europe therefore accounted in 1971 for 26.8 per cent of exports. Trade with the Arab countries is small but growing under official encouragement. Exports to Arab countries reached 8.2 per cent of the total in 1971 and imports 7 per cent.

There was normally a surplus on the current account of invisible trade which helped to redress part of the deficit on merchandise trade, but this surplus was turned into a deficit after the closure of the Suez Canal in June 1967 and the decline in tourist revenue. Canal dues received were £E86.2 million in 1965, £E95.3 million in 1966 and £E47.0 million in (the first five months of) 1967. Payments and receipts for shipping and insurance have been fairly balanced at about £E10 million each way. Interest and dividends acquired were £E12.6 million in 1971, according to provisional estimates, compared with £E14.1 million in 1970. The servicing of foreign loans rose from £E29.4 million in 1970 to £E32.5 million in 1971, and government expenditure abroad reached £E35.7 million in 1971. The Central Bank estimated the deficit on current transactions at £E211.1 million in 1971, compared with £E200.7 million in 1970.

ECONOMIC POLICY

According to the Permanent Constitution of 1971 the economy of Egypt is one based on socialism with the people controlling all means of production. In practice this means that the Government owns or controls practically every economic unit in the economy worth controlling. Although the doctrine of socialism was invoked from the first land reform in 1952, the economy remained largely in private hands

until 1961, except for the nationalization of the Suez Canal company in 1956 and that of British and French property during the Suez attack. During 1961, all cotton exporting firms were nationalized, and the Alexandria futures market was closed; 275 industrial and trading concerns were taken over by the state in whole or in part; taxation was made so progressive that individual income was virtually limited to the official maximum of £E5,000; the maximum limit on land ownership was reduced from 200 to 100 feddans (before it was reduced again in 1969); individual shareholding was limited to £E10,000; 25 per cent of the net profits of industrial companies was to be distributed to the workers, who were to be represented on the boards of directors, and to work only a 42-hour week.

Other nationalization measures followed, so that the only sectors of the economy remaining outside complete government ownership are agriculture and urban real estate, but even these are overwhelmingly regulated by laws and decrees. Concerns are grouped under boards and boards under Chairmen and Ministers, and a constant stream of directives helps to bring the activities of all the controlled units in line with Government policies.

After 1967 the Government introduced yet more restricting measures aiming at curbing consumer demand including a variety of taxes, forced savings and compulsory contributions out of wages and salaries. Now, however, the trend is towards "denasserization", the sequestrations of the 1960s have been ruled illegal, new laws are being passed to allow private-sector participation in former state preserves like exporting and importing and transport, and foreign investment is seen as the key to development.

TRANSPORT

The Government is aiming to expand both the Mediterranean and Red Sea port capacities as well as reviving Port Said, Ismailia and Suez to cope with traffic passing through the reopened Suez Canal. Alexandria port is being expanded and a completely new port is planned, west of Alexandria, at Dakheila, which by 1978 should be commissioned with a capacity of 20 million tons a year, compared with Alexandria's present capacity of 13 million tons. Safaga on the Red Sea is also being developed but mainly to handle mineral imports and exports.

River transport is being expanded to relieve the load on roads and railways for internal distribution. Navigable waterways total about 3,100 km., of which about half is the Nile and the rest canals. Canals such as the Nubariya canal in the delta and the Bahr Youssef between Fayoum and Asiut make it possible to link Alexandria with Upper Egypt through Cairo.

Egypt was one of the first countries to have a railway—in 1851—and a good network was built up at an early stage of its development. Now with over 4,000 kilometres of track modernization is urgently needed. A project using loans from various sources of up to $165 million is to be undertaken to modernize the railway system and expand its carrying capacity, as well as to draw up a comprehensive national transport survey.

Good roads connect Cairo with Alexandria, the canal towns and Upper Egypt. There are plans to expand the output both of locally produced goods vehicles and of vehicles from joint-venture projects set up with foreign companies such as British Leyland, Honda or Yamaha.

EgyptAir, the state airline, has recently been in difficulties because it has been starved of funds by the Government and because, for political reasons, it was persuaded to buy eight Soviet TU-154s which the Egyptian pilots refused to fly because they claimed they were unreliable. Some of these problems have been resolved with the decision to acquire 10 Boeings as a replacement for the Soviet planes which have been returned.

STATISTICAL SURVEY

AREA AND POPULATION

AREA (sq. km.)		POPULATION (Census of May 30th, 1966)					
Total	Inhabited	Total	Cairo	Alexandria	Giza	Port Said	Suez
1,001,449	55,039	30,075,858	4,219,853	1,801,056	1,650,381	282,977	264,098

Total Population (estimated): 37,000,000 (March 1975).
Population of Greater Cairo* (estimated): 6,588,000 (mid-1974).
Population of Alexandria (estimated): 2,259,000 (mid-1974).

* Includes Cairo City, Shubra El Khaima and Giza City.

EMPLOYMENT
(1973—'000 workers)

Agriculture	4,179
Industry	1,160
Construction	359
Electricity	41
Transport, Communication and Storage .	409
Trade and Finance	860
Housing	138
Utilities	41
Social Development Services . . .	1,789
TOTAL	8,976

GOVERNORATES*
(1965)

GOVERNORATE	AREA (sq. km.)	CAPITAL	GOVERNORATE	AREA (sq. km.)	CAPITAL
Cairo . .	214.2	Cairo	Munufia . . .	1,532.1	Shibin el-Kom
Alexandria . .	2,679.4	Alexandria	Behera . . .	4,589.5	Damanhur
Port Said . .	72.1	Port Said	Giza	1,009.6	Giza
Ismailia . .	1,441.6	Ismailia	Beni Suef . . .	1,321.7	Beni Suef
Suez . . .	17,840.4	Suez	Fayum . . .	1,827.2	Fayum
Damietta . .	589.2	Damietta	Menia . . .	2,261.7	Menia
Dakahlia . .	3,470.9	Mansura	Asyut . . .	1,553.0	Asyut
Sharkia . .	4,179.6	Zagazig	Suhag . . .	1,547.2	Suhag
Kalyubia . .	1,001.1	Benha	Kena . . .	1,850.7	Kena
Kafr el-Sheikh . .	3,437.1	Kafr el-Sheikh	Aswan . . .	678.5	Aswan
Gharbia . .	1,942.2	Tanta			

* Excluding the four sparsely-populated "frontier districts".

AGRICULTURE
PRINCIPAL CROPS

	AREA ('ooo feddans*)				PRODUCTION ('ooo metric tons)			
	1969/70	1970/71	1971/72	1972/73	1969/70	1970/71	1971/72	1972/73
Wheat	1,312	1,356	1,246	1,249	1,519	1,732	1,618	1,838
Maize	1,508	1,526	1,538	1,656	2,397	2,344	2,421	2,508
Millet	500	494	483	487	874	854	831	853
Barley	88	76	97	86	84	77	109	97
Rice	1,142	1,137	1,146	997	2,605	2,534	2,507	2,274
Clover	2,748	2,770	2,819	2,874	45,177	46,327	n.a.	n.a.
Beans†	302	262	337	272	278	257	362	273
Lentils	47	65	67	74	33	50	54	62
Onions†	47	56	49	45	451	583	490	530
Sugar Cane . . .	186	193	202	198	6,934	7,486	7,701	7,349

* 1 feddan = 1.038 acres.   † Dry crop and the production of onions includes interplanted crop.

Livestock: (1972 estimates—'ooo) Cattle 2,129, Buffaloes 2,098, Camels 117, Goats, 1,234, Sheep 2,013, Horses 30, Donkeys 1,430.

Eggs: (1973) 1,606 million

Honey: Production (1973) 6,682 tons.

AREA AND PRODUCTION OF RAW COTTON

	1970–71		1971–72		1972-73	
	'ooo feddans*	'ooo kantars†	'ooo feddans*	'ooo kantars†	'ooo feddans*	'ooo kantars†
Menoufi . . .	363	1,916	305	1,742	289	1,436
Dandara . . .	117	723	102	722	109	802
Ashmouni . . .	137	838	104	672	91	613
Others . . .	908	5,527	1,041	5,892	1,111	5,832
TOTAL . .	1,525	9,004	1,552	9,028	1,600	8,683

* 1 feddan = 1.038 acres.   † 1 metric kantar = 157.5 kg.

MINING AND INDUSTRY
('ooo metric tons)

COMMODITY	1970	1971	1972	1973
Crude oil	16,388†	17,100†	10,720	8,479
Benzine	360	695	859	961
Kerosene	490	740	970	1,158
Mazout	1,624	2,572	3,212	3,050
Asphalt	58	73	113	143
Phosphate . . .	582	712	563	553
Manganese . . .	4	4	2	3
Common salt . . .	444	425	381	454
Iron ore . . .	453	473	427	656
Refined sugar . . .	547	675	604	634
Cottonseed oil . . .	126	118	145	131
Super phosphate . .	411	487	518	419
Caustic soda . . .	20	18	16	14
Cement	3,259	3,921	3,822	3,617
Woollen fabrics . .	3	3	9*	9*
Cotton yarn . . .	164	171	179	183
Cotton cloth . . .	110	114	116	118
Electricity (million kWh.) .	7,592	7,995	8,057	7,979

* Million metres.   † 'ooo cubic metres.

PRODUCTION CO-OPERATIVES

			1970	1971	1972*
Agriculture	.	.	4,978	4,997	4,948
Sea Food	.	.	57	58	60

* Preliminary.

FINANCE

1,000 millièmes = 100 piastres = 5 tallaris = 1 Egyptian pound (£E).

Coins: 1, 2 and 5 millièmes; 1, 2, 5 and 10 piastres.

Notes: 5, 10, 25 and 50 piastres; 1, 5 and 10 pounds.

Exchange rates (July 1975): £1 sterling = 854.3 millièmes; U.S. $1 = 390.6 millièmes.

£E100 = £117.06 sterling = $256.00.

Note: From September 1949 to May 1962 the Egyptian pound was valued at U.S. $2.87156 ($1 = 348.24 millièmes). Between May 1962 and February 1973 the pound's value was $2.30 ($1 = 434.78 millièmes). The present official selling rate (£E1 = $2.56) has been effective since February 1973. From November 1967 to August 1971 the exchange rate was £1 sterling = £E1.0435; from December 1971 to June 1972 it was £1 sterling = £E1.1328.

BUDGET ESTIMATES
(£E million)

CURRENT BUDGETS

REVENUE				1973	1974	EXPENDITURE				1973	1974
State revenue	.	.	.	618.1	714.7	Administration	.	.	.	n.a.	872.5
Other current revenue		.	.	1,514.1	1,927.2	Public authorities	.	.	.	n.a.	1,365.5
						Economic organizations	.	.	.	n.a.	645.8
						Special finance funds	.	.	.	n.a.	25.4
TOTAL	.	.	.	2,132.2	2,641.9	TOTAL	.	.	.	2,237.0	2,909.2

INVESTMENT BUDGETS

REVENUE			1973	1974	EXPENDITURE				1973	1974
Finance from own resources	.		54.0	78.2	Administration	.	.	.	66.0	49.7
Foreign facilities	.	.	128.8	216.4	Public authorities	.	.	.	111.7	114.0
Loans from domestic savings	.		249.7	225.4	Economic organizations	.	.		218.5	338.3
					Special finance funds	.	.		0.1	0.4
					Public treasury investments	.	.		36.2	17.6
TOTAL	.	.	432.5	520.0	TOTAL	.	.	.	432.5	520.0

Source: National Bank of Egypt *Economic Bulletin*, Vol. XXVII, No. 1, 1974.

RESERVES AND CURRENCY IN CIRCULATION
(at December 31st)

	1971	1972	1973	1974
Gold Reserves (U.S. $ million) . . .	92	92	103	104
Currency in Circulation (£E million) . .	558.7	631.4	777.2	947.6

BALANCE OF PAYMENTS
(U.S. $ million)

	1972	1973	1974
Current account:			
Exports f.o.b.	901.9	1,010.6	1,667.4
Imports f.o.b.	1,426.0	1,586.9	3,194.6
Visible trade balance . . .	−524.1	−576.3	−1,527.2
Invisibles	7.6	6.8	168.7
Current balance	−516.5	−569.5	−1,358.5
Financial grants	326.9	646.9	1,033.3
Current balance plus grants . . .	−189.6	77.4	− 325.2
Capital account:			
Inflow	509.7	693.4	1,130.2
Outflow	340.9	474.8	728.0
Net capital transactions . . .	168.8	218.6	402.2
Allocation of SDRs	24.0	—	—
Overall balance of payments surplus . .	3.2	296.0	77.0

Source: The Economist, June 28th, 1975.

EXTERNAL TRADE
(£E million)

	1969	1970	1971	1972	1973	1974
Total Imports . . .	277.3	342.0	400.0	390.8	361.1	919.2
Total Exports . . .	323.9	331.2	343.2	358.8	444.2	593.3

PRINCIPAL COMMODITIES

IMPORTS	£E MILLION			
	1970	1971	1972	1973
Cereals and Milling Products . .	30.5	70.7	51.8	68.2
Animal and Vegetable Oils . .	16.9	23.2	31.0	16.8
General Grocery	11.1	6.2	6.2	4.8
Tobacco	7.5	8.1	9.9	11.2
Textiles and Textile Articles . .	19.2	16.1	16.6	16.9
Paper and Paper Products . .	12.2	13.8	13.4	11.8
Pottery and Glassware . . .	3.4	3.9	4.0	3.6
Clocks, Watches, Scientific Apparatus	2.8	2.7	2.5	4.1
Mineral Products	35.4	36.4	28.7	10.8
Chemical Products	41.9	47.4	52.4	53.6
Wood, Hides and Rubber . .	23.9	24.6	37.0	24.9
Machinery and Electrical Apparatus	57.1	55.1	53.5	51.7
Transport Equipment . . .	32.6	40.5	30.9	35.9
Crude Petroleum	7.2	13.0	26.4	3.6
Iron and Steel	24.9	28.2	30.9	25.3

PRINCIPAL COMMODITIES—*Continued*]

EXPORTS	1971		1972		1973	
	'ooo tons	£E million	'ooo tons	£E million	'ooo tons	£E million
Cotton, raw	333	175.0	295	162.0	n.a.	192.0
Cotton Yarn . . .	42	35.6	47	42.6	45	44.2
Cotton Piece Goods . . .	22	17.5	21	17.5	17	16.7
Rice	515	24.5	456	22.1	298	26.1
Potatoes	61	2.0	77	3.2	108	6.6
Onions	92	5.8	107	5.4	89	9.2
Edible Fruits . . .	145	9.4	90	5.4	260	17.0
Manganese and Phosphates . .	282	1.2	212	1.0	n.a.	n.a.
Crude Oil	529	1.9	5,225	20.3	9,681	36.9
Benzine, Kerosene and Mazout .	41	0.3	314	1.8	169	1.5
Cement	1,362	5.9	799	3.7	564	4.6

EXPORTS OF COTTON
(kantars; one kantar=99.05 lb.)

PRINCIPAL COUNTRIES	1972	1973	VARIETIES	1972	1973
Bulgaria	48,268	72,351	Giza 45	601,204	506,441
Czechoslovakia . .	464,957	362,905	Menoufi	1,560,150	1,264,346
German Democratic Repub.	62,418	62,090	Giza 68	1,052,808	993,539
Greece	110,554	114,715	Giza 69	664,829	818,102
Hungary . . .	130,617	61,088	Giza 67	1,497,844	1,535,406
Poland . . .	151,689	163,588	Dandara	156,719	142,808
Romania . . .	294,823	300,430	Giza 66	207,897	172,687
Spain . . .	170,171	236,562	Others	158,092	262,275
U.S.S.R. . . .	1,547,118	1,260,519			
Yugoslavia . . .	108,381	236,562	TOTAL . . .	5,899,543	5,695,604

PRINCIPAL COUNTRIES
(£E million)

IMPORTS	1970†	1971	1972	1973
Saudi Arabia	0.6	0.5	0.4	n.a.
U.S.S.R.	34.9	54.0	51.9	25.6
Czechoslovakia	13.6	17.7	13.0	11.9
German Democratic Republic . .	8.4	15.8	16.5	18.0
Yugoslavia	8.9	6.2	4.7	2.2
United Kingdom	13.5	14.1	15.4	13.6
Germany, Federal Republic . .	26.6	28.1	25.8	28.3
Italy	22.6	22.3	13.9	16.9
Japan	5.2	5.1	4.8	5.5
India	27.2	19.2	12.8	10.0
U.S.A.	20.9	22.2	33.9	45.2
Poland	9.9	8.6	6.6	9.2
Romania	11.3	9.9	12.9	16.3
France	25.3	20.7	28.5	30.7
China, People's Republic . . .	6.7	7.7	11.2	10.2

† Excludes crude petroleum.

EXPORTS	1970	1971	1972	1973
U.S.S.R.	122.4	136.2	126.0	145.9
Czechoslovakia	15.8	17.7	21.0	26.2
German Democratic Republic	19.7	11.2	15.4	17.4
Yugoslavia	8.2	4.1	3.7	4.6
United Kingdom	6.2	7.1	8.0	14.8
Germany, Federal Republic	8.9	9.6	10.7	14.0
Italy	11.0	9.7	11.2	19.5
Japan	10.6	13.3	15.3	22.8
India	18.0	20.9	18.9	13.3
U.S.A.	2.7	2.9	5.2	6.7
Saudi Arabia	1.6	1.6	1.9	3.1
Poland	7.5	12.4	17.4	15.1
Romania	8.1	7.6	9.4	11.3
France	6.5	5.6	7.9	10.7
China, People's Republic	7.7	11.5	11.0	7.6

TRANSPORT

RAILWAYS

	1970–71	1971–72
Total Freight (million ton km.)	3,340	2,976
Total Passengers (million passenger km.)	6,772	7,306
Track Length (km.)	4,233	4,385

ROADS
(Licences issued at end of each year)

	1971	1972	1973
Buses	7,358	8,081	7,933
Lorries	27,351	31,111	31,538
Cars	148,022	158,644	167,378
Motor Cycles	27,494	32,215	37,221

SHIPPING
SUEZ CANAL TRAFFIC

	VESSELS	NET TONNAGE ('000)	PASSENGERS ('000)	RECEIPTS (£E '000)
1964	19,943	227,991	270	77,697
1965	20,289	246,817	291	85,792
1966	21,250	274,250	300	95,187
1967: Jan.–May	9,652	127,825	157	44,000

The Suez Canal was reopened on June 5th, 1975.

CIVIL AVIATION
(tons)

	1969	1970	1971	1972	1973*
Cargo	14,512	15,269	17,433	21,608	18,775
Mail	1,379	1,151	1,201	1,299	1,437

* Preliminary.

TOURISM

	TOTAL VISITORS	ARABS	EUROPEANS	AMERICANS	OTHERS	TOTAL (guest-nights) ('ooo)
1969 . .	345,343	193,977	85,463	32,769	33,134	4,396
1970 . .	357,661	230,803	65,985	25,427	35,446	4,574
1971 . .	428,062	260,169	94,540	30,051	43,302	5,988
1972 . .	540,880	313,960	132,012	44,062	50,846	6,626

Tourism was affected by the October war in 1973 when the number of tourists fell to 534,000, but the total number of visitors to Egypt in 1974 was 700,000.

Tourist Accommodation (1974–75): 16,000 beds, estimated to rise to 33,000 by 1976–77.

EDUCATION

(1971–72)

	CLASSES	TEACHERS	PUPILS
Primary	90,022	99,351	3,873,297
General and Technical Preparatory . .	23,216	27,888	927,703
General Secondary	8,135	14,359	312,489
Technical Secondary . . .	8,502	14,300	289,812
Teacher Training	782	2,172	27,247
Higher Education	n.a.	5,378	241,690

Sources: Central Agency for Public Mobilization and Statistics, Cairo; Research Department, National Bank of Egypt, Cairo; International Monetary Fund.

THE CONSTITUTION

The Permanent Constitution of the Arab Republic of Egypt was approved by referendum on September 11th, 1971. There are six chapters with 193 articles, many of them based on the 1964 Interim Constitution, but chapters 3 and 4 show a considerable degree of liberalization of the former statutes.

CHAPTER 1

The State

Egypt is an Arab Republic with a democratic, socialist system based on the alliance of the working people and derived from the country's historical heritage and the spirit of Islam.

The Egyptian people are part of the Arab nation, who work towards total Arab unity.

Islam is the religion of the State; Arabic is its official language and the Islamic code is a principal source of legislation. The State safeguards the freedom of worship and of performing rites for all religions.

Sovereignty is of the people alone which is the source of all powers.

The protection, consolidation and preservation of the socialist gains is a national duty: the sovereignty of law is the basis of the country's rule, and the independence of immunity of the judiciary are basic guarantees for the protection of rights and liberties.

The Arab Socialist Union is the political organization of the State which represents the alliance of the working forces of the people; the farmers, workers, soldiers, the intelligentsia and national capitalism.

CHAPTER 2

The Fundamental Elements of Society

Social solidarity is the basis of Egyptian society, and the family is its nucleus.

The State ensures the equality of men and women in both political and social rights in line with the provisions of Moslem legislation.

Work is a right, an honour and a duty which the State guarantees together with the services of social and health insurance, pensions for incapacity and unemployment.

The economic basis of the Republic is the socialist based on sufficiency and justice. It is calculated to prevent exploitation and to level up differences between classes.

The people control all means of production and regulate the national economy according to a comprehensive development plan which determines the role of Arab and foreign capital.

Property is subject to the people's control.

Property shall be expropriated only by law and against fair compensation. Nationalization shall also be by law for public interest considerations or socialist objectives.

Agricultural holding may be limited by law.

The State follows a comprehensive central planning and compulsory planning approach based on quinquennial socio-economic and cultural development plans whereby the society's resources are mobilized and put to the best use.

The public Sector assumes the leading role in the development of the national economy. The State provides absolute protection of this Sector as well as the property of co-operative societies and trade unions against all attempts to tamper with them.

CHAPTER 3
Public Liberties, Rights and Duties

All citizens are equal before the law. Personal liberty is a natural right and no one may be arrested, searched, imprisoned or restricted in any way without a court order.

Houses have sanctity, and shall not be placed under serveillance or searched without a court order with reasons given for such action.

The law safeguards the sanctities of the private lives of all citizens; so have all postal, telegraphic telephonic and other means of communication which may not therefore be confiscated, or perused except by a court order giving the reasons, and only for a specified period.

Public rights and freedoms are also inviolate and all calls for atheism and anything that reflects adversely on divine religions is prohibited.

The freedom of opinion, the press, printing and publications and all information media are safeguarded.

Press censorship is forbidden, so are warnings, suspensions or cancellations through administrative channels. Under exceptional circumstances as in cases of emergency or in war time, censorship may be imposed on information media for a definite period.

Egyptians have the right to permanent or provisional emigration and no Egyptian may be deported or prevented from returning to the country.

Citizens have the right to private meetings in peace provided they bear no arms. Egyptians also have the right to form societies which have no secret activities or are hostile to the government. Public meetings are also allowed within the limits of the law.

CHAPTER 4
Sovereignty of the Law

All acts of crime should be specified together with the penalties for the acts.

Recourse to justice, it says, is a right of all citizens, and those who are financially unable, will be assured of means to defend their rights.

Arrested persons may protest against their detention and their protests should be decided upon within a prescribed period otherwise they should be released.

CHAPTER 5
System of Government

The President, who must be at least 40 years old, is nominated by at least one-third of the members of the People's Assembly, approved by at least two-thirds, and elected by popular referendum. His term is for six years and he 'may be re-elected for another subsequent term.' He may take emergency measures in the interests of the state but these measures must be approved by referendum within 60 days.

The People's Assembly, elected for five years, is the legislative body and approves general policy, the budget and the development plan. It shall have 'not less than 350' elected members, at least half of whom shall be workers or farmers, and the President may appoint up to ten additional members. In exceptional circumstances the Assembly, by a two-thirds vote, may authorize the President to rule by decree for a specified period but these decrees must be approved by the Assembly at its next meeting.

The Assembly may pass a vote of no confidence in a Deputy Prime Minister, a Minister or a Deputy Minister, provided three days' notice of the vote is given, and the minister must then resign. In the case of the Prime Minister, the Assembly may "prescribe" his responsibility and submit a report to the President: if the President disagrees with the report but the Assembly persists, then the matter is put to a referendum: if the people support the President the Assembly is dissolved; if they support the Assembly the President must accept the resignation of the government. The President may dissolve the Assembly prematurely, but his action must be approved by a referendum and elections must be held within 60 days.

Executive Authority is vested in the President, who may appoint one or more vice-presidents and appoints all ministers. He may also dismiss the vice-presidents and ministers. The President has 'the right to refer to the people in connection with important matters related to the country's higher interests.' The Government is described as 'the supreme executive and administrative organ of the state'. Its members, whether full ministers or deputy ministers, must be at least 35 years old. Further sections define the roles of Local Government, Specialized National Councils, the Judiciary, the Higher Constitutional Court, the Socialist Prosecutor General, the Armed Forces and National Defence Council and the Police.

CHAPTER 6
General and Transitional Provisions

No law shall normally have retroactive effect, but this may be changed, except in criminal matters, with the approval of a majority of the Assembly. Articles of the constitution may be revised, at the suggestion of the President or one-third of the Assembly, but the revision must be submitted for approval by a public referendum. The term of the present President shall date from his election as President of the United Arab Republic.

THE GOVERNMENT

THE PRESIDENCY

President: Col. MUHAMMAD ANWAR SADAT.

Vice-President: Lt.-Gen. MUHAMMAD HOSNI MUBARAK.

COUNCIL OF MINISTERS

(July 1975)

Prime Minister: Gen. MAMDOUH MUHAMMAD SALEM.

Deputy Premier and Minister of Higher Education: Dr. MUHAMMAD HAFEZ GHANEM.

Deputy Premier and Minister of War: Gen. MUHAMMAD ABDUL GHANI AL-GAMASSI.

Deputy Premier and Minister of Foreign Affairs: MUHAMMAD ISMAIL FAHMI.

Minister of Labour: ABDEL LATIF BAITIYA.

Minister of Electric Power: AHMED SULTAN.

Minister of Tourism: IBRAHIM NEGUIB.

Minister of Social Affairs: Dr. (Mrs.) AICHA RATEB.

Minister of Agriculture and Relations with Sudan: Dr. OSMAN ALI BADRAN.

Minister of War Production: Lt.-Gen. AHMED KAMEL EL-BADRI.

Minister of Culture and Information: YOUSSEF EL-SEBAI.

Minister of Health: AHMED FUAD MOHIEDDIN.

Minister of Petroleum: AHMAD IZZEDIN HASAN HILAL.

Minister of State for Foreign Affairs: MUHAMMAD MAHMOUD RIYAD.

Minister of State for Council of Ministers Affairs: ABDEL FATTAH ABDULLAH.

Minister of State for Parliament Affairs: ALBERT BARSOUM SALAMA.

Minister of Building and Reconstruction: OSMAN AHMED OSMAN.

Minister of Insurance: MUHAMMAD ABDEL FATTAH IBRAHIM.

Minister of Education: Dr. MUSTAFA KAMAL HELMI.

Minister of Local Administration: MUHAMMAD HAMED MAHMOUD.

Minister of Supply: ABDEL RAHMAN EL-CHAZLI.

Minister of Justice: ADEL YOUNES.

Minister of Marine Transport: Gen. MAHMOUD ABDUL RAHMAN FAHMI.

Minister of Planning and Administrative Development: IBRAHIM HELMI ABDUL RAHMAN.

Minister of Interior: SAYED HUSAIN FAHMI.

Minister of Commerce: ZAKAREYA TEWFIK ABDEL FATTAH.

Minister of Irrigation: ABDEL AZIM ABU EL ATA.

Minister of Industry: ISSA CHAHINE.

Minister of Scientific Research: Dr. MUHAMMAD EL-GEBEILI.

Minister of Finance: Dr. AHMED ABOU ISMAIL.

Minister of Economy and Economic Co-operation: Dr. MUHAMMAD ZAKI CHAFEI.

Minister of Telecommunications: MUHAMMAD GAMALEDDIN HASSANEIN.

Minister of Wakfs: Dr. MUHAMMAD EL-DAHABI.

Minister of Transport: GAMALEDDIN MUHAMMAD SEDKI.

Minister of Aviation: HAMDI ABU-ZAID.

PEOPLE'S ASSEMBLY

ELECTIONS

ELECTIONS OCTOBER 27th AND NOVEMBER 3rd, 1971

Of the 360 seats (10 appointed and 350 elected), 53 per cent were won by farmers and workers.

Speaker: SAYED MAREI.

Deputy Speakers: GAMAL AL-OTAIFI, ALI AS-SAYED ALI.

POLITICAL ORGANIZATION

Arab Socialist Union (ASU): Cairo; f. 1961 as the alliance of all working people's forces; Chair. President SADAT; First Sec. of Central Committee RIFAAT AL-MAHGOUB; the Higher Exec. Cttee. has 10 mems.; the Central Cttee. has 230 mems., 200 elected from ASU Governorates' Conferences, and 30 appointed members (2 to represent the police, 2 the students and 4 the armed forces). The National Congress is the largest representative body of the ASU. At the end of May 1975 President Sadat appointed a 30-man committee to supervise the restructuring of the ASU.

DIPLOMATIC REPRESENTATION

EMBASSIES ACCREDITED TO EGYPT

(In Cairo, unless otherwise stated)

(E) Embassy.

Afghanistan: 59 Sh. Oruba (Heliopolis) (E); *Ambassador:* Dr. ABDUL WAHAB KARIM.

Albania: 29 Sh. Ismail Muhammad (Zamalek) (E); *Ambassador:* ZIKI AGOLLI.

Algeria: 14 Sh. Brazil (Zamalek) (E); *Ambassador:* (vacant).

Argentina: 8 Sh. As-Saleh Ayoub (Zamalek) (E); *Ambassador:* OMAR M. VAQUIR.

Australia: 1097 Corniche el Nil (Garden City) (E); *Ambassador:* CHARLES ROBIN ASHWIN.

Austria: 21 Sh. Sadd El-Aaly (Dokki) (E); *Ambassador:* Dr. OTTO MASCHKE.

Bahrain: 13A Sh. Sadd El-Aaly (Dokki) (E); *Ambassador:* ABDEL AZIZ SAAD EL-SHAMLAN.

Bangladesh: 18 Souria St., Madinet El Mohandessine (Dokki) (E); *Ambassador:* MUHAMMAD ATA ELRAHMAN.

Belgium: 20 Kamel El Shnaoui St. (Garden City) (E); *Ambassador:* PIERRE ANCIEUX HENRI DE FAVEAUX.

Bolivia: 6 Rue Nawal (Dokki) (E); *Ambassador:* (vacant).

Brazil: 1125 Corniche El Nil (Maspiro) (E); *Ambassador:* LUIZ BASTIAN PINTO.

Bulgaria: 36 El Messaha St. (Dokki) (E); *Ambassador:* Dr. PETAR VUTOV.

Burma: 24 Rue Muhammad Mazhar (Zamalek) (E); *Ambassador:* U THA TUN.

Burundi: 8 Abdel Rahman El Rafei St. (Dokki) (E); *Ambassador:* PROTAIS MANGONA.

Cambodia: 2 Tahawia St. (Giza) (E); *Ambassador:* SARIN CHHAK.

Cameroon: 42 Babel St. (Dokki) (E); *Ambassador:* MBOMBO NJOUYA IBRAHIM.

Canada: 6 Sh. Muhammad Fahmy El Sayed (Garden City) (E); *Ambassador:* JEAN FOUCHETTE.

Central African Republic: 10 Sh. Sadd El-Aaly (Dokki) (E); *Ambassador:* MICHEL ADAMA TAMBOUX.

Chad: 26 Sh. El Korum-Midan El Nasr (Dokki) (E); *Ambassador:* MARWAN HAIMARI.

Chile: 5 Sh. Chagaret El-Dorr (Zamalek) (E); *Ambassador:* RAMÓN VIVEROS DURAN.

China, People's Republic: 14 Sh. Bahgat Aly (Zamalek) (E); *Ambassador:* CHANG TUNG.

Colombia: 15 Sh. Aboul Feda (Zamalek) (E); *Ambassador:* (vacant).

Congo People's Republic: 12 Midan El Nasr (Dokki) (E); *Ambassador:* GABRIEL EBENGOU.

Cuba: 2 Al Anab St. (Dokki) (E); *Ambassador:* Dr CARLOS ALFARAS.

Cyprus: 23a Ismail Muhammad St. (Zamalek) (E); *Ambassador:* ANTIS G. SOTERIADES.

Czechoslovakia: 43 Sh. Muhammad Mazhar (Zamalek) (E); *Ambassador:* LUMIR HANAK.

Denmark: 12 Sh. Hassan Sabri (Zamalek) (E); *Ambassador:* KJELD V. MORTENSEN.

Ecuador: 8 Salamlek St. (Garden City) (E); *Ambassador:* JOSÉ MONTERO TORO.

El Salvador: Madrid, Spain (E).

Ethiopia: 12 Midan Bahlawi (Dokki) (E); *Ambassador:* ATO GETACHEV MEKASHA.

Finland: 2 El-Malek El-Fadel (Zamalek) (E); *Ambassador:* JOEL PEKURI.

France: 29 Sh. Giza (E); *Ambassador:* BRUNO DE LEUSSE.

German Democratic Republic: 13 Sh. Hussein Wassef (Dokki) (E); *Ambassador:* HANS-JOACHIM RADDE.

Germany, Federal Republic: 20 Boulos Hanna St. (E). *Ambassador:* HANS-GEORG STELTZER.

Ghana: Villa 24, Sh. 22 (Dokki) (E); *Ambassador:* Maj.-Gen. CLENLAND COFIE BRUCE.

Greece: 18 Sh. Aïcha El-Taïmouria (Garden City) (E); *Ambassador:* GEORGES PAPADOPOULOS.

Guatemala: Rome, Italy (E).

Guinea: 47 Sh. Muhammad Mazhar (Zamalek) (E); *Ambassador:* KALIL FOFANA.

Hungary: 36 Sh. Muhammad Mazhar (Zamalek) (E); *Ambassador:* LAJOS S. NAGY.

India: 5 Aziz Abaza St. (Zamalek) (E); *Ambassador:* ASHOK BALKRISHNA BHADKAMKAR.

Indonesia: 13 Sh. Aïcha El-Taïmouria (Garden City) (E); *Ambassador:* MOHAMED SHARIF PADMADISASTRA.

Iran: 11 Sh. Okba (Dokki) (E); *Ambassador:* KHOSROW KHOSROVANI.

Iraq: 9 Sh. Muhammad Mazhar (Zamalek) (E); *Ambassador:* SAMIR ABDUL AZIZ AL-NAJM.

Italy: 15 Sh. El Salamlik (Garden City) (E); *Ambassador:* GIAN LUIGI FERRETI.

Japan: 14 Sh. Ibrahim Naguib (Garden City) (E); *Ambassador:* TSUTOMU WADA.

Jordan: 6 Sh. El-Gohainy (Dokki) (E); *Ambassador:* FAWAZ SALIM ABOU EL GHONM.

Kenya: 8 Madina El Munawara (Dokki) (E); *Ambassador:* OMAR AHMED FAKIH.

Korea, Democratic People's Republic: 6 El Saleh Ayoub St. (Zamalek) (E); *Ambassador:* KIM BYONG HO.

Kuwait: 4 Montaza St. (Zamalek) (E); *Ambassador:* HAMAD ISSA EL-RUJAIE.

Lebanon: 5 Sh. Ahmed Nessim (Guizeh) (E); *Ambassador* MOHAMED SABRA.

Liberia: 7 El Batal Ahmed St. (Dokki) (E); *Ambassador:* MARTINUS L. JOHNSON.

Libya: 7 Sh. Saleh Ayoub (Zamalek) (E); *Ambassador:* MILOD EL SEDIK RAMADAN.

Malaysia: 7 Wadi El Nil St. (Agouza) (E); *Ambassador:* SHAHUDDIN MUHAMMAD TAIB.

Mali: 36 Bhagat Ali St. (Zamalek) (E); *Ambassador:* BOUBACAR DIALLO.

Mauritania: 31 Souria St. (Dokki) (E); *Ambassador:* ISMAIL OULD MOULOUD.

Mexico: 5 Dar El Chifa (E); *Ambassador:* ROBERTO DE ROSENWEIG DIAZ.

Mongolia: 3 Midan El Nasr (Dokki) (E); *Ambassador:* TSEVEENGOMBYE DEMIDDAGVA.

Morocco: 10 Sh. Saleh El Dine (Zamalek) (E); *Ambassador:* ABDELLATIF LARAKI.

Nepal: 19 Rue Tiba (Madinet El Kodah) (E); *Ambassador:* BISHWA PRADHAN.

Netherlands: 18 Sh. Hassan Sabri (Zamalek) (E); *Ambassador:* GERRIT WILLIEM VAN BARNWELD KOOY.

Nigeria: 13 Sh. Gabalaya (Zamalek) (E); *Ambassador:* HARUNA BIN MUSA.

Norway: 8 Gezira St. (Zamalek) (E); *Ambassador:* TANCRED IBSEN (also accred. to Ethiopia, Jordan, Lebanon and Sudan).

Oman: 30 Montaza St. (Zamalek) (E); *Ambassador:* MALALLAH ALI HABIB.

Pakistan: 8 El Saluli St. (Dokki) (E); *Ambassador:* AHMED SAEED KIRMANI.

Panama: 8 Salamlek St., Apt. 41 (E); *Ambassador:* (vacant).

Peru: 9 Shagaret El Dorr St. (E); *Ambassador:* ENRIQUE DE LOS HEROS RIQUELME.

Philippines: 5 Sh. Ibn El-Walid (Dokki) (E); *Ambassador:* (vacant).

Poland: 5 Sh. Aziz Osman (Zamalek) (E); *Ambassador:* TADEUSZ OLECHOWSKI.

Portugal: 15a Mansour Muhammad St. (Zamalek) (E); *Ambassador:* Dr. DUARTE VAZ PINTO.

Qatar: 10 El Semar St. (Dokki) (E); *Ambassador:* ALI SOLTAN AL ALEY.

Romania: 6 Sh. El Kamel Muhammad (Zamalek) (E); *Ambassador:* PETRU BURLACU.

Saudi Arabia: Villa 12, Sh. El Kamel Mohamed (Zamalek) (E); *Ambassador:* Shaikh FUAD AHMAD NAZIR.

Senegal: 2 Sh. Ahmed Ragheb (Garden City) (E); *Ambassador:* MAMADOU IBRA NGOM.

Sierra Leone: 56 Sh. Amman (Dokki) E); *Ambassador:* Alhaji SHEKH GIBRIL.

Singapore: 40 Babel St. (Dokki) (E); *Ambassador:* KURBA RAM VUJ.

Somalia: 38 Rue El Shahid Abdel Moneim Riad (Dokki) (E); *Ambassador:* ABDULLAHI ADAN AHMED.

Spain: 28 Ahmed Hechmat St. (Zamalek) (E); *Ambassador:* MANUEL ALABARAT.

Sri Lanka: 8 Sh. Yehia Ibrahim (Zamalek) (E); *Ambassador:* H. O. WIJEGOONAWARDENA.

Sudan: 4 Sh. El Ibrahimi (Garden City) (E); *Ambassador:* AHMED SALAH BOKHARI.

Sweden: 4 Sh. Sadd El Aali (Dokki) (E); *Ambassador:* LARS PETRUS FOLKE VON CELSING.

Switzerland: 10 Sh. Abdel Khalek Saroit (E); *Ambassador:* DANIEL GAGNEBIN.

Syria: 14 Ahmad Hechmat St. (Zamalek) (E); *Ambassador:* EZZEDINE NEISEE.

Tanzania: 9 Abdel Hamid Lotfi St. (Dokki) (E); *Ambassador:* CHRISTOPHER P. NGAIZA.

Thailand: 2 Sh. El Malek El Afdal (Zamalek) (E); *Ambassador:* SUNTHORN SUWANSARAN.

Trinidad and Tobago: Beirut, Lebanon (E).

Tunisia: 26 Sh. El Guezira (Zamalek) (E); *Ambassador:* SALAH EDDINE ABDELLAH.

Turkey: Avenue El Nil (Giza) (E); *Ambassador:* FAHIR ALACAM.

Uganda: 9 Midan El Missaha (Dokki) (E); *Ambassador:* Lt.-Col. JACK W. BUNYENYEZI.

U.S.S.R.: 95 Sh. El Giza (Giza) (E); *Ambassador:* VLADIMIR POLIAKOV.

United Arab Emirates: 55 Rue Mohammad Mazhar (E); *Ambassador:* TARYAM OMRAN TARYAM.

United Kingdom: Ahmed Ragheb St. (Garden City) (E); *Ambassador:* Sir PHILIP ADAMS.

U.S.A.: 5 America El Latinia St. (Garden City) (E); *Ambassador:* HERMANN EILTS.

Uruguay: 6 Sh. Loutfallah (Zamalek) (E); *Ambassador:* SILVIO A. CORRADI IRISARRI.

Vatican City: 5 Sh. Muhammad Mazhar (Zamalek) (Apostolic Nunciature); *Nuncio:* Mgr. ACHILLE GLORIEUX.

Venezuela: 5 Sh. Mansour Muhammad (Zamalek) (E); *Ambassador:* Col. JESÚS MANUEL PÉREZ MORÁLES.

Viet-Nam, Democratic Republic: 21 Sh. Giza (Giza) (E); *Ambassador:* NGUYEN HUY THU.

Viet-Nam, Provisional Revolutionary Government of South: 24 Mossadek St. (Dokki) (E); *Ambassador:* TRAN VAN HOA.

Yemen Arab Republic: 28 Sh. Amin El Rafei (Dokki) (E); *Ambassador:* HUSSEIN M. EL MASWARI.

Yemen, People's Democratic Republic: Soliman Abaza St. (Dokki) (E); *Ambassador:* ABDEL-MALIK ISMAIL MUHAMMAD.

Yugoslavia: 33 Sh. El Mansour Muhammad (Zamalek) (E); *Ambassador:* AUGUSTIN PAPIC.

Zaire: 5 Mansour Mohammad St. (Zamalek) (E); *Ambassador:* GIALO BINA TE WAPINDA.

Zambia: 13 Souria St. (Madinet El Mohandessine) (E); *Ambassador:* MATIYA NGALANDE.

Egypt also recognizes Costa Rica, Gabon, the Gambia, Guinea-Bissau, Guyana, Haiti, Honduras, Iceland, Ireland, the Ivory Coast, Lesotho, Madagascar, Malta, Mauritius, Mozambique, New Zealand, Nicaragua, Niger, Rwanda, Swaziland, Togo and the Upper Volta.

JUDICIAL SYSTEM

The Courts of Law in Egypt are basically divided into four categories as follows:

1. *The Supreme Court* (called *The Court of Cassation*)
2. *The Courts of Appeal*
3. *The Primary Tribunals*
4. *The Summary Tribunals*

Each Court contains criminal and civil chambers.

1. The Supreme Court

The highest Court of Law in Egypt. Its sessions are held at Cairo and its jurisdiction covers the whole Egyptian territory.

Final judgements rendered in criminal and civil matters may be referred to the Supreme Court—by the accused or the Public Prosecution in criminal matters, and by any of the litigants in civil matters—in cases of misapplications or misinterpretations of the law as applied by the competent court in final judgement, as well as in cases of irregularity in the form of the judgement or the procedures having effect on that judgement.

The Supreme Court is composed of the Chief Justice, four Deputy-Chief Justices and thirty-six Justices.

2. Courts of Appeal

There are six Courts of Appeal situated in the more important Governorates of Egypt: Cairo, Alexandria, Asyut, Mansura, Tanta, and Beni Suef. Each of these courts contains a criminal chamber, *The Assize Court*, to try cases of felonies, and a civil chamber to hear appeals filed by any of the litigants in civil matters against a judgement rendered by the primary tribunal, where the law so permits.

President in Cairo: M. MAHMOUD ABD-EL-LATIF.

3. Primary Tribunals

In each Governorate, there is a Primary Tribunal, each of which contains several chambers. Each chamber is composed of three Judges. Some of these chambers try criminal cases, whilst others hear civil litigations.

Primary Tribunals sit as Courts of Appeal in certain cases, according to circumstances.

4. Summary Tribunals

Summary Tribunals are branches of the Primary Tribunals and are situated in the different districts of Egypt. Each of these tribunals is composed of a single Judge.

Summary Tribunals hear civil and criminal matters of minor importance according to certain details.

The Public Prosecution

The Public Prosecution is headed by the Attorney-General and consists of a large number of Attorneys, Chief Prosecutors and Prosecutors, who are distributed among the various districts of Egypt. The Public Prosecution is represented at all criminal Courts and also at litigation in certain civil matters. Furthermore, the enforcement of judgement rendered in criminal cases is controlled and supervised by the Public Prosecution.

Attorney-General: AHMAD MUSA.

The Supreme Judicial Council

This Council exists to guarantee the independence of the judicial system from outside interference. Under the presidency of the Chief Justice, the Supreme Judicial Council contains the following members:

the Chief Justice

two Deputy Chief Justices

the Under-Secretary of State for the Ministry of Justice

the Attorney-General

the President of the Court of Appeal in Cairo

the President of the Primary Tribunal in Cairo.

All matters concerning the promotion, discipline or otherwise of the members of the judicial system are referred to this Council.

An Arbitration Bureau was set up in 1966 to investigate cases between state and public sector organizations.

RELIGION

Over 90 per cent of Egyptians are Muslims, and almost all of these follow Sunni tenets. The four tenets are represented in Egypt and all follow the Holy Koran and the Sunna. Villagers adhere strictly to Islamic rites and teachings. Since the Fatimide dynasty Egyptians have attached great importance to the decoration of their mosques. St. Mark is considered to be the first founder of the Coptic Church after Jesus. The Coptic Church is known historically as the Church of Alexandria or the Egyptian Coptic Orthodox Church, and is still considered the main Eastern church. There are over a million Copts in Egypt forming the largest religious minority, there is no discrimination of any kind against them, and they have contributed greatly to the cultural life of Egypt. Besides the Copts there are other Christian minorities numbering about a quarter of a million and consisting of Greek Orthodox, Roman Catholics, Armenians and Protestants. There is also a small Jewish minority.

Grand Sheikh of Al Azhar: Dr. ABDEL-HALIM MAHMOUD.

Grand Mufti of Egypt: Sheikh KHATIR MUHAM MUHAMMAD.

Coptic Orthodox Church: Anba Ruies Building, Ramses St., Abbasiya, Cairo; f. A.D. 61; Leader Pope SHENOUDA III; about 8 million followers in Egypt, Sudan, N. America, Canada, Australia.

Coptic Catholic Church: Patriarch Cardinal STEPHANOS I. SIDAROUSS, 34 Sh. Ibn Sandar, Koubbeh Bridge, Cairo; 4 dioceses; 120,000 mems.; publ. *Al Salah.*

Greek Catholic Patriarchate: P.O.B. 50076 Beirut, Lebanon; 16 rue Daher, Cairo; Patriarch of Antioch, of Alexandria and of Jerusalem His Beatitude MAXIMOS V HAKIM; 750,000 mems. in the Middle East.

Greek Orthodox Church: Patriarch NIKOLAUS VI.

Armenian Apostolic Church: 179 Ramses Ave., Cairo, P.O.B. 48-Faggala; Archbishop MAMPRE SIROUNIAN.

Armenian Catholic Patriarchate: 36 Mohammed Sabri Abou Alam Street, Cairo; Archbishop RAPHAEL BAYAN.

Maronite Church: 15 Hamdi Street, Daher, Cairo; Archbishop JOSEPH MERHI.

Jewish Community: Office of the Chief Rabbi, Rabbi HAIM DOUEK; 13 Sebil-el-Khazindar St., Abbassia, Cairo.

THE PRESS

Despite a high illiteracy rate the Egyptian press is well developed. Cairo is the biggest publishing centre in the Middle East.

Newspapers were placed under the control of the National Union by a decree of President Nasser in May 1960. Journalists were obliged to obtain licences from the National Union and publishing houses, hitherto free, were placed under its control. All the important newspapers and magazines are now owned by the Government, although the four big publishing houses of al-Ahram, Dar al-Hilal, Dar Akhbar al-Yom and Dar al-Gomhouriya, operate as separate entities and compete with each other commercially. Dar al-Hilal is concerned only with magazines and publishes *al-Mussawar, Hawa'a* and *al-Kawakeb.* Dar Akhbar al-Yom publishes the daily newspaper *al-Akhbar,* the weekly newspaper *Akhbar al-Yom* and the weekly magazines *Akher Saa* and *Al Guil el Gedid.*

Dar al Gomhouriya publishes the daily *al-Gomhouriya,* the daily English language paper *Egyptian Gazette,* the daily French newspaper *Le Progrès Egyptien* and the afternoon paper *al-Misaa.*

The most authoritative daily newspaper is the very old established *al-Ahram.* Other popular large circulation magazines are *Rose al-Youssef, Sabah al-Kheir* and *al Izaw w'al Television.*

In February 1974 President Sadat ended press censorship, except on military matters, and foreign correspondents in Cairo were relieved of the duty of submitting their reports, except those on military matters, for censorship.

In May 1975 President Sadat set up the Supreme Press Council, under the Chairmanship of the First Secretary of the Arab Socialist Union, to supervise the activities of journalists.

DAILIES

ALEXANDRIA

Barid al-Charikat: P.O.B. 813; f. 1952; Arabic; evening; commerce, finance, insurance and marine affairs, etc.; Editor S. BENEDUCCI; circ. 15,000.

al-Ittihad al-Misri: 13 Sharia Sidi Abdel Razzak; f. 1871; Arabic; evening; Propr. ANWAR MAHER FARAG; Dir. HASSAN MAHER FARAG.

Journal d'Alexandrie, Le: 1 Sharia Rolo; French; evening; Editor CHARLES ARCACHE.

Phare Egyptien, Le: 26 Avenue Hourriya; f. 1926; Greek-owned, French language; morning; independent; Editor ANTOINE GERONIMO.

Réforme, La: 8 Passage Sherif; f. 1895; French; noon; Propr. Comte AZIZ DE SAAB; circ. 7,000.

al-Safeer: 4 El-Sahafa St.; f. 1924; Arabic; evening; Editor MOSTAFA SHARAF.

Tachydromos-Egyptos: 4 Sharia Zangarol; f. 1882; Greek; morning; liberal; Publisher PENY COUTSOUMIS; Editor DINOS COUTSOUMIS; circ. 11,000.

CAIRO

al-Ahram (*The Pyramids*): Gallaa St.; f. 1875; Arabic; morning; independent; Editor ALI HAMDI EL GAMAL; circ. 400,000.

al-Akhbar: Dar Akhbar al-Yom, Sharia al-Sahafa; f. 1952; Arabic; independent; Editor MUSTAFA AMIN; circ. 695,000.

Arev: 3 Sharia Soliman Halaby; f. 1915; Armenian; evening; Editor AVEDIS YAPOUDJIAN.

Egyptian Gazette: 24 Sharia Galal; f. 1880; the only English daily; morning; Editor Dr. AMIN MOHAMED ABOUL-ENEIN; circ. 10,000.

al-Gomhouriya (*The Republic*): 24 Sharia Zakaria Ahmed; f. 1953; Arabic; morning; official organ of the Arab Socialist Union; Chief Editor M. B. BADAWI; circ. 250,000.

Houssaper: Armenian; circ. 1,500.

Journal d'Egypte, Le: 1 Borsa Guédida St.; f. 1950; French; morning; Propr. and Editor EDGARD GALLAD; circ. 13,000.

al-Misaa: 24 Sharia Zakaria Ahmed; Arabic; evening; Editor ABDEL MONEIM EL LAWI.; circ. 40,000.

Phos: 14 Zakaria Ahmed St.; f. 1896; Greek; morning; Editor S. PATERAS; Man. BASILE A. PATERAS; circ. 20,000.

Progrès Egyptien, Le: 24 Sharia Zakaria Ahmed; f. 1890; French; morning including Sundays; Editor MAURICE YACCARINI; circ. 14,500.

PERIODICALS

ALEXANDRIA

al Ahad Al Gedid: 88 al-Tatwig Street; Editor-in-Chief MAHMUD ABDEL MALAK KORITAM; General Manager MUHAMMAD KORITAM.

Alexandria Medical Journal: 4 G. Carducci; English, French and Arabic; quarterly; publ. by Alexandria Medical Asscn.; Editor AMIN RIDA; circ. 1,500.

Amitié Internationale: 59 Avenue Hourriya; f. 1957; publ. by Asscn. Egypt. d'Amitié Inter.; Arabic and French; quarterly; Editor Dr. ZAKI BADAOUI.

L'Annuaire des Sociétés Egyptiennes par Actions: 23 Midan Tahrir; f. 1930; annually in December; French; Propr. ELIE I. POLITI; Editor OMAR EL-SAYED MOURSI.

L'Echo Sportif: 7 rue de l'Archevêché; French; weekly; Propr. MICHEL BITTAR.

L'Economiste Egyptien: 11 rue de la Poste, Alexandria; P.O. Box 847; f. 1901; weekly; Propr. MARGUERITE HOSNY.

Egypte-Sports-Cinéma: 7 Avenue Hourriya; French; weekly; Editor EMILE ASSAAD.

Egyptian Cotton Gazette: P.O.B. 433; organ of the Alexandria Cotton Exporters Association; English; twice yearly; Chief Editor Dr. FOUAD A. TAWFIK.

Egyptian Cotton Statistics: English; weekly.

Gazette d'Orient, La: 5 rue de l'Ancienne Bourse; Propr. MAURICE BETITO.

Guide des Industries: 2 Sharia Adib; French; annual; Editor SIMON A. BARANIS.

Informateur des Assurances: 1 Sharia Adib; f. 1936; French; monthly; Propr. ELIE I. POLITI; Editor SIMON A. BARANIS.

Médecine d'Egypte: 298 rue Port Said, Cléopatra; Editor HUBERT DE LEUSSE; French.

Réforme Illustrée, La: 8 Passage Sherif; f. 1925; French; weekly; Propr. Comte AZIZ DE SAAB; circ. 20,000.

Répertoire Permanent de Législation Egyptienne: 27 Ave. El Guesch, Chatby-les-Bains; f. 1932; French and Arabic; Editor V. SISTO.

Revue des Questions Douanières: 2 Sharia Sinan; Arabic; monthly; economics and agriculture; Propr. ALY MUHAMMAD ALY.

Revue Economique Trimestrielle: c/o Banque de Port-Said, 18 Talaat Harb St., Alexandria; French (f. 1929) and Arabic (f. 1961) editions; quarterly; Editor: MAHMOUD SAMY EL ADAWAY.

Sanaet El-Nassig (*L'Industrie Textile*): 5 rue de l'Archevêché; Arabic and French; monthly; Editor PHILIPPE COIAS.

L'Universitaire—Science et Techniques: 298 Sharia Port Said, Cléopatra; French; scientific and technical; quarterly; Editor HUBERT DE LEUSSE.

Voce d'Italia: 90 Sharia Farahde; Italian; fortnightly; Editor R. AVELLINO.

CAIRO

Actualité: 28 Sharia Sherif Pasha; French; weekly; Dir. and Propr. GEORGES TASSO.

Akhbar al-Yom: 6 Sharia al-Sahafa; f. 1944; Arabic; weekly (Saturday); Editor-in-Chief IHSAN ABDEL KODDOUS; Editing Man. SAID SONBOL; circ.1,102,000.

Akher Saa: Dar Akhbar al-Yom, Sharia al-Sahafa; f. 1932; Arabic; weekly (Wednesday); independent; Editor-in-Chief ANIS MANSOUR; circ. 184,500.

al-Ahd al-Goumhouri: 132 Sharia Kalaa; Editor ABDEL-KHALEK TAKIA.

al Ahram Al Iqtisadi: United Arab Press, Gallaa St.; economic and political affairs; owned by *Al Ahram*; circ. 12,000.

al-Azhar: Sharia al-Azhar; Arabic; Dir MUHAMMAD FARID WAGDI.

al-Doctor: 8 Hoda Shaarawy St.; f. 1947; Arabic; monthly; Editor Dr. AHMAD M. KAMAL; circ. 30,000.

al-Fussoul: 17 Sharia Sherif Pasha; Arabic; monthly; Propr. and Chief Editor MUHAMMAD ZAKI ABDEL KADER.

al-Garida al-Togaria al-Misriya: 25 Sharia Nubar Pasha; f. 1921; Arabic; weekly; circ. 7,000.

al-Hilal: Dar al-Hilal, 16 Sharia Muhammad Ezz El-Arab; f. 1895; Arabic; monthly; Editor SALEH GAWDAT.

al-Hurriya: Arabic; weekly; published by Arab Socialist Union; Editor-in-Chief MUHAMMAD SUBAIH.

al-Izaa wal-Television: 13 Sharia Muhammad Ezz El-Arab; f. 1935; Arabic; weekly; Editor RAGA EL AZABI; circ. 120,000.

al-Kawakeb (*The Stars*): Dar al-Hilal, 16 Sharia Muhammad Ezz El-Arab; f. 1952; Arabic; film magazine; Editor KAMAL EL-NAGMI; circ. 38,500.

al-Mukhtar: Dar Akhbar al-Yom, Sharia al-Sahafa; f. 1956; Arabic edition of *Readers' Digest*; Editor MOHAMED ZAKI ABDEL KADER; circ. 50,000.

al-Mussawar: Dar al-Hilal, 16 Sharia Muhammad Ezz El-Arab; f. 1924; Arabic weekly; Editor FIKRY ABAZA; circ. 162,000.

al-Sabah: 4 Sharia Muhammad Said Pasha; f. 1922; Arabic; weekly; Editor MOSTAFA EL-KACHACHI.

al-Tahrir: 5 Sharia Naguib-Rihani; Arabic; weekly; Editor ABDEL-AZIZ SADEK.

al-Talia (*Vanguard*): f. 1965; left wing; monthly.

Ana Wa Inta: Sharia Central; Arabic; monthly; Editor MOHAMED HASSAN.

Arab Observer: published by the Middle East News Agency, 11 Sh. Sahafa; f. 1960; weekly international news magazine; English; has now incorporated *The Scribe*; Editor-in-Chief Dr. ABDEL HAMID EL-BATRIK.

Contemporary Thought: University of Cairo; quarterly; Editor Dr. Z. N. MAHMOUD.

Echos: 15 Sharia Mahmoud Bassiouni; f. 1947; French; weekly; Dir. and Propr. GEORGES ORFALI.

Egyptian Chamber of Commerce Bulletin: 4 Midan Falaki.

Egyptian Directory, The: 19 Sharia Abdel Khalek Sarwat, B.P. 500; f. 1887; French and English; annual; Man. and Editor TAWHID KAMAL.

Egyptian Mail: 24 Sharia Zakaria Ahmed; f. 1910; English; weekly; Editor Dr. AMIN ABOUL-ENEIN.

Femme Nouvelle, La: 48 Sharia Kasr-el-Nil; French; twice yearly; Editor DORIA SHAFIK.

German-Arab Trade: 2 Sharia Sherif Pasha; German, English, Arabic; Editor DIETER SCHIERLOH; circ. 6,000.

Ghorfet al-Kahira (*Journal of Cairo Chamber of Commerce*): 4 Midan Falaky; Arabic; monthly.

Hawa'a (*Eve*): Dar al-Hilal, 16 Sharia Muhammad Ezz El-Arab; women's magazine; Arabic; weekly.

Images: Dar Al-Hilal, 16 Sharia Muhammad Ezz El-Arab; French; illustrated; weekly; Editors EMILE and CHOUCRI ZEIDAN.

Industrial Egypt: P.O.B. 251, 26A Sharia Sherif Pasha, Cairo; f. 1924; Bulletin of the Federation of Egyptian Industries; English and Arabic; quarterly; Editor Eng. GAMIL EL-SABBAN.

Industry and Trade Information: 13 Sharia Abdel Hamid Said; English; weekly; commercial and industrial bulletin; Dir. and Propr. NICOLAS STAVRI; Editor N. GHANEM.

Informateur Financier et Commercial: 24 Sharia Soliman Pasha; f. 1929; weekly; Dir. HENRI POLITI; circ. 15,000.

Kitab al-Hilal: 16 Sharia Muhammad Ezz El-Arab; monthly; Proprs. EMILE and CHOUKRI ZEIDAN.

Lewa al-Islam: 11 Sharia Sherif Pasha; Arabic; monthly; Propr. AHMED HAMZA; Editor MUHAMMAD ALY SHETA.

Lotus Magazine (*Afro-Asian Writings*): 104 Kasr El Eini St.; f. 1968; quarterly; English, French and Arabic; Editor YOUSSEF EL SEBAI.

Magalet al-Mohandeseen: 28 Avenue Ramses; f. 1945; published by The Engineers' Syndicate; Arabic and English; ten times a year; Editor and Sec. MAHMOUD SAMI ABDEL KAWI.

Medical Journal of Cairo University: Manyal University Hospital, Sharia Kasr el-Aini; Kasr el-Aini Clinical Society; English; quarterly.

Megakkah al-Zerayia: monthly; Arabic; agriculture; circ. 30,000.

The Middle East Observer: 8 Chawarby St.; f. 1955; weekly; English; specializing in economics of Middle East and African markets; also publishes supplements on law, foreign trade and tenders; Man. Owner AHMED FODA; Chief Editors A. W. MORSI, AHMED SABRI; circ. 30,000.

Progrès Dimanche: 24 Sharia Galal; French; weekly; Editor M. YACCARINI.

Riwayat al-Hilal: 16 Sharia Muhammad Ezz El-Arab; Arabic; monthly; Proprs. EMILE and CHOUKRI ZEIDAN.

Rose el Youssef: 89A Kasr el Ainei St.; f. 1925; Arabic; weekly; political; circulates throughout all Arab countries, includes monthly English section, Chair. KAMEL ZOHEIRY; Editor ABDUL RAHMAN AL-SHARQAWI; Editor English section IBRAHIM EZZAT; Man. ABDEL GHANI ABDEL-FATTAH; circ. 35,000.

Sabah al-Kheir: 18 Sharia Mohamed Said; Arabic; weekly; light entertainment.

Tchehreh Nema: 14 Sharia Hassan El-Akbar (Abdine); f. 1904; Iranian; monthly; political, literary and general; Editor MANUCHEHR TCHEHREH NEMA MOADEB ZADEH.

Up-to-Date International Industry: 10 Sharia Galal; Arabic and English; foreign trade journal.

NEWS AGENCIES

Middle East News Agency: 4 Sharia Sherrifin, Cairo; f. 1955; regular service in Arabic, English and French; Chair. MOHAMED ABDEL GAWAD.

Misr Egyptian News Agency: 43 Sharia Ramses, Cairo.

FOREIGN BUREAUX

Agence France Presse: 33 Kasr El Nil St., Cairo; Chief JEAN-PIERRE JOULIN.

ANSA: 19 Sh. Abdel Khalek Sarwat, Cairo; Chief MARIO RISPOLI.

AP: 33 Kasr El Nil, Cairo; Chief HARRY A. DUNPHY.

Bulgarian Telegraph Agency: 13 Sh. Muhammad Kamel Morsi, Aguza, Cairo; Chief DIMITER MASLAROV.

Četeka (Czechoslovak News Agency): 7 Sh. Hasan Asem, Zamalek, Cairo.

Deutsche Presse Agentur (dpa): 33 Kasr el Nil St., Apt. 13/4, Cairo.

Kyodo News Service: Flat 12, 33 Abdel Khalek Tharawta, Cairo; Chief HIDEO YAMASHITA.

Reuters: Apt. 43, Immobilia Bldgs., 26 Sh. Sherif Pasha, Cairo, P.O.B. 2040.

UPI: 4 Sh. Eloui, P.O.B. 872, Cairo; Chief RAY N. MOSELEY.

PUBLISHERS

Egyptian General Organization for Publishing and Printing: 117 Corniche el Nil St., Cairo; affil. to Min. of Culture.

ALEXANDRIA

Alexandria University Press: Shatby.

Artec: 10 Sharia Stamboul.

Dar Nashr ath-Thagata.

Egyptian Book Centre: A. D. Christodoulou and Co., 5 Sharia Adib; f. 1950.

Egyptian Printing and Publishing House: Ahmed El Sayed Marouf, 59, Safia Zaghoul; f. 1947.

Maison Egyptienne d'Editions: Ahmed El Sayed Marouf, Sharia Adib; f. 1950.

Maktab al-Misri al-Hadith li-t-Tiba wan-Nashr: 7 Nobar St.; also at 2 Sherif St., Cairo; Man. AHMAD YEHIA.

CAIRO

Akhbar El Yom Publishing House: 6 Sharia al-Sahafa; f. 1944; publishes *al-Akhbar* (daily), *Akhbar al-Yom* (weekly), and colour magazine *Akher Saa*; Pres. ALI AMIN; Dir.-Gen. Dr. SALIB BOUTROS.

Al-Hilal Publishing House: 16 Sharia Muhammad Ezz El-Arab; f. 1895; publishes *Al-Hilal, Riwayat Al-Hilal, Kitab Al-Hilal* (monthlies); *Al Mussawar, Al Kawakeb, Hawa* (weeklies).

Dar al-Gomhouriya: 24 Sharia Galal; publications include the dailies, *al-Gomhouriya, al-Misaa, Egyptian Gazette* and *Le Progrès Egyptien*; Pres. ABDEL MONEIM EL LAWI.

Dar al-Hilal: Al Hilal Bldg., 16 Sharia Mohammed Ezz El-Arab; f. 1892; publishes magazines only, including *al-Mussawar, Hawa'a* and *al-Kawakeb*; Pres. FIKRI ABAZA.

Dar al Kitab al Arabi: Misr Printing House, Sharia Noubar, Bab al Louk, Cairo; f. 1968; Man. Dir. Dr. SAHAIR AL KALAMAWI.

Dar al Maaref Egypt: 1119 Cornich El-Nil St.; f. 1890; Arabic books in all fields; distributor of books in English, French and German; Man. Dir. Dr. SAYED ABUL NAGA.

Documentation and Research Centre for Education (Ministry of Education): 33 Falaky St.; f. 1956; Dir. Mrs. ZEINAB M. MEHREZ; bibliographies, directories, information and education bulletins.

Editions Horus: 1 Midan Soliman Pasha.

Editions le Progrès: 6 Sharia Sherif Pasha; Propr. WADI CHOUKRI.

Editions et Publications des Pères Jésuites: 1 rue Boustan al Maksi, Faggala; scientific and religious publications; Dir. H. DE LEUSSE.

Editions Universitaires d'Egypte, Les: Alla El-Dine El-Chiati and Co.; 41 Sharia Sherif Pasha.

Higher University Council for Arts, Letters and Sciences: University of Cairo.

Imprimerie Argus: 10 Sharia Galal; Propr. SOCRATE SARRAFIAN.

Lagnat al Taalif Wal Targama Wal Nashr (*Committee for Writing, Translating and Publishing Books*): 9 Sharia El-Kerdassi (Abdine).

Librairie La Renaissance D'Egypte (Hassan Muhammad & Sons): 9 Adly St., P.O.B. 2172; f. 1930; Man. HASSAN MUHAMMAD; religion, history, geography, medicine, architecture, economics, politics, law, children's books, atlases, dictionaries.

Maktabet Misr: P.O.B. 16, Faggalah, Cairo; f. 1932; publ. wide variety of fiction, biographies and textbooks for schools and universities; Man. AMIR SAID GOUDA A SAHHAR.

Middle East Publishing Co.: 29 Rue Abdel Khalek Sarwat.

Mohamed Abbas Sid Ahmed: 55 Sharia Nubar.

National Library Press (*Dar al Kutub*): Midan Ahmed Maher; bibliographic works.

New Publications: J. Meshaka and Co., 5 Sharia Maspero.

The Public Organization for Books and Scientific Appliances: Cairo University, Orman, Ghiza; f. 1965; state organization publishing academic books for universities, higher institutes, etc.; also imports books, periodicals and scientific appliances; Chair. KAMIL SEDDIK; Vice-Chair. FATTHY LABIB.

Senouhy Publishers: 54 Sharia Abdel-Khalek Sarwat; f. 1956; Dirs. LEILA A. FADEL, OMAR RASHAD.

Other Cairo publishers include: *Dar al-Fikr al-Arabi, Dar al-Fikr al-Hadith Li-t-Tab wan-Nashr, Dar wa Matabi, Dar al-Nahda al-Arabiya, Dar al-Misriya Li-t-Talif wat-Tardjma, Dar al-Qalam, Dar ath-Thagapa, Majlis al-Ala Li-Riyyat al-Funun, Maktaba Ain Shams, Maktaba al-Andshilu al-Misriya, Maktabat al-Chandshi, Maktabat al-Nahira al-Hadith, Markaz Tasjil al-Athar al-Misriya, Matbaat ar-Risala, al-Qaumiya li-t-Tibaa wan-Nashr-Wizarat az-Ziraa Maslahat al-Basatin.*

RADIO AND TELEVISION

Egyptian Radio and Television Corporation: Cairo; f. 1971; supervised by Dep. Prime Minister and affil. to Ministry of Culture and Information.

Société Egyptienne de Publicité: 24-26 Sharia Zakaria Ahmed, Cairo; f. 1906; handles all advertising media in Egypt, including radio, TV and Suez Canal advertising panels; affil. to Al Tahrir Printing and Publishing House; Dep. Dir. Gen. KHEDR MOHAMED ABDEL SALEM.

RADIO

Egyptian Broadcasting Corporation: Corniche el Nil, Cairo; f. 1928; 169 hours daily; Chair. MOHAMED MAHMOUD SHAABAN; Dir.-Gen. Arabic Programmes SAFIA EL MOHANDES; Dir.-Gen. Foreign Programmes MOHAMED ISMAIL MOHAMED.

Home service programmes in Arabic, English, French, Armenian, German, Greek and Italian; foreign services in Hebrew, Persian, Spanish, Bengali, Turkish, Folani, Malawi, Shona, Lingala, Yoruba, Dankali, English, Swahili, Urdu, Indonesian, Hindi, Somali, Russian, Sosotho, Sindebek, Amharic, Wolof, French, Hausa, German, Siami, Pushtu, Portuguese, Italian, Zulu, Nianja, Thai, Bambra, Arabic. *Broadcasting and TV* (weekly), *Broadcasting Art* (quarterly).

Middle East Radio: Société Egyptienne de Publicité, 24-26 Sharia Zakaria Ahmed, Cairo; f. 1964; commercial service with 500-kW. transmitter; U.K. Agents: Radio and Television Services (Middle East) Ltd., 21 Hertford St., London, W.1.

In 1973 there were 30 million radio receivers and 15 million television sets.

TELEVISION

Egyptian Television Organization: Corniche el Nil, Cairo; f. 1960; 150 hours weekly (two channels); Chair. ABDEL HAMID YOUNES; Dir.-Gen. Programmes Mrs. SAMIHA AB EL-RAHMAN.

FINANCE

BANKING

(cap.=capital; p.u.=paid up; dep.=deposits; m.=million; amounts in £ Egyptian)

The whole banking system was nationalized in 1961.

CENTRAL BANK

Central Bank of Egypt: 31 Sharia Kasr-el-Nil, Cairo; f. 1961; cap. 3.0m., dep. 576m. (December 1973) Governor AHMED ZANDO.

COMMERCIAL BANKS

Arabic Real Estate Bank: Cairo; Vice-Pres. HANAFY LABIB HUSEIN.

Egyptian Real Estate Bank: Cairo; Gov. MOHAMED KAMEL ABASS.

Bank of Alexandria, S.A.E.; 6 Salah Salem St., Alexandria; f. 1864; p.u. cap. 3m., dep. 270m. (December 1973); 80 brs.; incorporated Industrial Bank 1971; Pres. AHMED ABDEL GHAFFAR.

Banque du Caire: 22 Adly St., P.O.B. 1495, Cairo; f. 1952; cap. 2.5m., dep. 215m. (Dec. 1973); Chair. HASSAN ZAKI AHMED; Gen. Mans. and Dirs. MUHAMMAD ABDEL LATIF DAHABA, MAHMOUD FAHMY LABAN, MUHAMMAD SADEK ALI.

Banque Misr, S.A.E.: 151 Sharia Mohamed Farid, Cairo; f. 1920; nationalized 1960; incorporated Bank of Suez and Banque Collectivité Financière 1964; absorbed Banque de Port Said 1971; 197 brs.; cap. 4m., res. 37.8m. (December 1973); Chair. and Man. Dir. AHMED FOUAD; publ. *Economic Bulletin.*

National Bank of Egypt, S.A.E.; 24 Sharia Sherif Pasha, Cairo; f. 1898; nationalized 1960; handles all Egyptian import and export operations; cap. and reserves 14.0m., dep. 345.9m. (December 1973); 89 brs.; Chair. Dr. HAMED A. EL SAYEH; publ. *Quarterly Economic Bulletin.*

DEVELOPMENT BANKS

Arab African Bank: 44 Abdel-Khalek Sarwat St., Cairo; f. 1964; cap. 20m.; undertakes all types of foreign trade finance, investment in development projects in Arab and African countries; Chair. and Man. Dir. SULAIMAN AHMED EL HADDAD (Kuwait); Dep. Chair. and Man. Dir. MAHMOUD BAHIR ONSY (Egypt); Founders and shareholders: Ministry of Finance and Oil (Kuwait); Central Bank of Egypt (Egypt); Rafidain Bank (Iraq); Ministry of Finance (Qatar); Central Bank of Algeria (Algeria); Ministry of Finance (Jordan) etc.; branches in Beirut, Dubai, Muscat and Abu Dhabi.

Arab International Bank: 35 Abdel Khalek Sarwat St., Cairo; f. 1971 as Egyptian International Bank; aims to promote trade and investment in Egypt, Libya and other Arab states; Chair. ABDUL-MONEIM KAISSOUNI.

Egyptian General Agricultural and Co-operative Organisation: 110 El-Kasr El-Eini St., Cairo; f. 1964; formerly *Agricultural Credits and Co-operative Bank.*

OTHER BANK

Nasser Social Bank: 35 Kasr El Nil St., Cairo; f. 1971; interest-free savings and investment bank for social and economic development.

STOCK EXCHANGES

Cairo Stock Exchange: 4A Cherifein St., Cairo; f. 1883; Pres. SHOUHDI AZER.

Alexandria Stock Exchange: Pres. M. HASSAN HAGGAG.

INSURANCE

Misr Insurance Company: 7 Sharia Talaat Harb, Cairo; Chair. FATHI MOHAMED IBRAHIM.

Al Chark Insurance Company, S.A.E.: Cairo; 15 Sharia Kasr-el-Nil; f. 1931; Chair. AHMED ZAKI HELMI; general and life; incorporates *Nile Insurance Co., Al Mottahida Insurance Co.,* and *Africa Insurance Co.*

Commercial Insurance Company of Egypt, S.A.E.: 7 Midan E. Tahrir, Cairo; f. 1947; life, fire, marine, accident; Managing Dir. AHMED ZAKY HELMY.

The Egyptian Reinsurance Company, S.A.E.: 28 Talaat Harb St., P.O.B. 950, Cairo; f. 1957; Chair. MOHAMED SAID ELEZABY.

L'Epargne, S.A.E.: Immeuble Chemla Sharia 26 July, P.O.B. 548, Cairo; all types of insurance.

Al Iktisad el Shabee, S.A.E.; 11 Sharia Emad El Dine, P.O.B. 1635, Cairo; f. 1948; Man. Dir. and Gen. Man. W. KHAYAT.

Al Mottahida: 9 Sharia Soliman Pasha, P.O.B. 804, Cairo; f. 1957.

National Insurance Company of Egypt, S.A.E.: 33 Sharia Nabi Danial, P.O.B. 446, Alexandria; f. 1900; cap. 750,000; Chair. MOSTAFA EL-SAYED EL-ESNAWY.

Provident Association of Egypt, S.A.E.: 9 Sharia Sherif Pasha, P.O.B. 390, Alexandria; f. 1936; Man. Dir. C. G. VORLOOU.

TRADE AND INDUSTRY

CHAMBERS OF COMMERCE

ALEXANDRIA

Egyptian Chamber of Commerce, Alexandria: El-Ghorfa Eltegareia St.; Pres. ABDEL HAMIED SERRY; Vice-Pres. ABEDEL SATTAR ARAFAH, MOSTAFA KAMAL BARAKAT; Treas. ALY ALY EL KATA, TAWFIC EL MELEIGY; Sec. AHMED EL ALFI MUHAMMAD; Gen. Dir. MUHAMMED FATHY MAHMOUD.

Camera di Commercio Italiana di Alessandria: P.O.B. 1763; f. 1885; 173 mems.; Pres. Cav. LUIGI F. POLVARA; Vice-Pres. Ing. ROBERT MITROVICH, Sig. EMILIO LINDI;

Sec. of Council Ing. CARLO SCARPOCCHI; Treas. PIER LUCA CAPPIEILO; Sec.-Gen. PIERO FAZZI; publ. *Rivista degli Scambi Italo-Egiziani.*

Chambre de Commerce Hellénique: 19 Sharia Sherif Pasha; f. 1901; Pres. YANKO CHRYSSOVERGHI; Vice-Pres. C. GEORGIAFENDIS, C. NANOPOULOS; Treas. CHR. KOKKINOS; Hon. Sec. ALEX M. CASULLI.

Chambre de Commerce Turque: 9 Sharia Sherif Pasha; Hon. Pres. TAHA CARIM; Pres. ILHAMI CAKIN; Vice-Pres. IZZET LEVENDER and KASSIM KUTAY; Treas. HABIB ALEX. DIAB; Sec.-Gen. ZIYA SÖNMEZ.

CAIRO

Cairo Chamber of Commerce: 4 Midan El Falaki St.; f. 1913; Pres. MUHAMMAD ALI SHETA; Vice-Pres. ABDEL-MOHSEN HELAL SHETA, KAMAL HAFIZ RAMADAN; Sec.-Gen. Y. YOUSSIF FAHMI; Treas. AHMED NAIM; Gen. Dir. SAID EL-BARRAD; publ. *Monthly Bulletin*.

Camera di Commercio Italiana per l'Egitto: 33 Sharia Abdel Khalek Sarwat, P.O. Box 19 1947; Pres. Ing.; BENITO GIANCRISTOFARO; Vice-Pres. Gr. Uff. LUIGI DE LUCA; Gen. Sec. Dr. ERNESTO RAVISA; 120 mems; publs. *Rivista degli Scambi Italo-Egiziani* (every four months).

Chambre de Commerce Hellénique du Caire: 17 Sharia Soliman El Halabi; f. 1923; Pres. P. ARSLANOGLOU; Vice-Pres. C. B. STAVROU; Sec. A. VLASSOPOULOS.

German-Arab Chamber of Commerce: 2 Sharia Sherif Pasha, Cairo; f. 1951; Pres. RUDI STAERKER; Sec.-Gen. KARLGERD QUINK; publ. *German Arab Trade*.

Representation of Federal Chamber of Foreign Trade of Yugoslavia: 47 Sharia Ramses, P.O.B. 448, Cairo; f. 1954; Sec.-Gen. D. STANKOVIĆ.

OTHER TOWNS

Egyptian Chamber of Commerce for Aswan Governorate: Abtal El-Tahrir St., Aswan.

Egyptian Chamber of Commerce for Asyut Governorate: Asyut.

Egyptian Chamber of Commerce for Behera Governorate: Gomhouriya St., Damanhoru.

Egyptian Chamber of Commerce for Beni-Suef Governorate: Mamdouh St., Moqbel El-Guedid, Beni-Suef.

Egyptian Chamber of Commerce for Dakahlia Governorate, Mansura: El-Saleh Ayoub Square, Mansura.

Egyptian Chamber of Commerce for Damietta Governorate: Damietta.

Egyptian Chamber of Commerce for Fayum Governorate: Fayum.

Egyptian Chamber of Commerce for Gharbia Governorate: Tanta.

Egyptian Chamber of Commerce for Giza Governorate: El-Saa Square, Giza.

Egyptian Chamber of Commerce for Ismailia Governorate: Ismailia.

Egyptian Chamber of Commerce for Kafr-el-Sheika Governorate: Kafr-el-Sheikh.

Egyptian Chamber of Commerce for Kena Governorate: El-Gamil Street, Kena.

Egyptian Chamber of Commerce for Menia Governorate: Menia.

Egyptian Chamber of Commerce for Manufia Governorate: Sidi Fayed Street, Shibín-El-Kom.

Egyptian Chamber of Commerce for Port Said Governorate: Port Said.

Egyptian Chamber of Commerce for Kalyubia Governorate: Benha.

Egyptian Chamber of Commerce for Sharkia Governorate: Zagazig.

Egyptian Chamber of Commerce for Suez Governorate: Suez.

Egyptian Chamber of Commerce for Suhag Governorate: Suhag.

NATIONALIZED ORGANIZATIONS

General Organization under the Ministry of War:

Armed Forces: 90 Sh. Al-Azhar, Cairo.

General Organizations under the Ministry of Industry, and Mineral Wealth:

Egyptian General Organization for Food Industries: 6 Salem and Salem St., Agouza, Cairo; 26 companies; products include most basic foodstuffs, tobacco, sugar, soft and alcoholic drinks, confectionary, essential oils, essences, soap, perfumery, cosmetics, etc.; 90,000 workers; Dir. Prof. Dr. HASSAN ASHMAWI.

Egyptian General Organization for Spinning and Weaving: 5 Tolobat St., Garden City, Cairo; 28 companies.

Egyptian General Organization for Engineering, Electric and Electronic Industries: 28 Talaat Harb St., Cairo; 22 companies.

Chemical Industries: 49 Kasr El Nil St., Cairo; 29 companies.

Building Materials and Ceramics: 49 Kasr El Nil St., Cairo; 13 companies.

Metal Industries: 5 July 26th St., Cairo; 9 companies.

Geological Survey of Egypt and Mining Authority: Pres. RUSHDI SAID; Dir. Gen. GALAL EL DIN MOSTAFA.

General Organization under the Ministry of Military Production:

Egyptian General Organization for Military Factories and Industries of Aviation: 8 Gemaee St., Garden City, Cairo.

General Organizations under the Ministry of Marine Transport:

Maritime Transport: 8 Nasser St., Alexandria; 7 affiliated companies.

General Organization under the Minister of Treasury:

Social Insurance General Organization: 126 July St., Cairo.

General Organizations under Ministry of Economy and Foreign Trade:

Egyptian General Organization of Foreign Trade: 2 companies for exporting agricultural products, 2 for engineering and one for cars.

Egyptian General Organization of Cotton: 19 El Gomhouria St., Cairo; 25 El Horria Ave., Alexandria.

General Organization under Ministry of Health:

Egyptian General Organization for Drugs, Chemicals and Medical Equipment: 11 companies.

General Organizations under Ministry of Housing and Construction:

Egyptian General Organization of Housing and Rehabitation: 4 Latin America Street, Garden City, Cairo; 10 companies.

General Organization of Co-operative Housing and Construction: Nasr City, Cairo.

Civil Contracting Company: 14 Talaat Harb, Cairo.

General Organizations under Ministry of Culture and Information:

Egyptian General Organization for Tourism and Hotels: 4 Latin America St., Garden City, Cairo.

Egyptian Broadcasting and T.V. Corporation: Corniche el Nil, Cairo.

General Organizations under the Ministry of Land Reclamation:

General Egyptian Organization of Land Reclamation: Dokki; 6 companies.

Executive Council of Desert Projects.

General Organizations under Ministry of Agriculture:

Co-operative Agriculture: Misr Insurance Bldg., Giza; Dir.-Gen. ABDUL MAKSOUD EZZAT MOHAMED EZZAT.

Poultry: Misr Insurance Bldg., Giza.
Meat: 14 El Gamhouria Sq., Abdin, Cairo.
Maritime Wealth.

General Organization under Ministry of Aviation:
Misr Organization for Aviation.

General Organizations under the Suez Canal Authority:
7 affiliated companies.

OIL

Egyptian General Petroleum Corporation: P.O.B. 2130, Cairo; State supervisory authority generally concerned with the planning of policies relating to petroleum activities in Egypt with the object of securing the development of the oil industry; has entered into 50-50 partnership agreements with a number of foreign companies; Pres. Eng. MOHAMED RAMZY EL-LETHY; Gen. Man. Dr. MOUSTAFA EL AUOTY.

Compagnie Orientale des Pétroles d'Egypte: 155 Muhammad Farid St., Cairo; f. 1957; capital equally shared between EGPC and International Egyptian Oil Co., which is a subsid. of ENI of Italy; exploration and production of crude oil.

Delta Petroleum Co. (DELPCO): P.O.B. 2048, Cairo; f. 1973; capital equally shared between EGPC and Int. Egyptian Oil Co. (subsid. of ENI of Italy); development and production operations of Abo-Madi Gas Field.

General Petroleum Company (GPC): P.O.B. 743, Cairo; f. 1962; wholly owned subsidiary of EGPC; operates mainly in Eastern Desert and produced approx. 26,500 barrels per day in 1973.

Gulf of Suez Petroleum Company (GUPCO): 1097 Sharia Corniche El Nil, Cairo; f. 1965; partnership between EGPC and Amoco-Egypt Co., U.S.A.; developed the El Morgan oilfield in the Gulf of Suez, also holds other exploration concessions in the Gulf of Suez and the Red Sea.

Fayoum Petroleum Company (FAPCO): P.O.B. 2400, Cairo; f. 1972; partnership between EGPC and Amoco-Egypt; developed the Abu El Gharadig oil and gas field in the Western Desert, also holds other exploration concessions in the Western Desert.

Nile Petroleum Company (NIPO): P.O.B. 2400, Cairo; f. 1972; partnership between EGPC and Amoco-Egypt; developed the Razzak oilfield in the Western Desert, also holds other exploration concessions in the Nile valley.

Western Desert Petroleum Company (WEPCO): P.O.B. 412, Alexandria; f. 1967 as partnership between EGPC and Phillips Petroleum; developed Alamein and later, Yidma fields in the Western Desert, producing approx. 13,000 barrels per day in early 1975; Chair. Eng. HASSAN EL DEWY.

Numerous foreign oil companies are prospecting for oil in Egypt under agreements with EGPC.

EMPLOYERS' ORGANIZATIONS

Federation of Egyptian Industries: P.O.B. 251, 26A Sharia Sherif Pasha, Cairo, and P.O.B. 1658, 65 Horia Rd., Alexandria; f. 1922; Pres. Dr. Eng. MAHMOUD ALY HASSAN; represents the industrial community in Egypt.

AFFILIATED ORGANIZATIONS

Chamber of Food Industries: 26A Sherif St., Cairo; Pres. Prof. Dr. HASSAN ASHMAWI.

Chamber of Building Materials and Construction: Pres. Eng. HASSAN MUHAMMAD HASSAN.

Chamber of Cereals and Related Products Industry: Pres. Dr. FAWZI YOUSSEF REFAI.

Chamber of Chemical Industries: Pres. Dr. HASSAN IBRAHIM BADAWI.

Chamber of Engineering Industries: Pres. Eng. MUHAMMAD ABDEL BAKI EL-KOSHEIRY.

Chamber of Leather Industry: Pres. Dr. HASSAN IBRAHIM EL-SISSY.

Chamber of Metallurgical Industries: P.O.B. 251, 13 Sherif St., Cairo; Dir. Eng. ADEL A. SHOEIB.

Chamber of Petroleum and Mining: Pres. Dr. HAMED HASANEIN AMER; Dir. ABDALLAH ABDELRAHIM.

Chamber of Printing, Binding and Paper Products: Pres. Eng. YOUSSEF MOUSTAFA BAHGAT.

Chamber of Spinning and Weaving Industry: Pres. HAMED EL-MAAMOUN HABIB.

Chamber of Woodworking Industry: Pres. HASSAN SOLIMAN MUHAMMAD.

TRADE UNIONS

Egyptian Federation of Labour (EFL): 90 El Galaa St., Cairo; f. 1957; 16 affiliated unions; 2.5 million mems.; affiliated to the International Confederation of Arab Trade Unions and to the All-African Trade Union Federation; Pres. SALAH GHARIB; Sec. SAEED GOMAA; publ. *El Omal* (weekly, Arabic).

Arab Federation of Food Workers (AFFW): P.O.B. 877, Cairo; 500,000 mems.; Gen. Sec. SAAD MUHAMMAD AHMED.

Federation of Arab Engineers: 28 Ramses St., Cairo; Sec. MUHAMMAD SAKR.

General Trade Union of Agriculture: 31 Mansour St., Bab al-Louk, Cairo; 350,000 mems.; Pres. SALAH AL DIN ABU AL-MAGI; Gen. Sec. NASR AL DIN MUSTAPHA.

General Trade Union of Banking and Insurance: 2 Al Qadi al Fadl St., Cairo; 32,000 mems.; Pres. MUHAMMAD FATHI FOUDA; Gen. Sec. MUNIR HABASH.

General Trade Union of Building Industries: 9 Emad el Din St., Cairo; 46,000 mems.; Pres. ABD AL MUTALE SALEM; Gen. Sec. HAMED HUSSAIN BARAKAT.

General Trade Union of Business and Management Services: 387 Port Said St., Bab al Khalk, Cairo; 46,000 mems.; Pres. AWAD ABD AL QADER; Gen. Sec. ABL AL RAHMAN KHEDR.

General Trade Union of the Chemical Industries: 76 Gomhouria St., Cairo; 60,000 mems.; Pres. MUHAMMAD ASAAD RAGEH; Gen. Sec. HAMYA ALI MAHJOUB.

General Trade Union of Workers in Engineering, Metal and Electrical Industries: 90 El Galaa St., Cairo; 130,000 mems.; Pres. SAEED GOMAA ALI; Gen. Sec. GAMAL TARABISHI.

General Trade Union of Nutritional Industries: 3 Hosni St., Qubba al Hadaek, P.O.B. 2230, Cairo; 125,000 mems.; Pres. MOHAMED ABDOU GOMAA; Vice-Pres. MAHMOUD EL ASKHRI.

General Trade Union of Railways: 47 Al Tera al Boulaquiya St., Cairo; 46,000 mems.; Pres. MUHAMMAD ATITO; Gen. Sec. AHMAD FAWZI ALI.

General Trade Union of Textiles: 327 Shoubra St., Cairo; f. 1960; 250,000 mems.; Pres. SALAH GHARID.

TRANSPORT

RAILWAYS

Egyptian Railways: Cairo; f. 1852; length and gauge 4,855 km., 1,435 mm.; 2,598 km., 1,435 mm. auxiliary lines; 25 km. electrified; Chair. Eng. MAHMOUD KAMEL MORTAGY.

Alexandria Passenger Transport Authority: 21 Saad Zaghloul Square, P.O.B. 466, Alexandria; controls City Tramways (28 km.), Ramleh Electric Railway (16 km.), suburban buses (201 km.); Chair. Eng. ALY HOSNY MAHMOUD; Tech. Dir. Eng. MOHAMED ABDEL-LATIF NASSEF.

Heliopolis Company for Housing and Inhabiting: 28 Ibrahim El Lakkany St., Heliopolis, Cairo; 50 km., 148 railcars; Gen. Man. ABDEL MONEIM SEIF.

A 6¼-mile underground railway is under consideration in Cairo, and a 430 km. line to carry iron ore from the Bahariya mines to the Helwan iron and steel works was opened in August 1973. The railway service between Cairo and Ismailia, which had been closed since 1967, was re-opened in March 1974.

ROADS

Egyptian General Organization of Inland Transport for Provinces Passengers: Sharia Kasr-el-Aini, Cairo; Pres. HASAN MOURAD KOTB.

There are good metalled main roads as follows: Cairo-Alexandria (desert road); Cairo-Benna-Tanta-Damanhur-Alexandria; Cairo-Suez (desert road); Cairo-Ismailia-Port Said or Suez; Cairo-Fayum (desert road); in 1970 there were over 13,000 miles of good metalled roads.

Automobile et Touring Club D'Egypte: 10 rue Kasr-el-Nil, Cairo; f. 1924; 622 mems.; Hon. Pres. Ing. HASSAN NAGI; Pres. Maj.-Gen. Dr. MOHAMMED ABDEL HAMID MORTAGHI.

SHIPPING

Egyptian Maritime Co.: 3 rue de l'Ancienne Bourse, Alexandria; f. 1930; services Alexandria/Europe, Canada, Black Sea, Adriatic Sea and Africa; fleet of 39 vessels; Chair. M. Y. RAMADAN.

American Eastern Trading and Shipping Co., S.A.E.: 17 Sharia Sesostris, Alexandria; Pres. M. E. WAGNER; Manager, Egypt, AHMED LABIB TAHIO.

Egyptian Stevedoring and Shipping Co., S.A.E.: 17 Sharia Sesostris, Alexandria; f. 1946; Pres. J. H. CHALHOUB; Manager MUHAMMAD FAHMY TAHIO.

Thebes Shipping Agency: P.O. Box 45, 41 Sharia Neb; Daniel, Alexandria; maritime transport.

THE SUEZ CANAL

Suez Canal Authority (*Hay'at Canal Al Suess*): 6 Lazokhli St., Garden City, Cairo; Pres. Eng. MASHHOUR AHMED MASHHOUR.

Length of Canal: 162.5 km.; maximum permissible draught: 38 ft.; maximum width (at water level): 660 ft.; minimum width (at depth of 36 ft.): 295 ft. The Canal was closed between June 1967 and June 1975.

CIVIL AVIATION

EgyptAir: Head Office: Cairo International Airport, Heliopolis, Cairo; f. 1932 as Misr Airwork; operates internal services in Egypt and external services throughout the Middle East, Far East, Africa and Europe; Pres. Gen. GAMAL ERFAN; fleet of eight Boeing 707, four Comet 4C.

The following foreign airlines serve Egypt: Aeroflot, Air France, Air India, Alia, Alitalia, AUA, British Airways, British Caledonian, ČSA, Cyprus Airways, Ethiopian Air Lines, Garuda, Ghana Airways, Interflug, Iraqi Airways, JAL, JAT, Libyan Arab Airlines, KLM, Kuwait Airways, LOT, Lufthansa, MALÉV, MEA, Olympic Airways, Pan Am, PIA, Qantas, Sabena, SAS, Saudia, Sudan Airways, Swissair, TAROM, TWA and UTA.

TOURISM

Ministry of Tourism: 110 Sh. Kasr-el-Aini, Cairo; f. 1965; branches at Alexandria, Port Said, Suez, Luxor and Aswan; Minister of Tourism IBRAHIN NAGUIB IBRAHIM.

General Organization for Tourism and Hotels: 4 Latin America St., Garden City, Cairo; f. 1961; affiliated to the Ministry of Tourism.

Authorized foreign exchange dealers for tourists include the principal banks and the following:

American Express of Egypt Ltd.: 15 Kasr-el-Nil St., Cairo; f. 1919.

Thomas Cook and Son: 4 Sharia Champollion, Cairo.

CULTURAL ORGANIZATION

Ministry of Culture: Cairo; Minister YOUSSEF EL SEBAI.

PRINCIPAL THEATRES AND ORCHESTRA

Pocket Theatre: Cairo; f. 1961.

Egyptian General Organization of Cinema, Theatre and Music: Ministry of Culture and Information.

Departments include the following: **Opera Lyric Troupe, Opera Ballet, Opera Chorale, Cairo Symphony Orchestra.**

Members frequently take part in performances with visiting opera companies.

National Puppet Theatre: Cairo.

NATIONAL DANCE TROUPES

National Folklore Dance Troupe: Cairo; frequently performs on tours abroad.

Reda Folklore Dance Troupe: 50 Kasr-el-Nil St., Cairo; f. 1959; frequently performs on tours abroad; Dirs. MAHMOUD REDA, ALI REDA; Principal Dancers FARIDA FAHMY, MAHMOUD REDA; Composer and Conductor ALI ISMAIL.

ATOMIC ENERGY

Atomic Energy Organization: Dokki, Cairo; f. 1955; Dir. Dr. SALAH HEDAYET. First reactor with 2,000 kW. power, opened at Inchass in 1961.

Regional Radioisotope Centre: Cairo; f. 1957; eleven laboratories for research and development in scientific, medical, agricultural and industrial fields; in 1963 the Centre was transformed into a Regional Centre for the Arab countries of the Middle East, in co-operation with UN I.A.E.A.

DEFENCE

Supreme Commander of the Armed Forces: President ANWAR EL-SADAT.

Minister of War and Commander-in-Chief: Gen. MUHAMMAD ABDUL GHANI AL-GAMASSI.

Chief of Staff of the Army: Lieut.-Gen. MUHAMMAD ALI FAHMI

Commander of the Air Force: General MAHMOUD CHAKER ABDUL MONEIM.

Commander of Air Defence: Gen. HILMI AFISI MORSI.

Commander of the Navy: Vice-Admiral MUHAMMAD AHMAD ZIKRI.

Defence Budget 1974-75: £E1,225 million.

Military service: 3 years.

Total armed forces: 323,000: army 280,000; navy 15,000; air force 28,000. Reserves 534,000. Paramilitary forces: 100,000 (National Guard etc.).

EDUCATION

Great importance has been attached to the development of educational facilities by the Egyptian Government since 1952. Its educational policy states that education is free and should play an indispensable part in the life of every citizen. It was realised that the first and most essential step in the programme of educational expansion was the construction of an adequate number of new schools. In 1952 a Ten Year Plan was inaugurated whereby an organization known as "The Schools Premises Foundation" was given the responsibility of constructing 400 new schools each year. Education, particularly technical education, has continued to be a primary concern of the Government and in the 1971–72 budget £E170 million was allocated to education, culture and national guidance.

Primary Education

This is extended to all children between the ages of six and twelve, and is free and compulsory. Four hundred primary schools are being constructed annually. The number of pupils in the primary stage in the year 1952 amounted to 1,540,202 (997,490 boys and 541,708 girls), compared with 3,873,297 in 1971–72. In the latter year the pupils were organized into 90,022 classes.

Preparatory Education

This is an intermediate stage between primary and secondary education. There were two main different types of preparatory school, general and technical, but the technical schools are being phased as separate institutions at this level. In 1971–72 there were 23,216 preparatory classes attended by about 928,000 children (two-thirds being boys).

Secondary Education

(*a*) General schools: here the emphasis is placed on academic studies. The aim is to develop the abilities of pupils best qualified for a university education. The number of students in 1971–72 was 312,489.

(*b*) Technical Schools: a vocational training is given in these schools, in agriculture, industry or commerce. In 1971-72 there were 289,812 pupils in technical schools of various kinds. There were also about 27,000 pupils in teacher training establishments.

University Education

In addition to the old and famous Al-Azhar University, which opened its gates to women students in 1962, there are the universities of Cairo, Alexandria, Ain Shams and Assiut.

Cairo University was founded privately in 1908; in 1928 it became the State University. The American University at Cairo was founded in 1919, Alexandria University in 1942, and Ain Shams in 1950. Another university has been founded at Assiut, and was opened in time for the academic year 1957–58. Most universities include the following faculties: Agriculture, Commerce, Dental Surgery, Medicine, Pharmacy, Engineering, Law, Arts and Science.

The East of the Delta University was founded in 1972 from the Mansoura branch of Cairo University, and the Mid-Delta University was founded in 1972 from the Tanta Branch of the University of Alexandria.

In addition there are various post-graduate courses of study, and many students are sent abroad to complete their higher education. More, however, come from other countries to study in Egypt. In terms of student numbers the leading universities are amongst the world's largest (65,000 students at Cairo University) but the facilities are mostly very overcrowded. It was estimated that there were nearly 200,000 university students in Egypt in 1975. A plan to place university campuses in rural areas was announced in August 1974.

Adult Education

A campaign to promote literacy and adult education is being directed and financed by the Ministry of Education, supported by the continuous co-operation of UNESCO. In 1970–71 new councils for literacy and adult education were formed, consisting of members representing the following sectors of the community: planning, production, local administration and the Arab Socialist Union. The Ministry of Education and the Arab League are co-operating on a Regional Literacy project.

UNIVERSITIES

Ain Shams University: Kasr el Zaafran, Abbasiyah, Cairo; 1,025 teachers, 38,200 students.

Alexandria University: Shatby, Alexandria; 2,350 teachers, 49,284 students.

Al-Azhar University: Cairo 1,354 teachers, 31,867 students.

American University in Cairo: 113 Sh. Kasr el Aini, Cairo; 175 teachers, 1,500 students.

East of the Delta University: Mansoura.

Mid-Delta University: Tanta.

University of Assiut: Assiut; 13,177 students.

University of Cairo: Orman, Ghiza; 3,302 teachers, 61,953 students.

BIBLIOGRAPHY

GENERAL

ABDEL-MALEK, ANWAR. Egypte, société militaire (Paris, 1962).
Idéologie et renaissance nationale/L'Egypt moderne (Pari 1969).

AHMED, J. M. The Intellectual Origins of Egyptian Nationalism (London, Royal Institute of International Affairs, 1960).

ALDRIDGE, JAMES. Cairo: Biography of a City (Macmillan, London, 1970).

AYROUT, H. H. The Egyptian Peasant (Boston, 1963).

BADDOUR, ABD. Sudanese-Egyptian Relations. A Chronological and Analytical Study (Nijhoff, The Hague, 1960).

BADEAU, J. S. The Emergence of Modern Egypt (New York, 1953).

BAER, GABRIEL. A History of Landownership in Modern Egypt 1800–1950 (Oxford University Press, London, 1962).
The Evolution of Landownership in Egypt and the Fertile Crescent, the Economic History of the Middle East 1800–1914 (University of Chicago Press, Chicago and London, 1966).
Studies in the Social History of Modern Egypt (University of Chicago Press, Chicago and London, 1969).

BERGER, MORROE. Bureaucracy and Society in Modern Egypt: a Study of the Higher Civil Service (Princeton University Press, 1957).
Islam in Egypt Today: Social and Political Aspects of Popular Religion (Cambridge University Press, 1970).

BERQUE, JACQUES. Egypt: Imperialism and Revolution (Faber, London, 1972).

BOKTOR, AMIN. The Development and Expansion of Education in the U.A.R. (The American University, Cairo, 1963).

COULT, LYMAN H. An Annotated Bibliography of the Egyptian Fellah (University of Miami Press, 1958).

CROMER, EARL OF. Modern Egypt (2 vols., London, 1908).

DODWELL, H. The Founder of Modern Egypt (Cambridge, 1931, reprinted 1967).

DRIAULT, E. L'Egypte et l'Europe (5 vols., Cairo, 1935).

ELISOFAN, E. The Nile (New York, 1964).

GARZOUZI, EVA. Old Ills and New Remedies in Egypt (Dar al-Maaref, Cairo, 1958).

HARRIS, C. P. Nationalism and Revolution in Egypt: the Role of the Muslim Brotherhood (Mouton and Co., The Hague, 1964).

HARRIS, J. R. (Ed) The Legacy of Egypt (2nd ed. Oxford University Press, 1972).

HOLT, P. M. Egypt and the Fertile Crescent (Longmans, London, 1966).

HOPKINS, HARRY. Egypt, The Crucible (Secker and Warburg, London, 1969).

HURST, H. E. The Nile (London, 1952).
The Major Nile Projects (Cairo, 1966).

LACOUTURE, JEAN and SIMONNE. Egypt in Transition (London, Methuen, 1958).

LANDAU, JACOB M. Parliaments and Parties in Egypt (Israel Publishing House, Tel-Aviv, 1953).

LAUTERPACHT, E. (Editor). The Suez Canal Settlement (Stevens and Sons, London, 1960, under the auspices of the British Institute of International and Comparative Law).

LENGYE, EMIL. Egypt's Role in World Affairs (Public Affairs Press, Washington, D.C., 1957).

LITTLE, TOM. Modern Egypt (Ernest Benn, London, 1967, Praeger, New York 1967).

LLOYD, LORD. Egypt since Cromer (2 vols., London, 1933–34).

MAHMOUD, ZAKI NAGIB. Modern Egyptian Thought (London, 1946).

MARLOWE, J. Anglo-Egyptian Relations (London, 1954).

MORINEAU, RAYMOND. Egypte (Lausanne, 1964).

NASSER, ABDEL GAMAL. Egypt's Liberation: The Philosophy of the Revolution (Washington, 1955).

NEGUIB, MOHAMMED. Egypt's Destiny: A Personal Statement (New York, 1955).

OWEN, ROBERT and BLUNSUM, TERENCE. Egypt, United Arab Republic, The Country and its People (Queen Anne Press, London, 1966).

RIAD, HASSAN. L'Egypte Nassérienne (Editions de Minuit Paris, 1964).

RUSSELL PASHA, Sir THOMAS. Egyptian Service, 1902-1946 (London, 1949).

STEVENS, GEORGIANA G. Egypt Yesterday and Today (New York, 1963).

STEWART, DESMOND. Cairo (Phoenix House, London, 1965).

VAUCHER, G. Gamal Abdel Nasser et son Equipe, 2 vols. (Brill, Leiden, 1950)

VIOLLET, ROGER and DORESSE, JEAN. Egypt (New York, Cromwell, 1955).

WATERFIELD, GORDON. Egypt (Thames & Hudson, London, 1966).

WATT, D. C. Britain and the Suez Canal (London, Royal Institute of International Affairs, 1956).

WAVELL, W. H. A Short Account of the Copts (London, 1945).

WILBUR, D. N. The United Arab Republic (New York, 1969).

WILSON, JOHN A. The Burden of Egypt (Chicago, 1951).

WYNN, WILTON. Nasser of Egypt: The Search for Dignity (Cambridge, Mass., 1959).

YOUSSEF BEY, AMINE. Independent Egypt (London, 1940).

ANCIENT EGYPT

ALDRED, CYRIL. Egypt to the End of the Old Kingdom (Thames and Hudson, London, 1965).

BREASTED, JAMES HENRY. A History of Egypt from the Earliest Times to the Persian Conquest (Harper and Row, New York, 1959).

DE LUBICZ, A. S. The Temples of Karnak (2 vols., London, 1961).

ERMAN, ADOLF. The Ancient Egyptians; a Sourcebook of their Writings (trans. A. M. BLACKMAN, Harper, New York, 1966).

FISCHEL, WALTER J. Ibn Khaldun in Egypt (University of California Press, 1967).

FORSTER, E. M. Alexandria: a History and a Guide (Doubleday, New York, 1961).

GARDINER, Sir ALAN HENDERSON. Egypt of the Pharaohs (Clarendon Press, Oxford, 1961).

GLANVILLE, S. R. K. (editor). The Legacy of Egypt (Oxford, 1942).

GREENER, L. The Discovery of Egypt (Cassell, London 1966, Viking Press, New York, 1967).

JOHNSON, ALLAN C. Egypt and the Roman Empire (Ann Arbor, 1951).

MEYER-RANKE, PETER. Der Rote Pharao (Christian Wegner Verlag, Hamburg, 1964).

MONTET, PIERRE. Das Leben der Pharaonen (Frankfurt/ Berlin/Vienna, 1970).

PIRENNE, JACQUES. Histoire de la Civilization de l'Egypte antique (Neuchâtel, 1966).
La Religion et la Morale de l'Egypte antique (La Baconnière, Neuchâtel, 1966).

POSENER, G. (Ed.). A Dictionary of Egyptian Civilization (Methuen, London, 1962).

MODERN HISTORY

AVRAM, BENNO. The Evolution of the Suez Canal State 1869-1956. A Historico-Juridical Study (Librairie E. Droz, Libraire Minard, Geneva, Paris, 1958).

BARAWAY, RASHED EL. The Military Coup in Egypt (Cairo, Renaissance Bookshop, 1952).

BARRACLOUGH, GEOFFREY, Ed. Suez in History (London, 1962).

BLUNT, WILFRED SCAWEN. Secret History of the English Occupation of Egypt (Martin Secker, London, 1907).

CONNELL, JOHN. The Most Important Country. The Story of the Suez Crisis and the Events leading up to It (Cassell, London, 1957).

EFENDI, HUSEIN. Ottoman Egypt in the Age of the French Revolution (trans. and with introduction by Stanford J. Shaw) (Harvard Univ. Press, Cambridge, 1964).

FARNIE. D. A. East and West of Suez. The Suez Canal in history, 1854-1956 (Clarendon Press, Oxford, 1969).

HEIKAL, MUHAMMAD. The Road to Ramadan (Collins, London, 1975).

HILL, R. Egypt in the Sudan 1820-1881 (Oxford University Press, London and New York, 1959).

HOLT, P. M. Political and Social Change in Modern Egypt (Oxford University Press, 1967).

HUSSEIN, MAHMOUD. La Lutte de Classes en Egypte de 1945 à 1968 (Maspero, Paris, 1969).

ISSAWI, CHARLES. Egypt in Revolution (Oxford, 1963).

JOESTEN, JOACHIM. Nasser: The Rise to Power (London, Odhams, 1960).

KINROSS, LORD. Between Two Seas: The Creation of the Suez Canal (John Murray, London, 1968).

LACOUTURE, JEAN. Nasser: A Biography (Secker and Warburg, London, 1973).

LANE-POOLE, S. History of Egypt in the Middle Ages (4th edn., reprinted, Frank Cass, London, 1967).

LOVE, K. Suez: the Twice-fought War (Longman, 1970).

MANSFIELD, PETER. Nasser's Egypt (Penguin Books London, 1965).
Nasser (Methuen, London, 1969).
The British in Egypt (Weidenfeld and Nicolson, London, 1971).

MARLOWE, JOHN. Cromer in Egypt (Elek Books, London, 1970).

NUTTING, ANTHONY. No End of a Lesson; the Story of Suez (Constable, London, 1967).
Nasser (London, Constable, 1972).

O'BALLANCE, E. The Sinai Campaign 1956 (Faber, London, 1959).

ROYAL INSTITUTE OF INTERNATIONAL AFFAIRS. Great Britain and Egypt, 1914-51 (London, 1952).

SADAT, ANWAR AL. Revolt on the Nile (London, Allen Wingate, 1957).

SAFRAN, NADAV. Egypt in Search of Political Community. An analysis of the intellectual and political evolution of Egypt, 1804-1952 (Harvard University Press, Cambridge, Mass., Oxford University Press, London, 1961).

SAYYID, AFAF LUTFI AL. Egypt and Cromer: A Study in Anglo-Egyptian Relations (John Murray, London, Praeger, New York, 1968).

SCHONFIELD, HUGH A. The Suez Canal in Peace and War, 1869-1969 (Vallentine, Mitchell, London, 2nd revised edn., 1969).

SHAW, STANFORD J. Ottoman Egypt in the Eighteenth Century (Harvard University Press, 1962).

STEPHENS, R. Nasser (Allen Lane The Penguin Press, London, 1971).

TIGNOR, R. L. Modernization and British Colonial Rule in Egypt 1882-1914 (Princeton, 1966).

VATIKIOTIS, P. J. A Modern History of Egypt (Praeger, New York, 1966: Weidenfeld and Nicolson, London, 1969).
The Egyptian Army in Politics (Indiana University Press, Bloomington, 1961).

ZAKI, ABDEL RAHMAN. Histoire Militaire de l'Epoque de Mohammed Ali El-Kebir (Cairo, 1950).

ECONOMY

EL GHONEMY, M. RIAD. Economic and Industrial Organization of Egyptian Agriculture since 1952, Egypt since the Revolution (Allen and Unwin, London, 1968).

EL KAMMASH, M. M. Economic Development and Planning in Egypt (London, 1967).

HANSON, BENT and MAZOUK, GIRGIS. Development and Economic Policy in the U.A.R. (Egypt) (North Holland Publishing Co., Amsterdam, 1965).

KARDOUCHE, G. S. The U.A.R. in Development (Praeger, New York, 1967).

MABRO, ROBERT. The Egyptian Economy 1952-1972 (Oxford University Press, London, 1974).

MEAD, DONALD C. Growth and Structural Change in the Egyptian Economy (Irwin, Homwood, Ill., 1967).

O'BRIEN, PATRICK. The Revolution in Egypt's Economic System 1952-65 (Oxford, 1966).

RADWAN, SAMIR. Capital Formation in Egyptian Industry and Agriculture 1882-1967 (St. Antony's Middle East Monographs, published by Ithaca Press, London, 1975).

SAAB, GABRIEL S. The Egyptian Agrarian Reform 1952-1962 (Oxford University Press, London and New York, 1967).

WARRINER, DOREEN. Land Reform and Economic Development (Cairo, 1955).
Land Reform and Development in the Middle East—A Study of Egypt, Syria and Iraq (2nd ed. Oxford University Press, London, 1962).

Iran
(Persia)

PHYSICAL AND SOCIAL GEOGRAPHY

W. B. Fisher

SITUATION

The kingdom of Iran is bounded on the north by the Caspian Sea and by the Transcaucasian and Turkistan territories of the U.S.S.R., on the east by Afghanistan and Pakistan, on the south by the Persian Gulf and Gulf of Oman, and on the west by Iraq and Turkey.

PHYSICAL FEATURES

Structurally, Iran is an extremely complex area; and owing partly to political difficulties and partly to the difficult nature of the country itself, complete exploration and investigation have not so far been achieved. In general, it can be stated that Iran consists of an interior plateau, from 3,000–5,000 ft. in height, that is ringed on almost all sides by mountain zones of varying height and extent. The largest mountain massif is that of the Zagros, which runs from the north-west of Iran, where the frontiers of Iran, Russia, Turkey and Iraq meet, first south-westwards to the eastern shores of the Persian Gulf, and then eastwards, fronting the Arabian Sea, and continuing into Baluchistan. Joining the Zagros in the north-west, and running along the southern edge of the Caspian Sea, is the narrower but equally high Elburz range; whilst along the eastern frontier of Iran are several scattered mountain chains, less continuous and imposing than either the Zagros or the Elburz, but sufficiently high to act as a barrier.

The Zagros range begins in north-west Iran as an alternation of high tablelands and lowland basins, the latter containing lakes, the largest of which is Lake Urmia. This lake, having no outlet, is saline. Further to the south-east the Zagros becomes much more imposing, consisting of a series of parallel hog's-back ridges, some of which reach over 14,000 ft. in height. In its southern and eastern portions the Zagros becomes distinctly narrower, and its peaks much less high, though a few exceed 10,000 ft. The Elburz range is very much narrower than the Zagros, but equally, if not more, abrupt, and one of its peaks, the volcanic cone of Mt. Damavand (18,700 ft.), is the highest in the country. There is a sudden drop on the northern side to the flat plain occupied by the Caspian Sea, which lies nearly 90 ft. below sea-level, and is shrinking rapidly in size. The eastern highlands of Iran consist of isolated massifs separated by lowland zones, some of which contain lakes from which there is no outlet, the largest being the Hirmand Basin, on the borders of Iran and Afghanistan.

The interior plateau of Iran is partly covered by a remarkable salt swamp (termed *kavir*) and partly by loose sand or stones (*dasht*), with stretches of better land mostly round the perimeter, near the foothills of the surrounding mountains. In these latter areas much of the cultivation of the country is carried on, but the lower-lying desert and swamp areas, towards the centre of the plateau, are largely uninhabited. The Kavir is an extremely forbidding region, consisting of a surface formed by thick plates of crystallized salt, which have sharp, upstanding edges. Below the salt lie patches of mud, with, here and there, deep drainage channels—all of which are very dangerous to travellers, and are hence unexplored. Because of this great handicap from the presence of an unusually intractable "dead heart", it has proved difficult to find a good central site for the capital of Iran—many towns, all peripheral to a greater or lesser degree, have in turn fulfilled this function, but none has proved completely satisfactory. The choice of the present capital, Teheran, dates only from the end of the eighteenth century.

Iran suffers from occasional earthquakes, which can cause severe loss of life, damage to property and disruption of communications. A particularly bad example occurred in the north-eastern Khurasan province in August and September 1968; estimates placed the toll from this disaster at up to 20,000 deaths and severe damage over 750 square miles.

The climate of Iran is one of great extremes. Owing to its southerly position, adjacent to Arabia and near the Thar Desert, the summer is extremely hot, with temperatures in the interior rising possibly higher than anywhere else in the world—certainly over 130°F. has been recorded. In winter, however, the great altitude of much of the country and its continental situation result in far lower temperatures than one would expect to find for a country in such low latitudes. Minus 20°F. can be recorded in the north-west Zagros, and 0°F. is common in many places.

Another unfortunate feature is the prevalence of strong winds, which intensify the temperature contrasts. Eastern Iran in particular has a violent visitation in the so-called "Wind of 120 Days", which blows regularly throughout summer, reaching at times over 100 m.p.h. and often raising sand to such an extent that the stone walls of buildings are sometimes scoured away and turn to ruins.

Most of Iran is arid; but in contrast, parts of the north-west and north, receive considerable rainfall—up to 80 inches along parts of the Caspian coast, producing very special climatic conditions in this small region, recalling conditions in the lower Himalayas. The Caspian shore has a hot, humid climate and this region is by far the most densely populated of the whole country. Next in order of population density comes the north-west Zagros area—the province of Azerbaizhan, with its capital, Tabriz, the second city of Iran. Then, reflecting the diminished rainfall, next in order come the central Zagros area, and adjacent parts of the interior plateau, round Isfahan, Hamadan, Shiraz, and Kermanshah, with an extension as far as Teheran. The extreme east and south, where rainfall is very scanty, are practically uninhabited.

ECONOMIC LIFE

Owing to the difficulties of climate and topography there are few districts, apart from the Caspian plain, that are continuously cultivated over a wide area. Settlement tends to occur in small clusters, close to water supplies, or where there are especially favourable conditions—a good soil, shelter from winds, or easy communications. Away from these cultivated areas, which stand out like oases among the barren expanses of desert or mountain, most of the population live as nomads, by the herding of animals. The nomadic tribesmen have had great influence on the life of Iran. Their principal territory is the central Zagros, where the tribal system is strongly developed; but nomads are found in all the mountain zones, though their numbers are very few in the south and east. Reza Shah (see "History") made considerable efforts to break the power of the nomadic tribes and to force them to settle as agriculturalists; but since his death there has been a recrudescence of tribal activity. However, the Iranian oilfields lie within tribal territories, and an important change is taking place as nomads accept employment as labourers in the oil industry. This may in time accomplish much of what Reza Shah attempted to do.

Economic activity has suffered from the handicaps of topography and climate, prolonged political and social insecurity (with constant pressure by foreign powers), and widespread devastation in the later Middle Ages by Mongol invaders, from which Iran has never fully recovered. Agricultural methods in particular are primitive, so that yields are low; but the drawbacks to efficient production mentioned in the general introduction to this volume—archaic systems of land tenure, absentee landlords, lack of education, and shortage of capital—are gradually being overcome. In the north and west, which are by far the most productive, a wide variety of cereals (including wheat, barley, and rice) and much fruit are grown, but in the south and east the date is the principal source of food. Some Iranian fruit is of remarkable quality (especially the apricots and grapes) and melons of over 100 lbs. weight are known.

Iran has a number of mineral resources, some of which are exploited on a commercial scale. The newly discovered copper deposits at Sar Cheshmeh could be among the largest in the world. Iranians have always had a high reputation as craftsmen—particularly in metal work and in carpet-making; and Reza Shah attempted to develop modern mechanized industry by placing state-owned factories in most of the big towns.

Some of these have proved successful, others not, but bazaar manufactures still remain the more important. Teheran has now become a sizeable manufacturing centre, with brick- and cement-making, light engineering, processing of foodstuffs and manufacture of consumer goods as chief activities. Carpet making remains important in Iran owing to considerable demand from the U.S.A. and Europe (especially West Germany) where Persian rugs are a status symbol.

The adverse nature of geographical conditions has greatly restricted the growth of communications in Iran. The country is very large in relation to its size of population—it is 1,400 miles from north-west to south-west—and because of the interior deserts, many routes must follow a circuitous path instead of attempting a direct crossing. Then, too, the interior is shut off by ranges that are in parts as high as the Alps of Europe, but far less broken up by river valleys. Road construction is everywhere difficult, but since the mid-1960s increasing effort has gone into providing an all-weather surface set of trunk routes between major cities: special allocations are made in the Five-Year Plans. An important link is the railway constructed with great effort before the Second World War between the Caspian coast, Teheran and the Persian Gulf. Other rail links with bordering countries have already and are still being built: from Teheran there are now direct links with the U.S.S.R., and more recently with Turkey, whilst a line is being pushed southeastwards that could one day link with Pakistan. Though there are mountain streams, many flowing in deep, inaccessible gorges, only one, the Karun river, is at all navigable. The Caspian ports are subject to silting, whilst in the south most harbours are either poorly sheltered or difficult of access from the interior. However, the last few years have seen a deliberate focusing of development on the Gulf, in response to the enhanced economic and political status of the region, now one of the wealthiest parts of the world. As well, the improvement of the frontier with Iraq, negotiated during 1975, will help Iranian development in the Shatt al-Arab. Small ports like Bushire and Lingeh, resorts such as Chah Behar and other centres are being developed as part of Iran's drive towards greater contacts in the Gulf and Indian Ocean.

RACE AND LANGUAGE

Iran has numerous ethnic groups of widely differing origin. In the central plateau there occurs a distinctive sub-race, termed by some anthropologists Iranian or Irano-Afghan. The distinguishing qualities are a moderate to rather tall stature, a moderately round head, pronounced features, but less so than among Armenoids, and a colouring generally lighter than that of many surrounding peoples. In the mountain districts there are many other smaller groups of separate racial composition. A number of nomads, including the Bakhtiari tribes, would seem to be of Kurdish stock; whilst Turki (Mongoloid) strains are apparent in others, such as the Qashqai tribes. Smaller groups from the Caucasus (Georgians and Circassians) are represented in Azerbaijan and the Caspian provinces, whilst Turki influence is again apparent in the racial composition of the eastern districts of Iran, especially round Meshed. The Southern Zagros near the Arabian Sea has a small population that tends to be of mixed Iranian, Afghan, and Hindu stock. Some observers have suggested that in this region there may also be representatives of a primitive negrito race, related to the hill-tribes of India and of south-east Asia.

With so many differing ethnic groups, it is not surprising to find that several languages are current in Iran. Persian, an Indo-Aryan language related to the languages of western Europe, is spoken in the north and centre of the country, and is the one official language of the State. As the north is by far the most densely peopled region of Iran, the Persian language has an importance somewhat greater than its territorial extent would suggest. Various dialects of Kurdish are current in the north and central Zagros mountains, and alongside these are found several Turki-speaking tribes. Baluchi occurs in the extreme south-east. English and French are spoken by most of the educated classes.

HISTORY

EARLY HISTORY

The Achaemenid empire, the first Persian empire, was founded by Cyrus who revolted against the Median empire in 533 B.C. After the defeat of the Median empire Babylon was taken in 539 B.C., and in 525 B.C. under Cambyses, the successor of Cyrus, Egypt was conquered. The period of conquest was rounded off by Darius who reduced the tribes of the Pontic and Armenian mountains and extended Persian dominion to the Caucasus. The main work of Darius, however, lay not in the conquest but in the organization which he gave to the empire. During his reign wars with Greece broke out and in 490 B.C. the Persian army suffered a major defeat at Marathon; an expedition under Xerxes, the successor of Darius, which set out to avenge this defeat was, after initial successes, defeated at Salamis in 480 B.C. The empire was finally overthrown by Alexander who defeated the Persian army at Arbela in 331 B.C. and then burnt Persepolis, the Achaemenid capital; the last Darius fled and was killed in 330 B.C. Alexander thereafter regarded himself as the head of the Persian empire. The death of Alexander was followed by a struggle between his generals, one of whom, Seleucus, took the whole of Persia, apart from northern Media and founded the Seleucid empire. About the year 250 B.C. a reaction against Hellenism began with the rise of the Parthian empire of the Arsacids. Although by origin nomads from the Turanian steppe, the Arsacids became the wardens of the north-east marches and were largely preoccupied in defending themselves in the east against the Scythians who, with the Tocharians and Sacae, repeatedly attacked the Parthian empire, while in the west they were engaged in fending off attacks by the Romans.

The Arsacids were succeeded by the Sasanians, who, like the Achaemenids, came from Fars and, like them, were Zoroastrians. Ardashir b. Babak, after subduing the neighbouring states (c. A.D. 212), made war on the Arsacid, Artabanus V, whom he eventually defeated. The empire which he founded largely continued the traditions of the Achaemenids, although it never equalled the Achaemenid empire in extent. The monarchy of the Sasanian period was a religious and civil institution. The monarch who ruled by divine right was absolute but his autocracy was limited by the powers of the Zoroastrian hierarchy and the feudal aristocracy. In the reign of Qubad (A.D. 488–531) a movement of revolt, partly social and partly religious, led by Mazdak, gained ground. Under Qubad's successor Anushiravan (531–679) orthodoxy was restored, but at the cost of the imposition of a military despotism. Like the Arsacids before them the Sasanians were occupied in the west with wars with Rome and in the east with repelling inroads of the nomads from Central Asia.

MUSLIM PERSIA

By the beginning of the seventh century A.D. Persia had been greatly weakened by these wars, and when the Muslim Arabs attacked, little effective resistance was offered. The decisive battles were fought at Qadisiyya (A.D. 637) and Nihavand (c. A.D. 641). Persia did not re-emerge as a political entity until the sixteenth century A.D., although with the decline of the Abbasid empire semi-independent and independent dynasties arose in different parts of Persia and at times even incorporated under their rule an area extending beyond the confines of present day Persia. As a result of the Arab conquest Persia became part of the Muslim world. Local administration remained largely in the hands of the indigenous population and many local customs continued to be observed. In due course a new civilization developed in Persia, the unifying force of which was Islam.

With the transfer of the capital of the Islamic empire from Damascus to Baghdad (c. A.D. 750) Persian influence began to be strongly felt in the life of the empire. Islam had already replaced Zoroastrianism and by the tenth century modern Persian, written in the Arabic script and including a large number of Arabic words in its vocabulary, had established itself. Its emergence was of immense importance; the literary tradition for which it became the vehicle has perhaps more than any other factor kept alive a national consciousness among the Persians and preserved the memory of the great Persian empires of the past, however much the details became blurred and even distorted in the course of transmission.

By the eighth century A.D. the Abbasid caliphate had begun to disintegrate and when in the eleventh century control of the north-eastern frontiers broke down, the Ghuzz Turks invaded Persia. This movement, of which the Seljuqs became the leaders, was ethnologically important since it altered the balance of population, the Turkish element from then on being second only to the Persian in numbers and influence. Secondly, it was in the Seljuq empire that the main lines of the politico-economic structure, which was to last in Persia in a modified form down to the twentieth century A.D., were worked out. The basis of this structure was the land assignment, the holder of which was often virtually a petty territorial ruler, who was required, when called upon to do so, to provide the ruler with a military contingent. This system was to some extent forced upon the Seljuqs and others after them, because they were unable to establish an effective system of direct administration or to exercise financial control over their military forces and because they could not integrate the settled and semi-settled elements of the population: the weakness of the system was that whenever the central control slackened, the empire tended to split up into independent or semi-independent units.

The Seljuq empire itself broke up in the twelfth century into a number of succession states; the thirteenth century saw the Mongol invasion and in 1258 Hulagu, the grandson of Chinghiz (Jenghiz) Khan, sacked Baghdad and destroyed the caliphate. For some years the Ilkhan dynasty, founded by Hulagu, ruled Persia as vassals of the Great Khan in Qaraqorum, but from the reign of Abaqa (1265–1281) onwards they became virtually a Persian dynasty. Their empire, like that of the Seljuqs before them— and for very much the same reason—broke up at the beginning of the fourteenth century into a number of succession states. Towards the end of the century Persia again fell under the dominion of a military conqueror, when Timur, who had started his career as the Warden of the marches in the Oxus-Jaxartes basin against the nomads of Central Asia, undertook a series of military campaigns against Persia between 1381 and 1387. The kingdom founded by him was shortlived and rapidly disintegrated on the death of his son Shahrukh, the western part falling first to the Turkomans of the Black Sheep and then to the Turkomans of the White Sheep, while Transoxania passed into the hands of the Uzbegs.

THE PERSIAN MONARCHY

The sixteenth century saw the foundation of the Safavid empire, which was accompanied by an east-ward movement of the Turkomans from Asia Minor back into Persia. For the first time since the Muslim conquest Persia re-emerged as a political unit; her frontiers became more or less fixed, although there was a general movement of contraction in the eighteenth and nineteenth centuries notably in the north-west and north-east. The foundations of the Safavid empire were laid by Isma'il Safavi (1502–24). He deliberately fostered a sense of separateness and of national unity vis-à-vis the Ottoman Turks with whom the Safavids were engaged in a struggle for supremacy in the west, and the main weapon he used to accomplish his purpose was Shi'ism. Not only the

Turks but the majority of his own subjects were at the time Sunni—nevertheless he imposed Shi'ism upon them by force and created among the population of his dominions, many of whom, especially among his immediate followers, were Turks, a sense of national unity as Persians. Apart from a brief inter-lude under Nadir Shah, Shi'ism has since then re-mained the majority rite in Persia and is the official rite of the country at the present day. Under Shah Abbas (1587–1629) the Safavid empire reached its zenith and Persia enjoyed a power and prosperity which she has not since achieved.

GREAT POWER RIVALRY

During the Safavid period, intercourse with Europe increased. Various foreign embassies interested mainly in the silk trade reached the Safavid court via Russia and via the Persian Gulf. In the latter area in the early years of the sixteenth century a struggle for supremacy developed between the British and the Dutch. "Factories" were established by the East India Company in the Gulf from the early sixteenth century.

Under the later Safavids internal decline set in and from 1722–30 Persia was subject to Afghan invasion and occupation while in the west and north she was threatened by Turkey and Russia. After the death of Peter the Great there was a temporary slackening of Russian pressure, but the Turks continued to advance and took Tabriz in 1725, peace being eventually made at Hamadan in 1727. The Afghans were finally evicted by Nadir Shah Afshar whose reign (1736–47) was remarkable chiefly for his military exploits. The Afsharids were succeeded by Karim Khan Zand (1750–79) whose relatively peaceful reign was followed by the rise of the Qajars who continued to reign until 1925. Under them the capital was transferred from Isfahan to Teheran. During the Qajar period events in Persia became increasingly affected by Great Power rivalry until not only Persia's foreign policy was dominated by this question, but her internal politics also.

With the growth of British influence in India in the late eighteenth and early nineteenth centuries the main emphasis in Anglo-Persian relations, which during the sixteenth and seventeenth centuries had been on commerce, began to shift to strategy. Persia and the Persian Gulf came to be regarded as one of the main bastions to India and the existence of an independent Persia as a major British interest. In the early nineteenth century fear of a French invasion of India through Persia exercised the mind of the British in India and Whitehall. French envoys were active in Persia and Mesopotamia from 1796 to 1809, and to counter possible French activities Captain (after-wards Sir John) Malcolm was sent to Persia in 1800 by the Governor-General of India; he concluded a political and commercial treaty with Fath Ali Shah, the main purpose of which was to ensure that the Shah should not receive French agents and would do his utmost to prevent French forces entering Persia. With the defeat of Napoleon in Egypt the matter was no longer regarded as urgent and the agreement was not ratified. Subsequently the French made proposals to Persia for an alliance against Russia and in 1807 Persia concluded the Treaty of Finkenstein with France after which a military mission under General Gardanne came to Persia. In 1808 another British mission was sent under Malcolm. Its object was "first, to detach the Court of Persia from the French alliance and to prevail on that Court to refuse the passage of French troops through the territories subject to Persia, or the admission of French troops into the country. If that cannot be obtained, to admit English troops with a view of opposing the French army in its progress to India, to prevent the creation of any maritime post, and the establishment of French factories on the coast of Persia". Malcolm's task was complicated by the almost simultaneous arrival of a similar mission from Whitehall. In 1809 after the Treaty of Tilsit, which debarred the French from aiding the Shah against Russia, Gardanne was dismissed.

WARS WITH RUSSIA AND TURKEY

Meanwhile the formal annexation of Georgia by Russia in 1801 had been followed by a campaign against Russia. This proved disastrous to Persia and was temporarily brought to an end by the Treaty of Gulistan (1813) by which Persia ceded Georgia, Qara Bagh and seven other provinces. British policy continued to be exercised over the possibility of an invasion of India via Persia and in 1814 the Treaty of Teheran was concluded with Persia by which Great Britain undertook to provide troops or a subsidy in the event of unprovoked aggression on Persia. Although the treaty provided for defence against any European power it was primarily intended to provide against the designs of Russia. In fact it proved ineffective and when the Perso-Russian war recommenced in 1825 Great Britain did not interfere except as a peacemaker and discontinued the subsidy to Persia, who was technically the aggressor. The war was concluded in 1828 by the Treaty of Turkomanchai, under the terms of which Persia ceded Erivan and Nakhjivan and agreed to pay an indemnity; in addition, she was prohibited from having armed vessels on the Caspian.

During this period Persia was also engaged in hostilities with Turkey. Frontier disputes in 1821 culminated in the outbreak of war, which was concluded by the Treaty of Erzerum (1823).

By the nineteenth century the Persian Government had ceased to exercise effective control over the greater part of Khurasan. Russian policy, which became conciliatory towards Persia during the twenty-five years or so after the Treaty of Turkomanchai, encouraged the Shah to reimpose Persian rule on the eastern provinces. British policy, on the other hand, having come to regard Afghanistan as an important link in the defence of India, urged moderation upon the Persian Government. Nevertheless a Persian expedition set out, took Quchan and Sarakhs and laid siege to Herat; on the death of Abbas Mirza, the heir apparent and commander of the Persian

forces in the east at the time, the siege was raised. After the accession of Muhammad Shah in 1834, a new expedition was sent against Herat. The sending of this, too, was encouraged by Russia while the Barakzai chiefs of Kandahar also offered the Persians assistance against their Saduzai rivals in Herat. The siege of Herat began in 1837 but was raised when the Shah was threatened with British intervention. Subsequently local intrigues headed by Sa'id Muhammad had enabled the Persians to enter Herat, and when Muhammad Ysuf Saduzai seized Herat some years later in 1855 and put Sa'id Muhammad to death, relatives of the latter went to Teheran to enlist the support of the Shah who thereupon ordered the governor of Meshed to march on Herat. The seizure of the city by Persia led to the outbreak of the Anglo-Persian war in 1856, which was terminated by the Treaty of Paris (1857) after a British force had occupied the island of Kharg in the Persian Gulf.

In the second half of the century the subjection of the Turkoman tribes by Russia, her capture of Marv in 1854, and the occupation of the Panjeh, meant that Russian influence became dominant in Khurasan in the same way as the advance of Russia to the Araxes after the Persian wars in the early part of the nineteenth century had made Russian influence dominant in Azerbaizhan.

INCREASED FOREIGN INTERVENTION

Internally the second half of the nineteenth century was remarkable chiefly for the beginnings of the modernist movement, which was stimulated on the one hand by internal misgovernment and on the other by increased intervention in the internal affairs of the country by Russia and Britain. Towards the end of the century numerous concessions were granted to foreigners largely in order to pay for the extravagances of the court. The most fantastic of these was the Reuter concession. In 1872 a naturalized British subject, Baron de Reuter, was given by the Shah a monopoly for seventy years of railways and tramways in Persia, all the minerals except gold, silver and precious stones, irrigation, road, factory and telegraph enterprises, and the farm of customs dues for twenty-five years. Eventually this concession was cancelled and permission instead given for the foundation of a Persian state bank with British capital, which was to have the exclusive right to issue banknotes; and accordingly in September 1889 the Imperial Bank of Persia began business. In the same year Dolgoruki obtained for Russia the first option of a railway concession for five years. In November of the following year the railway agreement with Russia was changed into one interdicting all railways whatsoever in Persia. In 1889 after negotiations for foreign loans Belgian officials were put in charge of the customs administration. By the turn of the century there had been "a pronounced sharpening of Anglo-Russian hostility as a consequence of a whole series of Russian actions, not only in northern Persia where Russian ascendancy to a large extent had to be admitted, but as well in southern and eastern Persia which had hitherto been predominantly British preserves". In 1900 a Russian loan was given, to be followed by another in 1902 secured on the customs (excluding those of Fars and the Gulf). Subsequently various short-term advances and subsidies from the Russian treasury including advances to the heir apparent, Muhammad Ali, were made so that by 1906 some £7½ million were owing to the Russians. Under the 1891 Russo-Persian tariff treaty, trade between the two countries had increased, and when under the 1901 Russo-Persian commercial treaty a new customs tariff was announced in 1903, Russian exports to Persia were considerably aided and up to 1914 Russian commerce with Persia continued to grow.

The grant of these various concessions to foreigners and the raising of foreign loans gave rise to growing anxiety on the part of the Persian public. Further, large numbers of Persians had fled the country and were living in exile. When a tobacco monopoly was granted to a British subject in 1890, various elements of the population, including the intellectuals and the religious classes, combined to oppose it. Strikes and riots threatened and the monopoly was rescinded. No effective steps, however, were taken to allay popular discontent. In 1901 protests were made against the loans and mortgages from Russia which were being contracted to pay for Muzaffar ud-Din Shah's journeys to Europe. By 1905–6 the demand for reform had grown in strength and finally on August 5th, 1906, after 12,000 persons had taken sanctuary in the British legation, a constitution was granted. A long struggle then began between the constitutionalists and the Shah. The Cossack Brigade, formed during the reign of Nasir ud-Din Shah, which was under Russian officers and was the most effective military force in the country, played a major part in this struggle and was used by Muhammad Ali Shah to supress the National Assembly in 1908. Civil war ensued and Muhammad Ali Shah's abdication was forced in 1909.

Meanwhile in 1907 the Anglo-Russian convention had been signed. The convention, which included a mutual undertaking to respect the integrity and independence of Persia, divided the country into three areas, that lying to the north of a line passing from Qasri Shirin to Kakh where the Russian, Persian and Afghan frontiers meet in the east, that lying to the south of a line running from Qazik on the Perso-Afghan frontier through Birjand and Kerman to Bandar Abbas on the Persian Gulf, and that lying outside these two areas. Great Britain gave an undertaking not to seek or support others seeking political or economic concessions in the northern area; Russia gave a similar undertaking with reference to the southern area. In the central area the freedom of action of the two parties was not limited and their existing concessions (which included the oil concession granted to D'Arcy in 1901) were maintained. The conclusion of this convention—which had taken place partly because of a change in the relative strength of the Great Powers and partly because the British Government hoped thereby to terminate Anglo-Russian rivalry in Persia and to prevent further Russian encroachments—came as a shock to Persian opinion which had hoped much from the support which the British Government had given to the constitutional movement. It was felt that Persian interests had been bartered away by Great Britain for a promise of Russian support in the event of a European war. In fact, the convention failed in its object. Russian pressure continued to be exercised on Persia directly and indirectly. In 1909, 1911 and 1912 Russian troops occupied Tabriz and other towns in north Persia; and in 1911 as a result of Russian pressure the National Assembly was suspended and the resignation forced of the American Administrator-General of the Finances, Shuster, who had been appointed in the hope of bringing order into the finances of Persia.

THE FIRST WORLD WAR

During the 1914–18 War Persia was nominally neutral but in fact Turkish; British and Russian forces and German agents were active in the country, and on the conclusion of the armistice between Russia and Turkey in 1917 two British expeditionary forces set out for Russia through Persia on what proved to be abortive missions. By the end of the war the internal condition of Persia was chaotic. To the British Government the restoration of order was desirable and with this end in view the Agreement of 1919 was drawn up whereby a number of men were to be lent to reorganize the Persian army and to reform the Ministry of Finance and a loan of £2 million was to be given. There was opposition to this agreement in the U.S.A. and France and in Persia, and the treaty was not ratified. A *coup d'état* took place in 1921, Reza Khan (later Reza Shah) becoming Minister of War. In February 1921 the Soviet-Persian Treaty was signed whereby the U.S.S.R. declared all treaties and conventions concluded with Persia by the Tsarist Government null and void. Under Article VI the U.S.S.R. was permitted "to advance her troops into the Persian interior for the purpose of carrying out the military operations necessary for its defence" in the event of a third party attempting "to carry out a policy of usurpation by means of armed intervention in Persia, or if such a Power should desire to use Persian territory as a base of operations against Russia. . . ." In a letter dated December 12th, 1921, from the Russian diplomatic representative at Teheran to the Persian Minister for Foreign Affairs, it was stated that this article was intended to apply "only to cases in which preparations have been made for a considerable armed attack upon Russia or the Soviet Republics allied to her, by the partisans of the régime which has been overthrown or by its supporters among those foreign Powers which are in a position to assist the enemies of the Workers' and Peasants' Republics and at the same time to possess themselves, by force or by underhand methods, of part of the Persian territory, thereby establishing a base of operations for any attacks—made either directly or through the counter-revolutionary forces—which they might meditate against Russia or the Soviet Republics allied to her".

REZA SHAH 1925-1941

In 1923 Reza Khan became Prime Minister and finally in 1925 the crown of Persia was conferred upon him. His first task was to restore the authority of the central government throughout the country, and the second to place Persia's relations with foreign countries on a basis of equality. All extra-territorial agreements were terminated from 1928. Lighterage and quarantine duties on the Persian littoral of the Persian Gulf, hitherto performed by Great Britain, were transferred to the Persian Government in 1930. The Indo-European Telegraph Company, which had been in operation since 1872, had almost entirely been withdrawn by 1931 and the British coaling stations were transferred from Basidu and Henjam to Bahrain in 1935.

In 1932 the cancellation of the Anglo-Persian Oil Company's concession was announced by Persia. The original concession obtained by D'Arcy in 1901 had been taken over by the Anglo-Persian Oil Company (later the Anglo-Iranian Oil Company) in 1909 and the British Government had acquired a controlling interest in the company in 1914. Thenceforward the main emphasis of British policy towards Persia had been on oil rather than strategy, though from 1941 onwards the strategic aspect again became important. The Persian Government's action in cancelling the concession was referred to the League of Nations. Eventually an agreement was concluded in 1933 for a new concession whereby the concession area was materially reduced and the royalty to be paid to the Persian Government increased. The concession was to run to 1993.

Internally Reza Shah's policy aimed at modernization and autarchy, In the later years of his reign the Government became increasingly totalitarian in its nature. Compulsory military service was introduced and the army much increased in size. Communications were greatly improved; the construction of a trans-Persian railway was begun. Education was remodelled on western lines. Women were no longer obliged to wear the veil after 1936. Foreign trade was made a state monopoly, currency and clearing restrictions were established. These arrangements fitted in with the economy of Germany and by the outbreak of World War II, Germany had acquired considerable commercial and political influence in Persia.

On the outbreak of war Persia declared her neutrality. In 1941 the Allies demanded a reduction in the number of Germans in the country, and when no satisfaction was obtained sent another communication demanding the expulsion of all German nationals, except such as were essential to Persian economy and harmless to the Allies. This demand was not complied with and on August 26th, 1941, Persia was invaded. Hostilities lasted some two days. On September 16th Reza Shah abdicated in favour of his son Muhammad Reza. In January 1942 a Tripartite Treaty of Alliance was concluded with Great Britain and the U.S.S.R. whereby Great Britain and the U.S.S.R. undertook jointly and severally "to respect the territorial integrity, sovereignty and political independence of Persia" and "to defend Persia by all means in their command from aggression" and the Persian Government undertook to give the Allies for certain military purposes the unrestricted right to use, maintain and guard, and in the case of military necessity, to control, all means of communications in Persia. Allied forces were to be withdrawn not later than six months after the conclusion of hostilities between the Allied Powers and Germany and her associates. In so far as the establishment of communications with the U.S.S.R. was concerned the Treaty was effective; its operation in other respects was less satisfactory. In the Russian zone of occupation the Persian authorities were denied freedom of movement and effective administration made impossible. American advisers were appointed by the Persian Government in 1942 and 1943 in the hope of reorganizing certain aspects of the administration. Their efforts were for a variety of reasons in no case attended by more than a limited measure of success and in due course their services were terminated.

In 1943 a British company applied for an oil concession in south-east Persia and in 1944 the Socony Vacuum and Sinclair Oil Companies made various proposals to the Persian Government. In September the Persian Cabinet issued a decree deferring the grant of oil concessions till after the war. The U.S.S.R. meanwhile asked for an oil concession in the north and brought heavy, though unavailing, pressure to bear on the Persian Government to accede to this demand. Persian security forces were prevented by Soviet forces from entering Azerbaizhan or the Caspian Provinces and an autonomous government was set up in Azerbaizhan with Russian support in December 1945. In January 1946 the Persian Government had recourse to the Security Council. In March the Tripartite Treaty expired and British and American forces evacuated Persia, Soviet forces remaining. The Persian Government again presented a note to the Security Council. In April an oral understanding, confirmed by an exchange of letters between the Persian Prime Minister and the Soviet Ambassador, was arrived at whereby a joint Soviet-Persian company to exploit the oil in the northern provinces was to be formed. In May Soviet forces evacuated the country. Soviet pressure, however, continued to be exerted through the Tudeh party, the Democrat movement in Azerbaizhan, and the Kurdish autonomy movement, and the Persian Government was unable to re-enter Azerbaizhan until December. In the following October, the Soviet Oil Agreement was presented to the National Assembly but was not ratified. In October 1947 an agreement was signed with America, providing for a U.S. military mission in Persia to co-operate with the Persian ministry of war in "enhancing the efficiency of the Persian army".

NATIONALIZING THE OIL INDUSTRY

Meanwhile unrest and discontent at internal misgovernment increased, culminating in the Nationalist movement of 1950/51. In July 1949 a Supplemental Oil Agreement with the Anglo-Iranian Oil Company was initialled. Opposition to this agreement (whereby

Persia was offered considerable financial gains) was strong. In November 1950 the oil commission of the National Assembly recommended its rejection. Meanwhile Persia had received a loan of $25 million from the Export & Import Bank of Washington and a grant of $500,000 under the Point IV allocation. Subsequently in 1952 the Point IV aid programme was expanded. In April 1951 the National Assembly passed a Bill for the nationalization of the oil industry, and in May, Dr. Muhammad Musaddiq, who had led the campaign for nationalization of oil, became Prime Minister. The Company and the British Government severally filed petitions with the International Court, the former asking the Court to declare Persia bound by the 1933 agreement to agree to accept the Company's request for arbitration and the latter asking the Court to nominate an arbitrator. The Persian Government declined to recognize the Court's jurisdiction. Eventually the British Government referred the dispute to the Security Council, which decided on October 19th, 1951, to defer consideration of the Persian case pending a final pronouncement of the International Court. The *status quo*, however, could not be maintained in Persia and the Anglo-Iranian Oil Company evacuated the country, being unable to continue operations.

On July 22nd, 1952, the International Court found that it had no jurisdiction in the oil dispute. This decision, however, was not a decision on the merits of the case. The Company accordingly maintained its claim to be entitled to all crude oil and oil products derived from the area covered by its concession agreement, and stated its intention to take such action as was necessary to protect its interests. American policy showed an increasing interest in Persian affairs. During the period August to October 1952, considerable correspondence passed between the British, American and Persian Governments in the oil dispute, culminating in a joint offer by Sir Winston Churchill and President Truman, making proposals concerning the assessment of the compensation to be paid to the Anglo-Iranian Oil Company and the re-starting of the flow of oil to world markets. The Persian Government rejected these proposals and put forward counter proposals which were unacceptable. On October 22nd the Persian Government broke off diplomatic relations with Great Britain. Further Anglo-American proposals for an oil settlement were put forward in February 1953, which the Persian Government rejected. Meanwhile dissension between Musaddiq and some of his supporters broke out, and a rift also developed between him and the Shah. The economic situation of the country began to deteriorate rapidly, culminating in the overthrow of Mussadiq by General Zahedi in August 1953. Musaddiq was tried and sentenced to three years solitary confinement for trying to overthrow the régime and illegally dissolving the *majlis*.

The new government resumed diplomatic relations with Great Britain in December 1953, and negotiations with British and American oil interests began for the solution of the oil problem. In September 1954 an agreement was signed, and ratified by the *majlis* and senate in October, granting a concession to a consortium of eight companies (subsequently increased to seventeen) on a percentage basis.

It was also agreed that the claims of the Anglo-Iranian Oil Company and the Persian Government against each other were to be settled by the payment of a lump sum to the Company, which was also to receive compensation from the other members of the consortium. The profits arising within Persia from the oil operations were to be equally shared between the Persian Government and the consortium. The agreement was for a period of twenty-five years with provision for three five-year extensions, conditional upon a progressive reduction of the original area. The National Iranian Oil Company was to operate the Naft-i Shah oilfield and the Kermanshah refinery to meet part of Persia's own needs and to handle the distribution of oil products in Persia and to be responsible for all facilities and services not directly part of the producing, refining, and transport operations of the two operating companies set up under the agreement. The greater part of the cost of these facilities and services, which would include industrial training, public transport, road maintenance, housing, medical care, and social welfare, would be recovered by the NIOC from the operating companies.

GROWING POWER OF THE SHAH

Internally order was restored. The Tudeh party was proscribed, but continued to exist underground, and in January and August 1954, Tudeh conspiracies were uncovered. The failure of the Government to push forward actively with reform, however, led in due course to a reappearance of unrest and discontent. In April 1955 Zahedi resigned and was succeeded by Ala, the Shah henceforward taking a more active part in the administration. In October, Persia joined the Baghdad Pact. The change of government, however, did not materially lessen the mounting discontent, and in November an attempt was made on the Prime Minister's life. Meanwhile, the country had not recovered from the financial difficulties brought on by the Musaddiq régime, in spite of the considerable financial aid granted to Persia by the U.S. to enable the country to carry on until oil revenues began to come in. U.S. aid has continued during the years that oil revenues have been coming in, and over 800 million U.S. dollars were poured into Iran between the end of the Second World War and September 1960. On March 5th, 1959, a bilateral defence agreement was signed in Ankara between the United States and Iran. Under the agreement the Government of the United States "will, in case of aggression, take such appropriate action, including the use of armed force, as may be mutually agreed, and as envisaged in the Joint Resolution to promote peace and security in the Middle East". (The Joint Resolution refers to the "Eisenhower Doctrine".)

Relations with the U.S.S.R. in the years following the fall of Musaddiq were not cordial, but in December 1954 an agreement providing for (1) the repayment by the U.S.S.R. of her war debts to Persia for goods supplied and services rendered, and (2) mapping of the revised frontiers was signed. In 1956 the Shah made a state visit to the U.S.S.R. The joint Soviet-Iranian frontier demarcation commission, which began working in August 1955, completed its task in April 1957, when protocols were signed defining the frontiers in detail.

On April 3rd, 1957, Hussein Ala resigned and was succeeded as Prime Minister by Dr. Manoutchehr Egbal, who formed a new government. Immediately after taking office Dr. Egbal issued a decree ending martial law and declared his intention of forming a democratic two-party system, in accordance with the desires of the Shah. In February 1958, the formation Government-Nation-Party was announced. An Opposition-People's-Party had been formed in 1957. Elections contested by both these political parties were held for the first time in August 1960, but after accusations that electoral irregularities had enabled the government party to secure an overwhelming majority the Shah declared the elections annulled, and the Prime Minister, Dr. Egbal, resigned. A new cabinet was formed under the leadership of Jafar Sharif Emami, the former Minister of Mines and Industries. New elections were held in January 1961 but National Front supporters alleged that the elections had again been rigged. Dr. Emami was again elected Prime Minister, but it was generally agreed that the existing electoral law was unsatisfactory and the Shah, in his speech to the new *majlis*, stated that its first task must be the passing of a new electoral law.

In May 1961, however, Dr. Emami resigned as a result of criticism of his handling of a teachers' strike, and the Shah called upon Dr. Ali Amini, the leader of the opposition, to form a new government.

Dr. Amini quickly took stern measures to halt the political and economic chaos in Iran. A drive against corruption in the Government and civil service was coupled with policies of land reform, decentralization of administration, control of government expenditure and limitation of luxury imports. Both Houses of Parliament were dissolved pending the passing of a new electoral law which would make free and fair elections possible. Postponement of elections in July 1962, led to disorder in Teheran, and the added difficulty of producing a reasonably balanced budget led Dr. Amini to tender his resignation.

A new government was quickly formed by Mr. Assadollah Alam, the leader of the *Mardom* (People's) Party. Mr. Alam, one of Iran's largest landowners and administrator of the Pahlevi Foundation, had previously distributed much of his land voluntarily amongst the peasants. He stated that Iran would remain closely linked to the West, and that he would continue the land reform programme and the struggle against internal political corruption. A reform programme was approved by a national referendum held in January 1963. Presenting the new budget in April, Mr. Alam announced that elections restoring the country to a parliamentary government would be held in June or July 1963.

REFORMS OF THE SHAH

Since 1950 the Shah has been distributing his estate amongst the peasants. By the end of 1963 he had disposed of all his Crown Properties and the Shah now receives only the sums allotted in the civil list. The Pahlevi Foundation was established in 1958 and has received considerable gifts from the Shah for the purpose of improving standards of education, health and social welfare amongst the poorer classes. In October 1961 the Shah created the £40 million Pahlevi Dynasty Trust, the income of which is being used for social, educational and health services for the Iranian people.

In January 1963 a referendum was held, as a result of which overwhelming approval was given to the Shah's six-point plan for the distribution of lands among the peasants, the promotion of literacy, the emancipation of women, etc. The break-up of great estates began almost immediately, and the programme was finally completed in September 1971; another important measure was the formation of the Literacy Corps (and later of the Health Corps), in which students could serve their period of national service as teachers, working in the villages. This aspect of the Shah's reforms was widely publicized, and in September 1965 an international anti-illiteracy conference was held in Teheran, attended by a number of Ministers of Education. In May 1966 the Shah donated £250,000 or one day's defence expenditure, to the world campaign against illiteracy.

A court statement of March 14th, 1958, announced the divorce of the Shah and Queen Soraya. The Shah and the Queen, who were childless, were married in 1951. The announcement said that the Shah had been unanimously advised by his Privy Councillors that the heir to the throne must be in direct descent from the Sovereign, in order to safeguard national interests. The Shah has a daughter by his previous marriage to Princess Fawzia of Egypt which was dissolved in 1948. In December 1959, the Shah married Farah Diba, an Iranian architectural student, and in October 1960 Riza Kurush, a son and heir, was born. A daughter, Princess Maasoumeh Farahnaz, was born in March 1963, another son in April 1966 and another daughter in March 1970.

The elections scheduled for July 1963 eventually took place in September of that year. The result was an overwhelming victory for the National Union of Mr. Alam; his party was in fact a coalition of several political groups, all pledged to support the reform programme of the Shah. The elections, in which for the first time women were allowed to vote, were held in the face of strenuous opposition from the left-wing parties of Iran, notably the National Front and the Communist Tudeh party, which called unsuccessfully for a boycott. The new Parliament—the first since both houses were dissolved by Dr. Amini in May 1961—was opened in October; in a speech from the throne, the Shah called on Parliament to inaugurate a new 20-year programme of economic and social reform and political development; he stressed the importance of drastic judicial and administrative reorganization, of educational expansion, and of a system of democratic local government. These reforms, said the Shah, were vital to the future existence of the nation. He announced a second phase of the land reform programme, whereby it was hoped that another 20,000 villages would be added to the 10,000 already handed over to the tenants. Queen Farah accompanied the Shah at the opening—the first Queen ever to do so. The Alam government continued until March 1964, when without tendering any reason, Mr. Alam resigned. The new leader was Hassan Ali Mansur, a former Minister and founder of the Progressive Centre, which had played a prominent part in the coalition of Mr. Alam the previous year. In December 1963 he had formed the New Iran Party, which by now had the support of some 150 members of the *majlis*. In his policy statement, Dr. Mansur said that the major objectives of his party would be the implementation of the Shah's reform programme, the protection and expansion of home industries, and the diversification of Iran's export trade, which hitherto had consisted of little more than oil. The second stage of the land reform plan was placed before the *majlis* in May; this aimed to break down the great estates more thoroughly; the maximum permissible size was to be from 120 hectares in arid regions to 30 hectares in more fertile areas. In spite of fears that the necessary credit would not be forthcoming, the programme was pressed forward by the knowledge that there was impatience among the peasantry and some lack of enthusiasm to undertake new works by landlords who were to be dispossessed.

REGIONAL CO-OPERATION

After preliminary talks by their Foreign Ministers in Ankara, the three Heads of State of Iran, Turkey, and Pakistan met on July 21st–22nd, 1964, in Istanbul and issued a statement which affirmed the need for increased regional co-operation between the three countries, and announced the formation of a new tripartite scheme of collaboration to be known as "Regional Co-operation for Development". The scheme provided for regular thrice-yearly meetings between the Foreign Ministers of the countries concerned, with the possible addition at a later date of Afghanistan; there would be close collaboration in the economic and technical spheres, and many projects could be undertaken together in the fields of communications, agriculture, industry, education, health, tourism and regional development; cultural links, based on the common Islamic heritage of the three nations, would be strengthened, especially at University level. It was emphasized that although the scheme was to exist independently of the Central Treaty Organization, it was not intended to usurp its functions; a large area existed outside the province of CENTO in which collaboration on national projects was possible.

On January 21st, 1965, Mr. Mansur was the victim of an armed attack in Teheran, by a young man who fired four shots at him at point-blank range; he died five days later in hospital. The assassin, Muhammad Bokharai, was arrested on the spot, together with two alleged accomplices. The three men, together with another who was said to have incited them to the crime, and nine others who were also implicated, were all members of the extreme right-wing religious sect Fedayan Islam, which was strongly opposed to the liberal policies of the Mansur government. There was no suggestion that the murder was other than an internal affair. The accused men were tried *in camera* by a military tribunal in Teheran and on May 9th the four principal accused were sentenced to death by firing squad. The others received varying terms of imprisonment.

Amir Abbas Hoveida, the Finance Minister, was immediately appointed Acting Premier, and became Prime Minister on the day following Mr. Mansur's death, retaining his post at the Finance Ministry. He pledged himself to the continuation of his predecessor's policies, and was given the massive support of the *majlis*. More active than some of his predecessors, he made a particular point of visiting the provinces in order to study their problems at first-hand. Mr. Hoveida has continued as Prime Minister right through into 1975, although elections took place in 1967, 1971 and 1975 and several Cabinet reorganizations and party political changes have been made.

In April 1965 an attempt was made on the Shah's life. The trial of the six people accused of organizing the attempt attracted world wide publicity; two received a death sentence, but these sentences were eventually reduced to life imprisonment. All six were apparently members of a militant Communist sect.

Several more trials followed; 55 men were accused of plotting armed insurrection, and their leader was sentenced to death; thirteen former Tudeh leaders were sentenced to death *in absentia*; and in February 1966 Khalil Maleki, a former Tudeh leader who broke away to form a moderate socialist group, was sentenced to three years' imprisonment in another public trial. In April 1966 the discovery of another Tudeh network was announced.

FOREIGN RELATIONS

The good relations between Iran and the Soviet Union have continued since 1964–65, when various mutually beneficial trading and technical agreements were signed, and a regular air service between Teheran and Moscow was inaugurated. It had been an avowed part of Mr. Mansur's policy that Iran should be as much interested in maintaining links with the Soviet Union as with the West. In June 1965 the Shah visited Moscow, and in October an agreement was signed for the construction by Soviet engineers of a steel mill. Relations with other countries were mainly commercial, including the U.S.A., Federal Germany, Japan, Romania, Hungary and Czechoslovakia.

The Shah also took seriously his role as a mediator, remaining firmly neutral in the Pakistan-India dispute of September 1965, and discussing the Viet-Nam situation with Averell Harriman in January 1966. Only with Iraq were relations strained during the winter, when the long-standing disagreement over the Shatt-al-Arab erupted into a series of border incidents, protest notes and popular demonstrations. By the spring of 1966 the situation had eased, discussions expected to start in April were postponed by the death of President Arif.

The policy of strengthening international relations continued throughout 1966 and 1967, with visits by the Shah to Yugoslavia and Morocco in June 1966, and Bulgaria, Hungary and Poland in September, and by the Prime Minister to Romania in November; these resulted in economic and cultural agreements. In April 1967 the King and Queen of Thailand paid a state visit to Iran, and in May the Turkish Prime Minister and King Hussein of Jordan both visited Teheran. At the end of May the Shah and the Queen paid a visit to West Germany, where in spite of elaborate precautions by the police, Iranian students succeeded in carrying out demonstrations of protest. This was followed by a visit to France, cut short because of the Middle East crisis. On May 31st the Government issued a statement of support for the claims of the Palestinian Arabs in accordance with the principles laid down by the United Nations. A large number of countries from West and East Europe, Asia and America have participated in various aspects of Iran's economic development.

The most publicized event of 1967 was the coronation of the Shah on October 26th, twenty-six years after his accession to the throne. An appropriate atmosphere had been built up by frequent stress in publicity inside and outside Iran on the claim that the Iranian monarchy was the oldest in the world, having been established 2,500 years ago. The long-delayed coronation was also hailed as the crowning glory of the "white revolution" inaugurated by the Shah in 1963. Immediately after placing the crown on his head, the Shah crowned Queen Farah—the first woman to receive this honour in Iranian history—in an act symbolizing the emancipation of Iranian women. By an earlier act of a Constituent Assembly, meeting on September 7th, the Queen had been nominated as Regent in the event of the Shah being unable to carry out his duties before the Crown Prince's twentieth birthday.

The stability of Iran was emphasized, not only by economic development and expansion and by the organization of international gatherings ranging from the Regional Co-operation Organization for Development (in which Iran continued to be an active partner) to the International Congress of Iranian Art and Archaeology, but also by the formal ending on November 29th of United States economic aid under the "Point Four" scheme. Iran, which had been the first country to accept this aid in 1951, was now the second (after the Republic of China) to find herself able to dispense with it. Military aid, however, was to continue. At the same time economic co-operation with the U.S.S.R. was developed, and an agreement was made for the purchase of £40,000,000 of munitions, the first time the Soviet Union had concluded an arms transaction with a member of the Western bloc.

In January 1968 the British Government announced its decision to withdraw all its forces from the Gulf by the end of 1971. Since these forces had apparently helped to preserve the local status quo, a revival of the ancient rivalry between Arabs and Persians over supremacy in the Gulf then seemed a likely prospect following their removal. The Iranian Government's reiteration of its claim to Bahrain in February 1968 did not help relations with the Arab world, and the Shah's official visit to Saudi Arabia was abruptly cancelled later that month. However, the political climate in the Gulf improved as the year progressed, partly owing to Iran's reduction of emphasis on the Bahrain question and to its cautious welcome for the proposed Federation of Arab Emirates (which it was thought would incorporate Bahrain). In October the Government signed an agreement with Saudi Arabia delineating the continental shelf between the two countries; this was hailed as a major step forward as the ownership of the shelf had become an important issue since the discovery of large offshore oil deposits in 1965.

The Bahrain dispute was submitted to the United Nations early in 1970, and a special mission visited the island in the spring. As was generally expected, it found that the large Arab majority overwhelmingly preferred full independence to joining Iran or remaining a British protectorate. Iran had previously agreed to accept the mission's findings, and it did so without complaint, though expressing concern for the future of Iranians in the Gulf states. In June 1970 a dispute with other Gulf states also arose over Iran's claim to the islands of Abu Musa and the Tumbs belonging to Sharjah and Ras al Khaimah respectively. The dispute was only settled at the beginning of December 1971. The Sheikh of Sharjah agreed to share his island of Abu Musa with Iran. The Sheikh of Ras al Khaimah was less accommodating, so Iran invaded his possesions of the Greater and Lesser Tumbs and took them by force. Seven people were killed and all the Arab inhabitants expelled to the mainland. Britain's treaty of protection with Ras al Khaimah was about to expire, as a prerequisite of the formation of the United Arab Emirates, and the British therefore took no action, causing strong reactions from Iraq and Libya in particular. Since occupying Abu Musa and the Tumbs Iran has been developing them as military bases to command the straits of Hormuz which lie at the neck of the Gulf. Iran regards maintaining freedom of passage through the Straits of Hormuz as vital to her strategic and economic interests, and it is for this reason that she has been building up military forces in the region and has also been sending troops to help the Sultan of Oman in his struggle against the rebels of the Popular Front for the Liberation of Oman (PFLO). In February 1974 the Shah described the Persian Gulf as Iran's "jugular vein" and pointed out that Iran could not survive the presence of "any forces of subversion, destruction, chaos and murder which might come close to the entrance to the Gulf".

Relations with the more radical Arab states have been less friendly. These states have long been suspicious of Iran's close ties with the West, and especially of the generous American military aid to the powerful Iranian armed forces. The Iranian attitude to Israel is now, for them, an even greater cause for concern. Though no formal diplomatic ties exist, Iran maintains normal trading links with Israel, of which oil supplies and landing rights for Israeli airlines are thought to be particularly important. Since the October 1973 war between the Arabs and Israel, however, Iran has tended to re-emphasize her Islamic connection with the Arab world, although still maintaining a tacit liaison with Israel.

Iran's only frontier with an Arab state is with Iraq. Near the Gulf the border is delineated by the Shatt al-Arab waterway, and, by the terms of the 1937 treaty, it actually runs along the eastern, i.e. Iranian bank; thus Iraq legally has sovereignty over the whole waterway. Iran has long resented this position and in April 1969 it decided to abrogate the treaty by sending Iranian vessels flying the national flag through the waterway, whilst heavy naval forces stood by. The aim was apparently to force a re-negotiation of the treaty. In September 1969, there were further armed clashes on the border—reports differed as to the extent of the casualties. In January 1970, Iraq accused the Iranian Government of backing the abortive *coup* in Iraq, and diplomatic relations between the two countries were broken. The situation both on the border and at governmental level remained tense throughout 1970. Iraq expelled some 15,000 Iranian residents over this period, and Iran was widely thought to be giving aid to the Kurdish rebels in northern Iraq. Iraq again broke off diplomatic relations in December 1971 in protest against Iranian actions in the Gulf, and more than 60,000 Iranians were expelled from Iraq, including some 4,000 who considered themselves Iraqi nationals. Relations with Iraq continued to be strained, and there were several border clashes in the early months of 1973, when Iran was very critical of Iraq's role in the Iraq-Kuwait border dispute.

Diplomatic relations between Iran and Iraq were restored soon after the outbreak of the Arab-Israeli war in October 1973, and the Iranian Government gave assurances to Iraq that it would not exploit the absence of Iraqi forces on the Syrian front. After the October war fighting again broke out on the border with Iraq, and it was particularly severe in February 1974. A United Nations Mediator was appointed, and in March 1974 a ceasefire was arranged which gave a temporary respite until more border incidents occurred in August. Further clashes occurred in December 1974, and secret talks in Istanbul in January 1975 between the Foreign Ministers of Iran and Iraq failed to prevent fresh clashes in February. It was therefore something of a surprise when, at the OPEC meeting in Algiers in March 1975, it was announced that the Shah and Sadam Hussein Takriti (the Vice-President of the Iraqi Revolution Command Council) had signed an agreement which "completely eliminated the conflict between the two brotherly

countries". Not only did this agreement settle the outstanding border differences, but it also deprived the Kurds in Iraq of the help which they had been receiving from Iran in their struggle against the Iraqi Government, thus causing a Kurdish collapse and a virtual end to the Kurdish war.

The border agreement provided that Iran and Iraq would define their frontiers on the basis of the Protocol of Constantinople of 1913 and the verbal agreement on frontiers of 1914 and that the Shatt al-Arab frontier would be defined according to the Thalweg Line (i.e. the middle of the deepest shipping channel). The treaty giving effect to this agreement was signed on June 15th, 1975.

Internally, signs of opposition to the Shah's régime, never far from the surface of Iranian life, became more and more evident as the celebrations for the 2,500th anniversary of the Persian monarchy were in preparation for October 1971. The combination of the very unequal distribution of the enormous earnings from oil and the suppression of any sign of dissent was made more politically explosive as the lavishness of the celebrations (estimates of the cost range from $50 million to $300 million) and the massiveness of the security precautions (600–1,000 people were interned in the few months before October) began to make their impact. The underground opposition movement carried out a series of guerrilla attacks, most notably assassinating the Chief of Military Justice, Zia Farsiou, in April 1971. The Government response became even more draconian and gave some indication of the seriousness of the guerrilla threat to the Government. In 1971, 13 people were executed before verdicts in their cases were even announced. In October 1973 an alleged attempt to kidnap or kill the Shah, Empress Farah and Crown Prince Reza was revealed by the Government security authority, SAVAK.

In March 1975 the Shah, dissatisfied with the current structure of party politics in Iran and wanting to weld together all those who supported the principles of his "White Revolution" policy, announced the formation of a single party system, the Iran National Resurgence Party (*Rastakhiz*), with the Prime Minister, Amir Abbas Hoveida, as Secretary-General. At elections held towards the end of June 1975 it was thought that as many as 80 per cent of those elected to the 268-seat Majlis were new members. Thirty senators were also elected to the Senate. The new Majlis contains more women and more representatives of the professional and workers' guilds than its predecessor.

Iran expected to receive £7,600 million in oil revenues in 1974, compared with £1,650 million in 1973. Rapid industrialization is now taking place, and details of Iran's oil, and the economic progress resulting from it, can be found in the Economic Survey.

ECONOMIC SURVEY

At the census of 1966 the population was returned as 25,788,722. Of this total, some 9,800,000 were urban residents, of whom 2,700,000 were located in Teheran and some 1,500,000 in the major cities of Isfahan, Meshed, Tabriz and Shiraz. With a growth rate of 3 per cent per annum, the population had risen to an estimated 32,496,000 by 1974 and is expected to rise to 36 million by 1978. Since the mid-1930s there has been an accelerating migration from rural to urban areas. The population of Teheran reached an estimated 4,000,000 in 1973. Much of the population is concentrated in the fertile northern areas of the country and the central desert lands are sparsely populated. The rise in the rate of population growth is attributable chiefly to the reduction in deaths due to malnutrition and famine and great advances in public health, particularly the virtual eradication of malaria over wide areas. The size of the nomadic population, now between 3 and 4 million, has declined since the 1940s, as a result of Government attempts to settle the nomads in villages. These tribes are in fact semi-nomadic, moving between traditional winter quarters in the plains, and summer pastures in the mountains.

Whereas the urban population had achieved over 65 per cent literacy by the beginning of the 1970s, the rural population had reached only 15 per cent literacy. However, the Literacy Corps programme under which high school graduates spend part of their military service teaching children in villages to read and write, has helped to achieve a substantial drop in the rural illiteracy rate since the programme was started in 1962. The number of rural primary schools has risen from 8,000 in 1962 to nearly 22,000.

Since 1963 when the Shah launched his "White Revolution" programme, per capita income has risen from $200 to $1,274 in 1975. During the Fourth Plan, 1968–73, G.N.P. rose at an average of 11.2 per cent a year at fixed prices. Over the period of the current Plan, 1973–1978, it is expected that G.N.P. will rise in real terms from $17,000 million to $55,000 million and that per capita income will grow to $1,520. The growth rate in 1973–74 was 34 per cent and could be over 50 per cent in 1974–75, with the full effects of the oil price rises being felt. For the remainder of the Plan period, an annual growth rate of 16 per cent is envisaged.

AGRICULTURE

Out of a total surface area of 165 million hectares, 19 million (11.5 per cent) are under cultivation and over half is classified as uncultivable, non-agricultural land. About 5.3 million hectares of agricultural land are fed with perennial irrigation water supplies from modern water-storage systems or from the ancient system of qanats (underground water channels), although these have fallen into disrepair in recent years. Rain-fed agriculture is important in the western provinces of Kermanshah, Kurdestan and Azerbaizhan. Agriculture is the principal economic activity of the Iranian people. However, whilst agriculture employs some 40 per cent of the total labour force, it accounts for only 13 per cent of G.N.P., and as a result the incomes of farm workers remain low. The average annual income of each peasant is about $200, compared with $1,000 for people in the towns. The structure of agriculture has remained basically unchanged in the twentieth century, although there has been a general tendency over the past forty years away from subsistence farming to the production of cash crops. A large variety of crops are cultivated in the diverse climatic regions of Iran. Grains are the chief crops, including wheat (the major staple), barley and, in the Caspian provinces, rice. Cotton, sugar-beet, tea, almonds, pistachios and dates are of commercial importance and olives and a variety of fruits and vegetables, as well as tobacco, are also grown. A scheme intended to make Iran self-sufficient in sugar was launched late in 1973. Cane sugar is being grown at Haft Teppeh, in the southern province of Khuzestan and a paper plant has been established in association with the plantation, which produced 110,000 tons of sugar in 1972–73. The world's largest sugar refinery is to be built in Iran by a Dutch firm; it will begin operating in 1977. With the aim of raising rice production, the Government has launched a project under which farmers will be provided with seeds of new high-yield strains, fertilizers at low prices, easy credits and loans.

The agricultural sector remains the least developed sector of the economy despite its importance and it is estimated that nearly 90 per cent of Iran's peasants are still subsistence farmers. The chief factors limiting the size of agricultural production are inadequate communications, limiting access to markets; poor seeds, implements and techniques of cultivation; lack of water and under-capitalization, which is a result chiefly of the low income of the peasant. The Fifth Plan gives greater emphasis to agriculture, partly as an attempt to deal with serious domestic shortages of meat, sugar and other foodstuffs, and also as part of the overall rural development policy. During the Fourth Plan (1968–73) the agricultural sector grew at under 3 per cent per annum. A growth rate of 7 per cent is envisaged for the period of the Fifth Plan (1973–78); nevertheless, by the end of the Plan, agriculture's contribution to G.N.P. will be only 8 per cent.

In 1974 Iran had to import 2.5 million metric tons of wheat (total domestic consumption 6 million tons) and 70,000 tons of meat. Food requirements, as a result of improved living standards and increased population, are growing at over 11.5 per cent a year. Prices of foodstuffs rose by about 12 per cent during 1973, contributing greatly to the accelerating rate of inflation. Although land reform and the introduction of mechanization and fertilizers has contributed to an increase in the size of harvests over recent years, much of this increase has been a result of increasing the area under cultivation.

Before the Land Reform Act of 1962 about 70 per cent of the fertile land was owned by a small number of large landowners. This led to a situation in which a share-cropping peasant cultivated the land on behalf of an absentee landlord. Until 1962 various attempts at land reform failed because of the dominance of the landlord element in the *Majlis*. In 1962, during the absence of a *Majlis*, a new land reform law was promulgated, limiting landholding to one village. All land above this was to be sold to the peasants. It was recognized that many peasants would lack the knowledge and capital to work their own land independently, so the project was accompanied by a drive to organize the peasants into co-operatives through which state land might be channelled. The second phase of reform was implemented from 1965 and involved the redistribution of all land in excess of a maximum varying according to soil fertility between 30 and 150 hectares (hectare— 2.5 acres approx.). The effect of the programme was somewhat cushioned by escape clauses which allowed landlords, for a transitional period, to keep up to 500 hectares of "mechanized land" and an unlimited further amount of land if it could be shown that this had been virgin land which the farmer had himself brought under mechanization. These measures had the double advantage of softening the blow for the richer landlords, and encouraging the continued use of mechanized farming with hired labour. The government would also pay to the landlord one-third of the price of any land sold to a peasant, in cash, which was to be repaid by the peasant over 14 months; and there were further financial inducements to landlords designed to speed the process of changeover. The first and second phases, which were concerned largely with land redistribution, were followed by a third phase, implemented slowly from 1967 onwards and aimed at encouraging mechanization and the consolidation of fragmented holdings. In 1971, when the land reform programme was officially completed, the government claimed that 761,931 families had benefited from phase I of the reform and 1,535,510 from phase II. By 1975, 2,800 co-operatives with a membership of 2.3 million persons had been set up. The Fifth Plan provides for better credit facilities for co-operatives and more Government help in the form of tractors, seeds and fertilizers. The number of members should rise to 3 million by the end of the Plan period, but the number of co-operatives will be reduced, with the object of consolidating them into larger units. Individual farmers with more than 200 hectares of land or groups of smaller farmers who join together as a company will also be given special subsidies for seed and fertilizers. Local training centres for farmers are also planned, but severe lack of trained personnel will make it difficult for these projects to be realized. About 65 farm corporations, joint stock companies in which the peasants are shareholders, have been established by the Government. At present, 23,000 people belong to these corporations which, because of their size, are able to obtain credit and to farm intensively with a high degree of mechani-

zation. The Government plans to increase their number to 143 by the end of the Fifth Plan.

The Government is encouraging the development of related industries with investment of 35,000 million rials under the Fifth Plan. By the end of 1978, 300,000 hectares, or 8 per cent of irrigated land, will be devoted to the agro-industry sector. Schemes include sugar plantations, almond plantations, meat complexes, dairy complexes and fodder production plants, and in many cases are joint ventures with foreign companies. In 1974 there were 220 schemes under way, and foreign companies were involved in 25 of these.

The principal products of the nomad sector of Iranian agriculture are livestock products—dairy produce, wool, hair and hides. In 1972 there were about 5.5 million head of cattle, 26 million sheep, 14.7 million goats and 110,000 camels. About 40 per cent of sheep and goats are raised by semi-nomadic tribal herdsmen. Production is limited by the prevalence of animal pests and the apparently inevitable lower productivity of pastoral as compared with domestic stock breeding, although account must be taken of the fact that most of the land grazed by the nomads' herds is land which could not be made economically viable in any other way. During the reign of Reza Shah (1923–41) the Iranian Government tried to enforce settlement on the nomads but the tribes rebelled. Since the early 1960s, Government policy has been to "encourage" settlement and has been achieving gradual success.

About 11.5 per cent of Iran is under forest or woodland, including the Caspian area—the main source of commercial timber—and the Zagros Mountains. Forestry in an economic sense is a recent activity and it is only since the nationalization of forest land in 1963 that effective attempts have been made under the Forestry Commission at protection, conservation and reafforestation.

Although Iran has direct access to both the Caspian Sea and the Gulf, fishing remains poorly developed in both areas. The Caspian fisheries are chiefly noted for an annual production of over 200 tons of caviar. Production in the Gulf amounts to about 5,000 tons per year and is largely consumed by the fishing community itself. The relative importance of caviar as a fishery export has been increasing in recent years to account for nearly 90 per cent by value of total fish exports. The biggest customer for Iranian caviar is the U.S.S.R. which in 1972 took 81 tons of the 196 ton yield. Production is expected to rise to 250 tons by the end of the Fifth Plan and could reach 400 tons a year by 1983. Pollution and the steadily falling water-level of the Caspian Sea are two serious problems being tackled under a Soviet-Iranian agreement signed in 1973. The Government intends to increase the fishing fleet and build canning and fish-meal plants along the Gulf coast. One survey has estimated that when fully developed, Iran's southern fisheries could earn as much as U.S. $200 million annually, chiefly from high-grade shrimp and prawn. In October 1973 the Iranian Government declared that it had extended its fishing limits to 50 miles, in order to safeguard its expanding fisheries industry from unfair competition from foreign, particularly Japanese, fleets.

PETROLEUM

The major industry of Iran is the petroleum industry, to which the large town of Abadan owes its entire existence. The history of commerical exploitation dates back to 1901, when W. K. D'Arcy was granted a sixty-year monopoly of the right to explore for and exploit oil in Iran, with the exception of the five northern provinces, which fell within the sphere of Russian influence. Oil was eventually discovered in commercial quantities at Masjid-i-Sulaiman in 1908 and in 1909 the Anglo-Persian Oil Company was formed. The Company was renamed Anglo-Iranian in 1935. A long series of disputes between the Iranian Government and Anglo-Iranian ended with the nationalization of the oil industry by Iran in 1951 and the replacement of Anglo-Iranian by what is generally known as the Consortium. The Consortium is an amalgam of interests (British Petroleum 40 per cent; Royal Dutch Shell 14 per cent; Gulf Oil, Socony Mobil, Exxon, Standard Oil of California and Texaco each with 7 per cent; *Compagnie Française des Pétroles* 6 per cent; Iricon Agency 5 per cent) formed to produce oil in the area of the old Anglo-Iranian concession as redefined in 1933. The Consortium's concession was to have lasted until 1979 with the possibility of a series of extensions under modified conditions for a further fifteen years. The revenues derived from the Consortium have formed by far the greatest part of Iran's oil revenue. Ownership of oil deposits throughout Iran and the right to exploit them or to make arrangements for their exploitation is vested in the National Iranian Oil Company, an Iranian State enterprise.

Until 1973 Iran had a leasing agreement* with the Consortium, but at a time when Middle Eastern governments were seeking participation agreements with commercial oil companies, the Iranian Government gave the Consortium an ultimatum: under no circumstances would Iran extend its lease, and the companies could either continue under existing arrangements until 1979 and then become ordinary arms-length buyers, or negotiate an entirely new "agency" agreement immediately.

The Consortium opted for the latter plan, and on 24th May, 1973 a contract was signed in Teheran under which the National Iranian Oil Company (NIOC) formally took over full ownership and control of the oil industry in the Consortium area, agreeing to provide all investment capital for expansion, while the Consortium was to set up a new operating company, Iranian Oil Services, which would act as production contractor for NIOC. In return the western companies were granted a 20-year supply of crude as privileged buyers, which they would take in proportion to their shareholding in the Consortium.

---

* For an explanation of the various types of agreements between oil companies and governments *see* Oil in the Middle East and North Africa, pages 69-102.

The National Iranian Oil Company participates in several other joint-venture companies, usually with a 50 per cent share (*see* p. 355) but these account for only about 10 per cent of total Iranian production.

In 1974, Iran's total output of crude petroleum was 302 million tons, representing 24.8 per cent of total Middle East production. Falling world demand for oil has resulted in a drop in Iranian output, from 5.9 million barrels per day at the end of 1974 to 5.6 million barrels per day in March 1975. Output in April 1975 was 9.7 per cent less than in the previous April. Iran is a member of the Organization of Petroleum Exporting Countries (OPEC) and is its second largest producing member. Its proven reserves, published in 1973, total 8,219.2 million tons, or 9.2 per cent of known world reserves.

The aim of NIOC is to acquire a stake in downstream operations in purchaser countries and eventually to become a major company engaged in all aspects of the oil industry, with the help of foreign participation. It intends to do this on a barter system, agreeing to a long-term supply of crude oil in return for a substantial share in refining and distribution operations in the purchasing country, or in return for participation by the purchasing country in the construction of refineries and in related projects in Iran. Negotiations have begun, and in some cases initial agreement has been reached, on a number of joint ventures, including the following: with West Germany, for the construction of a $500 million oil refinery at Bandar Bushehr on the Gulf, with most of the annual 25 million ton output being earmarked for West German consumption; with the U.K., guaranteeing an extra 8 million tons of crude a year, in return for goods including military equipment; with Japan, for the construction of a $1,000 million refinery; with Ashland Oil of the U.S.A., giving NIOC a 50 per cent share in the company's refining and distribution operations in New York State in return for a long-term supply of crude oil; with ENI, the Italian state hydrocarbons company, for participation in ENI's distribution operations in Europe and in eight African countries. Negotiations on participation agreements have also been opened in connection with refineries in India and Greece.

NIOC's refinery at Shiraz was opened in November 1973 with an initial output of 40,000 b.p.d., or 2 million tons a year. The Abadan refinery, the largest in the world, reached a record output of 484,800 b.p.d. in March 1974. NIOC is planning to build a refinery in the Neka region of Mazandaran with a 330,000 b.p.d. capacity which will probably begin operating in 1977 or 1978. The project will involve building a pipeline to Neka from the existing Ahwaz-Teheran pipeline. A new 83,000 b.p.d. refinery is planned at Tabriz, to start operations in 1977, and others are planned for Isfahan and Ahwaz.

NATURAL GAS

Iran's natural gas reserves are unofficially estimated at some 270 trillion cubic feet, which makes them greater than those of the U.S.A. and second only to reserves in the Soviet Union. Exploitation is in the hands of the National Iranian Gas Company (NIGC), a subsidiary of NIOC. Pure gas is found in fields offshore from Bushehr in the Gulf and at Sarrakhs in the north-east. In the past, much of the associated gas found in the southern oilfields was flared but in the late 1960s a pipeline, known as the Iranian Gas Trunkline (IGAT) was constructed from Ahwaz in the south-west to Astara on the Russian border. The gas was sold at the low price of 21 cents a cubic foot to the Soviet Union as part of an agreement signed in 1965, whereby the Russians constructed the Isfahan steel mill, a heavy machine plant at Arak and a machine tool factory at Tabriz, as well as providing a certain amount of light military equipment. About 1,600 cubic feet a day are pumped to the Soviet Union.

Domestic requirements are supplied through a network of spur lines to main cities from the IGAT line and plans for a second trunkline are being studied. By the end of the current Plan period it is expected that natural gas will be supplying 31 per cent of Iran's energy requirements, compared with the present 11 per cent.

Iran's first liquefaction plant is to be built near the offshore fields of pure gas near Bushehr and will begin operating in 1977. A new company, Kalingas, has been set up for this purpose and foreign participants include American, Japanese and Norwegian firms. The project will involve investment of about $700 million in Iran. Negotiations are under way for a second liquefaction plant on Kharg Island, with the participation of Phillips and Tokyo Electric. As part of a $3,000 million package deal agreed with France in June 1974, France is to build a liquefaction plant in Iran, a gas pipeline and twelve liquid natural gas carriers.

Iran hopes to become the major supplier of natural gas to western Europe. In April 1975 Iran signed an agreement with West Germany and the U.S.S.R. for 13,000 million cubic metres per year to be piped through the Soviet Union to Germany. The scheme will involve the construction of a new gas trunkline from southern Iran to the Soviet border. Studies are also being carried out on possible schemes for pumping gas to a Turkish port for liquefaction and shipment, for a transcontinental pipeline via Turkey, Greece, Yugoslavia and Italy.

Although under the new agreement with the former Consortium Iran has the right to exploit the gas within the agreement area, if it is unable to pump all the gas from the fields, member companies of the Consortium may, subject to Iran's approval, establish liquefaction plants and export liquefied natural gas from terminals on the Gulf.

OTHER MINERALS

The mineral resources of Iran have not been surveyed completely. Lead-zinc is mined at Bafq near Yazd, at Khomein, west of Isfahan and at Ravanj near Qum, with a combined potential of 600 tons of concentrates daily, though current plans for development are limited to Bafq. Chrome from the Elburz mountains and near Bandar Abbas, red oxide from

Hormuz in the Persian Gulf and turquoise from Nishapur are all produced for export. Sulphur and salt are produced on the coast of the Gulf, near Bandar Abbas and Iran is the leading sulphur exporter in the region. Coal deposits at Kerman, where output is some 25,000 tons a month, are used in the Isfahan steelworks, 700 kilometres to the north-west. Three coal mines in the Elburz Mountains were producing a total of 20,500 tons a day in 1973. There are iron ore deposits in the Elburz Mountains, at Yazd, Kerman and Isfahan. Iron ore from Bafq near Yazd is carried 540 kilometres by a specially developed railway to the Isfahan steel plant.

Deposits of copper ore have been found in Azerbaizhan, Kerman and in the Yazd and Anarak areas. About 10,000 tons of copper ore is mined annually in Azerbaizhan; it is planned to treble production in the next few years.

A number of very important deposits have been discovered since 1967 in the Kerman area south-east of Iran, the most important being at Sar Cheshmeh. It is predicted that Iran could soon become the world's seventh largest copper producer. The Government has invited foreign companies to participate in joint ventures on a 40/60 per cent basis, the foreign firm paying all exploration costs. A Japanese consortium provided the capital outlay for a privately-owned mine at Qal'eh Zari in eastern Iran and in return they get 80 per cent of the mine's annual output of 20,000–25,000 tons of copper concentrate. A number of foreign companies have been prospecting in several areas but in most cases deposits have turned out to be very low grade and the companies have returned the mines to the Government.

The Sar Cheshmeh deposits are to be exploited by Iran alone. The mine's projected output is expected to provide 145,000 tons of blister copper per year during the first ten years and its lifespan could be between 30 and 50 years. Reserves are estimated at over 400 million tons averaging 1.12 per cent copper content, with another 400 million tons of lower grade beneath. The giant project includes the construction of road and rail links to be built under the Fifth Plan to link the mine with Bandar Abbas 400 kilometres away on the Gulf, a training school, and a new town for the families of the 3,000 men who will work the mine. The cost of production in this remote and arid area has proved a formidable obstacle, but with direct Government participation it is hoped that smelting can begin in 1977.

INDUSTRY

Looking ahead to the time when its oil supplies will dry up, Iran is determined to become a major industrial power by the end of the century. In order to achieve this, the Government has concluded a number of trade and joint venture agreements with the governments of industrialized countries, for the transfer of technology and skills to Iran on a massive scale. Major "package" deals of this type have been made with the U.S.A., France, the United Kingdom, Italy and the U.S.S.R. The industry and mining sector of the Iranian economy has grown extremely rapidly since 1963, first with the help of fairly large foreign loans and now with the investment of huge oil revenues. The average annual growth of this sector has been 20 per cent in the period 1963 to 1974 and it employs over 2 million people. However, by the end of the Fifth Plan non-oil industry will contribute only 16 per cent of gross national product.

Industry concentrated initially on transforming local or imported raw materials into goods for the home market. These industries can be divided into three groups: textiles, food processing and construction materials. The largest cotton-producing area is Isfahan and this is the centre of cotton textile production, followed by Shahi in Mazanderan and Behshahr in Gurgan. Isfahan is also the centre of woollen production, drawing supplies from the nomad producers of the area. Tabriz, in Azerbaijan, is also a big woollen centre. Jute and silk are produced in Mazanderan. Persian carpets are still entirely the products of a handicraft industry. In 1972–73, over $100 million was brought in by the countless thousands of carpet-makers. Carpets are Iran's chief non-oil foreign exchange earner and by the end of the Fifth Plan exports of carpets are expected to be worth $500 million. However, there is an alarming trend towards shoddy workmanship and inferior materials which the Government is anxious to check, in order to save the reputation of the Persian carpet. Food processing includes sugar refining, flour milling and canning. The Fifth Plan lays great emphasis on agro-industries which will include the processing of meat and dairy products. With industrial development, the rapid growth of new urban centres, and the Government's social development policy involving the building of schools and housing, the building industry has been expanding fast in recent years. Cement production has grown rapidly in recent years to about 4 million tons a year and the Government plans to raise this level to 20 million tons by 1978. During the Fifth Plan, building materials in general are expected to grow by 23.3 per cent per annum.

The Government's declared policy is to spread industrial development widely throughout the country by exploiting local sources of raw materials, but it is only recently that new industrial centres have been created in the provinces. In 1960, of 4,430 factories in Iran, nearly half were in Teheran. Main industrial growth points are now Isfahan, Tabriz and Arak, and the secondary ones are Rasht, Meshed and Shiraz. The Fourth Plan placed emphasis on small industries and set up a new industrial estate at Zazvin, with 135 factories. The Fifth Plan, although it will grant loans and credit to about 10,000 small industrial enterprises, concentrates more on a heavy industrial base.

The petrochemical industry in Iran began with the opening in 1961 of a fertilizer plant at Shiraz. State-run activities in the petrochemicals field are the responsibility of the National Petrochemical Company (NPC), a subsidiary of NIOC. The Government is now planning an ambitious programme of development for

this sector during the Fifth Plan period and at the same time it is anxious to attract foreign capital for participation in joint-venture projects. Among major projects is a giant complex to be built at Bandar Shapur with a 50 per cent share held by Japanese interests. The complex will produce olefins and aromatics, from which final products are derived. The olefin unit will use hydrocarbon gases produced at the Marun and Mahwaz oilfields to produce ethylene, propylene and butadiene. The aromatics unit will use naphtha from the Abadan refinery to produce benzene and mixed xylenes. A salt electrolysis unit at the complex will produce chlorine and caustic soda. The various units are expected to begin operating in stages from early 1977. Between 50 and 60 per cent of the plant's output will be exported and the remainder will be used for Iran's domestic requirements.

Fertilizers are produced at Shiraz and Bandar Shapur, with output just covering present domestic requirements of around 400,000 tons a year. By 1978 consumption is expected to have doubled and the increase in requirements will be largely met by expanding the capacity of the Bandar Shapur plant, totally owned by NPC. PVC is manufactured at Abadan. The Kharg Island project, a joint venture in which the American firm AMOCO has a 50 per cent share, produces sulphur, liquid petroleum gas and natural gas liquids. A $280 million plant producing polyester and acrylic fibres is to be set up at Isfahan in a joint venture with the American firm E.I. Du Pont de Nemours and will start operating in 1976. Initial output will be 100,000 tons a year. The Government has approved a number of joint ventures with foreign companies for the manufacture of a wide range of petrochemical end products.

Iran's first steel mill was established at Isfahan under a $286 million credit agreement concluded in 1965 with the Soviet Union. The Arya Mehr plant began operating in March 1973, after a number of teething troubles and lack of suitable coal supplies. Present capacity is 700,000 tons a year and it has been agreed to expand this, with Soviet participation, to 1.9 million tons as part of the Government's programme for a heavy industrial base during the Fifth Plan period. A heavy-equipment plant may also be added to the complex. Local consumption for steel has been growing at 20 per cent a year and will probably reach 5 million tons by 1978, by which time national output should be 6 million tons. The Isfahan complex is run by the National Iranian Steel Corporation. The Arya Mehr project has included the building of the steel mill itself, development of iron ore and coal mines and the building of a new town at Arya Shah which will eventually house 300,000 people. A second blast furnace with a capacity of about 2,500 tons a day and a cold sheet rolling mill are planned. By 1980 Isfahan should be producing hot-rolled sheets.

France is to participate in the construction of a special steels plant with an annual capacity of 250,000 tons costing about $250 million. An aluminium plant with an annual capacity of 50,000 tons went into production at the beginning of 1973. Partners in the projects are the Iranian and Pakistani Governments and Reynolds Metals.

A well-established industry is that of motor manufacturing, which mainly comprises assembly plants. Until recently, parts were all imported but these are increasingly being manufactured in Iran. The industry began in 1957 and by 1974 total production reached 60,000 cars a year. Output by the end of the current Plan should be 600,000 vehicles per year. Already, Iran is selling buses to Egypt and Yugoslavia. In 1968, 30 per cent of Iran's passenger cars were imported, but by 1973 this proportion had dropped to 8 per cent, largely as a result of strong protective measures employed by the Government.

The largest of Iran's twelve motor manufacturers, Iran National, produces a version of the Hillman Hunter under licence from Chrysler UK, called the Peykan, which is Iran's best-selling car. A version of the Citroen Dyane, called the Jyane, is also manufactured and other models include versions of Chevrolet and Mazda cars, and Land Rovers. Buses and lorries are made under licence from Leyland Motors, Volvo and Daimler-Benz. General Motors is to set up a huge lorry plant to produce 100,000 vehicles per year by 1980. Iran National has launched a $100 million project to build its own engines, which will eventually lead to the production of an all Iranian car.

Diesel engines by British Leyland and Daimler-Benz are made at Tabriz and Massey Ferguson is soon to start assembling tractors there. Electrical goods and machine tools are also manufactured. During the Fifth Plan period, target annual growth rates for mechanical machinery, motor vehicles and electrical goods are 28.2 per cent, 19.2 per cent and 15.9 per cent respectively. Projects for underground railway systems for Teheran and other cities, and for the electrification of Iranian railways, were included in a financial agreement signed with France in June 1974.

Electricity generating capacity is at present about 2,206 mW and this is expected to increase to 6,300 by 1978. A number of new dams are to be constructed and the Reza Shah the Great Dam is expected to be completed in 1975. Iran agreed in principle in February 1974 to order five nuclear power stations from France, each with a generating capacity of 5,000 mW, at a total cost of some $1,200 million.

TRADE AND COMMUNICATIONS

Iran's imports of goods and services during 1974 were worth some U.S. $10,000 million. In the first half of the Iranian year 1353 (March 1974–March 1975), imports were up by almost 62 per cent on the same period the previous year. By 1982 Iran's import bills could total U.S. $40,000 million. If purchases of military equipment are included, the U.S.A. is the leading supplier, with West Germany second, but the positions are reversed if military purchases are not taken into account. Japan is in third place (14 per cent), followed by the U.K. (11.6 per cent), France (4.7 per cent), Italy (4.4 per cent) and the Soviet

Union (2.7 per cent). The EEC countries together account for nearly 42 per cent of Iran's total imports.

The share of industrial goods in Iran's exports doubled during the period of the Fourth Plan, but they still account for less than a quarter of all non-oil exports, with two-thirds of the total represented by "traditional" goods: carpets, cotton, fresh and dried fruit, hides and caviar. "New" industrial products include knitwear, textiles, clothes, pharmaceuticals, chemicals, soaps, detergents and shoes. Processed foodstuffs and vehicles are also exported. Non-oil exports as a whole increased in the first half of 1974–75 by only 8.25 per cent. Main customers for Iran's non-oil exports are West Germany, the U.S.S.R., the U.S.A., Japan, the United Kingdom, France, Italy and Kuwait.

Iran's principal imports, excluding military equipment, are machinery and equipment, iron and steel goods, chemical products, synthetic fibres and foodstuffs. Imports of vehicles have been declining in recent years, as Iran builds up its own industry.

Iran is pressing for the conclusion of a preferential trading agreement with the EEC.

There have been a number of important developments in Iran's external communications recently. Under the auspices of CENTO, railway lines are planned, or have been constructed, to link the Iranian system to the European system by building a line from Sharafkhaneh in West Iran to Mus in East Turkey and to the South Asian system by building a line from Yazd to Zahedan. The $90 million link with Turkey was inaugurated in 1971 and it is hoped to complete the extension to join the Pakistani network by 1976. In addition two roads are under construction to link Iran with Pakistan, one from Kerman to Quetta and the second from Bandar Abbas to Karachi via Mekran, to be part of the Asian Highway. The Sari-Shah Pasand, the Quchan-Meshed and the Mashad-Islam Qaleh sections had been completed by 1971. The agreement with the U.S.S.R. in December 1962 to re-open the old land route through Russia for Iran's trade with Europe will also have important consequences, shortening the distance by 3,000 miles.

FINANCE

Expenditure under the 1975–76 consolidated budget is expected to total 2,445,000 million rials. General budget spending is envisaged at 1,788,700 million rials (11.6 per cent more than in the revised 1974–75 budget). Of this, 29.4 per cent is for defence (41 per cent more than in the previous year). Oil and gas revenues are expected to provide 83 per cent of the total, at about U.S. $21,900 million. In 1973–74 they provided 53 per cent of total revenue.

Iran's foreign exchange position is healthy, with total official reserves at the end of February 1975 amounting to $9,992 million. The balance of payments at the end of the year 1972–73 showed a deficit of just over $11 million. However, by the end of the current Five-Year Plan, the Government expects there to be a surplus on current account of $20,600 million. It envisages a deficit on capital account of about $13,300 million, due mainly to loan repayments, totalling some $6,500 million and investments and lending abroad amounting to about $11,500 million. Therefore, at the end of the Plan period there would be a net surplus on capital and current account of just over $7,000 million. Experts predict that by 1978 Iran may again become a net borrower.

In February 1973 the rial was in effect revalued against the U.S. dollar by 11.1 per cent and by a further 1.1 per cent in June. The rial became convertible in September 1974. In February 1975 the Government decided to value the rial in terms of the IMF Special Drawing Right (SDR) instead of the U.S. dollar.

Inflation, which by 1975 was running at an annual rate of over 20 per cent, is now one of the major political and economic issues in Iran. Land prices have risen rapidly and wholesale prices at the beginning of 1974 were 12.5 per cent higher than a year before. The Government, in a number of anti-inflationary measures, has attempted to peg prices by creating a Price Supervision Council and has launched a major programme of bond issues to help to absorb excess liquidity.

During 1974, Iran provided a total of $7,000 million (6 per cent of its G.N.P.) in aid to more than 30 countries. It has also recycled some of its oil revenues by purchasing about $350 million of World Bank bond issues and by placing about $700 million at the disposal of the International Monetary Fund. It has also contributed $280 million to the UN special fund set up to ease the balance of payments problems of the least developed countries, hit by high oil prices. Iran's total investments in foreign industrial

enterprises or property, total some $500 million. It expects to recycle, through investments or loans abroad, $40–50,000 million of the total $100,000 million of oil revenues accruing during the Plan period.

FIFTH DEVELOPMENT PLAN

In March 1973 Iran embarked upon her Fifth Development Plan (1973–78). Whereas the main thrust for the Fourth Plan had been concentrated on oil and industry, the emphasis in the Fifth Plan is on improved living standards, education and training, closely followed by agriculture. Total expenditure was originally planned at U.S. $35,500 million, which was greater than the combined investment of the previous four plans put together. However, total anticipated oil revenues, originally estimated at $24,600 million for the period of the Plan, are now put at some $100,000 million. Total Plan expenditure was therefore raised to $68,600 million in August 1974. The largest single allocation will go to housing, followed by industry. In the latter sector, the emphasis is on developing the hydrocarbons and steel industries. Agriculturally-based industries will also receive special attention. The original target of the Plan was for an average annual growth rate of 14 per cent, but for the remaining period of the Plan, this rate is now expected to be nearly 26 per cent in real terms. Annual growth rates of 52 per cent are projected for the oil and gas sector, 18 per cent for industry and mining, 16 per cent for services and 7 per cent for agriculture.

Lack of adequate infrastructure and shortage of trained manpower and technical expertise are likely to be a major constraint on the implementation of the Plan in all sectors.

STATISTICAL SURVEY

(The Iranian year begins in March)

AREA AND POPULATION

AREA	POPULATION			
	Census (November 1st–20th, 1966)			Estimate (1974)
	Males	Females	Total†	
1,648,000 sq. km.*	13,355,801	12,432,921	25,788,722	32,496,000

* 636,300 square miles.

† Including nomadic tribes and other unsettled population (709,799).

CHIEF TOWNS

POPULATION (1974 estimates)

Greater Teheran*	.	3,931,000	Ahwaz	.	350,000	Khorramshar	.	130,000
Isfahan	.	601,000	Kermanshah	.	253,000	Yazd	.	118,000
Meshed	.	586,000	Rasht	.	187,000	Kerman	.	114,000
Tabriz	.	559,000	Qom	.	169,000	Qazvin	.	110,000
Shiraz	.	410,000	Rezaiyah	.	152,000	Dezful	.	104,000
Abadan	.	361,000	Hamadan	.	141,000			

* Sample survey.

ECONOMICALLY ACTIVE POPULATION*

(1971 sample survey)

	MALES	FEMALES	TOTAL
Agriculture, Forestry, Hunting and Fishing .	3,108,700	301,700	3,410,400
Mining and Quarrying	873,900	517,900	1,391,800
Manufacturing			
Construction	507,000	1,900	508,900
Electricity, Gas, Water Supply . . .	98,300	2,100	100,400
Commerce	633,600	8,900	642,500
Transport, Storage and Communications .	272,600	4,600	277,200
Services	663,300	170,000	833,300
Others (not adequately described) . .	72,800	6,100	78,900
TOTAL IN EMPLOYMENT . .	6,230,200	1,013,200	7,243,400
Unemployed	779,000	107,900	836,900
TOTAL	7,009,200	1,121,100	8,130,300

* Excluding nomadic tribes and other unsettled population.

INDUSTRIAL EMPLOYMENT 1972

	ESTABLISH-MENTS	EMPLOYEES
Food Manufacturing	28,853	181,118
Beverages	89	4,880
Tobacco	3	5,708
Textiles, Carpets, etc. . . .	49,577	715,964
Clothing	47,462	223,542
Wood and Furniture	14,324	92,467
Paper and Cardboard . . .	297	8,707
Printing and Binding . . .	1,239	15,026
Leather and Hides	1,497	20,300
Rubber and Rubber Products . .	1,244	13,491
Chemicals	1,447	37,012
Non-metallic Minerals . . .	6,655	72,203
Petroleum	15	37,700
Base Metals	944	31,415
Metal Products	29,058	107,595
Non-electrical Machinery . .	1,653	16,194
Electrical Machinery . . .	3,924	33,704
Transport Equipment . . .	13,788	74,902
Miscellaneous	7,077	23,402
TOTAL	209,146	1,715,330

AGRICULTURE

PRODUCTION
('ooo metric tons)

	1971-72	1972-73	1973-74†
Wheat . . .	3,700	4,546	4,600
Barley . . .	900	1,009	923
Rice (paddy) . .	1,050	1,200	1,334
Cotton (raw) . .	444	600	615
Sugar Beet . .	3,980	3,918	4,240
Oil Seed . .	46	54	57
Tea (green) . .	64	88	93

† Provisional

LIVESTOCK
('ooo)

	1971	1972
Sheep	24,292	25,040
Goats	13,950	13,460
Cattle	5,515	5,607

Fishing: Persian Gulf 14,000 tons, Caspian Sea 3,250 tons (incl. 2,000 tons of sturgeon and over 200 tons of caviar) —annually.

MINING
('ooo metric tons)

	1969–70	1970–71	1971–72
Iron Ore . .	10.0	150.0	98.0
Copper Ore . .	2.6	2.8	3.0
Lead . .	89.0	99.0	77.0
Zinc . .	97.0	66.0	89.0
Chromite . .	222.0	152.0	120.0
Barite . .	77.0	79.0	80.0
Coal . .	530.0	600.0	1,000.0

OIL
NET CRUDE OIL PRODUCTION
('ooo cubic metres)

	1969	1970	1971	1972	1973
Iranian Oil Exploration and Producing Company	179,924	202,884	240,500	266,000	312,900
National Iranian Oil Company (Naft-e-Shah) .	541	594	700	856	965
Irano-Italian Oil Company (SIRIP) . . .	1,547	1,854	3,335	4,900	4,100
Iran-Pan American Oil Company (IPAC) . .	6,023	5,372	7,246	7,900	7,400
Lavan Petroleum Company	6,924	8,267	7,801	9,800	10,700
Iranian Marine International Oil Company (IMINOCO)	888	3,210	3,856	4,600	4,000
TOTAL	195,847	222,181	263,438	294,056	340,065

('ooo barrels)

	1969	1970	1971	1972	1973
Iranian Oil Exploration and Producing Company	1,131,200	1,276,600	1,512,800	1,662,300	1,968,000
National Iranian Oil Company (Naft-e-Shah) .	3,400	3,700	4,100	5,400	6,000
Other oil companies	96,700	119,200	140,100	168,100	170,400
TOTAL	1,231,800	1,399,500	1,657,000	1,835,800	2,144,400

OIL EXPORTS
('ooo barrels)

	1969	1970	1971	1972	1973
Crude	1,039,308	1,205,902	1,452,431	1,657,000	1,920,100
Refined . . .	113,525	115,510	110,606	108,800	100,500
TOTAL . .	1,152,833	1,321,412	1,563,037	1,765,900	2,020,600

INDUSTRY

		1971-72	1972-73	1973-74	1974-75
Vegetable Ghee	'ooo metric tons	164	183	188	247
Sugar	,, ,, ,,	666	669	697	700
Cigarettes and cigars . . .	million	13,452	12,923	13,449	14,400
Paints	'ooo metric tons	18.8	21.2	24.6	n.a.
Cement	,, ,, ,,	2,882	3,372	3,489	4,500
Refrigerators	'ooo	171	196	257	500
Heaters	,,	139	159	216	n.a.
Gas Stoves	,,	228	319	313	n.a.
Radios	,,	159	222	281	n.a.
Televisions	,,	158	185	242	n.a.
Vehicles	,,	54	70	77	85

FINANCE

100 dinars = 1 Iranian rial.

Coins: 5, 10, 25 and 50 dinars; 1, 2, 5 and 10 rials

Notes: 5, 10, 20, 50, 100, 200, 500, 1,000, 5,000 and 10,000 ials.

Exchange rates (July 1975): £1 sterling = 145.74 rials; U.S. $1 = 66.64 rials.

1,000 Iranian rials = £6.86 = $15.01.

Note: From December 1946 to May 1957 the official exchange rate was U.S. $1 = 32.25 rials (1 rial = 3.1008 U.S. cents) but other rates were in operation for certain commercial transactions. From 1956 the trade rate was $1 = 75.75 rials (1 rial = 1.3201 U.S. cents) and this was the official parity from May 1957 to February 1973, despite the devaluation of the U.S. dollar in December 1971. In terms of sterling, the exchange rate was £1 = 181.80 rials from November 1967 to August 1971; and £1 = 197.38 rials from December 1971 to June 1972. In February 1973 a new par value of $1 = 68.175 rials was established but in February 1975 the direct link with the dollar was broken and the rial has since been tied to the IMF Special Drawing Right (initially at 82.24 rials per SDR), whose value is determined by changes in a weighted "basket" of 16 national currencies.

BUDGET
(million rials, 12 months ending March 20th)

REVENUE	1971/72	1972/73	1973/74	1974/75
Direct taxes	30,587	36,771	48,415	67,767
Indirect taxes	55,430	60,829	71,735	103,171
Monopolies, ownership rights . . .	147,197	188,041	235,932	501,057
Government service revenues . .	7,941	17,020	23,666	28,374
Miscellaneous	115,068	84,255	109,000	45,776
Profit-making and commercial agencies affiliated to government	125,203	161,620	203,985	600,930
TOTAL	481,426	548,536	692,733	1,347,075

EXPENDITURE	1971/72	1972/73	1973/74	1974/75
General affairs	32,528	36,539	67,949	88,407
Defence and security	77,499	100,941	133,754	215,067
Social affairs	66,179	83,104	104,873	155,757
Economic affairs	123,958	138,140	133,544	230,693
Debt repayments	57,979	28,192	61,766	77,507
Profit-making and commercial agencies affiliated to government	125,203	161,620	203,985	600,930
TOTAL	483,346	548,536	705,871	1,368,361

OIL REVENUES

Total oil revenues received by Iran, in U.S. $ million: (1971) 1,902.7, (1972) 2,430.5, (1973) 4,000, (1974) 20,000 approx.

FIFTH DEVELOPMENT PLAN 1973-78
('000 million rials)

	Original March 73	Revised August 74
Agriculture	121	239.6
Water	106	160.0
Industry	180	352.1
Mining	46	62.0
Oil	130	333.0
Gas	24	51.0
Power	53	240.0
Communication	177	404.0
Telecommunication	36	91.4
Rural development	36	60.0
Urban development	32	45.0
Government building	91	320.0
Housing	90	230.0
Education	127	130.0
Arts and culture	5	10.0
Tourism	7	11.0
Health	24	43.0
Welfare	5	9.0
Sports	9	15.0
Provincial development	0	10.0
Public affairs	0	32.0
TOTAL GOVERNMENT EXPENDITURE	1,299	2,848.1
Expenditure by government companies		445.0
Estimated expenditure by private sector		1,570.0
Less government loans to private sector		—229.0
TOTAL (NET)		4,364.0

Source: The Royal Road to Progress, Ministry of Information, Teheran, 1974.

EXTERNAL TRADE
(million rials, 12 months ending March 20th)

	1970-71	1971-72	1972-73	1973-74
Imports	128,260	157,658	193,652	253,190
Exports (excluding oil)	21,192	26,270	33,863	42,840
Oil Exports	163,746	176,272	248,912	375,901

Source: Bank Markazi Iran.

OIL EXPORTS
('000 long tons)

	1970	1971	1972	1973
Crude Oil	165,300	198,600	225,300	263,500
Crude Oil Run to Abadan Refinery	21,000	21,100	20,800	21,600

COMMODITIES
(million rials)

PRINCIPAL IMPORTS	1971–72	1972–73	1973–74
Iron and Steel	29,402	20,778	45,620
Motor Vehicles and Parts . . .	10,362	10,486	20,007
Electrical Machinery and Apparatus . .	19,300	14,388	20,101
Boilers and other Machinery . .	33,807	31,885	52,741
Chemicals and Pharmaceuticals . .	6,694	6,217	20,116
Textiles	5,962	6,369	12,518
Wool and Animal Hair . . .	2,414	2,867	4,759
Animal and Vegetable Fats . . .	3,471	2,223	4,106
Paper, Paperboard, etc. . . .	3,497	3,155	5,934
Rubber and Products	2,769	2,972	5,239
Sugar and Confectionery . . .	869	1,620	5,141
Cereals	7,752	4,052	7,413

PRINCIPAL EXPORTS (excl. Oil)	1971–72	1972–73	1973–74
Raw cotton	5,142	2,761	10,463
Wool	41	38	117
Hides and leather . . .	1,311	1,496	1,943
Fruit	2,880	2,338	6,388
Gum Tragacanth . . .	361	231	1,100
Carpets	5,761	4,785	7,353
Mineral ores	1,259	1,183	1,504
Oil-bearing seeds	610	700	695

PRINCIPAL COUNTRIES
(million rials)

	1971/72		1972/73		1973/74	
	Imports	Exports (excl. Oil)	Imports	Exports (excl. Oil)	Imports	Exports (excl. Oil)
Czechoslovakia . . .	2,151	1,104	1,863	1,634	1,537	778
France	7,199	725	9,119	664	12,173	1,609
Germany, Federal Republic .	29,809	3,910	35,713	4,548	49,583	7,184
India	2,170	495	3,130	432	3,737	378
Italy	7,235	737	8,525	782	9,544	1,574
Japan	21,090	1,620	27,099	1,737	37,159	2,910
U.S.S.R.	10,819	5,269	5,347	7,902	14,491	6,889
United Kingdom . . .	17,440	821	22,476	1,120	23,793	1,983
United States . . .	22,416	2,118	32,186	3,112	33,017	3,696

TRANSPORT

RAILWAYS

		1972	1973
Passengers . . .	('000)	4,097	4,209
Passenger-kilometres .	(millions)	2,054	2,188
Freight tons carried .	('000)	3,693	4,448

ROADS
('000)

		1972	1973
Cars	.	393.9	404.2
Goods Vehicles (incl. Buses) .	.	113.6	117.3
Motor Cycles and Scooters .	.	239.1	241.9

SHIPPING

		1971	1972
Ships entered		1,916	2,061
Freight loaded .	('000 m. tons)	1,120	1,187
Freight unloaded	('000 m. tons)	4,112	4,144

CIVIL AVIATION

		1971	1972
Passenger-km.	('000)	607,000	711,000
Cargo . .	('000 ton-km.)	3,886	4,301

POST AND TELECOMMUNICATIONS
(1974-75—'000, estimated)

Number of telegrams:	
Internal	12,000
Abroad	660
Telephone calls:	
Internal	12,000
Abroad	100
Letters despatched:	
Internal	320,000
Abroad	45,000
Parcels despatched:	
Internal	650
Abroad	55

TOURISM

	1973	1974
Visitors	373,515	420,000*
Approximate Money Spent (million U.S. $) .	50.0	58.0

* estimate

EDUCATION
(1973/74)

	SCHOOLS	PUPILS ('000)
Elementary . . .	18,719	3,144
Literacy Corps . . .	15,234	508
Orientation Course .	3,728	907
Secondary . . .	2,222	748
Technical and Vocational .	339	70
Primary Teacher Training .	114	34
Universities and Colleges .	148	123

Sources (except where otherwise stated): Statistical Centre of Iran, Teheran.

THE CONSTITUTION

On August 15th, 1906, an Imperial Decree was issued to convoke a Constituent Assembly. This Assembly adopted the Constitution of Iran on December 30th of that year.

THE EXECUTIVE POWER

The executive power rests in the Shah. He appoints the Prime Ministers, who must be approved by the *Majlis*. In addition to their individual responsibility for their departments, ministers have a joint responsibility for the affairs of the country.

In 1949 an amendment to the Constitution was made whereby the Shah was granted the right to dissolve the *Majlis* when it was deemed necessary, provided that a new election was ordered to take place soon afterwards.

THE LEGISLATIVE POWER

According to the Constitutional Law the legislative power comprises the Senate and the National Consultative Assembly (the *Majlis*). The latter Assembly consists of over 200 members elected for four years; the number of members rises with the growth of the population and by the July 1971 elections had reached 268. The Senate, which was convened for the first time in February 1950, comprises 60 Senators: 30 elected and 30 nominated by the Shah, 15 representing Teheran, and 15 representing the provinces. Senators must be Muslims. Their term of office is four years. There are also Senators from the minority religious groups.

PROVINCIAL DIVISIONS

According to the latest state division (March 1974), Iran is divided into 21 provinces (*Ostans*), two independent Governorate-Generals, 153 counties (*Shahrestan*) and 461 municipalities (*Bakhsh*).

All towns have a municipal administration, the director of which is chosen by the town council. The nomination must be approved by the Ministry of the Interior.

THE GOVERNMENT

THE HEAD OF STATE

H.I.M. Mohammad Reza Pahlavi Aryamehr, Shahanshah of Iran
(succeeded to the throne on the abdication of his father, September 16th, 1941).

THE CABINET
(July 1975)

Prime Minister: Amir Abbas Hoveida.

Minister of Foreign Affairs: Abbas Ali Khalatbari.

Minister of Defence: Gen. Reza Azimi.

Minister of the Interior: Dr. Jamshid Amouzegar.

Minister of Economic and Financial Affairs: Dr. Hooshang Ansari.

Minister of Information and Tourism: Gholam Reza Kianpour.

Minister of Education: Ahmad Hooshang Sharifi.

Minister of Science and Higher Education: Abdol Hosain Samii.

Minister of Mines and Industries: Farrokh Najmabadi.

Minister of Co-operatives and Rural Affairs: Reza Sadaghiani.

Minister of Posts, Telephones and Telegraphs: Karim Motamedi.

Minister of Trade: Ferreidoon Mahdavi.

Minister of Housing and City Planning: Homayoun J. Ansari.

Minister of Social Affairs: Sheikhol-Eslamzadeh.

Minister of Agriculture and National Resources: Mansur Rouhani.

Minister of Energy: Iraj Vahidi.

Minister of State and Head of Plan and Budget Organization: Abdul Majid Majidi.

Minister of Roads: Javad Shahrestani.

Minister of Health: Anushirvan Puyan.

Minister of Arts and Culture: Mehrdad Pahlbod.

Minister of Justice: Sadeq Ahmadi.

Minister of Labour: Amir Ghasem Moini.

Ministers without Portfolio: Ezatollah Yazdanpanah, Manuchehr Kalali.

Minister of State and Executive Assistant to Prime Minister: Hadi Hedayati.

Minister of State: Safi Asfia.

PARLIAMENT

THE SENATE

President: Eng. Ja'afar Sharif-Emami.

The Senate consists of 60 members, 30 of which are appointed by the Shah, and 30 are elected (15 from Teheran and 15 from the Provinces). The term of office is four years.

NATIONAL CONSULTATIVE ASSEMBLY
(The Majlis)

President: Eng. A. Riazi.

Elections to the 24th session of the Majlis were held in June 1975, under the new single party system. Over 80 per cent of those elected to the Majlis were new members.

POLITICAL PARTY

Iran National Resurgence Party (*Restakhiz*): Teheran; f. 1975 by decree of the Shah; aims to unite all those who support the principles of the "White Revolution"; Sec.-Gen. Amir Abbas Hoveida.

Before the formation of the Iran National Resurgence Party, the main political parties had been the governing party, the Iran Novin Party and the Mardom Party.

DIPLOMATIC REPRESENTATION

EMBASSIES ACCREDITED TO IRAN
(In Teheran unless otherwise stated)
(E) Embassy.

Afghanistan: Pahlavi Ave. (Yussefabad), 16 Ebn-Sina Ave., Kucheh Rassia (E); *Ambassador:* ZALMAY MAHMUD-GHAZI.

Algeria: Ave. Roosevelt (Nord), rue No. 8, No. 13 (E); *Ambassador:* HAFID KERAMANE.

Argentina: Pahlavi Ave. (Tajrish), No. 560 (E); *Ambassador:* (vacant) (also accred. to Afghanistan).

Australia: 23 Ave. Arak, P.O.B. 3408 (E); *Ambassador:* IVOR G. BOWDEN.

Austria: Takhte Jamshid, Forsat Ave. (E); *Ambassador:* Dr. ALBERT FILZ.

Bahrain: 31 Ave. Vozara (E); *Ambassador:* ABDUL AZIZ ABDULRAHMAN BUALI.

Bangladesh: Ave. Kakh No. 350-352 (E); *Ambassador:* A. R. S. DOHA.

Belgium: Ave. Takht-e-Tavous, 41 Ave. Daryaye Noor (E); *Ambassador:* PIERRE VAN HAUTE (also accred. to Afghanistan).

Brazil: Pahlavi Ave., Tajrish No. 69 (E); *Ambassador:* ALUYSIO REGIS BITTENCOURT (also accred. to Afghanistan).

Bulgaria: Aramehr Ave., Ave. Taghe Bostan, No. 23 (E); *Ambassador:* KIRIL SHTEREV.

Burma: Islamabad, Pakistan (E).

Canada: Takhte Jamshid Ave. Forsat, P.O.B. 1610 (E); *Ambassador:* JAMES GEORGE (also accred. to Bahrain, Kuwait, Oman and Qatar).

Chad: Moscow, U.S.S.R. (E).

Chile: Ave. Park, Ave. Passargade No. 30 (E); *Ambassador:* ARTURO YOVANE ZUNIGA.

China, People's Republic: Ave. Saltanatabad, Ave. Golestan 1, No. 51 (E); *Ambassador:* Madame MU HSIAO.

Czechoslovakia: Sarshar No. 61 (E); *Ambassador:* Dr. VLADIMIR POLACEK.

Denmark: Copenhagen Ave. 13 (E); *Ambassador:* OLE BERNHARD OLSEN (also accred. to Afghanistan).

Egypt: 123 Ave. Abassabad, Ave. Park, P.O.B. 22 (E); *Ambassador:* EZZAT IBRAHIM SOLIMAN.

Ethiopia: Ankara, Turkey (E).

Finland: Ave. Gandhi, corner of 25th St. (E); *Ambassador:* KURT D. UGGELDAHL.

France: France Ave. (E); *Ambassador:* ROBERT DE SOUZA.

Gabon: address unavailable (E); *Ambassador:* BARTH-ELÉMY MOUAPA BEOTSA.

German Democratic Republic: (E); *Ambassador:* FERDINAND THUN (also accred. to Afghanistan).

Germany, Federal Republic: Ferdowsi Avenue (E); *Ambassador:* Dr. HANS-GEORG WIECK.

Ghana: Islamabad, Pakistan (E).

Greece: Kheradmand Ave., Kucheh Salm. No. 43 (E); *Ambassador:* PANAYIOTIS ECONOMOU (also accred. to Afghanistan and Pakistan).

Guinea: Jeddah, Saudi Arabia (E)

Hungary: Television Ave. No. 7, Rue Sizdahom (E); *Ambassador:* BALINT GAI (also accred. to Afghanistan).

Iceland: Bonn, Federal Republic of Germany (E).

India: N. Saba Ave. No. 166 (E); *Ambassador:* RAMCHANDRA DATTATRAYA SATHE.

Indonesia: Shah Abbas Kabir Ave., Magnolia Ave. No. 1 (E); *Ambassador:* H. A. A. ACHSIEN.

Iraq: Ave. Pahlavi (E); *Ambassador:* MIDHAT JUMAA.

Italy: France Ave. 81 (E); *Ambassador:* LUIGI COTTAFAVI.

Japan: Northern Saba Ave. 53 (E); *Ambassador:* KATSUICHI IKAWA.

Jordan: Bukharest Ave. No. 16th Ave. No. 55 (E); *Ambassador:* SALEH AL-KURDI (also accred. to Afghanistan).

Korea, Democratic People's Republic: Ave. Tavanir No. 87 (E); *Ambassador:* LI YUN HO.

Korea, Republic: Kakh Ave., Heshmatoddowleh No. 427 (E); *Ambassador:* SI HAK HYUN.

Kuwait: Maikadeh Ave., 3-38 Sazman-Ab St. (E); *Ambassador:* Shaikh NASSER MUHAMMAD AHMAD AL-JABER AL-SABAH (also accred. to Afghanistan).

Lebanon: Bukharest Ave. No. 12 (E); *Ambassador:* KHALIL AL-KHALIL (also accred. to Afghanistan).

Lesotho: Ave. Gandhi, rue 11, No. 11 (E); *Ambassador:* MOOKI V. MOLAPO.

Malaysia: Bukharest Ave. No. 8 (E); *Ambassador:* MUHAMMAD YUSOFF BIN ZAINAI (also accred. to Afghanistan and Turkey).

Malta: London, U.K. (E).

Mexico: Ankara, Turkey (E).

Mongolia: Prague, Czechoslovakia (E).

Morocco: Dorahiye Yussofabad, Muhammad Reza Shah Ave. (E); *Ambassador:* BADREDDINE SNOUSSI (also accred. to Afghanistan and Turkey).

Nepal: Islamabad, Pakistan (E).

Netherlands: Takhte Tavous, Near Pahlavi Ave., Rue Moazami Rue Jahansouz No. 36 (E); *Ambassador:* P. A. E. RENARDEL DE LAVALETTE (also accred. to Afghanistan).

Nigeria: address unavailable (E); *Ambassador:* Brig. GEORGE KURUBO.

Norway: Aban Ave. 3 (E); *Ambassador:* NILS ANTON JORGENSEN (also accred. to Afghanistan, Bahrain, Kuwait and Qatar).

Oman: Ave. Abbas-Abad, Ave. Bukharest, 17th Ave. No. 10 (E); *Ambassador:* ISMAIL KHALIL AL-RASSASI.

Pakistan: Ave. Aryamehr. Jamshidabad Chomali, Ave. Khorshid, No. 9 (E); *Ambassador:* MUHAMMAD ASLAM KHAN KHATTAK.

Peru: New Delhi, India (E).

Philippines: Islamabad, Pakistan (E).

Poland: 140 Takhte Jamshid Ave. (E); *Ambassador:* BOGUSLAW PASZEK.

Portugal: Rodsar Ave. No. 41; *Ambassador:* PAULO FRANCISCO MENDES DA LUZ.

Qatar: Ave. Abbas Abad, Ave. Télévision, Second Ave. 14-16 (E); *Ambassador:* AHMED HAMD AL-ATEYAH (also accred. to Afghanistan).

Romania: Fakhrabad Ave. 12 (E); *Ambassador:* ALEXANDRU BOABĂ (also accred. to Afghanistan and Oman).

Saudi Arabia: Ave. Aban, P.O.B. 2903 (E); *Ambassador:* IBRAHIM S. BAKR.

Senegal: Ave. Vozara, 8th St. No. 4 (E); *Ambassador:* MASSAMBA SARRE (also accred. to Afghanistan, Bahrain and Turkey).

Singapore: New Delhi, India (E).

350

Spain: Fisherabad Ave., Khoshbin St. 29 (E); *Ambassador:* CARMELO MATESANZ (also accred. to Afghanistan).

Sri Lanka: Islamabad, Pakistan (E).

Sudan: Ave. Vozara, Ave. 23, No. 3 (E); *Ambassador:* SALAH-EDDINE OSMAN HASHIM.

Sweden: Takhte Jamshid Ave., Forsat Ave. (E); *Ambassador:* BENGT ODHNER (also accred. to Afghanistan).

Switzerland: Pasteur Ave. (E); *Ambassador:* CHARLES-ALBERT WETTERWALD (also accred. to Afghanistan).

Syria: Ave. Muhammad Reza Shah, Ave. 34, No. 9 (E); *Ambassador:* ALI MOHSEN ZEIFA.

Thailand: Bou Ali Sina Ave. Park Amine-Dowleh No. 4 (E); *Ambassador:* Maj.-Gen. BULRIT DARDARANANDA.

Trinidad and Tobago: Beirut, Lebanon (E).

Tunisia: Abbas Abad, Ave. Park No. 131 (E); *Ambassador:* TAOUFIK SMIDA.

Turkey: Ferdowsi Ave. No. 314 (E); *Ambassador:* SADI ELDEM.

U.S.S.R.: Churchill Ave. (E); *Ambassador:* V. Y. EROFEEV.

United Arab Emirates: Ave. Vozara, 8th St. (E); *Ambassador:* Sheikh AL-MAKTOUM.

United Kingdom: Ferdowsi Ave. (E); *Ambassador:* Sir ANTHONY PARSONS.

U.S.A.: Takhte Jamshid Ave., Roosevelt Ave. (E); *Ambassador:* RICHARD M. HELMS.

Vatican: France Ave. 97 (Apostolic Internunciature); *Ambassador:* Mgr. Dr. ERNESTO GALLINA.

Venezuela: Aban Ave. No. 90 (E); *Ambassador:* (vacant).

Yemen Arab Republic: Ave. Bukharest, rue 6, No. 23 (E); *Ambassador:* MUHAMMAD ALI IBRAHIM.

Yugoslavia: Ave. Arak, rue Shahrivar (E); *Ambassador:* MUHAMMAD HADZIC.

Zaire: Ave. Vozara, rue 3 (E); *Ambassador:* DONGO YEMO MOBUTU.

JUDICIAL SYSTEM

Chief Justice of the Supreme Court: NASSER YEQANEH.
Prosecutor-General: AHMAD FALLAH RASTEQAR.

SUPREME COURT

The jurisdiction of the Supreme Court in Teheran includes disputes about the competence of Government departments in relation to the existing laws, and it also acts as a Court of First Instance when ministers are prosecuted, either for personal offences or in respect of the affairs of their department. It is also the highest court of appeal. In exceptional cases, at the request of the Prosecutor-General, the Supreme Court deals with criminal cases.

PROVINCIAL COURTS

Courts of Appeal and Central Criminal Courts are established in each province.

OTHER COURTS

There are Courts of First Instance in the towns. The Arbitration Council was established in 1966 to examine and rule on all petty offences. The courts of lowest jurisdiction are those of the Justices of the Peace, which are established in most villages and small towns and deal with small civil cases and petty offences. On June 30th, 1966, the Arbitration Council was added to the judicial organs of the state. This Council is competent to deal with all complaints and petitions filed by businessmen and craftsmen, claims for damages and losses sustained in driving accidents, and domestic disputes, up to a claimed amount of ten thousand Rials in all cases. The Arbitration Council also examines and rules on petty offences (misdemeanour and felony) for which punishment does not exceed two months and/or one thousand two hundred Rials fine. Trials and examinations in such cases are undertaken free of charge.

SPECIAL TRIBUNALS

Special tribunals include Ecclesiastical Courts, which have a limited jurisdiction on matters of marriage and personal status; the Civil Servants' Criminal Court, in Teheran; and Permanent and Temporary Military Courts. Permanent Military Courts exist in all provinces and deal with treasonable offences; Temporary Military Courts are established whenever martial law is declared in a region, and are competent to hear certain cases which are normally within the jurisdiction of the ordinary courts.

RELIGION

According to the Constitution the officially recognized religions of Iran are Islam, Zoroastrianism, Christianity and Judaism.

MUSLIMS

The great majority of the Iranian people are Shi'i Muslims, and Iran with Iraq and the Yemen Arab Republic are notable as the only countries in the world where Shi'i adherents are in a majority. About five per cent of the population are Sunni Muslims, but there is complete religious toleration. Iran is thus in many ways the centre of the Shi'i faith, and pilgrimage to Iranian shrines is an important activity; Qum and Meshed are in particular regarded as holy cities.

ZOROASTRIANS

There are about 21,000 Zoroastrians, a remnant of a once widespread sect. Their religious leader is MOUBAD. Zoroastrianism was the official religion of pre-Islamic Iran. Many adherents were compelled by Arab persecution to emigrate, and the main centre of their faith is now Bombay.

OTHER COMMUNITIES

Communities of Armenians, and somewhat smaller numbers of Jews, Assyrians, Greek Orthodox, Uniates and Latin Christians are also found as officially recognized faiths. The Baha'i faith, which originated in Iran, has about 60,000 adherents.

Baha'i faith: Shirkat-i-Nawnahalan, Manuchehri Avenue, Teheran; 1,854 centres, 1 school.

Roman Catholic Archbishop of Urmia, Bishop of Salmas and Metropolitan of Iran: Khalifagari Kaldani Katoliq, Rezaieh; (vacant); Patriarchal Administrator Most Rev. YOUHANNAN SEMAAN ISSAYI, Archbishop of Teheran.

Anglican Bishop in Iran: Rt. Rev. HASSAN BARNABA DEHQANI-TAFTI, Bishop's House, P.O.B. 12, Isfahan. Diocese founded 1912.

Synod of the Evangelical (Presbyterian) Church in Iran: Assyrian Evangelical Church, Khiaban-i Shapur, Khiaban-i Aramanch, Teheran; Moderator Rev. ADLE NAKHOSTEEN.

THE PRESS

The working of the Iranian Press is set out in the 1955 Press Law as modified in 1963. This legislation defines the qualities of education and character required in persons intending to publish newspapers; and stipulates that no newspaper may be banned without a court order, except for criticism of religion or the monarchy, for disclosing military information or for provoking the people to oppose government troops. With the exception of scientific, cultural and government publications, newspapers with less than 3,000 circulation and magazines with less than 5,000 are illegal.

In 1965 the cabinet approved the Reporters' Code of Journalism which required reporters to be licensed by the Ministry of Information, prevented them accepting government service and prohibited the reporting or photography of specified military areas and closed court sittings, etc. All communist publications are prohibited in Iran.

Teheran dominates the press scene as many of the daily papers are published there and the bi-weekly, weekly and less frequent publications in the provinces generally depend on the major metropolitan dailies as a source of news. In the city are published some 20 daily and 21 weekly newspapers, and 27 weekly and 44 monthly magazines. There are at least 85 registered provincial papers.

With the exception of a small number of political organs and official publications, all newspapers are owned by private individuals.

The major dailies also publish other papers and periodicals thus forming small publishing groups which are still largely family concerns. The *Ettela'at Group* (Prop. ABBAS MASSOUDI) includes *Ettela'at* with two foreign language daily and two weekly newspapers and four popular weekly magazines, including one for women and two for children. The *Kayhan Group* (Prop. Dr. M. MES-BAZADEH) includes *Kayhan* with its English daily, a weekly sports paper, two popular weekly magazines and a medical magazine. The *Echo of Iran Group* (Prop. JAHANGIR BEHROUZ) includes the daily, weekly and monthly *Echo of Iran*, the monthly *Iran Trade* and the annual *Almanac and Iran Who's Who*, all in English.

PRINCIPAL DAILIES

Alik: Naderi Ave., Teheran; f. 1931; morning; political and literary; Armenian; Prop. Dr. R. STEPANIAN; circ. 10,000.

Ayandegan: Shah Ave., 322 Guiti Sq., Teheran; morning; political; Prop. Dr. H. AHARI.

Azhang: Roosevelt St., Teheran; f. 1954; airmail edition *Azhang Havaii*; Editor KAZEM MASOUDI; circ. 10,000.

Bourse: Kh. Sevom Esfand, Ku. Mobarshakat, Teheran; f. 1961; financial; Editor Dr. Y. RAHMATI.

Echo of Iran: Hafiz Ave., (Behjatabad), Kuche Khalkhali No. 4, P.O.B. 2008, Teheran; f. 1952; English; political, social and economic; Editor JAHANGIR BEHROUZ; circ. 6,000.

Ettela'at: Khayyam Ave., Teheran; f. 1925; evening; political and literary; Editor HASSAN SADR HAJ SAYYED JAVADI; circ. 100,000.

Ettela'ate Hawaei: Air edition of above; Editor HAMID MASHOUR; circ. 6,000.

Farman: 69 Manuchehri Ave., Teheran; political; Editor A. SHAHANDEH; circ. 15,000.

Iran Presse: Ave. Kheradmand, Ku. Tahbaz No. 19, Teheran; French; Editor S. FARZAMI.

Le Journal de Tehran: Kayyam Ave., Teheran; f. 1934; morning; French; Editor HOSSEIN KASMAI; circ. 8,000.

Kayhan Hava: Political and social; Editor M. SEMSAR; circ. 250,000.

Kayhan International: Ferdowsi Ave., Kuche Atabak, Teheran; political; morning; English; circ. 15,000; Editor KAZEM ZARNEGAR.

Keyhan: Ferdowsi Ave., Teheran; evening; political; Propr. Dr. M. MESBAHZADEH.

Khorassan: Meshed; f. 1948; Owner and Editor MUHAMMAD SADEGH TEHRANIAN; circ. 30,000.

Koushesh: Forughi Ave., Teheran; morning; political and scientific; Editor SHOKRULLAH SAFAVI.

Mahde Azadi: Tabriz; political and social; Prop. ESMAIL PEYMAN.

Marde Mobarez: Kh. Manouchehri; political and social; Propr. ASSAD RAZMARA.

Mehre Iran: Zhaleh Ave., Teheran; formerly affiliated to Mardom Party; morning; Editor MOHSEN MOVAGHAR.

Nedaye Iran-Novin: Fisherabad Ave. 41, Sepand St., Teheran; formerly affiliated to New Iran Party; Editor M. A. RASHTI.

Peyghame Emrouz: Kh. Qavam Saltaneh, Teheran; evening; political and social; Dr. ABDOLRASUL AZIMI; circ. 23,000.

Poste Teheran: Kh. Shahabad, Teheran; political evening; circ. 8,000; Editor MUHAMMAD ALI MASSOUDI.

Sedaye Mardom: Kh. Hafez, Teheran; f. 1945; political and literary; morning; Publisher MUHAMMAD HUSSEIN FARIPOUR; Editor FEREIDOON FARIPOUR.

Tehran Journal: Kayyam Ave., Teheran; f. 1954; morning; English; Editor KHOSROW FOROUGHI; circ. 10,000.

PRINCIPAL PERIODICALS

Aftabe Shargh: Meshed; weekly; political; Prop. Mrs. NARGESS AMOOZEGAR.

Al-Akha: Khayyam Ave., Teheran; f. 1960; Arabic; weekly; Dir. Sen. ABAS MASSOUDI; Editor NAZIR FENZA.

Around Iran: published by The Echo of Iran, Hafiz Ave., Teheran; English, tourist; Man. Editor J. BEHROUZ.

Bourse Monthly: Sevom-Esfand Ave., Kuche Bakht 15, Teheran; f. 1963; economic; Editor Dr. Y. RAHMATI.

Daneshkade Pezeshki: Faculty of Medicine, Teheran University; medical magazine; monthly; Editor Dr. M. BEHESHTI.

Donya: Istanbul Ave., Teheran; weekly; Editor A. K. TABATABA'I.

Donyaye Varzesh: Khayyam Ave., Teheran; f. 1970; weekly sport magazine; Editor BIJAN RAFIEI.

Ettela'at Banovan: Kayyam Ave., Teheran; women's weekly magazine; Editor Mrs. PARI ABASALTI; circ. 40,000.

Ettela'at Javanan: Khayyam Ave., Teheran; f. 1958; youth weekly; Editor R. ETTEMADI.

Ettela'at Kodekan: Khayyam Ave., Teheran; f. 1957; teenage weekly; Editor NADER AKHVAN HEYDARI.

Ferdowsi: Bahar Ave., Teheran; weekly; Editor N. JAHAN-BANOIE; circ. 26,000.

Film-Va-Honar: Roosevelt Ave., Teheran; weekly; Editor A. RAMAZANI.

Iran Economic Service: Hafiz Ave., Behjatabad, 4 Kucheh Khalkali; P.O.B. 2008, Teheran; weekly, economic.

Iran Trade and Industry: Echo of Iran, P.O.B. 2008, Hafiz Ave., Teheran; f. 1965; monthly economic periodical; Editor J. BEHROUZ; circ. 10,000.

Javanan: Ave. Sepah, Teheran; weekly magazine for young people; circ. over 10,000.

Kayhan Bacheha: Kh. Ferdowsi, Teheran; children's magazine weekly; Editor DJAAFAR BADII; circ. 95,000.

Kayhan Varzeshi: Kh. Ferdowsi, Teheran; sport weekly; Editor Dr. M. MESBAZADEH; circ. 60,000.

Khandaniha: Kh. Ferdowsi; f. 1939; weekly; circ. 25,000; Editor A. A. AMIRANI.

Music Iran: 1029 Amiriye Ave., Teheran; f. 1951; monthly; Editor BAHMAN HIRBOD; circ. 7,000.

Navaye-Khorasan: Meshed; political; weekly; Prop. H. MAHBODI.

Pars: Shiraz; twice weekly; circ. 3,500; Editor F. SHARGI.

Rahnejat: Darvazeh Dowlat, Isfahan; political and social weekly; Prop. N. RAHNEJAT.

Sepahan: Baharestan Square, Teheran; literary; weekly.

Sepid va Siyah: Kh. Ferdowsi; popular monthly; Editor Dr. A. BEHZADI; circ. 30,000.

Setareye Cinema: Lalezar-Now Ave., Teheran; film weekly; Editor P. GALUSTIAN.

Setareye Esfahan: Isfahan; political; weekly; Prop. A. MIHANKHAH.

Sobhe Emroug: Ferdowsi Ave., Teheran; Editor Mrs. AMIDI-NURI.

Sokhan: Hafiz Ave., Zomorrod Passage, Teheran; f. 1943; literary monthly; Editor Dr. P. N. KHANLARI; circ. 5,000.

Sport: P.O.B. 342, Ebne Sina St., Park Aminodoleh, Kakhe Markazi Taj; Teheran; sports, weekly.

Teheran Chamber of Commerce Monthly Journal: Teheran; Farsi; circ. 5,000; also **Weekly Bulletin**, circ. 5,000; both distributed mainly to members.

Tehran Economist: 99 Sevom Esfand Ave., Teheran; f. 1953; Persian and English; weekly; Editor Dr. B. SHARIAT; circ. 15,000 Persian, 4,500 English.

Tehran Messavar: Ave. Jaleh, Teheran; popular weekly; Editor ABDULLAH VALA; circ. 50,000.

Zan-E-Ruz (*Women Today*): Kh. Ferdowsi, Teheran; women's weekly; circ. 150,000; Editor Mrs. F. MESBAZADEH.

NEWS AGENCIES

International Press Agency of Iran: Teheran Ghvamsaltaneh Square, P.O.B. 1125, Teheran.

Pars News Agency: General Department of Publications and Broadcasting, Maidan Ark, Teheran; f. 1936; Pres. HOSEINQHOLI JAVANSHIR.

FOREIGN BUREAUX

A.F.P.: P.O.B. 1535, Teheran; Correspondent JEAN-CLAUDE BRARD.

A.N.S.A.: Ave. Hafez, Kuche Hatef 11, Teheran; Chief EMIRA GIULIANA PIZZUTO.

A.P.: 7 Fifth St., Television Ave., Teheran; Correspondent PARVIZ RAEIN.

Reuter: P.O.B. 1607, Teheran; Correspondent ALI MEHRAVARI.

Tass: Kheyaban Hamid, Kouche Masoud 73, Teheran; Correspondent VLADIMIR DIBROVA.

U.P.I.: P.O.B. 529, Teheran; Correspondent YOUSOF MAZANDI.

PUBLISHERS

Ali Akbar Elmi: Shahabad Ave.; Dir. ALI AKBAR ELMI.

Amir Kabir: 235 Avenue Saadi, Teheran; f. 1950; historical, social, literary, and children's books; Dir. ABDULRAHIM JAFARI.

Boroukhim: Avenue Ferdowsi, Teheran; dictionaries.

Bungah Tarjomeh va Nashr Ketah: Teheran; affiliated to the Pahlavi foundation.

Danesh: 357 Ave. Nasser Khosrow, Teheran; f. 1931 in India, transferred to Iran in 1937; literary and historical (Persian); imports and exports books; Man. Dir. NOOROUAH IRANPARAST.

Ebn-e-Sina: Meydane 25 Shahrivar, Teheran; f. 1957; educational publishers and booksellers; Dir. EBRAHIM RAMAZANI.

Eghbal Publishing Co.: Shahabad Ave., Teheran; Dir. DJAVAD EGHBAL.

Franklin Book Programs Inc.: 2 Alborz Ave., Shahreza Ave., Teheran; f. 1952; a non-profit organization for International Book Publishing Development; main office in New York; Dir. ALI ASGHAR MOHAJER.

Ibn-Sina: Shahabad St. Teheran.

Iran Chap Company: Ave. Khayyam, Teheran; f. 1966; newspapers, books, magazines, colour printing and engraving; Man. Dir. FARHAD MASSOUDI.

Kanoon Marefat: 6 Ave. Lalehzar, Teheran; Dir. HASSAN MAREFAT.

Khayyam: Shahabad Avenue; Dir. MOHAMMAD ALI TARAGHI.

Majlis Press: Avenue Baharistan, Teheran.

Nil Publications: Mokhberoddowleh Sq., Koutcheh Rafahi, Teheran. Dir. A. AZIMI.

Pirouz: Shahabad Avenue; Dir. MIRMOHAMMADI.

Safiali Shah: Baharistan Square; Dir. MANSOUR MOSHFEGH.

Taban Press: Ave. Nassir Khosrow, Teheran; f. 1939; Propr. A. MALEKI.

Teheran Economist: Sevom Esfand Ave. 99, Teheran.

Teheran University Press: Avenue Shah-Reza.

Towfigh: Istanbul Ave., Teheran; publishes humorous Almanac and pocket books; distributes humorous and satirical books; Dir. Dr. FARIDEH TOWFIGH.

Zawar: Shahabad Avenue; Dir. AKBAR ZAWAR.

RADIO AND TELEVISION

National Iranian Radio and Television: P.O.B. 33-200, Teheran; semi-autonomous governmental authority; f. 1971 by merger of Radio Iran and National Iranian Television; 5,000 employees.

> **Radio:** covers entire area of Iran; in addition the Voice of Iran reaches half Europe and the whole of Asia and Africa; medium-wave and short-wave regional broadcasts in local languages and dialects; foreign broadcasts in English, French, Arabic, Russian, Armenian, Pashtu, Kurdish, Urdu, Turcoman and Baluchi; 60 transmitters.
>
> Number of radio receivers: 8 million (1973).

Television: production centres in Teheran (2), Abadan, Bandar Abbas, Isfahan, Kerman, Kermanshah, Mahabad, Meshed, Rasht, Rezaieh, Sanandaj, Shiraz, Tabriz, Zahedan, Latian Dam; 79 relay stations; black and white at present, with colour facilities being tested.

> Number of TV receivers: 1.7 million (1973).

American Forces Radio and Television: Teheran; f. 1954; recordings and films of American programmes; 68 hours weekly.

FINANCE

(cap. = capital; p.u. = paid up; dep. = deposits; m. = million; all figures stated in Rials)

BANKING

CENTRAL BANK

Bank Markazi Iran: Ferdowsi Ave., Teheran; f. 1960; central note-issuing bank of Iran, government, commercial and specialized banking; cap. 5,000m., dep. 446,000m. (Oct. 1974); Gov. MOHAMMED YEGANEH; Deputy Gov. JALIL SHORAKA.

Bank Asnaf Iran (*Guilds Bank of Iran*): Baharestan Square, Teheran; f. 1957; cap. p.u. 100m.; Chair. Gen. ALI AKHBAR ZARGHAM; Gen. Man. SOLIMAN AGHAIE.

Bank Bazargani Iran: Maidan Sepah, P.O.B. 2258, Teheran; reps. abroad in London, England and Hamburg, German Federal Republic; f. 1950; cap. p.u. 1,500m., dep. 29,116m. (March 1974); 225 brs.; Chair. Dr. DJAVAD SADR; Man.-Dir. Senator MOSTAFA TADJADOD.

Bank Bimeh Iran (*Iran Insurance Bank*): Teheran; under auspices of government-sponsored Sherkate Sahami Bimeh Iran (Insurance Company of Iran); cap. p.u. 400m.; 10 brs. and 4 sub-brs. in Teheran, 19 brs. in other towns; Chair. and Man. Dir. MOHAMMED REZA TEHRANI.

Banque Etebarate Iran (*Iran Credit Bank*): 50 Ave. Sevom Esfand, Teheran; f. 1958; cap. p.u. 700m., dep. 7,557m. (March 1973); Chair. and Man. Dir. H.E. AHMED CHAFIK.

Bank Etebarat Sanati (*Industrial Credit Bank*): Khiaban Ateshkadeh, Teheran; f. 1956; stock owned by the Govt.; cap. p.u. 4,319m., dep. 1,217m. (Oct. 1974); Chair. and Man.-Dir. ALINAGHI FARMANFARMAIAN; Dep. Man.-Dir. AHMAD ZIAI.

Bank Kar: Ave. Hafez, Teheran; f. 1958; cap. 1,030m., dep. 3,219m.; Man. ARSEN BARKHORDARIAN.

Bank Kargosha'i Iran (*Pawn Bank*): Moulavi Ave., Teheran; cap. provided by Bank Melli Iran; Principal Officer ESMAIEL TAHERI.

Bank Melli Iran (*The National Bank of Iran*): Ferdowsi Ave., Teheran; state-owned bank; brs. abroad in Frankfurt, Sharjah, Paris, Bahrain, Jeddah, Hong Kong, London, Hamburg, New York, Tokyo, Munich, Muscat and Dubai; f. 1928; cap. and res. 6,108m., dep. 274,928m., total assets 363,423m. (January 1975); affiliation Bank Tedjarat Kharedji Iran; 1,423 brs. throughout Iran; Pres. YOUSSOF KHOSHKISH.

Bank of Iran and the Middle East: Kucheh Berlin, Ave. Ferdowsi, P.O.B. 1680, Teheran; f. 1959; brs. at Khorramshar, Abadan and Teheran (18); The British Bank of the Middle East owns 35 per cent of the issued capital; 65 per cent is held by Iranian interests; cap. p.u. 1,000m., dep. 5,973m.; Chair. Dr. G. H. KHOSHBIN; Dir. and Adviser K. V. R. JEFFERIES; Gen. Man. M. H. VAKILY.

Bank of Teheran: 25 Pahlavi Ave., Teheran; f. 1952; cap. p.u. 3,000m., dep. 43,210 (March 1975); Pres. MOSTAFA FATEH; Man.-Dir. BAHMAN BEHZADI.

Bank Omran (*Development Bank*): Teheran; f. 1952 to provide technical guidance and financial support to farmers of distributed Crown villages; also acts as a commercial bank; 144 brs.; Pres. HOUSHANG RAM.

Bank Pars: Avenue Takht-Jamshid, Teheran; f. 1952; cap. p.u. 500m. (March 1974); Chair. and Pres. E. NIKPOUR; Managing Dir. MEHDI LALEH.

Bank Rahni Iran (*The Mortgage Bank of Iran*): Ferdowsi Street, Teheran; f. 1939; Government bank (affiliate of Ministry of Development and Housing) which grants loans for building houses; cap. p.u. 5,538m., total assets 24,827m. (March 1974); Chair. and Man. Dir. Eng. A. BEHNIA.

Bank Refah Kargaran (*Workers' Welfare Bank*): 125 Roosevelt Ave., Teheran; f. 1960; cap. p.u. 1,000m.; 65 brs.; state-owned bank; Chair. MUHAMMAD MAJIDI.

Bank Russo-Iran: Jonoobe Parke Shahr, Teheran; cap, p.u. 600m.; branch in Isfahan.

Bank Saderat Iran (*The Export Bank of Iran*): 124 Ave. Shah, Teheran; P.O.B. 2751; f. 1951; cap. p.u. 3,000m.; dep. 95,308m. (March 1974); 3,000 brs. in Iran; brs. in Dubai, Abu Dhabi, Fujaireh, Ras Al Khaimah, Ajman, Sharjah (United Arab Emirates), Qatar, Bahrain; offices in London, Hamburg, Paris, Beirut; agency in New York; Man. Dir. Eng. M. A. MOFARAH.

Bank Sepah (*Army Bank*): Ave. Sepah, Teheran; f. 1925; state-owned bank; cap. p.u. 1,500m., dep. 53,160m. (March 1974); 455 brs.; Pres. MANOUTCHEHRE NIKPOUR; Deputy Pres. DJALIL SASSINI.

Bank Shahryar: 1/99 Sepahbod Zahedi Ave., Teheran; cap. p.u. 5.000m; Chair. ALI REZAI; Man. Dir. MANOUCHEHR HEMANI.

Bank Taavon Keshavarzi Iran (*Agricultural Cooperative Bank of Iran*): Khiaban Park Shahr (North), Teheran; f. 1933; cap. 21,059m. (April 1975); government bank; Pres. HASSAN EMAMI.

Distributors' Co-operative Credit Bank: 37 Ave. Ferdowsi, Teheran; f. 1963; cap. 600m., dep. 4,472 (1973); Chair. SEIFULLAH RASHIDIAN; Pres. ASSADULLAH RASHIDIAN.

Foreign Trade Bank of Iran (*Bank Tedjarat Kharedji Iran*): Avenue Saadi, Teheran; f. 1960; jointly owned by Bank Melli Iran, Bank of America, Banca Comerciale Italiana and Deutsche Bank A.G.; cap. 700m., dep. 9,481m., reserves 420m. (March 1974); Chair. YOUSSEF KHOSHKISH; Man. Dir. ASHOT SAGHATELIAN.

Industrial and Mining Development Bank of Iran (IMDBI): 133 Hafez St., P.O.B. 1801, Teheran; f. 1958; 84 per cent of shares held by more than 3,100 Iranian individuals and institutions, 16 per cent held by France, U.K., Netherlands, Italy, Japan, U.S.A. and Federal Germany; to develop, encourage and stimulate private industrial, mining and transportation enterprises in Iran; cap. 3,150m., total assets 40,997m. (March 1974); Man.-Dir. A. GASEM KHERADJOU.

Industrial Credit Bank: Ateshkadeh Ave., Teheran; provides medium and long-term industrial credit.

International Bank of Iran and Japan: 750 Ave. Saadi, P.O.B. 1837, Teheran; f. 1959; cap. 2,000m. (July 1975); 35 per cent Japanese owned; Chair. MOSTAFA MESBAH-ZADEH; Pres. A. SALMANPOUR.

Iranians' Bank: 184 Takht Jamshid Ave., Teheran; f. 1960; cap. 1,000m., dep. 9,719m. (1975); associated with First National City Bank; Chair. A. H. EBTEHAJ; Pres. NADER AKRAMI.

Irano-British Bank: Avenue Saadi, P.O.B. 1584, Teheran; f. 1959; affiliated with the Standard and Chartered Banking Group Ltd.; cap. p.u. 1,000m.; Gen. Man. W. T. WATSON.

Mercantile Bank of Iran and Holland: Ave. Saadi, P.O.B. 1522, Teheran; f. 1959; affiliated with Algemene Bank Nederland N.V., Amsterdam; cap. p.u. 500m., dep. 5,791m.; 12 brs. in Teheran, 1 in Ahwaz, 1 in Isfahan, 1 in Khorramshahr; Chair. SOLEYMAN VAHABZADEH; Man. Dir. AHMAD VAHABZADEH; Resident Dir. W. M. BROUWER.

FOREIGN BANKS

The following banks have representative offices in Teheran: Bank of America N.T. & S.A., Bank of Tokyo, Banque de Bruxelles, Banque de Paris et des Pays-Bas, Bayerische Vereinsbank, Berliner Bank, Chase Manhatten Overseas Corporation, Commerzbank, Deutsche Bank, Dresdner Bank, Vereinsbank in Hamburg.

Iranian Bankers' Association: 41 Daryay-e-Noor St., Takht-e-Tavous Ave., Teheran; Man. Dir. JALAL ABDOH.

STOCK EXCHANGE

Teheran Stock Exchange: Taghinia Bldg., Saadi Ave., Teheran; f. 1968; Chair. of Council M. YEGANAH; Publs. *Monthly Bulletin* and *Annual Report*.

INSURANCE

Sherkate Sahami Bimeh Iran (*Iran Insurance Co.*); Avenue Saadi, Teheran; f. 1935; state-owned insurance company; all types of insurance; cap. p.u. 200m.; Chair. and Man. Dir. AMIR HUSHANG KATUZIAN.

Alborz Insurance Co. Ltd.: Alborz Bldg., 250 Sepahbod Zahedi Ave., Teheran; f. 1959; most classes of insurance except livestock insurance; five brs.; p.u. cap. 400m.; Management Habibollah Nahai and Brothers.

Omid Insurance Co. Ltd.: 99 South Kheradmand Ave., Corner of Salm St., Teheran; f. 1960; cap. and dep. 800m.; Man.-Dir. Eng. AMIR MOEZZI.

Pars, Société Anonyme d'Assurances: Avenue Saadi, Teheran; f. 1955; fire, marine, motor vehicle and personal accident insurance; Gen. Man. MADJID MALEK; Tech. Man. YERVANT MAGARIAN.

Sherkate Sahami Bimeh Arya (*Arya Insurance Co. Ltd.*): 213 Soraya Ave., Teheran; f. 1952; cap. 100m.; Chair. Dr. G. H. JAHANSHAI; Deputy Man. Dir. MEHRAB BARZEGAR.

Sherkate Sahami Bimeh Asia (*Asia Insurance Co. Ltd.*): Takht Jamshid Ave., Fisherabad Corner, Teheran; f. 1960; Man.-Dir. R. SHAMS.

Sherkate Sahami Bimeh Melli (*The National Insurance Co. Ltd.*): Shah Reza/Villa Ave., P.O.B. 1786, Teheran; f. 1956; all classes of insurance; Chair. H. E. AHMED CHAFIK; Managing Dir. EDWARD JOSEPH.

Sherkate Sahami Bimeh Omid: Boulevard Karimkhan Zand, Ave. Kheradniand Jonoubi 99, Teheran; f. 1960.

All insurance companies are members of the Syndicate of Iranian Insurance Companies.

OIL

National Iranian Oil Company (NIOC), Takhte Jamshid Ave. (P.O.B. 1863), Teheran
A state organization controlling all oil and gas operations in Iran.

NIOC

The National Iranian Oil Company (NIOC) was incorporated April 1951 on nationalization of oil industry to engage in all phases of oil operations; auth. cap 100,000 million rials, in 10,000 shares, 50 per cent paid up; all shares held by Iranian Government and are non-transferable; Chair. of Board and Managing Dir. H.E. Dr. MANOUTCHEHR EGHBAL; Deputy Chair. and Gen. Managing Dir. (International Affairs) H.E. Dr. R. FALLAH; Dirs. H.E. A. K. BAKHTIAR, B. MOSTOWFI, T. MOSSADEGHI, Dr. P. MINA, Dr. M. A. NABEGH, M. T. DIBA, A. A. RAFIEE, M. JALINOOS; Alternate Dirs. H. ENTEKHABI, A. FALLAH, M. MODIR, K. NARAGHI, F. NOORI.

In October 1954 an agreement was concluded between the Iranian Government and NIOC on the one hand and eight major oil companies (subsequently increased to fourteen) on the other, to operate the southern oilfields (as defined) on behalf of NIOC. These companies were collectively known as the Consortium, for which *see below*. The agreement was for twenty-five years with provision for three five-year extensions, at the option of the Consortium under specific terms and conditions, NIOC being responsible for non-industrial activities in the agreement area. It directly operates the Naft-i-Shah oilfield, the Kermanshah refinery, the Teheran refineries, the Shiraz refinery and the Abadan refineries; it also carried out exploration and drilling in all parts of the country not subject to special agreements. NIOC is solely responsible for internal distribution of petroleum products and has laid over 4,570 km. of pipeline throughout Iran. The Petroleum Act of 1957 empowered NIOC to divide Iran into 27 petroleum districts, to invite bids for their exploitation, and to sign agreements. NIOC signed a series of agreements: in 1957 with AGIP Mineraria (an Italian company); in 1958 with Pan American Petroleum Corpn.; in 1965 with several groups for exploration of offshore areas. In all eight of the companies formed, NIOC had 50 per cent participation. In September 1966 agreement was reached with the French state organization Entreprise des Recherches et d'Activités Pétrolières (ERAP) to operate as a contractor on behalf of NIOC in exploration both on and offshore. At present ERAP is active only in 3,294.5 sq. km. offshore areas.

In December 1966 the Consortium relinquished one-quarter of the Agreement Area, comprising three parcels totalling 25,069 sq. miles, one in the north-west and two in the south-east, to NIOC. NIOC signed a further two contract type agreements in 1969: one with a group of five companies (ERAP, Agip, Hispanoil, Petrofina and O.e.M.V.) and the other with Continental Oil Company of U.S.A. and Phillips Petroleum Company. Continental Oil Co. later sold 50 per cent of its interest to Cities Service. Also in 1972 three joint venture agreements were signed; with four Japanese and one U.S. oil companies; with Amerada Hess Corpn. (now dissolved); with Mobil Oil Corporation.

A major change took place in 1973, however, when the Consortium was issued with an ultimatum—the oil companies could either remain in the country until the existing 25-year contract expired in 1979 (with the proviso that they doubled production), after which they would get no more preferential treatment than any other foreign company, or alternatively, the Consortium could agree to be taken over immediately and then make preference agreements with the Government on a long-term basis. The latter course was agreed in March, and under a preliminary agreement signed in June 1973 between Iran and the Consortium, the Consortium is guaranteed a supply of oil over a 20-year period. The Iranian Oil Exploration and Producing Company was liquidated and the Oil Service Company of Iran was established, which operates as a contractor to the National Iranian Oil Company. The operation of Abadan refinery has passed to NIOC who will sell the products to the oil companies.

The decision was due partly to the Iran Government's need for greatly increased funds for the Fifth Development Plan, but also to its aim to gain as much control over foreign oil companies as had been achieved by other Arab states such as Kuwait, Qatar and Saudi Arabia in October 1972.

The company has formed two subsidiaries to represent it in two associated fields—The National Iranian Petrochemical Company and The National Iranian Gas Company. The latter has signed an agreement to supply the Soviet Union with large quantities of natural gas.

During 1974 Iran invited bids for a large amount of new acreage, both onshore and offshore, and contracts were concluded with five companies: Compagnie Française des Pétroles (France), Ultramar (U.K.), Deminex (West German consortium), Ashland Oil Partnership (U.S.A. and Canada) and AGIP (Italy).

Société Irano-Italienne des Pétroles (SIRIP): Ave. Abbas Abad 30, P.O.B. 1434, Teheran; f. 1957: owned jointly by NIOC and AGIP S.p.A.; Man. Dir. Dr. A. Angelucci.

Iran-Pan American Oil Co. (IPAC): 315 Takhte Jamshid Avenue, Teheran; f. 1958; owned jointly by NIOC and Amoco Iran Oil Co.; to exploit Persian Gulf offshore deposits in their agreement area; Man. Dir. M. T. Razaghnia.

Iranian Marine International Oil Company (IMINOCO): 128 Roodsar Ave., Teheran; f. 1965; formed with National Iranian Oil Co. on the one hand and Phillips Petroleum Co., AGIP (a subsidiary of the Italian ENI) and Hydrocarbons India Pvt. Ltd. (a subsidiary of the Oil and Natural Gas Commission of India); Chair. R. Kalhor; Man. Dir. C. Trampini.

Lavan Petroleum Company (LAPCO): 3 Elizabeth II Boulevard, Teheran; f. 1965; formed with Atlantic Richfield, Murphy Oil Corporation, Sun Oil Co., and and Union Oil Co. of California, who own 50 per cent interest, and the National Iranian Oil Co., who own the remaining 50 per cent; Man. Dir. N. E. Dietzel.

Iranian Offshore Petroleum Company (IROPCO): P.O.B. 3257, Teheran; f. 1965; formed with CEPSA, and Cities Service Co., Kerr-McGee Corpn., Atlantic-Richfield Co., Skelly Oil Co., Superior Oil Co., and Sunray D.X. Oil Co.; Chair. A. Vaziri-Tabar; Man. Dir. Bruce Vernor.

Phillips Petroleum Company Iran: P.O.B. 3184, Teheran; assumed operations of area previously operated by CONOCO under agreement signed with NIOC in April 1969 for exploration and development of a 5,000 sq. mile area in South Iran; Vice-Pres. and Man. Dir. William B. Belknap.

Sofiran: P.O.B. 3220, Teheran; French and Japanese oil interests.

European Group of Companies (EGOCO): Teheran; ERAP holds a 32 per cent share in a consortium exploring a 10,000 square mile area in Fars province; ENI has a 28 per cent share, Hispanoil 20 per cent, Petrofina 15 per cent and OMV of Austria 5 per cent.

Iran Nippon Petroleum Company (INPECO): 130 Ave. Shah Abbas Kabir, Teheran; f. 1971; partnership—50 per cent NIOC, 50 per cent Japanese group; Man. Dir. Sh. Hikata.

Hormoz Petroleum Company (HOPECO): 290 Ave. Villa, IBM Building, Teheran; f. 1972; partnership—50 per cent NIOC, 50 per cent Mobil; Chair. Dr. A. Fallah; Man. Dir. R. A. Wilson.

Bushehr Petroleum Company (BUSHCO): 41 Ave. Daryaye Noor, between Takhte Tavoos and Abbasabad, Teheran; f. 1971; partnership—50 per cent NIOC, 50 per cent Amerada Hess; Man. Dir. M. Qadimi Nawai.

THE CONSORTIUM

Consortium members, with percentage shareholdings: Gulf Oil Corporation (7%), Mobil Corporation (7%), Exxon (7%), Standard Oil Co. of California (7%), Texaco Inc. (7%), The British Petroleum Co. Ltd. (40%), Bataafse Petroleum Maatschappij N.V. (14%,) Compagnie Française des Pétroles (6%), the remaining 5 per cent being divided amongst the following six American companies: The American Independent Oil Co., The Atlantic Richfield Co., Charter Oil Co., Getty Oil Co., The Standard Oil Company (Ohio), and Continental Oil Co.

TRADE AND INDUSTRY

CHAMBERS OF COMMERCE

Iran Chamber of Commerce, Industries and Mines: 254 Ave. Takht-Jamshid, Teheran; f. 1970; supervises the affiliated 17 Chambers in the provinces; Pres. Sen. Dr. TAHER ZIAI.

R.C.D. Joint Chamber of Commerce: Teheran; f. 1965 with Pakistan and Turkey under auspices of Regional Co-operation for Development.

EMPLOYERS' ASSOCIATION

Association des Employeurs Industriels de l'Iran: Teheran.

LABOUR ORGANIZATIONS

All Trade Unions were dissolved in 1963, and syndicates of workers must be registered with the Government. In March 1963 there were 67 syndicates representing various trades, of which the largest included the *National Iranian Oil Company Workers' Syndicate* with 6,000 members.

CO-OPERATIVES

Central Organization for Rural Co-operatives of Iran (C.O.R.C.): Teheran; Man. Dir. GHOLAMHOSEIN TAVASSOLI. Following the implementation of the Land Reform Act, the C.O.R.C. was established by the Government in 1963. The aim of the organization is to offer educational, technical and credit assistance to rural co-operative societies and their unions. The C.O.R.C. will gradually transfer its stocks to rural co-operative unions and become the national body for rural co-operatives. By March 1975 2,839 amalgamated rural co-operatives with a membership of 2,472,226 had availed themselves of C.O.R.C. facilities. The share capital of the societies is 4,418m. rials, the reserves is 1,460m. rials and the number of villages under operation is 43,422. At the same time 134 rural co-operative unions with 2,774 member societies, share capital of 2,191m. rials and reserves of 232m. rials, had benefited from C.O.R.C. operations.

TRADE FAIR

Iran International Fairs and Exhibitions Corpn.: P.O.B. 33-22, Tajrish, Teheran; Dir.-Gen. M. SHEEDFAR; publ. *Exhibition News.*

TRANSPORT

RAILWAYS

Iranian State Railway: Head Office: Teheran; f. 1938; Deputy Minister for Transport Affairs and Man. of the Railways H. MOUSSAVIAN, Technical Vice-Pres. A. NADJAFIAN, Commercial Vice-Pres. K. ATABAKI, Financial Vice-Pres. H. MOBASHER, Admin. Vice-Pres. R. MOSTOFI.

The Iranian railway system includes the following main routes.

Trans-Iranian Railway runs 1,392 km. from Gorgan, in the north, through Teheran, and south to Bandar Shahpur on the Persian Gulf.

South Line links Teheran to Khorramshahr via Ghom, Arak, Dorood, Andimeshk and Ahwaz; 937 km.

North Line links Teheran to Gorgan via Garmsar, Firooz Kooh and Sari; 499 km.

Teheran-Tabriz Line linking with the Azarbaijan Railway (736 km.).

Garmsar-Meshed Line connects Teheran with Meshed via Semnan, Damghan, Shahrud and Nishabur; 812 km.

Ghom-Zahedan Line when completed will be an intercontinental line linking Europe and Turkey, through Iran, with India. Zahedan is situated 91.7 km. west of the Baluchistan frontier, and is the end of the Pakistani broad gauge railway. The section at present links Ghom to Zarand via Kashan, Sagsi, Yazd and Bafgh; 847 km. A branch line from Sagsi was opened in 1971 via Esfahan to Aryamehr steel mill at Zarrinshahr; 112 km.

Ahwaz-Bandar Shahpur Line connects Bandar Shahpur with the Trans-Iranian railway at Ahwaz (123 km.).

Azarbaizhan Railway extends from Tabriz to Julfa (146.5 km.), meeting the Caucasian railways at the Soviet frontier. A line from Sharaf-Khaneh to the Turkish frontier at Razi was opened in 1971.

The total length of main lines is 4,519 km.

ROADS

Ministry of Roads: Ministry of Roads and Communications, Teheran; Minister Eng. J. SHAHRESTANI.

There are about 45,000 km. of roads, of which some 12,500 km. had asphalt or paved surfaces by 1973. The Asian (CENTO) Highway provides a two-lane asphalt highway from the Turkish border at Bazergan and the Iraq border at Qasr-e-Shirin to the Afghanistan border at Tayebat. The road connecting Teheran to the border with Pakistan is under construction from Kerman to the border.

MOTORISTS' ORGANIZATIONS

Touring and Automobile Club of Iran: 37 Varzesh Ave., Teheran; f. 1935; Gen. Man. M. R. SAFFARI.

INLAND WATERWAYS

Principal waterways:

Lake Rezaiyeh (Lake Urmia) 50 miles west of Tabriz in North-West Iran; and River Kharun flowing south through the oilfields into the River Shatt al Arab thence to the head of the Persian Gulf near Abadan.

Lake Rezaiyeh: From Sharafkhaneh to Golmankhaneh there is a twice-weekly service of tugs and barges for transport of passengers and goods.

River Karun: Regular cargo service is operated by the Mesopotamia-Iran Corpn. Ltd. Iranian firms also operate daily motor-boat services for passengers and goods.

SHIPPING

Persian Gulf: Principal ports are Khorramshahr, Bushire, Bandar Abbas, Bandar Shahpur. Oil exports from the Abadan refinery are now handled by the new Mahshahr installations (opened December 1967) and Kharg Island terminal in the Persian Gulf. Bushire is being developed to supplement the facilities at Khorramshahr, while the capacity of Bandar Abbas has recently been increased.

Caspian Sea: Principal port Bandar Pahlavi.

Arya National Shipping Lines: 2 Pahlavi Ave., Khorram-shahr; 26 vessels; liner services between the Persian Gulf and Europe.

CIVIL AVIATION

Iran National Airlines Corporation (*Iran Air*): Iran Air Building, Mehrabad Airport, Teheran; f. 1962; replaces Iranian Airways Co.; serves Iran, the Middle East and Europe, Karachi, Kabul and Bombay; Chair. Gen. M. KHATAMI; Man. Dir. Lt.-Gen. ALI M. KHADEMI; fleet of three Boeing 707, four Boeing 727, four Boeing 737 and two DC-6; three Concordes, two Boeing 747 and three Boeing 727 are on order.

Teheran is also served by the following foreign lines: Aeroflot, Air France, Air India, Alia, Alitalia, Ariana Afghan Airlines, British Airways, CSA, El Al, Iraqi Airways, JAL, KLM, Kuwait Airways, Lufthansa, MEA, PAA, Qantas, Sabena, SAS, Swissair, Syrian Arab Airlines.

The first phase of a new Teheran airport should be completed by 1980.

TOURISM

Ministry of Information and Tourism: 174 Elizabeth Blvd., Teheran; f. 1974; Minister Dr. GHOLAM REZA KIANPOUR. The former Iran National Tourist Organization (INTO) was established in 1963 and became the new Ministry of Information and Tourism in 1974. Publications: *Iran Travel News* (monthly), *Monthly Statistics Bulletin*, brochures, guide books, road maps, posters, etc.

During 1973 402,703 tourists visited Iran, showing an increase of 30,629 (about 7.5 per cent) over 1972. The estimated income from tourists over this period was U.S. $60 million.

CULTURAL ORGANIZATIONS

Ministry of Culture and Arts: Kh. Kamal-ol-Molk, Teheran; f. 1964 to replace the Fine Arts Administration; 7 Deputy Ministers are responsible for the following areas: (i) Planning and Projects; (ii) Parliamentary Affairs; (iii) Administration and Financial Affairs; (iv) Cinematographic Affairs; (v) Cultural Relations Affairs; (vi) Research and Protection of Cultural Heritage; (vii) Artistic Affairs.

The High Council of Culture and Arts, Board of Trustees of Secretariat for Libraries, Artistic Higher Educational Institutions, National Library, Royal Foundation of Iranian Academies, Rudaki Hall, and International Film Festival are directly responsible to the Minister of Culture and Arts MEHRDAD PAHLBOD.

Teheran Symphonic Orchestra: Kh. Kamal-ol-Molk, Teheran; 75 mems.; Music Dir. FARHAD MESHKAT.

Fine Arts Theatre Group: c/o Ministry of Culture, Teheran; produces weekly programmes for television.

Music Council of Radio Iran: Maidan Ark, Teheran; supervises all music programmes, both Persian and Western (popular and classical), broadcasts on two AM stations and one FM station in Teheran; also serves in advisory capacity all provincial stations; Chair. Dr. H. FARHAT.

Shiraz-Persepolis Festival of Arts: Shiraz; f. 1967; plays, films and music representing both Eastern and Western culture; held for a short fortnight at end of Aug. and beginning of Sept.; partly staged in the ruins at Persepolis; Pres. R. GHOTBI; publs. various books and brochures in Persian on music and drama, festival brochure annually.

ATOMIC ENERGY

Atomic Energy Organization of Iran: Teheran; f. 1974; set up to utilize atomic rays and energy in industries and agriculture and other services, to provide desalination plants, to produce primary materials required for atomic industries and to set up the necessary scientific and technical infrastructure to implement such projects, as well as to provide harmonious co-ordination and supervision over all matters related to atomic energy in Iran; Pres. A. ETEMAD.

Teheran University Nuclear Centre: P.O.B. 2989, Teheran; f. 1958; research in nuclear physics, electronics, nuclear chemistry, radiobiology and health physics; training and advice on nuclear science and the peaceful applications of atomic energy; a 5-MW pool-type research reactor on the new campus of Teheran University went critical in November 1967; a 3-MeV Van de Graaff-type accelerator became operational in 1972; Dir. Dr. B. PARSA.

DEFENCE

Defence Budget 1974-75: 215,100 million rials.

Military service: 2 years.

Total armed forces: 238,000: army 175,000; navy 13,000; air force 50,000.

EDUCATION

Primary and Secondary Education

When compulsory primary education was established by Reza Shah the Great in the 1930s there were no more than 36,000 children attending school. In 1973-74 over five million children were attending many thousands of primary and secondary schools all over the country. The figure represents a sevenfold increase during the past 18 years. This does not include Literacy Corps schools and literacy classes.

Primary education for five years is compulsory for all children, and along with a three years' guidance period, was declared free in 1974. An increasing number of children are now proceeding to secondary schools after obtaining their primary education certificate.

During the past few years the Government has taken steps to encourage private investment in education and as a result thousands of primary schools and hundreds of privately-owned secondary schools have come into being in Teheran and in the major provincial centres.

The Government is now helping to create city and provincial organizations which will take over, under overall Government control, the entire secondary schooling machinery of their region.

Higher Education

Iran has eight universities, three in Teheran and respectively one in Shiraz, Tabriz, Ahwaz, Meshed and Isfahan. There are also twelve institutes of higher education, four teachers' training colleges, a college of advanced technology in Abadan and colleges of agriculture in Karaj, Rezaiyeh and Kerman. Vocational training schools also exist in Teheran, Shiraz, Tabriz, Rasht and other cities.

Over 115,000 students were in 1974 attending graduate and postgraduate courses at these universities, while a further 30,000 were studying abroad, chiefly in Europe and North America.

In recent years much emphasis has been put on improving higher education facilities as well as expanding research. A Ministry of Science and Higher Education was established in 1967 to streamline and co-ordinate the affairs of universities, colleges and research institutes.

In 1968 the principles of the educational reforms which formed part of the "White Revolution", were formulated at a meeting presided over by the Shah. Since then these reforms have been carried out, with the result that the quality of higher education has improved considerably. In recent years the Government has been working on several plans to expand vocational training schools and re-orienting universities towards the training of skilled personnel and technicians required by Iran's rapidly expanding industries.

UNIVERSITIES

University of Azarabadegan: Tabriz; 502 teachers, 6,998 students.

University of Ferdowsi: Meshed; 227 teachers, 4,005 students.

University of Isfahan: Isfahan; 255 teachers, 4,663 students.

Jundi-Shapur University: Ahwaz, Khouzestan Province; 232 teachers, 2,961 students.

National University of Iran: Evin, Teheran; 309 teachers, 6,272 students.

Pahlavi University: Shiraz; 396 teachers, 4,050 students.

University of Teheran: Ave. Shah Reza, Teheran; 1,236 teachers, 17,617 students.

Arya Mehr University of Technology: Eisenhower Blvd., Teheran; 261 teachers, 2,688 students.

BIBLIOGRAPHY

GENERAL

ABDALIAN, S. Damavand (Iran) (Teheran, 1943).

BARTH, F. Nomads of South Persia (London, 1961).

CAMBRIDGE HISTORY OF IRAN.
Volume I: The Land of Iran.
Volume V: The Saljuq and Mongol Periods.
(Both Cambridge University Press, 1968).

CURZON, Lord. Persia and the Persian Question (2 vols., London, 1892).

DE PLANHOL, X. Recherches sur la Géographie humaine de l'Iran Septentrional (Paris, 1964).

ELWELL-SUTTON, L. P. Modern Iran (London, 1941).
A Guide to Iranian Area Study (Ann Arbor, 1952).
Persian Oil: A Study in Power Politics (London, 1955).

ENGLISH, P. W. City and Village in Iran (Wisconsin, 1967).

ESKELUND, KARL. Behind the Peacock Throne (Alvin Redman, New York, 1965).

FIELD, HENRY. Contributions to the Anthropology of Iran (Chicago, 1939).

FRYE, RICHARD N. Persia (Allen and Unwin, London, 3rd ed. 1969).

FURON, RAYMOND. L'Iran (Paris, 1952).
Géologie du Plateau iranien (Paris, 1941).
La Perse (Paris, 1938).

GAIL, MARZIEH. Persia and the Victorians (London, 1951).

GRAVES, PHILIP. The Life of Sir Percy Cox (1941).

GROSECLOSE, ELGIN. Introduction to Iran (New York, 1947).

HAAS, WILLIAM S. Iran (New York, 1946).

HANDLEY-TAYLOR, GEOFFREY. Bibliography of Iran (Fifth Edition, St. James Press, London, 1969).

HUOT, JEAN LOUIS. Persia Vol. I (Muller, London, 1966).

IQBAL, MUHAMMAD. Iran (London, 1946).
Iran Almanac (Echo of Iran, Teheran, annually).
Iran: A Selected and Annotated Bibliography (Washington, 1951).

KEDDIE, NIKKI R. Historical Obstacles to Agrarian Change in Iran (Claremont, 1960).

KEMP, N. Abadan (London, 1954).

LAMBTON, A. K. S. Landlord and Peasant in Persia (New York, 1953).
Islamic Society in Persia (London, 1954).
A Persian Vocabulary (Cambridge, 1961).
The Persian Land Reform 1962-66 (Clarendon Press, Oxford, 1969).

MARLOWE, JOHN. Iran, a Short Political Guide (Pall Mall Press, London and New York, 1963).

MEHDEVI, A. S. Persian Adventure (New York, 1954).
Persia Revisited (London, 1965).

MILLSPAUGH, A. C. Americans in Persia (Washington, 1946).

MOTTER, T. H. VAIL. The Persian Corridor and Aid to Russia (Washington, 1952).

RAMAZANI, ROUHOLLAH K. The Persian Gulf: Iran's Role (Charlottesville, University Press of Virginia, 1972).

SANGHVI, RAMESH. Aryamehr: The Shah of Iran (Macmillan, London, 1968).

SHAH OF IRAN. Mission for My Country (Hutchinson, London 1961).

SHEARMAN, I. Land and People of Iran (London, 1962).

SIRDAR, IKBAL ALI SHAH. Persia of the Persians (London, 1929).

SMITH, A. Blind White Fish in Persia (New York, 1953).

STARK, FREYA. The Valleys of the Assassins (London, 1934).
East is West (London, 1945).

THARAUD, JÉRÔME. Vieille Perse et Jeune Iran (Paris, 1947).

VREELAND, H. H. Iran (Human Relations Area Files, 1957).

WARD, PHILIP. Touring Iran (Faber & Faber, London, 1971).

WICKENS, G. M. and SAVORY, R. M. Persia in Islamic Times, a practical bibliography of its history, culture and language (Institute of Islamic Studies, McGill University, Montreal, 1964).

WILBER, DONALD N. Iran: Past and Present (Princeton University Press, 1955).
Iran: Oasis of Stability in the Middle East (Foreign Political Association, Inc., New York, 1959).

ZABIH, SEPEHR. The Communist Movement in Iran (University of California Press 1967).

CIVILIZATION AND LITERATURE

ARBERRY, A. J. (ed.). The Legacy of Persia (London and New York, 1953).
Shiraz: The Persian City of Saints and Poets (Univ. of Oklahoma Press, 1960).
Tales from the Masnavi (London, 1961).
More Tales from the Masnavi (London, 1963).
(ed.). The Cambridge History of Iran (Cambridge University Press 1969).

BAUSANI, A. Der Perser: von den Anfängen bis zur Gegenwart (Kohlhammer, Stuttgart, 1965).

BELL, GERTRUDE L. Persian Pictures (London, 1928).

BROWNE, E. G. A Literary History of Persia (4 vols., Cambridge, 1928).

COLLEDGE, M.A.R. The Parthians (Thames and Hudson, London, 1968).

CULICAN, WILLIAM. The Medes and the Persians (1965).

DUCHESNE-GUILLEMIN, JACQUES. The Hymns of Zarathustra (trans. with commentary) (Beacon, L. R., Boston, Mass., 1963).

ELWELL-SUTTON, L. P. Colloquial Persian (London, 1941).
Persian Proverbs (London, 1954).
Elementary Persian Grammar (Cambridge, 1963).

GHIRSHMAN, R. L'Iran: des Origines à Islam (Paris, 1951).
Iran from the Earliest Times to the Islamic Conquest (London, 1954).
Arts of Ancient Persia from the Origins to Alexander the Great (London, 1963).
Iran (New York, 1964).

HERZFELD, E. Iran in the Ancient East (Oxford, 1941).

KAMSHAD, H. Modern Persian Prose Literature (Cambridge, 1966).

LEVY, REUBEN. The Persian Language (New York, 1952).
Persian Literature (1928).

LOCKHART, L. Famous Cities of Iran (London, 1939).
The Fall of the Safavi Dynasty and the Afghan Occupation of Persia (Cambridge University Press, 1958).

MONTEIL, V. Les Tribus du Fars et la sédentarisation des nomades (Mouton, Paris and The Hague, 1966).

OLMSTEAD, A. T. History of the Persian Empire, Achaemenid Period (Chicago, 1948).

POPE, ARTHUR. Survey of Persian Art from Prehistoric Times to the Present. Vols. 1–6 (Oxford University Press, 1938–58).

RICE, CYPRIAN. The Persian Sufis (Allen and Unwin, London, 1964).

ROSS, Sir DENISON. Eastern Art and Literature (London, 1928).
The Persians (London, 1931).

STOREY, C. A. Persian Literature (London, 1927).

SYKES, Sir PERCY. Persia (Oxford, 1922).
A History of Persia (2 vols.; 3rd edition, with supplementary essays) (London, 1930).

WIDENGREN. Die Religionen Irans (Kohlhammer, Stuttgart, 1965).

WULFF, H. E. The Traditional Crafts of Persia (M.I.T. Press, Cambridge, Mass., 1966).

RECENT HISTORY

BANANI, AMIN. The Modernization of Iran, 1921–1924 (Stanford, 1961).

BUNYA, ALI AKBAR. A Political and Diplomatic History of Persia (Teheran, 1955).

COTTAM, R. W. Nationalism in Iran (Pittsburgh University Press, 1964).

FATEMI, NASROLLAH S. Diplomatic History of Persia 1917–1923 (New York, 1952).

HAMZAVI, A. H. K. Persia and the Powers: An Account of Diplomatic Relations, 1941–46 (London, 1946).

ISSAWI, CHARLES. The Economic History of Iran, 1800–1919 (University of Chicago Press, 1972).

LENCZOWSKI, GEORGE. Russia and the West in Iran (Cornell Univ. Press, 1949).

NAKHAI, M. L'Evolution Politique de l'Iran (Brussels, 1938).

RAMAZANI, ROUHOLLAH K. The Foreign Policy of Iran 1500–1941 (University Press of Virginia, Virginia, 1966).

SKRINE, Sir CLARMONT. World War in Iran (Constable, London, 1926).

STEPPAT, FRITZ. Iran zwischen den Grossmächten, 1941-48 (Oberursel, 1948).

UPTON, JOSEPH M. The History of Modern Iran: An Interpretation (Harvard University Press, 1960).

ECONOMY AND OIL

ABOLFAZI, ADLI. Aussenhandel und Aussenwirtschaftspolitik des Iran (Duncker and Humblot, Berlin, 1960).

AMUZEGAR, JAHANGIR. Technical Assistance in Theory and Practice: the Case of Iran (Praeger Special Studies in International Economics, New York, 1966).

AMUZEGAR, JAHANGIR and ALI FEKRAT, M. Iran: Economic Development under Dualistic Conditions (University of Chicago Press, 1971).

BALDWIN, GEORGE B. Planning and Development in Iran (Johns Hopkins Press, Baltimore, 1967).

BHARIER, JULIAN. Economic Development in Iran 1900-1970 (Oxford University Press, London, 1971).

FATEH, MOUSTAFA KHAN. The Economic Position of Persia (London, 1926).

GHOSH, SUNIL KANTI. The Anglo-Iranian Oil Dispute (Calcutta, 1960).

GORELIKOV, SEMEN GERASIMOVICH IVAN. A study in the Geography and Economics of Persia (Russian text), (Moscow, 1961).

GUPTA, RAJ NARAIN. Iran: An Economic Study (New Delhi, 1947).

I.L.O. SECRETARIAT. Labour Conditions in the Oil Industry in Iran (Geneva, 1950).

MASON, F. C. Iran: Economic and Commercial Conditions in Iran (H.M.S.O., London, 1957).

NAHAI, L. and KIBELL, C. L. The Petroleum Industry of Iran (Washington: U.S. Department of the Interior, Bureau of Mines, 1963).

NIRUMAND, BAHMAN. Persien, Modell eines Entwicklungslande, oder Die Diktatur der freien Welt (Rowohlt-Verlag, Reinbek-bei-Hamburg, 1967).

SOTOUDEH, H. L'Evolution Economique de l'Iran et ses Problèmes (Paris, 1957).

WILLIAMSON, J. W. In a Persian Oilfield (London, 1930).

MODERN IRAN

ARASTEH, REZA. Educational and Social Awakening in Iran (E. J. Brill, Leiden, 1962).
Man and Society in Iran (Leiden, 1964).

AVERY, PETER. Modern Iran (Benn, London, 1967).

BINDER, LEONARD. Iran, Political Development in a Changing Society (University of Calif. Press, 1962).

VON BLÜCHER, WIPERT. Zeitenwende in Iran: Erlebnisse und Beobachtungen (Biberach an der Riss, 1949).

BROWNE, E. S. The Press and Poetry of Modern Persia (Cambridge, 1914).
A Year Amongst the Persians (London, 1950).

GRAEFE, A. VON. Iran, Das neue Persien (Berlin, 1937).

NIRUMAND, BAHMAN. Iran: the new imperialism in action (Modern Reader Paperbacks, New York and London, 1971).

RAJPUT, A. B. Iran Today (Lion Publications, 1946).

RODKIN, ANGELA. Unveiled Iran (London, 1942).

WILBER, D. N. Contemporary Iran (New York, 1963).

WOODSMALL, RUTH. Moslem Women Enter a New World (London, 1936).

Iraq

PHYSICAL AND SOCIAL GEOGRAPHY

W. B. Fisher

Iraq is bounded on the north by Turkey, on the east by Iran, on the south by Kuwait and the Persian Gulf, on the south-west by Saudi Arabia and Jordan, and on the north-west by Syria. The actual frontier lines present one or two unusual features. In the first place, there exists between Iraq, Kuwait, and Saudi Arabia a "neutral zone", rhomboidal in shape, which was devised to facilitate the migrations of pastoral nomads, who cover great distances each year in search of pasture for their animals and who move regularly between several countries. Hence the stabilization or closing of a frontier could be for them a matter of life and death. Secondly, the frontier with Iran in its extreme southern portion below Basra follows the course of the Shatt al-Arab channel, but from 1936 until March 1975 the frontier was at the left (east) bank, placing the whole of the river within Iraq. This situation had become increasingly unacceptable to Iran, and in March 1975 the border was restored to the Thalweg line in the middle of the deepest shipping channel in the Shatt al-Arab estuary. Thirdly, the inclusion of the northern province of Mosul within Iraq was agreed only in 1926. Because of its oil deposits, this territory was in dispute between Turkey, Syria and Iraq. Again the presence of large numbers of migratory nomads journeying each season between Iran, Turkey, Syria and Iraq was a further complicating factor.

PHYSICAL FEATURES

The old name of Iraq (Mesopotamia=land between the rivers) indicates the main physical aspect of the country—the presence of the two river valleys of the Tigris and Euphrates, which merge in their lower courses. On the eastern side of this double valley the Zagros Mountains of Persia appear as an abrupt wall, overhanging the riverine lowlands, particularly in the south, below Baghdad. North of the latitude of Baghdad the rise to the mountains is more gradual, with several intervening hill ranges, such as the Jebel Hamrim. These ranges are fairly low and narrow at first, with separating lowlands, but towards the main Zagros topography becomes more imposing, and summits over 10,000 ft. in height occur. This region, lying north and east of Baghdad, is the ancient land of Assyria; and nowadays the higher hill ranges lying in the extreme east are called Iraqi Kurdistan, since many Kurdish tribes inhabit them.

On the western side of the river valley the land rises gradually to form the plateau which continues into Syria, Jordan, and Saudi Arabia, and its maximum height in Iraq is about 3,000 ft. In places it is possible to trace a cliff formation, where a more resistant bed of rock stands out prominently, and from this the name of the country is said to be derived (Arabic *Iraq*=cliff). There is no sharp geographical break between Iraq and its western neighbours comparable with that between Iraq and Iran; the frontier lines are artificial.

THE RIVERS

It remains to describe the valley region itself and the two rivers. The Tigris, 1,150 miles in length (1,850 km.), rises in Turkey, and is joined by numerous and often large tributaries both in Turkey and Iraq. The Euphrates, 1,460 miles in length (2,350 km.), also rises in Turkey and flows first through Syria and then Iraq, joining the Tigris in its lower course at Qurna, to form the stream known as the Shatt al-Arab, which is 115 miles (185 km.) in length. Unlike the Tigris, the Euphrates receives no tributaries during its passage of Iraq. Above the region of Baghdad both rivers flow in well-defined channels, with retaining valley-walls. Below Baghdad, however, the vestiges of a retaining valley disappear, and the rivers meander over a vast open plain with only a slight drop in level—in places merely 8 or 10 feet in 100 miles. Here the rivers are raised on great levees, or banks of silt and mud (which they themselves have laid down), and now lie several feet above the level of the surrounding plain. One remarkable feature is the change in relative level of the two river beds—water can be led from one to the other according to the actual district, and this possibility, utilised by irrigation engineers for many centuries, still remains the basic principle of present-day development. At the same time, the courses of both rivers can suddenly alter. A flood may breach the wall of the levee, and the water then pours out on to the lower-lying plain, inundating many square miles of territory. Ultimately, the river finds a new course and builds a fresh levee. Old river channels, fully or partially abandoned by the river, are thus a feature of the Mesopotamian lowland, associated with wide areas of swamp, lakes, and sandbars. The Tigris, though narrower than the Euphrates, is swifter, and carries far more water.

As the sources of both rivers lie in the mountains of Turkey, the current is very fast, and upstream navigation is difficult in the middle and upper reaches. In spring, following the melting of snows in Asia Minor, both rivers begin to rise, reaching a maximum in April (Tigris) and May (Euphrates). The spring is a very anxious time, since floods of 12 to 20 feet occur, and 32 feet is known—this in a region where the land may fall only 10 feet or less in level over 50 miles. Immense areas are regularly inundated, levees often collapse, and villages and roads, where these exist, must be built on high embankments. The Tigris is particularly liable to sudden flooding, and can rise at the rate of one foot per hour. Contrasts with the Nile of Egypt will be noted. The latter river is confined in a steep-sided valley over most of its length, and floods do not spread far away from the river. In lower Iraq, on the other hand, wide expanses are inundated every year, e.g. as in early 1954 when a flood of 30 ft. occurred and many thousands were rendered homeless.

CLIMATE AND ECONOMIC ACTIVITY

The summers are overwhelmingly hot, with shade temperatures of over 110°F.; and many inhabitants retire during the heat of the day to underground rooms. Winters may be surprisingly cold: frost, though very rare at Basra, can be severe in the north. Sudden hot spells during winter are another feature in the centre and south of Iraq. Rainfall is scanty over all of the country, except for the north-east (Assyria), where 15 to 25 inches occur—enough to grow crops without irrigation. Elsewhere farming is entirely dependent upon irrigation from river water. The great extent of standing water in many parts of Iraq leads to an unduly high air humidity, which explains the notorious reputation of the Mesopotamian summer.

The unusual physical conditions outlined present a number of obstacles to human activity. The flood waters are rather less "manageable" than in Egypt, and there is less of the regular deposition of thick, rich silt that is such a feature of the Nile. The effects of this are strikingly visible in the relatively small extent of land actually cultivated—at most, only one-sixth of the potentially cultivable territory and 3 per cent of the total area of the country. The population, of about 10 million, is about 30 per cent that of Egypt. Because of the easy availability of agricultural land, wasteful, "extensive" farming methods are often followed, giving a low yield. On the whole, Iraq is underpopulated, and could support larger numbers of inhabitants.

A feature of the last few years has been the use of oil royalties (ID 547 million in 1973) for development schemes, particularly in irrigation. Various Plans allocated up to £30 million annually, but this was not always used. Now, with higher oil revenues, the figure has been revised upward, and more extensive development is planned. A further favourable factor is the discovery in 1975 of a major new oilfield, which could make Iraq third Middle Eastern producer

The unusual physical conditions have greatly restricted movement and the development of communications of all kinds. In the upper reaches of the rivers boat journeys can only be made downstream, whilst nearer the sea the rivers are wider and slower but often very shallow. Roads are difficult to maintain because of the floods, and the railways have two differing gauges—standard and metre; the latter is however in process of replacement and with decreasing risk of flooding, standard gauge has been laid between Baghdad and Basra via Kut. The effect has been to leave in isolation many communities that have differing ways of life and even differing languages and religious beliefs. Numerous minority groups are hence a feature of Iraq.

THE PEOPLE

In the marshes of the extreme south there are communities of Arabs who spend most of their lives in boats and rafts. Other important minorities live in, or close to, the hill country of the north: the Kurds, who number over one million and migrate extensively into Syria, Turkey and Iran (*see* Recent History); the Yazidis of the Jebel Sinjar; the Assyrian Christians (the name refers to their geographical location, and has no historical connection); and various communities of Uniate and Orthodox Christians. As well, there were important groups of Jews—more than in most other Muslim countries—though since the establishment of the State of Israel much emigration has taken place. It should also be noted that whilst the majority of the Muslims follow Shi'a rites, the wealthier Muslims are of Sunni adherence.

Ethnically, the position is very complicated. The northern and eastern hill districts contain many racial elements—Turki, Persian, and proto-Nordic, with Armenoid strains predominating. The pastoral nomads of western Iraq are, as might be expected, of fairly unmixed Mediterranean ancestry, like the nomads of Syria, Jordan, and Saudi Arabia; but the population of the riverine districts of Iraq shows a mixture of Armenoid and Mediterranean elements. North of the Baghdad district the Armenoid strain is dominant, but to the south, it is less important, though still present.

Arabic is the official and most widely used language. Kurdish and dialects of Turkish are current in the north, whilst variants of Persian are spoken by tribesmen in the east. An estimate, probably over-generous to the Arabic speakers, puts the relative numbers at: Arabic 79 per cent, Kurdish 16 per cent, Persian 3 per cent, and Turkish 2 per cent of the total population.

HISTORY

Iraq was one of the earliest centres of civilization. Before 3000 B.C. the Sumerians, a people of problematical origin, had established a complete civilization in the marshy alluvial areas at the head of the Persian/Arabian Gulf. Here a number of city states developed, cities like Eridu, Uruk, Ur, Kish and Lagash. These states were supported by a highly developed agricultural economy, based on an intricate irrigation system.

Around 2500 B.C., Lagash gained ascendency over several other cities, until, not long afterwards, Lugalzaggisi, the governor of Umma, overran Uruk and embarked on a career of widespread conquest. Lugalzaggisi was in turn defeated by Sargon of Agade, who united the whole of Mesopotamia under Akkadian rule and conquered Elamite Susa, and whose armies penetrated as far as the Mediterranean. Akkadian dominions were extended even further under his successors, but the Sumerians of the south took every opportunity to revolt and attacks by Elamites and mountain tribesmen, the Gutians, caused the empire to collapse around 2200 B.C. After a period of chaos, a new Sumerian kingdom, centered at Ur (the Third Dynasty of Ur) established supremacy over the south, lasting through the twenty-first century B.C. It was finally sacked by invaders from Elam, and by the Amorites from the north-west, and was never again of great historical importance.

The Amorites were Semites, whose homeland was Arabia. They came into conflict with the Elamites in Sumer, and in the eighteenth century B.C. Hammurabi created an extensive empire famous for the splendour of its civilization. Pressure from the Caucasian tribes, Hurrians and Kassites, was increasing, but the empire finally crumbled before the onslaught of the Hittites, who sacked Babylon in the seventeenth century B.C.

In the north, new powers were emerging, notably the Mitanni, who occupied northern Iraq. At last their rule disintegrated under constant pressure from the Hittites of Asia Minor, whose influence, in the years following the reign of their great king Subbiluliuma (*c.* 1390–1350 B.C.), was advanced almost to the Persian/Arabian Gulf. Meanwhile, on the higher reaches of the Tigris, the warlike Assyrians, who hastened the decline of the Mitanni and the Hittite empire, embarked from time to time on a career of conquest destined to be of brief duration, as under Adad-nirari I (*c.* 1300 B.C.) and Tiglath-pileser I (*c.* 1200 B.C.). In the reign of Ashur-nasir-pal II (883–859 B.C.) Assyrian ambition burst forth once more, re-establishing control over northern Mesopotamia. Syria and Cilicia were subdued under Shalmaneser III (860–825 B.C.) and the Assyrian empire in its heyday comprised Van and other Armenian territories, Babylonia, Syria, Egypt and large areas of Persia. An army of unprecedented efficiency, mass deportations on a vast scale, relentless cruelty, a régime of rigid and despotic centralization—these features of Assyrian rule evoked the bitter enmity of the subject peoples, who, when the empire weakened as a result of incessant warfare and of Scythian

invasion from the north, rose in combined revolt and sacked Nineveh in 612 B.C. Iraq now became the centre of a neo-Babylonian state which, under Nebuchadnezzar (604–562 B.C.) included much of the Fertile Crescent, but was soon to fall before the Persians, who seized Babylon in 539–538 B.C.

Thereafter, Iraq was a mere province of the vast Achaemenid empire, which extended from Asia Minor to the Punjab in north-west India and from southern Russia to Egypt. Alexander the Great brought Persian rule to an end in a series of brilliant campaigns (334–327 B.C.). After his death in 323 B.C., one of his generals, Seleucus, controlled most of the Asiatic lands which the conqueror had dominated. The Seleucids maintained their hold on Iraq for more than a hundred years and then, in the course of prolonged warfare, lost it to the Parthians, who during the third and second centuries B.C. founded a powerful state in Persia.

Under the Parthians Iraq was a frontier province over against the might of Rome. To the north and west of Mesopotamia a line of strong fortresses, e.g., Carrhae (Harran), Edessa (modern Urfa), Diyarbakir, Dara, Nisibin, marked the ground where the rival armies fought. At Carrhae, in 54 B.C., the Parthian horsemen severely defeated the Romans but from the time of Augustus until the reign of the Emperor Trajan there was no major war between the two states. Between A.D. 113 and 117, Trajan conquered much of Iraq, yet his successor, Hadrian, felt that it would be too expensive to defend the new territories and so abandoned them. Rome resumed the offensive under Marcus Aurelius (162–166), Septimius Severus (195–199) and Caracalla (216–218), her rule being now extended from the middle Euphrates to the Khabur river.

The Parthian domination came to an end in 224 owing to internal revolt in Persia; the emergence of the Sasanid régime now began. In 260 Sapor I crushed the Romans in battle near Edessa and captured the Emperor Valerian. The endless frontier hostilities flared out once more into violent war under Diocletian, Constantius and Julian (third–fourth centuries), the Romans being forced back behind the line of the Euphrates. The conflict then died down for more than a hundred years and was not resumed on a large scale until the Sasanid state recovered much of its old vigour under Kobad I (488–531) and Khusran Anushirvan (531–579). The prolonged warfare of the sixth–seventh centuries came to an end with the brilliant campaigns of the Byzantine Emperor Heraclius in Armenia and Iraq (622–628). Byzantium and Persia were by now exhausted and in the meantime a formidable danger had arisen in the far south.

THE RISE OF ISLAM

The prophet Muhammad (d. 632) had created at Mecca and Medina a religious and political organization that aroused powerful forces long latent in Arabia.

The Arab nomads of the great desert, united within the community of Islam, were forbidden to pursue their ancient tribal feuds. The restless energy thus concentrated in the Muslim state found an outlet in war outside Arabia and the Arabs overran Syria and Egypt. By 634 the Arab warriors had begun the conquest of Iraq. The battle of Qadisiya in 635 led to the fall of the Persian capital, Ctesiphon, in June of that year. A further battle at Jalula in 637 marked the end of Sasanid power in Iraq, although resistance continued in the north until the Arabs took Mosul in 641. Kufa and Basra became the two great garrison cities on which Muslim rule in Iraq was to be based for the next hundred years.

The murder of the Caliph 'Uthman in 656 brought about a civil war between his successor, 'Ali, and Mu'awiya, a kinsman of 'Uthman, who had long been governor of Syria. After an indecisive battle at Siffin in 657 the two rivals had recourse to arbitration, as a result of which, at Adhruh in January 659, both men were deposed from their respective positions, a judgment which deprived 'Ali of his real status as Caliph and Mu'awiya of a pretension to that office which as yet he had not ventured openly to avow. The outcome of the conflict remained uncertain during the next two years, until at length the murder of 'Ali at Kufa in January 661 left the way clear for Mu'awiya to become Caliph. The war revealed that effective power within the new empire was passing from Mecca and Medina to the great garrison cities where the main Arab armies were stationed. 'Ali had been obliged to go from the Hijaz to Iraq, his chief support coming from Kufa. Mu'awiya relied for his success on the strength of Syria. The real issue had been whether Iraq or Syria should be the metropolitan province of the empire. With the emergence of Mu'awiya as Caliph in 661, the question was decided, for almost a hundred years, in favour of Syria.

During the period of the Umayyad dynasty (661–750) Iraq became the centre of the movement known as Shi'atu 'Ali, i.e. "the party of 'Ali". Born amongst the Arabs themselves, it assumed at first the form of a "legitimist" opposition to Umayyad rule, asserting that the Caliphate should of right belong to the descendants of 'Ali, the son-in-law of the Prophet. As a purely Arab and political faction, resting to a large degree on the bitter dislike of Iraq for the hegemony of Syria, it was to meet with failure, for the armies of Kufa and Basra could not overcome the military pre-eminence of the Syrians. At Karbala, in October 680, Husain, the son of 'Ali, fell in battle against the Umayyad forces in Iraq. This event, by giving to the Shi'a an illustrious martyr, inaugurated a new and rapid growth of the party, not on the political level but as a religious sect.

UMAYYAD RULE

The Umayyad state was based on the fundamental assumption that a vast subject population, non-Muslim and non-Arab, would continue indefinitely to yield tribute to a dominant Arab and Muslim warrior aristocracy, the revenues derived from the conquered territories and from the *jizya*, i.e. the poll-tax imposed on those who did not belong to the faith of the Prophet, being shared out amongst the members of that aristocracy. Whether from a genuine acceptance of the new religion or from motives of self-interest, e.g. to escape the poll-tax and to secure the financial, economic and social privileges of the Arab Muslims, the subject peoples began to adopt Islam. The revenues of the state fell and the decline could not be made good through the acquisition of rich new lands, for the age of rapid conquest was over. Since Muhammad had declared all Muslims to be equal, the new converts, or Mawali, demanded that the Arabs concede to them a due participation in the rewards of empire. When it became clear that the Arab aristocracy meant to defend its pensions, privileges and other exclusive rights—the available resources of the state were insufficient to meet the claims of the ever-increasing numbers of Mawali—a crisis of the first magnitude threatened the Umayyad régime.

The Mawali now gave their allegiance to the Shi'a, transforming the movement into a means for the expression of their social and economic grievances against the established order and, at the same time, remoulding it as a religious sect which embraced ideas not of Muslim origin but derived from their previous Christian, Jewish and Zoroastrian traditions. This radical change in the Shi'a was already visible in the years 685–687, when a serious revolt occurred at Kufa in the name of Muhammad ibn al-Hanafiya, a son of 'Ali by a wife other than Fatima, the daughter of the Prophet.

The Umayyad Caliph 'Umar II (717–720) introduced a series of financial reforms designed to conciliate the Mawali, a policy which met only with a transient success, for the ultimate effect of his measures was to increase the expenditure and lower the revenue of the state. Disillusionment grew apace amongst the non-Arab Muslims. An efficient propaganda machine, known under the name of the Hashimiya, made its appearance in Iraq, its task being to disseminate extreme Shi'i ideas. In 716 control of this organization fell into the hands of Muhammad ibn 'Ali ibn al- 'Abbas, descended from an uncle of the Prophet. Its chief centre of activity was in the great frontier province of Khurasan, in north-east Persia, where Arab colonies from Basra and Kufa had settled in about 670. Abu Muslim, a Persian Mawla of Iraq, was sent to Khurasan as confidential agent of the Hashimiya in 743 and there raised the standard of revolt against the Umayyads. Syria, long since weakened by fierce tribal feuds amongst the Arabs, could not withstand the storm. In 750 Umayyad rule came to an end and was replaced by that of the 'Abbasid dynasty, while Iraq at last achieved her ambition of becoming the dominant province of the empire.

'ABBASID RULE

The 'Abbasid caliphs had now an immediate and urgent task to perform. It was impossible for them to govern as the representatives of the more advanced elements in the Shi'a, when most of their Muslim subjects were of the Sunni or orthodox faith. The second 'Abbasid, al-Mansur (754–775), the real founder of the new régime, therefore abandoned the extremists who had done so much to bring his house to power. He also built a new garrison city in Iraq for his main army, the hard core of which consisted largely of regiments from Khurasan. This capital of the 'Abbasid empire, Baghdad, soon developed into a great emporium of trade and a political centre of vast importance. An autocratic caliph, claiming divine authority for his power, which rested on regular armed forces and was exercised through a paid bureaucracy; a cosmopolitan ruling class of officials and landowners, of merchants and bankers; the 'Ulama, i.e. the hierarchy of religious scholars, jurists, teachers and dignitaries—these were the main characteristics of the 'Abbasid Caliphate, which for a time brought to Iraq and, indeed, to the Islamic state as a whole a splendid prosperity derived from a flourishing agriculture and industry and from the lucrative transit trade between India and the Mediterranean.

It was in regard to political unity that the 'Abbasid empire proved most vulnerable. The relative cohesion which the Muslim state had enjoyed owing to the dominance of the Arab warrior aristocracy did not survive the revolution of 750. The new dynasty sought to use the Muslim faith itself as a means of binding together the varied ethnic and social elements of the population, but the attempt was soon shown to be a failure. After the death of Harun ar-Rashid (786–809), whose reign marked the apogee of 'Abbasid power as well as fostering a great flowering of Arabic culture, civil war broke out between his sons Amin and Ma'mun, the former depending largely on the support of Iraq, the latter on the strength of Persia and, above all, on the troops of Khurasan. The conflict was, in one sense, a battle between Persia and Iraq for pre-eminence within the empire. Ma'mun conquered Baghdad in 813, but for a time considered the idea of making Marv in Khurasan his capital, a project which he abandoned only when he realized that it would lead to repeated revolt in Iraq. In August 819 he returned to Baghdad.

Persia, disappointed in its hopes, now began to break away from the caliphs of Baghdad. Local dynasties made their appearance in the east, the Tahirids in 820, the Saffarids in 867, the Samanids in c. 892. A similar process occurred in the west, Spain after 756, Morocco after 788, Tunisia after 800 being virtually independent of Baghdad. In 868 the dynasty of the Tulunids arose in Egypt. The more extreme elements of the Shi'a were also active, especially in Persia and the neighbouring regions, inspiring repeated insurrections against the 'Abbasid régime. Southern Iraq suffered heavily in the Zanj Rebellion (869–883), when one Ali ibn Muhammad founded a state of Negro slaves at Basra, which was sacked in 871. The Qarmatians, a religious movement of communistic and revolutionary tendencies, founded a strong régime of their own in the province of Bahrain (now called al-Hasa) and for most of the tenth century carried out frequent raids into Iraq. Meanwhile, at Baghdad, the power of the army was growing. The corps gathered for the Caliph's protection consisted of slaves (mamluks), mostly of Turkish origin, commanded by free officers. Since the reigns of al-Mu'tasim (833–842) and al-Wathiq (842–847), their officers had also been Mamluks. As power fell more and more into the hands of the army, the Mamluks were able to appoint and depose the caliphs at will. Iraq fell at length under the domination of Daylamite mountain dwellers from the region south of the Caspian Sea, Shi'i in religion and led by a family of *condottière* chieftains, the Buwaihids, who, after subduing most of western Persia, occupied Baghdad in 945. Buwaihid rule—a period of the deepest degradation for the Caliphate, since the Commander of the Faithful was now a mere puppet obedient to the orders of a Shi'i—lasted until 1055. It then collapsed before the assault of Turks from the steppe lands beyond the Oxus, who, led by the Seljuqs, a family also of *condottière* origin, overran Persia and then seized Baghdad under Tughril Beg. The Seljuq Turks were Sunni Muslims and their success was not unwelcome amongst the orthodox, who regarded it as a liberation from the yoke of the Shi'i Buwaihids. Yet the Caliph, although treated with deference, was still only in name the head of the state, all effective power being concentrated in the hands of the Seljuq Sultan.

After the death of Malik Shah in 1092, dynastic dissension and revolt amongst the Turkish tribesmen brought about a rapid decline of the new régime and the rise of succession states ruled by princes or by officers of the Seljuq house. In Iraq a series of nine Seljuq sultans ruled from 1118–94, almost all of them fated to die a violent death in conflict with rival claimants or with their Atabegs, i.e. amirs, who were the most powerful figures in the land. Some of these Atabegs established independent principalities of their own, e.g. the Zangid dynasty at Mosul, which played an important role in arousing the Muslims to defend Islam against the Christian Crusaders in Syria. The last Seljuq Sultan of Iraq, Tughril (1177–94), was defeated in battle with the Turkish ruler of Khwarizm (the region of Khiva, south of the Aral Sea). The victor, Takash (1172–1200), and his successor, 'Ala'ad-Din Muhammad (1200–20), sought to extend his rule over Iraq, but, before this ambition could be realised, the Mongols destroyed the power of the Khwarizm shahs.

THE MONGOL INVASIONS

By 1220 the great conqueror Jenghiz Khan had overrun all Transoxania and was threatening to invade Persia. His death in 1227 led to a long pause in the Mongol advance. In 1253 Hülakü, a grandson of Jenghiz Khan, moved westward in force, captured Baghdad in 1258 and thus made an end of the Abbasid caliphate. Subordinated henceforth to the Mongol Khan of Persia, Iraq became a mere frontier province, bereft of all its former wealth and splendour and much neglected by its rulers. On the death of the Mongol Khan Abu Sa'id in 1335, Iraq, after a brief period of confusion, passed into the hands of a new dynasty, the Jala'irids, who ruled over the land until the early years of the fifteenth century. During this period Iraq was again overrun by Mongols and in

1401 Timur Beg sacked Baghdad with merciless severity. The Jala'irid régime did not long outlast the death of Timur in 1405.

To the north of Iraq, around Lake Van, a powerful Turcoman confederation, known as the Black Sheep (Kara Koyunlu) was rising into prominence. The Turcomans defeated the last Jala'irid, Ahmed, and created a new state which, under Jihan Shah (1444–67), extended from Tabriz to the Shatt al-'Arab. The power of the Kara Koyunlu soon collapsed in war with a rival Turcoman confederation, that of the Ak Koyunlu (White Sheep), who, led by their famous chieftain, Uzun Hasan (1423?–78), crushed Jihan Shah and took over the territories which he had ruled. Dynastic quarrels brought about a rapid disintegration of the White Sheep ascendancy.

In the years 1499–1508 the now crumbling Ak Koyunlu régime was destroyed by the Safavid, Isma'il. (His ancestors were hereditary masters of a powerful religious order notable for its advanced Shi'i teaching and, from their main centre at Ardabil near the Caspian Sea, had fashioned their numerous adherents amongst the Turcoman tribes of Asia Minor into a formidable military movement). Isma'il made himself Shah of Persia and also conquered Iraq. To the Ottoman Sultan, the dissemination of Shi'i beliefs among the tribes of Anatolia was a menace which had to be eliminated, for it threatened to undermine his own control in that region, the Ottomans being Sunni, i.e. orthodox Muslims. Selim I made war on Shah Isma'il in 1514 and so began a protracted conflict between the Ottomans and the Safavids which was to last, with long intervals of precarious peace, until 1639. Sultan Suleyman, in the course of his first campaign against Persia, conquered Baghdad in 1534–35.

OTTOMAN IRAQ

The Ottomans were to find Iraq a most difficult and expensive province to administer. Religious animosities proved to be a constant source of trouble. Northern Iraq and Kurdistan followed largely the Sunni faith; Baghdad itself was divided in its allegiance between Sunni and Shi'i Islam; southern Iraq was a region under strong Shi'i influence. The task of restraining nomad tribes from raiding the settled lands was an endless and wearisome business. Moreover, the tribes of the delta marshlands and of the mountainous areas close to the frontier with Persia were ever liable to rise in revolt against the administration. From time to time Iraq was the scene of warfare between the Ottomans and the Safavids, e.g., in the years 1578–90, and indeed came once more under Persian control, when Shah Abbas (1587–1629) seized Baghdad in 1623 and retained it in the face of a determined Ottoman counter-offensive in 1625/26. After a second attempt at reconquest in 1629/30 had failed, the Ottomans at last recovered Baghdad in 1638 and in the next year made peace with the Safavids.

As the Ottoman state fell into decline, the Sultan at Istanbul became less able to dominate the course of events in so distant a province as Iraq. From about 1625 until 1668, Basra and the Delta marshlands were in the hands of local chieftains independent of the Ottoman administration at Baghdad, a state of affairs which recurred in the period 1694–1701. The appointment of Hasan Pasha to command at Baghdad in 1704 marked a new phase in the history of Ottoman Iraq. The pashalik was to pass from himself to his son, then to the husbands of his grand-daughters, and thereafter to a series of Mamluk governors raised and trained in the household of his immediate successors. From 1704 to 1831, therefore, the Sultan failed to enforce at Baghdad an appointment of his own choice.

Hasan Pasha died in 1723, just at the moment when the Ottomans had become involved in a new war against Persia. The last of the Safavids had been deposed in 1722 by the Afghan Mir Mahmud. Hasan Pasha's son, Ahmed Pasha, occupied Kermanshah, which Hasan himself had seized in the first stage of the conflict, and then overran Hamadan and Luristan, but these lands were lost once more to Persia when Nadir Shah, in the years after 1729, drove out the Afghans and invaded Iraq. Baghdad itself withstood a siege in 1733 and Mosul underwent the same experience in 1743. The war brought much suffering to Iraq, the province falling, as a result of frequent revolt amongst the restless tribesmen and the devastation caused by repeated campaigns, into a state of anarchy. None the less, Ahmed Pasha remained throughout this period in firm control of Baghdad and Basra and also exercised a strong influence over the affairs of Mosul and Kirkuk. He lived to see peace made with Persia in 1746 on terms which restored the general position to what it had been before the war. A few months later in 1747, he died, leaving no son to succeed him.

The palace household which his father had created and which he himself had further developed contained Mamluks recruited for the most part from Georgia, converted to Islam and trained in their youth for subsequent service in the administration of Iraq. After a brief interval of confusion, in which the Porte tried to impose its own nominee but soon had to admit failure, Suleyman Agha, one of the Mamluks whom Hasan Pasha had bought and educated, became the governor of Baghdad and Basra, an office which he held with great success for twelve years until his death in 1762. Yet another Mamluk, 'Umr Agha, ruled Iraq from 1764 to 1775. Internal strife and a frontier war which led to a Persian occupation of Basra marked the period immediately following his death.

At length, in 1780, the most famous of the Mamluk pashas, Suleyman the Great, assumed the government of Baghdad and Basra. Much of his time was spent in curbing the Kurdish chieftains in the north and the Arab tribes, above all the powerful Muntafiq confederation in the south of Iraq. From about 1790 he had to face the enmity of the formidable Wahhabi state recently founded in central Arabia. The raids of the Wahhabi tribesmen into Iraq intensified until in 1801 the great Shi'i sanctuary of Karbala was taken and sacked. The death of Suleyman in the next year threw Iraq into even greater confusion. There were further Wahhabi *razzias*, e.g. against Najaf in 1803 and Basra in 1804, and constant trouble with the tribes along the Persian border. It was only in 1817 that the last of the Mamluk pashas, Da'ud, secured control of the province and restored some semblance of order by repeated punitive campaigns against the Kurds and the nomads of the desert lands.

Meanwhile, reforms were being introduced at Istanbul which foreshadowed the end of the Mamluk régime in Iraq. Selim III (1789–1807) and Mahmud II (1808–39) sought to refashion the administration and the military forces of the empire on European lines. The moment when the Ottoman Sultan would attempt to end the Mamluk system and regain direct possession of Iraq was now at hand. Mahmud II sent 'Ali Ridha Pasha to perform this task in 1831. A severe outbreak of plague crippled the resistance of the Mamluks, Da'ud Pasha was deposed and the Mamluk regiments were at once exterminated. A new phase in the history of Iraq was about to begin.

WESTERN INFLUENCE

Although some of the European nations had long been in contact with Iraq through their commercial interests in the Persian/Arabian Gulf, western influences were slow to penetrate into the province. By 1800 there was a British Resident at Basra and two years later a British Consulate at Baghdad. France also maintained agents in these cities. French and Italian religious orders had settlements in the land. It was not, however, until after 1831 that signs of more rapid European penetration became visible, such as steam-boats on the rivers of Iraq in 1836, telegraph lines from 1861 and a number of proposals for railways, none of which was to materialise for a long time to come. The Ottoman government did much in the period between 1831 and 1850 to impose direct control over Kurdistan and the mountainous areas close to the Persian border, but the introduction of reforms was not, in fact, begun until in 1869 Midhat Pasha arrived at Baghdad. Much of his work, performed in the brief space of three years, proved to be superficial and ill-considered, yet he was able to set Iraq on a course from which there could be no retreat in the future. A newspaper, military factories, a hospital, an alms-house, schools, a tramway, conscription for the army, municipal and administrative councils, comparative security on the main routes and a reasoned policy of settling tribesmen on the land—these achievements, however imperfect, bear solid witness to the vigour of his rule. After his departure in 1872, reform and European influence continued to advance, although slowly. Postal services were much developed, a railway from Baghdad to Samarra was completed in 1914 (part of the projected *Baghdad-bahn*, which betokened the rapid growth of German interest in the Ottoman Empire) and the important Hindiya Barrage on the Euphrates was rebuilt between 1910 and 1913. The measures of reform and improvement introduced between 1831 and 1914 must indeed be judged as belated and inadequate—the Iraq of 1900 differed little from that of 1500—yet a process of fundamental change had begun, which no régime, however inept, could reverse.

In November 1914 Britain and the Ottoman Empire were at war. British troops occupied the Shatt al-Arab region and, under the pressure of war needs, transformed Basra into an efficient and well-equipped port. A premature advance on Baghdad in 1915 ended in the retreat of the British forces to Kut, their prolonged defence of that town and, when all attempts to relieve it had failed, the capitulation to the Ottomans in April 1916. A new offensive launched from Basra in the autumn of that year brought about the capture of Baghdad in March 1917. Kirkuk was taken in 1918, but, before the Allies could seize Mosul, the Ottoman government sought and obtained an armistice in October. For two years, until the winter of 1920, the Commander-in-Chief of the British Forces, acting through a civil commissioner, continued to be responsible for the administration of Iraq from Basra to Mosul, all the apparatus of a modern system of rule being created at Baghdad—e.g., departments of Land, Posts and Telegraphs, Agriculture, Irrigation, Police, Customs, Finance, etc. The new régime was Christian, foreign and strange, resented by reason of its very efficiency, feared and distrusted no less by those whose loyalties were Muslim and Ottoman than by important elements who desired self-determination for Iraq.

The last phase of Ottoman domination in Iraq especially during the years after the Young Turk Revolution in 1908, had witnessed a marked growth of Arab nationalist sentiment. Local circles in Iraq now made contact with the Ottoman Decentralization Party at Cairo, founded in 1912, and with the Young Arab Society, which moved from Paris to Beirut in 1913. Basra, in particular, became a centre of Arab aspirations and took the lead in demanding from Istanbul a measure of autonomy for Iraq. A secret organization, al-'Ahd (the Covenant) included a number of Iraqi officers serving in the Ottoman armies. The prospect of independence which the Allies held out to the Arabs in the course of the war strengthened and extended the nationalist movement. In April 1920 Britain received from the conference at San Remo a mandate for Iraq. This news was soon followed by a serious insurrection amongst the tribesmen of the south. The revolt, caused partly by instinctive dislike of foreign rule but also by vigorous nationalist propaganda, was not wholly suppressed until early in the next year. In October 1920 military rule was formally terminated in Iraq. An Arab Council of State, advised by British officials and responsible for the administration, now came into being and in March 1921 the Amir Faisal ibn Husain agreed to rule as King at Baghdad. His ceremonial accession took place on August 23rd, 1921.

The Najdi (Saudi Arabian) frontier with Iraq was defined in the Treaty of Mohammara in May 1922. Saudi concern over loss of traditional grazing rights resulted in further talks between Ibn Saud and the U.K. Civil Commissioner in Iraq, and a Neutral Zone of 7,000 sq. km. was established adjacent to the western tip of the Kuwait frontier. No military or permanent buildings were to be erected in the zone and the nomads of both countries were to have unimpeded access to its pastures and wells. A further agreement concerning the administration of this zone was signed between Iraq and Saudi Arabia in May 1938.

MODERN IRAQ

Despite the opposition of the more extreme nationalists, an Anglo-Iraqi Treaty was signed on October 10th, 1922. It embodied the provisions of the mandate, safeguarded the judicial rights of foreigners and guaranteed the special interests of Britain in Iraq. Subsidiary agreements were to be made covering military co-operation, the status of British officials and also matters of justice and finance. An Electoral Law, published in May 1922, prepared the way for the choice of a constituent assembly, which met in March 1924 and, in the face of strong opposition by the nationalists, ratified the treaty with Britain. It accepted, too, an Organic Law declaring Iraq to be a sovereign state with a constitutional hereditary monarchy and a representative system of government. In 1925 the League of Nations recommended that the *vilayet* of Mosul, to which the Turks had laid claim, be incorporated into the new kingdom, a decision finally implemented in the treaty of July 1926 between the interested parties, Britain, Turkey and Iraq. By this year a fully constituted Parliament was in session at Baghdad and all the ministries, as well as most of the larger departments of the administration, were in effective control. Moreover, the state now possessed a competent judicial organization, a small army of about 7,500 men and a police force well equipped to deal with the refractory desert tribesmen. In 1930 a new treaty was signed with Britain, which established between the two countries a close alliance for a period of 25 years. The agreement provided for full consultation in foreign affairs and mutual aid in time of war. Iraq undertook to grant free passage for British troops and all other needful facilities, recognizing the importance to Britain of its "essential communications" in the region. British forces were also to hold two air bases at Shu'ayba and Habbaniya. On October 3rd, 1932 Iraq entered the League of Nations as an independent power, the mandate being now terminated.

The difficulties which confronted the Kingdom in the period after 1932 required much time and effort for their solution: e.g. the animosities between the Sunni Muslims and the powerful Shi'i tribes on the Euphrates, which tended to divide and embitter political life; the problem of relations with the Kurds, some of whom wanted a state of their own, and with other minorities like the Assyrians; the complicated task of reform in land tenure and of improvement in agriculture, irrigation, flood control, public services and communications. As yet the Government itself consisted of little more than a façade of democratic forms concealing a world of faction and intrigue. The realities of the political scene were a xenophobe press often ill-informed and irresponsible; "parties" better described as cliques gathered around prominent personalities; a small ruling class of tribal sheikhs; landowners; and the intelligentsia—lawyers, students, journalists, doctors, ex-officers—frequently torn by sharp rivalries. It is not surprising, therefore, that the first years of full independence showed a rather

halting progress towards efficient rule. The dangerous nature of the tensions inside Iraq was revealed in the Assyrian massacre of 1933 carried out by troops of the Iraq army. Political intrigue from Baghdad had much to do with the outbreak of tribal revolt along the Euphrates in 1935/36. The army crushed the insurrection without much trouble and then, under the leadership of General Bakr Sidqi and in alliance with disappointed politicians and reformist elements, brought about a *coup d'état* in October 1936. The new régime failed to fulfil its assurances of reform, its policies alienated the tribal chieftains and gave rise to serious tensions even within the armed forces, tensions which led to the assassination of Bakr Sidqi in August 1937.

Of vast importance for Iraq was the rapid development of the oil industry during these years. Concessions were granted in 1925, 1932 and 1938 to the Iraq, Mosul and Basra Petroleum Companies. Oil had been discovered in the Kirkuk area in 1927 and by the end of 1934 the Iraq Petroleum Company was exporting crude oil through two 12-inch pipelines, one leading to Tripoli and the other to Haifa. Exploitation of the Mosul and Basra fields did not begin on a commercial scale until after World War II.

In 1937 Iraq joined Turkey, Persia and Afghanistan in the Sa'dabad Pact, which arranged for consultation in all disputes that might affect the common interests of the four states. A treaty signed with Persia in July 1937 and ratified in the following year provided for the specific acceptance of the boundary between the two countries as it had been defined in 1914. Relations with Britain deteriorated in the period after 1937, mainly because of the growth of anti-Zionist feeling and of resentment at British policy in Palestine. German influence increased very much at this time in Iraq, especially amongst those political and military circles associated with the army group later to be known as the Golden Square. Iraq severed her diplomatic connections with Germany at the beginning of World War II, but in 1941 the army commanders carried out a new *coup d'état*, establishing, under the nominal leadership of Rashid 'Ali al-Gaylani, a régime which announced its non-belligerent intentions. A disagreement over the passage of British troops through Iraq left no doubt of the pro-German sympathies of the Gaylani government and led to hostilities that ended with the occupation of Basra and Baghdad in May 1941. Thereafter Iraq co-operated effectively with the Allied war effort and became an important base from which aid was sent northward through Persia to Russia. In 1943 Iraq declared war on the Axis powers and in 1945 signed the Charter of the United Nations.

Iraq, during the years after World War II, was to experience much internal tension and unrest. Negotiations with Britain led to the signing at Portsmouth in January 1948 of a new Anglo-Iraqi agreement designed to replace that of 1930 and incorporating substantial concessions, amongst them the British evacuation of the airbases at Shu'ayba and Habbaniya and the creation of a joint board for the co-ordination of all matters relating to mutual defence. The animosities arising from the situation in Palestine called forth riots at Baghdad directed against the new agreement with Britain, which were sufficiently disturbing to oblige the Iraqi Government to repudiate the Portsmouth settlement.

ARAB-ISRAEL WAR 1948

With anti-Jewish and anti-Western feeling so intense, it was inevitable that troops should be sent from Iraq to the Arab-Israeli war which began on May 15th, 1948. The Iraqi troops shared in the hostilities for a period of just over two months, their participation terminating in a truce operative from July 18th. Their final withdrawal from Palestine did not commence, however, until April 1949. Subsequently, there was a considerable emigration of Jews from Iraq to Israel, especially in the years 1951–52.

The expense of the war against Israel, bad harvests, the general indigence of the people—all contributed to bring about serious tensions resulting in rioting at Baghdad in November 1952 and the imposition of martial law until October 1953. None the less, there were some favourable prospects for the future—notably a large expansion of the oil industry. New pipelines were built to Tripoli in 1949 and to Banias in Syria in 1952; the oil-fields of Mosul and Basra were producing much crude petroleum by 1951–52. A National Development Board was created in 1950 and became later, in 1953, a national ministry. An agreement of February 1952 gave to the Iraq Government 50 per cent of the oil companies' profits before deductions for foreign taxes. Abundant resources were thus available for development projects of national benefit (e.g. the flood control and irrigation works opened in April 1956 on the Tigris at Samarra and on the Euphrates at Ramadi).

THE BAGHDAD PACT

Iraq, in the field of foreign relations, was confronted during these years with a choice between the Western powers, eager to establish in the Middle East an organized pattern of defence, and the Soviet Union, entering at this time into a diplomatic propaganda and economic drive to increase her influence in the Arab lands. Baghdad, in February 1955, made with Ankara an alliance for mutual co-operation and defence. Britain acceded to this pact in the following April, agreeing also to end the Anglo-Iraqi agreement of 1930 and to surrender her air bases at Shu'ayba and Habbaniya. With the adherence of Pakistan in September and of Iran in October 1955 the so-called Baghdad Pact was completed: a defensive cordon now existed along the southern fringe of the Soviet Union. It was resolved, in November 1955, to form a permanent Council of the Baghdad Pact and, in April 1956, to create an organization which would counter Communist penetration and activities in the Middle East. The U.S.A. also declared its wish to enter into close political, military, economic and technical liaison with the Council of the Baghdad Pact and its subordinate committees.

CONSEQUENCES OF THE SUEZ CRISIS

The outbreak of hostilities between Israel and Egypt on October 29th, 1956, and the armed intervention of British and French forces against Egypt (October 31st–November 6th) led to a delicate situation in Iraq, where strong elements were still opposed to all connections with the Western Powers. Iraq, indeed, broke off diplomatic relations with France on November 9th and announced that, for the immediate future at least, it could give no assurance of taking part in further sessions of the Council of the Baghdad Pact, if delegates from Britain were present.

The attitude of the Baghdad Government during the Suez crisis had provoked unrest in Iraq. Disturbances at Najaf and Mosul resulted in some loss of life. Student demonstrations against the Anglo-French intervention in Egypt and the Israeli campaign in Sinai led the Iraqi Government to close colleges and schools. Martial law, imposed on October 31st, 1956, was not raised until May 27th, 1957.

The tension born of the Suez crisis persisted for some time to come. President Eisenhower, concerned over the flow of Soviet arms to Syria and Egypt, sought from Congress permission to use the armed forces of the United States to defend nations exposed to danger from countries under the influence of international communism. He also requested authorization to disburse 200 million dollars in economic and military aid to the Middle East states prepared to co-operate with the West. This programme received the formal approval of the Congress and Senate of the United States in March 1957. On March 16th the U.S.A. pledged some $12,500,000 of the funds available under the "Eisenhower Doctrine" to the Muslim members of the Baghdad Pact and also made it known that it would participate actively in the work of the military committee of the Pact.

RELATIONS WITH SYRIA AND JORDAN

At the time of the Suez crisis there had been sharp tension between Iraq and Syria. Pumping-stations located inside Syria and belonging to the Iraq Petroleum Company were sabotaged in November 1956 with the result that Iraq suffered a large financial loss through the interruption in the flow of oil to the Mediterranean coast. Not until March 1957 did Syria allow the Iraq Petroleum Company to begin the repair of the pipelines.

Since the Suez crisis of 1956 troops of Iraq and Syria had been stationed in Jordan as a precaution against an Israeli advance to the east. Iraq, in December 1956, announced that her troops would be withdrawn; the Syrian forces, however, still remained in Jordan. The fear that Syria might intervene in favour of the elements in Jordan opposed to King Hussein brought about further recriminations between Baghdad and Damascus. The danger of an acute crisis receded in April 1957, when the U.S.A. declared that the independence of Jordan was a matter of vital concern and underlined this statement by sending its Sixth Fleet to the eastern Mediterranean. In February

1958 King Faisal of Iraq and King Hussein of Jordan joined together in the Arab Federation, but the Federation still embryonic in form, came to an end with the *coup* in Iraq in July 1958.

OVERTHROW OF THE MONARCHY

King Faisal II, together with the Crown Prince of Iraq and General Nuri as-Sa'id, lost their lives in the course of a *coup d'état* begun on July 14th, 1958, by units of the Iraqi Army stationed near Baghdad. Iraq was now to become a Republic. Power was placed in the hands of a council of sovereignty exercising presidential authority and of a cabinet led by Brigadier 'Abd al-Karim Kassem, with the rank of Prime Minister. By the first week in August the new régime in Iraq had received international recognition from most states, whether of the East or of the West.

A struggle for power was now to develop between the two main architects of the July *coup d'état*—Brigadier (later General) Kassem, the Prime Minister, and Colonel (later Field-Marshal) Abd al-Salam Muhammad Aref, the Deputy Prime Minister and Minister of the Interior. Colonel Aref was associated with the influential Baath Party and had shown himself to be a supporter of union between Iraq and the United Arab Republic. Now, in September 1958, he was dismissed from his offices and, in November, was tried on a charge of plotting against the interests of Iraq. As reconstituted in February 1959 the new régime might be described as hostile to the United Arab Republic and inclined to favour a form of independent nationalism with left-wing tendencies. In March 1959 a rebellion in Mosul was suppressed almost immediately.

General Kassem announced the withdrawal of Iraq from the Baghdad Pact on March 24th, 1959. Since the revolution of July 1958 Iraq's adherence to the Pact had been little more than nominal. One result of this withdrawal was the termination of the special agreement existing between Britain and Iraq since 1955 under the first article of the Baghdad Pact. On March 31st it was made known that the Royal Air Force contingent at Habbaniyah would be recalled.

PROBLEMS OF THE KASSEM RÉGIME

Earlier in 1959 the Communist elements in Iraq had been refused representation in the government. The Communists operated through a number of professional organizations and also through the so-called People's Resistance Force. Communist elements had infiltrated into the armed forces of Iraq and into the civil service. General Kassem now began to introduce measures which would limit Communist influence inside the government and administration of the country. In July 1959 fighting occurred at Kirkuk between the Kurds (supported by the People's Resistance Force) and the Turcomons, with considerable loss of life. General Kassem, accusing the Communists of being responsible for this outbreak, now disarmed and disbanded the People's Resistance Force. How strong the internal tensions had become in Iraq was underlined when, on October 7th, 1959, an attempt was made on the life of General Kassem.

General Kassem, in June 1961, laid claim to Kuwait on the ground that Kuwait, in former times, had been included in the Ottoman province of Basra. Reports of Iraqi troop movements in the region of Basra induced the Shaikh of Kuwait to appeal for armed assistance from Great Britain. At the beginning of July 1961 the Security Council of the United Nations met to consider a complaint from Kuwait to the effect that Iraq was threatening her independence and territorial integrity.

REBELLION OF THE KURDS

Much more important for the government at Baghdad was the fact that, in March 1961, a considerable section of the Kurdish population in northern Iraq rose in rebellion under Mustafa Barzani, the President of the Democratic Party of Kurdistan—a party established in 1958 after the return of Barzani from an exile occasioned by an earlier unsuccessful revolt in 1946. The refusal of the central régime at Baghdad to grant the reiterated Kurdish demands for an autonomous status had contributed greatly to bring about the new insurrection. Mustafa Barzani in March 1961 proclaimed an independent Kurdish state. By September 1961 the rebels controlled some 250 miles of mountainous territory along the Iraqi-Turkish and Iraqi-Persian frontiers, from Zakho in the west to Sulaimaniya in the east. The Kurds were able to consolidate their hold over much of northern Iraq during the course of 1962. Military operations tended, in these years, to follow a regular pattern—a spring and summer offensive by the government forces, with the ground then won being lost again to the Kurds in the autumn and winter. The Kurds used guerrilla tactics with much success to isolate and deprive the government garrisons in the north of supplies. By December 1963 Kurdish forces had advanced south towards the Khanaqin area and the main road linking Iraq with Iran. The government troops found themselves in fact confined to the larger towns such as Kirkuk, Sulaimaniya and Khanaqin. Negotiations for peace began near Sulaimaniya in January 1964 and led to a cease-fire on February 10th. The national claims of the Kurds were to be recognized in a new provisional constitution for Iraq. Moreover, a general amnesty would be granted by the Iraqi Government. The Kurdish tribesmen, however, refused to lay aside their arms until their political demands had been given practical effect. Despite the negotiation of this settlement it was soon to become clear that no final solution of the Kurdish problem was as yet in sight.

FALL OF KASSEM

A military *coup* carried out in Baghdad on February 8th, 1963, overthrew the régime of General Kassem, the General himself being captured and shot. The *coup* arose out of an alliance between nationalist army officers and the Baath Party. Colonel Aref was now raised to the office of President and a new cabinet created under Brigadier Ahmed al-Bakr. The Baath Party, founded in 1941 (in Syria) and dedicated to the ideas of Arab unity, socialism and freedom, drew its main support from the military elements, the intellectuals and the middle classes. It was, however, divided in Iraq into a pro-Egyptian wing advocating union with the United Arab Republic and a more independent wing disinclined to accept authoritarian control from Egypt. The coup of February 1963 was followed by the arrest of pro-Kassem and of Communist elements, by mass trials and a number of executions, by confiscations of property and by a purge of the officer corps and of the civil service.

A number of efforts were made, during the years 1963–65, to further the cause of Arab unification. An agreement signed at Cairo on April 17th, 1963, envisaged a federation of Egypt, Syria and Iraq. On September 2nd a communiqué stated that Syria and Iraq would create new committees to hasten defence co-operation between the two states. A Supreme Defence Council for the forces of Syria and Iraq was in fact established on October 8th with General Ammash (Defence Minister of Iraq) as Commander-in-Chief. On May 26th, 1964, Iraq signed with the U.A.R. an agreement establishing a Joint Presidency Council, with a secretariat at Cairo. Later in the same year, on October 16th, President Aref of Iraq and President Nasser of the U.A.R. made it known that a unified political command would be created between their two states. The subsequent course of events in 1965 was to demonstrate that these measures to advance the cause of Arab unification had little prospect of achieving much immediate practical effect.

MANOEUVRES OF THE BAATH PARTY

These same years saw in Iraq itself a conflict for control between the extremist and the more moderate Baath elements. At the end of September 1963 the extremists dominated the Baath Regional Council in Iraq. An international Baath Conference held at Damascus in October 1963 strengthened the position of the extremists through its support of a federal union between Syria and Iraq and its approval of more radical social and economic policies. A further Baathist conference at Baghdad in November 1963 enabled the moderates to elect a new Baath Regional Council in Iraq with their own adherents in control. At this juncture the extremists attempted a *coup d'état*, in the course of which air force elements attacked the Presidential Palace and the Ministry of Defence.

On November 18th, 1963, President Aref assumed full powers in Iraq, with the support of the armed forces, and a new Revolutionary Command was established at Baghdad. Sporadic fighting occurred (November 18th–20th) between the government troops and the pro-Baathist National Guard. A main factor in the sudden fall of the Baathists was the attitude of the professional officer class. Officers with Communist, Kassemite or pro-Nasser sympathies, or with no strong political views, or of Kurdish origin, had all been removed from important commands and offices. The privileged position of the National Guard caused further resentment in the army. The long drawn-out operations against the Kurds, the known dissensions within the Baathist ranks in Iraq and the

intervention of Baath politicians from abroad in Iraqi affairs also contributed to discredit the extreme elements amongst the Baathists. On November 20th, 1963, a new Cabinet was formed at Baghdad, consisting of officers, moderate Baathists, independents and non-party experts.

THE ARAB SOCIALIST UNION

On July 14th, 1964, President Aref announced that all political parties would be merged in a new organization known as the "Iraqi Arab Socialist Union". At the same time it was revealed that all banks and insurance companies, together with thirty-two important industrial concerns, would undergo nationalization. The firms now nationalized included steel, cement and tobacco concerns, flour mills, food industries, building material firms and tanneries.

In July 1965 a number of pro-Nasser ministers handed in their resignations. At the beginning of September 1965 a new administration came into being with Brigadier Aref Abd al-Razzaq as Prime Minister. The Brigadier, reputed to be pro-Nasser in his sympathies, attempted to seize full power in Iraq, but his attempted *coup d'état* failed and, on September 16th, he himself, together with some of his supporters, found refuge in Cairo. On April 13th, 1966, President Abd al-Salam Aref of Iraq was killed in a helicopter crash. His brother Major-General Abd al-Rahman Aref succeeded him as President with the approval of the Cabinet and of the National Defence Council. In late June 1966 Brigadier Aref Abd al-Razzaq, who had staged the unsuccessful *coup d'état* of September 1965, led a second abortive coup, which was foiled by the prompt action of President Aref.

KURDISH NATIONALISM

The war against the Kurds, halted only for a short while by the cease-fire of February 1964, dragged out its inconclusive course during 1964–66. Some of the fighting in December 1965 occurred close to the Iraq-Iran border, leading to a number of frontier violations which gave rise to sharp tension between the two states during the first half of 1966. In June of 1966 Dr. Abd al-Rahman al-Bazzaz, Prime Minister of Iraq since September 1965, formulated new proposals for a settlement of the conflict with the Kurds. Kurdish nationalism and language would receive legal recognition; the administration was to be decentralized, allowing the Kurds to run educational, health and municipal affairs in their own districts; the Kurds would have proportional representation in Parliament and in the Cabinet and the various state services; the Kurdish armed forces (some 15,000 strong) were to be dissolved. Mustafa Barzani, the Kurdish leader, declared himself to be well disposed towards these proposals.

This entente was implemented only to a limited extent. The cabinet formed in May 1967 contained Kurdish elements, and President Aref, after a visit to the north in late 1967, reaffirmed his intention to make available to the Kurds appointments of ministerial rank, to help with the rehabilitation of the war-affected areas in Kurdistan, and to work towards effective co-operation with the Kurds in the Government of Iraq. This state of quiescence was, however, broken in the first half of 1968 by reports of dissension amongst the Kurds themselves, with open violence between the adherents of Mustafa Barzani and the supporters of Jalal Talabani, who had co-operated with the Government.

RAPPROCHEMENT WITH IRAN

Relations with Iran, always strained, had not been helped by the Kurdish conflict. During the second half of 1966, however, there was a marked improvement in the relations between Iraq and Iran. Incidents on the common frontier of the two states died down with the lull in the fighting between Iraqi troops and the Kurdish insurgents. President Aref of Iraq made an official state visit to Teheran in March 1967. A communiqué of March 19th declared that the two countries had agreed to continue negotiations for a joint oil exploration in the Naft Khaneh and Naft-i Shah border regions. Details of agreements on other issues, e.g. navigation rights and the collection of tolls in the Shatt al-Arab, demarcation of the Gulf continental shelf (important for the control of potential oil resources) and the status of Iranian nationals in Iraq, would be worked out by a joint committee. A cultural and trade agreement was also to be concluded between the two states.

OIL DISPUTES AND THE JUNE WAR

The winter of 1966–67 witnessed a dispute between Syria and the Iraq Petroleum Company—a dispute which was to have a serious effect on the oil revenues accruing to Iraq. The government at Damascus claimed that it had not been receiving from the IPC the full amount of revenue due to it under an agreement reached in 1955. To compensate for the alleged loss of revenue, levied on oil carried across Syria from the IPC fields in northern Iraq to ports on the Mediterranean coast, the Damascus Government demanded large back payments, increased the transit charges, and envisaged also the imposition of a surcharge. The Iraqi Government was also considering a request to the IPC that oil production in Iraq be raised 10 per cent. It was embroiled, moreover, in a long argument with the IPC over concession areas confiscated from the company five years earlier, but as yet unsettled by the national oil organization created to take them over. On December 8th, 1966, Syria impounded the property of the Iraq Petroleum Company within its territories. The assets impounded embraced some 300 miles of pipeline, several pumping stations and the terminal installations at Banias on the coast of Syria. On December 12th–13th Iraqi oil ceased to flow across Syria to Banias and to Tripoli. Iraq was thus confronted with a potential loss of revenue amounting to about £8 million per month. Several delegations from Baghdad went to Damascus in order to urge that a settlement be found for the dispute. Not until the beginning of March 1967, however, was a new agreement signed between the IPC and the

Syrian Government. It was announced early in May 1967 that the IPC had also reached agreement in principle with the Iraqi Government on the royalties payable for the first quarter of 1967, when the pipeline across Syria was out of use.

When the Arab-Israeli war broke out in June 1967, the movement of Iraqi oil was again affected. Problems connected with its production and export constituted a major preoccupation of the Baghdad Government during the period immediately following the war. Iraq had at the outset severed diplomatic relations with the U.S.A. and Britain after Arab charges that the two states had aided Israel in the war and she also banned the export of oil to them. When, at the end of June, supplies of Iraqi oil began to be moved once more from the pipeline terminals on the Mediterranean, this embargo remained. In August Iraq, Syria and the Lebanon resolved to allow the export of Iraqi oil to most of the countries of Europe, the United Kingdom being still subject, however, to the embargo.

Relations with the West improved slightly during the autumn and winter of 1967. The remaining oil embargoes were gradually removed, and in December General Sabri led a military delegation to Paris. This was followed by President Aref's official visit to France in February 1968, and in April France agreed to supply Iraq with 54 Mirage aircraft over the period 1969–73. In May diplomatic relations with the United Kingdom were resumed.

THE 1968 COUP AND ITS AFTERMATH

Throughout the first half of 1968 the régime conspicuously lacked popular support, being commonly thought to be both corrupt and inefficient, and the sudden bloodless *coup d'état* of July 17th did not surprise many observers. General Ahmed Hassan al-Bakr, a former Prime Minister, became President; the deposed President Aref went into exile and his Prime Minister, Taher Yahya, was imprisoned on corruption charges. The new government, though still composed of Baath Party members, was expected to follow a moderate line within the Arab context, and the coup elicited a hostile reaction from Cairo and Damascus. Two ministers were influential Kurds, which was also thought to be a significant development.

Nothing came of this, however, for on July 30th the entire cabinet was dismissed by the President, who accused it of "reactionary tendencies". He then appointed himself Prime Minister and Commander-in-Chief and chose a new cabinet in which Generals Hardan Takriti and Saleh Ammash (formerly Interior Minister) were seen as the other major figures.

During the second half of 1968 the internal political situation deteriorated steadily. By November there were frequent reports of a purge directed against opponents of the new régime, and freedom of verbal political comment seemed to have disappeared. Numerous Western teachers and professional people were expelled. A former Foreign Minister, Dr. Nasser al-Hani, was found murdered, and a distinguished former Prime Minister, Dr. al-Bazzaz, and other members of former governments were arrested as "counter-revolutionary leaders"; most were later given long jail sentences. Open hostilities with the Kurds broke out in October 1968 for the first time since the June 1966 ceasefire, and continued on an extensive scale throughout the winter. Early in March 1969 the rebels shelled the IPC's installations at Kirkuk, inflicting considerable damage. Iraqi army and air force attempts to enforce the writ of the Baghdad Government had little success; the régime claimed that the rebels were receiving aid from Iran and Israel. Fighting continued unabated through 1969, the Kurds demanding autonomy within the state and asking for UN mediation.

When, in January 1969, fourteen men were sentenced to death for spying for Israel it became clear that the life for the Jewish minority in Iraq had become steadily more difficult since the rise of Zionism and the establishment of the State of Israel. The community numbered some 250,000 in 1939, widely spread throughout Iraq both geographically and occupationally; thirty years later estimates put its size at a mere 2,500 people, virtually confined to a ghetto in Baghdad. Large-scale emigration, mainly to Israel had taken place in the early 1950s.

SETTLEMENT WITH THE KURDS

The most important event of 1970 was the settlement with the Kurds when, in March, a fifteen-article peace plan was announced by the Revolutionary Command Council and the Kurdish leaders. The plan conceded that the Kurds should participate fully in the Government; that Kurdish officials should be appointed in areas inhabited by a Kurdish majority; that Kurdish should be the official language, along with Arabic, in Kurdish areas; that development of Kurdish areas should be implemented; and that the provisional constitution should be amended to incorporate the rights of the Kurds.

The agreement was generally accepted by the Kurdish community and fighting ceased immediately. The war had been very expensive for Iraq, in terms of both lives and money, and it had seriously delayed the national development programme. It had also absorbed a large part of Iraq's army, which consequently became available for service on Israel's eastern front—joining the Iraqi force already stationed in Jordan—or for defensive duties on the Iranian frontier.

Although Mustafa Barzani retained his 15,000 troops as an official Iraqi frontier force, the legal status of Kurdistan still remained to be settled. A census should have been held to determine which parts of northern Iraq had a predominantly Kurdish population to qualify for the promised autonomy, but this was postponed. The Kurds claimed that this was to allow Arabs to emigrate to the rich oil-bearing area of Kirkuk. The Government, on its side, pointed to the thousands of Kurds who returned from Iran when hostilities ceased.

The Kurdish settlement, although not entirely satisfactory, did introduce an element of stability into life in Iraq and allowed a number of reforms to be initiated. In October 1970 the state of emergency, in operation almost continuously since July 1958, was lifted. Many political detainees, including former ministers, were released. Censorship of mail was abolished at the end of the year, having lasted for over thirteen years, and a month later the censorship of foreign correspondents' cables was brought to an end after a similar period.

At the same time, however, the Government maintained its ruthless attitude towards possible new opponents. Salah Umar Ali, Minister of Information and Culture and member of the Council of Command of the Revolution was dismissed in July 1970; Vice-President Hardan al Takriti in October. Both dismissals arose from internal policy differences, and only hints of the wranglings inside the Baath Party at the time reached the outside world. "Reactionaries" and communists alike were the victims of press campaigns or purges.

Kurdish unity was boosted in February 1971 by the decision of the Kurdish Revolutionary Party to merge with the Kurdish Democratic Party of Mustafa Barzani and in July 1971 a new provisional constitution was announced, which embodied many of the points contained in the 1970 settlement. The Kurds were directed by the Supreme Committee for Kurdish Affairs to give up their arms by August 1971 and the situation in the north continued to be normal.

Evidence of unrest, however, was growing both in Kurdistan and in the Government itself. In July 1971 an attempted coup by army and air force officers was put down by the Government but dissatisfaction continued to be reported. The Kurds were beginning to show discontent with the delays in implementing the 1970 agreement. Their demand for participation in the Revolutionary Command Council was refused and in September 1971 an attempt was made on Barzani's life. Also in September, while President Bakr was in hospital, another coup was said to have been attempted but this was denied. Vice-President Salih Mahdi Ammash and the Foreign Minister, Abd-al-Karim Shaikhli, were dismissed soon afterwards, indicating the extent of the power struggles within the Council.

THE CONTINUING KURDISH PROBLEM

During 1972, possibly because of increasing preoccupation with foreign affairs, dissension within the Government was less in evidence. Clashes with the Kurds, however, became more frequent and there was another plot to assassinate Barzani in July. The Baath Party's deteriorating relations with the Kurds brought a threat from the Kurdish Democratic Party to renew the civil war. One of the main Kurdish grievances was that the census agreed upon in 1970 had still not taken place. The two sides met to discuss their differences, the Kurdish side pointing to the unfulfilled provisions of the 1970 agreement and the Baath reiterating the various development projects carried out in Kurdish areas. In December 1972, a break appeared in the Kurdish ranks when it was reported that a breakaway party was to be set up in opposition to Barzani's party.

FOREIGN RELATIONS 1968-71

The more radical section of the Arab world had initially greeted the July 1968 coup with disfavour and the new régime was at pains to prove itself as militant an exponent of Arab nationalism as its predecessor. The régime gradually became an accepted member of the nationalist group, but there was some Arab criticism of its policies, notably the public hangings and their effect on world opinion. In March 1969, a joint Eastern Command was established comprising Jordan, Syria and Iraq. This was made possible by changes in the Syrian leadership in the spring of 1969, the Damascus régime having previously had very poor relations with Iraq.

Like Algeria, on the opposite flank of the Arab world, Iraq took a hard line on the Palestinian problem (having moved substantial forces into Jordan on the outbreak of war in 1967). All peace proposals—American, Egyptian and Jordanian—were rejected. In theory total support was given to the Palestine liberation movement but, despite a threat to the Jordanian Government at the beginning of September 1970 to intervene in Jordan on behalf of the Palestinian guerrillas, the Iraqi forces stationed there did not take part in the fighting. In January 1971, most of Iraq's 20,000 troops were withdrawn from both Jordan and Syria. In March it was reported in Cairo that Iraq's monthly contribution to the Palestine Liberation Army had ceased. Iraq's attitude to Middle East peace proposals opened up a rift with Egypt even before President Nasser's death and her contempt for the proposed Egypt-Libya-Syria federation, as well as for any negotiated settlement with Israel, kept her well isolated from Egypt and almost all the other Arab states. In July 1971 there were signs that Iraq wished to reduce her isolation, offering to co-operate again with the Arab states if they abandoned attempts to negotiate with Israel, but the renewal of hostilities between the Jordanian Government and the guerrillas caused a break in relations with Jordan. Iraq closed the border, called for Jordan's expulsion from the Arab League and banned her from participating in the Eighth International Baghdad Fair. Sudan broke off relations after Iraq's recognition of the short-lived revolutionary take-over at the end of July 1971 and there were differences with Syria. A certain rapprochement was, however, achieved with Kuwait.

Meanwhile, relations with Iran continued to be poor. Iraq frequently accused the Teheran Government of assisting the Kurdish rebellion and had responded by mass expulsions of Persians resident in Iraq. In April 1969 the Shatt al-Arab waterway again caused a minor confrontation. Iraq has benefited by a 1937 treaty (engineered by the British Government which then effectively controlled Iraq, but not Iran) which gave it control of the waterway. Iran tried to force a re-negotiation of the treaty by illegally sending through vessels flying the Iranian flag. Being unwilling (or politically unable) to yield any of its sovereignty, and unable to challenge Iran militarily, Iraq was obliged to accept this situation. Iraq proposed referring the dispute to the International Court of Justice, but Iran rejected the suggestion. Minor border clashes between the two sides' forces continued to occur sporadically. The Shah's Government was generally thought to have been a party to the attempted coup in January 1970, some of whose leaders were apparently in exile in Teheran. In December 1970, it was the turn of the Iranians to accuse Iraq of sponsoring an attempt to stage a coup in Teheran. Not surprisingly, the two countries were also divided on policy towards the Gulf States. Iraq broke off diplomatic relations with Iran (and Britain) after Iran's seizure of the Tumb Islands in the Persian/Arabian Gulf in November 1971. The deportation of ever larger numbers of Iranians from Iraq was reported at the end of 1971 and their expulsion continued into 1972.

Relations with the Western world, and the U.S.A. in particular, remained poor, several people arrested or expelled in late 1968 being accused of spying for the Americans. The friendship with the Soviet Union remained the major factor in Iraq's foreign policy, particularly since the U.S.S.R. was supplying the bulk of Iraq's military equipment. Partly as an extension of this friendship and partly as a gesture of disapproval for the German Federal Republic's relationship with Israel, Iraq recognized the German Democratic Republic at ambassador level in May 1969.

THE PROBLEM OF OIL

Relations between the Government and the IPC had continued to be strained, the Government continually maintaining its intention of eventually exploiting its own oil resources. An agreement reached in March 1972 provided for a 20 per cent Government participation in the concessions of the Iraq, Basra and Mosul Petroleum Companies but the details of the agreement were left for further negotiation. The North Rumeila field, expropriated from the IPC in 1962, started production in April 1972, its development having been financed by a Russian loan. Nevertheless, Iraq was still dependent on Western oil interests and the Government was anxious that output should be maintained at a high level in order to safeguard revenues. Thus the cutback in production from the northern oilfields in early 1972 caused the Government to protest. In June 1972 IPC's interests were nationalized and the company immediately announced that it would take legal action to prevent the marketing of the oil.

It had been assumed that Iraq's oil exports would be very seriously affected by the difficulties of finding markets for oil after the nationalization. In the event, Iraq was able to make a number of agreements almost immediately for the sale of oil. Among them were, as might have been expected, a number of barter deals with Eastern Bloc countries and the Soviet Union, and several agreements to repay loans in crude oil.

Immediately after the break with IPC, Iran concluded an agreement with France for the sale of 23.75 per cent of oil from the nationalized Kirkuk field. This was, the Government explained, in token of France's continued friendly attitude towards the Arab World. Contacts were also made with Spain, Italy, Greece, India, Japan and Brazil. By the end of 1972 it was clear that Iraq was maintaining sales, although the situation was marred by a dispute over transit dues for use of the IPC pipeline which Syria had nationalized on June 2nd, 1972. Syria was insisting on higher rates than those originally paid by IPC and an agreement was only reached in January 1973.

Meanwhile, contacts between IPC and the Government to determine compensation had continued, and IPC had repeatedly postponed its deadline for beginning legal proceedings. With the mediation of Nadim Pachachi of OPEC and Jean Duroc-Danner of CFP, an agreement was finally reached on February 28th, 1973. The company agreed to settle Iraqi claims for back royalties by paying £141 million, and to waive its objections to Law No. 80 under which the North Rumeila fields were seized in 1961. The Government agreed to deliver a total of 15 million tons of crude from Kirkuk, to be loaded at Eastern Mediterranean ports, to the companies as compensation. The Mosul Petroleum Company agreed to relinquish all its assets without compensation and the Basrah Petroleum Company, the only one of the group to remain operational in Iraq, undertook to increase output from 32 million tons in 1972 to 80 million tons in 1976. This agreement was regarded on the whole as a victory for the Iraqi Government, although the companies were by no means net losers by it.

With the IPC dispute out of the way, Iraq showed its unwillingness to continue indefinitely with exporting oil on a barter basis to the Eastern Bloc countries. The Government made it clear that it would press for a cash basis to future agreements.

FOREIGN RELATIONS 1972–73

The nationalization of IPC brought expressions of approval from a number of countries, including Arab States and the Soviet Union. The 15-year friendship treaty with the Soviet Union, signed in March 1972, was ratified in July and Iraq's relations with the Eastern Bloc states continued to be good. President Bakr visited Moscow in September for talks on increased economic and military aid and in October Iraq applied to join COMECON. Despite this, however, the Government was well aware of the dangers of too close and exclusive a relationship with the Soviet Bloc. France was specifically singled out as the Western country most friendly towards the Arabs and the President's fourth anniversary speech in July revealed that Iraq would not be unwilling to open up friendly relations with Western countries. Although diplomatic relations with the United States were still severed, the U.S.A. established an "interests section" in Baghdad.

In March 1973 there was a clash with Kuwait, arising out of Iraq's desire to safeguard the military base at Um Qasr and the narrow oil export routes via the Gulf. Iraqi forces occupied the border port of Sameta, but later withdrew.

CONSTITUTIONAL CHANGE

In July 1973 an abortive *coup* took place, led by the Security chief, Nazim Kazzar, in which the Minister of Defence, General Hammad Shehab, was killed. It is thought that it was an attempt by a civilian faction within the Baath Party to get rid of President Bakr and the military faction. One result of the attempted *coup* was an amendment to the constitution giving more power to the President, and the formation of a National Front between the Baath Party and the Iraq Communist Party. There seemed a possibility at this time that the Kurdistan Democratic Party might be persuaded to join the National Front, but later events were to prove these hopes groundless.

CLIMAX AND END OF KURDISH WAR

According to the agreement made between the Iraq Government and the Kurds in March 1970 the deadline for implementation of the agreement was March 11th, 1974. An uneasy peace between the Kurds and the Iraqis had existed between those two dates. When March 11th, 1974, arrived Sadam Hussein Takriti, the Vice-President of the Revolution Command Council and the "strong man" of the régime, announced the granting of autonomy to the Kurds. Barzani and his Kurdish Democratic Party felt that the Iraqi offer fell short of their demands for full government representation, which included membership of the Revolution Command Council. A minority of Kurds, who belonged to Abdel Satter Sharif's Kurdish Revolutionary Party welcomed the proposals, however. Barzani and his militia, the Peshmerga, began armed resistance in north Iraq. In April 1974 the Iraqi Government replaced five Kurdish Ministers known to support Barzani by five other Kurds who supported the Government plan for giving the Kurds a measure of autonomy. Later in April the Iraqi Government appointed a Kurd, Taha Moheddin Marouf, as Vice-President of Iraq, but since he had long been a supporter of the Baghdad Government, it seemed unlikely that this would pacify the Kurds of the K.D.P.

By August 1974 the Kurdish war had reached a new level of intensity. The Baghdad Government was directing large military resources against the *Pesh Merga*, as Barzani's forces were called, and were deploying tanks, field guns and bombers. About 130,000 Kurds, mainly women, children and old men, took refuge in Iran. The *Pesh Merga* were able to keep up their resistance in Iraq only with the help of arms and other supplies from Iran. When, therefore, an agreement to end their border dispute was signed by Iraq and Iran at the OPEC meeting in Algiers on March 6th, 1975, both countries also agreed to end "infiltrations of a subversive character" and the Kurdish rebellion collapsed. Barzani felt that he could not continue his struggle without Iran's aid, and fled to Teheran. A ceasefire was arranged on March 13th, and Iraq announced that an amnesty would be granted to all Kurds who surrendered by April 1st. About 200,000 Kurds fled to Iran when the rebellion collapsed, but only between 50,000 and 60,000 were expected to settle permanently in Iran. The amnesty was later extended for two months, and by late June 1975 the number of Kurds living in exile in Iran was estimated at 97,000.

Although the Kurdish war appeared to be over, deteriorating relations between Syria and Iraq over the Euphrates waters and rivalry between factions of the Baath Party made it possible in the middle of 1975 that Syria would take up the cause of the Kurds.

FOREIGN AFFAIRS 1973–75

On the outbreak of the October 1973 war between the Arabs and Israel, Iraq sent considerable land forces to the Syrian front and took advantage of Iran's offer to resume diplomatic relations. The Iraqi Government, however, had taken offence because President Sadat had not consulted Iraq in advance, and because of this Iraqi forces were withdrawn from Syria as soon as the ceasefire went into effect, and Iraq boycotted the Arab summit meeting in Algiers in November.

Relations deteriorated with Iran in the early months of 1974, when frontier fighting broke out, and it was only after the appointment of a UN Mediator in March that "normal" relations on the frontier were restored, and they deteriorated again in August in spite of talks in Istanbul between Iraqi and Iranian diplomats. Further border clashes took place in December 1974, and secret talks in Istanbul between the Iraqi and Iranian Foreign Ministers in January 1975 failed to prevent the outbreak of fresh clashes in February. It was therefore something of a surprise when at the OPEC meeting at Algiers in March 1975 it was announced that Sadam Hussein Takriti, Vice-President of the Iraqi Revolutionary Command Council, and the Shah of Iran had signed an agreement which "completely eliminated the conflict between the two brotherly countries". This agreement also ended the Kurdish war (*see* above), and was embodied in a treaty signed between the two countries in June 1975. The frontiers were defined on the basis of the Protocol of Constantinople of 1913 and the verbal agreement on frontiers of 1914. The Shatt al-Arab frontier was defined according to the Thalweg Line, which runs down the middle of the deepest shipping channel.

In April 1974 diplomatic relations with Britain, broken off in 1971 when Iraq accused Britain of collusion with Iran's seizure of the Tumb Islands in the Persian Gulf, were restored. In common with other Middle Eastern Countries Iraq achieved greater control of her oil industry between 1973 and 1975. These developments are dealt with in the Economic Survey below, and in the article "Oil in the Middle East and North Africa", pages 69–102.

ECONOMIC SURVEY

Iraq is traditionally an agricultural country, but its economic development has been largely attributable to its oil industry, which accounts for four-fifths of the country's foreign exchange receipts (and over nine-tenths of its export earnings), two-thirds of government revenue and one-fifth of gross domestic product. Accordingly Iraq's chief opportunity for development consists in the large revenues accruing from the operations of the oil companies in her territory. These revenues were stagnant in the early sixties at ID120–135 million but in the year ending March 31st, 1972 they had risen to ID354 million as a result of increased production and revised agreements with the oil companies. This rapid rise is attributed to revisions to agreements with the oil companies together with a sharp increase in production. The improvement in oil revenues was short-lived, however, for on June 1st, 1972, the long-standing disputes between Iraq and the oil companies culminated in the nationalization of the assets of the Iraq Pertoleum Company (IPC) the largest producing company in Iraq.

The nationalization move and the events leading up to it resulted in a severe loss of production throughout 1972 and necessitated a temporary curtailment of the development programme. The programme was reinstituted on the announcement of the settlement of the dispute on February 28th, 1973. Partly as a result of this settlement and the consequent increased production, but particularly due to increased oil prices in the latter part of the year, oil receipts in 1973 were estimated at ID547 million. With the higher posted prices and with revised agreements negotiated with the oil companies these revenues were expected to reach a massive ID1,540 million in 1974. Iraq's economic potential remains great for alone of the oil-producing countries of the Middle East she has enough land and water to enable her to spend her oil revenue in a productive manner.

Iraq is also an underpopulated country which, according to both historical evidence and present estimates of possible expansion could support a population of, perhaps, twice the size of her present ten million. She has millions of acres of cultivable land that could be irrigated from the generous (though in the past dangerously undisciplined) waters of the Tigris and the Euphrates.

These great advantages have indeed certain limitations placed upon them by the nature of the country and the degree of social evolution attained by its people. Salination of the soil and the spreading of malaria as a result of big irrigation projects are dangers that have to be guarded against. The two great rivers, the Tigris and Euphrates, which must be the basis of the country's entire system of irrigation, are, in the words of Lord Salter "temperamental and difficult to control". In addition, the country, with the exception of its northern area, is extremely flat and only a little above sea-level. This makes drainage and irrigation difficult and explains why most of the land at present consists largely of either desert or swamps. On the human side there may be a shortage of labour, and, particularly at the present moment, of the skilled labour that will be required to accomplish and operate the vast and up-to-date schemes of agricultural and industrial development that are contemplated or actually in process of execution.

The total population was estimated at 10.8 million in 1974, mostly living in the alluvial plain of the Tigris and Euphrates or the foothills of the north-east. Between 1965 and 1972 the population increased by 3.3 per cent annually. The working population was estimated at 3 million in 1970. Though many women work in agriculture, women are not generally employed elsewhere and at the present time cannot be regarded as making a substantial contribution to the non-agricultural labour force. Some idea of the employment situation may be formed from the table in the Statistical Survey.

Iraq's gross domestic product rose from ID 826 million in 1964 to ID 1,484 million in 1971, the latest year for which estimates are available. This increase represents an annual average growth of 8.7 per cent. Per capita G.D.P. amounted to 139 dinars in 1971.

AGRICULTURE

Agriculture is the main source of employment and, next to oil, the most important sector. Although the country's latest development plan (1974–79) gives high priority to the oil industry, agriculture remains important; the aim is to produce an agricultural surplus for export by reducing dependence on weather conditions and solving the salinity problems which affect irrigated land. Iraq has a total area, including territorial waters and counting half the neutral zone, of 438,446 square kilometres. Of this the North Desert, South Desert and Al-Jazira Desert comprise about 200,000 square kilometres, so that the total area of the fourteen Liwas (administrative units) of urban and agricultural land into which the country is divided is 238,000 square kilometres, or 95,000,000 dunums. At present about 23 million dunums of this total are utilized for agricultural purposes.

The land tenure system is extremely complex, embracing privately owned land, public land (mainly desert), waqfs (religious endowments), and three types of government-owned land. By far the greater part of registered land is that which is government-owned and previously without established tenancy.

The effect of the land registration programme, which lasted from 1932 until 1958, was to create a large landowner class and a landless peasantry. Despite the fertility of many areas of the country, the development of agricultural techniques and productivity has been inhibited by the lack of security in rural areas arising from the disruptive activities of large landowners and, more recently, the land reform agencies.

The first attempts to reform the system of land tenure resulting from the 1932 legislation concentrated upon the distribution of government land among peasant smallholders with the aim of creating communities of landowners with an improved standard of living and practising agriculture by modern methods. In October 1958 the Government announced a new and more radical land reform project. This provided for the break-up of large estates whose owners were to be compelled to forfeit their "excess" land to the Government which would redistribute the land to new peasant owners. Under the terms of the reform the largest holding permitted on flow-irrigated land is 1,000 dunums (about 600 acres), on land watered by rainfall it is 2,000 dunums. The estates broken up were to be allotted to farmers in holdings of a maximum of 60 or 120 dunums, according to the type of land, and the formation of agricultural co-operatives was planned to help the new owners with capital, machinery and technical advice. Landowners losing land were to be compensated in state bonds (in 1969 all the state's liabilities to recompense landowners were cancelled). It was hoped that the reform would take only five years to complete but the application of the law was initially mismanaged and the expropriation of land consistently ran ahead of the ability of the administration to distribute it. By the end of 1972 some 4.73 million dunums had been requisitioned from landlords and distributed to 100,646 families, but considerable areas of land remain awaiting distribution. The Government has been promoting the growth of co-operatives and collective farms since 1967.

The general system of cultivation is fallow farming and crop rotations are rare. Despite changes in recent years, the most common type of farm operation is by share tenancy, the farmer surrendering to the landowner a share of his crop—usually 50 per cent in return for pump irrigation, water and other facilities. Other forms of operation are: (1) plantation farming, when the landowner or tenant of a rented farm employs paid labour; and (2) individual peasant proprietorships, when the farmer owns or rents his land and works it himself with his family.

The farm worker is concerned primarily with subsistence and grows crops and keeps animals to provide for himself and his family. Cash crops are grown by plantation farmers and peasant proprietors. Types of agriculture vary considerably but the largest and most commonly grown crops are barley and wheat. Together with lentils, vetch and linseed they constitute the main winter crops. Normally Iraq produces an exportable surplus of barley, though in years of low rainfall barley exports are not possible. After several years poor harvest there was a successful cereal crop in 1972 with a total of 3.5 million tons of cereals being harvested of which 1.75 million tons were exported. Summer crops are much smaller but in recent years have all shown healthy increases in size. The principal summer crops include rice, dates, tobacco and sesame, and these are grown much more extensively where better irrigation is available, as in the northern zone between Fallujah, Baghdad and Diyalah. Among fruit trees the date palm is by far the commonest and the best. Year by year Iraq alternates with Egypt as the world's largest date-producing country. In 1972 Iraq exported 265,416 tons of dates earning the country ID 8.1 millions; dates are, after oil, the biggest export earner. In 1974 Iraq made new agreements for the export of dates to Australia and China. Also an agreement has been signed for 1,200 tons of Iraqi tobacco to be sold to Egypt. Cotton is also grown on a small scale in central Iraq. Around the major towns a comparatively sophisticated market gardening organization has developed.

Generally, agricultural output varies according to rainfall, flooding and political disturbances. In recent years harvests have proved poor, the weather has been unfavourable and fears of massive land collectivization by the Government have caused uncertainty, while the Government's promises of greatly increased aid for agricultural development have not been fulfilled.

Wheat and barley production have been falling in recent years, and the area under barley has contracted considerably. The average yield of wheat has fallen from 228.2 kg. per meshara in 1968 to 175.7 kg. per meshara in 1970. The average yield of barley fell from 274.6 kg. per meshara in 1968 to 253.6 kg. per meshara in 1970. As an indication of the problems of the agricultural sector, some 200,000 tons of Australian wheat was imported in 1971. However there was a good harvest in 1972 of 2.62 million tons of wheat compared with 822,000 tons in 1971, saving the country ID 8.1 million in imports. The successful harvest is thought to be largely due to the new high yielding varieties of seed used. Despite these plans, however, Iraq has signed a three-year agreement with Canada to import between 3.7 million and 11 million bushels of wheat in exchange for which Canada is to buy oil and dates. 1973 wheat production was only 857,000 tons. In the 1974–75 development budget ID 190 million has been allocated for agriculture compared with ID 65 million in 1973–74 and ID 70 million in 1972–73. The funds are to be directed into projects for the production of poultry, eggs and meat as well as for the construction of dams and the improvement of agricultural mechanization. A number of sugar mills are to be built and production of sugar from dates is planned. Another proposal costing ID 17.5 million involves setting up seven poultry farms designed to produce 70 million eggs annually by 1977. At the same time a project worth ID 11.52 million has been started with French and West German companies to raise production of chickens by 12 million a year by 1977. In May 1973 the World Bank granted a $40 million loan for grain storage projects. In order to promote the fishing industry Iraq is to form a co-operative fishing company with Russia with 51 per cent of shares owned by Iraq and 49 per cent owned by Russia.

In the latest development plan Iraqi agriculture is to receive U.S. $11,500 million over the next five years. The aim is to achieve self-sufficiency in food supply and envisages a 25 per cent increase in cultivated land from 16 million dunums to 20 million dunums. This represents an increase from 55 per cent to 68 per cent of the country's cultivable total.

The cost of imports of food and live animals in 1974 reached U.S. $600 million, or the equivalent of nearly one-tenth of the official oil receipts. In 1974 food imports accounted for 30 per cent of all imports. The main suppliers of cereals in 1974 were the U.S.A. (392,300 tons) and Australia (116,400 tons) and this tonnage and the price is expected to be even higher in 1975. Rice imports will also rise as production was only 200,000 tons in 1974 compared with 306,000 tons in 1971. Sugar is another expensive import and, according to a recent agreement signed with Cuba in April 1975, 100,000 tons will be supplied for five years; but the Cubans are to assist in the development of Iraq's sugar cane production and refining.

RIVER CONTROL AND IRRIGATION

River control policy in Iraq has three main objects: the provision of water for irrigation, the prevention of devastating floods, and the creation of hydro-electric power. It is southern and central Iraq that are affected in all three cases, since northern Iraq is rain-fed and for the most part the terrain is unsuitable for large-scale irrigation from the stored water of major dams. Minor local reservoirs and tube wells are enough to supplement the rain in the north.

At present the main systems providing flow irrigation are based on the Euphrates (serving nearly 3 million dunums), the Tigris (1.7 million dunums), the Diyalah River and the LesserZab River. Pumps are used extensively along both the Euphrates and the Tigris. Four dams, barrages or reservoirs (at Samarra, Dokan, Derbendi Khan and Habbaniyah) provide security against flood dangers. When the waters of the Euphrates and Tigris are fully utilized through dams and reservoirs, the area of cultivated land in Iraq will be almost doubled.

Great importance has been placed on the country's need for improved irrigation and an agreement has been signed with the U.S.S.R. for joint co-operation in irrigation affairs. Soviet experts are studying the Bakhma, Hindujah, Haditha, Fallujah and Kirkuk irrigation projects. The current development plan envisages further outlays on a number of other major water storage and control schemes of which the most important are the Euphrates dam, the Himrin dam, the Eski-Mosul dam and the Bekhme dam, while work on smaller scale canal, drainage and diversion works will also form a continuing element in the overall water control programme. By the end of 1974 the first phase of the Kirkuk irrigation project will begin. The first phase will last five years and has been allocated ID 70 million. Following phases will take a further seven years with the ultimate objective of irrigating 500,000 square metres. Also in 1974 a contract was awarded to a Greek firm to improve the existing irrigation canals in the Hilla, Dawaniya and Dalmaj districts. Construction of the Tharthar-Euphrates canal and the Halapcha storage schemes has begun. Work has begun on the lower Al-Khalis irrigation scheme at an estimated cost of ID 21.3 million (half of which will be provided by the World Bank). An area of 362,000 dunums will be supplied with water and 50,000 peasant families will benefit from this scheme.

Irrigation will receive U.S. $3,500 million under the new plan, and these dozen major dams and irrigation projects should give an additional 11 to 12 million dunums of irrigated land. The Kirkuk dam will irrigate 400,000 dunums by 1980 and will eventually supply water for 1.5 million dunums. The Mosul dam on the Tigris will extend irrigation over an area of 1.2 million dunums as well as generating electricity. Two other schemes of flood control and irrigation are the Lower Khalis and the Tharthar projects. The latter is due for completion in 1976 with the work having been done by the Soviet Union, who were also involved with the Falluja dam which will irrigate 900,000 dunums along the Euphrates. The Lower Khalis (supported by the World Bank) will increase irrigation by 625,000 dunums. In addition, the Diwaniya-Dalmaj irrigation project is due for completion within three years and four other schemes— the Abu Ghuraib, Al-Ishaqi, Dujaila and Nahr Saad—will also increase irrigation facilities as well as being interlocked with general agricultural development.

OIL

The oil industry is the country's principal source of wealth and provides the bulk of capital for all state and municipal industries. In 1970 Iraq was the eighth largest oil producer in the world. This production has hitherto come almost exclusively from the Iraq Petroleum Company (IPC) and its associated companies, the Mosul Petroleum Company and the Basra Petroleum Company. The IPC group represents a consortium of British, Dutch, French and American oil companies together with the Gulbenkian interest. Under an agreement signed on February 28th, 1973 the IPC group conceded the nationalization of its assets in Iraq with the exception of the BPC operation which remains independent. However, influenced by the Arab-Israeli war in October 1973 Iraq nationalized the U.S. and Dutch interests in BPC, thus gaining a 38 per cent in BPC which was increased to 43 per cent when the Portuguese Gulbenkian Foundation's five per cent stake was nationalized (because of the Portuguese attitude to Arab nations in the October war). At the time of writing the ownership of BPC assets has not been determined but it is expected that Iraq will eventually demand a 60 per cent share in the BPC company.

The major oil field previously controlled by the IPC group is at Kirkuk with subsidiary production from the Jambur and Bai Hassan fields. Export from these and from the small fields previously controlled by MPC at Ain Zalah and Butmah is by pipeline, through Syria and the Lebanon, to the port terminals of Banias (890 km. from Kirkuk) and Tripoli (854 km. from Kirkuk) on the East Mediterranean coast. The output of BPC is from its Rumaila and Zubair fields in southern Iraq and exports are piped to the Gulf and shipped from the deep water terminal at Khor al-Amaya and from Fao. There is also a pipeline from Kirkuk to Baghdad, completed in 1966, which carries natural gas and liquid petroleum gas for use in Baghdad's power stations and industries. Production from the state-owned North Rumaila field began in

the second quarter of 1972 and present annual production is estimated at 10 million tons. Upon completion of the second stage of development in 1974 it is expected that production from this field will rise to 18 million tons, with further expansion to 42 million tons planned by mid-1975.

Of the total IPC group output in 1970, 73.3 million tons was exported (56.2 million tons by pipeline to the Mediterranean coast) and 3.3 million tons was delivered to oil refineries owned and operated by the Iraqi Government. In 1971–72 Iraq's oil refining output totalled 943 million imperial gallons of oil products. In August of 1971 the Soviet Union undertook to construct a refinery in Mosul capable of handling 30,000 barrels a day. In April 1974 the Basra refinery was opened; this has a capacity of 3.5 million tons per annum of oil products and will supply Southern Iraq, with the surplus being exported. The U.S.S.R. is to build an oil products pipeline between Basra and Baghdad at an estimated cost of ID 11 million.

The IPC concession in Iraq dates from 1925. Relations between the oil companies and the Government were first comprehensively formalized in 1952. The companies undertook to pay the Government 50 per cent of their theoretical profit (based on posted prices) as well as certain other revenues, and guaranteed revenue and production minima. In December 1961, after prolonged negotiations for a revision of concession agreements had broken down, the Government passed Law No. 80, under which the companies' area of operations was restricted to their producing oilfields, equivalent to less than 0.5 per cent of their previous area, and the remainder of their concessions withdrawn. Negotiations over the revision of Law No. 80 resulted in a draft agreement concluded in 1965, but never ratified, which reportedly provided for the oil companies to retain their current producing areas and as much acreage again (including the newly discovered North Rumaila field).

However, by Law No. 97 of 1967, the Government's oil policy changed direction. Under this law the Iraq National Oil Company (INOC), a state oil company formed in 1964, was given exclusive rights over all areas except those left to IPC in Law 80. INOC was to be allowed to operate jointly in association with foreign companies, if it wished, as long as no concession was awarded. Accordingly, a contract was signed between INOC and *l'Entreprise de Recherches et d'Activités Petrolières* (ERAP), a French state company. The French company acts as contractor in four areas where oil has not been proven. INOC will contribute financially only if oil is found. All oil will belong to INOC, while ERAP will be permitted to buy a share at a privileged price. ERAP began drilling in 1968 near Basra and has since discovered oil at Buzurgan, Abu Gharab and Siba. The development of these fields was delayed for some two years by disputes between ERAP and the Iraqi Government, but in May 1973 a contract was signed complementing the 1968 agreement and which allowed for the export of 8 million tons of crude oil a year from the Abu Gharab and Buzurgan fields as soon as the deep-water terminal at Fao is completed. Agreements regulating production and accounting procedures were also signed in November 1973. Exploration of other areas allocated to ERAP in 1968 will continue until the end of 1974.

Despite negotiations with several foreign companies, INOC finally announced, early in 1968, that it would develop the rich field of North Rumaila by itself. This field, discovered by IPC but expropriated under Law 80, is thought to be capable of 42 million tons per year. The Alrafidain Bank agreed to extend a loan of ID 6 million to INOC to finance the first stage of the exploitation of the field which is now producing 10 million tons of crude oil a year. In mid-1975 the first stage of the deep-water terminal at Fao will be completed. This terminal will handle oil from the North Rumaila field initially at the rate of 50 million tons a year but increasing to 80 million tons a year by the end of 1975. In July 1969 the U.S.S.R. and Iraq signed an agreement under which Soviet aid worth some £28 million would be given to INOC to develop North Rumaila and other proven oilfields. In August 1971 a new protocol on economic and technical co-operation was signed in Moscow. It was agreed to proceed with the second stage of the North Rumaila field, so as to achieve an annual output of 18 million tons, to explore other new fields, and to link the Nahr Umr field to the pipeline from North Rumaila to Fao. The Soviet Union also agreed to participate in a major project to link the new fields in southern Iraq with the Mediterranean port-terminals by a pipeline of 1,250 km. in length and 48 inches in diameter; it has been suggested that the pipeline would have an annual capacity of 50 million tons and would cost some $420 million. Work is being carried out to increase the capacity of the Kirkuk-Banias pipeline by 10 million tons a year to facilitate increased production from the Kirkuk oilfields (presently producing 70 million tons a year). In 1972 production began on the North Rumaila field, at an initial rate of 5 million tons a year which has now risen to 10 million tons a year. INOC has been active in the past year negotiating long term trade agreements for its crude oil output.

Recent contracts of note include an agreement with France to supply at least 12.5 million tons a year for ten years and in addition Iraq is to supply Japan with 160 million tons of crude oil and petroleum products in return for $100 million in credits which will be used for building petro-chemical factories and refineries. Such barter arrangements for oil are an increasing feature of Iraq's international trade. There are similar agreements with Austria, Italy and several Eastern Bloc countries as well as India, Sweden, Spain and Bangladesh.

INOC's activities extend beyond the exploration for and production of crude oil. In 1972 it established a Directorate of Crude Oil Tankers as an autonomous company, to be responsible for the operation and management of a tanker fleet. Five of seven tankers ordered from Spanish yards have been delivered. In March 1974 Iraqi Oil Tankers Company (IOTC) awarded a Swedish firm a contract to build four tankers of 154,000 tons to be delivered between December 1976 and October 1977. This will bring the IOTC fleet to eleven tankers capable of carrying four million tons a year. Also in March INOC awarded a contract to a Japanese firm to build one tanker of 144,000 d.w.t. and another four of low draught at 120,000 tons each to carry oil to any Gulf or Mediterranean port. When all the tankers have been delivered Iraq will have a total of sixteen with a combined deadweight of 1.7 million tons. A state-owned sulphur recovery plant has been operating at Kirkuk since 1968 producing 120,000 tons per year of sulphur from associated gas from the Kirkuk field. The by-product gases are sent by pipeline to Baghdad.

Total oil production in Iraq was 22 million tons in 1957 and 47.3 million tons in 1960. By 1970 output had reached 76.4 million tons, only marginally more than the previous year, but in 1971 it increased sharply to 83.8 million tons following agreements between the Government and the oil companies on higher production targets for the southern oilfields. A sharp decline in production in 1972 to 72 million tons was caused by the disputes between IPC and the Government. With the dispute settled and aided by the output from the new field at North Rumaila, production reached an estimated 92 million tons in 1973.

In February 1971 Iraq participated in the Teheran agreement between the Western oil companies and the six oil-producing companies of the Gulf. The agreement provided for a 35 cents per barrel increase in posted prices on oil shipped from the Gulf as well as for a higher (55 per cent) tax rate on relevant company profits, and also incorporated escalation clauses to take account of the rise in the price of petroleum products on world markets and of changes in the terms of trade experienced by the oil-producing countries.

In June 1971 the Iraqi Government reached an agreement with IPC, after protracted negotiations, whereby the posted price of all Iraqi oil shipped from the Mediterranean terminals was to be raised; additionally the tax rate on the companies operating in northern Iraq was also raised to 55 per cent, and the companies agreed to monthly instead of quarterly tax and royalty payments.

In January of 1972 the signatories of the Teheran agreement, meeting at Geneva, agreed to a further increase (of 8.57 per cent) in posted prices at the Gulf to offset the effect of the dollar devaluation that resulted from the currency realignment of December 1971. The postings for Iraqi and Saudi Arabian crude oil at East Mediterranean terminals were similarly increased. The additional payments would be linked to an index reflecting changes in the values of nine industrial countries' currencies and would vary with the appreciation or depreciation of the dollar as measured by this index. The oil producing countries later claimed payments in excess of this index which they contended did not sufficiently account for the effects on their revenue of the currency realignments of February 1973. The oil companies finally agreed to meet the full demands of the producing countries early in June 1973.

Since this agreement the situation has changed considerably, mainly because of the October war. Iraq is opposed to OAPEC's (the Organisation of Arab Petroleum Exporting Countries) policy of oil cuts, and has even increased sales to friendly countries. Iraq did follow OAPEC's policy in embargoing supplies to the U.S.A. and Holland and nationalized unfriendly countries' oil interests in Iraq. In spite of warnings against consumer backlash because of increased price rises (this was after the seventy per cent price rises in October 1973) Iraq raised its prices by a further 134 per cent in January 1974. This massive price rise, combined with increased oil production means that revenues from oil in 1973 reached ID 547 million, and are expected to reach ID 1,540 million in 1975. These figures show a huge increase over the estimated revenues in 1972 to 1973 of ID 354 million.

The already poor relations between the Government and the oil companies deteriorated when the companies further cut back production in the northern fields by 45 per cent in March and April 1972 compared with the two preceding months. IPC claimed that the cut-back was necessitated, for purely commercial reasons, by the widened cost differential between crude oil shipped from East Mediterranean and Gulf terminals which followed the June 1971 agreement on Mediterranean posted prices. Compared with an average difference in tax burden of around 35 cents per barrel between oil shipped through the Mediterranean and through the Gulf, the difference in freight rates is only some 10 cents per barrel in favour of the Mediterranean terminals. This difference was further widened by higher tax payments to Syria and the Lebanon for transit dues to East Mediterranean terminals.

This cut-back revived, with increased bitterness, the disputes which had continued since 1961, and on June 1st, 1972, the Iraqi Government announced that by decree Law No. 69 the assets of IPC had been nationalized. The Syrian Government then announced that it had similarly nationalized all IPC assets in Syria. After protracted negotiations an agreement was finally announced in Baghdad on 28th February, 1973 which settled all outstanding disputes between the Government and the IPC group. Under the settlement the IPC conceded the loss of its Kirkuk oilfields in return for a total of 15 million tons of crude oil, worth some £128 million, to be loaded at Eastern Mediterranean ports, free of all charges and at the rate of at least one million tons a month starting on March 1st, 1973. The IPC agreed to waive its objection to Law 80 under which the North Rumaila fields were seized in 1961 and also agreed to pay the Government the sum of £141 million as settlement of all Government claims on the group. The agreement further announced that the MPC had agreed to hand over all its assets and installations to the Government as of March 31st, 1973 without seeking any compensation.

The IPC pipeline and port facilities in the Lebanon were also scheduled to be handed over to the Iraq Government but Lebanon refused to allow this and a subsequent agreement, signed in Beirut on March 5th, 1973, provided for a Lebanese takeover of the pipeline and loading installations.

The terms of the agreement also require BPC, the only member of the IPC group to remain operational in Iraq, to increase output from the 1972 level of 32 million tons to 80 million tons in 1976. In addition BPC is to relinquish its concession in the Mosul field without compensation. Following the Arab-Israeli war in October 1973 Iraq obtained a 43 per cent stake in BPC by nationalizing the U.S. and Dutch interests representing 38 per cent together with the Gulbenkian 5 per cent. It is thought likely that Iraq will increase its interests to 60 per cent in the near future.

INDUSTRY

Iraq has not the same impelling reasons for rapid and large-scale industrialization as countries with a surplus and increasing population that is too large to be supported by agriculture. The policy of the Government and the Ministry of Planning aims therefore at an industrial development that will not be so accelerated as to outrun seriously the available surplus of skilled labour required. It also prescribes that the industries to be encouraged should be carefully selected as based upon domestic resources and assured of a domestic market.

Apart from oil (which stands in a category by itself) Iraq has few industries of any size. In greater Baghdad the larger enterprises are electricity and water supply, brick and cement manufacture. In addition there is a large number of smaller-unit industries concerned with food and drink processing (date-packing, breweries, etc.), cigarette-making, spinning and weaving, chemicals, furniture, shoe-making, jewellery and various metal manufacturers. The Government controls most of manufacturing industry and mining through the General Industrial Organization, set up in 1964.

Major state factories include a bitumen plant at Qaiyarah, south of Mosul, which produces 60,000 tons of asphalt per year and employs 250 workers; a £3 million textile factor at Mosul, equipped with 644 looms, employing 1,200 workers, and producing 25 million square yards per year of calico from locally grown cotton; and two cement factories, each with a daily output of 350 tons. The Fujallah cement factory is to be expanded while a new cement works is planned for the Badoosh area which will have a minimum capacity of 1 million tons a year. Total output at present is some 1 million tons which more than covers Iraqi demand. A sugar factory with an annual production of 35,000 tons is in production at Mosul and further expansion is planned. Two further plants at Kerbela and Sulaimaniyah are under construction. A fertilizer factory at Basra has an initial output of 120,000 tons of ammonium sulphate as well as uric and sulphuric acid. It uses sulphur from the Kirkuk plant and natural gas from the Rumaila field. Other projects include a paper board factory at Basra. A rayon plant at Hindiyah opened in 1968 and another is planned. Shoe and cigarette factories serve the domestic market. Projects under construction include a car tyre and tubes plant, a chemical fertilizer plant and a wire and cable plant. In addition ID 16 million have been allocated for four flour mills in Nineveh, Kirkuk, Basra and Baghdad.

The Soviet Union has assisted with the construction of eleven factories, including a steel mill and an electrical equipment factory at Baghdad, a drug factory at Samarra and an agricultural machinery plant at Musayib. A large share of industrial development is expected to take place in co-operation with Eastern bloc countries and several agreements have been signed. These include loans from Bulgaria, to pay for complete industrial plants and technical aid in mineral exploration, which will be repaid in crude oil shipments, and a loan from Hungary, some two-thirds of which is also repayable in oil. The U.S.S.R. is to receive oil to the value of ID 50 million in return for services in connection with industrial projects and, on a similar contract, Czechoslovakia is to build an oil refinery at Basra. In addition, the U.S.S.R. has provided a ID 80 million loan to finance Russian-built projects including an oil refinery and pipeline, two hydro-electric power stations, a phosphate mine and a fertilizer plant, while contracts, each valued at ID 7 million have been signed under which the U.S.S.R. will provide agricultural and road-building equipment.

Two trade agreements have been completed with China. Under the terms of the first, Iraq will supply 100,000 tons of sulphur each year over a five-year period while China will make available ID 14 million to Iraq for the purchase by China of 250,000 tons a year of chemical fertilizer from the Basra fertilizer plant.

There are deposits of iron ore, chromite, copper, lead and zinc in the north, where test drilling is now being carried out, and important deposits of lime-stone, gypsum, salt, dolomite, phosphates and sulphur have also been located. The main sulphur deposit, discovered at Mishraq in North Central Iraq, is to be developed by the state Iraq National Minerals Company, which awarded the contract to the Polish state firm, Centrozap. The plant was commissioned early in 1972; output will begin at a rate of 250,000 tons a year and a rate of 1.5 million tons annually is the eventual target. New port facilities, designed particularly for handling liquid sulphur, are being built at Um Qasr, and when completed in 1975, should allow sulphur exports to be doubled. Recently contracts have been signed for sulphur exports to Egypt, India and China. In total some 16,000 tons of sulphur have been shipped in the first four months of 1974 compared with 170,000 tons in 1973. A large proportion of the electricity generated by the new hydro-electric station on the Samarra barrage will be utilized by the Mishraq sulphur complex; a power line costing ID 2.3 million will directly connect Samarra and Mishraq. Polish help will also be given to develop Iraqi phosphate deposits in return for phosphate fertilizers and crude oil deliveries to Poland.

Many new industrial plants have been started or are planned for the future. A steel rolling mill is to be constructed at Khor-Al-Zubair at a cost of ID 30 million. The planning board has given permission for a petrochemical plant at Basra which will produce 120,000 tons of plastic annually. This plant will use the by-product gas from crude oil production in Southern Iraq, most of which is now burnt off. The new sulphur plant at Kirkuk started production in May 1972 at a capacity of 400 ton/day. The sulphur output supplies the Basra fertilizer plant, and the Hindujah artificial fibres factory. While desulphurized gas will be sent to al-Taji in dry gas and LPG form for domestic and industrial use. Gas will also be available for power stations and in other industry in Baghdad. There are plans to construct an aluminium smelter in the Basra area which would also use waste oilfield gas.

Along with growth in the industrial base there is a continuing increase in the generation and consumption of electricity. In the years 1953–65 consumption of electricity rose substantially from 343 to 1,200 million kWh. Consumption in Baghdad rose from 206.4 million kWh. in 1960/61 to 1,383.5 million kWh. in 1968/69. The capacity of the power station on the Lesser Zab, near Kirkuk, will eventually be raised to 150,000 kW., when it will supply Mosul, Kirkuk, Arbil and Sulaimaniyah. Baghdad's power station is similarly raising its capacity to 200,000 kW. There are other hydro-electric stations at Basra, and based on the Samarra barrage, and more are planned at Dokan and Derbendi. In March of this year ID 24 million was awarded for the first stage of an ID 35 million rural electrification programme. This project will provide electricity for 9,000 villages.

The commercial banks (which were nationalized in 1964) provide short-term credit, while longer term credit and aid for industry and agriculture is provided by several state-owned agencies—the Industrial, Agricultural, Mortgage and Co-operative banks. The Industrial Bank, whose board is appointed by the Council of Ministers, is a shareholder in several large plants and in the private Light Industries Company which is establishing plants for the manufacture or assembly of kerosene heaters, cookers, radio sets, animal fodder, bicycles and electric wire.

COMMUNICATIONS

The Public Works Department is responsible for the control and maintenance of public roads in Iraq, but major road and bridge construction is the responsibility of the Ministry of Planning. The main artery runs from the Jordanian frontier through Baghdad to the Iranian border but the road system is under complete reconstruction with the assistance of a World Bank loan of $23 million as part finance for a $54 million building programme. The 1973/74 investment programme envisages the construction of 10 bridges at a cost of ID 17.5 million and recently bids have been invited for road-building contracts worth a total of ID 63 million including a new 475 kilometre road connecting Kirkuk with Rutba which will cost ID 35 million.

Iraq's main port is at Basra; a new port has been constructed at Um Qasr and also BPC is going ahead with building offshore and onshore loading facilities at the Khor-al-Amaya terminal. A new terminal is to be built at Fao at an estimated cost of ID 36 million, with a further £ sterling 64 million contract for the land facilities of the deep water terminal. The terminal will deal with the expected increase in INOC's output. The continuing dispute with Iran over the approaches to Basra on the Shatt el Arab river has made it increasingly necessary to develop Um Qasr as an alternative post and military base. Iraq has been extremely anxious to secure the approaches to Um Qasr which lies at the head of a lagoon whose entrance is controlled by Kuwait. River navigation is of some importance, particularly on the Tigris between Basra and Baghdad.

There are major international airports at Basra and Baghdad and civil airports at Mosul (which is being developed to take international services) and Kirkuk, as well as an IPC field at Kirkuk. A new airport is being constructed at Baghdad.

The Railways Administration is a semi-autonomous body operating under a Director-General who is responsible to a government-appointed board. The principal lines run from Baghdad through Mosul to Tel Kotchek (529 km.) and from Basra to Baghdad (569 km.). In 1971 work was completed, with Russian assistance, on the realignment and conversion of the latter to standard gauge. A line is being built to link Shaiba and Um Quasr and work is to begin on a line from Kirkuk to Salaimaniyah. Eventually the Government hopes to expand the railway system to provide links with Kuwait, Saudi Arabia, Lebanon and Iran. In the 1974-79 plan, expenditure on the railway system is expected to reach ID 268 million, notably on the construction of links between Kirkuk–Baghdad and Baghdad–Ramadi, a new station at Baghdad, and to purchase new locomotives and rolling stock.

Improvements are planned for the telecommunications system. The Government has been granted a World Bank loan of $27.5 million towards a major plan, costing $61 million, which includes the provision of subscriber-trunk-dialling services, a micro-wave link between major towns and the establishment of a satellite ground station.

FINANCE

Development spending is a potential cause of inflation but until the past three years the rate of price increase, as measured by available indices, was very modest. At the end of 1968 consumer prices were less than 3 per cent higher than their level of five years earlier. Since then prices have risen comparatively sharply, partly as a result of the poor performance of the agricultural sector, and by the first half of 1971 inflation was a cause of some concern to the Government, anxious for its political popularity. Increased imports and tighter price controls resulted in a fall in prices in the second half of 1971 and by the end of that year inflation appeared to be under control, or at

least not significantly in excess of other comparable economies.

The budgeting procedure has been rationalized in recent years and a consolidated account consisting of the Ordinary Budget, the Development Plan Budget, and the Budget for the Autonomous Agencies, is now presented. Despite the receipt of 50 per cent of all state oil revenues the budget has tended to show a deficit, but with the expected vast increases in oil revenues a budget surplus can be anticipated at least for the next few years. In the 1972–73 budget, Government revenue was estimated at ID 331 million in the Ordinary Budget and ID 243 million in the Development Budget, together showing an increase of ID 39 million or seven per cent over the previous year, almost all attributable to increased oil revenues. Expenditure during 1972–73 was estimated at ID 347 million in the Ordinary Budget and ID 243 million in the Development Budget. The Government has just ratified a total budget expenditure for 1974–75 of ID 2,933 million which includes ID 1,169 for investment purposes. This budget is well over double the 1973–74 budget expenditure of ID 1,375 million.

On external account Iraq usually runs a deficit on trade (excluding oil) which is more than offset by foreign exchange earnings from the oil sector. The payments surplus generated by the oil industry is needed to meet payments on foreign borrowing for Iraq's development programme. The trade balance for the oil sector in 1972 shows a surplus of ID 204 million giving an overall trade surplus of ID 127 million. The strengthening external position is indicated by the rise in gold and foreign exchange reserves held by the Iraq Central Bank from $781 million at the end of 1972 to $3,025 million in October 1974.

DEVELOPMENT AND PLANNING

The bulk of financing for development comes from the Government's oil revenues, supplemented by the net profits from government agencies and by external loans. In recent years Eastern bloc countries have been an increasingly important source of external finance; the Soviet Union has been the major lender here, but other communist countries have provided sizeable loans; an East German loan amounting to $84 million was granted in 1969 to be repaid over a twelve-year period at an interest rate of 2.5 per cent, in Iraqi commodities and crude oil. It will be used to finance cement, starch and sugar factories.

The 1970–74 five-year development plan had an investment allocation of ID 1,000 million with priority being given to the agricultural sector. This plan terminated in March 1974 and was replaced by a new five-year plan. The total expenditure under the new 1974–79 plan is expected to be about $7,500 million with priority given to investment in the oil sector. This amount will probably be revised upwards as Iraq will receive considerably more revenue from oil sales than had been anticipated. ID 225 million will be invested in industry with priority for iron, steel and petrochemical plants, while ID 178 million is destined for agricultural developments with priority given to irrigation projects and meat and poultry production. Iraq should now be entering a phase of rapid expansion owing to her increasing oil revenues and the next few years should see a rise not only in the value of exports but also in the amount and cost of imports. It has been announced that imports in 1974–75 will cost in the region of ID 1,134 million compared with ID 415 million in 1973–74. From December 1974, 212 categories of imported goods are to be handled exclusively by state organiza-

tions demonstrating Iraq's determination to control her import bill and maintain a balance of trade surplus.

The latest budget, for the nine months between April and December 1975, calls for an expenditure of U.S. $14,000 million, an increase of 35 per cent over 1974. The budget allocates U.S. $3,650 million for development, of which one-third will go to the industrial sector, $700 million for housing and utilities, $800 million for agriculture and $680 million for transport and communications.

STATISTICAL SURVEY

AREA AND POPULATION

TOTAL AREA	ARABLE	POPULATION (1974)	BAGHDAD (capital)	MOSUL	BASRA
438,446 sq. km.	75,364 sq. km.	10,765,000	2,800,000	857,000	854,000

A neutral zone of 7,000 sq. km. between southern Iraq and northern Saudi Arabia is administered jointly by the two countries. Nomads move freely through it, but there are no permanent inhabitants.

POPULATION BY PROVINCE (MUHAFADHA)
(1974)

Nineveh	892,299		Babylon	577,781
Sulaimaniya	537,738		Kerbela	557,866
Arbil	475,733		Qadisiyah	414,317
Kirkuk	586,249		Maysan	360,931
Diala	485,601		Thi-Qar	544,159
Anbar	378,302		Basra	915,257
Baghdad	3,342,477		Muthanna	150,936
Wasit	380,352		Dhok	165,726

EMPLOYMENT
(1973 estimate)

Agriculture	1,540,400
Mining	18,500
Manufacturing	170,000
Electricity, Gas and Water	14,300
Construction	73,000
Commerce	164,000
Transport	162,000
Services	330,000
Others	380,400
Unemployed	200,100
TOTAL LABOUR FORCE	3,052,700

AGRICULTURE
AREA AND PRODUCTION OF PRINCIPAL WINTER CROPS

	1972		1973		1974	
	AREA ('000 dunums)	PRODUCTION ('000 tons)	AREA ('000 dunums)	PRODUCTION ('000 tons)	AREA ('000 dunums)	PRODUCTION ('000 tons)
Wheat	7,658.0	2,625.0	4,624.0	957.0	6,624.0	1,339.0
Barley	2,902.0	979.0	1,856.0	461.8	2,185.0	533.0
Linseed	23.8	3.7	4.2	9.0	6.0	0.9
Lentils	43.8	7.1	17.1	2.4	16.0	2.6
Vetch (Hurtman) . . .	3.9	0.8	3.1	0.8	3.0	0.4
Broad Beans	59.7	14.9	59.8	14.9	n.a.	n.a.

AREA AND PRODUCTION OF PRINCIPAL SUMMER CROPS

	1972		1973		1974	
	AREA ('000 dunums)	PRODUCTION ('000 tons)	AREA ('000 dunums)	PRODUCTION ('000 tons)	AREA ('000 dunums)	PRODUCTION ('000 tons)
Rice	376.3	267.8	255.8	156.6	130.0	69.0
Sesame	52.7	7.0	52.6	5.7	58.0	6.0
Green grams . . .	52.6	9.8	37.9	7.2	n.a.	n.a.
Millet	18.0	4.1	9.6	2.1	n.a.	n.a.
Giant millet . . .	29.7	6.4	24.3	6.5	n.a.	n.a.
Maize	53.0	17.7	42.8	19.1	n.a.	n.a.

Livestock (1971): Sheep 4,736,241; Goats 1,521,661; Cattle 1,200,499; Donkeys 456,520; Horses 85,230; Buffaloes 111,889; Camels 38,349; Chickens 11,860,577.

DATE CROP
(tons)

1970-71	1971-72	1972-73	1973-74
300,000	450,000	310,000	390,000

AREA AND PRODUCTION OF COTTON

	1972	1973	1974
Area (dunums) .	146,800	143,270	113,000
Production (tons) .	50,800	45,310	40,000

IRRIGATION

	1969-70	1970-71	1971-72	1972-73
Number of Pumps . .	13,769	14,135	15,484	15,734
Total Horse Power . .	366,751	350,335	368,885	364,458

OIL
PRODUCTION OF CRUDE OIL
('000 barrels)

	1971	1972	1973	1974*
Total production . .	618,375	536,502	736,588	700,000

* Estimate

INDUSTRY
('000 units)

	1968	1969	1970	1971	1972
Leather tanning:					
Upper leather (sq. ft.) .	6,738.6	n.a.	9,003.1	n.a.	n.a.
Toilet Soap (tons) . . .	7.6	7.3	6.1	15.3	19.1
Vegetable oil (tons) . .	52.9	58.0	62.0	84.1	72.4
Woollen textiles:					
Cloth (metres) . . .	835.6	n.a.	1,319.6	1,001.1	n.a.
Blankets (number) .	447.5	611.0	623.8	577.8	653.0
Cotton textiles (metres) .	31,805.7	32,447.0	48,321.3	59,326.1	71,000.0
Beer (litres)	6,064.1	n.a.	8,214.1	8,983.8	10,238.0
Matches (gross) . . .	1,371.0	1,686.4	1,959.4	1,629.3	1,861.0
Cigarettes (million) . .	5.1	5.2	6.6	6.2	6.3
Shoes (pairs) . . .	5,619.5	n.a.	4,445.1	n.a.	n.a.

FINANCE

1,000 fils=20 dirhams=1 Iraqi dinar (I.D.).

Coins: 1, 5, 10, 25, 50 and 100 fils.

Notes: 250 and 500 fils; 1, 5, and 10 dinars.

Exchange rates (July 1975): £1 sterling=647.47 fils; U.S. $1=296.05 fils.

100 Iraqi dinars=£154.45=$337.78.

Note: From September 1949 to August 1971 the par value of the Iraqi dinar was U.S. $2.80 ($1=357.14 fils). Between December 1971 and February 1973 the dinar's value was $3.04 ($1=328.95 fils). The present dollar valuation became effective in February 1973. The Iraqi dinar was at par with the pound sterling until November 1967, after which the exchange rate was £1=857.14 fils (1 dinar=£1.167) until June 1972.

Ordinary Budget, April-December 1975: Expenditure I.D. 3,640 million.

Investment Budget 1975: Total expenditure I.D. 1,076 million (Industry I.D. 448 million, Agriculture I.D. 207 million, Transport and Communications I.D. 166 million, others 255 million).

CENTRAL BANK RESERVES
(U.S. $ million at December 31st)

	1970	1971	1972	1973	1974
Gold	143.5	155.8	155.8	173.1	175.7
IMF Special Drawing Rights .	—	12.7	25.2	24.2	28.2
Reserve Position in IMF . .	—	—	18.7	32.9	33.4
Foreign Exchange . .	318.7	431.9	581.8	1,322.9	3,035.9
TOTAL . . .	462.2	600.4	781.5	1,553.1	3,273.2

CONSUMER PRICES INDEX (IFS)
(1963=100)

1968	1969	1970	1971	1972	1973	1974
105.9	111.9	116.8	121.0	127.3	133.5	144.6

EXTERNAL TRADE

TOTAL TRADE
('000 I.D.)

YEAR	IMPORTS	EXPORTS*	RE-EXPORTS	TRANSIT
1970.	181,651	22,566	2,164	27,942
1971.	247,870	22,780	n.a.	33,801
1972.	234,680	28,614	2,394	65,485
1973.	270,317	32,523	272	56,095

* Exports of crude oil are not included.

EXPORTS OF CRUDE OIL
('000 I.D.)

1969	1970	1971	1972	1973
346,185	368,065	523,191	523,000	523,200

PRINCIPAL COMMODITIES
('000 I.D.)

IMPORTS	1971	1972	1973
Tea	6,072	7,600	4,712
Sugar	12,278	11,000	14,599
Pharmaceutical products	8,805	8,224	1,270
Clothing	422	404	191
Boilers and engines	35,098	44,446	47,898
Automobiles and parts	12,115	10,474	10,867
Timber	3,182	2,836	2,235

EXPORTS	1971	1972	1973
Barley	n.a.	515	n.a.
Dates	6,905	9,080	10,016
Straw and fodder	94	103	371
Raw wool	1,403	1,549	611
Raw cotton	74	467	84
Hides and skins	1,822	2,633	3,657
Cement	2,712	2,607	3,402

OIL REVENUES
(U.S. $ million)

1964	.	353	1970	.	521
1965	.	375	1971	.	340
1966	.	394	1972	.	575
1967	.	361	1973	.	1,500*
1968	.	476	1974	.	7,200*
1969	.	483			

* Estimate

PRINCIPAL COUNTRIES
('ooo I.D.)

IMPORTS	1971	1972	1973
Australia	15,444	734	1,314
Belgium	6,338	7,598	11,599
Bulgaria	3,631	3,923	—
Canada	16,293	890	596
China, People's Republic . . .	7,446	6,531	10,843
Czechoslovakia	12,496	16,321	14,931
Egypt	2,789	3,020	1,801
France	15,344	14,658	22,664
German Democratic Republic . .	3,665	7,923	6,358
Germany, Federal Republic . .	8,218	11,342	10,767
India	4,184	5,522	5,443
Italy	7,972	11,478	8,816
Japan	7,482	10,581	18,191
Lebanon	5,484	6,333	4,373
Malaysia	7,822	4,956	6,323
Netherlands	3,257	6,037	4,270
Pakistan	4,253	2,510	2,585
Poland	7,044	6,092	4,975
Sri Lanka	4,997	4,937	
Sweden	6,873	7,302	4,928
U.S.S.R.	29,605	17,030	23,773
United Kingdom	22,626	22,735	23,350
U.S.A.	12,096	9,554	15,024

EXPORTS (excluding oil)	1971	1972	1973
China, People's Republic . . .	1,070	2,623	1,861
India	1,197	1,514	1,429
Kuwait	3,002	4,113	4,054
Lebanon	2,829	3,386	4,687
Syria	3,809	2,430	3,741
U.S.S.R.	1,194	2,285	2,244
U.A.R. (now Egypt) . . .	3,299	3,166	1,597

TRANSPORT

RAILWAYS

	1970–71	1971–72	1972–73
Passenger km. ('ooo)	469,023	538,475	603,582
Freight ton km. ('ooo)	1,310,028	1,513,628	1,371,195

ROADS
LICENSED VEHICLES ('ooo)

	1970	1971	1972	1973
Cars . . .	67.4	71.8	75.5	77.3
Goods Vehicles .	32.7	33.7	45.5	46.1
Buses . .	9.2	10.9	11.2	11.6
Motor Cycles .	6.9	7.5	7.8	8.2

Source: International Road Federation.

INLAND WATERWAYS

	1970–71	1972	1973
Total net reg. tonnage . .	140,380	109,667	50,149
Number of Vessels . . .	1,264	1,099	1,272

SHIPPING
Movement of Ocean-going Merchant Vessels at the Ports of Basra and Um Qasr.

	No. of PASSENGERS (Arrivals and Departures)*	No. of VESSELS		TONNAGE OF CARGO (excluding Crude Oil)	
		Loaded (Entered and Cleared)	In Ballast (Entered and Cleared)	Imported	Exported
1970 . .	5,610	661	395	945,931	279,914
1971 . .	5,396	659	658	2,132,086	230,964
1972 . .	6,213	—	—	1,884,954	454,953
1973 . .	3,928	643	699	1,510,509	1,031,591

* Port of Basra only.

In 1972 passenger arrivals at Basra were 2,956 and departures 3,257.

SHIPPING OF CRUDE OIL
Export by tanker from all ports.

	1970	1971	1972
Crude oil ('000 tons) . . .	17,038	29,690	34,205

CIVIL AVIATION
Flights through Baghdad and Basra Airports.

	FLIGHTS		PASSENGERS			CARGO (kg.)	
	Iraqi Airways	Total	Disembarked	Embarked	Transit	Off-Loaded	Loaded
1970 . . .	1,527	3,198	110,172	111,841	8,071	2,615,722	528,542
1971 . . .	2,346	4,031	127,404	126,760	n.a.	2,463,596	820,156
1972 . . .	3,197	4,549	158,451	154,929	n.a.	2,680,818	855,637
1973 . . .	4,329	5,782	197,305	199,866	9,787	3,064,383	1,003,455

TOURISM

	1971	1972	1973
Visitors . . .	589,857	536,717	488,248

EDUCATION
(1973–74)

	SCHOOLS	PUPILS
Primary . . .	6,731	1,408,929
Secondary (General) .	1,093	388,624
Vocational . . .	65	16,010
Teacher Training . .	n.a.	n.a.
Universities . . .	5	55,140
Colleges and Technical Institutes . . .	8	3,211

Source: Central Statistical Organization, Ministry of Planning, Baghdad.

THE CONSTITUTION

The following are the principal features of the Provisional Constitution issued on September 22nd, 1968:

The Iraqi Republic is a popular democratic and sovereign state. Islam is the state religion.

The political economy of the state is founded in socialism.

The state will protect liberty of religion, freedom of speech and opinion. Public meetings are permitted under the law. All discrimination based on race, religion or language is forbidden. There shall be freedom of the Press, and the right to form societies and trade unions in conformity with the law is guaranteed.

The Iraqi people is composed of two main nationalities: Arab and Kurds. The Constitution confirms the nationalistic rights of the Kurdish people and the legitimate rights of all other minorities within the framework of Iraqi unity.

The highest authority in the country is the Council of Command of the Revolution, which will promulgate laws until the election of a National Assembly. The Council of Command of the Revolution has six members including the President and the Vice-President. The Council exercises its prerogatives and powers by a two-thirds majority.

Two amendments to the constitution were announced in November 1969. The President, already Chief of State and head of the government, also became the official Supreme Commander of the Armed Forces and President of the Command Council of the Revolution. Membership of the latter body was to increase from five to a larger number at the President's discretion.

Earlier, a Presidential decree replaced the 14 local government districts by 16 governates, each headed by a governor with wide powers.

The fifteen-article agreement which aimed to end the Kurdish war was issued on March 11th, 1970. In accordance with this agreement a form of autonomy was offered to the Kurds in March 1974, but some of the Kurds rejected the offer and fresh fighting broke out. The new Provisional Constitution was announced in July 1970. Two amendments were introduced in 1973 and 1974.

The President and Vice-President are elected by a two-thirds majority of the Council. The President, Vice-President and members of the Council will be responsible to the Council. Vice-Presidents and Ministers will be responsible to the President.

In July 1973, President Bakr announced a National Charter as a first step towards establishing the Progressive National Front. A National Assembly and People's Councils are features of the Charter.

THE GOVERNMENT

HEAD OF STATE
President: Field-Marshal AHMED HASSAN AL-BAKR.
Vice-President: TAHA MOHEDDIN MARUF.

REVOLUTIONARY COMMAND COUNCIL
President: Field-Marshal AHMED HASSAN AL-BAKR
Vice-President: SADAM HUSSAIN TAKRITI.
Members: The President, the Vice-President, Gen. SAADOUN GHAIDAN, Dr. IZZAT MUSTAFA, IZZAT AL-DOURI, TAHA AL-JEZRAWI.

COUNCIL OF MINISTERS
(July 1975)

Prime Minister and Minister of Defence: Field-Marshal AHMED HASSAN AL-BAKR.

Minister of Health: Dr. IZZAT MUSTAFA.

Minister of the Interior: IZZAT AL-DOURI.

Minister of Industry and Minerals and Acting Minister of Planning: TAHA AL-JAZRAWI.

Minister of Communications: SAADOUN GHAIDAN.

Minister of Oil: TAYEH ABDUL-KARIM.

Minister of Youth: NAIM HADDAD.

Minister of Higher Education and Scientific Research: GHANEM ABDUL-JALIL.

Minister of Education: MUHAMMAD MAHJOUB.

Minister of Information: TAREQ AZIZ.

Minister of Foreign Affairs: Dr. SAADOUN HAMMADI.

Minister of State for Foreign Affairs: Dr. HISHAM AL-SHAWI.

Minister of Economy: HIKMAT AL-AZZAWI.

Minister of Public Works and Housing: Dr. RASHID AL-RIFAI.

Minister of Labour and Social Affairs: ANWAR ABDUL-QADAR AL-HADITHI.

Minister of Finance: Dr. SAADI IBRAHIM.

Minister of Transport: ADNAN AYUB SABRI.

Minister of Justice: Dr. MUNZIR AL-SHAWI.

Minister of Agriculture and Agrarian Reform: Dr. HASSAN FAHMI JUMAA.

Minister of Municipal Affairs: ABDUL-SATTAR TAHER SHARIF.

Minister of Irrigation: MAKRAM AL-TALBANI.

Ministers of State: Dr. AHMAD ABDUL-SATTAR AL-JAWARI, HAMED AL-JEBOURI, Dr. ABDULLAH AL-KHODEIR, AMER ABDULLAH, AZIZ SHERIF, ABDULLAH ISMAIL AHMAD, OBEIDULLAH AL-BARZANI.

NATIONAL ASSEMBLY

No form of National Assembly has existed in Iraq since the 1958 revolution which overthrew the monarchy. The existing provisional constitution contains provisions for the election of a new assembly at a date to be determined by the Government. The members of the Assembly are to be elected from all political, social and economic sectors of the Iraqi people. A Kurdistan Legislative Council was set up at Arbil in March 1974. The Council sits for a three-year term and has 80 members.

POLITICAL PARTIES

National Progressive Front: Baghdad; f. July 1973, when Arab Baath Socialist Party and Iraqi Communist Party signed a joint manifesto agreeing to establish a comprehensive progressive national and nationalistic front. In 1975 representatives of Kurdish parties and organizations and other national and independent forces joined the Front; Sec.-Gen. NAIM HADDAD (Baath).

    Arab Baath Socialist Party: Baghdad; revolutionary Arab socialist movement founded in Damascus in 1947; has ruled Iraq since July 1968, and since July 1973 in alliance with the Iraqi Communist Party in the National Progressive Front; Regional Sec.-Gen. AHMED HASSAN AL-BAKR; Vice-Regional Sec.-Gen. SADAM HUSSAIN TAKRITI.

Iraqi Communist Party: Baghdad; f. 1934; became legally recognized in July 1973 on formation of National Progressive Front; First Sec. AZIZ MOHAMMED.

Kurdistan Democratic Party: Kurdish party which accepted terms of autonomy offered in March 1974 and joined the National Progressive Front; Sec.-Gen. AZIZ AQRAWI.

Kurdistan Democratic Party: represents the Kurds who rejected autonomy offered in March 1974; Chair. MULLAH MUSTAFA BARZANI (now in Iran); the resistance of the KDP of MULLAR MUSTAFA BARZANI virtually collapsed after the agreement between Iraq and Iran in March 1975.

DIPLOMATIC REPRESENTATION

EMBASSIES ACCREDITED TO IRAQ

(In Baghdad unless otherwise stated)

(E) Embassy.

Afghanistan: 27/1/12 Waziriyah (E); *Ambassador:* Prof. KHALILLULLAH KHALILI (also accred. to Bahrain, Kuwait and the United Arabs Emirates).

Algeria: Karradat Mariam (E); *Ambassador:* (also accred. to Turkey).

Argentina: Damascus, Syria (E).

Australia: Beirut, Lebanon (E).

Austria: 27/7/35 Masbah (E); *Ambassador:* Dr. NOREBERT LINHART.

Bangladesh: 13H/9/35 Masbah (E); *Ambassador:* KHONDHER GALAIM MUSTAPHA (also accred. to the People's Democratic Republic of Yemen).

Belgium: Saddun St. (E); *Chargé d'Affaires:* RAYMOND VAN ROY.

Brazil: 39A/21/4 Al Wathiq Square (E); *Ambassador:* MARIO LOUREIRO DIAS COSTA.

Bulgaria: 35/1 Karradat Mariam (E); *Ambassador:* SPAS NIKOLOV GOSPODOV.

Canada: Beirut, Lebanon (E).

Central African Republic: (E); *Ambassador:* SYLVESTRE SANA.

Chad: 97/4/4 Karradet Mariam (E); *Chargé d'Affaires:* AHMAT TITINBAYE.

China, People's Republic: Karradat Marian (E); *Ambassador:* CHAO HSING-CHIH.

Cuba: (address unavailable) (E); *Ambassador:* ADALBERTO QUINTANA SUÁREZ.

Cyprus: Cairo, Egypt (E).

Czechoslovakia: 1/7 Karradat Mariam (E); *Ambassador:* MIROSLAV JURASKA.

Denmark: Ankara, Turkey (E).

Egypt: 6/31/4 Karradat Mariam (E); *Ambassador:* ABDEL MONEIM EL-NAGAR.

Ethiopia: Cairo, Egypt (E).

Finland: Masbah 37/7/35 (E); *Chargé d'Affaires:* JOUKO LAAMANEN.

France: Kard el Pasha 9G/3/1 (E); *Chargé d'Affaires:* YVES SAILLARD.

German Democratic Republic: Masbah 34/33/32 and 52/53/54/354 (E); *Ambassador:* GÜNTER SCHURATH.

Germany, Federal Republic: (E); *Ambassador:* HEINZ VOIGHT.

Greece: Damascus, Syria (E).

Guinea: Cairo, Egypt (E).

Hungary: 22/1/12 Karradat Mariam (E); *Ambassador:* JÓZSEF FERRÓ (also accred. to Kuwait).

India: Taha St., Najib Pasha, Adhamiya (E); *Ambassador:* R. BHANDARI.

Indonesia: 24/6/33 Alwiya, Wathiq Square (E); *Ambassador:* MALIKSWARI MUKTAR (also accred. to Kuwait).

Iran: Karradat Mariam (E); *Ambassador:* HUSSEIN SHAHIDZADA.

Italy: 3/4 Nidhal St. (E); *Chargé d'Affaires:* TORQUATO CARDILLI.

Japan: 40/7/35 Masbah (E); *Ambassador:* SEIICHI SHIMA.

Jordan: 17 July St., Karradat Mariam; *Ambassador:* DHIYAB AL-ORAN.

Kenya: Cairo, Egypt (E).

Korea, Democratic People's Republic: Al Fatih Square (E); *Ambassador:* KIM QYO NAM.

Kuwait: Karradat Mariam (E); *Ambassador:* KHALID A. L. AL-MUSALLAM.

Lebanon: 13/21/5D Husamuddin St. (E); *Ambassador:* SUHAIL SHAMMAS.

Libya: Al Mansour (E); *Ambassador:* SALEH AL-SENUSS. ABDUL SAYED.

Mauritania: (E); *Ambassador:* AHMED BIN AL-TILBEH.

Mongolia: Prague, Czechoslovakia (E).

Morocco: 4/266 Karradat Mariam (E); *Ambassador:* MOHAMED NACIRI.

Netherlands: *Chargé d'Affaires:* Dr. MEIHUIZEN (also accred. to Oman).

Nigeria: Cairo, Egypt (E).

Norway: Ankara, Turkey (E).

Pakistan: Karradat Mariam (E); *Ambassador:* MU'IZZIDDIN AHMAD.

Poland: Karrada al-Sharkiya, Masbah (E); *Ambassador:* LUCJAN LIK.

Qatar: Mansour (E); *Ambassador:* AHMED ALI MAARIFIYA.

Romania: 52/5/35 Masbah (E); *Ambassador:* VASILE GEORGE.

Saudi Arabia: Waziriyah (E); *Ambassador:* ALI A. EL-SUGAIR.

Somalia: 49/5/35 Masbah (E); *Ambassador:* JAMI ILMI.

Spain: 12/9/21 Masbah (E); *Ambassador:* AMELIO MARTINE.

Sri Lanka: 10 B/6/12 Alwiyah (E); *Ambassador:* FEISAL JUNAID.

Sudan: 51/5/35 Masbah (E); *Ambassador:* ABBAS MUSA MUSTAFA.

Sweden: 23A/2 Al Nidhal St. (E); *Chargé d'Affaires:* HANS ANDERSSON.

Switzerland: 21/2/1 Karrada al Sharqiya, Zuwiya (E); *Chargé d'Affaires:* JEAN-LOUIS BERTHOUD.

Syria: 37/2J Saadoun Park (E); *Ambassador:* MUNIR AL-KHAIR.

Tunisia: Mansour 34/2/4 (E); *Ambassador:* ZUHAIR AL SHILLI.

Turkey: 2/8 Waziharyi (E); *Ambassador:* NASIF CUHURK.

U.S.S.R.: 140 Mansour St., Karradat Mariam (E); *Ambassador:* ANATOLY BARKOVSKY.

United Arab Emirates: (E); *Ambassador:* RASHID SULTAN AL-MUKHAWI.

United Kingdom: Sharia Salah Ud-Din, Karkh (E); *Ambassador designate:* J. A. N. GRAHAM, C.M.G.

Vatican: 20/4 Karradat Mariam (Apostolic Nunciature); *Apostolic Pro-Nuncio:* JEAN RUPP.

Venezuela: Cairo, Egypt (E).

Viet-Nam, Democratic Republic: Damascus, Syria.

Yemen, Arab Republic: 2/33/4 Karradat Mariam (E); *Chargé d'Affaires:* ABDUL KARIM EL QUDDUS.

Yemen, People's Democratic Republic: Masbah 18/9/21 (E); *Ambassador:* HAFIDH QAYID FARI.

Yugoslavia: 10/11/1 Asfar Quarter, Battaween (E); *Ambassador:* DANILO PURIC.

Zambia: Cairo, Egypt (E).

Iraq also has diplomatic relations with Bahrain, Malta and Tanzania.

JUDICIAL SYSTEM

Courts in Iraq consist of the following: The Court of Cassation, Courts of Appeal, First Instance Courts, Peace Courts, Courts of Sessions, Shara' Courts and Penal Courts.

The Court of Cassation: This is the highest judicial bench of all the Civil Courts; it sits in Baghdad, and consists of the President and a number of Vice-Presidents and not less than fifteen permanent judges, delegated judges and reporters as necessity requires. There are four bodies in the Court of Cassation, these are: (*a*) The General body, (*b*) Civil and Commercial body, (*c*) Personal Status body, (*d*) The Penal body.

A Technical Bureau has been established which is related to the Court of Cassation and is carrying out the work of abstracting and classifying the legal principles which are contained in the judgments issued by it.

Courts of Appeal: The country is divided into five Districts of Appeal: Baghdad, Mosul, Basrah, Hilla, and Kirkuk, each with its Court of Appeal consisting of a President, Vice-Presidents and not less than three members, who consider the objections against the decisions issued by the First Instance Courts of first grade.

Courts of First Instance: These courts are of two kinds: Limited and Unlimited in jurisdiction.

Limited Courts deal with Civil and Commercial suits, the value of which is five hundred Dinars and less; and suits, the value of which cannot be defined, and which are subject to fixed fees. Limited Courts consider these suits in the final stage and they are subject to Cassation.

Unlimited Courts consider the Civil and Commercial suits irrespective of their value, and suits the value of which exceeds five hundred Dinars with first grade subject to appeal.

First Instance Courts consist of one judge in the centre of each *Liwa*, some *Qadhas* and *Nahiyas*, as the Minister of Justice judges necessary.

Revolutionary Courts: These deal with major cases that would affect the security of the state in any sphere: political, financial or economic.

Courts of Sessions: There is in every District of Appeal a Court of Sessions which consists of three judges under the presidency of the President of the Court of Appeal or one of his Vice-Presidents. It considers the penal suits prescribed by Penal Proceedings Law and other laws. More than one Court of Sessions may be established in one District of Appeal by notification issued by the Minister of Justice mentioning therein its headquarters, jurisdiction and the manner of its establishment.

Shara' Courts: A Shara' Court is established wherever there is a First Instance Court; the Muslim judge of the First Instance Court may be a *Qadhi* to the Shara' Court if a special *Qadhi* has not been appointed thereto. The Shara' Court considers matters of personal status and religious matters in accordance with the provisions of the law supplement to the Civil and Commercial Proceedings Law.

Penal Courts: A Penal Court of first grade is established in every First Instance Court. The judge of the First Instance Court is considered as penal judge unless a special judge is appointed thereto. More than one Penal Court may be established to consider the suits prescribed by the Penal Proceedings Law and other laws.

One or more Investigation Court may be established in the centre of each *Liwa* and a judge is appointed thereto. They may be established in the centres of *Qadhas* and *Nahiyas* by order of the Minister of Justice. The judge carries out the investigation in accordance with the provisions of Penal Proceedings Law and the other laws.

There is in every First Instance Court a department for the execution of judgments presided over by the Judge of First Instance if a special President is not appointed thereto. It carries out its duties in accordance with the provisions of Execution Law.

RELIGION

ISLAM

Over 90 per cent of the population are Muslims. The Arabs of northern Iraq, the Bedouins, the Kurds, the Turkomans, and some of the inhabitants of Baghdad and Basra, are mainly of the Sunni sect, the remaining Arabs south of the Diyala, belong to the Shi'i sect. Leaders: Mr. ALWAIDH (Sunni), Prof. ABDUL QASSEM AL MOUSAWI AL KHOUI (Shi'i).

CHRISTIANITY

There are Christian communities in all the principal towns of Iraq, but their principal villages lie mostly in the Mosul district. The Christians of Iraq fall into three groups. (a) the free Churches, including the Nestorian, Gregorian, and Jacobite; (b) the churches known as Uniate, since they are in union with the Roman Catholic Church including the Armenian Uniates, Jacobite Uniates, and Chaldeans; (c) mixed bodies of Protestant converts, New Chaldeans, and Orthodox Armenians.

Catholic:

Latin Rite: Archbishop of Baghdad: P.O.B. 2090, Baghdad: Most Rev. ERNEST NYARY; approx. 2,000 adherents.

Armenian Rite: Archbishop of Baghdad: P.O.B. 2344, Baghdad: Most Rev. JEAN KASPARIAN.

Chaldean Rite: Patriarch of Babylon of the Chaldeans: His Beatitude PAUL II CHEIKHO, with 15 Arch-

bishops and Bishops in Iraq, Iran, Syria, Turkey and Lebanon. Approx. 475,000 adherents.

Syrian Rite: Archbishop of Mosul: Most Rev. CYRIL EMANUEL BENNI; Archbishop of Baghdad: Most Rev. ATHANASE J. D. BAKOSE; approx. 32,000 adherents.

Orthodox Syrian Community: 12,000 adherents.

Orthodox (*Gregorian*) **Community:** 12,000 adherents, mainly Armenians; Acting Bishop of Baghdad KRIKOR HAGOPIAN.

JUDAISM

The Jewish community numbered some 250,000 in 1939, but most Jews have left the country since the Second World War, particularly during the nineteen-fifties; unofficial estimates put the present size of the community at 2,500, almost all living in Baghdad.

OTHERS

About thirty thousand Yazidis and a smaller number of Turcomans, Sabeans, and Shebeks make up the rest of the population.

Sabean Community: 20,000 adherents; Head Sheikh DAKHIL, Nasiriyah; Mandeans, mostly in Nasiriyah.

Yazidis: 30,000 adherents; TASHIN BAIK, Asifni.

THE PRESS

DAILIES

Baghdad Observer: P.O.B. 257, Karantina, Baghdad; f. 1967; English; Editor-in-Chief FUAD YOUSIF QAZANCHI; circ. 7,000.

al Jumhuriya (*The Republic*): Karantina, Baghdad; f. 1963, re-founded 1967; Editor-in-Chief SA'AD QASSIM HAMMOUDI; circ. 25,000.

al Riyadhi (*Sportsman*): Baghdad; f. 1971; published by Ministry of Youth.

al Taakhi (*Brotherhood*): P.O.B. 5717, Baghdad; re-founded 1968; Kurdish paper; Editor-in-Chief AZIZ AQRAWI; circ. 25,000.

Tarik al Shaab (*People's Path*): Sadoun, Baghdad; f. 1973; organ of Iraqi Communist Party.

al Thawra (*Revolution*): Aqaba bin Nafi's Square, P.O.B. 2009, Baghdad; f. 1968; organ of Baath Party; Chief Editor TARIK AZIZ; circ. 70,000.

WEEKLIES

al-Fikr al-Jadid (*New Thought*): f. 1972; weekly; literary; Editor HUSAIN QASIM AL-AZIZ; circ. 30,000.

Alif Ba (*Alphabet*): Karantina, Baghdad; Editor-in-Chief AMIR MA'ALA.

al-Mutafarrij: Rashid St., Hayderkhana, P.O.B. 409, Baghdad; f. 1965; Editor MOUJIB HASSOON.

L'Opinion de Baghdad: Dar El-Jamaheer de Presse, P.O.B. 4074, Baghdad; f. 1970; bi-monthly, political, French; Editor-in-Chief ALI SMIDA; circ. 5,000.

Saut al Fallah (*Voice of the Peasant*) Baghdad; f. 1968; organ of General Federation of Peasant Societies; Editor-in-Chief LATIF AL-DILAIMI; circ. 15,000.

Waee Ul-Omal (*The Workers' Consciousness*): Headquarters of General Federation of Trade Unions in Iraq, Gialani St., Senak, P.O.B. 2307, Baghdad; Iraq Trades Union organ; Chief Editor MOHMMAD AYESH; circ. 25,000.

PERIODICALS

al Adib al-Muasser (*Contemporary Writer*): Baghdad; published by Iraqi Union of Writers.

al Aqlam (*The Pen*): Baghdad; literary; monthly; Ministry Information; f. 1964.

Commerce: Chamber of Commerce, Baghdad; f. 1938; quarterly; commercial and economic; circ. 2,500; also a weekly bulletin dealing in commodity prices and market conditions; circ. 3,000.

al-Funoon al-Ida'aiya: Iraqi Broadcasting, Television and Cinema Establishment, Salihiya, Baghdad; supervised by Broadcasting and TV Training Institute; engineering and technical; every two months.

al-Idaa'h Wal-Television: Iraqi Broadcasting, Television and Cinema Establishment, Salihiya, Baghdad; radio and television programmes and articles; weekly.

Iraq Academy Journal: Iraq Academy, Waziriyah, Baghdad; f. 1947; scientific and cultural, deals with Arabic and Islamic civilization.

Iraq Government Gazette, The: Ministry of Information, Baghdad; f. 1922; Arabic edition irregular, English edition weekly; legal and official; circ. Arabic 4,000, English 500.

Journal of the Faculty of Medicine, The: College of Medicine, University of Baghdad, Baghdad; f. 1941; quarterly; Arabic and English; medical and technical; published by the Faculty of Medicine, Baghdad; Edited by Prof. YOUSIF D. AL NAAMAN, M.D., D.SC.

Majallat-al-Majma al-'Ilmi al-Iraqi: Iraqi Academy, Waziriyah, Baghdad; f. 1947; quarterly; scholarly magazine on Arabic Islamic culture.

Majallat al-Thawra al-Ziraia (*Magazine of Iraq Agriculture*): Baghdad; quarterly; agricultural; published by the Ministry of Agriculture.

al-Masrah Wal-Cinema: Iraqi Broadcasting, Television and Cinema Establishment, Salihiya, Baghdad; artistic, theatrical and cinema; monthly.

al-Mu'allem al-Jadid: Ministry of Education, Baghdad; f. 1935; quarterly; educational, social, and general; owned and published by the Ministry of Education; Editor KHALIL AL-SAMARRAI.

al-Muthaqaf al-Arabi (*The Informed Arab*): Baghdad; f. 1964; literary monthly; Editor-in-Chief ARSHAD TAWFIQ; circ. 5,000.

Al Naft Wal Aalam (*Oil and the World*): publ. by Iraq National Oil Co., Baghdad; f. 1973; Editor-in-Chief MOHAMMED SA'ID AZIZ; monthly.

Sawt al-Talaba (*The Voice of Students*): Baghdad; f. 1968; organ of Nat. Union of Iraqi Students; bi-monthly; circ. 25,000.

al-Sinai (*The Industrialist*): P.O.B. 5665, Baghdad; publ. by Iraqi Federation of Industries; Arabic and English; quarterly.

Sumer: Directorate-General of Antiquities, Jamal Abdul Nasr Street, Baghdad; f. 1945; archaeological, historical journal; publ. by the Directorate-General of Antiquities; Chair. of Ed. Board Dr. ISA SALMAN (Dir.-Gen. of Antiquities); annual.

al-Thaquafa (*Culture*): Baghdad; f. 1970; Marxist; Editor-in-Chief SALAH KHALIS; monthly; circ. 2,000.

al-Thaquafa al-Jadida (*The New Culture*): Baghdad; f. 1969; pro-Communist; Editor-in-Chief SAFA AL-HAFIZ; monthly; circ. 3,000.

al-Turath al-Sha'abi (*Folklore Heritage*): Ministry of Information, Baghdad; specializes in Iraqi folklore; monthly.

NEWS AGENCIES

Iraqi News Agency: Abu Nawwas St., P.O.B. 3084, Baghdad; f. 1959; gathers and circulates news and photographs for use at home and abroad; independent in financial and administrative affairs; has contracts and agreements with various international commercial agencies and government news agencies; issues daily and weekly bulletins circulated to the radio and TV stations and to local newspapers, against subscription fees; Board of Directors includes Dir.-Gen. of Iraqi News Agency (Chair.), reps. from Ministries of Information, Foreign Affairs, Dir. of Military Intelligence, Dir.-Gen. of Broadcasting and TV, of P.T.T., representatives of Revolutionary Command Council, Chair. of Al-Jamahir Press House, two I.N.A. Directors and two workers' representatives; offices in Beirut, Cairo and Kuwait and correspondents in Algiers, Tunis, Khartoum, Tripoli, Sana'a, Aden, Abu Dhabi, Damascus, Rabat, Moscow, Cyprus, Madrid, Sri Lanka, New Delhi and New York; Dir.-Gen. TAHA YAEEN AL-BASRI.

FOREIGN BUREAUX

AFP (*France*): P.O.B. 5699, South Gate, Baghdad; Chief NAGIB FRANGIEH.

MENA (*Egypt*): Rasheed Str., al-Morabaa, Zaki Gamil Building, P.O.B. 2, Baghdad.

D.P.A. and Tass also have offices in Baghdad.

PUBLISHERS

al Ahliya: Mutanabi St., Baghdad.

Dar al Basri: Amin Square, Rashid Street, Baghdad.

Dar al Bayan: Mutanabi Street, Baghdad.

al Hurriyah Printing Establishment: Baghdad; f. 1970; largest printing and publishing establishment in Iraq; controls al Jumhuriyah (see below).

al Jumhuriyah Printing and Publishing Co.: Waziriya, Baghdad; f. 1963; the principal Iraqi publishers of newspapers and books.

al Ma'arif Ltd.: Mutanabi Street, Baghdad; f. 1929; publishes periodicals and books in Arabic, Kurdish, Turkish, French and English.

al-Muthanna: Mutanabi St., Baghdad; f. 1936; booksellers and publishers of books in various languages; also in Basrah; Man. MOHAMED K. M. AR-RAJAB.

al Nahdah: Mutanabi St., Baghdad; politics, Arab affairs.

Dar al Nathir: North Gate, Baghdad.

National House for Publications, Distribution and Advertisement: Wathba Square, Baghdad; f. 1972; attached to Ministry of Information; publishes and distributes books in Arabic and other languages; sole importer and distributor of newspapers, magazines and periodicals.

al-Thawra Printing and Publishing House: Baghdad; f. 1970.

RADIO AND TELEVISION

RADIO

Broadcasting Station of the Republic of Iraq: Iraqi Broadcasting and Television Establishment, Salihiya, Baghdad; home service broadcasts in Arabic, Kurdish, Syriac and Turkuman; foreign service in French, German, English, Russian, Persian, Swahili, Turkish and Urdu; there are 4 medium wave and 13 short wave transmitters; Dir.-Gen. LATEEF AL-DELAIMY.

Idaa'h Baghdad: f. 1936; 22 hours daily.

Idaa'h Sawt Al-Jamahir: f. 1970; 21 hours daily.

Number of radio receivers (1973): 2.7 million.

TELEVISION

Baghdad Television: Ministry of Information, Iraqi Broadcasting and Television Establishment, Salihiya, Karkh, Baghdad; f. 1956; government station operating 7 hours daily; Dir.-Gen. LATEEF AL-DELAIMY.

Kirkuk Television: f. 1967; government station; commercial; 6 hours daily.

Mosul Television: f. 1968; government station; commercial; 6 hours daily.

Basrah Television: f. 1968; government station; commercial; 6 hours daily.

Missan Television: f. 1974; government station; commercial; 6 hours daily.

Kurdish Television: f. 1974; government station; commercial; 6 hours daily.

Muthanna and Um Qasir stations are under construction.

Number of TV receivers (1973): 350,000.

FINANCE

All banks and insurance companies, including all foreign companies, were nationalized in July 1964. The assets of foreign companies were taken over by the state.

(cap. =capital; p.u. =paid up; dep. =deposits; res. =reserves; m. =million; amounts in Iraqi dinars.)

BANKING

CENTRAL BANK

Central Bank of Iraq: Banks St., Baghdad; f. 1947 as National Bank of Iraq; brs. in Mosul and Basra; has the sole right of note issue; cap. p.u. 25m., dep. 187.7m. (Dec. 1974); Gov. Dr. FAWZI AL-KAISSI; publs. *Quarterly Bulletin, Annual Report.*

COMMERCIAL BANKS

Rafidain Bank: New Banks St., P.O.B. 35, Baghdad; f 1941; Commercial Bank of Iraq was merged with Rafidain Bank, June 1974; 132 brs.; cap. p.u. 10m., res. 9m., dep. 412m. (Nov. 1974); Pres. and Chair. ADNAN AL-TAYYAR; publs. *Al-Masarf* (monthly), *Al-Masrafi* (weekly).

SPECIALIZED BANKS

Agricultural Bank of Iraq: Rashid St., Baghdad; 24 branches; cap. p.u. 6.4m.; Gen. Man. ABDUL RAZZAK AL-HILALI.

Estate Bank of Iraq: Hassan ibn Thabit St., Baghdad; f. 1949; 19 branches; gives loans to assist the building industry; cap. p.u. 34m.; acquired the Co-operative Bank in 1970; Dir.-Gen. LABEED AL-KARAGULLY.

Industrial Bank of Iraq: Industrial Bank Building, Bagdad; 5 branches; f. 1940; cap. p.u. 10m.; Gen. Man. KAMEL I. AL-AZZAWI; publ. *Annual Report.*

INSURANCE

Iraqi Life Insurance Co.: Shabander Bldg., New Banks' St., Baghdad; f. 1960; cap. p.u. 356,000; Chair. and Gen. Man. BADI AHMED AL-SAIFI.

Iraq Reinsurance Company: Reinsurance Building, Khullani Square, P.O.B. 297, Baghdad; f. 1961; to transact reinsurance business on the international market; Chair. and Gen. Man. Dr. MUSTAFA RAJAB; London Office: 5 Fenchurch St., E.C.3.

National Insurance Co.: Al-Aman Bldg., Al-Khulani St., P.O.B. 248, Baghdad; f. 1950; cap. p.u. 1m.; state monopoly for all direct non-life insurance; Chair. and Gen. Man. ABDULBAKI REDHA.

OIL AND GAS

Iraq National Oil Company (INOC): P.O.B. 476, Kullani Square, Baghdad; f. in 1964 to operate the oil industry at home and abroad; one of the main objectives of the July 1968 Revolution was to establish an oil industry capable of fostering the national economy, through direct development and exploitation of crude petroleum; it was decided that national oil development should start at Rumaila fields, Basra.

Iraq Company for Oil Operations (ICOO): Arrapha, Kirkuk; f. 1972; ICOO undertook responsibility for operation of nationalized Iraq Petroleum Co. in Iraq. The company's sphere of activities include drilling, production, processing and transportation of crude oil by pipelines to terminals at Banias in Syria and Tripoli in the Lebanon.

In March 1973, a comprehensive settlement was reached with the international oil companies embracing full compensation for the nationalized assets and surrender to the Government of Iraq of the Mosul Petroleum Co. concession. MPC fields are now maintained and operated by ICOO, which became responsible for the operation of the five producing fields, three near its centre of operations in Kirkuk (Kirkuk, Bai Hassan and Jambur), and two (Ain Zalah and Butmah) in Nineva Governorate; Chair. ABDUL SATTAR F. AL-RAWI.

Basrah Petroleum Company Ltd.: Office: 33 Cavendish Square, London, W1M 0AA; Chair. and Man. Dir. G. G. STOCKWELL; Exec. Dir. I. G. MACPHERSON.

The company operates in southern Iraq. Oil is produced from the Zubair and Rumaila fields and exported via a deep-water loading terminal at Khor-al-Amaya, 24 miles from Fao. Production in 1973 was approximately 35 million tons.

Entreprise des Recherches et d'Activités Petrolières (ERAP): signed a contract with INOC in 1968 under which it acts as contractor to INOC. This contract was amended in 1973 and development of the Abu Ghirab and Buzurgan fields is now underway. Production is expected to be on stream towards the end of 1975 at the initial rate of 10 m.t.y.; meanwhile ELF-ERAP is still conducting exploration work in the assigned areas.

Oil Products Distribution Administration: Baghdad; is responsible for distribution and marketing of all distillates, lubricating oils, greases, natural gas and liquid gas all over Iraq.

Government Oil Refinery Administration: Baghdad; operates refineries at Baghdad, Khanaqin, Kirkuk, Hadithah, Qayarah and Basrah with a total capacity of 180,000 BPSD and sulphur recovery plant at Kirkuk that utilizes associated gas of Kirkuk field to produce sulphur, natural gas and liquid gas. Two gas lines were laid between Kirkuk and Baghdad where gas is processed at Taji Plant (12,000 BPSD); total capital investment I.D. 80m.; annual turnover I.D. 50m. approx.

Iraq Petroleum Company Ltd.: Office: 33 Cavendish Square, London, W1M 0AA; Chair. and Man. Dir. G. G. STOCKWELL; Exec. Dir. I. G. MACPHERSON.

Until June 1972 the company produced and exported oil from northern Iraq. In June 1972 the Iraq Government took over the company's assets and operations in Iraq. A settlement between the company and the Government relating to this take-over was reached in February 1973.

TRADE AND INDUSTRY

CHAMBERS OF COMMERCE

Federation of Iraqi Chambers of Commerce: Mustansir St., Baghdad; f. 1969; all Iraqi Chambers of Commerce are affiliated to the Federation; Pres. ABDUL-WAHAB AL-KASAB; Sec.-Gen. KADHIM A. AL-MHAIDI; publs. *Iraq Trade Directory, Annual Trade Report, Monthly Economic News Bulletin, Wholesale Price Bulletin,* other trade and economic publications and brochures.

Amarah Chamber of Commerce: Al-Amarah; f. 1950; Pres. HAJ J. AL-AMMAR; Sec. R. AL-SAFFAR.

Arbil Chamber of Commerce: Arbil; f. 1966; Pres. SHEKHEEL HAJ HASSAN; Sec. MUHAMMAD DAZAH (ad interim).

Baghdad Chamber of Commerce: Mustansir St., Baghdad; f. 1926; 23,709 mems.; Pres. ABDUL WAHAB AL-KASAB; Sec. MOHAMMAD NAYEF AL-SHIBLI; Dir.-Gen. MUNIR SAID; publs. *Weekly Bulletin, Commerce* (quarterly magazine), *Trade Directory.*

Basra Chamber of Commerce: Basra; f. 1926; Pres. AMER AL-TIKRITI; Sec.-Gen. HARITH AL-MAKZOMY; publ. *al Tajir* (monthly).

Diwaniya Chamber of Commerce: Diwaniya; f. 1961; Pres. ABDULLAH AL-KHAFAJI; Sec. AMIN AL-ASADI.

Diyala Chamber of Commerce: Diyala; f. 1966; Pres. ADNAN AL-SARAH; Sec. ABDUL SATTAR HILMI.

Hillah Chamber of Commerce: Hillah; f. 1949; Pres. SAMI ALI AL-SULTAN; Sec. SHAHID AL-KHRIBAWI.

Karbala Chamber of Commerce: Karbala; f. 1952; Pres. MUDHIR SAAD QUANDI; Sec. RASHEED ABUDAGAH; Man. SAHIB H. HILME.

Kirkuk Chamber of Commerce: Kirkuk; f. 1957; Pres. HASSANI AL-HADITHI; Sec. SAMI BUNI.

Mosul Chamber of Commerce: Khalid ibn Al-Waleed, P.O.B. 35, Mosul; f. 1926; 7,526 mems.; Pres. ABDUL GHANI AL ANNAZ; Vice-Pres. MUMTAZ AL YAWER; Sec. ABDUL MAJEED AL NAFOUSSI; publ. *Bulletin.*

Najaf Chamber of Commerce: Najaf; f. 1950; Pres. MUHAMMAD ALI AL-BALAGHI; Sec. ABDUL MAHDI SHLAL.

Nasiriya Chamber of Commerce: Nasiriya; f. 1958; Pres. SHAIL ABID AL-YASIN; Sec. SATTR SALMON.

Sulaimaniya Chamber of Commerce: Sulaimaniya; f. 1967; Pres. SHAFIQ AHMED AL-CHALABI; Sec. AMIN MOLOOD.

EMPLOYERS' ORGANIZATION

Iraqi Federation of Industries: Iraqi Federation of Industries Bldg., Al-Khulani Square, Baghdad; f. 1956; 4,450 mems.; Pres. HATAM ABDUL RASHID; publs. *Al Sinai* (quarterly), Directory of Iraqi Industries and monthly reports.

INDUSTRIAL ORGANIZATIONS

General Establishment for Industry: Baghdad; state organization controlling most of Iraq's industry; organized into 5 departments covering (1) Clothing, Hides and Cigarettes, (2) Construction industries, (3) Weaving and Textiles, (4) Chemicals and Foodstuffs, (5) Engineering.

Iraqi Dates Organization: Baghdad; responsible for date exports; Acting Dir. JAWAD K. AL-HILIFI.

National Iraqi Minerals Co.: P.O.B. 2330, Alwiyah, Baghdad; f. 1969; 1,210 mems.; responsible for exploiting all minerals in Iraq except oil; Pres. Dr. SHAKIR AL-SAMARRAI.

TRADE UNIONS

General Federation of Trade Unions of Iraq: Abu Nawas St., Baghdad; f. 1964; 12 General Unions with a membership of 1,750,000 are affiliated to the General Federation and registered with the Ministry of Labour and Social Security Affairs; Pres. MOHAMMED AYESH; Sec.-Gen. BEDAN FADHIL; publ. *Wai al-Ummal.*

Union of Teachers: Baghdad; Pres. IBRAHIM MARZOUK.

Union of Palestinian Workers in Iraq: Baghdad; Sec.-Gen. SAMI AL SHAWISH.

There are also unions of doctors, pharmacologists, jurists, artists, and a General Federation of Iraqi Women.

CO-OPERATIVES

By the end of 1972 there were 1,167 co-operative societies. There were over 120 joint agricultural co-operatives and 60 local co-operatives outside the agrarian reform areas. The total number of peasants affiliated to the co-operatives is 175,000.

PEASANT SOCIETIES

General Federation of Peasant Societies: Baghdad; f. 1959; has 734 affiliated Peasant Societies.

TRADE FAIR

Baghdad International Fair: Damascus St., Al Mansoor, Baghdad; administered by Iraqi Fairs Administration; held annually in October; f. 1964; 52 countries participated in the 1974 Fair.

TRANSPORT

RAILWAYS

Iraqi Republic Railways: Baghdad Central Station Building, Baghdad; total length of track (1971): 2,528 km., consisting of 1,234 km. of standard gauge, 1,294 km. of one-metre gauge; Dir.-Gen. SUHAIL M. SALEH.

A metre-gauge line runs from Basra through Baghdad, Khanaqin and Kirkuk to Erbil. The standard gauge line covers the length of the country from Rabiyah on the Syrian border via Mosul, Baghdad and Basra to Um-Qasr. From here it is proposed to extend the track through Kuwait to Dhahran in Saudi Arabia, thus connecting Europe with the Persian Gulf. The standard gauge line between Baghdad and Basra is eventually intended to replace the metre gauge line between the two cities. Most trains are now hauled by diesel-electric locomotives. As well as the internal services there is also a regular express between Baghdad and Istanbul.

ROADS

The most important roads are: Baghdad–Mosul–Tel Kotchuk (Syrian border), 521 km.; Baghdad–Kirkuk–Arbil–Zakho (border with Turkey), 544 km.; Kirkuk–Sulaimaniya, 109 km.; Baghdad–Amara–Basra–Safwan (Kuwaiti border), 595 km.; Baghdad–Rutba–Syrian border (to Damascus), 555 km.; Baghdad–Babylon–Diwaniya, 181 km.

Under the 1970–75 Development Plan $91 million have been allocated to rebuilding and extending the present road system. The World Bank has made a $19 million loan towards the project. In 1972 a total of 9,240 km. of paved road had been completed and a further 1,368 km. were under construction.

Iraq Automobile and Touring Association: Al Mansoor, Baghdad; f. 1931; 4,200 mems.; Chair. AHMAD HUSAIN ALI; Sec.-Gen. HASHIM ABDULLA TAHA.

SHIPPING

Iraqi Ports Administration: Basra; Dir.-Gen. ABDUL JABBAR SAADI.

The Ports of Basra and Um Qasr are the commercial gateway of Iraq. They are connected by various ocean routes with all parts of the world, and constitute the natural distributing centre for overseas supplies. The Iraqi Maritime Company maintains a regular service between Basra, the Gulf and north European ports. Other shipping lines operate cargo and passenger services from Basra and Um Qasr to all parts of the world. There are fast mail and passenger services from Basra to Bombay via Khorramshahr, Bushire, and Karachi, connecting at Bombay with the Peninsula and Orient Mail Services to England, Australia, South Africa, and the Far East.

At Basra there is accommodation for 12 vessels at the Maqal Wharves and accommodation for 7 vessels at the buoys. There are 1 silo berth and 2 berths for oil products at Muftia and 1 berth for fertilizer products at Abu Flus. There is room for 3 vessels at Um Qasr.

In 1971–73 the revenue of the Iraqi Ports Administration was I.D. 14,973,697 against a general expenditure of I.D. 10,620,226 (including capital works). Expenditure on planning schemes was I.D. 2,528,475. In 1974 the port of Basra was visited by 1,237 ships; the total tonnage exported (excluding crude oil) was 641,685 and imported tonnage totalled 2,079,793. Um Qasr port handled 136 vessels, imports were 87,813 tons and exports 259,510.

There are deep-water tanker terminals at Fao and Khor Al-Amaya for 4 and 3 vessels respectively. In 1974 41,153,017 tons of crude oil was exported from Khor Al-Amaya.

For the inland waterways, which are now under the control of the Iraqi Ports Administration, there are 1,036 registered river craft, 48 motor vessels and 105 motor boats.

Iraqi Maritime Transport Co.: P.O.B. 3052, Baghdad; f. 1952; 6 cargo vessels; total g.r.t. 47,105.64 (1973); Dir.-Gen. (acting) EDGAR SARKIES.

CIVIL AVIATION

A new international airport, ten miles from Baghdad, was opened in January 1970. Another airport at Bamerni, in the province of Dhok was opened in August 1972. There is also an international airport at Basra. Internal flights connect Baghdad to Basra and Mosul.

Iraqi Airways: Al Kharkh, Baghdad; f. 1945; Dir.-Gen. ABDUL MUHSEN ABUE AL KHAIL; regular services from Baghdad to Amman, Bahrain, Basra, Beirut, Berlin, Cairo, Copenhagen, Damascus, Dhahran, Doha, Dubai, Frankfurt, Geneva, Istanbul, Karachi, Kuwait, London, Moscow, Mosul, New Delhi, Paris, Prague, Sofia, Teheran, Vienna, Warsaw; fleet: 3 Tridents, 3 Viscounts, 3 Boeing 707, 2 Boeing 737.

In 1974 the following airlines also operated services to Iraq: Aeroflot, Air France, Ariana Afghan, Balkan, British Airways, ČSA, Egyptair, Interflug, KLM, Kuwait Airways, LOT, Lufthansa, MEA, PIA, Saudia, Swissair, Syrian Arab.

TOURISM AND CULTURE

Ministry of Information, Tourism and Resorts Administration: Khulani Sq., Baghdad; f. 1956; Dir.-Gen. Dr. ALI GHALIB AL-ANI; publs. *Tourism in Iraq* (bimonthly), guide books, posters, tourist maps and pamphlets.

THEATRE GROUPS

OFFICIALLY SPONSORED

National Ensemble for Folk Arts: Baghdad; Folkore group providing dancing and singing concerts.

National Group for Acting: Iraqi Broadcasting, Television and Cinema Establishment, Salhiya, Baghdad; f. 1968; 56 actors of both sexes.

PRIVATE

Baghdad Theatre Group: Baghdad; f. 1967.

Contemporary Theatre Group: Baghdad; f. 1966.

Folklore Group: Baghdad; f. 1965.

Free Theatre Group: Baghdad; f. 1965.

14 July Theatre Group: Baghdad; f. 1966.

Theatre Arts Group: Baghdad; f. 1967.

United Artists' Group: Baghdad; f. 1967.

ATOMIC ENERGY

Atomic Energy Commission: Baghdad; f. 1956; Sec.-Gen. Dr. MOYASSAR YAHIA ALMALLAH; an atomic reactor (IRT-2000), built with Soviet aid at Tuwaitha, south of Baghdad, was inaugurated in 1968. The reactor provides isotopes for application in agriculture, medicine, industry and scientific research.

DEFENCE

Estimated defence expenditure 1974-75: 236 million dinars.

Military service: 2 years.

Total armed forces: 112,500; army 100,000; navy 2,000; air force 10,500. Reserves: 268,000. Paramilitary forces: 19,000.

EDUCATION

Since the establishment of the Republic in 1958 there has been a marked expansion in education at all levels. Spending on education has increased substantially since 1958, reaching I.D. 123.3 million in the 1974 budget. During 1974-75 two decisions were promulgated which constitute a landmark in the history of the Iraqi educational System. The first was a decision of the Revolutionary

Command Council announcing free education in all stages from pre-primary to higher. The second decision abolished private education and transferred all existing private schools into state schools. Pre-school education is expanding although as yet it reaches only a small proportion of children in this age group. Primary education, lasting six years, is now officially compulsory, and there are plans to extend full-time education to nine years as soon as possible. At present, secondary education, which is expanding rapidly, is available for six years. In 1970 French was officially adopted as the second language to be taught in schools.

Science, Medical and Engineering faculties of the universities have undergone considerable expansion, although technical training is less developed. Two branches of Baghdad University at Basra and Mosul became independent universities in 1967.

UNIVERSITIES

University of Baghdad: Baghdad; 1,509 teachers, 19,274 students.

Basra University: Basra; 126 teachers, 3,213 students.

al Mustansiriya University: Baghdad; 450 teachers, 9,716 students.

Mosul University: Mosul; 149 teachers, 3,275 students.

University of Sulaimaniya: Sulaimaniya; 74 teachers, 1,130 students.

BIBLIOGRAPHY

GENERAL

BELL, Lady FLORENCE (Ed.). The Letters of Gertrude Lowthian Bell (2 vols., London, 1927).

BURGOYNE, ELIZABETH (Ed.). Gertrude Bell, from her personal papers, 1914-26 (London, 1961).

HARRIS, GEORGE L. Iraq, Its People, Its Society, Its Culture (HRAF Press, New Haven, 1958).

LLOYD, SETON F. H. Iraq: Oxford Pamphlet (Bombay, 1943).
Twin Rivers: A Brief History of Iraq from the Earliest Times to the Present Day (Oxford, 1943).
Foundations in the Dust (Oxford, 1949).

LONGRIGG, S. H. and STOAKES, F. Iraq (Ernest Benn, London, 1958).

QUBAIN, FAHIM I. The Reconstruction of Iraq 1950-57 (Atlantic Books, London, 1959).

SALTER, Lord, assisted by PAYTON, S. W. The Development of Iraq: A Plan of Action (Baghdad, 1955).

STARK, FREYA. Baghdad Sketches (John Murray, London, 1937).

STEWART, DESMOND, and HAYLOCK, JOHN. New Babylon: a Portrait of Iraq London, (Collins, 1956).

VERNIER, B. L'Irak d'Aujourd'hui (Paris, 1962).

ANCIENT HISTORY

BRAIDWOOD, R. J. and HOWE, B. Prehistoric Investigation in Iraqi Kurdistan (Chicago, 1961).

CAMBRIDGE ANCIENT HISTORY (Vols. I and II, New Ed., Cambridge, 1962).

CHATERJI, S. Ancient History of Iraq (M. C. Sarkar, Ltd. Calcutta, 1961).

FIEY, J. M. L'Assyrie Chrétienne (Imprimerie Catholique, Beirut, 1965).

FRANKFORT, H. Archæology and the Sumerian Problem (Chicago, 1932).
The Birth of Civilization in the Near East (Anchor, New York, 1951).

LLOYD, SETON F. H. The Art of the Ancient Near East (London, 1961).
Ruined Cities of Iraq (Oxford, 1945).
Mesopotamia (London, 1936).
Mounds of the Near East (Edinburgh, 1964).

MALLOWAN, M. E. L. Early Mesopotamia and Iran (Thames and Hudson, London, 1965).

OATES, E. E. D. M. Studies in the Ancient History of Northern Iraq (British Academy, London, 1967).

OPPENHEIM, A. LEO. Ancient Mesopotamia (Chicago U.P., 1964).
Letters from Mesopotamia (Chicago U.P., 1967).

PARROT, A. Nineveh and Babylon (London, 1961).
Sumer (London, 1961).

PIGGOTT, S. (Ed.) The Dawn of Civilization (London, 1962).

ROUX, GEORGES. Ancient Iraq (London, 1964).

SAGGS, H. W. F. The Greatness that was Babylon (Sidgwick and Jackson, London, 1962).

STARK, FREYA. Rome on the Euphrates (John Murray, London, 1966).

WOOLLEY, Sir C. L. Abraham (London, 1936).
Mesopotamia and the Middle East (London, 1961).
The Sumerians (Oxford, 1928).
Ur of the Chaldees (London, 1950).
Ur Excavations. 8 vols. (Oxford, 1928-).

ISLAMIC PERIOD

CRESWELL, K. A. C. Early Muslim Architecture (3 vols., Oxford, 1932-50).

HITTI, P. K. A History of the Arabs (2nd ed., London, 1940).

LE STRANGE, GUY. The Lands of the Eastern Caliphate (Cambridge, 1905).

LOKKEGAARD, FREDE. Islamic Taxation in the Classical Period, with a Special Reference to Circumstances in Iraq (Copenhagen, 1950).

RECENT HISTORY

ADAMSON, DAVID. The Kurdish War (London, 1964).

AL-MARAYATI, ABID A. A Diplomatic History of Modern Iraq (Speller, New York, 1961).

DANN, URIEL. Iraq under Qassem: A Political History 1958-63 (Praeger, New York, 1969).

FOSTER, H. A. The Making of Modern Iraq (London, 1936).

GALLMAN, W. J. Iraq under General Nuri (Johns Hopkins Press, 1964).

HALDANE, Sir J. A. L. The Insurrection in Mesopotamia, 1920 (Edinburgh, 1922).

HASANI, ABDUL RAZZAQ. Ta'rikh al-'Iraq al-Siyasi al-Hadith (Political History of Modern Iraq) (Sidon, 1948).

KHADDURI, MAJID, Independent Iraq 1932-58, A Study in Iraqi Politics (2nd edition, Oxford University Press, 1960).
Republican Iraq: A study in Iraqi Politics since the Revolution of 1958 (Oxford University Press, 1970).

LONGRIGG, S. H. Four Centuries of Modern Iraq (Oxford, 1925).
Iraq 1900-1950: A Political, Social and Economic History (London, 1953).

MILLAR, RONALD. Kut: The Death of an Army (London, 1969).

MOBERLY, F. J. The Campaign in Mesopotamia, 1914-1918 (4 vols., London, 1923-27).

PAIFORCE: the official story of the Persia and Iraq Command, 1941-1946 (London, 1948).

WILSON, Sir A. T. Loyalties: Mesopotamia, 1914-17 (London, 1930).
Mesopotamia, 1917-20: a Clash of Loyalties (London, University Press, 1931).

ZAKI, SALIH. Origins of British Influence in Mesopotamia (New York, 1941).

ECONOMY

AINSRAWY, ABBAS. Finance and Economic Development in Iraq (Praeger, New York, 1966).

DLADEN, HORST. Eine sozio-ökonomische Betrachtung (Leske, Opladen, 1969).

JALAL, FERHANG. The Role of Government in the Industrialization of Iraq 1950–1965 (Frank Cass, London, 1972).

LANGLEY, KATHLEEN M. The Industrialisation of Iraq (Harvard University Press, 1961).

LONGRIGG, S. H. Oil in the Middle East (London, 1954).

MINORITIES

ARFA, HASSAN. The Kurds (Oxford University Press, Oxford, 1966).

BADGER, G. P. The Nestorians and their Rituals (2 vols., London, 1888).

BLUNT, A. T. N. Bedouin Tribes of the Euphrates (2 vols., London, 1879).

DAMLUJI, S. The Yezidis (Baghdad, 1948) (in Arabic).

DROWER, E. S. Peacock Angel (Being some account of Votaries of a Secret Cult and their Sanctuaries) (London, 1941).
The Mandeans of Iraq and Iran (Oxford, 1937).

EMPSON, R. H. W. The Cult of the Peacock Angel. (A Short Account of the Yezidi Tribes of Kurdistan) (London, 1928).

FIELD, H. Arabs of Central Iraq: Their History, Ethnology, and Physical Characters (Chicago, 1935).
The Anthropology of Iraq (4 vols., 1940, 1949, 1951, 1952, Chicago (first 2 vols.), Cambridge, Mass. (last 2 vols.).

KINNANE, DIRK. The Kurdish Problem (Oxford, 1964).
The Kurds and Kurdistan (Oxford, 1965).

LUKE, Sir H. C. Mosul and its Minorities (London, 1925).

O'BALLANCE, EDGAR. The Kurdish Revolt 1961–1970 (Faber and Faber, London, 1974).

SALIM, S. M. Marsh Dwellers of the Euphrates Delta (New York, 1961).

THESIGER, WILFRED. The Marsh Arabs (London, 1964).

Israel

PHYSICAL AND SOCIAL GEOGRAPHY

W. B. Fisher

The pre-1967 frontiers of Israel are defined by armistice agreements signed with neighbouring Arab states, and represent the stabilization of a military front as it existed in late 1948 and early 1949. These boundaries are thus in many respects fortuitous, and have little geographical basis. It may be pertinent to recall that prior to 1918 the whole area now partitioned between Syria, Israel and the kingdom of Jordan formed part of the Ottoman Empire, and was spoken of as "Syria". Then after 1918 came the establishment of the territories of the Lebanon, Syria, Palestine, and Transjordan—the frontier between the last two lying for the most part along the Jordan river.

The present State of Israel is bounded on the north by the Lebanon, on the north-east by Syria, on the east by the Hashemite Kingdom of Jordan, and on the south and south-west by the Gulf of Aqaba and the Sinai Desert, now an occupied territory. The so-called "Gaza strip", a small piece of territory some 25 miles long, formed part of Palestine, but was, under the Armistice Agreement of February 1949, then left in Egyptian control. The territories occupied after the war of June 1967 are not recognized as forming part of the State of Israel, although it seems unlikely that she will give up her annexation of the Old City of Jerusalem. The geographical descriptions of these territories are, therefore, given in the chapters on the countries which controlled them before June 1967*.

Because of the nature of the frontiers, which partition natural geographical units, it is more convenient to discuss the geography of Israel partly in association with that of its neighbour, Jordan. The Jordan Valley itself, which is divided territorially between the two states, is dealt with in the chapter on Jordan, but the uplands of Samaria-Judaea, from Jenin to Hebron, and including Jerusalem, which form a single unit, will be discussed below, though a large part of this territory lies outside the frontiers of Israel.

PHYSICAL FEATURES

The physical geography of Israel is surprisingly complex and though the area of the state is small, a considerable number of regions are easily distinguished. In the extreme north the hills of the Lebanon range continue without break, though of lower altitude, to form the uplands of Galilee, where the maximum height is just under 4,000 ft. The Galilee hills fall

away steeply on three sides: on the east to the well-defined Jordan Valley (see Jordan), on the west to a narrow coastal plain, and to the south at the Vale of Esdraelon or "Emek Yezreel". This latter is a rather irregular trough formed by subsidence along faults, with a flat floor and steep sides, and it runs inland from the Mediterranean south-eastwards to reach the Jordan Valley. At its western end the vale opens into the wide Bay of Acre, 15 to 20 miles in breadth, but it narrows inland to only a mile or two before opening out once again where it joins the Jordan Valley. This lowland area has a very fertile soil and an annual rainfall of 16 inches, which is sufficient, with limited irrigation, for agriculture. Formerly highly malarial and largely uncultivated, the vale is now very productive. For centuries it has been a corridor of major importance linking the Mediterranean coast and Egypt with the interior of south-west Asia, and has thus been a passage-way for ethnic, cultural, and military invasions.

South of Esdraelon there is an upland plateau extending for nearly 100 miles. This is a broad upfold of rock, consisting mainly of limestone and reaching 3,000 ft. in altitude. In the north, where there is a moderate rainfall, the plateau has been eroded into valleys, some of which are fertile, though less so than those of Esdraelon or Galilee. This district, centred on Jenin and Nablus, is the ancient country of Samaria, until 1967 part of Jordan. Further south rainfall is reduced and erosion is far less prominent; hence this second region, Judaea proper, stands out as a more strongly defined ridge, with far fewer streams and a barer open landscape of a more arid and dusty character. Jerusalem, Bethlehem and Hebron are the main towns. Towards the south-east rainfall becomes scanty and we reach the Wilderness of Judaea, an area of semi-desert. In the extreme south the plateau begins to fall in altitude, passing finally into a second plateau only 1,000 to 1,500 ft. above sea level, but broader, and broken by occasional ranges of hills that reach 3,000 ft. in height. This is the Negev, a territory comprising nearly half of the total area of Israel, and bounded on the east by the lower Jordan Valley and on the west by the Sinai Desert. Agriculture, entirely dependent on irrigation, is carried on in a few places in the north, but for the most part the Negev consists of steppe or semi-desert. Irrigation schemes are now being developed in those areas where soils are potentially productive.

Between the uplands of Samaria-Judaea and the Mediterranean Sea there occurs a low-lying coastal plain that stretches southwards from Haifa as far as the Egyptian frontier at Gaza. In the north the plain is closely hemmed in by the spur of Mount Carmel (1,800 ft.), which almost reaches the sea; but the plain soon opens out to form a fertile lowland—the

---

* For the state of the de facto boundaries after the disengagement agreements of 1974 with Egypt and Syria, see maps. p. 63.

Plain of Sharon. Further south still the plain becomes again broader, but with a more arid climate and a sandier soil—this is the ancient Philistia. Ultimately the plain becomes quite arid, with loose sand dunes, and it merges into the Sinai Desert.

One other area remains to be mentioned—the Shephelah, which is a shallow upland basin lying in the first foothills of the Judaean plateau, just east of the Plain of Sharon. This region, distinguished by a fertile soil and moister climate, is heavily cultivated, chiefly in cereals.

CLIMATE

Climatically Israel has the typical "Mediterranean" cycle of hot, dry summers, when the temperature reaches 90° to 100° F., and mild, rainy winters. Altitude has a considerable effect, in that though snow may fall on the hills, it is not frequent on the lowlands. Jerusalem can have several inches of snow in winter, and Upper Galilee several feet. The valleys, especially Esdraelon and adjacent parts of the upper Jordan, lying below sea-level, can become extremely hot (over 100°) and very humid.

Rainfall is very variable from one part of Israel to another. Parts of Galilee receive over 40 inches annually, but the amount decreases rapidly southwards, until in the Negev and Plain of Gaza, it is 10 inches or less. This is because the prevailing southwesterly winds blow off the sea to reach the north of Israel, but further south they come from Egypt, with only a short sea track, and are hence lacking in moisture.

RACE AND LANGUAGE

Discussion over the racial affinities of the Jewish people has continued over many years, but there has been no unanimity on the subject. One view is that the Jewish people, whatever their first origin, have now taken on many of the characteristics of the peoples among whom they have lived since the Dispersal—e.g., the Jews of Germany were often closely similar in anthropological character to the Germans; the Jews of Iraq resembled the Arabs; and the Jews of Abyssinia had a black skin. Upholders of such a view would largely deny the separateness of ethnic qualities amongst the Jews. On the other hand, it has been suggested that the Jews represent

an intermixture of Armenoid and other Middle-Eastern racial strains, with the former predominating—and evidence for this may be found in the head-form and facial appearance of many Jews, which are often strongly Armenoid. The correctness of either viewpoint is largely a matter of personal interpretation.

Under British mandatory rule there were three official languages in Palestine—Arabic, spoken by a majority of the inhabitants (all Arabs and a few Jews); Hebrew, the ancient language of the Jews; and English. This last was considered to be standard if doubt arose as to the meaning of translation from the other two.

Since the establishment of the State of Israel the relative importance of the languages has changed. Hebrew is now dominant, Arabic has greatly declined following the flight of Arab refugees, and English is also less important, though it remains the first foreign language of most Israelis.

Hebrew, once widely current in biblical days, underwent considerable eclipse after the dispersal of Jewish people by the Romans, and until fairly recently its use was largely restricted to scholarship, serious literature and religious observance. Most Jews of Eastern and Southern Europe did not employ Hebrew as their everyday speech, but spoke either Yiddish or Ladino, the former being a Jewish-German dialect current in East and Central Europe; the latter being a form of Spanish. Immigrants into Israel since 1890 have, however, been encouraged to use Hebrew as a normal everyday speech, and Hebrew is now the living tongue of most Israeli Jews. The revival has been a potent agent in the unification of the Israeli Jewish people because, in addition to the two widely different forms of speech, Yiddish and Ladino, most Jewish immigrants usually spoke yet another language according to their country of origin, and the census of 1931 recorded over sixty such languages in habitual use within Palestine.

It is only by a revival of Hebrew that the Jewish community has found a reasonable *modus vivendi*—yet this step was not easy, for some devout Jews opposed the use of Hebrew for secular speech. Furthermore, there was controversy as to the way Hebrew should be pronounced but the Sephardic pronunciation was finally adopted.

HISTORY

Tom Little

(with revisions for the 1975–76 edition by the Editor)

For most Jews the creation of the State of Israel in 1948 was the fulfilment of Biblical prophecy; to some in this more secular age it is a country justifiably won by political skill and force of arms in a world that denied them one for nearly 2,000 years; but, however regarded, it is seen as the fulfilment of Jewish history.

Although clearly a more ancient people from east of the Euphrates, the Jews trace their descent from Abraham, the first of the Patriarchs, who departed from Ur, the centre of the ancient Chaldean civilization, about 2,000 years B.C. Oral tradition as recorded in the Old Testament states that he was instructed by God to leave Chaldea with his family and proceed to Canaan (Phoenicia), or Palestine, the land of the Philistines, where he would father a great nation which would play an important part in human history. The authors of the Old Testament were primarily concerned to establish the descent of the Jewish people from Abraham under the guidance of God but in so doing they preserved the ancient history of the Jews which archaeology has tended to confirm within a debateable chronology.

Abraham's nomad family eventually reached Canaan and grazed their flocks there for a time before crossing Sinai to the richer pastures of Egypt. They remained in Egypt probably about 400 years and multiplied greatly, but their separateness in race, religion and customs at last excited the fears of the pharaohs, who enslaved them. Moses, who had escaped this slavery because he was brought up an Egyptian, fled with the Jews from the country (c. 1,200 B.C.) and gave them his law (the Torah) proclaiming the absolute oneness of God and establishing the disciplines of His worship.

They wandered for some decades in the wilderness before reaching the river Jordan. Moses' successor, Joshua, led some of the families (or tribes) across it and conquered Canaan. It was a stormy occupation of constant conflict with the indigenous peoples until the warrior Saul triumphed and became the first 'king'. His successor, David, completed the subjugation of the Israelites' enemies and briefly united all the tribes. King Solomon, his son, raised the country to its peak and built the Temple of Jerusalem which came to be recognized as the temple of all the Jews and the focal point of worship. His magnificence burdened the people, and this and his tolerance of the worship of idols provoked a successful revolt of the ten northern tribes under Jereboam who established Israel as his own kingdom. This division into two parts, Israel and Judah (which contained Jerusalem), was disastrous, for Israel was soon overcome by the Assyrians and its people were taken into captivity and lost to history. About 100 years later Judah fell

victim to the Babylonians and its people were also taken captive, but their community endured to become an important element in the future of Judaism. The Babylonians destroyed Solomon's temple.

When the Persian leader Cyrus conquered Babylon he gave the Jews permission to return to Jerusalem, and some did so. There they set about rebuilding the Temple which was completed about 500 B.C. and in 200 years of relative tranquility their religion was consolidated by a series of great teachers. Palestine was in turn conquered by Alexander the Great and it and the Jews became part of his empire; but Alexander was tolerant, as were his successors in Egypt, the Ptolemies, with the result that Alexandria became the centre of a learned school of Hellenic Judaism.

The results were tragic in the successor Roman empire. The Jews rebelled against the oppressive Roman rule and Nero sent his greatest general, Vespasian, and his son, Titus, to suppress them. The conquest was completed by Titus, Jerusalem and the second temple were destroyed (c. 70 A.D.), and the Diaspora which began with the Assyrian conquest of Israel was complete. A small community of Jews remained in Jerusalem and the surrounding countryside, and devoted themselves to their religion, producing their version of the Talmud, the repository of Judaic history, learning and interpretation which, with the Torah and the Old Testament, became the essence of the faith, but it was the version of the Talmud produced by the Babylonian scholars which became the accepted document.

Scattered across the world, throughout Arabia, Asia as far as China, North Africa and Europe as far as Poland and Russia, Jewish communities continued to exist, sometimes powerful, often persecuted, but held in their exclusiveness and survival by religion and certain central themes: their belief in the oneness of God, his promise to Abraham, the promise of the 'return', and the Temple as the temple of all Jews. In terms of time their occupation of Palestine was relatively short and for even less of that time did they hold or rule it all, but the scattered communities continued to look towards Jerusalem.

THE ZIONIST MOVEMENT

In the late nineteenth century there were affluent and even powerful groups of Jews in Europe but the people as a whole were usually treated as second-class citizens in the countries where they lived. The large, pious and orthodox groups in Eastern Europe, in particular, were subject intermittently to persecution, and in 1881 there was a series of pogroms in Russia which stirred the conscience of world Jewry into forming plans for their escape. For the eastern

Jews there could be only one destination: Palestine. The pogroms lead directly to the formation in Russia of a movement called the Lovers of Zion (*Hovevei Zion*), and within that movement another was formed, called the *Bilu*, by a large community of young Jews in the Kharkov region. In 1882 a *Bilu* group in Constantinople issued a manifesto demanding a home in Palestine. They proposed that they should beg it from the Sultan of Turkey, in whose empire Palestine lay, and that if he would not give them absolute possession he should at least let them have an autonomous 'State within a larger State.'

The word Zionism was coined by a Russian about a decade later as a spiritual-humanitarian concept but Theodor Herzl, who became the leader of the movement, defined its aim specifically at the Basle Congress of 1897 (*see* Documents on Palestine, p. 48): 'Zionism', he said, 'strives to create for the Jewish people a home in Palestine secured by public law'. He wrote in his journal after the congress: 'At Basle I founded the Jewish State . . . perhaps in five years, and certainly fifty, everyone will know it'. He is recognized as the founder of political Zionism.

He was concerned essentially with the creation of a safe refuge for the suffering communities of Eastern Europe and thought that their migration and settlement could and should be financed by prosperous Jews. When he failed to get help from the Sultan he considered other possible 'homes' as far apart as Uganda and Latin America, but even safe places could never have the appeal to orthodox Jews as had Palestine, sanctioned in their scriptures and 'promised' to them by God. Some of the Jews of Russia and Poland escaped persecution to make their own way to Palestine and became the earliest immigrant communities there.

When the Turkish empire was destroyed by Allied forces in the 1914–18 war new possibilities of getting their 'home' or State in Palestine opened up before the Zionists. In the years 1915–16 Sir Mark Sykes for Britain and M. Charles Georges-Picot for France had, in fact, drafted an agreement (*see* Documents on Palestine, p. 48) in which, while undertaking 'to recognize and protect an independent Arab State or Confederation of Arab States', the two powers in effect carved the Middle East into their respective spheres of influence and authority pending the time of its liberation from Turkey. Influential Zionists, notably Dr. Chaim Weizmann, saw their opportunity to press Britain for a commitment to provide a home for the Jews in Palestine and secured the help of Judge Louis Brandeis, a leading United States Zionist and principal adviser to President Woodrow Wilson, in bringing the U.S. into the war on the side of the Allies in April 1917. The outcome was the Balfour Declaration (*see* Documents on Palestine, p. 49) which was contained in a letter from Arthur James Balfour to Lord Rothschild on behalf of the Zionist Federation, dated November 2nd, 1917. It stated:

"His Majesty's Government view with favour the establishment in Palestine of a national home for the Jewish people, and will use their best endeavours

to facilitate the achievement of this object, it being clearly understood that nothing shall be done which may prejudice the existing civil and religious rights of existing non-Jewish communities in Palestine, or the rights and political status of Jews in other countries".

The San Remo Conference decided on April 24th, 1920 to give the Mandate under the newly formed League of Nations to Britain (the terms of which were approved by the United States, which was not a member of the League) before they were finally agreed by the League Council on July 24th, 1922. The terms (*see* Documents on Palestine, p. 52) included a restatement of the Balfour Declaration and provided that "an appropriate Jewish agency" should be established to advise and cooperate with the Palestine Administration in matters affecting the Jewish national home and to take part in the development of the country. This gave the Zionist Organization a special position because the Mandate stipulated that it should be recognized as such an agency if the mandatory authority thought it appropriate. Britain took over the Mandate in September 1923.

THE MANDATE

Herzl's first aim had thereby been achieved: the national home of the Jewish people had been "secured by public law"; but major obstacles were still to be overcome before the home, or State, became a reality. When the Mandate was granted, the Arabs constituted 92 per cent of the population and owned 98 per cent of the land in Palestine, and it could clearly not be a home unless the demography and land ownership were changed in favour of the Jews. It was to these ends that the Zionist movement now directed itself, but Britain and it had different views concerning what was meant by "favouring" the establishment of the home, both in the matter of boundaries and immigration, even though Britain was consistently sympathetic to the enterprise. This was important, for although she was nominally under the supervision of the Mandates Commission of the League, she was able to run Palestine very much as a Crown Colony and administered it through the Colonial Office.

The World Zionist Organization had presented a memorandum to the Paris Peace Conference in 1919 setting forth its territorial concept of the home, as follows:

The whole of Palestine, southern Lebanon, including the towns of Tyre and Sidon, the headwaters of the Jordan river on Mount Hermon and the southern portion of the Litani river; the Golan Heights in Syria, including the town of Quneitra, the Yarmuk river and Al-Himmeh hot springs; the whole of the Jordan valley, the Dead Sea, and the eastern highlands up to the outskirts of Amman, thence in a southerly direction along the Hedjaz railway to the Gulf of Aqaba; in Egypt, from El-Arish, on the Mediterranean coast, in a straight line in a southerly direction to Sharm as-Sheikh on the Gulf of Aqaba.

The League of Nations and the Peace settlement did not accept these boundaries but the mandate given to Britain included Transjordan, the territory East of the river and beyond Amman. Britain allotted Transjordan as an Emirate to Emir Abdullah in 1921 and with the grant of full independence in 1946 it became a kingdom.

The Arabs bitterly opposed the Balfour Declaration and Jewish immigration and called for the prohibition of land sales to Jews. Britain would neither accede to their demands nor to Jewish claims to a majority in Palestine. There were intermittent outbreaks of Arab violence, notably in 1922 and 1929, which brought the Arabs into conflict with the mandatory government and there were four British Commissions of Inquiry and two White Papers were issued (*see* Documents on Palestine, p. 53) on the situation before 1936, none of which envisaged a Jewish majority. In 1936 there was an effective six-months general strike of the Arab population followed by a large scale rebellion which lasted until the outbreak of the Second World War and in 1939 another Commission issued the third White Paper (*see* Documents on Palestine, p. 55) which stated that Britain would not continue to develop the Jewish national home beyond the point already reached, proposed that 75,000 more Jews should be admitted over five years and then Jewish immigration would cease. Finally, it proposed that self-governing institutions should be set-up at the end of the five years. This would have preserved the Arab majority in the country and its legislature.

THE BILTMORE PROGRAMME AND AFTER

The world emotional context at that time was conditioned by the horrifying Nazi policy of exterminating Jews—a policy which was to reach even more frightful proportions after the outbreak of war. Zionists and Jews generally regarded the White Paper as a betrayal of the terms of the Mandate and when Mr. Ben Gurion, Chairman of the Jewish Agency Executive, was in New York in 1942 an Extraordinary Zionist Conference held at the Biltmore Hotel utterly rejected the White Paper and reformulated Zionist policy. The declaration of the conference (*see* Documents on Palestine, p. 56) issued on May 11th, 1942 concluded as follows:

> The conference urges that the gates of Palestine be opened; that the Jewish Agency be vested with control of immigration into Palestine and with the necessary authority for upbuilding the country, including the development of its unoccupied and uncultivated lands; and that Palestine be established as a Jewish Commonwealth integrated into the new structure of the democratic world.

This policy brought the Jews into head-on collision with the Palestine Government before the war was over. Those in Europe who escaped the Nazi holocaust were herded into refugee camps and some who could do so with organized Zionist help tried to reach Palestine, but the British authorities, in accordance with the 1939 policy, tried to prevent their entry.

The British failed. The Jewish population which had been 56,000 at the time of the Mandate was 608,000 in 1946 and was estimated to be 650,000 on the eve of the creation of Israel, or about two-fifths of the entire population. Further, the Jewish Agency had formed its own military organizations, the Haganah and its units of shock troops, the Palmach, which were strengthened by those Jews who had fought on the side of the British during the war, and supported by two smaller extremist groups, the Irgun Zvaei Leumi and the Stern Gang. Towards the end of the war they embarked on a policy of violence designed to impose the Biltmore programme. They successfully made the Mandate unworkable and Britain referred it to the United Nations (which had replaced the League) on April 2nd, 1947.

The UN General Assembly sent a Special Commission (UNSCOP) to Palestine to report on the situation and its report issued on August 31st, 1947 proposed two plans: a majority plan for the partition of Palestine into two States, one Jewish and one Arab, with economic union; and a minority plan for a federal State. The Assembly adopted the majority plan (*see* Documents on Palestine, p. 57) on November 29th by 33 votes for and 13 against, with ten abstentions. The plan divided Palestine into six principal parts, three of which, comprising 56 per cent of the total area were reserved for the Jewish State and three, with the enclave of Jaffa, comprising 43 per cent of the area, for the Arab State. It provided that Jerusalem would be an international zone administered by the UN as the holy city for Jews, Moslems and Christians. The Arabs refused to accept this decision and in the subsequent disorders about 1,700 people were killed. In April 1948 the Jewish forces swung into full-scale attack and by the time the Mandate was terminated on May 14th, 400,000 Arabs had evacuated their homes to become refugees in neighbouring Arab countries.

THE STATE ESTABLISHED

The Mandate was relinquished by Britain at 6 p.m. Washington time; at 6.01 the State of Israel was officially declared by the Jewish authorities in Palestine; at 6.11 the United States accorded it recognition and immediately afterwards Russia did likewise. Thus Israel came into existence only one year late on Herzl's 50-year diary prophecy. The Arab States belatedly came to the help of the Palestinian Arabs but their attempt to overthrow it failed and Israel was left in possession of more territory than had been allotted to her under the UN partition plan. It included new (non-Arab) Jerusalem and she rejected the proposed internationalization of the city, for the Jews considered the return to Jerusalem to be at the heart of the divine promise to them.

A provisional government was formed in Tel-Aviv the day before the Mandate ended with Ben Gurion as Prime Minister and other members of the Jewish Agency Executive in leading ministerial posts. The constitution and electoral laws had already been prepared and the first general elections were held in January 1949 for a single-chamber Knesset (or parliament) elected by proportional representation. This enabled several parties to gain representation with Mapai usually in the majority but never predominant. The result has been that government was conducted afterwards by uneasy coalitions—except when military confrontation with the Arabs was involved.

After the war another 400,000 Arabs fled from the additional territory conquered by Israel and in the course of another year about 300,000 more left the impoverished Arab West Bank for Transjordan. (In 1950 King Abdullah held a referendum in which the West Bank Arabs agreed to be part of his kingdom which then became known as Jordan.) The Israeli Government maintained the mandatory military control, established in the earlier disorders, over those Arab populations which remained within its territory but allowed "co-operative" Arabs to be elected to the Knesset; four were elected to the first parliament.

A gigantic programme of immigration was launched immediately the Provisional Government took over and within three years the Jewish population was doubled. This result, unparalleled in history, was assisted by Iraq which expelled the larger part of its age-old Jewish communities. The 1961 census gave Israel's population as 2,260,700, of whom 230,000 were Arabs. The two-millionth Jew arrived in May 1962 and the three-millionth early in 1972. A massive plan for land development to provide for the new people was executed concomitantly with the early immigration programme; the Jewish National Fund took over 3,000,000 dunums of former Arab land and used heavy mechanical equipment to bring it rapidly back into production. This was made possible by the stupendous support from abroad which came in the form of private gifts from world Jewry, State loans and aid, and private Jewish investments. The United States was both privately and publicly the major contributor but by agreement at the Hague in 1952, West Germany agreed to pay reparations for Nazi crimes which amounted to £216 million in Deutsche Marks before payments were concluded in 1966. The effect of this influx of unearned money from all sources was to cause serious inflation which in 1962 forced devaluation of the Israel £ to one-fifth of its original value and was still a grave problem in 1975 (see Economic Survey).

Israel was admitted to the United Nations, albeit on conditions concerning Jerusalem and refugees which were contrary to her overall policy and were never fulfilled. Her relations with the Arab States were governed by a series of armistice agreements reached in Rhodes in 1949 which, in effect, established an unsteady truce without an Arab commitment to permanent peace. The Arabs continued to insist that the creation of Israel was a usurpation of Arab territory and right and a denial of UN principles. Defence policy therefore dominated Israel's political thinking and firmly established the principle that she would remain militarily superior to any combination of Arab States. In the early 1950s, however, it was the Palestinian refugees who caused intermittent frontier trouble, mainly from Syria and Jordan but

to some extent from the Gaza strip which, since the 1948 war, had been administered by Egypt.

Whenever one of the frontiers became too troublesome, Israel mounted a retaliatory raid *pour décourager les autres*. Acting on the principle that Nasser's Egypt was the only serious danger, Mr. Ben Gurion ordered a raid which on February 28th, 1955, wiped-out the small Egyptian garrison at Gaza and the reinforcements travelling by road to its support. The result was contrary to Ben Gurion's intention; Nasser determined to secure adequate military strength and to that end entered into the"Czech" arms agreement in August 1955 by which he bartered cotton and took credits from Russia for substantial quantities of arms and planes which began to arrive quickly. The threat to Israel was therefore increased.

SUEZ

On July 26th, 1956, Nasser nationalized the Suez Canal company of which Britain and France were the principal shareholders (*see* Egypt) and the two European powers prepared to retake control of it. Neither could expect any support from the two super-powers, or from world opinion in general, for open invasion, but in October Ben Gurion entered into a secret pact with them by which Israel would invade Sinai and thus justify Britain and France intervening to keep the combatants apart. The Israelis invaded on October 29th, with powerful armoured columns and rapidly advanced towards the canal and 24 hours later Britain and France issued their ultimatum that both sides should withdraw to 20 miles from the canal. Israel had by this time taken almost all of the Sinai, including the Gaza strip and Sharm as-Sheikh at the entrance to the Gulf of Aqaba, and she readily agreed to do so, but Egypt refused on the grounds that she was being asked to withdraw from her own territory.

The Anglo-French force thereupon invaded the Port Said area and advanced some miles along the Suez Canal. There it was halted by Sir Anthony Eden, the British Prime Minister, in face of the forthright condemnation of the UN and financial sanctions threatened by the U.S.; a decision which the French Prime Minister, M. Guy Mollet, reluctantly accepted. Both countries withdrew their troops before the year was out. This was a severe blow to Mr. Ben Gurion who had counted on holding at least a security buffer zone on a line from El Arish, on the Mediterranean coast, to Sharm as-Sheikh (the Zionist 1919 frontier proposal). Therefore Israel delayed her final withdrawal from Egypt until January, and from the Gaza strip until March 1957 when a UN Emergency Force proposed by Canada and accepted by Egypt, was completely established on the Sinai frontier and at Sharm as-Sheikh. Even so, Egypt kept detaining ships in the Suez Canal and confiscating cargoes bound for Israel, against which Mrs. Golda Meir, then Foreign Minister, strongly protested to the United Nations in September 1959.

A development of great consequence to Israel at this time was Russia's more active policy in the

Middle East, founded on relations with Egypt which had begun with bulk purchases of cotton and the arms deal in 1955. The U.S.S.R. took no less than 50 per cent of Egyptian exports in 1957 and in 1958 agreed to finance the foreign currency requirements of the mammoth High Dam at Aswan and to direct the building of it. In keeping with this policy Russia adopted a strongly pro-Arab and anti-Israeli line and steadily rearmed Nasser's forces.

Mr. Ben Gurion resigned "for personal reasons" in June 1963 and was succeeded by Mr. Levi Eshkol, his Finance Minister and continuously a minister since he joined the provisional government from the Jewish Agency in 1948. He was in modern terminology a "dove", inclined to a more conciliatory policy which he hoped would in time erode Arab enmity. This was opposed by many in the ruling hierarchy, notably the veteran Ben Gurion and Moshe Dayan, who had commanded the Israeli forces in their brilliant victory in 1956 and was now in the cabinet. Ben Gurion emerged from retirement to become Minister of Defence early in 1967 intent to counter Egypt's President Nasser, whom he considered the serious menace to Israel's security. There had also been a notable increase in Arab guerrilla activity across the frontiers of Egypt, Jordan and Syria and the Palestinians had formed a guerrilla organization called Al-Fatah for which the Syrian premier had publicly declared his support in 1966.

Israel countered with occasional massive "strikes", notably one against the Jordanian village of Samu in November 1966. The Syrian frontier became more active in January and the situation became serious enough for the UN Secretary-General, U Thant, to seek—unsuccessfully—to reconvene the lapsed Syrian-Israeli Mixed Armistice Commission. The border clashes took on even graver proportions in April, with aircraft engaged on both sides, and in May Israel warned that it would invade Syria to overthrow its Baathist Government if guerrilla raids did not cease.

President Nasser warned that he would have to activate the Egypt-Syrian Joint Defence Agreement if Israel's "aggression" did not cease. In May, King Hussein brought Jordan into the agreement and in that same month Nasser received information, which proved later to be untrue, that Israeli troops were massing on the Syrian frontier. In response Nasser ordered the withdrawal of the United Nations Emergency Force from the Gaza strip, the Sinai Desert and Sharm as-Sheikh. U Thant immediately obeyed, and Nasser then imposed a total blockade on Israeli shipping in the Straits of Tiran, although Israel had always made it plain that this would be considered a *casus belli*.

U Thant flew to Cairo on May 22nd, but by that time Nasser had already strengthened his forces in the Sinai and called up his reserves. Israel, Jordan and Syria had also mobilized. Israel formed a national government by bringing to the cabinet one representative of each of the three opposition parties. General Moshe Dayan, the victor of the 1956 Sinai campaign, was brought in as Defence Minister.

THE JUNE WAR

Israel made its pre-emptive strike in the early hours of June 5th when her armoured forces moved into Sinai. At 0600 hours GMT Israeli planes attacked 25 airfields in Egypt, Jordan, Syria and Iraq, destroying large numbers of planes on the ground and putting the runways out of action, thus effectively depriving the Egyptian and Jordanian ground forces of air cover. There were some fierce armoured battles in the Sinai but Israeli forces were in position along the Suez Canal on June 8th. They took Sharm as-Sheikh without a fight. On the eastern front, they reached the Jordan river on June 7th and entered and conquered Old (Arab) Jerusalem on the same day. Their main forces destroyed, President Nasser and King Hussein accepted a cease-fire on the 8th. Israel then turned its attention to the Syrian fortifications on the Golan Heights from which Israeli settlements were being shelled. In a brilliant but costly action, armour and infantry captured the heights. Syria accepted a cease-fire on the 9th but Israel ignored it until the 10th, by which time her troops were in possession of Quneitra, on the road to Damascus. The "six-day war", as it became known, was over; Israel had achieved a victory more sweeping even than that of 1956.

Israel had recovered Jerusalem and access to the Western Wall of the Temples of Solomon and Herod, which were the most sacred places of worship for all Jews but to which they had been denied access since the division of the city between the Arabs and Israel in 1948. Israel immediately tore down the barriers, reunited the city, put the administration of Arab Jerusalem under her existing city administration, and effectively annexed it. The UN General Assembly passed a resolution on July 4th, which Israel disregarded, calling on her to rescind all the measures taken and to desist from any further action that would change the status of the holy city. Israel made it plain from the beginning that there could be no question of returning Old Jerusalem to Arab possession in any peace settlement.

The United Nations and the world powers busied themselves with the search for peace. On August 29th the heads of the Arab States began a Summit conference in Khartoum at which they decided to seek a political settlement but not to make peace with or recognize Israel or to negotiate directly with her and meanwhile "to adopt necessary measures to strengthen military preparation to face all eventualities". The UN Security Council agreed to Resolution 242 after many attempts on November 22nd which stated that the establishment of a just and lasting peace in the Middle East should include the application of the following principles:

(i) withdrawal of Israeli armed forces from territories occupied in the recent conflict; and (ii) termination of all claims or states of belligerency and respect for and acknowledgement of the sovereignty, territorial integrity, and political independence of every State in the area, and their right to live in peace within secure and recognized boundaries free from threats or acts of force. The

Council affirmed also the necessity for (*a*) guaranteeing freedom of navigation through international waterways in the area, and (*b*) achieving a just settlement of the refugee problem.

The Secretary-General designated Ambassador Gunnar Jarring of Sweden as Special Representative to assist the process of finding a peaceful settlement on this basis.

The essential ambiguity of the Council resolution was contained in the phrase "withdrawal . . . from territories occupied . . ." (which in the French translation became "les territoires"), and the Israeli Government has contended ever since that it meant an agreed withdrawal from some occupied territories "to secure and recognized boundaries". This was, in Israel's view, precluded by the Arab States' Khartoum resolution and their insistence that Resolution 242 meant total withdrawal from the 1967 occupied territories. Further, Israel insisted that she would only negotiate withdrawal directly with Egypt and the Arab States as part of a peace settlement and that the function of Jarring was to bring this about and not to initiate proposals of his own for a settlement.

UNEASY SECURITY

Meanwhile Israel based her policy on retention of the occupied territories as warranty of her security. The 1967 defeat had severely damaged Russia's prestige in the Arab world and to repair her position she began immediately to restore the Egyptian armed forces, including the air force. Meanwhile President de Gaulle imposed in 1967 an arms embargo on Israel and refused to deliver 50 supersonic Mirage IV fighters which Israel had ordered and paid for. Israel therefore turned to the United States, arguing that the balance of military power must, for her security, be maintained in her favour. This point was conceded by the U.S. in 1968 with a contract to deliver 50 Phantom jet fighter-bombers, which brought Cairo within range and were more powerful than any MiGs in Egypt.

Russia established powerful artillery West of the canal with which Nasser began in 1968 a "war of attrition" in order to force Israel to accept his terms. Relatively heavy casualties were caused to the Israeli troops, notably in July and October, and throughout the period Israel retaliated punitively with air and artillery attacks which forced Egypt to evacuate the canal zone towns. Suez and its oil refineries were destroyed. The zone remained disturbed until 1970, reaching a climax in February when 80 civilians were killed in an Israeli bombing raid on Soviet SAM-II missile installations.

Israel's Prime Minister, Levi Eshkol, died on February 26th, 1969, and was succeeded in the following month by Mrs. Golda Meir, who had been Minister for Foreign Affairs from 1956 to 1966.

President Nixon, who had taken office in the United States, supported an initiative by his Secretary of State, William Rogers, "to encourage the parties to stop shooting and start talking". This was announced on June 25, 1970, and was unfavourably received in the Arab world. Nasser flew to Moscow with a proposal to accept it on condition that Russia supplied SAM-III missiles capable of destroying low-flying aircraft. He returned to Cairo and stunned Egypt and the Arab world with an unconditional acceptance of the Rogers plan and its related canal zone 90 day ceasefire. King Hussein immediately associated Jordan with Nasser's acceptance. Israel accepted the Rogers plan on August 7th but immediately complained that Egypt had broken the ceasefire agreement by moving SAM-III missile sites into the 30-mile wide standstill area along the canal.

President Nasser died suddenly on September 28th, 1970, but President Sadat, who succeeded him, sustained his policy. Although he only agreed to extend the ceasefire for another 90 days, it continued indefinitely. The American effort was directed towards securing an interim agreement by which Israel would withdraw from the Suez Canal and allow it to be reopened but Israel, again on the basic principle of her security, would only consider a limited withdrawal and would not agree that Egyptian troops should cross the canal, terms which Egypt would not accept. U.S.-Israeli relations, vital to Israel, were uneasy during most of 1971 while the State Department pressed the Tel-Aviv Government to concede unacceptable terms of withdrawal from the canal. President Sadat gave the end of the year as a deadline for "peace or war", but before the year was out Mrs. Golda Meir secured a commitment to Israeli security from President Nixon firmer than any obtained in the past; the Rogers plan thereupon died but 1972 dawned without the threatened outbreak of war from Egypt.

An upsurge of Palestinian guerrilla activity disturbed Israel after the 1967 war. People in frontier villages and settlements were forced to sleep in underground shelters. Although security was more than adequate to secure the State, it could not prevent isolated raids and terrorist acts which reached their peak in 1969, but in the end the problem was largely solved by the disunity within the Palestinian movement itself. Two left-wing guerrilla groups, the Popular Front for the Liberation of Palestine (PFLP) and its offshoot, the Popular Democratic Front (PDFLP) embarked on a series of terrorist acts against Israeli planes and passengers at European airports and challenged the authority of King Hussein within Jordan. The King proceeded to drive the guerrillas out of his country, an operation which was not finally concluded until July of the following year (*see* Jordan). Israel's troubles along the Jordan frontier thereupon ceased. There were intermittent raids from Syria and Lebanon but Israel was able to control these disturbances by retaliatory attacks and the dangers within the country greatly declined. In May 1972 the PFLP returned to the airport terrorist acts, and a three-man Japanese "Red Army" suicide squad sent by the PFLP landed at Lod in an Air France plane and indiscriminately shot to death 28 people in the airport and wounded 80 before two of them were killed and the third captured. A new Palestinian terrorist group calling itself Black September (*see* Jordan) seized the

Israeli team at the Munich Olympics on September 5th; eleven of the team and four terrorists were killed in a battle with West German police who captured the remaining three terrorists. There were a number of letter-bomb attacks on Israelis in Europe in the last quarter of the year but it soon became evident that Israeli security services were retaliating when fourteen PLO members were killed or wounded by similar attacks in the space of a few weeks. It developed into a silent war between the Palestinian terrorists and a terrorist wing of the Israeli secret service, and by mid-1973 five Arabs and five Israeli agents had been murdered in European capitals and Cyprus.

Punitive raids were made on the Syrian Golan Heights in January 1973 and on February 21st an Israeli Phantom shot down a Libyan airliner which had strayed over Sinai, causing 108 deaths, including some French crew members. This caused a world outcry which was muted ten days later when eight Palestinians seized the Saudi Arabian Embassy in Khartoum and held the retiring U.S. Ambassador and his successor, the Belgian Chargé d'Affaires, the Saudi Ambassador and the Jordanian Chargé d'Affaires as hostages for the release of Palestinians in several countries. They killed the American and European diplomats before surrendering to the Sudanese authorities.

The stated objective of Israeli punitive raids on Syria and Lebanon was to compel both countries to prevent the Palestinian resistance groups from mounting raids from within their borders, whether against Israel or in other countries. This objective seemed most successfully achieved in Lebanon on April 10th by a daring commando raid into the heart of Beirut, where the raiders killed three resistance leaders, while other commando units attacked two refugee camps outside the city and destroyed the PDFLP headquarters, killing one of its leaders. The Israeli authorities were able to make a number of arrests in the occupied territories from information gained in this raid. It caused a political crisis in Lebanon and led to open conflict between Palestinian groups and the Lebanese Army, which only came to an end when the Palestinian leaders agreed to revise the Cairo agreement of 1970, by which they had had virtual autonomy within the refugee camps.

THE OCCUPIED TERRITORIES

About 380,000 Arabs fled from the West Bank to Jordan, but nearly a million remained under Israeli occupation; of these, the 70,000 in East (Arab) Jerusalem, which was annexed, were treated as Israeli citizens and the remainder brought under military administration. This was of necessity strict for the first three years because of help given to Palestinian guerrillas by the Arabs in the occupied territories and, in some instances, in Israel proper. The Gaza strip was by far the most troublesome and it was not until the end of 1971 that Israeli security operations, including the clearance of one large refugee camp which had proved particularly difficult, brought the area under control. It was announced in March 1973 that the strip would be incorporated into Israel, that Jewish settlement in the strip would continue and that Arab inhabitants could circulate freely in Israel during the day. Higher living standards enjoyed by the Arabs under the occupation, 60,000 of whom found work in Israel itself, the inevitable growth of collaboration with the Israeli authorities and, finally, the disarray in which the Palestinian movement found itself by late 1970 rendered the security problem inside the country minimal during 1971. In March of the following year the Israeli military authorities successfully held elections for the mayors and municipalities in the main Arab towns, despite guerrilla threats of reprisals against any Arabs taking part.

Government policy was officially that in a peace settlement there would be substantial territories returned to the Arabs but there was no clear consensus in the Government or the country as to what they would amount to, except to the extent that Israel should have "secure frontiers". However, statements by Ministers made it clear that in addition to East Jerusalem and the Gaza strip, which had been effectively annexed, the Golan Heights of occupied Syria and parts of the Jordanian West Bank would not be returned. There was also increasing evidence on the ground. An extensive building programme to house immigrants was rapidly being executed in and around Jerusalem; 42 settlements had been established by January 1973 although, according to Israeli figures, only 3,150 Israeli civilians had been allowed to take up permanent residence in the areas.

Israel radio announced on August 18th, 1973 that another 35 settlements would be built in the occupied territories, bringing the total to 77. The Jewish National Fund and the Israeli Lands Administration had between them acquired 15,000 acres of Arab land and the army was in occupation of another 20,000 acres. A plan advanced by Deputy Prime Minister Yigal Allon, although not publicly approved by the Government, seemed to be in process of *de facto* execution. He proposed that a chain of Israeli settlements should be established along the Jordan river, which was effectively being done, a second chain along the Samarian Hills on the West bank, and a third along the road from Jerusalem to Jericho, in order to establish Israel's security. The rest of the West Bank and the main towns, excepting Jericho, would then be returned to Jordan.

The virtue of the Allon plan for most Israelis was that it would absorb few Arabs, for the core of the dispute within Israel remained the question of demographic balance between Arabs and Jews which would be changed in the Arabs' favour by the absorption of territory in which there were many of them resident. For that reason, the Government refused the request, submitted by the newly elected mayors of the Arab towns on the West Bank, that those Arabs who had fled the area after the 1967 war should be allowed to return. To restore the population balance the Jewish Agency, which was responsible for organizing immigration, concentrated upon Jews in Soviet

Russia who were the largest reservoir of would-be immigrants. Russia began to relax its stringent opposition to Jewish emigration in 1971, with the result that thousands of Soviet Jews began to arrive in Israel. Of the 57,000 immigrants in the year 1972–73, 33,000 were from the Soviet Union.

THE YOM KIPPUR WAR

The failure to strike against Israel created great difficulties for President Sadat with his own people throughout 1972 and increased the over-confidence that had existed in Israel ever since the brilliant victory of 1967. It was believed firmly that Egypt was afraid to go to war again and that the Bar-Lev defences along the eastern bank of the Suez Canal could not be overcome, but in fact, Sadat was working steadily towards war against the advice of his Soviet ally. He secured the financial support of King Faisal of Saudi Arabia to buy arms for hard currency, the agreement of Syrian President Hafez Assad to a limited war for the recovery of territories lost in 1967, made his peace with King Hussein of Jordan and finally secured the arms required from Russia.

By the late Summer of 1973 he was ready for war on two fronts, Syria and Egypt, with King Hussein standing aside to tie-up a part of Israeli forces facing Jordan. His order to his Minister of War to prepare the offensive had been given as early as November 1972. The Israeli Government wasted £4.5 million in May 1973 by mobilizing reserves on a report of imminent war which proved to be false and in the first two days of October they rejected a call from the army High Command to remobilize. There was confusion about conflicting reports from Israeli and American intelligence services and the Government discounted the danger.

At 2 p.m. on October 6th—the most important religious festival in Israel, Yom Kippur—the Egyptians launched their attack, breaking down the assumed impregnable sand banks of the Bar-Lev line with powerful water-jets, throwing pontoon bridges across the Suez Canal and breaking into Sinai. The line was undermanned. By midnight that day, the Egyptians had 500 tanks and missiles across the canal and destroyed 100 Israeli tanks. Almost simultaneously the Syrians had broken through the Israeli lines on the Golan heights.

Israel began the rapid mobilization of its reserve forces, the highly trained and numerically most important part of its defensive system, but before they could play an effective part the Egyptians had occupied the East bank of the canal to a depth of several miles and by the third day were advancing to the strategic Mitla pass in Sinai. At this point the counter-attacking Israeli armour faced a new and secret Russian anti-tank weapon—a gun fired from the shoulders of the enemy infantry and it caused further losses. The Syrian forces had by that time reached five miles from the Israeli frontier in Golan.

While fierce tank battles raged in Sinai, said to be bigger than any in the second World War, Israel halted the Syrians on its vulnerable northern frontier and counter-attacked successfully, driving the Syrians in a fighting retreat back over the 1967 cease-fire lines to within 20 miles of Damascus, where its forces were halted on the Syrian second line of defence. The Egyptians held their positions in Sinai but did not reach the Mitla pass. By this time an Iraqi armoured division, Iraqi Migs, and a crack Jordanian armoured brigade had reinforced the Syrian Eastern flank.

The Egyptian High Command blundered on the twelfth day when it allowed a small Israeli commando force to cross to the West bank of the Suez Canal near Deversoir at the northern end of the Great Bitter Lake. The Israelis were able to reinforce the bridgehead with a force strong enough to swing southwards to Suez and endanger the Egyptian Third Army on the East bank. Losses were very heavy on both sides.

The UN Security Council started discussing the war on October 8th but only agreed on a ceasefire resolution, jointly submitted by the United States and Russia, on the 22nd. Fighting continued on both fronts, during which the Israeli forces on the Suez West bank advanced to take the town of Suez and cut off the Egyptian Third Army. Two more Security Council resolutions were passed before the ceasefire became precariously effective on October 25th but even then it was honoured more in the breach than observance until the end of the year.

U.S. Secretary of State, Dr. Henry Kissinger, did much to maintain a peace-making momentum by tours of the Arab countries to secure negotiations for a permanent settlement in Geneva on December 18th. He visited Morocco, Tunisia, Egypt, Jordan and Saudi Arabia between November 5th and 9th. His Assistant Secretary Joseph Sisco saw Israeli leaders on his behalf on November 8th, and that day Israel accepted "in principle" the terms of an agreement Dr. Kissinger had reached with President Sadat for the "scrupulous" observance of the ceasefire. This agreement secured the evacuation of civilians from, and the supply of food and medicines to, Suez town, the removal of impediments to the movement of non-military supplies to the Egyptian Third Army, the hand-over of Israeli check-points on the Cairo-Suez road to the UN peace-keeping personnel and the exchange of all war prisoners. Dr. Kissinger made a second tour in mid-December as a result of which Egypt, Jordan and Israel sent high-calibre representatives to Geneva for negotiations on December 21st. Syria refused to attend.

They were adjourned to an unspecified date in January 1974 to allow time for the Israeli general elections, which had been postponed from October 30th to December 31st because of the war. Dr. Henry Kissinger returned to the Middle East in January and after days of intensive diplomatic activity, shuttling back and forward between Israel and Egypt, he secured the agreement of both countries to a disengagement of their forces which was announced on January 17th (*see* Documents on Palestine, p. 61) Israel agreed to withdraw its troops in Sinai to a line approximately 20 miles from the Suez Canal and Egypt to reduce its forces on the East bank. There was to be a neutral buffer zone between the two armies manned by troops of the UN Emergency Force. The agreement was signed on January 24th.

Agreement for the disengagement of forces on the northern front was not signed until May 31st (*see* Documents on Palestine, p. 62), and then only after Dr. Kissinger had flown back and forward between Jerusalem and Damascus almost daily between the 16th and 29th. Israel and Syria agreed to withdraw their troops to lines on each side of the 1967 cease-fire line, and the ruined town of Kuneitra, capital of the Golan Heights, was handed back to Syria. Both countries then handed over the prisoners they had taken in the 1973 war.

Two important factors weakened the Israeli position. In the last days of the war the Arab oil producing States banned the supply of oil to the United States and Holland and reduced supplies to Western Europe. (Britain and France were exempted but in fact were unable to get their full supplies.) This, combined with steep increases in oil prices which caused serious balance-of-payment problems for the European countries—although this had nothing to do with the war—led the EEC to issue a joint declaration in the Arab favour (*see* Documents on Palestine, p. 61. Even more damaging to Israel was the confrontation which almost developed between Russia and the United States when they both began heavy supplies of war equipment to the Arabs and Israel respectively. Dr. Kissinger made it clear to Israel that the United States would continue to support Israel, but not to the extent that would end the *détente* with Russia. It was unquestionably a form of pressure on Israel, although this was denied. Whatever anxiety Israel felt was allayed, at least in part, when President Nixon gave his blessing to any undertakings his Secretary of State had entered into by making a tour of Egypt, Saudi Arabia, Syria, Israel and Jordan in June. Shortly afterwards Israel's Finance Minister, Shimon Peres visited Washington and the outcome was the conversion of a $500 million loan into a gift and an undertaking to supply a powerful force of warplanes to ensure Israel's security.

THE AFTERMATH

The war had a profoundly disturbing effect on Israeli public opinion. The country had never suffered such losses before: nearly 3,000 dead and missing which was a substantial proportion of so small a population. The ease with which the Egyptians had crossed the canal and over-run the Bar-Lev line and the firmness with which the Syrians held the second line of defence 20 miles from Damascus were not off-set in Israeli eyes by the fact that Israeli troops had broken through and recrossed the canal and had made territorial gains in Syria; the Arab forces had fought with hitherto unknown determination and had used their sophisticated Soviet weaponry with great skill. The public's total confidence in the overwhelming superiority of their own army and air force was severely shaken with the result that a sharp division of opinion occurred between those who thought the war emphasized the need to keep defensible frontiers at all costs and those, less numerous, who viewed it as an argument for a more diligent search for a permanent peace. There was widespread dissatisfaction with the Government and a public debate ensured over the failure to anticipate the outbreak of war and the breakdown of military intelligence. There were mutual recriminations among the generals and Defence Minister Moshe Dayan's popularity in the country slumped. General Ariel Sharon whose forces had made the break-through and canal crossing in Egypt, resigned from the army to join the right-wing Likud Party—the "hawks" of Israeli politics.

This confusion was reflected in the elections. The Labour alignment, led by Mapai, which had ruled ever since the State came into existence, emerged as the strongest party with 51 seats but lost five. Likud, the main opposition, made substantial gains and won 39 seats but at the far left, the New Communists won 4 seats and the Civil Rights list 3. The religious parties lost some ground. Mrs. Golda Meir reformed her coalition government but resigned on April 11th when the report on the 1973 war was published. General Yitzhak Rabin, who had been Chief of Staff in 1967, became Prime Minister on June 3rd—the first time a native-born Sabra had held the office. Despite the fact that he was a member of the Labour Alignment, his Government effectively marked a break with the Mapai caucus which had dominated the Jewish community in Palestine ever since the Jewish Agency during the mandate. Mrs. Meir, Abba Eban (who had been Foreign Minister since 1966) and Moshe Dayan were not in the cabinet but Mrs. Meir's Government remained in office until the completion of the disengagement agreement with Syria, when General Rabin took office. Both he and his Foreign Minister, Yigal Allon, were willing to make territorial sacrifices to achieve a settlement with the Arabs.

The internal security achieved in 1971 no longer existed after the war, partly because the better showing of the Arab forces encouraged resistance among Israeli Arabs and made penetration by the Palestine Liberation Organization groups easier. These groups also became more fanatical and in May 1974 began to launch into Israel "suicide missions" consisting of from three to six men. They had two admitted objectives: to secure the release of PLO members held in Israeli prisons and to cause a breakdown of the proposed Arab-Israeli peace negotiations. Palestinian raids into Israel, including an attack on the village of Maalot in which 27 Israeli schoolchildren were killed, continued throughout the summer of 1974 and provoked large-scale Israeli reprisals against guerrilla bases in the Lebanon.

In October Dr. Kissinger renewed his quest for a further settlement but talks broke down in the following month and throughout November war with Syria seemed imminent. Israel's attitude had been hardened by two events: Arab recognition of the PLO as "sole representative of the Palestinian people" at the Rabat summit, and the status afforded the PLO by the United Nations in the following month. Mr. Rabin firmly restated Israel's refusal to negotiate with people whom he regarded as no more than terrorists bent on Israel's destruction.

The peace momentum was regained with a further Kissinger mission in March 1975 but hopes for a settlement faded with Israel's insistence that any withdrawal from the Sinai peninsula should be accompanied by an Egyptian guarantee of non-belligerency. American displeasure at Israeli intransigence was obvious, while the Arab countries demanded an early return to the Geneva conference with a PLO delegation representing the Palestinians. However, in June 1975 Mr. Rabin reopened negotiations aimed at an interim settlement in Sinai, expressing Israel's apparent willingness to withdraw to the eastern end of the Mitla and Giddi passes and to return the Abu Rudais oilfields to Egypt, in return for a limited non-belligerency pact. As an expression of good intent Israel had reduced her forces in the limited armament zone in Sinai, three days before the re-opening of the Suez Canal on June 5th. By mid-August a second interim agreement with Egypt seemed imminent.

In May 1975 the mandate for the UN Disengagement Observation Force (UNDOF) on the Golan Heights was renewed for a further six months although Israel and Syria were no closer to a settlement. Israel has consistently refused to surrender the strategic Heights without firm political guarantees from Syria. The Government's continuing policy of establishing civilian settlements in Golan and, more particularly, on the West Bank has provoked the widespread belief that Israel has effectively annexed some of the occupied territories and would be unwilling to return them in any peace settlement. (A more detailed account of the peace negotiations can be found in "The Arab-Israeli Confrontation", page 34.)

Although Mr. Rabin's refusal to make territorial concessions without firm political commitments from the Arab countries caused considerable international criticism, it greatly enhanced his authority within Israel. The Government was strengthened in October 1974 by the re-entry into the Cabinet of three members of the National Religious Party and in March 1975 Mr. Rabin's firmness in resisting American pressure for a settlement won him the grudging support of the opposition Likud party. By July 1975, with the opposition in disarray, Mr. Rabin was able to negotiate any agreement from a position of strength despite the Government's small parliamentary majority.

ECONOMIC SURVEY

The continuous flow of immigrants, as well as the hostility of both the natural and human environment in the eastern Mediterranean have not only affected Israel's political progress. They have also left a deep imprint on her economy and its development.

Large-scale immigration calls not only for heavy financial outlay to transport the future citizen to the shores of the new state and to maintain him during the early period of his stay, but also for extensive capital investments in order to absorb him into the economic life of the country. Similar problems have had to be overcome with respect to the establishment of a productive agricultural—and later industrial—economy.

The continued tension between Israel and her Arab neighbours entails the maintenance of a costly defence system. At the same time, the boycott operated through the Arab League reinforces a certain intrinsic isolation from world markets—interfering with Israel's lines of communication, hampering her foreign trade, and restricting the natural outlets for her products and services.

Yet despite these difficulties, Israel's economy has expanded at a very rapid rate and shows substantial achievements in practically every branch of production: agriculture and fisheries, industry and mining, building and construction, transport and communications, trade and services. At the same time, a high rate of capital formation has been sustained.

One of the basic problems of Israel's economy, however, has been a tendency towards overheating—inflation—and in turn, towards too rapid contraction. In 1971 and 1972 inflation ran at 12–13 per cent per annum, stimulated primarily by a large increase in money supply. This trend accelerated in later years, with consumer prices rising by 26.4 per cent in 1973 and by 50.1 per cent in 1974. There were particularly sharp price rises in February and November 1974, the latter caused by the devaluation of the currency. The last low point in Israel's economic cycle occurred in 1966 and early 1967 when economic growth fell to nil. Unemployment increased sharply, as did emigration.

By mid-1967, however, it was evident that the economic picture was improving; this trend was confirmed by the war "boom" which followed the Arab-Israeli fighting of that year. Production and employment returned to their former levels, helped by large military orders, as well as by the revival of the home market. The occupied territories provided additional markets as well as a labour source. As a result economic growth showed an 11 per cent rise in 1968 and 12.3 per cent in 1969.

Some signs of a falling off of this high level of economic expansion were discernible in 1970, when the overall G.N.P. growth rate fell to 9 per cent, largely because sufficient financial or human resources were not available to sustain further increases.

Capital inflow and immigration have been maintained through 1971, 1972 and 1973 with the result that growth in real terms continued at an annual rate of 9 per cent. But in 1974 immigration declined by 23,000 to 32,000 and emigration rose to 18,000.

AREA AND POPULATION

The total area of the State of Israel within its 1948 armistice frontiers amounts to 7,993 square miles; the territories occupied in 1967 (i.e. Sinai, the West Bank and the Golan Heights) multiplied fourfold the original area of Israel. This compares with the area of Palestine under British mandate which totalled 10,249 square miles. By the end of 1974 the population of Israel proper (excluding East Jerusalem) was 3,318,000, including about 2,750,000 Jews.

In addition there were one million persons in the area brought under Israeli administration as a result of the 1967 and 1973 wars.

The population density of Israel was 156 per square kilometre in 1973. The population is heavily concentrated in the coastal strip, with about three-quarters of the Jewish and nearly two-thirds of the non-Jewish population located between Ashkelon and Naharia. The Tel-Aviv—Jaffa area, which had a population of over 1,000,000 in 1973, is the most densely populated area of the country and accounts for 33 per cent of the total population. A further 18 per cent live in the central area between Tel-Aviv and Jerusalem, 15 per cent around Haifa, 15 per cent in the northern area and some 11 per cent around Jerusalem. Large desert areas are uninhabited except for nomadic Bedouin tribes numbering about 40,000 people in 1973. Approximately 85 per cent of the population was classified as urban in 1973, the urban population being made up of 2,535,000 Jews and 210,000 non-Jews.

The main reason for the growth of the Jewish population was immigration. Immigration accounted for 60 per cent of the yearly increase in the Jewish population between 1958 and 1970. In 1970, 54 per cent of the Jewish population had been born abroad. Twenty-eight per cent was born in Europe and America, 14 per cent in Africa and 12 per cent in Asia. Of the 1,182,800 Israeli-born Jews, only 17 per cent were second generation Israelites. Immigration up to 1948 totalled 452,158 persons, of whom nearly 90 per cent came from Europe and America. The biggest wave of immigrants—over 576,000—arrived during the first six years of the new State. These were refugees from war-torn Europe, followed by Jews emigrating from the Arab States. Large numbers have come from North Africa as a result of political developments there and during 1955–64 a total of over 200,000 emigrated from Africa into Israel. Since 1956 immigration from Eastern Europe has been resumed. After the mid-1960s immigration began to decline, falling from 54,716 in 1964 to 14,327 in 1967, but the level of immigration picked up considerably after the 1967 war bringing the total numbers of immigrants between 1965 and 1972 to over 200,000. The bulk of these came from Europe and America and this source accounted for 55 per cent of the 36,928

immigrants in 1970. The level of immigration rose to 45,000 in 1971, and to 55,900 in 1972, but declined slightly in 1973 to 54,700 and fell to 32,000 in 1974.

The Jewish birth rate was around 27 per thousand in 1973 compared with a rate almost twice as high for non-Jews, but the infant mortality rate was much higher for the latter. The total yearly rate of increase (including immigration) of the Jewish population was 5.0 per cent in 1972, compared with a peak annual rate of increase of 23.7 per cent during 1948-51.

The Israeli civilian labour force in 1973 totalled 1,088,400, or slightly below 50 per cent of the population aged 14 years and over, and was made up of roughly 30 per cent women and 70 per cent men. The growth in the labour force from 735,800 in 1960 has been due chiefly to the rise in total population, since the participation rate has declined slightly.

An important characteristic is the relatively high proportion of dependents in the population, with one-third aged 14 years and under. As a result of this, the ratio of the labour force to total population—under 35 per cent—is low by European and American standards.

In 1973 some 24 per cent were employed in manufacturing and mining, 8 per cent in agriculture and about 13 per cent in commerce.

As is apparent from these figures, only about half of the labour force is employed in the truly "productive" branches of the economy. Efforts are being made to improve this distribution, which is considered unsatisfactory and which, to a certain extent, is the result of a tendency of many of the immigrants to continue, if possible, in their former professions—mostly in the field of trade and services. Large-scale building projects and public works and the compulsory national service for both sexes in the armed forces have also taken a large share of the labour supply available, while the availability of economic assistance and other forms of unilateral transfers from abroad has also prevented the weeding-out of "non-productive" economic branches.

AGRICULTURE

The agriculture sector is relatively small, accounting for just over 6 per cent of domestic product and employing 8 per cent of the labour force. In spite of this, Israeli agriculture has attracted a great deal of international attention. Agriculture, more than any other sector of the economy, has been the focus of ideological pressure. For centuries Jews in the Diaspora were barred from owning land and the Zionist movement therefore saw land settlement as one of the chief objectives of Jewish colonization. Since the establishment of the State, government agricultural policy has centred chiefly on the attainment of self-sufficiency in foodstuffs, in view of military considerations and Israel's possible isolation from its chief foreign food supplies; on the saving of foreign exchange through import substitution and the promotion of agricultural exports; and on the absorption of the large numbers of immigrants in the agricultural sector. In line with these objectives, the promotion of mixed farming and of co-operative farming settlements has also been an important element in government policy. Although the increase in agricultural production has resulted in Israel becoming largely self-sufficient in foodstuffs—it is seriously deficient only in grains, oils and fats—and important savings have been made in foreign exchange, government intervention in the agricultural sector has been criticized as having resulted in a misallocation of resources and in impairment of the economic efficiency of agriculture.

Cultivation has undergone a profound transformation and from an extensive, primitive and mainly dry-farming structure it has developed into a modern intensive irrigated husbandry. A special feature of Israel's agriculture is its co-operative settlements which have been developed to meet the special needs and challenges encountered by a farming community new both to its surroundings and its profession. While there are a number of different forms of co-operative settlements, all are derived from two basic types: the *moshav* and the *kibbutz*. The *moshav* is a co-operative smallholders' village. Individual farms in any one village are of equal size and every farmer works his own land to the best of his ability. He is responsible for his own farm, but his economic and social security is ensured by the co-operative structure of the village, which handles the marketing of his produce, purchases his farm and household equipment, and provides him with credit and many other services.

The *kibbutz* is a collective settlement of a unique form developed in Israel. It is a collective enterprise based on common ownership of resources and on the pooling of labour, income and expenditure. Every member is expected to work to the best of his ability; he is paid no wages but is supplied by the *kibbutz* with all the goods and services he needs. The *kibbutz* is based on voluntary action and mutual liability, equal rights for all members, and assumes for them full material responsibility.

During the years following the establishment of the State a large-scale expansion of the area under cultivation took place. This was caused by the heavy influx of immigrants and the recultivation and rehabilitation of the area from which the Arabs had been forced to flee. The cultivated area increased from 400,000 acres in the crop year 1948–49 to over one million acres in 1972–73, of this some 480,000 acres are irrigated. Total water consumption at present amounts to 1,500 million cubic metres, of which 1,200 million cubic metres is consumed by agricultural users.

Without taking into consideration the cost or availability of irrigation water, it is estimated that the land potential ultimately available for farming under irrigation is 5,284 million dunums, while 4,096 dunums is the figure given for the area potentially available for dry farming. There are also 8.5 million dunums available for natural pasture and 0.9 million dunums for afforestation.

The main factor limiting agricultural development is not land, but the availability of water.

Since on average 800 cubic metres of water are needed per annum to irrigate one dunum of cultivated area, it is obvious that Israel must harness all water resources. For this reason, the Government established a special Water Administration headed by a Water Commissioner who has statutory powers to control and regulate both the supply and the consumption of water.

The Water Administration has been charged, among other tasks, with the implementation of the national water project. The purpose of this project is to convey a substantial part of the waters of the Jordan River and of other water sources from the north to southern Judea and to the Negev, to store excess supplies of water from winter to summer and from periods of heavy rainfall to periods of drought, and to serve as a regulator between the various regional water supply systems. The backbone of the national water project is the main conduit from Lake Tiberias to Rosh Haayin (near Tel-Aviv), known as the National Water Carrier, which has an annual capacity of 320 million cubic metres. Two other large schemes, also in operation, are the Western Galilee-Kishon and the Yarkon-Negev projects. Small desalination plants have been built at Eilat and elsewhere, and will be used more extensively if costs are eventually reduced. Desert farming in the Negev, using brackish water found underground, has achieved considerable success on an experimental basis. The 1972–73 season was one of very low rainfall, in consequence the Ministry of Agriculture paid I£4 million in compensation for crop losses as a result of the drought. Some 80,000 dunums were affected in the Negev, and 50,000 dunums in the Beisan, Gilboa and Lower Galilee.

Cultivation of citrus fruits is one of the principal agricultural branches and produces the main export crop. The varieties grown are "shamouti" oranges, "late" oranges, grapefruit, lemons, tangerines, and citrons. A Citrus Marketing and Control Board supervises all aspects of the growing and marketing of the fruit, particularly exports. The area under cultivation continued to expand as a result of new plantings, the total area reached 431,000 dunums for the 1972–73 season, and with the stress laid on modern methods and techniques both in the groves and packing houses the yield increases each year.

The 1972–73 citrus crop was some 1,688,600 tons, of which somewhat less than 900,000 tons were exported. Chief markets were West Germany, the United Kingdom and France. The total value of Israeli citrus fruit exports in 1971 was $114 million.

Of the remaining area under cultivation at the beginning of 1973—some 4,360,000 dunums—about 2,680,000 dunums were producing field crops, 870,000 were planted with other fruit crops, 390,000 dunums were being used for assorted vegetables, potatoes, melons and pumpkins, 245,000 dunums were devoted to fishponds and the remainder for miscellaneous purposes. Of the last, increasing emphasis is being laid on the growing of floral plants, produce from which is exported directly to Western Europe as cut flowers.

There has been a steady increase in the number of cattle, raised mainly for dairy farming. However, government policy from 1970 through 1972 led to a shift towards increasing beef cattle production, this in turn created a shortage of milk. Government controls on dairy herds were relaxed, and grants of I£50 million made available to farmers for improving and increasing their dairy herds. Milk production for 1973 totalled 295 million litres against a demand of 550 million litres. At the end of 1973 cattle in Israel totalled 280,000 head, of which 75,000 were beef animals. The keeping of poultry has become one of the basic branches of agriculture: laying hens, geese, ducks and turkeys in Israel now total about 10,450,000 and poultry now provides the main source of animal protein for the population. It is of particular importance for the absorption of new immigrants as the raising of poultry is eminently suitable for new settlers who have as yet little experience of farming.

Supplies of fish are derived from three sources: Mediterranean Sea fishing (trawling, in-shore and deep-sea fishing), lake fishing (Lake Tiberias) and fish breeding ponds. Sea fishing has been expanding in recent years and Israeli fleets operate from the Canary Islands to the Indian Ocean, and also off the South African Cape. Breeding of fish in ponds has become highly developed and provides the largest part of the total catch. In 1973, the fish catch totalled 15,300 tons, about half of which came from Israeli ponds.

INDUSTRY

Israel derives more of its national income—some 27 per cent—from industry than does any other Middle Eastern country and the relative importance of industry is steadily increasing. From 1950 to 1970 industrial production rose by over 500 per cent—or over 10 per cent per year—and the value of industrial output in 1972 reached I£19,100 million, compared with I£15,700 million in 1971. Industrial growth has been particularly vigorous since 1967. Output in the period 1968–72 in real terms rose by 80 per cent while exports have risen over five years by 124 per cent. The expansion has been particularly rapid in the more sophisticated industries—electrical and electronic equipment, transport equipment, machinery and metal products.

In 1973 there were some 19,200 industrial establishments in Israel (including self-employed persons) of which about 244 employed more than 100 persons and about 117 more than 300 persons. Whilst over two-thirds of the industrial labour force was employed in establishments employing over 30 persons, nearly 12 per cent worked in establishments employing fewer than 5 persons and which accounted for nearly 70 per cent of the total number of industrial establishments.

Israel's industry originally developed by supplying such basic needs as soap, oil and margarine, bread, ice, printing and electricity. It used raw materials available locally to produce citrus juices and other citrus by-products, canned fruit and vegetables, cement, glass and bricks. In order to save foreign exchange, imports of manufactured goods were curtailed, thus giving local industry the opportunity of adding local labour value to the semi-manufactures imported from abroad.

To stimulate investment and encourage the inflow of foreign capital the Law for the Encouragement of Capital Investments was enacted in 1950, broadened in 1959 and amended in 1967. The Law sets up an Investment Centre and provides for the approval of projects contributing to the development of industrial potential, the exploitation of natural resources, the creation of new sources of employment—particularly in development areas—and to the absorption of new immigrants. Among the concessions granted to approved projects, particularly those financed in foreign currency, are remittance of profits and withdrawal of capital, and tax benefits in respect of income tax, indirect taxes and depreciation allowances.

Although most of Israel's industrial production, about 85 per cent, still goes for home consumption, industrial exports now constitute about half of all Israeli exports. Here again there has been a very rapid expansion as a result of tax and investment incentives from the Government. Israeli industrial exports, worth $18 million in 1950, had risen to $946 million by 1972. A 1975 agreement with the EEC will phase out tariffs on Israel's industrial exports by July 1977.

Israel's most important industrial export product is diamonds, most of the expertise for the finishing of which was supplied by immigrants from the Low Countries. In 1973 Israel exported some $575 million worth of diamonds; the country's share of international trade in polished diamonds has risen to 30 per cent and as high as 80 per cent in medium-sized stones, in which she specializes.

Israel Aircraft Industries, employing some 14,000, is Israel's largest single industrial enterprise. At its main plant adjacent to Lod Airport it produces the first wholly Israeli-designed aircraft—the Arava, a twin-turboprop passenger/cargo transport—and the Commodore Jet, a 10-place twin-jet executive aircraft, as well as the Gabriel sea-to-sea missile.

The food, beverage and tobacco industries account for about 15 per cent of manufactures and employ some 35,000 persons. About 90 per cent of output is sold on the local market; the rest, such as juices, wines, chocolate and coffee, goes abroad.

The textiles and clothing industry, which was developed chiefly because of its low capital-labour ratio, accounts for about 15 per cent of total industrial production and employs some 50,000 persons. In 1970, it exported goods worth some $96 million—about 15 per cent of total output.

There is also a small but rapidly expanding electronics industry, specializing in equipment for military and communications purposes. Exports by this sector have been increasing by some 20 to 30 per cent a year and in 1970 were worth in the area of $14,623,000.

In view of the heavy power needs of irrigation and the water installations, agriculture as well as industry are large-scale consumers of electricity. As both irrigation and industry have been expanding, sales of electric power are constantly increasing. By the end of 1972, generating capacity had increased to over 1,500,000 kW. This was further increased to 2,070,000 kW at the end of 1973 when the first unit of the Eshkol C power station came into operation.

MINERALS

The Petroleum Law of 1952 regulates the conditions for the granting of licences for oil prospecting, divides the country into petroleum districts and fixes a basic royalty of 12.5 per cent. Oil was discovered in 1955 at the Heletz-Bror field on the coastal plain and later at Kokhav, Brur and Negba. Although 34 wells in Israel are now producing, their output is less than 100,000 tons a year. The current level of production in Egyptian territory occupied by Israel is about 5 million tons a year: estimates of potential production range as high as 40 million tons a year. In 1971 Israel made a major oil strike in the occupied Egyptian area of the Gulf of Suez. Estimates of the size of output varied from 24,000 to 70,000 barrels per day.

Output of gas from Rosh-Zohar in the Dead Sea area, Kidod, Hakanaim and Barbur is transported through a 29 km. 6-inch pipeline to the Dead Sea potash works at Sodom and through a 49 km. 4-inch and 6-inch line to towns in the Negev and to the Oron phosphate plant.

Despite these finds, Israel has in the past lacked large resources of fuel and power and has been dependent on imports (mainly crude oil and fuel oil) amounting in 1970 to over $70 million a year. The imported crude oil is refined at the Haifa oil refinery, which has a capacity of over 6.0 million tons per year. Actual throughput in 1973 was 6.2 million tons, of which 912,000 tons were exported. Roughly a third of its output is exported. Dependent on the Haifa refinery is a growing petrochemicals industry, which represents an investment of some $20 million. A new chemical terminal was inaugurated at the end of 1972. The terminal covering an area of 200 dunums is reserved for the import of liquified chemicals and was built at a cost of I£5 million. Further expansion is planned.

The closure of the Suez Canal and the new oil supplies encouraged the Israeli authorities to go ahead with a scheme for a new large 42-inch pipeline, 160 miles in length, from Eilat to Ashkelon on the Mediterranean coast. The first crude oil flowed through the pipeline early in 1969. Initial throughput was about 13 million tons, this was increased to 25 million tons in 1972, and to 40 million tons in 1973. Provision has been made for an eventual increase in the line's capacity to 60 million tons a year. The source of the crude oil put through the pipeline is thought to be Iran, though some may come from the Sinai fields. A refinery with a capacity of 3.5 million tons per year has been built at Ashdod, ten miles north of the pipeline terminal at Ashkelon. Initial production started in early 1973. An Israeli-owned tanker fleet is now under construction, gross tonnage totalled over 1.0 million tons by the end of 1972 and rose to 1.8 million tons in 1973.

The Dead Sea, which contains potash, bromides, magnesium and other salts in high concentration, is the country's chief source of mineral wealth. The potash works on the southern shore of the Dead Sea, are owned by Dead Sea Works Ltd. The works are linked by road to Beersheba, from where a railway runs northward. Production capacity by the end of 1972 stood at 1.4 million tons.

Phosphates are mined at Oron in the Negev. New plant has improved the concentration of the ore to 38 per cent. The plant has now a production capacity of 600,000 tons a year and a new railway line from the Oron phosphate area to Eilat is planned. New deposits of phosphates estimated at 8 million tons have been found in the Arava of the Negev. Production from Oron and Arava amounted in 1973 to 1.2 million tons.

At Timna, in the southern Negev near Eilat, geological surveys have located proven reserves of 20 million tons of low-grade copper ore (about 1.5 per cent Cu) and a further 50 million tons of probable reserves. The building of a mill to make use of these ores and for producing copper-cement was completed in 1958. The capacity was recently doubled to 3,000 tons per day. The ore is mined by open-cast and underground methods. In 1973, copper production from the Timna complex reached 11,900 tons.

FINANCE

The problems confronting Israel make a certain degree of inflationary financing unavoidable, and it is reflected in the country's financial statistics. In the early years of the State, when the Government financed its deficits through the printing press and banks expanded their credits, efforts were made to maintain a low level of prices by means of controls and rationing. The result was a large surplus of purchasing power in the hands of the public. The attempt of the public to expand this surplus gave rise to a black market in controlled goods and to a sharp rise in the prices of uncontrolled goods and services.

Government deflationary measures and a credit squeeze were not effective in slowing down the rise in prices until 1967. In November 1967, the occasion of the British devaluation of sterling was taken for a further devaluation of the Israeli pound. The Israeli pound was devalued again in August 1971, following the imposition by the U.S. of an import surcharge. The U.S. in fact was forced to devalue the dollar in December 1971 amidst considerable international currency uncertainty, which culminated in a further devaluation of the U.S. dollar in February 1973 along with the currencies of other countries including Israel. In November 1974 the Israeli pound was devalued by 30 per cent against the U.S. $. On June 17th, 1975, the Israeli pound was devalued by about 2 per cent, with a further devaluation of 1.9 per cent on August 5th. The June 17th official exchange rate was I£6.12 per U.S. $, but the black market rate was I£17.65 per U.S. $. The official August rate was $1=I£6.24.

The size and composition of the Israeli budget reflect, perhaps better than any other economic indicator, the special conditions and problems confronting Israel's economy. To begin with, the Israeli budget generally accounts for more than 40 per cent of the national income—a situation made possible on the one hand by the direct receipt from abroad of grants-in-aid, reparations and loans; and on the other, because it has been the practice to channel these very large revenues directly into development projects.

The 1973–74 Israeli budget lists expenditures of I£26,860 million, with nearly half of revenues deriving from property and income tax as well as from taxes on expenditure, the remainder being made up of War bond sales, gifts and transfers.

Main items of revenue outlay are defence and security, social services and "economic purposes". Reflecting yet another of the problems of inflationary financing is expenditure on debt servicing and repayment.

That the Israeli payments position was ever in surplus (some I£142 million in 1972) was the result of capital movements to Israel totalling more than $10,000 million since the establishment of the State. Against these funds may be set the inevitable loss on current account ($1,265 million estimated in 1973). Transfer payments—proceeds from the United Jewish Appeal and similar campaigns, personal restitutions, as well as institutional and personal remittances—comprised about 70 per cent of this total, the remainder coming from overseas short and long-term loans and investments, including about $80 million from the sale of State of Israel bonds.

Israel's foreign debt at the end of 1974 amounted to over U.S. $7,300 million, following heavy borrowing in 1970–74 (a net increase in the period of U.S. $5,000 million). Foreign exchange reserves were worth U.S. $1,151 million (against U.S. $1,695 million at the end of 1973).

TRADE

Israel's balance of trade inevitably shows a heavy deficit, reflecting its dependence on foreign consumer and capital goods—if not foodstuffs—and raw materials. Although exports have increased dramatically, from $28 million in 1949 to $199 million in 1959 and $1,800 million in 1974, imports have remained well ahead. In 1949, Israel's imports were worth $252 million, in 1959, $427 million; in 1974 Israel imported goods and services to a total value of $4,200 million. The trade deficit of $2,400 million in 1974 shows a dramatic reversal of the slight improvement sustained in 1972 over 1971, when the deficit was reduced to $855 million from $896 million.

Imports of consumer goods amounted to some $212 million (or 10.8 per cent of the total) in 1972. Capital goods amounted to some $478 million (or 24.5 per cent of the total) in 1972. However, when aircraft and ships are excluded imports of capital goods total $415 million. By far the largest import sector, however, was that which covered raw materials and production inputs at $1,258 million. This includes the import of diamonds which amounted to $336 million in 1972.

The focus of Israel's foreign trade is mainly Europe and North America. Thus the progress towards regional economic integration in Western Europe is of considerable concern. In May 1964, a three-year agreement was concluded with the European Eco-

nomic Community providing for tariff reductions of from 10 to 40 per cent on about 20 items, mostly industrial goods. This expired in 1967, but a five-year preferential trade agreement with the EEC was signed in June 1970. This agreement included a 45 per cent cut in EEC tariffs on certain agricultural and industrial items, a 40 per cent cut for citrus fruit and a 300 ton per year quota for textiles. In return, Israel is granted tariff cuts of from 10 to 25 per cent on industrial and processed agricultural imports. It has also been agreed with the EEC that Israeli access to the United Kingdom (which became a member of the EEC on January 1st, 1973) shall remain on the pre-entry basis while further agreements are negotiated for 1974-75.

The draft budget for the year beginning April 1975 was presented in February. It called for an increase of 40 per cent over the current budget to an expenditure of over I£56,300 million. Of the total expenditure 40 per cent was allocated to defence and 9 per cent for the repayment of foreign debt.

BANKING, TRANSPORT AND TOURISM

Israel possesses a highly-developed banking system, consisting of the central bank (the Central Bank of Israel), 28 commercial banks, 14 credit co-operatives and 35 other financial institutions. Long-term credits are granted by mortgage banks, the Israel Agricultural Bank, the Industrial Development Bank and the Maritime Bank. As of mid-1971, the amount of outstanding bank credit to the public was I£6,739 million. The Bank of Israel policy in 1973 was one of restraint in an effort to reduce the volume of outstanding bank credit. To prevent unemployment from reaching 6 per cent the money supply rose by 22 per cent in the six months to June 1975.

The function of the Central Bank is to issue currency, to accept deposits from banking institutions in Israel (and extend temporary advances to the Government), act as the Government's sole fiscal and banking agent, and manage the public debt. Its Governor supervises the liquidity position of the commercial banks and regulates the volume of bank advances.

The continued severance of all lines of communication with her Arab neighbours has not only intensified Israel's dependence on sea and air communications, but has also given great impetus to the establishment of a national merchant marine and airline.

Since 1949, Israel has operated its own international air carrier—El-Al Israel National Airlines Ltd. Regular scheduled services to West Europe, U.S.A., Cyprus, Iran, and parts of Africa and Asia are maintained; in addition, some 14 international airlines call at Ben Gurion Airport, Lod, Tel-Aviv.

Domestic services are provided by Arkia, a national carrier which in 1972 carried over 400,000 passengers from Tel-Aviv to Jerusalem, Eilat, Haifa, Rosh Pina and Massada, as well as to points in the occupied territories.

Israel's merchant navy has been undergoing expansion, and Israel Shipyards Ltd., at Haifa, can build ships up to 10,000 tons d.w. In the north, the port of Haifa and its Kishon harbour extension provide Israel's main port facilities. The south is served by the port of Eilat—Israel's only non-Mediterranean port—at the head of the Gulf of Aqaba, and by a new deep-water port at Ashdod, some 30 miles south of Tel-Aviv.

About I£70 million have so far been invested in Israel's railways, which by 1970 operated some 416 miles of main lines and 205 miles of branch lines. The service extends from Nahariya, north of Haifa, to Jerusalem, and then southwards through Beersheba. In 1965 it reached Dimona and in 1970 the phosphate works at Oron; ultimately, an extension to Eilat is envisaged. Traction is wholly by diesel locomotives. In 1971–72 traffic consisted of 38 million passenger-kilometres and 490 million ton-kilometres of freight.

Roads are the chief means of transport. In 1972 there were some 2,600 miles of paved roads in Israel, 92 miles of which were four-lane motorways, and 1,786 miles of which were main or regional roads. Travelling them were 147,000 private vehicles—nearly 49 per thousand of the Israeli population.

In 1972, some 727,500 tourists visited Israel, bringing foreign exchange earnings from tourism to $212.7 million, an increase of 19 per cent on 1971. The country has more than 300 hotels graded from five-star to one-star, and including guest-houses at the *kibbutzim*, pilgrims' hospices and youth hostels. Overall administration of Israeli tourism is carried out by the Ministry of Tourism, which maintains 20 offices abroad. It is also in charge of regulating tourist services in Israel, including the arrangement of "package" tours and the provision of multilingual guides.

STATISTICAL SURVEY

AREA AND POPULATION

AREA	POPULATION December 31st, 1974	BIRTH RATE (per '000) 1974	MARRIAGE RATE (per '000) 1974	DEATH RATE (per '000) 1974
20,700 sq. km.*	3,318,000	27.6†	9.5†	7.2†

* 8,000 square miles.

† These figures include the population of the Old City of Jerusalem and the surrounding areas (area 70 sq. km., population 85,000 at December 31st, 1974), which Israel annexed in 1967.

ADMINISTERED TERRITORIES*
(1972)

	AREA (sq. km.)	POPULATION
Golan . . .	1,150	n.a.
Judea and Samaria . .	5,879	639,300
Gaza	378	} 390,700
Sinai	61,181	
TOTAL . .	68,588	n.a.

* The area and population of the Administered Territories have changed as a result of the October 1973 war.

POPULATION OF CHIEF TOWNS
(Dec. 1974)

Jerusalem (capital)	.	344,200	Holon	. . .	110,300
Tel-Aviv—Jaffa	.	357,600	Petach-Tikva	. .	103,000
Haifa . .	.	225,000	Beersheba .	. .	93,400
Ramat Gan .	.	120,000	Bene Beraq	. .	81,000

GROWTH OF POPULATION AND JEWISH IMMIGRATION, 1960–73

END OF YEAR	PERMANENT POPULATION	JEWS	OTHERS	IMMIGRATION
1960 . . .	2,150,400	1,911,200	239,200	24,510
1961 . . .	2,234,200	1,981,700	252,500	47,638
1962 . . .	2,331,800	2,068,900	262,900	61,328
1963 . . .	2,430,100	2,155,500	274,600	64,364
1964 . . .	2,525,600	2,239,000	286,400	54,716
1965 . . .	2,598,400	2,299,100	299,300	30,736
1966 . . .	2,657,400	2,344,900	312,500	15,730
1967* . . .	2,773,900	2,383,600	390,300	14,327
1968* . . .	2,841,100	2,434,800	406,300	20,544
1969* . . .	2,919,200	2,496,600	422,700	23,510
1970* . . .	3,001,400	2,561,400	440,000	20,624
1971* . . .	3,095,100	2,636,600	458,500	41,930
1972* . . .	3,200,500	2,723,600	476,900	55,888
1973* . . .	3,307,500	2,810,400	497,100	54,886

* These figures exclude the population of the areas occupied by Israel since June 1967 and now known in Israel as the "Administered Territories" (*see* above), but include the population of the Old City of Jerusalem and the surrounding areas, which Israel annexed in 1967 and regards as Israeli territory (the UN Security Council and General Assembly have declared this annexation invalid).

EMPLOYMENT
('000)

	1970	1971	1972*	1973*	1974*
Agriculture, Forestry and Fishing . .	84.8	84.5	83.5	81.4	70.7
Mining, Quarrying and Manufacturing .	233.3	239.6	248.4	269.8	273.9
Electricity, Gas and Water . . .	11.3	11.0	9.0	10.4	10.4
Construction	80.1	88.3	99.3	96.1	87.7
Trade, Restaurants and Hotels . .	125.0	126.4	137.1	138.9	131.6
Transport, Storage and Communications .	72.2	74.0	76.9	78.9	83.5
Financing, Insurance and Business Services .	49.7	56.7	60.2	68.0	70.0
Community, Social and Personal Services .	303.8	314.1	328.7	341.6	354.4
Others	3.0	2.5	4.4	3.3	7.0
TOTAL	963.2	997.1	1,047.4	1,088.4	1,089.2

* Averages.

AGRICULTURE
AGRICULTURAL LAND USAGE
('000 dunums or '00 hectares)

	1970–71	1971–72	1972–73	1973–74	1974–75
Field Crops . .	2,660	2,650	2,672	2,739	2,800
Fruit incl. citrus . .	835	845	861	870	875
Vegetables, potatoes, etc.	370	396	354	376	390
Nurseries, flowers, fish ponds, etc. .	275	274	283	285	285
TOTAL Cultivated Area	4,140	4,165	4,170	4,270	4,350

PRODUCTION
(metric tons)

	1969–70	1970–71	1971–72	1972–73	1973-74
Wheat	125,000	199,500	301,400	241,500	274,000
Barley	13,600	17,600	32,800	17,900	30,200
Sorghum	10,900	20,600	40,400	29,700	34,200
Hay	137,300	141,200	132,500	126,800	138,000
Groundnuts	18,700	21,200	19,800	14,600	18,000
Cotton Lint . . .	35,300	36,700	40,300	37,400	49,800
Cottonseed	58,600	69,000	67,400	63,400	84,000
Sugar Beet . . .	237,000	258,600	248,500	217,300	116,700
Melons and Pumpkins . .	131,500	132,900	161,700	127,000	124,000
Vegetables	472,300	490,400	502,000	532,700	496,200
Potatoes	137,100	142,000	143,100	165,100	152,400
Citrus Fruit . . .	1,261,900	1,513,500	1,552,800	1,688,600	1,698,000
Other Fruit . . .	288,800	307,700	359,800	297,000	337,300
Milk (kl.) (incl. sheep and goat milk)	487,700	497,500	519,200	565,900	590,900

PRODUCTION OF CITRUS FRUIT
(metric tons)

	1970–71	1971–72	1972–73	1973-74
Grapefruit . . .	361,300	334,300	390,800	395,500
Lemons . . .	46,400	39,900	45,400	36,500
Oranges: Shamouti .	746,500	842,200	817,000	834,400
Lates	298,100	273,500	362,600	358,500
Other varieties . .	61,200	62,900	72,800	73,100
TOTAL . .	1,513,500	1,552,800	1,688,600	1,698,000

LIVESTOCK
('000)

	1972	1973	1974
Cattle	260	280	300
Poultry . . .	10,000	11,000	12,000
Sheep	185	185	197
Goats	124	138	138

FISHERIES
(tons)

1970–71	1971–72	1972–73	1973-74
26,100	27,100	26,500	22,700

INDUSTRIAL OUTPUT
(I£ million at market prices)
(Establishments employing 5 or more people)

	1968	1969	1970	1971	1972
Non-Metallic Mineral Products . .	362	395	503	634	780
Foodstuffs, Beverages and Tobacco . .	1,724	1,966	2,257	2,762	3,373
Textiles and Clothing . . .	1,116	1,255	1,515	1,860	2,400
Metals and Machinery . . .	1,263	1,583	1,863	2,332	2,928
Chemicals and Petroleum Products .	537	590	714	902	1,138
Diamond Industry . . .	614	563	518	644	810
Wood and Wood Products . .	315	329	379	486	644
Transport Equipment . . .	353	441	657	815	1,078
Electrical and Electrical Equipment .	399	625	776	961	1,317
Rubber and Plastics . . .	356	408	479	608	720
Printing and Publishing . .	215	246	275	336	439
Leather and Leather Products . .	90	104	109	122	158
Mining and Quarrying . .	181	222	264	327	397
Paper and Cardboard . . .	201	209	265	351	423
Miscellaneous . . .	92	106	117	153	207

FINANCE

100 agorot (singular, agora)=1 Israeli pound (I£).
Coins: 1, 5, 10, 25 and 50 agorot; 1 pound.
Notes: 1, 5, 10, 50 and 100 pounds.
Exchange rates (August 1975): £1 sterling=I£13.16; U.S. $1=I£6.24.
I£100=£7.60 sterling=$16.03.

Note: Multiple exchange rates were in operation between 1952 and mid-1955. From July 1955 to February 1962 the official exchange rate was U.S. $1=I£1.80. Between February 1962 and November 1967 the exchange rate was $1=I£3.00. From November 1967 to August 1971 the rate was $1=I£3.50 (I£1=28.57 U.S. cents). It was $1=I£4.20 (I£1=23.81 U.S. cents) from August 1971 to November 1974; $1=I£6.00 (I£1=16.67 U.S. cents) from November 1974 to June 1975; and $1=I£6.12 (I£1=16.34 U.S. cents) from June to August 1975. The exchange rate was £1 sterling=I£8.40 from February 1962 to August 1971; and £1 sterling=I£10.944 from December 1971 to June 1972.

CENTRAL GOVERNMENT BUDGET
(I£ million, twelve months ending March 31st)

REVENUE	1972/73	1973/74	1974/75*	1975/76*
Ordinary Budget:				
Income Tax and Property Tax	3,815.7	4,915.2	9,066.0	10,770.0
Customs and Excise	3,356.9	5,449.6	7,842.0	9,920.0
Purchase Tax	1,314.0	1,691.5	2,812.0	3,740.0
Other Taxes	574.6	680.6	1,086.0	1,395.0
Interest	621.8	838.5	753.0	1,083.0
Loans	1,239.8	1,713.4	2,861.0	3,630.0
Other Receipts	651.9	814.1	7,495.5	13,982.0
TOTAL	11,574.7	16,102.9	31,915.5	44,520.0
Development Budget:				
Foreign Loans	3,100.0	8,079.3	8,918.0	13,350.0
Internal Loans	2,969.6	5,723.2	4,100.0	5,900.0
Other Receipts	965.2	1,109.8	—4,283.5	—7,470.0
TOTAL	7,034.8	14,912.3	8,734.5	11,780.0
TOTAL REVENUE	18,609.5	31,015.2	40,650.0	56,300.0

EXPENDITURE	1972/73	1973/74	1974/75*	1975/76*
Ordinary Budget:				
Ministry of Finance	135.8	169.6	193.5	302.0
Ministry of Defence	5,889.3	15,340.0	16,289.0	22,306.0
Ministry of Health	358.7	587.5	699.0	1,177.0
Ministry of Foreign Affairs	124.6	182.2	190.2	269.0
Ministry of Education and Culture	1,098.3	1,603.3	2,008.4	3,415.0
Ministry of Police	215.7	301.4	378.5	697.5
Ministry of Social Welfare	126.8	202.3	480.0	589.0
Other Ministries	604.9	875.1	1,002.6	1,508.9
Interest	1,774.6	2,237.1	3,465.5	5,000.0
Transfers to Local Authorities	568.0	794.6	1,018.5	1,765.0
Subsidies	1,346.2	2,286.8	2,900.0	4,300.0
Other Expenditures	910.3	812.1	3,298.3	3,190.6
TOTAL	13,153.2	25,392.0	31,923.5	44,520.0
Development Budget:				
Industry and Crafts	304.2	387.0	326.0	468.5
Transport	234.5	229.5	302.0	336.5
Communications	307.0	358.8	468.0	540.0
Housing	937.5	1,061.5	2,289.0	3,485.0
Public Buildings	332.7	516.1	699.9	1,054.4
Debt Repayment	2,087.2	2,866.4	3,851.5	5,180.0
Other Expenditures	782.3	413.1	790.1	715.6
TOTAL	4,985.4	5,832.4	8,726.5	11,780.0
TOTAL EXPENDITURE	18,138.6	31,224.4	40,650.0	56,300.0

* Estimates.

GENERAL CONSUMER PRICE INDEX
(1969 = 100)

1970	1971	1972	1973	1974	1975*
106.1	118.8	134.1	160.9	224.8	308.2

* Average for May.

MONEY SUPPLY
(million I£ at year end)

	1970	1971	1972	1973	1974
Currency held by the public	1,282	1,584	1,974	2,716	3,173
Current deposits	2,104	2,757	3,613	4,677	5,549
TOTAL MONEY SUPPLY . . .	3,386	4,341	5,587	7,393	8,722

EXTERNAL TRADE
('000 U.S.$)

	IMPORTS	EXPORTS	BALANCE
1967 * . . .	756,935	517,245	239,690
1968 * . . .	1,093,192	602,105	491,087
1969* . . .	1,304,376	688,697	615,679
1970* . . .	1,433,497	733,622	699,875
1971* . . .	1,811,605	915,061	896,544
1972* . . .	1,961,362	1,099,838	861,524
1973* . . .	2,968,579	1,391,821	1,576,758
1974* . . .	4,197,856	1,736,577	2,461,279

* Excluding trade with the administered territories.

COMMODITIES
('000 U.S. $)

IMPORTS	1971	1972	1973	1974
Diamonds, rough . . .	240,264	336,589	488,017	442,960
Boilers, machinery and parts .	197,818	242,198	279,724	325,052
Electrical machinery .	96,342	127,959	158,828	212,718
Iron and steel . . .	144,672	151,162	226,055	450,881
Vehicles	96,972	133,445	196,008	263,417
Chemicals . . .	117,520	134,627	180,800	293,971
Crude oil . . .	84,589	97,308	208,816	616,180
Cereals	83 908	77,077	140,915	226,972
Textiles and textile articles .	74,201	72,980	102,368	130,911
Ships, boats, aircraft, etc. . .	189,850	64,516	204,019	150,507

EXPORTS	1971	1972	1973	1974
Diamonds, worked . . .	303,379	426,867	617,109	641,146
Edible fruits . . .	124,474	123,372	127,854	136,721
Textiles and textile articles .	119,154	121,364	142,838	160,234
Fruit and vegetable products .	50,120	62,202	73,399	88,654
Resins and plastics . . .	9,858	12,163	16,905	33,225
Fertilizers . . .	29,801	29,699	34,191	67,246
Rubber, including synthetic .	18,772	20,847	17,898	26,144
Organic chemicals . .	15,296	17,746	25,744	59,287
Mineral products . .	41,654	42,317	48,095	90,164
Plywood . . .	6,412	6,287	9,503	6,654

COUNTRIES
('ooo U.S. $)

	1972		1973		1974	
	IMPORTS	EXPORTS	IMPORTS	EXPORTS	IMPORTS	EXPORTS
Australia and New Zealand . .	7,203	7,865	5,582	14,005	8,595	20,592
Austria	13,124	8,706	25,057	15,144	31,568	21,711
Belgium-Luxembourg . . .	122,351	46,249	150,610	75,063	142,209	105,775
Canada	27,313	18,704	32,470	21,503	33,234	27,831
Denmark	8,822	5,728	12,052	7,477	16,694	7,545
Finland	20,920	7,902	24,283	9,099	34,868	9,326
France	95,155	55,390	129,682	63,068	154,066	83,451
Germany, Federal Republic . .	229,332	103,655	527,110	135,061	687,438	136,666
Hong Kong	2,592	60,888	371	96,887	5,925	118,580
Iran	2,258	44,610	2,600	36,848	4,916	63,178
Italy	166,291	28,496	150,029	35,718	225,560	69,166
Japan	47,286	71,610	59,207	87,312	130,487	69,114
Netherlands	82,827	67,437	164,954	97,517	223,317	138,621
Romania	25,304	10,693	39,643	14,150	47,977	25,414
South Africa	11,591	8,816	27,489	11,966	38,356	28,736
Sweden	37,200	13,798	61,821	15,960	61,821	19,489
Switzerland	70,299	62,706	84,825	87,651	112,615	105,021
Turkey	13,683	2,809	13,951	4,110	6,034	9,843
United Kingdom	365,362	111,251	484,556	140,632	543,415	156,758
U.S.A.	373,235	223,475	560,888	267,641	754,201	300,016
Yugoslavia	18,905	7,907	16,187	9,312	19,736	14,251

TRANSPORT

RAILWAYS

	1972	1973	1974
Passengers ('ooo) .	4,430	4,072	3,720
Freight ('ooo metric tons) .	3,136	3,475	3,658

ROADS 1974
MOTOR VEHICLES ('ooo)

Private Cars	267.4
Trucks, Trailers . . .	94.8
Buses	5.6
Taxis	4.3
Motorcycles, Motorscooters .	33.0
Other Vehicles	3.22
TOTAL . . .	408.3

SHIPPING
('ooo tons)

	1972	1973	1974
Cargo Loaded . .	3,469	3,317	3,720
Cargo Unloaded .	4,915	5,577	6,250

CIVIL AVIATION (El Al revenue flights only)
('ooo)

	1971	1972	1973
Kilometres flown .	31,825	31,982	33,077
Passenger-km. .	3,213,940	3,550,100	3,490,500
Cargo ton-km. .	404,000	425,000	454,000
Mail (tons) .	745	746	738

TOURISM
TOURIST ARRIVALS

1969	409,000
1970	441,294
1971	656,756
1972	727,532
1973	661,651
1974	627,727

COMMUNICATIONS MEDIA

	1972	1973	1974
Radio receivers .	680,000	n.a.	n.a.
TV licences .	370,000	n.a.	n.a.
Telephones .	620,000	698,800	751,700
Daily Newspapers .	26	26	27

EDUCATION
(1974–75)

JEWISH:	SCHOOLS	PUPILS	ARAB:	SCHOOLS	PUPILS
Kindergarten	4,279	139,625	Kindergarten	254	15,934
Primary Schools	1,213	375,443	Primary Schools	287	105,373
Secondary Schools	206	54,878	Secondary Schools	77	12,860
Vocational Schools	306	64,505	Vocational	24	1,456
Agricultural Schools	27	5,877	Agricultural Schools	2	687
Teachers' Training	49	10,356	Teachers' Training	2	723
Others (Evening, Handicapped)	487	75,412	Others (Evening, Handicapped)	42	9,228

Source: Central Bureau of Statistics, Jerusalem.

THE CONSTITUTION

There is no written Constitution. In June 1950, the Knesset voted to adopt a State Constitution by evolution over an unspecified period. A number of laws, including the Law of Return (1950), the Nationality Law (1952), the State President (Tenure) Law (1952), the Education Law (1953) and the "Yad-va-Shem" Memorial Law (1953) are considered as incorporated into the State Constitution. Other constitutional laws are: The Law and Administration Ordinance (1948), the Knesset Election Law (1951), the Law of Equal Rights for Women (1951), the Judges Act (1953), the National Service and National Insurance Acts (1953), and the Basic Law (The Knesset) (1958).

The President

The President is elected by the Knesset for five years.

Ten or more Knesset Members may propose a candidate for the Presidency.

Voting will be by secret ballot.

The President may not leave the country without the consent of the Government.

The President may resign by submitting his resignation in writing to the Speaker.

The President may be relieved of his duties by the Knesset for misdemeanour.

The Knesset is entitled to decide by a two-thirds majority that the President is incapacitated owing to ill-health to fulfil his duties permanently.

The Speaker of the Knesset will act for the President when the President leaves the country, or when he cannot perform his duties owing to ill-health.

The Knesset

The Knesset is the parliament of the State. There are 120 members.

It is elected by general, national, direct, equal, secret and proportional elections.

Every Israel national of 18 years or over shall have the right to vote in elections to the Knesset unless a court has deprived him of that right by virtue of any law.

Every Israel national of 21 and over shall have the right to be elected to the Knesset unless a court has deprived him of that right by virtue of any law.

The following shall not be candidates: the President of the State; the two Chief Rabbis; a judge (*shofet*) in office; a judge (*dayan*) of a religious court; the State Comptroller; the Chief of the General Staff of the Defence Army of Israel; rabbis and ministers of other religions in office; senior State employees and senior Army officers of such ranks and in such functions as shall be determined by law.

The term of office of the Knesset shall be four years.

The elections of the Knesset shall take place on the third Tuesday of the month of Cheshven in the year in which the tenure of the outgoing Knesset ends.

Election day shall be a day of rest, but transport and other public services shall function normally.

Results of the elections shall be published within fourteen days.

The Knesset shall elect from among its members a Chairman and Vice-Chairman.

The Knesset shall elect from among its members permanent committees, and may elect committees for specific matters.

The Knesset may appoint commissions of inquiry to investigate matters designated by the Knesset.

The Knesset shall hold two sessions a year; one of them shall open within four weeks after the Feast of the Tabernacles, the other within four weeks after Independence Day; the aggregate duration of the two sessions shall not be less than eight months.

The outgoing Knesset shall continue to hold office until the convening of the incoming Knesset.

The members of the Knesset shall receive a remuneration as provided by law.

The Government

The Government shall tender its resignation to the President immediately after his election, but shall continue with its duties until the formation of a new Government.

After consultation with representatives of the parties in the Knesset, the President shall charge one of the Members with the formation of a Government.

The Government shall be composed of a Prime Minister and a number of Ministers from among the Knesset Members or from outside the Knesset.

After it has been chosen, the Government shall appear before the Knesset and shall be considered as formed after having received a vote of confidence.

Within seven days of receiving a vote of confidence, the Prime Minister and the other Ministers shall swear allegiance to the State of Israel and its Laws and undertake to carry out the decisions of the Knesset.

THE GOVERNMENT

HEAD OF THE STATE

President of the State of Israel: Prof. EPHRAIM KATZIR.

THE CABINET

(August 1975)

Prime Minister and Minister of Communications: YITZHAK RABIN (Labour Party).

Deputy Prime Minister and Minister of Foreign Affairs: YIGAL ALLON (Labour Party).

Minister of Defence: SHIMON PERES (Labour Party).

Minister of Finance: YEHOSHUA RABINOWITZ (Labour Party).

Minister of Labour: MOSHE BARAM (Labour Party).

Minister of Education and Culture: AHARON YADLIN (Labour Party).

Minister of Police: SHLOMO HILLEL (Labour Party).

Minister of the Interior: Dr. YOSEPH BURG (National Religious Party).

Minister of Tourism: MOSHE KOL (Independent Liberal).

Minister of Justice: HAIM ZADOK (Labour Party).

Minister of Religious Affairs: Dr. YITZHAK RAPHAEL (National Religious Party).

Minister of Social Welfare: (vacant).

Minister of Health: VICTOR SHEMTOV (Mapam).

Minister of Immigration and Absorption: SHLOMO ROSEN (Mapam).

Minister of Commerce and Industry: HAIM BAR-LEV (Labour Party).

Minister of Housing: AVRAHAM OFER (Labour Party).

Minister of Transport: GAD YAACOBI (Labour Party).

Minister of Agriculture: AHARON UZAN (Labour Party).

Ministers without Portfolio: ISRAEL GALILI (Labour Party), GIDEON HAUSNER (Independent Liberal).

PARLIAMENT

Speaker of the Knesset: YISRAEL YESHAYAHU.

The state of the parties in the 8th Knesset, following the General Election of December 1973, was as follows:

PARTY	VOTES	SEATS	PARTY	VOTES	SEATS
Labour-Mapam Alignment* . .	621,183	51	Independent Liberals . . .	56,560	4
Likud	473,309	39	New Communist List . . .	53,353	4
National Religious Party . .	130,349	10	Arab Lists (affiliated to Labour) .	48,961	3
Torah Front (Agudat Israel-Poalei Agudat Israel)	60,012	5	Civil Rights List*	35,023	3
			Moked-Maki	22,147	1

There was a 78 per cent poll from the 2,034,478 people eligible to vote in the 1973 elections. The Knesset is elected by proportional representation by universal suffrage for four years.

* In July 1975 Labour-Mapam Alignment seats numbered 50 after one member left to join the Civil Rights List, renamed Yaad, which now has four seats.

POLITICAL PARTIES

Israel Labour Party: P.O.B. 36, Tel-Aviv; formed in 1968 as a merger of the three former Labour groups, Mapai, Rafi and Achdut Ha'avoda; Zionist Social Democratic party, membership 300,000, including most of Kibbutz (collective) and Moshav (co-operative) villages. In 1973 elections, in alignment with another Zionist Socialist party, Mapam, gained 60.2 per cent in Histadrut (General Federation of Labour) and, together with affiliated Arab and Druze factions, 54 out of 120 Knesset (Parliament) seats. Holds all central cabinet positions and heads almost all important municipalities, though not Tel-Aviv; Sec.-Gen. MEIR ZARMI.

Likud: Tel-Aviv; f. September 1973 under an agreement between Gahal (a merger of Herut and the Liberal Party), the State List, the Free Centre and the Labour Movement for the Land of Israel; party with largest membership in Israel Defence Forces; aims: territorial integrity (advocates retention of all territories occupied in the 1967 war as

essential to future security of Israel); absorption of newcomers; a social order based on freedom and justice, elimination of poverty and want; development of an economy that will assure a decent standard of living; improvement of the environment and the quality of life; reforms in local government; assurance of democracy through the formation of a strong political force, as an alternative of the ruling party. Appears as a bloc in the Knesset, municipal and local councils, and the Histadrut, but the constituent parties maintain their own autonomous organization. Joint Chairmen MENACHEM BEGIN (Herut), Dr. E. S. RIMALT (Liberal Party of Israel).

Gahal (the Herut Movement and Liberal Party Bloc) formed in 1965 as the result of an agreement between

The Herut (*Freedom*) **Movement:** P.O.B. 23062, Tel-Aviv; was founded in 1948 by the Irgun Zvai Leumi, which played an activist part in the underground struggle against the British in the closing years of the Mandate.

The Herut Party strives to extend the present frontiers of Israel to its historic boundaries extending on both sides of the Jordan. The party stands for private initiative; 61,000 mems.; Founder and Chair. MENACHEM BEGIN, M.K.

The Liberal Party of Israel: 68 Ibn Gvirol St., Tel-Aviv; f. 1961 by merger of the General Zionists' and Progressive Parties; "Includes all strata of Israel's society. Its basic principles are those of the liberal philosophy. It strives for: national unity, political and economic consolidation of the state, safeguarding its security and integrity; unceasing efforts to achieve a durable peace with Israel's neighbours; a community based on democracy and social justice; ensuring freedom of the individual and his liberties; stimulation of private enterprise; reform of the tax system; narrowing the social and educational gap between the various strata of the nation; extensive immigration and complete material and social integration of newcomers; equal rights and chances for all citizens of the state." Party Chair. Dr. E. S. RIMALT; Exec. Chair. S. EHRLICH.

The State List: f. 1969 by former members of Rafi (Labour group); Sec.-Gen. YIGAL HOROWITZ.

Free Centre: f. 1967 by dissidents from Herut; Chair. SHMUEL TAMIR.

National Religious Party: f. 1956; stands for strict adherence to Jewish religion and tradition, and strives to achieve the application of the religious precepts of Judaism in everyday life. It is also endeavouring to establish the constitution of Israel on Jewish religious law. Element in government coalition with 10 knesset seats and 3 cabinet posts.

The United Workers' Party—Mapam (*Mifleget Hapoalim Hameuchedet*): P.O. Box 1777, Tel-Aviv; f. January 1948.

Mapam is a left-wing Socialist-Zionist party, participating in the coalition government; membership: urban workers, professionals, 75 *Kibbutzim;* aims: public-owned enterprise, guaranteed real wages, progressive taxation, independence of labour movement from state control, large-scale Jewish immigration, equal rights for Arabs, neutralist foreign policy, atomic demilitarization of Israel-Arab region, a negotiated Israel-Arab peace; fully supported disengagement agreements with Egypt and Syria; branches in North and South America, Europe and Australia; since January 1969 grouped in an "alignment" (*Ma'arach*) with the Israel Labour Party (*see* above) which appeared as a common list in the December 1973 elections.

The Kibbutz Artzi Federation of collective settlements (affiliated with Mapam) maintains *Hashomer Hatzair*, which educates Jewish youth to pioneer life in Israel, and operates *Sifriat Poalim* (*The Workers' Library*) and *Hadfus Hehadash* (*The New Press*).

Daily newspaper *Al Hamishmar*; weeklies in Arabic, Yiddish and Romanian.

Gen. Sec. MEIR TALMI; Political Sec. NAFTALI FEDER; Organizing Sec. ARIEH JAFFE; International Sec. YONA GOLAN.

Independent Liberal Party: P.O.B. 23076, Tel-Aviv; f. 1965 by 7 Liberal Party Knesset members after the formation of the Herut Movement and Liberal Party Bloc; four seats in Knesset; 20,000 mems.; Chair. MOSHE KOL; Gen. Sec. ITZHAK BARKAI; publs. *Temurot* (Hebrew, monthly), *Die Liberale Rundschau* (German, monthly), *Igeret* (Hebrew, quarterly).

Meri: 3 Gordon St., Tel-Aviv; f. 1973 by Ha'olam Hazeh (New Force); supports an Israeli-Palestinian co-existence, separation of religion and state, civil rights and freedom of speech and the press; Pres. URI AVNERY.

Communist Party of Israel (MAKI): P.O.B. 1843, Tel-Aviv; f. 1919; opposes important aspects of present Soviet policy; aims include non-alignment of Israel; peace with the Arab States based on mutual recognition of the just national rights of Israeli and Arab peoples, and of the right to self-determination of the Israeli and the Palestinian people; defence of working class interests and formation of Left alignment for social progress; in 1973 formed an electoral bloc, "Moked—for Peace and Socialist Transformation"; has one seat in the 8th Knesset. Publishes the Hebrew weekly *Kol Haam*; monthlies in Yiddish, Bulgarian, English and French.

New Communist List of Israel: broke away from the Communist Party of Israel in 1965; draws its main support from the Arab Community; favours full implementation of UN Security Council resolution 242 of 1967.

Civil Rights List: Tel-Aviv; f. 1973; breakaway movement from the Labour Party; aims: women's liberation; greater freedom for the individual from the influence of the religious "establishment"; electoral reform. A new Socialist Party named Yaad was formed on May 20th, 1975, by Llova Eliav together with most of the Civil Rights Movement led by Shulamith Aloni. Yaad now has four members in the Knesset.

Agudat Israel (f. 1912) and **Poalei Agudat Israel** (f. 1924) are also Orthodox Judaist parties, the membership of the Poalei Agudat Israel being drawn largely from wage-earners; formed the Torah Front for the December 1973 elections; has five seats in the 8th Knesset.

The official organ of Agudat Israel is the daily *Hamodia*; that of the Poalei Agudat Israel is the daily *Shearim*.

Pres. of Poalei Agudat Israel Dr. K. KAHANA.

Co-operation and Fraternity Party: an Arab party associated with the *Mapai* party.

Progress and Development Party: an Arab party associated with the *Mapai* party; has two seats in the 8th Knesset.

DIPLOMATIC REPRESENTATION

EMBASSIES AND LEGATIONS ACCREDITED TO ISRAEL

(E) Embassy; (L) Legation.

Argentina: 35 Sderot Shaul Hamelekh, Tel-Aviv (E); *Ambassador:* JORGE E. CASAL.

Australia: 145 Hayarkon St., Tel-Aviv (E); *Ambassador:* RAWDON DALRYMPLE.

Austria: 11 Hermann Cohen St., Tel-Aviv (E); *Ambassador:* Dr. JOHANNA NESTOR.

Barbados: London, United Kingdom (E).

Belgium: 76 Ibn Gvirol St., Tel-Aviv (E); *Ambassador:* FRANS WILLEMS.

Bolivia: 60 Shmaryahu Levin St., Jerusalem (E); *Ambassador:* ROBERTO PACHECO HERTZOG.

Brazil: 14 Hei Be'Yiar, Tel-Aviv (E); *Ambassador:* P. J. M. DA SILVA PARANHOS DO RIO BRANCO (also accred. to Cyprus).

Burma: 12 Mateh Aharon St., Ramat Gan (E); *Ambassador:* U BA NI.

Canada: 220 Hayarkon St., Tel-Aviv (E); *Ambassador:* T. PAUL MALONE (also accred. to Cyprus).

Chile: 10 Brenner St., Jerusalem (E); *Ambassador:* Dr. SAMUEL GEISER.

Colombia: 22 Jabotinsky St., Jerusalem (E); *Ambassador:* Dr. CARLOS ENRIQUE ARDILA ORDOÑEZ (also accred. to Cyprus).

Costa Rica: 7 Mordechai Caspi St., Jerusalem (E); *Ambassador:* Mrs. R. M. KARPINSKY DE MURILLO.

Denmark: 23 Bnei Moshe St., Tel-Aviv (E); *Ambassador:* SVEN EBBESEN.

Dominican Republic: 3 Bustanay St., Jerusalem (E); *Ambassador:* JOSÉ VILLANUEVA.

Ecuador: 37 Jabotinsky St., Jerusalem (E); *Ambassador:* Dr. HUGO JATIVA-ORTIZ.

El Salvador: Kiryat Wolfson, Diskin St., Villa No. 4, Jerusalem (E); *Ambassador:* Col. NAPOLEON ARMANDO GUERRA.

Finland: 224 Hayarkon St., Tel-Aviv (E); *Ambassador:* MATTI KAHILUOTO.

France: 112 Tayeleth Herbert Samuel, Tel-Aviv (E); *Ambassador:* JEAN HERLY.

Germany, Federal Republic: 16 Soutine St., Tel-Aviv (E); *Ambassador:* PER FISCHER.

Greece: 44 Hei Beiyar, Kikar Hamedina, Tel-Aviv (L); *Diplomatic Representative:* SOTIRIOS CONSTANTOPOULOS.

Guatemala: 3 Azza St., Jerusalem (E); *Ambassador:* Col. RAMIRA GEREDA ASTURIAS (also accred. to Greece).

Haiti: 16 Kovshei Katamon St., Jerusalem (E); *Ambassador:* MUSSET PIERRE-JEROME.

Honduras: Paris, France (E).

Iceland: Oslo, Norway (E).

Ireland: Berne, Switzerland (E).

Italy: 24 Huberman St., Tel-Aviv (E); *Ambassador:* FAUSTO BACCHETTI.

Japan: 10 Huberman St., Tel-Aviv (E); *Ambassador:* KAZUHIDE KOMURO.

Korea, Republic: Rome, Italy (E).

Laos: Paris, France (E).

Malawi: Addis Ababa, Ethiopia (E).

Malta: London, United Kingdom (E).

Mexico: 14 Hei Beiyar St., Tel-Aviv (E); *Ambassador:* Dr. BENITO BERLIN.

Nepal: Paris, France (E).

Netherlands: Beith Yoel, 33 Yaffo St., Jerusalem (E); *Ambassador:* (vacant).

Nicaragua: Rome, Italy (E).

Norway: 21 Hess St., Tel-Aviv (E); *Ambassador;* ODD G. JAKOBSEN.

Panama: 6 Yeshayahu Press St., Jerusalem (E); *Ambassador:* ELIO V. ORTIZ.

Peru: 19 Weizmann St., Tel-Aviv (E); *Ambassador:* BERNARDO ROCA REY.

Philippines: 14 Hei Beiyar St., Kikar Hamedina, Tel-Aviv (E); *Ambassador:* Dr. RAFAELITA SORIANO.

Romania: 24 Adam Hacohen St., Tel-Aviv (E); *Ambassador:* ION COVACI.

South Africa: 2 Kaplan St., Tel-Aviv (E); *Ambassador:* Dr. CHARLES FINCHAM.

Sweden: 198 Hayarkon St., Tel-Aviv (E); *Ambassador:* (vacant).

Switzerland: 228 Hayarkon St., Tel-Aviv (E); *Ambassador:* JACQUES BERNARD RUEDI (also accred. to Cyprus).

Thailand: Rome, Italy (E).

Turkey: 20 Bialik St., Tel-Aviv (L); *Chargé d'Affaires:* AHMET ASIM AKYAMAC.

United Kingdom: 192 Hayarkon St., Tel-Aviv (E); *Ambassador:* ANTHONY ELLIOTT.

U.S.A.: 71 Hayarkon St., Tel-Aviv (E); *Ambassador:* MALCOLM TOON.

Uruguay: 20 Uziya St., Katamon, Jerusalem (E); *Ambassador:* (vacant).

Venezuela: 28 Rachel Imenu St., Jerusalem (E); *Ambassador:* NAPOLEÓN GIMÉNEZ.

Israel also has diplomatic relations with Jamaica, Lesotho, Singapore and Swaziland.

THE JEWISH AGENCY FOR ISRAEL

P.O.B. 92, Jerusalem.

Organization:

The governing bodies are the Assembly which determines basic policy, the Board of Governors which manages the Agency between Assembly meetings and the Executive responsible for the day to day running of the Agency.

Chairman of Executive: (vacant).

Chairman of Board of Governors: MAX M. FISHER.

Director-General: MOSHE RIVLIN.

History:

Article Four of the League of Nations' Mandate provided for the establishment of a Jewish agency to co-operate with the administration in the economic and social development of the Jewish national home. The Zionist Organization served as this agency until 1929, when the Jewish Agency was finally constituted, with the admission of non-Zionists as well as Zionists to its Council. The Zionist Congress of 1925 bound the Agency to the following "inviolable principles": a continuous increase in the volume of Jewish immigration, the recovery of the land as Jewish public property, agricultural colonization based on Jewish labour, and the promotion of the Hebrew language and Hebrew culture.

When the State of Israel was established in 1948, the provisional Government was formed from the members of the Executive of the Va'ad Leumi (the representative organ of Palestinian Jewry) and members of the Jewish Agency Executive resident in Palestine at the time. The division of tasks between the Jewish Agency and the Government was defined in the Status Law of 1952 and in a Covenant entered into in 1954.

During 1967-71 discussions on reconstituting the Jewish Agency were conducted between the World Zionist Organization and the fund raising organizations of World Jewry. In June 1971, an agreement for the reconstitution of the Agency came into force, separating the functions of the World Zionist Organization from those of the Agency.

Functions:

According to the Agreement of 1971, the Jewish Agency undertakes the immigration and absorption of immigrants in Israel, including absorption in agricultural settlement and immigrant housing, social welfare and health services in connection with immigrants, and education, youth care and training.

Revenue and Expenditure:

The Jewish Agency's chief source of revenue are the voluntary fund-raising campaigns throughout the world. Approximately two-thirds of the campaign income is derived from the U.I.A. Inc. in the United States, and the rest from campaigns conducted under the auspices of or in co-operation with the Foundation Fund (Keren Hayesod). The Agency also received 18 per cent of German Reparations from 1952–66.

Expenditure apart from debt service, includes transport of immigrants, aid to Jewish education and cultural activities as well as purchases of equipment and stocks for the new settlements established by the Agency.

Budget: (1975/76) U.S. $42 million.

JUDICIAL SYSTEM

The law of Israel is composed of Ottoman law, British law, Palestine law, applicable in Palestine on May 14th, 1948, when the independence of the State of Israel was declared, the substance of the common law and doctrines of equity in force in England, as modified to suit local conditions, and religious law of the various recognized religious communities as regards matters of personal status, in so far as there is nothing in any of the said laws repugnant to Israeli legislation and subject to such modifications as may have resulted from the establishment of the State of Israel and its authorities, and also of the laws enacted by the Israeli legislature. The pre-1948 law is increasingly being replaced by original local legislation.

CIVIL COURTS

The Supreme Court is the highest judicial instance in the State. It has jurisdiction as an Appellate Court from the District Courts in all matters, both civil and criminal (sitting as a Court of Civil Appeal or as a Court of Criminal Appeal), and as a Court of First Instance (sitting as a High Court of Justice) in matters in which it considers it necessary to grant relief in the interests of justice and which are not within the jurisdiction of any other court or tribunal. This includes applications for orders in the nature of *habeas corpus*, *mandamus*, prohibition and *certiorari*, and enables the court to review the legality of acts of administrative authorities of all kinds.

President of the Supreme Court: S. AGRANAT.

Permanent Deputy President of the Supreme Court: Y. SUSSMAN.

Justices of the Supreme Court: M. LANDAU, Z. BERINSON, A. WITKON, H. COHN, E. M. MANNY, I. KISTER, M. ETZIONI, I. KAHAN.

The District Courts: Jerusalem, Tel-Aviv-Jaffa, Haifa, Beersheba, Nazareth. They have unlimited jurisdiction as Courts of First Instance in all civil and criminal matters not within the jurisdiction of a Magistrates' Court, all matters not within the exclusive jurisdiction of any other tribunal, and matters within the concurrent jurisdiction of any other tribunal so long as such tribunal does not deal with them, and as an Appellate Court in appeals from judgments and decisions of Magistrates' Courts and judgments of Municipal Courts and various administrative tribunals.

Magistrates' Courts: There are 27 Magistrates' Courts, having criminal jurisdiction to try contraventions and misdemeanours, and civil jurisdiction to try actions concerning possession or use of immovable property, or the partition thereof whatever may be the value of the subject matter of the action, and other civil actions where the amount of the claim, or the value of the subject matter, does not exceed I£10,000.

Labour Courts: Established in 1969. Regional Labour Courts in Jerusalem, Tel-Aviv, Haifa and Beersheba, composed of Judges and representatives of the Public. A National Labour Court in Jerusalem, presided over by Judge Z. Bar-Niv. The Courts have jurisdiction over all matters arising out of the relationship between employer and employee; between parties to a collective labour agreement; matters concerning the National Insurance Law and the Labour Law and Rules.

Municipal Courts: There are 5 Municipal Courts, having criminal jurisdiction over any offences against municipal regulations and by-laws and certain other offences, such as town planning offences, committed within the municipal area.

RELIGIOUS COURTS

The Religious Courts are the Courts of the recognized religious communities. They are competent in certain defined matters of personal status concerning members of their community. Where any action of personal status involves persons of different religious communities the President of the Supreme Court will decide which Court shall have jurisdiction. Whenever a question arises as to whether or not a case is one of personal status within the exclusive jurisdiction of a Religious Court, the matter must be referred to a Special Tribunal composed of two Justices of the Supreme Court and the President of the highest court of the religious community concerned in Israel.

The judgments of the Religious Courts are executed by the process and offices of the Civil Courts.

Jewish Rabbinical Courts: These Courts have exclusive jurisdiction in matters of marriage and divorce of Jews in Israel who are Israeli citizens or residents. In all other matters of personal status they have concurrent jurisdiction with the District Courts with the consent of all parties concerned.

Muslim Religious Courts: These Courts have exclusive jurisdiction in matters of marriage and divorce of Muslims who are not foreigners, or who are foreigners subject by their national law to the jurisdiction of Muslim Religious Courts in such matters. In all other matters of personal status they have concurrent jurisdiction with the District Courts with the consent of all parties concerned.

Christian Religious Courts: The Courts of the recognized Christian communities have exclusive jurisdiction in matters of marriage and divorce of members of their communities who are not foreigners. In all other matters of personal status they have concurrent jurisdiction with the District Courts with the consent of all parties concerned. But neither these Courts nor the Civil Courts have jurisdiction to dissolve the marriage of a foreign subject.

Druze Courts: These Courts, established in 1963, have exclusive jurisdiction in matters of marriage and divorce of Druze in Israel, who are Israeli citizens or residents, and concurrent jurisdiction with the District Courts in all other matters of personal status of Druze with the consent of all parties concerned.

MILITARY COURTS

Courts-Martial: A Court-Martial is competent to try a soldier within the meaning of the Military Justice Law, 1955, who has committed an act constituting a military offence, without prejudice to the power of any other Court in the State to try him for that act if it constitutes an offence under any other law. A Court-Martial is also competent to try a soldier for any offence which is not a military offence, but the Attorney General may order that he be tried by another Court if he is of the opinion that the offence was not committed within the framework of the Army or in consequence of the accused's belonging to the Army.

RELIGION

JUDAISM

Judaism, the religion evolved and followed by the Jews, is the faith of the great majority of the population. Its basis is a belief in an ethical monotheism.

There are two main Jewish communities: the Ashkenazim and the Sephardim. The former are the Jews from Eastern, Central, or Northern Europe, while the latter originate from the Balkan countries, North Africa and the Middle East. Although they have separate synagogues, and differ somewhat in their ritual and pronunciation of Hebrew, there is no doctrinal distinction. The prevailing influence is that of the Ashkenazim Jews, who are more modern and westernized, but the recent Hebrew revival has been based on the Sephardi pronunciation of the ancient Hebrew tongue.

The supreme religious authority is vested in the Chief Rabbinate, which consists of the Ashkenazi and Sephardi Chief Rabbis and the Supreme Rabbinical Council. It makes decisions on interpretation of the Jewish law, and supervises the Rabbinal Courts. There are 8 regional Rabbinical Courts, and a Rabbinical Court of Appeal presided over by the two Chief Rabbis.

According to the Rabbinical Courts Jurisdiction Law of 1953, marriage and divorce among Jews in Israel are exclusively within the jurisdiction of the Rabbinical Courts. Provided that all the parties concerned agree, other matters of personal status can also be decided by the Rabbinical Courts.

There are 195 Religious Councils, which maintain religious services and supply religious needs, and about 405 religious committees with similar functions in smaller settlements. Their expenses are borne jointly by the State and the local authorities. The Religious Councils are under the administrative control of the Ministry of Religious Affairs. In all matters of religion, the Religious Councils are subject to the authority of the Chief Rabbinate. There are 365 officially appointed rabbis. The total number of synagogues is about 7,000, most of which are organized within the framework of the Union of Israel Synagogues.

Head of the Ashkenazi Community: H.E. The Chief Rabbi SHLOMO GOREN.

Head of the Sephardic Community: H.E. The Chief Rabbi OVADIA YOSSEF.

Two Jewish sects still loyal to their distinctive customs are:

The Karaites, a sect which recognizes only the Jewish written law and not the oral law of the Mishna and Talmud. The community of about 12,000 many of whom live in or near Ramla, has been augmented by immigration from Egypt.

The Samaritans, an ancient sect mentioned in 2 Kings xvii, 24. They recognize only the Torah. The community in Israel numbers about 500; about half of them live in Holon, where a Samaritan synagogue has been built, and the remainder, including the High Priest live in Nablus, near Mt. Gerizim, which is sacred to the Samaritans.

ISLAM

The Muslims in Israel are in the main Sunnis, and are divided among the four rites of the Sunni school of Muslim thought: the Shafe'i, the Hanbali, the Hanafi, and the Maliki. Before June 1967 they numbered approximately 175,000; in 1971, approximately 343,900.

CHRISTIAN COMMUNITIES

The Greek Catholic Church, P.O.B. 279, Haifa; numbers about 35,000 and Haifa is the seat of the Archbishop of Acre, Haifa, Nazareth and all Galilee; Archbishop JOSEPH M. RAYA; publ. *Ar-Rabita* (Arabic monthly; circ. 4,000).

The Greek Orthodox Church in Israel has approximately 22,000 members. The Patriarch of Jerusalem is His Beatitude BENEDICTOS.

The Latin (Roman Catholic) Church has about 10,000 native members in Israel plus about 2,000 Polish and Hungarian Catholic refugees. The Latin Patriarch of Jerusalem is His Beatitude JAMES JOSEPH BELTRITTI; Representative in Israel H.E. Bishop HANNA KALDANY.

The Maronite Community, with approximately 4,000 members, has communal centres in Haifa, Jaffa, Jish, Nazareth and Jerusalem. The Maronite Patriarch resides in the Lebanon.

The Evangelical Episcopal Church in Israel, which belongs to the Anglican Communion, has 1,000 members and was officially recognised by Israel in April 1970; it comes under the jurisdiction of the Archbishop in Jerusalem and is now being reorganized (Temporary Vicar-Gen., the Most Rev. Dr. ROBERT STOPFORD, St. George's Close, Jerusalem).

Other denominations include the *Armenian Church* (900 members), the *Coptic Church* (700 members), the *Russian Orthodox Church*, which maintains an Ecclesiastical Mission, the *Ethiopian Church*, and the *Baptist Lutheran* and *Presbyterian Churches*.

THE PRESS

Tel-Aviv is the main publishing centre, only three dailies being published in Jerusalem. Largely for economic reasons there has developed no local press away from these cities; hence all papers regard themselves as national. Friday editions, Sabbath eve, are increased to up to twice the normal size by special weekend supplements, and experience a considerable rise in circulation. No newspapers appear on Saturday.

Most of the daily papers are in Hebrew, and others appear in Arabic, English, French, Polish, Yiddish, Hungarian and German. The total daily circulation is 500,000–600,000 copies, or twenty-one papers per hundred people, although most citizens read more than one daily paper.

Most Hebrew morning dailies have strong political or religious affiliations. *Lamerhav* is affiliated to Achdut Ha'avoda, *Al Hamishmar* to Mapam, *Hatzofeh* to the National Religious Front—World Mizrahi. *Davar* is the long-established organ of the Histadrut. Mapai publishes the weekly *Ot* but no daily. Although the revenue from advertisements is increasing, very few dailies are economically self-supporting; most depend on subsidies from political parties, religious organizations or public funds. The limiting effect on freedom of commentary entailed by this party press system has provoked repeated criticism.

The Jerusalem Arabic daily *Al Anba* has a small circulation (10,000) but an increasing number of Israeli Arabs are now reading Hebrew dailies. The daily, *Al Quds*, was founded in 1968 for Arabs in Jerusalem and the West Bank; the small indigenous press of occupied Jordan has largely ceased publication or transferred operations to Amman.

There are around 400 other newspapers and magazines including some 50 weekly and 150 fortnightly; over 250 of them are in Hebrew, the remainder in eleven other languages.

The most influential and respected dailies, for both quality of news coverage and commentary, are *Ha'aretz*, characterized by its sober but proudly independent editorials, and the Union paper, *Davar*, which frequently has articles by government figures. These are the widest read of the morning papers, exceeded only by the popular afternoon press, *Ma'ariv* and *Yedioth Aharonoth*. The *Jerusalem Post* gives detailed and sound news coverage in English.

The Israeli Press Council, established in 1963, deals with matters of common interest to the Press such as drafting the recently published code of professional ethics which is binding on all journalists.

The Daily Newspaper Publishers' Association represents publishers in negotiations with official and public bodies, negotiates contracts with employees and purchases and distributes newsprint, of which Israel now manufactures 75 per cent of her needs.

DAILIES

Al-Anba: P.O.B. 428, 7 Habikma St., Jerusalem; f. 1968; published by Jerusalem Publications Ltd.; Editor YAACOV HAZMA; circ. 10,000.

Al Hamishmar (*The Guardian*): Hamishmar House, 4 Ben Avigdor St., Tel-Aviv; f. 1943; morning; organ of the United Worker's Party (Mapam); Editors MARK GEFEN, HAIM SHUR; circ. 25,000.

Al Quds (*Jerusalem*): P.O.B. 19788, Jerusalem; f. 1968; Arabic; Editor ABU ZALAF.

Chadshot Hasport: Tushia St., P.O.B. 20011, Tel-Aviv 61200; f. 1954; Hebrew; sports; independent; circ. 30,000.

Davar (*The Word*): P.O.B. 199, 45 Sheinkin St., Tel-Aviv; f. 1925; morning; official organ of the General Federation of Labour (Histadrut); Editor HANNAH ZEMER; circ. 50,000.

Ha'aretz (*The Land*): 21 Salman Schocken St., Tel-Aviv; f. 1918; morning; liberal, independent; Editor GERSHOM G. SCHOCKEN; circ. 55,000 (week-days), 75,000 (weekends).

Hamodia: Kikar Hacheruth, P.O.B. 1306, Jerusalem; organ of Agudat Israel; morning; Editor YEHUDA L. LEVIN; circ. 8,000.

Hatzofeh: 66 Hamasger St., Tel-Aviv; f. 1938; morning; organ of the National Religious Front; Editor S. DANIEL; circ. 11,000.

Israel Nachrichten: 52 Harakevet St., Tel-Aviv; f. 1974; morning; German; Editor J. E. PALMON; Publisher S. HIMMELFARB; circ. 20,000.

Israelski Far Tribuna: 113 Givat Herzl St., Tel-Aviv; Bulgarian.

Jerusalem Post: P.O.B. 81, Romema, Jerusalem; f. 1932; morning; independent; English; Editor (vacant); circ. 34,000 (weekdays), 45,000 (weekend edition); there is also a weekly overseas edition (*q.v.*).

Le Journal d'Israel: 26 Agra St., P.O.B. 28330, Tel-Aviv; independent; French; Dir.-Chief Editor J. RABIN; circ. 10,000; also overseas weekly selection; circ. 15,000.

Lamerhav: 1 Nahal Ayalon St., Tel-Aviv; f. 1954; morning; socialist; Chief Editor DAVID PEDAHZUR; circ. 18,000.

Letzte Nyess (*Late News*): 52 Harakevet St., Tel-Aviv; f. 1949; Yiddish; morning; Editor M. TSANIN; circ. 23,000.

Ma'ariv: Ma'ariv House, P.O.B. 20010, Tel-Aviv; f. 1948; evening; independent; Editor ARIE DISSENTSHIK; circ. daily 170,000, Friday 225,000.

Nowiny i Kurier: 52 Harakevet St., Tel-Aviv; f. 1952; Polish; morning; Editor S. HIMELFARB; circ. 15,000.

Omer: 45 Sheinkin St., Tel-Aviv; Histadrut popular vowelled Hebrew paper; f. 1951; Chief Editor MEIR BARELI; circ. 10,000.

Sha'ar: 4A Hissin St., Tel-Aviv 64284; economy and finance; Hebrew and English; Editor S. LARI.

Shearim: 64 Frichman St., Tel-Aviv; organ of Poalei Agudat Israel; Editor YEHUDA NAHSHONI; circ. 5,000.

UJ Kelet: 52 Harakevet St., Tel-Aviv; f. 1918; morning; Hungarian; independent; Editor Dr. G. MARTON; circ. 20,000.

Viata Noastra: 52 Harakevet St., Tel-Aviv; f. 1950; Romanian; supports the Israel Labour Party; morning; Editor MEIR ZAIT; circ. 30,000.

Yedioth Aharonoth: 5 Yehuda Mozes St., Tel-Aviv; f. 1939; evening; independent; Editor Dr. H. ROSENBLUM; circ. 140,000, Friday 195,000.

Yom Yom: P.O.B. 1194, Tel-Aviv; f. 1964; morning; economy and finance; Editor P. MERSTEN.

WEEKLIES AND FORTNIGHTLIES

Al Ta'awun: P.O.B. 303, Tel-Aviv; f. 1961; published by the Arab Worker's Dept. of the Histadrut and the Co-operatives Dept. of the Ministry of Labour; co-operatives quarterly; Editor TUVIA SHAMOSH.

Al Harriya: 38 King George St., Tel-Aviv; Arabic weekly of the Herut Party.

Al-Ittihad: P.O.B. 104, Haifa; f. 1944; Arabic; journal of the Israeli Communist Party; Chief Editor EMILE HABIBI.

Al Marsad: P.O.B. 736, 4 Ben Avigdor St., Tel-Aviv; Mapam; Arabic.

Bama'alah: P.O.B. 303, Tel-Aviv; journal of the young Histadrut Movement; Editor N. ANAELY.

Bamahane: Military P.O.B. 1013, Tel-Aviv; f. 1948; military, illustrated weekly of the Israel Army; Editor YOSSEF ESHKOL.

Bitaon Heyl Ha'avir (*Air Force Magazine*): Doar Zwai 2348; f. 1948; Editor M. HADAR; Managing Editor Y. OFFER; circ. 33,000.

Dvar Hashavua: 45 Sheinkin St., Tel-Aviv; f. 1946; popular illustrated; weekly; published by Histadrut, General Federation of Labour; Editor O. ZMORA; circ. 50,000.

Economic Review: 17 Kaplan St., Tel-Aviv; economic and social problems of immigration and absorption; Editors Dr. L. BERGER, CHAYA LAZAR; circ. English edition 3,500, Spanish edition (*Reseña Económica*) 2,000, French edition (*Revue Economique*) 2,000.

Ethgar: 75 Einstein Street, Tel-Aviv; twice weekly; Editor NATHAN YALIN-MOR.

Glasul Populurui: Eilath St., P.O.B. 2675, Tel-Aviv; weekly of the Communist Party of Israel; Romanian; Editor MEÏR SEMO.

Gold, Money, Commodities: 37, Harbour St., Haifa; f. 1969; fortnightly; English; hedged investments, investment advice, monetary developments.

Haolam Hazeh: P.O.B. 136, 3 Gordon St., Tel-Aviv; f. 1937; independent; illustrated news magazine; weekly; Editor-in-Chief URI AVNERY.

Harefuah: 39 Shaul Hamelech Blvd., Tel-Aviv; f. 1920; with English summary; fortnightly journal of the Israeli Medical Association; Editor I. SUM, M.D.; circ. 6,000.

Hed Hahinukh: 8 Ben-Saruk Street, Tel-Aviv; f. 1926; weekly; educational; published by the Israeli Teachers' Union; Editor ZVI ARAD; circ. 32,000.

Illustrirte Weltwoch: P.O.B. 2571, Tel-Aviv; f. 1956; Yiddish; weekly; Editor M. KARPINOVITZ.

The Israel Digest: P.O.B. 92, Jerusalem; f. 1957; independent; fortnightly digest of news and views; circ. 20,000; Editor ZVI SOIFER.

Jerusalem Post Overseas Weekly: P.O.B. 81, Romema, Jerusalem; f. 1959; English; Overseas edition of the *Jerusalem Post* (*q.v.*); circ. 35,000 to 95 countries.

Kol Ha'am (*Voice of the People*): 37 Eilath St., P.O.B. 2675, Tel-Aviv; f. 1947; organ of the Communist Party of Israel; Editor B. BALTI.

Laisha: P.O.B. 28122, 7 Fin St., Tel-Aviv; f. 1946; Hebrew; women's magazine; Editor DAVID KARASSIK.

Liawladina: Arabic Publishing House, P.O.B. 28049, Tel-Aviv; f. 1960; children's fortnightly; Board of Editors ELIAHU AGHASSI, DEEBEH GHABIN, MISHEL HADDAD, MUSTAFA MURAR, SAMIRA NAQQASH, NAZIR SHIMALLY.

Maariv Lanoar: 2 Carlebach St., Tel-Aviv; f. 1956; weekly for the youth; Editor AMMON BEI-RAV; circ. 26,000.

MB (*Mitteilungsblatt*): P.O.B. 1480, Tel-Aviv; f. 1932; German journal of the Irgun Olei Merkas Europa; Editor Dr. HANS TRAMER.

Min Hayesod: Tel-Aviv; fortnightly; Hebrew; news and political commentary.

Reshumot: Ministry of Justice, Jerusalem; f. 1948; Hebrew and Arabic; official Government gazette.

Sada-A-Tarbia (*The Echo of Education*): published by the Histadrut and Teachers' Association, P.O.B. 303, Tel-Aviv; f. 1952; Arabic; educational; fortnightly; Editor TUVIA SHAMOSH.

OTHER PERIODICALS

Al-Bushra: P.O.B. 6088, Haifa; f. 1935; monthly; Arabic; organ of the Ahmadiyya movement; Editor JALAL-UD-DIN QAMAR.

Al Hamishmar: 20 Yehuda Halevy Street, Tel-Aviv; Bulgarian monthly of United Workers' Party.

Al Jadid: P.O.B. 104, Haifa; Arabic; literary monthly; Editor HANA NAKARA.

Ariel: Cultural and Scientific Relations Division, Ministry for Foreign Affairs, Jerusalem; published by Youval Tal, P.O.B. 2160, Jerusalem; f. 1962; quarterly review of the arts and letters in Israel; edns. in English, Spanish, French and German; Editor YAEL LOTAN.

Avoda Ubituach Leumi: P.O.B. 915, Jerusalem; f. 1949; monthly review of the Ministry of Labour, and the National Insurance Institute, Jerusalem; Editor Z. HEYN; circ. 3,000.

Business Diary: 37 Harbour St., Haifa; f. 1947; monthly; English; news digest, trade, finance; Editor G. ALON.

Business Diary Trade Lists: 37 Harbour St., Haifa; f. 1947; weekly; English, Hebrew; shipping movements, import licences, stock exchange listings, business failures, etc.; Editor G. ALON.

Christian News from Israel: 23 Shlomo Hamelech St., Jerusalem; quarterly issued by the Ministry of Religious Affairs; in English, French, Spanish; Editor SHALOM BEN-ZAKKAI; circ. 20,000.

Dapim Refuiim: 101 Arlosoroff St., P.O.B. 16250, Tel-Aviv; f. 1935; eight times a year; medical; Hebrew with English and French summaries; circ. 5,000; Editor Dr. M. DVORJETSKI.

Divrei Haknesset: c/o The Knesset, Jerusalem; f. 1949; records of the proceedings of the Knesset, published by the Government Printer, Jerusalem; Editor D. NIV; circ. 300.

Dvar Hapoelet: P.O.B. 303, Tel-Aviv; f. 1934; monthly journal of the Council of Women Workers of the Histadrut; Hebrew; Editor ZIVIA COHEN; circ. 11,000.

Folk un Zion: P.O.B. 92, Jerusalem; f. 1950; monthly; current events relating to Israel and World Jewry; circ. 6,000; Editor SIMHA SNEH.

Frei Israel: P.O.B. 8512, Tel-Aviv; Yiddish, progressive monthly, publ. by Asscn. for Popular Culture.

Gazit: 8 Zvi Brook St., P.O.B. 4190, Tel-Aviv; f. 1932; monthly; Hebrew and English; art, literature; Publisher G. TALPHIR.

Goldene Keit, Die: 30 Weizmann St., Tel-Aviv; f. 1949; Yiddish; literary quarterly; published by the Histadrut; Editor A. SUTZKEVER; Co-Editor E. PINES; Man. Editor SHMUEL CHORESH.

Hameshek Hahaklai: 21 Melchett St., Tel-Aviv; f. 1929; agricultural; Editor ISRAEL INBARI.

Hamis'har (*Commerce*): P.O.B. 852, Tel-Aviv; f. 1932; quarterly; Hebrew; economic and commercial; Chamber of Commerce Tel-Aviv-Yafo; Editor Dr. E. W. KLIMOWSKY; circ. 50,000.

Hamizrah Hehadash (*The New East*): The Hebrew University of Jerusalem; f. 1949; quarterly of the Israel Oriental Society; Hebrew with English summary; Middle Eastern, Asian and African Affairs; Editor YEHOSHUA PORATH.

Hamlonai (*The Hotelier*): P.O.B. 11586, Tel-Aviv; f. 1962; monthly of the Israel Hotel Association; Hebrew and English; Editor Dr. K. LICHT.

Hapraklit: P.O.B. 14152 Tel-Aviv; f. 1943; quarterly; published by the Israel Bar Association; Editors A. POLONSKY, J. GROSS; circ. 6,500.

Hassadeh: 25 Lilienblum St., Tel-Aviv; f. 1920; monthly; review of mixed farming; English summaries; Editor J. M. MARGALIT; circ. 10,000.

Hed Hagan: 8 Ben Saruk St., Tel-Aviv; f. 1935; educational; Editor Mrs. ESTHER RABINOWITZ; circ. 3,500.

Israel Annals of Psychiatry: Jerusalem Academic Press, Givat Saul, P.O.B. 2390, Jerusalem; f. 1963; quarterly; Editor-in-Chief Prof. H. Z. WINNIK.

Israel Economist: P.O.B. 7052, 6 Hazanowitz St., Jerusalem; f. 1945; monthly; English; political and economic; independent; Editor J. KOLLEK, M.JUR.; also publishes *The Tel-Aviv Stock Exchange Information Card Service.*

Israel Exploration Journal: P.O.B. 7041, Jerusalem; f. 1950; quarterly; Editor Dr. D. BARAG; circ. 2,000.

Israel Export and Trade Journal, The: P.O.B. 11586, Tel-Aviv; f. 1949; monthly; English; commercial and economic; published by Israel Periodicals Co. Ltd.; Editor YOANNE YARON; Man. Dirs. F. A. LEWINSON and ZALMAN PELTZ.

Israel Industry and Commerce: P.O.B. 1199, Tel-Aviv; English; monthly; serves Israeli exporters; Editor SH. YEDIDYAH.

Israel Journal of Medical Sciences: P.O.B. 1435, Jerusalem; incorporating *The Israel Journal of Experimental Medicine* and *The Israel Medical Journal*; f. 1965; monthly; Editor-in-Chief Dr. M. PRYWES; circ. 5,500.

Israels Aussenhandel: 14 Chissin St., P.O.B. 11586, Tel-Aviv; f. 1967; monthly; German; commercial; Editor Z. PELTZ.

Kalkalan: 8 Akiva St., P.O.B. 7052, Jerusalem; f. 1952; monthly; Hebrew commercial and economic; independent; Editor J. KOLLEK, M.JUR.

Kirjath Sepher: P.O.B. 503, Jerusalem; f. 1924; bibliographical quarterly of the Jewish National and University Library, Jerusalem.

Labour in Israel: 93 Arlosoroff St., Tel-Aviv; periodic bulletin of the Histadrut; English, Swedish, French, German, Portuguese and Spanish.

Leshonenu: Academy of the Hebrew Language, P.O.B. 3449, Jerusalem; f. 1929; quarterly; for the study of the Hebrew language and cognate subjects; Editor S. ABRAMSON.

Leshonenu La'am: Academy of the Hebrew Language, P.O.B. 3449, Jerusalem; f. 1945; popular Hebrew philology; Editors E. ETAN, M. MEDAN.

Ma'arachot: Ha'Kirya Rechov Gimmel 1, Tel-Aviv; f. 1939; military; Editor Col. STZCHAK ZIV.

Mada: Weizmann Science Press of Israel, P.O.B. 801, Jerusalem; f. 1956; popular scientific bi-monthly in Hebrew; Editor-in-Chief KAPAI PINES; circ. 11,000.

Melaha Vetaassiya (*Trade and Industry*): P.O.B. 11586, Tel-Aviv; monthly review of the Union of Artisans and Manufacturers of Israel; Man. Dir. Z. PELTZ.

Mibifnim: 27 Sutin St., P.O.B. 16040, Tel-Aviv; f. 1924; quarterly of the United Collective Settlements (Hakibbutz Hameuchad); Editor ZERUBAVEL GILEAD; circ. 8,000.

Molad: P.O.B. 1165, Jerusalem; f. 1948; quarterly; independent political and literary periodical; Hebrew; published by Miph'ale Molad Ltd.; Editor EPHRAIM BROIDO.

Monthly Bulletin of Statistics: Israel Central Bureau of Statistics, P.O.B. 13015, Jerusalem; f. 1949.

Monthly Statistics of the Administered Territories: f. 1971; Hebrew and English.

Foreign Trade Statistical Quarterly: f. 1969; Hebrew and English.

Monthly Statistics of Tourism and Hotel Services: f. 1973; Hebrew and English.

Monthly Price Statistics: f. 1949; Hebrew.

Monthly Foreign Trade Statistics: f. 1950; Hebrew and English.

Immigration Statistics: f. 1970; monthly and quarterly; Hebrew.

Moznayim (*Balance*): P.O.B. 7098, Tel-Aviv; f. 1929; literature and culture; monthly; circ. 2,500; Editors B. Y. MICHALY, A. B. YOFFE.

Ner: Ihud, P.O.B. 451, Jerusalem; f. 1948; monthly on political and social problems; advocates Arab-Jewish reconciliation; Hebrew, English, Arabic; circ. 1,500.

New Outlook: 8 Karl Netter St., Tel-Aviv; f. 1957; Israeli and Middle Eastern Affairs; monthly; circ. 10,000; Editor SIMHA FLAPAN.

Proche-Orient Chrétien: B.P. 19079, Jerusalem; f. 1951; quarterly.

Quarterly Review of the Israel Medical Association (*Mif'al Haverut Hutz*—Non-resident Fellowship of the Israel Medical Association): 39 Shaul Hamelekh Blvd., Tel-Aviv; English; also published in French and Spanish; quarterly; Editor Dr. V. RESNEKOV.

Refuah Veterinarit: P.O.B. 18, Beit Dagan; f. 1943; quarterly review of veterinary medicine; Editor Dr. M. LANDAU.

La Revue de l'A.M.I. (Non-resident Fellowship of the Israeli Medical Association): 39 Shaul Hamelekh Blvd., Tel-Aviv; French, English and Spanish; quarterly; Editor Dr. S. ZALUD.

Scopus: Hebrew University of Jerusalem; f. 1946; published by Department of Information and Public Affairs, Hebrew University of Jerusalem; twice yearly; English; Editor D. A. SUSMAN.

Shituf (*Co-operation*): 24 Ha'arba St., Tel-Aviv, P.O.B. 7151; f. 1948; monthly; economic, social and co-operative problems in Israel; published by the Central Union of Industrial, Transport and Service Co-operative Societies; Editor L. LOSH; circ. 2,500.

Sinai: P.O.B. 642, Jerusalem; Torah, science and literature; Editor Dr. YITZCHAK RAPHAEL.

Sindbad: P.O.B. 28049, Tel-Aviv; f. 1969; children's monthly; Editors ELIAHU AGHASSI, WALID HUSSEIN.

Sulam: 2 Ben Yehuda St., Jerusalem; political; monthly; Editor Y. SHAIB.

Terra Santa: P.O.B. 186, Jerusalem; f. 1921; monthly; published by the Custody of the Holy Land (the official custodians of the Holy Shrines); Italian, Spanish, French, English and Arabic editions published in Jerusalem, by the Franciscan Printing Press, English edition in Washington, German edition in Vienna, Maltese edition in Valletta.

Tmuroth: 48 Hamelech George St., P.O.B. 23076, Tel-Aviv; f. 1960; organ of the Liberal Labour Movement; monthly; Editor D. SHLOMI.

Urim La-Orim: 93 Arlosoroff St., P.O.B. 303, Tel-Aviv; educational problems in the family; monthly; Editor HAYIM NAGID.

Vilner Pinkas: P.O.B. 28006, Tel-Aviv; f. 1968; periodical review of current affairs for Vilna-Jews the world over, and for the history of Yerushdayim Delito; Yiddish; Editor M. KARPINOVITZ.

WIZO Review: Women's International Zionist Organization, 38 Sderoth David Hamelekh, Tel-Aviv; English, Spanish and German editions; Editor SYLVIA SATTEN BANIN; circ. 20,000.

Yam: Israeli Maritime League, P.O.B. 706, 5 Habankim St., Haifa; f. 1937; review of marine problems; Editor Z. ESHEL; Pres. MOSHE M. POMROCK; circ. 5,500.

Zahrat-el-Shabab: Arabic Publishing House, P.O.B. 28049, Tel-Aviv; f. 1971; teenagers' monthly; Editors E. AGHASSI, R. BAYADSI, MUSTAFA MURAR, RASMI BAYADSI, ABDUL-GHAFFAR YUNIS.

Zion: P.O.B. 1062, Jerusalem; f. 1935; research in Jewish history; quarterly; Hebrew and English; Editors I. F. BAER, H. H. BEN-SASSON, S. ETTINGER.

Zraim: 7 Dubnov St., P.O.B. 40027, Tel-Aviv; f. 1953; journal of the Bnei Akiva (Youth of Hapoel Hamizrachi) Movement; Editor YEDIDIA COHEN.

Zrakor: 37 Harbour St., Haifa; f. 1947; monthly; Hebrew; news digest, trade, finance, economics, shipping; Editor G. ALON.

The following are all published by Weizmann Science Press Israel, P.O.B. 801, Jerusalem 91000; Exec. Editor L. LESTER.

Israel Journal of Botany: f. 1951; Editor Prof. LEONORA REINHOLD; quarterly.

Israel Journal of Chemistry: f. 1951; Editor Prof. Y. ELIEZER; bi-monthly.

Israel Journal of Earth-Sciences: f. 1951; Editor Y. WEILER; quarterly.

Israel Journal of Mathematics: f. 1951; Editors B. WEISS, A. PAZI; monthly, 3 vols. of 4 issues each per year.

Israel Journal of Technology: f. 1951; Editor Prof. D. ABIR; 6 issues per year.

Israel Journal of Zoology: f. 1951; Editor Y. L. WERNER; quarterly.

Journal d'Analyse Mathématique: f. 1955; Editor Prof. Y. KATZNELSON; irregular.

PUBLISHERS' ASSOCIATION

Daily Newspaper Publishers' Association of Israel: P.O.B. 2251, 4 Kaplan St., Tel-Aviv; safeguards professional interests and maintains standards, supplies newsprint to dailies; negotiates with trade unions, etc.; mems. all daily papers; affiliated to International Federation of Newspaper Publishers.

NEWS AGENCIES

Jewish Telegraphic Agency (JTA): Israel Bureau, Jerusalem Post Building, Romema, Jerusalem 94467; Dir. DAVID LANDAU.

ITIM, News Agency of the Associated Israel Press: 10 Tiomkin Street, Tel-Aviv; f. 1950; co-operative news agency; Dir. and Editor HAYIM BALTSAN.

FOREIGN BUREAUX

Agence France-Presse: 7 Schderot Kheu, Tel-Aviv; Chief NATHAN GURDUS.

ANSA: 25 Ibn Gvirol St., Tel-Aviv; Bureau Chief FABIO CANNILLO.

Middle East Bureau: Jerusalem Post Bldg. Jerusalem, 94 467.

The following are also represented: AP, DPA, North American Newspaper Alliance, Reuters, Tass.

PUBLISHERS

Achiasaf Ltd.: 13 Yosef Hanassi St., Tel-Aviv; f. 1933; general; Man. Dir. SCHACHMA ACHIASAF.

Am Hassefer Ltd.: 9 Bialik St., Tel-Aviv; f. 1955; Man. Dir. DOV LIPETZ.

"Am Oved" Ltd.: 22 Mazah Street, Tel-Aviv; f. 1942; fiction, scientific, sociology; textbooks, children's books; Man. Dir. N. URIELI.

Amichai Publishing House Ltd.: 5 Yosef Hanassi St., Tel-Aviv; f. 1948; Man. Dir. YEHUDA ORLINSKY.

Arabic Publishing House: 17A Hagra St., P.O.B. 28049, Tel-Aviv; f. 1960; established by the Histadrut (trade union) organization; periodicals and books; Dir. and Gen. Editor ELIAHU AGHASSI; Senior Editor MUSTAFA MURAR.

Bialik Institute, The: P.O.B. 92, Jerusalem; f. 1935; classics, encyclopaedias, criticism, history, archaeology, art, reference books, Judaica; Dir. CHAIM MILKOV.

Carta, The Israel Map and Publishing Co. Ltd.: Mazia St., P.O.B. 2500, Jerusalem; f. 1958; the principal cartographic publisher; Man. Dir. EMANUEL HAUSMAN.

Dvir Publishing Co. Ltd., The: 58 Mazah St., P.O.B. 149, Tel-Aviv; literature, science, art, education; Man. Dir. ALEXANDER BROIDO.

Eked Publishing House: 29 Bar-Kochba St., Tel-Aviv; f. 1959; poetry; Dirs. ITAMAR YAOZ-KEST, MARITZA ROSMAN.

Encyclopedia Publishing Co.: 1 King David St., Jerusalem; f. 1947; Hebrew Encyclopedia and other encyclopedias; Chair. Mrs. BRACHA PELI, ALEXANDER PELI.

Gazit: 8 Zvi Brook St., Tel-Aviv, P.O.B. 4190; art publishers; Editor GABRIEL TALPHIR.

Haifa Publishing Co. Ltd.: P.O.B. 407, Haifa; f. 1960; fiction and non-fiction.

Hakibbutz Hameuchad Publishing House Ltd.: P.O.B. 16040, 15 Nehardea St., Tel-Aviv; f. 1940; general; Dir. A. AVISHAI.

Hamenorah Publishing House: 24 Zangwill St., Tel-Aviv; f. 1958; books in Hebrew, Yiddish and English; Dir. MORDECHAI SONNSCHEIN.

Israeli Music Publications Ltd.: 105 Ben Yehuda St., P.O.B. 6011, Tel-Aviv; f. 1949; books on music and musical works; Dir. Dr. PETER E. GRADENWITZ.

Izre'el Publishing House Ltd.: 76 Dizengoff St., Tel-Aviv; f. 1933; Man. ALEXANDER IZREEL.

Jerusalem Academic Press: Givat Shaul, P.O.B. 2390, Jerusalem; f. 1959; scientific and technical publications; Gen. Man. ITZHAK LAHAD.

Jerusalem Publishing House: 39 Tchernechovski St., Jerusalem, P.O.B. 7147; f. 1967; history, archaeology, art and other reference books; Dir. SHLOMO S. GAFNI.

Jewish Agency Publishing Department: P.O.B. 704; Jerusalem; f. 1945; Palestinology, Judaism, scientific, classics, and publicity brochures; Dir. M. SPITZER.

Karni Publishers Ltd.: 11 Yehuda Halevi St., Tel-Aviv; f. 1951; children's and educational books; Dir. SAMUEL KATZ.

Keter Publishing House Jerusalem Ltd.: P.O.B. 7145, Givat Shaul B, Jerusalem; f. 1959; original and translated works in all fields of science and humanities, published in English, French, German, other European languages and Hebrew; publishing imprints: Israel Program for Scientific Translations, Israel Universities Press, Keter Books, Encyclopaedia Judaica; Man. Dir. YITZHAK RISCHIN.

Kiryath Sepher: 15 Arlosorov St., Jerusalem; f. 1933; dictionaries, textbooks, maps, scientific books; Dir. SHALOM SIVAN (STEPANSKY).

Koren Publishers Jerusalem Ltd.: P.O.B. 4044, Jerusalem; Bible, religion and Judaism.

Lewin-Epstein Ltd.: 9 Yavneh St., Tel-Aviv; f. 1930; general fiction, education, science; Man. Dir. ABRAHAM GOTTESMANN.

Magnes Press, The: The Hebrew University, Jerusalem; f. 1929; general studies; Dir. CHAIM TOREN.

Ministry of Defence Publishing House: Hakiriya, Tel-Aviv; f. 1939; military literature; Dir. AHARON NIV. MA'ARACHOT.

M. Mizrachi Publishers: 19 Y. L. Peretz, Tel-Aviv; f. 1960; children's books; Dir. MEIR MIZRACHI.

Otsar Hamoreh: 8 Ben Saruk, Tel-Aviv; f. 1951; educational; Dir. MENACHEM LEVANON.

Y. L. Peretz: 31 Allenby Rd., Tel-Aviv; f. 1956; mainly books in Yiddish; Man. Dir. MOSHE GERSHONOWITZ.

Rubin Mass: 11 Marcus St., P.O.B. 990, Jerusalem; f. 1927; Hebraica, Judaica; Dir. RUBIN MASS.

Schocken Publishing House Ltd.: P.O.B. 2316, Tel-Aviv; f. 1938; general; Dir. Mrs. RACHELI EDELMAN.

Shikmona Publishing Co. Ltd.: P.O.B. 4044, Jerusalem; Zionism, archaeology, art, fiction and non-fiction.

Sifriat-Ma'ariv Ltd.: Ma'ariv House, 2 Carlebach St., Tel-Aviv; f. 1954; general; Man. YAKIR WEINSTEIN; Editor NAFTALI ARBEL.

Sifriat Poalim Ltd.: 73 Allenby St., P.O.B. 526, Tel-Aviv 65-171; f. 1939; textbooks; Gen. Man. YAAKOV ZVIELI.

Sinai Publishing Co.: 72 Allenby Rd., Tel-Aviv; Hebrew books and religious articles; Dir. AKNAH SCHLESINGER.

Tarbut Ve'Hinuch Publishers: 93 Arlozorov St., Tel-Aviv; f. 1956; educational; Man. IZAAK KOTUNSKY.

Tarhish Books: P.O.B. 4130, 91-040 Jerusalem; f. 1940; plays, poetry, bibliophile, classics; Man. Dir. Dr. MOSHE SPITZER.

Weidenfeld and Nicolson Jerusalem Ltd.: 19 Herzog St., P.O.B. 7545, Jerusalem; branch of the London publishing company; established in Israel 1969; Editorial Dir. INA FRIEDMAN; Sales Man. R. FRANKLIN.

Weizmann Science Press of Israel: 33 King George Ave., P.O.B. 801, Jerusalem 91000; f. 1951; publishes scientific books and periodicals; Man. Dir. RAMI MICHAELI; Exec. Editor L. LESTER.

Yachdav United Publishers Co. Ltd.: 29 Carlebach St., P.O.B. 20123, Tel-Aviv; f. 1960; educational; Chair. MORDECHAI BERNSTEIN; Dir. BENJAMIN SELLA.

Yavneh Ltd.: 4 Mazeh St., Tel-Aviv; f. 1932; general; Dir. YEHOSHUA ORENSTEIN.

S. Zack and Co.: 2 King George St., Jerusalem; f. c. 1930; reference books, textbooks, dictionaries, judaica, children's books; Dirs. DAVID and MICHAEL ZACK.

Israel Book Publishers Association: 29 Carlebach St., P.O.B. 20123, Tel-Aviv; f. 1939; mems.: 74 publishing firms; Pres. MORDECHAI BERNSTEIN; Sec.-Gen. BENJAMIN SELLA.

Jerusalem International Book Fair: P.O.B. 1508, Jerusalem 91000; takes place in alternate years; 800 publishing firms from 30 countries were represented in 1973; the 1975 Book Fair took place April 28th-May 5th.

RADIO AND TELEVISION

RADIO

Israel Broadcasting Authority (I.B.A.): 21 Heleni Hamalka, Jerusalem; f. 1948; station, Jerusalem with additional studios in Tel-Aviv and Haifa; Dir.-Gen. I. LIVNI. I.B.A. broadcasts five programmes for local and overseas listeners on medium, shortwave and VHF/FM in thirteen languages: Hebrew, Arabic, English, Yiddish, Ladino, Romanian, Hungarian, Moghrabit, Persian, French, Russian, Georgian and Spanish.

Number of radio receivers: 680,000 (1972).

Galei Zahal: Tel-Aviv; f. 1951; Army broadcasting station for soldiers; station, Tel-Aviv with studios in Jerusalem; broadcasts one programme on medium wave in Hebrew.

TELEVISION

Israel Broadcasting Authority (I.B.A.): broadcasts began in 1968; station in Jerusalem with additional studios in Tel-Aviv; Dir.-Gen. I. LIVNI; one black and white network (VHF with UHF available in some areas); broadcasts in Hebrew and Arabic.

Instructional Television Centre: Ministry of Education and Culture, Tel-Aviv; f. 1963 by Hanadiv (Rothschild Memorial Group) as Instructional Television Centre; began transmissions in 1966; now broadcasts on a national scale to 1,300 schools with 540,000 pupils, 70 per cent of the high school population; the programmes form an integral part of the syllabus in a wide range of subjects.

Number of TV licences 370,000 (1972).

FINANCE

(cap. = capital; p.u. = paid up; dep. = deposits; m. = million; I£ = Israeli £; brs. = branches.)

BANKING

CENTRAL BANK

Bank of Israel: Mizpeh Building, 29 Jaffa Rd., Jerusalem, P.O.B. 780; f. 1954 as the Central Bank of the State of Israel; (Sept. 1974) cap. I£10m., reserves I£10m.; Gov. MOSHE SANBAR; Dir.-Gen. Dr. E. SHEFFER, Mans. M. HETH, J. SARIG, S. LEVI, Z. SUSSMAN, M. MEIRAV, S. PELED, O. MESSER; 2 brs.; publs. *Annual Report, Economic Review, Banking Statistics* (monthly).

ISRAELI BANKS

Arab Israel Bank Ltd.: 14 Hatishim Veshalosh St., Haifa; subsidiary of Bank Leumi le-Israel B.M.; f. 1959 to serve primarily the Arab sector of the economy; cap. p.u. I£3.5m., dep. I£132.2m. (Dec. 1974); Chair. J. ROSH; Gen. Man. E. ASHKENAZI

Bank Hapoalim B.M.: 50 Rothschild Blvd., Tel-Aviv; f. 1921; cap. p.u. I£228.8m., dep. I£18,898m. (Dec. 1974); Man. Dirs. J. LEVINSON (Chair.), E. AVNEYON, A BERGNER, B. RABINOW, M. OLENIK; over 225 brs.

Bank Kupat-Am Le-Israel Ltd.: 13 Ahad Ha'am St., P.O.B. 352, Tel-Aviv; f. 1918; cap. p.u., reserves and surplus I£12.3m., dep. I£337m. (Dec. 1974); Chair. B. YEKUTIELI; Man. Dir. M. OSTFELD; 16 brs.

Bank Lemelacha Ltd.: 18 Shocken St., Tel-Aviv; f. 1953; cap. p.u. I£25m., dep. I£171.4m. (Dec. 1974); Chair. YAACOV SALMAN; Man. Dir. A. FEIN; 16 brs.

Bank Leumi le-Israel B.M.: 24–32 Yehuda Halevy St., Tel-Aviv; f. 1902; cap. p.u. I£185.1m., dep. I£16,053m. (1973); Chair. Dr. E. LEHMANN; Man. Dir. and Chief Exec. E. I. JAPHET; 240 brs.; publ. *Review of Economic Conditions in Israel* (quarterly).

First International Bank of Israel Ltd.: 18/20 Lincoln St., P.O.B. 20185, Tel-Aviv; f. 1972 as a result of a merger between The Foreign Trade Bank Ltd. and Export Bank Ltd.; Chair. of Board MARK MOSEVICS; Man. Dir. DAVID GOLAN; 38 brs.

Israel American Industrial Development Bank Ltd.: 50 Rothschild Blvd., Tel-Aviv; f. 1956; cap. p.u. I£12m.; dep. I£351m. (Dec. 1974); Chair. M. OLENIK; Gen. Man. H. DUVSHANI.

Israel Bank of Agriculture Ltd.: 83 Hashmonayim St., Tel-Aviv; f. 1951; cap. p.u. I£234.8m., dep. I£653.6m. (March 1974); Chair. A. BRUM; Man. Dir. D. CALDERON.

Israel Discount Bank Ltd.: 27–29 Yehuda Halevy St., Tel-Aviv; f. 1935; cap. p.u. I£88m., dep. I£16,000m. (Dec. 1974); Chair. DANIEL RECANATI; Vice-Chair. RAPHAEL RECANATI; 152 brs.

Israel General Bank Ltd.: 28 Achad Ha'am St., Tel-Aviv; f. 1964; cap. p.u. I£6.1m., dep. I£388.4m. (Dec. 1974); Chair. Baron EDMOND DE ROTHSCHILD; Man. Dir. DAVID SHOHAM; 3 brs.

Israel Industrial Bank Ltd.: 13 Montefiore St., Tel-Aviv; f. 1933; cap. p.u. I£12.03m., dep. I£205.3m. (Dec. 1973); Chair. A. FROMCENKO; Man. Dir. A. D. KIMCHI; 9 brs.

Israel Loan and Savings Bank Ltd.: 21 Herzl St., Tel-Aviv; cap. I£10.3m.; Chair. E. AVEYNON; Man. Dir. I. GAFNI.

Japhet Bank Ltd.: 11 Rothschild Blvd., Tel-Aviv; f. 1933; subsidiary of Bank Hapoalim B.M.; cap. p.u. I£12m., dep. I£701m. (Dec. 1974); Chair. B. RABINOV; Man. Dir. U. COHEN; 14 brs.

Mercantile Bank of Israel Ltd.: 24 Rothschild Blvd., Tel-Aviv; f. 1924; subsidiary of Barclays Discount Bank; cap. p.u. I£2m., dep. I£156m. (Dec. 1974); Chair. DANIEL RECANATI; Gen. Man. SHLOMO MAGRISO.

Union Bank of Israel Ltd.: 6–8 Ahuzat Bayit St., P.O.B. 2428, Tel-Aviv; f. 1951; subsidiary of Bank Leumi le-Israel B.M.; cap. p.u. I£32.0m., dep. I£2,524m. (Dec. 1974); Chair. E. I. JAPHET; Gen. Mans. W. HAUCK, M. MAYER; 16 brs.; publ. *Newsletter* (monthly).

United Mizrahi Bank Ltd.: 48 Lilienblum St., Tel-Aviv; f. 1923; cap. p.u. I£47.6m., dep. I£1,922m. (Dec. 1974); Chair. N. FEINGOLD; Gen. Man. A. MEIR; 50 brs.

MORTGAGE BANKS

General Mortgage Bank Ltd.: 13 Ahad Ha'am St., Tel-Aviv; f. 1921; subsidiary of Bank Leumi le-Israel B.M.; cap. p.u. I£25.3m., dep. I£1,190m. (Dec. 1974); Chair. E. LEHMANN; Vice-Chair. S. TULCHINSKY; Gen. Mans. Y. BACH, M. KAHAN.

Housing Mortgage Bank Ltd.: 115 Allenby St., Tel-Aviv; f. 1951; subsidiary of Bank Hapoalim B.M.; cap. p.u. I£23.2m., dep. I£749.6m. (Dec. 1974); Chair. Y. RAVIM.

Israel Development and Mortgage Bank Ltd.: 16 Simtat Beit Hashoeva, Tel-Aviv; f. 1959; subsidiary of Israel Discount Bank Ltd.; Gen. Mans. K. REICH, A. VREEDENBURG.

Tefahot, Israel Mortgage Bank Ltd.: 9 Heleni Hamalka St., Jerusalem; f. 1945; cap. p.u. I£70m., dep. I£2,514m.; Chair. ZEEV SHAREF; Man. Dir. MOSHE MANN. *Affiliated Bank:* **Carmel Mortgage and Investment Bank Ltd.,** 207 Hameginim Blvd., Haifa.

Unico Investment Co. Ltd.: Shalom Tower, 9 Ahad Ha'am St., Tel-Aviv; f. 1961.

FOREIGN BANKS

Barclays Discount Bank Ltd.: 103 Allenby Rd., Tel-Aviv; f. 1971 in association with Israel Discount Bank Ltd. incorporating former brs. of Barclays Bank International Ltd.; cap. p.u. I£11m.; Chair. DANIEL RECANATI; Gen. Man. GIDEON LAHAV; 50 brs. *Affiliated Bank:* **Mercantile Bank of Israel Ltd.,** 24 Rothschild Blvd., Tel-Aviv.

Exchange National Bank of Chicago: 9 Ahad Ha'am St., Shalom Tower, Tel-Aviv 65251; also in Jerusalem; f. 1970; Vice-Pres. and Gen. Man. AVIEZER CHELOUCHE.

STOCK EXCHANGE

Tel-Aviv Stock Exchange: 113 Allenby Rd.; Chair. Dr. E. LEHMANN; Vice-Chair. D. RECANATI; Exec. Dir. D. OTENSOOSER; publs. *Official Quotations* (daily, monthly, annually), *Financial Structure and Performance of Companies Listed on the Tel-Aviv Stock Exchange* (annual).

INSURANCE

Ararat Insurance Company Ltd.: Ararat House, 32 Yavneh St., Tel-Aviv; f. 1949; Man. Dir. PHILIP ZUCKERMAN.

Aryeh Insurance Co. Ltd.: Shalom Tower, Tel-Aviv; f. 1948; Chair. AVINOAM M. TOCATLY.

Hassneh Insurance Co. of Israel Ltd.: 115 Allenby St., P.O.B. 805, Tel-Aviv; f. 1929; Chair. MICHAEL NUSSBAUM.

Israel Phoenix Assurance Company Ltd., The: 30 Levontin St., Tel-Aviv; f. 1949; Chair. of Board and Man. Dir. DAVID J. HACKMEY.

Israel Reinsurance Company Ltd., The: 7 Shadal St., P.O.B. 2037, Tel-Aviv; f. 1951; Chair. Board of Dirs. A. SACHAROV; Gen. Man. S. JANNAI.

Maoz Insurance Co. Ltd.: 36 Lilienblum St., Tel-Aviv; f. 1945; formerly Binyan Insurance Co. Ltd.; Chair. Y. GRUENGARD.

Mazada Insurance Service Ltd.: 3 Ahuzat Bait St., Tel-Aviv; f. 1932; Man. A. SPIGELMAN, M.A.

Menorah Insurance and Reinsurance Company Ltd.: Menorah House, 73 Rothschild Blvd., Tel-Aviv; f. 1935; Gen. Man. DAVID HIRSCHFELD.

Migdal-Binyan Insurance Co. Ltd.: 53 Rothschild Blvd., Tel-Aviv; f. 1934; Chair. E. LEHMANN; Man. Dir. J. GRUENGARD.

Palglass Palestine Plate Glass Insurance Co. Ltd.: 30 Achad Ha'am St., Tel-Aviv; f. 1934; Gen. Man. AKIVA ZALZMAN.

Sahar Insurance Company Ltd.: Sahar House, 23 Ben-Yehuda St., Tel-Aviv; f. 1949; Chair. and Man. Dir. A. SHAROV.

Samson Insurance Co. Ltd.: 27 Montefiore St., P.O.B. 29277, Tel-Aviv; f. 1933; Chair. M. NUSSBAUM.

Sela Insurance Co. Ltd.: 6 Ahuzat Bait St., Tel-Aviv; f. 1938; Man. Dir. S. P. LUSTIG.

Shiloah Company Ltd.: 2 Pinsker St., Tel-Aviv; f. 1933; Gen. Man. R. S. BAMIRAH; Man. Mme BAMIRAH.

Yardenia Insurance Company Ltd.: 22 Maze St., Tel-Aviv; f. 1948; Man. Dir. H. LEBANON.

Yuval Insurance Co. Ltd.: 27 Keren Hayesod, Jerusalem; f. 1962; Man. Dir. J. KAPLAN.

Zigug Glass Insurance Co. Ltd.: 34 Sheinkin St., Tel-Aviv; f. 1952; Chair. D. HIRSCHFELD.

Zion Insurance Company Ltd.: 120 Allenby Rd., Tel-Aviv; f. 1935; Chair. HAIM TAIBER.

THE HISTADRUT

Hahistadrut Haklalit shel Haovdim Beeretz Israel, 93 Arlosoroff Street, Tel-Aviv.

(GENERAL FEDERATION OF LABOUR IN ISRAEL)

Secretary-General: YERUHAM MESHEL.

The General Federation of Labour in Israel, usually known as the Histadrut, is the largest voluntary organization in Israel, and the most important economic body in the State. It is open to all workers, including members of co-operatives and of the liberal professions, who join directly as individuals. The Histadrut engages in four main fields of activity: trade union organization; economic development; social insurance based on mutual aid; and educational and cultural activities. Dues—between 2.5 per cent and 4.5 per cent of wages (up to I£1,000)—cover all its trade union, health and social services activities. The Histadrut was founded in 1920.

ORGANIZATION

In 1974 the Histadrut had a membership of 1,250,000, including over 150,000 in collective, co-operative and private villages (*kibbutzim* and *moshavim*) affiliated through the Agricultural Workers' Union, and 324,777 wives (who have membership status); 87,916 of the members were Arabs. In addition some 100,000 young people under 18 years of age belong to the Organization of Working and Student Youth, a direct affiliate of the Histadrut. The

main religious labour organizations, *Histadrut Hapoel Hamizrahi* and *Histadrut Poalei Agudat Israel*, belong to the trade union section and welfare services, which thus extend to 90 per cent of all workers in Israel.

All members take part in elections to the Histadrut Convention (*Veida*), which elects the General Council (*Moetsa*) and the Executive Committee (*Vaad Hapoel*). The latter elects the 19-member Executive Bureau (*Vaada Merakezet*), which is responsible for day-to-day implementation of policy. The Executive Committee also elects the Secretary-General, who acts as its chairman as well as head of the organization as a whole and chairman of the Executive Bureau. Nearly all political parties are represented on the Histadrut Executive Committee. Throughout Israel there are 72 local Labour Councils.

The Executive Committee has the following departments: Trade Union, Arab Affairs, Mutual Aid, Organization, International, Finance, Legal, Employment, Vocational Training, Absorption and Development, Academic Workers, Pensions, Religious Affairs and Higher Education.

TRADE UNION ACTIVITIES

Collective agreements with employers fix wage scales, which are linked with the retail price index; provide for social benefits, including paid sick leave and employers' contributions to sick and pension and provident funds; and regulate dismissals. Dismissal compensation, until recently fixed by collective agreements, is now regulated by law. The Histadrut actively promotes productivity through labour management boards and the National Productivity Institute, and supports incentive pay schemes.

There are unions for the following groups: clerical workers, building workers, teachers, engineers, agricultural workers, technicians, textile workers, printing workers, diamond workers, metal workers, food and bakery workers, wood workers, government employees, seamen, nurses, civilian employees of the armed forces, actors, musicians and variety artists, social workers, watchmen, cinema technicians, institutional and school staffs, pharmacy employees, medical laboratory workers, X-ray technicians, physiotherapists, social scientists, microbiologists, psychologists, salaried lawyers, pharmacists, physicians, occupational therapists, truck and taxi drivers, hotel and restaurant workers, workers in Histadrut-owned industry, garment, shoe and leather workers, painters and sculptors and industrial workers.

OFFICERS AND PUBLICATIONS

Secretary of Labour Economy (Hevrat Odim): EPHRAIM REINER.

Chairman of International Department: YERUHAM MESHEL.

Chairman of Trade Union Department: URIEL ABRAHAMOVICZ.

Chairman of Mutual Aid and Insurance Department: YAAKOV VILAN.

Chairman of Culture and Education Department: RAPHAEL BASH.

Chairman of Sports and Youth Department: SHMUEL BAHAT.

Treasurer: ISRAEL KEISAR.

Chairman of Organization Department: AHARON HAREL.

The principal newspapers and periodicals published by the Histadrut are as follows:

Davar (*The World*) (daily), *Omer* (daily), *Dvar Hashavua* (illustrated weekly), *Davar Liyeladim* (children's weekly), *Devar Hapoalet* (women's monthly), *Israel au Travail* (French), *Labour in Israel* (English), *Trabajo en Israel* (Spanish). (*See* also Press section.)

ECONOMIC ACTIVITIES

General Co-operative Association of Labour in Israel (*Hevrat Ovdim*): Every member of the Histadrut is simultaneously a member of Hevrat Ovdim, and therefore a part-owner in its economy, whether or not he works within its framework. This labour economy includes a variety of structural forms, falling into two main types: co-operative societies run by their own members, such as all *kibbutzim* and *moshavim* and the producer, service, transport and consumer co-operatives; and the collectively-owned enterprises which are initiated by Hevrat Ovdim.

SOCIAL WELFARE

All the Histadrut's social welfare institutions are based on the principal of mutual aid, and over 75 per cent of membership dues is allocated to them.

Kupat Holim (*The Workers' Sick Fund*): 14 Ben Ami Street, Tel-Aviv; the largest health organization in Israel; over 850 clinics, 14 hospitals, 17 convalescent homes; also conducts preventive health services; serves 77 per cent of the population.

Mishan: 27 Bloch St., Tel-Aviv; grants loans to needy members and maintains old-age homes and children's institutions.

Dor l'Dor: 27 Bloch St., Tel-Aviv; assists elderly workers, in particular those not covered by a regular pension scheme.

Matsiv: 27 Bloch St., Tel-Aviv; assists dependants of deceased members.

Seven central pension and provident funds operate within the Histadrut framework, with contributions coming from both their members and the employers. In addition to providing a wide range of benefits, these funds constitute the principal source of savings of the population. These long-term savings are directed to the development of the economy; moreover, by absorbing monies, they also act as an anti-inflationary influence. Accumulated funds total I£5 billion.

EDUCATION AND CULTURE

The Centre for Education and Culture: 93 Arlosoroff Street, Tel-Aviv; initiates, plans and co-ordinates activities on a national scale, among them immigrant education courses, evening courses for adults, a theatre company, and numerous choirs, folk-dance groups and popular art circles; arranges theatrical performances and concerts in rural centres, supplies films weekly to agricultural villages and produces its own films.

Amal: 93 Arlosoroff Street, Tel-Aviv; a special Histadrut department to operate and co-ordinate a network of 32 technical high schools.

The Organization of Working and Student Youth: 91 Hachashmonaim St., Tel-Aviv; for young people under the age of 18 who have commenced work or are still at secondary school; 100,000 mems.

Hapoel: 8 Haarba St., P.O.B. 7170, Tel-Aviv; f. 1926; the Histadrut sports organization; 600 brs. with 92,500 mems.

The Women Workers' Council (*Moetzet Hapoalot*) and **Union of Working Mothers** (*Irgun Imahot Ovdot*): 93 Arlosoroff Street, Tel-Aviv; cover both women workers and women members who do no paid outside work but actively help in the absorption of immigrants, the welfare of children of members, the promotion of education programmes for women, including the eradication of illiteracy, good citizenship courses and consumers' activities, etc.; 518 day-care centres for 16,900 children; vocational and agricultural training for 6,500 boys, girls and women; over 250 club rooms for both Jewish and Arab women.

INTERNATIONAL RELATIONS

The Histadrut is affiliated to the International Confederation of Free Trade Unions, is active in the International Labour Organization and the International Co-operative Alliance, and has active and friendly relations with labour movements all over the world. Most of its national unions are affiliated to their respective International Trade Secretariats.

International Institute for Development, Co-operation and Labour Studies: P.O.B. 16201, Tel-Aviv; est. by the Afro-Asian Institute of the Histadrut; has conducted courses for over 5,000 participants from 90 countries; annual international courses in English and French.

Centre for Labour and Co-operative Studies for Latin America: f. 1962; has conducted courses for some 1,500 participants from all the countries of Latin America, and from the Caribbean.

TRADE AND INDUSTRY

CHAMBERS OF COMMERCE

Joint Representation of the Israeli Chambers of Commerce: P.O.B. 501, Tel-Aviv; co-ordinates the Tel-Aviv, Jerusalem and Haifa Chambers of Commerce; Sec. F. B. WAHLE.

Jerusalem Chamber of Commerce: P.O.B. 183, Jerusalem 91000; f. 1908; about 300 mems.; Pres. M. H. ELIACHAR; Vice-Pres. A. ASHBEL, E. BODENKIN, A. DASKAL, A. P. MICHAELIS, Y. PEARLMAN; publ. *Bulletin* (Hebrew and English).

Haifa Chamber of Commerce and Industry (*Haifa and District*): P.O.B. 176, 53 Haatzmaut Rd., Haifa; f. 1921; 700 mems.; Pres. JOSEPH ROSH; Gen. Sec. A. MEHOULAL.

Chamber of Commerce, Tel-Aviv-Jaffa: P.O.B. 501, 84 Hachashmonaim St., Tel-Aviv; f. 1919; 1,500 mems.; Pres. A. BENYAKAR; Secs. D. GRAJCAR, F. B. WAHLE; publ. *Hamishar*.

Federation of Bi-National Chambers of Commerce with and in Israel: 82 Allenby Rd., Tel-Aviv; federates: Israel-America Chamber of Commerce and Industry; Anglo-Israel Chamber of Commerce; Australia-Israel Chamber of Commerce; Chamber of Commerce and Industry Israel-Africa and the Malagasy Republic; Chambre de Commerce Israel-Belgique-Luxembourg; Canada-Israel Chamber of Commerce and Industry; Israel-Danish Chamber of Commerce; Chambre de Commerce Israel-France; Chamber of Commerce and Industry Israel-Germany; Camera di Commercio Israel-Italia; Israel-Japan Chamber of Commerce; Israel-Latin America Chamber of Commerce; Netherlands-Israel Chamber of Commerce; Israel-Norway Chamber of Commerce; Handelskammer Israel-Schweiz; Israel-South Africa Chamber of Commerce; Israel-Sweden Chamber of Commerce; Chair. A. CHELOUCHE; Exec. Dir. H. ZUCKERMAN, O.B.E.; and also incorporates Bi-National Chambers of Commerce existing in 20 foreign countries with Israel.

Anglo-Israel Chamber of Commerce (Israel): 82 Allenby Rd., Tel-Aviv, P.O.B. 1127; f. 1951; 400 mems.; Joint Pres. Dr. A. S. ARNON, C.B.E., A. S. COHEN, C.B.E.; Chair. E. IZAKSON.

TRADE AND INDUSTRIAL ORGANIZATIONS

The Agricultural Union: Tchlenov 20, Tel-Aviv; consists of more than 50 agricultural settlements and is connected with marketing and supplying organizations, and Bahan Ltd., controllers and auditors.

Central Union of Artisans and Small Manufacturers: P.O.B. 4041, Tel-Aviv; f. 1907; has a membership of 40,000 divided into 70 groups according to trade; the union is led by a seventeen-man Presidium; Chair. JACOB FRANK; Gen. Sec. PINHAS SCHWARTZ; publ. *Hamlakha;* 30 brs.

Citrus Control and Marketing Boards: 69 Haifa Rd., Tel-Aviv; the government-established institution for the control of the Israel citrus industry; Boards made up of representatives of the Government and the Growers. Functions: Control of plantations, supervision of picking and packing operations; marketing of the crop overseas and on the home markets; shipping: supply of fertilisers, insecticides, equipment for orchards and packing houses and of packing materials, technical research and extension work; long-term financial assistance to growers.

Farmers' Federation: P.O.B. 209, Tel-Aviv; has a membership of 7,000 independent farmers, citrus and winegrape growers; Pres. AMARON FRANK; Chair. Central Cttee. IZCHAK-ZIV-AV; publ. *The Israeli Farmer* (monthly).

General Association of Merchants in Israel: 6 Rothschild Boulevard, Tel-Aviv; the organization of retail traders; has a membership of 30,000 in 60 brs.

Israel Diamond Exchange Ltd.: P.O.B. 3222, Ramat Gan; f. 1937; production, export, import and finance facilities; estimated exports (1973) U.S. $600m.

Israel Journalists' Association Ltd.: 4 Kaplan St., Tel-Aviv; Sec. MOSHE RON.

Manufacturers' Association of Israel: 13 Montefiore St., P.O.B. 29116, Tel-Aviv; Pres. MARK MOSEVICS; Gen. Man. Col. PELEG TAMIR; Gen. Sec. A. Z. CRYSTAL, F.C.C.S.; publ. *News Bulletin* (every two months).

TRADE UNIONS

Histadrut Haovdim Haleumit (*National Labour Federation*): 23 Sprinczak St., Tel-Aviv; f. 1934; 84,000 mems.; publs. *Hazit Ha'Oved, Lapid.*

Histadrut Hapoel Hamizrahi (*Mizrahi Workers' Organization*): 108 Ahad Haam St., Tel-Aviv; has 55,000 members in 75 settlements.

Histadrut Poalei Agudat Israel (*Agudat Israel Workers' Organization*): Geula Quarter, Corner Yehezkel St., Jerusalem; has 19,000 members in 12 settlements.

TRANSPORT

RAILWAYS

Israel Railways: P.O.B. 44, Haifa; a department of the Ministry of Transport. All its lines are managed and operated from Haifa. The total length of mainline and sidings track in operation is 809 km.

The main flow of traffic is from Haifa Port and from the oil installations and industrial centres in the vicinity of Haifa and of minerals from Beersheba, Dimona and Oron, to the north. The bulk of freight traffic consists of grain, cement and building materials, heavy bulk imported commodities, minerals, phosphates and potash, and oils. Passenger traffic is operated between the main towns: Jerusalem, Tel-Aviv, Haifa, Beersheba, Dimona and Nahariya.

Gen. Man. Zvi Tsafriri; Principal Asst. Lea Steinmetz.

Underground Railways

Haifa Underground Funicular Railway: Haifa; opened 1959; 2 km. in operation; Man. D. Scharf.

Tel-Aviv Rapid Transit: Municipal Offices, Tel-Aviv-Jaffa Municipality; a feasibility study has been made on the possibility of building a 48 km. rapid transit line (11 km. underground).

ROADS

Ministry of Labour, Public Works Dept., Jerusalem.

There are 3,700 km. of metalled main roads not including roads in towns and settlements. Under a five-year plan ending in 1975 the following works will be completed:

One hundred km. new roads to be built, 25 km. additional two-lanes for existing roads, 400 km. widening and improving existing roads.

Automobile and Touring Club of Israel (ATCI): 19 Petah Tiqva Rd., P.O.B. 36144, Tel-Aviv 66183; f. 1949; over 11,000 mems.; Sec.-Gen. Mrs. C. Nahmias; publ. *Memsi* (monthly).

SHIPPING

The Israel Ports Authority: Maya Building, 74 Petah Tiqva Rd., Tel-Aviv; f. 1961; to plan, build, develop, administer, maintain and operate the ports. In 1975–76 investment will amount to I£390m. for the Development Budget in Haifa, Ashdod and Eilat Ports. Cargo traffic in 1974-75 amounted to 10.2m. tons (oil excluded).

ZIM Israel Navigation Co. Ltd.: 209 Hameginim Ave., P.O.B. 1723, Haifa; f. 1945; runs cargo services in the Mediterranean and to N. Europe, N. and S. America, Far East, Africa and Australia; Chair. M. Tzur; Man. Dir. M. Kashti.

Cargo Ships "El-Yam" Ltd: P.O.B. 182, Haifa; f. 1952; Man. Dir. Raphael Recanati; a world-wide cargo tramp service.

Maritime Fruit Carriers Co. Ltd.: 53 Shderot Hameginim, P.O.B. 1501, Haifa; refrigerated cargo services; Chair. Yaacov Meridor; Man. Dir. Mila Brener.

Haifa and Ashdod are the main ports in Israel. The former is a natural harbour, enclosed by two main breakwaters and dredged to 37 ft. below mean sea-level. An auxiliary harbour was opened in 1955. In 1965 the new deep water port was completed at Ashdod which has a capacity of about 4 million tons per year.

Israel has a merchant fleet of 107 ships, with a displacement of over 1,600,000 tons.

The port of Eilat is Israel's gate to the Red Sea. It is a natural harbour, operated from a wharf. A new port, to the south of the original one, started operating in 1965.

CIVIL AVIATION

El Al Israel Airlines Ltd.: P.O.B. 41, Ben Gurion Airport, Lod, Tel-Aviv; f. 1949; daily services to most capitals of Europe; over twenty flights weekly to New York; services to Johannesburg, Teheran, Nairobi, Nicosia, Istanbul, Bucharest and Montreal; fleet of two Boeing 720B, three Boeing 707-420, three Boeing 707-320B, two Boeing 707-320C, three Boeing 747B; Pres. M. Ben-Ari.

Arkia, Israel Inland Airlines Ltd.: 88 Ha'Hashmonaim St., Tel-Aviv; f. 1950; scheduled services from Tel-Aviv and Jerusalem to Eilat, Rosh Pina, Haifa, Massada, Abu Rodes, Ophira (Sharm-el-Sheikh) and Santa Katarina; fleet of six Viscounts, four Heralds; Man. Dir. L. Bigon.

The following airlines also serve Israel: Air France, Alitalia, AUA, British Airways, Canadian Pacific, Cyprus Airways, KLM, Lufthansa, Olympic Airways, Sabena, SAS, Swissair, Tarom, THY, TWA.

TOURISM

Ministry of Tourism: P.O.B. 1018, Jerusalem; information offices at Jerusalem, Tel-Aviv, Haifa, Nazareth, Zefat, Ben Gurion International Airport, Beersheba, Tiberias, Ashqelon, Arad, Bethlehem, Ramallah, Allenby Bridge, Akko, Netanya, Nahariyya and Eilat; Minister of Tourism Moshe Kol; Dir.-Gen. Gviton.

There are also offices in the following countries: England (London), France (Paris), German Federal Republic (Frankfurt), Italy (Rome), Netherlands (Amsterdam), Switzerland (Zürich), Sweden (Stockholm), U.S.A. (New York, Chicago, Beverly Hills, Atlanta), Argentina (Buenos Aires), Canada (Toronto), Denmark (Copenhagen), Belgium (Brussels), South Africa (Johannesburg), Australia (Sydney).

CULTURAL ORGANIZATIONS

The Israel Festival: 5th Flr., Shalom Tower, Ahad Ha'am St., Tel-Aviv, P.O.B. 29874; organizes the Isreal Festival which takes place in July/August in Caesarea, Jerusalem and Tel-Aviv; Dir. A. Z. Propes.

Israel Music Institute: P.O.B. 11253, Tel-Aviv; f. 1961; publishes and promotes Israeli music, educational music and musicological works abroad; member since 1969 of International Music Information Centre; Chair. Uri Toeplitz; Man. Dir. William Elias.

The National Council of Culture and Art: Hadar Daphna Bldg., Shaul Hamelech Blvd., Tel-Aviv.

PRINCIPAL THEATRES

Cameri Theatre: Tel-Aviv; f. 1944; public trusteeship; repertory theatre; tours abroad.

Habimah National Theatre of Israel: P.O.B. 222, Tel-Aviv; f. 1918 in Russia, moved to Palestine 1928; Jewish, classical and modern drama.

Israel National Opera and Israel National Opera Ballet: 1 Allenby St., Tel-Aviv; f. 1947 by Edis de-Philippe (Dir.); classical and modern opera and ballet; open 50 weeks of the year.

PRINCIPAL ORCHESTRAS

Haifa Symphony Orchestra: 50 Pevsner St., Haifa; Music Dir. SAMUEL FRIEDMAN.

Israel Chamber Orchestra: 103 Ibn Gvirol St., Tel-Aviv; f. 1965; 42 mems.; Artistic Dir. GARY BERTINI.

Israel Philharmonic Orchestra: Frederic R. Mann Auditorium, Tel-Aviv; f. 1936 by Bronislaw Huberman; 106 mems.; frequent tours abroad; 35,000 subscribers; Musical Adviser ZUBIN MEHTA; Concertmasters CHAIM TAUB, URI PIANKA.

The Jerusalem Symphony Orchestra: Israel Broadcasting Authority, Y.M.C.A. Building, Jerusalem; f. 1938; 90 mems.; Dir. YEHUDA FICKLER; Chief Conductor LUKAS FOSS.

DANCE TROUPES

Bat-Dor Dance Company: 30 Ibn Gvirol St., Tel-Aviv; contemporary repertory dance company; owns theatre in Tel-Aviv; frequent tours abroad; Producer BATSHEVA DE ROTHSCHILD; Artistic Dir. JEANNETTE ORDMAN.

Batsheva Dance Company: 9 Sderot Hahaskala, Tel-Aviv.

Inbal Dance Theatre: 74 Arlosoroff St., Tel-Aviv; f. 1949; modern Israeli dance theatre specializing in their traditional folk art, with choreographic themes from the Bible; frequent tours abroad; Founder and Artistic Dir. SARA LEVI-TANAI.

FESTIVALS

Israel Festival of Music and Drama: Caesarea; international festival of music, dance and drama; f. 1961; one month annually July-August; organized by Israeli Festival Association.

Ein Gev Music Festival: Kibbutz Ein Gev, Kinneret; international festival; annually for one week at Passover.

Zimriya: World Assembly of Choirs, comprising Israeli and international choirs; f. 1952; triennial; next assembly 1976.

ATOMIC ENERGY

Israel Atomic Energy Commission: 26 Rehov Ha Universita, Ramat Aviv, Tel-Aviv; and P.O.B. 17120, Tel-Aviv; f. 1952; advises the Government on long term policies and priorities in the advancement of nuclear research and development; supervises the implementation of policies approved by the government; represents Israel in its relations with scientific institutions abroad and international organizations engaged in nuclear research and development (Israel is a member of IAEA); Chair. The PRIME MINISTER; Dir.-Gen. SHALHEVETH FREIER.

The Atomic Energy Commission has two research and development centres: the Soreq Nuclear Research Centre and the Negev Nuclear Research Centre near Dimona. The main fields of research are: nuclear physics and chemistry, reactor physics, reactor engineering, radiation research and applications, application of isotopes, metallurgy, eletronics, radiobiology, nuclear medicine, nuclear power and desalination. The centres also provide national services: health physics including film badge service, isotope production and molecule labelling, activation analysis, irradiation, advice to industry and institutions, training of personnel, technical courses, documentation.

Soreq Nuclear Research Centre: Yavne; f. 1952; equipped with a swimming pool type research reactor IRR-1 of 5 MW thermal; Dir. A ROTH (acting).

Negev Nuclear Research Centre: Dimona; equipped with a natural uranium fuelled and heavy water moderated reactor IRR-2 of 26 MW thermal; Dir. ABRAHAM SEROUSI.

Weizmann Institute of Science: Rehovot; Department of Nuclear Physics engaged in research and graduate teaching in experimental nuclear structure and elementary particle physics, as well as in theoretical and applied physics; a new *14 UD Pelletron* accelerator is to be completed in 1975; Head Prof. I. TALMI.

Department of Isotope Research engaged in research and teaching in a broad area, ranging from environmental research to brain chemistry, using isotope techniques; it also operates a product on-scale plant for the separation of o^{17} and o^{18} from o^{16}; Head J. R. GAT.

The Hebrew University of Jerusalem: Jerusalem; engages in atomic research and teaching in chemistry, physics biology and medicine.

Technion: Israel Institute of Technology: Haifa; the Dept. of Physics engages in undergraduate teaching in physics and engineering, as well as graduate teaching and research mainly in nuclear physics, high energy physics, foundations of quantum mechanics, atomic physics, relativity and astrophysics and related fields; the Dept. of Nuclear Engineering undertakes teaching and graduate work in applied nuclear science and engineering; research groups work in the fields of theoretical and experimental nuclear reactor physics, neutron physics, nuclear desalination, heat transfer, nuclear radiations; Head, Nuclear Engineering Dept. Prof. N. SHAFRIR; Chair., Dept. of Physics Prof. P. SINGER.

DEFENCE

The General Staff

This consists of the Chiefs of the General Staff, Manpower, Logistics and Intelligence Branches of the Defence Forces, the Commanders of the Air Force and the Navy, and the officers commanding the three Regional Commands (Northern, Central and Southern). It is headed by the Chief of Staff of the Armed Forces.

Chief of Staff of the Armed Forces: Lt.-Gen. MORDECHAI GUR.

Commander of the Air Force: Maj.-Gen. BINYAMIN PELED.

Commander of the Navy: Maj.-Gen. BINYAMIN TELEM.

Defence Budget (1974–75): I£22,500 million.

Military Service (Jewish population only): Men under 29 and women under 26 are called for regular service of up to 36 months for men and 24 months for women. Physicians may be called up to the age of 34.

Total Armed Forces: 115,000: 30,000 regular cadre and 85,000 conscripts, this can be raised to 300,000 by mobilizing reservists within 48–72 hours; army 11,500 regular, 83,000 conscripts (275,000 when fully mobilized); navy 3,500 regular, 1,000 conscripts (5,000 when fully mobilized); air force 15,000 regular, 1,000 conscripts (20,000 conscripts when fully mobilized).

Paramilitary Forces: 9,000.

EDUCATION

The present-day school system is based on the Compulsory Education Law (1949), the State Education Law (1953) and on some provisions of the 1933 Education Ordinance dating back to the British Mandatory Administration. The former introduced free compulsory primary education for all children between the ages of 5 and 15 (one kindergarten, eight years elementary schooling); in addition, those aged 14–18 who have not completed their elementary schooling may attend special evening classes until they reach the necessary standard.

The State Education Law abolished the old complicated Trend Education System, and vested the responsibility for Primary Education in the Government, thus providing a unified State-controlled elementary school system. The law does, however, recognise two main forms of Primary Education—(a) State Education; (b) Recognised Non-State Education. State Education may be sub-divided into two distinct categories of schools—State Schools and State Religious Schools for Jews, and State Schools for Arabs. Schools and kindergartens of the State system are in the joint ownership of the State and the Local Authorities, while the recognized non-State institutions are essentially privately-owned, although they are subsidised, and supervised by the State and the Local Authorities. The standard curriculum for all elementary schools is laid down by the Ministry of Education and Culture, but supplementary subjects, comprising not more than 25 per cent of the syllabus, may be included at the discretion of the school authorities, subject to prior approval by the Minister.

The two largest non-State school systems are the Agudat Israel Schools (of an ultra-orthodox religious character) and the boarding schools, mostly agricultural, for young immigrants, run by various voluntary bodies.

State Primary Education is financed by a partnership of the Central Government and the Local Authorities. Since 1953 the salaries of all teachers and kindergarten mistresses of State Schools have been paid by the Central Government, whilst the cost of maintenance and of maintenance services, and the provision of new buildings and equipment have been the responsibility of the Local Authorities. The State does not impose an Education Tax but local authorities may, with the Ministry's approval, levy a rate on parents for special services.

School supervision is the prerogative of the Ministry of Education and Culture through the Director-General of the Ministry, and there are six District Inspectors and a varying number of School Inspectors. Two "Pedagogical Secretariats", one for primary and one for post-primary schools, co-ordinate educational work and deal with problems arising in the various branches of the Educational System.

The State provides different schools for the Jewish and Arab children, because of the distribution of population and the language difference. Nevertheless many Arab children attend Jewish primary, secondary, vocational, agricultural and even teacher-training colleges. In the Jewish sector there is a distinct line of division between the secular State schools and the Religious State Schools, which are established on the demand of parents in any locality, provided that a certain minimum number of pupils have first been enrolled. In the Arab Schools all instruction is in Arabic, and there is a special department for Arabic Education in the Ministry of Education and Culture. Some 90 per cent of the Arab children attend school regularly.

Particular attention is paid to retarded children, and special classes are provided for them in the ordinary schools, besides the moderate-sized schools for backward and handicapped children which have been established by the Ministry.

Working Youth Schools are provided for boys and girls, between the ages of 14–17, who have not completed their primary education. These schools provide a four-year course, their grades corresponding to grades 5–8 in the primary schools, but there are also two preparatory classes for beginners, mostly for the children of new immigrants.

Post Primary Education is of three main types: Secondary, Vocational and Agricultural. Secondary Education is under the jurisdiction of the Ministry of Education and Culture. The other two categories were administered by the Ministries of Labour and Agriculture respectively, but passed over to the Ministry of Education in September 1960.

Secondary Schools. In 1973-74 the Ministry of Education and Culture had under its supervision 207 Hebrew and 75 Arab secondary schools, with 53,696 and 11,397 pupils respectively. No direct financial aid is given by the State to secondary schools, except building loans. On the other hand the central government and local authorities assist children who have passed a preliminary test to pay their school fees. This assistance is given on a sliding scale according to the parents' means and obligations, and may even cover the total cost. An official proposed syllabus has been published by the Ministry, for use in these schools.

Vocational Training. There are three types of training available in this section of the Education System: Vocational Schools, Apprenticeships and Vocational Training Courses for Adults.

In the school year 1973-74 there were 302 Hebrew and 24 Arab vocational schools with 64,068 and 1,456 pupils respectively. Almost all the courses extend over a period of three or four years, and the students are boys and girls between the ages of 14 and 18. The curriculum consists of some 20 hours practical training, and 24 hours instruction on industrial and general subjects, each week.

Apprenticeship is regulated by the Apprenticeship Act of 1953, and all apprentices must attend apprenticeship schools one day a week. There is no apprenticeship in agriculture; most trades require 3–4 years apprenticeship, which normally applies to youths from 14–18 years of age.

A programme of Pre-Vocational Training for pupils in the last two grades of the Government Primary Schools was launched in 1955. This programme includes training in various trades, handicrafts and agriculture, and was intended to enable pupils continuing in the Vocational Schools to begin their studies in the second year of those schools. In fact they are now absorbed in the two-year secondary schools and thus get four years of a mixed general and vocational education. The training is given in addition to the Primary School curriculum.

Vocational training for adults is divided into two sections: basic trade courses (day courses) which are intended for persons who have had no previous vocational training or have to change their occupation (mostly new immigrants), and supplementary training courses (evening classes), intended for the further education of already skilled workers. The courses are from 3–18 months.

Agricultural Schools: there are various kinds of schools offering training in agriculture, ranging from the Faculty of Agriculture of the Hebrew University, and the Rupin Institute courses for adults to the agricultural secondary schools and other training centres for youth.

In 1973-74 there were 30 agricultural schools of which two were for Arab pupils, including a fishing school, a school of horticulture, and an agricultural technical institute providing a diploma-course. Five of these (including the fishing school and the technical institute) are government schools; the others are financed by various organizations such as the Women Workers' Council, Women's International Zionist Organization, etc.

In 1973-74 there were 6,464 Hebrew and 603 Arab pupils. Most schools have well-developed farms in which the pupils work for 3–4 hours a day. A 3-year course is usual and only a few have a 4-year course. Some 2-year courses are being opened in regional schools for farm-youth.

Teachers' Training. As the enrolment in schools throughout the country increases by about 20,000 pupils each year, the need for additional teachers is keenly felt. There are 45 Hebrew and two Arab teacher training colleges with 8,656 Hebrew and 587 Arab students respectively. To qualify as a teacher the student must have taken 14 years of study. Pupils normally complete the 12-year secondary school course and then go to a teachers' training college for a further two years. In these two years the student has practical teaching experience before sitting for the examination of the Ministry of Education and Culture.

Adult Education. Numerous facilities for adult education are offered both by institutions of higher learning and by various organizations. Special attention is being paid to the study of the Hebrew language and new immigrants have the opportunity to study Hebrew in intensive 5–6 month courses (*ulpanim*) some of which are conducted in agricultural settlements where students work for half the day to cover their living expenses.

The Occupied Territories. The educational system in the occupied parts of the adjacent Arab countries has been taken over with few changes. In 1973-74 the West bank had 970 schools (86 run by UNRWA) with 207,729 pupils. In the Gaza strip were 149 state and 126 UNRWA schools with 2,476 teachers and an enrolment of 123,556. Many of the textbooks have been replaced where material critical of Jews, Zionism or the State of Israel was discovered; at first, teachers and students refused to return to schools under Israeli control, but this school strike gradually lost force and within a year of the occupation most schools in the occupied territories were operating more or less normally.

UNIVERSITIES

Bar-Ilan University: Ramat-Gan; 850 teachers, 8,000 students.

Ben Gurion University of the Negev: P.O.B. 2053, Beersheba; 385 teachers, 3,200 students.

Haifa University: Mount Carmel, Haifa; 778 teachers, 5,500 students.

The Hebrew University of Jerusalem: Jerusalem; 1,955 teachers, 16,000 students.

Tel-Aviv University: Ramat-Aviv, Tel-Aviv; 2,208 teachers, 16,752 students.

Technion, Israel Institute of Technology: Haifa; 1,500 teachers, 6,260 undergraduate, 3,300 graduate students.

Weizmann Institute of Science, Feinberg Graduate School: Rehovot; 500 students.

BIBLIOGRAPHY

GENERAL

AVI-HAI, AVRAHAM. Ben Gurion, State Builder (Israel Universities Press, 1974).

AVNERY, URI. Israel without Zionists (Collier-Macmillan, London, 1969).

EDELMAN, MAURICE. Ben Gurion, a Political Biography (Hodder and Stoughton, London, 1964).

GLUECK, NELSON. The River Jordan (Philadelphia, 1946.) Rivers in the Desert (London, 1959).

HILLEL, MARC. Israel en danger de paix (Fayard, Paris, 1969).

KOHN, HANS. Nationalism and Imperialism in the Hither East (London, 1932).

KOLLEK, TEDDY, and PEARLMAN, MOSHE. Jerusalem, Sacred City of Mankind (Weidenfeld and Nicholson, London, 1968).

MALLISON, W. T. (Jr.) The Zionist-Israel Juridical Claims to Constitute "The Jewish People" Nationality Entity and to Confer Membership of it. (*George Washington Law Review*, Vol. 32, No. 4-June 1964).

MARMORSTEIN, EMILE. Heaven at Bay: The Jewish Kulturkampf in the Holy Land (Oxford University Press, 1969).

ORNI, E. and EFRAT, E. The Geography of Israel (Darey, New York, 1965).

ORON, YITZHAK. Middle East Record, Vol. II (Daniel Davey and Co., New York, 1966).

PARKES, J. W. The Emergence of the Jewish Problem, 1878-1939 (Oxford, 1946).
A History of Palestine from A.D. 135 to Modern Times (Gollancz, London, 1949).
End of Exile (New York, 1954).
Whose Land? A History of the Peoples of Palestine (Pelican, Harmondsworth, 1970).

PATAI, R. Israel Between East and West (Philadelphia, 1953).
Culture and Conflict (New York, 1962).

SHAPIRO, HARRY L. The Jewish People: a biological history (UNESCO, 1960).

TOYNBEE, ARNOLD J. Survey of International Affairs, Vol. I (London, 1925).

TUCHMAN, BARBARA W. Bible and Sword (Redman, London, 1957; Minerva, New York, 1968).

WEINGROD, ALEX. Reluctant Pioneers, Village Development in Israel (Cornell University Press, New York, 1966).

ZANDER, WALTER. Israel and the Holy Places of Christendom (Weidenfeld and Nicolson, 1972).

ANCIENT HISTORY

DE VAUX, R. Ancient Israel: Its Life and Institutions (New York, 1961).

ORLINSKY, H. M. Ancient Israel (Cornell University Press).

SMITH, Sir G. A. Historical Geography of the Holy Land (24th ed., London, 1931).

YADIN, YIGAEL. Message of the Scrolls (Grosset and Dunlap, New York).
Masada (Weidenfeld and Nicolson, London, 1966).

YEWIN, S. A Decade of Archaeology in Israel 1948-58 (Istanbul, 1960).

RECENT HISTORY

ALLON, YIGAL The making of Israel's Army (Vallentine, Mitchell, London, 1970).

BARBOUR, NEVILL. Nisi Dominus: a survey of the Palestine Controversy (Harrap, London, 1946, reprinted by the Institute for Palestine Studies, Beirut, 1969).

BENTWICH, NORMAN and HELEN. Mandate Memories, 1918-1948 (Hogarth Press, London, 1965).

BERMANT, CHAIM. Israel (Thames and Hudson, London, 1967).

BERGER, EARL. The Covenant and the Sword, Arab-Israel Relations 1948–56 (University of Toronto Press, Toronto, 1965).

BURNS, E. L. M. Between Arab and Israeli (Harrap, London, 1962; Astor-Honor, New York, 1963).

CATTAN, HENRY. Palestine, the Arabs and Israel (Longmans Green, London, 1969).

CHURCHILL, RANDOLPH and WINSTON. The Six Day War (Heinemann/Penguin, London, 1967).

CROSSMAN, R. H. S. Palestine Mission (London, 1947).

DOUGLAS-HOME, C. The Arabs and Israel (Bodley Head, 1968).

DRAPER, T. Israel and World Politics: Roots of the Third Arab-Israeli War (Secker and Warburg, London, 1968).

ESCO FOUNDATION FOR PALESTINE, Palestine: A Study of Jewish, Arab and British Policies (2 vols., New Haven, 1947).

GABBAY, RONY E. A Political Study of the Arab-Jewish Conflict, the Arab Refugee Problem (Geneva and Paris, 1959).

HADAWI, SAMI, Palestine, Loss of Heritage (San Antonio, Texas, 1963).

HOWARD, M., and HUNTER, R. Israel and the Arab World (Institute of Palestine Studies, Beirut).

HUTCHISON, Cmdr. E. H. Violent Truce (New York, Devin-Adair, 1956).

JIRYIS, SABRI. The Arabs in Israel (Institute for Palestine Studies, Beirut, 1968).

KADER, RAZZAK ABDEL. The Arab-Jewish Conflict (1961).

KHALIDI, WALID. From Haven to Conquest: Readings in Zionism and the Palestine Problem until 1948 (Institute for Palestine Studies, Beirut, 1971).

KIMCHE, JON. Palestine or Israel (Secker & Warburg, London, 1973).

KIMCHE, JON and DAVID. Both Sides of the Hill: Britain and the Palestine War (Secker and Warburg, London, 1960).

KOESTLER, ARTHUR. Promise and Fulfilment: Palestine, 1917-1949 (London, 1949).
Thieves in the Night (New York and London, 1946).

LANDAU, JACOB M. The Arabs in Israel (Oxford University Press, London, 1969).

LAQUEUR, WALTER. The Road to War 1967 (Weidenfeld and Nicolson, London, 1968).

The Israel-Arab Reader (Weidenfeld and Nicolson, London, 1969).

LILIENTHAL, ALFRED M. The Other Side of the Coin: An American Perspective of the Arab-Israeli Conflict (New York, 1965).

LORCH, N. The Edge of the Sword: Israel's War of Independence 1947-49 (Putnam, New York, 1961).

MARLOWE, JOHN. The Seat of Pilate, An Account of the Palestine Mandate (Cresset, London, 1959; Dufour, Philadelphia, 1958).

O'BALLANCE, E. The Arab-Israeli War (New York, Praeger, 1957).

The Third Arab-Israeli War (Faber & Faber, London, 1972).

PERETZ, DON. Israel and the Palestine Arabs (The Middle East Institute, Washington, 1958).

RIZK, EDWARD. The Palestine Question, Seminar of Arab Jurists on Palestine, Algiers, 1967 (Institute for Palestine Studies, Beirut, 1968).

RODINSON, MAXIME. Israel and the Arabs (Penguin Books, Harmondsworth, 1968; Pantheon, New York, 1969).

ROULEAU, ERIC and HELD, JEAN-FRANCIS. Israel et les Arabes (Editions du Seuil, Paris, 1967).

ROYAL INSTITUTE OF INTERNATIONAL AFFAIRS. Great Britain and Palestine 1915-45 (London, 1946).

SHARABI, HISHAM B. Palestine and Israel: The Lethal Dilemma (Van Nostrand Reinhold, New York, 1969).

SYKES, CHRISTOPHER. Crossroads to Israel (Collins, London, 1965).

TEVETH, SHABTAI. Moshe Dayan (Weidenfeld and Nicolson, London, 1972).

ZURAYK, C. N. Palestine, the Meaning of the Disaster (Beirut, 1956).

THE STATE

BADI, JOSEPH. Fundamental Laws of the State of Israel (New York, 1961).

BARUTH, K. H. The Physical Planning of Israel (London, 1949).

BEN GURION, D. Rebirth and Destiny of Israel (New York, 1954).

Israel: A Personal History (London, New English Library, 1972).

BENTWICH, NORMAN. Fulfilment in the Promised Land 1917-37 (London, 1938).

Judæa Lives Again (London, 1944).

Israel Resurgent (Ernest Benn, 1960).

The New-old Land of Israel (Allen and Unwin, 1960).

Israel, Two Fateful Years 1967–69 (Elek, London, 1970).

BENTWICH, J. S. Education in Israel (Routledge and Kegan Paul, London, 1965).

BERNSTEIN, MARVER H. The Politics of Israel (London, 1958).

BRECHER, MICHAEL. The Foreign Policy System of Israel (Oxford University Press, London, 1972).

COMAY, JOAN. Everyone's Guide to Israel (New York, 1962).

Introducing Israel (London, Methuen, 1963).

COMAY, JOAN and PEARLMAN, MOSHE. Israel (New York, 1965).

CROSSMAN, R. H. S. A Nation Reborn (London, Hamish Hamilton, 1960).

DAVIS, MOSHE (Ed.). Israel: its Role in Civilisation (New York, 1956).

DAYAN, SHMUEL. The Promised Land (London, 1961).

DE GAURY, GERALD. The New State of Israel (New York, 1952).

DRABKIN-DARIN, H. Housing in Israel (Tel-Aviv, Gadish Books, 1957).

EBAN, A. The Voice of Israel (New York, Horizon Press. 1957).

The Story of Modern Israel (Weidenfeld & Nicolson, London, 1973).

HALPERIN, HAIM. Changing Patterns in Israel Agriculture (London, 1957).

THE ISRAEL ECONOMIST. Jerusalem (annual).

JANOWSKY, OSCAR I. Foundations of Israel: Emergence of a Welfare State (Anvil Nostrand Co., Princeton, 1959).

KRAINES, O. Government and Politics in Israel (Allen and Unwin, London, 1961).

LIKHOVSKI, ELIAHU S. Israel's Parliament: The Law of the Knesset (Oxford, Clarendon Press, 1971).

MEDDING, PETER. Mapai in Israel: Political Organisation and Government in a New Society (Cambridge U.P., London, 1972).

MEIR, GOLDA. This is our Strength (New York, 1963).

PATINKIN, D. The Israel Economy; the first decade (Jerusalem, 1960).

PEARLMAN, Lt.-Col. MOSHE. The Army of Israel (New York, 1959).

PREUSS, W. Co-operation in Israel and the World (Jerusalem, 1960).

RUBER, A. The Economy of Israel (Frank Cass, London, 1960).

SACHAR, H. M. ALIYAH, The Peoples of Israel (New York, 1962).

SAFRAN, NADAV. The United States and Israel (Harvard U.P., 1963).

SAMUEL, The Hon. EDWIN. Problems of Government in the State of Israel (Jerusalem, 1956).

SEGRE, V. D. Israel: A Society in Transition (Oxford U.P., London, 1971).

SHATIL, J. L'économie Collective du Kibboutz Israëlien (Paris, Les Editions de Minuit, 1960).

SITTON, SHLOMO. Israël: Immigration et Croissance 1948-58 (Editions Cujas, Paris, 1963).

WAAGENAAR, S. Women of Israel (New York, 1962).

ZIONISM

BEIN, ALEX. Theodor Herzl (East and West Library, London, 1957).

COHEN, ISRAEL. A Short History of Zionism (London, Frederick Muller, 1951).

FRANKL, OSCAR BENJAMIN. Theodor Herzl: The Jew and Man (New York, 1949).

GOLDWATER, RAYMOND (ed.). Jewish Philosophy and Philosophers (McGraw, London, 1962).

LAQUEUR, WALTER. A History of Zionism (Weidenfeld & Nicolson, London, 1972).

LIPSKY, L. A Gallery of Zionist Profiles (New York Farrar, Straus and Cudahy, 1950).

LOWENTHAL, MARVIN (ed. and trans.) Diaries of Theodor Herzl (Grosset and Dunlap, New York, 1965).

PETUCHOWSKY, J. J. Zionism Reconsidered (Twayne, New York, 1966).

SCHECHTMAN, J. Rebel and Statesmen: the Jabotinsky Story (New York, Thomas Yoseloff, 1956).

SOKOLOW, NAHUM. History of Zionism (2 vols., Longmans, London, 1919; Ktav, New York, 1969).

STEIN, LEONARD and YOGEV, GEDILIA (Editors). The Letters and Papers of Chaim Weizmann; Volume I 1885-1902 (Oxford University Press, 1968).

SOKOLOW, NAHUM. History of Zionism (2 vols., London, 1919).

WEISGAL, MEYER, and CARMICHAEL, JOEL. Chaim Weizmann—a Biography by Several Hands (London, Weidenfeld and Nicolson, 1962).

WEIZMANN, Dr. CHAIM. The Jewish People and Palestine (London, 1939).

Trial and Error: the Autobiography of Chaim Weizmann (Hamish Hamilton, London, 1949; Schocken, New York, 1966).

OFFICIAL PUBLICATIONS

Report of the Palestine Royal Commission, 1937 (Cmd. 5479), London.

Report of the Palestine Partition Commission, 1938 (Cmd. 5854), London.

Statement of Policy by His Majesty's Government in the United Kingdom (Cmd. 3692), London, 1930; (Cmd. 5893), London, 1938; (Cmd. 6019), London, 1939; (Cmd. 6180), London, 1940.

Government Survey of Palestine (2 vols., 1945-46), Jerusalem. Supplement, July 1947, Jerusalem.

Report of the Anglo-American Committee of Enquiry, Lausanne, 1946.

Report to the United Nations General Assembly by the UN Special Committee on Palestine, Geneva, 1947.

Report of the UN Economic Survey Mission for the Middle East, December 1949 (United Nations, Lake Success, N.Y.; H.M. Stationery Office).

Annual Yearbook of the Government of Israel.

Israel Government. The Arabs in Israel (1952).

Jewish Agency for Palestine. Documents Submitted to General Assembly of UN, relating to the National Home (1947).

The Jewish Plan for Palestine (Jerusalem, 1947).

Statistical Survey of the Middle East (1944).

Statistical Abstract of Israel. Central Bureau of Statistics (annual).

Jordan

PHYSICAL AND SOCIAL GEOGRAPHY

W. B. Fisher

The Hashemite Kingdom of Jordan (previously Transjordan) came officially into existence under its present name in 1947 and was enlarged in 1950 to include the districts of Samaria and part of Judaea that had previously formed part of Arab Palestine. The country is bounded on the north by Syria, on the north-east by Iraq, on the east and south by Saudi Arabia, and on the west by Israel. The total area of Jordan is approximately 37,500 sq. miles (The territory west of the Jordan river—some 2,165 sq. miles—has been occupied by Israel since June 1967).

PHYSICAL FEATURES

The greater part of the State of Jordan consists of a plateau lying some 2-3,000 ft. above sea-level, which forms the north-western corner of the great plateau of Arabia (see "Saudi Arabia"). There are no natural topographical frontiers between Jordan and its neighbours Syria, Iraq, and Saudi Arabia, and the plateau continues unbroken into all three countries, with the artificial frontier boundaries drawn as straight lines between defined points. Along its western edge, facing the Jordan Valley, the plateau is uptilted to give a line of hills that rise 1-2,000 ft. above plateau-level. An old river course, the Wadi Sirhan, now almost dry with only occasional wells, breaks up the plateau surface on the south-east and continues into Saudi Arabia.

The Jordanian plateau consists of a core or table of ancient rocks, covered by layers of newer rock (chiefly limestone) lying almost horizontally. In a few places (e.g. on the southern edge of the Jordan Valley) these old rocks are exposed at the surface. On its western side the plateau has been fractured and dislocated by the development of two strongly marked and parallel faults that run from the Red Sea via the Gulf of Aqaba northwards to the Lebanon and Syria. The narrow zone between the faults has sunk, to give the well-known Jordan rift valley, which is bordered both on the east and west by steep-sided walls, especially in the south near the Dead Sea, where the drop is often precipitous. The valley has a maximum width of 14 miles.

The floor of the Jordan Valley varies considerably in level. At its northern end it is just above sea-level; the surface of Lake Tiberias (the Sea of Galilee) is 686 ft. below sea-level, with the deepest part of the lake 700 ft. lower still. Greatest depth of the valley is at the Dead Sea (surface 1,300 ft. below sea level, maximum depth 1,298 ft.).

Dislocation of the rock strata in the region of the Jordan Valley has had two further effects: firstly, earth tremors are still frequent along the valley (Jerusalem has minor earthquakes from time to time); and secondly, considerable quantities of lava have welled up, forming enormous sheets that cover wide expanses of territory in the State of Jordan and southern Syria, and produce a desolate, forbidding landscape. One small lava flow, by forming a natural dam across the Jordan Valley, has impounded the waters to form Lake Tiberias.

The River Jordan rises just inside the frontiers of Syria and the Lebanon—a fruitful source of dispute between the two countries and Israel. The river is 157 miles long, and after first flowing for 60 miles in Israel it lies within Jordanian territory for the remaining 95 miles. Its main tributary, the Yarmuk, is 25 miles long, and close to its junction with the Jordan forms the boundary between Jordan State, Israel and Syria. A few miles from its source, the River Jordan used to open into Lake Huleh, a shallow, marshfringed expanse of water which was for long a breeding ground of malaria, but which has now been drained. Lake Tiberias, also, like Huleh, in Israel, covers an area of 122 sq. miles and measures 14 miles from north to south, and 16 miles from east to west. River water outflowing from the lake is used for the generation of hydro-electricity.

The river then flows through the barren, inhospitable country of its middle and lower valley, very little of which is actually, or potentially, cultivable, and finally enters the Dead Sea. This lake is 40 miles long and 10 miles wide. Owing to the very high air temperatures at most seasons of the year evaporation from the lake is intense, and has been estimated as equivalent to $8\frac{1}{2}$ million tons of water per day. At the surface the Dead Sea water contains about 250 grams of dissolved salts per litre, and at a depth of 360 feet the water is chemically saturated (i.e. holds its maximum possible content). Magnesium chloride is the most abundant mineral, with sodium chloride next in importance; but commercial interest centres in the less abundant potash and bromide salts.

Climatically, Jordan shows close affinity to its neighbours. Summers are hot, especially on the plateau and in the Jordan Valley, where temperatures up to 120° F. have been recorded. Winters are fairly cold, and on the plateau frost and some snow are usual, though not in the lower Jordan Valley. The significant element of the climate of Jordan is rainfall. In the higher parts (i.e. the uplands of Samaria and Judaea and the hills overlooking the eastern Jordan Valley) 15 to 25 inches of rainfall occur, enough for agriculture; but elsewhere as little as 8 inches or less may fall, and pastoral nomadism is the only possible way of life. Only about 25 per cent of the total area of Jordan is sufficiently humid for cultivation.

Hence the main features of economic life in Jordan are subsistence agriculture of a marginal kind, carried on in Judaea-Samaria and on the north-eastern edge of the plateau, close to Amman, with migratory herding of animals—sheep, goats, cattle and camels—over the remaining and by far the larger portion of the country. As a result, the natural wealth of Jordan is small and tribal ways of life exist in many parts. Before the June 1967 War tourism (with which must be included religious pilgrimage, mainly to the Holy Christian places of Jerusalem) had developed into a very important industry but this has been seriously jeopardized by the Israeli occupation of the West Bank territory and annexation of Jerusalem.

RACE AND LANGUAGE

A division must be drawn between the Jordanians living east of the River Jordan, who in the main are of pure Mediterranean stock, ethnically similar to the desert populations of Syria and Saudi Arabia, and the Arabs of the Jordan Valley and Samaria-Judaea. These latter are slightly taller, more heavily built, and have a broader head-form. Some authorities suggest that they are descendants of the Canaanites, who may have originated far to the north-east, in the Zagros area. An Iranian racial affinity is thus implied—but this must be of very ancient date, as the Arabs west of the Jordan Valley have been settled in their present home for many thousands of years. Besides the two groups of Arabs there are also small colon-

ies of Circassians from the Caucasus of Russia, who settled in Jordan as refugees during the nineteenth and twentieth centuries A.D.

Arabic is spoken everywhere, except in a few Circassian villages, and, through the contacts with Britain, some English is understood in the towns.

HISTORY

Jordan, as an independent State, is a twentieth-century development. Before then it was seldom more than a rugged and backward appendage to more powerful kingdoms and empires, and indeed never had any separate existence. In Biblical times the area was covered roughly by Gilead, Ammon, Moab and Edom, and the western portions formed for a time part of the kingdom of Israel. During the sixth century B.C. the Arabian tribe of the Nabataeans established their capital at Petra in the south and continued to preserve their independence when, during the fourth and third centuries, the northern half was incorporated into the Seleucid province of Syria. It was under Seleucid rule that cities like Philadelphia (the Biblical Rabbath Ammon and the modern Amman) and Gerasa (now Jerash) rose to prominence. During the first century B.C. the Nabataeans extended their rule over the greater part of present-day Jordan and Syria; they then began to recede before the advance of Rome, and in A.D. 105–6 Petra was incorporated into the Roman Empire. The lands east of the Jordan shared in a brief blaze of glory under the Palmyrene sovereigns Odenathus (Udaynath) and Zenobia (al-Zabba') in the middle of the third century A.D., and during the fifth and sixth centuries formed part of the dominions of the Christian Ghassanid dynasty, vassals of the Byzantine Empire. Finally, after fifty years of anarchy in which Byzantine, Persian and local rulers intervened, Transjordania was conquered by the Arabs and absorbed into the Islamic Empire.

For centuries nothing more is heard of the country; it formed normally a part of Syria, and as such was generally governed from Egypt. From the beginning of the sixteenth century it was included in the Ottoman *vilayet* of Damascus, and remained in a condition of stagnation until the outbreak of the Great War in 1914. European travellers and explorers of the nineteenth century rediscovered the beauties of Petra and Gerasa, but otherwise the desert tribes were left undisturbed. Even the course of the war in its early stages gave little hint of the upheaval that was to take place in Jordan's fortunes. The area was included in the zone of influence allocated to Britain under the Sykes-Picot Treaty of May 1916 (*see* Documents on Palestine, p. 48), and Zionists held that it also came within the area designated as a Jewish National Home in the promise contained in the Balfour Declaration of November 1917. Apart from these somewhat remote political events the tide of war did not reach Jordanian territory until the capture of Aqaba by the Arab armies under Faisal, the third son of King Hussein of the Hijaz, in July 1917. A year later, in September 1918, they shared in the final push north by capturing Amman and Deraa.

The end of the war thus found a large area, which included almost the whole of present-day Jordan, in Arab hands under the leadership of Faisal. To begin with, the territory to the east of the River Jordan was not looked on as a separate unit. Faisal, with the assistance of British officers and Iraqi nationalists, set up an autonomous government in Damascus, a step encouraged by the Anglo-French Declaration of November 7th, 1918, favouring the estab-

lishment of indigenous governments in Syria and Iraq. Arab demands, however, as expressed by Faisal at the Paris Peace Conference in January 1919, went a good deal further in claiming independence throughout the Arab world This brought them sharply up against both French and Zionist claims in the Near East, and when in March 1920 the General Syrian Congress in Damascus declared the independence of Syria and Iraq, with Faisal and Abdullah, Hussein's second son, as kings, the decisions were denounced by France and Britain. The following month the San Remo Conference awarded the Palestine Mandate to Britain, and thus separated it effectively from Syria proper, which fell within the French share. Faisal was forced out of Damascus by the French in July and left the country.

THE KINGDOM OF TRANSJORDAN

The position of Transjordania was not altogether clear under the new dispensation. After the withdrawal of Faisal the British High Commissioner informed a meeting of notables at Es Salt that the British Government favoured self-government for the territory with British advisers. In December 1920 the provisional frontiers of the Mandates were extended eastwards by Anglo-French agreement so as to include Transjordania within the Palestine Mandate, and therefore presumably within the provisions regarding the establishment of a Jewish National Home. Yet another twist of policy came as the result of a conference in Cairo in March 1921 attended by Winston Churchill, the new British Colonial Secretary, Abdullah, T. E. Lawrence and Sir Herbert Samuel, High Commissioner for Palestine. At this meeting it was recommended that Faisal should be proclaimed King of Iraq, while Abdullah was persuaded to stand down in his favour by the promise of an Arab administration in Transjordania. He had in fact been in effective control in Amman since his arrival the previous winter to organize a rising against the French in Syria. This project he now abandoned, and in April 1921 was officially recognized as *de facto* ruler of Transjordan. The final draft of the Palestine Mandate confirmed by the Council of the League of Nations in July 1922 contained a clause giving the Mandatory Power considerable latitude in the administration of the territory east of the Jordan (*see* Documents on Palestine, p. 52). On the basis of this clause a memorandum was approved in the following September expressly excluding Transjordan from the clauses relating to the establishment of the Jewish National Home, and although many Zionists continued to press for the reversal of this policy, the country thenceforth remained in practice separate from Palestine proper.

Like much of the post-war boundary delineation, the borders of the new state were somewhat arbitrary. Though they lay mainly in desert areas they frequently cut across tribal areas and grazing grounds with small respect for tradition. Of the three or four hundred thousand inhabitants only about a fifth were town-dwellers, and these confined to four small cities ranging in population from 30,000 to 10,000. Nevertheless Transjordan's early years were destined to be comparatively peaceful. On May 15th, 1923, Britain formally recognized Transjordan as an independent constitutional State under the rule of the Amir Abdullah with British tutelage, and with the aid of a British subsidy it was possible to make some slow progress towards development and modernization. A small but efficient armed force, the Arab Legion, was built up under the guidance of Peake Pasha and later Glubb Pasha; this force distinguished itself particularly during the Iraqi rebellion of May 1941. It also played a significant role in the fighting with Israel during 1948. Other British advisers assisted in the development of health services and schools.

The Amir Abdullah very nearly became involved in the fall of his father, King Hussein, in 1924. It was in Amman on March 5th, 1924, that the latter was proclaimed Caliph, and during the subsequent fighting with Ibn Sa'ud Wahhabi troops penetrated into Transjordanian territory. They subsequently withdrew to the south, and in June 1925, after the abdication of Hussein's eldest son Ali, Abdullah formally incorporated Ma'an and Aqaba within his dominions. The move was not disputed by the new ruler of the Hijaz and Najd, and thereafter the southern frontier of Transjordan has remained unaltered.

INDEPENDENCE

In February 1928 a treaty was signed with Great Britain granting a still larger measure of independence, though reserving for the advice of a British Resident such matters as financial policy and foreign relations. The same treaty provided for a constitution, and this was duly promulgated in April 1928, the first Legislative Council meeting a year later. In January 1934 a supplementary agreement was added permitting Transjordan to appoint consular representatives in Arab countries, and in May 1939 Britain agreed to the conversion of the Legislative Council into a regular Cabinet with ministers in charge of specified departments. The outbreak of war delayed further advances towards independence, but this was finally achieved in name at least by the Treaty of London of March 22nd, 1946. On the following May 25th Abdullah was proclaimed king and a new constitution replaced the now obsolete one of 1928.

Transjordan was not slow in taking her place in the community of nations. In 1947 King Abdullah signed treaties with Turkey and Iraq and applied for membership of the United Nations; this last, however, was thwarted by the Russian veto and by lack of American recognition of Transjordan's status as an independent nation. In March 1948 Britain agreed to the signing of a new treaty in which virtually the only restrictive clauses related to military and defence matters. Britain was to have certain peace-time military privileges, including the maintenance of airfields and communications, transit facilities and co-ordination of training methods. She was also to provide economic and social aid.

Transjordan had, however, not waited for independence before making her weight felt in Arab affairs in the Middle East. She had not been very active before the war, and, in fact her first appearance on the international scene was in May 1939, when Transjordanian delegates were invited to the Round Table Conference on Palestine in London. Transjordan took part in the preliminary discussions during 1943 and 1944 that led finally to the formation of the Arab League in March 1945, and was one of the original members of that League. During the immediately following years it seemed possible that political and dynastic differences would be forgotten in this common effort for unity. Under the stresses and strains of 1948 however, the old contradictions began to reappear. Abdullah had long favoured the project of a "Greater Syria", that is, the union of Transjordan, Syria, and Palestine, as a step towards the final

unification of the Fertile Crescent by the inclusion of Iraq. This was favoured on dynastic grounds by various parties in Iraq, and also by some elements in Syria and Palestine. On the other hand it met with violent opposition from many Syrian nationalists, from the rulers of Egypt and Saudi Arabia—neither of whom were disposed to favour any strengthening of the Hashemite house—and of course from the Zionists and the French. It is in the light of these conflicts of interest that developments subsequent to the establishment of the State of Israel must be seen.

FORMATION OF ISRAEL

On May 14th–15th, 1948, British troops were withdrawn into the port of Haifa as a preliminary to the final evacuation of Palestine territory, the State of Israel was proclaimed, and Arab armies entered the former Palestinian territory from all sides. Only those from Transjordan played any significant part in the fighting, and by the time that major hostilities ceased in July they had succeeded in occupying a considerable area. The suspicion now inevitably arose that Abdullah was prepared to accept a *fait accompli* and to negotiate with the Israeli authorities for a formal recognition of the existing military boundaries. Moreover, whereas the other Arab countries refused to accept any other move that implied a tacit recognition of the *status quo*—such as the resettlement of refugees—Transjordan seemed to be following a different line. In September 1948 an Arab government was formed at Gaza under Egyptian tutelage, and this was answered from the Transjordanian side by the proclamation in December at Jericho of Abdullah as King of All-Palestine. In the following April the country's name was changed to Jordan and three Palestinians were included in the Cabinet. In the meantime armistices were being signed by all the Arab countries, including Jordan, and on January 31st, 1949, Jordan had at last been recognized by the United States.

On the three major problems confronting the Arab States in their dispute with Israel, Jordan continued to differ more or less openly with her colleagues. She refused to agree to the internationalization of Jerusalem, she initiated plans for the resettlement of the Arab refugees, and she showed a disposition to accept as permanent the armistice frontiers. In April 1950, after rumours of negotiations between Jordan and Israel, the Arab League Council in Cairo succeeded in getting Jordan's adherence to resolutions forbidding negotiations with Israel or annexation of Palestinian territory. Nevertheless in the same month elections were held in Jordan and Arab Palestine, the results of which encouraged Abdullah formally to annex the latter territory on April 24th, 1950. This step was immediately recognized by Britain.

At the meeting of the Arab League that followed, Egypt led the opposition to Jordan, who found support, however, from Iraq. The decisions reached by the Council were inconclusive; but thereafter Jordan began to drift away from Arab League policy. Jordan supported the United Nations policy over Korea, in contradistinction to the other Arab states, and signed a Point Four agreement with the United States in March 1951. Though there was at the same time constant friction between Jordan and Israel the unified opposition of the Arab States to the new Jewish State seemed to have ended, and inter-Arab differences were gaining the upper hand.

ABDULLAH ASSASSINATED

On July 20th, 1951, King Abdullah was assassinated in Jerusalem. Evidence brought out at the trial of those implicated in the plot showed that the murder was as much as anything a protest against his Greater Syria policy, and it was significant that Egypt refused to extradite some of those convicted. Nevertheless the stability of the young Jordan-ian State revealed itself in the calm in which the King's eldest son Talal succeeded to the throne, and the peaceful elections held shortly afterwards. In January 1952 a new constitution was promulgated. Even more significant, per-haps, was the dignity with which, only a year after his accession, King Talal, whose mental condition had long been giving cause for anxiety, abdicated in favour of his son, Hussein, still a minor. In foreign policy Talal had shown some signs of a reaction against his father's ideas in favour of a *rapprochement* with Syria and Egypt, one step being Jordan's signature of the Arab Collective Security Pact which she had failed to join in the summer of 1950.

This policy was continued during the reign of his son, King Hussein, notably by the conclusion of an economic and financial agreement with Syria in February 1953, and a joint scheme for the construction of a dam across the Yarmuk River to supply irrigation and hydro-electric power. At the same time Hussein maintained the family ties with Iraq, state visits being exchanged with King Faisal II immediately after the former's formal accession in May 1953.

During the year there was a recrudescence of trouble along the frontier with Israel. A temporary agreement reached under UN auspices in June seemed to have eased matters, but in October an Israeli attack on the Jordanian village of Qibya aroused violent emotions in the Arab countries. In March, 1954, the position was reversed with an Arab attack on an Israeli bus in the Scorpion Pass, an incident that led to a temporary breakdown in the truce arrangements and to a series of further frontier violations. Another problem that still remained unsolved was the elaborate scheme sponsored by the United States for the sharing of the Jordan waters between Jordan, Iraq, Syria and Israel, which could make no progress in the absence of political agreement. In May, amid mounting tension, the cabinet of Fawzi al-Mulqi resigned, and a new govern-ment was formed by Tawfiq Abu'l-Huda, which was re-organized on October 25th, 1954, after the elections of October 16th.

During December a financial aid agreement was signed in London with the United Kingdom, and the opportunity was taken to discuss the revision of the Anglo-Jordanian Treaty of 1946. Agreement over this was not possible owing to British insistence that any new pact should fit into a general Middle East defence system. In May 1955 Abu'l-Huda was replaced by Sa'id al-Mufti, while an exchange of state visits with King Sa'ud hinted at a *rapprochement* with Saudi Arabia. Nevertheless, in November Jordan declared its unwillingness to adhere either to the Egyptian-Syrian-Saudi Arabian bloc or to the Baghdad Pact.

DISMISSAL OF GLUBB PASHA

On December 15th, following a visit to General Sir. G. Templer, Chief of the Imperial General Staff, Sa'id al-Mufti resigned and was replaced by Hazza al-Majali, known to be in favour of the Baghdad Pact. The following day there were violent demonstrations in Amman, and on December 20th Ibrahim Hashim became Prime Minister, to be succeeded on January 9th by Samir Rifai. In February 1956 the new Prime Minister visited Syria, Lebanon, Iraq, Egypt and Saudi Arabia, and shortly after his return, on March 2nd, King Hussein announced the dismissal of Glubb Pasha, commander-in-chief of the Jordanian armed forces, and replaced him by Major-General Radi 'Annab. The Egyptian-Syrian-Saudi Arabian bloc at this juncture offered to replace the British financial subsidy to Jordan; but the latter was not in fact withdrawn, and King Hussein and the Jordanian government evidently felt that they had moved far enough in one direction, and committed

themselves to a policy of strict neutrality. In April, however, the King and the Prime Minister paid a visit to the Syrian President in Damascus, and in May Major-General Annab was replaced by his deputy, Lt.-Colonel Ali Abu Nuwar, generally regarded as the leader of the move-ment to eliminate foreign influence from the Jordanian army and government. This coincided with the reappoint-ment of Sa'id al-Mufti as Prime Minister. During the same period discussions culminated in agreements for military co-operation between Jordan and Syria, Lebanon and Egypt, and in July Jordan and Syria formed an economic union. At the beginning of the same month al-Mufti was replaced by Ibrahim Hashim.

RELATIONS WITH ISRAEL AND WITH THE OTHER ARAB STATES

Meanwhile relations with Israel, including the problem of the Arab refugees, the use of Jordan waters, the defini-tion of the frontier, and the status of Jerusalem, continued to provide a standing cause for anxiety. Early in July there was a further series of frontier incidents, which lasted well into the autumn. October saw the development of military relations with Iraq; however a plan to move Iraqi troops into Jordan was stopped by the stiff reaction of the Israeli government. Tension between Jordan and Israel was further increased after the Israeli, British and French military action in Egypt. A new cabinet, headed by Suleiman Nabulsi, had taken office early in October, and new elections were followed by the opening of negotiations for the abrogation of the Anglo-Jordanian Treaty of 1948, and the substitution of financial aid from the Arab coun-tries. At a conference held in Cairo on January 18th and 19th, 1957, between King Sa'ud, King Hussein, President Nasser and the Syrian and Jordanian Prime Ministers, an agreement was signed providing for an annual payment of £E 12,500,000 (£12,800,000 sterling) to Jordan over the next ten years. Saudi Arabia and Egypt were each to con-tribute £E 5,000,000 and Syria £E 2,500,000. Owing to subsequent political developments, however, the shares due from Egypt and Syria were not paid. On March 13th, 1957, an Anglo-Jordanian agreement was signed abro-gating the 1948 treaty, and by July 2nd the last British troops had left. In the meantime Nabulsi's evident lean-ings towards the Soviet connection, clashing with the recently-enunciated Eisenhower doctrine, led to his breach with King Hussein and his resignation on April 10th. Two weeks of cabinet crises, demonstrations and riots preceded the formation of a new government under Ibrahim Hashim. All political parties were suppressed, and plans to establish diplomatic relations with Russia were dropped. Gen. Ali Abu Nuwar was removed from the post of Commander-in-Chief, and the United States announced its determination to preserve Jordan's inde-pendence—a policy underlined by a major air-lift of arms to Amman in September in response to Syria's alignment with the Soviet Union. In May Syrian troops serving under the joint Syro-Egypto-Jordanian command were with-drawn from Jordanian territory at Jordan's request, and in June there was a partial rupture of diplomatic relations with Egypt.

On January 18th, 1958, an agreement was reached between Israel and Jordan for the implementation of the 1948 agreement on the Mount Scopus demilitarized zone.

On February 14th, the merger of the Kingdoms of Iraq and Jordan in a federal union to be known as the Arab Federation was proclaimed in Amman by King Faisal of Iraq and King Hussein. This new federation, made in response to the formation of the United Arab Republic a fortnight before, was dissolved by decree of King Hussein on August 2nd, following the revolution in Iraq. Samir Rifai became Prime Minister of Jordan in May, on the

resignation of Ibrahim Hashim who took up the appoint-
ment of Vice-Premier in the short-lived Arab Federation.
On July 22nd, Hashim was assassinated by the mob in
Baghdad during the rioting that followed the revolution.

British troops were flown to Amman from Cyprus on
July 17th, in response to an appeal by King Hussein. They
had all been withdrawn by the beginning of November—
under UN auspices—and in the two years that followed
Jordan settled down to a period of comparative peace.
Hazza' al-Majali succeeded Rifai at Prime Minister on
May 6th, 1959. Firm measures were taken against communism and subversive activities (defence and internal
security accounted for rather more than half of the
1960–61 budget) and collaboration with the West was, if
anything, encouraged by the country's isolation between
Iraq, Israel and the two halves of the United Arab Republic. American loans continued to arrive at the rate of
about $50,000,000 a year, and there was also technical
aid of various kinds from Britain, Western Germany and
other countries. An important development was the official
opening of the port of Aqaba on the Red Sea, virtually
Jordan's only outlet.

Relations with Jordan's Arab neighbours continued to be
uneasy, though diplomatic relations with the United
Arab Republic, broken off in July, 1958, were resumed
in August 1959. Incidents on the Syrian border were
almost as frequent as on the Israeli, and there were no
signs of a rapprochement with Iraq. In January 1960,
both the King and the Prime Minister condemned the
Arab leaders' approach to the Palestine problem, and
in February Jordanian citizenship was offered to all Arab
refugees who applied for it. On the other side of the balance
sheet, King Hussein paid a flying visit to King Saud in
February, 1960, and in March strongly anti-Zionist statements appeared in the Jordanian press. Nevertheless there
seemed to be no change in the general position that
Jordan wished for formal recognition of her absorption
of the Palestinian territory west of the Jordan, while the
United Arab Republic and other Arab countries favoured
the establishment of an independent Palestine Arab
government.

On August 29th, 1960, the Jordanian Prime Minister,
Hazza al-Majali, was assassinated by the explosion of a
time-bomb in his office. Jordan was quick to attribute
the outrage to persons in the United Arab Republic. A
curfew was imposed, but after a cabinet reshuffle comparative stability was restored, with Bahjat Talhouni as
Prime Minister.

United States aid continued to reach Jordan on a substantial scale, and relations with the United States were
further strengthened by the visit of King Hussein to New
York in October 1960, when he addressed the United
Nations Assembly and talked with President Eisenhower,
and by a trade agreement in February 1961.

INTERNAL DEVELOPMENTS

The calm and even enthusiasm with which the King's
marriage to an English girl in May 1961 was received by
the Jordanian population was generally seen as a sign of
the strength of the Throne. In January 1962, Wasfi al-Tal
had taken over the premiership, and in December after
the completion of elections, the formation of political
parties was once again permitted.

Mr. Al-Tal's government was short-lived. In March 1963
he was replaced by Samir Rifai, a nominee of the King.
But shortly after the news of a plan to federate Egypt,
Syria and Iraq, rioting broke out against Mr. Rifai who
resigned on April 20th after only twenty-three days in
office. A transitional government was appointed by the
King with the task of dissolving the Lower House and
holding new elections; these were duly held in July, when

the caretaker government of Sherif Hussein bin Nasser, the
king's great-uncle, was confirmed in office. The relaxing of
tension at home was followed by a conciliatory policy
abroad. In January 1964 King Hussein himself represented
Jordan at the Cairo conference held to discuss joint Arab
measures to deal with the Jordan waters dispute, which had
flared up again with the rumour of Israeli plans to take
unilateral action in the continued absence of any international agreement.

In July 1964 King Hussein demonstrated his personal
control over the Government when Hussein bin Nasser
resigned, and Bahjat Talhouni was asked to take over
once again. Talhouni, who had previously been head of the
Royal Cabinet and the official representative of the King
since the Arab summit conference in January 1964, stated
that his government would work "in accordance with the
spirit of the Arab summit conference and based on King
Hussein's instruction". Also in July, Jordan recognized the
Republican régime in the Yemen, and relations with the
United Arab Republic were improved by an exchange of
visits between the U.A.R. First Vice-President, Abdul
Hakim Amer, and King Hussein. In August Jordan
signed the Arab Common Market agreement, and in
September the King attended the Arab Summit Conference in Alexandria, at which the problem of the Jordan
waters was one of the main topics of discussion. Talhouni
resigned in February 1965, and was replaced by Wasfi
al-Tal. In April a constitutional uncertainty was resolved,
with the nomination of the King's brother Hassan as
Crown Prince; the infant son of the formerly British
Princess Muna was thus excluded.

WAR WITH ISRAEL

During the latter part of 1966 Jordan's foreign relations
became increasingly worsened by the widening breach with
Syria. Charges and counter-charges were made of plots to
subvert each other's governments, and while the U.A.R.
and the U.S.S.R. supported Syria, Jordan looked for backing to Saudi Arabia and the U.S. This situation made it
increasingly difficult for Jordan's relations with Israel to
be regularized. In July 1966 Jordan suspended support for
the Palestine Liberation Organization, accusing its secretary Shukairy of pro-Communist activity, and this move
was copied by Tunisia in October. In November an Israeli
reprisal raid aroused bitter feeling in Jordan and elsewhere.
While Jordan introduced conscription and Saudi Arabia
promised military aid, Syria and the Palestine Liberation
Organization called on the Jordanians to revolt against
King Hussein. Negotiations to implement the resolution
of the Supreme Council for Arab Defence that Iraqi and
Saudi troops should be sent to Jordan to assist in her
defence broke down in December. This was followed by
clashes on the Jordan/Syria frontier, by PLO-sponsored
bomb outrages in Jordan (resulting in the closure of the
PLO headquarters in Jerusalem), and by worsening
relations between Jordan and the U.A.R. and a ban by
the latter on aircraft carrying British and American arms
to Jordan. In retaliation Jordan withdrew recognition of
the Sallal régime in Yemen, and boycotted the next meeting of the Arab Defence Council. On March 5th Wasfi
al-Tal resigned and was succeeded by Hussein bin Nasser
at the head of an interim government.

As the prospect of war with Israel drew nearer, King
Hussein composed his differences with Egypt, and personally flew to Cairo to sign a defence agreement. Jordanian
troops, together with those of the U.A.R., Iraq and Saudi
Arabia, went into action immediately on the outbreak of
hostilities in June. By the end of the Six Days War, however, all Jordanian territory west of the River Jordan had
been occupied by Israeli troops, and a steady stream of
West Bank Jordanians began to cross the River Jordan to

the East Bank. Estimated at between 150,000 and 250,000 persons, they swelled Jordan's refugee population and presented the government with intractable social and economic problems. In August, although Jordan had reached no settlement with Israel, a small percentage of the refugees were enabled to return to the West Bank under an agreement mediated by the International Red Cross. By June 1968 about 105,000 of the new refugees remained in temporary camps. Jordan had so far refused to ask UNRWA to extend its mandate to the refugees of the June war.

King Hussein formed a nine-man Consultative Council in August 1967, composed of former premiers and politicians of varying sympathies, to meet weekly and to participate in the "responsibility of power". Later a Senate was formed consisting of fifteen representatives from the inhabitants of the west bank area, and fifteen from eastern Jordan. Several changes of government took place. Saad Jumaa had succeeded as Prime Minister on April 23rd, 1967, after general elections, and on July 15th, after first resigning, was entrusted with the formation of a new cabinet. On October 7th, however, he resigned again, and was succeeded by Bahjat Talhouni; a feature of this reconstruction was that the King took over personal command of the country's armed forces. King Hussein was also active in the diplomatic field, visiting Britain, the United States, France, Italy, Turkey, Pakistan and the U.S.S.R. to gain sympathy and support for his country's cause. U.S. arms shipments to Jordan were resumed on February 14th, 1968.

Meanwhile the uneasy situation along the frontier with Israel persisted, aggravated by the deteriorating economic situation in the country. Reprisal actions by Israel after numerous commando raids directed against her authority in Jerusalem and the West Bank and operating from Jordanian territory culminated in a major attack in March with the object of destroying an alleged guerrilla camp at Karameh. Further major attacks were made at Irbid and Essalt in June and August respectively; following the latter attack, Jordan appealed for UN intervention. In June 1969 Israeli commandos blew up the diversion system of the Ghor Canal, Jordan's principal irrigation project.

THE GUERRILLA CHALLENGE

The instability in Amman after the June War was reflected in the short life of Jordanian cabinets—it became rare for one to remain unchanged for more than three months. A careful balance had to be struck between the Palestinians and the King's traditional supporters. Thus, in the new cabinet announced after the June 1970 crisis, Palestinians were given more of the key ministries, including that of the Interior. Abdul Munem Rifai, Jordan's senior diplomat, became Prime Minister for the second time.

The main factor in Jordan's internal politics between June 1967 and 1971 was the rivalry between the official government and the guerrilla organizations, principally Al Fatah. These organizations gradually assumed effective control of the refugee camps and commanded widespread support amongst the Palestinian majority of Jordan's present population. They also received arms and training assistance from other Arab countries, particularly Syria, and finance from the oil-rich Gulf states. Some camps became commando training centres, the younger occupants of these, almost all unemployed, welcoming the sense of purpose and relief from idleness and boredom that recruitment into a guerrilla group offered. The fedayeen movement virtually became a state within a state. Its

leadership has stated that "We have no wish to interfere in the internal affairs of Jordan provided it does not place any obstacles in the way of our struggle to liberate Palestine". In practice, however, its popularity and influence represented a challenge to the government, whilst its actions attracted Israeli reprisals that did serious damage to the east bank, now the only fertile part of Jordan, and generally reduced the possibilities of a peace settlement on which Jordan's long-term future depended.

A major confrontation between the two forces occurred in November 1968, after massive demonstrations in Amman on the anniversary of the Balfour Declaration. Extensive street fighting broke out between guerrillas and the army, which, being mainly Bedouin, has little in common with the Palestinians anyway, and for a short period a civil war seemed possible, but both sides soon backed down. Some sources attributed the trouble to the government's attempt (subsequently abandoned) to disarm the refugee camps; others pointed out that small extremist groups had led the fighting which was discouraged by the more responsible Al Fatah leadership. Similar confrontations followed in February and June 1970, and on both occasions the Government was forced to yield to Palestinian pressures. In February the cabinet soon had to abandon an attempt to restrict the carrying of arms by guerrillas. June saw the most serious crisis. A week's fighting in Amman and the surrounding district resulted in an estimated 100 deaths, an assassination attempt on the King and a partial evacuation of the Western community in the capital. King Hussein and Yasser Arafat, the Al Fatah leader (whose own position was threatened by the rise of small extremist groups in Jordan), jointly drew up and signed an agreement redefining their respective spheres of influence. The guerrillas appeared to have granted little or nothing, but Hussein was forced to dismiss his Commander-in-Chief and a cabinet minister, both relatives. These were regarded as the leaders of the anti-fedayeen faction, which remained strong amongst the Bedouin sheikhs. Despite the agreement, the tension between the government and the guerrillas continued, aggravated by opposition to the government's concessions from hard-line army officers.

A new and dangerous stage in the relations between the two sides in Jordan was reached in July with the acceptance by the government of the American peace proposals for the Middle East. The guerrilla groups, with few exceptions, rejected these, and, as the cease-fire between the U.A.R. and Israel came into operation on August 7th, it was clear that the Jordanian Government was preparing for a full-scale confrontation with them. The top command of the army was strengthened and measures were taken to bolster the defences of Amman. At the same time there was fighting between some of the guerrillas themselves over attitudes to the Rogers Plan.

CIVIL WAR

Bitter fighting between government and guerrilla forces broke out at the end of August. In the first part of September the violence was increased by two factors: the assassination attempt on King Hussein and the hijackings by PLFP of four Western Airliners. The threat of intervention on the side of the commandos by Iraq and Syria; the transference of Libyan aid from the Jordanian government to the guerrillas; a succession of cease-fire agreements between the two sides; the release of all but 54 hostages taken from the aircraft to secure the release of Palestinian commandos held by Western governments; none of these developments were enough to prevent the escalation into full civil war in the last half of the month, and thousands of deaths and injuries. (Estimates of deaths up to the first week in October vary between 500 and 3,500.) The continued detention of any hostages by the PFLP was a direct challenge to the government's authority. On September 16th a military cabinet was formed under Brig. Muhammad Daoud—in any case martial law had been in force since the end of the June 1967 war—and immediately Field Marshal Habis Majali replaced as Commander-in-Chief Lt.-Gen. Mashour Haditha, who had been sympathetic to the commandos and had tried to restrain their severest opponents in the army.

In the fighting that followed the guerrillas claimed full control in the north, aided by Syrian forces and, it was later revealed, three battalions of the Palestine Liberation Army sent back by President Nasser from the Suez front. The Arab states generally appealed for an end to the fighting. Libya threatened to intervene and later broke off diplomatic relations; Kuwait stopped its aid to the government; but the Iraqi troops stationed on the Eastern front against Israel notably failed to intervene. On the government side talks were held with the U.S.A. about direct military assistance—on what scale is not known, but there were rumours of a plan for joint American and Israeli intervention if Hussein looked in danger of being overthrown. In the event such a dangerous widening of the Palestinian confrontation was avoided by the scale of the casualties in Jordan and by the diplomacy of Arab heads of state (reinforced by President Nasser's reported threat to intervene on the guerrillas' behalf) who prevailed upon King Hussein and Yasser Arafat to sign an agreement in Cairo on September 27th ending the war. A follow-up committee of three members was established under the Tunisian premier, Bahi Ladgham, to oversee the implementation of the agreement. The previous day a civilian cabinet had been restored under Ahmed Toukan. Five military members were retained.

A definitive agreement, very favourable to the liberation organizations, was signed by Hussein and Arafat on October 13th in Amman, but this proved to be simply the beginning of a phase of sporadic warfare between the two parties, punctuated by new agreements, during which the commandos were gradually forced out of Amman and driven from their positions in the north back towards the Syrian frontier. At the end of October a new government, still containing three army officers, was formed under Wasfi al-Tal. By January 1971 army moves against the Palestine guerrillas had become so blatant that Ladgham threatened to resign from the follow-up committee and the U.A.R., Syria and Algeria all issued strong protests at the Jordanian Government's attempt to "liquidate" the liberation movements. All but two brigades of Iraqi troops were, however, withdrawn from Jordan.

By April the Jordanian Government seemed strong enough to set a deadline for the guerrillas' withdrawal of their remaining men and heavy armaments from the capital. Later in the month King Hussein was able to state that "security" had been restored, and to ban trade unions, student unions and other organizations backed by the guerrillas. Isolated outbreaks of fighting between government and commando forces were still being reported from the north, however. More important was the declaration issued on June 5th by seven commando organizations, including even the more moderate Fatah, calling for the overthrow of Hussein. However, it was the Jordanian authorities who in July moved first to resolve the contest for political power in Jordan. On July 13th a major Government attack began on the guerrillas entrenched in the Jerash-Aljoun area. Four days later it was all over. The Government claimed that all the bases had been destroyed and that 2,300 of 2,500 guerrillas in them had been captured. About 100 sought refuge in Israeli-occupied territory. Most of the Palestinians taken prisoner by the Jordanian government were released a few days

later, either to leave for other Arab states or to return to normal life in Jordan.

The "solution" (in King Hussein's word) of the guerrilla "problem" provoked strong reaction from other Arab governments. Iraq and Syria closed their borders with Jordan; Algeria suspended diplomatic relations; and Egypt, Libya, Sudan and both Yemens voiced public criticism. Relations with Syria deteriorated fastest of all. In August there were three days of clashes on the border between Syrian and Jordanian tanks and artillery, which appeared to have been the result of a simple mistake escalating out of all proportion, and Syria broke off diplomatic relations. The closure of the border was more serious for Jordan than the actual breach in relations, because the trade route through Syria from Beirut was now denied and all Jordan's imports had to be directed to her only port, Aqaba, on the Red Sea. However, Iraq soon began to ease the restrictions on movements across her border and airspace, and by February 1972 normal trading relations between her and Jordan had resumed.

In the meantime, Saudi Arabia had been attempting to bring together guerrilla leaders and Jordanian Government representatives to work out a new version of the Cairo and Amman agreements. Meetings did take place in Jeddah but were fruitless, and the Palestinians responded in their own way to the events of July. Three unsuccessful attemps were made in September to hijack Jordanian airliners. Then, on September 28th, 1971, Wasfi al-Tal, the Prime Minister and Defence Minister, was assassinated by members of a secret Palestinian guerrilla group, the Black September Organization.

In December 1971 the Black September Organization made two further assassination attempts. In one the Jordanian Ambassador to the United Kingdom, Zaid al-Rifai, escaped with a wounded hand from a gun attack in London. In the other the Jordanian Ambassador to Switzerland was sent a parcel bomb which exploded when opened by police, seriously injuring three people.

HUSSEIN'S ANSWER

Throughout the period since the liquidation of the guerrillas in July 1971 Hussein had been seeking to strengthen his political position. In August he announced the creation of a tribal council—a body of sheikhs or other notables, appointed by him and chaired by the Crown Prince—which was to deal with the affairs of tribal areas. A month later the formation of the Jordanian National Union was announced. This (renamed Arab National Union in March 1972) was to be Jordan's only legal political organization. It was not to be a party in the usual sense; proponents of "imported ideologies" were debarred from membership; the King became President and the Crown Prince Vice-President; and appointed the 36 members of the Supreme Executive Committee.

However, the King's boldest political move, and an obvious attempt to regain his standing in the eyes of Palestinians, was his unfolding of plans for a United Arab Kingdom in March 1972. This kingdom was to federate a Jordanian region, with Amman as its capital and also federal capital, and a Palestinian region, with Jerusalem as its capital. Each region was to be virtually autonomous, though the King would rule both and there would be a federal council of ministers.

Outside Jordan there was almost universal criticism of this plan from interested parties—Israel, the Palestinian organizations and Egypt, which in the following month broke off diplomatic relations. Jordan's isolation in the Arab world had never been more complete.

Throughout the rest of 1972 and the first half of 1973 Hussein continued to stand by his original plans for a

United Arab Kingdom, but at the same time insisting that peace with Israel can only come within the framework of UN Resolution 242 (*see* Documents on Palestine, page 58) and hotly denying suggestions from other Arab states that he was considering signing a separate peace treaty with Israel.

The internal security of Jordan was threatened in November 1972 when an attempted military coup in Amman by Major Rafeh Hindawi was thwarted. It was alleged that the attempted coup had the support of Libya and the Palestinian guerrillas. In February 1973 Abu Daoud, one of the leaders of Al Fatah, and 16 other guerrillas were arrested on charges of infiltrating into Jordan for the purpose of subversive activities.

The latter affair took place while King Hussein was on a visit to the U.S.A. requesting defence and financial aid. President Nixon agreed to provide two squadrons of F.5 fighter bombers. On his return he commuted the death sentences passed on the guerrillas by a Jordanian military court and previously confirmed by himself, to life imprisonment. In May 1973 Hussein's Prime Minister, Ahmed Lauzi, resigned for health reasons and a new government under Zaid al-Rifai was formed. Rifai is known to be firmly against the Palestinian guerrillas and was the target of a bomb attack when he was Ambassador to London in 1971.

In September 1973 Hussein attended a "reconciliation summit" with President Sadat of Egypt and Assad of Syria. This was Jordan's first official contact with the two states since they had broken diplomatic relations, and they were restored after the summit. The meeting was condemned by Al Fatah, Libya and Iraq but Jordan regained some stature in the Arab world after Hussein's general amnesty for all political prisoners; among those released was Abu Daoud.

During the Middle East War in October 1973 Jordan sent troops to support Syria on the Golan Heights but was otherwise not actively involved, and did not open a third front against the Israelis as in the 1967 War. Jordan was represented at the Geneva talks in December 1973. During February 1974 there was considerable unrest among sections of the army though this was settled by increases in pay ordered by Hussein who was out of the country when the disturbances started. In April Hussein announced that the Arab National Union, which remains the sole political organization in Jordan, was to be reorganized with an executive and council of reduced numbers.

During most of 1974 the main characteristic of Hussein's policy towards the PLO and the status of the West Bank was extreme ambiguity. He continued to try to preserve the West Bank as part of his kingdom despite strong pressure from other Arab states and the increasing influence of the PLO. In September 1974 after a meeting between Egypt, Syria and the PLO expressing support for the PLO as the "only legitimate representative of the Palestinian people", Jordan refused to participate in further Middle East peace talks. However, in October 1974 at the Arab Summit Conference at Rabat (*see* Documents on Palestine, page 64), representatives of twenty Arab heads of state unanimously recognized the PLO as the sole legitimate representative of the Palestinians, and its right to establish a national authority over any liberated Pal-

estinian territory. Effectively ceding Jordan's claim to represent the Palestinians and re-incorporate the West Bank, when recaptured, into the Hashemite Kingdom, Hussein reluctantly assented to the resolution. He said that Jordan would continue to strive for the liberation of the West Bank and recognize the full rights of citizenship of Palestinians in Jordan. The prospect of a separate, independently ruled Palestinian state was strongly condemned by Israel.

Following the Rabat Conference Hussein was given more extensive powers in revisions to the Jordanian constitution approved by parliament in November. He was allowed to rule without parliament for a year and reorganize his Kingdom in order to lessen the numbers of Palestinians in the executive and legislative branches of government, his 1972 plan for a United Arab Kingdom now being wholly defunct. Parliament was dissolved and a new government formed in November, with Zaid al-Rifai remaining Prime Minister. Palestinian representation was decreased, and the question of citizenship of the estimated 800,000 Palestinians on the East Bank became contentious. Elections in Jordan were postponed in March 1975.

The success of the PLO at the Rabat Conference had, despite internal feuds (*see* Palestine Organizations, page 65), considerably strengthened its position. This was further the case when the UN acknowledged the PLO as the legitimate representative of the Palestinians by an overwhelming majority in November. The PLO was also granted observer status at the UN.

In January 1975 Jordan, Egypt, the PLO and Syria held talks, agreeing on the principle of future regular meetings, though nothing of substance was achieved. Whilst reaffirming his recognition of the PLO and, in a later interview with *Le Monde* (January 21st), saying he would recognize a PLO government in exile headed by Yasser Arafat, Hussein refused to agree to re-establishment of guerrilla bases or to attend a future session of the Geneva talks. In the same month, the failure of Dr. Henry Kissinger's peace mission to the Middle East made tension in the area still more acute.

In March Jordan announced that it was sending troops and donating fighter aircraft to the Sultanate of Oman to support its fight against guerrilla forces backed by Southern Yemen. Continuing its relations with Taiwan and its close ties with Western countries, especially the United States, Jordan's foreign policy has remained conservative, though in April 1975 the Romanian President visited Jordan, the first Communist leader to do so.

In May Hussein declared Jordan's willingness to fight if a new war against Israel broke out, a large arms order from the United States was reported, together with a conciliatory speech urging Israel's withdrawal from occupied territories in return for recognition of its right to exist. President Sadat visited Jordan in May and President Assad in June of 1975. Jordan's acceptance of the status of the PLO on the West Bank had, by mid-1975, removed a major obstacle to Arab unity, ensured that Jordan would receive more aid from oil-rich states, and that Jordan had a good chance of close relations with other Arab countries from which it had been estranged for so long.

ECONOMIC SURVEY

Jordan's economy has twice been completely disrupted by war between the Arabs and the Israelis, first in 1948, and then in 1967. While Jordan in 1948 acquired some 2,165 square miles of new territory—the vast salient which juts out into Israel west of the River Jordan—the country's population also increased more than threefold. In 1948, before the war broke out, the country's population was perhaps 400,000. The number of those living on the West Bank of the River Jordan in the territory acquired in 1948 was well over 800,000. This territory was occupied by the Israelis in 1967, but perhaps 350,000 of the inhabitants fled to non-occupied Jordan. The disruption caused by the October 1973 war between the Arabs and Israel was by no means as severe, since Jordanian territory was not directly involved. According to the latest estimates, the population of Jordan in 1974 was 2,646,000, of which about 40 per cent lived in the Amman district.

The absorption of the refugees of 1948 and of 1967 into Jordan's economy has presented the country with problems for which few precedents could be found in modern times. These problems were accentuated by ethnic, cultural and religious differences. Jordanians before 1948 were mainly Bedouin and mostly engaged in pastoral, and even nomadic, activities. They therefore had little in common with the Palestinians, many of whom established themselves in Jordan as traders and professional men. The vast majority of the country's original inhabitants were Sunni Muslims, but until 1967 at least there were also 180,000 Christians. Also in 1967 some 53 per cent of the population was classified as urban.

Again, the loss of the West Bank of the Jordan to Israel in the summer of 1967 created a whole series of new problems. For the result was the loss not only of some efficiently farmed agricultural land, but also of the important and growing tourist industry, and the large sums in foreign exchange received from the people who annually visited the old city of Jerusalem and Bethlehem. Some of the immediate problems brought by the war of 1967 were met by aid from Arab countries, but Jordan's economic future in the long run will obviously depend on the nature of any settlement which may be reached with Israel.

The area of the country, including the 2,165 square miles of the West Bank territory, was about 25,000 square miles. A large part of it however consisted of desert which spreads eastwards from a narrow, fertile strip of country running south from the Syrian frontier to Ma'an, and probably no more than about 5 per cent of the country's total area was cultivable. East of the Jordan river the country is mostly plateau, averaging about 2,000 ft. above sea level. The climate is of the Mediterranean variety, but, owing perhaps to the height above sea level, the extremes of heat and cold are greater than on the Levantine littoral. West of the Hedjaz railway there is an abundant and fairly regular rainy season, beginning in October or November and ending in April, and following the same pattern as in Israel. East of the railway line the annual rainfall tends to decrease very rapidly. From May to September there is generally no rainfall at all.

AGRICULTURE

Agriculture is the most important sector of the economy, accounting for between 14 and 20 per cent of the gross domestic product and employing about 40 per cent of the total labour force. Great improvements were achieved in the years prior to the 1967 war but the war and subsequent events on the East Bank resulted in almost complete disruption. In recent years, however, the economic situation on the East Bank has stabilized and agricultural production is again showing steady progress.

The size of the average agricultural holding varies according to its location. In the Jordan Valley, which is worked by nearly a third of the country's economically active population, the average plot is under five acres, whereas in the highland region above the valley, where yields are much lower, farms tend to be large, sometimes exceeding 500 acres. Crop cultivation peters out altogether as the semi-arid lands east of the valley give way to desert and the sparse vegetation on the desert fringes serves only as grazing for sheep and goats belonging to the Bedouin nomads. Attempts to intensify farming have centred on irrigation schemes in the Jordan Valley, based on the diversion of rivers flowing directly into the Jordan from the eastern highlands into canals along the valley floor. The valley is administered by a special authority and has its own development scheme, drawn up in 1972. Irrigation targets are being met mainly by extensions to the East Ghor canal and by the Zarqa river project. The East Ghor canal runs parallel to the Jordan carrying water diverted from the Yarmuk river. Work on the scheme began in 1958 and by 1963 it had added 300,000 acres to the country's irrigated area, but the installations were severely damaged by Israeli bombardment in 1967 and repairs were not carried out until after the 1970 civil war. By the end of 1975 it is hoped that the canal will have been extended to bring another 52,000 acres under irrigation. The Zarqa river project hinges on the construction of the King Talal dam to divert the river water and increase the irrigated area still further. As well as irrigation, crop-raising has also been improved by the introduction of special strains of seed, inorganic fertilizers and mechanization. There were 2,856 tractors in use on the East Bank alone at the end of 1971, compared with 2,000 in the whole of Jordan in 1966.

Cereals, fruit and vegetables are the mainstays of Jordan's agriculture and 1974 was a record year for the cereal crop, with production of wheat, at 244,500 tons, and barley, at 40,200 tons, reaching its highest since Jordan lost one-quarter of its cereal acreage with the Israeli occupation of the West Bank. The combined wheat crop from both banks in 1964 had totalled 294,700 tons and the barley crop 97,200 tons. The success of the East Bank harvest in 1974 was particularly welcome after the serious drought of 1973 which had reduced wheat production to only 50,400 tons and barley production to 5,900 tons, levels comparable with those of 1970 when civil war had lowered output. However, even when the harvest is good, cereal production is not adequate to feed the country. The bulk of Jordan's grain requirements has always to be imported. Cereal imports in 1973 rose to JD 6.5 million from JD 3.7 million in 1972, and the 1974 figures, with wheat and wheat flour imports costing JD 7.1 million, gave no indication of a reverse trend.

The loss of the West Bank had a serious effect on cereal production but its effect on fruit and vegetable cultivation was disastrous, lopping off some 80 per cent of the fruit-growing area and 45 per cent of the area under vegetables and depriving Jordan of an important and expanding source of some of its major export commodities. Production of fruit and vegetables on the East Bank has fluctuated violently, partly because of the weather and partly as a result of political instability in 1969 and 1970. In 1974, however, a reasonably good year, tomato production totalled 133,500 tons compared with 259,700 tons in 1967 and vegetables other than tomatoes (mainly aubergines) reached 141,300 tons compared with 282,200 tons in 1967. Olives stood at 40,100 tons against 64,000 tons in 1967, grapes at 17,800 tons against 71,600, citrus fruits at 33,900 tons against 61,400, melons at 45,800 tons against 118,400 and other fruits at 17,500 tons against 64,800 tons in 1967.

INDUSTRY AND MINING

Industry, which is almost entirely of recent origin and accounts for about 12 per cent of the gross domestic product, is concentrated around Amman and in Nablus on the West Bank. About 65 per cent of all factories produce food products or clothing but the major industrial income derives from the three heavier industries—phosphate extraction, cement manufacture and petroleum refining. Most plant is small and industry is mostly concerned with assembly and processing rather than manufacturing.

The country's mineral wealth lies predominantly in its phosphate reserves which cover 60 per cent of Jordanian territory and are estimated at around 1,000 million tons. However, the existence of about 55 million tons of good quality copper ore in the Wadi Araba in southern Jordan was announced in March 1974 and French specialists began studies of the deposits in September that year, aiming to start excavation on a commercial scale in 1976. Other minerals include gypsum, manganese ore, abundant quantities of glass sand and the clays and feldspar ore required for ceramics manufacture. Foreign investors have been found to finance the establishment of companies to produce ceramics and sheet glass and also to exploit potash deposits in the Dead Sea. A concession for oil prospection, granted to a Canadian firm in 1972, was withdrawn nine months later with no positive results having been reached, but the possibility of a big oil strike near Ramalla on the Israeli-occupied

West Bank was announced by Israeli geologists in January 1975 and in April the Jordanian Government awarded a 30-year 8,400-square-kilometre concession to a United States-based exploration company. Under the agreement this company will bear all the exploration and exploitation expenses, recouping these from its share of any eventual liftings of oil. The Jordanian Government will remain sole owner of all reserves in the concessionary area.

Rich beds of phosphates exist at Rusaifa, a few miles north-east of Amman, and have been exploited since 1963 by a local company financed partly by the Government. Other deposits in the Wadi Hasa area, south of Amman, have been developed by American and Italian interests. By 1968 the country's total production of natural phosphates was 1,162,000 tons, more than five times the production in 1956. Production fell, however, to 651,000 tons in 1971, mainly as a result of the closure of the Syrian borders to Jordanian traffic, but rose again to 715,000 tons in 1972 and 1,674,800 tons in 1974, surpassing for the first time the record set in 1968. Phosphates are Jordan's biggest single export commodity. They earned JD 19.5 million in 1974, compared with JD 4 million in 1973, JD 2.2 million in 1970 and JD 4.2 million in 1968. By 1978 Jordan is hoping for additional income of about JD 20 million a year from sales of phosphoric acid fertilizers. It was announced in March 1975 that a United States company would build a 600,000-tons-a-year fertilizer plant at Aqaba. The project, costing an estimated $180 million, will be run by a new enterprise in which the Jordanian Government, the local phosphate mining company, the International Finance Corporation, the Abu Dhabi Fund for Arab Economic Development, the United States contractor and private investors will all hold shares.

Output of petroleum products from Jordan's only oil refinery at Zarqa has increased steadily from 445,800 tons in 1970 to 748,400 tons in 1974, and production capacity is being raised to 2.9 million tons per year. Plans to form a joint venture with Romania to build a second refinery in the south were agreed in April 1975. There are also long-term plans for a second cement plant in the south but in the meantime the existing plant at Fuheis near Amman is undergoing an expansion programme which will raise output capacity from 620,000 tons a year in 1975 to 1.2 million tons a year in 1978. Cement production, badly hit by the troubles of 1970, rose to its peak in 1972 at 661,600 tons, but declined to 596,200 tons in 1974. Other goods produced in Jordan include batteries, cigarettes, detergents, pharmaceutical products, paper, spirits and alcoholic drinks and leather. There is also potential for the development of a flourishing fishing industry centred on the Gulf of Aqaba.

TRANSPORT

The development of the Jordanian economy has, in the past, been hampered by the difficulty of communication. Recognizing this the Government paid attention to immediate transport needs in the Three-Year Development Plan (1973-75) and in January 1975 commissioned a firm of consultants to draw up recommendations for a five-year investment programme and a ten-year development strategy. Future developments under these programmes will have to be guided by the fact that Jordan has only one port, at Aqaba on the Red Sea, over 200 miles from the capital, Amman. Though there is a good road from Amman to Beirut through Syria, transport costs on this route are heavy and overland routes from Jordan northwards were cut three times between 1972 and 1973. The re-opening of the Suez Canal on June 5th, 1975, has also had important repercussions on the amount of trade passing through Aqaba, especially with the congested state of most Eastern Mediterranean ports.

A vital railway link between Aqaba and the Al-Hasa phosphate mines has been built with financial backing from Federal Germany, and a road between the port and the agricultural and mining installations of the southern Ghor is under construction. Iraq is expected to invest in the construction of a desert road to facilitate the transit of Iraq-bound goods from Aqaba through Jordan. Cargo handled at Aqaba declined in the years immediately following 1967, falling from an average 100,000 tons a month in 1966 to 32,000 tons in 1970 but this figure rose again to 104,000 tons in 1973 although Aqaba was closed for a month during the Arab-Israeli war. It reached a monthly average of 124,000 tons in 1974, of which phosphate exports accounted for 71 per cent. Future road schemes will include the construction of a network of roads inside Amman and a motorway from Rum, near Aqaba, through Ras al-Naq to Maan. The latter will be financed by a United States loan. What was formerly Jordan's only railway, the single-track Hedjaz line, used to run through Maan northwards to Damascus and south to Mecca and Medina in Saudi Arabia, and, though the Jordanian section of the railway is the only one still in operation, plans exist to reconstruct the section between Damascus and Al-Hasa.

The state airline is taking over a growing role in handling the country's freight and passenger transport. Having made a net profit in 1973 for the first time in its 10-year existence, and increased this profit in 1974, the airline set up an air freight company in April 1975 to operate on routes to other Middle Eastern capitals, Europe and the Far East.

EXTERNAL TRADE

The war of 1967 disrupted the country's foreign trade less, perhaps, than might have been expected. By 1970 imports had recovered to JD 65.9 million, roughly the level of 1966, and by 1974 they had more than doubled to JD 156.5 million. Income from domestic exports received a sudden boost in 1974 when phosphate prices on world markets were raised fourfold by Morocco, the world's biggest phosphate exporter. The value of exports of all goods for the year increased by 250 per cent to reach JD 49.8 million, against less than JD 19 million in 1973, although the volume of phosphates exported increased by only 55 per cent during the same period. There are plans to treble phosphate production to an annual level of

five million tons by 1976, a target which at current prices could mean an income from phosphates alone of some JD 60 million. Such a figure may go some way to reducing Jordan's consistently chronic trade deficit, which rose to JD 106.8 million in 1974 from JD 89.3 million in 1973.

Phosphate exports in 1974 accounted for 49.5 per cent of the export total, against 21 per cent in 1973. Fruit, mainly oranges, and vegetables, mainly tomatoes, made up another 24 per cent. Cement, which in 1972 accounted for 15 per cent of the total, declined to 10 per cent in 1974 although the value of cement sales at some JD 4 million was more than twice that achieved two years earlier. By far the greatest proportion of Jordan's exports used to be sold to Iraq, Lebanon and Syria which together absorbed as much as 89 per cent of exports in 1953. By 1971, however, Saudi Arabia and Kuwait had become Jordan's two biggest customers and in 1974 exports to India headed the list accounting for 16.7 per cent of the total, with Japan in fourth place taking 9.6 per cent.

Jordan's imports, which in the years between 1965 and 1970 ranged between JD 55 million and JD 68 million jumped suddenly to JD 95 million in 1972 and to JD 156.5 million in 1974. Owing mainly to the loss of the West Bank and other war effects, the largest single import category in 1974, as in previous years, was food and live animals. The value of such imports reached JD 46.1 million in 1974 or 29.4 per cent of the import total. In 1973 the largest single item of imports was metallic minerals, mainly iron and steel, which at nearly JD 16 million represented about 10 per cent of total imports. In most years machinery and transport equipment and manufactured goods together form a large part of total imports.

Jordan's biggest supplier in 1974, as in the three previous years, was the United States, but its clear lead over other suppliers has dwindled. From providing 24 per cent of all Jordan's imports in 1971 the United States supplied 11 per cent in 1974. Federal Germany accounted for 9 per cent of all imports in 1974, Britain accounted for 7.7 per cent and Japan for 4.7 per cent. The importance of the United States and Federal Germany during the first half of the 1970s was a direct reflection of changing aid patterns as these two countries sought to replace Britain as the main Western providers of aid and consequently of imports. The proportion of imports from Arab countries hovered between 17 and 20 per cent in the years 1972 to 1974, while the value of imports from Japan, China, India, Czechoslovakia, Romania, Hungary and Bulgaria increased significantly.

FINANCE

Before 1967 net earnings from the tourist trade and income from private donations constituted the only important invisible export. Many people visited Bethlehem (now occupied by Israel) and the Old City of Jerusalem (now annexed by Israel) and religious and charitable organizations abroad sent money to help maintain the various foundations. After 1967 income from tourism and private transfers fell dramatically and the JD 6 million surplus on the travel account in 1966, when tourism earned JD 11.3 million, was already reduced to a deficit by 1968. In 1974, however, the Jordanian Government decided to allow its visitors to cross over to the West Bank and the number of tourists arriving in the country that year rose by 79 per cent on the 1973 total to reach 554,913, nearly regaining the 1966 level of 617,000, while income from tourism exceeded it, reaching JD 17.3 million. Oil transit dues, on the other hand, though almost back to pre-1967 levels by 1972, suffered a set-back in 1974 when the Trans-Arabian Pipeline Company (Tapline) which pumps Saudi oil through Jordan to Zahrani in south Lebanon attempted to raise the price of its annual supplies of five million barrels of oil to the Zarqa refinery from $2.27 to $13.64 a barrel. Jordan suspended its payments for the oil and Tapline its payment of transit royalties, worth about JD 2.4 million a year. Talks to settle the dispute began following the Tapline shutdown in February 1975.

For many years Jordan's increasing trade deficit has been made good mainly by capital imports and subventions. Before 1967 these used to come principally from Britain and the United States but since 1967 there have been similar payments from Saudi Arabia and other Arab states (*see* below). These subventions have enabled the country's exchange reserves to be maintained and even increased. At the end of 1974 net foreign assets stood at JD 118.4 million, compared with JD 65.3 million at the end of 1966, and international reserves stood at $349.7 million compared with $167.7 million at the end of 1966.

As the country's economy was, until 1956, mainly financed by the United Kingdom, it was natural that Jordan should remain a member of the sterling area.

Money supply at the end of February 1975 was JD 176.29 million. The Arab Bank, which possesses branches in most of the countries that are members of the Arab League has its head office in Amman. Other commercial banks are British, namely Grindlays and the British Bank of the Middle East, but it was announced in May 1975 that Chase Manhattan Bank of the U.S. would open a branch in Amman. There is also a Development Bank of Jordan and an Agricultural Bank and the Government has interests in both of these.

Before 1967 most of Jordan's financial support had come from the United Kingdom and the United States. After the June 1967 war Kuwait, Saudi Arabia and Libya undertook to pay Jordan quarterly sums of $112 million. These budgetary grants were suspended in the autumn of 1970 in protest against the Government's treatment of Palestinian guerrillas, and the revenue from foreign grants fell from JD 37.6 million in 1969 to JD 33 million in 1970, the only two years when subventions to the Government were exclusively from Arab sources. The United States, whose direct budgetary support ceased altogether in 1967, one year after Britain's, stepped in again in 1971 to make up the deficit. Budget support from Arab

sources sank still further to JD 19.9 million in 1971 but had risen again by 1974 to JD 38.7 million against only JD 14.2 million from the United States. Development loans worth a further JD 8.9 million brought total foreign aid in 1974 to just under JD 62 million. These were provided by West Germany (JD 4.5 million), Kuwait, the International Development Association of the World Bank, Qatar, Denmark, Iran and Britain. Jordan's 1975 budget allowed for JD 60.4 million in foreign support, including grants of JD 2.5 million from the United States, JD 12.9 million from Saudi Arabia and JD 12 million from Kuwait. Saudi Arabia and Kuwait provided JD 14.9 million and JD 12.5 million in budget support respectively in 1974. Additional income of $300 million a year for defence was promised to Jordan by leaders of the Arab oil-producing states at the Arab summit conference in Rabat in October 1974. Saudi Arabia paid the first instalment of this aid in January 1975 with a cheque for $51.6 million and Kuwait and Qatar followed with contributions worth $50 million and $9 million in February 1975.

State expenditure, which was running at about JD 70 million a year immediately before the 1967 war, rose to JD 105 million in 1972 and JD 166 million in 1974. Spending under the 1975 budget was put at JD 218 million, including JD 92.4 million (or 42 per cent) for development projects, more than double the JD 44.8 million allocation to development in 1974, and JD 55.2 million (or 25 per cent) for defence and security. Defence expenditure in the years immediately preceding 1972 accounted for 45 per cent of total spending, but this proportion had decreased to around 27 per cent by 1974. Budget receipts in 1974 reached JD 125 million according to preliminary figures issued by the Central Bank. Of these JD 63.2 million consisted of domestic revenue, with 58 per cent coming from indirect taxation. Since 1969 the Government has resorted to domestic borrowing to help meet cash shortages, mainly in the form of sales of Treasury Bills and Government bonds. This accounted for an estimated JD 13 million of income in 1974. The 1975 budget allowed for a JD 11.9 million deficit, with revenues from all sources projected at JD 206 million.

Economic development in Jordan has been severely handicapped by the 1948 and 1967 wars with Israel, and by the civil war of 1970. The war of October 1973 did not have such a severe effect. The hundreds of thousands of refugees from the Israelis are the ultimate responsibility of the United Nations Relief and Works Agency (UNRWA), which pays out about JD 3.3 million a year for rations for them, and also employs probably the largest number of people in Jordan, some 2,500. But Jordan has still had to devote most of her own scanty resources to the solution of pressing short-term problems. The 1966-73 Seven-Year Plan was suspended after the 1967 war and a new Three-Year Plan covering the period 1973-75 was outlined to a conference of aid givers and supporters in Amman in November 1972. The JD 179 million development plan was ambitious but well thought out and offered incentives to both local and foreign investors (*see* Statistical Survey). The public sector was due to provide 55.6 per cent of total investment of which more than half would come from foreign grants and loans. This was thought to be a reasonable aim given the support expressed by the West, especially the United States and West Germany The Government answered misgivings about the ability of the Jordanian private sector to provide JD 79.4 million towards investment with projections that gross private fixed capital formation should have reached JD 30.9 million by 1975, rising from JD 25.6 million in 1974 and JD 22.9 million in 1973. These estimates were based on figures for previous years when gross private fixed capital formation had reached JD 22.7 million in 1969, fallen to JD 17.9 million in 1970 but risen again to JD 21.9 million in 1971.

The plan aimed at creating 70,000 new jobs, increasing the gross domestic product by 8 per cent a year to JD 273.5 million in 1975, developing the socio-economic superstructure, raising the ratio of domestic revenues to total state revenues from 42 per cent in 1972 to 57 per cent in 1975, strengthening the balance of payments and reducing the deficit in the trade balance. The three-year plan is to be followed by a five-year development programme beginning in 1976 and aiming at expenditure of JD 750 million. The new plan is expected to include some projects carried over from the previous one.

The external public debt rose to JD 79.7 million at the end of 1974 and another JD 64.3 million had been committed by foreign governments and international institutions but undisbursed. Of the total debt 23 per cent was owed to West Germany, 19.6 per cent to Britain, 13 per cent to Kuwait, 12.3 per cent to the United States, 8.9 per cent to the International Development Association (IDA) and 5.9 per cent to Saudi Arabia. Of the undisbursed loans JD 18.97

million was to come from West Germany, JD 7.86 million from Iran, JD 7.39 million from Britain, JD 7.14 million from Kuwait, JD 6.3 million from the IDA and JD 5.6 million from the United States. Additional commitments made by mid-1975 included $12.3 million from the Arab Fund for Economic and Social Development (AFESD) and $5 million from the IDA for the second stage of the Hussein thermal power station, other World Bank loans of $3 million for the Industrial Development Bank, $7.5 million for agricultural development, $6 million for education projects and $1 million for potash mining. The U.S. Agency for International Development (AID) had also agreed to lend $6 million for the potash project, the IDA had promised another $6 million for education and the AFESD had also offered to finance a $25 million road scheme in Amman. Britain had committed £3.47 million for a water supply project, Iraq had offered a loan for port expansion and the United States had undertaken to grant a $10 million loan (from the Middle East Contingency Fund set up under the 1974 U.S. Foreign Aid bill) to finance road construction. United States economic aid earmarked specifically for Jordan under the 1974 Foreign Aid Bill was set at $77 million. A Saudi donation of $47 million for "urgent requirements" and $10 million for army housing was reported in January 1975, shortly after Iran had promised a $10 million loan for the army housing scheme.

According to the Central Bank's preliminary estimates, consumption expenditure and gross capital formation for 1973, the last year for which figures are available, totalled JD 356.28 million and income from exports of goods and services was JD 46.18 million, while the cost of imports was JD 138.46 million. Net factor income from abroad at JD 23 million meant that the Gross National Product for the year stood at JD 287 million.

STATISTICAL SURVEY

AREA AND POPULATION
(East and West Banks)

TOTAL AREA	ARABLE LAND	PASTURES	FOREST	POPULATION (1974 est.)
95,396 sq. km.	10,695 sq. km.	75,000 sq. km.	1,250 sq. km.	2,660,000

Population of the East Bank (1974 est.): 1,891,000.
Amman (capital) (1974 est.): 615,000.
1974 (East Bank only): Births 81,490, Deaths 6,445, Marriages 12,513.

AGRICULTURE
(East Bank only)
PRINCIPAL CROPS

	AREA ('ooo dunums)			PRODUCTION ('ooo metric tons)		
	1972	1973	1974	1972	1973	1974
Barley . . .	605.6	531.7	648.7	34.0	5.9	40.2
Maize . . .	2.5	2.0	2.6	0.3	0.2	0.4
Sesame . . .	12.5	6.9	7.6	0.3	0.1	0.1
Wheat . . .	2,236.7	2,441.8	2,462.0	211.4	50.4	244.5
Broad Beans . .	2.7	2.9	4.5	0.1	0.1	0.7
Chick Peas . .	30.9	73.4	124.9	2.0	1.9	8.3
Kersenneh . .	71.0	80.6	78.2	6.8	2.3	6.6
Lentils . . .	284.1	241.9	215.6	22.4	4.8	29.5

FRUIT AND VEGETABLES
(East Bank only)
('ooo metric tons)

	1972	1973	1974		1972	1973	1974
Almonds . . .	1.0	0.2	0.8	Tomatoes . . .	152.7	83.1	133.3
Apples and Pears .	2.9	0.4	4.0	Eggplants . . .	32.5	14.7	32.4
Apricots . .	0.4	—	1.5	Onions and Garlic .	0.7	3.8	1.8
Citrus Fruits . .	20.9	15.4	33.6	Cauliflowers and Cabbages	13.2	10.4	15.9
Figs . . .	2.2	1.0	1.2	Watermelons and Melons .	63.0	56.0	46.6
Bananas . . .	6.7	2.3	4.4	Potatoes . . .	0.9	0.4	3.9
Plums and Peaches .	0.1	—	0.3	Broadbeans (green) .	5.1	1.8	3.4
				Cucumbers . . .	17.7	10.4	17.5

LIVESTOCK
(East Bank only)
('ooo Heads)

	1971	1972	1973	1974
Camels	17.3	16.1	18.2	13.7
Cattle	38.8	45.9	46.3	42.2
Sheep and Goats . .	1,051.9	1,128.2	1,351.6	1,190.2

FORESTRY
(East Bank only)

	1973	1974
Area newly planted ('ooo dunums)	12.2	25.0
Timber production (cu. metres) .	603	568.0

FISHING
(East Bank only)

	1972	1973	1974
Quantity of fish landed at Aqaba and on Jordan and Yarmuk rivers (tons) .	134.8	90.5	91.6

INDUSTRY
(East Bank only)
('ooo tons)

	1971	1972	1973	1974
Phosphates . . .	651.1	714.9	1,088.6	1,674.8
Cement . . .	418.9	661.6	616.8	596.2
Alcohol ('ooo litres) .	192.6	208.2	260.5	190.3
Beer ('ooo litres) .	1,734.7	1,753.4	2,156.4	2,544.2
Tobacco (Kg.) . .	8,224.0	7,517.0	7,692.0	661.2
Cigarettes (Kg.) . .	1,533,291.0	1,511,336.0	2,160,391.0	1,972,275
Electricity (million kWh.)	210.1	248.9	280.6	n.a.

FINANCE

1,000 fils=1 Jordanian dinar (J.D.).
Coins: 1, 5, 10, 20, 25, 50, 100 and 250 fils.
Notes: 500 fils; 1, 5 and 10 dinars.
Exchange rates (July 1975): £1 sterling=702.96 fils; U.S. $1=321.43 fils.
100 Jordanian dinars=£142.25=$311.11.

Note: The Jordanian dinar was introduced in July 1950, with a value of £1 sterling, then equal to U.S. $2.80 ($1=357.14 fils). This valuation in terms of U.S. currency remained in effect until February 1973. The dinar's present par value of $3.111 became effective in February 1973, although the market rate fluctuates above and below this value. In March 1975 the market rate was 1 J.D.=$3.22. The dinar was at par with the pound sterling until November 1967, after which the exchange rate was £1=857.14 fils (1 dinar=£1.167) until August 1971. The rate was £1=930.61 fils (1 dinar=£1.075) from December 1971 to June 1972.

BUDGET 1972
(East and West Banks)
(J.D. '000)

REVENUE		EXPENDITURE	
Internal Revenue	37,770	Defence and Police	45,070
Foreign Grants	44,460	Administration	29,060
Foreign Borrowing	10,210	Social Services	11,580
Internal Borrowing	5,000	Economic Services	15,150
Loans Repaid	—	Transport and Communications	5,010
TOTAL	97,440	TOTAL	105,870

1973 Budget: Balanced at J.D. 148.6 million.

1974 Budget: Revenue J.D. 153.1 million; Expenditure J.D. 165.7 million.

1975 Budget: Revenue J.D. 206 million; Expenditure J.D. 218 million.

NATIONAL ACCOUNTS
(million J.D.)

	1970	1971	1972
GROSS DOMESTIC PRODUCT (at factor cost)	189.56	202.58	224.16

DEVELOPMENT EXPENDITURE ESTIMATES
1973-75
(million J.D.)

Agriculture	13.020
Irrigation	14.636
Mining and Industry	26.120
Tourism and Antiquities	7.170
Electricity	9.781
Transportation	35.812
Communications	6.712
Trade	0.775
Education	10.914
Public Health	1.480
Social Welfare and Labour	1.455
Housing and Government Buildings	34.890
Municipal and Village Affairs	14.758
Miscellaneous	1.477
TOTAL	179.000

Source: National Planning Council.

EXTERNAL TRADE
('ooo J.D.)

	1970	1971	1972	1973	1974
IMPORTS	65,882	76,627	95,310	108,248	156,507
EXPORTS	12,170	11,440	17,005	18,984	49,752

COMMODITIES
('ooo J.D.)

IMPORTS	1972	1973	1974
Animals and Products .	5,574.8	7,549.9	9,161.9
Grains and Legumes .	4,580.6	8,221.3	9,545.6
Vegetables . .	719.5	1,403.9	1,499.5
Fruits . . .	2,552.4	3,616.1	5,582.7
Spices . .	1,858.4	2,459.9	2,209.8
Other Agriculture .	2,248.5	2,494.3	2,942.3
Forestry Products .	837.7	1,161.4	964.1
Mining and Quarrying .	4,973.9	3,522.3	3,930.9
Food Manufactures .	12,675.2	8,068.4	15,165.8
Textiles . .	8,081.1	8,388.0	9,763.5
Clothing . .	1,762.4	1,799.6	2,390.6
Wood and Cork .	564.9	1,002.6	1,182.7
Paper and Products .	1,902.3	1,967.7	4,300.8
Printing and Publishing	406.1	382.2	509.1
Rubber and Products .	1,137.0	1,254.5	2,296.2
Chemical Products .	6,089.5	7,076.8	9,806.5
Petroleum (refined) .	1,193.0	763.1	1,553.3
Non-Metallic Minerals .	1,401.2	1,939.2	2,490.0
Metallic Minerals .	7,300.6	10,095.0	16,018.8
Non-Electric Machines .	4,988.5	6,342.2	10,909.4
Electric Machines .	3,989.4	4,072.1	6,276.8
Transport Equipment .	6,473.7	6,621.3	18,051.3

EXPORTS	1972	1973	1974
Phosphates . .	3,497.1	4,020.4	19,531.3
Tomatoes . .	724.3	915.7	1,836.2
Lentils . .	918.8	451.7	1,540.5
Water Melons . .	38.5	28.3	191.4
Other vegetables and fruit .	2,145.0	2,708.7	5,333.0
Cigarettes . .	397.7	546.2	711.3
Bananas . .	105.9	35.6	46.7
Raw Hides and Skins .	130.1	260.9	272.5
Electric Accumulators .	432.7	408.7	495.5
Olive Oil and Prepared Olives .	367.2	120.7	655.9

COUNTRIES
('ooo J.D.)

IMPORTS	1972	1973	1974
United Kingdom .	8,645.2	9,031.2	12,035.6
U.S.A. . .	16,887.3	11,265.1	17,583.2
Germany, Fed. Repub. .	8,693.3	8,699.6	14,514.1
Lebanon . .	5,045.5	6,388.4	8,336.1
Japan . .	4,598.0	5,348.3	7,380.8
Syria . .	4,143.7	7,799.5	5,806.5
Saudi Arabia .	3,379.0	3,427.3	3,692.8
Italy . .	2,677.6	3,426.3	5,868.3
China, People's Repub. .	1,997.2	2,089.9	4,327.4
France . .	2,284.3	2,550.1	3,718.4
U.S.S.R. . .	1,117.4	744.1	978.9
Netherlands .	2,441.9	3,353.9	4,489.5
Egypt . .	2,446.1	2,753.9	7,108.1
India . .	1,396.5	1,415.3	2,968.0
Romania . .	1,886.5	1,152.0	2,886.1

EXPORTS	1972	1973	1974
Kuwait . .	1,685.2	1,572.7	2,777.3
Iraq . .	1,504.9	1,007.7	1,616.7
Lebanon . .	1,529.8	1,390.5	4,001.1
Saudi Arabia .	2,140.5	2,560.0	5,540.4
India . .	1,404.9	1,191.4	7,267.0
Syria . .	1,611.9	2,585.2	2,873.7
Yugoslavia . .	201.2	163.4	1,201.4
Turkey . .	247.5	306.4	1,625.7
China . .	—	0.1	
Czechoslovakia .	210.6	183.9	708.6

TRANSPORT

RAILWAYS
(East Bank only)

	1972	1973	1974
Passengers carried .	n.a.	33,234	80,125
Freight carried (tons) .	56,305	51,917	65,807

ROADS
(East Bank only)

	1972	1973	1974
Cars (private) . .	11,173	12,802	16,101
Taxis . . .	4,785	5,725	6,949
Buses . . .	470	502	529
Lorries and Vans .	5,243	5,777	6,470
TOTAL (incl. others) .	24,320	27,622	33,256

SHIPPING
(East Bank only)
(Aqaba port)

	1972	1973	1974
Number of vessels calling .	327	304	299
Freight loaded ('000 tons) .	704.9	811.2	1116.2
Freight unloaded ('000 tons)	518.6	433.8	367.4

CIVIL AVIATION
(East Bank only)

	1972	1973	1974
Passengers (number)	120,100	163,400	243,355
Freight ('000 tons) .	2,463.0	2,625.1	3,844.0

TOURISM
(East Bank only)

	1972	1973	1974
Visitors to Jordan .	292,041	307,744	554,913

COMMUNICATIONS MEDIA
(East Bank only)

Number of telephones (1973) . .	21,461
Number of radio sets (1974) .	200,000
Number of cinemas (1973) . .	36

EDUCATION

	SCHOOLS (East Bank)	TEACHERS (East Bank)	PUPILS (East and West Bank)
1971–72 . .	1,712	13,136	630,235
1972–73 . .	1,892	14,421	688,698
1973–74 . .	2,062	16,205	501,468*

* East Bank only.

Source: Department of Statistics, Amman.

THE CONSTITUTION

(Revised Constitution approved by King Talal I on January 1st, 1952)

THE Hashemite Kingdom of Jordan is an independent, indivisible sovereign state. Its official religion is Islam; its official language Arabic.

Rights of the Individual. There is to be no discrimination between Jordanians on account of race, religion or language. Work, education and equal opportunities shall be afforded to all as far as is possible. The freedom of the individual is guaranteed, as are his dwelling and property. No Jordanian shall be exiled. Labour shall be made compulsory only in a national emergency, or as a result of a conviction; conditions, hours worked and allowances are under the protection of the State.

The Press, and all opinions, are free, except under martial law. Societies can be formed, within the law. Schools may be established freely, but they must follow a recognized curriculum and educational policy. Elementary education is free and compulsory. All religions are tolerated. Every Jordanian is eligible to public office, and choices are to be made by merit only. Power belongs to the people.

The Legislative Power is vested in the National Assembly and the King. The National Assembly consists of two houses: the Senate and the House of Representatives.

The Senate. The number of Senators is one-half of the number of members of the House of Representatives. Senators must be unrelated to the King, over 40, and are chosen from present and past Prime Ministers and Ministers, past Ambassadors or Ministers Plenipotentiary, past Presidents of the House of Representatives, past Presidents and members of the Court of Cassation and of the Civil and Sharia Courts of Appeal, retired officers of the rank of General and above, former members of the House of Representatives who have been elected twice to that House, etc. . . . They may not hold public office. Senators are appointed for four years. They may be re-appointed. The President of the Senate is appointed for two years.

The House of Representatives. The members of the House of Representatives are elected by secret ballot in a general direct election and retain their mandate for four years. General elections take place during the four months preceding the end of the term. The President of the House is elected by secret ballot each year by the Representatives. Representatives must be Jordanians of over 30, they must have a clean record, no active business interests, and are debarred from public office. Close relatives of the King are not eligible. If the House of Representatives is dissolved, the new House shall assemble in extraordinary session not more than four months after the date of dissolution. The new House cannot be dissolved for the same reason as the last.

General Provisions for the National Assembly. The King summons the National Assembly to its ordinary session on November 1st each year. This date can be postponed by the King for two months, or he can dissolve the Assembly before the end of its three months' session. Alternatively, he can extend the session up to a total period of six months. Each session is opened by a speech from the throne.

Decisions in the House of Representatives and the Senate are made by a majority vote. The quorum is two-thirds of the total number of members in each House. When the voting concerns the Constitution, or confidence in the Council of Ministers, "the votes shall be taken by calling the members by name in a loud voice". Sessions are public, though secret sessions can be held at the request of the Government or of five members. Complete freedom of speech, within the rules of either House, is allowed.

The Prime Minister places proposals before the House of Representatives; if accepted there, they are referred to the Senate and finally sent to the King for confirmation. If one house rejects a law while the other accepts it, a joint session of the House of Representatives and the Senate is called, and a decision made by a two-thirds majority. If the King withholds his approval from a law, he returns it to the Assembly within six months with the reasons for his dissent; a joint session of the Houses then makes a decision, and if the law is accepted by this decision it is promulgated. The Budget is submitted to the National Assembly one month before the beginning of the financial year.

The King. The throne of the Hashemite Kingdom devolves by male descent in the dynasty of King Abdullah Ibn al Hussein. The King attains his majority on his eighteenth lunar year; if the throne is inherited by a minor, the powers of the King are exercised by a Regent or a Council of Regency. If the King, through illness or absence, cannot perform his duties, his powers are given to a Deputy, or to a Council of the Throne. This Deputy, or Council, may be appointed by *Iradas* (decrees) by the King, or, if he is incapable, by the Council of Ministers.

On his accession, the King takes the oath to respect and observe the provisions of the Constitution and to be loyal to the nation. As head of the State he is immune from all liability or responsibility. He approves laws and promulgates them. He declares war, concludes peace and signs treaties; treaties, however, must be approved by the National Assembly. The King is Commander-in-Chief of the Navy, the Army and the Air Force. He orders the holding of elections; convenes, inaugurates, adjourns and prorogues the House of Representatives. The Prime Minister is appointed by him, as are the President and members of the Senate. Military and civil ranks are also granted, or withdrawn, by the King. No death sentence is carried out until he has confirmed it.

Ministers. The Council of Ministers consists of the Prime Minister, President of the Council, and of his Ministers. Ministers are forbidden to become members of any company, to receive a salary from any company, or to participate in any financial act of trade. The Council of Ministers is entrusted with the conduct of all affairs of State, internal and external.

The Council of Ministers is responsible to the House of Representatives for matters of general policy. Ministers may speak in either House, and, if they are members of one House, they may also vote in that House. Votes of confidence in the Council are cast in the House of Representatives, and decided by a two-thirds majority. If a vote of "no confidence" is returned, the Ministers are bound to resign. Every newly-formed Council of Ministers must present its programme to the House of Representatives and ask for a vote of confidence. The House of Representatives can impeach Ministers, as it impeaches its own members.

Amendments. Two amendments were passed in November 1974 giving the King the right to dissolve the Senate or to take away membership from any of its members, and to postpone general elections for a period not to exceed a year, if there are circumstances in which the Council of Ministers feels that it is impossible to hold elections.

THE GOVERNMENT

HEAD OF STATE

King HUSSEIN IBN TALAL; proclaimed King by a decree of the Jordan Parliament on August 11th, 1952; crowned on May 2nd, 1953.

Chief of Royal Cabinet: MUDAR BADRAN.

CABINET

(July 1975)

Prime Minister, Minister of Defence, Minister of Foreign Affairs: ZAID AL-RIFAI.

Minister of Development and Reconstruction: SUBHI AMIN AMR.

Minister of Culture and Information: SALAH ABU-ZAID.

Minister of Transport: KHALED AL-HAJ HASAN.

Minister of Education: THUGAN EL-HINDAWI.

Minister of Social Welfare: SAMI AYYUB.

Minister of Finance: SALEM EL-MASA'DEH.

Minister of Tourism: GHALEB BARAKAT.

Minister of Communications: AHMAD EL-SHOBAKI.

Minister of Provisions: ALI HASAN AUDEH.

Minister of Agriculture: MARWAN EL-HMOUD.

Minister of Islamic Affairs: Sheikh ABDEL-AZIZ EL-KHAYYAT.

Minister of State for Foreign Affairs: SADEK EL-SHARI'.

Minister of Public Works: MAHMOUD EL-HAWAMDEH.

Minister of Interior: THARWAT EL-TALHOUNI.

Minister of State for Prime Ministry Affairs: RAKAN 'INAD EL-JAZI.

Minister of Justice: NAJI HASAN EL-TARAWNEH.

Minister of Health: TRAD SAUD EL-KADI.

Minister of Interior for Municipal and Rural Affairs: MUHAMMAD GHDOUB EL-ZABIN.

Minister of Commerce and Industry: RAJA'I EL-MU'ASHER.

ADMINISTRATIVE PROVINCES (LIWAS)

Province	Location
Ajlun	Northern Jordan, between the River Yarmuk and Wadi Zerqa.
Balqa	Between Wadi Zerqa and Wadi Mujib.
Kerak	Between Wadi Mujib and the edge of the desert.
Ma'an	Southern Jordan, including Aqaba on the Red Sea.
Nablus*	Includes the towns of Tulkarm and Jenin.
Jerusalem Governorate*	Includes Jerusalem, Ramallah, Jericho and Bethlehem.
Hebron*	Central Jordan.
Amman Governorate	Includes Amman and Zarka.

* Indicates a province which has been occupied by Israel since the war of June 1967.

PARLIAMENT

THE SENATE

(HOUSE OF NOTABLES)

President: BAHJAT TALHOUNI.

The Senate consists of 30 members, appointed by the King. A new Senate was appointed by the King in November 1974, containing 7 Palestinians compared with 15 in the previous Senate.

HOUSE OF REPRESENTATIVES

Elections to the 60-seat House of Representatives took place in April 1967. There were no political parties. Parliament (the House of Representatives) was dissolved by Royal Decree on November 23rd, 1974.

POLITICAL PARTIES

Political parties were banned before the elections of July 1963. In September 1971 King Hussein announced the formation of a Jordanian National Union. This is the only political organization allowed. Communists, Marxists and "other advocates of imported ideologies" are ineligible for membership. In March 1972 the organization was renamed the Arab National Union. It is estimated that there are about 100,000 members. It has been reported that in April 1974 King Hussein dissolved the executive committee of the Arab National Union, and accepted the resignation of the Secretary-General.

DIPLOMATIC REPRESENTATION

EMBASSIES AND LEGATIONS ACCREDITED TO JORDAN

(E) Embassy, (L) Legation.

Afghanistan: Jeddah, Saudi Arabia (E).

Algeria: Amman (E); *Ambassador:* ABDESSAMI BEN AL Sheikh AL HUSSEIN.

Argentina: Beirut, Lebanon (E).

Austria: Beirut, Lebanon (E).

Belgium: Beirut, Lebanon (E).

Brazil: Beirut, Lebanon (E).

Bulgaria: Amman (E).

Canada: Beirut, Lebanon (E).

Chad: Beirut, Lebanon (E).

Chile: Amman (E).

China (Taiwan): Amman; *Ambassador:* Gen. CHEN YI-FAN.

Czechoslovakia: Amman (E).

Denmark: Beirut, Lebanon (E).

Egypt: Amman; *Ambassador:* FATHI ABDUL HALIM KANDIL.

Finland: Beirut, Lebanon (E).

France: Amman; *Ambassador:* DOMINIQUE CHARPY.

German Democratic Republic: Damascus, Syria (E).

Germany, Federal Republic: Amman (E); *Ambassador:* Dr. HORST SCHMIDT-DORNEDDEN.

Greece: Damascus, Syria (E).

Guinea: Cairo, Egypt (E).

Haiti: Amman (E).

Hungary: Damascus, Syria (E).

India: Amman; *Ambassador:* Dr. AMRIK S. MEHTA.

Indonesia: Jeddah, Saudi Arabia (E).

Iran: Amman; *Ambassador:* FEREIDUN MOVASSAGHI.

Iraq: Amman (E); *Ambassador:* KHALID MAKKI.

Italy: Amman (E); *Ambassador:* Dr. DANTE MATACOTTA.

Japan: Amman (E); *Ambassador:* MINAO TSUCHIYA.

Korea, Republic: Jeddah, Saudi Arabia (E).

Kuwait: Amman; *Ambassador:* AHMED GHEYTH ABDUL-LAH.

Lebanon: Amman (E); *Ambassador:* ABDEL RAHMAN SOLH.

Malaysia: Jeddah, Saudi Arabia (E).

Morocco: Amman (E); *Ambassador:* MUHAMMAD TAZI.

Nepal: Cairo, Egypt (E).

Netherlands: Beirut, Lebanon (E).

Nigeria: Jeddah, Saudi Arabia (E).

Norway: Cairo, Egypt (E).

Pakistan: Amman (E); *Ambassador:* MAHDI MASUD.

Poland: Amman (E).

Portugal: Beirut, Lebanon (E).

Qatar: Amman; *Ambassador:* Sheikh HAMAD BIN MOHAMMAD BIN JABER AL-THANI.

Romania: Amman (E); *Ambassador:* VASILE GANDILA.

Saudi Arabia: Amman (E); *Ambassador:* Sheikh AHMED AL-KUHEIMY.

Senegal: Jeddah, Saudi Arabia (E).

Somalia: Jeddah, Saudi Arabia (E).

Spain: Amman (E); *Ambassador:* JAIME AGUIRRE DE CÁRCER.

Sri Lanka: Cairo, Egypt (E).

Sweden: Beirut, Lebanon (E).

Switzerland: Amman; *Ambassador:* PIERRE DUMONT.

Syria: Amman (E); *Ambassador:* ABDUL KARIM SABBAGH.

Turkey: Amman (E); *Ambassador:* SAHIN UZGÖREN.

U.S.S.R.: Amman (E); *Ambassador:* ALEXEI VORONIN.

United Arab Emirates: Amman; *Ambassador:* Dr. FAISAL BIN KHALID AL-QASIMI.

United Kingdom: Amman (E); *Ambassador:* HUGH BALFOUR PAUL.

U.S.A.: Amman (E); *Ambassador:* THOMAS R. PICKERING.

Uruguay: Beirut, Lebanon (E).

Vatican: Jerusalem, Israel (L).

Venezuela: Beirut, Lebanon (E).

Yugoslavia: Damascus, Syria (L).

JUDICIAL SYSTEM

With the exception of matters of purely personal nature concerning members of non-Muslim communities, the law of Jordan was based on Islamic Law for both civil and criminal matters. During the days of the Ottoman Empire, certain aspects of Continental law, especially French commercial law and civil and criminal procedure, were introduced. Due to British occupation of Palestine and Trans-Jordan from 1917 to 1948, the Palestine territory has adopted, either by statute or case law, much of the English common law. Since the annexation of the non-occupied part of Palestine and the formation of the Hashemite Kingdom of Jordan, there has been a continuous effort to unify the law. This process of unification is now virtually completed, with the promulgation of new laws to replace older laws on both sides of the River Jordan.

Court of Cassation. The Court of Cassation consists of seven judges, who sit in full panel for exceptionally important cases. In most appeals, however, only five members sit to hear the case. All cases involving amounts of more than J.D. 100 may be reviewed by this Court, as well as cases involving lesser amounts and cases which cannot be monetarily valued. However, for the latter types of cases, review is available only by leave of the Court of Appeal, or, upon refusal by the Court of Appeal, by leave of the President of the Court of Cassation. In addition to these functions as final and Supreme Court of Appeal, the Court of Cassation also sits as High Court of Justice to hear applications in the nature of habeas corpus, mandamus and certiorari dealing with complaints of a citizen against abuse of governmental authority.

Courts of Appeal. There are two Courts of Appeal, each of which is composed of three judges, whether for hearing of appeals or for dealing with Magistrates' Courts judgments in chambers. Jurisdiction of the two Courts is geographical, with the Court for the Western Region sitting in Jerusalem (which has not sat since June 1967) and the Court for the Eastern Region sitting in Amman. The regions are separated by the River Jordan. Appellate review of the Courts of Appeal extends to judgments rendered in the Courts of First Instance, the Magistrates Courts, and Religious Courts.

Courts of First Instance. The Courts of First Instance are courts of general jurisdiction in all matters civil and criminal except those specifically allocated to the Magistrates' Courts. Three judges sit in all felony trials, while only two judges sit for misdemeanor and civil cases. Each of the seven Courts of First Instance also exercises appellate jurisdiction in cases involving judgments of less than J.D. 20 and fines of less than J.D. 10, rendered by the Magistrates' Courts.

Magistrates' Courts. There are fourteen Magistrates' Courts, which exercise jurisdiction in civil cases involving no more than J.D. 250 and in criminal cases involving maximum fines of J.D. 100 or maximum imprisonment of one year.

Religious Courts. There are two types of Religious Court: The Sharia Courts (Muslims); and the Ecclesiastical Courts (Eastern Orthodox, Greek Melkite, Roman Catholic and Protestant). Jurisdiction extends to personal (family) matters, such as marriage, divorce, alimony, inheritance, guardianship, wills, interdiction and, for the Muslim community, the constitution of Waqfs (Religious Endowments). When a dispute involves persons of different religious communities, the Civil Courts have jurisdiction in the matter unless the parties agree to submit to the jurisdiction of one or the other of the Religious Courts involved.

Each Sharia (Muslim) Court consists of one judge (Qadi), while most of the Ecclesiastical (Christian) Courts are normally composed of three judges, who are usually clerics. Sharia Courts apply the doctrines of Islamic Law, based on the Koran and the Hadith (Precepts of Muhammad), while the Ecclesiastical Courts base their law on various aspects of Canon Law. In the event of conflict between any two Religious Courts or between a Religious Court and a Civil Court, a Special Tribunal of three judges is appointed by the President of the Court of Cassation, to decide which court shall have jurisdiction. Upon the advice of experts on the law of the various communities, this Special Tribunal decides on the venue for the case at hand.

RELIGION

Over 80 per cent of the population are Sunni Muslims, and the King can trace unbroken descent from the Prophet Muhammad. There is a Christian minority, living mainly in the towns, and smaller numbers of non-Sunni Muslims.

Prominent religious leaders in Jordan are:

SHEIKH ABDULLAH GHOSHEH (Chief Justice and President of the Supreme Muslim Secular Council).

SHEIKH MOHAMMED FAL SHANKITI (Director of Sharia Courts).

SHEIKH ABDULLAH QALQILI (Mufti of the Hashemite Kingdom of Jordan).

THE PRESS

DAILIES

Al-Destour (*The Constitution*): P.O.B. 591, Amman; f. 1967; Arabic; publ. by the Jordan Press and Publishing Co.; circ. 14,000.

Al-Rai: Amman; government-controlled.

PERIODICALS

Amman al Masa'a: P.O.B. 522, Amman; f. 1961; Arabic; weekly; political and cultural; circ. 12–15,000; Editor ARAFAT HIGAZI.

Al Aqsa: Amman; armed forces magazine; weekly.

Huda El Islam: Amman; f. 1956; monthly; Islamic; scientific and literary; published by the Department of Islamic Affairs; Editor ABDULLAH KALKELI.

Huna Amman (*Amman Calling*): f. 1961; monthly; published by the Television Corporation; circ. 5,000.

Jordan: P.O.B. 224, Amman; f. 1969; published quarterly by Jordan Tourism Authority; circ. 5,000.

Military Magazine: Army Headquarters, Amman; f. 1955; quarterly; dealing with military and literary subjects; published by Armed Forces.

Official Gazette: Amman; f. 1923; weekly; circ. 8,000; published by the Jordan Government.

Rural Education Magazine: P.O.B. 226, Amman; f. 1958; published by Khadouri Agricultural College, Teachers' Training College at Beit Haninah and Teachers' Training College at Howwarah (jointly).

Sharia: P.O.B. 585, Amman; f. 1959; fortnightly; Islamic affairs; published by Sharia College; circ. 5,000.

Al Usra: Amman; Arabic; monthly; women's magazine.

NEWS AGENCIES

Jordanian News Agency: P.O.B. 6845, Amman; f. 1969; Government-controlled; Dir. Gen. N. MAJALI.

FOREIGN NEWS BUREAUX

Reuters: P.O.B. 667, Amman.

D.P.A. and Tass maintain bureaux in Amman.

PUBLISHERS

Jordan Press and Publishing Co. Ltd.: Amman; f. 1967 by owners of the former *al-Manar* and *Falastin*; cap. J.D. 100,000, of which 25 per cent held by government; publishes *al-Destour*.

Other publishers in Amman include: *Dairat al-Ihsaat al-Amman, George N. Kawar, al-Matbaat al-Hashmiya* and *The National Press.*

RADIO AND TELEVISION

The Hashemite Jordan Broadcasting Service (H.B.S.): P.O.B. 909, Amman; f. 1959; station at Amman broadcasts daily 19½ hours in Arabic to the Arab World, 7 hours in English to Europe and 1 hour in Arabic to Europe; Dir.-Gen. MARWAN DUNIN.

Jordan Television Corporation: P.O.B. 1041, Amman; f. 1968; government station broadcasting for 48 hours weekly in Arabic and English; advertising accepted; Dir.-Gen. M. KAMAL; Dir. Engineering T. NASEREDDIN.

Number of radio receivers 200,000, number of TV receivers 29,000 (East Bank only).

FINANCE

(cap. = capital; p.u. = paid up; dep. = deposits; m. = million; J.D. = Jordan dinars.)

BANKING
CENTRAL BANK

Central Bank of Jordan: P.O.B. 37, Amman; f. 1964; cap. J.D. 2m.; dep. 25.2m. (1973); Gov. Dr. SAID NABULSI; Deputy Gov. HUSAYN EL-KASIM.

NATIONAL BANKS

Agricultural Credit Corporation: P.O.B. 77, Amman; f. 1970; government-owned credit institution; Dir.-Gen. M. O. QUR'AN.

Arab Bank Ltd.: King Faisal St., P.O.B. 68, Amman; f. 1930; cap. p.u. and reserves J.D. 17.1m.; dep. 276m.; total assets 452.1m. (December 1974); brs. in several Arab countries, and in U.K.; affiliates and sister institutions in London, Paris, Hong Kong, Switzerland, Luxembourg and Nigeria; Chair. ABDUL MAJEED SHOMAN.

Bank of Jordan Ltd.: P.O.B. 2140, Jabal Amman on 3rd Circle, Amman; f. 1960; cap. p.u. J.D. 533,360; dep. 9.2m. (December 1974); Chair. and Gen. Man. HUSNI SIDO AL-KURDI.

Cairo Amman Bank: P.O.B. 715, Prince Hassan St., Amman; f. 1960; cap. J.D. 750,000; dep. 14.1m. (1972); 7 brs.; Chair. JAWDAT SHASHA'A; Gen. Man. HAIDAR CHUKRI; associated with Banque du Caire, Cairo, and succeeded their Amman Branch.

Industrial Development Bank: Amman; f. 1965; cap. J.D. 3m. of which J.D. 1m. owned by the government.

Jordan National Bank S.A.: P.O.B. 1578, Amman; f. 1956; cap. p.u. J.D. 1m.; dep. J.D. 18.6m. (Dec. 1974); 11 brs. in Jordan, 3 brs. in Lebanon; Chair. and Gen. Man. H.E. SULEIMAN SUKKAR; Deputy Gen. Man. H.E. ABDUL-KADER TASH.

FOREIGN BANKS

British Bank of the Middle East: 20 Abchurch Lane, London, EC4N 7AY; P.O.B. 444, Amman; f. 1889; Chair. A. MACQUEEN; Area Man. T. V. HUNT.

National and Grindlays Bank: 23 Fenchurch St., London EC3M 3DD; P.O.B. 3, King Hussein St., Amman; acquired the Ottoman Bank interests in Jordan in 1969; brs. in Amman (7 brs.), Aqaba, Irbid (sub-branch in Northern Shouneh), Zerka (sub-branch in Russeifeh); Gen. Man. in Jordan J. C. HENDRY.

Rafidain Bank: Baghdad; Amman; f. 1941; Chair. and Gen. Man. ATTA AL-DHAHI.

INSURANCE

Al-Chark Insurance Co.: Abujaber Bldg., P.O.B. 312, Prince Muhammad St., Amman.

Jordan Insurance Co. Ltd.: P.O.B. 279, King Hussein St., Amman; cap. p.u. J.D. 350,000; brs. in five Arab countries and the U.K.

Many of the larger British and American insurance companies have branches or agents in Jordan.

TRADE AND INDUSTRY
CHAMBERS OF COMMERCE

Chamber of Commerce, Amman: P.O.B. 287, Amman; f. 1923; Pres. MUHAMMAD ALI BDEIR; Dir. SAID MATOUK.

Chamber of Commerce, Irbid: P.O.B. 13; f. 1950; Pres. MUFLEH HASSAN GHARAIBEH; Dir. HASSAN M. MURAD.

CHAMBER OF INDUSTRY

Chamber of Industry: P.O.B. 1800, Amman; Pres. W. ASFOUR.

PUBLIC CORPORATION

East Ghor Canal Natural Resources Authority: P.O.B. 878, Amman; the 50-mile canal is now completed, and work is in progress on the irrigation system; the U.S.A. has provided $12m. towards the cost of the canal; the project provides irrigation for some 20,000-30,000 acres. An additional 6 miles of main canal and irrigation system have been completed with an additional irrigated area of 5,000 acres, financed by Kuwait Government grants of $3m. Under the fourth stage of the project, due for completion in November 1976, 12,000 acres will be permanently irrigated, and a South Korean company will extend the canal by 11 miles, build the first spraying irrigation network in the Jordan valley, and build a canal to take water from the King Talal Dam to the East Ghor Canal.

TRADE UNIONS

The General Federation of Jordanian Trade Unions: Wadi as-Sir Rd., P.O.B. 1065, Amman; f. 1954; 33,000 mems.; member of Arab Trade Unions Confederation; Gen. Sec. AHID QUNTAR.

There are also a number of independent unions, including:

Drivers' Union: P.O.B. 846, Amman; Sec.-Gen. SAMI MANSOUR.

Union of Petroleum Workers and Employees: P.O.B. 1346, Amman; Sec.-Gen. BRAHIM HADI.

PHOSPHATE

Jordan Phosphate Mines Co. Ltd.: P.O.B. 30, Amman; engaged in production and export of rock phosphates; production (1973): 1.1 million tons.

TRANSPORT
RAILWAYS

Hedjaz Jordan Railway: (administered by the Ministry of Transport): P.O.B. 582, Amman; f. 1902; length of track 480 km.; Gen. Man. M. R. QOSEINI.

This was formerly a section of the Hedjaz railway (Damascus to Medina) for Muslim pilgrims to Medina and Mecca. It crosses the Syrian border and enters Jordanian territory south of Dera'a, and runs for approximately 366 km. to Naqb Ishtar, passing through Zarka, Amman, Qatrana and Ma'an. Some 844 km. of the line, from Ma'an to Medina in Saudi Arabia, have been abandoned for the past fifty years. Reconstruction of the Medina line, begun in 1965, was scheduled to be completed in 1971 at a cost of £15 million, divided equally between Jordan, Saudi Arabia and Syria. However, the reconstruction work has been suspended at the request of the Arab States concerned, pending further studies on costs. The line between Ma'an and Saudi Arabia (114 km.) is now completed, as well as 15 km. in Saudi Arabia as far as Haret Ammar Station. A new 115 km. extension to Aqaba is being financed by a J.D. 12 million loan from the Federal Republic of Germany; this line is scheduled to be completed during 1975. The extension will mainly be used for transporting phosphates and will connect Aqaba to Beirut.

As at the end of 1972 there were 17 locomotives, 344 goods wagons, 45 oil tank wagons and 8 passenger cars.

ROADS

Ministry of Public Works: Amman.

Amman is linked by road with all parts of the kingdom and with neighbouring countries. In addition, several thousand km. of tracks make all villages in the kingdom accessible by motor transport in summer. At the end of 1973 Jordan had 1,751 km. of main roads, 1,548 km. of secondary roads and 2.582 km. of other roads; 83 per cent of the roads are metalled.

Royal Automobile Club of Jordan: P.O.B. 920, Jebel Lweibdeh, Amman; Head Office: Wadi Seer Cross Roads; f. 1953; affiliated to the F.I.A., A.I.T.; Pres. of Honour H.M. King HUSSEIN; Gen. Man. D. H. LEDGER.

SHIPPING

The port of Aqaba is Jordan's only outlet to the sea and has two general berths of 340 metres and 215 metres, with seven main transit sheds, covered storage area of 4,150 sq. metres, an open area of 50,600 sq. metres and a phosphate berth 210 metres long and 10 meters deep.

PIPELINES

Two oil pipelines cross Jordan. The Iraq Petroleum Company pipeline, carrying petroleum from the oilfields in Iraq to Haifa, has not operated since the Arab-Israeli hostilities commenced. The 1,067-mile pipeline, known as the Trans-Arabian Pipeline (TAPLINE) carries petroleum from the oilfields at Dhahran in Saudi Arabia to Sidon on the Mediterranean seaboard in Lebanon. It traverses

Jordan for a distance of 110 miles and Jordan receives about £1½ million per annum in royalties. Tapline has frequently been cut by hostile action.

CIVIL AVIATION

In addition to Jordan's international airport of Amman, a new airport at Aqaba was opened in May 1972. Work has begun on a new international airport in Amman.

Alia (The Royal Jordanian Airline): Head Office: P.O.B. 302, Arab Insurance Building, First Circle, Jabal, Amman; f. 1963; government-owned; services to Middle East, Europe and Far East; fleet of one Caravelle, three Boeing 707, two Boeing 720, three Boeing 727; Chair. and Pres. ALI CHANDOUR.

Arab Wings Co. Ltd.: P.O.B. 3038, Amman; wholly owned subsidiary of Alia; executive jet charter service; Chair. and Man. Dir. ALI CHANDOUR.

Jordan World Airlines: f. 1975; subsidiary of Alia.

The following airlines also serve Jordan: EgyptAir, Euroflot, Iraqi Airways, KLM, Kuwait Airways, MEA, Saudia.

TOURISM

Jordan Tourism Authority: P.O.B. 224, Amman; f. 1952; Chair. GHALEB BARAKAT; Dir. IGOR FARRADJ; publ. *Jordan* (quarterly).

CULTURAL ORGANIZATION

The Department of Culture and Arts: Ministry of Culture and Information, P.O.B. 6140, Amman; aims to encourage artistic movements throughout the Kingdom, promote growth of talents and prepare specialists in all fields of culture and fine arts. Consists of seven sections:

Culture: publishes books, issues quarterly literary magazine (*Afkar*), arranges regular lectures by specialists in all subjects and collaborates with men of letters in the Kingdom.

Folklore: issues quarterly journal covering all aspects of folklore of various countries, popular tales and traditions; carries out research and promotes traditional folklore customs, and organizes folklore festivals.

Theatre: produces local and other plays, encourages playwrights and trains actors.

Institute of Fine Arts: aims to promote painting and sculpture and gives regular courses; offers assistance to improve and widen talents and arranges exhibitions in Jordan and abroad.

Jordan Conservatory of Music: aims to develop musical talents; three-year courses.

Folklore Dancing Troupe of Jordan: revives folk dancing in Jordan, organizes festivals in Jordan and takes part in international festivals abroad.

Public Relations: responsible for all foreign and local relations.

DEFENCE

Commander-in-Chief of the Armed Forces: Field-Marshal HABIS MAJALI.

Chief of Staff of the Armed Forces: Major-General ZAID BIN SHAKAR.

Defence Budget (1974): 44.2 million dinars.

Military Service: voluntary.

Total Armed Forces: 74,850: army 70,000; navy 250; air force 4,600.

Paramilitary Forces: 22,000 (7,000 Public Security Force and 15,000 Civil Militia).

In July 1975 it was reported that the Jordanian armed forces were to be increased to a strength of 122,000.

EDUCATION

Education in Jordan is both centralized and decentralized. The Ministry of Education prescribes textbooks and curricula for all schools, both public and private. On the other hand, Jordan is divided into 15 districts of education, called directorates (5 are located in the West Bank), each headed by a Director who takes many decisions without reference to the Ministry of Education.

Ministry of Education schools and institutes of higher education accommodated about 68 per cent of total school enrolment in 1973-74. One per cent of school enrolment was in the schools of the Ministry of Defence, Ministry of Public Health, Ministry of Social Affairs and Labour, and the Ministry of Religious Affairs and Inalienable Properties (AWQAF). The University of Jordan offered education for about 5 per cent of total student enrolment, while UNRWA provided education for about 21 per cent of the student population. Foreign and national private schools took about 10 per cent of the school enrolment. Most of the foreign private schools are run by religious bodies, while the national private schools are run by secular as well as religious bodies.

Children normally start the six years of elementary education at the age of seven. The elementary cycle is followed by three years of the preparatory cycle (junior high). The nine years of the elementary and preparatory cycles are compulsory. At the end of the compulsory years of education, all students sit for the Public Preparatory Education Examination. According to the Education Act of 1964, education terminates for those who do not pass the examination. Those who do pass are entitled to pursue their education in the three-year secondary cycle education schools (senior high) depending upon the number of vacancies available in the tenth grade (the first secondary year) in the various districts.

Higher secondary education is provided either by secondary general schools or secondary vocational schools. Students of both types of secondary schools sit for the public secondary education examination. Those who pass are entitled to pursue their education in institutes of higher learning, both in Jordan and abroad.

For the year 1972 the Ministry of Education budget was J.D. 7.13 million, or 6.7 per cent of the total national budget. For details of number of pupils, etc., *see* Statistical Survey.

UNIVERSITY

University of Jordan: near Jubaiha, P.O.B. 1682, Amman; 218 teachers, *c.* 3,600 students.

BIBLIOGRAPHY

ABDULLAH OF TRANSJORDAN, KING. Memoirs, trans. G. Khuri, ed. P. Graves (London and New York, 1950).

ABIDI, A. H. H. Jordan, a Political Study, 1948–1957 (Asia Publishing House, Delhi, 1966).

CROSS, FRANK M. (Jr.). Ancient Library of Qumran (Anchor Books, New York).

DEARDEN, ANN. Jordan (Hale, London, 1958).

GLUBB, J. B. The Story of the Arab Legion (London, 1948).
A Soldier with the Arabs (Hodder and Stoughton, 1957).
Britain and the Arabs: A Study of Fifty Years 1908–1958 (Hodder and Stoughton, London, 1959).
War in the Desert (London, 1960).
The Middle East Crisis—A Personal Interpretation (London, 1967).
Syria, Lebanon, Jordan (London, 1967).
Peace in the Holy Land (London, 1971).

GOICHON, A. M. L'Eau: Problème Vital de la Région du Jourdain (Brussels, Centre pour l'Etude des Problèmes du Monde Musulmane Contemporain, 1964).

GRANQVIST, HILMA. Birth and Childhood among the Arabs: Studies in a Muhammadan Village in Palestine (Helsinki, 1947).
Family Life among the Arabs.
Marriage Conditions in a Palestinian Village.

HACKER, JANE M. Modern Amman: a social study (Durham, 1960).

HARRIS, G. L. Jordan, Its People, Its Society, Its Culture (Human Relations Area Files, New Haven, 1958).

HUSSEIN, HIS MAJESTY KING. Uneasy Lies the Head (London, 1962).

HUTCHISON, Cmdr. E. H., Violent Truce (New York, Devin-Adair, 1956).

INTERNATIONAL BANK FOR RECONSTRUCTION AND DEVELOPMENT. The Economic Development of Jordan (Baltimore, Johns Hopkins Press, 1957).

JARVIS, C. S. Arab Command: the Biography of Lt.-Col. F. W. Peake Pasha (London, 1942).

JOHNSTON, CHARLES. The Brink of Jordan (London, Hamish Hamilton, 1972).

KENNEDY, Sir ALEXANDER. Petra: Its History and Monuments (London, 1925).

KENNEDY, Sir ALEXANDER. Petra: Its History and (Frederick Praeger, New York, 1960).

KOHN, HANS. Die staats- und verfassungsrechtliche Entwicklung des Emirats Transjordanien (Tübingen, 1929).

KONIKOFF, A. Transjordan: An Economic Survey (2nd edn., Jerusalem, 1946).

LUKE, Sir HARRY C., and KEITH-ROACH, E. The Handbook of Palestine and Transjordan (London, 1934).

LYAUTEY, PIERRE. La Jordanie Nouvelle (Juilliard, Paris, 1966).

MINISTRY OF FOREIGN AFFAIRS, AMMAN. Jordan: Some aspects of its growing importance in the Middle East (Amman, 1951).

MORRIS, JAMES. The Hashemite Kings (Faber, London, 1959).

PALESTINE GOVERNMENT. Memorandum on the Water Resources of Palestine (Jerusalem, 1947).

PATAI, R. The Kingdom of Jordan (Princeton, 1958).

PEAKE, F. G. History of Jordan and Its Tribes (Univ. of Miami Press, 1958).

PEROWNE, STEWART. The One Remains (London, 1954). Jerusalem and Bethlehem (A. S. Barnes Ltd., South Brunswick, New Jersey, 1966).

PHILLIPS, PAUL G. The Hashemite Kingdom of Jordan: Prolegomena to a Technical Assistance Programme (Chicago, 1954).

SANGER, RICHARD H. Where the Jordan Flows (Middle East Institute, Washington, 1965).

SHWADRAN, B. Jordan: A State of Tension (Council for Middle Eastern Affairs, New York, 1959).

SMITH, Sir G. A. Historical Geography of the Holy Land (24th ed., London, 1931).

SNOW, PETER. Hussein: A Biography (London, Barrie and Jenkins, 1972).

SPARROW, GERALD. Hussein of Jordan (the authorized biography) (Harrap, London, 1961).
Modern Jordan (Allen and Unwin, 1961).

TOUKAN, BAHA UDDIN. A Short History of Transjordan (London, 1945).

U.S. GOVERNMENT PRINTING OFFICE. Area Handbook for the Hashemite Kingdom of Jordan (Washington, D.C., 1970).

VATIKIOTIS, P. J. Politics and the Military in Jordan 1921-57 (Praeger, New York, 1967).

VERDES, JACQUES MANSOUR. Pour les Fidayine (Paris, 1969).

Kuwait

PHYSICAL AND SOCIAL GEOGRAPHY

Kuwait lies at the head of the Persian Gulf, bordering Iraq and Saudi Arabia. The area of the State of Kuwait is 17,818 sq. km., including the Kuwaiti share of the Partitioned Zone (see below).

For long it was generally held that the Gulf extended much further north, but geological evidence suggests, first, that the coastline has remained broadly at its present position and, second, that the immense masses of silt brought down by the Tigris and Euphrates cause irregular downwarping at the head of the Gulf. Local variation in the coastline is therefore likely, with possible changes since ancient times. Kuwait grew up because it has a zone of slightly higher, firmer ground that gives access from the Gulf inland to Iraq, and because it has a reasonably good and sheltered harbour in an area that elsewhere has many sandbanks and, further south, coral reefs. In recent years, owing to Kuwait's rapid economic development, Kuwait City has been almost totally rebuilt on a much grander scale.

The territory of Kuwait is mainly almost flat desert with a few oases. With an annual rainfall of 1 to 37 centimetres, almost entirely between November and April, there is a spring "flush" of grass. Summer shade temperature may reach 123°F., though in January, the coldest month, temperatures range between 27° and 85°, with a rare frost. There is little drinking water within the state, and supplies are largely distilled from sea water, and brought by pipeline from the Shatt al-Arab.

Kuwait's population has increased very rapidly in recent years. It is unofficially estimated to have been 152,000 in 1950 but recent census results have produced totals of 206,473 (February 1957), 321,621 (May 1961), 467,339 (April 1965) and 738,662 (April 1970). By mid-1974, according to official estimates, the population had reached 929,000. Between 1963

and 1970 the average annual increase in Kuwait's population was 10.0 per cent, the highest growth rate recorded in any independent country.

Much of Kuwait's population growth has resulted from immigration, though the country also has one of the highest natural increase rates in the world. Between 1957 and 1970 the non-Kuwaiti population grew from less than 93,000 (45 per cent of the total) to more than 391,000 (53 per cent), most of them from other Arab states. In 1973 the natural increase of the population was 4.0 per cent, with 40,165 recorded births (45.5 per 1,000 inhabitants) and only 4,601 deaths (5.2 per 1,000). The high birth rate is particularly remarkable in view of the unequal distribution of the sexes, owing to the preponderance of males among the immigrant population. In 1970 the non-Kuwaitis comprised 244,368 males and 146,898 females. Among the 347,396 Kuwaiti citizens, by contrast, there were 175,513 males and 171,883 females. The birth rate for the Kuwaiti population alone exceeded 50 per 1,000 in some recent years.

At the 1970 census Kuwait City, the capital and principal harbour, had a population of 80,405, though the largest town was Hawalli, with 106,542 inhabitants. Other sizeable localities, all in Hawalli Governorate, were Salmiya (67,346), Abraq Kheetan (38,015) and Farawaniya (37,250).

Immediately to the south of Kuwait, along the Gulf, is a Partitioned Zone of 5,700 sq. km. which is divided between Kuwait and Saudi Arabia. Each country administers its own half, in practice as an integral part of the state. However, the oil wealth of the whole Zone remains undivided and production from the on-shore concessions in the Partitioned Zone is shared equally between the two states' concessionaires (Aminoil and Getty).

HISTORY

Although Kuwait is situated on the fringe of the Mesopotamian basin it has always belonged rather to the nomadic desert of Arabia than to the settled populations of the plains watered by the Euphrates and Tigris rivers. Thus the successive rule of the 'Abbasid Caliphate of Baghdad (750–1258), the Mongols (1258–1546) and the Ottoman Turks (1546–1918) had little direct influence on the area around Kuwait.

The origin of the present town of Kuwait is usually placed about the beginning of the 18th century, when a number of families of the famous Anaiza tribe migrated from the interior to the Arabian shore of the Gulf. These migrants included such important families as as-Sabah, al-Khalifa, az-Zayed, al-Jala-

hima and al-Ma'awida, from whom many of the present Kuwaitis are descended.

The foundation of the present Sabah ruling dynasty dates from about 1756, when the settlers of Kuwait decided to appoint a Sheikh to administer their affairs, provide them with security and represent them in their dealings with the Ottoman Government. The town prospered and in 1765 it was reported to contain some 10,000 inhabitants possessing 800 vessels and living by trading, fishing and pearling.

In 1776 war broke out between Persia and Turkey and the Persians captured Basra, which they held until 1779. During this time the East India Company moved the southern terminal of its overland mail route to Aleppo from Basra to Kuwait, and much of the trade of Basra was diverted to Kuwait. Sheikh Abdullah bin Sabah was reported to have been well disposed to the British, who for their part held him in high regard as being a man of his word.

About this time Kuwait was repeatedly threatened by raids from the Wahhabis, fanatical tribesmen from central Arabia, and the need for protection against these enemies led to closer contacts with the East India Company, who had a depot in the town. Ottoman dominion over the mainland was accepted in return for recognition of British trading interests over the route from the Mediterranean to India through the Gulf. The depredations of pirates and the threat from the Wahhabis caused Kuwait's prosperity to decline in the early years of the 19th century, but the British Navy restored peace to the Gulf, and by 1860 prosperity had returned.

In order to retain their autonomy the Kuwaitis had to maintain good relations with the Turks. Although not under direct Turkish administration the Sheikh of Kuwait recognised a general Ottoman suzerainty over the area by the payment of tribute and Sheikh Abdullah bin Sabah al-Jabir (1866–92) accepted the title of *Qa'immaqam* (Commandant) under the Turkish *Vali* (Governor) of Basra in 1871. His successor, Sheikh Mubarak "the Great", feared that the Turks would occupy Kuwait, and in 1899, in return for British protection, he signed an agreement with the British not to cede, mortgage or otherwise dispose of parts of his territories to anyone except the British Government, nor to enter into any relationship with a foreign government other than the British without British consent. This agreement prevented Germany securing Kuwait as a terminal for her projected Berlin to Baghdad railway.

The reign of Sheikh Mubarak from 1896 to 1915 marked the rise of Kuwait from a Sheikhdom of undefined status to an autonomous state. In 1904 a British political agent was appointed, and in 1909 Great Britain and Turkey opened negotiations which, although never ratified because of the outbreak of the First World War, in practice secured the autonomy of Kuwait.

Sheikh Mubarak's second son, Sheikh Salim, who succeeded to the Sheikhdom in 1917, supported the Turks in the World War, thus incurring a blockade of Kuwait. Sheikh Salim was succeeded in 1921 by his nephew, Sheikh Ahmad al-Jabir. Kuwait prospered under his rule and by 1937 the population had risen to about 75,000.

Under Sheikh Ahmad the foundation of Kuwait's great oil industry was laid. After considerable prospecting, he granted a concession in 1934 jointly to the Gulf Oil Corporation of the U.S.A. and the Anglo-Persian Oil Co. of Great Britain who formed the Kuwait Oil Co. Ltd. Deep drilling started in 1936, and was just beginning to show promising results when war broke out in 1939. The oil wells were plugged in 1942 and drilling was suspended until the end of the war.

After the war the oil industry in Kuwait was resumed on an extensive scale (*see* Economic Survey)

and in a few years the character of Kuwait town was changed from an old-fashioned dhow port to a thriving modern city supported by the revenues of the oil industry. In 1950 Sheikh Ahmad died and was succeeded by Sheikh Abdullah as-Salim. His policy was to use the oil revenues substantially for the welfare of his people, and in 1951 he inaugurated a programme of public works and educational and medical developments which has turned Kuwait into a planned and well-equipped country.

THE MODERN STATE

The economic aspects of post-war development are dealt with in the survey following. Here it should be noted that Kuwait has gradually built up what are probably the most comprehensive welfare services in the world, very largely without charge, at least to native Kuwaitis. Education is completely free in Kuwait, and this includes free food and clothing for students. Medical attention is also free to all and the health service is generally considered to be of a very high standard. A heavily subsidized housing programme has now provided accommodation for most residents meeting the country's generous criteria of "poverty". Even local telephone calls are free.

In June 1961 the United Kingdom and Kuwait terminated the 1899 agreement which had given the U.K. responsibility for the conduct of Kuwait's foreign policy, and Kuwait therefore became a fully independent state. The ruling Sheikh took the new title of Amir. In July Kuwait was admitted as a member of the Arab League.

Shortly after attaining independence, Kuwait was threatened by an Iraqi claim to sovereignty over the territory. British troops landed in Kuwait in response to a request from the Amir for assistance. The Arab League met in July and agreed that an Arab League Force should be provided to replace the British troops as a guarantee of Kuwait's independence. This force, composed of contingents from Saudi Arabia, Jordan, the United Arab Republic and the Sudan, arrived in Kuwait in September 1961. The United Arab Republic contingent was withdrawn in December 1961, and those of Jordan, Saudi Arabia and the Sudan before the end of February 1963. On May 14th, 1963, Kuwait became the 111th member of the United Nations.

In December 1961, for the first time in Kuwait's history, an election was held to elect 20 members of the Constituent Assembly (the other members being Ministers). This Assembly drafted a new Constitution which was published on November 11th, 1962. Under the new Constitution a National Assembly of 50 members was elected in January 1963, and the first session was held on January 29th, with Sheikh Sabah as-Salim as-Sabah, brother of the Amir and Heir Apparent, as the Prime Minister of a new Council of Ministers.

In October 1963 the new Iraqi government announced that it had decided to recognize Kuwait's complete independence; Iraq wanted to clear her relations with Kuwait and remove the atmosphere created by the Kassem régime. Kuwait is thought to have made a substantial grant to Iraq to improve relations at this juncture. In February 1964 an agreement (never implemented) was subsequently signed whereby Iraq would supply to Kuwait 120 million gallons of water daily; and in November the two countries concluded a Trade and Economic Agreement which virtually abolished customs duties between them.

In January 1965 a constitutional crisis, reflecting the tension between the paternalist ruling house and the democratically-minded National Assembly, resulted in the formation of a strengthened cabinet under the Heir Apparent, Sheikh Sabah as-Salim. In May that year Kuwait was one of ten Arab countries which broke off diplomatic relations with West Germany as a consequence of the formal establishment by that country of diplomatic relations with Israel. Two months later Kuwait decided not to ratify the agreement to set up an Arab Common Market with Iraq, Jordan, Syria and the U.A.R. There was strong feeling in the National Assembly that such an association would be disadvantageous to Kuwait.

On November 24th, 1965, Sheikh Abdullah died and was succeeded by Sheikh Sabah. His post as Prime Minister was taken over by another member of the ruling family, Sheikh Jabir al-Ahmad, who became Heir Apparent in May 1966.

In the developments of 1966 and 1967 within the Arab community Kuwait continued to play a neutral role, and in particular tried to act as mediator in inter-Arab disputes such as the Yemen and South Arabian problems. Sheikh Sabah paid visits to Iraq and Lebanon, and Kuwait supported Syria in the dispute with the Iraq Petroleum Company.

Kuwait declared her support for the Arab countries in the 1967 war with Israel, and joined in the oil embargo on the U.S.A. and the United Kingdom. No Kuwaitis had, however, reached any theatre of war before the ceasefire was announced. The Government donated KD 25 million to the Arab war effort. At the Khartoum Conference in September 1967 Kuwait joined Saudi Arabia and Libya in offering financial aid to the U.A.R. and Jordan whilst their economies recovered from the June war. The Kuwaiti share of this amounted to KD 55 million annually.

On May 13th, 1968, it was announced that the agreement of June 1961—whereby Britain had undertaken to give military assistance to Kuwait if asked to do so by her ruler—would terminate on May 13th, 1971. This followed an earlier announcement that Britain would withdraw all troops from the Gulf region by the end of 1971. After the election of a Conservative government in June 1970, however, Britain investigated the possibility of reconsidering this decision, but the Kuwaiti Government stressed its belief that there was no need for the presence of British forces in the Gulf region. In this connection, Kuwait continually encouraged the formation of a federation of Bahrain, Qatar and the Trucial States but her qualities as a go-between were insufficient to persuade the first two states to join what eventually became the United Arab Emirates.

Since the June 1967 war Kuwait has no longer been a frequent target of radical Arab criticism. Its financial support for the countries hit by the war and other generous economic assistance have no doubt contributed to this, while the lavish financing of the Palestinian guerrillas has been even more important. A factor behind this assistance is the large Palestinian community, said to be over 70,000 strong, in Kuwait; many of the most able and educated Palestinians have made a career in the country in recent years. Financial aid to Jordan, however, was cut off in September 1970 following the war between government and guerrilla forces; although resumed in December, it was again suspended in January 1971 as fighting in Jordan continued, but was later resumed once more.

During the 1960s the Kuwaiti leadership's policies led to extensive redistribution of income, through the use of oil revenues in public expenditure and through the land compensation scheme. At the same time, however, there was popular discontent about corruption and inefficiency in public services and the manipulation of the Press and the National Assembly.

In response to public opinion, the ruling family permitted the Assembly elections of January 1971 to be held on the basis of a free vote, though women, illiterates and all non-Kuwaitis still have no voting rights. There was a lively election campaign, with 184 candidates contesting the 50 seats, despite the non-existence of political parties, which are still illegal. Several members and supporters of the Arab Nationalist Movement, founded in the 1950s by Dr. George Habash (now leader of the Popular Front for the Liberation of Palestine), were elected. This radical group, led by Dr. Ahmad al-Khatib, is generally regarded as the principal opposition to the Government.

After the 1971 elections the Crown Prince was re-appointed Prime Minister and formed a new Cabinet. The representation of the ruling family was reduced from five to three and, for the first time, the Cabinet included two Ministers drawn from the elected members of the National Assembly. After the elections in January 1975 a 16-member cabinet was appointed with the Crown Prince continuing as Prime Minister. Seven new Ministers were appointed, a new post of Deputy Prime Minister was created and the functions of the former Ministry of Oil and Finance were separated.

The main domestic problem is the difference in status between native-born Kuwaitis and immigrants, the latter comprising 53 per cent of the population in 1975. Whilst the living conditions of the immigrants are very good by Arabian standards, most senior positions are reserved for Kuwaitis, as is the suffrage and free use of some welfare services. The creation of sufficient employment opportunities to avoid the unsettling effects of idleness and boredom, a social problem even with generous unemployment benefits, is a major difficulty now confronting the Government.

In March 1973 Iraqi troops and tanks occupied a Kuwaiti outpost at Samtah, on the 100-mile border with Iraq. Iraq later withdrew her troops, but by July

1974 the border dispute was still unsettled. In May 1973 it was announced that Kuwait was to buy arms worth almost £200 million from the U.S.A. in order to strengthen her defensive position in the Gulf.

In January 1973, in common with several other Middle East countries, the Kuwait Government signed a participation agreement with the country's main oil-producing concern, the Kuwait Oil Company (KOC), owned equally by British Petroleum (BP) and Gulf Oil. KOC produced over 90 per cent of Kuwait's oil output in 1972. The agreement would have given the Government an initial 25 per cent share in KOC and a 51 per cent (controlling) interest by 1982. These terms, however, were subject to ratification by the National Assembly, where strong opposition prevented adoption of the agreement. Some members demanded nationalization of the oil industry and others wanted new participation talks leading to immediate majority control. In June the Government announced its intention to renegotiate the January agreement.

During the Arab-Israeli war of October 1973 Kuwaiti forces stationed along the Suez Canal were involved in fighting. Kuwait also contributed to the Arab cause by giving considerable financial aid, totalling KD 100 million, to other Arab states. While the war was still in progress, Kuwait called for a meeting of OAPEC to draw up a common Arab policy for the use of oil as a weapon to put pressure on Western countries, particularly the U.S.A., to force an Israeli withdrawal from occupied Arab territory. This meeting took place in Kuwait, where OAPEC's ten member-states decided to reduce petroleum production by at least 5 per cent progressively each month. Kuwait was also one of the Arab countries which imposed a total embargo on oil shipments to the U.S.A. and, later, to the Netherlands.

Immediately before the OAPEC meeting, Kuwait joined other Gulf states in announcing a unilateral increase of 70 per cent in the posted price of crude petroleum (the reference price used for tax and royalty purposes) from November 1st, 1973. This followed similar moves by Algeria, Indonesia and Venezuela.

In November, at a further meeting in Kuwait, Oil Ministers from the Arab states agreed on an extra 5 per cent reduction in output for November, with the combined effect of the embargoes and production cutbacks expressed as an overall drop in supply of 25 per cent compared with September levels, to be followed by further reductions in the future. Later in November the Arab group in OPEC agreed on the next 5 per cent cut for December, but exempted EEC countries except the Netherlands.

At the next OAPEC meeting, held in Kuwait in December, an additional 5 per cent cut, without exemptions, was agreed for January 1974. A second December meeting, also in Kuwait, partly reversed earlier decisions to reduce oil production. Just before this, the Gulf states belonging to OPEC had agreed on a further sharp increase in the posted price of oil, effective from January 1st, 1974.

Kuwait played a leading part in all these moves and made considerable reductions in national oil output. Monthly production (in million metric tons) fell from 13.4 in September 1973 to 12.0 in October and 9.8 in November. There was later a reversal in this trend and monthly output was more than 10 million tons in the first half of 1974.

Following the conclusion in January of a disengagement agreement between Egypt and Israel and the consequent improvement in Arab relations with the U.S.A., seven of the Arab oil-producing states (including Kuwait) agreed in March to lift the embargo on supplies to the U.S.A. In July 1974 the Arab countries also lifted the oil embargo on the Netherlands. Kuwait's policy of conserving her oil reserves, and the fall in the world demand for oil, has meant that production fell during 1974. Official Kuwait figures released in June 1975 revealed that production in 1974 was 15.7 per cent lower than in 1973. In May 1975, Kuwait Oil Company's output fell to 1.69 million b/d, the lowest level since June 1967 when supplies were cut off because of the Arab-Israeli war.

While the fuel crisis was developing, negotiations continued between the Government and KOC for new participation terms. Agreement was reached in January 1974 for the acquisition by the Government of a 60 per cent share, with the right to acquire the remaining 40 per cent in 1979. Although this gave Kuwait an immediate controlling interest in KOC, some members of the National Assembly, encouraged by the nationalization of foreign-owned oil companies in Iraq and Libya, demanded a third round of negotiations to achieve 100 per cent ownership. Finally, in May, the Assembly voted to accept the second agreement, with retroactive effect from January 1st. It was reported that this would cost the Government $112 million in compensation.

In June 1974 the Kuwait Oil, Gas and Energy Corporation (KOGEC) was formed, followed in August 1974 by the Supreme Council for Petroleum Resources. The Supreme Council formulates general oil policy, and KOGEC, a state-owned company, acts as the executive arm of the Supreme Council. The company will manage all aspects of the oil industry in Kuwait pending the formation of a new government body to assume control of all oil affairs.

After the National Assembly elections in January 1975 the Ministry of Finance and Oil was divided and oil affairs became the sole responsibility of the Ministry of Oil. This presaged Kuwait's take-over of the remaining 40 per cent of the Kuwait Oil Company's assets in March 1975, the details of which were still under negotiation in July 1975.

Until 1973 Kuwait's financial support for the leading Palestinian organizations had protected the country from active involvement in the guerrilla struggle. However, the activities of extremist groups, lacking such links with Kuwait, have resulted in incidents which embarrassed the Kuwait Government. In September 1973 Arab gunmen occupied the Saudi Arabian Embassy in Paris and later flew to Kuwait with five hostages. The gunmen surrendered to the Kuwaiti authorities, who later handed them over to the Palestine Liberation Organization (PLO), which had condemned the incident.

In December 1973 the perpetrators of a terrorist attack on an airliner in Rome were also flown to Kuwait, where they surrendered. For political reasons the Government was reluctant to place the terrorists on trial or extradite them to Italy. In March 1974 the Kuwaiti authorities handed the prisoners over to the PLO and they were flown to Cairo.

In February 1974 another Palestinian group occupied the Japanese Embassy in Kuwait and held the staff as hostages in return for the release of four Palestinians captured after an abortive incident in Singapore. The Japanese Government complied with the Palestinians' demands and both groups were flown to Aden. The Kuwaiti authorities fear that such incidents will encourage extremists to regard Kuwait as a safe refuge.

ECONOMIC SURVEY

The State of Kuwait has an area of 17,818 square kilometres. It consists mainly of desert with no natural land frontiers. There is practically no rainfall, and the humidity is lower than it is farther down the Gulf. The temperature is exceedingly high in spring and summer; there is occasionally a frost in winter. Until oil was produced, the only town was the harbour of Kuwait on the Gulf. But for some 150 years this port was of some significance because it was a centre for pearl fishing and the building of dhows or "booms"; and several of the plans for building a railway across Mesopotamia envisaged Kuwait as the eastern terminus.

The rapid development of the oil industry since about 1950 has dramatically changed all this. In 1971 Kuwait had more than 13 per cent of the world's proven reserves. In 1974, despite a fall in production, Kuwait's oil output was the sixth largest in the world. The revenue from oil, estimated to reach U.S. $9,000 million in 1974, has brought to the area a prosperity unimaginable twenty-five years ago. In May 1975 a study compiled by the Union Bank of Switzerland revealed that Kuwait had a G.N.P. of U.S. $11,000 per head, the highest in the world.

The population, estimated at 990,000 in April 1975, has been growing at the rate of 10 per cent per annum as the result of immigration from the surrounding countries, resulting from higher wages and better working conditions than anywhere else in the Middle East; of the total of 738,662 recorded at the 1970 census, less than half, some 347,000, were Kuwaitis. An important part of the annual revenue from oil has been spent on health, education and other social services such as the distillation of fresh water from sea water, and as a result the standard of living in Kuwait is at present among the highest in the world. Most of the social services, such as education and health, are free; it has been said that, as a welfare state, Kuwait now probably has no parallel. In recent years the Government has distributed some of its wealth to other parts of the Arab world by loans and grants.

OIL

In 1933 the Anglo-Persian Oil Company, now the British Petroleum Company Limited, and Gulf Oil Corporation applied jointly to the Ruler of Kuwait for a concession to explore the territory. The two companies formed an operating unit, the Kuwait Oil Company, each holding 50 per cent of its share capital, and a concession was granted for 75 years in December 1934, extended for a further 17 years in 1951. A large oilfield was discovered at Burgan, about 25 miles south of the town of Kuwait, in 1938, but the onset of World War II delayed development until 1945. By 1948 six million tons were produced, but the main impetus to speed up development was supplied by the Abadan affair in 1951, which in effect denied Iranian production to the rest of the world for three years. By 1956 Kuwait's production had increased to 54 million tons, and was then the largest in the Middle East. Further fields were found by the company, notably at Raudhatain, north of Kuwait, and the company's production had reached over 148 million tons by 1972, although large areas of the original concession have been relinquished to the State in accordance with the Agreement. To handle this vast production, a huge tanker port has been constructed at Mina al-Ahmadi, not far from the Burgan field, which from a terminal some 10 miles offshore can now handle the largest tankers. At Ahmadi there is also a town of more than 20,000 inhabitants, of whom about 5,000 are employees of the company, and there is a refinery with an annual throughput capacity of 12 million tons.

Beginning in October 1973, Kuwait joined other Arab countries in a campaign of restricting oil production. The total 1973 oil output in Kuwait (excluding the Partitioned Zone) was 138 million metric tons, a fall of 8.4 per cent from the 1972 figure—and the first decline in the country's oil production since exploitation began in 1946. Production in 1974 was restricted even further and was 15.7 per cent lower than in 1973. In 1974 the Kuwait Government acquired a 60 per cent interest in the Kuwait Oil Company and in March 1975 the Kuwait Government took over the remaining 40 per cent, although details of the take-over were still under negotiation in July 1975 (*see* also History, page 473).

Two other companies have been permitted by Kuwait and Saudi Arabia to operate in the Partitioned Zone, and produce oil. These are Aminoil, which has a joint operating agreement with Getty Oil Co. under which Aminoil and Getty bear one half of certain expenses such as drilling; and Arabian Oil Company in which Japanese interests own 80 per cent of the share capital, the governments of Kuwait and Saudi Arabia each holding 10 per cent. So far the production of these companies is small compared with that of the Kuwait Oil Company. The Royal Dutch-Shell group has a concession to explore for oil offshore, but its operations have been held up by the problem, so far unsolved, of determining what are Kuwaiti waters. A Spanish state oil company, Hispanoil, was granted a concession in Kuwait during 1967 on territory relinquished by the Kuwait Oil Company. Of this concession, the Kuwait National Petroleum Company (KNPC) owns 51 per cent, but KNPC is not obliged to pay any of the costs of exploring until oil is discovered in commercial quantities. In addition KNPC markets in Kuwait oil products produced by the Kuwait Oil Company, and owns a refinery at Shuaiba. In 1973 the company produced 6,035,000 tons of various products, representing an increase in refining throughout of 9.6 per cent over 1972. Exports in 1973 totalled 7,085,500 tons, including 5,830,000 tons from the Shuaiba refinery.

Kuwait formerly derived its income from the oil industry through the so-called fifty-fifty agreements signed by the operating companies with many host countries in the early 1950s. The principle of these agreements was that when the operating company exported its crude oil, it paid a royalty to the host government amounting to $12\frac{1}{2}$ per cent of the value of the oil at the "posted" price less the cost of production, then paying income tax at $37\frac{1}{2}$ per cent of the total value of the oil at that price, the host government thus receiving 50 per cent of the value. As the companies were free to fix the posted price they exerted their right to reduce it when the price at which they were able to sell the oil fell below the posted price. This, of course, had the effect of unilaterally diminishing the revenues of the host governments, although because the realized price was lower than the posted price, the host governments were receiving more than 50 per cent of the actual revenue per barrel.

The outcry in the Middle East against this practice was such that the last time the posted price was reduced was in August 1960. In order to increase their "take", the host countries, Kuwait among them, persuaded the companies to agree in 1964 that the $12\frac{1}{2}$ per cent should be "expensed". This meant that, in addition to the cost of production, the amount of the royalty was to be deducted from the posted price, but the tax of 50 per cent was to be charged on the balance, thus increasing the payment to the host country from 50 to $56\frac{1}{4}$ per cent of the posted price. But as the price realized by the companies continued, almost uninterruptedly, to fall below the posted price, the division of profits grew nearer to 70–30, the latter being the companies' share. However, so great was the increase in Kuwait's production that its 1971-72 revenue, estimated at KD 370 million, was double that of 1958. The cooperation between the host countries referred to above was achieved largely through the Organization of Petroleum Exporting Countries (OPEC), formed in 1960. Of this body Kuwait was a founder-member. Kuwait was also a founder-member of the Organization of Arab Petroleum Exporting Countries (OAPEC), formed in 1968, which has its headquarters in Kuwait, and has grown rapidly in membership.

In November 1970, the Kuwait Oil Company agreed to an increase of 9 U.S. cents in the posted price of crude oil, bringing it to $1.68 per barrel, and to an increase of 5 per cent in the rate of income tax payable. However, following the OPEC conference held in Caracas in December, tough negotiations began between OPEC and the major oil companies regarding further price increases. A settlement was reached on February 14th, 1971, when it was agreed to stabilize the rate of income tax at 55 per cent and to increase the posted price by a uniform 35 cents per barrel, with a new system of gravity differentials and an allowance for upward adjustments in four of the five years of the agreement. From June 1971 the terminal price of the Kuwait Oil Company's crude oil was $2.187 per barrel. To offset the effects of the dollar devaluations, agreements were reached in Geneva in January 1972 and June 1973 to raise the posted price to $2.776 per barrel.

During the Arab-Israeli war in October 1973 the Gulf states, including Kuwait, unilaterally announced a 70 per cent increase in the posted price of crude petroleum, thereby abandoning the formula agreed in February 1971 and subsequently modified (see above). This decision took effect on November 1st, 1973, when the posted price per barrel increased to about $5.11, of which about $3 (an increase of $1.25) was payable by the oil companies to the government of the host country. In December the Gulf states agreed on a further increase, aimed at raising the "take" of each host country to $7 per barrel for standard quality petroleum. This became effective on January 1st, 1974, when the posted price was more than doubled to $11.65 per barrel. In Kuwait the "buy-back" price for the state's share in oil output was set at $10.95 per barrel for July to September 1974.

OTHER INDUSTRIES

The government has done much to foster the growth of other industries in order to diversify the economy and to provide an alternative source of employment to oil. A law of 1965 empowers it to grant exemption from import duties on capital goods, subsidized rates for water and power, and preference in government purchases for locally manufactured products. An Industrial Development Committee assists the development of local industry. A Petrochemical Industries Company was formed in 1963 to manufacture fertilizers, and in 1964 a larger concern, Kuwait Chemical Fertilizer Company, was set up. An industrial area has been developed at Shuaiba, between Kuwait City and Ahmadi, close to KNPC's refinery. With a new fertilizer plant at Shuaiba owned by KNPC, Kuwait now has a potential production capacity of 1.5 million tons a year.

There are several factories in Kuwait supplying consumer requirements, such as processed food and soft drinks, and there is a flour mills company. The construction industry is of some importance, owing to the vast amount of house and office building there has been in the last decade, not to mention the construction of public works such as roads, power stations, schools and hospitals, much of this work having been undertaken, however, by foreign contractors.

At the 1970 census there were more than 32,000 persons (13.7 per cent of the working population) employed in manufacturing, compared with only 5,746 (less than 2.5 per cent) in the production of crude petroleum and natural gas. In 1972-73 manufacturing accounted for 3 per cent of G.D.P., and crude oil, natural gas and other mining and quarrying accounted for 63.7 per cent.

PUBLIC UTILITIES

To support the increase of population brought by the development of oil, a vast infrastructure of public works had to be created. There are desalination plants in Kuwait City and the Shuaiba industrial area, and production of potable water averaged 27 million gallons a day in 1972. Important sources of fresh water have been found at Raudhatain and Al Shigaia. In 1973 Kuwait produced 3,668 million kWh. of electric energy for public use. The harbour of Kuwait City has been completely reconstructed; four deep-water berths have been provided, and an international airport has been built. There is a national airline with an international service, Kuwait Airways Corporation, which is owned by the State. All these facilities were created at the expense of the Government, the oil ports at Mina al-Ahmadi and nearby at Mina al-Abdullah having been made by the Kuwait Oil Company. However, there are several shipowning companies owned by the private sector, including Kuwait Oil Tanker Company, which, by 1976, will have a fleet capacity totalling some 1.8 million deadweight tons. Kuwait Shipping Company is also rapidly expanding its fleet

AGRICULTURE AND FISHERIES

Owing to the present lack of water, little grain is grown, and most of the food consumed in Kuwait has to be imported. In 1974 the total cultivable area was about 3 per cent of the whole, estimated at 27,000 dunums. Of this, vegetables and crops occupied about 6,000 dunums, with another 1,000 devoted to orchards and timber. However, the Government has done much to encourage animal husbandry, the main activity (before the development of the oilfields) of the bedouin, who still rear camels, sheep and goats. There is an experimental farm of 90 acres owned by the Government, and in the private sector there is a growing poultry and dairy industry. Fishing, on the other hand, is of some importance, because the Gulf, and particularly Kuwait's territorial waters, abound in sea creatures, notably prawns (some of which are exported to the U.S.A.) and shrimps. There were four fishing companies based on the abundance of fish in Kuwait's territorial waters, until they were amalgamated into Kuwait United Fisheries in 1972.

FOREIGN TRADE AND BALANCE OF PAYMENTS

Well over 90 per cent of the value of Kuwait's exports consists of oil. Total exports in 1974 were

valued at KD 3,183 million, having shown an uninterrupted and very substantial increase since oil was first produced. About two thirds of the volume of the oil exported goes to European destinations. In 1973 over 16 per cent of the Kuwait Oil Company's exports went to Japan, about 15 per cent to the United Kingdom, just under 15 per cent to France, about 13 per cent to the Netherlands and 8 per cent to Italy.

The total value of imports in 1970 dropped slightly to KD 223 million, having risen steadily for many years except in 1964, when there was something of a recession owing apparently to overstocking. Imports in 1972 totalled KD 262 million, and in 1973 KD 311 million. The most important item is machinery and transport equipment which accounted for 34 per cent of total imports by value in 1973. Manufactured goods in that year accounted for 21 per cent and food and live animals 17 per cent. Kuwait's principal suppliers in 1973 were Japan, the U.S.A. and the United Kingdom, who supplied 18 per cent, 14 per cent and 10 per cent respectively of total imports by value.

According to the fourth Annual Report of the Central Bank of Kuwait, the balance of payments of Kuwait during the fiscal year ending March 1973 revealed a payments surplus of KD 166 million, which is the change in the net foreign assets of monetary authorities and the banking system. The foreign assets of the Ministry of Finance and Oil rose from KD 441 million in March 1971 to KD 689 million in March 1972 and KD 789 million in March 1973.

CURRENCY, BANKING AND FINANCE

The currency in circulation is the Kuwaiti dinar, details of which are given in the Statistical Survey.

The only foreign bank previously allowed to operate in Kuwait, the British Bank of the Middle East, was taken over by the Government in 1971 and now manages the Bank of Kuwait and the Middle East under agreement. However, there are a number of commercial banks financed by local capital, and the management of one of these, the Al Ahli Bank, is provided by the French Credit Lyonnais. Of the local banks, by far the largest is the National Bank of Kuwait, founded in 1953, the total assets of which amounted to KD 448 million at the end of 1974. The other banks include the Gulf Bank and the Commercial Bank of Kuwait, founded respectively in 1960 and 1961. The United Bank of Kuwait, founded in London in 1966, represents the National Bank, the Commercial Bank and the Gulf Bank, which hold part of its share capital. The net foreign assets of the commercial banks at March 31st, 1974, amounted to KD 390 million. In 1960 the Government founded a Savings and Credit Bank. Its paid-up capital in 1975 was KD 31 million, all provided by the State, to promote savings and to provide finance for small industries, agriculture, property and small businesses.

There is now an active stock market in Kuwait, and for some time the State has been active in encouraging investment. In 1962 a Kuwait Investment Company was created, of which the State owns half the capital, to engage in portfolio investment and in property dealing in Kuwait. A similar concern, the

Kuwait Foreign Trading & Investment Company, was established by the State, which owns 98 per cent of the share capital, to undertake business transactions abroad, and reference has already been made to the reserves of the State overseas. There is no official information about the amount of private portfolio investment overseas by Kuwaitis, but it is known to be substantial, and the estimate of the country's balance of payments for 1972–73 puts the income derived therefrom in that year at KD 65 million.

PUBLIC FINANCE

The budgeted expenditure for the fiscal year 1974-75 was set at KD 959 million (about U.S. $3,300 million). There was an allocation of KD 385 million (about U.S. $1,500 million) to the state's general reserve, part of which would be used for capital participation in mixed-sector companies or for loans to private-sector enterprises. This would leave KD 574 million (just under U.S. $2,000 million) for general expenditure. Oil revenues, however, were expected to be about U.S. $9,000 million and, after deduction of grants to Arab confrontation states, a surplus of between U.S. $6,000 and U.S. $7,000 was expected.

At some KD 180 million the development budget for 1975-76 was about the same as that for 1974-75. The main projects were in the field of power-generation extensions and new school buildings.

In recent years Kuwait has become a significant financial power and the state has invested a large amount overseas. Government investment income from foreign assets totalled KD 60 million in 1972-73. Nevertheless, Kuwait has played a leading role in aiding less prosperous countries in the region. At the end of 1961 the Government established the Kuwait Fund for Arab Economic Development (KFAED) to provide loan capital for development projects in the other Arab countries. KFAED has an authorized capital of KD 1,000 million, and it was increased to this figure from KD 200 million in 1974. Also, the fund's loan area was extended from the Arab world to all developing countries, and, in 1974, loans granted totalled KD 134.2 million. Kuwait also subscribed KD 30 million to the Arab Fund for Economic and Social Development and about U.S. $130 million to the Islamic Development Bank as well as participating in the Arab-African Oil Assistance Fund, the Arab Bank for African Industrial and Agricultural Development and the Organization of Arab Oil Exporting Countries (OAPEC). In 1974 Kuwait was estimated to have deployed 71 per cent of its surplus to Arab and other developing countries in aid and investments.

DEVELOPMENT

The efforts of the last few years to diversify the economy have had some success. In 1963 the G.D.P. of Kuwait was estimated to be KD 500 million. Of this KD 444 million, or 89 per cent, was provided by the oil industry. For the year 1972-73 the G.D.P. was estimated to be KD 1,579 million, of which KD 1,002 million, or 63.5 per cent, was from mineral production. During the last few years, it is true, there have been slight setbacks to those parts of the economy which do not depend directly on oil, and the years 1968 to 1970 are regarded as a period of relative recession. The cause of this lay mainly in the June 1967 war, after which Kuwait undertook to pay large subsidies to Egypt and Jordan. At the same time, the slowing down of the growth in oil production necessitated restraints in public spending. The greatly increased oil revenues of the 1970s have brought Kuwait out of this period of stagnation. All the same, efforts to diversify the economy and maximize the increase in G.D.P. have continued.

STATISTICAL SURVEY

AREA AND POPULATION

AREA	POPULATION (Census of April 19th, 1970)†				
	Total	Kuwaitis	Foreigners	Males	Females
17,818 sq. km.*	738,662	347,396	391,266	419,881	318,781

Estimated Population: (April 1975) 990,389 (469,120 Kuwaitis; 521,269 non-Kuwaitis).

* Including the Kuwaiti portion of the Partitioned Zone, shared with Saudi Arabia.

† Including 754 Kuwaiti nationals abroad.

Principal Towns (1970 Census): Kuwait City (capital) 80,405; Hawalli 106,542; Salmiya 67,346.

ECONOMICALLY ACTIVE POPULATION*

(1970 Census)

	MALES	FEMALES	TOTAL
Agriculture, Hunting, Forestry and Fishing .	4,051	9	4,060
Oil and Natural Gas, Mining and Quarrying .	6,455	716	7,171
Manufacturing	31,973	115	32,088
Electricity, Gas and Water Supply . .	7,236	16	7,252
Construction	33,606	68	33,674
Trade, Restaurants and Hotels . .	28,954	329	29,283
Transport, Storage and Communications .	11,997	141	12,138
Finance, Insurance, Property and Business Services	3,506	242	3,748
Community, Social and Personal Services .	89,320	14,816	104,136
Other Activities (not adequately described) .	797	30	827
TOTAL IN EMPLOYMENT . .	217,893	16,478	234,371
Unemployed	4,782	118	4,900
TOTAL	222,675	16,596	239,271

* Including Kuwaiti nationals outside the country.

OIL

KUWAIT (Kuwait Oil Co.)

	Production (long tons)
1970 . .	135,494,480
1971 . .	144,468,129
1972 . .	148,711,076
1973 . .	142,090,000
1974 . .	112,800,000

KUWAIT/SAUDI ARABIA PARTITIONED ZONE
(American Independent Oil Co. and Getty Oil Co.)

	Production (long tons)
1970 . .	8,940,000
1971 . .	9,910,000
1972 . .	8,190,464
1973 . .	7,320,000
1974 . .	8,520,823

KUWAIT/SAUDI ARABIA PARTITIONED ZONE OFFSHORE
(Arabian Oil Co.)

	Production (long tons)
1969 . .	16,150,000
1970 . .	16,960,000
1971 . .	18,690,000
1972 . .	20,000,000*
1973 . .	19,992,000

* Approximate.

OIL EXPORTS
(1973)

DESTINATION	CRUDE OIL*		REFINED PRODUCTS INCLUDING LIQUEFIED PETROLEUM GAS	
	million U.S. barrels	%	million U.S. barrels	%
Western Europe . . .	535.8	55.4	15.8	10.7
Asia and Oceania . . .	376.2	38.2	81.4	55.2
North and South America . .	46.7	4.8	6.5	4.4
Arab and Other Countries . .	7.9	0.9	43.7	29.7
TOTAL . . .	966.6	100.0	147.4	100.0

* Excludes American Independent Oil Company production of crude oil, which is included in the refined products figure for the company.

KUWAIT OIL COMPANY CRUDE OIL EXPORTS BY DESTINATION

	1970		1971		1972		1973	
	tons	%	tons	%	tons	%	tons	%
United Kingdom .	25,236,126	21.2	25,842,332	20.2	24,070,928	17.9	18,904,421	15.3
Japan . . .	15,353,896	12.9	17,783,685	13.9	22,465,540	16.7	20,182,806	16.4
Netherlands .	10,812,790	9.1	12,015,376	9.4	14,872,166	11.0	16,182,877	13.1
Italy . .	12,374,513	10.4	11,954,502	9.3	13,526,299	10.0	10,290,436	8.4
France . .	10,697,850	9.0	11,117,512	8.7	16,599,045	12.3	17,793,022	14.4
Ireland . .	10,515,043	8.8	10,445,691	8.2	6,668,442	5.0	5,626,124	4.6
Singapore .	4,377,414	3.7	6,183,626	4.8	7,884,940	5.9	6,531,488	5.3
South Korea .	2,416,540	2.0	5,894,861	4.6	5,380,114	4.0	2,950,036	2.4
Federal Germany .	4,110,392	3.4	4,427,435	3.5	4,360,783	3.2	3,201,748	2.6
Taiwan . .	2,764,286	2.3	3,166,073	2.5	2,813,214	2.1	1,865,238	1.5
Belgium . .	2,958,250	2.5	2,555,098	2.0	496,908	0.4	261,786	0.2
Other Countries .	17,521,860	14.7	16,671,833	12.9	15,563,501	11.5	19,427,000	14.8
TOTAL . .	119,138,960	100.0	128,058,024	100.0	134,701,880	100.0	123,216,982	100.0

ARABIAN OIL COMPANY
CRUDE OIL EXPORTS BY DESTINATION, 1972
(long tons)

Europe	667,000
Japan	8,801,000
Australia	111,000

AMERICAN INDEPENDENT OIL COMPANY
EXPORTS OF REFINED PRODUCTS
(barrels)

1969 . . .	12,805,358
1970 . . .	28,640,259
1971 . . .	30,551,116
1972 . . .	29,308,905
1973 . . .	26,712,271

KUWAIT NATIONAL PETROLEUM COMPANY PRODUCTION FOR LOCAL CONSUMPTION
(barrels)

	1971	1972	1973
Super Premium . .	94,302	145,607	270,824
Gasoline Premium . .	2,790,690	2,952,465	2,946,417
Aviation Kerosene . .	298,114	300,178	267,417
Gas Oil . . .	1,036,761	1,055,710	1,149,567
Fuel Oil . . .	234,616	226,700	281,306
Diesel Oil . . .	25,921	20,343	28,805
Asphalt . . .	158,951	131,861	87,891
Others . . .	21,744	19,764	892
TOTAL . .	4,661,099	4,852,628	5,033,119

NATURAL GAS PRODUCTION
(million cu. ft.)

	GAS PRODUCED	USED BY COMPANIES	USED FOR INJECTION	USED BY STATE	TOTAL GAS USED
1970 . .	570,376	90,000	45,342	52,707	188,048
1971 . .	643,710	93,830	69,469	63,224	226,522
1972 . .	647,808	95,904	65,903	85,741	247,548
1973 . .	581,065	100,947	79,043	85,098	265,088

INDUSTRY

		1971	1972	1973
Motor Spirit	'000 metric tons	578	596	783
Kerosene and Jet Fuel . . .	,, ,, ,,	805	906	1,032
Distillate Fuel Oils . . .	,, ,, ,,	7,118	3,569	3,447
Residual Fuel Oil . . .	,, ,, ,,	11,570	10,878	10,208
Ammonium Sulphate . . .	metric tons	65,450	92,179	118,795
Electricity Generated . . .	million kWh.	2,636	3,295	3,668
Potable Water	million galls.	7,675	8,584	9,291
Brackish Water	,, ,,	5,507	5,397	6,495
Sodium Chloride . . .	tons	4,731	4,977	10,030
Chlorine	,,	1,674	1,723	3,865
Caustic Soda	,,	1,890	1,944	4,361
Hydrochloric Acid . . .	galls.	126,774	140,786	193,928
Lime-Sand Bricks . . .	cubic metres	196,446	230,451	148,383
Milling (Kuwait Flour Mills Co.) . .	tons	95,504	96,480	98,297

FINANCE

1,000 fils=10 dirhams=1 Kuwaiti dinar (KD).

Coins: 1, 5, 10, 20, 50 and 100 fils.

Notes: 250 and 500 fils; 1, 5 and 10 dinars.

Exchange rates (July 1975): £1 sterling=628.5 fils; U.S. $1=287.4 fils.

100 Kuwaiti dinars=£159.12=$348.00.

Note: The Kuwaiti dinar was introduced in April 1961, replacing the Persian Gulf Indian rupee. The dinar's initial value of U.S. $2.80 ($1=357.14 fils) remained in force until August 1971. Between December 1971 and February 1973 the dinar's par value was $3.04 ($1=328.95 fils). From February 1973 to March 1975 it was $3.3778 ($1=296.05 fils) but a fluctuating market rate was also in operation. The Kuwaiti dinar was at par with the pound sterling until November 1967, after which the exchange rate was £1=857.14 fils (1 dinar=£1.167) until June 1972. Since March 1975 the dinar's value has been determined in relation to a weighted group of currencies of the country's main trading partners.

BUDGET
(1972–73)

Revenue	'000 KD	Current Expenditure	'000 KD
Income Tax	386,680	Head of State	8,000
Production and Consumption Taxes and Fees	129,967	Information	6,347
		Public Works . . .	13,688
Services Revenues . . .	26,405	Posts, Telegraphs and Telephones	6,798
Miscellaneous Revenues and Dues .	4,123	Education	45,121
Incidental Revenues . . .	1,095	Foreign Affairs . . .	3,406
		Interior	28,455
		Defence	32,043
		Public Health . . .	20,912
		Social Affairs and Labour . .	7,107
		Electricity, Water, Power and Water Distillation Plant and Chlorine Plant.	14,644
		Finance and Oil, including Customs and Ports and Housing . . .	12,877
		Unclassified and Transferable .	104,119
		Other Expenditure . . .	12,199
TOTAL	548,470	TOTAL	315,712

1973–74: Revenue 568.1m.; Expenditure 339.9m. (est.).

1974–75: Revenue 959.9m.; Expenditure 574.5m. (est.).

EXTERNAL TRADE
(million KD)

	1966	1967	1968	1969	1970	1971	1972	1973	1974
Imports c.i.f. . .	165.3	211.9	218.3	230.8	223.3	232.3	262.2	310.6	448.4
Exports f.o.b. . .	479.4	484.4	513.5	550.1	590.9	893.8	981.3	1,129.8	3,183.2

COMMODITIES
('000 KD)

	IMPORTS			EXPORTS*		
	1971	1972	1973	1971	1972	1973
Food and Live Animals . . .	40,924	46,133	53,066	6,561	6,902	9,094
Beverages and Tobacco . .	6,094	6,512	7,650	913	1,424	2,457
Crude Materials, inedible, except fuels	4,015	3,956	5,478	748	914	1,944
Mineral Fuels, Lubricants and Related Materials	2,154	2,597	2,875	339	232	—
Animal and Vegetable Oils, Fats .	1,117	1,040	1,061	36	46	50
Chemicals	10,684	12,736	13,507	6,484	12,333	19,738
Manufactured Goods . . .	51,340	56,316	65,514	4,194	8,949	13,306
Machinery and Transport Equipment	77,501	85,552	106,928	12,537	14,288	17,097
Miscellaneous Manufactured Articles	37,980	46,822	51,153	1,968	3,850	6,021
Others	497	514	3,363	602	657	66

* Excluding crude petroleum and petroleum products.

PRINCIPAL COUNTRIES

('ooo KD.)

IMPORTS	1971	1972	1973	EXPORTS*	1971	1972	1973
Australia . . .	6,475	7,466	8,613	Bahrain . . .	1,069	1,335	1,830
Belgium and Lux'bourg	3,610	3,238	5,005	Egypt . . .	800	530	294
China, People's Republic	7,629	8,456	10,797	India . . .	654	3,222	3,688
France . . .	14,002	11,016	8,236	Iran . . .	2,501	3,745	5,870
Federal Germany . .	17,598	21,762	24,311	Iraq . . .	3,814	2,730	2,765
India . . .	7,384	7,595	7,792	Jordan . . .	1,277	490	775
Iran . . .	4,047	3,754	4,513	Lebanon . . .	2,360	2,557	1,911
Italy . . .	9,782	11,258	13,161	Pakistan . . .	1,131	2,158	1,964
Japan . . .	32,789	41,967	55,542	Qatar . . .	923	1,597	2,769
Lebanon . . .	10,654	13,545	13,337	Saudi Arabia . .	6,803	12,252	18,580
Netherlands . .	5,649	6,678	7,435	United Arab Emirates .	2,491	3,833	7,306
Switzerland . .	3,429	3,537	4,153	United Kingdom .	2,523	3,716	1,673
United Kingdom .	26,841	26,613	31,743	U.S.A. . . .	1,159	725	1,653
U.S.A. . . .	33,622	34,328	43,794				

* Excludes oil exports (*see* OIL *above*).

TRANSPORT

Shipping (1973): *Arrivals:* 1,161 ships; passenger arrivals 20,992; passenger departures 22,793.

Vehicles: Total (1970) 149,150; (1971) 157,876; (1972) 175,087; (1973) 198,222.

Civil Aviation: Kuwait Airport, total aircraft movements (1970) 14,088; (1971) 13,998; (1972) 13,549; (1973) 14,768.

EDUCATION*

(1973/74)

	SCHOOLS	TEACHERS	STUDENTS
Kindergarten	53	971	11,959
Primary	100	4,164	75,499
Intermediate . . .	81	3,909	53,386
Secondary . . .	31	2,642	24,107
Commercial . . .	3	175	938
Industrial College . .	1	215	786
Religious Institute . .	1	37	251
Special Training Institutes	11	939	1,644
Teacher Training Colleges .	4	155	847

* Data for government schools only; in 1973/74 there were 1,811 teachers, 37,670 pupils at private schools.

Sources: Central Statistical Office, Planning Board, Kuwait; Ministry of Finance and Oil, Kuwait; Ministry of Education, Kuwait; National Bank of Kuwait, S.A.K.; Kuwait Oil Co. Ltd., Ahmadi, Kuwait.

THE CONSTITUTION

(Promulgated November 16th, 1962)

The principal provisions of the Constitution are as follows:

SOVEREIGNTY

Kuwait is an independent sovereign Arab State; her sovereignty may not be surrendered, and no part of her territory may be relinquished. Offensive war is prohibited by the Constitution.

Succession as Amir is restricted to heirs of the late MUBARAK AS-SABAH, and an Heir Apparent must be appointed within one year of the accession of a new Amir.

EXECUTIVE AUTHORITY

Executive power is vested in the Amir, who exercises it through a Council of Ministers. The Amir will appoint the Prime Minister "after the traditional consultations", and will appoint and dismiss Ministers on the recommendation of the Prime Minister. Ministers need not be members of the National Assembly, though all ministers who are not Assembly members assume membership *ex-officio* in the Assembly for the duration of office. The Amir also lays down laws, which shall not be effective unless published in the *Official Gazette*. The Amir sets up public institutions. All decrees issued in these respects shall be conveyed to the Assembly. No law is issued unless it is approved by the Assembly.

LEGISLATURE

A National Assembly of 50 members will be elected for a four-year term by all natural-born literate Kuwait males over the age of 21, except servicemen and police, who may not vote. Candidates for election must possess the franchise and be over 30 years of age. The Assembly will sit for at least eight months in any year, and new elections shall be held within two months of the last dissolution of the outgoing Assembly.

Restrictions on the commercial activities of Ministers include an injunction forbidding them to sell property to the Government.

The Amir may ask for reconsideration of a Bill passed by the Assembly and sent to him for ratification, but the Bill would automatically become law if it were subsequently passed by a two-thirds majority at the next sitting, or by a simple majority at a subsequent sitting. The Amir may declare Martial Law, but only with the approval of the Assembly.

The Assembly may pass a vote of no confidence in a Minister, in which case the Minister must resign. Such a vote is not permissible in the case of the Prime Minister, but the Assembly may approach the Amir on the matter, and the Amir shall then either dismiss the Prime Minister or dissolve the Assembly.

An annual budget shall be presented, and there shall be an independent finance control commission.

CIVIL SERVICE

Entry to the Civil Service is confined to Kuwait citizens.

PUBLIC LIBERTIES

Kuwaitis are equal before the law in prestige, rights and duties. Individual freedom is guaranteed. No one should be seized, arrested or exiled except within the rules of law.

No punishment shall be administered except for an act or abstaining from an act considered a crime in accordance with a law applicable at the time of committing it, and no penalty shall be imposed more severe than that which could have been imposed at the time of committing the crime.

Freedom of opinion is guaranteed to everyone, and each has the right to express himself through speech, writing or other means within the limits of the law.

The Press is free within the limits of the law, and it should not be suppressed except in accordance with the dictates of law.

Freedom of performing religious rites is protected by the State according to prevailing customs, provided it does not violate the public order and morality.

Trade unions will be permitted and property must be respected. An owner is not banned from managing his property except within the boundaries of law. No property should be taken from anyone, except within the prerogatives of law, unless a just compensation be given.

Houses may not be entered, except in cases provided by law. Every Kuwaiti has freedom of movement and choice of place of residence within the state. This right shall not be controlled except in cases stipulated by law.

Every person has the right to education and freedom to choose his type of work. Freedom to form peaceful societies is guaranteed within the limits of law.

THE GOVERNMENT

HEAD OF STATE

Amir of Kuwait: His Highness Sheikh SABAH AS-SALIM AS-SABAH
(succeeded on the death of his brother, November 24, 1965).

COUNCIL OF MINISTERS

(August 1975)

Prime Minister: Sheikh JABER AL-AHMAD AL-SABAH.

Deputy Prime Minister and Minister of Information: Sheikh JABER AL-ALI AL-SALEM AL-SABAH.

Minister of Education: JASEM KHALID AL-MARZUQ.

Minister of Housing: HAMAD MUBARAK AL-AYYAR.

Minister of Public Works: HAMAD YOUSSEF AL-NISF.

Minister of Interior and Defence: Sheikh SAAD AL-ABDUL-LAH AL-SALEM AL-SABAH.

Minister of Social Affairs and Labour: Sheikh SALEM AL-SABAH AL-SALEM AL-SABAH.

Minister of Communications and Transport: SULAIMAN HUMUD AL-ZAID AL-KHALID.

Minister of Foreign Affairs: Sheikh SABAH AL-AHMAD AL-JABER AL-SABAH.

Minister of Finance: ABDEL-RAHMAN SALEM AL-ATIQI.

Minister of Health: Dr. ABDEL-RAHMAN ABDULLAH AL-AWADI.

Minister of State for Cabinet Affairs: ABDEL-AZIZ HUSAIN.

Minister of Justice and Waqfs: ABDULLAH IBRAHIM AL-MUFFARIJ.

Minister of Power and Water: ABDULLAH YOUSSEF AL-GHANIM.

Minister of Oil: ABDEL-MUTTALEB AL-KAZIMI.

Minister of Trade and Industry: ABDEL-WAHHAB YOUSSEF AL-NIFISI.

PROVINCIAL GOVERNORATES

Ahmadi: Sheikh JABIR ABDULLAH JABIR AL-SABAH.
Hawalli: Sheikh NAWAF AL-AHMAD AL-JABIR.
Kuwait: Sheikh NASSER SABAH AL-NASSER AL-SABAH.

NATIONAL ASSEMBLY

In elections held for the fourth time under the new Constitution on January 27th 1975, 260 candidates were nominated for the 50 seats (5 seats in each of 10 districts). There are no official political parties, the candidates standing as individuals. In the 1975 elections, however, several opposition leaders were re-elected. The vote is limited to natural-born Kuwaiti males over 21 who are able to read and write (about 40,000 voters).

Secretary: IBRAHIM AL-KHREIBIT.

Speaker: KHALID SALIH AL-GHUNAIM.

Deputy-Speaker: AHMAD SAADOUN.

DIPLOMATIC REPRESENTATION

EMBASSIES ACCREDITED TO KUWAIT

(In Kuwait City unless otherwise indicated)

(E) Embassy.

Afghanistan: Baghdad, Iraq (E), *Chargé d'Affaires a.i.* in Kuwait; MUHAMMAD ANWAR.

Algeria: Istiqlal St. (E); *Chargé d'Affaires a.i.:* KHOUDIR SALHI.

Argentina: Cairo, Egypt (E).

Austria: Beirut, Lebanon (E).

Bangladesh: Istiqlal St., Dasmah, Area No. 4, House No. 19 (E); *Ambassador:* Lt.-Gen. KHAWAJA WASIUDDIN.

Belgium: Mohammed Al-Ghunaiman Villa, Damascus St. (E); *Ambassador:* GUY COPETTE (also accred. to Bahrain and Oman).

Brazil: Istiqlal St. (E); *Ambassador:* MURILLO YURGEL VALENTE.

Bulgaria: Cairo St., Mansuria (E); *Ambassador:* (vacant).

Canada: Teheran, Iran (E).

China, People's Republic: Sheikh Ahmed Jaber Bldgs., Dasman (E); *Ambassador:* SUN CHIENG-WEI.

Colombia: Beirut, Lebanon (E).

Costa Rica: Beirut, Lebanon (E).

Czechoslovakia: No. 14, Diyya Quarter, Cairo St. (E); *Chargé d'Affaires:* TOMAS STRAKOS.

Denmark: Jeddah, Saudi Arabia (E).

Egypt: Mussa'ed al Saleh Bldg., Istiqlal St. (E); *Ambassador:* IZZ-AL ARAB AMIN IBRAHIM.

Finland: Beirut, Lebanon (E).

France: Qabazard Bldg., Istiqlal St. (E); *Ambassador:* JOSE PAOLI.

German Democratic Republic: Shuwaikh (E); *Ambassador:* GÜNTER SCHURATH.

Germany, Federal Republic: Al-Sour St. (E); *Ambassador:* Dr. JOHANNES LOHSE (also accred. to Bahrain).

Greece: Beirut, Lebanon (E).

Guinea: Jeddah, Saudi Arabia (E).

Hungary: Baghdad, Iraq (E).

India: 34 Shara, Istiqlal (E); *Ambassador:* R. AXEL-KHAN.

Indonesia: Baghdad, Iraq (E).

Iran: Haj Abdulla Dashti Bldg., Istiqlal St. (E); *Ambassador:* Dr. FEREYDUN ZAND-FARD.

Iraq: 37 Istiqlal St. (E); *Ambassador:* (vacant).

Italy: Villa No. 6, F. Omar Ben Al-Khatab, Mulla Bldgs., Sharq (E); *Ambassador:* Dr. GERARDO ZAMPAGLIONE (also accred. to Bahrain, Oman and the United Arab Emirates).

Japan: Al-Sour St. (E); *Ambassador:* SHOTARO TAKAHASHI (also accred. to Bahrain and Oman).

Jordan: Mansour Qabazard Bldg., Istiqlal St. (E); *Chargé d'Affaires a.i.:* AWAD ABU OBEID.

Kenya: Cairo, Egypt (E).

Lebanon: Istiqlal St. (E); *Ambassador:* SAMIH AL-BABA (also accred. to Bahrain).

Libya: Istiqlal St. (E); *Chargé d'Affaires a.i.:* MUHAMMAD ALI BA'REH.

Malaysia: Mansuria (E); *Ambassador:* JAMALUDDIN BIN HAJI.

Mali: Cairo, Egypt (E).

Malta: Tripoli, Libya (E).

Mauritania: Villa No. 5, Sheikh Salman Duaij, Riad St. (E); *Ambassador:* ISMAIL W. MAWLOOD.

Morocco: Shuwaikh Area B (E); *Ambassador:* AHMAD BEN AL-MALEEH (also accred. to Bahrain and Oman).

Nepal: Cairo, Egypt (E).

Netherlands: Al-Sour St. (E); *Ambassador:* Jonkeer J. A. BEELAERTS VAN BLOKLAND (also accred. to Bahrain and the United Arab Emirates).

Nigeria: Jeddah, Saudi Arabia (E).

Norway: Teheran, Iran (E).

Oman: Istiqlal St. (E); *Chargé d'Affaires:* ABDULLA A. AL-NAJJAR.

Pakistan: Hamza St., Daiya (E); *Ambassador:* NIJMUL SAQEB KHAN.

Poland: Third Ring Rd., Rawdah (E); *Chargé d'Affaires:* STANISLAW MAKSYMOWICZ.

Qatar: Istiqlal St. (E); *Ambassador:* MUHAMMAD M. AL-KHELAIFI.

Romania: Sheikh Duaij Ibrahim Bldg., Istiqlal St. (E); *Ambassador:* Dr. CONSTANTIN CARUNTU.

Saudi Arabia: Istiqlal St. (E); *Ambassador:* HUMOID FAHAD AL-ZAID.

Senegal: P.O.B. 23892, Al Nougra, Safat (E); *Ambassador:* MOUSTAPHA CISSE.

Somalia: Nasir St., Shuwaikh "B" (E); *Ambassador:* MUSA ISLAM FARCH.

Spain: Abdullah Salem District (E); *Ambassador:* RAMÓN ARMENGOD (also accred. to Bahrain, Oman and the United Arab Emirates).

Sudan: Istiqlal St. (E); *Ambassador:* AHMAD S. AL-HABEEB (also accred. to Bahrain).

Sweden: Hilali St. (E); *Chargé d'Affaires:* THORD BENGTSON (Ambassador resident in Jeddah).

Switzerland: Amman, Jordan (E).

Syria: No. 33 Diiyah District (E); *Ambassador:* (vacant).

Tunisia: Ibn Battuta St., Shamia (E); *Ambassador:* REDA BASH-BAWAB (also accred. to Bahrain and Oman).

Turkey: Brieid Al-Gar (E); *Ambassador:* ISMAIL B. OLGACAY (also accred. to Bahrain).

U.S.S.R.: Sheikh Ahmad al-Jaber al-Sabah Bldg., No. 5 Dasman District (E); *Ambassador:* NIKOLAI N. SIKAT-CHEV.

United Arab Emirates: Istiqlal St. (E); *Ambassador:* SAIF BIN JAHWAN.

United Kingdom: Arabian Gulf St. (E); *Ambassador:* ALBERT THOMAS LAMB.

U.S.A.: Bneid Al-Gar (E); *Ambassador:* WILLIAM A. STOLLFUS, JR.

Venezuela: Beirut, Lebanon (E).

Yemen Arab Republic: Abdullah Al-Salem Area, Morocco St. (E); *Ambassador:* ABDULLAH ALI AL-DHABI (also accred. to Bahrain).

Yugoslavia: Al-Mansour St., Shuwaikh "B" (E); *Ambassador:* LAZAR ZIVULJ.

Zaire: Damascus St. (E); *Ambassador:* NDEZE MATABARO.

Zambia: Cairo, Egypt (E).

Kuwait also has diplomatic relations with Australia, Bahrain, Cuba, Guinea-Bissau, Guyana, Ireland, Madagascar, Peru, Tanzania, Trinidad and Tobago, Uganda and the Upper Volta.

JUDICIAL SYSTEM

There is a codified system of law based largely upon the Egyptian system. In criminal matters, minor contraventions are dealt with by Magistrates Courts, felonies by Criminal Assize Courts. Appeal in the case of misdemeanours is to a Misdemeanours Court of Appeal.

Civil cases are heard by a General Court within which are separate chambers dealing with commercial cases, other civil cases and matters of personal status. Appeal is to a High Court of Appeal. Matters of personal status may go beyond the High Court of Appeal to a Court of Cassation.

In criminal cases, investigation of misdemeanours is the responsibility of the police, while responsibility for the investigation of felonies lies with the Attorney-General's Office.

RELIGION
MUSLIMS

The inhabitants are mainly Muslims of the Sunni and Shiite sects.

CHRISTIANS

Anglican Chaplain in Kuwait: Rev. JOHN PRAGNELL, c/o Kuwait Oil Co. Ltd., 3 Ninth Avenue, Ahmadi 6, Kuwait.

Roman Catholic: Right Rev. Mgr. V. SAN MIGUEL, O.C.D., Administrator Apostolic of Kuwait, Bishop's House, P.O.B. 266, Kuwait.

National Evangelical Church in Kuwait: Rev. YUSEF ABDUL NOOR, Box 80, Kuwait; a United Protestant Church founded by the Reformed Church in America; services in Arabic, English and Malayalam.

There are also Armenian, Greek, Coptic and Syrian Orthodox Churches in Kuwait.

THE PRESS
DAILIES

Akhbar al-Kuwait (*Kuwait News*): P.O.B. 1747, Shuwaikh, Kuwait; f. 1961; Arabic; independent; Editor ABDUL-AZIZ FAHAD AL-FULAIJ; circ. 4,000.

Al-Qabas: P.O.B. 21800, Airport Rd., Shuwaikh, Kuwait; f. 1972; Arabic; Editor JASSIM AHMAD AL-NUSUF; Gen. Man. ZULFICAR KOBEISSI; circ. 20,000.

Al-Siyasa: P.O.B. 2270, Kuwait; f. 1965; Arabic; political; Editor AHMED AL-JARALLAH; circ. 19,000.

Ar Rai al-Amm (*Public Opinion*): P.O.B. 695, International Airport Road, Shuwaikh Industrial Area, Kuwait; f. 1961; Arabic; political, social and cultural; Editor YOUSEF AL-MESSAEED; circ. 30,000.

Daily News: P.O.B. 695, International Airport Rd., Shuwaikh Industrial Area, Kuwait; f. 1963; English; political, independent; Editor-in-Chief YOUSEF AL-MESSAEED; circ. 10,000.

Kuwait Times: P.O.B. 1301, Fahed Al Salem Ave., Kuwait; f. 1961; English; political; Owner and Editor-in-Chief YOUSUF ALYAN; circ. 6,000.

WEEKLIES AND PERIODICALS

Kuwait Al-Youm (*Kuwait Today*): P.O.B. 193, Kuwait; f. 1954; Sunday; the "Official Gazette"; Amiri Decrees, Laws, Govt. announcements, decisions, invitations for tenders, etc.; published by the Ministry of Information; circ. 5,000.

Adhwa al-Kuwait: P.O.B. 1977, Kuwait; f. 1962; literature and arts; Arabic; weekly; free advertising magazine; Editor MYRIN AL HAMAD; circ. 5,000.

Al-Arabi: P.O.B. 748, Kuwait; f. 1958; Arabic; science, history, arts; monthly; published by the Ministry of Information; Editor Dr. AHMED ZAKI; circ. 125,000.

Al-Balagh: Kuwait; weekly.

Al-Hadaf (*The Aim*): P.O.B. 1142, Al Sur St., Kuwait; weekly; f. 1961; Arabic; political and cultural; Editor-in-Chief M. M. SALEH; Proprietor D. M. SALEH; circ. 8,000 (also monthly supplement: *Economic Review*).

Al-Ittihad: P.O.B. 13189, Kuwait; monthly organ of the National Association of Kuwait Students.

Al Kuwaiti: Ahmadi; fortnightly journal of the Kuwait Oil Co. Ltd.; circ. 6,000; Arabic.

Al-Mujtama'a: P.O.B. 4850, Kuwait; f. 1969; Arabic weekly issued by the Social Reform Society.

Al Nahdha (*The Renaissance*): P.O.B. 695, International Airport Rd., Shuwaikh Industrial Area, Kuwait; f. 1967; weekly; social and political; Arabic; Editor YOUSSUF AL-MASSAEED; circ. 40,000.

Ar-Raid (*The Pioneer*): P.O.B. 11259, Cairo Rd., Kuwait; f. 1969; weekly; issued by Kuwaiti Teachers' Association; circ. 4,000.

Ar Ressaleh (*The Message*): P.O.B. 2490, Shuwaikh, Kuwait; f. 1961; weekly; Arabic; political, social and cultural; Editor JASSIM MUBARAK.

At-Tali'a: P.O.B. 1082, Mubarak al-Kabir St., Kuwait; f. 1962; weekly; Arabic; Editor SAMI AHMED AL-MUNAIS; circ. 10,000.

Al-Watan (*The Homeland*): P.O.B. 1774, Kuwait; f. 1964; political weekly circ. 1,000.

Al-Yaqza (*The Awakening*): P.O.B. 6000, Kuwait; f. 1966; political pan-Arab weekly; circ. 25,000.

Hayatuna (*Our Life*): P.O.B. 1708, Kuwait; f. 1968; medicine and hygiene; Arabic; fortnightly; published by Al-Awadi Press Corporation; Editor Dr. ABDUL RAHMAN AL-AWADI; circ. 6,000.

Journal of the Kuwait Medical Association: P.O.B. 1202, Kuwait; f. 1967; English; quarterly; published by Medical Asscn.; Editor Dr. ABDUL RAZZAK AL YUSUF; circ. 1,500.

Kuwait Chamber of Commerce and Industry Magazine: P.O.B. 775, Kuwait; f. 1959; monthly; circ. 5,000.

Kuwaiti Digest: Ahmadi; English; quarterly; journal of Kuwait Oil Co.; circ. 5,000.

Mejallat al-Kuwait (*Kuwait Magazine*): P.O.B. 193, Kuwait; news and literary articles; Arabic; fortnightly illustrated magazine; published by Ministry of Information.

Saut al-Khaleej (*Voice of the Gulf*): P.O.B. 659, Kuwait; f. 1962; political weekly; Editor BAQER KHRAIBITT; circ. 9,000.

Usrati (*My Family*): P.O.B. 2995, Kuwait; women's magazine; Arabic; fortnightly; Editor Mrs. GHANIMA AL-MARZOOG; circ. 10,000.

NEWS AGENCIES
FOREIGN BUREAUX

AFP: Sayyid Nabeel Shami, P.O.B. 193, Kuwait.

Hsinhua: P.O.B. 22168, nr. Dasman Palace, Kuwait.

Middle East News Agency: P.O.B. 1927, Fahd El-Salem St.

Reuters: Gulf St., Behbehani compound, Flat No. 21, P.O.B. 5616, Kuwait.

Tass: P.O.B. 1455, Kuwait.

RADIO AND TELEVISION
RADIO

Kuwait Broadcasting Station: P.O.B. 397, Kuwait; f. 1951; broadcasts in Arabic, English and Urdu; short wave (4 × 250 kW), medium wave (3 × 750 kW and 2 × 100 kW), and F.M. Stereo (5 kW) transmitters; Asst. Under-Sec. for Broadcasting Affairs ABDUL AZIZ MOHAMED JA'FFER; Asst. Under-Sec. for Engineering Affairs ABDUL-RAHMAN IBRAHIM AL-HUTY.

Number of radio receivers (1974): 210,000.

TELEVISION

Television of Kuwait, Ministry of Information: P.O.B. 621, Kuwait; f. 1961; broadcasts in Arabic; three transmitters are used, and broadcasts reach Saudi Arabia, southern Iraq, and other Gulf States; advertising is accepted, and colour television is planned; Asst. Under-Sec. of TV Affairs MUHAMMAD SANOUSSI; Programme Controller IBRAHIM AL-YUSUF.

Number of television receivers (1974): 130,000.

FINANCE

(cap.=capital; p.u.=paid up; dep.=deposits; m.=million; amounts in Kuwait Dinars)

BANKING
NATIONAL BANKS

Central Bank of Kuwait: P.O.B. 526, Kuwait; f. 1969; replaced Currency Board in administering currency and credit policies; cap. 2m., reserves 3m.; Governor HAMZAH ABBAS HUSSAIN; publ. *Annual Report*.

National Bank of Kuwait, S.A.K.: Abdullah Al-Salim St., P.O.B. 95, Kuwait; f. 1952; cap. and res. 24.9m., total assets 448.1m. (Dec. 1974); 29 brs.; Chair. YACOUB YOUSUF AL HAMAD; Chief Exec. and Gen. Man. C. D. FEARS.

Alahli Bank of Kuwait K.S.C.: Commercial Centre 5, P.O.B. 1387, Kuwait; 10 brs.; cap. p.u. 2.5m.; dep. 169.8m.; Chair. SAOUD AL ABDUL RAZZAK; Gen. Man. PHILIPPE DUJARDIN.

Bank of Kuwait and the Middle East K.S.C.: P.O.B. Safat 71, Kuwait; 49 per cent owned by the Government; began operations in Dec. 1971 when it took over former branches of the British Bank of the Middle East; cap. p.u. 2m.; Chair. FAHAD AL BAHAR; Gen. Man. L. J. McLEAY.

Commercial Bank of Kuwait, S.A.K.: Mubarak Al Kabir St., P.O.B. 2861, Kuwait; cap. and res. 8.6m., dep. 219m. (Dec. 1974), 21 brs.; Chair. ABDUL AZIZ AL AHMAD AL BAHAR; Gen. Man. H. J. KWANT.

Gulf Bank K.S.C.: P.O.B. Safat 3200, Abdullah Al-Salim. St., Kuwait; f. 1961; cap. p.u. 3,267m. (March 1975); 14 brs.; Chair. KHALID YUSIF AL-MUTAWA; Gen. Man. R. SINCLAIR.

Kuwait Real Estate Bank K.S.C.: P.O.B. 22822, Safat, Kuwait; Man. Dir. SAAD ALI AL-NAHED; Gen. Man. F. W. DIEPENBROCK.

Savings and Credit Bank: Arabian Gulf St., P.O.B. 1454, Kuwait; f. 1960; cap. p.u. 31m., dep. 29.1m. (March 1973); Chair. AHMED Z. AL-SERHAN; Dir.-Gen. YOUSEF M. SHAIJI.

United Bank of Kuwait: Head Office 3 Lombard St., London; f. 1966; Chair. ABDLATIF Y. AL-HAMAD.

INSURANCE
NATIONAL COMPANIES

Al Ahleia Insurance Co., S.A.K.: P.O.B. 1602, Ali Al-Salim St., Kuwait; f. 1962; covers all classes of insurance; cap. K.D. 1m.; Chair. MUHAMMAD Y. AL-NISF; Man. Dir. ABDULLA A. AL-RIFAI; Gen. Man. Dr. RAOUF H. MAKAR.

Gulf Insurance Co. K.S.C.: P.O.B. 1040, Kuwait; f. 1962; cap. 1m.; Gen. Man. ELIAS N. BEDEWI.

Kuwait Insurance Co.: Abdullah Al-Salim St., P.O.B. 769, Kuwait; f. 1960; cap. p.u. 1m.; Gen. Man. SHAKIB S. SHAKHSHIR; Deputy Gen. Man. FOUAD A. AL-BAHAR.

FOREIGN COMPANIES

Some 20 Arab and other foreign insurance companies are active in Kuwait.

OIL

Kuwait National Petroleum Co., K.S.C.: P.O.B. 70, Kuwait; f. 1960; 60 per cent state-owned; to be taken over by KOGEC; refining, exploring and marketing company; a large refinery at Shuaiba opened in May 1968; p.u. cap. 15m. (1973); Chair. YOUSEF IBRAHIM AL-GHANIM; publ. *Al-Wataniah* (monthly).

Kuwait Oil, Gas and Energy Corporation: Kuwait; f. 1974, reorganized 1975; will manage all aspects of the oil industry in Kuwait pending the formation of a new government body to assume full control of all oil affairs; under control of Minister of Oil.

Kuwait Oil Co.: Ahmadi, Kuwait; f. 1934; state-owned; 691 wells producing at end of December 1974; oil production in 1974 was 112.8 million long tons.

Kuwait Shell Petroleum Development Co. (*Royal Dutch Shell*): Fahad al-Salim St., Kuwait; has concession, signed January 1961, of 5,595 sq. km. offshore from Kuwait; operations suspended pending clarification of the offshore boundary disputes with Iraq, Iran and Saudi Arabia.

Kuwait Spanish Petroleum Co.: P.O.B. 20467, Kuwait; f. 1968; 51 per cent owned by Kuwait National Petroleum Co., 49 per cent by Hispanoil of Spain; holds concessions of 910,000 hectares (about half the land area of Kuwait) for a period of 35 years from 1968; drilling began in 1970.

American Independent Oil Co.: Main Office 50 Rockefeller Plaza, New York, N.Y.; Kuwait Office P.O.B. 69, Kuwait; shares with Getty Oil Co. (from Saudi Arabia) concessions in Kuwait/Saudi Arabia Partitioned Zone onshore; combined oil production in 1974 was 8,520,823 long tons.

Arabian Oil Co.: Head Office Tokyo; Kuwait Office P.O.B. 1641, Kuwait; Field Office Ras Al-Khafji, Kuwait Partitioned Zone; a Japanese company which has concessions offshore of the Partitioned Zone; there are 56 producing wells as well as four flow stations in operation; in 1974 crude oil production averaged 82,000 barrels per day.

TRADE AND INDUSTRY

CHAMBER OF COMMERCE

Kuwait Chamber of Commerce and Industry: P.O.B. 775, Chamber's Bldg., Ali Salem St., Kuwait State; f. 1959; 4,300 mems.; Pres. ABDUL AZIZ AL-SAGER; Vice-Pres. YOUSEF AL-FULEIJ and MOHAMAD A. AL-KHARAFI; Gen. Sec. HAYTHAM MALLUHI; publs. *Monthly Magazine* (circ. 5,000) and annual economic and administrative reports.

DEVELOPMENT

Kuwait Foreign Trading, Contracting and Investment Co.: P.O.B. 5665, Kuwait; f. 1965; overseas investment company; 80 per cent government holding; cap. and res. KD 27.9m., total assets KD 37.2m. (1973); Chair. and Man. Dir. ABDULWAHAB A. AL-TAMMAR.

Kuwait Fund for Arab Economic Development: Mubarak Al-Kabir, P.O.B. 2921, Kuwait; cap. KD 1,000m.; wholly Government owned; assists other Arab governments with development loans; Chair. ABDULREHMAN SALEM AL-ATEEQY; Dir. Gen. ABDLATIF Y. AL-HAMAD.

Kuwait Investment Co. S.A.K.: P.O.B. 1005, Kuwait; f. 1961; total resources KD 55m. (December 1974); investment banking institution owned 50 per cent by the Government and 50 per cent by Kuwaiti nationals; international banking and investment; Chair. and Man. Dir. BADER ALI AL-DAWOOD.

Kuwait National Industries Company: Kuwait; f. 1960; 51 per cent Government owned company with controlling interest in various construction enterprises.

Kuwait Planning Board: Kuwait City; f. 1962; supervises long-term development plans; through its Central Statistical Office publishes information on Kuwait's economic activity; Dir.-Gen. AHMED ALI AL DUAIJ.

Petrochemical Industries Co. K.S.C.: P.O.B. 1084, Kuwait; f. 1963; owns and operates a chemical fertilizer division for the manufacture of ammonia, urea, sulphuric acid, ammonium sulphate and chlorine plant.

Shuaiba Area Authority: P.O.B. 4690, Kuwait; f. 1964; an independent governmental authority to supervise and run the industrial area and Port of Shuaiba. It has powers and duties to direct and develop the area and its industries which include an oil refinery, cement factory, fishing plant, power stations and distillation plants, chemical fertilizer and petrochemical industries.

TRANSPORT

ROADS

Roads in the towns are metalled and the most important are dual carriageway. There are metalled roads to Ahmadi, Mina Al-Ahmadi and other centres of population in Kuwait, and to the Iraqi and Saudi Arabian borders. A four-lane trunk road to Damman in Saudi Arabia is under construction.

Automobile Association of Kuwait and the Gulf: P.O.B. Safat 2100, Kuwait; f. 1964; Pres. H. E. Sheikh NASSER ATHBI AL-SABAH.

Gulf Automobile Association: Al-Luheib Bldg. No. 2, behind Municipality Bldg., P.O.B. 827, Kuwait.

Kuwait Automobile and Touring Club: Airport Rd., Khaldiah, P.O.B. Safat 2100, Kuwait; f. 1956; Pres. H. E. Sheikh NASSER AL ATHBI AL SABAH.

Kuwait International Touring and Automobile Club: P.O.B. Safat 2100, Kuwait; f. 1966; Sec.-Gen. A. W. MONAYES.

Kuwait Transport Co. S.A.K.: Kuwait; provides internal bus service; regular service to Iran inaugurated December 1968.

SHIPPING

A modern port has been built at Shuwaikh, two miles west of Kuwait Town, which is capable of handling simultaneously up to eight large cargo ships and several smaller ships. Ships of British and other lines make regular calls.

A second port is under construction at Shuaiba to the south of Kuwait.

The oil port at Mina al-Ahmadi, 40 km. south of Kuwait Town is capable of handling the largest oil tankers afloat, and oil exports of over 2 million barrels per day.

Kuwait Oil Tanker Co. S.A.K.: P.O.B. 810, Kuwait; f. 1957; 1,500 shareholders; cap. KD 11.5m.; owns 6 vessels totalling 800,000 deadweight tons; tankers on order 1,344,000 deadweight tons; sole tanker agents for Mina al-Ahmadi and agents for other ports.

Kuwait Shipping Co. S.A.K.: P.O.B. Safat 3636, Kuwait; f. 1965; 76.9 per cent government owned; services to Europe, the Far East, East Africa and America; 47 vessels totalling 920,000 tons; fully paid cap. KD 18m.; Man. Dir. NOURI MUSAED AL SALEH; Gen. Man. D. H. TOD.

CIVIL AVIATION

Kuwait Airways Corporation: Al-Hilali St., P.O.B. 394, Kuwait; f. 1954; services to Abadan, Abu Dhabi, Aden, Athens, Baghdad, Bahrain, Beirut, Bombay, Cairo, Damascus, Delhi, Dahran, Doha, Dubai, Frankfurt, Geneva, Jeddah, Karachi, London, Muscat, Paris. Rome, Sana'a, Teheran, Prague; fleet of 5 Boeing 707; Chair. and Gen. Man. FAISAL SAOUD AL-FULAIJ; Man. Dir. JASSIM YOUSEF AL-MARZOOK; publs. *Al-Boraq* Magazine), *KAC News*.

Kuwait is also served by the following airlines: Air France, Air India, Alia, British Airways, CSA (Czechoslovakia), Democratic Yemen Airlines, EgyptAir, Gulf Aviation, Iranair, Iraq Airways, KLM, Lufthansa, MAS (Malaysian Air System), MEA, PIA (Pakistan), Saudia, Syrian Arab Airlines and Yemen Airways.

DEFENCE

The mainly British-equipped armed forces number over 10,000, and include 8,000 in the army and 2,000 in the air force. The navy consists of a coastguard force of 200 and there is a para-military force of 1,500. Defence expenditure amounted to KD 47 million in 1974.

EDUCATION

Within the last few years a comprehensive system of kindergarten, primary, intermediate and secondary schools has been built up, and compulsory education between the ages of 6 and 14, was introduced in 1966–67. However, many children spend two years before this in a kindergarten, and can go on to complete their general education at the age of 18 years. In 1973–74 more than 169,000 pupils attended 285 government schools staffed by over 13,000 teachers. The general policy of the Government is to provide free education to all Kuwaiti children from kindergarten stage to the University. Almost all Kuwaitis are Muslims and speak Arabic, so there is no language problem. Pupils are also provided, free of cost, with food, textbooks, clothing and medical treatment. In 1973–74 there were 37,670 pupils being taught by 1,811 teachers at private schools.

Children may spend two preliminary years at a kindergarten, and at the age of 6 commence their compulsory education at a primary school. This lasts four years, after which the pupils move on to an intermediate school where they stay for another four years. Secondary education, which is optional and lasts four more years, is given mainly in general schools, but there are also a technical college for boys, a technical school for boys and a religious institute (with intermediate and secondary stages). There are also eleven institutes for handicapped children. Adult education centres have 23,091 students.

Two-year courses at post-secondary teacher training institutes provide teachers for kindergartens and primary schools and the University provides for intermediate and secondary schools. The number of graduates is not enough to meet all the teaching staff requirements and so the Ministry of Education meets this shortage by recruiting teachers from other Arab countries.

Scholarships are granted to students to pursue courses which are not offered by Kuwait University, especially medicine, pharmacy and engineering. In 1972–73 there were 792 Kuwaiti scholarship students studying in Egypt, Lebanon, U.K. and the U.S.A. There were also 575 pupils from Arab, African and Asian states studying in Kuwait schools on Kuwait Government scholarships. Kuwait University also provides scholarships for a number of Arab, Asian and African students.

In 1973–74 the education budget totalled KD 54 million (this figure does not cover building new schools) representing 11.4 per cent of the total state budget.

UNIVERSITY

Kuwait University: P.O.B. 5969, Kuwait; f. 1966; 3,292 students (1973); 73 professors.

BIBLIOGRAPHY

BERREBY, JEAN-JACQUES. Le Golfe Persique; mer de légende-réservoir de pétrole (Payot, Paris 1959).

BUREAU OF FOREIGN COMMERCE. A Trade List of Kuwait Business Firms (Washington).

CENTRAL OFFICE OF INFORMATION. The Arab States of the Persian Gulf (London).

DANIELS, JOHN. Kuwait Journey (White Crescent Press, Luton, England, 1972).

DEPARTMENT OF SOCIAL AFFAIRS. Annual Report (Kuwait).

DICKSON, H. R. P. Kuwait and her Neighbours (Allen and Unwin, London, 1956).

EL MALLAKH, RAGAEI. Economic Development and Regional Co-operation: Kuwait (University of Chicago Press, 1968).

FREETH, Z. Kuwait was my Home (Allen and Unwin, London, 1956).

GOVERNMENT PRINTING PRESS. Education and Development in Kuwait (Kuwait).

Port of Kuwait Annual Report (Kuwait).

HAKIMA, A. A. The Rise and Development of Bahrein and Kuwait (Beirut, 1964).

HAY, Sir RUPERT. The Persian Gulf States (Middle East Institute, Washington, 1959).

INTERNATIONAL BANK FOR RECONSTRUCTION AND DEVELOPMENT. The Economic Development of Kuwait (Johns Hopkins Press, Baltimore, 1965).

KOCHWASSER, FRIEDRICH H. Kuwait. Geschichte, Weren und Funktion einer modernen Arabischen Staates (Tübingen, Eldmann, 1961).

KUWAIT OIL CO. LTD. The Story of Kuwait (London).

MARLOWE, JOHN. The Persian Gulf in the 20th Century (Cresset Press, London, 1962).

MEZERIK, AVRAHAM G. The Kuwait-Iraq Dispute, 1961 (New York, 1961).

SAMĪR SHAMMĀ. The Oil of Kuwait, Present and Future. Translated from Arabic. (Middle East Research and Publishing Centre, Beirut, 1959).

WILSON, Sir A. T. The Persian Gulf (Oxford University Press, 1928).

WINSTONE, H. V. F., and FREETH, ZAHRA. Kuwait: Prospect and Reality (Allen and Unwin, London, 1972).

Lebanon

PHYSICAL AND SOCIAL GEOGRAPHY

W. B. Fisher

The creation, after 1918, of the modern State of the Lebanon, first under French Mandatory rule and then as an independent territory, was designed to recognize the nationalist aspirations of a number of Christian groups that had lived for many centuries under Muslim rule along the coast of the eastern Mediterranean and in the hills immediately adjacent. At least as early as the sixteenth century A.D. there had been particularist Christian feeling that ultimately resulted in the grant of autonomy, though not independence, to Christians living in the territory of "Mount Lebanon", which geographically was the hill region immediately inland and extending some 20–30 miles north and south of Beirut. The territory of Mount Lebanon was later expanded, owing to French interest, into the much larger area of "Greater Lebanon" with frontiers running along the crest of the Anti-Lebanon mountains, and reaching the sea some miles north of Tripoli to form the boundary with Syria. In the south there is a frontier with Israel, running inland from the promontory of Ras an-Nakura to the head of the Jordan Valley. In drawing the frontiers so as to give a measure of geographical unity to the new State, which now occupies an area of 4,015 square miles, large non-Christian elements of Muslims and Druzes were included, so that at the present day the Christians of the Lebanon form only about half the total population. Many Christians have emigrated to North and South America, and the relatively higher birthrate of the non-Christian groups is a further factor in altering the balance of numbers.

PHYSICAL FEATURES

Structurally, the Lebanon consists of an enormous simple upfold of rocks that runs parallel to the coast. There is, first, a very narrow and broken flat coastal strip —hardly a true plain—then the land rises steeply to a series of imposing crests and ridges. The highest crest of all is Qurnet as-Sauda, just over 10,000 ft. high, lying southeast of Tripoli; Mount Sannin, north-east of Beirut, is over 9,000 ft. A few miles east of the summits there is a precipitous drop along a sharp line to a broad, troughlike valley, known as the Bekaa (Biqa), about 10 miles wide and some 70 to 80 miles long. The eastern side of the Bekaa is formed by the Anti-Lebanon mountains, which rise to 9,000 ft., and their southern continuation, the Hermon Range, of about the same height. The floor of the Bekaa Valley, though much below the level of the surrounding mountain ranges, lies in places at 3,000 ft. above sea-level, with a low divide in the region of Baalbek. Two rivers rise in the Bekaa— the Orontes, which flows northwards into Syria and the Gharb depression, ultimately reaching the Mediterranean through the Turkish territory of Antioch; and the River Litani (Leontes). This latter river flows southwards, and then, at a short distance from the Israeli frontier, makes a sudden bend westwards and plunges through the Lebanon mountains by a deep gorge. Plans are now partly complete to develop the waters of the Litani in this region for irrigation and hydro-electric power.

There exists in the Lebanon an unusual feature of geological structure which is not present in either of the adjacent regions of Syria and Israel. This is the occurrence of a layer of non-porous rocks within the upfold forming the Lebanon mountains; and, because of this layer, water is forced to the surface in considerable quantities, producing large springs at the unusually high level of 4,000 to 5,000 ft. Some of the springs have a flow of several thousand cu. ft. per second and emerge as small rivers; hence the western flanks of the Lebanon mountains, unlike those nearby in Syria and Israel, are relatively well watered and cultivation is possible up to a height of 4,000 or 5,000 ft.

With its great contrasts of relief, and the configuration of the main ranges, which lie across the path of the prevailing westerly winds, there is a wide variety in climatic conditions. The coastal lowlands are moderately hot in summer, and warm in winter, with complete absence of frost. But only 5 or 10 miles away in the hills there is a heavy winter snowfall, and the higher hills are covered from December to May, giving the unusual vista for the Middle East of snow-clad peaks. From this the name Lebanon (laban— Aramaic for "white") is said to originate. The Bekaa has a moderately cold winter with some frost and snow, and a distinctly hot summer, as it is shut off from the tempering effect of the sea.

Rainfall is on the whole abundant, but it decreases rapidly towards the east, so that the Bekaa and Anti-Lebanon are definitely drier than the west. On the coast, between 30 and 40 inches fall annually, with up to 50 inches in the mountains, but only 15 inches in the Bekaa. As almost all this annual total falls between October and April (there are three months of complete aridity each summer) rain is extremely heavy while it lasts, and storms of surprising intensity can occur. Beirut, for example, has slightly more rain than Manchester, but on half the number of rainy days. Another remarkable feature is the extremely high humidity of the coastal region during summer, when no rain falls. The sultry heat drives as many as can afford it to spend the summer in the hills.

ECONOMIC LIFE

The occurrence of high mountains near the sea, and the relatively abundant supplies of spring water have had a marked influence on economic development within the Lebanon. Owing to the successive levels of terrain, an unusually wide range of crops can be grown, from bananas and pineapples on the hot, damp coastlands, olives, vines and figs on the lowest foothills, cereals, apricots and peaches on the middle slopes, to apples and potatoes on the highest levels. These latter are the aristocrats of the Lebanese markets, since they are rarest, and, with the growing market in the oilfield areas of Arabia and the Persian Gulf, they fetch the highest price. Export of fruit is therefore and important item. Then, too, abundant natural water has led to the growth of pinewoods and evergreen groves, which add greatly to the already considerable scenic beauty of the western hill country. There has hence grown up an important tourist trade, centred in the small hill villages, some of which have casinos, luxury hotels, and cinemas. Main activity is during the summer months, when wealthy Middle Easteners and others arrive; but there is a smaller winter sports season, when ski-ing is carried on.

In addition, the geographical situation of the Lebanon, as a "façade" to the inland territories of Syria, Jordan, and even northern Iraq and southern Turkey, enables the

Lebanese ports to act as the commercial outlet for a very wide region. The importance of Beirut as a commercial centre is due in large part to the fact that the Lebanon is a free market. Over half of the volume of Lebanese trade is transit traffic, and the Lebanon handles most of the trade of Jordan. Her own exports are mostly agricultural products. Byblos claims to be the oldest port in the world; Tyre and Sidon were for long world-famous, and the latter is now reviving as the Mediterranean terminal of the Tapline (Trans-Arabian Pipe Line) from Saudi Arabia. Another ancient centre, Tripoli, is also a terminal of the IPC pipeline from Iraq. Beirut is now, however, the leading town of the country, and contains one-quarter of the total population. Though local resources are not in general very great (there are no minerals or important raw materials in the Lebanon) the city lives by commercial activity on a surprising scale, developed by the ingenuity and opportunism of its merchant class. The opening in 1951 of a commercial airport designed for jet airliners, before any such aircraft were actually in use in the world, is typical of the forward-looking attitude of many Lebanese.

Beirut has of recent years come to serve as a financial and holiday centre for the less attractive but oil-rich parts of the Middle East. Transfer of financial credit from the Middle East to Zürich, Paris, London, New York and Tokyo; a trade in gold and diamonds; and some connexion with the narcotic trade of the Middle East—all these give the city a very special function. In addition, the town provides discreet distraction for all types of visitor.

RACE AND LANGUAGE

It is difficult to summarize the racial affinities of the Lebanese people. The western lowlands have an extremely mixed population possibly describable only as "Levantine". Basically Mediterranean, there are many other elements, including remarkably fair individuals—Arabs with blonde hair and grey eyes, who are possibly descendants of the Crusaders. The remaining parts of the country show a more decided Armenoid tendency, with darker colouring, broader head-form, and more pronounced facial features. In addition, small refugee groups, who came to the more inaccessible mountain zones in order to escape persecution, often have a different racial ancestry, so that parts of the Lebanon form a mosaic of varying racial and cultural elements. Almost all Middle Eastern countries are represented racially within the Lebanon.

Arabic is current over the whole country, but owing to the high level of education (probably the highest in any Middle Eastern country) and to the considerable volume of temporary emigration, English, French and even Spanish are widely understood. French is probably still the leading European language (though English is tending to replace it) and some of the higher schools and one university teach basically in this language. In addition, Aramaic is used by some religious sects, but only for ritual—there are no Aramaic speaking villages as in Syria.

HISTORY

ANCIENT AND MEDIEVAL HISTORY

In the Ancient World the Lebanon was important for its pine, fir, and cedarwood, which neighbouring powers, poorly supplied with timber resources, coveted so much that during the long period of Egyptian, Assyrian, Persian, and Seleucid rule, the exploitation of the forests of the Lebanon was normally a royal privilege. The area was also mined for its iron and copper in the time of the Ptolemies and the Romans. Gradually the Lebanon came to have a distinct history of its own, for the mountainous character of the region prevented any complete subjugation to outside authority. It is probable that the Arab conquest of Syria did not include the "mountain", to which fled all those who, for one reason or another, were opposed to the Arab domination. The Caliph Mu'awiya (661–80) made some effort to assert a greater control, but the resistance of the native Aramaean Christians was reinforced by the arrival of the Mardaites from the fastnesses of the Taurus and the Amanus. These Christian nomads, led by Byzantine officers, made determined advances into the Lebanon, late in the seventh century, and seem to have united with the Maronite Christians who were later to become a Uniate Church of the Roman communion and to have a predominant role in the history of the Lebanon. The Caliph Abd al-Malik (685–705) paid tribute to Byzantium in return for a withdrawal of most of the Mardaite forces; but it is clear that the "mountain" had begun to assume its historic function of providing a sure refuge for racial and religious minorities.

The Lebanon maintained its Christian character until the ninth century when, amongst other elements, the Arab tribe of Tanukh established a principality in the region of al-Gharb, near Beirut, and acted as a counterpoise to the Maronites of the North Lebanon, and as a bulwark against Byzantine threats from the sea. Gradually, Islam and, more slowly still, the Arabic language penetrated the "mountain" where, however, Syriac lingered on in the Maronite districts until the seventeenth century (it is still spoken in three villages of the Anti-Lebanon). In the ninth and tenth centuries Muslim sects began to take root in the "mountain" as, for example, the Shi'i, known in the Lebanon under the name of Mitwali, and, in the eleventh century, the Druse faith, which won a firm hold in the South Lebanon.

The Crusaders established in this area the County of Tripolis and the lordships of Gibelet and Batron which enjoyed considerable support from the Christian population of the North Lebanon and were protected by a network of fortresses, the most famous of which is Hisn al-Akrad (Crac des Chevaliers). In the Mamluk period the rulers of the Lebanon continued to practise the art of political manoeuvring, thus maintaining for themselves a considerable degree of autonomy. The Tanukhid Amirs, after a long period in which they had played off the Crusaders against the Muslim amirates, had eventually taken the Mamluk side. In the North Lebanon the Maronites, under their bishop, maintained contact with the Italian Republics and also with the Roman Curia. Less fortunate were the Druzes and the Mitwali who, in the last years of the thirteenth century, took advantage of the Mamluk preoccupation with the Mongol threat from Persia and began a protracted revolt which led to widespread devastation in the Central Lebanon.

THE OTTOMAN PERIOD

In the sixteenth century the Turcoman family of Assaf and, after them, the Banu Saifa rose to prominence in the area from Beirut to the north of Tripoli; while in the south the Druze house of Ma'an supplanted the Tanukhid amirs.

After the conquest of 1516–17, the Ottoman Sultan Selim I had confirmed the amirs of the Lebanon in their privileges and had imposed only a small tribute; yet not infrequently there was open conflict with the Ottomans, as in 1584–5 when, after an attack on a convoy bearing the tribute from Egypt to Constantinople, the Sultan Murad III sent a punitive expedition to ravage the lands of the Banu Saifa and of the Druzes.

The power of the House of Ma'an now reached its zenith in the person of Fakhr ad-din II (1586–1635), who by every possible means—bribery, intrigue, foreign alliance, and open force—set out to establish an independent power over the whole of the Lebanon and parts of Palestine to the south. To this end he entered into close relations with the Grand Duke of Tuscany, negotiating in 1608 a commercial agreement which contained a secret military clause directed against the Sultan. In 1613 a naval and military expedition sent from the Porte compelled Fakhr ad-din to seek refuge with his Tuscan ally; but, returning in 1618, he rapidly restored his power and within a few years was virtual ruler from Aleppo to the borders of Egypt. The Sultan, heavily engaged in repressing revolt in Anatolia, and in waging a long struggle with Persia, could do no more than recognise the *fait accompli*. Fakhr ad-din now embarked on an ambitious programme of development for the Lebanon. He sought to equip a standing army with arms imported from Tuscany. Italian engineers and agricultural experts were employed to promote a better cultivation of the land and to increase the production of silk and olives. The Christian peasantry were encouraged to move from the North to the South Lebanon. Beirut and Sidon flourished as a result of the favour he showed to commerce; and religious missions from Europe—Capuchins, Jesuits, Carmelites—were allowed to settle throughout Syria, a development of great importance for France which strove to assert a "protectorate" over all the Catholic and other Christian elements in the Ottoman Empire. However, the ambitions of Fakhr ad-din were doomed to failure when by 1632 the Sultan Murad IV assumed effective control at Constantinople. The Pasha of Damascus, supported by a naval squadron, began a campaign to end the independent power of the Lebanon, and in 1635 Fakhr ad-din was executed at Constantinople.

In 1697, the Ma'an family became extinct, and was succeeded by the House of Shihab, which maintained its predominance until 1840. In the course of the eighteenth century, the Shihab Amirs gradually consolidated their position against the other factions of the "Mountain" and for a while recovered control of Beirut. While normally they took care to remain on good terms with the Turkish Pashas of Tripoli, Sidon and Damascus, the Pashas, for their part, strove to exercise an indirect control by fomenting the family rivalries and religious differences which always marked the course of Lebanese politics. With the advent of Bashir II (1788–1840) the House of Shihab attained the height of its influence. Not until the death of Ahmed Jazzar, Pasha of Acre (1804), was he free to develop his power, which he maintained by the traditional methods of playing off one Pasha against the other, and by bribing the officials of the Porte whenever it seemed expedient. In 1810 he helped the Ottomans to repel an invasion by the Wahhabi power of Arabia; but in 1831 he sided openly with Muhammad Ali of Egypt, when that ruler invaded Syria. Holding the Lebanon as the vassal of Egypt, he was compelled, however, to apply to the "Mountain" the unpopular policy imposed by Ibrahim Pasha, the son of Muhammad Ali, with the result that a revolt broke out, which, after the Egyptian withdrawal of 1840, led to his exile. The age of the Lebanese Amirs was now at an end, for the Ottomans assumed control of the "Mountain", appointing two Kaimakams to rule there, one Druze and the other Maronite, under the supervision of the Pashas of Sidon and Beirut.

The period of direct Ottoman rule saw the rapid growth, between the Druzes and the Maronites, of a mistrust already visible during the time of the Egyptian dominance, and now fostered by the Ottomans as the only means of maintaining their influence over the Lebanon. As a result of social and economic discontent, due to the slow disintegration of the old feudal system which had existed in the Lebanon since the Middle Ages, the Maronite peasantry revolted in 1858 and destroyed the feudal privileges of the Maronite aristocracy, thus clearing the way for the creation of a system of independent smallholdings. The Druze aristocracy, fearing the consequences of a similar discontent among their own Maronite peasantry, made a series of attacks on the Maronites of the North Lebanon, who, owing to their own dissensions, could offer no effective resistance. The dubious attitude of the Turkish Pashas, in the face of these massacres of 1860, led to French intervention, and in 1864 to the formation of an organic statute for the Lebanon, which was now to become an autonomous province under a non-Lebanese Ottoman Christian governor, appointed by the Sultan and approved by the Great Powers. He was to be aided by an elected administrative council and a locally recruited police force. The statute also abolished legal feudalism in the area, thus consolidating the position won by the Maronite peasantry in 1858. The period from 1864 to 1914 was one of increasing prosperity, especially among the Christian elements, who also played an important role in the revival of Arab literature and Arab national feeling during the last years of the nineteenth century.

THE FRENCH MANDATE

The privileged position of the Lebanon ended when the Turks entered the war of 1914–18; and by 1918 the coastal areas of the Lebanon were occupied by British and French forces. In September 1920 the French created the State of the Greater Lebanon which included not only the former autonomous province but also Tripoli, Sidon, Tyre and Beirut, some of which had in earlier times been under the control of the amirs of the Lebanon. The period from 1920–36 was for the Lebanon one of peaceful progress. A constitution was devised in 1926, which proved unworkable and was suspended in 1932, from which time the President of the Republic carried on the administration. He was, by convention, a Christian, while the Prime Minister was a Muslim, and both worked towards the achievement of a careful balance between the various religious communities of the new State. The Lebanon was not unaffected by the growth of the nationalist movement in Syria, some sections of which demanded the reduction of the Lebanon to its pre-war limits and even the abolition of its existence as a separate State. These demands found some support amongst the Sunni Muslims of the areas added to the Lebanon proper in 1920, with the result that the Syrian revolt of 1925–26 spread to parts of the southern Lebanon. The Maronite Christians, on the whole, supported the idea of a separate Lebanon, but were not united in their attitude towards France on the one hand, and the Arab States on the other. The Franco-Lebanese Treaty of 1936 differed little from that which France negotiated at the same time with Syria, the chief difference being that the military convention gave France wider military powers in the Lebanon than in Syria. A reformed constitution was promulgated in 1937; but the French refusal to ratify the treaty in 1938, and the advent of war prolonged a situation which, if outwardly calm, concealed a considerable discontent beneath the surface. In November 1941 the Free French Commander, General Catroux, formally proclaimed the Lebanon a sovereign independent State. In September

1943 a new Parliament which had a strong nationalist majority soon came into conflict with the French authorities over the transfer of the administrative services. When, in November 1943, the Lebanese Government insisted on passing legislation which removed from the constitution all provisions considered to be inconsistent with the independence of the Lebanon, the French Delegate-General arrested the President and suspended the constitution. The other Arab States, together with Great Britain and America, supported the Lebanese demands and in 1944 France began to transfer to Lebanese control all important public services, save for the *Troupes Spéciales*, i.e. local levies under French command, whose transfer the French authorities at first made conditional on the signing of a Franco-Lebanese Treaty. But in 1945 the *Troupes Spéciales* were handed over to the Lebanon without such conditions, and an agreement between France and the Lebanese Government in 1946 provided for the withdrawal of French troops.

MODERN HISTORY

Since 1946 the Lebanon has continued to view with great reserve all projects for a Greater Syria, or for the union of Syria and Iraq; and has striven to maintain a neutral role in those disputes which have rendered the unity of the Arab League largely illusory. Like the other Arab States, the Lebanon was at war with the new State of Israel from May 1948; but negotiated an armistice in March 1949. Just as in Syria the ill-success of the Arab arms had led eventually to the *coup d'état* of March 1949, so in the Lebanon the widespread disillusionment of Arab nationalist hopes prepared the ground for a conspiracy against the Government. This conspiracy was easily suppressed in June 1949 and its leader, Antun Sa'ade, was executed in July.

In internal affairs, the Lebanese Government had to face considerable economic and financial difficulties soon after the end of the 1939-45 war. When, in January 1948, France devalued the franc (to which both the Lebanese and the Syrian currencies were linked) the Lebanon, economically weaker than Syria, felt obliged to sign a new agreement with France (February 1948). Syria refused to do so and began a long and complicated dispute with the Lebanon over the precise nature of the economic and financial arrangements which were to exist between the two States. In March 1950 the Lebanese Government refused a Syrian demand for full economic and financial union between Syria and the Lebanon. The severance of economic relations which now ensued did not end until the signing, in February 1952, of an agreement which arranged for the division of royalties due from oil companies, and for the status, for customs purposes, of agricultural and industrial products passing between the two states.

In recent years American influence has increased in the Lebanon as in the other states of the Middle East and the Lebanon now receives considerable revenues from the oil companies whose pipe-lines bring the oil of Iraq and Saudi Arabia through Lebanese territory. Negotiations with the oil companies, in the spring of 1952, foreshadowed an increase in such revenues.

In September 1952 the Lebanon had to face a severe crisis in her internal affairs. Political and economic unrest brought about the fall of the Lebanese Government and the resignation of President al-Khuri, who had held office since 1943. Charges of corruption were made against the President. During his long tenure of power he had indeed used all the arts of political influence and manoeuvre in order to impose a real degree of unity on a state where the divergent interests of Maronites, Sunni and Shi'i Muslims, Druzes, and other religious communities underlined the need for firm and coherent rule.

To an even greater degree, however, the crisis was due to causes of an economic order. The Lebanon had attained its independence in the period of war-time prosperity. The end of the war meant a progressive diminution of foreign expenditure in the Lebanon, e.g., by the French and British forces stationed there, and the gradual disappearance of war shortages which had favoured Lebanese trade. The devaluation of the French franc, the unsuccessful war with Israel, and above all the economic rupture with Syria gave rise to further difficulties. The break with Syria hit the Lebanon hard, for Syria was the chief provider of agricultural goods to the Lebanon and the chief customer for Lebanese industrial products. The effect of these developments was the more serious in that the Lebanon has a permanent adverse balance of trade, her annual deficit being largely covered by the revenues accruing to her from a wide variety of financial, commercial and transit services and by royalties paid to her by the oil companies. By 1952 there was much discontent arising from the high cost of living and from considerable unemployment. It was in fact a loose coalition of all the elements of opposition, both political and economic which brought about the fall of the al-Khuri régime.

CONSTITUTIONAL REFORM

As a result of the crisis Camille Chamoun became the new President of the Republic. The new administration, with the Amir Khalid Chehab as Prime Minister, bound itself to introduce reforms, including changes in the electoral laws, the grant of the vote to women, revision of the Press laws and the reorganization of justice. The elections held in July 1953 led to the formation of a Chamber of Deputies, 44 in number and divided as follows: 13 Maronites, 9 Sunni Muslims, 8 Shi'i Muslims, 5 Orthodox Christians, 3 Greek Catholics, 3 Druzes, 2 Orthodox Armenians and one member for other minorities.

Negotiations between Syria and the Lebanon over common economic problems continued throughout these years. The agreement of February 1952 had been prolonged for a period of one year. This agreement was renewed for a further six months in February 1953 and again for a similar period in August 1953.

The elections held in the Lebanon during the summer of 1953 were carried out under the provisions of the electoral law of November 1952. Since the foundation of the republic, all seats in the Chamber of Deputies had been distributed among the various religious communities in proportion to their numerical strength. Parliament was thus an institution reflecting in itself the religious and social structure of the state and capable of harmonious function, provided that the electoral system which maintained a delicate balance between the communities suffered no violent and prejudicial change. At the same time, it contained a strong "feudal" element—the tribal and religious leaders who, with their trusted retainers, formed powerful groups within the Parliament and were often criticised as being "anti-national" in their aims and methods. To end or at least weaken this "feudalization" of Lebanese political life, without, however, impairing the vital equilibrium between the Muslim and Christian communities, had long been the purpose of those who advocated a reasonable and well-considered policy of reform. The law of 1952 created 33 electoral districts (during the previous life of the republic the number had been, as a rule, five) and allotted to eleven of them two seats, and to the remainder one seat each. Of the sum-total of 44 seats the Maronites were now to receive 13, the Sunni Muslims 9, the Shi'i Muslims 8, the Greek Orthodox Christians 5, the Druzes 3, the Greek Catholics 3, the Armenian Catholics 2 and the other confessions (Protestant, Jewish, Nestorian, etc.) 1 seat.

The election of 1953 did in fact bring defeat to some of the Shi'i lords of the south. It would seem, however, that something more than electoral reform will be needed, if the "feudal" aspects of the present régime are to be eliminated. In the course of time such a change might perhaps come about through the growth of well-organized political parties which cut across confessional lines. None the less it remains an open question whether a government more "national" in character would succeed in preserving Lebanese unity and concord as well as the old order, grounded in the traditions of the past, has so far been able to do.

FOREIGN RELATIONS 1953-56

In the period 1953–56 financial and economic relations with Syria remained on a provisional basis much the same as that which had prevailed in the years 1950–53, earlier short-term arrangements being renewed from time to time, as need arose. Discussions with Syria in November 1953 over problems of currency, loan policy, banks and exchange difficulties made no effective progress. The Lebanese Government was more successful, however, in its efforts to promote internal development. It was announced in August 1955 that the International Bank had granted to the Lebanon a loan of 27 million dollars for the Litani river scheme which, when completed, was expected to more than double the electric power available within the republic and also to irrigate a large acreage in the coastal region. The Lebanon signed a number of commercial treaties at this time, which bore witness to the growing penetration of Soviet influence into the Arab lands: with Russia itself in April 1954, with Eastern Germany in November 1955, with Communist China in December 1955 and with Poland in January 1956.

At the Asian-African conference held at Bandung in April 1955 the Lebanese delegates expressed themselves in terms unfavourable to Communism. Since that time the Beirut government has not allowed its relations with Russia and her allies to pass beyond the limits of normal commercial intercourse. In regard to the Baghdad Pact, concluded between Iraq and the Turkish Republic in February 1955, the Lebanon adopted a neutral attitude. When, in March 1955, Egypt, supported by Saudi Arabia and (although with some hesitation) by Syria, attempted to form an alliance of Arab states from which Iraq was to be excluded, the Lebanese Government declined to enter into the proposed scheme, but also assured Cairo that it did not intend to join the Baghdad Pact. Its efforts were in fact directed, and not unsuccessfully, towards allaying, at least for the immediate future, the sharp tension then existing between Egypt and Iraq. Moreover, as the visit of President Chamoun to Ankara at the end of March, and the return visit of President Bayar to Beirut in June revealed, the Lebanon, while anxious not to compromise the cause of Arab unity, saw no reason to avoid diplomatic endeavours which might bring about more amicable relations between the Turkish Republic and the Arab world.

THE EISENHOWER DOCTRINE

A state of emergency was declared in the Lebanon during the Sinai-Suez crisis at the end of October 1956. The Chamber of Deputies announced its support of Egypt, but the Lebanon did not break off diplomatic relations with Great Britain and France. In November there were disturbances, however, at Tripoli and Beirut against the attitude of the Government. Reports issued at this time intimated that the Egyptian military attaché at Beirut had been implicated in the recent disorders. The "Eisenhower Doctrine", a new programme, made known in January 1957, of financial, economic and military aid by the United States to those countries of the Middle East which were prepared to accept it, evoked a favourable response in Lebanese official circles. The Foreign Minister of the Lebanon declared that the government was willing to collaborate closely with the U.S.A. in the implementation of the programme. During the visit to Beirut in March of Mr. Richards, special adviser to President Eisenhower on Middle Eastern affairs, it was announced that the Lebanon would co-operate with the United States in the task of opposing the growth of Communist influence in the area and would receive, under the new programme, assistance to the amount of some 20 million dollars. The United States was also to help in the strengthening of the Lebanese armed forces. Some of the political groups in the Lebanon protested against this pro-Western alignment, asserting that it could not fail to isolate the Lebanon from the other Arab states and thus impair Arab solidarity. None the less, in April, the government obtained from the Chamber of Deputies a vote of confidence in its policies.

The problem of electoral reform had been under consideration in the Lebanon in the course of 1956. The main proposal now to be given effect was that the number of seats in the Chamber of Deputies should be raised from 44 to 66. As election time drew near in the summer of 1957, riots occurred in Beirut, the government being compelled to call out troops for the maintenance of order. According to reports current at this time more than one hundred Communists were arrested for their share in the disturbances. The tense electoral campaign of June 1957 was fought out between two blocs, the one supporting the government, the other opposing it in the form of a United National Front. When the election results were made known, it became clear that the government had won a marked triumph. A first provisional estimate suggested that it might count on the adherence of some three-quarters of the deputies in the new Chamber. Of the sum-total of 66 seats the Maronites now received 20, the Sunni Muslims 14, the Shi'i Muslims 12, the Greek Orthodox Christians 7, the Druzes 4, the Greek Catholics 4, the Orthodox Armenians 3, the Armenian Catholics 1 and the other religious minorities (Protestants, Jews, etc.) also 1 seat.

It was announced in July 1957 that the Lebanon would receive from the United States, under the Eisenhower Doctrine, economic and military aid to the value of approximately 15 million dollars in the course of the fiscal year 1958. Military equipment granted under the Doctrine had in fact begun to reach Beirut in June 1957. The Lebanese Government reiterated in August 1957 its firm desire to continue co-operation with the United States. In October, the King of Saudi Arabia and, in December, the Shah of Iran, visited Beirut, communiqués being issued, of which the first pledged Saudi Arabia and the Lebanon to support of the Arab cause, while the second gave assurances that both Iran and the Lebanon would work for peace in the Middle East.

There had been sharp disturbances in the Lebanon at the time of the elections held in June 1957. It became clear that unrest, especially amongst those elements of the population which opposed the pro-Western policies of the Lebanese Government and favoured an alignment with Egypt and Syria, was in no wise dead, when further incidents (bomb outrages, assassinations) occurred in November 1957. The government, in its desire to halt these subversive activities, now imposed a close control over all Palestine refugees in the Lebanon. Indeed, after renewed outbreaks of violence in December, the northern area of the Lebanon was declared to be a military sector. It was also announced in January 1958 that a national guard would be formed for the protection of important installations.

The Lebanese Government stated in March 1958 that it would not join the United Arab Republic (Egypt and Syria), the Arab Federation (Iraq and Jordan) or indeed any association which might limit its own independence and sovereignty. Large sections of the Muslim population, both in the north (at Tripoli) and in the south (at Tyre and Sidon), were inclined to be pro-Arab rather than pro-Lebanese in sentiment—a mood greatly stimulated by the emergence of the new United Arab Republic and by the propaganda emitted from Cairo and Damascus for the return to Syria of those predominantly Muslim areas which had been joined to the old Lebanon in the time of the French Mandate. There was conflict, too, between those who, although reluctant to see the Lebanon lose its separate political existence, were none the less strongly opposed to the pro-Western attitude of the Lebanese Government and those who, fearing the possible absorption of the Lebanon into the framework of a larger Arab state, felt themselves bound to support fully the policies of the Beirut régime. The danger was real that these complex tensions might explode in the form of a "confessional" conflict between Muslims and Christians, in which, if not the continued independence, then at least the entire political orientation of the Lebanon would be at stake.

THE CRISIS OF 1958

A reorganization of the government, carried out in March 1958 and designed to remove certain members who were critical of the pro-Western policies of the Lebanon and favoured closer co-operation with the United Arab Republic, brought no relief to the grave situation then developing. Serious disturbances, originating in Tripoli and the northern areas adjacent to the Syrian border, broke out in the second week of May and spread rapidly to Beirut and also to Tyre and Sidon in the southern Lebanon. The Druze population in the south-east was involved, too, in the disorders, being sharply divided into pro- and anti-government factions. Hostile demonstrations led to the destruction of the United States Information Service centres at Tripoli and Beirut. At the request of the Lebanese Government, the United States agreed to dispatch in all haste supplies of arms and police equipment and decided at the same time to reinforce the American 6th Fleet stationed in the Mediterranean. The U.S.S.R. now accused the United States of interference in Lebanese affairs and declared that Western intervention might have grave consequences. The Lebanese Government itself charged the United Arab Republic with interference in its internal affairs and appealed for redress to the Arab League which, meeting at Benghazi in June, failed to agree on a course of action. The problem was now brought before the United Nations which resolved to send an Observer Corps to the Lebanon. The Secretary General of U.N.O., Dr. Hammarskjöld, also visited the Middle East, conferring both with leaders in the Lebanon and with President Nasser at Cairo.

The Lebanese Government was now, in fact, confronted with a widespread insurrection, in which the Muslim elements in the population were ranged against the Christian elements. The forces opposed to the existing régime controlled parts of Beirut, Tripoli and Sidon, as well as large areas in the north and the south of the Lebanon. Attempts to negotiate a settlement led to no favourable result. The Prime Minister, Sami al-Sulh, gave an assurance that President Chamoun did not intend to ask for a constitutional amendment which would enable him to seek re-election to his office in September 1958, the date when his present tenure of it was due to end. To this assurance the leaders of the insurrection replied with a firm demand for the immediate resignation of the President, who made it clear, however, that he would not relinquish his office until September.

On July 14th—the date of the *coup d'état* which led to a change of régime in Iraq—President Chamoun requested the United States to send American troops into the Lebanon with a view to the maintenance of security and the preservation of Lebanese independence. By July 20th, some 10,000 men of the United States forces were stationed in and around Beirut. Meanwhile, Mr. Robert Murphy of the American State Department had come to the Lebanon with the aim of discussing the situation with leaders of both sides in the conflict. The United States also made it known that action on the part of forces under the control on the United Arab Republic against American troops in the Lebanon might lead to most serious consequences. At this juncture, the U.S.S.R. and the Chinese People's Republic made strong protests against the American intervention and asked for the prompt withdrawal of the United States forces landed in the Lebanon. In August 1958, the General Assembly of the United Nations met to discuss the problem. On August 18th, the United States gave a written undertaking to withdraw its troops, either at the request of the Lebanese Government, or in the event that the United Nations took appropriate measures to ensure the integrity and peace of the country. The General Assembly thereupon adopted a resolution, framed by its Arab members, which provided for the evacuation of American troops under the auspices of the United Nations and of the Arab League.

PRESIDENT CHEHAB, 1958-64

Meanwhile, the Lebanese Chamber of Deputies had, on July 31st, elected as the new President of State General Fuad Chehab, the Commander-in-Chief of the Lebanese Army—a choice supported by members from both sides involved in the internal conflict. He assumed office on September 23rd, in succession to President Chamoun and at once invited Rashid Karami, the leader of the insurgents at Tripoli, to become Prime Minister. An agreement was made on September 27th to the effect that the United States forces were to leave the Lebanon by the end of October.

In October 1959 the Lebanese Cabinet was increased from four to eight members, so that greater representation might be given to the various political groups. The Chamber of Deputies approved in April 1960 an Electoral Reform Bill, which imposed for the first time the principle of the secret ballot in Lebanese elections and also enlarged the Chamber itself from 66 to 99 deputies—a total figure that maintained the existing ratio (laid down in 1943) of six Christian to every five Muslim (including Druze) deputies in the Chamber. The Chamber was dissolved by the President of the Lebanon on May 5th, 1960, the government of Mr. Rashid Karami resigning nine days later. A general election was then held in four separate stages on June 12th, 19th and 26th and July 3rd, 1960.

The election took place in an atmosphere of complete calm, strict security measures being enforced throughout the various stages of the electoral process. In the new Chamber of Deputies there were 30 Maronite Christians, 20 Sunni Muslims, 19 Shi'i Muslims, 11 Greek Orthodox Christians, 6 Greek Catholics, 6 Druzes, 4 Armenian Orthodox Christians, 1 Armenian Catholic, 1 Protestant and 1 member representing other elements. A large number of the "rebel" personalities prominent in the events of 1958 and hitherto not seated in the Chamber were now returned as members. Of the Deputies who had formed the previous Chamber 31 (out of 66) retained their seats. Some of the traditional "feudal" notabilities also recovered their places in the Chamber.

President Chehab announced on July 20th, 1960, that he intended to resign his office. He was persuaded, however, to reverse his decision. A new government, under the leadership of Mr. Saeb Salam, took the oath of office on August 2nd, 1960. The Cabinet, which included several personalities active on one side or the other in the troubles of 1958, was prompt to reaffirm the traditional policies of non-expropriation, of minimal government intervention in private enterprise, of encouragement for private investment both foreign and domestic, and of currency convertibility. Economic trends during 1960 revealed that the Lebanon had recovered almost completely from the effect of the disturbances in 1958.

CABINET REFORM

It had come to be felt, since August 1960, that the Lebanese Cabinet, 18 members strong, was too large for the maintenance of an efficient administration. Internal dissension, having weakened the Cabinet for some time past, brought about a crisis leading to the resignation of six ministers on May 9–10th, 1961. On May 22nd, the Prime Minister established a new Cabinet consisting of eight ministers only. Mr. Salam, as the result of a dispute with some members of his government, notable amongst them being Mr. Jumblatt, the Druze leader, who was Minister of Works and Planning, resigned his office on October 24th, 1961. Mr. Rashid Karami, a former Prime Minister, formed a new government on October 31st, 1961.

Military elements, acting in conjunction with civilians described as supporters of the extremist National Social Party, made an unsuccessful attempt, on December 31st, 1961, to overthrow the Lebanese government. The National Social Party was in fact the old Parti Populaire Syrien founded in the 1930s by Antoine Saadé with the aim of uniting several Arab States into a Greater Syria. Its present leader, Dr. Abdallah Saadé, was now arrested and the party itself dissolved by the Lebanese government on January 1st, 1962. The rebels, failing in their purpose, fled towards the Metn region in the hope of finding assistance there, the National Social Party having enjoyed considerable favour in that area. The Lebanese government took firm action against all the elements suspected of implication in the revolt. Military operations continued throughout the first days of January 1962. By January 10th, the rebellion was over save for a few remnants of rebel resistance still to be found in the Akkar and Hermel mountains.

EXTERNAL AGREEMENTS

In February 1962 the Lebanese Government entered into an agreement with the Tunisian Government envisaging co-operation between the two states in the fields of educational, cultural and technical assistance. During the remainder of 1962 the Lebanon entered into various agreements with the Egyptian half of the United Arab Republic, Niger, Cameroon, Guinea and Senegal. These agreements were mainly on technical and cultural co-operation.

The dispute, now six years old, over payments connected with the pipelines passing oil through the Lebanon to the Mediterranean coast was at last brought to an end. At Beirut in August 1962 a settlement was made between the Lebanese Government and the Trans-Arabian Pipeline Company (Tapline), an American organization. In return for facilities relating to the transit of oil, to the loading of the oil and to the security of the pipelines the Lebanon was to receive about $4,500,000 (as against $1,250,000 under earlier agreements). The new and higher rate of payment included a sum of $500,000 in lieu of supplies of oil at reduced prices which Tapline had undertaken to make available to the national oil refineries in Syria and Jordan—the Lebanon itself does not possess such oil refineries. Tapline also promised to pay the sum of $12,500,000 in

settlement of all past claims made by the Lebanese Government. Of this latter amount $865,000, together with a portion of the new payments to be made to the Lebanon in respect of facilities for the loading of oil would be withheld until the full implications of a former agreement between the Lebanon and Syria had been made clear, such agreement having envisaged that whatever advantage the Lebanon might obtain in its relations with Tapline should be shared with Syria.

During the course of 1963 the government negotiated new economic and commercial agreements with Poland (April), the German Federal Republic (May), Sweden (October), and the U.S.S.R. (November). Syria and Lebanon agreed in September to ease restrictions in travel, employment, trade and finance between their respective territories and also reached an understanding in regard to their protracted dispute over the sharing of oil-transit dues. A brief period of sharp tension ensued, however, during the second half of October, as the result of a frontier clash between Syrian and Lebanese troops, which led to the death of several Lebanese soldiers. Syrian and Lebanese delegations met in January, 1964, to discuss questions relating to their common frontier and in particular the delimitation of certain areas hitherto not clearly demarcated.

On February 19th, 1964, the Cabinet led by Rashid Karami (which had held office for the last two years) resigned, after President Chehab had signed a decree dissolving the Chamber of Deputies (elected in 1960) and ordering elections to be held on four successive Sundays from April 5th, 1964 to May 3rd, 1964. A caretaker cabinet was appointed to supervise the elections for the new Chamber of Deputies.

PRESIDENT HÉLOU

General Chehab, whose six-year term of office as President of the Republic was due to end in September 1964, rejected all appeals that he should submit himself as a candidate for a second time. Even when the Chamber of Deputies passed a motion in favour of an amendment to the Constitution which would enable him to stand for a further term of office, General Chehab persisted (June 3rd, 1964) in his refusal. On August 18th, 1964, M. Charles Hélou, Minister of Education in the caretaker administration, succeeded General Chehab as President. M. Hélou pledged himself to follow the policies and reforms introduced under General Chehab.

On September 25th, 1964, Hussein Oweini, the Head of the caretaker Cabinet in office since February of that year, formed an administration at the request of President Helou. The new administration aroused dissatisfaction, however, in the Chamber of Deputies, since, deriving from the Cabinet appointed originally to act as a caretaker during the period of the 1964 elections, it was in fact composed wholly of non-members of the Chamber. Having resigned on November 13th, 1964, Oweini now, on November 18th, 1964, gathered together a new Cabinet which, save for himself and the Foreign Minister, consisted of members drawn from the Chamber of Deputies and reflected in itself all the main trends of opinion within the Chamber.

FOREIGN RELATIONS

On July 20th, 1965, the Prime Minister, Mr. Hussein Oweini, resigned. There had been much debate in the Chamber of Deputies about a proposed agreement to guarantee private American investment in the Lebanon against expropriation, war or revolution—an agreement construed in some political circles as giving to the United States a possible excuse for intervention, at need, in Lebanese affairs. Acrid discussion had also occurred in the

Chamber over bills intended to bring about reforms in the judicial system and in the civil service. On July 26th, Rashid Karami became the new Prime Minister, with nine Cabinet Ministers to assist him, all chosen from outside the Chambers of Deputies.

There was friction during the first months of 1965 between Federal Germany and the Arab States because of the decision by Bonn to enter into formal diplomatic relations with Israel. Anti-German demonstrations occurred at Tripoli and Beirut and on May 13th, 1965 the Lebanon broke off diplomatic relations with Federal Germany. In May 1965 Lebanon signed an agreement on trade and technical co-operation with the European Economic Community (EEC). There was some friction between Israel and the Lebanon over border incidents during the summer and autumn of 1965. Members of the Palestinian guerrilla organization, al-Fatah, raided into Israel, provoking Israeli reprisals against the Lebanese village of Noule.

FINANCIAL CRISIS

Rashid Karami modified his cabinet in December 1965 and January 1966, these changes arising from difficulties which hindered the full implementation of an administrative and judicial reform programme, one of the main advocates of which was President Hélou. A number of senior judges had to accept a forced retirement in December 1965, and a similar fate overtook several ambassadors and senior diplomats in January 1966. By the end of March an estimated 150 officials including 100 civil servants had been compelled to withdraw from public life. This sustained attempt to curb corruption and the abuse of office in government circles and to ensure efficient and honest administration inevitably caused considerable tension. There was strong pressure in the Chamber of Deputies for a return to a cabinet chosen mainly from the Chamber itself. This and other difficulties obliged Karami to offer his resignation to President Hélou who appointed Dr. Abdallah al-Yafi as the new Premier.

Dr. al-Yafi assembled a ten-man Cabinet drawn entirely from the Chamber of Deputies with the exception of himself and M. Philippe Takla, the new Foreign Minister. The constitution of the cabinet represented a balance between the various religious interests and, from the point of view of politics, between the left-wing and right-wing elements in the Chamber of Deputies.

In October 1966 the Intra Bank of the Lebanon was compelled to close its doors because of a run of withdrawals amounting to more than £11 million in the preceding month. The Lebanese Cabinet, on October 16th, met to discuss methods of ensuring that the banks of the Lebanon had available adequate supplies of liquid cash. It also ordered all Lebanese banks to discontinue operations for a period of three days. Later in the same month the Cabinet decided to place before Parliament a bill seeking special powers which would enable the government to take measures of safeguarding of the interests of small depositors at the Intra Bank. A crisis of confidence was a serious affair for a state where banking activities are of the highest importance. The bill presented to the Parliament envisaged the establishment of an insurance company, jointly owned by the government and the banks, to guarantee small deposits. A special commission would supervise the activities of the banks in the Lebanon. A further result of that financial crisis was that the Government resolved to discourage the creation of new commercial banks, foreign or Lebanese, for a period of five years. Hitherto there had been an almost complete freedom to establish new banks in the Lebanon and there had been a large expansion of the banking system based on the flow into the Lebanon of vast oil revenues from Saudi Arabia and from the states of the Persian Gulf.

On December 2nd the Prime Minister of the Lebanon, Dr. Abdullah al-Yafi, offered the resignation of his government to President Hélou. Mr. Rashid Karami formed a new administration on December 7th, 1966. It was composed of men drawn from outside Parliament, six of whom held ministerial posts for the first time.

In April 1967 the Lebanon obtained an increase of more than 50 per cent in the royalties which it received from the Iraq Petroleum Company for the transit and loading of Iraq oil.

In June 1967 the Lebanese Government aligned itself with the Arab states then engaged in war against Israel. On June 8th the Government asked the Ambassadors of Britain and the U.S.A. to leave the Lebanon. Pro-Egyptian demonstrations at Beirut in June caused some damage to British and American properties there. Some trouble was also reported from Tripoli, where a West German cultural centre was subjected to attack. However, the months following the war witnessed a gradual easing of the tensions arising out of the conflict, and in September 1967 the Lebanese Cabinet agreed to reinstate its ambassadors in Washington and London.

POLITICAL INSTABILITY

Rashid Karami's Cabinet resigned from office in February 1968. President Hélou then asked Dr. Abdallah al-Yafi to form an interim administration, whose main task was to be the preparation and conduct of the general election in March 1968. The two most successful parties elected in the Chamber of Deputies were the Maronite-dominated Triple Alliance, of a right-wing complexion, and the Democratic Block aligned further to the left. However, Dr. al-Yafi's interim administration remained in office until October, when it was forced to resign, owing to bitter rivalry between the two main political groups, the "Chamounists" and the "Chehabists" (both named after former Presidents), disputes over sectional representation in the Cabinet, and the Government's inability to command a majority in the Chamber of Deputies. After a week of confusion, during which the President, Charles Hélou, offered his own resignation, a new four-man government was announced on October 20th, still headed by Dr. al-Yafi. The political situation remained fluid; in November the new ministry offered to resign, apparently over student unrest, but withdrew the offer the following day.

THE GUERRILLAS AND ISRAEL

May 1968 had seen the first clash between Lebanese and Israeli forces on the border for over two years. But as the activities of the Palestinian guerrillas increased, so the Lebanon became more and more the scapegoat for Israel's grievances against the Palestinians. On December 26th an Israeli airliner was machine-gunned by Arab guerrillas at Athens airport, causing two casualties (one fatal). Two days later Israeli commandos raided Beirut airport and destroyed thirteen aircraft, all belonging to Lebanese lines, without loss of life. Israel said the raid should be seen as a reprisal for the Athens attack, a warning to the Arab world not to make any repetition of it, and a further warning to the Lebanon to police the activities of the fedayeen movement in the country more effectively. The financial cost to the Lebanon was relatively small as most were insured abroad. The major after-effects of the raid were, firstly, the widespread criticism it attracted even from countries normally favourable to Israel. The Lebanon was seen as a country which had taken little active part in the campaign against Israel, while the *fedayeen* within it were only enjoying the freedom available to them in Lebanon's open, tolerant society. The UN Security Council unanimously condemned Israel for the raid. The second effect was the fall of the Government on January 7th, 1969, its alleged lack of preparedness for Israeli aggression being the final blow to bring down a weak administration. After much political manoeuvring, a new ministry was formed on January 20th headed by Mr. Rashid Karami, Prime Minister for the seventh time.

This government was immediately confronted with the basic problems underlying the Lebanese situation. Foremost amongst these is the Christian-Muslim balance; in theory both religions are equally represented in the Lebanon, but no census has been held since 1939 mainly because the authorities fear that the balance has shifted to a 60 per cent Muslim predominance, which would seriously affect the political situation. The Christian community has a disproportionate share of the wealth and important positions, and is the mainstay of the modest armed forces; it is generally conservative by Arab standards and takes a moderate position on the Israel question. The less privileged Arab majority is more in favour of both domestic reform (Lebanon has, for example, only the beginnings of a welfare state) and of a more militant position towards Israel. Early in 1969 numbers of Syrian guerrillas entered the country and apparently spent as much time in action against the Lebanese army as against Israel. Unrest also appeared amongst the 260,000 Palestinian refugees in the Sidon camp; part of the frontier with Syria was eventually closed. Numerous strikes and demonstrations continued. The Karami government felt unable to maintain the necessary coalition from the two communities and their various factions and resigned on April 25th, but it continued to function as a caretaker administration as no stronger government could be formed.

In the late summer of 1969 a number of guerrilla groups were reported to have moved to new bases better sited for attacks on Israel, which continued to raid these bases in reprisal; the combination of these factors created some friction between the guerrillas and the Lebanese army. In October the army apparently attacked some of these camps in an attempt to restrict or direct their activities. This triggered off a crisis that continued through the second half of October and threatened to develop into a full-scale civil war. The caretaker government resigned, claiming that it had not authorized the army's actions, and the President and the armed forces administered the country directly. Radical elements and guerrillas took over Tripoli, the second largest city, for several days, and most of the Palestinian refugee camps became fully converted into military training and equipment centres. Militant support for the guerrillas was voiced throughout the Arab world, and there were threats of military intervention by Syria and Iraq. Despite the tension, no extensive fighting occurred and there were few deaths.

On November 2nd the Lebanese Commander-in-Chief and Yassir Arafat, the leader of Al Fatah, signed a ceasefire agreement in Cairo. This limited the guerrilla freedom of movement to certain areas; as further defined in January 1970, it also provided that camps had to be set up some distance from towns, that military training must cease in refugee camps, and that guerrillas must enter Israel before starting to shoot. The intention was not to prevent guerrilla attacks, but to stop innocent Lebanese getting hurt, or their property being damaged, by Israeli counter-attacks.

The calmer atmosphere that followed the ceasefire enabled Mr. Karami to form another cabinet towards the end of November. There was much concern about the weakness of the country's southern defences, and in January 1970 the new ministry felt strong enough to fire the Commander-in-Chief, appointing instead Brigadier Jean Njeim. In March there was a series of street battles in the Beirut area between the Palestinian guerrillas and militant right wing Falangist groups, but the Government and the army managed to avoid becoming involved. In May Israel launched a major air and ground attack on guerrilla positions in southern Lebanon, a substantial area being occupied for nearly two days. Syria sent air assistance for the small Lebanese air force. The result of the raid was as usual disputed.

POLITICAL CRISES

Sulaiman Franjiya was elected President in August 1970, and a new cabinet was formed by Saeb Salam. Some measures of political liberalization, such as the relaxation of press, radio and television censorship and the removal of the ban on extremist parties (the Lebanese Communist Party, Parti Populaire Syrien, pro-Iraq Baath Party, etc.), did little to curb domestic unrest. Strikes and demonstrations against unemployment and inflation, student disorders and fighting between Phalangists and the Parti Populaire Syrien continued throughout 1971. The parliamentary elections of April 1972 produced a marked swing towards left-wing political groups.

The Palestinian guerrillas remained Lebanon's major problem. Their bases in the refugee camps became more important following the expulsion of the guerrillas from Jordan in July 1971, and guerrilla operations against Israel produced violent Israeli reprisals in which both Palestinians and Lebanese suffered. The villages of southern Lebanon bore the brunt of Israeli raids, and their inhabitants secured a greater measure of Lebanese army control over guerrilla activities in March 1972. Arab terrorist actions still produced Israeli reprisals against Lebanon, even when there was little connection between the terrorists and Israel's vulnerable northern neighbour. The killing of Israeli athletes at the Olympic Games in Munich in September 1972 led to Israeli ground and air attacks on guerrilla bases, in which the Lebanese army suffered a number of casualties. The Lebanese Government was unable to persuade the guerrillas to suspend their activities against Israel, and there were several clashes between the Lebanese army and the guerrillas in December.

In February 1973 Israeli commandos attacked guerrilla training bases in refugee camps about 100 miles north of the Lebanese frontier, and escaped virtually unopposed. A further Israeli raid, in which three guerrilla leaders were shot in their homes in the centre of Beirut, and an attempt to blow up oil storage tanks at the Zahrani terminal, attributed to Palestinian extremists, resulted in the fall of the Salam Government. Mr. Salam resigned, dissatisfied with the inability of the Lebanese armed forces to prevent an Israeli military action in the capital, and Dr. Amin Hafez formed a new government. Several members of the Salam cabinet remained in office, the new government including representatives of most of the major political and religious groups.

Tension between the Lebanese army and the guerrillas culminated in May 1973 in Lebanese ground and air attacks on the refugee camps. An invasion by guerrillas based in Syria was repulsed, and a ceasefire was brought about by the mediation of other Arab states. The guerrillas apparently agreed to remove heavy weapons from the refugee camps, to stop their terrorist activities within Lebanon and to cease using the camps as bases for training guerrillas.

The Hafez Government lasted only seven weeks. The Prime Minister resigned on June 14th, unable to settle the Sunni Muslim claim for a greater share in the allocation of government posts, and it was not until July 8th that Takieddin Solh was able to form a new ministry. A moderate, Mr. Solh enjoyed the support of many Sunni factions, and his cabinet included representatives of all the main religious blocs. Outside Parliament, however, violent disorders continued, with industrial disputes and the claims of tobacco growers, for instance, resulting in demonstrations and clashes with police. The Phalange party maintained training camps for its own militia, and there appeared to be a danger that political conflicts might lead to the creation of private armies, clashing with each other as well as with the armed forces and the Palestinians.

The potential religious hostility within Lebanon, and the political implications of the division of government and administrative posts on a confessional basis were again demonstrated in February 1974. Civil service reforms, intended to overcome the sectarian nature of certain appointments, were opposed by Maronites who feared that they would lose posts traditionally reserved to their community. The National Liberal Party threatened to withdraw its three cabinet members, and the proposed reforms were also condemned by the Phalange and the Bloc National. The Shi'i Muslims of southern Lebanon also made demands for increased representation and more investment and development in the south. The Shi'i leader, Imam Moussa as-Sadr, implied that he would organize his followers and arm them as protection against Israeli raids, which he has since done.

Although Lebanon was not directly involved in the October 1973 Arab-Israeli war, southern regions had continued to serve as a guerrilla base and to suffer Israeli reprisals. Southern villages were shelled intermittently, and small-scale raids across the border and acts of terrorism became commonplace. In the first six months of 1974 there were three notable Israeli attacks on Lebanese targets, each following guerrilla outrages in Israel, despite Lebanese denials that the terrorists involved came from Lebanon. In April six villages in southern Lebanon were attacked, in May refugee camps were bombed by Israeli planes and shelled by Israeli gunboats. Three days of bombing in June killed 100 people and wounded 200 in villages and camps in the south.

In July there were clashes between Palestinians and Phalangists who continued to demand more government controls on guerrilla activities. Throughout 1974 and into 1975 Israeli shelling, air raids and incursions into Lebanon continued, together with guerrilla attacks against the Israelis. Consequently the situation on the border remained tense. In September 1974, unable to curb internal sectarian violence by its ineffective ban on the possession of fire-arms, Takieddin Solh's cabinet resigned. In October a new government was formed under Rashid Solh though violence continued, finally erupting in a bloody clash between troops and citizens of the port of Sidon. Almost 20 died and nearly 100 were wounded in the fighting which led to strikes and demonstrations that produced more violence. The cabinet split amid the granting of a Muslim demand to confer citizenship to long-time residents of the country. Letter bomb and dynamite explosions and further border fighting between the Israelis and guerrilla groups were followed by further fierce conflict between the Phalangists and Palestinians, in which over 150 died and 300 were wounded. Much damage was caused in Beirut and, after an agreement by Solh to normalize relations with the Palestinians and the fact that the security forces had not intervened in the fighting, the Phalangists appeared to be on the defensive.

However, another cabinet split followed and Rashid Sohl resigned in May 1975. He accused the Phalange of provoking the internal struggles and said that either the Palestinians should have a larger share of power in government or the sectarian basis of the construction of the Lebanese political system should be reviewed. As sporadic violence continued, the Phalangist leader, Pierre Gemayel, continued to emphasize the need for Lebanese Government authority over the whole country reflecting Christian fears of eventual Muslim domination. In May 1975 the situation deteriorated further, and sectarian strife caused over 100 deaths, with over 300 wounded. President Franjiya called on a retired brigadier, Noureddin Rifai, to form a military government which contained only one civilian. It took office on May 23rd, with support from the Phalange, but left-wing and centre groups, together with Syria's objections, forced its resignation on May 26th. Called on for the eighth time, Rashid Karami became prime minister designate. In May seven Lebanese troops were killed during an Israeli attack, the first such since September 1972.

The intensification of the split between the Muslim and Christian communities, represented at their extremes by party militias, has now placed in grave jeopardy the balance of government between the various religious groups in Lebanon. Hostility between the Socialists and the Phalange (allied to ex-President Camille Chamoun's National Liberal Party) has accentuated the difficulties in forming a representative government. Although traditionally the President is a Maronite Christian and the Prime Minister a Sunni Muslim, the population balance in Lebanon has altered considerably since the 1952 electoral law laid the basis for the country's government. The Christian community feels that its basic security is threatened, especially as successive Lebanese governments have been totally unable to exercise meaningful control over guerrilla bands in their raids on Israeli-held territory, which have led internally to endless sectarian strife. The Palestinian guerrilla forces have the advantage, not only of strong support from other Arab states, but also of backing from the large Muslim population in Lebanon and of the glaringly obvious weakness of the Lebanese armed forces to enforce law and order. The decision of Rashid Karami to stand for President in 1976 is a break with the pattern of compromise on which stability in Lebanon has previously depended, but the situation may well lead to a radical change in traditional patterns.

Towards the end of June 1975 the crisis intensified following more clashes between the Phalangists and Palestinians, with 250 dead and about 700 wounded and deadlock resulting between the various political factions. On July 1st Rashid Karami eventually succeeded in forming a new government which excluded Progressive Socialist and Phalangist representatives; by early July an uneasy peace left Lebanon facing an uncertain future.

ECONOMIC SURVEY

The Lebanon, which covers a surface area of 10,400 square kilometres, includes a coastal area, two mountain ranges that run from the north to the south separated by a fertile agricultural valley, the Bekaa, and semi-desert areas in parts of the extreme north- and south-east. There is also a rich cereal-growing plains area in Akkar province, in the far north, and a fertile agricultural area in the far south. Until the Second World War, the Lebanon was a part of Syria, administered by the French. After independence and the dissolution of an economic partnership between the Lebanon and Syria in 1950, fears were expressed about the economic viability of Lebanon once it was cut off from the Syrian hinterland. However, the country has not only managed to survive and to develop a small industrial sector but also to become a major commercial and financial centre of the Middle East.

The population of Lebanon, according to a survey carried out by the UN, was estimated to total about 2,870,000 in 1971. The annual growth rate is estimated to be above 2.6 per cent. Of the total population, more than a third live in the four big towns of Beirut, Tripoli, Sidon and Zahlé. In addition, there is a sizeable population of Palestinian refugees, estimated to total about 300,000, about 20 per cent of whom live in camps set up around the major towns and in rural areas. A new group of refugees, composed of those Lebanese who have fled from Israeli attacks on southern Lebanon, has also flooded the cities of Sidon, Beirut and Tripoli.

No proper census has been held since 1932 for fear of upsetting the delicate political balance between the various sects or confessions. All political and adminis-trative offices have been and are still allocated on the basis of the 1932 census which showed Christians in the majority by six to five over non-Christians. It is thought that the Muslims, however, now compose about 60 per cent of the total population, in part because of the higher ratio of Muslims in the Pales-tinian population in Lebanon and in part because the Muslims tend to have a higher birth rate and to emi-grate less than the Christians. Few of the existing political leaders favour holding a census, as this would disturb the delicate system of allocating offices on a sectarian basis under the terms of the National Pact adopted in 1943, but there have been widespread demands by trades unions, Muslim religious and charitable institutions and by certain members of parliament for taking a new census. Support for doing away with the National Pact altogether and for allo-cating political office by national elections without respect to sectarian considerations is also growing, particularly among the Shi'i Muslims who tend to be concentrated among the poorer sections of the community.

The Lebanese economy also suffers regularly from disruption for external reasons. 1973 was a worse year than most. Fighting between Lebanese and Pales-tinians in May 1973, disputes with Syria and Iraq leading to border closures or restrictions, the October war and continual Israeli raids all played havoc with the economic life of the country. In 1974 and 1975 the situation deteriorated further with violent internal clashes threatening the fabric of Lebanon's political structure and causing much economic disorder (*see* History).

The last survey of the labour force in the Lebanon, conducted by the Ministry of Planning in 1970, showed a total force of 572,000 in that year. The sur-vey showed that of that number, about 34,000, or 6 per cent, were unemployed. Of the active work force, about 55 per cent were working in the services sector, including Government administration, 18.9 per cent in agriculture and 17.7 per cent in industry. About 63.8 per cent were either illiterate or had not completed primary education.

In addition to the local labour force a large number of Palestinian refugees and Syrian immigrants are employed as skilled or unskilled labour. However, most of the Syrians, thought to total around 100,000, left the Lebanon during the fighting in 1975. As they traditionally work at the port of Beirut, or in the con-struction industry, these two sectors were particularly badly affected.

Of the total area of the country, just over half (52 per cent) consists of mountain, swamp or desert, and a further 7 per cent of forest. Only 23 per cent of the area is cultivated, but there is a further 17 per cent which it is considered could be cultivated given suitable conditions. The coastal strip enjoys a Mediterranean climate and is exceedingly fertile, producing mainly olives, citrus fruits and bananas. Many of the steep valleys leading up from the coastal plain are carefully terraced and very productive in olives and soft fruit, especially mulberries, and in the Zahlé and Shtaura regions there are well-known vineyards. Cotton, in particular, and onions are grown in the hinterland of Tripoli. The main cereal-growing district is the Bekaa, the fertile valley between the Lebanon and the Anti-Lebanon ranges. In the north of this valley is the source of the river Orontes. The river Litani also flows southwards through the Bekaa before it turns west near Marjayoun to flow into the Mediter-ranean just north of Tyre. This valley is particularly fertile, and cotton is now grown there with some success. Throughout the country the size of the average holding is extremely small and, even so, a small-holding, particularly in the mountains, may be broken up into several fragments separated from each other by a considerable distance.

AGRICULTURE

The country's principal grain crop is wheat, which in good years reaches 70,000 tons, but in bad years can fall to 40,000 tons. About 161,000 acres were planted with wheat during the 1973–74 season, and production was estimated by the International Wheat Council to have reached 65,000 metric tons, compared with 45,000 in 1972–73. The only other important cereal crop is barley which rarely exceeds about 30,000 tons in a good year, and which fell below 10,000 tons in the years 1969–71. The country is far from being self-supporting in cereals, and grain and flour continue to constitute one of the most important items which the Lebanon has to buy from abroad. It is also in this respect especially that the Lebanon has suffered from the economic divorce which has separated her from Syria, for in most years Syria has an exportable surplus of cereals.

Lebanon's production of fruit is almost more important to her economy than that of grain. Production has increased substantially over the last two decades and the citrus crop has risen from an annual average in the years 1948–52 of 75,000 tons to 307,000 tons in 1973. There was a rush to plant apple trees in the 1950s but overproduction led to reduced output in 1968–70. Production rose again to 154,000 tons in 1971 and reached an estimated 166,000 tons by 1973. The production of fresh grapes has flourished in recent years, and in 1973 amounted to 107,000 tons. That of figs amounts to about 15,000 tons a year, but bananas constitute perhaps a more important cash crop, production having increased from an annual average of 16,000 tons during the years 1948–52 to 29,000 tons in 1969. Much progress has recently been made in the production of sugar cane and sugar beet. Sugar beet production totalled 190,000 tons in 1972.

Other important vegetable crops are potatoes, onions, tomatoes, cucumbers and melons. Potato production reached an estimated 130,000 metric tons in 1974 compared with 117,000 metric tons in 1973 while the output of tomatoes rose to an estimated 70,000 metric tons in 1974 compared with 59,000 in 1973. Cotton and tobacco are also grown but tobacco production, which is grown primarily in southern Lebanon, has been badly affected by the Israeli attacks. The forests are well regulated, but have been greatly thinned by the ravages of the goat, as elsewhere in the region, and the number of the famous cedars of Lebanon has sadly diminished. Stock-raising is not so important in the Lebanon as elsewhere in the Middle East, as there is insufficient grazing land, but Lebanese dairy produce is now of excellent quality. There were about 67,000 head of cattle and 242,000 sheep in the Lebanon in 1971. Seasonal migration from winter to summer pastures in the mountains and vice versa continues to be one of the chief characteristics of stock-raising in the Lebanon, as elsewhere in the Middle East.

Poultry production has recently become a major source of agricultural income and, although modern methods are used, more primitive handling methods are said to be the cause of an 18 per cent death rate for newly hatched chickens. A record 24.9 million chicks were hatched in 1971 but only about 18 million of these survived. Of the total, 15.8 million were set aside for flesh and 2.1 million for egg laying. Egg production in 1971 reached 576 million of which 309 million eggs were exported. The difficulties of chicken production are a good example of the problems facing producers in all sectors of the Lebanese economy where modern production techniques are imported but the lack of know-how renders these techniques less efficient.

INDUSTRY

Several foreign oil companies have expressed interest in seeking oil exploration concessions in Lebanon, including two U.S. companies, Tripco and Milford Argosy, and an Italian-American group led by Agip of Italy's state ENI group. Techno-export of the Soviet Union, Auriol Oil & Gas and the French state-controlled Compagnie Française des Pétroles (CFP) have had talks with the Government about concessions but CFP withdrew a proposal after Tripco was granted a concession to prospect for oil off the Lebanese coast. The agreement, announced in April 1975, covered a period of 15 years and production, if commercially feasible, would be shared with the Government receiving 80 per cent of output up to 200,000 barrels a day and 85 per cent of anything over that. Tripco is expected to take an initial 40 per cent of production to cover exploration costs and will pay the Government $1 million before drilling starts. However, there is some doubt that the Tripco agreement will actually be implemented since about 90 per cent of Lebanese territory, both onshore and offshore, has already been legally conceded to three other companies, Lebanese Petroleum, Shahin and Shahin & Abdini Oil. Parliamentary approval is needed before any other concessions covering the 90 per cent could be granted legally.

The new interest in oil exploration in the Lebanon followed reports in 1974 that big oil reserves had been found in Akkar in the north, in the western part of the Bekaa valley and in an area along the central coast. The Government has not confirmed the reports, but a Romanian firm, Rompetrol, was asked by the Government to carry out a geological survey of the entire country after completing a preliminary study in the Bekaa area in the autumn of 1974. There are also thought to be important deposits of oil-bearing shale which, if exploited, could yield an estimated 215,000 million barrels according to some reports. However, it is likely that the major attraction of the Lebanon is that the four-fold rise in oil prices after the October 1973 Middle East War has now made such exploration economically promising.

Even before the new interest in oil, exploration in the Lebanon was of central importance to the oil industry. Two of the world's most important oil pipelines, one from the Kirkuk oil wells in Iraq to the Mediterranean Sea at Tripoli and the second from Aramco's oilfields in Saudi Arabia to Zahrani near Sidon, cross the country. There are two important refineries, one at the terminal of each of the pipelines, and the Lebanese and Saudi Governments have agreed to co-operate in building a third refinery. In the past the Government has received a royalty for use of the pipelines, which amounted to £L64.5 million in 1972. However, since then the royalty revenues have been declining because of disputes over the pipelines.

Revenues from the Kirkuk-Tripoli pipeline, which was run by the Iraq Petroleum Company (IPC), were reduced after both Iraq and Syria nationalized IPC assets in their countries on June 1st, 1972. This led to a dispute over ownership of the IPC refinery in Lebanon after the Iraqi Government and IPC reached a settlement of the nationalization issue in Iraq in March 1973. Last year the Lebanese Government was reported to have reached a tentative agreement with IPC providing up to £L75 million in compensation for the Government's take-over of the IPC refinery at the time of the Iraq-IPC settlement. Under the terms of the agreement, IPC would manage the refinery in return for a share of the profits. The Government would also benefit in that the price it pays for crude oil from the Iraqi fields remains at $2.54 a barrel net of transit charges, perhaps the lowest cost for oil in the world.

Settlement of the second dispute, concerning the Saudi Arabian-Zahrani pipeline, run by the Trans-Arabian Pipeline Company (Tapline), was delayed by the violence which plagued Beirut in the spring and summer of 1975 and the subsequent delays in naming a new Cabinet after the collapse of the military cabinet in May. Tapline had suspended its pumping operations in February, saying that oil tankers found it cheaper to lift oil directly from the Saudi Gulf terminal at Ras Tanura. But the company also has been demanding payment from the Lebanese Government for the higher cost of Saudi crude oil and has claimed that the Government owed it $100 million. The Government has paid a preferential price for Saudi crude refined for local use, about $5 a barrel, compared to the market price of about $10.42 a barrel. The dispute led Tapline to threaten a closedown of its operations in Lebanon in May 1975 while the Government has lost more than £L20 million in transit royalties.

The Government has also virtually taken over the refinery at the Zahrani terminal, which is run by the Mediterranean Refining Company (Medreco), jointly owned by Caltex and Mobil. Mobil, Caltex's two parent firms—Texaco and Standard Oil of California, and another big U.S. oil company, Exxon, also own Tapline and were the original owners of Saudi Arabia's major producer, the Arabian American Oil Company (Aramco). Medreco has threatened to close its refining operations if Tapline closes and is demanding that the Government allow it to charge higher prices for refined oil products. The Government, which has been seeking to maintain prices at existing levels, has been paying several million Lebanese pounds a month in state subsidies since the takeover to keep prices from rising. However, there is doubt that the Government can prevent this from happening sooner or later since any Saudi concessions on the price of oil it sells to either the refinery or directly to the Government would involve setting up a two-tiered pricing system, something the Saudi Government has so far been unwilling to do. More likely is the possibility that the Saudis will increase their aid to Lebanon to help it maintain the subsidies.

The two refineries processed slightly more than 2,300,000 tons of crude oil in 1973 and 1974 compared with just over 2,000,000 tons in 1972. Demand for kerosene, aircraft fuels and petrol is high in the Lebanon because of its importance as a communications and transit centre, and the big rise in oil prices, together with the increase in demand, has made the construction of a third refinery more pressing. Although the Saudi Government has agreed to help build it, actual progress on the plan is likely to be delayed until a settlement is reached on the price to be paid for Saudi crude oil pumped to the Lebanon.

Manufacturing industry has for many years been highly developed in Lebanon compared with other states in the Middle East, but suffers from political disruptions and strikes. Industrial investment doubled between 1970 and 1973 and stood at £L2,000 million at the end of 1973. Investments by private industrial firms rose even more spectacularly the following year, reaching £L155 million, or 34 per cent of total investment by private firms, compared with only £L31 million at the end of 1973. Total industrial production reached more than £L2,150 million by the end of 1973, compared with £L1,059 million in 1964, while the number of workers employed in industry rose to 120,000 in 1973 compared with only 70,000 in 1971. Industrial exports nearly doubled in 1974 and totalled £L846 million compared with £L444 million in 1973.

Industry in the Lebanon is traditionally a small-scale operation run by individuals who employ a handful of people. However, the number of limited liability companies has been growing and rose from 18 in 1973 to 44 in 1974. Food processing, yarn and textile firms account for about 44 per cent of industrial output and furniture and woodworking factories about 29 per cent. Mechanical industries account for only about 7 per cent of total production and the rest is divided among cement, ceramics, pharmaceutical and plastics industries. Eight per cent of the country's industrial establishments are located in Beirut or in the adjacent Mount Lebanon area. Raw materials are mainly imported. Imports by industrial establishments are estimated at about £L800 million a year, accounting for about 40 per cent of all imports. Of these imports, semi-processed commodities account for about 61 per cent, raw materials 24 per cent and machinery and equipment 15 per cent.

With the exception of the oil companies, the largest industrial employers are probably the food-processing industries, including sugar refineries and biscuit and confectionery factories. These are followed by the well developed textile industries. The building industry has been stimulated by the inflow into real estate of funds from Lebanese abroad, mainly those whose property was sequestrated in West Africa. This brought a sharp rise in land prices and construction activity in 1974. Lebanon's two cement plants produce a surplus for export, and a third plant now planned for Siblin should make the sector more competitive and reduce prices. The Government is exerting increasing efforts towards promoting industrial expansion and in March 1972, in a measure similar to one of 1954, all industries created between 1971 and 1976 were exempted from income tax for six years. Industries created before 1971 were to benefit from a partial tax holiday if they expanded their activities before the end of 1975. The Government has also been inviting foreign capital to participate in industrial development, especially through the creation of an industrial free zone at Beirut port. In addition, a new bank was set up in December 1971 to finance industrial expansion, the National Bank for Industrial and Touristic Development, with a capital of £L60 million of which 51 per cent is subscribed by the state.

The lack of adequate sources of power had hindered industrial development in the 1960s but Lebanon now has excess capacity and in 1972 started supplying power through a 100 million kWh line to southern Syria and was proposing to set up a similar line to supply central Syria. Production of electric power reached 1,975 million kWh in 1974 compared with 1,790 million kWh in 1973.

EXTERNAL TRADE

Lebanon has suffered from an adverse balance of visible trade for many years, and in 1973 exports covered only 48 per cent of imports. The value of imports increased from £L299 million in 1951 to £L3,349 million in 1973 while exports rose from £L90 million in 1951 to £L1,598 million in 1973. These figures do not include re-exports nor the highly important transit trade through the free port of Beirut to Syria, Jordan, Iraq, Saudi Arabia and the Gulf States.

The most important exports are precious stones, metals and coins, textiles, machinery and electrical goods, transport equipment and fruits and vegetables. The October 1973 war severely affected transit trade to the Arab hinterland and exports to Western Europe have been increasing at a higher rate, partly because of a preferential trade agreement signed with the EEC in December 1972 and partly because of the increasing importance of Lebanon's industrial exports. Saudi Arabia remained Lebanon's single most important customer in 1973 but other Arab countries such as Kuwait, Syria and Jordan fell behind Western Europe in importance. France was Lebanon's second most important customer in 1973 followed by the United Kingdom, both of whom tripled their imports. Libya moved into fourth place just ahead of Kuwait, which fell from second to fifth place.

The most important imports in 1973 were precious metals, stones, jewellery and coins, machinery and equipment, including electrical goods, textiles and textile products, metals, transport equipment, vegetable products, chemicals and pharmaceuticals. West Germany, the U.S.A., France, Italy and the United Kingdom were Lebanon's most important suppliers in order of importance.

Overall, imports rose by 21 per cent from £L2,901 million in 1972 while exports increased by 36.7 per cent from £L1,169 million. The trade deficit more than doubled in 1973 from £L629.6 million to £L1,187.2 million but invisible earnings from services, tourism, the transit trade and remittances by Lebanese working abroad in the U.S.A., South America and West Africa usually cover the deficit and help produce an overall surplus in the balance of payments. Trade remains Lebanon's chief contributor to G.D.P., however, averaging about 30 per cent of the total.

CURRENCY AND FINANCE

Gold and foreign exchange reserves, which amounted to U.S. $206.1 million at the beginning of 1964, steadily increased to U.S. $861.6 million by the end of 1973. In 1974 they rose spectacularly to U.S. $1,673.7 million, almost double the 1973 figure, largely because of deposits from Arab oil producing countries.

The importance of Beirut as the commercial and financial centre of the Middle East has derived from the almost complete absence of restriction on the free movement of goods and capital, and from the transference of the Middle Eastern headquarters of many foreign concerns from Cairo to Beirut after 1951. Moreover, large sums were being earned in the Gulf by Arabs who were seeking investment locally, especially in property, and for them Beirut was a convenient centre. Beirut's dominance has been strengthened by the massive increases in surplus oil revenues earned by the producing states, much of which is channelled through Lebanon. By June 1975 the number of representative offices opened by foreign banks in Beirut had reached 72 compared with 56 at the end of 1974. Among them are the British Bank of the Middle East, the Eastern Bank, the Moscow Narodny Bank, and several leading German and American banks.

Early in 1966 the Government introduced new regulations governing the establishment of new banks (notably a minimum capital of £L3 million) and subjected the opening of additional branches to the consent of the central bank. The failure of the Intra Bank, the largest purely Lebanese bank, in 1966 resulted in a thorough reform of the banking system, and some smaller commercial banks of local origin were merged into larger concerns. Foreign takeovers of Lebanese banks have increased over recent years, and by the end of 1972 only two of the leading 16 banks were still Lebanese-owned.

The stability of the Lebanese banking system resulted in an embarrassingly large liquidity surplus in 1974. Deposits had risen from £L3,357 million in 1969 to £L10,247 million at the end of 1974 with no equivalent increase in investment opportunities inside the country. Loans during 1969–74 rose from £L2,301 million to £L5,649 million. This same banking stability had led to increasing confidence in the Lebanese pound as a relatively stable international currency and for the first time at the end of 1972 a Lebanese currency loan was granted to a foreign borrower by Lebanese banks. Lebanese currency foreign loans had reached over £L240 million by the end of 1973 of which £L75 million was lent to the World Bank. Foreign loans absorbed some of the liquidity surplus, as did the reinvestment of Lebanese-currency deposits abroad in foreign currencies. However, since the October 1973 war the bank rate has fluctuated wildly—at one time it shot up to 35 per cent.

Lebanon's position as the natural repository for Arab oil funds is coming under increasing competition from European and Gulf financial centres, and the Government is considering legislation on a "banking free zone" to free foreign-currency deposits by non-residents from certain fiscal obligations in order to encourage the inflow of more deposits into the country. In conjunction with the banking secrecy law, under which numbered accounts are legal, this would make Beirut the most attractive financial centre in the Middle East.

Beirut's position in Middle East finance and its susceptibility to currency fluctuations in 1973 exacerbated internal inflationary pressures, resulting from the relative freedom of banks in granting loans and from the floating Lebanese pound. Inflation is thus the country's most pressing problem, and was a major factor in causing the internecine strife which paralysed many parts of the country in the spring and summer of 1975. At the end of 1974 the consumer price index for Beirut stood at 136.7, up 9.4 points over December 1973 (1966=100). For the country as a whole it stood at 142.4 in March 1975 compared with 134.1 in March 1974, but unofficial estimates of the inflation rate indicate it is rising even faster, more than 25 per cent a year. Price rises have been highest in food, clothing and rents and have had the strongest impact on those least to absorb them. Although the Government has tried to control food imports and prices paid by consumers it has achieved little success and an attempt to implement price controls on basic commodities in early 1975 was short-lived. The system of political patronage and the monopoly control of the import trade have so far effectively prevented price controls from being imposed effectively.

COMMUNICATIONS AND TOURISM

Beirut is the centre of communications for the whole Arab East. Both Middle East Airlines (MEA) and Trans-Mediterranean Airways (TMA) have recently added to their fleets. MEA has bought more Boeings, including Jumbos, and TMA ordered its eighth Boeing in September 1974. Both airlines provide Lebanon with sizable foreign currency earnings. MEA reported profits of £L6.9 million sterling in 1974, a rise of 9 per cent over 1973, despite the higher price and shortage of aircraft fuels. Freight through Beirut International Airport increased by 7.6 per cent in 1974 to a total of 118,431 metric tons.

Congestion at the port of Beirut has raised serious doubts about its ability to expedite freight through to the Arab hinterland. During the fighting in Beirut in 1975 more than 200 ships were waiting to unload and the chronic delays have also cut into Government revenue. Surcharges imposed by shipping conferences were up to 125 per cent, the highest anywhere, by August 1974, even before the 1975 troubles. The heavy development plans underway in Saudi Arabia and Kuwait and Iraq, however, are expected to increase demand although other nearby ports, particularly Latakia in Syria and Tripoli in northern Lebanon can take over some of the burden from Beirut. Traffic through the port in 1974 included 3,373 ships while cargo handled rose from 5.19 million metric tons in 1973 to 5.3 million metric tons in 1974.

Work to extend the port of Beirut has begun and a joint venture between a Lebanese firm and a British company was awarded a contract in January 1975 to extend the breakwater, build a new quay wall and carry out dredging. Other firms are improving port facilities and also carrying out designs to expand the port of Tripoli.

The World Bank is carrying out a study of Lebanon's road network, which includes the important overland Beirut-Damascus motorway, and the Bank is expected to contribute to plans to expand Lebanon's 7,100 kilometres of roads. A £L700 million project is planned to build a new motorway from Beirut to Syria via the mountain towns of Shtaura and Hammama.

Tourism, usually a big foreign currency earner, has been badly hit by the political disruptions which, in 1975, began at a time when tourism was just beginning to recover from the effects of the October 1973 War. As the fighting continued through the month of June many tourists, including those from the Gulf states who traditionally spend their summer in the mountain resorts of Lebanon, decided to go elsewhere. Hotel activity in Beirut was down by 80 per cent while in resort areas it had fallen almost 100 per cent in May 1975. Revenues of entertainment facilities and of restaurants are also expected to be badly affected in 1975. In the first quarter of 1975, before the disturbances, tourism had risen 10.5 per cent, from 537,000 tourists in the first quarter of 1974 to 594,000.

PUBLIC FINANCE AND DEVELOPMENT

The 1975 budget was still pending in July and action by Parliament to approve it was expected to be delayed until the autumn. Government offices were receiving temporary allocations based on their spending in 1974 and this was expected to result in a surplus at the end of the year. The draft 1975 budget totalled £L1,986 million, an increase of about 43 per cent over 1974. The biggest increase in expenditure was in funds allocated for food subsidies which are planned to rise tenfold to £L195 million. However, since there have been two new Cabinets formed in Lebanon since the draft budget was submitted it was highly likely that the draft budget would be revised before being finally approved by Parliament.

Except in the refugee camps, where Arabs driven out of Palestine are maintained largely by UNRWA, the general standard of living in the Lebanon is higher than in most of the other Arab countries of the Middle East.

According to the latest World Bank estimates, for 1971, GNP at market prices was $1,840 million. Though rising over 1965–71 at only 0.8 per cent, GNP per caput in Lebanon was, at $660, the highest in the Arab world outside the oil-exporting states.

Three attempts at fitting development within a plan framework have so far come to little. The major projects have their own authorities to run them, like the Green Plan (the state organization for rural development) and the Litani Office. Five major irrigation and land reclamation schemes are at various stages of planning or implementation, the combined cost of which could reach £L1,000 million. Both the UNDP and FAO are likely to provide finance. The biggest scheme—the Litani valley scheme—has been under discussion since 1961 and was given a go-ahead by the government only in August 1973. The other major projects are the expansion of Beirut port, for which the Iranian Government has promised assistance, the building of the Beirut–Tripoli motorway for which the Iranians have also promised help, as well as the World Bank and the construction of a third oil refinery, for which Saudi Arabia has promised assistance.

STATISTICAL SURVEY

AREA AND POPULATION

AREA
(hectares)

TOTAL	CULTIVATED	IRRIGATED	MARGINAL AND GRAZING	FOREST	WASTE
1,040,000	270,000	72,000	128,800	73,200	549,200

POPULATION

TOTAL* (1974)	BEIRUT* (capital—1972)	TRIPOLI* (1972)	BIRTHS* (1974)	MARRIAGES* (1974)	DEATHS* (1974)
3,100,000	800,000	150,000	73,244	20,001	13,175

* Estimate.

AGRICULTURE
PRINCIPAL CROPS

	AREA ('000 hectares)			PRODUCTION ('000 tons)			YIELD (tons per hectare)
	1971	1972	1973	1971	1972	1973	1973
Wheat	48.2	50.5	50.1	41.0	63.7	55.1	1.1
Barley	7.3	7.8	7.3	6.3	7.6	6.5	0.9
Sugar Beet	2.8	3.8	2.5	146.2	190.0	139.4	55.4
Potatoes	9.0	9.2	8.9	108.8	116.5	116.2	13.1
Onions	1.8	1.6	1.5	35.7	29.5	31.2	20.7
Tobacco	7.6	7.8	7.5	8.4	9.5	9.9	1.3
Citrus Fruit	11.9	11.9	11.9	278.4	296.2	307.3	105.8
Apples	13.0	12.8	12.3	154.5	220.4	166.1	15.1
Grapes	17.8	17.8	18.2	115.0	109.4	107.4	6.1
Olives	27.5	28.0	30.2	54.8	39.6	32.2	1.1
Tomatoes	4.9	4.6	4.4	67.0	72.6	59.1	13.6

LIVESTOCK
('000)

	1970	1971	1972	1973
Goats . . .	366	357	355	348
Sheep . . .	244	242	239	213
Cattle . . .	66	67	67	62
Donkeys . . .	27	28	28	25
Poultry . . .	18,260	19,234	20,164	17,463

INDUSTRY

	Unit	1971	1972	1973	1974
Tobacco Manufactures . .	tons	3,122	3,250	3,893	6,337
Timber	cu. metres	48,793	57,748	66,285	54,451
Cement	'ooo tons	1,499	1,626	1,659	1,744
Electricity . . .	million kWh.	1,375	1,548	1,791	1,975

OIL REFINING
('ooo tons)

	1968	1969	1970	1971	1972	1973	1974
Crude Oil intake .	1,803	1,849	1,992	2,001	2,039	2,329	2,328
Petrol . . .	347	347	374	397	446	517	814
Kerosene* . .	190	207	212	218	155	224	229
Gas Oil . . .	281	318	338	343	329	369.8	420.7
Fuel Oil . . .	897	884	958	947	1,082	895.1	910.7
Butane . . .	24	23	22	24	26	48.8	63.1

* Prior to 1972, figures include jet fuel.

FINANCE

100 piastres = 1 Lebanese pound (£L).

Coins: 1, 2½, 5, 10, 25 and 50 piastres.

Notes: 1, 5, 10, 25, 50 and 100 pounds.

Exchange rates (July 1975): £1 sterling = £L4.775; U.S. $1 = £L2.18.

£L100 = £20.94 sterling = $45.87.

Note: A basic official exchange rate of U.S. $1 = £L3.08 was introduced in January 1956. This remained in effect until February 1973, despite the devaluation of the U.S. dollar in December 1971. The official exchange rate was £1 sterling = £L7.392 from November 1967 to August 1971; and £1 sterling = £L8.026 from December 1971 to June 1972. However, the basic rate was used only for official exchange operations and for the valuation of official assets and customs duties. All commercial transactions take place on the basis of a fluctuating free market rate, established in November 1948. Prior to February 1973 the exchange rate in the free market usually fluctuated between £L2.97 and £L3.40 per U.S. dollar, with a "low" of £L3.50 in June 1967. In February 1973, when the U.S. dollar was again devalued, the Lebanese pound appreciated considerably on the free market. At the same time a new official rate of $1 = £L2.772 was introduced but this became inoperative in March 1973, since when official valuations have been based on an "effective" rate whose parity is adjustable from month to month. For converting the value of foreign trade transactions, the average rates (£L per U.S. dollar) were: 3.157 in 1968; 3.255 in 1969; 3.269 in 1970; 3.228 in 1971; 3.051 in 1972; 2.610 in 1973; and 2.328 in 1974.

ORDINARY BUDGET ESTIMATES
(Expenditure 1973—million £L)

Defence	246.7
Education	201.6
Public Works and Transport . . .	168.1
Ministry of the Interior . .	83.4
Debt Servicing	52.2
Hydro-electric Resources . . .	25.8
TOTAL (including others) .	1,080.8

1974 Budget: £L1,225 million.

1975 Budget: £L1,607 million.

NATIONAL ACCOUNTS

GROSS DOMESTIC PRODUCT
(million £L at current prices)

ECONOMIC ACTIVITY	1970	1971	1972
Agriculture, Hunting, Forestry and Fishing . . .	445	466	631
Mining, Quarrying and Manufacturing . . .	661	750	884
Electricity, Gas and Water	113	118	129
Construction	218	239	290
Wholesale and Retail Trade, Restaurants and Hotels .	1,527	1,723	2,009
Transport, Storage and Communication . . .	401	438	478
Finance, Insurance, Real Estate and Business Services	165	197	235
Owner-Occupied Dwellings	430	495	558
Community, Social and Personal Services . .	482	522	676
Public Administration and Defence . . .	424	451	477
TOTAL	4,866	5,399	6,365

EXTERNAL TRADE*
(£L'000)

	1968	1969	1970	1971	1972	1973
Imports	1,865,087	2,006,431	2,252,177	2,451,922	2,901,836	3,348,849
Exports	510,261	554,301	650,619	815,619	1,168,195	1,599,458
Transit Trade† . . .	1,532,938	1,348,894	1,272,105	2,429,687	1,350,430	1,345,294

* Based on the rate of free market prices of the U.S. dollar.

† Through the free port of Beirut; includes crude oil pumped through the Lebanon.

PRINCIPAL COMMODITIES
(£L '000)

IMPORTS	1972	1973	EXPORTS*	1972	1973
Precious Metals, Stones, Jewellery and Coins . . .	252,406	640,237	Vegetable Products . . .	136,720	145,354
Vegetable Products . . .	240,437	292,868	Precious Metals, Stones, Jewellery and Coins . . .	114,612	333,989
Machinery and Electrical Apparatus . .	402,660	479,325	Animals and Animal Products .	56,781	51,874
Textiles and Products . .	354,314	413,261	Machinery and Electrical Apparatus . . .	123,707	168,238
Non-precious Metals and Products	250,286	346,365	Non-precious Metals and Products	95,992	114,037
Transport Vehicles . .	248,657	322,734	Textiles and Products . .	122,307	172,662
Animals and Animal Products .	124,135	131,140	Beverages and Tobacco . .	81,400	87,559
Industrial Chemical Products .	239,331	259,480	Transport Vehicles . .	126,631	150,162
Mineral Products . .	169,658	187,469			
Beverages and Tobacco .	157,673	150,428			

* Including re-exports.

PRINCIPAL COUNTRIES
(£L '000)

IMPORTS	1971	1972	1973	EXPORTS	1971	1972	1973
Belgium . .	54,773	70,149	91,941	France . . .	13,896	52,750	161,912
Czechoslovakia .	41,384	56,463	70,057	Germany, Fed. Rep.	13,496	12,039	19,315
France . . .	266,549	300,434	361,915	Greece . . .	2,083	1,739	6,388
Germany, Fed. Rep.	264,295	316,107	380,839	Iraq . . .	68,641	69,440	50,075
Iraq . . .	98,017	121,819	119,919	Italy . . .	14,855	16,875	22,695
Italy . . .	187,269	246,474	293,724	Jordan . . .	37,843	23,513	51,020
Japan . . .	103,370	120,785	126,233	Kuwait . . .	88,690	110,621	105,497
Jordan . . .	13,895	16,605	21,021	Saudi Arabia . .	125,387	190,284	260,910
Netherlands . .	56,897	56,598	69,055	Spain . . .	1,207	3,023	5,294
Saudi Arabia . .	32,983	52,537	69,506	Syria . . .	75,654	83,366	77,403
Switzerland . .	228,307	189,587	141,886	U.S.S.R. . .	9,404	8,192	13,833
Syria . . .	35,312	69,125	51,544	United Kingdom .	26,508	44,962	148,288
Turkey . . .	56,574	38,664	55,225	U.S.A. . .	23,164	71,636	72,069
United Kingdom .	198,054	239,685	261,409				
U.S.A. . . .	250,408	322,355	377,542				

TRANSPORT

RAILWAYS

	PASSENGERS ('000)		GOODS ('000)		REVENUE ('000 £L)		
	Journeys	Passenger-Kms.	Tons	Ton-kms	Passengers	Goods	Total
1969 .	78	7,278	313	24,455	178	2,018	2,196
1970 .	76	7,430	258	20,082	187	1,916	2,103
1971 .	71	7,187	325	26,789	184	2,236	2,420
1972 .	55	5,004	417	33,116	134	2,313	2,447
1973	36	2,829	512	35,063	81	2,446	2,527

ROADS

	1969	1970	1971	1972	1973	1974
Motor cars (taxis and private) .	129,674	136,016	146,270	164,790	185,935	220,204
Buses	1,763	1,794	1,905	2,067	2,258	2,397
Lorries	14,473	14,795	15,656	17,130	19,151	20,983
Motor cycles . . .	12,004	9,800	9,731	10,734	12,036	13,179

SHIPPING IN BEIRUT

	SHIPS ENTERED		MERCHANDISE (Metric Tons)	
	Number	Tonnage	Entered	Cleared
1970 .	2,685	4,385,247	2,289,321	728,144
1971 .	2,910	4,790,713	2,456,517	626,384
1972 .	3,265	5,958,425	2,666,821	677,378
1973 .	3,098	5,112,983	2,819,534	717,870
1974 .	2,613	5,276,000	3,411,546	667,841

TRAFFIC THROUGH THE INTERNATIONAL AIRPORT IN BEIRUT

	AIRCRAFT USING AIRPORT	PASSENGERS USING AIRPORT	FREIGHT THROUGH AIRPORT (metric tons)
1970 .	41,553	1,558,246	57,691
1971 .	39,643	1,832,514	69,742
1972 .	38,735	2,090,634	87,991
1973 .	40,037	2,258,474	109,560
1974 .	48,070	2,747,972	118,431

TOURISM

	1971	1972	1973	1974
Total Foreign Visitors (except Syrians) .	1,015,772	1,048,159	884,997	1,510,260
of which:				
Visitors from Arab countries .	619,171	577,186	535,641	892,203
Visitors from Europe . .	213,698	250,932	171,338	316,080
Visitors from the Americas .	94,076	102,281	75,606	143,000
Syrian Visitors	1,241,633	1,233,903	1,019,498	1,498,131
TOTAL . . .	2,257,405	2,281,062	1,904,495	3,008,391

EDUCATION

(1972–73)

	SCHOOLS	PUPILS	TEACHERS
Public:			
Primary and kindergarten . .	740	202,913	
Upper primary . . .	549	77,161	} 17,077
Secondary	65	18,240	
Private:			
Primary and kindergarten . .	742	} 366,987	16,168
Upper primary and secondary	390		

Source: Direction Centrale de la Statistique, Ministère du Plan, and Direction Générale des Douanes, Beirut.

THE CONSTITUTION

(Promulgated May 23rd, 1926; amended by the Constitutional Laws of 1927, 1929, 1943 and 1947.)

According to the Constitution, the Republic of the Lebanon is an independent and sovereign State, and no part of the territory may be alienated or ceded. Lebanon has no State religion. Arabic is the official language. Beirut is the capital.

All Lebanese are equal in the eyes of the law. Personal freedom and freedom of the Press are guaranteed and protected. The religious communities are entitled to maintain their own schools, provided they conform to the general requirements relating to public instruction as laid down by the State. Dwellings are inviolable; rights of ownership are protected by law. Every Lebanese citizen who has completed his twenty-first year is an elector and qualifies for the franchise.

Legislative Power

Legislative power is exercised by one house, the Chamber of Deputies, with 99 seats, 53 of which are allocated to Christians and 45 to Muslims (for full details of allocation, *see* Parliament, p. 510). Its members must be over 25 years of age, in possession of their full political and civil rights, and literate. They are considered representatives of the whole nation, and are not bound to follow directives from their constituencies. They can be suspended only by a two-thirds majority of their fellow-members. Secret ballot was introduced in a new election law of April 1960.

The Chamber holds two sessions yearly, from the first Tuesday after March 15th to the end of May, and from the first Tuesday after October 15th to the end of the year. The normal term of the Chamber of Deputies is four years; general elections take place within sixty days before the end of this period. If the Chamber is dissolved before the end of its term, elections are held within three months of dissolution.

Voting in the Chamber is public—by acclamation, or by standing and sitting. A quorum of two-thirds and a majority vote is required for constitutional issues. The only exceptions to this occur when the Chamber becomes an electoral college, and chooses the President of the Republic, or Secretaries to the Chamber, or when the President is accused of treason or of violating the Constitution. In such cases voting is secret, and a two-thirds majority is needed.

Executive Power

The President of the Republic is elected for a term of six years, and is not immediately re-eligible. He and his ministers deal with the promulgation and execution of laws passed by the Chamber of Deputies. The Ministers and the Prime Minister are chosen by the President of the Republic. They are not necessarily members of the Chamber of Deputies, although they are responsible to it and have access to its debates. The President of the Republic must be a Maronite Christian and the Prime Minister a Sunni Muslim; and the choice of the other Ministers has to reflect the division between the communities in the Chamber.

The President himself can initiate laws. Alternatively, the President may demand an additional debate on laws already passed by the Chamber. He can adjourn the Chamber for up to a month, but not more than once in each session. In exceptional circumstances he can dissolve the Chamber and force an election. Ministers can be made to resign by a vote of no confidence.

THE GOVERNMENT

HEAD OF STATE

President of the Republic: SULAIMAN FRANJIYA (took office September 23rd, 1970).

THE CABINET

(August 1975)

Prime Minister and Minister of Defence, Finance and Information: RASHID ABDUL HAMID KARAMI (Sunni, Parliamentary Democratic Front).

Minister of Interior, Post Office and Telecommunications, Hydraulic and Electrical Resources: CAMILLE CHAMOUN (Maronite, National Liberal Party).

Minister of Justice, Public Works and Economy: ADEL OSSEIRAN (Shi'ite).

Minister of Agriculture, Housing and Health: MAJID ARASLAN (Druze).

Minister of Foreign Affairs, Education and Planning: PHILIPPE TAKLA (Greek Catholic).

Minister for Social Affairs and Labour, Tourism, Industry and Oil: GHASSAN TUENI (Greek Orthodox).

PARLIAMENT

CHAMBER OF DEPUTIES

The electoral reform bill of April 1960 maintained the existing ratio of 6 Christians to 5 Muslims in the Chamber of Deputies. It is the custom for the President of the Chamber of Deputies to be a Shi'i Muslim.

President of Chamber: KAMAL ASAAD.

Deputy president of Chamber: MOUNIR ABU FADEL.

RELIGIOUS GROUPS

Maronite Christians	30
Sunni Muslims	20
Shi'i Muslims	19
Greek Orthodox	11
Greek Catholics	6
Druzes	6
Armenian Orthodox	4
Armenian Catholics	1
Protestants	1
Others	1
TOTAL	99

There was a General Election in May 1972, but the diversity of allegiance in the Chamber makes a strict analysis by party groupings impossible. The distribution of seats among religious groups is laid down by law.

POLITICAL PARTIES

al-Baath: f. in Syria, 1940, by MICHEL AFLAK; secular party with policy of Arab union, branches in several Middle Eastern countries; 2 mems. in Chamber of Deputies; Sec. ABDUL MAJID RAFII, Chambre des Députés, Place de l'Étoile, Beirut.

Bloc National: f. 1943; policy of power-sharing and the exclusion of the military from politics; 5 mems. in the Chamber of Deputies; Leader RAYMOND EDDÉ; Sec.-Gen. EDOUARD IBRAHIM HONEIN, Chambre des Députés, Place de l'Étoile, Beirut.

ad-Dustour (Constitutional Party): f. 1943; led struggle against French mandate, established 1943 Constitution; party of the political and business élite; Leader MICHEL BECHARA AL-KHOURY, rue Michel Chiha, Kantari, Beirut.

al-Harakiyines al-Arab: Beirut; f. 1948 by GEORGES HABACHE; Arab nationalist party, with Marxist tendencies.

al-Hayat al-Wataniya: Beirut; f. 1964 by AMINE ARAYSSI.

al-Jabha al-Damukratiya al-Barlamaniya (Parliamentary Democratic Front): Beirut; mainly Muslim support; Leader RASHID ABDUL HAMID KARAMI, Chambre des Députés, Place de l'Étoile, Beirut.

al-Kata'eb (Phalanges Libanaises, Phalangist Party): P.O.B. 992, Place Charles Hélou, Beirut; f. 1936; nationalist, reformist, democratic social party; 70,260 mems.; Leader PIERRE GEMAYEL; Vice-Pres. JOSEPH CHADER; Gen. Sec. JOSEPH SAADE; 7 mems. in Chamber of Deputies; publs. *al-Amal* (Arabic daily), *Action—Proche Orient* (French political and scientific monthly).

Mouvement de l'Action Nationale: f. 1965; Founder and Leader OSMAN MOSBAH AD-DANA, P.O.B. 5890, Centre Starco, Bloc Sud, Beirut.

an-Najjadé: f. 1936; unionist; 3,000 mems.; Founder and Pres. ADNANE MOUSTAPHA AL-HAKIM, Sawt al-Uruba, P.O.B. 3537, Beirut; publ. *Sawt al-Uruba* (Arabic daily).

an-Nida' al-Kawmi: f. 1945; Founder and Leader KAZEM AS-SOLH, Ramlet al-Baïda, Imm. Chammat, Beirut.

Parti Communiste Libanais (Lebanese Communist Party): rue al-Hout, Imm. du Parti Communiste Libanais, Beirut; f. 1924; officially dissolved 1948–71; Marxist, much support among intellectuals; 1 mem. in Chamber of Deputies; Sec.-Gen. NICOLAS CHAOUI; publs. *an-Nida* (daily), *al-Akhbar* (weekly), *al-Tarik* (monthly), *Gantch* (Armenian weekly).

Parti Démocrate: f. 1969; supports a secular, democratic policy, private enterprise and social justice; Sec.-Gen. JOSEPH MUGHAIZEL; co-founder ÉMILE BITAR, rue Kantari, Imm. Labban, Beirut.

Parti National Liberal (al-Wataniyin al-Ahrar): f. 1958; liberal reformist party; 9 mems. and assocs. in Chamber of Deputies; Founder and Pres. CAMILLE CHAMOUN, Chambre des Députés, Place de l'Étoile, Beirut.

Parti Populaire Syrien (Social Nationalist Party); f. 1932, banned 1962–69; advocates a "Greater Syria", composed of Lebanon, Syria, Iraq, Jordan, Palestine and Cyprus; 1 supporter in Chamber of Deputies: MICHEL MAALOULI, Chambre des Députés, Place de l'Étoile, Beirut.

Parti Socialiste Progressiste (al-Takadumi al-Ishteraki): P.O.B. 2893, Zkak el-Blat, Beirut; f. 1948; progressive party, advocates constitutional road to socialism; over 16,000 mems.; 10 mems. in Chamber of Deputies; Founder and Pres. KAMAL JOUMBLATT; publ. *al-Anbla'* (weekly).

Parti Socialiste Révolutionnaire: Beirut; f. 1964; Leader YOUSSEF MOUBARAK.

Parti Tachnag: f. 1890; principal Armenian party; collective leadership; 5 mems. in Chamber of Deputies, including KHATCHIG BABIKIAN, Chambre des Députés, Place de l'Étoile, Beirut.

DIPLOMATIC REPRESENTATION

EMBASSIES AND LEGATION ACCREDITED TO LEBANON

(Beirut unless otherwise indicated)

(E) Embassy; (L) Legation.

Afghanistan: Rue Rachidin, Tallet el-Khayyat, Imm. Land and Construction No. 3, 7th Floor, Apt. 14 (E); *Ambassador:* ABDEL-WAHID KARIM.

Algeria: Jnah (opposite Coral Beach) (E); *Ambassador:* MUHAMMAD YAZID.

Argentina: 149 Ave. Fouad 1er (E); *Ambassador:* ALBERTO SUAYA (also accred. to Jordan and Saudi Arabia).

Australia: SFAH Bldg., Rue Kantari (E); *Ambassador:* PIERRE HUTTON (also accred. to Iraq and Jordan).

Austria: Quartier Sursock, Rue Négib Trad, Villa Nocolas Cattan (E); *Ambassador:* HANS WALSER (also accred. to Jordan, Kuwait and Syria).

Bahrain: Sami Fouad Hamzeh Bldg., Bir Hassan (E); *Ambassador:* ALI IBRAHIM AL MAHROUS.

Bangladesh: Rue Tabet (Verdun), Imm. Said Jaafar (E); *Ambassador:* KHONDKER GOLAM MUSTAFA.

Belgium: 15th Floor, Centre Verdun, Rue Dunant (E); *Ambassador:* HUBERT BEDUWE (also accred. to Cyprus and Jordan).

Bolivia: Place de l'Etoile, Imm. Tchatalbadjian (E); *Chargé d'Affaires:* NAJIB BICHARA GHOSN.

Brazil: Rue Verdun, Imm. Mahmassani (E); *Ambassador:* JORGE D'ESCRAGNOLLE TAUNAY (also accred. to Jordan).

Bulgaria: Blvd. Chiah-Hadath, Imm. Lati (E); *Ambassador:* GUEORGUI TANEV.

Cameroon: Cairo, Egypt (E).

Canada: Rue Hamra, Centre Sabbagh (E); *Ambassador:* LEOPOLD AMYOT (also accred. to Iraq and Jordan).

Chad: Blvd. Sami Solh, Forêt Kfoury, Imm. Kalot Frères (E); *Chargé d'Affaires:* NODJIMADJE N'GARTORI (also accred. to Jordan).

Chile: Rue Maamari, Imm. Lion's (E); *Ambassador:* General ALFREDO CANALES.

China, People's Republic: Rue 62, Nicolas Ibrahim Sursock, Ramlet El-Baida (E); *Ambassador:* HSU MING.

Colombia: Chouran, Imm. Jaber al-Ahmad al-Sabbah (E); *Ambassador:* ALBERTO LOSADA LARRA (also accred. to Kuwait).

Congo People's Republic: Cairo, Egypt (E).

Costa Rica: Rue Hamra (E); *Chargé d'Affaires:* RIAD ABDEL-BAKI (also accred to Kuwait).

Cuba: Rue Abdel Sabbah between Rue Sakiet el-Janzir and Rue de Vienne, Imm. Abdel Rahman et Bahjat Ghazal (E); *Ambassador:* MIGUEL BRUGUERAS DEL VALLE (also accred. to Greece).

Cyprus: Cairo, Egypt (E).

Czechoslovakia: Rue Fouad 1er, Imm. Kayssi (E); *Ambassador:* Dr. KAREL BLAZEK.

Denmark: Rue Clemenceau, Imm. Minkara (E); *Ambassador:* MOGENS WARBERG (also accred. to Cyprus and Jordan.

Dominican Republic: Raouché, Imm. Minkara (E).

Egypt: Rue Ramlat el-Baida (E); *Ambassador:* AHMAD LOUTFI MOUTAWALLI.

Ethiopia: Cairo, Egypt (E).

Finland: Centre Gefinor, Rue Clemenceau (E); *Ambassador:* HEKKI KALAHA (also accred. to Jordan and Kuwait).

France: Rue Clemenceau (E); *Ambassador:* HUBERT ARGOD.

German Democratic Republic: Ave. de Paris (E); *Ambassador:* Dr. BRUNO SEDLACZEK.

Germany, Federal Republic: Rue Hamra, Imm. Arida (E); *Ambassador:* RUEDIDER VON PACHELBEL.

Ghana: Jnah, Imm. Cheikh Sabah Ahmad Al-Sabah (E); *Ambassador:* Maj.-Gen. CLELAND COFIE BRUCE.

Greece: Rue de France (E); *Ambassador:* EUSTACHE KALAMIDAS (also accred. to Kuwait).

Guinea: Cairo, Egypt (E).

Haiti: Rue du Fleuve, Imm. Sarkis (E); *Ambassador:* PIERRE SARKIS.

Hungary: Jnah, Imm. Cheikh Salem Al-Sabah (E); *Ambassador:* JÁNOS VERES.

India: Rue Kantari, Imm. Samharini (E); *Ambassador:* SHILENDRA K. SINGH (also accred. to Cyprus).

Indonesia: Cairo, Egypt (E).

Iran: Jnah, Imm. Sakina Mattar (E); *Ambassador:* MANSOUR GHADAR.

Iraq: Jnah, Face Eden Rock (E); *Ambassador:* KHALED NOUR ISMAIL AL-WAIS (also accred. to Cyprus).

Italy: Rue Makdissi, Imm. Cosmidis (E); *Ambassador:* VINCENZI DE BENEDICTIS.

Ivory Coast: Avenue Sami Solh, Imm. Georges Tazbek (E); *Ambassador:* AMADOU BOCOUM.

Japan: Corniche Chouran, Imm. Olfat Nagib Salha (E); *Ambassador:* NOBORU SIGIURA (also accred. to Cyprus).

Jordan: Rue Verdun, Imm. Belle-Vue (E); *Ambassador:* WALID SALEH.

Kenya: Cairo, Egypt (E).

Kuwait: Bir Hassan, The Stadium Roundabout (E); *Ambassador:* MUHAMMAD YOUSSEF AL-ADASSANI.

Liberia: Rome, Italy (E).

Libya: Jnah, Imm. Cheikh Abdallah Khalifé Al-Sabbah (E); *Ambassador:* ABDEL-KADER GHOUKA.

Malaysia: Cairo, Egypt (E).

Mali: Cairo, Egypt (E).

Malta: Achrafié, Rue Marian Geahchan, Imm. Varkés Sarafian (L); *Chargé d'Affaires:* BERNARD FATTAL.

Mauritania: Cairo, Egypt (E).

Mexico: Rue Hamra, Imm. Arida (E); *Ambassador:* Dr. FRANCISCO APODACA (also accred. to Pakistan).

Morocco: Corniche Masraa, Imm. Chamat (E); *Ambassador:* DRISS BENNOUNA.

Nepal: Cairo, Egypt (E).

Netherlands: Rue Kantari, Imm. Sahmarani (E); *Ambassador:* ADRIANUS CORNELIS VROON (also accred. to Cyprus and Jordan).

Nigeria: Cairo, Egypt (E).

Norway: Cairo, Egypt (E).

Oman: Bir Hassan (E); *Ambassador:* ABDULLAH ALI AL-QUTABI.

Pakistan: 2699 Rue de Lyon (E); *Ambassador:* Dr. S. M. KORESHI (also accred. to Cyprus).

Panama: Corniche Mazraa, Imm. Saab (E).

Peru: Cairo, Egypt (E).

Poland: Furn el-Chebbak, Rue Asile des Vieillards, Imm. Haddad Frères (E); *Ambassador:* ANTONI PIERZCHALA.

Portugal: Rue Beyhum, Villa Omar Beyhum (E); *Ambassador:* (vacant) (also accred. to Jordan).

Qatar: Dibs Building, Chouran Street (E); *Ambassador:* MUHAMMAD BEN HAMAD AL THANI.

Romania: Avenue Sami el-Solh, 215 Forêt Kfouri, Imm. Boutros et Chammah (E); *Ambassador:* Dr. MIHAIL LEVENTE.

Saudi Arabia: Rue Bliss, Manara (E); *Ambassador:* Sheikh MUHAMMAD AL-MANSOUR AL-RUMAIH.

Senegal: Corniche Mazraa, Rue Ibn el-Assir, Imm. Kholy el-Kataby (E); *Ambassador:* ALPHONSE N'DIAYE.

Singapore: Cairo, Egypt (E).

Spain: Ramlet el Baida, Imm. White Sands (E); *Ambassador:* JOSÉ LUIS FLOREZ-ESTRADA.

Sri Lanka: Cairo, Egypt (E).

Sudan: Rue Mme Curie, Imm. Minkara (E); *Ambassador:* MIRGHANI SULAIMAN KHALIL.

Sweden: Rue Clemenceau, Imm. Moukarzel et Rubeiz (E); *Ambassador:* JEAN-JAQUES VON DARDEL (also accred. to Cyprus and Jordan).

Switzerland: Avenue Perthuis, Imm. Achou (E); *Ambassador:* CHARLES-ALBERT DUBOIS.

Thailand: Cairo, Egypt (E).

Tunisia: Ramlet el-Baida, Imm. Rock and Marble (E); *Ambassador:* MUHAMMAD AMAMOU.

Turkey: Bir Hassan (E); *Ambassador:* NECMETTIN TUNCEL.

U.S.S.R.: Rue Mar Elias el-Tina (E); *Ambassador:* ALEXANDER SOLDATOV.

United Arab Emirates: Jnah, Face Eden Rock, Imm. Wafic Tabbara (E); *Ambassador:* RASHED MAKKAWI.

United Kingdom: Avenue de Paris, Ain el-Mreissé (E); *Ambassador:* PETER WAKEFIELD, C.M.G.

U.S.A.: Ave. de Paris (Corniche), Imm. Ali Reza (E); *Ambassador:* MCMURTRIE GODLEY.

Uruguay: Rue Verdun, Fayoumé, Imm. Mohamad Hussein Ben Moutahar (E); *Ambassador:* RODOLFO COMAS AMARO (also accred. to Jordan and Syria).

Vatican: Rue Georges Picot; *Apostolic Nuncio:* Mgr. ALFREDO BRUNIERA.

Venezuela: Rue Kantari, Imm. Sahmarani (E); *Ambassador:* Dr. PEDRO J. BARRADAS (also accred. to Jordan and Kuwait).

Yemen Arab Republic: Blvd. Khaldé-Quzai, Imm. Ingénieur Ryad Amaiche (E); *Ambassador:* ABDUL-QUDDOUS AL-WAZIR.

Yemen, People's Democratic Republic: Ramlet el Baida, Imm. Ramlet el Baida (E); *Chargé d'Affaires a.i.:* AHMAD ALI MAISARI.

Yugoslavia: Imm. Daouk, Arts et Metiers Quarter (E); *Ambassador:* MILIC BUGARCIC.

Zaire: Cairo, Egypt (E).

Zambia: Cairo, Egypt (E).

Lebanon also has diplomatic relations with Albania, Cambodia, Central African Republic, Dahomey, Ecuador, El Salvador, Gabon, the Gambia, Guatemala, Honduras, Ireland, Luxembourg, Madagascar, Monaco, Nicaragua, Niger, Paraguay, the Philippines, Sierra Leone, Togo and the Upper Volta.

JUDICIAL SYSTEM

Law and justice in the Lebanon are administered in accordance with the following codes, which are based upon modern theories of civil and criminal legislation:

(1) Code de la Propriété (1930).

(2) Code des Obligations et des Contrats (1932).

(3) Code de Procédure Civile (1933).

(4) Code Maritime (1947).

(6) Code de Procédure Pénale (Code Ottoman Modifié).

(7) Code Pénal (1943).

(8) Code Pénal Militaire (1946).

(9) Code d'Instruction Criminelle.

The following courts are now established:

(*a*) Fifty-six "Single-Judge Courts", each consisting of a single judge, and dealing in the first instance with both civil and criminal cases; there are seventeen such courts at Beirut and seven at Tripoli.

(*b*) Eleven Courts of Appeal, each consisting of three judges, including a President and a Public Prosecutor, and dealing with civil and criminal cases; there are five such courts at Beirut.

(*c*) **Four Courts of Cassation**, three dealing with civil and commercial cases and the fourth with criminal cases. A Court of Cassation, to be properly constituted, must have at least three judges, one being the President and the other two Councillors. The First Court consists of the First President of the Court of Cassation, a President and two Councillors. The other two civil courts each consist of a President and three Councillors. If the Court of Cassation reverses the judgment of a lower court it does not refer the case back but retries it itself.

First President of the Court of Cassation: BADRI MEOUCHI.

(*d*) The Council of State, which deals with administrative cases. It consists of a President, Vice-President and four Councillors. A Commissioner represents the Government.

President of the Court of the Council of State: ABOU KHAIR.

(*e*) The Court of Justice, which is a special court consisting of a President and eight judges, deals with matters affecting the security of the State.

In addition to the above, Islamic, Christian and Jewish religious courts deal with affairs of personal status (marriages, deaths, inheritances, etc.).

There is also a Press Tribunal.

RELIGION

PRINCIPAL COMMUNITIES

	1958	1972*
Christians	792,000	n.a.
Roman Catholics . .	529,500	1,089,438
Armenian Rite . .	14,500	24,500
Chaldean Rite . .	n.a.	5,957
Greek (Melkite) Rite .	} 91,000 {	183,345
Latin Rite . . .		20,000
Maronite Rite . .	424,000	837,636
Syrian Rite . .	n.a.	18,000
Orthodox . . .	219,000	n.a.
Greek . . .	150,000	n.a.
Armenian . . .	69,000	n.a.
Protestant . .	14,000	n.a.
Muslims	624,000	n.a.
Sunni	286,000	n.a.
Shi'i	250,000	n.a.
Druzes	88,000	n.a.
Jews	6,600	n.a.

* The 1972 figures for members of the Roman Catholic churches are based on estimates by the curias of dioceses based in the Lebanon. National and diocesan boundaries do not necessarily correspond.

It will be seen that the largest single community in the Lebanon is the Maronite, a Uniate sect of the Roman Church. The Maronites inhabited the old territory of Mount Lebanon, i.e. immediately east of Beirut. In the south, towards the Israeli frontier, Shi'i villages are most common whilst between the Shi'i and the Maronites live the Druzes (divided between the Yazbakis and the Jumblatis). The Bekaa has many Greek Christians, whilst the Tripoli area is mainly Sunni Muslim. Altogether, of all the regions of the Middle East, the Lebanon probably presents the closest juxtaposition of sects and peoples within a small territory. As Lebanese political life is organized on a sectarian basis, the Maronites also enjoy much political influence, including a predominant voice in the nomination of the President of the Republic.

ROMAN CATHOLIC CHURCH

ARMENIAN RITE

Patriarchate of Cilicia: Patriarcat Arménien Catholique, Beirut; includes Patriarchal Diocese of Beirut; 23 priests, 24,500 Catholics; Patriarch IGNACE PIERRE XVI BATANIAN.

CHALDEAN RITE

Diocese of Beirut: Evêché Chaldéen-Catholique, B.P. 8566, Beirut; 8 priests, 5,957 Catholics; Bishop RAPHAEL BIDAWID.

LATIN RITE

Apostolic Vicariate of Beirut: Vicariat Apostolique, Villa Maria, B.P. 4224, Beirut; 240 priests, 25,000 Catholics; Vicar Apostolic PAUL BASSIM.

MARONITE RITE

Patriarchate of Antioch: Patriarcat Maronite, Bkerké (winter), Dimane (summer); includes Patriarchal Diocese of Gibail and Batrun; 200 priests, 184,763 Catholics; Patriarch ANTOINE KHORAICHE. The Maronite Rite includes the Archdioceses of Beirut, Tripoli and Tyre, and the Dioceses of Baalbek, Saida and Sarba.

MELKITE RITE

Patriarchate of Antioch: Patriarcat Grec-Melkite Catholique, B.P. 50076, Beirut; jurisdiction over the Melkites of Egypt and the Sudan, Jerusalem and Iraq; publs. *Sophia* (English), *Le Lien* (French); Patriarch of Alexandria, Antioch and Jerusalem MAXIMOS V HAKIM. The Melkite Rite includes the Metropolitan Archdioceses of Tyre, Beirut and Gibail, and the Archdioceses of Baalbek, Baniyas, Saida, Tripoli, and Zahleh and Furzol.

SYRIAN RITE

Patriarchate of Antioch: Patriarcat Syrien-Catholique, rue de Damas, P.B. 8879, Beirut; jurisdiction over Syrian Catholics of Palestine, Jordan, Lebanon and Turkey; Patriarch IGNACE ANTOINE II HAYEK.

Patriarchal Vicariate of the Lebanon: Vicariat Patriarcal Syrien, rue de Syrie, Beirut; 13 priests, 18,000 Catholics; Vicar Patriarchal FLAVIEN ZACHARIE MELKI.

Note: The statistics of priests and Catholics are estimates by the diocesan curias for the situation on December 31st, 1972.

OTHER RELIGIOUS GROUPS

Armenian Orthodox: Leader Mgr. KHOREN I PAROYAN, Catholicos of Cilicia and All the East, Catholicossat des Arméniens Orthodoxes, Antélias.

Greek Orthodox: Leader His Beatitude ELIAS IV MUAWAD, Patriarch of Antioch and All the East, Patriarcat Grec-Orthodoxe, P.O.B. 9, Damascus, Syria.

Syrian Orthodox: Leader Mgr. IGNATIOS III YACOUB, Patriarch of Antioch and All the East, Patriarcat Syrien Orthodoxe, Beirut.

Shi'i Muslims: Leader Imam SAYED MOUSSA AS-SADR, Pres. of the Supreme Islamic Council of the Shi'i Community of the Lebanon, Dar al-Iftaa al-Jaafari, Beirut.

Sunni Muslims: Leader S.G. Sheikh HASSAN KHALED, Grand Mufti of the Lebanon, Tarik Jadidé, rue Boustany, Beirut.

Druzes: Leader S.G. Sheikh MUHAMMAD ABOUCHACRA, Supreme Spiritual Leader of the Druze Community, rue Abou Chacra, Beirut.

Jews: Leader CHAHOUD CHREIM, Beirut.

Protestants: Leader Rev. Dr. FARID AUDEH, Pres. of Nat. Evangelical Union of the Lebanon, P.O.B. 5224, rue Maurice Barrès, Beirut.

Union of the Armenian Evangelical Churches in the Near East: P.O.B. 377, Beirut; Moderator Prof. Hov P. AHARONIAN; the Union includes some thirty Armenian Evangelical Churches in Syria, Lebanon, Egypt, Cyprus, Greece, Iran and Turkey.

THE PRESS

With 96 newspapers, some 40 of them dailies, serving a readership drawn from a population of only two and a half million, the Lebanese Press is highly competitive. It is also relatively free from external controls, compared with most of the other Middle East countries. Freedom of the press, along with freedom of expression and association, is guaranteed, within the limits of the law, by article 13 of the Constitution. However, the legal limitations on the expression of opinion are somewhat restrictive. The basic press law is that of 1948, under which all papers and periodicals have to be licensed by the Ministry of the Interior. The licence can be withdrawn if a paper ceases publication temporarily within six months of its inception, or if circulation drops below 1,500 for thirty days. The editor must have a university qualification, and must deposit a security. The 1948 law also made journalists subject to the judgements of a tribunal of discipline. After a period of conflict between the Government and the Press, the existing law was revised by the press law of 1958, which abolished the procedure for detaining journalists pending investigations, and, with certain exceptions, made it possible for persons convicted of infringement of press regulations to lodge an appeal.

The most important dailies are *al-Anwar* and *an-Nahar*, which have the highest circulations, *The Daily Star*, *al-Jarida* and *L'Orient-Le Jour*, the foremost French paper. The latter two are owned by Georges Naccache, former Lebanese ambassador to France, and tend to take a pro-government line. In a country where most of the élite speak French the other French daily, *Le Soir*, is also influential, and, for the same reason, the twice-weekly publication *Le Commerce du Levant* occupies an important place in the periodical press.

The Lebanese Press has benefited indirectly from Beirut's status as by far the most important base for foreign correspondents covering the Middle East. Long-distance communications have consequently been developed to a high standard.

DAILIES

al-Amal: P.O.B. 992, place Charles Hélou, Beirut; f. 1939; Phalangist Party; Arabic; circ. 14,000; Editor GEORGES OMEIRA.

al-Anba': P.O.B. 955, Beirut; f. 1948; Arabic.

al-Anwar: P.O.B. 1038, Beirut; f. 1959; independent; Arabic; Supplement, Sunday, cultural and social; published by Dar Assayad S.A.L.; circ. 75,200; Propr. SAID FREIHA; Editor ISSAM FREIHA.

Ararat: P.O.B. 756, Nor Hagin, Beirut; f. 1937; Communist; Armenian; circ. 3,000; Editor KRIKOR JABULIANO.

Ayk: P.O.B. 2623, Beirut; f. 1953; Armenian.

Aztag: P.O.B. 587, rue Zokak el-Blatt, Beirut; f. 1926; Armenian; circ. 4,500.

al-Baïraq: P.O.B. 1800, rue Monot, Beirut; f. 1911; Arabic; published by Soc. Libanaise de Presse; Editors ASSAD and FADEL AKL; circ. 3,000.

Baïrut: P.O.B. 7944, Beirut; f. 1952; Arabic.

Baïrut al-Massa: P.O.B. 1203, place des Capucins, Beirut; f. 1932; Arabic; Editor ABDULLAH MASHNUQ; circ. 6,000.

ach-Chaab: P.O.B. 5140, Beirut; f. 1961; Arabic; Nationalist; Propr. and Editor MUHAMMAD AMIN DUGHAN; circ. 7,000.

ach-Chams: P.O.B. 7047, Beirut; f. 1925; Arabic.

ach-Charq: P.O.B. 838, rue de la Marseillaise, Beirut; f. 1945; Arabic; Editor KHAIRY AL-KA'KI.

Daily Star: P.O.B. 11-987, rue al-Hayat, Beirut; f. 1952; independent; English; Chief Editor JIHAD KHAZEN; circ. 12,300.

ad-Dastour: P.O.B. 886, Beirut; f. 1968; Arabic; Owner and Editor AL- BALLOUT; circ. 53,400.

ad-Dunia: P.O.B. 4599, Beirut; f. 1943; Arabic; political; Chief Editor SULIMAN ABOU ZAID.

al-Hadaf: P.O.B. 212, rue Béchir, Imm. Esseilé, Beirut; f. 1969; Arabic.

al-Hadith: P.O.B. 5858, Beirut; f. 1927; Arabic.

al-Hayat: P.O.B. 11-987, rue al-Hayat, Beirut; f. 1946; independent; Arabic; circ. 32,538.

al-Jarida: P.O.B. 220, place Tabaris, Beirut; f. 1953; independent; Arabic; Editor ABDULLA SKAFF; circ. 22,600.

al-Joumhouria: P.O.B. 7111, Beirut; f. 1924; Arabic.

al-Khatib: P.O.B. 365, rue Georges Picot; Arabic.

al-Kifah: P.O.B. 1462, rue Mère Gelas, Beirut; f. 1950; Arabic; Editor RIAD TAHA; circ. 21,000.

Lissan-ul-Hal: P.O.B. 4619, rue Chateaubriand, Beirut; f. 1877; Arabic; Editor GEBRAN HAYEK; circ. 33,000.

al-Liwa': P.O.B. 2402, Beirut; f. 1970; Arabic.

al-Moharrer: P.O.B. 5366, Beirut; f. 1962; Arabic; nationalist; Editor TAUFIQ KHATTAB; circ. 4,000.

an-Nahar: P.O.B. 226, rue Banque Centrale du Liban, Press Co-operative Bldg., Beirut; f. 1933; Arabic; independent; Publisher and Editor-in-Chief GHASSAN TUENI; Co-Editor MICHEL ABOU JAOUDÉ; circ. 74,538.

an-Nass: P.O.B. 4886, Beirut; f. 1959; Arabic.

Nida: P.O.B. 4744, Beirut; f. 1958; Arabic; published by the Lebanese Communist Party; Editor KARIM MROUÉ; circ. 3,500.

Nida' al-Watan: P.O.B. 6324, Beirut; f. 1937; Arabic.

an-Nidal: P.O.B. 1354, Beirut; f. 1939; Arabic.

L'Orient-Le Jour: P.O.B. 2488, rue Banque du Liban, Beirut; f. 1942; French independent; Dir. PIERRE EDDÉ; Editor JEAN CHOUERI; circ. 21,500.

Raqib al-Ahwad: P.O.B. 467, rue Patriarche Hoyek, Beirut; f. 1937; Arabic; Editor SIMA'N FARAH SEIF.

Rayah: P.O.B. 4101, Beirut; Arabic.

ar-Ruwwad: P.O.B. 2696, rue Mokhalsieh, Beirut; f. 1940; Arabic; Editor BESHARA MAROUN.

Sada Lubnan: P.O.B. 7884, Beirut; f. 1951; Arabic.

Sadal Janoub: Beirut; f. 1936; Arabic.

as-Safa: P.O.B. 9192, Beirut; f. 1972; French; published by Soc. Nat. de Presse et d'Edition S.A.L.; Editor RENÉ AGGIOURI; circ. 15,000.

Sawt al-Uruba: P.O.B. 3537, Beirut; f. 1959; Arabic; an-Najjadé Party; Editor ADNANE AL-HAKIM.

Le Soir: P.O.B. 1470, rue de Syrie, Beirut; f. 1947; French; political independent; Dir. DIKRAN TOSBATH; Editor ANDRÉ KECATI; circ. 16,500.

at-Tayyar: P.O.B. 1038, Beirut; Arabic; independent; issued weekly for the time being; circ. 75,000.

Telegraf—Baïrut: P.O.B. 1061, rue Béehara el Khoury, Beirut; f. 1930; Arabic; political, economic and social; Editor TOUFIC ASSAD MATNI; circ. 15,500 (5,000 outside Lebanon).

al-Yawm: P.O.B. 1908, Beirut; f. 1937; Arabic; Editor WAFIC MUHAMMAD CHAKER AT-TIBY.

az-Zamane: P.O.B. 6060, rue Boutros Karameh, Beirut; f. 1947; Arabic; Editor ROBERT ABELA.

Zartonk: P.O.B. 617, rue de l'Hôpital Français, Beirut; f. 1937; Armenian; official organ of Armenian Liberal Democratic Party; Editor P. TOUMASSIAN.

WEEKLIES

Achabaka: Dar Assayad, P.O.B. 1038, Beirut; f. 1956; society and features; Arabic; Propt. SAID FREIHA; Editor GEORGE IBRAHIM EL-KHOURY; circ. 126,500.

al-Ahad: Rue Mère Gelas, P.O.B. 1462, Beirut; Arabic; RIAD TAHA; circ. 32,000.

al-Akhbar: Beirut; Arabic; published by the Lebanese Communist Party; circ. 21,000.

al-Anba': Rue Maroun Naccache, P.O.B. 2893, Beirut; Progressive Socialist Party; Arabic; Editor KAMAL JUMBLATT.

al-Anwar Supplement: P.O.B. 1038, Beirut; cultural-social; every Sunday; supplement to daily *al-Anwar*; Editor ISSAM FREIHA; circ. 90,000.

Argus: Bureau des Documentations Libanaises et Arabes, P.O.B. 11-3000, Beirut; twice-weekly news bulletin; circ. 1,000.

al-Ash-Shir': 144 Rue Gouraud, Beirut; f. 1948; Catholic; Arabic; Editor Father ANTOINE CORTBAWI.

Assayad: Dar Assayad, P.O.B. 1038, Beirut; f. 1943; Propt. SAID FREIHA; Editor RAFIQUE KHOURY; circ. 94,700.

al-Awassef: Homsi Bldg., P.O.B. 2492, Beirut; f. 1953; Arabic; political, independent; Dir. DAHER KHALIL ZEIDAN; circ. 10,500.

Combat: Beirut; French; Editor GEORGES CORBAN.

Le Commerce du Levant: P.O.B. 687, Kantari St., SFAH Bldg., Beirut; f. 1929; twice weekly; also publishes monthly edition; commercial; French; circ. 15,000; Editor: Société de la Presse Economique; Pres. E. S. SHOUCAIR.

Dabbour: Museum Square, Beirut; f. 1922; Arabic; Editors MICHEL RICHARD and FUAD MUKARZEL; circ. 12,000.

al-Dyar: P.O.B. 959, Verdun St., Bellevue Bldg., Beirut; f. 1941; Arabic; political; Editor YASSER HAWARI; circ. 46,000.

Gantch: Beirut; Armenian; published by the Lebanese Communist Party; circ. 2,200.

al-Hawadess: P.O.B. 1281, Beirut; f. 1911; Arabic; political; Chair. and Gen. Man. SALIM LOZI; Deputy Gen. Man. MAHMOUD MARAACHLI; Editor-in-Chief NABIL KHOURY; circ. 130,000.

al-Hurriya: P.O.B. 857, Beirut; f. 1960; voice of Arab Nationalist Movement; Arabic; Chief Editor MUHSIN IBRAHIM; circ. 12,000.

al-Iza'a: Rue Selim Jazaerly, P.O.B. 462, Beirut; f. 1938; politics, art, literature and broadcasting; Arabic; circ. 11,000; Editor FAYEK KHOURY.

al-Jamhour: Mussaïtbeh, P.O.B. 1834, Beirut; f. 1936; Arabic; illustrated weekly news magazine; Editor FARID ABU SHAHLA; circ. 45,000, of which over 30,000 outside Lebanon.

Kul Shay': Rue Béehara el Khoury, P.O.B. 3250, Beirut; Arabic.

al-Liwa: Rue Abdel Kaim Khalil, P.O.B. 2402, Beirut; Arabic; Propr. ABDEL GHANI SALAAM.

Magazine: Quartier Sursock, Achrafieh, P.O.B. 1404, Beirut; f. 1956; in French; political and social; Publ. Les Editions Orientales S.A.L.; Publisher GEORGE ABOU ADAL; Ed.-in-Chief ALINE LAHOUD; circ. 15,983.

Massis: Place Debbas, Beirut; f. 1949; Armenian; Catholic; Editor F. VARTAN TEKEYAN; circ. 2,000.

an-Nahda: Abdul Aziz St., P.O.B. 3736, Beirut; Arabic; independent; Man. Editor NADIM ABOU-ISMIL.

Middle East Economic Survey: Middle East Research and Publishing Centre, P.O.B. 11-1224, Beirut; f. 1957; oil topics; Editor and Publr. FUAD W. ITAYIM.

al-Ousbou' al-Arabi (Arab Week): Quartier Sursock, Achrafieh, P.O.B. 1404, Beirut; f. 1959; Arabic; political and social; Publishers Les Editions Orientales, S.A.L.; Publisher GEORGE ABOU ADAL; Editor-in-Chief ASSAD MOKADDEM; circ. 147,500 (circulates throughout the Arab world).

al-Rassed: P.O.B. 11-2808, Beirut; Arabic; Editor GEORGE RAJJI.

Revue du Liban: Rue Allenby, Beirut; f. 1928; French; Editor IBRAHIM MAKHLOUF; circ. 15,000.

Samar: P.O.B. 1038, Beirut; photorama magazine; circ. 50,000.

OTHER SELECTED PERIODICALS

Note: published monthly unless otherwise stated.

al-Adib: P.O.B. 878, Beirut; f. 1942; Arabic, artistic, literary, scientific and political; Editor ALBERT ADIB.

al-Afkar: Rue Mère Gelas, Beirut; international; French; Editor RIAD TAHA.

Alam Attijarat (*Business World*): Strand Bldg., Hamra St., Beirut; f. 1965 in association with Johnston International Publishing Corpn., New York; monthly; commercial; Editor NADIM MAKDISI; international circ. 17,500.

Arab Economist: Gefinor Tower, Clemenceau St., P.O.B. 11-6068, Beirut; monthly; published by Centre for Economic, Financial and Social Research and Documentation S.A.L.; Chair. Dr. CHAFIC AKHRAS; Man. Dir. Dr. SABBAN AL HAJ.

Arab Oil & Gas Journal: Arab Petroleum Research Centre, P.O.B. 7167, Beirut; Arabic (monthly), French and English (fortnightly); Publisher and Editor Dr. NICOLAS SARKIS.

L'Economie des Pays Arabes: B.P. 6068, Beirut; f. 1969; French; published by Centre d'Etudes et de Documentation Economiques Financières et Sociales S.A.L.; Pres. Dr. CHAFIC AKHRAS; Dir.-Gen. Dr. SABBAH AL HAJ; circ. 5,000.

al-Idary: P.O.B. 1038, Beirut; business management; Arabic; circ. 10,000.

International Crude Oil and Product Prices: Middle East Petroleum and Economic Publications, P.O.B. 11-1224, Beirut; f. 1971; twice yearly review and analysis of oil price trends in world markets; Publisher FUAD W. ITAYIM.

al-Intilak: c/o Michel Nehme, al-Intilak Printing and Publishing House, P.O.B. 4958, Beirut; f. 1960; literary; Arabic; Chief Editor MICHEL NEHME.

Lebanese and Arab Economy: Allenby St., P.O.B. 1801, Beirut; f. 1951; fortnightly; Arabic, English and French; Publisher Beirut Chamber of Commerce and Industry and SAMI N. ATIYEH; Editor and Dir. ABDEL-WAHAB RIFA'I.

Majallat al Izaat al Loubnaniat: Lebanese Broadcasting Corporation, Beirut; Arabic; broadcasting affairs.

Naft al Arab: Beirut; f. 1965; monthly; Arabic; oil; Publisher ABDULLAH AL TARIQI.

Nous Ouvriers du Pays: 144 Rue Gouraud, Beirut; Catholic; English-French; social welfare; Editor Father ANTOINE CORTBAWI.

Rijal al Amal (*Businessmen*): P.O.B. 220, Cornishe Square, Beirut; business magazine; Arabic, with special issues in English and French; Editor G. W. SKAFF; circ. 12,000.

Sawt al-Mar'ah: Dar al-Kitab, P.O.B. 1284, Beirut; Lebanese Women's League; Arabic; Editor: Mrs. J. SHEIBOUB.

Tabibok: P.O.B. 4887, Beirut; f. 1956; medical, social, scientific; Arabic; Editor Dr. SAMI KABANI; circ. 78,000.

al-Tarik: Beirut; cultural and theoretical; published by the Lebanese Communist Party; circ. 5,000.

al-'Ulum: Dar al Ilm Lil Malayeen, rue de Syrie, P.O.B. 1085, Beirut; scientific review.

Welcome to Lebanon and the Middle East: Tourist Information and Advertising Bureau: Starco Centre, North Block 711, P.O.B. 4204, Beirut; f. 1959; on entertainment, touring and travel; English; Editor SOUHAIL TOUFIK ABOU-JAMRA; circ. 6,000.

NEWS AGENCIES
FOREIGN BUREAUX

ANSA: rue Verdun, Immeuble Safieddine, B.P. 1525, Beirut; Correspondent EDOUARD SAAB.

AP: Antoine Massoud Building, Rue Mgr. Chebli, No. 12, Beirut; Chief of Middle East Services ROY ESSOYAN.

Četeka (Czechoslovak News Agency): P.O.B. 5069, Beirut; Chief Middle East Correspondent VLADIMIR OTRUBA.

Middle East News Agency: 72 Al Geish St., P.O.B. 2268, Beirut.

North American Newspapers Alliance: Palm-Beach Hotel, Beirut; Chief ANDREW J. NASH.

UPI: Press Co-operative Building, Rue Hamra, Beirut; Bureau Man. GERARD LOUGHRAN.

AFP, DPA, Iraq News Agency, Reuters and Tass also have offices in Beirut.

PRESS ASSOCIATIONS

Lebanese Press Syndicate: P.O.B. 3084, Beirut; f. 1911; 12 mems.; Pres. RIAD TAHA; Vice-Pres. FARID ABOU SHAHLA; Sec. MOHAMMAD BADIH SERBEY.

Foreign Press Syndicate: rue Clemenceau, Beirut; Pres. GEORGES BITAR.

PUBLISHERS

Arab Institute for Research and Publishing: Syria St. and Samadi Bldg., 5th Floor, P.O.B. 5460, Beirut; works in Arabic and English.

Dar al Adab: Beirut; literary and general.

Dar al Iim Lil Malayeen: Rue de Syria, P.O.B. 1085, Beirut; f. 1945; dictionaries, textbooks, Islamic cultural books; owners: MUNIR BA'ALBAKY and BAHIJ OSMAN.

Dar-Alkashaf: P.O.B. 112091, A. Malhamee St., Beirut; f. 1930; publishers of *Alkashaf* (Arab Youth Magazine), maps and atlases; printers and distributors; Propr. M. A. FATHALLAH.

Daral- Kitab al-Jadid: Hamra St., Hindi Building, P.O.B. 1284, Beirut; political studies; owner: FUAD BADR.

Dar al-Makshouf: Rue Amir Beshir, Beirut; scientific, cultural and school books; owner: Sheikh FUAD HOBEISH.

Dar Al-Maaref Liban S.A.L.: P.O.B. 2320, Esseily Bldg., Riad Al-Solh Square, Beirut; f. 1959; children's books and textbooks in Arabic; Gen. Man. JOSEPH NASHOU; Sales Man. ADEL HOSNI.

Dar Al-Mashreq (Imprimerie Catholique): P.O.B. 946, Beirut; f. 1853; religion, art, literature, history, languages, science, philosophy, school books, dictionaries and periodicals; Dir. PAUL BROUWERS, S.J.

Dar An-Nahar S.A.L.: B.P. 226, Beirut; f. 1967; publishes *Kadaya Moua'ssira* (quarterly); circ. 7,000; Pres. MOHAMED ALI HAMADÉ.

Dar Assayad S.A.L.: P.O.B. 1038, Beirut; f. 1943; publishes in Arabic *Al-Anwar* (daily), *Assayad* (weekly), *Al-Tayar* (weekly), *Achabaka* (weekly), *Samar* (weekly), *Dar-Assayad Yearbook*; has offices and correspondents in Arab countries and most parts of the world; Centre for Research, Studies and Archives; Chair. SAID FREIHA; Man. Dir. BASSAM FREIHA.

Dar Beirut: Librairie Beyrouth, Immeuble Lazarieh, rue Amir Bechir, Beirut; f. 1936; Prop. M. SAFIEDDINE.

Institute for Palestine Studies, Publishing and Research Department: Ashqar Bldg., Clémenceau St., P.O.B. 7164, Beirut; f. 1963; private non-profit Arab research organization; to promote better understanding of the Palestine problem; publishes books, reprints, research papers (English, Arabic, French), two annual documentary collections (English, Arabic) yearbook (in Arabic), *Bulletin* (fortnightly, Arabic), *Journal of Palestine Studies* (quarterly, English), *Knesset Debates* (annually, Arabic); library 12,000 vols.; Inter-Arab Board of Trustees: Chair. Prof. CONSTANTINE ZURAYK; Exec. Sec. Prof. WALID KHALIDI.

The International Documentary Center of Arab Manuscripts: Maqdissi St., Ras Beirut Hanna Bldg., P.O.B. 2668, Beirut; f. 1965; publishes and reproduces ancient and rare Arabic texts; Propr. ZOUHAIR BAALBAKI.

Khayat Book and Publishing Co. S.A.L.: 90–94 rue Bliss, Beirut; Middle East, Islam, oil, Arab publications and reprints; Man. Dir. PAUL KHAYAT.

Librairie du Liban: Riad Solh Sq., P.O.B. 945, Beirut; f. 1944; dictionaries, Middle East, travel, Islam; Proprs. KHALIL and GEORGE SAYEGH.

Middle East Publishing Co.: Beirut, Rue George Picot, Imm. El Kaissi; f. 1954; publishes *Medical Index* and *Revue Immobilière* (Real Estate); Man. Editor ELIE SAWAF.

New Book Publishing House: Beirut.

Rihani Printing and Publishing House: Jibb En Nakhl St., Beirut; f. 1963; Propr. ALBERT RIHANI; Man. DAOUD STEPHAN.

Other publishing houses in Beirut include: *Dar al-Andalus, Dar Majalaat Shiir, Imprimerie Catholique, Imprimerie Universelle, Al Jamiya al Arabi, Al Kitab al Arabi, Librairie Orientale, Al Mahtab al-Tijari, Middle East Stamps Inc., Mu'assasat al-Marif, Nofal and Bait at Hikmat, Saidar.*

RADIO AND TELEVISION

RADIO

Lebanese Broadcasting Station: rue Arts et Métiers, Beirut; is a part of the Ministry of Information; f. 1937; Dir.-Gen. K. HAGE ALI; Technical Dir. J. ROUHAYEM; Dir. of Programmes N. MIKATI; Head of Administration A. AOUN; Public Relations FAOUZI FEHMY.

The Home Service broadcasts in Arabic on short wave, the Foreign Service broadcasts in Portuguese, Arabic, Spanish, French and English.

Number of radio receivers: 605,000.

TELEVISION

Compagnie Libanaise de Télévision (C.L.T.): P.O.B. 4848, Beirut; f. 1959; commercial service; programmes in Arabic, French and English on four channels; Pres. Dir.-Gen. General S. NOFAL; Technical Man. M. S. KARIMEH; Programme Dir. PAUL TANNOUS.

Télé Orient: P.O.B. 5054, Beirut; f. 1960; Compagnie de Télévision du Liban et du Proche-Orient (S.A.L.); commercial service; programmes in Arabic, French and English on two channels (11 and 5); Acting Gen. Man. CLAUDE SAWAYA.

Number of TV receivers: 325,000.

FINANCE

(cap. = capital; p.u. = paid up; dep. = deposits; m. = million; L£ = Lebanese £; res. = reserves.)

Beirut has for long been the leading financial and commercial centre in the Middle East, as can be seen from the extensive list of banking organizations given below. However, public confidence in the banking system was strained by the closing of the Intra Bank, the largest domestic bank, late in 1966 when its liquid funds proved insufficient to cope with a run of withdrawals. The bank obtained enough guarantees to re-open in January 1968, though it is now an investment bank managed by a New York company. Before this crisis the government had passed a law stipulating a minimum capital of £L 3 million for all banks. This was followed in 1967 by a new law authorising a government take-over of a private bank facing difficulties threatening the interests and deposits of its clients; all depositors are to be paid in full by the State. This law was invoked in June 1968 when the Banque al-Ahli was taken over. The Bank Control Commission has taken over a number of small banks and assisted in the liquidation of several others. The major foreign-owned banks now have a much larger proportion of deposits than before the Intra crisis. In 1970 the decision was taken to grant no new licences (except for medium-term lending institutions) until 1976, and foreign banks have therefore been acquiring interests in Lebanese-owned banks to establish a foothold in Beirut.

BANKING ASSOCIATION

Association of Banks in Lebanon: P.O.B. 976, Riad el Solh Square, Beirut; f. 1959; serves and promotes the interests of the banking community in the Lebanon; mems.: over 100 banks and banking rep. offices.

CENTRAL BANK

Banque du Liban: P.O.B. 5544, rue Masraf Loubnane, Beirut; f. 1964; central bank; cap. L£15m.; res. L£31.6m. (Dec. 1972); Gov. ELIAS SARKIS.

DEVELOPMENT BANKS

National Bank for Industrial and Touristic Development: Tabariz Sq., Ave. Fouad Chehab, S.N.A. Bldg., 5th Floor, B.P. 8412, Beirut; f. 1973; cap. L£60m.; Chair. and Gen. Man. Dr. SALIM HOSS; Dir. of Loans Dr. ROY KARAOGLAN; Dir. of Research Dr. JOSEPH FULEIHAN.

Investment and Finance Bank (INFI): P.O.B. 13-5110, Fouad Chehab Ave., St. Nicolas Area, Beirut; f. 1974; loans for development projects; associated with Banque Audi; cap. L£15m., 60 per cent from Lebanese sources.

PRINCIPAL LEBANESE BANKS

Arab Libyan Tunisian Bank S.A.L.: Riad Solh Sq., Shaker & Oueni Bldg., P.O.B. 9575, Beirut; f. 1973; subsidiary of Libyan Arab Foreign Bank and Société Tunisienne de Banque; cap. p.u. L£10m.; Pres. and Gen Man. MOHAMED ABDEL JAWAD.

Bank Almashrek S.A.L.: Bank Almashrek Bldg., Riad El Solh St. 52, Beirut; Affil. with Morgan Guaranty Trust; cap. L£15m., dep. L£64.4m. (1973); Chair. FAHD ALBAHAR; Man. Dir. RODNEY B. WAGNER.

Bank of Beirut and the Arab Countries S.A.L.: Allenby St., P.O.B. 1536, Beirut; f. 1957; cap. L£5m., dep. L£138.2m. (1973); Chair. TOUFIC S. ASSAF; Vice-Chair. and Gen. Man. NASHAT SHEIKH EL-ARD; Joint Gen. Man. AMIN M. ALAMEH.

Banque al-Ahli (Banque Nationale) Foncière, Commerciale et Industrielle S.A.L.: Rue Foch, P.O.B. 2868, Beirut; f. 1953; cap. L£10m.; res. L£3.16m.; Pres. and Gen. Man. BOUTROS EL KHOURY (*see note above*).

Banque Audi S.A.L.: Fouad Chehab Ave., St. Nicolas Area, P.O.B. 2560, Beirut; f. 1928; cap. p.u. L£10m.; dep. L£173.2m. (1972); Chair. and Gen. Man. GEORGES OIDIH AUDI.

Banque de Crédit Agricole, Industriel et Foncier: Beirut; f. 1954; Dir.-Gen. Sheikh BOUTROS EL KHOURY; took over several banks in 1967–68, including Banque de l'Economie Arabe, Banque d'Epargne and Union National Bank.

Banque de Credit National S.A.L.: rue Allenby, P.O.B. 204, Beirut; f. 1959; cap. and reserves L£4.2m.; dep. L£25.8m. (Dec. 1973); Pres. and Gen. Man. EDMOND J. SAFRA; Deputy Gen. Man. HENRI KRAYEM.

Banque de l'Industrie et du Travail, S.A.L.: B.P. 11-3948, rue Riad Solh, Beirut; f. 1961; cap. L£10m.; dep. L£103m. (1973); Chair. LAURA EMILE BUSTANI; Man.-Dir. W. F. GOSLING, O.B.E.; Gen. Man. Dr. ASSAAD F. SAWAYA.

Banque du Liban et d'Outre-Mer (S.A.): Ajami Square, Beirut; f. 1951; cap. p.u. L£8m., dep. L£315.9m. (Dec. 1973); Chair., Gen. Man. Dr. NAAMAN AZHARI.

Banque Libano-Française-Beyrouth: 1 rue Riad El Solh, Beirut; f. 1968; cap. p.u. L£5m.; dep. L£381m. (Dec. 1973); Pres. and Chair. JEAN GIBERT; Dir. and Gen. Man. FARID RAPHAEL.

Banque de la Méditerranée S.A.L.: P.O.B. 348, Beirut; f. 1944; cap. L£5m.; dep. L£111m. (1973); Pres. Baron JACQUES DE DUMAST; Gen. Man. JOSEPH A. EL-KHOURY.

Banque Française pour le Moyen-Orient S.A.L.: P.O.B. 393, Imm. Starco, Rue Omar Daouk, Beirut; f. 1971 to take over branches in Lebanon of Société Centrale de Banque; affil. to Banque de l'Indochine; cap. L£5m.; total resources L£284.9m. (Dec. 1973); Pres. and Gen. Man. RENÉ BOUSQUET.

Banque Libanaise pour le Commerce S.A.L.: P.O.B. 1126, rue Riad El-Solh, Beirut; f. 1950; cap. L£5m.; res. L£15m. (Dec. 1973); Man. JEAN FARES SAAD ABI-JOUADE.

Banque Libano-Bresilienne S.A.L.: P.O.B. 3310, Maarad St., Beirut; f. 1962; cap. L£5m.; res. L£1.3m. (Dec. 1973); Pres. N. A. GHOSN; Gen. Man. J. A. GHOSN.

Banque Sabbag S.A.L.: P.O.B. 144, Sabbag Centre, Hamra, Beirut; f. 1880 as H. Sabbag et Fils, since 1950 a joint stock company with Banque de L'Indochine and Banca Commerciale Italiana; cap. L£6m.; dep. L£149m. (1974); Chair. PAUL-MARIE CRONIER.

Banque Saradar S.A.L.: Kassatly Bldg., Fakhry Bey St., P.O.B. 1121, Beirut; f. 1948; cap. L£5m.; dep. L£88.9m. (Oct. 1974); Pres.-Gen. Man. JOE MARIUS SARADAR; Asst. Gen. Man. ABDO I. JEFFI.

Banque G. Trad (Crédit Lyonnais) S.A.L.: P.O.B. 113, Weygand St., Beirut; f. 1951; cap. L£3m.; dep. L£329m. (Dec. 1973); Pres. G. A. TRAD.

Beirut-Riyad Bank S.A.L.: Beirut-Riyad Bank Bldg., Riad Solh St., P.O.B. 4668, Beirut; f. 1959; cap. p.u. L£12.5m.; dep. L£175m. (Dec. 1973); Pres. and Gen. Man. HUSSEIN MANSOUR.

British Bank of the Lebanon S.A.L.: rue Trablos, P.O.B. 11-7048, Beirut; f. 1971; dep. L£40.8m. (1973); subsidiary of British Bank of the Middle East; Chair. J. C. KELLY, O.B.E.; Man. Z. N. AUDEH.

Byblos Bank: P.O.B. 5605, Beydoun Bldg., al-Arz St., Beirut; f. 1962; cap. L£11m.; res. L£2.7m.; dep. L£226.4m. (Dec. 1973); Pres. SEMAAN M. BASSIL; Gen. Man. FRANÇOIS S. BASSIL.

Chemical Bank (Middle East) S.A.L.: Rabiya Metn, Beirut; subsidiary of Chemical Bank, New York.

Continental Development Bank, S.A.L.: Beydoun Bldg., Arz St., P.O.B. 3270, Beirut; f. 1961; subsidiary of Continental Bank, Chicago; cap. L£8m.; total resources L£178m. (1973); Chair. RICHARD K. O. CAREY.

Crédit Libanais S.A.L.: P.O.B. 1458, Riad el-Solh Square, Beirut; f. 1961; cap. L£12m.; dep. L£214m. (Dec. 1973); Chair. and Gen. Man. B. Y. OBÉGI; Gen. Man. H. Y. OBÉGI.

Federal Bank of Lebanon S.A.L.: Parliament Square, P.O.B. 2209, Beirut; f. 1952; cap. L£10m.; Pres. M. SAAB; Vice-Pres. A. FARID M. SAAB; Mans. G. A. KHOURY, A. B. ATAMIAN.

First National Bank of Chicago (Lebanon) S.A.L.: P.O.B. 1629, Riad el-Solh St., Beirut; f. 1958; wholly-owned subsidiary of First National Bank of Chicago, U.S.A.; cap. L£4m.; total resources L£159.1m. (Dec. 1973); Chair. and Gen. Man. ZIAD H. IDILBY.

Jammal Investment Bank, S.A.L.: Jallad Bldg., Riad el-Solh St., Beirut; f. 1963 as Investment Bank, S.A.L.; cap. p.u. L£10m.; dep. L£70m. (1974).

MEBCO BANK—Middle East Banking Co. S.A.L.: B.P. 3540, Beydoun Bldg., Beirut; f. 1959; cap. p.u. L£6.25m.; dep. L£53.5m. (1973); Chair. and Gen. Man. MOHAMED ALI CHALABI.

Rifbank S.A.L.: Head Office: P.O.B. 5727, rue Kantari, Beirut; f. 1965; in association with Commerzbank A.G., The National Bank of Kuwait S.A.K., The Commercial Bank of Kuwait S.A.K.; cap. p.u. L£4m.; dep. L£118m. (1973); Chair. A. A. BASSAM; Man. G. H. CLAYTON, F.I.B.

Royal Bank of Canada (Middle East) S.A.L.: St. Charles City Centre, Omar Daouk St., P.O.B. 11-250, Beirut; f. 1969; cap. L£5m.; dep. L£86m. (1973); Pres. BRUCE LAMONT; Gen. Man. EDWARD BROKES; Man. KHALIL KIKANO.

Société Bancaire du Liban S.A.L.: rue Allenby, Beirut; P.O.B. 11-435; f. 1899; cap. p.u. and reserves L£5m.; dep. L£68.6m. (Dec. 1973); Chair. S. S. LEVY.

Société Générale Libano-Européenne de Banque S.A.L.: Riad el-Solh St., P.O.B. 2955, Beirut; f. 1953; cap. p.u. L£5m.; dep. L£235m. (1973); Chair. A. M. SEHNAOUI; Gen. Man. GÉRARD GLORIEUX.

Société Nouvelle de la Banque de Syrie et du Liban S.A.L.: P.O.B. 957, Beirut; f. 1963; cap. p.u. L£10.4m.; res. L£4.2m. (Dec. 1973); Pres. GUY TRANCART.

Trans Orient: Beirut; f. 1966; cap. p.u. L£3m.; joint venture with the International Bank of Washington and Lebanese private investors.

Union Bank S.A.L.: Gefinor Centre, Beirut; f. 1974; merchant bank; cap. L£15m; Chair. Dr. MUHAMMAD ATALLAH; Vice-Chair. Mrs. NADIA EL-KHOURY.

PRINCIPAL FOREIGN BANKS

Algemene Bank Nederland N.V. (*General Bank of the Netherlands*): Amsterdam, Netherlands; P.O.B. 3012, Beirut.

Arab African Bank: Cairo, Egypt; Riad el-Solh St., P.O.B. 6066, Beirut.

Arab Bank Ltd.: Amman, Jordan; Beirut Main Branch: Riad Solh St., Beirut.

Banca Commerciale Italiana S.p.A.: Milan, Italy; P.O.B. 7481, Starco North Bldg. 706, Beirut.

Banco Atlántico S.A.: Barcelona, Spain; P.O.B. 7376, Beirut.

Banco di Roma S.p.A.: Rome, Italy; Beirut, Saida and Tripoli.

Bank of America (National Trust and Savings Asscn.): San Francisco, U.S.A.; P.O.B. 3965, Beirut; Man. C. HOLLANDER.

Banque Misr-Liban: Cairo, Egypt.

Bank of Nova Scotia: Halifax, Canada; Riad el-Solh St., P.O.B. 4446, Beirut; Man. A. J. BRIDI.

Bank of Tokyo: Tokyo, Japan; Arab Bank Bldg., P.O.B. 11-1187, Beirut; Reps. T. KOBAYAKAWA, K. KATO, M. TANI.

Bank Saderat Iran: Teheran, Iran; Beirut Branch, P.O.B. 5126, Beirut.

Bankers Trust Co.: New York, U.S.A.; Shaker Oueini Bldg., Place Riad Solh, P.O.B. 6239, Beirut; f. 1903; Vice-Pres. Resident Rep. WALID NIAZY.

Banque de l'Union Européenne S.A.: Paris, France; Beirut.

Banque Nationale de Paris S.A.: Paris, France; Beirut.

Banque Nationale de Paris Intercontinentale S.A.: Paris, France; Immeuble Fattal, rue Allenby, Beirut.

Bayerische Vereinsbank: Munich, Federal Republic of Germany; KLM Bldg., rue de l'Armée, Beirut; Rep. PETER SCHMID-LOSSBERG; also representing Berliner Bank A.G., Frankfurter Bank, Norddeutsche Kreditbank A.G., Westfalenbank A.G.

British Bank of the Middle East: London; Bab Edriss, Beirut; brs. at Ras Beirut, St. George's Bay, Mazra'a and Tripoli.

The Chartered Bank: London; P.O.B. 3996, Riad el-Solh St., Beirut; Man. in Beirut G. R. LOVELL.

Československá Obchodní Banka A.S. (*Commercial Bank of Czechoslovakia Ltd.*): Prague, Czechoslovakia; Middle East Office: B.P. 5928, Beirut.

Chase Manhattan Bank, N.A.: New York; P.O.B. 11-3684, Beirut; Vice-Pres. and Man. DONALD RICHTENBURG; Regional Rep., Investment Adviser ANTOINE ASFOUR; 2nd Vice-Pres. Petroleum ANTOINE COURBAGE; Asst. Rep. NIZAR OMARY.

Chemical Bank: 20 Pine St., New York, N.Y. 10015; P.O.B. 7286, Riad el-Solh St., Beirut; Rep. MICHAEL DAVIES.

Commerzbank A.G.: Düsseldorf, Federal Republic of Germany; P.O.B. 3246, Beirut; Rep. KLAUS TJADEN.

Continental Illinois National Bank and Trust Co.: Chicago, U.S.A.; f. 1975; P.O.B. 11-7239, Arab Bank Bldg., rue Riad Solh, Beirut.

Crédit Commercial de France S.A.: Paris, France; Aoueni Bldg., Riad el-Solh Square, Beirut; Rep. M. HEMAYA.

Credit Suisse: Zürich, Switzerland; P.O.B. 11-8244, rue Karamé 27-29, Beirut; Regional Rep. MAJED DAJANI. MAILA.

Deutsche Bank A.G.: Frankfurt am Main, Federal Republic of Germany; Beirut.

Dresdner Bank A.G.: Frankfurt/Main, Federal Republic of Germany; Imm. Starco, B.P. 4831, Beirut; Reps. M. S. HADDAD and REINER AURICH.

First National Bank of Boston: Boston, U.S.A.; Suite 501, Arab Bank Bldg., Riad el-Solh St., Beirut.

First National City Bank: New York, N.Y. 10022; P.O.B. 113648, Beirut; Resident Vice-Pres. MEHLI M. MISTRI.

Frankfurter Bank: Frankfurt am Main, Federal Republic of Germany; P.O.B. 3247, Beirut (*see* Bayerische Vereinsbank).

Habib Bank (Overseas) Ltd.: Karachi, Pakistan; Beirut.

Jordan National Bank, S.A.: Amman, Jordan; Beirut, Tripoli and Saida.

Lloyds Bank International: London, England; 1401 St. Charles City Centre, Omar Daouk St., P.O.B. 11-9716, Beirut; Rep. J. ANTOINE ZANANIRI.

Manufacturers Hanover Trust Co.: New York, U.S.A.; B.I.T. Bldg., Riad el-Solh St., Beirut; Rep. HASSAN HUSSEINI.

Morgan Guaranty Trust Co.: New York, U.S.A.; P.O.B. 5752, Beirut-Riyad Bank Bldg., rue Riyad Solh, Beirut; Rep. in Middle East FREDERICK H. S. ALLEN.

Moscow Narodny Bank Ltd.: Head Office: London, E.C.4; Beirut Branch: P.O.B. 5481, Beirut; Man. in Beirut T. ALIBEKOV.

Rafidain Bank: Head Office: Baghdad, Iraq; Beirut Branch: Bazirkan Souk, Beirut, P.O.B. 1891; f. 1941.

Saudi National Commercial Bank: Jeddah, Saudi Arabia; P.O.B. 2355, Beirut; f. 1938.

State Bank of India: Bombay, India; P.O.B. 7252, 5th Floor, Arab Bank Bldg., Riad el-Solh St., Beirut.

Swiss Bank Corporation: Basle, Switzerland; Beirut Riyad Bldg., Riad el-Solh St., Beirut; Rep. KASPAR SCHATTMEIER.

Trade Development Bank (*Banque pour le Développement Commercial*): Geneva, Switzerland; rue Allenby, Beirut.

Union Bank of Switzerland: Zürich, Switzerland; P.O.B. 5734, Starco South 1001-4, Beirut; Reps. B. FISCHER, G. E. SALAWI.

United California Bank: Los Angeles, U.S.A.; Beirut.

Association of Banks in Lebanon: Army St., P.O.B. 976, Beirut; f. 1959; 94 mems.; Pres. JOSEPH GEAGEA; Gen. Sec. Dr. PIERRE NASRALLAH; publ. studies of Lebanese economy, especially banking.

INSURANCE

NATIONAL COMPANIES

"La Phenicienne" (S.A.L.) (formerly *al Ahli*): Centre Géfinor, rue Clemenceau, P.O.B. 5652, Beirut; f. 1964; Chair., Gen. Man. ANTOINE K. FEGALY; Dep. Gen. Man. NICOLAS MAASSAB.

al-Ittihad al-Watani: Head Office: Immeuble Fattal, P.O.B. 1270, Beirut; Chair. JOE I. KAIROUZ.

Arabia Insurance Co. Ltd. S.A.L.: Arabia House, Phoenicia St., P.O.B. 11-2172, Beirut; Vice-Chair. and Gen. Man. BADR S. FAHOUM.

Commercial Insurance Co. S.A.L.: Starco Centre, P.O.B. 4351, Beirut; f. 1962; Chair. J. SABET; Gen. Man. R. M. ZACCAR.

Compagnie Libanaise d'Assurances (S.A.L.): Riad el-Solh St., P.O.B. 3685, Beirut; f. 1951; Man. Dir. ELIA F. S. ABOUJAOUDÉ; Man. BAHJAT DAGHER.

Libano-Suisse Insurance Co. (S.A.L.): Commerce and Finance Bldg., Rond-Point Kantari, Beirut; cap. p.u. L£2m.; agencies Jordan, Kuwait, Qatar, Saudi Arabia and United Arab Emirates; Pres. and Gen. Man. PIERRE J. SEHNAOUI; Vice-Pres. and Deputy Gen. Man. EMILE M. GHOSN; Man., Lebanon Branch, ANTOINE MAILA.

Some twenty of the major European companies are also represented in Beirut.

TRADE AND INDUSTRY

CHAMBERS OF COMMERCE AND INDUSTRY

Beirut Chamber of Commerce and Industry: Sanayeh, Spears St., Chamber of Commerce & Industry Bldg., P.O.B. 11801, Beirut; f. 1898; 10,000 mems.; Pres. ADNAN KASSAR; Gen. Dir. WALID AHDAB; publ. *The Lebanese and Arab Economy* (20 issues per annum).

Tripoli Chamber of Commerce and Industry: Tripoli.

Sidon Chamber of Commerce and Industry: Sidon.

Zahlé Chamber of Commerce and Industry: Zahlé; f. 1939; 497 mems.; Pres. ALFRED SKAFF.

EMPLOYERS' ASSOCIATIONS

Association of Lebanese Industrialists: Chamber of Commerce and Industry Bldg., Justinian St., P.O.B. 1520, Beirut.

Conseil National du Patronat: Beirut; f. 1965.

TRADE UNION FEDERATIONS

Confédération Générale des Travailleurs du Liban (C.G.T.L.): Beirut; confederation of the following four federations; Pres. GABRIEL KHOURY.

Federation of Independent Trade Unions: Central Bldg., rue Mère Galace, Beirut; f. 1954; estimated 6,000 mems. in 7 trade unions; affiliated to Confed. of Arab T.U.'s; Pres. MOHAMED EL-ASSIR; Sec.-Gen. ALI HOURANI; publ. *Sawt al 'Amel.*

Federation of Unions of Workers and Employees of North Lebanon: Al-Ahram Building, Abu-Wadi Square, Tripoli; f. 1954; affiliated to Confed. of Arab T.U.'s; 3,700 mems. in 14 trade unions; Pres. MOUSTAFA HAMZI; Sec.-Gen. KHALED BARADI; publ. *Al A'mel.*

Ligue des Syndicats des Employés et des Ouvriers dans la République Libanaise (*League of Trade Unions of Employees and Workers in the Lebanese Republic*): Immeuble Rivoli, Place des Canons, Beirut; f. 1946;

estimated 6,000 mems. in 21 trade unions; affiliated to ICFTU; Pres. HUSSEIN ALI HUSSEIN; Vice-Pres. HALIM MATTAR; Sec.-Gen. FOUAD KHARANOUH; Foreign Sec. ANTOINE CHIHA; Del. to ICFTU and mem. of Exec. Cttee. ANTOINE CHIHA; publ. *Al-Awassef.*

United Unions for Employees and Workers: Imm. Waqf Bzoummar, rue Béchara el Khoury, Beirut, B.P. 3636; f. 1952; affiliated to ICFTU; 16,000 mems. in 21 trade unions; Pres. GABRIEL KHOURY; Sec.-Gen. ANTOINE AOUN; publ. *La Gazette.*

RESEARCH CENTRE

ICFTU Trade Union Research Centre: P.O.B. 3180, Beirut; f. 1964.

TRANSPORT

RAILWAYS

Office des Chemins de Fer de l'Etat Libanais et du Transport en Commun de Beyrouth et de sa Banlieue: Head Office: P.O.B. 109, Souk el-Arwam, Beirut; since 1960, all railways in Lebanon have been state-owned. There are 335 km. of standard-gauge railway and 82 km. of narrow-gauge local lines; the coastal line between Israeli and Syrian frontiers is open only from Zahrani to Tripoli, due to political disturbances; Chair. ADEL HAMIE; Interim Dir.-Gen. ANTOINE BAROUKI.

ROADS

Lebanon has 7,100 km. of roads, of which 1,990 km. are main roads. Most are generally good by Middle Eastern standards. The two international motorways are the north-south coastal road and the road connecting Beirut with Damascus in Syria. Among the major roads are that crossing the Bekaa and continuing South to Bent-Jbail and the Chtaura-Baalbek road. Hard-surfaced roads connect Jezzine with Moukhtara, Bzebdine with Metn, Meyroub with Afka and Tannourine.

Automobile et Touring Club du Liban: Immeuble Fattal, rue du Port, P.O.B. 3545, Beirut.

SHIPPING

Beirut is the principal port of call for the main shipping and forwarding business of the Levant. Tripoli, the northern Mediterranean terminus of the oil pipeline from Iraq (the other is Haifa), is also a busy port, with good equipment and facilities. Saida is still relatively unimportant as a port.

There are many shipping companies and agents in Beirut. The following are some of the largest:

"Adriatica" S.p.A.N.: Rue Riad E. Solh, Immeuble Gellad, Beirut, P.O.B. 1472; Dir. ALDO SILLI.

American Lebanese Shipping Co. S.A.L.: P.O.B. 215, Imm. Fattal, rue du Port, Beirut; f. 1951; Pres. P. PARATORE.

American Levant Shipping & Distributing Co.: P.O.B. 1429, Rue Patriarch Hoyek, Immeuble Anwar Dassouki & Co.; agents for: Holland America Line, Lykes Bros. Steamship Co., Prudential Steamship Corpn., Ciro Pellegrino & Figlio, Bermare—Marittima di Navigazione; branches and correspondents throughout Middle East; Pres. E. SEAHOLM; Man. Dir. SAMIR ISHAK.

Arab Shipping and Chartering Co.: P.O.B. 1084; agents for China National Chartering Corpn., China Ocean Shipping Co., Kiu Lee Shipping Co. Ltd., Chinese-Tanzanian Joint Shipping Co.

Barrad Shipping Co. S.A.L.: P.O.B. 181, Beirut; refrigerated tramp services; 3 cargo reefer vessels; Chair. P. H. HELOU.

British Maritime Agencies (Levant) Ltd.: rue du Port, agents for: Ellerman and Papayanni Line Ltd., Ellerman's Wilson Line Ltd., Prince Line Ltd., etc.

Catoni & Co. S.A.L.: P.O.B. 800, rue du Port; f. 1960; Chair. H. J. BEARD; agents for: British Maritime Agencies (Levant) Ltd., Royal Netherlands Steamship Co., Lloyd's.

Ets. Derviche Y. Haddad: rue Derviche Haddad, P.O.B. 42; agents for: Armement Deppe, Antwerp and Compagnie Maritime Belge, Antwerp.

Daher & Cie. S.A.L.: Byblos Bldg., Place des Martyrs, P.O.B. 254; importer and distributor of cars and building materials. Agence Maritime Daher are agents for: Cie. de Navigation Daher, Concordia Line, Navale et Commerciale Havraise Peninsulaire, Société Maritime des Petroles B.P., Cie Navale des Petroles, Cie. Générale Transatlantique, Nouvelle Cie. de Paquebots, Sudcargos, Medcar, Stolt Nielsen Inc.

O. D. Debbas & Sons: Head Office: Sahmarani Bldg., Kantary St., P.O.B. 11-003, Beirut; Man. Dir. ELIE O. DEBBAS.

Fauzi Jemil Ghandour: P.O.B. 1084; agents for: Denizçilik Bankası T.A.O. (Denizyollari), D.B. Deniz Nakliyati T.A.Ş. (Dbcargo), Iraqi Maritime Transport Co.

T. Gargour & Fils: rue Foch, P.O.B. 371; f. 1928; agents for: Assoc. Levant Lines S.A.L.; Dirs. NICOLAS T. GARGOUR, HABIB T. GARGOUR.

Globe Shipping, Chartering and Tourist Co.: P.O.B. 6986, Beirut; agents for Hellenic Mediterranean Lines Piraeus Uiterwyk Shipping Co., Tampa Linea C, Genoa, Sintra S.p.a., Palermo, Lykiardopulo & Co., Livanos Shipbrokers, General Steam Navigation, etc.

Henry Heald & Co. S.A.L.: Im. Fattal, Rue du Port, P.O.B. 64; f. 1837; agents for: Canadian Pacific Lines, Nippon Yusen Kaisha, P. & O. Group, Royal Mail Lines, Scandinavian Near East Agency, Vanderzee Shipping Agency, Worms and Co.; Chair. J. L. JOLY; Dirs. G. HANI, M. J. H. MOFFETT.

Hitti Frères: Rue de Phenicie, P.O.B. 511; airlines and shipping agents.

Khedivial Mail Line: Rue du Port.

Raymond A. Makzoumé: rue de la Marseillaise, P.O.B. 1357; agents for: Jugoslav Lines, Italian Lines, Hellenic Lines Ltd. (N.Y.), Fenton Steamship Co. Ltd. (U.K.).

Mediterranean Maritime Co. S.A.L.: P.O.B. 1914, Bourse Bldg., Hoyek St., Beirut; managers for National Maritime Agencies Co. W.LL., Kuwait.

Mena Shipping and Tourist Agency: P.O.B. 11-884, Modern Bldg., El Arz St., Beirut; 5 cargo vessels; Man. Dir. W. LEHETA.

Messageries Maritimes: Rue Allenby, P.O.B. 880.

Rudolphe Saadé & Co. S.A.L.: Freight Office: P.O.B. 2279, Rue de la Marseillaise; Travel Office: Ave. des Français; agents for American Export Lines, Rosade Lines and Syrian Arab Airlines; f. 1964; Pres. JACQUES R. SAADE.

Union Shipping & Chartering Agency S.A.L.: P.O.B. 2856; agents for Yugoslav vessels.

CIVIL AVIATION

MEA (*Middle East Airlines, Air Liban*): MEA Bldgs., Airport Blvd., Beirut, P.O.B. 206; f. 1945; regular services throughout Europe, the Middle East and Africa; fleet of 3 Boeing 747, 3 Boeing 707/320C, 16 Boeing 720; Pres. and Chair. Sheikh NAJIB ALAMUDDIN; Gen. Man. ASAD NASR.

Trans-Mediterranean Airways (TMA): Beirut International Airport, P.O.B. 3018, Beirut; f. 1953; world-wide cargo services between Europe, Middle East, S.-E. Asia, the Far East and U.S.A., including a round-the-world cargo service; fleet of 7 Boeing 707/320C; Pres. and Chair. MUNIR ABU-HAIDAR; Exec. Vice-Pres. M. V. RICHMOND.

The following foreign companies also operate services to Lebanon: Aeroflot, Air Algérie, Air France, Air India, Alia, Alitalia, Ariana Afghan Airlines, AUA, British Airways, CSA, EgyptAir, Ethiopian, Garuda, Ghana Airways, Iberia, Interflug, Iranair, Iraqi Airways, JAL, JAT, KLM, Kuwait Airways, Libyan Arab Airlines, LOT, Lufthansa, Malev, Olympic Airways, Pan American, PIA, Sabena, SAS, Saudia, Sudan Airways, Swissair, Syrian Arab Airlines, Tarom (Romania), THY (Turkey), TWA, UTA, Varig, Viasa and Yemen Republic Airlines.

TOURISM

Ministry of Tourism: Beirut; f. 1966; official organization; Dir.-Gen. MITRI NAMMAR; Head International Relations Dept. ANTOINE ACCAOUI; Head Speleological Service SAMI KARKABI.

National Council of Tourism: P.O.B. 3544, rue de la Banque du Liban, Beirut; government-sponsored autonomous organization; overseas offices in New York, Paris, Frankfurt, Stockholm, Brussels and Cairo; Pres. CHEIKH HABIB KAYROUZ; Vice-Pres. SELIM SALAM.

Baalbeck International Festival: Beirut; Dir. WAGIH GHOSSOUB.

THEATRES

Baalbeck Festival Modern Theatre Group: Baalbeck; Dir. MOUNIR ABU-DEBS.

National Theatre: Beirut; Dir. NIZAR MIKATI.

DEFENCE

Commander-in-Chief of the Armed Forces: Gen. ISKANDER GHANEM.

Defence Budget (1974): L£300.17 million.

Military Service: At present voluntary, but in May 1974 the Cabinet approved a Bill to institute 18 months compulsory military service for all 18-year-old men. The law could be extended to include women.

Total Armed Forces: 15,250: army 14,000 (including 1 tank battalion, with 100 tanks); navy 250; air force 1,000 (with 18 combat aircraft). Para-military forces: 5,000 gendarmerie.

EDUCATION

Until 1952 facilities for public education were provided only at the primary stage and they were considerably outnumbered by foreign and private institutions. Since the end of the French mandate in 1944, public education has greatly developed and now reaches all levels of instruction. Free primary education was introduced in 1960, but private institutions still provide the main facilities for secondary and university education. Private schools enjoy almost complete autonomy except for a certain number which receive government financial aid and are supervised by the Ministry's inspectors.

The primary course lasts for five years. It is followed either by the four-year intermediate course or the three-year secondary course. The baccalaureate examination is taken in two parts at the end of the second and third years of secondary education, and a public examination is taken at the end of the intermediate course. Technical education is provided mainly at the National School of Arts and Crafts, which offers four-year courses in electronics, mechanics, architectural and industrial drawing, and other subjects. There are also public Vocational schools providing courses for lower levels.

Higher education is provided by twelve institutions, including five universities. In 1972–73 50,803 students attended these centres, of whom 45.7 per cent were Lebanese citizens. Teacher training is given at various levels. A three-year course which follows the intermediate course trains primary school teachers and another three-year course which follows the second part of the baccalaureate trains teachers for the intermediate school. Secondary school teachers are trained at the Higher Teachers' College at the Lebanese University. Two Agricultural Schools provide a three-year course for pupils holding the intermediate school degree.

For the year 1973 the budget of the Ministry of National Education amounted to L£201.5 million or 18.64 per cent of state expenditure. By 1972–73 there were altogether 1,354 public schools and 1,927 private schools, containing some 800,500 pupils and 39,000 teachers.

UNIVERSITIES

American University of Beirut: Beirut; 500 teachers, 4,250 students.

Beirut Arab University: Tarik El-Jadidé, P.O.B. 5020, Beirut; 163 teachers, 23,000 students.

Université Libanaise (*Lebanese University*): Bir Hassan, Beirut; 733 teachers, 14,826 students.

Université Saint Joseph: B.P. 293, Beirut; 65 teachers, 3,500 students.

Université Saint-Esprit De Kaslik: Jounieh; 117 teachers, 403 students.

BIBLIOGRAPHY

ABOUCHDID, E. E. Thirty Years of Lebanon and Syria (1917–47) (Beirut, 1948).

AGWANI, M. S. (Ed.). The Lebanese Crisis, 1958: a documentary study (Asia Publishing House, 1965).

ANSARI, A. Die Verfassungen des Libanon, der Vereinigten Arabischen Republik und des Irak (Metzner Verlag, Frankfurt am Main, Berlin, 1960).

ATIYAH, E. An Arab tells his Story (London, 1946).

BESOINS ET POSSIBILITÉS DE DÉVELOPPEMENT DU LIBAN, Étude Préliminaire, 2 Vols. (Lebanese Ministry of Planning, Beirut, 1964).

BINDER, LEONARD (Ed.). Politics in Lebanon (Wiley, New York, 1966).

BURCKHARD, C. Le Mandat Français en Syrie et au Liban (Paris, 1925).

CARDON, L. Le Régime de la propriété foncière en Syrie et au Liban (Paris, 1932).

CATROUX, G. Dans la Bataille de Méditerranée (Julliard, Paris, 1949).

CHAMOUN, C. Les Mémoires de Camille Chamoun (Beirut, 1949).

CORM, G. C. Politique Economique et Planification au Liban 1953–63 (Beirut, 1964).

DAGHER, J. Bibliographie du Liban (Beirut, 1945).

EDDÉ, JACQUES. Géographie Liban-Syrie (Beirut, 1941).

FEDDEN, R. Syria (London, 1946) (also covers the Lebanon).

FRANCE, Ministère des Affaires Etrangères. Rapport sur la Situation de la Syrie et du Liban (Paris, annually, 1924–39).

GHATTAS, EMILE. The monetary system in the Lebanon (New York, 1961).

GULICK, JOHN. Social Structure and Culture Change in a Lebanese Village (New York, 1955).

HACHEM, NABIL. Liban: Sozio-ökonomische Groundlagen (Opladen, 1969).

HACHETTE WORLD GUIDES. Lebanon (Hachette, Paris, 1965).

HADDAD, J. Fifty Years of Modern Syria and Lebanon (Beirut, 1950).

HARDING, G. LANKESTER. Baalbek, a New Guide (Beirut, 1964).

HARIK, ILIYA F. Politics and Change in a Traditional Society—Lebanon 1711–1845 (Princeton University Press, 1968).

HEPBURN, A. H. Lebanon (New York, 1966).

HIMADEH, RAJA S. The Fiscal System of Lebanon (Khayat, Beirut, 1961).

HITTI, PHILIP K. Lebanon in History (3rd ed., Macmillan, London 1967).

HOURANI, ALBERT K. Syria and Lebanon (London, 1946).

HUDSON, MICHAEL C. The Precarious Republic: Political Modernization in the Lebanon (Random House, New York, 1968).

JIDEJIAN, NINA. Byblos Through the Ages (Dar El-Mashreq, Beirut, 1968).

KATIN, VLADIMIR KONSTANTINOVICH. Lebanese Economy and Foreign Trade (Russian Text) (Vneshtorgizdats, Moscow, 1961).

LONGRIGG, S. H. Syria and Lebanon under French Mandate (Oxford University Press, 1958).

MILLS, ARTHUR E. Private Enterprise in Lebanon (American University of Beirut, 1959).

PEARSE, R. Three Years in the Levant (London, 1949).

PENROSE, S. B. L. That They Have Life: the story of the American University of Beirut 1866–1941 (Princeton, New Jersey, U.P., 1941).

PUAUX, G. Deux Années au Levant; souvenirs de Syrie et du Liban (Hachette, Paris, 1952).

QUBAIN, FAHIM I. Crisis in Lebanon (Middle East Institute, Washington, D.C., 1961).

RONDOT, PIERRE. Les Institutions Politiques du Liban (Paris, 1947).

SABA, ELIAS S. The Foreign Exchange Systems of Lebanon and Syria (American University of Beirut, 1961).

SAFA, ELIE. L'Emigration Libanaise (Beirut, 1960).

SALIBI, K. S. The Modern History of Lebanon (Praeger, New York, and Weidenfeld & Nicolson, London, 1964).

SAYIGH, Y. A. Entrepreneurs of Lebanon (Cambridge, Mass., 1962).

SIKSEK, SIMON G. Preliminary Assessment of Manpower Resources and Requirements in Lebanon (American University of Beirut, 1960).

STEWART, DESMOND. Trouble in Beirut (Wingate, London, 1959).

STUDIES ON THE GOVERNMENT OF THE LEBANON. (Compiled by the Dept. of Public Admin., American University of Beirut, 1956.)

SULEIMAN, M. W. Political Parties in Lebanon (Cornell University Press, Ithaca, N.Y., 1967).

SYKES, JOHN. The Mountain Arabs (Hutchinson, London, 1968).

THUBRON, C. The Hills of Adonis (Heinemann, London, 1968).

TIBAWI, A. L. A Modern History of Greater Syria, including Lebanon and Palestine (Macmillan, London, 1969).

WARD, PHILIP. Touring Lebanon (Faber and Faber, London, 1971).

ZIADEH, NICOLA. Syria and Lebanon (Praeger, New York, 1957).

Libya

PHYSICAL AND SOCIAL GEOGRAPHY

W. B. Fisher

Libya, until 1963 three Federated States, is bounded on the north by the Mediterranean Sea, on the east by Egypt and the Sudan, on the south and south-west by Chad and Niger, on the west by Algeria, and on the north-west by Tunisia. The three component areas of Libya are: Tripolitania, in the west, with an area of 110,000 sq. miles; Cyrenaica, in the east, area 350,000 sq. miles; and the Fezzan, in the south, area 220,000 sq. miles—total for Libya, 680,000 sq. miles. The independence of Libya was proclaimed in December 1951; before that date, following conquest from the Italians, Tripolitania and Cyrenaica had been ruled by a British administration, at first military, then civil; and the Fezzan had been administered by France. The revolutionary government which came to power in September 1969 has formally re-named the three regions: Tripolitania became known as the Western provinces, Cyrenaica the Eastern provinces, and the Fezzan the Southern provinces.

PHYSICAL FEATURES

The whole of Libya may be said to form part of the vast plateau of North Africa, which extends from the Atlantic Ocean to the Red Sea; but there are certain minor geographical features which give individuality to the three component areas of Libya. Tripolitania consists of a series of regions of different level, rising in the main towards the south, and thus broadly comparable with a flight of steps. In the extreme north, along the Mediterranean coast, there is a low-lying coastal plain called the Jefara. This is succeeded inland by a line of hills, or rather a scarp edge, that has several distinguishing local names, but is usually alluded to merely as the Jebel. Here and there in the Jebel occur evidences of former volcanic activity—old craters, and sheets of lava. The Jefara and adjacent parts of the Jebel are by far the most important parts of Tripolitania, since they are better watered and contain most of the population, together with the capital town, Tripoli.

South of the Jebel there is an upland plateau—a dreary desert landscape of sand, scrub, and scattered irregular masses of stone. After several hundred miles the plateau gives place to a series of east-west running depressions, where artesian water, and hence oases, are found. These depressions make up the region of the Fezzan, which is merely a collection of oases on a fairly large scale, interspersed with areas of desert. In the extreme south the land rises considerably to form the mountains of the central Sahara, where some peaks reach 12,000 ft. in height.

Cyrenaica has a slightly different physical pattern. In the north, along the Mediterranean, there is an upland plateau that rises to 2,000 ft. in two very narrow steps, each only a few miles wide. This gives a bold prominent coastline to much of Cyrenaica, and so there is a marked contrast with Tripolitania where the coast is low-lying, and in parts fringed by lagoons. The northern uplands of Cyrenaica are called the Jebel Akhdar (Green Mountain), and here, once again, are found the bulk of the population and the two main towns Benghazi and Derna. On its western side the Jebel Akhdar drops fairly steeply to the shores of the Gulf of Sirte; but on the east it falls more gradually, and is traceable as a series of ridges, only a few hundred feet in altitude, that extend as far as the Egyptian frontier. This eastern district, consisting of low ridges aligned parallel to the coast, is known as Marmarica, and its chief town is Tobruk.

South of the Jebel Akhdar the land falls in elevation, producing an extensive lowland, which except for its northern fringe, is mainly desert. Here and there occur a few oases—Aujila (or Ojila) Jalo, and Jaghbub in the north; and Jawf, Zighen, and Kufra (the largest of all) in the south. These oases support only a few thousand inhabitants and are of much less importance than those of the Fezzan In the same region, and becoming more widespread towards the east, is the Sand Sea—an expanse of fine, mobile sand, easily lifted by the wind into dunes that can sometimes reach several hundred feet in height and over 100 miles in length. Finally, in the far south of Cyrenaica, lie the central Saharan mountains—the Tibesti Ranges, continuous with those to the south of the Fezzan.

The climate of Libya is characterised chiefly by its aridity and by its wide alternation of temperatures. Lacking mountain barriers, the country is open to influences both from the Sahara and from the Mediterranean Sea, and as a result there can be abrupt transitions from one kind of weather to another. In winter, it can be fairly raw and cold in the north, with sleet and even light snow on the hills. In summer it is extremely hot in the Jefara of Tripolitania, reaching temperatures of $105°-115°$ F. In the southern deserts conditions are hotter still. Garian once (incorrectly) claimed the world record in temperature, but figures of over $120°$F are known. Several feet of snow can also occur here in winter. Northern Cyrenaica has a markedly cooler summer of $80°-90°$, but with high air humidity near the coast. A special feature is the *ghibli*—a hot, very dry wind from the sout 1 than can raise temperatures in the north by $30°$ or even $40°$ in a few hours, sometimes giving figures of $70°$ or $80°$ in January. This sand-laden, dry wind may blow at any season of the year, but spring and autumn are the most usual seasons. Considerable damage is done to growing crops, and the effect even on human beings is often marked.

The hills of Tripolitania and Cyrenaica receive annually as much as 15 to 20 inches of rainfall, but in the remainder of the country the amount is 8 inches or less. A special difficulty is that once in every five or six years there is a pronounced drought, sometimes lasting for two successive seasons. Actual falls of rain can also be unreliable and erratic.

ECONOMIC LIFE

Such conditions impose severe restriction on all forms of economic activity. Although oil has been found in considerable quantities in Libya, physical and climatic conditions make exploitation difficult, and until the closing of the Suez Canal in 1967 the remote situation of the country, away from the currents of international trade, was a further handicap. But production of crude oil has increased rapidly and in 1974, though production was cut back, it was 82.4 million metric tons. The availability of oil revenues has now begun to transform the economic situation of Libya. Plans for extensive development are being drawn up by foreign consultants, with the aim of improving housing, and the fostering of consumer goods industry. Roads, electricity, better water supplies and re-organized town planning are in process of being achieved.

In the better-watered areas of the Jafara, and to a smaller extent in northern Cyrenaica, there is cultivation of barley, wheat, olives, and Mediterranean fruit.

The Fezzan and the smaller oases in Cyrenaica are almost rainless, and cultivation depends entirely upon irrigation from wells. Millet is the chief crop, and there are several million date palms, which provide the bulk of the food. Small quantities of vegetables and fruit—figs, pomegranates, squashes, artichokes, and tubers—are produced from gardens. Along the northern coast, and especially on the lower slopes both of the Tripolitanian Jebel and the Jebel Akhdar, vines are widely grown, chiefly for wine-making. An edict imposing complete prohibition upon Libyan Muslims has, however, led to a restriction of production.

Over much of Libya pastoral nomadism, based on the rearing of sheep and goats, and some cattle and camels, is the only possible activity. In Cyrenaica nomads outnumber the rest of the population, but in Tripolitania the main emphasis is on agriculture, though herding is still important. The latter region also has a number of small local industries,

whilst there are very few of these in Cyrenaica, and none in the Fezzan.

The original population of Libya seems to have been Berber in origin, i.e. connected with many of the present-day inhabitants of Morocco, Algeria, and Tunis. The establishment of Greek colonies from about 650 B.C. onwards seems to have had little ethnic effect on the population; but in the ninth and tenth centuries A.D. there were large-scale immigrations by Arabic-speaking tribes from the Najd of Arabia. This latter group, of relatively unmixed Mediterranean racial type, is now entirely dominant, ethnically speaking, especially in Cyrenaica, of which it has been said that no other part of the world (central Arabia alone excepted) is more thoroughly "Arab".

A few Berber elements do, however, survive, mainly in the south and west of Libya; whilst the long-continued traffic in Negro slaves (which came to an end in the 1940s) has left a visible influence on peoples more especially in the south but also to some extent in the north.

Arabic, brought in by the tenth century invaders, is now current as the one official language of Libya, but a few Berber-speaking villages remain.

HISTORY

Until very modern times, the history of Libya consisted basically of a series of local histories of small cities, and it is difficult to obtain a clear conspectus of the history of the country as a whole.

Where harbours and roadsteads existed in Libya, which had more or less fertile immediate hinterlands, and which were conveniently sited with respect to the northern ends of caravan routes trading from the interior of Africa, those peoples of the Mediterranean who from time to time were active as seamen and traders, established, or maintained, "emporia"—small city colonies. These conditions existed in Libya only at the west and the east ends of the bleak and forbidding Gulf of Sirte where the desert reaches to the sea and separates the modern provinces of Tripolitania and Cyrenaica by a vacuum 250 miles across.

Where there was desert, there was nothing; where the semi-desert lay, and around the distant oases of the interior, there were the nomads and the semi-nomads, whose way of life changed little throughout the centuries and in whose history the main event was their conversion to Islam. Intolerant of all external controls, they seem perpetually to have resented the civilizing influences from without which clung to the two extremities of the Mediterranean coastline around Sabratha, Tripoli, Leptis at the west end, and ancient Cyrene, Barca, Berenice (now Benghazi) and Derna at the east. When the coastal cities were in strong hands, their civilizing influence was pushed inland to the limits of cultivable land. When they were in weak hands, their influence stopped at their city gates, and the very sands of the desert invaded what under stronger rulers of the cities bore crops of corn, olives and grapes.

From the evidence of Herodotus, and also from that of modern archaeological research, it appears that in the earliest historical times two races inhabited Libya—the "Libyans" and the "Ethiopians"—the former, of Mediterranean stock, inhabited the coastal areas; the latter, of negroid and African stock, inhabited the interior. They

used neolithic stone instruments. They knew how to cultivate. The Garamantes of the Fezzan raised cattle over a thousand years before Christ, when Phoenician sailors from the cities of Tyre and Sidon in Syria began to visit Libya to trade for gold and silver, ivory, apes, and peacocks. The perils of their voyages in little ships and the advantages of having emporia at or near the northern ends of the caravan routes led the Phoenicians eventually to establish permanent colonies on the coast, at Leptis, Uai'at (Tripoli) and Sabratha, where more or less safe roadsteads existed. Their most famous colony, Carthage, lay to the west of the boundary of what is now called Libya. But this city, in its maritime and commercial struggle with the ancient Greeks, extended its influence eastward and by 517 B.C. had incorporated the three cities into its Empire.

By this time the Greeks had colonized Cyrene (about 600 B.C.) and raised it to be a powerful city. The Carthaginians, sensitive to competition in Libya, not only drove off an attempt by the son of a Spartan King to found a colony near Leptis, but advanced to contact with Cyrene, where, some time about the beginning of the fourth century B.C., a firm frontier was established against the Cyrenaicans at the Mounds of Philainos, where Mussolini's "Marble Arch" now stands. Cyrene herself fell under the domination of Alexander the Great, and although he was never able to carry out his threat of marching against Carthage, Ptolemy I Soter, heir to Alexander's Egyptian conquests, conquered Cyrenaica for Egypt and extended his empire westwards as far as Sirte.

By about 250 B.C. Carthage was at the height of her power. Her monopolistic policy in commercial and foreign relations reduced the three "emporia" to political non-entity, although their agriculture flourished.

By this time the Romans had substituted themselves for the Greeks as the most powerful Europeans in the Mediterranean. During the struggle between Rome and Carthage which followed, the Tripolitanian half of Libya fell into the power of the Numidians under Massinissa, who allied himself with Rome. After the destruction of Carthage, the three emporia remained under nominal Numidian suzerainty, but in ever closer trading relationship with Italy, until Caesar's war against Pompey, when, after his victory at Thapsus over the Pompeians and their Numidian allies, Caesar created the Roman province of Africa Nova. Augustus set this province under a proconsul responsible to the Senate who also commanded the Legio III Augusta. Meanwhile Cyrenaica had passed under Roman sovereignty by the testament of the last of her Ptolemaic Kings—Ptolemy Apion—and was eventually created a province about 75 B.C.

The Pax Romana extended itself during the first century after Christ from the Mediterranean to the Fezzan. The second century was for Libya a period of prosperity, peace and civilization, the like of which she has never seen again. In particular under Septimius Severus, himself born in Leptis, and the successors of his family, the cities, and especially Leptis, attained the height of their splendour.

This condition did not last. Decline had set in by the middle of the fourth century. The general economic disease which was affecting Roman civilization affected also Africa. Christianity had challenged the spiritual values of the classical world but was itself too full of schisms to provide unity and strength. Libya itself was the scene of fierce internecine struggles caused by the Donatist heresy. Barbarians broke into the province, devastating the countryside, destroying its agricultural system, and spreading insecurity which caused depopulation through flight to the towns. In A.D. 431, Genseric and his Vandals appeared, overran the country, beat down the city walls, and brought ruin in their train. They were the first to introduce that piracy for which its harbours in a later age became notorious. A hundred years later the Emperor Justinian's general Belisarius found little difficulty in reconquering the country for the Byzantine Empire. There was a temporary revival of prosperity but continual rebellions by the Berber tribes soon reduced the country to anarchy.

THE MUSLIM PERIOD

In this condition the first Arab invaders found it. In the Caliphate of Omar, Amr ibn al-As, the conqueror of Egypt, overran the country as far as the Fezzan and Tripoli, the walls of which city he razed. This was in A.D. 643. There followed successive expeditions, mostly for booty, fiercely resisted by the Berbers, in the course of which Oqba ibn Nafi founded Qairawan (A.D. 670) and actually reached the Atlantic. The majority of the Berbers rapidly embraced Islam, but for the most part in its schismatic forms as Kharijites, Ibadites, and Shi'ites. An outlet for their turbulence was found in joining them with the Arabs in the invasion of Spain (A.D. 711).

Schism and continual rebellion induced the Caliph of Baghdad, Harun ar-Rashid, to appoint, in A.D. 800, Ibrahim ibn al-Aghlab as Governor with capital at Qairawan. He founded the Aghlabid dynasty, which became virtually independent of the Abbasid Caliph of Baghdad, but which brought little peace to Libya. A hundred years later a Shi'ite rising overthrew the Aghlabids and founded the Shi'ite Fatimid Dynasty, which from Tunisia conquered Egypt, transferred the seat of their Government to Cairo in A.D. 972, and made Bulukkin ibn Ziri Governor of Ifriqiya. He in turn set up a dynasty under which the land enjoyed considerable prosperity. But, at the beginning of the eleventh century, the Zirid Amir returned to orthodox Sunnism and acknowledged the sovereignty of the Caliph of Baghdad.

The Fatimid Caliph of Egypt, Al-Mustansir, reacted by sending against Libya two nomad Arab tribes which had been kept in Upper Egypt—the Banu Hilal and the Banu Suleim (A.D. 1049). This invasion was a final catastrophe for medieval Libya. The country was devastated, agriculture abandoned. The fortified cities, and in particular Tripoli, alone retained some vestiges of civilization. The next two centuries tell of little but intertribal wars, and the gradual fusion of the Arab and Berber races. Nor do the fourteenth and fifteenth centuries offer much more to record in "Ifriqiya". Murabit dynasts from Morocco contended with Muwahhid dynasts from the Balearic Islands. From these struggles emerged a dynasty in Tunisia called the Hafsids, whose power declined into a weak and anarchic state that attracted the attention of the new, crusading and imperialistic power of Christian Spain which could not overlook the fact that the cities of the northern coast of Africa had become dens of pirates.

Ferdinand the Catholic sent an expedition under Cardinal Ximenes and Don Pietro of Navarre which took Oran, Bugia, Algiers, and Tunis, and then, in 1510, Tripoli. These conquests produced a profound impression on the Muslim world, which at that time had become more united under the Ottoman Turks than it had been since the Abbasid Caliphs were at their zenith six hundred years earlier. The people outside the cities resisted the Spanish with Ottoman encouragement. Within the cities the Spanish were exposed to the dangers of conspiracy. Moreover they could make little effort to extend their power inland since, after the accession of the Emperor Charles V, Spain became heavily involved in European politics. The citizens of Tripoli intrigued unsuccessfully with the corsair Khair ad-Din, known as Barbarossa, who had made himself Lord of Algeria and had later become the Admiral of the Ottoman Sultan.

In these circumstances, the Emperor Charles V confided (A.D. 1530) the Lordship and the defence of Tripoli to the Knights Hospitallers of St. John (later to be known as the Knights of Malta) who had in A.D. 1522 lost Rhodes to the Ottoman Sultan, Suleyman the Magnificent. The Knights were able to maintain themselves there for only 21 years and then Sinan Pasha, who had been sent to reduce Malta but had failed in the attempt, invaded the town and forced the Knights to capitulate.

The Ottoman rulers of Constantinople now proceeded to organise their North African possessions into three Regencies—Algeria, Tunisia, and Tripoli, the last including also Cyrenaica and the Fezzan—each under a Pasha. But their organization contained from the first the germs of the disease to which it ultimately succumbed. The population of the interior was left almost unadministered. Tribute was levied and collected by a few regular troops, and by the "Maghzen" tribes from the remaining tribes, in return for the privilege of exemption from tithe and capitation tax. The system gave obvious opportunities for oppression and rebellion, and the division of the people into feudal lords and serfs. Worse still was the hardening of the professional soldiery of the garrisons, the Janissaries, of slave origin, into a military caste in which promotion was by seniority alone, and the retired officers of which had the right to a seat in the Pasha's Divan, or Council. The Janissaries became a power within the state. No less dangerous was the influence of the pirate captains—the corsairs. The Pashas subsidized them with arms and equipment and took their recognized share of their prizes. The Captains' Guild, called at-Ta'ifa, also became a power within the State. As early as A.D. 1595 the Divan was conceded by the Sultan the right of deciding foreign affairs and taxation. At the beginning of the seventeenth century the Janissaries introduced the custom of electing a "Dey" who sometimes reduced the Ottoman Pasha to a nonentity, sometimes shared with him the power, and sometimes was himself both Dey and Pasha. The history of the seventeenth and eighteenth centuries is one of intrigue, rebellion, sudden death, occasional outbreaks of pestilence, and of a country supported mainly by the depredations of the corsairs upon the merchant-fleets of Christian powers and the enslavement of their crews. In A.D. 1654 Admiral Blake was the first to bombard Tripoli in reprisal for such piracies. The great de Ruyter of Holland followed in 1669 and again in 1672.

In 1711 a local notable, Ahmed Karamanli, of Ottoman origin, and an officer of Janissaries, was proclaimed Dey. He succeeded not only in killing the former Dey and in defeating and killing the new Pasha sent from Constantinople, but also in persuading the Sultan Ahmed III to recognise him as Pasha. For the first time Libya had some sort of autonomous existence. The Karamanli dynasty lasted until 1835. Several of these rulers, and in particular the first and the last (Yusuf ibn Ali Karamanli, who was in power during the period of the Napoleonic wars) were men of strong personality, and capable statesmen who controlled the whole of Libya and improved the political and economic condition of the country. Like the former Pashas, they relied for much of their revenue on piracy. But the Karamanlis learned to make treaties with the maritime powers, bargaining with them to refrain from attacking their ships for a consideration, and for the most part restraining their Captains from breaking such treaties. When they failed to do so the powers would take strong action, as did the United States of America in 1805. The lesser powers naturally suffered most from the corsairs.

Such vast profits had the rulers of the Barbary coast made from piracy during the Napoleonic wars that the smaller powers made the abolition of piracy and of the enslavement of Christians points for discussion at the Congress of Vienna. England was entrusted with the suppression of these evils. It took ten years of naval and diplomatic action on the part of England and the Kingdom of the Two Sicilies to effect this. The suppression of piracy spelt the ruin of the Karamanlis. Yusuf Pasha fell into dire financial straits from which his expedients of adulterating the currency, of state trading, and of pledging in advance the already exorbitant taxes, so far from rescuing him served only to ruin both him and Libya. In 1830 French pressure compelled him to give up even the payments formerly exacted from Christian States for the right to maintain Consuls in Tripoli and for the right to unmolested navigation. In desperation, Yusuf demanded a special "aid" from both Jews and Muslims and this was the signal for revolt.

Probably through fear of the extension of French power in Algiers and Tunis, the Sultan decided to reoccupy Libya and to bring it once more under the direct rule of the Porte. This was in 1835. The rest of Libya's story in the nineteenth century is similar to that of most of the possessions of "The Sick Man of Europe"—corruption, oppression, revolts and their suppression—the towns alone being held by the Turks, with an occasional more energetic or more honest Governor. The period was, however, marked by the diffusion of Sanusi influence. The Sanusi were a religious brotherhood, founded by one Muhammad ibn Ali al Sanusi who settled in Cyrenaica on Jebel al Akhdar in 1834. From there the order spread, founding fraternities (*zawia*) throughout Libya and North Africa. In 1855 the Sanusi headquarters were transferred to Jaghbub to avoid opposition to the order of the Turks and, to some extent, Europeans. Al Sanusi was succeeded on his death in 1859 by his son Muhammad al Mahdi, who led the brotherhood until 1901.

ITALO-TURKISH CONFLICTS

On September 29th, 1911, Italy declared war on Turkey for causes more trivial than those which twenty-four years later led to her war with Ethiopia and her denunciation as an aggressor. After a short bombardment Italian troops landed at Tripoli on October 3rd. Italy knew the Turks to be involved in the Balkans, and knew, through her commercial infiltration of Libya, their weakness in Africa. But her attack on Libya was not the easy exercise she expected. The Turks withdrew inland. But the Libyans organized themselves and joined the Turks, to whom the Porte sent assistance in the form of arms and of two senior officers, Ali Fethi Bey and Enver Pasha. The presence in the Italian army of Eritrean troops was a spur to the pride of the Libyans. In October and November a number of actions were fought around Tripoli in which the Italians had little success. A seaborne Italian force then descended on Misurata and seized it, but could make no progress inland. At Ar-Rumeila they suffered a considerable reverse. Turkey, however, defeated in the Balkan War, was anxious for a peace, which was signed on October 18th, 1912. One of the conditions of this peace was that the Libyans should be allowed "administrative autonomy". This was never realized.

Peace with Turkey did not, however, mean peace in Libya for the Italians. Although most of the Tripolitanians submitted and were disarmed within two years, the Sanusiya of Cyrenaica under Sayyid Ahmad ash-Sharif, and their adherents in the Fezzan and Tripolitania, refused to yield. The Sanusiya maintained a forward post at Sirte under Sayyid Ahmad's brother, Sayyid Safi ad-Din as-Sanusi. What contact there was between this Sayyid and one Ramadan as-Sueihli of Misurata is obscure. Ramadan had been in the resistance to the Italians and two years later had appeared to be submissive. At all events, he found himself commanding Libyans in an action started by the Italians at Al-Qaradabia in 1914, to push back Sayyid Safi ad-Din. Ramadan and his Misuratis changed sides in this action to the discomfiture of the Italians. By the time that the First World War had started, the Italians held only the coast towns of Tripoli, Benghazi, Derna and Tobruk, and a few coast villages near Tripoli.

The First World War gave Turkey and her German allies the opportunity of fermenting trouble against Italy in Libya. Arms and munitions were sent by submarine. Nuri Pasha from Turkey and Abdurrahman Azzam (late Secretary-General of the Arab League) from Egypt joined Sayyid Ahmad ash-Sharif in Cyrenaica. Ramadan as-Sueihli became head of a government at Misurata. The Sultan, to prevent quarrels, sent as Amir Osman Fu'ad, grandson of Sultan Murad; and Ishaq Pasha as commander in chief in Tripolitania. The strategical objective of these efforts was to tie up Italian forces in Libya and British forces in the Western Desert. The climax of Nuri Pasha's efforts with the Sanusi was their disastrous action in the Western Desert against the British, as a result of which Sayyid Ahmad ash-Sharif handed over the leadership to Sayyid Muhammad Idris. He was compelled to make the treaty of az-Zawiatna with the British and the Italians who recognised him as Amir of the interior of Cyrenaica, provided he desisted from attacks on the coastal towns and on Egypt.

The end of the war in 1918 left Italy weak and the Libyans, deserted by the Turks, weary. The Tripolitanians attempted to form a republic with headquarters at Gharian and with Abdurrahman Azzam as adviser. The Italians made a truce with them at Suani ibn Adam, permitting a delegation to go to Rome and entertaining the idea of "administrative independence". Ramadan as-Sueihli visited Tripoli. In Cyrenaica, Sayyid Muhammad Idris as-Sanusi likewise attempted to come to terms. In 1921 at Sirte the Tripolitanian leaders agreed with him to join forces to obtain Libya's rights and to do homage to him as Amir of all Libya. Meanwhile the delegation to Rome had returned empty-handed and Ramadan as-Sueihli had been slain in a tribal fight.

ITALIAN COLONIZATION

The advent of the Fascists to power in Italy (1922) coincided with the appointment in Tripoli of a vigorous Governor, Count Volpi. Thereafter, it took them until 1925 to occupy and pacify the province of Tripolitania and disarm the population. In Cyrenaica, however, the famous Sayyid Omar al-Mukhtar, representing the Amir Muhammad Idris, whose health had broken down, kept up the struggle. The Italians realized that the only effective policy was to deprive the Sanusiya of their bases, the oases of the South. Jaghbub was occupied in 1925, Zella, Ojila and Jalo in 1927. In 1928 Marshal Badoglio was appointed Governor General and in 1929 he occupied Mizda in the Fezzan. Omar Mukhtar still resisted. The Italians removed into concentration camps at al-Aqeila the tribes of the Jebel Akhdar. In 1930 Graziani was appointed to Cyrenaica, and the famous barbed-wire fence was erected along the frontier of Egypt. Finally, in 1931, cut off from all support, Omar Mukhtar, now an aged man, was surrounded, wounded, captured, and hanged.

Starting in the early 1920s, the Italians proceeded to colonize, in the sense of that word which is now in disrepute, those parts of Libya which they had occupied, and which geographical and ecological conditions rendered profitable for development. They enlarged and embellished the coastal towns. They extended throughout the cultivable areas a most excellent network of roads. They bored wells. They planted trees, and stabilized sand-dunes. But their civilizing policy was weighted heavily in favour of their own race. The object was clearly the settlement in Africa of as much as possible of Italy's surplus peasant population. These were encouraged to come in large numbers. Skilled cultivators of olives, vines, tobacco, barley, they needed the best lands and were provided with them. The priority given to the progress of the Libyans was a low one. Primary education for the Libyans was encouraged and schools provided for them. But the main medium of instruction was Italian. Very few Libyans were accepted into Italian secondary schools. To prevent Muslim Libyans seeking higher education in Egypt and elsewhere, a small Muslim Higher College was founded in Tripoli. The Libyans avoided sending their children to school, although attempts at compulsion were made. They feared lest their children lose their Islamic faith and way of life.

INDEPENDENCE

There followed the Second World War, and the occupation in 1942 of Cyrenaica and Tripolitania by a British Military Administration and of the Fezzan by French Forces. Thereafter until 1950 the country was administered with the greatest economy on a care and maintenance basis. Its final fate was long in doubt, until the United Nations decreed its independence by 1952. On December 24th, 1951, Libya was declared an independent United Kingdom with a federal constitution under King Idris, the former Amir Muhammad Idris, hero of the resistance.

According to the Constitution promulgated in October 1951, the state of Libya was a federal monarchy ruled by King Muhammad Idris al-Mahdi al-Sanusi and his heirs, and divided into the three provinces of Tripolitania, Cyrenaica and the Fezzan. The Federal Government consisted of a bicameral legislature, i.e., a Chamber of Deputies, to which was responsible a Council of Ministers appointed by the King, and a Senate of 24 members, 8 for each province. The King had the right to nominate half the total number of Senators, to introduce and to veto legislation, and to dissolve the Lower House at his discretion. The Constitution also provided that Provincial Legislatures should be created for the subordinate provinces of the new realm.

On the attainment of full independence serious political, financial and economic problems confronted Libya. Not the least of these was the task of fostering amongst the population a sense of national identity and unity. The loyalties of the people were still given to the village and the tribe, rather than to the new federal state. Poor communications and the great spaces of desert land, together with the lack of trained personnel and lingering provincial rivalries, were great obstacles to the establishment of a stable and efficient modern administration.

These rivalries revealed themselves in the next two years. The Party of Independence, which supported the constitution, won control in the February 1952 elections for the Federal Chamber of Deputies. The National Congress Party of Tripolitania, however, was opposed to the federal principle and advocated a unitary state with proportional representation (which would have given Tripolitania the main voice). Disorders arising from this disagreement led to the outlawing of the Tripolitania party and the deportation of its leader al-Sa'adawi. A Legislative Council for Tripolitania was formed in 1952 but had to be dissolved in 1954 because of continued friction with the Federal Government and the King.

About 80 per cent of the population of Libya was engaged in agriculture; but owing to the low rainfall, the hot desert winds and primitive farming methods, the average yield was small. There were no important mineral resources and only a few industries, most of them in Italian hands. Since 1945 exports had sufficed to meet only about 50 per cent of the cost of imports, most of which had been in the form of consumer goods needed to maintain the already low standards of life, and not of capital equipment and machinery. Income from foreign military establishments had been estimated as being 50 per cent above the total value of exports.

Efforts were undertaken, with Western technical aid, to increase the economic resources of Libya, e.g., to improve irrigation and initiate schemes for water catchments, to extend reafforestation, to teach better methods of farming, and to explore the possibilities of extending industries which could process local products and raw materials such as edible oils, fruits, vegetables, fish, etc.

FOREIGN RELATIONS IN THE 1950s

The first important development in the sphere of foreign relations was the admission of Libya to the Arab League in March 1953. The second development reflected the economic difficulties of the new state and its close links with Western Europe. In July 1953 Libya concluded a twenty-year treaty with Britain. In return for permission to maintain military bases in Libya, Britain undertook to grant the new state £1 million annually for economic development and a further annual sum of £2,750,000 to meet budgetary deficits. The financial obligations of the treaty were subject to review after five years.

In September 1954 a similar agreement was signed with the United States. A number of air bases were granted to the U.S. in return for economic aid amounting to $40 million over twenty years, which amount was later substantially increased. Libya also consolidated relations with France and Italy, signing a friendship pact with France in 1955 and a trade and financial agreement with Italy in 1956. In addition Libya was attempting to cement relations with her Arab neighbours. In May 1956 Libya concluded a trade and payments pact with Egypt, arranging the exchange of Libyan cattle for Egyptian foodstuffs.

The critical problem for Libya was to ensure that enough funds from abroad should be available to meet the normal expenses of the Government and to pay for much-needed improvements. At this time, her strategic position was all Libya had to sell, hence her involvement with the Western military alliance and in particular with Britain, France, Italy, Italy, Turkey and the United States. The Libyan attitude to the Communist world was much more reserved. A Soviet ambassador was accredited to Tripoli in January 1955, but a Soviet offer of economic aid was rejected the following year. In 1955, too, Libya was admitted to membership of the United Nations.

Reliance on income from foreign military bases continued, therefore, to dominate foreign policy. In April 1958 the Prime Minister, Abd al Majid Kubar, who had taken office in May 1957 on the resignation of his predecessor, Mustafa ibn Halim, went to London to discuss the financial assistance that would be given to Libya during the five years 1958–63 under the terms of the Anglo-Libyan agreement signed in 1953. He announced to the Libyan Parliament in May 1958 that in the five-year period ending on April 1st, 1963, Great Britain would provide subsidies to the amount of £3,250,000 per annum, would make available light arms and equipment for 5,000 Libyan troops and would also continue the programme of free military training. He also stated that the British Government would no longer give £1 million per annum to the Libyan Development Agency, as it had done since 1953, and that the United States intended to contribute to the Agency $5.5 million during the next five years.

In September 1958 Libya became a member of the International Monetary Fund and of the International Bank for Reconstruction and Development. Official sources stated in May 1959 that Libya would henceforward receive financial aid from the United States, not through the various aid organizations of the United States, but directly from the United States Government. In June 1959 the U.S. Development Loan Fund made available to Libya $5 million for electric power generation and transmission facilities designed to serve Tripoli and the surrounding region. During the course of 1958 and 1959 a number of discoveries of oil were made in various areas of Libya.

In August 1960 the Libyan Government announced that the U.S.A. had agreed to pay $10 million per annum for the use of military bases in Libya. Aid was also obtained from Federal Germany at this time.

OIL DISCOVERIES

After 1955–56, when Libya granted concessions for oil exploration to several American companies, the search for oil resources became one of the main interests of the Libyan Government. By the end of 1959 some fifteen companies held oil concessions in Libya. An oilfield at Zelten in Cyrenaica was discovered in June 1959. Before the year was out, six productive wells had been found in Tripolitania, four in Cyrenaica and one in the Fezzan. On May 24th, 1960, the Libyan Government promulgated a law establishing a Council of Development (Majlis al-I'mār) to examine the natural resources of Libya and to consider projects and policies of an economic and social character By the beginning of July 1960 there were thirty-five oil wells in production, yielding altogether a little less than 93,000 barrels of oil per day. The development of the oilfields is dealt with in greater detail in the *Economic Survey* which follows this history.

In the month of August 1964 British Petroleum discovered large oil reserves in eastern Libya, not far from the Egyptian frontier, and stated that a pipeline would be built to Tobruk for the exploitation of this field. The Esso Libya corporation confirmed in November that it intended to construct a gas liquefaction plant at Mersa Brega. December 1964 witnessed the opening of a pipeline from the Hofra

oilfield to a new loading terminal at Ras Lanuf on the Gulf of Sirte. Oil production showed a tremendous increase in the 1962–66 period, with exports rising from 8 million tons in 1962 to over 70 million in 1966.

A UNITARY REALM

A general election was held in Libya on January 17th, 1960. Most of the 55 seats were contested, but there was no party system in operation. The election was fought mainly on a personal basis. Secret ballotting, limited in earlier elections to the urban areas, was now extended to the rural districts. The Prime Minister, Abd al Majid Kubar, and the other members of his Cabinet retained their seats.

Libya's increasing wealth was making the business of government more complex and several changes of administration ensued between 1960 and 1963. Finally, in March 1963, a new cabinet under the premiership of Dr. Mohieddin Fekini was appointed.

Dr. Fekini stated in April 1963 that his government intended to introduce legislation designed to transform Libya from a federal into a unitary state—a change which would mean increased efficiency and considerable economies in administration. On April 15th the Prime Minister presented to the Chamber of Deputies a Bill which contained a number of important reforms: (1) the franchise was to be granted to women; (2) Libya would have (as before) a bicameral parliamentary system, but henceforward the King was to nominate all the 24 members of the Senate (heretofore half nominated and half elected); (3) the Kingdom of Libya would cease to be a federal state comprising three provinces (Tripolitania, Cyrenaica and Fezzan), becoming instead a unitary realm divided into ten administrative areas; (4) the administrative councils established in each of the three provinces were to be abolished, the exercise of executive power residing now in the Council of Ministers. Libya became a unitary state by royal proclamation on April 27th, 1963.

THE REALITY OF INDEPENDENCE

In the field of foreign relations, Libya was by now helped by the prospect of financial independence and was making her voice heard in international affairs, particularly in Africa. As a result of decisions taken at the Addis Ababa conference of African Heads of State in May 1963 Libya closed her air and sea ports to Portuguese and South African ships. The signing of pacts with Morocco (1962) and Algeria (1963) meant that Libya now had closer links with all the Maghreb countries. Libya was also showing signs of throwing off her dependence on the West. The 1955 agreement with France had allowed France to retain in Libya certain military facilities—notably in the field of communications—for the defence of her African territories. The future of this agreement was raised by Dr. Fekini in November 1963. He expressed the view that the recently acquired independence (1960) of Libya's southern neighbours, Niger and Chad, rendered the agreement obsolete and he thought that the whole matter should be considered anew.

The question of foreign military bases in Libya now came to the fore. On January 22nd, 1964, Dr. Fekini resigned his office of Prime Minister after student demonstrations at Benghazi and Tripoli. The new Prime Minister was Mahmud Muntasser, hitherto Minister of Justice. The Government issued a statement on February 23rd to the effect that it did not propose to renew or extend its military agreements with Great Britain and the United States and that it supported the other governments of the Arab world in the resistance to imperialism. Mr. Muntasser defined the aim of his government as the termination of the existing agreements with Great Britain and the United States and the fixing of a date for the evacuation of the bases in Libya. The Chamber of Deputies now passed a resolution calling for the achievement of this aim and providing that, if negotiations were unsuccessful, the Chamber would pass legislation to abrogate the treaties and close the bases.

The Anglo-Libyan treaty of 1953 was due to expire in 1973. Under the treaty Great Britain maintained a Royal Air Force staging post near Tobruk, an Air Force detachment at Idris airport in Tripoli and Army District Headquarters at Tripoli and Benghazi. The American-Libyan agreement of 1954 was to expire in 1971. Near Tripoli was situated the largest American air-base outside the United States. Under the treaties Libya had received large amounts of financial, economic and military aid from the United States and from Great Britain. Libyan dependence on such aid had diminished, however, as a result of the swift development of the oil fields, which provided the state with increasing revenues. Great Britain offered to withdraw from her military positions in Tripolitania, the western region of the Kingdom.

At elections for the Libyan Parliament held in October 1964 moderate candidates won most of the 103 seats. Women received the right to vote in this election. King Idris dissolved the Parliament, however, on February 13th, 1965, as the result of complaints about irregularities in the election procedure of October 1964.

The Prime Minister resigned, to be succeeded by Husayn Maziq, Minister for Foreign Affairs. A new election for Parliament was held on May 8th, 1965, over two hundred candidates contesting the 91 seats, 16 members being returned unopposed.

The withdrawal of the British troops stationed in Tripolitania took place in February and March 1966. Britain retained for a time certain facilities at Idris airport near Tripoli, small detachments at Benghazi, Tobruk and the R.A.F. staging post of El Adem, to the south of Tobruk.

The outbreak of the six-day Arab-Israeli war in June 1967 was followed by serious disturbances in Tripoli and Benghazi, in which port and oil workers and students, inflamed by Egyptian propaganda, played a prominent part. The British and United States embassies were attacked and the Jewish minorities were subjected to violence and persecution which resulted in the greater part of them emigrating to Italy, Malta and elsewhere. The Prime Minister, Husayn Maziq, proved unable to control the situation and was dismissed by the King on June 28th. Firm measures by his successor, Abdul Qadir Badri, brought a return to order but the antagonisms he aroused forced him to resign in turn in October. He was succeeded as Prime Minister on October 28th by the Minister of Justice, Abdul Hamid Bakkush, a Tripoli lawyer.

An immediate result of the June war was a fall in the Libyan output of crude oil of about 80 per cent because of the boycott of oil supplies from Arab countries to Britain, the United States and Federal Germany. There was a gradual return to full production in the months following the conflict, however, and the ban on the export of oil was lifted in September. The closure of the Suez Canal brought about a considerable increase in Libya's oil exports and general prosperity, although the Libyan Government agreed to make annual aid payments totalling £30 million to the U.A.R. and Jordan to alleviate the consequences of the war. Libya's oil output increased by about 50 per cent in 1968 and the country became after only 7½ years the second largest producer in the Arab world with the great advantage, as a supplier to Europe, of being on the right side of the Suez Canal.

The new Prime Minister, Abdul Hamid Bakkush, was a progressive. His relatively young and well-educated administration immediately embarked on a programme of rapid change, seeking to modernize Libya's administration, reform the civil service and improve the educational system. He also sought to provide the armed forces with up-to-date equipment, and under a contract announced in April 1968 the purchase from a British firm of a surface-to-air missile defence system costing £100 million was arranged. An agreement to buy British heavy arms, notably the advanced Chieftain tanks, followed in spring 1969. In September 1968, however, Mr. Bakkush was replaced as premier by Wanis el Qaddafi, the pace of his reforms having apparently alienated some conservative elements. Both ministries enjoyed close relationships with the Western countries but played little part in Arab politics.

THE 1969 COUP

On September 1st, 1969, a military coup was staged in Tripoli whilst the King was in Turkey for medical treatment. Within a few days the new régime gained complete control of the entire country. The coup was remarkable for the absence of any opposition, relatively few arrests, virtually no fighting and no deaths at all being reported. The "Revolutionary Command Council" (RCC) initially remained anonymous but was soon revealed as a group of young army officers, the leader, Muammar Gaddafi, being only 27. The aged King refused to abdicate but accepted exile in Egypt when it became obvious that the revolution had been completely accepted by his people.

The provisional constitution announced in November stated that supreme power would remain in the hands of the RCC which appoints the cabinet; there was no mention of any future general election or of a National Assembly, and the royal ban on political parties continued. A largely civilian cabinet was appointed under close military supervision. The Ministers of Defence and of the Interior were accused of organizing an abortive counter-revolution in December, and were tried and sentenced in 1970. In January Col. Gaddafi himself became Prime Minister and several of his colleagues also joined the cabinet.

The principal force underlying the régime's policies was undoubtedly the professed one of Arab nationalism. Internally this led to the strict enforcement of the royal law requiring businesses operating in Libya to be controlled by Libyans—banks being particularly affected. The remaining British military establishment in Libya, requested to leave as soon as possible, was finally removed in March 1970, and the much larger U.S. presence at Wheelus Field followed suit in June. Most of the European and American managers, teachers, technicians and doctors were replaced by Arabs, mainly from Egypt. English translations disappeared from street signs, official stationery and publications, and most hoardings, the use of Arabic alone being permitted; similarly, the Islamic prohibitions on alcoholic drinks and certain Western clothes were officially revived. In July 1970 the property of all Jews and Italians still living in Libya—some 25,000 people—was sequestrated by the Government, and both communities were encouraged to leave without delay; some Jews were, however, offered compensation in government bonds. In the same month the three main oil marketing companies—Shell, Esso and an ENI subsidiary—had their distribution facilities nationalized.

Another anti-government plot was reported crushed in July 1970. In the autumn two ministers resigned and there were signs of a power struggle developing in the Revolutionary Command Council. The internal dissension apparently increased in the first part of 1970 over the proposed federation with the U.A.R., Syria and Sudan, and over President Gaddafi's promises of a constitution, and political institutions, including an elected president. A step towards introducing these was the announcement in June 1971 that an Arab Socialist Union was to be created as the state's sole party. Such a development would also presumably assist integration with the U.A.R. and Sudan.

FOREIGN POLICY AFTER THE COUP

The new régime almost immediately received recognition—indeed acclaim—from the radical Arab countries and the U.S.S.R., and the rest of the world also granted recognition within a few days. As would be expected from the Arab nationalist inspiration behind the revolution, the monarchy's close ties with the Western powers were abandoned in favour of close relations with the Arab world and Egypt in particular; this friendship became the basis of an important triple alliance announced late in 1969, the Sudan being the third member. The alliance was intended to develop both politically—as a strong bulwark against Israel and the West—and economically, in that the economies of the three countries complemented each other to a considerable extent. However, when a federation agreement was signed in April 1971, it was Syria which became the third member. Libya also adopted a militant position on the Palestine question, and this created some diplomatic problems regarding arms contracts.

The royal government's contract to buy a British missile defence system, implicitly aimed against Egypt, was duly cancelled; fulfilment of another major British contract, for the advanced Chieftain tanks, was delayed by Britain, which feared that the tanks might reach the Palestine front. Colonel Gaddafi's government itself ordered over 100 French Mirage jet fighters. There were widespread fears in the West that Egyptian pilots would fly the Mirages, which might then be used to escalate the campaign against Israel. Deliveries of Soviet tanks were reported in the summer of 1970.

Although in July 1970 the Libyan Government followed Egypt in accepting the American proposals for a cease-fire with Israel, it continued its militant statements on the Middle East problem. President Gaddafi stated that a peaceful solution was impossible and rejected the UN Security Council resolution on which the Rogers initiative was based. During the fighting between Palestine guerrillas and the Jordanian army in September 1970, Libya redirected its financial aid from the Government to the guerrillas and broke off diplomatic relations with Hussein's government.

Nearer home, the coup appeared to have reorientated Libya away from the Maghreb; in the summer of 1970 Libya withdrew from the Maghreb Permanent Consultative Committee. Relations with Tunisia improved in the last half of 1970, after initial concern in Tunis in 1969 at the radical leanings of the new régime, and President Gaddafi headed a delegation which visited Tunisia in February 1971. Relations with Morocco were severed in July 1971 after the Libyan Government prematurely gave its support to an attempt to overthrow King Hassan, which failed within twenty-four hours.

There was little evidence of any closer relationship with the communist power, although China was recognized in June 1971 and the U.S.S.R. was given due credit for its Middle East policies. But communism was regarded in Libya as a "foreign" ideology, antipathetic to more "progressive" Arab socialism (as in Sudan). Hence, in July 1971, Gaddafi was ready to help President Nemery of Sudan to regain power after a coup led by communists had ousted him. A regular BOAC flight from London to

Khartoum was forced down over Libya and two leaders of the coup, one of whom, Major al-Nur, was travelling back to become head of state, were taken from the plane and handed over to Sudan. They were almost immediately executed by the restored régime.

OIL POWER

In April 1971 the negotiations with the oil companies operating in Libya, which had begun soon after the 1969 coup, finally ended in a new five-year agreement raising the total posted price for Libyan crude to $3.447 per barrel. In the last stage of the negotiations, conducted in Tripoli, the Libyan Government also represented the interests of the Algerian, Iraqi and Saudi Arabian Governments. Threats of an embargo on the export of crude oil were used as a lever in the negotiations.

In ten years Libya's position had changed from one of penury and dependence to one of power based entirely on her ability to cut off oil supplies. The pronouncements of President Gaddafi were, therefore, by now of great moment to the West. In July 1971, the Deputy Prime Minister, Major Abd al Salam Jalloud, visited West Germany, France and Britain. Germany, which buys a particularly large proportion of its crude oil from Libya, needed to maintain good relations. France was anxious over the use to which Libya would put the Mirage jet fighters being supplied under the 1970 agreement. The same anxiety was revealed in Britain over the supply of armaments, but none of these countries could afford to alienate Libya.

In December 1971, avowedly in retaliation for Britain's failure to prevent the Iranian occupation of the Tumb islands in the Gulf, Libya nationalized the assets of British Petroleum. This began the process of nationalizing the foreign oil companies which is described in more detail in the Economic Survey.

Relations with Egypt and Syria were somewhat strained at the end of 1971, the cause of the friction being largely Gaddafi's uncompromising hard line on the Arab/Israel conflict. In October, President Sadat and Gaddafi met for talks on the problem and Gaddafi continued to press for all-out war.

Relations with Britain were also very much strained in the winter of 1971/72, not only because of the nationalization of BP but also because of Libyan intervention in the dispute over Malta over the British bases there. Libya had for some time been actively fostering relations with Malta, talks on possible Libyan aid being held in August 1971. In January 1972 the British naval training mission was ordered to leave Libya. And in February the 1954 agreement with the United States was abrogated.

Libya's attitude towards the Soviet Union had remained cool, and the Government was violently opposed to the Iraqi/Soviet treaty, signed in April 1972. Nevertheless, in February 1972, Major Jalloud visited Moscow and in March an agreement on oil co-operation was signed. It was also reported that the U.S.S.R. might supply arms to Libya.

At home, President Gaddafi continued to attempt to run the legislature and the Government entirely in accordance with Islamic principles. At the end of March 1972 the Arab Socialist Union held its first national congress. At subsequent sessions of the ASU resolutions were passed, clarifying its position and policies, and abolishing censorship of the Press, while at the same time maintaining financial control of newspapers.

In July 1972 disagreement within the RCC led to Maj. Jalloud taking over as Prime Minister from Gaddafi, a new cabinet being formed in which all but two of the ministers were civilians.

ARAB UNITY

A recurrent feature of President Gaddafi's foreign policy was the announcement of proposals for the union of Libya with neighbouring states, and their later collapse. The Tripoli Charter of December 1969 establishing a revolutionary alliance of Libya, Egypt (then the United Arab Republic) and Sudan was followed by gradual moves towards federation and the adhesion of Syria. Sudan withdrew, but in September 1971 referenda in Libya, Egypt and Syria approved the constitution of the Federation of Arab Republics, which officially came into existence on January 1st, 1972. The Federation was of little practical consequence, and his partners seemed to find President Gaddafi's public statements of revolutionary enthusiasm somewhat embarrassing.

The Federation was not Gaddafi's only attempt to export his ideals by means of merger. At the time of Malta's dispute with Britain over the use of bases, in 1971, he proposed a union of Malta with Libya, but was rebuffed. In December 1972, in a speech in Tunis, he proposed the union of Libya and Tunisia, much to the surprise of his audience, not least President Bourguiba, who immediately rejected the idea, making some pointed remarks about Gaddafi's inexperience.

A merger of Libya and Egypt was agreed in principle in August 1972, but as the date when it should come into force approached, certain difficulties became apparent. Gaddafi, who had recently launched his Cultural Revolution of April 1973, was seen as a reactionary Islamic puritan in Egypt, and he was openly critical of Egyptian moral laxity. Some 40,000 Libyans attempted to stage a "march on Cairo" in July 1973, to bring pressure to bear on the Egyptian Government. The marchers destroyed an Egyptian border post, but were halted some 200 miles from Cairo. This incident served only to increase Egyptian suspicion of Libyan revolutionary enthusiasm, which was seen as unsuitable for Egypt's more advanced and cosmopolitan society. The union nevertheless came into effect on September 1st, 1973, with the establishment, on paper, of unified political leadership and economic policy and a constituent assembly. The union soon fell apart, wrecked by Gaddafi's opposition to Egypt's conduct of the October 1973 Arab-Israeli war.

President Gaddafi's attitude towards the Palestine problem had long been a source of discord between Libya and other Arab states. He gave financial support to the Palestinian guerrillas, and a number of Libyan volunteers were sent to assist them, Gaddafi's objective being the complete destruction of Israel. He was extremely critical of what he saw as the lack of total commitment to the Palestinian cause on the part of Egypt and Syria, and frequently expressed the opinion that the Arab states could not, and did not deserve to defeat Israel. He accused Egypt and Syria of being more interested in the recovery of territory lost in the 1967 war than in aiding the Palestinian resistance movement, which was being "destroyed by the Arabs in co-operation with Israel". Gaddafi was not informed of the Egyptian and Syrian plan to attack Israel in October 1973, was strongly critical of their battle plan, and refused to attend the Algiers meeting of Arab heads of state after the war, declaring that it would only ratify Arab capitulation. Libya was nevertheless an enthusiastic proponent of the use of the Arab oil embargo against countries considered to be pro-Israel. During the war, Libya's participation had been limited to the supply of arms and equipment, and its conclusion seemed only to complete Gaddafi's disillusionment with the union with Egypt.

Presidents Gaddafi and Bourguiba announced the union of Libya and Tunisia on January 12th, 1974, following two days of talks. A referendum to approve the decision was to be held on January 18th, but was almost immediately postponed. The decision had been taken in absence of the Tunisian Prime Minister, Hedi Nouira. When he returned to Tunisia, the pro-merger foreign minister was dismissed, and Tunisia's attitude changed to one of indefinite deferment of the union. Gaddafi's impetuous action seemed to have produced a unified state, but Tunisia now treated the agreement as merely a declaration of principle, without any practical effect.

Gaddafi's enthusiasm for Arab unity continued unabated, but the failure of political mergers led him to propound a new course. His speeches attacked the Arab leaders who blocked unity and failed to "liberate" Palestine, and he spoke of Libyan aid for revolution and the achievement of Arab union by popular pressure on the governments of Tunisia, Egypt, Algeria and Morocco. Libya had for some time been providing money, arms and training for subversive or "liberation" organizations operating in Ireland, Eritrea, the Philippines, Rhodesia, Portuguese Guinea, Morocco and Chad, as well as providing aid for sympathetic countries such as Pakistan, Uganda, Zambia, Togo and, after May 1973, Chad. Now it appeared that Libya was supporting subversion in Egypt and Sudan. Attempted *coups* in Egypt in April and Sudan in May 1974 were believed to have had Libyan support, and relations between Libya and other Arab states became increasingly hostile. Gaddafi's failed mergers and his interference in the internal affairs of other countries were believed to have been major factors in his withdrawal from an active political role in April 1974, when it was seen that he had failed in his policy of exporting the ideals of the Libyan Cultural Revolution.

THE CULTURAL REVOLUTION

President Gaddafi's somewhat idiosyncratic political and social philosophy first obtained full expression in a speech in April 1973, when he called for the immediate launching of a "cultural revolution to destroy imported ideologies, whether they are eastern or western" and for the construction of a society based on the tenets of the Koran. The form which this revolution was to take was laid down in a five-point programme: "people's committees" would be set up to carry out the revolution, the "politically sick" would be purged, the revolutionary masses would be armed, a campaign would begin against bureaucracy and administrative abuses, and imported books which propagated Communism, atheism or capitalism would be burned. The people's committees set about their task of supervision of all aspects of social and economic life, criticizing and dismissing officials and business executives who failed to show the required revolutionary fervour, and offensive books and magazines were seized and destroyed.

In May 1973 Gaddafi presented his Third International Theory, "an alternative to capitalist materialism and communist atheism". In effect, it appeared to be a call for a return to Muslim fundamentalism, together with a rather confused combination of socialism and respect for private property, and much talk of tolerance and the rights of oppressed nationalities. Whilst the Cultural Revolution proceeded apace in Libya, Gaddafi seemed more concerned with foreign policy and his new-found role as revolutionary philosopher, who had put forward a universally applicable theory which would replace existing ideologies. Gaddafi concentrated on the formulation and propagation of his theory, and his erratic and unsuccessful attempts to export the Libyan revolution by merger or by subversion, while the mundane details of administration were increasingly left to Major Jalloud, the Prime Minister.

The return to the Koran and the rejection of external influences took several forms, some petty, such as the insistence upon the use of Arabic in foreigners' passports, some macabre, as in the revival of such features of Koranic law as the amputation of thieves' hands. The theory was also invoked in the disputes with foreign oil companies in 1973 (dealt with in detail in the Economic Survey), presented as an expression of Libyan independence. The revolution seemed to peter out as Gaddafi became more involved with foreign affairs, and it was rumoured that there was some discord within the RCC, some of whose members were dissatisfied with Gaddafi's eccentricities and the failure of his schemes for Arab union.

On April 5th, 1974 it was announced that Gaddafi, while remaining head of state and commander-in-chief, had been relieved of political, administrative and ceremonial duties, and was to devote himself to ideological and mass organization work. It appeared that, willingly or otherwise, Gaddafi had effectively been replaced by Prime Minister Jalloud. After a five-month withdrawal from active direction of the Government, Gaddafi re-emerged in the autumn of 1974 and it soon became apparent that he was more than ever in command. Relations with Egypt deteriorated after Gaddafi boycotted the Rabat summit of Arab Heads of State in October. Gaddafi was unhappy about the deci-

sion to recognize the PLO, under Yasser Arafat, as the sole legitimate representative of the Palestinians, and Gaddafi has subsequently shown his support for the "rejectionist front"—the wing of the Palestine guerrilla movement which rejects the idea of a possible settlement of the Arab-Israeli conflict under terms acceptable to Arafat and President Sadat.

The war of words with Egypt continued in 1975, with articles in the Libyan press containing bitter personal attacks on President Sadat and with the Egyptian press accusing Gaddafi of preparing to mount an invasion of Egypt. A delegation from the National Assembly of the Federation of Arab Republics, which visited Tripoli and Cairo in May, was able to bring about a temporary reconciliation, but at the end of May relations deteriorated again after reports that Libya was to allow the establishment of Soviet military bases on its territory in return for huge supplies of Soviet weapons. It later appeared that the arms deal did not include the establishment of Soviet military bases in Libya, and was in fact smaller than at first reported. Egypt, however, whose friendship since the October war has been transferred to the U.S.A. and away from the Soviet Union, viewed the whole deal with suspicion.

ECONOMIC SURVEY

Oil has transformed the Libyan economy. Before its discovery in commercial quantities in the 1950s, agriculture was the basis of the economy and domestic revenue covered only about half of the Government's ordinary and development expenditure. But between 1962 and 1968, national income increased from LD 131 million to LD 798 million and gross national product (G.N.P.) increased from LD 163 million to LD 909 million. Oil exports during the period increased by 835 per cent, accounting for 51 per cent of gross domestic product (G.D.P.) in 1968.

In foreign trade over 98 per cent of exports consist of petroleum and products and a healthy trade surplus is being maintained.

Since the 1969 revolution, state intervention in the economy has increased, in line with President Gaddafi's ideas of "Islamic socialism". The Government has at least a 51 per cent share in a number of sectors including banking and insurance, public transport, some sections of the construction industry and some manufacturing concerns. Apart, however, from the nationalization of distribution and marketing of oil in Libya in 1970, the Government refrained from directly taking over oil company assets until the dispute with BP in 1971.

Until the country's oil resources began to be exploited not more than 25 per cent of the population lived in the towns. This is no longer true, and the drift to the towns has caused a serious problem. Something like half of the non-urban population are settled in rural communities, and the other half are semi-nomads, who follow a pastoral mode of life. The majority of the population of Libya is Arab or Berber by race, with Negroid races predominating in the Fezzan (Southern Province). The 1973 census showed the total population to be 2,259,497.

AGRICULTURE

Agriculture dominated the economy until the discovery of oil. Even now the oil industry gives direct employment to no more than a small fraction of the population and the present Government regards the agricultural sector as of the first importance. At present only a very small proportion of the total area of the country is cultivable and of this a high percentage is used for grazing in some regions. In mid-1970 all Italian-owned land and property in Libya, including 37,000 hectares of cultivated land, was confiscated and plans were made to distribute the expropriated lands to Libyan farmers, with government credits for seed, fertilizers and machinery. The area under irrigation is increasing and, according to 1974 figures, had reached 275,000 hectares. A number of very large contracts has been awarded for reclamation and irrigation work in various scheduled areas. The best-known schemes are the Kufra Oasis project to irrigate 10,000 hectares; the Tawurgha project to reclaim 3,000 hectares; the Sarir reclamation project; the Jebel el-Akhdar project; the Jefara plain project; and the Wadi Qattera reclamation project. In 1974 an allocation of LD 3.4 million was announced for six more agricultural projects, covering over 10,000 hectares. All projects are meant to be fully integrated, providing for the establishment of farms, the building of rural roads, irrigation and drainage facilities and, in some cases, the introduction of agro-industries.

After a successful year in 1972–73, as far as the implementation of investment projects was concerned, the Government decided to make a great effort in agriculture, allocating to it a sum of LD 700 million over the 10-year period 1973–83 and it is now the major sector in Libya's development plan. In fact, allocations in the current three-year plan have been drastically revised upwards. The plan, as revised in February 1975, provides LD 566.9 million for agricultural development and agrarian reform.

In spite of the money poured into the sector, however, results in terms of production were largely unsatisfactory, certainly up to 1972. Climatic and soil factors will, it is hoped, cease to play such a large part in fluctuations of output, once irrigation projects are under way and the distribution and use of fertilizers is well established. There are signs in the production figures for 1973 that this is already happening. The other limiting factor, that of lack of trained technicians and administrators and poor education among the farming communities, are not so easily solved. Libya is obliged for the present to rely on foreign expertise. During 1974 and 1975 a number of agreements were concluded with countries who have experience in dealing with semi-desert conditions, notably Australia and India.

Animal husbandry is the basis of farming in Libya and is likely to remain so until irrigation and reclamation measures really start to take effect. Sheep and goats are used for meat, milk and wool. Cattle, like the donkeys and camels, were used mainly for draught and transport but in recent years breeding for dairy produce has been expanded and milk production is expected to reach 22 million litres a year by 1977. Livestock is being imported on an increasing scale from a number of sources. Breeding cattle have been supplied by the United Kingdom, and stock-raising co-operation agreements signed with Argentina, Romania and Australia. In 1974 contracts were awarded for fodder factories at Sebha, Zleiten and Zawia. Estimates of livestock numbers in 1973 showed a considerable rise in the sheep and cattle population as compared with 1970, but a corresponding drop in numbers of goats and camels, reflecting the current emphasis on meat and dairy production.

Of the cereal crops, barley, which is the staple diet of most of the population, is by far the most important. Production of both barley and wheat rose considerably in 1973, as did that of a number of fruit and vegetable crops. Olives and citrus fruit are grown mainly in Western Province, and other important food crops are tomatoes, almonds, castor beans, groundnuts and potatoes, also grown mainly in Western Province. Dates are produced in oases in Southern Province and on the coastal belt. Esparto grass, which grows wild in the Jebel, is used for the manufacture of high quality paper and bank-notes and was formerly Libya's most important article of export.

An interesting new development, only possible in an oil-rich economy, is the development of hydroponic farming. A contract was signed with a U.S. firm in 1974 to develop a number of hydroponic farms. Similar experiments are being carried out in the Arabian Gulf states but it is doubtful whether such methods will be employed on a large scale in Libya, in view of the scope for reclamation.

Some attempts have been made by the Government at reafforestation, including a successful small-scale experiment in 1971 to stabilize the soil with a synthetic rubber spray and then plant eucalyptus saplings. Since then, a number of co-operation agreements signed with other countries have included schemes for dune stabilization.

The offshore waters abound in fish, especially tunny and sardines, but most of the fishing is done by Italians, Greeks or Maltese. Of special importance are the sponge-beds along the wide continental shelf. These are exploited by foreign fishermen and divers, mainly Greeks from the Dodecanese. In 1975, a Romanian company completed a study of the fisheries potential of the Mediterranean coast. Co-operation with other Maghreb countries, coupled with the establishment of canning and processing industries, and proper marketing procedures, could make the industry reasonably profitable; but it has not been given a high position in development priorities.

OIL

That oil was present in both Tripolitania and Cyrenaica had long been suspected, and for several years after Libya became independent, a large number of the bigger oil companies carried out geological surveys of the country. In 1955 a petroleum law came into force setting up a petroleum commission, which was empowered to grant concessions on a fifty-fifty profit sharing basis, with parts of each concession being handed back to the Government after a given period. Under this law, concessions were granted to many American companies and to British, French and other foreign groups. By 1972 eleven groups, involving 21 companies, held concession rights.

Important oil strikes first began to be made in 1958, and ten years later Libya was already the fourth largest exporter in the world. The growth of the oil industry was particularly rapid after the closing of the Suez Canal in 1967, but it still employs only a relatively small proportion of the population.

Exports take place from five different ocean terminals connected to the various fields by pipelines built by the five groups which have made the major finds. The pipeline system and the terminals are, however, available to other groups. The first of the five terminals to be opened was that at Mersa Brega on the Gulf of Sirte, in 1961. The pipeline was built to Bir Zelten, some 200 miles south of Benghazi, where Esso Standard (Libya) had found oil in 1959. This group also operates a refinery at Mersa Brega and a gas liquefaction plant to prepare gas for shipment to Italy and Spain. The terminal for the Oasis group's Hofra field is at Ras el Sidr, to the west of Mersa Brega. The Mobil/Gelsenberg group also found oil near Hofra, but built another pipeline to Ras Lanuf, just east of Ras el Sidr. From a fourth terminal at Mersa el-Hariga, near Tobruk, a pipeline some 320 miles long runs to Sarir, then the BP/Bunker Hunt concession. The most recent terminal is at Zuetina, and was opened in 1968 to serve the Augila and Idris fields. Here an American company, Occidental, which did not even obtain its concession until early in 1966, had found oil in large quantities. The Amoseas group, which produces oil from the Nafoora field, not far from Augila, has a pipeline connected to the Ras Lanuf terminal.

In 1965 a law was passed bringing the arrangements under which the producing companies pay tax and royalties to the Libyan Government into line with those in force in the other Middle Eastern members of OPEC, which Libya joined in 1962. Hitherto the price used by the companies to calculate the profits on which tax was assessed had been the price they actually realized on world markets. The new law stipulated amongst other things that the price used should be the so-called posted price instead, which for many years had been much higher; this the operating companies eventually accepted. Negotiations began in the autumn of 1969 between the Government and the companies with the object of increasing the posted price, and came to fruition in April 1971 with the signing of the Tripoli agreements which raised the base posted price per barrel of 40° API crude to $3.07 with temporary adjustments bringing the total posted price per barrel to $3.447. The agreement also included annual incremental price rises until 1975; settlement of company income tax rates at 55 per cent (except for Occidental Oil); an assured reinvestment in exploration, secondary recovery or gas projects; and a guaranteed supply of crude to the Libyan National Petroleum Corporation (LINOCO) sufficient for local consumption.

Further adjustments were made in May 1972, when agreement was reached in principle on an 8.49 per cent increase in posted prices to offset the realignment of world currencies in December 1971. Detailed agreements on this issue had been concluded by early June 1972 with all the oil companies in Libya except Mobil/Gelsenberg and Esso. Libya's disagreement with the latter stemmed from the Government's argument, not accepted by Esso, that the 8.49 per cent price increase should apply also to liquefied natural gas produced from the Brega plant. Esso is believed to have lost as much as $200 million on the Brega project due to building and technical difficulties and price quarrels with the Government. The plant cost $350 million and was completed in June 1970, but deliveries to Spain, the first customer, did not begin until March 1971, and to Italy until the summer of 1971.

A further agreement on a new formula for adjusting oil prices was signed between Libya and the oil companies in Geneva in June 1973.

The October 1973 war with Israel caused further upheavals in the price situation and Libya doubled the posted price of 40°API crude to $18.768 a barrel, effective from January 1st, 1974. In March 1974 a three-tier price system was proposed, giving preference to Islamic countries, followed by developing countries, with the industrial powers paying the highest prices. In April and May 1974 cuts in prices to contract customers, and in the buy-back prices to companies with participation agreements, were announced. Reductions were reported in September 1974 and again in January 1975, when Libya also announced 5 per cent royalty increases on equity crude lifted by companies, bringing the rate to 65 per cent, in line with OPEC policy. Further cuts were made in February and June 1975. Reports varied as to the exact amounts by which prices were reduced, but it was generally agreed that competition from the cheaper Gulf crudes, combined with a fall in demand, had occasioned the cuts. Demand is, however, partly seasonal and, moreover, Libya supports the general principle of higher world oil prices to meet inflation. Monthly oil output, which averaged 13.3 million metric tons in 1970, fell to less than 4 million tons by the end of 1974.

Libya was a leader of those oil producers which demanded participation in oil company activities. In September 1972 it negotiated an agreement with ENI under which Libya received an immediate 50 per cent share in ENI's Libyan activities. ENI was induced to make this agreement by Libya's refusal to allow exports from Concession 100, the Italian company's first source of Libyan oil, and by the awarding of the Zawia refinery contract to an ENI subsidiary. Libya, for its part, reduced its initial demand, which was for a 51 per cent share.

Talks on participation began in earnest in January 1973. Agreements for 51 per cent participation were concluded with Occidental, Marathon, Continental and Amerada Hess, but the major oil companies, with interests elsewhere in the Arab world, proved recalcitrant, since any agreement concluded with Libya would inevitably affect those already made with, for example, the Arabian Gulf states. The result of a long round of negotiations was that the Government now holds a 51 per cent share in the Libyan operations of Agip, Continental/Marathon/Amerada Hess, Exxon, Mobil and Occidental, while it has completely nationalized the holdings of Amoseas, BP/Bunker Hunt, Shell, Texaco, California Asiatic and Atlantic Richfield.

In fact, for some time the Government refrained from any general nationalization measures, apart from the takeover of distribution in 1970. But in December 1971 it took over BP's Libyan interests in retaliation for the British Government's failure to prevent the Iranian occupation of the Arabian Gulf islands of Abu Musa and the Tumbs. British Petroleum had operated the 400,000 barrels-a-day (b/d) Sarir field with Bunker Hunt and Libya set up the Arabian Gulf Exploration Company to operate BP's half of the field. Production dropped to a little over 200,000 b/d and BP warned that it would take legal action against any buyer of crude from AGEC. Meanwhile, talks with the other partner in the Sarir field, Bunker Hunt, dragged on until in June 1973 Libya nationalized the company's assets. Both BP and Bunker Hunt brought a number of actions against companies who bought Sarir crude after nationalization and the dispute lasted for many months. In 1974, however, following a compensation agreement between Shell and the Libyan Government, agreement was finally reached with BP, although not with Bunker Hunt.

A new phase in exploration involving much greater

Government participation is now under way in Libya. Companies who signed agreements in 1974 included Exxon, AGIP, Mobil/Gelsenberg, Total, Petrobras, CFP and Elf-Aquitaine. Elf-Aquitaine's new El-Meheiriga field was due to go on stream early in 1975. Exploration expenditure was forecast at $504 million for the period 1974–78.

On the marketing side, Libya has up to now tended to conclude agreements involving the exchange of crude oil for specific goods or services. Poland agreed to exchange oil for ships and machinery; a similar agreement was made with Yugoslavia to supply tankers; France signed a long-term agreement to barter technical assistance for oil; Italy is supplying industrial goods in return for oil; and, perhaps most controversial, co-operation agreements were signed in 1974 with the U.S.S.R. which provided for arms supplies and development assistance.

Libya, however, in common with other large oil producers, would much prefer to refine and process its own oil, rather than export it in its crude state. In this respect, the country is rather behind the older-established producers, having one refinery at Zawai, opened in September 1974 and now being expanded, and two other small privately-owned plants. Three more refineries are planned: for Zuetina (400,000 b/d); Misurata (220,000 b/d) and Tobruk (220,000 b/d). Contracts were awarded in 1975 for the Tobruk plant. Libya plans to have enough refining capacity to refine all its crude production by 1978.

Libya is also investing in refining ventures abroad, notably the refinery at Koper in Yugoslavia and the Adriatic pipeline from Libya to Eastern Europe. Clauses covering refining and petrochemicals development are now being included in new exploration agreements.

The tanker fleet is currently being enlarged with three tankers ordered from Japan, two from Yugoslavia and four from Sweden. Sweden was also asked in 1974 to build a refinery in Libya but no agreement has yet been reached.

INDUSTRY

Manufacturing in Libya has been largely confined to the processing of local agricultural products and such traditional crafts as carpet weaving, tanning and leather working and shoe making. Plans were made several years ago for a whole range of factories to make such diverse articles as prefabricated construction materials, cables, glass, pharmaceuticals, woollen and synthetic textiles, among others. Most of these factories did not get past the tendering stage, but the Government is now settling down to getting Libyan development going again.

Contracts for industrial plant have in the past been awarded mainly to Western European and U.S. companies, but Japanese firms are becoming more active in Libya and links with Eastern Europe, particularly Yugoslavia are much closer. At the beginning of 1975 a joint venture agreement to manufacture carbon paper was signed with a Japanese firm and an aluminium plant is planned with Yugoslavian partici-

pation. Libya's first ready-made clothing factory at Derna, and a new tannery at Tajura, were opened in 1974. Other manufacturing projects planned are: a canning factory for Zawia; a tyre factory at Tajura; a hypodermic syringe plant; a soap factory, and a glass factory for Tripoli. President Gaddafi also said in January 1975 that Libya had plans for the establishment of a heavy industry sector involving vehicle and tractor assembly plants, shipbuilding and iron and steel works.

Iron ore reserves estimated at over 700 million tons were discovered in southern Libya, at Wadi Shatti in 1974 and plans for their exploitation are under way.

The construction work now being carried out under the development programme has given rise to a rapidly increasing demand for cement, which is imported in large quantities. Existing cement plants at Homs and Benghazi are being expanded and two more are being built at Souk el-Khemis and Derna, with others planned. It is hoped that production will reach 4 million tons a year once all the plants are fully operational.

The most impressive expansion is occurring in the oil-based industries. An industrial complex, including ethylene, ammonia and methanol plants is under construction at Marsa el-Brega. In addition, a synthetic fibres project is under study and urea and ammonia plants are planned as part of the petrochemicals programme.

Throughout 1974/75 the Government continued to award large contracts for power stations, some in association with desalination plants. A large contract was awarded in 1975 for the construction of a power/desalination plant in Tobruk, and a gas power station is planned for Misurata. Libya took further steps in 1975 towards the use of nuclear power; agreements were signed with the U.S.S.R. and India and a West German firm was given a contract to build a heavy water plant. Libya has signed the nuclear non-proliferation treaty.

As might be expected, the large and increasing volume of imports has led to severe congestion at the main ports of Tripoli and Benghazi, and Libya has an agreement with Tunisia to use facilities at Gabes and Sfax to relieve the situation. In addition, Derna and Misurata ports are being reconstructed. Both Tripoli and Benghazi are undergoing large-scale expansion. This is necessarily a long-term process and the development of rail, road and to some extent air freight is very important. There is an extensive road-building programme and the telecommunications network is constantly being expanded. The first major contract awarded to a Japanese firm in Libya went to Nippon Electric for the installation of a microwave network.

EXTERNAL TRADE

Until production of oil began, Libya's exports consisted almost entirely of agricultural products, and its imports of manufactured goods. In 1960, for instance, imports were valued at LD 60.4 million and exports at LD 4.0 million, leaving an adverse balance of LD 56.4 million (although LD 21 million of the total value of imports in 1960 was accounted for by goods imported for the account of the oil companies). Oil was first exported in the autumn of 1961, and by 1969 imports totalled LD 241.3 million and exports LD 773.9 million, of which LD 771.2 million or over 99 per cent, was accounted for by oil. The minute proportion of remaining exports were mainly hides and skins, groundnuts, almonds, metal scrap and re-exports.

Imports now consist of a wide variety of manufactured goods, such as textiles, motor vehicles and luxury consumer goods. In the last few years imports of timber, chemicals and raw materials and, in particular, cement and building materials, have been stepped up. In addition, many foodstuffs have to be imported, for example tea, sugar, coffee and, in years of drought, wheat and flour.

Libya's principal supplier in 1973 was Italy, with the United Kingdom, France, West Germany and Japan a long way behind. Eastern Bloc countries are likely to take a larger share of the market as more trade and co-operation agreements are signed. Libya's best oil customers in 1972 were the United Kingdom, France, West Germany, Italy and the U.S.A. Sales to Italy were stimulated by the ENI settlement and to the U.S.A. by the much-publicized American fuel crisis. However, the events of 1973, and the embargo on sales to America (since lifted) and the Netherlands, altered the pattern somewhat. The trade surplus was reduced to LD 623.1 million in 1972 because of the enlarged investment programme and cuts in oil output but rose again in 1973 to LD 656 million. Of the LD 540 million total imports in 1973, over one-third consisted of capital machinery and transport equipment.

FINANCE

Before the 1969 coup most Libyan banks were subsidiaries of foreign banks. However, amongst the first decrees issued by the Revolutionary Council was one which required 51 per cent of the capital of all banks operating in Libya to be owned by Libyans; the majority of directors, including the chairman, of each bank had to be Libyan citizens. The royal Government had followed a similar policy without compulsion, and a number of foreign banks had accordingly already "Libyanized" themselves. In December 1970, all commercial banks were nationalized, with government participation set at 51 per cent. There are now only five commercial banks in the country including one formed at the same time by the

amalgamation of the former commercial section of the central bank with two small Libyan banks.

The development of the oil industry has enabled Libya to maintain a high degree of stability in the external value of its currency. Until December 1971 Libya was a member of the Sterling Area, but the nationalization of BP and the withdrawal of deposits of £200 million from British banks resulted in her expulsion.

The massive growth in oil revenue has also allowed the Government to devote about half its income to development expenditure. It has even been able to give generous aid abroad, in particular to the Yemen P.D.R., Egypt, Syria and Jordan, although the Government is somewhat capricious in implementing aid agreements. Aid was cut off from the Jordanian Government in September 1970 when it attacked the Palestinian guerrillas. Egypt was criticized over its conduct of the war with Israel and in 1974 Libya demanded the return of a loan to the Sudan. There is no comparable organization in Libya to the Kuwait Fund for Arab Economic Development, but in 1974 Libya made a contribution to the Islamic Development Bank. In 1972 and 1973 Libya gave increased attention to the Mediterranean and Africa and aid has been granted to Malta, Chad, Uganda, Somalia, Zaire and others.

At the end of April 1972 the Government published a one-year development budget to cover the period ending March 31st, 1973, and a three-year development budget to end on March 31st, 1975. The one-year budget involved total spending of LD 367 million, a record figure (the 1970–71 budget totalled LD 300 million), and the three-year programme called for expenditure of LD 1,165 million. Despite the fact that many of the allocations in the 1972–73 budget were not spent (in some sectors probably less than half the funds available were utilized), the Government was sufficiently encouraged by its experience to revise the three-year plan dramatically. In the spring of 1973 the three-year budget was amended to provide for a LD 800 million increase in spending to bring the three-year total to LD 1,965 million, with increased emphasis placed on agriculture. A further increase in total spending, to LD 2,115 million, was approved in 1974. In February 1975 the allocations were revised yet again to give total expenditure of LD 2,571 million, with even more emphasis on agriculture. Power, transport, housing and education all received increased allocations, reflecting mainly the continued upsurge in construction activity and prestige projects such as the universities of Benghazi and Tripoli.

STATISTICAL SURVEY

AREA AND POPULATION

AREA (sq. km.)	POPULATION	
	1964 Census	1973 Census
1,759,540	1,564,369	2,259,497

POPULATION BY DISTRICT
(1973 Census)

Tripoli	. . .	709,117
Benghazi	.	331,180
Zawia (Zavia)	.	244,352
Misurata	.	179,316
Khoms	. .	162,673

Gharian	. . .	155,162
Jebel Akhdar	.	131,071
Derna	. . .	123,397
Sebha	. . .	113,211
Kalig	. . .	110,018

AGRICULTURE

LAND USE, 1971
('000 hectares)

Arable land	2,377
Land under permanent crops . .	144
Permanent meadows and pastures .	7,000
Forests and woodlands . . .	534
Other land	165,899
TOTAL . . .	175,954

LIVESTOCK
(Estimates—'000)

	1971	1972	1973
Sheep . . .	2,284	2,274	3,100
Goats . . .	1,141	1,109	1,000
Cattle . . .	101	106	121
Camels . . .	120	122	120

PRINCIPAL CROPS
(tons)

	1971	1972	1973
Barley . .	32,127	116,395	204,514
Wheat . .	17,726	41,585	67,327
Olives . .	5,000	94,533	149,313
Citrus Fruits .	24,918	27,138	20,046
Groundnuts .	11,075	13,692	11,000
Almonds .	3,560	4,515	4,850
Tomatoes .	130,816	170,038	175,516
Dates . .	66,190	59,544	61,670
Potatoes .	22,813	49,046	78,352

Tobacco leaf production (1972) 1,205 metric tons, manufactured tobacco production (1871) 179 metric tons. Grapes are also grown in quantity (about 11,000 metric tons in 1973).

INDUSTRY
(Value of Output in LD'000—Large establishments only)

	1971	1972
Food Manufacturing .	10,221	11,072
Beverage Industries .	2,252	3,218
Tobacco Manufactures .	11,286	13,585
Chemicals and Products .	4,916	5,086
Textiles . .	2,011	1,795
Cement and Products .	2,786	4,718
Fabricated Metal Products .	1,747	6,363
TOTAL (incl. others) .	38,323	45,837

OIL

CRUDE OIL PRODUCTION
(metric tons)

1967	83,477,000
1968	125,539,000
1969	149,900,000
1970	159,700,000
1971	132,600,000
1972	119,600,000
1973	104,900,000
1974	82,400,000

FINANCE

1,000 dirhams=1 Libyan dinar (LD).

Coins: 1, 5, 10, 20, 50 and 100 dirhams.

Notes: 250 and 500 dirhams; 1, 5 and 10 dinars.

Exchange rates (July 1975): £1 sterling=647.47 dirhams; U.S. $1=296.05 dirhams.

100 Libyan dinars=£154.45=$337.78.

Note: The dinar is equivalent to the former Libyan pound (of 1,000 milliemes), which it replaced in September 1971. The Libyan pound had been introduced in March 1952, with a value of U.S. $2.80 ($1=357.14 millièmes). This valuation remained in effect until August 1971. Between December 1971 and February 1973 the new Libyan dinar (replacing the pound) was worth $3.04 ($1=328.95 dirhams). The present dollar valuation became effective in February 1973. The Libyan pound was at par with the pound sterling until November 1967, after which the exchange rate was £1 sterling=857.14 millièmes or dirhams (Lib£1 or 1 dinar=£1.167 sterling) until June 1972.

ADMINISTRATIVE BUDGET EXPENDITURE 1975
(LD million)

Interior and police	36.1	Industry and mineral wealth		2.2
Foreign affairs	10.0	Oil		0.8
Education	31.4	Support of state corporations		31.2
Health	10.0	Miscellaneous		23.8
Communications authorities	5.0	Local administration		167.3
Social affairs and social insurance	3.0	Armed forces		60.0
Housing	2.8			
Agriculture and agrarian reform	3.6	TOTAL (incl. others)		437.3

DEVELOPMENT COUNCIL THREE-YEAR PLAN

In March 1972 a three-year development budget was published, to run until the end of March 1975. In the Spring of 1973 this budget was revised to bring the three-year total expenditure to LD 1,965 million. A further increase to LD 2,115 million was approved in 1974 and in 1975 total expenditure was raised yet again to LD 2,751 million.

EXTERNAL TRADE
(LD'000)

	1969	1970	1971	1972	1973
Imports	241,301	198,002	250,352	343,204	539,939
Exports	772,765	841,829	959,918	966,307	1,196,393

1974: Exports 2,331.5 million dinars.

SELECTED COMMODITIES
(LD'000)

IMPORTS	1971	1972	1973	EXPORTS	1971	1972	1973
Food and Live Animals	47,574	53,128	85,055	Crude Petroleum	959,392	948,230	1,161,666
Beverages and Tobacco	2,484	1,201	1,779	Groundnuts	235	408	—
Mineral Fuel	5,770	7,393	10,627	Hides and Skins	284	1,247	1,366
Animal and Vegetable Oils and Fats	5,539	2,786	9,515	Castor Oil Seed	3	16	10
Inedible Crude Materials excluding Fuel	8,307	9,980	24,535	Wool and other Animal Hair	—	311	972
Chemicals	15,123	16,646	21,244				
Manufactures	52,025	81,220	137,244				
Machinery	72,963	117,780	183,572				
Miscellaneous	40,557	53,069	66,367				

PRINCIPAL COUNTRIES
(LD'ooo)

IMPORTS	1970	1971	1972	1973
Italy	42,712	57,712	88,352	139,056
U.S.A.	27,307	17,323	21,635	28,623
U.K.	18,579	24,866	29,911	37,192
Germany, Federal Republic .	17,950	23,167	32,825	56,052
Netherlands . . .	6,190	7,600	10,135	13,128
France	12,724	21,402	24,206	44,102
Belgium	2,212	—		
Japan	11,116	15,193	19,930	34,391
China, People's Republic .	3,781	6,444	8,433	11,216
Lebanon	5,628	7,335	11,149	20,203
Other Countries . .	50,003	53,847	96,628	155,976

EXPORTS OF CRUDE OIL
(LD'ooo)

COUNTRY	1970	1971	1972	1973
U.K.	127,697	157,230	129,620	132,818
Germany, Federal Republic .	147,305	168,260	238,332	253,923
Italy	218,090	230,526	185,714	324,797
France	113,344	119,492	84,619	63,454
Netherlands . .	79,627	56,928	44,063	39,431
U.S.A.	22,251	57,746	74,587	92,116
Belgium	32,634	23,550	11,132	95,955
Spain	38,363	39,060	24,107	16,349
TOTAL (incl. others)	841,134	956,867	948,231	1,161,666

TRANSPORT
ROADS

	1970	1971	1972
Private Cars . .	95,762	110,312	144,225
Lorries . .	44,582	50,435	67,921
Buses . . .	820	877	1,009
Taxis . . .	4,367	4,703	7,115

SHIPPING

	SHIPS ('ooo N.R.T.)		CARGO ('ooo metric tons)	
	Entered	Cleared	Loaded	Unloaded
1970 .	4,381	4,357	39	2,600
1971 .	4,653	4,713	20	3,003
1972 .	5,450	5,433	22	5,649
1973 .	5,146	5,023	22	5,053

CIVIL AVIATION

	1971	1972	1973
Number of Passengers			
Entering . . .	128,005	274,243	283,088
Leaving . . .	124,356	237,548	295,794
Cargo Unloaded (tons) .	12,111	13,808	15,189
Cargo Loaded (tons) .	2,412	2,763	1,927

EDUCATION
(1973-74)

State Schools	Schools	Students	Teachers
Primary . .	1,837	489,882	20,580
Preparatory .	375	74,437	5,141
Secondary .	66	13,784	1,446
Teacher Training .	84	15,606	1,193
Technical . .	8	3,411	276

Source: Census and Statistical Dept., Ministry of Planning, Tripoli.

THE CONSTITUTION

A new provisional constitution of 37 articles was proclaimed in December 1969. The following is a summary of its principal features:

Libya is a democratic and free Arab Republic with sovereignty of the people who constitute part of the Arab nation and whose objective is comprehensive Arab unity.

The official religion of the state is Islam but the state guarantees religious freedom.

Supreme authority is vested in the Revolution Command Council which has power to appoint the Council of Ministers, to sign and modify treaties and to declare war. It retains power over the armed forces and the diplomatic corps.

All citizens are equal and the foundations of the country are built on family unity.

The state will aim to achieve socialism by means of social justice which forbids all forms of exploitation. It will work towards the liberation of the national economy from every foreign influence, guiding it towards productivity and stability.

The property of the state is also the property of the public. Private property cannot be exploited and is guaranteed by the state. It can only be expropriated as laid down by law.

Freedom of speech is guaranteed as long as it does not transgress the principles of the revolution.

The extradition of political prisoners is forbidden.

All titles, including those granted by the previous government, have been revoked.

Medical care is a guaranteed right for all citizens; education will be compulsory until the end of primary stage (now at the age of nine).

THE GOVERNMENT

REVOLUTION COMMAND COUNCIL

Chairman: Col. MUAMMAR AL-GADDAFI.

Members: Lt.-Col. ABU BAKAR YUNIS JABER, Maj. ABDUL SALAM JALLOUD, Maj. BASHIR AL SAGHIER HAWADY, Maj. ABDUL MONIEUM AL TAHER AL HUNY, Maj. AL KHOWEILDY AL HAMIDY, Maj. MUSTAFA AL KHARROBY, Maj. MUKHTAR ABDULLAH AL GERWY, Maj. MUHAMMED NAJIM, Maj. AWAD ALI HAMZA, Maj. OMAR AL-MEHESHI.

CABINET
(*August* 1975)

Prime Minister: Maj. ABDUL SALAM JALLOUD.

Minister of Foreign Affairs: Maj. ABDUL MONIEUM AL TAHER AL-HUNY.

Minister of the Interior: Maj. AL-KHOWEILDY AL-HAMIDY.

Minister of Planning and Scientific Research: Maj. OMAR ABDALLA AL-MEHEISHI.

Minister of Justice: MUHAMMAD ALI AL-GADI.

Minister of Health: Dr. MOFTAH AL-OSTA OMAR.

Minister of Labour and Civil Service: ABDUL ALI AL-OBEIDI.

Minister of Petroleum: EZZEDIN AL-MABROUK.

Minister of Agriculture and Agrarian Reform: MUHAMMAD ALI AL-TABU.

Minister of Housing: Eng. MUHAMMAD AL-MANKOUSH.

Minister of Communications: Eng. TAHA AL-SHERIF BEN AMER.

Minister of Economy: ABU BAKR ALI SHERIF.

Minister of Industry and Mineral Resources: Eng. JADALLA AZOUZ TALHI.

Minister of Treasury: MUHAMMAD ZAROUK RAJAB.

Minister of Education: Dr. MUHAMMAD SHERIF.

Minister of State for Agricultural Development: Eng. ABDUL-MEJEID AL-GO'UD.

Minister of Social Affairs and Social Security: Eng. ABDUL SALAM AL-FITURI.

Minister of State: MUHAMMAD ABUL-QASSIM ZUWAI.

Minister of State for Nutrition and Marine Resources: Dr. OMAR AHMAD AL-MAGSI.

Minister of Municipal Affairs: MOFTAH MUHAMMAD KEIBA.

Minister of Marine Transport: MANSOUR MUHAMMAD BADR.

Minister of Electric Power: Eng. JOMAA SALEM AL-ARBASH.

PARLIAMENT

The Senate and House of Representatives were dissolved after the *coup d'état* of September 1969, and the provisional constitution issued in December 1969 made no mention of elections or a return to Parliamentary procedure. However, in January 1971 Col. GADDAFI announced that a new Parliament would be appointed, not elected; no date was mentioned. All political parties other than the Arab Socialist Union are banned.

POLITICAL PARTY

Arab Socialist Union: f. 1971; the only legal party; at the General Conference held in November 1974 it was decided that the Arab Socialist Union should take charge, at all levels, of supervision and direction of people's committees (*see* Recent History); Sec.-Gen. Major BASHIR HAWADY.

DIPLOMATIC REPRESENTATION

EMBASSIES ACCREDITED TO LIBYA
(Tripoli unless otherwise stated)

(E) Embassy.

Afghanistan: Cairo, Egypt (E).

Algeria: Sharia Qayrouan 12 (E); *Ambassador:* BIN AUDA BIN MUSTAFA.

Argentina: Sharia Mouzafar al Aftas (E); *Ambassador:* OMAR MUHAMMAD VAQUIR.

Austria: Sharia al Amir Abdulkadir al Jazairi (E); *Ambassador:* Dr. OTTO PLEINERT.

Belgium: Sharia Sidi 'Isa (E); *Ambassador:* CHARLES LOODTS.

Brazil: Oasis Building (E); *Ambassador:* CARLOS F. LECKIE LOBO.

Bulgaria: Sharia Murad Agha (E); *Ambassador:* STOYAN KARASLAVOV.

Canada: Cairo, Egypt (E).

Chad: Sharia Bin 'Ashur (E); *Ambassador:* KAHLIL OTHMAN.

Chile: Cairo, Egypt (E).

China (Taiwan): Sharia al-Hadi Ka'bar (E); *Ambassador:* TSAI PA.

Czechoslovakia: Sharia Mahmud Shaltut (E); *Ambassador:* JOSEF VARHOLIK.

Denmark: Cairo, Egypt (E).

Egypt: Sharia Bin 'Ashur (Relations Office); *Acting Head:* SA'ADADDIN SARDANI.

Finland: Sharia Mustafa Kamel (E); *Chargé d'Affaires:* ANTON RATIA.

France: Sharia Huper (E); *Ambassador:* GUY GEORGY.

German Democratic Republic: (E); *Ambassador:* RONALD BÖTTCHER.

Germany, Federal Republic: Sharia Hassan al-Masha (E); *Ambassador:* Dr. GUNTHER F. WERNER.

Greece: Sharia Jalal Bayar, 18 (E); *Ambassador:* STEFANO ROCANAS.

Guinea: Cairo, Egypt (E).

Hungary: Sharia Talha Bin Ubaidallah (E); *Chargé d'Affaires:* GYULA BOGNAR.

India: Sharia Mahmud Shaltut (E); *Ambassador:* HOMI J. H. TALEYARKHAN.

Iran: Tunis, Tunisia (E).

Iraq: Sharia Nasser (E); *Ambassador:* (vacant).

Italy: Sharia 'Oran 1 (E); *Ambassador:* ALDO CONTE MAROTTA.

Japan: 37 Sharia Bin Ka'ab (E); *Ambassador:* ARAO OHTA.

Kuwait: Sharia Bin Yassir (E); *Chargé d'Affaires:* MUHAMMAD ABDUL AZIZ SALEH.

Lebanon: Sharia Bin Yassir (E); *Ambassador:* MUHAMMAD MALEK.

Mali: Cairo, Egypt (E).

Malta: Sharia Bin Ka'ab, 13 (E); *Chargé d'Affaires:* EVARIST SALIBA (also accred. to Tunisia).

Mauritania: Sharia Bin Ka'ab (E); *Ambassador:* AHMAD DUBBEH.

Morocco: Sharia Bashir al-Ibrahimi (E); *Ambassador:* IDRIS AL-FALLAH.

Netherlands: Sharia Jelal Bayar 20 (E); *Chargé d'Affaires:* Dr. J. J. DE ROOS.

Niger: Sharia Bin 'Ubaydallah (E); *Ambassador:* (vacant).

Nigeria: Sharia Ammar Ben Yaser (E); *Chargé d'Affaires:* ADAM JUMBA.

Norway: Rabat, Morocco (E).

Pakistan: Sharia al-Khitabi (E); *Ambassador:* Lt.-Gen. RAHMAN GUL.

Poland: Sharia Ben Ashur (E); *Ambassador:* JANUSZ LEWANDOWSKI.

Romania: Sharia Ben Ashur (E); *Ambassador:* NICOLAE VERES.

Rwanda: Hay al Andalus (E); *Chargé d'Affaires:* JEAN-MARIE SIBOMANA.

Saudi Arabia: Sharia al-Qayrouan 2 (E); *Ambassador:* ABD AL-MUSHIN AL-ZAYD.

Senegal: Cairo, Egypt (E).

Somalia: Sharia Khalid Ben Elwalid (E); *Ambassador:* MUHAMMAD HASHI ABDI.

Spain: Sharia al-Jazayri (E); *Ambassador:* CARLOS ROBLES.

Sri Lanka: Cairo, Egypt (E).

Sudan: Sharia Donato Suma (E); *Ambassador:* ABDUL AAL SANADA.

Sweden: Sharia Mugaryef (E); *Ambassador:* TORSTEN HYLANDER.

Switzerland: Sharia Jeraba (E); *Chargé d'Affaires:* HERMANN RIEDER.

Syria: Sharia Muhammed Rashid Rida, 4 (Relations Office); *Acting Head:* 'ALY HASAN.

Tunisia: Sharia Bashir al-Ibrahimi (E); *General Commissioner:* MAHMUD SHARSHUR.

Turkey: Sharia al-Fatah 36 (E); *Ambassador:* (vacant).

Uganda: Cairo, Egypt (E).

U.S.S.R.: Sharia Solaroli (E); *Ambassador:* IVAN N. YAKUSHIN.

United Arab Emirates: Sharia Ben Ashur (E); *Chargé d'Affaires:* SAIF ALY AL JARWAN.

United Kingdom: Tariq al-Fatah (E); *Ambassador:* D. F. MURRAY.

U.S.A.: Sharia al-Nasr (E); *Chargé d'Affaires:* ROBERT STEIN.

Venezuela: Sharia Abdulrahman Kwakby (E); *Ambassador:* (vacant) (also accred. to Morocco).

Yemen Arab Republic: Sharia Ubai Ibn Kaa'b 36 (E); *Ambassador:* (vacant).

Yemen, People's Democratic Republic: Sharia Bin 'Ashur (E); *Ambassador:* ALI AHMED AL-SULAMI.

Yugoslavia: Sharia Bashir al-Ibrahimi (E); *Ambassador:* BORIS RAFAJLOVSKI.

Zaire: Aziz al Masri (E); *Ambassador:* LOUYA LONDOALE.

Libya also has diplomatic relations with Burundi, Cambodia, Costa Rica, Cyprus, Dahomey, Gabon, the Democratic People's Republic of Korea, Malaysia, Panama and Togo.

JUDICIAL SYSTEM

President of the Supreme Court: MUHAMMAD ABDULKAREEM AZZUZ.

The law of the Judicial System of 1954 established the following courts: the Federal Supreme Court, the Courts of Appeal, the Courts of First Instance and the Summary Courts. Sittings are in public, unless the court decides to hold them *in camera* in the interests of decency or public order. Judgment is in all cases given in public. The language of the courts is Arabic, but there is a translation office attached to each Court to help non-Arabic speaking parties or lawyers.

In October 1971 the Revolution Command Council decreed that all legislation should conform with the basic principles of Islamic Law and set up committees to carry this out. In April 1973 Colonel Gaddafi declared that any egislation likely to impede the progress of the revolution or to defeat public interest must be repealed.

The **Supreme Court** consists at present of a Chief Justice and ten justices appointed by the Revolution Command Council.

Courts of Appeal exist in Tripoli, Benghazi and Missurata, consisting of a President, Vice-President and three judges; judgments must be given by three judges. Each Court of Appeal includes a Court of Assize consisting of three judges.

Courts of First Instance are set up in the provinces, consisting of a President, Vice-President and a number of judges; judgment in these courts is given by one judge.

Summary Courts, composed of one judge, exist within the territorial jurisdiction of every Court of First Instance.

The People's Court is a special court set up by decree in October 1969. It deals with any crimes the Revolution Command Council sees fit to refer to it, but is particularly concerned with cases of political or administrative corruption.

RELIGION

Muslims: The Libyan Arabs practically without exception follow Sunni Muslim rites.

Chief Mufti of Libya: Sheikh TAHER AHMED AL ZAWI.

Christians: The Christian community numbered about 35,000, mostly Italian Roman Catholics, before the 1969 revolution; its numbers have been greatly reduced by the departure of the Italians during 1970. The Roman Catholic Cathedral in Tripoli was transformed into a mosque in November 1970.

Roman Catholic Church: Apostolic Vicariates of Benghazi, Derna and Tripoli, Apostolic Prefecture of Misurata; 9 priests, 4,000 Catholics (1972).

THE PRESS

In October 1973 the Revolution Command Council decreed the nationalization of all private newspapers, which were to be handed over to the Public Press Organization.

DAILIES
TRIPOLI

Al-Fajr al-Jadid: Sharia Tariq; f. 1969; official journal; Editor NURI AL HUMAIDI.

Al Fateh.

Al Jihad: Editor SALIM WALIY.

PERIODICALS
TRIPOLI

Al Fateh: weekly; Editor ALY FAITURI.

The Libyan Arab Republic Gazette: published by the Ministry of Justice; legal; weekly.

Al Shura: monthly.

Al Taqafa al Arabiya: P.O.B. 4587; f. 1973; cultural; circ. 25,000.

Al Wahdah: monthly.

NEWS AGENCIES

Arab Revolution News Agency: P.O.B. 2303, Tripoli; f. 1865; attached to Ministry of Information and Culture. Serves the Libyan radio network, newspapers and government departments (name changed from Libyan News Agency, June 1973).

FOREIGN BUREAUX

DPA, Reuters and Tass have offices in Tripoli.

RADIO AND TELEVISION

General Organization of People's Revolution Broadcasting: P.O.B. 333, Tripoli; P.O.B. 274, Benghazi; f. 1957 (TV 1968); broadcasts in Arabic and English from Tripoli and Benghazi; from September 1971 special daily broadcasts to Gaza and other Israeli-occupied territory were begun; under the direction of the Minister of Information and Culture; Dir.-Gen. IBRAHIM EL BISHARY.

Number of radio receivers: 100,000 (1973).

A national television service was inaugurated in December 1968. Number of TV receivers: 15,000 (1973).

FINANCE

BANKING

(br.=branch; cap.=capital; p.u.=paid up; dep.=deposits; LD=Libyan Dinar; m.=million; res.=reserves)

CENTRAL BANK

Central Bank of Libya: Sharia al Malik Seoud, P.O.B. 1103, Tripoli; f. 1955; bank of issue and central bank carrying Government accounts and operating exchange control; commercial operations transferred to National Commercial Bank 1970; cap. LD 1m.; res. and dep. of commercial banks LD 86.5m. (March 1972); Governor K. M. SHERLALA.

OTHER BANKS

Libyan Arab Foreign Bank: 1st September St., P.O.B. 2542, Tripoli; government bank wholly owned by Central Bank of Libya; cap. p.u. LD 20m.

Masraf al Gumhouria: Giaddat Martyr Imhemmed Mgarief, P.O.B. 396, Tripoli; f. 1969 as successor to Barclays Bank International in Libya; government-owned; 24 brs. throughout Libya; cap. and legal res. LD 1.5m.; dep. 84.9m. (Dec. 1974); Chair. SHETWI K. ETTIR.

National Commercial Bank: Shuhada Square, P.O.B. 4647, Tripoli; f. 1970 to take over commercial banking division of Central Bank and brs. of Aruba Bank and Istiklal Bank; 18 brs.; cap. LD 2.5m.; dep. LD 175.6m.; res. LD 16m. (Dec. 1974); Chair. and Gen. Man. BASHIR M. SHARIF.

Sahara Bank: Sharia 1 September, P.O.B. 270, Tripoli; f. 1964 to take over br. of Banco di Sicilia; 12 brs.; Chair. and Gen. Man. FARAG A. GAMRA.

Umma Bank S.A.L.: 1 Sharia Omar Mukhtar, P.O.B. 685, Tripoli; f. 1969 to take over brs. of Banco di Roma; 12 brs.; cap. LD 500,000; dep. 105.5m.; res. LD 6.2m. (June 1974); Chair. and Gen. Man. YOUSEF I. AGHIL.

Wahda Bank: Jamal Abdul Nasser St., P.O.B. 452, Benghazi; f. 1970 to take over Bank of North Africa, Commercial Bank, S.A.L., Nahda Arabia Bank, Kafila Ahly Bank of Libya; 20 brs.; cap. and res. LD 4.7m.; dep. LD 113.4m. (Dec. 1974).

INSURANCE

Libya Insurance Co.: P.O.B. 2438, Tripoli; P.O.B. 643, Benghazi; all classes of insurance.

Al Mukthar Insurance Co.: 230 Muhammad Lemgare-St., P.O.B. 2548, Tripoli; all classes of insurance.

OIL

Petroleum affairs in Libya are dealt with entirely by the Ministry of Petroleum which is charged, in accordance with Article 2 of Law 120 of 1970, with organization, control, follow-up and supervision of petroleum resources within the limits of the State's general policy, development plan and regulations in force concerning petroleum matters. Since 1973 Libya has been entering into participation agreements with some of the foreign oil companies, and nationalizing others.

Ministry of Petroleum: P.O.B. 256, Tripoli.

NATIONAL COMPANIES

(Details of oil companies operating in Libya can be found in "Oil in the Middle East and North Africa, pages 69–102)

National Oil Corporation (NOC): P.O.B. 2655, Tripoli; f. 1970 as successor to the Libyan General Petroleum Corporation, to undertake joint ventures with foreign companies; to build and operate refineries, storage tanks, petrochemical facilities, pipelines and tankers; to take part in arranging specifications for local and imported petroleum products; to participate in general planning of oil installations in Libya; to market crude oil and to establish and operate oil terminals; Chair. SAID ALI JAMHOOR.

Arabian Gulf Exploration Co.: Chair. NURY SENOUSY.

Brega Oil Marketing Co.: Chair. ALI FITURY.

Um Al-Jawaby Petroleum Co.: Chair. HADI S. BELAZI.

National Drilling Co.: P.O.B. 1454, Tripoli; Chair. MUHAMMAD ATTIGA.

PARTICIPATION COMPANIES

Oasis Oil Co.: Chair. OMAR MUSTAFA MUNTASSER.

Esso Standard: Chair. ABDUSSALAM ZAGAAR.

Occidental of Libya: Chair. ABDULLATIF ZARRUG.

Mobil Oil Libya: P.O.B. 690, Tripoli; Chair. AZZEDIN CREUI; Pres. and Gen. Man. D. F. PENDLEY.

Agip Oil Co.: Chair. MESSEOUD GERNAZ.

FOREIGN COMPANIES

Aquitaine Libye: P.O.B. 282; Man. HENRY BATAI.

Amoco Libya: Man. JIM MACDONALD.

TRADE AND INDUSTRY

CHAMBERS OF COMMERCE

Tripolitania Chamber of Commerce, Industry and Agriculture: Al-Jomhourieh St., P.O.B. 2321, Tripoli; f. 1952; Pres. SALEM EL-SAGHIR GADDAH; Sec.-Gen. BASHIR K. EL-GENAYYEN; 40,000 mems.; publs. *Quarterly Bulletin, Trade Acquaintance* (bi-weekly) and *Commercial Directory* (annual, English and Arabic).

Benghazi Chamber of Commerce, Industry and Agriculture: P.O.B. 208-1286, Benghazi; f. 1953; Pres. HASAN H. MATAR; Sec.-Gen. MUHAMMAD H. ALGAZERI; 5,400 mems.

DEVELOPMENT

Industrial and Real Estate Bank of Libya: Tripoli and Benghazi; f. 1965; state industrial development and house-building finance agency, cap. LD 10m.; Dir. MOHAMED RABEI.

Kufrah and Sevir Authority: Council of Agricultural Development, Benghazi; f. 1972 to develop the Kufrah Oasis and Sevir area in south-east Libya.

National General Organization for Industrialization: P.O.B. 4388, Tripoli; f. March 1970; Chair. ABDEL SALAM JALOOD; Deputy Chair. ABU-BAKR SHERIF.

NATIONALIZED INDUSTRIES

General Tobacco Company: P.O.B. 696, Tripoli; develops the production and curing of tobacco; leaf production 1,000,000 kilos, manufactured tobacco production 2,800,000 kilos (1973).

TRADE UNIONS

National Trade Unions' Federation: (affiliated to ICFTU); P.O.B. 734, 2 Sharia Istanbul, Tripoli; f. 1952; Sec.-Gen. SALEM SHITA; 30,000 mems.; Publ. *Attalia* (weekly).

Union of Petroleum Workers of Libya: Tripoli; also branch in Benghazi.

TRADE FAIR

Tripoli International Fair: P.O.B. 891, Tripoli; under control of General Board of Tourism and Fairs; annual fair March 1st–20th; Chair. and Dir.-Gen. SALEH F. AZZABI.

TRANSPORT

ROADS

The most important road in Libya is the national coast road, 1,822 km. in length, which runs the whole way from the Tunisian to the Egyptian border, passing through Tripoli and Benghazi. This road has recently been widened and re-surfaced. It has a second link between Barce and Lamluda, which is 141 km. long. The other federal road completed (in 1962) runs from a point on the coastal road 120 km. south of Misurata through Sebha (capital of Fezzan) to Ghat near the Algerian border (total length of 1,250 km.). There is a branch 260 km. long running from Vaddan to Sirte. There is a new road crossing the desert from Sebha to the frontiers of Chad and Niger.

In addition to the national highways, the west of Libya has about 1,200 km. of black-top and macadamized roads and the east about 500 km. Practically all the towns and villages of Libya, including the desert oases, are accessible by motor vehicle, but the going is sometimes rough.

SHIPPING

Principal ports are Tripoli, Benghazi, Port Brega and the Oasis Marine Terminal at Es-Sider. Port Brega was opened to oil tankers in 1961. A 30-inch crude oil pipeline connects the Zelten oilfields with Marsa El Brega. Another pipeline joins the Sarir oilfield with Marsa Hariga, the port of Tobruk, and a pipeline from the Sarir field to Zuetina was opened in 1968. There is another oil port at Ras Lunuf. Libya also has the use of Tunisian port facilities at Sfax and Gabes, to alleviate congestion at Tripoli.

General Maritime Transport Organization: 10 Granata St., P.O.B. 4673, Tripoli; f. 1970 to handle all projects dealing with maritime trade.

The following shipping companies are among those operating services through Libyan ports:

Abdurrahman R. Kikhia and Co. (Shipping Division): f. 1968; offices in Tripoli: P.O.B. 401; Benghazi: P.O.B. 157; Tobruk: P.O.B. 16.

The Libyan Transport Co.: Benghazi; Sharia Omar El Mukhtar, P.O.B. 94; f. 1949; brs. at Beida, Tobruk, Marsa Brega and Cairo; Dirs. A. S. FERGIANI, A. T. BUZER, A. F. JIAFAR.

Giaber Agency: f. 1946; membership 25; Head Office: Tripoli, 12-16 Jebba St.

National Navigation Co. of Libya: Tripoli: 67 Bagdad St., P.O.B. 2437; Benghazi: P.O.B. 139; f. 1964; regular services from Tunisian, French, Spanish, Moroccan, Algerian, Turkish and Italian ports to Tripoli and Benghazi; Man. L. TAKTAK.

Tirrenia, Società per Azioni di Navigazione: Tripoli: c/o Libyan Shipping and Travel Agency, Sharia Istiklal, Badri Bldg., P.O.B. 985; Benghazi: G. Gabriel, c/o Libyan Transport Co., Sharia Omar El Mukhtar 19.

CIVIL AVIATION

There are four civil airports:

The International Airport, situated at Ben Gashir, 21 miles from Tripoli.

Benina Airport, 12 miles from Benghazi.

Sebha Airport.

Misurata Airport (domestic flights only).

Libyan Arab Airlines: P.O.B. 2555, Tripoli; f. 1965; passenger and cargo services from Tripoli and Benghazi to Rome, Paris, London, Geneva, Cairo, Athens, Khartoum, Tunis, Beirut, Algiers and Malta; domestic services throughout Libya; fleet of one Boeing 727-200, three Caravelle, two Fokker F-27, one Boeing 720-B on lease from M.E.A.; three Boeing 727-200 on order, delivery 1975; six Fokker F-27 on order, delivery 1975/76; Chair. AHMED ARABI ZAWI; Gen. Man. MASOOD ABOU AMER.

Linair (*Libyan National Airways*): 18 Sharia Enasser, P.O.B. 3583, Tripoli; f. 1962; domestic services, charter and oil-prospecting support operations; fleet of three Fokker F-27; Pres. Z. Y. LENGHI, Gen. Man. P. W. BAKKER.

Libya is also served by the following foreign airlines: Aeroflot, Air Algérie, Alitalia, British Caledonian, ČSA, EgyptAir, JAT, KLM, Lufthansa, Malta Airlines, Saudia, Sudan Airways, Swissair, Syrian Arab, Tunis Air, UTA.

TOURISM

General Board of Tourism and Fairs: Tripoli; f. 1964.

Tourism is being developed in Libya, but major potential attractions include the superb Roman remains at Leptis Magna, Sabratha and Cyrene, the fine climate, mountains and hundreds of miles of unspoilt beaches.

DEFENCE

Chief of Staff of Armed Forces: Maj. ABU BAKR YOUNIS.

Defence Budget (1974): LD 119 million.

Military Service: voluntary.

Total Armed Forces: 32,000: army 25,000; navy 2,000; air force 5,000.

EDUCATION

One of the consequences of Libya's long history of successive foreign occupations and subjugation to foreign domination has been the extreme paucity of educational facilities for the indigenous peoples.

In 1921 only four Arab primary schools were in existence in Tripolitania, with a total of 611 pupils, and there was a similar lack of development in respect of native education in Cyrenaica.

During the following years some expansion took place, and by 1939 there were in Tripolitania 70 Italo-Arab primary schools with 6,884 Arab and 170 Italian pupils, 13 girls' trades schools with 944 pupils, a secondary school, and an arts and crafts school with 85 students. In addition, evening classes were started for adult Arab illiterates, and in 1928 Arabs were permitted to join Italian secondary schools. Small numbers of Arabs also gained admittance to Italian and Egyptian universities. Koranic schools also increased in numbers from 52 with 1,792 pupils in 1921 to 496 schools with 10,165 pupils in 1939. For Jews there were 19 primary schools (2,645 students), 2 trade secondary schools with 101 pupils, and 15 private schools catering for 1,939 pupils.

Up to the year 1939 the educational system for Arabs in Cyrenaica was similarly under-developed. At that time not more than 37 elementary schools were in existence with a total of 2,600 Arab pupils, and for Jews there were 5 elementary schools with 621 students.

Due to the destruction of towns and communications and to the evacuation of many people to the interior during the Second World War, education was badly disrupted, and at the end of the war there was a great demand for educational facilities. Secondary education was no longer limited to the few places permitted in Italian schools and Libyan schools of all grades rapidly increased in number. A steady expansion of all educational services

occurred between 1943 and 1949, followed by a considerable acceleration after the United Nations' decision of November 21st, 1949.

The numbers attending kindergarten, primary and secondary schools increased from a total of 6,808 in 1943–44 to 607,624 in 1973–74. The number of teachers rose similarly, from 219 in 1943–44 to 29,101 in 1973–74. Elementary education is compulsory for children of both sexes. The above statistics do not include "Kuttabs"—self-efforts at small groups of children being educated collectively in villages.

In 1958 the University of Libya opened in Benghazi with Faculties of Arts and Commerce, followed the next year by the Faculty of Science near Tripoli. Faculties of Law, Agriculture, Engineering, Teacher Training, and Arabic Language and Islamic Studies have since been added to the University. The University was divided into two parts, to form the Universities of Tripoli and Benghazi, in 1973.

In the 1972–73 Ordinary Budget LD 51.8 million (22.5 per cent of the total) was allocated to education, and in the 1972–73 Development Budget education received LD 39.8 million (10.3 per cent of the total).

UNIVERSITIES

University of Benghazi: P.O.B. 1308, Benghazi; f. 1955; 170 teachers, 7,100 students.

University of Tripoli: Tripoli; f. 1973; *c.* 300 teachers, *c.* 5,300 students.

BIBLIOGRAPHY

ANSELL, MEREDITH O. and AL-ARIF, IBRAHIM M. The Libyan Revolution (The Oleander Press, London, 1972).

DI AGOSTINI, Col. ENRICO. La popolazione della Tripolitania (2 vols.; Tripoli, 1917).
La popolazione della Cirenaica (Benghazi, 1922-23).
Amministrazione Fiduciaria all'Italia in Africa (Florence, 1948).
Archivio bibliografico Coloniale (Libia) (Florence, 1915-21).

BARUNI, OMAR. Spaniards and Knights of St. John of Jerusalem in Tripoli (Arabic) (Tripoli, 1952).

BERLARDINELLI, ARSENIO. La Ghibla (Tripoli, 1935).

BLUNSUM, T. Libya: the Country and its People (Queen Anne Press, London, 1968).

CACHIA, ANTHONY J. Libya under the Second Ottoman Occupation, 1835-1911 (Tripoli, 1945).

CECCHERINI, UGO. Bibliografia della Libia in continuazione . . . . de F. Minutilli (Rome, 1915).

COLUCCI, MASSIMO. Il Regime della Proprieta Fondiaria nell'Africa Italiana: Vol. I. Libia (Bologna, 1942).

CORÒ, FRANCESCO. Settantasei Anni di Dominazione Turca in Libia (Tripoli, 1937).

CUROTTI, TORQUATO. Gente di Libia (Tripoli, 1928).

DESPOIS, JEAN. Géographie Humaine (Paris, 1946).
Le Djebel Nefousa (Paris, 1935).
La Colonisation italienne en Libye; Problèmes et Méthodes (Larose-Editeurs, Paris, 1935).

EPTON, NINA. Oasis Kingdom: The Libyan Story (New York, 1953).

EVANS-PRITCHARD, E. E. The Sanusi of Cyrenaica (London, 1949).

FARLEY, RAWLE. Planning for Development in Libya (Pall Mall, London, 1971).

FIRST, RUTH. Libya—the Elusive Revolution (Penguin, London, 1974).

FISHER, W. B. Problems of Modern Libya (*Geographical Journal*, June 1953).

FORBES, ROSITA. The Secret of the Sahara: Kufara (London, 1921).

FRANCA, PIETRO, and others. L'Italia in Africa: Incivilimento e Sviluppo dell'Eritrea, della Somalia, e della Libia (Rome, 1947).

HAJJAJI, S. A. The New Libya (Tripoli, 1967).

HERRMANN, GERHARD. Italiens Weg zum Imperium (Goldman, Leipzig, 1938).

HESELTINE, NIGEL. From Libyan Sands to Chad (Museum Press, London, 1960).

HILL, R. W. A Bibliography of Libya (University of Durham, 1959).

JONGMANS, D. G. Libie-land van de dorst (Boom, Meppel, 1964).

JUIN, A-P. Le Maghreb en Feu (French) (Paris, Librairie Plon, 1957).

KHADDURI, MAJID. Modern Libya, a Study in Political Development (Johns Hopkins Press, 1963).

KHALIDI, I. R. Constitutional Developments in Libya (Beirut, Khayat's Book Co-operative, 1956).

KUBBAH, ABDUL AMIR Q. Libya, Its Oil Industry and Economic System (The Arab Petro-Economic Research Centre, Baghdad, 1964).

LEBLANC, M. E. Anthropologie et Ethnologie (du Fezzan) (1944-45).

LEGG, H. J. Libya: Economic and General Conditions in Libya (London, 1952).

LETHIELLEUX, J. Le Fezzan, ses Jardins, ses Palmiers: Notes d'Ethnographie et d'Histoire (Tunis, 1948).

LINDBERG, J. A General Economic Appraisal of Libya (New York, 1952).

MICACCHI, RODOLFO. La Tripolitania sotto il dominio dei Caramanli (Intra, 1936).

MINUTILLI, FEDERICO. Bibliografia della Libia (Turin, 1903).

MURABET, MOHAMMED. Tripolitania: the Country and its People (Tripoli, 1952).

NORMAN, JOHN. Labour and Politics in Libya and Arab Africa (Bookman, New York, 1965).

OWEN, R. Libya: a Brief Political and Economic Survey (London, 1961).

PELT, ADRIAN. Libyan Independence and the United Nations (Yale U.P., 1970).

PICHOU, JEAN. La Question de Libye dans le règlement de la paix (Paris, 1945).

Lord RENNELL. British Military Administration of Occupied Territories in Africa during the years 1941-47 (London, H.M.S.O., 1948).

RIVLIN, BENJAMIN. The United Nations and the Italian Colonies (New York, 1950).

ROYAL INSTITUTE OF INTERNATIONAL AFFAIRS. The Italian Colonial Empire (London, 1940).

ROSSI, P. Libya (Lausanne, 1965).

RUSHDI, MUHAMMAD RASIM. Trablus al Gharb (Arabic) (Tripoli, 1953).

SCARIN, Prof. La Giofra e Zella (Florence, 1938).
L'Insediamento Umano nella Libia Occidentale (Rome, 1940).
Le Oasi Cirenaiche del 29° Parallelo (Florence, 1937).
Le Oasi del Fezzan (2 vols.; Florence, 1934).

SCHLUETER, HANS. Index Libycus (G. K. Hall, Boston, 1972).

SCHMEIDER, OSKAR and WILHELMY, HERBERT. Die faschistische Kolonisation in Nordafrika (Quelle and Meyer, Leipzig, 1939).

STEELE-GREIG, A. J. History of Education in Tripolitania from the Time of the Ottoman Occupation to the Fifth Year under British Military Occupation (Tripoli, 1948).

VILLARD, HENRY S. Libya: The New Arab Kingdom of North Africa (Ithaca, 1956).

WARD, PHILIP. Touring Libya. 3 vols. (1967–69).
Tripoli: Portrait of a City (1970).

WILLIAMS, G. Green Mountain, an Informal Guide to Cyrenaica and its Jebel Akhdar (London, 1963).

WILLIMOTT, S. G. and CLARKE, J. I. Field Studies in Libya (Durham, 1960).

WRIGHT, JOHN. Libya (Ernest Benn, London, and Praeger, New York, 1969).

Morocco

PHYSICAL AND SOCIAL GEOGRAPHY

The Kingdom of Morocco is the westernmost of the three North African countries known to the Arabs as Jeziret al Maghreb or "Island of the West". Intermediate in size between Algeria and Tunisia, it occupies some 172,000 square miles and has an extensive coastline facing both the Atlantic and the Mediterranean. However, as a result of both its position and the existence of massive mountain ranges within its borders, Morocco has remained relatively isolated from the rest of the Maghreb and has served as a refuge for descendants of the original Berber-speaking occupants of north-west Africa.

The population at the 1971 census was 15,379,259, and the overall density was 27 per square kilometre. About 35 per cent of the total are Berber-speaking peoples, living mainly in mountain villages, while the Arabic-speaking majority is concentrated in towns in the lowlands, particularly in Casablanca, which is the largest city in the Maghreb, in Marrakesh, the old southern capital, and in Rabat (population: 367,620), the modern administrative capital. There were some 450,000 Europeans living in Morocco before the country attained its independence from the French in 1956 but since then their number has greatly diminished.

PHYSICAL FEATURES

The physical geography of Morocco is dominated by the highest and most rugged ranges in the Atlas Mountain system of north-west Africa. They are the result of a phase of mountain-building that took place in the geologically recent Tertiary era when sediments deposited beneath an ancestral Mediterranean Sea were uplifted, folded and fractured. The mountains remain geologically unstable and Morocco is liable to severe earthquakes, such as the appallingly destructive one that took place at the port of Agadir in 1960.

In Morocco the Atlas Mountains form four distinct massifs which are surrounded and partially separated by lowland plains and plateaux. In the north, in the zone of the former Spanish Protectorate, the Rif Atlas comprise a rugged arc of mountains that rise steeply from the Mediterranean coast to heights of over 7,300 feet. Their limestone and sandstone ranges are difficult to penetrate and have functioned as an effective barrier to east-west communications. They are inhabited by Berber farmers who live in isolated mountain villages and have little contact with the Arabs of Tetuan (population: 139,105) and Tangier (population: 187,894) at the north-western end of the Rif chain.

The Middle Atlas lie immediately south of the Rif from which they are separated by the Col of Taza, a narrow gap which affords the only easy route between western Algeria and Atlantic Morocco. They rise to nearly 10,000 feet and form a broad barrier between the two countries. They also function as a major drainage divide and are flanked by the basins of Morocco's two principal rivers, the Oum er Rbia which flows west to the Atlantic and the Moulouya which flows north-east to the Mediterranean. Much of the Middle Atlas consists of a limestone plateau dissected by river gorges and capped here and there by volcanic craters and lava flows. Semi-nomadic Berber tribesmen spend the winter in valley villages and move to the higher slopes in summer to pasture their flocks.

Southward the Middle Atlas chain merges into the High Atlas, the most formidable of the mountain massifs, which rises to over 13,000 feet and is heavily snow-clad in winter.

The mountains are aligned in a chain from south-west to north-east, and they rise precipitously from both the Atlantic lowland to the north and the desert plain of Saharan Morocco to the south. The contrast between the two sides is very striking; the northern slopes are covered by forest and scrub while the southern slopes consist of bare, sunbaked rock. Eastward the chain loses height and continues into Algeria as the Saharan Atlas. The central part of the massif is made up of resistant crystalline rocks which have been eroded by former glaciers and present streams into a wilderness of sharp peaks and steep-sided valleys, but elsewhere limestones and sandstones give rise to more subdued topography. There are no easily accessible routes across the High Atlas, but numerous mountain tracks make possible the exchange of goods by pack animal between Atlantic and Saharan Morocco. A considerable Berber population lives in the mountain valleys in compact, fortified villages.

The Anti Atlas is the lowest and most southerly of the mountain massifs. Structurally it forms an elevated edge of the Saharan platform which was uplifted when the High Atlas were formed. It consists largely of crystalline rocks and is joined to the southern margin of the High Atlas by a mass of volcanic lavas which separates the valley from the river Sous, draining west to the Atlantic at Agadir, from that of the upper Draa, draining south-east towards the Sahara. On the southern side of the chain barren slopes are trenched by gorges from which cultivated palm groves extend like green tongues out into the desert.

The only extensive area of lowland in Morocco stretches inland from the Atlantic coast and is enclosed on the north, east and south by the Rif, Middle and' High Atlas. It consists of the Gharb plain and the wide valley of the River Sebou in the north and of the plateaux and plains of the Meseta, the Tadla, the Rehamna, the Djebilet and the Haouz farther south. Most of the Arabic-speaking people of Morocco live in this region.

CLIMATE

Northern and central Morocco experiences a "Mediterranean" type of climate, with warm wet winters and hot dry summers, but this gives way southward to semi-arid and eventually to desert conditions. In the Rif and the northern parts of the Middle Atlas mean annual rainfall exceeds 30 inches and the summer drought lasts only 3 months, but in the rest of the Middle Atlas, in the High Atlas and over the northern half of the Atlantic lowland rainfall is reduced to between 30 and 16 inches and the summer drought lasts for 4 months or more. During the summer intensely hot winds from the Sahara, known as the Sirocco or Chergui, occasionally cross the mountains and sweep across the lowland desiccating all that lies in their path. Summer heat on the Atlantic coastal plain is tempered however by breezes that blow inland after they have been cooled over the cold waters of the Canaries current offshore.

Over the southern half of the Atlantic lowland and the Anti Atlas semi-arid conditions prevail and rainfall decreases to between 16 and 8 inches a year. It also becomes very variable and is generally insufficient for the regular cultivation of cereal crops without irrigation. East and south of the Atlas Mountains, which act as a barrier to rain-bearing winds from the Atlantic, rainfall is reduced still further and regular cultivation becomes entirely dependent on irrigation.

VEGETATION

The chief contrast in the vegetation of Morocco is between the mountain massifs, which support forest or open woodland, and the surrounding lowlands which, when uncultivated, tend to be covered only by scrub growth of low, drought-resistant bushes. The natural vegetation has however been widely altered, and in many places actually destroyed, by excessive cutting, burning and grazing. This is particularly evident in the lowlands and on the lower mountain slopes where such scrub species as juniper, thuya, dwarf palm and gorse are common. There is little doubt that cork oak covered a large part of the Atlantic lowland but today only the "forest" of Mamora remains to suggest the former abundance of this valuable tree. The middle and upper slopes of the mountains are often quite well wooded, with evergreen oak dominant at the lower and cedar at the higher elevations. The lowlands to the east and south of the Atlas Mountains support distinctive types of steppe and desert vegetation, in which esparto grass and the argan tree (which is unique to south-western Morocco) are conspicuous.

Since Morocco gained its independence territorial disputes have arisen with Algeria, Mauritania and the Spanish Sahara. During the period of French occupation the south-eastern frontier with Algeria was never precisely defined and the Moroccan government has claimed an area beyond it which extends into all three neighbouring countries. The claim is based on the fact that in medieval times Moroccan rule was effective over much of the western Sahara and it is associated with the recent discovery of large iron ore deposits in the area together with the expectation of finding valuable reserves of oil. An agreement on the border with Algeria was finally ratified in May 1973.

D. R. H.

HISTORY

The Phoenicians and after them the Carthaginians established staging posts and trading factories on the coasts of Morocco. Still later, the Romans established in what is now northern Morocco the province of Mauritania Tingitana, the frontier or *limes* passing a little to the south of Rabat, Meknès and Fez. Muslim warriors raided into Morocco under Uqba b. Nafi in A.D. 684–85. It was not, however, until the first years of the eighth century that the Muslims began to bring Morocco under durable control, their forces, under Musa b. Nusair, reaching the Tafilalet and the Wadi Draa. The Berber tribesmen of Morocco rallied to the cause of Islam and had a large share in the Muslim conquest of Spain after A.D. 711. Religious ideas of a heterodox character—i.e., the ideas of the Khawarij, who constituted the first of the great schismatic movements inside Islam—won much support among the Berbers of Morocco. The spread of Kharijite beliefs, the fierce particularism of the Berbers and their refractoriness towards all forms of political control, led to a great rebellion in 739–40, which had as its chief consequence the fragmentation of Morocco into a number of small Muslim principalities.

It was Idris, a descendant of al-Hasan, the son of the Caliph 'Ali and of Fatima, the daughter of the Prophet Muhammad, who, fleeing westward after an unsuccessful revolt against the Abbasid Caliph in Iraq, founded the first of the great Muslim dynasties ruling in Morocco. The Idrisid régime lasted from 788–89 to 985–86. Idris, the founder of the new state, died in 792–93, after reducing most of Morocco and also Tlemcen to obedience with the aid of the Berber tribesmen who had rallied to his cause on his arrival in the western Maghreb. His son, Idris II, founded Fez, the capital of the Idrisids and a notable centre of Muslim life and civilisation in the Maghreb. After the death of Idris II (d. 828–29) the régime fell into decline. Morocco now endured for some two hundred years a long period of internecine conflict, of tribal revolt and of warring principalities. At the same time it had to face external danger in the form of pressures from the Umayad Caliphate of Cordoba in Spain (at the apogee of its power and splendour in the reigns of Abd al-Rahman III (912–61) and al-Hakam II (961–76)) and also from the Fatimid Caliphate established and consolidated in Ifriqiya (i.e. modern Tunisia and eastern Algeria) during the years 908–69.

It was after this long period of turmoil and fragmentation that Morocco entered into the most splendid phase of its medieval history. There now arose, amongst Berbers of

Sanhaja descent who followed a nomadic mode of life in the regions near the Senegal, the religious movement of the Almoravids (al-Murabitun—"people of the ribat", i.e., of a fortified abode devoted to spiritual retreat and also to jihad or war against the infidel). The chieftain of these Berbers, Yahya b. Ibrahim, brought back from Mecca Abd Allah b. Yasin to spread the true doctrine of Islam among his people. The Almoravids soon passed over from the pursuit of the ascetic life to war on behalf of the true faith. The tide of conquest in Morocco gathered momentum under the amir Abu Bakr and led, after his death, to the establishment of a vast Almoravid state in the time of Yusef b. Tashufin (d. 1106), who in 1062 founded Marrakesh and extended the domination of the Almoravids over all Morocco and much of Algeria. In 1086 he halted the southward advance of the Christian *riconquista* in Spain and then annexed the Muslim lands there to the Almoravid territories in North Africa. His successor Ali b. Yusuf (d. 1142) consolidated and maintained the empire, but thereafter the power of the Almoravids fell into a rapid decline. The Saharan nomads who had been the dynamic force behind the movement became absorbed, as it were, into the rich milieu of Andalusian Muslim civilization. Dynastic discord and incompetence among the Almoravid amirs hastened the collapse of the régime. The Christians in Spain took Saragossa in 1118 and began a new phase of their *riconquista*. And in the Atlas mountains of Morocco a new religious force was preparing to burst out over the Moroccan scene. Seven years later, in Morocco, the Almohads rose in revolt against the Almoravids and after 22 years of stubborn conflict took Marrakesh in 1147.

A religious leader, Muhammad b. Tumart (d. 1130), who had studied at Cordoba, Mecca and Baghdad, taught amongst the Masmuda Berbers of the High Atlas doctrines of a strict unitarian character and assumed for himself the designation of al-Mahdi, "the rightly guided one". Amongst the Masmuda he gathered around himself a nucleus of Berber adherents—the "Unitarians", i.e., al-Muwahhidun or Almohads. After the death of Ibn Tumart in 1130 one of his ardent disciples, a Berber of the Kumiya tribe named Abd al-Mumin, became the Khalifa of the Mahdi. Under the guidance of Abd al-Mumin (d. 1163) the Almohads took Marrakesh in 1147 and then in the years 1151–59 overran the rest of Morocco and the North African lands as far east as Tripolitania and Cyrenaica. The Almohads reached the summit of their splendour in the reign of al-Mansur (1184–98), who brought Muslim Spain under Almohad control and checked the menacing advance of the Christians at the battle of Alarcos (1196). Under his successor Muhammad al-Nasir (1199–1214) the Almohads suffered a serious defeat in battle against the Christians of Spain at Las Navas de Tolosa (1212). Thereafter the Almohad empire began to decline. The Hafsids made themselves independent in Ifriqiya (1235–56). Much of the Central Maghreb came under the control of the Abd al-Wadid amirs ruling at Tlemcen. At the same time a new Berber house—the Merinids, of Zenata Berber origin—rose into prominence, conquering Fez in 1248 and Marrakesh in 1269 and thus bringing to an end the last remnants of Almohad rule.

THE MERINIDS

The Merinids, whose effective power lasted for about one hundred years, came from eastern Morocco, overran first the northern regions of Morocco and then the lands in the south. Their attempts to reconstitute the empire of the Almohads met with no durable success. Revolt against their domination was not infrequent in the southern regions of Morocco. Several campaigns undertaken to regain control of the eastern Maghreb brought no more than transient gains, both Ifriqiya and Tlemcen escaping from their domination. Nor could the Merinids establish themselves in Spain, although their interventions there did hinder the Christian *riconquista* and gave the Muslim state of Grenada enough time to consolidate its resources and thus gain the strength to resist the Christians until 1492. The decline of the Merinid régime saw the culmination of a process long since in train. Nomadic tribes of Arab origin—the Hilal and the Sulaym—penetrated into the Maghreb during the course of the 11th and 12th centuries. Other Badawi elements infiltrated through the northern reaches of the Sahara during the later phases of Almohad rule. With the gradual disintegration of the Merinid state the Badawi tribes thrust westward through the Atlas mountains and penetrated into the heart-lands of Morocco. These Badawi invasions, although causing widespread disruption and confusion, contributed much to the arabisation of Morocco and the neighbouring lands. During the years of Merinid decline, dynastic quarrels led to political disintegration, with the result that rival states came into being at Fez and Marrakesh. Morocco, until 1465, was a prey to prolonged internal discords, which ended, at least in part, only with the emergence of another régime of Zenata Berber origin—the Wattasid régime (1465–1549). The Wattasids had no long pre-eminence, their failure to halt the progress of the Portuguese and the Spaniards, who had begun to establish themselves along the Atlantic and the Mediterranean shores of Morocco, being one of the main reasons for their rapid decline.

THE LINE OF SHARIFS

A new movement of resistance to the intrusions of the Spaniards, and, above all, of the Portuguese (by 1500 the masters of Ceuta, Tangier, Arcila, Agadir, Mazagan and Safi on the western coast of Morocco) was born amongst the religious confraternities, amongst the *marabouts* and the "shorfa" (descendants of the Prophet) in Morocco, who now led the Jihad, or war on behalf of the Muslim faith, against the Christians. Out of this situation arose the Saadian régime, originating in a line of Sharifs from the region of the Wadi Draa on the Saharan side of the Atlas mountains. The Saadians took Fez in 1520 and Marrakesh in 1548. Their prestige was due to their status as descendants of the Prophet and to their success in driving the Portuguese from most of their possessions on the Atlantic littoral of Morocco—a success which culminated in their defeat of the Portuguese at the battle of Alcazarquivir in 1578. The most famous of the Sharifs, Ahmad al-Mansur (1578–1603) resisted the pressure of the Ottoman Turks on his eastern frontier with Algeria and in 1591 sent out a large expedition which seized Timbuktu and Goa on the Western Sudan, returning with rich plunder in the form of slaves and gold. Al-Mansur, realising that his house had no strong tribal support, such as earlier dynasties had owned, organised the Saadian régime on a new foundation (the Makhzan)—a system under which various Arab tribes enjoyed exemption from taxes in return for armed service to the state. Much depended, in such a system, on the character of the Sultan. If he were strong and able, all might be well, but in practice the political influence of the sultans tended to fluctuate in accordance with their skill or incompetence. The tribal rivalries would break out anew, the endless tensions between the nomadic and the settled elements in the population became intensified whenever the central government was weak or ill-directed. At such times the "Bled as-Siba" (the areas of dissidence—in particular the Atlas Mountains) set their tribal autonomies against the forces of the "Bled al-Makhzan" (the controlled areas). The period of Saadian rule, which ended in 1668, was, however, one of considerable prosperity for Morocco. Sugar cane culture was encouraged; gold brought by caravan from the Sudan added to the resources of the régime; close commercial contact was made with the lands of southern and western Europe, amongst them England.

Yet another wave of popular religious sentiment brought to power a new house—known under the designations Alawi, Hasani or Filali—which still reigns in Morocco. The Alawi Sharifs had their origin amongst the Berbers located in the oases of Tafilalet, i.e., Saharan Morocco. Under the guidance of the Alawi house Berber forces took Fez in 1644 and Marrakesh in 1668. The reigns of Rashid II (1664–72) and, above all, of Mulai Ismail (1672–1727) established the Alawi régime on a firm basis and saw Morocco more thoroughly pacified and more solidly united than it was ever to be again until the time of the French occupation. Ismail used as one of his main instruments of rule a powerful corps of negro troops, some stationed close to his capital, Meknès, others established in a network of Qasbahs (fortresses) which covered most of the land. He also had at his command a strong force of European renegades. Among the main achievements of Mulai Ismail must be numbered the occupation, in 1684, of Tangier (English since 1662) and the capture, in 1689, of Larache (Spanish since 1610). Mulai Ismail concluded with France in 1682 a commercial agreement, which was confirmed later in 1787, precedence being then accorded to the consuls of France over the consuls of all other nations.

Mulai Ismail had managed to thrust back the pressure of the Sanhaja Berbers, who were beginning to move down from the Middle Atlas into the lowland areas of Morocco. His successors did not win the same degree of success, with the result that, after the death of Ismail in 1727, a period of confusion ensued in Morocco until the rise of yet another able prince, the Sharif Muhammad b. Abdallah (1757–1790). Muhammad founded Mogador in 1765 and drove the Portuguese from Mazagan in 1769. He entered into a pact of friendship and commerce with Spain in 1767. A brief period of conflict with Spain followed in 1774, but a new agreement was negotiated between Morocco and Spain in 1780.

Muhammad b. Abdallah and his immediate successors, Mulai Sulaiman (1792–1822) and Mulai Abd al-Rahman (1822–59) made strenuous efforts to maintain the control of the central régime in the face of tribal dissidence, and to ward off the possibilities of foreign intervention in the affairs of Morocco. The French conquest of Algiers in 1830 was bound, however, to have repercussions in Morocco. Mulai Abd al-Rahman gave assistance to Abd al-Qadir, the amir who led the Muslim resistance to France in Algeria during the years 1832–47. During the course of their campaigns against Abd al-Qadir the French met and defeated a Moroccan force at Wadi Isly in 1844.

A dispute over the limits of the Ceuta enclave, which was under Spanish rule, led in 1860 to a brief war between Morocco and Spain. Spanish troops under General O' Donnell defeated the Moroccans at Los Castillejos and seized Tetuan. A further engagement at Wadi Ras in March 1860 brought the war to a close. A peace settlement followed, under the terms of which the Ceuta enclave was enlarged and Spain was given indemnities amounting to 100 million pesetas. Morocco also granted to Spain a territorial enclave on the Atlantic coast opposite the Canaries (Santa Cruz de Mar Pequeña, now Ifni).

FRENCH RULE

France, with her hold on Algeria secure, began to turn her eyes towards the Western Maghreb—but the rivalries among the great Powers long hindered the establishment of a French protectorate over Morocco. In April 1904, however, Great Britain agreed to recognise the pre-eminence of French interests in Morocco in return for a similar recognition of English interests in Egypt. A convention between France and Spain in October 1904 assigned to Spain two zones of influence, one in northern and the other in southern Morocco. The Germans now sought to intervene in Moroccan affairs and at the conference of Algeciras in 1906 secured the adherence of the Great Powers to the economic "internationalisation" of Morocco. A sharp crisis in 1911, when the German gun-boat *Panther* appeared at Agadir, ended in a Franco-German settlement, the Germans now recognising Morocco as a French sphere of influence in return for territorial concessions in the Congo. In March 1912 Morocco became a Protectorate of France, with a French Resident-General empowered to direct foreign affairs, to control defence and also to introduce internal reforms. A new convention of 1912 between France and Spain revised the earlier agreement of 1904: Spain now received her zones of influence in Morocco (though somewhat diminished in extent)—but from France as the protecting power and *not* from the Sultan.

The first French Resident-General in Morocco was General Lyautey (1912–25). He established effective control, before 1914, over the plains and lower plateaux of Morocco from Fez to the Atlas mountains south of Marrakesh; then, before 1918, over the western Atlas, the Taza corridor connecting with Algeria and some areas of the northern highlands. French troops helped Spain to subdue the formidable rebellion (1921–26) of the Rif tribesmen under Abd al-Krim. This success meant the subjugation of the northern mountains and allowed the French to turn with unimpeded vigour to the reduction of the Middle Atlas and the Tafilalet—a task accomplished by 1934, when the pacification of the whole of Morocco could be regarded as complete.

It was at this time that nationalist sentiment began to make itself felt in Morocco. A "Comité d'Action Marocaine" now asked for a limitation of the protectorate. This "Comité" was dissolved in 1937, but nationalist propaganda continued against the French régime. Morocco rallied to the cause of France in 1939 and to the Free French movement in 1942. A Party of Independence (Istiqlal), formed in 1943, demanded full freedom for Morocco, with a constitutional form of government under Sultan Muhammad b. Yusuf, who supported the nationalist movement. The Istiqlal, strong in the towns, did not find great favour at this time among the conservative tribesmen of Morocco, who tended to concentrate their resistance to reform on western lines around Thami al-Glawi, the Pasha of Marrakesh. The tensions between the new and the old ideas in Morocco became much sharper in 1953. Sultan Muhammad b. Yusuf had long adhered to the aims of the Istiqlal movement. He had fallen into disagreement with the French administration, refusing to issue *dahirs* (decrees) authorising various measures that the French desired to see in force. In May 1953 a number of Pashas and Caids, with al-Glawi, the Pasha of Marrakesh, at their head, asked for the removal of the Sultan. Berber tribesmen began to converge in force towards the main urban centres in Morocco such as Rabat, Casablanca and Fez. On August 20th, 1953, the Sultan agreed to go into exile in Europe, but not to abdicate. Muhammad b. Arafa, a prince of the Alawi house, was now recognised as Sultan. Attempts to assassinate him occurred in September 1953 at Rabat and again in March 1954 at Marrakesh. The situation continued to be tense, with outbreaks of violence occurring here and there throughout Morocco in 1954–55 and nationalist fervour running high.

INDEPENDENCE—1956

Sultan Muhammad b. Arafa renounced the throne and withdrew to Tangier in 1955. Muhammad b. Yusuf, on November 5th in that year, was recognised once more as the legitimate Sultan. A joint Franco-Moroccan declaration of March 2nd, 1956, stated that the Protectorate agreement of 1912 was obsolete and that the French government now recognised the independence of Morocco. A Protocol of the same date covered the transitional phase before new agreements between France and Morocco, still to be negotiated, could come into effect. The Sultan would now have full legislative powers in Morocco. Henceforward a High Commissioner was to represent France in the new state. France undertook also to aid Morocco with the organization of its armed forces and to assist in the re-assertion of Moroccan control over the zones of Spanish influence, the sole legal basis for which was the Franco-Spanish convention of 1912. On November 12th, 1956, Morocco became a member of the United Nations.

In August 1956 the Istiqlal proclaimed the need to abrogate the Convention of Algeciras (1906), which had "internationalised" the economic life of Morocco, and also to secure the withdrawal of all foreign troops from the land. An international conference met at Fedala, near Casablanca, in October 1956, to consider the future of Tangier, administered since 1912 under an international régime. In October 1956 Tangier was restored to Morocco. A Royal Charter of August 1957 maintained in general the former economic and financial system in force at Tangier, including a free money market, quota-free trade with foreign countries and a low level of taxation. In 1959 Tangier lost its special status and was integrated financially and economically with Morocco, but a Royal decree of January 1962 made it once more a free port. The Istiqlal, in 1956, had envisaged the creation of a "Great Morocco" which, according to a map published in July of that year, would include certain areas in South-West Algeria, the Spanish territories in North-West Africa and also Mauritania, together with the French Sudan (i.e., the Republic of Mali). The Sultan of Morocco and his government reiterated these claims in the years which followed the achievement of Moroccan independence. Moreover, in 1958, a number of personalities prominent in the political life of Mauritania, amongst them the Amir of Trarza in the extreme south-west of the Republic, withdrew to Morocco and found a welcome there. Morocco began in 1960 an intensive propaganda and diplomatic campaign against Mauritania, asking, in August 1960, that the question of Mauritania be placed on the agenda of the United Nations. The Political Committee of the UN General Assembly debated the question in November, but without agreeing to a formal resolution.

The problem of the Spanish territories in North-West Africa also came to the fore at this time. During the course of a visit which Sultan Muhammad b. Yusuf made to Madrid in April 1956, soon after Morocco became independent, Spain had recognised the independence of Morocco, renouncing also the northern zone of the protectorate assigned to her in Morocco under the terms of the Franco-Spanish convention of 1912. One factor in the general situation was the existence in the western Sahara of irregular Moroccan forces (the "Armée de Libération du Grand Sahara") reputed to have some connection with the Istiqlal. These irregular forces attacked the Spanish enclave of Ifni in Southern Morocco on November 23rd, 1957, but after some stiff fighting had to withdraw in the first week of December. During the first three months of 1958 irregular bands also raided into the Spanish territories of Saguia al-Hamra and Rio de Oro and into the northern fringes of Mauritania. A combined Franco-Spanish operation cleared the irregulars from the Spanish territories and the adjacent lands by the beginning of March. The Moroccan government had declared that it was not responsible for these incursions. Negotiations between Morocco and Spain, held at Cintra in Portugal, led in April 1958 to an agreement under which Spain, in accordance with the settlement reached in April 1956, relinquished to Morocco the southern zone of her former protectorate.

KING HASSAN II AND ROYAL DOMINANCE OF GOVERNMENT

The dominant political force after independence remained the Istiqlal, which obtained a majority in the Government. At the same time Sultan Muhammad strengthened the position of the monarchy. In July 1957 Prince Moulai Hassan was proclaimed heir to the throne and in August the Sultan assumed the title of king. Istiqlal's efforts to reduce the power of the monarch were hampered by divisions within the party itself. Tension between the conservative and radical wings reached breaking-point in December 1958 when a Government was formed by Abdullah Ibrahim, a leader of the radical tendency. In the following months Ben Barka led a movement to establish a radical party organization independent of the conservative Istiqlal leadership of Allal El Fassi. In September 1959 this new organization became an independent party, the National Union of Popular Forces (UNFP). Although the UNFP supported Ibrahim's government, it became the object of repressive measures by the police and the army who were under the control of the king or of "king's men" in the cabinet. In May 1960 a new government was formed with the King himself as Prime Minister and Prince Hassan as his deputy, and the UNFP went into opposition. On the death of King Muhammad in February 1961 the prince ascended the throne as King Hassan II, and also became Prime Minister. In December 1962 a new constitution was approved by referendum, establishing a constitutional monarchy with guaranteed personal and political freedoms. In January 1963 a cabinet reshuffle deprived the Istiqlal leaders of their posts in the government, and when elections for the House of Representatives were held in May both Istiqlal and the UNFP appeared as opposition parties. The King was represented by the newly-formed Front for the Defence of Constitutional Institutions (FDIC). The election, by universal direct suffrage, failed to produce the expected clear majority for the government party, the results being: FDIC 69 seats; Istiqlal 41 seats; UNFP 28 seats; Independents 6 seats. In the following months repressive action was taken against both opposition parties. Several Istiqlal deputies were arrested for protesting against corruption and mismanagement of the election, leading the party to boycott further elections later in the year. Almost all the leaders of the UNFP were arrested in July 1963 in connection with an alleged *coup* attempt. Many of them were held in solitary confinement, tortured and eventually sentenced to death. In November the King gave up the post of Prime Minister, installing a Government of FDIC men devoted to his interests.

RELATIONS IN THE MAGHREB

Moroccan troops, in July 1962, entered the region south of Colomb-Béchar in Algeria—a region never officially demarcated. The Moroccan press also launched a strong campaign in support of the view that the Tindouf area in the extreme south-west of Algeria should belong to Morocco—a claim of some importance, since the area contains large deposits of high-grade (57 per cent) iron ore and also considerable resources of oil and natural gas.

In September 1963 Moroccan auxiliaries began to move southward from Tagounit into the region of Hassi-Beida and Tinjoub, about 250 miles south-west of Colomb-Béchar and 200 miles north-east of Tindouf. There was sharp fighting in this area from October 8th to November 4th, 1963. With the mediation of President Keita of Mali a ceasefire was signed at Bamako on October 30th. An arbitration commission was established by the OAU on November 18th, and Algeria and Morocco submitted evidence in support of their respective territorial claims. On February 20th, 1964, an agreement was reached on the establishment of a demilitarized zone.

A swift improvement in relations between the two countries followed. In April 1964, prisoners were exchanged and in May normal diplomatic relations were restored. At the same time a joint technical committee reached agreement on a number of points and it was decided to continue discussions on outstanding issues. A more amicable relationship also became evident between Morocco and Mauritania. The Ministers of Information of these two states met at Cairo in July 1964 during the course of an African Summit Conference. An understanding was reached to bring an end to the "war" of radio propaganda and criticism hitherto active between Morocco and Mauritania.

King Hassan II paid an official visit to Tunisia in December 1964—a visit which marked the full renewal, between Morocco and Tunisia, of the good relations disturbed when, in 1960, Tunisia had recognized the independence of Mauritania. Diplomatic relations between Morocco and Tunisia had been restored somewhat earlier in May 1964.

The general improvement in relations between the Maghreb states led to meetings in September and November 1964 at which it was agreed to encourage economic co-operation and to establish a permanent joint consultative committee of the Maghreb involving Morocco, Algeria, Libya and Tunisia. Until 1970, when Libya withdrew, this body met regularly to discuss a collective approach to economic problems.

INTERNAL UNREST

In August 1964 the Moroccan Government was reorganized, although it remained composed largely of FDIC members. The reshuffle was the preparation for an attempt to attract the opposition parties back into a coalition government, since the FDIC had an inadequate majority in the House of Representatives and was itself split into two factions, the Democratic Socialist Party (PSD) and the People's Movement. The weakness of the government contributed to the tense political situation which developed in the first half of 1965 as unemployment and rising prices generated discontent among the urban working class. In March an unpopular Ministry of Education circular led to student protests. On March 23rd student demonstrations in Casablanca developed into rioting with the participation of workers, and over a hundred people are estimated to have been killed when police and troops fired on the demonstrators. Meanwhile negotiations were going on between the King and political leaders of all parties in an attempt to form a government of National Union. As a conciliatory gesture the King declared an amnesty for all political prisoners on April 14th. He proposed a programme of industrial development and agrarian reform, plus a campaign against corruption in the administration. Both Istiqlal and the UNFP refused coalition, however, demanding democratic elections to be followed by the formation of a government by the majority party. Faced with continuing political deadlock, on June 7th King Hassan proclaimed a state of emergency, under which he himself assumed full legislative and executive power. New elections, it was stated, would be held after the constitution had been revised and submitted to a referendum. In October 1965 the UNFP leader Ben Barka disappeared in France never to be seen again. Gen. Oufkir, one of the King's sturdiest supporters, was found guilty in France in his absence of complicity in Ben Barka's disappearance. Relations between Morocco and France became very strained and there were anti-government protest strikes in Morocco.

In July 1967, King Hassan relinquished the post of Prime Minister to Dr. Mohammed Benhima, and in 1967 and 1968 there were eight major cabinet reshuffles. Considerable student and trade union unrest continued during this period, but the King won some popularity by extensive nationalization measures and a degree of land redistribution.

There was a gradual return to full political activity in 1969, though still under royal direction. Municipal and rural communal elections were held in October, although these were boycotted by opposition parties and the successful candidates mostly stood as independents. Following this Dr. Mohammed Benhima was replaced as Prime Minister by Dr. Ahmed Laraki, formerly Foreign Minister. A national referendum on a new constitution was at last held in July 1970; official figures claimed that over 98 per cent of the votes were affirmative, despite general opposition from the main political parties, trade unions and student organizations. Elections for a new single chamber legislature were held in August. Of the 240 members, 90 were elected by direct suffrage, 90 by local councils and 60 by an electoral college. The results were that 158 elected members were Independents, 60 were of the government party *Mouvement Populaire* and 22 from opposition parties.

In July 1971 there was an unsuccessful attempt by a section of the army to overthrow the King and establish a republic. The attempt was led by Gen. Mohammed Medbouh, Minister of the Royal Military Household and Col. Muhammad Ababou. Together with some 1,400 military cadets, they attacked the King's palace at Skhirate while he was celebrating his birthday with members of the government, foreign diplomatic corps and many other guests. Although the rebels at one point had captured the King and his ministers, and controlled the radio station and the Interior Ministry, they were soon overwhelmed. Many of their own men apparently rallied to the King, while the rest of the army counter-attacked quickly. The revolt was suppressed in under 24 hours. Over 150 of the rebels were killed in the fighting. The King escaped unhurt but some of his generals, a minister and an ambassador were among those killed, and other guests were wounded. The King later said that there had been foreign involvement in the abortive *coup*, which he described as "Libyan-style". A few hours after the revolt had begun,

the Libyan Government had alerted its armed forces to be ready to defend the Moroccan "revolution". Relations between the two countries were later severed. The *coup* attempt appeared to have been engineered by right-wing army officers, angered by the level of corruption in the royal administration and by the King's too lenient treatment of dissent on the left. The King's response was to reshuffle the cabinet, giving General Oufkir a much enhanced position, and to begin to attack corruption in the ranks of state employees, civil servants and former ministers. The leaders of the attack on the Skhirate Palace had been killed in the fighting or summararily executed immediately afterwards, but more than a thousand other army officers and men were brought before the military tribunal at Kenitra in January 1972 and charged with complicity, and they were sentenced to imprisonment lasting variously from one year to life.

During the months following the Skhirate *coup*, a series of conciliatory talks was held between the Government and members of Istiqlal and the UNFP who had united to form a National Front in July 1970. Meanwhile, the trial at Marrakesh of 193 UNFP supporters charged with treason, which had been in progress since early 1970 was completed in September 1971, and sentences passed included five of the death penalty and six of life imprisonment. Efforts to obtain National Front participation in government continued into 1972, by which time all but 30 of the UNFP detainees had been released, but both Istiqlal and the UNFP refused to compromise with government policies.

In February 1972 King Hassan announced a new Constitution, under which executive power would be vested in the Government and the Assembly, and two-thirds of the Assembly's members were to be elected by universal suffrage compared to half under the previous constitution. The National Front urged a boycott of the constitution referendum and accused the Government of rigging the results, according to which 93 per cent of voters took part and approved the constitution in 98.75 per cent of valid votes cast. The constitution was promulgated in March, and in April a new cabinet, substantially the same as its predecessor was appointed to organize elections. On April 30th, however, King Hassan announced that Parliament, which was due to be reopened, would remain dissolved, and that elections for the new assembly were being postponed until new electoral lists had been drawn up. In July a split occurred in the UNFP which seperated the Rabat section from the rest of the party. As a consequence the National Front became a dead letter.

In August 1972 King Hassan survived another attempt on his life, when fighter planes of his air force tried to shoot down the plane in which he was travelling and strafed the airport and the royal palace in Rabat. The assassination attempt had apparently been planned by General Oufkir, the Minister of Defence and Army Chief of Staff, whose death occurred immediately afterwards. The King himself took over the command of the armed forces and defence matters and did not appoint a new Defence Minister until March 1973. He approached the opposition parties again, asking for their co-operation in supervising general elections and collaboration with the Government. However, both Istiqlal and the UNFP demanded that a number of far-reaching reforms be introduced, which were unacceptable to the King, as they included curtailing the King's powers and guaranteeing political freedom. The elections, which had been postponed until October, were further postponed indefinitely, and a new cabinet was formed in November without opposition participation.

FOREIGN RELATIONS 1966-72

During 1966-67 Morocco viewed with unease the arrival, in Algeria ,of Soviet planes, guns and tanks. The Moroccan government felt that the flow of arms into Algeria was creating a serious military imbalance in North Africa. Some of the new equipment which Algeria had received from the U.S.S.R. had been sent, so it was said, to the western areas of Algeria, where the Tindouf region was still a matter of dispute between Morocco and Algeria. In November 1966 Morocco acquired from the U.S.A. a number of military jets which formed a counterpoise to Soviet planes known to have reached Algeria. The King visited the United States in February 1967. Reports current at the time intimated that the U.S.A. was prepared to make available arms worth some 15 million dollars in order to strengthen the defences of Morocco. In March 1967 King Hassan urged Algeria to discontinue its military programme and to enter into negotiations with Morocco or else to accept the suggestion that a United Nations disarmament commission should visit Morocco and Algeria.

In the Arab-Israeli war in June 1967, the Moroccan government gave voice to its support of the Arabs' anti-Zionist cause, but did not commit its troops to the fighting. After the Arab defeat brief outbursts of public demonstration were followed by an unofficial commercial boycott of the 70,000 strong Jewish community in Morocco. The government condemnation of this boycott was unpopular with trade unionists and was challenged by the General Secretary of the U.M.T., Mahjoub Ben Seddiq, who was promptly arrested and sentenced to eighteen months' imprisonment on a charge of undermining the respect due to the authority of the state.

One principal event of the undisturbed political scene after the Palestine war was the Spanish surrender of the small coastal enclave of Ifni. Spain's possession of Ifni, Ceuta, Melilla and the Spanish Sahara to the south of Morocco has long been a cause of friction between the two countries; the Moroccan Government has made much of the apparent inconsistency between the Spanish campaign against Gibraltar and Spain's determined retention of its African colonies. Ifni, held by Spain since 1860, is a poor territory with little obvious economic or strategic potential, and its Spanish population is small. It might well have been handed over before but for Moroccan insistence on negotiating on the other territories. Ceuta and Melilla are Spanish populated and the Sahara has rich phosphate deposits, so Spain is considerably less willing to give them up. Morocco officially took over Ifni on June 30th, 1969.

Moroccan diplomacy achieved several notable successes in the 1969–70 period. Rabat was host to both the Islamic summit conference held in September 1969 following the fire at the Al Aqsa mosque in Jerusalem, and to the fifth Arab summit conference in December 1969. Morocco did not take a very active part in either meeting—just as it did not participate in the hostilities in Palestine—but its official acceptance of Mauritania's presence in September was to lead to the dropping of her claim to that country later in the year. Full diplomatic recognition and an exchange of ambassadors followed in January 1970; in June 1970, a treaty of solidarity, good neighbourliness and co-operation was signed between the two countries. Relations with France improved following the general pattern in the Arab world, and the diplomatic missions in Paris and Rabat were returned to full ambassadorial status for the first time since the Ben Barka affair in 1966. Relations were further improved with the visit to Morocco by the French Foreign Minister, M. Schumann in December 1970. As a result of talks, a Franco-Moroccan intergovernmental commission was set up, to meet at least once a year.

In May 1970 final agreement was reached in the frontier dispute with Algeria, and a joint commission mapped out a delineation maintaining the boundaries of the colonial period. The disputed region of Gara-Djebilet, rich in iron ore deposits, thus became the property of Algeria, but Morocco will have a share in a joint company to be established to exploit these deposits. In June 1972 the OAU Heads of State Assembly was held in Rabat, and King Hassan was elected Chairman. At the close of this meeting the Algerian-Moroccan border was agreed by both heads of state, and the agreement was ratified on May 17th, 1973.

HASSAN IN CONTROL

At the end of 1972 King Hassan's position appeared precarious. He was politically isolated since the main political parties continued in opposition and the armed forces could no longer be relied upon to support him. Many observers doubted his ability to survive. However, the King took strong measures against dissidents and won support by adopting nationalist policies.

In January 1973, following a student strike and clashes with police, the Moroccan students' union (UNEM) was banned. Then, in March, the capture of what were described as Libyan-supported guerrillas in the Atlas mountains led to widespread arrests of radicals in the major towns, including some leaders of the Rabat section of the UNFP. In April the Rabat section was suspended by the Government and shortly afterwards decrees were issued controlling the right of assembly, limiting public meetings and imposing press censorship. 157 people, including UNFP militants, were brought before the Kenitra military tribunal in June accused of terrorist activities and plotting against the monarchical régime. Many were given heavy sentences and 15 were executed in November. A similar trial of alleged Marxist-Leninists at Casablanca resulted in further long prison sentences.

In March 1973 the King announced plans for the Moroccanization of parts of the economy in the course of the next two years. At the same time he reinforced his traditional support in the rural areas by ordering the confiscation of foreign-owned lands and their distribution among the peasantry. Since most of the landowners were French, relations between France and Morocco cooled and French aid was suspended pending an agreement on compensation. In the same month relations with Spain became strained when Morocco announced the extension of its territorial waters from 12 to 70 miles. Instrusions of Spanish trawlers into the new limits led to frequent confrontations until an agreement was reached between the two governments in January 1974 allowing a limited number of Spanish vessels to fish in Moroccan waters. The new nationalist policy also led Morocco to take a more active part than previously in the Arab-Israeli conflict. In February troops were despatched to the Syrian front and during the October War further detachments were sent to Egypt. The common cause produced a degree of rapprochement between Morocco and the more revolutionary Arab states.

In the early months of 1974 political trials continued. Another round of arrests followed the announcement in February of the discovery of a plot to free prisoners in Kenitra jail. The King, however, made some conciliatory gestures. In March he announced plans for university and judicial reforms, and in April several imprisoned UNFP leaders were released. Relations with France improved and French aid was resumed in February, but despite the settlement of the fishing dispute relations with Spain remained bad, since Morocco continued to press her claim to the Spanish Sahara. The growth of phosphate mining in the territory posed a threat to the Moroccan economy which was itself dependent on revenue from phosphate exports. The opposition parties, motivated by a mixture of anti-colonialism and nationalism, urged the government to take action. In July 1974 the King held consultations with military leaders, ministers and leaders of all the political parties to prepare an international campaign for the annexation of the Sahara. An extraordinary degree of national unity was achieved, opposition leaders agreeing to act as government envoys to foreign capitals. Discussions with Spain in August produced no result. The Spanish pursued their own plan for the decolonization of the Sahara, involving the establishment of an independent state closely linked with Spain. This project was contested not only by Morocco but also by Mauritania which re-asserted its old claim to the area. Both countries rejected Spain's plan to hold a referendum in the Sahara under UN supervision. In October the issue was debated in the UN General Assembly at the initiative of Morocco. Two months later the Assembly formally approved Morocco's suggestion that the matter be brought before the International Court of Justice at the Hague and the UN Special Committee on Colonialism was instructed to send a mission to the territory. The referendum proposed by Spain was to be postponed for the time being.

The situation in the territory itself developed rapidly. By early 1975 there were at least three political groups active in the Sahara, associated respectively with Morocco, Spain and the radical Arab States, Algeria and Libya. There were reports of guerrilla activities and incursions by Moroccan troops. In January 1975 Morocco increased tension by extending its campaign to include the Spanish

enclaves of Ceuta and Melilla. Spain responded by a show of military strength in the enclaves and an assertion of its determination to retain them. In May the World Court hearings began and the UN investigative mission arrived in the Sahara. Since Spain reiterated its readiness to withdraw from the Sahara, it became clear that the chief conflict was between the rival North African countries and liberation movements. After Morocco and Mauritania reached some agreement on the future division of the territory Algeria became the main butt of Moroccan invective, because of its support for a liberation movement hostile to Moroccan claims and close to the Algerian Government in ideology.

In the atmosphere of national unity produced by the Sahara issue in the second half of 1974 there was an effervescence of political activity. New parties were formed and existing parties reorganized. Most notably the split in the UNFP was confirmed, as the Rabat section of the party became the USFP. King Hassan once more promised elections for the following year, and once more postponed them indefinitely, but even the opposition were not enthusiastic about elections before the settlement of the Sahara dispute. Harassment of opposition parties did not cease and no opposition figures were invited into the Government, but some political prisoners were released. Social and political conflicts were temporarily obscured by a mist of nationalist sentiment.

ECONOMIC SURVEY

Morocco has a congenial climate, varied soils with good agricultural potential and important mineral resources. There is an emerging industrial sector, a small, but growing managerial class and the beginnings of an industrial force. The economic infrastructure (transport, communications, electric energy) is at an advanced stage. The beauty of the country and its climate offer opportunities for the growth of tourism. However, the movement out of the country of capital and trained personnel in the period immediately before and after independence was a severe setback to economic growth. A series of poor harvests also limited growth but favourable capital movements resulted in an average annual growth of 3.9 per cent in the Gross National Product between 1963 and 1969 to 16,110 million dirhams in 1969. The fastest growth was recorded in mining and industry (4.3 per cent). Agricultural production rose by less than 1 per cent annually over this period, as did the activity in the various service sectors while construction and public works showed a decline. The five-year development plan introduced in 1968 aimed at an annual rate of growth of 4.3 per cent, and a slightly bigger increase was achieved, despite a fall off in investment because of political instability and severe floods in early 1970. The G.N.P. in 1972, the final year of the plan, reached 20,600 million dirhams. Agriculture remained the most important sector of production and output increased by four per cent, but this was scarcely sufficient to offset population growth. Industry has a small but growing place in the economy. In 1972 industrial production reached 1,840 million dirhams compared with 1,420 million dirhams at the beginning of the plan period. The mining and power sectors also

registered favourable increases in production but growth in the building and public works sector was slower than in the first five-year plan.

The problems that Morocco has to face are familiar among developing countries. The fast-rising population, increasing by 3 per cent per annum, is supported for the most part by an out-of-date agricultural system, and any substantial increase in the country's productive capacity is dependent on foreign finance. The population in 1974 was estimated at 16.9 million and is expected to reach 28 million by 1990. Per capita income stood at $279 in 1973, but most of the wealth is distributed among landowners and a small number of urban industrialists and merchants. The rural masses and small but growing urban proletariat are much poorer than per capita income figures indicate.

The share of G.N.P. devoted to investments is about 13.5 per cent, a low level by world standards. Unemployment is a serious problem; it is estimated that 40 per cent of the population between the ages of 20 and 30 are unemployed. Inflation is also a growing problem. Casablanca's consumer price index (1970= 100) rose from 108 in 1972 to only 112.5 in 1973, but then jumped to 128.7 in 1974.

There are, however, a number of factors that should contribute significantly to the country's faster economic development. The value of the country's main export item, phosphates, has risen sharply as a result of a 50 per cent price increase in July 1974, and although this has not eliminated Morocco's trade deficit as had been hoped, it has allowed a substantial rise in investment allocations under the 1973–77 development plan. The plan gives priority to industry, agriculture and irrigation, tourism and vocational training. The emphasis in industry is on labour intensive light industry which will produce import substitutes and goods for export. Remittances from expatriate workers made an important contribution to the balance of payments although the rapid growth between 1972 and 1973 (54.9 per cent to 1.029 million dirhams) may have fallen off in the following year with recession and higher unemployment in Europe. Tourism is also an important source of income. The number of tourists entering Morocco increased rapidly to 1,487,412 in 1973, but then fell slightly to 1,338,024 in 1974. Nevertheless, income from tourism during the first 11 months of 1974 was 35 per cent up on the same period for 1973 at 681 million dirhams. The country also has the natural advantages of a convenient geographical position, considerable natural resources and an excellent communications system.

AGRICULTURE AND FISHERIES

Agriculture is the key to the economy of Morocco. Three-quarters of Morocco's population live in the countryside, and 55 per cent of the active labour force is engaged in agriculture, livestock-raising and fishing. Thus agriculture provides the means of livelihood of the majority of the population, supplies about 90 per cent of the country's domestic food requirements and in the region of 40 per cent of the country's total merchandise exports. In 1972 agriculture contributed about 30 per cent of total domestic production.

Changing climatic conditions cause substantial year-to-year variations in agricultural output. In years with bumper harvests the contribution of agriculture to the gross domestic product rises to over 30 per cent, whereas in years with particularly poor crops the corresponding contribution is in the region of 20 per cent.

The principal crops are cereals, especially wheat and barley, beans and chick peas and other legumens, canary seed, cumin and coriander, linseed, olives, almonds and citrus fruits. Esparto grass is put to several uses including the manufacture of vegetable horsehair and is exported for paper making. Recently, vast areas of esparto grass have been brought into economic use by the establishment of a pulp industry based on this grass and on the eucalyptus tree. Forest resources, almost entirely under state control, include cork (covering approximately 310,000 hectares), cedar, argon, oak and various conifers. Tizra wood is exported for tanning.

Livestock numbers have been declining and the quality of herds is generally poor. Drought in the 1972–73 season meant that production of dairy products fell far short of targets, but the Government has introduced a number of incentives, including increased prices and subsidies to encourage production.

In the past Morocco has been largely self-sufficient in foodstuffs, but a series of poor harvests and a growing demand for cereals, sugar and dairy products resulted in a rise in imports of foodstuffs of 76.3 per cent in volume and 72.5 per cent in value (to 1,078 million dirhams) during 1973. Imports of wheat rose from 382,411 metric tons costing 136.9 million

dirhams in 1972 to 904,936 metric tons costing 483.4 million dirhams in 1973. Sugar imports also rose by 25.2 per cent in quantity to 277,919 metric tons during 1973 and by 44.8 per cent in value to 245.1 million dirhams. In 1974 this upward trend continued. The total value of food imports rose by 70 per cent to 1,834 million dirhams. Wheat imports cost 708 million dirhams, 47 per cent more than in 1973, and the value of sugar imports nearly tripled, leaping to 632 million dirhams.

Foodstuffs also account for a substantial if fluctuating proportion of exports—47.7 per cent in 1971, 46.9 per cent in 1972, 48.6 per cent in 1973, but only 22 per cent in 1974. The main items are citrus fruits (mostly oranges), tomatoes, processed fish and vegetables. Citrus exports in 1974 were worth 388 million dirhams, a drop of 21 per cent from 1973, with France the biggest market. Morocco is the world's second largest exporter of citrus fruits, selling abroad 699,637 metric tons in 1973 out of a total 1972/73 crop of 880,000 metric tons. A fruit-processing industry is also being developed and exports of processed fruits rose to 50 million dirhams in 1974. Under its 1969 treaty of association with the EEC, Moroccan citrus fruits can enter the Community paying only a small duty. But stiff competition is provided by Spanish and Israeli fruit and in April 1973 Moroccan citrus sales to the EEC were suspended for a week in protest against alleged violations of EEC price regulations by Spain and Israel. Efforts to obtain further concessions from the EEC for exports of citrus fruits and vegetables have been blocked by Italy and this has proved a stumbling block in negotiations on a new treaty of association.

Fishing is an important industry and catches average about 200,000 tons of sardines, 10,000 tons of mackerel, 3,000 tons of tunny fish and 2,000 tons of anchovies a year. Agadir has taken over from Safi as the main fishing port although Casablanca and Eassaouira are also important. Most fish is processed before being consumed or exported, and about 70,000 tons of fish are canned each year. Exports of canned fish reached 244 million dirhams in 1974. Moroccan sardines are renowned on the world market for their flavour and high quality. There are also substantial exports of fish meal and other products for use as fertilizers and animal foodstuffs.

Fish catches had been declining up to 1972 and Moroccan fishermen blamed European boats, especially those from Spain, for catching too many fish and depleting stocks. In March 1973 King Hassan announced that Morocco was extending its jurisdiction over territorial waters from 12 to 70 miles. Foreign fishing vessels are no longer allowed into the 70-mile area unless their government has a fishing agreement with Morocco. Spain refused to accept this measure, and several incidents involving the Spanish and Moroccan navies occurred. In January 1974 an agreement was reached which did not include Spanish recognition of the new limit, but allowed 200 Spanish vessels to fish near the Moroccan coast as part of a joint Moroccan-Spanish fishing company, *Maropêche*. This company has a capital of 4.4 million dirhams and intends to operate a fleet which will include ocean-going tuna-fishing vessels. The success of such joint ventures would do much to ease a difficult situation. The extension of territorial waters and increasing world prices of fish products should mean that fishing will make an increasingly important contribution to the national economy.

The agricultural sector is one of contrasts: on the one side, a system of holdings inherited from European farmers, with an emphasis on cash and export crops; and, on the other, the Muslim farmers, who are much less prosperous, and who raise crops mainly for their own consumption. The traditional arable farming comprises 800,000 to 1,000,000 holdings covering approximately 4 million hectares and is characterized by the small size of the holdings, the legal complexity of rights governing their tenure, low productivity, and the predominance of cereals and stock-raising. Irrigation plans have not made great headway due to the conservatism of the farmers and the complexity of the legal situation. Much of farming and grazing land is owned by the state, tribes and religious communities. Individual ownership formalized by title deeds is still relatively unusual but is spreading. The last colonial lands were nationalized in March 1973 when King Hassan decreed that 250,000 hectares of land belonging to foreign farmers, mainly French, should be taken over by the State. Nearly 2,000 foreign settlers are believed to have been affected by the decree. The demands of French farmers for compensation from the Moroccan Government were not immediately dealt with. This resulted in some tension in Franco-Moroccan relations and French aid to Morocco was suspended. However, France agreed to give Morocco aid totalling 200 million French francs for 1974 when Morocco consented to transfer proceeds from the sale of the 1972–73 season crops of the expropriated farms to the former owners.

Cereals are grown on more than 80 per cent of cultivated land and this is being increased as part of attempts to offset falling production, while the Government has also called for a major effort to increase yield. The Government has pressed strongly for increases in sugar beet production, and by 1965 sugar beet was being grown on over 11,500 hectares. In 1973 the sugar beet crop came to 1,293,000 tons, producing 226,000 tons of refined sugar, 70 per cent of total domestic demand. Market gardening, especially in irrigated areas yields more income per unit of land than most other crops. Output of tomatoes and miscellaneous green vegetables is fairly constant, but potato output fluctuates widely from one year to another. A year of weak prices can be disastrous for small market gardeners, who are nevertheless unwilling to submit to output controls. Output of pulses especially broad beans and chick peas has expanded fairly steadily. In 1971 42,000 tons of dry peas were produced, 190,000 tons of broad beans, 100,000 tons of chick peas and 22,000 tons of lentils. Production of olive oil came to only 28,000 tons in the 1973–74 season, a drop of 7,000 tons on the production of the previous year.

A total sum of £63 million was allocated to dams and irrigation networks under the five-year plan (1968–72) with a view to increasing the irrigated area by 158,000 hectares. The first of a series of six dams to be built during the plan period was completed in November 1970. The dam, located at Ait Aidel on the River Tersaout, will increase the irrigated area in the Haouz plain from 3,000 to 30,000 hectares. A hydro-electric plant with a capacity of 60 million kWh. a year is also planned. In May 1972 the Mansour Eddahbi dam in southern Morocco was inaugurated and in April 1971 the Hassan Eddakhil Dam was finished, which should irrigate a total area of 40,000 hectares. By the end of the 1973–77 plan Morocco should have 671,000 hectares of land under irrigated cultivation and the ultimate aim is to raise this figure to one million hectares. A total of 23 dams have been, or are being, built for this purpose. In 1974 tenders were invited for construction of dams at Timinoutine, the Sidi Cheho dam over the Wadi Oir ar-Rbia and the Tleta dam south of Tangier. Irrigation projects benefiting from World Bank assistance include the $53.7 million expansion of the Gharb Sebou region and the Souss Valley project, for which a $14.5 million loan was approved in May 1975, and enlargement of the Dokkala irrigation canal is to receive a $4.8 million loan from the African Development Bank.

MINING AND INDUSTRY

The most important mineral deposits are phosphates —Morocco is the third most important producer and the largest exporter in the world—and they represent about 90 per cent of the value of total exports of minerals from Morocco. In addition, Morocco is the fourth largest world producer of cobalt. Morocco also possesses important deposits of lead, manganese and zinc and lesser resources of several other metals, including copper and tin.

The chief phosphate deposits are at Khouribga and Youssoufia and are controlled by the state *Office Chérifien des Phosphates* (OCP). National consumption of phosphates, however, is very small at the moment and is provided by a factory for super-phosphates and hyper-phosphates in the Safi complex near Casablanca, which produces about 100,000 tons a year. Exports account for the bulk of production and, as a result of major price rises, earnings reached 4,075 million dirhams in 1974, compared with 788.1 million dirhams in 1973 and 673.2 million dirhams in 1972. Surplus supply over demand had depressed prices for a number of years but, with rising demand, the price per ton increased from $14 to $42 in November 1973 and then by a further 50 per cent to $63 in July 1974. A further rise to $68 per ton was introduced in March 1975, with effect from the start of the year. In December 1974 a major agreement was signed with the Soviet Union for the exploitation of phosphate reserves at Meskalas which could be worth $5,000 million. The project involves the export to the Soviet Union of three to five million tons a year from 1980 to 1990 and up to 10 million tons beyond 1990, while total exports from these reserves may be even higher. A phosphoric acid plant being set up at Safi for Maroc Phosphore by Siemens of West Germany and Polimex of Poland was due to start operations before the end of 1975. A second complex is to be built at Safi, costing some $87.2 million, financed mainly by the World Bank ($50 million), West Germany ($29.2 million) and Morocco itself. Financial assistance is also expected from Kuwait and the United Arab Emirates for phosphate processing.

Most of the other mineral products have not fared as well as phosphates have since independence. Iron ore is mined in Ait Amar and Uixan. Production, 1,577,000 tons in 1960, was only 534,000 tons in 1974. The lack of a steel industry within the country has not encouraged high activity in this sector. Manganese is the chief dollar earner; 35 per cent of production is treated in the Sidi Marouf factory. Lead and zinc are often found together in deposits, e.g. at Boukber, Touissit, Aouli and Mikbladen. The output of zinc has dropped to 27,000 tons in 1974 from 101,000 tons in 1959. About 30 per cent of lead ore production is treated by the Oued al-Heimar lead foundry, and new discoveries made at Bediane have increased production to 142,000 tons in 1974 compared with just over 122,000 tons in 1971. Exports increased to 165 million dirhams in 1974 compared with 27.5 million dirhams in 1970. Cobalt is also produced at Bou Azzar and copper at Blida. A Moroccan-Japanese venture is to invest 70 million dirhams in exploiting the Blida copper deposits and production is expected to reach 225,000 tons of ore a year. The total value of mining exports was 4,513 million dirhams in 1974 compared with 1,041 million dirhams in 1973 and 877 million dirhams in 1972.

Morocco also has coal and small quantities of petroleum. The coal deposits are at Djerada south of Oujda and are controlled by the Government mining organization, BRPM. The theoretical production capacity of Djerada's anthracite mines is 600,000 tons per year and production increased to 574,000 tons in 1974. Big increases in oil prices in 1973 may mean that Morocco will rely more on domestic supplies of coal in preference to high-priced oil imports. In the past the coal industry had been affected by the concentration in electricity projects on hydro-electricity at the expense of thermal generation, although the Soviet Union agreed to build a 60 MW. anthracite-fired power station at Djerada to provide 1,150 million kilowatt hours by 1977 or 1978. The first stage of the project, producing 900 million kilowatt hours, was opened in June 1973. Thermal plants accounted for half of electricity production in 1953 but only for 10 per cent in 1965. Total production in 1972 came to just under 2,200 million kilowatt hours and in 1973 increased by about 11 per cent to 2,439 million kilowatt hours. Production and distribution are state-controlled through *Energie Electrique du Maroc*; the frequency is 50 cycles per second.

Oil price rises in 1973 and 1974 added new impetus to the Government's attempts to develop a domestic oil industry. Production in 1973 amounted to 42,000 tons but this fell to 24,000 tons in 1974. Unless new reserves are discovered, production will soon decline to nothing. Apart from small oil deposits, prospecting in the Doukkala, Draa and Tafaya regions has not produced any significant finds since 1962, when oil

was found at Sidi Rhalem in the Essaouira region. All Morocco's production is refined in the country at a topping unit built at Mohammedia by the Italian firm ENI. The refinery is now run by the Société Maroc-Italienne de Raffinage (SAMIR), of which the Moroccan Government took full control in August 1974. A great part of the refinery's need for crude oil is satisfied by imports and oil continues to be an expensive import item.

The Bureau of Mining Research and Participation (BRPM) is undertaking large-scale prospecting for hydro-carbons and other minerals both alone and in association with private partners. Esso Exploration Inc. started activity in 1967 on off-shore permits south of Agadir. Aquitaine, Burmah Oil, Shell and Exxon were all granted permits to explore for oil in 1972–73. It is hoped to sign further contracts for exploration along the Atlantic coast. Encouraging results have been found by Esso in the province of Tarfaya. In 1974 deposits of oil shale were discovered at Tamahdid in southern Morocco. The shale is estimated to contain between 8 and 10 per cent oil and could yield 5,000–7,000 million tons of oil, but it would be very expensive to exploit and would only be profitable if world oil prices increased to a very much higher level. Natural gas has also been discovered, in a wildcat drilling made near Rabat by BRPM. In early 1970 a team of Soviet technicians discovered a deposit of cobalt in the region of Ouarzazate. Two Japanese companies, Mitsui Metal and Mining and Nittetsu Mining, have agreed to form a consortium with the Moroccan Government and a French company (Omnium Nord Africain de France) to build a factory to process copper extracted from a mine 130 kilometres to the east at Casablanca. The factory will have a capacity to treat between 800 tons and 1,000 tons of ore per day and should have come into operation in mid-1972. The Japanese companies will import about half the factory's production.

Several projects are proceeding for the exploitation of deposits of copper ores, fluorine and silver, and notably the Upper Moulaya lead zinc mines to be opened up by Zellidja with the BRPM.

The mining industry has been placed on the list of industries which benefit under the new Investment Code introduced in July 1973 to promote private investments, and replacing the first decree published in December 1969. Another decree virtually abolished the export tax on minerals by lowering it from 5 per cent *ad valorem* to 0.5 per cent on iron, antimony, cobalt, manganese, barytine and fluorine ores, fullers earth, lead, zinc and silver metals. For lead, zinc and copper ores the tax is reduced on a variable scale related to world prices of these minerals.

Industry is perhaps the least stagnant sector of the economy and certainly promises the highest rate of growth in the immediate future. The growth of manufacturing in Morocco (5 per cent a year on average during 1960–68) has been directed largely towards the light industries. Although the majority of the population has very little purchasing power, there is nevertheless a fairly large market for many consumer goods among the two to three million people who are better off. Encouraged by government promotion, many new enterprises have been established to produce goods that formerly had to be imported. An export-orientated industry has also emerged during the past few years, particularly in the field of food-processing. This consists mainly of fruit juice plants and canneries (fish and vegetables) as well as the edible oil industry. Of special importance for the domestic market are the flour-milling, sugar refining and tobacco processing industries. Next to the food industries in importance are the textile and leather industries. A metal products industry is also well established, while in the chemical sector the most significant plants are a crude oil refinery and the Safi plant which processes Morocco's most important mineral, phosphate. There are plans to build two sulphuric acid units at Safi.

Several foreign companies contribute to the country's manufacturing capacity; for example, the General Tire and Rubber Co. of Morocco and the *Société Marocaine de Constructions Automobiles*. A new $17 million tyre plant has been completed by Goodyear near Casablanca. The Safi chemical complex helps to supply the country's great need for agricultural fertilizers. A 14 million dirham chemical plant built by the West German Hoechst concern was opened in Casablanca in May 1972 to produce plastics, medicines and other chemical goods. Morocco has its own car assembly company, which increased its output of cars by 17 per cent in 1973 to 20,769. Berliet is to build a plant to produce vehicle spare parts and accessories, and Motor Iberica is interested in setting up a lorry-assembly plant.

Morocco is at present heavily dependent on imported textiles but considerable investment (some of it from the World Bank) has been made in increasing the capacity of the local industry, especially in cotton cloth. Industrialization plans for the future include projects for the manufacture of vegetable oil, PVC, iron and steel, artificial fibres and fertilizer. Increased demand for fertilizers will justify the installation of a second chemical plant for the processing of ammonium phosphate. Particularly worthy of note is Morocco's long-term sugar plan which is designed to promote national sugar production in such a way as to bring about a steady reduction in imports. According to the plan, an integrated sugar industry will be formed, through the addition of sugar work to the existing refineries and through the development of sugar crops, notably beet, which is already being grown successfully in some parts of the country. There are at present seven sugar mills with several more planned, including the 35 million dirham Suncas refinery, and Morocco hopes eventually to become self-sufficient in sugar.

About half of the industrial labour force is concentrated in Casablanca. There is substantial unemployment and after the last shipments of agricultural exports this is swelled by the seasonal laying off of workers (packers, etc.). The 1971 census revealed that 8.6 per cent of the total labour force was unemployed. Many workers emigrate for lack of employment opportunities and recently the pace of this emigration

has stepped up, mostly to France. The remittance of these workers' wages helps to strengthen the balance of payments. Fez and Marrakesh contain most of the artisans.

The conditions under which Morocco's industrial development surged forward since 1945 explain to some extent the present structure of industry. Some sections such as fish canning and edible oils and fats are over-equipped, while others are under-equipped. The textile industry, for instance, meets only about 35 per cent of local demand. Often the equipment is not fully integrated or balanced; for example, textiles have had an imbalance between spinning and weaving capacity. Recent trends indicate that many of these problems are being faced. The latest modern equipment is being installed to improve quality and increase profits.

"Moroccanization" of the country's business is taking place gradually. In April 1971 King Hassan II outlined that several hundred enterprises owned by foreigners in Morocco would gradually be transferred to Moroccan control. The King has taken particular care to point out that Moroccanization does not mean nationalization. Instead he sees it as the negotiated transfer of private enterprises from foreign to Moroccan hands with adequate immunities paid. In March 1973 King Hassan indicated that the pace of Moroccanization was to be accelerated. In April the details were published of the requirements for a "Moroccan" company: the chairman, the managing director, a majority of the board and at least half of the shareholders must be Moroccan. Under a timetable published in May 1973 wholesale and retail businesses, import agencies and industrial concerns had to be Moroccanized by April 30th, 1974, and the banking and insurance sectors would be taken over within the following year. Ten of the foreign banks in Morocco anticipated the move by taking in Moroccan shareholders, two of them majority holdings. The deadline for completion of the first stage was later put back to December 1974.

TRADE AND PAYMENTS

Morocco runs a deficit in her trade with other countries. Chief exports are agricultural goods and minerals. Agricultural production is extremely sensitive to changes in the weather, and a bad year will have considerable adverse affect on the balance of trade. Mineral exports too are subject to fluctuation with changes in world demand. The sharp rises in mineral prices in 1973–74 helped boost the value of Morocco's mineral exports, particularly phosphates. Morocco is the world's biggest exporter of phosphates and with production increasing Morocco's balance of trade in 1974 showed some improvement over previous years, despite a big increase in the value of imports caused by rises in the price of manufactured goods and fuels, and by the need to import large quantities of foodstuffs. France still remains by far the largest customer and supplier. Other major trading partners include Federal Germany, the U.S.A. and Italy.

The slight fall in the trade deficit from 938 million dirhams in 1973 to 852 million dirhams in 1974 was almost entirely due to the rise in exports of phosphates from 788 million dirhams to 4,075 million dirhams. The Moroccan Government had expected the increase in the value of phosphate exports to produce a trade surplus, but imports also rose steeply in value, most notably foodstuffs from 1,078 million dirhams to 1,834 million dirhams, crude petroleum from 226 million dirhams to 990 million dirhams and industrial equipment from 799 million dirhams to 1,337 million dirhams. Still, the proportion of imports covered by exports rose to 90 per cent in 1974 compared with 83 per cent in 1972. The total value of imports grew from 4,684 million dirhams in 1973 to 8,292 million dirhams in 1974, while exports increased from 3,746 million dirhams to 7,440 million dirhams.

In 1969 Morocco concluded a treaty of association with the European Economic Community which provided for duty-free entry into the EEC of Moroccan goods. Restrictions were lowered on Moroccan exports of certain food products including citrus fruits, olive oil and fish. In return Morocco reduced duties on manufactured goods from the EEC. Tomatoes, wine and some preserved foods were excluded from the agreement. In February 1973 Morocco conducted an agreement amending its treaty with the EEC to take into account the entry into the Community of Britain, Denmark and Ireland. The enlarged EEC accounts for over half Morocco's imports and exports. Morocco's treaty with the EEC was due to expire in March 1974 but negotiation of a new agreement was delayed by internal problems in the EEC and delays in formulating a new approach by the enlarged EEC on links with associated countries. When negotiations began, it was in the context of a global Mediterranean policy decided by the EEC and involving initially six Mediterranean countries, including Morocco's Maghreb neighbours. Morocco's own negotiations became deadlocked towards the end of 1974 over Morocco's demand for further concessions for its citrus fruits and the right to conclude a separate trade agreement with France. Discussions on ways to ease the deadlock early in 1975 apparently met with little success.

More and more state control has been introduced into the export trade. The export of phosphates is controlled by the *Office Chérifien des Phosphates*, and the export of citrus fruit, other agricultural products, fish products and handicraft goods by the *Office Chérifien de Contrôle d'Exportation*.

TRANSPORT AND COMMUNICATIONS

The road network of Morocco is well developed, incorporating 25,414 kilometres of routes (86.3 per cent paved) at the end of 1973. Most of Morocco's roads are built to design standards well in advance of the traffic which they are currently carrying. Many of these were built by the French army, primarily for strategic purposes. In 1972, there were over 358,000 vehicles in Morocco. The tonnage transported on Moroccan roads in 1973 was 8.2 million tons. In October 1970 an agreement was concluded between the French Renault company and the Moroccan Government on the establishment of an assembly factory near Casablanca. A similar agreement was signed with the French Peugeot company in the same month. These decisions are the result of the growing demand for private and commercial vehicles in Morocco.

The *Société Marocaine de Construction Automobile* (Somaca) assembles Renault, Simca, Fiat, Opel and Chrysler vehicles and production is currently running at about 20,000 vehicles a year. Volvo lorries are also assembled in Morocco, and some are exported to China.

The country's railway network is good, there being 1,778 km. of track, 708 km. of which are electrified. Traction is by electric or diesel locomotives. Casablanca is connected by a track that continues through Algeria to Tunis. The only line that shows a profit, however, is the western network of the *Office Nationale des Chemins de Fer du Maroc* (ONCFM), which stretches from Sidi Kacem to Casablanca, Marrakesh and Safi. This is almost entirely on account of the large shipments of minerals, particularly phosphates.

Morocco currently has thirty commercial airfields, of which nine are open to international traffic, the most important being Tanger-Boakhalf, Casablanca-Nouaceur and Rabat-Salé. Substantial runway and terminal improvements are being carried out at major airfields to encourage the tourist industry. Moroccan air transport is now mainly provided by Royal Air Maroc, which is an autonomous corporation in which the Moroccan State has a 67.7 per cent share and Air France 17.53 per cent, the remainder being held either by private transportation companies or by individuals. The number of passengers carried has shown a steady upward trend, numbering 1,512,194 in 1974 compared with only 437,000 in 1967. A second air company, Royal Air-Inter, which serves only Morocco's internal lines, hitherto largely covered by Air France, came into operation in April 1970. Royal Air Maroc has an 80 per cent holding in the company.

On its 2,000 km. of coastline, Morocco has a dozen ports of greatly varying importance. The coast is generally not very favourable for port installations since it is particularly rocky and the Atlantic swell is one of the strongest in the world. In 1973, the ports handled over 25 million tons of cargo. Of this total over 70 per cent went through Casablanca and about 15 per cent through Safi. The volume of cargo shipped has increased steadily in recent years (although with considerable variations between the different ports). Morocco has two major phosphate ports, Casablanca and Safi. Mohammedia is the principal petroleum port at present, but Safi is being developed to take large tankers. Maritime passenger traffic is concentrated at Tangier and Casablanca, with most at the former being based on the ferry service across the Straits of Gibraltar, and most at the latter on cruise visitors on relatively short stays.

FINANCE AND FOREIGN AID

Morocco's budget has been substantially raised as a result of higher income from phosphates, although it continues to be run at a deficit and the need for foreign aid remains. Expenditure was projected to rise by 88.5 per cent from 9,480 million dirhams in 1974 to 18,564 million dirhams in 1975, and revenues from 8,640 million dirhams to 15,958 million dirhams. During 1974 the surplus on the balance of payments current account more than doubled from 431.4 million dirhams to 1,035.1 million dirhams, capital income rose from 506.9 million dirhams in 1973 to 1,145.5 million dirhams in 1974, while capital expenditure in 1974 rose to 1,643.8 million dirhams. Foreign debt repayment in 1973 amounted to 295.4 million dirhams.

The improvement in the payments situation is reflected in the provision of two foreign loans by Morocco in the first half of 1975, one of $15 million for Mauritania and another of $28 million for Gabon. Morocco continues, however, to receive substantial foreign assistance, though this dropped from 582.4 million dirhams in 1972 to 448.5 million dirhams in 1973, provided mainly by the World Bank and the United States. The World Bank agreed to loans totalling some 161 million dirhams during 1974 and $62.5 million during the first half of 1975. Increasing financial aid is coming from Middle East oil-producing states, including Saudi Arabia, which agreed in principle to provide $50 million for development projects, and Iran, which pledged some $30 million,

mainly for agriculture. Other financial assistance was pledged by the Kuwait Fund for Arab Economic Development (for the development of phosphates) and by Abu Dhabi and the African Development Bank.

DEVELOPMENT

The growth in income has also led to substantial increases in investment allocations under the 1973–77 development plans. Total investment is expected to rise by 50 per cent to 39,770 million dirhams compared with the previous figure of 26,300 million dirhams. It was not immediately clear what effect this was expected to have on growth targets which originally included an overall annual growth rate of 7.5 per cent with 3.6 per cent for the primary sector, 11 per cent for the secondary sector and 6.9 per cent for services. King Hassan announced in January 1975 that the increases would be concentrated mainly on irrigation, mineral prospecting, industry and vocational training. Under the original plan some 37.2 per cent of investment was allocated for industry, 15.8 per cent for agriculture, 23.6 per cent for social and cultural affairs and 8.6 per cent for infrastructure.

STATISTICAL SURVEY
AREA AND POPULATION

Area (sq. km.)	Population (Census of July 20th, 1971)		
	Total	Moroccans	Aliens
458,730	15,379,259	15,267,000	112,000

Estimated Population: 16,880,000 (July 1st, 1974).

ADMINISTRATIVE DISTRICTS
(1973 estimates)

	Area (sq. km.)	Population	Density (per sq. km.)
Provinces:			
Agadir	53,000	1,220,600	23.0
Al-Hocima . . .	3,555	257,000	72.3
Beni Mellal . . .	14,100	695,300	49.3
El Jadida . . .	6,000	618,000	103.0
Fes	17,940	1,137,800	63.4
Kénitra . . .	19,820	1,415,600	71.4
Khouribga . . .	4,250	350,900	82.6
Ksar-es-Souk . .	100,000	491,000	4.9
Marrakech . . .	27,850	1,642,300	58.9
Meknès . . .	13,500	806,300	59.7
Nador . . .	6,130	501,300	81.8
Ouarzazate . . .	55,700	542,400	9.7
Oujda . . .	42,400	679,400	16.0
Safi . . .	13,620	942,600	69.2
Settat . . .	12,100	701,600	57.9
Tanger . . .	365	236,300	647.4
Tarfaya . . .	34,150	25,600	0.8
Taza . . .	22,460	604,000	26.9
Tétouan . . .	10,060	844,000	83.9
Prefectures:			
Casablanca . . .	1,200	1,894,400	1,578.7
Rabat-Salé . . .	530	702,600	1,325.7
Total . .	458,730	16,309,000	35.5

AGRICULTURE

('ooo metric tons)

	1970–71	1971–72	1972–73
Wheat	2,188	2,162	1,574
Barley	2,572	2,466	1,255
Maize	390	368	217
Olives	195	250*	330*
Dates	90	92*	92*
Pulses	354	414	353
Tomatoes	460*	460*	460*
Potatoes	226	226*	226*
Citrus Fruit . . .	832	852	943
Sugar Beet . . .	1,584	1,677	1,293
Cotton	19	27	27
Grapes	276	264	300*

* FAO estimate.

LIVESTOCK

('ooo-FAO estimates)

	1970–71	1971–72	1972–73
Cattle	3,630	3,640	3,700
Sheep	16,300	16,300	16,500
Goats	8,550	8,870	8,900
Camels	230	233	233
Horses	400	420	420
Asses	940	950	950

Source: FAO *Production Yearbook 1973*

FISHING

(metric tons)

	1971	1972	1973	1974
Total Catch . . .	223,932	243,068	402,852	281,039
of which:				
Sardines . . .	183,053	185,025	345,558	n.a.

MINING

('ooo metric tons)

	1972	1973	1974
Phosphates . . .	15,105	17,077	19,749
Iron Ore	234	375	534
Coal	547	565	574
Manganese . . .	96	146	175
Lead	146	159	142
Petroleum . . .	28	42	24
Zinc	36	33	27
Cobalt	11	10	13

INDUSTRY*

	UNIT	1970	1971	1972	1973
Cement	'ooo metric tons	1,165	1,481	1,541	1,619
Processed Lead . . .	,, ,, ,,	27	20	18	n.a.
Refined Sugar . .	,, ,, ,,	399	424	458	n.a.
Soap	metric tons	28,771	22,515	29,646	n.a.
Paint	,, ,,	11,219	12,194	11,843	n.a.
Textiles . . .	,, ,,	40,446	39,369	40,915	n.a.
Electricity . . .	million kWh.	1,830	1,962	2,196	2,439
Cars† . . .	number	20,009	19,078	17,781	20,769
Tyres	,,	411,000	410,000	378,000	n.a.
Shoes	'ooo pairs	4,494	4,721	4,725	n.a.
Flour . . .	metric tons	818,000	817,000	n.a.	n.a.
Refined Petroleum . .	'ooo metric tons	1,506	1,473	1,917	n.a.
Superphosphate . .	,, ,, ,,	180	264	342	n.a.
Carpets . . .	number	n.a.	n.a.	202,000	249,000
Wine	'ooo hl.	1,253	1,150	1,146	1,200
Olive oil . . .	metric tons	26,000	34,800	39,000	51,000
Fertilizers . . .	,, ,,	111,900	164,399	166,070	n.a.

* Major industrial establishments only. † Assembly only.

1974 Production: Electricity: 2,602 million kWh; cement: 1,747,000 metric tons.

FINANCE

100 Moroccan francs (centimes) = 1 Moroccan dirham.

Coins: 1, 2, 5, 10, 20 and 50 francs; 1 dirham.

Notes: 5, 10, 50 and 100 dirhams.

Exchange rates (July 1975): £1 sterling = 8.25 dirhams; U.S. $1 = 3.77 dirhams.

100 Moroccan dirhams = £12.12 = $26.53.

Note: The dirham was introduced in October 1959, replacing the Moroccan franc at the rate of 1 dirham = 100 francs. At the same time the currency was devalued, with the former exchange rate (U.S. $1 = 420 Moroccan francs) being replaced by a new rate of $1 = 5.0605 dirhams (1 dirham = 19.761 U.S. cents), which remained in operation until August 1971. From December 1971 to February 1973 the official exchange rate was $1 = 4.661 dirhams (1 dirham = 21.455 U.S. cents). A new par value of $1 = 4.195 dirhams (1 dirham = 23.84 U.S. cents) was established in February 1973, although the market rate fluctuates widely above and below this value. The par value was used for calculating the value of foreign trade transactions until the end of 1974. In terms of sterling, the exchange rate between November 1967 and June 1972 was £1 = 12.145 dirhams.

BUDGET ESTIMATES

(million dirhams)

	1972	1973	1974
Revenue . .	5,799	6,175	7,273
Expenditure . .	6,197	6,632	8,159

FIVE-YEAR DEVELOPMENT PLAN, 1973–77

INVESTMENT (million dirhams)*

Agriculture	4,158
Industry	9,777
Infrastructure	2,254
Teaching and Training of Cadres . .	1,637
Social and Cultural Equipment . .	6,193
General Administration . . .	1,174
Regional Development	1,100
TOTAL	26,293

* These figures are the original estimates for the plan. Revised estimates suggest a final total investment of 39,770 million dirhams.

Currency in Circulation (million dirhams at December 31st): 2,944 in 1972; 3,411 in 1973; 4,063 in 1974.

BALANCE OF PAYMENTS—ALL FOREIGN COUNTRIES
(million dirhams)

	1973			1974		
	Credit	Debit	Balance	Credit	Debit	Balance
Goods and Services:						
Merchandise f.o.b.	3,739.8	4,240.6	−500.8	7,397.4	7,933.2	64.2
Gold for Industry	—	4.5	− 4.5	—	0.3	− 0.3
Transport and Insurance . . .	295.4	581.5	−286.1	483.1	1,127.8	−644.5
Travel	1,005.2	377.2	628.0	1,025.0	395.0	630.0
Income from Investments . . .	58.4	334.3	−275.9	116.9	338.9	−222.0
Government Transactions . . .	202.7	345.5	−142.8	214.9	449.7	−234.8
Other services	98.6	118.0	− 19.4	122.1	149.8	− 27.7
Transfer Payments . . .	1,374.1	341.2	1,032.9	1,934.4	464.0	1,470.4
TOTAL CURRENT ACCOUNT . . .	6,774.2	6,342.8	431.4	11,293.8	10,258.7	1,035.1
Capital and Monetary Gold:						
Public Sector:						
Commercial Credits	112.9	184.9	− 72.0	216.4	164.9	51.5
Foreign Exchange Loans . . .	191.8	92.0	99.8	391.1	153.4	237.7
Loans in Dirhams . . .	15.3	18.5	− 3.2	6.9	23.4	− 16.5
Others	15.4	30.4	− 15.0	35.5	20.3	15.2
Private Sector:						
Commercial Credits	38.8	183.0	−144.2	234.1	1,061.6	−827.5
Loans and Investments . . .	106.4	93.9	12.5	95.5	190.7	− 95.2
Others	26.3	192.3	−166.0	166.0	29.5	136.5
TOTAL CAPITAL ACCOUNT . . .	506.9	795.0	−288.1	1,145.5	1,643.8	−498.3
Special Drawing Rights . .	—	—	—	—	—	—
TOTAL	7,281.1	7,137.8	143.4	12,439.3	11,902.5	536.8

EXTERNAL TRADE
(million dirhams)

	1968	1969	1970	1971	1972	1973	1974
Imports .	2,790	2,844	3,471	3,532	3,577	4,684	8,292
Exports .	2,278	2,455	2,469	2,526	2,953	3,746	7,440

PRINCIPAL COMMODITIES
(million dirhams)

IMPORTS	1972	1973	1974
Food, drink and tobacco . . .	625	1,078	1,834
Wheat	137	483	708
Sugar	169	245	632
Tea	86	67	105
Dairy products	70	73	119
Energy and lubricants . . .	225	303	1,128
Crude petroleum . . .	172	226	990
Animal and vegetable products . .	410	551	1,005
Crude vegetable oils . . .	105	168	423
Timber	99	141	191
Minerals	58	67	130
Semi-finished products . . .	945	1,177	1,972
Iron and steel goods . . .	252	329	578
Chemical products . . .	120	146	247
Fertilizers	37	52	154
Plastics	69	91	145
Paper and cardboard . . .	53	69	130
Artificial fibre threads . .	105	133	160
Agricultural equipment . . .	40	51	88
Industrial equipment . . .	670	799	1,337
Machinery (non-electric) . .	402	503	801
Electrical machinery . . .	178	187	276
Consumer goods	561	652	799
Passenger cars and spares . .	172	200	253
TOTAL	3,577	4,684	8,292

PRINCIPAL COMMODITIES—[*continued*]

EXPORTS	1972	1973	1974
Food, drink and tobacco	1,384	1,827	1,647
Citrus fruit	429	494	388
Fresh tomatoes	179	229	183
Potatoes	47	56	82
Fresh vegetables	47	54	51
Pulses	138	181	158
Preserved vegetables	83	84	115
Preserved fruits and jam . . .	29	47	50
Wines, etc.	35	96	60
Preserved fish	134	190	244
Energy and lubricants . . .	6	20	52
Animal and vegetable products . .	259	296	376
Olive oil	111	101	147
Pulp for paper	20	33	68
Minerals	877	1,041	4,513
Phosphates	673	788	4,075
Lead ore	90	102	165
Semi-finished products . . .	188	238	374
Fertilizers	69	84	139
Agricultural equipment	3	10	2
Industrial equipment	27	43	45
Consumer goods	207	272	432
Carpets	59	81	89
Clothes	46	54	86
TOTAL	2,953	3,746	7,440

PRINCIPAL COUNTRIES
(million dirhams)

IMPORTS	1972	1973	1974
Algeria	89	109	254
Belgium/Luxembourg	82	129	224
Brazil	93	110	246
Dominican Republic	15	69	141
France	1,111	1,488	2,283
Germany, Federal Republic . . .	268	383	843
Iraq	1	9	259
Italy	200	216	352
Netherlands	111	150	224
Poland	50	46	127
Saudi Arabia	—	—	129
Spain	138	233	337
Sweden	111	114	165
U.S.S.R.	142	183	253
United Kingdom	160	158	227
U.S.A.	270	495	746

EXPORTS	1972	1973	1974
Algeria	98	119	182
Belgium/Luxembourg	121	157	444
Brazil	26	24	167
France	964	1,264	1,705
Germany, Federal Republic . . .	265	365	545
Italy	265	259	554
Japan	32	50	168
Mexico	17	21	148
Netherlands	110	157	236
Poland	66	75	377
Romania	7	36	211
Spain	164	181	411
U.S.S.R.	113	115	136
United Kingdom	136	176	443
Yugoslavia	50	81	247

TRANSPORT
RAILWAYS

	1972	1973	1974*
Passenger-kilometres (million) . . .	591	624	737
Freight ton-kilometres (million) . . .	3,062	3,308	3,315

* Provisional.

ROADS

	1971	1972
Tonnage Transported . .	5,843,000	4,798,000
Cars	242,036	260,411
Lorries and Vans . .	90,495	97,734
Motor Cycles . . .	14,857	15,024

SHIPPING

	Unit	1972	1973
Passenger arrivals .	number	524,167	550,963
Passenger departures .	,,	476,715	496,163
Freight loaded . .	'000 tons	16,367	19,327
Freight unloaded . .	,, ,,	4,871	6,066

CIVIL AVIATION

	1972	1973	1974
Passenger arrivals	654,419	735,222	738,390
Passenger departures . . .	690,586	785,138	773,804
Freight loaded and unloaded (metric tons)	14,462	18,403	19,157

TOURISM

Country of Origin	1971	1972	1973
Algeria . . .	66,632	91,578	105,258
Belgium . . .	21,775	25,906	36,827
Denmark . .	8,621	9,454	9,589
France . . .	188,175	210,625	265,570
Federal Germany .	70,702	95,272	90,299
Italy . . .	17,904	25,147	25,342
Spain . . .	42,789	76,107	175,346
Switzerland . .	12,591	19,091	24,518
United Kingdom .	80,882	107,733	134,614
U.S.A. . . .	136,677	194,071	185,835
Others . .	176,168	208,469	287,039
Total .	822,916	1,063,453	1,340,237
Cruise Passengers .	91,376	127,580	147,175
Grand Total .	914,292	1,191,033	1,487,412

Total tourist visits (1974): 1,338,024.
Hotel Capacity (1973): 37,611 beds.

EDUCATION

	Primary School Pupils	Secondary School Pupils	Students Engaged in Higher Education
1971–72 . .	1,232,936	313,424	15,148
1972–73 . .	1,275,857	334,952	22,382
1973–74 . .	1,337,931	361,725	25,525

Source (unless otherwise stated): Direction de la Statistique, Rabat.

THE CONSTITUTION

(Promulgated March 10th, 1972, after having been approved by national referendum.)*

Preamble: The Kingdom of Morocco, a sovereign Moslem State, shall be a part of the Great Maghreb. As an African State one of its aims shall be the realization of African unity. It will adhere to the principles, rights and obligations of those international organizations of which it is a member and will work for the preservation of peace and security in the world.

General Principles: Morocco shall be a constitutional, democratic and social monarchy. Sovereignty shall pertain to the nation and be exercised directly by means of the referendum and indirectly by the constitutional institutions. All Moroccans shall be equal before the law, and all adults shall enjoy equal political rights including the franchise. Freedoms of movement, opinion and speech and the right of assembly shall be guaranteed. Islam shall be the state religion.

The Monarchy: The Crown of Morocco and its attendant constitutional rights shall be hereditary in the line of H.M. King Hassan II, and shall be transmitted to the oldest son, unless during his lifetime the King has appointed as his successor another of his sons. The King is the symbol of unity, guarantees the continuity of the state, and safeguards respect for Islam and the Constitution. The King shall have the power to appoint and dismiss the Prime Minister and Cabinet Ministers and shall preside over the Cabinet. He shall promulgate legislation passed by parliament and have the power to dissolve the House of Representatives; is empowered to declare a state of emergency and to initiate revisions to the Constitution. The Sovereign is the Commander-in-Chief of the Armed Forces; makes appointments to civil and military posts; appoints Ambassadors; signs and ratifies treaties; presides over the Council for National Development Planning and the Supreme Judiciary Council; and exercises the right of pardon.

Parliament: Parliament shall consist of a single assembly, the House of Representatives, which shall comprise 240 members elected for a four-year term. Two thirds of the members shall be elected by direct universal suffrage, and one third by an electoral college composed of councillors in local government and employers' and employees' representatives. Parliament shall pass legislation, which may be initiated by its members or by the Prime Minister; authorize any declaration of war; and approve any extension beyond thirty days of a state of emergency.

Government: The Government shall be responsible to the King and the House of Representatives and shall ensure the execution of laws. The Prime Minister shall be empowered to initiate legislation and to exercise statutory powers except where these are reserved to the King. He shall put before parliament the Government's intended programme and shall be responsible for co-ordinating ministerial work.

Relations between the Authorities: The King may request further consideration of legislation by parliament before giving his assent; submit proposed legislation to a referendum by decree; and dissolve the House of Representatives if a Bill rejected by parliament is approved by referendum. He may also dissolve the House of Representatives by decree, but the succeeding House may not be dissolved within a year of its election. The House of Representatives may defeat the Government either by refusing a vote of confidence moved by the Prime Minister or by passing a censure motion; either eventuality shall involve the Government's collective resignation.

Judiciary: The Judiciary shall be independent. Judges shall be appointed on the recommendation of the Supreme Council of the Judiciary presided over by the King.

* For the most part the Constitution is unchanged from the one drawn up by King Hassan II and promulgated in 1962. This provided for two houses of parliament, one elected by universal suffrage and one by electoral colleges, and was superseded by that of June 1970, which introduced a unicameral parliament, of which one-quarter of the members were to be elected by universal suffrage, and increased the powers of the monarch.

THE GOVERNMENT

HEAD OF THE STATE

H.M. KING HASSAN II (*accession February 26th, 1961*).

CABINET

(*July* 1975)

Prime Minister: AHMED OSMAN.

Minister of State for Culture: Hadj M'HAMED BAHNINI.

Minister of State for Information: AHMED TAÏBI BENHIMA.

Minister of State for Foreign Affairs: Dr. AHMED LARAKI.

Minister of State for Co-operation and Professional Training: Dr. MOHAMED BENHIMA.

Minister of the Interior: MOHAMED HADDOU ECHIGUER.

Minister of Posts, Telegraphs and Telecommunications: Gen. DRISS BEN AOMAR EL ALAMI.

Minister of Administrative Affairs and Secretary-General of the Government: M'HAMED BENYAKHLEF.

Minister of Health: Dr. ABDERRAHMAN TOUHAMI.

Minister of Justice: ABBES KAISSI.

Minister of Waqfs and Islamic Affairs: DEY OULD SIDI BABA.

Minister of Finance: ABDELKADER BENSLIMANE.

Minister of Agriculture and Agrarian Reform: SALAH M'ZILI.

Minister of Tourism, Housing, Town Planning and the Environment: HASSAN ZEMOURI.

Minister of Trade, Industry, Mines and Merchant Shipping: ABDELLATIF GHISSASSI.

Minister of Public Works and Communications: AHMED TAZI.

Minister of Higher Education: ABDELLATIF BEN ABDEL-JALIL.

Minister of Primary and Secondary Education: MOHAMED BOUAMOUD.

Minister of Labour and Social Affairs: MOHAMED LARBI EL KHATTABI.

Secretaries of State: *Responsible to the Prime Minister:*
ABDALLAH GHARNIT, National Co-operation and Traditional Industry
ABDESLEM ZNINED, General Affairs

MOHAMED BELHAYAT, Economic Affairs
TAYEB BENCHEIK, Planning and Regional Development
MOHAMED TAHIRI JOTTI, Youth and Sports
Finance: KAMAL RAGHAYE
Trade, Industry, Mines and Merchant Shipping: MOUSSA SAADI
Housing, Tourism, Town Planning and the Environment: JALAL SAID
Interior: DRISS BASRI
Waqfs and Islamic Affairs: HASSAN LOUKACH
Foreign Affairs: AHMED CHERKAOUI

NATIONAL ASSEMBLY

Although the constitution of March 1972 provides for a new form of Assembly, a date has not yet been set for elections, and parliament remains dissolved.

POLITICAL PARTIES

Mouvement Populaire: Leader MAHJOUBI AHERDAN; had 60 seats in Chamber of Representatives.

Progrès Social: represents salaried workers' groups; 10 seats in former Chamber of Representatives.

Istiqlal: f. 1944; aims to raise living standards, to confer equal rights on all, stresses the Moroccan claim to Mauritania and the Spanish Sahara; 9 seats in former Chamber of Representatives; Sec.-Gen. M'HAMED BOUCETTA; publs. *Al Alam* (daily), and *L'Opinion* (daily).

Union National des Forces Populaires—UNFP: B.P. 747, Casablanca; f. 1959 by MEHDI BEN BARKA from a group within Istiqlal; left wing; opposition party; in July 1972 a split occurred between the Casablanca and Rabat sections of the party; Leader ABDULLAH IBRAHIM.

Union Socialiste des Forces Populaires—USFP: Rabat; f. 1974 by Rabat section of UNFP; left-wing opposition party; Leader ABDERRAHIM BOUABID.

Parti Démocratique Constitutionnel: Leader MOHAMMED HASSAN WAZZANI; 1 seat in former Chamber of Representatives.

Mouvement Populaire Constitutionnel et Démocratique—MPCD: breakaway party from *Mouvement Populaire*; Leader ABDELKRIM KHATIB.

Parti du Progres et du Socialisme—PPS: f. 1974; left-wing; advocates nationalization and democracy; Sec.-Gen. ALI YATA.

Parti Libéral Progressiste—PLP: Casablanca; f. 1974; advocates individual freedom and free enterprise; Leader AKNOUSH AHMADOU BELHAJ.

Parti de l'Action: Rabat; f. 1974; advocates democracy and progress; Sec.-Gen. ABDALLAH SENHAJI.

DIPLOMATIC REPRESENTATION

EMBASSIES ACCREDITED TO MOROCCO

(In Rabat unless otherwise stated)

Afghanistan: Cairo, Egypt.

Algeria: 46 blvd. Tariq Ibnou Ziad; *Ambassador:* NOUR-REDDINE DELLECI.

Argentina: 4 Avenue Moulay Hassan; *Ambassador:* EDUARDO HUGO FRANCISCO CRESPO.

Austria: 2 Rue de Tedders; *Ambassador:* JOHANNES WILLFORT.

Belgium: 6 Avenue de Marrakech; *Ambassador:* Baron ROLAND D'ANETHAN.

Brazil: 34 Zankat Al Ghazali (Orangers); *Ambassador:* EVERALDO DEYRELL DE LIMA.

Bulgaria: 32 Rue des Cadets de Saumur; *Ambassador:* DIMITAR SABEV.

Cameroon: Paris, France.

Canada: 13 bis Rue des Cadets de Saumur, Agdal; *Ambassador:* MARC BAUDOIN.

Chad: Cairo, Egypt.

Chile: Madrid, Spain.

China, People's Republic: 6 Rue Joachim du Bellay; *Ambassador:* SUNG HAN-YI.

Cuba: 18 Boulevard du Front d'Oued; *Ambassador:* JUAN ANTON Y GARCIA.

Czechoslovakia: 4 Abou Faris Al Marini; *Ambassador:* VÁCLAV JIZDNY.

Denmark: 4 Rue de Khemisset; *Ambassador:* ARNE BØGH-ANDERSEN.

Egypt: 31 Zankat El Jazair; *Ambassador:* EZZ-EL-DIN RAMZY.

Ethiopia: 6 Avenue Pasteur: *Chargé d'Affaires:* MOHAMED SALHI YASSIN.

Finland: Madrid, Spain.

France: Avenue Mohamed V; *Ambassador:* JEAN-BERNARD RAIMOND.

Gabon: 48 Avenue de France; *Ambassador:* JEAN ENCONE.

German Democratic Republic: 4 Avenue de Meknes; *Ambassador:* WILFRIED KITTLER.

Germany, Federal Republic: 7 Rue Mohamed El Fatih; *Ambassador:* HEINRICH HENDUS.

Greece: 9 Rue de Kairouan; *Ambassador:* A. PAPADOPOULOS.

Guatemala: Madrid, Spain.

Hungary: 12 Rue d'Agadir; *Ambassador:* LÁSZLÓ MOLNAR.

India: 10 Avenue de Champagne, Agdal; *Ambassador:* P. K. GUHA (also accred. to Tunisia).

Indonesia: Algiers, Algeria.

Iran: 7 Zankat Al Qassar; *Ambassador:* ABBAS NAYERI.

Iraq: 6 Avenue de la Victoire; *Ambassador:* HAMD DALLI AL-KARBOULI.

Ireland: Paris, France.

Italy: 2 Rue de Sebou; *Ambassador:* GIOVANNI LODOVICO BORROMEO.

Ivory Coast: 21 Rue de Tedders; *Ambassador:* AMADOU THIAM.

Japan: 22 Avenue Tarik Ibn Ziad; *Ambassador:* OSAMU KATAOKA.

Jordan: Route des Zaers, Souissi; *Ambassador:* HASHEM ABOU AMARA.

Korea, Republic: 23 Avenue de France, Agdal; *Ambassador:* WOONSANG CHOI.

Kuwait: 48 Avenue Pasteur: *Ambassador:* MUHALHEL MOHAMED AL-MUDHAF.

Lebanon: 5 Rue de Tedders; *Ambassador:* Dr. SAID AL-ASSAAD.

Libya: 1 Rue Lavoisier; *Ambassador:* ABDALLAH SHIBANI SWESI.

Malaysia: Angle Zankat Achafii et Zankat Hamzah, Agdal; *Chargé d'Affaires:* OMARDIN BIN ABDUL WAHAB.

Mauritania: 64 Zankat Oum Errabia; *Ambassador:* OULD CHEIKH TALEB BOUYA.

Mexico: Accra, Ghana.

Netherlands: 38 Rue de Tunis; *Ambassador:* JEAN STRENGERS.

Niger: Algiers, Algeria.

Nigeria: 77 Rue des Cadets de Saumur, Agdal; *Ambassador:* MUHAMMADU BAWA BULKACHUWA.

Norway: 20 Charia As-Saouira; *Ambassador:* OLAV IVAR LEIF PAUL MOLTKE-HANSEN (also accred. to Algeria).

Pakistan: 20 Avenue d'Alger; *Ambassador:* ANOUAR HUSSAIN HIDAYATULLAH.

Paraguay: Madrid, Spain.

Peru: Algiers, Algeria.

Poland: 25 Zankat Oqbah, Agdal; *Ambassador:* ZDZISŁAW PACHOWSKI.

Portugal: 45 Rue Maurice Pascouet; *Ambassador:* JOSÉ JOAQUIM DE MINAE MENDONQA.

Qatar: 21 Avenue de France; *Ambassador:* ABDALLAH YOUSSEF AL JIDA.

Romania: 10 Rue d'Ouezzane; *Ambassador:* Dr. OVIDIU CORNELIU POPESCU.

Saudi Arabia: 43 Place de l'Unité Africaine; *Ambassador:* FAKRI SHEIKH EL ARD.

Senegal: 11 Avenue de Marrakech; *Ambassador:* LAMINE DIAKHATE.

Sudan: 9 Rue de Tedders; *Ambassador:* RASHID NURELDDINE.

Sweden: 6 Rue d'Armagnac; *Ambassador:* AKE VALDEMAR SJOLIN.

Switzerland: Square Condo de Satriano; *Ambassador:* JEAN-JACQUES DE TRIBOLET-HARDY.

Syria: 27 Rue d'Oqbah, Agdal; *Ambassador:* GHALEB ABDOUN.

Tunisia: 6 Avenue de Fez; *Ambassador:* BECHIR MHEDHEBI.

Turkey: 19 Avenue de Meknes; *Ambassador:* HASAN ISTINYELI.

U.S.S.R.: 20 Avenue Annegai; *Ambassador:* DIMITRI GORUNOV.

United Arab Emirates: 8 Rue d'Ifrane; *Ambassador:* AHMED AL-TAJER.

United Kingdom: 28 bis Avenue Allal Bin Abdallah; *Ambassador:* JOHN DUNCAN, C.M.G.

U.S.A.: Avenue de Marrakech; *Ambassador:* ROBERT G. NEUMANN.

Venezuela: Tripoli, Libya.

Yugoslavia: 39 Avenue Mousser El Kadem; *Ambassador:* LJUPCO TAVCIOVSKI.

Zaire: 34 Avenue de la Victoire; *Ambassador:* CHARLES ATEMBINO TE BOMBO.

Zambia: Cairo, Egypt.

Morocco also has diplomatic relations with Albania, Costa Rica, Guinea-Bissau, Mongolia, Nepal, Oman and the Vatican City.

JUDICIAL SYSTEM

The **Supreme Court** (*Majlis el Aala*), created on September 27th, 1957, is responsible for the interpretation of the law and regulates the jurisprudence of the courts and tribunals of the Kingdom. The Supreme Court sits at Rabat and is divided into four Chambers:

    1 Civil Chamber (the First Chamber).
    1 Criminal Chamber.
    1 Administrative Chamber.
    1 Social Chamber.

First President and Attorney-General: BRAHIM KEDDARA.

There are 20 Counsellors and 4 General Advocates.

Three Courts of Appeal. The Fez Court covers all the former Southern Zone and comprises:

    8 Regional Tribunals.
    11 Sadad Tribunals and branch chambers.

The Court of Appeal at Marrakesh comprises:

    4 Regional Tribunals.
    7 Sadad Tribunals and branch chambers.

The Court of Appeal at Casablanca comprises:

    4 Regional Tribunals.
    9 Sadad Tribunals and branch chambers.

The **Sadad Tribunals** pass judgment, without possibility of appeal, in personal, civil and commercial cases involving up to 300 dirhams. These tribunals also pass judgment, subject to appeal before the Regional Tribunals, in the same cases up to 900 dirhams, in disputes related to the personal and successional statutes of Moroccan Muslims and Jews, and in penal cases involving misdemeanours or infringements of the law.

The **Regional Tribunals** deal with appeals against judgments made by the Sadad Tribunals; and pass judgment in the first and last resort in cases of personal property of 900 to 1,200 dirhams or property producing a yield of up to 80 dirhams. The Regional Tribunals also pass judgment, subject to appeal before the Court of Appeal, in actions brought against public administrations in administrative affairs, and in cases of minor offences in penal matters.

Labour Tribunals settle, by means of conciliation, disputes arising from rental contracts or services between employers and employees engaged in private industry. There are 14 labour tribunals in the Kingdom.

A special court was created in 1965 in Rabat to deal with corruption among public officials.

RELIGION

MUSLIMS

Most Moroccans are Muslims.

CHRISTIANS

There are about 400,000 Christians, mostly Roman Catholics.

Archbishop of Rabat: JEAN MARCEL CHABBERT, 1 rue de l'Evêché, B.P. 258, Rabat.

Archbishop of Tangier: CARLOS AMIGO VALLEJO; 55 S. Francisco, B.P. 2116, Tangier.

JEWS

There are between 60,000 and 80,000 Jews.

Grand Rabbi of Casablanca: 167 blvd. Ziraoui, Casablanca; CHALOM MESSAS, President of the Rabbinical Court of Casablanca, Palais de Justice, Place des Nations Unies.

THE PRESS

DAILIES
Casablanca

Al Bayane: 32 rue Ledru-Rollin, B.P. 152, Casablanca; Arabic and French; Dir. ALI YATA.

Maghreb Informations: 16 rue de Foucauld; f. 1966; organ of U.M.T.; suspended by government 1968–71, 1975–; Dir. BOUBKER MONKACHI.

Maroc Soir: 34 rue Mohammed Smiha; f. Nov. 1971 to replace *La Vigie Marocaine*, closed down by the Government; French; Dir. AHMED ALAOUI; circ. 30,000.

Le Matin: rue Mohammed Smiha; f. Nov. 1971 to replace *Le Petit Marocain*, closed down by the Government; French; Dir. AHMED ALAOUI; circ. 40,000.

Rabat

Al Alam (*The Flag*): ave. Allal Ben Abdullah 11; organ of the Istiqlal Party; f. 1946; Arabic; Dir. ABDELKRIM GHALLAB; circ. 30,000; also *Al Alam Book*.

Al Anba'a (*Information*): Zankat Al Medina, B.P. 65; Arabic; Dir. AHMED AL YAAKOUBI; circ. 15,000.

L'Opinion: ave Allal Ben Abdullah 11; f. 1965; Istiqlal party newspaper; French; Dir. ABDELHAFID KADIRI; circ. 60,000.

PERIODICALS
Casablanca

Annidal: 14 rue Dioina, Sidi Bousmara, Médina Kédima; weekly; Dir. BRAHIM AHMED NTIFI.

CAF Omnisports: ave. Jean Mermoz; twice monthly; French; Dir. MAX MICHEL.

Cedies Informations: blvd. Mohamed Abdou 23; weekly; French; Dir. ANDRE ROGALT.

Construire: 25 rue d'Azialal; weekly; French; Dir. BOUCHAIB TALAL.

Le Courrier Economique: 28 ave. de l'Armée Royale; weekly; French; Dir. MOHAMED TAHIRI.

Les Echos Africains: 27 ave. des F.A.R.; monthly; French; Dir. CHOUFANI AL FASSI.

L'Espoir: 167 ave. Hassan; twice monthly; French; Dir. IDRIS CHARAF.

Al-Ittihad ul Watani: 46 rue de la Garon; organ of UNFP; weekly; Arabic; Dir. AHMED SHAKUR.

Lamalif: 11 rue Mustapha al Maani; French; monthly; non-political features and cultural magazine; Dir. MOHAMED LAGHLAM.

Al Mabadie: rue Caporal Paul; monthly; Arabic; Dir. ABDESLAM BOURKIA.

Le Maroc Agricole: 10 ave. des F.A.R.; twice monthly; French; Dir. MOHAMED LAGHLAM.

Maroc Fruits: 44 rue Mohamed Smiha; weekly; French; Dir. AHMED BEN MANSOUR NEJJAI.

Maroc-Médical: Immeuble Liberté, 287 Bd. de la Liberté; f. 1920; French; monthly medical journal; Dir. Dr. J. CHENEBAULT.

Al Mouharir: 11 rue Soldat Roch; weekly; Arabic; organ of USFP; Dir. OMAR BENJELLOUN.

Nous les Bêtes: 42 ave. des F.A.R.; twice monthly; French; Dir. RAOUL FAYAUX.

La Quinzaine du Maroc: 8 rue Voltaire; twice monthly; French; Dir. GABRIEL GAUTHEY.

Revue Automobile Africaine: 38 blvd. de la Gironde; monthly; French; Dir. ROBERT PERRIER.

Revue Fiduciaire Marocaine: 81 rue Colbert; twice monthly; French; Dir. MAURICE BERNARD.

Réalités Magrebines: 69 rue Mohamed Smiha; monthly; French; Dir. MOHAMED MERGAOUI.

Revue Marocaine de Droit: 70 rue Allal ben Abdullah; monthly; Arabic; Dir. MEYLAN BENCHALEL.

Revue Mensuelle de la Chambre de Commerce et d'Industrie de Casablanca: B.P. 423; monthly; French; Dir. ABDELLAH SOUIRI.

Télé Sport: 8 rue Voltaire; weekly; French; Dir. GABRIEL GAUTHEY.

La Vie Economique: 5 boulevard Ben Yacine; f. 1921; French; weekly; Dir. FELIX GARAS.

La Vie Industrielle et Agricole: 142 blvd. Mohamed V; twice monthly; French; Dir. AHMED ZGHARI.

La Vie Touristique: 142 blvd. Mohamed V; weekly; French; Dir. AHMED ZGHARI.

Fez

Fes: rue Etats Unis; monthly; Arabic; Dir. MOHAMED SLAOUI.

Rabat

Al Aamak: 291 ave. Mohamed V; monthly; Arabic; Dir. EL WAKILI THAMI.

Achaab (*The People*): 2 rue Parmentier, B.P. 364; independent; twice weekly; Arabic; Founder and Editor M. MEKKI NACIRI; Dir. MUSTAPHA BELHAJ; circ. 25,000.

Achorta: B.P. 437; monthly; Arabic; Dir. Directeur de la Sûreté Nationale.

Al Aklam: B.P. 2229; monthly; Arabic; Dir. ABDERRAHMANE BEN AMAR.

Asdae: 10 rue Port Said; weekly; Arabic; Dir. HASSAN ARABI.

Attadamoun: 23 ave. Allal ben Abdellah; monthly; Arabic; Dir. ABDELMAJID SEMLALI EL HASANI.

Barid el Maghreb: 281 ave. Mohamed V; monthly; Arabic; Dir. MUSTAPHA ALAOUI.

Daouat Elhak: Ministry of Waqfs; monthly; Arabic; Dir. MOHAMED BEN ABDELLAH.

Al Iman: 11 rue Allal ben Abdellah; monthly; Arabic; Dir. BOUBKER AL KADIRI.

Al Irchad: Ministry of Waqfs; monthly; Arabic.

Al Kawalisse: 281 ave. Mohamed V; weekly; Arabic; Dir. MUSTAPHA ALAOUI.

Al Khansa: 154 ave. Souss Mohamedia; monthly; Arabic; Dir. ABOUZAL AICHA.

Al Maghreb al Arabi: Rue Moulay Abdelaziz; Arabic weekly; Dir. AMR ALOIQUOUTI.

La Vie Nouvelle: 8 Zankat al Amiral Khnata; weekly; French; Dir. ROGER CHATAIGNE.

Tangier

Actualités Touristiques: 80 rue de la Liberté; monthly; French; Dir. TAYEB ALAMI.

Hebdo: 8 calle de la Libertad; weekly; French; Dir. A. BENSLIMANE.

Le Journal de Tanger: 43 rue Shakespeare, B.P. 420; French, English and Spanish; weekly; Dir. AHMED BENCHEKROUNE.

Tanjah: 8 place de France, B.P. 1055; f. 1956; French and Arabic; weekly; Dir. MOHAMMED MEHDI ZAHDI.

NEWS AGENCIES

Maghreb Arabe Presse: 10 rue Al-Yamama, Rabat; f. 1959; Arabic, French and English; Government-owned; Casablanca, Tangier; Man. Dir. ABDULJALIL FENJIRO.

FOREIGN BUREAUX

AFP (*France*): place Mohammed V, B.P. 118, Rabat; f. 1920; French; Dir. FELIX NEGGAR; Sec. and Editor MANOUBI MEKNASSY.

ANSA (*Italy*): c/o "MAP", 10 rue Al-Yamama, Rabat; Chief (vacant).

Reuters: 7 rue de Baghdad, Rabat; *Representative:* STEPHEN HUGHES.

DPA, NCNA and Tass also have bureaux in Rabat.

PUBLISHERS

Dar El Kitab: Place de la Mosquée, B.P. 4018, Casablanca; philosophy, law, etc.; Arabic and French; Dir. BOUTALEB ABDELHAY.

Imprimerie Artistique: 31 avenue Es-Sellaoui, Fez.

Imprimerie de Fedala: rue Ibn Zaidoun, Mohammedia; f. 1949; all types of printing.

RADIO AND TELEVISION

Radiodiffusion Télévision Marocaine: 1 Zenkat Al Brihi, Rabat; government station; *Radio:* Network 1 in Arabic, Network 2 in French, Network 3 in Berber, Spanish and English; Foreign Service in Arabic, French and English; *Television:* began 1962; 60½ hours weekly; French and Arabic; carries commercial advertising; Dir.-Gen. ABDELLATIF KHALES; publ. *Sawt al Maghreb.*

Number of radios (1972): 2,000,000.

Number of televisions (1973): 319,278.

Voice of America Radio Station in Tangier: c/o U.S. Consulate General, Chemin des Amoureux, Tangier.

FINANCE

(amounts in dirhams unless otherwise indicated.)

BANKING

CENTRAL BANK

Banque du Maroc: 277 ave. Mohammed V, Rabat; f. 1959; cap. 20m.; dep. 486m. (Dec. 1971); Gov. Prince MOULAY HASSAN BEN MEHDI; Vice-Gov. AHMED BENNANI.

MOROCCAN BANKS

Algemene Bank Nederland (Maroc) S.A.: Place du 16 Novembre, Casablanca; branch in Tangier; f. 1948; wholly owned subsidiary of Algemene Bank Nederland N.V., Amsterdam, Netherlands; cap. 5m.; Man. B. HANSEN.

Banque Americano Franco-Suisse pour le Maroc: 26 ave. de l'Armée Royale, B.P. 972, Casablanca; f. 1951; affil. to Swiss Bank Corporation, Crédit Commercial de France and Continental Illinois National Bank & Trust Co. of Chicago; cap. 4.5m.; Man. ROLAND FREY.

Banque Commerciale du Maroc S.A.: 81 ave. de l'Armée Royale, Casablanca; f. 1911; affiliated to Crédit Industriel et Commercial, Paris, France; cap. 19m., dep. 865m. (Dec. 1974); Pres. R. BELIN; Gen. Man. A. ALAMI; 5 brs.

Banque Marocaine du Commerce Extérieur: 241 boulevard Mohammed V, Casablanca; f. 1959; took over Société de Banque du Maghreb, 1971, Banco Español en Marruecos, 1975; partly state-owned; cap. 20m., res. 29m. (Dec. 1972); Chair. and Chief Exec. HADJ ABDEL MAJID BENGELLOUN; Man. Dir. DRISS GUEDDARI; 50 brs. in Morocco, one in Paris, one in Tangiers Free Zone.

Banque Marocaine pour le Commerce et l'Industrie: 26 place Mohammed V, Casablanca, P.O.B. 573; f. 1964; cap. 12m., res. 19m. (Dec. 1972); Pres. HADJ AHMED BARGACH; Gen. Man. MOHAMED BENKIRANE; 23 brs.

Banque A Mas: 51 ave. Hassan-Seghir, Casablanca.

Banque Nationale pour le Développement Economique: B.P. 407, place des Alaouites, Rabat; f. 1959; cap. p.u. 3.2m.; Pres. and Gen. Man. MUSTAPHA FARES; publ. *Rapport annuel.*

British Bank of the Middle East (Morocco): 80 ave. Lalla Yacout, P.O.B. 880, Casablanca; f. 1948; 3 brs. in Casablanca, one in Tangier; Chair. C. E. LOOMBE, C.M.G.

Compagnie Marocaine de Crédit et de Banque S.A.: 1 ave. Hassan II, Casablanca; f. 1964; affiliated to Compagnie Française de Crédit et de Banque, Paris, France; cap. 14.5m., res. 5.4m.; Pres. ALI KETTANI; 46 brs.

Crédit du Maroc S.A.: B.P. 579, 48–58 blvd. Mohammed V, Casablanca; f. 1963; cap. 8m., res. 15m. (Dec. 1971); Pres. M. KARIM-LAMRANI; Dir.-Gen. JAWAD BEN BRAHIM.

Société Générale Marocaine de Banques: 84 blvd. Mohammed V, B.P. 90, Casablanca; f. 1962; cap. 11m., res. 7m. (Dec. 1971); Chair. HAMED BARGACH; Man. Dir. YVES BONDIL; 18 brs.

Société Marocaine de Dépôt et Crédit: 79 ave. Hassan II, Casablanca; Pres. ABDELKADER BENSALEM.

Unión Bancaria Hispano Marroquí: 69 rue du Prince Moulay Abdullah, Casablanca; f. 1958; cap. 16m., dep. 229m. (Dec. 1971); Pres. ANTONIO SAEZ DE MONTAGUT; Gen. Man. PEDRO LANDRA VELON; 15 brs.

FOREIGN BANKS

Arab Bank Limited: Amman, Jordan; Casablanca and Rabat.

Several Spanish banks have branches in Ceuta.

BANK ORGANIZATIONS

Groupement Professionnel des Banques du Maroc: 27 ave. Hassan II, B.P. 577, Casablanca; f. 1967; groups all commercial banks for organization, studies, inquiries of general interest, and connection with official authorities; Pres. Hadj ABDELMAJID BENGELLOUN.

Association Professionelle des Intermédiaires de Bourse: 27 ave Hassan II, B.P. 577, Casablanca; f. 1970; groups all banks and brokers in the stock exchange of Casablanca, for organization, studies, inquiries of general interest and connection with official authorities; Pres. Hadj ABDELMAJID BENGELLOUN.

STOCK EXCHANGE

Bourse des Valeurs de Casablanca: Chamber of Commerce Building, 98 boulevard Mohammed V, Casablanca; f. 1929; Dir. ABDERRAZAK LARAQUI; publ. *Bulletin de la Cote.*

INSURANCE

Atlanta: 243 blvd. Mohammed V, Casablanca; f. 1947; Dir. M. POIRRIER.

Cie. Africaine d'Assurances: 123 blvd. Rahal el Meskini, Casablanca; Dir. M. ROUTHIER.

Cie. Nordafricaine et Intercontinentale d'Assurances (C.N.I.A.): 157 ave. Hassan II, Casablanca; cap. 1.8m.; Pres. ABDELKAMEL RERHRHAYE.

Cia. Marroqui de Seguros: 62 rue de la Liberté, Tangier; Dir. M. BUISAN.

COMAR Paternelle-Prévoyance: 42 avenue de l'Armée Royale, Casablanca; cap. 3.1m.; Gen. Man. BERNARD PAGEZY.

L'Empire: 45 rue du Cdt. Lamy, Casablanca; Dir. M. LÓPEZ.

L'Entente: 2 rue Mohammed Smiha, Casablanca; f. 1960; Pres. ABDELKADER BEN SALAH; Dir.-Gen. CHRISTIAN FAUCON.

Mutuelle Agricole Marocaine d'Assurances: 14 rue Abou Faras El Marini, Rabat; Dir. Gen. YACOUBI SOUSSANE.

La Providence Marocaine: 1 rond-point St. Exupéry, Casablanca; Dir. M. DE ROQUEFEUIL.

La Royale Marocaine d'Assurance: 67 ave. de l'Armée Royale, Casablanca; cap. 1.1m.; Dir.-Gen. MAHOMED BEN JILALI BENNANI.

Es Saada, Cie Générale d'Assurances et de Réassuranees: 123 ave. Hassan II, Casablanca; f. 1961; cap. 5m.; Dir.-Gen. PAUL-LOUIS CAMIZON.

Société Centrale de Réassurance: B.P. 183, ave. des Forces Armées Royales, Casablanca; f. 1961; Dir. MOHAMED AIMARAH.

Société Marocaine d'Assurances: 1 rond-point Saint Exupéry, Casablanca; Dir. M. GIUSTINIANI.

Société Nationale d'Assurances: B.P. 420, Casablanca.

***

Fédération Marocaine des Sociétés d'Assurances et de Réassurances: 300 rue Mustafa el Maani, Casablanca; f. 1958; Pres. M'HAMED BEN JILALI BENNANI; Dir. SEBTI ABDELHAQ.

TRADE AND INDUSTRY

CHAMBERS OF COMMERCE

British Chamber of Commerce for Morocco: 80 ave. Lalla Yacout, Casablanca; Chair. GRAHAM ACRES.

Chambre de Commerce et d'Industrie de Casablanca: 98 blvd. Mohammed V, B.P. 423, Casablanca; Pres. ABDELLAH SOUIRA.

Chambre Française de Commerce et d'Industrie du Maroc (CFCI): 15 avenue Mers Sultan, B.P 73, Casablanca; Pres. J. F. BRANDENBURG; Dir. PIERRE ROUSSELOT.

La Fédération des Chambres de Commerce et d'Industrie du Maroc: B.P. 218, 11 ave. Allal Ben Abdullah, Rabat; f. 1962; groups the 15 Chambers of Commerce and Industry; Pres. ABDELLAH SOUIRA; publ. *Revue Trimestrielle.*

DEVELOPMENT ORGANIZATIONS

Bureau de Recherches et de Participations Minières (BRPM): 27 Charii Moulay Hassan, B.P. 99, Rabat; f. 1928; a state agency to develop the mining industry Dir.-Gen. ABDERRAFIH GUESSOUS.

Caisse Marocaine des Marchés (*Marketing Fund*): Casablanca.

Caisse Nationale de Crédit Agricole (*Agricultural Credit Fund*): B.P. 49, Rabat.

Crédit Immobilier et Hôtelier: 159 ave. Hassan II, Casablanca; f. 1920; cap. 20m.; Dir. Gen. MOHAMED BENCHEKROUN.

Office National Interprofessionelle des Céréales et des Legumineuses: Rabat; Dir. MOHAMED BRICK.

Office de Commercialisation et d'Exportation (OCE): 45 ave. des F.A.R., Casablanca; f. 1965; turnover (1973/74) 1,400m. Dirhams; takes part in productivity planning, industrialization and overseas trade; Dir. CHAMI HASSAN.

Office du Développement Industriel (ODI): 8 rue Ghandi, Rabat; f. 1958; a state agency to develop industry; Dir.-Gen. ABDELAZIZ BENJELLOUN.

Société de Développement de l'Agriculture (SODEA): 14 Zankat Tangea, Rabat; state agricultural development organization.

Société de Gestion des Terres Agricoles (SOGETA): 11 rue de Salé, Rabat; oversees use of agricultural land.

PRINCIPAL STATE ENTERPRISES

Complexe Textile de Fes (COTEF): B.P. 267, Fez; f. 1967; 90 per cent state participation; started full activity in Jan. 1972.

Office Chérifien des Phosphates (OCP): 305 ave. Mohammed V, Rabat; f. 1921; a state company to produce and market rock phosphates and derivatives; Dir.-Gen. MOHAMMED KARIM LAMRANI.

Office National de l'Eau Potable (ONEP): 6 *bis* rue Patrice Lumumba, Rabat; responsible for drinking-water supply.

Office National de l'Electricité: B.P. 498, Casablanca; state electrical authority.

Office National des Pêches: 13/15 rue Chevalier Bayard, Casablanca; state fishing organization.

Société d'Exploitation du Fer du Rif (SEFERIF): B.P. 14, Nador; mines began production 1914, nationalized 1967; two mines produce iron ore for export and for the projected Nador iron and steel complex.

EMPLOYERS' ORGANIZATIONS

Association Marocaine des Industries Textiles: 58 rue Lugherim, Casablanca; f. 1958; mems. 300 textile factories; Pres. MOHAMED DRISSI; publ. *Bulletin* (weekly).

Association des Producteurs d'Agrumes du Maroc (ASPAM): 44 rue Mohamed Smiha, Casablanca; links Moroccan citrus growers; has its own processing plants.

Confédération Générale Economique Marocaine (C.G.E.M.): 23 blvd. Mohammed Abdouh, Casablanca; Pres. MOHAMED AMOR; Sec.-Gen. M. FAYÇAL CHRAÏBI.

Union Marocaine de l'Agriculture (U.M.A.): rue Ghandi Rabat; Pres. M. NEJJAI.

TRADE UNIONS

Union Générale des Travailleurs du Maroc (U.G.T.M.): 9 rue du Rif, angle Route de Médiouna, Casablanca; f. 1960; associated with Istiqlal; supported by unions not affiliated to U.M.T.; 400,000 mems.; Sec.-Gen. ABDERRAZZAQ AFILAL.

Union Marocaine du Travail (U.M.T.): Bourse du Travail, 222 avenue de l'Armée Royale, Casablanca; left wing and associated with UNFP; most unions are affiliated; 700,000 mems.; Sec. MAHJOUB BEN SEDDIQ; publs. *Maghreb Informations* (daily).

Union Syndicale Agricole (U.S.A.): agricultural section of U.M.T.

Syndicat National Libre: blvd. Hansali (prolongé), Casablanca; f. 1958; 69,000 mems.; Sec.-Gen. MEEKI IBRAHIMY.

TRADE FAIR

Foire Internationale de Casablanca: 11 rue Jules Mauran, Casablanca; international trade fair; alternate years usually for two weeks in April–May; the most recent fair was in 1975.

TRANSPORT

RAILWAYS

Railways cover 1,778 km. of which 161 km. are double track; 708 km. of lines are electrified and diesel locomotives are used on the rest. All services are nationalized.

Office National des Chemins de Fer du Maroc (ONCFM): 19 ave. Allal Ben Abdallah, Rabat; f. 1963; runs all Morocco's railways; Pres. AHMED TAZI; Dir. MOUSSA MOUSSAOUI.

ROADS

There are over 25,000 km. of roads. In 1973 there were 14 km. of modern motorway and 7,141 km. of main roads.

Compagnie Auxiliaire de Transports au Maroc (C.T.M.): 303 blvd. Brahim Roudani, Casablanca; Agencies in Tangier, Rabat, Meknès, Oujda, Marrakesh, Agadir, El Jadida, Safi, Essouira, Ksar-Es-Souk and Ouarzazate.

MOTORISTS' ORGANIZATIONS

The Royal Moroccan Automobile Club: place des Nations Unies, P.O.B. 94, Casablanca; f. 1913; 10,000 mems.; offices at Kenitra, Meknès, Fez, Oujda, Tangier, El Jadida, Safi, Marrakesh, Agadir, Taza, Khouribga, Youssoufia and Tétuan; Pres. MOHAMMED M'JID.

Touring Club du Maroc: 3 ave. de l'Armée Royale, Casablanca; 645 mems., 10,021 associate mems.; Pres. LARBI LAMRANI.

SHIPPING

The chief ports of Morocco are Casablanca, Tangier, Safi, Mohammedia, Kenitra and Agadir. In January 1962 the port of Tangier became an International Free Zone. Tangier is the principal port for passenger services. Casablanca is the principal freight port, handling 70 per cent of Morocco's trade. A new port is being built at Nador.

Agence Gibmar S.A.: 3 rue Henri Regnault, Tangier; also at Casablanca; regular sea services from Tangier to Gibraltar.

Compagnie Chérifienne d'Armement: 5 ave. de l'Armée Royale, Casablanca; f. 1929; Pres. BENNANI-SMIRES; regular lines to North France and Europe.

Compagnie Marocaine d'Agences Maritimes: 65 ave. de l'Armée Royale, B.P. 60, Casablanca.

Compagnie Marocaine de Navigation: 28 rue de Lille, Casablanca; f. 1946; Pres., Dir.-Gen. A. BOUAYAD.

Limadet-ferry: 3 rue Henri Regnault, Tangier; f. 1964; operates between Malaga and Algeciras and Tangier; Dir. AZIZ BOUZOUBAA.

Mafer: 3 rue Henri Regnault, Tangier; operates between Algeciras and Tangier.

Transmediterranea S.A., Cia: 39 rue du Mexique, Tangier, and at Casablanca; daily services Algeciras to Tangier.

Voyages Paquet: 65 ave. de l'Armée Royale Casablanca; 21 ave. d'Espagne, Tangier.

CIVIL AVIATION

There are international airports at Casablanca, Rabat, Tangier, Marrakesh and Agadir.

NATIONAL AIRLINES

Royal Air Maroc: Aéroport International Casablanca, Nouasseur; f. 1953; 67.7 per cent owned by the Government; domestic flights and services to Algeria, Austria, Belgium, Canada, France, Federal Germany, Italy, Mauritania, Netherlands, Senegal, Spain, Switzerland, Tunisia, United Kingdom and U.S.A.; fleet of three Boeing 727, four Caravelles; Chair. AHMED LASKY; Gen. Man. SAID BEN ALI.

Royal Air Inter: Aéroport Casablanca-Anfa; f. 1970; operates domestic services from Casablanca to Agadir, Al Hoceima, Fez, Ksar-es-Souk, Marrakesh, Ouarzazate, Oujda, Rabat, Tangier and Tetouan; foreign services to Oran, Malaga and Gibraltar; fleet of two F-27; Dir.-Gen. HASSAN YACOUB- SOUSSANE.

Casablanca is served by the following foreign airlines: Aeroflot, Air Afrique, Air Algérie, Air France, Air Mali, Balkan, British Caledonian, Iberia, KLM, Lufthansa, Pan American, Sabena, Saudia, Swissair and Tunis Air. In addition, ČSA fly to Rabat, British Airways to Marrakesh and Agadir, and Gibair to Tangier.

TOURISM

Office National Marocain de Tourisme: B.P. 19, 22 ave. d'Alger, Rabat; f. 1946; Dir. ABDELLATIF AMOR; publ. *Maroc-Tourisme* (quarterly).

CULTURAL ORGANIZATIONS

Direction des Affaires Culturelles: Ministry of Education and Fine Arts, Jardin de la Mamounia, Rabat; consists of three departments: Cultural Activities, Fine Arts and Folklore, Historical Monuments and Antiquities, which together administer all national cultural activities; Publs. *Bulletin d'Archéologie Marocaine, Etudes et Travaux d'Archéologie Marocaine.*

Association des Amateurs de la Musique Andalouse: Casablanca; directed and subsidized by the Ministry of Education and Fine Arts; Dir. Hadj DRISS BENJELLOUN.

PRINCIPAL THEATRES

Théâtre National Mohammed V: Rabat; Morocco's national theatre with its own troupe, subsidized by the state; Dir. M. A. SEGHROUCHNI.

Théâtre Municipal de Casablanca: blvd. de Paris, Casablanca; f. 1922, reorganized 1934 and 1949; presents a large number of foreign and national productions; maintained by the Casablanca Municipality; Dir. TAIB SADDIKI; Gen. Administrator ALI KADIRI.

PRINCIPAL ORCHESTRAS

Orchestre Symphonique du Conservatoire National de Musique: Rabat; European classical music and Andalusian (Arabic) music; chamber orchestra.

Orchestre du Conservatoire de Tétouan: Tetuan; specializes in Andalusian (Arabic) music; Dir. M. TEMSEMANI.

Orchestre du Conservatoire Dar Adyel: Fez; specializing in traditional music; Dir. Hadj ABDELKRIM RAIS.

FESTIVAL

Folklore Festival: Marrakesh; national festival of folk dancing; annually April–May; organized by the Ministry of Tourism under the direction of the Ministry of Education and Fine Arts.

DEFENCE

Defence Budget: (1974): 816 million dirhams.

Military Service: 18 months.

Total Armed Forces: 56,000: army 50,000; navy 2,000; air force 4,000. Paramilitary Forces: 23,000 (8,000 Gendarmerie, 15,000 Auxiliaries).

EDUCATION

Since Independence in 1956 Morocco has had to tackle a number of educational problems: a youthful and fast-growing population, an urgent need for skilled workers and executives, a great diversity of teaching methods between French, Spanish, Muslim and Moroccan Government schools, and, above all, a high degree of adult illiteracy. Morocco spends one-fifth of her national budget on education of which a considerable proportion is devoted to constructing buildings for higher studies and technical education. In many small towns and villages, local craftsmen have co-operated together in the building of elementary schools.

In 1973-74 there were 1,337,931 pupils in primary schools. At this level nearly 95 per cent of instruction is given in government schools, where syllabuses have been standardized since 1967. Great progress was made in providing new schools between 1957 and 1964, but since then the increase in the number of places has slowed down.

A decree of November 1963 made education compulsory for children between the ages of seven and thirteen, and this has now been applied in most urban areas, but throughout the country only 51 per cent of the age-group attended school in 1970–71. That year there were 5,034 government primary schools with 32,050 teachers, all Moroccan, trained in the 18 regional teacher training colleges. Instruction is given in Arabic for the first two years and in Arabic and French for the next three years, with English as the first additional language.

Secondary education lasts for three or four years, depending on the type of course, and in 1973–74 provided for 361,725 pupils. Approximately a quarter of these pupils attended technical schools, where reforms have taken place since 1970 to attract more pupils and to provide relevant training to meet the country's need for technical manpower. In 1971 there were 12,364 qualified teachers in secondary schools, of whom just under half were Moroccan and most of the rest French. Instruction is given mainly in French, but about a third of teachers use Arabic, and this trend is increasing.

Higher education has a long history in Morocco. The Islamic University of Al Qarawiyin at Fez celebrated its eleventh centenary in 1959-60. The Mohammed V University opened in Rabat in 1957 and now has over 20,000 students in four faculties. In addition there are institutes of higher education in business studies, agriculture, mining, law, and statistics and advanced economics, An African Centre for Research into Administrative Training for Development opened in Tangier in 1964 with financial backing from UNESCO and the UN Economic Commission for Africa.

Adult education is being tackled through the means of radio, simplified type, a special newspaper for the newly literate, and the co-operation of every teacher in the country. Another notable development in recent years has been the increasing attention given to education for girls. There are now a number of mixed and girls' schools, and the proportion is growing every year, especially in urban areas.

UNIVERSITIES

Al Quarawiyin University: 27 rue St. Pierre et Miquelon, Rabat; f. A.D. 859; 640 students.

Université Mohammed V: ave. Moulay Chérif, Rabat; f. 1957; 20,112 students.

BIBLIOGRAPHY

AMIN, SAMIR. The Maghreb in the Modern World (Penguin, Harmondsworth, 1971).

ASHFORD, D. E. Political Change in Morocco (Princeton U.P., 1961).
Perspectives of a Moroccan Nationalist (New York, 1964).

AYACHE, A. Le Maroc (Editions Sociales, Paris, 1956).

BARBOUR, NEVILL. Morocco (Thames and Hudson, London, 1964).

BELAL, ABDEL AZIZ. L'investissement au Maroc (1912–1964) et ses enseignements en matière de développement économique (Mouton, Paris, 1968).

BEN BARKA, MEHDI. Problèmes de l'édification du Maroc et du Maghreb (Plon, Paris, 1959).
Option Révolutionnaire en Maroc (Maspéro, Paris, 1966).

BENNETT, NORMAN ROBERT. A study guide for Morocco (Boston, 1970).

BERNARD, STÉPHANE. Le Conflit Franco-Marocain 1943–1956, 3 vols. (Brussels, 1963; English translation, Yale University Press, 1968).

BERQUE, JAQUES. Le Maghreb entre deux guerres (Eds. du Seuil, Paris, 1962).

BIDWELL, ROBIN. Morocco under Colonial Rule: French Administration of Tribal Areas 1912–56 (Frank Cass, London, 1973).

BOVILL, E. W. The Golden Trade of the Moors (London, 1958).

CLASEN, DIRK. Stauffacher-Reiseführer Marokko (Stauffacher Verlag, Zürich, 1964).

COHEN, M. I., and HAHN, LORNA. Morocco: Old Land, New Nation (Praeger, New York, 1964).

COULAU, JULIEN. La paysannerie marocaine (Paris, 1968).

HALL, L. J. The United States and Morocco, 1776–1956 (Scarecrow Press, Metuchen, N.J., 1971).

HALSTEAD, JOHN P. Rebirth of a Nation: the Origins and Rise of Moroccan Nationalism (Harvard University Press, 1967).

KININMONTH, C. The Travellers' Guide to Morocco (Jonathan Cape, London, 1972).

LACOUTURE, J. and S. Le Maroc à l'épreuve (du Seuil, Paris, 1958).

LANDAU, ROM. The Moroccan Drama 1900–1955 (Hale, London, 1956).
Morocco Independent under Mohammed V (Allen and Unwin, London, 1961).
Hassan II, King of Morocco (Allen and Unwin, London, 1962).
The Moroccans—Yesterday and Today (London, 1963).
Morocco (Allen & Unwin, London, 1967).

LANDAU, ROM and SWANN, WIM. Marokko (Cologne, 1970).

LE TOURNEAU, ROGER. Evolution politique de l'Afrique du Nord musulmane (Armand Colin, Paris, 1962).

MAXWELL, GAVIN. Lords of the Atlas (Longmans, London, 1966).

METCALF, JOHN. Morocco—an Economic Study (First National City Bank, New York, 1966).

PERROUX, F. and BARRE, R. Développement, croissance, progrès—Maroc-Tunisie (Paris, 1961).

ROBERT, J. La monarchie marocaine (Librairie générale de droit et de jurisprudence, Paris, 1963).

SPENCER, WILLIAM. The Land and People of Morocco (Lipincott, Pennsylvania, 1965).

STEWART, CHARLES F. The Economy of Morocco 1912-1962 (Oxford Univ. Press, 1965).

TERRASSE, H. Histoire du Maroc des origines à l'établissement du protectorat français, 2 vols. (Casablanca, 1949–50) (English trans. by H. Tee, London, 1952).

TIANO, ANDRÉ. La politique économique et financière du Maroc indépendant (Presses universitaires de France, Paris, 1963).

TROUT, FRANK E. Morocco's Saharan Frontiers (Geneva, 1969).

WATERSON, ALBERT. Planning in Morocco (Johns Hopkins, Baltimore, 1963).

WATERBURY, JOHN. The commander of the Faithful. The Moroccan political élite (London, 1970).

WORLD BANK. The Economic Development of Morocco (Johns Hopkins Press, Baltimore, 1966).

ZARTMAN, I. W. Morocco: Problems of New Power (Atherton Press, New York, 1964).

Oman

GEOGRAPHY

The Sultanate of Oman lies on the east of the Arabian Peninsula and is flanked by the United Arab Emirates on the north and west, by Saudi Arabia on the west and by Southern Yemen on the south-west. Its sea coast extends for over 1,000 miles and its total area, including Dhofar, is about 107,000 square miles. The country's frontiers with its neighbours have never been clearly demarcated on the ground but agreement exists on their general lines.

No census has ever been held in Oman and estimates of the country's population are based on conjecture. Official estimates placed the mid-year total at 550,000 for each year between 1949 and 1958; at 565,000 between 1959 and 1966; and at 600,000 in 1972. Based on a mid-1965 estimate of 565,000, the UN Population Division has projected a total of 657,000 for mid-1970 and 766,000 for mid-1975. Preliminary surveys for a census were taken in 1975.

At Muscat the mean annual rainfall is 3.94 inches and the average mean temperature varies between 69°F and 110°F. Rainfall on the hills of the interior is somewhat heavier and the south-western province of Dhofar is the only part of Arabia to benefit from the summer monsoon. Although most of the country is arid, there is cultivation on the coastal plain of the Batinah and in a number of valleys in the interior irrigation has been developed. The *Rub Al Khali* (or empty quarter) on Oman's western border is a rainless unrelieved wilderness of shifting sand almost entirely without human habitation.

HISTORY

Oman was probably the land of Magan mentioned in Sumerian tablets with which cities like Ur of the Chaldees traded in the third millenium B.C. The province of Dhofar also produced frankincense in vast quantities which was shipped to markets in Iraq, Syria, Egypt and the West. Roman geographers mention the city of Omana, although its precise location has not been identified, and Portus Moschus, conceivably Muscat. Masirah was also known to Pliny as the Island of Turtles. Oman at various times came under the influence of the Himyaritic kingdoms of South Arabia and of Iran, to which the introduction of the falaj irrigation systems is probably attributable, though legend attributes it to Sulaiman bin Daoud (Solomon).

The people of Oman come from two main stocks, the Qahtan who immigrated from South Arabia, and the Nizar who came in from the North. Tradition attributes the first important invasion from South Arabia to the leadership of Malik ibn Faham after the final collapse of the Marib dam in the Yemen in the first or second century A.D. Oman was one of the first countries to be converted to Islam by Amr ibn al As, who later converted Egypt to Islam. Omanis of the tribe of al Azd played an important part in the early days of Islam in Iraq. They subsequently embraced the Ibadhi doctrine which holds that the caliphate in Islam should not be hereditary or confined to any one family and established their own independent Imamate in Oman in the eighth century A.D. Subsequently, though subject to various invasions from time to time by the Caliphate, Iranians, Moguls and others, Oman has largely maintained its independence.

During the 10th century Sohar became probably the largest and most important city in the Arab world and Omani mariners, together with those from Basrah and other Gulf ports, went as far afield as China. Sohar, though subject to decline and recovery, remained an important port until, and indeed after, the Portuguese conquests. When the Portuguese under Albuquerque arrived in 1507 on their way to India, they found the Omani seaport under the suzerainty of the King of Hormus, himself of Omani stock. The towns of Qalhat, Quryat, Muscat and Sohar were all then thriving and prosperous.

The arrival of the Portuguese in the Indian Ocean changed the balance of power in the area radically. Previously the Omanis had been ubiquitous on the seas and it was an Omani pilot who guided Vasco da Gama across from Malindi to Calicut in India. The Portuguese established themselves in the Omani ports, concentrating principally on Sohar and Muscat, where they built the two great forts, Merani (1587) and Jalali (1588). British and Dutch traders followed in the wake of the Portuguese, though they did not establish themselves by force of arms in Oman in the same way. In 1650 the Imam Nasir bin Murshid of the Yaariba dynasty, who also inaugurated a period of Omani renaissance during which learning flourished, effectively turned the Portuguese out of Muscat and the rest of Oman. The country's external power grew and by 1730 the Omanis had conquered the Portuguese settlements on the coast of East Africa, including Mogadishu, Mombasa and Zanzibar.

The country was, however, ravaged by civil war in the first half of the eighteenth century when the strength and authority of the Imam diminished. During this period the Iranians were called in to assist one of the contenders for the Imamate, but they were finally expelled by Ahmad bin Said who was elected Iman in 1749 and was the founder of the Al Bu Said dynasty, which still rules Oman. The Al Bu Said is thus one of the oldest dynasties in the Middle East. The country prospered under the new dynasty and its maritime importance again grew. In about 1786 the capital of the country was moved from Rostaq to Muscat, a move which led to a dichotomy between the coast and the interior, creating political problems between the two regions at various times.

The Imam Said bin Sultan ruled Oman from 1804 until 1856. He was a strong and much beloved ruler, who also gained the respect and friendship of European nations, in particular the British. Treaties providing for the exchange of consular relations were negotiated with the British in 1839 (there had been earlier treaties of friendship in 1798 and 1800), the United States in 1833, France in 1844 and the Netherlands in 1877. British relations with Oman were maintained for the greater part of the period from the early eighteenth century until the present day, whilst the relations of the other states concerned were somewhat spasmodic.

Said bin Sultan revived Omani interest in Zanzibar and during the latter part of his reign spent an increasing amount of his time there. He started the clove plantations which were later to bring the territory great wealth and was the founder of the dynasty which ruled in Zanzibar until the revolution in 1964. When he died, his dominions were split between two of his sons, one of whom became Sultan of Oman and the other of Zanzibar. Following British mediation Zanzibar, which was the richer part of the heritage, agreed to pay Oman an annual subsidy of $6,400. During Said's time, Omani dominions reached their greatest extent in modern times. Dhofar became one of the constituent parts of the Sultanate in 1829, which it has remained ever since.

The next half of the century was one of some difficulty for the Sultanate on account of the erosion of the basis of its former prosperity. Not only had it lost its East African possessions but the series of treaties with Britain by which the slave trade was curbed also assisted the decline as Muscat had been an important port for this lucrative traffic.

Britain's only formal links with the Sultanate have been a series of Treaties of Friendship, Commerce and Navigation signed in 1891, 1939 and 1951. Britain has, however, given military assistance to Oman on a number of occasions in the past and is continuing to do so, though this is not based on any treaty obligation.

Several insurrections took place towards the end of the nineteenth century and in 1913 a new Imam was elected in the Interior, the Sultan who ruled from Muscat not having been elected. This led to the expulsion of the Sultan's garrisons from Nizwa, Izki and Sumail. In the same year Sultan Faisal bin Turki, who had ruled since 1888, died and he was succeeded by his son Taimur. Efforts to come to terms with the rebels failed but in 1920 an agreement between the Sultan and the principal dissidents, led by Isa bin Salih, was reached providing for peace, free movement of persons between the Interior and the coast, limitation of customs duty and non-interference by the Government of the Sultan in the internal affairs of the signatory tribes. Relations between the Imam, Mohammad bin Abdullah al Khalili, and the Sultan remained good until the Imam died in 1954 when rebellion again broke out under the Imam's successor Ghalib bin Ali, who sought foreign help to establish a separate principality. In December 1955, forces under the Sultan's control entered the main inhabited centres of Oman without resistance. The former Imam was allowed by the Sultan to retire to his village but his brother, Talib, escaped to Saudi Arabia and thence to Cairo. An "Oman Imamate" office was set up there

and the cause of the Imam was supported by Egyptian propaganda. In the summer of 1957 Talib returned and established himself with followers in the mountain areas north-west of Niswa. The Sultan appealed for British help and fighting continued until early 1959 when the Sultan's authority was fully re-established. In October 1960 ten Arab countries secured the placing of the "question of Oman" on the agenda of the General Assembly of the United Nations, despite British objections. In 1961 a resolution calling for the independence of Oman failed to get the necessary majority, and in 1963 a UN Commission of Inquiry refuted the Imamate charges of oppressive government and strong public feeling against the Sultan. Nevertheless, a Committee was set up to study the "question of Oman" and after its report had been submitted to the General Assembly in 1965 a resolution was adopted which among other things demanded the elimination of British domination in any form. The question was raised again in the United Nations on several occasions until more than a year after Sultan Qaboos's accession, Oman became a member of the UN in October 1971.

THE SULTANATE SINCE 1970

By 1970 Sultan Said's government had come to be regarded as the most reactionary and isolationist in the area, if not the world—slavery was still common, and many mediaeval prohibitions were in force. The Sultan's refusal to use the oil revenues for any purpose other than the building up of his armed forces had particularly embarrassed Britain, the oil companies and most neighbouring states, and this attitude had provided ideal conditions for the rebellion which broke out in Dhofar province in 1964. On July 24th, 1970, the Sultan was deposed by a coup led by his son, Qaboos bin Said, at the royal palace in Salalah. Qaboos, aged 28 and trained at Sandhurst, thus became Sultan to general acclaim both within the Sultanate and abroad, including support from the army; reports of British complicity in the coup were strongly denied by London. The new Sultan announced his intention to transform the country by using the oil revenues for development, following the example of the Gulf sheikhdoms to the north. He asked the rebels for their co-operation in developing the country, but only the Dhofar Liberation Front reacted favourably. The Popular Front for the Liberation of the Occupied Arabian Gulf (reported to control much of Dhofar, and to be receiving Chinese aid through the Yemen P.D.R.) and its ally the National Democratic Front for the Liberation of the Occupied Arab Gulf appeared to think that the palace coup changed little.

In August 1970 "Muscat" was dropped from the title of the country, which became simply the "Sultanate of Oman". Sultan Qaboos appointed his uncle, Tariq bin Taimur, as Prime Minister, but he resigned his office in December 1971, since when the Sultan has himself presided over cabinet meetings and acted as his own Prime Minister, Minister of Defence and Minister of Foreign Affairs. Government policy is aimed at providing the basic social and economic infrastructure which the former Sultan was rigidly opposed to—housing, education, communications, health services, etc. (Before the coup there were only three primary schools and one hospital). In addition, restrictions on travel have been lifted, many prisoners released, and many Omanis have returned from abroad. However, nearly half the annual budget is still devoted to defence and to quelling the Dhofar insurgency.

Oman's admission to the UN was achieved in face of opposition from the Yemen P.D.R., which supports the Popular Front for the Liberation of Oman and the Arab Gulf (PFLOAG), formed in 1972 by the unification of the two nationalist liberation fronts. The name of this organization was changed in July 1974 to People's Front for the Liberation of Oman. Oman's relationship with Britain also compromised Oman's candidature for UN membership. Britain still supplies arms and ammunition to the Oman Government and officers on secondment or contract. The progress achieved since the palace coup of 1970 has had some impact on the insurgents' following, with a number of defections to the Sultan's forces, but fighting continues. Omani forces attacked the border area of the Yemen P.D.R. for the first time in May 1972, the guerrillas having increasingly operated from beyond the border as the Sultan's forces advanced into Dhofar. In 1973 Iranian troops entered the conflict on the side of the Sultan, who also received assistance from Jordan, Saudi Arabia, the U.A.E., Pakistan and India. The Sultan's forces have gradually been gaining the upper hand and development in the Jebel area of Dhofar has been considerable. In March 1974 the Arab League set up a conciliation commission to bring about a reconciliation between the Yemen P.D.R. and Oman. The commission was welcomed by Oman but rejected by both the Yemen P.D.R. and the PFLO.

ECONOMIC SURVEY

AGRICULTURE AND FISHERIES

About 70 per cent of the working population is engaged in agriculture and the Sultanate's long-term plans for development foresee a considerable increase in agricultural production. At present subsistence farming dominates Oman's agriculture: because of the very limited rainfall and the wide variations in rainfall from one year to another farming is heavily dependent on irrigation. The oases of the interior rely on a system of underground water channels known as *falages* to tap water tables above the level of cultivation. On the Batinah coast irrigation is by pump from wells. About half of the estimated 36,000 hectares under cultivation are planted with dates. Other crops include lucerne, limes, mangoes, melons and bananas. Onions are grown and local tomatoes and cucumbers are also coming onto the town markets. Some wheat is grown in the interior around Nizwa.

In encouraging agricultural development the Department of Agriculture (which is a part of the Ministry of Development) hopes to increase production of traditional export crops and to reduce the

level of food imports by producing more for the home market. The Department has five experimental and production farms and 19 extension centres throughout the country. A series of 5 surveys of water resources in Northern Oman by international consultants will provide the basis for future agricultural planning. A contract worth $6 million was given to the American Farm Machinery Corporation for the establishment of demonstration and experimental farms.

Agriculture in Dhofar is the responsibility of the Dhofar Development Department. Because the province enjoys monsoon rains from June to September, the agricultural scene differs markedly from that in Northern Oman. Cattle are raised on the hills north of Salalah and coconut palms and a wide variety of vegetables are grown on the coastal plain. Although the insurgency has delayed development on the hills, the increasing pacification of the Eastern Area is allowing the Government to establish administrative centres and drill for water. Further plans envisage the fattening of cattle on the plain for slaughter. The constraints on agricultural development in Dhofar are the shortage of labour and the distance from markets, rather than any lack of water.

Fishing is a traditional industry in Oman and employs about 10 per cent of the working population. The inshore waters are rich in fish which is the main source of protein in the diet of many Omanis. Most fishing is done from canoes equipped with outboard motors, but the Government has signed two agreements with the U.S. firm Mardela to develop commercial and indigenous fishing in the Gulf of Oman.

OIL

The economy of Oman is dominated by the oil industry which provides almost all Government revenue. In 1937 Petroleum Concessions (Oman) Ltd., a subsidiary of the Iraq Petroleum Co., was granted a 75-year oil concession extending over the whole area except the district of Dhofar. A concession covering Dhofar was granted in 1953 to Dhofar Cities Service Petroleum Corporation; it expires in 25 years from the date of commercial production, with option to renew for another 25 years.

In 1964 Petroleum Development (Oman) Ltd., re-formed in 1967 as a subsidiary of Royal Dutch Shell (with an 85 per cent interest), Compagnie Française des Pétroles (with 10 per cent) and Gulbenkian interests with their traditional 5 per cent, announced that drilling had proved sufficient reserves for the company to go into commercial production. The production of oil began in 1967 at a rate of 200,000 barrels per day and expanded to 360,000 barrels per day by the end of 1969. However, during late 1970 and early 1971 technical difficulties affected production and the 1971 production of 105.56 million barrels was 15 million down on 1970. Total oil exports in 1972 were 103.2 million barrels and in 1973, 106.9 million barrels. Total oil production for 1974 was 105.8 million barrels.

In 1973 the four connected oil fields at Fahud, Natih, Yibal and Al-Huwaisah together produced at an average rate of 292,947 barrels per day. The average will have risen to about 375,000 barrels per day from January 1975, when the three Ghaba fields start producing. Towards the end of 1976 the Saih Rawl field should increase daily production to around 400,000 barrels per day.

Petroleum Development (Oman) Limited is also drilling in the north of Dhofar where quantities of relatively heavy oil are known to exist. It is not yet clear whether this will be a commercial proposition.

Sun Oil Company heads a group exploring in off-shore areas south of Masirah Island, and in 1975 a concession was granted to Elf/Sumitomo to explore in the Butabul region. Neither of these groups has yet announced finds.

In December 1973 the Oman Government purchased a 25 per cent share in Petroleum Development (Oman), and increased this to 60 per cent in July 1974. The present distribution of the remaining shares is Royal Dutch Shell 34 per cent, Compagnie Française des Pétroles 4 per cent and Gulbenkian 2 per cent. Oman is not a member of the Organization of Petroleum Exporting Companies (OPEC), nor of the Organization of Arab Petroleum Exporting Countries (OAPEC), but under the terms of the concessions granted to the companies the Government of the Sultanate is assured of treatment equal to that received by members of OPEC.

INDUSTRY AND MINERALS

Before 1964 industry in Oman was confined to small traditional handicrafts. The development of oil generated activity in the construction sector, but it was not until the change of régime in 1970 that Government investment in infrastructure projects and private spending on housing started a boom in construction which still continues. Some small factories have been opened to manufacture building materials or bottle soft drinks, but large scale industrialization is likely to be based on oil or natural gas. A British firm was contracted in 1975 to build 19 diesel power stations. A cement factory with a capacity of 600,000 tons a year is planned for completion in 1976, while construction of a flour mill, a thermal power station and a desalination plant is also under way. The Government is examining the possibility of developing traditional craft industries.

At present no minerals other than oil are exploited commercially in Oman. A Canadian/Omani joint company, Prospection (Oman), is prospecting for minerals in the North of Oman and deposits of copper and asbestos have been found.

STATISTICAL SURVEY

Area: 120,000 square miles.

Population: 750,000 (estimate for mid-1973); Capital area (Muscat to Seeb) estimated 50,000. Estimated number of gainfully employed 150,000; agriculture 109,000; fisheries 15,000; government 10,000; construction 6,000; oil, banking, services 5,000; others 5,000 (1972.)

Agriculture: Land utilization 1971 (hectares): Batinah 13,800; Interior 19,920; capital area 1,080; Musandam 400; Dhofar 800. Crops include dates, lucerne, limes, onions, pomegranates, wheat, bananas, mangoes, tobacco, chickpeas and coconuts.

MINING

		1970	1971	1972	1973	1974
Crude petroleum . .	'000 metric tons	17,169	14,406	14,010	14,420	14,041

INDUSTRY

		1968	1969	1970	1971	1972
Cement	'000 metric tons	339	382	475	559	626
Electric energy . . .	million kWh.	n.a.	100	105	111	130

FINANCE

1,000 baiza = 1 rial Omani (formerly called the rial Saidi).

Coins: 2, 5, 10, 25, 50 and 100 baiza.

Notes: 100, 250 and 500 baiza; 1, 5 and 10 rials.

Exchange rates (July 1975): £1 sterling = 755.4 baiza; U.S. $1 = 345.4 baiza.

100 rials Omani = £132.38 = $289.52.

Note: The rial was introduced in May 1970, replacing the Persian Gulf Indian rupee at the rate of 1 rial = 21 rupees = £1 sterling. The initial value of the rial was U.S. $2.40 ($1 = 416.7 baiza), which remained in operation until August 1971. From December 1971 to February 1973 the rial's value was $2.6057 ($1 = 383.8 baiza). The present dollar valuation has been effective since February 1973. The rial was at par with the pound sterling until the latter was allowed to "float" in June 1972.

BUDGET
(1974—Omani rials)

Revenue		Expenditure	
Oil	211,568,282	Ministry of Development . . .	23,380,473
		Ministry of Health . . .	13,219,399
		Ministry of Education . . .	6,631,243
		Ministry of Communications and Public Services	35,444,830
		Ministry of Information and Tourism .	8,366,712
		Police Department . . .	7,403,000
		Defence Department . . .	58,453,190
		Dhofar	10,304,904
Total (inc. others) . .	220,000,000	Total (inc. others) . .	220,000,000

1975 Budget: planned expenditure is 521 million rials Omani, of which 168 million rials is allocated for development.

EXTERNAL TRADE
IMPORTS*

Countries (Omani rials)	1972	1973	Principal Products ('000 Omani rials)	1972	1973
Australia . . .	1,068,843	2,049,954	Rice	864	1,989
Germany, Fed. Repub. .	654,437	2,126,997	Wheat and flour . .	583	1,314
Japan	1,949,435	3,546,557	Fruit and vegetables .	489	1,165
India	1,124,468	2,015,349	Ghee, milk and milk products	818	2,411
Iran	429,003	618,863	Cement	576	1,550
Netherlands . . .	957,427	3,473,186	Other building material .	1,450	7,326
Pakistan	609,070	1,194,616	Machinery and parts . .	1,799	2,941
U.A.E.	3,469,874	9,168,063	Cars and parts . . .	2,273	4,093
United Kingdom . .	3,872,289	7,726,728	Electric appliances and radios . . .	1,107	2,618
U.S.A.	287,210	1,798,982	Textiles	1,403	1,618
Others	4,291,125	6,954,677	Petroleum products . .	910	2,398
	18,713,181	40,673,992			

* Total of non-oil and non-governmental imports up to July 1973, total imports after that date.

In 1974 total imports exceeded 135 million Omani rials.

EXPORTS

Oil exports (1973): 60.6 million Omani rials.

Non-oil exports consist mainly of limes, fish and tobacco:
(Omani rials) 1971 429,804; 1972 391,327; 1973 609,049.

EDUCATION

	PRIMARY		SECONDARY	
	BOYS	GIRLS	BOYS	GIRLS
1970–71 .	5,805	1,136	—	—
1971–72 .	13,382	1,950	—	—
1972–73 .	20,303	4,032	623	128
1973–74 .	27,172	7,658	23	—

In 1973–74 there were 1,225 teachers of whom 451 were Omanis.

THE GOVERNMENT

Head of State and Premier:
Sultan QABOOS BIN SAID.

CABINET
(*July* 1975)

Personal Adviser to the Sultan and Governor of Muscat: Sayyid THUWAINI BIN SHIHAB.

Minister of Diwan Affairs: Sayyid HAMAD BIN HAMUD.

Minister of Justice: Sayyid HILAL BIN HAMAD AL-SAMMAR.

Minister of State for Foreign Affairs: QAIS ABDUL MUNIM AL-ZAWAWI.

Minister without Portfolio and Special Representative of the Sultan: Dr. ASIM AL-JAMALI.

Minister of Information and Culture: Sayyid FAHD BIN MAHMOUD AL-SAID.

Minister of Communications: Eng. ABDUL HAFIDH SALIM RAJAB.

Minister of Education: Sayyid FAISAL BIN ALI AL-SAID.

Minister of Land Affairs: Sayyid MUHAMMAD BIN AHMED.

Minister of Social Affairs and Labour: KHALFAN BIN NASR AL-WAHAIBI.

Minister of Awkaf and Islamic Affairs: Sheikh WALID BIN ZAHIR AL-HINA'I.

Minister of Public Works: KARIM AHMED AL-HAREMI.

Minister of the Interior and Deputy Minister of Defence: Sayyid FAHR BIN TAIMUR AL-SAID.

Minister of Commerce and Industry: MUHAMMAD ZUBAIR.

Minister of Agriculture, Fisheries, Petroleum and Minerals: SAID AHMED AL-SHANFARI.

Minister of Health: Dr. MUBAREK AL-KHADDURI.

Governor of Dhofar and Minister without Portfolio: Sheikh BRAIK BIN HAMUD AL-GHAFARI.

The Sultan acts as his own Minister of Foreign Affairs and of Defence.

DIPLOMATIC REPRESENTATION

EMBASSIES ACCREDITED TO OMAN
(In Muscat unless otherwise stated)

Austria: Jeddah, Saudi Arabia.

Belgium: Kuwait City, Kuwait.

Brazil: Jeddah, Saudi Arabia.

Canada: Teheran, Iran.

Denmark: Kuwait City, Kuwait.

Egypt: P.O.B. 969; *Ambassador:* HASSAN ALI HASSAN SALIM.

France: P.O.B. 591; *Ambassador:* MEJID KEBAILI.

Germany, Federal Republic: Jeddah, Saudi Arabia.

Guinea: Jeddah, Saudi Arabia.

India: P.O.B. 77; *Ambassador:* NIRMAL JEET SINGH.

Iran: P.O.B. 702; *Ambassador:* Dr. B. ZAND.

Italy: Kuwait City, Kuwait.

Japan: Kuwait City, Kuwait.

Jordan: P.O.B. 990; *Ambassador:* Dr. YACOUB ABU GHOSH.

Korea, Republic: Jeddah, Saudi Arabia.

Kuwait: P.O.B. 892, *Ambassador:* AHMED ABDUL-AZIZ AL-JASSIM.

Morocco: Kuwait City, Kuwait.

Netherlands: Kuwait City, Kuwait.

Pakistan: P.O.B. 1005; *Ambassador:* HAKIM MUHAMMAD AHSAN.

Qatar: P.O.B. 802, Ruwi; *Ambassador:* MUHAMMAD SA'AD AL-FAHAID.

Romania: Teheran, Iran.

Saudi Arabia: P.O.B. 456; *Chargé d'Affaires:* AHMED ALI MIMESH.

Somalia: Jeddah, Saudi Arabia.

Spain: Kuwait City, Kuwait.

Sweden: Jeddah, Saudi Arabia.

Switzerland: Jeddah, Saudi Arabia.

Tunisia: Kuwait City, Kuwait (E).

Turkey: Jeddah, Saudi Arabia.

United Arab Emirates: *Ambassador:* HAMAD SULTAN AL-DARMAKI MAKBOUL VILLAS.

United Kingdom: P.O.B. 300; *Ambassador:* JAMES TREAD-WELL.

U.S.A.: P.O.B. 966; *Ambassador:* WILLIAM WOLLE.

Yemen Arab Republic: *Ambassador:* MUHAMMAD ABDUL JABER MUSAHAD.

Yugoslavia: Kuwait City, Kuwait.

Oman has diplomatic relations with all Arab States, except Iraq and the People's Democratic Republic of Yemen, and with a large number of West European States and many Asian and African countries.

JUDICIARY AND RELIGION

Legal System: Jurisdiction is exercised by the Sharia Courts, applying Islamic Law. Local courts are officered by *Qadhis* appointed by the Sultan. The Chief Court is at Muscat. Appeals from the Chief Court go to the Sultan.

Religion: The majority of the population are Ibadhi Muslims; about a quarter are Sunni Muslims.

PRESS

WEEKLY NEWSPAPERS

Al Watan (*the Nation*): P.O.B. 445, Muscat; Editor SULEIMAN BIN MUHAMMAD AL-TAI.

Oman: P.O.B. 600, Muscat; produced by Ministry of Education; Editor MUHAMMAD AMIN ABDULLAH.

ENGLISH LANGUAGE

Gulf Mirror: P.O.B. 455, Manama, Bahrain; covers area of the Southern Gulf; Editor STEPHEN KEMBALL.

Times of Oman: P.O.B. 183, Muscat; Editor RANA N. PARVEZE.

PERIODICALS

Al Aquida (*The Faith*): P.O.B. 691, Muscat; weekly illustrated magazine; Editor SAID AL-SAMHAN AL-KATHIRI.

Al Muzari: P.O.B. 467, Muscat; monthly illustrated magazine of the Ministry of Agriculture; Editor KHALID AL-ZUBAIDI.

Al Nahda (*The Renaissance*): P.O.B. 979, Muscat; fortnightly illustrated magazine.

Al Usra (*The Family*): P.O.B. 1440, Mutrah; weekly illustrated magazine; Editor MUHAMMAD JABR.

Jund Oman (*Soldiers of Oman*): P.O.B. 113, Muscat; monthly illustrated magazine of the Department of Defence; Supervisor: Deputy Minister for Defence.

Nahwa Tarbiya Afdal: P.O.B. 3, Muscat; monthly educational magazine; Editor SALIM AHMED JA'AFER.

Tijarat Oman (*Commerce of Oman*): P.O.B. 580, Muscat; quarterly trade magazine; Editor HABIB M. NASIB.

RADIO AND TELEVISION

Radio Oman: Muscat; f. 1970; transmits in Arabic 7 hours daily; Director: ABDULLAH SAKHR AL AMRI.

Radio Salalah: f. 1970; transmits daily programmes in Arabic and the Dhofari languages; Director: ABDUL AZIZ ROWAS.

A colour television station built at Qurm outside Muscat by the German Company Siemens A.G. was opened in November 1974. A colour television system for Dhofar is being constructed by Pye of Great Britain and Phillips of the Netherlands. It is due to open in 1975.

The British Broadcasting Corporation has built a powerful new medium-wave relay station on the island of Masirah, off the Oman coast. It is used to expand and improve the reception of the B.B.C.'s Arabic, Farsi and Urdu services.

FINANCE

BANKING

Arab African Bank: P.O.B. 1117, Mutrah.

Arab Bank Ltd.: P.O.B. 991, Muscat; Man. ABDUL KADER ASKLAM.

Arab European International Bank: Muscat.

Arab International Bank for Foreign Commerce and Development: Muscat.

Bank of Credit and Commerce Int. S.A.: P.O.B. 840, Muscat; Man. G. MIRZA.

Bank Melli Iran: P.O.B. 410, Muscat; Man. M. AMADI.

Bank of Oman, Bahrain and Kuwait: P.O.B. 920, Muscat; br. in Rumi; Man. H. G. FRY.

Banque de Paris et des Pays-Bas: P.O.B. 425, Muscat.

British Bank of the Middle East: London; f. 1889; P.O.B. 234, Muscat; handles government finance; branches in Mutrah, Mina Al-Fahal, Al Falaj Hotel, Saham, Salalah, Seeb International Airport, Sohar, Ruwi, Buraimi, Taqa, Thamarit and Nizwa; Man. R. LOUGH.

The Chartered Bank: P.O.B. 210, Muscat; Man. A. R. HOLDEN; brs. in Mutrah, Ruwi and Sur.

Chase Manhattan Bank: Muscat.

Grindlays Bank Ltd.: London; P.O.B. 91, Muscat; Man. R. MURRAY; brs. in Mutrah, Ruwi, Seeb and Salalah.

Habib Bank (Overseas) Ltd.: P.O.B. 1326, Mutrah; br. in Greater Mutrah; Man. R. ALVI.

National Bank of Oman: P.O.B. 1272, Mutrah; Man. S. M. SHAFI.

INSURANCE

Oman United Agencies Ltd: Muscat; representatives of several British insurance companies; subsidiary of Gray, MacKenzie and Co. Ltd.

OIL

Petroleum Development (Oman) Ltd.: P.O.B. 81, Muscat; f. 1937; since July 1974 60 per cent owned by Oman Government, 34 per cent by Shell, 4 per cent by Compagnie Française des Pétroles and 2 per cent by Gulbenkian interests; exports oil from the Fahud, Yibal and Natih and Al-Huwaisah oilfields via a pipeline to a terminal at Mina al Fahal, near Muscat; production in 1974 was 295,000 barrels a day.

Sun Oil: holds concession area of 13,000 square km. south of Masirah Island; consortium composed of Sun Oil, Home Oil of Canada, Canadian Industrial Gas and Oil and Deutsche Schachtbau; exploration is in progress.

Elf/Sumitomo: concession granted in 1975 for exploration in the onshore region of Butabul; area of 7,000 square km.; ownership is equally divided between the two companies.

TRANSPORT

The number of motor vehicles is rapidly increasing. In 1973 14,447 vehicles were registered, compared with 5,516 in 1971.

ROADS

A network of adequate graded roads links all the main centres of population and only a few mountain villages are not accessible by Land Rover. A rapid road construction programme began in 1970 and nearly 300 miles of tarmac road are completed in Northern Oman. A new coastal highway between Muscat and Mutrah is under construction and scheduled for completion in 1978. In Dhofar tarmac roads have been completed from Raysut through Salalah to Taqa. The construction of many tarmac roads is planned for the near future.

SHIPPING

The new port of Mina Qaboos which was completed in 1974 at a cost of R.O. 18.2 million provides eight deep-water berths, warehousing facilities and a harbour for dhows and coastal vessels. In 1974 361 vessels visited Mina Qaboos. A coastal harbour has been completed at Raysut with berths for five ships. The oil terminal at Mina al Fahal can accommodate the largest super-tankers on off-shore loading buoys. Similar facilities for the import of refined petroleum products exist at Mina al Fahal and Riyam (near Muscat).

About 350 vessels visited Mutrah and Muscat in 1973. There are regular services to Britain (Strick Line), Australia (P & O), India and Pakistan (Gulf Shipping Co.) and Japan (Showa Line).

Loading facilities for smaller craft exist at Sohar, Khaboura, Sur, Marbat and Salalah.

Oman United Agencies Ltd.: P.O.B. 70, Muscat; shipping, clearing and forwarding agents and general merchants; subsidiary of Gray, Mackenzie and Co. Ltd.

CIVIL AVIATION

All domestic and international flights now operate from Seeb International Airport. Its runway is being extended from the present 10,000 feet to 12,000 feet. Most towns of any size have small air strips. Gulf Aviation operate frequent flights to the Gulf States, Beirut, London, Iran, India and Pakistan, and return flights four times a week to Salalah. A modern civil airport is under construction at Salalah. Other airlines using Seeb include Alia, Air India, British Airways, Iran Air, Middle East Airlines, Pakistan International Airways and Saudia (passenger); and Trans Mediterranean Airways and Tradewinds (cargo).

Gulf Aviation Co. Ltd.: (*see* Bahrain).

DEFENCE

Commander-in-Chief: Major-General KENNETH PERKINS.

Defence Budget 1974: 58.5 million Omani rials.

Military service: voluntary.

Total armed forces: 9,700 (including some 600 foreign personnel, serving on contract or secondment): army 9,000; navy 200; air force 500, with 12 combat aircraft. Ten AB-205A helicopters are on order from Iran; 3 BAC 1-11 have been ordered for the transport flight.

Paramilitary forces: 2,100; 1,000 gendarmerie (2 battalions), 1,100 tribal Home Guard.

EDUCATION

Until 1970 there were only three schools in Oman and it has been estimated that as many as 80 per cent of Omanis are still illiterate. In the years since the accession of Sultan Qaboos emphasis has been placed on the expansion of educational facilities all over the country. The number of children attending primary schools has increased from around 6,000 in 1970 to over 34,000 in 1974. Secondary education is still extremely limited. The shortage of teachers is a major problem and considerable numbers have been brought in from other Arab countries, particularly Egypt, Jordan and the Sudan. Plans are being implemented for the development of technical and agricultural education and craft training at intermediate and secondary level. There are also programmes to combat adult illiteracy.

BIBLIOGRAPHY

ADMIRALTY. A Handbook of Arabia (London, 1916).

AITCHISON, C. V. (Ed.). Government of India Foreign Department—Collection of Treaties Relating to India and Neighbouring Countries. Volume XII (Calcutta 1932).

ALLFREY, P. F. Warlords of Oman.

BADGER, G. P. The History of the Imams and Sayyids of Oman, by Salilbin-Razik, from AD 661 to 1856 (Hakluyt Society 1871).

BUSCH, B. C. Great Britain and the Persian Gulf 1894–1914 (University of California Press, 1967).

DEPARTMENT OF INFORMATION, MUSCAT. Oman (London, 1972).

FACT SHEETS ON EASTERN ARABIA (Private Information Center on Eastern Arabia, Heldenplein 12, 1800 Vilvoorde, Belgium).

GIBB, H. A. R. Ibn Battuta—Travels in Asia and Africa 1325–1354 (London, 1929).

HAWLEY, D. F. The Trucial States (George Allen and Unwin, London, 1971).

HOLDEN, D. Farewell to Arabia (London, 1966).

HOPWOOD, D. (Ed.). The Arabian Peninsula: Society and Politics (London, 1972).

KELLY, J. B. Great Britain and the Persian Gulf, 1793–1880 (London).

KELLY, J. B. Eastern Arabia Frontier (Faber and Faber, London).

LANDEN, R. G. Oman Since 1856 (Princeton University Press, 1967).

LORIMER, J. C. Gazeteer of the Persian Gulf, Oman and Central Arabia, 2 vols. (Calcutta 1908 and 1915).

MILES, S. B. The Countries and Tribes of the Persian Gulf (3rd edition, Frank Cass, London, 1966).

MORRIS, JAMES. Sultan in Oman (Faber, London, 1957).

PHILLIPS, WENDELL. Unknown Oman (Longmans, London, 1966).
Oman. A History (Longmans, London, 1967).

ROYAL INSTITUTE OF INTERNATIONAL AFFAIRS. Sultanate and Imamate in Oman (Oxford University Press, 1959).

RUBINACCI, R. Religion in the Middle East (Ed. Arberry, A. J.) Vol. 2, Chapter 16 (Cambridge).

SKEET, IAN, Muscat and Oman: The End of an Era (Faber and Faber, 1974).

THESIGER, WILFRED. Arabian Sands (Longmans, London, 1959).

WILSON, Sir A. T. The Persian Gulf (London, 1928).

Qatar

GEOGRAPHY

The Emirate of Qatar is a peninsula roughly 100 miles in length, with a breadth varying between 35 and 50 miles, on the west coast of the Persian Gulf. The total area is 4,000 square miles. There are over 170,000 inhabitants, two-thirds of whom are concentrated in the town of Doha, on the east coast. Two other ports, Zakrit on the west coast and Umm Said on the east, owe their existence to the discovery of oil. Zakrit is a convenient, if shallow, harbour for the import of goods from Bahrain, and Umm Said affords anchorage to the deep-sea tankers and freighters.

Qatar is stony, sandy and barren; limited supplies of underground water are unsuitable for drinking or agriculture because of high mineral content. Over half the water supply is now provided by sea water distillation processes. The inhabitants have traditionally lived from pearl-diving, fishing and nomadic herding.

HISTORY

Owing to the aridity of the peninsula the early history of Qatar is of little interest, though archaeological expeditions have found evidence of inhabitation in the Stone and Iron ages and as early as 4,000 B.C. In 1916 Great Britain, in order to exclude other powers from the area, made an agreement with the Sheikh of Qatar, who undertook not to cede, mortgage or otherwise dispose of parts of his territories to anyone except the British Government, nor to enter into any relationship with a foreign government other than the British without British consent. Similar agreements had been concluded with Bahrain in 1880 and 1892, with the Trucial States in 1892 and with Kuwait in 1899. In return Britain undertook to protect Qatar from all aggression by sea, and to lend her good offices in case of an overland attack.

The discovery of oil in the 1930s promised greater prosperity for Qatar, but because of the Second World War production did not begin on a commercial scale until 1949 (see below). An ambitious development programme is now being put into operation with the revenues from the production and export of oil. The Sheikhdom took a leading part in moves towards the formation of a Gulf Federation; it also enjoys close relations with Saudi Arabia. In January 1961 Qatar joined the Organization of Petroleum Exporting Countries, and in May 1970 it also became a member of OAPEC (the Organization of Arab Petroleum Exporting Countries).

In April 1970 a provisional constitution was announced which, it was said, would assist Qatar's entry into the Federation of Arab Emirates. The first cabinet was formed in May; the Ruler became Prime Minister with responsibility for oil, and six of the other nine members were also members of the Royal Family. However, Qatar decided to remain outside a Gulf Federation and became independent on September 1st, 1971. Qatar, however, still feels enthusiastic about the idea of some form of enlarged Gulf Federation in the future. Qatar and the United Kingdom immediately signed a new treaty of friendship. In the same month Qatar was first admitted as a member of the Arab League, and then to membership of the United Nations. Sheikh Ahmad bin Ali al-Thani became Amir on September 4th, but apparently took little interest in affairs of the State. He was deposed on February 22nd, 1972, in a bloodless *coup* staged by his cousin Sheikh Khalifa bin Hamad al-Thani. Sheikh Khalifa seized power with the support of the ruling al-Thani family, although his avowed purpose included the curtailment of some of the family's long-held privileges. The *coup* also thwarted the ambitions of the deposed Amir's son, Sheikh Abdul Aziz, who went into exile.

Moves made immediately after the February coup, affecting salaries in the public sector, housing and Royal appropriations, indicated that the new ruler was about to introduce an era of steadier social and political reform. In accordance with the 1970 constitution, Sheikh Khalifa decreed the first Advisory Council, to complement the ministerial government. Its 20 members, initially appointed, should eventually be elected representatives. The Advisory Council's constitutional entitlements include power to debate legislation drafted by the Council of Ministers before ratification and promulgation. It also has power to request ministerial statements on matters of general and specific policy inclusive of the draft budget.

ECONOMIC SURVEY

Agriculture is still developing but outside the capital most of the population is employed in the oil industry, which is the state's principal source of wealth. Fishing, apart from shrimp fishing and processing, is carried on to supply local demands. Unlike many of the other Sheikhdoms, Qatar has no entrepôt trade.

Interest in the petroleum possibilities of Qatar was first stimulated by the entry of Standard of California into Bahrain in 1930. Shortly after this date the Anglo-Iranian Company received permission from the ruler to make a surface survey of his territories, and in 1935 they were granted a concession. This gave them exclusive petroleum rights in the Sheikhdom and its territorial waters for 75 years. Payments were to be 400,000 rupees upon signature; an annual rental of 150,000 rupees for the first 5 years and 300,000 rupees thereafter; and a royalty of 3 rupees per long ton. The concession was later transferred to Petroleum Concessions Ltd., which formed an operating company, Petroleum Development (Qatar) Ltd.

Petroleum Development started exploration in 1937 and oil was discovered in 1939. Field activities were interrupted during the war, but resumed in 1947.

By 1949 the company had completed a drilling programme, the laying of a pipeline system from the field of Dukhan, on the west coast to Umm Said, and the construction of terminal facilities. At the end of that year the first shipment was made from the Umm Said offshore berths. From 1963 to 1970 production stagnated at about nine million tons a year but expanded rapidly during 1971 to reach 10.4 million tons, and the increase was maintained when production reached 11.4 million tons in 1972 and 11.7 million tons in 1973. As demand fell in 1974, production was reduced to 10.3 million tons. In 1953 the name of the company was changed to Qatar Petroleum Company Ltd.

An offshore grant was awarded to the "Shell" Overseas Exploration Company in 1952. This covers an area of approximately 10,000 square miles and it expires in 2027. A down payment of over £260,000 was made and exploration started in 1953. The first and second exploratory wells failed to find oil and were abandoned in 1955 and 1956 respectively. The operating company, the Shell Company of Qatar Ltd., lost their original drilling platform in a storm in 1956. This was replaced and drilling operations recommenced in December 1959. Test production from the offshore field at Idd el Shargi through temporary facilities began in January 1964. Construction of permanent facilities on Halul Island, some 60 miles off the coast of Qatar, were completed early in 1966. This also enabled production to be commenced from Shell's second field in Maydam Mazam. Shell Qatar began commercial production of oil in 1966 at an annual rate of more than 5,000,000 long tons, and this had increased to 15.4 million tons by 1973, falling to 13.9 million tons in 1974. Production from a third field, Bul Hanine, began in 1972. In 1963 the Continental Oil Company of Qatar was granted a concession over land and offshore areas relinquished by the Qatar Petroleum Company and the Shell Company of Qatar, and over a strip of territory in the south of the peninsula not previously included in any concession. In March 1969 a Japanese consortium was granted an exploration concession in the southeastern offshore area, but discontinued its search and returned the concessionary rights to the Government in 1974. Also in 1969 Qatar and Abu Dhabi agreed on the joint exploration of the al-Bunduq field, which is shared by the two countries. This is being developed by the al-Bunduq Co. Ltd., which is owned by British Petroleum, Compagnie Française des Pétroles and Qatar Oil Japan.

In April 1972 the Amir signed a law to create the Qatar National Petroleum Co., with power to carry out a comprehensive range of production, refining and marketing functions. In January 1973 the Qatar Government signed participation agreements with both local crude-producing companies—Qatar Petroleum Co. Ltd. and Shell Company of Qatar Ltd.— whereby it acquired a 25 per cent share in the operations of each company, this to rise to a controlling interest by 1982. Following the Arab-Israeli war of October 1973, however, a movement developed in all the Arab oil-producing states towards increased

participation in the operations of the western-owned oil companies (*see* chapter *Oil in the Middle East and North Africa*). Accordingly, the Qatar Government held negotiations with Qatar Petroleum Company and Shell Company of Qatar in February 1974 and reached agreement on the immediate acquisition by the Government of a 60 per cent interest in each of the companies. Two months afterwards it was further agreed that the companies should buy back at least 60 per cent of the Government's 60 per cent share of production at an average price of 93 per cent of posted prices. After the first six months the price was to be subject to quarterly review. The Government retained its option to sell its remaining 40 per cent of production on world markets or to sell it to the two companies at the price agreed. Talks are in progress in 1975 whereby the Qatar Government is endeavouring to acquire a 100 per cent interest in QPC and Shell Co. of Qatar.

Equally significant results of the Arab-Israeli conflict were severe but temporary cut-backs in oil production among Arab states and sharp but sustained increases in oil prices. Between October 1973 and January 1974 the "take" of the governments of the Gulf producer states (which include Qatar) rose from $3 per barrel to $7. Qatari revenue, which was $197.8 million in 1971 and $254.8 million in 1972, was estimated to be $397 million in 1973 and $1,391 million in 1974.

In order to avoid complete dependence on oil the Government has encouraged the growth of other industries, and the proportion of the revenue from oil used to finance development projects has been rising steadily, particularly since the seizure of power by Sheikh Khalifa in 1972. Government capital expenditure, set at $90.1 million in 1973–74, was scheduled to rise to $156 million in 1974–75.

The most significant completed project so far is an ammonia and urea fertilizer plant, based on the conversion of waste gas, which came into operation at Umm Said in February 1973 with a planned output of 430,000 tons per annum. Other developments have been in diverse fields. The Qatar Flour Mills Co., which, though privately owned, was set up at the prompting of the Government, operates a mill, completed at Umm Said in 1972, that can process 100 tons of flour a day. The Qatar National Fishing Co., originally formed in 1966 as an extension of the local shrimp-fishing industry, now has refrigeration and processing plant near Doha harbour capable of handling seven tons of shrimps daily. The Qatar National Cement Manufacturing Co. at Umm Bab began production at a rate of 100,000 tons per year early in 1969; its capacity has since been expanded. The Department of Agriculture has already succeeded in making the country self-sufficient in vegetables, production of which was negligible as recently as 1960; fruit production and the planting of trees are making rapid progress. Some vegetables, mainly tomatoes, marrows and cucumbers, are now exported to other Gulf states. A natural gas liquefaction plant, begun by the Qatar Petroleum Company in 1971, became operational in 1974.

In 1975 it became clear that Qatar was planning to use its oil wealth by developing heavy industry. Projects planned include an iron and steel complex to be built at a cost of QR 800 million in conjunction with two Japanese firms, a petrochemical project built with the assistance of two French firms and expected to begin production in 1970, further natural gas projects, and a second cement plant. Preliminary talks have begun on a project for an aluminium smelter.

Considerable amounts of revenue have also been invested in infrastructural development. A 130-bed hospital, built in Doha at a total cost of £3.5 million, was said to be one of the most modern in the world. Plans were under way in 1975 for the construction of a 650-bed general hospital. A desalination plant, powered by natural gas, is expected to supply Doha with over two million gallons of piped water per day. A 30-MW power station is also powered by natural gas. Work was begun in 1973 on the construction of a new desalination/power plant at Wakrah to be completed by 1983. As for communications, Doha has an international airport and plans have been drawn up for a new one to be located outside Doha. An earth satellite communications station is also projected, and the road, rural electrification and port systems are all being developed.

In May 1973 the Monetary Agency of Qatar announced the issue of its own Qatari currency, the Qatar riyal (QR) with the same parity and exchange value as the old currency, the Qatar/Dubai riyal.

In November 1973 the metric system was introduced.

STATISTICAL SURVEY

AREA AND POPULATION

AREA	POPULATION (1975 Estimates)	
	TOTAL	DOHA (capital)
4,000 sq. miles	170,000	130,000

OIL

QATAR PETROLEUM COMPANY CRUDE OIL PRODUCTION
'000 long tons

1965	9,158	1970	8,882
1966	9,059	1971	10,400
1967	9,070	1972	11,368
1968	9,018	1973	11,676
1969	9,366	1974	10,325

SHELL QATAR CRUDE OIL PRODUCTION
'000 long tons

1971	9,900
1972	11,500
1973	15,400
1974	13,921

FINANCE

100 dirhams = 1 Qatar riyal (QR).

Coins: 1, 5, 10, and 50 dirhams.

Notes: 1, 5, 10, 50 and 100 riyals.

Exchange rates (July 1975): £1 sterling = 8.493 riyals; U.S. $1 = 3.883 riyals.

100 Qatar riyals = £11.775 = $25.752.

Note: Before June 1966 Qatar's currency was the Persian Gulf Indian rupee, valued at 1s. 6d. sterling (£1 = 13.33 rupees). When the Indian rupee was devalued in June 1966 Qatar adopted Saudi Arabian currency prior to the introduction of the Qatar/Dubai riyal (at par with the old rupee) in September 1966. This new currency was also used in the states of Trucial Oman (now the United Arab Emirates) except Abu Dhabi. The Q/D riyal was valued at 21 U.S. cents ($1 = 4.762 riyals) until August 1971. The riyal's value was 22.8 U.S. cents ($1 = 4.386 riyals) from December 1971 to February 1973; and 25.333 U.S. cents ($1 = 3.947 riyals) from February 1973 to March 1975. In terms of sterling, the value of the Q/D riyal between November 1967 and June 1972 was 1s. 9d. (8.75 new pence), the exchange rate being £1 = 11.429 riyals. When the United Arab Emirates adopted a national currency in May 1973 the Q/D riyal was superseded by the Qatar riyal, with the same value as the old currency. Since March 1975 the Qatar riyal has been linked to the IMF Special Drawing Right (1 riyal = 0.21 SDR), whose value is determined by changes in a weighted "basket" of 16 national currencies. Some figures in this Statistical Survey are still expressed in Q/D riyals.

BUDGET EXPENDITURE

(1975-76 million Qatar riyals).

Heavy industry	305
Public services	602
Transport and communications	477
Education, health, information	275
Justice, security	144
TOTAL	1,800

OIL REVENUES

('000 Q/D riyals)

	1970–71 (1390)	1971–72 (1391)
Payments by Qatar Petroleum Co.	327,985	517,911
Payments by Shell Qatar	267,016	429,200

EXTERNAL TRADE

IMPORTS ('000 Qatar riyals)

1971	515,869
1972	607,263
1973	778,440
1974	1,068,945

Exports: Non-oil exports are negligible, and the customs do not provide figures, but there is a flourishing re-export trade with other Gulf States.

PRINCIPAL TRADING PARTNERS
('ooo Q riyals)

IMPORTS	1971	1972	1973	1974
United Kingdom	193,213	160,575	214,361	149,676
U.S.A.	50,298	63,149	80,040	109,493
Japan	54,108	76,108	86,826	190,941
Germany, Federal Republic	23,532	31,856	42,230	n.a.
Lebanon	28,394	42,033	44,189	67,038
India	14,727	12,453	20,177	n.a.
Bahrain	8,421	11,871	17,941	n.a.
Iran	6,232	12,576	15,312	n.a.
France	12,343	50,682	38,650	n.a.
Netherlands	12,188	12,416	17,015	n.a.
Australia	10,194	18,273	22,845	n.a.
Kuwait	5,944	11,499	19,307	n.a.
China	7,859	11,384	16,284	n.a.

EXPORTS AND RE-EXPORTS	1972	1973
Saudi Arabia	37,366	37,017
United Arab Emirates	14,153	11,480
Iran	3,669	2,400
Kuwait	2,794	2,204
Bahrain	1,887	5,600
Oman	1,696	1,130
Lebanon	1,627	2,200
Japan	1,431	1,200

EDUCATION

	PUPILS/STUDENTS		TEACHERS	
	1970–71	1972–73	1970–71	1972–73
Primary	14,479	15,725	752	794
Preparatory General	2,537	3,026	141	197
Secondary General	911	1,123	80	112
Teacher Training	237	288	38	n.a.
Commercial School	66	69	10	n.a.
Technical School	143	125	34	n.a.
Religious Institutions	158	175	16	n.a.

In 1972–73 there were 16 kindergartens with 2,595 infants; 89 Qatari students graduated from foreign universities.

THE CONSTITUTION

A new provisional constitution came into effect in July 1970. Executive power is put in the hands of the Council of Ministers, appointed by the Head of State, and assisted by an Advisory Council of twenty members, whose term was extended for a further three years in May 1975. All fundamental democratic rights are guaranteed.

THE GOVERNMENT

HEAD OF STATE
Amir: Sheikh KHALIFA BIN HAMAD AL-THANI.

COUNCIL OF MINISTERS
(*July* 1975)

Prime Minister: Sheikh KHALIFA BIN HAMAD AL-THANI.

Minister of Finance and Petroleum: Sheikh ABDUL-AZIZ BIN KHALIFA AL-THANI.

Minister of Foreign Affairs: Sheikh SUHAIM BIN HAMAD AL-THANI.

Minister of Education, Culture and Youth Care: Sheikh JASIM BIN HAMAD AL-THANI.

Minister of Public Health: KHALED MUHAMMAD AL-MANI.

Minister of the Economy and Commerce: Sheikh NASSIR BIN KHALID AL-THANI.

Minister of Electricty and Water: Sheikh JASSIM BIN MUHAMMAD AL-THANI.

Minister of Justice: (vacant).

Minister of the Interior: Sheikh KHALID BIN HAMAD AL-THANI.

Minister of Industry and Agriculture: Sheikh FAISAL BIN THANI AL-THANI.

Minister of Public Works: KHALID BIN ABDULLAH AL-ATIYYAH.

Minister of Information: ISSA GHANIM AL-KAWARI.

Minister of Municipal Affairs: Sheikh MUHAMMAD BIN JABR AL-THANI.

Minister of Labour and Social Affairs: ALI BIN AHMAD AL-ANSARI.

Minister of Communications and Transport: ABDULLAH BIN NASSIR AL-SUWAIDI.

DIPLOMATIC REPRESENTATION

EMBASSIES ACCREDITED TO QATAR

(In Doha, unless otherwise indicated)

Afghanistan: Baghdad, Iraq.
Austria: Jeddah, Saudi Arabia.
Belgium: Kuwait City, Kuwait.
Canada: Teheran, Iran.
Egypt: P.O.B. 2899; *Ambassador:* SALEH ZAGLOOL NASR ELDIN.
Finland: Jeddah, Saudi Arabia.
France: P.O.B. 2699; *Ambassador:* BERNARD LOPINOT.
Germany, Federal Republic: *Ambassador:* HANS HELMUT FREUNDT.
Guinea: Jeddah, Saudi Arabia.
India: P.O.B. 2788; *Ambassador:* ARIF QAMARAIN.
Iran: P.O.B. 1633; *Ambassador:* SHANADIN SHAFFRA.
Iraq: *Ambassador:* DAHHAM AL-ALOUSI.
Italy: Kuwait City, Kuwait.
Japan: Kuwait City, Kuwait.
Jordan: P.O.B. 2366; *Ambassador:* JAWDAT AL-MOHESIN.
Kuwait: P.O.B. 1177; *Ambassador:* ABDEL HAMID A. EL-BUAIGAN.
Lebanon: P.O.B. 2441; *Ambassador:* MARCELLE NAMMOOR.
Malaysia: Kuwait City, Kuwait.

Mauritania: *Ambassador:* BA ALI BAMBI BA.
Morocco: *Ambassador:* MUHAMMAD EL-TAHER BANNANI.
Netherlands: Kuwait City, Kuwait.
Norway: Teheran, Iran.
Oman: *Ambassador:* AHMED MUHAMMAD EL-NABAHANI.
Pakistan: P.O.B. 334; *Ambassador:* HAKIM MUHAMMAD AHSAN.
Saudi Arabia: *Ambassador:* Sheikh AHMED BIN ALI AL-MUBARAK.
Senegal: Teheran, Iran.
Somalia: *Ambassador:* ABDULLAH HAJI ABDEL-RAHMAN.
Sudan: *Ambassador:* EISA MOUSTAFA.
Spain: Kuwait City, Kuwait.
Sweden: Jeddah, Saudi Arabia.
Switzerland: Jeddah, Saudi Arabia.
Syria: *Ambassador:* ABDUL AZIZ AL-RIFAI.
Tunisia: *Ambassador:* AMMAR EL-SUEDI.
Turkey: Jeddah, Saudi Arabia.
United Kingdom: P.O.B. 3; *Ambassador:* DAVID CRAWFORD.
U.S.A.: *Ambassador:* ROBERT PAGANELLI.
Yemen Arab Republic: *Ambassador:* ABDULLA HIJIRI.

JUDICIAL SYSTEM

Justice is administered by five courts (Higher Criminal, Lower Criminal, Civil, Appeal and Labour) on the basis of codified laws. In addition traditional Sharia courts apply the Holy Law in certain cases. Non-Muslims are invariably tried by a court operating codified law. Independence of the judiciary is guaranteed by the provisional Constitution.

RELIGION

The indigenous population are Muslims of the Sunni sect, most being of the strict Wahhabi persuasion.

PRESS

Al-Doha Magazine: Ministry of Information, P.O.B. 2324, Doha; f. 1969; monthly; Arabic; circ. 3,000.

Dar Al-Ouroba: P.O.B. 633, Doha; Newspaper Printing and Publishing, Doha; publ. daily Arabic newspaper *Al-Arab*, circ. 7,000; weekly Arabic magazine *Al-Ouroba*, circ. 12,000; and weekly English magazine *Gulf News.*

RADIO AND TELEVISION

Radio Qatar: P.O.B. 1414, Doha; f. 1968; government service transmitting for 15 hours in Arabic, Saturday to Thursday, and 18 hours on Friday; and in English for 12 hours daily.

Qatar Television: P.O.B. 1944, Doha; f. 1970; two 5 kW transmitters began beaming programmes throughout the Gulf in March 1972. A second phase of development, including colour transmission, began in mid-1974.

FINANCE

BANKING

Qatar Monetary Agency: P.O.B. 1234, Doha; f. 1966 as Qatar and Dubai Currency Board; became Qatar Monetary Agency 1973 when Qatar issued its own currency, the Qatar riyal; currency in circulation (Dec. 1973) QR 129 million; Governor MAJED AL-MAJED.

Qatar National Bank, S.A.Q.: P.O.B. 1000, Doha; f. 1965; cap. and res. Q. riyals 82m., dep. 530m. (1974); Chair. Sheikh ABDUL AZIZ BIN KHALIFA AL-THANI; Gen. Man. A. A. NORRIE.

Arab Bank Ltd.: Amman, Jordan; P.O.B. 172, Doha; Man. SHARIF AL-JA'ABARY.

Bank of Oman: Doha.

Bank Saderat Iran: P.O.B. 2256, Doha.

Banque de Paris et des Pays-Bas: Paris; P.O.B. 2636, Doha.

British Bank of the Middle East, The: P.O.B. 57, Doha; Man. R. R. REES.

Chartered Bank: London; P.O.B. 29, Doha.

Commercial Bank of Qatar Ltd.: P.O.B. 3232, Doha; Gen. Man. ALAN MITCHELL.

First National City Bank: P.O.B. 2309, Doha.

Grindlays Bank Ltd.: London; P.O.B. 2001, Doha; Man. L. B. CANT.

Al-Mashreq Bank: Doha.

Qatar Commercial Bank: P.O.B. 637, Doha.

United Bank of Pakistan: P.O.B. 242, Doha.

INSURANCE

Qatar Insurance Co.: P.O.B. 666, Doha; f. 1964; assets and reserves 10m. Q. Riyals (1973); branches in Dubai and Riyadh; Man. FATHI I. GABR.

COMMERCE

Qatar Chamber of Commerce: P.O.B. 402, Doha; f. 1963; 13 mems. appointed by decree; Pres. AHMED MUHAMMAD AL-SOWAIDI; Sec. KAMAL AL-SALEH.

OIL

Qatar General Petroleum Agency: f. August 1974, as successor to Qatar National Petroleum Co.; in line with OPEC policy the Government agreed a participation agreement with the Qatar Petroleum Company and Shell Qatar in January 1974 to secure Qatar's interest. On February 20th, 1974 the Government signed a further agreement which gives it a 60 per cent interest in QPC and Shell Qatar. The Qatar General Petroleum Agency controls the Arab Maritime Co. for Oil Transport, Arab Co. of Petrol Pipes, National Oil Distribution Co., Arab Co. for Shipbuilding and Repair; Chair. Sheikh ABDUL AZIZ BIN KHALIFA AL-THANI (Minister of Finance and Petroleum).

Qatar Petroleum Co.: Doha; 40 per cent shareholder in the operating Company producing and exporting crude oil and natural gas liquids from the Dukhan oilfield (onshore). Under a participation agreement signed in 1974 the Government became a 60 per cent interest holder in the QPC Concession and crude oil production facilities effective from January 1st 1974. The operations in Qatar have been carried out on behalf of the interest holders by QPC as interim operator. Total production from the Dukhan fields in 1974 was 81.4 million barrels.

Shell Company of Qatar: P.O.B. 47, Doha; holds an offshore concession. A Government participation agreement was signed in February 1974 (*see* above); Man. Dir. H. R. H. CREPET. Total production in 1974 was 13.9m. long tons.

Qatar Gas Company: Doha; f. 1974; natural gas; Qatar Government owns 70 per cent and Shell owns remaining 30 per cent; capital QR 400 million.

TRANSPORT

ROADS

There are some 600 miles of surfaced road linking Doha and the oil centres of Dukhan and Umm Said with the northern end of the peninsula. A 65-mile long road from Doha to Salwa was completed in 1970, and joins one leading from Al Hufuf in Saudi Arabia, giving Qatar land access to the Mediterranean. A 260-mile highway, built in conjunction with Abu Dhabi, links both states with the Gulf network. Road construction is a continual process throughout the peninsula.

PIPELINES

Oil is transported by pipeline from the oilfield at Dukhan to the loading terminal at Umm Said. Natural gas is brought by pipeline from Dukhan to Doha where it is used as fuel for a power station and water distillation plant.

SHIPPING

Qatar National Navigation and Transport Co. Ltd.: P.O.B. 153, Doha; shipping agents, lighterage contractors, ship chandlers, clearing and forwarding agents at the ports of Qatar.

Director of Ports: ALI AL-SAAD, P.O.B. 313, Doha.

Doha Port: A four-berth quay costing £10 million was completed in 1970; it is linked with Doha Town by a 3,600-ft. causeway. A new expansion project, estimated to cost QR 162 million is expected to add six more berths.

Umm Said Harbour: Although accommodating smaller tankers (up to 60,000 d.w.t.) Umm Said still has the country's main oil terminal. A 220,000 ton capacity tank farm is connected by a series of pipelines with QPC's three main gathering stations. A 700 ft. wide jetty is linked to a grain mill and a newly constructed fertilizer plant.

CIVIL AVIATION

Doha international airport is equipped to receive jumbo jets; its runway was extended to 15,000 ft. in 1970. Plans for a new civil airport, which will have one of the longest runways in the world (14,993 ft.) are under preparation.

Gulf Air Co. Ltd.: jointly owned by Bahrain, Qatar, Abu Dhabi and British Airways (*see* Bahrain—Civil Aviation).

Gulf Helicopters: P.O.B. 811, Doha; 74 per cent owned by Gulf Air, 26 per cent by a British Airways Group; fleet of four Sikorsky S.62A.

Doha is served by the following airlines: Air France, Alia (Jordan), British Airways, EgyptAir, Gulf Air, Iranian Airways, Iraqi Airways, Kuwait Airways, MEA, Pakistan International Airlines, Saudia, Syrian Arab Airlines, TMA, Yemen Airlines.

EDUCATION

All education within Qatar is free and numerous scholarships are awarded for study overseas. The state education system was inaugurated in 1956, when 1,388 boys attended 17 primary schools; by 1974–75 some 20,164 children (10,528 boys and 9,618 girls) attended primary school. The six-year primary stage is followed by a three-year preparatory stage (2,683 boys and 2,241 girls in 1974–75) and a further three-year secondary stage. General secondary education facilities are complemented by a teacher-training institute, a technical school, a school of commerce and an institute of religious studies. 1,399 boys and 816 girls received general secondary education in 1974–75, while there were 307 trainee teachers enrolled. A number of Qataris are at present enrolled in higher education institutions abroad, almost all in other Arab countries, Britain, or the U.S.A. The number of schools (97 in 1975) and of teachers (1,695), together with expenditure under the 1973–74 budget of about £380 per pupil indicates the importance given to education in Qatar. In October 1973 the first two Higher Teacher Training Colleges were opened providing education to university level. The Ministry of Education has made substantial efforts to mitigate the effects of social deprivation on equal educational opportunity.

BIBLIOGRAPHY

See Bibliography on Bahrain, p. 243, and United Arab Emirates, p. 774.

Saudi Arabia

PHYSICAL AND SOCIAL GEOGRAPHY OF THE ARABIAN PENINSULA

The Arabian peninsula is a strongly marked geographical unit, being delimited on three sides by sea—on the east by the Persian Gulf and Gulf of Oman, on the south by the Indian Ocean, and on the west by the Red Sea—and its remaining (northern) side is occupied by the deserts of Jordan and Iraq. This isolated territory, extending over more than one million square miles, is, however, divided politically into several states. The largest of these is Saudi Arabia, which occupies over 800,000 sq. miles; to the east and south lie much smaller territories where suzerainty and even actual frontiers are in some instances a matter of doubt. Along the shores of the Persian Gulf and Gulf of Oman there are first the State of Kuwait, with two adjacent patches of "neutral" territory; then, after a stretch of Saudi coast, the island of Bahrain and the Qatar peninsula, followed by the United Arab Emirates and the much larger state of Oman. The People's Democratic Republic of Yemen, composed of the former British colony of Aden and former (British) Protectorate of South Arabia, occupies most of the southern coastline of the peninsula. To the north of it, facing the Red Sea, lies the Yemen Arab Republic. The precise location of frontiers between these states and Saudi Arabia, which adjoins them all, is still in some doubt, and atlases show varying positions. The granting of oil concessions and continued discoveries of oil may ultimately lead to a more accurate delimitation.

PHYSICAL FEATURES

Structurally, the whole of Arabia is a vast platform of ancient rocks, once continuous with north-east Africa. In relatively recent geological time a series of great fissures opened, as the result of which a large trough, or rift valley, was formed and later occupied by the sea, to produce the Red Sea and Gulf of Aden. The Arabian platform is tilted, having its highest part in the extreme west, along the Red Sea; and it slopes gradually down from west to east. Thus the Red Sea coast is often bold and mountainous, whereas the Persian Gulf coast is flat and low-lying being fringed with extensive coral reefs that make it difficult to approach the shore in many places.

Dislocation of the rock strata in the west of Arabia has led to the upwelling of much lava, which has solidified into vast barren expanses known as *harras*. Volcanic cones and flows are also prominent along the whole length of the western coast as far as Aden, giving peaks that rise well above 10,000 ft. The maximum height of the mountains is attained in the south, in the Yemen Arab Republic, where summits reach 14,000 ft.; and the lowest part of this mountain wall occurs roughly half-way along its course, in the region of Jeddah, Mecca, and Medina. One main reason for the presence of these three towns is the geographical fact that they offer the easiest route inland from the coast, and one of the shortest routes across Arabia.

Further to the east the ancient platform is covered by relatively thin layers of younger rocks. Some of the strata have weathered away to form shallow depressions; others have proved more resistant, and now stand out as ridges. This central area, diversified by shallow vales and upstanding ridges and covered in many places by desert sand, is called the Najd, and is spoken of as the homeland of the Wahhabi sect, which now rules the whole of Saudi Arabia. Farther east still practically all the land lies well below 1,000 ft. in altitude, and both to north and south lie desert areas. The Nefud in the north has some wells, and even a slight rainfall, so life is possible for a few oasis cultivators and pastoral nomads. But south of the Najd lies the Rub' al-Khali, or Empty Quarter, a rainless, unrelieved wilderness of shifting sand, too difficult for occupation even by nomads.

Though most of the east coast of Arabia (termed al-Hasa) is low-lying, there is an exception in the imposing ridge of the Jebel Akhdar of Oman, which also produces a fjord-like coastline along the Gulf of Oman. One other feature of importance is the presence of several large river valleys, or *wadis*, cut by river action at an earlier geological period, but now almost, or entirely, dry and partly covered in sand. The largest is the Wadi Hadhramaut, which runs parallel to the southern coast for several hundred miles; another is the Wadi Sirhan, which stretches from the Nefud north-westwards into Jordan.

CLIMATE

Because of its land-locked nature, the winds reaching Arabia are generally dry, and almost all the area is arid. In the north there is a rainfall of 4 to 8 inches annually; further south, except near the coast, even this fails. The higher parts of the west and south do, however, experience appreciable falls—rather sporadic in some parts, but copious and reliable in the Yemen Arab Republic. There are even small, regularly flowing streams in the higher parts of the Yemeni mountains, but none manages to reach the sea. The Jebel Akhdar (Green Mountain) of Oman, as its name indicates, also has more rainfall than the surrounding districts.

Because of aridity, and hence relatively cloudless skies, there are great extremes of temperature. The summer is overwhelmingly hot, with maxima of over 120° F., which are intensified by the dark rocks, whilst in winter there can be general severe frost and even weeks of snow in the mountains—sheepskins are worn in the Yemen Arab Republic. Another feature, due to wide alternations of temperature, is the prevalence of violent local winds. Also, near the coast, atmospheric humidity is very high, and this makes living conditions extremely unpleasant. The coasts of both the Red Sea and Persian Gulf are notorious for their humidity.

Owing to the tilt of the strata eastwards, and their great elevation in the west, rainfall occurring in the hills near the Red Sea apparently percolates gradually eastwards, to emerge as springs along the Persian Gulf coast. This phenomenon, borne out by the fact that the flow of water in the springs greatly exceeds the total rainfall in the same district, would appear to indicate that water may be present underground over much of the interior. Hence irrigation schemes to tap these supplies have been developed, notably in Najd at al-Kharj. Results are, however, fairly limited.

ECONOMIC LIFE

Over much of Arabia life is dependent on the occurrence of oases. Many wells are used solely by nomads for watering their animals, but in some parts, more especially the south, there is some regular cultivation. The Yemen Arab Republic, in particular, has a well-developed agriculture, showing a gradation of crops according to altitude, with cereals, fruit, coffee and *qat* (a narcotic) as the chief products. Other agricultural districts occur in Aden and the Hadhramaut (in Yemen P.D.R.), in Oman, and in the large oases of the Hijaz (including Medina and Mecca). Despite this, however, it must be emphasized that in the main, conditions in Arabia are harsh, and human life depends for existence partly on resources brought in from outside—the revenues from pilgrimage, trading by dhow in the Indian Ocean, or trading in the East Indies. A major change in the economy of Saudi Arabia and the Gulf states has taken place following the exploitation of oil, the revenues from which are transforming these states, and *inter alia* allowing the import of food for Arab oil workers.

RACE

The inhabitants of the centre, north, and west are of almost unmixed Mediterranean stock—lightly built, long-headed, and dark. In coastal districts of the east, south, and south-west intermixture of broader-headed and slightly heavier peoples of Armenoid descent is a prominent feature; and there has been some exchange of racial type with the populations on the Persian shores of the Persian Gulf and Gulf of Oman. Owing to the long-continued slave trade, negroid influences from Africa are also widespread. On this basis it is possible to delimit two ethnic zones within Arabia: a northern, central and western area, geographically arid and in isolation, with a relatively unmixed racial composition; and the coastlands of the south, south-west, and east, showing a mixed population.

LANGUAGE

Arabic is the only language of Arabia. Unlike many other parts of the Middle East, European languages are not current.

HISTORY

ANCIENT AND MEDIEVAL HISTORY

Although there is some support for the belief that Arabia was at one time a land of great fertility, there is little evidence of this in historical times. For the most part Arabian history has been the account of small pockets of settled civilization, subsisting mainly on trade, in the midst of an ocean of nomadic tribes whose livelihood was derived mainly from camel-breeding and raiding. The earliest urban settlements developed in the south-west, where the flourishing Minaean kingdom is believed to have been established as early as the twelfth century B.C. This was followed by the Sabaean and Himyarite kingdoms, which lasted with varying degrees of power until the sixth century A.D. The term "kingdom" in this connection implies rather a loose federation of city states than a centralized monarchy. As an important trading station between east and west, southern Arabia was brought into early contact with the Persian and Roman empires, whence spread the influence of Judaism, Zoroastrianism, and later Christianity. Politically, however, the south Arabian principalities remained independent, though there was an abortive Roman expedition in A.D. 24, and two brief periods of Abyssinian rule in the fourth and sixth centuries A.D.

By the end of the sixth century the centre of gravity had shifted to the west coast, to the Hijaz cities of at-Ta'if, Mecca and Medina. While the southern regions fell under the somewhat spasmodic control of the Sasanid rulers of Persia, the Hijaz grew in independence and importance as a trade route between the Byzantine Empire, Egypt, and the East. From the fifth century onwards Mecca was dominated by the tribe of Quraish, through whose extensive commercial activities influences from Byzantine, Persian, Aramaic and Judaic sources began to make themselves felt. Meanwhile the central deserts remained obstinately nomadic, and the inhospitable east coast formed for the most part a corner of the Persian sphere of influence.

It is not necessary here to relate in detail the events that led to the spectacular outbreak of the Arabs from the Arabian peninsula and their political and social domination within a century of an area extending from Spain to northern India. Ostensibly the driving force behind this great movement was the Islamic religion preached by Muhammad, a humble member of the Quraish tribe; and so powerful was its appeal that not only was the faith itself widely adopted, but even the language of its holy book, the Koran, has left an indelible impression on the speech of all the peoples it reached.

But this flowering and development of Arabism was to proceed for the most part outside the confines of the Arabian peninsula itself. The Islamic unification of the Near and Middle East reduced the importance of the Hijaz as a trade route. Mecca retained a unique status as a centre of pilgrimage for the whole Muslim world, but Arabia as a whole, temporarily united under Muhammad and his successors, soon drifted back into disunity. The Yemen was the first to break away from the weakening Abbasid Caliphate in Baghdad, and from the ninth century onwards a variety of small dynasties established themselves in Sana'a, Zabid, and other towns. Mecca also had its semi-independent governors, though their proximity to Egypt made them more cautious in their attitude towards the Caliphs and the later rulers of that country, particularly the Fatimids of the tenth to twelfth centuries. In Oman in the south-east a line of spiritual Imams arose who before long were exercising temporal power; to the north the Arabian shores of the Persian Gulf provided a home for the fanatical Carmathian sect whose influence at times extended as far as Iraq, Syria, Mecca, and the Yemen.

THE OTTOMAN PERIOD

Arabia continued to be restless and unsettled until the beginning of the sixteenth century, when the whole peninsula came nominally under the suzerainty of the Ottoman Sultans at Istanbul. It was a hold that was never very strong, even in the Hijaz, while in Oman and the Yemen native lines of Imams were once again exercising unfettered authority before the end of the century. More important for the future of the peninsula was the appearance of European merchant adventurers in the Indian Ocean and the Persian/Arabian Gulf. The Portuguese were the first to arrive in the sixteenth century, and they were succeeded in the seventeenth and eighteenth centuries by the English, Dutch and French. By the beginning of the nineteenth century Britain had eliminated her European rivals and had established her influence firmly in the Gulf and to a lesser extent along the southern coast.

The political structure of Arabia was now beginning to take the shape it has today. The Yemen was already a virtually independent Imamate; Lahej broke away in the middle of the eighteenth century, only to lose Aden to Britain in 1839 and to become the nucleus of the Aden Protectorate. To the north of the Yemen was the principality of the Asir, generally independent, though both countries were occupied by the Turks from 1850 to the outbreak of the Great War. The Hijaz continued to be a province of the Ottoman Empire. In 1793 the Sultanate of Oman was established with its capital at Muscat, and during the nineteenth century all the rulers and chieftains along the Persian Gulf coast, including Oman, the sheikhdoms of the Trucial Coast, Bahrain and Kuwait, entered into close and "exclusive" treaty relations with the British Government. Britain was principally concerned to prevent French, Russian and German penetration towards India and to suppress the slave and arms trades.

Meanwhile the Najd in the centre of Arabia was the scene of another upheaval with religious inspirations. The puritanical and reforming Wahhabi movement, launched in the middle of the eighteenth century, had by 1800 reached such strength that its followers were able to capture Kerbela and Najaf in Iraq, Damascus in Syria, and Mecca and Medina in the Hijaz. They were defeated by Muhammad Ali of Egypt, acting in the name of the Ottoman Sultan, in 1811–1818 and again in 1838; but the Wahhabi ruling house of Sa'ud continued to rule in the interior. Towards the end of the century they were in danger of being eclipsed by the Shammar line of Rashid to the north, who had Turkish support; but in 1902 Abd al-Aziz ibn Sa'ud, the late ruler of Saudi Arabia, succeeded in recapturing the Wahhabi capital of Riyadh, and by the outbreak of the Great War was master of the whole of central Arabia, including the Hasa coast of the Persian Gulf. In 1910, with the aim of reviving the ideals of the Wahhabi movement, he established the *Ikhwan* or Brethren and proceeded to settle them in colonies throughout the Najd, thus forming the basis of a centralized organization that was to prove a powerful instrument in later years.

MODERN HISTORY

When Turkey entered the war on the side of Germany in October 1914 Arabia inevitably became a centre of intrigue, if not necessarily of military action. British influence was paramount along the eastern and southern coasts, where the various sheikhs and tribal chiefs from Kuwait to the Hadhramaut lost no time in severing their last slender connections with the Ottoman Empire. On the other hand, the Turks had faithful allies in Ibn Rashid of the Shammar to the north of the Najd, and in Imam Yahya of the Yemen; they also retained their garrisons along the west coast, both in the Asir, whose Idrisi ruler was impelled by his long-standing enmity with the Imam of the Yemen to intrigue against them, and in the Hijaz, where Sharif Hussein of Mecca still acknowledged Ottoman suzerainty. In the centre Ibn Sa'ud, who had accepted Turkish recognition in 1913 of his occupation of the Hasa coast, was in close and friendly relations with the Government of India.

British military strategy developed as the war dragged on into a two-pronged thrust against the Turks from both Egypt and the Persian Gulf. In the implementation of this plan opinions were divided on the extent to which use could be made of the Arab population. The Indian Government on the eastern wing, while favouring the pretensions of Ibn Sa'ud, preferred to see the problem in purely military terms, and opposed any suggestion of an Arab revolt. This, however, was the scheme favoured by the Arab Bureau in Cairo, whose views eventually prevailed in London. They were alarmed at the Ottoman declaration of a *Jihad* (Holy War) and possible repercussions in Egypt and North Africa. Negotiations were started at a very early stage with Arab nationalist movements in Syria and Egypt, but these met with comparatively little success. More progress was made when the British negotiators turned their attentions to the Sherif of Mecca, Hussein, member of the Hashimi family that had ruled in Mecca since the eleventh century A.D. The support of such a religious dignitary would be an effective counter to Turkish claims. Hussein was inclined to favour the Allied cause, but was reluctant to act independently, and it was only after he had elicited from the British (in the Mac-Mahon correspondence—*see* DOCUMENTS ON PALESTINE, p. 48) promises which he believed would meet Arab nationalist aspirations that he decided to move. On June 5th, 1916, he proclaimed Arab independence and declared war on the Turks. By November things had gone so well that he felt able to claim the title of King of the Hijaz. Military operations continued throughout the winter, and in July 1917 the port of Aqaba was captured and the Hijaz cleared of Turkish troops except for a beleaguered and helpless garrison in Medina.

Arabia thereafter remained comparatively peaceful, and was not even greatly disturbed by the complicated post-war political manoeuvres in the Middle East. Hussein played a somewhat ineffectual role in maintaining the Arab point of view at the peace conferences and over the allocation of mandates, and as a result forfeited the favour of the British Government. When, therefore, he was unwise enough to challenge the growing power of his old enemy Ibn Sa'ud, he found himself entirely without support. Ibn Sa'ud's stature had been steadily growing since the end of the war. In November 1921 he had succeeded in eliminating the house of Ibn Rashid and annexing the Shammar, and a year later he was recognized by the Government of India as overlord of Ha'il, Shammar and Jawf. On March 5th, 1924, King Hussein laid claim to the title of Caliph, vacant by the deposition of the Ottoman Sultan. His claims were nowhere recognized, and Ibn Sa'ud, declaring him a traitor, overran the Hijaz in a campaign of a few months, captured Mecca and forced Hussein's abdication. Hussein's eldest son, Ali, continued to hold Jeddah for another year, but was then driven out, and on January 8th, 1926, Ibn Sa'ud proclaimed himself King of the Hijaz, so formally marking the establishment of the Saudi Arabian kingdom.

THE KINGDOM OF SAUDI ARABIA*

Ibn Sa'ud's new status was recognized by Britain in the Treaty of Jeddah of 1927, while Ibn Sa'ud in his turn acknowledged his rival Hussein's sons, Abdallah and Faisal, as rulers of Transjordan and Iraq, and also the special status of the British-protected sheikhdoms along the Gulf coast. The northern frontier of his domains had previously been established by the Hadda and Bahra agreements of November 1925, which set the Mandate boundaries as the limit of his expansion; while the border war with Yemen

* For subsequent developments in the rest of the Arabian Peninsula, *see* separate chapters on Bahrain, Kuwait, Oman, Qatar, United Arab Emirates, Yemen Arab Republic and Yemen People's Democratic Republic.

was, after protracted negotiations and a brief war, settled in 1934. (For a fuller account of this, *see* the Yemen Arab Republic chapter, History.)

During the years that followed, the new king continued to be absorbed in his primary task of unifying and developing his country. The colonization policy begun in 1910 was pursued vigorously; land settlements were established and Bedouin unruliness was suppressed. A start was made at the modernization of communications, and the need for economic development along modern lines was emphasized by the falling-off in the pilgrimage during the early 1930s. The serious crisis that this produced might indeed never have been averted had it not been for the discovery of oil in Bahrain in 1932 and the subsequent extension of prospecting to the mainland.

Saudi Arabia's chief sufferings during the war were economic, though there was an Italian air raid on Dhahran (and also on Bahrain) in October 1940. The pilgrimage traffic dropped away almost to extinction, and in April 1943 it was found necessary to include Saudi Arabia in the benefits of Lease-Lend. Up to September 1946 $17,500,000 had been received, and in August of that year there was a further £10,000,000 from the Export-Import Bank. Two years later, however, as a protest against American policy over Palestine, an American loan of $15,000,000 was turned down. But by this time the oil industry alone was enough to establish the Saudi Arabian economy firmly on its feet.

In January 1944 the California Arabian Standard Oil Company, owned jointly by the Standard Oil Company of California and the Texas Company, was re-formed as the Arabian American Oil Company. This was reconstructed once more in December 1948 to include the Standard Oil Company of New Jersey and Socony Vacuum—a move that brought protests from the French Government. Under an agreement of 1928 shareholders in the Iraq Petroleum Company, who included the latter two American companies as well as French and British interests, had agreed not to secure rival concessions within an area including the Arabian peninsula. A settlement was finally reached at the end of 1948, by which this so-called "Red Line" clause was abandoned. Meanwhile production had been mounting steadily as new fields were developed; a refinery was opened at Ras Tanura in October 1945, and two years later work was started on a pipeline to connect the Arabian fields with the Mediterranean. In spite of a year's suspension owing to events in Palestine, the task was completed before the end of 1950, and oil first reached the Lebanese port of Sidon on December 2nd of that year. In the same month a new "fifty-fifty" agreement was signed with the Arabian American Oil Company which was to set an interesting example to other foreign oil interests in December 1951. In 1956 a government-owned National Oil Company was formed to exploit areas not covered by the Aramco concession.

Saudi Arabia was an original member of the Arab League formed in 1945, and to begin with played a loyal and comparatively inconspicuous part. Ibn Sa'ud sent a small force to join the fighting against

Israel in the summer of 1948. When the solidarity of the League began to show signs of cracking, it was natural that he should side with Egypt and Syria rather than with his old dynastic enemies, the rulers of Iraq and Jordan. In course of time, however, he began to turn once more to internal development, and to forget his political quarrel with the United States in his need for economic advice and aid. The $15,000,000 Export-Import Bank loan was finally taken up in August 1950; in January 1951 a Point Four Agreement was signed, and in June a Mutual Assistance Pact. But the real basis of development was the revenue from the ever-expanding oil industry. This was sufficient to justify the announcement in July 1949 of a $270,000,000 Four Year Plan, in which an ambitious programme of railway development was the main item. A railway now links the oilfields in the east with Riyadh in the centre, and extends to the port of Dammam. For the rest the King's policy was one of cautious modernization at home, and the enhancement of Saudi Arabian prestige and influence in the Middle East and in world affairs generally.

AFTER IBN SA'UD

On November 9th, 1953, King Ibn Sa'ud died at the age of 71, and was succeeded peacefully by the Crown Prince, Sa'ud. It was assumed that there would be no major changes, but the policy already adopted of strengthening the governmental machine and of relying less on one-man rule was continued by the formation of new ministries and of a regular cabinet. In March 1958 King Sa'ud conferred upon his brother, the Amir Faisal, full powers over the foreign, internal and economic affairs of Saudi Arabia, with the professed aim of strengthening the machinery of government and centralizing responsibilities. In December 1960, however, the Amir Faisal resigned, and the King took over the office of Prime Minister himself. In the following month a High Planning Council, with a team of international experts, was set up to survey the country's resources, and thereafter there has been slow but steady progress in the modernization of the country.

Throughout his reign the King had seen his role as that of a mediator between the conflicting national and foreign interests in the Arab Middle East. He refused to join either the United Arab Republic or the rival Arab Federation. Relations with Egypt ranged from the mutual defence pacts between Egypt, Syria and Saudi Arabia in October 1955 (to which Yemen and Jordan adhered the following year) to the open quarrel in March 1958 over an alleged plot to assassinate President Nasser. Subsequently, relations improved, and the King visited Cairo in September 1959. Contacts with the United States have always been close, owing to the extensive American oil interests. The Saudi Arabian Government also played a leading role in bringing the Arab governments together after Egypt's nationalization of the Suez Canal in July 1956 and the Israel, British and French military action in the Sinai peninsula in November. In 1961 Saudi Arabia supported the Syrians in their break with the United Arab Republic, and in general

relations with the U.A.R. deteriorated. By 1964, however, in spite of the tensions over the Yemen revolution, there were signs of improved relations. King Sa'ud attended the Cairo conference on the Jordan waters dispute in January, and in March, after a meeting in Riyadh, diplomatic relations with the United Arab Republic were resumed. In September Prince Faisal attended the Arab Summit Conference in Alexandria, and afterwards had talks with President Nasser on the Yemen situation.

THE REIGN OF KING FAISAL

Meanwhile, in March 1964 King Sa'ud had relinquished all real power over the affairs of the country to his brother, Crown Prince Faisal, who had again acted as Prime Minister intermittently during 1962, and continuously since the middle of 1963. The rule of Prince Faisal was expected to result in many concessions to "Westernization" such as more cinemas and television, with more profound social and economic reforms to follow. The division of the country into provinces, each with a thirty-man council, was under study early in 1964. The change of power, by which King Sa'ud retired as active monarch, was supported in a statement by the *ulema* council of religious leaders "in the light of developments, the King's condition of health, and his inability to attend to state affairs". In November 1964 Sa'ud was formally deposed, and Faisal became King, as well as head of the Council of Ministers with the exclusive power of appointing and dismissing Ministers. His younger brother Khalid was appointed Crown Prince. On August 24th, 1965, King Faisal confirmed his stature as an important Arab leader, when he concluded an agreement at Jeddah with President Nasser of the U.A.R. on a peace plan for the Yemen.

Although the Yemen problem remained unsolved, there was evidence of Saudi Arabia's genuine anxiety that a solution should be found, even though in April 1966 the construction of a military airfield near the frontier brought protests from the Yemeni Republican Government and the U.A.R. Representatives of Saudi Arabia and the U.A.R. met in Kuwait in August 1966 in an attempt to implement the Jeddah agreement. But relations with both the U.A.R. and the Arab League continued to be tense, and no progress was evident. Matters were not improved by the appearance in Cairo of ex-King Sa'ud, with a public declaration of his support for U.A.R. policy in Yemen.

During 1966 and 1967 King Faisal made extensive visits abroad. In the June 1967 Arab-Israeli war, Saudi forces collaborated with Jordanian and Iraqi forces in action against Israel. At a summit conference of Arab leaders held in Khartoum at the end of August 1967 Saudi Arabia agreed to put up £50 million of a total £135 million fund to assist Jordan and the U.A.R. in restoring their economic strength after the hostilities with Israel. At the same time an agreement was concluded with President Nasser on the withdrawal of U.A.R. and Saudi military support for the warring parties in the Yemen. By way of recompense for these concessions the Saudi Arabian Government persuaded the other Arab states that it was in their best interests to resume production of oil, shipments of which to western countries had been suspended for political reasons after the war with Israel.

EVENTS SINCE THE 1967 WAR

Though outwardly calm, the internal political situation was apparently disturbed by abortive coups in June and September 1969. Plans for both are presumed to have been discovered in advance, the only visible evidence of the attempts being the arrests of numbers of army and air force officers. A flight of private capital abroad was also reported. Some observers drew parallels with developments in Libya. In the Yemen the Royalist cause which the Saudi Government had strongly supported appeared to be within sight of victory early in 1968, but by mid-1969 its remaining adherents had largely been driven into exile and the civil war seemed to have come to an end, although further hostilities were reported during the 1969-70 winter. Dissension amongst the Royalists, which led to the withdrawal of Saudi assistance, was a principal factor in this decline. Discussions between Sana'a representatives and Saudi officials took place at Jeddah in March 1970, and the Yemen Republic was officially recognized in July. Relations with Southern Yemen deteriorated, however, and an extensive battle on the disputed frontier took place in December 1969, with Saudi Arabia apparently winning easily owing mainly to its superior air power.

The important relationship with Iran, under some strain at the beginning of 1968 over the Bahrain question, improved greatly later in the year. In October the two countries signed a treaty which at last delineated their offshore boundaries. In November the Shah paid a state visit to Saudi Arabia; the occasion, which included a pilgrimage, was acclaimed as symbolic of Muslim unity. The Saudi Government took a favourable view of the proposed Gulf federation, and gave financial assistance for the road linking the Trucial sheikhdoms. Together with Kuwait the government was closely involved in 1971 in the diplomatic efforts to secure Bahrain's and Qatar's membership of a nine-member Gulf federation, but the two sheikhdoms eventually decided to remain apart from the Trucial States, which formed the United Arab Emirates.

As principal guardian of Muslim interests, Saudi Arabia was particularly concerned by the fire at the Al Aqsa mosque in Jerusalem in August 1969, and hence it was the leading instigator of the Islamic summit conference held to condemn Israel in Rabat the following month.

Relations with Sudan have become closer since the communist-inspired *coup* attempt there in July 1971, and President Nemery visited Saudi Arabia in November 1971 and April 1972. Saudi Arabia also played an important role in attempting to bring about agreement between the Palestinian guerrillas and the Jordanian Government after the final confrontation between them in north Jordan in July 1971. Aided by Egypt, the Saudi Government managed to arrange a series of talks between the representatives of the two sides in Jeddah during the last half of the year.

In 1972 and 1973 Faisal visited a large number of countries, including Morocco, Italy, Algeria, Tunisia, Egypt, France, Uganda, Chad, Senegal, Mauritania and Niger. The growing tension in the Gulf area generally was illustrated by an agreement with the U.S.A. in May 1973 for the supply of Phantom jets to Saudi Arabia, and the signing of a £250 million contract in June 1973 for British Aircraft Corporation to supply Saudi Arabia with air defence support systems. Saudi Arabia, however, warned the United States that she might be prepared to withhold oil supplies unless the U.S.A. changed her attitude in the Arab-Israeli dispute.

The warning was prophetic but went unheeded. When the Arab-Israeli war of October 1973 broke out, therefore, and when United States aid to Israel continued, Saudi Arabia, despite her traditionally good relationship with the West, led a movement by all the Arab oil-producing countries to exert political pressure by cuts in oil production. Since there was no immediate response from the U.S.A., OPEC members placed an embargo on oil supplies to that country and to several other developed western countries as well. Supplies to the western world were not cut off entirely, but it was announced that production would be progressively reduced until attitudes towards support for Israel changed. The Arab states having thus made clear the strength of their determination to achieve a Middle East settlement more favourable to the Palestinian cause, there then began, in the closing months of 1973 and the first months of 1974, a period of extremely active negotiating for a settlement that would mean more than simply an end to Arab-Israeli hostilities. On the one hand the western nations attempted to repair their links with the oil-producing countries; on the other hand these latter debated among themselves how far they should wield the "oil weapon" to achieve their ends.

As the possessor of 40 per cent of Middle East oil reserves, and one quarter of world reserves, Saudi Arabia, together with Egypt, was in the very forefront of these negotiations. It soon became apparent, however, that the Saudis held views that differed from those of other producer nations (notably Libya, Algeria and Iran) on the extent to which oil could be safely used to put pressure on the West. It was feared in Riyadh that too much of this pressure would have economic repercussions that nobody wanted. The more radical OPEC members wanted to retain the oil embargo until a satisfactory outcome to the October hostilities was reached. At a meeting in March 1974, though, Saudi Arabia pressed for a resumption of supplies to the U.S.A. and, when this was agreed, resisted any moves to increase oil prices, which, by January 1974 had risen to nearly four times the pre-hostilities level. It was reported that, in order to achieve their aim, the Saudis threatened to leave OPEC and lower prices unilaterally. Reluctantly, therefore, the radical OPEC members agreed to a freeze on oil prices.

Meanwhile, in negotiations with consumer countries, the Saudis made it clear that the continued supply of oil was dependent not only on a change in attitudes towards supporting Israel but on assistance to Saudi Arabia itself in industrializing and diversifying its economy against the day when oil reserves become depleted. The U.S.A. in particular showed itself eager to satisfy these conditions and an important economic and military co-operation agreement was signed in May 1974.

In December 1974 Saudi Arabia concluded a £370 million arms deal with France and in January 1975 a £328 million arms contract with the U.S.A. was announced.

On March 25th, 1975, King Faisal was assassinated by one of his nephews, Prince Faisal ibn Masaed ibn Abdul Aziz. Although at first it was feared that the assassination was a deep-seated plot it soon became clear that the assassin, although not mentally deranged, had acted on his own. King Faisal was succeeded by his half-brother, Khalid, the Crown Prince, and Khalid's brother Prince Fahd became Crown Prince, retaining his post as Minister of the Interior. Prince Fahd also became First Deputy Prime Minister.

No major change of policy resulted from Khalid's succession. He quickly announced that Saudi Arabia would follow the late King Faisal's policies involving Islamic solidarity and the strengthening of Arab unity, and that the objectives remained "the recovery of occupied Arab territories" and the "liberation of the City of Jerusalem from the claws of Zionism". At a press interview in May 1975 King Khalid said that Saudi Arabia would concede Israel's right to exist in its pre-1967 borders in return for total Israeli withdrawal from Arab lands occupied in 1967 and the establishment of a Palestinian state between Israel and Jordan.

In domestic affairs the Saudi Government continues to allow social change to unfold organically and at a moderate pace, without using its huge wealth to force the pace. A significant event in May 1975 was the opening of the King Faisal Medical City on the outskirts of Riyadh. Because of the official belief in organic change, despite the great improvement in communications, welfare services and the standard of living in general over recent years, Saudi Arabia remains the most traditional and conservative of the Arab countries; the ancient restrictions on smoking, alcohol, dress, etc., are still very largely observed, as are the Muslim calendar and religious festivals.

ECONOMIC SURVEY

AREA AND POPULATION

The area of Saudi Arabia has been estimated at 830,000 square miles but the borders have not all been defined and therefore no precise figure can be arrived at. Estimates of the kingdom's population have been a subject of dispute for some years. An official estimate for January 1st, 1956, put the figure at 6,036,400. A census was held in 1962–63 but the results were officially repudiated. The UN Population Division estimated the mid-1965 population at 6,750,000 and projected figures of 7,740,000 for mid-1970 and 8,966,000 for mid-1975. Meanwhile, Saudi officials were still quoting figures of 5–6 million in 1975. However, a census had been completed by mid-1975, a necessary preliminary to the ambitious second five-year development plan (1975–80), and it was reliably reported to have arrived at a total of only 4.3 million native Saudis. Half the population is thought to be urban by now, with the other half about equally divided between farmers clustered around oases and the Bedouin.

Foreigners working in Saudi Arabia are thought to number at least one million, though the last official estimate put them at only 400,000. Most of them are Arabs from poorer states, such as Yemenis and Egyptians.

The population of Riyadh, the royal capital, is estimated at about 450,000 and that of Jeddah, the leading port and commercial centre nearly 500,000. The other main towns are the holy cities of Mecca (250,000) and Medina (150,000), the east coast commercial centres, Al-Khobar (100,000) and Dammam (100,000), two agricultural centres, Hofuf (150,000) and Haradh (100,000), the summer capital, Ta'if (100,000), Yanbo, Abha, Jizan, Dhahran and Ras Tanura.

AGRICULTURE

Agriculture contributes less than 3 per cent of G.D.P. although it employs about half the population. Cultivation is confined to oases and to irrigated regions, comprising a mere 0.2 per cent of the total land area: the remaining agricultural land is used for low-grade grazing. The chief crops cultivated on irrigated or cultivated soil are wheat, lucerne, millet and maize, while fruits of many varieties, particularly dates, grow in abundance in oases. Production of wheat, which is, after dates, the second largest crop, provided only 25 per cent of requirements in 1972–73. Experiments with new wheat varieties, undertaken in collaboration with the FAO, have, however, shown that yield can be doubled. Sheep and goats are bred extensively, both for meat and for wool; camels are also bred.

The Government has recognized the importance of developing agriculture as a means of reducing the dependence on imported food, and as a means of diversifying the economy and of raising rural living standards. Since scarcity of water constitutes the chief factor limiting the development of agriculture,

the Government has launched an ambitious programme to overcome this obstacle. Execution of this
programme—which includes surveys for underground
water resources, construction of dams, irrigation and
drainage networks, combined with distribution of
fallow land, settlement of Bedouin and the introduction of mechanization—is aimed at eventually
raising agricultural production to the level of near
self-sufficiency in food. Consequently, budgetary
allocations for the agricultural sector have increased
several times over during the period since 1964–65
when the figure was 149 million riyals. The first
development plan covering 1970–75 projected a total
outlay of 1,317.5 million riyals for agriculture and
water resources. The second five-year plan (1975–80)
projects spending on agriculture at 4,000 million riyals
and on water (mainly desalination plants) at no less
than 34,000 million. During the second plan, irrigated
farm land is to be expanded by 50,000 hectares over
its present area of 121,000 hectares, though success
in reaching this target will largely depend on studies
on the development of water resources.

During the 1960s, surveys were carried out over
393,800 square miles—45 per cent of the total area
of the country—on behalf of the Government by
foreign consulting firms. The reports indicated a large
potential for considerably increasing agricultural
production in nearly all areas under cultivation by
improving water distribution and drainage systems.
Four other important projects which have been
undertaken by the Government include the al-Hasa
irrigation scheme, the Faisal Model Settlement
scheme, the Wadi Jizan dam project and the Abha dam.

The al-Hasa irrigation and drainage scheme,
inaugurated in December 1971, was completed over
five years at a cost of 260 million riyals and will
result in the reclamation of 12,000 hectares. It is the
country's biggest agricultural scheme and about
50,000 persons will benefit from it. The Faisal Model
Settlement scheme which cost 100 million riyals, has
involved extensive land reclamation and irrigation
and has provided permanent farmland and housing
for 1,000 Bedouin families. The Wadi Jizan dam,
which was inaugurated in March 1971, has a reservoir
with a capacity of 71 million cubic metres of water
and was built at a cost of 42 million riyals. It constitutes the first stage in a plan for development of Wadi
Jizan which will increase the irrigated area by 8,000
hectares and will contribute about 8.8 million riyals
annually to agricultural and livestock production.
The Abha dam in the Asir region was opened in April
1974 with a reservoir capacity of 2.4 million cubic
metres.

During the 1975–80 plan, seawater desalination
capacity will be increased from 13 million gallons per
day to 145 million gallons per day. Eight desalination
plants will be built, seven will be expanded for a
second time and five for a third time. By 1980 there
should be 27 plants in the kingdom.

Government encouragement to farmers is substantial. Interest-free loans are available through the
Agricultural Bank, set up in 1963, and chemical
fertilizer, domestic or imported, is distributed at
half-price. There are also large subsidies or incentives
for irrigation pumps, farm machinery or imported
rearing stock.

OIL

The most important industry in Saudi Arabia is
the production of crude oil and petroleum products.
In 1974 the country produced more oil than any other
country in the Middle East and ranked third in world
crude oil output, following the U.S.S.R. and the
U.S.A. Proven Saudi oil reserves stood at 164,000
million barrels at the end of 1974 or about 23 per cent
of the world total.

In 1933 a Saudi concession was granted to Standard
Oil Company of California to explore for oil. The
operating company, the Arabian American Oil
Company (Aramco), began explorations for oil in 1933
and was soon drilling. It discovered oil in commercial quantities in 1938. By the end of the Second
World War it had discovered four oil fields and had
established the necessary facilities, including a large
refinery, to meet post-war demands for crude oil and
refined products.

At the end of 1974, Aramco's proven reserves of
crude oil were estimated to be 103,400 million
barrels.* Production comes from fourteen major oilfields: Ghawar, Abqaiq, Safaniya, Abu Hadriya, Abu
Sa'fah, Qatif, Fadhili, Manifa, Khursaniyah, Dammam, Berri, Marjan, Zuluf and Khurais. Of these the
three first-named are by far the most important.
Ghawar is generally accepted as the world's largest
oilfield and Safaniya is the world's largest offshore
field. Production has mounted steadily each year
since 1956 to reach 2,996 million barrels in 1974 but
fell steadily from the average 8.2 million barrels a
day in 1974 to an average of 6.5 million b/d over the
first half of 1975. The Ras Tanura refinery on the
Gulf, which was completed in 1945, processed 224
million barrels of crude oil, natural gasoline and raw
liquified petroleum gas in 1974.

A 30/31-inch pipeline system, 1,068 miles long, runs
from Aramco's oil fields to the Mediterranean port of
Sidon, Lebanon. It was brought into operation in
1950 and by 1958 its capacity was 470,000 barrels
per day. It is operated by the affiliated Trans-Arabian
Pipe Line Company (Tapline).

The oilfields contain vast quantities of natural gas
and Aramco has developed the capacity in the
Abqaiq and Ghawar fields to reinject 405,000,000
cubic feet per day in order to conserve the gas for
future use and to reinforce the underground pressure
necessary for oil recovery.

The area of Aramco's original concession was about
673,000 square miles. The company has, however,
agreed to relinquish progressively parts of its concession areas. Following relinquishments in 1960,
1963, 1968 and 1973, its concession has been reduced
to 85,000 square miles and is expected to be progressively reduced to 20,000 square miles by 1993.

In 1949 the Saudi Arabian government granted the
Getty Oil Corporation a 60-year exclusive concession

---

* 1 barrel = 42 U.S. gallons = 34.9726 Imperial gallons.

covering its undivided half interest in the Saudi Arabian-Kuwait Neutral Zone, now called the Partitioned Zone. Getty's production in 1974 averaged 82,000 b/d. In 1969 Japanese interests, which had obtained concessions from Saudi Arabia and Kuwait in 1957 and 1958 covering an offshore area of the neutral zone of the Gulf, found oil which is now being exploited by the Arabian Oil Co. Production in 1974 averaged 379,659 b/d, 3.6 per cent less than in 1973.

In 1965 the French state company Auxerap concluded an agreement for offshore exploration in the Red Sea. The agreement provided for the Saudi Arabian state organization Petromin (General Petroleum and Mineral Organization) to participate in exploitation of any commercial discoveries. In December 1967 two further agreements were signed. One was between Petromin and the Italian state oil corporation, Agip, and Phillips Petroleum of the U.S., by which the latter two firms were permitted to explore for oil during a period of six years in some 77,000 square km. of the Rub'al-Khali and 9,600 square km. in the Eastern Province. This concession was relinquished in 1973. The other was between Petromin and a group led by two American corporations, Sun Oil Co. and Natomas, under which the group was granted similar rights in the Red Sea area. In both cases the prospecting concerns were to act as contractors for Petromin which retained the legal title to the concessions.

Revenues from oil rose steadily throughout the 1960s, from $334 million in 1960 to $949 million in 1969. This process accelerated at the beginning of the next decade, however, and the Saudi Government received $1,885 million in 1971 and $2,734 million in 1972. By far the largest proportion of this sum derived from one company, Aramco, which contributed $2,633 million in 1972. As a result of a participation agreement, effective from January 1973, the Government acquired a 25 per cent share in Aramco, which was scheduled to rise to a controlling interest by 1982. But following the Arab-Israeli war oil prices were pushed up drastically, and the Arab oil-producing countries in general made moves to acquire controlling shares in the oil companies. The Saudi Government waited until June 1974 before following the example of other governments and acquiring a 60 per cent interest in Aramco, backdated to January of that year. As a result of these developments revenues from oil were expected to rise dramatically in the coming years. Aramco paid $4,195.0 million in 1973, but this leaped to $22,375 million in 1974 out of total Saudi oil revenue of $22,573.5 million.

OTHER INDUSTRIES

The development of modern industry is at an early stage, and most of the kingdom's manufacturing is geared to the local market—building materials, some consumer products and some oil-related activities. The big local enterprises are the Ras Tanura oil refinery, three private-sector cement plants, and several Petromin projects (*see* below). The smaller industries include cement and plastic pipes; brick, marble and tile; furniture; cotton textile and carpet

mills; a shoe factory; detergent, paint and chemical plants; and food processing and soft drink industries.

In terms of output, construction has been the most important industry after oil in recent years, contributing around 4.4 per cent to G.D.P. at current prices in 1972–73, about the same as manufacturing industry. Consumption of cement rose to 1,280,000 tons in 1973, with 78 per cent being produced domestically compared with 25 per cent in 1960. However, other branches of manufacturing have grown faster in recent years than the construction industry.

The chief instrument of industrial development is Petromin, set up in 1962 to implement the long-run objective of diversifying the economy through the establishment of industries based on hydrocarbons and other minerals. Petromin's existing industrial projects include a steel rolling mill in Jeddah which produces reinforcing bars. This started production in 1968 with an annual capacity of 45,000 tons, which will eventually be expanded to 300,000 tons. Petromin also set up an oil refinery in Jeddah, which came on stream in 1968 with a capacity of 12,000 barrels per day, since raised to 45,000 barrels a day, and a lubricating oil plant. Petromin also has a 51 per cent holding in the Saudi Arabian Fertilizer Company (SAFCO), whose plant at Dammam started producing fertilizer and sulphuric acid in 1969.

The big oil price increase of late 1973 made much more ambitious industrialization programmes possible, and in the second five-year plan investment in industrial projects in the Eastern Region will amount to SR 37,800 million ($10,900 million) and in the Western Region SR 10,800 million ($3,100 million). The nucleus of the plans for the Eastern Region is the $4,500 million gas gathering, treatment and distribution plant, announced in March 1974 and contracted to Aramco in March 1975. The plant will be designed to handle around 6,000 million cubic feet of gas a day, corresponding to an oil production level of 12 million b/d, and will produce around 12 million tons a year of natural gas liquids (NGL), of which Saudi Arabia expects to be the world's biggest exporter by 1977. The gas plant will feed petrochemical and industrial ventures, power an electricity network and supply Aramco's operations.

Pipeline projects by Petromin within the framework of the second five-year plan are a crude line from the eastern fields to Yanbo on the Red Sea, a gas liquids line along the same route to allow the export of NGL from Yanbo, and a 500,000-b/d spur line from Tapline to the Red Sea port of Duba.

Petromin also plans three export refineries, with an initial capacity of 750,000 b/d, rising to 1.5 million b/d. Two of these will be in the east and one in the west. Shell is to build one at Jubail on the east coast, and Mobil will probably be asked to build one at Yanbo. The third is likely to be built by either Mitsubishi or Gulf.

There are to be three petrochemical complexes in the east and one in the west, as well as two or three fertilizer plants. A consortium of U.S.-led firms has been formed to build a direct-reduction steel plant at

Jubail, but final agreement on the project is awaited. Most of the output of the plant, which would use imported iron ore, probably in slurry form from Brazil, would be exported. An aluminium plant has also been under consideration by Petromin since 1974.

The only minerals, apart from hydrocarbons, being produced at present are limestone (for cement production), gypsum, marble, clay and salt. Substantial iron ore deposits are known to exist, as well as copper, gold, lead, zinc, silver and some uranium. The Mining Code offers good incentives for foreign investors in this field. U.S., French and Japanese teams are working on mineral surveys at present.

Industry planned outside Petromin's control—as joint ventures between foreign companies and Saudi interests—include a car assembly plant to turn out 8,000 General Motors vehicles a year by mid-1976, an assembly plant for small trucks to produce 60,000 vehicles a year, and a steel-pipe plant. The last two ventures have Japanese partners.

TRANSPORT

Until 1964 the only surfaced roads, besides those in the oil network, where in the Jeddah-Mecca-Medina area. Since then roads have been given priority with 20 per cent of the development budget. There are now over 7,000 miles of asphalted roads, and over 8,000 miles of new surfaced roads are planned for the period 1975–80.

There are three chief ports: Jeddah and Yanbo on the Red Sea and Dammam on the Gulf. These ports have been undergoing expansion and improvement in recent years. Jeddah, for example, has been modernized with the construction of nine new piers at a cost of about 273 million riyals. Projects are in hand for the development of Jizan and Jubail ports. Major projects include the expansion of the annual capacities of Jeddah and Dammam ports to about two million tons each.

The chief international airports are Jeddah, Dhahran and Riyadh. Although both Jeddah and Riyadh have been considerably improved in recent years, schemes are under way for the expansion of Riyadh and the building of a new airport to the north of Jeddah at a total cost of SR 750 million and SR 1,045 million respectively. Medina and Bisha airports are being improved and a new airport is to be built at Abha. The Government operates the airline, Saudia, which links important Saudi cities, with regular flights to many foreign countries. The airline carried 880,500 passengers in 1972.

The Government operates a modern railway system connecting the port of Dammam on the Gulf with Riyadh, the capital, some 370 miles inland.

FOREIGN TRADE

The total value of the country's exports, which consist almost entirely of oil, amounted to 17,302 million riyals in 1971, 22,761 million riyals in 1972 and 33,501 million riyals in 1973. Western Europe is the major market for Saudi oil and accounted for 52.6 per cent of total exports in 1973, with 41.3 per cent going to EEC countries. Exports to Asia were about 24.4 per cent of the total, with 14.7 going to Japan. Other important sources of foreign exchange derive from the local expenditure of Aramco and from the Pilgrimage traffic.

In 1973 the total value of imports was 7,351 million riyals compared with 4,708 million in 1972. Imports cover a wide range of manufactured goods, particularly machinery, vehicles and transport equipment (accounting for 34 per cent of total imports in 1973) and foodstuffs (24 per cent). Other significant imports are building materials, chemical products and textiles and clothing. The pattern of imports reflects the Saudi development effort and the country's poor agricultural resources. The U.S.A. has been the leading exporter to Saudi Arabia in recent years, accounting for 19.1 per cent of Saudi imports in 1973, followed by Japan and U.K. (15.4 per cent and 7.1 per cent) and West Germany (6.9 per cent). Lebanon, which accounted for 11.7 per cent of imports in 1973, has an important entrepôt trade with Saudi Arabia. There was a deficit on current account in 1968 and 1969, but there has since been a surplus which rose to $9,982 million in 1973. The rapid rise in oil exports and other receipts (chiefly Aramco royalties and the pilgrimage traffic) since 1970 has greatly exceeded the rise in investment income payments and government expenditure abroad.

FINANCE

The currency is described in the Statistical Survey. The Saudi Arabian Monetary Agency, established in 1952, is the Central Bank, its total holdings of gold, foreign currencies and other international reserve assets standing at $20,500 million at the end of May 1975. This compared with $14,500 million at the end of 1974 and only $3,877 million at the end of 1973. Saudi reserves are surpassed only by those of West Germany.

There are 12 commercial banks in Saudi Arabia, with over 70 branches. The largest Saudi commercial bank, the National Commercial Bank, has branches in most of the principal towns. The Agricultural Bank, set up in 1964, granted 5,414 new loans totalling 36.3 million riyals in 1973/74, compared with 4,477 loans totalling 19.6 million riyals in 1972/73. The Saudi Credit Bank was set up in 1973 to advance interest-free loans to low-income families. An Industrial Development Fund and a Real Estate Development Fund were also set up in 1974/75 to provide interest-free loans for expanding or modernizing an industry or buying a house for personal use.

AID

Since the oil price rises of late 1973, Saudi Arabia has stepped up its aid enormously, mostly to other Arab and Muslim states. In addition to buying arms direct for Egypt, it is committed under the Rabat Arab summit decisions of 1974 to providing $1,000 million a year to Egypt, Syria, Jordan and the Palestine Liberation Organization. Saudi Arabia has been fairly generous with other gifts to Egypt, Syria and Jordan, and the Saudi Development Fund, set up in September 1974 with a capital of 10,000 million riyals has also promised Egypt loans totalling $161 million. So far the Fund has disbursed loans totalling about $167 million (579 million riyals) to Malaysia, Tunisia and the Sudan, as well as Egypt.

Saudi Arabia has tried to compensate for the effect of the big oil price increases in other ways too. It has supported the IMF's oil facility, lent the World Bank a total of $890.8 million, contributed to various UN agencies and been among the principal financial supporters of the Islamic Development Bank, founded at the instigation of the late King Faisal, and the various funds and banks set up by rich Arab states to help their poorer brethren in the rest of the Arab and Third Worlds.

BUDGET AND ECONOMIC DEVELOPMENT PLAN

Oil revenues traditionally provide over 90 per cent of the state's budget revenue. In the 1975/76 Saudi financial year expenditure exceeds revenue for the first time in years. Revenue is set at 95,850 million riyals and expenditure at 110,935 million riyals. The difference is apparently to be made up from the kingdom's vast monetary reserves (*see* above). Expenditure in the previous financial year was set at 45,743 million riyals, and the record level of spending envisaged in the current year reflects vastly increased outlays on development, as the new five-year plan gets under way, and on defence. Development and other projects have been allocated two-fifths of total expenditure and defence one-fifth.

Revenue is actually budgeted lower in the current year than last year, when the figure was 98,247 million riyals. King Khalid said in announcing the budget that revenue was based on an oil production level of 6.75 million barrels a day, compared with the allowable capacity of 8.5 million b/d. The King also said that total oil income would be 3.6 per cent lower than in the previous year.

Saudi Arabia ran a budget deficit as recently as 1969/70, since when it has found itself left with bigger and bigger budget surpluses at the end of each financial year. In 1974/75 the Government budgeted for a surplus for the first time—a massive 52,504 million riyals.

The second five-year development plan (1975–80) provides for expenditure of no less than 498,000 million riyals (about $142,000 million). Described by the Saudi Minister of State for Planning, Hisham Nazer, as an "experiment in social transformation", the plan aims at raising G.D.P. by 114 per cent from 148,000 million riyals to 318,000 million riyals, and to reduce the proportion of G.D.P. accounted for by oil from about 86 per cent to 82 per cent.

Sixty-three per cent of the plan total (314,000 million riyals) has been allocated to economic and social development, 18 per cent (89,600 million riyals) to defence, 8 per cent (39,800 million riyals) to administration and 11 per cent (54,700 million riyals) to other items, including foreign aid. Within the economic and social sector, education has been given 23 per cent (114,500 million riyals) of the total plan expenditure.

STATISTICAL SURVEY

AREA AND POPULATION

AREA (estimated)	MID-YEAR POPULATION (UN estimates)†					
	1969	1970	1971	1972	1973	1974
830,000 sq. miles*	7,524,000	7,740,000	7,965,000	8,199,000	8,443,000	8,697,000

* 2,149,690 square kilometres.

† A census was held in 1962–63 but the results have been officially repudiated.

PRINCIPAL TOWNS
(estimated population in 1974)

Riyadh (royal capital)	350,000
Jeddah (administrative capital) . .	300,000
Mecca	250,000
Medina	100,000
Dammam	60,000
Al-Khobar	60,000

SAUDI ARABIA-IRAQ NEUTRAL ZONE

The Najdi (Saudi Arabian) frontier with Iraq was defined in the Treaty of Mohammara in May 1922. Later a Neutral Zone of 7,000 sq. km. was established adjacent to the western tip of the Kuwait frontier. No military or permanent buildings were to be erected in the zone and the nomads of both countries were to have unimpeded access to its pastures and wells. A further agreement concerning the administration of this zone was signed between Iraq and Saudi Arabia in May 1938.

SAUDI ARABIA-KUWAIT PARTITIONED ZONE

A Convention signed at Uqair in December 1922 fixed the Najdi (Saudi Arabian) boundary with Kuwait. The Convention also established a Neutral Zone of 5,770 sq. km. immediately to the south of Kuwait in which Saudi Arabia and Kuwait held equal rights. The final agreement on this matter was signed in 1963. Since 1966 the Zone has been divided between the two countries and each administers its own half, in practice as an integral part of the state. However, the oil wealth of the whole Zone remains undivided and production from the on-shore oil concessions in the Partitioned Zone is shared equally between the two states' concessionaires (Aminoil and Getty).

AGRICULTURE

PRINCIPAL CROPS
('000 metric tons)

	1971	1972	1973
Wheat	150*	150	150
Barley	18	20*	18*
Millet	134	135*	130*
Sorghum	190	190*	175*
Seasame seed	16.0	16*	16*
Tomatoes	80	90*	100*
Onions (dry)	34*	34*	35*
Grapes	24*	25*	25*
Dates	251.5	250*	250*
Oranges	13	15*	15*

* FAO estimate.
Source: FAO, *Production Yearbook 1973.*

LIVESTOCK NUMBERS
(FAO estimates)

	1970-71	1971-72	1972-73
Cattle	295,000	300,000	300,000
Sheep	2,950,000	2,975,000	3,000,000
Goats	1,730,000	1,715,000	1,700,000
Asses	135,000	140,000	143,000
Camels	560,000	570,000	580,000
Chickens	6,500,000	7,300,000	8,000,000

Source: FAO, *Production Yearbook 1973.*

LIVESTOCK PRODUCTS
(FAO estimates, metric tons)

	1971	1972	1973
Beef and veal	10,000	10,000	10,000
Mutton, lamb and goats' meat	39,000	41,000	43,000
Other meat	23,000	24,000	25,000
Edible offals	12,545	13,066	13,569
Cows' milk	29,000	30,000	31,000
Sheep's milk	52,000	54,000	56,000
Goats' milk	45,000	46,000	48,000
Hen Eggs	5,600	5,800	6,100

Source: FAO, *Production Yearbook 1973.*

FISHING
('ooo metric tons)

	1965	1966	1967	1968	1969	1970	1971	1972	1973
Total catch	18.6	20.2	22.1	25.2	29.5	29.1	29.9	30.4	31.3

Source: FAO, *Yearbook of Fishery Statistics 1973.*

MINING

	1969	1970	1971	1972	1973	1974
Crude petroleum ('ooo metric tons)	148,846	176,850	223,414	285,583	364,300	395,900
Natural gas (million cubic metres)	2,590	2,852	3,000	n.a.	n.a.	n.a.

CRUDE OIL PRODUCTION BY COMPANY
(million barrels)

	TOTAL	ARAMCO	GETTY OIL	ARABIAN OIL
1938 . . .	0.5	0.5	—	—
1946 . . .	59.9	59.9	—	—
1955 . . .	356.6	352.2	4.4	—
1967 . . .	1,023.8	948.1	25.1	50.6
1968 . . .	1,114.0	1,035.8	23.2	55.0
1969 . . .	1,173.9	1,092.4	22.7	58.8
1970 . . .	1,386.3	1,295.3	28.3	62.7
1971 . . .	1,740.8	1,641.6	33.7	65.5
1972 . . .	2,201.7	2,098.4	28.3	75.0
1973 . . .	2,772.7	2,677.4	23.4	71.9
1974 . . .	3,095.1	2,996.5	29.8	68.7

OIL REVENUES BY SOURCE
(million U.S. $)

	TOTAL	ARAMCO	GETTY OIL	ARABIAN OIL	OTHER COMPANIES
1939 . . .	3.2	3.2	—	—	—
1946 . . .	10.4	10.4	—	—	—
1955 . . .	340.8	338.2	2.6	—	—
1967 . . .	909.1	859.4*	17.8	31.8	0.1
1968 . . .	926.8	872.0	13.6	34.3	6.9
1969 . . .	949.0	895.2	15.2	37.1	1.5
1970 . . .	1,214.0	1,148.4	17.2	40.3	3.8
1971 . . .	1,884.9	1,806.4	20.6	44.2	13.7
1972 . . .	2,744.6	2,643.2	28.0	68.7	4.7
1973 . . .	4,340.0	4,195.0	22.0	91.4	31.7
1974 . . .	22,573.5	22,375.0	53.3	113.6	31.6

* Including certain special payments.

INDUSTRY
SELECTED PRODUCTS

		1969	1970	1971	1972
Nitrogenous fertilizers	'ooo metric tons	—	23.0	34.6	69.0
Liquefied petroleum gas . . .	,, ,, ,,	1,138	1,461	1,536	1,361
Motor spirit (petrol)*	,, ,, ,,	3,040	4,422	4,044	4,499
Kerosene	,, ,, ,,	434	884	684	641
Jet fuel	,, ,, ,,	1,816	1,775	1,699	2,100
Distillate fuel oils	,, ,, ,,	2,611	2,992	3,168	3,260
Residual fuel oil	,, ,, ,,	12,366	18,046	17,361	16,957
Petroleum bitumen (asphalt) . .	,, ,, ,,	142	169	185	159
Quicklime	,, ,, ,,	9	8	9	12
Cement	,, ,, ,,	576	675	703	910
Electric energy†	million kWh	653	724	805	1,000

* Including naphtha.

† Public sector only, excluding industrial establishments generating electricity primarily for their own use.

FINANCE

100 halalah = 20 qursh = 1 Saudi riyal.

Coins: 1, 5, 10, 25 and 50 halalah; 1, 2 and 4 qursh.*

Notes: 1, 5, 10, 50 and 100 riyals.

Exchange rates (July 1975): £1 sterling = 7.63 Saudi riyals; U.S. $1 = 3.49 Saudi riyals.

100 Saudi riyals = £13.10 = $28.65.

* The coins of 1, 2 and 4 qursh are being gradually withdrawn from circulation.

Note: Prior to January 1960 the prevailing exchange rate was U.S. $1 = 3.75 Saudi riyals (1 riyal = 26.67 U.S. cents). From January 1960 to August 1971 the exchange rate was $1 = 4.50 riyals (1 riyal = 22.22 U.S. cents). Between December 1971 and February 1973 the rate was $1 = 4.145 riyals (1 riyal = 24.13 U.S. cents). It was $1 = 3.730 riyals (1 riyal = 26.81 U.S. cents) from February to August 1973; and $1 = 3.55 riyals (1 riyal = 28.17 U.S. cents) from August 1973 to March 1975, when the riyal's direct link with the dollar was ended and the currency was valued in terms of the IMF Special Drawing Right (based on a weighted "basket" of 16 national currencies since July 1974). Initially the exchange rate was fixed at $1 = 3.475 riyals (1 riyal = 28.78 U.S. cents) but this was later revised to $1 = 3.49 riyals (1 riyal = 28.65 U.S. cents). In terms of sterling, the exchange rate between November 1967 and June 1972 was £1 = 10.80 riyals.

BUDGET
(million riyals)

REVENUE	1973-74	1974-75	EXPENDITURE	1973-74	1974-75
Oil Royalties	5,336	37,561	Defence	1,711	2,418
Income Tax (inc. tax on oil			Interior	1,267	1,944
receipts)	15,930	56,871	Education	1,677	2,515
Customs	330	400	Health	499	727
Other Items	1,214	3,415	Development Projects . .	14,263	26,397
			General Budgetary Reserve .	452	2,000
			Other Items	2,941	9,742
TOTAL . . .	22,810	98,247	TOTAL . . .	22,810	45,743*

* In addition to the total given, a further 52,504 million riyals was allocated to the Second Development Plan.

PROJECTS BUDGET
(million riyals)

	1971–72	1972–73	1973–74	1974–75
Ministry of Communications	1,333.7	1,246.1	2,051.7	4,212.1
Civil Aviation	127.3	223.9	466.8	1,150.8
Ministry of Agriculture and Water Resources .	456.0	572.5	855.0	249.7
Ministry of Petroleum and Mineral Resources .	82.3	86.7	136.3	164.3
Ministry of Commerce and Industry . .	28.9	29.9	46.0	114.4
Ministry of Labour and Social Affairs . .	24.1	26.4	36.4	165.7
Ministry of Education and Educational Institutions	125.9	255.1	565.5	1,265.6
Ministry of Health	29.2	45.4	84.2	435.1
Ministry of Interior (Municipalities) . .	438.8	640.5	1,575.3	3,683.8
Ministry of Hajj and Awqaf . . .	28.2	45.7	57.5	103.8
Ministry of Information	48.8	82.2	158.5	205.3
Others	2,312.5	3,463.2	8,229.8	14,646.4
TOTAL	5,035.7	6,717.6	14,263.0	26,397.0

Five-Year Plan (1975-1980): Total allocation SR 498,000 million.

Currency in Circulation (million riyals): 1971-72, 1,788.2; 1972-73, 2,163.9; 1973-74, 2,751.5; 1974-75, 3,374.4; Oct. 1974, 3,620.1.

GROSS DOMESTIC PRODUCT
(million riyals at current prices, twelve months ending June 30th)

	1969–70	1970–71	1971–72	1972–73
Agriculture, Forestry, Fishing . .	984.1	1,015.5	1,058.7	1,138.7
Mining and Quarrying:				
Crude petroleum and natural gas .	8,106.3	12,581.3	16,931.5	26,284.3
Other	46.7	50.3	58.7	90.4
Manufacturing:				
Petroleum refining . . .	1,240.9	1,474.2	1,441.6	1,810.8
Other	431.2	483.6	543.0	617.1
Electricity, Gas and Water . . .	273.1	297.9	302.2	319.1
Construction	933.9	1,007.0	1,173.8	1,808.9
Wholesale and Retail Trade, Restaurants and Hotels . . .	1,007.5	1,067.5	1,177.0	1,553.5
Transport, Storage and Communication .	1,242.5	1,479.3	1,567.4	2,121.3
Finance, Insurance, Real Estate, Business Services:				
Ownership of dwellings . . .	661.0	727.0	800.0	1,000.3
Other	354.7	376.6	411.4	522.5
Community, Social and Personal Services .	238.3	265.4	297.1	338.9
SUB-TOTAL	15,520.2	20,825.6	25,762.4	37,605.5
Less Imputed Bank Service charge . .	—46.0	—49.6	—50.0	—51.0
SUB-TOTAL	15,474.2	20,776.0	25,712.4	37,554.5
Public Administration and Defence . .	942.1	992.7	1,076.4	1,362.6
Other Government Services . . .	736.3	812.4	1,068.5	1,170.5
TOTAL	17,152.6	22,581.1	27,857.3	40,087.6
Import Duties	246.0	340.1	400.0	463.5
GROSS DOMESTIC PRODUCT .	17,398.6	22,921.2	28,257.3	40,551.1

BALANCE OF PAYMENTS
(million riyals—estimates)

	1971	1972	1973
Receipts:			
Exports, f.o.b.	16,294	21,795	33,409
Oil royalties from companies other than Aramco	333	420	448
Pilgrimage	485	653	909
Miscellaneous	478	655	1,123
Total	17,610	23,523	35,889
Payments:			
Imports, c.i.f.	4,226	5,769	7,359*
Non-monetary gold	42	40	50
Investment income payments . .	6,446	8,496	12,350
Government expenditures abroad, n.e.s. .	1,232	1,240	2,986
Travel and personal transportation, n.e.s. .	649	793	1,050
Tapline expenditures abroad . .	212	195	180
Other services	798	1,138	1,932
Total	13,605	17,671	25,907
CURRENT BALANCE	4,005	5,852	9,982
Capital and Financing Account:			
Direct investment liability . .	−490	−1,487	−220†
Other foreign capital . . .	762	1,050	3,978
Gold, foreign exchange holdings, and investments of SAMA . . .	3,753	5,480	6,044
Commercial banks' net foreign position .	103	741	125
Errors and Omissions	57	68	55
CAPITAL BALANCE	4,005	5,852	9,982

* Includes aid granted by Saudi Arabia.

† Netted against compensation paid to Aramco for 25 per cent participation in its oil production facilities.

EXTERNAL TRADE

(million riyals—Muslim calendar)

	1966-67	1967-68	1968-69	1969-70	1970-71
Imports . .	2,288	2,212	2,804	3,213	3,465
Exports . .	7.654	7,853	8,953	9,449	10,600

(million riyals—Gregorian calendar)

	1970	1971	1972	1973*	1974*
Imports . . .	3,197	3,667	4,708	7,351.7	n.a.
Exports . . .	10,907	17,302	22,761	33,501.5	131,820

* Provisional.

PRINCIPAL COMMODITIES
(million riyals)

IMPORTS	1971	1972	1973	EXPORTS	1971	1972	1973
Foodstuffs . .	1,097	1,222	1,875	Crude Oil ⎱ Aramco	11,490	16,937	n.a.
Textiles and Clothing	203	344	657	Refined Oil ⎰ only	1,470	1,647	n.a.
Machinery, Transport	1,099	1,686	2,523				
Building Materials .	463	480	534				
Chemical Products .	240	244	397				
Miscellaneous . .	565	732	1,366				
TOTAL . .	3,667	4,708	7,352	TOTAL (incl. others)	17,302	22,761	33,502

PRINCIPAL COUNTRIES
(million riyals)

	IMPORTS		EXPORTS	
	1972	1973	1972	1973
North America	924.9	1,431.9	1,316.6	1,765.0
U.S.A. . . .	916.7	1,407.0	1,128.9	1,609.2
Western Europe . . .	1,345.5	2,085.5	12,622.4	17,651.8
Belgium . . .	85.5	171.9	274.6	595.4
France . . .	107.5	156.3	2,111.0	3,060.7
Germany, Federal Republic .	293.8	507.5	736.2	1,101.5
Italy	190.6	197.4	2,546.9	3,321.8
Netherlands . . .	198.0	316.2	2,708.2	3,111.2
Spain	12.9	13.1	955.2	2,040.1
United Kingdom . . .	345.0	525.5	1,845.7	2,657.2
Middle East . . .	1,036.6	1,559.8	858.8	1,259.3
Bahrain . . .	91.6	40.6	616.1	770.3
Jordan . . .	50.0	108.9	33.7	67.0
Lebanon . . .	578.9	860.6	81.6	107.6
Africa	180.2	175.4	357.4	493.8
Asia	1,033.1	1,685.5	5,536.9	8,222.6
India	83.6	87.3	230.5	343.4
Japan	675.7	1,132.6	3,443.9	4,938.5
Malaysia . . .	1.1	3.5	89.0	129.6
South America . . .	9.0	3.3	1,207.2	2,252.8

PILGRIMAGE TO MECCA

NUMBER OF PILGRIMS BY COUNTRIES
(Muslim years)

	1389 (1969–70)	1390 (1970–71)	1391 (1971–72)	1392 (1972–73)	1393 (1973–74)	1394 (1974-75)
Afghanistan	9,125	13,663	10,744	17,447	6,220	6,299
Egypt	10,875	11,490	29,171	39,606	36,452	89,617
Indonesia	10,615	14,633	22,753	22,659	40,668	68,872
India	16,057	16,470	16,657	18,306	19,879	21,874
Iran	15,132	48,367	30,299	45,298	57,230	57,314
Iraq	24,902	19,482	17,628	24,681	35,567	58,983
Jordan	6,376	10,909	15,933	25,819	12,851	19,391
Libya	13,547	11,835	16,861	23,774	30,705	30,715
Malaysia	8,353	10,361	10,650	10,395	12,983	15,366
Morocco	10,943	10,640	15,463	22,425	14,923	26,632
Nigeria	24,185	35,187	44,061	48,981	38,869	51,764
Pakistan	28,535	38,256	23,344	95,968*	65,875*	69,455*
Sudan	20,495	14,865	29,004	29,506	33,222	42,084
Syria	22,383	42,339	27,045	31,777	10,448	31,583
Turkey	56,578	13,269	23,922	27,235	36,258	106,045
Yemen	54,658	50,269	60,358	60,250	54,082	75,557
Others	73,554	69,245	85,476	101,055	101,523	147,226
TOTAL . . .	406,295	431,270	479,339	645,182	607,755	918,777

* Including 6,595 pilgrims in 1972-73, 5,187 in 1973-74 and 2,921 in 1974-75 from Bangladesh.

1394: Others included pilgrims from Algeria (49,025), Niger (7,030) and Tunisia (10,785).

Source: General Directorate of Passports and Nationality, Ministry of Interior.

TRANSPORT

RAILWAYS

	1968	1969	1970	1971
Passenger-kilometres (million) . .	60	43	34	39
Freight tonne-kilometres (million) . .	46	45	39	42

Source: United Nations, *Statistical Yearbook 1973.*

ROAD TRAFFIC

(motor vehicles in use)

	1967	1968	1969	1970
Passenger cars . . .	43,800	52,700	61,100	64,900
Commercial vehicles . . .	32,400	35,300	43,200	50,400

Source: United Nations, *Statistical Yearbook 1973.*

INTERNATIONAL SEA-BORNE SHIPPING

('000 metric tons)

	1968	1969	1970	1971
Goods loaded . . .	103,778*	117,500*	151,431	185,820*
of which: Ras Tanura . .	103,478*	117,500*	151,431	169,750*
Goods unloaded . . .	1,847	2,032	2,200	2,955*

* Provisional figures.

Source: United Nations, *Monthly Bulletin of Statistics.*

CIVIL AVIATION

(total scheduled services)

	1969	1970	1971	1972
Aircraft departures . . .	24,491	25,158	n.a.	n.a.
Kilometres flown ('000) . . .	14,304	14,612	16,011	17,000
Passengers carried ('000) . .	505.1	558.0	614	762
Passenger-kilometres (million) . .	472.0	499.8	623	777
Freight carried (metric tons) . .	5,221	4,460	n.a.	n.a.
Freight tonne-km. ('000) . .	5,130	4,487	11,615	15,100
Mail tonne-km. ('000) . .	707	736	855	900
TOTAL tonne-km. ('000) . .	50,779	53,065	68,555	86,000

EDUCATION

(Academic year 1973–74)

	SCHOOLS	TEACHERS	PUPILS
Kindergarten	53	260	9,275
Elementary	2,711	26,612	577,736
Intermediate	503	5,950	100,544
Secondary	108	1,628	27,268
Teacher Training	61	953	13,932
Technical	13	380	2,690
Schools for Deaf, Dumb, Blind . .	10	448	1,725
Adult Education	900	14*	69,082
University Education . . .	3	1,073	10,711†
College of Petroleum and Minerals .	1	220	1,240
Religious Education (higher level) . .	39	689	14,736
Night Schools	65	740	9,363

* Full-time teachers only.

† Including the teachers' training college for women at Riyadh.

Educational budget for financial year 1972–73: 1,585m. riyals.

THE CONSTITUTION

After Ibn Saud had finally brought the whole of present-day Saudi Arabia under his control in 1925, the territory was made into a dual kingdom.

Six years later, in 1932, the realm was unified by decree and became the Kingdom of Saudi Arabia. Saudi Arabia as a whole has in practice been developing, in the last six years or so particularly, from monarchical towards ministerial rule. The power of the Cabinet was further increased in May 1958, when several ministries were delegated to the Crown Prince. In December 1960, however, the Crown Prince resigned and King Saud assumed the Prime Ministership. In 1962, Prince Faisal resumed the Prime Ministership. In 1964 King Saud was relieved of his duties and his brother Prince Faisal was proclaimed King.

The organs of local government are the General Municipal Councils, the District Council and the tribal and village councils. A General Municipal Council is established in the towns of Mecca, Medina and Jeddah. Its members are proposed by the inhabitants and must be approved by the King. Functioning concurrently with each General Municipal Council is a General Administration Committee, which investigates ways and means of executing resolutions passed by the Council. There are also elected district councils under the presidency of local chiefs, consisting of his assistant, the principal local officials and other important persons of the district. Every village and tribe has a council composed of the sheikh, who presides, his legal advisers and two other prominent personages. These councils have power to enforce regulations.

The principal administrative divisions are as follows:

Najd: capital Riyadh. Najd is sub-divided as follows:
1. The principality of Riyadh, to which are associated Wadi al-Dawasir, al-Aflaj, al-Hariq, al-Kharj, al-'Aridh, al-Washm and Sudair.
2. The principality of al-Qasim, comprising 'Unaizah, Buraidah, al-Ras and their villages, and al-Mudhannab and its dependencies.
3. The Northern principality (capital Hayil). This includes the tribes of Shammar, 'Anzah, al-Dhafir and Mutair, the Town of Taima in the south and some northerly towns.

Hijaz: capital Mecca. Includes the principalities of Tabuk, al-'Ula, Dhaba, al-Wajh, Amlaj, Yanbu', Medina, Jeddah, al-Lith, al-Qunfundhah, Baljarshi and Tayif.

'Asir: capital Abha. Includes Abha, Qahtan, Shahran, Rijal Alma', Rijal al-Hajr, Banu Shahr, Mahayil, Bariq and Bisha.

Najran and its villages.

Eastern Province (*Al Hasa*): capital Dammam. Includes Hofuf, Al-Mubarraz, Qatif, Dhahran, Al-Khobar and Qaryat al-Jubail.

THE GOVERNMENT

HEAD OF STATE

H.M. KING KHALID IBN ABDUL AZIZ
(Acceded to the throne March 25th, 1975)
Crown Prince: FAHD IBN ABDUL AZIZ.

COUNCIL OF MINISTERS

(July 1975)

Prime Minister and Foreign Minister: H.M. King KHALID IBN ABDUL AZIZ.

First Deputy Prime Minister and Minister of the Interior: H.R.H. Prince FAHD IBN ABDUL AZIZ.

Second Deputy Prime Minister and Commander of the National Guard: H.R.H. Prince ABDULLAH IBN ABDUL AZIZ.

Minister of Finance and National Economy: H.R.H. Prince MUSA'ID IBN ABDUL RAHMAN.

Minister of Defence and Aviation: H.R.H. SULTAN IBN ABDUL AZIZ.

Minister of Oil and Mineral Wealth: Sheikh AHMED ZAKI YAMANI.

Minister of Agriculture and Water: Sheikh HASSAN AL MUSHARI.

Minister of Pilgrimage Affairs and Endowments: HASSAN KUTBI.

Minister of Communications: Sheikh MUHAMMAD UMAR TAWFIQ.

Minister of Education: Sheikh HASAN IBN ABDULLA AL ASH-SHAYKH.

Minister of Labour and Social Affairs: Sheikh ABDUL RAHMAN ABA AL-KHAYL.

Minister of Commerce and Industry: Sheikh MUHAMMAD ALI AL AWADI.

Minister of Justice: Sheikh MUHAMMAD AL-HARAKAN.

Minister of Health: ABDEL-AZIZ ABDULLA AL-KHUWAITIR.

Minister of Information: Sheikh IBRAHIM AL-ANGARI.

Minister of State for Finance and National Economy: Sheikh MOHAMED ALI ABA AL KHAIL.

Minister of State for Internal Affairs: H.R.H. Prince NAYEF IBN ABDUL AZIZ.

Minister of State for Foreign Affairs: H.R.H. Prince SAUD AL FAISAL.

Minister of State for Planning: HISHAM MUHYI AL DIN NAZIR.

Ministers of State without Portfolio: ABDUL WAHHAB AHMAD ABDUL WASI, SALIH BIN ABDUL RAHMAN AL HUSAIN.

DIPLOMATIC REPRESENTATION

EMBASSIES ACCREDITED TO SAUDI ARABIA

(In Jeddah, unless otherwise indicated)

Afghanistan: *Ambassador:* MUHAMMAD YOUNESSE (also accred to Jordan).

Algeria: *Ambassador:* MOHAMMAD KADRI.

Argentina: Beirut, Lebanon.

Australia: *Ambassador:* IAN HAIG.

Austria: P.O.B. 1706; *Ambassador:* Dr. HEINRICH WINTER (also accred. to Qatar and Yemen Arab Republic).

Belgium: *Ambassador:* JEAN FRANÇOIS TRINE (also accred. to the Yemen Arab Republic).

Brazil: *Ambassador:* MURILLO GURGEL VALENTE.

Cameroon: *Ambassador:* E. ALI MALOUMRY.

Canada: *Ambassador:* JACQUES GIGNIC.

Chad: *Ambassador:* SOULEIMAN OUTMAN.

China (Taiwan): *Ambassador:* HSUEH YU-CHI.

Denmark: *Ambassador:* TROELS MUNK (also accred. to Kuwait).

Egypt: Shareh El Mattar; *Ambassador:* OSMAN HUSSEIN NOURI.

Ethiopia: *Ambassador:* OSMAN MOHAMMED.

Finland: *Ambassador:* LASSILA CAROLUS (also accred. to Qatar).

France: *Ambassador:* ROBERT RICHARD.

Germany, Federal Republic: *Ambassador:* NORBERT MONTFORD.

Ghana: *Ambassador:* OSBORNE HENEY KWEST BREW.

Greece: *Ambassador:* GEORGIOS YANNIE KALITSOUNAKIS (also accred. to the Yemen Arab Republic).

Guinea: *Ambassador:* TOURÉ FODÉ MAMADOU (also accred. to Bahrain, Kuwait and Qatar).

India: *Ambassador:* Sri ZAHIR AHMED.

Indonesia: *Ambassador:* H. RUS'AN (also accred. to Jordan).

Iran: 116 Madina Rd.; *Ambassador:* JAAFAR RAED.

Iraq: *Ambassador:* AHMAD DHAFAR MAHMOUD AL-GHAILANI.

Italy: *Ambassador:* ALBERTO RAMASSO VALACCA.

Japan: *Ambassador:* TAKEO SUZUKI (also accred. to the Yemen Arab Republic).

Jordan: *Ambassador:* Sheikh MUHAMMAD AMIN SHANQITI.

Kenya: Cairo, Egypt.

Korea, Republic: *Ambassador:* KYONG DO-KOON (also accred. to Jordan and Oman).

Kuwait: *Chargé d'Affaires:* BADER MUHAMMAD AHMED AS-SABAH.

Lebanon: *Ambassador:* RASHID FAKHOURI.

Libya: El Sharifia; *Ambassador:* MOHIEDDIN MESSAUDI.

Malaysia: *Ambassador:* AHMAD BIN MOHAMED HASHIM (also accred. to Jordan).

Mauritania: *Ambassador:* MUHAMMAD OULD JIDDOU (also accred. to Kuwait).

Morocco: *Ambassador:* ABDUL RAHMAN BADU.

Netherlands: *Ambassador:* JACOPUS JOHANNES DERKSEN (also accred. to the Yemen Arab Republic).

Niger: P.O.B. 1394; *Ambassador:* OMAR AHMAD.

Nigeria: *Ambassador:* HAJ BELLO MALLABO (also accred. to Jordan and Kuwait).

Norway: *Ambassador:* TROELS MUNK (also accred. to the Yemen Arab Republic).

Oman: *Ambassador:* SULAIMAN BIN ALI-KHALILI.

Pakistan: *Ambassador:* SAIFUR REHMAN.

Philippines: *Ambassador:* LININDING P. PANGADAMAN.

Qatar: *Ambassador:* ABDUL-AZIZ BIN SA'AD AL-SA'AD (also accred. to the Yemen Arab Republic).

Senegal: P.O.B. 1394; *Ambassador:* HAMET DIOP (also accred. to Jordan).

Somalia: *Ambassador:* AHMAD SHEIKH MUHAMMAD ISSA (also accred. to Bahrain, Jordan and Pakistan).

Spain: *Ambassador:* ALBERTO DE MESTAS.

Sudan: *Ambassador:* AL KHITM AL-SANOUSSI.

Sweden: *Ambassador:* BENGT RÖSIÖ (also accred. to Oman, Qatar and the Yemen Arab Republic).

Switzerland: *Ambassador:* MAX CASANOVA (also accred. to Bahrain, Oman, Qatar, the United Arab Emirates and the Yemen Arab Republic).

Syria: *Ambassador:* ABDUL HAMID DARKAL.

Thailand: *Chargé d'Affaires:* ORACHUN TANAPHONG.

Tunisia: *Ambassador:* MUHAMMAD RUWAISI (also accred. to the Yemen Arab Republic).

Turkey: *Ambassador:* CILADET QIYASSI (also accred. to Qatar and the Yemen Arab Republic).

Uganda: *Ambassador:* Lt. Col. ASWA MUSA.

United Kingdom: *Ambassador:* ALAN KEIR ROTHNIE.

U.S.A.: *Ambassador:* JAMES E. AKINS.

Venezuela: *Ambassador:* FRANCISCO MILLAN DELPRETTI.

Yemen Arab Republic: *Ambassador:* ISMAIL AHMAD AL-JARAFI.

Zaire: *Chargé d'Affaires:* NDUKI ENANA II.

Saudi Arabia also has diplomatic relations with Bahrain, Burundi, Ireland, Mali, Mexico, Sri Lanka and the United Arab Emirates.

JUDICIAL SYSTEM

Justice throughout the kingdom of Saudi Arabia is administered according to Islamic law by a Chief Judge, who is responsible for the Department of Sharia Affairs. Sentences in the kingdom are given according to the Koran and the Sunna of the Prophet.

The judicial system provides for three grades of court and a Judicial Supervisory Committee:

The Judicial Supervisory Committee. The Committee consists of three members and a president appointed by the King. It supervises all the other courts and is situated at Mecca.

Chief Justice, Mecca: Sheikh ABDULLAH IBN HASSAN.

Courts of Appeal (Courts of Cassation). There are several courts of appeal in Hijaz and Najd, having jurisdiction to hear appeals from the *Mahkamat al-Sharia al-Koubra.*

Mahkamat al-Sharia al-Koubra. The competence of these courts extends to all cases not covered by the above. They are situated in Mecca, Medina and Jeddah. Appeal may be made to the Courts of Cassation.

Mahkamat al-Omour al Mosta'jalah. These courts, which are held throughout the country, deal with cases of minor misdemeanours and actions in which the value does not exceed S.R. 30. Other branches of these courts deal exclusively with affairs of the Bedouin tribes with the same competence. The decisions of these courts are final.

RELIGION

Arabia is the centre of the Islamic faith and includes the holy cities of Mecca and Medina. Except in the Eastern Province, where a large number of people follow Shi'a rites, the majority of the population are of the Sunni faith. The last fifty years have seen the rise of the Wahhabi sect, who originated in the eighteenth century, but first became unified and influential under their late leader King Ibn Saud. They are now the keepers of the holy places and control the pilgrimage to Mecca.

Mecca: Birthplace of the Prophet Muhammad, seat of the Great Mosque and Shrine of Ka'ba visited by a million Muslims annually.

Medina: Burial place of Muhammad, second sacred city of Islam.

Chief Qadi and Grand Mufti: (Vacant).

THE PRESS

Since 1964 most newspapers and periodicals have been published by press organizations administered by boards of directors with full autonomous powers, in accordance with the provisions of the Press Law. These organizations, which took over from small private firms, are privately owned by groups of individuals widely experienced in newspaper publishing and administration (*see* Publishers).

There are also a number of popular periodicals published by the government and by the Arabian American Oil Co. and distributed free of charge. The press is subject to no legal restriction affecting freedom of expression or the coverage of news.

DAILIES

al-Bilad: King Abdul Aziz St., Jeddah; f. 1934; Arabic; published by al-Bilad Publishing Corporation; Editor ABDULMAJID AL-SHUBUKSHI; circ. 20,000.

al-Jazirah: P.O.B. 354, Apt. 88, Municipality Bldg., Safat, Riyadh; Arabic; circ. 5,000.

al-Madina al-Munawara: Jeddah, P.O.B. 807; f. 1937; Arabic; published by al-Madina Press Establishment; Editor OSMAN HAFEZ; circ. 20,000.

al-Nadwah: Mecca; f. 1958; Arabic; published by Mecca Press and Information Organization; Editor HAMED MUTAWI'E; circ. 10,000.

Replica: P.O.B. 2043, Jeddah; English; daily newsletter from Saudi newspapers and broadcasting service; Man. Dir. MUHAMMAD SALAHUDDIN; Gen. Man. ADNAN KAMEL SALAH.

al-Riyadh: P.O.B. 851, Riyadh; Arabic; published by Yamamah Press Organization; Editor TURKI A. AL-SUDARI; circ. 10,000.

Saudi Gazette: Al Mina Street, P.O.B. 5576, Jeddah; f. 1975; English; published by Okaz Organization; Editor-in-Chief MOHAMMAD AL-FAWZAN.

al Ukadh: Jeddah; circ. 3,500.

WEEKLIES

Akhbar al-Dhahran (*Dhahran News*): Dammam; f. 1958; Editor 'ABD AL-AZIZ AL-ISA; circ. 1,500.

al-Dawa: Riyadh; Arabic.

al-Khalij al-'Arabi (*The Arabian Gulf*): Al-Khobar; f. 1958; Editor 'ABD ALLAH SHUBAT; circ. 1,200.

Arabian Sun: Aramco, Dhahran; English; published by the Arabian American Oil Co.

News from Saudi Arabia: Press Dept., Ministry of Information, Jeddah; f. 1961; news bulletin; English; Editor IZZAT MUFTI; circ. 22,000.

News of the Muslim World: Mecca; Arabic; published by Muslim World League; Editor H. M. HAFIZ.

Oil Caravan Weekly: Aramco, Dhahran; Arabic; published by the Arabian American Oil Co.

al-Qasim: Riyadh; f. 1959; Editor 'ABD ALLAH AL SANE' circ. 1,000.

al-Riyadhah: Mecca; f. 1960; for young men; Editor MUHAMMAD 'ABD ALLAH MALIBARI; circ. 500.

Umm al-Qura: Mecca; f. 1924; Editor HUSSAIN ABDULLAH AAQEEL; published by the Government; governmental industrial and social affairs; circ. 5,000.

al-Yamamah: Riyadh; f. 1952; Dir. AHMED EL-HOSHAN; circ. 1,000.

al-Yaum (*Today*): P.O.B. 565, Dammam; f. 1965; Dir. ABDUL AZIZ AL-TURKY.

PERIODICALS

al-Manhal: 44 Arafat Street, Jeddah; f. 1937; monthly; literary; Editor 'ABDUL QUADDOS ANARIS; circ. 6,000.

al-Mujtama: P.O.B. 354, Apt. 88, Municipality Bldg., Safat, Riyadh; f. 1964; Arabic; weekly; Dir.-Gen. SALEH SALEM.

al-Tijarah: Jeddah; f. 1960; monthly; for businessmen; Editor AHMAD ISA TAHKANDI; circ. 1,300.

Hajj (*Pilgrim*): Mecca; f. 1947; Arabic and English; Editor MUHAMMAD SAID AL 'AMOUDI; published by the Government Ministry of Pilgrimage and Endowments; circ. 5,000.

NEWS AGENCIES

Saudi Press Agency: c/o Ministry of Information, Riyadh.

BETA Company: Al Mufti Bldg., King Abdul Aziz St., P.O.B. 2011, Jeddah.

PUBLISHERS

al-Bilad Publishing Organization: King Abdul Aziz St., Jeddah; publishes *al-Bilad*; Dir.-Gen. ABDULLAH DABBAGH.

Dar al-Yaum Press and Publishing Establishment: P.O.B. 565, Damman; publishes *al-Yaum*; Dir.-Gen. OMAR ZAWAWI.

al-Jazirah for Press Printing and Publishing: P.O.B. 354, Riyadh; f. 1964; 29 mems.; publishes *al-Jazirah* (daily) and *al-Mujtama* (weekly); Dir.-Gen. SALEH AL-AJROUSH.

al-Madina Press Establishment: P.O.B. 807, Jeddah; publishes *al-Madina al-Munawara*; Dir.-Gen. AHMED SALAH JAMJOON.

Saudi Publishing and Distributing House: Al-Jauhara Building, Flats 7 and 12, Baghdadia, P.O.B. 2043, Jeddah; books in Arabic and English; Man. Dir. MUHAMMAD SALAHUDDIN; Gen. Man. ADNAN K. SALAH.

al-Yamamah Press Establishment: Riyadh; publishes *al-Riyadh*, *al-Yamamah* and *She*; Dir.-Gen. ABDULLAH QAR'AWI.

RADIO AND TELEVISION

RADIO

Saudi Arabian Broadcasting Co.: Ministry of Information, Airport Rd., Jeddah; three stations at Jeddah, Riyadh and Dammam broadcast programmes in Arabic and English; overseas service in Urdu, Indonesian, Persian and Swahili; Dir.-Gen. KHALID GHOUTH.

ARAMCO Radio: Dhahran; broadcasts programmes in English for the entertainment of employees of Arabian American Oil Company.

There are about 87,000 radio receivers.

TELEVISION

Saudi Arabian Government Television Service: Information Ministry, Riyadh; stations at Riyadh, Jeddah, Medina, Dammam, and Qassim operate 6 hours daily; major stations and relay points are under construction to serve all principal towns; Dir.-Gen. A. S. SHOBAIL.

Dharan-HZ-22-TV. Aramco TV: Arabian American Oil Co., Room 300, Administration Bldg., Dharan; non-commercial; started 1957, since 1970 English language film-chain operation only; Man. (Community Services) JOHN D. KRIESMER; Man. (Communications) M. M. ORSETH.

There are about 120,000 TV sets.

FINANCE

BANKING

The Saudi Arabian banking system consists of: the Saudi Arabian Monetary Agency, as central note-issuing and regulatory body; twelve commercial banks (two national and ten foreign banks); and two specialist banks (the Saudi Arabian Agricultural Bank and the Saudi Credit Bank, inaugurated in December 1973 to provide interest-free loans for specific purposes to Saudi citizens of moderate means).

The rising volume of oil revenues imposed a need for a central monetary authority and in 1952 the Saudi Arabian Monetary Agency (SAMA) was established in Jeddah. SAMA's functions include: bankers to the government; stabilization of the value of the currency; administration of monetary reserves; issue of coin and notes; and regulation of banking.

In June 1966, a Banking Control Law formalized SAMA's control of the commercial banking system. Commercial banks are obliged to maintain a certain proportion of their deposit liabilities (currently, 10 per cent of demand deposits, and 5 per cent of time and savings deposits) as statutory deposits with SAMA. They must also maintain liquid reserves equivalent to a certain proportion (currently 20 per cent) of their total deposit liabilities and are required to be Saudi Joint Stock Companies, and may not trade for purposes other than banking. Their paid-up capital must be not less than 2.5 million Saudi riyals; banks' total deposit liabilities may not exceed 15 times their paid-up capital and reserves; and banks must plough back 25 per cent of their undistributed profits in the form of reserves, until such reserves equal, as a minimum, their paid-up capital.

(cap. = capital; p.u. = paid up; dep. = deposits; m. = million; amounts in Saudi Riyals)

CENTRAL BANK

Saudi Arabia Monetary Agency: P.O.B. 394, Airport Rd., Jeddah; f. 1952; gold, foreign exchange and investments 70,202m. (Dec. 1974); Pres. and Gov. ABDUL AZIZ AL QURAISHI; Vice-Gov. Sheikh KHALID MOHAMMAD ALGOSAIBI; Controller-Gen. ABDUL WAHAB M. S. SHEIKH; publs. *Statement of Affairs* (fortnightly); *Annual Report; Statistical Summary* (twice per year), 10 brs.

SPECIALIST BANKS

Agricultural Credit Bank: Jeddah; f. 1964; cap. 31.5m.; Dir.-Gen. IZZAT HUSNI AL-ALI.

Saudi Credit Bank: Jeddah; f. 1973; provides interest-free loans for specific purposes to Saudi citizens of moderate means.

NATIONAL BANKS

National Commercial Bank: P.O.B. 3555, King Abdulaziz St., Jeddah; f. 1938; cap. and reserves 140m.; dep. and current account 2,941m. (Jan. 1975); Partners Sheikh SALEH ABDULLAH MOSA ALKAAKI, Sheikh ABDULAZIZ MUHAMMAD ALKAAKI, Sheikh SALIM BIN MAHFOOZ (Gen. Man.); 27 brs.

Riyad Bank Ltd.: P.O.B. 1047, Jeddah; f. 1957; cap. p.u. 37.5m., total resources 2,317m. (July 1974); Chair. H. E. Sheikh ABDULLAH BIN ADWAN; Man. Dir. H.E. Sheikh ABDUL RAHMAN AL-SHEIKH; Gen. Man. P. D. BREWER; 27 brs.

FOREIGN BANKS

Algemene Bank Nederland, N.V.: P.O.B. 67, Jeddah; Al-Khobar; Dammam; head office: Amsterdam, Netherlands.

Arab Bank Ltd.: Amman, Jordan; P.O.B. 344, Jeddah; 6 brs.

Bank Melli Iran: Ferdowsi Ave., Tehran; Jeddah.

Banque de l'Indochine: Paris; Jeddah; P.O.B. 1.

Banque du Caire: Cairo; P.O.B. 472, Jeddah; 2 brs.

Banque du Liban et d'Outre-Mer S.A.: Beirut, Lebanon; P.O.B. 482, Jeddah.

British Bank of the Middle East: head office: 20 Abchurch Lane, London EC4N 7AY; P.O.B. 109, Jeddah; Dammam; Al-Khobar.

First National City Bank: New York; Riyadh, P.O.B. 833, Al Batha St.; Man. W. L. ROBERTS, Jr.; Jeddah, P.O.B. 490; Man. M. Y. WYSKIEL; 2 brs.

National Bank of Pakistan: Karachi; P.O.B. 116, Jeddah; Senior Vice-Pres. in Jeddah Sheikh INAYAT ALI.

United Bank Ltd.: Karachi; Dammam.

INSURANCE COMPANY

Saudi National Insurance Co. Ltd.: P.O.B. 106, Al-Khobar; f. 1958; Pres. HAMAD AHMAD ALGOSAIBI; Gen. Man. A. A. ALGOSAIBI.

TRADE AND INDUSTRY

CHAMBERS OF COMMERCE

Chamber of Commerce and Industries: Jeddah, P.O.B. 1264; f. 1950; Pres. (vacant); Dir. YOUSUF M. BANNAN; publ. *Al-Tijara.*

Chamber of Commerce and Industry: S. G. Saleh Tuimi, P.O.B. 596, Riyadh; f. 1961; acts as "arbitrator" in business disputes; Chair. Sheikh ABDUL AZIZ MUQAIREN; publ. monthly journal.

Dammam Chamber of Commerce: P.O.B. 719, Dammam.

Mecca Chamber of Commerce: P.O.B. 2, Mecca; f. 1944; Pres. MUHAMMAD A. BOGARI; publ. *Al Tijarah Wassina'Ah.*

Medina Chamber of Commerce: P.O.B. 443, Medina.

OIL

General Petroleum and Mineral Organization (PETROMIN): P.O.B. 757, Riyadh; f. 1962 to establish oil and mineral industries and collateral activities in Saudi Arabia; Gov. Dr. ABDUL HADI TAHER.

The following projects have been set up by Petromin:

Arabian Drilling Co.: P.O.B. 932, Riyadh; f. 1964; shareholding 51 per cent, remainder French private capital; undertakes contract drilling for oil, minerals and water both inside and outside Saudi Arabia.

Arabian Geophysical Survey Co. (ARGAS): P.O.B. 2109, Jeddah; f. 1966; shareholding 51 per cent, remainder provided by *Cie. Générale de Géophysique*; exploration and discovery of natural resources; has set up a nation-wide geodetic survey network.

Arabian Marine Petroleum Co. (MARINCO): P.O.B. 50, Dharan Airport; f. 1968; shareholding 51 per cent, remainder held by McDermott Co. of New Orleans, U.S.A.; undertakes marine construction work (pipelines, rigs, sea terminals, etc.).

Jeddah Oil Refinery: P.O.B. 1604, Jeddah; f. 1968; shareholding 75 per cent, remainder held by Saudi Arabian Refining Co. (SARCO); the refinery at Jeddah, Japanese-built and American-staffed, has a capacity of 45,000 bbl./day; distribution in the Western Province is undertaken by Petromin's **Department for Distribution of Oil Products.**

Petromin Marketing: P.O.B. 50, Dharan Airport; f. 1967; wholly-owned by Petromin; operates the installations and facilities for the distribution of petroleum products in the Eastern, Central and Northern provinces of Saudi Arabia.

Petromin Lubricating Oil Co. (PETROLUBE): P.O.B. 1432, Jeddah; f. 1968; joint venture with Mobil to set up a blending plant which began production in 1971.

Petromin Sulphuric Acid Plant (PETROCID): P.O.B. 757, Riyadh; plant began production mid-1971; wholly-owned by Petromin; produces sulphuric acid at Dammam.

Petromin Tankers and Mineral Shipping Co. (PETROSHIP): P.O.B. 1600, Jeddah; f. 1968; wholly owned by Petromin; operates tanker fleet.

Riyadh Refinery: P.O.B. 3946, Riyadh; f. 1974.

Saudi Arabian Fertilizers Co. (SAFCO): P.O.B. 553, Dammam; f. 1965; 51 per cent shareholding, remainder open to public subscription; the plant at Dammam has a capacity of about 1,100 tons of urea and 35 tons of sulphur a day; construction and management have been undertaken by Occidental Petroleum Co. of U.S.A.

Sulb: P.O.B. 1826, Jeddah; wholly-owned by Petromin; steel rolling mill at Jeddah.

FOREIGN CONCESSIONAIRES

Arabian-American Oil Co. (Aramco): Dhahran; f. 1933; holds the principal working concessions in Saudi Arabia, covering approx. 85,000 square miles; production (1973) 2,677.4 million barrels; Saudi Government acquired 60 per cent participation, June 1974 and by February 1975 negotiations were almost completed by which the Saudi Government would effect complete nationalization; Pres. F. JUNGERS; Chair. L. F. HILLS.

Arabian Oil Co. Ltd.: P.O.B. 335, Riyadh; f. 1958; holds concession for offshore exploitation of Saudi Arabia's half interest in the Kuwait-Saudi Arabia Partitioned Zone; oil production (1974) 138.6m. barrels; natural gas production (1974) 56.7m. cubic feet; Chair. ATARU KOBAYASHI; Dir. in Saudi Arabia TAKASHI HAYASHI.

Getty Oil Co.: P.O.B. 363, Riyadh; office in Mina Saud; f. 1928; holds concession for exploitation of Saudi Arabia's half-interest in the Saudi Arabia-Kuwait Partitioned Zone, both on-shore and in territorial waters; total Zone production (1973) 23.5 million barrels; Pres. J. P. GETTY.

TRANSPORT

RAILWAYS

Saudi Government Railroad Organization: Dammam; Gen. Man. OMAR A. FAKIEH.

The Saudi Government Railroad is a single track, standard gauge line 610 km. long. The main line, 577 km. long, connects the Port of Dammam and the Gulf with the capital Riyadh. The Organization is an independent entity with a board of directors headed by the Minister of Communications. In addition to working the railways the Organization also manages the Port of Dammam.

The historic Hedjaz railway running from Damascus to Medina has been the subject of a reconstruction project since 1963; however, little progress has been made since the war of June 1967.

ROADS

Asphalted roads link Jeddah to Mecca, Jeddah to Medina, Medina to Yanbu, Taif to Mecca, Riyadh to al-Kharj, and Dammam to Hofuf as well as the principal communities and certain outlying points in Aramco's area of operations. Work is proceeding on various other roads, including one which will link Medina and Riyadh, and one from Taif to Jizan in the south, near the Yemeni border. 1967 saw completion of the trans-Arabian highway, which links Dammam, Riyadh, Taif, Mecca and Jeddah. In 1973 there were 10,007 kilometres of asphalted roads.

SHIPPING

The deep-water port of Jeddah is the main port of the kingdom and the port for pilgrims to Mecca. An expansion scheme providing for nine new piers for large ships, costing £20 million was completed in January 1973. Yanbo, the port of Medina, has been extended and modernized, with new docks, storage space and a special Pilgrim centre; other ports on the Red Sea are Muwaih, Wejh and Rabigh. On the Gulf there are the small ports of Al-Khobar, Qatif and Uqair, suitable only for small local craft, and a deep-water port at Ras Tanura built by the Arabian American Oil Co. for its own use. The deep-water Dammam Port, which was also built by the Arabian American Oil Co. and is operated by the Saudi Government Railroad, lies approximately 12 km. from the coast and is connected to the mainland by a railway causeway.

Saudi Lines: P.O.B. 66, Jeddah; regular cargo and passenger services between all Red Sea ports and transport of pilgrims from the Philippines, Bangkok and Thailand; 2 cargo and 3 passenger ships.

CIVIL AVIATION

In 1974 the government decided to construct a modern international airport at Jeddah.

Saudia-Saudi Arabian Airlines: Saudia Bldg., P.O.B. 620, Jeddah; f. 1945; regular internal services to all major cities of Saudi Arabia; regular international services to London, Paris, Geneva, Rome, Beirut, Casablanca, Algiers, Tunis, Tripoli, Dubai, Doha, Bahrain, Muscat, Port Sudan, Khartoum, Cairo, Kuwait, Baghdad, Damascus, Amman, Asmara, Karachi, Bombay, Istanbul, Shiraz; fleet of 19 aircraft, principally Boeing 707, 720B, 737, DC-3 and Convair 340; Dir.-Gen. Sheikh KAMIL SINDI; Exec. Vice-Pres. and Dep. Dir.-Gen. S. W. CHAMBERS; Vice-Pres. (External Affairs) RIDA HAKEEM.

Saudi Arabia is also served by the following foreign airlines: Air Algérie, Air France, ALIA, Alitalia, AUA, British Airways, CSA, EgyptAir, Iranair, Iraqi Airways, KLM, Lufthansa, MEA, PIA, Sabena, Sudan Airways, and Syrian Arab Airlines.

ATOMIC ENERGY

Saudi Arabia joined the International Atomic Energy Agency in January 1963. Radio isotopes are used in the oil industry and are being introduced into state-controlled agricultural schemes.

DEFENCE

Defence Budget (1974-75): 6,400m. riyals.

Military Service: voluntary.

Total Armed Forces: 43,000; army 36,000; navy 1,500; air force 5,500.

Paramilitary Forces: 26,000.

EDUCATION

The educational system in Saudi Arabia resembles that of other Arab countries. Educational institutions are run mainly by the government. The private sector plays a significant role at the first and second levels, but its total contribution is quite small compared with that of the public sector.

Pre-elementary education is provided on a small scale, mainly in urban areas. Elementary education is of six years' duration and the normal entrance age is 6+. Intermediate education begins at 12+ and lasts for three years. Secondary education begins at 15+ and extends for three years. After the first year, successful pupils branch into science or arts groups.

Industrial and commercial schools can be entered after the completion of the intermediate stage, and the duration of study is three years. Facilities exist for the training of teachers.

There are five universities (see below) and also the College of Education for Girls and the Higher Islamic Judicial Institute. Adult education is divided into two categories: (a) to combat illiteracy; (b) follow-up. The duration of study in each is 16 months.

Budgetary allocations in the fiscal year 1974-75 were SR 3,760 million out of total budget allocations of SR 45,743 million.

UNIVERSITIES

Imam Mohammed bin Saud Islamic University: Riyadh.

Islamic University: Medina; f. 1961; 172 teachers, 2,944 students.

King Abdulaziz University: P.O.B. 1540, Jeddah; f. 1967; Rector Dr. M. A. YAMANY; 330 teachers, 3,659 students.

University of Petroleum and Minerals: Dharan; f. 1963; 105 teachers, 974 students.

Riyadh University: Riyadh; f. 1957; 365 teachers, 6,000 students.

BIBLIOGRAPHY

ARMSTRONG, H. C. Lord of Arabia (Beirut, 1962).

ASSAH, AHMED. Miracle of the Desert Kingdom (Johnson, London, 1969).

BENDIST-MÉCHIN, S. Ibn Séoud ou la naissance d'un royaume (Albin Michel, Paris, 1955).

BROWN, E. HOAGLAND. The Saudi-Arabia-Kuwait Neutral Zone (Beirut, 1964).

BUTLER, GRANT C. Kings and Camels: An American in Saudi Arabia (The Devin-Adair Co., New York, 1960).

DE GAURY, GERALD. Faisal (Arthur Barker, London, 1966).

DEQUIN, HORST. Saudi Arabia's Agriculture and its Development Possibilities (Frankfurt, 1963).

GHARAYBEH, A. Saudi Arabia (London, 1962).

HOWARTH, DAVID. The Desert King: Ibn Sa'ud (McGraw Hill, New York, 1964).

LEBKICHER, ROY, RENTZ, GEORGE, and STEINCKE, MAX. Saudi Arabia (New York, 1952).

LIPSKY, GEORGE A., and others. Saudi Arabia: Its People, Its Society, Its Culture (New Haven, 1959).

PHILBY, H. ST. J. B. Arabia and the Wahhabis (London, 1928).
Arabia (London, Benn, 1930).
Arabian Jubilee (London, 1951).
The Empty Quarter (London, 1933).
The Land of Midian (London, 1957).
A Pilgrim in Arabia (London, 1946).
Saudi Arabia (London, 1955).

SOULIÉ, G. J. L., Le Royaume d'Arabie Séoudite face à l'Islam révolutionnaire 1953–64 (Armand Colin, Paris, 1966).

TWITCHELL, KARL S., with the co-operation of JURJI, EDWARD J. Saudi Arabia (Princeton, 1953).

VAN DER MEULEN, D. The Wells of Ib'n Saud (John Murray, 1957).

WILLIAMS, K. Ibn Sa'ud: the Puritan King of Arabia (London, Cape, 1933).

WINDER, R. BAYLY. Saudi Arabia in the Nineteenth Century (Macmillan, London, 1965).

Spanish North Africa

SPANISH SAHARA   CEUTA AND MELILLA

SPANISH SAHARA
GEOGRAPHY

The Spanish Sahara consists of an arid tract of country, some 266,000 sq. km. in area, extending from the southern boundary of Morocco along the Atlantic coast for over 800 km. to the Mauritanian frontier at Cape Blanc. Inland it reaches 450 km. into the Sahara to its eastern frontier with Mauritania. The territory has a fluctuating population (74,902 in November 1974), most of whom are nomadic pastoralists of Moorish or mixed Arab-Berber descent with some negro admixture. They are divided into a number of tribes and depend for their existence on herds of camels, sheep and goats which they move seasonally from one pasture to another. The only towns are the capital, al-Aaiún, and Villa Cisneros. The latter stands on a narrow peninsula half-enclosing the bay of Rio de Oro and its harbour suffers from severe silting.

The relief of most of Spanish Sahara is gentle. The coast is backed by a wide alluvial plain overlain in the south by extensive sand dunes aligned from south-west to north-east and extending inland over 250 km. Behind the coastal plain the land rises gradually to a plateau surface diversified by sandstone ridges that reach 300 m. in height. In the north-east, close to the Mauritanian frontier, isolated mountain ranges, such as the Massif de la Guelta, rise to over 600 m. There are no permanent streams in Spanish Sahara and the only considerable valley is that of the Saguia el Hamra which crosses the northernmost part of the country to reach the coast at al-Aaiún north of Cape Bojador. The whole of Spanish Sahara experiences an extreme desert climate. Nowhere does mean annual rainfall exceed 10 cm. and over most of the territory it is less than 5 cm. In 1964 a vast subterranean fresh-water lake was discovered which is thought to extend some 90 km. inland from Villa Cisneros. Vegetation is at present restricted to scattered desert shrubs and occasional patches of coarse grass in most depressions. Along the coast summer heat is tempered by air moving inland after it has been cooled over the waters of the cold Canaries current which flows off shore from north to south.

Spanish Sahara formerly extended in the north as far as the River Draa in southern Morocco, but this strip of territory was ceded to Morocco in 1958. Morocco, however, lays claim to the whole country. This claim is based on the fact that Moroccan rule was effective over the whole area in medieval times and the claim has been pressed more strongly since the discovery of phosphates in the territory.

HISTORY

Cape Bojador on the north-west coast of Africa is named in a Catalan map of 1375. The Portuguese rounded the Cape in 1434 and two years later discovered an inlet which became known to them as Rio do Ouro, i.e. in Spanish, the Río de Oro. The voyage of 1436 would seem to have been the first occasion when the Portuguese brought back to Europe negro slaves acquired from the Sanhaja Berbers. Thereafter the Portuguese began to penetrate into the interior, establishing a trading-post at Wadan, not far from Atar, in 1487. Spanish attempts thereafter to colonise the coastal area from the Canaries had little success. It was not until 1884 that Spain occupied Río de Oro itself, the site of the future Villa Cisneros, and claimed at the same time a protectorate over the coastal zone from Cape Bojador southward to Cape Blanco. An agreement of June 1900 between France and Spain marked out the frontier between Río de Oro and Mauritania, but the border lands in the direction of Morocco remained ill-defined. Two further conventions of 1904 and 1912 dealt with these lands. The southern frontier of Morocco was situated on the Wadi Draa. Beyond the Draa southward as far as latitude 27° 40′ N. the area known as Tarfaya became the southern zone of the Spanish Protectorate in Morocco. The region of Cape Juby was occupied in 1916; La Güera, in the extreme south of the Río de Oro, in 1920; and Smara in the interior only in 1934. It was in 1934 that Spain re-organized the territories lying beyond the southern zone of her Protectorate in Morocco—i.e. the Spanish Sahara. The region between 27° 40′ N. and 26° N. became known as Saguia el Hamra the main centres being the capital, al-Aaiún and Smara. All the lands south of it constituted the Río de Oro, with its capital at Villa Cisneros.

Between 1934 and 1958 the Spanish Sahara (i.e. Saguia el Hamra and Río de Oro) formed one centralized adminis-tration with Tarfaya and Ifni, under a military Governor located at Sidi Ifni, the capital of the Ifni enclave. Three delegates represented the Governor in the southern territories and local administration was in the hands of military officials called *interventores*. On January 14th, 1958, it was announced at Madrid that these territories would be formed into two provinces: Ifni and the Spanish Sahara. No mention was made of the Tarfaya region. The two provinces now came under the control of the Director-General of African Provinces at Madrid. Command over all the troops in Ifni and the Spanish Sahara was entrusted to the Captain-General of the Canaries, but each province had its own Governor-General with headquarters at Sidi Ifni and at al-Aaiún.

Morocco, which became independent in March 1956, laid claim thereafter to all the Spanish possessions in North-West Africa and also to the Islamic Republic of Mauritania. The existence in the western Sahara of Moroccan irregular forces soon gave rise to serious trouble. These irregular bands, which attacked Ifni in November-December 1957, made raids into Tarfaya, Saguia el Hamra and Río de Oro and also into the northern areas of Mauritania, finding some support amongst such nomads as the Riqaibat, the most powerful of the tribes in the western Sahara. Actions of some considerable size had to be fought near Villa Cisneros and near al-Aaiún in January 1958. A joint Franco-Spanish campaign was waged against the irregulars in February and by the beginning of March 1958 the western Sahara had been restored to order.

Spain, in April 1956, had renounced the northern zone of the Protectorate in Morocco assigned to her under the terms of the Franco-Spanish convention of 1912. And in April 1958, after discussions held at Cintra in Portugal, Spain relinquished to Morocco the southern zone of her

Protectorate (also assigned to her in 1912), i.e. the region of Tarfaya. Morocco, since that time, has continued to assert her claim to the territories still under Spanish control in North-West Africa. At the United Nations in December 1965 the Moroccan delegate expressed the hope that the Moroccan claim to the Spanish Sahara and to Ifni might be settled through amicable negotiation. On December 16th, 1965, the United Nations adopted a resolution calling on Spain to liberate the Spanish Sahara and Ifni, and to enter into negotiations which would decide their future. The situation was rendered more complex by the fact that Mauritania had in October 1964 informed the U.N. Special Committee on Colonization of its desire to initiate direct discussions with Spain over the territories constituting the Spanish Sahara—a demand which the Ambassador of Mauritania at Washington reiterated in February 1966. A further complication was discernible inside Morocco itself, where some of the political organizations, above all the right-wing Istiqlal, had long maintained that Mauritania itself was an integral part of Morocco. Indeed, the Istiqlal, during the troubles of February 1966 in Mauritania, urged the government of Morocco to intervene on behalf of the Muslims in what it described as "our usurped province".

In September 1967 the Foreign Minister of Morocco went to Madrid in order to discuss the future of the Spanish territories in North Africa. The following December, the United Nations passed a new resolution urging Spain to organize, in consultation with Morocco and Mauritania and under UN auspices, a referendum which would allow the people of Spanish Sahara to determine its future. The Spanish Government accepted the principle of self-determination, but a fundamental difference in approach to the problem became apparent at the meetings in May and June 1970 at Nouakchott and Rabat between the Spanish Foreign Minister and Moroccan leaders. Positions hardened later in the same month after riots at al-Aaiún were quelled with loss of life. Accusations of interference and oppression were made by both sides and in July Spain held military exercises along the Spanish Sahara coast.

In December 1970 the UN Committee on Trusteeship again called for a referendum in the territory and in February 1973 the General Assembly of the UN passed a resolution calling on Spain to grant the territory independence in consultation with Morocco and Mauritania.

These countries, together with Algeria, continued in their claims for the phosphate-rich territory and each supported one of the three rival liberation organizations formed by Saharan exiles: *Morehob*, the 'Blue Men', the *Front populaire de libération du Sahara* and the *Mouvement de 21 août*.

Tension between Morocco and Spain increased with Morocco seeking support from other Arab states and calling for "decisive action". As a result, the Spanish Government announced in August 1974 that it would organize a referendum in 1975 to enable the inhabitants of the Spanish Sahara to determine their future. This proposal was accepted by King Hassan on condition that the Spanish troops and administration were withdrawn first and that the people were not asked to vote for independence, as he felt that the Sahara should eventually be integrated with Morocco on historical and geographical grounds.

In 1974 three new liberation groups were formed: the *Front for the Liberation of Saquia el Hamra and Rio de Oro* (Frente Polisario), whose aim is complete independence, the *Front for Liberation and Unity (FLU)*, who wish for unity with Morocco and the *Saharan National Union Party* (SNUP), the only legally recognized party, supported by Spain.

The dispute between Morocco and Spain grew worse in 1975, with Spain pouring arms and men into the area and Morocco stationing troops along the Saharan border. Several incidents were reported and terrorist attacks spread to the Spanish enclaves of Ceuta and Melilla. A UN Decolonization Committee mission was sent to the area to examine the situation. In May the leader of SNUP announced that he had pledged his allegiance to Morocco because he felt that Spain was trying to maintain its hold on the territory. Influenced by this and by the fact that Morocco's claim, being heard together with that of Mauritania at the International Court of Justice, is supported by the OAU and many Arab states, Spain announced its intention of withdrawing from the Sahara and transferring sovereignty to its people in the near future. However, the dispute continued to grow worse, with Algeria, which has now dropped all claims to the area, being accused of collaborating with Spain, and with clashes between Spanish and Moroccan troops becoming more frequent.

ECONOMICS AND STATISTICS

Spanish Sahara is to a major extent a military territory, and policing operations by the forces stationed there account for a quarter of the province's budgetary expenditure. In 1961 the province received a considerable boost from petroleum exploration when the expenditure of the prospecting companies helped to offset the costs of maintaining the province. However, hopes of valuable petroleum finds have been disappointed and the main new element in the economic life of the area is the introduction of phosphate mining. There is also tourism, though this is at the moment on a very reduced scale.

In the Sahara the land is too poor and the population too small to generate any economic wealth. By 1970 the European population was estimated at 16,600 (the majority being Spanish soldiers), while the number of the indigenous population, most of whom have a nomadic way of life, was put at 60,000, though many more nomads enter the territory during the rainy season. The northern part of the province parallel to the River Draa on the northern boundary is fairly mountainous, but none of the rivers is of any permanence; most of the territory is desert.

Settled agriculture is consequently slight; small quantities of barley and maize are grown, but most of the population is engaged in animal husbandry. In 1974 there were 62,141 camels, 10,000 sheep and 1,600 asses. Live camels and animal skins are sometimes exported to the Canary Islands. From Cabo Bojador down to La Güera, lobsters and other fish are caught by the Canaries fleet and sometimes by the Huelva fleet and by members of the Imeraguen tribe. The tonnage landed in 1974 was 5,823. At La Güera, the centre of this activity, there are two fish-processing plants. This is virtually the only industrial activity except for local crafts and a U.S.-financed desalting plant producing flavoured mineral water for local consumption. The production of electricity was 63,654 thousand kWh. in 1974. Transport is still underdeveloped, there were only 6,500 km. of poor quality roads and 7,495 vehicles in 1974. There are also a number of small airports served by the Spanish airline Iberia, which carried 84,781 passengers to the country in 1974.

In 1961 the restrictions on foreign capital investment were modified and the Saharan province experienced a brief boom as a result of the lure of mineral wealth. Nine U.S. and three Spanish firms took up concessions for petroleum prospecting. However, by the end of 1963 nearly all of the companies ran down operations and the only ones to remain were Gulf Oil (allied with the Spanish CEPSA), Texaco of Spain Inc. and the State-controlled INI. By 1964 60 per cent of the area of the concessions had been investigated at an approximate cost of 5,000 million pesetas, with no favourable results. The discovery of oil in mainland Spain probably precludes any revival of interest in the Spanish Sahara for some time to come. Oil companies were thought to be holding on to the concessions there only to put themselves in a better position to compete for concessions in mainland Spain. The only mineral sources proved so far are iron, situated in the north of the province (the INI, which carried out the survey, claimed that there are 70 million tons of 65 per cent iron content) and phosphates, commercially workable deposits of which were found in 1963.

The phosphate deposits are now known to be amongst the richest in the world. In March 1967 the development contract was awarded to a consortium led by the International Minerals and Chemical Corporation of America (with a 25 per cent interest). French and German interests took 20 per cent, and the Spanish Government the remaining 55 per cent. However, early in 1968 the American interests withdrew from the project, mainly because Spain insisted on sending the phosphates to a new factory in Spain itself. The Spanish state-controlled company Empresa Nacional Minera del Sahara S.A. (ENMINSA) is now in complete control of the venture and has signed up several subcontractors from other European countries to construct the various facilities required, with financial guarantees provided by the Spanish Government. Desert roads have been cut, and Spain has built a village for 500 workers at Bu-Craa. A conveyor belt has been built to carry ore to the sea. Production started in 1972 and a total output of 3.5 million tons was forecast for 1975, making Spanish Sahara the world's fourth largest producer of phosphates.

It was announced from al-Aaiún in May 1966 that a commission was to be formed which would prepare a plan for the social and economic development of the Spanish Sahara. The opening up of the phosphate mines at Bu-Craa, near the Moroccan border, has increased the desire of both Morocco and Mauritania to annexe the Spanish Sahara. Morocco is herself an important producer of phosphates, and would suffer commercially from this development.

A potential source of income, which has been exploited only on a very small scale as yet, is the tourist trade. In 1973 there were 17,841 visitors to the country and these mostly came on day excursions from the Canary Islands, for the country has little hotel accommodation to offer. Probably the most important economic breakthrough of recent years was the discovery in 1964 of a vast subterranean lake of fresh water thought to extend some 90 km. inland from Villa Cisneros. Rationally tapped, this water opens up a number of development possibilities.

STATISTICS

Area: approx. 266,000 sq. km. (Sur 184,000 sq. km.; Nordeste 56,000 sq. km.; Norte 26,000 sq. km.).

Population (Census of November 1974): 74,902 of whom 73,497 are Saharans, 857 are residents and 548 are foreigners. There are also about 20,000 Spanish soldiers. Towns: Al-Aaiún (capital) 24,048 (12,238 non-Europeans, 11,180 Europeans); Villa Cisneros 5,454. The number of nomads entering the territory during the rainy season is variable.

Agriculture (1974—metric tons): Barley 7,000, Alfalfa 210, Palm Trees 700 (number).

Livestock (1974): 62,141 Camels, 10,000 Sheep, 1,600 Asses, 350 Pigs.

Fishing (1974): Weight of catch 5,823 tons.

Mining: Phosphate deposits at Bucraa estimated at 1,700 million tons are exploited by Fosfatos de Bucraa, S.A., a state-controlled company. In April 1972 the first shipment of phosphate ore was loaded at Al-Aaiún. Production exceeded 3m. tons in 1974.

Industry (1974): Production of electric energy: 63,654,000 kWh.; Buildings constructed: 552 (451 for habitation).

Finance: Spanish currency: 100 céntimos = 1 peseta. Coins: 10 and 50 céntimos; 1, 2½, 5, 25, 50 and 100 pesetas. Notes: 100, 500 and 1,000 pesetas. Exchange rates (July 1975): £1 sterling = 124.25 pesetas; U.S. $1 = 56.72 pesetas; 1,000 Spanish pesetas = £8.05 = $17.63.

Budget (1974): Expenditure 2,374,831,000 pesetas. The territory receives substantial aid from Spain.

External Trade (1974): Imports ('000 pesetas): 1,200,427 (Foodstuffs 467,943, Manufactures 732,484); Exports (Raw materials): 2,411,335.

Transport: *Roads:* 6,500 km. roads and tracks; 7,495 vehicles (1974); *Shipping* (1974): Passengers disembarked 1,550, freight entered 387,109 metric tons; *Civil Aviation* (1974): Passengers entered 84,781, Passengers leaving 88,381; Freight 11,532 metric tons.

Education (1974): *Primary:* 2,321 Spanish, 3,184 Saharan pupils, 2,103 adults; 144 Spanish and 60 Saharan teachers; *Secondary:* 796 Spanish, 446 Saharan pupils.

Tourism (1973): 17,841 tourists.

Health (1974): Hospital beds 257, doctors 29.

THE GOVERNMENT

Spanish Sahara was recognized as a Province in 1958. It is divided into three regions: Sur (184,000 sq. km.), Nordeste (56,000 sq. km.) and Norte (26,000 sq. km.). A *Yemáa* (General Assembly) of 103 members (Pres. JATRI ULD SAID ULD YUMANI) and a *Cabildo* or local council (Pres. SEILA ULD ABEIDA) are the main representative bodies of the province. The province is represented in the Spanish *Cortes* by 6 *procuradores*.

There was an election to the General Assembly in January 1971.

Governor-General: Gen. FEDERICO GÓMEZ DE SALAZAR Y NIETO.

Director-General for Promotion of the Sahara: Col. EDUARDO BLANCO RODRÍGUEZ.

Religion: Muslim; the Europeans are nearly all Catholics.

Radio: *Radio Sahara*, Ap. 106, Al-Aaiún; government station; Dir. CARLOS GUISASOLA ESTELAR.

Radio Villa Cisneros, Apt. 53, Villa Cisneros; government station; Dir. F. PATIÑO DÍAZ-HERRERA.

There were 16,000 radio receivers in 1974.

Television: retransmission stations in Al-Aaiún, Smara and Villa Cisneros.

There were 2,000 television receivers in 1974.

Transport: Airfields at Villa Cisneros (the chief seaport) and Al-Aaiún, with passenger services to Madrid and Las Palmas operated by Iberia. There are also landing-strips at Smara, La Güera, Hagunía, Auserd, Aargub, Bir Enzarán, Anech and Agracha. A 3,500 metre loading pier has been constructed at Al-Aaiún to handle phosphate exports. A 72-km. conveyor brings the phosphate ores from the mines at Bucraa.

CEUTA AND MELILLA

GEOGRAPHY

CEUTA

The ancient port and walled city of Ceuta is situated on a rocky promontory in north-western Morocco overlooking the Strait of Gibraltar. It was retained by Spain as a *plaza de soberanía* when Morocco became independent in 1956 and is administered as part of Cádiz Province. The Portuguese first established a fort at Ceuta in 1415 and it was ceded to Spain by Portugal in 1668. It developed as a military and administrative centre for the former Spanish Protectorate in Morocco and now functions as a bunkering and fishing port. In 1973 its population was 64,576.

MELILLA

Melilla is situated on a small peninsula jutting out into the Mediterranean in north-eastern Morocco. It was retained by Spain as a *plaza de soberanía* when Morocco became independent in 1956 and is administered from Málaga. It was annexed by Spain in 1471 and served as a military stronghold up to the present. In 1973 it had a population of 59,529 and it is an active port which exports over 1 million tons of iron ore annually from mines inland at Kelata, Morocco.

PEÑÓN DE VELEZ, PEÑÓN DE ALHUCEMAS AND CHAFARINAS

These three rocky islets, situated respectively just west and east of Alhucemas and east of Melilla off the north coast of Morocco, are governed as integral parts of Spain.

HISTORY

Ceuta, Melilla and the island dependencies are known as the Plazas de Soberanía—i.e. *presidios*, or fortified enclaves, over which Spain has full sovereign rights. Children born in these dependencies, whether Christian or Muslim, are Spanish citizens and subjects. Both Ceuta and Melilla have municipal councils (*ayuntamientos*). Since Morocco became independent in 1956, supreme civil power in the *presidios* has rested in the hands of the Governor-General of the Plazas de Soberanía, who is himself responsible to the Directorate-General of African Possessions. In respect of ecclesiastical and judicial affairs Ceuta is integrated with the province of Cádiz, and Melilla with the province of Málaga in Spain.

Morocco, since 1956, has laid claim on a number of occasions to the Spanish possessions in North-West Africa. Spain, indeed, renounced in April 1956 the protectorate in northern Morocco which had been assigned to her under the terms of the Franco-Spanish convention of November 1912. No mention was made, however, of Melilla. Two years later, in April 1958, after discussions held at Cintra in Portugal, Spain handed over the protectorate in southern Morocco (sometimes known as Tarfaya) which had also been allotted to her in 1912. Recent events have made it clear that Spain would be most reluctant to cede Ceuta and Melilla—towns which she has now held for some centuries and which are largely Spanish in population and character. The Moroccan government has drawn a parallel with the situation in Gibraltar and pointed to the apparent inconsistency in the policies of the Spanish government. Morocco's recent interest in the Spanish Sahara has now spread to these two enclaves and Moroccan forces have carried out several bombing raids on the area. The Spanish authorities have reacted by expelling 40 Moroccan families, detaining and questioning many suspects and asking all Moroccans to become Spanish or leave the enclaves.

CEUTA

Ceuta is situated on the African shore opposite Gibraltar, the Straits being here about 25 km. wide. The Portuguese took Ceuta in 1415. On the union of the crowns of Spain and Portugal in 1580 Ceuta passed under Spanish rule and in 1694, when Portugal was formally separated from Spain, asked to remain under Spanish control. During the sixteenth, seventeenth and eighteenth centuries Ceuta had to endure a number of sieges at the hands of the Muslims. Ahmad Gailan, a chieftain in northern Morocco, blockaded the town in 1648–55. The Sultan of Morocco, Mulai Ismail (1672–1727), attacked Ceuta in 1674, 1680 and 1694, after which he maintained a blockade against the town until 1720. Ahmad Ali al-Rifi, a chieftain from northern Morocco, made yet another unsuccessful assault in 1732. A pact of friendship and commerce was negotiated between Spain and Morocco at Aranjuez in 1780, a peaceful agreement following in the next year over the boundaries of the Ceuta enclave. There was in 1844–45 a sharp dispute once more about the precise limits of Ceuta. Further disagreement in 1859 led to the war of 1860. Spanish forces, after an engagement at Los Castillejos, seized Tetuán from Morocco. After another battle at Wadi Ras in March 1860 the conflict came to an end. A settlement was now made which enlarged the enclave of Ceuta and obliged Morocco to hand over to Spain 100 million pesetas as war indemnities. In 1874 the town became the seat of the Capitanía General de Africa.

MELILLA

Spain secured control of Melilla in 1496, the town being infeudated thereafter to the ducal house of Medina Sidonia, which was empowered to appoint the governor and seneschal with the approval of the Spanish Crown. The Rif tribesmen attacked Melilla in 1562–64. Later still, the Sultan of Morocco, Mulai Ismail (1672–1727) assaulted the town in 1687, 1696 and 1697. Sultan Muhammad b. Abdallah (1757–90) besieged Melilla in 1771 and 1774. An agreement concluded between Spain and Morocco in 1780 at Aranjuez led, however, in the following year, to a peaceful delimitation of the Melilla enclave. There was a brief period of tension in 1844 and then, in 1861, under the terms of an agreement signed at Madrid, after the Spanish-Moroccan campaign of 1860, Melilla received an extension of its boundaries. Trouble with the Rif tribesmen gave rise in 1893–94 to the so-called "War of Melilla", which ended with a settlement negotiated at Marrakesh. It was not until 1909 that Spanish forces, after a hard campaign, occupied the mountainous hinterland of Melilla between the Wadi Kert and the Wadi Muluya—a region in which, some ten miles behind Melilla, are situated the rich iron mines of Beni Bu Ifrur. In July 1921 the Rif tribes, under the command of Abd al-Krim, defeated a Spanish force near Anual and threatened Melilla itself. Only in 1926, with the final defeat of the Rif rebellion, was Spanish control restored over the Melilla region. Melilla was the first Spanish town to rise against the Government of the

Popular Front on July 17th, 1936, at the beginning of the Spanish Civil War. Since 1939 both towns have been ruled as integral parts of Spain.

OTHER POSSESSIONS

The Chafarinas Islands, lying about 2½ miles off the Cabo de Agua, came under Spanish control in 1847. Peñon de Alhucemas is situated some three-quarters of a mile from the coast opposite Ajdir. It was occupied in 1673. Peñon de Vélez de la Gomera, about 50 miles farther west, came under Spanish rule in 1508, was then lost not long afterwards and reoccupied in 1564.

ECONOMICS

CEUTA AND MELILLA

Ceuta and Melilla, both free ports, are in fact of little economic importance, while the other possessions, with a population of 530, mostly fishermen, are of negligible significance. The basic reason for Spanish retention of these areas is their overwhelmingly Spanish population. For instance, in the Melilla census of 1960 (the latest complete figures available), of a total population of 79,056 only 6,300 Muslims and 3,100 Jews were recorded. The 80,000 population of Ceuta was similarly composed. Ceuta's population has fallen to 64,576 since 1960 owing to the lack of economic opportunities in the town. The hinterland of the two cities is small: the total extent of Ceuta is 19 square kilometres, and of Melilla 12 square kilometres. Accordingly most of the population's food needs have to be imported, with the exception of fish which is obtained locally. Sardines and anchovies are the most important items, in an annual catch of about 16,000 tons. A large proportion of the tinned fish is sold outside Spain. More important to the economies of the cities is the port activity; most of their exports take the form of fuel supplied—at very competitive rates—to ships. Most of the petroleum fuels come from the Spanish refinery in Tenerife. Ceuta's

port is the busier but, apart from the ferries from Málaga in Spain, Melilla's port is not so frequented and its exports are correspondingly low. But it figures importantly as an export point for the iron ore mined in the Uixan mines of the Moroccan Rif. Ceuta exports wood, cork, foodstuffs and beverages. Industry is limited to meeting some of the everyday needs of the cities. In both cities less than two per cent of the working population are employed in agriculture. Most of the industry is located in the port area. The total labour force in Ceuta in 1962 numbered 13,080 (construction 2,083, textiles 1,276, fishing 1,384 and commerce 1,768). Unemployment in both towns is about 600–700. Business and port activity are sufficiently high to permit the municipalities budgets which, by Spanish standards, are high in relation to the numbers of population; in 1964 these were 70 million pesetas for Ceuta and 90 million pesetas for Melilla. More than a million tourists visit the enclaves each year, mainly attracted by the duty-free goods on sale.

In 1975 Spain granted 14 million pesetas for the development of facilities in the enclaves.

CEUTA

Area: 19 square km.

Population (1973): 64,576.

External Trade: Ceuta is a duty-free port. Trade is chiefly with Spain, the Balearic and Canary Islands and Melilla.

Transport: Much of the traffic between Spain and Morocco passes through Ceuta; there are ferry services to Algeciras, Spain.

Education: (1972-73): Primary: 215 schools, 10,038 pupils; Secondary: 2,838 pupils.

Government: A Mayor administers the town and he is also a member (under the title *Procurador*) of the Spanish Parliament in Madrid. Procurador SERAFINO BECERRA.

Religion: Most Africans are Muslims; Europeans are nearly all Catholics; there are a few Jews.

Radio: *Radio Ceuta*, Virgilio Oñate 1, Ceuta; commercial; owned by Sociedad Española de Radiodifusión; Dir. J. SOLERA.

MELILLA

Area: 12.3 square km.

Population (1973): 59,529.

External Trade: Melilla is a duty-free port. Most imports are from Spain but over 90 per cent of exports go to non-Spanish territories. Chief exports: fish and iron ore from Moroccan mines.

Transport: There is a daily ferry service to Málaga and

a weekly service to Almería. Melilla airport is served by a daily service to Málaga, operated by Iberia.

Education (1972-73): Primary: 232 schools, 7,028 pupils; Secondary: 3,048 pupils.

Government: A mayor administers the town.

Radio: *Radio Melilla*, O'Donell 26, Melilla; commercial; owned by Sociedad Española de Radiodifusión; Dir. G. PALAU.

OTHER POSSESSIONS

Peñón de Vélez de la Gomera and Villa Sanjurjo on the Mediterranean coast between Ceuta and Melilla—and the Chafarinas Islands lying east of Melilla near the Algerian border. Peñón de Vélez de la Gomera and Villa Sanjurjo are small towns. The Chafarinas Islands have no permanent inhabitants.

BIBLIOGRAPHY

AREILZA, J. MA. DE, and CASTIELLA, F. MA. Revindicaciones de España (Madrid, 1941).

BOUCHER, M. Spain in Africa (3 articles, *Africa Institute Bulletin*, May–July 1966).

CARO BAROJA, J. Estudios Saharianos (Madrid, 1955).

HABSBOURG, OTTO D. E. Européens et Africains: L'Entente Nécessaire (Hachette, Paris, 1963).

HERNÁNDEZ PACHECO, E. and F. El Sahara Español (Instituto de Estudios Africanos, Madrid, 1947).

LODWICK, J. The Forbidden Coast: the Story of a Journey to Río de Oro (London, 1956).

PACHECO, F. HERNANDEZ, and TORRES, J. MA. CORDERO. El Sahara Español (Madrid, 1962).

PÉLISSIER, RENÉ. Los Territorios Españoles de Africa (Madrid, 1964).

SERVICIO INFORMATIVO ESPAÑOL. España en el Sahara (Madrid, 1968).

The Sudan

PHYSICAL AND SOCIAL GEOGRAPHY

L. Berry

THE NILE

The Democratic Republic of the Sudan is the largest state in Africa (2,500,000 sq. km.), stretching across nearly 18° of latitude and from sub-equatorial forest to some of the driest desert in the world. These vast spaces of contrasting terrain are, however, linked by the unifying Nile. Any account of Sudan should perhaps start with the river, so vital is it to the republic. The Nile enters Sudan from Uganda in the south and the "Bahr el Jebel" is fed by a number of streams draining the south-west of the country. Some miles north of Mongalla, the river enters the Sudd region where seasonal swamps cover a large part of the area. The White Nile drains the Sudd region northward, though half of the flow is lost by irrigation in the Sudd. The Blue Nile drains a large part of the Ethiopian Highlands and joins the White Nile at Khartoum. The two rivers are very different. In August the Blue Nile is in flood and, rising seven metres above its low level, makes up nearly 90 per cent of the total discharge at Khartoum (7,000 cu. m. per sec.). At low water the more regularly flowing White Nile provides 83 per cent of the discharge and the Blue Nile is reduced to a mere 80 cu. m. per second. North of Khartoum the Nile is the focus of most agricultural activity and pump irrigation along its banks provides a green strip through the desert to Wadi Halfa and Lake Nasser. The Atbara, which is the only tributary north of Khartoum, flows for about six months of the year and then dries up into a series of pools.

PHYSICAL FEATURES

Away from the Nile the Sudan is mainly a plainland and plateau country, although there are a number of important mountain ranges such as the Imatong and the Nuba Mountains (rising to over 1,500 m.) in the south; Jebel Marra, a largely extinct volcano (over 3,500 m.) in the west; and the Red Sea Hill ranges (over 2,000 m.) in the north-east. Elsewhere the plainlands, diversified in places by smaller hill ranges, slope gently to the north and towards the Nile.

CLIMATE

Sudan has a range of tropical continental climates, with a marked climatic gradient from south to north and from the Ethiopian plateau north-westwards. In the south the rainy season lasts up to eight months, producing over 1,000 mm. of precipitation, while at Atbara, north of Khartoum, there is a one-month rainy season in August and only 50 mm. of rainfall. In the north high summer temperatures are common, mean daily maxima reaching about 104°F. in Khartoum in May and June, though there is usually a marked diurnal range (about 68°F.). In the south

temperatures are lower (average daily maxima 86°F.), the hottest months being February and March.

VEGETATION AND SOILS

Vegetation types are related to the climatic gradient. Tropical rain forest is found only in the uplands of the extreme south; and the south-east is dominated by a wooded-grassland complex, which merges northwards in Kordofan, Darfur and Blue Nile Provinces to a "low woodland savannah", dominated by acacia and with large areas of short grassland. Northward is a gradation through semi-desert to desert. The pattern is broken in the south by the large swamp grasslands of the Sudd area.

In the south-east areas from east of Khartoum to Juba alkaline clay soils dominate, and the south-western part of the country has red latosols, but elsewhere soils are predominantly sandy with pockets and strips of finer materials along the water courses.

POPULATION

The population of the Sudan at the census of April 1973 was 12,427,795, compared with 10,262,536 at the time of the previous population survey in January 1956. This increase, of just over 21 per cent in 17 years, is slow by African standards. The total population is small in relation to the size of the country, but there is a very uneven distribution, with over 50 per cent of the people concentrated in 15 per cent of the total national area. High densities occur along the Nile and around Khartoum, but parts of Kordofan near the railway line, the Nuba mountains and parts of Bahr el Ghazal and Darfur have average densities of 15 per sq. km. with much higher local concentrations. The people of northern Sudan are of mixed Arabic and African origin and traditionally are nomadic or semi-nomadic; in the south Nilotic peoples predominate, the Nuer, the Dinka and the Shilluk being the most important.

The major towns are the provincial centres, with the three towns of Khartoum, Omdurman and Khartoum North forming by far the largest urban centre. The Khartoum urban complex, with a population of about 700,000, is the main industrial, commercial, communication and administrative centre, and handles 90 per cent of the external trade. Of the other towns Atbara the centre of the railway industry, Wad Medani, first town of the Gezira, El Obeid and Juba, are the most important. Sudan has a well-developed railway system which now provides good links with the most populated parts of the country. The road system is poorly developed, and outside the main towns well maintained roads are rare. Communications suffered considerable damage in the civil war.

HISTORY
Muddathir Abdel Rahim

The geographic position of the Sudan, between the Mediterranean-Middle Eastern world on the one hand and Central Africa on the other, has played an important part in determining the character and politics of the country since Biblical times at least. In almost all the contacts between the Sudan and the outside world Egypt has been the most important link, and, especially since the rise of Islam, the dominant one. Thus the Pharaohs, the Persians, the Greeks, the Romans, the Arabs, the Turks and the British, all those who governed or conquered Egypt in the past, have in turn found it either necessary or desirable to extend their influence, if not their power, beyond the traditional boundaries of Egypt (between the first and second cataracts) into the lands which now constitute the Republic of Sudan. Conversely, the inhabitants of those lands, or at any rate those of them who lived in the northern parts of the country, have always had to choose between three alternative policies: domination by Egypt; independence from their neighbours; or conquest of Egypt; at one time or another each of these possibilities was actually realized. At no time, however, could either of the two countries ignore the other—a fact which, with modern Egyptian nationalists, became the justification for making the Unity of the Nile Valley for many years the *raison d'être* of Egyptian foreign policy.

ANCIENT AND MEDIEVAL

From the time of Tuthmosis I (1530–1520 B.C.) until the eighth century B.C. northern Cush (as the area as far as the Gezira was called in ancient times) was, for the most part, under the effective control of the Pharaohs. And even after the political supremacy of the Pharaohs had been completely shaken off the Cushites continued to be so thoroughly Egyptianized that, at times, they regarded themselves as the champions of true Egyptian culture.

The political mastery of the Pharaohs in Cush gradually diminished from the tenth century onwards, and by 725 B.C. the balance of power was finally turned by a series of competent Cushite leaders who established themselves as the twenty-fifth Pharaonic dynasty. The most renowned Pharaoh of this Cushite dynasty was Tirhaka (688–663 B.C.) under whose leadership the empire extended from Cush to Syria and whose wars in Syria and Judea are recorded in the Bible. Tirhaka's empire, however, did not last long; a number of setbacks led to his final defeat by the Assyrians in 666 B.C. The kingdom of Cush survived for a thousand years, during which it expanded to the south, the capital being transferred from Napata, near the fourth cataract, to Meroe, near Kaboshiya, about 100 miles north of Khartoum. But under the pressure of Nubian migrants from the south-west and the new power of Axum in the east, the Meroitic kingdom declined and there was little of its former glory left when the first Christian king of Axum raided the Nile valley in A.D. 350.

From this cataclysm emerged three Nuba kingdoms into which Christianity was introduced from Egypt under the patronage of the Empress Theodora early in the sixth century A.D.

By A.D. 639, when the Arab Muslims invaded Egypt, two Christian Nuba kingdoms occupied approximately the territory formerly covered by the Meroitic realm. With the more northerly of these the Arab invaders made a treaty which subsisted for six hundred years. There was little Arab penetration into the Nuba country and the Sudan as a whole until the rise in Egypt of the Bahri Mamluk Sultans about A.D. 1250. These both encouraged southern emigration by the Bedouin and interfered in the politics of the northern Nuba Kingdom, which eventually disintegrated through Arab infiltration and intermarriage. The more southerly kingdom survived until A.D. 1504, when it was overthrown by the invasion of Negroid newcomers from the south called the Funj, who also defeated the infiltrating Arabs.

The Islamic Sultanate of The Funj, otherwise known as "the Black Sultanate", was, in effect, a confederation of smaller Sultanates or tribal chieftainships, each ruled by a "mek", or prince, who owed allegiance to the Sultan at Sennar, the new capital city on the Blue Nile, about 170 miles south of Khartoum. The authority of the Sultan at Sennar was recognized throughout the former lands of Cush and Nubia, including the Gezira, but was contested in Kordofan by the dynasty of Sultan Suleiman Solong, which established itself in Darfur in 1596. Largely as a result of internecine warfare and wars with the Furs in the west and the Abyssinians in the east the energies of the Funj were sapped and, by the nineteenth century, when Muhammad Ali Pasha of Egypt challenged them, their Sultanate was already in decline.

THE NINETEENTH CENTURY

Muhammad Ali had two main objectives in the Sudan: gold and slaves, both of which he needed in order to build an Egyptian-Arab empire independent of that of the Sultan in Istanbul. His ambitions in this respect were frustrated by the European powers and his dreams about gold were proved to be false. But Muhammad Ali did succeed in establishing an empire in the Nile Valley which lasted from 1821, when the last of the kings of Sennar surrendered, until 1885 when Khartoum fell to the Mahdi. Kordofan and Darfur were subsequently added to Sennar and, under his successors, principally Khedive Ismail, the boundaries of the empire were extended to the Great Lakes, and by 1877 the Somali coast as far as Ras Hofun was also recognized as Egyptian territory under the suzerainty of the Sultan.

Within this vast but loosely organized empire the Sudan was, at first, viewed as a province of Egypt but its administration, centred on the new capital of Khartoum, was afterwards decentralized and put under a Hakimdar (or Governor General) to whom provincial governors were responsible. And the provinces were likewise divided into smaller units which tended to follow the traditional tribal and territorial boundaries of the Funj period. The personnel of the new regime was a mixture of Circassian, Turkish, European and Armenian officers of the Ottoman-Egyptian army who were assisted, especially at the lower levels, by Sudanese sheikhs and tribal leaders.

Like its counterparts in other parts of the later Ottoman empire the Sudan administration was corrupt and far from efficient. Its difficulties, arising from the general malaise of the declining empire, were further accentuated, on the one hand by frequent and arbitrary interference from Cairo and, on the other, by the policy of rapid but poorly organized expansion which was followed by Muhammad Ali's successors, especially Khedive Ismail. Ismail furthermore was determined to abolish slavery in his own lifetime. Slavery had been part of the social system throughout the Nile Valley including the southern Sudan. But trading rights in the newly opened south had been sold to armed adventurers, and searching for slaves was carried to extremes which were in many cases reminiscent of the barbarities of the triangular slave trade. Ismail hoped to mitigate these evils by administrative means and through the agency of European expatriates such as Sir Samuel Baker and General Charles Gordon. But the violent methods used by these men in order to abolish the slave trade alienated large sections of the population, caused considerable social and economic dislocation and to that extent weakened the government's control over the country and played into the hands of the Sudanese religious rebel Muhammad Ahmed Abdulla. In March 1881, Abdulla declared that he was the Mahdi and called upon the people to rally with him against the Turks and for the reformation of Islam. This was not, at first, taken seriously by the government. The Mahdi on the other hand showed remarkable skill in manoeuvre and organization, and under his able leadership the apparently minor rebellion was rapidly transferred into a nation-wide "jihad" which by January 1885 resulted in the fall of Khartoum. Thus began a new chapter in the history of the country during which the Sudan was governed by Sudanese; first under the Mahdi and after his death in June 1885, by the Khalifa Abdullahi whose rule lasted for more than thirteen years.

In the meantime Britain had occupied Egypt and assumed effective, but indirect, control of its government. Thus, in 1883, the Government of the Khedive, acting on what was officially described as the advice of the British Government, concluded that it could not hold the Sudan against the Mahdists and therefore decided to evacuate the country and concentrate, instead, on the development of Egypt's own resources. It was in order to execute this policy that Gordon was sent to Khartoum where he was killed when the town fell to the Mahdi. The Egyptian nationalists greatly resented this policy of evacuation which they felt was dictated by British, not Egyptian, interests.

Ten years later Britain, in order to safeguard its own position in Egypt and to ward off the Italians, the Belgians and, most importantly, the French—all engaged in the general scramble for Africa, including the Upper Nile—decided that the Sudan also should be brought under its effective control. But since conquest would have brought Britain in direct conflict with the French and the other European powers in Central Africa, the British Government decided that the conquest should be done in the name of the Khedive and Egypt who, it was contended, were now in a position to reaffirm their control over what was described as Egyptian territory which had been temporarily disrupted by the Mahdist rebellion. The reconquest, as it was called, was as unpopular with the Egyptian nationalists as the policy of evacuation had been ten years previously—and for the same reasons. Opposition notwithstanding, the reconquest was executed by combined Egyptian and British forces under the general command of General Herbert Kitchener. It took three years: from 1896 to 1898, when, on September 2nd, the last of the Mahdist forces were destroyed at the battle of Omdurman.

THE CONDOMINIUM

The Anglo-Egyptian Agreement of 1899 laid the foundations of the new régime in the Sudan. The important, but thorny question of sovereignty over the country was however deliberately left out of the Agreement. For, from Britain's point of view, the acceptance, as binding law, of the theory that the new régime was a restoration of the Ottoman—Egyptian régime overthrown by the Mahdi was undesirable because it would have left Britain without legal basis for its presence in the Sudan, while the alternative—the theory that Britain was sovereign or had a share in sovereignty over the Sudan—would have aroused the hostility, not only of the Egyptians and the Sultan, but also of the French and the other European powers, and was therefore similarly undesirable. While emphasizing the claims which accrued to Britain by virtue of her participation in the reconquest, therefore, the Agreement was silent as to the juridical positions of the two conquering powers in the Sudan. This allowed Britain considerable scope for political and diplomatic manoeuvre. Thus, when the French questioned Britain's presence in the Sudan the British government insisted that it was acting on behalf of the Khedive; when the Egyptian nationalists raised the same question they were reminded of Britain's role in the reconquest; and when they protested their inferior position in the administration of the country, though they had contributed the larger share of men and money during the reconquest and almost all the expenses of the administration, Britain maintained that this was only fair as the country was reconquered in the name of Egypt which, however, was unable to govern itself let alone the Sudan. This was perhaps illogical but from a practical point of view, it made little difference so long as Britain was in effective control of Egypt as well as the Sudan. After Egypt's independence in 1922 however, and especially after the abolition of the Caliphate, in whom sovereignty over the Sudan had theoretically resided during the

Ottoman-Egyptian régime, the silence of the Agreement as to the subject of sovereignty became a source of increasing embarrassment to Britain.

The juridical dispute aside, the Agreement established in the Sudan an administration which was nominally Anglo-Egyptian but was actually a British colonial administration. Like the Ottoman-Egyptian administration it was headed by a Governor-General in whom all civil and military authority was vested. He was appointed by Khedivial decree but on the recommendation of the British government, without whose consent he could not be dismissed. Nothing was mentioned in the Agreement about his nationality but it is not surprising that all the Governors-General of the Sudan—like the Province Governors and District Commissioners who assisted them—were British. The British character of the régime became more obvious after 1924, when the Egyptian troops, officers and civilians who had hitherto acted as intermediaries between the British and the Sudanese were evacuated from the Sudan following the murder in Cairo of Sir Lee Stack, the then Governor-General of the Sudan and Sirdar (i.e. C.-in-C.) of the Egyptian Army. The administration of the country was until then based on the principle of Direct Rule and was, especially before the First World War, carried out along military lines. This was necessitated by the fact that resistance to the new régime did not cease after the battle of Omdurman and risings against it occurred annually. By the end of the war, however, the process of pacification, except in the south, was completed, and the last stronghold of Mahdism was taken when, in 1916, Sultan Ali Dinar of Darfur was killed and his Sultanate made a province of the Sudan.

INDIRECT RULE

The evacuation of the Egyptians from the Sudan in 1924 was generally unpopular with the Sudanese, especially the non-Mahdists and the small but influential educated class, who sympathized with the Egyptians on grounds of common language and religion, and saw in Egypt a natural ally against the British. Demonstrations were therefore organized in order to show solidarity with the Egyptians, and a Sudanese battalion mutinied and clashed with British troops. The rising was however ruthlessly crushed. Relations between the Sudan government and educated Sudanese deteriorated rapidly and a period of intense bitterness began which lasted well into the 1930s and was much aggravated by the depression and the subsequent retrenchment of salaries.

It was against this background that Indirect Rule, through the agency of tribal sheikhs and chiefs, was introduced, which soon replaced Direct Rule as the guiding principle in administration. Tribalism, which had been greatly weakened during the Mahdiyya, was revived and encouraged not only for purposes of administrative decentralization but also, and more importantly, as an alternative to bureaucratic government which necessitated the creation and employment of more and more educated Sudanese. These, because of their education, however limited, were politically more conscious than tribal leaders and therefore more difficult to control. Simultaneously with the stimulation of tribalism and tribal institutions therefore, training centres such as the military college were closed down; courses for training Sudanese administrators were discontinued; and harsh discipline which "savoured strongly of the barracks" was introduced in the Gordon College—an elementary institution which had been opened in 1902 for the training of artisans and junior officials. In general, the period from 1924 to the mid-thirties may be described as the golden age of Indirect Rule, or Native Administration; but from the point of view of education—always, under the British, closely connected with policy and administration—it was, in the words of a distinguished British scholar, "a period of utter stagnation". Economically however it was notable for the development of the Gezira scheme (*see* Economic Survey).

The introduction of Native Administration in the Northern Sudan after 1924 was paralleled in the south, by the launching of the government's new "Southern Policy". Until then official policy in the south was, apart from the maintenance of law and order, largely limited to the provision of various forms of assistance to Christian missionary societies which, in the words of an official Annual Report, worked for the proselytization of the population and "teaching these savages the elements of common sense, good behaviour, and obedience to government authority". After the rising of 1924 which, incidentally, was led by an officer of southern (Dinka) origin, the "Southern Policy" was introduced. It had two main objectives: the prevention of the spirit of nationalism, which had already taken root in Egypt, from spreading across the Northern Sudan to the south and to other East African "possessions"; and the separation of the three southern provinces from the rest of the country with a view to their eventual assimilation by the government of neighbouring British territories which, it was hoped, would then emerge as a great East African Federation under British control. Accordingly, Muslim and Arabic speaking people in the south, whether they were of Egyptian, northern Sudanese or west African origins, were evicted from the region while stringent systems of permits and "Closed Districts" were introduced to prevent others from entering. Southerners, on the other hand, were discouraged from visiting or seeking employment in the north, and those among them who had adopted the Muslim religion or used Arabic names, clothes or language were persuaded, by administrative means (which sometimes involved the burning of Arab clothes) to drop them and use, instead, Christian, English or native equivalents. Whereas education was then stagnating in the north and had so far been neglected in the south it was now enthusiastically supported by the government—but along lines calculated to eradicate all traces of Islamic and Arabic culture, and thus gradually sever relations between the northern and southern provinces.

TOWARDS SELF-GOVERNMENT

As may be expected the Southern Policy, like Native Administration, was most unpopular with the nationalists who, by the mid-1930s, had recovered from the shocks they had suffered after the failure of 1924. Encouraged by the challenge which the Axis powers were then presenting to Britain and by the restoration of Egypt's position in the Sudan in 1936, itself largely the result of the changing international scene, they began to mobilize themselves and prepared to resume their offensive. The Graduates' Congress, representing the *literati* of the country, was established early in 1938. Stimulated by the war, the Atlantic Charter and the open competition of the Egyptian and Sudan governments for their sympathy and support, the graduates, in 1942, submitted to the government a famous Memorandum in which they demanded, *inter alia*, the abolition of the Closed Districts Ordinance; the cancellation of subventions to missionary schools and the unifications of syllabuses in the north and the south; an increase in the share of the Sudanese in the administration of their country and the issue of a declaration granting the Sudan the right of self-government directly after the war. The government rebuffed the graduates by refusing to receive their Memorandum but nevertheless proceeded to react, on the local level, by the gradual transformation of Native Administration into a modern system of local government and, in central government administration, by launching, in 1943, an Advisory Council for the Northern Sudan which was replaced, in 1948, by a Legislative Assembly for the Sudan as a whole. The development of local government, however, was a very slow process (the first comprehensive local government Ordinance being promulgated as late as 1951); and it was in any case peripheral to the main wishes of the nationalists. The Advisory Council and the Legislative Assembly on the other hand failed to satisfy them because among other things, they had very little power to exercise (in the case of the Council no power at all), while their composition, largely based on the principle of appointment rather than free elections, only partially reflected political opinion in the country.

The limitations of the Council and the Assembly notwithstanding, the promulgation of these institutions had the effect of accentuating differences within Congress and eventually splitting it into two rival groups. Some worried about Egypt's continued claims over the Sudan, and feeling that independence could best be achieved by co-operating with the government, thought that Congress should participate in the Council and the Assembly however defective they were. This group, led by the Umma Party, was supported by the Mahdists, and their motto was "The Sudan for the Sudanese". Others being more distrustful of the British, felt that independence could best be achieved through co-operation with Egypt which was an Arabic-speaking and Muslim neighbouring country and, like the Sudan, despite its formal independence, a victim of British imperialism. They therefore stood for "The Unity of the Nile Valley" and, supported by the Khatmiyya, the chief rival of the Mahdists among the religious fraternities, boycotted both the Council and the Assembly.

In the meantime successive negotiations between the British and Egyptian governments led from one deadlock to another and the unhappy schism between "the Unionists" and "the Independence Front" continued until the outbreak of the Egyptian Revolution in July 1952. The new régime promptly disowned the king and the Pasha class with whom "The Unity of the Nile Valley under the Egyptian Crown" was a basic article of political faith, and thus cleared the way for a separate settlement of the Sudan question. Neguib, Nasser and Salah Salem, all of whom had served in the Sudan and knew the Sudanese well, then staged a diplomatic *coup* which put the initiative in their hands.

The British had consistently justified their continued presence in the Sudan in terms of their desire to secure self-determination for the Sudanese as opposed to imposing on them a unity with Egypt which many Sudanese were prepared to resist by force of arms if necessary. Having got rid of the king the new Egyptian régime now declared that it was equally willing to grant the Sudanese the right of self-determination. On the basis of this declaration an Anglo-Egyptian Agreement was signed in 1953. This Agreement provided, among other things, for the Sudanization of the police and the civil service and the evacuation of all British and Egyptian troops in preparation for self-determination within a period of three years. Elections, held under the supervision of an international commission, resulted in the victory of the National Unionist Party, whose leader Ismail El Azhari became the first Sudanese Prime Minister in January 1954 and proceeded to put the terms of the Agreement into effect. The Egyptians had supported the NUP during the elections and it was naturally expected that Azhari would try to lead the country in the direction of union with Egypt. However, by the time the Sudanization programme was completed and the Egyptian and British troops had left the country, it was clear that he stood for independence. Several reasons led to this apparent reversal of attitude. Among these was the fact that the overwhelming majority of the NUP had looked upon solidarity with the Egyptians as a means for achieving the independence of the Sudan. Besides, the official opening of Parliament of March 1st, 1954, witnessed a violent demonstration by the Mahdists of their determination to split the country if the government wanted to lead the Sudan along the path of unity with Egypt rather than independence. Several people were killed and the ceremony to which guests from many countries, including Gen. Neguib, had been invited, was postponed. It then became obvious that independence would not only satisfy the aspirations of the Sudanese but would also save the country from civil war. One thing, however, could still frustrate the country's progress to independence: namely the mutiny of southern troops at Juba in August 1955. This was the prelude to an attempted revolt in the south in which nearly three hundred northern Sudanese officials, merchants and their families were massacred. The disorders, except for some sporadic outbursts, did not spread to the two provinces of Upper Nile and Bahr El Ghazal but were centred in Equatoria. Order was restored in due course but the political problem of the south which, springing from the geographic and social differences between the northern and southern provinces, had been greatly accentuated by the "Southern Policy" of the British administration, continued to present a serious challenge to the Sudanese and the unity of the Sudan. Before they could vote for independence southern members of Parliament insisted that their request for a federal form of government be given full consideration. This they were duly promised.

The agreement had prescribed a plebiscite and other protracted procedures for self-determination. Azhari, supported by all Sudanese parties, decided to side-step these arrangements, and on December 19th, 1955, Parliament unanimously declared the Sudan an independent republic and, at the same time, resolved that a committee of five elected by Parliament exercise the powers of the Head of State in place of the Governor-General. Faced with this *fait accompli* Britain and Egypt had no choice but to recognize the Sudan's independence, which was formally celebrated on January 1st, 1956.

INDEPENDENT SUDAN

Immediately after independence the Sudan sought to establish itself in the international field and was soon afterwards unanimously accepted as a member of the UN, and in regional organizations such as the Arab League and later the OAU. Internally, the social services were expanded; the University College of Khartoum was raised to full university status; railway extensions on the Blue Nile south of Sennar and from Darfur to El De'ain were completed; and the first stages of the Managil extensions began operating, in July 1958, with a gross irrigable area of 200,000 acres, the whole scheme, involving some 800,000 acres, being completed in 1961. The administration, despite the difficulties which inevitably followed the rapid Sudanization programme, overcame the increased responsibilities with which it was charged. But financial and economic problems arising from rapid expansion on the one hand and difficulty in selling the cotton crops of 1957 on the other began to embrace the whole country and, coupled with difficulties on the political plane, resulted, in 1958, in the replacement of parliamentary government by the military regime of General Ibrahim Abboud.

The political problems in which the country was involved soon after independence began with a split which took place within the ruling N.U.P. between the Khatmiyya and the non-sectarian elements in the party. This was accompanied by an agreement between the leaders of the two religious fraternities, the Mahdists and the Khatmiyya, which was reflected in the political field by the final replacement of Azhiri by a coalition government which was formed by the Umma Party, representing the Mahdists, and the newly formed People's Democratic Party, the political organ of the Khatmiyya. The new Prime Minister was Sayed Abdalla Khalil, the secretary of the Umma Party and a retired officer of the Sudan Defence Force.

The unprecedented coalition of Mahdists and Khatmiyya at first seemed to work reasonably well, but difficulties soon began to appear. With the country's financial reserves falling rapidly, severe and unpopular restrictions had to be imposed and foreign aid sought. But the P.D.P., already worried by what it considered was the unduly pro-Western foreign policy of the Prime Minister, opposed acceptance of American aid.

Elections held in February 1958 resulted in no change and the already strained Umma-P.D.P. coalition was restored to power. If either party had been able to win a sufficient number of seats to form a government of its own the course of subsequent events would have been different. After hard negotiations the N.U.P. and the Umma Party agreed, on November 16th, 1958, to form a new government. But Abdalla Khalil did not view this move with favour, and having been an officer and having therefore close relations with the army, he consulted with a group of senior officers about the possibility of an army *coup*.

MILITARY GOVERNMENT

The *coup d'état* was launched on November 17th, 1958. To the people in general it came as a relief after the wrangling and differences of the parties. Gen. Abboud assured the country that his aim was restoration of stability and sound administration at home, and the fostering of cordial relations with the outside world, especially the U.A.R.

The military régime made a good start in the economic field by following a realistic cotton sales policy which ensured the sale of both the carry-over from the past seasons and the new crop. Loans from various international institutions and aid from the U.S.A., the U.S.S.R. and other sources were successfully negotiated. The money was used to finance such projects as the completion of the Managil extension and the construction of the Roseires Dam on the Blue Nile and the Khashm Al Girba Dam on the Atbara, the latter being used for the purpose of irrigating an area for the resettlement of the people of Jalfa, whose ancient town has now been submerged by waters of the High Dam at Aswan.

In spite of these efforts discontent soon began to grow. Prompting this was the feeling that too many officers—encouraged by the absence of democratic procedures of control and accountability—had become corrupt and used public funds for private gain. The result was that when the country was again gripped by financial and economic difficulties in 1964 the public was convinced that this could not be accounted for in terms of the poor cotton crop of that year, nor in terms of over-ambitious economic development schemes; in a word, they no longer trusted the government.

In the field of administration other than financial, the military régime was again unfortunate. In July 1961 a new system of provincial administration not unlike Pakistan's "Basic Democracies" was inaugurated. This was crowned in 1962 by the creation of the Central Council which met for the first time in November 1963. The idea was to train the people in responsible self-government through institutions which, it was said, would be more suitable to their genius than imported ones such as Westminster-type parliaments and the administrative system inherited from the pre-independence era. While this was, to most people, perfectly acceptable in principle, the actual working of the new system—under the close supervision and control of military personnel—turned out to be very different from the professed ideal. Friction between army officers on the one hand, and civil servants and other professional administrators on the other, resulted in the alienation of this important section of Sudanese society. Therefore, when the civil service was called to join the judiciary, university staff, workers and others in the general strike which took place after the outbreak of the revolution in October 1964, the response was both complete and enthusiastic.

THE CIVILIAN COUP

The immediate cause of the revolution was the Government's heavy-handed administration in the southern provinces. This was based on the mistaken idea that the problem of the southern Sudan was a military, not a political, problem and that it was mainly the result of the activities of the missionaries who had participated in the implementation of the "Southern Policy" of the British administration. But the expulsion of the missionaries in February 1964 dramatized the problem for the outside world rather than helped to solve it, while military action against both the *Anya Nya* rebels and the civilian villagers who were sometimes obliged to give them food and shelter, had the effect of forcing thousands of southerners to live as refugees in neighbouring countries and convinced many that the only solution of the problem was for them to have a separate and independent state in the south. Concerned for the unity of the country, politicians, university students and others started campaigning for the view that the country could not be saved except by the removal of the military from authority and the restoration of democratic government. Orders forbidding public discussion of the southern problem and other political matters were issued but were defiantly disregarded by students. On October 21st the police, determined to break up such a discussion, opened fire on students within the precincts of the university. One of the students died, and thus the revolution was set into motion. A general strike brought the country to a standstill and General Abboud was forced to start negotiations with a Committee of Public Safety to which he subsequently agreed to surrender political power.

A transitional Government, in which all parties, including for the first time the Communist Party and the Muslim Brotherhood, were respresented, was sworn in on November 1st. The Prime Minister was Sirr Al Khatim Al Khalifa, of the Ministry of Education. He had worked for many years in the south and was much respected by southerners. The ministers of interior and communications were southerners. As a result of the inclusion as ministers of representatives of the communist-dominated Workers' and Tenants' Trades Unions and certain front organizations, the cabinet as whole was dominated by the Communist Party, which had played an active part in mobilizing opinion against the military régime.

After restoring the freedom of the press, raising the ban on political parties, and starting a purge of the administration (which was subsequently abandoned on account of its being carried along partisan lines), the new government turned to the most important problem facing it: the problem of the southern Sudan. One of the first acts of the government had been a declaration of a general amnesty in the south which was accompanied by an appeal to southern leaders inside and outside the country to help solve the problem by peaceful means.

On March 16th, 1965, a Round Table Conference in which northern and southern parties participated was opened in Khartoum. It was also attended by observers from seven African states. The northern parties proposed to set up a regional government in the south which would have its own parliament, executive, public service commission, development committee and university. The southern parties which attended the conference were divided. Some wanted federation; others a separate state; while the unionists (who were not represented in the conference because the two other groups threatened to boycott it if they were allowed to participate) favoured the status quo. The federalists and the separatists eventually agreed to demand a referendum to enable southern voters to choose between the three alternatives of regional government, federation and separation. By March 30th however no general agreement between the northern and southern parties was reached over the constitutional future of the country, and the subject was referred to a Twelve Man Committee, on which all parties (except the Southern Unionists) were represented.

Externally the transitional government broke with the traditional neutralism which had characterized Sudanese foreign policy since independence, and supported national liberation movements in Southern Arabia, in the Congo, and among the Eritreans in Ethiopia. But this, like the purging of the administration, was controversial and was especially disliked by the leaders of the two main traditional parties, the Umma and the N.U.P., who together with the Islamic Charter Front (at the core of which was the Muslim Brotherhood) formed a front against the more left-wing P.D.P. and the Communist Party. The former felt that elections should be held as soon as possible so that a representative and responsible government could be formed, while the latter, who could not hope to improve their position in the country through elections, favoured the continuation of the new policies.

Elections were held in June 1965. They were boycotted by the P.D.P. but were heavily contested by all other parties, including the Communists. The Umma Party won the greatest number of seats, 76, followed by the N.U.P. who won 53. Neither party was however in a position to form a government on its own. The Communists won 11 out of the 15 seats in the graduates' constituency and had the further distinction of having among their representatives the first Sudanese woman M.P.

COALITION GOVERNMENT

It was obvious that the new government had to be a coalition. After some discussion the Umma and N.U.P. agreed to form a government in which Mohamed Ahmed Mahgoub (Umma) became Prime

Minister and Azhari the permanent President of the Committee of Five which collectively acted as Head of State.

The new coalition at once ran into difficulties over the southern question. In July there was serious rebel activity at Juba and Wau, and large numbers of southerners were killed in the course of reprisals by Government troops. There were also severe difficulties in retaining southern representation on the Government; two members appointed by SANU, the leading southern nationalist party, were withdrawn when Buth Dieu, Secretary of the Southern Liberal Party, was appointed Minister of Animal Resources in August. Personal animosity between the President of the Supreme Council, Al Azhari, and the Umma Party, Premier Mahgoub, led to a crisis within the coalition in October, which was only solved by the mediation of the young Umma Party President, Sadik el Mahdi. Government policies meanwhile became increasingly right-wing, as when, in November 1965, the Communist Party was banned and its members unseated from the Assembly.

In order to pacify Ethiopian opinion, which had been provoked by the discovery in the Sudan of a consignment of arms from Syria destined for the Eritrean rebels, and the Chad Government, which was concerned about the possibility of a conspiracy being hatched against it on Sudanese soil, the new Prime Minister hastened to affirm his government's adherence to the Accra pledges of non-interference (in the case of Ethiopia signing a border pact in June 1966). This was followed by a number of visits to neighbouring countries with the purpose of confirming the new government's position in this respect and, at the same time, making arrangements whereby the return of Sudanese refugees from these countries would be facilitated.

SADIK EL MAHDI ELECTED PREMIER

In the meantime a serious split was developing between the right wing of the Umma Party, led by Imam el Hadi (Sadik's uncle), which supported Premier Mahgoub, and the younger and more moderate elements who looked to Sadik for more effective leadership. Sadik, however, was reluctant to accept the Premiership not only on account of his young age (30), but also because failure (which was likely, in view especially of the mounting financial and security problems of the country) would prejudice his political future. But events, particularly the growing split within his party, and the pressure of his supporters, finally obliged him to change his mind. After a heavy defeat in a vote of censure, on July 25th, 1966, Mahgoub resigned and Sadik was then elected Premier. His government was also a coalition of Umma and N.U.P. but included, as Minister of Finance an independent expert of Khatmiyya background, Hamza Mirghani, who in 1961 had resigned his post as Principal Under-Secretary of the Ministry of Finance, and had since worked with the IBRD. There were also two southern Ministers.

The new government at once addressed itself to the two major problems of the country. With the help of stringent controls, on the one hand, and loans from the IBRD and IMF, the economy gradually began to recover, and the country's reserves of foreign currency, which had dropped to the alarming level of £S14 million, began to improve. Meantime the Twelve Man Committee had made considerable progress towards the settlement of the southern problem on the basis of regional government. A "Parties Conference" continued the Committee's work and, in April 1967, submitted a report in which it also recommended a regional solution. By this time the long-awaited supplementary elections in the south had been held, bringing 36 members to the Constituent Assembly, of whom 10, led by William Deng, represented SANU, the leading southern party. It was now possible to speed up the process of drafting the permanent constitution and the settlement of the southern problem.

The relative success of Sadik's nine-month-old administration, however, coupled with the announcement that he would stand for the post of President under the proposed constitution, resulted in the break-up of the coalition between his wing of the Umma Party and the N.U.P., whose leader, Azhari, like the leader of the Ansar, Imam el Hadi, also aspired to the Presidency. Thus, on May 16th, 1967, Sadik was defeated in the Assembly (111 against 93) and Mahgoub was, once again, elected Premier.

MAHGOUB RETURNS TO POWER

Under his leadership the new coalition of NUP and El Hadi's branch of Umma pursued a vigorous foreign policy, particularly in the Middle East after the Six Days War. As a result, the first Arab Summit Conference after the war was convened in Khartoum (August 1967) and Mahgoub, together with Iraqi and Moroccan colleagues, was subsequently entrusted with the task of finding a formula for the settlement of the Yemeni dispute. Deterioration of relations with the Western Powers, culminating in the severance of diplomatic relations with the United Kingdom and the U.S.A. after the June War, was accompanied by the development of closer relations with the Eastern bloc, and the conclusion of an arms deal with the U.S.S.R. resulted in the lifting, without formal announcement, of the ban which had previously been imposed on the Sudanese Communist Party.

The internal affairs of the country, particularly the already precarious financial situation, had in the meantime been somewhat neglected. The result was that when the Constituent Assembly was reconvened after the prolonged recess which followed the outbreak of hostilities in the Middle East, the opposition under the vigorous leadership of Sadik El Mahdi and William Deng (who, together with the ICF, now formed the New Forces Congress), was able to defeat the Government on several occasions. This, together with the growing PDP and Communist opposition to the Draft Permanent Constitution based on Islam, regionalism and a strong executive on the presidential model, induced the Government to dissolve the Constituent Assembly on January 7th, 1968, following a mass resignation of government members in the Assembly. Sadik and his allies contested the constitutionality of this act in the courts.

Before any judgement was pronounced, however, new elections were held in April, which were contested for the first time since 1958 by the PDP now merged with the NUP in the new Democratic Unionist Party. This won the largest number of seats, 101, followed by Sadik's Umma, who won 38, and El Hadi's Umma, with 30 seats. As the DUP did not command a majority on its own, a new coalition, also with Imam El Hadi's faction of the Umma Party, and under the leadership of Mahgoub, was formed when the Assembly was convened on May 27th.

Mahgoub's third government, however, was unable to improve the economic and financial conditions of the country and the situation in the southern provinces continued to deteriorate. Mahgoub, moreover, fell ill and the situation was aggravated by the cabinet crisis of April-May over the reallocation of ministerial responsibilities between the Umma and Democratic Unionist Parties. In the circumstances few people were surprised when, on May 25th, 1969, the Government was overthrown by a group of officers led by Col. (later Maj.-Gen.) Jaafir al-Nemery.

NEMERY'S REVOLUTIONARY GOVERNMENT

(revised for this edition by the Editor)

The new régime which was thereby ushered in declared that it was committed to a policy of "Sudanese Socialism" and gave the country the new name of the "Democratic Republic of the Sudan". The Transitional Constitution, Supreme Council of State and Constituent Assembly were abolished. Pending the promulgation of a new constitution, power was vested in a Revolutionary Council headed by Gen. Nemery. The only civilian member of the Council, Babiker Awadallah, a former Chief Justice, was appointed Prime Minister of a twenty-one-man cabinet, of whom at least five were full members of the Sudanese Communist Party. But he was subsequently replaced as Prime Minister by Gen. Nemery who was also Chairman of the Revolutionary Council.

All political organizations were later dissolved and several former ministers were tried on charges of bribery and corruption rumours of which had been rife before the coup. The property of certain persons, including the Mahdi family, was confiscated. Following an attempt on the life of Gen. Nemery the chief source of opposition to the régime in its early days, the Imam al-Mahdi (who had for some time been gathering weapons and supporters at Aba Island in the White Nile) was eliminated in March 1970. Imam al-Mahdi himself was killed on his way to Ethiopia, and Sadik, who had previously been arrested, was exiled to Egypt. He later returned and was re-arrested. Azhari, who had also been arrested, died while awaiting trial in Khartoum.

The régime was now able to turn more of its attention to the reshaping of the economy and the administration in the light of its professed policy of Sudanese Socialism. Considerable attention was given to the problem of the southern Sudan in particular. In June 1969 Gen. Nemery declared his government's policy of solving the problem by introducing regional autonomy in the southern provinces. A special Ministry of Southern Affairs was subsequently created to spell out the details of this policy. The first Minister of Southern Affairs was Joseph Garang, a Catholic southern Sudanese and a member of the Communist Party. Under his leadership considerable effort was directed to the formation of political cadres, but a certain amount of progress was also achieved in reconstruction and development. Several southerners were also appointed to ministerial, ambassadorial and administrative posts.

With growing self-assurance, particularly towards the end of its second year in office, the régime began to reconsider the extensive and controversial purges which had been enforced—largely under the influence of the Communist Party—in the early days of the régime. And Gen. Nemery began to publicly criticize the manner in which nationalized firms were being run.

In the field of foreign affairs, the policies of the régime were, above all, characterized by its militant support for the Arab cause over the Palestine question and by close cooperation with Libya and Egypt in particular. Thus one of the first decisions taken by the régime was to recognize the German Democratic Republic because of its position over the Palestine issue, and to refuse considering the re-establishment of relations with either Federal Germany or the U.S.A. owing to their support of Israel. The Rogers Plan was accepted, the fighting in Jordan deplored and Gen. Nemery headed the conciliation committee which secured a ceasefire between the Jordanian army and the Palestinian Liberation Organization in September 1970. In the meantime closer diplomatic and trade relations were forged with China and, until the coup and counter-coup of July 1971, with the U.S.S.R. and her closer Eastern European allies.

The coup of July 19th, 1971, was apparently engineered by a group of left-wing officers (principally Maj. Hashim al-Atta, Col. Babiker al-Nour and Maj. Farouq Hamadallah) who had been dropped from the Revolutionary Council, and by the Communist Party. Some of the Party's leading members had joined Nemery and apparently accepted his advocacy of Sudanese Socialism, but the bulk of the Party (led by Secretary-General Abdel-Khaliq Mahgoub) refused to follow suit and were particularly critical of Nemery's decision, in November 1970, to unite the Sudan with Libya and Egypt into one federal Arab Republic. A swift mid-day operation personally led by Hashim al-Atta removed Nemery from office for three days during which supporters and opposers of the coup, within the armed forces and outside, fought each other. The collapse of the coup was partly brought about through the intervention of Col. Gaddafi of Libya. For while Col. al-Nour and Maj. Hamadallah were returning from London to take command of the revolution, the BOAC plane carrying them was forced to land in Libya. They were taken off and the Libyan Government later handed them over to President Nemery who had regained power in a counter-coup three days after being ousted. (An Iraqi plane bringing Baathist and other supporters of the coup to Sudan crashed on the way killing all aboard.) A massive purge of communists followed and fourteen people were executed. Apart from Maj. al-Atta, who set the coup in motion in Khartoum, and the two leaders back from London, the Communist Party's Secretary-General, Abdel-Khaliq Mahgoub, the Secretary-General of the Federation of Sudanese Workers Union, al-Shafie Ahmad al-Shaikh and Joseph Garang were executed after trials before a military tribunal.

The events of July 1971 constituted an important landmark in the internal development and foreign relations of the Sudan.

In the field of foreign relations, the manner in which Nemery dealt with his adversaries after his return to power brought condemnation in unusually strong terms from the Soviet and East European governments. This, coupled with the apparent enthusiasm, if not active support, of Soviet and East European diplomats working in Khartoum for the communist-inspired coup, strained relations between the Sudan and these countries, though diplomatic ties remained intact. Sudanese foreign policy became mainly directed to forming closer links with the more conservative Arab governments such as Abu Dhabi, Kuwait and Saudi Arabia and friendly African states. Iraq maintained a hostile stance. Relations with Western countries improved and ties with the U.S.A. became more accommodating, though diplomatic relations were not resumed until July 1972. Relations with both Libya and Egypt worsened considerably during 1972. Sudanese troops were withdrawn at Egypt's insistence from their positions on the Suez Canal, and President Nemery's detention of Libyan aircraft containing troops sent by Col. Gaddafi to aid Uganda against invasion by Tanzania led to an antagonism between the two countries which remained strong until Gen. Nemery's visit to Libya in November 1974.

In an election held in October 1971 to confirm Gen. Nemery's nomination as President he received almost four million votes against 56,000. A new government was formed, the Revolution Command Council dissolved, and the Sudanese Socialist Union (SSU) recognized as the only legal political body in the Sudan. The SSU's Political Bureau, Executive Committee and General Secretariat were formed in October 1972 and the Central Committee in November 1972. All political parties remained banned, strong action being taken against Communist Party supporters in particular.

The vitally important Addis Ababa Agreement between the Sudanese Government and the *Anya Nya* southern Sudanese rebels led by "General" Joseph Lagu was signed in April 1972. Preparations for the compromise agreement began in 1971 and considerable assistance was given by Emperor Haile Sellassie of Ethiopia and the World Council of Churches in arranging the discussions which led to the end of the 17-year old civil war. The South gained regional autonomy within a federal structure of government, and dropped its aim of secession. It was granted a Regional People's Assembly with a High Executive

Council, and with representation in the national People's Assembly. The Head of the High Executive Council, appointed by the Regional People's Assembly, would also be a Vice-President of the Republic. The agreement also provided for the cessation of hostilities, the return and rehabilitation of southern Sudanese refugees abroad, the re-integration of *Anya Nya* rebels into the Sudanese armed forces and the recognition of the special status of the Christian religion and of the English language in the South together with the Islamic religion and Arabic in the North. The ceasefire came into effect on March 12th, 1972, and was a considerable personal achievement for Gen. Nemery, though the proper implementation of the ceasefire proposals posed considerable problems.

During the 17 years of civil war vast numbers of refugees had fled from the southern Sudan to the neighbouring African countries and even greater numbers were rootless inhabitants in the war-ravaged forests, bush and swamps of the South. Estimates vary enormously, but the general estimates of refugees outside the country averaged around 300,000 and of the homeless in the Southern region around 800,000. The South suffers from an almost total lack of postal, radio and newspaper communications, extremely poor roads, a drastic shortage of trained manpower and pitifully inadequate medical facilities. The UN Commissioner for Refugees, Sadruddin Aga Khan, launched a massive programme of repatriation, and this was aided by numerous relief organizations, foreign governments and church relief agencies. By the middle of 1974 refugees from Zaire, Uganda, Ethiopia and the Central African Republic had been resettled, as had the displaced Sudanese in the Southern region, and aid missions from numerous countries were assisting in the rehabilitation of parts of the South. Under the Addis Ababa Agreement 12,000 troops are stationed in the southern Sudan, of which half are southerners. Elections to the Regional People's Assembly were held without incident in November 1973, and Abel Alier, Gen. Nemery's nominee, was elected unopposed as President. The smooth passage of the elections, essential to preserve the country's stability, was followed by elections to the People's Assembly in April 1974 and this body opened in May.

In March 1973 three foreign diplomats, including the American ambassador, were murdered by Black September terrorists in Khartoum. In September the Government declared a short State of Emergency after student unrest and a strike by railway workers led to two deaths, many arrests and trade union pressure on the Government. Student unrest continued, and in February 1974 the University of Khartoum was closed again. In contrast to its stance during the 1967 Middle East War, the Sudan played a far less active role in that of October 1973. However in February 1974 plans for a union between Egypt and the Sudan, dormant since the cooling of relations in 1972, were revived though by mid-1975 this project still lacked firm foundations. In March 1974 all political prisoners in the Sudan were released including the former Prime Minister Sadik el Mahdi. In June, relations with the U.S.A. deteriorated after Gen. Nemery commuted the sentences of eight Black September terrorists found guilty of the murders of three diplomats 15 months earlier, and allowed them to be flown out of the country and handed over to the Palestine Liberation Organization.

In October 1974 Gen. Nemery announced that a plot by some members of the armed forces to over-throw his government had been foiled. For the first time since the end of the civil war riots broke out in the southern Sudan during October over attempts to begin the long delayed irrigation canal project at Jonglei, in collaboration with Egypt. Rumours of the stationing of Egyptian troops in the South provoked violence, leading to two dead and numerous arrests, whilst the South was also badly hit by floods which

left an estimated 250,000 homeless. In March 1975 a minor mutiny occurred in the army, initiated by former *Anya Nya* rebels, and in May a reported Communist plot against Nemery failed. General Nemery has warned constantly of the dangers facing the country from left- and right-wing extremists which is evident in periodic disturbances and plots. However, with the success of the Addis Ababa Agreement and the remarkable reconciliation between the North and the South, he remains both strong internally and active in African diplomacy, especially as a mediator in disputes. He has announced his intention to stand for re-election as President in October 1977.

The Sudan is head of the OAU Committee of Seven formed in December 1973 to co-ordinate relations with Arab states.

ECONOMIC SURVEY
Ali Ahmed Suliman
(with revisions for the 1975 edition by the Editor).

THE MAIN CHARACTERISTICS OF THE ECONOMY

The Sudan is primarily an agricultural and pastoral country. Agriculture, including livestock and forestry products, contributed more than 30 per cent of the gross domestic product in 1971–72. Animal wealth, though very undeveloped, contributes about 10 per cent of the G.D.P. The significance of agriculture in the Sudanese economy is also reflected in the distribution of manpower among the different economic sectors. About 85 per cent of those economically active (according to 1955–56 figures) are engaged in primary production. Manufacturing industries contributed only about 2 per cent of the G.D.P. up to 1962–63, increasing to 7 per cent in 1973, while the share of minerals is less than 1 per cent. No important minerals have yet been found in the Sudan in significant enough quantities to be exploited economically. The Sudan not only depends on agriculture, but on one main crop for its exports. In fact the share of extra-long staple cotton in the exports of the Sudan reaches more than 70 per cent in some years. Such dependence on one major export crop, with wide fluctuations in price and quantity exported, has caused political, as well as economic, instability.

With such a traditional agricultural sector it is not surprising that the Sudan has a low per capita income, which was only U.S. $97 in 1963–64, rising a little to $109 in 1970–71 and $125 in 1971–72. From 1961–71 G.D.P. in the Sudan grew at an annual rate of 4 per cent in current prices but overall, economic growth has been negligible. The population was believed to have been growing annually at a rate of about 2.8 per cent but the results of the 1973 census suggest a much lower rate of increase.

The average density of population in Sudan is low and there is no population pressure on the available resources at present. Open unemployment is very insignificant. In fact, Sudan suffers from a shortage of labour, particularly during the cotton-picking season. Sometimes this problem is solved by immigrant labour from neighbouring countries. The Sudan is a large country with large unproductive areas. Unfortunately it is these vast unproductive parts which are close to the Red Sea, whereas the more productive regions are separated from the sea and from Port Sudan by distances ranging between 500 and 1,500 miles. Their remoteness was a major factor in retarding economic development in the past. For the present, inadequacy of transport is one of the important bottle-necks in the economy, and this has been worsened by the 17 years of civil war up to 1972, when there were only 8 miles of tarred road in the southern region.

Perhaps one of the most striking features of the Sudanese economy is the dominant role which is played by the public sector in all important economic activities. The government owns the majority of modern capital establishments in the economy. In the ten-year plan the share of the government was £S337 million out of the total investment of £S565 million. In the period 1955/56–1962/63 the share of the government in gross fixed capital formation ranged between a half and two-thirds. However, it seems that the role of the public sector as a whole in gross fixed capital formation declined in the 1970s. In 1970–71, out of a total of £S73.2 million of gross fixed capital formation, the share of the public sector was only £S20.6 million. The government is not only the chief investor in public utilities, but is the main promoter of industries such as sugar, cotton-ginning, food processing, tanning and printing. Governmental efforts to develop the country have expanded to such an extent that all large hotels in the various parts of Sudan are owned and managed by the government. With the nationalization of all commercial banks and several leading commercial firms in May and June 1970 the economic significance of the public sector has become even greater.

AGRICULTURE

The availability of water is the governing factor for agriculture in Sudan. In most parts of the rainlands of Sudan drinking water for humans and animals is a crucial factor, especially before the rainy season, when land is prepared for cultivation, and after it during harvest time. However, land does not impose any constraint on the agricultural development of the country. The cultivable land is estimated to be about 200 million feddans (one feddan=1.038 acres). Only about 8 per cent of this cultivable land is being utilized in agriculture, and less than four million feddans are under irrigation. Half of this area is in the Gezira scheme (with its Managil extension), and the rest is irrigated by the flood waters of two small rivers in eastern Sudan, Gash and Baraka, by the flood waters of the Nile and by pumps.

Prior to the Nile Waters agreement of 1959 the distribution of water between Sudan and the U.A.R. was governed by the Nile Waters agreement of 1929, which allocated four milliard cubic metres to Sudan. However, with the 1959 agreement and the construction of the Roseires and Khashm el Girba dams, the water problem has been solved. Sudan is now entitled to draw 18.5 milliard cubic metres at Aswan High Dam or the equivalent of about 20.5 milliard cubic metres in Sudan, and the way has been opened for considerable expansion of irrigated agriculture. At present Sudan is drawing about half of its entitlement—about ten milliard cubic metres annually—but with the development of new areas along the White and Blue Nile, Atbara River and the Main Nile, as well as the intensification of the Gezira scheme by reducing fallow, and its diversification by such crops as wheat, groundnuts and *philipesara* vegetables, Sudan is expected to utilize all its entitlement within the coming five years or so. In March 1974 preparations for the construction of the Jonglei Canal to conserve more of the Nile water, were being finalized though these were further delayed by riots in the South in October 1974. The joint Egyptian-Sudanese project would increase Egypt's share of the Nile water by 1,900 million cubic metres per year and cultivate an extra 300,000 feddans in both countries. One of the main development projects in Sudan is the Rahad project, which will need about four milliard cubic metres of water for an area of about half a million feddans. The Roseires Dam, built at a cost of £S60 million will serve this project. Of the area available, half will be given to cotton, a third to groundnuts and a third left fallow. A pump station at Meira on the Blue Nile will feed a supply canal 50 miles long across the Rahad. The project main canal will be 100 miles long. Railway construction, clearance of land and building of nearby villages are to be undertaken and finance is to be provided by the World Bank, the U.S.A. and Kuwait. In the first phase it is planned that 100,000 feddans should be ready for planting by June 1976 and the first phase will also settle 14,000 tenant farmers and provide seasonal work for 90,000 agricultural labourers. After five years the scheme is intended to cover 300,000 feddans and to have settled an estimated 70,000 people in 15,000 tenancies. The Sukki project, which has also started, may reach an area of 170,000 feddans, while the pump-irrigated areas of the Northern Province may increase by about 165,000 feddans within a few years to come.

In spite of the significant role played by irrigation (particularly gravity irrigation) in the economic development of Sudan, the rainlands are more important. In 1970–71 the total cropped area of main crops increased by 4.9 per cent from the previous year's level of 9,820,793 feddans to 10,305,118 feddans. Rain-grown and flooded areas under cultivation both decreased from 7,900,000 and 150,000 feddans in 1969–70 to 2,400,000 and 130,000 respectively in 1970–71. The total area under irrigation continued to increase and reached 2.8 million feddans in 1970–71. With the exception of cotton, pulses and a proportion of groundnuts, Sudan's foodstuffs and most exported agricultural products come from the rainlands. In fact Sudan is self-sufficient in the essential foods: millet, meat, edible oils and salt.

The agricultural sector of the Sudan does not face any serious land tenure problems. The rainlands, in particular, are very free from such problems, and also enjoy the advantage of relatively low production costs. The present government has already started an anti-thirst campaign and has promised the economic and social development of those areas. The Ten-Year Plan (1961/62–1970/71) was more concerned with the modern sector and the irrigated lands.

Sudan has animal wealth which contributes about 10 per cent of G.D.P. annually. It was estimated in 1971–72 as 12.9 million cattle, 10.9 million sheep, 7.8 million goats and 2.5 million camels, although FAO estimates are somewhat higher. Its annual share in Sudan's exports (animals, hides and skins) was over 4 per cent between 1971 and 1973.

In the year 1962–63 forest reserve estates, which are completely owned by the government, increased by 7,000 feddans to a total of 2,574,000 feddans. Beside gum arabic, the other important forest products are the various types of timber which are processed by the forest department of the ministry of agriculture. In 1972–73 the forest department produced 74,729 railway sleepers, 31,612 poles and 635,000 cubic metres of sawn timber. The main consumer of these products is the government itself.

Sudan is rich in fish and other aquatic resources. The inland fisheries cover more than 20,000 sq. km., while marine fisheries extend for a distance of about 700 km. along the Red Sea. It is estimated that the annual total value of the output of fish and aquatic resources in Sudan is about £S10 million. Potential output of fish from the Nile is 60,000 tons annually (1974) but only a small percentage of this wealth is utilized at present. Since the actual output of fish from inland fisheries is estimated at around 20,000 tons annually, therefore about 40,000 tons are not utilized.

Cotton is the most important crop in Sudan from the economic point of view. It is the major export crop, the chief exchange earner and the main generator of income in the Sudan. A proportion of it is consumed locally by the textile industry. Its average share of exports over the five years 1965–69 was 53 per cent, not including its by-products, and 63 per cent including them. The cotton is of two types: long-staple varieties, Skallarides and its derivatives (commonly known as *Sakel*), and short-staple varieties, which are mainly American types and are consumed locally. The *Sakel* varieties are exclusively for export and are grown in the large schemes of the Gezira and the Gash and Tokar deltas, while the American types are grown in the rainlands of Equatoria, the Nuba mountains, Gedaref and also in some of the pump schemes in the Northern Province. The volume of output of the American types fluctuates more than the *Sakel*, but is generally increasing at a faster rate. In 1970–71 the total production of *Sakel* was 618,314 tons, while the total production of American types was 108,212 tons.

Owing to competition from synthetic fibres the government are to reduce the area under cultivation for long-staple cotton in the Gezira by a third. This should slightly lessen the Sudan's dangerously high reliance on cotton which was highlighted by the poor export figures in 1974 due to low production and bad marketing arrangements for cotton. In 1973, 1.2 million bales were exported with a value of £S85 million and in 1974 this fell to half a million bales worth £S53.2 million.

The Sudan's main cereal crop is sorghum (durra). It is the most important staple food in Sudan and is mainly grown in the rainlands. Sudan produces annually about 1.5 million tons of durra, which is usually sufficient for domestic consumption.

With urbanization and social development the consumption of bread made out of wheat flour is increasing by about 10 per cent annually. There seems to be a shift in consumption from *kisra* made out of durra to bread made out of wheat. Wheat is grown mainly as a cash crop. A small proportion of rural people use wheat flour in their diet. To meet the rapidly expanding demand of the urban population the government is growing wheat in the Gezira scheme and other suitable areas. It is also paying a subsidy to encourage its production and at the same time keep the price of bread reasonably low. In March 1975 it was announced that the area for growing wheat in the Gezira was to be increased from 400,000 feddans to 600,000 feddans in 1976, and that for groundnuts was to rise from 370,000 to 600,000 feddans in the Gezira. The value of groundnut exports rose by 40 per cent to £S18.2 million in 1974.

Reductions in the government's sugar subsidy led to riots in Khartoum in 1974, and radical moves to increase sugar production. The U.K. firm Lonhro is co-operating with the Sudanese Government in a scheme near Kosti designed to produce 350,000 tons of white sugar annually by 1979 on 100,000 feddans of land. The cost is an estimated $180 million and is destined to provide 20,000 jobs. It is expected to be financed with loans from the United Kingdom, Japan and the Arab states. Plans for sugar refineries at Hassaheisa, Sennar, Melut (with Belgian aid) and Mongalla (with Czechoslovak aid) are part of a scheme to produce 815,000 tons of sugar annually by 1980.

Sudan gums have been known in trade for at least two thousand years. Gum arabic, which constituted about 10 per cent of Sudan's exports in 1969 and 5 per cent in 1973 was for many years the second export crop, until overtaken by groundnuts in 1971. In 1974, however, its share of exports rose to 12 per cent, valued at £S14.2 million. It is the most important forest product and, though collected in the traditional sector, it is a purely cash crop. It is almost entirely exported, as the confectionery industry manufactures only a very small percentage of it. Sudan is the world's largest source of gum arabic, producing about 92 per cent of the total world consumption (1962–66).

INDUSTRY

The ginning of cotton encouraged the beginning of industry in Sudan early in this century. With the expansion of cotton production the number of ginning factories have increased until the Gezira Board alone has the largest ginning enterprise under single management in the world. The processing of cotton has not gone beyond ginning. Cotton seeds are partly decorticated, while the exports of cotton-seed oil and oil cakes are increasing. Groundnuts are also shelled for export. In 1969 24,685 tons were exported in shell, while 57,456 tons were exported shelled. Minerals (copper, iron, mica and chromite), which constitute less than 1 per cent of exports, are exported in the crudest form.

With the exception of the soap, soft drinks and oil-pressing industries, large industries manufacturing import substitutes started only after 1960. The government was not involved in any industry until 1959, with the exception of the Zande scheme, which involved a cotton mill at Nzara for promoting the social development of the Zande tribe. From 1960 the involvement in industry began to increase and in 1962 the government formed the Industrial Development Corporation to look after the large factories of the public sector. By 1968 the Industrial Development Corporation was managing nine manufacturing factories. There are also factories in the public sector managed by the ministries, such as the government printing press and the mint.

The first factory to be established was the Guneid sugar factory, which, in response to the great increase in the consumption of sugar in the 1950s, came into production in November 1961 with a capacity of 60,000 tons of refined sugar annually. A second factory was needed to meet the local demand and in 1963 Khashm el Girba sugar factory was started, with a capacity similar to that of Guneid. In addition to a tannery, opened in November 1961, the government also has five food processing plants: one cannery and one date factory in Kareima, another cannery in Wau, an onion dehydrating plant in Kassala and a milk factory in Babanousa. What is very striking about these food processing industries is that the supply of raw materials is not high enough to match the productive capacity, and therefore, the weakness in these factories is not technical but agricultural.

The private sector has also played an important role in the industrial development of this country. In the period 1960–69 the private sector invested £S35.9

million in industries of which £S16.1 million was Sudanese and £S19.8 foreign capital. The foreign capital is mainly savings of foreign residents accumulated from the profits of the import and export trade. The bulk of the investment has gone into the textile, soap, oil-pressing, footwear, soft drinks, printing, packing, flour, and knitwear industries. In the 1970s, the role of the private sector increased. In 1970–71, the private sector invested £S52.6 million in fixed capital formation, of which £S22 million is transport and £S14.8 million is machinery and equipment. The private sector is increasingly tending to invest in transport because of the serious inadequacy of the present system of transport available in the Sudan.

The government has encouraged industrialization in Sudan by various means. The Approved Enterprises (Concessions) Act, 1959, gave generous concessions to infant industries. The Organisation and Promotion of Industrial Investment Act, 1967, has been even more generous to industry. It gives exemption from the business profits tax for a number of years, depending on the size of the invested capital, allows very high rates of depreciation, gives very fair treatment to losses, reduces import duties on imported machinery and materials, protects domestic production by high tariffs and import restrictions and allocates building lands at reduced prices. In addition to this, the Industrial Bank, which was established in 1961, assists in the financing of private industrial enterprises with up to two-thirds of the capital required. In 1972 the Ministry of Industry brought in new legislation to encourage industrial investment. Owing to the government's 1969–70 socialist programme this had fallen with the output in manufacturing industry dropping to £S23 million in 1972 from £S35.6 million in 1970. The new act is very similar to that of 1967. However, the Organization and Promotion of Industrial Investment Act of 1967 seems to favour large-scale investment, since under it enterprises whose capital is £S1 million or more are exempted from the Business Profits Tax for ten years, while under the 1972 act they are exempted for the first five years and during the second five years, 10 per cent of the profits only are free from taxation. This has gone a considerable way to restoring confidence in the private sector, which was hard hit after the nationalization and confiscation of foreign and domestic business in 1970. Many of these were British and their take-over led to a cooling in Anglo-Sudanese relations. During Pres. Nemery's visit to Britain in 1973 the U.K. granted the Sudan £15.7 million in aid, and compensation agreements on the nationalized British industries were finalized. Foreign banking facilities dealing in medium and long-term development and foreign trade are now allowed to open in the Sudan and the Chase Manhattan Bank has announced its intention of opening a branch in 1975.

In 1973 oil was discovered in commercially viable quantities in the Red Sea off the Sudan. An exploration concession covering 3,360,000 acres on the Red Sea coast and offshore, north and south of Port Sudan, had been granted to several international companies, mainly American, by mid-1975. The government has the right to a 50 per cent interest in the project and intends to build a further refinery at Port Sudan.

FOREIGN TRADE

The value of Sudan's exports rose from £S63.4 million in 1960 to £S124.4 million in 1972, while the value of imports rose from £S63.7 million to £S123.0 million. The balance of payments would have become a more serious problem if it had not been for the government's policy of clamping down on imports and encouraging exports. There are import restrictions and high import duties on a large number of goods, though in 1975 further categories were exempted, but export taxes are light and no licence is required for export, with the exception of goods consumed locally and in short supply.

Imports rose considerably in 1973 to £S166.9 million compared with exports of £S143.5 million, thus putting renewed strain on the balance of payments.

Owing to the poor cotton crop and low market prices for what was produced, the trade deficit widened enormously to £S77.6 million in 1974, the Sudan's heavy debts adding further to the serious economic situation.

Sudan's main exports are primary agricultural products, and since the establishment of the Gezira Scheme in 1925, cotton has dominated Sudan's exports. Between 1960 and 1971 the share of lint cotton alone ranged between 46 and 65 per cent. In 1971 the U.S.S.R. was the largest buyer of Sudan's cotton, followed closely by India, the People's Republic of China, whose share had doubled since the previous year, and the EEC. However, since the attempted *coup* in 1971 the U.S.S.R.'s purchases dropped to nil in 1973 when the People's Republic of China took the largest share, 51,903 tons, followed by Japan, Italy and India. A trade agreement with China in 1975 envisages that imports and exports should be £S36 million for that year, and guarantees a market for a large share of the Sudan's cotton crop, which had been hit by lower world market prices during 1974 and 1975. In the last ten years, due to the expansion of production in the traditional sector, the relative importance of oil seeds as exports has increased and in 1973 groundnuts formed the second most important export crop with a share of about 9 per cent of exports. The EEC is the largest buyer of Sudan's groundnuts (60 per cent). The east European countries buy about 20 per cent of the groundnuts and the rest go to various west European countries. Gum arabic was overtaken in importance by groundnuts in 1971 to become the third export product, making up nearly 5 per cent of total exports in 1973.

The major imports are vehicles, transport equipment, machinery, appliances and textiles, and in 1973 sugar imports greatly increased. In 1963 the Sudan produced only 61 per cent of its domestic sugar needs. There are new plans to expand the sugar industry, so as to produce a surplus for export in the late 1970s. The growth of industries which are manufacturing important substitutes has affected the pattern of imports since the mid-1960s. The imports of footwear and cigarettes are declining in relative and absolute terms.

Perhaps a more striking change has taken place in the pattern of suppliers and buyers, if the late 1960s are compared with the early 1950s. The U.K. used to be the largest seller and buyer from the Sudan (30–40 per cent before independence). In 1973 only 3.4 per cent of Sudan's exports went to the U.K., and only 16 per cent of imports were brought from the U.K. Trade with socialist countries increased since independence until 1971 as a result of several bilateral agreements. Their share in Sudan's trade has, with the exception of the People's Republic of China, drastically declined since the attempted coup in 1971. Exports to the U.S.S.R. fell from £S18,351,000 in 1971 to £S3,000 in 1973. Trade with the Arab countries has been expanding in recent years and exports to them have reached about 10 per cent, but imports from these countries form a smaller percentage. The Arab countries are a good market for Sudan's animal exports.

FOREIGN AID

The Ten-Year Plan of Economic and Social Development, 1961/62–1970/71, was the country's first experience in planning, although there had been three previous attempts to develop Sudan in a systematic manner: 1946–51, 1951–56 and the Managil extension programme. In contrast to the Ten-Year Plan, the development programmes were not comprehensive, being concerned only with some projects in the public sector and depending on finance from savings of the public sector.

The total gross investment of the plan was estimated to be £S565 million, of which 40 per cent (£S228 million) was to be sponsored by the private sector and 60 per cent (£S337 million) by the public sector. Out of the total investment £S415.9 million was to be financed by domestic savings and £S219.7 million from foreign financial assistance. The £S415.9 would consist of £S219.7 million public savings and £S196.2 million private savings.

The amount of foreign aid which was actually received in the period 1960–69 did not fall very much short of the target of the plan. While £S150 million of foreign aid was forecast for the period 1961/62–1970/71, £S141 million of aid in the form of grants, long-term and medium-term loans and in kind was received in the period 1960–69. However, in spite of the small difference between projected and realized foreign aid, the plan could not be properly implemented, mainly because of a shortage of domestic and foreign finance.

The Khashm el Girba and Roseires dams could not be utilized fully because the lack of finance prevented the associated works being completed. Additional reasons, such as wastage and corruption, also contributed to hampering the completion of projects of the public sector.

From the Eastern bloc, aid to the Sudan from Yugoslavia has included a tannery, a cardboard factory and three ships, which constitute the Sudan Shipping Line. By 1973 a second tannery at Khartoum had been completed and a third was to be built at Malakal. Romania was assisting the development of river transport and in prospecting for petroleum in 1973. The U.S.S.R. has provided the Sudan with two grain elevators, factories for processing agricultural and dairy products, a hospital and veterinary laboratories. The change in Sudanese foreign policy however since 1971 has led to more aid from Western countries and from the People's Republic of China. China has built a foundry, completed the construction of a textile mill at Hassaheisa in early 1974 and a conference hall in Khartoum, as well as a section of the Khartoum-Port Sudan highway. This will run from Wad Medani to Gedaref, with two bridges across the Blue Nile and Rahad rivers, and is due for completion in 1975.

By mid-1975 the Sudan appeared to be in a favourable position to benefit from Arab aid, with close relations with most Arab states. In 1975 the Arab Fund for Economic and Social Development (AFESD) announced a ten-year plan to double GDP in the Sudan, and in 1975 plans were being prepared for a massive investment of $6,000 million of Arab funds in the Sudan for a scheme which would produce a substantial amount of the food requirements of Arab countries by 1985. This would involve a projected annual growth rate in the Sudan of 5.8 per cent between 1975 and 1980 and 8 per cent between 1980 and 1985, with greatly increased production of cereals, meat and sugar. In 1960–69 Arab aid totalled about 30 per cent of the total received. In 1972 relations with Egypt and Libya deteriorated, and the Sudan received aid mainly from Kuwait and Saudi Arabia. In 1974 Saudi Arabia agreed to co-operate with the Sudan in developing the resources of the Red Sea as part of a reported Saudi Arabian investment aid programme in the Sudan of an estimated $2,000 million. In May 1974 work opened on a new refinery at Triad Naft, to be supplied with Saudi oil through a pipeline financed with aid from Kuwait, and which is scheduled for completion in mid-1976. Saudi Arabia also guaranteed a large loan on the Euro-dollar market over 10 years for the Sudan in February 1974, and the Sudan negotiated a further Euro-dollar loan of $20 million in June 1974. Saudi budgetary aid of $5 million was announced in April 1974. In 1973 Kuwait granted assistance for financing the construction of a sugar refinery at Sennar. Kuwait also agreed to finance excess cotton unsold in the 1974–75 season. In 1975 Kuwait increased its promised contribution to the important Rahad Project to $62 million, and the IDA promised an increase to $50 million with the AFESD contributing $9 million, the U.S. Government $11 million, and Saudi Arabia a loan of $39 million in June 1975. Relations with Egypt improved in 1974 and the Higher Ministerial Committee for Co-ordination and Integration between Egypt and the Sudan planned further mutual economic co-operation.

Aid from the United Kingdom and U.S. also has often been dependent on political circumstances. In 1973 the U.S.A. donated wheat worth £S3.6 million and made a loan of £S9.6 million to enable Sudan Airways to purchase two Boeings. The U.S.A. also made a contribution of £S3.9 million to the

Rahad Project and is assisting in the construction of a dry batteries factory to be completed in September 1975. The United Kingdom had contributed to the development of the electricity system in Juba and guaranteed £S10 million to help build the Sennar sugar refinery. Norway is to provide $4 million in general aid and the Norwegian Church Research Agency is to provide aid for the South. Belgium is assisting with the construction of a sugar refinery at Melut. The Netherlands and UNHCR collaborated in a project to build a bridge across the Nile which was completed in 1973. The Federal Republic of Germany has played an important role in financing the economic development of the country by contributing to the financing of the Rosieres Dam, and credit from German firms helped to finance the Guneid and Khashm el Girba sugar factories. In 1973 funds were loaned to the Sudan for railways, telecommunications aid and improvements in the television and veterinary services.

The benefits for the Sudan in aid from international organizations are considerable. For 1972-76 the UN has promised $88 million in aid. A $40 million grant for food research from the FAO, announced in April 1975 will, include the expansion of research facilities at Khartoum University. In May 1975 the World Bank offered a loan of $10 million for educational expansion, especially in the South, and the IDA also offered $10 million for a similar scheme particularly to benefit the South, as well as $23 million for the development of power resources. The World Bank has played a vital role in the Sudan's aid projects, contributing loans of $245 million under generous terms since 1958. The Bank has financed vital projects such as the Roseires Dam, mechanized farming, Sudan Railways extension and dieselization, and the Managil Extension.

In 1973 the Sudan was also granted loans of £S25.7 million from the World Bank for the Rahad scheme, railway improvements and electricity generation. IMF special drawing rights up to £S9 million were granted to support balance of payments stabilization. The vast relief operation to rehabilitate and resettle southern refugees was covered by aid from the UN which contributed over $20 million, aid organizations and foreign governments.

At the end of 1973 the net foreign debt in respect of government loans was £S102.6 million. In 1974-75 Sudan paid £S17.25 million in repayments to creditors which is a heavy burden on the economy, particularly with the current high trade deficit, and one which could become critical if the projected Arab aid fails to materialize.

PUBLIC FINANCE

The Sudan government, like governments in many other underdeveloped countries, depends heavily on indirect taxes as a major source of revenue. In the fiscal year 1972–73 indirect taxes contributed 43 per cent of the central government's revenue, while in 1968–69 they yielded about 50 per cent. In these three years the relative share of indirect taxes declined because of increased import restrictions, and also because of the increased revenue from direct taxes and proceeds from government agricultural enterprises, particularly in 1969-70. The main source of revenue from indirect taxation is import duties. Because of balance of payments deficits in recent years the government has been trying to restrict imports of consumer goods, particularly luxuries, and those which bear the highest rates. Excise duties are growing in importance because of the growth of industries producing import substitutes. Thus, the share of excise duties in revenue from indirect taxation, 5 per cent in 1964–65, rose to 18 per cent in 1966–67 This change is also reducing the rate of increase of revenue from indirect taxation.

The revenue from direct taxes was about 14 per cent of the total revenue of the central government in 1972–73, having been 2.7 per cent in 1963–64. The present direct taxes of Sudan (1973–74) are income taxes, and a stamp duty. The income taxes comprise a personal income tax on monetary earnings, fringe benefits and interest; a business profits tax; and a tax on income from rent (as laid down by the Income Tax Act, 1967). The top rate is 50 per cent, when total income reaches £S25,000. Dividends are not normally taxable in the Sudan, since companies pay a business profits tax; shareholders do not pay an income tax on their dividends. Nevertheless, a holding company which receives dividends from its subsidiaries pays a business tax on aggregate profits, after getting a tax credit for the tax paid by the subsidiary. An emergency tax was introduced in August 1969 to absorb part of the wage and salary increases given to employees in the public sector in 1968 by the previous government. The revenue for the fiscal year 1968-69 for all the units in the public sector was estimated at £S171,878,116, and the maximum limit of borrowing by the government from the Central Bank was fixed at £S24.5 million, while the actual borrowing of the government during that fiscal year was £S24.3 million. Revenue for all units in 1974-5 was £S277.5 million, and in 1975-76 it was estimated to be £S406 million.

Since the mid-1960s the Sudan government has been finding it more and more difficult to make all its local cash payments, whether wages and salaries or payment to contractors, in time. This seems to be the result of two main factors: underestimation of expenditure and ineffective financial control of government accounts. This problem of the illiquidity of the public sector has forced the government to seek various ways to increase revenue and reduce expenditure, but it has not yet been solved. Deficit finance from the Bank of Sudan has been increasingly used to finance the government expenditure, but this is reaching a critical limit and adding to the already existing inflationary pressure.

The expenditure of the central government has been rising very fast since independence in 1956. In 1949 the total current expenditure of the central government was £S10 million; by 1975-76 it was an estimated £S304.5 million. Besides the rise in prices and the normal expansion in government services, increased expenditure on education, national defence and the rise in wages and salaries of the employees of the public sector have accentuated the rate of increase of the total current expenditure in recent years. The expenditure of the Ministry of Defence increased from £S14.1 million in 1965–66 to £S35.8 million in 1974–75, while the expenditure of the Ministry of Education increased from £S5.8 million in 1965–66 to £S12.3 million in 1973–74.

LABOUR AND WAGES

The number of persons five years of age and over reported in the 1955–56 census, as mainly engaged in economic activity, was 3,800,000 out of a population of 10.2 million. In addition it was estimated, on the basis of detailed tabulations of the census returns, that 1,116,000 persons, whose main activity was not economic, took part in subsidiary economic activity. So the total number engaged to any degree in economic activity was approximately 4,916,000 or 48 per cent of the population. Sudan's labour force is overwhelmingly male. Men made up 56 per cent of the total economically active population, women 24.7 per cent, boys 14.4 per cent and girls 4.9 per cent.

Of all the males and females in the labour force 86.7 per cent were primary producers, 3.3 per cent secondary producers and 10 per cent tertiary producers. All these percentages of sex and industrial distribution of the Sudan's labour force have not, it is thought, changed very much since 1955–56.

Beyond 1956 it is difficult to get any reasonably accurate data in order to assess the labour situation in Sudan. However, the number of wage-earners at present is estimated to be about one million— excluding agricultural workers. In 1975 about half a million workers were engaged in the public sector and about the same number are employed by the private sector.

Until about 1965 one of the country's major problems was considered to be the shortage of skilled workers. There was heavy dependence on expatriates of Greek and Armenian descent, who filled a high proportion of skilled jobs and managerial and executive posts.

However, by 1965 the major development projects were finished. The most important factories in both private and public sectors, as well as Khashm el Girba and Roseires dams, were finished by that year. In the early 1960s institutes of technical education and training centres were established and by 1965 their graduates could meet the demand for skilled labour.

In fact, after 1965, unemployment began to appear among skilled workers in the towns, and some economists and businessmen began to believe that the shortage of skilled workers was no longer a serious problem to the industrialization of Sudan. Sudan has already started to export skilled workers, clerical staff and teachers to the Arab countries.

The only available figures on unemployment come from the registrations at employment exchanges in major towns. In 1967–68 31,919 were registered as unemployed. In 1970–71 registered unemployment totalled 58,022. However, it is obvious that this figure does not represent total open unemployment in Sudan. Not all the workers register themselves when they are unemployed, particularly unskilled workers. On the other hand, some workers may register more than once, while, when other workers find a job, neither they nor their employers report to the employment exchanges. Therefore, the present figures of unemployment in Sudan should be viewed with great caution.

As from October 1974 a legal minimum wage of £S11.5 per month has been introduced. It is to be paid by all enterprises in the private sector which employ ten workers or more for monthly employment in Khartoum and Gezira Provinces as well as all the large towns in the other provinces. However, in the public sector the minimum monthly wage paid for permanent employment is £S16.5. The daily minimum wage ranges between 25 and 50 piastres, depending on the region and the season. During the cotton-picking season in the Gezira the daily minimum wage may rise as high as 50 piastres per day. Wages and salaries are higher in the public sector than in the private sector, with the exception of modern and large firms in the private sector, who only employ a very small percentage of the labour force engaged in the private sector.

PLANNING AND DEVELOPMENT

The first development plan was a ten-year plan, 1961–62 to 1970–71. Then a five-year plan 1970–71 to 1974–75 was published in 1970 and later in the year it was revised. Because of nationalization, the share of the public sector in investment increased from £S200 million to £S215 million. The private sector's share in capital investment has been fixed at £S170 million. The major targets of the plan are: to increase G.D.P. at an average rate of 7.6 per cent annually; to increase the revenue of the Government to £S953 million compared to £S516.5 million for the previous five years; to increase the share of commodity production to 65 per cent in 1974–75 as against 61.1 per cent in 1969–70; to increase industrial production by 57.4 per cent, and to increase the volume of agricultural production by 60.8 per cent. In June 1974 it was announced that the Plan would be extended to June 1977 and named the Amended Five-Year Plan. The allocations to the 1974–75 development budget would total £S194 million though actual expenditure did not exceed £S65 million, of which £S43.8 million was provided by external sources. The estimated 1975-76 development budget is £S281.8 million, of which £S69.3 million has been allocated to industry, £S58.9 million to agriculture and £S58.9 million to transport and communications.

The general aim of the plan is to promote welfare through an increase in productivity, realization of full employment and an expansion of public services. The number of projects in the plan for the public sector was 276, of which 239 projects have actually been started. In 1970–71 40 projects (17 per cent of the total planned) were completed.

POWER AND TRANSPORT

The installed generating capacity of the Sudan in 1970 was 96,685 kW. thermal and 29,220 kW. hydro. The total power generated in 1972 was 503,899,000 kWh. The number of consumers is 68,529 residential and commercial, 558 agricultural and 844 industrial. All the main towns of Sudan are supplied with electricity and some of the small towns which lie near to the transmission lines, such as Kamlin, also enjoy this facility. Seventeen towns altogether are provided with electricity. In June 1975 it was announced that the World Bank was to provide $23 million out of a total of $40 million for a project to spread electricity in the Sudan. The African Development Bank has loaned $5 million.

The volume of electricity used by industry is 118,353,000 kWh. (1972), while the volume of electricity used by agriculture for pumps is 26,200,000 kWh. The electricity consumption of industry does not include that of ginning factories, the large oil mills and Guneid and Khashm el Girba sugar factories. All these generate their own electricity from by-products. The grain silos at Gedaref and Port Sudan have their own generating sets.

Sudan depends mainly on railways for transport. Steamers and motor transport play only a secondary role. All-weather roads are very limited. The total length of asphalt main roads in Sudan is 333 km. of which Khartoum Province has 225 km. The length of cleared tracks covered with gravel is 4,936 km. The length of just cleared tracks is 12,496 km. and these make up the main network of roads in Sudan. However, they are usually impassable immediately after the rains. Road bridges cross the Blue and White Niles at four points, and four dams on the river also carry traffic. The Civil War caused considerable damage to communications in the South where 1,600 km. of road and 70 bridges were destroyed. A major reconstruction programme is under way.

The rail transport facilities are still far from adequate. The length of the railway network is 4,756 km. and the average density of railways for the whole country is only 1.9 km. per 1,000 sq. km. The river fleet comprises 386 low-speed old steamers of various types. River transport is mainly used between Kosti and Juba (1,435 km.) and between Dongola and Kareima (187 km.); these routes are navigable all year round. The total length of the river navigation routes is about 4,068 km., of which 1,723 km. are open all the year and the rest are seasonal. River transport between Wadi Halfa and Shellal, which lies partly on Lake Nasser, is under development at present. As far as sea transport is concerned, the government company, the Sudan Shipping Line, one of the successful public enterprises, owns seven dry cargo ships of 5,000 tons each. Only a small percentage of exports and imports are carried by domestic vessels. In June 1975 Gen. Nemery said Sudan would enlarge Port Sudan to cope with increased traffic after the re-opening of the Suez Canal which is likely to benefit Sudan's economy.

The government-owned Sudan Airways, formed in 1947, operates internal and international services. It connects Khartoum with twenty important Sudanese towns as well as with Europe, the Middle East and Africa. In 1972 it carried 133,424 passengers and 1,203,000 kg. of freight.

STATISTICAL SURVEY

AREA AND POPULATION

TOTAL AREA	ARABLE LAND	PASTURE	FOREST	TOTAL POPULATION (April 3rd, 1973)
967,500 sq. miles*	71,000 sq. kilometres	240,000 sq. kilometres	914,999 sq. kilometres	12,427,795

* 2,505,813 sq. kilometres.

PROVINCES

(July 1st, 1973)

	AREA (sq. miles)	POPULATION*		AREA (sq. miles)	POPULATION*
Bahr el Ghazal	82,530	1,575,000	Khartoum	8,097	968,000
Blue Nile	54,880	3,483,000	Kordofan	146,930	3,103,000
Darfur	191,650	1,869,000	Northern	184,200	1,252,000
Equatoria	76,495	1,438,000	Upper Nile	91,190	1,415,000
Kassala	131,528	1,798,000	TOTAL	967,500	16,901,000

* Not revised in the light of the April 1973 census.

PRINCIPAL TOWNS

	POPULATION (July 1st, 1973)
Khartoum (capital)	321,666
Omdurman	305,308
Khartoum North	161,278
Port Sudan	123,000
Wadi Medani	81,904
El Obeid	74,109
Atbara	62,407

Because of the flooding of the Wadhi Halfa and adjacent areas by the Aswan High Dam, over 50,000 inhabitants have been resettled in Khashm el Girba, on the Atbara River.

TRIBAL DIVISIONS

(1956 Census)

	'000	%
Arab	3,989	39
Southerners (Nilotic, Nilo-Hamitic, Sudanic)	3,056	30
Western People	1,315	13
Beja	646	6
Nuba	573	6
Nubiyin	330	3
Miscellaneous	94	1

The remaining 2 per cent was made up of 260,000 foreigners.

Births and Deaths (1966): Registered births 143,052 (birth rate 10.1 per 1,000); registered deaths 13,416 (death rate 1.0 per 1,000). Birth registration is believed to be about 20 per cent complete and death registration 5 per cent complete. UN estimates for 1965–70 put the average annual birth rate at 48.9 per 1,000 and the death rate at 18.4 per 1,000. These figures indicate that the natural increase rate is just over 3.0 per cent per year, but the results of the 1973 census suggest a much lower increase rate.

Employment (1970): Total economically active population 5,016,000, including 4,007,000 engaged in agriculture (ILO and FAO estimates).

AGRICULTURE
COTTON CROP

	AREA (feddans†)			PRODUCTION (long kantars*)		
	1969–70	1970–71	1971–72	1969–70	1970–71	1971–72
Long Staple	824,662	828,306	822,754	4,004,064	4,390,032	3,810,000
Medium Staple	138,041	183,858	186,576	581,060	633,863	650,426
Short Staple	295,208	203,582	201,599	237,294	133,371	168,219
TOTAL	1,257,911	1,215,746	1,210,929	4,822,418	5,157,266	4,628,645

Production of lint (metric tons): 246,000 in 1970; 245,000 in 1971; 239,000 in 1972; 190,000 in 1973; 229,000 in 1974.

† 1 feddan = 1.038 acres = 4,201 sq. metres

* 1 long kantar = 312 lb.

OTHER CROPS
(metric tons)

	1970	1971	1972	1973
Wheat	115,000	163,000	143,000	149,000
Maize	37,000	14,000	21,000*	20,000*
Millet	460,000	325,000	355,000	268,000
Sorghum (Durra) . . .	1,529,000	2,142,000	1,300,000	1,498,000
Rice	6,000	7,000*	7,000*	7,000
Sugar Cane	780,000*	750,000*	750,000*	750,000*
Potatoes	26,000	26,000*	26,000*	26,000*
Sweet Potatoes . . .	450,000*	450,000*	450,000*	470,000*
Yams	114,000*	116,000*	120,000*	124,000*
Cassava (Manioc) . . .	1,050,000*	1,100,000*	1,100,000*	1,110,000*
Onions	20,000*	20,000*	20,000*	20,000*
Water Melons . . .	285,000*	292,000*	295,000*	305,000*
Dry Beans	6,000*	4,000	16,000	8,000*
Dry Broad Beans . . .	12,000*	13,000*	13,000*	13,000*
Chick-Peas	2,000*	2,000*	2,000*	2,000*
Other Pulses . . .	40,000*	46,000*	45,000*	47,000*
Oranges and Tangerines .	1,000*	1,000*	1,000*	1,000*
Other Citrus Fruit . .	47,000*	48,000*	50,000*	51,000*
Dates	72,000*	72,000*	72,000*	74,000*
Bananas	10,000*	10,000*	10,000*	10,000*
Groundnuts (in shell) . .	337,000	294,000	568,000	543,000
Cottonseed	460,000	466,000	454,000	358,000
Sesame Seed	297,000	278,000	340,000	245,000
Castor Beans	18,000	18,000*	17,000	11,000

1974 ('000 metric tons): Groundnuts 991; Cottonseed 432; Sesame Seed 271.

* FAO estimate.

Source: FAO, mainly *Production Yearbook 1973.*

LIVESTOCK
(FAO estimates in '000 head)

	1969–70	1970–71	1971–72	1972-73
Cattle . . .	13,800	14,300	14,700	15,200
Sheep . . .	12,700	12,400	12,000	12,000
Goats . . .	10,050	10,100	10,150	10,200
Pigs . . .	7	7	7	7
Horses . . .	20	20	20	20
Asses . . .	630	640	650	660
Camels . . .	3,000	3,100	3,200	3,400
Chickens . . .	18,500	18,800	19,000	19,200

Source: FAO, mainly *Production Yearbook 1973.*

1972/73 (Official estimates): Cattle 14 million; Sheep 11.9 million.

LIVESTOCK PRODUCTS
(FAO estimates, metric tons)

	1971	1972	1973
Beef and Veal	185,000	190,000	198,000
Mutton, Lamb and Goats' Meat . .	101,000	105,000	109,000
Poultry Meat	11,000	11,000	11,000
Other Meat	49,000	51,000	53,000
Edible Offal	57,216	59,110	61,398
Cows' Milk	1,380,000	1,400,000	1,420,000
Sheep's Milk	134,000	140,000	149,000
Goats' Milk	450,000	450,000	460,000
Butter	18,400	19,200	20,000
Cheese	24,000	24,000	24,000
Hen Eggs	17,000	17,000	17,500
Wool: greasy	8,000	8,000	8,500
clean	3,200	3,200	3,400
Cattle Hides	17,774	18,278	18,984
Sheep Skins	13,025	13,575	14,125
Goat Skins	1,100	1,140	1,160

1974 (FAO estimates, 'ooo metric tons): Beef and Veal 186; Mutton, Lamb and Goats' Meat 87.
Source: FAO, mainly *Production Yearbook 1973.*

FORESTRY
ROUNDWOOD REMOVALS
(Unofficial estimates, cubic metres)
Twelve months ending June 30th

1969–70	20,970,000
1970–71	21,040,000
1971-72	21,078,coo

Source: FAO, *Yearbook of Forest Products.*

GUM ARABIC PRODUCTION
(tons)

Season	Gum Hashab	Gum Talh	Total
1969–70 . .	42,680	5,980	48,660
1970–71 . .	41,588	2,767	44,355
1971–72 . .	37,311	2,638	39,949
1972–73 . .	19,882	1,312	21,194

TIMBER PRODUCTION

	Unit	1969–70	1970–71	1971–72	1972–73
Railway Sleepers . . .	number	99,872	66,311	28,449	74,729
Poles	,,	3,810	4,998	7,941	31,612
Bamboo Canes . . .	,,	236,000	891,665	642,452	785,966
Firewood . . .	cu. metres	162,608	85,705	105,331	623,238
Other Sawn Wood . . .	,, ,,	9,598	9,421	7,411	11,966

FISHING
(metric tons)

	1971	1972	1973
Inland waters . .	21,400	21,400	21,800
Sea	800	800	800
Total Catch .	22,200	22,200	22,600

Source: FAO, *Yearbook of Fishery Statistics 1973.*

MINING

PRODUCTION

	Unit	1968	1969	1970	1971
Iron Ore*	'ooo metric tons	10	—	10	—
Salt (unrefined) . . .	,, ,, ,,	50	51	63	55
Gypsum . . .	,, ,, ,,	10	n.a.	n.a.	—
Chromium Ore* . . .	metric tons	11,485	12,451	13,866	10,200
Magnesite (crude) . .	,, ,,	6,500	499	100	91
Manganese Ore* . . .	,, ,,	2,000	340	464	—
Gold	kilogrammes	6	n.a.	—	—

1972: Chromium Ore 12,800 metric tons, Gold 2 kilogrammes.

* Figures refer to the metal content of ores.

Source: United Nations, *Statistical Yearbook* and *The Growth of World Industry.*

INDUSTRY

PRODUCTION

	Unit	1968–69	1969–70	1970–71	1971–72
Cement	'ooo tons	140.7	194.0	229.0	200.6
Flour of Wheat	,, ,,	51.5	111.6	176.0	191.3
Sugar	,, ,,	82.1	75.3	72.5	93.0
Soap	,, ,,	19.3	23.7	27.9	28.2
Wine	'ooo litres	1,453.0	2,450.0	3,357.0	2,955.6
Beer	,, ,,	7,159.0	4,534.0	7,245.0	7,713.7
Cigarettes	'ooo kilos	532.0	660.9	741.8	522.4
Matches	'ooo million	3.9	4.9	4.4	3.2
Shoes	million pairs	10.7	6.7	8.5	14.7
Textiles	yards	101,350.0	n.a.	n.a.	n.a.
Alcohol	'ooo litres	464.0	n.a.	n.a.	n.a.
Oil	'ooo tons	46.0	n.a.	n.a.	n.a.

PETROLEUM PRODUCTS
(metric tons)

	1968	1969	1970	1971
Motor Spirit	62,000	70,000	90,000	95,000
Naphtha	12,000	25,000	26,000	28,000
Jet Fuels	70,000	} 76,000	82,000	90,000
Kerosene	53,000			
Distillate Fuel Oils . .	184,000	234,000	234,000	239,000
Residual Fuel Oils . . .	195,000	224,000	239,000	161,000
Liquefied Petroleum Gas . . .	1,000	2,000	2,000	2,000

Source: United Nations, *Statistical Yearbook 1973.*

ELECTRICITY OUTPUT

	Installed Capacity (kW.)	Units Generated ('ooo kWh.)	Units Sold ('ooo kWh.)
1969 . .	130,893	528,176	430,173
1970 . .	116,966	392,421	367,900
1971 . .	120,822	441,762	308,378
1972 . .	118,353	503,899	308,875

FINANCE

1,000 millièmes = 100 piastres = 1 Sudanese pound (£S).
Coins: 1, 2, 5 and 10 millièmes; 2, 5 and 10 piastres.
Notes: 25 and 50 piastres; £S1, £S5 and £S10.
Exchange rates (July 1975): £1 sterling = 761.61 millièmes; U.S. $1 = 348.24 millièmes.
£S100 = £131.30 sterling = $287.156.

Note: The Sudanese pound was introduced in April 1957, replacing (at par) the Egyptian pound, valued at U.S. $2.87156 since September 1949. This valuation has been maintained in the Sudan ever since, despite two devaluations of the U.S. dollar. Since March 1972 the effective exchange rate for foreign trade transactions, excluding exports of cotton and gum arabic, has been £S1 = U.S. $2.50 ($1 = 400 millièmes). The exchange rate was £1 sterling = 835.78 millièmes (£S1 = £1.1965 sterling) from November 1967 to August 1971; and £1 sterling = 907.42 millièmes (£S1 = £1.102 sterling) from December 1971 to June 1972.

BUDGET ESTIMATES FOR CURRENT REVENUE AND EXPENDITURE
(£S million, twelve months ending June 30th)

REVENUE	1971–72	1972–73	EXPENDITURE	1971–72	1972–73*
Direct Taxation	25.0	26.8	Defence and Security	47.4	50.3
Indirect Taxation	86.9	81.0	Education	14.7	18.0
Fees and Charges, etc.	13.0	26.3	Health	8.5	9.6
Proceeds from Government			Other Social Services	5.0	5.9
Enterprises	47.8	36.5	Ministry of Agriculture, Food and		
Interest and Dividends	3.4	3.3	National Resources	11.0	14.0
Pension Contributions	5.0	3.5	Ministry of Communications and		
Reimbursement and Inter-			Transport	6.8	8.8
Departmental Services	7.4	8.9	Other Economic Services	3.1	3.8
Other Sources	4.2	5.0	Local Government	27.8	25.0
			Debt Servicing	15.6	16.1
			Other Expenditure	32.0	39.2
TOTAL REVENUE	192.7	191.3	TOTAL EXPENDITURE	171.9	190.7

* Provisional.

1973-74 Budget Estimate: Revenue £S220.8m.; Expenditure £S217.1m.
1974-75 Budget Estimate: Revenue £S277.5m.; Expenditure £S268.3m.
1975-76 Budget Estimate: Revenue £S337.3m.; Expenditure £S304.5m.

EXTERNAL TRADE
(£S million)

	1969	1970	1971	1972	1973	1974
Imports c.i.f.*	89.3	100.1	115.4	123.0	151.8	223.6
Exports f.o.b.†	86.2	103.4	114.4	124.4	151.2	122.0

* Excluding imports of crude petroleum (£S5,250,000 in 1972).
† Excluding exports of camels (£S2,420,000 in 1971).

PRINCIPAL COMMODITIES
(£S '000)

IMPORTS	1971	1972	1973	EXPORTS	1971	1972	1973
Sugar	9,247	9,683	18,299	Animals	1,959	2,130	2,948
Tea	4,004	6,138	5,367	Cotton, Ginned	69,424	74,331	80,083
Coffee	1,635	1,869	2,004	Cotton Seed	1,422	630	611
Wheat Flour	226	164	1	Cotton Seed Oil	4,501	4,284	1,456
Textiles	26,462	21,133	18,920	Durra	1,136	1,590	3,053
Clothing	911	873	633	Groundnuts	9,324	9,212	13,053
Footwear	102	201	104	Gum Arabic	8,425	9,128	7,846
Sacks and Jute	3,694	4,948	5,563	Oilseed Cake	n.a.	5,278	6,778
Cement	70	8	91	Sesame	7,996	8,756	10,878
Fertilizers	1,937	2,496	3,775	Hides and Skins	1,806	3,197	5,440
Machinery, Apparatus,							
Vehicles	23,312	27,196	24,370				
Tyres	1,937	1,512	1,948				
Petroleum Products	8,918	8,770	9,913				
Pharmaceuticals	2,760	4,603	5,161				
Iron and Steel	4,794	3,814	7,885				

1974 (£S'000); Cotton 53,200, Groundnuts 18,160, Gum Arabic 14,240.

COTTON EXPORTS BY COUNTRIES
(tons)

	1971	1972	1973
Germany, Federal Republic . .	13,328	16,102	19,791
India	37,001	66,035	21,714
Italy	13,620	23,112	22,915
Japan	11,260	18,696	30,438
United Kingdom . . .	10,581	9,569	10,763
People's Republic of China .	35,221	40,143	51,903
U.S.A.	2,549	1,928	696
U.S.S.R.	39,158	1,469	—
Romania	7,437	1,931	4,756
France	4,834	5,971	2,943
Netherlands . . .	328	1,354	1,439
Hungary	4,983	5,051	2,561
Poland	6,593	5,889	3,334
TOTAL (all countries) . .	206,903	197,250	173,253

PRINCIPAL COUNTRIES
(£S '000)

	IMPORTS				EXPORTS*			
	1970	1971	1972	1973	1970	1971	1972	1973
Belgium	2,076	1,708	1,183	3,492	1,996	2,080	3,994	2,337
China, People's Republic . .	4,030	7,733	9,046	13,611	6,000	10,785	14,469	20,896
Egypt	5,323	6,814	5,018	3,830	4,981	5,700	7,267	5,755
France	1,716	4,234	5,209	6,156	2,223	3,090	4,274	8,701
Germany, Federal Republic .	7,802	7,069	7,131	10,457	9,855	8,779	10,198	12,552
India	14,226	22,677	19,741	11,579	14,226	11,997	22,078	8,368
Italy	2,430	2,351	2,680	4,938	10,190	9,775	11,941	16,202
Japan	5,629	4,796	4,565	8,592	9,250	8,332	9,472	16,654
Netherlands . . .	2,892	3,038	2,136	3,920	3,319	4,155	4,664	6,615
Poland	1,916	1,873	1,292	1,552	1,660	2,111	1,901	1,510
U.S.S.R.	8,328	7,858	5,596	9,162	17,242	18,351	473	3
United Kingdom . .	17,929	15,757	18,386	27,955	5,834	4,885	4,274	5,203
U.S.A.	2,822	2,910	4,980	12,385	4,026	3,014	3,826	2,692
Yugoslavia . . .	1,140	2,201	1,818	1,857	986	1,006	2,261	860
Others	30,774	24,417	34,304	47,462	9,827	20,314	23,379	35,175
TOTAL . . .	109,033	115,436	123,085	166,948	101,615	114,374	124,471	143,523

* Excluding re-exports.

1974 (£S '000): Imports from U.K. 35,900, Exports from U.K. 8,400.

TRANSPORT

RAILWAY TRAFFIC

	1969	1970	1971
Freight ton-kilometres (million)	2,398	2,684	2,636

ROAD VEHICLES IN USE

	1969	1970	1971
Passenger Cars . . .	30,100	27,400	30,000
Commercial Vehicles . . .	17,700	16,500	18,000

SHIPPING

	1968	1969	1970	1971	1972
Ships calling at Port Sudan . .	845	770	760	741	805
Total Inward Tonnage . . .	1,594,019	1,582,369	1,845,215	1,829,231	2,006,344
Total Outward Tonnage . . .	952,449	950,975	988,653	1,052,540	1,166,585

CIVIL AVIATION
(Sudan Airways—International Traffic)

	1968	1969	1970	1971	1972
Passengers	36,975	65,293	133,678	139,514	133,424
Freight (kg.)	344,338	837,966	1,397,000	1,277,000	1,203,000

EDUCATION
(1973-74)

| | TEACHERS | STUDENTS | | |
		MALE	FEMALE	TOTAL
Pre-Primary*	266	7,927	7,958	15,885
Primary	27,185	786,628	375,619	1,162,247
Secondary: General . . .	6,127	103,495	34,819	138,314
Higher . . .	2,121	33,973	10,416	44,389
Vocational	365	4,347	267	4,614
Teacher Training . . .	406	2,528	1,538	4,066
Tertiary	1,046	16,371	1,391	17,762

* 1969 figures.

Source: Department of Statistics, H.Q. Council of Ministers, Khartoum, except where otherwise stated.

THE CONSTITUTION

A Provisional Constitution was introduced by the Revolutionary Command Council in August 1971. A People's Council, including various categories of the people's working forces, was called to draft and ratify a permanent constitution. It was endorsed by the People's Assembly in April 1973 as the Permanent Constitution of the Sudan.

The President

The President must be a Sudanese of at least 35 years of age. He is nominated by the Sudanese Socialist Union, is Head of State, and is responsible for maintaining the Constitution. He may appoint Vice-Presidents, a Prime Minister and Ministers who are responsible to him. He is the Supreme Commander of the People's Armed Forces and Security Forces, and the Supreme Head of the Public Service.

If satisfied that a national crisis exists, the President may declare a State of Emergency, which may entail the suspension of any or all freedoms and rights under the Permanent Constitution other than that of resort to the courts. In the event of the President's death, the First Vice-President will temporarily assume office for a period not exceeding 60 days.

The People's Assembly

The President may appoint up to a tenth of the members of the Assembly. The duration of a sitting is four years and sittings are held in public. A quorum consists of half the number of members. Amendments to the Constitution may be proposed by the President or one third of the membership of the People's Assembly. An amendment to the Constitution must have a two-thirds majority of the People's Assembly and the assent of the President.

Judiciary

The State is subject to the rule of law which is the basis of government. The judiciary is an independent body directly responsible to the President and judges are appointed by the President.

Religion

Unrestricted freedom of religion is allowed and mention is specifically made of the Islamic and Christian religions.

Southern Region

Under the Regional Constitution for the Southern Sudan, the three southern provinces form a single region, with its own regional executive in Juba headed by a president who is also a Vice-President of the whole Republic. The regional executive is responsible for all matters except national defence, external affairs, economic and social development, education, currency and coinage, air and inter-regional river transport, communications and telecommunications, nationality and immigration, public audit, customs and foreign trade regulation except for border trade. The regional President is appointed by and responsible to a Regional People's Assembly. The Assembly may postpone legislation of the central Government which it considers adverse to the interests of the South, though the President is not compelled to accede to its request. The Regional Constitution can be amended only by a four-fifths majority of the central People's Assembly, where southerners are represented.

The People's Assembly has 250 seats, which include 70 for the people's working forces alliance, 30 for the administrative units to be filled both by election and selection, 25 appointed by the President and 125 for the geographical areas. The regional People's Assembly consists of 60 members of whom 30 represent the geographical areas, 21 the people's working forces alliance and 9 the administrative units. They are elected by direct secret ballot.

THE GOVERNMENT

President and Minister of Defence: Gen. JAAFIR MOHAMED AL-NEMERY (*elected October* 1971).

First Vice-President and Minister of the Interior: Maj.-Gen. MOHAMED EL BAQIR AHMED.

Vice-President and President of the High Executive Council for the Southern Region: ABEL ALIER.

MINISTERS
(*August* 1975)

Minister of Foreign Affairs: GAMAL MOHAMED AHMED.

Minister of Health and Social Welfare: Dr. EL NAZIR DAFALLA.

Minister of Culture and Information: AHMED ABDUL HALIM.

Minister for Egyptian Affairs in the Sudan: Lt.-Col. SALAH ABDEL AAL MABROUK.

Minister of Education: Dr. MANSOUR KHALID.

Minister of Finance and National Economy: MAMOUN BIHARI.

Minister of Agriculture, Food and Natural Resources: Maj. ABUL GASIM MOHAMED IBRAHIM.

Minister of Construction and Public Works: MUSTAFA OSMAN HASSAN.

Minister of Industry and Mining: BADR EDDIN SULIMAN.

Minister of Local Government, Housing and Community Development: KARRAR AHMED KARRAR.

Minister of Public Services and Administrative Reform: ABDEL RAHMAN ABDALLA.

Minister of Transport and Communications: Dr. BESHIR ABBADI.

Minister of Irrigation and Hydroelectric Power: YAHIA ABDEL MAGEED.

Minister of Presidential Affairs: ABDALLA EL HASSAN EL KHIDER.

Attorney-General: ABDEL MAGEED IMAM.

Ministry of Youth, Sports and Social Welfare: Maj. ZEIN EL ABDIN MOHAMED AHMED ABDEL GADER.

Chairman, National Council for Research: WADIE HABASHI.

President of the Supreme Court: KHALAFALLA EL RASHEED.

Auditor General: IBRAHIM HASSAN ALLAM.

Adviser to the Head of State for Foreign Economic Co-operation: MUZAMIL SULIMAN GHANDOUR

Adviser to the Head of State for Military and Aviation Affairs: Gen. AWAD KHALAFALLA.

Adviser to the Head of State for Review and Reform of Laws: Dr. ZAKI MUSTAFA.

MINISTERS OF STATE

Minister of State for Head of State Affairs: FAISAL MOHAMED ABDEL RAHMAN.

Minister of State for Research and Services: Dr. HUSSEIN IDRIS.

Minister of State for General Education: MOHAMED EL TOM EL TIGANI.

Minister of State for Information: BONA MALWAL.

Minister of State for Local Government: OTHWAN DAK.

Minister of State for Head of Government Affairs: Dr. BAHA EDDIN MOHAMED IDRIS.

Minister of State for Co-operation: GANDEIL IBRAHIM.

HIGH EXECUTIVE COUNCIL FOR THE SOUTHERN REGION

President: ABEL ALIER.

Regional Minister of Agriculture, Animal Resources and Forests: Dr. GAMA HASSAN.

Secretary-General: CLETO HASSAN.

Regional Minister of Co-operation and Rural Development: MADING DE GARANG.

Regional Minister of Roads and Communications: IZBONI MONDIRI.

Regional Minister of Finance, Planning and Economy: HILARY LOGALI.

Regional Minister of Culture and Information: Dr. TOBY MADOT.

Regional Minister of Health: Dr. JUSTIN YAC.

Regional Minister of Public Service and Administrative Reform: MOSAIS SHOL.

Regional Minister of Regional Administration and Legal Affairs: NATALI OLWAK.

Regional Minister of Education: MICHAEL TAWIL.

Regional Minister of Housing and Public Utilities: JOSEPH ODUHO.

Regional Minister of Affairs of the Presidency and the High Executive Council: LAWRENCE LUAL LUAL.

PROVINCE COMMISSIONERS*

Bahr El Ghazal: ISAIAH KULANG.
Blue Nile: MOHAMED EL HASSAN AWAD EL KARIM.
Equatoria: HENRY BAGU.
Gezira: AHMED BABIKER EISA.
Kassala: MOHAMED ABDEL GADER OMER.
Khartoum: MAHDI MUSTAFA EL HADI.
Nile: SAAD AWAD MOHAMED AHMED.
Northern: KAMIL MOHAMED SAEED.
Northern Darfur: EL TAYEB EL MARDI.
Northern Kordofan: ABBAS ABDEL MAGID.
Red Sea: KARAMALLA EL AWAD.
Southern Darfur: ABDEL RAHMAN SULIMAN.
Southern Kordofan: HASHIM HASSAN ABDALLA.
Upper Nile: PETER GATKUOTH.
White Nile: MOHAMED EL SAYED EL SHAAR.

* Also Provincial Secretaries of the Sudanese Socialist Union.

PEOPLE'S ASSEMBLY

A People's Assembly is provided for under the Permanent Constitution, and elections to it were held in April 1974. The Assembly was opened in May 1974.

Speaker: EL RASHEED EL TAHER BAKR.

Leader: Dr. GAAFAR MOHAMED ALI BAKHEIT.

REGIONAL PEOPLE'S ASSEMBLY

Formed after elections in November 1973. Represents the Southern Region.

Speaker: LOBARI RAMBA.

Secretary: ISKANDER NAGEEB.

POLITICAL ORGANIZATION

Sudanese Socialist Union: Khartoum; f. 1972; only recognized political organization; consists of National Conference, Central Committee, Political Bureau and Secretariat-General; Pres. and Sec.-Gen. JAAFIR AL-NEMERY; Deputy Secs. Dr. GAAFAR MOHAMED ALI BAKHEIT, OMER EL HAG MUSA.

Political Bureau (*August* 1975): Gen. JAAFIR AL-NEMERY, MOHAMED EL BAQIR AHMED, ABEL ALIER, Maj. ABUL GASIM MOHAMED IBRAHIM, BADR EDDIN MOHAMED AHMED SULIMAN, EL RASHEED EL TAHER BAKR, AHMED ABDEL HALIM, LUIGI ADOK, MAHDI MUSTAFA, ABDALLA EL HASSAN EL KHIDER, Gen. AWAD KHALAFALLA, Dr. GAAFAR MOHAMED ALI BAKHEIT, HILLARY PAULO LOGALI, JOSEPH ODUHO, LAWRENCE WOL, MANSOUR KHALID, OMER EL HAG MUSA, MAMOUN BIHEIRY, ABDEL RAHMAN ABDALLA, Maj. ZEIN EL ABDEEN MOHAMED AHMED ABDEL GADIR.

Secretariat General (*August* 1975): Gen. JAAFIR AL-NEMERY, Maj. ABUL GASIM MOHAMED IBRAHIM, BADR EDDIN MOHAMED AHMED SULIMAN, GAAFAR MOHAMED ALI BAKHEIT, OMER EL HAG MUSA, EL RASHEED EL TAHER BAKR, AHMED ABDEL HALIM, LUIGI ADOK, KHALIFA KHOGALI, EL TAYEB MIRGHANI SHAKAK, Dr. MOHAMED OSMAN ABU SAG, MAHGOUB MEKKAWI, Dr. AHMED ABDEL KARIM BEDRI, OMER TAHA ABU SAMRA, MOHAMED SUBARA EL AWAD, ABDEL GALIL HASSAN ABDEL GALIL, Col. HASSAN BANAGA, Miss RAWDA BUSHARA, Dr. ABDULLA AHMED GALANDER.

DIPLOMATIC REPRESENTATION

EMBASSIES ACCREDITED TO THE SUDAN

(In Khartoum unless otherwise stated)

Algeria: Junction Mek Nimr St. and 67th St., P.O.B. 80; *Ambassador:* ABDEL AZIZ BEN HUSAIN.

Austria: Cairo, Egypt (E).

Belgium: St. 3, New Extension, P.O.B. 969; *Chargé d'Affaires:* THÉO L. R. LANSLOOT.

Bulgaria: El Mek Nimr St. South 7, P.O.B. 1690; *Ambassador:* IVAN MARINOV GUNINSKI.

Central African Republic: Africa Rd., P.O.B. 1723; *Ambassador:* GILBERT BANDIO.

Chad: St. 17, New Extension, P.O.B. 1514; *Ambassador:* MOULI SAID.

China, People's Republic: 69 31st St., P.O.B. 1425; *Ambassador:* YANG SHOU-CHENG.

Czechoslovakia: House 39, Street 39, Khartoum 2, P.O.B. 1047; *Ambassador:* Dr. ZDENĚK PAV (also accred. to Somalia).

Egypt: Mogram St.; *Ambassador:* SA'AD AL FATATRI.

Ethiopia: 6, 11A St. 3, New Extension, P.O.B. 844; *Chargé d'Affaires a.i.:* RIDWAN ABDALLA.

France: 6H East Plot 2, 19th St., P.O.B. 377; *Ambassador:* JEAN PIERRE CAMPREDON.

German Democratic Republic: P4 (3) B2, Khartoum West, P.O.B. 1089; *Ambassador:* HERBERT DENZLER.

Germany, Federal Republic: Baladiya St., P.O.B. 970; *Ambassador:* MICHAEL JOVY.

Greece: Block 74, 31st St., P.O.B. 1182; *Ambassador:* EFTHYMIOS TZAFERIS.

Hungary: Block 11, Plot 12, 13th St., New Extension, P.O.B. 1033; *Chargé d'Affaires:* ISTVÁN FODOR.

India: El Mek Nimr St., P.O.B. 707; *Ambassador:* INDU PRAKASH SINGH.

Iran: Baladiya St.; *Ambassador:* ARSALAN NAYER NURI.

Iraq: St. 5, New Extension; *Ambassador:* NAZIM JAWAD EL ARIDH.

Italy: 39th St., P.O.B. 793; *Ambassador:* GIULIO BILANCIONI.

Japan: 14-16, Block 5HE, P.O.B. 1649; *Ambassador:* TOSHIO KAWASHIMA.

Jordan: 25 7th St., New Extension; *Ambassador:* ALI KHRAIS.

Korea, Democratic People's Republic: 2-10 BE, 7th St., New Extension, P.O.B. 332; *Ambassador:* PAK NEUNG IL.

Kuwait: 9th St., New Extension; *Ambassador:* MOHAMMED SALEM EL BALHAN.

Lebanon: 60 St. 49; *Ambassador:* BULIND BEYDOUN.

Libya: Africa Rd. 50, P.O.B. 2091; *Ambassador:* YUNIS ABU UQAYLAH.

Morocco: *Ambassador:* ABDEL LATIF LAKHMIRI.

Netherlands: P.O.B. 391; *Chargé d'Affaires a.i.:* P. F. C. KOCH (also accred. to Somalia).

Niger: St. 1, New Extension, P.O.B. 1283; *Ambassador:* EL HAG OMAROU AMADOU.

Nigeria: P.O.B. 1538; *Ambassador:* EL HAJI NUHU MOHAMMED.

Pakistan: 29, 9AE, St. 3, New Extension, P.O.B. 1178; *Ambassador:* S. A. H. AHSANI (also accred. to the Central African Republic).

Poland: 73 Africa Rd., P.O.B. 902; *Chargé d'Affaires:* TYBURA JAN.

Qatar: St. 15, New Extension; *Ambassador:* ALI ABDUL RAHMAN MUFTAH.

Romania: St. 47, Plot 67, P.O.B. 1652; *Ambassador:* FLORIAN STOICA (also accred. to the Yemen Arab Republic).

Saudi Arabia: Central St., New Extension, P.O.B. 852; *Ambassador:* ARAB SAEED HASHIM.

Somalia: Central St., New Extension; *Ambassador:* JAALLE MOHAMED HAGI NUIR.

Spain: 52 39th St., P.O.B. 2621; *Ambassador:* JOSE MANUEL DEL MORAL Y GRACIA SAEZ.

Switzerland: Cairo, Egypt (E); *Chargé d'Affaires:* (Khartoum): RÉMY GODET.

Syria: 3rd St., New Extension; *Chargé d'Affaires a.i.:* WAHIB JABR.

Tanzania: P.O.B. 6080; *Ambassador:* WAZIN JUMA.

Tunisia: Cairo, Egypt (E).

Turkey: 71 Africa Rd., P.O.B. 771; *Ambassador:* SELUK TARLAND.

Uganda: Cairo, Egypt.

U.S.S.R.: B1, A10 St., New Extension, P.O.B. 1161; *Ambassador:* FELIX FEDOTOV.

United Arab Emirates: St. 3, New Extension; *Ambassador:* KHALIFA AHMED ABDEL AZIZ AL MUBARAK.

United Kingdom: New Abulela Bldg., P.O.B. 801; *Ambassador:* JOHN F. S. PHILLIPS.

U.S.A.: Gumhouria Ave.; *Ambassador:* WILLIAM D. BREWER.

Vatican: El Safeh City, Shambat, P.O.B. 623; *Apostolic Pro-Nuncio:* UBALDO CALABRESI.

Yemen Arab Republic: St. 35, New Extension; *Chargé d'Affaires:* ABDALLAH SALIH AL MASAJDY.

Yemen, People's Democratic Republic: St. 51, New Extension; *Chargé d'Affaires a.i.:* MOHAMED AWAD EL TAHS.

Yugoslavia: St. 31, 79-A, Khartoum 1, P.O.B. 1180; *Ambassador:* LJUBOMIR DRNDIĆ.

Zaire: Gumhouria Ave.; *Ambassador:* LOSSO LISONGI.

The Sudan also has diplomatic relations with Afghanistan, Argentina, Australia, Bahrain, Bangladesh, Brazil, Cameroon, Canada, Chile, Cyprus, Denmark, Finland, Gabon, Guinea, Indonesia, Kenya, Malaysia, Mali, Mauritania, Norway, Portugal, Senegal, Sri Lanka, Sweden, the Democratic Republic of Viet-Nam and Zambia.

JUDICIAL SYSTEM

The administration of justice is the function of the judiciary, as a separate and independent department of state. The general administrative supervision and control of the judiciary is vested in the Higher Judiciary Council headed by the President of the Republic. The members are the President of the Supreme Court, his three deputies and the Attorney-General.

Civil Justice: is administered by the courts constituted under the Civil Justice Ordinance, namely the Supreme Court, Court of Appeal and Other Courts. The Supreme Court consists of a president and one or more vice-presidents and sufficient number of judges. It is the custodian of the constitution under the Permanent Constitution of the Sudan of 1973.

Criminal Justice: is administered by the courts constituted under the Code of Criminal Procedure, namely Major Courts, Minor Courts and Magistrates' Courts. Serious crimes are tried by Major Courts which are composed of a president and two members and have power to pass the death sentence. Major Courts are as a rule presided over by a judge of the High Court appointed to a Provincial Circuit, or a Province Judge. There is a right of appeal against any decision or order of a Major Court and all findings and sentences of a Major Court are subject to confirmation.

Lesser crimes are tried by Minor Courts consisting of three magistrates and presided over by a second class magistrate and by Magistrates' Courts consisting of a single magistrate, or a bench of lay magistrates.

Local Courts: try a substantial portion of the criminal and civil cases in the Sudan and work parallel to some extent with the State Courts.

Chief Justice: KHALAFALLA EL RASHEED.

ISLAMIC LAW COURTS

Justice in personal matters for the Muslim population is administered by the Law Courts, which form the Sharia Division of the Judiciary. These courts consist of the Court of Appeal, High Courts and Qadis' Courts. The religious Law of Islam is administered by these courts in matters of inheritance, marriage, divorce, family relationships and charitable trusts.

Mufti: AWADALLA SALIH.

RELIGION

The majority of Sudanese are vigorous followers of Islam, but some communities in the south practise animism or fertility worship. It is estimated that there are more than 9 million Muslims and over 400,000 Catholics. The government plans to create a Sudanese National Church.

MUSLIM COMMUNITY

(Mainly divided into the following sects:)

Qadria: Heads of important local sub-sections include:
Sheikh AHMED EL GAALI.
Sheikh IBRAHIM EL KABASHI.
YOUSIF EL SHEIKH OMER EL OBEID.
KHALIFA BARAKAT EL SHEIKH.
Sheikh HAMAD EL NIL ABD EL BAGI.
Sheikh ABD EL BAGI EL MUKASHFI.

Shadhlia: Heads of local sub-sections include:
Sheikh EL MAGDOUB EL BESHIR.
Sheikh GAMAR EL DAWLA EL MAGDOUB.

Idrisia: Heads of local sub-sections include:
Sheikh EL HASSAN EL IDRISI.

Khatmiya: MUHAMMAD OSMAN EL MIRGHANI.

Sammania: Sheikh FATEH GHARIBALLA.

Ismaila: Sayed JAYAL ASFIA EL SAYED EL MEKKI.

Ansari: (vacant after death of El Hadi El Mahdi in 1970).

CHRISTIAN COMMUNITIES

Coptic Orthodox Church: Bishop of Nubia, Atbara and Omdurman: Rt. Rev. BAKHOMIOS.
Bishop of Khartoum, S. Sudan and Uganda: Rt. Rev. ANBA YOUANNIS.

Greek Orthodox Church: Metropolitan of Nubia: Archbishop SINESSIOS.

Greek Evangelical Church.

Evangelical Church: P.O.B. 57, Khartoum; Chair. Rev. RADI ELIAS; about 1,000 mems.; runs schools, literature centre.

Episcopal Church of the Sudan: Clergy House, P.O.B. 110, Khartoum; Bishop in the Sudan: The Rt. Rev. ELINANA J. NGALAMU; Asst. Bishops: The Rt. Rev. YEREMAYA K. DOTIRO, The Rt. Rev. BUTRUS T. SHUKAI, The Rt. Rev. BENJAMIN W. YUGUSUK.

Catholic Church:

Roman Rite:

Archbishop of Khartoum: P.O.B. 49, Khartoum; Most Rev. Bishop AUGUSTINE BARONI.

Archbishop of Wau: P.O.B. 29, Wau; Most Rev. Bishop IRENEUS WIEN DUD.

Vicariate Apostolic of Juba: P.O.B. 32, Juba; Rt. Rev. PAOLINO DOGGALE, Apostolic Administrator.

Vicariate Apostolic of El Obeid: P.O.B. 386, El Obeid; Rt. Rev. Mgr. FRANCESCO CAZZANIGA, Apostolic Administrator.

Vicariate Apostolic of Rumbek: Catholic Church, Rumbek; Rev. Fr. DOMINIC MATONG, Vicar Del.

Prefecture Apostolic of Malakal: P.O.B. 27, Malakal; Rt. Rev. Mgr. PIUS YUKWAN DENG, Apostolic Administrator.

Prefecture Apostolic of Mupoi: Catholic Church, Tombora; Rt. Rev. JOSEPH GASI, Apostolic Administrator.

Maronite Church: P.O.B. 244, Khartoum; Rev. Fr. YOUSEPH NEAMA.

Greek Catholic Church: P.O.B. 766, Khartoum; Bishop PAUL ANTAKI (Egypt); Vicar Rev. JOSEPH SUCKARIEH (Sudan).

Presbyterian Church: Malakal.

Christian Council: P.O.B. 317, Khartoum.

Bible Society: P.O.B. 532, Khartoum.

Sudan Interior Mission: P.O.B. 220, Khartoum.

THE PRESS

The Press was nationalized on August 27th, 1970. A General Corporation for Press. Printing and Publications was set up. The two main publishing houses are El-Ayam and El-Sahafa. These two houses publish all the following newspapers and magazines with the exception of those produced by other ministries.

DAILIES

El-Ayam: P.O.B. 363, Khartoum; Arabic.

El-Sahafa: P.O.B. 1228, Khartoum; f. 1961; Arabic; Chief Editor Dr. GAAFAR MOHAMED ALI BAKHEIT.

PERIODICALS

El Guwat El Musallaha: armed forces publication; weekly.

Huna Omdurman: f. 1942; Arabic; weekly; Sudan Broadcasting Service Magazine; published by Ministry of Culture and Information.

Nile Mirror: English; weekly; publ. by Ministry of Culture and Information for the Southern Region.

Sudan Cotton Bulletin: P.O.B. 1672, Khartoum; English; monthly; published by Cotton Public Corporation.

Sudan Cotton Review: P.O.B. 1672, Khartoum; English; annually; published by Cotton Public Corporation.

Youth and Sports: P.O.B. 2361, Khartoum; Arabic; publ. by the Ministry of Culture and Information.

NEWS AGENCIES

Sudan National News Agency (SUNA): P.O.B. 1506, Gamaa

Ave., Khartoum; f. 1971; daily and weekly summaries in English and Arabic; Man. MUSTAFA AMIN.

FOREIGN BUREAUX

Middle East News Agency: Dalala Bldg., P.O.B. 740, Khartoum.

Tass and the New China News Agency also have bureaux in Khartoum.

PUBLISHERS

Ahmed Abdel Rahman El Tikeina: P.O Box 299, Port Sudan.

Arab Printing Press.

El-Ayam Press Co. Ltd.: Aboul Ela Building, United Nations Square, P.O. Box 363, Khartoum; f. 1953; Man. Dir. BESHIR MUHAMMAD SAID; newspapers, pamphlets and books.

Al Ghorashi Printing House.

El-Sahafa Publishing House: government publications and short stories.

El-Salam Co. Ltd.: P.O.B. 197, Khartoum.

Claudios S. Fellas: P.O. Box 641, Khartoum.

Fuad Rashed: Wadi Halfa.

Government Printing Press: government publishing office; publications include the *Sudan Almanac.*

Khartoum University Press: P.O.B. 321, Khartoum; f. 1967; scholarly works; Dir. (vacant).

RADIO AND TELEVISION

Sudan Broadcasting Service: P.O.B. 572, Omdurman; a government-controlled radio station which broadcasts daily in Arabic, English, and Somali; Dir. MOHAMED KHOGALI SALIHEEN.

There were an estimated 1,310,000 radio receivers in 1972. A radio station is to be constructed in the Southern Region.

In November 1974 an earth satellite station was opened

at Umm Haraz and this has given Sudan much improved telecommunication links.

Sudan Television: P.O.B. 1049, Omdurman; f. 1962; thirty-five hours of programmes per week; Dir.-Gen. Dr. AHMED ZEIN.

Gezira Television Station: Wad Medani; f. 1972.

There were 70,000 television receivers in 1972.
A network to extend television transmission was begun in 1975.

FINANCE

BANKING

(cap. = capital; p.u. = paid up; dep. = deposits; m. = million)

Under the Nationalization of Banks Act 1970, all banks have been nationalized and converted into limited companies fully owned by the Bank of Sudan.

CENTRAL BANK

Bank of Sudan: P.O. Box 313, Khartoum; f. 1960; acts as banker and financial adviser to the Government and has sole right of issue of Sudanese banknotes; cap. p.u. £S1.5m.; Gov. IBRAHIM MOHAMMED NIMIR; Dep. Gov. EL FAKI MUSTAFA; Gen. Man. MAURICE LOGA; 8 brs.; publs. *Economic and Financial Bulletin* (quarterly), *Foreign Trade Statistical Digest* (quarterly), *Annual Report.*

COMMERCIAL BANKS

El Nilein Bank: P.O.B. 466, Khartoum; f. 1965; fully owned by Bank of Sudan; 12 brs.; auth. cap. £S4.7m.; cap. p.u. £S3.3m.; Chair. IBRAHIM ELIAS; 8 brs.

Juba-Omdurman Commercial Bank: P.O.B. 408, Khartoum; f. 1973; formerly Juba Commercial Bank and Omdurman National Bank; cap. £S850,000; Gen. Man. MOHAMED SALIH YAHYA.

People's Co-operative Bank: P.O.B. 922, Khartoum; f. 1970; formerly the Misr Bank; 6 brs.; deals with all operations and facilities of the Sudan co-operative movement; Gen. Man. ABDEL RAHMAN SID AHMED.

State Bank for Foreign Trade: P.O.B. 1008, Khartoum; f. 1970; formerly Barclays Bank D.C.O.; cap. £S1.2m.; dep. £S54,561,000 (Dec. 1973); 24 brs.; Gen. Man. and

Chair. of Board HUSSEIN ABDEL GADIR; Deputy SALIH MOHAMED ALI SAKRAN.

Sudan Commercial Bank: P.O.B. 1116, Khartoum; f. 1960; cap. p.u. £S1,099,611; dep. £S13,575,830; Chair. and Gen. Man. FARID RUFAIL ELIAS; 7 brs.

DEVELOPMENT BANKS

Agricultural Bank of Sudan: P.O.B. 1363, Khartoum; f. 1957; cap. £S7m.; provides agricultural credit; Chair. and Man. Dir. MIRGHANI EL AMIN EL HAG; 14 brs.

Industrial Bank of Sudan: P.O.B. 1722, Khartoum; f. 1962; cap. £S2m.; to provide loans to private sector industrial projects and interest in industrial enterprises; Gen. Man. MAHDI AHMED.

Sudanese Estates Bank: P.O.B. 309, Khartoum; cap. £S4.9m.; mortgage bank to finance urban housing development in the private sector; Gen. Man. MOHAMMED MEKKI KANANI.

INSURANCE COMPANIES

There are over forty foreign insurance companies operating in the Sudan.

General Insurance Co. (Sudan) Ltd.: P.O.B. 1555, Khartoum.

Sudanese Insurance and Re-insurance Co. Ltd.: P.O.B. 2332, Khartoum.

TRADE AND INDUSTRY

Agricultural Reform Corporation: P.O.B. 1986, Khartoum; Dirs. ABBAS AHMED EL SAYED, MUKHTAR MOHAMED MUKHTAR.

Agricultural Research Corporation: P.O.B. 126, Wad Medani; Dirs. MOHAMED OSMAN MOHAMED SALIH, EL HADI EL NUR.

Cotton Public Corporation: P.O.B. 1672, Khartoum; f. June 1970; Man. TEWFIK EL QUSI; the Corporation now supervises all cotton marketing operations through the following four main cotton companies:

Alaktan Cotton and Trade: P.O.B. 2607, Khartoum; Gen. Man. ABDEL RAHMAN ABDEL MONEIM.

National Cotton and Trade Co. Ltd.: P.O.B. 1522, Khartoum; Gen. Man. GEORGE N. ZEHIL.

Port Sudan Cotton and Trade Co. Ltd.: P.O.B. 590, Khartoum; HASHIM SID AHMED; br. at P.O.B. 261, Port Sudan.

Sudan Cotton Trade Co. Ltd.: P.O.B. 2284, Khartoum; Gen. Man. ABDEL FATAH IBRAHIM.

Offices Abroad:

Democratic Republic of Sudan Consulates, Sudan Cotton Section, 3 rue de Marché, 1204 Geneva, Switzerland.

Sudan Cotton Centre, P.O.B. 152, Osaka, Japan.

Gezira Board: H.Q. Barakat; Sales Office, P.O.B. 884, Khartoum; Gov. EL SADIQ BEDRI; Deputy Gov. AWAD EL KARIM SINADA; Chair. and Man. Dir. Dr. ABBAS ABDEL MAGID SINADA.

The Gezira Board is responsible for Sudan's main cotton producing area.

The Gezira Scheme represents a partnership between the Government, the tenants and the Board. The Government, which provides the land and is responsible for irrigation, receives 36 per cent of the net proceeds; the tenants, about 100,000 in 1971, receive 49 per cent. The Board receives 10 per cent, the local Government Councils in the Scheme area 2 per cent and the Social Development Fund, set up to provide social services for the inhabitants, 3 per cent.

The total possible cultivable area of the Gezira Scheme is over 5 million acres and the total area under systematic irrigation is now almost 2 million acres. In addition to cotton, groundnuts, sorghum, wheat and millet are grown for the benefit of tenant farmers.

Publications: *Annual Report, Annual Statement of Accounts, El Gezira News* (weekly), *Weekly Bulletin.*

Industrial Production Corporation: P.O.B. 1034, Khartoum; Chair. MOHAMED EL BASHIR EL WAGIE (acting); Deputy Chair. MIRGHANI BABIKER; incorporates:

Food Industries Corporation: P.O.B. 2341, Khartoum; Man. ALI ABDEL HAMID.

Grouped Industries Corporation: P.O.B. 385, Khartoum; Man. BABIKER MOHAMED ALI.

Leather and Plastics Industries Corporation: P.O.B. 1639, Khartoum; Man. ALI ABDEL HAMID.

Sugar Corporation: P.O.B. 511, Khartoum; Man. MOHAMED EL BASHIR EL WAGIE.

Mechanised Farming Corporation: P.O.B. 2482, Khartoum; Dirs. Dr. A. OSMAN SHAZALI, BABIKER EL MALEK.

Public Agricultural Production Corporation: P.O.B. 538, Khartoum:

Equatoria Agricultural Corporation.

Gash Delta Agricultural Corporation.

Khashm el Girba Agricultural Corporation: Man. Dir. MOHAMED HASSAN KHEIRALLA; Deputy MUSTAFA ADAM MANDIL.

Nuba Agricultural Corporation.

Suki Agricultural Corporation: Man. Dir. ADBEL JALIL ABDEL JABAL.

Rahad Corporation: Man. Dir. EL TAYED ABDEL GADER.

The Rahad Project, financed by the World Bank, Kuwait and the U.S.A., is designed to irrigate 300,000 acres and settle 70,000 people in 15,000 tenancies by 1978.

The State Trading Corporation: P.O.B. 211, Khartoum; Gen. Man. MOHAMED ABDEL KARIM ABBAS.

Automobile Corporation: P.O.B. 221, Khartoum; importer of vehicles and spare parts; Gen. Man. MUBARAK MAHGOUB LOGMAN.

Engineering Equipment Corporation: P.O.B. 97, Khartoum; importers and distributors of agricultural, engineering and electronic equipment; Gen. Man. AMIR YOUSIF.

Silos and Storage Corporation: P.O.B. 62, Khartoum; stores and handles agricultural products; Gen. Man. ABDEL RAHMAN MEDANI.

Trade and Services Corporation: P.O.B. 215, Khartoum; largest importer of general merchandise and services in storage, shipping and insurance; Gen. Man. BUKHARI ABDALLA.

Sugar Trade General Establishment: f. 1974.

CHAMBER OF COMMERCE

Sudan Chamber of Commerce: P.O.B. 81, Khartoum; f. 1908; Pres. ABDEL SALAM ABOUL ELA; Hon. Treas. TH. APOSTOLOU; Hon. Sec. SAYED SALEH OSMAN SALEH.

DEVELOPMENT CORPORATION

Sudan Development Corporation: P.O.B. 710, Khartoum; f. 1974 to provide assistance for agriculture, animal production, irrigation, industry and mining and infrastructure and foreign trade, to initiate studies for new projects, assist their co-ordination through loans, guarantees and equity participations; Chair. and Man. Dir. SYD MOHAMED ABDUL-MAGID AHMED; Deputy Chair. and Deputy Man. Dir. SYD OSMAN HASHIM ABDUL-SALAM.

TRADE UNIONS

In 1971 all existing trade unions were dissolved and reconstituted according to the 1971 Trade Unions Act. Sec.-Gen. of Trade Unions: SAYED ABDEL MONIEM HASSAN MEDANI.

FEDERATIONS

Federation of Sudanese Workers' Unions (F.S.W.U.): P.O.B. 2258, Khartoum; includes 38 Trade Unions of public service workers and workers of the private sector with a total membership of roughly 290,000 members; affiliated to the International Confederation of Trade Union Federations and the All-African Trade Union Federation; Pres. ABDALLA NASR QINAWI; Sec. Gen. MOHAMMED OSMAN GAMMAA.

Agricultural Sector Workers' Trade Union: Workers' Club, Khartoum North; 30,000 mems.; Pres. AWAD WIDATALLA; Sec. MOHAMMED OSMAN SALIM.

Gezira Scheme Workers' Trade Union: Barakat;
11,500 mems.; Pres. IBRAHIM MOHAMMED AHMED EL
SHEIKH; Sec. EL SIR ABDOON.

Health Workers' Trade Union: Khartoum Civil
Hospital, Khartoum; 25,000 mems.; Pres. EL
TAYES EL AWAD; Sec. GAAFAR MOHAMMED SID
AHMED.

Local Government Workers' Trade Union: Workers'
Union, Khartoum; 25,000 mems.; Pres. ISMAIL
MOHAMMED FADL; Sec. SALEM BEDRI HUMAM.

Post, Telegraph and Telephone Workers' Trade Union:
Workers' Club, Khartoum; 8,463 mems.; Pres.
MANSOUL EL MANNA; Sec. YASSIN ABDEL GALIL.

Public Service Workers' Trade Union: Baladia St.,
Khartoum; 19,800 mems.; Pres. MOHIE EDDIN
BAKHEIT; Sec. ALI IDRIS EL HUSSEIN.

Railway Workers' Trade Union: Railway Workers'
Club, Atbara; 32,000 mems.; Pres. MOHAMMED EL
HASSAN ABDALLA; Sec. OSMAN ALI FADL.

Sudan Irrigation Workers' Trade Union: Ministry of
Education, Wad Medani; 19,150 mems.; Pres.
MOHAMMED HABIB; Sec. SAYED MOHAMMED
AHMED.

Taxi Workers' Trade Union: Workers' Union, Khartoum; 15,000 mems.; Pres. EL RAYAN YOUSIF;
Sec. EL TAYEB KHALAFALLA.

Federation of Officials' Unions: (under establishment);
includes 47 unions of professionals, public service
officials and officials of the private sector.

Bank Officials' Union: Peoples Bank, Khartoum;
Pres. AHMED ABDALLA; Sec. AHMED MOHAMMED
IBRAHIM.

Gezira Board Officials' Union: Barakat; Pres. MOHAM-
MED EL HASSAN NASR; Sec. EL RAYAH ABDEL
HAFEEZ.

Local Government Officials' Union: Ministry of Local
Government, Khartoum; Pres. GAMAL HAMAD
AHMED; Sec. AMIN ABU OIDEIRI.

Post, Telegraph and Telephone Officials: Post Office,
Khartoum; Pres. MOHAMMED HAG ABDU; Sec.
MUSA GEILANI AHMED.

Railway Officials' Union: Sudan Railways, Atbara;
Pres. MOHAMMED ARAFA EL SAYED; Sec. HASSAN
EL TOM ALI.

Teachers' Union: Teachers House, Khartoum; Pres.
ABDALLA ALI ABDALLA; Sec. ZEIN EL ABDEEN
ABBAS.

CO-OPERATIVE SOCIETIES

There are some 600 co-operative societies in the Sudan,
of which 570 are formally registered.

Central Co-operative Union: P.O.B. 2492, Khartoum;
largest co-operative union operating in 15 provinces.

TRANSPORT

RAILWAYS

Sudan Railways Corporation: Atbara; Chair. ABDEL
RAHMAN NADIM; Gen. Man. MOHAMMED ABDEL
RAHMAN WASFI.

The total length of railway in operation is 4,756 route-
kilometres. The main line runs from Wadi Halfa, on
the Egyptian border to El Obeid, via Khartoum Lines,
from Atbara and Sennar connect with Port Sudan on the
coast. There are lines from Sennar to Roseires on the Blue
Nile (225 km.) and from Aradeiba to Nyala in the south-
western province of Darfur (689 km.), with a 445 km.
branch line from Babanousa to Wau in the Bahr el Ghazal
Province.

ROADS

Ministry of Transport and Communications: P.O.B. 300,
Khartoum; Dir. of Roads and Bridges AHMED OMER
KHALAFALLA.

National Transport Corporation: P.O.B. 723, Khartoum;
Gen. Man. MOHI EL DIN HASSAN MOHAMED NUR.

Roads in the Northern Sudan, other than town roads,
are only cleared tracks and often impassable immediately
after rain. Motor traffic on roads in the Upper Nile Province
is limited to the drier months of January–May. There are
several good gravelled roads in the Equatoria and Bahr el
Ghazal Provinces which are passable all the year round,
but in these districts some of the minor roads become impassable after rain. Rehabilitation of communications in
the Southern Sudan is a major priority as the civil war
completely destroyed 1,600 km. of roads and 70 bridges.

In 1975 construction of a road began which will link
the White Nile to the Blue Nile, running from Wad
Medani south to Sennar and west to Kosti.

The through route from Juba to Khartoum is open from
mid-November to mid-April.

Over 48,000 km. of tracks are classed as "motorable",
but only 333 km. are asphalt.

INLAND WATERWAYS

Ministry of Transport and Communications: P.O.B. 300,
Khartoum.

River Transport Corporation: P.O.B. 284, Khartoum;
Chair. ABDEL RAHMAN AHMED EL MAHI.

The total length of navigable waterways served by passenger and freight services is 4,068 km. From the Egyptian
border to Wadi Halfa and Khartoum navigation is
limited by cataracts to short stretches but the White Nile
from Khartoum to Juba is navigable at almost all seasons.
The Blue Nile is not navigable. River transport was badly
hit by the Civil War.

The Sudan River Transport Corporation operates
2,500 km. of steamer services on the navigable reaches of
the Nile, touching Juba, Gambeila, Wau, Shellal (in
Egyptian territory), and Dongola. These services connect
with the Egyptian main railway services and the Nile
river services of Uganda.

It was announced in September 1974 that Egypt and the
Sudan are to be linked by a waterway from Aswan along
Lake Nasser to Wadi Halfa.

The construction of the Egyptian High Dam has flooded
the Wadi Halfa. The Sudan and Egypt operate river
services in the Wadi Halfa/Aswan reach by deep-draught
vessels suitable to sail in the big lake thus created.

SHIPPING

Port Sudan, on the Red Sea, 784 km. from Khartoum,
is the only seaport. There are eleven fully equipped berths,
with a total length of 7,461 metres, and two secondary
berths. There are also two berths with a total length of
1,560 metres.

Red Sea Shipping Corporation: P.O.B. 339, Khartoum;
Gen. Man. OSMAN AMIN.

River Navigation Corporation: Khartoum; f. 1970; jointly owned by the Egyptian and Sudan governments; operates services between Aswan and Wadi Halfa.

River Transport Corporation: P.O.B. 284, Khartoum; responsible for operating steamer services on the Nile and manages Port Sudan; Chair. ABDEL RAHMAN AHMED EL MAHI.

Sea Port Corporation: P.O.B. 2534, Khartoum; Administrator Brig. NASR EL DIN MUSTAFA.

Sudan Shipping Line: P.O.B. 426, Port Sudan; f. 1960; four vessels operating between the Red Sea, North Europe and the United Kingdom; Chair. ISMAIL BAKHEIT; Gen. Man. SALAH EDDIN OMER.

United African Shipping Co.: P.O.B. 339, Khartoum; Gen. Man. MOHAMED TAHA EL GINDI.

CIVIL AVIATION

The airports at Juba and Malakal in Southern Sudan are to be repaired and new airports built at Wau and Port Sudan.

Sudan Airways: Gumhouria Ave., P.O.B. 253, Khartoum; f. 1947; this airline is owned by the Sudan Government; regular services throughout the Sudan and external services to Bahrain, Egypt, Ethiopia, Federal Republic of Germany, Greece, Italy, Iraq, Lebanon, Libya, Saudi Arabia and the U.K.; Charter and Survey based at Khartoum; fleet of two Boeing 707, four Fokker F-27 and some smaller machines; they have contracted to buy two Boeing 737 aircraft in 1975; Chair. ABDEL BAGI MOHAMED; Gen. Man. MOHAMMED EL AMIR EL AMIN.

The Sudan is also served by the following foreign airlines: Aeroflot, Alitalia, British Airways, EgyptAir, Ethiopian, Interflug, Libyan Arab, Lufthansa, MEA, Saudia and Swissair.

TOURISM

Public Corporation for Hotels and Tourism: P.O.B. 326, Khartoum; Chair. OMER BABIKER EL SHAFI'E; Projects Man. MAJOUB ALI; incorporates:

Sudanese Tourist Corporation: P.O.B. 2424, Khartoum; Man. TAWFIQ EL DIN.

Sudanese Hotels Corporation: P.O.B. 272, Khartoum; owns four hotels; Man. OSMAN HUSSEIN.

Duty Free Shops Corporation: P.O.B. 1789, Khartoum; Chair. MOHAMED ATTA MANNAN.

DEFENCE

Total Armed Forces: 43,600 (1974-75); army 40,000; navy 600; air force 3,000. Some 6,000 former *Anya Nya* rebels are now attached to the armed forces stationed in the southern Sudan. There are 5,000 para-military forces including 4,500 border guards and a 500-strong National Guard. Military service is voluntary at present though proposals for compulsory service have been made.

Defence Budget: (1974-75 est.) £S35,777,277.

Commander-in-Chief of the People's Armed Forces: Gen. AWAD KHALAFALLA.

Chief of Staff of the People's Armed Forces Maj.-Gen. BASR MOHAMED ALI.

Commander of the Southern Region: Maj.-Gen. JOSEPH LAGU (former *Anya Nya* leaders).

Commander of the National Guard: ABU ADH-DHAHAB.

EDUCATION

A committee to review higher education was announced by Pres. Nemery in September 1973. The President's original education policy was in keeping with the ideals of the new Socialist State, but recent years have seen a rapid rise in the percentage of non-government secondary schools (45 per cent in September 1973). The administrative machinery of supervision and control is conducted through the Ministry of Education. General policy is executed through different technical and administrative bodies under the control of the Ministry. In the past education was mainly administered centrally with the delegation of certain powers to the regional directorates. The new policy has widened the authority of the regional directorates, and only matters of a technical, political, planning and financial nature remain the responsibility of the central machinery.

Under the Five-Year Plan 1970/71–1974/75, education was reconstructed and all curricula revised to relate the educational system more effectively to the new economic and social needs of the country. While the duration of formal schooling remains the same as before, i.e. 12 years. the Primary Level (*see* below) has been lengthened by two years; the six-year secondary stage comprises a lower level or General Secondary and an upper level or Higher Secondary, each of three years duration. The Higher Secondary Level is in turn divided into an Academic and a Vocational/Technical/Higher Secondary stage, the latter being one year longer than the former. In 1972/73 £S33.91 million was allocated for education representing 10.6 per cent of the National Budget. Over the whole Plan period, i.e. 1970/71–1974/75, £S9,800,000 has been granted to the Ministries of Education and Higher Education and Scientific Research representing 4.9 per cent of the total Five-Year Development Budget.

The new Four-Year Plan (1975-78) places great emphasis on reducing the level of illiteracy from 80 per cent in 1975 to 50 per cent. The Plan involves special concentration on those involved in the industrial and agricultural sectors, the government service and housewives. It is to be linked with the development projects and resettlement schemes and the target is to reach a million people per year.

Primary Education. Several important developments have taken place in primary education. The most important are those in connection with the implementation of the New Plan including the extension of this level from four to six years and the expansion of classes which by September 1973 had been largely achieved. As regards the curricula, notable features included the introduction of "Environmental Studies", "Citizenship Education" and "National Subjects" comprising civics, history and geography. There has recently been a notable increase in the number of pupils in primary education rising from 610,798 in 1969 to 1,162,247 in 1973-74. The number of teachers rose from 12,370 in 1969 to 27,185 in 1973-74. In the South primary school enrolment in state schools increased from 53,169 in 1971-72 to 95,973 in 1974-75.

Academic Secondary and Vocational Education. Two essential developments have taken place: firstly the introduction of the "Selective System" whereby students in the two final years specialize in one of three alternative groups of subjects: Literary, Science and Mathematics or Commercial subjects. The second change is that students sit only for those subjects included in their specialization whether literary, scientific or commercial. New curricula changes include the introduction of New Mathematics projects, Sociology and Psychology at the Higher Secondary level and French as an alternative foreign language.

Technical Education. In March 1970 a scheme for the reorganization of Technical Education was officially announced. The new system comprises schools for unskilled workers, skilled workers, technical assistants, technicians and professional engineers, etc. Higher Technical education is provided at the Khartoum Technical Institute and in other new post-secondary, two-year institutions, for different technical and vocational specializations throughout the country. Agricultural education is being stressed. Two new agricultural schools are being built. Several hundred Sudanese are given economic training annually under the UNDP in a drive to increase productivity, and UNESCO is backing a project to increase industrial knowledge.

Higher Education. The Policy regarding Higher Education has been guided by two main principles: co-ordination and centralization. With regard to the University of Khartoum, the Amended Law (1970) was passed which included basic changes in the role and administration of the University, for example, the Head of State now becomes the Chancellor with the right to appoint the Vice-Chancellor, greater participation by students and the public has been granted in the running of the University's internal affairs and more democratic means are utilized in the running of academic affairs including departments. In September 1973 President Nemery announced the establishment of a new committee to review higher education in the Sudan.

Teacher Training. A number of crash programmes for training new teachers have been implemented following the introduction of the New Plan. The raising of the status of sub-grade schools to primary schools status has created the need for at least 2,000 primary teachers who would be in charge of teaching the additional fifth class in the new primary schools. Student teachers are hence selected from the Secondary School Certificate holders. The new 1975-78 Plan involves increasing the number of teachers to 40,000 by 1980.

Adult and Non-Vocational Education. Projects for increasing literacy among adults have been in progress for several years. Experiments in the improvement of syllabuses have begun supervised by the National Council of Literacy and Adult Functional Education, and new Adult Education curricula will be introduced and taught in the teacher training institutes.

UNIVERSITIES

University of Khartoum: P.O.B. 321, Khartoum; f. 1956; 450 teachers, 6,000 students.

Cairo University Khartoum Branch: P.O.B. 1055, Khartoum; f. 1955; 80 teachers, 5,100 students.

BIBLIOGRAPHY

GENERAL

ABDEL RAHIM, MUDDATHIR. Imperialism and Nationalism in the Sudan: A Study in Constitutional and Political Developments 1899-1956 (Oxford University Press, 1969).

ALBINO, OLIVER. The Sudan, a southern viewpoint (Oxford, 1969).

AMMAR, ABBAS, and others. The Unity of the Nile Valley, its Geographical Basis and its Manifestations in History (Cairo, 1947).

BARBOUR, K. M. The Republic of the Sudan: A Regional Geography (University of London Press, London, 1961).

BESHIR, M. O. The Southern Sudan: Background to Conflict (C. Hurst, London, 1968, Praeger, New York, 1968).

BONN, GISELA. Das doppelte Gesicht des Sudan (F. A. Brockhaus, Wiesbaden, 1961).

BOUSFIELD, L. Sudan Doctor (London, 1954).

BUDGE, Sir E. A. T. W. The Egyptian Sudan: Its History and Monuments (2 vols., London, 1907).
By Nile and Tigris (London, 1920).

BUXTON, J. C. Chiefs and Strangers (Oxford, 1963).

EGYPTIAN SOCIETY OF INTERNATIONAL LAW. Documents of the Sudan 1899-1953 (Cairo, 1953).

FADL, EL S. H. Their Finest Days (Rex Collings, London, 1969).

FAWZI, S. ED DIN. The Labour Movement in the Sudan, 1946-55 (Oxford University Press, London, 1957).

GAITSKELL, ARTHUR. Gezira: A Story of Development in the Sudan (Faber, London, 1959).

HAMILTON, J. A. DE C. The Sudan: the Road Ahead (London, 1945).
The Anglo-Egyptian Sudan from Within (London, 1935).

HENDERSON, K. D. D. The Sudan Republic (Benn, London, 1965).

HERZOG, ROLF. Sudan (Kurt Schroeder, Bonn, 1958).

HILL, R. A Bibliography of the Anglo-Egyptian Sudan from the earliest times to 1937 (Oxford, 1939).
A Bibliographical Dictionary of the Anglo-Egyptian Sudan (new edition, Frank Cass, London, 1967).
Egypt in the Sudan 1820-1881 (Oxford University Press, London and New York, 1959).
Slatin Pasha (Oxford University Press, London, 1964, New York, 1965).
Sudan Transport: a History (London, 1965).

HODGKIN, R. A. Sudan Geography (London, 1951).

HURST, H. E. and PHILIPS, P. The Nile Basin, 7 vols. (London, 1932-38).

JACKSON, H. C. The Fighting Sudanese (London, 1954).
Sudan Days and Ways (London, 1954).

KNIGHT, R. L., and BOYNS, B. M. Agricultural Science in the Sudan (1950).

LANGLEY, M. No Woman's Country: Travels in the Anglo-Egyptian Sudan (New York, 1951).

LEBON, J. H. C. Land Use in Sudan (Geographical Publications Ltd., Bude, U.K., 1965).

NASRI, A. R. EL-. A Bibliography of the Sudan 1938–1958 (Oxford University Press, 1962).

NEWBOLD, Sir D. The Making of the Modern Sudan; the Life and Letters of Sir Douglas Newbold (London, Faber and Faber, 1953).

ODUHO, JOSEPH, and DENG, WILLIAM. The Problem of the Southern Sudan (Oxford University Press, 1963).

SUDANESE GOVERNMENT. Ten Year Plan of Economic and Social Development 1961-62—1971-72 (Khartoum, Ministry of Finance and Economics, 1962).

TRIMINGHAM, J. S. Islam in the Sudan (London, 1949).

ANTHROPOLOGY

CUNNISON, IAN. Baggara Arabs (Oxford University Press, New York, 1966).

EVANS-PRITCHARD, E. E. Kinship and Marriage among the Nuer (London, 1951).

The Nuer (London, 1940).

Witchcraft, Oracles and Magic among the Azande (London, 1937).

GRIFFITHS, V. L., and TAHA, ABDEL RAHMAN ALI. Sudan Courtesy Customs (Sudan Government, 1936).

HABER, HUGO. Das Fortleben nach dem Tode im Glauben westsudanischer Völker (Mödling, 1951).

NADEL, S. F. The Nuba: an Anthropological Study of the Hill Tribes of Kordofan (London, 1947).

PAUL, A. A History of the Beja tribes of the Sudan (Cambridge, 1954).

SELIGMAN, C. G. Pagan Tribes of the Nilotic Sudan (London, 1932).

HISTORY

ABBAS, MEKKI. The Sudan Question: the Dispute about the Anglo-Egyptian Condominium, 1884-1951 (London, 1952).

ARKELL, A. J. Outline History of the Sudan (London, 1938); History of the Sudan to 1821 (2nd. ed., London, 1961).

BOAHEN, A. ADU. Britain, the Sahara and the Western Sudan 1788-1816 (Oxford University Press, New York and London, 1964).

COLLINS, ROBERT O. The Southern Sudan 1883-1898 (Yale University Press, 1962).

COLLINS, ROBERT O and TIGNOR, R. L. Egypt and the Sudan (Prentice, New York, 1967).

CORBYN, E. N. Survey of the Anglo-Egyptian Sudan, 1898-1944 (London, 1946).

EPRILE, CECIL, War and Peace in the Sudan 1955-1972 (David and Charles, Devon, England, 1974).

FABUNMI, L. A. The Sudan in Anglo-Egyptian Relations (Longmans, London, 1965).

GRAY, RICHARD. History of the Southern Sudan 1839–89 (Oxford, 1961).

HASSAN, YUSUF FADL. The Arabs and the Sudan (Edinburgh University Press, Edinburgh, 1967).

HENDERSON, K. D. D. Survey of the Anglo-Egyptian Sudan, 1898-1944 (London, 1946).

HOLT, P. M. The Mahdist State in the Sudan: 1881–98 (Oxford University Press, 2nd edn., 1970).

A Modern History of the Sudan (Weidenfeld and Nicolson, London, 1962, Praeger, New York, 1963).

MACMICHAEL, Sir H. A. A History of the Arabs in the Sudan (2 vols., Cambridge, 1922; reprinted Frank Cass, London and Barnes & Noble, New York, 1967).

The Anglo-Egyptian Sudan (London, 1935).

The Sudan (London, 1954).

SABRY, M. Le Soudan Egyptien, 1821-98 (Cairo, 1947).

SANDERSON, G. N. England, Europe and the Upper Nile (Edinburgh University Press, Edinburgh, 1965).

SHIBEIKA, MEKKI. The Sudan in the Century 1819-1919 (Cairo, 1947).

British Policy in the Sudan: 1882–1902 (London, 1952).

The Independent Sudan: The History of a Nation (New York, 1960).

SHINNIE, MARGARET. A Short History of the Sudan up to A.D. 1500 (Khartoum, 1954).

SHINNIE, P. L. Meroe (Thames and Hudson, London, 1967).

THEOBALD, A. B. The Mahdiya: A History of the Anglo-Egyptian Sudan, 1881-1899 (New York, 1951).

Syria

PHYSICAL AND SOCIAL GEOGRAPHY

W. B. Fisher

Before 1918 the term "Syria" was rather loosely applied to the whole of the territory now forming the modern States of Syria, the Lebanon, Israel and Jordan. To the Ottomans, as to the Romans, Syria stretched from the Euphrates to the Mediterranean, and from the Sinai to the hills of southern Turkey, with Palestine as a smaller province of this wider unit. Though the present Syrian Arab Republic has a much more limited extension, an echo of the past remains to colour the political thinking of a few present-day Syrians and from time to time there are references to a "Greater Syria" as a desirable but possibly remote aspiration.

The frontiers of the present-day State are largely artificial, and reflect to a considerable extent the interests and prestige of outside Powers—Britain, France, and the United States—as these existed in 1918-20. The northern frontier with Turkey is defined by a single-track railway line running along the southern edge of the foothills—probably the only case of its kind in the world; whilst eastwards and southwards boundaries are highly arbitrary, being straight lines drawn for convenience between salient points. Westwards, the frontiers are again artificial, though less crudely drawn, leaving the headwaters of the Jordan river outside Syria and following the crest of the Anti-Lebanon hills, to reach the sea north of Tripoli.

PHYSICAL FEATURES

Geographically, Syria consists of two main zones: a fairly narrow western part, made up of a complex of mountain ranges and intervening valleys; and a much larger eastern zone that is essentially a broad and open platform dropping gently towards the east and crossed diagonally by the wide Euphrates Valley.

The western zone, which contains over 80 per cent of the population of Syria, can be further subdivided as follows. In the extreme west, fronting the Mediterranean Sea, there lies an imposing ridge rising to 5,000 feet, and known as the Jebel Ansariyeh. Its western flank drops fairly gradually to the sea, giving a narrow coastal plain; but on the east it falls very sharply, alsmost as a wall, to a flat-bottomed valley occupied by the Orontes river, which meanders sluggishly over the flat floor, often flooding in winter, and leaving a malarial marsh in summer. Farther east lie more hill ranges, opening out like a fan from the south-west, where the Anti-Lebanon range, with Mount Hermon (9,000 ft.), is the highest in Syria. Along the eastern flanks of the various ridges lie a number of shallow basins occupied by small streams that eventually dry up or form closed salt lakes. In one basin lies the city of Aleppo, once the second town of the Ottoman Empire and still close to being the largest city of Syria. In another is situated Damascus,

irrigated from five streams, and famous for its clear fountains and gardens—now the capital of the country. One remaining sub-region of western Syria is the Jebel Druse, which lies in the extreme south-west, and consists of a vast out-pouring of lava, in the form of sheets and cones. Towards the west this region is fertile, and produces good cereal crops, but eastwards the soil cover disappears, leaving a barren countryside of twisted lava and caverns, for long the refuge of outlaws, bandits, and minority groups. Because of its difficulty and isolation the Jebel Druse has tended socially and politically to go its own way, remaining aloof from the rest of the country.

The entire eastern zone is mainly steppe or open desert, except close to the banks of the river Euphrates, Tigris, and their larger tributaries, where local irrigation projects have allowed a little cultivation. The triangularly-shaped region between the Euphrates and Tigris rivers is spoken of as the Jezireh (Arabic *Jazira* = island), but it is in no way different from the remaining parts of the east.

The presence of ranks of relatively high hills aligned parallel to the coast has important climatic effects. Tempering and humid effects from the Mediterranean are restricted to a narrow western belt, and central and eastern Syria show marked continental tendencies: that is, a very hot summer with temperatures often above 100° or even 110° F., and a moderately cold winter, with frost on many nights. Very close to the Mediterranean, frost is unknown at any season, but on the hills altitude greatly reduces the average temperature, so that snow may lie on the heights from late December to April, or even May. Rainfall is fairly abundant in the west, where the height of the land tends to determine the amount received; but east of the Anti-Lebanon mountains the amount decreases considerably, producing a steppe region that quickly passes into true desert. On the extreme east, as the Zagros ranges of Persia are approached, there is once again a slight increase, but most of Syria has an annual rainfall of under ten inches.

ECONOMIC LIFE

There is a close relationship between climate and economic activities. In the west, where up to 30 or even 40 inches of rainfall occur, settled farming is possible, and the main limitation is difficult terrain; but from the Orontes Valley eastwards natural rainfall is increasingly inadequate, and irrigation become necessary. The narrow band of territory where annual rainfall lies between 8 and 15 inches is sometimes spoken of as the "Fertile Crescent", since it runs in an arc along the inner side of the hills from Jordan though western and northern Syria as far east as Iraq. In its normal state a steppeland covered with seasonal grass, the Fertile Crescent can often be converted by irrigation and efficient organization into a rich and productive territory. Such it was in the golden days of the Arab Caliphate; now, after centuries of decline, it is once again reviving. From the 1940s to the 1950s a marked change was seen and, thanks to small-scale irrigation schemes and the installation of motor pumps to raise water from underground artesian sources, large areas of the former steppe are producing crops of cotton, cereals and fruit. Syria has now a surplus of agricultural production, especially cereals, and this allows her to export to Jordan and the Lebanon, neither of which are self-sufficient in food-stuffs. Production will increase with the eventual doubling of Syria's irrigated area (by 640,000 hectares) as the Euphrates Dam at Tabqa (inaugurated 1973) develops fully.

Because of its relative openness and accessibility and its geographical situation as a "waist" between the Mediterranean and the Persian Gulf, Syria has been a land of passage, and for centuries its role was that of an intermediary, both commercial and cultural, between the Mediterranean world and the Far East. From early times until the end of the Middle Ages there was a flow of traffic east and west

that raised a number of Syrian cities and ports to the rank of international markets. Since the 1930s, following a long period of decline and eclipse resulting from the diversion of this trade to the sea, there has been a revival of activity due to the new elements of air transport and the construction of oil pipelines from Iraq.

RACE AND LANGUAGE

Racially, we can distinguish many elements in the Syrian people. The nomads of the interior deserts are unusually pure specimens of the Mediterranean type, isolation having preserved them from intermixture. To the west and north there is a widely varying mosaic of other groups: Armenoids, such as the Kurds and Turkish-speaking communities of the north, and the Armenians themselves, who form communities in the cities; groups such as the Druzes, who show some affinity to the tribes of the Persian Zagros, and many others.

As a result, there is a surprising variety of language and religion. Arabic is spoken over most of the country, but Kurdish is widely used along the northern frontier and Armenian in the cities. Aramaic, the language of Christ, survives in three villages.

HISTORY

ANCIENT HISTORY

From the earliest times, Syria has experienced successive waves of Semitic immigration—the Canaanites and Phoenicians in the third millennium B.C., the Hebrews and Aramaeans in the second, and, unceasingly, the nomad tribes infiltrating from the Arabian peninsula. This process has enabled Syria to assimilate or reject, without losing its essentially Semitic character, the alien invaders who, time and again, in the course of a long history, have established their domination over the land. Before Rome assumed control of Syria in the first century B.C., the Egyptians, the Assyrians and the Hittites, and, later, the Persians and the Macedonian Greeks had all left their mark in greater or lesser degree. Damascus is claimed to be the oldest capital city in the world, having been continuously inhabited since about 2000 B.C., and Aleppo may be even older. Under Roman rule the infiltration and settlement of nomad elements continued, almost unnoticed by historians, save when along the desert trade routes a Semitic vassal state attained a brief importance as, for example, the kingdom of Palmyra in the Syrian desert, which the Emperor Aurelian destroyed in A.D. 272 or, later still, when the Byzantines ruled in Syria, the Arab State of Ghassan, prominent throughout the sixth century A.D. as a bulwark of the Byzantine Empire against the desert tribes in the service of Sasanid Persia.

ARAB AND TURKISH RULE

When, after the death of the Prophet Muhammad in A.D. 632, the newly-created power of Islam began a career of conquest, the populations of Syria, Semitic in their language and culture and, as adherents of the Monophysite faith, ill-disposed towards the Greek-speaking Orthodox Byzantines, did little to oppose the Muslims, from whom they hoped to obtain a greater measure of freedom. The Muslims defeated the Byzantine forces at Ajnadain in

July 634, seized Damascus in September 635, and, by their decisive victory on the River Yarmuk (August 636), virtually secured possession of all Syria. From 661–750 the Umayyad dynasty ruled in Syria, which, after the conquest, had been divided into four military districts or junds (Damascus, Homs, Urdun, i.e. Jordan, and Palestine). To these the Caliph Yazid I (680–83) added a fifth, Kinnasrin, for the defence of northern Syria, where in the late seventh century, the Mardaites, Christians from the Taurus, were making serious inroads under Byzantine leadership. Under Abd al-Malik (685–705) Arabic became the official language of the State, in whose administration, hitherto largely carried out by the old Byzantine bureaucracy, Syrians, Muslim as well as Christian, now had an increasing share. For Syria was now the heart of a great Empire, and the Arab Army of Syria, well trained in the ceaseless frontier warfare with Byzantium, bore the main burden of imperial rule, taking a major part in the two great Arab assaults on Byzantium in 674–8 and in 717–18.

The new regime in Syria was pre-eminently military and fiscal in character, representing the domination of a military caste of Muslim Arab warriors, who governed on the basic assumption that a large subject population, non-Muslim and non-Arab in character, would continue indefinitely to pay tribute. But this assumption was falsified by the gradual spread of Islam, a process which meant the progressive diminution of the amount of tribute paid to the State, and the consequent undermining of the fiscal system as a whole. In theory, conversion meant for the non-Arab convert (*Mawla*; in the plural, *Mawali*) full social and economic equality with the ruling caste, but in practice it was not enough to be a Muslim, one had to be an Arab as well. The discontent of the *Mawali* with their enforced inferiority expressed itself in an appeal to the universal character of Islam, an appeal which often took the form of religious heresies, and which, as it became more widespread, undermined the strength of the Arab régime.

To the ever present fiscal problems of the Arab State and the growing discontent of the *Mawali* was added a third and fatal weakness: the hostility between those Arab tribes which had arrived in Syria with or since the conquest, and those which had infiltrated there at an earlier date. The Umayyad house strove to maintain a neutral position over and above the tribal feuds; but from the moment when, under the pressure of events, the Umayyads were compelled to side with one faction to oppose the other (battle of Marj Rahit 684), their position was irretrievably compromised.

When in A.D. 750 with the accession of the Abbasid dynasty the centre of the Empire was transferred to Iraq, Syria, jealously watched because of its association with the former ruling house, became a mere province, where in the course of the next hundred years, several abortive revolts, inspired in part by the traditional loyalty to the Umayyads, failed to shake off Abbasid control. During the ninth century Syria was the object of dispute between Egypt and Baghdad. In 878 Ahmad ibn Tulun, Governor of Egypt, occupied it and, subsequently, every independent ruler of Egypt sought to maintain a hold, partial or complete, over Syria. Local dynasties, however, achieved from time to time a transitory importance, as did the Hamdanids (a Bedouin family from Northern Iraq) who, under Saif ad-Daula, ruler of Aleppo from 946–967, attained a brief ascendancy, marked internally by financial and administrative ineptitude, and externally by military campaigns against the Byzantines which did much to provoke the great Byzantine reconquest of the late tenth century. By the treaty of 997, northern Syria became Byzantine, while the rest of the country remained in the hands of the Fatimid dynasty which ruled in Egypt from 969. Fatimid control remained insecure and from about 1027 a new Arab house ruled at Aleppo—the Mirdasids, who were soon to disappear before the formidable power of the Seljuq Turks. The Seljuqs, having conquered Persia, rapidly overran Syria (Damascus fell to them in 1075) but failed to establish there a united State. As a result of dynastic quarrels, the Seljuq domination disintegrated into a number of amirates: Seljuq princes ruled at Aleppo and Damascus, a local dynasty held Tripoli and, in the south, Egypt controlled most of the littoral.

This political fragmentation greatly favoured the success of the First Crusade which, taking Antioch in 1098 and Jerusalem in 1099, proceeded to organize four feudal States at Edessa, Antioch, Tripoli and Jerusalem, but did not succeed in conquering Aleppo, Homs, Hama, and Damascus. From the death of Baldwin II of Jerusalem in 1131, the essential weakness of the crusading States began to appear. Byzantium, the Christian State of Lesser Armenia, and the Latin principalities in Syria never united in a successful resistance to the Muslim counter-offensive which, initiated by the energetic Turkish general Zangi Atabeg of Mosul, developed rapidly in the third and fourth decades of the century. Zangi, who seized Aleppo in 1128, and the Latin State of Edessa in 1144, was succeeded in 1146 by his able son Nur ad-Din, who by his capture of Damascus in 1154 recreated in Syria a united Muslim Power. On Nur ad-Din's death in 1174, the Kurd Saladin, already master of Egypt, assumed control at Damascus and, in 1183, seized Aleppo. His victory over the Crusaders at Hattin (July 1187) destroyed the kingdom of Jerusalem. Only the partial success of the Third Crusade (1189–92) and, after his death in 1193, the disintegration of Saladin's Empire into a number of separate principalities, made it possible for the Crusaders to maintain an ever more precarious hold on the coastal areas of Syria. The emergence in Egypt of the powerful Mamluk Sultanate (1250) meant that the end was near. A series of military campaigns, led by the Sultan Baibars (1260–77) and his immediate suc-

cessors, brought about the fall of Antioch (1268) and Tripoli (1289), and, with the fall of Acre in 1291, the disappearance of the crusading States in Syria.

Before the last crusading States had been reduced, the Mamluks had to encounter a determined assault by the Mongols, in the course of which Aleppo and Hama were sacked, and Damascus besieged; until, in 1260, the Mongol army of invasion was crushed at the battle of Ain-Jalut, near Nazareth. The Mongol Il-Khans of Persia made further efforts to conquer Syria in the late thirteenth century, negotiating for this purpose with the Papacy, the remaining crusader States, and Lesser Armenia. In 1280 the Mamluks defeated a Mongol army at Homs; but in 1299 were themselves beaten near the same town, a defeat which enabled the Mongols to ravage northern Syria and to take Damascus in 1300. Only in 1303, at the battle of Marj as-Suffar, south of Damascus, was this last Mongol offensive finally repelled.

The period of Mamluk rule in Syria, which endured until 1517, was on the whole one of slow decline. Warfare, periodical famine, and not least, the plague (there were four great outbreaks in the fourteenth century, and in the fifteenth century fourteen more recorded attacks of some severity) produced a state of affairs which the financial rapacity and misrule of the Mamluk governors and the devastation of Aleppo and Damascus by Timur (1400–01) served only to aggravate.

The ill-defined protectorate which the Mamluks asserted over Cilicia and considerable areas of southern Anatolia occasioned, in the late fifteenth century, a growing tension with the power of the Ottoman Turks, which broke out into inconclusive warfare in the years 1485–91. When to this tension was added the possibility of an alliance between the Mamluks and the rising power of the Safavids in Persia, the Ottoman Sultan Selim I (1512–20) was compelled to seek a decisive solution to the problem. In August 1516 the battle of Marj Dabik, north of Aleppo, gave Syria to the Ottomans, who proceeded to ensure their continued hold on the land by conquering Egypt (1517). Turkish rule, during the next three centuries, although unjustly accused of complete responsibility for a decay and stagnation which appear to have been well advanced before 1517, brought only a temporary improvement in the unhappy condition of Syria, now divided into the three provinces of Damascus, Tripoli, and Aleppo. In parts of Syria the Turkish pashas in reality administered directly only the important towns and their immediate neighbourhood; elsewhere, the older elements—Bedouin emirs, Turcoman chiefs, etc.—were left to act much as they pleased, provided the due tribute was paid. The pashas normally bought their appointment to high office and sought in their brief tenure of power to recover the money and bribes they had expended in securing it, knowing that they might, at any moment, be replaced by someone who could pay more for the post. Damascus alone had 133 pashas in 180 years. As the control of the Sultan at Constantinople became weaker, the pashas obtained greater freedom of action, until Ahmed Jazzar, Pasha of Acre, virtually ruled Syria as an independent prince (1785–1804).

The nineteenth century saw important changes. The Ottoman Sultan Mahmud II (1808–39) had promised Syria to the Pasha of Egypt, Muhammad Ali, in return for the latter's services during the Greek War of Independence. When the Sultan declined to fulfil his promise, Egyptian troops overran Syria (1831–33). Ibrahim Pasha, son of Muhammad Ali, now gave to Syria, for the first time in centuries, a centralized government strong enough to hold separatist tendencies in check and to impose a system of taxation which, if burdensome, was at least regular in its functioning. But Ibrahim's rule was not popular, for the landowners resented his efforts to limit their social and political dominance, while the peasantry disliked the conscription, the forced labour, and the heavy taxation which he found indispensable for the maintenance of his regime. In 1840 a revolt broke out in Syria, and when the Great Powers intervened on behalf of the Sultan (at war with Egypt since 1839), Muhammad Ali was compelled to renounce his claim to rule there.

Western influence, working through trade, through the protection of religious minorities, and through the cultural and educational efforts of missions and schools, had received encouragement from Ibrahim Pasha. The French Jesuits, returning to Syria in 1831, opened schools, and in 1875 founded their University at Beirut. The American Presbyterian Mission (established at Beirut in 1820) introduced a printing press in 1834, and in 1866 founded the Syrian Protestant College, later renamed the American University of Beirut. Syria also received some benefit from the reform movement within the Ottoman Empire, which, begun by Mahmud II, and continued under his successors, took the form of a determined attempt to modernize the structure of the Empire. The semi-independent pashas of old disappeared, the administration being now entrusted to salaried officials of the central government; some effort was made to create schools and colleges on Western lines, and much was done to deprive the landowning classes of their feudal privileges, although their social and economic predominance was left unchallenged. As a result of these improvements, there was, in the late nineteenth century, a revival of Arabic literature which did much to prepare the way for the growth of Arab nationalism in the twentieth century.

MODERN HISTORY

By 1914 Arab nationalist sentiment had made some headway among the educated and professional classes, and especially among army officers. Nationalist societies like *Al-Fatat* soon made contact with Arab nationalists outside Syria—with the army officers of Iraq, with influential Syrian colonies in Egypt and America, and with the Sharif Husein of Mecca. The Husein-McMahon Correspondence (July 1915–January 1916) encouraged the Arab nationalists to hope that the end of the Great War would mean the creation of a greater Arab kingdom. This expectation was disappointed, for as a result of the Sykes-Picot Agreement, negotiated in secret between England, France, and Russia in 1916 (*see* Documents on Palestine, page 48), Syria was to become a French sphere of influence. At the end of the war, and in accordance with this agreement, a provisional French administration was established in the coastal districts of Syria, while in the interior an Arab government came into being under Amir Faisal, son of the Sharif Husein of Mecca. In March 1920 the Syrian nationalists proclaimed an independent kingdom of Greater Syria (including the Lebanon and Palestine); but in April of the same year the San Remo Conference gave France a mandate for the whole of Syria, and in July, French troops occupied Damascus.

By 1925 the French, aware that the majority of the Muslim population resented their rule, and that only amongst the Christian Maronites of the Lebanon could they hope to find support, had carried into effect a policy based upon the religious divisions so strong in Syria. The area under mandate had been divided into four distinct units; a much enlarged Lebanon (including Beirut and Tripoli), a Syrian Republic, and the two districts of Latakia and Jebel Druse. Despite the fact that the French rule gave Syria a degree of law and order which might render possible the transition from a medieval to a more modern form of society, nationalist sentiment opposed the mandate on principle, and deplored the failure to introduce full representative institutions and the tendency to encourage separatism amongst the religious minorities. This discontent, especially strong in the Syrian Republic, became open revolt in 1925-26, during the course of which the French twice bombarded Damascus (October 1925 and May 1926).

The next ten years were marked by a hesitant and often interrupted progress towards self-government in Syria, and by French efforts to conclude a Franco-Syrian treaty. In April 1928 elections were held for a Constituent Assembly, and in August a draft Constitution was completed; but the French High Commissioner refused to accept certain articles, especially Article 2, which, declaring the Syrian territories detached from the old Ottoman Empire to be an indivisible unity, constituted a denial of the separate existence of the Jebel Druse, Latakia, and the Lebanese Republic. After repeated attempts to reach a compromise, the High Commissioner dissolved the Assembly in May 1930 and, on his own authority, issued a new Constitution for the State of Syria, much the same as that formerly proposed by the Assembly, but with those modifications which were considered indispensable to the maintenance of French control. After new elections (January 1932) negotiations were begun for a Franco-Syrian treaty, to be modelled on that concluded between England and Iraq in 1930, but no compromise could be found between the French demands and those of the nationalists who, although in a minority, wielded a dominant influence in the Chamber and whose aim was to limit both in time and in place the French military occupation, and to include in Syria the separate areas of Jebel Druse and Latakia. In 1934 the High Commissioner suspended the Chamber indefinitely. Disorders occurred early in 1936 which induced the French to send a Syrian delegation to Paris, where the new Popular Front Government showed itself more sympathetic towards Syrian aspirations than former French governments had been. In September 1936 a Franco-Syrian treaty was signed which recognised the principle of Syrian independence and stipulated that, after ratification, there should be a period of three years during which the apparatus of a fully independent State should be created. The districts of Jebel Druse and Latakia would be annexed to Syria, but would retain special administrations. Other subsidiary agreements reserved to France important military and economic rights in Syria. It seemed that Syria might now enter a period of rapid political development; but the unrest caused by the situation in Palestine, the crisis with Turkey, and the failure of France to ratify the 1936 treaty were responsible, within two years, for the breakdown of these hopes.

In 1921 Turkey had consented to the inclusion of the Sanjak of Alexandretta in the French mandated territories, on condition that it should be governed under a special regime. The Turks, alarmed by the treaty of 1936, which envisaged the emergence of a unitary Syrian State including, to all appearance, Alexandretta, now pressed for a separate agreement concerning the status of the Sanjak. After long discussion the League of Nations decided in 1937 that the Sanjak should be fully autonomous, save for its foreign and financial policies which were to be under the control of the Syrian Government. A treaty between France and Turkey guaranteed the integrity of the Sanjak, and also the Turco-Syrian frontier. Throughout 1937 there were conflicts between Turks and Arabs in the Sanjak, and in Syria a widespread and growing resentment, for it was clear that sooner or later Turkey would ask for the cession of Alexandretta. The problem came to be regarded in Syria as a test of Franco-Syrian co-operation, and when in June 1939, under the pressure of international tension, Alexandretta was finally ceded to Turkey, the cession assumed in the eyes of Syrian nationalists the character of a betrayal by France. Meanwhile, in France itself, opposition to the treaty of 1936 had grown steadily; and in

December 1938 the French Government, anxious not to weaken its military position in the Near East, declared that no ratification of the treaty was to be expected.

Unrest in Syria led to open riots in 1941, as a result of which the Vichy High Commissioner, General Dentz, promised the restoration of partial self-government; while in June of the same year, when in order to combat Axis intrigues the Allies invaded Syria, General Catroux, on behalf of the Free French Government, promised independence for Syria and the end of mandatory rule. Syrian independence was formally recognized in September 1941, but the reality of power was still withheld, with the effect that nationalist agitation, inflamed by French reluctance to restore constitutional rule, and by economic difficulties due to the war, became even more pronounced. When at last elections were held once more, a nationalist government was formed, with Shukri al-Kuwatly as President of the Syrian Republic (August 1943).

Gradually all important powers and public services were transferred from French to Syrian hands; but conflict again developed over the *Troupes Spéciales*, the local Syrian and Lebanese levies which had existed throughout the mandatory period as an integral part of the French military forces in the Levant, and which, transferred to the Syrian and Lebanese Governments, would enable them to form their own armies. Other points of dispute were the so-called "Common Interests" (i.e. departments dealing with matters of concern to both Syria and the Lebanon), and the control of internal security, hitherto in French hands. Strongly supported by the newly-created Arab League, Syria refused the French demand for a Franco-Syrian Treaty as the condition for the final transfer of these administrative and military services which had always been the main instruments of French policy. In May 1945 disturbances broke out which ended only with British armed intervention and the evacuation of French troops and administrative personnel. The *Troupes Spéciales* were now handed over to the Syrian Government, and with the departure of British forces in April 1946 the full independence of Syria was at last achieved.

UNSTABLE INDEPENDENCE

Since the attainment of independence Syria has passed through a long period of instability. She was involved in a complicated economic and financial dispute with the Lebanon (1948–50) and also in various schemes for union with Iraq—schemes which tended to divide political opinion inside Syria itself and, in addition, to disrupt the unity of the Arab League. Syria, in fact, found herself aligned at this time with Egypt and Saudi Arabia against the ambitions of the Hashemite rulers of Iraq and Jordan. These rivalries, together with the profound disappointment felt at Damascus over the Arab failures in the war of 1948–49 against Israel, were the prelude to a series of *coups d'état* in Syria: in March 1949, under Colonel Husni Za'im; in August of the same year, under Colonel Sami Hinnawi; and in December 1949, under Lieut.-Colonel Shishakli. Dislike of continued financial dependence on France, aspirations towards a greater Syria, the resentments arising out of the unsuccessful war against the Israelis—all help to explain the unrest inside Syria.

The intervention of the army in politics was itself a cause of further tension. Opposition to the dominance of the army grew in the Syrian Chamber of Deputies to such an extent that yet another *coup d'état* was carried out in December 1951. Syria now came under the control of a military autocracy with Colonel Shishakli as head of the state. The Chamber of Deputies was dissolved in December 1951; a decree of April 1952 abolished all political parties in Syria. After the approval of a new constitution in July

1953 General Shishakli became President of Syria in August of that year. The formation of political parties was now allowed once more. Members of the parties dissolved under the decree of April 1952 proceeded, however, to boycott the elections held in October 1953, at which President Shishakli's Movement of Arab Liberation obtained a large majority in the Chamber of Deputies. Politicians hostile to the regime of President Shishakli established in November 1953 a Front of National Opposition, refusing to accept as legal the results of the October elections and declaring as their avowed aim the end of military autocracy and the restoration of democratic rule. Demonstrations at Damascus and Aleppo in December 1953 led soon to the flight of Shishakli to France. The collapse of his regime early in 1954 meant for Syria a return to the Constitution of 1950. New elections held in September 1954 brought into being a Chamber of Deputies notable for the large number of its members (81 out of 142) who might be regarded as independents grouped around leading political figures.

INFLUENCE FROM ABROAD

There was still, however, much friction in Syria between those who favoured union or at least close co-operation with Iraq and those inclined towards an effective *entente* with Egypt. In August 1955 Shukri al-Kuwatli became President of the Republic. His appointment was interpreted as an indication that pro-Egyptian influence had won the ascendancy in Syria. On October 20th, 1955, Syria made with Egypt an agreement for the creation of a joint military command with its headquarters at Damascus.

The U.S.S.R., meanwhile, in answer to the developments in the Middle East associated with the Baghdad Pact, had begun an intensive diplomatic, propaganda and economic campaign of penetration into the Arab lands. In the years 1954–56 Syria, the only Arab state where the Communist Party was legal, made a number of barter agreements with the Soviet Union and its associates in eastern Europe. A report from Cairo intimated, in February 1956, that Syria had joined Egypt in accepting arms from U.S.S.R.

At the end of October 1956 there occurred the Israeli campaign in the Sinai peninsula, an event followed, in the first days of November, by the armed intervention of Great Britain and France in the Suez Canal region. On October 30th the President of the Syrian Republic left Damascus on a visit to the Soviet Union. A state of emergency was declared in Syria. Reports from Beirut revealed on November 3rd that Syrian forces had put out of action the pipelines which carried Iraqi oil to the Mediterranean. The damage that Syrian elements had done to the pipelines earned the sharp disapproval of such Arab states as Iraq and Saudi Arabia, both of whom were now faced with a severe loss of oil revenues. The Syrian Government declared that it would not allow the repair of the pipelines until Israel had withdrawn her troops from Gaza and the Gulf of Aqaba. Not until March 1957 was it possible to restore the pipelines, Israel having in the meantime agreed to evacuate her forces from the areas in dispute.

In April 1957 a crisis took place in Jordan where the Palestinian elements in political circles, with some support from the army, sought to draw Jordan into alignment with Egypt and Syria. At the time of the Sinai-Suez crisis in November 1956 contingents of Syrian troops had been stationed in Jordan. These troops were still on Jordanian soil. There were also reports that reinforcements might be sent to the Syrian forces in Jordan. It seemed that a major intervention in the affairs of Jordan was imminent. On April 24th the U.S.A. announced that it regarded the independence and integrity of Jordan as a matter of vital concern. The United States Sixth Fleet was now ordered to the eastern Mediterranean with instructions to assist

Jordan, if aid were requested. At the same time the U.S. Government deplored the flow of Soviet arms and equipment to Egypt and Syria. In May 1957 Syria stated that, in compliance with a request from Amman, she would withdraw her forces from Jordan.

UNION WITH EGYPT

The Syrian National Assembly, in November 1957, passed a resolution in favour of union with Egypt. Earlier in the year there had been discussions concerning proposals for a customs union between the two countries and for the co-ordination of their currencies and of their economic policies. The formal union of Egypt and Syria to constitute one state under the title of the United Arab Republic received the final approval of the Syrian National Assembly on February 5th, 1958. President Nasser of Egypt, on February 21st, became the first head of the combined state. A central cabinet for the U.A.R. was established in October 1958, also two regional executive councils, one for Syria and one for Egypt. A further move towards integration came in March 1960, when President Nasser announced the formation of a single National Assembly for the whole of the U.A.R. The Assembly, consisting of 400 deputies from Egypt and 200 from Syria, held its first meeting at Cairo on July 21st, 1960.

The more extreme elements of the right and of the left— e.g. the conservative class of landowners and also the Communist following in Syria—had viewed with distrust the union of Syria and Egypt. Amongst the Baath Socialists, who had played an important role in bringing about the merger with Egypt in 1958, dissatisfaction grew as a result of the small progress made with schemes for the socialization of the Syrian economy. There was disillusionment, too, in the Syrian armed forces over the more and more frequent transfer of Syrian officers to Egypt and of Egyptian officers to Syria. Administrators and officials of Egyptian origin had come, moreover, to hold a large number of the most influential positions in the Syrian Region of the U.A.R. Syria still retained, however, at the end of 1960 and in the first months of 1961, a considerable measure of autonomy in most economic matters.

August 1961 saw the abolition of the regional executive councils for Syria and Egypt created in 1958. This attempt to hasten the integration of the two countries was the prelude to a new crisis at Damascus. On September 28th, 1961, there occurred in Syria a military *coup d'état* which aimed—successfully—at the separation of Syria from Egypt and at the dissolution of the United Arab Republic. Political figures representing most of the parties which existed in Syria before the establishment of the U.A.R. in 1958 met at Damascus and Aleppo on October 3rd, 1961, issuing a declaration of support for the new regime and calling for free elections to a new legislature. Syrian members of the National Assembly of the U.A.R. gathered at Damascus on October 4th to denounce the arbitrary and dictatorial character of the control previously exercised from Cairo over Syrian affairs. President Nasser now, on October 5th, recognized the *fait accompli*. Most foreign states made haste to grant formal recognition to the government at Damascus. On October 13th, 1961, Syria became once more a member of the United Nations. A provisional constitution was promulgated in November and elections for a Constituent Assembly took place on December 1st, 1961.

The regime thus established in Syria rested on no sure foundation. At the end of March 1962 the Syrian Army intervened once more, bringing about the resignation of Dr. Nazim Kudsi, the President of the Republic, and also of the ministers who had taken office in December 1961. After demonstrations at Aleppo, Homs and Hama in April 1962, Dr. Kudsi was reinstated as President, but further ministerial resignations in May of that year pointed to the existence of continuing tensions within the government.

THE REVOLUTION OF 1963

A military junta, styled the National Council of the Revolutionary Command, seized control in Damascus on March 8th, 1963. During March and April 1963 tension was visible between those elements which advocated a close association with Egypt and those Baathist circles which tended to oppose such a programme. In May 1963 the Baathists took measures to purge the armed forces and the administration of personnel known to favour a close alignment with Egypt. A new government, formed on May 13th and strongly Baathist in character, carried out a further purge in June and at the same time created a National Guard recruited from members of the Baath movement. These measures led the pro-Egyptian elements to attempt a *coup d'état* at Damascus on July 18th, 1963. The attempt failed, however, with a considerable loss of life. On July 27th Major-Gen. Amin al-Hafiz, Deputy Prime Minister and Minister of the Interior, became President of the National Council of the Revolutionary Command, a position equivalent to Head of State.

There were, in the second half of 1963, a number of moves designed to bring about some form of union between Syria and Iraq, but they were doomed to disappointment. A *coup d'état* at Baghdad in November 1963 swept aside the Baath régime in Iraq.

BAATH SOCIALISM

The Syrian Government, in May 1963, had nationalized all Arab-owned banks in Syria and in August of that year proceeded to order their reduction into fewer but larger units with new boards set in charge of them. Government decrees issued in April 1964 nationalized a number of textile factories at Aleppo. The factories would henceforward be under the control of elected representatives of the employees, together with representatives of the Government, of al-Baath and of the trade unions. The principle of "self-management" in industrial concerns, and also in agriculture, had received approval at the international Baath conference of October 1963.

The nationalization of the banks and of various industrial enterprises, also the transfer of land to the peasants—all had contributed to bring about much dissatisfaction in the business world and amongst the influential landed elements. The Baath regime depended for its main support on the armed forces (purged of the personnel opposed to the policies of the government). These forces, however, had been recruited in no small degree from the religious minorities in Syria, including adherents of the Shi'i (Alawi) faith—most Syrians being, in fact, of Sunni or orthodox Muslim allegiance. In general, conservative Muslims tended to oppose the Baath government under guidance of the *'ulama* and of the Muslim Brotherhood. The mass of the peasant population was thought to have some pro-Nasser sympathies; the working class (small in number) was divided between pro-Nasser and Baathist adherents; the middle and upper classes opposed the domination of al-Baath. The unease arising out of these frictions and antipathies took the form of disturbances at Banias and Homs (February 1964), at Aleppo (March 1964) and finally of open revolt—soon suppressed—at Hama (April 1964).

On April 25th, 1964, a provisional constitution had been promulgated, describing Syria as a democratic socialist republic forming an integral part of the Arab nation. A Presidential Council was established on May 14th, 1964, with General Hafiz as head of the state.

A government decree of December 23rd, 1964, nationalized the as yet undeveloped petroleum and other mineral resources of Syria. Early in January 1965 the Syrian Government placed under national control, wholly or in part, industrial concerns connected with cement, dyes, textiles, sugar, canning, food production, chemicals and soap. On January 7th, 1965, a special military court was created with sweeping powers to deal with all offences, of word or deed, against the nationalization decrees and the socialist revolution. These new measures evoked once more a series of demonstrations and a strike of shopkeepers in Damascus (January 24th, 1965). Further government decrees now confiscated the goods and properties of merchants held to be responsible for the disorders. General Hafiz denounced the 'ulama and the Muslim Brotherhood as being involved in the demonstrations. On February 19th, 1965, further decrees nationalized about forty pharmaceutical importing establishments at Damascus and Aleppo, together with a number of other trading companies. The official Importing and Exporting Organization was now alone able to import basic commodities such as tea, tinned meats, fish, rubber, iron, timber, textiles, tractors cars, drugs, fertilizers, salt, tobacco and paper.

The autumn of 1965 saw a number of important changes inside Syria. A National Council, almost one hundred strong, was established in August with the task of preparing a new constitution which would be submitted to a public referendum. Meeting for the first time on September 1st, 1965, it created a Presidency Council, of five members, which was to exercise the powers of a head of state.

RADICAL REACTION

The tensions hitherto visible in al-Baath were, however, still active. Two groups stood ranged one against the other—on the one hand the older more experienced politicians in al-Baath, less inclined than in former years to insist on the unrestrained pursuit of the main Baathist objectives, socialism and pan-Arab union, and on the other hand the extreme left-wing elements, doctrinaire in their attitude and enjoying considerable support amongst the younger radical officers in the armed forces.

The tensions thus engendered found expression in a new coup d'état on February 23rd, 1966. A military junta representing the extreme radical elements in al-Baath seized power in Damascus and placed under arrest a number of personalities long identified with al-Baath and belonging to the international leadership controlling the organization throughout the Arab world—amongst them Mr. Michael Aflaq, the founder of al-Baath; General Hafiz, the chairman of the recently established Presidency Council; and Mr. Salah al-Din Bitar, the Prime Minister of the displaced administration.

The new Prime Minister of Syria, Dr. Yusuf Zeayen, visited the U.S.S.R. in April 1966. Russia then granted Syria a loan of about £50 million for the construction of a great dam, about a mile long, on the River Euphrates at Tabqa in northern Syria. The dam—built with Soviet technical assistance—is a major factor in a long-term project of development designed to double Syria's irrigated area in 20 years and triple it by the end of the century and to make possible a notable increase in the production of cotton. The dam is also able to produce large quantities of hydro-electric power.

Reports current in July 1966 indicated that the government at Damascus had arrested a number of politicians, amongst them personalities associated with the former National and People's Parties. On September 6th the Syrian Government announced that it had discovered and foiled a conspiracy against itself. The conspiracy was said to have been prepared by Baathist elements representing the regime evicted from power in the coup d'état of

February 1966. Of the personalities charged with involvement in the conspiracy the most prominent were Mr. Michel Aflaq, the founder of al-Baath; Mr. Salah al-Din Bitar, a former Prime Minister; and Dr. Munif al-Razzaz, at one time the Secretary-General of the International Baathist Organization. Also said to be implicated in the conspiracy were military elements supporting General Hafiz, the head of the preceding regime.

A delegation led by Dr. Yusuf Zeayen, the Prime Minister of Syria, visited Cairo on November 1st, 1966. On November 4th the United Arab Republic and Syria entered into a defence agreement for military co-ordination between the two countries. The agreement stipulated that aggression against either state would be considered as an assault on the other, to be repelled by the armed forces of the U.A.R. and of Syria acting together. A defence council and a joint military command were to be established under the terms of the agreement.

ARAB-ISRAELI WAR OF 1967

The friction ever present along the frontier between Syria and Israel had flared out from time to time during recent years into violent conflict—e.g. in March 1962 (Lake Tiberias), August 1963 (Huleh), November 1964 (Dan), August 1965 (Khirbet, north of Lake Tiberias), February 1966 (al-Dardara), May 1966 (Lake Tiberias) and July 1966 (again in the region of Lake Tiberias). Now, in the winter of 1966–67, the tension along the border began to assume more serious proportions. Israel, in October 1966, complained to the Security Council of the United Nations about guerilla activities from Syria across the frontier into Israeli territory. There was renewed violence near Lake Tiberias in January 1967. U Thant, in this same month, urged Syria and Israel to act with restraint and suggested that a special meeting be arranged of the Syrian-Israeli mixed armistice commission. This commission—which had not been convened since 1959—began its new discussions on January 25th, 1967. With further incidents occurring along the border, these discussions made no significant progress and came to an end on February 17th, 1967. There was a more serious outbreak of violence during April 1967, tanks, mortars, cannon and air force units from Syria and Israel being involved in fighting south-east of Lake Tiberias.

The continuing tension on the Syrian-Israeli frontier was now to become a major influence leading to the war which broke out on June 5th, 1967, between Israel and her Arab neighbours Egypt, Syria and Jordan. During the course of hostilities which lasted six days Israel defeated Egypt and Jordan and then, after some stubborn fighting, outflanked and overran the Syrian positions on the hills above Lake Tiberias. With the breakthrough accomplished, Israeli forces made a rapid advance and occupied the town of Quneitra about forty miles from Damascus. On June 10th Israel and Syria announced their formal acceptance of the United Nations proposal for a cease-fire. UN observers were stationed on both sides of the line then existing between the Israeli and Syrian forces. The UN truce supervision control was established at Quneitra.

During the period following the war, Syria opposed all attempts to reach a compromise solution and in effect boycotted the Arab summit conference held at Khartoum in August 1967. In September, the Baath party of Syria rejected all idea of a compromise with Israel, expressed its full support for the Yemen Republic and for the Arab nationalists in South Arabia and called on the Arab states in general to maintain a diplomatic, economic and cultural boycott of the United States, the United Kingdom and the Federal Republic of Germany.

A British resolution urging the withdrawal of the Israelis from the lands occupied by them during the June war and the ending of the belligerency which the Arab governments had up till then maintained against Israel, was adopted by the U.N. Security Council in November 1967. However, the resolution was immediately rejected by Syria, which alone maintained its commitment to a reunified Palestine.

STRUGGLE FOR POWER 1968-71

The ruling Baath Party had for some years been divided into two main factions. Until October 1968 the dominant faction had been the "progressive" group led by Dr. Atassi and Dr. Makhous, the Premier and Foreign Minister respectively. This group was distinguished by its doctrinaire and Marxist-orientated public pronouncements (not always put into effect despite its control of the government) and by the strong support it received from the U.S.S.R. It held that the creation of a strong one-party state and economy along neo-Marxist lines was of paramount importance, overriding even the need for a militant stand towards Israel and for Arab unity.

By October 1968 the government felt particularly insecure, partly owing to a feud with the new Baath régime in Iraq, and at the end of the month a new cabinet was formed including several members of the opposing "nationalist" faction. This group took less interest in ideological questions and favoured a pragmatic attitude to the economy, improved relations with Syria's Arab neighbours and full participation in the campaign against Israel, including support for the fedayeen movement. Its leader was Lt.-Gen. Hafiz al-Assad, who assumed the all-important Ministry of Defence. His critical attitude to the powerful Soviet influence on the government, seen by some "nationalists" as tantamount to colonialism in restricting Syria's freedom of action, led to a prolonged struggle with the "progressive" leadership. Cabinet reshuffles took place in March and again in May, but both Dr. Atassi and General Assad retained their positions. During the spring of 1969 a number of Communists were arrested or sent into exile, and the leader of the Syrian Communist Party, still technically an illegal organization, flew to Moscow.

General Assad attempted to take over the government in February 1969 but was forestalled by Soviet threats that if he did so all military supplies (including spares), economic and technical aid, and trade agreements would end. This would have brought about a major disruption in the national economy and the armed forces, and the "nationalists" were obliged to yield. In May General Mustafa Tlas, the Army Chief of Staff and General Assad's right-hand man, led a military delegation to Peking to buy arms. Some Chinese weapons were reported to be delivered in July. The incident indicated a new independence of Moscow. Some observers also saw this independence in the creation of a joint military command with Iraq (with whom relations improved during the spring) and Jordan. Relations with the Lebanon worsened, owing to Syria's support of the Lebanese fedayeen movement, which has many Syrian members. In the 1968–70 period this appeared to direct much of its activity towards bringing down the precarious Lebanese Government, presumably in the hope that a more militantly anti-Israel ministry would take power. Syria did, however, grant diplomatic recognition to the German Democratic Republic (East Germany) in June, and refused to resume diplomatic relations with Britain and the U.S.A. In May it was announced that a general election would be held in September, the first for seven years, but in August the elections were postponed indefinitely.

During the year 1969–70 there was some revival of activity on the front with Israel. Several air battles took place, and there was an extensive surface conflict involving tanks in June 1970; as usual, both sides claimed sweeping victories. Syria consistently supported the guerrilla forces in their struggle with the Jordan government, although guerrillas on Syrian territory seem to be allowed little freedom to manoeuvre.

In the spring of 1970 the Syrian section of the Tapline pipeline was put out of action, apparently by an accident. Syria refused to allow repairs, claiming that these operations would be dangerous as the section affected lies near Israeli-occupied territory. Since the pipeline and the crude oil it transports are American owned, the refusal was commonly seen as an attempt to put pressure on the United States and its Middle East policy. There was no official American reaction, but Saudi Arabia, as the oil producer affected and in any case at the opposite extreme to Syria in ideology, responded by threatening to abandon the use of Tapline altogether. This would have lost Syria (and the Lebanon and Jordan) considerable sums in transit dues. In January Syria allowed repairs to the pipeline to be started, after increased transit fees had apparently been conceded by Tapline.

In November 1970, following a reported *coup* attempt backed by Iraq in August, the struggle between the two factions of the Baath Party came to a head when General Assad seized power. Dr. Atassi, who was in hospital at the time, was placed under guard and a retired General, Salah Jadid, Assistant Secretary-General of the Baath Party and leader of the civilian faction, was arrested. Other members of the civilian wing were arrested or fled to the Lebanon. The coup was precipitated by attempts of Jadid and his supporters (culminating at the emergency session of the Tenth National Pan-Arab Congress of the Party) to oust Assad and Tlas from their posts. This power struggle had become acute as a result of differences over support for the Palestine guerrillas during the fighting with the Jordanian army in September. Jadid and Yusuf Zeayen, a former Prime Minister, controlled the Syrian guerrilla organization, Saiqa, and supported the movement of tanks from Syria into Jordan to support the Palestinian guerrillas' efforts against the Jordanian army. This Assad and the military faction opposed. Their approach to the Palestinian problem was more akin to Nasser's and they wanted to avoid giving any provocation to Israel, because they considered the Syrian armed forces to be unready to offer adequate resistance.

ASSAD IN POWER

There was no obvious opposition to the army takeover. Ahmed Khatib became acting President and General Assad Prime Minister and Party Secretary-General. A new Regional Command of the Baath Party was formed. The old leaders were removed from their posts in a purge which stretched into the new year. Following amendments to the 1969 provisional constitution in February 1971, General Assad was elected President for a seven-year term in March. In the following month General Abdel Rahman Khlefawi became Premier and Mahmoud Ayoubi was appointed Vice-President. In February, the first legislative body in Syria since 1966, the People's Council, was formed. Of its 173 members, 87 represented the Baath Party.

The Nasserite leanings of the new régime in foreign policy soon became apparent (and presumably helped Assad establish some kind of *modus vivendi* with the U.S.S.R.). Although Syria continued to reject the November 1967 UN Security Council resolution, relations with the U.A.R. and Jordan improved, and Syria's isolation in the Arab world was soon reduced. Syria's willingness to join a union with the U.A.R., Sudan and Libya almost immediately became apparent and agreement on federation with Libya and the U.A.R. was reached in April 1971. In the same month the Syrian Government advised the Palestinian guerrillas not to initiate any more operations from the Syrian front.

In September the Federation of Arab Republics was established, following a referendum covering all three countries. The Federation, however, has had little practical effect.

Since coming to power, the Assad régime had increased the army's control over Saiqa. In April 1971 guerrilla operations against Israeli positions from the Syrian front were banned by the Government. Then, at the beginning of July, some guerrilla units were forced out of Syria into south Lebanon and arms destined for them and arriving from Algeria were seized by the Syrian authorities. Yet after the Jordanian Government's final onslaught on the Palestinian guerrillas in north Jordan in July Syria closed her border and in August broke off diplomatic relations when the tension had become so great that tank and artillery clashes developed between the two armies. Egyptian mediation reduced the chances of any more serious conflict developing but diplomatic links remained severed with Jordan until October 1973. Relations with the U.S.S.R. improved during the last half of 1971 and in 1972, and in May Marshal Grechko, the Soviet Defence Minister, visited Damascus. Syria was not prepared, however, to sign a friendship treaty with the U.S.S.R. like Egypt and Iraq. On the other hand, the Syrian Government, which had been broadened in March 1972 to include representatives of parties other than the Baath like the communists, did not follow Egypt's example in July and expel its Soviet advisers.

At the beginning of June 1972, a few hours after the Iraq Government nationalized the Iraq Petroleum Company, the Syrian Government nationalized all IPC installations in Syria and demanded increased payments from the Iraq Government for oil pumped accross Syria by pipeline. A new price agreement was finally negotiated in January 1973.

In December 1972 Maj.-Gen. Khlefawi resigned from the post of Prime Minister for health reasons and a new Government was formed by Mahmoud al-Ayoubi, the Vice-President, with 16 out of 31 government portfolios going to the Baath Party. At the end of January 1973 a draft Constitution was approved by the People's Council and confirmed by a referendum in March. The Sunni Muslims were dissatisfied that the Constitution did not recognize Islam as the State religion, and as a result of their pressure an amendment was passed declaring that the President must be a Muslim. Under the Constitution freedom of belief is guaranteed, with the State respecting all religions, although the Constitution recognizes that Islamic jurisprudence was "a principal source of legislation". In 1972 a National Charter, creating a National Progressive Front, a grouping of the Baath party and its allies, came into being. In May 1973 elections were organized for the new People's Council under the aegis of the Front and 140 out of the 186 seats were won by the Progressive Front while 42 seats were won by Independents and 4 by the Opposition.

Syria helped to improve relations with Jordan by closing down, on September 16th, the "Voice of the Palestine Revolution" radio station, operated by Palestine guerrillas at Deraa, on the Jordanian border. Resumption of diplomatic relations between Syria and Jordan followed in October 1973.

THE FOURTH ARAB-ISRAELI WAR AND ITS AFTERMATH

On the afternoon of October 6th, 1973, Egyptian and Syrian forces launched war against Israel in an effort to regain territories lost in 1967. On both the Egyptian and Syrian fronts complete surprise was achieved, giving the Arabs a strong initial advantage, much of which they subsequently lost. The course of the war is described in "The Arab-Israeli Confrontation 1969–74", pages 34–45. Although Egypt signed a disengagement agreement with Israel on January 18th, 1974, fighting continued on the Syrian front in the Golan Heights area until a disengagement agreement was signed on May 31st, after much diplomacy and travel by the U.S. Secretary of State, Dr. Henry Kissinger. By the terms of the disengagement agreement (*see* "Documents on Palestine" pages 62–64), Syria regained the town of Quneitra, occupied by Israel since 1967. The town is a ruin and remains uninhabited. How it was destroyed remains one of the most bitterly controversial aspects of the aftermath of the war, owing to Syrian claims (backed by a UN investigation which called for a special committee to examine the devastation in November 1974) that Israel had systematically destroyed the town before agreeing to abandon it.

Syria is maintaining a "hard line" policy in the Middle East, especially regarding the Palestinian question, and since the 1973 war it has received vast amounts of Soviet military aid which has fully re-equipped its forces. Contact with Moscow and Eastern European states is extremely close. Syria's strong support for the PLO was vindicated in October 1974 at the Arab Summit in Rabat, Morocco, where the PLO's claim to the West Bank was recognized. Diplomatic relations with the U.S.A., broken off after the 1967 war, were resumed after President Nixon's visit to Damascus in June 1974. Relations with the Federal Republic of Germany were renewed in August 1974. Relations with Jordan, long under severe strain, improved considerably in 1975 after King Hussein visited Damascus in April and Assad visited Amman in June. Jordan and Syria signed a trade pact in July 1975. Syria is attempting to mediate between the warring Christian and Muslim factions in neighbouring Lebanon.

During 1975 the rival Ba'athist régimes of Syria and Iraq were involved in a dispute over the sharing of the waters of the Euphrates River where the giant Euphrates Dam project could, according to Iraq, threaten the water supply of three million Iraqis. Following a Syrian promise to guarantee Iraq's water supply, it was reported in August 1975 that the two governments had reached agreement after mediation by Saudi Arabia.

Since the October 1973 war there has been perpetual tension with Israel along the Golan Heights. The 1,200 UN observers had their mandate renewed in November 1974 and May 1975 for six-month periods amid mounting tension. Syria has openly distrusted Dr. Henry Kissinger's step-by-step method of finding a solution to the problems of a Middle East settlement; its reliance remains on maintaining considerable military power and also subjecting Israel to the maximum amount of diplomatic pressure internationally.

ECONOMIC SURVEY

Syria has been in a constant state of war since independence shortly after World War II. But no war did as much damage to Syria as the October 1973 war with Israel. The Israeli Defence Minister at the time, General Moshe Dayan, is reported to have said that he aimed to finish with Syria once and for all. In an attempt to break the back of Syrian resistance to the Israeli thrust towards Damascus, wave after wave of Israeli warplanes and Israeli warships bombarded targets on the coast—the port of Latakia and the oil terminals of Banias and Tartous—and power and oil refining installations—especially the huge Homs complex in central Syria which is the home of Syria's only refinery and which generates more than 40 per cent of Syria's power needs. Militarily, Syria was not brought to its knees. But economically, these three days of intensive attack in mid-October are estimated to have caused damage worth $1,800 million. The reconstruction effort needed after the war was immense. But Syria was lucky in being a country whose economy is still primarily agricultural with a population whose basic needs are relatively unsophisticated. It was also lucky in that the great majority of its industry, being light and agro-industrial, was spread widely over the country and, outside the Homs complex, it was difficult to pinpoint a target whose importance compensated for the heavy losses in aircraft sustained by the raiders. The exception, of course, was the newly completed Euphrates Dam in the far north east of the country. This was not attacked since its destruction would have been impossible to justify on military grounds as it had not yet made any impact on the economy.

The 1973 war may prove to have been a watershed for the Syrian economy. Three years of political continuity had by the time the war broke out brought to the country the first taste of economic wellbeing whose promise 25 years of political and economic instability had consistently frustrated. If the post-1973 understanding between the State and private enterprise continues, this first taste may develop into a boom. The completion of the huge Euphrates hydro-electric project will consolidate Syrian agriculture. Oil production, although small in comparison with other producers, especially in the Gulf, should help correct the chronic trade deficit. A reduction in military expenditure, if a peace settlement is reached, will free the State of much of the burden which in 1975 was expected to eat up one quarter of overall budget expenditure.

Syria had always been a land of rich agricultural, entrepreneurial and artisan skills and had always been considered of great economic promise. But instability since independence meant that periods of economic boom, usually coinciding with good agricultural harvests, were hastily replaced by lengthy slumps. Each new Government would attempt to repair what it thought were the mistakes of the previous Government. Economic chaos meant a loss of confidence in the country's economic future which led to a mass exodus of capital and skills and a state of lethargy among those who remained. Syrians are hoping now that the tide has turned. They accept State control of the "dominant heights" of the economy and feel that the era of inexperience, ineptitude and inefficiency in the state sector is on its way out and that the state is sincere in its advocacy of co-operation with an independent and protected private sector working within the framework of well-defined limits and policies. Defeat in the face of Israeli successes had checked self-confidence but a new patriotism has developed out of the 1973 war which in economic terms has meant a resurgence of the private sector. Confidence was further enhanced with Government measures early in 1974 aimed at encouraging the return of repatriated Syrian capital and its owners. Guarantees against nationalization and confiscation which, although limited, were available to foreign investors and traders, were expanded and extended to Syrian expatriates. The growing mood of economic self-confidence, already widespread in 1974, had to be weighed against a still relatively top-heavy bureaucracy, a still weak payments position, a heavy defence expenditure burden and some traces of inter-communal conflict. But these were felt to be problems of "form rather than substance" and that solutions to them could be found reasonably quickly now that economic confidence had been restored.

AREA AND POPULATION

Syria covers an area of about 72,000 square miles (185,180 sq. km.), under three-quarters of the size of England, Wales and Scotland. About 45 per cent of the total area is considered arable and the rest consists of bare mountain, desert and pastures suitable only for nomads. Of the total cultivable area of 8.7 million hectares, only 5.9 million hectares, or 68 per cent was cultivated in 1970, making the area under cultivation only 32 per cent of the total area. Official figures put the mid-1974 population (including Palestinian refugees) at 7,121,000. This compares with census totals of 4,565,121 in September 1960 and 6,304,685 in September 1970. Syria's population is growing by 3.3 per cent a year. Of the total population in 1973, 35.9 per cent were aged under 10 and roughly half were under the age of 15.4 years. There has been a continuing movement from village to town, reflected in a 60 per cent increase in the urban population between 1959, when 35 per cent of the population were classified as urban, and 1969, when 40 per cent came in this category. This movement is amply illustrated by the growth of shanty towns along the edges of the large urban centres such as Damascus and Aleppo. The population in Damascus rose from 475,399 in 1959 to 837,000 in 1970 and that of Aleppo rose from 466,026 to 639,000. The total labour force rose from 1,524,552 in September 1970 to 1,688,564 in December 1973, when it was equivalent to 25 per cent of the Syrian population. Of the 1973 labour force, agriculture, forestry, hunting and fishing employed 50.8 per cent (against 49 per cent in 1970), manufacturing and mining employed 10.7 per cent (against 12.5 per cent), trade, catering and hotels 9.3 per cent (against 9.1 per cent) and transport and communications employed 4 per cent, as in 1970.

AGRICULTURE

Agriculture is still the mainstay of the Syrian economy in spite of the existence of a traditionally strong trading sector and relatively successful efforts at industrialization in recent years. It accounts for at least one fifth of the G.D.P. and employs about half the labour force. The main areas of cultivation are a narrow strip of land along the coast from the Lebanese to the Turkish frontiers which enjoys a Mediterranean climate, is exceedingly fertile and produces fruit, olives, tobacco and cotton. East of this strip lies the northward continuation of the Lebanon range of mountains, which falls sharply on the east to the Orontes River valley whose marshes were recently reclaimed to form one of Syria's most fertile areas. This valley joins in central Syria the 100-mile wide steppe-plain which runs from the Jordanian borders northeastwards towards the Euphrates valley and is separated by a range of hills from the plain's northern reaches. The plain is traditionally Syria's major agricultural area, mainly grains-producing, in which are located the main cities, Damascus, Homs, Hama and Aleppo. The importance of this plain is now being rivalled by the Jezira area which lies between the Euphrates in Syria and the Tigris in Iraq. Although fertile lands along the banks of the Euphrates and its tributaries in Syria had previously been cultivated, the Jezira only came into its own in the early 1950s when large scale cotton cultivation was introduced in former pasture lands. This area will vastly increase in importance as the long-term irrigation and land reclamation projects linked with the Euphrates Dam project are carried out.

Agriculture in general has, however, experienced a decline on two fronts, the area of land under cultivation and productivity. Agriculture's share of the G.D.P. fell from 32.2 per cent in 1962 to 25.6 per cent in 1972 despite that year's bumper cereal harvest. Indices collated by the Food and Agriculture Organization of the United Nations (FAO) show that total agricultural production actually fell from 166 to 131 between 1962 and 1972 (base of 100 calculated on average yearly production 1952-6). Calculated on a per caput basis the index fell from 132 to 87 over the same period. The gross product of the agricultural sector rose to £S2,352 million in 1972 from £S1,380 million in 1970, but sank again to £S1,709 million in 1973 (the last year for which figures are available), as a result of poor harvests. The main factors affecting the decline in agriculture have been political. They stem from political instability and the resulting reluctance of farmers to invest in their land, and

even in some cases to cultivate their land. The basic reason has been the suspicion of Government intentions in relation to land ownership since the first agrarian reform law of 1958 and the inadequacy of credit and other facilities where the traditional channels, the large land-owners in the villages and the money-lenders in the towns, have been suppressed. The situation has improved recently with the more liberal interpretation of the agrarian reform law of 1958 and later amendments by the Assad régime leading to a relative stabizalition of the situation in the countryside. But the major problem facing Syrian agriculture remains unresolved: that of the under-use of potential. Traditionally between one quarter and one-third of cultivable land is kept fallow every year for purposes of conservation and crop rotation. The additional area of unused cultivable land, however, remains large by any standard. It increased from 1,892,000 hectares in 1963 to 2,825,000 hectares, or 32.5 per cent of total cultivable area, in 1970. This adds up to a staggering 62 per cent of the cultivable land remaining unused for different reasons in 1970. Some of this land does suffer from the lack of water resources in years of drought and this problem could be partly solved with the coming availability of water from the Euphrates Dam, and from the Government drive to find and extract underground reserves.

The Government appears to realize that the economic well-being of the state is closely linked to the development of agriculture. The Third Five-Year Plan (1971-75) allocated £S2,241 million, or 34.8 per cent of total investment, to agricultural projects, although the Euphrates Dam project (see below under Economic Development), which took the lion's share of appropriations, is not of exclusively agricultural interest since it will provide for much of Syria's future power needs. The Plan also aimed at the reclamation of 38,700 hectares over the five-year period and the addition of 100,000 hectares to the area under cultivation in 1970.

Cotton has for some years replaced grains as Syria's most valuable crop for although the area under cotton in 1970, for example, was one tenth of the area sown with grains, the value of cotton production was more than double that of grains and cotton provided almost half of Syria's total export earnings. Medium-staple cotton has been grown in the country for many years, but the high price of cotton after the Second World War, especially during the Korean War, gave a great stimulus to cotton production in the early fifties and the previously neglected Jezira area was opened up for large-scale agriculture on a new capital intensive basis relatively free from the traditional agricultural relations, still semi-feudal in the rest of the country. Cotton production grew from 38,000 tons in 1949 to 100,000 tons in 1950 and 220,800 tons in 1954. The area under cotton grew from 25,300 hectares in 1949 to 78,000 hectares in 1950 and 217,400 hectares in 1951, levelling off after that and even decreasing in recent years. The amount of irrigated land under cotton cultivation fell from 195,430 hectares in the 1973-74 season to an estimated 181,258 hectares in 1975-76, or less than 77 per cent of the corresponding figure for 1969. The total area under cotton, including non-irrigated land, was put at 142,078 hectares for 1975-76, compared with 240,000 hectares in 1972-73. Ginned cotton production in 1974-75 was around 147,000 tons and by June 1975 export commitments had accounted for 100,000 tons and domestic mill requirements had accounted for another 45,000 tons. In 1973, 119,200 tons of raw cotton were exported, earning £S448.3 million or 33 per cent of the export total. Sales of cotton yarn and textiles that year brought cotton income up to £S503 million but, though this figure rose substantially to reach £S760.8 million in 1974, cotton's share of the total dropped to 26 per cent from 42 per cent only two years earlier.

The grain crop is of great importance, for bread is the country's staple diet and in normal years there is an exportable surplus of grains. The size of the harvest, however, depends heavily on weather conditions and lack of adequate rainfall in several recent years resulted in disastrous droughts and grains had to be imported in large quantities. By 1970 the relative return of agricultural stability had pushed the area under cereals up to the level of the early sixties, reaching 2,476,000 hectares or just under half the total sown area, but this area has continued to fluctuate, dropping again to 1,960,000 hectares in 1972. The year 1972 nevertheless saw a bumper cereal crop with wheat production reaching an unprecedented 1,808,000 tons. This was followed by a very poor harvest in 1973 when only 593,000 tons of wheat were produced. Another good year in 1974 saw wheat output up to 1,630,000 tons and the 1975 harvest was expected to exceed this, matching the 1972 level. Barley production in 1972 reached 710,000 tons, shrank to 102,000 tons in 1973 and rose again to 655,480 tons in 1974. 1974 was also a good year for maize, with output up to 19,200 tons from 15,400 tons in 1973.

Syria does not depend only on cotton and cereals. Abundant quantities of dry legumes, fruit, vegetables and tobacco are also produced. Of total agricultural production (excluding livestock and dairy produce) worth £S1,320 million at current prices in 1973, cereals accounted for 21 per cent, industrial crops, mainly cotton, for 18 per cent, vegetables for 35 per cent, fruit for 14 per cent and dry legumes for 4 per cent. Stock raising is another important branch of agriculture and there are large flocks grazed by nomads in the pasture lands along the edges of the Syrian Desert. There were 5.3 million sheep in 1974, 684,000 goats and 524,000 head of cattle. Chicken numbered 5.4 million. Sheep and goats are exported for meat but raw hides and leather are also an important export item, earning £S34 million in 1973.

OIL

Syria was at one time thought to have no oil. The Iraq Petroleum Company group had rights throughout Syria which it abandoned in 1951 after failing to find oil in commercial quantities. A concession was granted in 1955 to an independent American operator who discovered the Karachuk field in the north-eastern corner of the country. The oil was of extremely low quality, a density of 19° API and a sulphur content of 4.5 per cent. The operator's concession was cancelled later to make way for state exploitation of the find but commercial production has not yet started on a significant scale. Another concession was granted in 1956 to a West German-led consortium which discovered the richer Suweidiya field whose deposits, although of low quality also, are at 25° API and 3.5 per cent sulphur content a much better commercial proposition than Karachuk oil. A third field was discovered at Rumelan, not far from Suweidiya, but Suweidiya is so far the only field producing significant quantities of crude. The concession of the German consortium was also cancelled later and in 1964 the Government decided that concessions should only be granted to the state-owned agency, the General Petroleum Authority and its offshoot, the Syrian General Petroleum Company.

In 1968 the Syrian company carried out seismic surveys in the Jbeisseh area, between Hassakeh and the Iraqi border, where IPC had formerly found only gas, and in May 1975 a promising new field in the area was formally opened, producing high-quality oil with a gravity of 40.5° API and a 0.62 per cent sulphur content. The inauguration of the Jbeisseh field coincided with a clear shift in the Government's policy on awarding concessions. The same month the final details of a 26-year offshore production-sharing agreement were signed with a United States group. The group has undertaken to invest $20 million in prospection, to give the Syrian Government 88 per cent of any eventual liftings and to set up a joint venture with Syria to manage oil production operations. In June 1975 the Government took its new policy a stage further by offering a dozen onshore oil concessions for international bidding.

Syria's four main existing oil-producing areas were developed with Soviet assistance. Oil production on a commercial basis first began at Suweidiya in July 1968 and output that year totalled 1 million metric tons, of which 833,000 tons were exported. Output in 1969, when the Karachuk field went into operation, failed to reach expectations, totalling 3.2 million tons, with exports accounting for 2.3 million tons, and production targets in subsequent years were not achieved. The October war in 1973 reduced output from a level of 6.3 million tons the previous year to just 5.4 million tons and production in 1974 reached some 5.7 million tons against an 8 million-ton target. Output in 1975 is nevertheless expected to top 10 million tons.

The failure to reach aims in oil production and exports is mainly attributable to difficulties in marketing the Syrian crude abroad, although the Suweidiya crude is suitable for blending with lighter crudes originating in Algeria or Libya to produce fuel oils. The high sulphur content of the Karachuk crude makes it especially suitable for the production of good quality asphalt. In its marketing efforts, Syria has concentrated mainly on sales to Western Europe in order to acquire sorely needed hard currencies. One of the main reasons for Syria's lack of success in marketing its crude in the West had been the reluctance of the major oil companies, which control most of the sales outlets, to allow the success of the Syrian experiments in state exploitation of oil reserves, the first of its kind in the Middle East. But no such difficulties should face Syria again, now that participation is the norm in most major oil-producing States and as a result of the growth of these States' national oil companies and their entry into the field of marketing.

In spite of disappointments in the short history of Syria's oil industry, oil is now a major export commodity and in May 1975 Syria was nominated for membership of the Organisation of Petroleum Exporting Countries (OPEC). Crude oil exports in 1973, amounting to just over 4 million tons, earned £S291.2 million, compared with earnings of £S200 million in 1972 and £S176 million in 1971. Oil revenue estimates for 1974 stood at more than £S900 million and were expected to rise by another 80 per cent in 1975. January 1975 saw the capacity of Syria's only refinery at Homs restored to its former level of 2.5 million tons a year, following its virtual destruction by Israeli bombardment in October 1973. A project to expand the refinery's capacity by a further 1.7 million tons a year is under way and additional plants which could bring Syria's total refining capacity to over 13 million tons a year are planned. Romanian firms have started work on one, a six-million-tons-a-year refinery at Banias.

Royalties for the transit of foreign crude through Syrian territory were for many years more important than indigenous oil production. One pipeline, built in 1934 from the Iraq Petroleum Company installations at Kirkuk, crosses Syria to a terminal at Tripoli in Lebanon, but a parallel line, completed in 1952, branches off at Homs in central Syria to a terminal on the Syrian coast at Banias. The other pipeline is that of the Trans-Arabian Pipeline Company (Tapline) which carries 24 million tons of Saudi Arabian crude a year to a terminal near Sidon in Lebanon and crosses about 100 miles of Syrian territory, much of which was occupied by Israel in 1967. Under agreements signed in 1971, royalties received from the two pipelines were to reach £S342 million a year. Iraq took over payment of the royalties due from IPC when the company was nationalized in both countries on June 1st, 1972, and, after lengthy negotiations, Syria and Iraq signed an oil transit agreement in January 1973 designed to give Syria some £S400 million in transit revenues that year. Total revenue from oil transit dues in 1974 was £S608 million. Work on increasing the capacity of the Kirkuk-Banias pipeline from 1.2 million to 1.4 million barrels a day has been carried out and the annual capacity of the Banias terminal is being raised from 33 million to 42 million tons.

INDUSTRY

A remarkable industrial boom, mainly based on textiles, occurred in Syria shortly after independence and was the main cause of the dissolution of the customs union with Lebanon in 1950, since the protectionist policies adopted by the Syrian Government to safeguard this growth came into direct conflict with Lebanon's free-trade tradition. Since then the industrial sector has grown steadily until in 1970, for the first time, the manufacturing and mining sector replaced agriculture as the main generator of wealth with this sector accounting for 20.5 per cent of the gross domestic product compared with 20.3 per cent for agriculture. Industrial production has more than trebled since the early 1950s and, in money terms, the index of industrial production rose to 360.3 in 1970, taking 1953 as a base year. In 1971 gross industrial output was valued at £S2,621 million, of which 33 per cent was contributed by food processing and tobacco, 32 per cent by textiles, yarn and clothing, nine per cent by chemicals and 6.5 per cent by mining and quarrying.

The importance attached by the Government to industrial growth is clear from the allocation of £S2,532 million for development spending on industry and mining in 1975, more than half the development budget for the year. Priorities for investment, apart from oil, are phosphate mining, electricity generation, cement, petrochemicals, fertilizers, iron and steel and sugar refining. Production of phosphates started from mines in the Palmyra area in 1972 and reached 650,000 tons in 1975. The 1975 output target was set at 1.35 million tons, to earn a projected $60 million in hard currency. The increases in electricity generation, the key to much of the country's future industrial development, will be provided mainly by the Euphrates Dam, which, on completion in late 1976, will have a capacity of 800 MW. Another important power plant is planned for Mehardeh on the Orontes. Four new cement plants, at Tartous, Aleppo, Hama and Adra, are under construction by East Germany and the aim is to reach an overall production level of 6 million tons of cement a year by 1980, compared with an estimated 2.5 million tons in 1975 and an actual 1 million tons in 1972. Talks on building a petrochemicals plant have been held with West Germany, which is believed to have offered to help finance the project as part of a loan agreement signed in April 1975. West German firms are also building a steel works for semi-finished products at Hama, under a contract won in February 1975. The plant will be situated next to the existing Polish-built iron-bar factory. Syria's own reserves of iron ore have been estimated at 100 million tons and a contract to survey these and other mineral deposits, including uranium, was awarded to a British firm in June 1975. Developments in the fertilizer industry include the construction by Romania of a superphosphate plant at Homs, due for completion in 1977, and the construction of ammonia and urea plants to be carried out under the 1976-80 Development Plan. Syria already has a nitrogenous fertilizer factory at Hama. In the field of sugar refining, four new refineries are to be built, two of them by a Belgian company. Established industries include rubber and paper manufacture, and the assembly of vehicles, refrigerators and television sets.

The principal industries centre around the major towns, Damascus, Aleppo and Homs and the port of

Latakia, and these centres, with the exception of Homs and the addition of Tartous, are also the site of Syria's five free zones, set up to encourage foreign investment in the establishment of light industries, assembly plants and warehouses.

EXTERNAL TRADE

Commerce has traditionally been a major occupation of Syria's towns, especially Damascus and Aleppo as they lie on the main east-west trade route. It has declined in importance with the increasing role played by Government in economic affairs and the resulting exodus of leading merchants and their firms who have transferred the centre of their activities, mainly to Beirut. But the country's foreign trade in general has been expanding rapidly. The value of exports increased from £S271 million in 1951 to £S721 million in 1961 but stabilized during the next decade, reaching £S743 million in 1971. The following year saw an unprecedented jump to £S1,098 million and in 1973 exports earned £S1,340 million, despite the October war. The total value of exports in 1974 more than doubled to £S2,914 million. Increased import costs, however, have out-stripped export performance. From £S291 million in 1951, imports rose to £S644 million in 1961, £S1,677 million in 1971 and £S4,570.9 million in 1974.

Raw cotton, as mentioned above, has for many years been Syria's principal export and, at £S448.3 million in 1973, it amounted to over a third of total exports. Crude oil exports in 1973 accounted for 22 per cent of the total, compared with 10 per cent in 1969. Grain is usually exported but in some years drought has resulted in large net imports of this commodity. Drought in 1973 drastically reduced wheat and barley production and cereal exports in 1974 consequently earned only £S0.4 million compared with £S47 million in 1973.

The main imports are usually industrial raw materials and machinery. The largest single import category in 1974 was metal and metal products at £S858 million, followed by machinery and equipment costing £S601.7 million. Imports of fuels and lubricants cost £S275.4 million and cereal imports at £S269 million reached an unprecedented level. They had totalled only £S92.7 million in 1973. Vehicle imports in 1974 cost £S232.5 million and fruit and vegetables £S122.8 million.

The trading pattern has seen some radical changes since the fifties. By 1970 the Communist countries, mainly the Soviet Union, had become Syria's leading suppliers. In 1974, however, West Germany was clearly in the lead providing 12 per cent of the total, followed by Italy, France and Lebanon, with the Soviet Union taking fifth place. A geographical breakdown of Syrian trade shows that in 1973 the countries of the European Economic Community (EEC) accounted for 37.3 per cent of Syria's total imports and 25.2 per cent of exports, while the seven Warsaw Pact countries together with China and Yugoslavia provided 19.8 per cent of the import total and took 34.2 per cent of exports. The importance of this group as a market for Syrian goods seems to

have risen still further in 1974 with exports to China up by 46 per cent and those to the Soviet Union more than doubled—the increase in the latter case being attributable mainly to sales of crude oil and to a lesser extent cotton and wollen textiles. The Arab countries in 1973 accounted for 14.5 per cent of Syrian imports and 21.4 per cent of exports. The United States supplied 4 per cent of imports but bought only 0.7 per cent of exports.

Syria's chief export aim is to reduce its exports of local raw materials, particularly cotton, replacing them with exports of processed or semi-processed products. Other aims originally outlined in a five-year foreign trade plan for the years 1971-75 have been undermined by economic liberalization measures introduced early in 1974. The plan sought to impose strict limits on the annual growth of imports but these virtually doubled between 1973 and 1974.

FINANCE

The sudden increase in Syrian exports from 1972 onwards was one of the major results of a reform in the foreign exchange regulations. All exports other than cotton and crude oil were shifted to the parallel (free) market which meant a *de facto* devaluation of Syrian currency in relation to most transactions. (For details of changes in the exchange rate, *see* the Statistical Survey, following). Figures published by the Central Bank show a balance of payments deficit of £S288 million in 1971. This had been reduced to £S84.5 million by June 1972. The commitment by Saudi Arabia, Kuwait and other Gulf states to provide subsidies to Syria along the lines of those provided to Egypt and Jordan since 1967 have also helped the balance of payments position. Massive pledges of aid have been made to Syria since the October war. Members of the Organization of Peroleum Exporting Countries promised Syria $783 million in 1974 and Arab oil producers attending the Rabat summit conference in October 1974 committed annual payments of $1,000 million to Syria for defence against Israel.

The inflow of foreign finance since the October 1973 war has been reflected in the striking upsurge in state expenditure under the 1974 and 1975 budgets. Ordinary budget expenditure in 1975 was estimated at £S4,595 million, including an allocation of £S2,639 million to defence, compared with ordinary expenditure of £S2,968 million in 1974, of which more than £S1,618 million was spent on defence. These figures compare with projected ordinary budget spending of £S1,670 million in 1973, £S552 million in 1962 and £S205 million in 1953. For the first time in 1973, the development budget was allocated more than the ordinary budget, but the £S1,743 million target for development spending that year was not reached, actual expenditure standing at £S1,074 million. The 1974 target, however, was exceeded, with £S4,018 million being spent on development against the original allocation of £S3,570.8 million. Under the 1975 budget development expenditure was set at £S5,850 million, bringing the general budget total to £S10,445 million.

Banking, like other major economic activities, has been nationalized and the Commercial Bank of Syria is responsible for all trade transactions. There is also an Industrial Bank, an Agricultural Bank, a Real Estate Bank and a Popular Credit Bank.

ECONOMIC DEVELOPMENT

The most ambitious of the projects contained in the current five-year plan (1971-75) is the Euphrates Dam project, under construction since 1968. Most of the country's future industrial and agricultural development depends on this scheme and, with this in mind, the Government allocated 24.7 per cent of public investment over the plan period to its implementation, with £S950 million earmarked for the dam itself and £S643 million for land reclamation and development in the Euphrates basin. The project involved the construction of a dam 4.6 kilometres long and 60 metres high with a width of 500 metres at the bottom. The reservoir thus created, Lake Assad, has been designed to hold 12,000 million cubic metres of water. The whole complex will eventually include eight turbines, the last of which are due for installation by the end of 1976, with a capacity of 800 MW. It will make possible the long-term irrigation of 640,000 hectares of land, some 550,000 of these by 1990. The scheme was undertaken with the help of 1,200 Soviet technicians and about £S600 million in Soviet financial assistance, under an agreement reached with the Soviet Union in April 1966. A West German offer of up to DM 350 million in credit for the scheme was dropped in 1965. In July 1973 the first stage was completed, with the diversion of the Euphrates River, and early in 1974, some months ahead of schedule, the dam's first turbines began to operate. By mid-1975 Lake Assad was one-third full, 20,000 hectares of the pilot project had been irrigated and the year's electricity supply from the dam was about 1,600 million kWh. Despite its advantages, the dam has underlined the urgent need for a permanent settlement on the sharing of Euphrates water between the three riparian states, Turkey, Syria and Iraq. Turkey opened its own Keban dam on the river in 1974 and the effect of this and the filling of Lake Assad led Iraq to protest early in 1975 that the lives and livelihoods of three million Iraqi peasants in the Euphrates basin were threatened by drought. However, it was reported in August 1975 that the dispute had been settled.

Syria's Fourth Five-Year Development Plan is due to run from 1976 to 1980. Its major objective is expected to be an increase in national revenue from exports of oil, other locally available minerals and agricultural products, sufficient to finance future development if and when foreign aid is reduced.

STATISTICAL SURVEY

AREA AND POPULATION

TOTAL AREA	ARABLE LAND	PASTURES	FOREST	POPULATION*
185,180 sq. km.	79,450 sq. km.	64,970 sq. km.	4,810 sq. km.	7,174,000

* July 1st, 1974.

REGISTERED BIRTHS, MARRIAGES AND DEATHS

	BIRTHS	MARRIAGES	DEATHS
1972	231,505	70,676	34,329
1973	254,299	67,771	33,036
1974*	269,925	65,910	31,556

* Estimate.

CHIEF TOWNS
(Population at September 23rd, 1970)

Damascus (capital)	836,668*	Latakia	125,716
Aleppo	639,428	Deir-ez-Zor	66,000
Homs	215,423	Hasakeh	33,000
Hama	137,421		

* Including suburbs, population was 923,253.

AGRICULTURE
AREA AND PRODUCTION OF PRINCIPAL CROPS

	1972		1973		1974	
	Hectares	Metric tons	Hectares	Metric tons	Hectares	Metric tons
Wheat . . .	1,354,000	1,808,000	1,476,000	593,000	1,537,220	1,629,896
Barley . . .	593,000	710,000	914,000	102,000	696,952	655,480
Maize . . .	11,500	15,000	11,600	15,400	13,500	19,220
Millet . . .	33,800	26,500	21,600	12,500	26,300	14,203
Lentils . . .	115,100	96,200	92,100	23,700	85,411	83,369
Cotton . . .	238,200	418,900	200,400	404,300	205,474	386,534
Tobacco . .	15,400	11,600	16,600	10,900	n.a.	n.a.
Sesame . .	33,000	9,500	15,200	5,100	34,000	13,186
Grapes . .	67,000	208,000	74,000	147,000	80,536	249,598
Olives . .	149,000	161,000	175,000	73,000	179,834	215,010
Figs . . .	21,000	38,000	21,000	31,000	20,767	37,998
Apricots . .	11,000	39,000	10,000	29,000	10,537	32,912
Apples . . .	10,000	42,400	14,000	41,100	15,571	44,322
Sugar beet .	9,600	248,900	7,700	152,400	6,500	138,900
Pomegranates .	3,300	21,100	3,200	13,900	3,431	16,882
Onions . .	6,900	80,800	6,800	98,600	8,700	133,122
Tomatoes . .	21,800	315,900	20,700	269,000	29,883	395,467
Potatoes . .	7,800	119,100	8,300	110,500	8,414	104,820

LIVESTOCK
('ooo head)

	1972	1973	1974
Cattle . .	488	493	524
Horses . .	62	63	60
Camels . .	9	6	8
Asses . .	242	248	242
Sheep . .	5,166	4,840	5,295
Goats . .	697	608	684
Hens and chickens .	5,162	4,614	5,401

DAIRY PRODUCE

		1972	1973	1974
Milk . .	'ooo tons	458	394	500
Cheese .	tons	26,640	24,084	26,000
Butter .	,,	1,353	1,092	1,267
Honey .	,,	289	183	340
Ghee .	,,	7,836	6,166	7,991
Eggs .	'ooo	324,000	370,000	404,316

INDUSTRY

		1972	1973	1974
Cotton Yarn	'ooo tons	27.9	28.5	30.4
Silk and Cotton Textiles . .	,, ,,	29.7	31.1	35.1
Woollen Fabrics . . .	tons	960.0	102.7	134.7
Cement	'ooo tons	1,004.0	848.0	865.0
Natural Asphalt . . .	,, ,,	21.1	26.5	34.9
Glass	,, ,,	15.8	22.2	24.7
Soap	,, ,,	25.9	27.8	28.3
Sugar	,, ,,	137.2	142.0	148.0
Salt	,, ,,	49.5	35.1	40.0
Edible Oils . . .	,, ,,	27.4	28.6	25.3
Manufactured Tobacco . .	,, ,,	4.7	5.3	5.8
Electricity . . .	million kWh.	1,223.0	1,154.0	1,366.0
Beer	'ooo litres	3,784.8	4,795.0	5,799.0
Wine	,, ,,	306.0	261.8	370.4
Arak	,, ,,	881.5	532.2	573.6

FINANCE

100 piastres = 1 Syrian pound (£S).

Coins: 2½, 5, 10, 25 and 50 piastres; 1 pound.

Notes: 1, 5, 10, 25 50, 100 and 500 pounds.

Exchange rates (July 1975): £1 sterling = £S8.037; U.S. $1 = £S3.675.

£S100 = £12.44 sterling = $27.21.

Note: The official basic exchange rate of U.S. $1 = £S2.19, established in 1949, is inoperative for all practical purposes. Prior to July 1962 the official selling rate, used for calculating the value of foreign trade, was U.S. $1 = £S3.58 (£S1 = 27.97 U.S. cents). From July 1962 to February 1973 the buying rate was $1 = £S3.80 and the selling rate was $1 = £S3.82 (£S1 = 26.18 U.S. cents). Exchange rates were adjusted frequently between February and July 1973. From July 1973 to February 1974 the buying rate was $1 = £S3.75 and the selling rate $1 = £S3.80. Since February 1974 the buying rate has been $1 = £S3.65 and the selling rate $1 = £S3.70. From January 1964 to July 1973 a "parallel" free market was also in operation. From early 1970 to February 1973 the free rates were $1 = £S4.30 (buying) or £S4.32 (selling). The official exchange rates were £1 sterling = £S9.12 (buying) or £S9.168 (selling) from November 1967 to August 1971; and £1 sterling = £S9.902 (buying) or £S9.954 (selling) from December 1971 to June 1972.

ORDINARY BUDGET
(£S million)

	1972	1973	1974
National defence	780.5	778.5	1,590.9
Cultural and social affairs . .	354.7	348.8	468.4
Communications and public works .	31.2	22.8	23.4
Economic affairs and planning . .	266.3	339.4	324.9
Administrative affairs	160.9	180.5	474.5
TOTAL	1,593.6	1,670.0	2,882.1

1975 Ordinary Budget: £S4,500 million.

CONSOLIDATED BUDGET
(£S million)

A new consolidated budget has been issued incorporating both ordinary and development budgets

	1972	1973	1974
Justice and Public Authorities . .	71.6	81.2	86.7
National Security	795.0	786.3	1,618.4
Culture and Information . . .	364.3	408.0	592.3
Social Welfare	84.1	70.1	69.7
Economy and Finance . . .	282.2	404.4	499.2
Agriculture and Land Reclamation . .	536.5	600.7	654.1
Industry and Mining	500.3	594.7	1,585.4
Public Works, Utilities and Communications	473.7	416.6	1,055.3
Other Expenditure and Revenue . .	80.3	50.9	319.4
TOTAL	3,188.0	3,412.9	6,480.5

1975 Consolidated Budget: £S10,500 million.

THIRD FIVE-YEAR PLAN
(1971–75—£S million)

	INVESTMENT (Public Sector)	%
Euphrates Dam Project .	1,593.0	24.7
Irrigation and Land Improvement	211.7	3.3
Agriculture . . .	436.1	6.8
Industry . . .	1,173.0	18.2
Power and Fuel . . .	1,013.8	15.7
Transport and Communications . . .	783.0	12.1
Towns and Buildings . .	585.9	9.1
Public Services . .	525.8	8.2
Local Trade . . .	124.7	1.9
TOTAL . .	6,447.0	100.0

OIL

FLOW OF OIL ACROSS SYRIA
('000 long tons)

	TOTAL	To BANIAS	To SIDON (Lebanon)	To TRIPOLI (Lebanon)
1970 . .	60,679	29,977	8,036	22,666
1971 . .	64,544	27,712	16,407	20,425
1972 . .	50,477	22,213	21,053	7,193
1973 . .	71,528	29,224	20,106	22,198
1974 . .	49,790	22,670	10,810	16,310

EXTERNAL TRADE
(£S '000)

	1969	1970	1971	1972	1973	1974
Imports . . .	1,411,324	1,374,637	1,677,038	2,060,648	2,342,068	4,570,879
Exports . . .	789,918	775,343	743,353	1,097,601	1,341,276	2,913,960

COMMODITIES (£S million)

IMPORTS	1971	1972	1973	1974
Cotton textiles, other textile goods and silk	112.2	202.3	223.3	310.9
Mineral fuels and oils	102.3	91.4	106.2	275.4
Lime, cement and salt	27.6	28.0	43.4	97.4
Cereals	231.7	96.8	92.7	269.0
Vegetables and fruit	81.3	81.0	102.9	122.8
Oilseeds and medical plants	6.0	8.3	11.5	12.8
Machinery, apparatus and electrical materials	222.2	374.8	417.3	601.7
Precious metals and coins	3.5	2.7	3.1	2.5
Base metals and manufactures	201.2	308.1	312.7	858.0
Vehicles	50.1	65.0	110.8	232.5
Chemical and pharmaceutical products	74.5	112.0	101.0	140.2
Preserved foods, beverages and tobacco	141.1	169.0	220.3	525.5
Other products	423.3	521.2	624.5	1,122.1

EXPORTS	1971	1972	1973	1974
Cotton (raw, yarn, textiles)	325.2	418.6	503.2	760.8
Other textile goods	86.9	117.6	200.6	214.1
Cereals	0.1	94.9	47.1	0.4
Vegetables and fruit	39.1	51.2	35.0	37.1
Precious metals	0.5	0.3	0.9	0.4
Preserved foods, beverages and tobacco	35.8	63.4	69.8	94.2
Live animals	25.2	60.0	50.1	12.2
Dairy products	0.9	2.1	1.0	0.4
Other Products	229.6	289.5	433.5	1,794.3

Oil Exports: (1971) £S176 million; (1972) £S200 million; (1973) £S291.2 million; (1974—estimate) £S400 million

COUNTRIES (£S million)

IMPORTS	1971	1972	1973	1974
Belgium	31.1	50.3	89.7	154.8
Cuba	52.3	86.4	58.9	14.5
France	99.0	119.6	167.4	400.5
Germany, Federal Republic	107.7	160.0	246.0	550.8
Iraq	101.6	83.7	101.1	154.3
Italy	116.4	166.3	186.1	408.8
Japan	72.9	130.8	85.2	151.7
Lebanon	143.5	138.4	141.1	359.7
Netherlands	42.5	48.1	53.6	104.6
U.S.S.R.	104.9	154.3	167.1	178.0
United Kingdom	55.5	99.0	106.1	143.5
U.S.A.	112.1	92.4	86.2	133.5

EXPORTS	1971	1972	1973	1974
China	24.2	70.3	109.4	160.2
Czechoslovakia	9.2	24.7	25.9	76.1
France	29.0	35.7	54.5	24.3
Germany, Federal Republic	29.3	33.3	68.0	441.1
Italy	208.8	116.7	173.5	90.4
Japan	20.9	16.3	7.6	5.8
Jordan	15.0	18.5	36.6	41.8
Kuwait	9.9	13.9	13.4	8.9
Lebanon	55.8	150.5	111.6	200.6
Romania	4.5	7.6	20.9	47.3
Saudi Arabia	14.7	24.6	40.7	53.9
U.S.S.R.	112.4	221.3	205.6	416.0
United Kingdom	3.3	22.0	17.9	284.5
U.S.A.	5.8	7.5	10.0	9.3

TRANSPORT

RAILWAYS

	1973	1974
Passenger-km. . .	68,992	101,282
Freight, 'ooo tons .	828	1,055

ROADS

		1972	1973
Passenger Cars .	.	31,571	34,741
Buses .	.	2,518	2,525
Lorries, Trucks, etc.	.	18,144	19,837
Motor-cycles .	.	8,681	9,656

SHIPPING
PORT OF LATAKIA

			1970	1971	1972	1973
Number of steam vessels entering harbour	.	.	1,642	1,629	1,856	1,701
Number of sailing vessels entering harbour	.	.	258	134	92	117
Cargo unloaded ('ooo tons) . .	.	.	1,847	1,717	1,645	1,529
Cargo loaded ('ooo tons)	.	.	478	264	518	312

CIVIL AVIATION
(Damascus Airport)

							1971		1972		1973	
							ARRIVE	DEPART	ARRIVE	DEPART	ARRIVE	DEPART
Aircraft . .	.	.	.	.	.	.	5,282	5,284	6,777	6,779	6,132	6,141
Passengers . .	.	.	.	.	.	.	139,598	139,633	176,372	191,720	176,682	199,394

TOURISM

	JORDANIANS AND LEBANESE	TOTAL VISITORS
1970	504,692	870,276
1971	943,011	1,322,862
1972	719,601	1,038,543
1973	413,982	709,626
1974	477,037	921,854

Tourist Accommodation: 20,085 tourist hotel beds (1973).

EDUCATION
(1973–74)

		PUPILS		TEACHERS	
		Public Sector	Private Sector*	Public Sector	Private Sector*
Pre-School . .	.	—	28,563	—	876
Primary . .	.	1,100,636	32,879	29,664	1,186
Preparatory . .	.	285,900	11,776	} 17,267†	1,860
Secondary . .	.	97,948	10,416		
Vocational . .	.	19,605	—	2,207	—
Teacher Training .	.	5,368	—	378	—
Universities . .	.	53,369	—	—	—

* Excluding UNRWA schools.   † Including administrative staff.

Source: Central Bureau of Statistics, Office of the Prime Minister, Damascus.

THE CONSTITUTION

A new and permanent constitution was endorsed by 97.6 per cent of the voters in a national referendum on March 12th, 1973. The 157-article constitution defines Syria as a "Socialist popular democracy" with a "pre-planned Socialist economy". Under the new constitution, Lt.-Gen. al-Assad remains President, with the power to appoint and dismiss his Vice-President, Premier and Government Ministers, and also becomes Commander-in-Chief of the armed forces, secretary-general of the Baath Socialist Party and President of the National Progressive Front. This is the country's first permanent constitution since 1961, when Syria ended its union with Egypt. The provisional constitution introduced in 1969 was never formally promulgated.

THE GOVERNMENT

HEAD OF STATE

President: Lt.-Gen. HAFIZ AL-ASSAD (elected March 12th, 1971, for a seven-year term).
Vice-President: MAHMOUD AL-AYOUBI.

CABINET

(July 1975)

(B) Baath, (SU) Socialist Union, (ASU) Arab Socialist Union.

Prime Minister: MAHMOUD AL-AYOUBI (B).

Deputy Prime Minister and Minister of Foreign Affairs: ABDEL HALIM KHADDAM (B).

Deputy Prime Minister and Minister of Economic Affairs: MOHAMMED HAIDAR (B).

Minister of Agriculture and Reclamation: MOURSEL ABOU OMAR (B).

Minister of Housing and Public Utilities: ABDEL RAZZAK ABDEL BAKI (SU).

Minister of Justice: ADIB AL-NAHAWI (ASU).

Minister for the Euphrates Dam: Ing. SOBHI KAHALE (Independent).

Minister of Education: Dr. SHAKER AL-FAHAM (B).

Minister of Defence: Lt.-Gen. MUSTAFA TLAS (B).

Minister of Health: Dr. MADANI AL KHYAMI (Independent).

Minister of Information: AHMED ISKANADAR AHMED (B).

Minister of the Interior: ALI ZAZA (B).

Minister of Supply and Internal Trade: Ing. AHMED KABALAN (B).

Minister of Public Works and Water Resources: ABDLE-GHANI KANNOUT (ASU).

Minister of Higher Education: Dr. MOHAMED ALI HASHEM (B).

Minister of Petroleum and Mineral Resources: Dr. ADNAN MOUSTAFA (B).

Minister of Finance: MOHAMED AL-SHARIF (B).

Minister of Culture and National Guidance: FAWZI KAYYALI (ASU).

Minister of Labour and Social Affairs: HUSSEIN AHMED KOUEIDER (B).

Minister of Local Administration: ADIB MELHEM (B).

Minister of Industry: SHTEWI SEIFO (B).

Minister of Wakfs: Sheikh ABDEL SATTAR AL-SAYED (Independent).

Minister of Communications: Ing. OMAR AL-SIBAALEE (Communist).

Minister of Tourism: ABDALLAH AL KHANI (Independent).

Minister of Electricity: Ing. HANEE AL-SAWAAF (Independent).

Minister of Transport: Ing. NAAMAN ZEIN (B).

Minister of State for Planning: Dr. NOURALLAH NOURALLAH (Independent).

Minister of the Economy and External Trade: Dr. MOHAMMED IMMADI (B).

Minister of State for the Premiership: FAYEZ NASIR (B).

Ministers of State: ZOUHAIR ABDEL SAMAD (Communist), ANWAR HAMADEH (ASU).

PEOPLE'S COUNCIL

A new People's Council was elected in May 1973 under the terms of the new Constitution. 140 out of the 186 seats were won by the Progressive Front, a grouping of the parties listed below, 42 seats were won by Independents, and the remainder by the Opposition.

Speaker: MOHAMMED ALI EL-HALABI.

POLITICAL PARTIES

The National Progressive Front, headed by President Assad, was formed in March 1972 by the grouping of the five parties listed below:

Arab Socialist Renaissance (Baath) Party: Arab socialist party; in power since 1963; supports militant Arab unity; Sec.-Gen. Pres. HAFIZ AL-ASSAD.

Syrian Arab Socialist Union: Nasserite; Leader Dr. JAMAL ATASI; Sec.-Gen. FAUZI KAYYALI.

Socialist Union: Leader SAMI SOUFAN.

Arab Socialist Party: a breakaway socialist party; Leader ABDEL GHANI KANNOUT.

Communist Party of Syria: Sec.-Gen. KHALID BAGDASH.

DIPLOMATIC REPRESENTATION

EMBASSIES ACCREDITED TO SYRIA

(In Damascus unless otherwise stated)

Algeria: Raouda, Imm. Noss; *Ambassador:* OTHMAN EL SAADI.

Argentina: Raouda, Rue Ziad ben Abi Soufian, Imm. Ab Kérim Abul; *Ambassador:* ENRIQUE LUPIZ (also accred. to Iraq).

Austria: Beirut, Lebanon.

Belgium: Rue Ata Ayoubi, Imm. Hachem; *Ambassador:* LUC SMOLDEREN.

Brazil: 76 Rue Ata Ayoubi; *Ambassador:* VICTOR JOSÉ SILVEIRA.

Bulgaria: 4 Rue Chahbandar; *Ambassador:* METODI POPOV.

Chile: 43 Rue Al Jala'a; *Ambassador:* MANUEL MOTT.

China, People's Republic: 83 Ata Ayoubi; *Ambassador:* TSAO KE-CHIANG.

Cuba: 81 Avenue Al Jala'a; *Ambassador:* ARTURO BARBER OROZCO.

Czechoslovakia: Place Aboul-Alaa; *Ambassador:* MIROSLAV POKORNY.

Denmark: Beirut, Lebanon; *Ambassador:* MOGENS WARBERG.

Egypt: Rue Misr, Imm. Malki; *Ambassador:* HASAN FEHMI ABDEL MAJID.

France: Rue Ata Ayoubi; *Ambassador:* (vacant).

German Democratic Republic: 60 Avenue Adnan el Malki; *Ambassador:* WOLFGANG KONSCHEL (also accred. to Jordan).

Germany, Federal Republic: 47 Rue Ibrahim Hanano; *Ambassador:* ULRICH VON RHAMM.

Greece: 57 Rue Ata Ayoubi; *Ambassador:* (vacant) (also accred. to Iraq and Jordan).

Hungary: 13 Rue Ibrahim Hanano (Imm. Roujoulé); *Ambassador:* (vacant) (also accred. to Jordan).

India: 40/46 Avenue Al Malki; *Ambassador:* KHALEK AHMAD NIZAMI.

Indonesia: 19 Rue Al-Amir Ezzeddine; *Ambassador:* ZAIN AREFIN OTHMAN.

Iran: Rue Kawakbi; *Ambassador:* MUHAMMAD POURSARATIP.

Iraq: Avenue Al Mansour; *Ambassador:* AUDA AHMED AL-BAYATI.

Italy: 82 Avenue Al Mansour; *Ambassador:* MAURIZIO BUCCI.

Japan: Malki, Rue Kurd Ali; *Ambassador:* MINORU IMAI.

Jordan: Abou Roumaneh; *Ambassador:* NABIH AMRO AL-NEMR.

Korea, Democratic People's Republic: 89 Avenue Al Jala'a; *Ambassador:* HAN SU IK.

Kuwait: Rue Ibrahim Hanano; *Ambassador:* AHMED HUSSEIN.

Libya: Place Al Malki, 10 Avenue Mansour; *Ambassador:* AHMAD ABDULSALAM BEN KHAYAL.

Mauritania: Malki, Malek ben Marwan, Apt. 6, Tabba Bldg.; *Ambassador:* OULD DADAH.

Morocco: Abou Roumaneh No. 2; *Ambassador:* AHMED IDRISSI.

Netherlands: Place Abou Ala'a Al-Maarri; *Ambassador:* JOHN B. E. P. VAN HOEVE.

Norway: Cairo, Egypt.

Pakistan: Avenue Al Jala'a; *Ambassador:* MUHAMMAD SALIMALLA.

Poland: Rue Georges Haddad, Imm. Chahine; *Ambassador:* STEFAN BOZYM.

Qatar: Abou Roumaneh; *Ambassador:* HAMAD ABDUL AZIZ AL-KAWARI.

Romania: Rue Ibrahim Hanano; *Ambassador:* EMILIAN MANCIUR.

Saudi Arabia: Avenue Al Jala'a; *Ambassador:* MUHAMMAD ABDULLA AL-MUTLAQ.

Somalia: Avenue Ata Ayoubi; *Ambassador:* YOUSSEF JAMA BOURALLE.

Spain: 81 Avenue Al Jala'a; *Ambassador:* GABRIEL NANUECO DE LECEA (also accred. to Cyprus).

Sudan: Rue Hanano; *Ambassador:* MUHAMMAD OSMAN MUHAMMAD el-AWAD.

Sweden: Abdul M. Ben Marwan, Abou Roumaneh; *Ambassador:* BENGT GUSTAV JEAN JACQUES DARDEL.

Switzerland: Malki, 31 Rue M. Kurd Ali; *Ambassador:* ALBERT DUBOIS.

Tunisia: Rue Rashid, Imm. Jabi; *Ambassador:* AL HABIB NOUIRA.

Turkey: 58 Avenue Ziad Bin Abou Soufian; *Ambassador:* SEFIK FENMEN.

U.S.S.R.: Boustan El-Kouzbari, Rue d'Alep; *Ambassador:* NOUREDDIN MOHIEDDINOV.

United Arab Emirates: Rue Raouda; *Ambassador:* MUHAMMAD ABDER-RAHMAN AL-BAKR.

United Kingdom: Malki; Rue Muhammad Kurd Ali; *Ambassador:* DAVID ARTHUR ROBERTS.

U.S.A.: Rue Al Mansour 2; *Ambassador:* RICHARD W. MURPHY.

Uruguay: Beirut, Lebanon.

Vatican City: 82 Rue Misr (Apostolic Nunciature): *Chargé d'Affaires a.i.:* Mgr. PABLO PUENTE.

Venezuela: Abou Roumaneh, Rue Nouri Pacha; *Chargé d'Affaires a.i.:* Dr. EUGENIO OMANA MURILLO.

Viet-Nam, Democratic Republic: 9 Avenue Malki; *Ambassador:* LONG THUAN PHUOC (also accred. to Iraq).

Yemen Arab Republic: 43 Rue Al Jala'a; *Ambassador:* (vacant).

Yugoslavia: Avenue A. Jala'a; *Ambassador:* VOJISLAV PEKIC (also accred. to Jordan).

Syria also has diplomatic relations with Afghanistan, Colombia, Cyprus, Finland, Guyana and Tanzania.

JUDICIAL SYSTEM

Court of Cassation: Damascus; is the highest court of appeal.

Courts of Appeal: 30 Courts of Appeal in the 30 Prefectures try all criminal cases subject to appeal, as well as all other cases within their competence by virtue of the law in force; some of them are composed of several chambers; decisions are given by three judges, one of them being the President.

Summary Courts: 110 Summary Courts try civil, commercial and penal cases within their competence; a Summary Court is constituted by one judge known as a "Judge of the Peace".

First Instance Courts: 41 First Instance Courts, constituted by one judge, deal with all cases other than those within the competence of special tribunals. In some Prefectures are several Chambers.

Chief Justice of Syria: IBRAHIM AL FARAJI.

PERSONAL STATUS COURTS

For Muslims: each court consists of one judge, the "Qadi Shari'i", who deals with marriage, divorce, etc.

For Druzes: one court consisting of one judge, the "Qadi Mazhabi".

For non-Muslim Communities: for Catholics, Orthodox, Protestants, Jews.

OTHER COURTS

Courts for Minors: their constitution, officers, sessions, jurisdiction and competence are determined by a special law.

Military Court: Damascus.

RELIGION

In religion the majority of Syrians follow a form of Sunni orthodoxy. There is also a considerable number of religious minorities: Muslim Shi'ites; the Ismaili of the Salamiya district, whose spiritual head is the Aga Khan; a large number of Druzes, the Nusairis or Alawites of the Jebel Ansariyeh and the Yezidis of the Jebel Sinjar.

MUSLIMS

Grand Mufti: AHMAD KUFTARO.

Most Syrians are Muslims. Nearly all are Sunnites with a small number of Ismailis and Shi'ites.

CHRISTIANS

Greek Orthodox Patriarch: His Beatitude ELIAS IV MUAWAD, Patriarch of Antioch and all the Orient; P.O.B. 9, Damascus.

Greek Catholic Patriarch: H.B. MAXIMOS V HAKIM; Bab-Sharki, Damascus; P.O.B. 50076, Beirut, Lebanon; one million mems.; publ. *Le Lien* (monthly, in French).

Syrian Orthodox Patriarch: His Holiness IGNATIUS YACOB III.

THE PRESS

Since the coming to power of the Baath Arab Socialist Party the structure of the press has been modified according to socialist patterns. Most publications are published by organizations such as political, religious, or professional associations, trade unions, etc. and several are published by government ministries. Anyone wishing to establish a new paper or periodical must apply for a licence.

The major dailies are *al-Baath* (the organ of the party) and *al-Thawrah* in Damascus, *al-Jamahir al-Arabia* in Aleppo, and *al-Fida* in Hama.

PRINCIPAL DAILIES

Aravelk: Aleppo; Armenian; morning; Editor Dr. A. ANGYKIAN; circ. 3,500.

al-Baath (*Renaissance*): rue el Barazil, Damascus; Arabic; morning; organ of the Baath Arab Socialist Party; circ. 20,000.

Barq al-Shimal: rue Aziziyah, Aleppo; Arabic; morning; Editor MAURICE DJANDJI; circ. 6,400.

al-Fida: rue Kuwatly, Hama; political; Arabic; morning; Publishing concession holder OSMAN ALOUINI; Editor A. AULWANI; circ. 4,000.

al-Jamahir al-Arabia: El Ouedha Printing and Publishing Organization, Aleppo; political; Arabic: Chief Editor MORTADA BAKACH; circ. 10,000.

al-Shabab: rue al Tawil, Aleppo; Arabic; morning; Editor MUHAMMAD TALAS; circ. 9,000.

al-Thawrah: El Ouedha Printing and Publishing Organization, Damascus; political; Arabic; morning; circ. 20,000.

WEEKLIES AND FORTNIGHTLIES

al-Ajoua: Compagnie de l'Aviation Arabe Syrienne, Damascus; aviation; Arabic; fortnightly; Editor AHMAD ALLOUCHE.

Arab Press Digest: Syrian Documentation Papers, P.O.B. 2712, Damascus.

al-Esbou al-Riadi: ave. Firdoisse, Tibi Bldg., Damascus; sports; Arabic; weekly; Publisher MOUNIR BAKIR; Dir. and Editor KAMEL EL BOUNNI.

Hadarat al-Islam: B.P. 808, Jadet Halbouni, Jadet El Raby, Damascus; religious; Arabic; fortnightly; Publisher MOUSTAPHA ESSIBAI; Dir. AHMAD FARHAT; Editor MUHAMMAD ADIB SALEH.

Homs: Homs; literary; Arabic; weekly; Publisher and Dir. ADIB KABA; Editor PHILIPPE KABA.

Jaysh al-Shaab: P.O.B. 3320, blvd. Palestine, Damascus; f. 1946; army magazine, Arabic; weekly; published by the Political Department.

Kifah al-Oummal al-Ishtiraki: Fédération Générale des Syndicats des Ouvriers, Damascus; labour; Arabic; weekly; Published by General Federation of Trade Unions; Editor SAID EL HAMAMI.

al-Majalla al-Batriarquia: B.P. 914, Syrian Orthodox Patriarchate, Damascus; f. 1962; religious; Arabic; monthly; Dir. and Editor SAMIR ABDOH; circ. 3,000.

al-Masira: Damascus; political; weekly; published by Federation of Youth Organizations.

al-Maukef al-Riadi: El Ouehda Organization, Damascus; sports; Arabic; weekly; Published by El Ouehda Printing and Publishing Organization; circ. 5,000.

al-Nass: B.P. 926, Aleppo; f. 1953; Arabic; weekly; Publisher VICTOR KALOUS.

Nidal al-Fellahin: Fédération Générale des Laboureurs, Damascus; peasant workers; Arabic; weekly; Published by General Federation of Workers; Editor MANSOUR ABU EL HOSN.

Revue de la Presse Arabe: 67 Place Chahbandar, Damascus; French; twice weekly.

al-Riada: B.P. 292, near Electricity Institute, Damascus; sports; Arabic; weekly; Dir. NOUREDDINE RIAL; Publisher and Editor OURFANE UBARI.

al-Sakafe al-Isboui: B.P. 2570, Souak El Sakr, Damascus; cultural; Arabic; weekly; Publisher, Dir. and Editor MADHAT AKKACHE.

al-Talia (*Vanguard*): B.P. 3031, the National Guard, Damascus; Arabic; fortnightly; Editor SOHDI KHALIL.

al-Tamaddon al-Islami: Darwichillé, Damascus; religious; Arabic; fortnightly; Published by Tamaddon al-Islami Association; Dir. MUHAMMAD EL KHATIB; Editor AHMAD MAZAR EL ADME.

al-Thawrah al-Ziraia (*Agricultural Revolution Review*): Ministry of Agrarian Reform, Damascus; f. 1965; agriculture; Arabic; monthly; circ. 7,000.

al-Yanbu al-Jadid: al-Awkaf Bldg., Homs; literary; Arabic; weekly; Publisher, Dir. and Editor MAMDOU EL KOUSSEIR.

MONTHLIES

al-Dad: rue El Tital, Wakf El Moiriné Bldg., Aleppo; literary; Arabic; Dir. RIAD HALLAK; Publisher and Editor ABDALLAH YARKI HALLAK.

Ecos: P.O.B. 3320, Damascus; monthly review; Spanish.

Flash: P.O.B. 3320, Damascus; monthly review; English and French.

al-Irshad al-Zirai: Ministry of Agriculture, Damascus; agriculture; every two months.

al-Kalima: Al-Kalima Association, Aleppo; religious; Arabic; Publisher and Editor FATHALLA SAKAL.

al-Kanoun: Ministry of Justice, Damascus; juridical; Arabic.

al-Maarifa: Ministry of Culture and National Guidance, Damascus; f. 1962; literary; Arabic; Editor SAFWAN KUDSI.

al-Majalla al-Askaria: P.O.B. 3320, blvd. Palestine, Damascus; f. 1950; official military magazine; Editor NAKHLI KALLAS.

al-Majalla al-Toubilla al-Arabilla: Al-Jalla's St., Damascus; Published by Arab Medical Commission; Dir. Dr. SHAMSEDDIN EL JUNDI; Editor Dr. ADNAN TAKRITI.

Majallat Majma al-Lughah al-Arabiyyah: Arab Academy of Damascus; P.O.B. 327, Damascus; f. 1921; Islamic culture and Arabic literature.

Monthly Survey of Arab Economics: B.P. 2306, Damascus and B.P. 6068, Beirut; f. 1958; English and French editions; published Centre d'Etudes et de Documentation Economiques, Financières et Sociales; Dir. Dr. CHAFIC AKHRAS.

al-Mouallem al-Arabi (*The Arab Teacher*): Ministry of Education; Damascus; f. 1948; educational and cultural; Arabic.

al-Mouhandis al-Arabi: Abdul Malek bin Marwan St., Damascus; published by Syrian Engineering Syndicate; scientific and cultural; Dir. SAMIH FAKHOURY; Editor Dr. AHMAD OMAR YOUSSEF; bi-monthly.

al-Moujtama al-Arabi al-Ishtiraki: Ministry of Social Affairs, Damascus; social security; Arabic; Editor SAMI ATFE.

al-Oumran: Ministry of Municipal and Rural Affairs, Damascus; fine arts; Arabic.

Rissalat al-Kimia: B.P. 669, El Abid Bldg., Damascus; scientific; Arabic; Publisher, Dir. and Editor HASSAN EL SAKA.

Saut al-Forat: Deir-Ezzor; literary; Arabic; Publisher, Dir. and Editor ABDEL KADER AYACH.

al-Shourta: Directorate of Public Affairs and Moral Guidance, Damascus; juridical; Arabic.

Souriya al-Arabilla: Ministry of Information, Damascus; publicity; in four languages.

Syrie et le Monde Arabe: P.O.B. 3550, Place Chahbandar, Damascus; economic, statistical and political survey.

al-Yakza: Sisi St., Al Yazka Association, Aleppo; f. 1935; Dir. and Editor PAUL GENADRI.

QUARTERLY

Les Archives Littéraires du Moyen Orient: Syrian Documentation Papers, P.O.B. 2712, Damascus.

ANNUALS

Bibliography of the Middle East: Syrian Documentation Papers, P.O.B. 2712, Damascus.

General Directory of the Press and Periodicals in the Arab World: Syrian Documentation Papers, P.O.B. 2712, Damascus.

PRESS AGENCIES

Agence Arabe Syrienne d'Information: Damascus; f. 1966; supplies bulletins on Syrian news to foreign news agencies.

FOREIGN BUREAUX

ANSA: P.O.B. 827, rue Salhié, Immeuble Tibi-Selo; f. 1962; Chief KHALIL NABKI.

Reuters: P.O.B. 3525, Ijl, Omary and Kassas Bldg., Damascus.

UPI: 3 Argentine St., Hafez Bldg.; Chief ADNAN INAYEH. DPA, Reuter and Tass also have bureaux in Damascus.

PUBLISHERS

Arab Advertising Organization: 28 Moutanabbi St., P.O.B. 2842 and 3034, Damascus; f. 1963; publishes Directory of Commerce and Industry, Damascus International Fair Guide and Daily Bulletin of Official Tenders; Dir.-Gen. GEORGE KHOURY.

Bureau des documentations syriennes et arabes: B.P. 451, 67 place Chahbander, Damascus; f. 1948; affiliated with the *Office arabe de presse et de documentation* (see below) in 1966, Dir.-Gen. SAMIR A. DARWICH, publs. include *Répertoire Permanent des Lois et Réglements Syriens, Tarif Permanent des Douanes de Syrie, Recueil des Accords Internationaux conclus par la Syrie* and monographs, legislative texts and other documents concerning Syria and the Arab world.

Damascus University Press: Damascus; art, geography, education, history, engineering, medicine, law, sociology, school books.

Office Arabe de Presse et de Documentation: P.O.B. 3550, Damascus; f. 1964; numerous periodical books and surveys on political and economic affairs; Dir.-Gen. SAMIR A. DARWICH. Has two affiliated branches: *Office Arabe-Etudes de Marchés* (market surveys and services) and *Office Arabe des Renseignements Commerciaux* (Commercial enquiries on firms and persons in Syria and Lebanon).

al-Ouedha Printing and Publishing Organization (*Institut al-Ouedha pour l'impression, édition et distribution*): Damascus and Aleppo; published *al-Jamahir al-Duroubah* and *al-Thawrah* (dailies) and *al-Maukef al-Riadi* (weekly).

Syrian Documentation Papers: P.O.B. 2712, Damascus; f. 1968; publishers of *Bibliography of the Middle East* (annual), *General Directory of the Press and Periodicals in the Arab World* (annual), *Les Archives Littéraires du Moyen Orient* (quarterly), *Arab Press Digest* (weekly), and numerous publications on political, economic and social affairs and literature and legislative texts concerning Syria and the Arab world; Dir.-Gen. LOUIS FARÉS.

al-Tawjih Press: P.O.B. 3320, Palestine St., Damascus.

Other publishers include: *Dar El-Yakaza El-Arabia, Dar El-Hahda El-Arabia, Dar El-Filez, Dar El-Fatah, Dubed, El-Mouassassa El-Sakafieh.*

RADIO AND TELEVISION

General Directorate of Broadcasting and Television: Omayyad Square, Damascus; f. 1945; Gen. Dir. KHODR AL SHA'AR; Dirs. KHODR AMRAN, SAMI JANO, MICHEL BARAH, GEORGE BOULAD; publ. *Here is Damascus* (fortnightly).

RADIO

Director of Broadcasting: KHUDR AMRAN.

Broadcasts in Arabic, French, English, Russian, German, Spanish, Polish, Turkish, Bulgarian.

There were 878,200 receivers in use at the end of 1974.

TELEVISION

Director of Television: AHMAD HULWANI.

Services started in 1960.

There were 223,700 receivers in use at the end of 1974.

FINANCE

BANKING

(cap.=capital;   p.u.=paid up;   dep.=deposits;   m.= millions; amounts in £S)

CENTRAL BANK

Central Bank of Syria: 29 Ayar Square, Damascus; f. 1956; cap. 10m.; total resources 6,962m. (Dec. 1973); Gov. NASSOUH DACCAK; 7 brs.

OTHER BANKS

Agricultural Bank: Baghdad St., Damascus; f. 1924; Dir.-Gen. Dr. HANNA KHOURY.

Commercial Bank of Syria S.A.: P.O.B. 933, Moawia St., Damascus; f. 1967; 20 brs.; cap. 50m.; total resources 3,073m. (June 1974); Pres. and Gen. Man. Dr. DIB ABU ASSALI.

Industrial Bank: Damascus; f. 1959; nationalized bank providing finance for industry; cap. 12.5m., dep. 53.4m., total investments (Feb. 1971) 106.8m.; brs. in Aleppo and Homs; Chair. and Gen. Man. Dr. A. S. KANAAN.

Popular Credit Bank: Darwishieh, Harika, P.O.B. 2841, Damascus; f. 1967; governmental bank; cap. 3m., dep. 95m. (Dec. 1973).

Real Estate Bank: Damascus; f. 1966; cap. 25m.

INSURANCE

Société d'Assurances Syrienne: Taghiz St., Damascus; f. 1953; a nationalized company; operates throughout Syria, with branches in Jordan and Lebanon; Chair. and Gen. Man. Dr. AZIZ SAKR.

TRADE AND INDUSTRY

CHAMBERS OF COMMERCE

Damascus Chamber of Commerce: B.P. 1040, Mou'awiah St., Damascus; f. 1914; 3,800 mems.; Pres. BADRED-DINE SHALLAH; Gen. Dir. MUHAMMAD THABET Gh. MAHAYNI; publ. *Economic Bulletin* (quarterly).

Aleppo Chamber of Commerce: Al-Moutanabbi Str., Aleppo; f. 1885; Pres. KASSEM NOUR-EL-DINE; Dir. FADEL ANIS.

Hama Chamber of Commerce and Industry: Sh. Bachoura, Hama; f. 1934; Pres. ABDUL-HAMID KAMBAZ.

Homs Chamber of Commerce and Industry: Aboul-of St., Homs; f. 1938; Pres. YUSUF AL-IKHOUAN; Dir. SELIM AL-MUSANNEF.

Latakia Chamber of Commerce: Sh. Al-Hurriyah, Latakia; Pres. JULE NASRI.

CHAMBERS OF INDUSTRY

Aleppo Chamber of Industry: Sh. Wara el-Jameh, Aleppo; Pres. SAMI AL-DAHR.

Damascus Chamber of Industry: P.O.B. 1305, Harika-Mouawiya St., Damascus; Pres. SHAFIC SOUCCAR; Gen. Man. ABDUL HAMID MALAKANI; publ. *Al Siniye* (Industry) (irregularly).

EMPLOYERS' ORGANIZATIONS

FEDERATIONS

Fédération Générale à Damas: Damascus; f. 1951; Dir. TALAT TAGLUBI.

Fédération de Damas: Damascus; f. 1949.

Fédération des Patrons et Industriels à Lattaquié: Latakia; f. 1953.

TRADE UNIONS

Ittihad Naqabat al-'Ummal al-'Am fi Suriya (*General Federation of Labour Unions*): Qanawat Street, Damascus; f. 1948; Pres. FAWZI BALI; Sec. MAHMUD FAHURI.

TRADE

Foire Internationale de Damas: 67 blvd. de Baghdad, Damascus; held annually from July 25th to August 20th.

OIL

General Petroleum Company: P.O.B. 2849, Damascus; f. 1958; state agency; holds the oil concession for all Syria; exploits the Suwadiyah, Karachuk and Rumaila oilfields; production in 1973 4.5 million metric tons; also organizes refining, storage and distribution of petroleum; Dir. Engineer GHASSAN MOUHANNA.

TRANSPORT

RAILWAYS

Syrian Railways: Registered Office: B.P. 182, Aleppo; Pres. of the Board of Administration Ing. OMAR SIBAI; Gen. Man. ABDELJABBAR KOUNDAKJI.

The present railway system is composed of the following network:

Meydan Ekbez (Turkish frontier)–Aleppo; Çoban-bey (Turkish frontier)–Aleppo; Qamishliya (Turkish frontier)–Jaroubieh (Iraq frontier); Aleppo–Homs; Koussair (Lebanese frontier)–Aleppo; Homs–Akkari (Lebanese frontier); there are 555 km. of normal gauge and 313 km. of narrow gauge track. Lines from Latakia to Aleppo (partially completed) and Djezira are under construction, and work on a line between Homs and Damascus (204 km.) has begun.

Syrian Railways: Northern Lines: 248 km, Southern Lines: 295 km.

Hejaz Railways (narrow gauge): 301 km. in Syria; the historic railway to Medina is the subject of a reconstruction project jointly with Jordan and Saudi Arabia, but little progress has been made since the June 1967 war.

ROADS

Arterial roads run across the country linking the north to the south and the Mediterranean to the eastern frontier. The main arterial networks are as follows: Sidon (Lebanon)-Quneitra-Sweida-Salkhad-Jordan border; Beirut (Lebanon)-Damascus - Khan Abu Chamat - Iraq border - Baghdad; Tartous - Tell Kalakh - Homs - Palmyra; Banias - Hama - Salemie; Latakia-Aleppo-Rakka-Deirezzor-Abou Kemal-Iraq border; Tripoli (Lebanon)-Tartous-Banias-Latakia; Turkish border - Antakya; Amman (Jordan) - Dera'a - Damascus-Homs-Hama-Aleppo-Azaz (Turkish border); Haifa (Israel) - Kuneitra - Damascus - Palmyra - Deirezzor-Hassetche-Kamechlie.

Asphalted roads: 6,000 km, macadam roads: 1,300 km, earth roads: 6,000 km.

Touring Club de Syrie: P.O.B. 28, Aleppo; f. 1950; the principal Syrian motoring organization; Pres. ALFRED GIRARDI.

PIPELINES

The oil pipelines which cross Syrian territory are of great importance to the national economy, representing a considerable source of foreign exchange. One of the pipelines runs from the installations at Kirkuk in Iraq to Tripoli in the Lebanon, cutting through approximately 300 miles of Syrian territory. Another line also crosses Syria *en route* to Sidon (Lebanon). Another line, completed in 1968, runs from Karatchouk, through Homs to a terminal at Tartous.

Following the Iraq Government's nationalization of the Iraq Petroleum Company, the Syrian Government nationalized the IPC's pipelines, pumping stations and other installations in Syria, setting up a new company to administer them:

Syrian Company for Oil Transport (SCOT): Dir.-Gen. HANNA HADDAD.

SHIPPING

The port of Latakia has developed and the construction of a deep water harbour was completed in 1959. A new port at Tartous is under construction.

The Iraq Petroleum Company has built a harbour at Banias to handle the oil transported in underground pipelines from Kirkuk.

CIVIL AVIATION

A new international airport for Damascus was opened in the summer of 1969.

Syrian Arab Airlines: P.O.B. 417, Red Crescent Bldg., Yousef-Al-Azmeh Square, Damascus; f. 1946, refounded 1961 after revocation of merger with Misrair forming U.A.A.; domestic services and routes to Abu Dhabi, Algiers, Athens, Baghdad, Benghazi, Budapest, Cairo, Casablanca, Copenhagen, Delhi, Dhahran, Doha, Dubai, East Berlin, Jeddah, Karachi, Kuwait, London, Moscow, Munich, Paris, Prague, Sana'a, Sofia, Teheran, Tripoli and Tunis; fleet of four Caravelles and two Boeing 707 on lease; Chair. Major-Gen. ASSAD MOUKAYED; Man. Dir. Air Brig.-Gen. AHMAD ANTAR.

The following foreign airlines serve Syria: Aeroflot, Air France, Alitalia, Ariana Afghan Airlines, Balkan (Bulgaria), British Airways, ČSA, EgyptAir, Interflug, Iraqi Airways, KLM, Kuwait Airways, Lufthansa, Malev, Pan American, Pakistan International Airlines, Qantas, SAS, Saudia and Swissair.

TOURISM

Ministry of Tourism: Abou Firas El-Hamadani St., Damascus; f. 1972; Minister of Tourism ABDALLAH KHANI; Vice-Minister B. KASSAB HASSAN; Dir. of Tourist Relations IHSAN CHICHAKLI.

Youth Tourism and Travel Organization: Av. 29 Mai, B.P. 201, Damascus; f. 1966; Dir. MOHAMED D'ADOUCH; 3 brs.

DEFENCE

Minister of Defence and C.-in-C. of the Armed Forces: Maj.-Gen. MUSTAFA TLAS.

Chief of Staff of the Armed Forces: Maj.-Gen. YUSUF SHAKKUR.

Defence Budget (1974): £S 1,618 million.

Military Service: 30 months (Jewish population exempted).

Total Armed Forces: 137,500: army 125,000; navy 2,500; air force 10,000.

Paramilitary Forces: 9,500 (8,000 Gendarmerie, 1,500 Desert Guard (Frontier Force).

EDUCATION

Compulsory schooling lasts six years up to the age of 14, and text books are issued free in the primary sector. Both primary and secondary education are expanding rapidly.

Technical schools prepare students mainly for work in agriculture and are open to the sons of peasants. Higher education is provided by the Universities of Damascus, Aleppo and Latakia, and the Damascus Institute of Technology.

The main language of instruction in schools is Arabic, but English and French are widely taught and are used for instruction in the University of Aleppo.

The budget for Culture and Information in the fiscal year 1974 was £S592 million.

UNIVERSITIES

University of Aleppo: f. 1960; 431 teachers; 13,926 students.

Damascus University: Damascus; f. 1923; 702 teachers; 37,407 students.

University of Latakia: f. 1971; 50 teachers; 2,153 students.

BIBLIOGRAPHY

ABU JABER, KAMAL S. The Arab Baath Socialist Party (Syracuse University Press, New York, 1966).

ASFOUR, EDMUND Y. Syrian Development and Monetary Policy (Harvard, 1959).

DIRECTORY OF COMMERCE AND INDUSTRY FOR THE SYRIAN ARAB REPUBLIC (Arab Advertising Organization, Damascus, 1969).

FEDDEN, ROBIN. Syria: an Historical Appreciation (London, 1946).
Syria and Lebanon (John Murray, London, 1966).

GLUBB, J. B. Syria, Lebanon, Jordan (Thames and Hudson, London, 1967).

HADDAD, J. Fifty Years of Modern Syria and Lebanon (Beirut, 1950).

HELBAOUI, YOUSSEF. La Syrie (Paris, 1956).

HITTI, PHILIP K. History of Syria; including Lebanon and Palestine (New York, 1951).

HOMET, M. L'Histoire secrète du traité franco-syrien (New Ed., Paris, 1951).

HOPWOOD, DEREK. The Russian presence in Syria and Palestine 1843–1914 (Oxford, 1969).

HOURANI, ALBERT H. Syria and Lebanon: A Political Essay (New York, 1946).

INTERNATIONAL BANK FOR RECONSTRUCTION AND DEVELOPMENT, THE. The Economic Development of Syria (Baltimore, 1955).

LLOYD-GEORGE, D. The Truth about the Peace Treaties, Vol. II (London, 1938).

LONGRIGG, S. H. Syria and Lebanon Under French Mandate (Oxford University Press, 1958).

PETRAN, TABITHA. Syria (Benn, London, 1972).

RABBATH, E. Unité Syrienne et Devenir Arabe (Paris, 1937).

RUNCIMAN, STEVEN. A History of the Crusades (London, Vol. I 1951, Vol. II 1952).

SAUVAGET, J. Les monuments historiques de Damas (Beirut, 1932).

SEALE, PATRICK. The Struggle for Syria (London, 1965).

SHARIF, A. A. Sources of Statistics in Syria (B.D.S.A., Damascus, 1964).

SPRINGETT, B. H. Secret Sects of Syria and the Lebanon (London, 1922).

STARK, FREYA. Letters from Syria (London, 1942).

SULTANOV, A. F. Souremennaya Siriya (Izdatel'stvo Vostochnoi Literaturni, Moscow, 1958).

THUBRON, C. A. Mirror to Damascus (Heinemann, London, 1967).

TIBAWI, A. L. Syria (London, 1962).
American Interests in Syria 1800–1901 (Oxford University Press, New York, 1966).
A Modern History of Syria (Macmillan, London, 1969).

TORREY, GORDON H. Syrian Politics and the Military (State University, Ohio, 1964).

TRITTON, A. S. The Caliphs and their Non-Muslim Subjects (London, 1930).

WEULERSSE, J. Paysans de Syrie et du Proche Orient (Paris, 1946).

YAMAK, L. Z. The Syrian Social Nationalist Party (Harvard University Press, Cambridge, Mass., 1966).

ZIADEH, N. Syria and Lebanon (New York, Praeger, 1957).

Tunisia

PHYSICAL AND SOCIAL GEOGRAPHY

D. R. Harris

Tunisia is the smallest of the three countries that comprise the "Maghreb" of north Africa but it is more cosmopolitan than either Algeria or Morocco. It forms a wedge of territory, 163,610 square kilometres in extent, between Algeria and Libya. It includes the easternmost ridges of the Atlas Mountains but most of it is low-lying and bordered by a long and sinuous Mediterranean coastline that faces both north and east. Ease of access by sea and by land from the east has favoured the penetration of foreign influences and Tunisia owes its distinct national identity and its varied cultural traditions to a succession of invading peoples: Phoenicians, Romans, Arabs, Turks and French. It was more completely Arabized than either Algeria or Morocco and remnants of the original Berber-speaking population of the Maghreb are confined, in Tunisia, to a few isolated localities in the south.

In 1974 the population was 5,641,000 and the overall density was 34.5 per square kilometre. Most of the people live in the more humid, northern part of the country and in 1966 one-seventh of the total were concentrated in the sprawling city of Tunis and its suburbs. Situated strategically where the Sicilian Channel links the western with the central Mediterranean and close to the site of ancient Carthage, Tunis combines the functions of capital and chief port. No other town approaches Tunis in importance but on the east coast both Sousse (population 90,000) and Sfax (population 100,000) provide modern port facilities, as does Bizerta (population 70,000) on the north coast, while some distance inland the old Arab capital and holy city of Kairouan (population 50,000) serves as a regional centre.

The principal contrasts in the physical geography of Tunisia are between a humid and relatively mountainous northern region, a semi-arid central region of low plateaux and plains and a dry Saharan region in the south. The northern region is dominated by the easternmost folds of the Atlas mountain system which form two separate chains, the Northarn and High Tell, separated by the valley of the River Medjerda, the only perennially flowing river in the country. The Northern Tell, which is a continuation of the Algerian Tell Atlas, consists mainly of sandstone and extends along the north coast at heights of between 300 and 600 metres. South of the Medjerda valley the much broader Tell Atlas, which is a continuation of the Saharan Atlas of Algeria, is made up of a succession of rugged sandstone and limestone ridges. Near the Algerian frontier they reach a maximum height of 1,544 metres in Djebel Chambi, the highest point in Tunisia, but the folds die away eastward towards the Cape Bon peninsula which extends north-east to within 145 kilometres of Sicily.

South of the High Tell or Dorsale ("backbone") central Tunisia consists of an extensive platform sloping gently towards the east coast. Its western half, known as the High Steppe, is made up of alluvial basins rimmed by low, barren mountains, but eastward the mountains give way first to the Low Steppe, which is a monotonous gravel-covered plateau and ultimately to the flat coastal plain of the Sahel. Occasional watercourses cross the Steppes but they only flow after heavy rain and usually fan out and evaporate in salt flats, or sebkhas, before reaching the sea.

The central Steppes give way southward to a broad depression occupied by two great seasonal salt lakes or shotts. The largest of these, the Shott Djerid, lies at 16 metres below sea-level and is normally covered by a salt crust. It extends from close to the Mediterranean coast near Gabès almost to the Algerian frontier and is adjoined on the north-west by the Shott el Rharsa which lies at 21 metres below sea-level. South of the shotts Tunisia extends for over 320 kilometres into the Sahara. Rocky, flat-topped mountains, the Monts des Ksour, separate a flat plain known as the Djeffara, which borders the coast south of Gabès, from a sandy lowland which is partly covered by the dunes of the Great Eastern Erg.

The climate of northern Tunisia is "Mediterranean" in type with hot, dry summers followed by warm, wet winters. Average rainfall reaches 150 cm. in the Kroumirie Mountains, which is the wettest area in north Africa, but over most of the northern region it varies from 40 to 100 cm. The wetter and least accessible mountains are covered with forests in which cork oak and evergreen oak predominate, but elsewhere lower rainfall and overgrazing combine to replace forest with meagre scrub growth. South of the High Tell rainfall is reduced to between 20 and 40 cm. annually, which is insufficient for the regular cultivation of cereal crops without irrigation, and there is no continuous cover of vegetation. Large areas of the Steppes support only clumps of wiry esparto grass, which is collected and exported for paper manufacture. Southern Tunisia experiences full desert conditions. Rainfall is reduced to below 20 cm. annually and occurs only at rare intervals. Extremes of temperature and wind are characteristic and vegetation is completely absent over extensive tracts. The country supports only a sparse nomadic population except where supplies of underground water make cultivation possible, as in the famous date-producing oasis of Tozeur on the northern edge of the Shott Djerid.

HISTORY

Although the creation of the present-day independent Republic of Tunisia has been a phenomenon of the post-war period, the history of this small but important part of North Africa has displayed a certain continuity since the earliest times. From the early days of Phoenician settlement in the course of the ninth century B.C., the region has alternated between being itself a focus of political control (the Carthaginian Empire, or the period of medieval Islam, for example) reaching out to colonize or dominate the adjacent shores of the Mediterranean; and being the object of imperial aggrandizement (Rome, the Ottoman Empire, France) on the part of the dominant Mediterranean power of the time. On top of this pattern must be superimposed the conquest of North Africa by the Arabs in the course of the seventh century A.D., which has determined the basic characteristics of Tunisia ever since.

The history of Tunisia may be said to begin with the establishment there of colonies of Phoenician settlers, and the rise of the Carthaginian Empire. Emerging, in the course of the sixth century B.C., from the mists of its legendary foundation by the semi-mythical Queen Dido, by *c.* 550 B.C. Carthage had reached a position of commercial and naval supremacy in the Mediterranean, controlling part of Sicily, and with trading colonies established as far as what is now southern Portugal. The empire reached its height in the course of the fourth century, but shortly afterwards became involved with the rising power of the Roman Republic in a bitter struggle for the hegemony of the Mediterranean. The Punic Wars (264–241; 218–201; 149–146), of which the second is memorable for Hannibal's invasion of Italy, ended in the utter destruction of Carthage as a political entity, and the incorporation of its domains within the growing empire of Rome.

After one and a half centuries of abandonment, the ancient site of Carthage was rebuilt by Augustus at the dawn of the Christian era: intensive colonization from this time onward brought to what had become the Province of Africa a new prosperity, and the blessings of Roman civilization. During the first two centuries A.D. Carthage was generally accounted the second city of the Empire after Rome, but with the decline of the Empire in the west in the course of fourth century, the great days of Roman Carthage were over. In A.D. 439 the city was lost to the Vandals, a nomadic people of Germanic origin, and became the capital of their ephemeral state, to be recovered for the Byzantine Empire in 533–34.

For the next two hundred and fifty years the history of Tunisia cannot be separated from the larger account of North Africa. Although Byzantine rule was better established in Tunisia than in the rest of the area, it was by no means secure. The tendency of the local governors to free themselves of the control of Constantinople was echoed by religious dissensions among the native population, who, largely Berber in origin, adopted various Christian heresies as tokens of their opposition to Imperial rule.

It was from another quarter, however, that the final challenge to Byzantine rule was to come The foundation in Arabia of the power of Islam, and its rapid expansion after the death of the Prophet (632), led quickly to the Arab conquest of Egypt and Syria, and to the shattering of the precarious unity of the Byzantine Empire. The first Arab raids into North Africa soon followed (647). After a confused period, in which the Arabs, the Berbers, and the forces of Byzantium all contested for the control of North Africa, Arab control over the area was finally established (698) with the conquest of Carthage, and the foundation of the town of Tunis. Islam now spread rapidly amongst the Berbers, but did not prevent them from making further attempts to regain their independence, merely providing them with new and more convenient pretexts for revolt in the shape of new Islamic religious heresies. The greater part of the eighth century is taken up with Berber-supported Kharijite risings, manifestations of extreme left-wing Islam against the central government, and with constant revolts among the occupying Arab forces. In the last years of the Umayyad dynasty (overthrown 748–50) Tunisia escaped completely from Imperial control: the new dynasty of the Abbasids, ruling from Iraq, made strong efforts to recapture the province. Kayrawan, founded in 670 as the centre of Arab rule in the Maghreb, was retaken, but lost in 767, when a period of complete anarchy ensued. After a period of rule by petty chieftains, Tunisia was restored to Abbasid control in the year 800, in the person of Ibrahim ibn Aghlab. As a reward for his services, and as a means of maintaining the form if not the actuality of imperial control over the area, the caliph Harun al-Rashid thereupon appointed him as tributary ruler of al-Ifrikiya—corresponding more or less to the Roman Province of Africa, and to the present-day state of Tunisia.

The period of Aghlabid rule is one of great importance for the history of Tunisia. For the major part of the ninth century the country enjoyed a relatively stable and prosperous existence, while the importance of the dynasty was early recognized by the arrival of an embassy from the Emperor Charlemagne. Some years later, returning in a different way the interest of Europe, Aghlabid forces began the conquest of Sicily (827–39). The middle of the ninth century was the zenith of Aghlabid rule, and was signalized by the emir Ahmed with the construction of great mosques in the major cities, and the building of an elaborate system of dams and reservoirs to supply the capital of Kayrawan. From 874 the power of the Aghlabid state began to decline; despite the virtual completion of the conquest of Sicily (878) the dynasty was finally overthrown in the course of a religious revolution from the west. Between 905 and 909 Tunisia was brought under the control of the Fatimids, adherents and fanatical propagators of the heretical doctrines of Shi'ism. Established in their new capital of Mahdiya, on the Tunisian coast, the Fatimids pursued a vigorous policy of expansion and conquest. Expeditions were sent against Egypt, and Sicily was once more ruled from North Africa, while by 933 Fatimid rule was established throughout the Maghreb. A serious threat to the regime, posed in 943–47 by the terrible Berber revolt led by "the man with the donkey", was overcome, and for the next twenty-five years Tunisia enjoyed a certain degree of prosperity. Fatimid power meanwhile was expanding in the east. In 969–70 the dynasty gained control of Egypt and Syria: three years later the caliph al-Muizz abandoned Mahdiya for his new capital of Cairo, and handed over the government of Tunisia to the Zirids, a family of Berber princes who had long supported the Fatimid regime. Under Zirid rule Tunisia enjoyed great prosperity, in which the arts and sciences, commerce and industry, all flourished, but this golden age was suddenly brought to an end in 1050 by the Zirids transferring their allegiance from Cairo to the orthodox caliph at Baghdad. Fatimid revenge was terrible. In 1051 hundreds of thousands of Hilali Arab nomads were sent against Ifrikiya from Egypt. Under the devastating impact of these marauding nomads the economy crumbled, along with the political power of the Berbers, and the country as a whole lapsed into political fragmentation. Further troubles now came from another quarter. In 1087 forces from the rising Italian city-states of Pisa and Genoa took Mahdiya, allowing the Zirids, who had held out there against the Hilali invasion, to continue as its rulers. Early in the twelfth century the Zirids renewed their loyalty to Cairo, and attempted to restore the shattered fragments of their state, but were interrupted by the Normans, who, having previously conquered Sicily and Malta, in 1148 drove the last Zirid from Mahdiya.

Norman rule in Tunisia was short-lived. By 1160 they had been ejected from their last coastal stronghold, and for the next fifty years Tunisia formed part of the empire of the caliphs of Marrakesh (the Almohads). With the thirteenth century the authority of Baghdad was briefly restored over Tunisia. In 1207 the Abbasid caliph al-Nasir set up a strong provincial government under a member of the Berber family of the Hafsids, who, having held the governorship of Tunis since 1184, were to continue as the main political force in the area until the Ottoman conquest late in the sixteenth century

For the most of the thirteenth century the Hafsids ruled over North Africa from Tripoli to central Algeria, and maintained close diplomatic and commercial relations with the trading ports and city-states of the northern shores of the Mediterranean. European interest in Tunisia had never disappeared since the temporary Norman conquest of the twelfth century: with the weakening of Hafsid rule in face of tribal and Arab unrest, Jerba came once more into Christian hands (1284–1337). In the reign of Abu'l-Abbas (1370–94) the fortunes of the dynasty once more improved, and further Christian attempts to seize

coastal places were repelled. His son held off repeated Sicilian and Catalan attempts to capture Jerba, and in 1428 went on the offensive, becoming involved in operations against Malta. The last Hafsid ruler of note was Abu Amr Uthman (1435–88). Shortly after his death the Hafsid Empire began to disintegrate, and at the same time Tunisia became involved in the wider struggle between the resurgent forces of the newly-unified Spanish monarchy and the Ottoman Empire for control of the Mediterranean, the outcome of which conflict was to determine the future of Tunisia for the next four centuries, and to mark its emergence as a definite political entity.

OTTOMAN RULE

With the completion of the *reconquista* in 1492 by the incorporation of the Muslim kingdom of Granada, Spain turned her attentions to the conquest of Muslim North Africa. The first place in the crumbling Hafsid territories to fall under her control was Bougie, in 1510, and then Tripoli, in the same year. Ten years later the strategic place of Jerba also fell. But these events had already produced a reaction. In 1516 Algiers had come into the possession of the Turkish corsair Aruj. His brother, Khayr ed-Din Barbarossa, who had succeeded him in 1518, had in 1533 been summoned to Istanbul to act as high admiral of the Ottoman fleet. In this new capacity he drove the compliant Emir al-Hasan from Tunis (1534), and placed the town under Ottoman control. In the following year a great Ottoman naval expedition retook the town, and al-Hasan returned as the Emperor's vassal, handing over la Goleta to Spain as the price of his restoration. Further coastal strongholds subsequently passed into Spanish hands, while in 1542 al-Hassan was deposed by his son Ahmed, who, with the not disinterested help of the Turkish corsair chiefs, made a final attempt to reunite Tunisia against Spain. After a long drawn-out struggle Ahmed fell at the siege of Malta, 1565, which, together with the Spanish naval victory of Lepanto six years later, marks the climax and virtual end of their struggle with the Ottomans for control of the sea. As far as Tunisia was concerned, the sole beneficiaries of the struggle were the Ottomans. Already well established at Algiers, in 1569 the Pasha of Algiers, Uluj Ali, placed a garrison in Tunis, only to be driven out briefly (1572) in the aftermath of the Spanish victory at Lepanto. The unfortunate Hafsid was restored for the last time as nominal ruler, but in 1574 an Ottoman expedition put an end to Spanish power in Tunis, and to the Hafsid dynasty itself.

Direct Ottoman rule in Algiers lasted only seventeen years. The provincial administration set up in 1574 took its orders at first from Algiers, and later from the Porte itself, but a military revolt in 1591 reduced the power of the Pasha, the actual representative of the sultan, to a cypher, and the affairs of the state were taken over by one of the forty *deys* or high officers of the Ottoman army of occupation. By *c.* 1600 a situation had arisen analogous to that in Algiers, the *diwan*, or governing council, coming to share a pre-eminent place with the *taifa*, or guild of the corsair chiefs. By 1606 the *de facto* independence of Tunisia had been recognized by the dispatch of a French embassy, under orders to negotiate commercial privileges with Tunis without reference to the Porte. Nevertheless, for the next two and a half centuries and more, Tunisia was regarded as part of the Ottoman Empire, a convenient fiction both flattering to the government at Istanbul, and useful to the *deys* in safeguarding their rule and bolstering their reputation with outside powers.

In the first half of the seventeenth century the situation of Tunis was fairly flourishing. Trade and commerce, especially with Marseilles and Livorno, prospered, while commercial relations were entered into with states as far distant as England and the Netherlands. From *c.* 1650 the power of the *deys* declined, and authority in the state gradually passed to the *beys*, originally subordinate in rank. Hammuda, *bey* from 1659 to 1663, became master of the entire country, and assured the maintenance of power in his family—the Muradids—until 1702. This was a period of decline, with tribal unrest away from Tunis, and incursions from the direction of Algiers. With the accession of Huseyn Ali Turki in 1705 a new line of *beys* brought some semblance of order to the country. The remainder of the eighteenth century passed fairly uneventfully for Tunisia, with a certain amount of quiet prosperity, despite the uncertainty of relations with Algeria, and the growing naval power of Europe in the Mediterranean.

With the aftermath of the Napoleonic Wars came the first real impact of Europe on Tunisia. The European powers, in congress at Vienna and Aachen (1815–17) forced upon the *bey* Mahmud (1814–24) the suppression of the corsairs and their piratical activities, which had provided a considerable part of the revenues of the state. The French occupied Algiers in 1830, and subsequently reduced the whole of Algeria to colonial status. The next fifty years witnessed desperate but unavailing efforts by Tunisia to avoid the same fate. Increasingly the influence of France and Britain, and later Italy, came to be manifest through the activities of their consuls. The *bey* Ahmed (1837–55) attempted to reform the army on western lines, and to liberalize the institutions of society: his efforts merely increased the financial dependence of Tunisia on France. Under Muhammad (1855–59) a proclamation of reform and equality based on the Ottoman Hatti-Sherif of 1839 was promulgated under European pressure: his successor Muhammad al-Sadik (1859–82) promulgated a Constitution (suspended 1864) which attempted to separate executive from legislative power, to codify the laws, and to guarantee the independence of the judiciary.

Nevertheless, Tunisia's position deteriorated. Increased taxes, imposed from the mid-fifties, provoked tribal rebellion, and the growing dependence on foreign loans led to foreign intervention. Annual debt charges eventually exceeded revenue and in 1869 the *bey* was obliged to accept international financial control by France, Britain and Italy. By 1881 the imminence of financial collapse decided France to intervene, especially as at the Congress of Berlin three years earlier Britain, confronted by French hostility to the Cyprus Convention between Britain and Turkey, had indicated that it would not contest French influence in Tunisia, which Germany actually encouraged. French forces invaded Tunisia in April 1881, the immediate occasion being incidents on the frontier with Algeria. They encountered no serious resistance and the *bey* was forced to accept the terms of the Treaty of Kassar Said (also known as the Treaty of Bardo) under which he remained the nominal ruler of his country while French officials took over the direction of military, financial and foreign affairs.

FRENCH PROTECTORATE

The French presence once established, French control was soon extended. In 1883 Ali IV, the successor to Muhammad al-Sadik, was forced to sign the Treaty of Mersa, which formally established a French protectorate over Tunisia and brought the actual government of the country under French control. Although the office of *bey* was preserved, the real power passed to the French Resident-General. The international control commission was abolished in 1884, the currency was reformed on French lines in 1891, and the extra-territorial privileges of other Europeans were abrogated. Encouraged by large-scale grants of land, there was a considerable influx of settlers from France, and also from Italy, especially after 1900. Besides being confronted with the task of sustaining the economy by something better than the proceeds of piracy, which they tackled by investment in the development of the country's resources, the French were faced with rivalry from Italy, whose ambitions in North Africa were not extinguished until the collapse of the Fascist regime in the Second World War, and with the rise of Tunisian nationalism.

Tunisian cultural and political life absorbed many French ideas but was also influenced by movements in other parts of the Islamic world. An attempt to emulate the Young Turk reformers in the Ottoman Empire was seen in the Young Tunisian movement (1908) which called for the restoration of the authority of the *bey* together with reforms on democratic lines. The achievement of independence in eastern Arab countries after the First World War, and the example of the nationalist movement in Egypt, inspired Tunisians with a greater national consciousness and in 1920 the Destour (Constitution) movement was formed under the leadership of Shaikh al-Tha'libi, one of the founders of the pre-war Young Tunisians.

The Destour called for a self-governing constitutional regime with a legislative assembly. French attempts to conciliate opinion by administrative reforms, beginning in 1920 with economic councils on which Tunisians were represented, did not satisfy the more radical elements, however, and in the face of further nationalist activity repressive measures were resorted to. Shaikh al-Tha'libi was exiled in 1923 and in 1925 the Destour movement was broken up. It revived in the years after the Depression but soon split, the old Destour leaders being accused of collaboration with France by younger members eager for political action on a broad front. In 1934, led by Habib Bourguiba, a Tunisian lawyer, these created the Néo-Destour (New Constitution) Party. The new party employed methods of widespread political agitation as a result of which Bourguiba was exiled. With the victory of the Popular Front in France in 1936 he returned to Tunisia but little was achieved in direct negotiations with the new French government, from which much had been expected in the way of reforms. The Néo-Destour was built up into a powerful organization, its influence extending into all parts of the country, and its strength was proved in a successful general strike in 1938. Widespread clashes with the police followed, martial law was proclaimed, some 200 nationalists were arrested and both the Destour and Néo-Destour parties were dissolved.

When the Second World War broke out in the following year Tunisian opinion rallied in favour of France and when Italy entered the war some 23,000 Italians in Tunisia were interned. With the fall of France Tunisia came under Vichy rule and Bizerta, Tunis and other ports were used by Germany and Italy to supply their armies in Libya. The country became a theatre of war until the defeat of the Axis forces by the Allies in 1943 brought about the eventual restoration of French authority. The *bey*, Muhammad al-Monsif, was accused of collaboration with the Axis powers and deposed; he was replaced by his cousin, Muhammad al-Amin, who reigned until Tunisia became a republic in 1957.

GROWING AUTONOMY

The virtual restoration of peace-time conditions in 1944 brought a relaxation of political restrictions and the years immediately following saw renewed agitation for political changes. French action to repress this obliged Habib Bourguiba to remove himself to Cairo in 1945 but his chief lieutenant, Salah ben Youssef, was able to remain in Tunisia. The French authorities turned their attention to political reforms and by Beylical decrees in 1945 the Council of Ministers and the Grand Council (an elected body with equal French and Tunisian representation) were reorganized, the authority of the latter being extended. These moves did not satisfy the nationalists, however, who in August 1946 at a national congress unequivocally demanded complete independence. Later in the year a ministry was formed under Muhammad Kaak which included an increased number of Tunisians (moderate leaders being appointed, the Destour and Néo-Destour having refused to participate); the French retained overriding control.

Bourguiba returned to Tunisia in 1949. In April 1950 Néo-Destour proposals were put forward for the transfer of sovereignty and executive control to Tunisian hands, under a responsible government with a Prime Minister appointed by the *bey* and an elected National Assembly which would draw up a democratic constitution. Local French interests would be protected by representation on municipal councils, and Tunisia would co-operate with France on terms of equality. These proposals were met with a reasonable response in France and a new Tunisian government was formed in August 1950, composed of an equal number of Tunisian and French ministers, with Muhammad Chenik as Chief Minister and Salah ben Youssef Minister of Justice. The object of the new Government was stated to be the restoration of Tunisian sovereignty in stages, in co-operation with France. Despite strong opposition to these developments from the European settlers (some 10 per cent of the population), who opposed all concessions to nationalist demands, further reforms were effected in September 1950 and February 1951, when French advisers to the Tunisian ministers were removed and the Resident-General's control over the Council of Ministers was diminished.

Peaceful progress towards autonomy came to a halt, however, with growing settler opposition, procrastination on the part of the French government and consequent alienation of the nationalists. Franco-Tunisian negotiations in 1951 came to nothing and Tunisian resentment erupted in strikes and demonstrations early in 1952. In February 1952 Bourguiba and other Néo-Destour leaders were arrested on the order of a new Resident-General, de Hautecloche, and a wave of violence spread throughout the country, culminating in the arrest and removal from office of the Chief Minister and the imposition of French military control.

A new Government was formed under Salaheddine Baccouche, a French-inspired scheme of reforms designed to lead to eventual internal autonomy was announced in April, and a temporary easing of tension followed, although the now-proscribed Néo-Destour took their case to Cairo and the UN General Assembly. Against a background of increasing terrorism, countered by French repressive action, and in face of opposition from both the Néo-Destour and the settlers, little in the way of reform could be achieved. The *bey* at first refused to sign French reform decrees and when he yielded in December 1952 under the threat of deposition the proposals were promptly repudiated by the Néo-Destour.

Terrorist activities continued and a secret settler counter-terrorist organization, the "Red Hand", came into prominence. The situation, which approached civil war in 1953, with bands of *fellagha* active in the western highlands and around Bizerta, and terrorism and counter-terrorism in the towns, did not improve until July 1954, when the newly-formed Mendès-France government in France offered internal autonomy for Tunisia with responsibility only for defence and foreign affairs being retained by France. The French proposals were accepted and in August a new Tunisian government headed by Tahar ben Ammar, which contained moderate nationalists but also three Néo-Destour members, was formed. Negotiations with the French government began at Carthage in September 1954 and although they had reached deadlock when the Mèndes-France government fell in February 1955 they were resumed in March and a final agreement was signed in Paris on June 2nd.

The agreement gave internal autonomy to Tunisia while at the same time protecting French interests and preserving the close links with France. France retained responsibility for foreign affairs, defence (including the control of frontiers) and internal security.

Although it was supported by a majority of the Néo-Destour, the extremist wing, headed by the exiled Salah ben Youssef, and the old Destour and Communist elements, opposed it, as also did the settlers' organizations. An all-Tunisian cabinet was formed in September 1955 by Tahar ben Ammar, with Néo-Destour members holding six of the twelve posts.

Habib Bourguiba had returned from three years' exile in June 1955, to be followed by Salah ben Youssef in September. In October, however, ben Youssef was expelled from the party for opposition to the recent agreement and for "splitting activities". A Néo-Destour party congress at Sfax in November 1955 confirmed the expulsion and re-elected Bourguiba as party president. The congress accepted the agreement but at the same time reaffirmed that it would be satisfied only with independence and demanded the election of a constituent assembly. Clashes between "Bourguibist" and "Youssefist" factions followed and in December a conspiracy to set up a terrorist organization to prevent the implementation of the agreement was discovered. Salah ben Youssef fled to Tripoli in January 1956 and many suspected "Youssefists" were placed in detention. At the same time *fellagha* activity revived, rebel bands becoming active in the remoter parts of the country and acts of terrorism being committed against both Frenchmen and members of the Néo-Destour.

INDEPENDENCE

Against the background of these events a Tunisian delegation led by Bourguiba began independence negotiations with the French Government in Paris on February 27th, 1956. In a protocol signed on March 20th France formally recognized the independence of Tunisia and its right to exercise responsibility over foreign affairs, security and defence, and to set up a national army. A transitional period was envisaged during which French forces would gradually be withdrawn from Tunisia, including Bizerta.

Elections for a Constituent Assembly, immediately held on March 25th, resulted in all 98 seats being won by candidates of the National Front, all of whom acknowledged allegiance to the Néo-Destour. The elections were boycotted by the "Youssefist" opposition. The ministry of Tahar ben Ammar resigned and Habib Bourguiba became Prime Minister on April 11th, leading a government in which 16 of the 17 ministers belonged to the Néo-Destour.

In the early years of independence Tunisia's relations with France were bedevilled by the question of the evacuation of French forces. A Tunisian demand for their withdrawal was rejected in July 1956 by a French government preoccupied with a deteriorating situation in Algeria. Bourguiba visited Paris in September in an attempt to promote a mediated settlement in Algeria based on French recognition of Algeria's right to independence but hopes of progress in this direction were shattered by the French kidnapping in October of five leading Algerian nationalists on their way from Morocco to Algeria. Tunisia immediately severed diplomatic relations with France, anti-French riots broke out and there were clashes between French troops and Tunisian demonstrators resulting in deaths on both sides.

Moves were made early in 1957 to strengthen Tunisia's relations with her neighbours. In January a treaty of good-neighbourliness was signed with Libya and proclaimed to be a step towards establishing a "Greater Arab Maghreb", and in March, at the end of a visit by Bourguiba, a twenty-year treaty of friendship was concluded with Morocco.

The *bey*, Muhammed al-Amin, had for long been the object of criticism from Tunisian nationalist leaders who saw him as having been unwilling to participate actively in the struggle for independence and apt to rely on French support. After independence his remaining powers were whittled away and on July 25th, 1957, the Constituent Assembly decided to abolish the monarchy, proclaim Tunisia a republic and invest Bourguiba with the powers of Head of State.

RELATIONS WITH FRANCE

Although diplomatic relations with France had been resumed in January 1957, differences between the two governments in connection with the Algerian revolt soon worsened. In May France suspended economic aid; Tunisia retaliated by abrogating the customs union with France and concluding trade agreements with Yugoslavia and Switzerland. In the same month French troops in Tunisia attempted to drive back into Algeria several thousand Algerian refugees who had crossed the border. Clashes between French forces and Tunisian national guards followed and Bourguiba called for negotiations for the withdrawal of all French troops to Bizerta. The French government's proposal to withdraw 10,000 out of the 25,000 French troops in Tunisia was cautiously welcomed, but at the same time the French claimed, and in September began to exercise, the right to pursue Algerian rebel bands across the Tunisian frontier. Bourguiba, now President, declared a state of emergency along the border with Algeria on September 9th and relations with France once more neared breaking point.

A further difference arose over the question of arms supplies. A French refusal in May 1957 to supply military equipment to Tunisia led President Bourguiba to look elsewhere. French attempts to prevent Tunisia from obtaining arms from any country other than France proved unsuccessful and in November the United States and Britain announced, to French protests, that they would proceed with deliveries.

During October and November 1957 discussions between President Bourguiba, the King of Morocco and Algerian rebel leaders resulted in an offer by Tunisia and Morocco of their good offices in an attempt to achieve a settlement which would combine sovereignty for Algeria with the safeguarding of French interests. This was accepted by the rebel leaders but rejected by the French government.

The most serious Franco-Tunisian incident of the Algerian war occurred in February 1958 when French aircraft from Algeria attacked the Tunisian border village of Sakhiet Sidi Youssef, the scene of several clashes the previous month, killing 79 people, injuring

130 and destroying many buildings. The Tunisian government's reaction was to break off diplomatic relations with France, to forbid all French troop movements in Tunisia, to demand the immediate evacuation of all French bases, including Bizerta, and to take the matter before the UN Security Council. French troops were blockaded in their barracks and the extra-territorial status of Bizerta, from which French warships were banned, was abolished. In addition some 600 French civilians were expelled from the frontier area and five of the seven French consulates closed.

British and United States mediation was accepted and on April 15th it was agreed that all French troops would be evacuated in accordance with a jointly-agreed timetable and Tunisian sovereignty over Bizerta recognized; at the same time the French consulates would be reopened and the cases of the expelled French civilians examined. When further clashes between Tunisian and French forces occurred in May, a state of emergency covering the whole country was proclaimed and Tunisia again took the matter to the Security Council and also requested further arms supplies from the United States and Britain.

A new phase in Franco-Tunisian relations began with the accession to power of General de Gaulle in June 1958. An agreement was concluded on June 17th under which French troops stationed outside Bizerta were to be withdrawn during the next four months, while negotiations for a provisional agreement on Bizerta were to follow. Restrictions on French troops were removed and diplomatic relations resumed. By October the only French troops remaining in Tunisia were in Bizerta.

Further elimination of French interests had mean-while commenced. In June the French-owned transport services and in August the electricity services of Tunis were nationalized. On November 29th President Bourguiba announced proposals for purchasing by 1960 all agricultural land in Tunisia owned by French citizens, for distribution to landless Tunisians.

POLITICAL CONSOLIDATION

With the improvement of relations with France the Tunisian government felt free to consolidate its internal position, by reforming the party structure of the Néo-Destour and by taking court proceedings against members of the former regime and "Youssefist" opponents. Prince Chadly, the eldest son of the ex-*bey*, and the former Prime Ministers, Tahar ben Ammar and Salaheddine Baccouche, were among those tried in the latter part of 1958 on charges which included the misuse of public funds and collaboration with the French authorities; sentences imposed ranged from heavy fines to imprisonment and loss of civic rights. Salah ben Youssef (*in absentia*) and 54 of his supporters were charged with plotting the death of President Bourguiba, smuggling arms from Libya, and aiming to overthrow the government; ben Youssef and several others were sentenced to death and most of the remainder received long prison sentences.

This trial reflected a widening breach between Tunisia and the United Arab Republic, from where ben Youssef had been conducting his activities. In October 1958 Tunisia had joined the Arab League, only to withdraw from a meeting of its Council ten days later after accusing the U.A.R. of attempts at domination. Diplomatic relations with the U.A.R. were severed the same month on the grounds of Egyptian complicity in the "Youssefist" attempt to assassinate President Bourguiba, and on the eve of ben Youssef's trial the President announced the capture of Egyptian officers who had secretly entered Tunisia to assist subversive elements to overthrow his government.

A further step in the establishment of a presidential system of government was taken with the promulgation on June 1st, 1959, of a new constitution for Tunisia, which provided for the election of the President for five years and permitted his re-election for three consecutive terms. The President was empowered to lay down the general policy of the state, choose the members of the government, hold supreme command of the armed forces and make all appointments to civil and military posts. The constitution also provided for the election of a National Assembly for five years and required the approval of the Assembly for the declaration of war, the conclusion of peace and the ratification of treaties. In elections which followed on November 8th President Bourguiba was unopposed and all 90 seats in the Assembly went to the Néo-Destour, their only opponents being the Communists.

THE BIZERTA CRISIS

During 1959 and 1960 Tunisian relations with France gradually improved. A trade and tariff agreement was signed on September 5th, 1959, and further agreements on technical co-operation and the transfer of French state property in Tunisia to the Tunisian government were concluded. In October 1959 President Bourguiba announced his support for President de Gaulle's offer of self-determination for Algeria, and Tunisia was subsequently able to act as intermediary between France and the Algerian rebels in moves towards a negotiated settlement. A meeting in Paris in February 1961 between Presidents Bourguiba and de Gaulle, at the latter's invitation, was regarded as a significant step forward in relations between the two countries.

At the same time the Tunisian claim for the handing-back of the Bizerta base was maintained and the issue came to a head on July 5th, 1961, when President Bourguiba made a formal demand for its return and repeated the claim, first put forward in 1959, to Saharan territory in Algeria adjacent to the south-western part of Tunisia. Demonstrations then took place against the continued French occupation of Bizerta and on July 17th President Bourguiba referred in the National Assembly to plans to "express our will to restore the Tunisian soil in both north and south".

Fighting between Tunisian and French troops began around the Bizerta base and in the disputed area of the Sahara on July 19th, 1961, diplomatic relations were again severed, and Tunisia called for a meeting of the UN Security Council. The fighting ended on July 22nd with the French in firm control of the base and town of Bizerta, over 800 Tunisians having been killed. In the south a Tunisian attempt to seize the fort of Garat el-Hamel also failed. A subsequent visit to Bizerta by the UN Secretary-General, Mr. Hammarskjöld, in an attempt to promote a settlement, was unsuccessful. A French statement on July 28th said that France wished to continue to use the base whilst a state of international tension persisted but was prepared to negotiate with Tunisia about its use during this period.

The immediate results of the Bizerta crisis were a rapprochement between Tunisia and other Arab states, a cooling of relations with the West and an improvement of relations with the Communist bloc.

The final settlement of the Bizerta dispute occupied the remainder of 1961 and much of 1962, talks being held in both Rome and Paris. The Algerian cease-fire in March 1962 had an immediately beneficial effect on Franco-Tunisian relations and the French base installations at Menzel Bourguiba, near Bizerta, were handed over to Tunisia on June 30th. In March 1963 agreement was reached on the transfer of some 370,000 acres of French-owned agricultural land to the Tunisian government. Other agreements, on trade and finance, were designed to reduce Tunisia's balance of payments deficit with France.

Although Algerian independence had been warmly welcomed by Tunisia the extremist doctrines of the new state conflicted with Tunisian moderation and relations quickly deteriorated. In January 1963 the Tunisian ambassador was recalled from Algiers on the grounds of alleged Algerian complicity in an unsuccessful attempt the previous month on the life of President Bourguiba in which "Youssefists" in Algeria, as well as supporters of the old Destour and army elements, were implicated. Moroccan mediation led to a conference of the Maghreb states in Rabat in February 1963 at which the Tunisians demanded the cessation of "Youssefist" activities in Algeria, and after further negotiations a frontier agreement between Tunisia and Algeria was signed in July. Algerian, and also Egyptian, leaders attended celebrations in December of the final French evacuation of Bizerta which had taken place two months earlier.

EXPROPRIATION

Despite agreement with France in February 1964 on the provision of loans and credits, it was claimed that the March 1963 agreement on the transfer of French-owned land had placed too great a strain on Tunisian financial resources and had also resulted in over-exploitation of the land held by settlers, who had been given up to five years before relinquishing it. On May 11th the Tunisian National Assembly enacted legislation authorizing the expropriation of all foreign-owned lands; this affected the proprietors of some 750,000 acres. The French immediately suspended, then cancelled, all financial aid.

This nationalization of foreign-owned land was also seen as a step towards the development of socialism in the agrarian sector of the economy. The Néo-Destour's commitment to "Tunisian socialism" was emphasized in the change of the party's name to the Parti Socialiste Destourien (PSD) at the time of the presidential and general elections in November 1964, in which President Bourguiba was again elected unopposed and the PSD, the only party to present candidates, filled all 90 seats in the National Assembly. Subsequent cabinet changes included the appointment of the President's son, Habib Bourguiba, Jr., as Foreign Minister.

From 1964 onwards internal political conditions became more settled and the attention of the government was turned to the tasks of economic development. The hold of the PSD on the country was strengthened and President Bourguiba's dominating position was unchallenged. In 1966 the setting-up was announced of a Council of the Republic, consisting of members of the government and of the political bureau of the PSD, to ensure continuing stability, one of its functions being to nominate an interim President in the event of the President's death.

FOREIGN POLICIES

Tunisia's relations with the world beyond the Arab states and Africa after 1964 tended to be influenced by the need for foreign aid, most of which was received from Western countries (particularly from the United States but also from Federal Germany) where the moderation of Tunisian policies inspired confidence. Towards the Communist world Tunisian gestures were cautious. Some economic assistance was obtained from the Soviet Union without Tunisia having shifted her non-aligned stance and, although a visit by Chou En-lai in January 1964 was followed by the establishment of diplomatic relations between Tunisia and the People's Republic of China, President Bourguiba publicly criticized Chinese policies, including the encouragement of revolution in Africa. On African issues Tunisia took a moderate line and inside the Organization of African Unity exercised a responsible influence. In 1965, in the course of a tour of French-speaking African states, President Bourguiba suggested the formation of a francophone African "Commonwealth"; the idea had a mixed reception, however, and interest soon waned.

Relations with the rest of the Arab world continued to be President Bourguiba's main foreign preoccupation and here his initiatives resulted in bitter controversy. In April 1965 he openly criticized Arab League policy on Palestine and advocated a more flexible approach, with direct negotiations with Israel on the UN partition plan of 1948. This provoked severe attacks from the U.A.R. and other Arab states (excepting Morocco, Libya and Saudi Arabia), and after violent demonstrations in Cairo and Tunis both countries withdrew their ambassadors. Tunisia's refusal at the end of April to follow the example of other Arab League states in breaking off relations with Federal Germany, which had exchanged ambassadors with Israel, increased the rift. A conference of Arab heads of state at Casablanca in May at which Tunisia was not represented, categorically rejected President

Bourguiba's proposal that Israel should be asked to cede territory to the Palestine refugees in return for recognition by the Arab states, and reaffirmed their determination to bring about the complete overthrow of Israel. In an open letter to those attending, President Bourguiba accused President Nasser of attempting to use the Arab League as an instrument of U.A.R. national policy and of interfering in the affairs of every Arab state; Tunisia was not prepared to take part in the debates of the Arab League in the light of this situation. In October 1966, after accusations by President Bourguiba that the U.A.R. was waging a campaign of insults against Tunisia, the severance of diplomatic relations with the U.A.R. was announced.

The six-day war between Israel and the Arab states in June 1967 brought immediate reconciliation in the Arab world despite long-standing differences. Tunisian troops were dispatched to the front but the Israeli success was so swift and the cease-fire came so soon that they were recalled before they had reached the scene of the fighting. Diplomatic relations between Tunisia and the U.A.R. were resumed and Tunisia was represented at the Arab summit meeting in Khartoum in September, which agreed not to recognize nor to negotiate with Israel. Untrue allegations of United States and British intervention on the side of Israel, made by Egypt and Jordan at the time of the Arab-Israel hostilities, resulted in serious rioting in Tunis where the British Embassy was sacked. Strict measures were taken by the Tunisian authorities to deal with the rioters and a student leader was subsequently sentenced to twenty years' imprisonment. After further disorders in March 1968, when his appeal was heard, 134 students and lecturers were arrested. They were tried in September on charges of plotting against the security of the state and attempting to overthrow the government. Most of them were given prison sentences.

The reconciliation between Tunisia and other Arab countries was short-lived. In May 1968, following an attack on President Bourguiba by the Syrian Prime Minister, who charged him with having betrayed the Arab struggle in Palestine, the Syrian chargé d'affaires and his staff in Tunis were accused of inciting Tunisian citizens to undertake subversive activities and ordered to leave the country. The Arab League, at a meeting in Cairo on 1st September refused to hear a statement from the Tunisian delegate criticising the Arab attitude over Israel, and particularly that of the U.A.R. On 26th September the Tunisian Government announced its intention of boycotting future meetings of the League. The statement reproached the U.A.R. with having sought to dictate to the Arab states and with having followed policies which had led to successive defeats at the hands of the Israelis and excessive dependence on communist countries. Nevertheless, Tunisian support for the Palestinian guerrilla movement was reaffirmed.

Earlier, there had been an improvement in Tunisia's relations with Algeria and an agreement had been signed in April 1968 on the demarcation of their common frontier. In May, however, the Algerians criticized statements made by President Bourguiba on the Arab-Israeli question and on the growth of Soviet naval forces in the Mediterranean, and in June the Tunisian Government granted asylum to the former Algerian Chief of Staff, Colonel Tahar Zbiri, who stood accused of leading an unsuccessful *coup d'état* against President Boumedienne. An exchange of visits by the Foreign Ministers of the two countries in the spring of 1969 brought about an improved climate for negotiation on the boundary question and on economic matters, especially those arising from the nationalization by each country of property owned by nationals of the other. On January 6th, 1970, a treaty of Co-operation and Friendship was signed, settling all outstanding issues between the two countries. It provided notably for collaboration in the exploitation of the El Borma oil-field which straddles the Tunisia-Algeria border.

THE FALL OF AHMED BEN SALAH

Between 1964 and 1969 the chief issue in internal affairs was the drive to collectivize agriculture, carried out under the leadership of Ahmed Ben Salah, Minister of Finance and Planning. The programme was carried out in the face of massive opposition in affected areas and disagreement within the ruling party itself. At the beginning of 1969 it was announced that collectivization would be completed by the end of that year, but in September in a sudden *volte-face* Ben Salah was transferred to the Ministry of Education and his agricultural policy abandoned. Ben Salah's subsequent fall was spectacular. Once generally regarded as the most brilliant member of the cabinet and a possible successor to the ageing President, he was stripped of all office, arrested and tried on a variety of charges. Found guilty in May 1970, he was sentenced to ten years' hard labour. However, he escaped from prison in February 1973 and has taken refuge in Europe, from where he has issued statements condemning President Bourguiba for acting against the people in the interests of a privileged class.

Ben Salah was the first of several ministers to experience a sharp reversal of fortune. After his re-election in November 1969, President Bourguiba spent much of his time receiving medical treatment abroad. There was speculation that the Prime Minister, Bahi Ladgham, would be his successor, especially as he ran Tunisia for six months in the President's absence. Ladgham was chairman of the committee set up to supervise the implementation of the Cairo agreement between King Hussein of Jordan and the Palestine Liberation Organization, and as such received wide publicity throughout the Arab world. However, on the pretext that Ladgham's duties in Jordan kept him too long out of the country, President Bourguiba replaced him as Premier by Hedi Nouira in October 1970. A year later the President declared that Nouira would be his successor when the time came. In March 1973 Ladgham resigned from all his political posts. Ahmad Mestiri was the next minister to fall into disgrace. As Minister of the Interior in 1970 and 1971, he demanded the liberalization of government. Consequently he was dismissed from the cabinet in September 1971, expelled from the party in 1972 and from the National Assembly in May 1973. When a revision of the constitution was finally proposed in March 1973 it included almost none of the measures suggested by Mestiri to modify the presidential nature of the régime. Indeed, during the next two years President Bourguiba and Prime Minister Nouira strengthened their grip on the country. In September 1974 the ninth party congress of the PSD elected Bourguiba as President-for-Life of the party and confirmed Nouira in the post of Secretary-General. Bourguiba appointed a new political bureau of 20 members, including 14 ministers, confirming a tendency to draw party and government closer together. In November Bourguiba was re-elected President of Tunisia unopposed and National Assembly elections saw all 112 PSD candidates returned, also without opposition. The new Assembly voted amendments to the constitution designating the Prime Minister as the President's successor and allowing for the appointment of a President-for-Life, a post to which the Assembly elected Bourguiba in March 1975.

If these formal assertions of presidential authority and popularity had little substance, there could still be no doubt of Bourguiba's hold on Tunisia. Opponents of the régime received short shrift. In August 1974 prison sentences were passed on 175 people, mostly Marxist students, for belonging to unauthorized organizations and plotting against the state, and other trials and arrests took place in late 1974 and the first half of 1975. There were student demonstrations in April 1973, but these have had no sequel and workers' strikes are still uncommon.

LIBYAN MERGER

In June 1970 the President's son, Habib Bourguiba, Jr., was replaced as Foreign Minister by Mohamed Masmoudi. From that date relations with the more radical Arab states and with radical powers outside the area improved. Normal relations were resumed with the U.A.R. and Syria, and Tunisia again took up membership of the Arab League. Diplomatic relations were established with North Viet-Nam and the Royal Government of Cambodia, and closer ties were made with China. In May 1973 Bourguiba launched a major diplomatic initiative on the Arab-Israeli dispute. He emphasized the need for dialogue and the rights of all peoples in the area to self-determination, including both Palestinians and Israelis. Many Arab states rejected the initiative as defeatist, while Jordan broke off relations with Tunisia after suggestions that King Hussein had no right to control the lands of the Palestinians. During the October War Tunisia ranged itself beside the other Arab states and sent a small contingent of troops to the front. After the ceasefire, however, President Bourguiba pointed out the continued military inferiority of the Arabs and returned to calls for a compromise solution. He continued to support the Palestinians, but relations with Jordan were re-established in March 1974.

On January 12th, 1974, after a meeting between President Bourguiba and Colonel Gaddafi, the Libyan leader, it was announced that Tunisia and Libya were to form a union. The announcement was greeted with general surprise for, despite an improvement in relations between the two countries in previous years, President Bourguiba had always shown himself to be hostile to union. Bourguiba was to be president of the new state, with Gaddafi as his deputy. It would seem that the union agreement was managed by Mohamed Masmoudi, who was present at the meeting, without the consent of the Prime Minister, Hedi Nouira, who was out of the country at the time. Nouira returned swiftly to Tunisia and on January 14th Masmoudi was dismissed from his post. The proposed referendum on the merger was postponed, and by February Libya and Tunisia were involved in an acrimonious exchange over the failure to implement the agreement. On February 11th Masmoudi was also relieved of his post in the party. He claimed that the U.S. Government was behind his dismissal, since Washington disliked his pro-Palestinian policy and his good relations with Communist countries. The proposed merger seems to have aroused little or no popular enthusiasm in Tunisia.

Apart from a certain tension with Libya in the aftermath of this confused affair, Tunisia's relations with its neighbours and with other Arab states continued to improve. Tunisia at last reached general agreement with other Arab nations on the Palestinian question, when Jordan acknowledged the need for an independent Palestine and the more radical Arab states accepted the existence of Israel. Trade and financial contacts with Arab countries grew.

For the rest, Tunisia's pro-Western orientation remained, reflecting the basic ideological choices of the régime and its dependence on aid from Western sources. Nevertheless, relations with socialist countries were friendly and the Government encouraged the growth of trade with the Soviet bloc and China. In 1975 Hedi Nouira went to both the U.S.A. and China, while the Soviet Premier, Aleksey Kosygin, visited Tunisia.

Bourguiba can depend on the continued support of Western powers and their capital as long as Tunisia maintains its favourable terms for foreign companies and its conservative attitude in world affairs. Ill-health and old-age remain the only real menace to the President's power and the political stability of the country.

ECONOMIC SURVEY

Tunisia covers an area of 163,610 square kilometres. At the last census in 1966 the population was 4,533,351 (excluding under-enumeration of about 4 per cent) and in 1974 it was estimated at 5,641,000, with over half under 25 years old. The annual rate of increase in the population in recent years has averaged 2.2 per cent, with emigration offsetting a natural rate of increase slightly above this rate. Most of the towns, and also the greater part of the rural population, are concentrated in the coastal areas. In the centre and the south, the land is infertile semi-desert, the population scattered, the standard of living very low, and the rate of growth of the population even higher than in the north.

The capital and main commercial centre is Tunis (population, including suburbs, around 800,000) which, together with the adjacent La Goulette, is also the chief port. There are about 50,000 Europeans in Tunis, mainly French and Italians, their numbers having decreased rapidly since independence. Other towns of importance are Sfax (100,000), which is the principal town in the south, the second port and the centre for exports of phosphates and olive oil, Sousse (90,000), Bizerta (70,000) and Kairouan (50,000). Approximately 65 per cent of the population depend directly on the agricultural sector, and of the total workforce of some 1.4 million (1972) about 50 per cent are employed in agriculture, which contributed only 20 per cent of the total gross domestic product in 1974. Much of agricultural employment is seasonal, bearing a large body of unskilled labourers without employment for part of the year. In 1972 about 200,000 Tunisians were employed abroad, thus relieving the domestic employment situation and providing a source of foreign exchange earnings through workers' remittances from overseas.

Tunisia is not lacking in natural resources. However, until recently, they have been poorly exploited. Agricultural production, still the mainstay of the economy, is subject to fluctuations in output which have repercussions on the rest of the domestic economy and on foreign trade. The very severe floods in September 1969 and the preceding three years of drought caused grave economic damage reflected in a worsening balance of trade and a sharp increase in the rate of inflation, which the Government had to restrain by direct price controls. However, in 1971 and in 1972 Tunisia had two exceptionally good harvests with cereal and fruit crops showing an overall increase of 50 per cent and 60 per cent respectively. Principally as a result of the exceptional harvests, but also because of production increases in manufacturing, transport, telecommunications and tourism, G.D.P. increased by 16.8 per cent in 1972, almost double the rate of growth achieved in 1971. After the exceptional growth year in 1972, poorer harvests and generally decreased mineral output resulted in an increase of only 2.8 per cent in 1973, but growth in 1974 probably surpassed the 9 per cent figure anticipated. High prices for phosphates, petroleum and olive oil were

responsible for this success. In the new four-year plan (1973–76) it is hoped to achieve an annual economic growth rate of 7.6 per cent.

Mineral resources are large and there is plenty of room for development. Phosphates and petroleum are the most important minerals, followed by iron ore. Generally speaking, with the exception of the Djerissa iron mines where the high metal content of the ore and ease of working have favoured exploitation, mining concerns in the past have often been under-equipped and frequently only exploited inter-mittently. There are substantial undeveloped deposits of iron, lead and zinc. A major hope for the future is petroleum, first found in commercial quantities in 1964. Production began in 1966, and an estimated 3.9 million metric tons were produced in 1973 (somewhat less than in 1972 because of production difficulties). Several important new discoveries have been made and the Ashtart offshore field began production in December 1973. Total crude oil production in 1974 was estimated at over 4 million metric tons. A natural gas field was discovered at Abder Rahmane in Cap Bon with reserves of 200 million cubic metres, which are sufficient to supply Tunis for 20 years.

Industry generates only a small part of national income, its development having been retarded by Tunisia's dependence on France and her market. The Government's policies on development are contained in the plans for 1962–64, 1965–68, 1969–72 and, currently, 1973–76. Encouragement is given to public and private sectors, with the latest plan emphasizing the Government's concern to attract private foreign capital for investment in export-orientated industries. Private investment from abroad has been encouraged by the remarkably liberal law of April 1972, granting extensive tax exemptions (*see* the section on Planning). Tunisia normally runs a considerable trade deficit which is covered by tourism receipts, remittances from abroad, and by foreign grants and loans of which the principal donors are the U.S.A., Federal Germany, Canada, France and the World Bank. Tunisia has, however, been successful in attracting aid from a large number of multilateral and bilateral sources. The servicing of foreign loans in recent years has required about 25 per cent of the gross receipts from exports and services. Though autonomous development is the ultimate aim, Tunisia continues to welcome foreign aid from any source. Without it, the successful implementation of the plan would be impossible.

The Tunisian economy is at a decisive stage in its development. Having suffered several setbacks over the last few years, the outlook is now much more favourable and there seems to be a more determined effort to formulate an economic policy which will stimulate growth and reduce the trade deficit. Attention is being focused towards industries which promise a quick return on investment and away from large and problematical projects. Recent oil finds also give grounds for optimism in the longer term.

AGRICULTURE

About two-thirds of the total area of Tunisia is suitable for farming and half the population earn their livelihood from the land. Agriculture contributed about 20 per cent of the national income in 1974 and this proportion is declining, even though the agricultural population is rising. For agricultural purposes the country is composed of five different districts—the north with its mountains, having large fertile valleys; the north-east including the Cap Bon, where the soil is especially suitable for the cultivation of oranges and other citrus fruit; the Sahel where the olives grow; the centre with its high tablelands and pastures; and the south with oases and gardens where dates are prolific. Harvests vary considerably in size, depending on the uncertain rainfall, since cultivation is largely by dry farming and irrigation is as yet limited. The main cereal crops are wheat, barley, maize, oats and sorghum; fruit is also important—grapes, olives, dates, oranges and figs are grown for export as well as for the local market.

In good years there is a surplus of cereal for export but in the late 1960s a series of poor harvests necessitated wheat and flour imports. In 1970 agricultural production increased by 3 per cent, which represented a satisfactory recovery from the devastation of the previous year's floods. Exceptional weather conditions and improved irrigation in 1971 and 1972 resulted in excellent agricultural yields with cereal production up some 50 per cent and orange production up 60 per cent, while the olive crop more than doubled. Since 1972 cereal production has continued to rise steadily despite the flooding of the Medjerda valley in the 1972/73 season. Olive oil production in 1972/73, at 70,000 metric tons, was considerably below the record levels of the 1971/72 season, partly because of the two-year flowering cycle of the olive trees and partly for climatic reasons. In the 1973/74 season production recovered sharply to 135,555 metric tons. Citrus fruits repeated this pattern with 107,000 metric tons produced in 1973/74, compared with 75,000 tons in the previous season. Over the period of the 1973–76 plan the Government hopes for a 22 per cent increase in production.

Under the 1969–72 plan the Government allocated 21 per cent of total investment to agriculture. It is hoped that the country will become self-sufficient in foodstuffs and that expansion in agriculture will be sufficient for the sector not to act as a drag on the rest of the economy. The means by which this should be achieved has been the cause of political conflict in the past decade. From 1960 until 1969, under the Minister of Planning, Ahmed Ben Salah, the basis of the Government's agrarian reform programme lay in the formation of collective "agricultural units". These units, consisting of 500 hectares at least, were to be operated as collectives in order to consolidate small peasant holdings and, later, to exploit land expropriated from French farmers or to be acquired eventually from owners of large or medium-sized farms. Usually each unit was divided up between various crops, such as hard-wheat, soft-wheat, olives and almonds, as well as livestock and fallow. It was

aimed to introduce water and electricity as resources allowed and to provide other communal facilities. The system was controlled through credits provided by the Agricultural Bank. By 1968 some 220 state co-operatives were in existence and several hundred more were being put together. However, there was then a pause for consolidation as "bottlenecks" and rural opposition were becoming widespread while political pressure was mounting from owners of the larger estates whose turn was now coming for collectivization. Questions were raised about the efficiency of the system and there were revelations of unsatisfactory performance, heavy debts and misappropriation of state funds. These discoveries were instrumental in the downfall and disgrace of Ben Salah, whose position was weakened by the displeasure of foreign aid donors with his agricultural policies (especially the World Bank which had previously given some support, including an $18 million loan in 1967).

Following Ben Salah's downfall farmers were given a chance to opt out of the state system which was soon dismantled. Nonetheless a law was passed providing for the eventual break-up of large private estates which cover about 750,000 hectares. They are to be split among individual farmers or private co-operatives over which the state intends to maintain some control through agricultural advisers and central marketing agencies. The Government has also taken a number of measures to stimulate output, including providing funds for mechanization, reducing taxes, and subsidizing fertilizers and seed purchases. In mid-1970 approximately half the cultivated area was in private hands, a further 30 per cent was worked by co-operative farm groups and the remainder was in large estates or under forest. In April 1974 a "supervised credits scheme" was announced, whereby small and medium-sized farms could be given supervised credits on a short-term basis to improve farming methods. To qualify for this scheme the farmer must belong to the Agricultural Mutual Assurance Society, which will act as an intermediary between the farmer and the bank giving credit. This Plan will be available to 90 per cent of Tunisian farmers and will thus affect about 3 million of the country's 45 million hectares under cultivation. It is hoped that the plan will encourage the use of modern diversified crops rather than the traditional staple crops.

The Government has also taken steps to encourage the fishing industry. Sfax is the main centre of the industry which landed 31,500 metric tons of fish in 1973, compared with less than 12,000 tons in 1956. The International Development Association has advanced $2 million to help replace sailing vessels with motorized boats. Early in 1972 the Government signed an agreement with Libya to establish a joint fishing company. Tunisia is giving some priority to fishing under the provisions of the 1973–76 development plan.

Tunisia's main crops are wheat, barley, grapes, olives, citrus fruit and dates.

Grown in a belt across the northern part of the

country, wheat is the most important cereal crop. In good years, wheat is exported but in bad years imports of wheat become necessary. The Government guarantees the price to the grower and, amongst other incentives, pays the transport costs of merchants. Wheat is now sold at world market prices, which have been lower than the prices that used to be obtained in the French market. In the 1972/73 season Tunisia produced 797,000 metric tons of wheat, a considerable improvement on the 591,000 tons produced in the 1971/72 season. This enabled wheat imports to be reduced from 295,000 tons in 1972 to 216,000 tons in 1973. The Government has encouraged the spread of the Mexican dwarf wheat and this variety now accounts for over one-tenth of output.

Production of barley fluctuates according to the rainfall, and in recent years has been only about half the record level (261,000 metric tons) reached in 1963. However, in the 1972/73 season barley production almost equalled the earlier levels at 232,000 tons.

Grapes are grown around Tunis and Bizerta. Wine production reached a peak of 1,986,000 hectolitres in 1963, but output declined in subsequent years, reaching its lowest level, of 600,000 hectolitres, in 1970. Production later increased to 1,000,000 hectolitres per year in 1972 and 1973. In March 1969 an agreement was signed between the EEC and Tunisia which allowed Tunisia partial association to the Community. Favourable concessions were granted to olive oil, fruit and vegetable exports, but wine is excluded from Community preferences although it receives privileged access to the French market. Wine used to represent Tunisia's second most important export, but in 1971 it ranked only seventh. In 1972 the value of wine exports trebled to TD 3 million from the 1971 figure. Wine exports trebled again in 1973 when they were valued at TD 9 million.

The size of olive harvests varies considerably, partly due to the two-year flowering cycle of the tree. In 1971 there was a dramatic rise over 1970 to well over 100,000 tons. In 1972 there was an exceptionally good crop of 167,000 tons of which 129,000 tons were exported, earning TD 46.3 million in foreign exchange compared with about 90,000 tons and TD 21 million in 1971. Thus olive oil temporarily displaced petroleum oil as the country's main export earner in 1972. In 1973 only 50,500 tons were exported, but world prices for olive oil rose so that exports were valued at TD 25.7 million, only 40 per cent lower than in 1972. Olive oil was Tunisia's second most important export. The much improved 1973/74 harvest should ensure that olive oil remains an important export earner in 1974. Domestic trade in olive oil is controlled by a State monopoly but the private sector is involved in export sales.

Citrus fruit is grown on the north-eastern coast. Citrus fruit production in the 1971/72 season amounted to 104,600 metric tons, of which 30,500 tons were exported in 1972, and fell to 75,000 tons in 1972/73, with 24,800 tons exported in 1973. A better crop is expected in 1973/74, and exports should improve. Date production fell from 39,000 metric tons in the

1971/72 season to 22,000 tons in 1972/73, with exports steady at 7,000 tons per year. Experimental planting of cotton and sugar beet has been tried. Sugar beet is used by the sugar refinery near Beja, which has a capacity of 1,850 tons per day. Other crops being tried include bananas, strawberries and pistachio nuts.

Tunisia's livestock includes some 3.2 million sheep, 680,000 cattle, 98,000 horses, 60,000 mules and 180,000 camels. The Government is anxious to improve cattle-stock and milk production. In 1971 an agreement was signed with Austria for technical and financial assistance in setting up a cattle-rearing scheme at Bou Salem. Of the TD 135 million to be spent on agriculture in the 1973–76 plan a significant amount is allocated to livestock breeding in order to keep pace with the increased demand for meat. Some 20,000 hectares of grazing land in the North will be improved and a further 50,000 hectares of grazing land created.

Some progress has been made in the last decade towards the diversification of crops, mechanization, irrigation and increased use of fertilizers. Two new irrigation schemes should improve output; the Oued Nebhana dam, near Kairouan, which cost 23 million dinars, will irrigate 5,000 hectares and assist in flood prevention; and in 1971 work began on the Bou Heurtma dam in Jendouba. Federal Germany is providing finance for this latter project which will irrigate 20,000 hectares when it reaches completion, probably in 1976. The World Bank is to lend Tunisia $23 million for a water project to be undertaken by SONEDE, the national water supply company. The project will improve the existing water supply scheme and ensure drinking water supplies for the town of Sfax. The Council of Ministers has approved investments totalling TD 50 million for water and irrigation projects and by 1975 the total area of irrigated land had increased to 80,000 hectares. It is believed that the maximum area for potential irrigation is more than 200,000 hectares.

The World Bank is providing $8 million for several schemes aimed at increasing milk production, and wheat output, providing farm machinery and developing date plantations and a new oasis in the south. In January 1973 a U.S. loan of $11 million was announced for financing agricultural projects. In addition it was announced that the U.S. Agency for International Development agreed to lend Tunisia TD 1.4 million to be used for a water purification plant in Tunis and for irrigation in the Shanshou region.

Fishing. Fishing employs 13,807 men and over 4,000 boats. In October 1962 territorial waters were extended from 3 to 6 miles and fishing limits to 12 miles off shore. The fishing industry is being expanded—the catch rose to 23,000 tons in 1962, nearly double the 1956 figure, but the subsequent rate of expansion has varied. The 1973 catch was about 31,000 tons. Exports of sea food were unable to keep pace with demand in 1972 and reached TD 2.2 million, rising to TD 2.7 million in 1973.

MINERALS

Tunisia has several rich mineral deposits and is one of the world's largest producers of phosphates. Although their quality is not as good as Morocco's, phosphates are nevertheless one of the country's most important exports. Iron ore is also mined and lead, zinc, potash and salt. Oil was discovered close to the Algerian border in May 1964 and gas has also been found. Some 13,000 persons are employed in the mining industry.

The current plan recognizes the present importance of the mining industry to the economy. It encourages the processing of minerals in Tunisia, which at present are exported in their raw state, particularly phosphates. The plan also proposes the exploitation of the iron ore deposits at Djebel Ank and further exploration for minerals. Production of phosphates and iron ore is expected to show a rising trend while output of lead and zinc ores may fall. Recent discoveries indicate a bright future for the petroleum industry. Considerable expansion in mineral production has taken place in the last decade, but there have been fluctuations in output, especially when operations were interrupted by the floods, in 1969. Output was again disappointing in 1972 and showed a continuing downward trend in 1973. The amount of crude oil produced was 97,000 metric tons less than in 1972, but natural phosphate production increased by 2.6 per cent. Comparing 1973 with 1972, production of ferrous and most non-ferrous metals dropped, 8 per cent less iron was produced, steel production fell by 31.8 per cent, zinc production by 24.8 per cent. Lead output decreased from 20,900 metric tons in 1971 to 19,900 in 1972 and 15,600 in 1973. The *Office National des Mines* is responsible for exploration for fresh mineral deposits, for the reactivation of deposits which have ceased production, for the carrying out of an elaborate modernization programme in mining methods and in the improvement of productivity. A further task is to promote exploration for oil.

Tunisia is the fourth largest producer in the world of calcium phosphates, which are mined mainly from six large deposits in central Tunisia. Production recovered after the floods to 3 million tons in 1970, and increased to 3.2 million tons in 1971, to 3.4 million in 1972 and to 3.5 million in 1973. Phosphate exports (including superphosphates and hyperphosphates) were valued at TD 20 million in 1972, rising to TD 23.8 million in 1973, due mainly to an increase in world prices. 1974 phosphate production is likely to be affected adversely by the floods which caused the shutdown of the mines at Sfax-Gafsa in December 1973. Export values should nevertheless rise as Tunisia, following the Moroccan initiative, increased the price of exported natural phosphates in December 1973, from $13 to $39 per metric ton. The domestic price remains unchanged. Some 60 per cent of Tunisian phosphate exports are for Western markets, particularly France, while the balance goes to Eastern European countries and China. The Tunisian phosphate industry is undergoing some major changes in policy under the new 1973–76 plan. The main objectives under the new policy plan are to develop new resources and to concentrate efforts on the local manufacture of highly profitable fertilizer and phosphoric acid. Phosphoric acid exports increased dramatically from 24,000 metric tons, valued at TD 679,000, in 1972, to 191,000 tons, worth TD 4.9 million, in 1973. Phosphate is used by the fertilizer industry to produce hyperphosphate, superphosphate and triple superphosphate. Phosphate mining is now concentrated in the hands of a single concern, the Sfax-Gafsa Co., which operates under the overall financial control of the Government. The company has announced a wide range of plans of modernization of output and new refining projects, as well as changes in the location of mining activities. New mechanical processes are to be introduced in order to speed up the growth of productivity. The Sfax-Gafsa Co. is in the process of opening two new mines, one at M'rata to replace the Moularies mine and one at Ste'Barba to succeed the Kalaa Jerda mine. The M'rata mine is expected to allow easy working with an annual output of some 1 million tons—double that of the Moularies. The Ste'Barba scheme, currently under study, is expected to cost around 1 million dinars in investment expenditure.

The long-term plan now laid down by the company includes development of a new deposit at Sehib, also in southern Tunisia. Reserves are now reported to be over 60 million tons. Preliminary work on this new deposit began in December 1970, and capital investment of 14 million dinars is expected, creating 1,200 new jobs.

Tunisia has numerous deposits of rich non-phosphorous iron ore; the two main deposits are at Djerissa and Douaria. Gross production in 1972 declined by 5 per cent over 1971, to 890,000 metric tons, falling further in 1973 to 809,000 tons. Exports were valued at TD 1.4 million in 1973, going mostly to markets in Italy, the United Kingdom and Greece. When current studies have been concluded, other deposits may be exploited. Japan, Brazil and the Federal Republic of Germany are to act in a joint venture with Tunisia to build a $55 million sponge iron plant with an annual capacity of 1 million metric tons.

Lead ore is extracted in the northern coastal region. Production of lead ore fell from 19,900 metric tons of contained lead in 1972 to 15,600 metric tons of contained lead in 1973. Exports of lead and lead manufactures were valued at TD 2.01 million in 1972, rising to TD 2.64 million in 1973. Zinc ore is mined in the north-western corner of Tunisia and production in 1972 equalled the 1971 level of 11,400 metric tons contained zinc. Mine production of zinc ore fell by an estimated 22.4 per cent in 1973 from the 1972 level. Most zinc exports used to be taken by France, but the French share is falling. Zinc exports were valued at TD 773,000 in 1973. About 90 per cent of the salt produced by COTUSAL (300–320,000 tons a year) is exported, chiefly to Japan. 1972 salt exports were valued at TD 575,000, rising to TD 783,000 in 1973.

Intensive exploration for petroleum has been carried out since the discovery of oil in neighbouring Algeria. In May 1964 the subsidiary of the Italian

State Hydrocarbons Agency (ENI) found oil at El Borma in the south near the Algerian border. Recoverable reserves were estimated to be 53 million tons in 1971. The field went into production in mid-1966 and in 1972 output reached 3.6 million tons. It was expected, however, that the output from this field would fall to 2.5 million tons in 1973 because of loss of pressure.

In 1968 a second field came into operation at Douleb, 125 miles north of El Borma. This field is operated by a joint French-Tunisian company SEREPT and had an output of 100,000 tons in 1972.

The Tunisian Government took a 50 per cent share in the El Borma operating company when oil was found. Crude oil is taken from El Borma via a spur pipeline which links with the pipeline from the oil fields at Zarzaitine and Edjeleh in Algeria to the terminal at La Skhirra on the Gulf of Gabès. Thence the crude is taken to the refinery at Bizerta (capacity 1.2 million tons per year). A second refinery is planned for Gabès, with an annual capacity of 10–12 million tons.

The *Société de Recherches et d'Exploitations des Pétroles en Tunisie* (SEREPT), in which French interests both public and private have a large share, together with *Aquitaine-Tunisie* (a wholly owned subsidiary of the French company SNPA) works the field at Douleb. A six-inch pipeline has been built to the port of La Skhirra. Production began in May 1968 and totalled 220,000 tons in that year. A small field, named Tamesmida on the Algerian border south-west of Douleb, was joined to the Douleb–La Skhirra pipeline in 1969 and will produce some 30,000 tons per year in order to supply a paper pulp plant at nearby Kasserine. Companies are showing a keen interest in exploration in Tunisia. *Aquitaine* with 4,000 square kilometres is a major exploration permit holder as is SITEP. The French company, *Cie Française des Pétroles* was awarded in 1968 a permit covering 15,000 square kilometres onshore and offshore in the Gulf of Gabès. SEREPT also operates a small gas field in the Cap Bon area which supplies Tunis. Production at Cap Bon amounts to nearly 10 million cubic metres annually. The same company in conjunction with the *Société Nationale des Pétroles d'Aquitaine* found gas at Douleb south-west of Tunis in 1966. A second gas field has been discovered at Bir Ali ben Khalifa near Sfax by a group of U.S. companies. The production rate from one well is estimated at 2.7 million cubic metres annually.

The Ashtart field in the Gulf of Gabès, in a concession held by Aquitaine and Elf/Erap, began production in December 1973 and is expected to produce 2 million tons a year by 1975. Two other fields became operational in 1972, the Bhirat and the Sidi al-Itayem fields, with annual production targets of 600,000 tons and 500,000 tons respectively.

Total Tunisian oil production in 1970 was 4.2 million metric tons. In 1971 there was a 1 per cent decline in output, but oil receipts rose comparatively sharply as a result of the increase in posted prices, and oil remained the principal export for the third year running, accounting for 25 per cent of export revenue.

Total output in 1972 was 4 million tons, but although this was less than in the previous two years, revenues rose by 31 per cent to TD 38 million as a result of increased crude oil prices. Production difficulties resulted in a reduced output of 3.9 million tons in 1973, although the export value of the same volume as in 1972 increased to TD 52 million as a result of the vastly increased oil prices of the end of 1973. Tunisia refined 1.2 million metric tons of crude oil for local consumption in 1972. Total oil production reached an estimated 4.1 million tons in 1974, a lower figure than had been expected, but prospects for the oil industry are promising. Offshore and onshore operations round the Gulf of Tunis are proceeding and there are hopes of further finds in the Gulf of Gabès. In 1972 the National Assembly passed a bill to set up a state company for petroleum activities, and the Government now has a 50 per cent participation in all the operating fields except for Douleb. Apart from the State oil company and SONATRACH (the Algerian state oil company which has agreed to help in efforts to inject pressure into the El Borma field) five foreign companies are prospecting in Tunisia and together are scheduled to spend TD 47 million on prospecting and TD 22.6 million on development of existing wells.

INDUSTRY

Industrial production in 1973 showed an increase of about 3.4 per cent over the 1972 level, which had, in turn, increased by 8.8 per cent over 1971. It is expected that higher growth rates will be achieved in the next few years, under the impetus of increased industrial investment. TD 135 million was invested in 1973, including TD 50 million for export-oriented industries. The textile industry received 34 per cent of the total investment, the construction industries 26 per cent, the remainder being shared among the engineering, chemical and food industries.

Industry consists of the processing of local raw materials, minerals, wool (two factories in the Sousse region are under construction), leather and foods—the last being the most important. There are 20 major flour mills with a total annual milling capacity of 380,000 tons. Vegetable oil processing is also important and a canning industry is being developed —already over 20 canning factories process fish of all kinds, mostly destined for export. There is a TD 2 million project to modernize the fishing industry. Two hundred and fifty coastal fishing vessels are to be constructed in Tunisia over the next five years, and new fishing ports are to be built, using a TD 4 million loan from the Kuwaiti Fund for Arab Economic Development. At Beja is a sugar refinery capable of refining 1,850 tons per day, sufficient to cover the country's needs in the near future, though some sugar beet has to be imported. Other factories pasteurize milk and make butter, cheese and yoghurt. Other industries include, amongst other construction materials plants, two cement factories. Production in 1973 was 528,000 metric tons, which did not meet Tunisia's domestic requirements, necessitating the importation of 151,000 tons. A similar level of imports is anticipated for 1974. A new cement factory with an annual output of 700,000 tons is to be built at Gabès by a French company, at a cost of TD 29 million. Production should commence in 1977, and is intended for local consumption. Two similar plants are planned at Bizerta and Thala. In addition, factories manufacture glass, metal furniture, batteries, paint and varnish, leather and shoes, clothing, various textiles, biscuits, chocolates, etc. There is also a motor vehicle assembly plant and three small metal foundries. The industrial sector, however, is expanding fast. There is an oil refinery ,with a capacity of one million tons, at Bizerta which supplies all local needs in petroleum products except aviation spirit. Built at a cost of 100 million francs, it is owned by *Société Tuniso-Italienne de Raffinage* (STIR), a joint Government/ENI company. A cellulose factory and a paper paste plant at Kasserine uses locally grown esparto grass as raw material. The first phase of a rubber factory near Sfax was opened in March 1973 with a work force of 200, scheduled to reach 450 when the second phase is completed.

Industrial projects include a $30 million nitrogenous fertilizer plant and an ammonium monophosphate plant at Gabès and a superphosphates plant at Sfax. The triple superphosphate fertilizer plant was initially backed by the IFC and Swedish and American Companies and is run by N.P.K. Engrais, S.A.T. The plant was designed for a capacity of 180,000 tons of triple superphosphate which was to be produced from local phosphates and imported sulphur and which was all to be exported. Shipments have been made to more than twenty countries including Sweden under long-term sales contracts. The company's production was 165,000 tons in 1970, and target output was 200,000 in 1972. The latest development plan emphasizes the need for expansion of the fertilizer industry in order to obtain full benefits in terms of added value for the country's phosphates deposits. Another major project, the steel complex at Menzel-Bourguiba is supplied with iron ore from Tamera and Djerissa and when it began operations in 1965, had an initial capacity of 120,000 tons of iron bars, wire and small sections. Other industrial capacity includes the glassworks at Megrine, a vehicle (Peugot) and tractor assembly plant, electrical equipment plant and a centre for manufacture of precision tools.

The Government is taking an active interest in the development of the south. Here the first plant producing phosphoric acid in Tunisia came into production at Ghannouch early in 1972, and by the end of the year its exports had earned TD 680,000. The plant is owned by Maghreb Chemical Industries and has a capacity of 120,000 tons a year; its output will be mainly for export. A second plant was to commence production in 1974. French and Swiss firms are to participate in a fluorspar processing plant being built at Ghannouch by Industries Chimiques Maghrebines. The plant will eventually employ 700. Ninety per cent of the TD 4.7 million it is expected to cost will be met by loans from France under an agreement signed in December 1973.

Production of electricity in 1973 was 963 million kWh., most of which was produced by thermal means; hydro-electric power is of lesser importance. Power production from this source varies considerably, depending on the availability of water. Altogether there are eighteen power stations. A 40 megawatt power station is being built in the Ghonnouch area and IBRD has approved a loan of $12 million for use in the project by *Société Tunisienne de L'Electricité et du Gaz*. A French company has won a TD 2.6 million contract to build a 42 megawatt power station in the southern suburbs of Tunis. The Arab Fund for Economic and Social Development is contributing TD 2.2 million to the project.

Plans have been drawn up for building a nuclear reactor costing 15 million dinars at Gabès. It is expected to produce 20,000 cubic metres of desalinized water and 50 megawatts of electricity per day.

In 1971 the World Bank granted Tunisia a loan of 5.2 million dinars to lay a gas pipe from Al-Burmah to the proposed power station at Gabès. The Bank will grant 3.9 million dinars at an interest rate of 7 per cent while the Kuwaiti Fund for Arab Economic Development will provide the remainder. The Italian state oil company ENI has signed an agreement with the Tunisian Government for the construction of a 180-mile natural gas pipeline across Tunisia, forming part of a 1,600-mile pipeline from Algeria to Sicily. Outlets will be built to fuel Tunisian industries.

Tunisia inherited a relatively modern system of road and rail communications from the period of colonial rule. As part of an overall transport and communications agreement announced in June 1974, Libya and Tunisia are to co-operate in the building of a railway line between Gabès and Tripoli. The agreement also covers co-operation by the two national airlines and port and maritime facilities. At present the rail network has approximately 2,100 km. of track and there are 18,774 km. of road. A loan of $24 million from IBRD is to be spent on a major road improvement scheme in the south. In February 1973 the Minister of Planning announced that TD 165 million would be spent on transport in the next four years, of which TD 70 million has been allocated to road transport. In September 1971, the first oil tanker of the Tunisian Navigation Company was delivered from Spain. The tanker was built at a cost of $2 million. A recent measure taken by the Government to encourage exports should benefit industry. An agency has been established which will assist new companies producing for export. Valuable tax concession, for periods of ten years or longer, will be granted.

The overall index of industrial production (monthly average) for 1973 stood at 150.2 (base 100 in 1968), an increase of some 3.4 per cent over the 1972 monthly average of 145.3, which was itself some 9 per cent greater than the 1971 index. The reduced rate of increase is attributed to falls in the production of superphosphates and construction materials, combined with a 2 per cent reduction in capital equipment output and a 7.5 per cent fall in tourist arrivals. Consumer goods production increased by 4.8 per cent and energy production by 10.2 per cent.

FINANCE

The *Banque Centrale de Tunisie* is the sole bank of issue of the dinar; it performs all the normal central banking functions. Transfers of foreign exchange to all countries have been subject to control since 1959. Apart from the commercial banks, there are financial institutions such as the *Société Nationale d'Investissement* which specialize in providing finance for investment purposes. SNI, established as a development finance company by the Government in 1959 with assistance from the IFC, was reorganized in 1965 into a privately controlled development finance company. Its objectives are to invest capital, both loan and equity, in private and public enterprise in manufacturing and tourism. The World Bank had by 1973 contributed loans to the value of $49 million to help finance SNI's activities. In June 1970, SNI joined with the IFC and other foreign investors in establishing COFITOUR, a tourism investment holding company.

Tunisia's currency is the dinar, introduced in November 1958. It was devalued by 20 per cent in September 1964 because French financial aid ceased after the nationalization of French-owned farms, but Tunisia did not devalue with the Franc zone in August 1969 and maintained the gold parity of the dinar after the currency realignments of December 1971, when the par value of the dinar rose from $1.905 to $2.068. As a result of the February 1973 currency crisis the dinar was further revalued to $2.298. Subsequent developments are detailed in the Statistical Survey. Foreign exchange reserves held by the central bank (including gold, SDR's and Tunisia's IMF position) rose from $59.6 million at the end of 1971 to $444.9 million by November 1974.

Gross National Savings are more than 17 per cent of G.N.P. while capital formation is consistently over 20 per cent of G.N.P. Investments in 1974 exceeded forecasts and amounted to one-third of total G.N.P. The availability of local savings for investment has meant firstly that foreign borrowings have been unnecessary and secondly that the local financial markets have expanded and become more sophisticated to meet the demand for loans. In the fourth Four-Year Plan (1973–76) an annual average of $750 million will be invested.

The current budget usually shows a surplus which is directed to capital expenditure. Direct taxation normally accounts for 20 per cent of total revenue and indirect taxes for over 50 per cent. Other sources of Government revenue are profits from state monopolies and receipts from state property and forests; oil is a growing source of Government income. In 1971 the ordinary budget was balanced at 155 million dinars only marginally up from the 1970 level. The 1972 budget increased expenditure by 15 per cent to TD 189 million and in 1973 a further 8 per cent increase in total expenditure to TD 215 million was set. The 1974 ordinary budget was balanced at TD 247 million, an increase of 14.9 per cent on the 1973 budget. The additional TD 32 million expenditure includes increased allocations for wages of state employees and debt repayments. Additional revenue

will be raised by increasing direct taxes by 9.6 per cent overall and indirect taxes by 10.7 per cent. Public companies will also make increased contributions to budget revenue. Of the 1974 budget 51.5 per cent expenditure is for social services and education. In an attempt to reduce dependence on the agricultural sector, the output of which can vary drastically according to weather conditions, the 1974 budget continues the policy set out in 1973, placing increased emphasis on the development of industry, particularly labour-intensive concerns orientated to both domestic and foreign markets.

Prices are distorted by subsidies. Direct subsidies in 1974 reached TD 50 million, mainly on sugar (TD 10 million), fertilizers (TD 10 million) and cereals (TD 18 million). The Government claims that inflation has been contained to less than 5 per cent. Consumer prices are said to have risen by only 17 per cent from 1970 to 1974 while wages rose by nearly 30 per cent. Unofficial estimates put inflation at 15 per cent in 1974.

PLANNING

It was not until 1961, when the Ten-Year Perspective Plan was formulated, that the Government laid down comprehensive plans for development. The broad lines of policy put forward in the Perspective Plan were embodied in the first three-year plan (1962–64), and then in successive four-year plans (1965–68, 1969–72, and, currently, 1973–76). The 1969–72 plan aimed at a 6 per cent growth rate compared with the 3.5–4 per cent rate achieved during the years 1962–68. Total investment was put at $1,200 million, of which $246 million was allocated to agriculture and some $300 million for industrial projects. The overall emphasis was on reducing unemployment, increasing productivity and improving the balance of payments. The plan's objectives were not fully met—not least because of the 1969 floods.

Two of the major difficulties facing the planners are rapid population growth, and the consistent, heavy trade deficit, which has meant that 40 per cent of development expenditure over the last decade has been financed by foreign aid. The main objectives of the 1973–76 plan are to ensure the profitability of investments under earlier plans; to concentrate on short-term productive investments, particularly in export industries; and to encourage private investment. Total expenditure during the four years covered by the new plan will be TD 1,000 million, almost the same as the total expenditure in the ten-year period 1962–72. Investments will begin at the rate of TD 200 million in 1973 rising to TD 290 million in 1976. A determined effort will also be made to reduce Tunisia's dependence on foreign aid to 20 per cent of development expenditure, a total of no more than $600 million over the four-year period.

Bizerta will continue to be the main industrial zone with its port, oil refinery and steel complex at Menzel Bourguiba, and other lesser enterprises. The Government hopes to establish a new industrial complex in the south where underemployment is severe. A new port, a fertilizer plant and a power station are planned. The Gabès port development is particularly significant. This will represent Tunisia's most important port complex and will in fact comprise three adjacent ports and an industrial estate. These three ports will be specially built to handle general merchandise, petroleum and other minerals respectively. Costs will be covered in part by development credits from Italy and the World Bank.

There has been a notable change in Tunisian policy regarding foreign private investment since the fall of Ben Salah and Ladgham, who were widely reputed to favour economic policies tending towards socialism. The law of April 27th, 1972, virtually abdicated a portion of Tunisian sovereignty in the eager pursuit of foreign capital. Stressing the availability of cheap labour and the absence of social conflict, the Tunisian Government has voluntarily entered the ranks of countries, such as the Ivory Coast, where development is carried out by, and for the benefit of, foreign investors. This law applies exclusively to manufacturing industries producing solely for export, which protects such local industry as already exists, although the Tunisian market would be too small and too poor to attract industry producing for domestic consumption. Factories can be set up anywhere in Tunisia, and businesses set up under the law benefit from a ten-year exemption from corporation tax, with a 10 per cent reduction in tax payments for the second period of ten years. For twenty years they pay no tax on the rental value of premises, no customs duties or turnover tax on capital goods, tools, spares, raw materials, semi-finished products and consumables necessary for production, imported or bought on the local market. They have complete freedom to recruit foreign executive and supervisory personnel, and, most important, there are no restrictions on the repatriation of income. During the first year of the law's operation, 33 projects were created with a total investment capital of TD 5.2 million, 27 of them in the textile industry. For twenty years Tunisia will receive nothing from this arrangement, no government revenue, no significant training and development of management expertise given the free entry of alien staff, no creation of local sources of capital, as profits are repatriated. The only conceivable benefit is the creation of jobs for unskilled labour, a commodity so plentiful and cheap that some 15,000 Tunisians leave for Europe every year. Rather than emigrating to become the proletariat of industrial Europe, the Government is bringing foreign industry to these unemployed Tunisians, who can now become an indigenous proletariat, while the profits flow out of the country unchecked.

EXTERNAL TRADE

Tunisia's foreign trade deficit has risen steeply in recent years. By 1972 the deficit had reached TD 72 million, and in 1973 it rose still further to TD 97 million. Exports have risen steadily but are heavily dependent on sales of agricultural and mineral products, and thus on the success of the harvest and the condition of world mineral markets. The 1972 trade figures were exceptional, with imports (c.i.f. value) rising to TD 222 million, exceeding TD 200 million for the first time, and exports to TD 150 million. In 1973 exports showed a further 12 per cent rise to TD 169 million, but this was more than offset by an increased import bill of TD 266 million, almost 20 per cent up on 1972. Crude oil sales accounted for 31 per cent of 1973's increased export earnings, with a slight decrease in sales volume being more than compensated for by higher world prices. Other major contributions to exports came from phosphates and other minerals, all benefiting from higher world prices for raw materials. There would have been an even greater improvement in export earnings but for a reduction in olive oil sales, worth 44 per cent less than in 1972 despite higher prices. There was a setback in the recent rapid rise in tourism, with 7.5 per cent fewer tourists than in 1972, but tourism still made a significant contribution to the overall payments position.

Crude petroleum, phosphates and olive oil are Tunisia's major export earners. Olive oil held the leading position in 1972 with record sales of 126,159 metric tons, valued at TD 46.06 million, but poor crops in 1973 resulted in much lower export sales of 50,517 tons. Increased world prices ensured that receipts fell only 44 per cent to TD 25.79 million. Crude petroleum again became the leading export earner in 1973, with sales worth TD 52.09 million, an increase attributable to higher prices over the TD 38.76 million earned in 1972, achieved despite a fall in volume of some 25,000 to 3.67 million tons. With production now under way at the Ashtart offshore oilfield, petroleum production in 1974 reached an estimated 4.1 million tons, with a consequent further rise in revenues despite a levelling off in prices. In 1973 phosphate exports, including superphosphates and hyperphosphates, were valued at TD 23.76 million, compared with TD 19.99 million in 1972, another increase attributed to a rise in price rather than volume. Phosphoric acid exports showed a notable increase in 1973, with a volume of 191,000 tons, worth TD 4.86 million, against 24,000 tons and TD 0.68 million in 1972. Other major exports included iron, lead, almonds, citrus fruits and wine, exports of which have expanded considerably in recent years. In 1971 wine exports amounted to only TD 1.32 million, rising to TD 3.06 million and a volume of 58,769 metric tons in 1972 and to 139,471 tons worth TD 9.04 million in 1973.

The increased import bill in 1973 could be attributed particularly to the raw material and semi-manufactured products sectors, where imports increased by 25 per cent over 1972 levels to TD 102 million. Capital equipment and vehicle imports rose by about 22 per cent to TD 80 million, foodstuffs by 14.5 per cent to TD 48.8 million. The increase in food imports occurred despite improved agricultural yields and a fall in tourist numbers, but was again due, in part at least, to higher world prices.

By the end of 1974 Tunisia's international reserves were more than $400 million (or the equivalent of five months' imports). The trade deficit of nearly 10 per cent of G.N.P. in the early 1960s has been subsequently reduced to less than 3 per cent. The improvement in the trade position allows Tunisia considerable scope to plan an increase in imports of capital goods to expand industrial capacity.

France remains Tunisia's principal supplier, with 36 per cent of all imports, worth TD 97.4 million, in 1973, compared with 35 per cent in 1971 and 1972. The U.S.A. was the second largest supplier in 1973 (TD 24.75 million), followed by the Federal Republic of Germany (TD 23.56 million) and Italy (TD 21.32 million). In 1973 France replaced Italy as Tunisia's largest export market, taking goods worth TD 46.7 million, followed by Italy with TD 26.76 million, the U.S.A. with TD 24.94 million (only TD 5.50 million in 1972), and Federal Germany with TD 11.73 million. The EEC supplied 62 per cent of Tunisian imports (TD 166 million) and accounted for 55 per cent of exports (TD 92 million) in 1973.

Much of Tunisia's trade takes place within the framework of bilateral agreements with other countries. Trade and co-operation agreements have been signed with Federal Germany, Italy, Sweden, Canada, the U.S.A., the Netherlands, Hungary, the German Democratic Republic, Yugoslavia and Libya, amongst others, and an association agreement with the EEC is being negotiated to facilitate Tunisian exports of agricultural and other goods. Over recent years discussions have been held with many countries, particularly in western Europe, on investment in Tunisia, notably in light industrial projects.

TOURISM

Between 1961 and 1972 total tourist arrivals grew at a rate of 30 per cent a year. Tourism became the nation's largest foreign currency earner in 1968 and receipts in 1972 were estimated at TD 70 million, representing just under half of total export earnings. In 1973, however, the number of tourists visiting Tunisia fell to about 721,000, some 7.5 per cent fewer than the 1972 record level. Receipts showed a marginal increase from TD 70 million in 1972 to TD 72 million in 1973, but this represents a decline in real money values, taking inflation into account. The reduced tourist trade has been attributed to poor marketing, problems in infrastructure development and a global downturn in foreign holidays influenced by currency and exchange rate uncertainties. Federal Germany is the principal contributor to tourist earnings, followed by France and the United Kingdom. There are four main centres for tourists: Hammamet, Sousse, Djerba and Tunis. Foreign private investment in the tourist industry is steadily growing and in 1971 Federal German and French companies spent 6 million dinars on hotel construction. In February 1973 a West German development bank granted the Tunisian National Tourism Office a TD 6.5 million loan most of which is to be used for tourist infrastructural projects. This loan was in addition to $12.4 million granted in September 1972 also for tourist infrastructure development. The International Finance Corporation (IFC) is to invest $1.9 million in a $11.4 million tourist project at Skanes. This is a joint British/Tunisian venture in

which IFC will have a 10 per cent stake, Tunisian Holidays 40 per cent and Tunisian investors 50 per cent. The project should provide between 460 and 480 jobs and brings IFC's investment in Tunisia to $16.6 million. The World Bank is to lend Tunisia $5.6 million to help finance a $12.3 million project training workers for the tourist industry. Three hotels will be built to serve as training centres which, it is hoped, will fill 27 per cent of the demand for staff for tourism. The *Compagnie Financière et Touristique* (COFITOUR), set up in 1970 with initial capital resources of $39 million, promotes and finances three types of ventures: new hotel construction; modernization of existing hotels; and other activities related to tourism such as transport, housing and real estate.

FOREIGN AID

The principal sources of economic aid for Tunisia continue to be Western countries and international institutions. The U.S.A. has been the major donor, with aid totalling some $528 million between 1957 and 1967, but since then increasingly important roles have been assumed by other countries, notably Federal Germany and the Gulf States, and institutions such as the World Bank. Aid from the U.S.S.R. and Eastern Europe has so far been on a limited scale.

The World Bank Group (IBRD, IDA and IFC) has been the most important multilateral donor, providing loans and credits for investment in a variety of projects—including participation in the *Société Nationale d'Investissement* (SNI) and in COFITOUR. The World Bank agreed in 1972 to provide SNI with TD 5 million, and an additional $14 million loan in 1973 for the purchase of imports necessary for the development of industry and tourism. In August 1973 a further World Bank loan of TD 72 million was agreed, and in 1974 $23 million was lent for the SONEDE water supply project. Still more loans were expected in 1974 to finance transport, family planning and agricultural projects. Between 1964 and 1973 World Bank loans to Tunisia totalled $155.6 million.

French aid was resumed in 1967 with a major contribution (loans of 93 million francs) being made for development of the Gabès industrial complex. In 1971, following a further easing in relations between Tunisia and France, a 40 per cent increase in the flow of French aid was announced, returning it to near the 1963 level. In 1972 France agreed to lend 15 million francs for investment in small enterprises, and further loans of 17 million and 15 million francs were arranged in 1973. France gave Tunisia 25,000 tons of wheat in 1973, and was to make a similar gift in 1974. The French Central Fund for Economic Co-operation granted a loan of 45 million francs in 1974, to finance imports of industrial, agricultural and mining equipment from France.

It was announced in 1974 that Federal Germany had agreed to lend Tunisia a total of DM 185 million (about TD 31 million), of which DM 155 million would be financial aid and DM 30 million in the form of technical assistance, to be made available half-yearly to correspond with development plan finance. In addition the Federal German Development Bank is to lend DM 7 million for agricultural projects. Previous Federal German aid in the form of long-term credits totalled DM 436 million (about TD 73 million)— DM 158 million for agriculture, DM 128 million for infrastructure projects, DM 85 million for capital goods imports and DM 65 million for industry and tourism.

After long negotiations, agreement was reached in 1969 between the European Economic Community and Tunisia under which Tunisia was granted partial association. Full association, which would include aid provisions and the free movement of labour, was thus postponed. Under the partial association agreement, which ran for 5 years, the EEC countries removed all custom duties and quotas on virtually all industrial exports from Tunisia (at present some 60 per cent of Tunisian exports to the EEC). However, there remained a quota of 100,000 tons of petroleum products exported to the EEC without tariff. Custom duties on olive oil and fish were reduced and preference given to hard wheat and various processed agricultural products. Limited preference was given to citrus fruit. In return Tunisia gave tariff reductions, equivalent to 70 per cent of the preference previously given to French goods, on 40 per cent of its imports from the EEC. Tunisia is unhappy about the terms of the present agreement (the trade gap with the EEC increased from TD 3.9 million in 1969 to TD 57 million in 1972 and to TD 74 million in 1973 with the enlarged community) and hopes to negotiate favourable revisions. The current agreement expired in August 1974, but it remains in force while negotiation of a new agreement is under way. Tunisia hopes to obtain better terms for exports of agricultural produce and light industrial goods.

In the meantime progress towards economic co-operation between the Maghreb countries is slow, though a Maghreb Permanent Consultative Committee and an Industrial Studies Centre have been established. One of the aims is to co-ordinate the four countries' development plans. Co-operation with Libya in the petrochemical industry is expected, following a 1968 agreement under which Tunisia will concentrate on production of superphosphates and phosphoric acid while Libya will devote its efforts to the production of ammonia and its derivatives; joint production of sulphuric acid is envisaged. The recently established joint venture in the fishing industry is a small step in the direction of co-operation.

A number of important bilateral and multilateral agreements have been signed in recent years. Tunisia is to co-operate with the Netherlands in establishing several manufacturing plants (to produce bicycles, shirts and shoes), and is to receive aid for agricultural projects. A $6.8 million loan from the U.S.A. was agreed in 1972 to enable Tunisia to purchase 10,000 tons of soya bean oil and 60,000 tons of wheat. A similar loan, for $12 million, had been granted in November 1971. Other major loans agreed in 1972-73 included a TD 1.6 million loan from Sweden for development in olive-growing regions, and a loan of TD 4 million from U.S. AID to be used for transport and irrigation projects. Sweden agreed in 1974 to supply an additional 47 million kronor (about TD 4.7 million) in credits, part of which was for the purchase of Swedish goods and services. Iran granted a TD 2 million loan for the Sidi Saad dam in July 1973. The Arab Fund for Economic and Social Development is to lend TD 2.9 million for the construction of a new power station, the Kuwaiti Fund for Arab Economic Development TD 4 million for fishing ports. Various projects in the 1973–76 development plan will be financed by TD 20 million in aid from four Gulf States: 8.2 million from Saudi Arabia, 6.6 million from the United Arab Emirates, 1 million from Abu Dhabi and 4.2 million from Qatar. Canada is to provide C$9 million (about TD 3.8 million) for agricultural development, in addition to the sum of C$29 million agreed in 1973.

STATISTICAL SURVEY

AREA AND POPULATION

AREA (sq. km.)	POPULATION			1971	1972	1973
	Total (July 1st, 1974)	Tunis (capital) (1966 census)	Births . .	182,749	198,785	194,760
			Deaths* .	48,762	43,391	43,716
			Marriages .	37,642	45,036	43,212
163,610	5,641,000	468,997				

* Death registration is estimated to be 65 per cent complete.

Other Towns: Sfax 100,000, Sousse 90,000, Bizerta 70,000, Kairouan 50,000, Gabes 40,000, Monastir 40,000, Menzel-Bourguiba 35,000.

AGRICULTURE

PRINCIPAL CROPS
('000 metric tons)

	1970	1971	1972	1973
Soft wheat	150	200	262	200
Hard wheat . . .	299	400	652	490
Barley	151	140	236	210
Esparto grass . . .	84	79	75	75
Potatoes	68	91	100	71
Tomatoes . . .	165	167	177	227
Peppers	58	86	81	92
Dates	19	46	39	42
Olives	400	900	350	675
Oranges	64	44	75	41
Other citrus fruit . .	37	33	51	34
Apricots	19	20	22	19
Almonds (in shell) . .	13	13	15	20
Grapes	n.a.	151	120*	130*
Melons and water melons .	107	138	162	171
Sugar beet . . .	40	36	24	31

* FAO estimate.

LIVESTOCK
(1973, FAO estimates—'000)

HORSES, DONKEYS	CATTLE	GOATS	SHEEP	CAMELS
287	680	460	3,200	180

Source: FAO *Production Yearbook 1973*

Fishing: Total catch including Shellfish (1970) 24,376 tons, (1971) 27,500 tons, (1972) 28,100 tons, (1973) 31,500 tons.

MINING
('000 metric tons)

	1969	1970	1971	1972	1973
Iron Ore	945	744	940	890	809
Lead Ore* . . .	23.9	22.0	20.9	19.9	15.6
Calcium Phosphate . .	2,599	3,021	3,162	3,387	3,474
Zinc Ore* . . .	9.2	11.8	11.4	11.4	8.8
Crude Petroleum . .	3,708	4,151	4,096	3,975	3,878
Natural Gas (million cu. metres) .	1	1	1	20	114

* Metal content of ore.

INDUSTRY

		1970	1971	1972	1973
Superphosphates	'ooo metric tons	382	422	413	400
Cement	,, ,, ,,	546	584	629	528
Lead	,, ,, ,,	22	19	25	26
Electric power	million kWh.	680	768	869	963
Town gas	'ooo cubic metres	19.1	17.6	18.6	19.0
Beer	'ooo hectolitres	201	280	331	340
Cigarettes	millions	3,286	3,549	4,205	n.a.
Wine	'ooo hl.	559	966	992	1,096
Olive oil	'ooo metric tons	90	167	70	130
Semolina	,, ,, ,,	n.a.	168	168	186
Flour	,, ,, ,,	195	194	211	224
Esparto pulp	,, ,, ,,	19	20	22	23
Refined sugar	,, ,, ,,	46	47	52	52
Cast iron and bar iron	,, ,, ,,	307	255	377	389
Lime	,, ,, ,,	166	166	158	187
Petrol	,, ,, ,,	94	100	94	94
Kerosene	,, ,, ,,	64	72	62	73
Diesel oil	,, ,, ,,	300	302	329	314
Fuel oil	,, ,, ,,	447	426	449	441

FINANCE

1,000 millimes = 1 Tunisian dinar.
Coins: 1, 2, 5, 10, 20, 50, 100 and 500 millimes.
Notes: 500 millimes; 1, 5 and 10 dinars.

Exchange rates (May 1975): £1 sterling = 873.2 millimes U.S. $1 = 377.8 millimes.

100 Tunisian dinars = £114.52 = $264.69.

Note: The Tunisian dinar was introduced in November 1958, replacing the Tunisian franc at the rate of 1 dinar = 1,000 francs. During 1957 the exchange rate had been fixed at $1 = 420 Tunisian francs, so the initial rate for the new currency was $1 = 420 millimes (1 dinar = $2.381). From December 1958 the relationship to French currency was 1 dinar = 1,175 old francs (11.75 new francs from January 1960). These rates remained in force until September 1964, when the dinar was devalued by 20 per cent. Between September 1964 and August 1971 the official exchange rate was $1 = 525 millimes (1 dinar = $1.905), with the dinar valued at 9.40 French francs until August 1969 and at 10.575 French francs thereafter. From December 1971 to February 1973 the par value was $1 = 483.55 millimes (1 dinar = $2.068). In terms of sterling, the exchange rate between November 1967 and June 1972 was £1 = 1.26 dinars. In February 1973 a new par value of $1 = 435.2 millimes (1 dinar = $2.298) was established but in March 1973 the French authorities ceased to maintain the franc-dollar rate within previously agreed margins. Tunisia retained its currency link with France, thus allowing its exchange rate against the dollar to vary widely from the par value. In January 1974 the Tunisian authorities announced that the franc-dinar rate would henceforth take into account the daily quotations of the Deutsche Mark in terms of francs on the Paris exchange market. For converting the value of foreign trade transactions, the average rates were: $1 = 477.2 millimes in 1972; $1 = 420.0 millimes in 1973; and $1 = 436.5 millimes in 1974.

STATE BUDGET
('ooo dinars)

REVENUE	1972	1973	EXPENDITURE	1972	1973
Income tax	42,637	48,337	Current expenditure	188,953	215,079
Indirect taxes	120,570	138,886	*of which:*		
Capital receipts	72,166	95,816	Public debt	13,361	13,805
			Staff	68,106	76,858
			Investment and management	13,433	13,922
			Subsidies to public establishments	46,790	53,219
			Capital budget	28,500	34,800
			Capital expenditure	77,007	101,337
			Direct investment	38,308	48,114
			Financial operations	17,346	29,206
			Debt payments	21,353	24,017
TOTAL (incl. others)	271,192	320,810	TOTAL	265,960	316,416

Current Expenditure: (estimate): 247 million dinars (1974).

NATIONAL ACCOUNTS
(million dinars at current prices)

Economic Activity	1971	1972	1973	1974
Agriculture and Forestry	146.2	209.5	207.0	250.8
Fishing	5.6	6.6	7.3	8.0
Crude Petroleum and Petroleum Products .	40.0	43.2	43.1	56.0
Other Mining and Quarrying . . .	10.1	10.2	11.3	57.7
Manufacturing*	71.9	97.2	105.1	157.4
Electricity, Gas and Water Supply . .	14.6	15.4	17.7	18.2
Construction	53.8	61.4	71.7	98.4
Wholesale and Retail Trade . . .	99.0	129.0	139.0	157.0
Transport and Communications . .	48.8	56.6	59.1	67.4
Tourism	29.4	36.6	39.8	39.8
Owner-occupied Dwellings . . .	53.6	55.0	56.3	57.8
Public Administration and Defence . .	111.1	120.2	135.6	164.3
Other Producers and Services† . .	63.3	72.6	73.3	77.0
Gross Domestic Product at Factor Cost	747.4	913.5	966.3	1,209.8
Indirect Taxes‡	121.4	141.8	} 151.0	176.3
Less Subsidies	7.1	11.6		
Gross Domestic Product in Purchasers' Values	861.7	1,043.7	1,117.3	1,386.1
Imports of Goods and Services . .	230.2	282.9	328.4	483.0
Less Exports of Goods and Services .	212.4	270.6	300.0	464.0
Available Resources . . .	879.5	1,056.0	1,145.7	1,405.1
Government Final Consumption . .	138.1	152.9	171.8	201.4
Private Final Consumption . . .	559.9	674.5	736.5	881.8
Increase in Stocks	9.3	31.8	—	—
Gross Fixed Capital Formation . .	172.2	196.8	237.4	321.9

* Excluding petroleum products.
† Including financial institutions, business services and community, social and personal services.
‡ Including import duties (million dinars): 14.8 in 1971; 18.5 in 1972.

EXTERNAL TRADE
('ooo dinars)

	1967	1968	1969	1970	1971	1972	1973
Imports	137,087	114,497	139,777	160,396	179,958	222,219	265,947
Exports	78,355	82,829	86,960	95,804	113,304	150,327	168,635

PRINCIPAL COMMODITIES
('ooo dinars)

Imports	1971	1972	1973
Milk, butter and cheese . . .	3,920	4,260	4,457
Wheat and meslin (unmilled) . . .	11,810	10,158	12,147
Sugar (raw and refined) . . .	6,012	8,630	8,255
Soybean oil	5,475	7,753	5,652
Crude petroleum	3,676	7,886	9,917
Pharmaceutical products . . .	5,272	6,437	6,759
Wood	5,467	3,897	6,135
Textile yarn and thread . . .	7,237	8,450	9,846
Iron and steel	3,337	6,020	10,002
Machinery (non-electric) . . .	28,618	31,732	38,363
Electric machinery	10,345	12,208	14,921
Tractors	3,605	4,894	3,636
Road motor vehicles . . .	6,755	8,351	8,929
Car bodies and chassis . . .	3,884	3,924	4,177
Aircraft and air equipment . . .	n.a.	4,446	7,392
Optical and scientific equipment . .	2,374	3,254	4,366
Total (incl. others) . . .	179,958	222,219	265,947

PRINCIPAL COMMODITIES—*continued*]

EXPORTS	1971	1972	1973
Dates	2,228	2,581	2,437
Citrus fruits	2,141	1,990	1,573
Almonds	1,362	1,326	3,924
Olive oil	24,019	46,057	25,788
Preserved fruit and vegetables . .	1,272	1,672	2,722
Wine	967	3,056	9,036
Natural phosphates	11,554	10,281	11,170
Iron ore	2,834	2,196	1,146
Crude petroleum	28,733	38,764	52,090
Phosphoric acid	—	679	4,856
Superphosphates	9,634	9,644	12,509
Paper pulp	1,889	1,603	1,905
Cotton fabrics	738	1,555	2,325
Carpets	1,876	2,416	2,646
Iron bar and sections . . .	1,817	2,928	5,153
Refined lead	1,923	2,010	2,644
TOTAL (incl. others) . . .	113,304	150,327	168,635

PRINCIPAL COUNTRIES
('ooo dinars)

IMPORTS	1971	1972	1973
Austria	4,676	3,902	2,014
Belgium/Luxembourg . . .	3,674	5,326	7,883
Brazil	3,249	5,366	5,115
Canada	4,178	4,342	5,149
France	64,827	79,229	97,412
Germany, Federal Republic . .	12,239	18,990	23,563
Greece	131	642	6,225
Iraq	3,216	352	4,576
Italy	15,497	22,473	21,324
Netherlands	3,742	4,688	6,932
Saudi Arabia	396	4,870	5,193
Spain	4,002	2,694	5,451
Sweden	2,500	1,851	3,758
Turkey	2,223	3,686	3,885
U.S.S.R.	2,140	2,706	3,476
United Kingdom	5,836	7,457	7,437
U.S.A.	26,230	26,618	24,750
TOTAL (incl. others) . . .	179,958	222,219	265,947

EXPORTS	1971	1972	1973
Algeria	1,724	1,691	2,641
Bulgaria	3,158	1,526	2,272
France	21,884	31,740	46,720
Germany, Federal Republic . .	14,857	12,603	11,727
Greece	2,283	1,783	6,648
Italy	22,146	44,552	26,756
Libya	11,212	7,618	8,960
Netherlands	846	744	2,654
Poland	3,459	3,769	2,128
Spain	6,801	14,534	4,001
Switzerland	2,558	2,075	1,863
Turkey	921	951	2,116
U.S.S.R.	3,721	4,286	3,524
United Kingdom	1,770	2,951	3,850
U.S.A.	1,544	5,498	24,941
TOTAL (incl. others) . . .	113,304	150,327	168,635

TRANSPORT

RAILWAYS

	1971	1972	1973
Passenger-km. (million) .	470	506	527
Freight ton-km. (million) .	1,372	1,442	1,392

ROADS
Vehicles in Use

	1971	1972	1973*
Private cars . .	72,056	80,393	90,238
Buses . .	2,239	2,451	2,546
Commercial vehicles .	39,389	43,838	50,181
Motor cycles . .	10,063	11,022	11,200

* Provisional.

SEA-BORNE SHIPPING

	1971	1972	1973	1974
Vessels ('000 net registered tons):				
Total entered and cleared*	25,137	27,236	25,933	28,256
Passenger journeys	252,200	302,502	246,625	223,618
Total goods loaded ('000 metric tons)† . .	14,083	19,406	17,241	n.a.
La Skhirra†	9,039	14,251	12,187	n.a.
Other ports	5,043	5,155	5,055	5,187
International goods loaded ('000 metric tons)† .	12,465	18,479	16,425	n.a.
La Skhirra†	8,161	14,141	12,113	n.a.
Other ports	4,304	4,338	4,312	n.a.
Coastwise goods loaded ('000 metric tons) .	1,618	927	816	n.a.
Total goods unloaded ('000 metric tons) .	3,499	3,885	4,184	5,030
International shipping . . .	1,883	2,958	3,212	n.a.
Coastwise shipping	1,616	927	972	n.a.

   * Excluding the petroleum port of La Skhirra.

   † Including Algerian crude petroleum. The total of such cargo loaded at La Skhirra for international shipping was (in metric tons): 5.2 million in 1971; 10.4 million in 1972.

CIVIL AVIATION

	1970	1971	1972
Passenger ('000) . .	785.0	1,047.2	828*
Freight (metric tons)	4,475	4,756	4,645
Mail (metric tons) .	896	921	n.a.

  * Not including passengers in transit.

TOURISM
PRINCIPAL NATIONALITIES OF VISITORS
('ooo)

	1970	1971	1972	1973
Algeria	8.9	11.8	14.6	18.6
Belgium	18.8	26.5	38.2	37.6
Denmark	8.1	10.1	14.0	14.1
France	106.6	132.4	152.3	171.7
Germany, Federal Republic .	77.3	153.8	168.9	104.8
Italy	27.1	38.5	37.2	39.7
Libya	36.4	54.4	64.2	63.1
Netherlands . . .	9.1	14.5	19.7	21.6
Sweden	16.9	22.0	24.4	19.1
Switzerland . . .	16.8	25.8	31.0	30.6
United Kingdom . . .	35.9	60.6	141.3	124.1
U.S.A.	14.0	12.8	16.2	13.1
TOTAL (incl. others) .	410.7	608.2	780.3	721.9

Tourist Visits: (1974) 716,003.
Tourist Accommodation: (1974) 56,292 tourist beds.
Tourist Nights: (1973) 5,882,497, (1974) 5.6 million.
Tourist Spending: (1972) 68m. dinars, (1973) 72m. dinars, (1974) 81m. dinars.

EDUCATION

| | INSTITUTIONS | PUPILS | | TEACHERS | |
	1974-75	1973-74	1974-75	1973-74	1974-75
Primary	2,277	865,786	898,464	20,961	21,706
Secondary	161	179,050	178,997	7,966	8,575
of which:					
Secondary Technical . . .	n.a.	52,748	54,366	n.a.	n.a.
Teacher Training . . .	12	4,974	3,027	271	222
University of Tunis . . .	15	11,540	13,723	n.a.	1,019

The percentage of girls is 38 per cent in primary schools, 31 per cent in secondary schools and 25 per cent at the university.

Sources: Bulletin mensuel de statistique, Institut national de la Statistique, Tunis; *Rapport annuel*, Banque centrale de Tunisie, Tunis.

THE CONSTITUTION

Tunisia, which had been a French Protectorate since 1881, achieved full internal autonomy in September 1955, and was finally recognized as a fully independent sovereign State by the Protocol of Paris of March 20th, 1956, by which France abrogated the former treaties and conventions.

NATIONAL ASSEMBLY

The Constitution was proclaimed by the Constituent Assembly on June 1st, 1959. Tunisia is a free, independent and sovereign republic. Legislative power is exercised by the National Assembly which is elected (at the same time as the President) every five years by direct universal suffrage. Every citizen who has had Tunisian nationality for at least five years and who has attained twenty years of age has the vote. The National Assembly shall hold two sessions every year, each session lasting not more than three months. Additional meetings may be held at the demand of the President or of a majority of the deputies.

HEAD OF STATE

The President of the Republic is both Head of State and Head of the Executive. He must be not less than forty years of age and is not permitted to serve more than three terms consecutively. The President of the Republic is also the Commander-in-Chief of the army and makes both civil and military appointments.

In December 1974 the provisions of the Constitution relating to the Head of State were amended to allow Habib Bourguiba to become President-for-Life. A further amendment empowered the Prime Minister to assume the Presidency in the event of the death, resignation or total incapacity of the incumbent.

COUNCIL OF STATE

Comprises two judicial bodies: (1) an administrative body dealing with legal disputes between individuals and State or public bodies; (2) an audit office to verify the accounts of the State and submit reports.

ECONOMIC AND SOCIAL COUNCIL

Deals with economic and social planning and studies projects submitted by the National Assembly. Members are grouped in seven categories representing various sections of the community.

THE GOVERNMENT

HEAD OF STATE

President-for-Life: HABIB BOURGUIBA.

THE CABINET

(*July* 1975)

Prime Minister: HEDI NOUIRA.

Minister responsible to Prime Minister: MOHAMED SAYAH.

Minister, Director of the President's Office: CHEDLI KLIBI.

Minister of Justice: SLAHEDDINE BALI.

Minister for Foreign Affairs: HABIB CHATTI.

Minister of the Interior: TAHAR BELKHODJA.

Minister of Defence: MOHAMED HÉDI KHEFACHA.

Minister of Finance: MOHAMED FITOURI.

Minister of the Economy: ABDELAZIZ LASRAM.

Minister of Agriculture: HASSAN BELKHODJA.

Minister of Education: DRISS GUIGA.

Minister of Cultural Affairs: MAHMOUD MESSADI.

Minister of Public Health: MOHAMED MZALI.

Minister of Public Works: LASSAAD BEN OSMAN.

Minister of Social Affairs: MOHAMED ENNACEUR.

Minister of Transport and Communications: ABDALLAH FARHAT.

Minister of Youth and Sport: FOUAD MBAZAA.

Minister at the Prime Minister's Office with Responsibility for Planning: MUSTAPHA ZAANOUNI.

Secretary of State for the National Economy: MEKKI ZIDI.

Secretary of State for Education: HEDI ZGHAL.

Secretaries of State for Supply: ABDEL-HAMID SASSI and LARBI MALLAKH.

Secretary of State for Defence: AHMAD BENNOUR.

Secretary of State for Information: MUSTAFA MASMOUDI.

Secretary of State for Foreign Affairs: MONGI KOOLI.

NATIONAL ASSEMBLY

President: SADOK MOKADDEM.

First Vice-President: FERDJANI BELHADJ AMMAR.

ELECTION, NOVEMBER 1974

All 112 seats were won by the Destour Socialist Party. There were no opposition candidates.

POLITICAL PARTIES

Parti Socialiste Destourien—PSD: 10 rue de Rome, Tunis; f. 1934 by Habib Bourguiba, as a splinter party from the old *Destour* (Constitution) Party; moderate left-wing republican party, which achieved Tunisian independence; 9th Congress held Sept. 1974; there is a political bureau of 20 members, including 14 ministers, and a central committee of 60 elected by the party congress; Sec.-Gen. HEDI NOUIRA; Chairman-for-Life HABIB BOURGUIBA.

DIPLOMATIC REPRESENTATION

EMBASSIES ACCREDITED TO TUNISIA

(In Tunis unless otherwise indicated)

Algeria: 18 rue de Niger; *Ambassador:* TIDJENI HADDAM.

Argentina: Algiers, Algeria.

Austria: 17 ave. de France; *Ambassador:* ERICH BINDER.

Bangladesh: Algiers, Algeria.

Belgium: 47 rue du 1er Juin; *Ambassador:* JACQUES GÉRARD.

Brazil: 15 rue Es-Sayouti, El Menzah; *Ambassador:* ADOLPHO J. BEZERRA DE MENEZES.

Bulgaria: 16 rue El Moutanabi; *Ambassador:* BOGOMIL NONEV.

Cameroon: 17 rue Jacques Cartier, Belvédère; *Ambassador:* FERDINAND LÉOPOLD OYONO.

Canada: 3 rue Didon, Notre Dame de Tunis, Cité al Mahdi; *Ambassador:* JACQUES GIGNAC.

Central African Republic: Algiers, Algeria.

Chad: Cairo, Egypt.

China, People's Republic: 41 ave. Lesseps; *Ambassador:* HOU YEH-FENG.

Costa Rica: Madrid, Spain.

Czechoslovakia: 98 rue de la Palestine; *Ambassador:* (vacant).

Denmark: 138 ave. de la Liberté; *Ambassador:* HANS MOLLEV.

Egypt: 1 rue Es-Soyouti, El Menzah; *Ambassador:* HASSEN ABDEL NAYEL.

Finland: 23 rue Baudelaire, El Omrane; *Ambassador:* SUNNELL JUHANI OSSI.

France: pl. de l'Indépendance; *Ambassador:* PHILIPPE REBEYROL.

Gabon: Paris, France.

German Democratic Republic: 16 rue Es-Soyouti, El Menzah; *Ambassador:* HEINZ DIETER WINTER.

Germany, Federal Republic: 18 rue Félicien Challaye; *Ambassador:* Dr. HEINZ NAUPERT.

Ghana: 103 ave. de la Liberté; *Ambassador:* ANTHONY W. EPHSON.

Greece: 4 rue El Jahedh, El Menzah: *Ambassador:* GEORGES J. GAVAS.

Guinea: Algiers, Algeria.

Hungary: Algiers, Algeria.

India: Rabat, Morocco.

Indonesia: Algiers, Algeria.

Iran: 10 rue Dr. Burnet, Belvédère; *Ambassador:* AKBAR DARAI (also accred. to Libya).

Iraq: 128 ave. de la Liberté; *Ambassador:* MEDLOUL NAJI EL MUHANNA.

Italy: 37 rue Abdennasser; *Ambassador:* SALVATORE SARACENO.

Ivory Coast: 1 pl. Pasteur; *Ambassador:* CHARLES AILLOT ABOUT.

Japan: 16 rue Jugurtha; *Ambassador:* YASUO YANO.

Jordan: 16 rue El Moutanabi, El Menzah; *Ambassador:* (vacant).

Korea, Republic: 7 rue Teymour, El Menzah; *Ambassador:* KYU SAP CHUNG.

Kuwait: rue Jacques Cartier, Belvédère; *Ambassador:* MOJRANE AHMED EL HAMAD.

Lebanon: 4 Impasse Ibn Chabbat, rue El Moezz, El Menzah; *Ambassador:* JOSEPH SALAMA.

Libya: 48bis rue du 1er Juin; *Commissioner General:* ABDEL-HAMID AS-SIDI AZ-ZINTANI.

Madagascar: Algiers, Algeria.

Mali: Paris, France.

Malta: Tripoli, Libya.

Mauritania: 4 rue Apollo XI; *Ambassador:* SOUMARE GAYE FILLY.

Mexico: Rome, Italy.

Morocco: 5 rue Didon, Notre Dame; *Ambassador:* GHALI BENHIMA.

Netherlands: 2 rue d'Artois; *Ambassador:* J. D. VAN DEN BRANDELER.

Niger: Algiers, Algeria.

Nigeria: Paris, France.

Norway: 7 ave. Habib Bourguiba; *Ambassador:* OLAV MOLTKE HANSEN.

Oman: 129 ave. de Lesseps; *Chargé d'Affaires:* MOHAMED EL HARITHI.

Pakistan: 20 rue Imam Muslim, El Menzah; *Ambassador:* N. KHAN KHATTAK.

Peru: Algiers, Algeria.

Poland: 12 rue Didon, Notre Dame; *Ambassador:* EDWARD WYCHOWANIEC.

Portugal: *Ambassador:* HENRIQUE GUILHERME AUGUSTE DE FIGAREDO SILVA MARTINS.

Qatar: *Ambassador:* ALI OMEIR NAIMI.

Romania: 6 rue Magon, Notre Dame; *Ambassador:* MARIN RADOI.

Saudi Arabia: 16 rue de l'Autriche; *Ambassador:* ABDEL-RAHMAN EL BASSAM.

Senegal: 122 ave. de la Liberté; *Ambassador:* PASCAL ANTOINE SANE.

Spain: 75 ave. Taieb Mehiri; *Ambassador:* ROMÁN OYARZÚN.

Sudan: Cairo, Egypt.

Sweden: 17 ave. de France; *Ambassador:* MARC GIRON.

Switzerland: 17 ave. de France; *Ambassador:* AUGUSTE HURNI.

Syria: 128 ave. de Lesseps; *Chargé d'Affaires:* ALI MUSTAPHA.

Thailand: Madrid, Spain.

Turkey: 47 ave. Mohamed V; *Ambassador:* (vacant).

U.S.S.R.: 31 rue du 1er Juin; *Ambassador:* BORIS L. KOLOKOLOV.

United Arab Emirates: *Ambassador:* AISSA AL ALAILI.

United Kingdom: 5 pl. de la Victoire; *Ambassador:* JOHN MARNHAM.

U.S.A.: 144 ave. de la Liberté; *Ambassador:* TALCOTT WILLIAMS SEELYE.

Venezuela: 61 ave. Mohamed V; *Ambassador:* Dr. PEDRO BARRADAS.

Viet-Nam, Democratic Republic: 23 rue Jacques Cartier; *Ambassador:* LE VAN TUAN.

Yemen Arab Republic: Algiers, Algeria.

Yugoslavia: 4 rue du Libéria; *Ambassador:* DRAGOMIR PETROVIC.

Zaire: 5 rue du Niger; *Ambassador:* GEYRO TE KULE.

Tunisia also has diplomatic relations with Afghanistan, Albania, Cambodia, Ireland, Kenya, Monaco, Panama, Somalia, Uganda, the Upper Volta and the Vatican City.

JUDICIAL SYSTEM

Cour de Cassation: Tunis; has three civil and one criminal sections.

There are three Courts of Appeal, at Tunis, Sousse and Sfax, and thirteen courts of First Instance, each having three chambers except the Court of First Instance of Tunis which has eight chambers.

Cantonal Justices have been set up in 48 areas.

RELIGION

The Constitution of 1956 recognizes Islam as the State religion, with the introduction of certain reforms, such as the abolition of polygamy. Minority religions are Jews (20,000), Roman Catholics (20,000), Greek Orthodox and a number of French and English Protestants.

Grand Mufti of Tunisia: Sheikh MOHAMMED HEDI BEL-CADHI.

Roman Catholic Prelature: 4 rue d'Alger, Tunis; *Titular Archbishop of Mossori:* Mgr. MICHEL CALLENS.

THE PRESS

DAILIES

TUNIS

L'Action: Maison du Parti, blvd. du 9 avril; f. 1932; organ of the Destour Socialist Party; French; Chief Editor ABDELHAY SEGHAÏER; circ. 32,000.

al-Amal (*Action*): 15 rue de 2 Mars 1934; f. 1934; organ of the Destour Socialist Party; Arabic; Chief Editor LARBI ABDERRAZAK; circ. 25,000.

Assabah (*The Echo*): 4 rue Ali Bach-Hamba; f. 1951; Arabic; Dir. HABIB CHEIKHROUHOU; circ. 50,000.

La Presse de Tunisie: 6 rue Ali Bach-Hamba; f. 1936; French; Dir. ABDELHAKIM BELKHIRIA; Chief Editor NOUREDDINE TABKA; circ. 35,000.

PERIODICALS

TUNIS

ach-Chaab: Place M'Hamed Ali; Trade union publication; Arabic; fortnightly.

ach-Chabab: 10 rue de Rome; publ. of the Union of Tunisian youth; Arabic language; monthly.

Assada: 4 rue Ali Bach-Hamba; weekly; Arabic.

Bulletin Annuel: Institut National de Statistique, B.P. 65.

Bulletin de la Chambre de Commerce de Tunis: 1 avenue Habib Thameur, Palais Consulaire; monthly; Dir. SLIMANE AGHA.

Conjoncture: Banque Centrale de Tunisie, 7 place de la Monnaie; economic and financial surveys; quarterly.

Il Corriere di Tunisi: 4 rue de Russie; Italian; weekly; Dir. M. FINZI.

Etudiant Tunisien: B.P. 286, 13 rue Gamal Abdel Nasser; f. 1953; French and Arabic; Chief Editor MOUNIR BEJI.

al-Fikr (*Thought*): B.P. 556; f. 1955; cultural review; Arabic; monthly; Dir. MOHAMED MZALI.

Ibla: 12 rue Jamâa el Haoua; f. 1937; social and cultural review on Maghreb and Muslim-Arab affairs; French; twice yearly; Dir. A. DEMEERSEMAN.

al-Idhaa wa Talvaza (*Radio and Television*): 71 ave. de la Liberté; broadcasting magazine; Arabic language; fortnightly; Editor ABDELMAJID ENNAIFAR; circ. 15,000.

al-Jaich: National Defence publication; Arabic language.

Journal Officiel de la République Tunisienne: Km. 2, Route de Radès, Radès; the official gazette; f. 1860; French and Arab editions published twice weekly by the Imprimerie Officielle (The State Press); Pres./Gen. Man. HAMED ZGHAL.

al-Maraa (*The Woman*): 56 boulevard Bab Benat; f. 1961; issued by the National Union of Tunisian Women; Arabic; political, economic and social affairs; monthly; circ. 10,000.

Le Sport: 9 ave. de la Liberté; French language; weekly; Pres. MAHMOUD ELLAFI; circ. 20,000.

Statistiques Financières: Banque Centrale de Tunisie, 7 place de la Monnaie; statistical tables; monthly.

Tunisie Actualités: Centre de Documentation Nationale, 9 rue Hooker Doolittle, Belvédère; f. 1966; quarterly; French; official journal.

La Tunisie Economique: 32 rue Charles-de-Gaulle; French; every 2 months; published by the Union Tunisienne de l'Industrie, du Commerce et de l'Artisanat; circ. 2,000.

NEWS AGENCIES

Tunis Afrique Presse (TAP): 25 ave. Habib Bourguiba, Tunis; f. 1961; cap. TD 500,000 with participation of the state, the press and employees; Pres. and Dir.-Gen. MAHMOUD TRIKI.

FOREIGN BUREAUX

Agence France-Presse (*France*): 45 ave. Habib Bourguiba, Tunis; Chief ROGER PIERARD.

ANSA (*Italy*): 8 rue Caracella, Tunis; Representative NICOLA RIENZA.

Associated Press (*U.S.A.*): 35 rue Garibaldi, Tunis; Chief F. VENTURA.

Novosti (*U.S.S.R.*): APN office, 108 ave. de la Liberté, Tunis; Chief O. BOGUSHEVICH.

Reuters (*U.K.*): 45 ave. Habib Bourguiba; Chief GUSTAVE DEJEANNE.

Tanjug (*Yugoslavia*): 4 rue du Libéria, Tunis.

TASS (*U.S.S.R.*): 2 rue Gounot, Tunis; Chief NADIRIAN VARTAN.

United Press International (*U.S.A.*): 28 rue Gamal Abdul Nasser, Tunis; Chief MICHEL DEURE.

Visnews: 33 rue Lénine, Tunis.

PUBLISHERS

Coopérative Ouvrière Publication Impression "C.O.O.P.I.": rue du Marché and ave. Taieb M'hiri, Sfax.

Dar Al Kitab: 5 ave. Habib Bourguiba, Sousse.

Dar Assabah: 4 rue Ali Bach-Hamba, Tunis; f. 1951; 200 mems.; publishes daily and weekly papers which circulate throughout Tunisia, North Africa, France, Belgium, Luxembourg and West Germany.

En Najah—Editions Hedi ben Abdelgheni: 11 ave. de France, Tunis; Arab and French books, oriental reviews.

Maison Tunisienne d'Edition (M.T.E.): 54 ave. de la Liberté, Tunis.

Institut National de la statistique: Tunis; publishes a variety of annuals, periodicals and papers concerned with the economic policy and development of Tunisia.

S.L.I.M. (**Société Librairie Imprimerie Messagerie**): blvd. Président Bourguiba, El Kef.

Société Anonyme de Papeterie et Imprimerie: 12 rue de Vesoul, Tunis.

Société d'Arts Graphiques, d'Edition et de Presse: 15 rue 2 mars 1934, la Kasbah, Tunis; f. 1966; publishes daily papers, magazines, books, etc.

Société Nationale d'Edition et de Diffusion: 5 ave. de Carthage, Tunis.

RADIO AND TELEVISION

RADIO

Radiodiffusion Télévision Tunisienne: 71 ave. de la Liberté, Tunis; government station; broadcasts in Arabic, French and Italian; Dir.-Gen. SLAHEDDINE BEN HAMIDA.

Number of radio receivers: 400,000 in 1972.

TELEVISION

Television was introduced in northern and central Tunisia in January 1966, and by 1972 transmission reached all the country. A relay station to link up with European transmissions was built at El Haouaria in 1967.

Number of television receivers 147,104.

FINANCE

(cap. = capital, p.u. = paid up, dep. = deposits, m. = million)

BANKING

CENTRAL BANK

Banque Centrale de Tunisie: 7 Place de la Monnaie, Tunis; f. 1958; cap. 3.0m. dinars, assets 355m. dinars (Dec. 1974); Gov. MOHAMED GHENIMA; Dir.-Gen. MOHAMED BOUSBIA; publs. *Conjoncture* (quarterly), *Statistiques Financières* (monthly), *Rapport Annuel*.

Banque de Développement de l'Economie de la Tunisie: 68 ave. Habib Bourguiba, Tunis; f. 1959; development bank, now the main source of long term and equity finance for industrial and tourist enterprises; received $35m. loan from World Bank in 1967; cap. 14m. dinars; Pres. and Gen. Man. HABIB BOURGUIBA, Jr.

Banque Franco-Tunisienne: 13 rue d'Alger, Tunis; Gen. Man. HABIB BEN YOUSSEF.

Banque Nationale de Tunisie: 19 ave. de Paris, Tunis; f. 1959; cap. 4m. dinars, dep. (1973) 44,291m. dinars; Pres./Gen. Man. MONCEF BELKODJA; Dir.-Gen. TAHAR FARAH; 30 brs.

Banque du Sud: 14 ave. de Paris, Tunis; f. 1968; cap. 2.5m. dinars, dep. 35.7m. dinars (Dec. 1974); Pres. SAÏD CHENIK; Sec.-Gen. MONGI BEN OTHMAN; publs. *Rapport annuel, Bulletin trimestriel*.

Banque de Tunisie: 3 avenue de France, Tunis; f. 1884; cap. 1.5m. dinars, dep. 33.35m. dinars (Dec. 1973); Pres. BOUBAKER MABROUK; Gen. Man. ABDERRAZAK RASSAA.

Caisse d'Epargne Nationale Tunisienne: blvd. 9 Avril 1938, Tunis.

Compte Chèques Postaux: blvd. 5 Avril 1938, Tunis.

Société Tunisienne de Banque: 1 ave. Habib Thameur, Tunis; f. 1958; cap. p.u. 3m. dinars (July 1972); Chair. M. HASSEN BELKHODJA.

Union Bancaire pour le Commerce et l'Industrie: 7-9 rue Gamal Abdel Nasser, Tunis; f. 1961; cap. p.u. 1.65m. dinars, dep. 33.6m. dinars; incorporates Banque d'Escompte et de Crédit à l'Industrie en Tunisie; Pres. and Dir.-Gen. ABDESSELAM BEN AYED.

Union Internationale de Banques: 65 ave. Habib Bourguiba, Tunis; f. 1963 as a merging of Tunisian interests by the Société Tunisienne de Banque with the Crédit Lyonnais and other foreign banks; cap. 2m. dinars; Pres. and Gen. Man. TAWFIK TORGEMAN.

FOREIGN BANKS

Arab Bank Ltd., Tunis Branch: Amman, Jordan; 21 rue Al-Djazira, Tunis.

British Bank of the Middle East: London; 70 avenue Habib Bourguiba, Tunis.

Crédit Foncier et Commercial de Tunisie: 13 ave. de France, Tunis.

Société Marseillaise de Crédit: Marseilles; 12 avenue de France, Tunis.

A national Stock Exchange was opened during 1967.

INSURANCE

Astrée, Compagnie Franco-Tunisienne d'Assurances Tous Risques et de Réassurances, S.A.: 43-45 ave. Habib Bourguiba, Tunis; f. 1950; Pres. ABDERRAZAK RASSAA; Dir.-Gen. MOHAMED HACHICHA.

Caisse Tunisienne d'Assurances Mutuelles Agricoles et Mutuelle Générale Assurances: 6 ave. Habib Thameur, Tunis; f. 1912; Pres. MOKTAR BELLAGHA, Dir.-Gen. SLAHEDDINE FERCHIOU.

Lloyd Tunisien: 7 ave. de Carthage, Tunis; f. 1945; Pres. M. ZERZERI; fire, accident, liability, marine, life.

Société Tunisienne d'Assurances et de Réassurances: ave. de Paris, Tunis; f. 1958; Pres./Dir.-Gen. HEDI ENNIFER; all kinds of insurance.

FOREIGN COMPANIES

About thirty of the major French, Swiss and British insurance companies are represented in Tunisia.

TRADE AND INDUSTRY

CHAMBERS OF COMMERCE

Chambre de Commerce de Tunis: Palais Consulaire, 1 ave. Habib Thameur, Tunis; f. 1925; 25 mems.; Pres. MAHMOUD ZERZERI; publ. *Bulletin* (monthly).

Chambre de Commerce du Centre: rue Chadly Khaznadar, Sousse; Pres. HÉDI BOUSLAMA; Sec.-Gen. TOUHAMI EL HEDDA; publ. *Bulletin Economique* (every two months in French and Arabic).

Chambre de Commerce du Nord: 12 rue Ibn Khaldoun, Bizerte; f. 1903; 8 mems.; Pres. MOHAMED TERRAS; Sec.-Gen. Mme SFAXI RACHIDA; publ. *Bulletin Economique*.

Chambre de Commerce du Sud: 21-23 rue Habib Thameur, Sfax; f. 1895; 8 mems.; publ. *Bulletin Economique* (monthly).

Chambre de Commerce et d'Industrie Franco-Tunisienne: 14 rue de Vesoul, Tunis; f. 1974; Pres. HABIB BOURGUIBA, Jr.

ECONOMIC ORGANIZATION

Union Tunisienne de l'Industrie, du Commerce et de l'Artisanat (U.T.I.C.A.): 32 rue Charles-de-Gaulle, Tunis; f. 1946 by FERDJANI BEN HADJ AMMAR; mems. about 250,000 in 13 regional unions and 12 national federations; Pres. FERDJANI BEN HADJ AMMAR; First Vice-Pres. HABIB MAJOUL; publs. *La Tunisie Economique* (monthly), *Economic Yearbook* (annual).

TRADE UNIONS

Union Générale des Etudiants de Tunisie (U.G.E.T.): 11 rue d'Espagne, Tunis; f. 1953; 600 mems.; Pres. MEKKI FITOURI; publ. *L'Etudiant Tunisien*.

Union Générale Tunisienne du Travail (U.G.T.T.): 29 place M'Hamed Ali, Tunis; f. 1946 by FARHAT HACHED; affiliated to ICFTU; mems. 150,000 in 23 affiliated unions; Sec.-Gen. HABIB ACHOUR.

Union Nationale des Femmes de Tunisie (U.N.F.T.): 56 blvd. Bab-Benat, Tunis; f. 1956; 35,000 mems.; Pres. Mme. FATHIA MZALI; Sec.-Gen. Mme. DORDANA MASMOUDI.

TRADE FAIR

International Fair in Tunis: Mohammed V St., Tunis; May 16th-June 1st, 1976.

TRANSPORT

RAILWAYS

Société Nationale des Transports: Tunis; controls the electrified line from Tunis to La Marsa (19½ km.); operates 72 local and 169 long-distance domestic and international bus routes.

Société Nationale des Chemins de Fer Tunisiens: 67 ave. Farhat Hached, Tunis; f. 1957; State organization controlling all Tunisian railways; an agreement was signed with the Libyan Government in June 1974 for the construction of a line from Gabès to Tripoli; Pres. M. A. SOUISSI; publs. monthly and annual reports.

In 1972 the total length of railways was 2,089 km.

ROADS

In 1973 there were 18,774 km. of roads. Of these 10,551 km. were main roads and 5,898 km. secondary roads.

SHIPPING

Tunisia has 4 major ports: Tunis–La Goulette, Bizerta, Sousse and Sfax. There is a special petroleum port at La Skhirra. A complex of three ports, with separate facilities for general merchandise, minerals and oil, is under construction at Gabès.

Compagnie Tunisienne de Navigation: P.O.B. 40, 5 avenue Dag Hammarskjoeld, Tunis; brs. at Bizerta, Gabès, La Skhirra, La Goulette, Sfax and Sousse.

CIVIL AVIATION

There are two international airports, Tunis-Carthage and Tunis-El Aouina. Other airports are at Jerba, Monastir, Sfax, Gabès and Tozeur.

Tunis Air (*Société Tunisienne de l'Air*): 113 ave. de la Liberté, Tunis; f. 1948; flights to Algeria, Belgium, France, Fed. Rep. of Germany, Italy, Libya, Luxemberg, Morocco, Netherlands, Saudi Arabia, Switzerland and U.K. and internal flights; fleet of five Boeing 727, four Caravelles, one Nord 262; Pres. ABDEL-AZIZ ZNAÏDI.

Société Tunisienne de Réparations Aéronautiques et de Constructions: Aérodrome de Tunis-Carthage, Tunis; f. 1952; internal charter flights for oil companies.

FOREIGN AIRLINES

Aeroflot, Air Afrique, Air Algérie, Air France, Air India, Alitalia, Austrian Airlines, Balkan, British Caledonian, CSA, EgyptAir, Interflug, JAT, KLM, Libyan Arab, LOT, Lufthansa, Malev, Royal Air Maroc, Sabena, SAS, Swissair, Tabso, TWA, and UTA also serve Tunis.

TOURISM

Office National du Tourisme et du Thermalisme: 1 ave. Mohammed V, Tunis; Dir.-Gen. A. BOURAOUI.

Direction de l'Information: 2 rue d'Alger, Tunis; Dir. ABDELKRIM MOUSSA.

Voyages 2000: 2 ave. de France, Tunis; Dir. Gen. AMOURI OMRANE; publ. *Voyages 2000*.

CULTURAL ORGANIZATIONS

Ministry of Cultural Affairs: Tunis; departments organize all national cultural events; Minister MAHMOUD MESSADI.

International Cultural Centre: Hammamet; f. 1962; has built an amphitheatre at Hammamet and maintains a summer drama school for actors and students; Dir. TAHAR GUIGA.

PRINCIPAL THEATRES

Théâtre Municipal de Tunis: Tunis; subsidized by the state.

Hammamet Theatre: Hammamet; open air theatre built 1963; organized by International Cultural Centre of Tunis.

CULTURAL FESTIVALS

Carthage Festival: Ministry of Cultural Affairs, Tunis; international festival of arts; held every year at the site of the ancient city and in Tunis; next Festival October, 1974.

Maghreb Theatre Festival: Monastir; f. 1964; open to theatrical groups from Algeria, Libya, Morocco and Tunisia.

ATOMIC ENERGY

Institut de Recherche Scientifique et Technique: Tunis-Carthage; f. 1969; attached institute of the University of Tunis; Dir. TAOUFIK BEN MENA.

DEFENCE

Estimated Defence Expenditure (1974): 17,500,000 dinars.
Military Service: 1 year (selective).
Total Armed Forces: 24,000: army 20,000; navy 2,000; air force 2,000.
Paramilitary Forces: 10,000 (5,000 Gendarmerie, 5,000 National Guard).

EDUCATION

Tunisia has better educational facilities than most developing countries. Approximately 70 per cent of children of school age receive an education. In 1974/75 there were almost 900,000 pupils in primary education and almost 180,000 in all secondary education.

Arabic only is used in the first year of primary school, but in the higher grades French becomes progressively more important and is used almost exclusively in higher education. About 14,000 Tunisians receive some higher education in the country, and about 3,000 go abroad for University courses. The University of Tunis was opened in 1961/62. It has 15 faculties and institutes.

UNIVERSITY

Université de Tunis: 94 blvd. du 9 Avril 1938, Tunis; f. 1960; 1,019 teachers, 13,723 students.

BIBLIOGRAPHY

ANTHONY, JOHN. About Tunisia (London, 1961).

ARDANT, GAVRIEL. La Tunisie d'Aujourd'hui et Demain (Paris, 1961).

ASHFORD, DOUGLAS E. Morocco-Tunisia: Politics and Planning (Syracuse University Press, 1965).

BASSET, ANDRÉ. Initiation à la Tunisie (Paris, 1950).

BOURGUIBA, HABIB. La Tunisie et la France (Paris, 1954). Hadith al-Jamaa (*Collected Broadcasts*) (Tunis, 1957).

BRUNSCHVIG, ROBERT. La Tunisie au haut Moyen Age (Cairo, 1948).

CAMBON, HENRI. Histoire de la régence de Tunisie (Paris, 1948).

DE MONTETY, HENRI. Femmes de Tunisie (Paris, 1958).

DESPOIS, JEAN. La Tunisie, ses Régions (Paris, 1959).

DUVIGNAUD, JEAN. Tunisie (Editions Rencontre, Lausanne, 1965).

DUWAJI, GHAZI. Economic Development in Tunisia (Praeger, New York, 1967).

GARAS, FELIX. Bourguiba et la Naissance d'une Nation (Paris, 1956).

GERMANN, RAIMUND E. Verwaltung und Einheitspartei in Tunisien (Europa Verlag, Zürich, 1968).

GUEN, MONCEF. La Tunisie indépendente face à son économie (Paris, 1961).

KNAPP, W. Tunisia (Thames and Hudson, London, 1972).

LAITMAN, LEON. Tunisia Today: Crisis in North Africa (New York, 1954).

LING, DWIGHT D. Tunisia, from Protectorate to Republic (Indiana University Press, 1967).

MENSCHING, HORST. Tunisien eine geographische Landeskunde (Darmstadt, 1968).

MICAUD, C. A. Tunisia, the Politics of Moderation (New York, 1964).

MOORE, C. H. Tunisia since Independence (University of California Press, Berkeley, 1965).

NERFIN, M. Entretiens avec Ahmed Ben Salah (F. Maspero, Paris, 1974).

PERROUX, F. and BARRE, R., Editors. Développement, croissance, progrès: Maroc-Tunisie (Paris, 1961).

RAYMOND, ANDRÉ. La Tunisie (Series *Que sais-je*, No. 318) (Paris, 1961).

ROMERIL, PAUL E. A. Tunisian nationalism: a bibliographical outline (*Middle East Journal* 1960, pages 206-215).

RUDEBECK, LARS. Party and People: A Study of Political Change in Tunisia (C. Hurst, London, 1969).

RUF, WERNER KLAUS, Der Burgismus und die Aussenpolitik der unabhängigen Tunesien (Freiburg, 1969).

SYLVESTER, ANTHONY. Tunisia (Bodley Head, London, 1969).

TLATLI, SALAH-EDDINE. Tunisie nouvelle (Tunis, 1957).

TUNISIA-SECRÉTARIAT D'ÉTAT AU PLAN ET À L'ECONOMIE NATIONALE. Plan Quadriennal 1965–68 (3 vols.) (Tunis, 1965). Perspectives Décennales de Développement 1962–71 (Tunis, 1962).

ZIADEH, NICOLA A. The Origins of Tunisian Nationalism (Beirut. 1962.)

Turkey

PHYSICAL AND SOCIAL GEOGRAPHY

W. B. Fisher

Turkey is in a remarkable sense a passage land between Europe and Asia. Nearly one-half of her 1,630 miles of land frontier is with European States—Greece, Bulgaria, and Soviet Russia; and the remainder with Iran, Iraq, and Syria. The richest and most densely populated west of Turkey looks towards the Aegean and Mediterranean Seas and is very conscious of its links with Europe; whilst in culture, racial origins, and ways of life there are frequent reminders of Turkey's geographical situation primarily as a part of Asia.

Turkey consists essentially of the large peninsula of Asia Minor, which has strongly defined natural limits: sea on three sides (the Black Sea in the north, the Aegean in the west, and the Mediterranean on the south), and high mountain ranges on the fourth (eastern) side. The small region of European Turkey, containing the cities of Istânbul (Constantinople) and Edirne (Adrianople) is on the other hand defined by a purely artificial frontier, the exact position of which has varied considerably over the last century, according to the fluctuating fortunes and prestige of Turkey herself. Another small territory, the Hatay, centred on Iskenderun (Alexandretta) and lying as an enclave in Syrian territory, was acquired as a diplomatic bargain in 1939.

PHYSICAL FEATURES

The geological structure of Turkey is extremely complicated, and rocks of almost all ages occur, from the most ancient to most recent. Broadly speaking, we may say that Turkey consists of a number of old plateau blocks, against which masses of younger rock series have been squeezed to form fold mountain ranges of varying size. As there were several of these plateau blocks, and not just one, the fold mountains run in many different directions, with considerable irregularity, and hence no simple pattern can be discerned—instead, one mountain range gives place to another abruptly, and we can pass suddenly from highland to plain or plateau.

In general outline Turkey consists of a ring of mountains enclosing a series of inland plateaus, with the highest mountains on the east, close to the U.S.S.R. and Iran. Mount Ararat, overlooking the Soviet frontier, is the highest peak in Turkey, reaching 16,915 feet, and there are neighbouring peaks almost as large. In the west the average altitude of the hills is distinctly lower, though the highest peak (Mount Erciyas or Argaeus) is over 13,000 ft. The irregular topography of Turkey has given rise to many lakes, some salt, and some fresh, and generally more numerous than elsewhere in the Middle East. The largest, Lake Van, covers nearly 4,000 sq. kilometres (1,100 sq. miles).

Two other features may be mentioned. Large areas of the east, and some parts of the centre of Asia Minor have been covered in sheets of lava which are often of such recent occurrence that soil has not yet been formed—consequently wide expanses are sterile and uninhabited. Secondly, in the north and west cracking and disturbance of the rocks has taken place on an enormous scale. The long, indented coast of the Aegean Sea, with its numerous oddly shaped islands and estuaries, is due to cracking in two directions, which

has split the land into detached blocks of roughly rectangular shape. Often the lower parts have sunk and been drowned by the sea. The Bosphorus and Dardanelles owe their origin to this faulting action, and the whole of the Black Sea coast is due to subsidence along a great series of fissures. Movement and adjustment along these cracks has by no means ceased, so that at the present day earthquakes are frequent in the north and west of Turkey, occasioning at times severe loss of life—most recently in the disaster of March 1970.

Because of the presence of mountain ranges close to the coast, and the great height of the interior plateaus (varying from 2,500 ft. to 7,000 ft.) Turkey has special climatic conditions, characterised by great extremes of temperature and rainfall, with wide variation from one district to another. In winter conditions are severe in most areas, except for those lying close to sea level. Temperatures of minus 20° to minus 40° F. can occur in the east, and snow lies there for as many as 120 days each year. The west has frost on most nights of December and January, and (again apart from the coastal zone), has an average winter temperature below that of the British Isles. In summer, however, temperatures over most of Turkey exceed 85° or 90° F., with 110° F. in the south-east. There can hence be enormous seasonal variation of temperature—sometimes over 100° F., among the widest in the world.

Rainfall too is remarkably variable. Along the eastern Black Sea coast, towards the Soviet frontier, over 100 inches fall annually (as much as in the wettest parts of the English Lake District, or the Western Isles of Scotland); but elsewhere, amounts are very much smaller. Parts of the central plateau, being shut off by mountains from the influence of sea winds, are arid, with annual totals of under 10 inches, and expanses of salt steppe and desert are frequent. Like Iran, Turkey also has a "dead heart", and the main towns of Anatolia, including Ankara, the capital, are placed away from the centre and close to hills, where rainfall tends to be greater.

It is necessary to emphasize the contrast that exists between the Aegean coastlands, which climatically are by far the most favoured regions of Turkey, and the rest of the country. Round the Aegean, winters are mild and fairly rainy, and the summers hot, but tempered by a persistent northerly wind, the Meltemi, or Etesian wind, which is of great value in ripening fruit, especially figs and sultana grapes.

ECONOMIC LIFE

The variety of geographical conditions within Turkey has led to uneven development, and this unevenness has been intensified by poor communications, due to the broken nature of the topography. Roads are relatively few, railways slow and often roundabout, and whole districts—sometimes even considerable towns—are accessible only by bridle track. Many rivers flow in deep gorges near their sources and either meander or are broken by cascades in their lower reaches, so that none are navigable.

Thus we find that the west of Turkey, situated close to the Aegean Sea, is by far the most densely peopled and the most intensively developed. Since 1923, however, attempts have been made to develop the Anatolian plateau and the districts in the extreme east, which, following the expulsion and massacre of the Armenians in 1914-18, for a time supported only a very scanty population. Development in the central plateau has been aided by the exploitation of several small but on the whole valuable mineral deposits, and by irrigation schemes to improve agriculture. A certain degree of industrialisation (mainly undertaken by state-sponsored and owned organisations) has also grown up, based on Turkish-produced raw materials—cotton, wool, mohair, beet-sugar, olive-oil, and tobacco. The eastern districts present a more intractable problem, and development so far has been slower.

Of recent years, the considerable annual increase of population, now about 2.7 per cent—slightly less than 10 years ago—has led to intensification of settlement and the bringing in of all available land for cultivation. Henceforth a principal problem for Turkey must be to improve yields from agriculture and industry. Because of the strategic importance of the country, there has been a considerable programme of road-building, largely financed by the U.S.A. and CENTO.

RACE AND LANGUAGE

Racially, the bulk of the Turkish people show an intermixture of Mediterranean and Armenoid strains. In the western half of the country Mediterraneans and Armenoids are more or less equally represented; but further east the proportion of Armenoids steadily increases, until towards the Soviet and Iranian borders, they become almost universal. We can in addition note less important racial elements: there would seem to be small numbers of proto-Nordics in the north and west, and some authorities suggest a racial relationship between Galatia (the modern district of Ankara) and ancient Gaul. The Ottoman Turks were in the main of Turki (western Mongoloid) ancestry, but in the view of some authorities their contribution to the ethnic stocks of Turkey would seem to have been small, since they were really an invading tribal group that became an aristocracy and soon intermarried with other peoples. There are also numbers of Caucasians—particularly Circassians and Georgians—who have contributed to the racial structure of Turkey; and during 1951 a further element was added by the arrival of many thousands of Bulgarian Muslims who had been deported from their own country.

The Turkish language, which is of central Asiatic origin, is spoken over most, but by no means all of the country. This was introduced into Turkey in Seljuq times, and was written in Arabic characters, but as these are not really well adapted to the sound of Turkish, Roman (i.e. European) script has been compulsory since 1928. As well, there are a number of non-Turkish languages. Kurdish has a wide extension in the south-east, along the Syrian and Iraqi frontiers; and Caucasian dialects, quite different from either Turkish or Kurdish, occur in the north-east. Greek and Armenian were once widespread, but following the deportations of the last forty years both forms of speech are now current only in the city of Istanbul, where considerable numbers of Greeks and Armenians still live.

HISTORY

ANCIENT HISTORY

The most ancient written records so far found in Asia Minor date from the beginning of the second millennium B.C. They are in Assyrian, and reveal the existence of Assyrian trading colonies in Cappadocia. These documents, together with a growing amount of archaeological evidence, show an important Copper Age culture in Central Anatolia in the third and early second millennia. Later in the second millennium the greater part of Asia Minor fell under the rule of the Hittites. This people has long been known from references in the Old Testament and other ancient texts, but its full importance was first revealed by the excavations at Boğazköy, the site of the ancient Hittite capital of Hattushash. The Hittite Empire flourished from about 1600 to about 1200 B.C., and reached its apogee in the fourteenth and thirteenth centuries, when it became one of the dominant States of the Middle East. One of the sources of Hittite strength was iron, which was first worked in Anatolia. The production of iron was for long a monopoly of the Hittite kings, but the use of iron implements eventually spread to other parts, and revolutionised agriculture, industry and war.

After the break-up of the Hittite Empire, Asia Minor was split up among a number of dynasties and peoples—Phrygians, Cimmerians, Lydians and others—about whom not very much is known. Towards the end of the Hittite period the Greeks began to invade the Aegean coast, and entered on a long struggle with the native states that is reflected in the story of the Trojan war. Greek culture spread in western Anatolia, which was gradually incorporated into the Hellenic world. A series of political changes, of which the most important are the Persian conquest in 546, the conquest of Alexander in 334, and the constitution of the Roman province of Asia in 133 B.C., did not impede the steady spread of Greek language and culture in the cities.

In A.D. 330, the Emperor Constantine inaugurated the new city of Constantinople, on the site of the old Greek trading settlement of Byzantium. This city at once became the capital of the East Roman and then of the Christian Byzantine Empire. Asia Minor was now the metropolitan province of a great Empire, and grew in wealth, prosperity and importance. Under Byzantine rule Greek Christianity, already firmly established in Roman times, spread over most of the peninsula.

SELJUQS AND OTTOMANS

At the beginning of the eleventh century a new conquest of Anatolia began—that of the Turks. The early history of the Turkish peoples is still obscure. Some references in the ancient biography of Alexander show them to have been established in Central Asia at the time of his conquests, and Turkish tribal confederacies played an important part in the invasions of Europe from late Roman times onwards. The name "Turk" first appears in historical records in the sixth century A.D., when Chinese annals speak of a powerful empire in Central Asia, founded by a steppe people called Tu-Kiu. It is from this state that the oldest surviving Turkish inscriptions have come. From the seventh century onwards the Central Asian Turks came into ever closer contact with the Islamic peoples of the Near East, from whom they adopted the Islamic faith and the Arabic script, and with them much of the complex civilisation of Islam. From the ninth century Turks entered the service of the Caliphate in increasing numbers, and soon came to provide the bulk of its armies, its generals, and eventually its rulers.

From the tenth century whole tribes of Turks began to migrate into Persia and Iraq, and in the eleventh, under the leadership of the family of Seljuq, the Turks were able to set up a great empire comprising most of the eastern lands of the Caliphate. The Muslim armies on the Byzantine frontier had long been predominantly Turkish, and in the course of the eleventh century they began a great movement into Anatolia which resulted in the termination of Byzantine rule in most of the country and its incorporation in the Muslim Seljuq Sultanate. A Seljuq prince, Suleyman ibn Kutlumush, was sent to organize the new province, and by the end of the twelfth century his successors had built up a strong Turkish monarchy in Anatolia, with its capital in Konya (the ancient Iconium). Under the rule of the Anatolian Seljuqs, which in various forms lasted until the fourteenth century, Anatolia gradually became a Turkish land. Masses of Turkish immigrants from further east entered the country, and a Turkish, Muslim civilisation replaced Greek Christianity.

In the late thirteenth century the Sultanate of Konya fell into decay, and gradually gave way to a number of smaller principalities. One of these, in north-western Anatolia, was ruled by a certain Osman, or Othman, from whom the name Ottoman is derived. The Ottoman State soon embarked on a great movement of expansion, on the one hand in Anatolia, at the expense of its Turkish neighbours, on the other in the Balkans. Ottoman armies first crossed to Europe in the mid-fourteenth century, and by 1400 they were masters of much of the Balkan peninsula as well as of almost all Anatolia. The capital was moved first from Bursa to Edirne and then, in 1453, to Constantinople, the final conquest of which from the last Byzantine Emperor completed the process that had transformed a principality of frontier-warriors into a new great empire. Constantinople, called Istanbul by the Turks, remained the capital of the Ottoman Empire until 1922. The wave of conquest was by no means spent. For more than a century Ottoman arms continued to advance into Central Europe, while in 1516–17 Sultan Selim I destroyed the Mamluk Sultanate and incorporated Syria and Egypt into the Empire. During the reign of Sultan Suleyman I (1520–66), called the Magnificent in Europe, the Ottoman Empire was at the height of its power. In three continents the Sultan held unchallenged sway over vast territories. A skilled and highly-organised bureaucracy secured for the peoples of the Empire peace, justice and prosperity; literature, scholarship and the arts flourished; and the Ottoman armies and fleets seemed to threaten the very existence of Western Christendom.

The decay of the Empire is usually dated from after the death of Suleyman. In the West great changes were taking place. The Renaissance and the Reformation, the rapid development of science and technology, the emergence of strong, centralised nation states with constantly improving military techniques, the deflection of the main routes of international trade from the Mediterranean to the open seas, all combined to strengthen Turkey's Western adversaries while leaving her own resources unchanged or even diminished, and helped to relegate her into a backwater of cultural and economic stagnation. An imposing military façade for a while masked the internal decay that was rotting the once all-powerful Empire, but by the end of the seventeenth century the weakness of the Ottoman State was manifest. Then began the struggle of the Powers for pickings of Turkish territory and for positions of influence in the Empire. During the eighteenth century it was Austria and Russia that made the main territorial advances in the Balkans and in the Black Sea area, while England and France were content with commercial and diplomatic privileges. In a succession of wars one province after another was lost, while internal conditions went from bad to worse. During the nineteenth century England and France began to play a more active role. British policy was generally to support the Turks against their impatient heirs. In 1854

Britain and France went to war at the side of Turkey in order to check Russian aggression, and in 1877–78 British diplomatic intervention was effective to the same end. Meanwhile the ferment of nationalist ideas had spread from the West to the subject peoples of the Empire, and one by one the Serbs, Greeks, Romanians and Bulgarians succeeded in throwing off Ottoman rule and attaining independent statehood.

More significant for Turkish history were the first stirrings of a new spirit among the Turks themselves. The first serious attempts at reform were made during the reign of Selim III (1789–1807), and during the nineteenth century a series of reforming sultans and ministers worked on a programme of reform and modernisation which, though it fell short of its avowed objectives, nevertheless transformed the face of the Ottoman Empire and began a process of change, the effects of which are still visible. In 1878 the reforming movement came to an abrupt end, and from that year until 1908 the Empire was subjected to the iron despotism of Abdul-Hamid II, who ruthlessly repressed every attempt at liberal thought and reform. In 1908 the secret opposition group known as the Young Turks seized power, and in a wave of revolutionary enthusiasm inaugurated a constitution, parliamentary government, and a whole series of liberal reforms. Unfortunately the Young Turks had little opportunity to follow up their promising start. First internal dissension, then foreign wars, combined to turn the Young Turk regime into a military dictatorship. In 1911 the Italians suddenly started a war against Turkey which ended with their gaining Libya and the Dodecanese Islands; in 1912–13 a Balkan alliance succeeded in wresting from the dying Empire most of its remaining possessions on the continent of Europe. Finally, in October 1914, Turkey entered the war on the side of the Central Powers. During the reign of Abdul-Hamid German influence had been steadily increasing in Turkey, and the process continued under the Young Turks. It was certainly helped by the growing friendship between the Western Powers and Russia, which threw the Turks into the arms of the only power that seemed ready to support them against Russian designs. German officers reorganised the Turkish Army. German business-men and technicians extended their hold on the economic resources of the country, and German engineers and financiers began the construction of the famous Baghdad railway which was to provide direct rail communication between Germany and the Middle East.

The Turkish alliance was of immense military value to the Central Powers. The Turkish armies, still established in Syria and Palestine, were able to offer an immediate and serious threat to the Suez Canal and to the British position in Egypt. By their dogged and successful defence of the Dardanelles they prevented effective co-operation between Russia and the Western Powers. Their Balkan position assured the supremacy of the Central Powers in that important area. Their position as the greatest independent Muslim State and their prestige among Muslims elsewhere created a series of problems in the British and French Empires.

Despite their weakness and exhaustion after two previous wars, the Turks were able to wage a bitter defensive war against the Allies. At last, after two unsuccessful attempts, one on the Dardanelles and the other in Mesopotamia, a new British attack from Egypt and from India succeeded in expelling the Turks from Palestine, Syria, and most of Iraq. Defeated on all sides, cut off from their allies by the Salonica Expedition, the Turks decided to abandon the struggle, and signed an armistice at Mudros on October 30th, 1918. The outlook for Turkey seemed black. Allied forces controlled Istanbul and the Straits— British forces were in control of the Arab countries, and in 1919 French, Italian and British forces occupied strategic positions in parts of Anatolia itself. In the capital the Young Turk leaders had fled, and a new Government was formed, subservient to the will of the occupying Powers.

For some time the victorious Powers were too busy elsewhere to attend to the affairs of Turkey, and it was not until the San Remo Conference of April 1920 that the first serious attempt was made to settle the Turkish question. Meanwhile the victors were busy quarrelling among themselves. Partly, no doubt, with the idea of forestalling Italian ambitions, the British, French, and American Governments agreed to a Greek proposal for a Greek occupation of Izmir and the surrounding country, and on May 15th, 1919, a Greek Army, under cover of allied warships, landed at Izmir. Second thoughts on the wisdom of this step appeared in the allied camp, and in October 1919 the Inter-Allied Commission in Istanbul condemned it as "unjustifiable" and as "a violation of the terms of the Armistice". The consequences of the invasion for Turkey were momentous. Now it was no longer the non-Turkish subject provinces and the Ottoman superstructure of the Turkish nation that were threatened, but the Turkish homeland itself. Moreover, the Greeks, unlike the Western Allies, showed that they intended to stay, and that they were aiming at nothing less than the incorporation of the territories they occupied into the Greek kingdom. The Turkish reaction to this danger was vigorous and immediate. The Nationalist movement, hitherto limited to a small class of intellectuals, became the mass instrument of Turkish determination to preserve the integrity and independence of the homeland. A new leader appeared to organise their victory.

THE RISE OF ATATÜRK

Mustafa Kemal, later surnamed Atatürk, was born in Salonica, then an Ottoman city, in 1880. After a promising career as a regular army officer, he achieved his first active command in Libya in 1911, and thereafter fought with distinction in the successive wars in which his country was involved. After his brilliant conduct of the defence of Gallipoli, he fought on various fronts against the Allies, and at the time of the Armistice held a command on the Syrian front. A month later he returned to Istanbul, and at once began to seek ways and means of getting to Anatolia to organise national resistance. At length he was successful, and on May 19th, 1919—four days after the Greek landing in Izmir—he arrived at Samsun, on the Black Sea coast, ostensibly in order to supervise the disbanding of the remaining Turkish forces. Instead he set to work at once on the double task of organising a national movement and raising a national army.

Meanwhile the Allied Powers were at last completing their arrangements for the obsequies of the Sick Man of Europe. After a series of conferences, a treaty was drawn up and signed by the Allied representatives and those of the Sultan's Government at Sèvres, on August 10th, 1920. The Treaty of Sèvres was very harsh—far harsher than that imposed on Germany. The Arab provinces were to be placed under British and French Mandates, to prepare them for eventual independence. In Anatolia, Armenian and Kurdish States were to be set up in the east, the south was to be divided between France and Italy, and a truncated Turkish Sultanate confined to the interior. The Straits were to be demilitarised and placed under Allied administration, with a Turkish Istanbul surrounded by Allied forces. The rest of European Turkey was to be ceded to Greece, while the Izmir district was to be under "Ottoman sovereignty and Greek administration".

This treaty was, however, never implemented. While the Allies were imposing their terms on the Sultan and his government in Istanbul, a new Turkish State was rising in the interior of Anatolia, based on the rejection of the treaty and the principles on which it was founded. On July

23rd, 1919, Mustafa Kemal and his associates convened the first Nationalist Congress in Erzurum, and drew up a national programme. A second Congress was held in September in the same year, and attended by delegates from all over the country. An executive committee, presided over by Mustafa Kemal, was formed, and chose Ankara, then a minor provincial town, as its headquarters. Frequent meetings were held in Ankara, which soon became the effective capital of the Nationalist movement and forces. It was there that they issued the famous National Pact, the declaration that laid down the basic programme of the Kemalist movement, renouncing the Empire and the domination of the non-Turkish provinces, but demanding the total and unconditional independence of all areas inhabited by Turks. This declaration won immediate support, and on January 28th, 1920, was approved even by the legal Ottoman Parliament sitting in Istanbul. The growth of the Nationalist movement in Istanbul alarmed the Allies, and on March 16th British forces entered the Turkish part of the city and arrested and deported many Nationalist leaders. Despite this setback, followed by a new anti-Nationalist campaign on the part of the Sultan and his political and religious advisers, the Kemalists continued to advance. On March 19th, 1920, Mustafa Kemal ordered general elections, and at the end of April a National Assembly of 350 deputies met in Ankara and voted the National Pact. The Sultan and his government were declared deposed, a provisional Constitution promulgated, and a government set up with Mustafa Kemal as President.

There remained the military task of expelling the invaders. The Greco-Turkish war falls into three stages, covering roughly the campaigns of 1920, 1921 and 1922. In the first the Nationalists, hopelessly outmatched in numbers and material, were badly defeated, and the Greeks advanced far into Anatolia. Turkish resistance was, however, strong enough to impress the Allies, who, for the first time, accorded a certain limited recognition to the Nationalist Government and proclaimed their neutrality in the Greco-Turkish war. The second campaign began with Greek successes, but the Turks rallied and defeated the invaders first at İnönü—from which İsmet Pasha, who commanded the Turkish forces there, later took his surname—and then, on August 24th, 1921, in a major battle on the Sakarya River, where the Turkish forces were under the personal command of Mustafa Kemal. This victory considerably strengthened the Nationalists, who were now generally realised to be the effective Government of Turkey. The French and Italians withdrew from the areas of Anatolia assigned to them, and made terms with the new Government. The Soviets, now established on Turkey's eastern frontier, had already done so at the beginning of the year.

A period of waiting and reorganization followed, during which the morale of the Greek armies was adversely affected by political changes in Greece. In August 1922 the third and final phase of the war of independence began. The Turkish Army drove the Greeks back to the Aegean, and on September 9th reoccupied Izmir. Mustafa Kemal now prepared to cross to Thrace. To do so he had to cross the Straits, still under Allied occupation. The French and Italian contingents withdrew, and, after a menacing pause, the British followed. On October 11th an armistice was signed at Mudanya, whereby the Allied Governments agreed to the restoration of Turkish sovereignty in Eastern Thrace. In November the Sultan's Cabinet resigned, and the Sultan himself went into exile. Turkey once more had only one government, and Istanbul, the ancient seat of Empire, became a provincial city, ruled by a governor appointed from Ankara.

The peace conference opened in November 1922. After many months of argument the treaty was finally signed on July 24th, 1923. It recognised complete and undivided

Turkish sovereignty and the abolition of the last vestiges of foreign privilege. The only reservation related to the demilitarisation of the Straits, which were not to be fortified without the consent of the Powers. This consent was given at the Montreux Conference in 1936.

THE TURKISH REPUBLIC

The military task was completed, and the demands formulated in the National Pact had been embodied in an international treaty. There remained the greater task of rebuilding the ruins of long years of war and revolution—and of remedying those elements of weakness in the Turkish State and society that had brought Turkey to the verge of extinction. Mustafa Kemal saw the solution of Turkey's problems in a process of Westernisation—in the integration of Turkey, on a basis of equality, in the modern Western world. To do this it was not sufficient to borrow, as other reformers had done, the outward forms and trappings of Western civilisation. It was necessary to change the very basis of society in Turkey, and to suppress, ruthlessly if need be, the opposition that was bound to come from the entrenched forces of the old order. Between 1922 and 1938, the year of his death, Kemal carried through a series of far-reaching reforms in Turkey. These may be considered under various headings.

The first changes were political. After the deposition of Sultan Vahdeddin in November 1922, a brief experiment was made with a purely religious sovereignty, and Abdul-Mejid was proclaimed as Caliph but not Sultan. The experiment was not successful. Abdul-Mejid followed his predecessor into exile, and on October 29th, 1923, Turkey was declared a Republic, with Kemal as President. The regime of Kemal Atatürk was effectively a dictatorship—though without the violence and oppression normally associated with that word in Europe. A single party—the Republican People's Party—formed the main instrument for the enforcement of Government policy. The Constitution of April 20th, 1924, provided for an elected Parliament which was the repository of sovereign power. Executive power was to be exercised by the President and a Cabinet chosen by him.

The next object of attack was the religious hierarchy, already weakened by the removal of the Sultan-Caliph. In a series of edicts the Ministry of Religious Affairs was abolished, the religious orders disbanded, religious property sequestrated, religious instruction forbidden. With the religious leaders in retreat, the attack on the old social order began. Certainly the most striking reforms were the abolition of the fez and the Arabic alphabet, and their replacement by the hat and the Latin alphabet. But these were probably less important in the long run than the abrogation of the old legal system and the introduction of new civil and criminal codes of law adapted from Europe. In 1928 Islam itself was disestablished, and the Constitution amended to make Turkey a secular State.

Not the least of the problems that faced Mustafa Kemal was the economic one. Turkey is naturally a very rich country, but her resources were for the most part undeveloped, and what development there was had been in foreign hands. To restore the devastation of war, replace the departed foreign investors, and raise the low standard of living of the country, much capital was needed. Rather than risk the independence of Turkey by inviting foreign capital in a time of weakness, Kemal adopted the principle of *Étatisme*, and made it one of the cardinal doctrines of his régime. From 1923 to 1933 the State made its main effort in railway construction, nearly doubling the length of line in that period. At the same time a start was made in establishing other industries. The major effort of industrialization began in 1934, with the adoption of the first five-year plan —completed in 1939. While often wasteful and inefficient,

State-sponsored industry was probably the only form of development possible at the time without recourse to foreign aid. The progress achieved stood Turkey in good stead in the critical years that were to follow.

The foreign policy of the Republic was for long one of strict non-involvement in foreign disputes, and the maintenance of friendly relations with as many Powers as possible. In 1935-36, however, Turkey co-operated loyally in sanctions against Italy, and thereafter the growing threat of German, and more especially Italian, aggression led to closer links with the West. In 1938 steps were taken to strengthen economic links between Turkey and Britain. A British credit of £16 million was granted to Turkey, and a number of contracts given to British firms by Turkey.

The death of Kemal Atatürk in November 1938 was a great shock to Turkey. Perhaps the best testimony to the solidity of his achievement is that his régime was able to survive that shock, and the stresses and strains of the war that followed shortly after.

He was succeeded as President by İsmet İnönü, who announced his intention of maintaining and carrying on the work of his predecessor. The new President was soon called upon to guide his country through a very difficult time. As early as May 12th, 1939, a joint Anglo-Turkish declaration was issued, stating that "the British and Turkish Governments, in the event of an act of aggression leading to war in the Mediterranean area, would co-operate effectively and lend each other all the aid and assistance in their power". This prepared the way for the formal Anglo-French-Turkish Treaty of Alliance signed October 19th, 1939. It had been hoped that this Treaty would be complemented by a parallel treaty with the U.S.S.R., but the equivocal attitude of the Soviet Government, followed by the Stalin-Hitler Agreement of August 1939, made this impossible, and the Turks proceeded with the Western alliance in the face of clearly expressed Soviet disapproval. They protected themselves, however, by Protocol II of the Treaty, stipulating that nothing in the Treaty should bind them to any action likely to involve them in war with the U.S.S.R.

TURKEY DURING THE SECOND WORLD WAR

The fall of France, the hostile attitude of the Soviet Government, and the extension of German power over most of Europe, led the Turkish Government to the conclusion that nothing would be gained by provoking an almost certain German conquest. While continuing to recognize the Alliance, therefore, they invoked Protocol II as a reason for remaining neutral, and in June 1941, when German expansion in the Balkans had brought the German armies within 100 miles of Istanbul, the Turks further protected themselves by signing a friendship and trade agreement with Germany, in which, however, they stipulated that Turkey would maintain her treaty obligations to Britain.

The German attack on the U.S.S.R., and the consequent entry of that country into the Grand Alliance, brought an important change to the situation, and the Western Powers increased their pressure on Turkey to enter the war. On December 3rd, 1941, President Roosevelt extended lease-lend aid to Turkey; in February 1943, Mr. Churchill visited Turkey and met Turkish statesmen at Adana; in December 1943, President İnönü went to Cairo to meet the British and American leaders. The main consideration holding Turkey back from active participation in the war was mistrust of Russia, and the widespread feeling that Nazi conquest and Soviet "liberation" were equally to be feared. Turkish statesmen foresaw the fate of the East European countries occupied by the Red Army, and evinced no desire to share it. While stopping short of actual belligerency, however, the Turks, especially after 1942, entered into closer economic and military relations with the West and aided the Allied cause in a number of ways. In August 1944 they broke off diplomatic relations with Germany, and on February 23rd, 1945, declared war on Germany in order to comply with the formalities of entry to the United Nations Conference in San Francisco.

The war years subjected Turkey to severe economic strains. These, and the dangers of armed neutrality in a world at war, resulted in the imposition of martial law, of closer police surveillance, and of a generally more authoritarian form of government. An unfortunate impression was made by the discrimination practised against foreigners and non-Muslim citizens in the assessment and collection of the Capital Levy imposed in 1942 to meet the growing financial strain. This measure, which occasioned much criticism both in Turkey and abroad, was quietly abandoned in 1943. And then, between 1945 and 1950, came a further series of changes, no less remarkable than the great reforms of Atatürk. When the Charter of the United Nations came up for ratification in the Turkish Parliament in 1945, a group of members, led by Celâl Bayar, Adnan Menderes, Fuad Köprülü and Refik Koraltan, tabled a motion suggesting a series of reforms in the law and the Constitution which would effectively ensure inside Turkey those liberties to which the Turkish Government was giving its theoretical approval in the Charter. The motion was rejected by the Government, and its sponsors forced to leave the party. In November 1945, however, under pressure of a by now active and informed public opinion, President İnönü announced the end of the single-party system, and in January 1946 the opposition leaders registered the new Democratic Party. Numerous other parties followed, including the National Party (formed July 1948 and reconstituted as the Republic National Party in 1954).

TURKEY UNDER THE DEMOCRATIC PARTY

In July 1946 new elections gave the Democrat opposition 70 out of 416 seats, and there can be little doubt that completely free elections would have given them many more. During the years that followed, the breach in the dictatorship grew ever wider, and a series of changes in both law and practice ensured the growth of democratic liberties. Freedom of the Press and of association were extended, martial law ended, and, on February 15th, 1950, a new electoral law was approved, guaranteeing free and fair elections. In May 1950 a new general election was held, in which the Democrats won an overwhelming victory. Celâl Bayar became President, and a new Cabinet was formed, with Adnan Menderes as Prime Minister and Fuad Köprülü as Foreign Minister. The new régime adopted a more liberal economic policy, involving the partial abandonment of *Étatisme* and the encouragement of private enterprise, both Turkish and foreign. For a while, the stability and progress of the republic seemed to be threatened by the growing activities of groups of religious fanatics, whose programme appeared to require little less than the abrogation of all the reforms achieved by the Turkish revolution. After the attempt on the life of the liberal journalist Ahmet Emin Yalman in November 1952, the government took more vigorous action against what were called the "forces of clericalism and reaction". Many arrests were made, and in the summer of 1953 the National Party, accused of complicity in reactionary plots, was for a time outlawed and legislation was passed prohibiting the exploitation of religion for political purposes. The relations between the two main parties, after a temporary improvement in the face of the common danger of reaction, deteriorated again in the course of 1953-54, though not to

such an extent as to imperil national unity. On May 2nd, 1954, in Turkey's third general election since the war, the Democrats won a resounding victory.

Encouraged by this overwhelming reaffirmation of popular support, the Government proceeded to adopt a number of measures which were criticised by the opposition as undemocratic. These included new civil service laws giving the Government greatly increased powers of dismissal and compulsory retirement, and an electoral reform restricted coalition candidatures. These laws, following on the new Press law of March 7th, 1954, embittered relations between Government and opposition. A number of prosecutions of opposition journalists followed, and in September the well-known journalist Hüseyin Cahit Yalçin was fined and condemned to imprisonment. This case aroused widespread indignation both at home and abroad, and despite official insistence that Yalçin had been tried and condemned by due process of law, he was amnestied by the President. Charges against some other opposition journalists were also dropped. Some Republican People's Party leaders, notably Nihat Erim, responded to this more conciliatory attitude of the Government, and on April 17th there was a meeting and an exchange of views between the Prime Minister and the Republican leader İsmet İnönü. Others, however, found the concessions of the Government inadequate, and by the summer, relations between Government and opposition had again been strained by new Press prosecutions. The opposition parties, however, remained active. On June 10th, 1955 the Republican Party organ *Ulus*, which had ceased publication in December 1953, reappeared under the editorship of Hüseyin Cahit Yalçin, and in the same month the National Party held a party congress in Ankara. both opposition parties decided to boycott the provincial council and municipal elections (September and November 1955 respectively), in which therefore the Democrats were opposed only by the very small Peasant Party and by Independents. These were able to score some successes.

In view of the smallness and weakness of the opposition parties, and the immense parliamentary majority of the Democratic Party, it was inevitable that sooner or later splits would appear within it. In October 1955 a serious crisis culminated in the dismissal or resignation from the party of nineteen deputies. These were later joined by some others and formed a new party, the Freedom Party.

Meanwhile, in September 1955, anti-Greek outbreaks occurred in Istanbul and Izmir. Turco-Greek relations had been growing steadily worse because of the Cyprus question, and the riots appeared to have been touched off by a report, later proved false, that Atatürk's house in Salonica had been blown up by a bomb. The riots, which affected other non-Turkish and non-Muslim elements besides the Greeks, did immense damage to property, though injury to persons was very limited. Martial law was at once proclaimed in Istanbul, Izmir and Ankara, several senior officers and officials relieved of their duties, and several cabinet changes made. A new Cabinet, the fourth since the Democrat victory in 1950, was presented to the assembly on December 9th.

These events, and the growing economic difficulties of the country, brought new political tensions, and in the summer of 1956 new amendments to the Press law (June 7th), the law for the protection of the national economy (June 6th) and the law of public assembly (June 27th) again aroused bitter opposition criticism.

Conflict between the Government and Opposition was sharpened by the decision taken to advance the date of the general elections by more than eight months, to October 27th, 1957. The three Opposition parties—Republicans, Freedom and National Parties—first intended to present a united front, but the electoral law was changed to make this impossible. They were therefore obliged to present separate lists in each constituency, and so, although the combined votes won by Opposition candidates were slightly more than 50 per cent of the total, the Democrats again emerged triumphant, though with a diminished majority.

In the new Assembly the themes of debate continued to centre on the economic condition of the country and what the Opposition considered inroads on liberty. A Bill was passed in December 1957 amending the rules of the Assembly, and laying down a new scale of penalties for their infraction. At the same time a proposal to channel all newspaper advertisements through a single organisation was interpreted as another device for ensuring Government control over the Press. The editors of the political weekly *Akis*, the managing editor and a writer on the staff of *Ulus*, and the managing editor of *Zafer* (a Government paper), were among journalists who suffered imprisonment.

At the end of 1959 the law claimed a victim well known abroad—Mr. Ahmet Yalman, the 71-year old editor of *Vatan*. His offence—shared with other editors—was to have reprinted an article strongly critical of the Government which had appeared in an American newspaper. Mr. Yalman was in Pakistan when sentence was passed on him, and on his return duly went to jail, whence he and other journalists emerged after the *coup d'état* of May, 1960. There is no doubt that its running fight with the Press contributed much to the downfall of the Menderes régime. The new régime, while not immediately sweeping away the old bans, encouraged newspaper owners and editors to draw up a "code of self-control" which was worked out with the assistance of the International Press Institute.

FOREIGN AFFAIRS 1945-60

In foreign affairs, both the People's Party and the Democrat Governments followed a firm policy of unreserved identification with the West in the cold war. Since May 1947 the United States has extended economic and military aid to Turkey on an increasing scale, and in 1950 a first indication of both the seriousness and the effectiveness of Turkish policy was given with the despatch of Turkish troops to Korea, where they fought with distinction. In August 1949 Turkey became a member of the Council of Europe, and early in 1952 acceded to full membership of the North Atlantic Treaty Organisation, in which she began to play an increasingly important part. Thereafter other arrangements were made by which Turkey accepted a role in both Balkan and Middle Eastern defence. On February 28th, 1953 a treaty of friendship and collaboration was signed in Ankara with Greece and Yugoslavia, which prepared the way for a subsequent alliance, and on April 2nd, 1954 a mutual aid pact was signed in Karachi between Turkey and Pakistan, with the blessing of the United States.

Despite her economic problems and her failure to secure the 300 million U.S. dollar loan which she had requested from the United States, Turkey resisted the temptation to follow the example of some other states and play the great powers off against one another. In spite of efforts from both north and south to detach her, Turkey remained faithful to the northern tier alliance, and on November 21st-22nd, 1955, the Turkish Prime Minister attended the inaugural meeting of the council of the Baghdad Pact, in which Turkey thereafter played a major role.

During the Sinai-Suez crisis of November 1956 the representatives of the Turkish Government, meeting with those of the other three Muslim members of the Baghdad Pact (Iraq, Iran and Pakistan), welcomed the withdrawal of the Anglo-French forces from Egypt. In December the Turkish Foreign Minister declared that the Pact had done much to limit and circumscribe the threat to peace in the Middle East. The President of the United States announced in January 1957 a new programme of economic and military assistance for those countries of the area which were willing to accept it. At a further meeting held in Ankara the Muslim states belonging to the Baghdad Pact expressed their approval of this "Eisenhower Doctrine". The United States, in March 1957, made known its decision to join the military committee of the Baghdad Pact. Mr. Richards, special adviser to the President of the United States, carried out a tour of the Middle East in March/April 1957 in order to explain the new doctrine and to distribute the funds assigned to its fulfilment. At the close of his visit to Ankara in March a joint communiqué was issued to the effect that Turkey would co-operate with the United States against all subversive activities in the Middle East and that financial aid would be forthcoming from Washington for the economic projects previously discussed between the members of the Baghdad Pact.

At the time of the Jordan crisis in April 1957 there was a period of tension when Turkish troops were held in readiness for action near the frontier with Syria. The outbreak of civil war in Lebanon in May 1958, and, still more, the *coup d'état* in Iraq of July 14th, gave Turkey fresh cause for anxiety. The events in Iraq took place on the eve of a meeting in Istanbul of Moslem members of the Baghdad Pact, but had the immediate consequence of withdrawing Iraq, in practice if not in name, from membership of the Pact. The staff of the Pact Council, secretariat and military planning organization were subsequently transferred to Ankara. Iraq withdrew formally from the Pact on March 24th, 1959. The Pact had, however, been strengthened a few weeks before by new defence agreements between Turkey, Iran, Pakistan and the United States of America signed on March 5th.

Fidelity to NATO and CENTO remained the basis of Turkey's foreign policy through the next two years. By the beginning of 1960, Turkey, following the examples of some of her allies, decided that such a policy need not be incompatible with less frigid relations towards Russia, and in April a visit to Moscow by Mr. Menderes was announced for July. Before it could take place the Menderes régime was overthrown, but his successors continued a more flexible policy. Soon after the revolution a cordial letter from Mr. Khrushchev to Gen. Gürsel received a cordial reply, in which, however, Turkey's need for active allies was once more emphasised.

THE CYPRUS QUESTION

Early in 1957 Great Britain had decided to release Archbishop Makarios from detention in the Seychelles islands. The leaders of the Turkish community in Cyprus visited Ankara in April. Their view was that, ultimately, partition alone would provide an adequate solution for the Cyprus problem. The Archbishop had meanwhile rejected all participation of the Cypriot Turks in future negotiations regarding the island. The Turkish Government itself remained firm in its determination not to allow Cyprus to be handed over unreservedly to the Greeks.

British efforts for a solution of the Cyprus problem increased as conditions inside the island deteriorated. The meeting of the Baghdad Pact Council at Ankara in January 1958, which was attended by the U.S. Secretary of State and the British Foreign Minister, was made the occasion for informal talks. The new Governor of Cyprus, Sir Hugh Foot, arrived to take part in these, but while they were in progress there was serious rioting by Turkish Cypriots in Nicosia and Limassol.

In June 1958 the British Government published a new plan for Cyprus, involving the association of the Greek and

Turkish communities directly with the government of the island. Initial Turkish reaction was cold, but in the end it was accepted that the plan was workable, and not incompatible with the eventual solution of partition, which the Turkish Government then favoured.

The winter of 1958–59 saw a period of intense diplomatic activity and exchanges between Athens and Ankara, as a result of which there began in Zürich on February 5th, 1959, bilateral negotiations between the Prime Ministers and Foreign Ministers of Greece and Turkey. Both countries emphasised that the Zürich conference was called on joint Greco-Turkish initiative. On February 11th, the two Prime Ministers initialled an agreement on the basic structure of a new independent Republic of Cyprus, with a Greek Cypriot President and a Turkish Cypriot Vice-President. There were to be ten Ministers in the Cabinet, three of them Turkish, and a House of Representatives, 30 per cent of whom should be Turkish. The possibility of the union of Cyprus with any other state, or of the partition of it into two independent states, was expressly excluded. On February 11th the two Foreign Ministers came to London from Zürich for preliminary discussions with the British Foreign Secretary, and it was then decided to invite Archbishop Makarios and Dr. Fazıl Küçük, the leader of the Turkish Cypriots, to a conference in London. On February 18th a conference of Prime Ministers, Foreign Ministers and the two Cypriot leaders opened at Lancaster House, London, and it ended on February 19th with the acceptance by all parties of the new Constitution for Cyprus.

Prolonged negotiations to implement the London and Zürich agreement were finally completed in Cyprus on July 1st, 1960. Elections were to be held at the end of the month, and Cyprus became an independent republic on August 16th. Turks filled fifteen out of the fifty seats in the House of Representatives, and a detachment of Turkish troops was stationed in the island.

THE 1960 REVOLUTION

Economic difficulties continued to be one of the main preoccupations of the Turkish Government. The development plans envisaged since 1950 had been carried forward with financial aid from the United States and from such bodies as the International Bank; farm mechanization, roads, communication facilities, port development and grain-storage projects were among the chief items of the programme. These policies had been accompanied by inflationary pressures, an unfavourable trade balance, decreased imports, a shortage of foreign exchange and, since the agricultural population was in receipt of subsidies from the Government, a higher demand for consumer goods which aggravated the prevalent inflation. Social and economic unease tended to reveal itself in a drift of people from the villages to the towns, the population of centres like Ankara, Istanbul, Izmir, Bursa and Adana being considerably increased during recent years.

The influences which led to the revolution had been long at work. Hostility between the Democrats in power and the People's Party in opposition grew steadily more marked, and was sharpened towards the end of 1959 by suspicions that the Democrats were planning to hold fresh elections in the near future ahead of time. It was feared that these would, if necessary, be rigged to keep the Democrats in power indefinitely.

In May, 1959, political tension between the two main parties had already broken into violence during a political tour of Anatolia conducted by the opposition leader İsmet İnönü. The Government banned all political meetings. Blows were struck in the Grand National Assembly, and the Opposition walked out.

Much the same pattern of events ushered in the final breakdown a year later. At the beginning of April, 1960, İsmet İnönü undertook another political tour of Anatolia. At one point troops were called on to block his progress. Three of the officers involved in this incident took the strong step of resigning. The Opposition tried, but failed, to force a debate in the Assembly. On their side the Democrats set up a commission of enquiry, composed entirely of their own supporters, to investigate "the destructive and illegal activities of the P.R.P." Again the Grand National Assembly was the scene of violence, and all political activity was suspended for three months.

At this point the students took a hand. The universities had for some time been a focus of anti-government feeling, and in consequence had, like the newspapers, found their liberties attacked. On April 28th students in Istanbul demonstrated against the Menderes Government. Troops were called on to fire, and martial law was declared in Ankara and Istanbul.

As administrator of martial law the Turkish Army found itself, contrary to its traditions, involved in politics. A group of officers decided that their intervention must be complete if Turkey was to return to Kemalist principles. In the early hours of May 27th they struck. President Bayar, Mr. Menderes, most Democratic Deputies and a number of officials and senior officers were arrested. The Government was replaced by a Committee of National Union headed by General Gürsel, a much respected senior officer who had fought with Atatürk at Gallipoli.

The *coup* was immediately successful and almost bloodless, though Dr. Gedik, former Minister of the Interior, committed suicide after his arrest The accusation against the Menderes régime was that it had broken the constitution and was moving towards dictatorship. The officers insisted that they were temporary custodians of authority and would hand over to the duly constituted civilians. A temporary constitution was quickly agreed, pending the drafting of a final new one. During this interval legislative power was vested in the Committee of National Unity, and executive power in a Council of Ministers, composed of civilians as well as soldiers. On August 25th, however, ten of the eighteen Ministers were dismissed, leaving only three civilians in the Government. General Gürsel was President of Republic, Prime Minister and Minister of Defence. The courts were declared independent. Commissions were set up to inquire into the alleged misdeeds of the Menderes regime.

Although the new régime did not fail to meet political opposition, particularly among the peasants and around Izmir, a stronghold of Mr. Menderes, the main problems facing it were economic. The former régime was shown to be heavily in debt in every field. Austerity measures, including restrictions on credit, had to be put into operation and an economic planning board was set up to work out a long-term investment plan with the aid of foreign experts.

THE COMMITTEE OF NATIONAL UNITY

The Committee of National Unity, which originally consisted of 37 members, was reduced to 23 on November 13th, 1960. The 14 officers dismissed represented a group led by Colonel Turkeş, who had been pressing for the army to retain its post-revolutionary powers and to introduce radical social reforms.

This purge completed, preparations for a return to political democracy continued. A new Assembly, to act as a temporary parliament, was convened at the beginning of January 1961. It consisted of the National Unity Committee of 23, acting jointly with a House of Representatives of 271 members, both elected and nominated. In this the People's Party predominated. At the same time party politics were again legalised and a number of new parties emerged. Some of them proved short-lived, but one, the Justice Party founded by General Ragıp Gümüşpala, who had been Commander of the Third Army at the time of the *coup d'état*, was destined to become formidable by attracting the support of many former adherents of the Democratic Party, now declared illegal.

A special committee of the Assembly framed a new constitution which had some significant changes from the 1924 version. It provided for a court to determine the constitutionality of laws, for a two-chambered legislature, and it included a reference to "social justice" as one of the aims of the State.

THE YASSIADA TRIALS

These constitutional developments took place against the background of the trial of the accused members of the Menderes régime. The trial was held on the little island of Yassiada in the Bosphorus, where the accused had been confined after arrest. It began on October 14th, 1960, and continued until August 14th, 1961, thus becoming one of the largest and longest political trials in history. By the end the court, presided over by Judge Selim Basol, had held 203 sittings and heard 1,068 witnesses.

In the final session of the court 633 accused appeared in the dock, of whom nearly 100 had earlier been liberated but not formally acquitted. The prosecutor asked for 228 death sentences, including eight for Mr. Menderes and four for Mr. Bayar. Then followed a month's adjournment, and during this interval an attempt was made to close the national ranks. On September 5th leaders of the five principal parties signed a joint declaration undertaking to avoid destructive speeches and to preserve national unity during the electoral campaign. After a five-day round-table conference, presided over by General Gürsel, they further agreed to reject the "Democrat mentality" and to eschew the coming Yassiada sentences as a subject for public discussion. On September 6th leading newspaper editors followed suit. The sentence of the court was pronounced on September 15th. There were fifteen death sentences, twelve of which, including that on Mr. Bayar, were commuted to life imprisonment. Adnan Menderes, Fatin Zorlu, the former Foreign Minister, and Hasan Polatkan, the former Minister of Finance, were duly hanged.

The trial inevitably absorbed the attention of the country, and there were many reminders that sympathy for the former régime and its leaders was far from dead. In March General Gürsel, who had suffered a slight stroke at the end of November, warned the Opposition parties that they were "playing with fire". There were rumours of a plot to rescue Mr. Menderes from prison, and on May 9th–10th 123 people were arrested and charged with "armed resistance to the régime". The most serious setback for the authorities, however, appeared in the results of the referendum on the new constitution. This was approved by 6,348,191 votes against 3,934,370, and the large minority was taken as an indication of continuing loyalty to the Democrats.

It was to electioneering that the country, still stirred by the execution of Mr. Menderes and his colleagues, turned in the autumn. The campaign, perhaps because Yassiada was ruled out as a subject for discussion, proved unexpectedly quiet. On October 15th, 1961, the elections gave the People's Party 173 seats and the Justice Party 158 seats in the National Assembly, and 36 and 70 respectively in the Senate.

These figures were a blow to the hopes of the People's Party that they would achieve an overall working majority. A coalition became necessary. The election results were also further evidence of latent support for the Democrats.

THE NEW GOVERNMENT

On October 25th, 1961, Parliament opened and the transfer of power from military to civilians was made. The revolutionaries had kept their word and a new epoch began. The next day General Gürsel, the only candidate, was elected President. But forming a government proved a much harder process. On November 10th Mr. İsmet İnönü, leader of the People's Party, was asked to form a government, and after much hesitation and strong pressure from the Army, the Justice Party agreed to join forces with its rival. A Cabinet was formed with Mr. İnönü as Prime Minister, Mr. Akıf İyidoğan, of the Justice Party, as Deputy Prime Minister, and ten more Ministers from each of the two coalition parties.

Restlessness in the country and within the Army was not, however, at an end. On February 22nd, 1962, there was an abortive revolt by a group of officers inside the Ankara Garrison. This appeared to be the act of some of those who feared that, with the Justice Party sharing power, the revolution was in danger of surrendering to those it had set out to overthrow. The Government remained, as Mr. İnönü said, exposed to a double fire— from those who thought the Army did too much (i.e. that civil liberties were still circumscribed) and those who thought it did too little (i.e. that it did not crush all signs of counter-revolution). The resignation of Mr. İnönü at the end of May weakened the extremists in the Justice Party, who had wanted to grant an amnesty to former supporters of Mr. Menderes. They were now face to face with the Army, the original movers of the 1960 revolution, and many of them felt it wise to moderate their demands.

By the end of June Mr. İnönü had formed a new coalition government composed of twelve Ministers from the Republican People's Party, six from the New Turkey Party, four from the Republican Peasants' Nation Party, and one Independent Minister.

The new government's programme expressed attachment to the principles of Western democracy and to the NATO alliance. It covered almost every sphere of the national life, including education, taxation, employment, and the problems of a rapidly rising birth-rate and an adverse balance of trade.

The somewhat uneasy political balance persisted against a background of rumours of further army intervention, and at times it seemed that only Mr. İnönü's skill and prestige kept Turkey on her chosen parliamentary course. As it was, the second half of 1962 saw scuffles break out on more than one occasion in the Assembly and Senate. The most controversial legislation concerned an amnesty for those convicted at Yassiada. A Bill was passed in October which cut sentences by four years. This automatically released those serving sentences of four years or less. Those with sentences of up to six and a half years were also given their freedom. On October 18th, 280 prisoners were set free. They were allowed to practise their professions but not to take part in public life. This act of clemency did not prevent the Opposition from pressing for a complete amnesty for all still detained, including Celal Bayar.

The Republican People's Party, like the country as a whole, found itself divided between those who favoured caution and those who insisted that the pace of reform should be faster. At its congress in October three leading members of the party, including its former secretary-general, Mr. Kasim Gülek, were expelled for a year. There were in addition some signs of a growing but largely uninformed interest in socialism. A Socialist Cultural Association, composed of politicians, intellectuals and journalists, was formed in December. But an article on socialism in *Cumhuriyet* brought its author arrest—a sign that the identification of socialism with communism was still prevalent.

1962 saw the publication of Turkey's long-awaited first Five-Year Plan (see below, *Economic Survey*). Before the Plan was published there had been considerable controversy over how the amount should be raised (about £2,400 million sterling). Four leading members of the planning organization, who favoured more drastic taxation of landowners and agriculturalists, including the director, Mr. Osman Torun, resigned in September. In January 1963 Mr. Attila Sönmez, director of economic planning, likewise resigned, on the grounds that serious inflation would result if the Plan were carried out as the Government intended. A working group set up in July by OECD in Paris was one answer to the problem of outside contributions to the Plan. This reached agreement in June 1963 and formal signature followed on September 12th. The agreement provided for the association of Turkey with the Common Market in two phases. The first, preparatory, phase was to last from five to nine years, and during it the Turkish economy would be prepared for a customs union by aid, amounting to $175 million, from the Six. Certain staple Turkish exports would, during the period, have privileged entry to Common Market countries. The second, transitional, phase would last twelve years. During it Turkish tariffs would be gradually reduced, leading ultimately to a full customs union. In April 1964 Turkey received a loan from Britain of £3 million.

POLITICAL UNREST

The political climate during 1963 remained unsettled. In February the leading radical of the original Committee of National Unity, Colonel Turkeş, who had been in unofficial exile abroad, returned with plans to set up a new political organization. More immediately threatening to the régime were the disturbances which marked the temporary release of the former President, Celal Bayar, from the prison in Kayseri where he had been since his sentence. A convoy of hundreds of cars escorted the 80-year-old politician to Ankara, where he was welcomed on March 24th by large and enthusiastic crowds. The reception appeared as a direct challenge to the revolution and was countered by violent protests, in which students and members of the armed forces participated, denouncing Mr. Bayar and his supposed supporters in the Justice Party. The Ankara offices of the party and its newspaper were attacked. After five days of liberty Mr. Bayar was taken back into custody, first in hospital and then again to his old prison at Kayseri. He was released again in November, 1964, by which time only a handful of those sentenced with him were left in gaol.

In the early hours of May 21st, 1963, Ankara was the scene of yet another abortive *coup d'état*. The instigator was Colonel Aydemir, who had been responsible for the attempted revolt in February 1962. On this occasion his resort to arms, in which some of the cadets at the Military Academy were involved, was quickly suppressed. Colonel Aydemir was executed in July, 1964. One result of the attempted *coup* was the imposition of martial law in Ankara, Istanbul and Izmir. Originally proclaimed for one month, martial law was repeatedly prolonged.

Although the Bayar incident and Aydemir *coup* produced divisions inside the ranks of the Justice Party, it showed considerable successes at the local elections in November, the first to be held since 1954. These successes were mainly at the expense of the New Turkey Party and the Republican Peasants' Nation Party, Mr. İnönü's two junior partners in the coalition. They resigned from the government, and after General Gümüşpala, the leader of the Justice Party, had tried and failed to form a Ministry,

the President called again on Mr. İnönü, who on December 23rd formed a minority government drawn from members of his own Republican Party and some independents. It received a vote of confidence in the Assembly.

The first months of 1964 were overshadowed by an attempt on the life of Mr. İnönü in February, and by the situation in Cyprus, where the fate of the Turkish minority created strong feeling in the mainland. Mr. İnönü's critics claimed that he had "missed the bus" by failing to intervene on the island with force when the trouble started.

RAPPROCHEMENT WITH U.S.S.R.

This, and other diplomatic efforts towards a solution, failed, and public opinion grew more irritated, not only with Greece, but also with Turkey's western allies, in particular America and Britain, who were accused of being lukewarm in their support for Turkey's case. In August this irritation caused a violent explosion in Izmir, when rioters wrecked the American and British pavilions at the trade fair. Mr. İnönü, though moving with characteristic caution, gave a warning that the alliance with the west, the basis of Turkey's foreign policy since the war, was in danger. To reinforce his warning came several steps designed to improve relations with the U.S.S.R. When the Cyprus problem first flared up again it had appeared that the Soviet Government took the side of Greece, and the Soviet trade pavilion had also been a target for the Izmir hooligans. But feelers were out in both Moscow and Ankara, and at the end of October 1964 Mr. Erkin visited the U.S.S.R.—the first Turkish Foreign Minister to make this journey for twenty-five years. Before leaving he invoked the memory of the early days of friendship between Atatürk and Lenin, and the same precedent was made much of by his hosts, who tactfully did not try to press Turkey into premature neutralism, as they had done in the past. On Cyprus, the U.S.S.R. appeared to have moved closer to the Turkish point of view, the communiqué which ended Mr. Erkin's talks speaking favourably of a solution "by peaceful means on the basis of respect for the territorial integrity of Cyprus, and for the legal rights of the two national communities".

Mr. Erkin's journey was followed up in January 1965 by the visit to Ankara of a Soviet parliamentary delegation. A trade pact between the two countries followed in March. In May, Mr. Gromyko, the Soviet Foreign Minister, paid a five-day visit to Turkey, and in August, Mr. Ürgüplü, the Prime Minister, paid a return visit to the U.S.S.R. Both occasions were the first of their kind for a generation, and produced a good deal of cordiality. The Soviet Government promised to supply Turkey with credits worth £71 million for a steel works, an oil refinery, and other industrial enterprises. But over Cyprus it was less forthcoming. Friendly references to the banned Turkish Communist Party at the Communist Party Congress in Moscow in March 1966 revived old suspicions of Soviet motives.

FALL OF MR. İNÖNÜ

For all this, Cyprus continued to give the Opposition ammunition with which to harass the İnönü government. At the Senate elections in June, 1964, the Justice Party won 31 out of the 51 seats contested, thus increasing its already large majority in this House. Its success was clouded by the death of the Party's leader, General Gümüşpala. In November Mr. Süleyman Demirel, aged 40, a trained engineer and a former Director General of the state water organization, was elected leader in his place, though he was without a seat in Parliament. Mr. İnönü survived more than one narrow vote of confidence, but was finally brought down on February 13th, 1965, by an adverse vote (225 to 197) in the Assembly on the

Budget—the first that the life time of a Turkish government had been ended in this way. There was some speculation whether the Army would allow the Opposition to form a government: the previous November General Sunay, Chief of Staff of the Armed Forces, had warned Justice Party Deputies against criticizing the army. After a short delay, however, a coalition government was formed, made up from the four parties which had been in Opposition—the Justice Party, the New Turkish Party, the Republican Peasant's Party, and the National Party. An independent senator, Mr. Suat Ürgüplü, who had spent much of his previous career in diplomacy, headed the team as Prime Minister. Mr. Hasan İşik, recently appointed as Ambassador to Moscow, was brought in as Foreign Minister, thereby indicating that the new government intended to continue pursuing better understanding with Russia.

Turkey suffered a bitter blow when, in December, the General Assembly of the United Nations passed a resolution urging all states to refrain from intervention in Cyprus. This was seen as directly aimed at Turkey's aid for the Turkish minority there. The Government in Ankara denounced the resolution as being "against right, law, and international agreements". However, in the early months of 1966 the position improved somewhat. Direct contacts between Ankara and Athens led to renewed hopes of a negotiated settlement. Unfortunately nothing had been achieved by the early summer of 1967, when the military *coup* in Athens led to Turkish fears that Greece was entering a new phase of instability and nationalism.

1965 was election year. The general election of October 11th confirmed the growing popularity of the Justice Party. Winning 240 seats in an Assembly of 450, it achieved a majority over all its rivals. The People's Party was reduced to 134 seats, followed by the extreme right-wing National Party with 31, the New Turkish Party with 19, the Turkish Workers' Party with 15, and the Republican National Peasants' Party with 11 seats. The emergence of an organized party of the left was perhaps even more remarkable than the triumph of the Justice Party, heirs of the Menderes tradition.

DEMİREL CABINET

Mr. Süleyman Demirel formed his cabinet from members of his own party. Introducing his government to the Assembly, Mr. Demirel declared that its most important task would be to withstand communism "by the realization of social justice and measures of social security". Emphasis was to be put on industrialization. "We have to catch up three centuries in three decades", he said.

In spite of its working majority the Demirel Government proved hardly more successful than its predecessors in getting things done. The Justice Party blamed its poor record of legislation on the obstructionist tactics of the Opposition. There had been filibusters, and several ugly scenes of violence on the floor of the Assembly. However, elections in June 1966 for a third of the seats in the Senate showed that the Justice Party was not losing popularity.

To some extent this success was attributable to the innate conservatism of the Turkish peasantry, who may have been alarmed by Mr. İnönü's statement that the People's Party was left of centre. This position was not approved by all the party—some thought it went too far, others not far enough. A convention of the party in October showed a victory for the left-wingers. Mr. Bülent Ecevit, 41 years old and a former Minister of Labour, was elected general secretary of the party, with the declared intention of turning it into a party of democratic socialism. Six months later 48 senators and congressmen, led by Mr. Turhan Feyzioğlu, a former Minister, resigned from the party on the grounds that it was falling into a "dangerous

leftist adventure". This was denied by Mr. Ecevit and Mr. İnönü, who supported him. They claimed that, on the contrary, their progressive policies took the wind out of other left-wing parties' sails, and so was the best barrier against communism.

In May 1967 a majority of dissidents came together to form the new Reliance Party, which proclaimed its opposition to socialism and its belief in the "spiritual values of the Turkish nation." In June Mr. Ecevit forced a fresh election of the People's Party executive, and by securing the elimination of two left-wing representatives on it he was able to emphasise that his party remained left of centre rather than left wing.

The National Party also found itself in trouble when 8 of its 31 deputies resigned. But the real threat to all parties other than the governing Justice Party was the new electoral law. This, which was finally passed in March 1968 against the protests of a united opposition, did away with the so-called "national remainder system"—a change which threatened the electoral chances of all the smaller parties but was thought to be particularly aimed at the Turkish Workers' Party, which was accused by the Government of using communist tactics. Earlier a battle had been fought over the party's stormy petrel, Çetin Altan. In July 1967 a vote was taken to lift his parliamentary immunity so that he could stand trial on a charge of distributing communist propaganda. This decision was quashed by the constitutional court in August.

In March 1966 President Gursel, whose health had deteriorated (he died in September), was succeeded by Senator Cevdet Sunay.

FOREIGN POLICY 1966-1969

Turkey's relations with her allies in 1966 deteriorated. There were various demonstrations against the Americans, culminating in March 1966 in a riot in Adana, during which American buildings were attacked and American cars overturned. This was touched off by rumours that American servicemen, of whom there were large numbers near the town, had made improper advances to Turkish women. But in effect it was the consequence of a long campaign in the press against America's military presence, which reflected a general increase in xenophobia.

Parallel with these manifestations against Turkey's formerly most stalwart ally went an effort by the Demirel Government to make its whole foreign policy more flexible. This flexibility was symbolized by many official visits, given and received, between Turkey on the one hand, and Romania, Bulgaria, Egypt, Yugoslavia and Morocco. One outcome of the exchanges with Arab leaders was that at the time of the June war with Israel the Turkish Government expressed its sympathy with the Arab cause. But perhaps the state visit which attracted most attention was that of President Sunay—the first Turkish head of state to be so welcomed since Sultan Abdul Aziz exactly 100 years before.

As usual the touchstone of Turkey's foreign relations continued to be Cyprus. In 1967 this perennial problem oscillated between near settlement and near war. The military régime brought to power in Athens by the *coup* of April 1967 seemed ready to negotiate, but no agreement was reached.

Later in the year the situation suddenly deteriorated as a result of attacks by Greek Cypriots on the Turkish enclaves on the island on November 15th. Two days later the National Assembly voted by 432 votes to 1 to authorize the Government to send troops to foreign countries—in other words, to fight in Cyprus. There were daily Turkish flights over the island and the prospects of war seemed real. As a result of strong intervention by American and UN go-betweens the worst was avoided. On December 3rd the Greeks undertook to withdraw their troops from the island and the Turks to take the necessary measures to ease tension. By February 1968 the situation had been so far restored that direct efforts to agree on a negotiated settlement for Cyprus were once again under way.

The principal event affecting foreign policy in 1968 was the state visit paid by General de Gaulle in October. The visit aroused considerable popular interest, and was widely seen as an attempt to restore the French language and culture to its former pre-eminence amongst European influences in Turkey. Since the Second World War it has largely been replaced by Anglo-American influences, and English is now the main foreign language taught in Turkey. A new defence agreement with the U.S. was signed in March 1969, which increased and clarified Turkish control over the American bases.

MILITARY INTERVENTION

Süleyman Demirel's Justice Party Government was faced with the growing problem of political violence from early 1968 onward. Disorders in the universities, springing from non-political educational grievances and from clashes between political extremists of the right and the left, took an increasingly violent form. Students staged anti-American riots, and in June 1969 troops had to be called in to prevent extremists disrupting examinations. The fighting between right and left factions became more serious in 1970, firearms and petrol bombs being used, and a number of political murders taking place.

Parliamentary politics also became rather confused. Elections in October 1969 produced an enlarged majority for the Justice Party, but the party soon split, a number of Mr. Demirel's right-wing opponents forming the Democratic Party. Party strengths became almost impossible to calculate, as factions and alliances formed and dissolved, and on crucial votes the support of Government and the combined Opposition parties was almost equally balanced. A new party, the National Order Party, with right-wing policies and theocratic tendencies, was formed in January 1970 by Professor Necmettin Erbakan.

The Turkish armed forces began to take an unusually close interest in political questions as internal disorders became more serious and it became apparent that factional bickering was preventing the Government from taking effective action. In May 1969 it was feared that the army would intervene to prevent the restoration of civil rights to members of the Menderes régime, and in 1970 the air force commander, General Muhsin Batur, was reported to be pressing for political and economic reforms and a return to the ideals of Atatürk. The student violence of 1970 and clashes between rival trade union organizations prompted General Tagmaç, Chief of the General Staff, to warn that the armed forces would consider it their duty to suppress disorders threatening Turkish national integrity and Atatürk's reforms. The year 1971 opened with intensified terrorism, and a wave of strikes and protests by public employees. There was a wave of bomb attacks on American-owned property, bank robberies and kidnappings of Americans, carried out by left-wing extremists, to which were added separatist agitation among the Kurds and reported Syrian encouragement for a separatist movement among the Arabs of Hatay province. It was at this stage that the armed forces intervened.

On March 12th, 1971, the Chief of the General Staff and the Army, Navy and Air Force Commanders delivered a memorandum to the President. Alleging that "Parliament and the Government, through their sustained policies, views and actions, have driven our country into anarchy, fratricidal strife and social and economic unrest; made the public lose all hope of reaching a level of contemporary civilization, a goal set by Atatürk; failed to realize the reforms stipulated by the Constituion; and placed the future of the Turkish republic in grave danger", they felt that it was "essential that, within the context of democratic principles, a strong and credible government should be formed which would neutralize the current anarchical situation". If this were not done quickly, they threatened, "the armed forces are determined to take over the administration of the State in accordance with the powers vested in them by the laws to protect and preserve the Turkish Republic". Later that day the Demirel Cabinet resigned.

MILITARY DOMINATION OF POLITICS

A new Government was formed by Dr. Nihat Erim, with the support of both the Justice Party and the Republican People's Party (RPP). Bülent Ecevit, the RPP secretary-general, resigned from office and refused to collaborate. Dr. Erim's programme promised sweeping reforms in taxation, land ownership, education, power and industry, but the Government's attention was first directed to the suppression of political violence. The military ultimatum was followed by further bombings, kidnappings and clashes between right and left-wing students and between students and police. On April 28th, 1971, martial law was proclaimed, initially for one month, in eleven provinces, including Ankara and .stanbul.

Newspapers were suppressed, strikes were banned and large numbers of left-wingers were arrested. The National Order Party was dissolved in May 1971, the Turkish Labour Party in July. The murder of the Israeli consul-general in Istanbul by the so-called Turkish People's Liberation Army provided the military authorities with an opportunity to round up nearly one thousand suspects in Istanbul alone, including many journalists, writers and intellectuals. In September 1971, Dr. Erim introduced a number of amendments to the Constitution, limiting individual civil rights and the autonomy of universities, radio and television, placing restrictions on the press and trade unions and giving the Government powers to legislate by decree. Dr. Erim's proposal to use the new powers to introduce sweeping social and economic reforms, supported by the armed forces, was opposed by the Justice Party. A Cabinet crisis in October and December 1971 led to the formation of a new coalition Cabinet, again headed by Dr. Erim, but his proposals for taking further executive powers were opposed by the four major parliamentary parties, and in April 1972 he resigned. A Cabinet formed by Suat Ürgüplü was rejected by President Sunay, and in May a Government drawn from the Justice Party, National Reliance Party and RPP, headed by Ferit Melen, was approved. There was a swing to the left within the RPP in May; the veteran party leader İsmet İnönü resigned after 34 years as chairman, and was replaced by Bülent Ecevit. Meanwhile, the terrorist activities of the Turkish People's Liberation Army continued, and martial law was prolonged at two-month intervals.

In July 1972, dissident RPP members, opposing the dominance of the left wing led by Mr. Ecevit, formed the Republican Party. In November the RPP withdrew its support from the Melen coalition Government, but its five ministers preferred to leave the party, and stay in the Cabinet. This caused further resignations from the RPP, including that of İsmet İnönü and 25 other deputies and senators. A number of these dissidents, together with the National Reliance Party and the Republican Party which had earlier broken from the RPP over allegedly excessive left-wing tendencies, formed the Republican Reliance Party in February 1973. The RPP, without its right wing, began actively to oppose the Melen Government, which it considered to be dominated by the armed forces, and martial law, under which, it was alleged with increasing frequency, arbitrary arrest and torture were practised. In March 1973, for the first time, the RPP voted against the prolongation of martial law, following a heated debate in which the Minister of the Interior disclosed that in the two years of martial law 1,383 persons had been sentenced by military courts, 553 acquitted, and that 179 trials were then taking place and 2,991 were in preparation.

President Sunay's term of office expired in March 1973, and the Grand National Assembly began the process of electing a new president. General Gürler resigned his post as Chief of Staff in order to stand for election, his candidature receiving the strong support of the armed forces. He was opposed by members of the Justice and Democratic Parties, while the RPP decided to abstain from voting, as a protest against the military interference in the election and the censorship of electoral news in Ankara. Despite obvious military support for General Gürler, 14 ballots failed to produce a result, and eventually the Justice Party, RPP and Republican Reliance Party agreed on a compromise candidate, Senator Fahri Korotürk, former Commander-in-Chief of the Navy, who had not belonged to any political party. He was elected President on April 6th, 1973. The following day Mr. Melen resigned, and was succeeded as Prime Minister by Naim Talû, an independent senator, who formed a Cabinet with Justice Party and Republican Reliance Party participation.

The Talû Government, although considered to be merely a caretaker administration to last until the general election, due in October 1973, brought about a number of reforms, and during its term of office the armed forces gradually withdrew from political affairs. A land reform law, distributing some 8 million acres to 500,000 peasants, was passed in June 1973, and measures were taken to prevent foreign domination of the mining and petroleum industries. A strong element within the armed forces felt that the time had come to return to a strictly military role, and that martial law had achieved its objective of crushing extremism. General Sancar, who became Chief of Staff when General Gürler resigned to make his unsuccessful attempt to become President, was opposed to military intervention in politics, and retired 196 senior officers. Many close associates of General Gürler were transferred to politically insignificant posts, and the retirement of General Batur, the Air Force Commander, removed the last of the officers who had signed the armed forces' memorandum of March 1971. Martial law was gradually lifted from the affected provinces, and came to an end in September 1973.

ECEVIT GOVERNMENT

General elections for the National Assembly and for 52 Senate seats were held on October 14th, 1973. In the National Assembly the RPP, with 185 seats, replaced the Justice Party as the largest party, but failed to win an overall majority. The RPP was believed to have won many votes from former supporters of the banned Turkish Labour Party, while the Justice Party lost support to the Democratic Party and a new organization, the National Salvation Party (MSP). The latter, led by Professor Necmettin Erbakan, was founded in 1972 to replace his banned National Order Party, and shared its traditionalist, Islamic policies, and became the third largest party in the new National Assembly. Prime Minister Talû resigned, but then continued in office for a further three months while negotiations on the formation of a coalition government dragged on. Despite this parliamentary crisis, the armed forces remained aloof from politics. Eventually, on January 25th, 1974, a Government was formed by the RPP and MSP, with Bülent Ecevit as

Prime Minister and Necmettin Erbakan as his Deputy. The Cabinet had 18 RPP members and seven from the MSP.

The new Government, an apparently unlikely coalition of the left-of-centre RPP and the reactionary MSP, proclaimed its reforming intentions, but made concessions to the demands of its Muslim supporters which tended to deviate from Atatürk's strictly secular principles. In March 1974, Turkey was for the first time represented at an Islamic Summit Conference. The appointment of an MSP deputy as Minister of the Interior brought about a number of petty manifestations of Islamic puritanism, but the main lines of the Ecevit Government's policy seemed to be of a reforming, liberal nature, intended to remove the more excessive manifestations of the police state created during the period of military intervention.

The land reform passed by the Talû administration came into operation in a pilot project in Urfa province, and in July the ban on opium production introduced under American pressure in 1972 was rescinded, but the Government's attention in the first six months of the Ecevit ministry was concentrated on the amnesty of political prisoners. In May the Government granted an amnesty to some 50,000 prisoners, including both common criminals and political prisoners arrested under martial law, as a belated gesture marking the fiftieth anniversary of the foundation of the republic. The more liberal political climate was shown by the creation of a new left-wing party, the Turkish Socialist Workers' Party, in June, with policies and leaders similar to those of the Turkish Labour Party. The success of the invasion of Cyprus and the way in which Mr. Ecevit ignored American protests against the removal of the ban on opium cultivation served to increase Mr. Ecevit's popularity and to strengthen his position with regard to his MSP coalition partners. The differences between the MSP and the RPP had been submerged during the Cyprus crisis, but once more became apparent in September. On September 16th, 1974, Mr. Ecevit announced that he had decided to resign, as the coalition was no longer viable. He was expected to form an interim government without the MSP, and announced that he would ask the President to hold elections in December 1974. It appeared likely that the popular acclaim he had won by his handling of the Cyprus and opium disputes would give the RPP a considerable electoral advantage, and that the removal of the constraint of coalition with the traditionalist MSP would allow the RPP to carry out its more radical policies of internal reform.

Following the resignation of the Cabinet of Bülent Ecevit on September 18th, 1974, Turkey remained for over six months without a government having parliamentary approval. Professor Sadi Irmak attempted unsuccessfully to form an interim coalition in November to prepare for new elections in 1975, but remained in office in a caretaker capacity whilst efforts were made to form a new government. Internal unrest increased during the lengthy government crisis, with serious clashes between opposing political factions and between students. It was reported in March 1975 that an incipient anti-Government *coup* by junior officers in Ankara had been suppressed by their superiors. No further details were available.

In March 1975 Mr. Süleyman Demirel returned to power, leading a right-wing coalition, the Nationalist Front, consisting of four parties: Mr. Demirel's Justice Party (the biggest), the National Salvation Party (MSP), the Republican Reliance Party (CGP) and the neo-fascist National Action Party (MHP). Of the cabinet of 30 the Justice Party occupied 16 of the seats, the MSP eight, the CGP four, and the MHP two. The coalition did not have an overall majority in the National Assembly, but support from other parties was virtually assured. It was, however, thought unlikely that the coalition would be strong enough to deal with the country's pressing problems.

CYPRUS

The traditional hostility between Turkey and Greece revived following the Greek announcement in February 1974 that oil had been found in Greek territorial waters in the Aegean. This led to a dispute over the extent of national jurisdiction over the continental shelf and territorial waters, with both sides making warlike moves in Thrace and the Aegean area. Turkey began a hydrographical survey of the continental shelf in this area, claiming oil exploration rights in the eastern Aegean. The potentially tense situation in the Aegean was overshadowed by the *coup* in Cyprus* on July 15th.

This *coup* was carried out by the Cypriot National Guard, led by officers from Greece, apparently with the support of the Greek military régime. Declaring its intention of protecting the Turkish community in Cyprus and preventing the union of Cyprus with mainland Greece, the Turkish Government proclaimed a right to intervene as a guarantor state under the Zürich agreement of 1959. On July 20th Turkish troops landed in Cyprus, and rapidly won control of the area around Kyrenia on the northern coast. The Turkish intervention in Cyprus was followed by negotiations in Geneva between Turkey, Greece and the United Kingdom. Turkey pressed for the creation of an independent federal Cypriot state, with population movements to give the Turkish community their own sector in the north. The intransigence of both Greeks and Turks, and Greece's rejection of a possible cantonal solution put forward by Turkey, led to a further successful advance by the Turkish forces in Cyprus. When a second ceasefire was called on August 16th, Turkey controlled about one-third of the total area of Cyprus.

The sector under Turkish control, all of Cyprus north of a line running from Morphou through Nicosia to Famagusta, contained more than half the livestock, citrus plantations and mineral reserves of Cyprus, with access to two major seaports. The flight of Greek Cypriot refugees from the north left the Turks a free hand to take over the administration and economy, and establish an effective partition of the island. Mr. Ecevit claimed that the Turkish military success had laid the foundation of a federal state with two autonomous administrations, allowing the Turkish Cypriot community to concentrate in the conquered area and establish their own government. On February 13th, 1975, the Turkish Cypriots unilaterally declared a Turkish Federated State in Northern Cyprus and continued pressing for the establishment of a bi-regional federal state system in Cyprus. The State was described by the Turkish Cypriot leader, Mr. Denktaş, as the federal wing of the Republic of Cyprus, although no such Federal Republic yet existed. Greek and Turkish Foreign Ministers held talks in Rome in May 1975 on outstanding disputes between the two countries, with the future of Cyprus among the main topics. The Greek-Turkish Aegean dispute was also discussed, including the issue of who held the rights over oil exploration in the area, the equitable division of the Aegean continental shelf and the question of air space control in the area. The dispute was submitted to the International Court of Justice. In May 1975 Turkey began reinforcing its troop strength along the Aegean coast and in Thrace to counter an alleged military build-up by Greece.

The U.S. imposed an embargo on military aid and the supply of arms to Turkey in February 1975 on the grounds that American military equipment had been used in the Turkish invasion of Cyprus in July 1974 and that Turkey had failed to make substantial progress towards resolving the Cyprus crisis. Relations between Turkey and the U.S. became further strained when, in July 1975, Turkey implemented counter-measures against the announced continuation of the U.S. arms ban, including the take-over of U.S. bases in Turkey by the Turkish Armed Forces and the abrogation of all Turkey's defence agreements with the U.S.A.. The Turkish decision did not directly affect NATO since the status of the NATO base in Turkey remained unchanged and alliance sources saw the situation as "a bilateral problem between Turkey and the U.S.". Concern had already been expressed by the alliance at the hostility between Turkey and Greece—both NATO members—and a call for a "cooling off" in the situation was expected.

---

* For full details of the Cyprus situation *see* Cyprus, page 251.

ECONOMIC SURVEY

Turkey is about 1,449 km. long and some 483 km. wide, covering an area of 779,452 sq. kilometres. The 1970 census recorded a population of 35,666,549, an increase of 2.7 per cent annually since 1965. By the middle of 1974 the population was 38,270,000. Two-thirds of the population live in rural areas. Of the twenty cities with a population of more than 100,000 the largest and best known are the former capital of Istanbul (2.4 million), the port of Izmir (591,000) on the Aegean Sea, and the capital Ankara (1.5 million, 1973 estimates). The average population density was 49 per sq. kilometre in 1974. In September 1973 649,454 Turks were working abroad, more than 500,000 of them in Federal Germany.

The country possesses great natural advantages: the land yields good grain and a wide variety of fruit and other products; it is rich in minerals; and it has a number of natural ports. The climate is varied and, on the whole, favourable, but communications are hindered by the mountain ranges that ring the Anatolian plateau to the north, east and south.

When the republic was founded in 1923, industrial development was undertaken, and textiles, cement and paper were among the first industries to be established. Between 1923 and 1941 the number of industrial establishments increased from 118 to 1,052. During this period the government's policy was one of "*étatisme*", aimed chiefly at the development of heavy industry. Its main instruments were two state "holding" companies, the Etibank and the Sümerbank, and much was achieved through them. In the post-war years there was a marked decline in economic impetus; it was not until after the victory of the Democratic Party in 1950 that the situation began to be transformed.

Under the Menderes régime, free enterprise was encouraged and there was a considerable private investment in industrial undertakings. Some government monopolies were returned to private hands, and state economic undertakings went into partnership with new enterprises formed with both domestic and foreign private capital. At the same time, there was large-scale official investment in public works schemes, notably in expanding electric power production and communications, with the result that the pace of development was greatly increased.

The Government made great efforts to speed up development and put through a vast industrialization programme. But the consequences of such rapid development with its high level of investment, were serious. Difficulties first made themselves felt in the autumn of 1952, and a severe economic crisis had arisen by the end of 1955. Capital development outran resources, and large imports of heavy industrial goods and machinery, not offset by a corresponding expansion in exports, produced a series of foreign trade deficits, with a consequent acute shortage of foreign exchange, in spite of considerable financial assistance from the United States. At home this led to strong inflationary pressure and high prices. The situation was aggravated by a succession of indifferent harvests and by low export prices for chromium and copper. Another contribution to Turkey's difficulties was the high prices paid to farmers, resulting in wheat and other agricultural produce being offered at higher than world prices. To this must be added the fact that Turkey had met heavy defence commitments, nearly 40 per cent of recent budgetary expenditure having been devoted to this purpose.

In an endeavour to combat inflation and reduce pressure on the country's slender reserves, the Government introduced a number of restrictive measures in 1955 and 1956. These included tight controls over liquidity, credit and foreign trade and strict profit margins. However, inflation continued and the trade position deteriorated still further so that in 1958 further controls were introduced. The 1958 stabilization programme was aimed at correcting the external imbalance by restricting imports and fighting inflation. The most important measures were credit restrictions, the reduction of non-essential investment and the effective devaluation of the Turkish lira. However, the Government's heart was not in its policies and they were not fully applied or completely effective. The Revolutionary Government showed more determination, imposed even more stringent controls and in August 1960 devalued the Turkish lira.

The stabilization programme was continued after 1961 with some success; restrictive measures were gradually being relaxed, though some imports were still limited. Investment policy was then co-ordinated in the Five-Year Plan (1962–67), which called for an annual investment of 18 per cent of gross national product (against an average of under 16 per cent in recent years) to a final total investment of TL59,646 million. It aimed at an annual increase in the Turkish national income of some 7 per cent a year. A second Five-Year Plan (1968–72) followed, again aiming at a 7 per cent annual rise in the gross national product: total investment in it was set at TL111,500 million in annual instalments rising to TL29,000 million by the last year of the Plan. A third Five-Year Plan (1973–77) commenced in 1973 with a target increase in the Turkish gross national product of 7.9 per cent per annum. Total investment is planned at TL281,000 million, of which manufacturing industry is to receive some TL187,000 million.

From 1963 until 1970 growth in G.N.P. averaged 6.5 per cent annually. There was a downturn in 1969 which, because of bad harvests and the effects on industry of acute shortages of foreign exchange, became more pronounced in 1970. In 1971 the growth rate was 9.2 per cent in real terms, while for 1972 the growth rate of G.N.P. was 7.6 per cent. In 1973 an increase in growth in real gross national product of 5.5 per cent was disappointing. In 1974 real growth recovered to 7.5 per cent which is only just below the target of 7.9 per cent in the current Third Plan. However, growth measured by real G.N.P. per head of population is lower—4.8 per cent—due to rapid population increase.

AGRICULTURE

Turkey is still predominantly an agricultural country; in 1970, 65 per cent of the employed population were engaged in agriculture, forestry, hunting and fishing. In spite of the heavy dependence on agriculture, this sector accounted for only 23 per cent of G.D.P. in 1973. In 1972 259,430 sq. km. was under cultivation, 33 per cent of the total area, a proportion which has been rising continuously since 1967. Most of the farms are small and the average size of a family farm is only 19 acres (7.7 hectares). In good years the country is basically self-sufficient in foodstuffs, except for wheat. Agricultural products accounted for 63 per cent by value of exports in 1973, the chief items being cotton, tobacco and nuts, which alone made up over half of the export trade in 1972. The value of agricultural exports fell by 10 per cent in 1973 due to a poor harvest, and although the 1974 total harvest was up by 6.1 per cent the value of agricultural exports did not increase substantially due to the decline in world demand.

During the period 1963–70, the agricultural growth rate was only 2.5 per cent per annum compared with a target rate of 4.2 per cent under the first five-year plan. This failure is attributed to the insufficient emphasis placed on agriculture in both plans. Agriculture was allocated 17.7 per cent of total investment under the first plan, 15.2 per cent under the second and 12 per cent under the current third plan. In fact, actual fixed investment under the first plan amounted to only 15.5 per cent of the national total and this pattern of under-achievement was repeated during the first three years of the second plan. There were indications by 1971 that this relative neglect would cease, with land reform aimed at the limitation of individual land-holdings, redistribution of land to farmers in co-operatives and the improved utilization of land, machinery and farmer education resources. In fact agricultural production in 1971 increased by some 30 per cent. In 1972 total agricultural production was worth TL59,000 million, in 1973 nearly TL67,000 million. If the potential for agricultural develop-ment is to be exploited, then along with land reform a larger share of government expenditure must be allocated to agriculture than it has received hitherto. Nevertheless, the foundations for the modernization of agriculture have been laid under the first and second plans: for example, the consumption of fertilizer increased from 430,000 tons in 1963 to over 3 million tons in 1971 and the land area under irriga-tion was increasing at an average rate of 100,000 hectares per annum.

A Land and Agrarian Reform Bill was passed in 1973, which should ultimately redistribute some 8 million acres to 500,000 peasants, over 15 years. 3.5 million acres of arable State property, 2.5 million acres of uncultivated State land which will be made arable and 2 million acres of private land which will be nationalized for free distribution make up the area covered by the bill. This area, 37,670 sq. kilometres, is significantly large compared with the total 250,730 sq. kilometres under cultivation in 1972. Many Turkish peasants own very little land, and about one-tenth of all farming families have no land at all. The reform came into operation in 1974 in a pilot project in Urfa province. The maximum holding for each family was set at 80 acres of irrigated or 250 acres of unirrigated land, the excess to be expropriated and paid for by the State. In Urfa, this excess should total 620,000 acres, to which will be added 250,000 acres of State land, all of which will be distributed to landless peasants in parcels large enough to provide a family revenue of TL22,500 a year at 1973 prices. 25,000 families of landless tenant-farmers should benefit from this redistribution in Urfa, and will be organized into co-operatives with State grants and loans to provide capital. The other 12,000 landless families will be diverted from agriculture, mainly to the textile and food industries. To complement the land reform, the State is to make heavy investments in industry and encourage private industry, and carry out large-scale improvements in roads, water supplies, sanitation and schools.

In 1972 51 per cent of the cultivated area was devoted to cereals, the most important of which, wheat, accounted for over 60 per cent of the total grain production. The principal wheat-growing area is the central Anatolian plateau, but the uncertain climate causes wide fluctuations in production. Barley, rye and oats are other important crops grown on the central plateau. Maize is grown along the Black Sea coastal regions, and leguminous crops in the Izmir hinterland. Rice, normally sufficient for domestic needs, is grown in various parts of the country. In 1971, thanks to favourable weather conditions, the wheat crop increased by 35 per cent to a new record level of 13.5 million tons, but this was

not repeated in 1972, or 1973 when the wheat crop fell to 10 million tons.

Cotton has only recently been taken seriously by Turkey, but its cultivation, mainly in the Izmir region and in the district round Adana, in southern Turkey, has been successful and great hopes are placed in it. Production has risen from under 200,000 tons in 1960 to 598,000 tons in 1974, with the result that cotton has become Turkey's single most profitable agricultural export: in 1973, cotton earned TL5,091 million, or approximately 31 per cent of total exports.

Turkey produces a particularly fine type of tobacco. The three principal producing regions are the Aegean district, the Black Sea coast, and the Marmara-Thrace region. The bulk of the crop is produced in the Aegean region, where the tobacco is notable for its light golden colour and mild taste. The finest tobacco is grown on the Black Sea coast, around Samsun. Although a traditional Turkish export, its relative position as an export has been declining in recent years. Exports in 1973 were worth TL1,783 million, or 10 per cent of total exports, most of which went to buyers in the United States and East European countries. The size of the crop fluctuates considerably: in 1974 it reached a record level of 196,000 metric tons, a considerable increase over the previous year's crop of 149,000 metric tons.

The coastal area of the Aegean, with mild winters and hot, dry summers produce the grape, fig and the olive. The outstanding product, however, is the sultana type of raisin, which is grown also in Cali-fornia and elsewhere. Turkey normally ranks second in the world as a sultana producer, but in good years such as 1970 (when the crop was 128,000 tons) becomes the largest producer in the world. In 1971, some 70,000 tons of sultanas were exported, with a total value of $20 million, which fell to $13.1 million in 1972, with a dramatic recovery to $56 million in 1973.

The Black Sea area, notably around the Giresun and Trabzon, produces the greatest quantity of hazel nuts (filberts) of any region in the world: in 1973—which was nearly a record year—a total of 251,000 tons of hazel nuts were harvested. Exports in 1973 amounted to $122 million. Substantial amounts of walnuts and almonds are also grown.

Tea is grown at the eastern end of the Black Sea, around Rize, and in other areas. Production from state tea plantations reached a record 46,000 tons in 1974.

Turkey is also an important producer of oilseeds, the principal varieties grown being sunflower, cotton, sesame and linseed. Output has expanded considerably, reaching 1.5 million tons in 1972.

Turkey was until 1972 one of the seven countries with the right to export opium under the UN Com-mission on Narcotic Drugs. Much opium was, how-ever, exported illegally, particularly to the U.S. and Iran; partly as a result of pressure from the U.S. Government, the Turkish Government made opium cultivation illegal in 1972, but the ban was lifted in July 1974.

Sheep and cattle are raised on the grazing lands of

the Anatolian plateau. Stock-raising forms an important branch of the economy. The sheep population of about 36.6 million (1973) is mainly of the Karaman type and is used primarily as a source of meat and milk. The bulk of the clip comprises coarse wool suitable only for carpets, blankets and poorer grades of clothing fabric, but efforts have been made in recent years to encourage breeding for wool and there are some 200,000 Merino sheep in the Bursa region.

The Angora goat produces the fine, soft wool known as mohair. Turkey is the second largest producer of mohair in the world; production averages 9,000 tons per annum.

Livestock production accounts for around 30 per cent of agricultural output and roughly 10 per cent of G.N.P. Increased production is aimed at under the five-year plans to cater for expected growth in home demand and also in export markets.

MINERALS

Turkey has a diversity of rich mineral resources, including large quantities of bauxite, borax, chrome, copper, iron ore, manganese and sulphur. Mining and quarrying employed 103,725 workers in 1970, and contributed only 1.5 per cent of the 1973 G.D.P. Mineral products amounting to $58.1 million were produced in 1972, accounting for 6 per cent of total exports. In spite of the importance of mining—particularly as a foreign exchange earner—investment in mining under the second five-year plan was set at TL4,100 or only 3.7 per cent of total planned allocations. This is attributed partly to the absence of an overall development strategy for the mining industry, where output is divided between the private and public sectors, and to the uneasy balance which has prevailed between the two sectors. The failings of the second plan have to some extent been ameliorated by the planned growth of 17 per cent a year to 1977 in the mining sector. The planned investment has been more than doubled to TL1,113 million. About 60 per cent of all mineral output and all coal production is carried out by State enterprises. The most important state enterprise in the mining sector is Etibank, which works through its subsidiaries, Eregli Coal Mines, East Chromium Mines, Turkish Copper, Keban Lead Mines and Keçiborlu Sulphur Mines. The state enterprises increased their predominance over the private sector during the early 1960s with an investment programme backed by the Mining Investment Bank, which was set up in 1962. The policy of encouraging the private sector to play a greater part in the mining industry through the establishment of the Turkish Mining Bank Corporation (TMBC) in 1968 has failed to overcome the general reluctance on the part of private investors to view mining as a worthwhile area for long-term investment, with the result that the private sector is undercapitalized. An additional factor militating against the development of mining has been the long-held suspicion of foreign investment in mining. An important development in the light of these considerations was that in early 1972 there was a bill before the Turkish Parliament for the

nationalization of boron minerals and lignite and for the prohibition of foreign investment in mining. When the bill was passed in May 1973, it had been amended merely to restrict foreign participation.

Bituminous coal is found at and around Zonguldak on the Black Sea coast. The seams are steeply inclined, much folded, and strongly faulted. The coal is generally mined by the longwall system or a variation of it. These mines constitute the Etibank's largest operation, and the coalfield is the largest in this part of the world, including the Balkans. Most of the seams are of good coking quality, the coke being used in the steel mills at nearby Karabük. Production of coal has risen from 3,772,000 tons in 1961 to 4,642,400 tons in 1973, lignite production from 1,594,000 tons in 1961 to 4,574,500 tons in 1973. It is thought that coal reserves may become exhausted by the mid-1980s when Turkey will become dependent on its lignite reserves. Lignite is found in many parts of central and western Anatolia. Seams located in western Turkey are operated by the West Lignite Mines, whose marketable production now exceeds 2,000,000 tons. Their reserves are estimated at some 1,500 million tons. The main mines, in addition to those operated by West Lignite Mines are at Soma, Degirmisaz and Tunçbilek. The domestic production of mineral energy (mainly petroleum and lignite) continues to increase. Several large-scale projects are being carried out to exploit these resources. These include the Keban Dam on the Euphrates river that is nearing completion, and a lignite plant in Elbistan (funded by the World Bank and the European Investment Bank) that will add significantly to the country's energy supply.

Practically all of Turkish iron ore comes from the Divrigi mine situated between Sivas and Erzurum in the north-east of the country and run by the Turkish Iron and Steel Corporation. The average grade of ore is from 60 to 66 per cent: reserves have been put at 28 million tons. Output varies with the needs of the Turkish iron and steel industry. Output of iron ore in 1973 amounted to 2,537,000 tons and is expected to register a significant increase when reserves in southern Turkey begin to be worked to serve the country's third major steelworks which is being built at Iskenderun.

Turkey is one of the world's largest producers of chrome. The richest deposits are in Guleman, south-eastern Turkey, in the vicinity of Iskenderun; in the area around Eskisehir, north-west Anatolia; and between Fethiye and Antalya on the Mediterranean coast. The Güleman mines, producing 25 per cent of the country's total, are operated by East Chromium Mines under Etibank. Other mines are owned and worked by private enterprise. Little chromium is used domestically and the mineral is the greatest foreign-exchange earner among mining exports. Chrome production in 1973 was 512,000 tons, and exports were worth $13.1 million.

Copper has been mined in Turkey since ancient times. Present-day production, conducted entirely by Etibank, comes from the Ergani Mines situated at Maden in Elâzığ, and the Morgul Copper Mine at

Borçka in Çoruh province. The latter mine is smaller, but is equipped with more modern plant. Output of pure copper came to 18,000 tons in 1973, while production of blister copper amounted to 22,500 tons, most of which was exported to West Germany, the United Kingdom and the United States. Known reserves of copper ore are put at 90 million tons, on which basis an annual production rate of some 50,000 tons is foreseen by the mid-1970s. Studies carried out by MTA have revealed the presence of a promising copper belt along the Black Sea coast, with possible reserves of 300 million tons of medium quality ore.

Eskişehir in north-west Anatolia is the world's centre of meerschaum mining. Meerschaum, a soft, white mineral which hardens on exposure to the sun and looks like ivory, has long been used by Turkish craftsmen for pipes and cigarette-holders, to which may now be added various items of costume jewellery.

Manganese, magnesite, lead, sulphur, salt, asbestos, antimony, zinc and mercury are important mineral resources. Of these, manganese ranks first in importance. Deposits, worked by private enterprise, are found in many parts of the country, but principally near Eskisehir and in the Eregli district. Production of manganese in 1973 amounted to 5,600 tons. Lead is mined at Keban, west of Elazig. Development of a new lead/zinc mine and electrolytic smelter in the Zantanti/Kayseri district is being undertaken by CINKUR, a private company 35 per cent owned by Etibank. It is planned that 40,000 tons of electrolytic zinc and 2,500 tons of refined lead will be produced annually by 1975. Production of sulphur from the Keciborlu mine in Isparta province was 23,600 tons in 1971. Antimony is mined in small quantities near Balikesir and Nigde.

The Uludag (Bursa) wolfram deposits have been calculated at 10,000 tons of tungsten ore, carrying an average grade of 0.43 per cent WO_3. These reserves are among the richest in the world. Etibank and the German firm of Krupp have entered into an agreement on the development of the deposits.

Turkey's bauxite deposits are about to be developed for the first time. An aluminium complex at Seydisehir, scheduled for completion by the end of 1972, is still under construction, and experiencing further delays. When completed, the plant, built with Soviet aid, will produce 60,000 tons of aluminium and 25,000 tons of semi-finished products. Bauxite will be supplied from the deposits located in Seydisehir, where the reserves are estimated at 30 million tons. When the plant is fully operational 80,000 tons of alumina will be available for export.

Oil was first struck in Turkey in 1950 and all subsequent strikes have been in the same area in the south-east of the country. Production of crude petroleum rose from 2,401,000 tons in 1966 to 3,505,000 tons in 1973; it now meets about half of Turkey's requirements. Four companies produce oil: (1) the Turkish Petroleum Corporation (TPAO), a 51 per cent state-sponsored Turkish company, at Garzan and Ramandag, with recently discovered deposits at Magrip, Batıraman and Kurtalan and the smaller fields at Kurtalan and Çelikli; (2) Mobil

at Bulgurdag, Silivanka and Selmo; (3) Shell at Kayaköy, Kurkan, Beykan and Sahaban; and (4) Ersan, a small private Turkish company, at Kahta. In 1973 the largest producer was Shell accounting for 58 per cent of output, followed by TPAO and Mobil. Ersan accounted for only around 50,000 tons. Recent discoveries are reported by the Turkish Government to have raised the country's reserves to some 500 million tons.

The largest oil refinery in Turkey, at Mersin, came on stream in June 1962. Built at a cost of $50 million, it has a capacity of 4,500,000 tons. It is operated by the Anatolian Refinery Company (ATAS), a Turkish-registered company owned by Mobil, Shell and BP. Fifteen per cent of the crude oil processed comes from the Mobil field at Bulgurdag and the Shell field at Karaköy; the remainder is imported from Iraq and Libya. The one million ton refinery at Izmit which came on stream in 1961, is wholly TPAO-owned, following the sale of Caltex's 49 per cent share to TPAO in 1972. The capacity of this refinery is being raised from 2.2 million to 5.5 million tons per annum. The TPAO operates a 660,000 tons per annum refinery at Batman, near Diyarbakır, connected by pipeline to both Garzan and Ramandag. Its capacity is being expanded to 800,000 tons per annum. A fourth refinery, with a 3 million ton per annum capacity, was under construction at Izmir in 1971 with Soviet aid. At present, two further refineries are planned, at Thrace, and at a site on the Black Sea.

TPAO operates a 310-mile, 18-inch diameter pipeline running from the oilfields around Batman to Dörtyol on the Gulf of Iskenderun. Daily throughput capacity is around 10,000 tons, but this may be increased to 16,000 tons. Other companies use the pipeline on a tariff basis.

INDUSTRY

The leading role in the process of inaugurating industrialization has been played by the state economic enterprises. Since 1950, however, private enterprise has been encouraged: although the state enterprises have not been denationalized, by the beginning of the 1970s the private sector accounted for about two-thirds of industrial output and its rate of capital investment had become almost equal to public sector investment. The share of industry in the economy is increasing: whereas in 1952 industry accounted for 12 per cent of domestic product this had increased to 18 per cent by 1970. Manufacturing accounted for 21.2% of G.D.P. in 1973. Simultaneously there has been a change in the structure of industry, away from the production of consumer goods to the production of secondary and even of capital goods. Whereas in 1962 consumer goods industries accounted for over two-thirds of industrial production, by 1969 its share had fallen to under 55 per cent. In the same period the share of the secondary goods industries increased from 17 to 30 per cent and that of capital goods from 12.9 to 14.1 per cent. Turkish industrial development has been protected from overseas competition by tariff and quota restrictions, with the result that Turkish industry is geared principally to the needs of the home market and manufactured goods account for only around 4 per cent of total exports. 1,263,624 workers, 9.41 per cent of the total employed population, were engaged in manufacturing industry in 1970.

The textile industry is Turkey's largest, employing around 275,000 persons and contributing about 16.5 per cent of industrial production at the beginning of the 1970s. The private sector accounts for 35 per cent of textile output. Production in the cotton industry has risen rapidly under the five-year plans, from 98,500 tons of yarn and 547.5 million metres of fabrics in 1962 to 200,000 tons and 950 million metres respectively in 1971. Yarn production for 1974 is estimated at 280,000 tons. During the same period, exports of cotton yarn and fabrics rose from $0.9 million to $28.4 million. There were 1.7 million cotton spindles in 1972 and this should reach 2.5 million by 1976 with yarn exports rising to $55–60 million and fabric exports to $26–30 million by 1977–78, by which time Turkey may begin to compete with developing countries such as Pakistan and Hong Kong. In comparison the development of the wool weaving industry has been slow with output rising from 20,000 tons of yarn and 23.6 million metres of fabrics in 1962 to 28,500 tons and 28 million metres respectively in 1969. Production declined to 27,000 tons in 1973.

The iron and steel works at Karabük, north-west Anatolia, are run by the state-controlled Turkish Iron and Steel Corporation. Capacity is 570,000 tons. A second iron and steel complex, at Eregli in west Anatolia, produces hot and cold rolled sheets, steel strip and tinplate. Production was disrupted at this plant during 1972 as a result of work to install an additional blast furnace and sintering plant. This should be completed by mid-1974 when plant capacity will be expanded from 600,000 to 1,250,000 tons. A new steel mill with a capacity of 1.2 million tons being built at Iskenderum under a credit agreement·with the Soviet Union is planned for completion also in 1974. In 1972 the merger of the Karabük works, the Divigri iron mine and the Iskenderum works was approved by the Turkish Parliament. Forty-nine per cent of the shares of the projected corporation will be sold to the public.

There are 31 cement factories with an annual capacity of nearly 10 million tons; more are under construction or planned. Production has been increasing steadily over recent years and in 1973 amounted to 8,948,000 tons, twice the figure for 1967.

Among food industries, the state-controlled sugar beet industry is the most important. Sugar production in 1973 totalled 724,000 tons. Production costs are very high and exports have to be heavily subsidized by the domestic market, except when the international price is very high.

The paper and board industry is dominated by the government-owned SEKA corporation which has one old established mill at Izmir with an annual capacity of 126,000 tons of paper and board plus three mills which were opened during 1971 with a combined annual capacity of 226,000 tons. SEKA's output in 1971 amounted to 154,000 tons, or 47 per cent of total paper and board production. Three further mills were opened during 1973.

The motor vehicle industry was established after 1956 as an import substitute industry and by 1971 had become the largest industrial employer after the textile industry. However, it accounted for only around 5 per cent of total industrial output. The total output of 25,000 trucks, pick-ups and buses and 46,000 saloon cars is fragmented between 15 enterprises with resulting loss of economies of scale. The process of merging of firms (there were 22 in 1967) is expected to continue under the impact of heavier taxation.

Turkey's first petro-chemicals complex, situated at at Izmit, began production in 1970 in ethylene, polythene, PVC, chlorine and caustic soda. In 1971 plans were under consideration for a second one, also at Izmit. Commercial fertilizer production has increased rapidly in recent years, reaching 1,673,000 tons in 1972, but falling to 572,000 tons in 1973. The state-owned Turkish Nitrates Corporation (TNC) has a nitrates plant at Kutahya with an annual capacity of 350,000 tons of nitrates, as well as a 220,000 tons triple superphosphates plant at Samsun and a superphosphates plant at Elazig also with 220,000 tons annual capacity. The Mediterranean Fertilizer Corporation's phosphates-nitrates complex at Mershin, based on by-products of the refinery there, began trial production in 1972. The TNC has plans for a plant with 1 million tons capacity in the Marmara region. In the private sector the capacities of the phosphates plants at Iskenderun and Yarimca were doubled in 1971 to 200,000 tons per annum each and converted to triple superphosphates.

Other manufacturing industries include tobacco, chemicals, pharmaceuticals, construction, metal working, engineering, leather goods, glassware and ferro-chrome.

Expansion is planned into a variety of fields, including aircraft production, dairy products and fruit-juice extraction.

There has been an extensive development of electrical energy; production in 1974 totalled 13,477 million kWh., of which 75 per cent was supplied by thermal sources and the remainder by hydroelectric plants.

Turkey's most ambitious power project, the Euphrates dam at Keban began production in 1973. The 670 ft. high dam will hold back a lake 70 miles long at the confluence of the two main branches of the Euphrates. The plant will have an initial capacity of 620,000 kW., rising to 1,240,000 kW. The power generated will go firstly through a 400-mile grid system to the industries of the north-western part of the country; but it is intended that the dam will also serve as the power basis for the development of the eastern part of Turkey, which in the past has lagged in industrial and agricultural wealth. The Gökçekaya hydro-electric station was completed in 1973 and the plant at Ambarli near Istanbul is being extended. There are many opportunities for further industrialization, but limitations are imposed by the slow growth of investment, the weak balance of payments that restricts the imports of capital equipment, and the large deficit incurred by the State Economic Resources. In 1973 industrial growth was 12.8 per cent, and in 1974 8.1 per cent.

FINANCE

The Central Bank (Merkez Bankasi), the sole bank of issue, started its operations on October 3rd, 1931. It controls exchange operations and ensures the monetary requirements of certain state enterprises by the discounting of bonds issued by these establishments and guaranteed by the Treasury. Other banks are described in the Finance section on page 753.

The monetary unit is the kuruş (piastre) by the law of April 1916. The Turkish lira (pound), which is, in practice, employed as the monetary unit, is made up of 100 kuruş.

The principal sources of budgetary revenue are income tax, import taxes and duties, production taxes, taxes and fees on services and revenues from State monopolies. From the beginning of 1962 agricultural incomes were taxed for the first time in recent history.

For the fiscal year 1973 (March 1st, 1973, to February 28th, 1974) general total budgetary revenue was TL61,056 million, and expenditure was TL62,143 million. According to provisional figures, the 1974 expenditure was TL75,229 million—an increase of 21.1 per cent in current expenditure—while revenues totalled TL73,381 million, a rise of 20.2 per cent.

The excess of spending over current budget appropriations was financed directly by the Central Bank. The money supply rose sharply in 1973 but was cut back sharply in the first half of 1974. Some indication of the growth rate which these figures reflect may be seen by comparing them with the fiscal year 1970 in which expenditures were TL28,860 million and revenue TL31,295 million. Taxes have been increased by unprecedented amounts over recent years, partially to counteract the traditional budget deficit, and to reduce the volume of deficit financing. The structural limits on expanding domestic production together with rising import prices led to high price increases. The wholesale price index rose by 32 per cent from July 1973 to July 1974 while the consumer price index rose by 17.6 per cent during 1974.

EXTERNAL TRADE

Before and during World War II, Turkish foreign trade figures showed a surplus of exports over imports. Since 1947 this position has been reversed, and the demands of Turkey's economic development, especially since 1950, have inflated the imports bill without making equivalent short-term additions to the country's exporting strength: in 1973 exports were only TL18,037 million compared with imports of TL29,265 million, giving a trading deficit of TL11,228 million. The trade deficit greatly increased in 1974, with imports (TL52,311 million) exceeding exports (TL21,197 million) by a record TL31,114 million. This visible trade deficit, equivalent to

U.S. $2,245 million in 1974, was partly offset by a net surplus on invisible items of $1,516 million in the same period. Turkish workers abroad sent back remittances worth $1,426 million. Due to the decline in economic activity in Western Europe and the consequent fall in recruitment of Turkish workers, remittances from overseas were expected to decrease in 1975. This, together with the high prices of imports, resulted in a fall in official reserves from $2,262 million at the end of July 1974 to $1,188 million at the end of April 1975. As a consequence of these developments the Turkish Government, which had revalued the lira in May 1974, was forced to devalue in September and again in April and July 1975.

The main exports by value in 1973 were cotton, fruit and nuts, tobacco, cattlecake and foodstuff residues, cereals and iron, chrome, manganese and other ores. The principal imports were machinery, chemicals, base metals, mineral products, vehicles, plastic and rubber. 46 per cent of Turkey's 1973 exports went to the EEC, 37 per cent to the original six members, and 10 per cent to the U.S.A. and Canada. By far the most important single customer was the Federal Republic of Germany, which is also the principal supplier of imports. 55 per cent of imports came from the EEC, 10 per cent from the U.S.A. and Canada.

An agreement with the European Economic Community was signed in September 1963 under which Turkey entered into a preparatory association with the Community. Turkey received $175 million in loans and preferential tariff quotas to help strengthen its economy to enable Turkey to meet the obligations involved in developing its association with the EEC. Early in 1973 Turkey entered into the second stage of its Association Arrangement with the EEC, the long-term aim being full membership in 1995.

PLANNING

During the years of the First Plan (1962–67) a real growth rate of 6.6 per cent per annum was achieved. Over 90 per cent of the scheduled investment targets were reached, private sector investment exceeding its target share of 40 per cent of total investment by a considerable margin.

The Second Five-Year Plan, covering the years 1968 to 1972, envisaged an annual growth rate of 7 per cent—the same as that targeted for the First Plan. This growth target was almost exactly achieved. Investment was planned to reach TL17,000 million in 1969 and to rise by some 11 per cent annually to nearly TL29,000 million by 1972. Total investment through the Second Plan was expected to be TL111,500 million from both the public and the private sectors. Foreign aid increased to $2,338 million by the end of 1970, a lower rate of increase than during the First Plan. Overseas loans of some $247 million in 1968 fell to $230 million in 1972. The long-term target of self-sustained economic growth, i.e. independent of foreign loans, is a prominent aim of the Third Five-Year Plan (1973–77). In addition, a substantial increase in revenues from foreign exchange is sought; for this reason heavy emphasis is now placed on export opportunities and import substitution.

The emphasis of the Second Plan was on industrial development and the reduction of the dependence of agriculture on weather conditions. Of total investment 22.4 per cent was allocated to manufacturing industry, a sum double the amount realized between 1963 and 1967 when certain projects were delayed. The Third Plan also places the emphasis on industrial develop-

ment, almost 45 per cent of the total investment being allocated to the mining and manufacturing industries. Priority is to be given to providing a modern heavy industry base to promote export opportunities and import substitution.

Government investment will concentrate on the infrastructure and education and health. Manufacturing industry will be mainly the responsibility of the private sector but the government will help out, if the private sector proves reluctant.

STATISTICAL SURVEY

AREA AND POPULATION

TOTAL AREA	THRACE	ANATOLIA	ESTIMATED POPULATION (July 1st, 1974)	WORKERS ABROAD (Sept. 27th, 1973)
779,452 sq. km.	23,764 sq. km.	755,688 sq. km.	38,270,000	649,454

CHIEF TOWNS
POPULATION (1973 estimate)

Ankara (capital)	.	1,461,346	Diyarbakir	. .	180,236
İstanbul	. .	2,376,296	Erzurum	. .	151,590
İzmir	. .	590,996	Samsun	. .	150,941
Adana	. .	383,045	Sivas	. .	150,267
Bursa	. .	318,209	Maraş	. .	149,603
Gaziantep	. .	274,999	Malatya	. .	144,248
Eskişehir	. .	243,327	İzmit	. .	141,681
Konya	. .	227,887	Mersin (İçel)	. .	130,256
Kayseri	. .	183,128	Elâziğ	. .	127,003

EMPLOYMENT*
(1970)

	MALE	FEMALE	TOTAL
Agriculture, Forestry, Hunting and Fishing .	4,249,184	4,513,539	8,762,723
Mining and Quarrying	101,684	2,041	103,725
Manufacturing Industries . .	1,004,596	259,028	1,263,624
Construction	409,796	2,267	412,063
Gas, Electricity and Water . .	16,551	453	17,004
Distributive Trades, Restaurants and Hotels .	706,346	30,720	737,066
Transport, Storage and Communications .	380,322	18,932	399,254
Financial, Insurance, Real Estate and Business Services	154,283	35,935	190,218
Community, Social and Personal Services .	1,448,514	207,448	1,655,962
Activities not Adequately Defined . .	117,328	15,416	132,744

* Based on a 1 per cent sample of the 1970 census results.

WORKERS ABROAD (September 27th, 1973)

Germany, Federal Republic	. .	528,200
Belgium	. .	10,000
Netherlands	. .	31,013
Austria	. .	26,931
Switzerland	. .	9,497
TOTAL (incl. others)	.	649,454

Remittances sent back to Turkey by workers abroad:

1969	U.S. $140,636,057	1972	U.S. $740,106,000
1970	U.S. $273,020,778	1973	U.S. $1,183,255,037
1971	U.S. $471,370,427	1974	U.S. $1,426,300,000

AGRICULTURE
UTILIZATION OF LAND

	AREA ('ooo hectares)				
	1969	1970	1971	1972	1973
Area under cultivation	24,672	24,296	24,527	25,073	25,013
Meadows and grazing lands*	n.a.	n.a.	n.a.	n.a.	n.a.
Market gardens and truck farms, orchards, olive groves, vineyards, etc.	2,960	3,043	3,082	3,183	3,276
Forests	18,273	18,273	18,273	18,273	19,136

* 26,135,000 hectares in 1967.

PRINCIPAL CROPS

CROP	AREA ('ooo hectares)			PRODUCTION ('ooo metric tons)		
	1972	1973	1974	1972	1973	1974
Wheat	8,700	8,850	8,750	12,200	10,000	11,000
Spelt	68	65	n.a.	75	80	82
Rye	625	610	600	755	690	560
Barley	2,530	2,550	2,580	3,725	2,900	3,330
Oats	295	280	275	396	380	380
Maize	617	625	620	1,030	1,100	1,200
Millet	38	38	30	52	31	40
Rice (paddy)	51	60	n.a.	203	265	n.a.
Mixed grain	222	225	n.a.	280	259	n.a.
Dry beans	106	100	100	159	148	145
Chick peas	178	186	175	183	185	195
Vetch	168	166	n.a.	152	131	n.a.
Potatoes	175	180	185	2,200	2,200	2,275
Onions (dry)	60	62	60*	575	610	635
Tomatoes	77*	78*	80*	2,000	2,050	2,160
Cabbages	26*	22*	n.a.	598	420	n.a.
Melons and water-melons . .	205	210*	n.a.	3,550	3,600*	n.a.
Aubergines (eggplants) . . .	33*	34*	n.a.	520	524*	n.a.
Cotton (lint)	} 760	677	838	{ 544	513	598
Cottonseed				870	821	957
Tobacco	352	323	377	180	130	179
Sugar beet	149	153	184	5,896	5,094	5,707
Sesame seed	63	48	46	33	26	29
Sunflower seed . . .	495	481	425	560	560	420
Olives	} 75,150†	77,530†	78,500†	{ 1,019	332	840
Olive oil				176	53	130
Tea	29	25*	26*	47	43	46

* FAO estimate.   † Number of trees.

FRUIT AND NUTS
(metric tons)

	1971	1972	1973	1974
Pears . . .	175,000	196,000	195,000	230,000
Apples . . .	780,000	850,000	850,000	920,000
Figs, Fresh . .	195,000	216,000	190,000	156,356
Grapes . . .	3,853,000	3,434,000	3,344,000	3,344,680
Walnuts . . .	110,000	113,000	98,000	110,000
Lemons . . .	141,500	149,000	137,000	265,000
Oranges . . .	460,000	467,000	470,000	500,000
Other Citrus Fruit .	92,000	112,000	99,000	135,000
Peaches . . .	84,000	140,000	120,000	160,000
Hazel-nuts (Filberts) .	166,000	190,000	251,000	244,000

LIVESTOCK
('ooo head at December*)

	1971	1972	1973		1971	1972	1973
Horses . .	1,027	962	936	Sheep . .	36,760	38,806	36,608
Asses . .	1,760	1,701	1,616	Goats . .	18,863	18,463	18,007
Mules . .	301	312	302	Buffaloes. .	1,026	1,039	1,023
Cattle . .	12,653	13,045	12,408	Camels . .	29	25	21
Chickens . .	34,612	36,361	38,329	Pigs . .	18	12	n.a.

* Poultry numbers refer to October.

MINING
PRODUCTION
('ooo metric tons)

MINERAL	1971	1972	1973	1974
Iron Ore (gross weight) . .	2,421	1,989	2,537	2,245
Chrome	926	688	512	694
Copper (Blister)† . .	18	17	32	29
Sulphur (Pure)† . .	24	21	18	19
Manganese . .	13.9	15.1	5.6	n.a.
Coal† . . .	4,639	4,641	4,642.4	4,973
Lignite† . . .	4,224	4,786	4,894	5,512
Crude Petroleum . .	3,453	3,388	3,505	3,209

† Public sector only. Total production of lignite was 5,336,000 metric tons in 1972.

INDUSTRY
SELECTED PRODUCTS

ITEM	UNIT	1971	1972	1973	1974
Paper . . .	'ooo tons	135	259	304	301
Cotton Yarn* . .	,, ,,	37	51	51.7	49
Woollen Yarn† . .	,, ,,	3.1	3.0	3.1	4
Cotton Fabrics‡ . .	million metres	216.4	227.3	218.8	209.9
Woollen Fabrics§ . .	,, ,,	5.0	4.7	4.5	5.5
Raki . . .	'ooo litres	9,118	10,754	12,059	14,648
Beer . . .	,, ,,	55,618	53,677	57,718	42,664
Tobacco . . .	'ooo tons	47	46	49	56
Pig Iron . .	,, ,,	880	1,134	896	1,200
Steel Ingots . .	,, ,,	1,117	1,442	1,163	1,458
Cement . .	,, ,,	7,553	8,425	8,948	8,931
Sugar . .	,, ,,	724	794	723	758
Commercial Fertilizers .	,, ,,	839	1,431	1,212	1,462
Sulphuric Acid (100%).	,, ,,	29	28	n.a.	n.a.
Electrolytic Copper .	,, ,,	7.1	7.3	8.8	9.9
Aluminium Sheets .	,, ,,	3.0	2.5	3.0	3.2
Polyethylene . .	,, ,,	10.2	12.4	22.0	28.4
Coke . . .	,, ,,	1,457	1,451	1,432	1,398
Motor Spirit . .	,, ,,	1,152	1,516	1,901	1,940
Kerosene . .	,, ,,	483	506	576	516
Distillate Fuel Oils .	,, ,,	2,081	2,518	3,055	3,004
Residual Fuel Oils .	,, ,,	4,022	4,710	5,612	5,564
Hydro-electricity .	million kWh.	2,587	3,209	2,619	3,356
Thermal Electricity .	,, ,,	7,114	8,033	9,679	10,121

* Public sector only. Total factory production in 1970 was 185,000 tons.

† Public sector only. Total production in 1971 was 26,500 metric tons.

‡ Public sector only. Total production in 1967 was 694 million metres, of which 27 per cent was produced by the public sector.

§Public sector only. Total production in 1970 was 30 million metres.

FINANCE

100 kuruş=1 Turkish lira (TL) or pound.

Coins: 5, 10, 25 and 50 kuruş; 1 and 2½ liras.

Notes: 5, 10, 20, 50, 100 and 500 liras.

Exchange rates (July 1975): £1 sterling=31.05 liras; U.S. $1=14.25 liras (export rate).

100 Turkish liras=£3.22=$7.02.

Note: Between June 1947 and August 1960 the exchange rate was U.S. $1=2.80 liras (1 lira=35.71 U.S. cents). From August 1960 to August 1970 the rate was $1=9.00 liras (1 lira=11.11 U.S. cents). Between August 1970 and December 1971 the mid-point rate was $1=15.00 liras (1 lira=6.67 U.S. cents), with an export (buying) rate of $1=14.85 liras and an import (selling) rate of $1=15.15 liras. From December 1971 to May 1974 the export rate was $1=14.00 liras (1 lira=7.14 U.S. cents) and the import rate was $1=14.30 liras. The rates were $1=13.50 liras (export) or 13.77 liras (import) from May-Sept. 1974, and $1=13.85 liras (export) or 14.13 liras (import) from September 1974 to April 1975. From April to July 1975 the export rate was $1=14.00 liras. In terms of sterling, the exchange rate between November 1967 and August 1970 was £1=21.60 liras; from August 1970 to December 1971 the mid-point rate was £1=36.00 liras; from December 1971 to June 1972 the export rate was £1=36.48 liras and the import rate £1=37.26 liras. Since June 1972, when sterling was allowed to "float", the exchange rates have been adjusted frequently.

GENERAL BUDGET

(TL million, fiscal year beginning March 1st)

REVENUE	1972*	1973*	EXPENDITURE	1972*	1973*
Tax Revenue	39,857	51,369	Finance	20,753	24,565
Taxes on Income	15,510	20,961	Defence	8,124	11,100
Income Tax	11,698	15,674	Education	7,069	8,922
Corporation Tax	2,100	2,996	Public Works, Health and Social		
Wealth Taxes	1,813	2,356	Welfare	2,158	2,543
Production	7,535	9,464	Agriculture	881	1,081
Expenditures	1,529	1,924	Rural Affairs	1,535	2,179
Services	4,539	5,667	Gendarmerie	871	1,283
Imports	8,931	10,997	Others	6,893	8,231
Other Normal Revenues	5,337	3,504			
Special Revenues and Funds	940	1,407			
			TOTAL EXPENDITURE	50,312	61,023
TOTAL REVENUES	46,134	56,280			

* Provisional figures. Revised totals (in TL million) are: Revenue 50,132 in 1972, 61,056 in 1973, 73,381 in 1974; Expenditure 49,868 in 1972, 62,143 in 1973, 75,229 in 1974.

NATIONAL ACCOUNTS

(TL million, at current prices)

	1971	1972	1973	1974
Agriculture and Livestock	50,144.4	59,332.5	66,874.8	112,552.7
Forestry	1,160.8	1,126.2	1,557.8	1,817.9
Fishing	316.8	392.1	496.0	747.0
Mining and Quarrying	3,234.8	3,794.3	4,197.3	5,502.7
Manufacturing	35,943.4	45,777.7	59,349.9	83,485.3
Electricity, Gas and Water Supply	2,846.8	3,069.6	3,526.0	5,570.0
Construction	10,311.3	12,621.1	16,076.8	20,365.0
Wholesale and Retail Trade	21,367.8	27,007.5	34,591.4	51,759.5
Transport and Communications	14,382.0	17,148.3	22,141.4	33,002.5
Financial Institutions	5,217.5	6,308.0	8,042.7	11,718.2
Private Professions and Services	9,583.8	11,759.3	14,358.1	21,108.3
Ownership of Dwellings	8,776.6	10,279.9	12,387.2	15,236.3
Less Imputed Bank Service Charge	2,932.3	3,489.4	4,449.0	6,482.2
DOMESTIC PRODUCT OF INDUSTRIES	159,753.7	195,127.1	239,150.4	356,383.2
Government Services	19,419.3	24,608.1	29,201.8	37,815.3
SUB-TOTAL	179,173.0	219,735.2	268,352.2	394,158.5
Import Duties	7,493.6	9,330.8	11,476.9	15,666.0
GROSS DOMESTIC PRODUCT	186,666.6	229,066.0	279,829.1	409,864.5
Net Factor Income from Abroad	5,469.0	8,694.4	15,056.8	17,351.3
GROSS NATIONAL PRODUCT	192,135.6	237,760.4	294,885.9	427,215.8

GOLD RESERVES AND CURRENCY IN CIRCULATION
(TL million, at year end)

	1970	1971	1972	1973	1974
Gold Reserves	1,886	1,820	1,904	2,114	2,049
Currency in Circulation . . .	11,850	13,917	15,978	20,700	26,151

CONSUMER PRICE INDEX
(Ankara—1968 = 100)

	1970	1971	1972	1973	1974
Food	118.2	134.7	149.5	179.4	213.7
Clothing	120.1	142.2	166.9	209.3	262.5
Household Expenditures . . .	114.2	135.3	154.5	182.4	225.7
Medical and Personal Care . .	104.1	119.6	131.6	146.2	156.0
Transportation	118.6	131.2	135.6	159.5	194.8
Cultural and Recreational Expenditures .	124.4	149.4	164.7	178.6	216.5

BALANCE OF PAYMENTS
(U.S. $ million)

	1971	1972	1973	1974
Exports f.o.b.	679	885	1,320	1,532
Imports f.o.b.	—1,058	—1,407	—1,880	—3,395
MERCHANDISE TRADE BALANCE . . .	—379	—522	—560	—1,863
Services (net)	301	590	1,110	1,387
Transfers (net)	102	56	75	69
CURRENT BALANCE	24	124	625	—408
Long-term capital (net) . . .	245	251	327	—4
Short-term capital (net) . . .	—66	629	—452	—266
CAPITAL BALANCE	179	880	—125	—270
Net errors and omissions . .	49	—250	35	319
TOTAL (net monetary movements) . .	252	753	534	—358
IMF Special Drawing Rights . .	16	17	—	—
Change in reserves, etc. . . .	268	771	534	—358

Source: IMF, *International Financial Statistics.*

EXTERNAL TRADE
(TL million)

	1968	1969	1970	1971	1972	1973	1974
Imports c.i.f. .	6,934.0	6,785.3	9,598.1	16,474.4	21,564.1	29,265.1	52,310.9
Exports f.o.b. .	4,467.8	4,831.5	6,407.7	9,090.0	11,875.9	18,037.4	21,197.3

COMMODITIES
(TL '000)

IMPORTS	1972	1973	1974
Live Animals and Animal Products . . .	20,690	62,172	46,935
Vegetable Products	162,999	554,009	3,866,905
Animal and Vegetable Oils and Fats . . .	254,485	42,570	293,765
Foodstuffs, Beverages and Tobacco . . .	32,820	35,494	961,065
Mineral Products	2,482,259	3,468,341	11,346,386
Chemicals	3,556,857	5,206,353	6,147,783
Plastic and Rubber	796,872	1,017,654	1,898,441
Hides and Skins	32,370	51,752	105,592
Wood	10,638	59,883	60,489
Paper-making Material	362,781	374,749	606,351
Textiles	777,344	754,076	1,469,724
Glassware, Ceramics	287,999	291,552	295,250
Base Metals	2,786,581	4,609,748	9,303,705
Machinery	7,137,340	9,058,688	11,404,006
Vehicles	2,359,402	3,038,232	3,457,767
Measuring Instruments . . .	461,319	588,451	766,887
All Other Products	41,315	49,623	279,801
TOTAL	21,564,071	29,263,347	52,310,852

EXPORTS	1972	1973	1974
Livestock	227,621	343,512	659,689
Fish	126,562	153,719	193,431
Fruit and nuts	2,524,877	3,420,011	3,964,401
Cereals	273,316	344,651	1,145
Oilseeds	192,914	250,044	165,236
Tannin materials, gums . . .	13,447	9,559	9,565
Cattlecake and foodstuff residues . .	370,743	552,292	550,328
Tobacco	1,701,555	1,782,960	2,838,146
Iron, chrome, manganese and other ores .	229,316	265,212	517,395
Hides and skins	43,423	56,536	16,150
Mohair, wool	94,248	180,342	75,206
Cotton	3,021,440	5,091,416	4,730,479
Copper and products . . .	11,411	81,772	305,633
All other products	3,045,003	5,505,404	7,170,483
TOTAL	11,875,876	18,037,430	21,197,287

PRINCIPAL COUNTRIES
(TL '000)

	IMPORTS			EXPORTS		
	1972	1973	1974	1972	1973	1974
Belgium/Luxembourg . . .	485,081	974,313	1,476,415	385,936	588,266	936,756
Czechoslovakia	176,218	157,720	228,544	180,885	143,163	234,186
France	1,467,631	1,878,396	3,386,383	682,488	995,325	918,367
Federal Germany . . .	3,957,941	5,824,646	8,074,167	2,495,360	3,044,297	4,738,285
German Democratic Republic .	116,172	136,994	109,512	98,059	93,699	116,336
Italy	2,356,718	2,416,127	3,786,135	718,749	1,577,483	1,251,681
Japan	464,206	841,407	2,798,069	133,971	223,056	251,961
Netherlands	626,541	1,400,891	1,625,536	371,616	564,358	725,111
Poland	101,023	116,846	413,125	63,340	86,805	137,303
Switzerland	1,046,645	1,781,266	2,960,027	1,018,961	1,585,854	1,303,438
U.S.S.R.	1,716,183	1,789,022	1,341,905	551,861	677,944	1,070,449
United Kingdom . . .	2,381,284	3,137,475	3,702,425	608,215	1,370,802	1,127,851
U.S.A.	2,494,341	2,545,112	4,813,474	1,374,858	1,797,120	1,997,625

Imports from Iraq (TL million): 747 in 1971; 431 in 1972; 476 in 1973.
Imports from Saudi Arabia (TL million): 318 in 1971; 743 in 1972; 1,201 in 1973.
Exports to Lebanon (TL million): 513 in 1971; 527 in 1972.

TOURISM

	1970	1971	1972	1973
Foreign Visitors to Turkey .	724,784	926,019	953,419	1,338,206
Income from Tourism ($'000) .	46,503	59,832	99,478	166,163

Foreign Visitors: 1,110,300 in 1974.

Tourist Accommodation (June 1974): 374 registered hotels, motels, boarding houses and holiday villages, with 20,811 rooms and 38,846 beds.

TRANSPORT

RAILWAYS
(millions)

	1972	1973	1974
Passenger kilometres .	5,337	5,215	5,753
Net ton-kilometres .	7,218	7,222	7,039

ROADS
(December 31st—'000)

	1972	1973	1974
Passenger Cars . .	185.3	234.6	303.8
Trucks . . .	142.2	159.4	175.0
Buses . . .	44.7	51.5	55.8
Motor Cycles . .	73.9	79.9	83.6

SHIPPING

		1971	1972	1973	1974
Vessels Entered*	('000 gross reg. tons)	13,704	16,538	18,376	15,942
Vessels Cleared*	(,, ,, ,, ,,)	13,550	16,827	18,169	15,942
Goods Loaded .	('000 metric tons)	3,957	4,999	4,798	4,305
Goods Unloaded	(,, ,, ,,)	11,189	12,231	16,074	17,630

* Includes vessels entered and cleared in ballast and loaded, but excludes coastal shipping.

CIVIL AVIATION
Turkish Airlines.
('000)

	1971	1972	1973	1974
Kilometres Flown . .	15,702	17,081	20,275	19,183
Passenger-kilometres . .	966,583	1,148,017	1,648,466	1,444,324
Cargo ton-kilometres . .	84,260	100,475	142,924	127,351
Mail ton-kilometres . .	1,432	1,393	1,527	1,479

EDUCATION
(1973–74)

	SCHOOLS	TEACHERS	PUPILS
Primary . .	40,342	156,717	5,327,089
Secondary .	3,020	40,351	1,231,433
Technical and Vocational .	977	16,848	285,447
Universities and Colleges . .	165	11,773	185,285

COMMUNICATIONS MEDIA

	1972	1973	1974
Telephones . .	473,462	531,367	588,000
Radio Licences .	3,958,767	4,033,478	4,091,142
TV Licences . .	157,226	266,922	455,752

Sources: State Institute of Statistics, Prime Minister's Office, Ankara, and *Review of Economic Conditions* (Türkiye İş Bankası A.Ş., Economic Research Dept., Ankara).

THE CONSTITUTION

PART ONE

Articles 1–9

The Turkish Republic is a nationalistic, democratic, secular and social State governed by the rule of law, based on human rights.

The Turkish State is an indivisible whole comprising the territory and people. Its official language is Turkish. Its capital is the city of Ankara.

Sovereignty is vested in the nation without reservation and condition. Legislative power is vested in the Turkish Grand National Assembly.

The right to exercise such sovereignty shall not be delegated to any one person, group or class.

The executive function shall be carried out by the President of the Republic and the Council of Ministers within the framework of law.

Judicial power shall be exercised by independent courts on behalf of the Turkish Nation.

Laws shall not be in conflict with the Constitution.

The provision of the Constitution establishing the form of the State as a republic shall not be amended.

PART TWO

Articles 10–62

Every individual is entitled, in virtue of his existence as a human being, to fundamental rights and freedoms, which cannot be usurped, transferred or relinquished.

All individuals are equal before the law irrespective of language, race, sex, political opinion, philosophical views, or religion or religious sect.

Status of aliens, personal immunities, freedom of communication, travel, residence, thought, belief, press and publications.

Right to controvert and rebut, to congregate, demonstrate and form associations.

Protection of individual rights.

PART THREE

Articles 63–66. Grand National Assembly

The Grand National Assembly of Turkey is composed of the National Assembly and the Senate of the Republic.

The two bodies meet in joint session in such instances as are provided in the Constitution.

The Grand National Assembly is empowered to enact, amend and repeal laws, to debate and adopt the bills on the State budget and final accounts, to pass resolutions in regard to minting currency, proclaiming pardons and amnesties, and to the carrying out of definitive death sentences passed by courts.

Articles 67–69. National Assembly

The National Assembly is composed of 450 deputies elected by direct general ballot. Election qualifications: elections shall be held every four years. The Assembly may hold new elections before the end of the four-year period.

Articles 70–73. The Senate

The Senate of the Republic is composed of 150 members elected by general ballot and 15 members appointed by the President of the Republic. Election qualifications: term of office is six years, one-third of members shall be re-elected every two years.

Articles 74–94. Elections, Members, Debates, Laws, Expenditure

Articles 95–101. The President of the Republic

The President of the Turkish Republic shall be elected for a term of seven years from among those members of the Turkish Grand National Assembly who have completed their fortieth year and received higher education; election shall be by secret ballot, and by a two-thirds majority of the plenary session. In case this majority is not obtained in the first two ballots, an absolute majority shall suffice.

The President is not eligible for re-election.

The President elect shall dissociate himself from his party, and his status as a regular member of the Grand National Assembly shall be terminated.

The President of the Republic is the head of the State. In this capacity he shall represent the Turkish Republic and the integrity of the Turkish Nation.

The President of the Republic shall preside over the Council of Ministers whenever he deems it necessary, shall dispatch the representatives of the Turkish State to foreign states, shall receive the representatives of foreign states, shall ratify and promulgate international conventions and treaties and may commute or pardon on grounds of chronic illness, infirmity or old age the sentences of convicted individuals.

The President of the Republic shall not be accountable for his actions connected with his duties.

All decrees emanating from the President of the Republic shall be signed by the Prime Minister, and the relevant Ministers. The Prime Minister and the Ministers concerned shall be responsible for the enforcement of these decrees.

The President of the Republic may be impeached for high treason upon the proposal of one-third of the plenary session of the Turkish Grand National Assembly, and conviction of high treason shall require the vote of at least a two-thirds majority of the joint plenary session of both legislative bodies.

Articles 102–109. The Council of Ministers

The Council of Ministers shall consist of the Prime Minister and the Ministers.

The Prime Minister shall be designated by the President of the Republic from among the members of the Turkish Grand National Assembly.

The Ministers shall be nominated by the Prime Minister, and appointed by the President of the Republic from among the members of the Turkish Grand National Assembly, or from among those qualified for election as deputies.

As head of the Council of Ministers, the Prime Minister promotes co-operation among the Ministries, and supervises the implementation of the Government's general policy. The members of the Council of Ministers are jointly and equally responsible for the manner in which this policy is implemented.

Each Minister shall be further responsible for the operations in his field of authority and for the acts and activities of his subordinates. The Ministers are subject to the same immunities and liabilities as the members of the Turkish Grand National Assembly.

Articles 110–111. National Defence

The office of the Commander-in-Chief is integrated in spirit in the Turkish Grand National Assembly and is represented by the President of the Republic.

The Council of Ministers shall be responsible to the Turkish Grand National Assembly for ensuring national security and preparing the armed forces for war.

The Chief of the General Staff is the Commander of the armed forces.

The Chief of the General Staff shall be appointed by the President of the Republic upon his nomination by the Council of Ministers, and his duties and powers shall be regulated by law. The Chief of the General Staff is responsible to the Prime Minister in the exercise of his duties and powers.

The National Security Council shall consist of the Ministers as provided by law, the Chief of the General Staff, and representatives of the armed forces.

The President of the Republic shall preside over the National Security Council, and in his absence this function shall be discharged by the Prime Minister.

Articles 112–125. Administration

Articles 126–131. Economic and Fiscal Provisions

The budget, accounts, development projects, natural resources.

Articles 132–136. The Judiciary

Judges shall be independent in the discharge of their duties. They shall pass judgment in accordance with the Constitution, law, justice and their personal convictions.

No organ, office, agency or individual may give orders or instructions to courts or judges in connection with the discharge of their judicial duty, send them circulars or make recommendations or suggestions.

No questions may be raised, debates held, or statements issued in legislative bodies in connection with the discharge of judicial power concerning a case on trial. Legislative and executive organs, and the administration are under obligation to comply with ruling of the courts. Such organs and the administration shall in no manner whatsoever alter court rulings or delay their execution.

Article 137. The Public Prosecutor

Article 138. Military Trial

Article 139. Court of Cassation

The Court of Cassation is the court of the last instance for reviewing the decisions and verdicts rendered by courts of law. It has original and final jurisdiction in specific cases defined by law.

Article 140. Council of State

The Council of State is an administrative court of the first instance in matters not referred by law to other administrative courts, and an administrative court of the last instance in general.

The Council of State shall hear and settle administrative disputes and suits, shall express opinions on draft laws submitted by the Council of Ministers, shall examine draft regulations, specifications and contracts of concessions, and shall discharge such other duties as prescribed by law.

Article 141. Military Court of Cassation

The Military Court of Cassation is a court of the last instance to review decisions and verdicts rendered by military courts. Furthermore, it shall try specific cases as a court of the first and last instance involving military matters as prescribed by law.

Article 142. Court of Jurisdictional Disputes

The Court of Jurisdictional Disputes is empowered to settle definitively disputes among civil, administrative and military courts arising from disagreements on jurisdictional matters and verdicts.

Articles 143–144. Supreme Council of Judges

Articles 145–152. The Constitutional Court

AMENDMENTS

Article 73 concerning membership of the Senate of the Republic, and Article 131 concerning the preservation of forests, were amended on April 17th, 1970.

Article 56 concerning financial aid to political parties, and Article 82 concerning the monthly allowances of members of the National Assembly were amended on June 30th, 1971.

On September 22nd, 1971, thirty-five articles were amended and nine temporary articles added. These amendments were aimed at preventing the abuse of liberties by making use of gaps existing in the Constitution, and at providing greater clarity in certain articles.

Five articles (30, 57, 136, 138 and 148) were changed and two temporary articles were added on March 15th, 1973. The addition to Article 36 set up State Security Courts.

THE GOVERNMENT

THE HEAD OF STATE

President: Admiral FAHRI KORUTÜRK (elected April 1973).

Principal Secretary of President's Office: FUAT BAYRAMOĞLU.

COUNCIL OF MINISTERS

(July 1975)

Prime Minister: SÜLEYMAN DEMIREL.

Deputy Prime Ministers: Prof. NECMETTIN ERBAKAN, TURHAN FEYZIOĞLU, Col. ALPARSLAN TÜRKEŞ.

Ministers of State: SEYFI ÖZTÜRK, HASAN AKSAY, MUSTAFA KEMAL ERKOVAN, GIYASETTIN KARACA.

Minister of Justice: ISMAIL MÜFTÜOĞLU.

Minister of National Defence: FERIT MELEN.

Minister of Interior: OĞUZHAN ASILTÜRK.

Minister of Foreign Affairs: IHSAN SABRI ÇAĞLAYANGIL.

Minister of Finance: YILMAZ ERGENEKON.

Minister of National Education: AL NAILI ERDEM.

Minister of Public Works: FEHIM ADAK.

Minister of Commerce: HALIL BAŞOL.

Minister of Health and Social Welfare: Dr. KEMAL DEMIR.

Minister of Customs and Monopolies: ORHAN ÖZTRAK.

Minister of Food, Agriculture and Husbandry: Prof. KORKUT ÖZAL.

Minister of Communications: NAHIT MENTEŞE.

Minister of Labour: AHMET TEVFIK PAKSU.

Ministry of Industry and Technology: ABDULKERIM DOĞRU.

Minister of Energy and Natural Resources: SELÂHATTIN KILIÇ.

Minister of Tourism and Information: LÜFTÜ TOKOĞLU.

Minister of Housing and Reconstruction: NURETTIN OK.

Minister of Rural Affairs and Co-operatives: VEFA POYRAZ.

Minister of Forestry: TURHAN KAPANLI.

Minister of Youth and Sport: ALI ŞEVKI EREK.

Minister of Culture: RIFKI DANIŞMAN.

Minister of Social Security: AHMET MAHIR ABLUM.

GRAND NATIONAL ASSEMBLY

(Seats as at June 1975)

SENATE

President: TEKIN ARIBURUN.

PARTY	SEATS
Justice Party	82
Republican People's Party . . .	43
Republican Reliance Party . . .	7
Democratic Party	3
National Salvation Party . . .	3
National Action Party	2
Turkish Workers' Party . . .	—
Nation Party	—
Independents	7
Presidential Appointees . . .	13
Life Senators	18
Vacant	6
Ex-Presidents of the Republic . .	1
TOTAL	185

NATIONAL ASSEMBLY

President: KEMAL GÜVEN.

PARTY	SEATS
Justice Party	149
Republican People's Party . . .	189
Republican Reliance Party . . .	10
Democratic Party	26
National Salvation Party . . .	49
National Action Party	3
Turkish Workers' Party . . .	—
Nation Party	—
Independents	18
Vacant	6
TOTAL	450

Elections to the Senate and National Assembly last held in October 1973.

POLITICAL PARTIES

Adalet Partisi (*Justice Party*): Ankara; f. 1961; Leader SÜLEYMAN DEMIREL; Sec.-Gen. NIZAMETTIN ERKMEN; supports private enterprise within a mixed economy.

Cumhuriyet Halk Partisi (*Republican People's Party*): Ankara; f. 1923 by Kemal Atatürk; Leader BÜLENT ECEVIT; Sec.-Gen. ORHAN EYUPOĞLU; favours a considerable degree of State enterprise along with continuing private enterprise. In recent years the party has moved to the left of centre.

Demokratik Parti (*Democratic Party*): Ankara; f. 1970 by deputies and senators expelled from the Justice Party; nationalist and traditionalist; Leader FERRUH BOZBEYLI.

Republican Reliance Party (C.G.P.): Ankara; f. 1967 as the National Reliance Party by 45 members of Parliament from the Republican People's Party, who broke away as a result of this party's "left of centre policies"; merged with Republican Party 1973; Leader Prof. TURHAN FEYZIOĞLU.

Nation Party (M.P.): Ankara; f. 1962; traditional and religious in character; Leader CEMAL TURAL.

National Action Party (M.H.P.): 3 Cadde 47, Bahçelievler, Ankara; f. 1948; favours integrity, secularism, nationalism, communal progress, increased scientific activities and development; supports close co-operation between the public and private sectors; Leader ALPARSLAN TÜRKES; Sec.-Gen. OSMAN ALBAYREK; publs. *Devlet* (weekly), *Tore* (monthly).

Turkish Unity Party (T.B.P.): Ankara; f. 1968; Conservative; Leader MUSTAFA TIMISI.

National Salvation Party (M.S.P.): Ankara; f. 1972; traditionalist, Islamic; took place of National Order Party which was closed down by order of the Constitutional Court; joined coalition government with Republican People's Party January 1974; leader NECMETTIN ERBAKAN.

Turkiye Sosyalist İşci Partisi (*Turkish Socialist Workers' Party*): Ankara; f. 1974; supports nationalization of major sectors of the economy, withdrawal from NATO and CENTO; Chair. AHMET KACMAZ; Sec.-Gen. YALCIN YUSUFOĞLU.

DIPLOMATIC REPRESENTATION

EMBASSIES AND LEGATIONS ACCREDITED TO TURKEY

(In Ankara unless otherwise stated)

Afghanistan: Çankaya, Cemal Nadir Sok. No. 25; *Ambassador:* MUHAMMED SAID.

Algeria: Çankaya, Cinnah Cad. 90/9-10; *Chargé d'Affaires:* MOHIEDDINE ABED.

Argentina: Rıza Şah Pehlevi Caddesi 57/1; *Ambassador:* JORGE GASTON BLANCO VILLALTA.

Australia: Gaziosmanpaşa, Nenehatun Cad. 83; *Ambassador:* J. M. MCMILLAN.

Austria: Atatürk Bulvarı 197; *Ambassador:* Dr. FRANZ HERBATSCHEK.

Belgium: Şehit Ersan Caddesi 42/1-2-4; *Ambassador:* JEAN DE BASSOMPIERRE.

Brazil: Çankaya, Alaçam Sokak, 10/4-5; *Ambassador:* Dr. WAGNER PIMENTA-BUENO.

Bulgaria: Atatürk Bulvarı 120; *Ambassador:* MARIN VATCHOV.

Cameroon: Cairo, Egypt.

Canada: Nenehatun Cad. No. 75, Gaziosmanpaşa; *Ambassador:* K. B. WILLIAMSON.

Chad: *Ambassador:* JOSEPH CHÉDID.

Chile: Çankaya, Abdullah Cevdet Sokak 20/2; *Ambassador:* RUDI GEIGER.

China, People's Republic: Yukarı Ayrancı 8, Durak Hoşdere Cad. 147; *Ambassador:* LIU CHUN.

Czechoslovakia: Ataturk Bulvarı 261; *Ambassador:* Dr. PETR BRUDNAK.

Denmark: Kırlangıç Sokak 42, Gaziosmanpaşa; *Ambassador:* S. SANDAGER JEPPESEN.

Dominican Republic: London, England.

Egypt: Atatürk Bulvarı 30; *Ambassador:* AHMED HAMDY.

El Salvador: Bonn, Federal Republic of Germany.

Ethiopia: Alabaş Sokak 2/10, Çankaya; *Ambassador:* Col. BALACHEW JAMANEH.

Finland: Galip Dede Sokak 1/20, Farabi; *Ambassador:* WILHELM SCHRECK.

France: Paris Cad. 70, Kavaklıdere; *Ambassador:* ROGER VAURS.

Ghana: Rome, Italy.

Greece: Fatma Aliye Sokak 1, Kavaklidere; *Ambassador:* DIMITRI COSMADOPOULOS.

Hungary: Gazi Mustafa Kemal Bulvarı 10; *Ambassador:* KAROLY KAPCSOS.

Iceland: Copenhagen, Denmark.

India: Kıbrıs Sokak 24, Çankaya; *Ambassador:* NEDYAM BALACHANDRAN MENON.

Indonesia: Abdullah Cevdet Sokak No. 12, Çankaya; *Ambassador:* Brig.-Gen. MUKHLAS ROWI.

Iran: Tahran Cad. 10; *Ambassador:* DJAMCHID GHARIB.

Iraq: Turan Emeksiz Sokak 11, Gaziosmanpaşa; *Ambassador:* Dr. MAHMOUD ALI EL-DAOUD.

Ireland: Rome, Italy.

Israel: Farabi Sokak 32, Çankaya; *Chargé d'Affaires:* SHMUEL DIVON.

Italy: Atatürk Bulvarı 118; *Ambassador:* GIORGIO SMOQUINA.

Japan: Gazi Osman Pasa, Resit Galip Cad. 81; *Ambassador:* TATSUO HIROSE.

Jordan: Dede Korkut Sokak 18, Çankaya; *Ambassador:* ZUHEYR EL MUFTI.

Korea, Republic: Cinnah Caddesi Alaçam Sokak 9; *Ambassador:* HAN LIM LEE.

Kuwait: Cinnah Caddesi 88/3-4, Çankaya; *Ambassador:* JASEM M. BOURISLY.

Lebanon: Cinnah Caddesi 11/3, Çankaya; *Ambassador:* FAIÇAL SULTAN.

Libya: Ebuzziya Tevfik Sokak 5, Çankaya; *Ambassador:* SAADEDDIN M. ABUSHWERB.

Malaysia: Teheran, Iran.

Mexico: Abdullah Cevdet Sokak 20/1, Çankaya; *Ambassador:* ALFONSO CASTRO-VALLE.

Morocco: Atatürk Bulvarı No. 223/9; *Ambassador:* Dr. AHMED BENABUD.

Nepal: Islamabad, Pakistan.

Netherlands: Şehit Ersan Cad. 4, Çankaya; *Ambassador:* C. TH. R. VAN BAARDA.

Nigeria: Farabi Sok. 8, Çankaya; *Ambassador:* Brig.-Gen. GEORGE T. KURUBU.

Norway: Bölük Cad. 14, Gaziosmanpaşa; *Ambassador:* DITLEF KNUDSEN.

Pakistan: Rıza Şah Pehlevî Caddesi No. 1; *Ambassador:* ALTAF AHMED SHEIKH.

Peru: Vienna, Austria.

Philippines: Rome, Italy.

Poland: Atatürk Bulvarı 251; *Ambassador:* IGNACY LOGA-SOWIŃSKI.

Portugal: Cinnah Caddesi 28/3; *Ambassador:* ANTONIO PINTO DE MESQUITA.

Romania: Bükreş Sok. 4, Çankaya; *Ambassador:* Dr. GEORGE MARIN.

Saudi Arabia: Abdullah Cevdet Sok. 18, Çankaya; *Ambassador:* MOHAMMAD SAID BASRAWI.

Senegal: Teheran, Iran.

Spain: Abdullah Cevdet Sokak No. 8, Çankaya; *Ambassador:* EMILIO GARRIGUES DIAZ-CAÑABATE.

Sudan: Teheran, Iran.

Sweden: Kâtip Çelebi Sok. 5; *Ambassador:* M. L. S. MATHEUS LUNDBORG.

Switzerland: Atatürk Bulvarı 263; *Ambassador:* CHARLES MASSET.

Syria: Çankaya, Abdullah Cevdet Sok. 7; *Ambassador:* Dr. SALAH EADINE TARAZI.

Thailand: Cinnah Caddesi 7/12, Kavaklıdere; *Ambassador:* SONDHI DHANASUNTHON.

Tunisia: Farabi Sokak 48/5-6; *Ambassador:* SALAH LADGHAM.

U.S.S.R.: Karyağdı Sokak 5, Çankaya; *Ambassador:* ALEXEI ALEXEIEVICH.

United Kingdom: Çankaya, Şehit Ersan Cad. 46/A; *Ambassador:* Sir HORACE PHILLIPS.

U.S.A.: Atatürk Bulvarı 110; *Ambassador:* WILLIAM B. MACOMBER.

Vatican: Gaziosmanpaşa Reşit Galip Cad. 94 (Apostolic Internunciature); *Apostolic Internuncio:* Mgr. SALVATORE ASTA.

Venezuela: Kavaklıdere Cad. 23/6; *Ambassador:* LUIS ALBERTO OLAVARRIA.

Yugoslavia: Paris Cad. 47, Kavaklıdere; *Ambassador:* EDUARD KLUJN.

Zaire: Cairo, Egypt.

Turkey also has diplomatic relations with Barbados, Cuba, Guinea, Laos, Malawi, Mauritania, Mongolia, Qatar, Sierra Leone, Somalia, Uruguay and the Yemen Arab Republic.

JUDICIAL SYSTEM

Until the foundation of the new Turkish Republic, a large part of the Turkish civil law—the laws affecting the family, inheritance, property, obligations, etc.—was based on the Koran, and this holy law was administered by special religious (Sharia) courts. The legal reform of 1926 was not only a process of secularization, but also a radical change of the legal system. The Swiss Civil Code and the Code of Obligation, the Italian Penal Code, and the Neuchâtel (Cantonal) Code of Civil Procedure were adopted and modified to fit Turkish customs and traditions.

Constitutional Court: Consists of fifteen regular and five alternate members. Reviews the constitutionality of laws passed by the Turkish Grand National Assembly. Sits as a High Council empowered to try senior members of state. The rulings of the Constitutional Court are final. Decisions of the Court are published immediately in the Official Gazette, and shall be binding on the legislative, executive, and judicial organs of the State.

Court of Cassation: The court of the last instance for reviewing the decisions and verdicts rendered by courts of law. It has original and final jurisdiction in specific cases defined by law. Members are elected by the Supreme Council of Judges.

Council of State: An administrative court of the first instance in matters not referred by law to other administrative courts, and an administrative court of the last instance in general. Hears and settles administrative disputes and expresses opinions on draft laws submitted by the Council of Ministers.

High Military Administrative Court: A military court for the judicial control of administrative acts concerning military personnel.

Military Court of Cassation: A court of the last instance to review decisions and verdicts rendered by military courts.

Court of Jurisdictional Disputes: Settles disputes among civil, administrative and military courts arising from disagreements on jurisdictional matters and verdicts.

Supreme Council of Judges: Consists of eighteen regular and five alternate members. Decides all personnel matters relating to judges.

Public Prosecutor: The law shall make provision for the tenure of public prosecutors and attorneys of the Council of State and their functions.

The Chief Prosecutor of the Republic, the Chief Attorney of the Council of State and the Chief Prosecutor of the Military Court of Cassation are subject to the provisions applicable to judges of higher courts.

Military Trial: Military trials are conducted by military and disciplinary courts. These courts are entitled to try the military offences of military personnel and those offences committed against military personnel or in military areas, or offences connected with military service and duties. Military courts may try non-military persons only for military offences prescribed by special laws.

State Security Courts: Set up by supplement to Article 136 of Constitution in March 1973 to prosecute offences against integrity of the State. Consist of presiding judge, four regular and two substitute judges, a public prosecutor and assistant public prosecutors.

RELIGION

MUSLIMS

Diyanet İsleri Reisi (*Head of the Muslim Faith in Turkey*): LÛTFI DOĞAN (ad interim).

Over 98 per cent of the Turkish people are Muslims, mainly Sunnis. Under the Republic, from 1923 onwards, action was taken to reduce the influence of religion on state affairs: e.g., its association with the schools was curtailed, mosques and churches were sometimes closed and facilities denied to their adherents, both Muslim and Christian. The Muslim faith was also disestablished. After 1950 there was a change, and religious life was to a certain extent revived. The revolution of 1960 brought about a return to the more secular republic of Atatürk but the formation of the Ecevit coalition Government in 1974 once again established links between church and state. The National Salvation Party, the junior members of the coalition, are committed to a return to the traditions and values of Islam, and government aid was promised for the building of mosques.

ROMAN CATHOLIC CHURCH

ARMENIAN RITE

Patriarchate of Cilicia: Patriarchat Arménien Catholique, Beirut, Lebanon; Patriarch IGNACE PIERRE XVI BATANIAN.

Archbishopric of Istanbul: Sakızağacı Cad. N. 31, P.K. 183, Beyoğlu, Istanbul; f. 1830; 3 secular priests, 6 religious priests, 7,400 Catholics (1974); Archbishop JEAN TCHOLAKIAN.

BYZANTINE RITE

Apostolic Exarchate of Istanbul: Beyoğlu, Hamalbaşı Cad. 44, Istanbul; f. 1860; 1 secular priest, 80 Catholics (1974); Exarch: (vacant).

CHALDEAN RITE

Archbishopric of Diarbekir: Archeveché Chaldéen, Beyoğlu, B.P. 280, Istanbul; 6 secular priests, 10,000 Catholics (1972); Archbishop GABRIEL BATTA.

Bishopric of Mardin: (vacant).

LATIN RITE

Metropolitan See of Izmir: Atatürk Cad. 210/6, P.K. 267, Izmir; 12 priests, 2,760 Catholics; Metropolitan JOHN HENRY BOCCELLA.

Apostolic Vicariate of Asia Minor: JOHN HENRY BOCCELLA.

Apostolic Vicariate of Istanbul: Satirci Sok. 2, Pangelti, Istanbul; 6 secular priests, 45 religious priests, 5,500 Catholics (1974); Apostolic Administrator Mons. PIERRE DUBOIS, O.F.M.

Mission of Trabzon: Katolik Kilisesi, P.K. 5, Samsun; 2 priests, 177 Catholics (1974); Superior Rev. P. GERMANO DA VERICA.

OTHER RELIGIONS

Mainly Greek Orthodox and Jews.

THE PRESS

Under the Constitution of 1961, "the press is free within the limits of the law". Provision is made for recourse to a constitutional court in issues involving laws affecting the Press.

Following the Revolution of 1960 and the new Constitution, which also introduced a measure of protection for editors, came the Law for Preventive Measures of March 1962. This law provided penalties of imprisonment with forced labour for persons criticizing the 1960 Revolution or for defending the pre-1960 or pre-Atatürk régimes, or suggesting that Turkey is unable to thrive as a democracy.

Political offences affecting the Press and the protection of the State and civil order are treated in Articles 141 and 142 of the Penal Code, the latter providing penalties of up to 15 years imprisonment for Communist propaganda. Articles 158 and 159 penalize defamation of the President, the Republic, the nation and institutions such as the army, parliament and the courts.

A further measure of press control is provided by the Board of Official Announcements which supervises the distribution of government announcements and advertising, which serve as an essential subsidy to the Press. The period of military rule from 1971 to 1973 was marked by the closure of many left-wing newspapers and magazines, as part of the repressive measures taken under martial law. The popular newspaper *Akşam* was closed by the military authorities for deriding the decisions of military courts, and military censorship was imposed on Turkish news agencies. The withdrawal of the armed forces from political affairs has brought about a larger measure of freedom.

It is almost impossible to produce a correct list of the numerous provincial newspapers, which tend to be small in circulation and rather short-lived. In all, there are some 372 daily papers, 260 weeklies and magazines, over 200 fortnightly and monthly and about 25 quarterly, six-monthly and annually published magazines. The estimated total circulation of all the daily papers is 1,353,000.

Formerly most newspapers were family businesses, but recently companies have emerged and newspaper groups are beginning to develop. *Hürriyet*, *Milliyet* and *Hayat* each head a group of papers. The Hürriyet Group includes *Hürriyet*, *Günaydın* and several weekly and monthly papers and its own news agency. The Hayat Group, which is the largest group owning periodicals, includes *Hayat*, *Ses* (the cinema and arts magazine), and several children's periodicals. Most papers are politically independent. A small number, while not being political organs, are indirectly associated with political parties. Noteworthy among these are *Barış*, which supports the Republican People's Party, and *Son Havadis*, which supports the Justice Party.

Almost all Istanbul papers are also printed in Ankara and İzmir on the same day, and some in Adana. Among the most serious and influential papers are the dailies *Milliyet* and *Cumhuriyet*. *Akbaba* is noted for its political satire. The most popular dailies are the Istanbul papers *Hürriyet*, *Milliyet*, *Tercüman*, *Son Havadis*, *Günaydın* and *Cumhuriyet*; *Yeni Asır*, published in İzmir, is the best selling quality daily of the Aegean region. A major popular weekly is the illustrated magazine *Hayat*.

PRINCIPAL DAILIES

ADANA

Çukurova: Kızılay Cad.; f. 1961; political; Editor MEHMET OLGUNBAŞ; circ. 1,950.

Vatandaş: Dörtyolağzı 117 Sok. 11; f. 1951; political; Editor MİTHAT GÜLYAŞAR; circ. 1,700.

Yeni Adana: Kızılay Cad. 65; f. 1918; political; Editor ÇETİN R. YÜREGİR; circ. 2,000.

ANKARA

Adalet: Agâh Efendi Sok.; f. 1962; morning; political, supports the Democratic Party; Editor TURHAN DİLLİGİL; circ. 16,500.

Ankara Ekspres: Rüzgârlı Sok. 3; f. 1968; political; Editor YAŞAR AYSEV; circ. 4,150.

Ankara Ticaret Postası: Rüzgârlı Sok., O.W. Han; f. 1954; commercial; Editor CAHİD BAYDAR; circ. 3,000.

Barış: Şinasi Sok., Ulus; f. 1971; morning; political, supports the Republican People's Party; Editor CEMALETTİN ÜNLÜ; circ. 15,700.

Başkent: Rüzgârlı Sok. 21/2; f. 1968; political; Publisher İSMET ÖZKAN; circ. 4,100.

Ekonomide Egemenlik: Atatürk Bulvarı 137/2; f. 1970; commercial; Editor FEHMİ ANLAROĞLU.

Halkçı: Rüzgârlı Sok. 39; f. 1956; evening; Editor ERDOĞAN TOKATLI; circ. 4,100.

Hür Anadolu: Rüzgârlı Sok. 21; f. 1967; political; Editor MUSTAFA ÖZKAN; circ. 4,050.

İktisadi İnkılâp: Plevne Sok. 12, Ulus; f. 1957; commercial; Editor ÜNSAL ÖZMEN; circ. 1,600.

İktisat ve Piyasa: İzmir Cad. 22/9; f. 1964; commercial; Proprietor ÜLKÜ BİLGİN; circ. 1,900.

İş ve Ekonomi: Rüzgârlı Sok., O.W. Han; f. 1964; Publisher-Editor COŞKUN BÖLÜKBAŞIOĞLU; circ. 2,000.

Memleket: Rüzgârlı Sok. 21/3; f. 1970; political; Editor ŞEMSİ BELLİ.

Resmi Gazete: Başbakanlık Neşriyat, ve Müdevvenat Genel Müdürlüğü; f. 1920; official gazette.

Tasvir: Ulus Han, Kat 5, Ulus; f. 1960; political; Propr. ŞAHIN AYMETE; Man. Dir. ŞAHAP GENSOY; circ. 8,500.

Turizm Ticaret: Çelikkale Sok. 8/12, Kızılay; f. 1970; commercial; Editor MEHMET EREN.

Turkish Daily News: Konur Sok. 16, Yenişehir; f. 1961; English language; Publisher-Editor İLHAN ÇEVİK; circ. 5,500.

Turkiye İktisat Gazetesi: Karanfil Sok. 56, Bakanlıklar; f. 1953; commercial; Editor SELAHATTIN TEDMAN.

Vatan: İbrahim Müteferrika Sok. 2/2; f. 1940; evening; Publisher NAİM TİRALİ; Editor MÜFİT DURU; circ. 5,500.

Yenigün: Rüzgârlı Sok. 45/8, Ulus; f. 1968; political; Editor KEMAL YAZGAN; circ. 4,000.

Yeni Tanin: Agâh Efendi Sok. 2/A, Ulus; f. 1964; political; Editor KEMAL YAZGAN; circ. 4,000.

Zafer: Çankırı Cad. 14; f. 1963; morning; political; Proprietor MUAMMER KIRANER; circ. 11,000.

BURSA

Bursanın Sesi: Yeniyol, Ersan İşhanı; f. 1969; political; Editor NECATİ AKGÜN; circ. 800.

Haber: Kümbet Sok. 7; f. 1964; political; Editor TURHAN TAYAN; circ. 1,200.

Hakimiyet: Başak Cad. 5; f. 1950; political; Editor MUSTAFA TAYLA; circ. 5,500.

Millet: Ankara Cad. 59; f. 1960; political; Editor FATMA MAT; circ. 900.

ESKİŞEHİR

İstikbal: Çarşı, Değirmen Sok. 15/A; f. 1950; political; Editor İRFAN UĞURLUER.

Milli İrade: Uygur Sok. 1; f. 1968; political; Editor ERDOĞAN KÂHYA.

Sakarya: Hacet Sok. 3; f. 1947; political; Editor BOZKURT ÜNÜGÜR.

ISTANBUL

Akşam: Mollafenari Sok. 30; f. 1918; independent; Editor İRFAN DERMAN; circ. 42,000; (closed down by the military authorities in February 1972).

Apoyevmatini: Suriye Çarşısı 10, Beyoğlu; f. 1925; Greek language; Publisher TAKVOR ACUN; circ. 3,500.

Babıalide Sabah: Sultanahmet, Adliye Bitişiği; f. 1965; political; Editor SABRİ YILMAZ; circ. 7,300.

Bizim Anadolu: Şeref Efendi Sok., Cağaloğlu; f. 1969; political; Editor ABDÜLKADİR BİLLURCU.

Cumhuriyet: Halkevi Sok. 39, Cağaloğlu; f. 1924; morning; independent political; Editor OKTAY KURTBÖKE; circ. 90,000.

Dünya: Narlıbahçe Sok. 15, Cağaloğlu; f. 1952; morning; political; Editor TEKİN GÜZELBEYOĞLU; circ. 14,500.

Ekonomi: Cemal Nadir Sok. 22, Cağaloğlu; f. 1944; commercial; Editor SAFA ÇELİKER; circ. 1,500.

Ekspres: Şeref Efendi Sok. 44, Cağaloğlu; f. 1962; evening; Editor COŞKUM ÖZER.

Embros: Galip Dede Cad. 103, Tünel; f. 1953; Greek language; evening; Editor MİHAL VASILIYADIS; circ. 1,000.

Günlük Ticaret: Çemberlitas Palas, Çemberlitas; f. 1947; political; Editor NESRİN TUNÇBİLEK; circ. 1,700.

Günaydın: Alây köşkü Sok. 2; f. 1968; political; Editor RAHMİ TURAN; circ. 272,600.

Haber: Şeref Efendi Sok. 44, Cağaloğlu; f. 1934; Editor M. LÜTFİ BALLISOY; Publisher DÜNDAS ENGIN; circ. 8,100.

Hergün: Cemal Nadir Sok. 9, Cağaloğlu; f. 1947; evening; Editor UĞUR GÜRTUNCA; circ. 8,300.

Hürriyet: Babıali Cad. 15-17, Cağaloğlu; f. 1948; morning; independent political; Publisher EROL SİMAVİ; Editor SALİM BAYER; circ. 650,000.

İstanbul Postası: Çatalçeşme Sok. 17, Cağaloğlu; f. 1946; commercial; Editor ÇETİN A. ÖZKIRIM; circ. 2,250.

Jamanak: İstiklâl Cad., Narmanlı Yurdu, Beyoğlu; f. 1908; Armenian; Chief Editor MARDIROS KOÇUNYAN; circ. 2,100.

Kelebek: Babıali Cad. 15-17, Cağaloğlu; f. 1972; morning; daily home magazine; Publisher EROL SİMAVİ; Editor ZEYNEP AVCI; circ. 260,000.

Marmara: İstiklâl Cad. 360/12, Tünel; f. 1941; Armenian language; Editor R. HADDECİYAN; circ. 1,700.

Milliyet: Nuruosmaniye Caddesi 65; f. 1950; morning; political; Editor ABDİ İPEKÇİ; circ. 329,000 (weekdays), 355,000 (Sunday).

Son Havadis: Şeref Efendi Sok. 44, Cağaloğlu; f. 1951; supports the Justice Party; Editor CAN KAYA İSEN; circ. 34,500.

Son Saat: Çemberlitaş Palas Kat 1, Cağaloğlu; f. 1956; evening; Editor SELİM BİLMEN; circ. 8,700.

Tercüman: Nuruosmaniye, Cağaloğlu; f. 1961; political; Editor-in-Chief SAADETTIN ÇULCU; Editor ÜNAL SAKMAN; circ. 415,000.

Yeni Asya: Şeref Efendi Sok. 32, Cağaloğlu; f. 1970; political; Editor A. RAHMİ ERDEM; circ. 9,400.

Yeni İstanbul: Dr. Emin Paşa Sok. 20, Cağaloğlu; f. 1950; independent political; Editor DOĞAN KOLOĞLU; circ. 29,200.

İZMİR

Ege Ekonomi: 2 Beyler Sok. 45/A; f. 1968; commercial; Editor KÂZIM YENİSEY; circ. 2,200.

Ege Telgraf: Atatürk Cad. 150; f. 1960; evening; political; Editor Süha Sükâtî Tekil.

Ekspres: 856 Sok. No. 46; f. 1952; political; Editor İşlthan Esen; circ. 52,000.

Ticaret: Gazi Bulvarı 18; f. 1942; commercial and political news; Editor Sezaİ Güven; circ. 7,600.

Yeni Asır: Gazi Osman Paşa Bulvarı 13/A; f. 1895; political; Editor Cemİl Devrİm; circ. 65,000.

Konya

Yeni Konya: İş Bankası bitişiği 4; f. 1949; political; Editors Gültekİn and Ayhan Gücüvener; circ. 2,500.

Yeni Meram: Mevlâna Cad. Sağlık Pasajı; f. 1949; political; Editor A. Rıdvan Bülbül; circ. 1,660.

WEEKLIES

Ankara

Ekonomi ve Politika: Tunus Cad. 12/3 Bakanlıklar; f. 1966; economic and political; Publisher Zİya Tansu.

Hız: Necatibey Cad., Sezenler Sok.; f. 1965; labour news; Publisher Şerafettİn Akova; Editors İsmaıl S. Gaşan, Necmi Ertez; circ. 10,000.

Outlook: Konur Sokak 27/7, Kizilay P.K. 210; f. 1967; English language; Editor M. A. Kışlalı.

Türkiye Ticaret Sicili: Karanfil Sok. 56, Bakanlıklar; f. 1957; commercial; Editor Oktay Dİzdaroğlu.

Yarın: İnkılap Sok. 25/2, Yenişehir; f. 1963; political; Publisher-Editor Müfİt Duru.

Yanki: Konor Sokak 27/7, P.K. 210, Kizilay; f. 1970; Editor Mehmet Alİ Kışlali.

Istanbul

Akbaba: Klodfarer Cad. 8-10, Divanyolu; f. 1923; satirical; Editor Kadrİ Yurdatap.

Doğan Kardeş: Türbedar Sok. 22, Cağaloğlu; f. 1945; illustrated children's magazine; Editor Şevket Rado; circ. 40,000.

Durum: Nuruosmaniye Cad., Atasaray İş Hanı, Kat 1.3, no. 102-302; f. 1964; political; Editor Mİthat Perİn.

Geçit: Nuruosmaniye Cad., Atasaray Han 408; f. 1966; political; Publisher Fürüzan Tekİl.

Hayat: Türbedar Sok. 22, Cağaloğlu; f. 1956; general interest illustrated magazine; Publisher Şevket Rado; circ. 130,000.

Hayat Spor: Türbedar Sok. 22, Cağaloğlu; f. 1974; illustrated sport magazine; weekly; Editor Mehmet Rado; circ. 90,000.

Istanbul Ticaret: Istanbul Chamber of Commerce, Eminönü-Unkapanı Cad.; f. 1957; commercial news; Publisher Dr. Yıldırım Kılkış.

La Vera Luz: Tahtakale Cad., Prevuayans Han 12; f. 1951; Jewish news; Publisher İlyazer Menda.

Pazar: Ankara Caddesi, Cemal Nadir Sok. 7; f. 1956; illustrated; Publisher Haldun Sİmavİ.

Resimli Roman: Türbedar Sok. 22, Cağaloğlu; f. 1965; weekly; illustrated; Editor Şevket Rado; circ. 90,000.

Şalom: Bereket Han 24/5, Karaköy; f. 1948; Jewish; Publisher Avram Leyon.

Ses: Türbedar Sok. 22, Cağaloğlu; f. 1962; illustrated film, TV, music magazine; Editor Şevket Rado; circ. 90,000.

Tutum: Nuruosmaniye Cad. 54; f. 1967; political; Editor Erdoğan Akkurt.

Yeni Gavroş: Billûr Sok. 10, Karaköy; f. 1945; Armenian news weekly; Publisher Boğos Artur.

PERIODICALS

Ankara

Adalet Dergisi: Adalet Bakanlığı; f. 1909; legal journal published by the Ministry of Justice; Editor Hüseyİn Ergül; circ. 3,500.

Ankara Barosu Dergisi: f. 1944; monthly; journal of the Ankara Bar.

Azerbaycan Türk Kültür Dergisi: P.K. 165; f. 1949; literary and cultural periodical of Azerbaizhanian Turks; Editor Dr. Ahmet Yaşat.

Bayrak Dergisi: Necatibey Cad., Karakimseli Han; f. 1964; Pub. and Editor Hami Kartay.

Çiftlik Dergisi: P.K. 43, Bakanlıklar-Ankara; f. 1960; agricultural; monthly; Publisher Vasfİ Hakman; circ. 10,000.

Devlet Opera ve Balesi Genel Müdürlüğü: f. 1949; State opera and ballet; Gen. Dir. Mİthat Fenmen.

Devlet Tiyatrosu: Devlet Tiyatrosu Um. Md.; f. 1952; art, theatre.

Dost: Menekşe Sok. 16/13, Yenişehir; f. 1947; literary; Editor Salİm Sengİl.

Elektrik Mühendisliği Mecmuası: Ihlamur Sokak 10/1, Yenişehir; f. 1954; published by the Chamber of Turkish Electrical Engineers.

Halkevleri Dergisi: Atatürk Bulvarı 104; f. 1966; art, literary; Publisher Kadrİ Kaplan.

Hisar: P.K. 501; f. 1950; literary; monthly; Editor-in-Chief Mehmet Çınarli; Editor İlhan Geçer.

İdare Dergisi: İçişleri Bakanliği; administrative.

Ilk Öğretim: Milli Eğitim Bakanliği; educational.

İller ve Belediyeler Dergisi: Mithat Paşa Cad. 45/2; f. 1945; monthly journal of the Turkish Municipal Asscn.; Pres. İsmet Sezgİn.

Karinca: Mithat Paşa Cad. 38/A, Yenişehir; f. 1934; monthly revue published by the Turkish Co-operative Society; circ. 6,000.

Maden Tetkik ve Arama Enstitüsü Dergisi: İnönü Bulvarı; f. 1935; bi-annual; publ. by Mineral Research and Exploration Institute of Turkey; English Edition *Bulletin of the Mineral Research and Exploration Institute* (bi-annual).

Mesleki ve Teknik Öğretim: Milli Eğitim Bakanlığı, Eğitim Araçları ve Teknik İşbirliği Genel Müdürlüğü, Ankara; f. 1942; published by a department of the Ministry of Education; educational.

Mühendis ve Makina: Sümer Sokak 36/1, Kızılay; f. 1957; engineering monthly; Publ. Chamber of Mechanical Engineers; Dir. and Editor Muzaffer Gürel.

Onasya Dergisi: P.K. 605; f. 1965; monthly; cultural; Publisher Sadİ Bayram; circ. 5,000.

Resmi Kararlar Dergisi: Ministry of Justice, Adalet Bakanliği; f. 1966; legal; Editor Avnİ Özenç; circ. 3,500.

T. C. Merkez Bankası Aylık Bülten: Merkez Bank; monthly.

Türk Arkeoloji Dergisi: General Directorate of Antiquities and Museums, Eski Eserler ve Müzeler Genel Müdürlüğü; archaeological.

Turk Dili: Türk Dil Kurumu, Atatürk Bulvarı 221, Kavaklıdere; f. 1951; monthly; literary.

Türk Kültürü: Tunus Cad. 16; f. 1962; cultural studies; Editor Prof. Dr. AHMET TEMİR.

Turkey—Economic News Digest: Karanfil Sok. 56; f. 1960; Editor-in-Chief BEHZAT TANİR; Man. Editor SADİK BALKAN.

Türkiye Bankacılık: P.K. 121; f. 1955; commercial; Publisher MUSTAFA ATALAY.

Türkiye Bibliyografyası: Millî Kütüphane Genel Müdürlüğü, Yenişehir; f. 1934; quarterly; Turkish national bibliography; published by the Bibliographical Institute of the Turkish National Library; Dir. FİLİZ BAŞBUĞOĞLU.

Türkiye Makaleler Bibliyografyası: Millî Kütüphane Genel Müdürlüğü, Yenişehir; f. 1952; quarterly; Turkish articles bibliography; published by the Bibliographical Institute of the Turkish National Library; Dir. FİLİZ BAŞBUĞOĞLU.

Yen Yayınlar, Aylık Bibliyografya Dergisi (*New Publications, Monthly Bibliographic Journal*):P.K. 440, Kızılay, Ankara; f. 1956; Published by Asscn. of Univ. Library School Graduates; Dir. ÖZER SOYSAL.

Ziraat Dergisi: Posta K. 305; f. 1950; monthly; agriculture.

Ziraat Dünyası: Posta K. 127; f. 1950; monthly; agriculture.

ISTANBUL

Arkitekt: Anadolu Han 32, Eminönü; f. 1931; quarterly; architecture, city planning and tourism; Chair. Dr. Arch. ZEKİ SAYÂR; Sec. KETİ ÇAPANOĞLU.

Bakiş: Cağaloğlu Yokuşu; f. 1945; Editor AVNİ ALTINER.

Banka ve Ekonomik Yorumlar: Erçevik Işhani 316, Sultanahmet, Istanbul; f. 1964; banking, economic, social and management subjects; Publisher NEZİH H. NEYZİ; circ. 2,500.

Deniz: Rıhtım Cad., Veli Alemdar Han, Kat 6/23, Karaköy; f. 1955; monthly; maritime news; Publisher EMEL KAZANLIOĞLU.

Filim: P.K. 307, Beyoğlu; f. 1970; cinema; Editor ONAT KUTLAR.

Iktisadi Yükseliş: P.K. 317; f. 1949; economic; Publisher ŞEMSETTİN CURA.

Istanbul, A Handbook for Tourists: Şişli Meydanı, 364; f. 1968; quarterly; published by the Touring and Automobile Club of Turkey; Publisher NURİ PERE; Editor ÇELİK GÜLERSOY.

İstanbul Barosu Dergisi: f. 1926; monthly; published by the Istanbul Bar.

İstanbul Ticaret Odası Mecmuası: İstanbul Ticaret Odası Gümüşpala Cad., Eminönü; f. 1884; every three months; journal of the Istanbul Chamber of Commerce; Turkish and English; Editor Dr. YILDIRIM KILKIŞ.

Kadın: Nuruosmaniye Cad., Benice Han 54, Cağaloğlu; f. 1947; serious, political, women's magazine; Publisher İFFET HALİM ORUZ.

Kemalizm: Bankalar Cad., Ankara H. 16; f. 1962; Publisher HÜSEYİN SAĞIROĞLU.

Kulis: Cağaloğlu Yokuşu 10/A; f. 1947; fortnightly arts magazine; Armenian; Publisher HAGOP AYVAZ.

Musiki Mecmuası: P.K. 666, Istanbul; f. 1948 monthly; music and musicology; Editor ETEM RUHİ ÜNGÖR.

Pirelli Mecmuası: Büyükdere Cad. 117, Gayrettepe; f. 1964; monthly; Publisher Türk Pirelli Ticaret A.S.; Editor U. CANAL; circ. 10,000.

Polis Dergisi: Kuledibi, Emniyet Sarayı, Karaköy; f. 1954; Publisher ADNAN KİRMAN.

Polis Magazin: Istiklâl Cad. 364/18, Beyoğlu; f. 1958; Publisher MİTHAT ENGİN VİRANYALI.

Ruh ve Madde Dergisi: P.K. 1157; f. 1959; organ of the Metapsychic and Scientific Research Society of Turkey; Publisher ERGÜN ARIKDAL.

Sağlık Âlemi: Divanyolu Cad. Ersoy Pasajı 1, Cağaloğlu; f. 1964; health; Editor ATİLÂ YÜCEL.

Sevgi Dünyası (*World of Love*): Larmartin Cad. 26/3, Taksim; f. 1963; Publisher Dr. R. KAYSERİLİOĞLU; circ. 10,000.

Söz: Piyerloti Cad. 7, Divanyolu; f. 1966; political; Editor GENÇAY GÜN.

Tıb Dünyası: Ankara Cad. 31/3 Küçük Han, Cağaloğlu, P.K. 192; f. 1927; monthly; organ of the Turkish Mental Health and Social Psychiatry Society; Editor Dr. FAHRETTİN KERİM GÖKAY.

Türk Anglo-Amerikan ve Almanya Postası: P.K. 192, Beyoğlu; f. 1947; commercial; Publisher KEMAL ERKAN.

Türk Folklor Araştırmaları: P.K. 46, Aksaray; f. 1949; arts and folklore; publ. by Turkish Folklore Association; Gen. Man. and Editor İHSAN HINÇER.

Türk Ticaret Almanağı: Mollafenarî Sok. 25, Cağaloğlu; commercial; Editor REŞAT TOPALOĞLU.

Turkish Trade Directory and Telex Index: Peykhane Caddesi 14, Daire 1, Çemberlitas; f. 1962; annual; Publisher CIRO COSTAMTE, COSTANTE BASIN AJANSI.

Türkiye Turing ve Otomobil Kurumu Belleteni: Halaskargazi Cad. 364, Şişli Meydanı; f. 1930; every two months; published by the Touring and Automobile Club of Turkey; Publisher NURİ PERE; Editor: ÇELİK GÜLERSOY.

Türkiyede ve Dünyada Tarım: P.K. 578; f. 1964; agricultural news; Publisher KEMAL BAYKAL.

Ülkücü Öğretman: Divanyolu Cad. 64, Cağaloğlu; f. 1965; education; Publisher HALİD BERK; Editor-in-Chief TEVFİK MARAL.

Varlık: Cağaloğlu Yokuşu 40; f. 1933; monthly; literary; Editor YAŞAR NABİ NAYIR.

Yeditepe: P.K. 77, Cağaloğlu, Mengene Sok., Yeni Han 21; f. 1950; literary and cultural; monthly; Editor HÜSAMETTİN BOZOK.

Yelken: P.K. 639, Karaköy; f. 1955; arts; Editor RÜKNETTİN RESULOĞLU.

Yeni Sanayi Dünyası: P.K. 515, Beyoğlu; f. 1963; Editor NURETTİN ÖZŞIMŞEK.

İZMİR

İzmir Barosu Dergisi: f. 1967; monthly; journal of the İzmir Bar; Editor CİHANGİR KUTLAY; Propr. NECDET ÖKLEM; circ. 1,000.

İzmir Ticaret Odası Dergisi: Atatürk Cad. 126; f. 1925; monthly; commercial.

KONYA

Çağrı Dergisi: P.K. 99; f. 1957; literary; monthly; Editor FEYZİ HALICI.

NEWS AGENCIES

Anatolian News Agency: Ankara and Istanbul; f. 1920; Gen. Man. ATTILA ONUK; publ. *Weekly Economical Bulletin.*

Hurriyet Haber Ajansı: Babıali Cad. 15-17 Kat 3, Cağaloğlu; f. 1963; Dir.-Gen. AYDOĞAB ÖNOL.

İKA Economic and Commercial News Agency: Tunus Cad. 12/3, Bakanlıklar, Ankara; f. 1954; Dir. ZİYA TANSU; publs. *Daily Economic and Commercial Bulletin, Investment and Finance Bulletin* (both English and Turkish), *Labour, Law and Social Insurance Bulletin, Ekonomi ve Politika.*

Türk Haberler Ajansi (*Turkish News Agency*): Basın Sarayı Kat 4, Cağaloğlu, Istanbul; f. 1950; 11 brs. in Turkey; Dir.-Gen. KADRİ KAYABAL; Editor-in-Chief HASAN YILMAER.

FOREIGN BUREAUX

AFP (*France*): P.K. 30. Cankaya-Ankara, Günes Sok. 14; Corr. VINCENT LATÈVE.

ANSA (*Italy*): Gelincik Sok. 7A/6, Ankara; Corr. ROMANO DAMIANI.

AP (*U.S.A.*): Konur Sok. 16, Kizilay, Ankara; Corr. NICHOLAS S. LUDINGTON.

DPA (*Federal Germany*): Ahmet Mithat Efendi Sok. 20/1; Cankaya-Ankara.

Reuters: P.K. 239, Kizilay, Ankara.

UPI (*U.S.A.*): Basın Sarayı, Cağaloğlu; Bureau Chief JOHN LAWTON.

AFP also has representatives in Istanbul and İzmir. Reuters (*U.K.*) and TASS (*U.S.S.R.*) are also represented in Turkey.

PRESS ASSOCIATION

Editörler Derneği (*Editors' Union*): Ankara Cad. 64, Istanbul; f. 1950; Pres. RAMAZAN ARKIN; Sec. RAKIM ÇALAPALA.

PUBLISHERS

Ağaoğlu Yayınevi: Selvilimesçit Sokak 2, Kurt İş Hanı, Cağaloğlu, Istanbul; translations and literary books; MUSTAFA KEMAL AĞAOĞLU.

Akgün Matbaası: Istanbul.

Ark Ticaret Ltd. ŞTİ: P.K. 577, Ankara; f. 1962; imports technical books and exports all kinds of Turkish books, periodicals and newspapers; Gen. Man. ATILAN TÜMER; European Branch: Erich Ollenhauer Str. 32/A-04, 6202 Wiesbaden-Biebrich, Federal Republic of Germany.

Arkın Kitabevi—Bir Yayınevi: Ankara Cad. 60, P.K. 11, Istanbul; f. 1949; encyclopedias, atlases, children's books, reference; Pres. and Man. RAMAZAN GÖKALP ARKIN.

Atlas Kitabevi Yayınevi: Nuruosmaniye Caddesi, Mengene Sokak 7-9, Istanbul: literary.

Ayyıldız Matbaası: Ankara.

Başkent Yayınevi: Anafartalar Caddesi, Nilüfer Sokak 5A, Istanbul; literary.

Bateş Bayilik Teşkilâtı A.Ş.: Molla Fenari Sokak 1, Cağaloğlu, Istanbul; f. 1960; books and periodicals.

Bedir Yayınevi: P.O.B. 1060, Istanbul; Islamic and Turkish books.

Berkalp Kitabevi: Şehir Bahçesi 7/8, Kızılay, Ankara.

Cumhuriyet Mat. ve Gaze T.A.Ş.: Halkevi Sokak 40/41, Cağaloğlu, Istanbul.

De Yayınevi: Vilâyet Han, Kat. 3, Cağaloğlu, Istanbul; literary.

Depas: 56 Cumhuriyet Bulvarı, Izmir.

Elif Kitabevi: Sahaflar Çarşısı 4, Beyazit, Istanbul; f. 1956; all types of publications, especially historical, literary, political, drama and reference; publ. *Elif Yayınları Kitap Belleten* (twice monthly).

Forum Yayınları: Ankara; literary and artistic books.

Gerçek Yayınevi: Istanbul; economic.

İnkılâp Kitabevi: Ankara Caddesi 95, Istanbul; Dir. NAZAR FİKRİ.

İnkilâp ve Aka Kitabevleri Kollektif Şirketi: Ankara Caddesi 95, Istanbul; Dir. KARABET FİKRİ.

Kanaat Kitabevi: Ilyas Bayar Halefi, Yakup Bayar, Ankara Caddesi 133, Istanbul; f. 1896; textbooks, novels, dictionaries, posters, maps and atlases.

Kanaat Yayınları Ltd. Şti: Ankara Cad. 133/1, Istanbul; f. 1951; maps, school books; Dir. YAKUP BAYAR.

Kültür Kitabevi: Ankara Cad. 62, Sirkeci, Istanbul; f. 1945; technical books, school books, language books, etc.; Dirs. İZİDOR and RENE KANT.

Neşriyat A.Ş.: Mollafenari S.1, Cağaloğlu, Istanbul; classics, children's books, novels.

Nil Yayınevi: Istanbul; literary translations.

Nişantaşı Deniz Kitabevi: Nisantas, Istanbul; poetry.

Öğretim Yayınevi: Ankara Cad. 62/2, Sirkeci, Istanbul; f. 1959; English, French, German, Italian and Dutch language courses, guides and dictionaries, phrase books for tourists; Dir. İZİDOR KANT.

Remzi Kitabevi: Ankara Caddesi 93, Istanbul; f. 1930: school textbooks, fiction, children's, science and reference books; Dir. REMZİ BENGİ.

Sermet Matbaası: Şeref Efendi Sok. 28, Cağaloğlu, Istanbul; f. 1950; books on medicine, statistics, economics, mathematics, dictionaries; Gen. Man. SERMET ARKADAŞ.

Tifdruk Matbaacılık Sanayii Anonim Şirketi: Davutpaşa Caddesi 101, Topkapı, Istanbul; f. 1955; novels, magazines, encyclopaedia.

Türk Dil Kurumu: Atatürk Bulvarı, 221 Kavaklidere, Ankara; f. 1932; non-fiction.

T.T.K. Basımevi: Ankara.

Turkish National Library: Bibliographical Institute, Milli Kütüphane Genel Müdürlüğü, Yenişehir, Ankara; publish Turkish national and articles bibliographies; Dir. FİLİZ BAŞBUĞOĞLU.

Türkiye Yayınevi: P.K. 611, Ankara Caddesi 36, Istanbul.

Varlik Yayınevi: Cağaloğlu Yokuşu 40, Istanbul; f. 1946; fiction and non-fiction books; Dir. YAŞAR NABİ NAYİR.

Yeditepe Yayınları: P.K. 77, Cağaloğlu, Mengene Sok., Yeni Han 21, Istanbul; publishes literature, poetry, translations, etc. and also *Yeditepe* (monthly).

Yeni Üniversite Kitabevi: Cağaloğlu, Ankara Caddesi 80, Istanbul.

Yeni Zaman Kitabevi: Ankara Caddesi 155, Istanbul; f. 1970; Dir. ROZİN İULİA FİKRİ.

RADIO AND TELEVISION

RADIO

Türkiye Radyo Televizyon Kurumu (T.R.T.): Nevzat Tandoğan Caddesi No. 2, Kavaklıdere, Ankara; f. 1964; controls Turkish radio and television services; Dir.-Gen. Prof. NEVZAT YALÇINTAŞ.

Home Service:

There are local radio stations in Ankara (3), Antalya, Çukurova, Diyarbakır, Istanbul (2), Erzurum, İzmir (2), Kars, Van, Gaziantep, Trabzon and Hakkari.

Foreign Service (Voice of Turkey):

Ankara I : SW, 100 kW.

Ankara II: SW, 250 kW. Nine daily short-wave transmissions in the following languages: Arabic, Bulgarian, English, French, German, Greek, Romanian, Serbo-Croat, Turkish; Dir. ESİN ÇELİKKAN.

American Forces Radio and Television Service:

Network Headquarters, Communications Facility Radio Network, Tuslog Det. 124, A.P.O., N.Y. 09289, U.S.A.; MW, 0.01 kW. transmitter at Adana, relay at Diyabakir.

KCFR Radio, A.P.O., N.Y. 09324, U.S.A.; MW, 0.01 kW. transmitter at Karamursel.

Ankara Türkiye Polis Radyosu: Ankara; SW, 1 kW.

Cinarli Sanat Enstitusu Deneme Radyosu (*Schools Education*): Izmir; MW, 0.5 kW.; SW, 0.25 kW.; Man. A. KIRDAR; Technical Dir. G. UYSAL.

İstanbul Teknik Üniversitesi Radyosu (*Istanbul Technical University*): Teknik Universitesi, Elektrik Fakültesi, Yüsek Frekans Teknigi Kürsüsü, Istanbul; SW, 1 kW.; FM, 0.25 kW.; Dir.-Gen. Prof. A. ATAMAN.

İstanbul Üniversitesi Fen Fakültesi Radyosu (*Faculty of Science, Istanbul University*), Tatbiki Fizik Merkezi, Istanbul; experimental station SW, 1.75 kW.; Dir.-Gen. Prof. Dr. F. YENICAY; Station Man. Y. KAINI.

İstanbul Yüksek Teknik Okulu Radyosu (*Technical School of Istanbul*): Yildiz, Istanbul; SW, 1.6 kW.; language lessons and music.

Turkish State Meteorological Service: P.O.B. 401, Ankara; SW, 2.5 kW.; music and weather reports; Dir.-Gen. Prof. Dr. U. E. CÖLASAN; Station Man. T. TUNA.

In 1973, 4,033,478 licenced radio receivers were in use.

TELEVISION

Türkiye Radyo Televizyon Kurumu (Ankara TV): Nevzat Tandoğan Cad. 2, Kavaklıdere, Ankara. A limited television service was set up in 1965, and regular broadcasts for Ankara began in 1968, now transmitting programmes seven days a week, averaging 50 hours a week. New studios are to be established in Ankara, Istanbul and İzmir; Head of Television Dept. YILMAZ DAĞDEVİREN; Programme Dir. TARIAN GÜNENÇ; Technical Dir. COŞKUN ARSLAN.

In 1974 approx. 250,000 licenced television receivers were in use.

FINANCE

(cap. = capital; p.u. = paid up; dep. = deposits; m. = million; brs. = branches)

(Amounts in Turkish liras, except where otherwise stated. Figures given for capital and deposits are for the end of the calendar year stated, except where otherwise stated.)

The Central Bank of the Republic of Turkey was originally founded in 1931, and constituted in its present form after the revolution of 1960. The Central Bank is the bank of issue and is also responsible for public deposits, and medium and long-term borrowings of the banks. In addition, all international payments go through the Bank, and all foreign exchange is held by the Bank.

There are some 50 other banks functioning in Turkey. Thirteen were created by special laws to fulfil specialized services for particular industries. The Sümerbank directs the operation of a number of state-owned factories; Etibank operates primarily in the extractive industries and electric power industries; the Agricultural Bank makes loans for agriculture; the Maritime Bank operates government-owned port facilities, the merchant marine and its own fleet of ships; the Real Estate Credit Bank participates in industrial undertakings and the construction of all types of building. Other specialized banks deal with tourism, municipalities and mortgages, etc.

The largest of the private sector Turkish banks is the Türkiye İş Bankası which operates over 500 branches. The private banks borrow at medium- and long-term mainly from the State Investment Bank.

There are three foreign banks operating branches in Turkey. Apart from these the Ottoman Bank, which was

founded in 1863 and is the oldest bank in Turkey, has strong British and French interests, while the Turkish Foreign Trade Bank is partly owned by the Bank of America and the Banca d'America e d'Italia.

There are several other credit institutions in Turkey, including the Industrial Development Bank of Turkey, which encourages private investment in industry by acting as underwriter in the issue of share capital. The Turkiye Sınai Kalkınma Bankası is a privately owned development finance company founded in 1950 with the assistance of the World Bank to stimulate industrial growth in the private sector.

There are numerous co-operative organizations, and in the rural areas there are Agricultural Sale Co-operatives and Agricultural Co-operatives. There are also a number of savings institutions.

BANKING

STATE BANKS

Türkiye Cumhuriyet Merkez Bankası (*Central Bank of the Republic of Turkey*): Bankalar Caddesi 48, Ankara; f. 1931; bank of issue; part of the share capital is owned by the State; cap. p.u. 25m.; dep. 20,955m. (1973); Gov. MEMDUH GÜPGÜPOĞLU; 18 brs.

Denizçilik Bankası T.A.O. (*Turkish Maritime Bank*): Rihtim Caddesi, Posta K. 1387, Istanbul; f. 1952; semi-public corporation; nominal cap. 1,750m., of which 51 per cent is subscribed by the Government, the rest by private investors and organizations; dep. 418.7m. (1973); operates a shipping line (*see* Shipping); Gen. Man. CELALETTIN EROL.

Devlet Yatırım Bankası (*State Investment Bank*): Ankara; f. 1964; loans and guarantees to State enterprises; cap. 2,000m.; Gen. Man. NEDİM R. AKSAL.

Etibank: (Banking Dept.) Sihhiye Cihan Sokak 2, Ankara; f. 1935; State economic enterprise active in mining, metallurgy, the chemical industry and banking; cap. 2,000m.; dep. 1,640m. (1973); Gen. Man. NEZİHİ BERKKAM; 67 brs.

İller Bankası (*Municipal Bank*): Atatürk Bulvarı, Ankara; f. 1933; Government Municipalities Bank; cap. 1,200m.; dep. 73.2m. (1973); Chair. of Board and Gen. Dir. MAZHAR HAZNEDAR.

Sümerbank: Ulus Meydanı 2, Ankara; f. 1933; Holdings Bank for governmental industrial undertakings; cap. 2,000m.; dep. 279m. (1973); Gen. Man. HIZIR GEYLAN.

Türkiye Cumhuriyeti Turizm Bankası A.Ş.: Ankara; f. 1960; state bank to develop tourism; authorized cap. 600m., cap. p.u. 514.7m. (1974); Gen. Man. İLHAN EVLİYAOĞLU.

Türkiye Cumhuriyeti Ziraat Bankası (*Agricultural Bank of the Republic of Turkey*): Bankalar Caddesi, Ankara; f. 1863; State Agricultural Bank; 855 branches; cap. p.u. 1,160m.; dep. 21,291m. (1974); Gen. Man. NEVZAT ALPTÜRK.

Türkiye Emlâk Kredi Bankası A.O. (*Real Estate Credit Bank of Turkey*): Atatürk Bulvarı 15, Ankara; f. 1926: cap. 1,000m.; dep. 2,988m. (1973); 170 brs.; Pres. and Gen. Man. MIRAÇ AKTUĞ.

Türkiye Sınai Kalkınma Bankası A.Ş. (*Industrial Development Bank of Turkey*): Meclisi Mebusan Cad. 137, P.O.B. 59, Fındıklı, Istanbul; f. 1950; cap. 193,373,000; loans and investments 3,061,000 (Dec. 1973); 4 brs.; Chair. SELAHATTİN KARAHAN; Gen. Man. REŞİD EGELİ.

Türkiye Vakıflar Bankası T.A.O.: Bankalar Caddesi 52, Ankara; f. 1954; cap. 100m.; cap. p.u. 62.5m.; dep. 3,501m. (1974); 168 brs.; rep. office in Frankfurt; Chair. ZİYA KAYLA; Gen. Man. CAVİD ORAL.

PRINCIPAL COMMERCIAL BANKS

Afyon Terakki Servet Bankası T.A.Ş.: f. 1926; cap. 1m.; dep. 842,000 (1973).

Akbank T.A.Ş.: Maclisi Mebusan Cad. 65-69, Findikli, Istanbul; f. 1948; cap. p.u. 225m., dep. 10,154m. (Dec. 1974); 450 brs.; Chair. BÜLENT YAZICI; Gen. Man. MEDENÎ BERK.

Anadolu Bankası A.Ş.: İstiklâl Caddesi 108, Beyoğlu, Istanbul; f. 1962; cap. p.u. 45m., deposits 794m. (1973); successor to Türk Ekspres Bank and Buğday Bankası; Gen. Man. A. ORHAN GİRAY.

Çaybank A.Ş.: f. 1958; cap. 2.75m.; dep. 4.1m. (1973).

Demirbank T.A.Ş.: 44-46 Bankalar Caddesi, Karaköy, Istanbul; f. 1953; cap. 12m., dep. 97.8m. (1973); Pres. TEVFİK ERENGÜL; Gen. Man. NURİ CINGILLIOĞLU.

Denizli İktisat Bankası T.A.Ş.: f. 1927; cap. 5m.; dep. 11.1m. (1973).

Egebank A.Ş.: Atatürk Avenue 80, P.K. 251, İzmir; f. 1928; cap. p.u. 5m., dep. 36.6m. (1973); Chair. SEVKET FİLİBELİ.

Elâzığ İktisat Bankası T.A.Ş.: f. 1929; cap. 10m.; dep. 9.8m. (1973).

Eskişehir Bankası T.A.Ş.: f. 1927; cap. 15m.; dep. 109.5m. (1973).

İşçi Kredi Bankası T.A.Ş.: f. 1954; cap. 3m.; dep. 48.1m. (1973).

İstanbul Bankası T.A.Ş.: Beyoğlu İstiklâl Caddesi, Mısır Apart. 309, Galatasaray, Istanbul; f. 1953; cap. p.u. 50m., dep. 497.5m. (1973); Pres. KEMAL HASOĞLU; Gen. Man. EROL TOKSÖZ.

İstanbul Emniyet Sandığı: f. 1868; res. 15.7m.; dep. 686.8m. (1973).

Kocaeli Bankası T.A.Ş.: f. 1927; cap. 5m.; dep. 48.1m. (1973).

Millî Aydın Bankası T.A.Ş.: f. 1913; cap. 8m.; dep. 15.6m. (1973).

Osmanlı Bankası (*Ottoman Bank*): Bankalar Caddesi, Karaköy, Istanbul; f. 1863; authorised cap. 10m., cap. p.u. 8m., dep. 2,027m. (1974); Dir.-Gen. J. JEULIN; Turkish Dir.-Gen. REŞAT AKSAN; 93 brs. in Turkey; Paris and London offices.

Pamukbank T.A.Ş.: İstiklal Caddesi 261, Galatasaray, Istanbul; f. 1955; cap. p.u. and reserves 38m., dep. 728.4m. (1974); 70 brs.; Chair., Pres. MEHMET E. KARAMEHMET; Gen. Man. S. BERAT AKERMAN.

Sağlık Bankası A.Ş.: f. 1928; cap. 500,000; dep. 14,000 (1973).

Şekerbank T.A.Ş.: Atatürk Bulvarı 55, Ankara; f. 1953; cap. p.u. 40m., dep. 1,031m. (1973); 106 brs.; Chair. of Board HALİL ATALAY; Gen. Man. ÖMER SUNAR.

Türk Diş Ticaret Bankası A.Ş. (*Turkish Foreign Trade Bank*): Cumhuriyet Caddesi 199-201, Harbiye, P.K. 11, Şişli, Istanbul; f. 1964; cap. p.u. 10m., dep. 327m. (1974); jointly owned by Bank of America, Türkiye İş Bankası and Banca d'America e d'Italia; brs. in Ankara, Istanbul (three) and İzmir; Chair. A. ÜSKÜDARLI; Gen. Man. ORAL ÇOBANOĞLU.

Türk Ticaret Bankası A.Ş. (*Turkish Commercial Bank*): Iskele Caddesi, Hayri Efendi Sokak, Bahçekapı, Istanbul; f. 1913; cap. 125m., dep. 5,405m. (1974); 282 brs.; Gen. Man. TURGUT SIZMAZOĞLU.

Türkiye Bağcilar Bankası A.Ş.: f. 1917; cap. 5m.; dep. 23.2m. (1973).

Türkiye Garanti Bankası A.Ş.: 43-45 Yeni Postahane Caddesi, Istanbul; f. 1946; cap. 160m., dep. 3,011m. (1973); 210 brs.; Chair. CABIR S. SELEK.

Türkiye Halk Bankası A.Ş.: Anafartalar Caddesi 41, Ankara; f. 1938; cap. 1,000m., dep. 3,311.6m. (1974); 261 brs.; Gen. Man. RAHMI ÖNEN.

Turkiye İmar Bankası T.A.Ş.: Karakoy, Istanbul; f. 1928; cap. p.u. 5m., dep. 174.9m. (1973); Gen. Man. FAHRETTIN ÜLAŞ.

Türkiye İş Bankası A.Ş.: Ulus Meydanı, Ankara; Foreign Dept.: Voyvoda Caddesi 27, Karaköy, Istanbul; f. 1924; cap. p.u. 40m., dep. 22,499m. (1974); 700 brs., including 2 in Cyprus; Offices in Frankfurt/Main and London; Chair. İ. RÜŞTÜ AKSAL; Gen. Man. SELAHATTIN KARAHAN; publs. annual review, economic report, two-monthly economic review.

Türkiye Öğretmenler Bankası T.A.Ş.: f. 1959; cap. 30m.; dep. 1,052m. (1973).

Türkiye Tütüncüler Bankası A.Ş.: Halit Ziya Bulvarı No. 45, İzmir, P.K. 239; f. 1924; 5 brs.; cap. p.u. 7m., dep. 101.4m. (1973); Chair. REŞAT EKINCİ; Gen. Man. ISMAİL AKSOY.

Uluslararası Endüstri ve Ticaret Bankası A.Ş.: Bankalar Cad. 69, Karakoy, Istanbul; f. 1888; cap. p.u. 2.65m., res. 32.4m., dep. 592.0m. (1974); Chair. and Chief Exec. FAHRETTİN ULAŞ; Gen. Man. TURGUT ATASAĞUN.

Yapi ve Kredi Bankasi A.Ş.: Istiklâl Cad., Korsan Çikmazi 1, Beyoğlu, Istanbul; f. 1944; cap. p.u. 300m., dep. 12.6m. (1974); 486 brs.; Chair. and Man. Dir. FAHRETTİN ULAŞ.

FOREIGN BANKS

Banka Komerçiyale İtalyana: Istanbul branch: Bankalar Cad. 53, Karaköy; Head Office: Milan, Italy; cap. p.u. 2.5m., dep. 158.5m. (1973).

Banco di Roma: Hayri Efendi Caddesi, Bahçekapi, P.O.B. 464, Istanbul; Head Office: Rome, Italy: cap. 1.5m., dep. 167.8m. (1973); Man. in Istanbul CARLO CAPPI.

Holantse Bank-Üni N.V.: Istanbul branch: P.K. 34, Karaköy; Head Office: Amsterdam, Netherlands: cap. p.u. 7.6m., dep. 70m. (1974); Man. in Istanbul D. VISSERMAN.

Deutsche Bank A.G. and Dresdner Bank A.G. have representative offices in Istanbul.

STOCK EXCHANGE

Borsa-Komiserliği: Menkul Kıymetler ve Kambiyo Borsası, 4 Vakıf Han, Bahçekapı, Istanbul; f. 1873; 323 mems.; Pres. REFİK T. SELİMOĞLU; publ. *Borsa*.

INSURANCE

Milli Reasürans T.A.Ş.: P.K. 359, Istanbul; f. 1929; state-owned with monopoly of re-insurance; supervises private insurance companies; Chair. SALİH COŞKUN; Gen. Man. SEBATİ ATAMAN.

Sosyal Sigortalar Kurumu: Ankara; Social Insurance Organization.

PRIVATE INSURANCE

Anadolu Anonim Türk Sigorta Şirketi (*Anatolia Turkish Insurance Society*): Rıhtım Caddesi 57, P.O.B. 1845, Karaköy, Istanbul.

Ankara Sigorta Şirketi (*Ankara Insurance Society*): Bankalar Cad. 80, Ankara Sigorta Hanı, Istanbul; f. 1936; Dir. KEMAL SARİGÖLLÜ.

Atlantik Sigorta A.Ş.: Bankalar Cad. No. 2, Karaköy, Istanbul; f. 1964; fire, marine, accident; Chair. EMİN ANSEN; Gen. Man. ENGİN ASAL.

Destek Reasurans T.S.A.Ş.: Cumhuriyet Caddesi 6a/2, Istanbul; f. 1943; Pres. BÜLENT KOZLU.

Doğan Sigorta A.Ş.: Doğan Sigorta Binası, Karaköy, Istanbul; f. 1942; Chair. EMİN ANSEN; Managing Dir. NAİL MORALI; Gen. Man. ENGİN ASAL; fire, marine, accident and life.

Güven Türk Anonim Sigorta Şirketi: Karaköy, Istanbul; f. 1925; Chair. and Gen. Man. A. FETHİ SOYSAL.

Halk Sigorta T.A.Ş.: Galata, Halk Sigorta Hanı, Söğüt Sokak, Istanbul; f. 1944; Man. SAFFET DEMİR.

İmtaş İttihadı Millî Türk Anonim Sigorta Şirketi (*Imtaş Insurance Company*): Karaköy, Ünyon Han, Istanbul, P.K. 107; f. 1918; Man. NURETTİN YAMANLAR.

Istanbul Umum Sigorta, Anonim Şirketi (*General Insurance Society of Istanbul*): Bankalar Cad. 31/33, Karaköy, Istanbul; f. 1893; Pres. CÂBİR SELEK; Man. HAŞIM EKENER.

Şark Sigorta Türk Anonim Şirketi: P.O.B. 111, Karaköy, Bankalar Cad., Şark Han, Istanbul; f. 1923; Chair. IZZET AKOSMAN.

Şeker Sigorta Anonim Şirketi: Meclisi Mebusan Cad. 325, Şeker Sigorta Hanı, P.O.B. 187, Fındıkh, Istanbul; all types of insurance and reinsurance.

Tam Hayat Sigorta A.Ş.: Büyükdere Cad., Tamhan, Şişli, Istanbul; general life assurance.

Tam Sigorta A.Ş.: Büyükdere Cad. 15, Tamhan, Şişli, Istanbul; all types of insurance except life.

Türkiye Genel Sigorta Anonim Şirketi: Yeni Postahane Karşışı, Istanbul; f. 1948; Pres. MEHMET E. KARA-MEHMET; Gen. Man. ÖMER ERÜL.

TRADE AND INDUSTRY

CHAMBERS OF COMMERCE AND INDUSTRY

Union of Chambers of Commerce, Industry and Commodity Exchanges of Turkey: 149 Atatürk Bulvarı, Bakanlıklar, Ankara; Pres. SEZAİ DIBLAN.

There are Chambers of Commerce and Industry in all towns of the Republic. Among the most important are the following:

Adana Chamber of Commerce: Adana; f. 1893; Pres. KÂZIM KÖSEOĞLU; Sec.-Gen. Â. İRFAN TUĞBERK; 4,000 mems.; publ. *Gazetesi*.

Adana Chamber of Industry: Adana; f. 1966; Pres. SAKIP SABANCI; 230 mems.

Ankara Chamber of Commerce: Şehit Teğmen Kalmaz Caddesi 20; Pres. NECDET ESEN; Gen. Sec. Dr. AGAH OKTAY GÜNER; publ. *Bulletin* (monthly).

Ankara Chamber of Industry: İzmir Caddesi 22/2; Pres. HAMİ KARTAY.

British Chamber of Commerce of Turkey (Assoc.): P.O.B. 190, Karaköy, Istanbul; f. 1887; 380 mems.; Sec. and Treas. N. COVEY, M.B.E.; publ. *Trade Journal* (3 to 4 issues a year).

Bursa Chamber of Commerce and Industry: Bursa; f. 1926; 4,582 mems.; Pres. SELAHATTIN AKTAR; Sec.-Gen. ERGUN KAĞITCIBAŞİ; publ. *Bursa Ticaret Haberleri*, weekly.

Chamber of Industry for the Aegean Region: Cumhuriyet Blv. 136, İzmir; f. 1954 succeeded to the İzmir Chamber of Industry; Pres. ŞİNAŞİ ERTAN; Sec.-Gen. NAİM KARAOSMAN; publs. *News Bulletin* (weekly), *Quarterly Review*.

Istanbul Chamber of Commerce: Ragıp Gümüspala Cad., Eminönü, Istanbul; f. 1882; 43,400 mems.; Pres. Exec. Board CELÂL UMUR; Sec.-Gen. Prof. Dr. İSMAİL ÖZASLAN; publs. *Istanbul Ticaret Odasi Mecmuası* (bi-monthly), *Istanbul Ticaret* (weekly), *Statistical Abstract* (in English).

İstanbul Chamber of Industry: Eminönü, Istanbul; Pres. NURULLAH GENGİZ.

Izmir Chamber of Commerce: Atatürk Caddesi 126, İzmir; f. 1885; 8,124 mems.; Pres. DÜNDAR SOYER; Sec.-Gen. ABDULLAH ASIM İĞNECİLER; publ. *Izmir Ticaret Odasi Dergisi* (monthly).

Mersin Chamber of Commerce and Industry: P.O.B. 212, Mersin; f. 1886; 1,711 mems.; Pres. MUSTAFA NİHAT SÖZMEN; Sec.-Gen. SUPHİ GÜZELOĞLU.

Samsun Chamber of Commerce and Industry: Samsun: f. 1923; 9 mems.; Pres. ABDULLAH ÖNCEN; Gen. Sec. NECAT GÖKTÜRK.

TRADE UNIONS

CONFEDERATION

Türk-İş (Türkiye İşçi Sendikaları Konfederasyonu) (*Confederation of Turkish Trade Unions*): Bayındır Sok. 10, Yenişehir, Ankara; f. 1952; affiliated to I.C.F.T.U.; 29 national unions and 6 federations with 1,200,000 employees; Pres. HALİL TUNÇ; Sec. Gen. SADIK ŞİDE; Financial Sec. ÖMER ERGÜN; Organizing Sec. ETHEM EZGÜ; Education Sec. KAYA ÖZDEMİR; publ. *Türk-İş*.

PRINCIPAL UNIONS

Unions affiliated to Türk İş with a membership of over 5,000.

Agaç-İş (Türkiye Ağaç Sanayii İşçileri Sendikası) (*Wood and Lumber*): Necatibey Cad. No. 20/22-23, Yenişehir, Ankara; f. 1949; 8,000 mems.; also affil. to IFBWW; Pres. ÖMER DENİZ; Gen. Sec. OSMAN NOGAY

Basın-İş (Türkiye Gazeteciler ve Basın Sanayii şçileri Sendikası) (*Journalists and Press Technicians*): Necatibey Cad. 61/12, Yenişehir, Ankara; f. 1964; 15,000 mems.; Pres. İSMAİL ÖZKAN; Gen. Sec. CEVDET NARİN.

Besin-İş (Türkiye Et Ekmek ve Besin Sanayii İşçileri Sendikası) (*Food Workers' Union*): Çankırı Cad. Barışta Işhanı No. 5, Ulus, Ankara; f. 1958; Pres. DEMİRHAN TUNCAY; Gen. Sec. NAŞİT ALTAY.

Çimse-İş (Türkiye Çimento, Seramik ve Toprak Sanayii İşçileri Sendikası) (*Cement, Ceramic and Soil*): Necatibey Cad. 22/11-12, Yenişehir, Ankara; f. 1963; 15,000 mems.; also affiliated to IFPCW; Pres. HASAN TÜRKAY; Gen. Sec. ABUZER UÇAR.

Deri-İş (Türkiye Deri, Debbağ, Kundura ve Saraciye Sanayii İşçileri Sendikası) (*Leather and Shoe*): Gençtürk Caddesi 17, Birlik İşhanı Aksaray—Istanbul; f. 1948; 5,000 mems.; also affiliated to ISLWF; Pres. MUSTAFA ŞAHİN; Gen. Sec. ADNAN GÜRKULE.

Dok Gemi-İş (Türkiye Liman Dok ve Gemi Sanayii İşçileri Sendikası) (*Port, Dock and Ship Building*): Ordu Caddesi, 285, Kat-6, Aksaray, Istanbul; f. 1947; 6,000 mems.; also affiliated to IMF; Pres. ASLAN SİVRİ; Gen. Sec. GÜNGÖR TARI.

Dyf-İş (Türkiye Demiryolları İşçi Sendikaları Federasyonu) (*Railways*): Necatibey Cad., Sezenler Sok. 5/4, Yenişehir, Ankara; f. 1952; 35,000 mems.; also affiliated to ITF; Pres. ŞERAFETTİN AKOVA; Gen. Sec. AHMET ÇATAKÇİNLER.

Genel-İş (Türkiye Genel Hizmetler İşçileri Sendikası) (*Public Services*): Süleyman Sırrı Sokak No. 2, Kat-1, Yenişehir, Ankara; f. 1962, 35,000 mems.; also affiliated to PSI; Pres. ABDULLAH BAŞTÜRK; Gen. Sec. HASAN OKYAR.

Ges-İş (Türkiye D.S.İ. Enerji, Su ve Gaz İşçileri Sendikası) (*State Energy, Gas, Water-Workers*): Süleyman Sırrı Sokak No. 2/14-15, Yenişehir, Ankara; f. 1961; 17,000 mems.; also affiliated to PSI; Pres. (vacant); Gen. Sec. EROL AYKAŞ.

Harb-İş (Türkiye Harb Sanayii ve Yardımcı İşkolları İşçileri Sendikası) (*Defence Industry and Allied Workers*): Yüksel Caddesi 8, Kızılay, Ankara; f. 1956; 26,000 mems.; also affiliated to PSI; Pres. KENAN DURUKAN; Gen. Sec. İLHAMİ AÇIKSÖZ; publ. *Türk harb-iş*.

Koop-İş (Türkiye Tarım Kredi Kooperatifleri Personeli Sendikası) (*Agricultural Credit Co-operative Employees*): Talâtpaşa Bulvarı No. 157/5, Cebeci, Ankara; f. 1964; 6,000 mems.; Pres. İBRAHİM ÇAPAN; Gen. Sec. M. ALİ KIRIKOĞLU.

Likat-İş (Türkiye Liman ve Kara Tahmil-Tahliye İşçileri Sendikası) (*Loading and Unloading Workers*): Necatibey Cad. 13/11-12, Yenişehir, Ankara; f. 1963; 14,770 mems.; also affiliated to ITF; Pres. AHMET KURT; Gen. Sec. YAŞAR ATICI.

Maden-Is (Turkiye Maden, Madeni Eşya ve Makina Sanayii İşçileri Sendikası) (*Metal, Metal Goods and Machine Industry Workers' Union of Turkey*): Barbaros Bulvarı 58, Kat 2-3-4-5, Beşiktaş, Istanbul; f. 1947; 55,000 mems.; Pres. KEMAL TÜRKLER; Gen. Sec. MEHMET ERTÜRK; publ. *Maden-Iş* (fortnightly).

Metal-İş (Türkiye Metal, Çelik, Mühimmat, Makina, Metalden Mamul Eşya ve Oto Sanayii İşçi Sendikaları Federasyonu) (*Federation of Turkish Metal, Steel, Metal Goods, Ammunition, Machines and Automobile Industry Workers' Unions*): Gazi Mustafa Kemal Bulvarı No. 40/1-2, Maltepe, Ankara; f. 1962; 61,428 mems. in 20 mem. unions; Pres. ENVER KAYA; Gen. Sec. MUSTAFA ÖZBEK.

OLEYIS (Türkiye Otel Lokanta ve Eğlence Yerleri İşçileri Sendikası) (*Hotel, Restaurant and Places of Entertainment*): Akay Cad. No. 24, Bakanlıklar, Ankara; f. 1969; 26,970 mems.; also affiliated to IUF; Pres. MUKBİL ZIRTILOĞLU; Gen. Sec. NUSRET AYDIN.

Petrol-İş (Türkiye Petrol, Kimya, Azot ve Atom İşçileri Sendikası) (*Oil, Chemical, Nitrogen and Atomic*): Yildiz Posta Cad., Ajlan Buhaları Sitesi, Evren Apt. D-Blok, Gayrettepe, Istanbul; f. 1950; 1,0200 mems.; also affiliated to IFPCW; Pres. İSMAİL TOPKAR; Gen. Sec. ÖZKAL YİCİ; publ. *Petrol-Iş* (weekly).

Sağlık-İş (Türkiye Sağlık İşçileri Sendikası) (*Health Employees*): Necatibey Cad., Başkent Apt. 1-2, Yenişehir, Ankara; f. 1961; 11,400 mems.; also affiliated to PSI; Pres. MUSTAFA BAŞOĞLU.

Şeker-İş (Türkiye Şeker Sanyii İşçileri Sendikası) (*Sugar Industry*): Mithatpaşa Cad. 13/3, Yenişehir, Ankara; f. 1947; 22,000 mems.; Pres. A. YAŞAR DOĞUALP; Gen. Sec. İLHAMI PARLAKDEMİR; publ. *Şeker-Iş* (newspaper, fortnightly).

Selüloz-İş (Türkiye Selüloz ve Mamulleri İşçileri Sendikası) (*Celluloid Industry*): Hürriyet Caddesi, Işılay Apt. Kat-1, Kocaeli; f. 1952; 8,400 mems.; Pres. NECATİ CANSEVER; Gen. Sec. SALİH GÜNGÖRMEZ.

Tarım-İş (Türkiye Tarım ve Tarım Sanayii İşçileri Sendikası) (*Agricultural Workers*): Necatibey Cad. 22/9-12, Yenişehir, Ankara; f. 1961; 65,000 mems.; affiliated to IUF and IFPAAW; Pres. BİNALİ YAĞİŞAN.

Tekgıda-İş (Türkiye Tütün, Müskirat Gıda ve Yardımcı İşçileri Sendikası) (*Tobacco, Drink, Food and Allied Workers' Union of Turkey*): 4 Levent Konaklar Sokak, P.K. 98, Istanbul; f. 1952; 151,300 mems.; also affiliated to IUF and Türk-İş; Pres. İBRAHİM DENİZCİER; Gen. Sec. NAZM CEYLANDAĞ.

Teksif (Türkiye Tekstil, Örme ve Giyim Sanayii İşçileri Sendikası) (*Textile, Knitting and Clothing*): Ziya Gökalp Cad. 80, Yenişehir, Ankara; f. 1951; 100,000 mems.; also affiliated to ITGWF; Pres. ŞEVKET YILMAZ; Gen. Sec. VAHAP GÜVENÇ.

Tes-İş (Türkiye Enerji, Su, Gaz ve Devlet S.I. İşçi Sendikaları Federasyonu) (*Energy, Water, Gas and State Water Department*): Meşrutıyet Cad. Karanfil Sokak, Beton

Apt. No. 34, Kat-2, Bakanliklar, Ankara; f. 1963; 17,000 mems.; Pres. ORHAN ERÇELİK; Gen. Sec. FARUK BARUT.

Tümtis (Türkiye Motorlu Taşıt İşçileri Sendikası) (*Motor Transport*): Yeniselim Paşa Sok. 62, P.K. 292, Aksaray, Istanbul; f. 1949; 7,163 mems.; also affiliated to ITF; Pres. MEHMET INHANLI; Gen. Sec. D. ZEKİ DEMİREL.

Türk Deniz Ulaş-İş (Türkiye Deniz Taşıtmacılığı İşçi Sendikaları Federasyonu) (*Water Transport*): Necatibey Cad., Şeref Han 401, Karaköy, Istanbul; f. 1959; 12,478 mems.; also affiliated to ITF; Pres. FERİDUN ŞAKİR ÖĞÜNÇ; Gen. Sec. KERİM AKYÜZ.

Türkiye Maden-İş (Türkiye Maden İşçileri Sendikaları Federasyonu) (*Mine Workers*): Mithatpaşa Cad. 10/11-12, Yenişehir, Ankara; f. 1958; 87,731 mems.; also affiliated to IMF; Pres. KEMAL ÖZER; Gen. Sec. MUSTAFA ORHAN.

Yapı-İş (Türkiye Yapıcılık Genel Hizmetleri Sanayii İşçileri Sendikası) (*General Construction Services Industry*): Ziya Gökalp Cad. 20/12, Yenişehir, Ankara; f. 1964; 31,005 mems.; also affiliated to IFBWW; Pres. TAHİR ÖZTÜRK; Gen. Sec. EMRULLAH AKDOĞAN.

Yol-İş (Türkiye Karayolu Yapım-Bakım ve Onarım İşçi Sendikaları Federasyonu) (*Highways Construction, Maintenance and Repair Workers*): İzmir Cad. No. 22/7, Yenişehir, Ankara; f. 1963; 29,759 mems.; also affiliated to PSI; Pres. HALİT MISIRLIOĞLU; Gen. Sec. R. RAFET ALTUN.

TRADE FAIR

İzmir Enternasyonal Fuarı (*Izmir International Fair*): Kültürpark, İzmir; f. 1929; August 20th–September 20th annually.

TRANSPORT

RAILWAYS

Türkiye Cumhuriyeti Devlet Demiryolları İşletmesi—TCDD (*Turkish Republic State Railways*): Ankara; f. 1924; operates all railways and connecting ports; the Railway Administration acquired the status of a public corporation in July 1953; Gen. Dir. ZÜHTÜ ORAL; Gen. Sec. FAHİR BİLCE; publ. *Demiryol* (monthly).

The total length of the railways operated within the national frontiers is 9,831 km. (1972), of which 272 km. are electrified. Five-Year Plans for modernizing the railway system were introduced in 1963, with dieselization and electrification projects having since been carried out. A third Five-Year Plan (1973–77) has been prepared and submitted to the Ministry of Communications; it aims at the further rationalization and modernization of the railways.

A rail link built under a CENTO agreement between Turkey and Iran was put into service in September 1971. Soon afterwards, a direct line to Bulgaria (Pehlivanköy to Edirne) was completed and opened.

ROADS

General Directorate of Highways: Ankara; Dir.-Gen. CELÂLEDDİN DURSUN.

At the beginning of 1975 the total length of expressways was 67 km., the total of all-weather roads was 132,176 km., comprising 32,696 km. of national, 18,480 km. of provincial and 81,000 km. of village roads. A 43-km. Istanbul–Gebze highway was completed as a four-lane expressway early in 1975. Construction of a 3.5-km. expressway between Istanbul–Edirne has also been started. Gebze–İzmit and Pozantı–Tarsus highways, 50 km. and 70 km. respectively, were under construction as freeways. The third bridge across the Golden Horn was opened to traffic in 1975, which completed the Istanbul peripheral highways and the Bosphorus Bridge System.

MOTORISTS' ASSOCIATION

Türkiye Turing ve Otomobil Kurumu (*Touring and Automobile Club of Turkey*): Halaskargazi Cad. 364, Şişli, Istanbul; f. 1923; 9,000 mems.; Dir.-Gen. ÇELİK GÜLERSOY.

SHIPPING

Denizcilik Bankası T.A.O. (*Turkish Maritime Bank*): Genel Müdürlük, Karaköy, Istanbul; f. 1952; capital of TL 2,000m.; four maritime establishments operate passenger, cargo and ferry-boat lines on inter-city, coastal, Adriatic, Aegean and Mediterranean Sea routes; four Port Administrations offer loading, unloading, transfer and warehousing facilities; five ship-yards and dry docks have repair and construction facilities for ships up to 20,000 tons; international concerns such as ship salvage and coastal security; other assets include: six hotels; 73,562 gross tons of shipping, 19 ships and 44,493 gross tons of inter-city communication, 68 ferries.

D.B. Deniz Nakliyati T.A.Ş.: Meclisi Mebusan Cad. 93–97, Fındıklı, Istanbul; associated company of Denizcilik Bankası T.A.O., operating R.C.D. joint services to U.S. Atlantic and Gulf ports; regular liner services to Continent and Mediterranean ports; Gen. Man. CEZMI BIREN; 49 cargo ships, 9 tankers, 25 vessels under construction.

PRIVATE COMPANIES

Denizcilik Anonim Şirketi: Meclisi Mebusan Caddesi, Fındıklı Han Kat 4, Fındıklı, Istanbul; f. 1952; tanker owners and shipbuilders up to 8,000 t.d.w., repair and dry-docking at company's shipyard in Istanbul; Chair. Board of Dirs. HAYRETTIN BARAN; Man. Dir. SABAHATTIN ÜLKÜ; 2 tankers.

Koçtuğ Denizcilik İşletmesi D.İ.: Bankalar Caddesi, Bozkurt-General Han Kat 5, Karaköy, P.K. 884, Istanbul; cargo services to and from Europe and the U.S.A.; Owners S. KOÇMAN, S. GÖKTUG; 6 cargo vessels.

Marmara Transport A.S.: Meclisi Mebusan Cad. No. 7, Salıpazarı Han Kat. 9, Fındıklı, Istanbul; shipbuilding, 2 slipways, capacity 10,000 d.w.t., output 25,000 d.w.t.; tanker services; Chair. A. KUNT; Man. Dir. S. BIGAT; 2 tankers.

Sadikzade Rusen Oğulları Akıf, Talat Sadıkoğlu Kollektif Şirketi: Arzu Han Kat 2, Rhıtım Caddesi, Tophane, İstanbul; cargo services to Europe; Chair. T. SADIKOGLU; Man. Dir. ADNAN ALDORA; 1 cargo vessel.

CIVIL AVIATION

There are airports for scheduled international and internal flights at Yeşilköy (Istanbul), Esenboğa (Ankara) and Adana, while international charter flights are handled by Antalya and Cigli (Izmir). Seventeen other airports handle internal flights only.

Türk Hava Yollari A.O. (THY) (*Turkish Airlines Inc.*): Cumhurivet Caddesi 199-201, Harbiye, Istanbul; f. 1933; 97.35 per cent state-owned; Pres., General REMZI YELMAN; extensive internal network and flights from Ankara and Istanbul to Amsterdam,

Athens, Beirut, Brussels, Copenhagen, Frankfurt, Geneva, London, Milan, Munich, Nicosia, Paris, Rome, Tel-Aviv, Vienna and Zurich; fleet of five Boeing 707, four Boeing 727, seven DC-9, two DC-10 and three F-28.

Turkey is also served by the following foreign airlines: Aeroflot, Air France, Alia, Alitalia, Ariana, AUA, Balkan, British Airways, ČSA, Cyprus Airways, El-Al, Iran National, Iraqi Airways, JAT, KLM, LOT, Lufthansa, MALÉV, MEA, Olympic, Pan American, Pakistan International, Sabena, Saudia, SAS, Swissair and TAROM.

TOURISM

Ministry of Tourism and Information: Gazi Mustafa Kemal Bulvarı 33, Ankara; Dir.-Gen. of Tourism TURGUT BOLU; Dir.-Gen. of Information SELÇUK BAKKALBAŞI.

TOURISM AND INFORMATION OFFICES

Austria: Mahlerstr. 3,1010 Vienna.

Belgium: 42 rue d'Arenberg, Brussels.

France: 102 avenue des Champs-Elysées, Paris 8.

Germany (Federal Republic): Baseler Str. 35-37, Frankfurt-am-Main; Karlsplatz 3/1, 8-Munich-2.

Iran: Khiyabani Ferdowsi, Teheran.

Italy: Piazza Della Repubblica 56, Rome.

Lebanon: rue Alhamra, Imm. du Prince Abdurrahman Bin Abdulaziz 635, ler. étage, Beirut.

Sweden: Kungsgatan 3 S-11, 143 Stockholm.

Switzerland: Limmatquai 72, 4e. étage, Zürich.

United Kingdom: 49 Conduit St., London W.1.

U.S.A.: 500 Fifth Ave., New York, N.Y. 10036.

CULTURAL ORGANIZATIONS

Fine Arts General Directorate (*Güzel Sanatlar Akademisı Genel Müdürlüğü*): Education Ministry, Bakanlıklar, Ankara; Dir.-Gen. MÜKERREM KEYMEN.

Department of Cultural Affairs: (*Kültür Müsteşaeliği*): Undersecretary MEHMET ÖNDER.

PRINCIPAL THEATRES

State Theatre General Directorate (*Devlet Tiyatrosu Genel Müdürlüğü*): part of the above; runs eight playhouses; Dir.-Gen. CÜNEYT GÖKÇER.

Büyük Tiyatro (*Great Theatre*): Ankara.

Küçük Tiyatro (*Small Theatre*): Ankara.

Devlet Opera ve Balesi: Ankara; state opera and ballet; permanent classical and modern ballet company of 65 dancers; Gen. Dir. MITHAT FENMEN.

There are three other state theatres in Ankara, and five private companies. Istanbul has thirteen private companies.

Istanbul City Opera: Taksim, Istanbul (burned down, being rebuilt); Dir. MUHSIN ERTUĞRUL.

ORCHESTRAS

Istanbul State Symphony Orchestra: Taksim, Istanbul; Gen. Dir. MUKERREM BERK.

Presidential Symphony Orchestra: Ankara.

ATOMIC ENERGY

Turkish Atomic Energy Commission: Prime Minister's Office, Bestekar Sokak 29, Ankara; f. 1956; controls the development of peaceful uses of atomic energy; 10 mems.; Chair. Hon. DOĞAN KITAPLI; Sec.-Gen. İBRAHIM DERİNER; publs. *Activity Reports, Research Reports*, etc.

There are nuclear research centres at Çekmece, near Istanbul, and at Ankara.

Technical University of Istanbul: İ.T.Ü. Institute for Nuclear Energy, Istanbul; f. 1961; graduate school of nuclear engineering; Dir. Prof. NEJAT AYBERS; publs. *External Research Reports, Bulletin*, Books.

Institute of Radiobiology: University of Ankara; sub-critical assembly.

Co-operation. Turkey is a member of the International Atomic Energy Agency (IAEA) and the European Nuclear Energy Agency (ENEA). IAEA is providing assistance which includes equipment and technical aid for the universities of Ankara and Istanbul.

Power: Turkey's first nuclear power station, with a capacity of 400 MW, is planned for completion in 1977.

DEFENCE

Chief of General Staff: Gen. SEMIH SANCAR.

Defence Budget (1974-75): 13,427 million liras.

Military Service: 20 months.

Total Armed Forces: 453,000: army 365,000 men, with 1,800 medium tanks, 3 battalions with surface-to-

surface missiles; navy 48,000 men, includes 15 submarines; air force 48,000 men, 290 combat aircraft.

Paramilitary Forces: 75,000 Gendarmerie.

In July 1975 there were an estimated 33,000–40,000 Turkish troops in Cyprus.

EDUCATION

One of the greatest problems confronting the new Republic was that of modernising and extending the educational system, for at that time only 11 per cent of the population were literate. New schools had to be built and equipped in towns and villages; teachers and inspectors trained, and suitable schemes of training devised for them; technical courses provided to equip skilled workers for industry and agriculture; and, above all, training in reading and writing had to be provided for the millions of peasants who had received no schooling.

Under the Ottoman Empire there had been a dual system of education—religious schools existing side by side with others in which ordinary educational subjects were taught, although religious instruction played a large part. Unity of education was recognised as the first requisite; the theological schools were converted into theological seminaries for the training of clergy, or abolished; the others were secularised. The Ministry of Education was declared the sole authority in all educational matters.

One of the main obstacles to literacy was the Arabic script, which required years of study before proficiency could be attained. In 1928, therefore, a Turkish alphabet was introduced, using Latin characters. At the same time the literary language was simplified, and purged of some of its foreign elements. By 1973–74 the education budget amounted to over TL 15,737 million, around 19.4 per cent of the state budget.

People's Schools

This change of script created a need for schools in which reading and writing in the new alphabet could be taught to adults. Temporary institutions known as "people's schools" or "national schools" were set up everywhere. During the winter months these schools gave instruction in reading and writing and other basic subjects to men and women beyond the normal school age. Between 1928 and 1935 some 2 million people received certificates of proficiency. Since then education in Turkey has made big advances, but although literacy is estimated at 65 per cent in towns, it is still much lower in the villages (30.3 per cent in 1960).

Primary Education

A compulsory school attendance law had been passed in 1913, but only under the Republic were measures taken to enforce this. Primary education is now entirely free, and co-education is the accepted basis for universal education. The number of schools has risen from 12,511 in 1950 to 40,577 in 1973, and the number of teachers from 27,144 to 149,084. In 1973–74, over 5.3 million children were attending primary schools.

Secondary Education

The reorganization of the system of secondary education began in the early 1920s. Before the reorganization there were two types of secondary schools: state schools, providing one or two educational stages, and local schools corresponding approximately to the modern middle schools. In 1926 the system of co-education was adopted in day schools of the middle-school group.

Present Organization. This period of education lasts six years, and is free.

The secondary schools are divided into two stages: middle schools and *lycées*, and students who intend to proceed to higher educational institutions must pass through both stages, spending three years in the middle school and three in the *lycée*.

The middle school, although complementary to the *lycée*, is a separate unit, designed to give a definite and complete education to those students who at the end of the course will proceed directly to work. The state examination is taken by all students at the end of the third year. Graduates of a middle school are qualified either to take up an unskilled occupation or to enter upon a vocational course at a school of a higher grade.

The *lycée* takes the student up to the age of 17 or 18 years, and those who wish to proceed to an institute of higher education must pass the state matriculation examination. The study of a modern language (English, French or German) is compulsory in middle schools and *lycées*. In addition, Latin and Greek have been taught in some *lycées* since 1940. The number of secondary schools has increased from 343 in 1950 to 3,235 in 1973, including the *lycées*. The number of students in these schools in the 1973–74 school year totalled 1,255,312.

Adult Education. Since 1932, reading-rooms have been established in every town and many villages. They are centres of social and cultural life and provide evening classes. Their libraries, meeting-halls and recreational facilities are open to all. In the towns there are also evening trade schools which provide technical training for adults, and travelling courses are sent out to the villages.

Higher Education. Higher educational institutions in Turkey were founded, and are administered, by the State. These institutions include the universities and the higher professional schools. There are now 12 universities and 70 institutes of higher education (including teacher training colleges). Three of the universities specialize in scientific and technical subjects. The number of students at universities and other institutes of higher education rose to nearly 190,000 in the academic year 1973–74.

Technical Education. The events of the past thirty years have shown that vocational education is an all-important factor in the life and progress of all nations, and the 1931 programme of the People's Party therefore accepted the desirability of setting up in Turkey professional and trade schools. The problem of technical education began to be seriously considered first in 1926; specialists were invited from Europe and America, and a plan was drawn up for perfecting the existing vocational schools and for founding new ones to meet the economic needs of each region. In addition, plans were made for evening schools to train craftsmen and for the founding of teachers' technical training colleges. There are two such colleges in Ankara, one for men and one for women. The number of technical and vocational schools and colleges in 1973–74 was 846, the number of instructors was 13,055 and 256,725 students were enrolled.

Teachers' Training. There are five types of teachers' training colleges in Turkey, excluding the universities.

Normal Schools. Graduates of the normal schools are appointed to positions in the primary schools, and are eligible by examination for admission to certain higher teachers' training institutions. There are two types of normal schools—seven-year schools, grades 6–12, following the primary school, and four-year schools following the middle school. All normal schools are boarding schools, but day students are accepted. There were 89 normal schools in 1973–74, with a total of 63,074 students.

Secondary Teachers' Training Schools and Pedagogical Institutes. There are 17 secondary teachers' training schools and pedagogical institutes. These schools are normally boarding schools; the following subjects can be studied at one or other of these institutions—literature, science, music, drawing and handicrafts, physical education, German, French, English. The graduates of the pedagogy departments are appointed to be primary school inspectors, or teachers of professional subjects in the normal schools.

Lycée Teachers' Training Colleges. There are three *lycée* teachers' training colleges, in Istanbul, Izmir and Ankara, offering courses in thirteen subjects—Turkish language and literature, history, geography, philosophy, French, English, German, mathematics–astronomy, mathematics–physics, chemistry–physics, physics–chemistry, natural sciences, and commerce. *Lycée* and commercial *lycée*

graduates are admitted to these colleges, and graduates teach in *lycées* and vocational schools of *lycée* standard.

Technical Teachers' Training Colleges for Men and Women. There are two, one for men and one for women; both are in Ankara; the courses are four-year, and graduates to the colleges teach either at boys' trade schools and institutes, or at girls' schools of domestic science and girls' trade schools and institutes.

Commercial Teachers' Training College. The College is at Ankara; it offers a four-year course, and prepares teachers for the commercial *lycées* and commercial middle schools.

Students from the Universities of Istanbul and Ankara may qualify for a teaching certificate by following certain courses, including one on pedagogy.

UNIVERSITIES

Ankara Üniversitesi (*University of Ankara*): Ankara; 1,886 teachers, 17,979 students.

Atatürk Üniversitesi (*Atatürk University*): Erzurum; 584 teachers, 3,428 students.

Boğaziçi Üniversitesi (*Bosporus University*): Istanbul; f. 1971; formerly Robert College; 125 teachers, 1,259 students.

Ege Üniversitesi (*University of Ege*): Bornova, Izmir; 800 teachers, 16,000 students.

Hacettepe Universitesi (*University of Hacetteppe*): 1,057 teachers, 5,000 students.

Istanbul Üniversitesi (*Istanbul University*): Beyazit, Istanbul; 1,654 teachers, 28,478 students.

Istanbul Teknik Üniversitesi (*Istanbul Technical University*): Taksim, Istanbul; 679 teachers, 7,418 students.

Karadeniz Teknik Üniversitesi (*Karadeniz Technical University*): Trabzon; 172 teachers, 2,158 students.

Orta Doğu Teknik Üniversitesi (*Middle East Technical University*): Yenişehir, Ankara; 734 teachers, 7,099 students.

BIBLIOGRAPHY

GENERAL

ALLEN, H. E. The Turkish Transformation (Chicago, 1935).

ARMSTRONG, H. C. Grey Wolf: Mustafa Kemal: an Intimate Study of a Dictator (London, 1937).

AUBOYNEAU & FEVRET. Essai de bibliographie pour l'Empire Ottomane (Paris, 1911).

BAHRAMPOUR, FIROUZ. Turkey, Political and Social Transformation (Gaus, New York, 1967).

BEAN, G. E. Aegean Turkey (Benn, London, 1966). Turkey's Southern Shore (Benn, London, 1968).

BERKES, NIYAZI. The Development of Secularism in Turkey (McGill University Press, Montreal, 1964).

BIRGE, J. K. A Guide to Turkish Area Study (Washington, 1949).

BISBEE, ELEANOR. The New Turks (Philadelphia, 1951). The People of Turkey (New York, 1946).

BRIDGE, ANN. The Dark Moment (New York, 1952). The Falcon in Flight (New York, 1951).

COHN, EDWIN J. Turkish Economic, Social and Political Change (New York, Praeger, 1970).

COOKE, HEDLEY V. Challenge and Response in the Middle East: The Quest for Prosperity, 1919-1951 (New York, 1952).

DODD, C. H. Politics and Government in Turkey (Manchester University Press, 1969).

EDGECUMBE, Sir, C. N. E. Turkey in Europe (Barnes and Noble, N.Y., 1965).

EKREM, SELMA. Turkey: Old and New (New York, 1947).

EREN, NURI. Turkey Today and Tomorrow (New York, 1964).

FREY, F. W. The Turkish Political Elite (M.I.T. Press, Cambridge, Mass., 1965).

GÖKALP, ZIYA. Turkish Nationalism and Western Civilisation (London, 1960).

GÜNTEKİN, REŞAT NURİ (trans. Sir WYNDHAM DEEDES). Afternoon Sun (London, 1950).

The Autobiography of a Turkish Girl (London, 1949).

HARRIS, GEORGE S. The Origins of Communism in Turkey (Hoover Institution, Stanford, Calif., 1967).

HAYIT, B. Turkestan im XX Jahrhundert (Darmstadt, C. W. Leske Verlag, 1956) (in German).

HEYD, URIEL. Foundations of Turkish Nationalism: the Life and Teachings of Ziya Gökalp (Luzac and Harvill Press, London, 1950).

Language Reform in Modern Turkey (Jerusalem, 1954).

HOTHAM, DAVID. The Turks (John Murray, London, 1972).

JACKH, ERNEST. The Rising Crescent (New York, 1950).

JÄSCHKE, GOTTHARD. Der Islam in der Neuen Türkei: eine Rechtsgeschichtliche Untersuchung Die Welt des Islams (N.S., Vol. I, Nos. 1-2).
Die Türkei in den Jahren 1942-51 (Wiesbaden, 1954).

KARPAT, KEMAL. Turkey's Politics, The Transition to a Multi-Party System (Princeton, 1959).

KAZAMIAS, A. M. Education and the Quest for Modernity in Turkey (Allen and Unwin, London, 1967).

KELLY, MARIE NOËLE. Turkish Delights: Travels and Impressions of the Turkish Scene, 1946-1949 (London, 1951).

KINNANE, DIRK. The Kurds and Kurdistan (Oxford, 1965).

KINROSS, Lord. Within the Taurus (London, 1954).
Europa Minor: Journeys in Coastal Turkey (London, 1956).
Turkey (303 photogravure illustrations, London, 1960).
Atatürk (Weidenfeld, London, 1964).

KIŞLALI, AHMET TANER. Forces politiques dans la Turquie moderne (Ankara, 1967).

KORAY, ENVER. Türkiye Tarih Yayınları Bibliografyası 1729-1950; A Bibliography of Historical Works on Turkey (Ankara 1952).

KÜRGER, K. Die Türkei (Berlin, 1951).

LAMB, HAROLD. Suleiman the Magnificent: Sultan of the East (New York, 1951).

LEWIS, BERNARD. Turkey Today (London, 1940).
The Emergence of Modern Turkey (Oxford University Press, London and New York (rev. edition 1970).

LEWIS, G. L. Turkey ("Nations of the Modern World" series) (London, 1955) (3rd edn., Praeger, N.Y., 1965).

LINKE, L. Allah Dethroned (London, 1937).

LUKACH (LUKE), Sir HARRY CHARLES. The Old Turkey and the New (Geoffrey Bles, London, 1955).

MANGO, ANDREW. Turkey (Thames and Hudson, London, 1967).

MARFORI, TERENZIO. La Constituzione della Repubblica Turca (Florence, 1947).

MAYNE, PETER. Istanbul (Dent, London, 1967).

MELLAART, JAMES. Earliest Civilizations of the Near East (Thames and Hudson, London, 1965).
Çatal Hüyük (Thames and Hudson, London, 1967).

MOOREHEAD, A. Gallipoli (New York, Harper, 1956).

MUNTZ, T. G. A. Turkey (New York, 1951).

NEWMAN, BERNARD. Turkish Crossroads (London, 1951).
Turkey and the Turks (Herbert Jenkins, London, 1968).

ORGA, IRFAN and MARGARETE. Atatürk (London, 1962).

PARKER, J., and SMITH, C. Modern Turkey (London, 1940).

PLATE, HERBERT. Das Land der Türken (Verlag Styria, Graz, Wien, Köln, 1957).

ROBINSON, RICHARD D. The First Turkish Republic (Harvard University Press, 1963).

SALTER, CEDRIC. Introducing Turkey (Methuen, London, 1961).

STARK, FREYA. Ionia (London, 1954).
Lycian Shore (London, 1951).
Riding to the Tigris (London, 1956).

STEINHAUS, KURT. Soziologie der turkischen Revolution (Frankfurt, 1969).

STEWART, DESMOND. Turkey (Life World Library Series Time Inc., N.Y., 1965).

SZYLIOWICZ, JOSEPH S. Political Change in Rural Turkey: Erdemli (Mouton, The Hague, 1966).

TOYNBEE, A. J. The Western Question in Greece and Turkey (Constable, London, 1923).

TOYNBEE, A. J., and KIRKWOOD, D. P. Turkey (London, 1926).
Lycian Shore (London, 1956).

TUNAYA, T. Z. Atatürk, the Revolutionary Movement and Atatürkism (Baha, Istanbul, 1964).

UNESCO. Emancipation of the Turkish Woman (Columbia University Press, New York).

VALI, FERENC A. Bridge across the Bosphorus: the Foreign Policy of Turkey (Johns Hopkins Press, 1970).

WARD, BARBARA. Turkey (Oxford, 1942).

WARD, ROBERT E., and RUSTOW, OANKWART A. (eds.). Political Modernizations in Japan and Turkey (Princeton University Press, 1964).

WEBSTER, D. E. The Turkey of Atatürk: Social Progress in the Turkish Reformation (Philadelphia, 1939).

WILLIAMS, GWYN. Turkey: A Travellers Guide and History (Faber and Faber, London, 1967).

YALMAN, A. E. Turkey in my time (University of Oklahoma Press, 1956).

HISTORY

AHMAD, FEROZ. The Young Turks (Oxford University Press, 1969).

ALDERSON, A. D. The Structure of the Ottoman Dynasty (Oxford, 1956).

ALLEN, W. E. D., and MURATOFF, P. Caucasian Battlefields: A History of the Wars on the Turco-Caucasian Border, 1828-1921 (Cambridge, 1953).

CAHEN, CLAUDE. Pre-Ottoman Turkey (Sidgwick and Jackson, London, 1968).

CASSELS, LAVENDER. The Struggle for the Ottoman Empire, 1717-1740 (John Murray, London, 1967).

COLES, PAUL. The Ottoman Impact on Europe (Thames and Hudson, London, 1968; Brace and World, New York, 1968).

DAVIDSON, RODERIC H. Turkey (Prentice-Hall, New York, 1968).

DUDA, HERBERT W. Vom Kalifat zur Republik (Vienna, 1948).

GURNEY, O. R. The Hittites (London, 1952).

JASCHKE, G. Die Türkei in den Jahren 1952-61 (Otto Harrassowitz, Wiesbaden, 1965).

KEDOURIE, ELIE. England and the Middle East: The Destruction of the Ottoman Empire, 1914-1921 (Cambridge, 1956).

LEWIS, BERNARD. Istanbul and the Civilization of the Ottoman Empire (University of Oklahoma Press, 1963).

LEWIS, GEOFFREY. La Turquie, le déclin de l'Empire, les réformes d'Ataturk, la Republique moderne (Verviers/Belgique, 1968).

LIDDELL, ROBERT. Byzantium and Istanbul (London, 1956).

LLOYD, SETON. Early Anatolia (London, 1956).

MANTRAN, ROBERT. Histoire de la Turquie (Paris, 1952).

MILLER, WILLIAM. The Ottoman Empire and its Successors, 1801-1927 (Cambridge, 1934).

OSTROGORSKY, G. History of the Byzantine State (Oxford, 1956).

PALLIS, A. A. In the Days of the Janissaries (London, 1951).

PFEFFERMANN, HANS. Die Zusammenarbeit der Renaissance Päpste mit den Türken (Winterthur, 1946).

PRICE, M. PHILIPS. A History of Turkey: From Empire to Republic (London, 1956).

RAMSAUR, E. E. The Young Turks and the Revolution of 1908 (Princeton University Press, 1957).

RICE, DAVID TALBOT. Art of the Byzantine Era (Frederick A. Praeger, New York, 1963).
Byzantine Art (Penguin, London, 1962).

RICE, TAMARA TALBOT. The Seljuks (London, 1962).

RUNCIMAN, Sir STEVEN. The Fall of Constantinople, 1453 (Cambridge University Press, 1965).

SUMNER, B. H. Peter the Great and the Ottoman Empire (Oxford, 1949).

THOMAS, L. V., and FRYE, R. N. The U.S.A. and Turkey and Iran (Oxford University Press, 1952).

VAUGHAN, DOROTHY. Europe and the Turk: A Pattern of Alliances, 1350-1700 (Liverpool, 1954).

VERE-HODGE, EDWARD REGINALD. Turkish Foreign Policy, 1918-1948 (2nd (revised) edition, London, 1950).

WALDER, DAVID. The Chanak Affair (Hutchinson, London, 1968).

ECONOMY

The Economy of Turkey: an Analysis and Recommendations for Development Program: Report of the Mission sponsored by the International Bank for Reconstruction and Development; in collaboration with the Government of Turkey (Baltimore, 1951).

HERSHLAG, Z. Y. Turkey: the Challenge of Growth (Leiden, 1968).

SHORTER, FREDERIC C. (ed.). Four Studies on the Economic Development of Turkey (Cass, London, 1967; Kelley New York, 1968).

THORNBURG, MAX, SPRY, GRAHAM, and SOULE, GEORGE. Turkey: an Economic Appraisal (New York, 1949).

United Arab Emirates

ABU DHABI   DUBAI   SHARJAH   RAS AL KHAIMAH   UMM AL QUWAIN   AJMAN
FUJAIRAH

GEOGRAPHY

The coastline of the seven United Arab Emirates extends for nearly 400 miles from the frontier of the Sultanate of Oman to Khor al-Odaid on the Qatar Peninsula in the Persian Gulf. The area is one of extremely shallow seas, with offshore islands and coral reefs, and often an intricate pattern of sandbanks and small gulfs as a coastline. In contrast to the Mediterranean, there is a large tide. The waters of the Gulf contain relatively abundant quantities of fish, large and small, hence fishing plays some part in local life. The climate is arid, with very high summer temperatures; and except for a few weeks in winter, air humidity is also very high. The total area of the U.A.E. has been estimated at approximately 32,000 square miles and it has a rapidly growing population estimated at 350,000, now concentrated in the oil boom areas of Abu Dhabi, the capital of the U.A.E., and Dubai. Many inhabitants are nomadic or settled Arabs. In the coastal towns live also many Persians, Indians, Pakistanis, Baluchis and Negros, the latter being descended from slaves carried from Africa during the course of several centuries of slave trading. The most important port is Dubai and this has a population of at least 95,000. Its significance derives from its position on one of the rare deep creeks of the area, and it now has a very large transit trade.

HISTORY

In the early 16th century the Portuguese commercial monopoly of the Gulf area began to be challenged by other European traders eager for a share in the profits from the Eastern trade, first by the Dutch, later by the British. By the end of the century the Portuguese ascendency in the East had declined and in 1650 the Portuguese evacuated Oman losing their entire hold on the Arabian shore. Then followed a period of commercial and political rivalry between the Dutch and the British during which the initial Dutch predominance weakened and in 1766 came practically to an end, while the British were consolidating their supremacy in India.

Both European and Arab pirates were very active in the Gulf during the 17th, 18th and early 19th centuries. Lawlessness reached its height at the beginning of the 19th century when the seafaring Arab tribes were welded together and incited to pillage by Wahhabi emissaries who had established their supremacy over the whole Arabian coast of the Gulf. Attacks on British-flag vessels led to British expeditions against the pirates in 1806 and 1809 and, finally, in 1818 against the pirate headquarters at Ras al Khaimah and other harbours along the 150 miles of "Pirate Coast". In 1820 a General Treaty of Peace for suppressing piracy and slave traffic was concluded between Great Britain and the Arab Tribes of the Gulf. Among the signatories were the principal Sheikhs of the Pirate Coast and the Sheikhs of Bahrain. A strong British squadron was stationed for some time at Ras al Khaimah to enforce the treaty.

Many piratical acts continued to be committed and accordingly, in 1835, the Sheikhs were induced to bind themselves by a "Maritime Truce" not to engage, in any circumstances, in hostilities by sea for a period of six months (i.e. during the pearl-diving season). The advantages of this were so marked that they were easily persuaded to renew the truce and continually did so for increasing periods until, in May 1853 a Treaty of Maritime Peace in Perpetuity was concluded between all the Sheikhs of the "Trucial Coast"—as it was henceforth called—establishing a "perpetual maritime truce". It was to be watched over and enforced by the British Government, to whom the signatories were to refer any breach. The British, however, did not interfere in wars between the Sheikhs on land.

The British concern in stopping the slave trade had also led to contacts with the Trucial Coast, where the Sheikhs had been engaged in carrying slaves from Africa to India and Arabia. By agreements signed with the British in 1838–39 and 1847 the Sheikhs undertook to prohibit the carriage of slaves on board vessels belonging to them or their subjects, and consented to the detention and search of such vessels and to their confiscation in case of guilt.

Towards the end of the 19th century France, Germany and Russia showed increasing interest in the Gulf area and in 1892 Britain entered into separate but identical "exclusive" treaties with the Trucial rulers concluded on different dates, whereby the Sheikhs undertook not to cede, mortgage nor otherwise dispose of parts of their territories to anyone except the British Government, nor to enter into any relationship with a foreign government other than the British without British consent. Britain had already undertaken to protect the states from outside attack in the Perpetual Maritime Treaty of 1853.

In 1820 when the General Treaty was signed, there were only five Trucial States. In 1866, on the death of the Chief Sheikh of Sharjah, his domains were divided amongst his four sons, the separate branches of the family being established at Sharjah, Ras al Khaimah, Dibah and Kalba.

In 1952, Kalba was incorporated into Sharjah when its ruler undertook to accept all the treaties and agreements in force between the United Kingdom and the other Trucial States. These undertakings included recognition of the right of the U.K. Government to fix state boundaries, to settle disputes between the Trucial Sheikhdoms and to render assistance to the Trucial Oman Scouts, a British-officered Arab force set up in 1952. The Ruler of Fujairah also accepted these undertakings when his state was recognized as independent in 1952.

In 1952 on British advice a Trucial Council was established at which all seven rulers met at least twice a year under the chairmanship of the Political Agent in Dubai. It was formed with the object of inducing the rulers to adopt a common policy in administrative matters and in the hope that an eventual federation of the states would ensue.

The advent of commercial production of oil in mid-1962 gave Abu Dhabi a great opportunity for development. The deposition of the Ruler, Sheikh Shakhbut, in 1966 removed a major obstacle to implementing this opportunity, and the history of this sheikhdom since then is a classic example of a society being transformed almost overnight by the acquisition of immense wealth. Dubai has also benefited greatly from the oil boom.

In June 1965 Sheikh Saqr of Sharjah was deposed. In spite of an appeal to the UN Secretary-General, supported by Iraq and the United Arab Republic, the accession of his cousin, Sheikh Khalid, passed off without incident. There was an unsuccessful attempt on the Sheikh's life in July 1970.

After June 1966 Britain gradually built a substantial military base at Sharjah, with the object of replacing Aden as the major base in the Middle East; by July 1968 the force of 3,000 men was also larger than Bahrain's and Sharjah had become the principal base in the Gulf. Early in 1968 the British Government announced that all its forces would be withdrawn from the area by the end of 1971. The Trucial Oman Scouts, a force of some 1,600 men officered and paid for by Britain and based in Sharjah, was proposed as the nucleus of a federal security force after British withdrawal in 1971, but some states, notably Abu Dhabi, were already creating their own defence forces.

It was feared that friction might be aroused by disputes over the ill-defined state borders; those between Qatar, Abu Dhabi and Dubai were settled early in 1970, the settlement being disputed by Saudi Arabia, whose claimed territory overlapped that of Abu Dhabi to a considerable extent. In July 1970 King Faisal requested that a plebiscite be held in the Buraimi district now ruled by Abu Dhabi. Further down the Gulf, offshore rights also caused trouble. Rival claims over the island of Abu Musa were made by both Sharjah and Iran when petroleum exploration began in 1970, but in 1971 an agreement was reached to split the profits from any oil production on the island.

The original proposals for the formation of a federation on the departure of British influence included Bahrain and Qatar, as well as the seven Trucial States, but negotiations on the participation of the larger and more developed states eventually broke down in 1971, and they opted for separate independence. On December 1st, 1971, Britain terminated all existing treaties with the Trucial States. The following day Abu Dhabi, Dubai, Sharjah, Umm al Quwain, Ajman and Fujairah formed the United Arab Emirates and a treaty of friendship was made with Britain.

Ras al Khaimah refused to join the Union until February 1972, when it had become clear that neither Britain or any Arab government was prepared to take action on Iran's seizure of the two Tumb islands in the Gulf belonging to the sheikhdom. In December 1971 the U.A.E. became members of both the Arab League and the United Nations.

In January 1972 the Ruler of Sharjah, Sheikh Khalid, was killed by rebels led by his cousin, Sheikh Saqr, who had been deposed as Ruler in 1965. The rebels were captured, and Sheikh Sultan succeeded his brother as Ruler. Sheikh Sultan soon confirmed that he would rule according to the relatively liberal principles of his brother and retain Sharjah's membership of the U.A.E.

Although the U.A.E. remained one of the most conservative Arab states, it gave considerable support to the Arab cause in the October War of 1973 and participated in the oil cut-backs and boycotts associated with it. It was the first state to operate a total ban on oil exports to the U.S.A. The Abu Dhabi budget makes provision for 3,500 million dirhams in international aid, mainly for Arab countries, in the period 1975-76.

In December 1973 the separate Abu Dhabi Government was disbanded and, in a cabinet reshuffle, some of its members became federal ministers. Most notably the Abu Dhabi oil minister, Mani Said al-Otaiba, became the first federal oil minister. The government reorganization involved a considerable extension of central authority and was a further step towards integration of the seven sheikhdoms. Abu Dhabi was using its economic power to encourage its partners to accept a greater degree of unity, although some seemed reluctant to abandon more of their personal authority. In May 1975, at a session of the Supreme Council, the seven Emirs gave their consent in principle to further steps for centralization. Police regulations are to be unified and a committee of experts is studying the question of a merger of defence forces.

ECONOMIC SURVEY

The economy of the U.A.E. is totally dominated by oil production which since the 1960s has turned this sparsely populated and underdeveloped part of the world into one of the richest of all countries in terms of per capita income. This new-found wealth has, since federation in 1971, been spread from the oil-rich Emirates of Abu Dhabi and Dubai to the other less-favoured states. Massive capital investment in ports and roads, and the development of social services, are changing the face of the Emirates. The financial and commercial sectors have expanded rapidly, but industrial development is hampered by a lack of manpower and raw materials. The U.A.E. leaders have been anxious to diversify the economy, so the traditional activities of fishing and agriculture have been encouraged and modernization projects undertaken to improve yields.

ABU DHABI

Abu Dhabi is the U.A.E.'s largest oil producer, the rate of production in 1974 being 1,415,000 b/d. Abu Dhabi Petroleum Company is largely responsible for exploitation of onshore deposits and Abu Dhabi Marine Areas for offshore. Export of petroleum began in 1963 and has increased continuously ever since. In 1971 revenue from oil was 431 million U.S. dollars, but by 1974 it had risen to 4,896 million U.S. dollars. Oil production fell during the first half of 1975 owing to price increases and a fall in world demand for oil. A state oil company, the Abu Dhabi National Oil Company has been created to represent the Government on the boards of foreign companies. It has been given a monopoly of oil-distribution in the country and is responsible for oil installations and oil-based industries. Until 1974 Abu Dhabi was a member of OAPEC, when it was replaced by the U.A.E. (For further information on Oil please see the section "Oil" under Trade and Industry in this chapter, and the chapter Oil in the Middle East and North Africa, pp. 69-102).

The population was estimated at around 17,000 before 1966, but with the considerable number of immigrants since then it was thought to have reached 95,000 in 1974. This explosive growth has inevitably led to shortcomings in such facilities as water and power supplies, accommodation and transport, though money is available to solve these problems. In 1968 Abu Dhabi initiated its first National Plan which envisaged a total expenditure of BD 316.97 million ($662 million) of which over 90 per cent was to be spent on social services and industrial and agricultural projects during the period 1968-73. The pace and pressure of development led to a minor crisis in late 1969 when expenditure began to exceed revenues, partly because the Government had authorized more projects than it could immediately pay for, especially as inflation had driven up the cost of all construction. A policy of consolidation was introduced at the end of 1969, with a resultant slowdown in the rate of develop-

ment. In the 1970 budget development expenditure was reduced by 35 per cent from the level envisaged under the five-year plan. After the 1969–70 "freeze" the Government continued a more cautious policy of "controlled expansion" until 1972. Then the development budget was once more allowed to grow, so that in 1973 it stood at 945 million dirhams compared with only 333 million in 1970. Following an industrial survey to examine ways of reducing the state's dependence on oil production, a $30 million refinery with a capacity of 15,000 barrels a day is to be constructed in Umm Al Nar for the newly established national oil company. A liquefied gas plant is under construction on Das Island and a cement works with an initial annual output of 200,000 tons is being built. The construction industry is booming as government money flows into housing projects and improved transport facilities. Abu Dhabi's development has been made more difficult by the poor port facilities—most trade comes through Dubai as the Gulf waters surrounding Abu Dhabi are extremely shallow. To overcome this dependence on Dubai, Abu Dhabi is being provided with an artificial deepwater harbour, Port Zayed, of which the first section is now in operation. The extension of the road network is continuing apace. The Government is studying the possibilities for creation of a tourist industry in the U.A.E. Agriculture is difficult but experiments are being carried out in cultivation under arid conditions, particularly on Sadiyat Island where a research centre was set up in 1967 by the Abu Dhabi Government and the University of Arizona.

In May 1973 the U.A.E. brought uniform currency into circulation, replacing the Bahrain dinar used in Abu Dhabi and the Qatar/Dubai riyal used in Dubai and the other northern states. The new denomination, the dirham, is equal to one Q/D riyal or one-tenth of the Bahrain dinar.

DUBAI

The Dubai Petroleum Company (DPC) operates a concession offshore of Dubai. The ownership of DPC is given in the chapter "Oil in the Middle East and North Africa", page 97, but in July 1975 it was announced that negotiations had been concluded on a 100 per cent participation agreement between Dubai and the oil companies concerned. The offshore concessionaires announced in 1966 that oil had been discovered in commercial quantities, and production started in 1969 at the rate of 30,000 barrels per day, rising to 100,000 b/d in early 1971 and a rate of 241,000 b/d for 1974, earlier estimates of reserves having been far exceeded. By 1974 annual oil revenues had reached an estimated U.S $640 million, almost five times as much as in 1973.

Dubai has long been the principal commercial centre and entrepôt port for the Emirates, and in consequence has benefited greatly from the oil boom in the area. The basis of the supremacy has been the relatively good facilities for shipping offered by Dubai

Creek; this lead has now been consolidated by the construction of a £24 million deep water harbour. This harbour, known as Port Rashid, which was completed in 1972, is the largest harbour in the Middle East and Dubai is to become a free port. Work began in 1973 on a dry-dock scheme for Dubai which will make it the largest supertanker complex in the Gulf. A tunnel and two new bridges will be built under and over the channel. A cement plant producing 500,000 tons a year is to be completed by 1975. Dubai's official import figures are the most reliable index of economic activity in the Emirates; imports have risen from 761 million dirhams in 1968 to 4,816 million in 1974. The sheikhdom has all the characteristics of a boom economy, albeit not in such an extreme form as Abu Dhabi. Massive construction projects absorb most of the local labour force, and immigrants, whose numbers have now had to be restricted, already outnumber natives. All food and manufactured articles have to be imported. Traditional occupations have declined— in Dubai these mainly consisted of fishing and smuggling. Dubai's low tariffs and absence of official restrictions have fostered smuggling to states with higher tariffs in the Gulf, and to India and Pakistan. This used to be particularly true of gold, still thought to be smuggled into India on a large if declining scale; the apparent decline is due to both increasingly vigilant Indian policing and to the safer and equally profitable opportunities now available in legal trade.

THE SMALLER SHEIKHDOMS

Until very recently the other Trucial States had only a traditional and very impoverished economy based on fishing and pearling. Red oxide deposits are exploited in Sharjah and Ras al Khaimah possesses an Agricultural Trials Station operated under British supervision. A cement works producing 700 tons a day is to be built in Sharjah, which has particularly good limestone resources. Another cement plant, with an annual output of 200,000 tons, has been constructed in Ras Al Khaimah; it is the first industry of any size to be introduced into the state. Several sheikhdoms have produced colourful series of postage stamps and attempted to tap the world philatelic market, with varying success. All have now signed oil agreements which give the rulers a limited income whilst exploration continues. In 1973 Crescent Petroleum discovered oil in commercial quantities off Abu Musa Island, which is disputed between Sharjah and Iran. The countries are to share oil revenue equally between them. Production began in 1974 and it was hoped to reach 100,000 b/d, but during the first quarter of 1975 it reached only 43,000 b/d. This concession is operated by Buttes Oil and Gas.

Sharjah is the most developed of these five states, owing to the former presence of a British R.A.F. station and the progressive attitude of the late Ruler, Sheikh Khalid. A British withdrawal has meant loss of an important source of revenue and employment, although it may develop into a repair complex for commercial aircraft, and there are plans to exploit the rich fishing grounds from Sharjah's enclave on the Gulf of Oman, around Khor Fakkan. Sharjah port, known as Mina Khalid, is being expanded to take large ocean-going vessels. Improved communications should encourage a profitable expansion of fisheries.

STATISTICAL SURVEY
AREA AND POPULATION

AREA (sq. miles)		POPULATION (1974 estimates)			
Total	Abu Dhabi (estimate)	Total	Abu Dhabi	Dubai	Sharjah
32,000	25,000	350,000*	95,000	100,000	55,000

Population estimates (1974) for the other sheikhdoms are as follows: Ras al Khaimah 45,000, Fujairah 15,000, Ajman 8,000 and Umm al Quwain 7,000.

* 1975 Estimate.

OIL
PRODUCTION OF CRUDE OIL

	ABU DHABI MARINE AREAS LTD. (long tons)	ABU DHABI PETROLEUM CO. LTD. (long tons)	DUBAI PETROLEUM COMPANY (metric tons)
1970 . .	12,686,029	20,079,903	4,306,000
1971 . .	16,933,168	27,160,258	6,252,000
1972 . .	20,827,096	28,833,735	7,727,000
1973 . .	23,938,949	37,564,329	11,047,000
1974 . .	21,812,871	43,308,610	12,000,000*

* Estimate.

FINANCE

1,000 fils = 10 dinars = 1 U.A.E. dirham.

Coins: 1, 5, 10, 25, 50 and 100 fils.

Notes: 1, 5, 10, 50, 100 and 1,000 dirhams.

Exchange rates (July 1975): £1 sterling = 8.633 dirhams; U.S. $1 = 3.947 dirhams.

100 U.A.E. dirhams = £11.584 = $25.333.

Note: Before June 1966 the currency used by the states of Trucial Oman (now the United Arab Emirates) was the Persian Gulf Indian rupee, valued at 1s. 6d. sterling (£1 = 13.33 rupees). When the Indian rupee was devalued in June 1966, Abu Dhabi adopted the Bahrain dinar (of 1,000 fils) while the other states used Saudi Arabian currency prior to the introduction of the Qatar/Dubai riyal (at par with the old rupee) in September 1966. The Bahrain dinar, equal to 10 old rupees, was valued at U.S. $2.10 ($1 = 476.19 fils) until August 1971; at $2.28 ($1 = 438.60 fils) from December 1971 to February 1973; and at $2.533 ($1 = 394.74 fils) from February 1973. The Q/D riyal, also used in Qatar was valued at 21 U.S. cents ($1 = 4.762 riyals) until August 1971; at 22.8 U.S. cents ($1 = 4.386 riyals) from December 1971 to February 1973; and at 25.33 U.S. cents ($1 = 3.947 riyals) from February 1973. Between November 1967 and June 1972 the Bahrain dinar was valued at 17s. 6d. sterling (87½ new pence) and the Q/D riyal at 1s. 9d. (8.75 new pence), the exchange rates being £1 = 1.143 dinars = 11.43 riyals. In May 1973 the U.A.E. adopted a common currency, the dirham, which was at par with the Q/D riyal (renamed the Qatar riyal) and thus valued at 25.33 U.S. cents. The original dollar valuation remains in effect.

FEDERAL BUDGET EXPENDITURE
(1975–76—'000 U.A.E. dirhams)

Ministry of Health	267,000
Ministry of Education . . .	457,000
Ministry of Interior	343,500
Ministry of Information and Culture .	93,800
Ministry of Communications . .	53,300
Ministry of Social Affairs . .	84,800
Ministry of Public Works . .	188,800
Ministry of Agriculture and Fisheries .	65,700
Ministry of Housing . . .	79,500
Ministry of Electricity and Water .	256,000
TOTAL (incl. others) . .	2,778,234

ABU DHABI BUDGET
(1975–76—'000 U.A.E. dirhams)

Current Expenditure	3,277,745
Development Budget . . .	3,500,000
Support of Federal Budget . . .	2,000,000
International Aid	3,500,000
Capital Payments	600,000
TOTAL (incl. others) . .	13,083,652

EXTERNAL TRADE

Dubai

IMPORTS
('000 U.A.E. dirhams)

COMMODITIES	1971	1972	1973	1974
Household goods	208,137	274,178	345,722	
Foodstuffs	150,080	198,766	282,843	
Garments	134,140	215,236	388,559	
Machinery	192,001	249,841	400,321	Reclassified
Building materials	142,154	153,032	326,414	
Electrical, radio and allied goods .	54,970	66,834	98,318	(*see*
Stationery	7,314	11,108	16,514	
Photographic goods . . .	3,773	7,600	9,614	Table on
Cosmetics	8,986	12,758	20,715	
Medicines and chemicals . . .	19,263	16,095	30,844	page 768)
Fuel and oil	26,710	84,311	121,291	
Arms and ammunition . . .	10,078	4,847	9,541	
Oil field materials	90,347	165,295	272,845	
Liquor and wine	11,063	14,754	17,423	
TOTAL	1,059,021	1,474,662	2,341,010	4,816,586

PRINCIPAL COUNTRIES—*continued*]

PRINCIPAL COUNTRIES	1971	1972	1973	1974
Australia	17,986	22,130	44,001	75,285
China	33,887	46,535	81,065	167,819
France	16,373	33,492	70,415	124,800
Germany, Federal Republic . . .	36,252	43,259	85,982	218,506
Hong Kong	35,562	57,604	98,704	140,340
India	47,010	54,026	77,639	181,993
Iran	19,773	14,029	81,745	260,150
Japan	181,699	308,157	528,573	942,229
Kuwait	6,925	12,085	58,276	161,896
Netherlands	32,018	41,518	42,126	97,801
Pakistan	25,282	29,336	51,769	124,681
Saudi Arabia	22,792	77,399	16,104	36,126
Switzerland	93,724	110,249	104,158	136,173
United Kingdom	186,450	191,314	280,847	576,541
U.S.A.	127,394	200,483	328,719	580,088

EXPORTS AND RE-EXPORTS
(U.A.E. dirhams)

1972	. .	179,115,368
1973	. .	222,507,616
1974	. .	303,132,196

IMPORTS
('ooo U.A.E. dirhams)

Food and live animals	661,885
Beverages and tobacco	87,782
Crude materials (inedible) except fuels .	101,510
Mineral fuels, lubricants, etc. . .	435,255
Animal and vegetable oils and fats .	31,349
Chemicals	153,113
Basic manufactures	1,327,902
Machinery and transport equipment .	1,037,598
Miscellaneous manufactured articles .	538,101
Oil field materials	412,220
Other commodities	29,865
TOTAL	4,816,585

There is a large and officially authorized trade in gold which is not, however, included in the official trade statistics for Dubai. Gold exports: (1970) 258 tons, (1971) 216 tons.

Abu Dhabi

IMPORTS
('ooo U.A.E. dirhams)

COMMODITIES	1973
Machinery and transport equipment .	557,824
Manufactured goods . . .	213,658
Food and live animals . . .	75,312
Petroleum and petroleum products .	36,051
Chemicals	31,217
TOTAL (including others) .	1,018,944

('ooo U.A.E. dirhams)

COUNTRIES	1972	1973
Australia	14,440	26,229
Dubai	54,800	n.a.
France	55,690	63,937
Germany, Federal Republic .	43,570	71,776
Italy	20,020	20,349
Japan	117,860	123,627
Lebanon	21,520	25,458
Netherlands	21,340	28,740
United Kingdom . . .	181,380	280,359
U.S.A.	103,950	202,698

TOTAL IMPORTS
('ooo U.A.E. dirhams)

1970	. .	352,453
1971	. .	469,416
1972	. .	757,620
1973	. .	1,018,944

EDUCATION

United Arab Emirates

	1970–71	1971–72	1972–73	1973–74
Schools . . .	66	74	128	147
Students . . .	27,745	32,871	40,193	44,272
Teachers . . .	1,198	1,585	2,386	2,957

Source: Ministry of Education *Annual Report 1973-74.*

THE CONSTITUTION

A provisional constitution for the U.A.E. was set up in December 1971. This laid the foundation for the federal structure of the Union of the seven sheikhdoms, previously known as the Trucial States.

The highest federal authority is the Supreme Council which comprises the rulers of the seven Emirates. It elects a president and vice-president from among its members. The president appoints a prime minister and a cabinet. There is a National Federal Council composed of 34 members appointed separately by each Emirate.

In June 1974 the Ministry of Justice was instructed to draft a permanent federal constitution to replace the provisional constitution.

THE GOVERNMENT

HEAD OF STATE

President: Sheikh ZAYED BIN SULTAN AL-NHAYYAN (Ruler of Abu Dhabi).
Vice-President: Sheikh RASHID BIN SAID AL-MAKTUM (Ruler of Dubai).

SUPREME COUNCIL OF THE UNION
(with each ruler's date of accession)

Ruler of Sharjah: Sheikh SULTAN BIN MUHAMMAD AL-QASIMI (1972).

Ruler of Ras al Khaimah: Sheikh SAQR BIN MUHAMMAD AL-QASIMI (1948).

Ruler of Umm al Quwain: Sheikh AHMAD BIN RASHID AL-MU'ALLA, M.B.E. (1929).

Ruler of Ajman: Sheikh RASHID BIN HUMAID AL-NU'AIMI (1928).

Ruler of Dubai: Sheikh RASHID BIN SAID AL-MAKTUM (1958).

Ruler of Abu Dhabi: Sheikh ZAYED BIN SULTAN AL-NHAYYAN (1966).

Ruler of Fujairah: Sheikh HAMAD BIN MUHAMMAD AL-SHARQI (1974).

CABINET
(*August* 1975)

Prime Minister: Sheikh MAKTUM BIN RASHID AL-MAKTUM.

Deputy Prime Minister: KHALIFAH BIN ZAYED AL-NHAYYAN.

Minister of Finance and Industry: HAMDAN BIN RASHID AL-MAKTUM.

Minister of Public Works: HAMDAN BIN MUHAMMED AL-NHAYYAN.

Minister of the Interior: MUBARAK BIN MUHAMMED AL-NHAYYAN.

Minister of Defence: MUHAMMAD BIN RASHID AL-MAKTUM.

Minister of Communications: MUHAMMAD SAEED AL-MULLA.

Minister of Foreign Affairs: AHMAD KHALIFAH AS-SUWAIDI.

Minister of Economy and Commerce: Sultan BIN AHMAD AL-MU'ALLA.

Minister of Health: SAIF BIN MUHAMMAD AL-NHAYYAN.

Minister of Labour and Labourers: MUHAMMAD BIN SULTAN AL-QASIMI.

Minister of Education: ABDULLAH IMRAN TARYAM.

Minister of Petroleum and Mineral Resources: MANI' SAID AL-OTAIBA.

Minister of Social Affairs: ABDUL AZIZ BIN RASHID AL-NU'AIMI.

Minister of Electricity and Water: ABDULLAH BIN HUMAID AL-QASIMI.

Minister of Justice: AHMAD BIN SULTAN AL-QASIMI.

Minister of Information and Culture: AHMAD BIN HAMED.

Minister of Agriculture and Fisheries: SAEED SALMAN (acting).

Minister of Housing: SAEED SALMAN.

Minister of Islamic Affairs and Awqaf: THANI BIN ISA BIN HAREB.

Minister of Youth and Sports: RASHID BIN HUMAID.

Minister of Planning: MUHAMMED AL-KINDI.

Minister of State for the Supreme Council's Affairs: ABDUL MALEK KAYED AL-QASIMI.

Minister of State for Cabinet Affairs: OTEIBA BIN ABDULLAH AL-OTEIBA.

Minister of State for Interior Affairs: HAMMUDAH BIN ALI.

Minister of State for Foreign Affairs: SAIF SAID GHUBASH.

Minister of State for Information: SAID AL-GHAITH.

Ministers of State: HAMAD BIN SAIF ASH-SHARQI, AHMAD BIN SULTAN BIN SLAYYEM.

Minister of State for Financial and Industrial Affairs: MUHAMMAD HABWISH.

ASSEMBLY

U.A.E. NATIONAL FEDERAL COUNCIL

Formed under the provisions of the temporary constitution, it is composed of 44 members from the various Emirates. Each Emirate appoints its own representatives separately. The Council studies laws proposed by the Council of Ministers and can reject them or suggest amendments.

DIPLOMATIC REPRESENTATION

EMBASSIES ACCREDITED TO THE UNITED ARAB EMIRATES

(Abu Dhabi unless otherwise stated.)

Afghanistan: Baghdad, Iraq.

Bangladesh: *Ambassador:* A. W. SHAMS-UL-ALAM.

Egypt: P.O.B. 4026; *Ambassador:* MOHAMED ALI KAMEL.

France: P.O.B. 4014; *Ambassador:* PAUL MARTIN.

Gabon: *Ambassador:* ABU BAKR BUKUKU.

Germany, Federal Republic: *Ambassador:* KARL HEINZ KUNZMANN.

India: P.O.B. 4090; *Ambassador:* S. E. H. RIZVI.

Iran: *Ambassador:* MANOUCHEHR BENHAM.

Iraq: P.O.B. 4030; *Ambassador:* TAWFIQ AL MOUMEN.

Italy: Kuwait City, Kuwait.

Japan: P.O.B. 2430; *Ambassador:* MASANAO ODAKA.

Jordan: P.O.B. 4024; *Ambassador:* MANSOUR BATAINEH.

Kuwait: P.O.B. 926; *Ambassador:* SULEIMON MAJID AL SHAHIN.

Lebanon: P.O.B. 4023; *Ambassador:* HASSIB AL-ABDULLAH.

Libya: P.O.B. 2091; *Ambassador:* MUHAMMAD BASHIR AL-MUGHAYRIBI.

Mauritania: *Ambassador:* YAHDIYA BIN SAYYID AHMAD.

Morocco: *Ambassador:* HASSAN AL FASSI AL FIHRI.

Netherlands: Kuwait City, Kuwait.

Pakistan: *Ambassador:* JAMIL EDDIN HASAN.

Saudi Arabia: *Ambassador:* ABDULLA KHAYYALI.

Somalia: *Ambassador:* ABDI NUR ALI YUSSUF.

Spain: Kuwait City, Kuwait.

Sudan: P.O.B. 2227; *Ambassador:* HASHIM MUHAMMAD SALEH.

Switzerland: Jeddah, Saudi Arabia.

Syria: P.O.B. 4011, *Ambassador:* MOUNIB AL RIFAI.

Tanzania: Cairo, Egypt.

Tunisia: *Ambassador:* AL HASHIMI WANAS.

United Kingdom: P.O.B. 248; *Ambassador:* DANIEL JOHN MACCARTHY, C.M.G.

United States: P.O.B. 4009; *Ambassador:* MICHAEL STERNER.

Yemen Arab Republic: P.O.B. 2095; *Ambassador:* MUHAMMAD SAID QUBATI.

Zaire: *Ambassador:* KABIKA MWENE-NGABWE DEDE.

The U.A.E. also has diplomatic relations with Bahrain and Oman.

JUDICIAL SYSTEM

U.A.E. subjects and citizens of all Arab and Muslim states are subject to the jurisdiction of the local courts.

In the local courts the rules of Islamic law generally prevail. A modern code of law is being produced for Abu Dhabi.

In Dubai there is a court run by a *qadi*, while in some of the other states all legal cases are referred immediately to the Ruler or a member of his family, who will refer to a *qadi* only if he cannot settle the matter himself. In Abu Dhabi a professional Jordanian judge presides over the Ruler's Court.

The 95th article of the provisional constitution of 1971 provided for the setting up of a Union Supreme Court and Union Primary Tribunals.

The Union has exclusive legislative and executive jurisdiction over all matters that are concerned with the strengthening of the Federation such as foreign affairs, defence and Union armed forces, security, finance, communications, construction, traffic control, education, public health, currency, measures, standards and weights, electricity, matters relating to nationality and emigration, Union information, etc.

The individual emirates maintain jurisdiction in all matters not assigned to the exclusive jurisdiction of the Union as stated in the constitution. In May 1974 the Minister of Justice proposed a draft law which would establish federal courts throughout the country and transfer jurisdiction over many matters from local to federal courts.

RELIGION

Most of the inhabitants are Muslims of the Sunni and Shi'ite sects.

THE PRESS

Abu Dhabi Chamber of Commerce Review: P.O.B. 662, Abu Dhabi; monthly; Arabic, some articles in English.

al-Ittihad (*Unity*): P.O.B. 17, Abu Dhabi; f. 1972; first daily paper in the U.A.E.; Editor-in-Chief KHALED MUHAMMAD AHMAD.

al-Wahdah: P.O.B. 4234, Abu Dhabi; f. 1973; independent; daily; Man. Editor RASHID AWEDA.

U.A.E. News: Ministry of Information and Culture, P.O.B. 791, Abu Dhabi; weekly; English.

U.A.E. and Abu Dhabi Official Gazette: P.O.B. 899, Abu Dhabi; Arabic.

Akhbar Dubai: Department of Information, Dubai Municipality, P.O.B. 1420, Dubai; f. 1965; weekly; Arabic.

Dubai External Trade Statistics: P.O.B. 516, Dubai; monthly; English.

Dubai Official Gazette: P.O.B. 516, Dubai; Arabic and English; quarterly or as necessary.

Gulf Weekly Mirror: P.O.B. 290, Dubai; branch office of the Gulf weekly newspaper; English; Rep. T. EDGAR.

---

al Sharooq (*The Sunrise*): Sharjah; f. 1970; monthly; Dir.-Gen. TAREEM OMRAN; Editor YOUSEF AL HASSAN; circ. 3,000.

Akhbar Ras al Khaimah: Ras al Khaimah; monthly; Arabic.

Ras al Khaimah: P.O.B. 87, Ras al Khaimah; Chamber of Commerce magazine; quarterly; Arabic.

RADIO AND TELEVISION

There are radio stations in Abu Dhabi, Dubai, Ras al Khaimah and Sharjah and television stations in Abu Dhabi and Dubai. Colour television is in operation in Abu Dhabi and Dubai.

Voice of the United Arab Emirates: f. 1972; stations in Abu Dhabi, Dubai, Ras al Khaimah and Sharjah; broadcasts daily in Arabic over a wide area ; commercial. It is estimated that there are 50,000 radio receivers and 16,000 television receivers in the U.A.E.

FINANCE

BANKING

United Arab Emirates Bankers' Association: P.O.B. 240, Abu Dhabi; Chair. R. G. GOSSIP (Chartered Bank); Vice-Chair. J. R. WILLIAMSON (National Bank of Dubai, P.O.B. 777, Dubai).

PRINCIPAL BANKS

Al Ahli Bank: P.O.B. 1719, Dubai.

Ajman Arab Bank: Ajman.

Algemene Nederlandse Bank: Dubai.

Arab Bank: Amman, Jordan; P.O.B. 875, Abu Dhabi; P.O.B. 1650, Dubai; P.O.B. 130, Sharjah; P.O.B. 20, Ras al Khaimah; Ajman.

Arab-African Bank: P.O.B. 1049, Dubai; and Sharjah.

Bank of Baroda: P.O.B. 2303, Abu Dhabi; Man. A. A. NEMAZIE, also Dubai.

Bank of Cairo: P.O.B. 533, Abu Dhabi.

Bank of Credit and Commerce International S.A.: P.O.B. 4021, Abu Dhabi; Dubai, Sharjah and Ajman.

Bank of Oman Ltd.: P.O.B. 2111, Dubai; f. 1967; cap. p.u. 6.7m. dirhams (May 1974); brs. at Abu Dhabi, Al Ain, Ajman, Hor-Al-Anz, Naif Rd. and Dubai Side; Gen. Man. ABDULLAH AL-GHURAIR.

Bank of Paris and the Netherlands: P.O.B. 4012, Abu Dhabi.

Bank of Sharjah: P.O.B. 1394, Sharjah.

British Bank of the Middle East, The: London; brs. in Dubai, Sharjah, Khor Fakkhan, Ras al Khaimah, Abu Dhabi, Fujairah, Kalba, Diba, Ajman and Umm al Quwain.

Chartered Bank: London; P.O.B. 240 and 1000, Abu Dhabi; P.O.B. 999 and 1125, Dubai; P.O.B. 5, Sharjah; P.O.B. 1240, Al Ain.

Commercial Bank of Dubai: P.O.B. 1709, Dubai; f. 1969; owned by Chase Manhattan Bank, Commerzbank A.G. and the Commercial Bank of Kuwait; brs. in Deira (3), Jumeriah (1), Ras al-Khaimah (1), Abu Dhabi (1), Sharjah (1).

Distributors Co-operative Credit Bank: P.O.B. 888, Abu Dhabi.

Dubai Bank: P.O.B. 2545, Deira, Dubai; f. 1970; control is held by local interests, but British, French and American banks are also participating; p.u. cap. 11.5m. dirhams; Chair. ABDUL RAHIM BIN IBRAHIM GALADARI; Gen. Man. P. J. REYNOLDS.

Dubai Islamic Bank: Dubai.

First National Bank of Chicago: P.O.B. 1655, Dubai.

First National City Bank: New York; P.O.B. 749, Dubai; P.O.B. 346, Sharjah; P.O.B. 999, Abu Dhabi.

Grindlays Bank Ltd.: London; P.O.B. 241, Abu Dhabi; P.O.B. 225, Ras al Khaimah; P.O.B. 357, Sharjah; P.O.B. 4166, Dubai; P.O.B. 1100, Al Ain.

Habib Bank (Overseas): Karachi; P.O.B. 888, Dubai; P.O.B. 897, Abu Dhabi; 9 other brs. in United Arab Emirates.

Melli Bank (Iran): P.O.B. 1894, Dubai; P.O.B. 459, Sharjah.

National Bank of Abu Dhabi: P.O.B. 4, Abu Dhabi; f. 1968; auth. cap. Dh. 10m.; res. Dh. 7.5m.; dep. Dh. 600m.; Gen. Man. D. G. SUTCLIFFE.

National Bank of Dubai: P.O.B. 777, Dubai; brs. in Abu Dhabi and Umm al Quwain; cap. p.u. Dh. 18.3m.; Gen. Man. D. W. MACK, M.B.E.

National Bank of Kuwait: Sharjah.

Rafidain Bank (Iraq): P.O.B. 273, Ras al Khaimah.

Sedarat Bank (Iran): P.O.B. 700, Abu Dhabi; P.O.B. 4182, Dubai; other brs. at Sharjah, Ajman, Fujairah and Ras al Khaimah.

Toronto Dominion Bank: Abu Dhabi and Dubai.

United Arab Emirates Development Bank: P.O.B. 2449, Abu Dhabi; participates in development of real estate, agriculture, fishery, livestock and light industries; cap. p.u. Dh. 500m.

United Bank: P.O.B. 1000, Dubai; P.O.B. 237, Abu Dhabi; eight other brs.

INSURANCE

Abu Dhabi National Insurance Co.: Omair Bldg., Sh. Khalifa St., P.O.B. 839, Abu Dhabi; f. 1972; cap. 5m. dirhams subscribed 25 per cent by the Government of Abu Dhabi and 75 per cent by United Arab Emirates nationals; Gen. Man. HISHAN ABDULRAZAK.

Arab Commercial Enterprises (Abu Dhabi) Ltd.: P.O.B. 585; Man. MANSOUR ABDUL RAHMAN.

Arab Commercial Enterprises (Dubai) Ltd.: P.O.B. 1100, Dubai; Man. TOUFIC H. BARAKEH.

Arabia Insurance Co. Ltd.: P.O.B. 1050, Dubai; Rep. WALEED H. JISHI.

Dubai Insurance Co.: P.O.B. 3027, Dubai; Chair. MAJID AL FUTTAIM; Gen. Man. FAROUK HUWAIDI.

Sharjah Insurance Co.: P.O.B. 792, Sharjah; f. 1970; monopoly of local insurance business; cap. 2.5m. dirhams, half subscribed by the Sharjah Government.

CHAMBERS OF COMMERCE

Abu Dhabi Chamber of Commerce and Industry: P.O.B. 662, Abu Dhabi; f. 1969; mems. 1,700; Pres. AHMED MASSOUD; publ. monthly magazine in Arabic, some articles in English.

Dubai Chamber of Commerce: Gamal Abdul Nasser Square, P.O.B. 1457, Dubai; f. 1965; 2,300 mems. Pres. SAIF AHMED ALGHURAIR.

Ras al Khaimah Chamber of Commerce, Industry and Agriculture: P.O.B. 87, Ras al Khaimah; registers trademarks in Ras al Khaimah; publ. quarterly magazine in Arabic and English.

Sharjah Chamber of Commerce and Industry: P.O.B. 580, Sharjah; f. 1970; Pres. MOHAMMED BIN OBAID AL-SHAMSI.

DEVELOPMENT

Capital Projects include inter-state roads, urban water and electricity schemes, housing and other urban development, rural water supplies, agricultural extension schemes and harbour works. Investigations into water resources, mineral prospects, soil, agricultural marketing and fisheries have been conducted.

Abu Dhabi Fund for Arab Economic Development (ADFAED): P.O.B. 814; f. 1971 with a capital of BD 50 million to provide development aid to Arab countries; in May 1974 the scope of aid was broadened and the capital was quadrupled to 2,000 million dirhams; Dir. Dr. HASAN ABBAS ZAKI.

National Bank for Investment and Development: P.O.B. 2449; f. 1974; development bank to finance private projects in industry, construction and fisheries; cap. 500m. dirhams; brs. in all seven emirates.

Planning Department: P.O.B. 12, Abu Dhabi; supervises Abu Dhabi's Development Programme; Chair. MUHAMMAD BIN KHALIFA AL-KINDA; Dir. ANIS ZAKI HASSAN.

OIL

In September 1974 the Government acquired a 60 per cent interest in ADPC and ADMA, and early in 1975 an increase of this interest to 100 per cent was under consideration. In the Spring of 1975 Abu Dubai withdrew from pressing for 100 per cent interest, but in July 1975 it was announced that Dubai had successfully concluded

a 100 per cent participation with the companies represented offshore and onshore in Dubai.

Ministry of Petroleum and Mineral Resources: P.O.B. 9, Abu Dhabi; Minister MANI SAID AL OTAIBA.

ABU DHABI

Abu Dhabi Marine Areas (ADMA): P.O.B. 303, Abu Dhabi; operates a concession 60 per cent owned by the Abu Dhabi National Oil Co. and 40 per cent by Abu Dhabi Marine Areas Ltd., Britannic House, Moor Lane, London, EC2Y 9BU, England (BP-Japan Oil Development Co. Ltd. 26⅔ per cent; Compagnie Française des Pétroles 13⅓ per cent). The concession lies in the Abu Dhabi offshore area and currently produces oil from Zakum and Umm Shaif fields; also acts as operator on behalf of al-Bunduq Co. Ltd., expected to come on stream late 1975; production (1974) 168,489,679 barrels (21,812,871 long tons); Chief Rep. and Gen. Man. Dr. A. J. HORAN.

Abu Dhabi Gas Liquefaction Company: owned by Abu Dhabi National Oil Co., 51 per cent; the British Petroleum Co., 16⅛ per cent; Compagnie Française des Pétroles, 8 1/16 per cent; Mitsui and Co., 22 1/20 per cent; Bridgestone Liquefied Gas Co., 2 9/20 per cent; to utilize natural gas produced in association with oil from offshore fields, the liquefied gas facilities are planned to come on stream in mid-1976 at an estimated cost of $400 million.

Abu Dhabi National Oil Company (ADNOC): Abu Dhabi; state company represents government's interests on the boards of Western oil companies, is responsible for all oil distribution in U.A.E.; is building its own refinery on Umm al Nar island and is responsible generally for oil installations and oil-based industries; is to form the Abu Dhabi Company for Oil Installations with the Arab International Contractor's Company; Gen. Man. MAHMOUD HAMRA-KROUHA.

Abu Dhabi Oil Company (Japan) (ADOCO): Abu Dhabi; consortium of three Japanese oil companies, Maruzen, Daikyo and Nihon Kogyo; holds offshore concession; oil strikes reported in September 1969 and January 1970; export of oil from Mubarraz Island terminal began in June 1973; production estimated 13,000 b/d; in 1973 announced plans to build an industrial complex in Abu Dhabi.

Abu Dhabi Petroleum Company Ltd. (ADPC): P.O.B. 270, Abu Dhabi; engaged in exploration, production and export of crude oil from onshore areas of Abu Dhabi. Export started from Bab field in December 1963. In 1965 the Bu Hasa field was brought on stream, to be followed in 1973 by the Asab field. Crude oil from Asab, Bu Hasa and Bab is exported from Jebel Dhanna Terminal. In 1975 there is a production capacity of 1.3 m.b/d; production (1974) 335,020,096 barrels; Man. Dir. G. G. STOCKWELL; U.A.E. Government-nominated Dir. MANI' SAID AL-OTAIBA; Gen. Man. A. J. A. GILLAN.

Phillips Petroleum: P.O.B. 6, Abu Dhabi; heads consortium with the Italian AGIP Co. (each with a 50 per cent interest); holds 7,126 sq. km. concession on land; Gen. Man. W. R. ELLIS.

Total Abu al Bukhoosh: Abu Dhabi; owned by Compagnie Française des Pétroles, Amerada Hess, Sunningdale Oils and Nepco Eastern; began production from the Abu al-Bukhoosh offshore field in June 1974; average production of 60,000 b/d in 1975.

Other concessions are held by Amerada Group and Sunningdale.

DUBAI

Department of the Ruler's Affairs and Petroleum Affairs:
P.O.B. 207, Dubai; government supervisory body;
Dir. MAHDI AL TAJIR.

Dubai Petroleum Company: Dubai; subsidiary of Continental Oil Co. (U.S.A.) in partnership with Compagnie Française des Pétroles, Hispanoil (Spain), Sun Oil Co. (U.S.A.), Deutsche Texaco AG (Germany), Wintershall AG (Germany); holds offshore concession which began production in 1969; production in 1972 7.7m. tons; 1973 10.8m. tons.

Texas Pacific Oil Co.: Dubai.

SHARJAH

Crescent Petroleum: Sharjah; operated by Buttes Gas and Oil of California; owned by Buttes (25 per cent), Ashland Oil (25 per cent), Shell Oil (25 per cent), Kerr McGee (12.5 per cent), Juniper Petroleum (2.5 per cent) and Cities Services (10 per cent); began exploration in 1969, made significant off-shore find in Abu Musa in 1973, began production in July 1974; a production rate of 100,000 b/d is eventually expected.

For details of concessions in the other Emirates *see* Oil in the Middle East and North Africa, pages 97–98.

TRANSPORT

ROADS

Until very recently there was no proper system of roads except in Dubai town, but the desert tracks are often motorable. In 1965 plans were made for a £1 million all-weather metalled road to be built from Dubai to Ras al Khaimah, to be financed by the Trucial States Development Office. The Dubai/Sharjah section of this was opened in September 1966. Work has now been completed on the Sharjah/Ras al Khaimah section at the expense of the Saudi Arabian Government. In 1968 Abu Dhabi opened a £1 million bridge linking the town with the mainland. The town is also linked with the Buraimi Oasis by a dual-carriageway motor road built mainly for political reasons. The oil companies have constructed roads in the area in which they operate. An underwater tunnel linking Dubai Town and Deira with a dual carriageway and pedestrian subway is almost complete (1975). There is a road linking Dubai and Abu Dhabi, and also a road between Fujairah and Khor Fakkan. Roads between Dhaid (Sharjah) and Fujairah, between Qatar and Abu Dhabi and between Abu Dhabi and the Liwa oasis are under construction.

SHIPPING

Dubai has been the main commercial centre in the Gulf for many years. In 1968 work was begun on a new artificial deep-water port to supplement the traditional harbour. Completed ahead of schedule in 1972, Port Rashid has 15 deep-water berths and several coastal berths. It makes Dubai harbour the largest in the Middle East. In 1974 1,883,624 tons of goods were unloaded from ocean vessels. In June 1974 a £65 million extension of 22 new berths was planned. Abu Dhabi has also become an important port since the opening of the first section of its artificial harbour, Port Zayed. Eventually it is planned to create 17 deep-water berths and extensive storage facilities. There are smaller ports in Sharjah and Ras al-Khaimah. Work on a dry-dock scheme for Dubai began in 1973. It will have two docks capable of handling 500,000-ton tankers, seven repair berths and a third dock able to

accommodate 1,000,000-ton tankers. This will make Dubai the biggest supertanker complex in the Gulf. In 1974 contracts were awarded for the building of six deep-water berths at Sharjah and plans were announced for a further doubling of Dubai's harbour capacity.

The British India Steam Navigation Co. Ltd. maintains a weekly scheduled service to Dubai on the Bombay–Basra run. The ships of British India Line and F. Strick & Co. call at Dubai and Abu Dhabi several times a month. Other lines which call regularly are D. D. G. Hansa, Johnson Line, Holland–Persian Gulf, Maersk Line, and Jugolinÿa.

CIVIL AVIATION

The new air terminal at Dubai was opened in 1971 by Sheikh Rashid. The £4m. terminal was the first in the Middle East to have facilities for handling Jumbo Jets. There is also an international airport at Abu Dhabi and a smaller one at Sharjah and an international airport is being built at Ras al Khaimah. A new airport for Abu Dhabi on the mainland is scheduled to be completed by 1981.

Gulf Air Dubai: Dubai National Air Travel Agency, P.O.B. 1515, Dubai; Omeir Travel Agency, Abu Dhabi; Sharjah Aircraft Handling Agency, Sharjah; daily service Bahrain—Doha–Abu Dhabi–Muscat; thrice weekly to Bander Abbas, Shiraz, Kuwait, Cairo; twice weekly to Bombay, Karachi and Salalah; four times weekly to Beirut; five times weekly to London; once a week to Athens and Baghdad.

Gulf Air Sharjah: Sharjah Aircraft Handling Agency, P.O.B. 8; Oman Travel Agency, P.O.B. 15; Kanoo Travel Agency; weekly flight Shiraz–Muscat, weekly flight Abu Dhabi–Doha–Bahrain–Sharjah.

Alia, Air France, Air India, British Airways, Egypt Air, Iran Air, Kuwait Airways, Middle East Airlines, PIA, KLM, Gulf Air, Iraqi Airways, Saudia, Syrian Arab Airlines and TMA all serve Dubai and Abu Dhabi, while Gulf Air and TMA serve Sharjah.

TOURISM

Ministry of Information and Culture: Government of the United Arab Emirates, P.O.B. 592, Abu Dhabi.

Ministry of Information and Culture: Government of the United Arab Emirates, P.O.B. 67, Dubai.

Ministry of Information and Culture: Government of the United Arab Emirates, P.O.B. 55, Sharjah.

Dubai Information Department: P.O.B. 1420, Dubai (local government).

Ras Al Khaimah Information Department: P.O.B. 200, Ras Al Khaimah (local government).

DEFENCE

Armed Forces: Union Defence Force 1,600; Abu Dhabi 8,850; Dubai 1,000; Ras al Khaimah 300; Sharjah 250.

Talks are in progress on the question of merging the separate defence forces.

EDUCATION

The U.A.E. is engaged in an expansion of education which is seen as a unifying force for the future of the federation. In 1971 there were about 28,000 pupils in the

U.A.E., and by 1973 the number had increased to an estimated 37,000. There are primary and secondary schools in all the states and further education in technical fields is available in the more advanced areas. Teachers from other Arab countries, most notably Kuwait, Egypt and Jordan, supplement the U.A.E.'s inadequate native teaching staff. Many students receive higher education abroad. Work on a university is to begin in 1976.

BIBLIOGRAPHY

ALBAHARNA, H. M. The Legal Status of the Arabian Gulf States (Manchester University Press, May 1969).

BUSCH, B. C. Britain and the Persian Gulf 1894–1914 (University of California Press, 1967).

DANIELS, JOHN. Abu Dhabi: A Portrait (Longman, London, 1974).

FACT SHEETS ON EASTERN ARABIA (Private Information Center on Eastern Arabia, Heldenplein 12, 1800 Vilvoorde, Belgium).

HAWLEY, DONALD FREDERICK. Courtesies in the Trucial States (1965).
    The Trucial States (George Allen and Unwin, London, 1971).

HAY, Sir RUPERT. The Persian Gulf States (Middle East Institute, Washington, 1959).

MANN, CLARENCE. Abu Dhabi: birth of an Oil Sheikhdom (Khayats, Beirut, 1964).

MARLOWE, JOHN. The Persian Gulf in the 20th Century (Cresset Press, London, 1962).

MILES, S. B. The Countries and Tribes of the Persian Gulf (3rd edition, Cass, London, 1966).

SADIQ, MUHAMMAD T., and SNAVELY, WILLIAM P. Bahrain, Qatar and the United Arab Emirates: Colonial Past, Present Problems, and Future Prospects (Heath, Lexington, Mass., 1972).

WILSON, Sir A. T. The Persian Gulf (1928).

Yemen Arab Republic

GEOGRAPHY

The Yemen Arab Republic lies at the south-west corner of the Arabian peninsula and comprises two well-defined areas—the highlands inland, and the coastal strip along the Red Sea. The climate of the highlands is considered the best in all Arabia since it experiences a régime rather like that of East Africa, with a warm temperate and rainy summer, and a cool, moderately dry winter with occasional frost and some snow. As stated below (*see* Yemen P.D.R.) these conditions are thought to be produced by an upper air current that brings very moist air from the Atlantic, giving rise to a minor monsoonal effect of heavy summer rainfall. As much as 35 inches of rain may fall annually on the higher parts of the interior, with 15–20 inches over much of the plateau; but the coast receives under 5 inches generally, and in the form often of irregular downpours. There is therefore the phenomenon of streams and even rivers flowing perennially in the highlands, but failing to reach the coast.

Because of this climatic gradation, from desert to temperate conditions, the Yemen has a similar gradation of crops and vegetation. The highest parts appear as "African", with scattered trees and grassland. Crops of coffee, qat, cereals and vegetables are grown, whilst lower down, "Mediterranean" fruits appear, with millet, and where irrigation water is available, bananas. Finally, near the coast, the date palm becomes the only tree.

The area of the Yemen is approximately 75,000 square miles and its population has been estimated at 6 million. The capital is Sana'a (on the d'El Jehal plateau, altitude 7,260 ft.).

HISTORY

In classical times the Yemen formed part of the south-eastern area of Arabia Felix. One of the best-known kingdoms in that region was that of Sheba, which lasted from 950 to 115 B.C. From then until the sixth century A.D. Arabia Felix was ruled by the Himyarite dynasty, from whom the modern Imams claim descent. In A.D. 525 the Ethiopians conquered the Himyarite Kingdom, and they in turn were overthrown by a Persian invasion in 575. During the seventh century the country nominally accepted Islam and the Sunnis of the Shafi'i rite established their power in the Tihama (the coastal region), and the Zaidis, a moderate branch of the Shia, held the highlands.

During the ninth century the Zaidi Imam Yahya al-Hadi ila'l-Haqq founded the Rassid dynasty of the Yemen, which has survived, with some interruptions, to the present time.

In 1517 the Yemen was conquered by the Ottoman Turks, but their power was continually contested by other European powers, and their authority was not great. Fierce tribal and religious warfare led the Turks to establish in 1872 a full occupation of the country under a Turkish *Vali*. This occupation lasted until the Mudros armistice of 1918, but in 1911 the Imam Yahya had led a full-scale revolt which secured a treaty confirming Turkish suzerainty, but dividing administrative control between the Imam in the highlands and the Turks in the Tihama and on the coast.

During the First World War the Imam had supported the Turks, and the British had therefore supported Idrisi invaders from the small state of the Asir to the north of the Yemen. A succession dispute broke out in the Asir in 1923 in the course of which Imam Yahya of the Yemen had occupied the port of Hodeida and the coastal areas. By the Treaty of Mecca in October 1926 the Sheikh of the Asir was placed formally under the protection of Ibn Sa'ud; this position, however, was never enthusiastically accepted by the Imam, who continued to bait the new king of Arabia and also to encroach on the British-protected territory of the Aden Protectorate. In these activities he seemed to have had the support of Italy, with whom he signed a treaty of friendship in 1926; and a Soviet trade delegation made a brief appearance in the country at this time. In 1930 following on a dispute over his Hijaz borders he encouraged the Sheikh of the Asir to revolt against Ibn Sa'ud; the latter attempted to settle the dispute by peaceful means, and negotiations dragged on until 1934. In April of that year, however, Ibn Sa'ud decided on more drastic action; marching on the Yemen, he drove the Yemeni troops out of Hodeida, and in a bloodless campaign of a month forced them back into Sana'a. The peace treaty of Ta'if allotted Tihama and Najran to Ibn Sa'ud but otherwise left the boundaries of the Yemen undisturbed—a policy of moderation that won him considerable prestige. At the same time Britain formally recognized the independence of the Yemen by treaty, and ended for a time a long series of frontier disputes.

The despotic and conservative Imam Yahya continued to rule until February 1948, when an attempted *coup d'état* by Sayyid Abdullah al-Wazzir resulted in his murder; his eldest son, Saif al-Islam Ahmad, however, succeeded to the throne and drove out the insurgent. Since then the Yemen has been co-operating in international affairs; in January 1951 a start was made on the development of the country with British, American and French technical aid, and at the same time full diplomatic relations were established for the first time with foreign powers, including Britain, the U.S.A. and Egypt.

In the winter of 1953 Yemen, with Arab support, began pressing before the United Nations her claims to Aden and the territories of the Aden Protectorate, and throughout the summer of 1954, and again in 1955, there was a series of frontier incidents.

In April 1955 an attempted *coup d'état* against the Imam Ahmad was defeated, and the royal conspirators executed; but one consequence may have been the Imam's decision in August of that year to set up a formal cabinet. During 1956 relations were established with the Soviet Union and a military pact was concluded with Egypt, Saudi Arabia and Syria.

The frontier dispute between Britain and the Yemen was continued late in December 1956 and in 1957, when Yemeni tribesmen were reported to have attacked villages in the Aden Protectorate. The Crown Prince visited London for talks in November 1957, but hostilities flared up again in the spring of 1958 and the political committee of the Arab League denounced the actions of Great Britain in the Aden territories. Two bomb incidents in Aden itself led to the enforcement in May 1958 of a temporary state of emergency. Unsuccessful talks to settle the dispute were held in July 1958 and May 1959. (For a fuller account of the border dispute see the chapter on Southern Yemen.)

A Yemeni delegation, headed by the Crown Prince, visited Cairo in February 1958 for negotiations which led to a federal union between the United Arab Republic and the Yemen, established by an agreement signed in Damascus on March 8th. The new union was named the United Arab States, and was to have a unified defence and foreign policy, and later a Customs union and common currency. Few practical steps were taken to that end and although, in November 1961, the Yemen renewed the agreement for a further three years, the Federation was formally dissolved by the United Arab Republic in December 1961.

In May 1959 disorders followed the departure of the Imam Ahmad to Europe and the Crown Prince Muhammad al-Badr introduced various reforms, including the innovation of a Representative Council. This policy was reversed on the return of the Imam in August.

CIVIL WAR 1962—1969

In March 1961 there was an unsuccessful attempt to assassinate the Imam, who was wounded in the shoulder. The Imam died in September 1962, and was briefly succeeded by his son Muhammad Badr. But a week later a revolt broke out, led by Colonel Abdullah Sallal, supported by troops from the U.A.R. The new Imam fled into the hills after a series of attempts to regain the capital, and Republican forces gained control of most of the country. The Republic was soon recognized by the U.S.S.R. and the United States, and early in 1963 was admitted to the United Nations. Britain, however, continued to give recognition to the Royalist régime, and stated on a number of occasions that she would only recognize the Republic when U.A.R. forces were withdrawn. Fighting continued throughout the year and did not cease until the summer of 1969, having been particularly severe during the winter of 1963–64 and much of 1968. An Observer Mission dispatched by the United Nations found that an agreement for simultaneous withdrawal of U.A.R. troops and Saudi Arabian military supplies had not been implemented by either side. The Mission operated from July 1963 to September 1964.

The rapprochement between U.A.R. and Saudi Arabia in February 1964 suggested that a solution would not be long delayed, and recognition by Jordan of the Republican régime was a further important step towards complete acceptance of the Revolution and its consequences. Britain, nevertheless, maintained her stand in support of the Royalists; the interest of the U.A.R. in driving British influence out of South Arabia (the Yemen Republican leaders were less vehement in this aim than their Egyptian colleagues) only strengthened the determination of the United Kingdom Government.

In May 1964 a new Republican Government was announced under the terms of a new Constitution published in April. The Prime Minister, Hamud Al Jaifi, soon displayed his command of the situation, which was emphasised by the frequent absences of the President for medical treatment in Cairo and Europe. In a policy statement in June a programme of school, hospital and road building was announced, and in July an agreement was signed in Cairo to establish a U.A.R./Yemen co-ordinating council and a joint military command; 90 per cent of the expenses of these ventures would be provided by Egypt,

which had already sent an estimated 40,000 troops into the country in support of the Republicans.

In September the UN military observers left the country, while at the same time Sallal was attending the Arab Summit Conference in Alexandria. Following this meeting President Nasser and King Faisal discussed the Yemen situation, and this led in November to a meeting at Erkwit in the Sudan, at which republican and royalist delegations agreed to a cease-fire and the convening of a national congress. Differences over procedure forced the postponement of this, and in December the royalists resumed the offensive. During January the Imam al-Badr proclaimed a constitutional charter. This military and political offensive led to dissensions in the republican cabinet, culminating in the fall of Hamud Al Jaifi in January 1965, and his replacement by Lieut.-Gen. Hassan Al-Amri with a mandate to stiffen the war effort. In April, however, Lieut.-Gen. Amri resigned, and was replaced by the moderate Muhammad Ahmad Noman, who embarked on a policy of conciliation. The long postponed National Congress met in May in the village of Khamer, though without the participation of the royalists, and on May 9 the text was published of an interim constitution, setting up a supreme Consultative Assembly with power to make laws, remove members of the Republican Council, and nominate the President. Despite the energetic efforts of Mr. Noman to achieve a peace settlement, it was not long before his sympathy for the Baathist cause ran him into opposition from the Egyptian authorities, who retained a measure of financial control over the Yemen. In July Noman resigned and after a few days of uncertainty President Sallal announced a new cabinet headed by Lieut.-Gen. Amri. The return to prominence of the military, pro-Egyptian element coincided with a number of important Royalist advances, and relations between the U.A.R. and Saudi Arabia worsened dangerously as each accused the other once again of complicity in the civil war.

THE SEARCH FOR A SETTLEMENT

In late summer events took a more hopeful turn when President Nasser agreed to discuss the Yemen situation with King Faisal at Jeddah. On August 24th, after their two-day conference, the two leaders concluded an agreement on a plan to bring the war to an end and to establish, within fifteen months, a Yemeni government free from outside interference. The agreement stipulated that a cease-fire was to be declared immediately; Saudi Arabia was to stop supplying arms to the Royalist forces; an interim government of moderate politicians, excluding both the Imam al-Badr and President Sallal, was to be set up within three months; after which the Egyptian forces, numbering about 50,000, were to be withdrawn during the ten-month period ending September 23rd, 1966. By November 23rd, 1966, a plebiscite would be held to enable the Yemenis to choose the political form they wished their state to assume.

Although the immediate effects of the Jeddah agreement were hopeful, including the establishment of a more representative Presidency Council for the Republic, and of a U.A.R./Saudi Arabian Peace Committee, the good intentions of the participants to the agreement were soon eroded. In November 1965 a conference of Republican and Royalist envoys meeting at Haradh reached deadlock over the next steps to be taken, and through 1966 the implementation of the agreement seemed less and less likely as relations between Egypt and Saudi Arabia deteriorated. Egyptian troop numbers in the Yemen, far from being reduced, were built up; despite a further U.A.R./Saudi meeting in August in Beirut, chaired by Kuwait, a solution seemed no nearer. Worse still, in September 1966 friction between Lt.-Gen. Amri and President Sallal came into the open when the latter returned to Sana'a. A large delegation, led personally by the Premier, then flew to Cairo to demand complete independence from U.A.R. for the Yemen régime, and the permanent removal of the President. The U.A.R. response to this was to arrest the members of the delegation, and Sallal himself assumed the duties of the premiership. This was followed by a drastic purge of the republican armed forces and administration, and a wave of riots, trials and executions. The dissident republican elements took refuge in the mountains to the north of Sana'a.

During the latter months of 1966 republican and royalist operations began to escalate. Egyptian aircraft were in action, and on several occasions air raids were made on the Saudi Arabian towns of Jizan and Najran. In January allegations were made of the use of poison gas, a charge denied by the U.A.R.

Meanwhile there was considerable diplomatic activity. In January Sallal formed the Popular Revolutionary Union at a meeting attended by Makkawi (*see* Southern Yemen). Outside Yemen, a Union of Popular Forces was formed, led by Ibrahim al-Wazir, who visited Riyad and Geneva calling for an Islamic State of Yemen, the withdrawal of Egyptian troops, and the ending of Saudi Arabian aid. On February 11th, 1967, Tunisia and Jordan withdrew their recognition of the Sallal régime. However, Jordanian recognition was subsequently restored, in consequence of the diplomatic rapprochement with Egypt at the time of the Arab-Israel war of June 1967.

In July, following a major government reorganization, the Royalists took advantage of the run-down in Egyptian troops to stage one of the fiercest land offensives for two years. Republican forces were driven from Haradh and the port of Maydi, and refugees from the coastal town of al-Luhayya had to be evacuated to the British-administered island of Kamaran. Later in July the Egyptian military build-up was resumed, and these localities were retaken. At the end of the month a Royalist spokesman complained to the United Nations of persistent poison gas attacks by Egyptian forces. U.A.R. denials of the use of poison gas were discredited by an independent International Red Cross inquiry in May 1967, which confirmed the use of such gas in a raid on May 10th.

THE EGYPTIAN WITHDRAWAL

Early in August 1967, on the occasion of the meeting of Foreign Ministers at Khartoum to prepare an agenda for an Arab summit conference, the U.A.R. delegate announced that the Egyptian Government was once again prepared to put into effect the agreement drawn up with King Faisal of Saudi Arabia at Jeddah in August 1965. The supervision of the withdrawal of troops would be entrusted to a committee of three Arab states. According to Radio Sana'a, a principal factor influencing this change of heart by the Egyptians was the British decision on a definite date for the withdrawal of troops from Aden, in January 1968. The implication appeared to be that Egypt saw no further need for the presence of her forces in Yemen after the British withdrawal from South Arabia had taken place. The fact that the U.A.R. was now partially dependent on financial aid from more conservative Arab countries, notably Saudi Arabia, was not mentioned.

On August 31st an agreement on these terms was finally reached by King Faisal and President Nasser at the Arab leaders' conference at Khartoum. Egyptian troops were to be withdrawn within three months; a plebiscite to determine the political future of the Yemen was to be held within a further six months; President Sallal was to lead a transitional government; the whole agreement to be carried out under the supervision of representatives of three independent Arab states, Iraq, Morocco and Sudan.

Although President Sallal immediately protested against the peace plan, his opposition did not prove an obstacle.

The Egyptian army, with an estimated strength of up to 80,000 men, had effectively colonized the Republican-held sector of the Yemen, and was in general neither popular nor well regarded for its military prowess. Thus its withdrawal, which was completed by January 1968, was not altogether unwelcome although it naturally encouraged the Royalist forces to become bolder. It also led to the deposition of President Sallal in November, carried out while he was on an official visit to Iraq, and the institution of a three man Presidency Council headed initially by Abdul Rahman al-Iriani. In December 1967 General Hassan Al-Amri, a militant republican, replaced the moderate Muhammad Noman on the Council; shortly afterwards he also became Prime Minister, again replacing a more moderate man. The National Liberation Front, the left-wing force that had come to power in the newly independent territory of Southern Yemen, also came to possess considerable influence in the Yemen at this time.

The Royalist army continued to make progress early in 1968, and for some time the Republican capital of Sana'a was virtually besieged. Its defendants claimed that the Imam was still receiving generous aid from Saudi Arabia, while much of their own equipment had been taken by the Egyptians. In January the Iraqi, Sudanese and Moroccan foreign ministers arranged a peace meeting in Beirut, but it proved abortive as the rival factions could not even agree to meet. By April the pressure on Sana'a had relaxed somewhat; a left-wing plot to overthrow the Al-Amri government was unsuccessful. In June the Royalist leader, Imam Muhammad al-Badr, was deposed by his followers in favour of his son (his cousin according to some accounts), Muhammad bin Hussein. A ministerial delegation from Southern Yemen met the leaders of the Republican government in July, apparently for talks regarding the rebels in the hinterland of both countries.

THE END OF THE CIVIL WAR

During the 1968–69 period it became evident that the Royalist military effort was in decline after its major offensive following the Egyptian withdrawal; some accounts claimed that the Royalists ceased to exist as a regular fighting force after a defeat at Hajja in December 1968. By the summer of 1969 the leading members of the Royalist camp were all in exile, and their followers had apparently accepted the Sana'a government. The principal cause of this swift collapse appeared to be a feud within the royal family following the deposition of the Imam. The Saudi Arabian Government's confidence in the Royalists, already weakened by their failure to capture Sana'a, thus diminished further; eventually the Saudis ceased their financial and military assistance on which the Royalists had depended. Since the Republicans were apparently in receipt of substantial arms supplies from other Arab countries and the U.S.S.R. their success was assured.

Nevertheless, there was a short-lived revival of military activity in the north-east during the winter of 1969-70. Rebel tribesmen, said to be opposed to rule from Sana'a rather than positive supporters of the Imam, surrounded the town of Saada for some weeks. This development, plus the massive economic problems faced by the government, led to the resignation of the Prime Minister, Abdallah Kurshoumi, in February 1970, only six months after he had succeeded General Al-Amri. Muhsin Al-Aini, the Ambassador in Moscow, was then appointed Prime Minister.

In March 1970 the Premier and the Foreign Minister met Saudi Arabian officials privately during the Islamic Foreign Ministers Conference at Jeddah. Although no formal announcement of the outcome was made, it appeared that an informal peace settlement was agreed upon. As a result, the leading Royalists, apart from the Imam and the royal family itself, returned to Sana'a in May 1970 and were offered a number of posts in the administration. Ahmed Al Shami, the former Royalist foreign minister, joined the Presidential Council, four Royalists joined the cabinet, and others were given high diplomatic or civil service posts or became members of the National Assembly.

The government was said to be anxious to open relations with the Western countries which had recognized the Royalist régime; in July 1969 diplomatic relations with Federal Germany were restored at a time when several Arab states followed an opposite policy in recognizing the G.D.R. (East Germany). One result was a generous offer of economic and financial aid from Bonn. In July 1970 Saudi Arabia formally opened diplomatic relations with the republic, followed, within a few days, by Britain and France. Drought created a widespread famine in the summer of 1970, and offers of food and medical supplies were received from many countries.

In December 1970, a new constitution was promulgated, providing for a Consultative Council to replace the National Assembly. Elections were held in March 1971.

In July 1971 there were rumours of an attempt by senior army officers to overthrow the Government, and several officers were dismissed. In September the Prime Minister, Lt.-Gen. Hassan Al-Amri, went into exile (until 1975) after reportedly murdering a man in his office. Tension between Sana'a and Aden increased in the first half of 1972 as supporters of FLOSY and the South Arabian League, opponents of the Aden Government, amassed on the borders between the two states.

Serious fighting broke out on the border in September, but an Arab League mission was able to mediate and a ceasefire became effective in October. A peace agreement and an agreement on eventual unification of the two Yemens were signed in Cairo on October 28th. Further details were discussed in Tripoli (Libya) in November by the Presidents of the two Yemens, and it was agreed that the people of Yemen would establish a single state, to be known as the Yemen Republic, with Sana'a as its capital, Islam as the State religion and Arabic as the official language. Committees were set up to discuss details of the unification. In January 1973 it appeared that certain obstacles had arisen in the progress towards union, but in February a new political organization, the Yemeni Union, was formed in Sana'a in anticipation of the forthcoming union. At the end of May fighting again broke out on the border between the two Yemens, and on May 30th, Sheikh Muhammad al-Othman, a member of the three-man Presidential Council, was assassinated by unknown gunmen. Although this incident temporarily soured relations between the two Yemens, it was announced in June that talks on unity would continue.

In December 1972 Mohsin al-Aini resigned as Prime Minister and a new government was later formed under Abdullah al-Hajari. The Government of Abdullah al-Hajari had to contend with a great deal of violence, particularly in the south of the country, and in September 1973 President Iriani and President Salem Rubai Ali of South Yemen met in Sana'a and decided to extend the one year period originally decided upon for the unification of their two countries, and to concentrate on suppressing terrorism and sabotage.

A new Government under Hassan Makki took office in March 1974, pledged to continue the policies of the former Prime Minister, Abdullah al-Hajari, and in particular to work for unification with South Yemen. On June 13th, however, a bloodless *coup* took place in which a seven-man military junta, under the leadership of pro-Saudi Colonel Ibrahim al-Hamadi, suspended the Constitution and Consultative Council and dissolved the armed forces high command and the Yemeni National Union. Colonel Hamadi later stated that the *coup* had been necessary to remedy economic and administrative chaos. The former President, Qadi Abdul Rahman al-Iriani, later left for Damascus. A provisional constitution was issued on June 19th and on June 21st a new Government was formed under Mohsin al-Aini. The policy of the new Government was stated to include openness to all Arab States, support for non-alignment and adherence to the Arab League Charter and the UN Charter. The goal of ultimate unity with South Yemen was to be preserved although outside observers now believe that the possibility of achieving this unity has become even more remote.

In January 1975 Mohsin al-Aini was relieved of his post of Prime Minister and replaced by the former Chairman of the central bank, Abdel-Aziz Abdel-Ghani. Although it was hoped that a return to constitutional government would be made in June 1975 (after one year of military rule), Col. Hamadi merely announced in May 1975 that he would nominate a commission to supervise the election of a Popular Assembly which would in turn amend the constitution.

Relations with Yemen P.D.R. deteriorated during 1975, with accusations of "acts of sabotage" by southern Yemenis coming from the North Yemen Government.

ECONOMIC SURVEY

M. Jibb

AGRICULTURE

Yemen contains some of the most fertile land in the Arabian Peninsula, both in the highlands, where agriculture has always been extensively practised, and in the dry coastal plain of the Tihama. Yemen's best-known crop is coffee, grown mainly in the hills behind the Tihama, although it is cultivated in various degrees all over the country. It used to be Yemen's largest foreign exchange earner, but the amount of land devoted to it has decreased, partly because of fluctuations in demand on the world market, partly because the farmers found the narcotic, qat, to be a more profitable crop. In 1972, however, the Government announced measures to limit the growing of qat, whereby its cultivation was banned on state-owned land or on *Waqf* (religious endowment) land. In any case, cotton has now replaced coffee as the main cash crop.

Yemen's major cereal crop is sorghum (durra), grown at any altitude up to 9,000 feet. The annual harvest of sorghum and millet is usually about one million tons but it fell to 720,000 tons in 1973/74.

Other cereals are wheat, barley and maize. Although a comparatively large area is allocated to cereals, the yield is poor and Yemen relies on imports of staple foods. A prolonged drought in the years 1968 to 1970 caused the failure of many crops and the resultant famine obliged the Government to import even larger quantities of wheat and cereals. The 1971 season saw increased yields, but recovery is proving a slow process, and it is unlikely that Yemen will be able to rely on natural rainfall for its future needs.

The highland areas also produce many fruits and vegetables, citrus fruits, apricots, peaches, grapes, tomatoes and potatoes being the main crops; but others, such as cauliflowers, lettuces, peas, cucumbers and water melons are being introduced at the instigation of the Ministry of Agriculture. The Government is seeking finance from the United Arab Emirates and the World Bank to develop agriculture further in the central highlands.

The hot Tihama plain produces dates, and tobacco and cotton plantations are being established there to form the basis for local industries. Cotton in particular is assuming some importance as a cash crop; in 1971-72, the first year in which cotton and cotton seeds were exported, their value was 9.9 million riyals and in 1972-73 it amounted to 10.8 million riyals. In 1973, raw cotton exports were worth 17.8 million riyals and export of cottonseeds 2 million riyals.

The Government plans to introduce Friesian cattle to the upland regions to improve the local stock, and breeding stations are being built in Sana'a, Taiz and Hodeida. In 1975 an agreement was made with U.S. interests to establish a poultry farm project.

Because droughts are so frequent, Yemen's major concern is to achieve efficient irrigation systems and water storage schemes and to utilize the ground water which exists in the Tihama.

The largest project now in hand is the $17.5 million agricultural scheme for the Tihama region, assisted by the United Nations, the International Development Association (IDA) and the Kuwait Fund for Arab Economic Development (KFAED). The scheme involves irrigation works in the Wadi Zebid area, the development of 60,000 hectares at Wadi Mawr, the establishment of a Tihama Development Authority and provision of credit schemes and various other services. Output of cotton and vegetables in the area should almost double when the project is completed and substantially increased yields of cereals and oilseeds are expected. Other UN schemes are a pilot project for the development of a sugar cane industry and the expansion of the government-run model farm near Taiz into an agricultural advisory centre.

In 1974/75 British firms undertook development studies, including agricultural projects, in areas such as Al-Jawf, Beida, Taiz and Maarib. The rebuilding of the ancient Maarib dam is still under discussion. The schemes under consideration are expected to cost about $100 million. Yemen is also receiving agricultural aid from the Netherlands, China and other Arab states.

INDUSTRY

The existing and projected new industries are mainly based on the traditional occupations such as textiles, leather work, basketry, jewellery and glass-making, and, where possible, local raw materials. The Government's aim is to become self-sufficient in food processing, clothing and construction industries, that is, those sectors which could be made independent of imported raw materials. There is a state-owned spinning and weaving factory at Sana'a, established under an agreement of 1958 between Yemen and China, and completed in 1967. The plant, the Sana'a Textile Factory, employs 1,500 workers, many of them women. China is continuing to make aid available for the textile industry, with plans to set up a mill in Hodeida. The Bajil textile factory, set up by French and Syrian interests in the 1950s, encountered financial difficulties and never went into production. A United Nations report of 1968 recommended its urgent rehabilitation and repair, and a Dutch firm conducted a study. Modernization is to go ahead under the Three-Year Plan. In addition, there are two cotton-cleaning plants in Hodeida, and one in Zebid, and a cotton seed oil and cake plant in Hodeida; these are privately owned. The textile industry is clearly the most promising line of industrial development in Yemen. The Yemen Cotton Company, owned 51 per cent by the Government, 30 per cent by the Yemeni Bank for Reconstruction and Development and 19 per cent by private interests, provides the plants with raw cotton, over which it has monopoly rights. In 1974 a new factory making school, police and military uniforms was opened and a similar plant for medical clothing is under consideration.

The rock salt factory at Salif, managed by the Ministry of Economy, utilizes local salt deposits, estimated to contain at least 25 million tons. The salt, which is of high quality, is all exported to Japan. The Salt Company has invested about $400,000 to raise production to 500,000 tons a year and the KFAED provided a loan to extend bulk-loading facilities at Salif port. A further KFAED loan of KD 1.2 million was agreed upon in 1972 to exploit the salt deposits further and to raise production to 1 million tons a year by 1974. A Canadian company is developing the mines.

The salt at Salif is the only mineral at present exploited in Yemen on any scale. There are also salt deposits at Marib in the east and at Qumah, near Salif. A mineral resources survey has been started by the U.S. Agency for International Development (AID). Other minerals known to exist in Yemen are: coal, copper (at Hamoura, near Taiz), iron, sulphur, lead, zinc, silver, gold and uranium. The exploitation of copper deposits at Hamoura, near Taiz, is being studied by KFAED experts. Talks are being held with South Yemen on the working of copper deposits in the Beida area. The Government has plans to exploit marble deposits in the Mawzah region.

The Yemen Petroleum Company, a joint venture between the Government and the YBRD, has the monopoly of imports, storage and distribution of oil products.

In 1970 a joint company, the Yemen Oil and Mineral Industrial Company, was formed by the Yemeni Government with the Algerian state-owned oil concern, SONATRACH. It was announced in 1972 that oil had been found in the Tihama but in the same year the company had to be dissolved because of lack of capital. The Government made it known that it would welcome foreign firms who wished to prospect for oil. In January 1974 an agreement was signed with Shell (Hamburg) to prospect for oil in the northern territorial waters, the company also having the right to refine any oil found. American and Japanese companies showed interest in 1974/75 and the Government is optimistic about the prospects of finding oil. A refinery is now being built at Hodeida and another is proposed for Salif.

Other industries include soft drinks factories, a cigarette plant at Hodeida, built with Italian aid, an oxygen plant, originally set up by the U.S.S.R. and now state-operated, and a plant making aluminium products. An IDA credit of $2.3 million to set up a pilot industrial project in Sana'a was announced in 1974. Through this scheme, the establishment of an iron foundry and plants manufacturing building fixtures and fitting, tools, clothing, and water pumps, among other things, will be attempted. Technical aid is being provided by the United Nations. The Yemeni Company for Industrial Development was formed to develop light industry, particularly in Sana'a, Taiz and Hodeida but industrialization is progressing very slowly, even with the increased aid which has been made available.

The Soviet-built cement factory at Bajil, which uses local limestone deposits is one of the more successful ventures. It should eventually achieve an output of 100,000 tons a year, which is thought to be sufficient to meet local demand for the time being. A Ccechoslovak firm won a contract in 1975 to set up a brickworks.

COMMUNICATIONS

It is only since the revolution in 1962 that Yemen has established regular links with the outside world, and that good roads have been built connecting the main towns. Road construction now has high priority in development plans. The Sana'a–Hodeida road, completed in 1962, was built by Chinese engineers and is a spectacular achievement. The Sana'a–Saada road, also built with Chinese aid, was due for completion in 1974. The Sana'a–Taiz, the Mocha–Taiz and the Sana'a–Ibb–Taiz roads were built with American aid. The World Bank and KFAED are financing the Taiz–Turbah road and Dutch aid is being provided for the Dhamar–Rada road. The repair and maintenance of these roads is proving a problem, since neither the equipment nor the personnel are available locally. Altogether there were estimated in 1973 to be about 3,400 km. of roads, of which only 600 km. are asphalted. In addition there are a number of gravel feeder roads under construction. These are of great im-

portance for the transport of agricultural produce which otherwise cannot reach centres of distribution. More asphalting is being done, especially around Sana'a, and a number of hard-surfaced roads are planned, notably the Amran–Hajja road. World Bank aid has been requested for the surfacing of the Taiz–Mocha and Dhamar–Rada roads.

Improvement in the roads system is reflected in the increasing imports of motor vehicles, both commercial and private.

There are three ports in Yemen: Hodeida, Mocha and Salif, of which the most important is Hodeida. A new harbour, completed in 1962 by the U.S.S.R., has since been deepened and is now being expanded still further with Iraqi aid. Mocha cannot be used by ships of any size at present, but in 1973 the Government allocated 2.5 million riyals for its improvement with Italian assistance. With the expansion of salt mining at Salif, the harbour is being rebuilt to enable it to take ships of up to 5,000 tons and a bulk petrol plant is also planned.

There are airports at Sana'a, Hodeida and Taiz and smaller airstrips in other towns. Sana'a airport, built by the U.S.S.R. and equipped by West Germany, is capable of taking large aircraft, and both Hodeida and Taiz can take international flights. Facilities for air travel are poor by international standards. A proper international airport is now under study for Sana'a.

Much work is now being done on providing Yemen with a telecommunications system, one of the Development Plan priorities. The three main towns, Sana'a, Taiz and Hodeida are linked by a 600 km. telephone line, built by East German experts, and are also connected to a number of other towns where telephone exchanges are in operation: Bajil, Ibb, Dhamar, Yerim, Manakha, Zebid, Beit-el-Faqih and Hais. East Germany also helped to found a Communications College at Sana'a. A six-channel microwave scatter system linking Sana'a and Taiz is being implemented by the United Nations and Sana'a is linked via Aden with the rest of the world. There are radio transmitters at Sana'a and Taiz and various small wireless communications posts scattered throughout the country. Work has started on a television network to operate from Sana'a.

FOREIGN TRADE

Yemen's trade is characterized by an ever-growing deficit which had reached 528 million riyals by 1973. There is every prospect that the deficit will increase still further as development projects get under way.

Yemen's exports consist almost entirely of agricultural produce: cotton, coffee, salt, skins and products of the artisan industries. The principal import is food and this has contributed most to the large trade gap in recent years. Food imports rose from 30 million riyals in 1966 to over 100 million riyals in 1970 because of the drought and famine experienced during that period. Although in 1971 food imports fell to 66 million riyals, the trend is for them to increase, partly because of rises in the world price of wheat. In 1973 food imports were worth 271 million riyals. A substantial proportion of the remainder of Yemen's imports is made up of finished goods, vehicles, electrical machinery and petrol. Increased imports of machinery and building equipment are expected between 1974 and 1977 to implement development projects, but Yemen cannot as yet utilize imported raw materials.

Yemen used to import most from Australia, which supplies foodstuffs, and the Soviet Union, but in 1972–73 a change in the pattern of trade took place and Japan became the principal supplier, especially of motor vehicles. Figures for trade with Yemen P.D.R. are inflated due to the volume of transit trade *via* Aden, but with the development of Hodeida as a port capable of handling all Yemen's trade, the importance of Aden is declining.

The amount of trade with the Eastern Bloc is increasing, with China and the Soviet Union taking deliveries of Yemen cotton and coffee in return for aid with industrial projects and the supply of machinery. This has tended to stimulate the production of coffee and cotton and qat exports dropped sharply in 1972–73.

FINANCE AND FOREIGN AID

During the civil war there was a considerable inflow of foreign exchange from Saudi Arabia and Egypt. This, coupled with continued remittances from Yemenis living abroad, tended to soften the effects of the decline in agriculture which took place after 1966. These flows resulted, however, in a rise in liquidity which, with increasing government expenditure, led in turn to inflation, a sharp rise in imports and the depreciation of the Yemeni riyal.

Yemen has a very large budgetary deficit, which in 1968–69 amounted to 70 million riyals and reached 83 million riyals in 1971–72 quite apart from foreign loan commitments. The instability of the Government in 1971 meant that no firm measures were taken to deal with the situation. In July 1971 the Government of Muhammad Ahmed Noman resigned because of its inability to deal with the state's financial difficulties. The administration under Mohsin al-Aini announced that it would make a sharp reduction in government spending, would do all it could to attract foreign investment and would try to establish light industry in Yemen. Subsequent administrations have pursued much the same policies, but the budget deficit continues to grow, not least because the defence allocation is so large—266 million riyals in 1974/75. The 1975/76 deficit was expected to be 210 million riyals. Saudi Arabia has consistently made available budgetary aid to Yemen, including a payment of 120 million Saudi riyals in June 1974.

After the civil war the country had to rely more and more on foreign assistance for development. Extensive aid was offered by China, the Soviet Union and the United Nations and smaller amounts by Hungary, Yugoslavia, Bulgaria and Romania. Western aid came mainly from the United States and West Germany. The richer Arab countries, notably Algeria and Kuwait, also started to take an interest in Yemen, Algeria in oil and mineral exploitation, and Kuwait in the agricultural sector through loans from the Kuwait Fund for Arab Economic Development. Between 1962 and 1969 a total of $141 million was offered by China, the Soviet Union and the United Nations alone and Yemen had since 1956 accumulated a total debt of about $190 million. Even so, aid offered has been in excess of aid drawn and many development projects have been held up.

With the relative stabilization of the Government in 1971–72 foreign interests showed themselves more ready to invest in and aid Yemen, but political events in 1972 and 1973 had an unfortunate effect on the economy, the fighting with the South being most unlikely to inspire confidence in foreign investors. The unity agreement signed at the end of 1972 between North and South Yemen achieved only a pause in hostilities but at the end of 1973 the two countries were discussing economic integration and the outlook was more hopeful. The Government continued to reiterate its intention to pursue unification plans. Various economy measures such as the reduction of diplomatic representation abroad are being implemented. Oil price rises hit Yemen very hard and the Government has had to absorb increased costs.

Much practical aid in the fields of health, education and social welfare has flowed into Yemen, particularly from China, the Soviet Union, the World Health Organization and UNICEF. The Arab states appear to be increasingly ready to co-operate with Yemen in providing both financial and practical assistance. Kuwait and Saudi Arabia and, more recently, the United Arab Emirates, have provided schools, hospitals and clinics and many other Arab countries have sent teachers to Yemen. At the end of 1972, the UAE provided a loan of $19 million and further aid was expected in 1974. Qatar has provided aid for schools, hospitals and roads, and radio and television staff training. In 1974 Iraq announced aid for education, health and transport projects and is helping with the Hodeida port improvements. Aid given by the Arab states reflects the priorities of the Three-Year Plan: education, communications and road building.

THE THREE YEAR PLAN

Yemen's first development plan was drawn up in 1973 to cover the years 1973–76, and revised in 1974. The main emphasis was laid on the improvement of basic amenities and communications. Total allocations amounted to 936 million riyals, of which transport alone received 292 million riyals. Education allocations amounted to 195 million riyals, spending on industry to 91 million riyals and on agriculture to 138 million riyals. Health spending was cut to 48 million riyals in the revised plan. The plan is, of course, financed mainly by foreign investment, the largest source being the World Bank. Considerable support is also expected from the United Nations and the oil-rich Arab states, with some aid from the Eastern block, but on nothing like the scale received by the

PDRY. Much work still needs to be done in the social sphere to combat the effects of malnutrition, disease and ignorance and here the United Nations is helping by mounting programmes to teach the ordinary people the principles of nutrition and hygiene. Particular attention is being paid in the plan to the development of water resources, both for agriculture and in the towns. Water supply schemes are under way in Sana'a, Hodeida, Taiz and Hajja. An electricity scheme for the Taiz, Sana'a and Hodeida areas is being partly financed by the Arab Fund for Economic and Social Development.

STATISTICAL SURVEY

AREA AND POPULATION

Area	Total* (1975)	Sana'a (capital) (1972)	Taiz (1972)	Hodeida (1972)
200,000 sq. km.	6,471,893	121,000	80,000	90,000

* Provisional census result.

AGRICULTURE
PRINCIPAL CROPS
(July 1st to June 30th)

	1971–72		1972–73		1973–74	
	Area ('000 hectares)	Production ('000 metric tons)	Area ('000 hectares)	Production ('000 metric tons)	Area ('000 hectares)	Production ('000 metric tons)
Sorghum and Millet . . .	1,100	1,020	1,100	900	880	720
Wheat	50	54	50	50	70	71
Barley	143	178	143	164	191	230
Maize	50	80	50	80	52	84
Pulses	60	60	5	64	6	64
Potatoes	5	58	60	56	65	64
Vegetables	15	137	16	150	16	150
Grapes	7	35	7	35	8	31
Coffee	6	5	7	5	7.6	5
Cotton	15	15	20	18.5	20	20
Tobacco	4	5	4	5	4.2	5

LIVESTOCK
1973 ('000 head)

Cattle . . .		810
Sheep . . .	}	9,500
Goats . . .		
Camels . . .		100
Horses . . .		4
Donkeys . . .		600

Source: Ministry of Agriculture.

INDUSTRY

Industrial Production 1972

(firms with more than five workers)

('ooo riyals)

Mining and Quarrying . . .	3,597
Food Manufacturing	6,332
Soft Drinks	6,877
Tobacco and Cigarettes . . .	2,062
Textiles	25,352
Wood Products	2,260
Printing and Publishing . . .	1,042
Building Materials . . .	4,178
Metal Products	3,077
Electricity	9,256
Vehicle Maintenance . . .	3,751
Others	1,886

FINANCE

40 buqsha=1 Yemeni riyal.

Coins: ½, 1 and 2 buqsha.

Notes: 10 and 20 buqsha; 1, 5, 10, 20 and 50 riyals.

Echange rates (July 1975): £1 sterling=9.98 Yemini riyals; U.S. $1=4.56 Yemeni riyals.

100 Yemeni riyals=£10.02=$21.92.

Note: The Yemeni riyal was introduced in 1964, with an initial value of 6s. 8d. sterling (£1=3.00 riyals) or 93.33 U.S. cents (U.S. $1=1.071 riyals). Thereafter, the authorities allowed the currency to depreciate on the free market while applying a system of multiple official exchange rates. By 1970 the free rate was $1=5.50 riyals (£1=13.20 riyals). In June 1971 multiple practices were eliminated, leaving a single rate which held fairly stable at $1=5.00 riyals until February 1973, since when the Central Bank has set a selling rate of $1=4.50 riyals. It was announced in March 1975 that the riyal would be divided into 100 fils rather than 40 buqsha.

BUDGET

('ooo riyals, year ending June 30th)

	REVENUE	EXPENDITURE
1971–72 . .	151,274	233,803
1972–73 . .	199,021	271,458
1973–74 . .	281,565	391,023

Source: Ministry of Treasury and Central Bank of Yemen.

EXTERNAL TRADE

('ooo riyals)

	1970	1971	1972	1973
Imports . .	178,449	184,840	376,245	564,248
Exports . .	15,759	21,571	20,074	36,008

PRINCIPAL COMMODITIES
('ooo riyals)

IMPORTS	1970	1971	1972	1973
Food and live animals . . .	100,422	72,640	117,060	271,822
Beverages and tobacco . . .	15,952	9,057	11,558	13,472
Crude materials (inedible) except fuels	66	1,144	56	1,056
Mineral fuels, lubricants, etc. . .	6,228	11,665	18,227	28,067
Animal and vegetable oils and fats .	426	1,954	2,738	2,738
Chemicals	5,667	9,406	21,019	35,974
Basic manufactures . . .	21,623	34,145	69,130	96,301
Machinery and transport equipment .	16,668	29,550	48,928	68,983
Miscellaneous manufactured articles .	11,396	15,278	25,960	42,362
Unspecified items	—	—	1,066	2,134
TOTAL	178,449	184,840	376,245	564,248

EXPORTS	1970	1971	1972	1973
Dried fish	123	23	229	536
Biscuits	n.a.	n.a.	17	1,184
Potatoes	348	183	247	488
Coffee	8,086	8,582	5,343	6,016
Qat	4,338	2,798	1,031	67
Hides and skins	1,195	2,039	3,262	5,472
Cottonseed	n.a.	777	564	2,127
Raw cotton	n.a.	7,986	7,154	17,796
Salt	1,489	2,383	661	30
TOTAL (incl. others) . .	15,759	21,571	20,074	36,008

PRINCIPAL COUNTRIES
('ooo riyals)

IMPORTS	1970	1971	1972	1973
Australia	22,161	13,883	47,091	9,483
Belgium	219	287	2,505	22,689
China, People's Republic . .	3,794	5,216	14,913	21,578
Egypt	5,786	8,228	18,049	21,035
Ethiopia	2,250	1,985	2,411	21,300
France	21,167	6,458	28,701	35,895
French Territory of the Afars and the Issas	1,219	5,888	13,113	33,059
Germany, Federal Republic . .	1,982	7,672	26,272	25,776
Japan	10,236	17,373	38,440	76,092
Netherlands	2,700	5,483	4,916	24,853
Saudi Arabia	108	1,714	23,861	36,522
U.S.S.R.	21,447	13,475	14,818	14,804
United Kingdom	15,132	14,746	19,634	25,272
Yemen, People's Democratic Republic .	41,774	49,538	40,941	40,425

EXPORTS	1970	1971	1972	1973
China, People's Republic . .	n.a.	7,986	7,718	5,929
Italy	22	324	981	2,303
Japan	1,863	2,479	539	7,979
Saudi Arabia	20	208	2,308	4,169
Singapore	n.a.	n.a.	157	5,942
Sweden	n.a.	n.a.	n.a.	5,507
U.S.S.R.	5,003	1,900	1,828	2,056
Yemen, People's Democratic Republic .	8,178	7,306	4,403	4,585

Source: Central Bank of Yemen.

TRANSPORT

ROAD TRAFFIC 1973

Private cars 2,288, motor cycles 6,063, taxis 3,329, trucks 6,957.

SHIPPING

	VESSELS ENTERING HODEIDA PORT	TONNAGE UNLOADED
1972 . .	506	506,991
1973 . .	520	530,943

CIVIL AVIATION
(Yemen Airways)

	PASSENGERS CARRIED	FREIGHT (tons)
1972	48,600	567
1973	43,400	431

EDUCATION
(1972–73)

	INSTITUTIONS	TEACHERS	PUPILS Boys	PUPILS Girls
Primary	1,442	4,053	136,977	17,630
Preparatory . . .	59	387	7,212	94
Secondary . . .	8	157	2,248	19
Commercial . . .	1	8	124	—
Technical . . .	1	42	250	—
Teacher Training . . .	9	n.a.	201	738
University Colleges . . .	4	41	391	48

Source (except where otherwise stated): Yemen Arab Republic Central Planning Organization.

PROVISIONAL CONSTITUTION

(Published June 19th, 1974)

In the name of the people, the Chairman of the Command Council, having taken cognizance of Command Council Proclamation No. 1 for 1974, Command Council Proclamation No. 4 for 1974 suspending the Constitution, and Command Council Proclamation No. 5 for 1974 increasing the membership of the Command Council, and desiring to consolidate the bases of authority during the transitional period and to regulate the rights and duties of all employees in a manner conducive to fruitful production to raise the country to the level which we all hope it will attain, we announce in the name of the people that during the transitional period the country will be governed in accordance with the following rules:

Chapter One: General Principles: the State:

Article 1: Yemen is an Arab, Islamic, and independent state enjoying full sovereignty. Its system is republican. The Yemeni people are a part of the Arab nation.

Article 2: The people are the source of all authority.

Article 3: Islam is the state religion and Arabic the official state language.

Article 4: The Islamic Sharia is the source of all laws.

Article 5: Yemen is an indivisible whole and its defence is the sacred duty of all citizens.

Chapter Two: Rights and Duties:

Article 6: Yemenis have equal rights and general duties.

Article 7: Personal freedom is guaranteed in accordance with the provisions of the law.

Article 8: There shall be no crime and no penalty except as laid down by law and there shall be no penalty for acts except those committed after the promulgation of the law (applying to them).

Article 9: Homes are inviolate: it is therefore inadmissible to enter them except in such instances as prescribed by the law.

Article 10: The confiscation of funds is prohibited, except within the confines of the law.

Article 11: No person's property shall be expropriated except in the public interest, in the instances prescribed by the law, and with just compensation to the person.

Article 12: The citizens have the right to express their thoughts by means of speech, writing, or voting within the confines of the law.

Article 13: Places of worship and learning have immunity which cannot be violated except in instances required by security needs and as prescribed by the law.

Chapter Three: The System of Government:

Article 14: The Chairman of the Command Council shall assume the function of general sovereignty, particularly in taking the measures he deems necessary to protect the revolution and the republican régime.

Article 15: The Command Council shall assume the functions of the legislative and executive authorities of the state. It shall also have the power to lay down general policy and define its general framework.

Article 16: The Government is the executive and administrative body responsible for carrying out the state's general policy as laid down by the Command Council.

Article 17: The judiciary is independent, and there shall be no authority over it except for the law. Its verdicts shall be handed down and executed in accordance with the principles of the Sharia.

Chapter Four: Concluding Rules:

Article 18: All the rules determined by the laws, bylaws and decisions prior to the issuance of this constitutional

declaration shall remain in force unless they conflict with the rules of this declaration or unless they are amended or revoked.

Article 19: During the transitional period action shall be taken to restore constitutional and democratic life on sound bases in view of the need to provide the Yemeni people with a dignified life and a bright future.

Article 20: This constitutional declaration shall come into force from the date of its issuance and it shall be published in the Official Gazette.

THE GOVERNMENT

MILITARY COMMAND COUNCIL

Chairman: Lt.-Col. IBRAHIM MUHAMMAD AL-HAMADI.

Members: ABDEL-AZIZ ABDEL-GHANI, Lt.-Col. AHMAD AL-GHASHMI, Lt.-Col. DIRHAM ABU-LUHUM, Lt.-Col. YAHYA MUTAWAKKEL, Maj. ABDULLA ABDEL ALEM.

CABINET
(August 1975)

Prime Minister: ABDEL-AZIZ ABDEL-GHANI.

Minister of the Interior: Lt.-Col. YAHYA MUTAWAKKEL.

Deputy Premier for Foreign and Economic Affairs: YAHYA JAGHMAN.

Deputy Premier for Internal Affairs: ABDULLA HASAN BARAKAT.

Minister of Communications: Brig. ABDUL-LATIF DAIFULLA.

Minister of Finance: MUHAMMAD AHMED JUNAID.

Minister of Local Administration: ABDEL-MALEK AT-TAYEB.

Minister of Economy: ALI LUTF ATH-THAUR.

Minister of Foreign Affairs: ABDULLA ABDEL-MAJID ASNAG.

Minister of Information: AHMAD QASSEM DAHMASH.

Minister of Justice: Qadi ALI SAMMAM.

Minister of Education: HASAN AL-BUQTUMI.

Minister of Waqfs: MUHAMMAD LUTF AS-SABANI.

Minister of Supply: SAID MUHAMMAD AL-HABIBI.

Minister of Municipal Affairs: MUTTAHER NADER.

Minister of Health: ABDEL-MALEK MUHAMMAD ABDULLA.

Minister of Social, Labour and Youth Affairs: ABDULLA HUSAIN AL-HALALI.

Minister of Agriculture: MUHAMMAD AL-KHADEM AL-WAJIH.

Minister of Works: ABDULLA AL-KURSHUMI.

Ministers of State: AHMAD ABDOU SAID, ABDEL-KARIM AL-ANSI, SALAH MASRI, AMIN HASAN ABU-RAS.

CONSULTATIVE COUNCIL

A Consultative Council was established as the supreme legislative body under the 1970 Constitution. It consists of 179 members, of whom 20 are appointed by the President and the remainder elected by popular vote every four years. Elections were first held in March 1971. The Council was dissolved after the *coup* of June 1974, but re-established in November 1974.

Speaker: Shaikh ABDULLAH BIN-HUSAIN AL-AHMAR.

POLITICAL ORGANIZATION*

Yemeni Union: Sana'a; f. 1973 in anticipation of merging of two Yemens.

* Dissolved June 1974.

DIPLOMATIC REPRESENTATION

EMBASSIES ACCREDITED TO THE YEMEN ARAB REPUBLIC
(In Sana'a unless otherwise stated)

Algeria: Ali Abdul Moghni St.; *Ambassador:* SAADEDDINE NOUIOUAT.

Austria: Jeddah, Saudi Arabia.

Belgium: Jeddah, Saudi Arabia.

Bulgaria: Cairo, Egypt.

China, People's Republic: Zubairy St.; *Ambassador:* (vacant).

Czechoslovakia: Gamal Abdul Naser St.; *Ambassador:* LUMIR HANAK.

Egypt: Gamal Abdul Naser St.; *Ambassador:* AHMAD FOUAD ABDUL HAYE.

Ethiopia: Zubairy St.; *Chargé d'Affaires:* TESFAYE TAKLE-HAIMANOT.

France: Gamal Abdul Naser St.; *Ambassador:* GEORGES GALLIÉ.

German Democratic Republic: 26 September St.; *Chargé d'Affaires:* GERHARD STRIEGNITZ.

Germany, Federal Republic: Republican Palace St.; *Ambassador:* Dr. GÜNTER HELD (also accred. to Yemen P.D.R.).

Greece: Jeddah, Saudi Arabia.

Hungary: Cairo, Egypt.

India: Al-Amir Building, Gamal Abdul Naser St.; *Ambassador:* (vacant).

Iran: *Ambassador:* Dr. HASSAN SABETI.

Iraq: Building Mohamed Zehrah, Zubairy St.; *Ambassador:* HISSAM UD-DIN ABDUL-AZIZ (also accred. to Yemen P.D.R.).

Italy: Gamal Abdul Naser St.; *Ambassador:* LORENZO BARACCHI TUA DI PAULLO.

Japan: Jeddah, Saudi Arabia.

Jordan: *Ambassador:* Maj.-Gen. HAIDAR MUSTAFA.

Korea, Democratic People's Republic: Zubairy St.; *Ambassador:* PAK HWA-SU.

Kuwait: 26 September St.; *Ambassador:* SAYYID IBRAHIM GASIM AL-BAHWAH (also accred. to Yemen P.D.R.).

Lebanon: Airport Rd.; *Chargé d'Affaires:* HIKMAT NASIR (also accred. to Yemen P.D.R.).

Libya: Airport Rd.; *Ambassador:* ABDUL-RAZZAK OMAR.

Netherlands: Jeddah, Saudi Arabia.

Norway: Jeddah, Saudi Arabia.

Oman: *Chargé d'Affaires:* MUNTHER MA-JED AL-SAEED.

Pakistan: Cairo, Egypt.

Poland: Cairo, Egypt.

Qatar: Jeddah, Saudi Arabia.

Romania: Khartoum, Sudan.

Saudi Arabia: Arman Building; *Ambassador:* Sheikh MOUSSAID BIN AHMED AL-SUDAIRI.

Somalia: Hadda Rd.; *Ambassador:* UTHMAN JAMA ISSA.

Spain: Cairo, Egypt.

Sweden: Jeddah, Saudi Arabia.

Switzerland: Jeddah, Saudi Arabia.

Syria: Zubairy St.; *Ambassador:* MUHAMMAD ADNAN ALZEER (also accred. to Yemen P.D.R.).

Tunisia: Jeddah, Saudi Arabia.

Turkey: Jeddah, Saudi Arabia.

U.S.S.R.: 26 September St.; *Ambassador:* VASILI KORNEV.

United Arab Emirates: Ali Abdul Mughny St.; *Ambassador:* SAYYID SALIM AL SUWAIDI.

United Kingdom: 11/13 Republican Palace St.; *Ambassador:* D. C. CARDEN.

U.S.A.: Beit Al-Halali; *Ambassador:* THOMAS J. SCOTES.

Viet-Nam, Democratic Republic: Cairo, Egypt.

Yugoslavia: Mogadishu, Somalia.

JUDICIAL SYSTEM

President of the State Security Court: Qadhi GHALIB ABDULLA RAJEH (political cases).

Public Prosecutor: Lt.-Col. MUHAMMAD KHAMIS.

Sharia Court: Sana'a; f. 1964; to deal with political cases and to try senior government officials; but now deals with cases related to Islamic law.

Disciplinary Court: prosecution office for maladministration and misappropriation of public funds; Chair. MUHAMMAD ABDO NUMAN.

PRESS

DAILIES

Al Gumhuryyah (*The Republic*): Information Office, Taiz; Arabic; government-owned.

Al Thawra (*The Revolution*): Ministry of Information, Sana'a; Arabic; government-owned.

WEEKLY AND OTHER

Al Bilad: P.O.B. 1438, Sana'a; Arabic; weekly; inclined to right.

Mareb: Dar Al-Qalam, Taiz; Arabic; weekly; supports Nasserite ideas.

Al Risalah: 26 September St., Sana'a; Arabic; weekly.

As-Sabah: P.O.B. 599, Hodeida; Arabic; weekly; reformist.

As-Salam: P.O.B. 181, Sana'a; Arabic; weekly.

Sana'a: P.O.B. 193, Sana'a; Arabic; fortnightly; inclined to left.

Al Shab: Al-Andalus Bookshop, Sana'a; Arabic; weekly; slightly left-inclined.

Saut al-Yemen: P.O.B. 302, Sana'a; Arabic; weekly; supports Muslim brotherhood.

Al-Ta'wn: Al Ta'wn Building, Jubairi St., Sana'a; Arabic; weekly; supports co-operative societies.

Al-Yemen: Sana'a; Arabic; fortnightly; inclined to right.

NEWS AGENCIES

Middle East News Agency: Sana'a.

Saba News Agency: Sana'a; f. 1970; Dir. HASSAN AL-ULUFI.

Tass also has a bureau in Sana'a.

RADIO

Radio Hodeida: Hodeida; government-controlled local radio; broadcasts in Arabic, 4 hours daily.

Radio Sana'a: Sana'a; government-controlled station, broadcasts in Arabic, 15 hours daily; Dir.-Gen. ABDUL RAHMAN AL-MUTARIB.

Radio Taiz: Taiz; government-controlled station; broadcasts in Arabic, 4 hours daily.

There are 250,000 receiving sets.

FINANCE

Central Bank of Yemen: P.O.B. 59, Sana'a; f. 1971; cap. p.u. 10m. riyals; responsible for issuing currency, managing gold and foreign exchange reserves etc.; at end of December 1973 currency in circulation amounted to 457.5m. riyals; Gov. and Chair. (vacant); Deputy Gov. and Deputy Chair. ABDULLA SANABANI; Gen. Man. ABDULLAH A. AL-BARAKANI.

Yemen Bank for Reconstruction and Development: P.O.B. 541, Sana'a; f. 1962; cap. 10m. riyals; consolidated bank; 8 brs.; Chair. MOHSIN SIRRY.

Arab Bank Ltd.: P.O.B. 68, Amman, Jordan; Tahrir (Liberation) Square, Sana'a; br. in Hodeida.

British Bank of the Middle East: 20 Abchurch Lane, London, E.C.4; P.O.B. 3932, Hodeida: Man. D. C. HOWELLS; P.O.B. 4886, Taiz: Man. I. W. CUTRESS.

Habib Bank (Overseas) Ltd.: Karachi, Pakistan; Hodeida.

United Bank of Pakistan: Ali Abdul Mugni St., Sana'a.

TRADE AND INDUSTRY

CHAMBERS OF COMMERCE

Hodeida Chamber of Commerce: Tahrir (Liberation) Square, P.O.B. 3370, Hodeida.

Taiz Chamber of Commerce: 26th September St., P.O.B. 4029, Taiz.

NATIONALIZED ORGANIZATIONS

General Cotton Organization: Sana'a.

Hodeida Electricity and Water Company: P.O.B. 3363, Hodeida; affiliate of Yemen Bank for Reconstruction and Development.

National Tobacco and Matches Co.: P.O.B. 3571, Hodeida; f. 1964; monopoly importing and sales organization for tobacco and matches; cigarette manufacturers at Hodeida to use tobacco grown locally on the company's plantations; Chair. A. A. NAGI.

Yemen Company for Foreign Trade: Hodeida.

Yemen Petroleum Co.: YPC Bldg., P.O.B. 3360, Hodeida; the sole petroleum supplier in the Yemen; Chair. HUSSAIN ABDULLAH AL MAKDANI; Gen. Man. YEHIA ABDULLAH AL-DAILAMI.

Yemen Printing and Publishing Co.: P.O.B. 1081, Sana'a; f. 1970; publishes ten newspapers (including two government newspapers), and undertakes many kinds of commercial printing; Chair. AHMAD MUHAMMAD HADI.

TRANSPORT

Roads: There are about 1,650 km. of main roads, of which about 600 km. are asphalted and the rest gravelled. Highways run from Hodeida to Sana'a, and from Moka to Taiz, Ibb and Sana'a. A highway from Sana'a to Saada is being built with Chinese aid. The Sana'a-Khamir section was opened in February 1972.

Shipping: Hodeida is a Red Sea port of some importance, and the Yemen Navigation Company runs passenger and cargo services to many parts of the Middle East and Africa. Extension programmes are being carried out on the ports at Salif and Mocha.

Adafar Yemenite Line: Hodeida.

Hodeida Shipping Co.: P.O.B. 337, Hodeida.

Middle East Shipping Co.: P.O.B. 3700, Hodeida; br. in Mocha.

Civil Aviation: Three airports—Al Rahaba at Sana'a, Al Ganad at Taiz and Hodeida Airport—are classified as being of international standard and are being developed following the end of the civil war. Federal Germany gave financial assistance towards the construction of the new Sana'a airport, which opened in August 1973.

Yemen Airways: Sana'a; internal services to Sana'a, Hodeida, Taiz, Beida, Hareeb, Barat and Saada, external services to Abu Dhabi, Aden, Asmara, Cairo, Djibouti, Doha, Jeddah, Khartoum and Kuwait; now supervised by a ministerial committee headed by the Minister of Communications, Brig. ABDUL-LATIF DAIFULLA; Chair. and Pres. SHAIF MOHAMMED SAEED; fleet of two DC-6, one Boeing 737-15, three DC-3.

The following airlines also serve the Yemen: Aeroflot, Air Djibouti, Alyernda, Ethiopian Airlines, Kuwait Airways, Somali Airlines, Syrian Arab Airlines and Saudi Arabian Airlines in addition to charter flights by various carriers.

DEFENCE

Defence Budget: 266 million riyals (1974–75).

Military Service: 3 years.

Total Armed Forces: 26,900: army 22,000, navy 300, air force 1,600; para-military forces: 20,000 tribal levies.

EDUCATION

Education in Yemen is still provided mainly by traditional types of school. A modern graded school system has, however, been introduced recently, providing a six-year primary course, a four-year intermediate course and a three-year secondary course. The religious colleges are located in the mosques, the most important of these being at Bir Al-A'zab, Zabid and Dhamar. They provide tuition in Arabic, philosophy, commentaries on the Koran, Muslim Law, tradition and history for those students who wish to pursue further studies. There is one agricultural school and six vocational schools in the Yemen. There is also a Military Academy, a College for Radio Telecommunications and a College of Aviation.

UNIVERSITY

University of Sana'a: P.O.B. 1247, Sana'a; f. 1974; 49 teachers, 1,470 students.

BIBLIOGRAPHY

ANSALDI, C. Il Yemen nella storia e nella leggenda (Rome, 1933).

ATTAR, MOHAMED SAID EL-. Le sous-développement Economique et Social du Yémen (Editions Tiers-Monde, Algiers, 1966).

BALSAN, FRANÇOIS. Inquiétant Yémen (Paris, 1961).

BETHMANN, E. W. Yemen on the Threshold (American Friends of the Middle East, Washington, 1960).

COLONIAL OFFICE. Aden and the Yemen (H.M.S.O., London, 1960).

DEUTSCH, ROBERT. Der Yemen (Vienna, 1914).

DOE, BRIAN. Southern Arabia (Thames and Hudson, London, 1972).

FAROUGHY, A. Introducing Yemen (New York, 1947).

FAYEIN, CLAUDE. A French Doctor in the Yemen (Robert Hale, London, 1957).

HELFRITZ, H. The Yemen: A Secret Journey (Allen and Unwin, London, 1958).

HEYWORTH-DUNNE, G. E. Al-Yemen: Social, Political and Economic Survey (Cairo, 1952).

INGRAMS, HAROLD. The Yemen; Imams, Rulers and Revolutions (London, 1963).

MACRO, ERIC. Bibliography of the Yemen, with Notes on Mocha (University of Miami Press, 1959).
Yemen and the Western World since 1571 (C. Hurst, London, and Praeger, New York, 1968).

O'BALLANCE, EDGAR. The War in the Yemen (Faber, London, 1971).

PAWELKE, GUNTHER. Der Yemen: Das Verbotene Land (Econ. Verlag., Düsseldorf, 1959).

SCHMIDT, DANA ADAMS. Yemen, the Unknown War (Bodley Head, London, 1968).

SCOTT, H. In the High Yemen (Murray, London, 1942).

U.S.G.P.O. Geology of the Arabian Peninsula: Yemen (Washington, 1967).

WENNER, MANFRED W. Yemen: a selected Bibliography of Literature since 1960 (Library of Congress Legislative Reference Service, Washington, D.C., 1965).
Modern Yemen, 1918-1966 (Johns Hopkins Press, Baltimore, U.S.A., 1967).

People's Democratic Republic of Yemen

(Southern Yemen)

PHYSICAL AND SOCIAL GEOGRAPHY

W. B. Fisher

On November 30th, 1967, the People's Republic of Southern Yemen came into existence, formed from the former British Colony and Protectorate of Aden (75 sq. miles and 111,000 sq. miles respectively), together with the islands of Perim (5 sq. miles) and Kamaran (22 sq. miles). Socotra (1,400 sq. miles) elected to join the new state. The Kuria Muria group of islands were returned to Muscat by Britain but the new Republican government revoked this decision. In November 1970 the name of the Republic was changed to the "People's Democratic Republic of Yemen". The capital is Aden. The state is divided into seven governorates which replace Aden and the 20 states of the old South Arabian Protectorate. The Republic lies at the southern end of the Arabian peninsula, approximately between longitude 43° and 56°E., with Perim Island a few miles due west, in the strait marking the southern extremity of the Red Sea; Kamaran Island some 200 miles north of Perim; Socotra and the Kuria Muria groups in the extreme east, the former at the entrance to the Gulf of Aden, the latter near the coast of Oman. The Republic has frontiers with the Yemen Arab Republic, Saudi Arabia, and Oman, but none of these frontiers is fully delimited, and in some instances they are disputed. Atlases still show considerable variation in the precise boundaries of all four territories, or sometimes do not indicate them at all.

Physically, the Republic comprises the broken and dislocated southern edge of the great plateau of Arabia. This is an immense mass of ancient granites, once forming part of Africa, and covered in many places by shallow, generally horizontal layers of younger sedimentary rocks. The whole plateau has undergone downwarping in the east and elevation in the west, so that the highest land (over 10,000 ft.) occurs in the extreme west, near the Red Sea, with a gradual decline to the lowest parts (under 1,000 ft.) in the extreme east. The whole of the southern and western coasts of the Republic were formed by a series of enormous fractures, which produced a flat but very narrow coastal plain, rising steeply to the hill country a short distance inland. Percolation of molten magma along the fracture-lines has given rise to a number of volcanic craters, now extinct, and one of these, partly eroded and occupied by the sea, forms the site of Aden port.

An important topographic feature is the Wadi Hadhramaut, an imposing valley running parallel to the coast at 100–150 miles distance inland. In its upper and middle parts, this valley is broad, and occupied by a seasonal torrent; in its lower (eastern) part it narrows considerably, making a sudden turn south-eastwards and reaching the sea. This lower part is largely uninhabited, but the upper parts, where alluvial soil and intermittent flood water are available, are occupied by a farming population.

The details of climate in the Republic are simple to state, but extremely difficult to explain. Rainfall is everywhere scanty, but relatively more abundant on the highlands and in the west. Thus Aden itself has 5 in. of rain annually, entirely in winter (December–March), whilst in the lowlands of the extreme east, it may rain only once in five or ten years. In the highlands a few miles north of Aden, falls of up to 30 in. occur, for the most part during summer, and this rainfall also gradually declines eastwards, giving 15–20 in. in the highlands of Dhofar. Ultimately, to the north and east, rainfall diminishes to almost nil, as the edges of the Arabian Desert are reached. This unusual situation of a reversal in climatic conditions over a few miles is thought to be the result of two streams of air; an upper one, damp and unstable in summer, and originating in the equatorial regions of East Africa; and a lower current, generally drier and related to conditions prevailing over the rest of the Middle East. In this way the low lying coastal areas have a maximum of rainfall in winter, and the hills of both the Yemens a maximum in summer. Temperatures are everywhere high, particularly on the coastal plain, which has a southern aspect: mean figures of 76°F. (Jan.) to 89° (June) occur at Aden town, but maxima of over 100° are common.

Except on the higher parts, which have a light covering of thorn scrub (including dwarf trees which exude a sap from which incense and myrrh are derived), and the restricted patches of cultivated land, the territory of the Republic is devoid of vegetation. Cultivation is limited to small level patches of good soil on flat terraces alongside the river beds, on the floor and sides of the Wadi Hadhramaut, or where irrigation from wells and cisterns can be practised. The most productive areas are: Lahej, close to Aden town; two districts near Mukalla (about 300 miles east of Aden), and parts of the middle Hadhramaut. Irrigation from cisterns hollowed out of the rock has long been practised, and Aden town has a famous system of this kind, dating back many centuries.

HISTORY

ADEN COLONY

When the Portuguese first rounded the Cape of Good Hope (1497–98), Aden was a port of some commercial importance, acting as a rendezvous for ships bound from India to the Red Sea and at the same time enjoying an active local trade with the Persian Gulf and the coast of East Africa. In 1513 the Portuguese, under Albuquerque, tried to capture the town, though without success. The Ottoman Turks, in their endeavour to deny the Portuguese access to the Red Sea, seized Aden in 1538, but their hold on the Yemen proved to be precarious. There was a serious revolt against the Ottoman régime in 1547–51 and a still more dangerous rebellion in 1566–70. When in the course of the seventeenth century the Ottoman state fell into decline, the authority of the Sultan over this distant region became little more than nominal, effective power in the Yemen passing now into the hands of local chieftains, the most notable of whom, after 1735, was the Sultan of Lahej. The discovery of the Cape route to India had greatly diminished the prosperity of Aden as a commercial entrepot, but with the Napoleonic campaign in Egypt in 1798, Aden assumed strategic importance in Britain's plan of containment. In 1799 Britain occupied the island of Perim. Shortage of water compelled a withdrawal to the mainland where friendly relations were established with the Sultan of Lahej with whom later in 1902 a commercial treaty was concluded. However, the need to possess a base in these waters under the British flag doubled with the coming of the steamship. Negotiations began for the purchase of the island of Socotra, which in 1834 was temporarily occupied by the East India Company; they might have succeeded had not the relations with the Sultan suddenly deteriorated in 1837 following the plunder near Aden of a wrecked Indian vessel flying the British flag. The incident was followed by the despatch by the East India Company of a British force from Bombay, under the command of Captain Haines of the Indian navy, which, on January 16th, 1839, captured Aden. By the peace treaty, the Sultan was guaranteed an annual sum of 6,000 dollars and Aden became part of the British Empire, administered by the government of Bombay. The Sultan did not finally abandon his efforts to regain Aden until 1857 when permanent peace was established with Britain. Perim Island was ceded in the same year. The Kuria Muria Islands had already been acquired in 1854 from the Sultan of Oman. With the opening of the Suez Canal and the revival of the Red Sea route, Aden, which had been a free port since 1853, increased in importance. In the twentieth century, with the gradual replacement of coal by oil, Aden, closely linked to the Persian Gulf area, enhanced its historic position as a fuelling station. Aden's strategic value is also based on plentiful supplies of fresh drinking water from the artesian wells at Shaikh Othman.

In 1932, the administration of Aden passed to the Governor-General of India in Council; in April 1937, it was vested in a separately appointed governor, who was also commander-in-chief, and who was assisted by an Executive Council. Crown Colony status had in fact been granted two years previously by the Government of India Act 1935. A Legislative Council for Aden, granted in 1944, was inaugurated in 1947. In 1955 the Aden Colony (Amendment) Order came into force, providing for an elected element in the Council; the first elections were held in December of the same year. Further constitutional changes were made in 1959. On January 4th, 1959, voting took place for the choice of 12 elected members of the Legislative Council. Nine Arabs, 2 Somalis and 1 Indian were elected to the Council. Large numbers of the Arab population boycotted the election.

On January 16th, 1961, Sir Charles Johnston, the Governor of Aden, announced to the Legislative Council of Aden that the (then) Colonial Secretary, Mr. Macleod, had approved a ministerial system of government for Aden and that members of the Executive Council in charge of administrative departments would soon assume ministerial status. The Governor also spoke of a possible closer association with the West Aden Protectorate and in particular with the Federation of Arab Amirates of the South. The Federation was renamed the Federation of South Arabia in April 1962. On November 30th, 1967, Aden and the Protectorate of South Arabia achieved independence under the name of the People's Republic of Southern Yemen.

SOUTH ARABIAN PROTECTORATE

Behind Aden and stretching some 600 miles along the coast is the territory of 20 former states whose rulers, between 1882 and 1914, entered into protective treaty relations with the British Government and acknowledged the authority of the Governor of Aden as Governor of the Protectorate. Many of the States later entered into closer treaty relations, and, while retaining independent control in the internal affairs of their respective territories, the rulers accepted the advice on administration offered by British Agents and Political Officers appointed by the Governor. Britain guaranteed protection to the States and they agreed not to cede territory to foreign powers.

EASTERN PROTECTORATE STATES

Formerly named the Eastern Aden Protectorate, the region covered by the States comprised the Hadhramaut (consisting of the Qu'aiti State of Shihr and Mukalla, and the Kathiri State of Sai'un), the Mahra Sultanate of Qishn and Socotra, the Wahidi Sultanates of Balhaf and Bir'ali, and the Sheikhdoms of Irqa and Haura. At July 1st, 1966, the total population of the area was estimated at 326,000. The Qu'aiti Sultan first concluded a protectorate treaty with Britain in 1888. In 1918 following an agreement between the Qu'aiti and the Kathiri Sultans, the latter accepted the protectorate treaty as extending to his State. Both Sultans agreed by further treaties, signed in 1937 and 1939, to accept the advice of a British Agent in all matters except those concerning the religion and custom of Islam. The British Agent for the Eastern Protectorate States was stationed at Mukalla in the territory of the premier chief, the Qu'aiti Sultan of Shihr and Mukalla. Both he and the Kathiri Sultan were constitutional rulers and were assisted by State Councils. Close co-operation existed between the two states in constitutional and in economic matters.

In 1949 an advisory treaty was concluded with the Wahidi Sultan of Balhaf. The Mahra Sultan of Qishn and Socotra signed a treaty of protection with Britain in 1866 and by it the Island of Socotra and the Abd Alkuri and Brothers Islands came within the protectorate.

WESTERN PROTECTORATE STATES

The former Western Protectorate comprised 17 states. Population at July 1st, 1966, was estimated at 570,000. Five of the States, in 1944 and 1945, agreed by advisory treaties with Britain to accept the advice of the Governor of Aden on administrative affairs—the Fadhli, the Lower 'Aulaqi and the Lower Yafa'i Sultans, the Sherif of Beihan and the Amir of Dhala. In 1952 similar treaties were signed by the Upper 'Aulaqi Sheikh and the 'Audhali Sultan; and a joint advisory and protectorate treaty was accepted by the newly elected Sultan of Lahej. The British Political Officers and the Arab Assistant Political Officers for the Western Protectorate States were under the supervision of the Assistant High Commissioner whose headquarters were in Al Ittihad, the Federal capital.

The British authorities, in 1954 and again in 1956, had discussed a plan of federation with local rulers in the West Aden Protectorate. On February 11th, 1959, the rulers of six (out of 17) states in the Western Protectorate signed a Federal Constitution and also a Treaty of Friendship and Protection with Great Britain. The British Government promised financial and military aid which would assist the Federation (embracing 'Audhali, Lower Yafa'i, Fadhli, Dhala, Beihan and Upper 'Aulaqi) to become eventually an independent state. The members of the Federation bound themselves not to enter into foreign relations of whatsoever kind without the approval of Great Britain. Lahej joined the Federation in October 1959, and Lower 'Aulaqi, 'Aqrabi and Dathina in February 1960. The Wahidi States of Balhaf and Bir Ali in the Eastern Aden Protectorate joined in 1962. Aden Colony became a member in January 1963, and Haushabi and Shaib joined in April. In 1965 there were three further accessions: the 'Alawi and Muflahi Sheikhdoms, and the Upper 'Aulaqi Sultanate. The new Federal capital was Al Ittihad near Bir Ahmed.

The U.K. met the cost of defence, including the R.A.F. and Protectorate levy establishments. Beside the security forces maintained by the U.K. Government there were tribal guards in the Western States partially supported by the States, and the Mukalla Regular Army maintained by the Qu'aiti State.

At the end of November 1961 the British Government handed over control of the Aden Protectorate Levies to the Federation of Arab Amirates of the South. The Levies—which would be henceforth the Army of the Federation—had been formed in 1928 to protect Aden on the landward side and to provide garrisons for the Red Sea islands of Perim and Kamaran. An Arab force trained and commanded by British officers, the Levies consisted in 1961 of five infantry battalions, an armoured car squadron, and various signals and administrative units. The Levies came under the control of the Sultan of Lahej, who was Minister of Defence to the Federation, but command of the force still rested in the hands of a British officer as hitherto; for operational purposes the Levies were at the disposal of the G.O.C. Land Forces, Middle East.

ADEN AND THE YEMEN

Relations between the Protectorate and the neighbouring State of the Yemen were at all times delicate. Frequent encroachments led to the demarcation of frontiers which were accepted in a convention signed with the Ottoman government in March 1914. During the first World War, the Turkish troops from Yemen occupied the greater part of the Protectorate, and though in 1919 most of the chiefs resumed their treaty relations with Britain, the Imam of Sana'a, who exercised the principal religious authority in Yemen, being the most powerful of the Chieftains, maintained his claim to the entire territories. He sought to enforce it by occupying the Amiri district including the Radhfan tribes and parts of Haushabi, Sha'ibi and Upper Yafa'i territory, and the Audhali plateau. He also occupied territory not then within the Protectorate, the district of the Beidha Sultan. Britain continually repelled the Imam's advance and in 1928 he was compelled to withdraw from most of the Amiri territory. The Anglo-Yemenite treaty of peace and friendship was signed in February 1934, and was to be valid for 40 years; the two powers agreed to respect the *status quo*, and to negotiate for the classification of frontiers; Britain recognized the independence of the Yemen and the Imam agreed to evacuate the remainder of the Amiri district. In 1950 they agreed further to set up a frontier commission and to exchange diplomatic missions. In 1953 Yemen pressed her claims to the territories of the Aden Protectorate before the United Nations, and in subsequent years there was a series of border incidents. In December 1956 both tribesmen and Yemeni forces were reported to have raided villages in the Protectorate and made invasions into Western Aden. Similar incidents of varying degrees of importance continued until 1959. During this period there was a substantial flow of arms and technicians into the Yemen from the U.S.S.R. and its allies, and in March 1958 a formal union with the U.A.R. was announced. Britain sent troop reinforcements and R.A.F. units to repel these attacks, and in 1958 it established a separate military command in Aden. On two occasions the Yemen brought the dispute before the United Nations on the grounds that the U.K. was committing acts of aggression against her territory.

Incidents along the ill-defined frontier between Aden and the Yemen became less numerous in 1959.

The Governor of Aden paid a visit to Taiz in November 1959 which led to the conclusion of two informal agreements with the Yemen, the first covering civil aircraft flights between Aden and the Yemen, the second establishing local frontier commissions to settle border incidents. The first frontier commission met in February 1960.

In August 1962 the Yemen denounced the agreements reached at the London conference (discussed below), and reiterated its claim to the Aden territories. The revolution which broke out in the Yemen on September 27th, 1962, led to the establishment of a Republic of the Yemen. Colonel Sallal, the leader of the revolution, stated at this time that the new régime did not intend to press a claim to the Aden territories and hoped indeed for friendship with Britain. The U.S.S.R. and the U.A.R. recognized the republican régime almost immediately, and the United States followed suit in December, but Britain refused recognition. The new Yemen government frequently accused Britain of giving assistance to the Royalist resistance during the winter of 1962–63; the British legation at Taiz was closed, there were several minor conflicts in the border area, and another Yemen protest was made at the UN.

British and Federal forces carried out extensive military operations against dissident border tribesmen in 1964 and 1965; officials claimed these measures were necessary mainly because of unrest created by Yemeni agents. Direct clashes with Yemeni forces also occurred; the situation remained complex owing to the continuing presence of Royalist forces in the area. In 1964 Britain proposed that UN observers should patrol the border areas; the republican government, however, would not accept this, claiming that no frontier was necessary as Aden and the Federation all belonged by right to the Yemen. This attitude did not help relations during the independence negotiations or with the new Southern Yemen government.

CONSTITUTIONAL DEVELOPMENTS

In August 1960 Sir Charles Johnston became Governor of Aden in succession to Sir William Luce. The new Governor announced to the Legislative Council of the Aden Colony in January 1961 that a ministerial system was to be introduced into Aden— members of the Executive Council in charge of administrative departments (twelve in all) would soon assume ministerial status. Sir Charles Johnston also noted that efforts were in progress to promote constitutional development within Aden and in particular to bring about a closer association between the West Aden Protectorate and the Federation of Arab Emirates of the South.

A constitutional conference, which included five Ministers from Aden and five from the Federation, met in London (July–August 1962) under the chairmanship of Mr. Duncan Sandys, the Colonial Secretary. The Aden Trade Union Congress and its political wing, the People's Socialist Party (both counted much on the support of Yemenis who worked in Aden and aimed at the ultimate union of the Yemen, Aden, the Federation and the other territories of the West Aden Protectorate) denounced the conference held in London. On July 23rd, 1962, they called a strike to protest against the composition of the existing Legislative Council of Aden and to demand a general election and the establishment of an autonomous government in Aden before further progress should be made towards union with the Federation of Arab Emirates.

The discussions undertaken in August 1962 led to a White Paper recommending the incorporation of Aden into the Federation as a constituent state. It specified that Britain would retain sovereignty over Aden and responsibility for its defence and internal security. These proposals were the principal features of a draft treaty between Britain and the Federation (re-named the Federation of South Arabia); Perim and the Kuria Muria islands, although administered by the governor of Aden, were to be excluded.

There was considerable opposition in Aden to incorporation into the Federation. Several political parties opposed the move, and strikes and demonstrations directed against it occurred throughout 1962. Serious riots coincided with the Aden Legislative Council's passing of the draft treaty in September. Nevertheless, Britain and the Federation duly signed the agreement in January 1963 and Aden formally became a member of the Federation later that month.

ADEN'S INCORPORATION IN THE FEDERATION

Aden's new government consisted of a nine-member Council of Ministers, all Adenis except for the British Attorney-General. Since its principal economic support remained British forces expenditure—£20 million was spent on capital projects alone in the 1962–65 period—it could hardly expect to escape the suspicions of the radical Arab nationalist movements. In May 1963 representatives of the United Nations Committee on decolonization visited Yemen but were not allowed into Aden or the Federation. In July they issued a report—later adopted by the full committee and eventually the General Assembly—which claimed that most of the population disliked "the repressive laws and police methods" of the government; it accused Britain of attempting to prolong its control whilst most South Arabians wanted union with the Yemen. Britain, of course, rejected the report. In the meantime two more states—the Haushabi Sultanate and the Shaibi Sheikdom—had joined the Federation, now 14 strong; on April 1st all customs barriers were abolished within the Federation, Aden remaining a free port.

In December 1963 an attempt to assassinate the High Commissioner in Aden killed two people and injured over fifty; a state of emergency was declared and large numbers of political activists were detained. Although no charges were made, several weeks elapsed before many activists were released, and much opinion in Aden and beyond clearly thought this police treatment was too harsh.

MOVES TOWARDS INDEPENDENCE

In June 1964 a constitutional conference was held in London and an agreement was signed whereby the Federation of Saudi Arabia, inclusive of Aden, would become independent not later than 1968. Further discussions took place in London in August 1965, but the talks failed, and violence in Aden increased. It was estimated that between December 1963 and May 1966 60 people had been killed and 350 injured in Aden alone as a result of terrorism, one-third of the casualties being British. Meanwhile, in March 1965, Mr. Abd al-Qawi Makkawi became Chief Minister of Aden. However, in September 1965 the Aden Council of Ministers was dismissed, and the Colony's constitution suspended, because of mounting terrorism and the Council's failure either to condemn the terrorists or take any action against them.

POLITICAL REALIGNMENTS

The political scene in South Arabia, as viewed from the side of the nationalist elements, presented at this time an appearance of increasing confusion. The People's Socialist Party, led by Mr. Abdallah al-Asnag, had merged, in May 1965, with the Committee for the Liberation of Occupied South Yemen and with the South Arabian League to form the Organization for the Liberation of the Occupied South. A further development took place in January 1966, when the Organization for the Liberation of the Occupied South united with the National Front for the Liberation of the Occupied South, an extremist group operating from the Yemen with Egyptian support and responsible for the campaign of terrorism in Aden. Out of this new fusion of interests came the Front for the Liberation of Occupied South Yemen (FLOSY), in which political figures like Mr. Makkawi and Mr. al-Asnag now began to assume positions of prominence. The South Arabian League, however, declined to accept the prospect of complete absorption in a united nationalist movement and resumed its former independence. As an organization it held moderate nationalist views, rejecting the territorial claims of the Yemen, disapproving of terrorism and of influence emanating from Egypt, and aiming in general at a united state of South Arabia which should embrace Aden, the federal states and also the principalities of the East Aden Protectorate. Over against these various nationalist forces stood the "traditionalist" elements, embodied in the sheikhdoms and sultanates of the South Arabia Federation (and also of the East Aden Protectorate).

Of great importance too, as a factor influencing the affairs of South Arabia was the situation in the Yemen, itself divided between tribesmen loyal to the old Imamate and supported by Saudi Arabia, and the republican régime maintained and controlled by Egypt—a situation, in short, which reflected in itself the confrontation of Egypt and Saudi Arabia for a dominant voice in the affairs of Arabia as a whole.

NEW PROPOSALS FOR ADEN, 1966

The Federation of South Arabia made known in February 1966, proposals which, it was hoped, might serve as a basis for a constitution when South Arabia gained independence in 1968. At the request of the Federal Government in September 1965, two British experts, Sir Ralph Hone and Sir Gawain Bell, had undertaken the task of framing new proposals. Their recommendations now envisaged the creation of a United Republic of South Arabia (including the Hadhramaut area). The republic would be organized on federal lines. Aden, however, together with the federal capital al-Ittihad and the islands of Perim, Kamaran and Kuria Muria, would form within the republic a distinctive "capital territory".

THE DEFENCE QUESTION

In February 1966 the British Government issued a White Paper on Defence, which envisaged large reductions in the use of the armed forces of Great Britain overseas and in the general expenditure on them. The White Paper declared that, when Aden became independent in 1968, all British forces would be withdrawn and concentrated at Bahrain in the Persian Gulf; it also made known that the British Government did not propose to enter into defence agreements with the newly independent state of South Arabia.

This announcement gave grounds for alarm to the sheikhdoms and sultanates embraced within the Federation that the National Guard of the Federation might be confronted in the future with a Yemen able to call on large numbers of Egyptian troops. The federal authorities sent a delegation to London, hoping to persuade the British Government to at least assist with the rapid strengthening of the federal forces and with the provision of equipment. In June the British Government offered to contribute as much as £5,500,000 towards the capital cost of expanding and re-equipping the armed forces of the Federation. It also declared its readiness to continue its contribution (about £5,000,000) to the federal budget each year and to increase, to the extent of some £2,500,000, its share (hitherto about £4,600,000) in the maintenance of the federal troops. This aid was to continue for three years after independence, provided that no radical change occurred in the political situation of an independent South Arabia. The British Government still declined, however, to undertake the defence of South Arabia after it had won independence.

The extreme nationalist organizations had long advocated the acceptance in full of the UN resolutions passed in December 1963. Now, in May 1966, the Federal Government of South Arabia made known its readiness at last to take the resolutions as a basis for future action.

THE UN MISSION

In June 1966 the UN Committee on Colonialism urged that a United Nations Mission be sent to South Arabia to advise on the best means of giving effect to the UN resolutions of 1963 and 1965: resolutions which envisaged the granting of independence to South

Arabia, the withdrawal of British forces, the return of political leaders in exile or in detention and the holding of elections under international supervision. In August 1966 the British Government declared that it welcomed the appointment of such a mission, but it insisted that it could not abandon its responsibilities for the maintenance of good order in South Arabia and that it was bound to observe the agreements which it had made with the local states existing in the area.

Further violence and demonstrations in Aden in February 1967 perhaps hastened the actual appointment, on February 23rd, of the UN Mission to South Arabia, led by Señor Manuel Pérez Guerrero, of Venezuela. The commission led to no fruitful result.

PREPARATIONS FOR INDEPENDENCE

In April 1967 Lord Shackleton, Minister without Portfolio, was sent to South Arabia to assist the High Commissioner in examining the possibilities for the establishment of a "caretaker" régime representing all the interested elements in South Arabia. The nationalist organizations continued, however, to reject all appeals for co-operation with the British and the federal authorities.

On June 20th, 1967, the British Government made known the measures that it intended to bring into effect. The date of independence was to be January 9th, 1968. During the critical months following the grant of independence a naval force, including an attack carrier, was to be assigned to South Arabian waters; a number of V-bombers would also be stationed on the island of Masira, not far from the South Arabian territories. In addition, Great Britain promised financial aid (for aircraft, amongst other items) and undertook to re-equip the federal forces with more modern types of small arms, field guns and armoured cars. A military mission would also be sent from Great Britain to advise the federal authorities. In order to check the growing violence in South Arabia it was proposed to suspend trial by jury in respect of terrorist activities. On the other hand, the ban on the NLF was to be removed and consideration given to the possible release of some detainees. The British Government also declared that it would be willing to accept a draft constitution which the federal régime was now circulating to its member states. This constitution would prepare the ground for eventual elections on a basis of universal adult suffrage and for the establishment, as soon as circumstances allowed, of an administration representative of all the political elements in South Arabia. Regarding the problem of the uncommitted states in the East Aden Protectorate, Great Britain favoured their union with the Federation of South Arabia. It seemed improbable, however, that such a merger, if it did indeed come about, would occur before South Arabia attained its independence.

The tense situation prevailing in Aden became still more complicated when, on June 21st, 1967, some of the South Arabian federal troops mutinied and fought out with the British force a battle which involved considerable loss of life. This trouble was said to have arisen out of tribal rivalries affecting the federal forces, but the suspicion could not be excluded that, under the impact of nationalist sentiments, some of the troops might have weakened in their allegiance both towards the federal régime and towards the protecting power.

During July 1967 Britain continued her efforts to establish in Aden and the associated territories a broad-based provisional administration which should hold office until the moment of independence in January 1968. To facilitate the achievement of this aim the Federal Government consented to invite one of its own members, Mr. Bayumi, to form an interim administration with the aid, if possible, of FLOSY and the NLF. These nationalist organizations remained adamant, however, in their refusal to recognize the federal régime, which, in their view, reflected in its structure pre-eminently the interests of the local sultans. Mr. Bayumi's endeavour to gain the co-operation of the nationalist groups ended in failure and on July 27th the federal authorities relieved him of his appointment as Prime Minister designate.

Meanwhile, in South Arabia itself, during August to October 1967 the authority of the sultans crumbled rapidly before the advancing tide of nationalism. The NLF extended its control over the sheikhdom of Maflahi and over most of the other tribal states. On August 28th Sheikh Ali Musaid al-Babakri, speaking as chairman of the Supreme Council of the South Arabian Federation, admitted that the Federal Government and the Sultans had lost control of events and appealed to the armed forces of South Arabia to take command of the situation. This appeal—which marked in fact the virtual disintegration of the federal regime—was unsuccessful, the South Arabian Army refusing to accept the role thus offered to it. The swift advance of the NLF was due, not least of all, to the alignment on its side of a large measure of support amongst the local tribes against their traditional rulers, and also to the determination of the federal armed forces to maintain a neutral attitude. During September and October the NLF also moved into the territories of the Eastern Aden Protectorate, the sultanates of Qaiti, Kathiri and Mahra now passing under its influence. The High Commissioner announouced on September 5th that Britain was now prepared to recognize the nationalist forces in general as representative of the local populations and would be willing to enter into negotiations with them.

THE CLASH BETWEEN NATIONALISTS

The collapse of the federal régime left the main nationalist organizations face to face. There had been discussions between them, under Egyptian auspices, at Cairo and in the Yemen, but without much sign of ultimate agreement. Now, the notable success of the NLF had done much to diminish the prospect before the Front for the Liberation of the Occupied South Yemen. This latter organization was under the disadvantage that it operated largely under Egyptian guidance and not in South Arabia itself, but from the Yemen. Its chief support in Aden had come from the numerous Yemeni elements formerly working there. Of adverse effect, too, was the fact that its leaders, Abdallah al-Asnag and Abd al-Qawi Makkawi, had been working from the Yemen as exiles during the past two years. The imminence of an Egyptian withdrawal from the Yemen also contributed to a decline in its influence.

With the federal structure now in ruins, the immediate question was whether or not the two main nationalist groups could be brought into mutual cooperation. Conflict soon broke out, however, between them, and fierce fighting developed in the northern suburbs of Aden during September. The South Arabian Army was able to enforce a brief ceasefire, and the rival organizations met in Cairo in October, but without any agreement. Fresh fighting then began, FLOSY being finally defeated when the Army high command joined forces with the NLF.

The latter then insisted that Britain should regard it as the sole valid representative of the people of South Arabia—a course of action which the authorities in London agreed to take on November 11th, 1967. On November 14th it was announced at Aden that Qahtan al-Shaabi, one of the founders of the NLF, would lead a delegation to Geneva to hold discussions with the representatives of Britain.

The evacuation of British troops from Aden had begun earlier on August 25th, 1967. As the situation unfolded itself in Aden, the British Government resolved to hasten the withdrawal of its forces and to advance the independence of South Arabia from January 9th, 1968, to a date if possible in the second half of November 1967. On November 27th, after the British troops had made over large areas of Aden to the armed forces of South Arabia, the NLF proclaimed the creation of the People's Republic of Southern Yemen. At Geneva, Qahtan al-Shaabi announced on November 28th that agreement had been reached with Great Britain over the cession of Aden and its associated territories. The last British troops in Aden were withdrawn on November 29th, 1967. Qahtan al-Shaabi, with the approval of the NLF, was appointed the first President of the Republic on November 30th.

INDEPENDENCE

The prospect before the new Republic in December 1967 was still a most uncertain one. On the economic side there were great difficulties to be overcome. The withdrawal of the British troops meant a serious loss of revenue. To maintain the armed forces inherited from the era of British control would impose on the Republic a large expenditure. Moreover, the closure of the Suez Canal had brought about a great falling off in the entrepôt trade of Aden and in the bunkering of ships. The continuance, in the immediate future, of financial aid from Britain was therefore of prime importance to the new régime in Aden. During the negotiations in Geneva between Britain and the NLF in November 1967 the British representatives agreed to make available financial aid to South Arabia

for a period of six months (December 1st, 1967, to May 31st, 1968) at a rate amounting to about £2 million per month. Talks held in Aden in April 1968 between a British delegation and the government led only to the rejection of a new, though reduced, offer of further financial assistance from Britain.

There was disagreement also between the South Yemen and Britain over the Kuria Muria Islands. These islands, about 40 miles from the south coast of Arabia and 200 miles east of the border between the Republic of the Southern Yemen and the Sultanate of Muscat, had been handed over to Britain in 1854 and, though administered subsequently from Aden, had not been included formally within the Aden Protectorate. On November 30th, 1967, Britain had made known to the United Nations her intention to restore the Kuria Muria Islands to the Sultan of Muscat—a decision which gave rise to much bitterness amongst the members of the new government in Aden, which continued to claim these islands and also Perim and Kamaran.

INTERNAL DISSENSION

The administration of President al-Shaabi had to meet other serious difficulties also. In the first months of 1968 it had carried out a series of "purges" in the armed forces and the police of the Southern Yemen. Discontent amongst the armed forces increased after the annual conference of the NLF convened at Zinjibar, east of Aden, in March 1968. The more extreme elements in the NLF were reported to have put forward at the conference resolutions designed to force the Government of the Southern Yemen further to the left—amongst them resolutions calling for the appointment of political commissars to all army units, for the strengthening of the NLF militia and for the creation of "popular guards". A demand was also made, it would seem, at this conference, for the establishment of popular councils in all six of the governorates of the Southern Yemen—these provincial councils having the right to elect a supreme council which would control the affairs of the new Republic. There was in March 1968 a real danger of conflict between the moderate and the extreme elements in the NLF. On March 20th the army intervened to bring about the dismissal of several ministers identified with the more radical section of the Front. The extremists indeed had been taking matters into their own hands in the eastern areas of the Republic—above all in the fifth and sixth governorates which embrace the former sultanates of Qaiti, Kathiri and Mahra (i.e. the erstwhile Eastern Aden Protectorate). Here the radical elements had established popular councils of their own choice, ignoring the governors appointed from the central régime, ousting members of the armed forces and the police, and seizing the oil installations at Mukalla. The tensions thus generated showed no sign of a rapid abatement, and on May 15th, 1968, there was a short-lived rebellion in the region of Jaar, Abyan and Shuqra—i.e. in the third governorate to the north-east of Aden.

Another more serious uprising occurred at the end of July 1968, when two groups of armed rebels cut roads in the Radfan and Aulaqi districts north and east of Aden. The leaders of this rebellion were named as Colonel Abdullah Saleh al Aulaqi ("Colonel Sabaa"), formerly the NLF commander of security forces, and Brig. Nasser Buraik al Aulaqi, who until independence had been commander of the South Arabian Army. These risings were quickly crushed by NLF forces. Both FLOSY and the rival exiled political organization, the South Arabian League, claimed credit for this threat to the Government of President al-Shaabi. Although several members of the FLOSY High Command were captured during the campaign, the economic difficulties of the country continued to act as a serious threat to the stability of the new régime. These difficulties enforced drastic cuts in government expenditure during the summer of 1968, notably in the salaries of the armed forces and the civil service, which cannot have helped the régime's popularity. The President did succeed in getting offers of aid from Federal Germany, Yugoslavia and several Arab countries, but on a small scale compared with the pre-independence British assistance. All support from Federal Germany was in any case cancelled following Southern Yemen's recognition of the German Democratic Republic in July 1969.

NEIGHBOURING HOSTILITY

Relations with neighbouring states continued to be poor, and the government blamed all unrest within the country on elements operating from these states. FLOSY, operating from Yemen and now without its Egyptian support, the deposed sheikhs and sultans from the Federation (now mostly in Saudi Arabia), and the Sultan of Muscat and Oman with his British advisers were claimed to be the most important of these. There were reports of large supplies of Soviet military equipment reaching Aden, some of which has been displayed in military parades; units of the Soviet fleet frequently visit Aden, which is now rarely used by British or other Western naval vessels.

In June 1969 President al-Shaabi resigned following a reported power struggle; Salem Rubayi Ali, a former commando leader who had gone into semi-exile in the provinces after a dispute with the leadership, came to power as Chairman of a new five-man Presidential committee, and a new cabinet was formed which included several other exiles. The new régime was seen as even more left-wing and pro-Soviet than its predecessor.

In November 1969 the government announced the nationalization of 36 foreign firms, including shipping, insurance and commercial companies, but excluding the BP oil refinery at Little Aden.

At this time there were reports of Saudi troops massing on the ill-defined frontier with Southern Yemen, and Saudi sources claimed than an extensive battle took place in December, with Saudi Arabia emerging victorious. Some reports claimed that the clash took place over oil-bearing territory. This occurred again in March 1970 and coincided with a report of an attempted *coup d'état* in Aden.

In November 1970, a new Constitution was promulgated, changing the name of the country to the People's Democratic Republic of Yemen, with a view to possible Yemeni unity. However, relations with the other Yemen and with other neighbouring states failed to improve, and during 1972 the People's Democratic Republic seemed threatened on all sides. Omani forces attacked frontier posts of the Aden Government in its drive against the rebels in its Dhofar province. These are grouped under the Popular Front for the Liberation of Oman (PFLO) and are supported by the Aden Government, through whom they receive Chinese aid. Forces of FLOSY and the South Arabian League were also reported to be gathering on the Yemeni borders. Saudi Arabia, as well as the Yemen Arab Republic, gives refuge to dissidents from the People's Democratic Republic, mainly because of the Aden Government's ideology.

In March 1974 the Arab League Foreign Ministers, meeting in Tunis, set up a conciliation commission in an attempt to end the long-standing conflict between the People's Democratic Republic and Oman over the support given by the Yemen P.D.R. Government to PFLO rebels in Oman.

POSSIBLE YEMENI UNITY

Serious fighting broke out on the border with the Yemen Arab Republic in September 1972, but an Arab League mission was able to mediate and a ceasefire became effective in October. A peace agreement on eventual unification of the two Yemens was signed in Cairo on October 28th. Further details were discussed in Tripoli (Libya) in November by the Presidents of the two Yemens, and it was agreed that the people of the Yemen would establish a single state, to be known as the Yemeni Republic, with Sana'a as its capital, Islam as the state religion and Arabic as the official language. Committees were set up to discuss details of the unification. In January 1973 it appeared that obstacles had arisen in the progress towards union, but in June 1973 the People's Democratic Republic Foreign Minister received the heads of mission of all socialist, Asian and African countries represented in Aden and reiterated his government's determination to implement the Cairo and Tripoli agreements on union. By September 1973 the prospects for the union had become more remote, and President Rubayi Ali and President Iriani of the Yemen Arab Republic met in Sana'a and agreed to extend the one-year period originally decided upon for unification. The subsequent *coup* in the Yemen Arab Republic in June 1974, when a pro-Saudi military junta gained control, made the union seem even more unrealistic. Events in the following twelve months seemed to confirm this opinion, although the inter-Yemeni joint economic and financial committee met once again in Sana'a in February 1975. In the Spring of 1975, however, the North Yemen Government was accusing South Yemen of "acts of sabotage" over the frontier.

In June 1975 the Secretary-General of the ruling National Front announced that two of South Yemen's smaller political parties, the People's Vanguard Party (formerly Baathist) and the People's Democratic Union (Communist), would formally amalgamate with the National Front in September 1975, when the three parties would become known as the United National Front Political Organization.

ECONOMIC SURVEY

M. Jibb

The People's Democratic Republic of Yemen consists of the former British colony of Aden and the former Eastern and Western Aden Protectorates. It is now divided into seven governorates, or provinces, whose finances and administration are centrally controlled, although the provincial councils are responsible for planning and finance on a local level. The Governorates vary greatly in size, the smallest being the First Governorate in the west, consisting of Aden district and the offshore islands, and the largest being the Sixth Governorate, the former Mahra Sultanate, situated in the extreme east of the country. A new province, Revolution Province, was formed within the Fifth Governorate in 1973.

Most of the population is concentrated in the west and one of the Government's hardest tasks since independence has been to unite the various regions politically, administratively and economically. Whether political and economic union with the Yemen Arab Republic will be possible or successful is open to question. The Government, however, continued (in spite of the outbreak of hostilities) in 1973 and 1974 to reiterate its commitment to the principle of unity. At the end of 1973 it was agreed to set up an organization to co-ordinate both countries' agricultural, industrial and fisheries policies.

Under British rule, the country was sustained by the position of Aden on the main shipping route to Europe from the Far East, India and East Africa via Suez. The British Petroleum refinery, completed in 1954, was the focus of industry and trade. In addition, the British troops stationed in Aden and the many foreign visitors who came ashore from ships calling at the port provided a market for services and luxury goods which encouraged local merchants and entrepreneurs and brought plenty of foreign exchange into Aden. This prosperity was, in the main, confined to the then Aden Colony where there was a boom in construction work between 1955 and 1965. The British Government was more concerned with maintaining the Aden base and the port installations than with developing the hinterland although certain agricultural areas were developed during this period. The Abyan district, where development started in 1947, became one of the major cotton-producing areas and a similar scheme was carried out in Lahej in the 1960s. In the Hadhramaut, where there are fertile valleys in an otherwise barren area, the Governments of the states of Quaiti and Kathiri financed irrigation schemes and agricultural developments.

The closure of the Suez Canal in 1967 and the withdrawal of British troops in the same year, put an end to the Republic's commercial prosperity. Furthermore, British aid and military expenditure, which amounted to about £11 million in 1960 and had increased to £36 million by 1967 and had more than covered the visible trade deficit, was discontinued after withdrawal, making it impossible for the Government to cover the budget deficit. In such a situation the Republic had no choice but to turn to other countries for sources of finance and technical aid to assist it in the transition from a service economy to one based on agriculture and manufacturing. The favourable terms offered by the Communist countries, coupled with a seeming lack of interest on the part of the West, made it inevitable that the Aden Government should turn to the Eastern bloc.

In November 1969 a decree was issued nationalizing all important foreign assets in the Republic, with the exception of the BP refinery. This development, although a logical one in view of the régime's socialist leanings, nevertheless tended to frighten off firms which might otherwise have risked some investment, and made the Republic more than ever dependent on the Soviet Union, China and East Germany.

The Three Year Development Plan 1971–1974, although limited by shortage of funds, aims at the creation, firstly, of a communications network, secondly the expansion of agricultural production and, thirdly, the establishment of small-scale light industries, based on locally produced raw materials. Some progress was made, notably in telecommunications, and it was estimated that about 80 per cent of the total allocation was invested. A new Five-Year Plan 1974–79 began in April 1974. Total capital investment in the Plan was eventually set at 92 million dinars, preliminary allocations of 144 million dinars having been rejected as too ambitious, and special attention is being given to the development of fisheries. The Plan was drawn up with assistance from Soviet experts, and both the U.S.S.R. and China have promised extensive aid with projects. Czechoslovakia agreed to lend $6.3 million for Plan projects and discussions were held in 1974 with Cuba, Bulgaria and North Korea.

AGRICULTURE

Only about a quarter of the country's cultivatable land is used at present, and the most intensively cultivated areas are Abyan, east of Aden, and Lahej, north of Aden. The river valleys of the Hadhramaut area in the Fifth Governorate are also fertile and relatively well-developed. The Kuwait Fund for Arab Economic Development (KFAED) financed a pre-investment study of the Abyan delta and in May 1974 agreed to lend 4.2 million Kuwaiti dinars to help finance land reclamation and irrigation in the area. Bulgaria is also aiding the project. The Abyan Dam project began in 1974 and is due for completion by 1977.

Cotton is produced mainly in Lahej and Abyan. The government-controlled Abyan Board supervises the whole process of growing and marketing and has its own ginnery at El Kad. Cotton is also produced in other areas and the Cotton Producers' Associations were the most flourishing co-operatives in the country. The area under cotton is, however, declining, in spite of cash incentives offered to growers. It is also becoming harder to market and much work needs to be done to improve the varieties grown and to seek suitable export outlets.

The Republic is able, on the whole, to meet local demand for most vegetables but imports onions, potatoes and fruit. The main fruits and vegetables grown are tomatoes, carrots, salad vegetables, bananas and melons. Bananas in particular are produced in quantity and the Food and Agriculture Organization has recommended an expansion of banana-growing, provided export markets can be found. In 1972 the only foreign customer was China.

Wheat is grown mainly in the Hadhramaut and Beihan but is not enough for the country's needs. The balance is imported mainly from Australia. Other cereals produced include barley, millet and sorghum. Tobacco is grown in the coastal areas, mainly in the Ghail Ba Wazir area. Livestock production has remained fairly static for the last ten years and considerable numbers of sheep and goats have to be imported to satisfy local meat demand.

The resources available at present are not sufficient to finance agricultural development schemes over the whole country and efforts are being concentrated in the Lahej, Abyan, Beihan and Hadhramaut areas. In the east, the developments most likely to take place are the expansion of tobacco growing and the development of the fishing industry, with Mukalla as its centre.

FISHERIES

The Arabian Sea fishing grounds are the Republic's greatest potential source of wealth. Most of the 10,000 fishermen fish only in territorial waters, their equipment is often poor and efficient marketing of the catch is impossible with the present state of communications. The main species caught are: anchovy, tunny, sardine, Indian mackerel, crayfish and green turtle. At the beginning of 1973 exports of fish took a very encouraging turn and several foreign countries were involved in developing the industry.

The Soviet Union and Cuba provided modern fishing vessels as well as equipment and technical aid. A Japanese firm obtained a contract in 1969 to fish in the coastal waters, and a joint Polish/Yemeni company with a capital of $5 million was planned. Denmark lent $2 million to finance development of

Nakhtun port and construct refrigeration and storage facilities. In 1974 the Arab Fund for Economic and Social Development granted a loan of KD 3.2 million to build a fish meal plant and to improve facilities at Mukalla port. Tenders for the project, and for a new power station, were invited in 1975. Improvements at the port of Shihr are also being considered.

In January 1975 a joint company was set up with Iraq to operate a deep-sea fishing fleet. A canning project for fish and turtles at Lahej is also planned, as a joint venture with Libya.

INDUSTRY

The BP refinery accounts at present for over 80 per cent of the country's total industrial output. In spite of the closure of the Suez Canal, output at the refinery continued to expand, partly because of increased demand from Egypt, although exports of refined products to Egypt decreased in 1970. The Government intended to spend about YD 2 million on the oil sector, one of the main projects considered being the supplying of oil by pipeline from Aden to Mukalla.

Industrial developments are planned to take the form of agro-industries. The Three-Year Development Plan envisaged the establishment of a textile industry based on local cotton; fruit and vegetable processing and canning plants; a cigarette factory; fish-canning plants and a tanning industry. This last would be particularly suitable since skins are at present exported in the raw state and there is much wastage. Some progress has been made, with China building a textile factory and a cigarette factory going into operation in 1973. Although in the initial stages the tobacco for the factory will be imported from Britain, supplies will eventually come from the Hadhramaut.

Existing industries (in Aden) are: the manufacture of cement blocks, tiles and bricks; salt production; soft drinks bottling and dairy plants. In the western Governorates there are also cotton ginneries, flour mills and seed-crushing plants. The fishing industry (see above) centres on Mukalla. A cement plant is planned for the Third Governorate, possibly using the extensive limestone deposits reported to exist to the east of Aden. The German Democratic Republic is helping with the establishment of factories making flour, biscuits, vegetable oil and animal fodder.

Known mineral resources are few but the country has not yet been fully explored. The Government has announced its hopes of an oil strike and companies from Canada, France, Japan, Romania and Bulgaria are reported to be interested. A joint Yemeni/Algerian company has done some prospecting in the Hadhramaut, and concession bids have been invited for the Al-Ghaida area.

All mineral and raw material sources in the country were declared publicly-owned in August 1973.

FOREIGN TRADE

Aden port handles nearly all the Republic's trade, as well as some of that of the Yemen Arab Republic. Transit trade to Yemen however, is declining owing to the development of the port of Hodeida. The free port of Aden attracted a large volume of traffic and all the commercial activities associated with a large port flourished, providing comfortable livings for the Adeni merchants but contributing little to the development of the other sectors of the economy. The disadvantages of a free port in the changed situation after 1967, not least the hindrance to industrial development caused by the lack of protective tariffs, led the Government, after much deliberation, to remove Aden's free port status, although there is still a free zone for transit trade.

In view of the disastrous effect of Aden's stagnation on a precarious economy, the Government viewed the re-opening of the Suez Canal in June 1975 with a satisfaction verging on jubilation. Plans for the port include dredging, improvement of mooring and repair facilities; expansion of the duty-free shopping zone and the construction of tourist facilities. The scheme is being financed by the World Bank and the Arab Fund for Economic and Social Development.

The trade deficit continued to grow up to 1969. Government austerity measures and the lack of foreign exchange, reduced imports in 1970 by over £7 million but exports continued at much the same level. In 1971 and 1972 the volume of both imports and exports declined. The main commodities exported (excluding petroleum products) are cotton, hides and skins, dried fish, rice and coffee. The chief imports (excluding petroleum) are clothing, foodstuffs and livestock. The drop in petroleum trade was particularly significant, as it made reduction of activity at the refinery inevitable, with consequent repercussions on the whole fragile economy. In 1966, bunkering made up a third of total exports, but by 1970 this proportion had fallen to less than 7 per cent and petroleum exports were moving to markets in Africa and Asia rather than Europe.

FINANCE AND FOREIGN AID

The Republic's finances have deteriorated steadily since independence. In 1966, gold reserves amounted to $64.86 million. By the end of 1970, gold reserves had fallen to $600,000 and foreign exchange to $53.3 million. In the same period, the budget deficit grew from 100,000 dinars to over 4 million dinars. This deficit was substantially cut in 1971, largely because more foreign grants were obtained, but expenditure still had to be held down with adverse effects on development. The situation was considered to be so serious in 1972 that the salaries of many government employees were cut by anything from 15 to 50 per cent and restrictions were placed on foreign travel. By the end of 1973 the situation was a little better, gold reserves amounting to $720,000 and foreign exchange holdings to $61.33 million. In 1975 the International Monetary Fund agreed to the purchase of SDR 7.25 million to help with balance of payments problems and general inflation.

The abrupt cessation of British aid to the Republic after the withdrawal of troops in November 1967 caused a crisis which enabled the communist bloc to step into the breach. The Soviet Union, under an agreement of February 1969, which included aid specifically for fisheries, undertook to provide technical aid and experts for a number of development projects. A separate agreement, signed in August 1969, covered aid for agriculture and irrigation. The first agreement was extended in February 1970 to include aid in kind worth 5.5 million roubles and, most important of all, a low-interest loan of 7 million roubles repayable over 12 years. This loan was significant in that actual financial aid was offered rather than aid in the form of goods or technical assistance. The German D.R. agreed to a loan of $22 million in October 1969 and China granted a $18 million loan in 1970, both part of large aid and trade "package deals". Both covered a wide range of projects, including in the case of the German D.R., the construction of telephone facilities and the establishment of light industries; and in the case of China, help with the road-building programme. Most of the communist bloc countries have offered aid to the Republic, particularly for communications projects.

The richer Arab countries, too, are providing aid in certain sectors. The Kuwait Fund for Arab Economic Development is financing the Abyan Delta project and an economic survey of the whole country. Algeria, as well as participating in oil exploration, agreed to give $4 million worth of development aid. Libya in 1972 granted a loan of 5.8 million dinars and in 1974 approved a first payment of LD1.5 million under this agreement. Libyan aid in 1974 totalled LD 3 million. The Aden Government approached the Arab League on the subject of compensation for losses incurred as a direct result of the June War of 1967 but no actual financial compensation has so far been awarded. Iraq gave a $5 million interest-free loan in 1974, of which $3 million was repayable in goods and services. In January 1975 a further $10 million loan was announced. Also in 1975, the Government launched a diplomatic offensive to improve relations with the rich Gulf states. A grant of $5 million was forthcoming from Kuwait and the United Arab Emirates agreed to finance a minerals survey.

The Republic's relations with the West have deteriorated not only because of the British refusal to continue aid, but as a result of the rapprochement with the Eastern bloc countries. The main source of aid other than the socialist countries and the Arab states, has been the United Nations. However, in 1974/75, loans were obtained from the World Bank for the Saiwun–Mukalla road project. One of the country's main difficulties is lack of trained manpower, manifested in the shortage of staff to run statistical departments and to collect information on the economy. A number of countries have offered training schemes for Yemenis to study abroad and in 1974 the International Development Association approved a loan of $5.4 million to finance education projects, including vocational training centres. Work started on these schemes in 1975.

STATISTICAL SURVEY

AREA AND POPULATION
(Census of May 14th, 1973)

	GOVERNORATES							TOTAL
	First	Second	Third	Fourth	Fifth	Sixth	Thamoud	
Population ('000) .	291	273	311	162	451	61	41	1,590
Area (sq. miles) . .	2,695	4,929	8,297	28,536	32,991	25,618	27,000	130,066

Estimated Population: 1,633,000 (July 1st, 1974).

Capital: Aden (population 150,000 in 1964).

EMPLOYMENT
First Governorate
(1972)

TOTAL	AGRICUL-TURE AND FISHING	MINING AND QUARRYING	MANUFAC-TURING	CON-STRUCTION	ELECTRICITY, GAS AND WATER	COM-MERCE	TRANS-PORT	SERVICES	MISCEL-LANEOUS
43,668	1,137	53	6,297	201	1,539	7,943	9,695	15,564	1,239

In the rest of the country 90 per cent of the population are engaged in agriculture.

AGRICULTURE
PRINCIPAL CROPS

	AREA ('000 acres)			PRODUCTION ('000 tons)		
	1970–71	1971–72	1972–73	1970–71	1971–72	1972–73
Sorghum and Millet . . .	90.0	105.0	110.0	57.0	66.0	69.0
Wheat	18.0	22.0	24.0	12.5	15.5	16.8
Barley	3.0	3.0	3.0	2.0	2.0	2.0
Sesame	10.0	10.0	10.2	3.4	3.4	3.5
Cotton Lint . . . . }	28.1	25.0	29.7	13.9	12.2	11.7
Cotton Seed. . . . }						

LIVESTOCK NUMBERS
(FAO estimates, October to September)

	1969/70	1970/71	1971/72	1972/73
Cattle	90,000	92,000	93,000	96,000
Sheep	210,000	215,000	220,000	225,000
Goats	850,000	870,000	885,000	900,000
Asses	27,000	28,000	29,000	30,000
Camels	41,000	40,000	40,000	40,000

Source: FAO, *Production Yearbook 1973.*

LIVESTOCK PRODUCTS
(FAO estimates, metric tons)

	1970	1971	1972	1973
Mutton, lamb and goats' meat .	n.a.	9,000	10,000	10,000
Cows' milk	6,000	6,000	6,000	7,000
Sheep's milk	7,000	8,000	8,000	8,000
Goats' milk	42,000	45,000	47,000	48,000
Hen eggs	5,900	6,300	6,400	6,600

Source: FAO, *Production Yearbook 1973.*

FISHING
('000 metric tons, live weight)

	1968	1969	1970	1971	1972	1973
Marine fish . . .	46.0	52.5	114.4	113.0	113.6	126.8
Other sea creatures . .	0.3	0.4	0.6	5.2	9.0	6.7
Total Catch . .	46.3	52.9	115.0	118.2	122.6	133.5

Source: FAO, *Yearbook of Fishery Statistics 1973.*

MINING
('000 metric tons)

	1967	1968	1969	1970	1971	1972
Salt (unrefined) . . .	72	90	63	88	67	75

INDUSTRY
SELECTED PRODUCTS

	Unit	1969	1970	1971	1972
Salted, dried or smoked fish . .	metric tons	3,569	7,293	7,328	n.a.
Motor spirit (Petrol) . . .	'000 metric tons	283	189	211	459
Kerosene	,, ,, ,,	276	156	149	110
Jet fuel	,, ,, ,,	610	746	496	450
Distillate fuel oils . . .	,, ,, ,,	1,099	1,087	585	525
Residual fuel oil	,, ,, ,,	3,620	3,598	1,888	1,828
Construction: new dwellings* . .	number	815	4,035	1,542	n.a.
Electric energy* . . .	million kWh.	180	192	151	139

* Figures refer to Aden only.

Sources: United Nations, *Statistical Yearbook 1973* and *The Growth of World Industry.*

FINANCE

1,000 fils = 1 Yemeni dinar (YD).

Coins: 1, 5, 25 and 50 fils.

Notes: 250 and 500 fils; 1, 5 and 10 dinars.

Exchange rates (July 1975): £1 sterling = 755.4 fils; U.S. $1 = 345.4 fils.

100 Yemeni dinars = £132.38 = $289.52.

Note: Before independence (November 30th, 1967) the currency unit was the South Arabian dinar (SA dinar), introduced in April 1965 with a value of £1 sterling, then worth U.S. $2.80. On November 18th, 1967, the pound and dinar were both devalued to $2.40 ($1 = 416.67 fils). Following independence the SA dinar was replaced by the Southern Yemen dinar, with the same value. The exchange rate (1 dinar = $2.40) remained in force until August 1971. Between December 1971 and February 1973 the rate was 1 dinar = $2.6057 ($1 = 383.77 fils). The present dollar valuation has been effective since February 1973. The dinar was at par with the pound sterling until the latter was allowed to "float" in June 1972.

BUDGET

(million dinars)

	REVENUE	FOREIGN AID	EXPENDITURE
1967–68	8.94	16.49	23.68
1968–69	8.96	4.91	15.83
1969–70	11.11	0.21	15.44
1970–71	13.22	1.85	17.56

EXTERNAL TRADE

(million dinars)

	1968	1969	1970	1971	1972	1973
Imports c.i.f.	84.5	90.9	83.7	64.9	57.2	59.8
Exports f.o.b.	45.8	59.8	60.8	43.6	41.3	42.4

COMMODITIES

(dinars)

	IMPORTS			EXPORTS		
	1970	1971	1972	1970	1971	1972
Live Animals	1,427,340	1,161,038	1,035,865	—	80	11
Dairy Produce, Eggs	2,533,358	1,809,567	1,954,250	72,057	39,115	17,049
Cereals	8,058,942	3,494,381	3,769,189	1,214,378	425,314	9,682
Fruit and Vegetables	1,571,888	1,392,555	1,207,363	148,547	79,454	61,112
Sugar, etc.	2,220,512	1,953,892	2,904,058	163,418	124,926	123,917
Coffee, Tea, Cocoa, Spices	2,803,054	1,259,512	1,646,846	801,856	573,630	645,442
Beverages and Tobacco	1,147,535	1,201,517	1,190,801	37,848	27,090	20,654
Oilseeds, Oil Nuts, etc.	1,277,443	896,742	812,730	389,440	89,586	17,781
Petroleum and Petroleum Products	34,390,272	26,542,827	26,053,281	44,991,450	29,185,109	30,145,420
Chemicals	3,029,368	2,672,747	1,820,957	256,496	205,482	113,750
Textiles	8,210,356	7,013,164	4,046,131	1,768,661	2,720,600	694,337
Machinery	1,572,333	1,402,672	1,995,439	117,019	78,934	38,014
Electrical Machinery	1,265,284	1,013,143	908,982	113,386	125,937	30,734
Transport Equipment	1,517,064	1,375,953	1,523,798	88,413	125,129	52,061
Manufactured Goods	5,055,902	4,441,784	2,554,823	696,195	978,915	483,234

COUNTRIES
(dinars)

IMPORTS				1970	1971	1972
Iran	.	.	.	15,252,843	8,164,206	6,054,482
Kuwait	.	.	.	11,106,192	7,779,199	10,286,292
Japan	.	.	.	8,820,657	7,065,488	3,965,484
U.K.	.	.	.	4,579,634	5,036,636	3,662,160
India	.	.	.	3,470,064	2,300,619	1,595,721
Trucial States (now U.A.E.)				4,592,011	1,085,871	2,425,678
Hong Kong	.	.	.	2,239,319	1,988,311	903,821

EXPORTS*				1970	1971	1972
U.K.	.	.	.	14,945,217	5,108,144	3,550,450
Japan	.	.	.	8,724,919	4,198,226	4,810,885
Australia	.	.	.	3,664,670	4,019,298	1,518,936
Thailand	.	.	.	5,192,631	2,812,183	3,239,970
Canary Is.	.	.	.	3,041,468	1,212,941	1,426,316
Yemen A.R.	.	.	.	2,852,661	4,534,365	1,997,379

* Excluding the supply of ships' bunker oil (4,011,144 dinars in 1970, 3,292,660 dinars in 1971 and 3,038,397 dinars in 1972).

TRANSPORT

ROAD TRAFFIC 1972
(vehicles in use)

Private	.	.	.	11,361
Taxis	.	.	.	1,563
Buses	.	.	.	190
Commercial trucks	.	.	.	3,670
Motor cycles	.	.	.	1,782
Tractors and cranes	.	.	.	807
TOTAL	.	.	.	19,373

INTERNATIONAL SEA-BORNE SHIPPING

		1971	1972	1973
Vessels Entered ('000 net reg. tons)	.	6,512	5,695	5,542
Dry Cargo Imported ('000 long tons)	.	269	283	310
Dry Cargo Exported ('000 long tons)	.	88	40	65
Oil Cargo Imported ('000 long tons)	.	3,896	3,720	3,343
Oil Cargo Exported ('000 long tons)	.	3,138	3,100	2,724

CIVIL AVIATION
(1973)

AIRCRAFT MOVEMENTS	PASSENGERS			FREIGHT (kilos)	
	Arrivals	Departures	Transit	Inward	Outward
6,581	67,983	67,995	17,921	1,007,332	693,225

EDUCATION
NUMBER OF SCHOOLS
(1972–73)

Primary Schools	960
Intermediate Schools . . .	77
Secondary Schools	19
Teachers' Colleges for Males . .	2
Teachers' Colleges for Females . .	1
Technical Institute	1

Source (except where otherwise stated): Central Statistical Office, Central Planning Commission, Aden.

THE CONSTITUTION

Before the new constitution was drawn up existing ordinances and regulations remained in force, with Presidential authority replacing the powers of the British and Federal Governments. The National Liberation Front general command, which had 41 members, formed the interim legislative authority. The country is divided into seven administrative Governorates. The two-year term of office granted to the National Liberation Front expired on November 30th, 1969, and was formally renewed for another year. Following the adoption of the new constitution on November 30th, 1970, a Provisional Supreme People's Council took over legislative powers. The 101 members were selected from the NLF, armed forces, professions, etc., with 15 workers elected by trade unions.

THE GOVERNMENT

HEAD OF STATE

President and Supreme Commander of the Armed Forces: SALEM RUBAYI ALI.

PRESIDENTIAL COUNCIL

Chairman: SALEM RUBAYI ALI.

Member and NLF Secretary-General: ABDUL FATTAH ISMAIL.

Member: ALI NASIR MUHAMMAD HASANI.

CABINET

(*August* 1975)

Prime Minister, Minister of Defence and Minister of Education: ALI NASIR MUHAMMAD HASANI.

Minister of Foreign Affairs: MUHAMMAD SALIH MUTI AL YAFAI.

Minister of the Interior: (vacant).

Minister of Information: RASHED MUHAMMAD THABET.

Minister of Justice and Waqfs: ABDULLAH MOHAMED GHANEM.

Minister of Health: Dr. ABDEL AZIZ ADDALY.

Minister of Public Works: HAIDAR ABU BAKR AL-ATTAS.

Minister of Communications: ANIS HASAN YAHYA.

Minister of Housing: NASSER YASSING.

Minister of Labour and Civil Service: ALI ASSAD MUTANNA.

Minister of Finance: FADL MUHSIN ABDULLAH.

Minister of Agriculture and Agrarian Reform: MUHAMMAD SULAIMAN NASIR.

Minister of Economy and Industry: ABDEL-AZIZ ABDEL-WALI NASHER.

Minister of Culture and Tourism: ABDULLAH ABDEL RAZZAQ BADIB.

Minister of Trade and Supply: MAHMUD SAID MULI (acting).

Minister of Industry and Minister of Planning: ABDEL AZIZ ABDEL WALI (acting).

Minister of State Security: MUHAMMAD SAID ABDULLA MUHSEN (acting).

POLITICAL PARTY

National Liberation Front: Aden; f. 1963; socialist and Arab nationalist; Leader ABDUL FATTAH ISMAIL. The Central Committee has 31 members and 14 substitute members—all elected.

POLITICAL BUREAU

Secretary-General: ABDUL FATTAH ISMAIL.
Deputy Secretary-General: President SALEM RUBAYI ALI.
ALI SALIH UBAD.
ALI SALIM AL-BEIDH.
SALIH MUSLIH QASSEM.
MUHAMMAD SALIH MUTI AL YAFAI.
ALI NASIR MUHAMMAD HASANI.

DIPLOMATIC REPRESENTATION

EMBASSIES ACCREDITED TO THE PEOPLE'S DEMOCRATIC REPUBLIC OF YEMEN

(In Aden unless otherwise stated)

Algeria: Kuwait.

Austria: Cairo, Egypt.

Bangladesh: Baghdad, Iraq.

Belgium: Cairo, Egypt.

Bulgaria: Khormaksar; *Ambassador:* VELIKO ENTCHEV.

China, People's Republic: 145 Andalus Gardens, Khormaksar; *Ambassador:* TSUI TSIEN.

Cuba: 36 Socotra Rd., Khormaksar; *Ambassador:* JACINTO VÁZQUEZ DE LA GARZA.

Czechoslovakia: Cairo, Egypt.

Egypt: Relief Rd., Ma'alla; *Ambassador:* MAHMOUD FAWZI KAMEL.

France: Sayhut St., Khormaksar; *Ambassador:* HENRI PIOT.

German Democratic Republic: Khormaksar; *Ambassador:* GUNTHER SCHARFENBERG.

Germany, Federal Republic: Sana'a, Yemen Arab Republic.

Guinea: Addis Ababa, Ethiopia.

Hungary: Cairo, Egypt.

India: Bremjee Chambers, Tawahi; *Ambassador:* IMDAD ALI.

Iraq: Sana'a, Yemen Arab Republic.

Italy: Tawahi; *Ambassador:* (vacant).

Japan: Cairo, Egypt.

Korea, Democratic People's Republic: Khormaksar; *Ambassador:* KIM UNG.

Kuwait: Sana'a, Yemen Arab Republic.

Lebanon: Sana'a, Yemen Arab Republic.

Libya: Khartoum, Sudan.

Mongolia: Cairo, Egypt.

Pakistan: 34 Kassim Hilal, Khormaksar; *Chargé d'Affaires:* MANSOOR ALAM.

Poland: Cairo, Egypt.

Romania: Abyan Beach Rd., Plot No. 106, Khormaksar; *Ambassador:* CONSTANTIN BABEANU.

Somalia: Britannic Court, Dolphin Square, Ma'alla; *Ambassador:* ABDI ALI HUSSEIN.

Spain: Addis Ababa, Ethiopia.

Sudan: Mogadishu, Somalia.

Sweden: Addis Ababa, Ethiopia.

Switzerland: Addis Ababa, Ethiopia.

Syria: Sana'a, Yemen Arab Republic.

Uganda: Jeddah, Saudi Arabia.

U.S.S.R.: Abyan Beach Rd., Khormaksar; *Ambassador:* ALEXANDER SEMIOSHKIN.

United Kingdom: 28 Shara Ho Chi Minh, Khormaksar; *Chargé d'Affaires a.i.:* J. S. M. ROBERTS.

Viet-Nam, Democratic Republic: Cairo, Egypt.

Viet-Nam, South: Cairo, Egypt.

Yugoslavia: Mogadishu, Somalia.

Zambia: Cairo, Egypt.

The People's Democratic Republic of Yemen also has diplomatic relations with Albania, Ethiopia, Kenya and Tanzania.

JUDICIAL SYSTEM

The administration of justice is entrusted to the Supreme Court and Magistrates' Courts. In the former Protectorate States Muslim law and local common law (Urfi) are also applied.

President of the Supreme Court: ABD-AL-MAJID ABD-AL-RAHMAN.

RELIGION

The majority of the population are Muslim but there are small Christian and Hindu communities.

THE PRESS

DAILIES

14 October: P.O.B. 4227, Aden; not published on Saturdays; f. 1968; Editor SALEM OMAR HUSSAIN; circ. 6,000.

WEEKLY

Ath-Thawri: P.O.B. 4227, Aden; published on Saturday; mouthpiece of National Front.

MONTHLIES

al-Thaqafa Al-Jadida: P.O.B. 1187, Aden; f. Aug. 1970; a cultural monthly review issued by the Ministry of Culture and Tourism; Arabic; circ. 3,000.

NEWS AGENCY

Aden News Agency: Aden; Dir. SALEM OMAR HUSAIN.

RADIO AND TELEVISION

RADIO

Democratic Yemen Broadcasting Service: P.O.B. 1264, Aden; transmits 100 hours a week in Arabic; Dir.-Gen. for Broadcasting and TV: RASHED MOHAMED TABET; there are about 150,000 receivers in the country.

TELEVISION

Democratic Yemen Broadcasting Service: P.O.B. 1264, Aden; programmes for four hours daily, mainly in Arabic; other series in English and French. There are about 25,000 receivers.

FINANCE

CENTRAL BANK

Bank of Yemen: P.O.B. 4452, Aden; replaced Yemeni Currency Authority 1972; cap. p.u. 500,000 YD; Publ. *Annual Report*.

BANKS

All foreign banking interests were nationalized in November 1969 and thereafter amalgamated to form the National Bank of Yemen, the only commercial bank operating in the country.

National Bank of Yemen: P.O.B. 5, Crater, Aden; f. 1970 by nationalizing and amalgamating the local branches of the seven foreign banks then in Aden; cap. p.u. 1.5 million YD; Gen. Man. Ayoob Nazir A. Wahed; 20 brs.

INSURANCE

All foreign insurance interests were nationalized in November 1969.

TRADE AND INDUSTRY

National Chamber of Commerce and Industry: P.O.B. 473, Crater; Pres. Abdulrehman Al-Sailani; Sec. Hussein Ali Abdo.

Aden Merchants' Association: M. A. Luqman Rd., 1-11 Crater; f. 1932; 209 mems.; Pres. Pherozeshaw P. Patel; Secs. Sorabjee P. Patel, m.b.e., Ali A. Saffi.

National Company for Home Trade: Crater, Aden; f. 1969; importers of cars, electrical goods, agricultural machinery, building materials and general consumer goods; incorporates the main foreign trading businesses which were nationalized in 1970; Acting Gen. Man. Saleh Ahmed Saleh.

TRADE UNIONS

General Confederation of Workers of the People's Democratic Republic of Yemen: P.O.B. 1162, Ma'alla, Aden; f. 1956; affiliated to WFTU and ICFTU; 35,000 mems.; Gen. Sec. Abdul Razak Shaif; publ. *Sout A Omal* weekly, circ. approx. 4,500.

CO-OPERATIVES AND MARKETING

There are 65 co-operative societies, mostly for agricultural products; the movement was founded in 1965 and is now the responsibility of the Ministry for Agriculture and Agrarian Reform.

OIL

Yemeni National Petroleum Co.: P.O.B. 5050, Aden; sole oil concessionaire importer and distributor of oil products in Yemen P.D.R.; in receipt of technical and financial assistance from Algeria; Chair. and Gen. Man. Abdul Karim Thabet.

TRANSPORT

ROADS

Aden Bus Co. Ltd.: Adbusco Bldg., Ma'alla, P.O.B. 905, Aden; f. 1960; operates services within the Crater, Ma'alla, Steamer Point, Sheikh Othman and Al-Mansoura areas; Chair. and Gen. Man. Saeed Fara Salim.

A new state transport monopoly, the Yemen Land Transport Company, is being formed to incorporate the Aden Bus Company and all other local public transport.

Aden has 140 miles of roads, of which 127 have bituminous surfacings. There are approximately 2,680 miles of rough tracks passable for motor traffic in the hinterland, but most of the transport is by camel and donkey.

SHIPPING

National Shipping Company: P.O.B. 1228, Steamer Point, Aden; founded by the amalgamation and nationalization of five foreign shipping companies in November 1969; freight and passenger services; branches or agents in Mukalla, Berbera (Somalia) and Mocha and Hodeida (Yemen Arab Republic).

Port of Aden Authority: Aden; f. 1888; state administrative body; Aden remained a free port (except for tariffs on petrol, alcohol and tobacco) until 1970, though trade has greatly declined since 1967. Aden Main Harbour has twenty first-class berths. Three of them are Dolphin berths accommodating vessels drawing up to 39 ft., and the remaining seventeen are buoy berths for vessels drawing up to 42 ft. There are 4 second-class berths for vessels drawing up to 28 feet, and 4 third-class berths for vessels whose draught does not exceed 18 feet. In addition to the above, there is ample room to accommodate vessels of light draught at anchor in the 18-foot dredged area. There is also 800 feet of cargo wharf accommodating vessels of 300 feet length and 18 feet draught. Aden Oil Harbour accommodates four tankers of 57,000 tons and up to 40 feet draught.

With the re-opening of the Suez Canal in June 1975 the Aden Port Authority planned to spend U.S. $30.7 million on an all-round improvement scheme.

CIVIL AVIATION

Democratic Yemen Airlines Company: Aden; f. 1971 as wholly owned Corporation by the Govt.

Other companies operating services include the following: Aeroflot, Air Djibouti, Air India, EAAC, EgyptAir, Ethiopian Airways, Kuwait Airways, MEA, Pakistan International Airlines, Somali Airlines, Sudan Airways, Yemen Airlines.

Aden Civil Airport is at Khormaksar, 7 miles from the Port. It was established in 1952, and is operated by the Civil Aviation Department.

DEFENCE

Defence Expenditure: 10 million dinars (1972 estimate).

Total Armed Forces: 4,000: army 11,300, navy 200, air force 2,500.

EDUCATION

The educational system consists of four years of Primary, three years of Intermediate and four to six years of Secondary schooling. There are 225 Government Primary Schools, 29 Intermediate Schools and 6 Secondary Schools, and a Technical Institute at Ma'alla, Aden, with a branch at Little Aden. Other higher education is received abroad.

In addition there are 12 Government-Aided and 5 Private Primary Schools, and 10 Grant-Aided and 4 Private Intermediate Schools. Teacher-Training Centres provide over 200 places for men and women trainees while adult education is provided by evening classes.

BIBLIOGRAPHY

BRINTON, J. Y. Aden and the Federation of South Arabia (American Soc. of Int. Law, Washington, 1964).

CENTRAL OFFICE OF INFORMATION. Aden and South Arabia (London, H.M.S.O., 1965).

COLONIAL OFFICE. Accession of Aden to the Federation of South Arabia (London, H.M.S.O., 1962).

COLONIAL OFFICE. Treaty of Friendship and Protection between the United Kingdom and the Federation of South Arabia (London, H.M.S.O., 1964).

FEDERATION OF SOUTH ARABIA. Conference on Constitutional Problems of South Arabia (H.M.S.O., 1964).

GAVIN, R. J. Aden 1839–1967 (Hurst, London, 1973).

GEHRKE, Dr. ULRICH. Südarabien, Südarabische Föderation oder Süd-Jemen? (*Orient* Magazine, German Near and Middle East Association, Hamburg, 1967).

GOVERNMENT OF ADEN. Memorandum on the Five-Year Development Plan, 1952–53 to 1956–57 (Aden, 1958).

GOVERNMENT OF ADEN. Report of the Adenisation Committee, 1959 (London, 1959).

HARDING, H. LANKESTER. Archaeology in the Aden Protectorate (London, H.M.S.O., 1964).

HICKINBOTHAM, Sir TOM. Aden (London, Constable, 1959).

INGRAMS, DOREEN. A Survey of the Social and Economic Conditions of the Aden Protectorate (London).

INGRAMS, W. H. A Report on the Social, Economic and Political Conditions of the Hadhramaut, Aden Protectorate (London, 1936).

JOHNSTON, CHARLES. The View from Steamer Point (London, Collins, 1964).

KING, GILLIAN. Imperial Outpost–Aden (New York, Oxford University Press, 1964).

LITTLE, TOM. South Arabia (London, Pall Mall Press, 1968).

MAWER, JUNE KNOX. The Sultans Came to Tea (Murray, London, 1961).

PAGET, JULIAN. Last Post: Aden 1964–67 (Faber and Faber, London, 1969).

QAT COMMISSION OF INQUIRY. Report (Aden, 1958).

TREVASKIS, Sir KENNEDY. Shades of Amber, A South Arabian Episode (London, Hutchinson, 1967).

VAN DER MEULEN, DANIEL. Hadramaut: Some of Its Mysteries Unveiled (Leiden, 1932, reprinted 1964).

WATERFIELD, GORDON. Sultans of Aden (Murray, London 1968).

PART FOUR

Other Reference Material

WHO'S WHO IN THE MIDDLE EAST AND NORTH AFRICA

A

Aamiry, Mohammed Adib al-, B.A.; Jordanian politician, educationalist and writer; b. 1907, Palestine; ed. American Univ. of Beirut and Palestine Law Inst.
Teacher 30; Headmaster 34; Ministry of Educ. Insp. 43; Deputy Dir. of Broadcasting Station, Jerusalem 44; Gen. Sec., Ministry of Foreign Affairs 50; Dir. Imports Dept. 51; Under-Sec. at Ministry of Educ. 52, at Ministry of Reconstruction and Devt. 53; Dir. Civil Service Dept. 55-58; Minister of Foreign Affairs Aug.-Oct. 67, of Educ. Oct. 67-April 68; Amb. to U.A.R. May 68; Minister of Culture, Information, Tourism and Antiquities Dec. 68-69; mem. Jerusalem Scientific Org., Cairo, Friends of Archaeology, Amman; Al Kawkab Medal 1st Grade, Al Istiqlal Medal 1st Grade, Distinguished Medal of Educ. 74 and others.
Publs. *How to Keep Your Health* (2 vols.), *Ray of Light* (short stories), *General Science* (4 vols.), *Plant Families, Life and Youth* 67, *Jerusalem: The Arab Heritage* 70, *Palestine: The Arab Heritage* 72.
P.O. Box 1514, Amman, Jordan.

Aba el-Khayl, Sheikh Abdulrahman, B.A.; Saudi Arabian diplomatist and politician; b. 1927; ed. Cairo Univ.
Diplomatic Service 52-, Ministry of Foreign Affairs, Cairo, Beirut 52-58; Dir.-Gen. Ministry of Finance and Nat. Econ. Council 58-60; Senior Adviser, Ministry of Foreign Affairs 60; mem. Admin. Board, Arab Cement Co., Jeddah 60-61; Minister of Labour and Social Affairs 61-.
Ministry of Labour and Social Affairs, Riyadh, Saudi Arabia.

Abaza, Tharwat, LL.B.; Egyptian lawyer, editor and writer; b. 28 June 1927; ed. Monira Primary School, Farouk Secondary School and Cairo Univ.
Lawyer 50-54; Editor *Elmasri* daily newspaper 52-54, *Alkahira* 54-55; Publishing Consultant 56-57, 61-; mem. Cttee. on Fiction, Supreme Council for Arts, Literature and Social Sciences, and of its State Prizes Cttee.; State Prize for Fiction 59; State Decoration Grade I for Literature.
Publs. *Ibn Ammar* (Historical Fiction) 54, *Al Hayat Lana* (Life for Us—play) 55, *Hareb men Alayam* (An Escape from Fate—novel) 56, *Kasr Ala Elnil* (A Palace over the Nile—novel) 57, *Alayam Alkhadra* (Green Days—short stories) 58, *Thoma Toshrek Alshams* (Then the Sun Rises—novel) 60, *Zhekriat Baida* (Far Echoes—short stories) 61, *Leka Honak* (An Appointment There—novel) 62, *Aldabab* (The Fog—novel) 64, *Shaion men Alkhawf* (A Little Fear—novel) 65, *Hayat El Hayah* (Life of Life—play), *Hathihi Elloba* (This Toy—short stories), *Hina Yamil Al Mizan* (When the Scales are Unbalanced—short stories).
5 Nadi Street, Maadi, Egypt.

Abbadi, Beshir Ahmed, PH.D.; Sudanese politician; b. 1936, Omdurman; ed. Univ. of Khartoum and Northwestern Univ., U.S.A.
Lecturer, Faculty of Eng., Univ. of Khartoum, Head, Dept. of Mechanical Eng. 70-71; mem. Board of Dirs. Sudan Railways 68-69, Chair. Board of Dirs. Sudan Airways 69-70; Minister of Communications Oct. 71-, also of Transport May 73-.
Ministry of Transport and Communications, Khartoum, Sudan.

Abbas, Ferhat; Algerian politician; b. 1899; ed. Algiers Univ.
Formerly a chemist at Sétif; Leader of *Association des Etudiants musulmans* 26-31; took part in org. of the Algeria People's Union 38; published "Manifesto of the Algerian People" 43; founded Amis du Manifeste et de la Liberté (A.M.L.) 44; under detention May 45-March 46; took part in the formation of the Union Démocratique du Manifeste Algérien (U.D.M.A.) 46; elected rep. to French Constitutional Assembly 46, later mem. of French Union Assembly; elected to Algerian Assembly 48 and 54; Leader of U.D.M.A. 46-56; joined Nat. Liberation Front (FLN) 55; mem. FLN del. to Eleventh Gen. Assembly of UN 57; Prime Minister of Provisional Government of the Algerian Republic (GPRA) in Tunisia 58-61; Pres. of the Chamber of Algeria 62-63; detained July 64-June 65.
Publs. *Le jeune algérien* 31, *La nuit coloniale* 62.
Konba, Algiers, Algeria.

Abboud, Gen. Ibrahim; Sudanese officer and politician; b. 1900; ed. Gordon Memorial Coll., Khartoum and Military Coll., Khartoum.
Entered Sudan Defence Force; served 39-45 war with Sudanese contingent, British Army in Eritrea, Ethiopia and Libya; Dep. C.-in-C. Sudanese Army 54, C.-in-C. 56-64; Pres. Supreme Military Council, Prime Minister and Minister of Defence 58-64.
Suakin, Sudan.

Abdalla, Abdel Rahman; Sudanese politician; b. 1933; ed. Khartoum Univ. Coll. and New York Univ.
Joined Ministry of Interior, Sub-Mamour 56; Inspector, Tokar district, later of Kassala Province; joined Halfa People's Settlement Comm. 59; Dir. Inst. of Public Admin. 63-65; Dir. African Admin. Training and Research Inst., Morocco 65; Dir. Nat. Inst. of Public Admin., Libya; Deputy Minister of Local Govt. Aug. 71; Minister of Public Service and Admin. Reform Oct. 71-.
Ministry of Public Service and Administrative Reform, Khartoum, Sudan.

Abdalla, Dr. Ismail-Sabri, PH.D.; Egyptian economist; b. 25 Dec. 1924, Malawi; ed. Abdin and Khedive Ismail schools, Cairo and Paris Univs.
Lecturer, Alexandria Univ. 51-54, Cairo Univ. 54-56; Econ. Adviser, Econ. Devt. Org. 57-59; Chief Editor *Dar Al-Maarif* Publishing House 65-69; Dir.-Gen. Inst. of Nat. Planning 69-71, Chair. of Board 72-, Dir.-Gen. May 75-; Deputy Minister of Planning 71, Minister of State for Planning 72-74, Minister 74; mem. Board, Soc. Egyptienne d'Econ. politique, de statistique et de législation 72-; mem. Acad. Advisory Board, UN African Inst. of Devt. and Planning 71-.
Publs. *Economie et Structure Economique* 52, *Lectures in Economics* (Arabic) 54, *The Organization of the Public Sector* (Arabic) 69, *Confrontation with Israel* (Arabic) 69, *Political Papers* (Arabic) 72; various articles in French and Arabic.
Institute of National Planning, Nasr City, Cairo; Home: 6 Ibn Malek Street, Guizeh, Egypt.

Abdelkerim, Ahmad Ezzat, D.LITT.; Egyptian historian; b. 19 June 1909; ed. Cairo Univ.
Lecturer, Asst. Prof. of Modern History, Cairo Univ. until 50; Visiting Prof. Univ. of Damascus 46-49; Prof. of Modern History, Ain Shams Univ. 50-64, Dean of Faculty of Arts, Ain Shams Univ. 61-64, Vice-Rector 64-68, Rector 68-71; Visiting Prof., Woodrow School of Foreign Affairs, Univ. of Virginia 52, Univ. of Libya, Benghazi 60-61.
Publs. *History of Education in Egypt under Mohamed Ali* 38, *History of Education in Egypt (From the Reign of Mohamed Ali to the British Occupation*—3 vols.) 44, *Venice, an Aristotelian Republic* (trans. from French) 47, *Modern and Contemporary History of the Arab World* 55, *History of Syria in the 18th Century* 58, *Studies in Modern Arab Renaissance* 59.
Abbasiyah, Cairo, Egypt.

Abdel Meguid, Ahmed Esmat, PH.D.; Egyptian diplomatist; b. 22 March 1923, Alexandria; ed. Faculty of Law, Alexandria Univ. and Univ. of Paris.

Attaché and Sec. Egyptian Embassy, London 50-54; Ministry of Foreign Affairs, Head of British Desk 54-56, Asst. Dir. Legal Dept. 61-63, Head, Cultural and Technical Assistance Dept. 67-68; Counsellor, Perm. Mission to European Office of UN, Geneva 57-61; Minister Counsellor, Egyptian Embassy, Paris 63-67; Official Spokesman of Govt. and Head Information Dept. 68-69; Amb. to France 69-70; Minister of State for Cabinet Affairs 70-72; Perm. Rep. to UN 72-; mem. Int. Law Asscn., took part in UN confs. on the Law of the Sea 59, on Consular Relations 63 and on the Law of Treaties 69; Ordre National du Mérite, France 67; Grand Croix 71; 1st Class Decoration, Egypt 70. Publs. several articles in *Revue Egyptienne de Droit International.*

Permanent Mission of Egypt to the United Nations, 36 East 67th Street, New York, N.Y. 10021, U.S.A.
Telephone: 879-6300.

Abdel-Rahman, Ibrahim Helmi, PH.D.; Egyptian United Nations official; b. 5 Jan. 1919; ed. Univs. of Cairo, London, Edinburgh, Cambridge and Leiden.

Lecturer in Astronomy and Astrophysics, later Asst. Prof. Cairo Univ. 42-54; Sec.-Gen. Council of Ministers 54-58; Dir. Egyptian Atomic Energy Comm. 54-59; mem. and Sec.-Gen. Nat. Science Council 56-58; mem. Nat. Planning Comm. 57-60; Dir. Inst. of Nat. Planning 60-63; UN Commr. for Industrial Devt. 63-66; Exec. Dir. UN Industrial Devt. Org. (UNIDO) 67-74; Senior Adviser to the Prime Minister 75; Minister of Nat. Planning and Admin. Reform April 75-; mem. Egyptian Del. UNESCO Gen. Conf. 48, 52, 54; mem. U.A.R. Del. to Int. Atomic Energy Agency, Vienna 57; mem. numerous UN Missions.

Council of Ministers, Cairo, Egypt.

Abdessalam, Belaid; Algerian politician; b. July 1928, Dehemcha.

Former Hon. Pres. Union Générale des Etudiants Musulmans Algériens; Instructor FLN school, Oujda; in Cabinet of M. Abdelhamid Mehri, Tunisia 60; Political Adviser in Cabinet of M. Ben Khedda 61; in charge of Economic Affairs, FLN Provisional Exec. 62; Pres., Dir.-Gen. SONATRACH 64-65; Minister of Industry and Energy 65-; Chair Org. of Arab Petroleum Exporting Countries (OAPEC) 74.

Ministère de l'Industrie et de l'Energie, Algiers, Algeria.

Abdoh, Djalal, LL.D.; Iranian diplomatist; b. 1909; ed. Teheran and Paris Univs.

Assistant Dir. Ministry of Justice 37-39; Public Prosecutor, Court of Govt. Employees, Teheran 41-43; Dir.-Gen. Ministry of Justice 43-44; mem. Parl. 44-49; Deputy Perm. Rep. to UN 49-53; Dir.-Gen. of Political Affairs, Ministry of Foreign Affairs 54-55; Acting Head Del. to Bandung Conf. 55; Amb. and Perm. Rep. to UN 56; Act. Rep. Security Council 56; Chair. Iranian Del. Gen. Assembly 58-59; Minister of Foreign Affairs 59; UN Plebiscite Commr., British N. Cameroons 59-60; Amb. at Large 61; Administrator, UN Temporary Exec. Authority (UNTEA), West New Guinea (West Irian) 62-63; Prof., Teheran Univ. 64-65; Amb. to India 65-68, to Italy 68-72; Man. Dir. Iranian Bankers' Asscn. 72-; mem. Currency and Credit Council 72-, Perm. Court of Arbitration 46-; Pres. Iranian Asscn. for the UN 72, Iranian branch of Int. Law Asscn. 73-.

Publs. *Civil Procedure of Iran, Comparative Law, International Private Law, Eléments psychologiques dans les Contrats, Le Ministère Public, Le régime Pénitentiaire en Iran, The Political Situation in Africa* (Persian), *The Political Situation in The Middle East* (Persian); series of articles on UN in *World Affairs.*

Abdul-Ghani, Abdul-Aziz, M.A.(ECON.); Yemeni economist; b. 4 July 1939, Haifan, Yemen Arab Repub.; ed. Colorado Coll. and Colorado Univ.

Minister of Health 67-68, of Economy 68-69, 70-71; Chair. Technical Office, Board of Planning 69-70; Gov. Central Bank of Yemen 71-75; Prime Minister Jan. 75-.

P.O. Box 38, Sana'a, Yemen Arab Republic.
Telephone: 2116.

Abdulla, Rahmatalla; Sudanese diplomatist; b. 1922; ed. Trinity Coll., Cambridge Univ.

Ambassador to India and Japan 59-60, Nigeria 60-61, France, Netherlands, Belgium, Switzerland and Spain 61-65; Minister of Nat. Educ. 64-65; served as Head of the History Faculty, Sudan Inst. of Educ.; Exec. Sec. and later Asst. Gen. Man., Sudan Gezira Board; Dept. Under-Sec. for Foreign Affairs 65-67; Amb. to France, Netherlands, Switzerland and Spain 68-70, Zaire 70-72; Perm. Rep. to UN 72-74; served as Personal Envoy of the Govt. to a meeting of African Heads of State, Del. to many int. confs., including those of the UN, OAU, regional African meetings and the Arab League.

Permanent Mission of Sudan to the United Nations, 757 Third Avenue, 24th Floor, New York, N.Y. 10017, U.S.A.

Abdullah al Sheikh, Hassan; Saudi Arabian politician; b. 1932; ed. Shariah Coll., Mecca and Al Azhar Univ., Cairo.

Former mem. Judicial Supervisory Cttee.; Vice-Pres. Judicial Supervisory Cttee.; Minister of Education and Health 62, now Minister of Educ.; Chancellor Riyadh Univ.; Chief Dir. Council of Arts, Sciences and Literature 62-; Chancellor Univ. of King Abdelaziz; Dir. Archaeological Dept.

Publs. *Duwarna Fi Al-Kufah* (Our Turn in the Struggle), *Brave Ideas, Dignity of The Individual in Islam.*

Ministry of Education, Riyadh, Saudi Arabia.

Abdullah ibn Abdulaziz ibn Abdelrahman el Faisal el Saud, H.R.H. Prince; Saudi Arabian Prince and army officer; b. Aug. 1921.

Brother of late H.M. King Faisal; Commdr. of Saudi Arabian Nat. Guard 62-; Second Deputy Prime Minister March 75-.

c/o National Guard, Riyadh, Saudi Arabia.

Abouhamad, Khalil, L. EN D.; Lebanese lawyer and politician; b. 15 Nov. 1936, Beyrouth; ed. Univ. Saint Joseph, Beirut.

Called to Bar, Beirut 62; practising lawyer 62-70, 73-; Minister for Foreign Affairs 70-73; Grand Cordon, Order of Cedar of Lebanon; Grand Cordon Ordinis Piani of the Vatican; Grand Cordon, Order of Leopold, Belgium; Grand Cordon of Italy, Egypt, Saudi Arabia, Tunisia, Greece, Liberia; other awards.

Rue Allenby, Immeuble Khawan, Beirut, Lebanon.

Abou Nosseir, Mohamed, B.A.; Egyptian lawyer and politician; b. 1915.

Legal practice 36-39; Advocate, State Legal Dept. 39-44; Advocate, Legal Dept. of Cabinet 44-46; Asst. Councillor and Sec.-Gen. State Council 52; Councillor, State Council, Public Works Section 53; Supervisor, Admin. Contracts Section, State Council 54; Dep. Minister of Commerce and Industry 54; Head of trade mission to Indonesia and Japan 54; mem. official del. to Bandung Conf. for Afro-Asian Countries 55; Head of Trade Missions to China 55, to U.K. 56, and of Economic Mission to Syria 56; Minister of Commerce and Industry 56-58, of Municipal and Rural Affairs 58-61 (Egyptian Regional Govt.); Chair. Board of Dirs., Gen. Egyptian Housing and Urbanism Org. 61-; Minister of Housing and Public Utilities 64-66; mem. Gen. Secr., Arab Socialist Union 66-; Chair. Preparatory Cttee. New Perm. Constitution 66; Minister of Justice 68-69.

4 El Saleh Ayoub Street, Zamalek, Cairo, Egypt.

Abu-Izzeddin, Halim Said, B.A., LL.B., LL.D.; Lebanese diplomatist; b. 11 June 1918; ed. American Univ. of Beirut and Faculté de Droit, Univ. de Paris.
Consul-General Cairo 44-46, Counsellor 46-50; Dir. Political Dept., Ministry of Foreign Affairs 50-53, 64-66; Dir.-Gen. Ministry of Information 53-55; Asst. Sec.-Gen. Ministry of Foreign Affairs 55-57; Ambassador to India 57-59; Gov. Northern Lebanon 59-64; Amb. to Egypt 66-71; Amb., Perm. Del. to UNESCO 71-; numerous decorations.
Publs. *Lebanon and its Provinces* (English) 63, *The Foreign Policy of the Lebanon* (Arabic) 66.
UNESCO, 7 and 9 place de Fontenoy, Paris, France; and Abadyeh, Lebanon.

Abu Odeh, Adnan Sa'id; Jordanian politician; b. 1933, Nablus; ed. Univ. of Damascus, Syria.
Teacher, Jordan 54-58, Kuwait, Trucial States 60-66; Intelligence Officer 66-70; Minister of Culture and Information 70, 71-72, Jan.-Aug. 73, 73-74, concurrently Minister of Tourism and Antiquities 70, 71; Chief of Royal Cabinet Aug.-Nov. 73; Sec.-Gen. Arab Nat. Union 72-73; Istiqlal Medal (1st Class).
c/o Ministry of Culture and Information, P.O. Box 1854, Amman, Jordan.

Abu Zaid, Salah; Jordanian politician; b. 21 April 1925; ed. Syrian Univ., Damascus, and Syracuse Univ., New York.
Teacher, Irbid Secondary School 42; Chief, Publicity Dept., Statistical Dept., Amman 50; Sec. Jordan Devt. Bd. 53-56; Controller of Press, Press Dept. 56-57; Asst. Dir.-Gen. Hashemite Broadcasting Service 58-59, Dir.-Gen. 62-64; Asst. Dir.-Gen. Nat. Guidance and Information 59-60, Dir.-Gen. 62, Chief, National Guidance 62-64; Minister of Information 64-65, Culture and Information 67-68, Tourism and Antiquities 67-68; Amb. to the U.K. 69-70; Personal Adviser to H.M. King Hussein 71-72; Minister of Foreign Affairs 72; mem. Senate 73-74, Chair. Foreign Relations Cttee 73-74; Minister of Culture and Information Nov. 74-; Arab Renaissance Medal, Jordanian Star, Cedar of Lebanon and several other medals.
Publ. *Al Hussein bin Talal* 58.
Ministry of Culture and Information, Amman, Jordan.

Abushadi, Mohamed Mahmoud, PH.D., B.COM., A.C.I.P.; Egyptian banker; b. 15 Aug. 1913, Fayoum; ed. Cairo Univ., Chartered Inst. of Patent Agents, and American Univ., Washington, D.C., U.S.A.
Controller-Gen. Insurance Dept., Ministry of Finance 49-52; Dir.-Gen. Govt. Insurance and Provident Funds 53; Chair. and Man. Dir. Development and Popular Housing Co. 54-55; Sub.-Gov. Nat. Bank of Egypt 55-60, Man. Dir. 61-67, Chair. 67-70; Chair. Social Insurance Org. 56-57; Chair. and Man. Dir. Cairo Insurance Co. 56-57; Man. Dir. Cairo Bank 56-57; Chair. Union de Banques Arabes et Françaises, Paris 70-, UBAF Ltd., London 72-; Order of the Repub., 2nd Class, Order of Merit, 1st Class.
Publs. *The Art of Central Banking and its Application in Egypt* 52, *Central Banking in Egypt* 52.
Union de Banques Arabes et Françaises, 4 rue Ancelle, 92 Neuilly sur Seine; Home: 52 avenue Foch, Paris 16e, France.

Acet, Kamran; Turkish diplomatist; b. 2 March 1917; ed. School of Political Studies, Univ. of Ankara.
With Ministry of Foreign Affairs 41-; served Ankara 41-43, 45-47; Attaché Rio de Janeiro 43-45; Vice-Consul Mytilene, Greece 47-49; First Sec. Helsinki 49-51; Dir. of Section, Dept. of Trade and Trade Agreements 51-53; First Sec. and Counsellor Washington 53-59; Deputy Dir.-Gen. then Dir.-Gen. Dept. of Middle East, Africa and Asia, Ministry of Foreign Affairs 59-62; Amb. to Ghana 62-64, to Morocco 64-66, to Tunisia 67-70; Deputy Sec.-Gen. for Cyprus Affairs and Greece Nov. 70-Nov. 71; Dir.-Gen. Personnel

and Admin., Ministry of Foreign Affairs Dec. 71-; mem. Turkish del. to 15th Session of Gen. Assembly of UN and to several meetings of CENTO and NATO; Grand Cordon, Kingdom of Morocco.
c/o Ministry of Foreign Affairs, Ankara, Turkey.

Adams, Michael Evelyn, M.A.; British writer; b. 31 May 1920; ed. Sedbergh School and Christ Church, Oxford.
Commonwealth Fund Fellowship in U.S.A. 54-55; Middle East Corresp. *The Guardian* 56-62; Asst. to Dir. Voluntary Service Overseas 64-67; Dir. of Information, Council for the Advancement of Arab-British Understanding (CAABU) 68-; Editor *Middle East International*.
Publs. *Suez and After* 58, *Umbria* 64, *Voluntary Service Overseas* 68, *Chaos or Rebirth* 68, *Handbook to the Middle East* (Editor) 71, *Publish it Not . . .* (with Christopher Mayhew) 75.
Council for the Advancement of Arab-British Understanding, 104 Grand Buildings, Trafalgar Square, London, W.C.2, England.

Adams, Sir Philip George Doyne, K.C.M.G.; British diplomatist; b. 17 Dec. 1915, Wellington, New Zealand; ed. Lancing and Christ Church, Oxford.
Vice-Consul, Beirut 39-41; war service 41; Third Sec., Cairo 41-45; Second Sec., Jeddah 45-47; Foreign Office, London 47-51; First Sec., Vienna 51-54; Trade Commr., Khartoum 54-56; Regional Inf. Officer, Beirut 56-59; Foreign Office, London 59-63; Consul-Gen., Chicago 63-66; Amb. to Jordan 66-70; Asst. Under-Sec. Foreign and Commonwealth Office 70; Deputy Sec. Cabinet Office 71-72; Amb. to Egypt 73-75.
c/o British Embassy, Cairo, Egypt; and Foreign and Commonwealth Office, London, England.

Adams, Robert McCormick, A.M., PH.D.; American anthropologist and archaeologist; b. 23 July 1926; ed. Univ. of Chicago.
Archaeological field work at Jarmo, Iraq 50-51; joined staff of Univ. of Chicago 54, Dir. Oriental Inst. 62-68, Prof. of Anthropology 63-, Dean, Div. of Social Science 70-74; Field studies of irrigation and settlement patterns in central and southern Iraq 56-58, 60, 67, 68-69, Iran 60-61; excavations in Iran 63, Syria 70; Chair. Assembly of Behavioral and Social Sciences, Nat. Research Council 73-, American Oriental Soc.; Fellow, American Acad. of Arts and Sciences, American Anthropological Asscn., American Asscn. for the Advancement of Science; mem. German Archaeological Inst., Nat. Acad. of Science, Middle East Studies Asscn., American Philosophical Soc.
Publs. *City Invincible: a Symposium of Urbanization and Cultural Development in the Ancient Near East* (co-editor with C. H. Kraeling) 60, *Land Behind Baghdad: a History of Settlement on the Diyala Plains* 65, *The Evolution of Urban Society: Early Mesopotamia and Pre-hispanic Mexico* 66, *The Uruk Countryside* (with H. J. Nissen) 72.
The Oriental Institute, 1155 East 58th Street, Chicago, Illinois 60637; and 5201 South Kimbark Avenue, Chicago, Illinois 60615, U.S.A.

Adasani, Mahmoud, B.SC.; Kuwaiti engineer; b. 31 Jan. 1934; ed. Kuwait, American Univ., Beirut and Univ. of Southern California.
Assistant petroleum engineer, Kuwait Oil Co. 58-60, petroleum engineer 60, Dir. 60-; Technical Asst., Gen. Oil Affairs Dept., Ministry of Finance and Oil 60-63, Dir. of Technical Affairs 63-66, Asst. Under-Sec. for Oil Affairs 66-; Man. Dir. Salwa Construction Co.; Dir. Kuwait Metal Pipeline Co. 70-; mem. American Inst. Mechanical Engineers, Kuwait Soc. Engineers.
Publs. *Oil of Kuwait, The Greater Burgan Field, North Kuwait Oil Fields.*
Ministry of Finance and Oil, P.O.B. 5077, Kuwait.

Adib, Albert; Lebanese editor; b. 1 July 1908, Mexico.
Editor many magazines, Cairo 27-30, Beirut 30-38; Pres.
Acad. of Oriental Music, Beirut 33-38; Gen. Dir. Radio-
Levant Broadcasting Station, Beirut 38-43; Editor and
proprietor *Al-Adib* review, Beirut 42-; mem. various acads.
and foreign cultural insts.; Chevalier of the Order of the
Cedar.
Publ. *Liman* (poems) 52.
P.O. Box 11-878, Beirut, Lebanon.

Adly, Dr. Ibrahim; Syrian United Nations official; b. 3
Nov. 1921, Damascus; ed. Damascus Univ. and American
Univ., Washington D.C.
Head, Income Tax Dept., Ministry of Finance 52-54, Dir.
of Internal Revenue 54-58, Dir. Personnel 58-60; Dir.-Gen.
Pension and Insurance Fund Inst. 60-62; Chair. of Board,
Dir.-Gen. Banque de Syrie et d'Outre Mer 62-63; Vice-
Chair., Dir.-Gen. Arab World Bank, Damascus 63-65;
Resident Rep. of UNDP in Kuwait 66-72, in Libya 72-;
Lecturer Damascus Univ. and School of Finance, Ministry
of Finance 54-59; Syrian Merit Decoration for outstanding
achievements.
United Nations Development Programme, P.O. Box 358,
Tripoli, Libya.

Adwok Bong Gicomeko, Luigi; Sudanese schoolmaster
and public servant; b. 1929; ed. Rumbek Secondary School
and Inst. of Education, Bakht Er Ruda.
Schoolmaster 52-58; mem. Parl. March-Nov. 58; Head-
master Tembura Intermediate School 63-64; elected mem.
Supreme Council of State Dec. 64, re-elected June 65,
resigned June 65; mem. Central Exec. Cttee. Southern Front
Party 64-67; mem. Sudan Constituent Assembly 67-69;
Minister of Works 71; Commr. Upper Nile Province 71-72;
Mem. for Educ., High Exec. Council for the Southern
Region 72-73, for Public Service Aug.-Dec. 73; Alt. Asst.
Sec.-Gen., Sudanese Socialist Union 74-; mem. People's
Assembly 74-.
Secretariat-General, Sudanese Socialist Union, P.O. Box
1850, Khartoum, Sudan.

Afif, Ahmed Jaber; Yemeni government official; b. 1930;
ed. High School, Sana'a.
Director of Schools, Hodeida Province 52-56; Under-Sec.
for Educ. 56-58; Dir. Sana'a Hospital 58-60; Under-Sec.
for Health 60-63; Amb. to Lebanon and Syria 63-69; Pres.
Council of Petroleum Co. 69-; Minister of Educ. 70-74.
Al-rayni Street, Sana'a, Yemen Arab Republic.

Afshar, Amir Dr. Asian; Iranian government official; b.
21 Nov. 1922; ed. Berlin and Hindenburg Schools, and
Univs. of Berlin, Greifswald, Vienna and Geneva.
Joined Ministry of Foreign Affairs 47, Sec., The Hague
50-54; Del. to Bandung Conf., Indonesia 55; Eisenhower
Exchange Fellowship 55-56; mem. Parl. 56-61; Del. to
UN Gen. Assembly 57, 58 and 60; Adjutant to the Shah
59-66; Plenipotentiary Minister 63; mem. High Political
Council 63-66; Pres. Iranian Shipping Lines 60-67; Amb.
to Austria 67-70, to U.S.A. and Mexico 69-70, to Fed.
Repub. of Germany 73-; Chair. Board of Governors of the
Int. Atomic Energy Agency, Vienna 68-; numerous
decorations.
Publs. in German: *The Constitution of the Third Reich* 42,
The Administration of the Third Reich 42, *Possibilities for
the Economic Development of Iran* 43; in Persian: *The End
of the Third Reich* 48, *God Created the Universe and the
Dutch made Holland* 55; in English: *Report on America* 56.
Iranian Embassy, Kölnerstrasse 71, Bonn-Bad Godesberg,
Federal Republic of Germany.

Afshar, Amir Khosrow, K.C.M.G., L. EN D.; Iranian diplomatist; b. 1918, Teheran; ed. American Coll., Teheran,
Univs. of Paris and Geneva.
Joined Ministry of Foreign Affairs 41; First Sec., Washington 46; First Sec., Perm. Del. to UN 47; Dir. UN Dept.

Ministry of Foreign Affairs 49, Dir. Third Political Dept.
51, Fourth Political Dept. 53; Chargé d'Affaires, London
53, Minister Plenipotentiary 54; Dir.-Gen. for Political
Affairs, Ministry of Foreign Affairs 58; Parl. and Political
Under-Sec. 59; Amb. to Fed. Repub. of Germany 61, to
France 63; Deputy and Acting Minister for Foreign Affairs
67; Amb. to U.K. 69-74; Order of Homayoun; Order of the
Crown; Grand Officier, Légion d'Honneur; Commdr. Cross
of the Order of Merit (Fed. Germany).
c/o Ministry of Foreign Affairs, Teheran, Iran.

Aga Khan IV, H.H. Prince Karim; spiritual leader and
Imam of Ismaili Muslims; b. 13 Dec. 1936; ed. Le Rosey,
Switzerland, Harvard Univ., U.S.A.
Became Aga Khan on the death of his grandfather, Sir
Sultan Mohamed Shah, Aga Khan III, G.C.S.I., G.C.I.E.,
G.C.V.O. 57; granted title His Highness by Queen Elizabeth
II 57, His Royal Highness by the Shah of Iran 59; Commdr.
Ordre du Mérite Mauritanien 60; Grand Croix, Ordre Nat.
de la Côte d'Ivoire 65, Ordre Nat. de la Haute-Volta 65,
Ordre Nat. Malgache 66, Ordre du Croissant Vert des
Comores 66; Grand Cordon Ordre du Tadj de l'Empire
d'Iran 67; Nishan-I-Imtiaz, Pakistan 70; Hon. LL.D.
(Peshawar Univ.) 67, (Univ. of Sind) 70.
1 rue des Ursins, 75004 Paris, France.

Aga Khan, Prince Sadruddin; Iranian UN official;
b. 1933; ed. Harvard Univ. and Harvard Univ. Graduate
School for Arts and Sciences.
UNESCO Consultant for Afro-Asian Projects 58; Head
of Mission and Adviser to UN High Commr. for Refugees
59-60; UNESCO Special Consultant to Dir.-Gen. 61; Exec.
Sec. Int. Action Cttee. for Preservation of Nubian Monu-
ments 61; UN Dep. High Commr. for Refugees 62-65, High
Commr. 65-; Publ. *The Paris Review*; Founder and Sec.
Harvard Islamic Asscn.; Pres. Council on Islamic Affairs,
New York City; mem. Inst. of Differing Civilizations,
Brussels.
Office of UN High Commissioner for Refugees, Palais des
Nations, 1211 Geneva 10, Switzerland.

Agam, Yaacoy; Israeli artist; b. 1928, Rishon Letzon;
ed. Bezalel School of Art, Jerusalem, Atelier d'art abstrait,
Paris.
One-man exhbns. in Galerie Craven, Paris 53, Galerie
Denise René, Paris 56, 58, Palais des Beaux-Arts, Brussels
58, Tel-Aviv Museum 58, Suzanne Bollag Gallery, Zurich
59, 62, Drian Gallery, London 59, Marlborough Gerson
Gallery, New York 66, Galerie Denise René, New York 71;
travelling retrospective exhbn. Paris, Amsterdam, Düsseldorf, Tel-Aviv 72-73; numerous group exhbns. 54-.
Works include: *Transformes Musicales* 61, *Double Metamorphosis*, Shalom Liner 64, *Sculptures in the City*, Reims
70, sculpture and mural, President's mansion, Israel 71
Water Fire fountain, St. Louis 71, environment, Elysée
Palace, Paris 72, mobile wall, School of Science, Montpellier 72, design and realization of a square in defence
quarter, Paris, incl. water fountain and monumental
sculpture 73; films produced incl. *Recherches et Inventions*
56, *Le Désert chante, Micro-salon* (with I. Mambush) 57.
26 rue Boulard, Paris, France.

Agib, Ahmed Abdel Rahman El-, D.MECH.ENG.; Sudanese
engineer; b. 1932, Sudri, Kababish; ed. Khartoum Univ.
Coll., Imperial Coll., London, Glasgow Univ.
Trained with English Electric Co. and several Italian and
German companies; Technical Man. Sifrian Co. 59-62;
Lecturer, Univ. of Khartoum 59, Head, Dept. of Mechan-
ical Engineering 67-69, Dean, Faculty of Engineering
69-71, Prof. 70; Pres. Industrial Production Corpn. 71;
Minister of Industry and Mining 71-72.
Department of Mechanical Engineering, University of
Khartoum, Sudan.

Agranat, Shimon, LL.D.; Israeli judge; b. 1906, U.S.A.; ed. Chicago Univ.
Went to Palestine 30; Advocate in private practice 31-40; Magistrate 40-48; Pres. District Court, Haifa 48-50; Judge, Supreme Court, Jerusalem 50-, Dep. Pres. 61-65, Pres. 65-; Chair. of Inquiry Comm. on Yom Kippur War.
62 Nayot Street, Rehavia, Jerusalem; and The Supreme Court, Jerusalem, Israel.

Ahmad, Maj.-Gen. Mohammed al-Baqir; Sudanese army officer and politician; b. 1927, El Sofi; ed. Commercial Secondary School, Khartoum, Military Coll. and Cairo Univ. Commissioned 50; Chief of Staff, Southern Command 58; Mil. Gov. Upper Nile Province 59; Mil. Attaché, London 60-67; Dir. of Training and Chief of Staff, Southern Command 68; Commdr. Mil. Coll. 68-69; Under-Sec. Ministry of Defence June-Dec. 69; First Deputy Chief of Staff of Armed Forces Dec. 69-June 70, Chief of Staff 70-71; Minister of Interior Oct. 71-73, Jan. 75-; First Vice-Pres. of Sudan 72-; mem. Council, Univ. of Khartoum; del. to several int. confs.; several decorations.
Office of the First Vice-President, Khartoum, Sudan.

Ahmadi, Sadegh; Iranian lawyer; b. March 1920, Kermanshah; ed. Darol-Fonoon High School, Teheran, Univ. of Teheran.
Appointed Judge 46; Asst., Inspectorate Org. of the Prime Minister's Office, later Dir.-Gen.; Public Prosecutor of Teheran; First Asst., State Gen. Inspectorate; mem. Parl.; Under-Sec. in charge of Planning and Studies, Ministry of Justice, Parl. Under-Sec.; Minister of Justice Sept. 71-; mem. Parl. del. to U.S.S.R.; has studied judicial systems in European countries.
Ministry of Justice, Teheran, Iran.

Ahmed, S. Habib, B.A.; Pakistani United Nations official; b. 1 April 1915; ed. Univ. of Delhi.
Administration, Central Govt., India 35-41; Finance and Budget Officer, Tata Iron & Steel Co., India 41-47; Budget Officer, UN 49-50; Public Admin. Adviser UN Commr., Libya 50; UN Consultant Public Admin. Ethiopia and Iraq 51; Chief, African Middle East Unit, Div. Public Admin. 51-54; Chief Officer for Asia and the Far East, UN Technical Assistance Admin. 55-58; Chief Admin. Office UN Observers Group in the Lebanon 59; Deputy Dir. Bureau of Tech. Assistance Operations UN Headquarters 59-60; UN Admin., Kamina Mil. Base, Congo 60-61; Chief Admin. Officer, UN Operations in the Congo 61-62; Resident Rep. of Tech. Assist. Board, and Dir. of Special Fund Programme, Congo 62-64, Resident Rep. of UN Devt. Programme, Somalia 64-67, Libya 68-71, Syria 71-75; Consultant Organization and Methods Staff, UNDP, New York 75-.
c/o International Development Bureau, 49 D'Arcy Drive, Winnipeg, Canada.

Aini, Mohsin A. al; Yemeni diplomatist and politician; b. 1932; ed. Cairo Univ. and Univ. of Paris.
Schoolteacher, Aden 58-60; Int. Confederation of Arab Trade Unions 60-62; Minister of Foreign Affairs, Yemeni Republic Sept.-Dec. 62; Perm. Rep. to UN Dec. 62-65, 65-66, 67-69; Amb. to U.S.A. 63-65, 65-66; Foreign Minister May-July 65; Prime Minister Nov. 67; Personal Rep. of Chair. Republican Council 67; Amb. to U.S.S.R. 68-70; Prime Minister and Foreign Minister 70-Feb. 71; Amb. to France July-Sept. 71; Prime Minister, Minister of Foreign Affairs 71-72, June 74-June 75; Amb. to U.K. 73-74, to France 75-.
Embassy of the Yemen Arab Republic, ave. Paul Douma 25, Paris 11e, France.

Ajlouni, Brig. Mazen al-; Jordanian politician; b. 1924, Amman; ed. High School in Jordan and in U.K. Joined Jordanian Army 48; A.-D.-C. to King Hussein 55; Chief Aide-de-Camp 57; Mil. Attaché, Ankara 57-58;

Asst. for Admin., Amman Municipality 64; Gen. Insp., Public Security Dept. 69; Chief Aide-de-Camp 69; Deputy Prime Minister and Deputy Mil. Gov.-Gen. Sept. 70; Minister of State, Prime Minister's Office, Sept.-Oct. 70, 71-72; Minister of Interior Oct. 70-May 71; Senator 71-.
P.O. Box 5100, Amman, Jordan.

Akasheh, Farid, M.D., F.A.C.S., F.R.C.O.G.; Jordanian physician; b. 14 Sept. 1921, Karak; ed. Govt. schools, Jordan, St. Joseph Univ. of Beirut, Wayne State Univ., Detroit, U.S.A., St. Andrew's Univ., Scotland.
Medical Officer, Karak District 50-52, Amman District 52-56; Chief Surgeon, Dir. Govt. Maternity and Gynaecological Hospital 57-65; Minister of Social Welfare and Labour 67, of Health 72-73; private practice, gynaecology and obstetrics 73-; 1st Jordanian Star.
Publs. *Rupture of the Uterus* 68, *Hazard of Grand Multiparity, Electrical Induction of Labour.*
P.O. Box 2173, Amman, Jordan.

Akins, James E.; American diplomatist; b. 15 Oct. 1926, Akron, Ohio; ed. Akron Univ.
U.S. Navy 45-46; undertook relief work with non-profit org. 48-50; taught in Lebanon 51-52; asst. editor with research org. 53-54; entered Foreign Service 54; held numerous diplomatic posts in Paris 54-55, Strasbourg 55-56, Damascus 56-57, Kuwait 58-60, Baghdad 61-64; with Secr., Wash., D.C. 65-67, Acting Deputy Asst. Sec. Int. Resource Food Policy 69-70, Dir. Fuels and Energy Office 70-72; Amb. to Saudi Arabia 73-.
Publs. articles on oil affairs.
American Embassy, Jeddah, Saudi Arabia; and Department of State, Washington, D.C. 20521, U.S.A.

Akurgal, Ekrem, PH.D.; Turkish archaeologist; b. 1911, Istanbul; ed. Germany.
Lecturer, Univ. of Ankara 41-49, Prof. of Archaeology 49-; has conducted excavations at Smyrna, Sinope, Phokaia, Daskyleion, Pitane and Erythrai 53-, at Izmir 67-; Visiting Prof., Princeton Univ. 61-62; mem. Turkish Historical Soc., Turkish High Comm. for Ancient Monuments; mem. Austrian and German Archaeol. Insts., British, Austrian and Swedish Acads.; Hon. mem. Soc. for Promotion of Hellenic Studies, London, American Inst. of Archaeol.; Dr. h.c. (Bordeaux) 61.
Publs. *Griechische Reliefs aus Lykien* 42, *Remarques Stylistiques sur les reliefs de Malatya* 46, *Späthethitische Bildkunst* 49, *Phrygische Kunst* 55, *Die Kunst Anatoliens von Homer bis Alexander* 61, *Die Kunst der Hethiter* 61, *Orient und Okzident* 66, *Treasures of Turkey* (with Mango and Ettinghausen) 66, *Urartäische und Altiranische Kunstzentren* 68, *Ancient Civilizations and Ruins of Turkey* (3rd edn.) 73.
University of Ankara, Dil ve Tarih-Coğrafya Fakültesi, Ankara; Home: Vali Dr. Reşit cad. 90/5 Çankaya, Ankara, Turkey.

Akwaa', Brig. Mohammed Ali al-; Yemeni army officer, b. 1933, Sana'a; ed. secondary school, Mil. Coll., Sana'a. Participated in the movts. against last three Imams of Yemen, Free Yemenis Revolution 48, attempted coup 55; Revolution of 26 September 1962; leading figure in movt. which ousted Pres. al-Sallal 67; has held several posts in mil. and civil service including Asst. Mil. Commdr. Taiz District, Head Criminal Investigation Dept., Head Nat. Security (Intelligence) Dept.; Chief of Staff, Army Operations, Head S. Yemen Relief Office attached to Presidency; Minister of the Interior 73-74.
Bir Al-Azab, Sana'a, Yemen Arab Republic.

Alam, Amir Assadollah; Iranian agriculturalist and politician; b. 1919; ed. Karaj Agricultural College, Univ. of Teheran.
Gov.-Gen. of Baluchistan 45-48; Minister of the Interior

48, of Agriculture 49, of Labour 50; Superintendent of the Pahlavi Estates and mem. of the High Council for their disposal 51; Minister of the Interior 55-57; Leader, Mardom (*People's Party*) 56-60; Prime Minister 62-64; Minister of the Imperial Court 66-74; Sec.-Gen. Pahlavi Foundation; Chancellor Pahlavi Univ.
c/o Ministry of the Imperial Court, City Avenue Kakh, Teheran, Iran.

Alami, Musa; Jordanian philanthropist; b. 1897; ed. Trinity Hall Cambridge.
Crown Counsel 26-37; founded Arab Devt. Soc. 43; founded orphanage and farm in desert near Jericho 51; region under Israeli occupation June 67-.
Rabiya, Beirut, Lebanon.

Alamuddin, Sheikh Najib Salim, B.A.; Lebanese airline executive; b. 9 March 1909; ed. American Univ. of Beirut and Univ. Coll. of South West, Exeter, England.
Teacher of Engineering and Mathematics, American Univ. of Beirut 30-33; Insp. of Mathematics, Educ. Dept., Govt. of Trans-Jordan 33-36; Insp.-Gen. of Customs, Trade and Industry, Trans-Jordan 39-40; Chief Sec. Govt. of Trans-Jordan 40-42; founded Near East Resources Co. 42; Gen. Man. Middle East Airlines 52-56, Chair. and Pres. 56-; Minister of Information and Tourism 65; Minister of Public Works and Transport 66, 73; Fmr. mem. Exec. Cttee. of Int. Air Transport Asscn.; Trustee Emeritus, American Univ. of Beirut; Dir. several Lebanese companies; numerous decorations.
Middle East Airlines, Beirut International Airport, P.O. Box 206, Beirut, Lebanon.
Telephone: 272220, 316316.

Al-Azzawi, Hikmet: (*see* Azzawi, Hikmat al-).

Alfozan, Yusuf; Saudi Arabian diplomatist; b. 1913; ed. Bombay and Arabia.
Agent (Personal) to H.M. King Abdulaziz Ibn Saud (Bombay) 38; Saudi Arabian Consul-Gen., Palestine 39-41, Bombay 49-55; Editor *Shubban's Voice* 36-38; Saudi Arabian Minister to India 55-57; Saudi Arabian Ambassador to India 57-65, to Iran 66-68, to Spain 68-74, to India 74-.
Saudi Arabian Embassy, 1 Eastern Avenue, Maharani Bagh, New Delhi, India.

Ali, Ali Sayed; Egyptian trade union executive; b. 4 July 1925; ed. El Zaher Commercial School, Cairo.
District Sales Man. Nasr Petroleum Co. until 63; petroleum union exec. since 48; Gen. Sec. Arab Fed. of Petroleum, Mining and Chemical Workers 63-; Chair. Workers' Educ. Asscn. 64; mem. Nat. Assembly until 71; Minister of State June 64; ILO Expert on Workers' Educ.
The Arab Federation of Petroleum, Mines and Chemicals Workers, 5 Zaki Street, Tewfikia, Cairo, Egypt.

Ali, Salem Rubayi; Yemeni politician; b. 1934, Southern Arabia; ed. in Aden.
Formerly school-teacher and in private law practice; participated in activities of Nat. Front for the Liberation of Occupied Southern Yemen (FLOSY) 63-67; mem. Gen. Command of NLF Nov. 67; in exile 68-69; Chair. Presidential Council June 69-; Pres. and Supreme Commdr. of the Armed Forces.
Presidential Council, Aden, People's Democratic Republic of Yemen.

Alier, Abdel, LL.B., LL.M.; Sudanese politician; b. 1933, Bor District, Upper Nile Province; ed. Univs. of Khartoum, London, Yale.
Former advocate; District Judge in El Obeid, Wad Medani and Khartoum until 65; participant in Round Table Conf. and mem. Twelve Man Cttee. to Study the Southern problem 65; mem. Constitution Comms. 66-67, 68; fmr. mem. Law Reform Comm. and Southern Front; Minister of Supply and Internal Trade Oct. 69-June 70; Minister of

Works June 70-July 71; Minister for Southern Affairs July-Oct. 71; Vice-Pres. Oct. 71-; Pres. High Exec. Council for the Southern Region April 72-; mem. Board of Dirs., Industrial Planning Corpn.; mem. Nat. Scholarship Board.
People's Palace, Khartoum, Sudan.

Alikhani, Ali Naghi; Iranian economist and politician; b. 1929; ed. Alborz Coll., Teheran, Univ. of Teheran and Univ. of Paris.
Former Econ. Adviser to Nat. Iranian Oil Co. and other orgs.; Minister of Economy 63-69; Chancellor, Univ. of Teheran 69-71; private business 71-.
264, 28th Street, Park Avenue (Abbasabad), Teheran, Iran.

Alireza, Sheikh Mohamed Ibn Abdullah; Saudi Arabian merchant and industrialist; b. 1911; ed. Saudi Arabia and India.
Former Pres. Chamber of Commerce and Industries, Jeddah; mem. Admin. Council, Jeddah 46; Ex-Pres. Jeddah Benevolent Water Supply Cttee.; mem. Board of Trustees of the Benevolent Falah School 34; Leader Saudi Arabian del. to the Int. Islamic Econ. Conf., Pakistan 49; Chair. of Jeddah Port Trust Project 50; Minister of Commerce and Industries 54-58; Ambassador to U.A.R. March-June 64; Pres. Haji Abdullah Alireza & Co. Ltd., Haji Abdullah Alireza Libyan Trading Co., Arabian Italian Engineering Contractors S.p.A., Rome, Arabian Petroleum Supply Co. S.A.; now Amb. to France.
Embassy of Saudi Arabia, rue André-Pascal 1, Paris 16e, France.

Al-Jamali, Asim; (*see* Jamali, Asim al-).

Allegro, John Marco; British philologist and archaeologist; b. 17 Feb. 1923; ed. Wallington County Grammar School and Univ. of Manchester.
Royal Navy 41-46; Manchester Univ. 47-52; research in Hebrew dialects, Magdalen Coll., Oxford 52-53; British rep. on Int. Editing Team for Dead Sea Scrolls, Jerusalem 53-; Lecturer in Comparative Semitic Philology and Hebrew, Univ. of Manchester 54-62, in Old Testament and Intertestamental Studies 62-70; Adviser to Jordanian Govt. on Dead Sea Scrolls 61-; Trustee and Hon. Sec. Dead Sea Scrolls Fund 62-70.
Publs. *The Dead Sea Scrolls* 56, 64, *The People of the Dead Sea Scrolls* 59, *The Treasure of the Copper Scroll* 60, 64, *Search in the Desert* 64, *The Shapira Affair* 65, *Discoveries in the Judaean Desert* (Vol. 5) 68, *The Sacred Mushroom and the Cross* 70, *The End of a Road* 70, *The Chosen People* 71, *Lost Languages* 75.
Craigmore, Ballasalla, Isle of Man.

Allon, Brig.-Gen. Yigal; Israeli soldier, agriculturalist and politician; b. 10 Oct. 1918, Kfar Tabor, Lower Galilee; ed. Kadourie Agricultural Coll., Oxford, Hebrew Univ., Jerusalem.
Joined Hagana 31, Commdr. of Palmach Company 41, in Syria and Lebanon with Allies, Dep. Commdr. Palmach 43, C.-in-C. Palmach 45-48; charged with Hagana operations in Palestine 45-47; in command, Upper Galilee, Central Israel, Jerusalem Corridor, the Negev and N. Sinai 47-48; Maj.-Gen. (Reserves) Zahal (Israel Defence Forces); mem. and Co-Founder Kibbutz Genossar 37-; Minister of Labour 61-67; Minister for Absorption 67-69; Deputy Prime Minister 67-; Minister of Educ. and Culture 69-74, of Foreign Affairs June 74-; mem. Exec. Cttee. Hakibbutz Hameuchad; fmr. Sec.-Gen. Achduth Ha-avodah Socialist Party; mem. Labour Party and Labour-Mapam Alignment; mem. 3rd, 4th, 6th and 7th Knessets.
Publs. *The Story of Palmach* 51 (Book of Palmach), *Curtain of Sand* 60, *The Making of Israel's Army* (in English and German) 70, *Shield of David* (in English) 70, *Three Wars and one Peace* (trans. in Arabic), and many essays

and articles on political, military, education and cultural subjects in Hebrew, Yiddish, Arabic and English.
Deputy Prime Minister's Office, Ministry of Foreign Affairs, Jerusalem; Home: Kibbutz Genossar, Israel.

Al-Mhaidi, Kadhim Abdul Hamid; Iraqi businessman; b. 12 Feb. 1922; ed. College of Law, Baghdad, England and U.S.A.
Director-General Baghdad Chamber of Commerce, until 63; Gen.-Man. Exhibitions Org. 63; Gen.-Man. Bank of Baghdad 64-65 Minister of Econ. July-Sept. 65 Chair. of Board and the Gen. Trade Establishment 66; Minister of Economy 66-67; Econ. Adviser of the Baghdad Chamber of Commerce 68; Sec.-Gen. Fed. of Iraqi Chambers of Commerce April 69-.
Federation of Iraqi Chambers of Commerce, Munstansir Street, Baghdad, Iraq.

Almogi, Major Joseph; Israeli politician; b. 5 May 1910; ed. secondary school.
Came to Palestine 30; mem. Haganah Command 33-39; Prisoner of War, Germany 41-45; Gen. Sec. Labour Council, Haifa 45-59; Gen. Sec. Mapai Party 59-62; Minister of State 61-62; Minister of Housing and Development 62-65; joined Israel Labour List (Rafi Party) 65; Minister of Labour 68-74; Mayor of Haifa 74-.
120 Arlozorov Street, Haifa, Israel.

Aloni, Shulamit, LL.M.; Israeli lawyer and politician; b. 1928, Tel Aviv; ed. Teachers' Seminary, Hebrew Univ.
Editor radio programmes on legal matters and civil rights; Columnist *Ydiot Achoronot* (daily); mem. 6th Knesset (Parl.) for Mapai 65-69; Chair. Consumers' Council 66-70; founder and Pres. Citizens Rights Movement 73-; mem. 8th Knesset 73-; Minister without Portfolio June 74-.
Publs. *The Citizen and His State* 58, (7th edn. 74), *The Rights of Children in Israel* 61, *The Arrangement—From a Halachi State to a State of Law* 70.
The Knesset, Jerusalem; Home: Kfar Shmariahu, Israel.

Alpert, Carl; Israeli journalist and university official; b. 12 May 1913; ed. Boston Univ., U.S.A.
Editor *The New Palestine* 40-47; Nat. Pres. American Young Judaea 40-41; Nat. Dir. Educ. Dept. Zionist Org. of America 47-52; emigrated to Israel 52; Dir. Public Relations Dept., Technion Israel Inst. of Technology 52-68; Exec. Vice-Chair. Technion Board of Govs. 62-; Nat. Pres. Asscn. of Americans and Canadians in Israel 57-59; author int. syndicated weekly column in 42 newspapers.
Technion Israel Institute of Technology, Technion City, Haifa, Israel.

Amer, Subhi Amin, M.D.; Jordanian politician; b. 1912; ed. American Univ. of Beirut.
Physician, Transjordan 38-46, Palestine Govt. 47-48; Dir. Govt. Hospital, Nablus 48-53; Chief Physician, Nablus District 53-57; Asst. Under-Sec. to Minister of Health 57-62; Minister of Health five times 62-67; Minister of Health, Reconstruction and Devt. Oct.-Dec. 62, 68-70, of Health June-Sept. 70, of Reconstruction and Devt. Sept. 70-.
Ministry of Reconstruction and Development, Amman, Jordan.

Ameri, Nasser, M.ECONS.; Iranian economist; b. 1 Jan. 1929, Kerman; ed. Cornell Univ., Ithaca, N.Y.
Director Community Devt. and Deputy Gov.-Gen. Kerman Province 54-59; Dir. Rural Devt. Planning for Iran 60-62; Dir.-Gen. of Community Devt. 62-63; Vice-Gov. Cen. Bank of Iran 63-68; Pres. Agricultural Devt. Fund of Iran 68-73; Sec.-Gen. Mardom Party 73-74.
Teheran, Iran.

Amin, Mohamed el Amir; Sudanese airways official; b. 1 June 1919; ed. Gordon Memorial Coll., Khartoum.
Attached to Office of Civil Sec. (now Ministry of Interior) 38-48; Chief of Booking and Freight Office, Sudan Airways 48-54, Sales Supt. Sudan Airways 54-66; Gen. Man. Sudan Airways 66-68, 72-; Adviser-Gen. 68-72.
Sudan Airways, P.O. Box 253, Khartoum North, Sudan.

Amin, Samir, D.ECON.; Egyptian economist; b. 4 Sept. 1931, Cairo; ed. Univ. of Paris.
Senior Economist, Econ. Devt. Org., Cairo 57-60; Technical Adviser for Planning to Govt. of Mali 60-63; Prof. of Econs., Univs. of Poitiers, Paris and Dakar; Dir. UN African Inst. for Econ. Devt. and Planning 70-.
Publs. *Trois expériences africaines de développement, Mali, Guinée, Ghana* 65, *L'Economie du Maghreb* (2 vols.) 67, *Le développement du capitalisme en Côte d'Ivoire* 68, *Le monde des affaires sénégalaises* 68, *Maghreb in the Modern World* 70, *L'Accumulation à l'échelle mondiale* 70, *L'Afrique de l'Ouest bloquée* 71, *Le développement inégal* 73.
African Institute for Economic Development and Planning, B.P. 3186, Dakar, Senegal.

Amini, Ali, D.ECON. ET IUR.; Iranian politician; b. 1 July 1907; ed. Ecole de Droit, Grenoble, and Faculté de Droit, Paris, France.
Alternative Judge, Court of First Instance, and Penal Branch, Court of Appeal, Teheran 31; Asst. Dir. Opium Admin. Monopoly 33; Asst. Dir. Customs Admin. 34, Dir.-Gen. 36; Economic Dir.-Gen. Ministry of Finance 38, Under-Sec. 40; mem. Chamber of Deputies Teheran and Deputy Prime Minister 40; Iranian rep. Int. Narcotic and Opium Confs. 49 and 50; Minister of Finance 52; led Iranian del. in negotiations with Int. Oil Consortium 54; Minister of Justice 55; Ambassador to U.S.A. 56-58; Prime Minister 61-62.
Publ. *L'institution du monopole de commerce extérieur en Perse.*
Park Aminodoleh, Avenue Ebnecina, Teheran, Iran.

Amiran-Pougatchov, Emanuel; Israeli composer; b. 1909, Russia.
Arrived in Israel 24; teachers included Yoel Engel and Prof. David Shor (Russia), Prof. S. Rosowsky (Israel), Sir Granville Bantock and Alec Roley (England); co-founder with Prof. Leo Kestenberg of Music Teachers' Seminary, Tel-Aviv; Officer-in-Charge of musical activities Israel Defence Forces 48; Directing Supervisor of Music Educ. in Ministry of Educ. and Culture 48-; Founder and Chair. Les Jeunesses Musicales in Israel; mem. of Board ISME 68-.
Compositions include: *Hashomer* (The Guard) for orchestra, *Evel* (orchestra), *A Symphonic Movement*, *Achrei Moti* (After my death) cantata, *Nachamu Ami* (cantata for mixed choir and orchestra), piano pieces, music for the theatre, and numerous songs which include *Ki Mitsion* (Out of Zion), *Mayim, Mayim* (Water, Water), *Hagez* (Shearing song), *Halleluyah.*
Office: Ministry of Education and Culture, Hadar-Daphna Building, Shderoth Hamelech Shaul, Tel-Aviv; Home: 39 Harav Friedman Street, Tel-Aviv, Israel.

Ammash, Major-General Saleh Mahdi; Iraqi soldier and politician; ed. Military Coll.
Minister of Defence Feb.-Nov. 63; C.-in-C. Supreme Defence Council of Iraq and Syria Oct.-Nov. 63; Deputy Prime Minister and Minister of the Interior July 68-70; Vice-Pres. 70-71; Amb. to U.S.S.R. 71-74, to France Feb. 74-.
Embassy of Iraq, 53 rue de la Faisanderie, 75016 Paris, France.

Ammoun, Fouad; Lebanese jurist and politician; b. 26 Nov. 1899; ed. Beirut School of Law and Univ. de Lyon.
President, Court of Appeal and of Cassation, Lebanon 35-42, Attorney-Gen. 42-43; Commr. of Govt. attached to Council of State 43-44; Joined Ministry of Foreign Affairs

44, Legal Expert 44-45, Gen. Sec. 45-56, 60-63; mem. Cttee. drafting Covenant of League of Arab States and numerous int. treaties 44; Minister for Planning and Nat. Economy Feb.-March 64; Minister for Foreign Affairs 64-65; Judge Int. Court of Justice 65-, Vice-Pres. 70-; Chair. Lebanese Nat. Comm. UNESCO 45-55, 60-63 and Cttee. Int. Econ. Relations 60-63; mem. del. to UN seven sessions between 48-63; Dir. h.c. Univ. of Monrovia; Cordon of the Phoenix (Greece).

Publs. several juridical articles, notably a commentary on the *Code Correctionnel Libanais* (with Ph. N. Boulos and W. El Kassar).

International Court of Justice, The Hague, Netherlands.

Amouzegar, Jamshid, B.C.E., M.S., PH.D., Iranian politician; b. 25 June 1923; ed. Univs. of Teheran, Cornell, Washington.

United Nations Expert, Mission to Iran 51; Chief, Engineering Dept. 52-55; Deputy Minister of Health 55-58; Minister of Labour 58-59, of Agriculture 59-60; Consulting Engineer 60-64; Minister of Health 64-65, of Finance 65-74, of Interior and Employment 74-, also in Charge of Civil Service Comm.; Chair. Int. Civil Service Advisory Board of UN; Pres. Org. of Petroleum Exporting Countries (OPEC) 74-.

Tajrish, Teheran, Iran.

Amri, Gen. Hassan al-; Yemeni politician.

Took part in the Revolution against the Imamate 62; Minister of Transport Sept.-Oct. 62, of Communications Oct. 62-April 63; mem. Council of the Revolutionary Command 62-63; Vice-President of Yemen 63-66; mem. Political Bureau 63-66; Prime Minister Jan.-April 65, July 65-Sept. 66; C.-in-C. Yemen Armed Forces 67-71; mem. Presidential Council and Prime Minister April-July 69, Aug.-Sept. 71; in exile in Lebanon until Jan. 75; returned to Yemen A.R. Jan. 75.

Amuzegar, Jahangir, PH.D.; Iranian economist and politician; b. 13 Jan. 1920; ed. Univs. of Teheran, Washington and California.

Teaching Asst., Univ. of California, Los Angeles 51-53; Lecturer, Whittier Coll. 53, Univ. of Michigan 53-55; Asst. Prof. Pomona Coll., Claremont, California 55-56; Asst. Prof. Michigan State Univ., E. Lansing, Mich. 56-58; Assoc. Prof. Occidental Coll. and Univ. of Calif., Los Angeles 58-60; Brookings Research Prof. 60-61; Lecturer, Univ. of Maryland 63-73; Adjunct Prof. American Univ. 75-; Econ. Adviser, Plan Org., Govt. of Iran 56-57; Minister of Commerce, Iran 61-62; mem. Council of Money and Credit 61-62, High Econ. Council 61-62; mem. Board of Dirs. Bank Melli Iran 61-62; Chair. Board, Foreign Trade Co. (Iranian Govt. Org.) 61-62; Minister of Finance 62; Chair. High Council of Nat. Iranian Oil Co. 62; Amb.-at-Large, Chief of Iranian Econ. Mission, Washington, D.C. 63-73; Exec. Dir. Int. Monetary Fund, Washington, D.C. 73-.

Publs. *Technical Assistance in Theory and Practice: The Case of Iran* 66, *Iran: Economic Development under Dualistic Conditions* 71.

International Monetary Fund, 700 19th Street, N.W., Washington, D.C. 20431, U.S.A.

Amuzegar, Kuros, M.SC., PH.D., Iranian politician; b. 15 June 1927, Teheran; ed. Univ. of Teheran and in U.S.A.

Engineering Consultant to Karaj Dam; Technical Consultant to Planning Org.; Under-Sec., Ministry of Devt. and Housing, subsequently Ministry of Labour; mem. Board of Dirs. and Man. Dir. Org. of Social Security; Minister of Devt. and Housing 71-74.

c/o Ministry of Development and Housing, Teheran, Iran.

Anderson, Sir (James) Norman (Dalrymple), O.B.E., Q.C., M.A., LL.D., D.D., F.B.A.; British educationalist; b. 29 Sept. 1908; ed. St. Lawrence Coll., Trinity Coll., Cambridge.

Missionary, Egypt Gen. Mission 32-40; Capt. Libyan Arab Force 40-41; Major (Political Officer for Sanusi Affairs) 41; Lieut.-Col. (Sec. for Arab Affairs, Civil Affairs Branch, G.H.Q., M.E. 43, Political Sec. 43); Col. (Chief Sec., Civil Affairs Branch) 44-45; lectured on Islamic Law in Cambridge 47-50; Lecturer in Islamic Law, School of Oriental and African Studies, Univ. of London 47; Reader in Oriental Laws, Univ. of London 51; Prof. of Oriental Laws Univ. of London 53-; Head of Dept. of Law, School of Oriental and African Studies 53-71; Lecturer in Mohammedan Law, Council of Legal Educ. 53-; Visiting Prof., Princeton Univ. and New York Univ. Law School 58, Harvard Law School 66; Chair. U.K. National Comm. of Comparative Law 58-60; Dir. Inst. of Advanced Legal Studies, Univ. of London 59-; Dean, Faculty of Law, Univ. of London 64-69; Pres. Soc. of Public Teachers of Law 69-70; Chair. House of Laity, Gen. Synod of Church of England 70-; mem. Panel of Advisory Jurists to Northern Nigerian Govt. 58-62; Vice-Pres. Int. African Law Asscn.; mem. Int. Cttee. of Comparative Law 63-67; Libyan Order of Independence, Class II.

Publs. *The World's Religions* (Gen. Editor) 50, *Islamic Law in Africa* 54, *Islamic Law in the Modern World* 59, *Changing Law in Developing Countries* (Editor) 63, *Family Law in Asia and Africa* (Editor) 68, *Into the World: The need and limits of Christian involvement* 68, *Christianity: the Witness of History* 69, *Christianity and Comparative Religion* 70, *Morality, Law and Grace* 72, *A Lawyer among the Theologians* 73; contributions on Islamic Law, etc., to various learned journals.

12 Constable Close, London, N.W.11, England.

Aneizi, Dr. Aly Noureddin; Libyan economist and diplomatist; b. 1904, Benghazi; ed. Secondary Agricultural School of Percia (Tuscany, Italy), Agronomical Inst. of Florence, Univ. of Naples, Oriental Inst. of Naples and Inst. de Grenoble, Naples.

Secretary, Cyrenaica Govt. 33-35; Dir. "Auqat", Benghazi Prov. 35-41; Conucillor, Benghazi Prov. 37-41; fled to Egypt to join nat. movt. for independence of Libya 41-44; Sec. Arab League, Cairo 45-51; mem. Libya House of Reps. 52-55, Vice-Pres.; Finance Minister 53-55; Founder and First Gov. Central Bank of Libya 55-61; Amb. to Lebanon and Jordan 61-62; Petroleum Minister 63-64; Chair. Sahara Bank 64-70, Libya Insurance Co. 64-71, Nat. Navigation Co. May 64-; Pres. Intellectual Soc. of Libya 65-, Libyan Olympic Cttee. 67-69; Highest Libya Independence Decoration 54; High Lebanon and Jordan Decoration 62.

P.O. Box 3760, Tripoli; 2 Kairawan Street, Tripoli, Libya.

Ansari, Homayoun J., M.S.; Iranian civil servant; b. 20 Dec. 1929, Esfahan; ed. in Iran and U.S.A.

Senior Exploration Geologist, Nat, Iranian Oil Co. 56-59, Head of Studies and Co-ordination, Exploration and Production Dept. 59-62; Dir.-Gen. Petroleum Affairs, Ministry of Finance 62-64; Chair. and Man. Dir. Telephone Co. of Iran 64-71; Chair. and Man. Dir. Telecommunication Co. of Iran 71-74; Minister of Housing and Urban Devt. April 74-.

Publs. several scientific papers on petroleum exploration.

122 Sheibani Street, Darrus, Teheran, Iran.

Telephone: 771017.

Ansari, Dr. Hooshang, M.A.; Iranian politician; b. 1928; ed. England, U.S.A. and Japan.

Successively Special Reporter of Int. News Service and Int. News Photos; Press Attaché of Publication and Propaganda Dept. in Japan; Commercial Attaché in Japan, Econ. Attaché, Tokyo; Chief, Supervisory Comm. of Public Supplies, mem. High Council on Iranian Aviation; Technical Under-Sec., Ministry of Commerce; Special Ambassador in African countries; Abm. to Pakistan and Ceylon

65-66; Minister of Information 66-67; Amb. to U.S.A. 67-69; Minister of Economy 69-, concurrently of Finance 74-.
Ministry of Economy, Maidan Ark, Teheran, Iran.

Arafat, Yasser (*pseudonym* of Mohammed Abed Ar'ouf Arafat); Palestinian resistance leader; b. 1929, Jerusalem; ed. Cairo Univ.
Joined League of Palestinian Students 44, mem. Exec. Cttee. 50, Pres. 52-56; formed, with others, Al Fatah movt. 56; engineer in Egypt 56, Kuwait 57-65; Pres. Exec. Cttee. of Palestine Nat. Liberation Movement (Al Fatah) June 68-, Pres. Cen. Cttee., Head Political Dept. 73-; also Chair. Palestinian Nat. Council; Gen. Commdr. Palestinian Revolutionary Forces; addressed UN Gen. Assembly Nov. 74.
Palestine Liberation Organization, Colombani Street, Off Sadat Street, Dr. R. Nasr Building, Ras Beirut, Lebanon.

Araslan, Uajid: (*see* Arslane, Amir Majuid Toufik).

Aram, Abbas; Iranian diplomatist; b. 1906; ed. Teheran and Europe.
Entered diplomatic service 31; Asst. Chief, Third Political Div., Foreign Ministry 43; First Sec. Berne 45; First Sec., Counsellor, and Chargé d'Affaires, Washingotn 46, 49 and 50; Dir. Fourth Political Div., Foreign Ministry 51; Counsellor, Embassy, Baghdad 53; Chargé d'Affaires and Minister, Washington 53 and 54-56; Dir.-Gen. Political Affairs, Foreign Ministry 58; Ambassador to Japan 58, concurrently to Republic of China; Minister of Foreign Affairs 59-60; Ambassador to Iraq 60-62; Minister of Foreign Affairs 62-67; Ambassador to U.K. 67-69, to People's Repub. of China 72-75, also accred. to Dem. Repub. of Viet-Nam and Dem. People's Repub. of Korea.
Ministry of Foreign Affairs, Teheran, Iran.

Aref, Lt.-Gen. Abdul-Rahman Mohammed (brother of late Pres. Abdul Salam Aref); Iraqi army officer and politician; b. 1916; ed. Baghdad Military Acad.
Joined Army 36; took part in July 58 Revolution, Chief of Gen. Staff Armoured Corps Dept. 58-61; Commdr. 5th Div. Feb. 63-Nov. 63; assisted in overthrow of Gen. Kaasem 63; mem. Regency Council 65; Asst. Chief of Staff Iraqi Armed Forces Dec. 63-64; Acting Chief of Staff 64, Chief of Staff 64-68; Pres. of Iraq April 66-68; also Prime Minister 67.

Argod, Hubert Aymard, DIPL. SC. POL.; French diplomatist; b. 28 Aug. 1914, Bourg-de-Péage; ed. Ecole des Roches, Ecole Libre des Sciences Politiques.
With diplomatic service 41-; with French provisional govt. Algiers 43; First Sec. Del. to UN 46; First Sec. Beirut 47-50; at High Comm. in Germany 51; Dept. of European Affairs, Ministry of Foreign Affairs 57; Head, Levant Desk 58-61; Amb. to Chad 61; Minister Counsellor, Algiers 63, Deputy High Rep. 63; Amb. to Cambodia 64-68, to Senegal and the Gambia 69-73, to Lebanon 75-; Officier, Légion d'Honneur, Croix de Guerre.
French Embassy, rue Clémenceau, Beirut, Lebanon; Home: 2 boulevard des Sablons, 92.200 Neuilly, France.

Arian, Abdullah al-, LL.B., PH.D.; Egyptian diplomatist and lawyer; b. 21 March 1920, Damanhur; ed. Cairo, Harvard and Columbia (N.Y.) Univs.
Assistant District Attorney, Boheirah Provence 42-43; Lecturer in Law, Cairo Univ. 43-45, Asst. Prof. of Int. Law and Int. Org., Inst. of Public Admin., Cairo 59-61; Prof. of Int. Law, Div. of Legal Studies, Inst. of Arab Higher Studies, Cairo 59-; Counsellor, Office of Pres. of Egypt 55-56; Counsellor and Legal Adviser, Perm. Mission at UN 57-59; Dir. Dept. of Legal Affairs and Treaties, Ministry of Foreign Affairs 59-68; Amb. and Deputy Perm. Rep. to UN 68-71; Amb. to France 71-74;

Perm. Rep. to UN Office, Geneva 74-; mem. Int. Law Comm. 57-58, 61-65, 66-; del. to numerous UN and OAU confs. and several sessions in UN Gen. Assembly.
Publs. several books and articles on questions of international law and the UN.
Mission Permanente d'Egypte auprès des Nations Unies, 72 rue de Lausanne, Geneva, Switzerland.

Ariburun, Gen. Tekin; Turkish politician; b. 1905, Istip, Yugoslavia; ed. Kulei and Konya Mil. Schools, Harbiye (Mil.) Coll. and War Acad.
Staff Officer in Turkish Air Force; served as first Turkish Air Attaché in Germany, U.S.A.; promoted to rank of Brig.-Gen. 50, Gen. 59; Commdr. Turkish Air Force 59-60, retd.; Senator for Istanbul 64-; Speaker of Senate 70-; Candidate for Presidency 73; Justice Party.
The Senate, Ankara, Turkey.

Arkell, Rev. Anthony John, M.B.E., M.C., D.LITT., F.S.A.; British archaeologist; b. 29 July 1898; ed. Bradfield and Queen's Coll., Oxford.
2nd-Lieut. Royal Flying Corps 16; Flying Off. Royal Air Force 18; Sudan Political Service 20-38; Chief Transport Officer Sudan Govt. 40-44; Commr. for Archaeology and Anthropology, Sudan Govt. 38-48; Chair. and Editorial Sec. *Sudan Notes and Records* 46-48; Lecturer in Egyptology, Univ. Coll. London 48-53; Reader in Egyptian Archaeology, Univ. of London 53-63; Archaeological Adviser to Sudan Govt. 48-54; mem. German Archaeological Inst. 53-; British Ennedi Expedition 57.
Publs. *Early Khartoum* 49, *The Old Stone Age in the Anglo-Egyptian Sudan* 49, *Shaheinab* 53, *History of the Sudan* 55, (2nd edn.) 61, *Wanyanaga* 64.
Cuddington, Colam Lane, Little Baddow, Chelmsford, Essex, England.

Armouti, Mohamed Nazzal; Jordanian diplomatist; b. 12 Aug. 1924; ed. Amman Secondary School, Salt Secondary School, Univ. of Damascus, and Exeter Univ., England.
Former Sec.-Gen. Ministry of Interior, Houses of Notables and House of Reps.; fmr. Insp.-Gen. Income Tax Dept.; Legal Adviser to Ministry of Finance; Gov. of Irbid, Ma'an, Salt, Hebron, Nablus, Kerak and Amman Districts respectively 55-61; Under-Sec. Ministry of Interior 61-64, Minister of Interior 64-65; Ambassador to Tunisia, Algeria and Libya 65, to Kuwait 67-70; Chair. Nat. Econ. Devt. Co.; decorations from Jordan, Syria, Silver Knights Org. (Papal), and Holy Sepulchre.
c/o National Economic Development Co., P.O. Box 357, Amman, Jordan.

Arslane, Amir Majuid Toufik; Lebanese politician; b. 1905; ed. Beirut.
Minister of Defence 43, 60-64, 69-70, May 72-73; fmr. Minister of Agriculture; Minister of State 73-74; Minister of Agriculture, Housing and Health May 75-; Grand Cordon of the Libyan Order of Independence and several foreign decorations.
Ministry of Agriculture, Beirut, Lebanon.

Asfia, Safi; Iranian mining engineer and politician; b. 1916; ed. Polytechnic Inst., Ecole des Mines, Paris.
Professor of Economic Geology, Teheran Univ. 39-62; Deputy Dir. Plan Org. 54-61, Man. Dir. 61-68; Deputy Prime Minister 68-74; Minister of State for Econ. and Devt. 68-70; Minister of State 74-.
Office of the Minister of State, Teheran, Iran.

Asha, Rafik el, M.B.A.; Syrian diplomatist; b. 1910; Damascus; ed. American Univ. of Beirut and New York City Univ.
Former bank official and finance analyst; Prof. of Banking Econs. and Accounting, Baghdad 32-41; joined Syrian Civil Service 41 and served as Deputy Dir.-Gen. of Supplies, Ministry of Supplies, Damascus; Chargé d'Affaires, Cairo

44-45; Acting Consul-Gen., N.Y. 45-47, Consul-Gen. 47-52; First Counsellor, Syrian Embassy, Washington 52, Minister Plenipotentiary June 52, Chargé d'Affaires a.i. Aug. 52; Alternate Gov. Int. Bank for Reconstruction and Devt. 52-55; del. to UN Gen. Assembly 46-60; alternate rep. Security Council 47-48, Acting Perm. Del. 48-51, Chargé d'Affaires, Perm. Del. to UN 53-58; Pres. Trusteeship Council 56-57; Pres. Arab League Council 59; U.A.R. Dep. Perm. Rep. to UN 59-61; Ambassador to Romania 61, to U.S.S.R. 61-62; Sec.-Gen. Ministry of Foreign Affairs 62-64; Syrian Perm. Rep. to UN July 64-65; Senior Financial Adviser to Admin. of UNDP 68-.
c/o UNDP, P.O. Box 2317, Damascus, Syria.

Ashiotis, Costas, M.B.E.; Cypriot diplomatist; b. 1908; ed. Pancyprian Gymnasium, Nicosia, and London School of Economics.
Former journalist and editor; Govt. Service 42-; Asst. Commr. of Labour 48; Dir.-Gen. Ministry of Foreign Affairs 60; mem. Cypriot Dels. to UN and Int. Confs.; High Commr. in U.K. 66-; Hon. M.B.E.
Publ. *Labour Conditions in Cyprus During the War Years 1939-45.*
Cyprus High Commission, 93 Park Street, London, W1Y 4ET England.

Ashraf Ahmadi, Ali, LL.B.; Iranian judge and politician; b. 1910, Behbahan; ed. High School, Shiraz and Univ. of Teheran.
Chief Magistrate Province of Teheran 47-49; Chief Justice Province of Khoozistan 50; Chief Criminal Court, Teheran 51; Chief Justice, Province of Isfahan 53; Gov. Isfahan 53-55; Judge, Supreme Court 55; Deputy Prime Minister 56-60; Sec. Royal Council 56-61; Minister of State 60-61; Deputy Dir. Pahlavi Foundation 62; Chief 12th Branch Supreme Court 63; Senator 64-; Scientific Order, 1st Class, Taj, 2nd Class, Homayoun, 1st Class.
Publs. *Laws and Justice in Ancient Imperial Iran* 60, *Five Years in the Service of His Majesty the Shahanshah* (2 vols.), *Ten Years' Work and Endeavour, 12 Years of Efforts for Reconstruction of New Iran, Iran in the Past and Present.*
176 Television Avenue, Abbas Abad, Teheran, Iran.

Ashtal, Abdalla Saleh, M.A.; Yemeni diplomatist; b. 5 Oct. 1940; ed. Menelik II Secondary School, Addis Ababa, Ethiopia, American Univ. of Beirut, Lebanon, New York Univ.
Assistant Dir. of Sana'a Branch, Yemeni Bank for Reconstruction and Devt. 66-67; mem. Supreme People's Council, 5th Province 67-68; Editor *Ash-arava* (weekly) 67-68; mem. Exec. Cttee. of Gen. Command, Nat. Liberation Front 68-72; Political Adviser, Perm. Mission to UN 70, Senior Counsellor 72-73, Perm. Rep. May 73-; concurrently non-resident Amb. to Canada Oct. 74-.
Permanent Mission of People's Democratic Republic of Yemen to the United Nations, 211 East 43rd Street, Room 903, New York, N.Y. 10017, U.S.A.

Âşiroğlu, Vahap, L. EN D.; Turkish diplomatist; b. 14 Aug. 1916, Karamursel; ed. Galatasaray Lycée, Istanbul and Faculty of Law, Univ. of Istanbul.
Entered diplomatic service 43; served in Czechoslovakia, Turkish Ministry of Foreign Affairs and Perm. Mission of Turkey at UN 46; Head of Chancery of Turkish Mission to UN 53-59; Minister and Deputy Perm. Rep. to UN 62-65; Amb. to Denmark 65-68, to Indonesia 68-71; Sec.-Gen. Regional Co-operation for Devt. (RCD) 71-74; mem. UN Comm. on Human Rights 53-56; Leader, Turkish del. to ICAO Assembly 56; Chair. del., GATT Ministerial meeting, Tokyo 59; Chair. UN Conciliation Comm. for Palestine 62-65.
c/o Ministry of Foreign Affairs, Ankara, Turkey.

Asnag, Abdallah Al-Majid al-; Yemeni trade union official and politician; b. 1933.
Senior Reservation Officer, Aden Airways 51-62; leader, People's Socialist Party, Gen. Sec. Aden Trade Union Congress until Dec. 62, 63-65; imprisoned Dec. 62-Dec. 63; Head of Political Bureau, Front for Liberation of Occupied South Yemen (FLOSY); in Yemen Arab Republic since 65; Minister of Foreign Affairs Aug.-Sept. 71, of the Economy 71-74, of Foreign Affairs March-June 74, Jan. 75-; Deputy Premier for Communications June 74- Jan.75.
Ministry of Foreign Affairs, Sana'a, Yemen Arab Republic.

Assaad, Kamel el, L. EN D.; Lebanese politician; b. 1929; ed. Law Faculty, Beirut and Univ. de Paris.
Practising lawyer; Deputy 53-; Mayor of Marjéyoun; Minister of Education 61-64; Pres. Chamber of Deputies 64-65, Speaker 72-; Minister of Water Resources and Health 66.
Hazmieh, Imm. Haddad, Beirut, Lebanon.

Assad, Lt.-Gen. Hafiz al-; Syrian army officer and politician; b. 1928.
Minister of Defence and Commdr. of Air Force Feb. 66-Nov. 70; Prime Minister Nov. 70-April 71; Sec. Baath Party Nov. 70-; Pres. of Syria March 71-; mem. Pres. Council, Fed. of Arab Repubs. 71-; Pres. Syrian Nat. Progressive Front 72-; Commdr. in Chief of Armed Forces 73-.
Office of the President, Damascus, Syria.

Assar, Nasser; Iranian painter; b. 26 Sept. 1928, Teheran; ed. Univ. of Teheran and Ecole des Beaux-Arts, Paris.
Came to Paris 53-; one-man exhbns.: Galerie Prisme, Paris 55, Galerie Bellechasse, Paris 60, Lincoln Gallery, London 61, Galerie Smith, Brussels 62, 64, Galerie H. Le Gendre, Paris 63, Galerie l'Oeil Ecoute, Lyon 65, Upper Grosvenor Galleries, London 66, "Hepta" Musée Galliéra, Paris 67, Athens Gallery, Athens 68, Galérie du Triangle, Paris 72, Galérie de Bellechasse, Paris 75; paintings in numerous group exhbns. in France, Brussels, Seattle, U.S.A. and Iran; exhibited at Biennials of Paris 61, 63 and San Marino 65; paints mainly landscapes.
65 rue La Fontaine, Paris 16e, France.

Assar, Nassir; Iranian diplomatist; b. 1926; ed. Univ. of Teheran.
Ministry of Foreign Affairs 45-; Vice-Consul, Stuttgart 49, Hamburg 53; Deputy Dir. Dept. of Int. Org., Ministry of Foreign Affairs 53-55; First Sec. Iranian Embassy to Turkey 56, Counsellor 61; First Sec. Iranian Mission to UN 58, Counsellor 59; Deputy Dir. of Econ. Affairs, Ministry of Foreign Affairs 60; Deputy Prime Minister, Head of Iranian Public Trust and Endowments 64; Sec.-Gen. Central Treaty Org. (CENTO) 72-74.
c/o CENTO, Eski Büyük Millet Meclisi Binasi, Ankara, Turkey.

Atalla, Anton Abden-Nur; Jordanian lawyer, banker and politician; b. 18 Oct. 1897; ed. American Univ. of Beirut and Law School, Jerusalem.
Crown Counsel 24-27, Magistrate 28-31; Senior Magistrate 32-37, Judge of District Court, Palestine 37-43; Senior Partner A. & H. Atalla and Co., Advocates, Jerusalem 43-48; Regional Gen. Manager, Arab Land Bank, Jordan 48-73, Consultant 74-; mem. Jordan House of Reps.; Chair. House Finance Cttee 54-56; Minister of Foreign Affairs 63-64, June-Oct. 70; mem. Senate 63-74; mem. Bureau of Interpretation of Constitution 74-, Legal Cttee., Foreign Relations Cttee., Senate 74-; Gov. Rotary Int. District, East Mediterranean 66-67; Jordanian Renaissance and Star, First Degree; several foreign decorations.
Arab Land Bank, P.O. Box 6425, Amman, Jordan.

Atassi, Nureddin, M.D.; Syrian politician; b. 1929; ed. Damascus Univ.
Minister of the Interior Aug. 63; Deputy Prime Minister Oct. 64; mem. Syrian Presidential Council May 64-Dec. 65; Pres. of Syria 66-70, also Prime Minister 68-70; Sec.-Gen. Syrian Baath Party 66-Oct. 70; in exile in Libya.

Ateeqy, Abdulreham Salim al-; Kuwaiti diplomatist and politician; b. 5 April 1928; ed. High School, Kuwait.
Secretary-General, Police Dept., Kuwait 49-59; Dir.-Gen. Health Dept. 59-61; Del. to UN 60-61, to WHO, Geneva 61, to UN Gen. Assembly 61; Amb. to U.S.A. 62-63; Under-Sec. Ministry of Foreign Affairs 63-67; Minister of Finance 67-, and Oil Affairs 67-75; Chair. Kuwait Fund for Arab Econ. Devt.
Ministry of Finance, P.O. Box Safat 9, Kuwait.

Atiya, Aziz Suryal, M.A., PH.D., LITT.D., F.R.HIST.S.; Egyptian historian and writer; b. 7 July 1898; ed. Univs. of Liverpool and London.
Charles Beard Fellow and Univ. Fellow, Univ. of Liverpool 30-32; History Tutor, School of Oriental Studies, Univ. of London 33-34; Prof. of Medieval and Oriental History, Univ. of Bonn 35-38; Prof. of Medieval History, Cairo 38-42, Alexandria 42-54; President Higher Institute of Coptic Studies, Cairo; consultant to Library of Congress, Washington, D.C. 50-51; visiting lecturer U.S. Univs., Univ. of Zurich and Swiss Inst. of Int. Affairs 50-51; Medieval Acad. Visiting Prof. of Islamic Studies, Univ. of Michigan, Ann Arbor 55-56; Luce Prof. of World Christianity, Union Theological Seminary, and Visiting Prof. of History, Columbia Univ., New York 56-57; Visiting Prof. of Arabic and Islamic History, Princeton Univ. 57-58; mem. Inst. for Advanced Study, Princeton 58-59; Dir. Middle East Center, Utah Univ. 59-67; Distinguished Prof. of History, Utah 67-; corresp. mem. UNESCO Int. Comm. for the Scientific and Cultural History of Mankind; corresp. mem. Coptic Archaeological Soc.; mem. Medieval Acad. of America, Mediterranean Acad., Rome; Hon. D.H.L.
Publs. *The Crusade of Nicopolis* 34, *The Crusade in the Later Middle Ages* 38, *Egypt and Aragon—Embassies and Diplomatic Correspondence between 1300 and 1330* 38, *Ki-ab Qawanin al-Dawawin by Saladin's Wazir ibn Mammati* 43, *History of the Patriarchs of the Holy Church of Alexandria* 48, *Monastery of St. Catherine in Mt. Sinai* 49, *The Mt. Sinai Arabic Microfilms* 54, *Coptic Music* 60, *Crusade, Commerce and Culture* 62, *The Crusades—Historiography and Bibliography* 62, *History of Eastern Christianity* 68, etc. (all books in either English of Arabic).
1335 Perry Avenue, Salt Lake City, Utah, U.S.A.

Attar, Mohammed Said al-; Yemeni diplomatist; b. 26 Nov. 1927; ed. Ecole Pratique des Hautes Etudes à la Sorbonne, Inst. d'Etudes du Développement Econ. et Social (I.E.D.E.S.), Univ. de Paris.
Research I.E.D.E.S. 60-62; Dir.-Gen. Yemen Bank for Reconstruction and Devt. 62-65, Pres. 68-71; Minister of Econ. March-Aug. 65, 67-68; Pres. Econ. Comm. Oct. 65-Feb. 66; Pres. of Econ. High Comm. 66-68; Minister of Foreign Affairs Nov. 67-69; Vice-Pres. High Cttee. for Planning; mem. Int. Asscn. of Sociology; Perm. Rep. to the UN 69-71, 73-74; Deputy Premier for Financial Affairs, Minister of the Economy Aug.-Sept. 71; Exec. Sec. UN Econ. Comm. for Western Asia (ECWA) 74-.
Publs. *L'Industrie du gant en France* 61, *L'épicerie à Paris* 61, *Etude sur la croissance économique de l'Afrique Occidentale* 62, *Le marché industriel et les projets de l'Arabie Séoudite* 62, *Le sous-développement économique et social du Yemen (Perspectives de la Révolution Yemenite)* 64, Arabic edn. 65.
Economic Commission for Western Asia (ECWA), B.P. 4656, Beirut, Lebanon.

Attiga, Ali Ahmed, B.SC., M.SC., PH.D.; Libyan economist; b. Oct. 1931, Misurata; ed. Univ. of Wisconsin and Univ. of California, U.S.A.
Assistant Economic Adviser, Nat. Bank of Libya 59-60, Dir. of Research 60-64; Under-Sec. Ministry of Planning and Devt. 64-66, Dir. Econ. Research Div. 66-68; Minister of Planning and Devt. 68-69, concurrently of the Economy

69; Sec.-Gen. Org. of Arab Petroleum Exporting Countries (OAPEC) Sept. 73-; Gen. Man. Libya Insurance Co. 70-, Chair. 73-; Chair. Nat. Investment Co. 71-73, Libya Hotel and Tourism Co. 71-; mem. Board of Dirs., Arab Reinsurance Co., Beirut.
Organization of Arab Petroleum Exporting Countries (OAPEC), P.O. Box 20501, Kuwait; and P.O. Box 3717, Tripoli, Libya.

Attiyia, Mahmoud Ibrahim, B.SC.; Egyptian geologist; b. 1900; ed. Cairo and Imperial Coll. of Science and Technology, London.
Assistant Lecturer, School of Engineering, Giza 23-25; Geologist, Geological Survey of Egypt 29, Asst. Dir. 39, Dir. 49; Dir.-Gen. Mines and Quarries Dept. 54-56; Tech. Dir. Mineral Wealth Co. and Sinai Manganese Co., Cairo 56-62; delegated Prof. of Geology, Cairo Univ.; A.R.C.S. London 29; F.G.S. London 30; mem. Inst. d'Egypte 46-; mem. of the Board, Desert Inst. of Egypt 50; mem. Egyptian Acad. of Sciences 50, Pres. 68-; mem. Conseil d'Administration de la Société de Géographie d'Egypte 51; State Prize in Geological and Chemical Sciences; Order of the Republic (Egypt).
Publs. *Notes on the Underground Water in Egypt* 42, *The Barramiya Mining District* 48, *New Mode of Occurrence of Iron-Ore Deposits* 49, *Iron-Ore Deposits of Egypt* 50, *Ground-Water in Egypt* 53, *Deposits in the Nile Valley and the Delta* 54, *Iron-Ore Deposits of the District East of Aswan* 55, *Manganese Deposits of Egypt* 56.
10 Diwan Street, Garden City, Cairo, Egypt.

Aulaqi, Sheikh Mohamed Farid al-; see Farid al-Aulaqi.

Avci, Sabit Osman; Turkish politician; b. 1921, Vesir, Artvin Prov.
Head of several depts. of Forestry Operational Management, Artvin; studied forestry related subjects in U.S.A. 53; Deputy for Artvin 61-; Minister of Rural Affairs 65, of Forestry 69, of Power and Natural Resources 69-70; Speaker of Nat. Assembly 70-73; Vice-Chair. Justice Party in Nat. Assembly 67; Justice Party.
National Assembly, Ankara, Turkey.

Avidom (Mahler-Kalkstein), Menahem, B.A.; Israeli composer; b. 6 Jan. 1908; ed. American Univ. Beirut, and in Paris.
Lecturer on theory of music, Hebrew Conservatoire of Music, Tel-Aviv 36-, and Music Teachers' Training Coll. Tel-Aviv 45-; Sec.-Gen. Israel Philharmonic Orchestra 46-; Vice-Pres. Board of Dirs. Acum Ltd. (Composers and Authors Asscn.), Dir.-Gen. 56-; Dir. Arts Dept. Jerusalem Convention Centre 52; Art Adviser, Govt. Tourist Centre, Ministry of Commerce and Industry 54-; Pres. League of Composers 58; mem. Nat. Arts Council 62; Israel State Prize 61, Tel Aviv Municipality Prize 48, 56; Israel Philharmonic Prize 53; Authors' and Composers' Asscn. Prize 62.
Compositions include: *A Folk Symphony* 47, *Symphony No. 2 David* 48, *Mediterranean Sinfonietta* 51, *2 Piano Sonatinas* 49, *Concertino* for violinist Jascha Heifetz, *Concertino* for cellist Gregor Piatigorsky 51, *Alexandra Hashmonaith* (opera in 3 acts) 52, *Jubilee Suite, Triptyque Symphonique, The Crook* (opera in 2 acts) 65, *B-A-C-H* Suite for chamber orchestra, *Sinfonietta* 66, *Twelve Changing Preludes* for piano 68, *Symphonie Variée* for chamber orchestra 69, *The Farewell* (opera in 1 act) 70, concerto for strings and flute, music for strings, symphonies 3, 4, 5, 6 and 7, psalms and cantatas, septet for woodwind, piano and percussion, string quartet No. 2, quartet for brass instruments, *The Pearl and The Coral* (ballet) 72, *Spring* overture for symphony orchestra 73, *Six Inventions for Piano in Homage and on the name of Arthur Rubinstein* 73, *Passacaglia for Piano* 73, *Yemenite Wedding Suite* 74, *Piece on the name of SCHoEnBerG for Piano* 74.
30 Semadar Street, Ramat-Gan, Israel.

Avni, Tzvi; Israeli composer; b. 2 Sept. 1927, Germany.
Arrived in Israel as a child; studied with Abel Ehrlich, Paul Ben-Haim and Mordecai Seter, Tel-Aviv Acad. of Music, with Aaron Copland and Lukas Foss at Tanglewood, Mass., and electronic music at Columbia Univ.
Compositions include: *Songs for Soprano and Orchestra* 57, *Woodwind Quintet* 59, *Prayer* for string orchestra 61, *Summer Strings* for string quartet 62, *Chaconne for Harp* 62, *Capriccio* for orchestra 63, *Vocalise* (electronic music) 64, *Two Pieces for Four Clarinets* 65, *Meditations on a Drama* for chamber orchestra 66 (ACUM Prize), *Collage* for Mezzo Soprano, Fl., Perc. and electronic tape 67, *Yerushalayim Shel Ma'ala* for mixed choir and orchestra 68, *Churban Habayit* for mixed choir and orchestra 68, *Five Pantomimes* for eight players 68, *Akeda* for chamber groups and narrator 69, *String Quartet No.* 2 (Liberson Prize 69), *Requiem for Sounds* (ballet music), *Ein Der* (ballet music) 70, *Holiday Metaphors* for symphony orchestra 70 (Engel Prize 73), *All the King's Women* (ballet music) 71, *By the Waters of Babylon* (prelude for small orchestra) 71.
Office: Amli Central Music Library in Israel, 26 Bialik Street, Tel-Aviv; Home: 7 Zangwill Street, Tel-Aviv, Israel.

Avriel, Ehud; Israeli diplomatist; b. 19 Oct. 1917; ed. High School Vienna.
Israeli Minister to Czechoslovakia 48, concurrently to Hungary 49; Minister to Romania 50; Dir.-Gen. Prime Minister's Office, Jerusalem 51-57; Ambassador to Ghana and to Liberia 57-60; Ambassador to Congo 60-61; Dep. Dir.-Gen. Ministry of Foreign Affairs 61-65; Ambassador to Italy Feb. 66-68, concurrently accred. to Malta May 66-68; elected Chair. World Zionist Action Cttee., Jerusalem 69-; Diplomatic Adviser and Amb. Extraordinary, Ministry of Foreign Affairs 72; Consul General to Chicago and Midwest 75-; mem. Knesset 55.
Ministry of Foreign Affairs, Jerusalem; and Neoth 111 East Wacker Drive, Chicago, Ill. 60601, U.S.A.

Awad, Muhammad Hadi; Yemeni diplomatist; b. 5 May 1934; ed. Murray House Coll. of Educ.
Teacher 53-59; Educ. Officer 60-62; Chief Insp. of Schools 63-65; Vice-Principal As-Shaab Coll. 65-67; Perm. Rep. to Arab League 68-70, concurrently Amb. to U.A.R., also accred. to Sudan, Lebanon, Libya and Iraq; Perm. Sec. Ministry of Foreign Affairs 70-73; Amb. to U.K. 73-, concurrently non-resident Amb. to Spain and Sweden 74-, to Denmark 75-.
Embassy of the People's Democratic Republic of Yemen, 57 Cromwell Road, London, S.W.7, England.

Awadallah, Babikir; Sudanese jurist; b. 1917; ed. School of Law, Gordon Coll., Khartoum.
District Judge, El Obeid; resigned to become Speaker of Sudanese House of Representatives 54-57; Judge of the Supreme Court 57, Chief Justice Oct. 64-May 67; Prime Minister and Minister of Foreign Affairs May-Oct. 69; Minister of Foreign Affairs 69-70, of Justice 69-71; First Vice-Pres. of Sudan Oct. 71-May 72.
c/o Sudanese Socialist Union, Khartoum, Sudan.

Ayari, Chedly, L. EN D.; Tunisian economist and politician; b. 24 Aug. 1933.
Head of Admin., Tunisian Banking Soc. 58-59; Asst. Faculty of Law and Political and Econ. Sciences, Univ. of Tunis 59-60, Dean 65-67; Econ. Adviser, Perm. Mission to UN 60-64; Exec. Dir. Int. Bank for Reconstruction and Devt. (IBRD), Int. Devt. Asscn. (IDA), Int. Finance Corpn. (IFC) 64-65; Dir. CERES (Centre d'Etudes et de Recherches Economiques et Sociales) 67-69; Sec. of State in charge of the Nat. Plan 69-70; Minister of Educ., Youth

and Sport 70-71; Amb. to Belgium and Luxembourg Feb.-March 72; Minister of the Nat. Economy March 72-74, of Planning 74; Chair. Arab Bank for Devt. of Africa 75-. Pres. UN Industrial Cttee. 62; del. to UN Confs. on Commerce and Devt. 62, 64; Grand Cordon, Order of the Repub.
Publs. Numerous articles in economic journals.
Arab Bank for the Development of Africa, Khartoum, Sudan; and Gammarth, La Mousa, Tunis, Tunisia.

Ayyoubi, Mahmoud; Syrian politician; b. 1932.
Former Dir.-Gen. for Admin. Affairs, Euphrates Dept.; Minister of Educ. 69-71, and Deputy Prime Minister 70-71; Vice-Pres. of Syria April 71-; Prime Minister Dec. 72-.
Office of the Vice-President, Damascus, Syria.

Azimi, Gen. Reza; Iranian army officer and politician; b. 1913; ed. Mil. Acad., Teheran.
Joined Imperial Army 29; Commdr. Armoured Corps, Chief of Army Staff Dept., Commdr. Central Army No. 1, Deputy Commdr. Ground Forces, Commdr. Western Army, Officer Commdg. Ground Forces 60-66, Adjutant-Gen. to Shahanshah; Minister of Defence 71-; various army decorations.
Ministry of Defence, Teheran, Iran.

Azkoul, Karim, PH.D.; Lebanese former diplomatist; b. 15 July 1915; ed. Jesuit Univ. of St. Joseph, Beirut, and Univs. of Paris, Berlin, Bonn and Munich.
Professor of History, Arab and French literature, and Philosophy in various colls. in Lebanon 39-46; Dir. of an Arabic publishing house and of a monthly Arabic review, *The Arab World,* in Beirut 43-45; mem. of the Lebanese del. to UN 47-50; Acting Perm. Del. to UN 50-53; Head of UN Affairs Dept., Ministry for Foreign Affairs 53-57; Head of Perm. Del. to UN 57-59; Consul-General in Australia and N.Z. 59-61; Amb. to Ghana, Guinea and Mali 61-64, to Iran and Afghanistan 64-66; Prof. of Philosophy, Beirut Coll. for Women 68-72, Lebanese Univ. 70-72; mem. Emergency World Council, Hague 71-, PEN; mem. Board of Trustees, Board of Man., Theological School of Balamand, Lebanon; Order of Cedar (Lebanon), Order of Holy Sepulchre (Jerusalem), Order of St. Marc (Alexandria), Order of the Brilliant Star (Republic of China), Order of Southern Star (Brazil), Order of St. Peter and Paul (Damascus).
Publs. *Reason and Faith in Islam* (in German) 38, and a similar work in Arabic 46, *A Study on Freedom of Association* (French, English, Russian, Spanish) 68; transl. *Consciencism* (Nkrumah) 64; *Arabic Thought in the Liberal Age* (Albert Hourani). 69.
Union Building, Spears Street, Al-Sanayeh, Beirut, Lebanon.

Azzawi, Hikmat al-, B.A.COMM.; Iraqi politician; b. 1934, Diyalah; ed. Coll. of Commerce, Baghdad Univ.
Reserve Lieutenant 57-58; Supt. Cen. Bank of Iraq 58-63, First Supt. 63; Auditor, Dir. of Stores and Warehouses, Dir. of Marketing, State Co. for Electrical Instruments and Equipment 66-68; Dir.-Gen., Chair. Govt. Purchasing Board 68; Chair. General Trade Establishment 69; Under-Sec. Ministry of Econ. 69; mem. Board of Dirs. Cen. Bank of Iraq 69; Minister of Econ. 72-; Chief Ed. *Al-Iktisad* (Economist) magazine, Baghdad.
Ministry of the Economy, Baghdad, Iraq.

B

Babikian, Khatchik Diran; Lebanese lawyer and politician; b. 1924, Cyprus; ed. College Italien Beirut, Faculté Française de Droit Beirut, Faculté de Paris, Univ. of London.
Barrister; Deputy for Beirut 57, 60, 64, 68, 72; mem. Parl. Comm. on Justice; Pres. Traffic Comm., Parl. Comm.

on Planning, Lebanese Management Asscn. 72; Minister for Admin. Reform 60-61; Minister of Public Health 68-69; Minister of Tourism 69-70, of Information 72-73, of Planning 73; Pres. Armenian Nat. Assembly 72.
Rue Abrine, Achrafié, Beirut, Lebanon.

Bachi, Roberto; Israeli statistician; b. 16 Jan. 1909; ed. Univ. degli Studi, Rome.
Professor of Statistics in Italian universities including Palermo 36, Genoa 37; Prof. of Statistics and Demography, Hebrew Univ. of Jerusalem 45-, Head of Dept. of Statistics 47-60, Dean Faculty of Social Sciences 53-54, Pro-Rector 59-60; planned Central Bureau of Statistics, State of Israel; Govt. Statistician and Scientific Dir. Central Bureau of Statistics 48-71; Fellow, American Statistical Soc., Israel Acad. of Sciences and Humanities; mem. Int. Statistical Inst. and of many int. and nat. learned socs.; Szold Prize 67, Bublick Prize (Hebrew Univ.) 72.
Publs. *Mobility of Population in the Large European Towns* (Italian) 32, then about 160 papers and books in English, Italian, Hebrew, French and Spanish on statistical method, demography, health, social and geographical statistics; *Graphical Rational Patterns: a New Approach to Graphical Presentation of Statistics* 68.
Chovevey Zion Street, 19 Jerusalem, Israel.

Badeau, John Stothoff, B.SC., S.T.M., D.D., LL.D.; American educationalist; b. 24 Feb. 1903; ed. Union, Rutgers and Colombia Univs. and Union Theological Seminary.
Prof. of Philosophy, and Dean Faculty of Arts and Sciences, American Univ. at Cairo 36; Regional Chief, Middle East, O.W.I. 43; Pres. American Univ. at Cairo 45-53; Pres. Near East Foundation 53-61; Ambassador to United Arab Republic 61-64; Dir. Middle East Inst., Columbia Univ., New York City 64-67, Emer. Prof. 71-; Lecturer, School of Foreign Service, Georgetown Univ.; Special Consultant, Dept. of Health, Education and Welfare; Trustee, American Univ. of Cairo, Union Theological Seminary, Near East Foundation, and Middle East Inst., Washington, D.C., American Research Centre in Egypt.
Publs. *East and West of Suez* 43, *Emergence of Modern Egypt* 53, *The Lands Between* 57, *The American Approach to the Arab World* 68.
Middle East Institute, Columbia University, New York, N.Y., U.S.A.

Bahar, Abdul Aziz al-, B.A.; Kuwaiti businessman; b. 1929; ed. American Univ., Beirut.
Executive, Ministry of Public Works; Dir.-Gen. of Housing Dept. 55-60; Dir.-Gen. Kuwait Fund for Arab Econ. Devt. 61-62; Chair. Commercial Bank of Kuwait, S.A.K. 62-; Chair. Kuwait Nat. Industries 63-65; Dir. Rifbank, Beirut 67; Dir. United Bank of Kuwait 66-; Chair. Kuwait Foreign Trading, Contracting and Investment Co. 65-74; Acting Chair. Commercial Bank of Dubai 69-; Dir. Kuwait Chamber of Commerce 64-; Hon. Consul of Costa Rica.
P.O. Box 460, Kuwait City, Kuwait.

Bahnini, Hadj M'Hammed, L. EN D., L. ÈS L.; Moroccan politician; b. 1914, Fez; ed. Lycée Gouraud (now "Lycée Hassan II"), Rabat.
Sec. Royal Palace; Magistrate, Haut Tribunal Chérifien; Instructor, College Impérial and Private Tutor to H.R.H. Crown Prince Moulay El Hassan, Prince Moulay Abdallah, Princess Lalla Aïcha and Princess Lalla Malika; Dir. of the Imperial Cabinet 50-61; Del. Judge, Meknés 51; Exiled Dec. 52-July 54; Sec.-Gen. of the Cabinet 55-; Minister of Justice 58-60; Minister of Admin. Affairs 65-70; Minister of Nat. Defence 70-71; Minister of Justice 71; Vice-Premier and Minister of Justice April-Nov. 72; Minister of State for Culture April 74-.
Office of the Minister of State, Ministry of Culture, Rabat, Morocco.

Bakdash, Khalid; Syrian politician; b. 1912; ed. Damascus Inst. of Law.

Member of Parl. 54-58; Sec.-Gen. Syrian Communist Party; self-imposed exile in East Europe 58-66; returned to Syria April 66; mem. Cen. Cttee., Syrian Nat. Progressive Front 72-.
Ave. Akrad, Damascus, Syria.

Bakir, Anwar, D. en D.; Egyptian postal executive; b. 24 Nov. 1914; ed. Univs. of Cairo and Paris.
Former Dir. of Int. Services, Egyptian Postal Service; fmr. Dir. of Posts of Egypt, now mem. Admin. Council; mem. Board of Dirs., Egyptian Postal Org.; Sec.-Gen. Arab Postal Union; del. to numerous confs. of APU and int. postal confs.
General Secretariat, Arab Postal Union, 28 rue Adly, Cairo, Egypt.

Bakr, Field Marshal Ahmed Hassan al-; Iraqi army officer and politician; b. 1914; ed. Military Academy.
Army career 36-58; Commdr. First Infantry Brigade 57; Forced to retire from Iraq Army 58; Prime Minister of Iraq Feb. 63 and Nov. 63; Vice-Pres. of Iraq Nov. 63-Jan. 64; Amb. Jan.-Sept. 64; Pres., Prime Minister and C.-in-C. of Armed Forces July 68-, Minister of Defence 73-; promoted to rank of Field Marshal 69.
Office of the President, Baghdad, Iraq.

Bakri-Wahab, Laman, B.A.; Iraqi cultural official; b. 8 Jan. 1929; ed. Fine Arts Inst., Baghdad and Baghdad Univ.
Law practice 54-55; Social Asst. for girl students, Baghdad Univ. 55-59; Editor-in-Chief *New Iraq Magazine* 60-61; Supt. Press Dept., Ministry of Culture and Guidance 63-64; Man. Iraqi Nat. Symphony Orchestra 64-66; Dir. Nat. Museum of Modern Art 67; Dir. of Arts 69-73; Dir. Cultural Affairs, Foundation for Technical Institutes, Ministry of Higher Educ. 73-.
44/2/55 Sulikh, Ahdamia, Baghdad, Iraq.

Balafrej, Ahmed; Moroccan politician; b. 1908; ed. Univs. of Paris and Cairo.
Secretary-General in Istiqlal (Independence) Party 44-; later exiled by French, returned to Morocco 55; Minister of Foreign Affairs 55-58; Prime Minister May-Dec. 58; Ambassador-at-Large 60-61; Dep. Prime Minister June 61; Minister of Foreign Affairs 61-Nov. 63; Personal Rep. of King with rank of Minister 63-June 72.
c/o The Royal Palace, Rabat, Morocco.

Ballal, Musa Awad; Sudanese politician; b. 20 Jan. 1931, Elfashir; ed. Univs. of Khartoum and Pennsylvania.
Director of Admin., Productive Efficiency Centre 65-67; Deputy Gen. Man. Industrial Devt. Corpn. and Sec.-Gen. Higher Council of Public Sector Corps. 70; Minister of Supply 71-72, of Industry and Mining 72-Jan. 75.
Publs. *Industrialization and the Social Progress in Rural Areas of the Sudan* 71, *The Problems of Industrialization in the Southern Sudan* 71.
3 Baladia Avenue, Khartoum, Sudan.

Barakat, Lt.-Col Abdullah Hosain; Yemeni politician; b. 26 Jan. 1934, Sana'a; ed. Mil. Coll. Sana'a, Police Coll. Cairo, Ain Shams Univ. and Cairo Univ.
Director of Police, Security and Passports, Taiz 61, of Public Security 62-64; Deputy, Ministry of Interior 64; Minister of Agriculture 65, of Interior 67-71; Amb. to Sudan 71, to Algeria and Tunisia 72-74; Minister of Social Affairs, Labour and Youth 74; Deputy Prime Minister for Interior Affairs Jan. 75-.
Deputy Prime Minister's Office, Sana'a; Home: Alkharabah Airport Road, Sana'a, Yemen Arab Republic.

Barakat, Gamal Eddine, LL.B., B.LITT.; Egyptian diplomatist; b. 1921; ed. Cairo Univ., Acad. of Int. Law, The Hague and Oriel Coll., Oxford.
Third Sec., London 50-52; with Political Dept., Ministry of Foreign Affairs 53-55; Consul-Gen. Aleppo 55-58; Counsellor, Washington 58-60; Head of Service Training Dept., Ministry of Foreign Affairs 61-63; mem. Org. of African

Unity Expert Cttee., Addis Ababa 63-64; Ambassador to Uganda 64-68, and to Burundi 67-68; Amb. to Finland 68-73; Asst. to the President's Advisor on Nat. Security 73-74; Dir.-Gen. Dept. of Cultural Relations and Technical Co-operation, Ministry of Foreign Affairs 74-75; Order of Merit (4th Grade) 58, Order of the Republic (2nd Grade) 64, Order of the Lion (Finland) 73.
Publs. *Status of Aliens in Egypt* 49, *Lectures on Diplomacy and Diplomatic Terminology in Arabic* 62, on *Diplomatic History and Practice* 75.
c/o Ministry of Foreign Affairs, Cairo, Egypt.

Barakat, Ghaleb, B.A.; Jordanian civil servant; b. 1927; ed. American Univ. Beirut.
Teacher, Nat. Coll., Tripoli 49-50, Teachers' Coll., Tripoli 50-52, Asst. Dir. 51-52; Chief Clerk, Jordan Tourist Dept. 52-53, Press Attaché 53-54; Tourist and Press Attaché, Royal Jordan Embassy, Rome 54-60; Dir. of Tourism 60-; Dir. Jordan Pavilion, Brussels Exhbn. 58; Commr.-Gen. Jordan Pavilion, New York World's Fair 64; Pres. Arab Int. Tourist Union 64, 70; Dir.-Gen. Tourism Authority 66-; Dir.-Gen. Ministry of Tourism and Anti-quities 68; Minister of Tourism and Antiquities 72-, con-currently of Transport 72; Jordanian, Belgian and Vatican decorations.
Ministry of Tourism and Antiquities, P.O.B. 224, Amman; Home: P.O. Box 9064, Amman, Jordan.

Baramki, Dimitri Constantine, B.A., PH.D.; Jordanian archaeologist; b. 1909; ed. St. George's School, American Univ. of Beirut, Univ. of London.
Teacher, Jerusalem 25-26; Student Inspector of Anti-quities, Palestine 27-28, Inspector 29; Senior Archæo-logical Officer 45; Archæological Adviser and Librarian, American School of Oriental Research, Jerusalem 49-51; Curator of Museums 51-; Asst. Prof. of Ancient History, American Univ. of Beirut 51-53, Associate Prof. 53, Prof. 58-; UNESCO Expert in Prehistoric Archaeology, accred. to Libya 64-65; excavated numerous sites in Palestine.
Publs. Numerous articles in the Quarterly of the Dept. of Antiquities, Palestine and in other publications.
American University of Beirut, Beirut, Lebanon.

Bar-Ilan, Tuvia, PH.D., B.CH.E.; Israeli chemist and university administrator; b. 28 Dec. 1912; ed. Polytechnic Inst. of Brooklyn and Hebrew Univ., Jerusalem.
Emigrated to Palestine from U.S.A. 23; research worker, Weizmann Inst. of Science, Rehovot 36-43; War Dept. analyst and British army officer 43-46; Commdr. Scientific Corps, Jerusalem area, Israeli Defence Forces 47-48; manufacturer of plastic products 49-66; Dir. Bar-Ilan Univ., Ramat-Gan 58-63; Dir. Bar-Ilan Univ., Extension Div. (Ashkelon, Safed and Jordan Valley) 65-; Pres. B'nei-B'rith, Holon 59-62, 63-65; Chair. Exec. Cttee. Nat. Religious Party, Holon 63-66; mem. Board of Higher Studies 61-65; Town Councillor, Holon 69-74; mem. Cen. Cttee. for Colleges 72-74; AACI Henrietta Szold Award for Advancing Higher Educ. in Israel 62.
Publs. Articles and patents on organic chemistry and plastics.
3 Azar Street, Holon, Israel.

Barkovsky, Anatoly; Soviet diplomatist; b. 1921, Moscow; ed. Diplomatic Acad.
Attaché, Third Sec., Second Sec., First Sec., U.S.S.R. Embassy, Egypt 52-57, Counsellor 59-61; Consul Gen., Syria 1961; Amb. to Syria 61-68, to Cyprus 71-73, to Iraq 74-.
Embassy of the U.S.S.R., Mansour Street 140, Karradat Mariam, Baghdad, Iraq.

Bar-Lev, Lieut.-Gen. Haim; Israeli officer and politician; b. 1924, Austria; ed. Mikhev Israel Agricultural School, Columbia Univ. School of Econs. and Admin., U.S.A.
Joined Palmach Units 42; Platoon Commdr., Beith-

Ha'Arava 44; Commdr. D Co., Yesreel 45-46; Commdr. Palmach N.C.O.'s course and C.O. Eight Regt., Negev Brigade 47, Operations Officer 48; Commdr. Armoured Units 48; Instructor and later Commdr., Bn. Commdrs. course 49-52; Chief of Staff, Northern Command 52-53; C.O. Givati Brigade 54-55; Dir. G.H.Q. Training Div. 56; Commdr. Armoured Brigade during Sinai campaign; Commdr. Armoured Corps 65-71; made study tour of armoured corps of Western European countries and U.S.A. 61; visited U.S. army installations and the armies of the Philippines, Japan, Thailand and S. Viet-Nam; Dir. Gen. Staff, Operations Branch 64-66; Deputy Chief of Staff, Israel Defence Forces 67, Chief of Staff 68-72; Minister of Commerce and Industry 72-; Labour Party.
Ministry of Commerce and Industry, Tel-Aviv, Israel.

Barromi, Joel; Israeli (b. Italian) diplomatist; b. 1920; ed. Univ. of Rome Law School and Hebrew Univ., Jeru-salem.
Ministry of Foreign Affairs 51-; First Sec. and Counsellor, Buenos Aires, Chargé d'Affaires *a.i.*, Montevideo and Havana 55-61; Deputy Dir. W. European Div., Ministry of Foreign Affairs 61, Dir. Latin American Div. 62-63; Deputy Perm. Rep. to UN 63-69, concurrently Amb. to Haiti Sept. 63-69; Dir. Div. of Cultural and Scientific Relations, Ministry of Foreign Affairs 70-.
Division of Cultural and Scientific Relations, Ministry of Foreign Affairs, Tel-Aviv, Israel.

Bartur, Moshe; Israeli diplomatist; b. 27 Oct. 1919; ed. Germany and Palestine.
Went to Palestine 38; with Jewish Agency 46-48; joined Ministry of Foreign Affairs 48; Perm. Rep., Office of UN, Geneva 61-65; Amb. to Japan 66-71; Senior Adviser to Major int. and Israeli corpns., Ministry of Foreign Affairs 72-.
Ministry of Foreign Affairs, Jerusalem, Israel.

Barzani, Mullah Mustafa; Iraqi politician; b. 1904.
Founder and leader, Kurdish Democratic Party; led revolts in Kurdistan 34, 43, 45, 46; exiled to U.S.S.R. 46-58; returned at invitation of Gen. Kassem 58; led Kurdish rebellion 65 until settlement 70; resumed rebellion March 74-; in exile in Iran March 75-.

Basher, Sayed Taha; Sudanese medical doctor and politi-cian; b. 2 June 1922, Swakin; ed. Gordon Memorial Coll. and Univ. of Khartoum.
Assistant neurologist 54-56; dipl. in psychiatry, London Univ. 56; psychiatric specialist 57-59; Senior psychiatric specialist 59-69; Minister of Labour May 69-70; Minister of Health 70-71; mem. WHO Scientific Advisory Cttee., Exec. Cttee. of the Int. Union for Psychiatry, Sudanese Medical Board, Exec. Cttee. of Psychiatry Soc. of Africa, Sudanese Philosophical Soc. Council and Nat. Vocational Front.
c/o Ministry of Health, Khartoum, Sudan.

Basmacı, Ferid; Turkish banker; b. 13 Feb. 1911, Istanbul; ed. Faculty of Econs. and Commerce, Istanbul.
Treasurer, Türkiye İş Bankası 53-58, Vice-Pres. 58-60, Man. Galata Branch 60-66, Senior Vice-Pres. 66-67, Pres. 67-73, Dir. 73-; Chair. Sinaî Yatırım ve Kredi Bankası 67-, Industrial Devt. Bank of Turkey 69-.
Türkiye İş Bankası A.Ş., Ulus, Ankara; Home: Vali Dr. Reşit Caddesi 74, Çankaya, Ankara, Turkey.

Basri, Meer S.; Iraqi poet, writer and economist; b. 19 Sept. 1911; ed. Baghdad.
Official, Iraqi Ministry for Foreign Affairs; Chief of Section and Acting Dir. of the Protocol; Dir. *The Iraq Directory* 35; Sec., and later Dir., Baghdad Chamber of Commerce 35-45; Controller Commercial Exchange 37-38; Asst. Iraq Commr. Int. Paris Exhbn. 37; Editor *Chamber of Commerce Journal* 38-45; del. Intl. Business Conf., Rye N.Y. 44; Dir. Eastern Commercial Corpn.; Ltd. 45-49

mem. Iraqi PEN Club; mem. Gen. Council and Admin. Council, Baghdad; Dir. of Information, Date Asscn. of Iraq 47; Fellow, Royal Asiatic Soc., London 50; Dir. of various companies 53-.

Publs. *Essays on Iraqi Economy* (Arabic) 48, *Echoes of the Lyre* (poetry), *Men and Shadows* (short stories), *Dictionary of Economic Terms and Theories* (Arabic, English and French), *Travels of Nijeholt* (trans.), *Role of Arab Men of Letters* 69, *Leaders of Thought in Modern Iraq*; poetry, short stories, literary criticism, etc.

20A Sussex Mansions, Old Brompton Road, London, S.W.7, England.

Bayani, Mehdi, PH.D.; Iranian librarian; b. 1906; ed. Univ. of Teheran.

Librarian, Nat. Teachers' Coll., and Lecturer, Faculty of Literature, Teheran Univ. 33; Head of Education Dept., Ispahan Province 40; Special Inspector and Asst. Dir. of Education Dept., Ministry of Art and Industry 41; Dir. Nat. Library of Teheran 42; Dir. of Imperial Library 57-72; Dir.-Gen. The Nat. Library 57; Prof. Nat. Teachers' Coll. 61-; Prof. Faculty of Art 63-.

Editor: *Nimuneh-Sukhan-i-Farsi* 38, *Rahnemaye Ganjineh Koran* 48, *Specimens of Fine Writing from the National Library, Teheran* 48, *Specimens of Fine Writing from the Imperial Library of Iran* 51, *Ahval va Athare mir Emad* 52, *Khochnevissan* (vol. 1) 66.

Publs. *Three Essays of Sheikh Shahabod-din Suhrawardi* 38-40; *Essay Sawanih-fel-Eshq Ahmad Ghazzali* 43; *Badaya ol-Azman* (Tarikhe Afzal) 47.

c/o Imperial Library, Qolestan Palace, Teheran, Iran.

Bayar, Celal; Turkish politician; b. 1883.

Minister of Nat. Economy 21; Minister of Reconstruction and Settlement (when Turkish and Greek populations were exchanged in accordance with Treaty of Lausanne) 23; founded İş Bank 24; Minister of Nat. Economy 32; Prime Minister 37-39; Vice-Pres. Republican Peoples' Party during Presidency of Kemal Atatürk; undertook leadership of new Democratic Party founded 46; Pres. of the Republic May 50-60; arrested and detained May 60; death sentence passed and changed to life imprisonment 61; released Nov. 64; pardoned 66.

Ankara, Turkey.

Bayramoğlu, Fuat; Turkish diplomatist; b. 23 March 1912, Ankara; ed. School of Political Sciences (Mülkiye), Instanbul and Univ. of Liège.

Entered Diplomatic Service 39; mem. Gen. Directorate of Press and Publication Cttee. 43; Head of Secretariat Prime Minister's Office 44-46; Chair. Press Dept. Cttee. 46; Dir. in Foreign Ministry 48; Consul, Cyprus 49; Consul Gen., Jerusalem 51-53; Dir.-Gen. Consular and Claims Dept., Ministry of Foreign Affairs, Ankara 53-57; Ambassador to Norway 57-59, to Iraq 59-60, to Iran 60-62, to Italy 62-63; Sec.-Gen. Ministry of Foreign Affairs 63-64; Ambassador to Belgium 64-67, to Italy 67-69, to U.S.S.R. 69-71; Chair. Inspection Corps, Ministry of Foreign Affairs 71-72; Sec.-Gen. to the Pres. of Turkey 72-; Humayoun Order of Iran 62, Grand Croix de Mérite Civil (Spain) 63, Grande Croce (Italy) 69, Presidential and Ministry of Foreign Affairs Distinguished Service awards 73; Silver and Gold Medals from five int. philatelic exhibns.

Publ. *Rubaiat* book of poems; several legal and sociological articles; *Rubailer* (book of quatrains) 74; *Turk Cam Sanati ve Beykoz* İşleri (Turkish Glass Art) 74.

Presidential Palace, Ankara, Turkey.

Bayülken, Ümit Halûk; Turkish diplomatist; b. July 1921; ed. Ankara Univ.

Joined Ministry of Foreign Affairs 44, served Frankfurt, Bonn, Dir. Middle East Section 51-53; Political Adviser to UN Del. 53-59; mem. Turkish Del. to Cyprus Joint Cttee., London 59-60; Dir.-Gen. Policy Planning Group,

Ministry of Foreign Affairs 60-63, appointed Minister Plenipotentiary; Asst. Sec.-Gen. for Political Affairs 63-64; Sec.-Gen. Ministry of Foreign Affairs 64-66; Ambassador to U.K. 66-69; Perm. Rep. to UN 69-71; Minister of Foreign Affairs 71-74; Sec.-Gen. CENTO 75-; Head of several overseas dels. since 52, Order Isobel la Catolica (Spain), German Grand Cross of Merit, Hon. G.C.V.O. (U.K.) 67.

Publs. several papers on the Cyprus question.

Central Treaty Organization, Eski Büyük Millet Meclisi, Ulus, Ankara, Turkey.

Beaumont, Sir Richard Ashton, K.C.M.G., O.B.E.; British diplomatist (retd.); b. 29 Dec. 1912; ed. Repton Coll. and Oriel Coll., Oxford.

Entered Consular Service 36, served Beirut 36, Damascus 38; war service 41-44; joined Foreign Office 45, served Mosul 46-47; Chargé d'Affaires, Damascus 47-48; Consul-Gen., Jerusalem 48-49, Caracas 50-53, Baghdad 53-58; Imperial Defence Coll. 58-59; Head of Arabian Dept., Foreign Office 59-61; Amb. to Morocco 61-65; Amb. to Iraq 65-67, to Egypt (fmrly. U.A.R.) 69-73; Dir.-Gen. Middle East Asscn. 73-.

Middle East Association, 33 Bury Street, London S.W.1, England.

Becker, Aharon; Israeli labour leader; b. 28 Dec. 1906; ed. secondary school.

Came to Palestine 24; Sec. Histadrut, Ramat Gan 29-32; Sec. Textile Workers Union 33-34; mem. Exec. Labour Council, Tel-Aviv 34-43; Man. Dir. Industrial Dept. Co-op. Wholesale Soc. 43-47; Head, Supply Mission, Ministry of Defence 48-49; Chair. Histadrut Trade Union Dept. 49-61, Sec.-Gen. of Histadrut 61-69; mem. Labour Party Secretariat, Governing Body of ILO 56-70, Bank of Israel, Knesset, Exec. Cttee. Histadrut.

Publs. numerous articles and booklets on economic and labour problems.

66 Keren Kayemet Boulevard, Tel-Aviv, Israel.

Bedjaoui, Mohammed; Algerian politician; b. 21 Sept. 1929; ed. Univ. of Grenoble and Institut d'Etudes Politiques, Grenoble.

Lawyer, Court of Appeal, Grenoble 51; research worker at Centre National de la Recherche Scientifique (C.N.R.S.), Paris 55; Legal Counsellor of the Arab League in Geneva 59-62; Legal Counsellor Provisional Republican Govt. of Algeria in Exile 58-61; Dir. Office of the Pres. of Nat. Constituent Assembly 62; mem. Del. to UN 62; Sec.-Gen. Council of Ministers, Algiers 62-63; Pres. Soc. Nat. des chemins de fer algériens (S.N.C.F.A.) 64; Dean of the Faculty of Law, Algiers Univ. 64-; Minister of Justice and Keeper of the Seals 64-70; mem., special reporter, Comm. on Int. Law, UN 65-; Amb. to France 70-; Perm. Rep. to UNESCO 71-; Carnegie Endowment for Int. Peace 56; Ordre du Mérite Alaouite, Morocco; Order of the Repub., Egypt.

Publs. *International Civil Service* 56, *Fonction publique internationale et influences nationales* 58, *La révolution algérienne et le droit* 61, *Succession d'états* 70.

Embassy of Algeria, rue Hamelin 18, Paris 16e, France; and 39 rue des Pins, Hydra, Algiers, Algeria.

Begin, Menachem, M.JUR.; Israeli politician; b. 1913; ed. Warsaw Univ.

Active in Jewish Youth Movement "Betar"; Chair. "Betar" in Czechoslovakia 36, in Poland 39; confined in Siberian labour camp by Moscow Comm. of N.K.V.D. 40-41; came with Polish army to Palestine 42; C.-in-C. Irgun Zvai Leumi 43, leading revolt against British rule in Palestine; mem. 1st, 2nd, 3rd, 4th and 5th Knessets (Israel Parl.); Leader of the Opposition in Knesset 48-67, 69-; Minister without Portfolio 67-69; Founder and Chair. Herut (Freedom Movement); joint Chair. of Likud Bloc 73-.

Publs. *The Revolt, personal memoirs of the Commander of Irgun Zvi Leumi* 49, *The White Nights.*
Knesset Building, Jerusalem; and 1 Rosenbaum Street, Tel-Aviv, Israel.

Beheiry, Mamoun Ahmed, B.A.; Sudanese civil servant and politician; b. 1925; ed. Victoria Coll., Alexandria, and Brasenose Coll., Oxford.
Former Dep. Perm. Under-Sec. Ministry of Finance and Economics; fmr. Chair. Sudan Currency Board; fmr. Chair. Nat. Technical Planning Cttee. 62; First Gov. Central Bank of Sudan 58-63; Gov. IMF and IBRD for Sudan; Chair. Cttee. of Nine preparing for African Devt. Bank 63; Minister of Finance and Econs. 63-64, Jan. 75-; Pres. of African Devt. Bank 64-70; Pres. Board of Trustees, Special Fund for Southern Region 72-74; Chair. Parl. Devt. and Econ. Affairs Cttee., Jan. 75-.
Minister of Finance and National Economy, Khartoum, Sudan.

Behnia, Abolhassan; Iranian banker; b. 5 Jan. 1910; ed. Univ. of Paris.
Professor, Technical Faculty, Teheran Univ. 42-67; Dir.-Gen. Ministry of Roads and Communications 46-47; Chair. and Man. Dir. Irrigation Org. 50-55; Minister of Roads and Communications 60; Dir. of Technical Bureau of Plan Org. 61-64; Chair. and Man. Dir. Bank Rahni Iran 65-.
Bank Rahni Iran, Ferdowsi Street, Teheran; and 41 Avenue Heravi, Saltanatabad, Teheran, Iran.

Bekata, Hifzi Oğuz; Turkish politician; b. 17 March 1911; ed. Ankara Univ.
Deputy for Ankara 43-50, 57-60; mem. Constituent Assembly 61; Minister of State June-Oct. 62, of the Interior 62-63; Senator for Ankara 61-; Gen. Sec. Turkish Asscn. of United Nations; Republican People's Party.
Publs. *Aydın Din Adamları* 62, *Birinci Cumhuriyet* 60, *Dağların Ardi* 65, *Hükumet Hakkında Konusmalar* 67, *Türkiyenin Bungünkü Görünüşü* 69.
Atatürk Bulvari 237/9, Kavaklidere, Ankara, Turkey.

Bel Kacem, Cherif; Algerian politician; b. 31 July 1933, Beni Mellal, Morocco.
Former mem. Armée de Libération Nationale; Deputy for Tlemcen; Questeur, Nat. Ass.; Minister of Nat. Orientation 63-64; Minister of Education 64-65; mem. Revolutionary Council 65-75, Dir. of Information 65-67; mem. Bureau Politique, F.L.N. 65-67; Minister of Finance and Planning March 68-70; Minister of State 70-July 75.
c/o Palais du Gouvernement, Algiers, Algeria.

Belkhodja, Tahar; Tunisian engineer and diplomatist; b. 1931; ed. Ecole supérieure d'Agriculture, Tunis.
Students' del. to Political Bureau of Neo-Destour Party 58-59; mem. Tunisian del. to UN Gen. Assembly 59; Sec. of State at Foreign Ministry Oct. 59-Jan. 60, Dir. of Foreign Affairs Jan. 60-61; Chargé d'Affaires, Paris Jan.-July 61; Ambassador to Senegal, also accred. to Guinea, Mauritania and Ivory Coast 61-66, to Spain 70; Sec. of State, Ministry of Agriculture 71; Minister of Youth and Sports 72; Head Perm. Mission to UN, Geneva 72; Minister of Interior, 73-; Ordre de l'Indépendance, Ordre de la République Tunisienne and other decorations.
Ministry of Interior, avenue H. Bourguiba, Tunis, Tunisia.

Ben Abbes, Youssef, M.D.; Moroccan physician and politician; b. 15 Aug. 1921; ed. Marrakesh, Medical Coll. of Algiers and Paris.
Joined Public Health Service 49, Dir. several hospitals, then Insp.-Gen. of Health; Minister of Health 58-61, of Health and Educ. 61-62, of Educ. 62-65; Mayor of Marrakesh and Pres. Provincial Council; Senator for Marrakesh; Ambassador to U.A.R. 65-66, to Italy 67-69, to Algeria 69-70; Minister of Foreign Affairs Oct. 70-71; Amb. to Spain 71-72, to France Sept. 72-.
Embassy of Morocco, rue Le Tasse 3, Paris 16e, France.

Benabdallah, Abdel-Aziz; Moroccan professor; b. 28 Nov. 1923; ed. Univ. of Algiers.
General Dir. for the Conservation and Registry of Land Properties 57; Dir. of Higher Educ. for Scientific Research 58-61; Dir. of Nat. Arabization Centre 61-68; Dir.-Gen. Perm. Office for the Co-ordination of Arabization in the Arab World, Arab League, Rabat 69-; Prof., Faculty of Arts, Mohamed V Univ., Rabat and also Dar-el-Hadith Inst., al-Qarawiyine Univ., Rabat.
Bureau Permanent d'Arabization, 8 rue Angola, Rabat, Morocco.

Ben-Aharon, Yitzhak; Israeli administrator; b. 1906, Bukovina, Austria; ed. Berlin High School for Political Science and Econs.
Went to Palestine 28; founder of Kibbutz Givat Hayim; Sec. Tel-Aviv Labour Council 38-39; Lieut., British Army, Second World War, prisoner-of-war 41-45; mem. Knesset 49-62; Minister of Transport 59-62; mem. Knesset 69-; Sec.-Gen. Histadrut 69-73.
Publs. *Listen Gentile, Michtavim Leuni, Bepheta Temura.*
Kibbutz Givat Hayim (Meyuhad), Doar Hedera, Israel.

Ben Ammar, Hassib; Tunisian professor and politician; b. 11 April 1924; ed. Coll. Sadiki, Tunis and Faculty of Sciences, Paris.
Active mem. of Destour groups abroad 42-52; mem. Destour Fed., Tunis 54; Sec.-Gen. of the Econ. and Social Board 59; Sec.-Gen. of Destour Youth Movt. 60; Mayor of Tunis 63-65, Gov. 65-69; Amb. to Italy 69; Minister of Defence 70-71; mem. Cen. Cttee., Destour Socialist Party (DSP) 64; mem. Political Bureau DSP, Chair. 69-70, Supreme Cttee. DSP 70-, Council of Nat. Defence 71-; Grand Cordon, Order of Independence, Grand Cordon, Order of the Repub.
Parti socialiste destourien, 10 rue de Rome, Tunis, Tunisia.

Ben-Ari, Mordechai; Israeli (b. Transylvania) airline executive; b. Sept. 1920; ed. Hebrew Univ., Jerusalem.
Arrived in Palestine 40, joined Kibbutz; fought in Israel's War of Independence; later Dir. of Immigration Operations in Austria and E. Europe; joined El Al Israel Airlines 50, Man. of Freight and Mail Dept., Head of Commercial Div. 58, Vice-Pres. (Commercial) 60-67, Pres. of El Al Israel Airlines Ltd. July 67-.
El Al Israel Airlines Ltd., P.O. Box 41, Ben Gurion Airport, Lod, Israel.

Ben Bella, Mohammed; Algerian politician; b. 1916.
Warrant Officer in Moroccan regiment during Second World War (decorated); Chief O.S. rebel military group in Algeria 47; imprisoned 49-52 (escaped); directed Algerian nat. movement from exile in Libya 52-56; arrested Oct. 56; held in France 59-62; Vice-Premier, Algerian Nationalist Provisional Govt., Tunis 62; Leader, Algerian Political Bureau, Algeria 62; Premier of Algeria Sept. 62-June 65, President of Algeria Sept. 63-June 65, concurrently Minister of Interior Dec. 64-June 65; overthrown by military *coup* and imprisoned 65; Lenin Peace Prize 64.
Algiers, Algeria.

Bendor, Shmuel; Israeli educator and former diplomatist; b. 21 June 1909, Belfast; ed. Liverpool Univ.
Emigrated to Palestine 32; became English teacher, later Vice-Principal, Haifa Reali School 32-48; Military Service 48-49; with Ministry of Education 49; Dir. of U.S. Dept. Foreign Ministry 50-54; Counsellor, Paris 54-57; Minister to Czechoslovakia 57-59, to Rumania 59-61; Dir. Western European Dept., Foreign Ministry 61-63; Deputy Dir.-Gen. Prime Minister's Office 63-66, Dir. Foreign Relations Atomic Energy Comm. 66-69; Dir. Foreign Relations and Sec. Council for Higher Educ., Ministry of Educ. and Culture 69-72; Dir. Israel Acad. of Sciences and Humanities 72-74; Consultant, Planning and Grants Cttee., Council of Educ. 75-.
58 Harlap Street, Jerusalem, Israel.

Benedictos (Vassilios Papadopoulos); Greek orthodox ecclesiastic; b. 1892; ed. Greek Orthodox Hieratic School, Jerusalem, and Athens Univ.
Clerk, Patriarchal Offices, Jerusalem 14; ordained deacon 14; accompanied the then Patriarch to Damascus during World War I; studies in Law and Theological Schools, Athens Univ. 21-25; rep. of Patriarch of Jerusalem at World Christian Conf. of Faith and Order, Geneva 27; Exarch of the Holy Sepulchre in Athens 29-46; ordained priest and Archimandrite 46; mem. Holy Synod, Jerusalem Patriarchate 46-; Legal Adviser and Chair. Pending Property Cttee. 47; Chair. Financial Cttee. 50; rep. of Patriarch, Internationalisation of Jerusalem Trusteeship Conf. 50; Archbishop of Tiberias 51; Greek Orthodox Patriarch of Jerusalem 57-; Grand Cross of King George of Greece, Grand Cross and Cordon of Patriarchate of Antioch, Jordanian and Lebanese orders.
Publs. Numerous historical and legal works.
Greek Orthodox Patriarchate, P.O. Box 4074, Jerusalem, Israel.

Bengelloun, Ahmed Majid, L. EN D.; Moroccan lawyer and politician; b. 27 Dec. 1927, Fez; ed. Inst. of Political Science, Paris.
Public Prosecutor, Marrakesh 56, later Public Prosecutor of Mil. Tribunal, Meknés, Gen. Counsel, Supreme Court; Public Prosecutor Court of Appeal 60-64; Minister of Information 65-67; Sec.-Gen. Ministry of Justice 67; Minister at the Royal Cabinet 67-71, of Civil Service 71-72, of Information 72-74; Prosecutor-Gen. May 74-; fmr. Prof. Inst. des Hautes Etudes Juridiques; Prof. Law Faculty, Univ. of Rabat, Ecole Marocaine d'Admin.; mem. Comm. for the Drafting of the Penal Code and Penal Procedure Code; has attended numerous int. judicial confs.; Order of the Throne, and several foreign decorations.
Bureau du Procureur Général, Rabat, Morocco.

Ben-Haim, Paul; Israeli composer; b. 5 July 1897; ed. State Acad. of Music and Univ. of Munich.
Composer, pianist and conductor in various cities in Germany 20-33; moved to Palestine 33 and settled in Tel-Aviv teaching composition and piano; guest conductor, Jerusalem Radio Orchestra and Israel Philharmonic Orchestra; Dir. New Jerusalem Acad. of Music 49-54; Hon. Pres. Israeli Composers' Asscn.; awarded Engel Prize of Tel-Aviv Municipality for *1st Symphony* 45, and for *2nd Symphony* 53; awarded Israel State Prize 57 for symphonic work *The Sweet Psalmist of Israel*; Cross of Merit (1st Class) of the Fed. Repub. of Germany 68.
Works include two symphonies, *Evocation* for violin and orchestra, *Pastorale* for clarinet and strings, Concerto for piano and orchestra, Concerto for strings, *Liturgical Cantata, The Sweet Psalmist of Israel*, other symphonic works include a violin and a 'cello concerto, cantatas, chamber music, songs, etc.
Aharonovitz Street 11, Tel Aviv, Israel.

Benhima, Ahmed Tahibi (brother of Mohamed Benhima, *q.v.*); Moroccan diplomatist and politician; b. 13 Nov. 1927; ed. Univs. of Nancy and Paris.
Chargé d'Affaires, Paris 56-57, Ambassador to Italy 57-59; Sec.-Gen. of Ministry of Foreign Affairs 59-61; Perm. Rep. to UN 61-64; Minister of Foreign Affairs 64-66; Dir. Cabinet of the King 66-67; Perm. Rep. to UN 67-71; Minister of Foreign Affairs 72-74; Minister of State for Information April 74-.
Ministry of Information, Rabat, Morocco.

Benhima, Mohamed, M.D. (brother of Ahmed Benhima, *q.v.*); Moroccan physician and politician; b. 25 June 1924; ed. Faculté de Médecine de Nancy, France.
Chief Medical Officer, Had Court District 54-56; Chief of Central Service for Urban and Rural Hygiene 56-57; Head of Personal Office of Minister of Public Health 57-60; Sec.-Gen., Ministry of Public Health Jan.-June 60; Gov.

of Provinces of Agadir and Tartaya 60-61; Minister of Public Works 61-62, 63-65, 67-69, of Commerce, Industry, Mines, Handicrafts and Merchant Marine 62-63; Minister of Nat. Educ. 65-67; Prime Minister July 67-69; Minister of Agriculture and Agrarian Reform 69; Minister of Public Health 69-72; Minister of the Interior 72-73; Minister of State for Co-operation and Training 73-; decorations from Govts. of Belgium, Morocco, Sweden, Ethiopia, Tunisia, Liberia and Egypt.
Km. 5,500, Route des Zaërs, Rabat, Morocco.

Benjenk, Munir P., B.SC. (ECON.); Turkish public servant; b. 1924; ed. English Lycée and Robert Coll., Istanbul and London School of Economics.
Worked with B.B.C., Reading 49-51; served with Turkish Army in Korea 51-52; with OEEC (now OECD), Paris 53-63; mem. Perm. Mission to Washington of OEEC 55-57; Dir. Sardinian Village Devt. Project 59-60; Asst. Dir. Devt. Dept., OECD 62-63; with Int. Bank for Reconstruction and Devt. 63-; Head of Econ. Advisory Mission, Algeria 64; Head of North Africa Div. 65-67, Deputy Dir. Middle East and North Africa Dept. 67-68; Deputy Dir. Europe, Middle East and North Africa Dept. 68-69, Dir. 70-72, Vice-Pres. of Dept. 72-; Ordine al Merito della Repubblica Italiana, Order of the Cedars of Lebanon 73.
1308 28th Street, N.W., Washington, D.C. 20007; and International Bank for Reconstruction and Development, 1818 H Street, N.W., Washington, D.C. 20433, U.S.A.

Ben Khedda, Ben Yousef; Algerian politician; b. 1920.
Minister of Cultural and Social Affairs, Algerian Provisional Govt. 58-Jan 60; Missions, Moscow and Peking 60-61; Prime Minister Algerian Provisional Govt., Tunis 61-62, Algiers 62; placed under arrest July 64.

Ben Lamlih, Ahmed, B.A.; Moroccan diplomatist; b. 1916; ed. Univ. of Cairo.
Participated in nat. liberation movement at "The Maghreb Office" Cairo 41-56; Minister to United Arab Repub. 56-59; Head, Afro-Asian Dept. at Ministry of Foreign Affairs 59-61; Amb. to Iraq 61-62, to U.A.R. 62-63, to Iran and Turkey 65-68; Head, Middle East and Arab League Dept. at Ministry of Foreign Affairs 68-70; Amb. to Libya 71, to Kuwait, Bahrain and Oman 72-.
Embassy of Morocco, P.O. Box 784, Kuwait.

Ben Mansour, Abdelwahab; Moroccan radio official and politician; b. 1920; ed. Al Qarawiyin Univ., Fez.
Political prisoner before leaving school; returned to North Africa, Algeria after Second World War and acted as liaison officer between Algerian and Moroccan Nationalists before independence; after independence, teacher then Head of Arab Services, Radiodiffusion Marocaine; Dir. of Political Affairs, Ministry of the Interior 63; mem., then Head of Royal Cabinet 64; Dir.-Gen. Radiodiffusion Télévision Marocaine 65-74; attends numerous int. confs.; numerous awards including named "Historiographer of the Realm" 63.
Radiodiffusion Télévision Marocaine, 11 rue Al Brihl, Rabat, Morocco.

Ben-Natan, Asher; Israeli soldier and diplomatist; b. 15 Feb. 1921; ed. Geneva Univ.
Secretary and Treas. Medorot-Zeraim Kibbutz 38-44; Immigration organizer, Europe 44-47; Ministry of Foreign Affairs 48-51; Gen. Man. Red Sea-Inkodeh Co. 55-56; Rep. of Ministry of Defence 56-59; Dir.-Gen. Ministry of Defence 59-65; Amb. to Fed. Repub. of Germany 65-70, to France 70-; Officier, Légion d'Honneur, Commdr., Ordre Nat. (Ivory Coast), Commdr., Ordre de l'Etoile Equatoriale (Gabon).
Embassy of Israel, avenue de Wagram 143, Paris 17e, France; and 89 University Street, Tel-Aviv, Israel.

Ben Salah, Ahmed; Tunisian politician; b. 13 Jan. 1926; ed. Collège Sadiki, Tunis and Univ. of Paris.
Teacher, Lycée de Sousse 48-51; Del. Tunisian Trade Union Movement at Int. Confederation of Trade Unions, Brussels 51-54; Sec.-Gen. Union Générale Tunisienne du Travail 54-56; Sec. of State for Public Health and Social Affairs 57-60, for the Plan and Finance 61-64, for the Plan and Nat. Economy 64-69, for Educ. Sept. 69-70; Asst. Sec.-Gen. Destour Socialist Party 64-70; imprisoned 70, escaped Feb. 73.
c/o Ministry of Justice, Tunis, Tunisia.

Ben Seddik, Mahjoub; Moroccan trade union leader; b. 1925.
Secretary-General Union Marocaine du Travail 55-; Pres. All-African Trade Union Fed. 61, 64, 66, 71; mem. Secretariat-Gen. Union Nat. des Forces Populaires; imprisoned 52-53, July 67; mem. Admin. Council, ILO.
Union Marocaine du Travail, 222 avenue des Forces Armées Royales, Casablanca, Morocco.

Benslimane, Abdelkader; Moroccan politician; b. 1932; ed. Toulouse Univ., France.
Joined Ministry of Finance 57; Amb. to France 61-63; Dir.-Gen. Bureau d'Etudes et Participation Industrielle 63-66; Del. to Maghreb Perm. Consultative Cttee. 66-72; Amb. to Benelux and EEC 72; Minister of Trade, Industry, Mines and Merchant Marine 72-74, of Finance April 74-.
Ministry of Finance, Rabat, Morocco.

Bentov, Mordechai; Israeli journalist and politician; b. 28 March 1900; ed. Inst. of Technology, Warsaw Univ., Jerusalem Law Classes.
Founder and Chief Editor *Al-Hamishmar* 43-48 and 49-55; Signatory of Declaration of Independence 48; elected mem. Knesset (Israel Parl.) 49, 51, 55, 59, 61; Minister of Labour in Provisional Govt. 48-49; Minister of Development 55-61; Minister of Housing 66-69; mem. Jewish Agency Del. to UN, Lake Success 47; Del. to Zionist Congresses, Round Table Conf., London 38, World Jewish Congress, U.S.A. 44, Geneva 53; mem. Secretariat, United Workers' Party (Mapam); Chair. Economic Affairs Cttee. of the Knesset 51; mem. World Exec. Hashomer Hatzair; Exec. Histadrut and Zionist Action Cttee.; mem. Exec. World Jewish Congress.
Publs. *The Case for a Bi-National Palestine* 46, *Israel Economy at the Crossroads* 65, *Israel, The Palestinians and the Left* 71.
Kibbutz Mishmar Haemek, Israel.

Ben Yahya, Prince Abdul Rahman; Yemeni Royalist politician.
Deputy Prime Minister until 67; Prime Minister 67-68; mem. Imamate Council 67-68; in exile 68-.

Ben Yahya, Mohammed Sedik; Algerian diplomatist; b. 1934.
Closely associated with Ferhat Abbas in Tunisia and Yazd 59-62; Ambassador to U.S.S.R. 62-65; undertook several missions for President Ben Bella 63-65; Ambassador to U.K. 65; mem. Algerian Del. to UN 65-66; Minister of Information 66-70, of Higher Educ. and Research 70-.
Ministry of Higher Education, Algiers, Algeria.

Berenblum, Isaac, M.D., M.SC.; Israeli pathologist and experimental biologist; b. 26 Aug. 1903; ed. Bristol Grammar School and Leeds Univ.
Riley-Smith Research Fellow, Dept. Experimental Pathology and Cancer Research, Leeds Univ. Medical School 29-36; Beit Memorial Research Fellow, Dunn School of Pathology, Oxford Univ. 36-40; Departmental and Univ. Demonstrator in Pathology, Oxford Univ. 40-48; in charge of Oxford Univ. Research Centre of British Empire Cancer Campaign 40-48; Special Research Fellow, Nat. Cancer Inst., Bethesda, Md., U.S.A. 48-50; Head of Dept. of Experimental Biology, The Weizmann Inst. of Science, Rehovot, Israel 50-71; Visiting Prof. of Oncology, Hebrew

Univ., Jerusalem 50-56; mem. Israel Research Council 52-57; Jack Cotton Prof. of Cancer Research, The Weizmann Inst. of Science, Rehovot, Israel 62-71, Emer. Prof. 71-; Hon. Life Mem. New York Acad. of Sciences, World Acad. of Sciences, Israel Acad. of Sciences and Humanities; Weizmann Prize of Municipality of Tel-Aviv-Yaffo 59; Rothschild Prize for Biology 66; Israel Prize 74.
Publs. *Science versus Cancer* 46, *Man Against Cancer* 52, *Cancer Research Today* 67, *Carcinogenesis as a Biological Problem* 74.
33 Ruppin Street, Rehovot, Israel.

Berger, Morroe, PH.D.; American educator and writer; b. 25 June 1917; ed. Columbia Univ., New York.
Assistant Prof., Princeton Univ. 52-58, Assoc. Prof. 58-61, Prof. of Sociology 62-; Dir. Program in Near Eastern Studies, Princeton Univ. 62-68, 73-; mem., Chair. Joint Cttee. of Near and Middle East, of American Council of Learned Socs. and Social Science Research Council 62-69; Consultant to U.S. Office of Educ. 65-68; mem. Governing Boards, American Research Center, Egypt (Pres. 74-), American Research Inst., Turkey 64-; Pres. Middle East Studies Assen. 67; Chair. Council on Int. and Regional Studies, Princeton Univ. 68-, Chair. Dept. of Sociology 71-74.
Publs. *Equality by Statute* 52, 67, *Bureaucracy and Society in Modern Egypt* 57, *The Arab World To-day* 62, *Madame de Staël on Politics, Literature and National Character* 64, *Islam in Egypt Today* 70; Editor *New Metropolis in the Arab World* 63; numerous articles in learned journals and contributions to encyclopaedias.
Jones Hall, Princeton University, Princeton, New Jersey 08540, U.S.A.

Bergmann, Ernst David, PH.D.; Israeli chemist and university professor; b. 18 Oct. 1903; ed. Berlin Univ.
Lecturer Berlin Univ. 28-33; Immigrated to Palestine 33; Scientific Dir. Daniel Sieff Research Inst. (now Weizmann Inst. of Science), Rehovot 33-51; Prof. of Organic Chemistry, The Hebrew Univ., Jerusalem 53-; Dir. Scientific Dept. Ministry of Defence 48-66; Chair. Israel Atomic Energy Comm. 52-66; Chair. Science Section, Israel Acad. of Sciences and Humanities; Hon. Sc.D. (Haifa Inst. of Technology), Hon. Ph.D. (Univ. of Montpellier); Rothschild Prize 62; Israel Defence Prize 66; Israel Prize 68.
Publs. *Organic Chemistry* (with W. Schlenk), *Isomerism and Isomerisation, Acetylene Chemistry* and many articles in scientific journals.
14 Ayn Rogel Street, Jerusalem, Israel.

Berinson, Zvi, SC. DIP., B.A.; Israeli judge; b. 1907; ed. Scots Coll. (Safad, Israel), Jesus Coll. Cambridge, and Gray's Inn, London.
Lecturer, Scots Coll. 29-31; Legal Adviser and Dir. Municipal Dept. Gen. Fed. of Jewish Labour, Palestine 36-49; Dir-Gen. Ministry of Labour, Israel Govt. 49-53; Justice, Supreme Court 54-; Lecturer on Labour Law and Social Insurance, Hebrew Univ. 53-71; Chair. League of Societies for the Rehabilitation of Offenders in Israel, Council of Israel Opera; Hon. Pres. Public Council for the Prevention of Noise and Air Pollution in Israel; mem. Board of Dirs., Int. Prisoners' Aid Assen.; Head of Israeli Del. to Int. Labour Conf. 49-53, 58, 59.
The Supreme Court of Israel, Jerusalem; 18 Marcus Street, Jerusalem, Israel.

Berk, Medenî; Turkish politician.
Fmr. Dir.-Gen. Emlâk Kredi Bankası; Minister of Reconstruction and Town Planning 57-59; Deputy Prime Minister 59-60; arrested May 60; sentenced to life imprisonment, released 65; Dir.-Gen. Akbank T.A.Ş. 66-; Pres. Union of Chambers of Commerce, Chambers of Industry and Commodity Exchanges of Turkey 70-71.
Etiler, Çamlık Sokak 6, Istanbul, Turkey.

Berk, Mükerrem; Turkish musician; b. 1917; ed. Istanbul Conservatoire.
Joined Presidential Symphony Orchestra 37, Principal Flute and Woodwind leader 41-68, Admin. Dir. 60-68; Gen. Dir. State Opera and Ballet 69-74; Dir. Istanbul State Symphony Orchestra and Izmir State Symphony Orchestra 74-; many tours in U.S.A., United Kingdom, W. Europe, Scandinavia, Middle East, India, Pakistan and U.S.S.R.
Istanbul Devlet Senfoni Orkestrasi Atatürk Kültür Merkezi, Taksim, Istanbul; Home: Selimehatun Camii Sok. No. 42/8, Ayazpaşa-Taksim, Istanbul, Turkey.

Berk, Nurullah; Turkish artist; b. 1906; ed. Acad. of Fine Arts, Istanbul, Paris Acad. and Léger and Lhote studios, Paris.
Teacher and fmr. Dir., Acad. of Fine Arts, Istanbul; exhibited UNESCO Int. Art Exhbn., Paris 47, Exhbn. of Turkish Art, Musée Cernuschi, Paris 47, Exhbn. of Turkish Art, Amsterdam 48, Turin Art Club Exhbn. 50, Contemporary Turkish Painting, Univ. Art Gallery, New York 71, Peinture Turque Contemporaine, UNESCO, Paris 74; mem. Int. Comm. of Govt. Experts on Art, Council of Europe, Strasbourg 69-72.
Publs. *Turkish Sculpture, Leonardo da Vinci, Art in Modern Turkey, La Peinture Turque, Bellinis, Sandro Boticelli— Le Musée des Beaux-Arts d'Istanbul 73, Cinquante ans de Peinture en Turquie 74.*
Abacı Latif Sokak 10, Besiktas, Istanbul, Turkey.

Berkol, Faruk N., LL.D.; Turkish diplomatist; b. 9 Sept. 1917, Istanbul; ed. Univs. of Istanbul and Paris and School of Political Science, Paris.
Joined Ministry of Foreign Affairs 41; First Sec., Washington 45-50; Counsellor, later Chargé d'Affaires, London 52-56; Chef de Cabinet to Pres. of Turkey 56-60; Amb. to Tunisia 62-67, to Belgium 67-72; UN Under-Sec. Gen., UN Disaster Relief Co-ordinator 72-.
Publs. works in Turkish and French on the Balkan *entente*, Turkish economic expansion and the legal status of eastern Mediterranean ports.
UN Disaster Relief, Palais des Nations, Geneva, Switzerland.

Berque, Jacques, D. ès L.; French oriental sociologist b. 4 June 1910; ed. Univ. of Algiers and Univ. de Paris à la Sorbonne.
Early career as Admin. Officer in Morocco; UNESCO specialist in Egypt 53-55; Dir. of Studies, Ecole des Hautes Études, Sorbonne 55-; Prof. of Social History of Contemporary Islam, Coll. de France 56-; Commdr. du Ouissam Alaouite (Morocco), Chevalier Légion d'Honneur and Palmes académiques (France); Commdr. of Merit (Syria, Tunisia).
Publs. *Structures sociales du Haut-Atlas 55, Les Arabes 57, Les Arabes d'hier à demain 60, Le Maghreb entre deux guerres 62, Dépossession du monde 64, L'Egypte, impérialisme et révolution 67, L'Orient Second 70, Langages arabes du Présent 74.*
Collège de France, 11 Place Marcelin-Berthelot, Paris 5e, France.

Berrada, Abdeslam, DIP.SC.AGRI.; Moroccan agronomist; b. 3 Oct. 1931, Fez; ed. secondary schools, Fez, Ecole Nat. d'Agriculture de Grignon, Ecole Nat. des Eaux et Forêts, Nancy, France.
Several posts in Waters and Forests Admin., subsequently Dir. 65; Sec.-Gen. Ministry of Agriculture and Agrarian Reform 71-72, Minister 72-74; Exec. Vice-Pres. Soc. Cellulose du Maroc 72-; rep. to numerous regional and int. confs.
c/o Ministère de l'Agriculture et de la Réforme Agraire, Rabat, Morocco.

Bertini, Gary; Israeli conductor; b. 1 May 1927, Bessarabia; ed. Israel Univ. of Paris, Conservatorio Verdi, Milan, Conservatoire Nat. Paris and studies under Arthur Honegger.
Founder RINAT Chamber Choir 55; Founder Jeunesses Musicales d'Israel; teacher of conducting at Rubin Acad. of Music; Artistic Dir. and Conductor Israel Chamber Orchestra; Principal Guest Conductor Scottish Nat. Orchestra; Regular Guest Conductor Hamburg State Opera, Paris Opera, Scottish Opera, BBC, Israel Philharmonic Orchestra and Jerusalem Philharmonic Orchestra; has conducted many orchestras in Israel and abroad, and has premiered much contemporary Israeli music; composer of symphonic and chamber music, ballets, incidental music to more than 40 plays, and music for films and radio.
5 Basel Street, Tel-Aviv, Israel.

Besse, Antonin Bernard; French company director; b. 22 Feb. 1927.
Chairman Besse group of companies (import, export, finance, maritime affairs) 51-65; Chair. Besse Int. S.A. (finance); mem. Int. Council of United World Colls.; Chevalier de l'Ordre de la Couronne.
P.O. Box 8203, Beirut, Lebanon; 14 avenue de Verzy, Paris 17e, France.

Bilge, Ali Suat, LL.T.; Turkish professor of international law and politician; b. 1921, Istanbul; ed. Univs. of Ankara and Geneva.
Assistant, Faculty of Political Science, Univ. of Ankara 50, Assoc. Prof. 52, Prof. 60-; Hon. Legal Adviser, Ministry of Foreign Affairs 60, First Hon. Legal Adviser 65; Judge, European Court of Human Rights 66; mem. Perm. Court of Arbitration, The Hague 66; mem. UN Cttee. of Human Rights 70; mem. Int. Law Comm. 71-; Minister of Justice Dec. 71-72; Amb. to Switzerland Oct. 72-.
Publs. *Diplomatic Protection of Compatriots 53, International Politics 66.*
Embassy of Turkey, Lombachweg 33, Berne, Switzerland.

Binder, Leonard; American university professor; b. 20 Aug. 1927; ed. Boston Latin School, Harvard Coll. and Harvard Univ.
Assistant Prof. Univ. Calif., Los Angeles 56-61; Assoc. Prof. and Prof. Univ. of Chicago 61-, Chair. Dept. of Political Science 64-67, Chair. Cttee. on Near Eastern Studies 63-65; mem. New Nations Cttee. 61-; Fellow Center for Advanced Studies in the Behavioral Sciences 67-68; Field Research in Pakistan 54-55, in Iran 58-59, in Egypt 60-61, in Lebanon 64, in Tunisia 64, 65, 66, 69; Chair. Research and Training Cttee., Middle East Studies Asscn. Pres. Middle East Studies Asscn. 73-74; Dir. Middle East Center, Univ. of Chicago 73-.
Publs. *Religion and Politics in Pakistan 60, Iran: Political Development in a Changing Society 61, The Ideological Revolution in the Middle East 64,* Editor, *Politics in the Lebanon 65,* Co-author, *Crises and Sequences in Political Development 72;* also numerous articles in periodicals.
Department of Political Science, University of Chicago, Chicago, Illinois 60637, U.S.A.

Birgi, Muharrem Nuri, LL.B.; Turkish diplomatist; b. 1908; ed. School of Political Sciences, Paris, and Faculty of Law, Geneva.
Joined Ministry of Foreign Affairs 32; served Warsaw 35-39, Ministry of Foreign Affairs 39-41, Paris 41, Madrid 42; Co-Dir.-Gen. First Political Dept., Ministry of Foreign Affairs 44; Dir.-Gen. Dept. of Int. Affairs 45, Dept. of Co-ordination 46, Dept. of Consular Affairs 46, Second Political Dept. 50; Adjutant to Sec.-Gen. Ministry of Foreign Affairs 51; Under-Sec. Ministry of Foreign Affairs 52-54, Sec.-Gen. 54-57; Ambassador to Great Britain 57-60; Perm. Del. NATO 60-72, retd.; head of Turkish del. to London Conference on Suez 56.
Toprakli Sokak, 11 Salacak-Üsküdar, Istanbul, Turkey.

Bishara, Abdulla Yacoub; Kuwaiti diplomatist; ed. Cairo Univ. and Balliol Coll., Oxford.

Second Sec., Kuwait Embassy, Tunisia 63-64; Dir. Office of Ministry of Foreign Affairs, Kuwait 64-71; Perm. Rep. to UN Sept. 71-, concurrently Amb. to Brazil and Argentina 74-; del. to numerous int. confs.
Permanent Mission of Kuwait at United Nations, 235 East 42nd Street, 27th Floor, New York, N.Y. 10017, U.S.A.

Bitar, Salah Eddine el-; Syrian politician b. 1912; ed. Damascus and Univ. of Paris.
Secondary school teacher in Damascus 34-42; entered politics 42; co-founder, with Michel Aflak, of Arab Resurrection Party and Editor of party organ; left Syria after Shishekly *coup* 52; later returned and took part in merging of Renaissance and Socialist parties to form Baath Party; elected to Parliament after overthrow of Shishekly 54; Minister of Foreign Affairs 56; head of Syrian Del. to UN Gen. Assembly 57; Minister of Culture and Nat. Guidance, U.A.R. 58-59; Prime Minister of Syrian Arab Republic March-May 11, 63, May 13, 63-Nov. 63; concurrently Minister of Foreign Affairs May 63-Nov. 63; Vice-Pres. Council of Revolutionary Commd. Nov. 63-May 64; Prime Minister and Vice-Pres. Council of Presidency May-Oct. 64; Prime Minister and Foreign Minister Jan.-Feb. 66, expelled from Baath Party Oct. 66.
Pacific Hotel, Beirut, Lebanon.

Bitat, Rabah; Algerian politician; b. 1927.
Member Front de Libération Nationale (F.L.N.); imprisoned 55-62; fmr. Minister of State, Algerian Provisional Govt., Tunis, later Algiers; mem. Political Bureau (in charge of Party Org.) July 62-63; Dep. Premier Sept. 62-May 63; Third Deputy Premier May 63-Sept. 63; left Algeria July 64, returned Dec. 64; Minister of State July 65-66; Minister of State in Charge of Transport 66-.
Ministry of Transport, Algiers, Algeria.

Blickenstaff, David; American United Nations official; b. 20 May 1915, Laverne, Calif.; ed. Woodstock School, Landour, Uttar Pradesh, India, Manchester Coll., Indiana, Univ. of Chicago.
Director, Jt. Office for Refugees, Madrid 42-45 Asst. Head of Section, UN Preparatory Comm., London 45-46 Exec. Officer, Head Gen. Assembly Affairs and Admin. Section, Office of UN Sec.-Gen. 47-54; Deputy Principal Sec. UN Comm. in Eritrea 49; Political Officer, UN Mission on Kashmir 51; Principal Sec. UN Observation Group in Lebanon June-Dec. 58; Dir. UN Information Centre, Paris 54-59, New Delhi 60-64; Resident Rep. UN Technical Assistance Board, Dir. Special Fund Programmes, India 60-64; Regional Rep. UN Devt. Programme (UNDP), Malaysia, Brunei, Singapore 64-69, Residence Rep. UNDP, Indonesia 69-71, now Residence Rep. UNDP, Tunisia.
United Nations Development Programme, P.O. Box 863, Tunis, Tunisia.

Bouabid, Abderrahim, LIC. EN DROIT; Moroccan lawyer, b. 23 March 1920; ed. schools in Salé, Rabat and Univ. of Paris.
Student and Istiqlal Rep., Paris 45-50; mem. Exec. Comm. of Istiqlal, Dir. *Al Istiqlal* 50-52; Political Officer, Moroccan Trade Union Movt. 50-52; in prison 52-54; Istiqlal Rep. to France 54-55, to Aix-les-Bains Conf. 55; Minister of State, First Moroccan Govt. Nov. 55; mem. Moroccan del. to Independence Conf., Paris 56, Amb. to France April-No. 56; Minister of Finance 56-58; took part in left-wing split of Istiqlal, leader of Union Nat. des Forces Populaires (UNFP) 59-, party banned 73; elected mem. Gen. Secr. UNFP by 2nd Congress 62; Deputy for Kénitra 63; lawyer for UNFP in trial for plot against King Hassan II Nov. 63-April 64; Head UNFP del. to Govt. consultations 65; mem. Cen. Cttee., Nat. Front (Koutla Watania) 70; mem. of body negotiating with King Hassan Dec. 71-March 72.
Plateau de Bettana, Salé, Morocco.

Boudiaf, Mohammed; Algerian politician; b. 1929.
Founder mem., Front de Libération Nationale (F.L.N.); imprisoned 56-62; fmr. Minister of State, Algerian Provisional Govt., Tunis, Deputy Premier 61-62; mem. Political Bureau (Guidance and External Affairs); imprisoned June-Nov. 63; Pres. Nat. Cttee. for Defence of the Revolution 64-; sentenced to death *in absentia* 65.

Boulares, Habib; Tunisian journalist and politician; b. 1932.
Editor-in-Chief of *As Sabah* 55-60; Dir. Tunis Radio and Television 60-61; Dir. of Information, Agence Tunis-Afrique Presse 61-64; Chief of Press of Destour Socialist Party 64-65; studied in Paris 65-70; Minister of Information 70-71.
Publ. *Murad III* (drama).
c/o Ministry of Information, Tunis, Tunisia.

Boumedienne, Colonel Houari (real name: **Mohammed Boukharouba**); Algerian army officer and politician; b. 23 Aug. 1927; ed. Islamic Inst., Constantine, Al Azhar, Cairo, and Military Schools.
Former Teacher, Guelma; Commdr. Armée de Libération Nationale, Tunis 60-62, Algiers 62-; Minister of Nat. Defence 62-; First Vice-Premier 63-65; Head of Revolutionary Council June 65-; Prime Minister July 65-.
Office of the Prime Minister, Algiers, Algeria.

Boumendjel, Ahmed; Algerian politician; b. 1908.
Former lawyer; fmr. mem. Democratic Union of the Algerian Manifesto (U.D.M.A.); Political Adviser to Provisional Govt. of the Algerian Republic; Head, Algerian Del. Melun Conf. June 60, mem. Algerian Del. Evian Conf. May 61; fmr. mem. Algerian Nat. Revolutionary Cttee.; Minister of Reconstruction, Works and Transport Sept. 62-Dec. 64; Officer-in-Charge UN Inst. for Training and Research (UNITAR), Geneva Dec. 65.
Algiers, Algeria.

Bourguiba, Habib Ben Ali; Tunisian politician; b. 3 Aug. 1902; ed. Collège Sadiki, Lycée Carnot, Univ. of Paris, Ecole Libre des Sciences Politiques.
Active in politics and journalism since 28; mem. Destour Party 21, broke away and formed Néo-Destour Party (outlawed by the French) 34; imprisoned by the French 34-36 and 38-43; escaped to Middle East 45, travelled to promote Tunisian independence 45-49, world tour 51 during Tunisian negotiations with French Govt.; arrested 52, placed under surveillance at Tabarka (Jan.), imprisoned at Remada (March), in solitary confinement, Ile de la Galite (May) until 54; released 54, under surveillance in France 54-55, during negotiations; returned to Tunisia following Franco-Tunisian Agreements 55; Pres. Tunisian Nat. Assembly, Prime Minister, Pres. of the Council, 56-59, 59-, concurrently Minister of Foreign Affairs and Defence 56-59; Pres. of Republic 57-, Life Pres. March 75-; Pres. Destour Socialist Party, Life Pres. 74-; Ordre du Sang, Ordre de la confiance en diamants.
Publs. *Le Destour et la France* 37, *La Tunisie et la France* 54.
The Presidency, Tunis, Tunisia.

Bourguiba, Habib, Jr.; L. ès D.; Tunisian diplomatist and politician; b. 9 April 1927; ed. College Sadiki, Lycée Carnot de Dijon, Faculté de Droit, Paris and Grenoble Univs.
Collaborated in nat. liberation movement, especially 51-54; lawyer in training, Tunis 54-56; Counsellor, Tunisian Embassy, Washington 56-57; Ambassador to Italy 57-58, to France 58-61, to U.S.A. 61-63, concurrently to Canada and Mexico; Sec.-Gen. to Presidency of the Repub. 64; Asst. Sec.-Gen. Destour Socialist Party 64-69; mem. Nat. Assembly 64-; Sec. of State for Foreign Affairs 64-69, Minister of Foreign Affairs 69-70, of Justice June-Nov. 70;

Dir.-Gen. Banque de Développement Economique de Tunise 70-.
Banque de Développement Economique de Tunisie, Avenue Habib Bourguiba, Tunis; Home: Villa Al Mahroussa, Avenue Salammbo, Tunis, Tunisia.

Boustany, Elie J., LIC. EN DROIT; Lebanese lawyer and diplomatist; b. 20 Aug. 1918; ed. Univ. of Saint-Joseph, Beirut.
Chef de Bureau, Office of Pres. of the Repub. 42, Head of Youth Dept. 43; Sec. Lebanese Embassy, Paris 44-45; Head of Legis., Ministry of Justice 47; Counsellor, Lebanese Embassy, Rome 56-58, 62-64, Madrid 58-60, London 60-62; Head Litigation Dept., Ministry of Foreign Affairs 64-66; Amb. to Senegal 66-71, concurrently accred. to Mali, Guinea, The Gambia; Dir. Int. Relations, Ministry of Foreign Affairs 71; Amb. to People's Repub. of China May 72-; Officer Order of Merit of the Repub. (Italy) 58, Commdr. Order of Civil Merit (Spain) 60, Grand Officer Nat. Order (Senegal) 71.
Publs. *Les codes libanais annotés et traduits* (7 vols.), *Recueil des traités* (2 vols.), *Législation libanaise* 1954-56; contribs. to Lebanese magazines and periodicals.
c/o Ministry of Foreign Affairs, Beirut, Lebanon.

Boustany, Fouad Ephrem, DR.-ÈS-LETTRES; Lebanese scholar; b. 15 Aug. 1906; ed. Deir-el-Kamar Coll. and Univ. St. Joseph, Beirut.
Teacher in Arab Literature, Islamic Insts. and History of Arab Civilization, Institut des Lettres Orientales 34-45; Dir. Ecole Normale 42-53; Prof. of Near Eastern History and Civilizations, Inst. des Sciences Politiques 45-55; Prof. of Arab Literature, Islamic Philosophy and Arab History, Acad. Libanaise des Beaux-Arts 47-53; Rector Univ. Libanaise 53-70; Sec.-Gen. Lebanese Nat. Comm. for UNESCO 48-55, Int. Comm. for Translation of Classic Works 49-, Acad. Libanaise; Dr. h.c. Univs. of Lyon 57, Austin, Texas 58, Georgetown, Washington, D.C. 58; decorations from: Lebanon, France, Vatican, Spain, Italy, Iran, Tunisia, Morocco and Senegal.
Publs. *Au temps de l'Emir* 26, *Ar-Rawae* (critical studies) 27, *Pourquoi* 30, *Histoire du Liban sous les Chéhab* of Amir Haïdar Chéhab (with Dr. A. Rustem) 33-35, *Bagdad, capitale des lettres abbassides* 34, *Le rôle des chrétiens dans l'établissement de la dynastie Omayyade* 38, *Le style orale chez les Arabes préislamiques* 41, *Al-Magani al Haditah* (5 vols.) 46-50, *Cinq jours à travers la Syrie* 50, *Les dits desmois* 73, *Encyclopedia Arabica* (10 vols.) 56-73.
Université Libanaise, Beirut, Lebanon.

Boutaleb, Abdelhadi; Moroccan politician; b. 23 Dec. 1923, Fez; ed. Al Qarawiyin Univ., Fez.
Professor of Arabic History and Literature, and Tutor to Prince Moulay Hassan and Prince Moulay Abdallah; Founder-mem. Democratic Party of Independence 44-51; campaigned, through the Party, for Moroccan independence, and for this purpose attended UN Session, Paris 51, and Negotiating Conf. at Aix-les-Bains 54-56; Minister of Labour and Social Questions in Bekkai Govt. 56; Chief Editor of journal *Al Rayal Am* 56-61; Amb. to Syria Feb. 62; Sec. of State, Ministry of Information Nov. 62, Ministry of Information, Youth and Sports Jan. 63; Minister of Information, Youth and Sports June 63; Interim Minister in Charge of Mauritania and Sahara Nov. 63; Minister of Justice 64-67, of Nat. Educ. and Fine Arts 67; Minister of State 68; Minister of Foreign Affairs 69-70; Pres. of Parl. 70-71; Amb. to U.S.A. Jan. 75-; Prof. of Constitutional Law and Political Insts., Mohamed V Univ., Rabat; decorations from Morocco, France, Spain, Italy, Tunisia and Egypt include Commdr. of the Throne of Morocco, Grand Cordon of the Republic of Egypt and Commdr. du Mérite Sportif, France.
Publs. Many cultural and literary works.
Moroccan Embassy, 1601 21st Street, N.W., Washington, D.C. 20009, U.S.A.

Boutaleb, Abdelhafid, L. ès L., L. ès D.; Moroccan politician; b. 30 June 1928; ed. Lycée de Fès, Lycée Louis-le-Grand, Paris, the Sorbonne and Faculté de Droit, Paris.
Director-General Ministry negotiating Independence for Morocco 55-56; Lawyer at Casablanca 57-58; Dir. Civil Service Dept. 59-60; Dir. of Admin., Municipal and Local Affairs, Ministry of the Interior 60-64; Dir. Royal Cabinet 64; Under-Sec. of State for the Interior Aug. 64-June 65; Minister of Work and Social Affairs 65-68; Minister of Public Works and Communications 68-69, of Justice 69-70; Minister of Labour, Employment and Professional Training Sept. 70; decorations from Fed. Repub. of Germany, Ghana, Tunisia, Egypt and Liberia.
8 rue Tedders, Rabat, Morocco.

Bouteflika, Abdul Aziz; Algerian politician; b. 1935; ed. Morocco.
Former Capt. Nat. Liberation Army (A.L.N.) and Secretary Gen. Staff; Minister of Sports 62-63; Minister of Foreign Affairs Sept. 63-; mem. F.L.N. Political Bureau 64-; mem. Revolutionary Council 65-; Pres. 29th Session, UN Gen. Assembly 74.
Ministry of Foreign Affairs, Algiers, Algeria.

Boutros, Fouad; Lebanese lawyer and politician; b. 1918; ed. Coll. des Frères, Beirut and Univ. of Lyon.
Judge, Civil and Mixed Commercial Court, Beirut 43-46; Judge Mil. Tribunal 45-46; Court Lawyer 47-; Govt. Lawyer 51-57; Minister of Nat. Educ. and of the Plan 59-60; mem. Chamber of Deputies 60-, Deputy Speaker 60-61; Minister of Justice 61-64; Vice-Pres. of the Council, Minister of Educ. and Defence 66, Minister of Foreign Affairs and of Tourism Feb.-Oct. 68; numerous decorations and honours.
Damascus Street—Al Kamal Building, P.O. Box 5848, Beirut; Home: Sursock Street, Fouad Boutros Building, Beirut, Lebanon.

Bouvet, Jacques Etienne; French engineer; b. 15 Jan. 1909; ed. Ecole Polytechnique and Ecole des Ponts-et-Chaussées.
Assistant Dir. Public Works, Cameroon 34-40, Dir. Martinique 40-43; Chief Engineer Hydraulic Service, Oran, Algeria 43-46; Engineer with Seine Navigation 46; Dir. S.A.C.T.A.R.D. (Soc. Auxiliaire de Co-ordination des Travaux d'aménagement du Rhone a Donzère-Mondragon) 47-53; Dir. E.G.T.H. (Entreprise des Grands Travaux Hydrauliques) 53-57; Prés. Dir.-Gén. S.O.P.E.G. (Soc. Pétroliere de Gérance) 57-72; Prés. Dir.-Gén. S.O.T.H.R.A. (Soc. de Transport du Gaz Naturel d'Hassi-er'Mel à Arzew) 60-67, Dir.-Gén. 67-72; Prés. Dir.-Gén. S.E.T.R.E.L. (Soc. d'études pour le transport du Gaz d'Hassi-er'Mel par Canalisations Transméditeranséennes) 60-64; Pres., Dir.-Gen. Soc. du Pipe-line Méditerranée-Rhône (S.P.M.R.) 69-; Chevalier Légion d'Honneur, Chevalier du Mérite Saharien.
Major engineering works include: enlargement of dry-dock at Fort de France, Martinique; improvement of the fall at Donzère-Mondragon and Montelimar power stations; 24 × 22 inch pipeline Haoud-el-Hamza-Bougie and 24 × 20 inch pipeline Hassi-er-r'Mel/Arzew.
9 rue Philibert-Delorme, Paris 17e, France.

Bouziri, Najib; Tunisian diplomatist; b. 1925; ed. Paris Univ. and Inst. d'Etudes politiques.
Joined Néo-Destour Party (now Destour Socialist Party) 41, mem. Central Cttee. 64-; practised law in France; mem. Tunisian del., autonomy negotiations 54-55; served with Home and Foreign Ministries 55-56; Chargé d'Affaires, Paris 56; Chef de Cabinet, Foreign Ministry 57-58; Ambassador to Italy 58-61, to Fed. Repub. of Germany 61-64; Sec. of State for P.T.T. Feb.-Nov. 64; 2nd Vice-Pres. Nat. Assembly 64-65; Amb. to U.S.S.R. March 65-70, concurrently to Poland Feb. 67; Amb. to Belgium and Luxembourg 70-72, to Morocco 72-73, to Algeria 73-75, to

Spain Feb. 75-; Leader, Tunisian del. to confs. on Maritime Law, Geneva 60, Diplomatic Relations, Vienna 61, Consular Relations, Vienna 63; Chair. Admin. and Budgetary Cttee. of UN Gen. Assembly 65.

Embassy of Tunisia, Méndez Núñez 17, Madrid, Spain.

Bozbeyli, Ferruh; Turkish lawyer and politician; b. 21 Jan. 1927, Pazarcik, Maras Prov.; ed. Univ. of Istanbul. Practised law until 65; mem. Parl. (Justice Party—JP) 61-70; fmr. Vice Pres. JP Parl. Group; Deputy Speaker Nat. Assembly, Speaker 65-70; founded Democratic Party (DP) 70; Leader DP Dec. 70-; Candidate for Presidency 73.

Democratic Party, Ankara, Turkey.

Brahimi, Lakhdar; Algerian diplomatist; b. 1934; ed. Medersa Algiers, Institut des Sciences Politiques, Algiers, and Ecole des Sciences Politiques, Paris.

Student Leader 53-56; Perm. Rep. of F.L.N. and later of Provisional Govt. of Algeria in South East Asia 56-61; Gen. Secretariat Ministry of External Affairs 61-63; Amb. to U.A.R. and Sudan 63-70; Perm. Rep. to Arab League 63-70; Amb. to U.K. July 71-.

Algerian Embassy, 6 Hyde Park Gate, London, S.W.7, England.

Burg, Yosef, DR. PHIL.; Israeli politician; b. 31 Jan. 1909; ed. Univs. of Berlin and Leipzig, Pedagogical Inst., Leipzig, Rabbinical Seminary Berlin, and Hebrew Univ. of Jerusalem.

Directorate, Palestine Office, Berlin 36; Nat. Exec. Mizrachi; Zionist Gen. Council 39-51; mem. Exec. Hapoel Hamizrachi 44-; Deputy Speaker First Knesset (Israeli Parl.) 49-51; Minister of Health, Govt. of Israel 51-52; Minister of Posts and Telegraphs 52-58; Minister of Social Welfare 59-70, of Interior 70-; Nat. Religious Party.

6 Ben Maimon Street, Jerusalem, Israel.

Burgan, Salih Khalil, M.D.; Jordanian politician; b. 1918; ed. American Univ. of Beirut.

Physician, Transjordan Frontier Forces 43-46, Dir. of Arab Physicians, T.F.F. 46-48; Private Physician, Zerka 48-63; M.P. 61-63; Minister of Health April 63-July 64, of Social Affairs and Labour Feb. 66, Sept. 66, 67-69, of Public Health Sept. 66-Aug. 67, of Social, Labour, Home, Municipal and Rural Affairs April 67-69; mem. of Senate 63-69; Regional Dir. ILO, Beirut 69-75, Asst. Dir.-Gen. ILO June 75-; Al Kawkab Medal (1st Grade); Grand Knight of the Holy Tomb.

Case Postale 500, CH-1211 Geneva 22, Switzerland.

Burns, Norman, M.A.; American economist and educationalist; b. 14 Nov. 1905; ed. Wittenberg Univ., Ohio, Yale Univ. and Univ. of Montpellier, France.

Assistant Prof. of Econs. American Univ. of Beirut 29-32; U.S. Govt. Service as Foreign trade economist, U.S. Tariff Comm., Dir. Foreign Service Inst. of State Dept., Dep. Dir. for Near East and South Asia, Int. Co-operation Admin., Econ. Adviser, UN Relief and Work Agency, Beirut, Dir. United States Operations Missions, Amman 34-61; Pres. American Univ. of Beirut 61-65; Board of Dirs. American Near East Refugee Inc., Washington 68-; mem. Board of Govs. Middle East Inst., Washington; Hon. LL.D. (Wittenberg Univ.); Commdr. Order of Cedar of Lebanon 65.

Publs. *The Tariff of Syria* 33, *Government Budgets of Middle East Countries* (Editor) 56, *Planning Economic Development in the Arab World* 59, *Education in the Middle East* 65, *Application of Technology and the Cultural Heritage* 65, *Management Factor in Economic Development* 70, *The Challenge of Education in the Developing Countries* 73, *The Energy Crisis and U.S. Middle East Policy* 73.

3813 North 37th Street, Arlington, Va. 22207, U.S.A.

Bydany, Abdulrahman al-; Yemeni politician and diplomatist; b. 1926; ed. Univs. of Cairo and Bonn.

Minister to German Fed. Repub. 55-59, to Sudan 59-60; resigned and resided in Cairo 60-62; after Yemen Revolution was Vice-Pres. of Revolutionary Council, Prime Minister, Minister of Economy, Minister of Foreign Affairs, Deputy C.-in-C. 62-63; in Cairo 63-66; Amb. to Lebanon 66-70.

Publs. *Secrets of Yemen, Economy of Yemen.*

c/o Ministry of Foreign Affairs, Sana'a, Yemen Arab Republic.

C

Çağlayangil, Ihsan Sabri; Turkish politician; b. 1908; ed. Faculty of Law, Univ. of Istanbul.

Formerly with Ministry of Interior; Gov. of Antalya 48-53, of Çannakale 53-54, of Sivas 54, of Bursa 54-60; Senator for Bursa 61-; Minister of Labour Feb.-Oct. 65, of Foreign Affairs 65-71, April 75-; Pres. Senate Foreign Affairs Cttee. 72; Justice Party.

Kennedy Caddesi 64/2, Ankara, Turkey.

Cahen, Claude Louis Alfred, D. ès L.; French university professor; b. 1909; ed. Sorbonne, Ecole des Langues Orientales and Ecole Normale Supérieure, Paris.

Professor, Faculty of Letters, Univ. of Strasbourg 45-59, Sorbonne, Paris 59-; Lecturer, Ecole des Langues Orientales, Paris 37-54; Dir. *Journal of the Economic and Social History of the Orient*; mem. Inst. de France 73; Schlumberger Prize 45.

Publs. *La Syrie du Nord au temps des Croisades* 40, *Le régime féodal de l'Italie normande* 40, *Histoire générale des Civilisations* III, *Le Moyen Age* (chapitres sur l'Islam), *Pre-Ottoman Turkey* 68, *Der Islam* (Fischer Weltgeschichte) 68, French edn. *L'Islam* 70; various studies in Turkish history, Islamic economic and social history, and history of the Crusaders.

62 avenue Carnot, Savigny s. Orge (S.et.O.), France.

Cappelletti, Luciano, J.D., PH.D.; Italian United Nations official; b. 22 Nov. 1930; ed. Univs. of Padua, Ferrara, Bologna and (Berkeley) Calif.

Associate Prof., Univ. of Bologna 60-63; joined UN Devt. Programme (UNDP) 63, has worked in India, Burma, Uganda, Pakistan; now Resident Rep. UNDP, Sudan.

Publs. *Burocrazia e Società* 68, and several articles on public administration in professional journals.

United Nations Development Programme, P.O. Box 913, Khartoum, Sudan.

Carton, Paul Georges; French diplomatist; b. 30 March, 1920; ed. Ecole Libre des Sciences Politiques and Ecole des Hautes Etudes Commerciales.

Joined diplomatic service 43, served Délégation Générale au Levant 43-45, Paris 46, Rabat 46-47, Tangier 47-48, Kabul 48-51, Amman 51-54, Tabriz 54, Ankara 54-55, Jeddah 55-56, Khartoum 56-58, Marrakesh 58-59; Consul-Gen. Aden 59-64; Counsellor, Washington 64-68; Amb. to Kuwait 68-74, concurrently to Qatar, Bahrain, United Arab Emirates 72-74, and Oman 72-74; Officier, Légion d'Honneur, Lebanese decorations.

c/o Ministère des Affaires Étrangères, Quai d'Orsay, Paris, France.

Cayer, Rt. Rev. John Aimé, D.D.; Canadian ecclesiastic; b. 1900; ed. Quebec and Montreal Colls. and Innsbruck Univ., Austria.

Ordained priest 26; missionary in Edmonton, Alberta 27-36; apptd. Rector of St. Anthony's Coll., Edmonton 30; Prof. of Theology, R.C. Seminary, Regina, Sask. 40-45; elected Commissary Provincial for the Franciscan Fathers 45, Minister Provincial for the Order in Canada 48; consecrated Bishop of Alexandria and Vicar Apostolic of Egypt, Sept. 49-, and Admin. of the Apostolic Vicariate of Port Said 57-.

Publ. *Mère Marie de Bethanie Beghian* 60.
Archbishop's Residence, 10 Sidi Metwalli, Alexandria, Egypt.

Chaker, Abdelmajid; Tunisian politician.
Secretary of State for Agriculture 62-64, for Information 64-66; Ambassador to Algeria 66-70; mem. Néo Destour, later Socialist Destour Party, Dir. until Nov. 64, mem. Bureau Politique Nov. 64-71, mem. Cen. Cttee. 71-; Amb. to Yugoslavia 70-73, to Sweden 73-.
Tunisian Embassy, 73c Drottninggatan, Stockholm, Sweden.

Chakkour, Lieut.-Gen. Youssef; Syrian army officer; b. 1926, Homs; ed. Jesuit Coll., Syrian Mil. School, Syrian Acad. of Staff, Foroshelov Acad.
Commander, S.W. Front and S.W. Region 63; Chief Commdr. Army Artillery 63; Commdr. Security Forces 64-67; Chief Operations Branch, Gen. H.Q. 67; Deputy Chief of Staff 68-72, Chief of Staff 72-74; Deputy Defence Minister 74-; Knight of Syrian, Egyptian and Palestinian Legions of Hon.; Moroccan and Syrian Orders of Merit; Commdr. Order of the Cedar of Lebanon.
c/o Ministry of Defence, Damascus, Syria.

Challah, Anwar S., M.S., M.B.A.; Syrian industrialist; b. 1910; ed. American Univ., and Univ. of California.
Former Pres. Syrian Oil Refining and Distribution Co., Damascus Chamber of Industry, Trustee Syrian Univ.; Pres. Juvenile Soc.; Trustee Savings Hospital; mem. Rotary Int.; Pres. Arab World Trade Promotion Centre.
P.O. Box 1618, Beirut, Lebanon.

Chamoun, Camille, LL.D.; Lebanese lawyer; b. 3 April 1900; ed. Coll. des Frères and Law School, Beirut.
Qualified as lawyer 24; mem. Parl. 34-; Minister of Finance 38; Minister of Interior 43-44; Minister to Allied Governments in London 44; Head of Del. to Int. Civil Aviation Conf., Chicago 44, UNESCO Conf. and UN Preparatory Comm. 45; Del. to UN Gen. Assembly, London and N.Y. 46; Lebanese rep. Interim Comm., UN 48; Pres. Lebanese Republic 52-58; leader Liberal Nationalist Party 58-; Minister of Interior, of Post Office and Telecommunications, of Hydraulic and Electrical Resources May 75-.
Ministry of the Interior, Beirut; Home: Saadyat, Lebanon.

Chanderli, Abdelkader; Algerian diplomatist; b. 1915; ed. Univ. of Paris.
Former Foreign Correspondent and Editor; Chief, Public Relations Div. UNESCO 49-55; Rep. of Algerian Front de Libération Nationale (FLN) in U.S.A. 56-62; Perm. Rep. of Algeria to UN 62-64; Vice-Pres. ECOSOC 64-65; Dir.-Gen. Centre for Industrial Studies and Technology, Algiers; Pres. and Gen. Man. CAMEL Petroleum Co.
c/o Ministry of Industry and Energy, Algiers, Algeria.

Chatti, Habib; Tunisian diplomatist; b. 1916; ed. Sadik Coll., Tunis.
Journalist 37-52, Editor *Ez-Zohra* 43-50, *Es-Sabah* 50-52; imprisoned 52, 53; Head, Press Cabinet of Pres. of Council 54-55, Head, Information Service 55; mem. Nat. Council, Néo-Destour Party 55; Dir. *Al Amal* 56; Vice-Pres. Constituent Nat. Assembly 56; Ambassador to Lebanon and Iraq 57-59, to Turkey and Iran 59-62, to U.K. 62-64, to Morocco 64-70, to Algeria 70-72; Dir. of the Presidential Cabinet 72-74; Minister of Foreign Affairs Jan. 74-; mem. Political Bureau and Cen. Cttee. Destour Socialist Party 74-; Deputy to Nat. Assembly 74-; Grand Cordon Ordre de la Répub. Tunisienne, several foreign decorations.
Ministry of Foreign Affairs, Tunis, Tunisia.

Chaudhuri, Kamal Reheem, F.R.S.A.; Bangladesh administrator; b. 1 March 1923; ed. Calcutta Univ., Presidency Coll., Aligarh Muslim Univ., Imperial Agricultural Research Inst. and Edinburgh Univ.

Governor Imperial Coll. of Science and Technology 57-65; Chair. British Commonwealth Scientific Offices, London 58; Assessor British Cttee. for Int. Nature Conservation 58-65; Chair. Commonwealth Agricultural Bureaux 61; Alt. Gov. IAEA 63; Head UNESCO Regional Science Office for the Arab States 70-; del. to numerous int. scientific and agricultural confs.; Egyptian Order of Merit 72.
Publs. include *Science and Ourselves* 60.
UNESCO Regional Science Office for the Arab States, 8 Salamlik Street, Garden City, Cairo, Egypt.

Chéhab, Amir Khalid; Lebanese diplomatist and politician; b. 1890; ed. Patriarchal Coll. Damascus.
Mem. comm. for drawing up Lebanese Constitution 26; Minister of Finance 27; elected Deputy 28-55, 60-; Pres. Chamber of Deputies 35; Prime Minister 38; Minister of State 43; Minister to Jordan 47; Prime Minister and Minister of the Interior Oct. 52-April 53; Leader Dar el Fatwa.
Rue de Damas, Beirut, Lebanon.

Chéhab, Amir Maurice; Lebanese archaeologist and historian; b. 1904; ed. Univ. St. Joseph, Beirut, Ecole du Louvre, and Ecole des Hautes Etudes Historiques, Paris.
Conservator, Lebanese Nat. Museum 28, Chief of Antiquities Service 37, Dir. 44; Prof. of the History of Architecture, Lebanese Acad. of Fine Arts 42, of Lebanese History, Ecole Normale 42, of Diplomatic and Gen. History, Ecole des Sciences Politiques 45; Prof. of Oriental Archæology, Inst. of Oriental Literature 46; Dir. Tyre and Anjar Excavations 50; Prof. of History and Archæology, Univ. of the Lebanon 53-59; Curator of Lebanese Gen. Antiquities 53-59, Dir.-Gen. of Antiquities 59-.
Direction des Antiquités, rue de Damas, Beirut, Lebanon.

Chelli, Tijani; Tunisian politician; b. 23 March 1931, Nabeul; ed. Collège Sadiki, Tunis and in France.
Engineer, Ministry of Public Works, Kef 59-60; Deputy Chief Engineer of Roads and Bridges 60; Dir. of Transport 61; Dir. of Sea and Air Transport 62; Pres., Dir.-Gen. Société Nationale des Chemins de Fer Tunisiens 65-67; Dir. of Industry, Dept. of the Plan and Nat. Economy 67-69; Pres., Dir.-Gen. Industries Chimiques Maghrébines (ICM) Jan.-Nov. 69; Minister of Public Works 69-70, of the Economy 70-72; Pres., Dir.-Gen. Agence de Promotion des Investissements Jan. 73-.
Agence de Promotion des Investissements, 18 avenue Mohamed V, Tunis, Tunisia.

Christofides, Andreas N., M.A.; Cypriot broadcasting official; b. 20 Aug. 1937; ed. Pancyprian Gymnasium, Nicosia, Athens Univ. and Columbia Univ., New York.
Teacher at Pancyprian Gymnasium 58-63; Dir. of Radio Programmes of Cyprus Broadcasting Corpn. 64-67; Dir.-Gen. of Cyprus Broadcasting Corpn. 67-; first Nat. Award Prize for *Points of View III*.
Publs. include: Essays: *Letters from New York* 65, *Points of View I* 66, *Points of View II* 69 (First Nat. Award Prize), *Introduction to Propaganda* 66, *Love Songs from Cyprus* 64, *An Anthology of Poetry from Cyprus* (with K. Montis) 69, *An Anthology of Short Stories* (with P. Ioannides) 71, *Points of View III;* Poems: *A Strange Illustration* 69, *Analytical Propositions* 70.
Cyprus Broadcasting Corporation, P.O. Box 1824, Nicosia, Cyprus.

Christophides, Ioannis; Cypriot politician; b. 21 Jan. 1924, Nicosia; ed. Pancyprian Gymnasium, Nicosia, Gray's Inn Law School, London.
Barrister-at-Law; joined family banking and insurance firms 48, Chief Exec. 54-72; Chair. of several private cos. 54-72; Chair. Cyprus Telecommunications Authority 66-72; Vice-Chair. Commonwealth Telecommunications Board 70-72; Minister of Foreign Affairs 72-74, Jan. 75-; Pres. Nicosia Branch, Cyprus Red Cross 64-72.
25 El. Venizelos Street, Nicosia, Cyprus.

Clerides, Glavkos John, B.A., LL.B.; Cypriot lawyer and politician; b. 1919; ed. Pancyprian Gymnasium, Nicosia, Univ. Tutorial Coll., London, King's Coll., London Univ., Gray's Inn, London.
Served with R.A.F. 39-45; shot down and taken prisoner 42-45 (mentioned in despatches); practised law in Cyprus 51-60; Head of Greek Cypriot Del., Constitutional Comm. 59-60; first Minister of Justice of the Republic 59-60; mem. House of Representatives 60-, Pres. of the House 60-; Acting Pres. of Repub. July-Dec. 74; Minister of Defence, Interior and Foreign Affairs Aug.-Dec. 74; Chair. Selection. Public Accounts and Attendance of Members cttees.; Rep. to Consultative Assembly of the Council of Europe; mem. Political Cttee. and Standing Cttee.; leader of Unified Party; Gold Medal Order of the Holy Sepulchre.
56 Metochio Street, Nicosia; House of Representatives, Nicosia, Cyprus.

Cohn, Haim H.; Israeli lawyer; b. 11 March 1911; ed. Univs. of Munich, Hamburg and Frankfurt-am-Main, Germany, Hebrew Univ. of Jerusalem, and Govt. Law School, Jerusalem.
Admitted to Bar of Palestine 37; Sec. Legal Council, Jewish Agency for Palestine, Jerusalem 47; State Attorney, Ministry of Justice, Hakirya 48, Dir.-Gen. 49; Attorney-Gen., Govt. of Israel 50; Minister of Justice and Acting Attorney-Gen. 52; Attorney-Gen. 52-60; Justice, Supreme Court of Israel 60-; mem. Perm. Court of Arbitration, The Hague 62-, UN Comm. on Human Rights 65-67; Deputy Chair. Council of Higher Educ., Israel 58-71; mem. Board of Govs., Int. Inst. of Human Rights, Strasbourg; Chair. Exec. Council Hebrew Univ. of Jerusalem; Visiting Prof. of Law, Univ. of Tel-Aviv; mem. Int. Comm. of Jurists, Geneva 73-.
Publs. *The Foreign Laws of Marriage and Divorce* (English) 37, *Glaube und Glaubensfreiheit* (German) 67, *The Trial and Death of Jesus* (Hebrew) 68, English edn. 71, *Jewish Law in Ancient and Modern Israel* 72.
Supreme Court of Israel, Jerusalem; and 36 Tchernihovsky Street, Jerusalem, Israel.

Colocassides, Michael G., B.SC.(ECON.); Cypriot economist; b. 9 Sept. 1933; ed. Pancyprian Gymnasium, Nicosia, London School of Econs., Univ. of London.
Posts in family business 55-72; Dir. Cyprus Devt. Bank 63-70, Chair. 68-70; Chair. Cyprus Tourism Org. 69-72; Minister of Commerce and Industry 72-74, 75-.
4 Aetolon Street, Nicosia I II, Cyprus.

Comay, Michael, B.A., LL.B.; Israeli diplomatist; b. 17 Oct. 1908; ed. Cape Town Univ., South Africa.
Major South African Army 40-45; Special Rep. South African Zionist Fed., attached to Political Dept. Jewish Agency, Jerusalem 46-48; mem. Israel del. to UN 48-, Chair. 60-67; has represented Israel at a number of int. confs.; Dir. British Commonwealth Div., Israel Foreign Ministry 48-51, Asst. Dir.-Gen. 51-53; Amb. to Canada 53-57; Asst. Dir.-Gen. Ministry for Foreign Affairs 57-59; Perm. Rep. to UN 60-67; Political Adviser to Foreign Minister and Amb.-at-Large 67-70; Amb. to U.K. 70-73; Special Adviser to Minister of Foreign Affairs Oct. 73-.
Ministry of Foreign Affairs, Jerusalem, Israel.
47 Harav Berlin Street, Jerusalem, Israel.

Coobar, Abdulmegid; Libyan politician; b. 1909; ed. Arabic and Italian schools in Tripoli, and privately.
With Birth Registration Section, Tripoli Municipal Council and later its Section Head, Adviser on Arab Affairs for the Council 43-44; resigned from Govt. Service 44; mem. Nat. Constitutional Assembly 50, and mem. its Cttee. to draft the Libyan Constitution; mem. of Parl. for Eastern Gharian 52-55, Pres. of Parl. Assembly 52-55; Dep. Prime Minister and Minister of Communications 55-56; again elected for Eastern Gharian to the new Chamber of Deputies 55, Pres. 56; mem. of Council of Viceroy 56;

Dep. Prime Minister and Minister of Foreign Affairs 57; Prime Minister 57-60, concurrently Minister for Foreign Affairs 58-60; Independence Award (First Class).
Asadu el-Furat Street 29, Garden City, Tripoli, Libya.

Crawford, William R., Jr., M.A.; American diplomatist; b. 22 April 1928; ed. Harvard Coll. and Univ. of Pennsylvania, U.S.A.
Political Officer, Jeddah, Saudi Arabia 51; Consul, Venice. Italy 53; Chargé d'Affaires, Taiz, Yemen 57; Principal Officer, Aden; Officer-in-Charge Lebanon-Israel Affairs, Washington, D.C. 62; Counsellor, Political Officer, Rabat, Morocco 64; Deputy Head of Mission to Cyprus 68; Amb. to Yemen Arab Repub. 72-74, to Cyprus 74-; Meritorious Service Award (U.S. Dept. of State) 59, William A. Jump Award 63.
c/o American Embassy, Nicosia, Cyprus.

Cunbur, Fatma Müjgân, DR. PHIL.; Turkish librarian; b. 1926; ed. Lycée and Univ. of Ankara.
Librarian of Faculty of Letters, Univ. of Ankara 52-55, Lecturer in Library Science 60-; Librarian Nat. Library 55-59, Acting Dir. 59, Chief of rare books and manuscripts section 60-65, Gen. Dir. 65-; mem. Turkish Librarians' Asscn., Turkish Language Asscn., Asscn. for Studying Social Life of Women.
Publs. *Türk Kadın Yazarları Bibliyografyasi* (Bibliography of Turkish Women Authors) 55, *Fuzuli hakkında bir bibliyografya denemesi* (A Preliminary Bibliography of the Turkish Poet Fuzuli) 56, *Fuzuli divan* (Collected Poems of Fuzuli) 58, *Yunus Emre'nin gönlü* (The Heart of Yunus Emre) 59, *Yusuf Ağa Kütüphanesi Vakfiyesi* (The Endowment of Yusuf Ağa Library) 63, *I. Abdülhamid vakfiyesi ve Hamidiye Kütüphanesi* (The Endowment of Abdülhamid I and the Hamidiye Library) 65, *Başaklarin sesi, Türkhalk sairleri, hayatlari ve eserleri* (The Sounds of Corn Ears, Turkish folk poets, their lives and works).
Turkish National Library, Yenişehir, Ankara, Turkey.

D

Daccak, Nassouh, L. EN D.; Syrian financial administrator; b. 1916, Damascus; ed. Damascus Univ.
Head Dept. of Foreign Trade, Ministry of Econ. 47-50; Dir. of Trade, Ministry of Econ. 50-51, Dir. of Econ. Affairs 51-59; Chair. Board of Dirs., Gen. Man. Industrial Bank 59-62; Gen. Sec. Ministry of Labour and Social Affairs 62-63; Chair. Board of Credit and Money 71-; Gov. Cen. Bank of Syria 71-; Alt. Gov. IMF, Arab Fund for Social and Econ. Devt.; mem. Board of Dirs., European Arab Bank.
Central Bank of Syria, Damascus, Syria.

Dafaaila, El Nazeer; Sudanese veterinary scientist and educationist; b. 1 Jan. 1922, El Obeid; ed. Univ. of Khartoum.
Veterinary Officer, Govt. Research Laboratories, Khartoum 46-50, Senior Research Officer 55-56; Univ. of Khartoum, Senior Lecturer Bacteriology 56-57, Dean, Faculty of Veterinary Science 58-62, Deputy Vice-Chancellor 60-62, Vice-Chancellor 62-68; Exec. Vice-Pres. Asscn. of African Univs. 68-69; Provost for Agriculture and Veterinary Medicine, Ahmadu Bello Univ., Zaria, Nigeria 71-72; Speaker of the People's Assembly 72-74; Minister of Health and Social Welfare Jan. 75-; Hon. Assoc. Royal Coll. of Vetinerary Surgeons, London 63; Hon. Fellow, Hanover Veterinary Univ. 63; Gold Medal, Balazan Foundation, Italy 63; Hon. Dr. Biological Sciences, Charles Univ., Prague 66.
Publs. numerous papers in the field of vetinerary and biological sciences and education.
Ministry of Health and Social Welfare, Khartoum, Democratic Republic of the Sudan.

Dagher, Abdallah, S.J.; Lebanese ecclesiastic and university rector; b. 1 June 1914; ed. Secondary School of Univ. St. Joseph, Oriental Seminary of Beirut and Univ. de Paris à la Sorbonne.
Entered Jesuit Noviciate 32; ordained priest 45; Prefect Arabic Studies, Secondary School of Univ. St. Joseph; Dir. Oriental Seminary (Maronite) of Beirut; Rector Maronite Seminary of Ghazir, Lebanon 51-57; Jesuit Provincial for the Near East 57-65; Rector Univ. St. Joseph 65-72, Coll. Notre-Dame de Jamhour 72-; Consultant of Roman Congregation for the Non-Christian Religious (Islam); Officier de la Légion d'Honneur, du Mérite Libanais.
Collège Notre-Dame de Jamhour, P.O. Box 2904, Beirut, Lebanon.

Dajani, Ali Taher, B.A.; Jordanian administrator; b. 1911; ed. English Coll., Jerusalem, American Univ. of Beirut.
Assistant Information Officer, Public Information Office, Jerusalem 36-43; Sec. Arab Chamber of Commerce, Jerusalem 43-47; Asst. Commr. of Commerce and Industry, Palestine Govt. 47-48; Admin. Sec. Amman Chamber of Commerce and Industry 50-55; Dir. Amman Chamber of Industry 62-; with Daily Star, Beirut; Jordan Corresp. of *Al-Hayat*, Beirut; mem. of Parl. July 63-Dec. 66; Minister of Communications Feb.-July 65; mem. Scientific Research Council, Jordan; Lecturer, Labour Educ. Inst.; Hon. Consul of Japan 72-74; Star of Jordan 1st Class.
Publs. in Arabic: *Pilgrimage to Mecca* 44, *The Economy of Jordan* 55, *Jerusalem: Faith and Struggle* 73, *Industry of Jordan* 69, 73; in English: *Industry of Jordan* 65, 67.
P.O. Box 1791, Amman, Jordan.

Dakhqan, Omar Abdullah, B.SC.; Jordanian politician; b. 1927, Amman.
Assistant Under-Sec. Ministry of Public Works 54; Dir.-Gen. Jordan-Hijaz Railway 56; Dir.-Gen. Central Water Authority 64-66, also Dir. of Geological and Mining Research 65-66; Dir.-Gen. and Deputy Pres. Natural Resources Authority 66-69; Dir.-Gen. Jordan Phosphate Co. 69-70; Minister of Agriculture 70-72.
Amman, Jordan.

Dalley, Christopher Mervyn, C.M.G., M.A., F.INST.PET., C.ENG.; British petroleum executive; b. 26 Dec. 1913; ed. Epsom College and Queens' Coll., Cambridge.
Royal Navy 39-45; British Petroleum Co. 46; Iranian Oil Operating Companies in Iran 54, Asst. Gen. Man. Dir. 58; Iraq Petroleum Co., Abu Dhabi Petroleum Co., Qatar Petroleum Co. and other associated companies 62, Man. Dir. 63; Pres. Inst. of Petroleum 70; Chair. Iraq Petroleum Co. 70-73; Chair. Oil Exploration Holdings Ltd. and Viking Jersey Equipment Ltd. 73-; Order of Homayoun (Iran) 63.
6 Godfrey Street, London, S.W.3, England.

Daoud, Lt.-Gen. Mohammad (cousin of fmr. King Mohammad Zahir Shah); Afghan army officer and politician; b. 18 July 1909; ed. Habibia Coll. Kabul, Pre-cadet School Kabul, and in France.
Governor of Kandahar 32; Gov. and C.-in-C. Eastern Provinces 34; C.-in-C. Central Forces and Mil. Schools 37; suppressed revolt of 45; Prime Minister 53-63, concurrently Minister of Defence and of the Interior; led *coup* deposing King Mohammad Zahir Shah July 73; Pres., Prime Minister Repub. of Afghanistan July 73-, concurrently Minister of Defence and of Foreign Affairs; renounced royal title July 73.
Office of the President, Kabul, Afghanistan.

Daouk, Ahmed bey; Lebanese engineer, diplomatist and politician; b. 1893; ed. Univ. of Aix-en-Provence.
Engineer with Sucreries et Raffineries d'Egypte 15-19; technical mission for King Hussein of Hedjaz 19-20;

consultant 20-27; held various directorships 27-40; Prime Minister 41, 42, May-Aug. 60; Pres. Nat. Congress 43; Ambassador to France 44-58, to Spain; Head of Missions to U.S.A., South America and Africa; Rep. to Arab League; mem. Dels. to UN and UNESCO 44-58; Pres. Admin. Council of Banks and Socs. 60-; Leader of official dels. overseas 60-; Prime Minister 60; Pres. Ogero Radio-Orient 73-; holder of several Lebanese and foreign decorations.
Rue Omar Daouk, Beirut, Lebanon.

Darwish, Dr. Ahmed el Sayed; Egyptian physician; ed. Cairo Univ.
Lecturer, Alexandria Coll. of Medicine until 64, Dean 64-; fmr. Minister of Tourism; Minister of Health and Social Affairs Sept. 71-Jan. 72; Adviser to the Pres. Jan. 72-.
The Presidency, Cairo, Egypt.

Dawalibi, Marouf; Syrian professor and lawyer; b. 1907; ed. Aleppo, Damascus, and Univ. of Paris.
Lawyer Court of Appeal Aleppo 35-39; Prof. Law Faculty, Damascus 47; Minister of Nat. Economy 49-50; Pres. Chamber of Deputies 51; Prime Minister and Minister of Defence 51; Minister of Nat. Defence 54; Prime Minister 61-62; mem. Exec. Council Motamav al Alam al Islami (World Muslim Congress) 65; living in Saudi Arabia 66.
Publs. *La Jurisprudence dans le Droit Islamique* 41, *Introduction au Droit Romain* 47, *Introduction à la science des sources du Droit Musulman* 49, *Précis du Droit Romain* 2 vols. 61, *Histoire Générale du Droit* 61.

Dayan, Gen. Moshe, LL.B.; Israeli soldier and politician; b. 20 May 1915, Degania; ed. agricultural high school, Nahalal, and Staff Coll., Camberley.
Trained in Haganah (Jewish militia) 29; second in command to Capt. Orde Wingate 37; imprisoned by British when Haganah declared illegal 39; released for training as intelligence scout in Syria 41; Colonel after 45; took leading part in war with Arabs 48-49; promoted to Gen. and Commdr. Southern Region Command 50; Commdr. Northern Region Command 51; Chief of Staff 53-58; Minister of Agriculture 59-64; Minister of Defence 67-74; fmr. mem. Mapai Party; joined Rafi Party (Labour List) 65; elected to the Knesset 59, 65, 69 (Maarach List).
Publs. *Diary of the Sinai Campaign* 66, *Mapa Hadasha, Yahassim Aherim* 69.
Yoav Street 11, Zahala, Tel-Aviv, Israel.

de Garang, (Enok) Mading; Sudanese politician; b. 1 Jan. 1934, Kongor, Bor; ed. Malak Altar Intermediate School, Rumbek Secondary School, Manchester Coll. of Science and Technology, Inst. of Educ., London Univ.
Member of Southern Nationalist Movement 56-; co-founder Sudan African Nat. Union, Manchester, U.K. 63; ed. *Voice of Southern Sudan*, Manchester, U.K. 63; man. Spearhead Press, Malakal 63; ed. *Light* 63-65; Asst. Production Man., Haile Selassie Printing Press, Ethiopia 65-67; studied then taught at Africa Lit. Centre, Kitwe, Zambia 67-69; co-founder Southern Sudan Asscn., London, Later Dir.; ed. *Grass Curtain*, London 70-72; External Spokesman, South Sudan Liberation Movement 70-March 72; mem. High Exec. Council for Southern Region, for Information, Culture, Youth and Sports, Tourism and Wildlife, Social Services April 72-73, for Rural Devt. and Co-operatives 73-; mem. Regional People's Assembly for Bor; mem. Cen. Cttee. Sudan Socialist Union; First Class Medal (Two Niles) for Peace.
Ministry of Rural Development and Co-operatives, Juba; Home: Bor District, Upper Nile Province, Sudan.

Deif, Nazih Ahmed, B.COM., M.A., PH.D.; Egyptian economist; b. 4 March 1923; ed. Cairo Univ. and Univ. of Chicago, Ill., U.S.A.
Member Expert Group collaborating with Arthur D. Little Group on Industrialization of Egypt 53; Dir. Econ.

Statistics, Ministry of Finance 54; Senior Research Officer, Nat. Planning Comm. 57, Dir.-Gen. 58; Under-Sec. Ministry of Planning, U.A.R. 61-64; Gov. Int. Monetary Fund, U.A.R. 64-66; Ministry of Treasury, Egypt 64-68; Prof. Inst. of Statistical Studies and Research, Cairo Univ. 69-70; Exec. Dir. for Middle East IMF Sept. 70-. Publs. numerous papers on national planning issues, particularly national accounting, and various UN publs. International Monetary Fund, Washington, D.C.; and 2 Rollins Court, Rockville, Md. 20852, U.S.A.

Demirel, Süleyman; Turkish hydraulic engineer and politician; b. 1924, Istâmköy, Isparta Prov.; ed. High School, Afyon and Istanbul Technical Univ.
Qualified engineer; worked in U.S.A. 49-51, 54-55; with Dir.-Gen. Electrical Studies, Ankara 50-52; in charge of building various hydro-electric schemes 52-54; Head of Dept. of Dams 54; Dir.-Gen. of Water Control 54-55; first Eisenhower Fellow for Study in U.S.A. 54; Dir. State Hydraulics Admin. 55-60; private practice including Consultant to Morrison-Knudsen, and lecturer Middle East Technical Univ. 61-65; Pres. Justice Party 64-; Deputy Prime Minister Feb.-Oct. 65; Prime Minister 65-71, April 75-.
Office of the Prime Minister, Ankara; and Adalet Partisi Genel Müdürlüğü, Ankara, Turkey.

Denktaş, Rauf; Cypriot lawyer; b. 27 Jan. 1924; ed. English School, Nicosia, and Lincoln's Inn, London.
Legal practice, Nicosia 47-49; Crown Counsel and Acting Solicitor-Gen., Attorney-Gen.'s Office 49-58; Chair. Fed. of Turkish Asscns. 58-60; Pres. Turkish Communal Chamber 60-; Vice-Pres. Turkish Cypriot Admin. 67-73; Pres. 73-75; Pres. Turkish Federated State of Cyprus 75-; Publs. *Secrets of Happiness* (1st edn. 43, 2nd edn. 73), *Hell Without Five* 44, *A Handbook of Criminal Cases* 55, *Five Minutes to Twelve* 66, *The AKRITAS Plan* 72, *A Short Discourse on Cyprus* 72; *The Cyprus Problem* 73.
The Residence of the Vice-President, Nicosia, Cyprus.

Diba, H.I.M. Queen Farah (*see* under Pahlavi, H.I.M. Queen Farah).

Dimechkié, Nadim, M.A.; Lebanese diplomatist; b. 5 Dec. 1919; ed. American Univ. of Beirut.
Director-General Ministry of Nat. Economy 43-44; Lebanese del. Joint Supply Board for Syria and Lebanon 42-44; Counsellor, Lebanese Embassy, London 44-49; Consul-Gen., Ottawa 50; Dir. Econ. and Social Dept., Ministry of Foreign Affairs 51-52; Chargé d'Affaires, Cairo 52, Minister 53-55; Minister to Switzerland 55-57; Amb. to U.S.A. 58-62; Dir. Econ. Affairs, Ministry of Foreign Affairs 62-66; Amb. to U.K. 66-; Lebanese Order of Cedars, Syrian Order of Merit, Tunisian Order of Merit, Greek Order of Phoenix, Egyptian Order of Ismail, etc.
Lebanese Embassy, 21 Kensington Palace Gardens, London, W.8, England.

Dimitrios I (**Dimitrios Papadopoulos**); Archbishop of Constantinople and Ecumenical Patriarch; b. 8 Sept. 1914, Istanbul; ed. Theological School of Halki, Heybeliada-Istanbul.
Ordained Deacon 37; Ordained Priest 42; Preacher in Edessa, Greece 37-38; Preacher, Parish of Feriköy-Istanbul 39-45; Priest of Orthodox Community, Teheran 45-50; Head Priest, Feriköy 50-64; Bishop of Elaia, Auxiliary Bishop of the Patriarch Athenagoras in Istanbul 64-72; Metropolitan of Imvros and Tenedos 72; Archbishop of Constantinople and Ecumenical Patriarch 72-.
Rum Ortodoks Patrikhanesi, Fener, Istanbul, Turkey.

Dimitriou, Nicos George, F.C.I.S.; Cypriot merchant banker, industrialist and diplomatist; b. 16 July 1920; ed. Larnaca Commercial Lyceum, Greek Gymnasium, Athens, and Maiden Erlegh Private School, Reading, England.

Manager and Sec. N. J. Dimitriou Ltd., Merchant Bankers 52-62, Man. Dir. 62-; Man. Dir. Larnaca Oil Works Ltd. 63-; dir. several Cyprus companies; Dir. Bank of Cyprus Ltd. 60-62; Chair. Cyprus Chamber of Commerce 60-63; Pres. Chamber of Commerce and Industry, Larnaca 63-68, Pezoporicos Club, Larnaca 57-68; Pres. Cyprus Soc. of Inc. Secretaries 68; Consul-Gen. of Denmark 61-; mem. Council Cyprus Chamber of Commerce and Industry 63-68; Chair. Cyprus Devt. Corpn. Ltd. 66-68; Minister of Commerce and Industry 68-70; Chair. Electricity Authority of Cyprus 70-73, Advisory Board Nat. and Grindlays Bank Ltd. 70-73; Amb. to U.S.A. 73-; Commdr. Order of Cedar of Lebanon; Commdr. Order of Dannebrog.
Publ. *Chambers of Commerce—their Objects and Aims*.
Embassy of Cyprus, 2211 R Street, N.W., Washington, D.C., U.S.A.; and Artemis Avenue 39, Larnaca, Cyprus.

Dinitz, Simcha, M.S.; Israeli politician; b. 23 June 1929; ed. Univ. of Cincinnati and School of Foreign Service and Graduate School, Georgetown Univ.
Director, Office of the Dir.-Gen., Ministry of Foreign Affairs 61-63; Political Sec. to Minister of Foreign Affairs 63-66; Minister, Embassy of Israel, Rome 66-68, Washington 68-69; Political Adviser to the Prime Minister 69, later Dir.-Gen. Office of the Prime Minister; Amb. to U.S.A. 73-; mem. Israeli del. to the UN 63, 64, 65.
Publ. *The Legal Aspect of the Egyptian Blockade of the Suez Canal* (Georgetown Law Journal) 56.
Embassy of Israel, 1621 22nd Avenue N.W., Washington, D.C. 20008, U.S.A. Home: 40 Nayot, Jerusalem, Israel.

Djamalzadeh, Mohamed Ali, LIC. EN DROIT; Iranian writer; b. 1896, Ispahan; ed. Univ. of Dijon, France.
Member, Cttee. of Iranian Nationalists, Berlin; worked for Int. Labour Org. 31; Cultural Attaché, Iranian Embassy, Geneva.
Publs. *Kaveh*, *Yéki bond-o-yéki nabond* (Once upon a time) 21, *Gandjé Cháyégan* (Economy of Iran), *History of Russo-Persian Relations*, *Elm-o-Honar* (Science and Art), *Caractères des Iraniens*, *Guide pour les écrivains et les nouvellistes*, and several novels and articles; translations in French, German, Russian, Hebrew, etc.
78F Florissant, 1206 Geneva, Switzerland.

Doğramaci Ihsan, M.D.; Turkish pediatrician and educator; b. 3 April 1915; ed. Istanbul, Harvard, Washington Univs.
Associate Prof. of Pediatrics, Ankara Univ. 49-54, Prof. of Child Health and Head of Dept. 54-63; Dir. Inst. of Child Health, Ankara 58-63; Prof. of Pediatrics and Head of Dept. Hacettepe Faculty of Medicine 63-, Dean of Faculty June 63-Nov. 63; Pres. Ankara Univ. 63-65; Pres. Hacettepe Science Centre, Ankara 65-67; mem. UNICEF Exec. Board 60-, Chair. 68-70; Chair. Board of Trustees, Middle East Technical Univ. 65-67; Pres. Hacettepe Univ. 67-75; Pres. Int. Pediatric Asscn. 68-; mem. Standing Cttee. Standing Conf. of Rectors and Vice-Chancellors of the European Univs. 69-; Dir. Int. Children's Centre (Paris) 70-; Fellow, Royal Coll. of Physicians (London) 71; Corresp. mem. Acad. Nat. de Médecine, France 73-; hon. mem. several foreign pediatric socs.; Hon. LL.D. (Nebraska and Glasgow Univs.), Dr. h.c. (Nice Univ.); Chevalier, Légion d'Honneur 73; Editor *The Turkish Journal of Pediatrics*, Consulting Editor *Clinical Pediatrics*.
Publs. *Annenin Kitabi* (Mother's Handbook on Child Care) 7 edns. 52-71, *Premature Baby Care* 54, *Porphysis in Childhood* 64, *Care of Mother and Child* 67, various monographs and articles on child health and pediatric topics.
c/o Hacettepe University, Ankara, Turkey.

Dostrovsky, Israel, PH.D.; Israeli scientist; b. 1918, Odessa, U.S.S.R.; ed. Univ. Coll., London.
Engaged in research work, Univ. Coll., London 40-43; Lecturer in Chem., Univ. Coll. of N. Wales 43-48; Joined

staff of Weizmann Inst. of Science 48; Head of Isotope Research Dept., Weizmann Inst. 48-65; mem. Isra Atomic Energy Comm. and first Dir. of Research 53-57; Chair. Nat. Council of Research and Devt. 59-61; Senior scientist, Brookhaven Nat. Laboratory, U.S.A. 61-64; Dir.-Gen. Israel Atomic Energy Comm. 65-71; Vice-Pres. Weizmann Inst. 71-73, Pres. 73-; Ramsay Medal, U.K. 44; Weizmann Prize, Israel 52; Dr. h.c. (Tel-Aviv Univ.) 73.
Neve Weizmann, Rehovot, Israel.

Douri, Izzat al-; Iraqi politician; b. 1942, al-Dour Shire; ed. secondary schools.
Editor *Voice of the Peasant* 68; Head Supreme Cttee. for People's Work 68-70; Minister of Agrarian Reform 70-74; Vice-Pres. Supreme Agric. Council 70-71; Head 71-; Minister of Agriculture 73-74; Minister of Interior 74-; mem. Revolutionary Command Council; Arab Baath Socialist Party.
Ministry of Interior, Baghdad; Home: Karkh, Baghdad, Iraq.

Driss, Rachid; Tunisian journalist and diplomatist; b. 27 Jan. 1917; ed. Sadiki Coll., Tunis.
Joined Néo-Destour Party 34; journalist exiled in Cairo, and with President Bourguiba founder mem. Bureau du Maghreb Arabe 46-52; returned to Tunisia 52; Editor *El Amal;* Deputy, Constitutional Assembly 56; Sec. of State Post Office and Communications 57-64, mem. Nat. Assembly 59-, Political Bureau Destour Socialist Party 58-; Amb. to the U.S.A. and Mexico 64-70; Perm. Rep. to UN 70-; Pres. Econ. and Social Council 71; Grand Cordon de l'Ordre de l'Indépendance de la République Tunisienne and foreign decorations.
Permanent Mission of Tunisia to UN, 40 East 71st Street, New York, N.Y. 10021, U.S.A.

Duaij, Ahmad Ali al-, B.A.; Kuwaiti civil servant; b. 25 Dec. 1937; ed. Shuwaikh Secondary School, Kuwait, Reading Technical Coll. and Keele Univ., England.
Joined Ministry of Foreign Affairs 62; joined Planning Board as Sec. 62, Sec.-Gen. 63, Dir.-Gen. with rank of Perm. Under-Sec. 64-; Head of Govt. Scholarships Cttee.; mem. Board, Univ. of Kuwait.
Publs. Regular articles in Kuwait, Lebanese and British Press.
The Planning Board, P.O. Box 15, Kuwait.

Dultzin, Leib (Leon Aryeh); Israeli business executive; b. 31 March 1913, Minsk, Russia.
Lived in Mexico 28-56, Israel 65-; mem. of the executive, Jewish Agency, Treas. 68, Chair. Exec. Cttee. 73-74; Minister without Portfolio, Govt. of Israel 70-73; Gov. Pal Land Devt. Co. Ltd., Bank Leumi le-Israel; Dir. Rassco Ltd., Yakhim Hakal Co. Ltd., Otzar Hataasiya; mem. World Directorate, Keren Hayesod; mem. of numerous Zionist orgs.
11 Mapu Street, Tel-Aviv, Israel.

Dupont-Sommer, André Louis; French university professor; b. 23 Dec. 1900; ed. Univ. of Paris.
Secretary, Collège de France 34-40; Dir. of Studies, School of Higher Studies 38-; Prof., Univ. of Paris 45-63; Pres. of Inst. of Semitic Studies, Univ. of Paris 52-; Prof. Collège de France 63-71, Hon. Prof. 72; mem. Institut de France 61-; Secrétaire Perpétuel de l'Académie des Inscriptions et Belles-Lettres 68-; Foreign mem. Accad. dei Lincei (Rome); Corresp. mem. Austrian Acad. of Sciences; Officier de la Légion d'Honneur Commandeur des Palmes académiques.
Publs. *La Doctrine gnostique de la lettre wâw...* 46, *Les Araméens* 49, *Les inscriptions araméennes de Sfiré* 48, *Aperçus préliminaires sur les manuscrits de la mer Morte* 50, *Nouveaux aperçus sur les manuscrits de la mer Morte* 53, *Les Ecrits esséniens découverts près de la mer Morte* 59, 60, 64, and others.
Palais Mazarin, 25 quai de Conti, Paris 6e, France.

Duval, H.E. Cardinal Léon-Etienne; Algerian (b. French) ecclesiastic; b. 9 Nov. 1903; ed. Petit Séminaire, Roche-sur-Foron, Grand Séminaire Annecy, Séminaire français Rome, and Pontifica Universitas Gregoriana.
Ordained priest 26; Prof. Grand Séminaire Annecy 30-42; Vicar-Gen. and Dir. of works, Diocese of Annecy 42-46; consecrated Bishop of Constantine and Hippo 46; Archbishop of Algiers 54-; created Cardinal 65; took Algerian nationality 65; Officier Légion d'Honneur.
Publs. *Paroles de Paix* 55, *Messages de Paix 1955-1962* 62, *Laïcs, prêtres, religieux dans l'Eglise selon Vatican II* 67.
Archbishop's House, 13 rue Khelifa-Boukhalfa, Algiers, Algeria.

E

Eban, Abba, M.A.; Israeli politician; b. (as Aubrey Solomon) 2 Feb. 1915, South Africa; ed. Queens' Coll., Cambridge.
Apptd. Liaison Officer of Allied H.Q. with the Jewish population in Jerusalem 40; Chief Instructor at the Middle East Arab Centre in Jerusalem; entered service of Jewish Agency 46; apptd. Liaison Officer with UN Special Comm. on Palestine 47; apptd. by the Provisional Govt. of Israel as its rep. to the UN 48, permanent rep. with rank of Minister 49; Ambassador to U.S.A. 50-59; Minister without Portfolio 59-60; Minister of Educ. and Culture 60-63; Deputy Prime Minister June 63-66; Minister of Foreign Affairs 66-74; mem. of Knesset 74-; Guest Prof. Columbia Univ. 74, Haifa Univ. 75; Pres. Weizmann Inst. of Science 58-66; Hon. Dr. New York, Maryland, Boston, Chicago, Cincinnati Univs.; foreign mem. American Acad. of Arts and Sciences 60.
Publs. *Maze of Justice* 46, *Social and Cultural Problems in the Middle East* 47, *The Toynbee Heresy* 55, *Voice of Israel* 57, *Tide of Nationalism* 59, *Chaim Weizmann: A Collective Biography* 62, *Israel in the World* 66, *My People* 68, *My Country* 73.
The Knesset, Jerusalem, Israel.

Ebtehaj, Abol Hassan; Iranian banker and administrator; b. 1899; ed. Lycée Montaigne, Paris, and Syrian Protestant Coll., Beirut.
Joined Imperial Bank of Iran 20; Govt. Inspector Agricultural Bank and Controller of State-owned companies 36; Vice-Gov. Bank Melli Iran 38; Chair. and Man. Dir. Mortgage Bank 40; Gov. and Chair. Bank Melli Iran (National Bank of Iran) 42-50; Chair. Iranian Del. Middle East Financial and Monetary Conf., Cairo 44; Chair. Iranian Del. Bretton Woods Conf. 44; Iranian Ambassador to France 50-52; Adviser to Man. Dir. Int. Monetary Fund 52-53; Dir. Middle East Dept. Int. Monetary Fund 53; Man. Dir. Plan Org. (Development Board), Teheran 54-59; Chair. and Pres. Iranians' Bank (Private Bank) 59-.
Iranians' Bank, 184 Takhte Jamshid Avenue, Teheran, Iran.

Ecevit, Bülent, B.A.; Turkish journalist and politician; b. 28 May 1925, Istanbul; ed. Robert Coll., Ankara, London and Harvard Univ.
Government official 44-50; Turkish Press Attaché's Office, London 46-50; Foreign News Editor, Man. Editor later Political Dir. *Ulus* (Ankara) 50-61, Political Columnist, *Ulus* 56-61; M.P. (Republican People's Party) 57-60, Oct. 61-; mem. Constituent Assembly 61; Minister of Labour 61-65; Political Columnist *Milliyet* 65; Sec.-Gen. Republican People's Party 66-71, Chair. 72-; Prime Minister Jan.-Nov. 74.
Publs. *Ortanin Solu* (Left of Centre) 66, *Bu Düzen Değismelidir* (The System Must Change) 68, *Atatürk ve Devrimcilik* (Atatürk and Revolution) 70; Translations into Turkish: *Gitinjali* (R. Tagore) 41, *Straybirds* (R. Tagore) 43, *Cocktail Party* (T. S. Eliot) 63.
Bade Sokak, Bade Apt 22/25 Küçükesat, Ankara, Turkey.

Echiguer, Mohammed Haddou; (*see* Shiguer, Mohamed Haddou).

Eddé, Raymond, L. en D.; Lebanese lawyer and politician; b. 1913; ed. Univ. Saint Joseph, Beirut.
Member of Parl. 53-57-60-65-68-72; Leader, Nat. Bloc Party 49-; Minister of Interior, of Public Works, of Social Affairs, and of Posts, Telegraphs and Telephones 58-59; stood for Presidency 58; Minister of Public Works, Agriculture, Planning, Water and Power 68-72.
Publs. *Loi sur les Immeubles de Luxe, Loi sur le Secret Bancaire, Loi sur le compte joint.*
Rue Emile Eddé, Quartier Arts et Métiers, Beirut, Lebanon.

Eghbal, Manouchehr, M.D.; Iranian physician and politician; b. 1908; ed. Iran and Univs. of Montpellier and Paris.
Professor of Infectious Diseases, Medical Faculty, Univ. of Teheran 38-53; fmr. Under-Sec. of State for Public Health and acting Minister of Public Health; Minister of Public Health 46; Minister of Posts and Telegraphs 47, of Nat. Education 48; Minister of Roads and Communications, of Health and of Interior 49; Gov.-Gen. of Azerbaijan 50; Teheran Senator 53; Rector, Univ. of Tabriz 51, Univ. of Teheran 54; Minister of the Imperial Court 56-57; Prime Minister 57-60; Prof. Teheran Univ. 60-61; Perm. Iranian Rep. to UNESCO 61-; Chair. of Board and Gen. Managing Dir. Nat. Iranian Oil Co. Oct. 63-; corresp. mem. Acad. of Medicine, Paris; mem. Board of Trustees of several insts., Board of Dirs. of numerous nat. companies and socs.; Dr. h.c. (Lafayette Coll., U.S.A., Paris, Bordeaux, Punjab Univs.); 33 decorations including Grand Croix, Légion d'Honneur; Grand Cross, Order of Danebrog; Order of Merit (China); Order of the Rising Sun (Japan); Grosses Verdienstkreuz mit Schulterband; and many Iranian decorations.
Office: National Iranian Oil Co., Ave. Takhte Jamshid, P.O. Box 1863; Home: Elahieh, Teheran, Iran.

Eilts, Hermann Frederick, M.A., LL.D.; American diplomatist; b. 23 March 1922, Germany; ed. Ursinus Coll., Johns Hopkins Univ. School of Advanced Int. Studies, Univ. of Pa., Nat. War Coll.
Counsellor and Deputy Chief of Mission, American Embassy, Libya 64-65; Amb. to Saudi Arabia 65-70; Diplomatic Adviser, U.S. Army War Coll. 70-73; Amb. to Egypt 73-; Arthur F. Fleming Distinguished Govt. Service Award 59; U.S. Army Decoration for Distinguished Civilian Service 73.
American Embassy, Cairo, Egypt.

Eisenstadt, Shmuel N., M.A., PH.D.; Israeli professor of sociology; b. 10 Sept. 1923, Warsaw, Poland; ed. Hebrew Univ., Jerusalem and London School of Economics.
Chairman, Dept. of Sociology, Hebrew Univ., Jerusalem 51-68, Prof. of Sociology 59-, Dean, Faculty of Social Sciences 66-68; Fellow Center for Advanced Studies in the Behavioral Sciences, Stanford Univ. 55-56; Visiting Prof., Univ. of Oslo 58, Univ. of Chicago 60, Harvard Univ. 66, 68-69; Carnegie Visiting Prof., Mass. Inst. of Technology 62-63; Chair. Council on Community Devt., Israel 62-66; Israeli Sociological Soc. 69-72; Visiting Prof., Univ. of Michigan 70, Univ. of Chicago 70, Univ. of Zurich 75, Harvard Univ. 75; mem. Advisory Board *International Encyclopedia of the Social Sciences;* Fellow, Netherlands Inst. of Advanced Studies 73; mem. Israel Acad. of Sciences and Humanities , Int. Sociological Soc., American Sociological Asscn.; Foreign Hon. mem. American Acad. of Arts and Sciences, American Philosophical Soc.; Hon. Fellow, London School of Econs.; McIver Award, American Sociological Asscn.
Publs. *The Absorption of Immigrants* 54, *Political Sociology* (editor) 55, *From Generation to Generation* 56, *Essays on Sociological Aspects of Economical and Political Development* 61, *The Political Systems of Empires* 63, *Essays on Comparative Institutions* 65, *Modernization, Protest and Change* 66, *Israeli Society* 68, *The Protestant Ethic and Modernization* 68, *Political Sociology of Modernization* (in Japanese) 68, *Comparative Perceptives on Social Change* (editor) 68, *Charisma and Institution Building: Selections from Max Weber* (editor) 68, *Ensayos sobre el Cambio social y la Modernización* (Spanish) 69, *Modernização e Mudança Social* (Portuguese) 69, *Political Sociology* (editor) 71, *Social Stratification and Differentiation* 71, *Tradition, Change and Modernity* 73.
The Hebrew University, Jerusalem; Home: Rechov Radak 30, Jerusalem, Israel.

El-Assad, Nassir El-Din, M.A., PH.D.; Jordanian administrator; b. 14 Dec. 1922; ed. Arab Govt. Coll., Jerusalem, and Cairo Univ.
Cultural Attaché League of Arab States, Cairo 54-59; Dean, Faculty of Arts and Educ., Univ. of Libya, Benghazi 59-61; Prof. of Arabic, Univ. of Jordan 62; Pres. Univ. of Jordan 62-68; Cultural Counsellor, League of Arab States, Cairo 68-; Corresp. mem. Arabic Language Acads. in Cairo and Damascus; Istiqlal Decoration, First degree.
Publs. *Sources of Pre-Islamic Poetry and their Historic Value* 56, *Modern Literary Trends in Palestine and Jordan* 57, *Singing and Singing Girls in Pre-Islamic Arabia* 60, *Modern Poetry in Palestine and Jordan* 61, *Diwan Kais Ibn El-Khatim* 62.
League of Arab States, Midan El-Tahrir, Cairo, Egypt.

Elath, Eliahu, PH.D.; Israeli diplomatist; b. 30 July 1903; ed. Hebrew Univ. of Jerusalem and American Univ. of Beirut.
Jewish Agency 34; Jewish Agency observer to San Francisco Conf. 45; Head of Jewish Agency's Political Office in Washington, D.C.; Israeli Amb. to U.S.A. 48-50; Minister to U.K. 50-52, Amb. 52-59; Adviser, Ministry of Foreign Affairs 59-60; Pres. Hebrew Univ., Jerusalem 61-67; Vice-Pres. Jewish Colonization Asscn.; Pres. Israel Oriental Soc.; Chair. Afro-Asian Inst., Tel-Aviv; Hon. Ph.D.
Publs. *Bedouin, their Life and Manners* 34, *Trans-Jordan* 35, *Israel and Her Neighbours* 57, *The Political Struggle for the inclusion of Elath in the Jewish State* 67, *San Francisco Diary* 71, *British Routes to India* 71, *Zionism and the Arabs* 74.
17 Bialik Street, Beth Hakerem, Jerusalem, Israel.

Elazar, Lieut.-Gen. David; Israeli army officer; b. 1925, Yugoslavia; ed. Hebrew Univ.
Went to Israel 40; entered Palmach 46; served in War of Liberation, Sinai Campaign; Commdr. Armoured Corps 61; Officer-in-Charge, Northern Command 64; commanded forces of Northern Command during six-day War June 67; Chief. Gen. Staff Branch 69; Chief of Staff and C.-in-C. Israeli Armed Forces 71-74; Pres., Chair. Board of Dirs. ZIM (Israel Navigation Co. Ltd.) 74-.
ZIM, 9 Palyam Avenue, P.O. Box 1723, Haifa, Israel.

Elias IV Mouawad; Greek ecclesiastic; b. 1914, Lebanon; ed. Theological School of Halki, Istanbul.
Greek Orthodox Patriarch of Antioch (Antakya) and all the East Sept. 70-.
Greek Orthodox Patriarchate, P.O. Box 9, Damascus, Syria.

Eliraz, Israel, M.A.; Israeli playwright and teacher; b. 24 March 1936, Jerusalem; ed. Hebrew Univ., Jerusalem, Tel-Aviv Univ., Sorbonne, Paris.
Plays produced in Israel, Paris, London, New York, Belgium and Germany; first libretto commissioned and performed by Hamburgische Staatsoper 71; Teacher in Jerusalem; Lecturer, Hebrew Univ.; awarded two first prizes by Nat. Council for Culture and Art, Israel.
Publs. novels: *Tin Swings, Last Birds, Golden Summer;* plays: *Far from the Sea—Far from the Summer, The Bear,*

The Banana, Round Trip, Three Women in Yellow, The Persian Protocoles; libretti: *Ashmedai, Massada 967, The Experience.*
6 Jabotinsky Street, Jerusalem, Israel.

Elmandjra, Mahdi, PH.D.; Moroccan international official; b. 13 March 1933; ed. Lycée Lyautey, Casablanca, Putney School, Vermont, U.S.A., Cornell Univ., London School of Economics and Univ. de Paris.
Head of Confs., Law Faculty, Univ. of Rabat 57-58; Adviser Ministry of Foreign Affairs, and to Moroccan Del. to UN 58-59; Dir.-Gen. Radiodiffusion Télévision Marocaine 59-60; Chief of African Div., Office of Relations with mem. States, UNESCO 61-63; Dir. Exec. Office of Dir.-Gen. of UNESCO 63-66; Asst. Dir.-Gen. of UNESCO for Social Sciences, Human Sciences and Culture July 66-Dec. 69; Visiting Fellow, Centre for Int. Studies, London School of Econs. and Political Sciences 70; Asst. Dir.-Gen. of UNESCO for Pre-Programming 71-75, Special Advisor for the Dir.-Gen. 75-; Chevalier, Ordre des Arts et Lettres (France).
Publ. *The United Nations System: An Analysis* 73.
Office UNESCO, place de Fontenoy, Paris 7e; Home: 12 rue Dufrenoy, 75016 Paris, France, and 20 rue Chenier, Casablanca, Morocco.

Epikman, Refik; Turkish artist and writer; b. 1902; ed. Acad. of Fine Arts, Istanbul and Paris.
Teacher in Gazi Pedagogic Inst., Ankara; exhibited in Exhbns. of Turkish Art, Amsterdam, Paris, Linz and Vth Teheran (Regional) Biennale; f. the Asscn. of Independent Turkish Painters and Sculptors 28; mem. Int. Asscn. of Art Critics.
Publs. *Classical Painters* 45, *17th, 18th and 19th Century World Art* 46, *Tiziano Vecellio's Art* 47, *The Art of Rubens* 51, *Turkish Artist and Archaeologist, The Art of Osman Hamdi* 69.
Gazi Osmanpasa Mahallesi, Nenehatun Cad. 114/1, Kavaklıdere, Ankara, Turkey.

Eralp, Orhan, B.A., LL.B., PH.D.; Turkish diplomatist; b. 28 Jan. 1915; ed. Robert Coll. Istanbul, Univ. Coll., London, and London School of Economics.
Ministry of Foreign Affairs 39-; Sec. Washington 42-48; Adviser to Turkish Del., UN Conciliation Comm. for Palestine 49-51; Perm. Rep. to European Office of UN, Geneva 51; Counsellor, London 52; Dir.-Gen. Second Dept., Ministry of Foreign Affairs 52-56; Ambassador to Sweden 57-59, to Yugoslavia 59-64; Perm. Rep. of Turkey to UN, New York 64-69; Sec.-Gen. Foreign Ministry 69-72; Perm. Rep. of Turkey to NATO 72-.
Permanent Delegation of Turkey to NATO, NATO, 1110 Brussels, Belgium.

Erbakan, Necmettin; Turkish politician; b. 1926, Sinop; ed. Inst. of Mechanics, Technical Univ. of Istanbul and Technische Universität, Aachen, Germany.
Assistant Lecturer Inst. of Mechanics, Technical Univ. of Istanbul 48-51; Engineer, Firma Deutz 51-54; Prof. Technical Univ. of Istanbul 54-66; Chair. Industrial Dept., Turkish Asscn. of Chambers of Commerce 66-68, Chair. of Asscn. 68; mem. Nat. Assembly 69-; f. Nat. Order Party 70 (disbanded 71); Chair. Nat. Salvation Party Oct. 73-; Deputy Prime Minister Jan.-Sept. 74, April 75-; Minister of State Jan.-Sept. 74.
Office of the Deputy Prime Minister, Ankara, Turkey.

Erdem, Hasan Hüsnü; Turkish theologian; b. 1889; ed. Univ. of Istanbul.
Teacher of Religion, Royal Middle School, Antalya; Prof. of Theology and Headmaster, Ankara Dârü'l-Hilâfe; Teaching mem. Ministry of Canonical and Pious Endowments; Teacher, Antalya High School; mem. Advisory Cttee. Religious Affairs Dept.; Lecturer in Exegesis and History of Exegesis, Faculty of Divinity, Ankara Univ.; Head of Religious Affairs Dept., Turkish Republic 61-64; mem. Supreme Cttee. of Religious Affairs, Dept. of Religious Affairs 66-.
Publs. Numerous translations from Arabic, and biographical and theological Islamic treatises.
Diyanet İşleri Başkanlığı, Din İşleri Yüksek Kurulu Üyesi, Ankara, Turkey.

Erim, Nihat, PH.D.; Turkish politician; b. 1912, Kandira, Kocael Province; ed. Lycée of Galatasaray, Istanbul, and Univ. of Istanbul Law School and Univ. of Paris.
Professor of Constitutional and Int. Law, Univ. of Ankara and Legal Adviser, Ministry of Foreign Affairs 42; mem. Parl. 45-50; Minister of Public Works, concurrently Deputy Prime Minister 48-50; Publr. and Editor *Ulus* (organ of the Republican People's Party) 50, subsequently Publr. and Editor of *Halkçi;* mem. for Turkey, European Human Rights Comm.; mem. Parl. 61-; Deputy Chair. Republican People's Party Nat. Assembly Group 61-71; mem. Turkish Parl. Group, Council of Europe 61-70; Prime Minister March 71-March 72; Senator 72-.
Publs. several books on law.
The Senate, Ankara, Turkey.

Erkmen, Hayrettin; Turkish economist, lawyer and politician; b. 1915; ed. Univs. of Ankara, Lausanne and Geneva.
Reporter, Board of Financial Research, Ministry of Finance 48; Asst. Prof. of Economics, Univ. of Istanbul 49; Minister of Labour 53-55; Pres. Parliamentary Group of Democratic Party; Minister of Labour Nov. 57-58; Minister of Commerce 58-60; Acting Minister of Reconstruction Dec. 59-May 60; arrested 60, sentenced 61, released 65; mem. Management Cttee. Turkish Central Bank 67-74.
Publs. *La Participation des Salariés à la Gestion de l'entreprise* 48; trans. in Turkish: J. Marchal, *Le mécanisme des prix,* R. Ramadier, *Le Socialisme et l'exercice de pouvoir.*
Istiklal Cad. Terzi Han 378, Beyoğlu, Istanbul, Turkey.

Erkmen, Nizamettin; Turkish politician; b. 1919, Giresun.
Director of Legal Affairs, Samsun; mem. Parl. for Giresun 61-; Sec.-Gen. Justice Party until 74; Minister of State Deputy Prime Minister 73-74; Justice Party.
Office of the Member for Giresun, National Assembly, Ankara, Turkey.

Erofeyev, Vladimir Yakovlevich; Soviet diplomatist; b. 24 May 1909, Moscow; ed. Moscow Machine Tool Inst.
Diplomatic Service 39-; Deputy Dir. and Chief. of Consular Dept., State Cttee. for Foreign Affairs 39-40; Counsellor to Turkey 40-42; Deputy Chief, Second European Dept., Ministry of Foreign Affairs 42-48, Head of Dept. for Latin American countries 48-49; Counsellor, London 49-52; Counsellor Ministry of Foreign Affairs 52-54; Minister Counsellor, Paris 54-55; Chief. of Second European Dept., Ministry of Foreign Affairs 55-58, of Near East Dept. 58-59; Amb. to the U.A.R. 59-65; on staff Ministry of Foreign Affairs 65-68; Amb. to Iran 68-.
U.S.S.R. Embassy, Churchill Avenue, Teheran, Iran.

Essaafi, M'hamed; Tunisian diplomatist; b. 26 May 1930; ed. Collège Sadiki and Univ. of Paris.
Secretariat of Foreign Affairs, Tunis 56; Tunisian Embassy, London 56-57; First Sec., Washington 57-60; Dir. of American Dept., Secr. of Foreign Affairs, Tunis 60-62, American Dept. and Int. Conf. Dept. 62-64; Amb. to U.K. 64-69; Sec.-Gen. Foreign Affairs, Tunis 69-70; Amb. to U.S.S.R. 70-74, to Federal Repub. of Germany May 74-; Grand Officier de l'Ordre de la République Tunisienne.
Tunisian Embassy, Bonn-Bad Godesberg, 103 Kölner Strasse, Federal Republic of Germany.

Ete, Muhlis, M.A., PH.D.; Turkish economist; b. 23 Oct. 1904.
Asst. Instructor 30, later Asst. Prof. Faculty of Law and Economics Istanbul Univ.; Teacher of Statistics School of Political Science, Istanbul, and of Money and Exchange, Higher School of Commerce and Economics Istanbul; Prof. of Business Economics, later of Gen. Principles of Economics, Ankara School of Political Science 40-50; Minister of State Enterprises 50-51; Minister of Economy and Commerce 51-52; Turkish Rep. Council of Europe, Vice-Pres. 53; Pres. Turkish Economic Asscn. and Turkish European Movement; fmr. Chief Editor *Türk Ekonomist;* Pres. of Control Board of State Enterprises 58-61; Minister of Commerce June 62-June 63; mem. of Parl.; Dir. of School of Econs., Istanbul 67-.
Publs. *Transportation, Money and Exchange, Lessons in Business Economics, Administration of Temporary and Permanent Exhibitions, Commerce, Banking and Exchanges, Probleme der Assoziierung der Türkei mit der Europäischen Wirtschaftsgemeinschaft* 63; and numerous translations.
Istanbul, Götztepe, Yeşil Ceşme Sok 30/8, Turkey.

Etemadi, Noor Ahmad; Afghan diplomatist; b. 22 Feb. 1921, Kandahar; ed. Istiqlal Lycée, Kabul, and Kabul Univ.
Joined Ministry of Foreign Affairs 46, Asst. Chief of Protocol, Dir. for Econ. Relations, Dir.-Gen. for Political Affairs 57; diplomatic posts in London and Washington; Deputy Minister of Foreign Affairs 63; Amb. to Pakistan 64; Minister of Foreign Affairs 65-71, Prime Minister 67-71; Amb. to Italy 72-73, to U.S.S.R. 73-74.
c/o Ministry of Foreign Affairs, Kabul, Afghanistan.

Etemadi, Tooryalay, M.A.; Afghan educationist; b. Aug. 1923; ed. Esteklal High School, Kabul, Indiana Univ., U.S.A.
Director of Foreign Cultural Relations, Sec. Afghan Nat. Comm. for UNESCO 53-60; Dean, Colls. of Science, Engineering and Agriculture 56-58, of Agriculture and Engineering 58-60; Pres. Cultural Office, Washington, D.C. 60-63; Pres. of Secondary Educ., Ministry of Educ. 63-64; Pres. Inst. of Educ. 64-65, Kabul Univ. 65-67, Acting Pres. 68-69; Cultural Rep., Beirut 67-68; Cultural Counsellor, Afghan Embassy, Bonn and W. Europe 69-70; Amb., Chef de Cabinet of the Minister of Foreign Affairs 71-; Grosses Verdienstkreuz mit Stern, and several other decorations; Hon. LL.D.
Publs. papers and articles on education.
The Secretariat, Ministry of Foreign Affairs, Kabul, Afghanistan.

Ettinghausen, Richard, PH.D.; American educationist and art curator; b. 5 Feb. 1906; ed. Univs. of Munich, Cambridge and Frankfurt a.M.
Asst. Islamic Dept., State Museum, Berlin 31-33; Asst. to Editor *A Survey of Persian Art* 33-34; Research Assoc., American Inst. for Persian Art and Archæology, N.Y. 34-37; Lecturer on Islamic Art, Inst. of Fine Arts, N.Y. Univ. 36-38; mem. Inst. of Advanced Study, Princeton, N.J. 37-38; Assoc. Prof. of Islamic Art, Univ. of Mich., Ann Arbor 38-44; Assoc. in Near-Eastern Art, Freer Gallery of Art, Smithsonian Inst., Washington, D.C. 44-58, Curator of Near Eastern Art 58-61, Head Curator 61-66; Research Prof. of Islamic Art, Univ. of Mich. 48-67; Editor *Ars Islamica* 38-51; Near-Eastern Editor *Ars Orientalis* 51-58; Editorial Board *The Art Bulletin* 40-, *Kairos* 59-, Assoc. Prof. of Islamic Art, Inst. of Fine Arts, New York Univ. 62-67, Adjunct Prof. of Fine Arts 60-67, Prof. of Fine Arts 67-; Asst. Curator, Near Eastern Art, Los Angeles County Museum of Art 67-; Consultative Chair. Islamic Dept., Metropolitan Museum of Art, N.Y. 69-.
Publs. *The Unicorn (Studies in Muslim Iconography I)* 50, *The Paintings of Emperors and Sultans of India in American Collections* 61, *Persian Miniatures in the Bernard Berenson Collection* 63, *Arab Painting* 62; Editor and contributor: *A Selected and Annotated Bibliography of Books and Periodicals in Western Languages dealing with the Near and Middle East, with special emphasis on Medieval and Modern Times* 52, *Aus der Welt der Islamischen Kunst* 59, *Turkish Miniatures from the 13th to the 14th Century* (editor) 65, *Treasures of Turkey* (co-author) 66.
Office: Institute of Fine Arts, New York University, 1 East 78th Street, New York, N.Y. 10021; Home: 24 Armour Road, Princeton, N.J. 08540, U.S.A.

Evenari, Michael; Israeli botanist; b. 9 Oct. 1904; ed. Univ. of Frankfurt.
Staff of Botany Dept., Univ. of Frankfurt 27-28, German Univ., Prague 28-31; Staff of Technische Hochschule, Darmstadt 31-33, Lecturer 33; External Teacher, Hebrew Univ., Jerusalem 34-37, Instructor 37-44, Lecturer 44, Chair. Dept. of Botany 45-, Prof. 51-; Vice-Pres. Hebrew Univ., Jerusalem 53-59; Fellow Linnean Soc.; Hon. Fellow American Botanical Soc.; mem. German Acad. of Science; Major Research on ancient desert agriculture and its modern application and studies in germination, physiology and ecology of desert plants.
Publ. *The Negev—The Challenge of a Desert* 71.
Department of Botany, Hebrew University of Jerusalem, Jerusalem, Israel.

Eytan, Walter, M.A.; Israeli public official; b. 24 July 1910; ed. St. Paul's School, London, Queen's Coll. Oxford.
Lecturer in German, Queen's Coll., Oxford 34-46; Principal, Public Service Coll., Jerusalem 46-48; Dir.-Gen., Ministry for Foreign Affairs, Israel 48-59; Ambassador to France 60-70; Political Adviser to Minister of Foreign Affairs 70-72; Chair. Israel Broadcasting Authority 72-.
Publ. *The First Ten Years* 58.
18 Balfour Street, 92 102 Jerusalem, Israel.

F

Fahd ibn Abdulaziz, H.R.H. Prince; Saudi Arabian politician; b. 1922.
Brother of the late King Faisal; Minister of Education 53, of the Interior 62-; Second Deputy Prime Minister 68-75, First Deputy Prime Minister March 75-; became Crown Prince 75.
Ministry of the Interior, Jeddah, Saudi Arabia.

Fahmi, Ismail; Egyptian diplomatist and politician; b. 1922; ed. Cairo Univ.
Entered diplomatic service 45; Counsellor to Egyptian Del. to UN 57, and later in charge of UN Affairs, Ministry of Foreign Affairs; Chair. Political Cttee. of UN, New York until 68; Amb. to Austria 68-71; Under-Sec. of State for Foreign Affairs 71-72; Amb. to Fed. Repub. of Germany 72-73; Minister of Tourism March-Oct. 73, of Foreign Affairs Oct. 73-; Vice-Pres. Council of Ministers April 75-.
Ministry of Foreign Affairs, Cairo, Egypt.

Fakhreddine, Mohamed; Sudanese diplomatist; b. 12 Oct. 1924; ed. Gordon Memorial Coll., Khartoum, and Univ. of Durham.
Chief of Protocol, Head of UN Section, Ministry of Foreign Affairs, Khartoum 56-58; Counsellor, London 58-60; Ambassador to Pakistan and Afghanistan 60-64, concurrently Ambassador to People's Repub. of China 64-65; Perm. Rep. to UN 65-71; Under-Sec. for Foreign Affairs Nov. 70-71; Deputy Minister 71; Amb. to U.S.S.R. 73-75, to Ethiopia Feb. 75-.
Embassy of Sudan, P.O. Box 1110, Addis Ababa, Ethiopia.

Farhan, Ishaq Ahmad, M.SC., M.A., ED.D.; Jordanian educationalist; b. 1934, Ein Karem; ed. American Univ., Beirut, and Columbia Univ., New York.

Science teacher 58-64; with Ministry of Educ., Amman 64, Dir. of Pedagogical Services and Head, Syllabi Section 69, Dir. of Syllabi 69-70; Minister of Educ. 70-73, of Endowments and Islamic Shrines 73.

Publs. several school textbooks and articles in scientific and pedagogical journals.

c/o Ministry of Endowments and Islamic Shrines, Amman, Jordan.

Farhat, Abdallah; Tunisian politician; b. 28 Aug. 1914, Ouerdenine; ed. Ecole Supérieure de langue Arabe, Tunis. Member Parti Néo-Destour 34-; successively Dir. Fédération Nationale des P.T.T. (Post and Telecommunications), Dir. Fédération Générale des Fonctionnaires and Treas.-Gen. Union Générale des Travailleurs Tunisiens 48-56; elected to 2nd Political Bureau 52, re-elected 55; Vice-Pres. Constituent Assembly 56-59; Deputy Nat. Assembly 59-; Dir. Cabinet of the Pres. 56-63, 70-71, Oct. 71-Aug. 72; Pres. and Dir.-Gen. Société Nationale d'Investissement 63-64; Sec. of State for Post and Telecommunications (P.T.T.) 64-69; Sec. of State for Agriculture Sept.-Nov. 69, Minister for Agriculture 69-71, for Nat. Defence 72-74, for Public Works Jan.-Sept. 74, for Transport and Communications Sept. 74-; Grand Cordon Ordre de l'Indépendance, Ordre de la République; many foreign decorations.

Ministère du Transport, Tunis, Tunisia.

Farid al-Aulaqi, Sheikh Mohammed; Yemeni politician; b. 1929; ed. Aden Protectorate Coll. for Sons of Chiefs, Government Secondary School, Aden, and Queen's Coll., Oxford.

Joined Protectorate Govt. Service as Asst. Political Officer 50; Political Officer 56-59; Minister of Finance, Fed. of S. Arabia 59-63; Minister of External Affairs 63-67; mem. Presidential Council June 69.

Upper Aulaqi, Fourth Governorate, People's Democratic Republic of Yemen.

Faris, Mustapha, DIPL.ING.; Moroccan engineer; b. 17 Dec. 1933; ed. Ecole Nat. des Ponts et Chaussées, Paris. Government Civil Engineer, Dept. of Public Works 56-61; Dir. of Supply, Nat. Irrigation Office 61-65; Dir.-Gen. of Hydraulic Engineering 65-69; Sec. of State for Planning attached to Prime Minister's Office 69-71; Minister of Finance 71-72; Pres., Dir.-Gen. Banque Nationale pour le Développement Economique Dec. 72-; fmr. Vice-Pres. Int. Comm. on Large Dams; Gov. IBRD (World Bank), African Devt. Bank; Ordre du Trône.

Banque Nationale pour le Développement Economique, B.P. 407, Rabat, Morocco.

Farmanfarmaian, Khodadad, M.A., PH.D.; Iranian economist and banker; b. 5 May 1928, Teheran; ed. American Univ. of Beirut, and Stanford and Colorado Univs. Instructor and Research Asst., Dept. of Econs., Colorado Univ. 52-53; Instructor, Dept. of Econs., Brown Univ. 53-55; Research Fellow, Center for Middle Eastern Studies, Harvard Univ. 55-57; Research Assoc., Dept. of Econs. and Oriental Studies, Princeton Univ. 57-58; Dir. Econ. Bureau, Plan Org. 58-61; mem. Tax Comm., Ministry of Finance 58-60; mem. High Econ. Council 59-62; Deputy Man. Dir. Plan Org. 61-62, Man. Dir. 70-73; Deputy Gov., Bank Markazi Iran (Central Bank of Iran) 63-68, Gov. 68-71; Chair. Board of Dirs., Bank Sanaye Iran 73-; medals from govts. of Iran and Belgium.

Publs. *Social Change and Economic Behaviour in Iran, Exploration in Entrepreneurial History* 56, *How can the World Afford OPEC Oil?* 75; has contributed to *Middle Eastern Journal*.

c/o Bank Sanaye Iran, Avenue Sepahbod Zahedi, No. 106, Teheran, Iran.

Fasi, Mohammed el; Moroccan university rector; b. 2 Sept. 1908; ed. Al Qarawiyin Univ., Fez, Univ. de Paris à la Sorbonne and Ecole des langues orientales, Paris.

Teacher, Inst. des Hautes Etudes Marocaines 35-40; Head Arab manuscript section, Bibliothèque Gén., Rabat 40; Tutor to Prince Moulay Hassan 41-44, 47-52; Rector Al Qarawiyin Univ. 42-44, 47-52; Vice-Pres. Conseil des Uléma 42-; Founder-mem. Istiqlal Party 44; under restriction 44-47, 52-54; Minister of Nat. Educ. 55-58; Rector of the Univ. of Morocco 58; Pres. Moroccan Del. to Gen. Conf. of UNESCO 56, 58, 60, 64, Vice-Pres. 62, leader of numerous UNESCO Confs. in the Arab World, Pres. Exec. Board of UNESCO 64; Pres. Conseil d'Administration de l'Association des Universités Partiellement ou Entièrement de Langue Française (AUPELF) 66; Pres. Conseil Exécutif de l'Association des Universités Africains 67; Minister for Cultural Affairs and Nat. Educ. 68; Pres. Conseil Exécutif de l'Association des Universités Islamiques 69; mem. Acad. of Arabic Language, Cairo 58, Acad. of Iraq; Dr. h.c. Univ. of Bridgeport 65, Lagos 68, Jakarta 68.

Publs. Numerous works including *L'évolution politique et culturelle au Maroc* 58, *La Formation des Cadres au Maroc* 60, *Chants anciens des femmes de Fès* 67.

12 rue Louis Chatelain, Rabat, Morocco.

Fatemi, Nasrollah, M.A., PH.D.; (b. Iranian); American professor.

Formerly Ed. Bakhtar newspaper, Gov. of Fars, mem. of Majlis, Mayor of Shiraz, and del. to UN (adviser to perm. Iranian del.); Visiting Prof. Asia Inst. and Princeton Univ. 50-55; Prof. of Social Sciences, Fairleigh Dickinson Univ. 55-61, Chair. Social Sciences Dept. 61-65, Dean of the Graduate School 65-71, Distinguished Prof. of Int. Affairs and Dir. of Graduate Inst. of Int. Studies 71.

Publs. *Biography of Hafiz* 36, *Persian Literature in the 16th and 17th centuries* 37, *Modern Persian Literature* 39, *Diplomatic History of Persia* 51, *Oil Diplomacy* 54, *The Dollar Crisis* 64, *The Roots of Arab Nationalism* 65, *Humanities in the Age of Science* 67.

Fairleigh Dickinson University, Teaneck, N.J., U.S.A.

Fawzi, Ahmad; Jordanian politician and engineer; b. 1927; ed. U.S.A. and Baghdad Univ.

District Engineer, Public Works 50-53, Asst. Under-Sec. 53-57, Under-Sec. 57-64; Mayor of Amman 64-; Minister of Interior for Municipal and Rural Affairs 67-68, and Minister without Portfolio 67-68; Minister of Public Works April 68-Aug. 69; Sec. Civil Eng. Union; mem. Devt. Board; Chair. Housing Corpn. Board; Chair. Municipal and Rural Loan Fund; Chair. Hidjaz Railway Reconstruction Cttee.; mem. Arab Cities Org. Exec. Office; Orders of Al-Kawkab (first rank), Al-Istiklal (first rank), Al-Nahda (second rank), Al-Jalalah Asharefah (first rank, Morocco), Tunisian Repub. (first rank), Mallizia, Ethiopian Emperor (first rank).

c/o Municipality of Amman, Amman, Jordan.

Fawzi, Mahmoud; Egyptian diplomatist and politician; b. 1900, Cairo; ed. Univs. of Cairo, Rome, Liverpool and Columbia.

Vice-Consul, N.Y. and New Orleans 26-29; Consul, Kobe, Japan 29-36; Dir. Dept. of Nationalities, Ministry of Foreign Affairs 39-41; Consul-Gen., Jerusalem 41-44; Egyptian rep. Security Council, UN 46; alternate rep. UN Gen. Assembly, N.Y. 47; Perm. Rep. of Egypt to UN 49-51; Ambassador to Great Britain 52; Minister of Foreign Affairs Dec. 52-58; U.A.R. Minister of Foreign Affairs 58-64; mem. Presidency Council 62-64; Dep. Prime Minister of Foreign Affairs 64-67, Vice-Pres. and Presidential Asst. for Foreign Affairs 67-68; Prime Minister 70-72; Vice-Pres. 72-74.

Cairo, Egypt.

Fawzi, Gen. Mohammed; Egyptian army officer; ed. Military Acad.

Former Dir. Mil. Acad. and Commdr. United Arab Repub. Expeditionary Forces in Yemen; Commdt. of Syrian-

Egyptian forces under Defence Pact 67; Chief of Staff of Army and Sec.-Gen. for Mil. Affairs, Arab League until 67; C.-in-C. Joint U.A.R. Forces 67-68; Minister of War 68-70; charged with high treason July 71; sentenced to imprisonment Dec. 71; released Feb. 74.
c/o Ministry of Defence, Cairo, Egypt.

Feinberg, Nathan, DR.IUR.UTR.; Israeli university professor; b. 6 June 1895; ed. Univ. of Zürich and Graduate Inst. of Int. Studies, Geneva.
Head of Dept., Ministry of Jewish Affairs, Lithuania 19-21; Sec. Cttee. of Jewish Dels., Paris 22-24; law practice in Palestine 24-27 and 34-45; Lecturer, Univ. of Geneva 31-33; Lecturer, Hebrew Univ., Jerusalem 45-49, Assoc. Prof. 49-52, Prof. of Int. Law and Relations 52-66, Dean of Faculty of Law 49-51, Prof. Emer. 65-; Lectured at Acad. of Int. Law, The Hague 32, 37, 52; mem. Perm. Court of Arbitration; mem. Inst. of Int. Law; Fellow of the Int. Inst. of Arts and Letters; mem. Board of Governors, Hebrew Univ.
Publs. *La Question des Minorités à la Conférence de la paix de 1919-1920 et l'action juive en faveur de la Protection Internationale des Minorités* 29, *La Juridiction de la Cour Permanente de Justice Internationale dans le Système des Mandats* 30, *La Juridiction de la Cour Permanente de Justice dans le Système de la Protection Internationale des Minorités* 31, *La Pétition en Droit International* 33, *Some Problems of the Palestine Mandate* 36, *L'Admission de Nouveaux Membres à la Société des Nations et à l'Organisation des Nations Unies* 52, *The Jewish Struggle Against Hitler in the League of Nations (Bernheim Petition)* (Hebrew) 57, *The Legality of a "State of War" after the Cessation of Hostilities* 61, *Palestine under the Mandate and the State of Israel: Problems of International Law* (Hebrew) 63, *The Jewish League of Nations Societies* (Hebrew) 67, *The Arab-Israel Conflict in International Law* 70, *On an Arab Jurist's Approach to Zionism and the State of Israel* 71, etc.; co-editor: *The Jewish Year Book of International Law* 49; Editor *Studies in Public International Law in Memory of Sir Hersch Lauterpacht* (in Hebrew) 62.
6 Ben Labrat Street, Jerusalem, Israel.

Fernea, Robert Alan, PH.D.; American anthropologist; b. 25 Jan. 1932; ed. Reed Coll., Portland, Oregon, and Univ. of Chicago.
Assistant, Assoc. Prof. of Anthropology, American Univ. in Cairo 59-65, Social Research Center, American Univ. in Cairo 61-65; Dir. Nubian Ethnological Survey 61-65; Visiting Lecturer, Univ. of Alexandria 63, 64; Consultant, Ford Foundation in U.A.R. 63-65; Post-doctoral Fellow, Harvard Univ. 65-66; Prof. of Anthropology, Univ. of Texas at Austin 66-, Dir. Middle East Center, 66-73; Fellow, American Anthropological Asscn., Founding Fellow, Middle East Studies Asscn. of N. America; Univ. of Chicago Fellow 54, Nat. Science Foundation Fellowship 56, 57, Danforth Fellow 54-59, Faculty Fulbright-Hays Fellow (Afghanistan) 67, (Morocco) 71-72.
Publs. *Symposium on Contemporary Egyptian Nubia* 67, *Shaykh and Effendi* 70, *Nubians in Egypt: Peaceful People* 73, and numerous anthropological articles.
University of Texas at Austin, Middle East Center, 2609 University Avenue, Social Work Building, Room 326, Texas 78712, U.S.A.

Feyzioğlu, Turhan, LL.D.; Turkish university professor and politician; b. 19 Jan. 1922; ed. Galatasaray Lycée, Istanbul Univ., and Ecole Nat. d'Administration, Paris.
Assistant Prof. Ankara Political Science School 45-47, Assoc. Prof. 47-54; Research, Nuffield Coll., Oxford 54; Co-editor *Forum* 54-58; Prof. Ankara Univ. 55; Dean, Political Science School, Ankara 56; M.P. 57, 61, 65-; mem. Nat. Exec. Cttee. Republican People's Party 57-61; Pres. Middle East Technical Univ. 60; mem. Constituent Assembly 60; Minister of Education 60; Minister of State

61; Deputy Prime Minister 62-63; mem. Turkish High Planning Council 61-63, Asst. Sec.-Gen. Republican People's Party 64, Vice-Pres. Parl. Group 65-66; founded Nat. Reliance Party (now Republican Reliance Party) 67, Pres. 67-; mem. Consultative Assembly (now Parliamentary Assembly), Council of Europe 64-66, 72-75, Vice-Pres. 74-75; Deputy Prime Minister April 75-.
Publs. *Administration Law* 47, *Judicial Review of Unconstitutional Laws* 51, *Les Parties Politiques en Turquie* 53, *The Reforms of the French Higher Civil Service* 55, *Democracy and Dictatorship* 57, *The Communist Danger* 69.
Office of the Deputy Prime Minister, Ankara, Turkey.

Field, Henry, B.A., M.A., D.SC.; American anthropologist; b. 15 Dec. 1902; ed. Eton Coll., and New Coll., Oxford.
Asst. Curator of Physical Anthropology, Field Museum of Natural History (Chicago) 26-34, Curator 34-41; Field Museum Expeditions, Near East 25-26, 27-28, 34; engaged in Govt. research work in Washington 41-45; Research on Anthropology of S.W. Asia 46-47; Univ. of Calif. African Expedition 47-48; Peabody Museum-Harvard Expedition to Near East 50, and to West Pakistan 55; Honorary Associate in Physical Anthropology, Peabody Museum, Harvard 50-; Research in India 69, in Mongolia 73; Annandale Medal, Asiatic Soc. of Bengal 66.
Publs. *Arabs of Central Iraq: their History, Ethnology and Physical Characters* 35; *Contributions to the Anthropology of Iran* 39; *The Anthropology of Iraq, Part I, No. 1* 40, Nos. 2-3 49; *Part II, No. 1* 51, Nos. 2, 3 52; *Contributions to the Anthropology of the Faiyum, Sinai, Sudan and Kenya* 52; *Contributions to the Anthropology of the Caucasus* 53; *The Track of Man* 53; *Ancient and Modern Man in Southwestern Asia* I 56, II 61; *Bibliographies on S.W. Asia*, I-VII 53-63; *An Anthropological Reconnaissance in West Pakistan* 59; *North Arabian Desert Archaeological Survey 25-50*, 60; *"M" Project for F.D.R.: Studies on Migration and Settlement* 62; Editor *Peabody Museum Russian Translation Series*, Vols. I-V 59-70, *Contributions to the Anthropology of Saudi Arabia* 72.
3551 Main Highway, Coconut Grove, Miami 33, Florida; Office: Peabody Museum, Harvard University, Cambridge, Mass., U.S.A.

Filali, Abdelaziz, LL.D.; Moroccan judge and administrator; b. 10 June 1924; ed. Lycée Gouraud, Rabat, Lycée Lyautey, Casablanca, Ecole Nat. d'Org. Economique et Sociale, Paris, Grenoble Univ. and Inst. des Hautes Etudes, Rabat.
Practised at the Bar, Casablanca 51-55; First Pres. Int. Tribunal of Tangier, Court of Appeal Tangier and Court of Appeal Rabat 55-; Lecturer Inst. des Hautes Etudes Marocaines, Ecole Marocaine d'Administration, then Asst. Dir. Ecole Marocaine; Pres. Centre Africain de Formation et de Recherche Administratives pour le Développement (C.A.F.R.A.D.), Tangier 64-; mem. Comm. for Arabization of Code of Civil Procedure 63, Comm. for Arabization of Code of Obligations and Contracts 64; Pres. Comm. for Arabization of Code of Commercial Law 65; designated Conciliator and Arbitrator, Int. Centre for Settlement of Investment Disputes, Washington, D.C., U.S.A.; Dr. h.c. Univ. of Grenoble.
Publs. *Marriage in Moroccan Law* (in Arabic), *Notes Judiciaires* (in French).
Cour d'Appel, Casablanca, Morocco.

Fisher, Sydney Nettleton, M.A., PH.D.; American university professor and editor; b. 1906; ed. Oberlin Coll., Univ. of Illinois, Princeton Univ. and Univ. of Brussels.
Tutor in Mathematics and English, Robert Coll., Istanbul 28-31, 36-37; Instructor in History, Denison Univ., Granville, Ohio 35-36; Instructor in History, The Ohio State Univ. 37-42, Asst. Prof. 42-47, Assoc. Prof. 47-55, Prof. 55-72, Prof. Emer. 72-; Co-ordinator, Graduate Inst. for World Affairs 62-65; Dir. Near and Middle East Program

67-71; Assoc. Chief, Econ. Analysis Section, Middle East Div., Foreign Econ. Admin., Washington, D.C. 43-44, Country Specialist, Commercial Policy Div., Dept. of State 44-46; Lecturer on World Affairs, Chautauqua Inst., Chautauqua, N.Y. 40, 41 and 42; Visiting Prof. of History and Govt., Stetson Univ., DeLand, Fla. 49; Dir. of Publs. of The Middle East Inst. and Editor *The Middle East Journal*, Washington, D.C. 52-53; Visiting Prof. of History, Univ. of S. Calif., Los Angeles 54, 61; mem. American Historical Asscn., The Middle East Inst., Royal Historical Soc., London, Accademia del Mediterraneo, Asscn. for North American Middle East Studies, etc.
Publs. *The Foreign Relations of Turkey, 1481-1512* 48, *Evolution in the Middle East* 53, *Social Forces in the Middle East* 55, *The Middle East: A History* 59, 69, *The Military in the Middle East* 63, *France and the European Community* 65, *New Horizons for the United States in World Affairs* 66.
P.O. Box 162, Worthington, Ohio 43085, U.S.A.

Fisher, William Bayne, B.A., DR. DE L'UNIV. (Paris); British university professor; b. 24 Sept. 1916; ed. Univs. of Manchester, Louvain, Caen and Paris.
Research Fellow 37-40; served in Royal Air Force 40-46, commissioned 41, O.C. R.A.F. Liaison Unit, Syria and Lebanon 44-45; Lecturer, Univ. of Manchester 46; Senior Lecturer, Dept. of Geography, Aberdeen Univ. 47-53; Reader and Head of Dept. of Geography, Univ. of Durham 54-56, Prof. 56-, Dir. Inst. of Middle Eastern and Islamic Studies 62-65, Principal Graduate Coll. 65-; Consultant H.M. Govt., Govt. of Libya and Harvard Univ., U.S.A.; Leader Univ. Expedition to Libya 51.
Publs. *The Middle East—a Physical, Social and Regional Geography* 50, 71, *Spain* (with H. Bowen-Jones) 57, *Malta* (with H. Bowen-Jones and J. C. Dewdney), Editor Vol. I *The Cambridge History of Iran* (Land and People) 68, *Populations of the Middle East and North Africa* (with J. I. Clarke) 72.
Abbey View, 42 South Street; and 38 Old Elvet, Durham, England.

Fitouri, Mohamed, L. EN D.; Tunisian politician; b. 4 April 1925, Kairouan; ed. Lycée Carnot, Tunis, Inst. des Hautes Etudes, Tunis and Faculté de Droit, Paris.
Called to the Bar 52; mem. Council, Nat. Asscn. of Lawyers 60; Advocate, Court of Cassation 62; mem. Econ. and Social Council; City Counsellor, Tunis 69; Deputy to Nat. Assembly Nov. 69-; Minister of Justice 70-71, of Finance Oct. 71-; Grand Cordon, Ordre de la République, Ordre de l'Indépendance.
Ministry of Finance, Tunis; and 17 rue Slaheddine El Ayoubi, Tunis, Tunisia.

Franjiya, Sulaiman; Lebanese politician; b. 14 June 1910, Zgharta; ed. coll. at Zgharta, near Beirut.
Elected to Parl. as Independent mem. 60 and 64; Minister of Posts, Telegraphs and Telephones and Minister of Agriculture 60-61; Minister of the Interior 68; Minister of Justice, Minister of Econ., Minister of Public Works, Minister of Nat. Econ. 69-70; head, trade del. to negotiate Soviet-Lebanese trade and payments agreement; Pres. of Lebanon Sept. 70-.
Office of the President, Beirut, Lebanon.

Frei, Ephraim Heinrich, D.PHIL.; Israeli professor; b. 2 March 1912, Vienna, Austria; ed. Vienna and Hebrew Univs.
Broadcasting Engineer, British Army and attached to British Embassy, Athens 42-46; Head Electronics Section Scientific Dept., Ministry of Defence, Israel 48-50; with Weizmann Inst. of Science 53-, Prof. and Head Dept. of Electronics 61-; mem. Inst. for Advanced Study, Princeton, N.J. 52; Int. Research Fellow, Stanford Research Inst., Calif. 60; mem. Board of Dirs. Yeda, Advisory Board, Jerusalem School of Applied Science; mem.

Board, Silver Inst. of Bio-Medical Engineering; Chair. I.E.E.E. Comm. on Magnetics in Life Sciences; Fellow, I.E.E.E.; Weizmann Prize 57.
Publs. scientific papers on electronics and physics.
5 Ruppin Street, Rehovot, Israel.

Freiha, Said; Lebanese newspaper proprietor; b. 1903.
Chairman Board Dar Assayad S.A.L. which publishes *Assayad* (weekly) 43-, *Achabaka* (weekly) 56-, *Al-Anwar* (daily) 59-.
Dar Assayad, Hazmié, P.O.B. 1038, Beirut, Lebanon.

Freund, Mrs. Miriam Kottler, M.A., PH.D.; American Zionist leader; b. 17 Feb. 1906; ed. Hunter Coll., New York Univ.
Teacher high schools, N.Y.C. to 44; Vice-Pres. Women's Comm., Brandeis Univ. 50-52; Nat. Board Hadassah, Women's Zionist Organization 40-, Vice-Pres. 53-56, Pres. 56-60; Chair. Nat. Youth Aliyah 53-56; mem. Actions Cttee., World Zionist Organization 56-; Chair. Exec. Cttee. American Zionist Council 60-; mem. Nat. Board Jewish Nat. Fund and Keren Hayesod 47-48; del. 21st Orientalist Congress, Moscow 60; Editor *Hadassah* magazine 66-71, Nat. Ed. Chair. 71-; mem. American Asscn. of Univ. Women, Jewish History Soc., Nat. Council of Nat. Planning Asscn. 70; Vice-Pres. American Zionist Fed. 70-72; mem. Exec. World Council of Synagogues.
Publs. *Jewish Merchants in Colonial America* 36, *Jewels for a Crown: The Chagall Windows* 63.
575 Park Avenue, New York, N.Y. 10021, U.S.A.

Frye, Richard Nelson, PH.D.; American orientalist; b. 10 Jan. 1920; ed. Univ. of Ill., Harvard Univ., and School of Oriental and African Studies, London.
Junior Fellow, Harvard 46-49; visiting scholar, Univ. of Teheran 51-52; Aga Khan Prof. of Iranian, Harvard 57-; Visiting Prof., Oriental Seminary, Frankfurt Univ. 58-59; Hamburg Univ. 68-69; assoc. Editor *Central Asian Journal* and *Indo-Iranica;* Hon. mem. German Archaeological Inst.
Publs. *Notes on the early coinage of Transoxiana* 49, *History of the Nation of the Archers* 52, *Narshakhi, The History of Bukhara* 54, *Iran* 56, *The Heritage of Persia* 62, *The Histories of Nishapur* 65, *Bukhara, the Medieval Achievement* 65, *Corpus Iranian Inscriptions* 68, 71, *Qasr-i Abu Nasr Excavations* 73, *The Golden Age of Persia* 75; Editor: *Bulletin Asia Institute* (monographs), *Cambridge History of Iran Vol. IV*.
546 Widener Library, Cambridge 38, Mass., U.S.A.

G

Gaballah, Sayed; Egyptian politician; ed. Cairo and Wisconsin Univs.
Teacher, Cairo Univ., Head Agricultural Econ. Section; Under-Sec. of State for Planning 63-71; Minister for Planning 71-74.
c/o Ministry of Planning, Cairo, Egypt.

Gaddafi, Col. Moamar al-; Libyan army officer and political leader; b. 1941, Misurata; ed. Univ. of Libya, Benghazi.
Served with Libyan Army 65-; Chair. Revolutionary Council and C.-in-C. of Armed Forces of Libya Sept. 69-; Prime Minister 70-72; Minister of Defence 70-; mem. Pres. Council, Fed. Arab Repubs. 71-.
Revolutionary Command Council, Tripoli, Libya.

Gaddafi, Wanis; Libyan politician and diplomatist.
Head of Exec. Council in Cyrenaican Provincial Govt. 52-62; Minister of Foreign Affairs Jan. 62-63, of Interior 63-64, of Labour 64; Ambassador to Fed. Repub. of Germany 64-65; Minister of Planning and Devt. 66-68; Minister of Foreign Affairs 68; Prime Minister Sept. 68-69; imprisoned for two years Nov. 71.
Tripoli, Libya.

Galili, Israel; Israeli politician; b. May 1911, Brailov, Ukraine; ed. Ahad Ha'am Primary School.
Went to Palestine 15; later worked on buildings and in printing; f. Asscn. of Working Youth 24; helped establish Kibbutz Na'an 30; Haganah activities 35-48; Deputy Minister of Defence, Israel Govt. 48; mem. Knesset; Minister without Portfolio (in charge of Information Services) 66-69; Minister without Portfolio 69-; Achdut Ha'Avoda.
The Knesset, Jerusalem; Kibbutz "Na'an", Israel.

Gat, Dr. Joel R., M.SC., PH.D.; Israeli professor of isotope research; b. 17 Feb. 1926, Munich, Germany; ed. Hebrew Univ., Jerusalem.
Department of Physical Chem., Hebrew Univ. 49-50; Ministry of Defence Laboratories, Jerusalem 50-52; Israel Atomic Energy Comm., Rehovot 52-59; Fellow ISNSE, Argonne Nat. Laboratories and Enrico Fermi Inst., Univ. of Chicago, Ill. 55-56; Fellow, Scripps Inst. of Oceanography, Univ. of Calif. San Diego at La Jolla 64-65; Acting Head, Isotopes Dept., Weizmann Inst. of Science 66-70, 74-; Prof. Isotope Research 71-; Deputy Chair. Scientific Council 72-; Walter P. Reuther Chair in the Peaceful Uses of Atomic Energy 68.
3 Hagrast, Rehovot, Israel.

Gazit, Mordechai, M.A.; Israeli diplomatist; b. 5 Sept. 1922; ed. Hebrew Univ., Jerusalem.
Minister, Embassy of Israel to U.S.A. 60-65; Asst. Dir.-Gen. Ministry of Foreign Affairs 65-67; Deputy Dir.-Gen. Ministry of Immigrant Absorption 69-70; Asst. Dir.-Gen. Ministry of Foreign Affairs 70-72, Dir.-Gen. 72-73; Dir.-Gen., Political Adviser Prime Minister's Office 73-.
Office of the Prime Minister, Jerusalem; Home: Kiryat Wolfson, Building 2 (Appartment 30), Jerusalem, Israel.

Gazit, Maj.-Gen. Shlomo; Israeli army officer; b. 1926, Turkey; ed. Tel-Aviv Coll., Tel-Aviv Univ.
Joined Palmach 44, successively served in 8th Co., Sixth Regt., and as Co. Commdr. Harel Brigade; Editor *Maarachot* (Army monthly) 49-51; Regimental Commdrs.' course 51; Dir. Office of the Deputy Chief of Staff until 53; Dir. Chief of Staff's Office 53-55; Deputy Regimental Commdr. G'Vati Brigade 55; Liaison Officer with French Army Del., Sinai Campaign 56; Asst. to Mil. Attaché, France 57; Instructor Israeli Defence Forces Staff and Command Coll. 58-59; with Gen. Staff 60-61; Deputy Commdr. Golani Brigade 62; co-founder and Instructor, Nat. Defence Coll., Jerusalem 63; served in senior posts, Intelligence Branch, Gen. Staff 64-67; Dir. Dept. of Mil. Govt. 67; Co-ordinator of Administered Areas, Ministry of Defence 67-74; Rank of Maj.-Gen. 73; Head Intelligence Branch, IDF April 74-; Israeli Defence Forces, General Staff, IDF April 74-.
Israeli Defence Forces, General Staff, 9 Itamar Ben-Avi Street, Tel-Aviv, Israel.

Geghman, Yahya Hamoud; Yemeni diplomatist; b. 24 Sept. 1934; ed. Law Schools, Cairo, Paris, Damascus and Boston and Columbia Univs.
Teacher of Arabic Language and Literature, Kuwait 57-59; Dir.-Gen. Yemen Broadcasting System, Special Adviser, Ministry of Foreign Affairs 62-63; Deputy Perm. Rep. to UN 63-66, 67-68; Minister Plenipotentiary, Yemen Arab Repub. (Y.A.R.) Embassy to U.S.A. 63-67; Minister of Foreign Affairs 68; Minister of State, Personal Rep. of the Pres. 69; Deputy Prime Minister 69-71; Amb. Extraordinary and Plenipotentiary, Perm. Rep. to UN 71-73; Amb. to U.S.A. 73-74; Deputy Prime Minister for Foreign and Econ. Affairs Jan. 75-; Pres. Supreme Council for Youth Welfare and Sport 70; Gov. for Y.A.R., Int. Bank for Reconstruction and Devt., Int. Monetary Fund 70-; mem. of del. to Conf. of Arab Heads of Govts. 65, 69, to U.S.S.R. 68, to UN General Assembly 62-; has represented Y.A.R. at many int. functions

Publs. articles on politics, economics and literature in various Arabic journals.
Office of the Deputy Prime Minister, Sana'a, Yemen Arab Republic.

Gelb, Ignace Jay, PH.D.; American university professor; b. 14 Oct. 1907; ed. Univ. of Rome.
Travelling Fellow, later Instructor, Univ. of Chicago 29-41; Asst. Prof. 41-43, Assoc. Prof. 43, 46-47, Prof. of Assyriology 47-65; Frank P. Hixon Distinguished Service Prof. 65-; U.S. Army 43-45; Guggenheim Fellow 60-61; Colvin Research Prof. 62-63; Editor *Chicago Assyrian Dictionary* 47-; Hon. mem. Société Asiatique, Paris, Societas Orientalis Fennica, Helsinki, Indian Oriental Soc., Hyderabad; Foreign mem. Accad. Nazionale dei Lincei, Rome; Fellow of the American Academy of Arts and Sciences; Pres. American Name Soc. 63-; Pres. American Oriental Soc. 65-.
Publs. *Hittite Hieroglyphs I-III* 31-42, *Inscriptions from Alishar* 35, *Hittite Hieroglyphic Monuments* 39, *Hurrians and Subarians* 44, *A Study of Writing* 52, *Sargonic Texts from the Diyala Region* 52, *Old Akkadian Writing and Grammar* 52, *Glossary of Old Akkadian* 57, *Sequential Reconstruction of Proto-Akkadian* 69.
Oriental Institute, University of Chicago, Chicago, Ill. 60637; and 5454 Woodlawn Avenue, Chicago, Ill., U.S.A.

Gemayel, Sheikh Pierre; Lebanese politician; b. 1905; ed. Univ. St. Joseph, Beirut and Cochin Hospital, Paris.
Trained as a pharmacist; founded Parti Démocrate Social Libanais—Les Phalanges (Kataeb Party) 36, leader 37-; imprisoned 37, 43; organized general strike 32; established the first Labour Code 44; Minister of Public Works 60, of Finance 60-61, of Communications 60, of Public Health 60, 61; Minister of Public Works May 61-Feb. 64; Minister of the Interior 66-67; Deputy for Beirut 60-; Lebanese, Polish and Egyptian decorations.
Rue de l'Université St. Joseph, Beirut, Lebanon.

Georgy, Guy-Noël; French diplomatist; b. 17 Nov. 1918, Paris; ed. Faculty of Law, Bordeaux and Paris.
Chief of Cabinet and Head of Information Dept., Cameroun 45-49; Attaché, Ministry for French Overseas Territories 50; Head of North-Cameroun District, Maroua 51-55; Chief of Cabinet, Ministry for French Overseas Territories 55; Gen. Sec. to Gabon 56; Gen. Man. of Econ. Affairs and Plan, Equatorial Africa 57, West Africa 58; High Commr. in Congo 59; High Commr. Congo (Brazzaville) 60; Amb. to Bolivia 61-64, to Dahomey 64-69, to Libya 69-.
French Embassy, Sharia Huper, Tripoli, Libya; 9 avenue Franco-Russe, Paris 7e, France.

Germanus Gyula, Julius, PH.D., D.LITT.; Hungarian orientalist and linguist; b. 1884; ed. Univs. of Budapest, Istanbul, Vienna and Leipzig.
Lecturer at Eastern Acad. of Commerce 12, Univ. of Political Economy, Dept. of Oriental Sciences 29, Univ. of Santineketan, Bengal 29-32; Prof. of Arab Language, Budapest Univ. 48-65; numerous journeys in Near East, pilgrimage to Mecca 35; Visiting Lecturer, Turkish, Egyptian and Indian Univs.; Independent mem. Hungarian Parl. 58-67; Corresp. mem. Arab Acad. of Cairo, Arab Acad. of Damascus, Acad. of Baghdad; mem. Accad. del. Mediterraneo; fellow, Inst. for Cultural Research, London 71.
Publs. *Allah Akbar* 36, *A félhold fakó fényében* (The Half-Moon's Dim Light) 58, and numerous articles on Arab literature including *History of Arab Literature, Anthology of Arab Poetry, Modern Poetry of South Arabia*.
Petőfitér 3, Budapest V, Hungary.

Ghaffari, Abolghassem, DR. SC. MATH., PH.D.; Iranian mathematician; b. 1909; ed. Darolfonoun School and Univs. of Nancy, Paris, London and Oxford.
Associate Prof., Teheran Univ. 37-42, Prof. of Mathematics 42-; Mathematics Research Asst. King's Coll., London

47-48; Research Fellow, Harvard 50-51, Research Assoc., Princeton 51-52; mem. Inst. for Advanced Study, Princeton 51-52; Senior Mathematician, Nat. Bureau of Standards, Washington, D.C. 56-57; aeronautical research scientist 57-64; Professorial Lecturer, American Univ., Washington 58-62; aerospace scientist, Goddard Space Flight Center, Greenbelt, Md. 64-; Visiting Prof. of Mathematics, Arya-Mehr Univ. of Technology, Teheran 74-75; has lectured at Univs. of Harvard, Maryland, Princeton and Columbia and at Massachusetts Inst. of Technology; mem. American, French and British Mathematical Societies; Fellow Washington Acad. of Sciences, New York Acad. of Sciences, American Asscn. for the Advancement of Science; mem. Iranian Higher Council of Education 54-58; Iranian Del. to 5th Pakistan Science Conf. Lahore 53, to Int. Congresses of Mathematicians, Amsterdam 54, Edinburgh 58, Stockholm 62; mem. Iranian Comm. for UNESCO 54; mem. American Astronomical Soc.; Orders of Homayoun and of Danesh (first class) and of Sepass (first class); U.S. Special Apollo Achievement Award.
Publs. *Sur l'Equation Fonctionelle de Chapman-Kolmogoroff* 36, *The Hodograph Method in Gas Dynamics* 50.
7109 Connecticut Avenue, Washington, D.C. 20015, U.S.A.; and Shah Reza Avenue, 31 Ladan Street, Teheran, Iran.

Ghaidan, Gen. Saadoun; Iraqi army officer and politician; b. 1930; ed. secondary educ. in Ramadi and Military Coll.
Commissioned 2nd Lieut. 53; Commdr. Repub. Body-Guard Forces 68; mem. Revolutionary Command Council 68; Minister of the Interior April 70-74, of Communications 74-.
Ministry of Communications, Baghdad, Iraq.

Ghaleb, Mohamed Murad; Egyptian diplomatist and politician; b. 1 April 1922, Cairo.
Under-Sec. for Foreign Affairs 59-60; Amb. to Congo Republic (Léopoldville) 60, to U.S.S.R. 61-71; Minister of Foreign Affairs 71-72, of Information 73-74; Amb. to Yugoslavia June 74-.
Embassy of Egypt, Andre Nikolića 12, Belgrade, Yugoslavia; and 78 El Nil Street, Gueza, Cairo, Egypt.

Ghanem, Gen. Iskander A.; Lebanese army officer; b. 10 Oct. 1913; ed. Coll. du Sacré Coeur, Mil. Acad., Homs, and Gen. Staff Coll., Leavenworth, Kan., U.S.A.
Promoted to rank of Capt. in Lebanese Army 45; Artillery Battalion Commdr., Artillery Insp. 47-58; Lieut.-Col. 53, Col. 59; Deputy Chief of Staff 59-66; Brig. 64; Commdr. Northern Region 66, 68; Armed Forces Attaché, Washington, D.C. 66-67; Head Mil. Court 67; Commdr. Beirut Region 67-68, 68-69; C.-in-C. Lebanese Army 71-Sept. 75, on leave of absence Sept. 75-, Gen. 71; Minister of Hydroelectric Resources, and of Nat. Defence 75; War Medal, Lebanese Merit Medal, Cedars Medal of High Ranking Officers, The Highest Mil. Cedars Medal, French Proficiency Medal, Portuguese Proficiency Medal, and several other decorations.
Mar Takla Hazmieh, Beirut, Lebanon.

Ghanem, Ismail, D. EN D.; Egyptian lawyer; b. 24 May 1924, Alexandria; ed. Alexandria Univ., Faculté de Droit, Paris and Inst. of Comparative Law, New York Univ.
Member Staff, Faculty of Law, Alexandria Univ. and Ain-Shams Univ. 51-; Dean Faculty of Law, Arab Univ. of Beirut, Lebanon 62-63; Dean, Faculty of Law, Ain-Shams Univ. 66-68, Vice-Rector 68-70, Rector 71-74; Amb. and Perm. Del. to UNESCO, Paris 70-71; Minister of Culture May-Sept. 71, of Higher Educ. and Scientific Research 74-75; mem. Exec. Board, Cairo Governorate; mem. Board, Acad. for Scientific Research; Chair. Council for the Social Sciences 71.
Publs. *Le Droit du Travail* 62, *La Vente* 63, *Le Droit*

Subjectif 63, all in Arabic; *Les Droits réels principaux*, 2 vols., 62, *La Théorie générale des Obligations* 66-67.
c/o Ministry of Higher Education, Cairo, Egypt.

Ghanem, Mohamed Hafez, PH.D.; Egyptian lawyer and government official; b. 28 Sept. 1925; ed. Cairo Univ. and Univ. de Paris.
Lecturer, Faculty of Law, Alexandria Univ. 49; Prof. of Public Int. Law and Vice-Dean, Faculty of Law, Ain Shams Univ. 60-68; Minister of Tourism 68-69, of Educ. 69-71; Sec.-Gen. Arab Socialist Union 73; Deputy Premier and Minister of Higher Educ. April 75-; Hon. Sec. Egyptian Soc. of Int. Law; mem. Arbitration, Conciliation and Meditation Comm. of Org. of African Unity (OAU) 66-71; mem. Legal Consultative Comm. for Afro-Asian Countries 58-65; State Prize for best publ. in field of Int. Law and Political Science 60.
Publs. *Public International Law* (Arabic) 64, *International Organization* 67.
Office of the Deputy Premier, Cairo; and 3 Sharia El Bergass, Garden City, Cairo, Egypt.

Gherab, Mohamed Habib; Tunisian UN official.
Former Amb. to Spain; Special Adviser to Tunisian Sec. of State for Foreign Affairs 67-69; mem. del. to XXIII session of UN Gen. Assembly; Asst. Sec.-Gen. of UN and Dir. of Personnel March 69-.
Office of Personnel, UN Secretariat, New York, N.Y., U.S.A.

Ghirshman, Roman, D. ÈS L.; French professor and archaeologist; b. 3 Oct. 1895; ed. Sorbonne, Ecole des Hautes-Etudes, Ecole du Louvre.
Director, French archaeological mission in Iran 31-67, in Afghanistan 41-43; mem. Acad. des Inscriptions et Belles-Lettres; Pres. Asscn. pour l'avancement des études iraniens; Dir. *Iranica Antiqua* review; Fellow British Acad.; Dr. h.c. (Teheran); Cmmdr. Légion d'Honneur; Grand Officer Homayoun and Tadj (Iran); Croix de St. Georges; Medal of Freer Gallery of Art.
Publs. *Fouilles de Tépé Giyan* 31-32, *Fouilles de Sialk* (2 vols.) 33-37; *Bégram, Histoire des Kouchans* 46, *Les Chionites-Hephtalites* 48, *Iran, des Origines à l'Islam* 51, *Village perse-achéménide* 54, *Bîchâpour II, mosaïques sassanides* 56, *Bîchâpour I* 70, *Iran, Parthes et Sassanides* 62, *Perse, Proto-Iraniens, Mèdes, Achéménides* 64, *Tchoga Zanbil, La Ziggourat*, vol. I 66, *Tchoga Zanbil, Temenos, Temples, Palais, Tombes* vol. II 68, *Iran, Immortal Kingdom* 70, *Les Terrasses sacrées de Bard-è Néchandeh et Masjid-i Solaiman, depuis le VIIIe siècle avant notre ère au Ve siècle de notre ère* 75; 300 articles in reviews.
96 rue La Fontaine, 75016, Paris, France.

Ghorbal, Ashraf, PH.D.; Egyptian diplomatist; ed. Washington Univ.
Joined Egyptian Del. to UN 49; Head Egyptian Interests Section, Indian Embassy, Washington 68-73; Press Adviser to the Pres. Feb.-Nov. 73; Amb. to U.S.A. Nov. 73-.
Embassy of Egypt, 2310 Decatur Place, N.W., Washington, D.C. 20008, U.S.A.

Ghorra, Edward A., L. EN D.; Lebanese diplomatist; b. 1913; ed. Patriarchal Coll., Beirut, American Univ. of Beirut, French Law School (Univ. St. Joseph), Beirut and Univ. of Pittsburgh, U.S.A.
Mem. of staff, American Univ. of Beirut 39-41; barrister 41-45; Consul-Gen. for Lebanon, New York 45-50, Sydney 50-55; attached Ministry of Foreign Affairs as Head Occidental Section 56-57; mem. Lebanese Del. to Economic and Social Council and UN Gen. Assembly 47-49; Dir. of Political Affairs and Int. Relations Dept. 57-58; del. to UN Gen. Assembly 58, 63; Ambassador to U.S.S.R. 59-63; Dir. Dept. for Lebanese Overseas, Ministry of Foreign Affairs 63-65; Amb. to Czechoslovakia and Poland 65-68; Perm. Rep. to UN 68-, concurrently Amb. to Jamaica 73-;

Rep. to Human Rights Comm. 69-, Social Comm. 69-71, Econ. and Social Council 71-73; Vice-Pres. Econ. and Social Council, Chair. Co-ordinating Cttee. 72-; Vice-Pres. UN Gen. Assembly 68, 74; foreign decorations.
Permanent Mission of Lebanon to the United Nations, 866 United Nations Plaza, Room 533-535, New York, N.Y. 10017, U.S.A.

Ghosheh, Abdallah Shehadeh; Jordanian judge; b. 21 Oct. 1905; ed. Rawdah Coll., Jerusalem, Jerusalem Law Inst.
Teacher 29-34; Chief Clerk, Shariya Hebron Court 34-38; Judge in Vaffa, Nazareth, Hebron and Nablus 38-46; mem. Shariya Court of Appeal 46-48; mem. Cttee. for Unification of Laws in Amman 50; Chief Justice 50; Chief Justice and Minister of Justice 50-51; Acting Minister of Educ. 51; Chief Islamic Higher Cttee. 51; mem. Supreme Council for Educ. in Jordan 53; mem. Devt. Cttee. for Al Aksa Mosque 54; Chief Justice and Head of Al Awkaj Council and Islamic Affairs March 64-; mem. Royal Consultative Body Aug. 67; Minister of Awkaj and Islamic Affairs and Holy Places Dec. 68; Kadi Kuda Nov. 69; Chief of Cttee. for collecting of money for rebuilding of Holy Mosque of the Rock 54, 62; Al Kawkab Medal Grade I, Al Nahda Medal Grade I.
Office of the Chief Justice of the Muslim Religious Courts, Amman, Jordan.

Ghoussein, Talat al-; Kuwaiti diplomatist; b. 1924; ed. American Univ. of Cairo.
Foreign News Editor *As-Shaab* (Jaffa, Palestine) 46-47; Controller, Arab Bank Ltd., Jaffa, Palestine 47-48; Editor Foreign News and Dir. of English Section, Broadcasting Station of Jordan 48-49; Dir. Press and Public Information Ministry of Foreign Affairs, Yemen 49-53; Sec.-Gen., Development Board, Kuwait 53-60; Dep. Private Sec. to Amir of Kuwait 60-61; Minister-Counsellor, Kuwait Embassy, Washington 62-63, Amb. to U.S.A. 63-70, concurrently to Canada 65-70; Amb. to Morocco 70-71, to Japan 71-.
Embassy of Kuwait, 13-12, Mita 4-chome, Minato-ku, Tokyo, Japan.

Ghozali, Sid Ahmed; Algerian industrialist; b. 31 March 1937, Marnia; ed. Ecole des Ponts et Chaussées, Paris.
Formerly Dir. of Energy, Ministry of Industry and Energy; Adviser, Ministry of the Economy 64; Under-Sec., Ministry of Public Works 64-65; Pres., Dir.-Gen. Société nationale de transports et de commercialisation des hydrocarbures (SONATRACH) 66-; mem. Org. technique de mise en valeur des richesses du sous-sol saharien 62-.
SONATRACH, Immeuble le Maurétanie, Algiers, Algeria.

Ghunaim, Khalifa Khalid al; Kuwaiti diplomatist and politician; b. 1921; ed. American Univ. of Beirut.
Deputy Chair Nat. Bank of Kuwait; mem. Kuwait Tanker Co., Kuwait Currency Board, Kuwait Development Board, Kuwait Chamber of Commerce; Ambassador to U.K. 61-62; Minister of Commerce 63-65; now Speaker, Nat. Assembly.
National Assembly, Kuwait.

Glubb, Lieut.-Gen. Sir John Bagot, K.C.B., C.M.G., D.S.O., O.B.E., M.C.; British officer; b. 16 April 1897; ed. Cheltenham and Royal Military Acad. Woolwich.
2nd Lieut. Royal Engineers 15, served France; served Iraq 20; Admin. Inspector Iraq Govt. 26; Officer Commdg. Desert Area (Transjordan) 30; Officer Commdg. Arab Legion, Transjordan (now Jordan) 38-56.
Publs. *Story of the Arab Legion* 48, *A Soldier with the Arabs* 57, *Britain and the Arabs* 59, *War in the Desert* 60, *The Great Arab Conquests* 63, *The Empire of the Arabs* 63, *The Course of Empire* 65, *The Lost Centuries* 67, *Syria, Lebanon, Jordan* 67, *A Short History of the Arab Peoples* 69, *The Life and Times of Muhammad* 70, *Peace in the Holy Land* 71, *Soldiers of Fortune* 73, *The Way of Love* 74.
West Wood St. Dunstan, Mayfield, Sussex, England.

Godik, Giora; Israeli theatre producer; b. 5 May 1921; ed. Magnus Krynski, Warsaw and Stefan Batory Univ., Wilna.
Fought with Polish Army during Second World War; settled in Israel 48; with Israeli Army 48-55; opened artists' agency Giora Godik Productions Ltd. 55; opened Giora Godik Theatre, Alhambra Theatre, Tel-Aviv 65; productions include *Barefoot in the Park, Fiddler on the Roof, The King and I, Kazablan, Hello Dolly, I Like Mike, Long Live the Horses, The Witch.*
Office: 10 Glikson Street, Tel-Aviv; Home: 53 King David Blvd., Tel-Aviv, Israel.

Goldmann, Nahum; Lithuanian-born Zionist leader; b. 10 July 1895; ed. Heidelberg, Berlin and Marburg Univs.
Editor and Publisher German Hebrew Encyclopedia Judaica 22-34; mem. Zionist Political Comm. 27; Act. Chair. Zionist Action Cttee. 33; escaped from Germany 34; Rep. of Jewish Agency to L. of N.; in U.S. 41; Rep. Jewish Agency for Palestine in U.S.A. during Second World War; Pres. World Jewish Congress 51-, World Zionist Org. 56-68, Conf. on Jewish Claims against Germany, Memorial Foundation for Jewish Culture; Chair. Cttee. on Jewish Claims against Austria 50-.
Ahad Haam 18, Jerusalem, Israel; 12 avenue Montaigne, Paris, France.

Goldstein, Rabbi Israel, M.A., D.D., D.H.L., LITT.H.D., LL.D., PH.D.; American Rabbi; b. 18 June 1896; ed. Univ. of Pennsylvania, Jewish Theological Seminary of America and Columbia Univ.
Rabbi Congregation B'nai Jeshurun N.Y.C. 18-60, Rabbi Emeritus 61-; Pres. Jewish Conciliation Board of America 29-68 (now Hon. Pres.), Jewish Nat. Fund of America 33-43 (now Hon. Pres.); Pres. Synagogue Council of America 42-44, Zionist Organization of America 44-46; Chair. World Confed. of Gen. Zionists 46-72 (now Hon. Pres.); United Palestine Appeal 47-49; Co-Chair. United Jewish Appeal 47-49; Treas. Jewish Agency 47-49; Pres. Amidar Israel Nat. Housing Co. for Immigrants 48-49; mem. World Jewish Congress Exec. 48-, and Chair. of its Western Hemisphere Exec. 50-60, Hon. Vice-Pres. 59-; Pres. American Jewish Congress 51-58; now Hon. Pres.; Pres. World Hebrew Union; mem. Jewish Agency for Palestine Exec. 48-72; World Chair. Keren Hayesod-United Israel Appeal 61-71; mem. Board of Govs. Hebrew Univ. of Jerusalem, Weizmann Inst. of Science; Univ. of Haifa; Founder Brandeis Univ. 46; Chair. Jerusalem Artists' House 65-70; Chair. in Zionism at Hebrew Univ. of Jerusalem, Synagogue of Hebrew Univ. of Jerusalem; Chair. in Practical Theology, Jewish Theological Seminary of America; Hon. Chair. Asscn. of Americans and Canadians in Israel.
Publs. *A Century of Judaism in New York* 30, *Towards a Solution* 40, *Mourner's Devotions* 41, *Brandeis University* 51, *American Jewry Comes of Age* 55, *Transition Years* 62, *Israel at Home and Abroad* 73.
12 Pinsker Street, Jerusalem, Israel.

Gomaa, Mohamed Sharawy; Egyptian politician; b. 25 July 1920; ed. Military Coll.
Governor of Suez 61-64; Minister and mem. U.A.R.-Iraq Joint Presidency Council 64; Cabinet State Minister 65-66; Minister of the Interior 66-71; Deputy Prime Minister 70-71; charged with high treason July 71, sentenced to imprisonment Dec. 71.
c/o Ministry of the Interior, Cairo, Egypt.

Goodarzi, Dr. Manouchehr; Iranian administrator; b. 1925; ed. Princeton Univ. and Univ. of S. Calif., U.S.A.
Lecturer, Princeton Univ.; Lecturer in Public Admin., Teheran Univ.; Founding Dir. Org. and Management Bureau 56-57, Dir. Dept. of Social and Municipal Devt. 57-60, Deputy Man. Dir. 60-62, Plan Org.; Deputy Prime Minister, Sec.-Gen. State Org. for Admin and Employment

Affairs 62-69; Minister of Agricultural Products and Consumer Goods 69-70; Minister in charge of Nat. Transport Co-ordination 70-71; Special Adviser to the Prime Minister 71-73; Pres., mem. of Board, Arj Mfg. Corpn. 73-; decorations from Iran, Repub. of Korea and Philippines.
Arj Corporation, P.O. Box 3427, Teheran, Iran.

Goren, Maj.-Gen. Shlomo; Israeli Rabbi; b. 1917, Poland; ed. Hebrew Univ., High Theological Seminar, Jerusalem.
In Israel 25-; co-founder Kfar Hassidim; Chief Chaplain, Israel Defence Forces 48-71; Chief Rabbi of Tel-Aviv (elected June 68); Ashkenazi Chief Rabbi of Israel Oct. 72-; Rabbi Kook Prize, State of Israel Prize.
Publs. *Nezer Hakodesh* (on Maimonides), *Shaarei Tahara, Talmud Yerushalmi Meforash, Torath Ha Moadim, Piskei Hilchoth Tzavah Hagrah Vehavushalmi, Responsa: Mashiv Milchama;* works on religion in military life, prayers for soldiers, etc.
Chief Rabbinate, Hechal Shlomo, Jerusalem; Private Office: 35 Shaul Hamelech Boulevard, Tel-Aviv, Israel.

Goulli, Slaheddine el, LL.D.; Tunisian diplomatist; b. 22 June 1919, Sousse; ed. Collège de Sousse and Université de Paris.
Tunisian Bar 47; in private industry 49-56; active in Tunisian Nat. Liberation Movement, Europe 47-56; Gen. Consul, Marseilles 56-57; Counsellor, Washington 58, Minister, Washington 59-61; Alt. Exec. Dir. World Bank 61; Amb. to Belgium, also accred. to Netherlands and Luxembourg 62, concurrently Perm. Rep. to EEC; Perm. Rep. to UN 69; Amb. to U.S.A. 69-73, concurrently to Mexico 70-73, to Venezuela 72-73; Grand Cordon de l'Ordre de la République Tunisienne 66, also decorations from Belgium, Netherlands and Luxembourg.
c/o Ministry of Foreign Affairs, Tunis, Tunisia.

Graham, John Alexander Noble, C.M.G.; British diplomatist; b. 15 July 1926, Calcutta, India; ed. Trinity Coll. Cambridge.
British Embassy, Amman 53-54, Belgrade 57-60, Benghazi 60-61, Kuwait 66-69; Principal Private Sec. to Foreign and Commonwealth Sec. 69-72; Head of Chancery, British Embassy, Washington 72-74; Amb. to Iraq 74-.
British Embassy, Baghdad, Iraq; and Foreign and Commonwealth Office, King Charles Street, London, S.W.1, England.

Guiga, Driss, L. EN D.; Tunisian politician; b. 21 Aug. 1924, Testour; ed. Sadiki Coll., Tunis.
Tunisian Bar; Chef de Cabinet, Ministry of Public Health 52; Dir. Nat. Security until 63; Dir.-Gen. of Tourism and Thermal Affairs 63; Sec. of State for Public Health Sept.-Nov. 69; Minister of Public Health 69-73, of Nat. Educ. 73-; mem. Destour Socialist Party 43-, has held several party posts, currently mem. Cen. Cttee.
Ministère de l'Education Nationale, Tunis, Tunisia.

Guillaumat, Pierre L. J.; French civil servant; b. 5 Aug. 1909; ed. Prytanée Militaire, La Flèche and Ecole Polytechnique.
Chef du Service des Mines, Indochina 34-39, Tunisia 39-43; Dir. of Carburants 44-51; Admin.-Gen. Atomic Energy Comm. 51-58; Pres. Petroleum Research Bureau 45-58; Minister of the Armies 58-60; Minister attached to Prime Minister's Office 60-62; Minister of Education (*a.i.*) 60-61; Pres. Union Générales des Pétroles 62-65, Electricité de France 64-66, Entreprise de Recherches et d'Activités Pétrolières 65-, Soc. Nat. des Pétroles d'Aquitaine 65-; Pres. Conseil d'Admin. Ecole Polytechnique 71-74; Grand Officier de la Légion d'Honneur, Croix de Guerre.
7 rue Nélaton, Paris 15e, France.

Gülek, Dr. Kasim, B.SC.(COM.), PH.D., LL.D.; Turkish politician, economist and farmer; b. 1910; ed. Robert Coll., Ecole des Sciences Politiques, Paris, Columbia, Cambridge, London, Berlin and Hamburg Univs.
Member of Parl. 40-; mem. Central Exec. Council of People's Republican Party 42; Chair. Cttee. on Commerce 43; del. to Int. Labour Conf. 44; Minister of Public Works 47; Minister of Communications 48, of State 49; Vice-Pres. Council of Europe 62; Chair. UN Comm. on Korea; Sec.-Gen. Republican People's Party 50-59, resigned from Republican People's Party 67; mem. Constituent Assembly 60-61; Pres. North Atlantic Assembly 69; Gov. Atlantic Inst. 69; Senator 69.
Publs. *Development of Economically Backward Countries* 32, *Development of Banking in Turkey* 33, *Democracy Takes Root in Turkey* 51.
B. Evler, 50 Sokak no. 3, Ankara, Turkey.

Gunter, John Wadsworth, M.A., PH.D.; American economist; b. 17 Feb. 1914; ed. Univ. of North Carolina.
Worked in U.S. Treasury Dept. 40-48, Treasury Rep. in Middle East 43-44, in London 46-48, Deputy Dir. Office of Int. Finance 48; Assoc. Prof. of Int. Trade, Univ. of Texas 48-49; U.S. mem. Greek Currency Cttee., Bank of Greece 49-51; Alt. mem. Comm. on German Debts, London 51-53; Asst. Dir. Middle Eastern Dept., Int. Monetary Fund 53, Deputy Dir., Acting Dir. 58-.
International Monetary Fund, Washington, D.C. 20431, U.S.A.

Gur, Lieut.-Gen. Mordechai; Israeli army officer; b. 5 May 1930; ed. Hebrew Univ.
Served in Haganah; Co. Commdr. during Independence War; Deputy Commdr. Paratroop Corps 57; Instructor, Command and Staff Coll. 58; C.O. Golani Brigade 61-63; in charge of Command and Staff Coll. 65-66; C.O. Paratroop Brigade during Six-Day War 67; mem. Israeli Del. to UN Emergency Session 67; C.O. Israeli Forces in Ghaza and N. Sinai, Northern Command 67-72; Mil. Attaché, Washington 72-73; C.O. Northern Command during Yom Kippur War Oct. 73; Chief Mil. Negotiator at Geneva Peace Conf. Dec. 73; Chief of Staff April 74-.
Publs. several children's books.
Ministry of Defence, Tel-Aviv, Israel.

Gürler, Gen. Faruk; Turkish army officer; b. 1913, Üsküdar, Istanbul; ed. War School, War Acad. for Land Forces.
Commander, Artillery and Infantry Units; Staff Officer, High Defence Council; Instructor War School and War Acad., later Acting Commdr.; Intelligence Officer, NATO; Deputy Chief of Staff of Army Corps, Deputy Artillery Commdr. of Div. and Army Corps, later Army Corps Commdr.; Chief of Staff of Land Forces Command; Acting Under-Sec. of State, then Under-Sec. of State, Ministry of Nat. Defence; promoted to rank of Gen. 68; Deputy Chief of Gen. Staff, Commdr. of Land Forces 68-72; Chief of Staff 72-73; Senator and unsuccessful Candidate for Presidency 73.
The Senate, Ankara, Turkey.

Gurney, Oliver Robert, M.A., D.PHIL.; British assyriologist; b. 28 Jan. 1911; ed. Eton Coll. and New Coll. Oxford.
Army Service 39-45; Shillito Reader in Assyriology, Oxford Univ. 45-, Prof. 65-; Fellow of British Acad. 59-, Magdalen Coll. Oxford 63-; Editor *Anatolian Studies* 59-.
Publs. *The Geography of the Hittite Empire* (with J. Garstang) 59, *The Hittites* 52, 72, *The Sultantepe Tablets I and II* (with J. J. Finkelstein and P. Hulin) 57, 64, *Ur Excavations—Texts VII* 74.
Bayworth Corner, Boars Hill, Oxford, England.

Gürün, Kâmuran; Turkish diplomatist; b. 1924, Çengelköy (Istanbul); ed. studied political science.
Entered diplomatic service 48; posted to Turkish Embassy,

Bonn 51; subsequently held various posts at Ministry of Foreign Affairs and diplomatic missions abroad; Dir.-Gen. Dept. for Admin. Affairs 61, subsequently Perm. Sec. to the Inter-Ministerial Cttee. on External Econ. Relations, Dir.-Gen. Dept. for Econ. and Commercial Affairs, Deputy Sec.-Gen. for Econ. Affairs and Sec.-Gen. Inter-Ministerial Econ. Council; Amb. to Romania 67-70; Perm. Rep. of Turkey at OECD 70-72; Amb. to Greece 74-.
Embassy of Turkey, 8 Odos Vassileos Gheorghiou II, Athens, Greece.

Gvati, Chaim; Israeli farmer and politician; b. 29 Jan. 1901; ed. Vilna, Poland, and Russian Univ.
Migrated to Palestine 24; mem. Kibbutz 24-, mem. Kibbutz Meuchad Central Cttee. 42-45; Chair. Security and Econ. Cttees. of The Agriculture Centre 46-49; Dir.-Gen. Ministry of Agriculture 50-57; Sec. Ichud Hakvutzot Veakibutzim 59-62; Sec. Federation of Kibbutz Movement 63-64; Minister of Agriculture 64-74; Mapai.
Kibbutz Yifat, Israel.

H

Habash, George, M.D.; Palestinian resistance leader; b. 1925, Lydda, Palestine; ed. American University of Beirut.
Member Youth of Avengeance 48 and Arab Nationalists' Movement early 50s; practised as doctor 50s; leader of Popular Front for the Liberation of Palestine Nov. 67-.
c/o Palestine Liberation Organization, Colombani Street, Off Sadat Street, Dr. Raji Nasr Building, Ras Beirut, Lebanon.

Habashi, Wadie; Sudanese agricultural economist and politician; b. 14 Aug. 1917, Merwi; ed. Univ. of Khartoum and Oxford Univ.
Worked on the Al Aalyab, Burgaeg and White Nile devt. schemes; Agricultural Insp. for Khartoum Province and later for Merwi, Dongla and Halfa; Technical Adviser to the Minister of Agriculture; Asst. Dir. for Planning and Devt., Dept. of Agriculture, Dir. 55-66; Rep. of Sudan to FAO Conf. 56, to Int. Tobacco Conf., Rhodesia 63; Chair. Admin. Council of El Gash Scheme Comm.; Dir. Production Section, Equatoria Schemes Comm.; Head, Advisory Comm. for Agricultural Research; mem. Gezira Scheme Admin. Council; mem. Studies Comm., Faculty of Agriculture, Univ. of Khartoum; with FAO 66-71, Dir. Joint Econ. Comm. of Africa and the UN, Addis Ababa; joined Int. Bank and Kuwait Fund of Arab Devt. Oct. 71, Minister of Agriculture 71-73, of Agriculture, Food and Natural Resources 73-74; Pres. Nat. Council for Research July 74-, OAU Scientific Council for Africa May 75-.
National Council for Research, Khartoum, Sudan.

Haddad, Amin Farid, PH.C., M.SC.; Lebanese university professor; b. 1911; ed. Nat. Coll. of Shwayfat, American Univ. of Beirut, Philadelphia Coll. of Pharmacy and Science.
Chief Pharmacist, The English Pharmacy, Khartoum, Sudan 33-36; Univ. Pharmacist and Instructor in Pharmacy, American Univ. of Beirut 36-42, Adjunct Prof. of Pharmacy 42-49, Assoc. Prof. of Pharmacy and Acting Dir. School of Pharmacy 49-52, Assoc. Prof. School of Pharmacy 52-, Prof. and Dir. 55-; also Dir. Pharmaceutical Service of Univ. Hospital 49-67; mem. American Pharmaceutical Asscn., American Soc. of Hospital Pharmacists, Int. Pharmaceutical Fed., Scientific Section; mem. Expert Advisory Panel on the Int. Pharmacopoeia and Pharmaceutical Preparation (WHO); Sec. High Comm. on Drugs, Lebanon 64-68; Chair. Scientific Cttee, Lebanese Order of Pharmacists 52-67; Temp. Adviser to WHO (Eastern Mediterranean Region) on pharmaceutical educ. 68-70,

71-74; Editor Lebanese Pharmaceutical Journal 53-63; Hon. Fellow, Univ. of Wisconsin, Madison, U.S.A. 58-59.
American University of Beirut, Beirut, Lebanon.

Haddad, Prof. Ghassan, D.ECON.SC.; Syrian educationist and politician; b. 26 Jan. 1926, Lattakia; ed. secondary schools, Latakia and Damascus, Mil. Acad., and U.S.S.R. Served in various mil. posts 48-61; promoted to rank of Gen. 63; mem. Higher Nat. Council of the Revolution, mem. of Gen. Leadership of the Army and Armed Forces 63; Minister of Planning 63-65, later Pres. Parl. Planning Cttee.; carried out scientific research 66-68; Conf. Prof. Univ. of Damascus, Planning Inst. for Social and Econ. Devt. 69-75; Econ. Adviser, Ministry of Planning, Iraq 75-; Founder and Pres. Board of Dirs., Arab Progress Publishers; mem. Union of Arab Writers, Union of the Arab Economists; several decorations including Médaille de Mérite de Hors Classe, Médaille de la Loyauté de Premier Classe.
Publs. many articles and works.
Ministry of Planning, Baghdad, Iraq.

Haddad, Sulaiman Ahmed el; Kuwaiti banker and politician; b. 1930; ed. Kuwait Aazamieh Secondary School, and Cairo Univ.
Secretary of Educ. Council of Kuwait; fmr. Financial Asst., Ministry of Educ. and mem. Constituent Assembly for formation of Kuwaiti Constitution; mem. National Assembly 63-; Chair. Arab African Bank.
Arab African Bank, 44 Abdel Khalek Sarwat Street, Cairo, Egypt.

Hadid, Mohammed Haj Hussein, B.SC. (ECON.); Iraqi economist; b. 1906; ed. American Univ. of Beirut, and London School of Economics.
Finance Inspector 31; in charge of Statistics Section, Min. of Finance 32, of Commerce Section 34, Acting Dir. of Commerce 35, Acting Dir.-Gen. of Revenue 36; elected deputy for Mosul 37, 48, 54; Vice-Pres. Nat. Democratic Party 46-54; Minister of Supply 46; Minister of Finance 58-60; Founder of Nat. Progressive Party 60; now Man. Dir. Consolidated Modern Enterprises Co.
Saadun, Baghdad, Iraq.

Hadithi, Murtada al-; Iraqi politician; b. 1939, Ramadi; ed. Higher Teachers' Training Inst. and Univ. of Baghdad.
School Teacher, Fallouja 66-67; mem. Revolutionary Command Council 67; Chair. Kurdish Affairs Bureau and Peace Cttee. 67; mem. World Peace Cttee.; Minister of Labour March 70-Oct. 71; Minister of Foreign Affairs 71-74; Amb. to U.S.S.R. 74-75.
Ministry of Foreign Affairs, Baghdad, Iraq.

Hadjioannou, Kyriacos, F.R.A.I., PH.D.; Cypriot teacher and diplomatist; b. 1909; ed. Famagusta Gymnasium, Athens Univ. and Oxford Univ.
Greek Master, Kyrenia Gymnasium 32-35, Famagusta 36-45; Principal, Famagusta Gymnasium 46-48, 57-60, 63-69; Amb. to U.A.R. 60-63; Lecturer, Teachers' Training Coll., Morphou 48-53; Principal, Morphou Gymnasium 53-57; Pres. United Nat. Solid Front 57-59; Founder and Pres. Philological and Scientific Soc. of Famagusta 60-61, 64-; Fellow, Royal Anthropological Inst. of Great Britain and Ireland 46-; Grand Cordon of the Repub. (Egypt).
Publs. *The Loan-words of Medieval and Modern Greek Cypriot Dialect* 36, *Cypriot Fables* 48, *Literary Texts of the Medieval and Modern Greek Cypriot Dialect with Introductions and Commentaries* 61, *Ta en Diaspora* 69, *Diplomacy and machinations in the Courts of the Lusignan Kings of Cyprus* 70, *Ancient Cyprus in Greek Sources*: Vol. I, *Legendary Traditions, History and Ethnology from Prehistoric Times to the Year 395 A.D.* 71, Vol. II, *Mythology and Religion, Geography and Geology* 73, Vol. III, Part I, *Letters, Sciences, Arts and Crafts from Homeric Times to*

the Year 395 A.D. 75, and articles in Greek, German, English, French and Belgian journals.
Ay. Spyridon 8, Famagusta 58; for the time being a regufee in Limassol, Cyprus.

Hafez, Maj.-Gen. Amin el; Syrian army officer and politician; b. 1911.
Former Military Attaché in Argentina; took part in the revolution of March 1963; Dep. Prime Minister, Mil. Gov. of Syria and Minister of Interior March-Aug. 63; Minister of Defence and Army Chief of Staff July-Aug. 63; C.-in-C. of Armed Forces July 63-64; Pres. of Revolutionary Council July 63-May 64; Pres. Presidency Council May 64-Feb. 66; Prime Minister Nov. 63-May 64, Oct. 64-Sept. 65; sentenced to death *in absentia* Aug. 71; living in exile.

Haidar, Mohamed Haider, LL.B.; Syrian politician; b. 1931; ed. secondary schools, Lattakia, Univ. of Damascus.
Teacher, Lattakia, Hama, Damascus 51-60; with Ministry of Agrarian Reform 60-63; Dir. Agrarian Reform Inst., Hama 63; Dir. Agrarian Reform, Damascus, Daraa, Al-Suaida 64; Dir. Legal and Admin. Affairs, Ministry of Agriculture and Agrarian Reform 65; Gov. Al-Hasakeh 66; mem. Command, Damascus Branch of Arab Socialist Baath Party 67, Temporal Regional Command 70, now Regional and Nat. Commands, mem. Cen. Command Progressive Nat. Front of Syria; now Deputy Prime Minister, Minister of Agriculture and Agrarian Reform until 73, of Econ. Affairs Sept. 73-.
Ministry of Economic Affairs, Damascus, Syria.

Haikal, Yusuf, PH.D., D. EN DROIT; Jordanian diplomatist; b. 15 Aug. 1912; ed. Arab Coll. Jerusalem and Univs. of London and Paris.
Gen. Inspector of Awqaf (Moslem Public Properties in Palestine); District Judge (Palestine) 43-45; Mayor of Jaffa 45-48; Minister to U.S.A. 49-53; Chief Jordan Del. with Mixed Armistice Comm., Jerusalem 53-54; Ambassador to Great Britain 54-56, to France 56-57, 62-64, to U.S.A. 57-58, 59-62, to Republic of China 64-65; Hutchinson Silver Medal, London School of Econ. and Political Science 37, Istiqlal Medal (1st class) 53.
Publs. include (in French) *The Prime Minister and the Evolution of the Parliamentary System* 37, *The Dissolution of Parliament* 35 (in Arabic), *The Palestine Problem* 37, *Towards Arab Unity* 43, *The Forefathers of the Prophet* 47, *Palestine Before and After* 71.
c/o Byblos Hotel, Georges Picot Street, Beirut, Lebanon.

Haithem, Muhammad Ali; Yemeni politician; b. 1940, Dathina, Southern Arabia.
Formerly school teacher; Minister of Interior 67; mem. Presidential Council of S. Yemen 69-71; Chair. Council of Ministers 69-70; mem. Nat. Front Gen. Command.
c/o Council of Ministers, Aden, People's Democratic Republic of Yemen.

Hajari, Al-Qadi Abdullah Ahmed Al-; Yemeni politician; b. 1917.
Minister of Communications and Culture before revolution (Sept. 62); Amb. to Kuwait 62-72; mem. Pres. Council 72-73; Prime Minister 73-74.
c/o Office of the Prime Minister, Sana'a, Yemen Arab Republic.

Hakim, George: (*see* Maximos V Hakim).

Hakim, Georges, M.A., L. en D.; Lebanese diplomatist; b. 1913; ed. American Univ., Beirut, and Univ. St. Joseph.
Appointed Adjunct Prof. of Economics, American Univ., Beirut 43; mem. of several advisory govt. cttees. on economic and financial questions 42-46; appointed alternate del. of Lebanon to Economic and Social Council of UN 46, Chief Del. 49; Counsellor Lebanese Legation Washington, D.C. 46-52, Chargé d'Affaires 48 and 51; Minister of Finance, Nat. Economy and Agriculture 52-53; represented Lebanon at numerous int. confs. including Int. Health

Conf. N.Y. 46, UN Conf. on Trade and Employment, London 46, Geneva 47, Havana 47-48, etc.; Board of Govs. of the Int. Bank for Reconstruction and Development and the Int. Monetary Fund 47-50; Vice-Chair. Economic and Financial Cttee. UN 49; Chair. Group of Experts on economic development of underdeveloped countries, apptd. by Sec.-Gen. of UN Feb.-May 51; Minister of Foreign Affairs and of Economy 53; Deputy Sec.-Gen. Ministry of Foreign Affairs Mar.-July 55; Minister to German Fed. Republic July 55-57, Ambassador 57-58; Minister of Nat. Economy Mar.-June 56; Perm. Rep. to UN 59-65, 66; Chair. UN Comm. on Human Rights 62; Deputy Prime Minister and Minister of Foreign Affairs July 65-Feb. 66, Dec. 66-67; Vice-Pres. American Univ. of Beirut 68-.
American University of Beirut, Beirut, Lebanon.

Hakim, Tewfik al-; Egyptian writer; b. 1902.
Leading playwright; mem. Acad. of the Arabic Language, Higher Council of the Arts, etc.; Grand Cordon of the Nile.
Publs. *The Return of the Sow* 33, *The Confused Sultan* 59, *Scheherezade, Pygmalion, The Cave-Dweller, You Who are Climbing the Tree* 63, *A Magistrate's Diary, Solomon the Wise, Bird of Lebanon, The Return of Consciousness, Fate of a Cockroach* 72.
c/o Al-Ahram, Sharia Lal-Galaa, Cairo, Egypt.

Halabi, Mohammed Ali el-; Syrian politician; b. 1937, Damascus; ed. Teachers Training School.
Teacher 54-62; mem. Command Baath Party, Damascus; Mayor of Damascus; mem. Assembly of the Arab Union; Speaker of People's Council June 73-.
People's Council, Damascus, Syria.

Halefoğlu, Vahit M., K.C.V.O., M.A.; Turkish diplomatist; b. 1919; ed. Antakya Coll. and Univ. of Ankara.
Turkish Foreign Service 43-, served Vienna, Moscow, Ministry of Foreign Affairs, London 46-59; Dir.-Gen. First Political Dept., Ministry of Foreign Affairs 59-62; Ambassador to Lebanon 62-65, concurrently accred. to Kuwait 64-65; Ambassador to U.S.S.R. 65-66; Ambassador to the Netherlands 66-70; Deputy Sec.-Gen. for Political Affairs, Ministry of Foreign Affairs Dec. 70-Feb. 72; Amb. to Fed. Repub. of Germany 72-; Lebanese, Finnish, British, Greek, Italian, German and Spanish decorations.
Embassy of Turkey, Utestrasse 47, Bonn-Bad Godesberg, Federal Republic of Germany.

Halkin, Simon, B.A., M.A., D.H.L.; American Hebrew scholar and author; b. 30 Oct. 1899, Dovsk, Russia; ed. N.Y. City Coll., Chicago, New York and Columbia Univs.
Instructor in Hebrew, Hebrew Union School for Teachers, New York City 24-32; Teacher, Geulah High School, Tel-Aviv 32-39; Lecturer in Bible, Jewish, Sociology and Modern Hebrew Literature, Chicago Coll. of Jewish Studies 40-43; Prof. of Hebrew and Hebrew Literature, Jewish Inst. of Religion, New York City 43-49; Assoc. Prof. of Hebrew Literature, Hebrew Univ. of Jerusalem 49-56, Prof. and Head of Dept. 56-68; Visiting Prof., Univ. of Calif. 54-55, Jewish Theological Seminary, N.Y. 65-66; Emer., Hebrew Univ. of Jerusalem 69; mem. Acad. of Hebrew Language; Pres. Israel PEN Club; Tchernichovsky Prize for translation (of Whitman) 53; Bialik Prize for Literature 68.
Publs. *Yehiel Ha-Hagri* (novel) 28, *Arai va-Keva* 43, *Ad Mashber* 45, *Al Haiy* (collected poems) 46, *Ma'avar Yabok* (collected poems), *Modern Hebrew Literature: Trends and Values* 51, *Literatura Hebrea Moderna* 68, *Collected Literary Essays and Studies* (3 vols., Hebrew) 70, *Adrift, Collected Short Stories* 73, and numerous others; translations of Shakespeare, Maeterlinck, Whitman, Shelley, Jack London, etc.
5 Radak Street, Jerusalem, Israel.

Hall, Harvey Porter, M.A.; American executive; b. 16 Nov. 1909; ed. Union Coll. and Harvard Univ.
Instructor, American Univ. of Beirut 30-33, Robert Coll., Istanbul 36-41; Dept. of State, Washington, D.C. 45-46; Dir. of Publs., The Middle East Inst. and Editor *The Middle East Journal* 46-56; Ford Foundation Fellowship 52-53, Programme Assoc. Ford Foundation 56-64, 71-, Assoc. Dir. Middle East-Africa Programme 64-67, Assoc. Rep., Beirut 67-71.
Publ. *American Interests in the Middle East* (Foreign Policy Asscn. Headline Series) 48.
Ford Foundation, P.O. Box 2379, Beirut, Lebanon.

Hamad, Abdlatif Yousef al-; Kuwaiti economist.
Director-General Kuwait Fund for Arab Econ. Devt. 63-; Dir. Kuwait Investment Co.; Chair. Prefabricated Buildings Co. of Kuwait, United Bank of Kuwait Ltd., London, Middle East Int. Fund; Dir. American Express Int. Fund; Exec. Dir. Arab Fund for Econ. and Social Devt.; Chair. Cie Arabe et Int. Investissements; Trustee Kuwait Inst. of Econ. and Social Planning in the Middle East; mem. Perm. Cttee. for Aid to the Arabian Gulf and Yemen.
Kuwait Fund for Arab Economic Development, P.O.B. 2921, Kuwait City, Kuwait.

Hamada, Sabri; Lebanese politician; b. 1902.
Former Speaker, Chamber of Deputies; Deputy Prime Minister, Minister of the Interior 47; Minister of Public Works and Transport May 72-73, of Agriculture July 73-74.
c/o Ministry of Agriculture, Beirut, Lebanon.

Hamadi, Col. Ibrahim Mohamed El-; Yemeni army officer; b. 1943.
Joined Army 62; attended mil. coll.; in charge of Parachute Corps; fmr. Commdr. Western and Cen. Regions; Deputy Prime Minister for Internal Affairs until Dec. 72; Deputy Chief of Staff 72-74; Chair. of Command Council June 74-.
Command Council, Sana'a, Yemen Arab Republic.

Hamed, Abdul Samad, PH.D.; Afghan politician; b. 8 Jan. 1930, Khoguiany (Djelalabad); ed. Nedjat High School and in Switzerland.
Director-General, Training Dept., Univ. of Kabul 57; Legal Adviser to Parl. 57-63; Pres. Secondary Educ. Dept., Ministry of Educ. 62; mem. Drafting Cttee. of the Constitution 63, Constituent Assembly 63; Gov. Parwan Province 64; Pres. Univ. of Kabul 65; Minister of Planning 66, 67; Sec.-Gen. Afghan Red Crescent Soc. 67; Deputy Prime Minister and Pres. of Tribal Affairs 71-72.
c/o Office of the Deputy Prime Minister, Kabul, Afghanistan.

Hammadi, Sadoon; Iraqi economist and politician; b. 22 June 1930, Karbala; ed. in Beirut, Lebanon and U.S.A.
Professor of Econs., Univ. of Baghdad 57; Deputy Head of Econ. Research, Nat. Bank of Libya, Tripoli 61-62; Minister of Agrarian Reform 63; Econ. Adviser to Presidential Council, Govt. of Syria 64; Econ. Expert, UN Planning Inst., Syria 65-68; Pres. Iraq Nat. Oil Co. (INOC) 68; Minister of Oil and Minerals 68-74, of Foreign Affairs 74-.
Publs. *Towards a Socialist Agrarian Reform in Iraq* 64, *Views About Arab Revolution* 69.
Ministry of Foreign Affairs, Baghdad, Iraq.

Hare, Raymond Arthur, A.B.; American diplomatist; b. 3 April 1901; ed. Grinnell Coll.
Instructor, Robert Coll., Constantinople 24-27; Exec. Sec. American Chamber of Commerce for Levant 26-27; Clerk, later Vice-Consul, U.S. Consulate-Gen., Constantinople 27-28; Language Officer, Paris 29, also Vice-Consul 31; Sec. in Diplomatic Service and Vice-Consul, Cairo 31; Beirut 32; Third Sec. and Vice-Consul, Teheran 33, Consul 35; Second Sec. Cairo 39, also at Jeddah 40-44, also Consul, Cairo 40; Second Sec., later First Sec. and Consul, London

44; Dept. of State 46; Nat. War Coll. 46-47; Chief, Div. of S. Asian Affairs 47 ; Deputy Dir. Office of Near East and African Affairs 48; Deputy Asst. Sec. State for Near East, S. Asian and African Affairs Oct. 49; Ambassador to Saudi Arabia and Minister to Yemen 50-53; Ambassador to Lebanon 53-54; Dir.-Gen. U.S. Foreign Service 54-56; Ambassador to Egypt 56-58, to United Arab Republic 58-59, also Minister to Yemen 59; Dep. Under-Sec. of State for Political Affairs 60-61; Ambassador to Turkey 61-65; Asst. Sec. of State for Near Eastern and South Asian Affairs 65-66; Pres. Middle East Inst. 66-69, Nat. Chair. 69-.
Middle East Institute, 1761 N. Street, N.W., Washington, D.C. 20036; 3214 39th Street, N.W., Washington, D.C. 20016, U.S.A.

Harkavy, Rabbi Zvi, B.A., M.A., TH.D.; Israeli (b. Russian) author and bibliographer; b. 1 Feb. 1908; ed. Inst. in U.S.S.R., Jerusalem Teachers' Seminary, Haifa Technion, Hebrew Univ. of Jerusalem, Petach Tikva Yeshiva, C.S.R.A.
Leader in Zion underground in U.S.S.R.; repatriated to Palestine 26; schoolmaster and lecturer Jerusalem Teachers' Seminaries 30-; Dir. Eretz Yisrael Publishing House 35-; Chaplain in Israeli Army 48-49; Dir. Dept. of Refugees in Ministry of War Casualties and later Editor of Ministry of Religious Affairs *Monthly* 49-53; Dir. Central Rabbinical Library of Israel 53-68; Editor *Hasefer* 54-; participated in world congresses; Visiting Prof., Yeshiva Univ., N.Y. 59; lectured at U.S.S.R. Acad. of Sciences, Leningrad 62; initiator of Religious Univ. (Bar-Ian) in Israel; one of the founders of the Religious Academics and Authors Orgs. and fmr. Chair.; Leader, Hapoel Hamizrachi, "Great Israel" Movement; an Editor of the *General Encyclopaedia* and of many periodicals and books; Komemiut, Hamishmar, Haganah, Ale, Hagana-Yerushalayim and Etziony Medals.
Publs. Biographies: *Rambam, Rabbi Shmuel Strashun, Rabbi Mates Strashun, Rabbi I. M. Pines, Professor Simcha Assaf, A. E. Harkavy, Rabbi Reuven Katz—Chief Rabbi of Petach Tikva, The Family Maskil L'eytan, The Family Harkavy*; Essays: *Jews of Salonica, The Jewish Community of Ekaterinoslav; Scepticism of Pascal; The Man, The Plant, The Animal, Inorganic Nature; The Secret of Happy Marriage, Sexual Hygiene from the Religious and Scientific Viewpoint; Shomrei Hagachelet—Responsa of Soviet Rabbis* 66, *My Father's Home* 68, *Autobibliography* 71, *Ein Roe* 72; *Book of Ekaterinoslav-Dnepopetrovsk* 73, *The Works of A. E. Harkavy* (20 vols.); also 1,100 articles and papers on Rabbinics, bibliography, theology, philosophy, archaeology, philology, history and Dead Sea Scrolls.
P.O. Box 7031, 7 Haran Street, Jerusalem 91070, Israel.

Harman, Avraham, B.A.; Israeli diplomatist; b. 1914; ed. Oxford Univ.
Moved to Palestine 38; held posts in Jewish Agency 38-48; Deputy Dir. Govt. Information Bureau 48-49; Consul-Gen. Montreal 49-50; Dir. Israel Information Office, N.Y. 50-53; Consul-Gen. Washington 53-55; Ministry of Foreign Affairs 55-56; Exec. Jewish Agency 56-59; Ambassador to the U.S.A. 59-68; Pres. Hebrew Univ. 68-.
The Hebrew University, Jerusalem, Israel.

Hart, Parker T.; American business executive; b. 28 Sept. 1910; ed. Dartmouth Coll., Harvard and Georgetown Univs., Institut Universitaire de Hautes Etudes Internationales, Geneva, and School of Foreign Service.
Translator, Dept. of State 37-38; Foreign Service Officer 38-69, served Vienna, Pará (Brazil), Cairo, Jeddah, Dhahran 38-47; Dept. of State 47-49; Consul-Gen. Dhahran 49-51; Nat. War Coll. 51-52; Dir. of Near Eastern Affairs, Dept. of State 52-55; Dep. Chief of Mission and Counsellor, Cairo 55-58; Consul-Gen., Damascus 58; Dep. Asst. Sec. of State, Near East and South Asia Affairs 58-61; Ambassador

to Saudi Arabia 61-65, concurrently Minister to Kingdom of Yemen 61-62 and Amb. to Kuwait 62-63; Amb. to Turkey 65-68; Asst. Sec. of State for Near Eastern and South Asian Affairs 68-69; Dir. Foreign Service Inst. 69; Pres. Middle East Inst., Washington, D.C. 69-73; Special Rep. for Middle East and North Africa, Bechtel Corpn. 73-; Co-Pres. American-Turkish Soc., N.Y.; mem. Board of Trustees, American Univ. of Beirut, Board of Advisers, Industrial Coll. of the Armed Forces; mem. Visiting Cttee. on Middle East Civilizations, Harvard Univ.; Royal Central Asian Soc.
4705 Berkeley Terrace, N.W., Washington, D.C. 20007, U.S.A.

Hasani, Baqir Husain, B.SC., LL.B.; Iraqi diplomatist; b. 15; ed. Columbia Univ., New York and Baghdad Law Coll.
Dir. of Commerce and Registrar of Companies, Iraq Ministry of Econs. 47-51; Dir.-Gen. of Contracts and Econ. Affairs, Development Board 51-54; Dir.-Gen. of Income Tax, Ministry of Finance 56-57; Dir.-Gen. and Chair. of Board of Dirs., Tobacco Monopoly Admin. 57-59; Minister to Austria 59-62, Ambassador 62-63; Chair. Board of Govs. Int. Atomic Energy Agency (IAEA) 61-62, Special Adviser to Dir.-Gen. 63-.
c/o International Atomic Energy Agency, Vienna 1010, Kaerntnerring 11, Austria; and Masbah, Karradah, Baghdad, Iraq.

Haseeb, Dr. Khair El-Din, M.SC., PH.D.; Iraqi economist and statistician; b. 1 Aug. 1929, Mosul; ed. Baghdad Univ. London School of Econs., Cambridge Univ.
Civil Service 47-54; Head of Research and Statistics Dept., Iraq Petroleum Co. 59-60; Lecturer, Baghdad Univ. 60-61, part-time lecturer 61-63; Dir.-Gen. Iraqi Fed. of Industries 60-63; Gov. Central Bank of Iraq 63-65; Actg. Pres. Econ. Org. 64-65; Pres. Gen. Org. for Banks 64-65; Assoc. Prof., Baghdad Univ. 65-71, Prof. of Econs. 71-74; Chief of Natural Resources and Science and Technology Dir., UN Econ. Comm. for Western Asia 74-; Gov. for Iraq, IMF 63-65; Alt. Gov. IBRD 63-65; Chair. of Board, Centre for Development of Industrial Management 63, Social Security Org. 63-65, Central Bank of Iraq 63-65; Dir. Iraq Nat. Oil Co. 67-68; fmr. mem. of Board of several orgs.
Publs. *The National Income of Iraq, 1953-1961* 64, *Workers' Participation in Management in Arab Countries* 71, *Sources of Arab Economic Thought in Iraq 1900-1971* 73, and several articles in English and Arabic on economic and development planning problems.
15/18/4, Al-Mansoor, Baghdad, Iraq.

Hashim, Maj. Abu al Qassim; Sudanese army officer and politician; b. 22 Nov. 1935; ed. Military Coll.
Commissioned 57; mem. Revolutionary Command Council May 69; Minister of Youth July 70-Oct. 71; Minister of State for the Presidency of the Repub. 71-72; Minister of Planning 72-73.
c/o Ministry of Planning, Khartoum, Sudan.

Hashim, Jawad M., PH.D.; Iraqi politician; b. 10 Feb. 1938; ed. London School of Econs. and Political Science, Univ. of London.
Professor of Statistics, Univ. of Baghdad 67; Dir.-Gen. Cen. Statistical Org. 68; Minister of Planning 68-71, 72-74; mem. Planning Board and Econ. Office, Revolutionary Command Council.
Publs. *Capital Formation in Iraq 1957-1970, National Income—Its Methods of Estimation, The Evaluation of Economic Growth in Iraq 1950-1970,* and eighteen articles.
Ministry of Planning, Baghdad, Iraq.

Hassan II, King of Morocco; 17th Sovereign of the Alouite dynasty; b. 9 July 1929; ed. Bordeaux Univ.
Son of Mohammed V; invested as Crown Prince Moulay Hassan 57; C.-in-C. and Chief of Staff of Royal Moroccan Army 57; personally directed rescue operations at Agadir earthquake disaster 60; Minister of Defence May 60-June

61; Vice-Premier May 60-Feb. 61; Prime Minister Feb. 61-Nov. 63, June 65-67; succeeded to throne on death of his father, 26 Feb. 1961; Minister of Defence, Commdr.-in-Chief of the Army Aug. 71-; Chair. Org. of African Unity 72-73.
Royal Palace, Rabat, Morocco.

Hassan, Abdullah el-, DIP.ARTS; Sudanese diplomatist and politician; b. 1925; ed. Gordon Secondary School, Khartoum Univ. Coll.
District Officer and Commissioner 49-56; Consul Gen. to Uganda 56-58; Head Political Section, Ministry of Foreign Affairs 58-64; Amb. to Ghana 60-64; Dir. Gen. Ministry of Information 65; Amb. to France 65-67, to Ethiopia 67-69; Under-Sec. Ministry of Foreign Affairs 69-70; Amb. to U.S.S.R. 71, to U.K. 72; Minister of Rural Devt. 72-73, of Interior 73-75; Sec. Gen. to the Presidency 75-; mem. Political Bureau, Sudan Socialist Union 72-; mem. numerous dels.; Order of the Republic, First Class, numerous foreign decorations.
Office of the Cabinet, Khartoum, Sudan.

Hassan, Ahmed Mohammed al-, D.PATH.; Sudanese pathologist and politician; b. 1930; ed. Univs. of Khartoum, Edinburgh and London.
Doctor 55-57; Research Asst., Univ. of Khartoum 58-60, Lecturer in Pathology 62-63, Senior Lecturer and Head of Dept. 65-66, Prof. 66-, Dean, Faculty of Medicine 69-71, Deputy Vice-Chancellor 71; Minister of Higher Educ. and Scientific Research 71-72; Chair. Medical Research Council, Nat. Council for Research; Pres. Sudan Philosophical Soc.
Medical Research Council, P.O. Box 2404, Khartoum, Sudan.

Hassan, Ignatius Gama, PH.D.; Sudanese politician; b. 12 Dec. 1941, Aradi Madi Torit Equatoria; ed. Rumbek Secondary School, Milan Univ.
With Research Div., Pesticides Devt. Div., Montecatini Edison Co., Milan 67-68, Entomologist for Eastern Africa 68-71, Chief, Pesticides Promotion Div., East and Central Africa 71-72; Minister of Agriculture, Irrigation, Forestry and Animal Production, Regional Prov. Gov. of Southern Sudan 72-73, Higher Exec. Council for the Southern Region 73-; mem. People's Regional Assembly 73-; Order of Kuwait, First Class, Order of the Two Niles, First Class.
Ministry of Agriculture, Irrigation, Forestry and Animal Production, Juba, Southern Region, Democratic Republic of Sudan.

Hassan, Mahmoud Ali, PH.D.; Egyptian engineer; b. 17 July 1915; ed. Cairo and Zürich Univs.
Director-General Industrial Control Dept. 56-59; Under-Sec. of State for Industry 59-61; Chair. Org. for Engineering Industries 61-66; Pres. Fed. of Egyptian Industries, Org. for Metallurgical Industries; Order of Trade and Industry (1st Class).
Publs. *Druckverlüste in Abzweigen von quadratischen Kanälen, Anwendungen der elektrolytischen Methode auf die Betzsche Theorie der Spaltverlüste an Schaufelgittern.*
45 Road 15 Maadi, Cairo, Egypt.

Hassan Rial, Cleto; (*see* Rial, Cleto Hassan).

Hassouna, Mohammed Abdel-Khalek; Egyptian diplomatist; b. 28 Oct. 1898; ed. Cairo Univ. and Cambridge Univ.
Began as lawyer 21; then joined Diplomatic Corps, served in Berlin 26, Prague 28, Brussels 28, Rome 30, Ministry for Foreign Affairs Cairo 32-39; Under-Sec. of State, Ministry of Social Affairs 39; served in Diplomatic Service in Belgium, Italy, Germany, Czechoslovakia; Gov. of Alexandria 42; Under-Sec. of State for Foreign Affairs 48; Minister of Social Affairs, Sirry Cabinet Nov. 49-Jan. 50; Minister of Education, Maher Cabinet Jan.-March 52; Minister of Foreign Affairs, Hilaly Cabinet March-June,

July 52; Sec.-Gen. League of Arab States 52-72; Grand Cordon Order of the Nile (Egypt); Nile Collar (Egypt) 72; Legion of Honour (France); decorations conferred by Belgium, China, Italy and Ethiopia.
3 Sharia Rifaa, Manchiet El-Bakry, Cairo, Egypt.

Hatem, Mohammed Abdel Kader, M.SC., PH.D.; Egyptian politician; b. 1918, Alexandria; ed. Military Acad., Univs. of London and Cairo.
Member, Nat. Assembly 57; Adviser to the Presidency, subsequently Deputy Minister for Presidential Affairs 57; Minister of State responsible for broadcasting and television 59; Minister for Culture, Nat. Guidance and Tourism 62; Deputy Prime Minister for Cultural Affairs and Nat. Guidance 65; Deputy Prime Minister and Minister for Culture and Information 71-74; Pres. Adviser on Nat. Council Affairs 74-75; Chair. of Board *Al-Ahram* 74-; mem. Gen. Secr. Arab Socialist Union; two hon. doctorates from French Univs.
c/o *Al Ahram*, Gallaa Street, Cairo, Egypt.

Hawari Ahmed, Mahmoud el-; Egyptian journalist; b. 12 April 1921; ed. Polytechnic School, Cairo.
Director, Arab Information Center Press Office, New York 55-58; Man. Editor Middle East News Agency, Cairo 58-65, now Chair. of Board; Dir. Magazine Dept., Nat. Publishing House 65-67; Chair. Nat. Distributing Co. 67; Publishing Man. Al-Katib Al-Arabi Publishing House 67-69; Adviser, Editing and Publishing Org. 69-71; Dir.-Gen. Egyptian Book Org. 71-72; Gold Cross, Order of King George I of Greece 60.
Middle East News Agency, 4 Sherifeen Street, Cairo; Home: Isis Building, Garden City, Cairo, Egypt.

Hawley, Donald Frederick, C.M.G., M.B.E.; British diplomatist; b. 22 May 1921; ed. Radley and New Coll. Oxford.
H.M. Forces 41; Sudan Political Service 44; joined Sudan Judiciary 47; called to Bar, Inner Temple 51; Chief Registrar, Sudan Judiciary, and Registrar-Gen. of Marriages 51; resigned from Sudan Service 55; joined British Foreign Service 55, Foreign Office 56; Political Agent, Trucial States in Dubai 58, Head of Chancery, British Embassy, Cairo 62; Counsellor and Head of Chancery, Lagos 65; Visiting Fellow, Dept. of Geography, Durham Univ. 67; Counsellor (Commercial), Baghdad 68-71, Chargé d'Affaires in Iraq 69, 70; Consul-Gen., Muscat 71, Amb. to Oman 71-75; Asst. Under Sec., Foreign Office, London 75-.
Publ. *The Trucial States* 71.
Foreign and Commonwealth Office, London, England.

Hayek, His Beatitude Ignace Antoine, D.PHIL., D. ÈS SC., Syrian ecclesiastic; b. 14 Sept. 1910: ed. Séminaire Patriarcal, Charfé, Lebanon, Pontifical Coll. of Propaganda Fide, Rome, and Oriental Pontifical Inst., Rome.
Ordained priest 33; successively or concurrently Dir. of School, Curate and Vicar-Gen., Aleppo; Archbishop of Aleppo 59-68; Syrian Patriarch Antioch 68-.
Patriarcat Syrien Catholique d'Antioche, rue de Damas, B.P. 8879, Beirut, Lebanon.

Hedayati, Hadi; Iranian educationalist and politician; b. 1923; ed. Teheran Univ., Faculté de Droit, Paris Univ., and Sorbonne, Paris.
Assistant Prof. Teheran Univ. 52-62, Prof. 62-; Legal Counsellor, Iran Insurance Co. 52-57; Counsellor, High Council of Econs. 57-60; High Counsellor, Ministry of Commerce 60; Exec. Man. Bimeh (Insurance) Bank 60-62; Deputy to Majlis 63-; Advisory Minister 63; Minister of Educ. 64-68; Advisory Minister 68-73; Minister of State 73-, Exec. Asst. to Prime Minister 74-; Homayoun Medal, Palme Académique (France); Imperial Award for best book of the year 58, 59.
Publs. *History of the Zand Dynasty in Iran*, *A Study of Iranian Handwritten Works in the 13th Hegyra Century*,

Cyrus the Great; translations into Persian: *History of Herodotus*, *The Principles of Administrative Management*.
Iranshahr Avenue, Kamyar Street, Teheran, Iran.

Hedayati, Mohammad Ali; Iranian lawyer and politician; b. 1912; ed. Teheran and Geneva Univs., Geneva Inst. of Int. Studies and Inst. of Criminology of Faculty of Law, Univ. of Paris.
Military service 35; joined Iranian Judicial Service 36, mem. Dept. of Legislative Revisions 37, Dep. Public Prosecutor of Teheran 37-38, Interrogator for Teheran 38-40, Judge of the Court of Appeal (Teheran) 40, Advocate in Courts of Justice 40; transferred to Ministry of Education 40, Assoc. Prof., Faculty of Law, Teheran Univ. 40-45, Prof. of Law of Criminal Procedure 45-73, Dean Faculty of Law 63-73; Minister of Justice 58-61; Counsellor, Lawyer, Ministry of Foreign Affairs; mem. 16th and 19th Sessions of Majlis; Order of Homayoun (First Class) 60.
Publs. *Les Mesures de Sûreté* (French), *The Law of Criminal Procedure* (Persian), *Economics* (Persian), *Situation politique et sociale de l'Iran*, *International Criminal Law* (Persian) *Economie mixte* (Persian), *Sanctuaire de Rey* (Persian), *Souvenir d'un Voyage à Mecque*.
11 Fifteenth Street, Amirabad Road, Teheran, Iran.

Hedda, Ali; Tunisian diplomatist; b. 30 Oct. 1930, Sousse; ed. Inst. des Sciences Politiques, Paris.
Attaché, Tunisian Embassy, Washington 56; Sec. Ministry of Foreign Affairs 57; with Secr. of State for Planning and Nat. Econ. 58-66; Minister, Tunisian Embassy, Rome 66; Amb. to Senegal 70-72, also accred. to Mali, Mauritania, Guinea, Liberia, Sierra Leone and The Gambia; Dir. Int. Co-operation, Ministry of Foreign Affairs 72; Dir. Cabinet of the Prime Minister 73; Amb. to U.S.A. Nov. 73-, concurrently to Mexico and Venezuela 74-; Grand Officer, Ordre de la République Tunisienne, Order of the Republic, Italy.
Tunisian Embassy, 2408 Massachusetts Avenue, N.W., Washington, D.C., U.S.A.

Hegazy, Abdel Aziz, D.PHIL.; Egyptian economist and politician; b. 3 Jan. 1923; ed. Fuad Univ., Cairo, Birmingham Univ., England.
Dean, Faculty of Commerce, Ain Shams Univ. 66-68; mem. Nat. Assembly 69-; Minister of the Treasury 68-73; Deputy Prime Minister, Minister of Finance, Econ. and Foreign Trade 73-74; First Deputy Prime Minister April-Aug. 74, Prime Minister 74-75.
Cairo, Egypt.

Heikal, Mohammed Hasanein; Egyptian journalist; b. 1923.
Reporter Akher Saa Magazine 44; Editor *Al-Akhbar* 56-57; Editor-in-Chief *Al-Ahram* daily newspaper 57-74; Editor and Chair. Establishment Board 60-74; mem. Central Cttee. Arab Socialist Union 68-; Minister of Nat. Guidance 70.
Publs. *Nahnou wa America* 67, *Nasser: The Cairo Documents* 72, *The Road to Ramadan* 75.
c/o Arab Socialist Union, Cairo, Egypt.

Helaissi, Sheikh Abdulrahman al-; Saudi Arabian diplomatist; b. 24 July 1922; ed. Cairo Univ. and Univ. of London.
Official at Ministry of Foreign Affairs; Secretary Embassy London 47-54; Under-Sec. Ministry of Agriculture 54-57; Rep. to UN 47, and at conferences on Health, Agriculture, Wheat, Sugar and Locusts; Head of Del. to FAO 55-61; Amb. to Sudan 57-60; Del. to Conference of Non-Aligned Nations, Belgrade 61; Amb. to Italy 61-66, concurrently to Austria; Amb. to U.K. 66-, concurrently to Denmark 66-69.
Publ. *The Rehabilitation of the Bedouins* 59.
Embassy of Saudi Arabia, 27 Eaton Place, London, S.W.1, England.

Helms, Richard M.; American government official; b. 30 March 1913; ed. high schools in U.S.A., Switzerland and Germany, and Williams Coll.
Worked for United Press and *The Indianapolis Times* 35-42; joined U.S. Navy 42, in Office of Strategic Services, Second World War; Central Intelligence Group 47-49, Central Intelligence Agency 49-73, Deputy Dir. for Plans 62, Deputy Dir. 65, Dir. 66-73; Amb. to Iran 73-.
United States Embassy, Takhte Jamshid Avenue, Roosevelt Avenue, Teheran, Iran.

Hélou, Charles; Lebanese lawyer and journalist; b. 1911; ed. St. Joseph (Jesuit) Univ. and Ecole Française de Droit, Beirut.
Barrister at Court of Appeal and Cassation Beirut 36; founded newspaper *L'Eclair du Nord* at Aleppo Syria 32; founded *Le Jour* Beirut 34; was Political Dir. of the latter until apptd. Lebanese Minister to the Vatican 47; fmr. Pres. Cercle de la Jeunesse Catholique Beirut; fmr. Sec.-Gen. Catholic Action of Lebanon; Minister of Justice and Health Sept. 54-May 55; Minister of Education Feb.-Sept. 64; President of Lebanon 64-70; Pres. Asscn. des Parlementaires de Langue Française 73-.
Kaslik, Jounieh, Lebanon.

Herzog, Gen. Haim, LL.B.; Israeli lawyer and military expert; b. 17 Sept. 1918, Belfast, N. Ireland; ed. Wesley Coll., Dublin, London and Cambridge Univs., Lincoln's Inn, London.
Went to Palestine 35; served in British Army, World War II; rank of Maj.; Dir. Intelligence, Israeli Defence Forces 48-50; Defence Attaché, Israeli Embassy, Washington, Ottawa 50-54; Field Commands 54-59; Dir. Mil. Intelligence 59-62; Gen. 61; Man. Dir. G.U.S. Industries 62-72; Gov. West Bank of the Jordan 67; Senior Partner, Herzog, Fox and Neeman 72-; Perm. Rep. to UN Sept. 75-; Hon. K.B.E. 70.
Publs. *Israel's Finest Hour* (Hebrew and English) 67, *Days of Awe* (Hebrew) 73, *The War of Atonement* 75 and numerous articles in foreign journals.
Permanent Mission of Israel to the United Nations, 800 Second Avenue, New York, N.Y. 10017, U.S.A.; Home: Zahala, Tel-Aviv, Israel.

Hewedy, Amin; Egyptian diplomatist; b. 1921; ed. Military and Staff Colls., Egypt, and General Staff Coll., Fort Leavenworth, U.S.A., and Press Coll., Egypt.
Former Army Officer; fmr. Ambassador of United Arab Republic to Morocco; Ambassador to Iraq 58, 63-66; Minister of State 66-67, of War 67-68, of State 69-70.
Publs. *Speeches in Strategy* 55, *Sun-Tso* 57.
Cairo, Egypt.

Hillel, Shlomo; Israeli politician; b. 23 April 1923, Baghdad, Iraq; ed. Herzliah School, Tel-Aviv, Hebrew Univ., Jerusalem.
Settled in Palestine 30s; mem. 2nd, 3rd Knessets (Parl.) 53-59; Amb. to Guinea 59-61, to Ivory Coast 61-63, concurrently to Dahomey, Upper Volta and Niger; mem. Perm. Mission to UN 64-67; Asst. Dir.-Gen. Ministry of Foreign Affairs, in charge of Middle East Affairs 67-69; Co-ordinator of Political Contacts with the Arab leadership in the Administered Territories 70; mem. 8th Knesset; Minister of Police 74-; Commdr. Nat. Order of the Repubs. of the Ivory Coast, Upper Volta, Dahomey.
Ministry of Police, Jerusalem, Israel.

Himadeh, Sa'id B., B.COMM., M.A.; Lebanese university professor; b. 3 April 1894; ed. American Univ. of Beirut and Columbia Univ., U.S.A.
Lecturer in Applied Economics, American Univ. of Beirut 20, Assoc. Prof. 23, Prof. of Applied Economics 39-59, Head, Dept. of Economics 35-48, of Dept. of Commerce 35-59, Emer. Prof. of Applied Economics 59-; Section Dir., Social Science Research 47-50; part-time Economic

Adviser to Lebanese Ministry of Nat. Economy 47; Gen. Sec. Higher Economic Advisory Council of Lebanese Govt. 46-48; Alternate Del. to UNESCO Gen. Conf. 48; Lebanese Govt. Del. First U.N. Social Welfare Seminar for Arab States of the Middle East 49, U.N. Economic Expert, U.N. Social Welfare Seminars 50 and 52; Chief Editor *Social Studies Series* (in Arabic) 45-47 and of its successor, *Al-Abhath* (quarterly journal of American Univ. of Beirut) 48-59, mem. Economic Development Board of Lebanon 53-; FAO Consultant and Discussion Leader, Centre on Land Problems in the Near East 55; mem. UNESCO Nat. Cttee. of Lebanon 55-59; Minister of Economy and Agriculture 66-68; mem. Editorial Advisory Board, Int. Encyclopaedia of Social Sciences 61-63; mem. Board of Dirs., Industry Inst. 62-67, Lebanese Govt. Housing Board 63-; mem. Board of Trustees, Inst. for Palestine Studies; Chair. Advisory Cttee. Bank of Lebanon 66; Order of the Cedar and other decorations.
Publs. *Monetary and Banking System of Syria (including Lebanon)* 35, *Economic Organisation of Iraq* 38; editor and co-author: *Economic Organisation of Syria (including Lebanon)* 36, *Economic Organisation of Palestine* 38; many articles on Middle East economy.
American University of Beirut, Beirut; Home: Manara (Ras Beirut), Beirut, Lebanon.

Hindawi, Dhaugan, ED.M.; Jordanian politician; b. 18 Feb. 1927; ed. Arab Coll., Jerusalem, Univ. of Cairo, Univ. of Maryland, U.S.A.
Principal, Teachers' Training Coll., Bet Hannina, Jerusalem 56-60; Supervisor of Educ. 60-63; Cultural Attaché, Cairo 64; Under-Sec. Ministry of Information 64-65; Minister of Information 65, of Educ. 65-70; Amb. to Kuwait 71-73; Minister of State for Prime Minister's Affairs 73; Minister of Finance 73-74, of Educ. 74-; many decorations from Jordan, Tunisia, France, Fed. Repub. of Germany and Malaysia.
Publ. *Palestinian Issue* (textbook).
Ministry of Education, Amman; and P.O. Box 7295, Amman, Jordan.

Hitti, Philip Khuri, B.A., PH.D.; American orientalist; b. 24 June 1886; ed. American Univ. of Beirut, Columbia Univ.
Lecturer, Oriental Dept., Columbia Univ. 15-19; Prof., American Univ. of Beirut 19-26; Asst. Prof. Semitic Literature, Princeton 26-29, Assoc. Prof. 29-36; Chair. Dept. of Oriental Languages 44; Dir. Programme in Near-Eastern Studies 47-54; mem. American Oriental Society, American Historical Asscn., etc.; Hon. Litt.D. (Princeton) 66, Hon. L.H.D. (Amer. Univ. Beirut) 69.
Publs. *The Origins of the Islamic State* 16, *The Semitic Languages Spoken in Syria and Lebanon* 22, *The Syrians in America* 24, *Characteristics of Moslem Sects* 24, *Syria and the Syrians* 26, *An Arab-Syrian Gentleman and Warrior in the Period of the Crusaders* 29, *The Origins of the Druze People and Religion* 29 (new edn. 64), *Kitab al I'tibar li-Usamah* 30, 64, *History of the Arabs* 37 (revised edn. 70), *The Arabs* 43-44 (revised edn. 67), *History of Syria, including Lebanon and Palestine* 51, 57, *Lebanon in History* 57 (revised 67), *Syria (A Short History* 59, *The Near East in History* 61, *Islam and the West* 62, *Short History of Lebanon* 65 (revised 68), *Short History of the Near East* 66, *A Short History of Syria* 67, *Makers of Arab History* 68, *Islam: A Way of Life* 70, *Capital Cities of Arab Islam* 73.
144 Prospect Avenue, Princeton, N.J., U.S.A.

Horowitz, David; Israeli banker; b. Feb. 1899; ed. Vienna and Lwów.
Member Exec. Cttee. Gen. Fed. of Jewish Labour 23; journalist and writer; Econ. Adviser and Sec. American Econ. Cttee. for Palestine 32-35; Dir. Econ. Dept. of Jewish Agency for Palestine; mem. various Govt. Cttees. under Mandatory Regime, and dir. various enterprises 35-48; Liaison Officer to UN Special Cttee. on Palestine 46; mem.

Jewish Del. to Lake Success 47; Head of Israel Del. to Econ. Survey Comm. of UN 48; Head of Israel Del. Financial Talks on Sterling Releases between Israel and Great Britain, London 49, and in negotiations between Israel and Great Britain on econ. and financial affairs in connection with termination of the Mandate; Dir.-Gen. Ministry of Finance 48-52; Gov. Designate, Bank of Israel 52-54, Gov. 54-71, Chair. Advisory Cttee. and Council 71-; Gov. (for Israel) Int. Bank for Reconstruction and Devt., Int. Devt. Asscn. and Int. Finance Corpn.; Chair. Board of Dirs., the Eliezer Kaplan School of Econs. and Social Sciences, Hebrew Univ.; mem. State Council for Higher Educ., Board of Govs. Hebrew Univ., Exec. Council Weizmann Inst. of Science, Board of Trustees of the Truman Center for the Advancement of Peace; Head, Israel Del. to UN Conf. on Trade and Devt., Geneva 64; Hon. Pres. Istituto per le Relazioni Internazionali (Rome); Dr. h.c. (Hebrew Univ. and Tel-Aviv Univ.); Israel Prize for Social Sciences 68.

Publs. *Aspects of Economic Policy in Palestine* 36, *Jewish Colonisation in Palestine* 37, *Economic Survey of Palestine* 38, *Jewry's Economic War Effort* 42, *Postwar Reconstruction* 42, *Palestine and the Middle East*, *An Essay in Regional Economy* 43, *Prediction and Reality in Palestine* 45, *State in the Making* 53, *Anatomie unserer Zeit* 64, *Hemispheres North and South* 66, *The Economics of Israel* 67, *The Abolition of Poverty* 69, *Anatomia de Nuestro Tiempo* 69, *The Enigma of Economic Growth—The Case Study of Israel* 72, and several publs. in Hebrew.

4 Halamed Hé Street, Jerusalem; and Bank of Israel, Jerusalem, Israel.

Hoveida, Amir Abbas, M.A., PH.D.; Iranian diplomatist, business executive and politician; b. Feb. 1919; ed. Univs. of Brussels and Paris.

Ministry of Foreign Affairs 42-58, served Federal Germany, Teheran, United Nations, New York, Ankara; mem. Board of Dirs. and Head of Admin., Nat. Iranian Oil Co. 58-64; founder mem. New Iran Party 63-75; Minister of Finance 64-65; Prime Minister 65-; Sec.-Gen., Pres. Exec. Cttee., Nat. Political Resurrection Movement March 75-. Office of the Prime Minister, Teheran; Home: No. 5 Kh. Cyrus Ehteshamieh, Darrous, Teheran, Iran.

Hoveyda, Fereydoun, LL.D.; Iranian diplomatist; b. 21 Sept. 1924, Damascus; ed. Univ. of Paris.

Various positions, Imperial Iranian Embassy, Paris 46-51; Programme Specialist, Mass Communications Dept., UNESCO 52-64; Under-Sec. of State for Int. and Econ. Affairs, Ministry of Foreign Affairs 65-71; Perm. Rep. to UN Aug. 71-; del. to various int. confs. including UN Gen. Assembly 48, 51, 65, UNESCO Confs. 66, 68, 70 and ECOSOC sessions 66-69; Léopold Senghor Prize, French Language Cultural and Technical Soc. for novel *Les Neiges du Sinai* 73.

Permanent Mission of Iran at United Nations, 622 Third Avenue, 34th Floor, New York, N.Y. 10016, U.S.A.

Howard, Harry Nicholas, A.B., M.A., PH.D.; American historian; b. 19 Feb. 1902; ed. Univs. of Missouri and California.

Gregory Fellow in History Univ. of Missouri 26-27; Research Asst. in Modern European History Univ. of California 28-29; Asst. Prof. History Univ. of Oklahoma 29-30; Associate Prof. History, Miami Univ. 30-37, Prof. 40-42; Lecturer Contemporary Problems, Univ. of Cincinnati 37-42; served Dept. of State as Head, East European Unit 42-44, mem. U.S. Del. UN Conf. on Int. Orgs. 45, Chief, Near East Branch Research Div. 45-47, Adviser Div. of Greek, Turkish and Iranian Affairs 47-49, UN Adviser, Dept. of State, Bureau of Near East, S. Asian and African Affairs 49-56; Acting U.S. Rep. Advisory Comm. UNRWA, Beirut 56-61; Special Asst. to Dir. of UNRWA 62-63; Adviser U.S. Del. UN Balkan Comm.

47-50; Prof. of Middle East Studies, School of Int. Service, American Univ., Washington, D.C. 63-68, Adjunct Prof. 68-; Chair. Middle East Program, Foreign Service Inst., Dept. of State 66, 71-72; Faculty Adviser FSI 66-67; Reserve Consultant, Dept. of State 67-; Assoc. Editor *Middle East Journal* 63-; mem. Board of Govs. Middle East Inst. 63-; Consultant, Middle East, Cincinatti Council on World Affairs 68-69; mem. Board of Dirs. ANERA 68-; Lecturer, Middle East, U.S. Army War Coll., Pa. 70-72; Visiting Prof. Missouri, Indiana, Calif. (Berkeley), Columbia and Colorado Univs.; Order of the Phoenix (Greece).

Publs. *The Partition of Turkey, A Diplomatic History 1913–1923* 31, *Military Government in the Panama Canal Zone* 31 (with Prof. R. Kerner), *The Balkan Conferences and the Balkan Entente* 30-35, *A Study in the Recent History of the Balkan and Near Eastern People* 36, *The Problem of the Turkish Straits* 47, *The United Nations and the Problem of Greece* 47, *The General Assembly and the Problem of Greece* 48, *Yugoslavia* (co-author) 49, *Soviet Power and Policy* (co-author) 55, *The King-Crane Commission* 63.

6508 Greentree Road, Bradley Hills Grove, Bethesda, Md. 20034, U.S.A.; and American University, Washington, D.C., U.S.A.

Humaidan, Dr. Ali; diplomatist; b. 20 Sept. 1931, Bahrain; ed. Univs. of Baghdad and Paris.

Deputy Rep. of Kuwait to UNESCO 67-69; Prof. of Political Science, Univ. of Kuwait 69-70; Legal Adviser to the Abu Dhabi Govt. 71-72; Perm. Rep. of the United Arab Emirates to UN 72-.

Permanent Mission of the United Arab Emirates to the United Nations, 866 Second Avenue, New York, N.Y. 10017, U.S.A.

Hussain, Abdul Aziz; Kuwaiti politician; b. 1921; ed. Teachers' Higher Inst., Cairo and Univ. of London.

Head, Kuwait Cultural Bureau, Cairo 45-50; Gen. Dir. of Education, Kuwait 52-61; Ambassador to Egypt 61-62; Minister of State for Cabinet Affairs 63-65, 71-.

Publ. *Arab Community in Kuwait* 60.

Ministry of State for Cabinet Affairs, Kuwait.

Hussein, Aly Hamdy, M.COM.; Egyptian diplomatist; b. 20 Dec. 1915; ed. Univ. of Cairo and Univ. of Madrid.

Commercial Counsellor 48-57; Counsellor to Foreign Office 58; Consul-Gen. in São Paulo 60-64; Amb. to Bolivia 64-65; Dir. of Econ. Dept. of Foreign Office, Cairo 66-68; Amb. to Belgium and Luxembourg 68-.

Embassy of Egypt, 2 avenue Victoria, 1050 Brussels, Belgium.

Hussein ibn Talal, King of Jordan; b. 14 Nov. 1935; ed. Victoria Coll., Alexandria, Egypt, Harrow School and R.M.A. Sandhurst (both in England).

Succeeded his father August 11th, 1952; came to power May 2nd, 1953; married 55, Princess Dina, daughter of Abdel-Hamid Aoun of Saudi Arabia; daughter Princess Alia, b. 56 (marriage dissolved); married 61, Antoinette Gardiner (assumed name of Muna el Hussein); sons, Prince Abdullah, b. 62, Prince Feisal, b. 63; twin daughters, Princess Zein, Princess Aisha, b. 68 (marriage dissolved); married 72, Alia Toukan, daughter of Baha'uddin Toukan *q.v.*; daughter Princess Haya, b. 74; Order of Al-Nahda, of Al-Kawkab, of Al-Istiqlal; Istiqlal Medal, and many other decorations.

Publs. *Uneasy Lies the Head* 62, *My War with Israel* 67.

Royal Palace, Amman, Jordan.

Huzayin, Soliman Ahmed, M.A., PH.D., LL.L.; Egyptian university professor; b. 1909; ed. Cairo, Liverpool and Manchester Univs.

Lecturer, Cairo Univ. 35; Dir.-Gen. Cultural Relations, Ministry of Educ., Cairo 50; Under-Sec. of State for Educ., Cairo 54; Rector, Univ. of Assiut 55-65; Minister of Culture

Oct. 65-66; mem. Institut d'Egypte 47-, Pres. Institut d'Egypte 54, Int. Council for the Study of the Geography of Africa and Asia 56-, Perm. Cttee. for Social Affairs, League of Arab States.
Publs. *Some Contributions of the Arabs to Geography* 32, *Some New Light on the Beginnings of Egyptian Civilization* 37, *The Place of Egypt in Prehistory* 41, *Arabia and the Far East* 42, numerous articles.
c/o Institut d'Egypte, 13 Sh. Sheikh Rihane, Cairo, Egypt.

I

Ibrahim, Abdel Aziz el Sayed, PH.D.; Egyptian educationist; b. 30 April 1907; ed. Teachers' Coll. and Higher Inst. of Educ., Cairo and Ohio State Univ., U.S.A.
Formerly Lecturer in Mathematics, Mil. Coll., Cairo; Prof. of Educ., Head of Dept., Ain Shams Univ.; Vice-Rector Cairo Univ., Rector Khartoum Branch, Cairo Univ.; Rector Alexandria Univ.; Minister of Higher Educ., later of Educ.; Visiting Prof. Columbia Univ., U.S.A.; now Dir.-Gen. Arab Educational, Cultural and Scientific Org., Arab League; mem. Arabic Language Acad. (Egypt), Scientific Acad. (Iraq); decorations from Egypt, Lebanon, Morocco, Tunisia, Jordan, German Democratic Repub.
Publs. *The Slide Rule for Military Cadets* 39, *The Preparation of Teachers in Arab States* 54, *The University and Culture* 60.
Arab Educational, Cultural and Scientific Organization, Arab League, Cairo; Home: 52 Merghani Street, Heliopolis, Cairo, Egypt.

Ibrahim, Major Abul Gasim Mohammed; Sudanese army officer and politician; b. 1937, Omdurman; ed. Khartoum Secondary School and Military Coll.
Commissioned 61; mem. Revolutionary Council 69; Minister of Local Govt. 69; Asst. Prime Minister for Services July 70; Minister of Interior Nov. 70; Minister of Health 71-74, and of Social Welfare 73-74, of Agriculture, Food and Natural Resources July 74-; Deputy Sec.-Gen. Sudanese Socialist Union.
Ministry of Agriculture, Khartoum, Sudan.

Ibrahim, Wing Commdr. Hassan; Egyptian businessman and former air force officer and politician; b. 1917; ed. Egyptian Mil. Coll. and Egyptian Air Force Coll.
Served Egyptian Air Force 39-52; mem. Revolutionary Council 52-56; Minister for Presidency and for Production 54-56; Chair. Economic Development Organization 57-59; Pres. El Nasr Company (pencil and graphite production) 58-61, Paints and Chemicals Industries 59-61; mem. Presidential Council 62-64; Vice-Pres. of U.A.R. 64-65; business exec. 66-; Pres. Middle East Financing and Consultation Co., Egyptian Catering and Contracting Co., Egyptian Catering Co.; Nile Collar of Egypt; various orders and decorations from Syria, Yugoslavia, Cameroon, Niger, Yemen, Bulgaria, Poland, Lebanon, G.D.R., Morocco, Malaysia, Libya.
10 Abdel-Rahman Fahmy Street, Garden City, Cairo; Home: 6 Khartoum Street, Heliopolis, Cairo, Egypt.

Ibrahim, Sid Moulay Abdullah; Moroccan politician; b. 1918; ed. Ben Youssef Univ., Marrakesh and the Sorbonne, Paris.
Mem. Istiqlal (Independence) Party 44-59; mem. Editorial Cttee. *Al Alam* (Istiqlal organ) 50-52; imprisoned for political reasons 52-54; Sec. of State for Information and Tourism, First Moroccan Nat. Govt. 55-56; Minister of Labour and Social Affairs 56-57; Prime Minister and Minister of Foreign Affairs Dec. 58-May 60; leader Union National des Forces Populaires 59-, suspended from party 72.
c/o Union National des Forces Populaires, B.P. 747, Casablanca, Morocco.

Idelson, Beba; Israeli statistician; b. 14 Oct. 1895; ed. Kharkov.
Teacher 12-15; Statistician in Russian Govt. depts. 16-22; Berlin 24-25; manual work as pioneer in Palestine 26-29; Statistician, Jewish Agency, Jerusalem 29-30; Gen. Sec. of Moetzet Hapoalot (Council of Women Workers in Israel) 30-72; mem. Council of State 48-; mem. and Deputy Speaker of Knesset (Israel Parl.) 48-65; mem. of the Exec. of the Labour Party 35-, of Fed. of Labour.
22 Rembrandt Street, Tel-Aviv, Israel.

Idris I (Sayyid Muhammad Idris as-Sanusi); former King of Libya; b. 1889.
Son of Sayyid Muhammad al-Mahdi; succeeded his uncle, Sayyid Ahmed Sherif as-Sanusi, in charge of affairs of the Senusiya Order 16; became Amir of Cyrenaica; proclaimed King of Libya Dec. 2nd 50; ascended the throne 24 December 51; deposed by military coup Sept. 69; sentenced to death *in absentia* 71; granted Egyptian nationality April 74.

Imady, Dr. Mohammed; Syrian economist and politician; b. 1 Dec. 1930, Damascus; ed. Damascus Secondary School, Damascus Univ. and New York Univ.
Deputy Minister of Planning 68-72, Minister 72; Minister of Economy and Foreign Trade Dec. 72-; Founders Day Award (New York Univ.).
Publ. *Economic Development and Planning* (textbook in Arabic for Damascus Univ.) 68, revised 69, 71.
Ministry of Economy and Foreign Trade, Damascus; Home: Mohajareen, Jareer 87, Damascus, Syrian Arab Republic.

Ioannides, George X.; Cypriot lawyer and politician; b. 1924, Ktima, Paphos; ed. Greek Gymnasium, Paphos.
Clerk, Civil Service 41-45; did correspondence course in commerce and accountancy; studied law, Middle Temple, London, and called to Bar 47; lawyer, Paphos 48-70; mem. House of Reps. (Patriotic Front Group) 60-70; Minister of Justice 70-June 72, of the Interior and Defence 72-74.
c/o Ministry of the Interior, Nicosia, Cyprus.

Ioannides, Odysseus A.; Cypriot surgeon and politician; b. 1927, Nicosia; ed. Pancyprian Gymnasium, Medical School, Athens Univ.
Private surgical practice, Nicosia 56-; Leader Progressive Front 70-; Minister of Agriculture and Natural Resources 72-74, of Health July-Aug. 74; Chair. Nicosia School Cttee. 65-66, 71-72.
c/o Ministry of Health, Nicosia, Cyprus.

Iran (Persia, Shah of; *see* Pahlavi, Mohammad-Reza).

Iryani, Sheikh Qadi Abd al Rahman al-; Yemeni religious and political leader; b. 18 July 1917.
Member of Revolutionary Council 62-74; Minister of Justice 62-63; Vice-Pres. Exec. Council Oct. 63-Feb. 64; mem. Political Bureau 64-74; mem. Presidency Council 65-74, Chair. 69-74; Chair. Peace Cttee. set up after Khamer Peace Talks May 65; leader of Zaidi (Shi'a) sect. Sana'a, Yemen Arab Republic.

Işik, Hasan Esat; Turkish diplomatist and politician; b. 1916, Istanbul; ed. Lycée of Galatasaray, Faculty of Law, Univ. of Ankara.
Ministry of Foreign Affairs 40-; Consulate-Gen., Paris 45-49; Head of Section, Dept. of Commerce and Econ. Affairs, and Dept. of Int. Econ. Relations 49-52; staff of Perm. Turkish Del. to European Office of UN, Geneva 52-54; Dir.-Gen. of Dept. of Commerce and Commercial Agreements, Ministry of Foreign Affairs 54-57; Asst. for Econ. Affairs to Sec.-Gen. of Ministry of Foreign Affairs, Sec.-Gen. Econ. Co-operation Int. Org. 57-62; Ambassador to Belgium, led negotiations for Turkey's entry to EEC 62-64, to U.S.S.R. 64-65, 66-68; Minister of Foreign Affairs

65; Amb. to France 68-73; mem. Nat. Assembly 73; Minister of Defence 74.
c/o Ministry of National Defence, Ankara, Turkey.

Ismail, Abdul Fattah; Yemeni politician.
Member Exec. Cttee., Nat. Liberation Front (NLF), Sec.-Gen. 71-; mem. of dels. of NLF and FLOSY (Front for the Liberation of Occupied South Yemen) 67; Sec.-Gen. Afro-Asian Solidarity Org. 73.
Presidential Council, Aden, People's Democratic Republic of Yemen.

Ismail, Abdul Malek; Yemeni diplomatist; b. 26 Nov. 1937, Aden; ed. Tawahi and Crater, Aden, Tech. School, Maalla, Khediwi High School, Cairo and Cairo Univ. Faculty of Commerce.
Member, United Nat. Front; Editor *A-Nour* and *Hakikah* (newspapers) 61-63; Vice-Chair. Gen. Union of Petroleum Workers 61-62, Chair. Petroleum Workers Union 62-64; Vice-Pres. Arab Fed. of Petroleum Workers 62-65; leading mem. Arab Nationalist Movement 56-63; leading mem. Nat. Liberation Front for Southern Yemen (NLF) 63-65; Dir. Nat. Front Office, Cairo 65-66; mem. Gen. Command of Nat. Liberation Front 66-68; Minister of Labour and Social Affairs 67-68; Minister of Econs., Commerce and Planning 68-70; Perm. Rep. to UN 70-73.
c/o Ministry of Foreign Affairs, Aden, People's Democratic Republic of Yemen.

Ismail, Ahmed Sultan, B.SC.; Egyptian mechanical engineer; b. 14 April 1923, Port Said; ed. Cairo Univ.
Worked as shift engineer, maintenance engineer at various power stations 45-64; mem. Exec. Board Electrical Projects Corpn. 64-; Nat. Defence Coll. 67; Gov. Menufia Prov. 68-71; Minister of Power 71-; Order of Repub., First Class.
43 Ahmed Abdel Aziz Street, Dokki, Cairo, Egypt.

Ismail, Gen. Mohamed Hafez; Egyptian soldier and diplomatist.
Assistant Under-Sec. of Foreign Affairs 60-64; Ambassador to United Kingdom 64-65; Amb. to Italy 67-69; Adviser to the Pres. on Nat. Security 71-74; Head of Pres. Cabinet 73-74; Amb. to U.S.S.R. 74-.
Egyptian Embassy, 56 Ul. Gertsena, Moscow, U.S.S.R.

Issawi, Charles Philip, M.A.; American economist; b. 1916; ed. Victoria Coll. Alexandria and Magdalen Coll. Oxford.
Sec. to Under-Sec. of State, Ministry of Finance, Cairo 37-38; Head of Research Section, Nat. Bank of Egypt, Cairo 38-43; Adjunct Prof. American Univ. of Beirut 43-47; UN Secretariat Economic Affairs Officer 48-55; Visiting Lecturer, Harvard Univ. 50, Johns Hopkins 67, Princeton Univ. 74; Prof. Columbia Univ. 51-; Pres. Middle East Spitues Asscn. of N. America 73-.
Publs. *Egypt: an Economic and Social Analysis* 47, *An Arab Philosophy of History* 50, *Egypt at Mid-Century* 54, *Mushkilat Qaumia* 59, *The Economics of Middle East Oil* (co-author) 62, *Egypt in Revolution* 63, *The Economic History of the Middle East 1800–1914* 66, *The Economic History of Iran 1800–1914* 71, *Oil, the Middle East and the World* 72, *Issawi's Laws of Social Motion* 73.
Columbia University, New York, N.Y., U.S.A.

J

Jabbur, Jibrail S., M.A., PH.D.; Lebanese university professor; b. 1904; ed. American Univ. of Beirut, Egyptian Univ. and Princeton Univ.
Vice-Principal, Homs Nat. Coll. 25-26; Instructor in Arabic, American Univ. of Beirut 26-29, 30-35, Asst. Prof. 35-42, Assoc. Prof. 42-46, 47-48, Prof. 48-50, Chair. Arabic Dept. 50-60, Margaret Weyerhauser Jewett Prof. of

Arabic 50-; Gold Medal (Merit) of Nat. Education and Public Instruction 51, Officer, Nat. Order of Cedars (Lebanon).
Publs. *Ibn Abd Rabbihi and his 'Iqd.* 33, *Al-Hayah al-'Arabiyyah fi al mi'at sanah al-'Ula ba'd wafat al-Nabi al 'Arabi* 34, *Umar Ibn Abi Rabiah,* Vol. I 35, Vol. II 39, Vol. III 70, *Fi al-Adab al-Andalusi* 49; Editor *Al-Kawakib al-Sa'irah,* Vol. I 45, Vol. II 49, Vol. III 59, *Kitab al 'Id* 67; translated and wrote with Philip Hitti and Edward Jurji, *Tarikh al-'Arab (al Mutawwal)* 3 vols. 49-51.
American University of Beirut, Beirut, Lebanon.

Jabre, Jamil Louis; Lebanese writer; b. 1924; ed. Univ. Saint-Joseph, Beirut.
Director of *Al-Hikmal* Revue; Cultural Counsellor for dailies *Al Jaryda* and *L'Orient* and United Unions for Employees and Workers; Founder-mem. Lebanese P.E.N. Club, Amis du Livre, Club du Roman, Club de la Jeunesse Vivante.
Publs. include: *Fever, After the Storm, Agony* (3 vols.), *May Ziadé, Amine Rihani, Gébrane Khalil Gébrane, Tagore, May: Authoress, Jahiz and the Society of His Times, Views on Contemporary American Literature* (essays), *Dream of Nemrod.*
Secteur Chalhoub, Immeuble Nassim Audi, Zalka, Beirut, Lebanon.

Jabre, Kamal Rachid; Lebanese commercial official; b. 1898.
Member Chamber of Deputies 37-39; Vice-Pres. Asscn. des Industriels Libanais; Pres. Beirut Chamber of Commerce and Industrial 64-74; Vice-Pres. Banque de Crédit Agricole, Industriel et Foncier; Founder Dir. Soc. de Filature et de Tissage; also founder of several industrial socs. and banks; Commdr. Ordre National du Cèdre.
Beirut Chamber of Commerce and Industry, P.O.B. 1801, Beirut, Lebanon.

Jaffar, Khalid Mohammed; Kuwaiti diplomatist; b. 12 June 1922; ed. Mubarakia School, Kuwait.
Teacher, Kuwait 40-42; Chief Cashier, Kuwait Municipality 43-45; Kuwait Oil Co., rose to Supt. of Public Relations 45-61; Lord Chamberlain to His Highness The Amir of Kuwait 61-62; Ambassador, Foreign Affairs, Kuwait May-Dec. 62, concurrently Head of Press and Culture Div., Ministry of Foreign Affairs; mem. Delegation to UN before admission of Kuwait as a mem. 62; deputized for Under-Sec. of State at the Ministry of Foreign Affairs 62-63; Amb. to U.K. 63-65, to France 65-67, concurrently to Lebanon 65-70, to Turkey 68-73, concurrently to Bulgaria, Greece 71-73.
c/o Ministry of Foreign Affairs, Kuwait City, Kuwait.

Jahanshahi, Abdol Ali, PH.D.; Iranian economist; b. 1924; ed. Univ. de Paris.
Ministry of Justice 46-57; Univ. of Teheran 57; Bank Melli Iran 57-60; Vice-Gov. Bank Markazi Iran 62-63; Minister of Educ. 64; Minister of State 64-65; Chancellor, Nat. Univ. of Iran 65-66; Alt. Exec. Dir. World Bank 66-71; Gov. Bank Markazi Iran (Central Bank of Iran) 71-73; Amb. Extraordinary, Head of Mission to European Communities March 74-.
Avenue Louise 166, 1050 Brussels, Belgium.

Jalallar, Mohammed Khan; Afghan politician; b. 6 Dec. 1936, Andkhoi; ed. Commerce Vocational School, Kabul and Kabul Univ.
Member Finance Dept., Ministry of Planning 58-63, Dir. Co-ordination Dept. 63-67, Pres. Financial Section 67-71; Deputy Minister of Finance 71-72; Minister of Finance 72-73 of Commerce Jan. 74-; Golden Minapal Award.
Ministry of Commerce, Kabul; and c/o Barat Ali, Afzal Market, Kabul, Afghanistan.

Jalloud, Major Abdul Salam Ahmed; Libyan politician; b. 15 Dec. 1944; ed. Secondary School, Sebha, Mil. Acad., Benghazi.

Member Revolutionary Command Council (RCC); Minister of Industry and the Econ., Acting Minister of the Treasury until 72; Prime Minister July 72-.
Office of the Prime Minister, Tripoli, Libyan Arab Republic.

Jamal, Jasim Yousof; Qatar diplomatist; b. 17 Sept. 1940; ed. Northeast Mo. State Univ., Kirksville, Mo., U.S.A. and Univ. of New York.
Ministry of Educ., Dir. Admin. Affairs 58-63, Cultural Adviser, U.S.A. 63-68; Dir. of Cultural Affairs 68-72; Perm. Rep. to UN 72-; non-resident Amb. to Canada, Brazil and Argentina.
Permanent Mission of Qatar to the United Nations, 747 Third Avenue, 22nd Floor, New York, N.Y. 10017, U.S.A.

Jamali, Asim al-; Omani politician; b. 15 Jan. 1935, Muscat; ed. Univ. of Karachi Medical Coll., Univ. of London.
Medical Officer of Health, Dubai 60-63; at London School of Hygiene and Tropical Medicine 64-65; Health Adviser to Trucial States Council, Dubai 65-70; Minister of Health, Oman 70-74, Minister without Portfolio and Special Rep. of the Sultan 74-; Renaissance Medal 74, Medal of the First Order.
The Diwan, Muscat, Sultanate of Oman.

Jamil, Sharif Husain ben; Jordanian politician.
Former Minister of Royal Court; Prime Minister April 63-July 64; Chief of the Royal Cabinet 67; mem. Consultative Council 67; C.-in-C. Armed Forces 69-70; Great Uncle of King Hussein.
The Royal Palace, Amman, Jordan.

Jamjoom, Ahmed Salah, B.COM.; Saudi Arabian businessman and politician; b. 1925; ed. Fouad Univ. Cairo and Harvard Law School.
Joined Arab Bank, Jeddah 50; Minister of State and mem. Council of Ministers 58-59; Supervisor of Economic Dept. 59-60; Minister of Commerce 60; Minister of Trade and Industry 61-62; Dir. and Partner, Mohd. Nour Salah Jamjoom & Bros. 62-; Dir. Jamjoom Vehicles and Equipment and Jamjoom Construction.
Publs. *An Approach to an Integrated Economic Development* 60, *Economics of Mecca* 67.
Mohamed Nour Salah Jamjoom and Brothers, Riyadh, and P.O. Box 1247, Jeddah, Saudi Arabia.

Jaq, Dr. Said Ahmed el-, M.A., PH.D.; Sudanese politician; b. 1930, Khartoum; ed. Univ. of Khartoum and in U.S.A.
Worked in Ministry of Works 54-56, later in consultative and design engineering; lecturer in Civil Eng., Univ. of Khartoum; worked on water and electricity projects for Shendi and Berber towns; founder and board mem. Sudanese Engineers Trade Union; helped to found Sudanese Teachers Asscn., Univ. of Khartoum; Minister of Works 69-70; Minister of Transport and Communications 70-71; mem. American Eng. Soc., Sudanese Engineers Soc.
c/o Ministry of Transport and Communications, Khartoum, Sudan.

Jarring, Gunnar, PH.D.; Swedish diplomatist; b. 12 Oct. 1907; ed. Lund Univ.
Associate Prof. Turkic Languages Lund Univ. 33-40; Attaché Ankara 40-41; Chief Section B Teheran 41; Chargé d'Affaires a.i. Teheran and Baghdad 45, Addis Ababa 46-48; Minister to India 48-51, concurrently to Ceylon 50-51, to Persia, Iraq and Pakistan 51-52; Dir. Political Div. Ministry of Foreign Affairs 53-56; Perm. Rep. to UN 56-58; rep. on Security Council 57-58; Amb. to U.S.A. 58-64, to U.S.S.R. 64-73, and to Mongolia 65-73; Special Rep. of Sec.-Gen. of UN on Middle East situation Nov. 67-; Grand Cross, Order of the North Star.
Publs. *Studien zu einer osttürkischen Lautlehre* 33, *The Contest of the Fruits—An Eastern Turki Allegory* 36, *The Uzbek Dialect of Qilich, Russian Turkestan* 37, *Uzbek Texts from Afghan Turkestan* 38, *The Distribution of Turk Tribes in Afghanistan* 39, *Materials for the Knowledge of Eastern Turkestan* (Vols. I-IV) 47-51, *An Eastern Turki-English Dialect Dictionary* 64.
Karlavägen 85, S-114 59 Stockholm, Sweden.

Jezrawi, Taha al; Iraqi politician; b. 1938, Mosul; ed. schools in Mosul and Military Coll.
Former army officer; mem. Regional Leadership, Arab Baath Socialist Party; Head, Arab Affairs Office, Revolutionary Command Council Nov. 69; Minister of Industry March 70-, Acting Minister of Planning 75.
Ministry of Industry, Baghdad, Iraq.

Jordan, King of (*see* Hussein ibn Talal).

Joukhdar, H.E. Mohammed Salen, B.A., M.A.; Saudi Arabian economist; b. 1932; ed. Univs. of California and Southern California.
Economic Consultant to Directorate-Gen. of Petroleum and Minerals, Saudi Arabia 58; Govt. Rep. Supervisory Cttee. for Expenditure and Purchasing, Arabian Oil Co. 61, Dir. 61-66; Sec.-Gen. Org. of Petroleum Exporting Countries (OPEC) 67-68; Deputy Minister of Petroleum and Mineral Resources 69-; mem. American Soc. of Economists.
Ministry of Petroleum and Mineral Resources, P.O. Box 247, Riyadh, Saudi Arabia.

Joumblatt, Kamal; Lebanese politician and hereditary Druse chieftain; b. 1919.
Fmr. Minister of Nat. Economy; Pres. Social Progress Party of Lebanon; Minister of Education and Fine Arts 60-61; Minister of State for the Interior and Planning Services 61-64; Minister of Public Works and P.T.T. 66-67; Minister of the Interior April-June 70; Pres. Parti Socialiste Progressive; Lenin Peace Prize 71.
Publ. *The Truth about the Lebanese Revolution* 59.
Chamber of Deputies, Beirut; and Zodak el Blat, Beirut, Lebanon.

Juffali, Ahmad; Saudi Arabian businessman; b. 15 Oct. 1924; ed. Saudi Arabia and United Kingdom.
Managing Dir., E. A. Juffali & Bros. 45-; mem. Board of Dirs. Saudi Electric Co. 52-; Man. Dir. Saudi Cement Co. 58, Medina Electric Co. 58-; Hon. Danish Consul 59-.
E. A. Juffali & Bros., King Abdul Aziz Street, P.O.B. 1049, Jeddah, Saudi Arabia.

Juma, Midhet (brother of Saad Juma, *q.v.*); Jordanian diplomatist; b. 19 Aug. 1920; ed. Cairo Univ.
Attaché to Arab League, Cairo 45-47; First Sec. and Counsellor, Cairo 47-52; Counsellor and Chargé d'Affaires, London 52-53; Minister to Pakistan 53-55; Chief of Protocol, Royal Palace Amman 56; Under-Sec. for Press and Broadcasting 56-58; Ambassador to the U.S.A. 58-59, to Morocco 59-62, to Federal Repub. of Germany 62-65, to Lebanon 65-67, to U.K. 67-69, to Tunisia 69-70, to Spain Sept. 71-; numerous decorations.
Embassy of Jordan, 44 Avenida Generalísimo, Madrid, Spain.

Juma, Saad (brother of Midhet Juma, *q.v.*); Jordanian diplomatist; b. 1916; ed. Syrian Univ., Damascus.
Civil Service for twenty-six years; Dir. Press and Publicity; Chief Censor; Sec. to Prime Minister; Perm. Under-Sec., Gov. of Amman; Under-Sec. for Foreign Affairs; Ambassador to Syrian Arab Republic 62, to U.S.A. 62-65; Minister of the Royal Court 65-67; Prime Minister and Minister of Nat. Defence April-Oct. 67; mem. Consultative Council 67; Amb. to U.K. 69-70; fmr. Personal Rep. to H.M. King Hussein; mem. Senate; honours from Jordan, Iran, Syria, Italy and China (Taiwan).
Publs. *Conspiracy and the Battle of Destiny, Hostile Society*.
Royal Palace, Amman, Jordan.

Jumeia'an, Mikhael; Jordanian administrator; b. 1915; ed. American Univ., Cairo.
Interpreter 40-43; Teacher 43-45; Govt. Agency Sec. 45-47; Asst. Chief Accountant 47-50; Registrar of Patents, Trademarks and Cos. 50-55; Asst. Div. Head, Civil Service 55-57, Div. Head 57-62, Asst. Under-Sec. 62-65, Under-Sec. 65-68; Dir. of Antiquities 68-70; Dir. Inst. of Public Admin. 70-; del. to many Arab and int. confs.
Publs. *International Laws of Chess* (transl. into Arabic), *Fundamentals of Supervision* (in Arabic) 64, *Fundamentals of Public Administration* 69, and many papers on public administration.
Institute of Public Administration, P.O. Box 13055, Amman, Jordan.

K

Kaddori, Fakhri Yassin, DR.RER.POL.; Iraqi economist; b. 28 Aug. 1932; ed. Adhamiya Intermediate School and Central Secondary School, Baghdad, Coll. of Commerce and Econs. (Univ. of Baghdad), State Univ. of Iowa, Cologne Univ., Int. Marketing Inst. (Harvard Univ.).
Director of Internal Trade, Ministry of the Economy 64-68; Minister of the Economy 68-71, now Chair. Bureau of Econ. Affairs, Revolutionary Command Council; Pres. Iraqi Economist Asscn.
Bureau of Economic Affairs, Revolutionary Command Council, National Council Building, Baghdad, Iraq.

Kader, Yehia Abdel; Egyptian diplomatist; b. 1920, Alexandria; ed. Univ. of Cairo.
Secretary, Counsellor Egyptian Embassies in Belgrade, Khartoum, Milan; Amb. to Saudi Arabia 64-68, to Yugoslavia 68-71; Chair. Egyptian Radio and Television 71; Amb. to U.S.S.R. 71-74.
c/o Ministry of Foreign Affairs, Cairo, Egypt.

Kahale, Noureddin, B.S., M.S.; Syrian engineer; b. 1911, ed. Robert Coll., Istanbul, and Purdue and Illinois Univs., U.S.A.
With Ministry of Public Works and Communications 41-51, Head Irrigation Section 41-43, Acting Dir. of Irrigation 43-46, Dir.-Gen. 47, Sec.-Gen. 48-51; Chair. Board and Dir. Latakia Port Co. 51-58; Minister of Public Works, Syrian Region, United Arab Republic 58-60, concurrently Pres. Syrian Exec. Council, Acting Minister of Planning, and Minister of State, Central Govt.; Vice-President U.A.R. and Minister of Planning, Central Govt. 60-61; Vice-President U.A.R. in charge of Production Sector 61; Chair. and Dir.-Gen. Euphrates Project Authority 61-; Sec. Asscn. of Syrian Engineers 43-49; Pres. Damascus Asscn. of Chartered Engineers 61-62; Pres. Supreme Council of Engineering Asscns. of U.A.R. 61; Syrian Rep. to various Int. Confs.; decorations from Govts. of Syria, Khmer Repub., Denmark, Ethiopia, Greece, Morocco, Spain, Sudan and Yugoslavia.
Principal works: design and execution, Hama Irrigation Scheme 45-46; planning and execution, Latakia Harbour 51-58; planning Tartousse Harbour 58-60, Euphrates Dam, Power Plant and Irrigation Project, Habur Dam and Irrigation Project 62-.
Publs. *The Solution of the Water Supply Shortage in Aleppo* 47, *The Latakia Harbour Project* 55 (Papers presented to Pan-Arab Engineers Confs.).
West Adnan Malki, Mohammed Kurd-Ali Street, Damascus, Syria.

Kaid, Ahmed (Commandant Slimane); Algerian politician; b. 1924.
Joined Nat. Liberation Army (ALN) 56; mem. of Ghardimaou Gen. Staff, and ALN Rep. to Evian talks 62; Deputy for Tiaret 62-; Minister of Tourism 63-64; Minister of Finance 65-68; Sec.-Gen. FLN Dec. 67-72; mem. Revolutionary Council 65-72.
c/o Council of the Revolution, Algiers, Algeria.

Kaissouni, Abdel Moneim, B.COM., B.SC., PH.D.; Egyptian financial administrator and politician; b. 1916; ed. Univ. of Cairo and London School of Economics.
With Barclays Bank, England 42-43; Lecturer and Asst. Prof. of Econs., Univ. of Cairo 44-46; Dir. Middle East Dept. Int. Monetary Fund, Washington, and later Chief Technical Rep. in Middle East 46-50; with Nat. Bank of Egypt 50-54; Minister of Finance, Economy and Deputy Prime Minister 54-56, 68; Chair. Arab Int. Bank 71-; Chair. European Arab Holding, Luxembourg 72; mem. Higher Econ. Council, Egypt 74; Chair. IMF and IBRD annual meetings 55; Pres. Cairo Conf. on Devt. 62; Pres. UN Conf. on Trade and Devt. 64; Grand Cordon of the Repub. (Egypt).
23 Sesostris Street, Heliopolis, Cairo, Egypt.

Kalali, Manouchehr, D.ECON.; Iranian politician; b. 1925; ed. Teheran Univ. and Paris, France.
Joined Ministry of Labour and Social Services, later Perm. Under-Sec.; mem. Parl for Mashad 65-; founder mem. "Kanoon Motara Ghi" (later Iran Novin Party), Sec.; mem. Exec. Board, Iran Novin Party; Asst. to Sec.-Gen. Iran Novin Party, Deputy Sec.-Gen., Sec.-Gen. 69-74; Minister of State 71; Minister without Portfolio 74-.
The Majlis, Teheran, Iran.

Kamel, Hassan, LL.D.; Egyptian diplomatist and administrator; b. 6 Sept. 1907; ed. Univs. of Montpellier, Cairo and Paris.
Member Mixed Bar 30-36; Lecturer, Admin. Law, High Coll. of Police and Admin. 36-37; Ministry of Foreign Affairs 37, served in several countries including France, Italy, Iran, Syria, Portugal, Switzerland, Libya, Argentina, Turkey and Hungary until 59; Legal Adviser, Govt. of Qatar 60, Dir.-Gen. 61-67, Adviser 67-; Perm. Rep. of Qatar to UN 71-72; Adviser of several dels. to UN and Rep. on numerous Int. Confs.; mem. several Law Asscns.; mem. Board of Dirs. Shell (Qatar) Ltd., Qatar Petroleum Ltd.; Officier, Légion d'Honneur, Commdr., Ordre Nat. du Mérite.
Publs. numerous legal articles.
P.O. Box 636, Doha, Qatar.

Kamel, Dr. Mostafa, LL.B.; Egyptian diplomatist; b. 27 Oct. 1908; ed. Univs. of Cairo and the Sorbonne.
Professor of Constitutional and Admin. Law, Univ. of Cairo; Govt. Observer, Summit Conf., Geneva 55; mem. Egyptian Del. to first Asian-African Conf., Bandung 55; Ambassador of Egypt to India 55-58; Amb. of U.A.R. to U.S.A. 58-67, to Belgium and Luxembourg 67-68.
Publs. Textbooks on constitutional, administrative and penal law.
Al-Shams Building, 94 Sarwat Street, Apt. 15, Al-Orman, Cairo, Egypt.

Karageorghis, Vassos, PH.D., F.S.A.; Cypriot archaeologist; b. 29 April 1929, Trikomo; ed. Pancyprian Gymnasium, Nicosia, Univ. Coll., and Inst. of Archaeology, London Univ.
Assistant Curator, Cyprus Museum 52-60, Curator 60-63, Acting Dir., Dept. of Antiquities, Cyprus 63-64, Dir. 64-; Vice-Pres. Council of Soc. for Cypriot Studies; mem. Governing Body, Cyprus Research Centre; Fellow, Soc. of Antiquaries, London, Univ. Coll. London; Corresp. Fellow, British Acad.; Corresp. mem. Archaeological Soc., Athens, Acad. of Athens; mem. German Archaeological Inst., Berlin, Royal Soc. for Humanistic Studies, Lund; Dr. h.c. (Univs. of Lyon, Göteborg, Athens, Birmingham); Chevalier de l'Ordre de la Légion d'Honneur.
Publs. *Treasures in the Cyprus Museum* 62, *Nouveaux Documents pour l'Etude du Bronze Récent à Chypre* 64,

Corpus Vasorum Antiquorum I 63, and *II* 65, *Sculptures from Salamis I* 64, *II* 66, *Excavations in the Necropolis of Salamis I* 67, *II* 70, *III* 73, *Cyprus* (Archaelogia Mundi) 68, *Salamis-New Aspects of Antiquity* 69, *Altägäis und Altkypros* (with H.-G. Buchholz) 71, and *Cypriot Antiquities in the Pericles Collection, Larnaca* 73, *Excavations at Kiton I: The Tombs* 74, and articles in German, American, English and French journals.
Cyprus Museum, P.O. Box 2024, Nicosia; Home: 12 Kastorias Street, Nicosia, Cyprus.

Karami, Rashid; Lebanese politician; b. 1921; ed. Fuad I Univ., Cairo.
Minister of Nat. Economy and Social Affairs 54-55; Prime Minister and Minister of the Interior Sept. 55-March 56; Prime Minister Sept. 58-May 60; Minister of Finance, Economy, Defence and Information Oct. 58-Oct. 59, of Finance and Defence Oct. 59-May 60; Prime Minister and Minister of Finance Oct. 61-April 64; Prime Minister 65-66, 66-67, 67-68, 69-70, May 75-, also Minister of Defence, Finance and Information May 75-.
Office of the Prime Minister, Beirut; and Rue Karm Ellé, Beirut, Lebanon.

Karim, Amin Abdul; Iraqi politician; b. 1921, Baghdad; ed. Coll. of Law.
Entered Govt. service March 43; has held various govt. posts including Dir. Gen. of Finance and Revenues, and Pres. State Org. of Banks -68; Min. of Finance 68-75.
c/o Ministry of Finance, Baghdad, Iraq.

Karim-Lamrani, Mohammed; Moroccan economist; b. 1 May 1919, Fez.
Chairman and Dir. of several cos. in Morocco; Gen. Man. Office Chérifien des Phosphates 67-; Chair. Crédit du Maroc; Econ. Adviser to H.M. the King; Minister of Finance 71; Prime Minister 71-72.

Karlin, Dr. Samuel, PH.D.; American mathematician; b. 8 June 1924, Poland; ed. Ill. Inst. of Technology and Princeton Univ.
California Inst. of Technology, Bateman Research Fellow 47-48, Asst. Prof. 49-51, Assoc. Prof. 51-55, Prof. 55-56; Visiting Asst. Prof., Princeton Univ. 50; Prof., Stanford Univ. 56-70; Guggenheim Fellow to Israel and France 60-61; Guest Mathematical Soc. of Japan 64; Head, Dept. of Pure Mathematics, Weizmann Inst. of Science, Rehovot, Israel 70-; Consultant Rand Corpn., Santa Monica; Chief Editor, *Theoretical Population Biology;* Editor or Assoc. Editor of *Journal of Mathematical Analysis, Logistics Journal, Journal of Applied Probability, Journal d'Analyse, Journal of Mathematics and Mechanics, Journal of Mathematical Biosciences, Journal of Approximation Theory and Advances in Mathematics;* Fellow, Inst. of Mathematical Statistics 56; fmr. mem. Int. Statistics Inst., American Acad. of Arts and Sciences and Council of American Mathematical Soc.; mem. of American Mathematical Soc., Inst. of Mathematical Statistics, Applied Mathematics panel, Nat. Research Council, U.S. Acad. of Sciences; Procter Fellow, Princeton Univ. 46; Wald Memorial Lecturer 57; Henry and Bertha Benson Chair. of Mathematics 71.
Publs. over 150 articles in various journals on topics of pure and applied probability theory, game theory, decision theory and statistical methodology, mathematical analysis and mathematical biology.
Meonot Shine 13, Rehovot, Israel.

Kassab, Adnan Ali; Iraqi civil servant; b. 1934; ed. Higher Inst. of Industrial Engineering.
Resident Engineer to Army Canal Project 61-63; Dir. of Admin. in Industrial Govt. Projects 63-64; later arrested and underwent political imprisonment; Dir.-Gen. of Iraqi Ports Admin. 68-71; Pres. Iraq Nat. Oil Co. 71-72; Pres. State Constructional Contracting Co. Sept. 72-.
State Constructional Contracting Co., Insurance Building, Rashid Street, Baghdad, Iraq.

Katz, Mindru; Israeli (b. Rumanian) pianist; b. 3 June 1925; ed. Bucharest Acad. of Music.
First public recital 31; first public concert with Bucharest Philharmonic Orchestra 47; extensive tours of E. Europe 47-, U.K. 58-, South and East Africa 60, 62, Far East, Australia, New Zealand and S. America 61; has also played in France, Germany, Portugal, Denmark, Sweden and Turkey; settled in Israel 59; Prizewinner, Berlin, Prague, Bucharest Int. Piano Competitions 51, 53, Rumanian State Prize.
45 Hanassi Street, Herzliya, Nof-Yam, Israel.

Katzir, Ephraim Katchalski, M.SC., PH.D.; Israeli professor of biophysics and Head of State; b. 16 May 1916, Russia; ed. Hebrew Univ., Jerusalem.
Professor, Dept. of Biophysics, Weizmann Inst. of Science 51-; Chief Scientist, Ministry of Defence 66-68; Pres. of Israel 73-; Visiting Prof., Hebrew Univ. 53-61; Guest Scientist, Harvard Univ. 57-59; Senior Foreign Scientist Fellowship, Univ. of California, Los Angeles 64; Chair. Weizmann Inst. Cttee. for Katzir Centre; mem. Board of Govs., Hebrew Univ.; mem. Israel Acad. of Sciences and Humanities, Biochemical Soc. of Israel, Israel Chemical Soc., Nat. Acad. of Sciences, U.S.A., American Acad. of Arts and Sciences (Foreign Hon. mem.), Leopoldina Acad. of Science, German Democratic Repub., American Soc. of Biological Chemists (Hon.), Ciba Foundation, Int. Union of Biochemistry and many other orgs.; mem. Board, *Analytical Biochemistry, Archives of Biochemistry and Biophysics, Biopolymers, Excerpta Medica* and Amino Acids and Proteins Section of *European Journal of Biochemistry;* Tchernikhovsky Prize 48, Weizmann Prize 50, Israel Prize Natural Sciences 59, Rothschild Prize Natural Sciences 61; Linderstram-Lang Gold Medal 69, Hans Krebs Medal 72.
Publs. numerous papers and articles on proteins and polyamino acids.
Office of the President, Jerusalem, Israel.

Kayla, Ziya; Turkish economist; b. 28 Dec. 1912; ed. School of Political Sciences, Istanbul.
Ministry of Finance 34-63, Asst. Inspector, Inspector and Chief Inspector of Finance 34-60; Deputy Minister of Finance 60-63; Chair. Board of Dirs. and Dir.-Gen. Central Bank of Turkey 63-66; Alternate Gov. for Turkey of Int. Bank for Reconstruction and Development 61-66; Pres. Banks' Asscn. of Turkey 63-66; Sec.-Gen. Comm. of Regulation of Bank Credits 63-66, Head of Foreign Investment Encouragement Cttee. 63-66; mem. Board of Controllers of the Prime Ministry 66-70; Pres. Council of Administrators, Türkiye Vakıflar Bankası 71-.
Publs. *Emission Movements in Turkey* 67, *Treasury and Central Banks Relations* 70.
Mesnevi sokak 8/8, Ankara, Turkey.

Kayra, Cahit; Turkish civil servant and diplomatist; b. 13 March 1917; ed. Univ. of Ankara.
Inspector of Finance 42-50; Counsellor, Gen. Dir. of Finance 50-55; private financial adviser 55-59; Head of Foreign Trade Dept., Ministry of Trade 59-60; Head of Turkish Perm. Del. to Gen. Agreement on Tariffs and Trade (GATT) 60-63; Deputy Under-Sec. of State to Min. of Finance 63-64; Head of Turkish Del. to OECD 64-67; Head of Research Dept., Ministry of Finance 67-73; Minister of Energy and Natural Resources 74; mem. Nat. Assembly for Ankara; Republican People's Party.
Publs. *Middle Eastern Oil* 53, *A Guide to the Turkish System of Taxation* 57, *Import Policy in Turkey* 63.
Research Department, Ministry of Finance, Ankara, Turkey.

Kazemzadeh, Hossein, LL.B.; Iranian lawyer and politician; b. 1923, Shiraz; ed. Univ. of Teheran and Princeton Univ., U.S.A.
Assistant Lecturer, Inst. of Business and Admin., Teheran Univ.; Deputy Man. Dir. Planning Org.; Deputy Prime Minister; Dir. Budget Dept.; Consulting Minister and Sec.-Gen. Org. for Admin. Affairs and Employment; Minister of Science and Higher Educ. until 73.
c/o Ministry of Science and Higher Education, Teheran, Iran.

Kedourie, Elie, B.SC.(ECON.); British university teacher.
Assistant Lecturer, then Lecturer in Politics and Public Admin., London School of Economics 53-60; Reader in Political Studies with special reference to the Middle East, London Univ. 61-65; Prof. of Politics, London Univ. 65-; Editor *Middle Eastern Studies* 64-.
Publs. *England and the Middle East: the Destruction of the Ottoman Empire* 56, *Nationalism* 60, *Afghani and Abduh* 66, *The Chatham House Version* 70, *Nationalism in Asia and Africa* 71, *Arabic Political Memoirs and Other Studies* 74.
London School of Economics, Houghton Street, Aldwych, London, W.C.1, England.

Kelani, Haissam; Syrian diplomatist; b. 6 Aug. 1926, Hamah; ed. Mil. Coll., Air Gen. Staff Coll., Paris and High Mil. Air Acad., Paris.
General Pilot 61-62; Amb. to Algeria 62-63, to Morocco 65-67; Sec.-Gen. Ministry of Foreign Affairs 67-69; Amb. to the German Democratic Repub. 69-72; Perm. Rep. to UN 72-; Hon. Dr. Contemporary History; twelve medals.
Publs. ten books, many articles in Arab reviews.
Permanent Mission of Syria to the United Nations, 150 East 58th Street, Room 1500, New York, N.Y. 10022, U.S.A.

Kellou, Mohamed; Algerian lawyer and diplomatist; b. 27 March 1931; ed. Univs. of Algiers and Montpellier.
Lawyer, Algiers; fmr. Vice-Pres. Union Générale des Etudiants Musulmans Algériens (U.G.E.M.A.) (in charge of Foreign Affairs); Front de Libération Nationale (F.L.N.) Rep. in U.K. 57-61; Chief of Provisional Govt. of Algeria Diplomatic Mission to Pakistan 61-62; Chief of Africa-Asia-Latin America Div., Ministry of Foreign Affairs, Republic of Algeria 62-63; Amb. to U.K. 63-64, to Czechoslovakia 64-70, concurrently to Hungary 65-70, to Poland 66-70, to Argentina 70-, concurrently to Chile, Uruguay, Bolivia and Peru.
Embassy of Algeria, Calle Montevideo 1889, Buenos Aires, Argentine; Home: 40 boulevard des Martyres, Algiers, Algeria.

Kemal, Yaşar; Turkish writer and journalist; b. 1923; self-educated.
Publs. *Memed, My Hawk* 61, *The Wind from the Plain* 63, *Anatolian Tales* 68, *They Burn the Thistles* 73, *Iron Earth Copper Sky* 74, *The Legend of Ararat* 75; novels, short stories and essays in Turkish; books translated into several languages.
P.K. 14, Basinköy, Istanbul, Turkey.

Kenter, Ayşe Yıldız; Turkish actress and producer; b. 1928; ed. State Conservatoire.
Worked in State Theatre for eleven years, playing about forty parts; Rockefeller Fellowship in Dramatic Art; teacher of Dramatic Art, State Conservatoire; now acting and producing independently; twice awarded Iskender Prize for best performance of the year.
Ihlamur Cad. Kuyulu bostan Sokak No. 31/5 Nişantaş, Istanbul, Turkey.

Kenyon, Dame Kathleen Mary, D.B.E., D.LITT., D.LIT., L.H.D., F.B.A., F.S.A.; British archaeologist; b. 5 Jan. 1906; ed. St. Paul's Girls' School and Somerville Coll., Oxford.
Sec. Inst. of Archaeology 35-48, Council for British

Archaeology 44-49; Lecturer Univ. of London Inst. of Archaeology 48-62; Principal St. Hugh's Coll. Oxford 62-73; Dir. British School of Archaeology in Jerusalem 51-66; Dir. Joint U.K.-Canadian Expedition in Jerusalem; has participated in and directed numerous excavations in U.K. and Middle East.
Publs. *Excavations at the Jewry Wall, Leicester* 48, *Samaria-Sebaste I* 42, *III* 57 (joint author), *Beginning in Archaeology* 54, *Digging up Jericho* 57, *Excavations at Jericho I* 60, *II* 66, *Archaeology in the Holy Land* 60, *Amorites and Canaanites* 66, *Jerusalem* 68, *Royal Cities of the Old Testament* 71, *Digging up Jerusalem* 74.
Rose Hill, Erbistock, Wrexham, Clwyd, LL13 0DE, Wales.

Khaddam, Abdel Halim; Syrian politician.
Deputy Prime Minister and Minister of Foreign Affairs April 71-; mem. Regional Command, Baath Party May 71-.
Ministry of Foreign Affairs, Damascus, Syria.

Khadduri, Majid, B.A., PH.D.; Iraqi educationist and writer; b. 27 Sept. 1909; ed. American Univ. of Beirut and Univ. of Chicago.
Sec.-Treas. Baghdad P.E.N. Club; mem. American Society of Int. Law; Iraqi Del. to the 14th Conf. of the P.E.N. Clubs in Buenos Aires 36; adviser to the Iraq Delegation at the San Francisco Conf. 45; Visiting Lecturer in Near Eastern History at Indiana Univ. 47-48; fmr. Prof. Modern Middle Eastern History at the Higher Teachers' Coll., Baghdad, Iraq 48-49; taught Middle East politics at Chicago and Harvard Univs. 49-50; Prof. Middle East Studies, Johns Hopkins Univ. 50-, Distinguished Research Prof. 70-; Dir. of Research and Education, Middle East Inst. 50-; Visiting Middle East Prof., Columbia Univ.; mem. American Pol. Science Asscn.; Pres. Shaybani Soc. of Int. Law Washington D.C.
Publs. *The Liberation of Iraq from the Mandate* (in Arabic) 35, *The Law of War and Peace in Islam* 41, *The Government of Iraq* 44, *The System of Government in Iraq* (in Arabic) 46, *Independent Iraq* 51, *War and Peace in the Law of Islam* 55, *Islamic Jurisprudence* 61, *Modern Libya* 63, *The Islamic Law of Nations* 66, *Republican Iraq* 69, *Political Trends in the Arab World* 70, *Arab Contemporaries* 73.
Office: 4454 Tindall Street, N.W., Washington 16, D.C., U.S.A.

Khal, Yusuf A. al-, B.A.; Lebanese writer and publisher b. 25 Dec. 1917; ed. American Univ. of Beirut.
Teacher of Arabic Literature, American Univ. of Beirut 45-47, 55-58; Editor *Sawt al Mar'at* women's monthly 46-48; Editor-Writer, Dept. of Public Information, UN Secretariat 48-50; Information Officer Libyan Mission to UN 50-52; Editor *Al Hoda* daily, New York 52-55; Founder and Editor *Shir* poetry magazine, *Adab* literary quarterly 57-; owner Gallery One, Beirut; Editorial Dir. Dar An-Nahar Publishing Co., Beirut 67-70, Soc. Co-operative Libanaise pour l'éditon et diffusion, Beirut.
Publs. *Al Hurriyat* (poetry) 44, *Herodiat* (poetical play) 54, *Al Bi'r al Mahjourat* (poetry) 58, *Quasa'id fil Arba'yn* (poetry) 60, *Collected Poems* 73; translations of works by T. S. Eliot, Auden, Pound, Sandberg, Frost and others; numerous essays and articles of literary criticism.
Rue Patriarcat, Beirut, Lebanon.

Khalatbary, Abbas Ali, PH.D.; Iranian diplomatist; b. 1912; ed. Univ. of Paris.
With Ministry of Foreign Affairs 42-; Dept. of Protocol and Third Political Div. 42; Second Sec., Berne 45, First Sec., Warsaw 47; Acting Head, Dept. of Int. Orgs. 50, Dir. 51; Counsellor, Iranian Embassy, Paris 53; Dir. Third Political Div. 57, Protocol Dept. 58; Amb. to Poland 59, concurrently Minister, Bucharest; Sec.-Gen. Central Treaty Org. (CENTO) 62-68; Deputy Minister of Foreign Affairs,

Under-Sec. for Political Affairs 68-70, Vice-Minister 70-71, Minister 71-; del. to various int. confs. including several sessions of UN Gen. Assembly (Head of Iranian Del. 71), summit of Islamic Conf., Lahore 74.
Imperial Iranian Ministry of Foreign Affairs, Teheran, Iran.

Khalid ibn Abd al-Aziz, H.M. King; Saudi Arabian Amir; b. 1913; ed. religious schools.
Appointed Asst. to his brother, Prince Faisal 34; Rep. of Saudi Arabia to various Int. Confs.; Vice-Pres. Council of Ministers 62-75; nominated Crown Prince 65; acceded to throne March 75; Prime Minister and Minister of Foreign Affairs March 75-.
Royal Palace, Riyadh, Saudi Arabia.

Khalid, Mansour, LL.D.; Sudanese diplomatist and lawyer; b. 17 Jan. 1931, Sudan; ed. Univs. of Khartoum, Pennsylvania and Paris.
Began his career as an attorney, Khartoum 57-59; Legal officer, UN, N.Y. 62-63; Deputy UN resident rep., Algeria 64-65; Bureau of Relations with Member States, UNESCO, Paris 65-69; Visiting Prof. of Int. Law, Univ. of Colorado 68; Minister of Youth and Social Affairs, Sudan 69-71; Chair. of Del. of Sudan to UN Gen. Assembly, Special Consultant and Personal Rep. of UNESCO Dir.-Gen. for UNWRA fund-raising mission 70; Perm. Rep. to UN for Sudan 71, Pres. Security Council 72; Minister of Foreign Affairs 71-75, of Educ. Jan. 75; Chair. OAU Ministerial Cttee. on Impact of Petroleum Price Increase in Africa 73-75.
Ministry of Foreign Affairs, Khartoum, Sudan.

Khalidi, Ismail Raghib, B.A., M.A., PH.D.; Saudi Arabian United Nations official; b. 13 Nov. 1916; ed. St. George's School and Govt. Arab Coll., Jerusalem, American Univ. of Beirut, Michigan Univ. and Columbia Univ., U.S.A.
Assistant Script Editor, Radio Arabic Desk, U.S. Office of War Information, New York 42-44; Sec.-Gen., Inst. of Arab-American Affairs, New York 44-47; New York Corresp. for *Al Misri* (Cairo daily) 46-47; Assoc. Dir. Asia Inst. for Arabic Studies, New York 47-48; Adviser to Saudi Arabian Del. UN 49; mem. UN Secretariat 49-, UN Mission to Libya 50-52, UN Observer, British N. Cameroons 60-61, Political Affairs Officer, UN Security Council Affairs Div. 55-; Principal Sec. UN Comm. for Unification and Rehabilitation of Korea (UNCURK) 62-65.
Publ. *Constitutional Development in Libya* 56.
121 Lorraine Avenue, Mount Vernon, N.Y. 10553, U.S.A.

Khalifa, Sheikh Hamed bin Isa al-; Heir Apparent to His Highness, Emir of Bahrain; b. 28 Jan. 1950; ed. Secondary School, Manama, Applegarth Coll., Godalming, Mons Officer Cadet School, Aldershot, England, and U.S. Army Command and Gen. Staff Coll., Fort Leavenworth, Kansas, U.S.A.
Founder, Commdr. Bahrain Defence Force, Head Defence Dept., Govt. of Bahrain 68-; mem. State Admin. Council 70-71; Minister of State for Defence 71-; awarded several foreign decorations.
Private Office of the Heir Apparent, Court of the Emir, Rifa'a Palace, Manama, Bahrain.

Khalifa, H.H. Sheikh Isa bin Sulman al-; Ruler of the State of Bahrain; b. 3 July 1933.
Appointed heir-apparent by his father, H.H. Sheikh Sulman bin Hamad al-Khalifah 58; succeeded as Sheikh on the death of his father Nov. 61.
Rifa'a Palace, Manama, Bahrain.

Khalifa, Sirr el Khatim, G.C.M.G.; Sudanese educationalist and politician; b. 1 Jan. 1919; ed. Gordon Coll., Khartoum. Former teacher, Gordon Coll., Khartoum, and Bakht-er-Ruda Inst.; Head, Khartoum Technical Inst. 60-64; Deputy Under-Sec. Ministry of Educ. 64; Prime Minister 64-65; Amb. to Italy 65-68, to United Kingdom 68-69;

Minister of Higher Educ. and Scientific Research 72-Jan. 75.
c/o Ministry of Higher Education and Scientific Research, P.O. Box 2081, Khartoum, Sudan.

Khalifa Abbas, El Obeid; Sudanese diplomatist; b. 1915; ed. Gordon Memorial Coll., Khartoum.
Sudan Railway Service 33-44, 48-54; Dep. Under-Sec. for Special Functions 55; Dep. Perm. Under-Sec. Ministry of Foreign Affairs 56-57; Ambassador to Ethiopia 57-59; Ambassador to Iraq, Lebanon, Jordan and Turkey 59-61, to U.S.A. 65-Jan. 66; Permanent Under-Sec. for Foreign Affairs March 66-69; Chair. Board of Dirs., Omdurman Nat. Bank 69-70; Diplomatic Adviser, Embassy of Qatar, London 72-.
Ministry of Foreign Affairs, Khartoum, Sudan; Suite No. 1027, Royal Lancaster Hotel, London, W.2., England.

Khalifa, Sheikh (*see* under Thani, Sheikh Khalifa bin Hamad al-).

Khalifah, Sheikh Khalifah bin Sulman al-; Bahrain politician; b. 1935.
Son of the late Sheikh Sulman and brother of the ruler, Sheikh Isa; Dir. of Finance and Pres. of Electricity Board 61; Pres. Council of Admin. 66-70; Pres. State Council 70-73, Prime Minister 73-.
National Assembly, Manama, Bahrain.

Khalil, Mohamed Kamal El-Din; Egyptian diplomatist. Lecturer in Int. and Public Law 41-56; Dir. of Research Dept., U.A.R. Ministry of Foreign Affairs 56-60; Minister Plenipotentiary, London 60-61; Dir. North American Dept., U.A.R. Ministry of Foreign Affairs 61-64; Ambassador to Jordan 64-66; Ambassador to Sudan 66-71; Under-Sec. of State for Foreign Affairs Sept. 71-74; Amb. to Belgium 74-.
Publ. *The Arab States and the Arab League* (2 vols.) 62.
Embassy of the Arab Republic of Egypt, 2 Avenue Victoria, 1050 Brussels, Belgium.

Khamri, Abdulla Ahmed al; Yemeni diplomatist; b. 2 June 1936.
Director, Nat. Liberation Front, Cairo; mem. NLF Exec. Cttee. until 68; Minister of Information and Culture; now Minister of State for Council Affairs, Personal Rep. of the Pres.
Council of Ministers, Aden, People's Democratic Republic of Yemen.

Khanlari, Parviz, PH.D.; Iranian historian and politician; b. 1913; ed. Teheran Univ. and Univ. of Paris.
Professor of Iranian Linguistics, Teheran Univ. 48-; Ed. *Sokhan* (literary monthly) 44-64, and of its *Scientific Supplement* 61-64; Dep. Minister of Interior 55; Senator 57; Minister of Education 62-64; Co-Founder *Mardom* Party 57; Gen. Sec. Imperial Foundation for Iranian Cultural Studies.
P.O. Box 984, Teheran, Iran.

Khatib, Ahmed al-; Syrian politician; b. 1931, Salkhad, Jabal al-Arab region.
Formerly Head, Syrian Teachers Asscn.; mem. Presidential Council Sept. 65-Feb. 66; Pres. of Syria Nov. 70-Feb. 71; Chair. People's Council Feb.-Dec. 71; Premier Fed. of Arab Repubs. Dec. 71-; mem. Baath Party, elected to Leadership Cttee. May 71.
People's Council, Damascus, Syria.

Khatib, Mohammed Fathalla el-, B.COMM., PH.D.; Egyptian politician; b. 1 Jan. 1927, Gharbiyah; ed. Univs. of Cairo and Edinburgh.
Director of Research and UN sections, Arab States Delegations Office, New York 58-61; Prof. of Comparative Govt., Univ. of Cairo 67-71; Dean of Faculty of Econs. and Political Science 68-71; Minister of Social Affairs May-Sept. 71; Adviser to the Pres. on Home, Econ. and Social

Affairs Sept. 71-72; Sec.-Gen. Arab Socialist Union Governorate of Cairo 71-72; Minister of Foreign Affairs, Fed. of Arab Repubs. Dec. 71-.
Publs. include *Power Politics in the UN* 62, *Local Government in U.A.R.* 64, *Studies in the Government of China* 65, *Studies in Comparative Government* 67, *Introduction to Political Science* 69.
11 Sh. Ibn Zinki-Zamalek, Cairo, Egypt.

Khayyal, Abdullah al; Saudi Arabian diplomatist; b. 1913; ed. Fuad I Univ., Cairo.
Private Sec. to Minister of Foreign Affairs, H.R.H. Prince Faisal 32; Dir.-Gen. of Schools, Eastern Saudi Arabia and Dir. A.H.S.A. Central School 41; Second Sec. Saudi Arabian Legation, Baghdad 43, First Sec. and Chargé d'Affaires 45; Minister to Iraq 47-55; Perm. Del. to UN 55-57; Ambassador to U.S.A. 55-63, concurrently Minister to Mexico 56-60, Ambassador 60-63; Pres. Islamic Center, Washington, D.C. 56-58; Dir. of Public Works 64-.
Department of Public Works, Jeddah, Saudi Arabia.

Khefacha, Mohamed El Hédi, L. ès L.; Tunisian politician; b. 11 Oct. 1916; ed. Coll. Sadiki, Lycée Carnot, Tunis and Faculté de Droit, Algiers.
Called to Bar, Tunis 42; Pres. Union of Young Lawyers of Tunisia 50-56; Gen. Inspector of Customs 56-58; Deputy 59; Sec. of State for Justice 58-66, concurrently Sec. of State for Finance 60-61; Sec. of State for Public Health 66-69, of the Interior 69-70, 71-73, of Public Works and Housing 73-74; Minister of Defence Jan. 74-; mem. Political Office, Destour Socialist Party 69-; Grand Cordon, Order of the Repub. 64, Grand Cordon, Order of Independence 66.
Ministry of Defence, Tunis, Tunisia.

Kheir, Ahmed Mohamed; Sudanese politician; ed. Gordon Memorial Coll., and Khartoum School of Law.
Advocate 44; mem. Sudan del. which negotiated Sudan's future 46; fmr. Vice-Pres. and Pres. of Nat. Cttee. for the Constitution; Minister of Foreign Affairs 58-64, of Mineral Resources 62-64.
Publs. (Arabic) *The Struggle of a Generation, Calamities of the British in the Sudan* (English), *Sudan Appeals to U.N.O.* Khartoum, Sudan.

Khene, Abderrahman, M.D.; Algerian doctor, politician and administrator; b. 6 March 1931; ed. Univ. of Algiers.
Secretary of State, Provisional Govt. of Algeria (G.P.R.A.) 58-60; Dir. of Political Affairs, Ministry of Interior, G.P.R.A. 60-61; Dir. of Cabinet, Ministry of Finances G.P.R.A. 61-62; Pres. of Technical Org. for Exploiting Wealth of Saharan Sub-Soil (l'Organisme Saharien) Sept. 62-Dec. 65; Pres. Electricité et Gaz d'Algérie (E.G.A.) July-Oct. 64; Pres. Industrial Co-operation Org. (O.C.I.) Jan. 66-Aug. 71; Minister of Public Works and Construction 66-70; Sec.-Gen. Org. of the Petroleum Exporting Countries (OPEC) 73-74; Exec. Dir. UN Industrial Devt. Org. (UNIDO) 75-.
United Nations Industrial Development Organization, Lerchenfelderstrasse 1, A-1070 Vienna, Austria.

Khiary, Mahmoud; Tunisian politician and trades union official; b. 1911; ed. Ecole Normale, Tunis.
Teacher 31-55; Sec.-Gen. Tunisian Union of Teachers 41-52; Pres. Gen. Fed. of Tunisian Officials 47-58; fmr. Sec.-Gen., Gen. Union of Tunisian Workers; fmr. Minister of Posts and Telegraphs; fmr. Minister of Agriculture; mem. Nat. Constituent Ass.; Chief, UN Civil Operations in the Congo 61-62; Pres. Dir.-Gen. Soc. Nat. Tunisienne de Cellulose, Soc. Nat. Tunisienne de Papier Alfa 63-72; Pres. Dir.-Gen. Société Nationale de Mise en Valeur du Sud (SONMIVAS) 72-74; Dir.-Gen. Entreprises Gén. des Travaux Publics et de Promotion de l'Habitat 74-.
20 rue du Koweit, Tunis, Tunisia.

Khlefawi, Gen. Abdel Rahman; Syrian army officer and politician; b. 1927, Damascus; ed. schools in Damascus, Military School, Homs.
Representative of Syria, Joint Arab Command, Cairo 64-67; Head, Armoured Forces Admin., Damascus 67-68; Head, Officers' Board, Ministry of Defence 68-70; Minister of the Interior Nov. 70-April 71; Prime Minister 71-72; mem. Regional Command, Baath Party.
c/o Office of the Prime Minister, Damascus, Syria.

Kholi, Hassan Sabri el-; Egyptian diplomatist; b. 25 Feb. 1922; ed. Univ. of Cairo, Mil. and Staff Colls.
Fought in Palestine War 48; Prof., Senior Officer Studies Inst.; opened Infantry School, Syria 57; Dir. Office for Palestine at the Presidency, Office for Public Affairs; Personal Rep. of the Pres. 64-75; has represented Egypt at UN, Arab League and Arab Summit Confs., numerous foreign decorations.
Publs. *The Palestine Case, Sinai, The Policy of the Imperialism and Zionism towards Palestine during the First Half of the Twentieth Century*, and several research papers on Palestine.
c/o The Presidency, Cairo, Egypt.

Khoshkish, Youssof; Iranian banker; b. 1906; ed. Teheran Secondary School and Sorbonne, Paris.
Bank Melli Iran 34-, Asst. Man., Org. Dept. 36-38, Man. Supply Dept. 38-39; Iranian del. Ministry of Finance, Europe 39-40, India 40-44; Vice-Pres. Bank Sepah 45-61; Pres. Bank Melli Iran 61-.
Bank Melli Iran, P.O. Box 41, Khiaban Ferdowsi, Teheran, Iran.

Khosrovani, Khosro, D.SC.; Iranian diplomatist; b. 16 June 1914; ed. Iran and England.
Foreign Service, served Ministry of Foreign Affairs, UN, Washington; later Deputy Minister of Nat. Economy; Chair. Board of Inspectorate N.I.O.C. 63; Ambassador to Turkey 63-65, to U.S.A. 65-67; High Insp. Ministry of Foreign Affairs 67; Pres. Council of Political Planning and Programmes 70; Amb. to Egypt 71-; Order of Homayoun, First Class.
11 Okbah Street, Dokki, Cairo, Egypt.

Khoury, Sheikh Maître Michel, LL.B.; Lebanese businessman and politician; b. 24 Nov. 1926; ed. Univ. St. Joseph, Beirut, Paris Univ. Faculté de Droit, Inst. d'Etudes Politiques and Coll. de France.
Political section, Ministry of Foreign Affairs 46-49; Contributor to *Le Jour* daily 44-; Dir.-Gen. Ets. Derwiche Youssef Haddad 53-; mem. Board Nat. Council of Tourism 62-66, Pres. 64-66; Minister of Defence and of Guidance, Information and Tourism Dec. 65-April 66; Minister of Planning and Tourism 66-68; Middle East Regional Editor *Columbia Journal of World Business*.
rue Michel Chiha, Kantari, Beirut, Lebanon.

Kianpour, Gholamreza, DR.ECON.; Iranian politician; b. 1929, Teheran; ed. Teheran Univ.
Economic Counsellor, Ministry of Finance; Judge, Ministry of Justice; Head of Office of Org., Plan Org., later Dir. of Finance; Dir. Bank Etebarat Sanati; Under-Sec. Ministry of Economy; Head of Admin. High Council; Gov.-Gen. of W. Azarbaijan; Gov.-Gen. of Isfahan; Minister of Information and Tourism April 74-; Taj Second Class, Homayoun First Class, Sepass First Class and several other decorations.
Publs. *Principle of Budget Preparation, Principle of Economies, Industrial Development, Training of Human Resources for Trade and Industry, Development of Economy and Technology, Principle of Banking.*
Ministry of Information and Tourism, Teheran, Iran.

Kikhia, Mansur Rashid; Libyan diplomatist; b. 1 Dec. 1931, Benghazi; ed. Faculty of Law, Univ. of Cairo and Paris.

Joined Diplomatic Service 57; Asst. in Nationality and Consular Affairs Section, Ministry of Foreign Affairs 57, Head, Treaties and Int. Confs. Section 58-60, 62-65; Second Sec. for Consular and Cultural Affairs, Libyan Embassy to France 60-62; Chargé d'Affaires, France Jan.-Aug. 62, Algeria Feb.-Aug. 63; Consul-Gen., Geneva 65-67; mem. Perm. Mission of Libya to UN 67-69; Under-Sec. Ministry of Unity and Foreign Affairs 69-72; Perm. Rep. to UN Feb.-July 72; Minister of Foreign Affairs July 72-73; has attended numerous int. confs., has represented Libyan Govt. at six sessions of UN Gen. Assembly, mem. Perm. Mission to UNESCO.
c/o Ministry of Foreign Affairs, Tripoli, Libya.

Kirk, George Eden, M.A.; American (b. British) author; b. 1911; ed. Cambridge, and Schools of Archaeology Athens and Jerusalem.
Epigraphist with Colt expedition, Palestine 35-38; Staff Officer (Int.) at G.H.Q Middle East Forces 40-45; Instructor Middle East Centre for Arab studies 45-47; M.E. specialist Royal Inst. of International Affairs 47-52; Assoc. Prof. Int. Relations, American Univ. of Beirut 53-57; Lecturer, Harvard Univ. Center for Middle Eastern Studies 57-66; Prof. of History, Univ. of Mass. 66-, Dir. of Graduate Studies in History 70-73.
Publs. *A Short History of the Middle East* 48 (definitive edn. 64), *The Middle East in the War* 52, *The Middle East, 1945-50* 55, *Contemporary Arab Politics* 61; contributed to: *The Military in the Middle East* (ed. Sydney N. Fisher) 63, *Forces of Change in the Middle East* (ed. Maurice M. Roumani) 71.
32 Cosby Ave., Amherst, Mass. 01002, U.S.A.

Kittani, Ismat T.; Iraqi United Nations official; b. 5 April 1929, Amadiya; ed. Knox Coll, Galesburg, Ill.
High School teacher, Iraq; joined Foreign Ministry 52; Attaché, Cairo 54-57; mem. Iraqi mission to UN 57, Acting Perm. Rep. 58-59; Perm. Rep. to European Office of UN 61-64; Chief, Specialized Agencies and Admin. Cttee. of Co-ordination Affairs, Dept. of Econ. and Social Affairs, UN Secr. 64; Sec. Econ. and Social Council 65-67; Principal Officer, later Dir. Exec. Office of Sec.-Gen. of UN 67-69; Deputy to Asst. Sec.-Gen. for Inter-Agency Affairs 69-70; Asst. Sec.-Gen. for Inter-Agency Affairs 71-73; Exec. Asst. to UN Sec.-Gen. Sept. 73-; fmr. del. of Iraq to various int. comms. and confs.; mem. Gov. Board ILO 59; alt. mem. Exec. Board WHO 61.
United Nations, New York, N.Y., U.S.A.

Klibi, Chadli; Tunisian politician.
Secretary of State for Information and Cultural Affairs 61, 64, for Cultural Affairs Nov. 64, also for Information and Guidance 66-69; Minister of Cultural Affairs and Information 69-73; Amb. to Egypt 73-74; Dir. Presidential Office Feb. 74-.
c/o Presidential Palace, Carthage, Tunisia.

Koç, Vehbi; Turkish businessman; b. 1901.
Opened first grocery shop in Ankara 17; formed Koç Trading Corpn. 37, General Elektrik Türk 49, and many other companies; assoc. with numerous major firms in U.S.A. and Europe; Chair. Koç Holding Corpn. 64-; manufactured Turkey's first passenger car (Anadol) 66, second (Murat, under licence from Fiat) 71; Founded Vehbi Koç Foundation 69, Turkish Educ. Foundation 69; Order of Merit (Fed. Repub. of Germany) 74.
Publ. *My Life Story* (in Turkish) 73.
Koç Holding Corporation, Fındıklı, Ankara, Turkey.

Kol, Moshe; Israeli educator and politician; b. 1911, Russia; ed. Hebrew Secondary School, Pinsk and Hebrew Univ. Jerusalem.
Co-Founder Hanoar Hazioni (Zionist Youth) movement in Poland and its Rep. on Cen. Cttee. of Zionist Org. in Poland; came to Israel and joined Hamefales pioneer group in Kfar

Saba 32; Del. to all Zionist Congresses 33-; mem. Histadrut Exec. 41-46; mem. Jewish Agency Exec. and Head of its Youth Aliya Dept. 46-66; mem. Provisional State Council 48, and Chair. of its Foreign Affairs Cttee.; Signatory mem. Declaration of Independence 48; mem. Knesset (Parl.) 49-66; Minister of Devt. and of Tourism 66-69, of Tourism 69-; Chair. Independent Liberal Party; Vice-Pres. Liberal Int. 69-; Co-Founder (in Israel), Oved Hazioni (Zionist Workers) Movement, World Confed. of Gen. Zionists; many Jewish Agency and govt. missions abroad; Hon. Treas. Israel Exploration Soc.
Publs. in Hebrew. *Arichim, Misholim Bezionout, Netivot Bechinouch Uveshikum, Morim Vechaverim, Youth Aliya* (also in English and French).
Ministry of Tourism, 24 King George Street, Jerusalem, Israel.

Kollek, Theodore (Teddy); Israeli politician; b. 1911; ed. Vienna.
Went to Palestine 34; mem. Kibbutz Ein-Gev. 37; with Zionist Youth groups in Europe and U.K. 38-40; Political Dept., Jewish Agency 42-47; Liaison with Jewish Underground in Europe 42-45; mem. Haganah mission to U.S.A. 47-48; Minister Plenipotentiary, Washington 51-52; Dir.-Gen. Prime Minister's Office, including Dept. for Applied Civilian Scientific Research, Bureau of Statistics, Govt. Press and Information Office, the devt. of broadcasting services, est. Israel Govt. Tourist Office, 52-64; Chair. Govt. Tourist Corpn. 56-65; Chair. Israel 10th Anniversary Celebrations; Mayor of Jerusalem 65-; Head of Nuclear Desalination of Water Project 64-66; Chair. Board of Governors, Israel Museum 65-; Rothschild Medal and Bublick Prize 75.
Publs. (with Moshe Pearlman) *Jerusalem: Sacred City of Mankind* 68, *Pilgrims to the Holy Land* 70, and numerous articles.
Municipality of Jerusalem, Jerusalem; Home: 6 Rashba Street, Jerusalem, Israel.

Komodromos, Epaminondas M.; Cypriot politician; b. May 1912, Drousha Village, Paphos District; ed. Ambetios School, Cairo and Athens Univ.
Lawyer 36-68; mem. Paphos School Cttee. 50-53; Minister of Interior and Defence 68-72.
c/o Ministry of Interior, Nicosia, Cyprus.

Koper, Daniş; Turkish politician and businessman; b. 19 Dec. 1908 Diyadin; ed. Ankara Lisesi and Munich Coll. of Technology.
Engineer Water Works Dept. 36-48; Dir. Provincial Bank 51; Gen. Man. Highways Admin. 51-56; Under-Sec. Ministry of Public Works 56-57; Minister of Public Works 60; Chair. Asscn. of Chamber of Engineering and Architecture 58-60; Chair. Turkish Airlines 59-60; Trustee Middle East Technical Univ., Ankara 59-60; mem. Constitutional Assembly 61; Partner Kuyaş Construction Co., and Bormak Ltd. 60-; Chair. Board and Exec. Cttee. Ereğli Iron and Steel Co. 61-68; Gen. Sec. Turkish Atomic Energy Comm. 70-71; Technical Counsellor Yapı ve Kredi Bank 72-; Chair. Board of Dirs. Bayurdirlek İşleri Corpn. 72-; mem. Board of Dirs. Black Sea Copper Works 72-; Chair. Board of Trustees, Middle East Technical Univ. 63-66; Chair. Board of Trustees, Ankara Koleji (High School) 63-68; Trustee, Hacettepe Univ. 70-71; Chevalier, Légion d'Honneur.
Office: 16/4 Gazi Mustafa Kemal Blv., Yenişehir, Ankara; Home: 6 Sokak Nr. 37, Bahçelievler, Ankara, Turkey.

Korutürk, Admiral Fahri S.; Turkish naval officer and diplomatist; b. 1903, Istanbul; ed. Naval Acad. and Naval War Coll.
Joined Navy 20; Naval Attaché, Rome 35-36, Berlin 37-38, Berlin and Stockholm 42-43; Commdr. of Submarine Fleet 47-50; Commdr. of Sea-Going Fleet 53-54; Chief of Intelligence, Armed Forces 54; Commdr. of the Fleet 55;

Commdr.-in-Chief, Straits Area 56; Commdr.-in-Chief of Navy and Commdr. of Allied Forces, Black Sea 57-60; Amb. to U.S.S.R. 60-64, to Spain 64-65; Senator apptd. by Pres. 68; Head Presidential Senate Group 71-73; Pres. of the Repub. 73-.
Office of the President, Ankara, Turkey.

Kotaite, Assad, LL.D.; Lebanese lawyer and aviation official; b 6 Nov. 1924; ed. French Univ. of Beirut, Univ. of Paris, Inst. des Hautes Etudes Internationales, Paris and Acad. of Int. Law, The Hague.
Practising barrister 48-49; Head, Legal Services, Int. Agreements and External Relations, Dir. of Civil Aviation, Ministry of Public Works and Transport 53-56; Rep. to Int. Civil Aviation Org. (ICAO) 56-70, Sec.-Gen. 70-; mem. UN Transport and Communications Comm. 57-59, Chair. 59; Chair. Air Transport Cttee., ICAO 59-62, 65-68; Golden Medal of Merit (Lebanon), Award of Air Law Soc. (Brazil), Gran Cruz del Merito Aeronautico (Spain).
International Civil Aviation Organization, 1000 Sherbrooke Street West, Montreal, Quebec, Canada.

Kouros, Andreas Kyriakou, M.A., PH.D.; Cypriot educationist; b. 6 Nov. 1918; ed. London and Oxford Univs., Int. Inst. of Educ. Planning, Paris.
Teacher 44-53; Insp. of Schools, Ministry of Educ. 53-59, Senior Insp. 59-61; Head Dept. of Primary Educ. 61-68; Head of Educ. Planning 68-70; Dir. of Educ. 70-72, Minister 72-74.
Publs. *The Construction and Validation of a Group Test of Intelligence for Greek Cypriot Children* 56, *Education in Cyprus under the British Administration* 59, *Electra* 68.
1 Souliou Street, Ayios Dhometios, Nicosia, Cyprus.

Kranidiotis, Nicos; Greek-Cypriot scholar and diplomatist; b. 25 Nov. 1911; ed. Pan Cyprian Gymnasium, Cyprus, Athens Univ., and Harvard Univ. Center for Int. Affairs.
Worked as schoolmaster in Cyprus; Dir. of *Hellenic Cyprus* (official political organ of Cyprus Ethnarchy) 49; Gen. Sec. Cyprus Ethnarchy 53-57, Councillor 57-60; Ambassador to Greece 60-, to Yugoslavia 63-, to Italy 64-, to Bulgaria and Romania 70-; Sec. of 2nd and 3rd Cyprus Nat. Assemblies 54, 55; Founder, Dir. and Editor (with others) of *Kypriaka Grammata* (Cyprus Literature), a literary magazine.
Publs. *Chronicles* (short stories) 45, *The Neohellenic Theatre* (essay) 50, *Studies* (poems) 51, *Forms of Myth* (short stories) 54, *The Poet G. Seferis* (essay) 55, *The National Character of the Cyprus Literature* 58, *Cyprus in her Struggle for Freedom* (history) 58, *An Introduction to the Poetry of George Seferis* 64, *Cyprus-Greece* 66, *Cyprus Poetry* 69.
Embassy of Cyprus, 16 Herodotos Street, Athens, Greece; Home: 16 Prometheus Street, Nicosia, Cyprus.

Kubar, Abd al-Majid (*see* Coobar, Abdulmegid).

Kubat, Ferit; Turkish politician; b. 1919, Diyarbakr; ed. American Coll. of Tarsus, Faculty of Law, Istanbul Univ.
Held various posts in local admin. until 64; Gov. of Edirne, Hatay and Muş successively; Under-Sec., Ministry of Foreign Affairs; Minister of the Interior 71-73.
National Assembly, Ankara, Turkey.

Küçük, Fazil, M.D.; Cypriot politician; b. 1906; ed. Istanbul and Lausanne Univs.
Owner and Editor *Halkın Sesi* (daily) 41-60; Leader, Cyprus Turkish Party (now Cyprus Turkish National Union) 43-; Chair. Evcaf High Council 56-60; Vice-Pres. Cyprus 60-73.
P.O. Box 339, Nicosia, Cyprus.

Kudsi, Nazem el, PH.D.; Syrian politician; b. 1906; ed. American Coll., Beirut, Damascus Univ. and Univ. of Geneva.

Barrister in Aleppo 30; Dep. for Aleppo 36, 47, 55; Minister Plenipotentiary, Washington 44-45; Prime Minister and Minister for Foreign Affairs 50; Pres. Council of Ministers 54-57; Leader, Populist Party; held no political office during United Arab Republic régime 58-61; Pres. of the Syrian Arab Republic 61-63, retired 63.
Aleppo, Syria.

Kuneralp, Zeki, DR.IUR.; Turkish diplomatist; b. 5 Oct. 1914; Istanbul; ed. Univ. of Berne.
Entered Diplomatic Service 40; Official, Ministry of Foreign Affairs, Turkey 41-42, 47-49; Attaché to Embassy Bucharest 43-47, Prague 49-52; Del. to NATO (Paris) 52-57; Asst. Sec.-Gen. Diplomatic Service 57-60, Sec.-Gen. 60; Ambassador to Switzerland Sept. 60-64, to U.K. Feb. 64-66; Sec.-Gen. Ministry of Foreign Affairs Aug. 66-69; Amb. to U.K. 69-72, to Spain 72-; Hon. G.C.V.O. 71.
Turkish Embassy, Monte Esquinza 48, Madrid, Spain.

Kurtbek, Col. Seyfi; Turkish army officer; b. 1906; ed. War Academy.
Commissioned Lieut. 23; Mil. expert, Disarmament Confs., Geneva 33; Mil. Attaché, Paris 33; Mil. Expert, Montreux Conf. (Straits) 36; Major, Chief of Operations Army Corps 39; Mil. Attaché, Athens 40; Lt.-Col., Dir. of the Mobilization Section of Gen. Staff, Ankara 44; Col. 48; resgnd. from the Army and elected Democratic Party Deputy for Ankara 50, re-elected 54; Minister of Communications 51-52; Minister of Defence 52-53; arrested 60, released 61; Vice-Pres. Justice Party 61-; Deputy for Sivas 65-; Chair. Parl. Foreign Affairs Comm. 65-; Medal of Independence.
Publs. (in Turkish) *War and Economy, Preparation of the Nation for Defence, Mobilization of Germany, To Arms, Women in National Defence.*
c/o Justice Party, Ankara, Turkey.

Kuwait, H.H. The Ruler of (*see* Sabah, Amir Sabah al Salem al).

Kyprianou, Spyros; Cypriot politician; b. 28 Oct. 1932; ed. City of London Coll. and Gray's Inn.
Qualified as barrister; mem. Cyprus Ethnarchy Secretariat, London 54-59; Cyprus observer at UN 57; headed del. to UN General Assembly 19, 20, 21 sessions; rep. Greek-Cypriot side in negotiations for tri-partite pact between Greece, Turkey and Cyprus 59; Minister of Justice Aug. 60; Minister of Foreign Affairs 60-72; several decorations.
3 Georghiou Tyrimou Street, Nicosia, Cyprus.

L

Labidi, Abdelwahab; Tunisian financier; b. 1929.
Former Gen. Man. Banque de Tunisie; Insp.-Gen. Banque Nat. Agricole de Tunisie; Man. Soc. Tunisienne de Banque; Man. Dir. Nat. Devt. Bank of Niger; Vice-Pres. African Devt. Bank June 69-70, Pres. 70-.
African Development Bank, B.P. 1387 Abidjan, Ivory Coast.

Ladgham, Bahi; Tunisian politician; b. 10 Jan. 1913, Tunis.
Joined Dept. of Interior 33, subsequently moved to Finance Dept.; Sec. of State for the Presidency and Sec. of State for Defence 56-69; Prime Minister of Tunisia 69-70; Chair. Arab Cttee. supervising the ceasefire between Jordanian Govt. and the Palestinian guerrillas in Jordan 70-71; fmr. personal rep. of Pres. Bourguiba; fmr. Sec.-Gen. Destour Socialist Party (fmrly. Néo-Destour Party).
c/o Destour Socialist Party, 10 rue de Rome, Tunis, Tunisia.

Laghzaoui, Mohamed; Moroccan politician; b. 27 Sept. 1906, Fez; ed. Coll. Moulay Idriss, Fez.
Former Minister of Economics; fmr. Director of National Security; Rep. of King Hassan to Algerian leaders Conf.

held by French Govt. 61-62; Dir.-Gen. Office Chérifien des Phosphates and Chief Co-ordinator of State Econ. Enterprises 63-65; Minister of Tourism, Industry and Mines 65; Pres. Afro-Asian Org. for Econ. Co-operation 66; Treas. Democratic Socialist Party (P.S.D.) 64-; Amb. to U.K. 69-71, to France 71-72.
Résidence Laghzaoui, Route de Suissi, Rabat, Morocco.

Lagu, Joseph; Sudanese army officer; b. 21 Nov. 1931; ed. Rumbek Secondary School, Mil. Acad., Omdurman.
Served in Sudanese Army 60-63; joined South Sudan Liberation Movt. 63, Leader SSLM 69; signed peace agreement with Govt. of Sudan March 72; Order of the Two Niles 72.
Publ. *The Anya-Nya—what we fight for* 72.
People's Armed Forces General Headquarters, Khartoum, Sudan.

Lalla Aicha, H.R.H. Princess; Moroccan diplomatist; b. 1930.
Eldest daughter of late King Mohammed V; Ambassador to United Kingdom 65-69, to Italy 69-71; Pres. Moroccan Red Crescent; Grand Cordon of Order of the Throne.
c/o Ministry of Foreign Affairs, Rabat, Morocco.

Landau, Moshe, LL.B.; Israeli judge; b. Danzig 1912; ed. London Univ.
Immigrated 33; called to Palestine Bar 37, Magistrate of Haifa 40, District Court Judge, Haifa 48, Justice Supreme Court, Jerusalem 53-.
The Supreme Court, Jerusalem, Israel.

Laraki, Moulay Ahmed, M.D.; Moroccan physician and diplomatist; b. 15 Oct. 1931, Casablanca; ed. Univ. of Paris.
With Ministry of Foreign Affairs 56-57; Perm. Rep. to UN 57-58; Head of Hospital Services, Casablanca 56-61; Ambassador to Spain 61-65, to U.S.A., concurrently accred. to Mexico, Canada and Venezuela 65-67; Minister of Foreign Affairs 67-69, April 74-; Prime Minister 69-71.
Ministry of Foreign Affairs, Rabat, Morocco.

Laskov, Haim; Israeli army officer; b. 4 April 1919; ed. Reali High School Haifa and St. Anthony's Coll. Oxford.
Guide to British Army units in Palestine 36-39; served with British Army (major) 41-46; Commdr. of Israel forces in capture of Nazareth and Upper Galilee 48; G.O.C. Training Command and Dir. Mil. Training 48-51; Air Officer Commanding, Israel Air Force 51-53; Dep. Chief of Staff and Dir. of Operations 55; Commdr. Armoured Forces, Sinai Campaign 56; G.O.C. Southern Command 57-58; Chief of Staff, Israel Defence Force 58-60; Dir.-Gen. Israel Ports Authority 61-70; Ombudsman to IDF 72-; mem. Inquiry Comm. into Yom Kippur War 73.
75 Einstein St., Tel-Aviv, Israel.

Lasky, Ahmed; Moroccan civil engineer and politician; b. 30 April 1932; ed. Casablanca High School, Ecole spéciale des travaux publics and Ecole nationale des ponts et chaussées, Paris.
Public Works Engineer, Casablanca 56; Chief Engineer Agadir Region 59; Chief Engineer Casablanca Region 60-62; Dir. Casablanca Harbour 62-65; Minister of Public Works and Communications 65-67; Chair. Royal Air Maroc 67-; Minister of Higher, Secondary and Technical Educ. 71-72; Officier, Ordre du Trône (Morocco), Ordre de George I (Greece), Commdr. Ordre de l'Istiqlal (Tunisia), Ordre Egyptien, Ordre Iranien.
Publs. numerous technical pamphlets about bridges and harbours in French and foreign magazines.
c/o Royal Air Maroc, Aéroport International Casablanca, Nouassenr; and 4 allée Montsouris, Casablanca, Morocco.

Lavon, Pinchas; Israeli politician; b. Poland 1904; ed. Lwów Univ.
Co-founder Gordonia (Zionist Youth Organization in Poland) 24; settled in Palestine 29; Sec. Mapai 35-37;

Exec. Cttee. Mapai and Histadrut 42-; mem. Knesset 49-; Minister of Agriculture 50-51; Minister of Defence 51-54; Minister without portfolio 54-55; Chair. Solel Boneh Ltd.; mem. Zionist Actions Cttee.; Sec.-Gen. Histadrut (Gen. Fed. of Labour in Israel) 56-61; Editor *Min Hayesod* 62-.
Publ. *Yesodot* (Foundation).
62 La Guardia Street, Tel-Aviv, Israel.

Lawzi, Ahmed Abdel Kareem al-; Jordanian politician; b. 1925, Jubeiha, nr. Amman; ed. Teachers' Training Coll., Baghdad, Iraq.
Teacher, 50-53; Asst. to Chief of Royal Protocol 53-56; Head of Ceremonies, Ministry of Foreign Affairs 57; mem. Parl. 61-62, 62-63; Asst. to Chief of Royal Court 63-64; Minister of State, Prime Minister's Office 64-65; mem. Senate 65; Minister of the Interior for Municipal and Rural Affairs 67; mem. Senate 67; Minister of Finance 70-71; Prime Minister 71-73; various Jordanian and foreign decorations.
The Senate, Amman, Jordan.

Ledwidge, Sir William Bernard John, K.C.M.G., M.A., A.M.; British diplomat; b. 9 Nov. 1915, London; ed. King's Coll., Cambridge Univ. and Princeton Univ.
Commonwealth Fund Fellow, Princeton Univ. 37-39; Mil. Service, H.M. Forces 40-46; First Sec., Foreign Office 48-49; British Consul, St. Louis, U.S.A. 49-52; First Sec., Kabul 52-56; Political Adviser, British Mil. Govt., Berlin 56-61; Counsellor, Foreign Office 61-65; Minister, U.K. Embassy, Paris 65-69; Amb. to Finland 69-72, to Israel 72-; C.M.G. 60.
54 rue de Bourgogne, Paris 7e, France; British Embassy, Tel-Aviv, Israel.
Telephone: 705-8026 (Home).

Lee, James E.; American oil executive; b. 13 Dec. 1921, Kiln, Mississippi; ed. Louisiana Polytechnic Inst., Ruston.
Gulf Oil Corpn. 42-, served in various engineering and supervisory posts 42-56; Project Adviser to Filoil Refinery Corpn., Manila 59; Area Rep. Manila, Exec. Vice-Pres., Gen. Man. Orient Gulf Oil Co. 62, Vice-Pres. of Refining, Pacific Gulf Oil Ltd., Japan 63; Area Rep. and Co-ordinator for Far East 64; Man. Dir. Kuwait, Kuwait Oil Co. 66; Pres. Gulf Oil Co. (Eastern Hemisphere) 69; Exec. Vice-Pres. Gulf Oil Corpn. 72, Pres., Dir. 73-; Trustee Carnegie-Mellon Univ. 73.
Gulf Oil Corporation, Gulf Building, Pittsburgh, Pa. 15230, U.S.A.

Léger, Jacques; Haitian international official; b. Port-au-Prince; ed. Faculty of Law, Univ. of Haiti.
Attached to Protocol Sec., Dept. of State 34-35; Sec. to Sec. of State for Foreign Affairs 35-36; service with legation in Venezuela; Dir. Haiti Service of Inter-American Affairs; Chargé d'Affaires, Venezuela 44-47; Amb. to Cuba 47-48, to Argentina and Brazil 48-50; Sec. of State for Foreign Affairs 50-51; Amb. to U.S.A. and Canada 52-56; Perm. Rep. to UN 56-57; research activities, N.Y. Public Library and Library of Congress 57-59; translator 59-63; UNDP Regional Rep., Ivory Coast 64-67, Democratic Repub. of Congo (now Zaire) 67-69, N.W. Africa 69-72, Kuwait 72-; Grand Officer, Légion d'Honneur, and other decorations.
United Nations Development Programme, P.O. Box 2193, Kuwait City, Kuwait.

Lehmann, Ernst, DR.RER.POL.; Israeli banker; b. 29 April 1902; ed. Berlin and Munich Univs.
Worked for several banks in Germany 24-35; emigrated to Palestine, apptd. Man. The Gen. Mortgage Bank of Palestine Ltd. 35; Man. Issue Dept., Anglo-Israel Bank Ltd. (now Bank Leumi le-Israel) dealt with issue of currency of Israel and admin. of Govt. Loans 48; Chair. Board of Dirs., Bank Leumi le-Israel B.M. 70-73, 74-, Bank Leumi Le-Israel (Schweiz), Bank Leumi Le-Israel (France), Migdal-Binyan Insurance Co. Ltd., Africa-Israel

Investment Ltd., Tel-Aviv Stock Exchange Ltd., Ihud Insurance Agencies Ltd.; mem. Board of Dirs. Bank Leumi (U.K.); Pres. Asscn. of Banks in Israel 70-; mem. Advisory Council, Advisory Cttee. Bank of Israel; Chair. Council Otzar Hityashvuth Hayehudim; Chair. United Israel Appeal.
Publs. various articles on financial and currency problems.
23 Benjamin Street, 52 512 Ramat-Gan, Israel.

Levanon, Chaim; Israeli politician; b. 25 March 1899; ed. Cracow Univ.
Went to Palestine 27; mem. Jewish Agency Exec.; Mayor Tel-Aviv-Jaffa 53-59; Chair. Exec. Council, Gen. Zionist Party (now Liberal Party) 53; Founder Tel-Aviv Univ.; Initiator, Freddy Mann Auditorium; Founder Havazelet Hasharon Settlement, Sharon.
18 Dubnov Street, Tel-Aviv, Israel.

Levinson, Jacob; Israeli banker; b. 1932; ed. Hebrew Univ., Jerusalem.
Member Kibbutz Rosh Hanikra 49-61; fmr. Sec. Hatnu'ah Hame'uhedet (United Youth Movement); fmr. Head Econ. Dept., Hevrat Ovdim (Gen. Co-operative Asscn. of Labour); now Chair. Board of Management, Bank Hapoalim B.M.; mem. Board of Management, Hevrat Ovdim, Advisory Board, Bank of Israel.
Bank Hapoalim B.M., 50 Rothschild Boulevard, Tel-Aviv; Home: Bar Kokhba 38, Ramat Gan, Israel.

Lewis, Bernard, B.A., PH.D., F.B.A., F.R.HIST.S.; British university professor; b. 31 May 1916; ed. Univs. of London and Paris.
Lecturer in Islamic History, School of Oriental Studies, Univ. of London 38; served R.A.C. and Intelligence Corps 40-41; attached to Foreign Office 41-45; Prof. of History of the Near and Middle East, Univ. of London 49-74; Cleveland E. Dodge Prof. of Near Eastern Studies, Princeton Univ. 74-, Long-term mem. School of Social Science, Inst. for Advanced Study 74-; Visiting Prof. of History, Univ. of California at Los Angeles 55-56; Columbia Univ. 60; Indiana Univ. 63, Princeton Univ. 64, Inst. for Advanced Study 69; Foreign mem. American Philosophical Soc.; Corresp. Fellow Inst. d'Egypte, Cairo; hon. mem. Turkish Historical Soc.
Publs. *The Origins of Isma'ilism* 40, *Turkey Today* 40, *British Contributions to Arabic Studies* 41, *Handbook of Diplomatic and Political Arabic* 47, *Land of Enchanters* (Editor) 48, *The Arabs in History* 50 (revised edns. 58, 64, 66, 70), *Notes and Documents from the Turkish Archives* 52, *The Kingly Crown* 61, *The Emergence of Modern Turkey* 61 (revised edn. 68), *Historians of the Middle East* (ed. with P. M. Holt) 62, 64, *Istanbul and the Civilization of the Ottoman Empire* 63, 68, *The Middle East and the West* 64, 68, *The Assassins* 67, *Race and Colour in Islam* 71, Co-editor *Encyclopaedia of Islam* 56-, *Cambridge History of Islam* 70, *Islam in History: Ideas, Men and Events in the Middle East* 73; *Islam from the Prophet Muhammad to the Capture of Constantinople* (2 vols.) 74, *History Remembered, Recovered, Invented* 75.
110 Jones Hall, Princeton University, Princeton, N.J. 08540, U.S.A.

Lifson, Shneior, PH.D.; Israeli scientist; b. 18 March 1914, Tel-Aviv; ed. Hebrew Univ.
Member of kibbutz 32-43; served in Science Unit, Israel Defence Forces 48-49; Weizmann Inst. of Science, attached to Polymer Dept. 49, Chair. Scientific Council 61-63, Head Chemical Physics Dept. 63-, Science Dir. 63-67; Rector Everyman's Univ., Israel 74; mem. Israel Science Teaching Center, Comm. of Molecular Biophysics of Int. Union of Pure and Applied Biophysics, European Molecular Biology Org., Advisory Board *Biopolymers* and Editorial Board

Journal of Statistical Physics (U.S.A.); Weizmann Prize 58, Israel Prize 69.
Publs. numerous scientific papers.
15 Neve Weizmann, Rehovot, Israel.

Liljestrand, Major-Gen. Bengt T:son, M.A., DIPL.C.E.I.; Swedish army officer; b. 26 Feb. 1919, Stockholm; ed. Uppsala Univ., Centre d'Etudes Industrielles, Geneva and Inst. Univ. de Hautes Etudes Internationales, Geneva.
Instructor, Royal Nat. Defence Coll. 60-62; Co-ordination Office, Defence Dept. 62-63; Defence Staff, Org. & Total Defence Section 64-66; Commdr. Boden Artillery Regt. 68-69; Chief of Staff, Western Region 69-73; Dir., Gen. Staff Coll. of Armed Forces 73-74; Chief of Staff UN Truce Supervision Org. in Palestine April 74-; Commdr. 1st Class Royal Swedish Order of the Sword; Kt. Finnish Order of Freedom.
Government House, Jerusalem; UNTSO, P.O. Box 490, Jerusalem, Israel.

Lloyd, Seton, C.B.E., M.A., F.B.A., F.S.A., A.R.I.B.A.; British archaeologist; b. 30 May 1902; ed. Uppingham and Architectural Asscn.
Asst. to Sir Edwin Lutyens, P.R.A. 27-28; excavated for Egypt Exploration Society, Egypt 29-30, for Oriental Inst., Univ. of Chicago in Iraq 30-37, for Univ. of Liverpool in Turkey 37-39; Technical Adviser, Govt. of Iraq, Directorate-Gen. of Antiquities 39-49; Dir. British Inst. of Archaeology in Ankara 49-61, Hon. Sec. 64-74, Pres. 74-; Prof. Emer. of Western Asiatic Archaeology, Univ. of London 62-69; Hon. M.A. (Edinburgh).
Publs. *Mesopotamia* 34, *Sennacherib's Aqueduct at Jerwan* 35, *The Gimilsin Temple* 40, *Presargonid Temples* 42, *Ruined Cities of Iraq* 42, *Twin Rivers* 43, *Foundations in the Dust* 48, *Early Anatolia* 56, *Alanya-Ala'iyya* 58, *Art of the Ancient Near East, Beycesultan* 62, *Mounds of the Near East* 63, *Highland Peoples of Early Anatolia* 67.
Woolstone Lodge, Faringdon, Oxon., England.

Logali, Hilary Nyigilo Paul; Sudanese politician; b. 1931, Juba, Equatoria Province; ed. Khartoum Univ., Yale Univ.
Official with Ministry of Finance; Sec.-Gen. Southern Front 64-; Minister of Public Works, then of Communications 65; Minister of Labour and Co-operatives 67-69; fmr. Man. Dir. Bata Nationalized Corpn.; apptd. to rank of Minister 71-; mem. for Finance, Econ. Planning and Agriculture, High Exec. Council for the Southern Region 72-73, for Finance and Econ. Dec. 73-.
High Executive Council for the Southern Region, Juba, Sudan.

Loizides, Andreas M.; Cypriot accountant and politician; b. 1932, Limassol; ed. Limassol Greek Gymnasium, and studied as a chartered accountant, Scotland.
Qualified as chartered accountant, Scotland 57; later partner in firms Metaxas, Christofides, Loizides and Scottis, and Touche Ross & Co.; founder mem. Inst. of Certified Public Accountants of Cyprus, later Pres.; mem. Council of Cyprus Employers' Consultative Asscn. 65-69; mem. Board Central Bank of Cyprus 68-70; Minister of Commerce and Industry July 70-72.
c/o Ministry of Commerce and Industry, Nicosia, Cyprus.

Loombe, Claude Evan, C.M.G.; British banker; b. 9 Aug. 1905.
Banking posts in Ceylon, India and China 32-41; Ministry of Finance, Iraq Govt. 41-45; with Bank of England 45-65, latterly as Adviser to Govs.; Chair. British Bank of the Middle East 67-74, Dir. 74-; mem. Currency Boards Jordan 48-65, Sudan 56-60, Kuwait 60-69, Libyan Currency Comm. 52-56; Order of Al-Rafidain, 4th Class (Iraq) 46, Order of Independence, 2nd Class 61, and Order of Jordanian Star, 1st Class 65.
64 Shepherds Way, Liphook, Hampshire, England.

Lourie, Arthur, M.A., LL.B.; Israeli diplomatist; b. South Africa 10 March 1903; ed. Univs. of Cambridge and Cape Town, and Harvard Univ.
In legal practice, also lecturer in Law, Witwatersrand Univ. 27-32; Political Sec. to Jewish Agency for Palestine, London 33; fmr. Dir. UN Office of the Jewish Agency, New York; liaison officer with Anglo-American Cttee. of Enquiry, Palestine 46; promoted to Minister Plenipotentiary and Envoy Extraordinary 50; fmr. Consul-Gen. of Israel in New York and Deputy Rep. of Israel to UN; Asst. Dir.-Gen. Ministry of Foreign Affairs, Jerusalem 54-57; Amb. to Canada 57-59, to U.K. 60-65; Chair. Israeli Del. to XIV Session UN; Deputy Dir.-Gen. Ministry of Foreign Affairs 65-73; Political Adviser to Minister of Foreign Affairs 72-75.
Ministry of Foreign Affairs, Jerusalem, Israel.

Luce, Sir William Henry Tucker, G.B.E., K.C.M.G.; British overseas administrator; b. 25 Aug. 1907; ed. Clifton Coll. and Christ's Coll. Cambridge.
Joined Sudan Political Service 30; Private Sec. to Gov.-Gen. 41-47, Deputy Gov. Equatoria Province 50-51, Gov. of Blue Nile Province and Dir. Sudan Gezira Board 51-53, Adviser to Gov.-Gen. on Constitutional and External Affairs 53-56; Gov. and C.-in-C. Aden 56-60, Political Resident, Persian Gulf 61-66; Dir. Eastern Bank 66-70, Tilbury Overseas Contractors and Gray, Mackenzie 67-70; Chair. Anglo-Arab Asscn. 68-70, Inchcape and Standard and Chartered Banking Group 73-; Special Rep. of U.K. to Persian Gulf States 70-72; Dir. Chartered Bank and Gray, Mackenzie 72-; Chair. Oryx Investments 74-.
Brook House, Fovant, Salisbury, Wiltshire, England.

Luqman, Ali Muhammad Ali, B.A.; Yemeni journalist, poet and politician; b. 6 Aug. 1918; ed. Univ. of Aligarh, India, and American Univ., Cairo.
Editor *Fatat-ul-Jezirah* (Arabic daily) 47-62, *Al Qalam al Adani* (Arabic weekly) 53-63, *Al Akhbar* (Arabic daily) 63-67; mem. Legislative Council, Aden 58-65; Trustee, Aden Port Trust, Aden 59-64; Sec. Aden Asscn. 49-58; Sec., Aden People's Congress, Aden 60-65; Aden Rep., Commonwealth Parl. Conf., London 61, Jamaica 64; Minister for Civil Aviation, Fed. of S. Arabia 64-65; Chair. Aden Electricity Corpn. 66-; Dir. Aden Press Agency 65-.
Publs. Poetry: *Alwatr Almaghmoor* 44, *Ashjan Fil Lail* 45, *Ala Rimal Sirah, Annat Shaab, Layali Ghareeb, Hadeer al Qafilah;* Poetical Drama: *Pygmalion, Ad Dhil Almanshood, Qais Laila, Al Adl al Mafqood, Samraa al Arab; Fatat-ul-Jezirah* (English) 48; Political: *Self Government* 49.
News House, Holkat Road, P.O. Box 435, Crater, Aden, People's Democratic Republic of Yemen.

Luqman, Muhammad Ali Ibrahim; Yemeni lawyer and journalist; b. 1898; ed. Aden and India.
Man. Clayton Ghaleb and Co. Ltd. 18-19; Man. English Pharmacy 21-22; Headmaster Govt. School Aden 24-28; Founder Arab Literary Club 24-30; Man. A. Besse (British Somaliland Branches) 32-34; Pres. Arab Reform Club 30-35, etc.; Pres. Poor Boys' Asscn.; Pleader of the Supreme Court Aden Colony; Ed. *Fatat-ul-Jezirah Newspaper* 40-; Minister of Civil Aviation 64-65; Sec.-Gen. People's Congress Party; Adviser to Aden Cultural Council; mem. Township Authority Exec. Cttee.
Publs. *Springs of European Progress* 33, *The British Nation* 40, *Saeed* 40, *Ardh Adhhaher* 45, *Kamla Devi* 47, *The French Revolution* 48, *Lahej Constitution* 52, *Aden Needs Self-Government* 53, *The Story of the Yemen Revolution* (joint editor) 62.
Esplanade Road, Crater, Aden, People's Democratic Republic of Yemen.

Lutfi, Ashraf Taufiq, B.A.; Kuwaiti petroleum consultant; b. 1 Jan. 1919; ed. Scots Coll., Safad, Palestine.
Teacher in elementary and secondary schools 38-46;

Welfare Officer 46-48; Sec. to State Sec. in Govt. Secr. 48-55, Asst. Sec. of State 55-61; Dir. of Office of Amir of Kuwait 61-64; Adviser on Oil Affairs, Ministry of Finance and Oil 64, 67-69; Sec.-Gen. Org. of Petroleum Exporting Countries (OPEC) 65-67; mem. Board Kuwait Nat. Petroleum Co. 61-71; Chair. Board Kuwait Aviation Fuelling Co. 62-71; Assoc. Dir. Petrolog Int., Beirut; retd.
Publs. *Arab Oil: A Plan for the Future* 60, *OPEC Oil: A Review of its Problems* 66.
79 Ulm/Donau, Gartenweg 3, Federal Republic of Germany.

M

Ma'ayani, Ami; Israeli composer; b. 1936, Tel-Aviv; ed. Tel-Aviv Univ., Haifa Technion and Columbia Univ., New York.
Studied music with Paul Ben-Haim and Prof. Vladimir Ussachevsky; Chair. League of Composers of Israel; Musical Dir. and Conductor of Nat. Youth Orchestra.
Works include: *Toccata for Harp* 59-60, *Concerto for Harp and Orchestra No. 1* 60, *Maquamat for Harp* 60, *Music for Strings* 62, *Teamin* 64, *Electronic Music* 64-65, *Concerto for Percussion and Eight Wind Instruments* 66, *Symphonic Concerto for Harp and Orchestra* 66, *Regalim* 66, *Concerto for Violin and Orchestra* 67, *Concerto for Violoncello and Orchestra* 67, *Concerto for Two Pianos and Orchestra* 69, *Qumran-Symphonic Metaphor* 70, *The War of the Sons of Light* (opera-oratorio in one act for solos, chorus, dancers and orchestra), chamber music, songs, etc.
8 Nahum Street, Tel-Aviv, Israel.

Mabrouk, Ezzidin Al-, LL.B., LL.M.; Libyan politician; b. 28 May 1932; ed. Cairo Univ. and Univ. Coll., London.
Public Prosecutor, Tripoli 56; subsequently Judge, Summary Court, Tripoli, Pres. Tripoli Court and Counsellor of Supreme Appeal Court; Senior Legal Adviser, Org. of Petroleum Exporting Countries (OPEC); Minister of Petroleum, Libya 70-.
Ministry of Petroleum, P.O. Box 256, Tripoli, Libya.

McDougall, James Forsyth; New Zealand international civil servant; b. 3 Oct. 1918; ed. Otago Univ.
Member of staff, Auckland Univ. 46-50, Educ. Dept., UNESCO, Paris 51-68; Assoc. Sec. Nat. Educ. Comm., Pakistan 59, Educ. Comm., India 64-66; Regional Dir. UNICEF, Eastern Mediterranean 68-.
Publs. various UNESCO publs. on education 53-64.
UNICEF, P.O. Box 5902, Beirut, Lebanon.

Mackenzie, Alfred H., M.A., B.A. (CANTAB.); Canadian United Nations official; ed. Cambridge and Toronto Univs.
War Service 40-46, Officer in Canadian Army; Prof. of Languages, Khaki Univ. 46; Asst. Sales Man. De La Rue Insulation 46-47; Co-Dir. United Plastics and Chemicals 47-48; Textile Firm Rep. for Cen. and S. America 48-50; joined UN, Head of UNESCO Latin America Desk 50-57; Regional Rep. for Cen. America, UN Technical Assistance Board 58-62, Resident Rep., Philippines 62-65; Resident Rep. UN Devt. Programme (UNDP), Morocco 65-69, Cyprus 69-73, Beirut, Lebanon 73-.
United Nations Development Programme, P.O. Box 3216, Beirut, Lebanon.

Macki, Ahmed al-Nabi; Omani diplomatist; b. 17 Dec. 1939, Muscat; ed. Cairo and Paris.
Member, Oman Del. to UNESCO 69-70; Dir. of Offices of Prime Minister and Minister of Foreign Affairs 70-71; First Perm. Rep. of Oman to UN 71-72; Under-Sec. Ministry of Foreign Affairs 72-73; Perm. Rep. to UN Nov. 73-, Amb. to U.S.A. Nov. 73-.
Permanent Mission of Oman to the United Nations, 605 Third Avenue, Room 3304, New York, N.Y. 10616, U.S.A.

Maghrabi, Mahmoud Soliman; Libyan politician; b. 1935; ed. George Washington Univ., U.S.A.
Helped to organize strikes of port workers June 67, for which he was sentenced to four years imprisonment and deprived of Libyan nationality; released Aug. 69; following the coup of Sept. 69 became Prime Minister, Minister of Finance and Agriculture, and of Agricultural Reform; dismissed from the Govt. 70; Perm. Rep. to UN 71-72; Amb. to U.K. 73-.
Embassy of Libyan Arab Republic, 58 Prince's Gate, London, SW7 2PW, England.

Maghur, Kamel Hassan; Libyan diplomatist; b. 1 Jan. 1935, Tripoli; ed. univs. of Cairo, Paris and Grenoble.
Assistant Counsellor, Admin. of Legislation, Tripoli 59-60; Counsellor, Court of Cassation and Deputy, Dept. of Casuistry and Legislation 60-69; Counsellor, Supreme Court 69-71; Perm. Rep. to UN 72-.
Permanent Mission of Libya to the United Nations, 866 United Nations Plaza, New York, N.Y. 10017, U.S.A.

Maguid, Yahya Abdel, C.ENG., A.M.I.C.E.; Sudanese politician; b. 7 Oct. 1925, Omdurman; ed. Gordon Memorial Coll. and Imperial Coll., London.
Received practical training in construction of irrigation projects with British companies specializing in this field; held various posts in Ministry of Irrigation, rising to Under-Sec. Sept. 69; part-time lecturer, Univ. of Khartoum; Minister of Irrigation and Hydro-electric Power 71; now Minister of State for Irrigation, Agriculture, Food and Natural Resources; mem. Int. Comm. for Hydraulic Law.
Ministry of Irrigation, Khartoum, Sudan.

Mahdavi, Fereidun, PH.D.; Iranian economist; b. 1933; ed. Hamburg Univ.
Financial and Econ. Adviser, Housing Org.; Economist Econs. Dept.; staff mem. Investment and Public Relations Dept.; Man. Econs. Dept. Asst. to Man. Dir., Industrial and Mining Devt. Bank of Iran, later Man. Dir. IMDBI; Minister of Trade April 74-.
Ministry of Trade, Teheran, Iran.

Mahdi, Saadik El (Great grandson of Imam Abdul-Rahman El-Madhi); Sudanese politician; b. 1936; ed. Comboni Coll., Khartoum and St. John's Coll., Oxford.
Son of the late Siddik El Mahdi; Leader, Umma Mahdist Party 61; Prime Minister 66-67; arrested on a charge of high treason 69; exiled April 70; returned to Sudan and arrested Feb. 72; released May 73.
Publ. *Problems of the South Sudan.*
Khartoum, Sudan.

Mahdi al Tajir, Mohamed; Dubai administrator; b. 26 Dec. 1931; ed. Bahrain Govt. School and Preston Grammar School, Lancs., England.
Department of Port and Customs, Govt. of Bahrain, Dir. 55-63; Dir. Dept. of His Highness the Ruler's Affairs and Petroleum Affairs March 63-; Dir. Nat. Bank of Dubai Ltd. 63-; Dir. Dubai Petroleum Co. April 63-; Chair. Dubai Nat. Air Travel Agency Jan. 66-; Dir. Qatar-Dubai Currency Board Oct. 66-; Chair. South Eastern Dubai Drilling Co. April 68-; Amb. of the United Arab Emirates to U.K. 72-; Dir. Dubai Dry Dock Co. 73-; Hon. Citizen of State of Texas, U.S.A. 63.
Department of H.H. The Ruler's Affairs and Petroleum Affairs, P.O. Box 207, Dubai; and Embassy of the United Arab Emirates, 30 Prince's Gate, London, S.W.7, England.

Mahfouz, Naguib; Egyptian author; b. 11 Dec. 1911; ed. University of Cairo.
Civil servant 34-, successively with Univ. of Cairo, Ministry of Waqfs, Dept. of Arts and Censorship Board; fmr. Dir.-Gen., now Adviser, Cinema Org. of Egypt; contributor to *Al-Ahram*; State Prize for 1st volume of *Bein el Kasrein* 57.

Publs. *Whisper of Madness* 38, *Play of Destiny* 39, *Radobis* 43, *Struggle of Tayiba* 44, *New Cairo* 45, *Khan el Khalil* 46, *Zuqaq el Madaq* 47, *The Mirage* 48, *Beginning and End* 49, *Bein el Kasrein* (trilogy) 52, *Children of our Quarter* 59, *Quails and Autumn* 62, *The Road* 64, *The Beggar* 65, *Small-talk on the Nile* 66, *Thief and Dogs, God's World, Sous L'Ombrelle* 69.
c/o Al-Ahram, Gala'a Street, Cairo, Egypt.

Mahgoub, Mansour; Sudanese accountant and politician; b. 1912, El Kowa; ed. Gordon Memorial Coll.
Joined Dept. of Finance 35; trained with various companies in England 50-51; Inspector, Auditory Dept., Sudan Dec. 51-Jan. 54; Asst. Dir. of Accounts, Ministry of Finance Jan. 54-March 55; Under-Sec. for Internal and Monetary Affairs March 55-58; Under-Sec. Ministry of Commerce, Industry and Supply 58, retd. 64; joined Sudan Commercial Bank as Asst. Dir. 64; Minister of the Treasury May 69-June 70; Minister of Economy, Trade and Supplies June 70-72.
c/o Ministry of Economy, Trade and Supplies, Khartoum, Sudan.

Mahgoub, Mohammed Ahmed; Sudanese lawyer and politician; b. 1908; ed. Gordon Coll. and Khartoum School of Law.
Qualified as an architect and lawyer; practising lawyer; mem. Legislative Assembly 48-54; accompanied Umma Party Del. to Lake Success 47; mem. Constitution Amendment Comm.; non-party candidate in Gen. Election 54; Leader of the Opposition 54-56; Minister of Foreign Affairs 56-58; practising solicitor 58-64; Minister of Foreign Affairs 64-Feb. 65; Prime Minister 65-66; Prime Minister and Minister of Foreign Affairs 67-68; Prime Minister and Minister of Defence 68-69.
Publs. *Democracy on Trial*, and several vols. of poetry (in Arabic).
60c Prince's Gate, Exhibition Road, London, S.W.7, England.

Mahmoud Aly, Dr. Abdel Halem; Egyptian religious leader; b. May 1910, Belbees, Sharkia; ed. Al-Azhar schools, Al-Azhar Univ., Sorbonne, Paris.
Professor of Philosophy, Al-Azhar Univ. 41-50, of Psychology 51-64; Dean Coll. of Religion 64-68; Sec.-Gen. Islamic Research Acad. 68-70; Under-Sec. of Al-Azhar 70-71; Minister of Al-Azhar Affairs 71-73; Grand Sheikh of Al-Azhar 73-.
Publs. several books on Islamic religion and Arabic scholars.
Office of the Grand Sheikh, Al-Azhar Administration, Cairo, Egypt.

Mahroug, Smail; Algerian economist; b. 21 Oct. 1926, Bougaa; ed. Univ. of Paris.
In Morocco 53-62, active in Front de Libération Nationale (FLN), also Dir. of Planning, Moroccan Govt.; returned to Algeria, Chef de Cabinet of Head of Econ. Affairs, Provisional Govt. 62; Econ. Counsellor to Pres. 63-70; Dir.-Gen. Caisse Algérienne de Développement 63-65; Dir.-Gen. Ministry of Finance 65-66; Minister of Finance 70-; Chair. Group of 24, IMF 74.
Ministère des Finances, Algiers, Algeria.

Majdalani, Nassim Mikail; Lebanese banker and politician; b. 1912, Beirut; ed. American Univ. of Beirut and Université de Lyon.
Barrister 37-44; Deputy for Beirut 57, 60, 64; Vice-Pres. of Council of Ministers and Minister of Justice 60-61, 64-65; mem. of Admin. Council of Bank N. Majdalani, Beirut; Minister of Economy 68-69; Minister of Foreign Affairs 69-71; Deputy Speaker, Chamber of Deputies Oct. 71-; Grand Cordon of Order of Tunisia; Medal of Order of St. Vladimir.
Chamber of Deputies, Beirut; Home: Rue Omar Ben Khattab, Beirut, Lebanon.

Majid, Abdul, PH.D.; Afghan diplomatist; b. 14 July 1914; ed. Cornell Univ. and Univ. of California (Berkeley).
Member Afghan Inst. of Bacteriology 41, Dir. 41-42; Prof. of Biology and Physiology, Kabul Univ. 40-46, Pres. of Univ. 46-48; Minister of Public Health 48-50; Minister of Education 50-56; Amb. to Japan 56-63, to U.S.A. 63-67, to U.K. 67-70; Minister of Justice 73-; Leader of Afghan del. to UN 66; Order of Educ. First Class 56, Sardar-i Ali 59, A. Haas Award (Univ. of Calif.) 66.
Ministry of Justice, Kabul, Afghanistan.

Majidi, Abdol-Majid, PH.D.; Iranian politician and lawyer; b. 11 Jan. 1929; ed. Teheran, Paris, Harvard and Illinois Univs.
Held posts in Export Devt. Bank and in Plan Org.; Head of Budget Bureau of Plan Org. 59-60; Financial and Admin. Asst. Man. Dir. of Plan Org. 62-64; Head of Budget Bureau formed in 1964; Deputy Prime Minister, Head of Cen. Budget Bureau, Plan Org. 66; Minister of Agricultural Products and Consumer Goods 67-68, of Labour and Social Affairs 68-73, of State in charge of Plan and Budget Org. 73-; mem. Arts and Culture High Council 68; Sec.-Gen. Red Lion and Sun Soc.
Plan and Budget Organization, Avenue Daneshkhadeh, Teheran, Iran.

Makarios III, Archbishop; Cypriot ecclesiastic and statesman; b. 13 Aug. 1913, Panayia, Paphos District; ed. Pancyprian Gymnasium, Nicosia, Theological Coll. of Athens Univ. and School of Theology, Boston Univ.
Ordained Deacon and Priest, Greek Orthodox Church 38; studied in Greece 38-43; mem. teaching staff Kykkos Abbey 43-46; ordained Archimandrite 46; studied in U.S.A. supported by World Council of Churches Fellowship 46-48; Bishop of Kitium 48-50; Archbishop of Cyprus and Ethnarch 50-; Cypriot national leader identified with *Enosis* (Union with Greece) movement; has travelled abroad to promote interest and support for *Enosis*; led negotiations with Sir John Harding, Gov. of Cyprus 55-56; deported to the Seychelles 56, released Mar. 57; in Athens until return to Cyprus March 59; President-elect 59-60; President of Cyprus 60-July 74, Dec. 74- (re-elected 68, 73); Rep. of Cyprus to Commonwealth Prime Ministers' Confs. 61, 62, 66, 69, 71; Hon. D.D. (Boston, Athens Univs.), Hon. LL.D. (Kerala, Salonica Univs., Jorge Tadeo Lozano Univ. of Bogotá, Royal Univ. of Malta); many foreign decorations.
Presidential Palace, Nicosia, Cyprus.

Makhebar, Albert; Lebanese politician; b. 1915.
Minister of Health 58; fmr. Minister of Foreign Affairs; Deputy Premier, Minister of State for Co-operatives and Housing Affairs May 72-73; Minister of State 73.
Beirut, Lebanon.

Makhous, Dr. Ibrahim; Syrian politician.
Member of Baath Party's Supreme Command 65; Deputy Prime Minister and Minister of Foreign Affairs 65, 66-68.
c/o Ministry of Foreign Affairs, Damascus, Syrian Arab Republic.

Makki, Dr. Hassan; Yemeni politician and diplomatist; ed. Univs. of Bologna and Rome.
Minister of the Economy 63-64, of Foreign Affairs 64, 66, 67-68, of Communications 65; Adviser to the Prime Minister 65-66; Amb. to Italy 68-70, to Fed. Repub. of Germany 70-72; Deputy Prime Minister 72-74; Prime Minister March-June 74; Deputy Prime Minister for Econ. Affairs June-Oct. 74; Perm. Rep. to UN Oct. 74-.
Permanent Mission of the Yemen Arab Republic to the United Nations, 211 East 43rd Street, Room 2402, New York, N.Y. 10017, U.S.A.

Maktum, H.H. Sheikh Rashid bin Said Al-; Ruler of Dubai; b. 1914; ed. privately.
Succeeded his father, Said bin Maktum, as 4th Sheikh 58; Vice-Pres. United Arab Emirates (UAE) Dec. 71-.
Royal Palace, Dubai.

Malek, Reda; Algerian diplomatist; b. 1931; ed. Univs. of Algiers and Paris.
Director of weekly *El Moudjahid*, Tunis 57-61; mem. F.L.N. Del. to Evian talks 61; Amb. to Yugoslavia 63-65, to France 65-70, to U.S.S.R. 70-.
Embassy of Algeria, Krapivinsky per. 1-A, Moscow, U.S.S.R.

Malik, Charles Habib, M.A., PH.D.; Lebanese philosopher, educationist and diplomatist; b. 1906, Btirram, Al-Koura; ed. American Univ. of Beirut, and Harvard and Freiburg Univs.
Instructor Maths. and Physics American Univ. Beirut 27-29; with *Al Hilal* Publ. House, Cairo 29-30; with Rockefeller Found. Exped., Cairo 30-32; Asst. in Philosophy Harvard 36-37; Instructor in Philosophy American Univ. Beirut 37-39; Adjunct-Prof. 39-43, Assoc. Prof. 43-45 Head of Dept. 39-45, on leave 45-55, Dean of Graduate Studies and Prof. of Philosophy 55-60, Distinguished Prof. of Philosophy 62-; E. K. Hall Visiting Prof., Dartmouth Coll. 60; Visiting Prof. Harvard Summer School 60; Minister of Lebanon to U.S.A. 45-53, to Cuba 46-55; Minister designate to Venezuela 47-48; Amb. to U.S.A. 53-55; Lebanese del. UN Conf. and Signatory UN Charter 45; mem. and Chair. Lebanese del. to UN 45-54; Pres. 13th Gen. Assembly UN 58-59; del. to Bandung Conf. 55; Minister for Foreign Affairs 56-58, for Nat. Education and Fine Arts 56-57; mem. of Parl. 57-60; Pres. Security Council 53, 54; Pres. Economic and Social Council 48; Chair. Human Rights Comm. 51, 52; Chair. Lebanese del. for Peace Treaty with Japan 51; Grand First Magistrate of the Holy Orthodox Church; Pres. World Council of Christian Educ. 67-71; Vice-Pres. United Bible Societies 66-72; Fellow Inst. for Advanced Religious Studies at the Univ. of Notre Dame, Indiana 69; Hon. life mem. American Bible Soc.; mem. Société européenne de Culture; Fellow American Asscn. for Advancement of Science, American Geog. Soc.; mem. American Philos. Assocn., American Philos. Soc., American Acad. of Arts and Sciences, Acad. of Human Rights, etc.; founding mem. Lebanese Acad.; Gold Medal, Nat. Institute of Social Sciences, N.Y.; Hon. Litt.D. (Princeton, James Millikin Univs.), Hon. LL.D. (Notre Dame, Brown, Denison, Fairfield, Syracuse, Harvard, Boston, Lehigh, Yale, Georgetown, Wash., Columbia, Ohio, Calif., Dartmouth, St. Mary's Halifax, Wesleyan Univs., Colby, Williams and Albright Colls. and others); Hon. Rector, Univ. Dubuque 51; decorated by governments of Lebanon, Italy, Jordan, Syria, Iraq, Cuba, Iran, Brazil, Dominican Repub., Austria, Greece, Rep. of China, Fed. Rep. of Germany, Denmark.
Publs. *War and Peace* 50, *Problems of Asia* 51, *Problem of Coexistence* 55, *Christ and Crisis* 62, *Man in the Struggle for Peace* 63, *God and Man in Contemporary Christian Thought* 70, *God and Man in Contemporary Islamic Thought* 72; numerous other published works and articles.
American University, Beirut, Lebanon; and Harvard Club, 27 West 44th Street, New York, U.S.A.

Malikyar, Abdullah; Afghan diplomatist; b. 1909; ed. Isteklal Coll., Kabul, and Franco-Persian Coll., Teheran.
Secretary and Gen. Dir. Prime Minister's Office 31-35; Head, Govt. Purchasing Office, Europe 36-40; Vice-Pres. Central Bank and Deputy Minister of Commerce 41-42; Gov. of Herat 42-47, 51-52; Minister of Communications 48-50; Pres. Hillmand Valley Authority Projects 53-62; Minister of Commerce 55-57, of Finance 57-64, Deputy Prime Minister 63-64; Acting Prime Minister 64; Amb. to

U.K. 64-67, to U.S.A. 67-, concurrently to Argentina, Brazil, Canada, Chile and Mexico; Sardar Ali Reshteen Decoration.
Afghan Embassy, 2001 24th Street, N.W., Washington, D.C., U.S.A.

Mallowan, Sir Max Edgar Lucien, Kt., C.B.E., M.A., D.LIT., F.B.A., F.S.A.; British archaeologist; b. 6 May 1904; ed. Lancing and New Coll. Oxford.
Expeditions Ur of the Chaldees 25-30, Nineveh 31-32, Arpachiyah 33, Chagar Bazar and Brak 34-38, Balikh Valley 38, Nimrud 49-57; Wing Commdr. R.A.F.V.R.; Adviser Arab Affairs, Tripolitania; Pres. British School of Archaeology, Iraq, and Editor of the journal *Iraq* 47-71; Pres. British Inst. of Persian Studies 62-; Prof. Western Asiatic Archaeology, Univ. of London 47-62, Prof. Emeritus 62-; Fellow of All Souls Coll., Oxford 62-71; corresp. mem. Arab Acad., Baghdad 54; Schweich Lecturer, British Acad. 55; Lucy Wharton Drexel Medal for Archaeological Research 57; Lawrence of Arabia Memorial Medal, Royal Central Asian Soc. 69; fmr. Editor of Near-Eastern and Western Asiatic Series of Penguin Books; foreign mem. Acad. des Inscriptions et Belles-Lettres 64, Royal Danish Acad. of Sciences and Letters 74; Trustee British Museum 73; Hon. Fellow, New Coll., Oxford 73.
Publs. *Prehistoric Assyria, Excavations at Chagar Bazar, Excavations in the Balikh Valley, Excavations at Brak, Excavations at Nimrud, Twenty-Five Years of Mesopotamian Discovery, Early Mesopotamia and Iran, Nimrud and Its Remains, Ivories in Assyrian Style, Furniture from Fort Shalmaneser.*
Winterbrook House, Wallingford, Oxfordshire, England.

Mammeri, Mouloud; Algerian writer; b. 28 Dec.1917; ed. Rabat, Algiers and Paris.
Director of Anthropological, Prehistoric and Ethnological Research Centre, Algiers; Prix des quatre jurys for *La colline oubliée* 53.
Publs. Novels: in French *La colline oubliée* 52, *Le Sommeil du juste* 55, *L'opium et le bâton* 65; Play: *Le Foehn* 67, *Le Banquet* 74; *Les isefra de Si Mohand* (collection of oral poems in Berber).
82 rue Laperlier, El-Biar, Algiers, Algeria.

Mansour, Ibrahim Moneim; Sudanese politician; b. 1933, Nuhud; ed. Alexandria Univ.
Formerly with Ministry of Commerce and The Agricultural Bank; Deputy Dir. Khartoum Textile Co. 64; Dir. Sudan Textile Factory; Gen. Man. Gulf Int. Corpn.; Minister of Economy and Trade 71-73, of Nat. Economy and the Treasury 73-Jan. 75.
Ministry of the National Economy, Khartoum, Sudan.

Marei, Sayed; Egyptian agriculturalist and politician; b. 26 Aug. 1913; ed. Faculty of Agriculture, Cairo Univ.
Worked on his father's farm after graduation; subsequently with import-export, pharmaceutical, seed, and fertilizer companies; mem. Egyptian House of Commons 44; Del. mem. Higher Cttee. for Agrarian Reform 52-; Chair. of Board, Agricultural Co-operative Credit Bank 55-56; initiated "Supervised Credit System"; Minister of State for Agrarian Reform 56-57; Minister of Agriculture and Agrarian Reform 57-58; Central Minister for Agricultural and Agrarian Reform in the U.A.R. 58-61; Dep. Speaker, Nat. Assembly and Man. Dir. Bank Misr, Cairo 62-67; Minister of Agriculture and Agrarian Reform 67-70; Deputy Premier for Agriculture and Irrigation 72-73; First Sec. Arab Socialist Union (ASU) 72-73; Personal Asst. to Pres. Sadat 73; Sec.-Gen. UN World Food Conf. Rome 74; Pres. UN World Food Council July 75-; Speaker, People's Assembly April 75-.
Publs. *Agrarian Reform in Egypt* 57, *U.A.R. Agriculture Enters a New Age* 60, *Food Production in Developing Countries* 68.
People's Assembly, Cairo; and 9 Sh. Shagaret El Dorr, Zamalek, Cairo, Egypt.

Martin, Jean-Pierre, PH.D.; French United Nations official; b. 2 Jan. 1926; ed. Univs. of Montpellier and Paris.
Economist, UN Dept. of Econ. and Social Affairs 49-60; Special Asst. to the Special Rep. of Sec.-Gen. of UN in Congo 60-61; Chief, Financial Policies and Institutions Section. UN Dept. of Econ. and Social Affairs 61-62; Chef de Cabinet of Under-Sec.-Gen. of UN for Econ. and Social Affairs 62-66; Dir. UN Econ. and Social Office, Beirut 66-74, Econ. Comm. for Western Asia (ECWA), Beirut 74-.
Publs. *Les Finances de Guerre du Canada* 51, *Les Finances publiques britanniques 1939-1955* 56; articles on financial and econ. subjects.
United Nations, B.P. 4656, Beirut, Lebanon.

Mashayekh Faridani, Mohammed Hossein, M.A., PH.D.; Iranian diplomatist and educationist; b. 1914; ed. Pahlavi Coll., Darolfonoon Coll. and Teheran Univ.
Lecturer in Literature and Philosophy, Teheran 40-44; Technical Inspector, Teheran Secondary Schools 44-46; Dir. of Cultural Dept., Ministry of Education 46; Editor, Education and Instruction Magazine 46; Cultural Counsellor, Karachi 48-52, New Delhi 52-55; Cultural Adviser, Ministry of Foreign Affairs 55-56; Dir. of Cultural Relations, Ministry of Foreign Affairs 57, Dir. of Public Relations and Editor of Magazine 57, Dir. Asian Countries Dept. 58; Minister-Counsellor, Baghdad 59-63; Ambassador to Iraq 63-64; Political Dir.-Gen., Ministry of Foreign Affairs 64; Amb. to Saudi Arabia 64-68, to Pakistan 69-73; several decorations from Iran, Pakistan, Holland and Jordan.
c/o Ministry of Foreign Affairs, Teheran, Iran.

Mashour, Ahmed Mashour; Egyptian engineer; b. April 1918; ed. Cairo Univ., Staff Officers Coll. U.K., and Fort Belvoir, U.S.A.
With Ministry of Transport 41; Army Engineer 42; Lecturer at Egyptian Acad. of War 48-52; Staff Officer Egyptian Corps of Engineers; Dir. of Transit, Suez Canal Authority 56; mem. Board of Dirs. Timsah Shipbuilding Co., Ismailia; Chair. and Man. Dir. Suez Canal Authority 65-; various decorations.
Suez Canal Authority, Ismailia, Egypt.

Masmoudi, Mohamed, LL.B.; Tunisian politician; b. 29 May 1925; ed. Tunis and Univ. of Paris.
Member of Tunisian Nationalist Movement 34-; Minister of State in Govt. negotiating Tunisian independence 53-55; Minister of the Economy 55-56; Amb. to France 56-58, 61-70; Minister of Information 58-61; Sec.-Gen. Destour Socialist Party 69-74; Minister of Foreign Affairs 70-74; assoc. with *Action*, later renamed *Afrique Action*.
La Manouba, Tunis, Tunisia.

Massoud-Ansari, Mohammad Ali, D. EN D.; Iranian diplomatist; b. 10 Oct. 1915; ed. Univ. of Paris, Ecole des Sciences Politiques, Paris.
Joined Ministry of Foreign Affairs 40; Second Sec., Embassy of Iran, Moscow 44-45; Second, then First Sec., London 48-50; Consul-Gen., Karbala and Baghdad, Iraq 53; Counsellor, Iranian Embassy, Stockholm 53-54; Acting Del. to UN Security Council 55-56; Chargé d'Affaires, Iranian Embassy, Ottawa 56; Amb. to Yugoslavia 59-62; Under-Sec. of State, Ministry of Foreign Affairs 62-64, Senior Counsellor 68-70; Amb. to Italy 64-68; Perm. Rep. to UN Office, Geneva 70-71; Amb. to Belgium and Luxembourg 71-74; mem. Iranian Del. to several sessions of UN Gen. Assembly.
c/o Ministry of Foreign Affairs, Teheran, Iran.

Massoudi, Abbas; Iranian publisher; b. 1901.
Founded daily *Ettela'at* 25; Propr. and Pres. of *Ettela'at* and its other publications; Vice-Pres. Iranian Senate; numerous articles.
Ettela'at, Kh. Kayyam, Teheran, Iran.

Mavrommatis, Andreas; Cypriot lawyer; b. 1932, Larnaca; ed. Greek Gymnasium, Limassol, and Lincoln's Inn, London.

Called to Bar 54; practised law, Cyprus 54-58; Magistrate, Paphos 58-60; District Judge 60; District Judge, Nicosia 64-70; Minister of Labour and Social Insurance 70-72; Special Legal Adviser to Ministry of Foreign Affairs 72-; Head Cyprus Del. to European Conf. on Security and Co-operation.
10 Plato Street, Nicosia 116, Cyprus.

Maximos V Hakim, (fmrly. **Archbishop George S. Hakim**), D.D.; Lebanese ecclesiastic; b. 18 May 1908; ed. St. Louis School, Tanta, Holy Family Jesuit School, Cairo and St. Anne Seminary, Jerusalem.
Teacher Patriarchal School, Beirut 30-31; Rector and Principal Patriarchal School, Cairo 31-43; Archbishop of Acre, Haifa, Nazareth and all Galilee 43-67; elected Patriarch of Antioch and all the East, Alexandria and Jerusalem Nov. 67; founded *Le Lien*, (French) Cairo 36, *Ar-Rabita* (Arabic) Haifa 43; Commdr. Légion d'Honneur; Dr. h.c. (Laval Univ. Canada and many U.S. univs.)
Publ. *Pages d'Evangile lues en Galilée* (transl. into English Dutch and Spanish) 54.
Greek Catholic Patriarchate, P.O. Box 50076, Beirut, Lebanon.

Mazar, Benjamin, D.PHIL.; Russian-born Israeli archaeologist; b. 28 June 1906; ed. Berlin and Giessen Univs.
Settled in Palestine 29; joined staff of Hebrew Univ. Jerusalem 43, Prof. of Biblical History and Historical Geography of Palestine 51-, Rector 52-61, Pres. 53-61, Pro-Rector 61-; Chair. Israel Exploration Soc.; Dir. excavations Ramat Rahel 32, Beth Shearim 36-40, Beth Yerah 42-43, Tell Qasile 48-50, 59, Ein Ged 60, 62, 64, 65, Old City of Jerusalem 68-73; Hon. mem. British Soc. for Old Testament Study, American Soc. of Biblical Literature and Exegesis; Hon. D.H.L. Hebrew Union Coll. (Jewish Inst. of Religion, U.S.A.), Jewish Theological Seminary of America.
Publs. *Untersuchungen zur alten Geschichte Syriens und Palästinas* 30, *History of Archaeological Research in Palestine* 36, *History of Palestine from the early days to the Israelite Kingdom* 38, *Beth Shearim Excavations 1936-40* 40 (2nd edn. 58), *Historical Atlas of Palestine: Israel in Biblical Times* 41, *Excavations at Tell Qasile* 51; Chair. Editorial Board *Encyclopaedia Biblica* 50, *Ein Gedi* 64, *The World History of the Jewish People Vol. II* 67, *The Western Wall and the Ophel Hill* 74.
Hebrew University of Jerusalem, Jerusalem; and 9 Abarbanel Street, Jerusalem, Israel.

Mazidi, Feisal, B.ECON.; Kuwaiti economist; b. 2 May 1933; ed. Kuwait and Univ. Coll. of N. Staffordshire, Keele, England.
Appointed to Dept. of Finance and Economy 59; Dir. State Chlorine and Salt Board; Dir. Kuwait Oil Co. Ltd. 60; Econ. Asst. to Minister of Finance and Economy 60; Chair. Econ. and Industrial Cttee. 61; Dir. Kuwait Fund for Econ. Development of Arab Countries 62; mem. Kuwait Univ. Higher Council 62-64; Chair. and Man. Dir. Kuwait Chemical Fertilizer Co. 64-71; Chair. Govt. Oil Concession Cttee. 63-65, Govt. Refinery Cttee. 64-66, Kuwait Maritime Mercantile Co. 65-70; Dir. Petrochemical Industries Co. 63-71, Kuwait United Fisheries Co. 71-; Pres. Kuwait Associated Consultants 71-; mem. Kuwait Econs. Soc.; Arab League Prize for paper on Natural Gas 63.
Publs. *Natural Gas in Kuwait and its Utilization* 63, *Kuwait as a Base for Petrochemicals* 65.
Kuwait Associated Consultants, P.O. Box 5443, Kuwait.

Mboro, Clement; Sudanese politician; b. *c.* 1920.
Joined Govt. Service 40, rose to Deputy Gov. Darfur Province 64; Minister of Interior 64-65; Minister of Industry and Mining 68-69; mem. and fmr. Pres. Southern

Front 64; mem. for Repatriation and Resettlement, High Exec. Council for the Southern Region 72-73.
c/o High Executive Council for the Southern Region, Juba, Sudan.

Mehr, Farhang, LL.M., PH.D., Iranian lawyer, economist and financial executive; b. 1924; ed. Univs. of Teheran, Southampton and London.
Professor of Law and Public Finance; Legal Adviser, Head of Industrial Relations Dept., Nat. Iranian Oil Co. 57; Adviser to High Council of Econs. and to Minister of Commerce 58; Dir.-Gen. Petroleum and Int. Affairs 59; Gov. for Iran, Org. of Petroleum Exporting Countries 63-68; Dir.-Gen. of Econ. Affairs 63; Chair. of several socs. including Ancient Iranian Cultural Soc. 63, Zoroastrian Anjuman 65; Deputy Minister of Finance 64-; Asst. Prime Minister 66-; Chair. of Board, Man. Dir. Iran Insurance Co. 67; Trustee, Teheran Coll. of Insurance, Kerman Univ., Computer Coll., Inst. of Int. Political and Econ. Studies; Chancellor Pahlavi Univ. 72-; Homayoun 2nd and 3rd Class, Taj 2nd Class, Sepas 1st Class, Kah 1st Class, Abadani va Pishraft 1st Class.
Publs. *Labour Law and Social Insurance* 60, *Government Corporation* 64, *Public Finance* 67.
Chancellor's Office, Pahlavi University, Shiraz, Iran.

Meir, Golda; Israeli politician; b. Kiev 3 May 1898; ed. Teachers' Seminary, Milwaukee, U.S.A.
Teacher and leading mem. Zionist Labour Party, Milwaukee; del. U.S. Section, World Jewish Congress until 21; emigrated to Palestine 21; joined Merhavia collective farm village; with Solel Boneh, Histadrut Contracting and Public Works Enterprise 24-26; Sec. Women's Labour Council of Histadrut 28; mem. Exec. and Secretariat, Fed. of Labour 29-34; Chair. Board of Dirs., Workers' Sick Fund 36; Head, Political Dept., Fed. of Labour; Mapai Del., Action Cttee., World Zionist Organization; mem. War Economic Advisory Council of Palestine Govt. 39; Head, Political Dept., Jewish Agency for Palestine, Jerusalem 46-48; Israel Minister to U.S.S.R. Aug. 48-April 49; Minister of Labour and Social Insurance 49-52, of Labour 52-56; Minister for Foreign Affairs June 56-66; Sec.-Gen. Mapai Feb. 66-68; Prime Minister 69-74; Acting Minister of Justice June-Sept. 72; Hon. LL.D. (Brandeis Univ.) 73.
8 Habaron Hirsch Street, Ramat-Aviv, Israel.

Melen, Ferit; Turkish politician; b. 1906, Van; ed. School of Political Science, Univ. of Ankara.
District Officer, Local Admin. 31-33; Auditor, Ministry of Finance 33-43, Dir.-Gen. of Incomes 43-50; Deputy for Van (Repub. People's Party) 50-64; Minister of Finance 62-65; Senator for Van 64-67; mem. Council of Europe 66-67; participated in formation of Nat. Reliance Party 67, now Deputy Leader; Minister of Nat. Defence 71-72, April 75-; Prime Minister May 72-73.
Republican Reliance Party, Ankara, Turkey.

Melikishvili, Georgy Alexandrovich; Soviet (Georgian) historian; b. 30 Dec. 1918; ed. Tbilisi Univ.
Works deal with the ancient history of the Near East and Transcaucasia; Prof. Tbilisi Univ.; Dir. Dept. of Ancient History, Historical Inst. of Georgian Acad. of Sciences; mem. Acad. of Sciences of Georgian S.S.R. 60-; Lenin Prize 57.
Publs. *Nairi-Urartu* 54, *Urartian Inscriptions in Cuneiform Characters* 60, *History of Ancient Georgia* 59.
Academy of Sciences, Tbilisi, Georgian S.S.R., U.S.S.R.

Mellink, Machteld Johanna, PH.D.; Netherlands archaeologist; b. 26 Oct. 1917; ed. Amsterdam and Utrecht Univs.
Field Asst. Tarsus excavations 47-49; Asst. Prof. of Classical Archæology Bryn Mawr Coll. 49-53, Assoc. Prof., Chair. Dept. of Classical and Near Eastern Archæology

53-62, Prof. 62-; staff mem. Gordion excavations organized by Pennsylvania Univ. Museum 50-, during which the putative tomb of King Midas was discovered 57; field dir. excavations at Karataş-Semayük in Lycia 63-, excavations of painted tombs in Elmali district 70-.
Publs. *Hyakinthos* 43, *A Hittite Cemetery at Gordion* 56; *Archaeology in Asia Minor* (reports in *American Journal of Archaeology*) 55-, editor *Dark Ages and Nomads c. 1000 B.C.*, *Frühe Stufen der Kunst* (with J. Filip) 74.
Department of Classical and Near Eastern Archaeology, Bryn Mawr College, Bryn Mawr, Pa. 19010, U.S.A.

Memmi, Albert; Tunisian writer; b. 15 Dec. 1920; ed. Lycée Carnot, Tunis, Univ. of Algiers and Univ. de Paris. Teacher of Philosophy in Tunis 55; Dir. Psychological Centre, Tunis 56; Researcher, Centre national de la recherche scientifique, Paris 59-; Asst. Prof. Ecole pratique des hautes études 59-66, Prof. 66-70; Prof. Univ. of Paris 70-; Commdr. Ordre de Nichan Iftikhar; Palmes Académiques.
Publs. include: *The Pillar of Salt* 53, *Strangers* 55, *Anthologie des écrivains nord-africains* 55, *Colonizer, Colonized* 57, *Portrait of a Jew* 62, *Le français et le racisme* 65, *The Liberation of the Jew* 66, *The Dominated Man* 68, *Le Scorpion* 69, *Jews and Arabs* 74.
5 rue Saint Merri, Paris 4e, France.

Menemencioğlu, Turgut; Turkish diplomatist; b. 1914; ed. Robert Coll., Istanbul, and Geneva Univ.
Turkish Ministry of Foreign Affairs 39-; Perm. Del., European Office UN, Geneva 50-52; Counsellor, Turkish Embassy, Washington 52; Dir. Gen. Econ. Affairs, Ministry of Foreign Affairs 52-54; Dep. Perm. Rep. to UN 54-60; Ambassador to Canada 60; Perm. Rep. to UN 60-62; Amb. to U.S.A. 62-66; High Political Adviser Ministry of Foreign Affairs 67; Sec.-Gen. Central Treaty Org. 68-71; Adviser, Ministry of Foreign Affairs 71-72; Amb. to U.K. Nov. 72-.
Turkish Embassy, 43 Belgrave Square, London SW1X 8PA; and 69 Portland Place, London, W.1, England.

Méouchi, Badri Selim, L. en D.; Lebanese judge; b. 1 Dec. 1902, Beirut; ed. Univ. of St. Joseph, Beirut.
Magistrate 27; Pres. of Court of First Instance 29-39; Judge, Court of Appeal, Beirut 39-46; Pres. Court of First Instance, Beirut 46; Pres. Court of Appeal, Beirut 46-50; First Pres. Court of Cassation 50-66; Pres. Conseil Supérieur de la Magistrature; Minister of the Interior and of Nat. Defence 66-68; Avocat à la Cour 68; Grand Officier, Ordre National de Cèdre; Grand Officier de Jordanie, de Haïti.
Rue Trabaud, Beirut, Lebanon.

Meridor, Yaacov; Israeli business executive; b. 1 Sept. 1913.
Joined Irgun Zevayi Leumi (IZL) 33, second in command 44-48; fmr. mem. Knesset (Parl.); founder, Chair. of Board, Maritime Fruit Carriers Ltd., Haifa.
Publ. *Long is the Road to Freedom.*
Maritime Fruit Carriers Ltd., 53 Shderot Hameginim, P.O. Box 1501, Haifa, Israel.

Merlin, Samuel; Israeli author and director of political studies; b. 17 Jan. 1910; ed. Lycée, Kishineff, Univ. of Paris.
Secretary-General World Exec., Zionist Revisionist and New Zionist Org. 34-38; Editor-in-Chief Yiddish daily *Di Tat*, Warsaw, Poland 38-39; Sec.-Gen. Hebrew Cttee. for Nat. Liberation 40-48; mem. First Knesset 48-51; Pres. Israel Press Ltd. 50-57; Dir. of Political Studies, Inst. for Mediterranean Affairs, N.Y. 57-; Lecturer, Middle East Studies, Fairleigh Dickinson Univ., N.J. 71-; Hon. mem. of Abu Gosh village near Jerusalem.
Publs. *The Palestine Refugee Problem* 58, *United States Policy in the Middle East* 60, *The Ascent of Man* (Co-Author) 63, *The Cyprus Dilemma* (Editor) 67, *The Big Powers and the Present Crisis in the Middle East* 68, *The Search for Peace in the Middle East* 69, *Guerre et Paix au Moyen Orient* 70.
Institute for Mediterranean Affairs, 1078 Madison Avenue, New York, N.Y. 10028, U.S.A.

Merzban, Mohammed Abdullah, M.A.; Egyptian politician; b. 20 Jan. 1918, Fayoum; ed. Fuad Univ. and Harvard Univ.
Lecturer, Faculty of Commerce, Cairo Univ. until 56; Sec.-Gen. Ministry of Industry 56-58; Gen. Man. Industrialization Authority 58-60; Chair. Al-Nasr Org. 60-61; Chair. Spinning & Weaving Org. 61-66; Chair. Bank of Cairo 66-68; Minister of Supply and Home Trade 68-70; Minister of Economy and Foreign Trade 70-73, also acting Minister of Supply and Home Trade 71-73; Deputy Prime Minister 72-73.
Publs. *Financial Management, Sales Management, Mathematics of Marketing.*
c/o People's Assembly, Cairo, Egypt.

Meshel, Yeruham; Israeli trade unionist; b. 24 Nov. 1912, Pinsk, Russia.
Immigrated to Palestine 33; Sec. Metal Workers' Union, Tel-Aviv, mem. Tel-Aviv Labour Council Exec. 45; mem. Trade Union Centre of Histadrut Exec. Cttee., Chair. Industrial Workers' Div. 50-60, mem. Central Exec. Bureau 60-, Chair. Trade Union Centre 61, Deputy Sec.-Gen. Histadrut 64-74, Head of Histadrut Social Security Centre and Arab Workers' Dept., Acting Sec.-Gen. Histadrut 73, Sec.-Gen. 74-; mem. Central Cttee. of Mapai 61, mem. Secr. Mifleget Ha'avoda 64; rep. to numerous int. labour confs.
Histadrut, 93 Arlosorof Street, Tel-Aviv, Israel.
Telephone: 267398.

Mesnil du Buisson, Robert du, Count, D. ès L., D. en D.; French archaeologist; b. 19 April 1895.
Dir. French Archaeological Missions in Syria, Egypt and France; Lecturer Ecole des Hautes Etudes 38-; Head Archaeological Mission, Centre Nat. de la Recherche Scientifique, Palmyra 65-; Pres. Société Nat. des Antiquaires de France 46-47; Pres. Société Historique et Archéologique de l'Orne 47-55, Hon. Pres. 56-; Pres. Soc. du Manoir d'Argentelles 57-; Dir. Centre Culturel et Touristique de l'Orne 67-; Vice-Pres. Fédération des Sociétés normandes 47-55, Pres. Soc. d'Ethnographie de Paris 69-; Commdr. of Legion of Honour 46; Lauréat Institut de France, Acad. des Inscriptions et Belles-Lettres 40, 63, Acad. des Beaux-Arts 58; Gold Medal Soc. d'Encouragement au Progrès 74.
Publs. *Les ruines d'El-Mishrifé au Nord-Est de Homs* 27, *La technique des fouilles archéologiques* 33, *Le site archéologique de Mishrifé-Qatna* 35, *Les noms et signes égyptiens désignant des vases* 35, *Souran et Tell Masin* 35, *Le site de Qadesh* 36, *Inscriptions juives de Doura-Europos* 37, *Inventaire des inscriptions palmyréniennes de Doura-Europos* 39, *Les peintures de la Synagogue de Doura 245-256 ap. J.-C.* 39, *Tessères et monnaies de Palmyre* 44, *Les ouvrages du siège a Doura-Europos* 45, *Le site archéologique d'Exmes (Uxoma)* 46, *Le sautoir d'Atargatis et la chaîne d'amulettes* 47, *Baghouz, l'ancienne Corsôté* 48, *Une voie commerciale de haute antiquité dans l'Orne* 51, *Les dieux et les déesses en forme de vase dans L'Antiquité Orientale, La palissade gauloise d'Alençon* 52, *L'alcôve royale dite "Lit de Justice d'Argentelles"* 53, *Un constructeur du Château de la Celle-Saint-Cloud, Jacques Jérémie Roussel* 54, *Les barques de la Grande Pyramide et le voyage au Paradis* 56, *Les enceintes gauloises d'Alençon* 58, *Inscriptions sur jarres de Doura-Europos* 59, *Une famille de Chevaliers de Malte, Les Costart* 60, *Le vrai nom de Bôl, prédécesseur de Bêl, à Palmyre* 61, *Les tessères et les monnaies de Palmyre de la Bibliothèque Nationale* 62, *Origine et évolution du Panthéon de Tyr, Les Chaussons de la*

Salle 63, *Les origines du Panthéon Palmyrénien* 64, *Le dieu-Griffon à Palmyre et chez les Hittites* 65, *Le dieu Ousô sur des monnaies de Tyr* 65, *Le drame des deux étoiles du matin et du soir dans l'antiquité orientale* 67, *Les origines du mythe animalier de la planète Vénus, Une ancienne famille de Normandie, les du Mesnil du Buisson* 68, *Etudes sur les dieux phéniciens* 70, *Nouvelles études sur les dieux et les mythes de Canaan* 73.
63 rue de Varenne, Paris 7e; and Château de Champobert, par Exmes (Orne), France.

Messadi, Prof. Mahmoud; Tunisian educationist and politician; b. 28 Jan. 1911, Tazarka; ed. Coll. Sadiki and Lycée Carnot, Tunis, Univ. of Paris.
Professor Lycée Carnot 36-38, Coll. Sadiki 38-48; Asst. Prof. Centre d'Etudes Islamiques, Univ. of Paris 48-52, Inst. des Hautes Etudes de Paris 48-55; Head Dept. of Secondary Educ., Tunis 55-58; Insp.-Gen. of Public Educ. 58-; Sec. of State for Nat. Educ. Youth and Sports 58-68; Minister of State 69-70; Minister of Cultural Affairs Dec. 73-; Deputy, Nat. Assembly; mem. Cen. Cttee. Destour Socialist Party; Grand Cordon Ordre de l'Indépendance, Ordre de la République.
Publs. *Essoud* (The Dam), *Haddatha Abou Houraira, Maouled en-Nassian* (Birth of Oblivion).
Ministère des Affaires Culturelles, Place du Gouvernement, Tunis, Tunisia.

Mestiri, Ahmed; Tunisian politician; b. 1925, Marsa.
Member of Central Cttee. of Néo-Destour Party 52-64, of Destour Socialist Party 64-68, 70; expelled from the Party 68, 71, Jan. 72; Ministerial Sec. 54-55; Sec. of State for Justice 56-58; Sec. of State for Finance and Commerce 58-60; Amb. to U.S.S.R., U.A.R., Algeria 60-66; Sec. of State for Defence 66-68; Minister of the Interior 70-71.
c/o Ministry of the Interior, Tunis, Tunisia.

Mestiri, Mahmoud; Tunisian diplomatist; b. 25 Dec. 1929; ed. Inst. d'Etudes Politiques, Univ. de Lyons.
Served in several Tunisian Dels. to UN 57; Alt. Rep. to UN 58, 59; Head of Tunisian special Diplomatic Mission to Congo (Léopoldville) 60; Asst. to Personal Rep. of UN Sec.-Gen. to Govt. of Belgium 61; Deputy Perm. Rep. of Tunisia to UN 62-65; Sec.-Gen. for Foreign Affairs, Tunis 65-67; Perm. Rep. to UN 67-69; Chair. UN Special Cttee. on the Situation with Regard to Implementation of Declaration on the Granting of Independence to Colonial Countries and Peoples 68; Amb. to Belgium Sept. 69, to Luxembourg Oct. 69, to EEC Nov. 69, to Germany 71-73, to U.S.S.R. 73-74, and to Poland Feb. 74-.
Embassy of Tunisia, Świętokrzyska 36/18, Warsaw, Poland.

Meulen, Daniel van der (*see* van der Meulen, Daniel).

Mhaidi, Kadhim Abdul Hamid al- (*see* Al-Mhaidi, Kadhim Abdul Hamid).

Mhedhebi, Béchir; Tunisian politician; b. 1912.
Ambassador to Lebanon, Kuwait, Libya 65-70; Sec.-Gen. Ministry of Foreign Affairs 70-71; Minister of Defence 71-72; Amb. to U.K. 72-74, to Morocco 74-; mem. Political Bureau, Destour Socialist Party Oct. 71-.
Tunisian Embassy, 6 Avenue de Fez, Rabat, Morocco.

Michałowski, Kazimierz; Polish archaeologist; b. 14 Dec. 1901.
Emeritus Professor of Mediterranean Archaeology, Warsaw Univ.; mem. Presidium, Polish Acad. of Sciences, Head Inst. of Mediterranean Archaeology; mem. numerous foreign acads. and scientific socs.; Vice-Dir. Warsaw Nat. Museum; in charge of Franco-Polish excavations, Egypt 37-39, Polish excavations, Crimea 56-58, Egypt 57-, Syria 59-, Sudan 62-, Cyprus 65-; Chair. Int. Working Group of Archaeologists and Landscape Architects, Abu Simbel; Pres. Soc. for Nubian Studies; Dir. of Polish Centre of Archaeology, Cairo; Prix de l'Acad. des Inscriptions et

Belles Lettres 33; State Prize 55, 66; Dr. h.c. (Strasbourg and Cambridge); Silver Cross Virtuti Militari, Cmmdr. Cross with Star of Order Polonia Restituta, Order of Banner of Labour, Cmmdr. Corona d'Italia, Officier Légion d'Honneur, numerous other Polish and foreign decorations.
Publs. *Les portraits hellénistiques et romains* 32, *Fouilles Franco-Polonaises à Tell Edfou* 37-50, *Mirmeki* 56, *Fouilles Polonaises à Palmyre* 60-64, *Fouilles Polonaises à Faras* 62-65, *Die Kathedrale aus dem Wüstensand* 67, *L'Art de l'Egypte Ancienne* 68 (English edn. 69), *Faras, Wall Paintings in the Collection of the National Museum in Warsaw* 74 (German and Polish edns. 74).
Sewerynów 6, Warsaw, Poland.

Mili, Mohamed; Tunisian civil servant; b. 4 Dec. 1917; ed. Ecole Normale Supérieure de Saint-Cloud and Ecole Nationale Supérieure des Télécommunications, Paris.
Telecommunications Engineer, Ministry of Posts 47-56; Dir.-Gen. of Telecommunications 57-65; Vice-Pres. Plan for Africa, Int. Telecommunication Union (ITU) 60-64; Pres. Admin. Council 64, Pres. Plan for Africa ITU 64-65, Vice-Sec.-Gen. ITU 65-66, Sec.-Gen. 66-; Commdr. Ordre de la République (Tunisia), Commdr. Order of Vasa (Sweden), Officier Ordre de l'Indépendance (Tunisia), Gran Cruz de la Orden de Duarte, Sánchez y Mella con Placa de Plata (Dominican Repub.).
International Telecommunication Union, Place des Nations, 1211 Geneva 20, Switzerland.

Minai, Ahmad, M.A., PH.D.; Iranian economist; b. 10 Sept. 1921; ed. Teheran Univ., Univs. of Glasgow and Oxford, American Univ., Washington, D.C.
Lecturer, London Univ. 49-50; joined Foreign Service 50; Third Sec., Washington, D.C. 53; First Sec., Ankara 60; Special Aide to Prime Minister with rank of Dir.-Gen., mem. High Econ. Council 61-62; Econ. Counsellor, Washington, D.C. 63; Vice-Gov. Agricultural Bank of Iran 65-66; Dir. Dept. of Econ. Affairs, Ministry of Foreign Affairs 66-67; Minister-Counsellor, Islamabad 67; Consul-Gen., Karachi 69; Minister-Counsellor, London 70; Dir. Fourth Political Dept., Ministry of Foreign Affairs 73; Amb. 74; Sec.-Gen. Regional Co-operation for Devt. May 74-.
Publs. several articles on econ. topics.
Office of the Secretary-General, Regional Co-operation for Development, 5 Los Angles Avenue, Teheran, Iran.

Mirfenderesky, Ahmad, LL.B.; Iranian diplomatist; b. 1918; ed. French Univ., Beirut.
Career with Ministry of Foreign Affairs 42-, served U.S.S.R., Netherlands, India, Turkey; Dir. Dept. of Econ. Affairs, Second Political Dept., Political Dir.-Gen. 62-64; Deputy Minister, Political and Parl. Depts. 64-65; Ambassador to U.S.S.R. Oct. 65-71; now Deputy Minister for Foreign Affairs.
Ministry of Foreign Affairs, Teheran, Iran.

Mirghani, Mohamed; Sudanese journalist; b. 1932; ed. Univ. of Besançon and London School of Journalism.
Foreign News Editor, Al Ayam Press House 49-58; Man. Regional News Services and Reuters, Khartoum 58-; Sudan Corresp. for Reuters and *Daily* and *Sunday Telegraph*, contributor to B.B.C. programmes.
Regional News Services, P.O. Box 972, Khartoum, Sudan.

Moalla, Mansour, L EN D., L. ÈS L., LL.D.; Tunisian economist; b. 1 May 1930, Sfax; ed. Inst. des Etudes Politiques, Ecole Nat. d'Administration, Paris.
Inspecteur des Finances 56; Technical Adviser, Ministry of Finance 57-58; Dir.-Gen. Banque Centrale de Tunisie 58-61; Dir. of Admin., Office of the Pres. 61-63, 68-69; Dir. Ecole Nat. d'Administration (ENA) 63-67; Under-Sec. of State, Ministry of Commerce and Industry 67-68; Sec. of State (then Minister) for Posts, Telegraphs and

Telecommunications (PTT) 69-70; Deputy Minister in charge of the Nat. Plan 70-71, Minister 71-74; mem. Cen. Cttee., Political Bureau, Destour Socialist Party 71-; Grand Cordon, Order of the Repub., Order of Independence.
32 avenue de la République, Carthage, Tunisia.

Mohammed Zahir Shah; fmr. King of Afghanistan; b. 15 Oct. 1914; ed. Habibia High School, Istiqlal Coll. (both in Kabul), Lycée Janson-de-Sailly and Univ. of Montpellier, France.
Graduated with highest honours; attended Infantry Officers' School, Kabul 32; married Lady Homira, Nov. 4th 1931; children, Princess Bilqis, Prince Ahmad Shah Khan, Princess Maryam, Prince Mohammed Nadir Khan, Prince Shah Mahmoud Khan, Prince Mohammed Daoud Jan, Prince Mirvis Jan; Asst. Min. in Ministry of Nat. Defence 32-33; acting Minister of Educ. 33; crowned King Nov. 8th, 33, deposed July 73; abdicated Aug. 73.

Mohieddin, Zakaria; Egyptian army officer and politician; b. May 1918; ed. Mil. Coll. and Staff Officers' Coll., Cairo.
Former lecturer Mil. Coll. and Staff Officers' Coll. and Dir.-Gen. Intelligence; Minister of the Interior 53-58; Minister of the Interior U.A.R. 58-62, Vice-Pres. U.A.R. and Chair. Aswan Dam Cttee. 61-62; mem. Nat. Defence Cttee. 62-69, Presidency Council 62-64; mem. Exec. Cttee. Arab Socialist Union 64-69; Deputy Prime Minister 64-65, June 67-68; Prime Minister and Minister of the Interior 65-66.
68 Khalifa al-Mamoun Street, Manchiet al-Bakri, Cairo, Egypt.

Moini, Amir-Ghassem; Iranian mechanical engineer and politician; b. June 1925; ed. Teheran Univ.
Ministry of Labour and Social Affairs 47-; Teheran Labour Dept.; Deputy Head Inspection Office; Acting Head of Fars Prov. Labour Dept., later Head; Deputy Head Teheran Branch of Workers' Social Insurance Org.; Deputy Dir.-Gen. Employment Services, later Dir.-Gen.; Sec.-Gen. Graduate Guidance Org.; Technical Under-Sec., Ministry of Labour and Social Affairs; mem. Board of Dirs. Social Insurance Org.; mem. Parl.; Acting Sec.-Gen. Iran Novin Party 71; Minister of Labour and Social Affairs 73-; Homayoun Order, First Class.
Ministry of Labour, 457 Avenue Eisenhower, Teheran, Iran.

Mokaddem, Sadok; Tunisian diplomatist; b. 1914; ed. Lycée Carnot, Tunis, Faculty of Sciences, Montpellier and Faculty of Medicine, Paris.
Physician, Tunis; mem. Néo-Destour 34-, mem. Political Bureau 52-; Sec. of State for Justice 54-55, for Public Health 55-56; mem. to Constituent Ass. 56-59, mem. Nat. Assembly 59-; Ambassador to Egypt 56-57; Sec. of State for Foreign Affairs 57-62; Ambassador to France 62-64; Pres. Nat. Assembly 64-69, 69-; Chair. Destour Socialist Party 70; Grand Cordon of Nat. Order of Independence, Grand Cordon, Nat. Order of the Repub.; several foreign decorations.
National Assembly, Palais du Bardo, Tunis, Tunisia.

Mosevics, Mark; Israeli industrialist; b. 22 Aug. 1920; ed. Dulwich Coll., London, Jesus Coll., Cambridge, England, Hebrew Univ. Jerusalem.
Chairman Board of Dirs., Israel Export Inst. 66-68; Chair. Board of Dirs., Israel Industrial Bank 68-72, mem. Board of Dirs. 72-; Chair. Board of Dirs., Elite Chocolate and Sweets Mfg. Co. Ltd., Co-ordinating Bureau of Econ. Orgs. 68-; Pres. Mfrs. Asscn. of Israel 69-; mem. Board of Dirs. Israel Corpn. Ltd. 70-; Chair. Board, First Int. Bank of Israel 73-; mem. Presidium, Prime Minister's 3rd Econ. Conf.; Hon. Pres. A'KIM (Appeal for Retarded Children) 72-.

Elite Chocolate and Sweets Manufacturing Co. Ltd., P.O. Box 19, Tel-Aviv; and 7 Wisotsky Street, Tel-Aviv, Israel.

Mostofi, Khosrow, M.A., PH.D.; Iranian professor; b. 8 July 1921; ed. Univs. of Teheran and Utah.
Assistant Prof. Political Science, Portland State Univ. 58-60, Univ. of Utah 60-65; Acting Dir. Inst. of Int. Studies, Univ. of Utah 62-63; Assoc. Prof., Univ. of Utah 65-70, Prof. 70-; Acting Chair. Dept. of Political Science 67; Dir. Middle East Center, Univ. of Utah 67-; Fulbright-Hays Fellow, Turkey and Iran 65-66; Board mem. American Inst. of Iranian Studies 68, CASA 73-; Co-Dir. American Center for Iranian Studies in Teheran 70; mem. N.D.F.L. Panel of Consultants, U.S.O.E. 68-70, American Asscn. of Univ. Profs., American Acad. of Political Sciences, Western Political Science Asscn., American Acad. for Advancement of Science.
Publs. *Suez Dispute: A Case Study of a Treaty* 57, *Aspects of Nationalism: The Sociology of Colonial Revolt* 64, *Parsee Nameh: A Persian Reader in 8 Vols.* Vol. I, II 63, 4th edn. Vol. I 69, *Iran in Encyclopaedia Britannica* 74, *Idries Shah* in *Studies in Art and Literature of the Near East* 74.
Room 19, Middle East Center, University of Utah, Salt Lake City, Utah 84112; Home: 2481 East 13th South Street, Salt Lake City, Utah 84108, U.S.A.

Moti, Mohammed Saleh (see Muti, Muhammad Salih).

Moulay Hassan Ben El Mehdi, H.R.H. Prince (Cousin of King Hassan II); Moroccan diplomatist; b. 1912.
Caliph Northern Zone of Morocco 25; Amb. to Great Britain 57-64, to Italy 64-67; now Gov. Banque du Maroc; decorations include, Ouissam Alaoui, Charles I Medal, Great Military Ouissam, Great Medal of Portugal, Great Dominican Medal, Great Naval Medal, Great Mahdaoui Medal, Great Houssni Medal.
Banque du Maroc, 277 avenue Mohammed V, Rabat, Morocco.

Mounayer, H.E. Eustache Joseph, D. en. L.; Syrian ecclesiastic; b. 6 June 1925; ed. Seminary of Benedictine Fathers, Jerusalem, Patriarchal Seminary, Charfé, Lebanon and Pontifical Univ. of Latran, Rome.
Ordained priest 49; Sec. of Archbishop of Damascus 54-59, concurrently Sec. of Apostolic Nunzio, Pres. ecclesiastical court; Sec. of Cardinal Tappouni 59-71; consecrated bishop 71; Patriarchal Auxiliary Bishop 71-.
Publs. *Les Synodes Syriens Jacobites* (in French), *Le Schihim* (in Arabic).
Patriarcat Syrien Catholique d'Antioche, Beirut, Lebanon.

Mousa, Omer el Haj; Sudanese army officer and politician; b. 1924, El Kawa; ed. Gordon Memorial Coll., Military Coll.
Joined the Co. Commdrs. course 53, staff course 63; worked in the Eastern, Western, Northern Commands, and the Signal Corps; later Dir. Armed Forces Admin.; Brig. 65; Dir. Gen. Staff Jan. 65-May 69; Minister of Nat. Guidance Oct. 69-71, of Information and Culture 71-75; Asst. Sec.-Gen. Sudanese Socialist Union 75-.
Sudanese Socialist Union, Khartoum, Sudan.

Moussalli, Paul Michel Négib, LIC. en D.; Lebanese lawyer and United Nations official; b. 9 April 1932; ed. Lycée français de garçons, Beirut, Faculty of Law, Beirut, Univ. of Lyons, France, Max Planck Inst. für Ausländisches Öffentliches Recht und Völkerrecht, Heidelberg, Germany, and Graduate Inst. of Int. Studies, Geneva, Switzerland.
Legal Adviser, Office of UN High Commr. for Refugees (UNHCR), Geneva 61-62; UNHCR Rep. for Tunisia 62; UNHCR Rep. at Tripartite Repatriation Comm. (Algerian refugees) 62; UNHCR Rep. for Algeria 62-63; UNHCR Legal Adviser, Geneva (questions relating to refugees in Africa and Asia) 63-66; UNHCR Regional Rep. for Africa

66-70; Acting Dir. of Admin. and Management, UNHCR, Geneva 71-74, Dir. 75-.
Office of United Nations High Commissioner for Refugees, Palais des Nations, Geneva, Switzerland.

Mubarak, Mousa al-, M.A.; Sudanese politician; b. 1932, Abu Si'id, Omdurman; ed. Univs. of London and Khartoum.
Former schoolteacher; Lecturer in History, Univ. of Khartoum; mem. Parl. (Nat. Unionist Party) 65-68, (Democratic Unionist Party) 68-69; Minister of Industry and Mineral Resources 69-70; Man., Chief Editor *Al-Ayam* 70-71; Minister of Labour Aug.-Oct. 71; Minister of State for Premiership Affairs 71-72; Minister of the Treasury 72.
P.O. Box 1701, Khartoum, Sudan.

Mubarak, Lt.-Gen. Muhammad Hosni; Egyptian air force officer and politician; b. 1929.
Commander, Air Force 72-75, Vice-Pres. of Repub. April 75-, Dir.-Gen. Egyptian Arms Procurement Agency April 75-.
Office of the Vice-President, Cairo, Egypt.

Müezzinoğlu, Ziya; Turkish civil servant and diplomatist; b. 5 May 1919; ed. Ankara Univ.
Inspector of Finance, Turkish Ministry of Finance 42-53; Adviser to Treasury, Ministry of Finance 53-59; Dir.-Gen. of Treasury 59-60; Dir.-Gen. of Treasury and Sec.-Gen. Org. for Int. Econ. Co-operation in Turkey 60; mem. Constituent Assembly 60; Chair. Interministerial Cttee. for Foreign Econ. Relations 62; Sec. of State of State Planning Org. 62-64; Amb. to Fed. Repub. of Germany 64-67; Amb., Perm. Del. to EEC 67; Minister of Finance May 72-73; mem. Nat. Security Council.
c/o Ministry of Finance, Ankara, Turkey.

Mufti, Said el-; Jordanian politician; b. 1898; ed. Turkish School, Damascus.
Governor of Amman 25, 39; Mayor of Amman 27, 38; mem. First Legislative Council 29, 31; Head of Treasury 39; Minister of Communications 44; Minister of Interior 44, 48; Minister of Finance and Communications 45; Deputy 47, 51 and 54; Minister of Commerce and Agriculture 47; Prime Minister and Minister of Foreign Affairs 55; Prime Minister 56; Deputy Prime Minister and Minister of Interior and Agriculture 57; Pres. of Senate 58; Deputy Prime Minister 63; Pres. of Senate 63-74; mem. Consultative Council 67; Jordan Medal of Independence First Class, Jordan Star First Class, and many others.
The Senate, Amman, Jordan.

Müftüoğlu, Sadık Tekin; Turkish politician; b. 1927, Çaycuma, Zonguldak.
Member of Parl. for Zonguldak 65-; Minister of Commerce 66-67, of State 67-69, of Finance 73-74; Justice Party.
c/o Ministry of Finance, Ankara, Turkey.

Muhammad Hasani, Ali Nasser; Yemeni politician; b. 1944, Dathina Rural District.
Active mem. of Nat. Liberation Front (NLF) 63-67; Gov. Second Province 67; mem. Nat. Front Gen. Command March 68; Minister of Local Govt. April 69, of Defence Dec. 69; mem. Front Exec. Cttee. 70; mem. Presidential Council of People's Democratic Repub. of Yemen 71-; Chair. Council of Ministers 71-; mem. Political Bureau of Nat. Front 72-; Minister of Educ. 74-.
Office of the Prime Minister, Aden, People's Democratic Republic of Yemen.

Mumcuoğlu, Hayri; Turkish lawyer; b. 1914, Istanbul; ed. secondary schools, Istanbul.
Assistant Judge, Bartın 37; Judge for Penal Affairs, Akçaabat, Saframbolu; Asst. Prosecutor, Ankara; Judge, Chief Prosecutor of the Repub.; Chief Prosecutor, Ministry of Justice; mem. Court of Cassation; mem. Parl. for Tekirdağ (New Turkey Party) 61; Minister of Housing and

Reconstruction 63; joined Repub. People's Party 67, resigned 72; Minister of Justice 73, 74-75; Independent.
National Assembly, Ankara, Turkey.

Muntasser, Dr. Omar Mahmud; Libyan politician and diplomatist; b. 28 July 1930; ed. Univs. of Florence and Oxford.
Minister, Libyan Embassy, Washington 60-61, London 61-62; Minister of Justice, Libya 62-63, 63-64, of Foreign Affairs 63; Ambassador to U.K., concurrently to the Netherlands 64-69, and Malta 66-69; now Under-Sec. for Petroleum.
Ministry of Petroleum, P.O. Box 256, Tripoli, Libya.

Muntasser, Saddiqh al; Libyan diplomatist; b. 17 Dec. 1913; ed. High School in Libya, and Oriental Univ., Naples, Italy.
Posts held include: District Officer of S. Desert Area, District Commr. of Misurata District, Provincial Commr. of E. Provinces, Under-Sec. of Communications of Govt. of Tripolitania, Governor-Gen., Rep. of King Idris I, Tripolitania; Amb. to U.S.A., Chief of Libyan Del. to UN, Amb. to U.A.R. and to Saudi Arabia, Chief of Libyan Del. to Arab League, Minister of Defence; business positions held include: Chair. Commercial Bank S.A.L., Tripoli, Libya Texas and Oil & Refining Co. Ltd., Gordon Woodroffe Co. Libya Ltd., Latco (Libyan Agency and Trading Co.), Lavco (Libyan Aviation Co.); Rep. of Richard Costain Civil Engineering Ltd., Costain and Press, Tripe and Wakeham; Amb. to Fed. Repub. of Germany 67-71, to Switzerland 68-71; decorations from Libya and Egypt.
c/o Ministry of Foreign Affairs, Tripoli, Libya.

Murphy, Richard William, B.A., A.B.; American diplomatist; b. 29 July 1929, Boston, Mass.; ed. Harvard Univ. and Emmanuel Coll., Cambridge.
United States Consul, Aleppo, Syria 60-63; Political Officer, U.S. Embassy, Jeddah 63-68, Amman 66-68; Country Dir. for Arabian Peninsula Affairs, U.S. Dept. of State 70-71; Amb. to Mauritania 71-74, to Syria 74-; Dept. of State Superior Service Award 69.
American Embassy, Damascus, Syria.
Telephone: 332315.

Muti, Muhammad Salih; Yemeni officer and politician; b. 16 June 1944, Aden; ed. Higher Technical Inst., Cairo.
Military Commdr. NLF Commandos in Aden 67; mem. High Command, Nat. Front 68-, Exec. Cttee. 70-, Politbureau March 72-; Minister of the Interior 69-73, of Foreign Affairs May 73-.
Ministry of Foreign Affairs, Aden, People's Democratic Republic of Yemen.

N

Nabi, Belkacem; Algerian oil executive.
Director of Energy and Oils, Ministry of Industry and Energy, Algeria until 66; Président-Directeur Général Soc. Nat. de Recherche et d'Exploitation des Pétroles en Algérie (S.N. REPAL) 66-; Adviser to Minister of Finance 66-70; Wali de Tlemcen 70.
S.N. REPAL, Algiers, Algeria.

Nabulsi, Omar, L. en D., M.A.; Jordanian politician; b. 1 April 1936, Nablus; ed. Cairo and Ain Shams Univs.
Legal Adviser, Sasco Petroleum Co., Libya 59-61; Political Attaché, Arab League 61-70; Asst. Head, Admin. Section, Royal Hashemite Court Jan.-Sept. 70; Minister of Nat. Economy 70-72; Amb., Ministry of Foreign Affairs 72; Amb. to U.K. 72-73; Minister of Agriculture 73, of Nat. Econ. 73-Jan. 75; Order of Al-Kawkab (First Class).
c/o Ministry of National Economy, Amman, Jordan.

Nabulsi, Suleiman; Jordanian diplomatist and politician; b. 1910; ed. American Univ. Beirut.
Bank official and Man. till 46; Minister of Finance and

Econs. 46-47 and 50-51; Amb. to London 53-54 (resigned); leader Nat. Socialist Party; Prime Minister and Foreign Minister 56-57; mem. Consultative Council 67; Chair. Jordanian Cttee. for Afro-Asian Solidarity; mem. World Peace Council; Orders of Nahda and of Istiqlal, Jordan Star.

c/o Ministry of Foreign Affairs, Amman, Jordan.

Naffah, Fouad Georges, LIC. EN DROIT; Lebanese lawyer; b. 1 March 1925, Zouk Mikhaël; ed. Inst. des Frères Maristes, Coll. d'Antoura, Univ. St. Joseph, Beirut.
Member of Parl. for Kesrouan 60, 72; Lecturer in Constitutional Law and Lebanese Constitution, Coll. de la Sagesse and Univ. Libanaise; Minister of Agriculture 72, of Finance 72-73, of Foreign Affairs 73-74.
c/o Ministère des Affaires Etrangères, Beirut; Home: Raouché, Beirut, Lebanon.
Telephone: 233561 (Office); 314333 (Home).

Naggar, Abd el Moneim el; Egyptian army officer and diplomatist; b. 1920; ed. Cairo Military Academy, Cairo Staff Academy, Cairo Univ. and Inst. de Hautes Etudes, Univ. of Paris.
Egyptian Army 39-57; Military Attaché, Paris 53-54, Madrid 55-57; Head of East European Dept., Ministry of Foreign Affairs, Cairo 58; U.A.R. Consul-General, Bombay 59-62, Hong Kong 62-63; Ambassador to Greece 63-64, to France 64-68; Minister of Foreign Affairs 69-71; Amb. to Iraq 72-; numerous decorations.
Embassy of Egypt, Karradat Mariam, Baghdad, Iraq.

Naguib Ibrahim, Ibrahim; Egyptian architect and politician; b. 24 June 1911; ed. Royal School of Engineering, Giza.
Chartered Structural Engineer, London 35; Architect State Bldg. Dept., Ministry of Public Works 31, Head Technical Dept. 44-52, Insp. N. Cairo Zone 52-55; Del. Lecturer, Alexandria Univ. 46-50, Ain Shams Univ. 54-62; Controller of Municipal and Village Affairs, Cairo Governorate 55-57; Dir.-Gen. of Technical Research and Inspection, Ministry of Municipal and Village Affairs 57-60; Deputy Minister of Housing and Public Utilities 62-67; mem. Cen. Cttee. Arab Socialist Union 68-72, Gen. Secr. 72-74; mem. People's Assembly, Vice-Chair. Services Cttee. 69-71; Minister of Tourism 71-72, of Tourism and Civil Aviation April 74-; Chair. Cttee. of Int. Experts in charge of project for salvaging Temples on Philae Island, Aswan, Cttee. for Urban Reconstruction; Pres. Afro-Asian Housing Org. 63-67; mem. Board, Egyptian Soc. of Engineers; mem. Inst. of Structural Engineers, London; Hon. Pres. Soc. of Architects; has participated in numerous int. scientific confs.
Publs. *Architectural Drawing* 40, *Buildings of Nubia* 45, *Code of Practice for Structural Engineering* 46, *Foundations of Buildings in Egypt and the Sudan* 51, *Village Buildings and the Farmer's House* 53, *The Nature of Soil, and Foundations in the City of Cairo* 59, *Housing in Developing Countries* 68, *Trends in Architecture in the Arab Countries* 69.
Ministry of Tourism, Cairo, Egypt.

Nahavandi, Houshang, L. EN D., DR. ECON. SC.; Iranian economist, educationist and politician; b. 1930; ed. Univ. of Paris.
Adviser to High Council of Econs. 58-61, to Ministry of Labour 59-61; Econ. Attaché, Iranian Embassy, Brussels 61-63; Deputy Head, Del. to European Econ. Community 62-63; Man. Dir. Foreign Trade Co. 63-64; Minister of Housing and Devt. 64-68; Chancellor Pahlavi Univ. 68-71, Univ. of Teheran 71-; Civil Aide-de-Camp to H.I.M. The Shahanshah Aryamehr; mem. Board of Trustees, Mashad Univ., Charity Foundation of H.I.H. Princess Shams, High Council of Nat. Soc. for the Protection of Animals, High Council for Nat. Educ.; Chevalier Légion d'Honneur (France); Commdr. Ordre de la Couronne (Belgium);

Homayoun Decoration 1st Class, 4th Class; Sepasse Decoration and several other awards.
Publs. numerous books and articles.
University of Teheran, Teheran, Iran.

Najar, Amiel Emile, LIC. en DR.; Israeli diplomatist; b. 6 Sept. 1912; ed. Univ. of Paris.
President of Exec., Zionist Fed. of Egypt 43-47; Dir. Western European Div., Ministry of Foreign Affairs 52-57, Asst. Dir.-Gen. Ministry of Foreign Affairs 57-58; Minister to Japan 58-60; Ambassador to Belgium and Luxembourg, Chief of Mission to the European Communities 61-68; mem. Israeli Del. to UN 48, 51-53, 55-57, 61, 64, 67, 70; Observer, Suez Conf., London 56; Amb. to Italy 68-74, concurrently to Malta 68-71; Amb. Extraordinary and Political Adviser to Minister of Foreign Affairs 74-.
Ministry of Foreign Affairs, Jerusalem, Israel.

Najjar, Joseph; Lebanese engineer and politician; b. 1908; ed. Univ. St. Joseph, Beirut, Ecole Nat. des Ponts et Chaussées, Paris.
Consultant to Ministry of Interior 33-38; Dir. Hydraulic Service 38-40; Sec. of State to Ministry of Finance 40-41; mem. Planning Council 52-64; mem. Admin. Council, Office of Electricity 59-64; Prof. of Higher Engineering School, Beirut 41-; Pres. Nat. Scientific Research Council 63-; Minister of Planning, Agriculture, Posts and Telegraphs July 65-66; Perm. Rep. to UNESCO 66-67; Minister of Posts and Telegraphs 67-68; Ordre du Mérite Libanais, 1er classe; Officier Légion d'Honneur, etc.
Conseil National de la Recherche Scientifique, Beirut, Lebanon.

Nakhai, Hossein Ghods, G.C.V.O.; Iranian diplomatist; ed. Coll. of Political Sciences, Teheran.
Counsellor, Iranian Embassy, Washington 34, London 42; Dir.-Gen. Ministry of Foreign Affairs 50; Deputy Minister and Acting Minister of Foreign Affairs 50; Iranian Ambassador to Iraq 51 and 53, to Japan 56-58, to Great Britain 58-61; Minister of Foreign Affairs 61-62; Amb. to U.S.A. 62-63; Minister of the Imperial Court 63-67; Amb. to Vatican 67-70; Homayoun Order (1st Class), and many foreign decorations.
Publs. *Rubaiyat* (in Persian and English), *God and Man, The Development of Personality, The Shahsavan's Daughter, Paradise, Lady of the Isles* (in English), *The Key to the Sacred Doors, Genii at Large* (in English).
c/o Ministry of Foreign Affairs, Teheran, Iran.

Nakib, Ahmed Abdul Wahab Al-; Kuwaiti diplomatist; b. 30 July 1933, Kuwait; ed. Adam State Coll., Colorado, U.S.A.
First Sec., Kuwait Embassy, London 62-63; Counsellor, first Perm. Mission of Kuwait to UN 63-66; Consul-Gen., Nairobi, Kenya 66-67; Amb. to Pakistan 67-70, to U.K. 71-.
Embassy of Kuwait, 40 Devonshire Street, London, W1N 2AX, England.

Nashashibi, Nasser Eddin; Jordanian (b. Palestine) editor and diplomatist; b. 1924; ed. Arab Coll., Jerusalem and American Univ. Beirut.
Arab Office, Jerusalem 45-47; Chief Chamberlain, Amman 51; Dir.-Gen. Hashemite Broadcasting 52; Roving Editor *Akhbar El Yom*, Cairo; Chief Editor *Al Gomhouria*, Cairo 59-65; Roving Rep. of the Arab League June 65-67; Roving Dip. Editor *Al-Ahram*, Cairo; now freelance writer and journalist in Europe and Middle East; Jordanian Independence Star, 1st degree.
Publs. *Steps in Britain* (Arabic) 48, *What Happened in the Middle East* 58, *Short Political Stories* 59, *Return Ticket to Palestine* 60, *Some Sand* (Arabic) 62, *An Arab in China* (Arabic and English) 64, *Roving Ambassador* (Arabic) 70.
38 Rue Athenée, Geneva, Switzerland.

Nasir, Mohammed, B.SC., M.A., ED.D.; Iraqi educator and diplomatist; b. 1911; ed. Teacher Training Coll., Baghdad, American Univ., Beirut and Columbia Univ., New York.

Schoolteacher 31-32; Prof. of Educ. and Dean of Coll. of Educ., Baghdad Univ. 41-45, 55-63; Cultural Attaché and Perm. Rep. of Iraq to Arab League Cultural Comm. 45-48; Cultural Attaché, Washington 48-54; Alternate Del. to UN 5th Gen. Assembly; Pres. Teachers Union of Iraq 63-64; mem. Council, Univ. of Baghdad 63-64; Minister of Educ. 64; Ambassador to U.S.S.R. Nov. 64-66; Minister of Culture and Nat. Orientation 66; Prof. of Educational Admin., and Chair. Dept. of Educ. Kuwait Univ. 67-.
Publs. include many school books in Arabic, *Arabic Readings* (2 vols., joint author) 40, *Civic Education* (joint author) 40, *Guide to Higher Education in the U.S.A.* 57, *Readings in Educational Thought*, Vol. I 73.
c/o Kuwait University, P.O. Box 5969, Kuwait.

Nassif, Albert; Lebanese lawyer and diplomatist; b. 1915; ed. Univs. of Cairo and Paris.
Studied Law and Political Economy, Paris, also journalist, Egypt, Lebanon, and French Equatorial Africa 36-44; ed. journal *Le Jour* 44-47; Lecturer, Faculty of Law, Beirut 45-47; 2nd Sec., Lebanese Legation, Vatican 47-50; 1st Sec., Lebanese Legation, Switzerland 50-53; Counsellor, Lebanese Embassy, France 53-55; Head of Social and Cultural Dept., Lebanese Ministry of Foreign Affairs 56; Counsellor, London 57-59; Ambassador to Liberia 59-61, to India 61-63, to Turkey 63-65; Dir. Int. Dept., Ministry of Foreign Affairs 66-69; Amb. to Tunisia 69-71, to Switzerland Nov. 71-; Commdr. Order of St. Grégoire; Chevalier Légion d'Honneur; Officer Order of the Cedar (Lebanon), Ordine al Merito della Repubblica Italiana, Chevalier, Ordre Humain de la Libération Africaine.
Publs. political, economic and legal studies.
Embassy of Lebanon, Alpenstrasse 24, Berne, Switzerland.

Nassiri, Gen. Ne'matollah; Iranian army officer; b. 1910; ed. Teheran Military Acad.
Early career in army posts including Chief, Mil. Police HQ 49, Commdr. Pahlavi Infantry Regiment 50, Imperial Guards 51; arrested Mossadegh under Shahanshah's orders 53; promoted to rank of Maj.-Gen. 58, Lt.-Gen. 62, Gen. 71; Deputy Mil. ADC to Shahanshah Aryamehr 60; Chief of Police 60-65; Mil. Gov., Teheran 63; Head, State Security and Intelligence Org. (SAVAK) and Asst. to Prime Minister 65-.
SAVAK, Teheran, Iran.

Natra, Sergiu; Israeli composer; b. 1924, Romania; ed. National Conservatoire, Bucharest.
Settled in Israel 61; G. Enesco Prize 45, State Prize 51, Engel Prize 69.
Works include: *March and Chorale* 44, *Suite for Orchestra* 48, *Sinfonia* 60, *Music for Violin and Harp* 60, *Toccata for Orchestra* 63, *Music for Harpsichord and Six Instruments* 64, *Sonatina for Harp* 65, *Voices of Fire* (ballet music), *Music for Oboe and Strings* 65, *Prelude for Narrator and Orchestra, Commentary on Nehemia, Song of Deborah for Mezzo-Soprano and Chamber Orchestra* 67, *Prayer for Harp* 70, *Trio in One Movement for Violin, Violoncello and Piano* 71, *Dedication: Two Poems for Mezzo-Soprano and Orchestra* 72, *A Book of Hebrew Songs for the Harp* 74, *Sacred Service* 75.
10 Barth Street, Ramat Aviv, Tel-Aviv, Israel.

Nawwar, Maj.-Gen. Ali Abu; Jordanian army officer and diplomatist.
Chief of Staff, Jordanian army 56; in exile in Egypt 57-64; Personal Rep. of King Hussein Oct. 70-Feb. 71; Amb. at Ministry of Foreign Affairs May 70; Amb. to France 71, also accred. to Belgium.
c/o Ministry of Foreign Affairs, Amman, Jordan.

Nebenzahl, Itzhak Ernst, DR.IUR.; Israeli administrator; b. 24 Oct. 1907; ed. Univs. of Frankfurt and Freiburg.
Settled in Palestine 33; Dir. Jerusalem Econ. Corpn. 47-61, Jerusalem Devt. Dept., Jewish Agency 48-50, Bank Leumi le-Israel Ltd. 56-61; Hon. Consul-Gen. of Sweden 52-62; Chair. Post Office Bank 54-61, of Advisory Cttee. and Council, Bank of Israel 57-62; State Comptroller of Israel 61, re-elected 66, 71-; Pres. Fifth Int. Congress of Int. Org. of Supreme Audit Insts. (INTOSAI) 65, Chair. 65-68, now mem. Gov. Board; Public Complaints Commr. (Ombudsman) 71-; fmr. mem. Petroleum Board, Anti-Trust Council, and several govt. inquiry cttees.; Partner, Hollander Concern (Stockholm, New York, London, Buenos Aires, Paris, Tokyo, etc.), Chair. Board of Dirs. 47-61; Chevalier (First Class), Royal Swedish Order of Vasa 57.
Office of the State Comptroller, P.O. Box 1081, Jerusalem; Home: 9 Batei Mahse Street, Old City, Jerusalem, Israel.

Ne'eman, Yuval, B.SC., DIP. ING., D.E.M., D.I.C., PH.D.; Israeli soldier and scientist; b. 14 May 1925; ed. Herzlia High School, Tel-Aviv, Israel Inst. of Technology, Haifa, Ecole Supérieure de Guerre, Paris, and London Univ.
Hydrodynamics Design Engineer 45; in Hagana 46; Captain, Israeli Defence Forces (Infantry) 48, Major 49, Lieut.-Col. 50, Col. 55; Defence Attaché, London 58-60; joined Israel Atomic Energy Establishments 60, Scientific Dir., Soreq Research Establishment 61-63; Head, Physics Dept., Tel-Aviv Univ. 62-, Prof. of Physics 64-; Research Fellow, Calif. Inst. of Technology 63, Visiting Prof. of Physics 64-65; Vice-Rector and Vice-Pres., Tel-Aviv Univ. 65-66, Pres. 71-; Senior Adviser and Chief Scientist, Ministry of Defence 75-; mem. Israel Atomic Energy Comm. 66-, Israel Nat. Acad. of Sciences 66-; known mainly for his co-discovery of Unitary Symmetry (The Eightfold Way) 61; Foreign Hon. mem., American Acad. of Arts and Sciences 70; Foreign Assoc. Nat. Acad. of Sciences, U.S.A. 72; Hon. Life mem. New York Acad. of Sciences 73; Hon. D.Sc.; Weizmann Prize for the Sciences 66, Rothschild Prize 68, Israel Prize for Exact Sciences 69; Albert Einstein Medal and Prize (U.S.A.) 70.
Publs. *The Eightfold Way* (with M. Gell-Mann) 64, *Algebraic Theory of Particle Physics* 67, *The Past Decade in Particle Theory* (with E. C. G. Sudarshan) 73; about 150 articles on physics, astrophysics and philosophy of science.
Department of Physics and Astronomy, Tel-Aviv University, Tel-Aviv, Israel.

Negahban, Ezatollah, B.A., M.A., PH.D.; Iranian archaeologist; b. 1 March 1925; ed. Teheran and Chicago Univs.
Assoc. Prof. Univ. of Teheran 56-62, Prof. 62-, Dir. Univ. Inst. of Archaeology 58-; Technical Dir. Iranian Archaeological Service 60-65; Technical Adviser to Ministry of Culture 65-; Hon. mem. German Archaeological Inst.; mem. Perm. Council, Congress of Pre- and Proto-historic Archaeology; excavated at Marlik 61-62, Haft Tepe; Dir. Iranian Archaeological (Iran Bastan) Museum 66.
Publs. *The Gold Treasures of Marlik* 62, *Preliminary Report on Marlik Excavation* 64.
Box 319, Teheran, Iran.

Neguib, Gen. Mohamed; Egyptian army officer; b. Khartoum 1901; ed. Sudan Schools, Gordon Coll., Khartoum, Royal Mil. Acad. and Egyptian Univ., Cairo.
Commissioned in infantry 17; served in Gen. Staff, Adjutant-Gen. and Q.M.-Gens'. departments during Second World War; Sub-Governor of Sinai and Governor of Red Sea Provinces in Frontier Corps; Col. Commdg. 2nd Machine Gun Bn.; Brig., 2nd in commd. of Egyptian troops in Palestine and commdg. successively 1st, 2nd, 3rd, 4th and 10th Inf. Bdes. during hostilities with Israel 48; Dir.-Gen. Frontier Corps 50, Dir.-Gen. Infantry 51, C.-in-C. Egyptian Army July 52; Prime Minister, Minister for War and Marine, C.-in-C. of the Army and Military Gov. of Egypt 52-53; Pres. of the Repub. of Egypt 53-54.
Cairo, Egypt.

Nekrouf, Younès, L. ès L.; Moroccan diplomatist; b. 1916; ed. Inst. des Hautes Etudes Marocaines, Rabat and Univs. of Bordeaux and Algiers.
Government Interpreter 35-39; School Teacher and Inspector of Schools 39-55; Dir. de Cabinet to Minister of Education 55-57; Cultural Counsellor, Moroccan Embassy, Paris, and Perm. Del. to UNESCO 57-59; Dir. Cultural Affairs and Technical Assistance, Ministry of Foreign Affairs 59-61; Counsellor, then Minister Plenipotentiary, Paris 61-64; Ambassador to Senegal 65-67, concurrently to the Gambia, Guinea and Liberia; Ambassador to Yugoslavia 67-68; Dir. Political Affairs, Ministry of Foreign Affairs 68-71; Amb. to India 71-74; del. to UN Gen. Assembly 65, 68-71; Moroccan Rep. to several int. confs.; Officier, Légion d'Honneur, Palmes Académiques, Commdr. Arts et Lettres, France; Officier Ouissame Alaouite, Ordre du Trône, Morocco; Grand Officer, Nat. Order of Yugoslavia, Order of Tudor Vladimirescu of Romania; Knight of Grand Cross, Order of Merit of the Repub. of Italy; Grand Officier Ordre du Mérite, Senegal.
Publ. *Méthode Active d'Arabe* (2 vols.) 58, various essays and articles on Portuguese colonization.
Ministry of Foreign Affairs, Rabat, Morocco.

Nemery, Maj.-Gen. Jaafar Mohammed al-; Sudanese army officer and political leader; b. 1 Jan. 1930, Omdurman; ed. Sudan Military Coll.
Former Commdr. Khartoum garrison; campaigns against rebels in Southern Sudan; placed under arrest on suspicion of plotting to overthrow the government; Chair. Revolutionary Command Council (R.C.C.) 69-71; C.-in-C. of Armed Forces 69-73; Prime Minister 69-73, Minister of Foreign Affairs 70-71, of Planning 71-72, of Defence 71-73; Pres. Political Bureau, Sec.-Gen. Sudanese Socialist Union 71-; Pres. of Sudan Oct. 71-.
Office of the President, Khartoum, Sudan.

Niamir, Kazem; Iranian diplomatist; b. 1914; ed. Sarvat Coll., Teheran, and Teheran and London Univs.
Court of Justice Teheran 34-37; Ministry of Foreign Affairs 38-; served London 40-46; Political Adviser to Iranian UN Mission 46; Ministry of Foreign Affairs 46-48; Counsellor New Delhi 49-52; Chief of Cultural Dept., Ministry of Foreign Affairs 52-54; Minister-Counsellor to Japan 54-58; Chief Third Political Dept. of Ministry of Foreign Affairs 59-63; Amb. to Jordan 63-65; mem. Ministry of Foreign Affairs High Political Council 66; Sec.-Gen. of the Iranian Asscn. for the UN 66-70; Amb. to Ethiopia 71-; numerous Iranian and foreign decorations.
Publs. *Treaty of Versailles and after* 37, *Demography* 37, *Political Organisation of Japan* 55.
Imperial Embassy of Iran, Ras Desta Damten Avenue, Addis Ababa, Ethiopia.

Nimir, Ibrahim Mohamed Aly, B.A., F.I.B.; Sudanese banker; b. 1922; ed. Gordon Memorial Coll. and Univ. of Wales.
Governor and Chair. Bank of Sudan 72-; Chair. Savings and Investment Council 73; mem. Ministerial Council for Nat. Econ. 73-74, Khartoum Univ. Council 74-, Islamic Univ. Council 74-, Board of Dirs. Sudanese Devt. Corpn. 74-; Alt. Gov. for Sudan, Int. Monetary Fund 72-.
Bank of Sudan, Khartoum, P.O. Box 313, Sudan.

Nissim, Isaac; Israeli Rabbi; b. 1896, Baghdad.
In Israel since 25; advocates consolidation of the various Jewish tribes into one single community; elected Rishon le Zion and Chief Rabbi (Sephardi) of Israel Feb. 55, installed March 55 until 72; Pres. Rabbinical High Court 55-72; Pres. Beth Hamidrash le Rabbanim Ule-Dayanim, Jerusalem.
Publs. *Yen Hatov, Canogah Zidkah Umishpat.*
7 Balfour Street, Jerusalem, Israel.

Nofal, Sayed, DR. ARTS; Egyptian international civil servant; b. 1910; ed. Cairo Univ.

Head of Literary Dept. *Al Sivassa* 35-38; Teacher, Cairo Univ. 38; later Dir. of Technical Secr., Ministry of Educ. and Ministry of Social Affairs; later Dir. of Legislative Dept., Upper House of Egyptian Parl.; later Dir. Political Dept., League of Arab States, Asst. Sec.-Gen. 60-.
Publs. include *Poetry of Nature in Arabic and Western Literature* 44, *Egypt in the United Nations* 47, *The Egyptian Parliament in a Quarter of a Century* 51, *The Political Status of the Emirates of the Arab Gulf and Southern Arabia* 59, *The Arab-Israeli Conflict* 62, *Arab Unity* 64, *Arab Nationalism* 65, *Arab Socialism* 66, *The Record of Israel* 66, *Joint Arab Action Book I* 68, *Book II* 71, *The Arab Gulf or The Eastern Borders of the Arab Homeland* 69, *An Introduction to Israeli Foreign Policy* 72.
League of Arab States, Midan Al Tahrir, Cairo; and 9 Khan Younis Street, Madinet al Mohandesseen, Dokki, Cairo, Egypt.

Noman, Ismail Said; Yemeni diplomatist; b. 1941, Aden; ed. Boston, Mass., U.S.A.
Instructor, Aden Coll. 67; Asst. Sec. Aden Electricity Corpn. 67-68; Amb. and Perm. Rep. to UN 68-70; Sales Man., Nat. Co. for Home Trade 70-72, Technical Man. 72-.
Khalifa Street Block 31/72, Al-Mansorah, Aden, People's Democratic Republic of Yemen.

Nouh Ahmed, Ahmed; Egyptian engineer and politician; b. 4 Dec. 1921; ed. Alexandria Univ. and Air Acad.
Lieutenant-General, Pilot Engineer, Gen. HQ Armed Forces; Technical Gen. Man. Misrair; fmr. Gen. Sec. Ministry of War, later Asst. Minister; Minister of State for Civil Aviation 71-72; Minister for Civil Aviation 72-74, concurrently of Tourism 73-74.
c/o Ministry of Civil Aviation, Cairo, Egypt.

Nouira, Hedi; Tunisian politician; b. 6 April 1911, Monastir; ed. High School, Sousse, and Paris.
Secretary of Gen. Confed. of Tunisian Workers 38; in detention 38-43; Sec.-Gen. of Néo-Destour Party 42-54, 69-; Minister of Commerce 54-55; Minister of Finance 55-58; Founder and Dir. of Central Bank of Tunisia 58-70; Minister of the Economy 70; Prime Minister Nov. 70-.
Office of the Prime Minister, Tunis, Tunisia.

Nowar, Ma'an Abu; Jordanian diplomatist; b. 26 July 1928, Salt; ed. London Univ.
Joined Jordanian Arab Army 43, Commdr. Infantry Brigade 57-63; Counsellor, Jordanian Embassy, London 63; Dir. Jordan Civil Defence 64-67, Jordan Public Security 67-69; Asst. Chief of Staff for Gen. Affairs 69-72; Minister of Culture and Information 72; Amb. to U.K. 73-; Jordanian Star 1st Class.
Royal Jordan Embassy, 6 Upper Phillimore Gardens, London, W8 7HB, England.

Nur, Abdul Mohsen Abu al-; Egyptian politician; b. 4 Aug. 1918; ed. Egyptian Military Acad.
Fought in Palestine war 48-49; took part in revolution 52; subsequently served as Mil. Attaché, Egyptian embassies in Sudan, Syria, Lebanon; Deputy Commdr. of the First Army 58; Gov. of Suez town; Minister of State for Land Reform 62, for Agrarian Reform and Land Reclamation 63; Deputy Prime Minister for Agriculture and Irrigation 64-68; Minister for Local Admin. 68; Deputy Sec.-Gen. Arab Socialist Union 67-70, Sec.-Gen. 70-May 71; sentenced to imprisonment for treason Dec. 71.
Cairo, Egypt.

Nurock, Mordekhai, O.B.E., M.A., LL.D. (HON.); Israeli diplomatist; b. 1893; ed. Dublin Univ.
With British Colonial Admin. Service, Palestine 20-36, Uganda 37-45; with British Control Comm., Germany and Austria 45-49; Adviser on Personnel to Israel Govt. 49-51; Financial Sec. Hebrew Univ. 51-52; Israel Minister to Australia and New Zealand 53-58; Israel Chargé d'Affaires, South Africa 59; mem. Board of Govs. Hebrew Univ. 63-

Editor Govt. Year Book 63-; ranking Ambassador 64-; Adviser on Publications, Foreign Ministry.
Publs. *Fruits of the Holy Land* (co-author), *Words of the Wise* (co-author).
201 Elm Tree Court, St. John's Wood, London, N.W.8, England; and Ministry for Foreign Affairs, Jerusalem, Israel.

Nuseibeh, Anwar Zaki, M.A.; Jordanian diplomatist and lawyer; b. 20 Jan. 1913; ed. Govt. Arab Coll., Jerusalem, and Queens Coll., Cambridge.
Land Officer, Palestine 36, Magistrate 37-42; Lecturer in Constitutional Law, Jerusalem Law Classes 36-48; fmr. mem. Jordan Parl. and Senator; Chief Arab Del., Jordan and Israel Mixed Armistice Comm. 51; Minister of Defence 53, of Educ. 54-55, of Reconstruction and Devt. 54-55; Gov. of Jerusalem, Jordan 61-62; Ambassador to U.K. 65-66; private business in Jordan 66-; Order of El Kawkab (1st Class); Assoc. Knight Order of St. John of Jerusalem; Knight of Order of Holy Sepulchre.
c/o Ministry of Foreign Affairs, Amman, Jordan.

Nuseibeh, Hazem, M.A., PH.D.; Jordanian politician; ed. Rawda Coll., Jerusalem, Victoria Coll., Alexandria, American Univ. of Beirut, Law School, Jerusalem, Woodrow Wilson School of Public and Int. Affairs and Princeton Univ.
Under-Secretary, Ministry of Nat. Econ. 57-59; Pres. Jordan Devt. Board 59-61; Minister of Foreign Affairs 62-63, 65-66; Minister of Royal Court 63-65; Prof. of Int. Affairs, Jordan Univ. 66-67; Minister of Reconstruction and Devt. 67-69; Amb. to Egypt 69-71, to Turkey 71-73, to Italy 73-, also accred. to Austria and Switzerland.
Publ. *Ideas of Arab Nationalism* 56.
Embassy of Jordan, Via Po 24, Rome, Italy.

Nutting, Rt. Hon. Sir (Harold) Anthony, Bt., P.C.; British politician and writer; b. 11 Jan. 1920; ed. Eton and Trinity Coll., Cambridge.
In British Foreign Service 40-45; mem. Parl. 45-56; Chair. Young Conservative and Unionist Movement 46, Nat. Union of Conservative and Unionist Asscns. 50, Conservative Nat. Exec. Cttee. 51; Parl. Under-Sec. of State for Foreign Affairs 51-54; Minister of State for Foreign Affairs 54-56 (resigned over British Suez policy); Leader, U.K. Del. to UN Gen. Assembly and UN Disarmament Comm. 54-56.
Publs. *I Saw for Myself* 58, *Disarmament* 59, *Europe Will Not Wait* 60, *Lawrence of Arabia* 61, *The Arabs* 64, *Gordon, Martyr and Misfit* 66, *No End of a Lesson* 67, *Scramble for Africa* 70, *Nasser* 72.
47 Addison Road, London, W.14, England.

O

Obeidi, Abdul Ati El-, M.SC.; Libyan politician; b. 10 Oct. 1939; ed. Libyan Univ., Manchester Univ., England.
Lecturer, Libyan Univ. 67-70; Minister of Labour 70-, of Civil Service 74-; Acting Minister of Foreign Affairs 70; decorations from Tunisia, The Philippines and Malaysia.
Ministry of Labour, Tripoli; Home: P.O. Box 2256, Benghazi, Libya.

Ofer, Avraham; Israeli politician; b. 1922.
With Israeli Navy, Lt.-Col. 48; founder and Dir.-Gen. Moetzet Halul 60; Asst. Dir. Ministry of Agriculture 60; mem. Del. for negotiations towards joining European Common Market; Gen. Man. Ashdod Corpn. Ltd.; mem. Knesset (Parl.) 69-; Minister of Housing June 74-; Labour Party.
Ministry of Housing, Jerusalem, Israel.

Okasha, Sarwat Mahmoud Fahmy, D. ÈS L.; Egyptian diplomatist, politician and banker; b. 1921; ed. Military Coll. and Cairo Univ.
Cavalry officer 39; took part in Palestine war 48-49; Mil. Attaché, Berne 53-54, Paris and Madrid 54-56; Attaché in

Presidency of Republic 56-67; U.A.R. Ambassador to Italy 57-58; Minister of Culture and Nat. Guidance and Pres. of Supreme Council for Literature, Art and Social Sciences 58-62; Chair. Board of Dirs. of Nat. Bank of Egypt 62; mem. UNESCO Exec. Board 62; mem. Nat. Assembly and Pres. Foreign Affairs Comm. 64-66; Deputy Prime Minister, Minister of Culture 66-68; Minister of Culture 68-71; Asst. to the Pres. 71-June 72; Pres. of Supreme Council for Literature, Art and Social Sciences; Pres. Egypt-France Asscn. 65-; numerous awards.
Publs. Nineteen works (incl. translations) since 42.
Villa 34, St. 14, Maadi, Cairo, Egypt.

Olcay, Osman; Turkish diplomatist; b. 17 Jan. 1924; ed. St. Joseph French Coll., Istanbul, and Faculty of Political Science, Univ. of Ankara.
Joined Ministry of Foreign Affairs, Turkey 45; Lieut., Turkish Army 46; Foreign Ministry 47; Vice-Consul, London 48-50, Second Sec., London 50-52; Chief of Section, Dept. of Econ. Affairs, Ministry of Foreign Affairs 52-54; First Sec. NATO, Paris 54, Counsellor and Deputy Perm. Rep. 58-59; Asst. Dir.-Gen. NATO Dept., Min. of Foreign Affairs, Ankara 59-60, Dir.-Gen. 60-63, Asst. Sec.-Gen. 63-64; Amb. to Finland 64-66, to India and Ceylon 66-68; Deputy Sec.-Gen. of NATO, Brussels 69-71; Minister of Foreign Affairs March-Dec. 71; Perm. Rep. to UN June 72-.
Permanent Mission of Turkey at the United Nations, 866 Second Avenue, 2 Hammarskjöld Plaza, 15th Floor, New York, N.Y. 10017, U.S.A.

Olsen, Bjørn; Danish United Nations official; b. 19 March 1930, Copenhagen; ed. Frederiksberg Gymnasium, Univ. of Copenhagen.
Worked for Asscn. for the Promotion of Int. Co-operation 54; joined Ministry of Foreign Affairs 55, served no. of posts including Principal Private Sec. to Minister of Foreign Affairs; Econ. Counsellor, Perm. Mission of Denmark to UN; Econ. Counsellor, Embassy of Denmark to U.S.A. -71; Resident Rep. UN Devt. Programme (UNDP) Afghanistan 71-.
United Nations Development Programme, P.O. Box 5, Kabul, Afghanistan.

Omran, Adnan; Syrian diplomatist; b. 9 Aug. 1934, Syria; ed. Univ. of Damascus, Moscow and Columbia, U.S.A.
Ministry of Foreign Affairs 62-63; mem. Perm. Mission to UN 63-66; First Sec., Moscow 66-68; Consul-Gen., Embassy in Berlin, German Dem. Repub. 68-70; Dir. Int. Org. and Conf. Dept., Ministry of Foreign Affairs 70-71, Palestine Dept. 71-72, Special Bureau Dept. 72-74, concurrently mem. Del. to UN 72-74; Amb. to U.K. 74-.
Embassy of the Syrian Arab Republic, 5 Eaton Terrace, London, SW1W 8EX, England.

Örek, Osman Nuri; Cypriot lawyer and politician; b. 1925; ed. Turkish Lycée, Nicosia, Univ. of Istanbul and Middle Temple, London.
Founder-mem. Cyprus-is-Turkish Asscn., London, Chair. 51-52; Sec. Nicosia Branch, Cyprus Turkish Nat. Union Party 53-55, Sec.-Gen. 55-July 60, Dep. Chair. July 60-; Dep. Chair. High Council of Evcaf 56-60; rep. Turkish Cypriot Community at London Conf. 59 and subsequent Joint Cttee.; Minister of Defence 59; mem. Exec. Council of Turkish Cypriot Provisional Admin. for Defence 67-74, concurrently for Internal Affairs 67-70, and External Affairs 67-74; mem. Exec. Council of Autonomous Turkish Cypriot Admin. for Vice-Presidency and Defence 74-75; Vice-Pres. Turkish Federated State of Cyprus Feb. 75-, Minister of Defence Feb. 75-.
Office of the Vice-President, Turkish Cypriot Administration, 9 Server Somuncuoglu Street, Nicosia; Home: 10 Ismail Beyoglu Street, Nicosia, Cyprus.

Orgad, Ben Zion; Israeli composer; b. 1926, Germany; ed. Acad. of Music in Jerusalem and Brandeis Univ., U.S.A.

Studied violin with Kinory and Bergman and composition with Paul Ben-Haim and Josef Tal; studied in U.S.A. under Aaron Copland and Irving Fine; now Supervisor of Musical Educ., Israel Ministry of Educ. and Culture; recipient of several awards for compositions.

Compositions include: cantatas: *The Story of the Spies* (UNESCO Koussevitsky Prize 52), *Isaiah's Vision*; works for orchestra, *Building a King's Stage, Choreographic Sketches, Movements on "A", Kaleidoscope, Music for Horn and Orchestra; Hatsvi Israel* (Symphony for baritone and orch.); *Out of the Dust* (for solo and instruments); *Ballada* (for violin), *Taksim* (for harp), *Monologue* (for viola); works for soloists and orchestra, songs, piano pieces, etc.

Ministry of Education and Culture, Hadar-Daphna Building, Tel-Aviv; Home: 14 Bloch Street, Tel-Aviv, Israel.

Osman, Ahmed, LL.D.; Moroccan diplomatist and politician; b. 3 Jan. 1930; m. Princess Lallah Nezh; ed. Royal High School, Rabat, Univ. of Rabat and Univ. of Bordeaux, France.

Member of Royal Cabinet (judicial matters) 56; joined Ministry of Foreign Affairs 57; Sec.-Gen. Ministry of Nat. Defence 59-61; Amb. to Fed. Repub. of Germany 61-62; Under Sec.-of-State for Industry and Mines 63-64; Pres. and Gen. Man. Moroccan Navigation Co. 64-67; Ambassador to U.S.A., Canada and Mexico 67-70; Minister of Admin. Affairs 70-71; Dir. of Royal Cabinet 71-72; Prime Minister 72-; participated in UN sessions 57, 58, 60, 61, Conf. on Maritime Law 58, Conf. of the League of Arab States 61.

Office of the Prime Minister, Rabat, Morocco.
Telephone: 245 54-33804.

Osman, Hassan Mutwakil Mohamed; Sudanese executive; b. Jan. 1918; ed. Coll. of Agriculture, Sudan.

Agriculturalist with Sudanese Dept. of Agriculture 42-48; Senior Officer Atbara Dairy 48-50; Insp. of Mechanized Crop Production 50-51; Insp. of Agriculture, Sennor and Fung Districts 51-54; Govt. Soil Conservation Officer 54-57; Asst. Dir. of Agriculture, Dept. of Agriculture 59-62, Deputy Dir. 63-65, Dir. Ministry of Agriculture 65-66; Dir. Sudan Gezira Board 64-66; mem. Council, Univ. of Khartoum and Board of Faculty of Agriculture 64-69; Man. Dir. and Chair. Sudan Gezira Board 66-70; Chair. Board of El Nilein Bank 70-73.

c/o El Nilein Bank, P.O. Box 466, Khartoum, Sudan.

Osman, Osman Ahmed, B.SC.; Egyptian civil engineer; b. 1917; ed. Cairo Univ.

Chairman The Arab Contractors (Osman Ahmed Osman & Co.) 52-, and of its assoc. companies, Saudi Enterprises, Kuwaiti Engineering Co., The Libyan Co. for Contracting and Devt.; Minister of Reconstruction Oct. 73-, and of Housing April 75-; Repub. Medal (First Class), Russian Hero of Labour Medal.

Chief works undertaken include: (in Egypt) Aswan High Dam, Suez Canal deepening and widening, Port Said Shipyard, Cairo Int. Airport, Salehaieh reclamation project, High Dam Electric Power Transmission Lines, Guiza Bridge, Ramses Bridge over the Nile; (in Saudi Arabia) Dhahran Airport, Riyadh Mil. Coll., Dammam Mil. Barracks; (in Kuwait) Municipality Centre, Kuwait drainage system; (in Libya) Benghazi drainage system, Benghazi Stadium; (in Iraq) Kirkuk Feeder Canal No. 2 and 3; (in Jordan) Khaled Ibn El-Walid Dam and Tunnels; (in Sudan) 200 bedroom First Class Hotel.

Publ. *The High Dam* (lecture) 66.

Ministry of Reconstruction and Housing, Ismailia, Egypt.

Osseyran, Adel; Lebanese politician; b. 1905, Saida; ed. American Univ. of Beirut.

Deputy for Southern Lebanon 43; Minister of Supplies in first Cabinet after Independence 43; mem. of Lebanese Del. to UN 47, 48; Deputy for Zahrani 53-; Pres. Chamber of Deputies 53, 57, 58; Minister of the Interior 68-69, of Justice, of Public Works, of Economy May 75-; Grand Cordon of the Order of the Cedar; several foreign decorations.

Chambre des Députés, Place de l'Etoile, Beirut, Lebanon.

Otaiba, Mana Saeed al; Abu Dhabi economist; b. 15 May 1946; ed. Univ. of Baghdad.

Chairman of Board, Abu Dhabi Nat. Oil Co.; mem. Abu Dhabi Planning Board; Pres. Dept. of Petroleum, Minerals and Industry; Chair. of Board, Abu Dhabi Gas Liquifaction Co.; Minister of Petroleum and Industry (Abu Dhabi) 72-73, of Petroleum and Mineral Resources (U.A.E. Fed. Govt.) Dec. 73-; mem. Board of six oil cos. in Abu Dhabi; has travelled on State visits, etc. throughout Arab countries, W. Europe, U.S.A., Canada.

Publs. *The Abu Dhabi Planning Board, The Economy of Abu Dhabi, Organization of the Petroleum Exporting Countries.*

Ministry of Petroleum, P.O. Box 9, Abu Dhabi, United Arab Emirates.

Othman as-Said, Muhammad; Libyan politician; b. Oct. 1922; ed. Sanusi religious institutions, Fezzan.

Head of Religious Court for Admin. Region of Brak 45; organized Libyan Nationalist Activity in Fezzan 47; imprisoned by French 48-50; Leader Fezzan Del. to Libyan Independence Comm. 50; mem. Constituent Assembly 50; mem. Advisory Comm. to UN in Libya 50; Minister of Health, Libya 51, later Minister of Public Health until 58; Deputy to Constituent Assembly 58; Minister for Econ. Affairs 60; Prime Minister 60-March 63; Deputy 64; private business 64-; numerous decorations.

Geraba Street 6, Tripoli, Libya.

Otten, Heinrich; German orientalist; b. 27 Dec. 1913. Professor and Dir. Oriental Seminar, Marburg Univ. 59-; mem. Acad. of Sciences and Literature, Mainz 59-; mem. German Archaeological Inst., Berlin 69-; corresp. mem. Vienna Acad. of Sciences 72.

Publs. several works on Hittitology and history of the Ancient Near East.

355 Marburg/Lahn, Sudetenstrasse 4, Federal Republic of Germany.

Ötüken, Adnan; Turkish librarian; b. 1911; ed. Lycée and Univ. of Istanbul, and Germany.

Asst. Turkish Language and Literature Dept., Univ. of Istanbul 40; Dir. of Publs., Asst. Dir.-Gen. of Fine Arts, Ministry of Education 52-54; Lecturer of Library Science, Univ. of Ankara; mem. Exec. Cttee. Turkish Nat. Comm. of UNESCO and Exec. Board Turkish Librarians' Assen.; Dir. Turkish Nat. Library 60-65; Under-Sec. for Culture, Ministry of Educ. 65-67; Lecturer in Turkish Language and Literature, Lycée Teachers' Training Coll., Ankara 67-; Gen. Sec. Turkish-Iraqi Standing Cttee. of Cultural Agreement; fmrly. Turkish Cultural Attaché in Germany.

Publs. *Bibliyotek bilgisi ve bibliyografi* (Library Science and Bibliography) 40, *Istanbul Üniversitesi Yayımları Bibliyografyası* (Bibliography of the Publs. of the Univ. of Istanbul) 41, *Seçme eserler bibliyografyası. 1. cilt* (Selected Bibliography, Vol. 1) 46, *Milli Kütüphane kurulurken* (Establishing the National Library) 46, *Istanbul Üniversities yayımları Bibliyografyası, 1933-45* (Bibliography of the Publs. of the Univ. of Istanbul, 1933-45, with Acaroğlu) 47, *Dünya edebiyatından tercemeler. Klâsikler Bibliyografyası, 1940-48* (Bibliography of classical and modern works translated and published by Turkish Ministry of Education, 1940-48) 47, (2nd edn.) *1940-50* 52, *Bibliyotekçinin el kitabı, 2 cilt* (Manual of the Librarian, 2 vols.) 47-48, *Milli Kütüphane Nasıl Kuruldu* (How the Turkish

National Library was founded) 55, *Türk dilinin Başına gelenler* (The Things that Happened to Turkish language, 2 vols.) 68, *Iki yilda 600 den fazla yazi* (bibliography) 69. Lycée Teachers' Training College, Ankara, Turkey.

Ouazzani, Thami; Moroccan diplomatist; b. 27 Dec. 1927, Fez; ed. Collège Moulay Idriss, Fez, Faculté de Droit, Paris and the Sorbonne.
Called to the Bar, Casablanca 51; Minister of Industry and Mines 55-56; mem. Conseil de l'Ordre des Avocats de Casablanca 59; Amb. to Yugoslavia and Greece 61; Sec. Gen. Charte de Casablanca 62; Minister of Labour and Social Affairs 63-64, of Public Works and Admin. Reform 65; Amb. to Algeria 65-67; Minister of Tourism 68; Minister in Royal Cabinet 68-69; Amb. to Tunisia 69-71; Amb. to U.K. 71-73; Grand Cordon Alaouite and decorations from Yugoslavia and Tunisia.
c/o Ministry of Foreign Affairs, Rabat, Morocco.

Özbek, Dr. Sabahattin; Turkish agronomist; b. 1915, Erzincan; ed. Secondary School, Istanbul, Faculty of Agriculture, Univ. of Ankara.
Lecturer, Faculty of Agriculture, Univ. of Ankara 38, Asst. Prof. 41, Prof. 53, Dean 55-57, 65-68; Visiting Prof. Univs. of Michigan and Calif. 50-51, 57-58; Minister of Nat. Educ. 72-73, of Communications 73-74; founded Atatürk Univ., Erzurum, later Co-Founder Faculty of Agriculture, Adana; Chair. Agricultural Cttee. for the preparation of First Five-Year Devt. Plan; mem. Turkish Atomic Energy Comm.; Prize of Professional Honour, Union of Agricultural Engineers; Independent.
Publs. 35 books in Turkish and foreign languages.
c/o Ministry of Communications, Ankara, Turkey.

Özel, Ahmet; Turkish engineer, educationist and politician; b. 1910; ed. Technical Univ. of Istanbul, and Paris Ecole Nat. Supérieure de Télécommunications.
Docent Technical Univ. of Istanbul and Factory Engineer 39, Prof. 49, Dir. Civil Aeronautical Inst. and Dean Electrical Faculty 52, Pres. 53-54; Dep. from Sıvas to Grand Nat. Assembly 54-57; Minister of Education 55-57; Pres. Atatürk Univ. 57-58, Prof. of Mathematics and Physics, Atatürk Univ. 58-67; Pres. Black Sea Technical Univ. 67, now Prof. of Electrical Engineering; mem. Democratic Party.
Publs. *Courses on Radio-Electricity, The Role of the Atmosphere on the Propagation of Electro-Magnetic Waves, The Application of Heaviside's Symbolic Computations of Electrotechnics, Electro-Magnetic Theory and Radiation, General Mathematics Courses.*
Department of Electrical Engineering, Black Sea University, Trabzon, Turkey.

Öztekin, Mukadder; Turkish politician; b. 1919, Niğde Prov.; ed. Galatasaray Lycée, Istanbul, Ankara Univ.
Joined Ministry of Interior 44; County Chief Officer in various districts, Insp.; Gov. of Adana 60; Senator for Adana 66; Minister of Public Works 71-73, of the Interior 73-74; Officier, Légion d'Honneur; Independent.
c/o Ministry of the Interior, Ankara, Turkey.

Öztrak, Ilhan, PH.D.; Turkish lawyer and politician; b. 1925, Ankara; ed. Faculty of Law, Ankara Univ. and Univ. of Neuchâtel, Switzerland.
Lecturer in Civil Law, Faculty of Political Sciences, Ankara Univ. 57, Asst. Prof. 61, Prof. 71; Dir. School of Journalism, Ankara 71; Minister of State 72-74.
Publs. several works on civil law.
c/o Ministry of State, Ankara, Turkey.

P

Pachachi, Adnan al, PH.D.; Iraqi diplomatist; b. 14 May 1923; ed. American Univ. of Beirut.
Joined Foreign Service 44, served Washington, Alexandria;

Dir.-Gen. of Political Affairs, Council of Ministers 57-58; Dir.-Gen. Ministry of Foreign Affairs 58-59; Perm. Rep. of Iraq to UN 59-65; Minister of State Dec. 65-66; Minister of Foreign Affairs 66-67; Perm. Rep. to UN 67-69; Minister of State, Govt. of Abu Dhabi, United Arab Emirates (UAE) 71-74; Personal Rep. of Head of State of the UAE and mem. Abu Dhabi Exec. Council 74-.
c/o Manhal Palace, Abu Dhabi, United Arab Emirates.

Pachachi, Nadim, A.R.S.M., PH.D.; Iraqi oil expert; b. 18 March 1914, Baghdad; ed. Imperial Coll., London.
Minister of Econs. 53-57; Minister of Finance 57-58; mem. of Parl. 52-58; Oil Adviser to the Libyan Govt. 60-64, to the Kuwaiti Govt. 66-68, to His Highness The Ruler of Abu Dhabi and the Govt. of Abu Dhabi 66-; Sec.-Gen. Org. of Petroleum Exporting Countries 70-72; Order of Rafidain, Hashemite Order.
c/o Organization of Petroleum Exporting Countries, Dr. Karl Lueger Ring 10, 1010 Vienna, Austria.

Pahlavi, H.I.M. Queen Farah (Shahbanou); Empress of Iran; b. 1938; ed. Italian School, Jeanne d'Arc School and Razi School, Teheran and Ecole Spéciale d'Architecture, Paris.
Married H.I.M. the Shah 21 Dec. 59; son Reza b. 31 Oct. 60, daughter Farahnaz b 12. March 63, son Ali Reza b. 28 April 66, daughter Leila b. 27 March 1970; Patron of 26 educ., health and cultural orgs. including Farah Pahlavi Asscn. (administration of orphanages in Iran), Iran Cultural Foundation; Foreign Assoc. Fine Arts Acad. of French Inst.
The Imperial Palace, Teheran, Iran.

Pahlavi, Mohammad-Reza; His Imperial Majesty the Shahanshah Aryamehr, Emperor of Iran; b. 26 Oct. 1919. Succeeded to throne on the abdication of his father, Reza Shah the Great, Sept. 16th, 41; married (1) Princess Fawzia, sister of King Farouk of Egypt; divorced Nov. 48; daughter, Princess Shahnaz Pahlavi; (2) Soraya Esfandiari, Feb. 12th, 51; divorced March 58; (3) Farah Diba, Dec. 21st, 59; sons: Prince Reza Pahlavi and Prince Ali Reza Pahlavi; daughters Princess Farahnaz and Princess Leila; Dr. h.c. Columbia, Michigan, Pennsylvania, California (U.C.L.A.), Harvard, New York, Washington Univs., U.S.A. and Univs. of Teheran, Punjab, Agra, Istanbul, Beirut, Rio de Janeiro, Bucharest, Sofia, Malaya, Bangkok, Madras, Nat. Univ. of Iran.
Publs. *Mission for My Country* 61, *The White Revolution* 61.
The Imperial Palace, Teheran, Iran.

Pahlbod, Mehrdad, B.SC.; Iranian politician; b. Teheran; ed. Univ. of Teheran and in France.
Official, Ministry of Educ.; Supervisor, Org. of Fine Arts; Deputy Prime Minister; now Minister of Culture and Art.
Ministry of Culture and Art, Teheran, Iran.

Pakravan, Gen. Hassan; Iranian army officer and diplomatist; b. 1911; ed. French Military Acad.
Assistant Mil. Attaché, Paris; Mil. Attaché, Pakistan 49-50; Head of Army Intelligence 50-53; Mil. Attaché, New Delhi 54-56; Deputy Chief, State Security and Intelligence Org. (SAVAK) 56-61; Asst. to Prime Minister and Head of SAVAK 61-65; Minister of Information Feb. 65-July 66; Amb. to Pakistan 66-69, to France 69-73, concurrently to Portugal 70-73; High Counsellor to the Imperial Court 73-; Order of Homayoun (1st Class), Taj (3rd Class); Grand Croix Légion d'Honneur, etc.
Ministry of the Court, Teheran, Iran.

Paoli, José; French diplomatist; b. 16 Dec. 1924, Epinal; ed. Ecole Nat. des Langues Orientales Vivantes, Paris, Faculté des Lettres, Sorbonne.
Secretary of Embassy, Cairo 51-54, Damascus 54-56, Moscow 58-61, Washington 61-64; Counsellor, Rabat 64-67, Tripoli, Libya 67-70; Asst. Dir. for Algerian Affairs,

Ministry of Foreign Affairs 70-75; Amb. to Kuwait 75-; Chevalier, Légion d'Honneur; Officier, Ordre Nat. du Mérite; Officier du Mérite egyptien; Wissam al Kuwait, First Class.

French Embassy, P.O.B. 1037, Kuwait City, Kuwait.

Papadopoulos, Tassos; Cypriot lawyer and politician; b. 1934; ed. Pancyprian Gymnasium, Nicosia, King's Coll., London, and Gray's Inn, London.
Law practice, Nicosia 55-59; fmr. mem. EOKA; mem. Constitutional Comm. drafting Cyprus Constitution 59-60; Minister of Interior *a.i.* 59-60; Minister of Labour and Social Insurance 60-70; Acting Minister of Agriculture 64-66, Minister of Health 60-70; M.P., Deputy Pres. House of Reps. July 70-.
House of Representatives, Nicosia, Cyprus.

Papaioannou, Ezekias; Cypriot journalist; b. 8 Oct. 1908; ed. American Acad., Larnaca, Cyprus.
Secretary-General, Progressive Party of the Working People (Anorthotikon Komma Ergazomenou Laou—AKEL) 49-; Deputy of AKEL, House of Reps. 60-; mem. Foreign Affairs Cttee., House of Reps. 60-, Chair. Communications and Works Cttee. 70-.
Akamas 8, P.O.B. 1827, Nicosia; and 8 Doiranis Street, Nicosia, Cyprus.

Parrot, André; French archaeologist; b. 15 Feb. 1901; ed. Univ. de Paris à la Sorbonne, Faculté de Théologie Protestante, Ecole du Louvre and Ecole Archéologique Française de Jerusalem.
Professor, Faculty of Protestant Theology, Univ. of Paris 37-55, Ecole du Louvre 37-; Head Keeper of Nat. Museums 46-65, Insp.-Gen. 65-; Dir. of Louvre Museum 68-72; Dir. of French archaeological expeditions to Mari (Syrian Arab Republic) and Larsa (Iraq); mem. Institut Français (Académie des Inscriptions et Belles-Lettres); mem. British Acad., Belgian Acad.; Commandeur Légion d'Honneur; Commandeur des Arts et des Lettres; Croix de Guerre 39-45; Grand Officer, Ordre Nat. du Mérite, Grand Cordon du Mérite Syrien.
Publs. *Mari, une ville perdue* 36, *Archéologie mésopotamienne* 46-53, *Tello-vingt campagnes de fouilles* 48, *Ziggurats et Tour de Babel* 48, *Découverte des Mondes ensevelis* 52, *Mari—le temple d'Ishtar* 56, *Mari—le Palais* (3 vols.) 58-59, *Les temples d'Ishtarat et Ninni—zaza* 67, *Le trésor d'Ur* 68, *Sumer* 60, *Assur* 61, *Abraham et son temps* 62, *Terre du Christ* 65, *Clés pour l'archéologie* 67, *Mari—capitale fabuleuse* 74.
11 rue du Val Grâce, Paris 75005, France.

Parsay, (Mrs.) Farrokhrou, M.D.; Iranian politician; b. March 1922; ed. Homa Primary School, Teheran, High Normal School, Teheran Univ.
Teacher 42-57; Principal of Secondary School, Teheran 57; mem. Parl. 63-; Under-Sec. Ministry of Educ. 65-68; Minister of Educ. 68-74; established Soc. of Woman Educators; Pres. Org. of Co-operation between Women's Socs., Soc. of Univ. Women; mem. Women's Sport Council; Chief, Educ. Cttee. of High Council of Iranian Women's Socs.
Publs. *Women in Ancient Iran* (in Persian), books on education, hygiene, nursing and motherhood.
The Majlis, Teheran, Iran.

Parsons, Sir Anthony Derrick, K.C.M.G., M.V.O., M.C., M.A. (OXON.); British diplomatist; b. 9 Sept. 1922, London; ed. King's School Canterbury, Balliol Coll., Oxford.
Army service 40-54; Asst. Mil. Attaché, Baghdad 52-54; Foreign Office 54-55; at British Embassy, Ankara 55-59, Amman 59-60, Cairo 60-61; Foreign Office 61-64; British Embassy, Khartoum 64-65; British Political Agent, Bahrain 65-69; with U.K. Mission to UN 69-71; Foreign and Commonwealth Office 71-74; Amb. to Iran 74-.
British Embassy, Teheran, Iran.

Partos, Oedeon; Israeli composer; b. 1907, Budapest; ed. in Budapest under Hubay (violin) and Kodaly (composition).
Founding mem. Int. Soc. for Contemporary Music; Leader of viola section, Israel Philharmonic Orchestra 38-56; Dir. Israel Acad. of Music, Tel-Aviv 51-; Prof. Tel-Aviv Univ. 61-; now devotes time to musical educ., composition and solo appearances.
Compositions include *Concerto* (for violin and orchestra), *Sinfonia Concertante* (for viola and orchestra), *Yiskor* (for strings), *Visions* (for flute, piano and strings), *Makamat* (for flute and string quartet), *Ein Gev* (symphonic fantasy, UNESCO Prize 52, Israel State Prize 54), *Images* (for orchestra), *Symphonic Movements*, *Five Israeli Songs*, *Tehilim* (for string quartet), *Agada* (for viola, piano and percussion), *Nebulae* (for woodwind quintet), *Iltur* (for 12 harps); piano pieces, etc.
The Israel Academy of Music, Tel-Aviv; 25 Tsimchei Hayehudim Street, Ramat Aviv, Tel-Aviv, Israel.

Patinkin, Don, PH.D.; Israeli economist; b. 8 Jan. 1922; ed. Univ. of Chicago.
Asst. Prof. of Economics, Univ. of Chicago 47-48; Research Assoc., Cowles Comm. for Economic Research 47-48; Assoc. Prof. of Economics, Univ. of Ill. 48-49; Lecturer, The Eliezer Kaplan School of Economics and Social Sciences, Hebrew Univ. 49, later Prof. of Economics; Dir. of Research, Maurice Falk Inst. for Economic Research in Israel 56-72; Pres. Econometric Soc. 74-; mem. Israel Acad. of Sciences and Humanities; Foreign Hon. mem. American Acad. of Arts and Sciences.
Publs. *Money, Interest and Prices: An Integration of Monetary and Value Theory* 56 (2nd edn. 65), *The Israel Economy: The First Decade* 59, *Studies in Monetary Economics* 72.
Chovevei Zion 5, Talbieh, Jerusalem, Israel.

Patsalides, Andreas, B.SC.ECONS.; Cypriot politician; b. 1922; ed. Greek Gymnasium, Limassol, School of Econs. and Political Science, London, and Harvard Univ., Mass.
Various posts in Public Service; Gen. Dir., Planning Bureau 59-68; Minister of Finance 68-74, Aug. 74-.
Ministry of Finance, Nicosia, Cyprus.

Pattichis, Nicos Kyriakou, LL.B., BARR.-AT-LAW; Cypriot politician; b. 20 Feb. 1916, Kato-Dhrys, Larnaca; ed. Pancyprian Gymnasium, Nicosia, Liverpool Univ. and Middle Temple, London.
District Judge 51-57; Vice-Pres. Cyprus Fed. of Chambers of Commerce and Industry 59-62; Mayor of Limassol 64-71; Pres. Chamber of Commerce and Industry, Limassol April-Aug. 74; Minister of Communications and Works Aug. 74-Jan. 75.
Despina N. Pattichis Str. 1, Limassol, Cyprus.

Pazhwak, Abdurrahman; Afghan civil servant; b. 7 March 1919.
Has been successively mem. Historical Section of Afghan Acad.; Dir. Foreign Publications Section of Afghan Press Dept.; Editor daily *Islah* and acting Dir.-Gen. of Bakhtar News Agency; Pres. Pashto-Tolana; Dir.-Gen. Publs. Section, Afghan Press Dept.; Press and Cultural Attaché, Afghan Embassy, London; mem. of Section of Information Dept. of ILO; Press and Cultural Attaché, Afghan Embassy, Washington; Dir. Section for East Asia and Dir. a.i., Section for UN, and Int. Confs., Afghan Ministry for Foreign Affairs; Dir.-Gen. Political Affairs in Ministry of Foreign Affairs 58; Perm. Rep. to UN 58-73; Amb. to Fed. Repub. of Germany 73, to India 73-; Pres. UN Human Rights Comm. 63, 21st Session of UN Gen. Assembly 66, 5th Special Session 66 and of Emergency Session of Gen. Assembly on Middle East 66; Special Envoy to Fourth Summit of Non-Aligned Countries, Algiers 73, to Summit of Islamic Conf., Lahore 74; Special Envoy to Pres. of Bangladesh.

Publs. *Aryana or Ancient Afghanistan, Pakhtunistan* (both in English), *Tales of the People* 58 (in Persian), and many other works.
c/o Ministry of Foreign Affairs, Kabul, Afghanistan.

Pazhwak, Niamatullah, PH.D.; Afghan educationist; b. 17 Aug. 1928; ed. Habibia High School, Kabul, Kabul Univ., Columbia Univ., U.S.A.
Director Teacher's Training School, Kabul 56, Habibia High School 58; Pres. Secondary Schools in Afghanistan 65; Cultural Counsellor, Royal Afghan Embassy to U.S.S.R. 68; Pres. of Compilation and Translation, Ministry of Educ. 70; Gov. Bamiyan Prov. March-Sept. 71, Kabul Prov. 71-72; Minister of the Interior 72-73, of Education 73-74.
Publs. articles on education in professional journals.
c/o Ministry of Education, Kabul, Afghanistan.

Peled, Natan; Israeli politician; b. 3 June 1913, Odessa; ed. secondary education.
Immigrated to Palestine 32; agricultural labourer in Kibbutz; Sec.-Gen. of Kibbutz Fed. 'Hashomer Hatzair' 50-55; Political Sec., Mapam Party 56-58; Minister of Israel to Bulgaria 58-60; Amb. to Austria 60-63; mem. Knesset 65-69; Minister of Immigrant Absorption 70-74.
Kibbutz Sarid, Israel.

Peres, Shimon; Israeli politician; b. 1923, Poland; ed. New York Univ., Harvard Univ.
Immigrated to Palestine 34; fmr. Sec. Hano'ar Ha'oved Movt.; mem. Haganah Movt. 47; Head of Israel Naval Service, Ministry of Defence 48; Head of Defence Mission in U.S.A.; Deputy Dir.-Gen. of Ministry of Defence 52-53, Dir.-Gen. 53-59, Deputy Minister of Defence 59-65; mem. Knesset 59-; mem. Mapai Party 59-65, founder mem. and Sec.-Gen. Rafi Party 65, mem. Labour Party after merger 68; Minister for Econ. Devt. in the Administered Areas and for Immigrant Absorption 69-70, of Transport and Communications 70-74, of Information March-June 74, of Defence June 74-.
Publs. *The Next Step* 65, *David's Sling* 70, and numerous political articles in Israeli and foreign publications.
Ministry of Defence, Tel-Aviv; 186 Arlosoroff Street, Tel-Aviv, Israel.

Perowne, Stewart Henry, O.B.E., K.ST.J., M.A., F.S.A.; British orientalist and historian; b. 17 June 1901; ed. Haileybury Coll., Corpus Christi Coll. Cambridge, and Harvard Univ.
English Lecturer, Govt. Arab Coll. Jerusalem 27-30; Asst. Sec. Palestine Govt. 30-32, Asst. District Commr. 32-34; Asst. Sec. Malta 34-37; Political Officer, Aden 37; Arabic Programme Organizer, B.B.C. 38; Information Officer, Aden 39-41; Public Relations Attaché, British Embassy, Baghdad 41-44, Oriental Counsellor 44-47; Colonial Sec. Barbados 47-50; Acting Gov. March-Oct. 49; Adviser, Ministry of Interior, Cyrenaica 50-51; Adviser on Arab Affairs, U.K. Del. UN Gen. Assembly 51; discovered ancient Aziris 51; Hon. Asst. Jerusalem Diocesan Refugee Organization 52; designed and supervised seven Arab refugee villages 52-56; Faculty mem. "College Year in Athens" 65-66.
Publs. *The One Remains* 54, *Herod the Great* 56, *The Later Herods* 58, *Hadrian* 60, *Caesars and Saints* 62, *The Pilgrim's Companion in Jerusalem and Bethlehem* 63, *The Pilgrim's Companion in Roman Rome* 63, *The Pilgrim's Companion in Athens* 65, *Jerusalem* 65, *The End of the Roman World* 66, *Death of the Roman Republic* 68, *Roman Mythology* 69, *The Siege within the Walls* 70, *Rome* 71, *The Journeys of Saint Paul* 73, *The Caesars' Wives: above Suspicion?* 74, *The Archaeology of Greece and the Aegean* 74, *Holy Places of Christendom* 75.
44 Arminger Road, London, W12 7BB, England.

Persia, Shah of (*see* Pahlavi, Mohammad-Reza).

Petrides, Frixos L.; Cypriot teacher and politician; b. 1915, Nicosia; ed. Pancyprian Gymnasium and Univ. of Athens.
In Athens during Second World War; teacher, Pancyprian Gymnasium after Second World War; Chair. Pancyprian Asscn. 47-60; Headmaster, Pancyprian Gymnasium 60; Chair. of Board, Cyprus Broadcasting Corpn. 60-70; Minister of Educ. 70-72; Chair. Cyprus Tourism Org. 72-.
Cyprus Tourism Organization, P.O. Box 4535, Nicosia, Cyprus.

Phanos, Titos; Cypriot politician; b. 23 Jan. 1929, Nicosia; ed. Pancyprian Gymnasium, Nicosia, Middle Temple, London.
Called to Bar 51; practised law during independence campaign 52-66; mem. EOKA fighters union; mem. of Cttee. of Human Rights of the Nicosia Bar Asscn.; arrested by British administration and served 16 months as political detainee 56-58; mem. Consultative Body to Archbishop Makarios 59-60; mem. House of Representatives for Nicosia 60-66; Parl. Spokesman (Floor Leader) of pro-government Patriotic Front 63-66; mem. Consultative Assembly of Council of Europe 63-65; Minister of Communications and Works 66-70; Amb. to Belgium, Head of Mission to EEC 71-, concurrently Amb. to Luxembourg and Netherlands 73-.
Embassy of Cyprus, 83-85 rue de la Loi, 1040 Brussels, Belgium.

Phillips, Sir Horace, K.C.M.G.; British diplomatist; b. 31 May 1917, Glasgow, Scotland; ed. Hillhead High School, Glasgow.
Inland Revenue Dept., London 35-39; Indian Army 40-47; Consul, Persia and Afghanistan 47-50; Foreign Office 51-53; Chargé d'Affaires, Saudi Arabia 53-56; Aden Protectorate Sec. 56-60; Counsellor, Teheran 60-64; Deputy Political Resident, Persian Gulf 64-66; Amb. to Indonesia 66-68; British High Commr. in Tanzania 68-72; Amb. to Turkey 73-.
Embassy of United Kingdom, Çankaya, Şehit Ersan Cad. 46/A, Ankara, Turkey.

Phillips, John Fleetwood Stewart, C.M.G., M.A.; British diplomatist; b. 16 Dec. 1917; ed. Worcester Coll., Oxford.
H.M. Forces 39-45; Sudan political service 45-54; First Sec., Foreign Office 55-56; Oriental Sec., Libya 57-60; H.M. Consul-Gen., Muscat 60-63; Counsellor, Amman 63-66; Imperial Defence Coll. 67; Deputy High Commr., Cyprus 68; Amb. to People's Democratic Republic of Yemen Feb. 69-70, to Jordan 70-72, to Sudan 73-; Fellow, Royal Commonwealth Soc., British Museum rep. on Board of Trustees, Palestine Archaeological Museum, Jerusalem 66.
c/o British Embassy, P.O. Box 801. Khartoum, Sudan; and Records Section, Foreign and Commonwealth Office, London, S.W.1, England.

Phillips, Wendell, A.B., PH.D., F.R.G.S., F.R.A.I., F.A.G.S., F.R.C.A.S., F.R.A.S.; American explorer and archaeologist; b. 25 Sept. 1921, Oakland, Calif.; ed. Univ. of Calif., Berkeley.
President and Dir. Philpryor Corpn. 51-58; Pres. Middle East American Oil Co. 55-56; Chair. P.T.P. Corpn., Reno, Nev. 62-, Phillips Pacific, Sacramento, Calif. 60-; Pres. American Foundation for Study of Man, Washington 49-; Dir.-Gen. Antiquities, Oman 53; Econ. Adviser and Rep. of H.M. Sultan of Oman 56-; mem. many scientific expeditions; Dir. African expedition 47-49, Sinai Expedition 50, Oman Geographical Expedition 61; excavations in Yemen 51-52, Sumhuram, Dhofar 52-53, Sohar, Oman 58; Prof. of Archaeology, Univ. of Wyoming 68; Pres. Wendell Phillips Oil Co., Wendell Phillips Oil Co. (Korea) Ltd.; mem. Overseer's Cttee. to visit Anthropology Dept., Harvard 74-76; Trustee, Hawaii Loa Coll. 68, San Francisco Theological Seminary 70; mem. several learned socs.;

Hon. Dr. Univs. of Redlands, Colorado, Trinity, Pacific, and Kyungpook Nat. Univ., Calvin Coolidge, Emporia, Sterling, and Whitworth Colls, Idaho Coll., Grand Canyon Coll., Miami, Calif. Baptist Coll., Emmanuel Coll., Florida Southern Coll., John Brown Univ., Eastern Coll., Union Coll., Utah, Fort Lauderdale Univ., Davis and Elkins Coll.; Hon. Sheikh of Bal-Harith tribe; Brussels Univ. Commemorative Medal 69, Gold Plate Award of American Soc. of Achievement 72, Explorers' Club Gold Medal Award 74.
Publs. *Qataban and Sheba* 55, *Unknown Oman* 66, *Oman, a History* 67.
Suite 1409, Bank of Hawaii, 2222 Kalakaua Avenue, Honolulu, Hawaii 96815, U.S.A.

Picard, Leo Yehuda, PH.D., D.SC.; Israeli geologist; b. 3 June 1900; ed. Freiburg, Bonn, Berlin, Zürich and London Univs.
Assistant, Univ. of Florence 24; emigrated to Palestine 24; Asst. Hebrew Univ. of Jerusalem Geology Dept. 25-33, Lecturer 34-63, Head of Dept. 36-37, Assoc. Prof. 37-39, Prof. 39-, now Emer; Research in Paris 26, London 29-30; Consultant to Argentine Govt. 45; Dir. Geol. Survey of Israel 50-54; Adviser to Israel Govt. 55-; Chair. Cttee. of Experts on Arid Regions, UNESCO 54; Adviser to Greek Govt. on groundwater 56-57; Chief Geological Cons. TAHAL Water Planning Israel 57-; Chair. Nat. Cttee., 6th World Petroleum Congress 62; Special Adviser to UN on groundwater exploration in Cyprus 63, Iran 64, and Bolivia 65; Dir. Groundwater Research Centre, Hebrew Univ. Jerusalem; Cons. in Oil Exploration to Finance Ministry 68; mem. Cttee. for Neotechnics and Pleistocene Stratigraphy (INQUA Congress, Paris) 69; mem. Israel Acad. of Sciences and Humanities; Foreign Corresp. Soc. Géol., France; Israel Prize for Natural Sciences 58.
Publs. numerous works on geology, palaeontology, hydrogeology, petroleum, and pure geological research.
Groundwater Research Centre, the Hebrew University, Jerusalem, Israel.

Pickering, Thomas Reeve, M.A.; American diplomatist; b. 5 Nov. 1931, Orange, N.J.; ed. Bowdoin Coll., Brunswick, Me., Fletcher School of Law and Diplomacy, Medford, Mass., Univ. of Melbourne, Australia.
Lieutenant U.S. Navy 56-59; joined Dept. of State 59-, Intelligence Research Specialist 60, Foreign Affairs Officer 61, Arms Control and Disarmament Agency 61-62; mem. U.S. Del. to Disarmament Conf., Geneva 62-64; Principal Officer, Zanzibar 65-67; Deputy Chief of Mission, Dar es Salaam 67-69; Deputy Dir. Bureau of Politico-Mil. Affairs 69-73; Exec. Sec. Dept. of State, Special Asst. to Sec. of State 73-74; Amb. to Jordan Feb. 74-.
Department of State, Washington, D.C. 20520, U.S.A.

Pirasteh, Said Mehdi, PH.D.; Iranian lawyer and politician; b. 1919; ed. Teheran Univ.
Successively clerk, Ministry of Justice, Public Prosecutor, Rep. of Public Prosecutor at Judicial Court, Asst. to Public Prosecutor of Supreme Court, Parl. Deputy, Under-Sec. Ministry of Interior, Gov.-Gen. of Fars and Southern Ports, Gov.-Gen. of Khuzistan; Minister of Interior 63-64; Amb. to Iraq 64-67, to Belgium 68-71.
c/o Ministry of Foreign Affairs, Teheran, Iran.

Pirenne, Jacques, Comte, LL.D., PH.D.; Belgian historian; b. 26 June 1891; ed. Ghent Univ.
Tutor to Prince Leopold (later King Leopold III) 20-24; Chargé de Cours Univ. of Brussels 21, Prof. 24-, Sec. Oriental Inst. 30-; scientific mem. Oriental Inst. of Prague 33; Michonis Prof. Coll. de France 35; awarded Quinquennial Prize for Historical Sciences for work 30-35; Lecturer Univ. of Cairo 39; Prof. Univ. of Grenoble 40, Univ. of Geneva 41-44; Head King Leopold's Secretariat with title "Secretary to the King" Aug. 45; Editor

Archives d'Histoire du Droit Oriental 35-, mem. Académie Royale de Belgique 45-, Acad. Septentrional (Paris) 59-; Grand Croix Ordre de la Couronne; Grand Officier Ordre de Léopold; Officier Légion d'Honneur.
Publs. *Histoire des Institutions et du Droit Privé de l'Ancienne Egypte* (3 vols.) 32-35, *La civilisation sumérienne* 44, *La civilisation babylonienne* 45, *Les Grands Courants de l'Histoire Universelle* (7 vols.) 44-56 (German, Italian, Spanish, Portuguese, English), *La Belgique devant le nouvel équilibre du monde* 45, *Civilisations Antiques* 50, *Histoire de la Civilisation de l'Egypte Ancienne* (3 vols.) 61-63 (Italian, Spanish), *Histoire de l'Europe de 1500 à 1955* (3 vols.) 60-62, *La Religion et la Morale dans l'Egypte Antique* 65, *La Société hebraïque d'après la Bible* 65, *Le Dossier du Roi Léopold III* 69, *Les Hommes d'Etat célèbres de l'Antiquité* 70.
49 Rue des Echevins, Brussels, Belgium; and Château de Hierges, par Aubrîves, 08 Ardennes, France.

Polyakov, Vladimir Porfirievitch, PH.D.; Soviet diplomatist; b. 1931; ed. Inst. of Oriental Studies, Moscow.
Diplomatic Service 56-; Counsellor, Syria 61-65; various posts in Ministry of Foreign Affairs 65-67; Counsellor-Minister, Egypt 68-71; Amb. to People's Democratic Repub. of Yemen 72-74, to Egypt May 74-.
Embassy of the U.S.S.R., 95 Sh. El Giza (Giza), Cairo, Egypt.

Popal, Ali Ahmad, PH.D.; Afghan teacher, politician and diplomatist; b. 22 Feb. 1916; ed. Nedjat Secondary School, Kabul, and Univ. of Jena.
Teacher and Dir., Nedjat School, Kabul 42-46; Dir. of Teachers Training Coll. 46-47; Head of Primary Educ. Dept., Ministry of Educ. 47-49, also Teacher and Dean in Faculty of Women, Kabul Univ. 47-49; Head of Gen. Educ. Dept., Ministry of Educ. 49-51, Deputy Minister of Educ. 52-56, Minister of Educ. 56-64, Second Vice-Premier 62-64; Amb. to German Fed. Repub., also accred. to Sweden and Switzerland 64-66; Amb. to Turkey 66-67; First Deputy Prime Minister 67-69; Minister of Educ. 67; Amb. to Pakistan, also accred. Sri Lanka and Thailand 69-74, to Japan 74-; Order of Maaref, 3rd Class 46, 1st Class 64, Order of Sardarie-Ahlie 58, and orders from Egypt, Yugoslavia and Federal Republic of Germany.
Publs. *Education in Afghanistan, A Comparison of Education in Europe (Germany) and America, The Republic of Turkey.*
Afghan Embassy, 31-21, Jingumae 6-chome, Shibuya-ku, Tokyo, Japan.

Pourhomayoun, Ali-Asghar, D. en D.; Iranian economist; b. 1912; ed. legal studies in Europe.
Assistant Prosecutor and Counsellor, Court of Appeal 37; Prof. of Econs., Law Faculty, Univ. of Teheran 43; Under-Sec. Ministry of Nat. Economy 50-53, Minister of Nat. Economy 53; Pres. Bd. of Dirs., Iran Insurance Co. 53, Pres. and Man. Dir. 53-55; Dir. Inst. for Public Admin., Faculty of Law 56-60; Minister of Commerce 60; Minister without Portfolio 61; Gov. Central Bank of Iran 61-65; Pres. Currency and Credit Council 61-63; mem. High Econ. Council 61-63; Grand Cross of Merit with Star (Germany); Grand Cross Order of Léopold II (Belgium).
Publs. *La Banque Nationale de l'Iran et son rôle dans le développement, Principles of Economics, Planning and Business Cycles.*
Shahreza Avenue, 21st Azar Street, Prof. Edward Brown Road, No. 10, Teheran, Iran.

Prem Chand, Lieut.-Gen. D.; Indian army officer (retd.) and United Nations official; b. 1916, Muzaffargarh, now West Pakistan; ed. Govt. Coll., Lahore and Staff Coll., Quetta.
Commissioned Indian Army 37; served in Gen. Staff, Army HQ, New Delhi 47, later apptd. Mil. Asst. to Chief of

Army Staff; commanded Regimental Centre of First Gurkha Rifles; Instructor, Defence Services Staff Coll., Wellington; subsequently apptd. Deputy Dir. of Mil. Training, Dir. of Personnel Services, Dir. of Mil. Intelligence, New Delhi; Chief of Staff, HQ Western Command, Simla 61, Commanded Div. in Western Command; Gen-Officer, Katanga Area, UN Operation in the Congo 62-63; Commanded Div. in Eastern Command, Chief of Staff, HQ Eastern Command, Calcutta; retd. 67 then held admin. post in industrial concern; Commdr. UN Force in Cyprus (UNFICYP) 69; rank of Lieut.-Gen. 75.
UNFICYP, P.O. Box 1642, Nicosia, Cyprus.

Pritchard, James Bennett, A.B., B.D., PH.D., S.T.D., D.D.; American orientalist; b. 4 Oct. 1909; ed. Asbury Coll., Drew Univ., Univ. of Pa. and Philadelphia Divinity School. Professor of Old Testament Literature, Crozer Theological Seminary 42-54; Annual Prof. American School of Oriental Research, Jerusalem 50-51, Archaeological Dir. 51, Visiting Prof. 56-57, 61-62; Prof. Old Testament Literature Church Divinity School of the Pacific 54-62; Prof. Religious Thought, Univ. of Pa. and Curator of Biblical Archaeology Univ. Museum 62-, Dir. 67-; Visiting Prof. of Archaeology, American Univ. of Beirut 67; mem. American Oriental Soc., Archaeological Inst. of America (Pres. 72-), Soc. for Biblical Literature; Editor *Journal of the American Oriental Soc.* 52-54.
Publs. *Palestinian Figures* 43, *Ancient Near Eastern Texts* 50, *The Ancient Near East in Pictures* 54, *Archaeology and the Old Testament* 58, *Gibeon, Where the Sun Stood Still* 62, *The Ancient Near East: Supplementary Texts and Pictures* 69, *The Ancient Near East Vol. II* 75.
University Museum, 33rd and Spruce Streets, Philadelphia 4, Pa., U.S.A.

Q

Qaboos bin Said (*see* under Said, Qaboos bin).

Qaddafi, Col. Moamar al- (*see* under Gaddafi, Col. Moamar al-).

Qadir, Maj. Zain al-Abdin Mohammed Ahmed Abdel; Sudanese politician; b. 7 May 1940, Tuti; ed. Military Coll. Commissioned 62; mem. Revolutionary Command Council May 69; Ombudsman 70; Minister of Animal Production Nov. 70; Asst. Prime Minister for Agricultural Sector Feb. 71; Minister of Communications and Transport Aug. 71; Minister of Transport 71-72.
c/o Ministry of Transport, Khartoum, Sudan.

Qassim, Awn al-Sharif, M.A., PH.D.; Sudanese politician; b. 15 Oct. 1933, Halfaiat al Molook; ed. Univs. of Khartoum, London and Edinburgh.
Lecturer, School of Oriental and African Studies, London Univ. 59-61; Lecturer, Dept. of Arabic, Univ. of Khartoum 61-64, Senior Lecturer 69, Dir. Translation Section 69-70; Minister of Waqfs and Religious Affairs Oct. 71-73.
c/o Ministry of Waqfs and Religious Affairs, Khartoum, Sudan.

Quddus, Ihsan Abdal (son of the late Rose al-Yussuf, famous actress and writer); Egyptian writer; b. 1 Jan. 1919; ed. Univ. of Cairo.
Practised in law 42; joined magazine *Rose al-Yussuf* 42, imprisoned for attack on govt. 45, released and became Chief Editor, again imprisoned 50, 51; first novel publ. 54; Editor *Akhbar al-Yom* until 74; writer for *Al-Ahram* May 74-.
Publs. include *I am Free* 54, *Do not Turn out the Sun* (two vols.) 60, *Nothing Matters* 63.
c/o Al-Ahram, Galaa Street, Cairo, Egypt.

Qusus, Jiryis; Jordanian educationalist and writer; b. 1913; ed. American Univ. of Beirut.

Teacher in various schools 36-51; Headmaster of Es-Salt Govt. Secondary School 51-53; Insp. of English, Ministry of Educ. 53-57; Asst. Under-Sec. and Senior Chief Insp. Ministry of Educ. 57-61; Asst. Under-Sec. Ministry of Communications 61; Ambassador in the Ministry of Foreign Affairs and Head of the Research and Studies Dept. 62, Consular Dept. 63-65, Under-Sec. 65, Ambassador and Head of Research Dept. 66-; Order of Istiqlal.
Publs. *Selected Poems* 53, *Selected English Prose* 56, *Applied Translation* (3 vols.) (co-author) 57, *Selected Verses* 58, *Fables from the Middle East* 60, *Education and Art* (co-translator), *The Genius of Shakespeare* (Arabic) 60.
Ministry for Foreign Affairs, Amman, Jordan.

R

Rabin, Maj.-Gen. Yitzhak; Israeli army officer and politician; b. 1 March 1922, Jerusalem; ed. Agricultural School, Kfar Tabor, and Staff Coll., England.
Palmach commands 43-48, including War of Independence; represented Israel Defence Forces (I.D.F.) at Rhodes armistice negotiations; fmr. Head of Training Dept., I.D.F.; C.-in-C. Northern Command 56-59; Head, Manpower Branch 59-60; Deputy Chief of Staff and Head, Gen. Staff Branch 60-64, Chief of Staff I.D.F. 64-68; Amb. to U.S.A. 68-72; Minister of Labour March-April 74; Prime Minister June 74-, and Minister of Communications 74-75; Leader Labour Party May 74-; Hon. Doctorates, Jerusalem Univ. 67, Dropsie Coll. 68, Brandeis Univ. 68, Yeshiva Univ. 68, Coll. of Jewish Studies, Chicago 69, Univ. of Miami 70, Hebrew Union Coll., Boston 71.
Office of the Prime Minister, Jerusalem, Israel.

Rabinowitz, Yehoshua; Israeli politician; b. 13 Nov. 1911; ed. Poland and Tel-Aviv School of Law and Econs. Management posts in Israeli Co-operative Movement 48-56; mem. Tel-Aviv Municipal Council 56-59, Deputy Mayor 59-61, Chair. Financial, Townbuilding and Planning Cttees. 61-69, Mayor of Tel-Aviv 69-74; Minister of Housing March-May 74, of Finance June 74-; Labour Party.
Ministry of Finance, Jerusalem, Israel.

Rachmilewitz, Moshe, M.D.; Israeli physician; b. Russia 2 Sept. 1899; ed. Univs. of Königsberg and Berlin.
Post-graduate studies as E. Libman Fellow, New York, Hamburg, Vienna, Amsterdam and Paris 27-31; came to Palestine 31; research in haematology and cardiology; Head Dept. Rothschild Hadassah Univ. Hospital "B", Jerusalem; Prof. School of Medicine, Hebrew Univ.
11 Ussishkin Street, Jerusalem, Israel.

Rafael, Gideon; Israeli diplomatist; b. Germany 5 March 1913; ed. Univ. of Berlin.
Emigrated 34; mem. Kibbutz 34-43; active in Haganah and war services 39-42; Jewish Agency, Political Dept. 43; in charge of preparation of Jewish case for Jewish Agency, Political Dept., Nuremberg War Crimes Trial 45-46; mem. of Jewish Agency Comm. to Anglo-American Comm. of Enquiry 46, and of Jewish Agency mission to UN Special Comm. for Palestine 47; mem. Israel Permanent Del. to UN 51-52; alternate rep. to UN 53; rep. at UN Gen. Assemblies 47-66; Counsellor in charge of Middle East and UN Affairs, Ministry for Foreign Affairs 53-57; Ambassador to Belgium and Luxembourg 57-60, to the European Econ. Community 59; Dep. Dir.-Gen. Ministry of Foreign Affairs 60; Head of Israel Del. Int. Conf. Law of the Sea, Geneva 60; Deputy Dir.-Gen. Ministry for Foreign Affairs 60-65; Perm. Rep. to UN, Geneva 65-66; Special Ambassador and Adviser to Foreign Minister May 66-67; Perm. Rep. of Israel to UN 67; Dir.-Gen. Ministry of Foreign Affairs 67-71; Senior Political Adviser to Minister of Foreign

Affairs 72-73; Amb. to U.K. Oct. 73-; Head of Del. to UNCTAD III 72.
Embassy of Israel, 2 Palace Green, Kensington, London, W8 4QB, England; and Kiryath Yovel, Jerusalem, Israel.

Rahal, Abdellatif; Algerian diplomatist; b. 1923.
Ambassador to France 63; then posts in Ministry of Foreign Affairs; Sec.-Gen. Ministry of Foreign Affairs until 70; Perm. Rep. to UN 70-.
Permanent Mission of Algeria at United Nations, 750 Third Avenue, 14th Floor, New York, N.Y. 10017, U.S.A.

Raphael, Yitzchak, M.A., PH.D.; Israeli politician; b. 5 July 1914; ed. Hebrew Univ.
Settled in Palestine 35; mem. Exec. Jewish Agency and Head, Emigration Dept. 48-54; mem. of 2nd, 3rd, 4th, 5th, 6th, 7th and 8th Knesset; Chair. Exec. Hapoel Hamizrachi (Nat. Religious Party); mem. World Exec. Nat. Religious Party Mizrachi; Chair. Legislative Cttee. Knesset; Chair. Mossad Harav Kook (Publishers); Deputy Minister of Health 62-64; Minister of Religious Affairs March-June 74; Chair. (Mosad) Yad Harav Maimon Judaic Studies Centre.
Publs. *Sefer Hachasidith, Rishonim v'achronim, Hachasidut v'Eretz Israel*; Ed. *Encyclopaedia of Religious Zionism* 59, 60.
P.O.B. 642, Jerusalem, Israel.

Rashid, Rashid A. al-, M.A.; Kuwaiti civil servant and diplomatist; b. 23 Dec. 1934; ed. Claremont Men's Coll., California, U.S.A., and Claremont Graduate School.
Assistant Technical Dir., Public Works Dept., Kuwait 59-61; Asst. Sec. for Kuwait Govt. Secretariat 61; Dir. of Political Dept., Ministry of Foreign Affairs, Kuwait until 63; Perm. Rep. of Kuwait to UN Sept. 63-67; Under-Sec. Ministry of Foreign Affairs, Kuwait March 67-.
Ministry of Foreign Affairs, Kuwait.

Rateb, Aisha, PH.D.; Egyptian politician; ed. Faculty of Law, Cairo Univ.
Junior Lecturer, Faculty of Law, Cairo Univ., Prof. of Int. Law; Minister of Social Affairs 71-; Chair. Legislative Affairs Cttee. 73-.
Ministry of Social Affairs, Cairo, Egypt.

Raya, His Grace Archbishop Joseph Marie; Israeli ecclesiastic; b. 15 Aug. 1917; ed. Lebanon and St. Anne Seminary, Jerusalem.
Parish Priest, Zahlé, Lebanon 41-45, Paterson, New Jersey 49-51, Birmingham, Alabama 51-68; Archbishop of St. Jean d'Acre, Haifa, Nazareth and all Galilee 68-.
Greek Catholic Archbishopric, P.O. Box 279, Haifa, Israel.

Razzaz, Ahmed Munif, M.B., B.CH.; Jordanian physician and politician; b. 1919; ed. Amman Secondary School, American Univ. of Beirut and Cairo.
Teacher 39-41; mem. Baath Party 49-, Jordan Regional Leadership 56-66, Sec. 60-66, Sec.-Gen. Baath Party 65-66; exiled to Syria 52-53; imprisoned 57-59, 61, 63-64; arrested Feb. 66; Arab League Prize 63.
Publs. *Features of New Arab Life* (in Arabic) 53, *Evolution of the Meaning of Nationalism* (in Arabic) 60, (English trans.) 63, *Freedom and its Problems in Underdeveloped Countries* 65.
Baath Party, rue Abdul Aziz 66, Damascus, Syria.

Razzek, Brig. Aref Abdel; Iraqi politician; b. 1914; ed. Military Acad.
Entered Air Force 36; became Commdr. Habbaniya base; Minister of Agriculture Nov. 63-Dec. 63; Commdr. of Air Forces Dec. 63-July 65; Prime Minister and Acting Minister of Defence Sept. 65; Abortive *coup d'état* Sept. 65, June 66; imprisoned June 66.
c/o Ministry of Justice, Baghdad, Iraq.

Recanati, Daniel; Israeli banker; b. 26 Oct. 1921, Greece.
Chairman Israel Discount Bank Bankholding Corpn. Ltd.;

Chair. and Man. Dir. Israel Discount Bank Ltd.; Chair. Board of Dirs. Barclays Discount Bank Ltd., Discount Bank Investment Corpn. Ltd.; dir. of several cos.
Israel Discount Bank, 27-29 Yehuda Halevy Street, Tel-Aviv, Israel.

Rechter, Zvi; Israeli business executive; b. 16 Nov. 1920, Vienna; ed. High School.
Emigrated to Palestine 40; mem. Kibbutz Ma'aleh Ha-Hamisha until 68; Man. Co-operative Centre for Bldg. 58-66; Treas. Solel Boneh Bldg. and Public Works Co. Ltd. 66-70, Man. Dir. 71-.
Solel Boneh Ltd., P.O. Box 1678, Tel-Aviv, Israel.
Telephone: (03) 62-53-11 (Office).

Reiner, Markus, D.TECH.; Israeli university professor; b. 5 Jan. 1886; ed. Technische Hochschule, Vienna.
Engineer, Austrian State Railways 11-18, Romanian State Railways 18-22; Civil and Structural Engineer, Govt. of Palestine 22-45; Research Prof., Lafayette Coll., Easton, Pa., U.S.A. 31-33; Scientific Adviser, Standards Inst. of Palestine 45-47; Head of Rheological Laboratory, Technion, Haifa 48-60; Prof. of Mechanics, Technion, Haifa 48-60; Research Prof., Israel Inst. of Technology 60-; mem. Israel Acad. of Sciences and Humanities; Hon. mem. Groupe Français de Rhéologie; Weizmann Prize for Township of Tel-Aviv 56; Israel Prize, Govt. of Israel 58; Rothschild Prize 63; Gold Medal, British Soc. of Rheology 66; D.Phil. h.c. (Jerusalem).
Publs. *Lectures on Theoretical Rheology* 60, *Deformation Strain and Flow* 60, *Advanced Rheology* 71, *Selected Papers on Rheology* 75.
Technion City, Haifa, Israel.

Remez, Brig.-Gen. Aharon; Israeli air force officer and diplomatist; b. 8 May 1919; ed. Herzliah Grammar School, Tel-Aviv, Harvard School of Business Administration, U.S.A., and Woodrow Wilson School of Public and International Affairs, Princeton, U.S.A.
Agricultural training in Kibbutz, Givat Haim 37-39; Emissary to Zionist Youth Movement, U.S.A. 39-41; Royal Air Force 42-47; mem. Kibbutz Kfar Blum 47-; Dir. of Planning and Operations, later Chief of Staff, Israel Air Force 48; Commdr.-in-Chief Israel Air Force 48-51; Head, Ministry of Defence Purchasing Mission, U.S.A. 51-53; Aviation Adviser to Minister of Defence 53-54; mem. Board of Dirs. Solel Boneh Ltd., Exec. Dir. Koor Industries Ltd. 54-59; mem. Knesset 56-57; Admin. Dir. Weizmann Inst. of Science, Rehovot 59-60; Dir. Int. Co-operation Dept., Ministry for Foreign Affairs 60-64, Adviser on Int. Co-operation to Minister for Foreign Affairs 64-65; Consultant to OECD 64-65; Chair. Nat. Aviation Council 63-65; Amb. to U.K. 65-70; Dir.-Gen. Israel Ports Authority 70-.
Israel Ports Authority, Maya Building, 74 Patah Tiqva Road, Tel-Aviv; Home: 8 San Martin Street, Jerusalem, Israel.

Rennie, Sir John Shaw, G.C.M.G., O.B.E.; British UN official; b. 12 Jan. 1917; ed. Glasgow Univ., Balliol Coll., Oxford.
Assistant District Officer, Tanganyika 40-49; District Officer 49-51; Deputy Colonial Sec., Mauritius 51-55; British Resident Commr., New Hebrides 55-62; Gov. and C.-in-C. of Mauritius 62-68, Gov.-Gen. and C.-in-C. 68; Deputy Commr.-Gen. UNRWA 68-71; Commr.-Gen. UNRWA 71-; Hon. LL.D. (Glasgow Univ.) 72.
UNRWA Headquarters, Museitbeh Quarter, Beirut, Lebanon.

Riad, Mahmoud; Egyptian diplomatist; b. 8 Jan. 1917; ed. Military Acad. and General Staff Coll.
Egyptian Rep. to Mixed Armistice Comm. 49-52; Dir. Dept. of Arab Affairs, Ministry of Foreign Affairs 54-55; Ambassador to Syria 55-58; President's Counsellor on

Foreign Affairs 58-62; Chair. Del. to UN Econ. Comm. for Africa 61; Ambassador and Perm. Rep. to UN 62-64; Minister of Foreign Affairs 64-72, Deputy Premier 71-72; Pres. Adviser Jan.-June 72; Sec.-Gen. League of Arab States June 72-.
League of Arab States, Midan al Tahrir, Cairo, Egypt.

Riad, Dr. Mahmoud Mohammed, PH.D.; Egyptian electrical and electronic engineer; b. 4 June 1918, Cairo; ed. Cairo Univ., Imperial Coll., London Univ.
Assistant Prof. of Telecommunications, Alexandria Univ. 43-56; Head Eng. Dept., Atomic Energy Org. 56-57; Dir.-Gen. Telecommunications Org. 57-64; Sec.-Gen. Arab Telecommunications Union 58-; Minister of Communications 64-65; Chair. Electricity Corpn. 65-66, Electrical and Electronic Industries Corpn. 66-68; Prof. of Electronics, Kuwait Univ. 68-71; Minister of Transport and Communications 71-April 75; Fellow, American Inst. of Electrical and Electronic Engineers, Inst. of Electrical Engineers, England.
Publs. various papers on science and engineering in technical journals.
Office of the Secretary-General, Arab Telecommunications Union, 83 Ramses Street, Cairo; and Ministry of Transport and Communications, Cairo, Egypt.

Rial, Cleto Hassan, B.SC., M.A.; Sudanese administrator; b. 1 Sept. 1935, Wau, Bahr El Ghazal; ed. Xavier Univ., Ohio, Univ. of Notre Dame, Indiana, Inst. of Social Studies, The Hague, Royal Inst. of Public Admin., London.
Executive Officer, Ministry of Local Govt. 58-59; Schoolmaster, Comboni Coll., Khartoum 59-60; Finance Insp. Ministry of Finance and Econs. 62-63; Lecturer Inst. of Public Admin. 63-72; Sec.-Gen. High Exec. Council for the Southern Region 72-; mem. Second Order of the Nile.
Publ. *Methods and Techniques of Community Development Programmes* 66.
Secretariat General, P.O. Box 17, Juba, Sudan.

Riazi, Abdollah; Iranian politician; b. 1906; ed. Univ. de Paris à la Sorbonne.
Assistant Dean, Technical Coll. 36-45, Dean 56-; Pres. of Majlis 64-.
The Majlis, Teheran, Iran.

Richmond, Sir John Christopher Blake, K.C.M.G.; British diplomatist; b. 7 Sept. 1909; ed. Lancing Coll., Hertford Coll., Oxford, and Univ. Coll., London.
On archæological expeditions, Beisan, Jericho, Tel El Duweir, Ithaca 31-36; H.M. Office of Works 37-39; served in Middle East in Second World War 39-46; Dept. of Antiquities, Palestine Govt. 46-47; British Foreign Service, Oriental Sec., Baghdad 47-51; Foreign Office 51-53; Counsellor, Amman 53-55; Consul-Gen. Houston, Texas 55-58; British Property Comm. Cairo 59; Political Agent, Kuwait Oct. 59-61, British Ambassador 61-63; Supernumerary Fellow, St. Antony's Coll., Oxford 63-64; Ambassador to Sudan 65-66; Lecturer in Modern Near East History, Durham Univ. 66-74; retired.
20 The Avenue, Durham City, Durham, England.

Riegner, Dr. Gerhart M.; Swiss administrator; b. 12 Sept. 1911, Berlin; ed. Univs. of Berlin, Freiburg, Heidelberg, Paris, Graduate Inst. of Int. Studies, Geneva, and Acad. for Int. Law, The Hague.
Legal Sec. World Jewish Congress 36-39, Dir. Geneva Office 39-48, mem. World Exec. 48-60, Dir. of Co-ordination 60-65, Sec.-Gen. 65-; Int. Chair. World Univ. Service 49-55; Pres. Conf. of non-Govt. Orgs. at UN 53-55, Conf. of non-Govt. Orgs. in Consultative Status with UNESCO 56-58.
Publs. articles on legal matters, Jewish affairs and Christian-Jewish relations.
World Jewish Congress, 1 rue Varembé, Geneva; Home: 25 Avenue Wendt, Geneva, Switzerland.

Rifaat, Kamal Eldin Mahmoud; Egyptian diplomatist and politician; b. 1921; ed. Military Academy.
Served in Armed Forces 42-55; mem. Nat. Ass. 57 Deputy Minister for Presidential Affairs 58; Minister of Labour 61, 67; mem. Presidential Council; Deputy Prime Minister for Scientific Affairs 64; mem. Gen. Secr. Arab Socialist Union 64; Amb. at Ministry of Foreign Affairs Nov. 70; Amb. to U.K. 71-74; Order of the Repub., Mil. Star, and decorations from Cameroon, Morocco, Tunisia, Yugoslavia.
Publs. *Strategy, The Social Experiment, The Third World and the Socialist Solution, National Liberation.*
c/o Ministry of Foreign Affairs, Cairo, Egypt.

Rifa'i, Abdul Munem; Jordanian diplomatist; b. 1917; ed. American Univ. of Beirut.
In service of King Abdullah 38; Chief Sec. of Govt. 40; Asst. Chief of Roya . Court 41-42; Consul-Gen. in Cairo, Lebanon and Syria 43-44; Del. to Treaty Conf. with Great Britain 46; Under-Sec. of Foreign Affairs 47; Minister to Iran and Pakistan 49; Amb. to United States and Perm. Rep. to UN 53-57, to Lebanon 57, to Great Britain 58; Chief of Nat. Guidance 59; Perm. Rep. to UN 59-66; Amb. to U.A.R. 66, 67-68; Minister of Foreign Affairs 68-69; Prime Minister March-Aug. 69; Deputy Prime Minister, Minister of Foreign Affairs and Senator 69-70; Prime Minister June 70-71; Personal Rep. to H.M. King Hussein 72-73; Perm. Rep. to Arab League 73; Amb. to Egypt Sept.-Dec. 73; Special Adviser to H.M. King Hussein on Int. Affairs Dec. 73-74, mem. Senate 74-; numerous decorations.
The Senate, Amman, Jordan.

Rifai, Rashid M. S. al-, M.S.ENG., PH.D., M.I.E.E.; Iraqi electrical engineer; b. 1 May 1929; ed. American Univ. of Beirut, Lebanon, Univ. of Bristol, England, Purdue and Rice Univs., U.S.A.
Chief Engineer, Gen. Co. for Electrical Industries 68; Minister for Presidential Affairs July-Aug. 68, of Oil and Minerals 68-70; Minister of State 70; Minister of Planning 71, of Communications 72-75, of Public Works and Housing 75; Acting Minister of Defence 73-74.
Ministry of Communications, Baghdad, Iraq.

Rifai, Yousuf Hashim Ahmed al-; Kuwaiti politician; b. 1932; ed. Shuwaikh Secondary School, Kuwait.
Director, Travel and Residence Dept. 61-63; mem. Nat. Assembly 63-, Sec. 63; Minister of Posts, Telegraphs and Telephones 64; Minister of State for Cabinet Affairs Nov. 64, also Chair. of Municipal Council 66.
c/o National Assembly, Kuwait.

Rifa'i, Zaid al-, M.A.; Jordanian diplomatist; b. 27 Nov. 1936, Amman (nephew of Abdul Munem Rifa'i, *q.v.*); ed. Victoria Coll., Cairo, and Harvard and Columbia Univs. Joined diplomatic service 57; served at embassies in Cairo, Beirut and London and at the Perm. Mission of Jordan at UN; Chief of Royal Protocol 65; Sec.-Gen. of Royal Court and Private Sec. to H.M. King Hussein 67; Chief of Royal Court 69-70; Amb. to U.K. 70-72; Political Adviser to H.M. King Hussein 72-73; Prime Minister May 73-; Minister of Foreign Affairs and Defence 73-.
Office of the Prime Minister, Amman, Jordan.

Rimalt, Elimelech, PH.D.; Israeli politician; b. 1 Nov. 1907, Poland; ed. Hebrew High School, Cracow, Poland, Univ. of Vienna and Rabbinical Seminary, Vienna, Austria.
Emigrated to Palestine from Austria 39, and served as Head of Schools in Ramat Gan, Israel and Dir. of Educ. Dept. of Ramat Gan Municipality; Deputy Mayor of Ramat Gan 55-59; Minister of Posts, Israel Govt. 69; Founder, Union of Gen. Zionist (now Liberal) Workers; mem. Knesset; Chair. Liberal Party in fifth Knesset; Co-Chair. Herut-Liberal Hoc (Gahal), Knesset 65-68; Past Chair.

and mem. of numerous Parl. Cttees; now Chair. Liberal Party of Israel, co-Chair. Likud bloc 73-.
Publs. Scientific work in the field of Semitic languages.
68 Ibn Gvirol Street, Tel-Aviv, Israel.

Rishtya, Kassim; Afghan writer and diplomatist; b. 1913; ed. Istiklal High School, Kabul, Banking Inst., Kabul.
Clerk in Press Section, Ministry of Foreign Affairs 31; Chief Clerk Foreign Relations Section, Ministry of Communications 32; mem. Kabul Literary Circle 33; Dir. Publs. Div. 36, Vice-Pres. 38; Editor *Kabul Almanach* and *Kabul Magazine* 36-38; Dir.-Gen. of Publs. Press Dept. 40-44, Vice-Pres. 44-47, Pres. 47-48; Pres. Govt. Econ. Planning Board 49, Govt. Co-operative Org. 49-52, Bakhtar News Agency 52-55; Minister of Information 56-59; Amb. to Czechoslovakia, Poland and Hungary 60-62, to Egypt, Greece, Sudan, Ghana 62-63; Minister of Information 63; Vice-Chair. Cttee. for Revision of Constitution 63; Minister of Finance 64-65; Rep. for Afghanistan at Second Conf. for the Support of the Arab People 69; Del. to UN Gen. Assembly 69; Amb. to Japan 70-73, also accred. to the Philippines.
Publs. *Afghanistan in the 19th Century*, *Jawani Afghan*, short stories, translations and several novels.
c/o Ministry of Foreign Affairs, Kabul, Afghanistan.

Rivlin, Moshe; Israeli administrator; b. 1925, Jerusalem; ed. Teacher's Seminary, Graduate Aluma Inst. for Jewish Studies, Mizrachi Teachers' Coll. and Hebrew Univ., Jerusalem.
Joined Haganah 40; Head, Council of Youth Movts., Jerusalem 44-46; Consul, New York 52-58; Dir. Information Dept., The Jewish Agency 58-60, Sec.-Gen. 60-66, Dir.-Gen. and Head of Admin. and Public Relations Dept. 66-71; elected Dir.-Gen. of reconstituted Jewish Agency 71; Assoc. mem. Exec., World Zionist Org. 71, Chair. Haganah veterans in Israel.
The Jewish Agency, P.O. Box 92, Jerusalem; 48 King George Avenue, Jerusalem, Israel.

Robert, Louis; French archaeologist; b. 15 Feb. 1904; ed. Paris Univ., Ecole Normale Supérieure.
Member French School, Athens 27-32; Dir. of Studies Ecole des Hautes Etudes 32-; Prof. of Greek Epigraphy and Antiquities Coll. de France 39-74; dir. excavations at Amyzon 49 and Claros (Temple of Apollo) 50-61; Officier Légion d'Honneur.
Publs. *Villes d'Asie Mineure, Etudes Anatoliennes, Les Gladiateurs dans l'Orient Grec, Etudes de Numismatique Grecque, Hellenica* (13 vols.), *Noms Indigènes dans l'Asie Mineure, La Carie* (with his wife, Jeanne Robert), *Monnaies antiques en Troade, Documents de l'Asie Mineure méridionale, La déesse de Hiérapolis Castabala, Monnaies Grecques, Opera Minora Selecta* (4 vols.), *Bulletin Epigraphique* (with his wife) 38- (annually).
31 avenue René Coty, Paris 14e, France.

Rosen, Pinhas Felix; Israeli lawyer and politician; b. 1 May 1887; ed. Univs. of Freiburg and Berlin.
Called to Bar, Germany 14; served in German Army First World War 14-18; Chair. Zionist Fed. in Germany 20-23; mem. Zionist Exec. London 26-31; went to Palestine 31; called to Palestine Bar 32; Municipal Councillor Tel-Aviv 35-46; Minister of Justice 48-51, 52-61; mem. Knesset (Parl.) 48-68.
10 Ramban Street, Jerusalem, Israel.

Rosen, Shlomo; Israeli politician; b. 21 June 1905.
Active in Histadrut, missions abroad; mem. Exec. Cttee., Jewish Agency; mem. Exec. Comm., Mapam (United Workers' Party); mem. Knesset (Parl.), Deputy Speaker 65-; Sec. Kibbutz Movement; Minister for Immigration and Absorption March 74-.
Ministry of Immigration and Absorption, Jerusalem, Israel.

Rosenne, Shabtai, LL.B., PH.D.; Israeli lawyer and diplomatist; b. 24 Nov. 1917; ed. London Univ. and Hebrew Univ. of Jerusalem.
Advocate (Israel), Political Dept., Jewish Agency for Palestine 46-48; Legal Adviser, Ministry of Foreign Affairs 48-66; Deputy Perm. Rep. to UN 67-71; Perm. Rep. to UN (Geneva) 71-74; Ministry of Foreign Affairs 74-; mem. Del. to UN Gen. Assemblies 48-74, Vice-Chair. Legal Cttee. 60; mem. Del. to Armistice Negotiations with Egypt, Jordan, Lebanon and Syria 49; mem. Del. to UN Conf. on Law of the Sea 58,60, Chair. Del. to UN Conf. on Law of Treaties 68, 69, mem. other UN confs.; Govt. Rep. before Int. Court of Justice in several cases; mem. Int. Law Comm. 62-71, UN Comm. on Human Rights 68-70; Assoc. Inst. of Int. Law 63-, Rapporteur, Termination and Modification of Treaties 65; Israel Prize 60, Certificate of Merit, American Soc. of Int. Law 68.
Publs. *International Court of Justice 57, The Time Factor in Jurisdiction of the International Court of Justice 60, The Law and Practice of the International Court* (2 vols.) 65, *The Law of Treaties: Guide to the Vienna Convention 70, The World Court: What it is and how it works 73*; and numerous articles, mainly on law.
Ministry of Foreign Affairs, Jerusalem, Israel.

Ross, John-Paul Beverley; British former United Nations official; b. 21 Nov. 1908; ed. Dragon School, Oxford, Repton School and Cambridge Univ.
Admitted as solicitor 38; worked for Ministry of Econ. Warfare, London 39-43, Combined Econ. Warfare Agency, Cairo and Caserta 43-45, later with Supreme Headquarters Allied Expeditionary Force (SHAEF), Versailles; mem. British del. to Council of Foreign Ministers, London, Paris, New York, Moscow 45-47, to Peace Conf., Paris 46; mem. Int. Secr., Preparatory Comm. for the OEEC 47; Deputy Dir. (later Dir.) German External Assets Div., Inter-Allied Reparations Agency, Brussels 47-52; Acting Resident Rep. UN Technical Assistance Board, Burma 52-53, Philippines 53-54, Pakistan 54-55, Deputy Resident Rep., Indonesia 55-59, Iran 59-64; Resident Rep. UN Devt. Programme (UNDP), Israel 64-73, retd.; mem. Law Soc., Royal Inst. of Int. Affairs.
Publ. trans. from French of *The Church of the Holy Sepulchre, Jerusalem* by Charles Coüasnon 74.
52 rue de Villeneuve, Thieux 77-230 par Dammartin-en-Goële, Seine et Marne, France.

Rossides, Zenon; Cypriot diplomatist; b. 8 Feb. 1895; ed. Limassol Coll. and Middle Temple, London.
Called to Bar 23; law practice in Cyprus 25-54; mem. Nat. Del. to London 29-31; mem. Ethnarchy Council 46-48 and 58-59; mem. Exec. 50-59; Greek Cypriot Rep. on Joint Cttee. in London, leading to Independence of Cyprus 59-60; Ambassador to U.S.A. 60-73; Perm. Rep. of Cyprus to UN 60-; Vice-Pres. UN Gen. Assembly 61-62, 63-64; Chair. UN Cttee. on Portuguese Colonies 62.
Publs. *The Island of Cyprus and Union with Greece 51, The Problem of Cyprus 58.*
Permanent Mission of Cyprus to the United Nations, 820 Second Ave., New York, N.Y. 10017, U.S.A.

Rouhani, Fuad, LL.M.; Iranian lawyer and executive; b. 23 Oct. 1907; ed. Teheran and London Univ.
Anglo-Iranian Oil Co., Legal and Administrative Branches 26-51; Chief Legal Adviser, Nat. Iranian Oil Co. 51-54, Dir. 54-, Deputy Chair. 56; Sec.-Gen. and Chair. Board of Govs., Organization of Petroleum Exporting Countries (OPEC) 61-64; Adviser to the Prime Minister 64; Sec.-Gen. Regional Co-operation for Devt. 64-68; Adviser to Prime Minister; now in private practice as expert on Iranian and int. law; D. en D. (Paris) 68.
16 Kh. Rasht (Behjatabad), Teheran, Iran.

Rouhani, Mansour, M.SC.; Iranian politician; b. 1921, Teheran; ed. Univs. of Teheran and London.

Chairman and Gen. Dir. Technical Dept., Teheran Water Supply Org.; Minister of Water and Power 65-71, of Agriculture 71-, and Natural Resources 74-.
Ministry of Agriculture and Natural Resources, Teheran, Iran.

Rouillon, Fernand; French diplomatist; b. 11 Dec. 1920, Condrieu (Rhône); ed. Tivoli Coll., School of Political Sciences, Bordeaux Univ.
With Ministry of Foreign Affairs 44-; Dept. of Econ. Affairs 44-47; Tunis, London (NATO) and Ottawa 47-56; Dept. of Eastern Europe 56-58, of Cultural Affairs 58-60; Rabat, New York (UN), and Athens 60-70; Asst. Dir. Dept. of Middle East 70-75; Amb. to Syria June 75-; Chevalier, Légion d'Honneur; Officier, Ordre National du Mérite.
French Embassy, Damascus, Syrian Arab Republic.

Roussos, Nicolaos S.; Cypriot civil engineer and politician; b. 1906, Lania Village, Limassol District, ed. Greek Gymnasium, Limassol, and Athens Technical Univ. Practised civil engineering in Greece, mainly road construction work 29-33; Municipal Engineer, Limassol 33-47; Senior Partner, N. S. Roussos & J. Pericleous (civil engineers and architects) 38-70; Minister of Communications and Works 70-72; mem. of Board, Cyprus Telecommunications Authority 60-68, Vice-Chair. 68-70, Chair. June 72-; Pres. Cyprus Civil Engineers and Architects Asscn. 46-62; Pres. UN Asscn. of Cyprus 70, Limassol Rotary 61-62, Limassol Wine Festival 64, 65.
Cyprus Telecommunications Authority, Nicosia; and P.O. Box 270, Limassol, Cyprus.

Rubayyi, Salem (*see* Ali, Salem Rubia).

Runciman, The Hon. Sir Steven (James Cochran Stevenson), Kt., M.A., F.B.A.; British historian; b. 7 July 1903; ed. Eton Coll. and Trinity Coll., Cambridge.
Fellow Trinity Coll., Cambridge 27-38; Lecturer Cambridge Univ. 31-38; Press Attaché, British Legation, Sofia 40-41; Prof. of Byzantine Studies, Istanbul Univ. 42-45; Rep. of British Council, Greece 45-47; Chair. Anglo-Hellenic League 51-67; Trustee, British Museum 60-67; Pres. British Inst. of Archaeology at Ankara 61-75; Fellow, British Acad. 57; Hon. Fellow, Trinity Coll., Cambridge 65; Hon. Litt.D. (Cambridge, London, Chicago, Durham, St. Andrews, Oxford, Birmingham), Hon. LL.D. (Glasgow), Hon. D.Phil. (Thessalonika), Hon. D.D. (Wabash, U.S.A.).
Publs. *The Emperor Romanus Lecapenus* 29, *The First Bulgarian Empire* 30, *Byzantine Civilization* 33, *The Medieval Manichee* 47, *History of the Crusades* (3 vols.) 51-54, *The Eastern Schism* 55, *The Sicilian Vespers* 58, *The White Rajahs* 60, *The Fall of Constantinople 1453* 65, *The Great Church in Captivity* 68, *The Last Byzantine Renaissance* 70, *The Orthodox Churches and the Secular State* 71.
Elshieshields, Lockerbie, Dumfriesshire, Scotland.

S

Saam, Mohammad, M.A., PH.D.; Iranian educationalist and politician; b. 1924, Kerman, Iran; ed. Univs. of Teheran, Nebraska and S. Calif., U.S.A.
Former teacher; Dir. Dept. of Educ.; Del. of Dept. of Educ. to Near East Inst.; Admin. Consultant to Cen. Bank of Iran; mem. Parl.; Gov. Gen. of Gilan and Isfahan; fmr. Minister of Information; Minister of Interior 72-74.
c/o Ministry of Interior, Teheran, Iran.

Saba, Elias, B.LITT.; Lebanese economist and politician; b. 1932, Lebanon; ed. American Univ. of Beirut and Univ. of Oxford.
Economic Adviser to Ministry of Finance and Petroleum, Kuwait and Kuwait Fund for Arab Econ. Devt. 61-62;

Chair. Dept. of Econs., American Univ. of Beirut 63-67; Assoc. Prof. of Econs., American Univ. of Beirut 67-69; Deputy Prime Minister of the Lebanon, Minister of Finance and Minister of Defence 70-72; Econ. and Financial Adviser to Pres. 72-73; Chair. and Gen. Man. St. Charles City Centre, S.A.R.L. 74-; Chair. and Chief Exec. Arab Int. Finance Co., Switzerland 74-.
Publ. *Postwar Developments in the Foreign Exchange Systems of Lebanon and Syria* 62.
Biarritz Building, P.O. Box 9500, Beirut, Lebanon.

Saba, Hanna, D. en D.; Egyptian jurist and diplomatist; b. 23 July 1909; ed. Coll. of Jesuit Fathers, Cairo, Faculté de Droit, Paris, and Ecole Libre des Sciences Politiques, Paris.
Ministry of Foreign Affairs, Cairo 42, Counsellor 46, Minister 52; Dir. of Treaties Div., UN Secr. 46-50; Juridical Adviser, UNESCO 50-67; Asst. Dir.-Gen. of UNESCO 67-71; Alt. Chair. UNESCO Appeal Board 73; Vice-Chair. Asscn. of French and Arab Jurists, Arbitration Comm. of Franco-Arab Chamber of Commerce; Grand Officer of Merit, Egypt; Officer of the Nile.
Publs. *L'Islam et la nationalité* 32, *L'évolution dans la technique des traités, Les droits économiques et sociaux dans le projet de pacte des droits de l'homme, Les ententes et accords régionaux dans la Charte des Nations Unies* (Course at Acad. of Int. Law, The Hague 52), *L'Activité quasi-législative des institutions spécialisées des Nations Unies* (Course at Acad. of Int. Law, The Hague 64).
3 boulevard de la Sassaye, Neuilly (Hauts de Seine), France.

Sabah, His Highness Sheikh Jabir al-Ahmed al-Jabir al-; Kuwaiti politician; b. 1928; ed. Almubarakiyyah School and privately.
Governor, Ahmedi and Oil Areas 49-59; Pres. Dept. of Finance and Economy 59; Minister of Finance, Industry and Commerce 63; Prime Minister 65-; appointed Crown Prince 66.
Office of the Prime Minister, Council of Ministers, Kuwait.

Sabah, Sheikh Saad al-Abdullah al-Salem al-; Kuwaiti politician.
Deputy Pres., Police and Public Security Dept. until 61; Minister of the Interior 61-65; Minister of the Interior and Defence Nov. 65-.
Ministry of the Interior, Kuwait.

Sabah, Sheikh Sabah al-Ahmed al-Jabir al-; Kuwaiti politician; b. 1929; ed. Mubarakiyyah National School, Kuwait and privately.
Member Supreme Cttee. 56-61; Head of Dept. of Social Affairs and Dept. of Printing, Press and Publications 61; Minister of Guidance of News 63; Minister of Foreign Affairs 63-, acting Minister of Oil 65-67; Minister of Oil Affairs 67.
Ministry of Foreign Affairs, Kuwait.

Sabah, Sheikh Sabah al-Salem al-; Amir of Kuwait, twelfth ruler of the Sabah dynasty; b. 1913; ed. privately.
Head of Police Dept. 38-59; mem. Supreme Exec. Cttee. 55-61; Deputy Prime Minister and Minister of Foreign Affairs 61-63; Prime Minister 63-65; succeeded his brother Sheikh Abdullah al-Salem al-Sabah as Amir of Kuwait Nov. 65.
Sief Palace, Amiry Diwan, Kuwait.

Sabah, Sheikh Salem al-Sabah al- (son of Sheikh Sabah al-Salem al-Sabah, Amir of Kuwait *q.v.*); Kuwaiti diplomatist; b. 18 June 1937; ed. Secondary School, Kuwait, Gray's Inn, London, and Christ Church, Oxford.
Joined Foreign Service 62; Head of Legal (later Political) Dept. Ministry of Foreign Affairs; Amb. to the U.K. 65-70, to U.S.A. 70-, also accred. to Canada; rep. of Kuwait to

confs. in Middle East and Africa, including Arab Summit Conf., Casablanca Oct. 65.
Embassy of Kuwait, 2940 Tilden Street, N.W., Washington, D.C., U.S.A.

Sabeti, Dr. Hassan, C.V.O., LIC.SC.POL., PH.D.; Iranian diplomatist; b. 1912, Mashad; ed. Teheran Univ., Univ. of Cologne.
Joined Govt. Service 42; with Ministry of Foreign Affairs 51-; Second Sec., Cologne 54-58; Under-Sec., 5th Political Dept., Teheran 58-60, Protocol Dept. 60-70; Counsellor, The Hague 70; in charge of Translations Section, Teheran 70-73; Amb. to Yemen Arab Repub. June 73-; Orders of Taj (Class V) 55, Homayoun (Class IV) 65, Homayoun (Class III) 69; Order of Merit (Fed. Germany) 58; Commdr. Order of the Rising Sun (Japan) 58.
Embassy of Iran, Sana'a, Yemen Arab Republic.

Sabir, Mohieddin, PH.D.; Sudanese politician; b. 1919, Dalgo; ed. Univ. of Cairo, Bordeaux Univ. and the Sorbonne, France.
Director, Ministry of Social Affairs 54; Editor-in-Chief *El Estglal* and *Sot El Sudan* (daily papers); Man. *El Zaman* (daily paper); UNESCO Expert and Head, Social Sciences Dept., Regional Centre for Social Devt., Sirra Llyan; mem. Constituent Assembly 68; Minister of Educ. 69-72.
c/o Ministry of Education, Khartoum, Sudan.

Sabri, Aly; Egyptian politician; b. 30 Aug. 1920; ed. Military Acad. and Air Force Acad.
Fought in Palestine War 48; Minister for Presidential Affairs, Egypt 57-58, U.A.R. 58-62; Pres. Exec. Council 62-64, Prime Minister 64-65; Vice-Pres. of Repub. Oct. 65-67; Sec.-Gen. Arab Socialist Union Oct. 65-67, 68-Sept. 69; Deputy Prime Minister 67 and Minister of Local Govt. 67-Oct. 67; Resident Minister for Suez Canal Zone Oct. 67-68; Vice-Pres. of Repub. 70-71; on trial for treason Aug. 71, sentenced to life imprisonment Dec. 71.
Cairo, Egypt.

Sa'd, Farid Ali, B.SC.; Jordanian economist; b. 1908; ed. American Univ. of Beirut, Lebanon.
Science Teacher, Principal, Insp. of Educ. in Transjordan and Palestine 28-35; District Officer, Palestine Govt. 35-43; Man. Arab Bank Ltd., Haifa 43-48; mem. War Econ. Advisory Council of Palestine Govt. 43-46; Senator 51-55; mem. Royal Fiscal Comm., Cttee. of Educ. Moslem Coll.; Minister of Finance; Chair., Man. Dir. Jordan Tobacco and Cigarette Co. Ltd., Jordan Bata Co.; Dir. Jordan Petroleum Refinery Co. Ltd.; Chair. Advisory Board, Nat. and Grindlays Bank Ltd.; mem. Arab Orphans Cttee., Board of Royal Jordanian Airlines; Vice-Mayor Amman Municipality; Trustee, Jordan Univ., American Univ. of Beirut.
P.O. Box 59, Amman, Jordan.

Sadaghiani, Reza; Iranian agriculturalist; ed. Karaj Agricultural Faculty, near Teheran, and Syracuse Univ., U.S.A.
Iranian Ministry of Agriculture 39, served as Technical Under-Sec. to Dept. of Forestry, Head of Karkheh Devt. Org. of the Plan Org., Head of Agriculture Div. of Plan Org., Dir. of Rural Devt., Under-Sec. for Research and Planning to Ministry of Agriculture, Deputy Chief of Central Bureau of Planning, Under-Sec. for Technical Affairs to Minister of Agriculture; Pres. Agricultural Bank of Iran; Minister of Co-operatives and Rural Affairs 74-.
Ministry of Co-operatives and Rural Affairs, Teheran, Iran.

Sadaka, Nagib, B.A., L. ès L., D. en D.; Lebanese diplomatist; b. 1915; ed. American Univ. of Beirut, French Faculty of Law, Beirut, and the Sorbonne.
Lecturer, Inst. of Political Science, French Faculty of Law, Beirut 46; Head of Western Political Section, Ministry of Foreign Affairs 47, Head of UN Service 49;

Counsellor, Paris 52; Dir.-Gen. Ministry of Educ. 52-55; Amb. to Switzerland and U.A.R. 58-60; Amb. to Belgium and Perm. Rep. to EEC 60-66; Sec.-Gen. Ministry of Foreign Affairs 66-.
Publs. *Paternal power in Moslem law* (in Arabic) 39, *La question syrienne pendant la guerre de 1914-1918* 40, *The Palestinian Question* (in Arabic) 46.
Ministère des Affaires Etrangères, rue Sursock, Beirut, Lebanon.

Sadat, Col. Muhammad Anwar es-; Egyptian officer and politician; b. 25 Dec. 1918; ed. Military Coll.
Commissioned 33; fmr. Gen. Sec. Islamic Congress; one of Free Officers who overthrew monarchy 52; Editor *Al Jumhuriya* and *Al Tahrir* 55-56; Pres. Egyptian Nat. Union 57-61; Pres. Afro-Asian Conf., Cairo 58; Speaker U.A.R. Nat. Assembly 61-69; mem. Presidency Council 62-64, Vice-Pres. of U.A.R. 64-67, 69-70; interim Pres. Sept.-Oct. 70, Pres. Oct. 70-; Chair. Pres. Council, Fed. of Arab Republics Oct. 71-; Chair. Arab Socialist Union (ASU); Prime Minister 73-74; Mil. Gov.-Gen. 73-.
The Presidency, Cairo, Egypt.

Sadawi, A. M. Suhail; Libyan oil executive; b. 1928, Beirut; ed. American Univ. of Beirut.
With Gulf Oil Corpn., Libya 58-61; Int. Labour Office, Geneva 62-63; Head, Gen. Econ. Section, Org. of Petroleum Exporting Countries (OPEC) 63; participated in negotiations for amendment of Libyan Petroleum Law 65; mem. Pricing Comm., Libya 67, Chair. 68; Asst. Under Sec., Libyan Ministry of Petroleum 68; Deputy Dir. Gen. Libyan Nat. Petroleum Corpn. 68; Sec.-Gen. Org. of Arab Petroleum Exporting Countries 70-73.
Arab Economists Petroleum Affairs (Consultants), P.O. Box 8840, Beirut, Lebanon.

Sadek, Gen. Mohammed Ahmed; Egyptian army officer; ed. Frunze Mil. Acad., U.S.S.R.
Served in Egyptian army, World War II, Palestine War 48, Suez Campaign 56; Mil. Attaché, Egyptian Embassy in Fed. Repub. of Germany 64; of Dir. Studies, Mil. Acad., Cairo 65-67; Dir. of Information, Army Intelligence Dept. 67; Chief of Staff of the Army 69; Minister of War and Mil. Production 71-72; Deputy Premier for Nat. Defence 72; mem. Supreme Council of the Armed Forces.
c/o Ministry of War, Cairo, Egypt.

Sadiq, Issa, PH.D.; Iranian educationist; b. 1894; ed. Univs. of Paris, Cambridge (England), and Columbia (N.Y.).
Directed various depts. Ministry of Education 19-30; mem. Nat. Constituent Assembly 25-49, 67; Pres. and Prof. Nat. Teachers' Coll.; Dean of Faculties of Arts and Science Teheran Univ. 32-41; Chancellor of Univ. 41; Minister of Education 41, 43, 45, 47 and 60-61; Senator for Teheran 49-52, 54-60, 63-67, 67-71; Vice-Pres. Iranian Acad. 37-70; mem. Board of Govs., Nat. Bank of Iran 37-52; Prof. of History of Educ., Univ. of Teheran 32-72; Pres. Persia-America Relations Soc. 49-53; mem. Royal Cultural Council 62-; Founder mem. Nat. Soc. for Physical Educ. 33-54, Soc. for Preservation of Nat. Monuments 44-, Nat. Soc. for Protection of Children 53-; mem. High Educational Council 34-41, 51-58, 72-, Iranian Acad. of Language 70-, High Council for Culture and Art 72-.
Publs. *Principles of Education, New Methods in Education, History of Education, Modern Persia and her Educational System* (in English), *A Year in America, The March of Education in Iran and the West, A Brief Course in the History of Education in Iran, History of Education in Persia from the Earliest Times to the Present Day, History of Education in Europe, Memoirs,* etc.
316 Avenue Hedayat, Valiabad, Teheran; and The University, Avenue Shah Reza, Teheran, Iran.

Sadr, Javad, PH.D.; Iranian diplomatist and politician; b. 1912; ed. Univ. de Paris à la Sorbonne.
Ministry of Interior 39, Ministry of Foreign Affairs 41; fmr. mem. Information and Legal Affairs Div., Ministry of Foreign Affairs, later First Sec. and Consul, Palestine; fmr. Chief of Secr. to Prime Minister; fmr. Minister in Yugoslavia; fmr. Deputy Minister of Interior and of Foreign Affairs; fmr. Ambassador to Japan; Minister of Interior 64-66; Minister of Justice 66-68; Foreign Office Adviser 68; Prof. Inst. of Political Sciences; Lecturer, Centre for Int. Studies of Teheran Univ.; Chair. Exec. Board Int. Law Asscn. (Iran Branch); Grand Officer Homayoun, Officer Tadj Order, Order of Merit for Justice, 8 foreign decorations.
Publs. *International Institutions* 71, *Diplomatic Law* 75 (both in Persian).
Zafaranieh Sadr Street 10, Tajrish, Teheran, Iran.

Saffar, Salman Mohamed al-, PH.D.; Bahrain diplomatist; b. 1931, Bahrain; ed. Baghdad Univ., Iraq and Sorbonne, Paris.
Primary school teacher, Bahrain 49-54, Secondary school teacher 59-60; with Ministry of Foreign Affairs, Bahrain; Perm. Rep. to UN Sept. 71-.
Permanent Mission of Bahrain to United Nations, 747 Third Avenue, 19th Floor, New York, N.Y. 10017, U.S.A.

Sagar, Abdul Aziz al-Hamad al; Kuwaiti businessman and politician; b. 1913; ed. Secondary School, Bombay.
Member Municipality Board 52-55, Devt. Board 52-55; Chair. Kuwait Chamber of Commerce 59-, Nat. Bank of Kuwait 59-65; Jt. Council 61-62; Chair. Kuwait Oil Tanker Co. 61-64, 65-; mem. Constituent Assembly 63-, Speaker 63-65; Minister of Health 63; Chair. Red Crescent Soc. 66-.
P.O. Box 244, Kuwait City, Kuwait.

Sahnoun, Hadj Mohamed, M.A.; Algerian diplomatist; b. 8 April 1931; ed. Lycée of Constantine, Univ. de Paris à la Sorbonne and New York Univ.
Director of African, Asian and Latin American Affairs Ministry of Foriegn Affairs 62-63, of Political Affairs 64; Del. to UN Gen. Assembly 62-63, 64-65; Asst. Sec.-Gen. Org. of African Unity (OAU) 64-.
Publ. *Economic and Social Aspects of the Algerian Revolution* 62.
OAU, P.O. Box 3243, Addis Ababa, Ethiopia.

Said, Faisal al-; Omani diplomatist; b. 1927, Muscat.
Attached to Ministry of Foreign Affairs, Muscat 53-57; lived abroad 57-70; Perm. Under-Sec. Ministry of Educ. 70-72; Minister of Econ. Affairs 72; Perm. Rep. to UN 72-73; Minister of Educ. Nov. 73-.
Ministry of Education, Muscat, Oman.

Said, Mostafa Tewfik el-, LL.B., LL.D., Egyptian lawyer and professor; b. 1908; ed. Mansourah Secondary School and Cairo Univ.
Public Prosecutor 29-38; Lecturer and Asst. Prof. of Criminal Law, Cairo Univ. 38-42; Prof. of Criminal Law, Alexandria Univ. 42; Dean of Faculty of Law, Alexandria Univ. 46; Attorney-Gen., Alexandria Court of Appeal 49, Prof. of Criminal Law, Cairo Univ. 50; Dean of Faculty of Law, Cairo Univ. 52; Rector of Alexandria Univ. 54-58; Rector of Cairo Univ. 58-61; Chair. of Supreme Council of the Univs.; Ambassador to Portugal 62-64, to Somalia 64-68, to German Democratic Repub. Feb. 72-.
Publs. *On the Scope and Exercise of Marital Rights* 36, *The Egyptian Penal Code Annotated,* 3rd edition 37, *Crimes of Forgery Under the Egyptian Law,* 4th edition 53, *Principles of Criminal Law,* 3rd edition 47, *The Expansion of Higher Education in the United Arab Republic* 60.
Egyptian Embassy, Warmbader Strasse 50/52, Berlin-Karlshorst, German Democratic Republic.

Said, Qaboos bin; Sultan of Oman; b. 18 Nov. 1940; ed. by British tutors and at Royal Military Coll., Sandhurst.
In Britain 58-66; served in British Army and studied local government; returned to Salalah 66; deposed his father Said bin Taimur 70; Sultan July 70-.
The Palace, Muscat, Sultanate of Oman.

Said Ansary, Alinaghi, M.RER.POL.; Iranian diplomatist; b. 18 Jan. 1920, Teheran; ed. Teheran Univ. and Faculty of Int. Relations, George Washington Univ., U.S.A.
Served in various political and admin. depts., Ministry of Foreign Affairs 47-49; First Sec., Iranian Embassy in U.S.A. 49-54; Asst. Head of Protocol, Ministry of Foreign Affairs 54-58; First Sec., Iranian Embassy in Italy 58-61; Consul-Gen., Milan 61-62; apptd. Sec.-Gen. Household of H.I.H. Princess Shams Pahlavi 62-66, concurrently Aide-de-Camp to H.I.M. the Shahanshah Aryamehr; Head of Protocol of the Imperial Court 66; apptd. Amb. 70; Amb. to Italy May 72-, concurrently to Albania.
Imperial Embassy of Iran, Via Nomentana 57, 00162 Rome, Italy.

Saif al-Islam, Abdullah ben Hassan; Yemeni politician.
Minister of the Interior April 67-69; mem. Mil. Council 67; Prime Minister *ad interim* June 68; in exile 68-.

Saif al-Islam, al-Hassan ben Yahya, H.H.; Yemeni politician.
Crown Prince of the Yemen 62-; Prime Minister 62-67; Head of Mil. Council 67; in exile 68-.

Saif al-Islam, Mohamed al-Badr, H.R.H.; Prince of the Yemen; b. 1927; ed. Coll. for Higher Education, Sana'a.
Son of King of the Yemen; Minister for Foreign Affairs 55-61, and Minister of Defence and C.-in-C. 55-62; succeeded to Imamate on the death of his father, Imam Ahmed Sept. 62; left Taiz following Republican *coup d'état* Sept. 62, leading Royalist resistance 62-68; replaced by Imamate Council May 68; in exile 68-.

Saif al-Islam, Mohammed ben Hussein; Yemeni politician; b. 1938.
Former diplomatic rep. to Fed. Germany; Vice-Pres. Imamate Council 67-May 68, Pres. of Council May 68; Commdr. of Royalist Armed Forces 67-68; in exile 68-.

Salah, Abdullah A.; Jordanian diplomatist; b. 31 Dec. 1922; ed. Bishop Gobat's School, Jerusalem, and American Univ. of Beirut.
Field Educ. Officer, United Nations Relief and Works Agency (UNRWA), Jordan 52-62; Ambassador to Kuwait 62-63, to India 63-64, to France 64-66, 67-70; Minister of Foreign Affairs 66-67, 70-72; Amb. to U.S.A. 73-, also accred. to Canada; several decorations.
Jordanian Embassy, 2319 Wyoming Avenue, N.W., Washington, D.C., U.S.A.

Salam, Saeb; Lebanese politician; b. 1905; ed. American Univ. of Beirut.
Elected Provisional Head Lebanese Govt. 43; deputy 43-47, 51; Minister of Interior 46, 60-61; Minister Foreign Affairs 46; Prime Minister 52, 53, 60-61, concurrently Minister of Defence 61; pioneer Lebanese civil aviation 45; Pres. Middle East Airlines Co., Beirut 45-56; Pres. Nat. Fats & Oil Co. Ltd., Beirut; Prime Minister 70-73.
Rue Moussaitbé, B.P. 206, Beirut, Lebanon.

Saleh, Jehanshah, M.D., F.I.C.S., F.R.C.O.G.; Iranian surgeon, gynaecologist and politician; b. 1905; ed. Syracuse Univ., N.Y.
Intern, St. Joseph's Hospital, Syracuse, N.Y. 33, Orange Memorial Hospital, N.J. 34, Resident Surgeon 35; Prof. of Anatomy, Teheran Univ. Faculty of Medicine 36-41, Prof. of Gynæcology 40-, Dean 47-54; Dir. and Chief of Gynæcological and Obstetrical Service, Vaziri Hospital, Teheran 36-37; Dir. and Chief Surgeon, Women's Hospital, Teheran 37; Minister of Public Health 50, 53, 54, 55, 60-61;

Minister of Educ. 61-63; mem. Board of Dirs. and Chief of Public Health Section, Red Lion and Sun (analogous to the Red Cross) 38-; Fellow, Int. Coll. of Surgeons; Pres. Iranian Asscn. of Obstetricians and Gynæcologists, and of Iran-America Medical Society; mem. American Medical Asscn., Iranian Central Council of Sanitation, Central Council for Education; Chancellor Teheran Univ.; WHO adviser in medical education and auxiliary branches 52-; Senator 69-; Hon. LL.D. (Syracuse Univ.), Hon. Sc.D. (Univ. of Bordeaux), Hon. F.R.C.O.G. (England), Hon. M.D. (Univ. of Vienna); Palmes Académiques, France; Grand Officier de l'Ordre Nat. du Mérite (France); Grand Officier de l'Ordre du Mérite Social (Belgium).
Publs. *The Relation of Diet to the Preservation of Teeth* 31, *Morphine Addiction and its Treatment* 32, *Diseases of Women* 41, *Normal and Abnormal Obstetrics* 42, *Recent Advances in Gynaecology* 60, *Text Book of Gynaecology* 64, 71.
Home: 10 W.Takht-i-Jamshid Avenue, Teheran; Office: University of Teheran, Avenue Shahreza, Teheran, Iran.

Salem, Mamdouh Mohamed; Egyptian civil servant and politician; b. 1918, Alexandria; ed. Police Acad.
Police Commdr., Alexandria 64-68; Gov. of Assiyut 68-70, of Alexandria 70-71; Deputy Premier, Minister of the Interior 71-75, Premier April 75-.
Office of the Premier, Cairo, Egypt.

Salih, Salih Mohammed; Sudanese banker; b. 1918; ed. Sudan Higher School.
Municipal Engineer, Govt. Survey Dept. 42, Agricultural Engineer 43-45, Chief Surveyor 45-51; Field Insp. Sudan Gezira Board 51-55, Group Insp. 55-56, Asst. Gen. Man. 56-62, Gen. Man. 62-64, Acting Man. Dir. 65-66; Chair. Board of Dirs., Gen. Man. Agricultural Bank of Sudan 67-73; mem. People's Council 72-, Head Finance and Audit Cttee.; Man. Dir. Sudan Oil Seeds Co. 74-.
People's Council, Khartoum, Sudan.

Salim, Khalil, B.A., DIP.ED., ED.D.; Jordanian educator, politician and banker; b. 1921; ed. American Univ. of Beirut, Inst. of Education, London and Columbia Univ.
Teacher in Secondary Schools 41-49; Lecturer Teachers Coll. 50; Dir. Cultural Affairs 52; Sec. Jordan Nat. Comm. for UNESCO 50-58; Asst. Under-Sec. of Educ. 55-62; Minister of Social Affairs 62; Minister of State, Prime Minister's Office 62-63; Chair. Authority for Tourism and Antiquities 62-63; Minister of Nat. Economy 62-63; Gov. Central Bank of Jordan 63; Chair. Board of Jordan Co-operation Union 65-68; Amb. to France 74-; mem. Jordan Devt. Board and mem. Board of Trustees, Univ. of Jordan; Deputy Chair. ALIA airline; Chair. Gen. Insurance Corpn.; Sec.-Gen. Royal Scientific Soc.; Chair. Inst. of Banking Studies; Deputy Chair. Council of Scientific Research; mem. Higher Exec. Cttee. Jordanian Nat. Union.
Publs. *Re-organization of Educational Administration in Jordan* 60, 15 textbooks on mathematics and numerous articles on mathematics, popular science, education, economics and banking.
Jordanian Embassy, 80 Boulevard Maurice Barrès, 92200 Neuilly, France.

Sallal, Marshal Abdullah; Yemeni army officer and politician; b. 1917; ed. in Iraq.
Returned to Yemen from Iraq 39; imprisoned 39; army service 40-48, 55-; imprisoned 48-55; Gov. of Hodeida 59-62; Chief of Staff to Imam Mohammed 62; Pres. of the Revolutionary Council and C.-in-C. 62-67; Prime Minister 62-64, 66-67, concurrently Minister of Foreign Affairs 63-64.
Cairo, Egypt.

Salzman, Pnina; Israeli pianist; b. 1923; ed. Ecole Normale de Musique and Conservatoire National de Musique, Paris.

Gave first concert in Paris at age of twelve; since then has given concerts in five continents; travels all over the world every year, playing with most of the major orchestras; over 300 concerts with Israeli orchestras.
20 Dubnov St., Tel-Aviv, Israel.

Sambursky, Shmuel, PH.D.; Israeli physicist; b. 28 Oct. 1900; ed. Univs. of Königsberg, Berlin and Utrecht.
Staff, Dept. of Physics, Hebrew Univ. Jerusalem 28-, Lecturer 34, Assoc. Prof. of Experimental Physics 49-60, Prof. and Head of Dept. of History and Philosophy of Science 60-; Exec. Sec. Palestine Board for Scientific and Industrial Research 45-48; Dir. Research Council of Israel 49-56, Vice-Chair. 56-59; mem. Exec. Cttee. of Nat. Comm. for UNESCO; Israeli del. UNESCO Gen. Confs. 49, 50, 51, 52, 54, 56, 58, 62; mem. Int. Advisory Cttee. on Scientific Research of UNESCO 54-57; Dean, Faculty of Science, Hebrew Univ. 57-59; Visiting Fellow, St. Catherine's Coll. Oxford 64-65; mem. Israel Acad. of Sciences and Humanities.
Publs. *The Physical World of the Greeks* 56, *Physics of the Stoics* 59, *The Physical World of Late Antiquity* 62.
c/o Hebrew University, Jerusalem, Israel.

Samii, Abdol Hossein, M.A., PH.D.; Iranian professor of medicine; b. 20 June 1930; ed. Univ. of Calif., Los Angeles, Cornell Univ.
Intern, Resident in Medicine, N.Y. Hosp., Peter Bent Brigham Hosp., Mass. Gen. Hosp.; Fellow, Rockefeller and Helen Hay Whitney Foundations; Prof. of Medicine, Nat. Univ. of Iran 63; Deputy Minister of Health 64; Chair. Dept. of Medicine, Medical Dir., Firouzgar Medical Centre 64; mem. Exec. Board, Social Insurance Org. 67; Dir. Pars Hosp. 70; Assoc. Prof. of Medicine, Univ. of Rochester 72; Adjunct Prof. of Medicine, Cornell Univ. 74; Minister of Science and Higher Educ. 74-; Chancellor of Reza Shah Kabir Univ.
Ministry of Science and Higher Education, Villa Avenue, Teheran, Iran.

Samii, Mohammad Mehdi; Iranian banker; b. 1918; ed. Inst. of Chartered Accountants in England and Wales.
Bank Melli Iran 45-51; National Iranian Oil Co. 51-53; Bank Melli Iran 53-59; Industrial and Mining Development Bank of Iran 59-63; Gov. Bank Markazi Iran (Central Bank of Iran) 63-68, 70-71; Man. Dir. Plan Org. 68-70; Adviser to the Prime Minister 71-73; Pres. Agricultural Devt. Bank of Iran 74-.
23 Takhte Jamshid Avenue, Teheran, Iran.

Samuel, 2nd Viscount, cr. 37, of Mount Carmel and of Toxteth, Liverpool, **Edwin Herbert Samuel, C.M.G.;** British lecturer and author; b. 1898; ed. Westminster School, Balliol Coll. Oxford, and Columbia Univ.
Served First World War; Palestine Civil Service 20-48; Visiting Prof. Dropsie Coll., Philadelphia 48-49, Graduate School of Public Affairs, Albany, New York 63, Univ. of Pittsburgh 70; Visiting Lecturer, Witwatersrand Univ., Johannesburg 53; European Dir. *The Conquest of the Desert* Exhibition, Jerusalem 51-53; Principal of the Inst. of Public Admin. in Israel; Dir. *Jewish Chronicle*, London, 51-70, Vallentine Mitchell (Publishers) Ltd., (London) 65-, Ellern Investment Corpn., Tel-Aviv 64-, Moller Textile Co., Nahariya 65-; Senior Lecturer in British Institutions, The Hebrew Univ., Jerusalem 54-69; Adviser, Magen David Adom (Israeli Red Cross) 57-.
Publs. *A Primer on Palestine* 32, *The Jewish Communal Villages of Palestine* 38, *The Theory of Administration* 46, *Problems of Government in the State of Israel* 56, *British Traditions in the Administration of Israel* 57, *The Structure of Society in Israel* 69, *Roots* (with Mordechai Kamrat) 69, *Anglo-Israel Relations 1948-1968: A Catalogue* 69, *A Lifetime in Jerusalem: Memoirs* 69, *See How they Run: the Administration of Venerable Institutions* 75; Short Stories:

A Cottage in Galilee 57, *A Coat of Many Colours* 60, *My Friend Musa* 63, *The Cucumber King* 65, *His Celestial Highness* 68, *The Man Who Liked Cats* 74.
House of Lords, London S.W.1, England; and 15 Rashba Road, Jerusalem, Israel.

Sanbar, Moshe, M.A.(ECON.); Israeli banker and economist; b. 29 March 1926, Kecskemét, Hungary; ed. Univ. of Budapest and Hebrew Univ., Jerusalem.
Emigrated to Israel 48; Project Dir., Israel Inst. of Applied Social Research and later Deputy Dir. 51-58; Lecturer in Statistics, Hebrew Univ., Jerusalem 57-61; Dir. Research Dept., Deputy Dir. Internal State Revenue Div., Ministry of Finance 58-63, Dir. of Budgets 63-68; Econ. Adviser to Ministry of Finance 63-68; Deputy Chair., and later Chair., Industrial Devt. Bank of Israel 68-71; Chief Econ. Adviser to Minister of Finance 69-71; Acting Deputy Minister of Commerce and Industry 70-71; Gov. Bank of Israel Nov. 71; Gov. for Israel, IBRD, IFC, IDA; Chair. Econ. Devt. and Refugee Rehabilitation Trust, Board of Dirs. Habimah Nat. Theatre.
Publs. *My Longest Year* (Yad Vashem Prize) 66; many articles and research studies on economic subjects.
Bank of Israel, Mizpan Building, Jerusalem; Home: 44 Pincas Street, Tel-Aviv, Israel.

Sançar, Ilhami, B.A.; Turkish lawyer; b. 1909, Gördes; ed. secondary school, Izmir, Univ. of Ankara.
Appointed bailiff 36; Attorney-Gen. for Menemen 36, for Urgüp 39; worked as lawyer in local govt. 39; practised as barrister 40; mem. Constitutional Assembly 61; Deputy for Istanbul 61, 65-; Minister of Defence 61-65, 73-74.
Tunalı Hilmi Caddesi No. 90/7 Kavaklıdere, Ankara, Turkey.

Sancar, Gen. Semih; Turkish army officer; b. 1911, Erzurum; ed. Artillery School, War Acad.
Served in Turkish Army as Commdr. of Artillery Battery and Battalion, Asst. Commdr. Army Corps Artillery, Dept. Chief, Branch Section Dir. in Land Forces and Gen. Staff H.Q.; then Instructor War Acad.; Dir. of Personnel, Dir. of Operations Turkish Gen. Staff; promoted to rank of Gen. 69; Commdr. of Gendarmerie 69; Commdr. 2nd Army; Commdr. Turkish Land Forces 72-73; Chief of Gen. Staff 73-.
General Staff Headquarters, Ankara, Turkey.

Sani'i, Gen. Asadollah; Iranian army officer and politician; b. 1904; ed. Officers' Training Coll.
Special Adjutant to Shahanshah; Deputy Minister of War 61, 62, Minister of War 63-70; Minister of Agricultural Products and Consumer Goods 70-71; Third, Second and First Order of Merit; Third, Second and First Order of Honour; Second and First Order of Homayoun; First Order of Service and several other decorations.
Teheran, Iran.

Sanusi, H.R.H. Prince Hassan Rida; Former Crown Prince of Libya; b. 1934.
Son of H.M. King Idris I; became Crown Prince on death of his Great Uncle, Ahmed Sherif as-Sanusi, Dec. 50; in exile 69-.

Sarc, Omer Celâl, DR.RER.POL.; Turkish professor and administrator; b. 1901; ed. Robert Coll., Istanbul, Handelshochschule, Berlin, and Univ. of Berlin.
Asst. Prof. of Econs., Univ. of Istanbul 26, Assoc. Prof. of Applied Econs. and Statistics 33, Prof. of Applied Econs. and Statistics 38-55, 57-, Dean of Faculty of Econs. 36-48, Rector of the Univ. 49-51, 63-65, Pro-Rector 51-53, 65-69; Visiting Prof. Columbia Univ., School of Int. Affairs 54-55, 67-68; Chief, Middle East Unit, Dept. of Econ. Affairs, UN, New York 55-56; Dir. Econ. and Social Affairs, Council of Europe 59-61; Hon. Dr. Jur. (Fuad I Univ., Cairo); Officer, Legion of Honour, Great Cross of Merit (Fed. Germany).

Publs. *Agricultural and Industrial Policy* 34, *Theory of Statistics* 35, *The Foundations of Turkish Economy* 50.
c/o University of Istanbul, Beyazit, Istanbul; Home: Kalipci Sok. 156-I, Divan AP, Tesvikiye, Istanbul, Turkey.

Sarrûf, Fûad, B.A., LL.D.; Lebanese author and university official; b. 1900; ed. Shwaifat Nat. Coll., and American Univ. of Beirut.
Teacher and Headmaster, Lebanon 19-22; Asst. Editor *Al-Muqtataf* (monthly), Cairo 22-27, Editor 27-44; Editor *Al-Mukhtar* (Arabic edition of *Reader's Digest*), Cairo 43-47; Columnist, *Al-Ahram* (daily), Cairo 48-51; Vice-Pres. in charge of Univ. Relations, American Univ., Beirut 52-68; started Dept. of Journalism, American Univ., Cairo 35-43; Pres. Lebanese Nat. Comm. for UNESCO; mem. Exec. Board of UNESCO 66-70, Vice-Pres. 70-72, Pres. 72-74; fmr. mem., later Sec., Vice-Pres. Egyptian Asscn. for Advancement of Science 30-52; mem. Lebanese Nat. Research Council, Baalbek Int. Festival Cttee.; Hon. LL.D. (Univ. of the Pacific, Calif.) 58; several decorations.
Publs. *Pillars of Modern Science* 35, *Horizons of Modern Science* 39, *The Conquest Goes On* 44, *Horizons Without End* 58, *Man and the Universe* 61, *Modern Science in Modern Society* 66, *Scientific Papers* 72, *The Eternal Fire*, numerous other books.
55 rue du Caire, Hamra, Beirut, Lebanon.

Sasson, Eliahu (Elias); Israeli diplomatist and politician; b. 2 Feb. 1902, Damascus; ed. St. Joseph Coll., Beirut.
Owner and Editor of Arab newspaper *Al Hayyat*, Damascus 19-21; corresp. and editor of various Hebrew and Arab newspapers, Jerusalem, Damascus, Beirut, Baghdad, Cairo and Tel-Aviv 24-31; Head of Div. for Arab Affairs, Political Dept., Jewish Agency 32-47; Head of Middle Eastern Dept. Israeli Ministry of Foreign Affairs 47-50; Minister to Turkey 50-53, to Italy 53-57, Ambassador 57-60, to Switzerland 60-61; Minister of Posts 61-67, of Police 67-69; mem. Knesset (Parl.) 69-; mem. Israeli del. at Israeli-Egyptian Armistice negotiations, Rhodes, and signatory of the Armistice Treaty 48-49; joint head of Israeli del. at Lausanne Conf. of Palestine Conciliation Comm. 49; mem. Israeli del. at UN 47-48; numerous foreign awards and honours.
24 Lincoln Street, Jerusalem, Israel.

Satir, Kemal; Turkish physician and politician; b. 1911, Adana; ed. Adana.
Practised as X-ray specialist; mem. Parl. for Adana (Republican People's Party) 43-60, 69-, for Elazig 61-69; Minister of Communications 48-50; private practice, Adana 50-57; Deputy Sec.-Gen. RPP, Sec.-Gen. 61-66; mem. Constituent Assembly; Deputy Prime Minister 63-65; resigned RPP 72; formed Republican Party which joined Nat. Reliance Party to become Republican Reliance Party, Pres. Council of RRP; Minister of State and Deputy Prime Minister 73-74.
Republican Reliance Party (C.G.P.), Ankara, Turkey.

Saudi Arabia, Royal Family of (*see* under first names, as Khalid (King).

Sayah, Mohamed; Tunisian politician; b. 31 Dec. 1933; ed. Sadikia, Sfax, and Training School for Higher Education, Tunis.
Joined Néo-Destour Party 49; mem. Gen. Union of Tunisian Students 52-62, mem. Exec. Bureau 57-62, Sec.-Gen. 60-62; Asst. Dir. Néo-Destour Party and Chief Editor *L'Action* 62-64, Gen. Sec. of Destourian Youth, Gen. Sec. of Tunisian Youth 63-64; mem. High Comm. SDP 70-; Deputy Nat. Assembly 64-; Minister of Information 69-70; Perm. Rep. to UN, Geneva 70; Minister Public Works and Housing 71-73, of Youth and Sports 73; Minister at the Prime Minister's Office Nov. 73-; mem. Central Cttee., then mem. Political Bureau and Dir. Destour Socialist Party 64.

Publs. Several books on the history of the National Tunisian Movement.

c/o Office of the Prime Minister, Tunis, Tunisia.

Sayegh, Yusef A., M.A., PH.D.; Palestinian economist; b. 26 March 1916; ed. American Univ. of Beirut and Johns Hopkins Univ.

At American Univ. of Beirut, Asst. Prof. of Econ. 53-54, 56-57, Assoc. Prof. 57-58, 62-63, Prof. 63-74; Dir. Econ. Research Inst. 57-59, 62-64; Econ. Adviser, Planning Board of Kuwait 64-65; Econ. Consultant, Jordan East Ghor Study 66-67; Consultant, Org. of Arab Petroleum Exporting Countries 74-; Chair. Planning Board, Nat. Fund of Palestine Liberation Org. (PLO); Grand Prix twice from Lebanese "Friends of the Book" Soc.

Publs. *Bread with Dignity: Socio-economic Content of Arab Nationalism* (Arabic) 61, *Enterpreneurs of Lebanon* 62, *Economics and Economists in the Arab World* 64, *Second Look at Lebanese Economy* (Co-Author) (Arabic) 66, *The Israeli Economy* (Arabic) 66, *The Strategy of Action for the Liberation of Palestine* (Arabic) 68, *Jordan: Country Study* (Mediterranean Development Project) (Co-Author).

Organization of Arab Petroleum Exporting Countries (OAPEC), P.O. Box 20501, Al-Soor Street, Kuwait.

Schaeffer, Claude Frédéric Armand, M.A.; French archaeologist; b. 6 March 1898; ed. Strasbourg and Paris Univs.

Curator Prehistoric, Roman and Early Medieval Museum, Palais Rohan, Strasbourg 21-32; Curator Coins and Medals Dept. Strasbourg Univ. 26-32; Curator French Nat. Museums 33-54; Dir. of Research at Nat. Centre of Scientific Research, Paris 46-54; Vice-Pres. Comm. des Fouilles, Direction Générale des Relations Culturelles, Ministry of Foreign Affairs; mem. French Inst. 53; Hon. Prof. Collège de France 54; Dir. expedition Ras Shamra, Syria 29- (discovered Canaanite alphabetic cuneiform records); Cyprus 32, 34, 35, 46, 47, 49-, Malatya, Turkey 46, 47, 48, 50; mem. Archaeological Cttee. Ministry of Education; Hon. Fellow St. John's Coll. Oxford; mem. Nat. Society of Antiquaries, France; corresp. mem. Belgian Royal Acad., Danish Royal Acad.; corresp. Fellow of British Acad.; Hon. Fellow Royal Anthropological Inst. of Great Britain and Ireland, etc.; hon. mem. Deutsche Morgenländische Gesellschaft; served as Capt. Corvette with Fighting French Naval Forces 40-45; D.Litt. h.c. (Oxon.), D.C.L. h.c. (Glasgow), Hon. F.S.A.; Gold Medal, Soc. of Antiquaries 58, Scientific and Philological Soc., Famagusta, Cyprus 65; Hon. Citizen of Latakia (Syria), Famagusta (Cyprus).

Publs. *Haches néolithiques* 24, *Tertres funéraires préhistoriques dans la forêt de Haguenau* (2 vols.) 26, 30, *Missions en Chypre* 36, *Ugaritica I* 39, *Cuneiform Texts of Ras Shamra-Ugarit* 39, *Stratigraphie comparée et Chronologie de l'Asie occidentale* 48, *Ugaritica II* 49, *Enkomi-Alasia* 52, *Ugaritica III* 56, *Ugaritica IV* 62, *Ugaritica V* 65, *Ugaritica VI* 69, *Alasia I* 72.

Le Castel Blanc, 16 rue Turgot, St. Germain-en-Laye; and l'Escale, B.P. 16, La Croix-Valmer (83), France.

Schnitzer, Moshe, M.A.; Israeli diamond exporter; b. 21 Jan. 1921; ed. Balfour High School, Tel-Aviv, Hebrew Univ. of Jerusalem.

Chairman, Asscn. of Diamond Instructors 43-46; Vice-Pres. Israel Diamond Exchange 51-66, Pres. 66-; Pres. Israel Exporters' Asscn. of Diamonds 62-; World Pres. Int. Fed. of Diamond Exchanges 68-72; partner, Diamond Export Enterprise 53-; mem. Consulting Cttee. to Minister of Commerce and Industry 68-; Editor *The Diamond;* Most Distinguished Exporter of Israel 64.

Publ. *Diamond Book* (in Hebrew) 46.

Israel Diamond Exchange, 3 Jabotinsky Road, Ramat Gan; and 78 Sharet Street, Tel-Aviv, Israel.

Schocken, Gershom; Israeli editor and publisher; b. Sept. 1912; ed. Univ. of Heidelberg and London School of Economics.

Joined staff of *Haaretz* (daily newspaper) 37, publisher and editor 39-; Dir. Schocken Publishing House Ltd.; mem. Knesset (Parl.) 55-59.

Haaretz Building, 21 Salman Schocken Street, P.O. Box 233, Tel-Aviv, Israel.

Scholem, Gershom, PH.D.; Israeli professor; b. 5 Dec. 1897, Berlin, Germany; ed. Berlin, Jena, Berne and Munich Univs.

Lecturer, Hebrew Univ. Jerusalem 25, Prof. of Jewish Mysticism 33-65; Dean, Hebrew Univ. 41-43, now Prof. Emer. Inst. of Jewish Studies; Visiting Prof., Jewish Inst. of Religion, New York 38, 49, Brown Univ., Providence, R.I. 56-57, Hebrew Union Coll., Cincinnati 66; Pres. Israel Acad. of Sciences and Humanities 68-74; mem. Netherlands Acad. of Sciences, American Acad. of Arts and Sciences, American Acad. for Jewish Research, Westfälische Akad. der Wissenschaften; Israel State Prize 55, Rothschild Prize 62, Reuchlin Prize 69, Harvey Prize 74, Lit. Prize, Bavarian Acad. of Arts 74; Dr. h.c. (Univs. of Jerusalem, Zürich).

Publs. several books on Judaism and Jewish Mysticism (in Hebrew, German and English), *Kaballah*.

The Israel Academy of Sciences and Humanities, P.O. Box 4040, Jerusalem; Home: 28 Abarbanel Street, Jerusalem, Israel.

Sebai, Youssef Mohamed; Egyptian writer; b. 10 June 1917, Cairo; ed. Military Acad. and Cairo Univ.

Began writing while at school; teacher of military history 43-52, Dir. Military Museum 52-53; Editor-in-Chief *Arissala al Gadida* 53-56; Sec.-Gen. High Council of Arts, Letters and Social Sciences 56, Afro-Asian People's Solidarity Org. 57-73; Editor-in-Chief *Akher Sa'ah* review 67-71; Pres. Board of Dirs. of *Dar Al Hilal* and Editor-in-Chief *Al Mosawwar* review 71-73; Minister of Culture 73-; Sec. Gen. Arab Writers' Union and several other writers' asscns.; Italian and Egyptian decorations; Ministry of Culture Prize for best film story (for *Rodda Qalbi* and *Gamila*) (*Rodda Qalbi* also won a prize for the best dialogue).

Publs. Novels: *Na'eb Azra'il, Ard el Nifaq* (Land of Hypocrisy), *Inny Rahila* (I am Going Away), *Bein el Atlal* (Among the Ruins), *El Sakka Mat* (Death of a Water Carrier), *Rodda Qalbi, Tarik el Awda* (The Return), *Nadia;* Short Stories: *Ya Ommatun Dahikat* (A Nation that Laughed), *A Night of Wine, Sheikh Zo'orob;* Plays: *Om Ratiba, Behind the Curtain, Stronger than Time.*

Ministry of Culture, Cairo; Home: Villa Sebai, Mokatam City, Cairo, Egypt.

Seelye, Talcott Williams; American diplomatist; b. 6 March 1922, Beirut; ed. Deerfield Acad., Amherst Coll. and George Washington Univ.

Army service 43-46; teacher, Deerfield Acad., Deerfield, Mass. 47-48; speech writer, Washington 48-49; joined State Dept. 49; served in Germany, Jordan, and Lebanon; Consul, Kuwait 56-60; Chargé d'Affaires, Saudi Arabia 65-66, Deputy Chief of Mission 66-68; Amb. to Tunisia 72-; White House Commendation; Hon. LL.D. (Amherst Coll.) 74.

Publs. articles in various journals.

American Embassy, 144 Avenue de la Liberté, Tunis, Tunisia.

Sela, Michael (Salomonowicz), M.SC., PH.D.; Israeli chemist; b. 6 March 1924, Tomaszow, Poland; ed. Hebrew Univ., Jerusalem and Geneva Univ.

Professor and Head, Dept. of Chemical Immunology, Weizmann Inst. of Science, Vice-Pres. 70-71, Dean Faculty of Biology 70-73, mem. Board of Govs. 70-; Chair. Board of Advisers, Basle Inst. for Immunology; mem. Israel Acad. of Sciences and Humanities 71-; mem. Council Int. Union of Immunological Socs., Vice-Pres. 74-; mem. Int. Union Pure and Applied Biophysics, Int. Cell Research Org.; Foreign mem. Max-Planck-Inst. für Immunobio-

logie; mem. Board of Trustees, Inst. de Biologie Physico-Chimique, Paris; Chair. Council European Molecular Biology Org. 75; serves on many editorial boards, including *European Journal of Immunology, European Journal of Biochemistry, and Immunogenetics*; Hon. mem. American Soc. Biological Chemists, American Asscn. of Immunologists; Foreign Hon. mem. American Acad. Arts and Sciences; Fogarty Scholar-in-Residence, Nat. Insts. of Health, Bethesda, Md. 73-74; Israel Prize Natural Science 59, Rothschild Prize for Chemistry 68, Otto Warburg Medal 68, Emil von Behring Prize 73.
Publs. over 400 in immunology, biochemistry and molecular biology; Ed. *The Antigens* (three vols. published).
Weizmann Institute of Science, Rehovot, Israel.

Senoussi, Badreddine, LL.M., M.H.; Moroccan politician; b. 30 March 1933, Fez; ed. Univ. of Bordeaux, Chamber of Commerce, Paris.
Adviser, "Haut Tribunal Chérifien", Rabat 56; Civil Service Admin., Ministry of State 57; Sec.-Gen. Nat. Tobacco Co. 58; Head, Royal Cabinet 63; Under-Sec. of State for Admin. Affairs 65; Minister of Post Office and Telecommunications 66, of Youth, Sports and Social Affairs 70-71; Amb. to U.S.A. 71-74, also accred. to Canada and Mexico; awarded many foreign decorations.
c/o Ministry of Foreign Affairs, Rabat, Morocco.

Seter, Mordecai; Israeli composer; b. 1916, Russia.
Studied Paris with Paul Dukas and Nadia Boulanger 32-37; Prof. Israel Acad. of Music, Tel-Aviv; Prix Italia 62; Israel State Prize 65.
Works include: *Sabbath Cantata* 40, *Festivals* 46, *Three Motets* 51, *Dithyramb* 66 (choral music); *Elegy* 54, *Ricercar* 56, *Espressivo* 71 (for strings); *Midnight Vigil* (oratorio) 62; *Sinfonietta, Variations, Fantasia* 65, *Judith* 62, *Jephthah's Daughter, Yemenite Suite* 65, *Meditation* 67, *Rounds* 68 (orchestral music); *Part Real, Part Dream* (with Martha Graham) 64 (ballet); *Jerusalem* 66 (symphony for choir and orchestra); *Partita* (violin and piano) 51, *Monodrama* (clarinet and piano)70, *Epigrams* 70, *Requiem* 70, *Intimo* 70, *Autumn* 70, *Quartet* 70, *Soliloquio, Janus* and *Sine Nomine* for piano 73, *Trio* 73, *Concertante* 73, *Trio* 74, *Events* 74, *Quintet* 75, *Ensemble* 75 (chamber music).
The Israel Academy of Music, Tel-Aviv, Israel.

Shaabi, Qahtan Muhammed as-; Yemeni politician; b. 1920; ed. school in Aden, and studied agricultural engineering, Khartoum Univ.
Director of Agriculture, Lahej State 55-58; joined South Arabian League 58, Public Relations Officer 59-60; Adviser to Ministry of South Yemen Affairs, Govt. of Yemen People's Repub. 63; founder-mem. Nat. Liberation Front (N.L.F.) 63, later Sec.-Gen.; mem. N.L.F. Del. to Geneva talks on independence of S. Arabia Nov. 67; Pres. of People's Repub. of Southern Yemen, also Prime Minister and Supreme Commdr. of Armed Forces Nov. 67, resigned June 69.
c/o National Liberation Front, Aden, People's Democratic Republic of Yemen.

Shafei, Col. Hussein; Egyptian army officer and politician; b. 1918; ed. Mil. Coll., Cairo.
Commissioned as 2nd Lieut. 38; took part in Palestine hostilities 48; graduated from Staff Officers' Coll. 53 and apptd. Officer-in-Charge Cavalry Corps; Minister of War and Marine April-Sept. 54, of Social Affairs Sept. 54-58; Minister of Labour and Social Affairs. U.A.R. 58-61; Vice-Pres. and Minister of Social Affairs and Waqfs 61-62; mem. Presidency Council 62-64; Vice-Pres. of U.A.R. (Egypt) 64-67, 70-75; Dep. Prime Min. and Min. of Waqfs 67-71.
c/o Office of the Vice-President, Cairo, Egypt.

Shafik, Doria (Ahmad); Egyptian journalist and feminist; b. 1919; ed. Univ. of Paris.
Studied abroad; on return became Editor *La Femme*

Nouvelle 45, *Bent el Nil* (in Arabic) 46-, *Katkout* and *Doria Shafik Magazine*; organized Bent el Nil Union (feminist movement) 48.
Publs. *La Bonne Aventure, l'Esclave Sultane, L'Amour Perdu, L'Art pour l'Art dans L'Egypte Antique, La Femme et l'Islam, La Femme Egyptienne, Voyage autour du Monde.*
6 Salah el Din, Zamalek, Cairo, Egypt.

Shafiq, Mohammad Moussa, LL.M., M.C.L., M.A.; Afghan scholar and politician; b. 30 May 1932, Kabul; ed. Ghazi High School, Al Azhar Univ., Cairo, and Columbia Univ., U.S.A.
Joined Ministry of Justice 57, Dir. Nat. Office for Legislation 57-62; Prof. of Int. Law, Kabul Univ., 57-68; Deputy Minister of Justice 63-64; Adviser, Ministry of Foreign Affairs 66-68; Amb. to Egypt, concurrently to Lebanon, Sudan and Ghana 68-71; Minister of Foreign Affairs 71, Prime Minister 72-73.
Kabul, Afghanistan.

Shah, Idries; author; b. 16 June 1924; ed. private and traditional Middle Eastern schools.
Studied in Middle East, Europe and S. America; Dir. of Studies, Inst. for Cultural Research 66-; Visiting Prof. Univ. of Geneva 72-73; author of numerous works on philosophy; Patron Cambridge Poetry Festival 75; Fellow, Royal Econ. Soc.; Life mem. British Asscn., The National Trust; mem. PEN, Club of Rome; Life Gov. Royal Hosp. and Home for Incurables; Gov. Royal Humane Soc.; Prof. h.c. (Univ. of La Plata) 74; Int. Community Service Award 73; six first prizes during UNESCO World Book Year 73; Gold Medal, Services to Poetry 75; subject of BBC documentary film 69, of vol. of collected papers in honour of Idries Shah 74.
Publs. *Oriental Magic* 56, *Secret Lore of Magic* 57, *Destination Mecca* 57, *The Sufis* 64, *Special Problems* 66, *Exploits of Nasruddin* 66, *Tales of the Dervishes* 67, *The Pleasantries* 68, *The Way of the Sufi* 68, *Reflections* 68, *Caravan of Dreams* 68, *Wisdom of the Idiots* 69, *The Dermis Probe* 69, *The Book of the Book* 69, *Thinkers of the East* 70, *The Magic Monastery* 72, *The Subtleties of the Inimitable Mulla Nasrudin* 73, *The Elephant in the Dark* 74, *Learning How to Learn* 74.
c/o Jonathan Cape Ltd., 30 Bedford Square, London, WC1B 3EL, England.

Shahgholi, Manouchehr, M.D.; Iranian physician and politician; ed. Univ. of Teheran and in New York.
Minister of Health 65-73, of Science and Higher Educ. 73-74.
Ministry of Science and Higher Education, Teheran, Iran.

Shakhbut bin Sultan bin Zaid, H.H. Sheikh; former Ruler of Abu Dhabi; b. 1905.
Succeeded to Sheikdom 28, deposed Aug. 66; sons Zaid b. 30, Sultan b. 36.
Manama, Bahrain.

Shalchian, Hassan; Iranian civil engineer and politician; b. 1913; ed. State Univ. of Belgium.
Ministry of Roads 39-, successively Dir. of Technical Dept., Dir. Chalus Road Dept., Dir. Dept. of Technical Inspectorate Dir.-Gen. of Roads, mem. Supervisory Board of Ministry of Roads; fmr. Head of Construction Dept. Ministry of Roads; fmr. Exec. for Implementation of Third Plan Projects; Perm. Under-Sec. Ministry of Roads 62; Technical Deputy Minister of Roads 63; Minister of Roads and Communications 63, 64-74; Chair. Technical Cttee. Training Centre; Man. Dir. Water and Power Authority, Azarbaijan Province 64; Univ. Lecturer 64-; mem. Exec. Board Queen Pahlavi Foundation 68; mem. High Council Ports and Shipping Org. 69-.
c/o Ministry of Roads and Communications, Teheran, Iran.

Shallon, Nessim, L. EN D.; American United Nations official; ed. Ecole Supérieure, Paris, Faculty of Law, Paris, Ecole Française de Droit.
First Sec. Fed. of Egyptian Industry; Export Consultant General Overseas Corpn., New York 45-46; served in U.S. Army 46; Liaison Officer UN 46, Officer for Econ. Affairs 48, Asst. to Dir. of Co-ordination for Specialized Agencies, Econ. and Social Affairs, Exec. Office of Sec.-Gen. 49-50; Technical Assistance Officer, UN Technical Assistance Board, New York 50-53, Asst. Dir. Field Co-ordination 53-; Deputy Resident Rep. UN Devt. Programme (UNDP) India 64-69, Iran 69-; Pres. Tanglewood Manor Inc. 56-64.
United Nations Development Programme, P.O. Box 1555, Teheran, Iran.

Shamgar, Meir; Israeli lawyer; b. 1925, Danzig; ed. Govt. law classes, and London Univ.
Settled in Palestine 39; detained by British Admin. for underground activities, deported to East Africa 44-48; Col. in Israeli Army 48-68; Mil. Advocate-Gen. 61-68; Attorney-Gen. 68-; Chair. Advisory Council, Inst. of Criminology, Tel-Aviv Univ., Inter-dept. Cttee. on Drugs; fmr. Law Lecturer, Hebrew Univ., Jerusalem, Tel-Aviv; mem. Israel Bar Council 61-68; mem. of Council, Int. Soc. of Mil. Law and Law of War.
Publs. various legal essays in Israeli and foreign journals.
Ministry of Justice, Jerusalem, Israel.

Shamir, Moshe; Israeli writer; b. 15 Sept. 1921; ed. Tel-Aviv Herzliya Gymnasium.
Former mem. Kibbutz Mishmar Haemek; in Haganah underground units 47-48; Capt. in Israel Army 48; Lit. Ed. *Maariv*; mem. Hebrew Acad.; Ussiskin Prize 48, Brenner Prize 53, Bialik Prize 55.
Publs. (novels) *He Walked in the Fields under the Sun, With his own Hands, King of Flesh and Blood, David's Stranger, Naked You Are, The Border, A Dove from an Alien Cote* 73; (plays) *He Walked in the Fields, The War of the Sons of Light, The Heir,* and others.

Shamloo, Ahmad (A. Bamdad); Iranian poet and writer; b. Dec. 1926, Teheran.
Former Editor *Ketabe hafte, Baroo, Khooshe* and other publs.
Publs. (poetry) *Fresh Air* 57, *Mirror Garden* 59, *Aida in Mirror* 63, *Aida, The Three Daggers and Memory* 66, *Phoenix in the Rain* 67, *Elegies of Earth* 69, *Springing in the Fog* 71, *Abraham in the Fire* 72, and 40 other volumes including translations; *Persian Folklore Encyclopaedia* (50 vols.).
Farhanguestane Zaban, Khiabane Iranshah, Teheran, Iran.

Shankiti, Sheikh Mohammed Amin; Jordanian politician and diplomatist.
Chief Justice, Muslim Religious Courts -59; Minister of Education 59-61; Ambassador to Saudi Arabia 63-, concurrently to the Sudan, to the Yemen Arab Repub. 71-; mem. Joint Comm. for Border Disputes 66-.
Embassy of the Hashemite Kingdom of Jordan, Jeddah, Saudi Arabia.

Shapiro, Jacob Shimshon, LL.B.; Israeli lawyer and politician; b. 1902; ed. Kharkov Univ. and Law School, Jerusalem.
Settled in Palestine (now Israel) 24; co-founder Kibbutz Givat Hashlosha; Attorney-Gen., Govt. of Israel 48-49; Minister of Justice 66-73; Chair. Cabinet Policy Cttee., East Jerusalem; mem. Labour Party.
c/o Ministry of Justice, Jerusalem, Israel.

Sharabi, Nizam B. al-, B.A., M.A.; Jordanian politician; b. 1 March 1916; ed. Birmingham Univ.
Lecturer, American Univ. at Beirut 38-41; Dir. of Social Affairs Dept., Gaza and Jaffa 42-47; Asst. Dir. Jordan Red Cross 48-49; Controller of Trade 49-51; Under-Sec. Ministry of Social Affairs 51-54; Snr. Man. Arab Bank 54-63; Asst. Dir.-Gen. 65-68, 69-; Minister of Finance Dec. 63, of Nat. Econ. and Finance 64, of Communications and Defence 64-65, of Nat. Economy Dec. 68-March 69; El-Kawkab El-Urdouii First Class.
c/o Arab Bank Ltd., King Faisal Street, P.O. Box 68, Amman, Jordan.

Sharaf, Abdul Hamid; Jordanian diplomatist.
Former Head, Arab and Palestine Affairs, Ministry of Foreign Affairs; Dir. Broadcasting Service 63-64; Dir. Political Dept., Ministry of Foreign Affairs; Asst. Chief of Royal Cabinet 64-65; Minister of Information 65-67; Amb. to U.S.A. 67-72, to Canada 69-72; Perm. Rep. to UN March 72-.
Permanent Mission of Jordan to the United Nations, 866 United Nations Plaza, Room 550-552, New York, N.Y. 10017, U.S.A.

Sharef, Ze'ev; Israeli politician; b. 1906, Bukovina, Romania.
Went to Palestine 25, worked as labourer; joined Kibbutz Givat Brenner 29; Sec. Israel Sports Org. of Gen. Fed. of Labour in Israel (Histadrut); active in Haganah 40; Sec. of Political Dept. of Jewish Agency 43-47; worked on admin. blueprint of Jewish State 47-48; Sec. of Israel Govt. 48-57; Dir.-Gen. of Prime Minister's Office 48-49; Civil Service Commr. 51-52; Dir. of State Revenue, Ministry of Finance 54-61; Special Adviser to Prime Minister 64-65; mem. Knesset 65-; Chair. of Ports Authority 62-66; Minister of Commerce and Industry 66-69, Minister of Finance Aug. 68-Dec. 69; Minister of Housing 69-74; Mapai.
Publ. *Shlosha Yamim* (Three Days).
c/o Ministry of Housing, Jerusalem, Israel.

Sharif, Omar (Michel Shalhoub); Egyptian actor; ed. Victoria Coll. Cairo.
Salesman, lumber-import firm; made first film *The Blazing Sun* 53; starred in 24 Egyptian films and two French co-production films during following five years; commenced int. film career with *Lawrence of Arabia*.
Films include: *Lawrence of Arabia, The Fall of the Roman Empire, Behold a Pale Horse, Ghengis Khan, The Yellow Rolls Royce, Doctor Zhivago, Night of the Generals, Mackenna's Gold, Funny Girl, Cinderella—Italian Style, Mayerling, The Appointment, Che, The Last Valley, The Horsemen, The Burglars, The Mysterious Island, The Tamarind Seed, Juggernaut, Funny Lady.*
c/o Carolyn Pfeiffer Ltd., Flat 2, 10 Connaught Place, London, W.2, England.

Sharif Emami, Jafar; Iranian engineer and politician; b. 8 Sept. 1910, Teheran; ed. primary and secondary studies in Teheran; Railway Central Coll., Brandenburg, Germany, and Government Technical High School, Boras, Sweden.
Joined Iranian State Railways 31; Technical Deputy Dir.-Gen. of Iranian Govt. Railways 42; Chair. and Man. Dir. of Irrigation Corpn. 46-50; Under-Sec. to Minister of Roads and Communications, Dir.-Gen. Iranian Govt. Railways and then Minister of Roads and Communications 50-51; mem. High Council of the Plan Org. 51-52; Man. Dir. of Plan Org. and Chair. High Council of Plan Org. 53-54; Senator from Teheran 55-57, 63-; Pres. of Senate 63-; Minister of Industries and Mines 57-60; Prime Minister 60-61; Deputy Custodian of Pahlavi Foundation 62-; mem. Board of Dirs. Royal Org. of Social Services 62-; Chair. Board of Dirs. Industrial and Mining Devt. Bank 63-; Pres. Iranian Asscn. of World Federalists 63-; mem. Board of Red Lion and Sun of Iran 63, Deputy Chair. 66-; Pres. Iranian Engineers, Assn. 66-; Pres. Third Constituent Assembly 67; mem. American Soc. of Civil Engineers 46-, Board of Trustees, Pahlavi Univ. Shiraz,

Nat. Univ. Teheran 62, and Aria Mehr Tech. Univ. 65, Queen Pahlavi's Foundation 66; mem. Founding Board, Soc. for Preservation of Nat. Monuments 66; Pres. 22nd Conf. of the Red Cross 73; decorations from Iran, Italy, Fed. Repub. of Germany, France, Sweden, Belgium, Austria, U.K., Japan, Romania, Thailand, Tunisia, Norway, Denmark, Morocco, Yugoslavia, Poland, Hungary, Pakistan, Ethiopia, Malaysia.
Darrooss Ehteshamieh 48, Teheran, Iran.

Sharifi, Ahmad-Hushang, PH.D.; Iranian educationist; b. 1925, Teheran; ed. France.
With Iranian Consulate, Paris; mem. Perm. Del. to UNESCO; French Language Translator, Teheran Univ. 57, Finance Teacher 58, Lecturer in Political Science 60, Prof. of Political Science 66; Financial and Admin. Adviser to Ministry of Educ. 64, Under-Sec. of Educ. 64; Principal, Teachers Training Coll. 68; Chancellor Nat. Univ., Teheran 73; Minister of Educ. 74-; mem. Iran Novin Party.
Ministry of Education, Teheran, Iran.

Sharon, Major-Gen. Ariel; Israeli army officer and politician; b. 1928.
Active in Hagana since early youth; Instructor, Jewish Police units 47; Platoon Commdr. Alexandroni Brigade; Regimental Intelligence Officer 48; Co. Commdr. 49; Commdr. Brigade Reconnaissance Unit 49-50; Intelligence Officer, Cen. Command and Northern Command 50-52; studies at Hebrew Univ. 52-53; in charge of Unit 101, on numerous reprisal operations until 57; studies Staff Coll., Camberley, U.K. 57-58; Training Commdr., Gen. Staff 58; Commdr. Infantry School 58-69; Commdr. Armoured Brigade 62; Head of Staff, Northern Command 64; law studies, Tel-Aviv Univ. 66; Head Brigade Group during Six-Day War 67; resigned from Army July 73; recalled as Commdr. Cen. Section of Sinai Front during Yom Kippur War Oct. 73, forged bridgehead across Suez Canal; with others formed Likud Front Sept. 73; mem. Knesset (Parl.) 73-74; joined army reserves Dec. 74.
Jerusalem, Israel.

Shazly, Lt.-Gen. Saad Mohamed al Hosseiny el-, M.POL.SC.; Egyptian army officer; b. 1 April 1922, Cairo; ed. Khedive Ismail Secondary School, Cairo, Cairo Univ., Mil. Coll., and in U.S.S.R.
Officer of the Guards 43-48; Platoon Commdr. Arab-Israeli War 48; Commdr. of Parachute School 54-56; Commdr. of Parachute Battalion 56-58; Commdr. United Arab Repub. Contingent, UN, Congo 59-60; Defence Attaché, London 61-63; Brig. Commdr. in Yemen Civil War 65-66; Commdr. Shazly Group, Egyptian-Israeli War 67; Commdr. of Special Forces 67-69; Commdr. Red Sea District 70-71; Chief of Staff of Egyptian Armed Forces 71-73; Amb. to U.K. 74-; holder of twenty-two decorations including Order of the Repub., 1st Class, Etoile d'Honneur, Médaille Mil. du Courage, Médaille du Congo, Knight, Syrian Order of Honour.
Embassy of Arab Republic of Egypt, 75 South Audley Street, London, W.1, England; and 39 Gamal Eldin Eldessuky, Heliopolis, Cairo, Egypt.

Sheaikhly, Abdul Karim Abdul Sattar al-; Iraqi politician; b. 1937, Baghdad.
Political emigré in Cairo 60-63; Asst. Attaché Iraqi Embassy, Beirut 63-68; mem. Revolutionary Command Council; Minister of Foreign Affairs 68-72; Perm. Rep. to UN Sept. 72-; Head of del. to UN Gen. Assembly 68-.
Permanent Mission of Iraq to the United Nations, 14 East 79th Street, New York, N.Y. 10021, U.S.A.

Shebani, Dr. Omar, M.A., PH.D.; Libyan educationist; b. 1930; ed. Cairo, Ain-Shams Univs. and Boston, George Washington Univs., U.S.A.
Assistant Dir. Teachers' Coll., Univ. of Libya (now Univ.

of Benghazi) 65, Dir. of Youth Dept. 68, Asst. Prof., Pres. 70-.
General Administration, University of Benghazi, Libya.

Shenouda III, Anba, B.A., B.D.; Egyptian ecclesiastic; b. 3 Aug. 1923.
Former Prof. of Theology and Patrology, Coptic Orthodox Theological School, Cairo; Pope of Alexandria and Patriarch of The See of St. Mark in all Africa and the Near East 71-.
St. Mark's Patriarchate, Anba Ruiess Building, Ramses Street, Abbasiya, Cairo, Egypt.

Sheriff, Noam; Israeli composer; b. 1935, Tel-Aviv; ed. Hebrew Univ., Jerusalem.
Arranger of folk and light music for Israeli Broadcasting Authority; Prof. of Orchestration, Israel Acad. of Music, Tel-Aviv; First Prize of Israel Philharmonic Orchestra 57, 60.
Works include: *Ashrei* 61, *Destination 5* 61, *Sonata for Piano* 62, *Heptaprisms* 65, *Confession* 66, *Piece for Ray* 66, *Arabesque* 66, *Invention for Flute* 67, *Invention for Harp* 68, *Invention for Horn* 68, *Metamorphosis on a Galliard* 67, *Chaconne* 68, *Two Epigrams* 68, etc.
22 Maoz Aviv, Tel-Aviv, Israel.

Shiguer, Mohamed Haddou; Moroccan politician; b. 1932; ed. Mohammed V Univ.
Taught for 12 years; mem. Nat. Assembly; Minister of Post and Telecommunications 64-66, of Agriculture 66-67, of the Royal Cabinet 67, of Defence 67-68, of Primary Educ. 68-72, of Nat. Educ. 72-73, of the Interior May 73-.
Ministry of the Interior, Rabat, Morocco.

Shlonsky, Avraham; Israeli poet; b. March 1900; ed. High School and Sorbonne.
Went to Palestine 21; mem. Editorial Board *Davar;* founder and Editor *Groovim, Toopim, Itim, Orlogin;* Literary Editor *Sifriat Hapoalim;* mem. Board, Mosad Bialik; mem. Hebrew Acad.
Publs. *Davai* (poems) 24, *Le-Aba Ima* 25, *Bagalgal* 26, *Be-Ele Hayamim* 29, *Avne Bohu* 34, *Yalkut Shirat Haamim, Al Milet, Shirei Hamapolet Vehapius, Avnei Gvil, Mishivei Hapkosdok Haarooch;* trans. several foreign works into Hebrew, including Shakespeare, Pushkin, Gogol, Brecht, Chekhov and Gorki.
50 Gordon Street, Tel-Aviv, Israel.

Shoukry, Mohammed Anwar; Egyptian egyptologist; b. 1905; ed. Cairo Univ. Inst. of Egyptology, Univ. of Göttingen.
Asst. Prof. of Egyptology, Cairo Univ. 48-52, fmr. Prof.; Chief Archæologist Cen. of Documentation of Egyptian Art and Civilization 56-59; Dir.-Gen. Dept. of Egyptian Antiquities 59-66; Asst. Under-Sec. of State, Ministry of Culture and National Guidance 61-70; Resident Archaeologist in Nubia 64.
Publs. *Die Grabstatue im Alten Reich, Egyptian Art from the Beginning till the End of the Ancient Kingdom* (in Arabic).
c/o Ministry of Culture, Cairo, Egypt.

Shragai, Shlomo Zalman; Israeli journalist; b. 31 Dec. 1899; ed. Jeshivoth-Talmudical Colls. in Poland.
Founder of Young Mizrachi Movement in Poland 17; founder of organization for training religious youth for Eretz Israel 19; elected mem. Jewish Nat. Council of Poland 20; Editor religious Zionist-Hebrew newspaper, *Hatechia* 20; migrated to Palestine and employed as builder in Jerusalem 24; elected exec. mem. Hapoel Hamizrachi Party 24-; exec. mem. Va'ad Leumi (Jewish Nat. Council) of Eretz Israel 29, Zionist Actions Cttee. 33; Chair. Broadcasting Services of Palestine 38; elected exec. mem. Jewish Agency, London 46; first Mayor of Jerusalem 50-52; Head of Immigration Dept. of Jewish Agency 53; Contrib. to Israeli daily *Hatzofe* and *Sinai-Monthly for Thora* and *Jewish History Research.*

Publs. *Vision and Fulfilment* (Hebrew) 25, *Tehumin, Beit Ushbitza, Tahalichey Hageula Vhatmura, Shaa Vanezach, Peame Geula, Zemanim, Besugiot Hador.*
8 Keren Kayemeth Street, Jerusalem, Israel.

Shukairy, Ahmed, M.A., LL.D.; Jordanian lawyer and politician; b. 1908; ed. American Univ., Beirut.
Former Minister of State for UN Affairs; Perm. Rep. of Saudi Arabia to the UN until 63; Chair. Palestine Liberation Org. 63-67.
19 Gabalaya Street, Zamalek, Cairo, Egypt.

Siassi, Ali-Akbar, P.HD.; Iranian psychologist and politician; b. 1896; ed. Persia and France.
Professor Univ. of Teheran 27-; Head Dept. of Advanced Studies of the Ministry of Educ. 32; Chancellor of the Univ. of Teheran 42; Minister of Educ. 43; drafted bill and law for national compulsory free education, and took necessary measures for its enforcement 43; Minister of State without portfolio 45, of Education 48-50, of Foreign Affairs 50; del. III Int. Congress of Persian Art and Archæology 35, UN Conf. San Francisco 45; Pres. Iranian del. UNESCO Conf. Paris 49, Int. Conf. of Univs. 50, UNESCO Conf. Paris 51, Int. Conf. of Univs., Mexico City 60, Royal Soc. Tricentenary Celebrations, London 60; Perm. mem. Iranian Acad.; Hon. Pres. Univ. of Teheran; Dr. h.c. Univ. of Charles 1st, Prague 47, Univ. of Strasbourg 65, etc.; mem. Int. Cttee. Scientific and Cultural History of Humanity; Pres. Iranian Council of Philosophy and Human Sciences, Iranian Psychological Asscn. of Iran; mem. Royal Cultural Council, etc.; Commdr. Légion d'Honneur; Commdr. Palmes Académiques, etc.
Publs. In French: *L'Education en Perse* 21, *La Perse au Contact de l'Occident* 31, *La Méthode des Tests* 31, *Le Génie et l'Art iraniens aux prises avec l'Islam* 35, *De l'Unesco à la Sorbonne* 53, *L'Iran au XIXe siècle* 55; In Persian: *Psychology* 38, *Educational Psychology for Teachers' Colleges* 41, *Introduction to Philosophy* 47, *Mind and Body* 53, *The Psychology of Avicenna and its similarities with the Modern Psychology* 54, *Logic* 56, *Ethics* 57, *Logic and Philosophy* 58, *Intelligence and Reason* 62, *Criminal Psychology* 64, *Psychology of Personality* 70, *Theories of Personality* 75.
President Roosevelt Avenue, Namdjou Street, Teheran, Iran.

Sidarouss, H.E. Cardinal Stephanos I; Egyptian ecclesiastic; b. 1904; ed. Jesuits' Coll. Cairo, Univ. de Paris, Faculté de Droit, and Ecole Libre des Sciences Politiques.
Barrister, Egypt 26-32; Vincentian Priest 39-; Prof. Seminaries at Evreux, Dax and Beauvais (France); Rector Coptic Catholic Seminary, Tahta 46, Tanta 47-53, Maadi 53-58; Auxiliary Bishop to the Patriarch of Alexandria 47-58, Patriarch 58-; created Cardinal 65.
34 Ibn Sandar Street, Koubbeh Bridge, Cairo, Egypt.

Sidi Baba, Dey Ould; Moroccan diplomatist; b. 1921, Mauritania.
Counsellor, Ministry of Foreign Affairs, Morocco 58, Head of African Div. 59; mem. Moroccan Dels. to UN Gen. Assembly 59-64; Acting Perm. Rep. of Morocco to UN 63-65, Perm. Rep. 65-67; Minister of Royal Cabinet 67-; Amb. to Saudi Arabia 71-72; Dir. Royal Cabinet 72-73; Minister of Educ. 73-74, of Waqfs and Islamic Affairs April 74-; Commandeur du Trône Alaouite; Niger Grand Order of Merit; Officer of Libyan Order of Independence; Commdr. of Syrian Order of Merit.
Ministère des Habous et Affaires Islamiques, Rabat, Morocco.

Sidky, Aziz, B.ENG., M.A., PH.D.; Egyptian politician; b. 1 July 1920; ed. Cairo Univ., Univ. of Oregon and Harvard Univ.
Minister of Industry 56-63; Deputy Prime Minister for Industry and Mineral Wealth 64-65; Adviser for Produc-

tion Affairs to Pres. of U.A.R. 66-67; Minister of Industry, Petroleum and Mineral Wealth 68-71; Deputy Prime Minister 71-72, Prime Minister 72-73; Personal Asst. to Pres. Sadat 73-April 75; has attended many int. confs. on industrial affairs.
c/o The Presidency, Cairo, Egypt.

Siemienski, Zbigniew; Polish banker; b. 1 June 1909; ed. Univ. of Warsaw.
With Bank of Poland 34-39, 42-45; Lecturer in Polish, Univ. Coll., London 46-51; Econ. Adviser, Devt. Bank of Ethiopia 52-53, Deputy Managing Dir. 54; Currency and Banking Adviser to Govt. of Yemen on behalf of UN T.A.B. 55; Currency Controller, Sudan Currency Board 56-59; Gen. Man. Bank of Sudan 60-66; Adviser Central Bank of Cyprus 66-67, of Kenya 67-70, Banque du Maroc 71-; Technical Dir. Qatar and Dubai Currency Board 66-73.
Publs. *Fixed Interest Bond* (in Polish) 35, and articles in Polish *Economist* 44-46, *Middle East Journal* (*Impact of Coffee Boom on Ethiopia*) 55.
c/o Banque du Maroc, Rabat, Morocco; and 12 Mount Park Crescent, London, W.5, England.

Siilasvuo, Lieut.-Gen. Ensio; Finnish army officer; b. 1 Jan. 1922, Helsinki; ed. Lycée of Oulu, Finnish Mil. Acad., Finnish Command and Staff Coll.
Platoon Commdr., Infantry Co. Commdr. and Chief of Staff, Infantry Regiment 11 41-44; Company Commdr., Infantry Regiment 1 45-50; attended Command and Staff Coll. 51-52; various staff appointments in mil. districts of N. Finland 53-57; Commdr. Finnish Contingent, UN Emergency Force 57; Mil. Observer, UN Observation Group in Lebanon 58; Finnish Defence Attaché in Warsaw 59-61; Staff Officer Third Div. 62-64; Commdr. Finnish Contingent, UN Force in Cyprus 64-65; Instructor, Nat. Defence Coll. 65-67; Chief, Foreign Dept. GHQ 67; Senior Staff Officer, UN Truce Supervision Org. in Palestine 67-70; Chief of Staff, UN Truce Supervision Org. in Palestine 70-73; Commdr. UN Emergency Force 73-; Commdr. Order of the Lion of Finland 1st Class; Finnish Cross of Freedom 3rd and 4th Class; Knight of the Order of the White Rose of Finland 1st Class.
United Nations Emergency Force, P.O. Box 172, Cairo, Heliopolis West, Egypt.

Simavi, Haldûn; Turkish journalist; b. 1925; ed. Kabataş Lisesi, Istanbul.
Publisher and Gen. Man. of daily newspapers *Günaydin, Gün, Saklambaç, Okey,* weekly mags. *Fotoroman, Pazar, Tarkan, Kara Murat,* etc.; co-owner Istanbul daily newspaper *Hürriyet.*
Veb Ofset, Ileri Matbaacılık A.S. Cağaloğlu, Istanbul, Turkey.

Simon, Ernst, PH.D., DR. THEOL. (h.c.); Israeli educationist; b. 15 March 1899; ed. Univs. of Berlin and Heidelberg.
Editor (with Martin Buber) *Der Jude* 23-24; Lecturer in Jewish subjects, Frankfurt-am-Main 22-28; taught at various schools in Germany and Palestine 28; Assoc. Dir. of Jewish Adult Education Centre of Germany 33-34; Lecturer Hebrew Univ. of Jerusalem 38-50, Assoc. Prof. of Educ. 50-55, Prof. 55-68, Prof. Emer. 68-; Visiting Prof. of Educ., Jewish Theological Seminary of America, N.Y. 47-48, 62; Visiting Prof. of Educ. at Univ. of Judaism, L.A., Calif. 56-57; mem. Research Board Leo Baeck Inst. of Jews from Germany; mem. Board Ihud Organization for Jewish-Arab Co-operation; mem. Board Religious Youth Village; co-Editor Pedagogical Encyclopaedia, 5 vols. (Hebrew); Israeli State Prize for Educ. 67; Buber-Rosenzweig Medal 69.
Publs. *Ranke und Hegel* 29, *Das Werturteil im Geschichtsunterricht* 31, *Bialik* 35, *Educational Meaning of Socratic Irony* (Hebrew) 49, *Pioneers of Social Education—Pestalozzi and*

Korczak (Hebrew), *The Teaching of Pestalozzi* 53 (Hebrew), *Jewish Adult Education in Nazi Germany as Spiritual Resistance, Franz Rosenzweig's Position in the History of Jewish Education* (Hebrew), *Freud the Jew* (Hebrew, German and English), *Martin Buber and the Faith of Judaism* (Hebrew), *Martin Buber and German Jewry* (English) 58, *Aims of Secondary Education in Israel* (Hebrew) 61, *Brücken* (Collected Essays—German) 65, *M. Buber's Correspondence* 3 vols. (German, with G. Schaeder), 72-75, *Buber's Political Philosophy and Practice* (Hebrew) 73.
35 Ben Maimon Avenue, Jerusalem, Israel.

Sinadah, Mubarek Osman; Sudanese politician; b. 1919, Omdurman; ed. El Higra School, Omdurman, Omdurman Intermediate School and Gordon Coll.
Former civil servant; Sec.-Gen. Town Planning Board 62-64; Commr. of Lands 64-69; Minister of Housing 69-71, of Housing and Public Utilities 71-73, of Construction and Public Works 73.
c/o Ministry of Construction and Public Works, P.O. Box 300, Khartoum, Sudan.

Sindi, Sheikh Kamil; Saudi Arabian airline executive; b. 3 Jan. 1932, Mecca.
Joined Saudi Arabian Airlines and Civil Aviation Org. 47; in charge of Operations and Maintenance Dept. 47; Sec. to Dir.-Gen. until 60; Dir.-Gen. of Civil Aviation 61-66; Dir.-Gen. Saudi Arabian Airlines (SAUDIA) 67-.
SAUDIA, P.O. Box 167, Jeddah, Saudi Arabia.

Slaoui, Driss; Moroccan politician and banker.
Minister of Commerce and Industry 59-61; Dir. of Royal Cabinet March 62; Minister of Public Works 62-63, of Finance 63-64, of Nat. Economy and Agriculture Nov. 63-64; Gov. Banque du Maroc (Central Bank) 64-68; Minister of Justice 68-69; Dir.-Gen. Royal Cabinet 69-71; Perm. Rep. to UN Sept. 74-; Rep. to Int. Court of Justice in Western Sahara case June-July 75.
Permanent Mission of Morocco to the United Nations, 757 Third Avenue, 23rd Floor, New York, N.Y. 10017, U.S.A.

Slim, Taieb; Tunisian politician and diplomatist; b. 1914; ed. Tunis Lycée and Univ. of Paris.
Member Néo-Destour Party, detained 41-43; Arab Maghreb Bureau, Cairo 46-49; Head, Tunisian Office, Cairo 49, established Tunisian offices, New Delhi, Jakarta, Karachi; Head, Foreign Affairs, Presidency of Council of Ministers 55-56; Ambassador to U.K. 56-62, also accredited to Denmark, Norway and Sweden 60-62; Perm. Rep. to UN 62-67, concurrently Amb. to Canada; Minister, Personal Rep. of the Pres. 67-70; mem. Nat. Assembly 69-; Amb. to Morocco 70-71; Minister of State 71-72; Amb., Perm. Rep. to UN, Geneva 73-; mem. Political Bureau Destour Socialist Party 71-.
Mission Permanente de Tunisie, Palais des Nations, Geneva, Switzerland.

Slimane, Commandant (*see* Kaid, Ahmed).

Smilanski, Izhar; Israeli writer; b. 1916; ed. Teachers' Seminary and Hebrew Univ.
Former teacher; mem. Knesset 48-; Brenner Prize for *Midnight Caravan*.
Publs. include: *Midnight Caravan, Hirbeth Hiza'a, The House on the Hill, Days of Ziklag* (2 vols.), *Stories of the Plain*.
14 Moskowitz Street, Rehovot, Israel.

Smith, Wilfred Cantwell, M.A., PH.D., D.D.; Canadian university professor; b. 21 July 1916; ed. Upper Canada Coll., Univ. of Grenoble, Univ. of Madrid, American Univ. Cairo, Univ. of Toronto, Cambridge and Princeton Univs.
Served as rep. among Muslims of the Canadian Overseas Missions Council, chiefly in Lahore 40-49; Lecturer in Indian and Islamic History, Univ. of the Punjab, Lahore 41-45; Prof. of Comparative Religion 49-63, and Dir. Inst.

of Islamic Studies, McGill Univ. 51-63; Pres. American Soc. for the Study of Religion 66-69; Prof. of World Religions and Dir. Center for the Study of World Religions, Harvard Univ. 64-73; McCulloch Prof. of Religion, Dalhousie Univ. 73-; Fellow, Royal Soc. of Canada, Dalhousie Univ. 64-73; Fellow, Royal Soc. of Canada (Pres. Humanities and Social Science Section 72-73), American Acad. of Arts and Sciences; Chauveau Medal, Royal Soc. of Canada 74.
Publs. *Modern Islam in India* 43 (revised edns. 47, 65), *Islam in Modern History* 57, *Meaning and End of Religion* 63, *Faith of Other Men* 63, *Modernisation of a Traditional Society* 66, *Questions of Religious Truth* 67.
6010 Inglis Street, Halifax, N.S., Canada.

Snoussi, Ahmed, LL.D.; Moroccan diplomatist; b. 22 April 1929; ed. Lycées at Meknes and Casablanca, Schools of Law and Political Sciences, Paris.
In Nationalist Movement; cabinet attaché to Minister of State in negotiations with France 56; Head, Press Div. Ministry of External Affairs 56; Sec.-Gen. Conf. on status of Tangiers; Moroccan Del. to UNESCO Conf. and UN; Dir.-Gen. Information; mem. Tech. Co-op. Mission to Congo and King's special envoy to Congo 58-59; UN Conciliation Mission to Congo 61; Sec.-Gen. Ministry of Information, Tourism Handicrafts and Fine Arts 61-65; Ambassador to Nigeria and Cameroon 65-67; Minister of Information 67-71; Amb. to Tunisia 71-73, to Algeria Nov. 73-; Editor numerous magazines, including *Maroc* (Ministry of External Affairs) and *Maroc Documents* (Ministry of Information); Officer Order of the Throne of Morocco, Cross of Courage and Endurance (Mission to Congo), decorations from Jordan and Yugoslavia.
Embassy of Morocco, 6 rue des Cèdres, Algiers, Algeria.

Solh, Takieddine; Lebanese politician and diplomatist; b. 1909; ed. American Univ. of Beirut, and Univ. Saint Joseph, Beirut.
Former Civil Servant; fmr. Counsellor, Embassy to United Arab Republic, and to the Arab League; mem. of Parl. 57, 64-; Pres. Foreign Affairs Comm. 64-; Minister of the Interior 65; Prime Minister, Minister of Finance 73-74; Pres. L'Appel Nat. Party (*Al Nida'a El Quaoumi*).
c/o Office of the Prime Minister, Beirut; and rue de Damas, Beirut, Lebanon.

Soliman, Mohammed Sidki; Egyptian army officer and politician; b. 1919; ed. Fuad I Univ., Cairo.
Colonel in U.A.R. Army -62; Minister for the High Dam Sept. 62-Sept. 66; Prime Minister 66-67; Deputy Prime Minister, Minister of Industry and Power 67-70; Pres. Soviet-Egyptian Friendship Soc.; Order of Lenin.
c/o Ministry of Industry, Cairo, Egypt.

Solomides, Renos; Cypriot business executive and politician; b. 1928; ed. Univ. of Paris.
Former Asst. Gen. Sec. Hellenic Mining Co., Commercial Man. Cyprus Textiles Ltd., Gen. Man. KEO Ltd. (wine firm and brewery); Minister of Finance 62-68; Financial Adviser, Research and Investments Bureau.
Research and Investments Bureau, P.O.B. 2444, Nicosia, Cyprus.

Soteriades, Antis; Cypriot lawyer and diplomatist; b. 10 Sept. 1924; ed. London Univ. and Gray's Inn, London.
In legal practice, Nicosia 51-56; detained on suspicion of assisting EOKA 56; escaped and became EOKA leader for Kyrenia district; mem. Exec., Edma Party May 59; High Commr. to U.K. Oct. 60-66; Ambassador to United Arab Repub. 66-, concurrently to Lebanon 67-, to Syria 67-74, to Iraq 73-; Knight of Order of St. Gregory the Great (Vatican) 63.
Embassy of Cyprus, 23A Ismail Mohammed Street Zamalek, Cairo, Egypt.

Sotoodeh, Fatholah, B.S., M.A.; Iranian engineer and politician; b. 1924; ed. Polytechnical Inst. of Teheran and New York Univ.

Engineer with Vanak Metalworks 45-46; studies in U.S.A., then Senior Engineer and Asst. to Prof. of Industrial Engineering, New York Univ., and consulting engineer 46-58; Consulting Engineer, Plan Org. of Iran 58; Man. Dir. Vanak Metalworks and Rubber Factory 59-64, Iran Fisheries 64-65; Minister of P.T.T. 65-74; Chair. Board of Dirs. Construction Bank, Iranian Nuclear Energy Co.; Prof. of Industrial Management, Teheran Polytechnical Inst.; Iran Novin Party.

Publs. research into the use of sunlight in water heaters, water distillators and sun-stoves.

c/o Ministry of Posts, Telegraphs and Telephones, Old Shimran Road, Teheran, Iran.

Soulioti, (Mrs.) Stella; Cypriot lawyer and politician; b. 1920; ed. Limassol, Victoria Girls' Coll., Alexandria, St. James' Secretarial Coll., London and Gray's Inn, London. Worked in Cyprus Govt. Public Information Office; in W.A.A.F. Middle East in Second World War; qualified as barrister after war; joined family practice; Minister of Justice Aug. 60-70, concurrently Minister of Health 64-66; Law Commr. 71-; Pres. Cyprus Red Cross Soc.; Chair. Scholarship Board; Vice-Pres. Cyprus Anti-Cancer Soc.; Hon. LL.D. (Nottingham Univ.) 72.

P.O. Box 4102, Nicosia, Cyprus.

Sowayel, Ibrahim 'Abd Allah al-; Saudi Arabian diplomatist; b. 31 Aug. 1916; ed. Saudi Inst., Mecca, and Cairo Univ.

Taught Arabic literature for a year in school for Preparation of (Student) Missions Abroad, Mecca; First Sec. Saudi Legation, Cairo 45; later Chargé d'Affaires, Beirut; Counsellor, Ministry of Foreign Affairs, Jeddah 54-56, Minister and Deputy Foreign Minister 56; Amb. to Iraq 57-60; Minister of Foreign Affairs 60-62; Head of Political Branch of Royal Diwan and Special Adviser to King with rank of Minister April-Sept. 62; Minister of Agriculture Oct. 62-Aug. 64; Amb. to U.S.A. 64-, concurrently to Mexico 65-.

Royal Embassy of Saudi Arabia, 2800 Woodland Drive, N.W., Washington, D.C., 20008, U.S.A.

Spanos, Marcos; Cypriot politician; b. 6 Aug. 1932, Lefkonico; ed. Famagusta Greek Gymnasium and American Acad., Larnaca, Gray's Inn, London.

Called to the Bar 56; practised law in Nicosia 57; Dir.-Gen. Office of the Pancyprian Cttee. of Human Rights 58, resident corresp. Int. League for the rights of Man 59; Rapporteur, Supreme Constitutional Court 62-64, Counsel of the Repub., Legal Dept. 64-67; seconded to Ministry of Labour to establish Arbitration Tribunal 67, Chair. Arbitration Tribunal 68; Minister of Labour and Social Insurance 72-74; founder mem. UN Asscn. of Cyprus; Chair. Consultative Cttee. to Cyprus Athletic Org. 69; mem. Cttee. School for Deaf Children.

c/o Ministry of Labour and Social Insurance, Nicosia, Cyprus.

Spuler, Bertold, DR. PHIL.; German university professor; b. 5 Dec. 1911; ed. Univs. of Heidelberg, Munich, Hamburg and Breslau.

Collaborator, Soc. for Silesian History 34-35; Asst. Dept. of East European History, Univ. of Berlin and Co-editor *Jahrbücher für Geschichte Osteuropas* 35-37; Asst. Dept. of Near Eastern Studies, Univ. of Göttingen 37-38; Dozent, Univ. of Göttingen 38-42; Full Prof. Univ. of Munich 42, Göttingen 45, Hamburg 48-; Ed. *Handbuch der Orientalistik* 49-, *Der Islam* 49-; Hon. Dr. Theol. (Berne); Hon. Dr. ès Lettres (Bordeaux).

Publs. include *Die europäische Diplomatie in Konstantinopel bis 1739* 35, *Die Minderheitenschulen der europäischen Türkei von der Reformzeit bis zum Weltkriege* 36, *Die Mongolen in Iran: Politik, Verwaltung und Kultur der Ilchanzeit 1220-1350* 39, 3rd edn., 68, *Die Goldene Horde, Die Mongolen in Russland, 1223-1302* 43, 2nd edn. 65, *Die Gegenwartslage der Ostkirchen in ihrer staatlichen und volklichen Umwelt* 48, 2nd edn. 69, *Geschichte der islamischen Länder im Überblick I: Chalifenzeit II: Mongolenzeit* 52-53, *Iran in frühislamischer Zeit: Politik, Kultur, Verwaltung und öffentliches Leben 633-1055* 52, *Regenten und Regierungen der Welt* 53, 2nd edn. 62-64 (with additions) 66, 72, *Wissenshaftl. Forschungsbericht: Der Vordere Orient in islamischer Zeit* 54, *The Age of the Caliphs* 60, 2nd edn. 68, *The Age of the Mongols* 60, 2nd edn. 68, *Geschichte der morgenländischen Kirchen* 61, *Les Mongols et l'Europe* (English edn. 71) 61, *Wüstenfeld-Mahlersche Vergleichungstabellen zur muslimischen, iranischen und orient-christlichen Zeitrechnung,* 3rd edn. 61, *Innerasien seit dem Aufkommen der Türken* 65, *Geschichte des Mongolen nach Zeugnissen des 13 u. 14 Jahrhunderts* (English edn. 71) 68, *Die historische und geographische Literatur Irans* 68, *Der Islam: Saeculum-Weltgeschichte III-VII* 66-72, *Kulturgeschichte des Islams* (*Östlicher Teil*) 71, *Die Kunst des Islam* (with J. Sourdel-Thomine) 73, *Die Orthodoxen Kirchen* (71 articles in *Int. Kirchl. Zeitschrift,* Bern) 39-74.

Mittelweg 90, Hamburg 13, German Federal Republic.

Spyridakis, Constantinos, PH.D.; Cypriot educationist and politician; b. 1903; ed. Pancyprian Gymnasium, Nicosia and Univs. of Athens and Berlin.

Teacher, Pancyprian Gymnasium, Nicosia 23-31, 34-35, Asst. Headmaster 35-36, Principal 36-60; Chair. Greek Board of Education 59-60; Pres. Greek Communal Chamber 60-65; Minister of Educ. 65-70; Corresp. mem. Acad. of Athens; Pres. Council of Soc. for Cypriot Studies; Pres., mem. and official of numerous academic and scientific orgs.; Dr. h.c. (Univ. of Salonika); Grand Cross of Royal Order of Phoenix (Greece); Gold Medal of Goethe Inst., Munich, Gold Medal of the Church of Cyprus, etc.

Publs. *Evagoras the First, King of Salamis* (German 35, Greek 45), *Cyprus Kings 4th Century B.C., An Outline of the History of Cyprus* 58, *The Kings of Cyprus* (Greek) 63, *A Brief History of Cyprus* 63 (Greek 64, new edn. 72, Arabic 70, English new revised edn. 74), *Studies, Lectures, Speeches, Articles* 72-74 (3 vols.).

St. Helen Street 8B, Nicosia, Cyprus.

Stark, Dame Freya Madeline, D.B.E.; British explorer and writer; b. 31 Jan. 1893; ed. School of Oriental Studies and privately.

Travelled in Middle East and Iran 27-39 and in South Arabia 34-35, 37-38; joined Ministry of Information Sept. 39, sent to Aden 39, Cairo 40, Baghdad as attaché to Embassy 41, U.S.A. and Canada 44; Hon. LL.D. (Glasgow Univ.) 52, Hon. D.Litt. (Durham) 70; C.B.E. 53; recipient of the Founders' Medal (Royal Geographical Soc.), of Mungo Park Medal (Royal Scottish Geographical Soc.), Richard Burton Memorial Medal (Royal Asiatic Soc.), and of Sir Percy Sykes Medal (Royal Central Asian Soc.).

Publs. *The Valley of the Assassins* 34, *The Southern Gates of Arabia* 36, *Baghdad Sketches* 37, *Seen in the Hadhramaut* 38, *A Winter in Arabia* 40, *Letters from Syria,* 42, *East is West* 45, *Perseus in the Wind* 48, *Traveller's Prelude* 50, *Beyond Euphrates* 51, *Winter in Arabia* 52, *Ionia* 54, *The Lycian Shore* 56, *Alexander's Path* 58, *Riding to the Tigris* 59, *Dust in the Lion's Paw* 61, *The Journey's Echo* (an anthology) 63, *Rome on the Euphrates* 66, *The Zodiac Arch, Time, Movement and Space in Landscape* 69, *The Minaret of Djam* 70, *Turkey, Sketch of Turkish History* 71, *Selected Letters* 74.

Asolo, Treviso, Italy; and c/o John Murray, 50 Albermarle Street, London, W.1, England.

Steel, David Edward Charles, B.A.; British company director; b. 29 Nov. 1916; ed. Rugby School and Univ. Coll., Oxford.
Officer, Q.R. Lancers, in France, the Middle East, N. Africa and Italy 40-45; Admitted as solicitor 48, worked for Linklaters and Paines 48-50; Legal Dept., British Petroleum Co. Ltd. 50-56, N.Y. 58, Pres. B.P. (N. America) Ltd. 59-61, Regional Co-ordinator, Western Hemisphere, B.P. Co. Ltd. 61-62; Man. Dir. Kuwait Oil Co. Ltd. 62-65, Dir. 65; Man. Dir. B.P. Co. Ltd. 65-, Deputy Chair. 72-; D.S.O. 40, M.C. 45.
37 Ormonde Gate, London, S.W.3, England.

Steltzer, Hans-Georg; German diplomatist; b. 30 April 1913, Braunschweig; ed. Realgymnasium, Rendsburg and Plön, Schleswig-Holstein, Univ. of Hamburg.
Military service 34-45; successively with Office of Cultural Affairs, Kiel 46, Bi-Zonal Admin. for Econ. Affairs 48-49, Ministry of Econ. Affairs 49-50; joined diplomatic service 50-, Vice-Consul 51; Pretoria 51-54, Second Sec. 53; Foreign Office, Bonn 54-57, First Sec. 55; New Delhi 57-60; Foreign Office 60-63, Counsellor 61; Amb. to Ghana 64-68; Minister Plenipotentiary 68; with Fed. Press and Information Office, Bonn 68-69; Dir.-Gen. Dept. for Cultural Relations, Foreign Office 70-72; Amb. to Egypt Aug. 72-; German Gold Cross, Fed. Cross of Merit 1st Class, Grand Cordon Egyptian Order of Merit.
Publs. on African affairs and int. cultural co-operation.
Embassy of the Federal Republic of Germany, 20 Boulos Hanna Street, Cairo-Dokki, Egypt.

Stephani, Christakis, B.COMM., F.C.A.; Cypriot banker; b. 28 Sept. 1926, Cyprus; ed. London School of Econs. and Political Science.
Accountant-General of the Repub. of Cyprus 60-65; Gov. Cen. Bank of Cyprus 65-.
Central Bank of Cyprus, P.O. Box 1087, 36 Metochiou Street, Nicosia, Cyprus.

Stino, Kamal Ramzy; Egyptian politician.
Minister of Supplies 59, 62-63; Dep. Prime Minister for Supply and Home Trade 64-66; mem. Gen. Secretariat Arab Socialist Union 66-.
27 Rifai Street, Giza, Cairo, Egypt.

Stylianou, Petros Savva; Cypriot politician; b. 8 June 1933; ed. Pancyprian Gymnasium and Univ. of Athens and Salonika.
Served with Panhellenic Cttee. of the Cyprus Struggle (PEKA) and Nat. Union of Cypriot Univ. Students (EFEK), Pres. EFEK 53-54; Co-founder Dauntless Leaders of the Cypriot Fighters Org. (KARI) joined liberation movement 55, detained 55, escaped; leader Nat. Striking Group; arrested 56 and sentenced to 15 years imprisonment; transferred to English prison, repatriated 59; mem. Central Cttee. United Democratic Re-creation Front (EDMA) 59; Deputy Sec.-Gen. Cyprus Labour Confederation (SEK) 59, Sec.-Gen. 60-62; founded Cyprus Democratic Labour Federation (DEOK) 62, Sec.-Gen. 62-; mem. House of Reps. 60-70, Sec. of House 60-62; Man. Editor *Ergatiki Foni* (Voice of the Working Class) 60-62; Man. Editor DEOK newspaper *Ergatikos* (The Workers' Struggle) 62-63; Man. Editor *Allagi* (Change) 63; mem. Co-ordination Cttee. of 28 associated vocational and scientific orgs. 64-66; Pres. Pancyprian Org. for the Disabled 66-; founder Pancyprian Olive Produce Org. 67; Man. Dir. *Kypriakos Logas* (Scientific Cypriot) 69-; Pres. Council of Cyprus Historical Museum and Archives Oct. 74-, Pancyprian Cttee. for Enclaved Greek Population 74-.
Publs. *The Kyrenia Castle* 66 *The Epic of Central Prisons* 67, *Hours of Resurrection* 67, *Problems on Education* 68, *Sean Macstiofain, Leader of the IRA and Adorer of Hellenism* 73, *Saint Demetrianos—Bishop of Chytri-Cyprus* 73, *Historical Data relating to the Ethnarchical Role of the Cyprus Church* 73, *Achievements and Targets in the Rehabilitation of the Disabled* 73, *Laographicon Minologion* 73, *Oi tris ftochoi Agioi tis Kythreas* 75, *To xerizoma* 75.
10 Kimon Street, Engomi, Nicosia, Cyprus.

Succar, Abdullatif Zeki; Syrian United Nations official; b. 27 Dec. 1924; ed. Coll. des Frères Maristes, Jounieh, Lebanon, American Univ. of Beirut and New York Univ.
With UN, New York 48-56; Consultant on Palestine Affairs, Syrian Ministry of Foreign Affairs 56-61; Deputy Civilian Officer, Katanga, UN Operation in the Congo, Senior Programme Officer 61-64; Deputy Resident Rep., UN Devt. Programme, Somalia 65-68; Resident Rep. UNDP, People's Democratic Repub. of Yemen 68-71; Regional Rep. UNDP, Saudi Arabia, Bahrain, Qatar, U.A.E. and Oman 71-.
United Nations Development Programme, P.O. Box 558, Riyadh, Saudi Arabia; and c/o United Nations Development Programme, New York, N.Y., U.S.A.

Sultan ibn Abdulaziz, H.R.H. Prince; Saudi Arabian politician; b. 1924.
Brother of the late King Faisal; fmr. Minister of Communications; Minister of Defence and Aviation 62-.
Ministry of Defence, Jeddah, Saudi Arabia.

Sunay, Cevdet; Turkish army officer and politician; b. 10 Feb. 1900; ed. Kuleli Military Lyceum, Istanbul and Military Acad.
With Turkish Army 16-66; served in Palestine 17, later under Atatürk; Capt. 30; Officer Operations Dept. Gen. Staff 33; Teacher Mil. Acad. 42-47; Commdr. Artillery Regt. 47; Chief Operations Dept. Gen. Staff; Gen. 59; Deputy Chief Gen. Staff Aug. 58-May 60; C.-in-C. Land Forces 60, Chief of Staff Aug. 60-66; Senator 66; Pres. of Turkey 66-73; Senator 73-; Hon. K.C.B. 67.
Akbaş sok. Botanik Apt. 2/5, Cankaya-Ankara, Turkey.

Sussmann, Joel, LL.B., DR.JUR.; Israeli judge; b. Poland 24 Oct. 1910; ed. Univs. of Frankfurt, Heidelberg, Berlin, and Cambridge.
In private legal practice 38-49; Mil. Prosecutor, Israel Defence Army 49; Judge, Supreme Court of Israel 53-70, Perm. Deputy Pres. 70-; Prof. Hebrew Univ., Jerusalem; Israel Prize 75.
Publs. *Wechsel- und Scheckrecht Palästinas, Bills of Exchange, Dine'i Staroth, Dine'i Borerut, Sidrei Hadin Haesrachi* (Law of Civil Procedure).
13 Balfour Street, Jerusalem; and The Supreme Court, Jerusalem, Israel.

T

Taba, Abdol Hossein, M.D.; Iranian physician; b. 1912; ed. Birmingham and London Univs.
Former Dir.-Gen. of Health, Teheran; Vice-Pres. World Health Assembly 51; Deputy Regional Dir. WHO Eastern Mediterranean Regional Office 52-57, Regional Dir. 57-.
World Health Organization Eastern Mediterranean Regional Office, P.O.B. 1517, Alexandria, Egypt.

Tabibi, Abdul Hakim, M.A., PH.D.; Afghan diplomatist; b. 7 Oct. 1924, Kabul; ed. Habibia High School, Kabul Univ., and George Washington and American Univs., U.S.A.
Entered Ministry of Foreign Affairs 54; First Sec. Perm. Mission to UN 56-58, Counsellor 59-61, Minister Counsellor 61-64; Amb. to Yugoslavia and Bulgaria 64-65; Minister of Justice and Attorney-Gen. 65-66; Amb. to Japan and the Philippines 67-70, to India, Nepal and Burma 70-73; Gov. Asian Devt. Bank 67-73; mem. UN Int. Law Comm. 71-73; del. to various UN and other int. confs.; decorations from Afghanistan, Yugoslavia and Japan.
Publs. *Law of the Sea and its Relation to the Countries*

without Sea Coast 59, *Free Access to the Sea for Land-locked Countries* 58, *The Right of Transit* 70, and various articles.
c/o Ministry of Foreign Affairs, Kabul, Afghanistan.

Taha, Mohammed Fathi; Egyptian meteorologist; b. 15 Jan. 1914, Cairo; ed. Cairo Univ. and Imperial Coll. of Science and Technology, London.
Under-Secretary of State and Chair. Board of Dirs. Egyptian Meteorological Authority 53-; Vice-Pres. IAF 65; mem. WMO Exec. Cttee. 55, Second Vice-Pres. 59-63, Pres. 71-75; Pres. Perm. Meteorological Cttee., Arab League 71-75; Chair. Nat. Cttee. on Geodesy and Geophysics; mem. High Comm. on Outer Space Research for Peaceful Uses, Nat. Comm. for Int. Council of Scientific Unions and many other cttees. dealing with scientific research in Egypt.
Egyptian Meteorological Authority, Koubry El-Quobba P.O., Cairo, Egypt.

Taher, Abdulhady H., PH.D.; Saudi Arabian government official; b. 1930; ed. Ain Shams Univ. Cairo and California Univ.
Entered Saudi Arabian Govt. service 55; Dir.-Gen. Ministry of Petroleum and Mineral Resources 60; Gov.-Gen. Petroleum and Mineral Org. (PETROMIN) 62-; Man. Dir. Saudi Arabian Fertilizers Co. (SAFCO); Dir. Coll. of Petroleum and Minerals, Saudi Arabian Railroads, Arabian Oil Co. (ARAMCO); Hon. mem. American Petroleum Engineers' Asscn.
Publ. *Income Determination in the International Petroleum Industry* 66.
PETROMIN, P.O.B. 757, Riyadh, Saudi Arabia.

Taimur al-Said, Tarikbin; Omani diplomatist; b. 2 July 1923; ed. English High for Boys, Istanbul, Robert Coll., Istanbul, and Germany.
Commissioned in Muscat Army 41-44; Chair., Administrator, Muscat Mutrah Municipality 45-57; in charge of Operational Area in Jabal War 58-59; self-exile 62-70; Prime Minister 70-71; Personal Adviser for Diplomatic Affairs to Sultan of Oman, Senior Amb. Extraordinary and Plenipotentiary 72-; Order of Oman 1st Class.
P.O. Box 202, Muscat, Oman; and Leuchtturmweg 21, 2000 Hamburg 56, Federal Republic of Germany.

Tajaddod, Mostafa; Iranian banker and politician; b. 1909; ed. secondary school, Teheran, and in Europe.
In Europe 33-45; Deputy Gov. Industrial Bank of Iran 45-50; Chair. Board of Dirs. Bank Bazargani Iran (Commercial Bank of Iran) 50-; fmr. mem. of Majlis, now mem. Senate; fmr. Minister of Commerce.
Bank Bazargani Iran, Maiden Sepah, Teheran, Iran.

Takieddine, Bahiqe Mahmoud; Lebanese politician; b. 1909, Baakline; ed. Université St. Joseph, Beirut.
Barrister 31-47; Deputy for Mont Liban 47; Minister of Agriculture 49; Deputy for Chouf 51, 53, 60, 64; Minister of Social Affairs and Health 53-60; fmr. Pres. Parl. Comm. on the Admin. of Justice; Minister of Economy 64-65; Minister of Information 68-69, of the Interior 73-74.
c/o Ministère de l'Intérieur, Beirut; Home: Rue Verdun, Beirut, Lebanon.

Takla, Philippe; Lebanese politician; b. 1915; ed. Univ. Law School, Beirut.
Law practice, Beirut 35-45; M.P. 45, 47; Minister of Nat. Economy and Communication 45-46, 48-49; Minister of Foreign Affairs 49, 61-64, 64-65; Gov. Bank of Lebanon 64-66, 66-67; Minister of Foreign Affairs and of Justice 66; Perm. Rep. to UN 67-68; Amb. to France 68-71; Minister of Foreign Affairs and of Educ. and Planning May 75-.
Ministry of Foreign Affairs, Beirut; and Rue Maarad, Beirut, Lebanon.

Takriti, Saddam Hussain; Iraqi politician; b. 1937, Tikrit; ed. Al-Karkh (Baghdad) and Al-Qasr al-Aini (Cairo) secondary schools, Cairo and Baghdad Univs.

Joined Arab Baath Socialist Party 57; sentenced to death for attempted execution of Gen. Kassem 59; in Egypt 62, joined Baath Party, Cairo; returned to Iraq 63; mem. 4th Regional Congress and 6th Nat. Congress, Baath Party 63, mem. Regional Leadership 63, mem. 7th Nat. Congress, Syria 64; arrested for plotting overthrow of Pres. Aref Oct. 64; mem. Nat. Leadership, Baath Party 65, 70-, Deputy Sec. Regional Leadership 66-68; played prominent role in July 68 *coup*; Vice-Pres. Revolutionary Command Council Nov. 69-.
Revolutionary Command Council, Baghdad, Iraq.

Tal, Josef; Israeli composer; b. 1910, Poland; ed. Berlin State Acad. of Music.
Went to Israel 34; taught piano and composition at Jerusalem Acad. of Music 37, Dir. 48-52; now Head, Dept. of Musicology, Hebrew Univ., Jerusalem; Dir. Israel Centre for Electronic Music 61-; has appeared with Israel Philharmonic Orchestra and others as pianist and conductor; concert tours of Europe, U.S.A., Far East; UNESCO Scholarship for research in electronic music.
Works include: *Saul at Ein Dor* 57, *Amnon and Tamar* 61, *Ashmedai* 69 (operas), Symphony No. 1 53, No. 2 60, *Concerto for Harpsichord and Electronics* 64, *Double Concerto* (for violin and violoncello) 70, *Masada 1967* 73, other cantatas, quintets, music for ballet and several books on the theory of music.
Department of Musicology, Hebrew University, Jerusalem; Home: 3 Dvora Haneviyah Street, Jerusalem, Israel.

Talal ibn Abdulaziz, Amir; Saudi Arabian Prince; b. 1930; ed. secondary school.
Son of the late King Abdul ibn Saud; half brother of former King Saud; Minister of Communications 53-54; Ambassador to France 55-56; Minister of Finance 61.
Cairo, Egypt.

Taleb-Ibrahimi, Ahmed, M.D.; Algerian doctor and politician; b. 5 Jan. 1932; ed. Univ. of Paris.
Son of Sheikh Bachir Brahimi, spiritual leader of Islam in Algeria; Dir. Jeune Musulman 52-54, Union Générale des Etudiants Musulmans Algériens 55-56, French Fed. of the FLN 56-57; imprisoned in France 57-62, in Algeria 64-65; Doctor, Hôpital Mustapha, Algiers 62-64; Minister of Nat. Educ. 65-70; mem. UNESCO Exec. Board; Minister of Information and Culture 70-.
Publs. *Contribution à l'histoire de la médecine arabe au Maghreb* 63, *Lettres de Prison* 66, *De la décolonisation à la révolution culturelle* 73.
Ministry of Information and Culture, 119 rue Didouche Mourad, Algiers, Algeria.

Taleghani, Khalil, B.SC.; Iranian civil engineer and politician; b. 13 Sept. 1913; ed. American Coll. of Teheran and Univ. of Birmingham.
Junior engineer, England 37-39; Engineer, Persian Army 39-41; Chief Engineer, Technical Dir., Dir. of Ebtekar and other construction companies and Golpayegan Water Co. 41-51; Minister of Agriculture Dec. 51-June 52, July 52-March 53 and 55-56; Minister of State June 56-59; Dir. Taleghani-Tashakori Co. (consulting engineers); Man. Karaj Dam Authority 54-59; Chair. Industrial and Mining Development Bank of Iran 60-62; Dir. Taleghani-Daftari (Consulting Engineers) 60-; Chair. B. F. Goodrich Tyre Manufacturing Co. 60-; Chair. Pars Paper Co. 67-, Iran-California Co. 70-, Manem Consultants 70-; mem. Iranian Asscn. of Consulting Engineers; Fellow A.S.C.E.; Tadj and Homayoun (1st Order) Medals.
Baghe-Bank Street Golhak, Tehran, Iran.

Talhouni, Bahjat, LL.B.; Jordanian politician; b. 1913, Ma'an; ed. Damascus Univ.
Lawyer 36-38; Judge, Kerak 38-52; Pres. Court of Appeals 52-53; Minister of Interior 53, of Justice 53-54; Chief Royal Cabinet 54-60, 63-64, June-Aug. 69, Nov. 73-; Prime

Minister 60-62, 64-65, 67-70, concurrently Minister of Foreign Affairs 67-68, of Defence 68-69, of Interior April-Sept. 68; mem. Senate 62-; Personal Rep. of H.M. King Hussein 67-69; mem. Consultative Council 67; Pres. Cttee. for Preparation of Civil Law 71; Trustee, Jordan Univ. 62-.
c/o Royal Palace, Amman, Jordan.

Talib, Maj.-Gen. Naji; Iraqi soldier and politician; b. 1917; ed. Iraqi Staff Coll. and Sandhurst, England.
Military Attaché, London 54-55; Commdr. Basra Garrison 57-58; Minister of Social Affairs 58-59; lived abroad 59-62; Minister of Industry March 63-Nov. 64; mem. U.A.R.-Iraq Joint Presidency Council May 64-65; Minister of Foreign Affairs Nov. 64-Sept. 65; Prime Minister and Minister of Petroleum Affairs 66-May 67.
Baghdad, Iraq.

Talû, Naim; Turkish banker and politician; b. 22 July 1919; ed. Faculty of Economics, Istanbul Univ.
Joined Türkiye Cumhuriyet Merkez Bankası (Central Bank of Repub. of Turkey) 46, Chief 52, Asst. Dir. of Ankara Branch 55-58, Dir. of Exchange Dept. 58-62, Asst. Gen. Dir. 62-66, Acting Pres. and Gen. Dir. 66-67, Pres. and Gen. Dir. 67-70, Gov. 70-71; Chair. Foreign Investment Encouragement Cttee. 67-68; Chair. Banks' Asscn. of Turkey 67-71; Sec.-Gen. Cttee. for Regulations of Bank Credits 67-70; Minister of Commerce 71-73; Prime Minister 73-74; mem. Ankara Educ. Foundation, Soc. for Protection of Children in Turkey.
Başbakan, Ankara, Turkey.

Tarazi, Salah el Dine, L. EN D., D. EN D.; Syrian diplomatist; b. 1919; ed. Coll. des. Frères, Damascus and Faculté Française de Droit, Beirut.
Lawyer 40-47; Lecturer and Asst. Prof. of Law, Damascus Univ. 46-48; Ministry of Foreign Affairs 49-50; Chargé d'Affaires, Brussels 51-53; Alternate Perm. Rep. to UN 53-56; Sec.-Gen. Ministry of Foreign Affairs 56-57; Ambassador to U.S.S.R. 57-58; Ambassador of United Arab Republic to Czechoslovakia 58-59, to People's Republic of China 59-61; Syrian Ambassador to People's Republic of China 61-62; Perm. Rep. of Syria to UN 62-65; Ambassador to U.S.S.R., also accredited to Poland 64; now Amb. to Turkey; Syrian, Belgian and Czech awards.
Publs. *Les Services Publics Libano-Syriens* 46; articles concerning law and political science in Arabic and French.
Syrian Embassy, Çankaya, Abdullah Cevdat Sok 7, Ankara, Turkey.

Tariki, Abdallah; Saudi Arabian oil executive; b. 1919; ed. Univs. of Cairo and Texas.
Studied at Univ. of Texas and worked as trainee with Texaco Inc. in W. Texas and California 45-49; Dir. Oil Supervision Office, Eastern Province, Saudi Arabia (under Ministry of Finance) 49-55; Dir.-Gen. of Oil and Mineral Affairs (Saudi Arabia) 55-60; Minister of Oil and Mineral Resources 60-62; Dir. Arabian American Oil Co. 59-62; Leader Saudi Arabian Del. at Arab Oil Congresses 59, 60; Independent Consultant 62-; adviser to Egyptian, Algerian and Kuwaiti Govts. on oil matters.
P.O. Box 22699, Kuwait.

Tartakower, Arie, DR. IUR., D.RER.POL.; Israeli (b. Polish) university professor; b. 24 Sept. 1897; ed. Univ. of Vienna.
Co-founder Zionist Labour Movement and Chair. Zionist Labour Party, Poland 22-39; Lecturer, Inst. of Jewish Sciences, Warsaw 32-39; Dir. Dept. of Relief and Rehabilitation of World Jewish Congress (U.S.A.) 39-46; fmr. Prof., Lecturer and Head, Dept. of Sociology of the Jews, Hebrew Univ., Jerusalem; Hon. Vice-Pres. World Jewish Congress; mem. Gen. Council World Zionist Org.; mem. World Secr. Zionist Labour Movement; Co-founder and fmr. Pres. Israel Asscn. for UN; Chair. World Asscn. for Hebrew Language and Culture.
Publs. include: *History of the Jewish Labour Movement,*

Jewish Emigration and Jewish Policy of Migration, The Jewish Refugee, Jewish Wanderings in the World, The Wandering Man, The Jewish Society, History of Jewish Colonization (2 vols.), *The Tribes of Israel* (3 vols.).
1 Ben Yehuda Road, Jerusalem, Israel.

Tawfiq, Mohammad 'Omar; Saudi Arabian politician; b. 1917; ed. Shari'a Coll. of Literature and Islamics, Medina. Former teacher; fmr. clerk, Post and Telegraph Dept. 41-58, rose to Chief Sec. Council of Ministers; retd. 58; business and press activities 58-62; Minister of Communications 62-, of Pilgrimage and Religious Endowment Affairs 63-70.
Ministry of Communications, Riyadh, Saudi Arabia.

Tekinel, Ismail Hakki; Turkish lawyer; b. 1925, Babaeski-Kirklareli, Edirne.
Served as judge in many provs.; private practice as solicitor; mem. Parl. for Istanbul 61; Deputy Chair. Justice Party; Chair. Justice Cttee. of Nat. Assembly; Minister of State 73-74; Justice Party.
T.B.M. Meclisi, Ankara, Turkey.

Tekoah, Yosef; Israeli diplomatist; b. 4 March 1925; ed. Université L'Aurore, China, and Harvard Univ.
Instructor in Int. Relations, Harvard Univ. 47-48; Dep. Legal Adviser, Ministry of Foreign Affairs 49-53; Dir. Armistice Affairs, and Head Israel Dels. to Armistice Comms. with Egypt, Jordan, Syria and Lebanon 53-58; Dep. Perm. Rep. to UN 58, Act. Perm. Rep. 59-60; Ambassador to Brazil 60-62, to U.S.S.R. 62-65; Asst. Dir.-Gen. Ministry of Foreign Affairs 66-68; Perm. Rep. to UN 68-75.
c/o Ministry of Foreign Affairs, Jerusalem, Israel.

Tewfik, Zakaria; Egyptian cotton executive; b. 1920; ed. Cairo Univ.
With Bank Misr; then Commercial Attaché, Belgium, Spain; Dir.-Gen. Exchange Control Office 61; Under-Sec. for Cotton Affairs, Ministry of Economy 61-; Dir.-Gen. Cotton Org. 61-; Egyptian Del. to many int. cotton confs.
General Organization for Cotton, 19 El-Gomhouriya Street, Cairo, Egypt.

Thacker, Thomas William, M.A.; British university professor; b. 6 Nov. 1911; ed. City of Oxford School, Univs. of Oxford and Berlin.
Goldsmiths' Research Scholar, Oxford and Berlin 33-35; Senior Research Student, Oxford 35-37; Lecturer in Semitic Languages, Univ. Coll. of Bangor, North Wales 37-38; Reader in Hebrew, Univ. of Durham 38-40; Foreign Office 40-45; Prof. of Hebrew and Oriental Languages, Univ. of Durham 45-51, Prof. of Semitic Philology and Dir. School of Oriental Studies, Univ. of Durham 51-; Foreign mem. Royal Belgian Acad.
28 Church Street, Durham, England.

Thani, Sheikh Abdul Aziz Khalifa al-, B.S.; Qatari politician; b. 12 Dec. 1948, Doha; ed. Indiana North and George Washington Univs., U.S.A.
Deputy Minister of Finance and Petroleum June-Dec. 72; Minister of Finance and Petroleum 72-; Chair. Board of Dirs. Qatar Nat. Bank 72-, Qatar Nat. Petroleum Co. 73-; Chair. Joint Management Cttee., QPC and Shell Qatar 73-; Gov. for Qatar, Int. Monetary Fund and World Bank 72-; Chair. State of Qatar Investment Board 72-; Rep. to numerous confs. of OPEC, OAPEC, UN, IMF, IBRD, Islamic Summit, Non-aligned confs., etc.
Ministry of Finance and Petroleum, P.O. Box 83, Doha, Qatar.

Thani, Sheikh Khalifa bin Hamad al-; Amir of Qatar; b. 1934.
Deputy Ruler of Qatar, Prime Minister and Minister of Finance and Petroleum Affairs Sept. 71-Feb. 72; deposed

his cousin Sheikh Ahmad and took office as Amir of Qatar Feb. 72.
The Royal Palace, Doha, Qatar.

Theocharis, Reghinos D., PH.D. (London); Cypriot economist and banker; b. 10 Feb. 1929; ed. Highest School of Economics, Athens, Univ. of Aberdeen and London School of Economics.
Inspector of Commercial Education, Cyprus 53-56; at London School of Economics 56-58; Chief, Economic Development Unit, Bank of Greece, Athens 58-59; Minister of Finance in Cyprus Provisional Govt. March 59-Aug. 60; Minister of Finance Aug. 60-62; Governor, Bank of Cyprus Ltd. 62-; Hon. Fellow, London School of Econs. and Political Sciences 71.
Publ. *Early Developments in Mathematical Economics* 61.
Bank of Cyprus Ltd., Nicosia, Cyprus.

Thesiger, Wilfred, C.B.E., D.S.O., M.A.; British traveller; b. 3 Jan. 1910; ed. Eton and Magdalen Coll., Oxford.
Explored Danakil country of Abyssinia 33-34; Sudan Political Service, Darfur and Upper Nile Provinces 35-39; served in Ethiopia, Syria and Western Desert with Sudan Defence Force and Special Air Service, Second World War; explored the Empty Quarter of Arabia 45-50; lived with the Madan in the Marshes of Southern Iraq 50-58; awarded Back Grant, Royal Geographical Soc. 36, Founders Medal 48; Lawrence of Arabia Medal, Royal Central Asian Soc. 55; David Livingstone Medal, Royal Scottish Geographical Soc. 61, Royal Soc. of Literature Award 64, Burton Memorial Medal, Royal Asiatic Soc. 66; Hon. D.Litt. (Leicester) 68.
Publs. *Arabian Sands* 58, *The Marsh Arabs* 64.
15 Shelley Court, Tite Street, London, S.W.3, England.

Tixier, Claude, L. ès L., D. ès D.; French economist; b. 22 Nov. 1913; ed. Arts and Law Faculties and Ecole des Sciences Politiques, Univ. of Paris.
Deputy Inspector of Finances 39, Inspector of Finances 42; Deputy Dir. to Ministry of Nat. Economy 45; Chief, Service of Economic Survey 46; Dir. Cabinet of Sec. of State for the Budget 47; Deputy Dir. Cabinet of Minister of Finances 48; Dir. Cabinet of Prime Minister (Finances) 48; Dir. Cabinet of Minister of Finances 49; Dir.-Gen. of Finances to the Algerian Ministry, Algiers 49-58; Vice-Pres. European Investment Bank July 58-62; Pres. Banque Industrielle de Financement et de Crédit 62-67; admin. Union Bancaire pour le Commerce et l'Industrie, Tunis, Lafarge-Maroc, Casablanca, CADEM, Meknes; Vice-Pres. Banque Worms 67-; Chevalier de la Légion d'Honneur.
45 Boulevard Haussmann, Paris 9e; and 5 square des Ecrivains Combattants, Paris 16e, France.

Tlass, Major-Gen. Mustapha el-; Syrian army officer and politician; ed. Military and Law Colls.
President of Damascus Mil. Tribunal 64, of Homs Mil. Tribunal; Chief of Staff of the Syrian Army 68; Deputy Minister of Defence 68, Minister and C.-in-C. of Syrian Armed Forces 71-; mem. Regional Bureau of Baath Party; Nat. Order of Cedar (Lebanon) 71.
Ministry of Defence, Damascus, Syria.

Tombazos, George; Cypriot politician; b. 2 Feb. 1919; ed. Pancyprian Gymnasium, Cyprus Coll., Dentists' School of Athens.
Worked as dentist at Morphou 50-66; M.P. for Nicosia 60-66; Chair. Board of Greek Education 59-60; Pres. Greek Communal Chamber of Cyprus 60-65; Minister of Education 65-66; Minister of Agricultural and Natural Resources 66-70; Head, Central Information Service 70-75; Minister of Communications and Works 75-; Gold Medal of Patriarchate of Jerusalem; Gold Medal of Goethe Inst. Munich; Grand Cross of Royal Order of Phoenix 66.
Ministry of Communications and Works, Nicosia, Cyprus.

Tomeh, Georges J., M.A., PH.D.; Syrian university professor and diplomatist; b. 1922; ed. American Univ. of Beirut and Georgetown Univ.
Attaché, London, and Alt. Del. to UNESCO 45-46; Syrian Embassy, Washington 47-52; Alt. Gov. Int. Monetary Fund 50; Dir. UN and Treaties Dept., Ministry of Foreign Affairs, Damascus 53-54; Asst. Prof. of Philosophy and Asst. to Dean of Arts and Sciences, American Univ. of Beirut 54-56; Dir. Research Dept., Ministry of Foreign Affairs, Damascus 56-57; Consul-Gen., New York 57-58, Minister Consul-Gen. of United Arab Republic in New York 58, Minister, New York 61; Consul-Gen. and Deputy Perm. Rep. of Syria to UN 61-63; Minister of Economy, Syrian Arab Repub. 63-64; Prof. of Philosophy, Syrian Univ. 64-65; Perm. Rep. to UN 65-72; Order of Syrian Merit, Commdr. Order of St. Paul and St. Peter.
Publs. (in Arabic) *The Idea of Nationalism* 54, *Philosophy of Leibnitz* 54, 65, *Making of the Modern Mind* (2 vols.) (trans. from English) 55-57, 65, *Arab Emigrants to the United States* 65; (in English) *Islam, Year Book of Education and Philosophy* 57, *Neutralism in Syria* 64, *Challenge and Response: A Judgement of History* 69.
c/o Ministry of Foreign Affairs, Damascus, Syria.

Toukan, Baha'ud-din, B.A.; Jordanian diplomatist; b. 1910; ed. American Univ. of Beirut.
Joined Arab Legion and Sec. to Officer Commdg. 32; transferred to Court of H.R.H. the Amir of Transjordan 37; joined staff of B.B.C., London 42; Income Tax Assessor, Transjordan Govt. April 45-46; Gov. of Belqa District July 46-47; Sec. to Transjordan Del. to negotiate Independence Treaty, London Feb. 46; Transjordan Consul-Gen. in Jerusalem 47-48; Jordan Minister to Egypt 48-51, to Turkey 51-54; Under-Secretary, Ministry of Foreign Affairs 54-56; Ambassador to U.K. 56-58; Permanent Rep. to UN 58, Feb. 71-72; Under-Sec. Ministry of Foreign Affairs 62-71; Amb. to Italy 72-73; mem. of Senate 73-; decorations include: First Order of Istiqlal, Grand Officer Lebanese Republic.
Publ. *Short History of Transjordan* (in English) 45.
The Senate, Amman, Jordan.

Toukan, Mohammed Ahmed, M.A.; Jordanian politician and banker; b. 15 Aug. 1903; ed. Oxford Univ.
Various teaching posts 30-48; Minister of Public Works, Devt. and Reconstruction 50, of Education 50-53; former Man. Nat. Bank of Jordan; Minister of State for Prime Ministry Affairs and Minister of Tourism Feb.-July 66; Minister of Communications 66; Minister of Foreign Affairs April 67-July 67; Deputy Prime Minister July 67-69; Minister of Defence Dec. 68-69; Al Istiqlal Medal, Al Kawkab Medal.
Amman, Jordan.

Toumazis, Panayiotis, M.SC.ENG.; Cypriot civil engineer; b. 1912, Famagusta; ed. Greek Gymnasium, Famagusta, and Nat. Metsovion Polytechnic, Athens.
Municipal engineer, Famagusta; later served as Pres. Famagusta Devt. Corpn., Famagusta Fed. of Trade and Industry, and Architects and Civil Engineers Council of Registration; mem. House of Reps. 60-70; Minister of Agriculture and Natural Resources 70-72; mem. Cyprus Civil Engineers' and Architects' Asscn.
5 Edisson Street, Famagusta, Cyprus.

Tsur, Yaakov; Israeli diplomatist; b. 18 Oct. 1906; ed. Hebrew Coll. Jerusalem, Univ. of Florence and Sorbonne.
Mem. staff daily newspaper *Haaretz*, Tel-Aviv 29; Dir. French Dept. and later Co-Dir. Propaganda Dept. Jewish Nat. Fund, Jerusalem 30; special Zionist missions, Belgium, Greece, France 34-35, Bulgaria and Greece 40; Dir. Publicity Dept. Jewish Agency Recruiting Council 42;

Liaison officer with G.H.Q. British Troops in Egypt 43-45; Head del. to Greece 45; Pres. Israeli Army Recruiting Cttee. Jerusalem 48; Minister to Argentina 49-53, Uruguay 49-53, Chile 50-53 and Paraguay 50-53; Ambassador to France 53-59; Dir.-Gen. Foreign Office 59; Chair. Zionist Gen. Council 61-68; Chair. Jewish Nat. Fund.
Publs. *Juifs en Guerre* 47, *The Birth of Israel* 49, *Preludio a Israel* 56, *Shaharit shel Etmol* (autobiography) 66, French trans.—*Prière du Matin* 67 (English ed. *Sunrise in Zion*), *An Ambassador's Diary in Paris* 68, *La Révolte Juive* (Italian, Spanish and Russian trans.) 70, *Portrait of the Diaspora* 75.
c/o P.O. Box 283, Jerusalem, Israel.

Tueni, Ghassan, M.A.; Lebanese newspaper editor and politician; b. 1926; ed. Harvard Univ.
Publisher and Editor-in-Chief, *An-Nahar* (daily newspaper); Deputy Prime Minister, Minister of Educ. and Information 70-71; fmr. Parl. Deputy; arrested and detained Dec. 73; Minister for Social Affairs and Labour, for Tourism, for Industry and Oil May 75-.
c/o An-Nahar, rue Banque du Liban, Hamra, Lebanon.

Tuhami, Hassan Muhammed el-; Egyptian politician; b. 1924; ed. Military Coll., Cairo.
Ambassador, Ministry of Foreign Affairs 61; Amb. to Austria 62; Sec.-Gen. of the Presidency 69; Minister of State 70-71; Adviser to the Pres. 71-75.
c/o The Presidency, Cairo, Egypt.

Tuna, Ahmet Nusret; Turkish politician; b. 1916, Mucur, Kireşehir.
Has worked as a teacher, lawyer and journalist; Senator for Kastamonu 61; Deputy Chair. of Justice Party, in Senate until 73; Minister of Agriculture 73-74; Justice Party.
c/o Ministry of Agriculture, Ankara, Turkey.

Turki, Brahim; Tunisian diplomatist; b. 13 Nov. 1930.
Teacher of Arabic until 56; Admin., Secr. of State for Foreign Affairs 56-59, Head Dept. of Econ. Affairs 59; econs. course UN Gen. Secr. 59-60; Counsellor Ministry of Foreign Affairs 60-61; Principal Private Sec. to Sec. of State for Foreign Affairs 61-62; rank of Minister Plenipotentiary 62; Consul-Gen., Paris 62-65; Minister, Tunisian Embassy, Algeria 65-67; Dir. Political Affairs, Ministry of Foreign Affairs 67-70; Amb. to The Netherlands 70-73, to U.K. March 74-; participated in many sessions of UN Gen. Assembly and OAU; Commdr. Order of Repub. of Tunisia; many foreign decorations.
Tunisian Embassy, 29 Prince's Gate, London, S.W.7, England.

Tutunji, Djamil, M.D.; Jordanian doctor and diplomatist; b. 1896; ed. Syrian Protestant Coll., Homs, American Univ. of Beirut and Medical Univ., Constantinople.
Medical Officer, Ottoman Army 18, Madeba District 19-22, Arab Legion 23; Royal Physician 23-40; Dir. of Health 40-50; Dep. Minister of Health 50-51, Minister 51-62; mem. Senate 62-63; Amb. to U.S.S.R. 64-65; Senator 67-71; Star of Jordan, Knight of St. John of Jerusalem, Knight of the Holy Sepulchre, Decoration of Revolution and of Independence.
P.O. Box 643, Amman, Jordan.

Tzur, Michael; Israeli shipping executive; b. 1 May 1923; ed. Tel-Aviv Univ.
Service with Ministry of Commerce and Industry and the Treasury 51-66; Dir.-Gen. Ministry of Commerce and Industry 58-66; Chair. of Board of Dirs. Zim Israel Navigation Co. 66-; Man. Israel Corpn. until 74.
Zim Israel Navigation Co. Ltd., 209 Hameginim Avenue, Haifa, Israel.

U

Ulay, Sitki; Turkish army officer; b. 1907; ed. War Acad. Ankara.
Has served as Military Attaché in Egypt and Afghanistan; Commandant, War School; Minister of Communications 60-Jan. 61; Minister of State 61-62; founder Social Democratic Party later incorporated with Republican People's Party; elected to Supreme Consultative Assembly of R.P.P.; mem. Senate; mem. Council of Admin., Vakıflar Bankası (Foundations Bank) 70.
Publ. *Harbiye Silah Başına (Alarm to War School)* 66.
Evkaf Apt. 1/3-3, Ankara, Turkey.

Ulfat, Gul Pacha; Afghan poet and writer; b. 1909; ed. private studies.
Staff writer *Anis* (daily) 35-36; Writers' Soc. 36; later mem. staff *Islah* (daily); Editor *Kabul Magazine* 46; Editor *Nangrahar* (weekly) 48; Chief of Tribal Affairs in Nangrahar Province; mem. House of Reps. from Jalalabad (Nangrahar), and Second Deputy to Pres. of House 49, mem. from Karghaie 52; Pres. of Afghan Acad. 56, Afghan-U.S.S.R. Friendship Soc. 59-63, Tribal Affairs (mem. Central Cabinet) 63-65; Rep. in Wolise Jerga (formerly House of Reps.) from Jalalabad 65-69.
Publs. Twenty-five books on literary, social and political subjects, and numerous essays.
Sher Shah Maina, Kabul, Afghanistan.

Umri, Gen. Hassan (see Amri, Gen. H.).

Uqaili, Maj.-Gen. Abdul Aziz al-; Iraqi army officer and politician; b. 1920; ed. Military Coll., Artillery School, Staff Coll., Baghdad, Staff Coll., Camberley, England, and Law Acad., Baghdad.
Army service 38-; Instructor, later Senior Instructor, Staff Coll., Baghdad; Ambassador to Iran Feb. 59; arrested in Mosul Revolt March 59, acquitted Sept. 59; Dir.-Gen. Iraqi Ports Admin. Feb.-April 63; rejected appt. of Ambassador to Japan July 63; Dir.-Gen. Iraqi Ports Admin. 63-65; Minister of Defence Sept. 65-66; under detention 69.
Publs. *History of the First Barzan Insurrection 1931* and articles in various journals.
Nassah No. 24/9/1, Adhamiah, Baghdad, Iraq.

Ürgüplü, Suat Hayri; Turkish diplomatist and politician; b. 1903; ed. Galatasaray Lycée and Univ. of Istanbul.
Lawyer; mem. Parl. 39-43; Minister of Customs and Monopolies in Sarajoğlu Govt. 43-46, resigned and left People's Party; re-elected to Grand Nat. Assembly 50 with support of Democratic Party which he subsequently joined; mem. and Vice-Pres. Council of Europe 50-52; Amb. to Fed. Repub. of Germany 52-55, to United Kingdom 55-57, to U.S.A. 57-60, to Spain 60; Independent Senator and Speaker of Senate 61-63; Prime Minister Jan.-Oct. 65, 72; Chair. Senate Foreign Affairs Cttee. 66-68, Culture and Art Foundation of Istanbul; Pres. Turkish Section, European League for Econ. Co-operation; Hon. mem. and Kt. of Mark Twain Soc.; Fed. Grand Cross of Merit with Star and Sash; Grand Cross, Order of Merit, Fed. Repub. of Germany.
Yapi ve Kredi Bankasi, Istanbul; Home: Sahil Cad. 19, Yesilyure, Istanbul, Turkey.

Ussoskin, Moshe; Israeli social worker; b. 8 March 1899, Moghileiv-Podolsk, Russia; ed. Cernauti Univ.
Zionist work in Bessarabia 17; Controller Bank Moldova Bucharest and Co-Dir. Branche Reni 18-28; Dir. American Joint Distribution Cttee. and Foundation for Hungary, Turkey and Balkan countries 28-41; Dir. Cen. Bank for Jewish Co-operatives in Romania 33-41; in Israel 41-; Senior Officer Migdal Ins. Co. Jerusalem 41-48; exec. comm. Union Credit Co-operatives 42-47; Dir.-Gen. and

Treas. *Keren Hayessod* United Israel Appeal 49-68; Vice-Chair. Tel-Aviv Devt. Co.; mem. Board Israel Land Devt. Co., Jerusalem Econ. Corpn., Binjaneh Haumah Ltd., and others; mem. Presidium of Credit Co-operatives in Palestine 42-47, of World Fed. of Bessarabian Jews; Board of Govs. Hebrew Univ. Jerusalem; has organized much relief work for refugees.

Publs. Co-Editor of co-operative monthly *Die Genossenschaft Czernowitz-Bukovina; Social Welfare among Jews in Bessarabia, Social Welfare among Jews in Saloniki (Greece)*, and many articles on co-operative, economic, zionist, and Jewish matters in many languages.
16 Arlosoroff Street, Jerusalem 92181, Israel.

Uzan, Aharon; Israeli agriculturist; b. Tunisia.
Emigrated to Israel 49; co-founder, settler, Moshav Ghilat, in Negev 49, Sec., later Head of supply network; mem. Knesset (Parl.) 65-69; Deputy Minister of Agriculture 66-69; Gen. Sec. Tnuat Hamoshavim 70-74; Minister of Communications March-June 74, of Agriculture June 74-; Labour Party.
Ministry of Agriculture, Jerusalem, Israel.

Uzuner, Ali Riza; Turkish politician; b. 1 April 1926, Of, Trabzon; ed. secondary school, Erzurum, and Faculty of Forestry.
Carried out research in various branches of forestry in Sweden for three years; Dir. Forestry Research Inst. until 61; mem. Parl. (Republican People's Party) 61-73; Minister of Labour 71-73; mem. Nat. Security Council; now engaged as Expert, Ministry of Forestry.
Republican People's Party, Uludag Sok. 13/6, Maltepe, Ankara, Turkey.

V

Vahidi, Iraj, C.E., D.P.H.E.; PH.D.; Iranian politician; b. 1927, Khorramshahr; ed. Univs. of Teheran and Durham.
Engineer, Ministry of Roads; mem. Board of Dirs., Independent Irrigation Inst., subsequently Man. Dir.; Technical Asst. to Ministry of Water and Power; Man. Dir. Khouzestan Water and Power Authority; Minister of Agriculture 71, of Water and Power 71-74, of Energy 74-.
Ministry of Energy, Teheran, Iran.

Vajda, Georges; French professor; b. 18 Nov. 1908; ed. Séminaire Rabbinique, Budapest, and Paris, Ecole des Langues Orientales and Sorbonne.
Prof., Séminaire Israélite de France 36-; Lecturer, Ecole Pratique des Hautes Etudes, Sorbonne 37, Dir. 54-; Head of Oriental Section, Inst. de Recherche et d'Histoire des Textes 40-; Prof. Univ. de Paris 70-; Sec. Société des Etudes Juives.
Publs. *Introduction à la Pensée Juive du Moyen Age* 47, *La Théologie ascétique de Bahya ibn Paquda* 47, *Répertoire des Catalogues et Inventaires de Manuscrits Arabes* 49, *Un Recueil de Textes Historiques Judéo-Marocains* 51, *Inventaire des Manuscrits Arabes Musulmans de la Bibliothèque Nationale* 53, *Juda ben Nissim Ibn Malka, philosophe juif marocain* 54, *Les certificats de lecture dans les manuscrits arabes de la Bibliothèque Nationale* 57, *L'amour de Dieu dans la théologie juive du moyen âge* 57, *Isaac Albalag* 60, *Recherches sur les relations entre la Philosophie et la Kabbale* 62, *Le Dictionnaire des Autorités de 'Abd al-Mu'min ad-Dimyati* 62, *Le commentaire d'Ezra de Gérone sur le Cantique* 69, *Deux commentaires Karaïtes sur l'Ecclésiaste* 71, *Revue des Etudes Juives* (Editor).
Institut de Recherche et d'Histoire des Textes, 40 avenue d'Iéna, 75016 Paris; and 51 rue Sainte-Placide, 75006 Paris, France.

Valian, Abdol-Azim, B.A., PH.D.; Iranian politician; b. 1925, Teheran; ed. Univ. of Teheran and Military Faculty of Teheran.
Commissioned army officer; Dir. Org. of Land Reform; official, Ministry of Agriculture; Minister of Land Reform and Rural Co-operatives 71-74.
c/o Ministry of Land Reform and Co-operatives, Teheran, Iran.

Vanden Berghe, Louis, PH.D.; Belgian oriental archaeologist; b. 24 Dec. 1923; ed. Univs. of Ghent, Brussels, Amsterdam and Leyden.
At Univ. of Ghent, Assoc. Prof. 53-57, Prof. of Western Asiatic Archaeology and Civilizations 57-; Prof. of History and Archaeology of Ancient Iran, Univ. of Brussels 58-; Curator of the Iran Dept. of Musées Royaux d'Art et d'Histoire, Brussels 66-; Visiting Prof., Rome Univ. 65; Dir. Belgian Archaeological Expedition in Iran 65-; explorations and excavations in S. Iran 51-64; discoveries include several new prehistoric cultures, unknown Elamite, Parthian and Sassanid Rock-Reliefs, the great Kunar Siah complex and other Sassanid Fire Temples; mem. Royal Acad. of Sciences, Letters and Arts, Belgium (Chair. 73); Corresp. mem. German Archaeological Inst., Berlin; Hon. Dr. Teheran Univ.; Iranian Orders of Homayoun and of Sepass; Officer of the Order of Leopold.
Publs. Co-Editor of *Iranica Antiqua*, Author of *Archéologie de l'Iran Ancien* 59, 66, *La nécropole de Khurvin* 64, *Art Iranian Ancien, préhistoire, protohistoire* 66, *Opgravingen in Pusht-i Kuh, I Kalwali en War Kabud* 68, *On the Track of the Civilizations of Ancient Iran* 68, and many publs. on the excavations in Luristan, Iran.
Department of Western Asiatic Archaeology and Civilizations, University of Ghent, Blandijnberg, 2 Ghent; Home: Oost-Nieuwkerke, Belgium.

van der Meulen, Daniel; Netherlands author and explorer; b. 1894; ed. Arnhem, and Univ. of Leyden.
Dutch East India Civil Service 15-23, 32-41, 45-48; Neths. Consul, Jeddah 26-31; Minister to Saudi Arabia 41-45; Adviser to Lieut. Gov.-Gen. van Mook, Java 45-48; organiser and leader Arabic broadcasts, Neths. Radio, Hilversum 48-50; exploration of S.W. Arabia 31, 39, 43, 52, 58-59, 62-63, 64, 67, 71, 72; hon. mem. Netherlands Royal Geographical Soc.; Patron's Medal, Royal Geographical Soc., London 47; Order Orange Nassau (Neths.).
Publs. *Hadhramaut, Some of its Mysteries Unveiled* 32, *Aden to The Hadhramaut* in English 47, Swedish and German, *Onbekend Arabië* 51, *Ontwakend Arabië* 53, *The Life Story of King Ibn Saud of Saudi Arabia* (in Indonesian, Dutch and English) 52, revised edn. 57, re-titled *The Wells of Ibn Saud, Faces in Shem* 61, *Ik Stond Erbij* 64, *Verdwijnend Arabie, Mijn Weg Naar Arabië en de Islam*.
9 Flierderweg, Gorssel, Netherlands.

W

Waely, Faisal el-, PH.D.; Iraqi professor and government official; b. 1922; ed. Teacher-Training Coll., Baghdad and Oriental Inst. of Chicago.
Professor, Baghdad Univ. (Coll. of Literature) 53-56; Dir.-Gen. of Technical Affairs, Ministry of Education, Baghdad 58-59; Prof. Cairo Univ. 59-63; Dir.-Gen. of Antiquities, Baghdad 63-.
Publs. Various articles in journal *Sumer*.
Directorate-General of Antiquities, Baghdad West, Iraq.

Wahrhaftig, Zorach, D. JUR.; Israeli lawyer and politician; b. Warsaw 2 Feb. 1906; ed. Univ. of Warsaw.
Private law practice, Warsaw 32-39; Vice-Pres. Mizrachi, Poland 26-39; mem. of exec., Keren Hayesod, Hechalutz

Hamizrachi, World Jewish Congress; Deputy Dir. Inst. of Jewish Affairs, New York 43-47; Vice-Pres. Hapoel Hamizrachi, U.S.A. 43-47; Dir. Vaad Leumi Law Dept. 47; mem. Provisional Council, Govt. of Israel 49; mem. of Knesset; Dep. Minister for Religious Affairs 56-59, Minister of Religious Affairs 62-74; Chair. Constitution, Law and Justice Cttee., Knesset; mem. Jewish Law Research Inst., Ministry of Justice 48; Lecturer on Talmudic Law, Hebrew Univ.; mem. American Soc. for Int. Law, Board of Trustees, Bar-Ilan Univ.
Publs. *Starvation over Europe* 43, *Relief and Rehabilitation* 44, *Where Shall They Go?* 46, *Uprooted* 46, *Hazaka in Jewish Law* 64, and many publs. in Hebrew on Israel Law and Religion.
The Knesset, Jerusalem, Israel.

Weckmann-Muñoz, Luis, PH.D., LL.D., M.A.; Mexican diplomatist and historian; b. 7 April 1923, Ciudad Lerdo, Durango; ed. Nat. Univ. of Mexico, Univs. of Paris and Calif., Inst. des Hautes Etudes Int. and Ecole des Chartes, Paris.
Successively Sec. of Legation and Chargé d'Affaires, Czechoslovakia, Sec. of Embassy and Chargé d'Affaires, France 52-59; Dir.-Gen. for Int. Educ. Affairs and Exec. Sec.-Gen. Mexican Nat. Council for UNESCO 59-64; Minister Plenipotentiary and Chargé d'Affaires, France 65-66; Amb. to Israel 67-69, to Austria 69-72, to Fed. Repub. of Germany 73-74; Special Rep. of UN Sec.-Gen. to Iran and Iraq April-June 74; Special Rep. of UN Sec.-Gen. in Cyprus 74-; Vice-Pres. 1st Interamerican meeting on Science and Technology, Washington; UNESCO's expert for Latin America on Cultural Exchanges.
Publs. *La Sociedad Feudal* 44, *Las Bulas Alejandrinas de 1943 y la Teoría Política del Papado Medieval* 49, *El Pensamiento Político Medieval y una nueva base para el Derecho Internacional* 50, *Les origines des Missions Diplomatiques Permanentes* 53, *Panorama de la Cultura Medieval* 62, *Les Relaciones Franco-Mexicanas (1823-1885)* vol. I 61, vol. II 63, vol. III 72.
United Nations Peace-Keeping Force in Cyprus, P.O. Box 1642, Nicosia, Cyprus.

Weisgal, Meyer Wolf; American journalist and executive; b. 11 Oct. 1894; ed. Columbia Univ.
National Secretary Zionist Org. of America 21-30; Dir.-Gen. Palestine Pavilion, World's Fair, New York 39-40; Personal Political Rep. Dr. Weizmann in U.S.A. 40-48; Organiser, American Section Jewish Agency for Palestine, Sec.-Gen. 43-46; Organizer and Exec. Vice-Chair. American Cttee. Weizmann Inst. 46-59; Chair. Exec. Council Weizmann Inst. of Science, Israel 49-66, Pres. of Inst. 66-69, Chancellor 70-; del. World Zionist Congress 24-; fmr. Editor *The New Palestine* (New York) 21-30, *Jewish Standard* (Toronto) 30-32.
Publs. *Chaim Weizmann: Statesman, Scientist, Builder of the Jewish Commonwealth* 44, *Chaim Weizmann, a Biography by Several Hands* 62, *Meyer Weisgal ... So Far: An Autobiography*, *The Letters and Papers of Chaim Weizmann* (editor) 73 and numerous Jewish and Zionist pamphlets, etc.
14 Neveh Weizmann, Rehovot, Israel; and 240 Central Park South, New York 19, N.Y., U.S.A.

Weitz, Raanan, PH.D.; Israeli rural development planner; b. 27 July 1913; ed. Hebrew Gymnasia, Jerusalem Hebrew Univ. and Univ. of Florence.
Agricultural Settlement Dept., Jewish Agency 37-, fmr. Village Instructor, now Head of Dept.; service with Intelligence Corps, British 8th Army, Second World War; fmr. mem. Haganah; mem. Exec., Zionist Org. 63-; Chair. Nat. and Univ. Inst. of Agriculture 60-66; Head, Settlement Study Centre 63-; Prof. of Rural Devt. Planning, Univ. of Haifa 73-.

Publs. *Agriculture and Rural Development in Israel: Projection and Planning* 63, *Rural Planning in Developing Countries* (Editor) 65, *Agricultural Development—Planning and Implementation* 68, *From Peasant to Farmer: A Revolutionary Strategy for Development* 71, *Rural Development in a Changing World* (Editor) 71, *Urbanization and the Developing Countries, Report on the Sixth Rehovot Conference* (Editor) 73.
Zionist Organization, P.O. Box 92, Jerusalem; Home: Moshav Ora, Mare-Yehuda Mobile P.O., Israel.

Weizman, Ezer; Israeli politician and air force officer (retd.); b. 15 June 1924; ed. Hareali School, Haifa and R.A.F. Staff Coll.
Served in first Israeli fighting squadron, War of Independence 48; founded Israeli Air Force Air Staff 52-53; commanded fighter wing 53-56, in Sinai Campaign 56-57; Head of Air Div., Israeli Air Force 57-58; Commdr. I.A.F. 58-66; Head of Gen. Staff Div., Israeli Defence Force 66-69; Minister of Transportation 69-70, resigned with other Gahal Ministers; Dir. Maritime Fruit Carriers Ltd. 70; Chair. Exec. Cttee., Herut Party 71-72.
28 Hageffen Street, Ramat, Hasheram, Israel.

Wise, George S.; American university professor; b. Poland 1906; ed. Columbia Univ.
Former lecturer in Sociology at Columbia Univ. and Univ. of Mexico; business interests in U.S.A., Mexico and Israel; Pres. Tel-Aviv Univ. 63-71, Chancellor 71-.
Tel-Aviv University, Ramat-Aviv, Tel-Aviv, Israel.

Witkon, Alfred, DR.JUR.; Israeli judge; b. 23 Feb. 1910; ed. Univs. of Bonn, Berlin and Freiburg, and Middle Temple, London.
Called to Middle Temple Bar 36, to Palestine Bar 37; practised law, Palestine 37-48; Pres. District Court, Jerusalem 48; Justice, Supreme Court of Israel 54-.
Publs. *Law and Society* 55, *The Law of Taxation* 69, *Law and Politics* 65.
17 Shmaryahu Lewin Street, Jerusalem, Israel.

Y

Yaacobi, Gad, M.SC.; Israeli politician; b. 1935, Moshav Kfar Vitkin; ed. Tel-Aviv Univ., School of Law and Econs Member Moshavim Movt. 60-67; Asst. to Minister of Agriculture, Head of Agriculture and Settlement Planning and Devt. Centre 60-66; mem. Cen. Cttee. Histadrut, Labour Union, Rafi Faction 66-; Chair. Econ. Council Rafi Faction 66-67; mem. Cen. Cttee., Secr. Labour Party; Asst. to Sec. Labour Party 66-70; mem. Parl. (Knesset) 69-, Parl. Finance Cttee. 69-70, Parl. Defence and Foreign Affairs Cttee. 74, Deputy Minister of Transport 70-74, Minister June 74-.
Publs. *The Quality of Power* 71, and many articles on economics and politics.
Ministry of Transport, Jerusalem, Israel.

Yadin (formerly Sukenik), **Lt.-Gen. Yigael,** M.A., PH.D.; Israeli soldier and archaeologist; b. 21 March 1917; ed. Hebrew Univ., Jerusalem.
Chief of Gen. Staff Branch, Haganah H.Q. 47; Chief of Operations, Gen. Staff, Israel Defence Forces 48 Chief of; Gen. Staff Branch 49, Chief of Staff 49-52; Archæological Research Fellow, Hebrew Univ. 53-54; Lecturer in Archæology, Hebrew Univ. 55-59, Assoc. Prof. 59-63, Prof. 63-; Dir. Hazor Excavations 55-58, 69, Bar Kochba Excavations 60-61, Megiddo Excavations 60, 66-67, 70-71, Masada Excavations 63-65; mem. Israel Acad. of Sciences and Humanities; corresp. mem. British and French Acads.
Publs. *The Scroll of the War of the Sons of Light against the*

Sons of Darkness 55, *The Message of the Scrolls* 57, *Hazor I: The First Season of Excavations*, *Hazor II: Second Season*, *Hazor III-IV: Third Season*, *A Genesis Apocryphon* (with N. Avigad) 56, *Warfare in Biblical Lands* 63, *Finds in a cave in the Judaean Desert* 63, *Masada: First Season of Excavations* 65, *The Ben-Sirah Scroll from Masada* 65, *Masada: Herod's Fort and the Zealots' Last Stand* 66, *Philacteries from Qumran* 69, *Bar-Kochba* 71, *Hazor* (Schweich Lectures) 72, *Hazor* 75.
47 Ramban Road, Jerusalem, Israel.

Yadlin, Aharon; Israeli politician; b. 17 April 1926; ed. Hebrew Univ.
Co-founder Kibbutz Hatzerim; fmr. mem. Presidium, Israel Scouts Movement; mem. Knesset (Parl.) 59-; Deputy Minister of Educ. and Culture 64-72; Gen. Sec. Israel Labour Party 72-; Minister of Educ. and Culture June 74-.
Ministry of Education and Culture, Jerusalem, Israel.

Yafi, Abdullah al-; Lebanese lawyer and politician; b. 1901; ed. Univ. of Paris.
Admitted to Beirut Bar 26; Prime Minister and Minister of Justice 38-39; Minister of Justice and Finance 47; mem. Lebanese del. to Preparatory Conf. for founding League of Arab States 44, to UN San Francisco Conf. 45; Prime Minister 54 and 56; in private practice 56-66; Prime Minister 66, also Minister of Finance and Information 66; Prime Minister 68-69.
Rue Fouad 1er, Beirut, Lebanon.

Yahia, General Tahir; Iraqi army officer and politician; b. 1915; ed. primary school, Tikrit, secondary school, Baghdad, Teachers' Training Coll. and Military Coll.
Former teacher, Mamounia School, Baghdad; mem. Nat. Movement 41; Commdr., Armoured Cars' Battalion, Palestine War 48; mem. Military Court, Habaniya 48; mem. Free Officers' Group 58, later Dir.-Gen. of Police; Chief of Staff, Iraqi Army Feb.-Nov. 63; Prime Minister 63-65; Deputy Prime Minister 67; Prime Minister and acting Minister of the Interior 67-68; Al-Khidma Medal, Al-Chaja Medal, Al-Rafidain Medal.
Baghdad, Iraq.

Yamani, Ahmed Zaki; Saudi Arabian politician; b. 1930, Mecca; ed. Cairo Univ., New York Univ. and Harvard Univ.
Saudi Arabian Govt. service; private law practice; Legal Adviser to Council of Ministers 58-60; Minister of State 60-62; mem. Council of Ministers 60-; Minister of Petroleum and Mineral Resources 62-; Dir. Arabian American Oil Co. 62-; Chair. Board of Dirs. Gen. Petroleum and Mineral Org. (PETROMIN) 63-, Coll. of Petroleum and Minerals, Dhahran 63-; Chair., Board of Dirs. Saudi Arabian Fertilizer Co. (SAFCO) 66-; Sec. Gen. Org. of Arab Petroleum Exporting Countries (OAPEC) 68-69; mem. several int. law asscns.
Publ. *Islamic Law and Contemporary Issues.*
Ministry of Petroleum and Mineral Resources, Riyadh, Saudi Arabia.

Yariv, Brig.-Gen. Aharon; Israeli army officer; b. 1920, Latvia; ed. French Staff Coll.
Emigrated to Palestine 35; Capt. British Army 41-46; Haganah 46-47; various posts with Northern Command, Israel Defence Forces 48-50, Operations Div., H.Q. 51; IDF Officers' Staff Coll. 52-56; Mil. Attaché, Washington and Ottawa 57-60; joined Mil. Intelligence 61, Dir. until 72; Special Adviser to the Prime Minister Oct. 72-73; mem. Knesset 74-; Minister of Transport March-June 74, of Information June 74-Jan. 75.
c/o Ministry of Information, Jerusalem, Israel.

Yasin, Abdul-Hamid; Jordanian educationist and administrator; b. 1908; ed. Teachers' Coll. Jerusalem and American Univ. Cairo.
Teacher 24-36; Broadcaster and translator, Jerusalem 36-42; Labour and Co-operatives Inspector, Jerusalem 42-46; mem. Arab Information Office, Jerusalem 46-47; Town Clerk, Jaffa 47-48; Registrar and instructor, American Univ. Cairo 48-52, Dean of Educ. Faculty 52-53; Principal, Teachers' Coll., Amman 53-60; UNESCO Adviser on Educ., Libya 60-62; Sec.-Gen. Jordan Univ. 62-64; Head of UNRWA Educ. Dept., Jerusalem 64-65; mem. Exec. Cttee. and Del. to Arab League, Palestine Liberation Org., Jerusalem and Cairo 65-66; Dir.-Gen. Housing Corpn., Amman 66-67; Dir.-Gen. Broadcasting 67-68; Counsellor, Ministry of Educ. 68-, Dir. Public Admin. Inst. Amman 68-70; Editor *Journal of Modern Education*, Cairo 52-53, *Teacher's Message*, Amman 56-60.
Publs. *Short Stories* (Arabic) 46, *10 Short Stories* (Arabic) 59; Translations: *Overstreet, The Mind Goes Forth* 60, and contributions on education to magazines, papers and broadcasts.
c/o Institute of Public Administration, Amman, Jordan.

Yasseen, Mustafa Kamil, D. EN D.; Iraqi international lawyer; b. 1920, Iraq; ed. Univs. of Baghdad, Cairo and Paris.
Member, Baghdad Bar 42; Lecturer in Private Int. and Penal Law 50, Asst. Prof. 54; Prof. and Head, Dept. of Int. Law, Univ. of Baghdad 59; Gen. Dir. Political Dept., Ministry of Foreign Affairs 59, Dept. of Int. Orgs. 64; Amb. and Perm. Rep. to Office of UN, Geneva 66; Gen. Dir. Dept. of Int. Orgs., Ministry of Foreign Affairs 71-; mem. Perm. Court of Arbitration; mem. UN Int. Law Comm. 60-, Pres. 66; Assoc. Inst. of Int. Law 61, mem. 71; mem. Curatorium, Hague Acad. of Int. Law; Corresp. mem. Acad. of Legislation, Toulouse; Iraqi rep. to several int. confs., to Vienna Conf. on the Law of Treaties 68, 69, Chair. of Drafting Cttee., to Council of UNCTAD 66-69, to Gov. Body, ILO 66-69, to UN Gen. Assemblies 58-, to various UN, ILO confs., etc.; Dr. h.c. (Nice) 70; Grand Cross of Civil Merit (Spain); Grand Officer, Nat. Order of Merit (France); Commdr. Order of the Crown (Morocco).
Publs. various books and articles on int. law.
Ministry of Foreign Affairs, Baghdad, Iraq.

Yassein, Mohammed Osman, B.SC.(ECON.); Sudanese international civil servant; b. 1915; ed. Khartoum and London School of Economics.
Joined Sudanese Political Service 45; Liaison Officer in Ethiopia 52-53; Gov. Upper Nile Province 54-55; Perm. Under-Sec. of Foreign Affairs 56-65; mem. Sudanese del. to UN 56; Del. to Independent African States Conf., Monrovia 59, to Accra Conf. on Positive Action for Peace and Security in Africa 60, to Independent African States Conf., Léopoldville 60; Special Adviser to UN on training of diplomatists 61-62; Special Envoy to Ethiopia and Somalia on border dispute; mem. African Unity Org. Comm. for Conciliation and Arbitration between Algeria and Morocco; Organizer, African Finance Ministers first Conf., Khartoum 63, Grading Structure and Salaries Comm. of Zambia 66; joined UN Office of Technical Co-operation 66; Resident Rep. UN Devt. Programme (UNDP), Jordan 70-; Hon. mem. Inst. of Differing Civilizations, Brussels; Kt. Great Band of Humane Order of African Redemption (Liberia), Grand Officer, Order of Menelik II, Republican Order (Egypt), Star of Yugoslavia, First Order of Independence (Jordan).
Publs. *The Sudan Civil Service* 54, *Analysis of the Economic Situation in the Sudan* 58, *Problems of Transfer of Power— the Administration Aspect* 61, *Germany and Africa* 62; in Arabic: *The Poets' Ballads*, *Tewfiq the Poet*.
United Nations Development Programme, P.O.B. 565, Amman, Jordan; Home: P.O. Box 2201, Khartoum, Sudan.

Yassin, Aziz Ahmed, PH.D., D.I.C., B.SC.; Egyptian consulting engineer; b. 13 Aug. 1918; ed. Abbassia Secondary School, Cairo Univ., and Imperial Coll., London. Ministry of Housing and Public Utilities, rising to Under-Sec. of State 39-59; Dir.-Gen., Vice-Chair. Building Research Centre 54-59, Chair., Pres. Tourah Portland Cement Co., Alexandria Portland Cement Co. 59-63; mem. Board of Dirs. Helwan Portland Cement Co., Sudan Portland Cement Co. 59-63; Chair. Egyptian Cement Cos. Marketing Board 59-63; Chair., Pres. Egyptian Gen. Org. for Housing and Public Building Contracting Cos. 63-65; Minister of Tourism and Antiquities 65-67, of Housing and Construction 66-68; mem. Board of Aswan High Dam Authority 66-68; External Prof. of Soil Mechanics, Cairo Univ. 51-, of Civil Engineering, Ain Shams Univ.; mem. Building Research and Technology Council, Egyptian Acad. of Science and Technology 72-; Sec.-Gen. Federation of Arab Engineers (FAE) 75; mem. several other scientific civil engineering and building orgs.; Order of the Repub. 1st Class, Order of the Banner (Hungary), Commdr.'s Cross with Star of Order of Resurrection of Poland. Publs. *Model Studies on the Bearing Capacity of Piles* 51, *Bearing Capacity of Deep Foundations in Clay Soils*, *Testing Sand Dry Samples with the Tri-axial Apparatus* 53, *Bearing Capacity of Piles* 53, *The Industry of Building Materials in Egypt* 57.
4 Waheeb Doas Street, Maadi, Cairo, Egypt.

Yazıcı, Bedi, M.SC.; Turkish business executive; b. 1917; ed. Robert Coll., Columbia Univ.
Fire and Marine Man. Nat. Reinsurance Co. 43-48; Prof. of Insurance, Business School of Istanbul 45-50; Man. Dir. The Credit Bank of Turkey 62-63, Porcelain Industries Inc. of Istanbul 62-63; Pres. The Gen. Insurance Co. of Turkey 48-63, Istanbul Chamber of Commerce 60-63; mem. Insurance Board, Ministry of Commerce 44-64; Chair. and Man. Dir. TAM Insurance Co. 64-74; TAM Life Insurance Co. 66-74; Chair. and Man. Dir. AKSIGORTA Insurance Co. 74-; Trustee, Robert Coll. 64-.
Aksu Han, Karakoy, Istanbul, Turkey.

Yazıcı, Bülent, M.S.; Turkish banker; b. 3 Feb. 1911; ed. Robert Coll., Istanbul, and Columbia Univ.
Ministry of Finance 34-38; Insp. 38-45; Financial Counsellor, Turkish Embassy, Washington 45-49; Dep. Gen. Dir. Dept. of the Treasury 49-50; Dep. Gen. Man. Industrial Development Bank of Turkey 50-60; Dir. and Gen. Man. Türkiye İş Bankası A.S. 60-67; Chair. American-Turkish Foreign Trade Bank 64-67, Union of Chambers of Commerce, Industry and Exchanges of Turkey 60-62; Vice-Chair. Asscn. of Banks of Turkey 60-67; Chair. Industrial Devt. Bank of Turkey 60-69, Man. Dir. 69-71; Dir. Tam Hayat Sigorta A.S. 67-; Advisory Bd. Unilever-İş Ticaret ve Sanayi, Sti 68-; Chair. and Man. Dir. Akbank TAŞ 71-; Chair. Akcimento A.Ş., Cimsa A.Ş., Turkish Management Educ. Foundation; Commodore, Deniz Klubu.
36 Devriye Sok., Moda, Kadıköy, Istanbul, Turkey.

Yeganeh, Mohammed, M.A.; Iranian economist; b. 5 May 1923; ed. Teheran Univ., Columbia Univ., New York.
Economic Affairs Officer, UN Middle East Studies Section 49-58; UNDP Adviser to Govt. of Tunisia 58-59; Head UN Industrial Section 59-64; Deputy Minister for Econ. Affairs 64-69; Minister of Devt. and Housing 69-70; Special Econ. Adviser to Prime Minister 70-71; Alt. Exec. Dir. for Middle East, Int. Bank for Reconstruction and Devt. 71-72; Exec. Dir. Int. Monetary Fund 72-73; Gov. Cen. Bank of Iran Aug. 73-; Homayoun Medal 66, Devt. Medal 67.
Publs. *Suspension of Penalties* 46, *Foreign Trade and Commercial Policies of Iran* 50, *Investments in the Petroleum Industry of the Middle East* 52, *Perspectives décennales des*

développements économiques en Tunisie 60, *Economics of the Middle Eastern Oil* (with Charles Issawa, *q.v.*) 62, *Reflections on the Teheran Oil Agreement* 71, *Possibilities for Co-operation among Developing Countries in Development Utilization of Natural Gas* 71.
Bank Markazi Iran, Ferdowsi Avenue, Teheran, Iran.

Yemen, Former King of the (*see* Saif Al-Islam Mohamed Al-Badr, H.M. The Imam).

Yeshayahu, Yisrael; Israeli politician; b. 14 April 1910, Yemen.
Settled in Israel 29; Head, Dept. for Yemenites and Eastern Communities, Histadrut 34-38; delegated by Histadrut and Israeli Govt. to organize operation "Magic Carpet" (mass airlift of Yemenite Jews to Israel) 48; mem. Labour Party 49-; founder of 45 co-operative settlements for Yemenite Jews; del. to Zionist congresses, to Assefat Hanivharim; perm. collaborator on Hapoel Hazair, Davar, etc.; Deputy Speaker of Knesset 55-66, 70-72, Speaker 72-, Chair. Knesset House Cttee. 70-72; Minister of Posts 66-69; mem. Cen. Cttee., Histadrut; mem. leading bodies of Labour Party, Sec.-Gen. Labour Party 71-72.
Publs. research in Yemenite folklore; *Miteiman le-Zion*, *Shvut Teiman*, *Shevatim ve-Edot be Kur Ha-Histadrut*; Editor: *Maslul*, *Shluhot* (periodicals).
The Knesset Building, Jerusalem; and 49, Homa u-Migdal Street, Holon, Israel.

Yetkin, Suut Kemal; Turkish scholar; b. 1903; ed. Univs. of Paris and Rennes.
Asst. Prof. of History of Art and Aesthetics, Univ. of Istanbul 33-36; Dir.-Gen. of Fine Arts, Ministry of Education 39-41; Prof. of History of Art and Aesthetics, Ankara Univ. 41-50, of History of Turkish and Islamic Arts 50-59; Rector Ankara Univ. 59-63; Prof. of Turkish Art, Columbia Univ. 63-64; Officier Légion d'Honneur; Republican Party.
Publs. (in Turkish) *Philosophy of Art* 34, *Courses in Aesthetics* 42, *Literary Doctrines* 43, *Speeches on Literature* 44, *The Art of Leonardo da Vinci* 45, *Art Problems* 45, *On Literature* 53, *Famous Painters* 55, *A. Gide: A Selection of his Critical Writings* 55, *History of Islamic Architecture* 59 (3rd edn. 65), *Problems in Art* 62, *Turkish Architecture* 65, *Currents in Literature* 67, *Essays* 72, *Baroque Art* 74, *Art in Islamic Countries* 74; (in French) *L'Architecture turque en Turquie* 62, *Ancienne Peinture Turque* 70.
Kavaklidere Sok., Güney Apartman 23/5, Ankara, Turkey.

Yoseph, Ovadya; Israeli Rabbi; b. Baghdad, Iraq.
Member, Sephard Rabbinical Court 45; Chief of Rabbinical Court of Appeals and Deputy Chief Rabbi of Egypt (Cairo) 47; mem. regional Rabbinical Court of Petach Tiqva 51, Jerusalem 58; mem. Grand Court of Appeals, Jerusalem 65; Pres. of Great Metivta, Jerusalem; Pres. "Yeshivat Thora Ve-horaa", Tel-Aviv; mem. Management "Yeshivat Porath" Jerusalem; Pres. Cttee. of Building Fund for Yeshivat "Porath Yoseph" in the Old City; Chief Rabbi and Chief of Rabbinical Court of Tel-Aviv May 68-; Sephardi Chief Rabbi of Israel Oct. 72-; Rabbi Kook Prize, Rabbi Uziel Prize.
Publs. *Yobia Omer*, several vols. of Responsa, *Hazon Ovadia*.
Chief Rabbinate, 51 Hamelech David Boulevard, Tel-Aviv, Israel.

Younes, Mahmoud; Egyptian engineer; b. 3 April 1912; ed. Royal Coll. of Engineers, Cairo Univ. and Staff Officers' Coll.
Engineer 37; M.Sc. 42; with Mil. Operations Directorate 43; Lecturer, Staff Officers' Coll. 44 and 47; Dir. Technical Affairs Office, G.H.Q. 52; Man. Dir. and Chair. Gen. Petroleum Authority 54; Counsellor, Ministry of Commerce and Industry for Mineral Wealth; Man. Dir. and Chair. Suez

Canal Authority 56; Chair. 57-65; Pres. Engineers' Syndicate 54-65; Dir. and Chair. Cie. Orientale des Pétroles d'Egypte et Soc. Coopérative des Pétroles 58-65; mem. Nat. Assembly 64-; Deputy Prime Minister for Transport and Communications 65-66; for Electric Power, Oil and Mining 66-67, for Petroleum and Transport 67-68; Consultant, ENI. GP 68; now in private consulting office in Beirut; Order of Merit (Class I), Order of the Nile (Class III), Military Star, Liberation Medal, Palestine Medal, Grand Cordon of the Order of the Yugoslav Standard, Grand Officer Order of Vasco Núñez de Balboa (Panama), Repub. Medal (Class III), Mil. Service Medal (Class I), Order of the Repub. (Class I).
P.O.B. 7272, Beirut, Lebanon; and 26 July Street 21, Cairo, Egypt.

Yussof, Dr. Mohammed; Afghan politician.
Former Minister of Mines and Industries; Prime Minister and Minister of Foreign Affairs 63-65; Amb. to Fed. Repub. of Germany, Switzerland, Sweden, Denmark 66-73.
c/o Ministry of Foreign Affairs, Kabul, Afghanistan.

Z

Zabarsky, Abraham; Israeli banker; b. 29 March 1897; ed. Kharkov Univ.
Town Councillor, Tel-Aviv 25-50; Treas. Israeli Defence Forces 47-49, mission to U.S.A. 48-49; fmr. Chair. and Man. Dir. Bank Hapoalim B.M.; Gen. Man. Israel-American Industrial Devt. Bank Ltd.; Chair. Housing Mortgage Bank Ltd.; mem. Advisory Cttee. Bank of Israel; mem. Gen. Council of Histadrut; mem. Editorial Board *Economic Quarterly*; Dir. of several companies and del. to numerous Zionist congresses.
Publs. *Jewish Cooperative Movement in Palestine and Abroad, Labour Economy in Israel*, and numerous articles.
11 Keren Kayemeth Boulevard, Tel-Aviv, Israel.

Zadok, Haim; Israeli lawyer and politician; b. 2 Oct. 1913, Poland; ed. Ukraine, Warsaw Univ. and Jerusalem Law School.
Immigrated 35; took up private practice as lawer 45; with Haganah and Jewish Settlement Police until 48; Major in Reserve I.D.F., War of Independence; Deputy Attorney-Gen. 49-52; in private law practice 52-65, 67-74; Lecturer, Tel-Aviv Univ. 53-61; mem. Knesset 59-; mem. Advisory Council, Bank of Israel; Chair. Income Tax Reform Cttee.; Israel Del. to Council of Europe 61-65; Minister of Commerce and Industry May 65-66, concurrently Minister of Devt. May 65-66; Chair. Knesset Foreign Affairs and Defence Cttee. 70-74, mem. Constitutional, Legal and Judicial Cttee. until 74; Minister of Justice March 74-, of Religious Affairs June-Nov. 74; Chair. Exec. Cttee. Hebrew Univ., Jerusalem 69-74; Mapai.
Knesset Building, Jerusalem; and 31 Hamitnader Street, Afeka, Tel-Aviv, Israel.

Zahedi, Ardeshir, B.SC.; Iranian diplomatist; b. 17 Oct. 1928; ed. in Teheran, American Univ. of Beirut and State Univ. of Utah (U.S.A.).
Treasurer, Iran-American Comm. 50-52; Civil Adjutant to His Imperial Majesty the Shah of Iran 54-; Iranian Amb. to U.S.A. 60-62, to U.K. 62-66, to U.S.A. and Mexico 73-; Minister of Foreign Affairs 67-71; Hon. LL.D., Utah State Univ., Chungang Univ., Seoul, East Texas Univ. 73; numerous decorations.
Imperial Iranian Embassy, 3005 Massachusetts Avenue, N.W., Washington, D.C. 20008, U.S.A.

Zahedi, Hassan; Iranian politician; b. 1913; ed. Teheran Univ. and Columbia Univ., U.S.A.
Entered Government Service 36, in Agricultural Bank until 45; in U.S. and posts with UN 45-58; in Ministry of Finance 58-61; Pres. Agricultural Bank, Teheran 61-68; Minister of Agriculture 68-70; Minister of the Interior 70-71; Gov.-Gen. of Khorassan 71-.
Alam Avenue-Alam Street, Tajrich, Teheran, Iran.

Zahir, Abdul; Afghan politician; b. 1909, Lagham; ed. Habibia High School, Kabul and Columbia and Johns Hopkins Univs., U.S.A.
Practised medicine in U.S.A. before returning to Kabul 43; Chief Doctor, Municipal Hospital, Kabul 43-50; Deputy Minister of Health 50-55, Minister 55-58; Amb. to Pakistan 58-61; Chair. House of the People 61-64, 65-69; Deputy Prime Minister and Minister of Health 64-65; Amb. to Italy 69-71; Prime Minister 71-72.
c/o Office of the Prime Minister, Kabul, Afghanistan.

Zaid bin Sultan Al-Nihyan, H.H. Sheikh; President of the United Arab Emirates and Ruler of Abu Dhabi; b. 1918.
Governor of Eastern Province 46-66; deposed his brother Sheikh Shakhbut and succeeded to Sheikhdom 66; Pres. Fed. of Arabian Emirates 69-71; Pres. United Arab Emirates (U.A.E.) 71-.
Amiri Palace, Abu Dhabi, Arabian Gulf.

Zaki, Hassan Abbas; Egyptian politician; b. 2 Jan. 1917; ed. primary and secondary schools and Cairo Univ.
Commercial Sec. U.A.R. Embassy, Wash. 52; Govt. Rep. in Stock Exchange Mina El Bassal 55; Dir.-Gen. Exchange Control Dept. Ministry of Econs.; mem. Nat. Assembly; Minister of the Treasury 58, of Economy and Supply 61; Head of Board of Dirs. Egyptian Org. for Insurance 65; Minister of Economy and Foreign Trade 66-70; Order of Merit (Fourth Class) and awards from Yugoslavia, Greece, Somalia and Romania.
Publs. Various articles on monetary, international trade and cotton policies.
23 Gabalia Street, Zamalek, Egypt.

Zalzalah, Abdul Hassan, M.SC., PH.D.; Iraqi banker and politician; b. 1926; ed. Coll. of Law, Univ. of Baghdad and Indiana Univ., U.S.A.
Director Loans and Investments Dept., Central Bank of Iraq 57, Foreign Exchange Dept. 57, Econ. Research Dept. 59-62; Deputy Gov. Central Bank of Iraq 62-63, Acting Gov. 62-63, Chair. of Board of Admin. 62-63; Amb. to Iran 63-64; Minister of Industry 64-65, of Planning 64-65; Acting Minister of Finance Aug. 65; Amb. to Austria 66, to Egypt (also accred. to Somalia) 66-68; Gov. Cen. Bank of Iraq 69-73.
Publs. Economic, political, literary and poetic works in Arabic and English in local and foreign newspapers and magazines.
c/o Central Bank of Iraq, Banks Street, Baghdad, Iraq.

Zayyat, Mohamed Hassan el-, M.A., D.PHIL.; Egyptian diplomatist; b. 14 Feb. 1915; ed. Cairo and Oxford Univs.
Lecturer and Asst. Prof. Alexandria Univ. 42-50; Cultural Attaché, Egyptian Embassy, Washington, D.C. 50-54, First Sec. and Counsellor 54; Counsellor, Egyptian Embassy, Teheran 55-57, Minister 57; Del. of Egypt on UN Advisory Council for Somaliland 57-60, Special Envoy and Ambassador of U.A.R. in Somaliland 60; Head of Dept. of Arab Affairs and Perm. Del. of U.A.R. to Arab League 60-62; Alt. Perm. Rep. of U.A.R. to UN 62-64; Ambassador to India, concurrently accred. to Nepal 64-66; Under-Sec. of State for Foreign Affairs 65-67; Deputy Minister, Chair. U.A.R. State Information Services and Govt. Spokesman 67-69; Perm. Rep. to UN 69-72; Minister

of State for Information 72, of Foreign Affairs 72-73; Adviser to the Pres. 73-April 75.
1 Midan al Nasr, Almaadi, Cairo, Egypt.

Zayyen, Dr. Yousef; Syrian politician; b. 1931; ed. Damascus Univ. and osteopathy study in the U.K.
Minister of Agrarian Reform Nov. 63-May 64; Ambassador-designate to U.K. Aug. 64; mem. Syrian Presidential Council 64; mem. Nat. Revolutionary Council 65; Prime Minister Sept.-Dec. 65, 66-68; Baath Party.
c/o The Baath Party, Damascus, Syrian Arab Republic.

Zeevy, Maj.-Gen. Rechavam; Israeli officer and government official; b. 20 June 1926, Jerusalem.
Service in Palmach 44-48; Intelligence Officer 48-49; Operations Officer 49; Battalion Commdr. 50-53; Staff Officer G.H.Q. 53-55; Chief of Staff, Southern Command 55-57; Chief of Org. Dept., G.H.Q. 57-59; U.S. Army Command and Gen. Staff Coll. 59-60; Chief of Staff Cen. Command 60-64; Asst. Chief of Operations, G.H.Q. 64-68; G.C.O. Cen. Command 68-73; Asst. Chief of Staff and Chief of Operations 73-74; Intelligence and Special Matters Adviser to the Prime Minister 74-.
Publs. several articles on the History of the Holy Land.
Office of the Prime Minister, Hakirya, Tel-Aviv; Home: Ramat-Hasharon, Israel.

Zekia, Mehmed; Cypriot judge; b. 1903; ed. Univ. of Istanbul and Middle Temple, London.
Member, Legislative Council of Cyprus 30; mem. Advisory Council of Cyprus 33; Chair. Cttee. on Turkish Affairs 48; Advocate 31-40; District Judge 40; Pres. District Court 47; Judge, Supreme Court 52; Judge, High Court of Justice 60; Judge, European Court of Human Rights 61-; Chief Justice of Cyprus 64-66.
The Supreme Court, Nicosia, Cyprus.

Zentar Mrani, Mehdi, L. en D.; Moroccan diplomatist; b. 6 Sept. 1929; ed. Coll. Moulay Idriss de Fez, Lycée de Meknes, and Faculté de Droit, Paris.
Called to Bar, Casablanca 55; Head of Office of Minister of State in Charge of Moroccan Independence Negotiations 56; Dir. African Affairs, Ministry of Foreign Affairs 57; Dir. of Tourism 58; Consul-Gen. Paris 59; Legal Adviser, Ministry of Foreign Affairs, Rabat 60-61, Dir. of Political Affairs 61-63; Ambassador to Algeria 63-64, to Yugoslavia 64-67, to U.A.R. May 67-71; Perm. Rep. to UN 71-Sept. 74; Vice-Pres. Moroccan Del. to Constitutional Conf. of Org. of African Unity (OAU) and signed Charter for Morocco; Commissaire at Conciliation Comm. of OAU; Pres. 48th Session of Arab League 67-68; Officer Order of the Throne, Morocco, Grand Cordon, Order of the Flag, Yugoslavia, Greek decoration.
c/o Ministry of Foreign Affairs, Rabat, Morocco.

Zhiri, Kacem; Moroccan diplomatist; b. 25 March 1920; ed. Inst. of Higher Studies, Rabat.
Detained for activities in independence movement of Morocco 36, 44, exiled and detained 52; fmr. Man. daily newspapers *Al-Maghrib* and *Al Alam*; Gen. Dir. Broadcasting Station of Morocco 56-59; Ambassador to Senegal 60-61, to Yugoslavia 62-64, to Algeria 64-65; Dir. of Information, Ministry of Foreign Affairs 66; Perm. Del. of League of Arab States to UN, Geneva 66-68; Minister of Secondary and Technical Educ. 68-69; Amb. to Mauritania 70-72, to People's Repub. of China 72-73; Founder, Free School in Al-Jadida; Moroccan and Yugoslav decorations.
Publs. *Biography of Mohammed V* 56, *The Gold of Sous* (novel) 55, Political commentaries 56-58, Social and historical studies.
61 rue de la Marne, Rabat, Morocco.

Ziai, Taher, B.SC., PH.D.; Iranian professor and politician; b. 1917; ed. American Coll. of Teheran, Technische Hochschule, Berlin and Univ. of Vienna.
Professor (Geology and Mining) Teheran Univ. 46-; Dir. Nat. Iranian Oil Co. 47; Under-Sec. Ministry of Nat. Econs. 55; Ministry of Industry and Mines 56; Minister of Industry and Mines 60-61, 62-63; mem. of the Senate 67-; Pres. Iran Chamber of Commerce, Industries and Mines 67-; Order of Homayoun; Grand Cross of Merit (Fed. Repub. of Germany).
Technical Faculty, University of Teheran, Teheran, Iran.

Ziaie, Abdul Hakim, PH.D.; Afghan judge; b. 15 Sept. 1915; ed. Esteqlal High School, Kabul, Tokyo Univ. and the Sorbonne.
Director higher and vocational educ. 43-45; Dean, Faculty of Law and Political Science 45-47; Pres. Dept. for Secondary Educ. 47-49; Educational Adviser, Ministry of Educ. 55-57, Pres. of its Planning Board 56-63; Deputy Pres. Kabul Univ. 57-58; Dean, Faculty of Econs. 57-60; Dean, Faculty of Law and Political Science 60-63; Acting Deputy Minister of Educ. 61. Deputy Minister 63-65; Minister of Planning 65-67; Chief Justice of Afghanistan 67-73; has participated in over 25 int. confs. throughout the world; Kabul Acad. Prize for Literature 35; Medal of Educ. 58; Medal of Stoor 62.
Publs. all 17 of which have been published in Afghanistan, France and Japan, include: *Educational Development in Afghanistan* 51, *Afghanistan's General Progress* 56, *The Rule of Education in securing Human Rights* 64.
c/o Judicial Council, Ministry of Justice, Kabul, Afghanistan.

Ziartides, Andreas; Cypriot trade unionist; b. 1919; ed. Pancyprian Gymnasium, Nicosia.
Trade unionist 37-; mem. Pancyprian Trade Union Cttee. 41, Gen. Sec. 43-47; Gen. Sec. Pancyprian Fed. of Labour 47-; mem. Central Cttee. Cyprus Working People's Progressive Party (AKEL); mem. House of Reps. Cyprus 60-; mem. Exec. Cttee. World Fed. of Trade Unions (WFTU).
Pancyprian Federation of Labour, 31-35 Archemos Street, Nicosia, Cyprus.

Ziv-Av, Itzhak; Israeli administrative official; b. 4 June 1907; ed. Inst. of Pedagogy, Smolensk.
In Palestine 26-; Man. Editor *Haboker* 35-48; Dir. Public Relations Div., Ministry of Defence and Gen. H.Q., Israel Defence Forces 48-52; Dir.-Gen. Israel Farmers' Federation 52-; Chair. Exec. Cttee., Co-ordinating Bureau, Israeli Econ. Orgs. 67-; Editor *Farmers of Israel* (monthly) 62-; mem. Board of Dirs. Jewish Nat. Fund; mem. Council, State Land Authority.
Publs. *The Unknown Land, I seek my Brethren, The Price of Freedom, Forever Ours, From Frontier to Frontier, A World to Live In, Another World,* and poetry for children.
Israel Farmers' Federation, P.O. Box 209, Tel-Aviv; Home: Ramat-Qan, Narkissiun Avenue 20, Tel-Aviv, Israel.

Zobu, Fazil, M.S.; Turkish business executive; b. 1915; ed. Robert Coll., Istanbul, and Purdue Univ., U.S.A.
Manager Turkish State Monopolies Cigarette Factories 43-48; Vice-Pres. (Production), State Monopolies 48-54; Gen. Man. Türkay Endüstri ve Ticaret A.Ş. 54-64, Dir. 64-; Pres. Chamber of Industry of Istanbul 63; Man. Dir. EVAL A.S. 68-; Dir. Industrial Devt. Bank of Turkey.
Çatalkaya Apt. 12, Topağaci-Nişantas, Istanbul, Turkey.

Zuayter, Akram; Jordanian educationist and diplomatist; b. 1909; ed. Al-Najah Coll., Nablus, American Univ. of Beirut, and School of Law, Jerusalem.
Teacher, secondary schools, Nablus and Acre 27-30; Chief Ed. *Mira'at-al-Shark* and *Al-Hayat*, Jerusalem 30-31; Prof.

of History, Training Coll., Baghdad 34-35; Sec. Palestinian Nat. Cttee. 36; exiled 37-50; Insp. of Education, Iraq 40-41; Pres. Arab Del. to Latin America for Palestine Cause 47-48; Minister of Education, All-Palestine Govt. 49; Counsellor, Syrian Del. to Arab League, mem. Perm. Palestine Cttee. 50; Jordan Del. to UN 61; Gen. Sec. Moslem Confs., Jerusalem 60-62; Ambassador of Jordan to Syria 62-63, to Iran 63-66, also accred. to Afghanistan 64-66; Minister of Foreign Affairs 66; Senator 66; Minister of the Royal Court 67-; mem. Consultative Council 67; Amb. to Lebanon March 71-; Al Kawkab Medal and Al Istiqlal Medal (Jordan), Hon. G.C.M.G., and orders from Iran, Libya, and Repub. of Korea.

Publs. *Our History* 35, *Arabic Readings* 39, *Recent History* 41, *Mission to a Continent* 50, *The Palestine Cause* 54, *An Essay in Federation* 55.

Jordanian Embassy, Beirut, Lebanon.

Zukerman, Pinchas; Israeli violinist; b. 16 July 1948, Israeli; ed. Israel Conservatory, Acad. of Music, Tel-Aviv, Juilliard School of Music, New York.

Studied with Ivan Galamian; debut in New York with New York Philharmonic 69, in U.K. at Brighton Festival 69; concert and recital performances throughout U.S.A. and Europe; directs, tours and plays with English Chamber Orchestra; has performed at Spoleto, Pablo Casals and Edinburgh Festivals; Leventritt Award 67.

c/o Harold Holt Ltd., 122 Wigmore Street, London, W1H oDJ, England.

Zurayk, Constantine Kaysar, M.A., PH.D.; Lebanese educationist; b. 18 April 1909; ed. American Univ. of Beirut, Univ. of Chicago and Princeton Univ.

Assistant Prof. of History, American Univ. of Beirut 30-42, Assoc. Prof. 42-45; First Counsellor, Syrian Legation, Washington 45-46; Syrian Minister to U.S.A. 46-47; Vice-Pres. and Prof. of History, American Univ. of Beirut 47-49; Rector, Syrian Univ. Damascus 49-52; Vice-Pres. American Univ. of Beirut 52-54, Acting Pres. 54-57; Distinguished Prof. of History, American Univ. of Beirut 56-; mem. Syrian Del. to UN Gen. Assembly and Alternate Rep. of Syria on Security Council 46-47; mem. Exec. Board UNESCO 50-54; Pres. Int. Asscn. of Univs. 65-70, Hon. Pres. 70-; mem. Int. Comm. for Scientific and Cultural History of Mankind; Corresp. mem. Iraq Acad., Arab Acad., Damascus; Hon. mem. American Historical Asscn.; Chair. Inst. for Palestine Studies 65-; Order of Merit, Distinguished Class (Syria) Educ. Medal, First Class (Lebanon); Commdr. Order of the Cedar (Lebanon).

Publs. *Al-Wa'y al Qawmi* (National Consciousness); *Ma'na al-Nakbah* (The Meaning of the Disaster); *Ayyu Ghadin* (Whither Tomorrow); *Nahnu wa-al-Tarikh* (Facing History); *Hadha al-'Asr al-Mutafajjir* (This Explosive Age); *Fi Ma'rakat al-Hadarah* (In the Battle for Culture); *Ma'na al-Nakbah Mujaddadan* (The Meaning of the Disaster Again), *More than Conquerors;* Editor, Ismai'l Beg Chol's *Al-Yazidiyyah qadiman wa hadithan* (Yazidis past and present), *Ibn al-Furat's History* Vols. VII-IX (partly with Najla Izzeddin); Editor and translator Miskawayh's *Tahdhib al-Akhlaq* (The Refinement of Character).

American University of Beirut, Beirut, Lebanon.

Calendars, Time Reckoning and Weights and Measures

Muslim Calendar

The Muslim era dates from July 16th, A.D. 622, which was the beginning of the Arab year in which the *Hijra*, Muhammad's flight from Mecca to Medina, took place. The Muslim or Hijra Calendar is lunar, each year having 354 or 355 days, the extra day being intercalated eleven times every thirty years. Accordingly the beginning of the Hijra year occurs earlier in the Gregorian Calendar by a few days each year. The Muslim year 1396 A.H. begins on January 3rd, 1976.

The year is divided into the following months:

1. Muharram	30 days		7. Rajab	30 days	
2. Safar	29 ,,		8. Shaaban	29 ,,	
3. Rabia I	30 ,,		9. Ramadan	30 ,,	
4. Rabia II	29 ,,		10. Shawwal	29 ,,	
5. Jumada I	30 ,,		11. Dhu'l-Qa'da	30 ,,	
6. Jumada II	29 ,,		12. Dhu'l-Hijja	29 or 30 days	

The Hijra Calendar is used for religious purposes throughout the Islamic world and is the official calendar in Saudi Arabia and the Yemen. In most Arab countries it is used side by side with the Gregorian Calendar for official purposes, but in Turkey and Egypt the Gregorian Calendar has replaced it.

PRINCIPAL MUSLIM FESTIVALS

New Year: 1st Muharram. The first ten days of the year are regarded as holy, especially the tenth.

Ashoura: 10th Muharram. Celebrates the first meeting of Adam and Eve after leaving Paradise, also the ending of the Flood and the death of Husain, grandson of Muhammad. The feast is celebrated with fairs and processions.

Mouloud (*Birth of Muhammad*): 12th Rabia I.

Leilat al Meiraj (*Ascension of Muhammad*): 27th Rajab.

Ramadan (*Month of Fasting*).

Id ul Fitr or **Id ul Saghir** or **Küçük Bayram** (*The Small Feast*): Three days beginning 1st Shawwal. This celebration follows the constraint of the Ramadan fast.

Id ul Adha or **Id al Kabir** or **Büyük Bayram** (*The Great Feast, Feast of the Sacrifice*): Four days beginning on 10th Dhu'l-Hijja. The principal Muslim festival, commemorating Abraham's sacrifice and coinciding with the pilgrimage to Mecca. Celebrated by the sacrifice of a sheep, by feasting and by donations to the poor.

Hijra Year				1394		1395		1396	
New Year	.	.	.	Jan. 25th,	1974	Jan. 14th,	1975	Jan. 3rd,	1976
Ashoura	.	.	.	Feb. 3rd,	,,	Jan. 23rd,	,,	Jan. 12th,	,,
Mouloud	.	.	.	April 5th,	,,	March 25th,	,,	March 13th,	,,
Leilat al Meiraj	.	.	.	Aug. 16th,	,,	Aug. 5th,	,,	July 24th,	,,
Ramadan begins	.	.	.	Sept. 18th,	,,	Sept. 7th,	,,	Aug. 26th,	,,
Id ul Fitr	.	.	.	Oct. 18th,	,,	Oct. 7th,	,,	Sept. 25th,	,,
Id ul Adha	.	.	.	Dec. 25th,	,,	Dec. 14th,	,,	Dec. 2nd,	,,

Note: Local determinations may vary by one day from those given here.

Iranian Calendar

The Iranian Calendar, introduced in 1925, is based on the Hijra Calendar, adapted to the solar year. Iranian New Year (*Nowruz*) occurs at the vernal equinox, which usually falls on March 21st Gregorian. The year 1354 began on March 21st, 1975.

The Iranian year is divided into the following months:

1. Favardine	31 days		7. Mehr	30 days	
2. Ordibehecht	31 ,,		8. Aban	30 ,,	
3. Khordad	31 ,,		9. Azar	30 ,,	
4. Tir	31 ,,		10. Dey	30 ,,	
5. Mordad	31 ,,		11. Bahman	30 ,,	
6. Chariver	31 ,,		12. Esfand	29 or 30 days	

The Iranian Calendar is used for all purposes in Iran and Afghanistan, except the determining of Islamic religious festivals, for which the lunar Hijra Calendar is used.

Hebrew Calendar

The Hebrew Calendar is solar with respect to the year, but lunar with respect to the months. The normal year has 353–355 days in twelve lunar months, but seven times in each nineteen years an extra month of 30 days (*Adar II*) is intercalated after the normal month of Adar to adjust the calendar to the solar year. New Year (*Rosh Hashanah*) usually falls in September of the Gregorian Calendar, but the day varies considerably. The year 5735 began on September 17th, 1974, and 5736 on September 6th, 1975.

The months are as follows:

1. Tishri	30 days		7. Nisan	30 days	
2. Marcheshvan	29 or 30 days		8. Iyyar	29 ,,	
3. Kislev	29 or 30 ,,		9. Sivan	30 ,,	
4. Tebeth	29 days		10. Tammuz	29 ,,	
5. Shebat	30 ,,		11. Ab	30 ,,	
6. Adar	29 ,,		12. Ellul	29 ,,	
(Adar II)	30 ,,				

The Hebrew Calendar is used to determine the dates of Jewish religious festivals only.

Standard Time

The table shows zones of standard time, relative to Greenwich Mean Time (G.M.T.). Many of the individual countries adopt daylight saving time at certain times of year.

Traditional Arabic time is still widely used by the local population in Saudi Arabia except in most of the Eastern Province. This system is based upon the local time of sunset when timepieces are all set to 12.

G.M.T.	1 HOUR AHEAD	2 HOURS AHEAD	3 HOURS AHEAD	3½ HOURS AHEAD	4 HOURS AHEAD	4½ HOURS AHEAD
Algeria Morocco Spanish Sahara	Tunisia	Cyprus Egypt Israel Jordan Lebanon Libya Sudan Syria Turkey	Bahrain Iraq Kuwait Yemen, P.D.R.	Iran	Oman Qatar United Arab Emirates	Afghanistan

Note: Saudi Arabia and the Yemen Arab Republic use solar time.

Weights and Measures

Principal weights and units of measurement in common use as alternatives to the Metric and Imperial systems

WEIGHT

UNIT	COUNTRY	METRIC EQUIVALENT	IMPERIAL EQUIVALENT
Charak	Afghanistan	1·764 kilos.	3·89 lb.
Hogga	Iraq	1·27 kilos.	2·8 lb.
Kharwar	Afghanistan	564·528 kilos.	1,246·2 lb.
Khord	Afghanistan	110·28 grammes	3.89 oz.
Maund	Yemen, P.D.R. / Saudi Arabia	37·29 kilos.	82·28 lb.
Qintar (Kantar) or Buhar	Cyprus / Egypt	228·614 kilos. / 44·928 kilos.	504 lb. / 99·05 lb.
Ratl or Rotl	Saudi Arabia / Egypt	0·449 kilo.	0·99 lb.
Seer	Afghanistan	7·058 kilos.	15·58 lb.
Uqqa or Oke	Cyprus / Egypt	1·27 kilos. / 1·245 kilos.	2·8 lb. / 2·751 lb.
Yeni Okka	Turkey	1 kilo.	2·205 lb.

LENGTH

UNIT	COUNTRY	METRIC EQUIVALENT	IMPERIAL EQUIVALENT
Busa	Saudi Arabia / Sudan	2·54 cm.	1 in.
Dirraa, Dra or Pic	Cyprus	60·96 cm.	2 ft.
Gereh-gaz-sha	Afghanistan	6·6 cm.	2·6 in.
Kadam or Qadam	Sudan	30·48 cm.	1 ft.

CAPACITY

Unit	Country	Metric Equivalent	Imperial Equivalent
Ardabb or Ardeb.	Saudi Arabia Sudan Egypt	198·024 litres	43·56 gallons
Kadah	Sudan Egypt	2·063 litres	3·63 pints
Keila	Cyprus	36·368 litres	8 gallons
	Sudan Egypt	16·502 litres	3·63 gallons
Ratel	Sudan	0·568 litre	1 pint

AREA

Unit	Country	Metric Equivalent	Imperial Equivalent
	Cyprus	1,335·8 sq. metres	0·33 acre
	Iraq	2,500 sq. metres	0·62 acre
Donum or Dunum	Israel Jordan	1,000 sq. metres	0·2471 acre
	Syria Turkey	919·04 sq. metres	0·2272 acre
Feddan	Saudi Arabia Sudan Egypt	4,201 sq. metres	1·038 acres
Yeni Donum	Turkey	10,000 sq. metres (1 hectare)	2·471 acres

METRIC TO IMPERIAL CONVERSIONS

Metric Units	Imperial Units	To Convert Metric into Imperial Units Multiply by:	To Convert Imperial into Metric Units Multiply by:
Weight			
Gramme	Ounce (Avoirdupois)	0·035274	28·3495
Kilogramme (kg.)	Pound (lb.)	2·204622	0·453592
Metric ton ('000 kg.)	Short ton (2,000 lb.)	1·102311	0·907185
	Long ton (2,240 lb.)	0·984207	1·016047
	(The short ton is in general use in the U.S.A., while the long ton is normally used in Britain and the Commonwealth.)		
Length			
Centimetre	Inch	0·3937008	2·54
Metre	Yard (=3 feet)	1·09361	0·9144
Kilometre	Mile	0·62137	1·609344
Volume			
Cubic metre	Cubic foot	35·315	0·0283
	Cubic yard	1·30795	0·764555
Capacity			
Litre	Gallon (=8 pints)	0·219969	4·54609
	Gallon (U.S.)	0·264172	3·78541
Area			
Square metre	Square yard	1·19599	0·836127
Hectare	Acre	2·47105	0·404686
Square kilometre	Square mile	0·386102	2·589988

SELECT BIBLIOGRAPHIES

BOOKS ON THE MIDDLE EAST

(See also Bibliographies at end of Chapters in Part II)

ABDEL MALEK, A. La Pensée Politique Arab Contemporaine (Editions du Seuil, Paris, 1970).

ABIR, MORDECHAI. Oil, Power and Politics: Conflict in Arabia, The Red Sea and The Gulf (Frank Cass, London, 1974).

ABU JABER, KAMEL S. The Arab Baath Socialist Party (Syracuse University Press, New York, 1966).

ABU-LUGHOD, IBRAHIM (ed.). The Transformation of Palestine: Essays on the Development of the Arab-Israeli Conflict (Northwestern University Press, Evanston, Ill., 1971).

ADAMS, MICHAEL (ed.). The Middle East: A Handbook (Anthony Blond, London, 1971).

ADAMS, MICHAEL and MAYHEW, CHRISTOPHER. Publish it Not . . . the Middle East Cover-up (Longman, London, 1975).

AFIFI, MUHAMMAD. The Arabs and the United Nations (Longmans, London, 1964).

ALDERSON. A. D, The Structure of the Ottoman Dynasty (New York, Oxford University Press, 1956).

AMERICAN ENTERPRISE INSTITUTE. United States Interests in the Middle East (Washington, D.C., 1968).

ANTONIUS, GEORGE. The Arab Awakening. 4th edition (Beirut, 1961).

ARBERRY, A. J. (ed.). Religion in the Middle East— Volume I Judaism and Christianity, Volume II Islam and General Summary (Cambridge University Press, 1969).

ATIYAH, EDWARD. The Arabs (Baltimore, 1955).

ATLAS OF THE ARAB WORLD AND THE MIDDLE EAST (Macmillan, London, 1960).

BASTER, JAMES. The Introduction of Western Economic Institutions into the Middle East (Royal Inst. of Int. Affairs and O.U.P., 1960).

BAER, GABRIEL. Population and Society in the Arab East (Routledge, London, 1964).

BE'ERI, ELIEZER. Army Officers in Arab Politics and Society (Pall Mall Press, London, 1969).

BELL, J. BOWYER. The Long War, Israel and the Arabs since 1946 (Englewood Cliffs, 1969).

BELYAEV, J. C. (ed.). Arabs, Islam and the Arab Caliphate in the early Middle Ages (Pall Mall Press, London, 1969).

BERGER, MORROE. The Arab World Today (Doubleday New York, 1962).

BERQUE, JACQUES and CHARNAY, J.-P. Normes et Valeurs dans l'Islam Contemporaine (Payot, Paris, 1966).

BETHMANN, ERICH W. A Selected Basic Bibliography on the Middle East (American Friends of the Middle East, Washington, 1964).

BIDWELL'S GUIDES TO GOVERNMENT MINISTERS, Vol. II, The Arab World 1900-1972. Compiled and edited by Robin Bidwell (Frank Cass, London, 1973).

BINDER, LEONARD. The Ideological Revolution in the Middle East (New York, 1964).

BIROT, P. & DRESCH, J. La Méditerranée et le Moyen Orient, Vol. II (Paris 1955).

BROCKELMANN, C. History of the Islamic Peoples (New York and London, 1947–48).

BULLARD, Sir R. Britain and the Middle East from the earliest times to 1952 (London, 1952).

BULLOCH, JOHN. The Making of a War: The Middle East from 1967–1973 (Longman, London, 1974).

CARRÉ, OLIVIER. L'Idéologie Palestinienne de Résistance (Armand Colin, Paris, 1972).

CATTAN, HENRY. Palestine and International Law: The Legal aspects of the Arab-Israeli Conflict (Longman, London, 1973).

CATTAN, J. Evolution of Oil Concessions in the Middle East and North Africa (Oceana, Dobbs Ferry, New York, 1967).

CLARKE, JOHN I. and FISHER, W. B. (Ed.). Populations of the Middle East and North Africa (University of London Press, 1972).

COOK, M. A. (ed.). Studies in the Economic History of the Middle East (Oxford University Press, 1970).

COOLEY, JOHN K. Green March, Black September: The Story of the Palestinian Arabs (Frank Cass, London, 1973).

COON, C. S. Caravan: the Story of the Middle East (New York, 1951, and London, 1952).
The Impact of the West on Social Institutions (New York, 1952).

COPELAND, MILES. The Game of Nations (Weidenfeld and Nicolson, London, 1969).

CRAGG, K. A. Counsels in Contemporary Islam (Edinburgh, 1964).

CREMEANS, CHARLES D. The Arabs and the World (London, Pall Mall Press, 1963).

DANIEL, NORMAN. Islam and the West (Edinburgh University Press, revised edition 1963).
Islam, Europe and Empire (Edinburgh University Press, 1964).

DODD, S. C. Social Relations in the Near East. 2nd revised and enlarged edition (London, New York, and Toronto, Oxford University Press, 1940).

EL-GHONEMY, MOHAMMED RIAD (ed.). Land Policy in the Near East (Rome, 1967).

ENCYCLOPAEDIA OF ISLAM, THE. 4 vols. and supplement (Leiden, 1913–38).

EL-ERIAN, TAHANY. References dealing with the Arab World: A selected and annotated list (Org. of Arab Students in the U.S.A. and Canada, New York, 1966).

ETTINGHAUSEN, RICHARD. Books and Periodicals in Western Languages dealing with the Near and Middle East (Washington, Middle East Institute, 1952).

FARIS, N. A. (ed.). The Arab Heritage (Princeton, N.J., Princeton University Press, 1944).

FIELD, HENRY. Bibliography on Southwestern Asia: VII, A Seventh Compilation (University of Miami, 1962).

FIELD, MICHAEL. $100,000,000 a Day—Inside the World of Middle East Money (Sidgwick and Jackson, London, 1975).

FINNIE, D. H. Desert Enterprise: The Middle East Oil Industry and its Local Environment (Cambridge, Mass., 1958).

FISHER, S. N. Social Forces in the Middle East (Cornell University Press, Ithaca, N.Y., 1955).
The Middle East: A History (Alfred Knopf, New York, 6th edition, 1971).

FISHER, W. B. The Middle East—a Physical, Social and Regional Geography (London, 3rd edition, 1954).

FRYE, R. N. (ed.). The Near East and the Great Powers (Harvard University Press, Cambridge, Mass., 1951, and Oxford University Press, London, New York, and Toronto, 1952).

GIBB, H. A. R. Mohammedanism (London, 1949).
Modern Trends in Islam (Chicago, 1947).
Studies on the Civilisation of Islam (London, 1962).

GIBB, H. A. R., and BOWEN, HAROLD. Islamic Society and the West (2 vols., London, 1950, 1957).

GILBERT, MARTIN. The Arab-Israeli Conflict: Its History in Maps (Weidenfeld and Nicolson, London, 1974).

GLUBB, Lt.-Gen. Sir JOHN. A Short History of the Arab Peoples (Hodder and Stoughton, London, 1969).

GRANT, D. (ed.). The Islamic Near East (University of Toronto Press, 1960).

GRUNDWALD, K., and RONALL, J. O. Industrialisation in the Middle East (Council for Middle East Affairs, New York, 1960).

GRUNEBAUM, GUSTAVE E. VON (ed.). Unity and Variety in Muslim Civilisation (Chicago, 1955).
Islam: Essays on the Nature and Growth of a Cultural Tradition (London, Routledge and Kegan Paul, 1961).
Modern Islam: the Search for Cultural Identity (London, 1962).

HAIM, SYLVIA G. Arab Nationalism: An Anthology (Berkeley, Calif., 1962).

HALL, HERVEY P. (ed.) The Evolution of Public Responsibility in the Middle East (Washington, 1955).

HALPERN, MANFRED. The Politics of Social Change in the Middle East and North Africa (Princeton University Press, N.Y., 1963).

HARTSHORN, J. E. Oil Companies and Governments (Faber, London, 1962).

HATEM, M. ABDEL-KADER. Information and the Arab Cause (Longman, London, 1974).

HAZARD. Atlas of Islamic History (Oxford University Press, 1951).

HERSHLAG, Z. Y. Introduction to the Modern Economic History of the Middle East (E. J. Brill, Leiden, 1964).

HERZOG, Maj.-Gen. CHAIM. The War of Atonement (London, Weidenfeld and Nicolson, 1975).

HIGGINS, ROSALYN. United Nations Peacekeeping 1946–67: Documents and Commentary, Volume I The Middle East (Oxford University Press, 1969).

HIRST, DAVID. Oil and Public Opinion in the Middle East (Praeger, New York, 1966).

HIRSZOWICZ, LUKASZ. The Third Reich and the Arab East (Routledge and Kegan Paul, London, 1966).

HITTI, PHILIP K. History of the Arabs (London, 1940, 10th edn., 1970).
A Short History of the Near East (New York, 1966).
Makers of Arab History (Macmillan, London, 1968).
Islam. A Way of Life (Oxford University Press, London, 1971).

HOARE, IAN, and TAYAR, GRAHAM (eds.). The Arabs. A handbook on the politics and economics of the contemporary Arab world (B.B.C. Publications, London, 1971).

HODGKIN, E. C. The Arabs (Modern World Series, Oxford University Press, 1966).

HOLLINGWORTH, CLAIRE. The Arabs and the West (London, 1952).

HOLT, P. M. Studies in the History of the Near East (Cass, London, 1973).

HOLT, P. M., LAMBTON, A. K. S., LEWIS, B. (eds.). The Cambridge History of Islam. Vol. I The Central Islamic Lands (Cambridge University Press, 1970); Vol. II The Further Islamic Lands, Islamic Society and Civilization (Cambridge University Press, 1971).

HOSKINS, H. A. Middle East: Problem Area (New York, 1954).

HOURANI, A. H. Minorities in the Arab World (London, 1947).
A Vision of History (Beirut, 1961).
Arabic Thought in the Liberal Age 1798-1939 (Oxford Univ. Press, 1962).

HUREWITZ, J. C. Unity and Disunity in the Middle East (New York, Carnegie Endowment for International Peace, 1952).
Middle East Dilemmas (New York, 1953).
Diplomacy in the Near and Middle East (Vol. I, 1535-1914; Vol. II, 1914-56; Van Nostrand, 1956).
Soviet-American Rivalry in the Middle East (ed.) (Pall Mall Press, London, and Praeger, New York, 1969).
Middle East Politics: The Military Dimension (Pall Mall Press, London, 1969).

AL-HUSAY, KHALDUN S. Three Reformers; A Study in Modern Arab Political Thought (Khayats, Beirut, 1966).

HUSSEIN, MAHMOUD. Les Arabes au présent (Seuil, Paris, 1974).

HUXLEY, J. From an Antique Land: Ancient and Modern in the Middle East (London, 1954).

INSIGHT ON THE MIDDLE EAST WAR (André Deutsch, London, 1974) (*Sunday Times* team of writers).

IONIDES, MICHAEL. Divide and Lose: the Arab Revolt 1955-58 (Bles, London, 1960).

INTERNATIONAL INSTITUTE FOR STRATEGIC STUDIES. Sources of Conflict in the Middle East (Adelphi Papers, International Institute for Strategic Studies, London, 1966).

IRELAND, P. W. (ed.). The Near East, Problems and Prospects (Chicago, 1942).

IRWIN, I. J. Islam in the Modern National State (Cambridge University Press, Cambridge, 1965).

ISSAWI, CHARLES (ed.). The Economic History of the Middle East, 1800-1914 (University of Chicago Press, 1966).

ISSAWI, CHARLES AND YEGANEH, MOHAMMED, The Economics of Middle Eastern Oil (Faber, London, 1963).

IZZEDDIN, N. The Arab World (Chicago, 1953).

JANIN, R. Les Eglises orientales et les Rites orientaux (Paris, 1926).

JANSEN, G. H. Non-Alignment and the Afro-Asian States (Praeger, New York, 1966).

JONES, DAVID. The Arab World (Hilary House, New York, 1967).

KARPAT, KEMAL H. Political and Social Thought in the Contemporary Middle East (Pall Mall Press, London, 1968).

KEDOURIE, ELIE. England and the Middle East (London, 1956).
The Chatham House Version and other Middle-Eastern Studies (Weidenfeld and Nicolson, London, 1970).
Arabic Political Memoirs and Other Studies (Frank Cass, London, 1974).

KELLY, J. B. Eastern Arabian Frontiers (Faber, London, 1963).

KERR, MALCOLM. The Arab Cold War 1958–1964 (Oxford University Press, 1965).

KHADOURI, M. Political Trends in the Arab World (Johns Hopkins Press, Baltimore, 1970).

KHADOURI, M. & LIEVESNY, H. J. (ed.). Law in the Middle East, Vol. I (Washington, 1955).

KHALIL, MUHAMMAD. The Arab States and the Arab League (historical documents) (Khayat's, Beirut).

KHAYAT, M. K. and KEATINGE, M. C. Food from the Arab World (Beirut, 1959).

KHOURI, FRED J. The Arab-Israeli Dilemma (Syracuse/ New York, 1968).

KINGSBURY, R. C. and POUNDS, N. J. G. An Atlas of Middle Eastern Affairs (New York, 1963).

KIRK, GEORGE E. The Middle East in the War (London, 1953).
A Short History of the Middle East: from the Rise of Islam to Modern Times (New York, 1955).
Contemporary Arab Politics (Methuen, London, 1961).

KUMAR, RAVINDER. India and the Persian Gulf Region (London, 1965).

KURZMAN, DAN. Genesis 1948: The First Arab/Israeli War (Vallentine, Mitchell, London, 1972).

LAHBABI, MOHAMED AZIZ. Le Personnalisme Musulmane (Presses Universitaires de France, Paris, 1964).

LALL, ARTHUR. The UN and the Middle East Crisis (New York/London, 1968).

LANDEN, R. G. (ed.). The Emergence of the Modern Middle East: Selected Readings (Van Nostrand Reinhold, New York, 1970).

LAQUEUR, W. Z. Communism and Nationalism in the Middle East (London and New York, 1957).
A History of Zionism (Weidenfeld and Nicolson, London, 1972).
The Struggle for the Middle East: The Soviet Union and the Middle East 1958-68 (Routledge and Kegan Paul, London, 1969).
Confrontation: The Middle-East War and World Politics (Wildwood, London, 1974).
(ed.) The Middle East in Transition (Routledge and Kegan Paul, London, 1958).
(ed.) The Israel-Arab Reader (New York/Toronto/ London, 1969).

LAWRENCE, T. E. The Seven Pillars of Wisdom (London, 1935).

LEIDEN, CARL (ed.). The conflict of traditionalism and modernism in the Muslim Middle East (Austin, Texas, 1969).

LENCZOWSKI, GEORGE. The Middle East in World Affairs (Ithaca, N.Y., Cornell University Press, 1956).
Oil and State in the Middle East (Cornell Univ. Press, 1960).

LENGYEL, EMIL. The Changing Middle East (New York, 1962).

LERNER, D. The Passing of Traditional Society: Modernising the Middle East (Glencoe, Illinois, 1958).

LEWIS, B. The Arabs in History (London, 1950 and 1954).
The Middle East and the West (London, 1964).
Race and Colour in Islam (London, 1971).
Islam in History (London, 1973).

LONGRIGG, S. H. Oil in the Middle East (London, 1954, 3rd edn., London, 1968).
The Middle East: a Social Geography (London, 2nd rev. edn., 1970).

MACDONALD, ROBERT W. The League of Arab States (Princeton University Press, Princeton, 1965).

MANNIN, ETHEL. A Lance for the Arabs (London, 1963).

MANSFIELD, PETER. The Ottoman Empire and Its Successors (Macmillan, London, 1973).
(ed.). The Middle East: A Political and Economic Survey, 4th edition (Oxford U.P., London, 1972).

MASON, HERBERT (ed.). Reflections on the Middle East Crisis (Paris/The Hague, 1970).

MICHAELIS, ALFRED. Wirtschaftliche Entwicklungsprobleme des Mittleren Ostens (Kiel, 1960).

MIKDASHI, ZUHAYR. The Community of Oil Exporting Countries (George Allen and Unwin, London, 1972).

MIQUEL, ANDRÉ. Islam et sa civilisation (Paris, 1968).

MONROE, ELIZABETH. Britain's Moment in the Middle East (Chatto and Windus, London, 1963).

MOSLEY, LEONARD. Power Play: The Tumultuous World of Middle East Oil 1890–1973 (Weidenfeld and Nicolson, London, 1973).

MUSREY, ALFRED A. An Arab Common Market: A Study in Inter-Arab Trade Relations 1920–67 (Praeger, New York, 1969).

NASR, SEYYED HOSSEIN. Science and Civilization in Islam (Harvard, 1968).

NEVAKIVI, JUKKA. Britain, France and the Arab Middle East 1914–20 (Athlone Press, University of London, 1969).

NUTTING, ANTHONY. The Arabs (Hollis and Carter, London, 1965).
No End of a Lesson, The Story of Suez (Constable, London, 1967).

O'BALLANCE, EDGAR. The Third Arab-Israeli War (Faber and Faber, London, 1972).

OXFORD REGIONAL ECONOMIC ATLAS. The Middle East and North Africa (Oxford University Press, 1960).

PANNIKKAR, K. M. The Afro-Asian States and their Problems (Allen and Unwin, London, 1960).

PARTNER, PETER. The Arab World (Pall Mall, London, 1962).

PEARSON, J. D. (ed.). Index Islamicus (Cambridge, 1967).

PENNAR, JAAN. The U.S.S.R. and the Arabs: The Ideological Dimension (Hurst, London, 1973).

PLAYFAIR, IAN S. O. The Mediterranean and the Middle East (History of the Second World War, H.M.S.O., London, 1966).

POLIAK, A. N. Feudalism in Egypt, Syria, Palestine, and the Lebanon, 1250–1900 (London, Luzac, for the Royal Asiatic Society, 1939).

POLK, W. R. The United States and the Arab World (Harvard University Press, 1965, rev. edn. 1970).
(ed. with CHAMBERS, R. L.) Beginnings of Modernization in the Middle East: the Nineteenth Century (University of Chicago Press, 1969).

PORATH, Y. The Emergence of the Palestinian Arab National Movement 1918–1929 (Frank Cass, London, 1974).

PROCTOR, J. HARRIS (ed.). Islam and International Relations (Pall Mall Press, London, 1965).

PURYEAR, V. J. France and the Levant from the Bourbon restoration to the Peace of Kutiah. (California, University of California Press, 1941).

QUBAIN, FAHIM I. Education and Science in the Arab World (Johns Hopkins Press, Baltimore, 1967).

RIVLIN, B., and SZYLIOWICZ, J. S. (eds.). The Contemporary Middle East—Tradition and Innovation (Random House, New York, 1965).

RODINSON, MAXIME. Islam and Capitalism (France, 1965, England 1974).

RONART, STEPHAN and NANDY. Concise Encyclopaedia of Arabic Civilization (Amsterdam, 1966).

RONDOT, PIERRE. The Destiny of the Middle East (Chatto & Windus, London, 1960).
L'Islam (Prismes, Paris, 1965).

ROUHANI, FUAD. A History of OPEC (Pall Mall Press, London, 1972).

SACHAR, HOWARD M. Europe Leaves the Middle East 1936–1954 (Allen Lane, London, 1973).

SVUVAGET, J. Introduction à l'histoire de l'orient musulman (Paris, 1943) (2nd edn. re-cast by C. CAHEN, Univ. of Calif. Press, 1965).

SEARIGHT, SARAH. The British in the Middle East (Weidenfeld and Nicolson, London, 1969).

SEGESVARY, VICTOR. Le Réalisme Khrouchtchévien: La politique soviétique au Proche-Orient (Editions de la Baconnière, Neuchâtel, Switzerland, 1968).

SHABAN, M. A. The Abbasid Revolution (Cambridge University Press, 1970).
Islamic History A.D. 600–750 (A.H. 132) A New Interpretation (Cambridge University Press, 1971).

SHARABI, H. B. Governments and Politics of the Middle East in the Twentieth Century (Van Nostrand, New York, 1962).
Nationalism and Revolution in the Arab World (Van Nostrand, New York, 1966).
Palestine and Israel: The Lethal Dilemma (Pegasus Press, N.Y., 1969).

SIMMONS, J. S. & OTHERS. Global Epidemiology, Vol. 3: The Near and Middle East (Philadelphia, 1954).

SIMON, JAN. Men and Medicine in the Middle East (World Health Organization, Alexandria, 1967).

SMITH, W. CANTWELL. Islam and Modern History (Toronto, 1957).

SOUTHERN, R. W. Western Views of Islam in the Middle Ages (Oxford, 1957).

SPENCER, W. Political Evolution in the Middle East (Philadelphia, 1962).

SPECTOR, IVAR. The Soviet Union and the Muslim World (Seattle, University of Washington Press, 1956).

STARK, FREYA. Dust in the Lion's Paw (London and New York, 1961).

STEVENS, GEORGINA G. (ed.). The United States and the Middle East (Prentice Hall, N.J., 1964).

STEWART, DESMOND. The Middle East: Temple of Janus (Hamish Hamilton, London, 1972).

STOCKING, G. W. Middle East Oil. A Study in Political and Economic Controversy (Vanderbilt University Press, Nashville, 1970).

SUMNER, B. H. Tsardom and Imperialism in the Far East and Middle East (London, Oxford University Press, 1940).

SWADRAN, BENJAMIN. The Middle East, Oil and the Great Powers (London, 1956).

THAYER, P. W. (ed.). Tensions in the Middle East (Baltimore, 1958).

THOMAS, D. WINTON (ed.). Archaeology and Old Testament Study (Oxford University Press, 1967).

THOMAS, L. V. and FRYE, R. N. The United States and Turkey and Iran (Cambridge, Mass., 1951).

TREVELYAN, HUMPHREY (Lord). The Middle East in Revolution (Macmillan, London, 1970).

TRIMINGHAM, J. SPENCER. The Sufi Orders in Islam (Clarendon Press, Oxford, 1971).

TUGENHADT, C. Oil: The Biggest Business (Eyre and Spottiswoode, London, 1968).

VATIKIOTIS, P. J. Conflict in the Middle East (George Allen and Unwin, London, 1971).

WADSMAN, P., and TEISSEDRE, R.-F. Nos Politiciens face au Conflict Israélo Arabe (Paris, 1969).

WAINES, DAVID. The Unholy War (Medina Press, Wilmette, 1971).

WARRINER, DOREEN. Land and Poverty in the Middle East (London, 1948).
Land Reform and Development in the Middle East: Study of Egypt, Syria and Iraq (London, 1962).

WATT, W. MONTGOMERY. Muhammad at Mecca (Clarendon Press, Oxford, 1953).
Muhammad at Medina (Clarendon Press, Oxford, 1956).
Muhammad, Prophet and Statesman (Oxford University Press, 1961).
Muslim Intellectual—Al Ghazari (Edinburgh University Press, 1962).
Islamic Philosophy and Theology (Edinburgh University Press, 1963).
Islamic Political Thought: The Basic Concepts (Edinburgh University Press, 1968).

YALE, WILLIAM. The Near East (University of Michigan Press, Ann Arbor, 1968).

YOUNG, T. C. (ed.). Near Eastern Culture and Society (Princeton, N.J., Princeton University Press, 1951).

ZEINE, Z. N. The Struggle for Arab Independence (Beirut, 1960).

BOOKS ON NORTH AFRICA

(See also Bibliographies at end of Chapters in Part III)

ABUN-NASR, JAMIL M. A History of the Maghrib (Cambridge University Press, 1972).

ALLAL EL-FASSI. The Independence Movements in Arab North Africa, trans. H. Z. Nuseibeh (Washington, 1954).

AMIN, SAMIR. L'Economie du Maghreb (2 vols., Editions du Minuit, Paris, 1966).
The Maghreb in the Modern World (Penguin Books, London, 1971).

BARBOUR, NEVILLE, Editor. A Survey of North West Africa (The Maghreb) (Royal Institute of International Affairs, Oxford University Press, 1959).

BERQUE, JAQUES. Le Maghreb entre Deux Guerres (2nd edn., Editions du Seuil, Paris, 1967).

BRACE, R. M. Morocco, Algeria, Tunisia (Prentice-Hall, Englewood Cliffs, N.J., 1964).

BROWN, LEON CARL (ed.). State and Society in Independent North Africa (Middle East Institute, Washington, 1966).

CAPOT-REY, R. Le Sahara Français (Paris, 1953).

CENTRE D'ETUDES DES RELATIONS INTERNATIONALES. Le Maghreb et la Communauté Economique Européenne (Editions F.N.S.P., Paris, 1965).

CENTRE DE RECHERCHES SUR L'AFRIQUE MÉDITERRANÉENNE D'AIX EN PROVENCE. L'Annuaire de l'Afrique du Nord (Centre Nationale de la recherche scientifique, Paris, annually).

CHARBONNEAU, J. Editor. Le Sahara Français (Cahiers Charles de Foucauld, No. 38, Paris, 1955).

DUCLOS, J., LECA, J., and DUVIGNAUD, J. Les Nationalismes Maghrébins (Centre d'Etudes des Relations Internationales, Paris, 1966).

ECONOMIC COMMISSION FOR AFRICA. Main Problems of Economic Co-operation in North Africa (Tangier, 1966).

FURLONGE, Sir GEOFFREY. The Lands of Barbary (Murray, London, 1966).

GALLAGHER, C. F. The U.S. and North Africa (Cambridge, Mass., 1964).

GARDI, RENÉ. Sahara, Monographie einer grossen Wüste (Kummerley and Frey, Berne, 1967).

GAUTIER, E. F. Le Passé de l'Afrique du Nord (Paris, 1937).

GORDON, D. C. North Africa's French Legacy 1954–62 (Harvard, 1962).

HAHN, LORNA. North Africa: from Nationalism to Nationhood (Washington, 1960).

HERMASSI, ELBAKI. Leadership and National Development in North Africa (University of California Press, 1973).

HESELTINE, N. From Libyan Sands to Chad (Leiden, 1960).

JULIEN, CH.-A. Histoire de l'Afrique du Nord (2nd Edition, 2 Vols., Paris 1951-52).
L'Afrique du Nord en Marche (Paris, 1953).
History of North Africa: From the Arab Conquest to 1830. Revised by R. Le Tourneau. Ed. C. C. Stewart (Routledge and Kegan Paul, London, 1970).

KHALDOUN, IBN. History of the Berbers. Translated into French by Slane (4 vols., Algiers, 1852-56).

LE TOURNEAU, ROGER. Evolution Politique de l'Afrique du Nord Musulmane (Paris, 1962).

LEVI-PROVENÇAL, E. Islam d'Occident (Etudes d'Histoire Médiévale, Paris, 1948).

LISKA, G. The Greater Maghreb: From Independence to Unity? (Center of Foreign Policy Research, Washington, 1963).

MARÇAIS, G. La Berberie Musulmane et l'Orient au Moyen Age (Paris, 1946).

MOORE, C. H. Politics in North Africa (Little, Brown, Boston, 1970).

MORTIMER, EDWARD. France and the Africans, 1944-1960 (Faber, London, 1969).

MUZIKÁR, JOSEPH. Les perspectives de l'intégration des pays maghrébins et leur attitude vis-à-vis du Marché Commun (Nancy, 1968).

NICKERSON, JANE S. Short History of North Africa (New York, 1961).

PARRINDER, GEOFFREY. Religion in Africa (Pall Mall Press, London, 1970).

POLK, WILLIAM R. (ed.). Developmental Revolution: North Africa, Middle East, South Asia (Middle East Institute, Washington, 1963).

RAVEN, SUSAN. Rome in Africa (Evans Brothers, London, 1970).

ROBANA, ABDERRAHMA. The Prospects for an Economic Community in North Africa (Pall Mall, London, 1973).

SAHLI, MOHAMED CHERIF. Décoloniser l'Histoire; introduction à l'histoire du Maghreb (Maspero, Paris, 1965).

SCHRAMM, JOSEF. Die Westsahara (Paunonia-Verlag, Freilassing, 1969).

STEEL, R. (ed.). North Africa (Wilson, New York, 1967).

TOYNBEE, Sir ARNOLD. Between Niger and Nile (Oxford University Press, 1965).

TRIMINGHAM, J. S., The Influence of Islam upon Africa (Longmans, London, and Librairie du Liban, Beirut, 1968).

TUTSCH, HANS E. Nordafrika in Gärung (Frankfurt, 1961). From Ankara to Marrakesh (New York, 1962).

UNESCO. Arid Zone Research, Vol. XIX: Nomades et Nomadisme au Sahara (UNESCO, 1963).

UNIONS, LABOUR AND INDUSTRIAL RELATIONS IN AFRICA; AN ANNOTATED BIBLIOGRAPHY. Cornell Research Papers in International Relations, 4 (Cornell University Press, New York, 1965).

WARREN, CLINE and SANTMYER, C. Agriculture of Northern Africa (U.S. Dept. of Agriculture, Washington, 1965).

ZARTMAN, I. W. Government and Politics in North Africa (New York, 1964).
(ed.) Man, State and Society in the Contemporary Maghrib (Pall Mall, London, 1973).

SELECT BIBLIOGRAPHY (PERIODICALS)

ACTA ORIENTALIA ACADEMIAE SCIENTIARUM HUNGARICAE. H-1363 Budapest, P.O.B. 502, Hungary; 1950; three times a year; text in English, French, German or Russian; Editor L. LIGETI.

ACTA ORIENTALIA. Publ. Munksgaard, Nørre Søgade 35, DK 1370 Copenhagen K, Denmark, by the Oriental Societies of Denmark, Norway, and Sweden; history, language, archaeology and religions of the Near and Far East; once or twice yearly; Editor Prof. SØREN EGEROD; Editorial Sec. Mrs. LISE SODE-MOGENSEN.

AFRICA. Dirección General de Promoción de Sahara, Sección de Archivo-Biblioteca y Documentación de Africa, Castellana 5, Madrid 1, Spain. Head of Section ASUNCIÓN DEL VAL.

AFRICA CONTEMPORARY RECORD. Rex Collings Ltd., 6 Paddington St., London, W1M 3LA; annual documented survey.

AFRICA RESEARCH BULLETINS. Africa Research Ltd., 1 Parliament St., Exeter, EX4 3DZ, Devon, England; f. 1964; monthly bulletins on (a) political and (b) economic subjects.

AFRICAN QUARTERLY. Indian Council for Cultural Relations, Azad Bhavan, Indraprastha Estate, New Delhi, India.

L'AFRIQUE ET L'ASIE MODERNES, 13 rue du Four, 75006 Paris, France; f. 1948; quarterly.

AL-ABHATH. Publ. American University of Beirut, Beirut, Lebanon; f. 1948; Editor MAHMUD A. GHUL; quarterly on Arab affairs.

ALAM ATTIJARAT (*The World of Business*). Johnston International Publishing Corpn. (New York), Beirut; Arabic; business; 10 issues per year; Editor NADIM MAKDISI.

AL-TIJARA AL-ARABIYA AL-INKLEEZYA (*Anglo-Arab Trade*). British Industrial Publicity Overseas Ltd., London W.C.2; Arabic; quarterly.

ANATOLIAN STUDIES. c/o British Academy, Burlington House, Piccadilly, London, W1V oNS, England; f. 1949; annual of the British Inst. of Archaeology at Ankara; Editor Prof. O. R. GURNEY.

ANATOLICA. Netherlands Historical and Archaeological Institute at Istanbul, Istiklâl Caddesi 393, Istanbul-Beyoğlu, Turkey; f. 1967; annual; Editors: Prof. Dr. A. A. KAMPMAN, HANDAN ALKIM, Dra. PAULINE H. E. DONCEEL-VOÛTE, Dr. E. J. VAN DONZEL, Dr. SEMRA ÖGEL.

ANNALES ARCHÉOLOGIQUES ARABES SYRIENNES. Direction Générale des Antiquités et des Musées, University St., Damascus, Syria; semi-annually.

ANNALES DE L'INSTITUT D'ÉTUDES ORIENTALES DE LA FACULTÉ DES LETTRES D'ALGER. Institut d'Études Orientales, Faculté des Lettres, Algiers, Algeria.

ANNUAIRE DE L'AFRIQUE DU NORD. Edited by the Centre de Recherches et d'Etudes sur les Sociétés Mediterranéennes, Faculté de Droit, Avenue Schuman, Aix en Provence; published by the Centre national de la Recherche Scientifique, 15 quai Anatole France, 75700 Paris, France; Dir. Prof. FLORY, France; f. 1962; contains special studies, chronologies, chronicles, documentation and bibliographies.

THE ARAB ECONOMIST. Centre for Economic, Financial and Social Research and Documentation SAL, Gefinor Tower, Clemenceau Street, Bloc B—P.O.B. 11—6068, Beirut, Lebanon; f. 1969; Chair. Dr. CHAFIC AKHRAS; monthly; circ. 7,300.

ARAB REPORT AND RECORD. 84 Chancery Lane, London, W.C.2, England; f. 1966; digest of Arab political, economic and social affairs; twice monthly; Editor PETER KILNER.

THE ARAB WORLD. The Anglo-Arab Association, 33 Cavendish Square, London, W1M 0AA; Social and cultural interests, non-political; quarterly.

ARABICA. c/o Départment d'Etudes Islamiques, Paris IV, Sorbonne, Paris 5e, France; Editor G. LECOMTE; three issues annually.

ARCHIV FÜR ORIENTFORSCHUNG. Graz, Austria; f. 1923; irregular; Editor and Publisher Dr. ERNST WEIDNER.

ARMENIAN REVIEW. Hairenik Association, Inc., 212 Stuart St., Boston, Mass. 02116, U.S.A.

ASIAN AFFAIRS. Royal Society for Asian Affairs, 42 Devonshire St., London, W.1, England; f. 1901; three times per year.

ASIAN AND AFRICAN STUDIES. Israel Oriental Society, The Hebrew University, Jerusalem, Israel; f. 1965; Editor GABRIEL BAER; annual.

L'ASIE NOUVELLE. 97 rue St. Lazare, Paris 9e, France; weekly and special issues; Dir. ANDRÉ ROUX.

ASIEN-BIBLIOGRAPHIE. Asien Bucherei, D-359 Bad Wildungen, German Federal Republic; quarterly.

BELLETEN. Türk Tarih Kurumu, Kizilay Sokak no. 1, Ankara, Turkey; f. 1931; history and archaeology; quarterly.

BIBLIOGRAPHY OF THE MIDDLE EAST. P.O.B. 2712, Damascus, Syria; f. 1968; annual.

BIBLIOTHECA ORIENTALIS. Published by Netherlands Institute for the Near East, Noordeindsplein 4-6, Leiden, Netherlands; f. 1943; Board of Dirs. E. VAN DONZEL, A. A. KAMPMAN (ed.), H. J. A. de MEULEN-AERE, C. NIJLAND; bi-monthly.

BULLETIN OF THE SCHOOL OF ORIENTAL AND AFRICAN STUDIES. School of Oriental and African Studies, University of London, London, W.C.1, England; three issues annually.

BULLETIN OF SUDANESE STUDIES. P.O.B. 321, Khartoum; Arabic; published by Sudan Research Unit, University of Khartoum; f. 1968; bi-annual; Editor AWN AL-SHARIF QASIM.

LES CAHIERS DE TUNISIE, B.P. 1128, Tunis; f. 1953; quarterly; Dir. MOHAMED TALBI, Editor-in-Chief BÉCHIR TLILI.

CHUTO TSUHO (The Middle East News). The Middle East Institute of Japan, Jutakukodan Bldg., Akasaka 8-10-21, Minato-ku, Tokyo, Japan; f. 1958; Editor H. IWANAGA; monthly.

LE COMMERCE DU LEVANT. Kantari St., SFAH Building, Beirut, Lebanon; two editions (bi-weekly and monthly).

COMUNITÁ MEDITERRANEA. Lungotevere Flaminio 34, Rome; law and political science relating to Mediterranean countries; Pres. E. BUSSI.

CULTURA TURCICA. T. K. Araştirma Enstitüsü, P.K. 14, Çankaya, Ankara, Turkey; f. 1964; articles in English, French and German; semi-annual; Editor Prof. Dr. AHMET TEMIR.

DEUTSCHE MORGENLÄNDISCHE GESELLSCHAFT; ZEITSCHRIFT. Deutsche Morgenländische Gesellschaft, 355 Marburg/Lahn, Postfach 642, Federal Republic of Germany; f. 1948; covers the history, languages and literature of the Orient; bi-annual.

L'ECONOMIE ET LES FINANCES DES PAYS ARABES. Centre d'Etudes et de Documentation Economiques, Financières et Sociales, S.A.L., B.P. 6068, Beirut, Lebanon; monthly. Pres. Dr. CHAFIC AKHRAS, Dir.-Gen. Dr. SABBAH AL HAJ.

EGYPTE CONTEMPORAINE. Société Egyptienne d'Economie Politique, de Statistique et de Législation, B.P. 732, Cairo, Egypt; f. 1909; quarterly in Arabic, French and English.

EUROPE OUTREMER. 6 rue de Bassano, Paris 16e, France; f. 1923; economic and political material on French-speaking states of Africa; monthly.

FRANCE-PAYS ARABES. Published by L'Association de Solidarité Franco-Arabe, 12-14 rue Augereau, 75007 Paris, France; politics, economics and culture of the Arab world; monthly.

FREE PALESTINE. P.O.B. 492, London, S.W.7; f. 1968; monthly; Editor AZIZ YAFI.

HAMIZRAH HEHADASH. Israel Oriental Society. The Hebrew University, Jerusalem, Israel; f. 1949; Hebrew with English summary; Middle Eastern, Asian and African affairs; quarterly; Editor YEHOSHUA PORATH.

HESPERIS-TAMUDA. Faculté des Lettres, Université Mohammed V, Rabat, Morocco; f. 1921; history, archaeology, civilization of Maghreb and Western Islam, special reference to bibliography.

HUNA LONDON (BBC Arabic Radio Times). BBC Arabic Service, Bush House, Strand, London, WC2B 4PH.

IBLA. Institut des Belles Lettres Arabes, 12 rue Jamâa el Haoua, Tunis, Tunisia; f. 1937; twice a year.

INDO-IRANIAN JOURNAL. D. Reidel Publishing Co., P.O.B. 17, Dordrecht, Netherlands; 306 Dartmouth Street, Boston, Mass. 02116, U.S.A.; f. 1957; semi-annually.

INTERNATIONAL CRUDE OIL AND PRODUCT PRICES. P.O. Box 1224, Beirut, Lebanon; f. 1971; six-monthly review and analysis of crude oil and product price trends in world markets.

INTERNATIONAL JOURNAL OF MIDDLE EAST STUDIES. Cambridge University Press, 200 Euston Rd., P.O.B. 92, London, NW1 2DB; Journal of the Middle East Studies Association of North America; first issue Jan. 1970; four times per year.

INTERNATIONALES AFRIKA FORUM. Weltforum Verlag, 8000 Munich 19, Hubertusstrasse 22/I, German Federal Republic; f. 1965; monthly.

IRANISTISCHE MITTEILUNGEN. Antigone-Verlag, 3559 Allendorf an der Eder, German Federal Republic; f. 1967; Editor HELMHART KANUS-CREDÉ.

IRAQ. British School of Archaeology in Iraq, 31–34 Gordon Square, London, W.C.1, England; f. 1932; semi-annually.

DER ISLAM. 4D2 Hamburg 13, Rothenbaumchaussee 36, German Federal Republic; two issues annually.

ISLAMIC CULTURE. Islamic Culture Board, Post Box 171, opp. Osmania University Post Office, Hyderabad 7, India; f. 1927; quarterly.

ISLAMIC QUARTERLY. The Islamic Cultural Centre, 146 Park Rd., London, N.W.8, England; f. 1954; quarterly; Publication Manager R. EL-DROUBIE.

IZVESTIA AKADEMII NAUK-OTEDELENIE LITERATURY I YAZYKA. Soviet Academy of Sciences, Moscow, U.S.S.R.; bi-monthly.

JEUNE AFRIQUE. Presse Africaine Associée, 51 av. des Ternes, Paris 17e, France; f. 1960; Publisher BECHIR BEN YAHMED; weekly.

JEWISH OBSERVER AND MIDDLE EAST REVIEW. 36 White-friars St., London, EC4Y 8BL, England; weekly; Editor H. CORNEY.

JOURNAL OF THE AMERICAN ORIENTAL SOCIETY. American Oriental Society, 329 Sterling Memorial Library, New Haven, Conn., U.S.A.; f. 1842; Biblical studies, Ancient Near East and Far East; quarterly.

JOURNAL ASIATIQUE. Journal de la Société Asiatique, 3 rue Mazarine, Paris 6e, France; f. 1822; Dir. D. GIMARET; covers all phases of Oriental research; quarterly.

JOURNAL OF NEAR EASTERN STUDIES. Oriental Institute, University of Chicago, 1155 East 58th St., Chicago, Ill. 60637, U.S.A.; devoted to the Ancient and Medieval Near and Middle East, archaeology, languages, history, Islam.

JOURNAL OF PALESTINE STUDIES. P.O.B. 7164, Beirut, Lebanon; f. 1971; Palestinian affairs and the Arab-Israeli conflict; Editor HISHAM SHARABI; circ. 5,000.

MAGHREB-MACHREK. Fondation Nationale des Sciences Politiques, La Documentation Française, 29–31 quai Voltaire, 75340 Paris Cedex 07, France; f. 1964; bi-monthly.

M.E.N. WEEKLY. Middle East News Agency, 4 Sharia Sheruffin, Cairo, Egypt; f. 1956; weekly news bulletin.

THE MIDDLE EAST. 17/18 Henrietta Street, London, WC2E 8QH, England; f. 1974; business, economic and political monthly; Editor RICHARD PURDY.

MIDDLE EAST ECONOMIC DIGEST. MEED Ltd., 84–86 Chancery Lane, London, W.C.2, England; f. 1957 weekly report on economic developments; Chair. and Editor-in-Chief ELIZABETH COLLARD; Editor JONATHAN WALLACE.

MIDDLE EAST ECONOMIC SURVEY. P.O.B. 1224, Beirut, Lebanon; f. 1957; weekly review of news and views on Middle East/North African oil.

MIDDLE EAST INTERNATIONAL. Room 105, Grand Buildings, Trafalgar Square, London WC2N 5EP; f. 1971; monthly; politics, economics and culture; Editor MICHAEL ADAMS.

THE MIDDLE EAST JOURNAL. Middle East Institute, 1761 N St., N.W., Washington, D.C. 20036, U.S.A.; journal in English devoted to the study of the modern Near East; f. 1947; quarterly; Editor WILLIAM SANDS.

MIDDLE EASTERN STUDIES. Frank Cass & Co. Ltd., 67 Great Russell St., London, WC1B 3BT, England; f. 1964; Editor ELIE KEDOURIE; three times yearly.

MIDEAST MARKETS. Chase World Information Corporation, 1 Chase Manhattan Plaza, New York, N.Y. 10015, U.S.A.; fortnightly.

MIZAN. Central Asian Research Centre, 1B Parkfield St., London N1, England; analyses Soviet and Chinese policies in the Middle East; six issues per year.

MUSLIM CHRONICLE. P.O.B. 700, London, W.2; f. 1970; weekly; Editor FAREED S. JAFRI.

THE MUSLIM WORLD. 55 Elizabeth St., Hartford, Conn. 06105, U.S.A.; f. 1911; Islamic studies in general and Muslim-Christian relations in past and present; quarterly; Editor WILLEM A. BIJLEFELD.

NARODY ASII I AFRIKI (Istoriya, Ekonomika, Kultura). Akad. Nauk S.S.S.R., Khokhlovsky per., 13, Moscow, U.S.S.R.; f. 1955; bi-monthly.

NEAR EAST REPORT. 1341 G St., N.W., Washington, D.C. 20005, U.S.A.; f. 1957; analyses U.S. policy in the Near East; circ. 34,000; weekly; Managing Editor SHEILA F. SEGAL, Assoc. Editor WOLF I. BLITZER, Contributing Editor MORRIS J. AMITAY.

NEW OUTLOOK. 8 Karl Netter Street, Tel-Aviv, Israel; f. 1957; Israeli and Middle Eastern Affairs; monthly; Editor SIMHA FLAPAN.

OEL (Zeitschrift für die Mineralölwirtschaft). 2 Hamburg 13, Alsterkamp 20, Federal Republic of Germany; f. 1963; monthly.

OIL AND GAS JOURNAL. Petroleum Publishing Co., 1421 S. Sheridan, Tulsa, Oklahoma 74112, U.S.A.; f. 1902; weekly.

ORIENS. International Society for Oriental Research, Frankfurt/Main, Federal Republic of Germany; f. 1948; articles in German, French and English, on the history and archaeology of the Near and Far East; annual; Editor Prof. Dr. R. SELLHEIM.

ORIENT. German Orient Institute, 2 Hamburg 13, Mittelweg 150, Federal Republic of Germany; f. 1960; current affairs articles in German, English and French; Documents, Book Reviews and Bibliographies; quarterly; Editors Dr. RAINER BÜREN, Dr. RAINER GLAGOW.

ORIENTE MODERNO. Istituto per l'Oriente, via A. Caroncini 19, Rome, Italy; f. 1921; chronicle of events, extremely useful for students of the modern Near East; monthly.

PALESTINE AFFAIRS. P.O.B. 1691, Beirut, Lebanon; studies of Palestine problem; f. 1971; monthly in Arabic; Editor Dr. ANIS SAYEGH.

PALESTINE EXPLORATION QUARTERLY. Palestine Exploration Fund, 2 Hinde Mews, London, W.1, England; f. 1865.

PALESTINE EXPLORATION QUARTERLY. Palestine Exploration Fund, 2 Hinde Mews, London, W.1, England.

PERSICA. Netherlands-Iranian Society; Molenstraat 27, The Hague, Leiden, Netherlands; f. 1963; annual; Editors Prof. Dr. A. A. KAMPMAN and Dr. C. NIJLAND.

PETROLEUM ECONOMIST (formerly Petroleum Press Service). 24 Ludgate Hill, London, EC4M 7DS, England; f. 1934; monthly, in English, French, Spanish, German, Arabic and Japanese editions.

PETROLEUM TIMES. IPC Business Press Ltd., 33/40 Bowling Green Lane, London, EC1R 0NE, England; f. 1899; fortnightly.

REVUE D'ASSYRIOLOGIE. Presses Universitaires de France, 12 rue Jean-de-Beauvais, Paris 5e, France; f. 1923; bi-annual; Editor JEAN NOUGAYROL.

LA REVUE BIBLIOGRAPHIQUE DU MOYEN ORIENTAL. Publisher L. FARÈS, B.P. 2712, Damascus, Syria.

REVUE DES ETUDES ISLAMIQUES. Librarie Orientaliste Paul Geuthner, 12 rue Vavin, 75006 Paris, France; f. 1927; ed. H. LAOUST.

RIVISTA DEGLI STUDI ORIENTALI. Scuola Orientale, Facoltà di Lettere, University of Rome, Rome, Italy; quarterly; Publisher GIOVANNI BARDI.

ROCZNIK ORIENTALISTYCZNY. Grójecka 17, Warsaw, Poland; f. 1915; Editor-in-Chief JAN REYCHAN; Sec. EDWARD TRYJARSKI; semi-annual.

ROYAL ASIATIC SOCIETY OF GREAT BRITAIN AND IRELAND JOURNAL. 56 Queen Anne Street, London, W1M 9LA, England; f. 1823; covers all phases of Oriental research.

AL SINAI (The Industrialist). Iraqi Federation of Industry, P.O.B. 5665, Baghdad, Iraq; f. 1960; articles in Arabic, and English; quarterly.

STUDIA ISLAMICA, G. P. Maisonneuve et Larose, 11 rue Victor-Cousin, Paris 5e, France; bi-annual.

STUDIES IN ISLAM. Indian Institute of Islamic Studies, Panchkuin Rd., New Delhi, India; quarterly.

SUMER. Directorate-General of Antiquities, Baghdad Iraq; archaeological; bi-annual.

TÜRK KÜLTÜRÜ. T. K. Araştırma Enstitüsü, P.K. 14, Çankaya, Ankara, Turkey; f. 1962; Turkish language articles on current affairs and history; Editor Dr. AHMET TEMIR; monthly.

TÜRK KÜLTÜRÜ ARAŞTIRMALARI. T. K. Araştırma Enstitüsü, P.K. 14, Çankaya, Ankara, Turkey; f. 1964; scholarly articles in Turkish; bi-annual.

DIE WELT DES ISLAMS. Publ. E. J. Brill, Oude Rijn 33a, Leiden, Netherlands; f. 1913; contains articles in German, English and French; Editor Prof. Dr. O. SPIES.

WIENER ZEITSCHRIFT FÜR DIE KUNDE DES MORGENLANDES. Oriental Institute of the University of Vienna, A-1010 Wien I, Universitätsstrasse 7/V, Austria; irregular.

WORLD PETROLEUM. 25 West 45th St., New York, N.Y. 10036, U.S.A.; f. 1930; monthly.

Research Institutes

Associations and Institutes Studying the Middle East and North Africa.

(*See also* Regional Organizations—Education in Part I)

AFGHANISTAN

The Asia Foundation: P.O.B. 257, Kabul.

ALGERIA

Centre de Recherches Africaines: Faculté des Lettres, Université d'Alger, 2 rue Didouche Mourad, Algiers.

Institut d'Etudes Arabes: Université d'Alger, 2 rue Didouche Mourad, Algiers.

Institut d'Etudes Orientales: Université d'Alger, 2 rue Didouche Mourad, Algiers; publ. *Annales*.

AUSTRIA

Afro-Asiatisches Institut in Wien: A-1090 Vienna, Türkenstrasse 3; f. 1959; seminars and language courses and other cultural exchange between African and Asian students in Vienna; library of 1,000 vols.; Gen. Sec. A. GRÜNFELDER.

Orientalisches Institut der Universität Wien: A-1010 Vienna, Universitätsstrasse 7/V; f. 1886; 50 mems.; library of 25,000 vols.; Pres. Prof. Dr. ARNE A. AMBROS, Prof. Dr. HANS HIRSCH, Prof. Dr. ANDREAS TIETZE; publ. *Wiener Zeitschrift für die Kunde des Morgenlandes* (irregular).

BELGIUM

Centre pour l'Etude des Problèmes du Monde Musulman Contemporain: 44 ave. Jeanne, 1050 Brussels; f. 1957; publs. *Correspondance d'Orient-Etudes* (half-yearly) and collections *Correspondance d'Orient* and *Le monde musulman contemporain—Initiations*.

Departement Oriëntalistiek: Faculteit van de Wijsbegeerte en Letteren Katholieke Universiteit te Leuven, Blijde Inkonststraat 21, B3000 Leuven; f. 1936; Pres. Prof. J. VERGOTE; 25 mems.; publs. *Orientalia Lovaniensia Analecta, Orientalia Lovaniensia Periodica, Bibliothèque du Muséon* (1929-68), *Orientalia et Biblica Lovaniensia* (1957-68).

Fondation Egyptologique Reine Elisabeth: Parc du Cinquantenaire, Brussels B1040; f. 1923 to encourage Egyptian studies; 750 mems.; library of 80,000 vols.; Pres. M. E. BONVOISIN; Dir. M. J. BINGEN; publs. *Chronique d'Egypte, Bibliotheca Aegyptiaca, Papyrologica Bruxellensia, Bibliographie Papyrologique sur fiches.*

Private Information Center on Eastern Arabia: Heldenplein 12, 1800 Vilvoorde; f. 1970; 3,500 documents on Bahrain, Qatar, Oman and the United Arab Emirates; Dir. M. VAN DAELE; Beirut office: P.O.B. 50050, Beirut; Dir. of Beirut office S. M. KARAM; publs. (monthly list of new acquisitions, fact sheets on Eastern Arabia).

CZECHOSLOVAKIA

Department of Oriental Studies of the Slovak Academy of Sciences: Slovak Academy of Sciences, Klemensova 27, Bratislava; f. 1960; 10 mems.; Pres. Dr. I. DOLEŽAL; Vice-Dir. Dr. M. GALIK; publ. *Asian and African Studies* (annual).

Oriental Institute: Prague I, Lázeňská 4; f. 1922; Head of library Mrs. VLASTA RUZKOVÁ; publs. *Archiv Orientální* (quarterly), *Nový Orient* (monthly).

DENMARK

Orientalsk Samfund (*Orientalist Association*): Scandinavian Inst. of Asian Studies, Kejsergade 2, Copenhagen K; f. 1915 to undertake the study and further the understanding of Oriental cultures and civilizations; 75 mems.; Pres. Prof. SØREN EGEROD; Sec. Prof. J. P. ASMUSSEN; publ. *Acta Orientalia* (annually).

EGYPT

Academy of the Arabic Language: 26 Sharia Mourad, Giza, Cairo; f. 1932; Pres. Dr. AHMED LOUTFI EL SAYED; Sec.-Gen. Dr. IBRAHIM MAKDOUR; publ. *Review*, collections of scientific and Koranic terms.

American Research Center in Egypt Inc.: 2 Midan Kasr el Doubara, Cairo, and 20 Nassau St., Princeton, N.J. 08540; f. 1948 by American universities to promote research by U.S. scholars in all phases of Egyptian civilization, including archaeology; 19 institutional mems. and 235 individual mems.; Pres. Prof. JOHN A. WILSON; Vice-Pres. Prof. MORROE BERGER; American Dir. LILY M. BROWN; Cairo Dir. JOHN DORMAN.

Deutsches Archäologisches Institut (*German Archaeological Institute*): 22 Sharia Gezira al Wusta, Zamalek, Cairo; Dir. Prof. Dr. WERNER KAISER.

Institut Dominicain d'Etudes Orientales: Priory of the Dominican Fathers, 1 Sharia Masma al-Tarabish, Abbasiyah, Cairo; f. 1952; Dir. Père G. C. ANAWATI; publ. *Mélanges* (yearly).

Institut d'Egypte: 13 Sharia Sheikh Rihane, Cairo; f. 1798; studies literary, artistic and scientific questions relating to Egypt and neighbouring countries; Pres. MUHAMMAD REDA MADWAR; Sec.-Gen. P. GHALIOUNGUI; publs. *Bulletin* (annual), *Mémoires* (irregular).

Institut Français d'Archéologie Orientale: 37 Sharia Sheikh Ali Youssef, Cairo; f. 1898; Dir. S. SAUNERON.

Société Archéologique d'Alexandrie: 6 Sharia Mahmoud Moukhtar, Alexandria; f. 1893; 100 mems.; Pres. MOHIE EL-DIN EL-SHAZILI; Sec.-Gen. D. A. DAOUD; Treas. A. SADEK; Editor MAX DEBBANE; publs. *Bulletins, Mémoires, Monuments de l'Egypte Gréco-Romaine, Cahiers, Publications Spéciales.*

Société Egyptienne d'Economie Politique, de Statistique et de Législation: B.P. 732, Cairo; f. 1909; 900 mems.; Pres. Dr. ABDEL HAKIM RIFAI; Sec.-Gen. Dr. GAMAL EL OTEIFI; publ. *Revue* (quarterly in Arabic, French and English).

Society for Coptic Archaeology: 222 Avenue Ramses, Cairo; f. 1934; 360 mems.; library of 8,500 vols.; Pres. MIRRIT BOUTROS GHALI; Sec. Dr. ANTOINE KHATER; Treas. Dr. BOUTROS BOUTROS GHALI; Librarian Dr. O. H. E. KHS-BURMESTER; publs. *Bulletin* (annual), *Fouilles, Bibliothèque d'Art et d'Archéologie, Textes et Documents et Divers.*

FINLAND

Suomen Itämainen Seura (*Finnish Oriental Society*): Helsinki, Snellmaninkatu 9-11; f. 1917; 200 mems.; Pres. Dr. E. SALONEN; Sec. Dr. I. KÄRKI; publ. *Studia Orientalia*.

FRANCE

Centre d'Etudes de l'Orient Contemporain: 13 rue du Four, Paris 6e; f. 1943; collaborates with la Documentation française and runs course on contemporary Arab World; Dir. Prof. CL. CAHEN.

Centre de Hautes Etudes sur l'Afrique et l'Asie Modernes: 13 rue du Four, 75006 Paris; f. 1936; Dir. G. MALECOT; publs. *L'Afrique et L'Asie* (quarterly), *Cahiers de l'Afrique et l'Asie* (irregular), *Langues et dialectes d'Outre-Mer* (irregular), *Recherches et documents du CHEAM* (irregular).

Centre de Recherches Africaines: 17 rue de la Sorbonne, Paris 5e.

Centre de Recherches et d'Etudes sur les Sociétés Méditerranéennes: Faculté de Droit, 3 ave. Robert Schuman, Aix-en-Provence; Dir. M. FLORY; publs. *Annuaire de l'Afrique du Nord, Collection du CRESM, Les Cahiers du CRESM*.

Fondation Nationale des Sciences Politiques: 27 rue Saint-Guillaume, Paris 7e; f. 1945; Administrator J. CHAPSAL; Centre d'Etudes des Relations Internationales, Dir. J. MEYRIAT; Arab World section has research team of 9 mems.; publs. include *Maghreb-Machrek* (bi-monthly).

Institut d'Etudes Arabes et Islamiques de l'Université de Paris: 13 rue de Santeuil, Paris 5e; Dir. Prof. CL. CAHEN.

Institut d'Etudes Iraniennes de l'Université de la Sorbonne Nouvelle (Paris): 22 ave. du Président Wilson, 75116 Paris; f. 1947; Dir. GILBERT LAZARD; publs. *Travaux, Studia Iranica* (journal).

Institut d'Etudes Sémitiques: 11 place Marcelin-Berthelot, 75005 Paris; f. 1930; publ. *Semitica*.

Institut d'Etudes Turques de l'Université de Paris: 13 rue du Four, Paris 6e; Dir. L. BAZIN.

Institut National des Langues et Civilisations Orientales: 2 rue de Lille, Paris 7e; attached to Univ. de la Sorbonne Nouvelle Paris III; f. 1795; faculties of languages and civilizations of West Asia and Africa; the Far East, India and Oceania; Eastern Europe; library of 600,000 vols. and 2,000 MSS.; over 8,000 students, 90 teachers, 170 lecturers; Pres. R. SIEFFERT; Sec. Mme J. FIATTE; publs. various Oriental studies.

Institut de Papyrologie: Université de Paris-Sorbonne, 1 rue Victor-Cousin, Paris 5e; Dir. JEAN SCHERER.

Société Asiatique: 3 rue Mazarine, Paris 6e; f. 1822; 500 mems.; library of 80,000 vols.; Pres. CLAUDE CAHEN; Vice-Pres. L. HAMBIS, J. FILLIOZAT; Secs. L. BAZIN, Y. HENROUET, M. SOYMIE; Dir. D. GIMARET; publs. *Journal Asiatique* (quarterly), *Cahiers de la Société Asiatique*.

FEDERAL REPUBLIC OF GERMANY

Altorientalisches Seminar der Freien Universität Berlin: 1 Berlin 45, Unter den Eichen 78/79; f. 1950.

Arbeitsgemeinschaft Vorderer Orient (AGVO): 2000 Hamburg 13, Mittelweg 150; consists of German research orgs. into politics, science and commerce of the Far and Middle East; 25 mem. insts. (1975); Sec. Dr. RAINER BÜREN.

Deutsche Afrika Gesellschaft: Bonn, Markt 10-12; publ. *Afrika Heute* (monthly).

Deutsche Morgenländische Gesellschaft: 355 Marburg/Lahn, Postfach 642; Sec. Dr. WOLFGANG VOIGT; publs. *Zeitschrift* (semi-annual), *Abhandlungen für die Kunde des Morgenlandes*, *Bibliotheca Islamica*, *Wörterbuch der Klassischen Arabischen Sprache*, *Beiruter Texte und Studien*, *Verzeichnis der orientalischen Handschriften in Deutschland*.

Das Deutsche Orient-Institut: 2000 Hamburg 13, Mittelweg 150; f. 1960 from the Nah-und Mittelostverein e.V.; since 1965 has been affil. to Deutsche Übersee-Institut; devoted to research in politics, science and commerce of Near and Middle East; Dir. Dr. RAINER BÜREN; publ. *Orient* (quarterly).

Internationale Gesellschaft fuer Orientforschung: 17/25 Mertonstrasse, Frankfurt; f. 1948; 400 mems.; Pres. Prof. R. SELLHEIM; publ. *Oriens* (annual).

Nah- und Mittelost Verein (*German Near and Middle East Association*): D2 Hamburg 13, Mittelweg 151; f. 1934; 600 mems.; Chair. HANS-OTTO THIERBACH; Gen. Sec. R.-E. FRHR. V. LÜTTWITZ.

Seminar für Orientalische Sprachen: Adenauerallee 102, 53 Bonn; institute attached to the University of Bonn; Dir. Prof. Dr. W. HOENERBACH.

HUNGARY

Magyar Tudományos Akadémia, Orientalisztikai Bizottsága (*Oriental Committee of the Hungarian Academy of Sciences*): Budapest V, Roosevelt tér. 9; publ. *Acta Orientalia Hung.* (three times a year).

INDIA

Asiatic Society of Bombay: Town Hall, Bombay 400 001; f. 1804; 1,511 mems.; library of 200,000 vols.; Pres. Sri K. T. DESAI; Hon. Sec. Sri RUSI J. DARUWALA; in 1973 the Society established the Dr. P. V. Kane Research Inst. to promote, encourage and facilitate research in Oriental studies; publishes critical annotated texts of rare Sanskrit and Pali MSS.

Indian Institute of Islamic Studies: Panchkuin Rd., New Delhi 1 and Tughlaqabad, New Delhi 62; f. 1963; library of 25,000 vols. and 1,000 MSS; Pres. HAKEEM ABDUL HAMEED; Dir. S. A. ALI; publ. *Studies in Islam* (quarterly).

Iran League: Navsari Bldg. (2nd floor), Dr. Dadabhai Navroji Rd., Fort, Bombay I; f. 1922; 500 mems.; Pres. Sir JAMSETJEE JEEJEEBHOY, Bart.; Sec. J. E. RANDERIA; publs. *Iran League Journal* and translations and commentaries in modern Persian of Avesta texts.

Iran Society: 12 Dr. M. Ishaque Rd., Calcutta 16; f. 1944; 176 mems.; Pres. Justice S. A. MASUD; Gen. Sec. M. A. MAJID; publs. *Indo-Iranica* (quarterly), etc.

IRAN

The Asia Institute: Pahlavi University, Shiraz; Dir. Dr. RICHARD N. FRYE; publs. *Bulletin of the Asia Institute, Monographs of the Asia Institute*.

British Institute of Persian Studies: 238 ave. Takhte Jamshid, P.O.B. 2617, Teheran 15; f. 1961; cultural institute, with emphasis on history and archaeology; 382 individual mems.; Pres. Sir MAX MALLOWAN, C.B.E., D.LIT., F.B.A., F.S.A.; Hon. Sec. J. E. F. GUERITZ; Dir. DAVID STRONACH, O.B.E., M.A., F.S.A.; publ. *Iran* (annual).

Regional Cultural Institute: 5 Los Angeles Ave., Teheran; f. 1966; Dir. Dr. SALIM NEYSARI; publs. *Journal* (quarterly), also publications on the history and culture of Iran, Turkey and Pakistan.

IRAQ

American School of Oriental Research: Baghdad; f. 1923; undertakes archaeological surveys and excavations; Dir. (vacant); publ. *Bulletin*, quarterlies and monographs.

Deutsches Archäologisches Institut: 71B/11 Hurriya Square, Karrada, Baghdad.

Instituto Hispano-Arabe de Cultura: Park Sa'adun, P.O.B. 256, Baghdad.

Iraq Academy: Waziriyah, Baghdad; f. 1947 to maintain the Arabic language, to undertake research into Arabic history and the history of Iraq, and to encourage research in the modern arts and sciences; Pres. ABDUL RAZZAQ MUHIDDIN; Sec. Dr. Y. IZZIDIEN; publ. *Literary Criticism in Iraq, Bulletin.*

ISRAEL

Academy of the Hebrew Language: P.O.B. 3449, Jerusalem; f. 1953; study of the Hebrew language and compilation of an historical dictionary; Pres. Prof. Z. BEN-HAYYIM; publ. *Zikhronot, Leshonenu, Leshonenu La'am,* monographs and dictionaries.

Albright Institute of Archaeological Research in Jerusalem: 26 Salah ed-Din, P.O.B. 19096, Jerusalem; f. 1900; research in Semitic languages, literature and history; archaeological research and sponsors excavations; Pres. G. ERNEST WRIGHT; Dir. W. DEVER; Publs. *Bulletin, Annual, Biblical Archaeologist.*

American Institute of Holy Land Studies: P.O.B. 1276, Jerusalem; f. 1959; Christian study centre; Pres. Dr. G. DOUGLAS YOUNG.

The Ben-Zvi Institute: Yad Izhak Ben-Zvi and the Hebrew University of Jerusalem; f. 1948; sponsors research in the history and culture of Jewish communities in the East; Chair. Prof. SHAUL SHAKED; Asst. Dir. JOSEPH HACKER.

British School of Archaeology in Jerusalem: P.O.B. 19/283, Jerusalem; f. 1920; archaeological research and excavation; hostel and library; Chair. Dame K. M. KENYON, D.B.E.; Dir. Mrs. C. M. BENNETT, F.S.A.; publ. *Levant.*

Couvent Saint Etienne des Pères Dominicains, Ecole Biblique et Archéologique Française: P.O.B. 178, Jerusalem; f. 1890; research, Biblical and Oriental studies, exploration and excavation in Palestine; Dir. R. P. TOURNAY; library of 55,000 vols.; publs. *Revue Biblique, Etudes Bibliques, Etudes Palestiniennes et Orientales, Cahiers de la Revue Biblique, Bible de Jérusalem.*

Historical Society of Israel: P.O.B. 1062, Jerusalem; f. 1925 to promote the study of Jewish history and general history; 850 mems.; Pres. Prof. B. DINUR; publ. *Zion* (quarterly).

Institute of Asian and African Studies: Hebrew University of Jerusalem, Jerusalem; f. 1926; studies of medieval and modern languages, culture and history of Middle East, Asia and Africa; Dir. Prof. MOSHE MAÓZ; publs. *Hebrew University, Oriental Studies and Manuscripts.*

Israel Exploration Society: 3 Shemuel ha-Nagid St., P.O.B. 7041, Jerusalem; f. 1913; excavations and historical research, congresses and lectures; 3,000 mems.; Chair. Prof. Y. YADIN; Pres. Prof. B. MAZAR; Hon. Sec. J. AVIRAM; publ. *Eretz Yisrael* (Hebrew annual), *Qadmoniot* (Hebrew quarterly), *Israel Exploration Journal* (English quarterly), various books on archaeology (in Hebrew and English).

Israel Oriental Society: The Hebrew University, Jerusalem; f. 1949; lectures and symposia to study all aspects of contemporary Middle Eastern, Asian and African affairs; Pres. E. ELATH; publ. *Hamizrah Hehadash* (Hebrew quarterly), *Oriental Notes and Studies* (irregular), *Asian and African Studies* (annual).

Near East School of Archaeology: Jerusalem; Dir. J. P. FREE.

Orientalisches Institut der Görres-Gesellschaft: P.O.B. 19424, Jerusalem; historical and archaeological studies.

Pontifical Biblical Institute: King David and Botta Streets, P.O.B. 497, Jerusalem; f. 1927; study of Biblical geography and archaeology, student tours, excavations; Dir. Rev. FRANCIS FURLONG, S.J.; publ. *Biblica, Orientalia.*

Shiloah Center for Middle Eastern and African Studies: Tel-Aviv University, Ramat Aviv, P.O.B. 39012; f. 1959; Dir. Dr. HAIM SHAKED; publs. *Middle East Record* (annual), etc.

Wilfrid Israel House for Oriental Art and Studies: Kibbutz Hazorea, Post Hazorea, near Haifa; f. 1947; opened 1951 in memory of late Wilfrid Israel; a cultural centre for reading, study and art exhbns.; houses Wilfrid Israel collection of Near and Far Eastern art and cultural materials; local archaeological exhibits from neolithic to Byzantine times; science and art library; Dir. Dr. U. R. BAER; Curator E. MEIRHOF.

ITALY

Istituto Italiano per il Medio ed Estremo Oriente (ISMEO) Palazzo Brancaccio, via Merulana 248, Rome; f. 1933; Pres. Prof. GIUSEPPE TUCCI; Gen. Sec. Rear-Admiral I. N. R. MARIANO IMPERIALI; Cultural Dir. Prof. ANTONIO GARGANO; publs. *East and West* (quarterly), *Rome Oriental Series, Nuovo Ramusio,* Archaeological Reports and Memoirs.

Istituto Italo-Africano: via Ulisse Aldrovandi 16, Rome; Pres. Avv. VITTORINO VERONESE, Sec.-Gen. PAULO TALLARIGO.

Istituto per l'Oriente: via Alberto Caroncini 19, Rome; f. 1921; Pres. Prof. F. GABRIELI; publ. *Oriente Moderno* (monthly), *Rassegna di Studi Etiopici* (annual), *Oriens Antiquus* (quarterly).

Istituto Universitario Orientale: Piazza San Giovanni Maggiore 30, Naples; f. 1888; library of 63,646 vols.; Dir. Prof. A. BOMBACI.

Istituto di Studi del Vicino Oriente: Universita degli Studi, Città Universitarià, Rome; Dir. Prof. P. MATTHIAE.

JAPAN

Ajia Keizai Kenkyusho (*Institute of Developing Economies,* formerly *Institute of Asian Economic Affairs*): 42 Ichigaya-Hommura-cho, Shinjuku-ku, Tokyo 162; f. 1958; 266 mems.; Chair. TAKEKAZU OGURA; Pres. NOBORU KANOKOGI; library of 123,000 vols.; publs. *Ajia Keizai* (Japanese, monthly), *The Developing Economies* (English, quarterly), occasional papers in English.

Chuto Chosakai (*Middle East Institute of Japan*): Jatakukodan Bldg., 10-21 Akasaka 8-chome, Minatoku, Tokyo; f. 1956; Chair. YUTAKA TSUCHIDA; Exec. Dirs. HIROSHI IWANAGA, NOBUO KUROKAWA; Publs. *Chuto Tsuho* (Middle East News—monthly), *Chuto Nenkan* (Yearbook of Middle East and North Africa), *Chuto Seji Keizai News* (Political and Economic News of the Middle East) (twice a month).

Nippon Orient Gakkai (*Society for Near Eastern Studies in Japan*): Tokyo Tenrikyokan, 9, 1-chome, Kanda Nishiki-cho, Chiyoda-ku, Tokyo; f. 1954; 438 mems.; Pres. H.I.H. Prince TAKAHITO MIKASA; publs. *Orient* (Japanese, twice-yearly), *Orient* (European languages annual).

LEBANON

Centre for Economic, Financial and Social Research and Documentation S.A.L.: Gefinor Centre, Bloc B, 500-502 Clemenceau St., P.O.B. 6068, Beirut; f. 1958; Pres. Dr. CHAFIC AKHRAS; Dir.-Gen. Dr. SABBAH AL HAJ.

Institut de Géographie du Proche et Moyen Orient: ave. de Damas, B.P. 2691, Beirut; f. 1946; Dir. M. LE LANNOU.

Institut de Recherches d'Economie Appliquée: Faculté de Droit et des Sciences Economiques, Université Saint Joseph, B.P. 293, Beirut; f. 1963; economic studies of the Lebanon and other countries of the Middle East; Dir. Prof. ELIAS GANNAGE; publ. *Proche-Orient, études économiques* (quarterly).

Institut Français d'Archéologie: rue Omar Daouk, B.P. 11-1424, Beirut; f. 1946; library of 24,000 vols. (Bibliothèque Henri Seyrig); Dir. ERNEST WILL; publ. *Syria, Revue d'Art et d'Archéologie* (annual), *Bibliothèque Archéologique et Historique*.

P.L.O. Research Centre: P.O.B. 1691, Beirut; f. 1964; studies Palestine problem; publs. irregular monographs, books and essays in Arabic, English and French.

MOROCCO

Faculté des Lettres et des Sciences Humaines: Université Mohammed V, Rabat; f. 1959; publs. *Hespéris-Tamucla La Revue de Géographie du Maroc, La Revue des Etudes Littéraires et Philosophiques*.

THE NETHERLANDS

Assyriologisch Instituut der Rijksuniversiteit: Rijksuniversiteit te Leiden, Noordeindsplein 4A, Leiden; Dir. F. R. KRAUS.

Netherlands Institute for the Middle East (*Midden Oosten Instituut*): 3 Spui, P.O.B. 10, The Hague; f. 1949; publ. *Barid Hollanda, Bulletin* (Press Digest).

Netherlands Institute for the Near East (*Nederlands Instituut voor het Nabije Oosten*): Noordeindsplein 4-6, Leiden; Dir. Prof. Dr. E. VAN DONZEL; library of 15,000 vols. and 500 periodicals; Publs. *Bibliotheca Orientalis Anatolica, Studia Scholten, Scholae de Buck, Publications d'Istanbul, Bibliographia Antiqua*.

NORWAY

Indo-Iransk Institutt: Niels Treschows Hus, Blindern, Oslo; f. 1920; studies Indian and Iranian languages, culture and history; library of 23,000 vols.; Pres. Prof. NILS SIMONSSON.

PAKISTAN

Institute of Islamic Culture: Club Rd., Lahore; f. 1950; Dir. Prof. M. SAEED SHEIKH; Admin. Officer and Sec. M. ASHRAF DARR; publs. *al-Maarif* (monthly), and about 135 publications on Islamic subjects in English and Urdu.

Islamic Research Institute: P.O.B. 1035, Islamabad; f. 1960; Dir. Dr. A. J. HALEPOTA.

POLAND

Polskie Towarzystwo Orientalistyczne (*Polish Oriental Society*): ul. Sniadeckich 8, Warsaw; f. 1922; mems. 260; Pres. TADEUSZ LEWICKI, JAN BRAUN, WLODZIMIERZ ZAJACZKOWSKI; Sec. LESZEK CYRZYK; publ. *Przeglad Orientalistyczny* (quarterly).

Research Centre for Mediterranean Archaeology: Palac Kultury i Nauki, Room 1909, Warsaw; f. 1956; documentation and publication of Polish excavations in the Middle East; Dir. Prof. Dr. KAZIMIERZ MICHALOWSKI; publs. *Travaux du Centre d'Archéologie Méditerranéenne, Palmyre-Fouilles Polonaises 1959-, Faras-Fouilles Polonaises 1961-, Etudes et Travaux I-VI, Deir el Bahari, Corpus Vasorum Antiquorum, Corpus Signorum Imperii Romani.*

Zaklad Orientalistyki P.A.N. (*Research Centre for Oriental Studies*): Freta 16, Warsaw; f. 1953; Dir. Prof. Dr. ANANIASZ ZAJĄCZKOWSKI.

PORTUGAL

Instituto de Linguas Africanas e Orientais: Rua da Junqueira 86, Lisbon 3; f. 1946; library; 10 teachers; specializes in African and Oriental studies.

SPAIN

Asociacion Española de Orientalistas: Juan XXIII 5, Madrid 3; publ. *Boletin* (annual).

Egyptian Institute of Islamic Studies: Francisco de Asis Mendez Casariego 1, Madrid 2; affiliated to Ministry of Higher Education, Cairo; f. 1950; Dir. Dr. AHMED HEIKAL; publs. *Magazine of the Egyptian Institute* and other educational books.

Instituto "Benito Arias Montano" de Estudios Hebraicos Sefardies y Oriente Próximo (*Institute of Hebrew, Sephardic and Near East Studies*): Duque de Medinaceli 4, Madrid 14; f. 1940; branch in Barcelona; 18 mems. Dir. FEDERICO PEREZ CASTRO; Sec. JOSÉ LUIS LACAVE RIAÑO; publ. *Sefarad* (quarterly) and books.

SWEDEN

Scandinavian Institute of African Studies: P.O.B. 2126, S-75002, Uppsala; information and documentation centre, organizes seminars and publishes wide range of books and pamphlets, also newsletters in Swedish, English and French; library of 16,000 vols.

Swedish Oriental Society: Stockholm.

SWITZERLAND

Centre d'Etudes Orientales: Université de Genève, rue de Candolle 3, Geneva; Dir. Prof. C. MAYSTRE.

Schweizerische Gesellschaft für Asienkunde: Zurich; publ. *Asiatische Studien* (bi-annual).

SYRIA

Institut Français d'Etudes Arabes: B.P. 344, Damascus, f. 1922; library of 35,000 vols., 300 periodicals; Dir. ANDRÉ RAYMOND; Gen. Sec. JEAN-PAUL PASCUAL; 8 scholars; publs. *Bulletin d'Etudes Orientales* (annually, 27 vols. published), monographs, translations and Arabic texts (100 vols. published), Islamic archaeology.

Near East Foundation: B.P. 427, Damascus.

TUNISIA

Institut des Belles Lettres Arabes: 12 rue Jamâa el Haoua, Tunis; f. 1930; cultural centre; Dir. A. DEMEERSEMAN; publ. *IBLA* (twice yearly) and special studies.

Mission Archéologique Française en Tunisie: 8 rue M'hamed Ali, Tunis; Dir. PIERRE CINTAS; Publications Dir. CL. POINSSOT; publ. *Karthago* (quarterly).

TURKEY

British Institute of Archaeology at Ankara: Büklüm Sokak 96, Kavaklidere, Ankara; f. 1948; archaeological research and excavation; Dir. D. H. FRENCH; publs. *Anatolian Studies* (annual), *Occasional Publications*.

Centri di Studi Italiani in Turchia: Adakale Sokak 8, Yenişehir, Ankara; Dir. Prof. BRUNO ARCURIO; Mesrutiyet Caddesi 161, Istanbul; Dir. Prof. GIOVANNI BATTAGLIA; Ataturk Caddesi, 280, Izmir; Prof. PIERO FERRARI.

Deutsches Archäologisches Institut: Sira Selvi 123, Taksim, Istanbul; Dir. Prof. Dr.-Ing. R. NAUMANN; publ. *Istanbuler Mitteilungen* (annual), *Istanbuler Forschungen, Beihefte zu Istanbuler Mitteilungen.*

Institut Français d'Archéologie: Istanbul; f. 1930; Dir. EMMANUEL LAROCHE.

Netherlands Historical and Archaeological Institute: Istiklâl Caddesi 393, Beyoğlu, Istanbul; f. 1958; library of 14,000 vols.; Dir. Dra. P. H. E. DONCEEL-VOÛTE; publs. *Publications de l'Institut Historique et Archéologique Néerlandais de Stamboul, Revue Anatolica.*

Österreichisches Generalkonsulat Kulturinstitut Istanbul: Belvedere Apt. 101/2, Tesvikiye, Istanbul; Dir. Prof. Dr. J. E. KASPER.

Türk Dil Kurumu (*Turkish Linguistic Society*): Ankara; f. 1932; 536 mems.; library of 20,000 vols.; Pres. Prof. MACIT GÖKBERK; Sec.-Gen. OMER ASIM AKSOY; publs. *Türk Dili* (monthly), *Türk Dili Arastırmaları-Belleten* (annual).

Türk Kültürünü Araştırma Enstitüsü (*Institute for the Study of Turkish Culture*): P.K. 14, Çankaya, Ankara; f. 1961; scholarly research into all aspects of Turkish culture; Dir. Prof. Dr. AHMET TEMİR; publs. *Türk Kültürü* (monthly), *Cultura Turcica* (semi-annual), *Türk Kültürü Araştırmaları* (semi-annual).

Türk Tarih Kurumu (*Turkish Historical Society*): Ankara; f. 1931; 41 mems.; library of 128,000 vols.; Pres. Ord. Prof. ENVER ZIYA KARAL; Gen. Dir. ULUĞ İĞDEMİR; publs. *Belleten* (quarterly), *Belgeler* (twice a year).

Türkiyat Enstitüsü (*Institute of Turcology*): University of Istanbul, Bayezit, Istanbul; f. 1924; research into Turkish language, literature, history and culture; library of 20,000 vols.; Dir. Dr. M. CAVID BAYSUN.

U.S.S.R.

Commission on Oriental Literature of the Department of Literature and Language, U.S.S.R. Academy of Sciences: Volkhonka 18/2, Moscow; Chair. Acad. N. I. KONRAD.

Institute of Asian Peoples of the Department of History, U.S.S.R. Academy of Sciences: Armyansky per. 2, Moscow, Dir. Acad. B. GAFUROV.

Institute of Oriental Studies of the Academy of Sciences of the Georgian S.S.R.: Tbilisi, Georgian S.S.R.

Institute of Oriental Studies, U.S.S.R. Academy of Sciences: Armyansky per. 2, Moscow; Dir. B. GAFUROV.

Research Institute of Oriental Studies of the Academy of Sciences of the Azerbaijanian S.S.R.: Baku, Azerbaijanian S.S.R.

Section of Oriental Studies of the Academy of Sciences of the Armenian S.S.R.: Erevan, Armenian S.S.R.

Section of Orientology and Calligraphy of the Academy of Sciences of the Tajik S.S.R.: Dushanbe, Tajik S.S.R.

UNITED KINGDOM

Anglo-Arab Association, The: 33 Cavendish Square, London, W1M 0AA; non-political.

Council for the Advancement of Arab-British Understanding (CAABU): Room 106, Grand Buildings, Trafalgar Square, London, WC2N 5EP; f. 1967; 1,300 mems.

Egypt Exploration Society: 3 Doughty Mews, London, WC1N 2PG; f. 1882; library of 4,000 vols.; Sec. MARY D. ST. B. CRAWFORD; publs. *Excavation Memoirs, Archaeological Survey, Graeco-Roman Memoirs, Journal of Egyptian Archaeology, Texts from Excavations, etc.*

Islamic Cultural Centre (and London Central Mosque): 146 Park Rd., London, N.W.8; f. 1944 to spread Islamic culture in Great Britain; library of 3,000 vols., mostly Arabic; Dr. MAHMOOD HOBALLAH; publ. *Islamic Quarterly.*

Middle East Association: Bury House, 33 Bury St., London, SW1; trade asscn. for Middle East and North Africa; Dir.-Gen. Sir RICHARD BEAUMONT, K.C.M.G., O.B.E.; Dep. Dir.-Gen. and Sec. R. GODDARD-WILSON.

Middle East Centre: Faculty of Oriental Studies, Sidgwick Ave., Cambridge CB3 9DA; Dir. Prof. R. B. SERJEANT, PH.D.; Sec. R. L. BIDWELL, PH.D.

Middle East Centre: St. Antony's College, 137 Banbury Road, Oxford OX2 6JF; f. 1958; Dir. Dr. D. HOPWOOD; library of 22,000 vols.; Publs. St. Antony's Middle East Monographs.

Palestine Exploration Fund: 2 Hinde Mews, London, W.1; f. 1865; 900 subscribers; Pres. The Archbishop of Canterbury; Hon. Sec. M. A. KNIBB, PH.D, B.D., S.T.M.; publ. *Palestine Exploration Quarterly.*

Royal Asiatic Society of Great Britain and Ireland: 56 Queen Anne St., London, W.1; f. 1823 for the study of the history, sociology, institutions, customs, languages and art of Asia; approx. 800 mems.; library of 100,000 vols. and 1,500 MSS.; branches in various Asian cities; Pres. Prof. E. H. S. SIMMONDS, M.A.; Sec. Miss D. CRAWFORD; publs. *Journal* and monographs.

Royal Society for Asian affairs: 42 Devonshire St., London, W.1; f. 1901; 2,000 mems. with past or present knowledge of the Middle East, Central Asia or the Far East; library of about 5,000 vols.; Pres. Lord SELKIRK; Chair. Sir STANLEY TOMLINSON, K.C.M.G., LL.D.; Sec. Miss M. FITZSIMONS; publ. *Journal* (three times a year).

School of African and Asian Studies: University of Sussex, Falmer, Brighton, Sussex BN1 9QN; Dean IEUAN LL. GRIFFITHS, B.SC.(ECON.), PH.D.

School of Oriental and African Studies, University of London: Malet St., London, WC1E 7HP; f. 1916; library of over 400,000 vols. and 2,000 MSS.; Dir. Prof. Sir CYRIL PHILIPS.

UNITED STATES OF AMERICA

Academy of Asian Studies: 431 Duboce Ave., San Francisco, Calif., 94117; Pres. Dr. EDSZEN N. LANDRUM.

American Friends of the Middle East, Inc.: 1717 Massachusetts Ave., N.W., Washington, D.C. 20036; f. 1951; a private, non-profit organization for furthering communication and understanding between the peoples of the Middle East and N. Africa and the people of the U.S.A. through educational and international programmes; offices in Washington D.C. and Egypt, Iran, Jordan, Lebanon, Morocco and Tunisia.

American Oriental Society: 329 Sterling Memorial Library, Yale Station, New Haven, Conn. 06520; f. 1842; 1,850 mems.; Sec. HUGH M. STIMSON; publ. *Journal.*

American Schools of Oriental Research: 126 Inman Street, Cambridge, Mass. 02139; f. 1900; approx. 2,000 mems.; support activities of independent archaeological institutions abroad: The Albright Institute of Archaeological Research, Jerusalem, Israel, and the American

Center of Oriental Research in Amman, Jordan; Pres. FRANK MOORE CROSS, Jr; Admin. Dir. THOMAS D. NEWMAN; publs. *Biblical Archaeologist* (quarterly), *Bulletin* (quarterly), *Journal of Cuneiform Studies* (quarterly), *Annual*.

Center for Middle Eastern Studies: University of Chicago, 1130 E. 59th St., Chicago, Ill. 60637; f. 1966; research into medieval and modern cultures of the Middle East from Morocco to Pakistan; Dir. LEONARD BINDER.

Center for Middle Eastern Studies: Harvard University, 1737 Cambridge St., Cambridge, Mass. 02138; research in social sciences and humanities.

Center for Middle Eastern Studies: The University of Texas at Austin, Tex. 78712; f. 1960; linguistic and social studies of Middle East languages and cultures; Dir. Dr. PAUL W. ENGLISH; Publs. monograph series on 19th and 20th century Middle East.

Center for Near East and North African Studies: University of Michigan, 144 Lane Hall, Ann Arbor, Mich. 48104; f. 1961; research into the ancient, medieval and modern cultures of the Near East and North Africa, Near Eastern languages and literature; Dir. Dr. WILLIAM D. SCHORGER.

The Dropsie University: Broad and York Streets, Philadelphia, Pa. 19132; f. 1907; Pres. A. I. KATSH.

Gustave E. von Grunebaum Center for Near Eastern Studies (formerly known as the Near Eastern Center): University of California, Los Angeles, 405 Hilyard Ave., Los Angeles, Calif. 90024; f. 1957; social sciences, culture and language studies of the Near East since the rise of Islam; a growing programme of Ancient Near Eastern Studies; library of over 100,000 vols. and outstanding MSS. collection in Arabic, Armenian, Hebrew, Persian and Turkish; Dir. SPEROS VRYONIS Jr.; Assoc. Dir. AMIN BANANI.

Hairenik Association, Inc.: 212 Stuart St., Boston, Mass. 02216; publ. *Armenian Review*.

Hoover Institution on War, Revolution and Peace: Stanford University, Stanford, Calif. 94305; f. 1919; contains important collection of materials on Middle East and North Africa; Dir. W. G. CAMPBELL; publs. about twenty books each year, plus six-volume survey of the Institution's library.

The Iran Foundation, Inc.: Empire State Bldg., New York, N.Y. 10001; project assistance relating to the advancement of health and education in Iran and other culturally related areas.

Institute for Mediterranean Affairs: 1078 Madison Ave., New York, N.Y. 10018; established under charter of the University of the State of New York to evolve a better understanding of the historical background and contemporary political and socio-economic problems of the nations and regions that border on the Mediterranean Sea, with special reference to the Middle East and North Africa; 350 mems.; Pres. Ambassador SEYMOUR M. FINGER; Chair. Prof. N. S. FATEMI; Vice-Chair. Prof. A. P. LERNER; Dir. SAMUEL MERLIN.

Israel Institute: Yeshiva University, Amsterdam Ave. and 185th St., New York, N.Y. 10033; f. 1954; research into modern Israel and her cultural and political problems, Jewish history and culture; Dir. Dr. SAMUEL K. MIRSKY; publ. *Sura, Talpioth*.

Joint Committee on the Near and Middle East: c/o Social Science Research Council, 605 Third Avenue, New York, N.Y. 10016; the Committee is co-sponsored by the American Council of Learned Societies and administers a programme of grants for research by individual scholars in the social sciences and humanities, and a programme of dissertation research fellowships for U.S. and Canadian citizens.

Middle East Center: University of Utah, Salt Lake City, Utah 84112; f. 1960; co-ordinated programme in Middle East languages and area studies in 12 academic departments; B.A. in Arabic or Persian, M.A. and Ph.D. in Middle East Studies with area of concentration in Arabic, Hebrew, Persian or Turkish; annual summer programme of Arabic Studies at Bourguiba Inst. for Modern Languages, Univ. of Tunis; student exchange with Univ. of Teheran, academic year programme, Univ. of Tel-Aviv; history of 100,000 vols.; Dir. Dr. KHOSROW MOSTOFI.

Middle East Institute: 1761 N. St., N.W., Washington, D.C. 20036; f. 1946; exists to develop and maintain facilities for research, publication and dissemination of information, with a view to developing in the United States a more thorough understanding of the countries of the Middle East; the Institute holds an annual conference on Middle East affairs; 1,600 mems.; National Chair. Hon. RAYMOND A. HARE; Pres. Hon. L. DEAN BROWN; Sec. MALCOLM C. PECK; Dir. of Publs. WILLIAM SANDS; publs. *Middle East Journal* (quarterly), *Middle East Monitor* (two per month), and occasional books.

Middle East Institute: Columbia University, 1113 International Affairs Bldg, New York, N.Y. 10027; f. 1954; a graduate training programme on the modern Middle East for students seeking professional careers as regional specialists, research into problems of economics, government and international relations of the Middle East countries, and their languages and history; library of more than 100,000 vols. in Middle East vernacular and equally rich in Western languages; Dir. Prof. J. C. HUREWITZ; publs. *Publications in Near and Middle East studies* (completed), *Modern Middle East Series* (irregular).

Middle East Studies Association: New York University, Washington Square, New York, N.Y. 10003; f. 1967 to promote high standards of scholarship and instruction and to facilitate communication on the area; membership open to all persons of scholarly attainment in the field of Middle Eastern studies; 1,500 mems.; Pres. (1975) Prof. RODERIC H. DAVISON; Vice-Pres. Prof. AFAF L. AL-SAYYID MARSOT; Exec. Sec. Prof. I. W. ZARTMAN; publs. *Bulletin* (quarterly), *International Journal of Middle East Studies* (quarterly).

Middle East Studies Centre: Portland State Univ., Portland, Ore. 97207; language and area studies in Arabic, Persian, Turkish and Hebrew; Dir. Prof. FREDERICK J. COX.

Near East College Association, Inc.: 40 Worth St., New York, N.Y. 10013; and 548 Fifth Ave., New York, N.Y. 10036.

Near East Foundation: 54 East 64th St., New York, N.Y. 10021, U.S.A.; f. 1930. Aims: to conduct educational programmes and agricultural projects in order to improve standards of living in underdeveloped areas of Asia and Africa, primarily the Near East; Hon. Chair. CLEVELAND E. DODGE; Vice-Chair. J. B. SUNDERLAND; Pres. HERRICK B. YOUNG; Exec. Dir. DELMER J. DOOLEY; publs. *Annual Report*, newspaper (semi-annually).

Near Eastern Studies: Indiana University, Bloomington, Indiana 47401; courses in Arabic, Hebrew and Turkish languages and literature both modern and classical, history, political science and religions of the area; Chair. WADIE JWAIDEH.

Oriental Institute: 1155 E. 58th St., Chicago, Ill. 60637; f. 1919; principally concerned with cultures and languages of the ancient Near East; extensive museum; affiliated to the University of Chicago; Dir. JOHN A. BRINKMAN.

Program in Near Eastern Studies: Princeton University, Jones Hall, Princeton, N.J. 08540; f. 1947; research in all aspects of the modern Near East; library of 120,000 vols.; Dir. MORROE BERGER; Associate Dir. JOHN H. MARKS; publs. _Proceedings of Annual Near East Conference_ (annual), _Princeton Studies on the Near East_ (irregular), _Princeton Near East Papers_ (irregular).

Semitic Museum: Harvard University, 6 Divinity Ave., Cambridge, Mass. 02138; f. 1889; sponsors exploration and research in Western Asia; contains collection of exhibits from ancient Near East; Curator Dr. CARNEY E. S. GAVIN.

VATICAN

Pontificium Institutum Orientalium Studiorum (_Pontifical Institute of Oriental Studies_): 7 Piazza Santa Maria Maggiore, 00185-Rome; f. 1917; library of 105,000 vols.; Rector Rev. GEORGES DEJAIFVE, S.J.; Sec. Rev. J. ŘEZÁČ, S.J.; publs. _Orientalia Christiana Periodica, Orientalia Christiana Analecta, Concilium Florentinum_ (_Documenta et Scriptores_), _Anaphorae Syriacae_.

10° | 90° 5° West of Greenwich 0° East of Greenwich 5° | 10° | 15° | 20° | 25°

SPAIN
Lisbon
PORTUGAL
C.St.Vincent
Seville
Granada
Cartagena
Str. of Gibraltar
Tangier
Gibraltar (Br.)
Ceuta (Sp.)
Melilla (Sp.)
Mina Hassan Tani
Rabat
Casablanca
Fez
Meknes
Safi
Essaoira (Mogador)
Marrakesh
High Atlas
Anti-Atlas
Sidi Ifni
Middle Atlas
M O R O C C O
Rif Mts.
Oran
Mostaganem
Médéa
El Asnam
Algiers
Tizi Ouzou
Constantine
Annaba (Bône)
Bizerta
Tunis
SICILY
Palermo
Sousse
Sfax
G. of Gabès
Djerba I.
Chott Djerid
Chott Melrhir
Setif
Batna
Aurès Mts.
Tlemcen
Tiaret
High Plateaux
Saharan Atlas
Atlas
Aïn Sefra
Béchar
Touggourt
Ghardaïa
Ouargla
Ft. Lallemand
Great Eastern Erg
Beni Abbès
Great Western Erg
Ft. MacMahon
Hamada of Dra
Dra
SPANISH SAHARA
Erg
Igidi
Tademaït Hamada
Tinrherta Hamada
Ain Salah
Sebkra Mekerrhane
Sebkra Azz el Matti
Hassi el Krenig
Ft. Flatters
Ft. de Polignac
Tassili-n-Ajjer
In Eker
TAHAT 9,840
Hoggar
Tamanrasset
Tamanrasset
Djanet
Gat
In Afaleleh
Gadames
El Homra Hamada
T R I P O L I T A N I A
Tripoli
Homs
Beni Ulid
Misurata
G. of Sidra
Benghazi
J el Akhdar
Beida
Tobruk
Mersa Brega
Sirte
C Y R E N A I C A
Jofra Oasis
Hon
Zella
Marada
Jalo Oasis
Siwa
Umm el Abid
Sebha
Murzuch
Zuila
Wau el Kebir
El Garun
F E Z Z A N
L I B Y A
Serir of Kalanshu
Ed Dacar
Birel Harash
Kufra
Oases
El Jauf
Rebiana
Gilf Keb Plateau
UWEINAT 6,259

A L G E R I A

Schech Erg
Tanezrouft
S A H A R A
Adrar of the Iforas
Tassili Oua-n-Ahaggar
Djado
10,709
10,335
Tibesti
Serir
Aozu
Sarra
EMI KOUSSI 11,201

MAURITANIA

MALI REPUBLIC
L.Faguibine
Timbuctu
Niafounké
L.Haogoundou
Niger
TAMGAK MTS. 9,900
Adar
Aïr or Azbine
Agadès
Tazililet
Faya
Mourdi Depression
Ennedi
C H A D
Bodélé Depression

UPPER VOLTA
Ouagadougou
White Volta
Niamey
Sokoto
Maradi
Zinder
Kano
L. Chad (Tchad)
Abéché
N'Djamena
D A R F U R
Geneina
El Fash
MARRA MTS. 10,130
El H
Mogororo
Abu Ma

GHANA
Tamale
L. Volta
ASHANTI
Kumasi
Obuasi
Akosombo Dam
Sekondi
Takoradi
Accra
Gold Coast
Coast
Lome
TOGO
DAHOMEY
Cotonou
Porto-Novo
Benin
Oyo
Ibadan
Abeokuta
Lagos
Slave Coast
Bight of Benin
N I G E R I A
Kaduna
Bauchi
Plateau Jos
Bauchi
Maiduguri
Makurdi
Enugu
Benue
Garoua
Sarh
CENTRAL AFRICAN REPUBLIC
Adamaoa
Massif N'Gaoundéré
Ft.Crampel
CAMEROON
Port Harcourt
Buea
Calabar
Victoria
Macias Nguema (Eq. Guinea)
Douala
Yaoundé
Bangui
Bondo
EQUATORIAL GUINEA
Gulf of Guinea
Bight of Bonny
Dja
CONGO (P. R.)
Libenge
Uele

Lisbon
Barcelona
CORSICA
Ajaccio
Rome
ITALY
Naples
Bari
Cagliari
SARDINIA
Majorca
Balearic Islands
Valencia
C. de la Nao
Tyrrhenian Sea
Pantelleria (It.)
MALTA
Ionian Sea
M E D I T E R R A N E A N
YUGOSLAVIA
Sofia
BULGARIA
Plovdiv
Skopje
Tiranë
ALBANIA
GREECE
Thessalonica
Athens
Piraeus
Adriatic Sea
Aegean Sea
Dardanelles
CRETE

0° East of Greenwich | 5° | 10° | 15° | 20° | 25°
Conical Orthomorphic Projection

Black Sea

U.S.S.R.

TURKMENISTAN

Istanbul
Bosporus
Zonguldak
Samsun
Batumi
Kutaisi
Tbilisi
Leninakan Kirovabad
AZERBAYDZHAN
Baku
Kara-Kum
Bukhara

Bursa
Eskişehir
Ankara
Sivas
Erzurum Yerevan
MT. ARARAT 16945
Tabrīz
Rasht
Alborz Mts.
Shāhrūd
Khorāsān
Ashkhabad
Koppeh Dagh
Meshed

TURKEY
L. Tuz
Kayseri 12369
Afyonkaharisar
Malatya 8570
Erzincan 11315
Diyarbakır Siirt
Reza'iyeh
L. Van
Sanandaj Hamadān
Qom
Garmsar
Darya-ye Namak
Dashte-Kavīr
Herat
AFGHANISTAN

Toros Mts. 11762
Adana
Mersin
G. of Antalya
Aleppo
Kirkūk
Mosul
Kermānshāh 11717
Teheran
14200 12783
Iṣfahān
IRAN (PERSIA)
Dasht-e-Lut
Zābol
Sīstān
PAKISTAN

odes
eece)
Nicosia
Banias
SYRIA
Hama
Homs
Deir ez Zor
Karbalā
Baghdād
Lorestān
Zagros Mountains
14920
Kermān
Zāhedān
Baluchistān
Makran

CYPRUS
LEBANON
Beirut
Damascus
Haditha
Hadithah
Ahwāz
Khūzestān
Fars
Shīrāz
Lārestān

SEA
ISRAELI OCCUPIED TERR.
Haifa
ISRAEL
Tel Aviv
Jaffa
Jerusalem
Amman
Al Wudyan
Basra
Abādān
Būshehr
Persian Gulf

xandria
Tanta
Port Said
Dead Sea
JORDAN
Ma'an
Al Hajara
Kuwait
Neutral Territ
Str. of Hormuz
OMAN
Gulf of 'Oman

Cairo
Ismailia
Suez
Eilat
Aqaba
Sakaka
Jauf
Summān
Dahna
Manama
Sharjah
Dubai
Muscat
J. AKHDAR 10,400
Ras al Hadd

YPT
Qena
Port Safaga
Tebuk
Jabal Shifa
Nafud
Hail
Buraida
'Anaiza
BAHRAIN
Doha
QATAR
Hufhuf
Abu Dhabi
Umm Said
UNITED ARAB EMIRATES

Dakhla Oasis
Luxor
Aswān 6552
Jabal Shammar
NAJD
Junaitha
Riyadh
Haradh
Jufura
Umm Samim
Masira

2nd Cataract
Wadi Halfa
Selima Oasis
Medina
Quwai'iya
Tuwaiq
SAUDI ARABIA
Sabkhat Matti
Sabkhat Minjora
Ras al Madraka

HERN
Nubian Desert
Muhammad Qol
Yanbu
Asir
Jeddah
Mecca
Rub' al Khali
Dhofar
Kuria Muria Is.
Salalah

Cataract
Port Sudan
Tihama
OMAN
Sabaloka Gorge

DAN
4th Cataract
Merowe
5th Cataract
Atbara
Farasan Is.
Jauf
Hadramaut
Mukalla
Ras Fartak
Socotra

KHARTOUM
Omdurman
Khartoum
Ed Damer
Kassala
Dahlak Arch.
Massawa
Kamaran Is.
YEMEN ARAB REPUBLIC
Sana'a
YEMEN PEOPLE'S DEMOCRATIC REPUBLIC
Saiwun

DOFAN
El Obeid
Khasm el Girba
Wad Medani
RAS DASHAN 15,158
ERITREA
Asmara
As Shaab
Aden
Abd al Kuri
The Brothers
Gulf of Aden

BLUE NILE
Er Roseires
Gondar
L. Tana
Choke Mts. 13,381
Dessye
FRENCH TERR. AFARS ISSAS
Djibouti
Perim
Bab el Mandeb
Berbera
Hargeisa
Hordio
C. Guardafui

Malakal
UPPER NILE
Addis Ababa
Harar
Abyssinian Plateau
Diredawa
SOMALIA
INDIAN OCEAN

QUATORIA
Juba
Nimule
L. Rudolf
Mega
KENYA
UGANDA
Obbia

Ft.	M.
16,000	4,800
10,000	3,000
6,000	1,800
3,000	900
1,500	450
1,000	300
600	180
300	90
Sea Level	
Land Depression	

Scale 1:19 m. 1 inch to 300 miles approx.